The New York Times
CROSSWORD PUZZLE
DICTIONARY

𝕿𝖍𝖊 𝕹𝖊𝖜 𝖄𝖔𝖗𝖐 𝕿𝖎𝖒𝖊𝖘

CROSSWORD PUZZLE DICTIONARY

By

Thomas Pulliam and Clare Grundman

A HUDSON GROUP BOOK

 QUADRANGLE/THE NEW YORK TIMES BOOK COMPANY

Produced in association with Morningside Associates.

Second printing December 1974

Library of Congress Catalog Card Number: 73-79912

International Standard Book Number: 0-8129-0382-x

(NOT —) FINITE CONDITIONAL
ABSOLUTELY YEA YES AMEN BONE COLD DEAD FAIR JUST PLAT SLAP PLAIN PLUMB STARK BARELY FAIRLY FLATLY SIMPLY WHOLLY SHEERLY ENTIRELY EVENDOWN
ABSOLUTION EXCUSE PARDON SHRIFT LOOSING SHRIVING
ABSOLUTISM CAESARISM DESPOTISM
ABSOLVE FREE QUIT CLEAR LOOSE REMIT ACQUIT ASSOIL EXCUSE EXEMPT FINISH PARDON SHRIVE UNBIND CLEANSE FORGIVE JUSTIFY RELEASE DISPENSE LIBERATE OVERLOOK
ABSORB EAT FIX SOP SUP SOAK SUCK TAKE AMUSE DRINK MERGE RIVET UNITE DEVOUR ENGAGE ENGULF ENWRAP IMBIBE INGEST INSORB INWRAP OCCUPY SPONGE STIFLE COMBINE CONSUME ENGROSS IMMERSE INVOLVE OCCLUDE SWALLOW
ABSORBED DEEP GONE LOST RAPT SUNK FIXED ABSENT BURIED ENRAPT HIPPED INTENT PLUNGED RIVETED WRAPPED IMMERSED
(— BY) ALL
ABSORBENT BASE FOMES SPONGY ANTACID SORBENT ANTIACID DRINKING
ABSORBER SNUBBER
(— OF MONEY) LICKPENNY
(SHOCK —) BUFFER DAMPER
ABSORBING
ABSORPTION AUTISM
(— UNIT) SABIN
ABSTAIN DENY FAST KEEP STAY AVOID CEASE SPARE SPURN WAIVE DESIST DISUSE ESCHEW FOREGO REFUSE REJECT FORBEAR REFRAIN RESTRAIN TEETOTAL WITHHOLD
(— FROM) FAST FORGO LEAVE ABJURE ESCHEW FOREGO REFRAIN
ABSTAINER TOTE RECHABITE
ABSTEMIOUS SOBER ACETIC SLENDER MODERATE
ABSTENTION CELIBACY CHASTITY
ABSTERGE WIPE BATHE CLEAN PURGE RINSE
ABSTINENCE ENCRATY
ABSTINENT SOBER ABSTEMIOUS
ABSTRACT CULL DEED DRAW NOTE PART PURE TAKE BRIEF IDEAL STEAL ABSORB DEDUCT DETACH DIVERT DOCKET PRECIS REMOVE ABRIDGE COMPEND EXCERPT ISOLATE PURLOIN SECRETE SUMMARY VIDIMUS ABSTRUSE ACADEMIC ARGUMENT BREVIATE DISCRETE SEPARATE SYLLABUS SYNOPSIS TABLEITY WITHDRAW
(NOT —) CONCRETE
(PL.) PARATITLA PARATITLES
ABSTRACTED REMOTE
ABSTRACTION STUDY ENTITY ABSTRACT QUODDITY
ABSTRUSE DARK DEEP HIGH HIDDEN

MYSTIC REMOTE SECRET SUBTLE CURIOUS OBSCURE RETIRED ABSTRACT ACROATIC ESOTERIC PROFOUND
ABSURD HOT RICH WILD DOTTY DROLL FALSE INANE INEPT SILLY SCREWY STUPID ASININE FATUOUS FOOLISH LAPUTAN DOGGEREL FABULOUS
ABSURDITY FATUITY FOOLERY FOPPERY WALTROT MAGGOTRY NONSENSE UNREASON
ABUNA METRAN
ABUNDANCE WON COPY FLOW MORT SONS WONE CHEAP DEPTH FOUTH POWER RIVER ROUTH ROWTH SCADS SONSE STORE WRECK BOUNTY FOISON GALORE LAVISH OODLES PLENTY POWDER RICHES TALENT UBERTY WEALTH FLUENCY LASHINS SATIETY BELLYFUL FULLNESS LASHINGS OPULENCE PLEURISY RIMPTION
(IN —) APLENTY
ABUNDANT FAT OLD FREE LUSH MUCH RANK RICH RIFE AMPLE FLUSH HEFTY LARGE OPIME ROUTH ROWTH STORE DEMOID GALORE HEARTY ROUTHY APLENTY COPIOUS FERTILE FULSOME LIBERAL PROFUSE REPLETE TEEMING UBERANT UBEROUS WEALTHY AFFLUENT FRUITFUL GENEROUS NUMEROUS
(NOT —) LIGHT SPARE
ABUNDANTLY RIFE WELL FREELY LARGELY HEARTILY
ABUSE MAR MOB TAX BUSE CALL DRUB FLAY GAFF HARM HURT LACK MAUL RAIL RUIN SLAM TEEN VAIN CRIME CURSE FAULT GRIEF SCOLD SLANG SNASH SPOIL BERATE DEFILE INJURE INSULT MALIGN MISUSE MUMBLE PUNISH RAVISH REVILE TANCEL TANSEL VILIFY YATTER AFFRONT BACKJAW BEDEVIL DECEIVE DESPITE FALSIFY MISBEDE MISCALL MISNAME OBLOQUY OUTRAGE PERVERT PROFANE SLANDER TRADUCE UPBRAID VIOLATE BALLARAG BUSINESS DISHONOR FRUMPERY LANGUAGE MALTREAT MISAPPLY MISTREAT REPROACH SLAPDASH
ABUSED DOWNTROD DOWNTRODDEN
ABUSIVE FOUL DIRTY SHREWD CORRUPT SATIRIC CHEATING INSOLENT LIBELOUS
ABUT BUTT JOIN REST TOUCH ADJOIN BORDER BUTTAL PROJECT
ABUTILON MALLOW
ABUTMENT CRIB PIER ALETTE BUTTRESS
ABUTTING FLUSH ADJACENT
ABYSM ABIME BISME DOWNFALL
ABYSMAL DEEP DREARY PROFOUND UNENDING WRETCHED
ABYSS PIT POT DEEP GULF HELL VOID ABYSM CHAOS CHASM DEPTH

GORGE BOTTOM VORAGO ABADDON GEHENNA SWALLOW DOWNFALL INTERVAL
ABYSSAL ABYSMAL BASSALIAN
ABYSSINIA AXUM ETHIOPIA
ABYSSINIAN SIDI ABASSIN
(— BANANA) ENSETE
ACACIA GUM JAM BABUL GIDYA MULGA MYALL SIRIS THORN TIMBE VEREK ARABIC BABLAH BINDER GIDGEA GIDGEE GIDYEA HASHAB LEGUME LOCUST MIMOSA WATTLE YARRAN BLUEBUSH BRIGALOW CHAPPARO IRONWOOD ROSEWOOD
ACADEMIC IVY RIGID FORMAL CLASSIC DONNISH ERUDITE LEARNED POMPIER
ACADEMY LYCEE CRUSCA LYCEUM MANEGE SCHOOL COLLEGE SOCIETY YESHIVA SEMINARY
(RIDING —) MANAGE MANEGE
ACADIAN CAJUN
ACAJOU CAJU CAJOO CAJOU
ACALEPH MEDUSA MEDUSAN
ACANA ALMIQUE
ACANTHA FIN SPINE THORN PRICKLE ACANTHON
ACAPU WALNUT WACAPOU CHAPERNO
ACARID NYMPH NYMPHA OCTOPOD DIBRANCH
ACAUDAL BOBBED ANUROUS ECAUDATE TAILLESS
ACAULESCENT STEMLESS
ACCEDE LET AGREE ALLOW ENTER GRANT YIELD ACCORD ASSENT ATTAIN COMPLY CONCUR CONCEDE CONFORM CONSENT
ACCELERATE GUN REV RUN HYPO JAZZ RACE URGE DRIVE FAVOR FORCE HURRY SPEED HASTEN ADVANCE FORWARD FURTHER QUICKEN ANTEDATE DISPATCH EXPEDITE INCREASE THROTTLE
ACCELERATION SPEEDUP
(— OF REACTION) CATALYSIS
(— UNIT) STAPP
ACCELERATOR GAS SPEEDER BETATRON THROTTLE
ACCENT BEAT BLAS BURR MARK TONE ACUTE GRAVE ICTUS PITCH PULSE SOUND THROB VERGE BROGUE LENGTH RHYTHM STRESS THESIS EMPHASIS
(DORIC —) PLATEASM
(IRISH —) BROGUE
(MUSICAL —) BEAT
(WITHOUT AN —) ATONIC
ACCENTED FZ SFZ TONIC STRONG MARCATO MARCANDO SFORZATO
ACCENTUATE ACCENT
ACCENTUATION DECLAMATION ENHANCEMENT
ACCEPT BUY EAT BEAR FANG HAVE HOLD JUMP TAKE ADMIT ADOPT AGREE ALLOW HONOR INFER MARRY ASSENT ASSUME AVOUCH POCKET APPROVE BELIEVE CONCEDE EMBRACE ESPOUSE RECEIVE

(— **AS ONE'S OWN**) NOSTRIFICATE
(— **AT RANDOM**) DRAW
(— **BETS**) BOOK
(— **EAGERLY**) LEAP
(— **INHERITANCE**) ADIATE
(— **READILY**) SWALLOW
(— **WITHOUT QUESTION**) ABIDE
ACCEPTABLE LIEF SIGHTLY
WELCOME GRACIOUS PASSABLE
PLEASANT
ACCEPTANCE PASS SNAFF ADITIO
TAQLID PASSAGE CREDENCE
CURRENCY
(— **OF INHERITANCE**) CERNITURE
(— **OF ORDER**) ALLOTMENT
ACCEPTED GOING VULGAR
POPULAR APPROVED CREDITED
ORTHODOX STANDARD
(**WIDELY** —) INVETERATE
ACCEPTOR BASE
ACCESS FIT WAY ADIT DOOR GATE
PATH ROAD ENTRY GOING ROUTE
ACCOST AVENUE COMING ENTREE
PORTAL STREET ADVANCE
APPROACH ENTRANCE PAROXYSM
RECOURSE
(— **OF DISEASE**) ATTACK
ACCESSIBILITY EXPOSURE
ACCESSIBLE NEAR OPEN HANDY
PATENT AFFABLE PRESENT
FAMILIAR PERVIOUS SOCIABLE
ACCESSION ENTER ALLUVIO
ILLAPSE ADDITION ALLUVION
ENTRANCE INCREASE
ACCESSORY HAT AIDE ALLY DOME
TOOL EXTRA SCARF HELPER
ABETTOR ADJUNCT ANCILLA
ENCLAVE FITTING FIXTURE ADDITIVE
HATSTAND
(PL.) ADDENDA FIXINGS STAFFAGE
ACCIACCATURA MORDENT
ACCIDENT HAP CASE LUCK EVENT
GRIEF CHANCE HAZARD INJURY
MISHAP FORTUNE QUALITY
CALAMITY CASUALTY DISASTER
FORTUITY INCIDENT
(**EUCHARISTIC** —**S**) SPECIES
ACCIDENTAL ODD CASUAL CHANCE
RANDOM EXTERNAL
ACCIPITER HAWK
ACCLAIM CRY CLAP FAME HAIL
LAUD ROOT CHEER CLAIM ECLAT
EXTOL SHOUT PRAISE APPLAUD
HOSANNA OVATION PLAUDIT
WELCOME APPLAUSE
(**NOISY** —) RIOT
ACCLAMATION CRY VOTE CHEER
SHOUT HOSANNA PLAUDIT
APPLAUSE
ACCLIMATE INURE HARDEN SEASON
ACCUSTOM
ACCLIMATIZE ADAPT HARDEN
SEASON
ACCLIVITY BANK BROW HILL RISE
GRADE PITCH SLANT SLOPE TALUS
ASCENT HEIGHT INCLINE
ACCOLADE EMMY KISS RITE SIGN
AWARD HONOR KUDOS MEDAL
OSCAR TOKEN SYMBOL EMBRACE

GARLAND CEREMONY
ACCOMMODATE AID BED BOW FIT
CAMP GIVE HELP HOLD LEND SORT
SUIT ADAPT BOARD DEFER FAVOR
HOUSE LODGE SERVE YIELD
ADJUST COMPLY FAVOUR OBLIGE
SETTLE CONFORM CONTAIN
FASHION ATTEMPER GARRISON
ACCOMMODATION LOAN BERTH
BERTHAGE GIFFGAFF
(— **BILL**) KITE
ACCOMPANIED FRAUGHT
ACCOMPANIMENT SON ALBA
BURDEN EXCORT OOMPAH ADJUNCT
DESCANT SUPPORT OBLIGATO
(PL.) FIXINGS
ACCOMPANIST JONGLEUR
ACCOMPANY SEE FARE FERE JOIN
LEAD TEND WAIT BRING PILOT
ASSIST ATTEND CONCUR CONVEY
CONVOY ESCORT FOLLOW SECOND
SQUIRE COEXIST CONDUCT
CONSORT SUPPORT CHAPERON
ACCOMPANYING FELLOW ADJUNCT
ACCOMPLICE PAL AIDE ALLY CHUM
BUDDY CRONY LOUKE SHILL TILER
BONNET COHORT FELLOW HELPER
ABETTOR FEODARY FEUDARY
HUSTLER PARTNER STEERER
ACCOMPLISH DO GO END WIN FILL
WORK ENACT EQUIP FETCH FORTH
SWING AFFORD ATTAIN EFFECT
FINISH FULFIL MANAGE ABSOLVE
ACHIEVE CHEVISE COMPASS
EXECUTE EXPLETE FULFILL FURNISH
OPERATE PERFECT PERFORM
REALIZE SUCCEED COMPLETE
CONTRIVE DISPATCH ENGINEER
OUTCARRY
ACCOMPLISHED APT ABLE DONE
ADEPT ENDED GREAT TERSE
BESEEN EXPERT HANDSOME
TALENTED
ACCOMPLISHMENT ART END DEED
FEAT PASS CRAFT SKILL EFFECT
TALENT EARNING QUALITY FRUITION
LEARNING
(**PRIOR** —) ANTICIPATION
ACCORD GIVE JIBE JUMP SUIT UNIT
AGREE ALLOW ATONE AWARD BEFIT
CHIME CHORD CORDE GRANT LEVEL
STAND TALLY UNITY ACCEDE
ADJUST ASSENT BESTOW BETEEM
COMPLY CONCUR SETTLE UNISON
COMPORT COMPOSE CONCEDE
CONCERT CONCORD CONSENT
CONSORT HARMONY RAPPORT
RESPOND UNANIME DIAPASON
SYMPATHY
(— **WITH**) SUIT
(**IN** —) ALONG
ACCORDANCE CONCERT CONSENT
(**IN** —) ALONG
ACCORDANT EVEN ATTUNED
AGREEING COHERENT SUITABLE
ACCORDING (— **TO ART**) SA
(— **TO LAW**) SL
(— **TO**) AD BY SEC EMFORTH
ENFORTH PURSUANT SECUNDUM

ACCORDINGLY SO THEN THUS
HENCE IGITUR
ACCORDION LANTUM FLUTINA
FLAUTINO
ACCOST BAIL HAIL MASH MEET
ABORD BOARD GREET SPEAK
ACCESS BROACH HALLOO SALUTE
ACCOAST ADDRESS SOLICIT
APPROACH GREETING
ACCOUCHEUR OBSTETRICIAN
ACCOUCHEUSE MIDWIFE
ACCOUNT TAB BILL BOOK DEEM
DRAW ITEM NICK NOTE RATE REDE
SAKE TAIL TALE TELL TEXT WORD
AUDIT BLAME CHALK COUNT JUDGE
SCORE STATE STORY VALUE
WORTH BATTEL CREDIT DETAIL
ESTEEM HORARY LEGEND PROFiT
REASON RECKON RECORD REGARD
RELATE RENDER REPORT REPUTE
TREATY ACCOMPT COMPOST
COMPUTE EXPLAIN JOURNAL
LEXICON NARRATE PROCESS
RECITAL TAILZIE BREVIARY
CONSIDER ESTIMATE TREATISE
(— **FOR**) SAVE EXPLAIN
(**ACCURATE** —) GRIFF GRIFFIN
(**CREDIT** —) TICK
(**LONG** —) ILIAD
(**TRAVEL** —) ITINERARY
ACCOUNTABILITY DETAIL LIABILITY
ACCOUNTABLE LIABLE AMENABLE
ACCOUNTANT CLERK SIRCAR
SIRKAR AUDITOR PESHKAR
PUTWARI KULKARNI MUTSUDDY
RECKONER
ACCOUNTANT-GENERAL DAFTARDAR
DEFTERDAR
ACCOUNTING TASK REASON
COSTING
ACCOUTER ARM RIG GIRD ARRAY
DRESS EQUIP ATTIRE CLOTHE
OUTFIT BEDIGHT FURNISH HARNESS
PROVIDE
ACCOUTERMENTS GEAR TIRE
DRESS ATTIRE GRAITH
ACCREDIT ALLOT VOUCH CREDIT
DEPUTE APPOINT APPROVE ASCRIBE
BELIEVE CERTIFY CONFIRM
ENDORSE LICENSE SANCTION
ACCRETION SUM GAIN GROWTH
DEPOSIT EXUDATE ADDITION
ADHESION INCREASE
(**INJURIOUS** —) RUST
ACCRUAL ACCRUE DEMERIT
ACCRUE ADD WIN EARN GAIN GROW
PILE ARISE ENSUE ENURE INCUR
INURE ISSUE MATURE RESULT
SPRING ACQUIRE COLLECT
REDOUND ACCRESCE CUMULATE
INCREASE
ACCUMULATE DRAW FUND GROW
HEAP HIVE MASS PILE SAVE AMASS
DRIFT HOARD STACK STORE TOTAL
ACCRUE GARNER GATHER MUSTER
SCRAPE COLLECT HARVEST
INCREASE
ACCUMULATION DRIP DUMP FUND
GAIN HEAP MASS PILE STACK

PREFACE

THE NEW YORK TIMES CROSSWORD PUZZLE DICTIONARY exceeds in completeness and scope all other puzzle dictionaries. No useful word has been omitted. Not only have puzzles themselves been combed for synonyms that are used over and over, but also a word-for-word reading of major unabridged dictionaries, both current and old, produced a thoroughly complete and extensive checklist.

Each of us has been solving and compiling puzzles for many years, and our chief purpose has been to design a practical and easy-to-use dictionary, in the belief that your needs and requirements for such a volume closely reflect our own. For example, the synonyms are arranged by the number of letters, and then alphabetized so you can quickly find the very word that fills the spaces in the puzzle. Another feature, one that seems obvious for a crossword puzzle dictionary but is not found in most of them, is that all words are printed in easy-to-read capital letters. The type has been chosen with great care for its legibility, and the three-column format not only provides a short line of type to scan, but also enables us to get a very large number of words on each page.

Synonyms of great length have been omitted to give room for the shorter, more useful words. The puzzler can always "fill in" the very long words provided he has a good supply of short common synonyms. We have placed, therefore, an arbitrary ceiling of eight-letter word-lengths, knowing this will satisfy almost all needs. Here and there, however, you will find occasional exceptions to this rule. These are synonyms of such frequent, interesting and normal usage that their omission might handicap the puzzler.

The "shaded boxes" scattered through the book are a notable and unique feature of THE NEW YORK TIMES CROSSWORD PUZZLE DICTIONARY. They collect under one heading a variety of categories and synonyms that you would have a hard time finding in other dictionaries. For example, when you are confronted by the clue "Brazilian river" merely turn to the shaded area marked BRAZIL, where you will find several excellent possibilities. Similarly, look for a "Philippine native" under PHILIPPINES, or a "Scottish measure" under SCOTLAND.

Another useful feature is the lavish listing of phrases. For instance, instead of being confronted by the simple clue "Sword," you may run up against "Double-edged sword." Under the entry word SWORD in this dictionary you will find ample phrases that qualify the entry word or more sharply specify its meaning. Also, given the definition "Turn aside," simply look under TURN and find that phrase, along with many others.

THE NEW YORK TIMES CROSSWORD PUZZLE DICTIONARY is a versatile reference book which you will want to keep on your desk or next to your

chair for help, not only with crossword puzzles, but also for a large variety of other puzzles and contests. In addition, it will be invaluable for writers, speakers, and the like, for (with more than ½ million words) it is one of the largest books of synonyms ever published. Its simple arrangement makes it far easier to use than the standard thesauri.

Our hope is that you will come to use this new word book as we might. Get to know it and be adventuresome! If the first entry you consult does not corner the exact word you are seeking, let any listing at that spot lead you to a cross-reference. Follow this track until you have the right word "treed."

A project of this scope may well have been beyond the ability of only two to accomplish. We have required and welcomed top-flight support during our work. Although many might be named, special note must be given to the efforts of Richard Martz and David House of Dartmouth College, who were responsible for much of the computerization; also, to Gorton Carruth and Robert O'Brien of Morningside Associates. Each made his individual contributions, which we gratefully acknowledge.

Happy word hunting!

Tom Pulliam
Clare Grundman

The New York Times
CROSSWORD PUZZLE
DICTIONARY

A AN AY HA AIR ARY PER ALFA EACH
ALPHA
(EVER —) ARROW
AA LAVA
AAL AL MULBERRY
AARDVARK ANTEATER EDENTATE
AARDWOLF HYAENID
AARON (BROTHER OF —) MOSES
(BURIAL PLACE OF —) HOR
(FATHER OF —) AMRAM
(SISTER OF —) MIRIAM
(SON OF —) ABIHU NADAB ELEAZAR
AARONIC LEVITIC LEVITICAL
AB HATI
ABA ABAYAH
ABACA HEMP FIBER LUPIS LINAGA
MANILA
ABACK SHORT
ABACUS SOROBAN
ABADDON PIT HELL ABYSS SATAN
APOLLYON
ABAFT AFT BACK BAFT ABAFF
ASTERN BEHIND REARWARD
(— THE BEAM) LARGE
ABALONE EAR PAUA AWABI NACRE
ORMER UHLLO ASSEIR MOLLUSK
ABANDON EGO CAST DROP FLEE
JUNK QUIT SINK ALLAY DITCH
EXPEL LEAVE PLANT REMIT SCRAP
WAIVE YIELD ABJURE BANISH
BETRAY DESERT DEVEST DISUSE
DIVEST EXPOSE FOREGO FORHOO
FORLET MAROON RECANT REFUSE
REJECT RELENT RESIGN SLOUGH
VACATE DEPLORE DISCARD FORLEIT
FORSAKE SCUTTLE ABDICATE
FORHOOIE FORSWEAR JETTISON
RASHNESS RENOUNCE SURCEASE
(WITH —) DESPERATELY
ABANDONED BAD LEFT LORN LOST
WICKED CORRUPT FORLORN
PROJECT DEPRAVED DERELICT
DESERTED DESOLATE FLAGRANT
FORSAKEN
ABANDONMENT BURIAL APOSTASY
(— OF RESTRAINT) LETUP
ABASE SINK VAIL AVALE AVILE
BLAME DEMIT DIMIT LOWER SHAME
ABJECT BEMEAN DEBASE DEFAME
DEJECT DEMEAN DEPOSE GROVEL
HUMBLE LESSEN MEEKEN REDUCE
DEGRADE DEPRESS MORTIFY
DIMINISH DISGRACE DISHONOR
ABASED ABAISSE DEJECTED
ABASH AWE COW BASH BAZE DASH
AVALE ESBAY SHAME HUMBLE
CONFUSE MORTIFY BEWILDER
BROWBEAT CONFOUND
ABASHED BLANK CHEAP SHAMED
ASHAMED FOOLISH SHEEPISH
ABASHMENT VERGOYNE
ABATE EBB END LOW CALM CURB
FAIK FALL MEND OMIT SLOW SOFT
VOID WANE ALLAY ANNUL BREAK
CHECK LOWER QUASH RELAX REMIT
SLAKE SWAGE ASLAKE DEDUCT
LESSEN PACIFY REBATE REDUCE
RELENT ABOLISH ASSUAGE
CASSARE CHANCER NULLIFY

QUALIFY SLACKEN SUBSIDE
DECREASE DIMINISH MITIGATE
MODERATE OVERBLOW PALLIATE
ABATEMENT DELF FALL ALLAY
DELFT DELPH LETUP GUSSET
MIOSIS DECREASE DISCOUNT
ABATIS OBSTACLE SLASHING
ABAXIAL DORSAL
ABBA FATHER
ABBE MONK CLERIC CURATE PRIEST
ABBESS AMMA VICARESS
ABBEY ABADIA ABBAYE PRIORY
CONVENT NUNNERY CLOISTER
ABBOT ABBAS COARB
(— OF MISRULE) BISHOP
ABBREVIATE CUT CLIP DOCK PRUNE
DIGEST ABRIDGE BOBTAIL CURTAIL
SHORTEN CONDENSE CONTRACT
TRUNCATE
ABBREVIATED SHORT BOBTAIL
CRYPTIC MUTILATE
ABBREVIATION LAPSE SIGLUM
SYMBOL
(PL.) SIGLA
ABC ALPHABET
ABDICATE CEDE QUIT DEMIT EXPEL
LEAVE REMIT DEPOSE DISOWN
FOREGO RESIGN RETIRE VACATE
ABANDON DISCLAIM RENOUNCE
ABDICATION DRIFT
ABDOMEN BOUK WOMB ALVUS
APRON BELLY MELON MIRAC PLEON
THARM PAUNCH VENTER STOMACH
ABDOMINAL HEMAL CELIAC
COELIAC VENTRAL VISCERAL
ABDUCT LURE TAKE STEAL ABDUCE
KIDNAP RAVISH SPIRIT CAPTURE
ABDUCTION APAGOGE RAPTURE
ABDUCTOR SPIRIT
ABEAM ABREAST
ABECEDARIAN TYRO NOVICE
LEARNER BEGINNER
ABECEDARIUS ABC
ABED SICK RESTING RETIRED
SLEEPING
ABEL (BROTHER OF —) CAIN SETH
(PARENT OF —) EVE ADAM
ABELMOSK MUSK MALLOW
ABERDEEN ANGUS BLACK DODDY
DODDIE
ABERRANT WILD CLAMMY DEVIANT
ABNORMAL STRAYING VARIABLE
ABERRATION SLIP WARP ERROR
FAULT LAPSE MANIA DELIRIUM
DELUSION INSANITY
ABESSIVE CARITIVE
ABET AID EGG BACK HELP BOOST
COACH ASSIST FOMENT INCITE
SECOND SUCCOR UPHOLD
COMFORT CONNIVE ESPOUSE
FORWARD FURTHER SUPPORT
SUSTAIN ADVOCATE BEFRIEND
ABETTING CONFEDERATE
ABETTOR FAUTOR ADVOCATE
PROMOTER
ABETO ACXOYATL
ABEYANCE ABEYANCY DORMANCY
ABEYANT LATENT
ABHOR UG IRK HATE SHUN AGRISE

DETEST LOATHE DESPISE DISLIKE
EXECRATE
ABHORRENCE HATE ODIUM HATRED
HORROR DISGUST DISLIKE
AVERSION LOATHING
ABHORRENT UGSOM HATEFUL
INFAMOUS
ABIDE BE WIN WON BEAR BIDE KEEP
LAST LEND LENG LIVE REST STAY
WAIT ABEAR AWAIT DELAY EXIST
HABIT PAUSE STAND SWELL TARRY
ENDURE HARBOR LINGER REMAIN
RESIDE SUBMIT INHABIT SOJOURN
SUBSIST SUSTAIN CONTINUE
TOLERATE
(— BY) HOLD
ABIDING FAST STABLE LASTING
ABIDINGNESS PERMANENCE
ABIES FIRS CONIFERS
ABIETATE SYLVATE
ABIGAIL MAID
(HUSBAND OF —) DAVID NABAL
ABIGEUS ABACTOR
ABIJAH (FATHER OF —) DAVID
(SON OF —) ASA
ABILITY G CAN MAY CLAY EASE
FORM HAND CLASS FLAIR FORCE
MIGHT POWER SKILL STUFF VERVE
ENERGY ENGINE MAUGHT STROKE
TALENT CALIBER CUNNING FACULTY
POTENCY APTITUDE CAPACITY
STRENGTH
(— TO ENTER) ACCESS
(— TO THROW) ARM
(BATTING —) STICKWORK
(CREATIVE —) IMAGINATION
(INVENTIVE —) CONTRIVANCE
(MENTAL —) INGENY BRAINPOWER
ABIPON CORONADO
ABJECT LOW BASE MEAN POOR
SUNK VILE HELOT PALTRY SORDID
SUPINE FAWNING FORLORN
IGNOBLE SERVILE SLAVISH
BEGGARLY CRINGING DEGRADED
DOWNCAST LISTLESS WRETCHED
ABJOINT ABSTRICT
ABJURE DENY NITTE SPURN ESCHEW
RECALL RECANT REJECT RESIGN
REVOKE ABANDON DISAVOW
EJURATE RETRACT ABNEGATE
DISCLAIM FORSWEAR RENOUNCE
ABLAUT APOPHONY
ABLAZE ALOW AFIRE ALOWE
ABLEEZE BURNING GLOWING
RADIANT GLEAMING INFLAMED
ABLE APT BIG CAN FIT FERE ADEPT
HABIL SMART THERE CLEVER
EXPERT FACILE FITTED HABILE
POTENT STRONG BASTANT
CAPABLE DOUGHTY DEXTROUS
POSSIBLE POWERFUL SKILLFUL
SUITABLE TALENTED VIGOROUS
(— TO WALK) FEERIE FEIRIE
ABLE-BODIED YAL YALD YAULD
ABLUTION BATH WIDU WUDU WUZU
LOTION BAPTISM BATHING WASHING
ABNAKI WABANAKI
ABNEGATE DENY ABJURE FOREGO
REFUSE REJECT DISAVOW DISCLAIM

FORSWEAR IMMOLATE RENOUNCE
ABNORMAL ENORM QUEER UTTER
ERRATIC UNUSUAL VICIOUS
ABERRANT ATYPICAL FREAKISH
ABNORMALITY ATAXY ATAXIA
LETHAL BROWNING DEMENTIA
ENORMITY
(**CATTLE** —) SAWDUST
ABOARD ON ONTO ACROSS
ATHWART
ABODE COT DAR HUT INN WON
BODE CELL FLAT HALL HOME NEST
OMEN REST SEAT TENT WOON
BEING BOWER DELAY HAUNT HOUSE
MANOR PITCH RESET SIEGE SUITE
ABIDAL BIDING ESTATE ADDRESS
COTTAGE HABITAT LODGING
MANSION SITTING CUNABULA
DOMICILE DWELLING RESIANCE
TENEMENT
(— **OF DEAD**) DAR AARU HELL
ARALU HADES ORCUS SHEOL
HEAVEN SHADES XIBALBA
(— **OF DELIGHT**) ELYSIUM
(— **OF EVIL POWERS**) ABYSS
(— **OF GODS**) MERU ASGARD
OLYMPUS
(— **OF LOST SOULS**) ABADDON
(— **OF SOULS**) LIMBO
(**ANIMAL** —) ZOO MENAGERIE
(**CELESTIAL** —) HEAVEN
(**FILTHY** —) STY STYE
(**MISERABLE** —) DOGHOLE
(**SHELTERED** —) SHADE
ABOLISH END BLOT KILL ABATE
ANNUL ERASE FORDO QUASH
CANCEL EFFACE FOREDO RECALL
REPEAL REVOKE VACATE DESTROY
NULLIFY RESCIND REVERSE
ABROGATE
ABOLITION EXTINCTION
ABOMA BOA BOM BOMA
ABOMASUM READ REED
ABOMINABLE VILE RUSTY ODIOUS
ROTTEN BEASTLY HATEFUL
HEINOUS MALEDICT
ABOMINABLY BEASTLY
ABOMINATE HATE ABHOR DETEST
LOATHE EXECRATE
ABOMINATION EVIL CRIME CURSE
HORROR PLAGUE DISGUST
AVERSION
ABONGO BABONGO
ABORAL DORSAL
ABORIGINAL ABO YAO FIRST NATAL
BINGHI NATIVE SAVAGE NATURAL
PRIMARY ORIGINAL
(— **WOMAN**) GIN
ABORIGINE KA KHA TODA ALFUR
BAIGA BLACK BOONG DASYU MAORI
MYALL ALFURO ARANDA ARANTA
ARUNTA BINGHI INDIAN KIPPER
KODAGA NATIVE SAVAGE ADIBASI
CHINHWAN WARRAGAL WARRIGAL
ABORT SLIP
ABORTION SLIP ABORT FAILURE
CASTLING FETICIDE MISBIRTH
ABORTIVE IDLE VAIN BLIND FUTILE
ABOUND SNY FLOW SNEE TEEM

COVER FLEET SWARM REDOUND
OVERFLOW
ABOUNDING RIFE FLUSH ROUTH
COPIOUS REPLETE TEEMING
ABUNDANT
ABOUT BY IN OF ON RE SAY AWAY
NEAR SOME UMBE UPON ANENT
ASTIR CIRCA ABROAD ACTIVE
ALMOST ANENST AROUND CIRCUM
TOWARD ENVIRON CIRCITER
ABOUT-FACE FLOP
ABOVE ON UP OER SUP ATOP OVER
PAST UPON ABEEN ABOON ABUNE
ALOFT SUPRA BEFORE BEYOND
HIGHER THEREUP OVERHEAD
SUPERIOR
(— **GENERAL LEVEL**) APART
ABRADE RAW RUB BARK FILE FRET
GALL RASP SAND WEAR CHAFE
ERASE GRATE GRAZE GRIND SCORE
TOUCH SCRAPE IRRITATE
ABRADER FILE RASP EMERY
SANDER ABRASER GRINDER
SCRAPER
ABRAHAM (**BIRTHPLACE OF** —) UR
(**BROTHER OF** —) HARAN NAHOR
(**CONCUBINE OF** —) HAGAR
(**FATHER OF** —) TERAH
(**GRANDFATHER OF** —) NAHOR
(**GRANDSON OF** —) ESAU
(**NEPHEW OF** —) LOT
(**SON OF** —) ISAAC MEDAN SHUAH
MIDIAN ZIMRAN ISHMAEL JOKSHAN
(**WIFE OF** —) SARAH KETURAH
ABRASION BURN GALL OUCH SCAR
SORE GRAZE BRUISE BLASTING
ABRASIVE SAND EMERY PUMICE
QUARTZ SILICA ALUNDUM ERODENT
ABRADANT CORUNDUM SCRUBBER
ABRAXAS GEM STONE AMULET
ABRASAX
ABREAST EVEN AFRONT BESIDE
HANGING
ABRET BREAD WAFER
ABRI SHED COVER DUGOUT SHELTER
ABRIDGE CUT DOCK LASK BRIEF
ELIDE LIMIT RASEE RAZEE BRIDGE
REDUCE SHRINK CURTAIL DEPRIVE
REWRITE SHORTEN ABSTRACT
BREVIATE COMPRESS CONDENSE
CONTRACT DIMINISH RETRENCH
SIMPLIFY
ABRIDGED TAIL
ABRIDGEMENT TAIL BRIEF DIGEST
PRECIS RESUME SKETCH COMPEND
EPITOME PANDECT SUMMARY
SUMMULA ABSTRACT BOILDOWN
BREVIARY SYNOPSIS
ABROAD OFF ASEA AWAY ABOUT
ASTIR FORTH ABREED AFIELD
ASTRAY WIDELY DISTANT OUTWARD
OVERSEA OFFSHORE
ABROGATE ANNUL QUASH REMIT
CANCEL REPEAL REVOKE VACATE
ABOLISH NULLIFY RESCIND
DISSOLVE OVERRULE
ABRUPT BOLD CURT DEAD FAST
RUDE BLUFF BLUNT BRIEF BRUSK
HASTY ICTIC QUICK ROUGH SHARP

SHEER SHORT STEEP STUNT SURLY
TERSE TOTAL CHOPPY CRAGGY
CRUSTY PROMPT RUGGED SUDDEN
ANGULAR BRUSQUE PRERUPT
VIOLENT HEADLONG VERTICAL
(**NOT** —) SOFT
ABRUPTLY BANG SHARP SHORT
STEEPLY SUDDENLY
ABSALOM (**FATHER OF** —) DAVID
(**SLAYER OF** —) JOAB
ABSAROKA CROW
ABSCESS BOIL MORO SORE ULCER
FESTER INCOME LESION QUINSY
VOMICA EXITURE GUMBOIL PARULIS
APOSTEME SQUINACY
ABSCISSA X COSINE
ABSCISSION APOCOPE
ABSCOND GO FLY RUN BOLT FLEE
HIDE QUIT ELOPE SCRAM SMOKE
DECAMP DEPART DESERT ELOINE
ESCAPE LEVANT WITHDRAW
ABSENCE CUT LACK VOID WANT
BLANK LEAVE DEFECT REMOVE
VACUUM DEFAULT FAILURE
VACANCY FURLOUGH
(— **FROM DUTY**) LIBERTY
(— **FROM ONE'S COUNTRY**) EXILE
(— **OF AN ORGAN**) AGENESIA
AGENESIS
(— **OF BIAS**) DETACHMENT
(— **OF CEREMONY**) FAMILIARITY
(— **OF FAMILIARITY**) DISTANCE
(— **OF FEELING**) APATHY
(— **OF FEVER**) APYREXY APYREXIA
(— **OF FORM**) ENTROPY
(— **OF GOVERNMENT**) ANARCHY
(— **OF INHIBITIONS**) ANIMALITY
(— **OF LIGHT**) BLACK DARKNESS
(— **OF MARRIAGE**) AGAMY
(— **OF MIND**) ABSTRACTION
(— **OF NAILS**) ANONYCHIA
(— **OF PAIN**) ANODYNIA
(— **OF PIGMENTATION**) ACHROMA
ACHROMIA
(— **OF SKULL**) ACRANIA
(— **OF TAIL**) ANURY
(— **OF TASTE**) AGEUSIA
(— **OF TRUMPS**) CHICANE
(— **OF TRUTH**) FALSEHOOD
ABSENT CUT OFF OUT AWAY AWOL
GONE LOST WANE DESERT MUSING
LACKING MISSING WANTING
ABSORBED DREAMING
(— **IN MIND**) ABSTRACT
ABSENTMINDED MUSING DISTRAIT
DREAMING
ABSENTMINDEDNESS STARGAZING
ABSINTHE AJENJO GENIPI
ABSOLUTE GOD ONE TAO TAT DEAD
DOWN FAIR FINE FREE MEAR MEER
MERE PLAT PLUM PURE RANK REAL
SELF TRUE VERY BLANK CLEAR
FIXED PLUMB SHEER STARK TOTAL
UTTER WHOLE ENTIRE SEVERE
SIMPLE SQUARE CERTAIN PERFECT
PLENARY ABSTRACT COMPLETE
DESPOTIC EVENDOWN EXPLICIT
IMPLICIT POSITIVE
(— **TEMPERATURE**) T

STORE ANLAGE BACKUP BUDGET
COLUMN DEBRIS GARNER BACKLOG
CUMULUS DEPOSIT DOSSIER
MORAINE DIVIDEND INTEREST
(— OF FLUID) EDEMA OEDEMA
ASCITES
(— OF FORCE) CHARGE
(— OF SNOW) ALIMENTATION
(— OF TRIFLES) FLOTSAM
(— ON CONCRETE) LAITANCE
ACCURACY NICETY FIDELITY
JUSTNESS
(HISTORICAL —) SYNCHRONISM
ACCURATE JUST LEAL NICE TRUE
CLOSE EXACT FLUSH RIGHT
NARROW PROPER SEVERE STRICT
CAREFUL CORRECT PRECISE
FAITHFUL PERQUEER PUNCTUAL
TRUTHFUL
(NOT —) IMPURE
(UNPLEASANTLY —) BRUTAL
ACCURATELY JUST FAIRLY JUSTLY
CLOSELY EXACTLY INSOOTH
ACCURSED FEY CURSED DAMNED
DOOMED FORBID SACRED WARIED
BLASTED MALEDICT
ACCUSATION BEEF WITE BLAME
CAUSE CRIME POINT WHITE APPEAL
ATTACK CHARGE THREAP THREEP
ACCUSAL SCANDAL DELATION
(FALSE —) SUGGESTION
ACCUSATORY WRAYFUL
ACCUSE TAX WRY CALL FILE NOTE
SHOW SLUR TASK WITE WRAY
ACOUP ARGUE BLAME PEACH TAINT
TOUCH WHITE APPEAL ATTACH
ATTACK BECALL BEWRAY CHARGE
DEFAME DELATE DETECT INDICT
INTENT MURMUR APPEACH ARRAIGN
ATTAINT CENSURE IMPEACH
IMPLEAD TRADUCE CHASTISE
DENOUNCE QUESTION REDARGUE
REPROACH
(— UNJUSTLY) SLANDER
ACCUSER CHARGER DELATOR
LIBELANT
ACCUSING CULPATORY
DENUNCIATORY
ACCUSTOM URE USE WIN WON
HAFT WONT ADAPT BREAK DRILL
ENURE FLESH HABIT HAUNT INURE
TRAIN ADDICT ADJUST CUSTOM
INDUCE SEASON CONSORT
EDUCATE TOUGHEN ACQUAINT
(— HORSE TO BIT) MOUTH
(— TO PASTURE) HAFT
ACCUSTOMED TAME USED WONE
WONT USANT USUAL INURED
CHRONIC CURRENT HABITED
CONSUETE
ACE AS ALS JOT ONE PIP TIB ATOM
CARD HERO MARK TOPS UNIT
ADEPT BASTO FLYER POINT BULLET
EXPERT AVIATOR BRISQUE
PARTICLE
(— OF CLUBS) BASTA BASTO
(— OF SPADES) SPADILLE SPADILLO
(— OF TRUMPS) TIB HONOR PUNTO
(THREE —S) GLEEK

ACEDIA SLOTH ACCIDIA ACCIDIE
ACEPHALOUS HEADLESS
ACER NEGUNDO
ACERB ACID HARD SOUR TART
ACRID HARSH SHARP BITTER
SEVERE
ACERBATE EMBITTER IRRITATE
ACERBITY ACRIMONY ASPERITY
SEVERITY TARTNESS
ACETABULUM PAN PYXIS CUPULE
ACETABLE HOLDFAST
ACETAL KETAL FORMAL KETATE
BUTYRAL
ACETALDEHYDE ETHYL ETHANAL
ALDEHYDE
ACETIC SOUR SHARP ZOONIC
ACETYLENE TOLAN ALKINE ALKYNE
ETHINE ETHYNE TOLANE
ACHE AKE NAG NIP ECHE GELL
HURT LONG PAIN PANG PINE RACK
WARK WERK HACHE SMART STANG
STOUN THROB THROE WARCH
DESIRE MISERY STITCH STOUND
TWINGE TWITCH ANGUISH EARACHE
SORENESS
ACHENE CYPSELA UTRICLE
ACHIEVE DO END GET WIN EARN
GAIN HACK HAVE MAKE FETCH
FORCE REACH SCORE AFFORD
ARRIVE ATTAIN EFFECT FINISH
OBTAIN CHEVISE COMPASS EXPLOIT
FULFILL PRODUCE REALIZE
SUCCEED TRIUMPH COMPLETE
CONCLUDE CONTRIVE
(— HARMONY) AGREE
(— ORIENTATION) ADJUST
ACHIEVEMENT ACT JOB DEED FEAT
WORK ACTION CAREER RESULT
EXPLOIT HARVEST FELICITY
ACHILLEA PTARMICA
ACHILLES PELIDES
(FATHER OF —) PELEUS
(FRIEND OF —) PATROCLUS
(HORSE OF —) XANTHUS
(MOTHER OF —) THETIS
(SLAYER OF —) PARIS
ACHIOTE OLEANA ACHUETE
ANNATTO ARNATTA ARNATTO
ACHRAS SAPOTA
ACHROMACYTE SHADOW
ACHROMATIC GRAY GREY NEUTRAL
ACICULAR SPLINTERY
ACID DRY YAR DIAL DOPA KEEN
PABA SOUR TART ACERB ACRID
ALGIN AMINO CERIN EAGER HARSH
LYSIN RHEIN SHARP ULMIC ABRINE
ALLIIN BITING BITTER GLYCIN
LYSINE PROLIN SERINE TWEAKY
VALINE ACERBIC ACETOSE CERASIN
FILICIN GLYCINE PROLINE STEARIN
VINEGAR
(NITRIC —) AQUAFORTIS
ACIDITY ACOR VERDURE ACERBITY
SOURNESS VERJUICE
ACKNOWLEDGE NOD OWN AVER
AVOW SIGN ADMIT ADOPT ALLOW
GRANT KITHE KYTHE THANK YIELD
ACCEDE ACCEPT AGNIZE ANSWER
ASSENT AVOUCH BEKNOW COUTHE

FATHER REWARD CONCEDE
CONFESS DECLARE OBSERVE
PROFESS DISCLOSE
ACKNOWLEDGEMENT GRANT
THANK AVOWAL CREDIT SHRIFT
APOLOGY AGNITION
ACLE AKLE IRUL JAMBA IRONWOOD
PYENGADU
ACLYS HURLBAT
ACME IT ACE CAP TOP APEX CULM
HIGH PEAK CREST PITCH POINT
STATE APOGEE CLIMAX COMBLE
CRISIS CULMEN HEIGHT HEYDAY
SUMMIT ZENITH CUMULUS SUBLIME
CAPSHEAF CAPSTONE PINNACLE
ACNE WHELK
ACOLYTE BOY HELPER NOVICE
SERVER LEARNER PATENER
ACOMIA BALDNESS
ACONITE BIKH ACONITUM NAPELLUS
ACORN NUT MAST GLAND OVEST
BELLOTA BELLOTE
(— CUPS) VALONIA
(PL.) MAST CAMATA PANNAGE
CAMATINA
ACORN-SHAPED BALANOID
ACOUSTICS SONICS PHONICS
ACQUAINT KNOW TELL TEACH
VERSE ADVISE INFORM NOTIFY
SCHOOL APPRISE APPRIZE POSSESS
RESOLVE
ACQUAINTANCE KITH HABIT
COUSIN FRIEND GOSSIP AFFINITY
FAMILIAR INTIMATE
(CLOSE —) HABIT INWARDNESS
(PRACTICAL —) PRACTICE PRACTISE
(PL.) KITH SOCIETY
ACQUAINTED ACQUENT VERSANT
ACQUIESCE BOW ABIDE AGREE
CHIME YIELD ACCEDE ACCEPT
ASSENT COMPLY CONCUR SUBMIT
CONCEDE CONFIRM CONFORM
CONSENT
ACQUIRE ADD BAG BUY GET WIN
EARN FORM GAIN GRAB HAVE MAKE
REAP ADOPT AMASS ANNEX BEGET
CHEVY CHIVY GLEAN LEARN REACH
SEIZE STEAL ATTAIN CHIVEY CHIVV
DERIVE EFFECT GARNER OBTAIN
SECURE SNATCH COLLECT
CONQUER DEVELOP PROCURE
RECEIVE CONTRACT
(— DESIRABLE QUALITY) AGE
(— KNOWLEDGE) LERE
ACQUISITION WIN GAIN LUCRE
ACQUEST ACQUIST GETTING
CONQUEST
(DISHONEST —) GRAFT
ACQUIT PAY FREE QUIT CLEAR
QUIET ASSOIL BEHAVE BESTOW
EXCUSE PARDON ABSOLVE
COMPORT CONDUCT RELEASE
REQUITE LIBERATE OVERLOOK
UNCHARGE
ACQUITTAL EXCUSE
ACQUITTANCE QUIETUS RELEASE
ACRE AKER LAND ACKER FIELD
STANG ARPENT COLLOP FARMHOL
(120 —S) HIDE

(2-3RDS —) COVER
(QUARTER —) ROOD
(PL.) ACREAGE
ACREMAN CARUCARIUS
ACRID HOT ACID BASK KEEN SOUR
HARSH ROUGH SHARP SURLY
BITING BITTER CAUSTIC PUNGENT
REEKING UNSAVORY VIRULENT
ACRIMONIOUS MAD ACID KEEN
ACRID ANGRY GRUFF HARSH IRATE
SHARP SNELL SURLY BITTER
CAUSTIC STINGING
ACRIMONY VIRUS PUNGENCY
SOURNESS
ACRISIUS (DAUGHTER OF —) DANAE
ACROBAT ZANY KINKER GYMNAST
TOPPLER TUMBLER BALANCER
ACROPOLIS FORT HILL POLIS
CADMEA CITADEL LARISSA
ACROSOME IDIOSOME IDIOZOME
ACROSS OVER SPAN YOND CROSS
ABOARD THWART ATHWART
OPPOSITE TRAVERSE
(CLEAN —) SHORT
ACROSTIC ABC AGLA DORA GAME
POEM TANAK PHRASE PUZZLE
TANACH
ACRYLIC PROPENOIC
ACT BE DO GO APE LAW LET ACTU
BILL COME DEAL DEED DORA FACT
FEAT HOCK JEST MAKE MOVE PART
PASS PLAY SKIT SLIM TAKE TURN
WORK ACTUS DRAMA EDICT EMOTE
ENTRY EXERT FEIGN GRACE KARMA
MODEL SCENE SHIFT STUNT ACTION
BEHAVE BESTIR DECREE DEMEAN
FACTUM MANAGE RAGMAN
COMPORT EXECUTE EXPLOIT
PERFORM PORTRAY PRETEND
STATUTE FUNCTION PRETENSE
SIMULATE
(— AFFECTEDLY) MIMP
(— AS WANTON) RIG
(— AWKWARDLY) HOCKER
(— BEFORE) ANTICIPATE
(— BLUNDERINGLY) BULL
(— DECEITFULLY) DOUBLE
(— DISHONESTLY) FUDGE
(— FOOLISHLY) FON FONNE FOLEYE
FOOTER FOOTLE
(— FRIVOLOUSLY) FRIVOL FRIBBLE
(— IN THEATER) GAFF
(— INDECISIVELY) DITHER
(— INDEPENDENTLY) SEVER
(— OF APPROVAL) EUGE
(— OF BEGGING) CADGE
(— OF CIVILITY) CURTSY DEVOIR
CURTSEY
(— OF KINDNESS) CARESS BENEFIT
(— OF LABOR) DILIGENCE
(— OF PRAYER) DEVOTION
(— OF STUPIDITY) BETISE
(— OF TRICKERY) COG
(— OUT) ENACT DRAMATIZE
(— PLAYFULLY) DALLY BANTER
(— QUICKLY) GIRD
(— RASHLY) RACKLE
(— SPORTIVELY) DAFF
(— SUDDENLY) FLASH

(— TIMIDLY) NESH
(— TOGETHER) AGREE COACT
CONCUR CONCORD
(— TRIFLINGLY) JANK
(— UP TO) EVEN
(— UPON) AFFECT HANDLE
(COMICAL —) JIG
(CONVENTIONAL —) AMENITY
(CORRUPT —) DEPRAVITY
(CRIMINAL —) INFAMY
(DARING —) ESCAPADE
(DECEITFUL —) ABUSE
(DECEPTIVE —) FEINT
(FAULTY —) PARAPRAXIS
(FOOLISH —) DIDO IDIOTISM
(FORBIDDEN —) CRIME
(FORMAL —) CEREMONY
(HABITUAL—) EXERCISE
(HASTY —) FLING
(HOSTILE —) BLOW
(INJURIOUS —) SPOIL
(LAUDATORY —) COUP
(LITURGICAL —) LAVABO
(LIVELY —) JIG
(MISCHIEVOUS —) DIDO CANTRAP
CANTRIP
(OFFENSIVE —) AFFRONT
(OFFICIAL —S) ACTA
(PLAYFUL —) RALLERY RAILLERY
(PRAISEWORTHY —) DEMERIT
(RUDE —) INCIVILITY
(SUDDEN VIOLENT —) BENSEL
BENSIL
(THOUGHTLESS —) FOLLY
(UNMANNERLY —) SOLECISM
(UNUSUAL —) STUNT
(VALOROUS —) WORSHIP
(VARIETY —) SKETCH
(WRONG —) DERELICT DERELICTUM
(PL.) DOINGS
ACTINAL ORAL
ACTING AGENT SERVING
(— AGAINST) ADVERSE
(— BY TURN) ALTERN
(— ODDLY) HAYWIRE
(— RAPIDLY) DRASTIC
(UNSKILLFUL —) BUNGLING
ACTINIAN OPELET VESTLET
ACTINOST RADIAL RADIALE
ACTINOZOAN SEAFLOWER
ACTION ACT AIR DAP JOB ACTO
CASE DEED FACT FRAY GEST PLAY
PLOY PUSH SHOW STEP SUIT WORK
ACTIO DOING EDICT FIGHT FLING
GESTE ISSUE THING TREAD VENUE
AFFAIR AGENCY BATTLE BEFOOT
COMBAT PRAXIS CONDUCT FACTION
GESTURE PROCESS TANQUAM
ACTIVITY BEHAVIOR BUSINESS
CONFLICT FUNCTION PRACTICE
PRACTISE
(— OF WIND) EOLATION
(ABSURD —S) BOSH
(ANTAGONISTIC —) ATOMISM
(BLAMEWORTHY —) WITE
(CAPRICIOUS —) FREAK
(COARSE —) HARLOTRY
(COOPERATIVE —) SYNERGISM
(COURT —) LAW SUIT ASSIZE

LAWSUIT QUERELA QUERELE
(CRUEL —) RUTH
(CUSTOMARY —) COURSE
(EXTEMPORE —) SCHEDIASM
(FINAL —) CATASTROPHE
(FOOLISH —) FOPPERY INEPTITUDE
(FRISKY —) FRISKIN
(FRIVOLOUS —) DALLIANCE
(IMPULSIVE —) STAMPEDE
(INITIAL —) LEADOFF INDUCTION
(JOINT —) COACTION
(LEGAL —) DEBT SUIT ACCOUNT
DETINET DETINUE
(MEAN —S) DOGGERY
(MILITARY —) SWEEP
(ODD —S) JIMJAMS
(PLAYFUL —) FUN FROLIC
(RASH —) HASTE
(REPEATED —) DRUM DOUBLE
(SUDDEN —) FLISK
(SYMBOLIC —) CHARADE
(TACTLESS —) GAUCHERIE
(UNAVOIDABLE —) FORCEPUT
(UNINTERMITTED —) HEAT
(VIOLENT —) HEAT AFFRAY
(WHIMSICAL —S) HUMORS
HUMOURS
(WILY —) WRINKLE
ACTIVATE SPARK ACTIFY ELICIT
ACTIVE UP YAL YAP YEP BUSY GAIN
LISH LIST PERT RASH SPRY TRIG
WHAT YALD YARE YEPE YERN
ABOUT AGILE ALERT ALIVE ASTIR
BRISK DEEDY FRESH LIGHT LINGY
LUSTY NIPPY PEART QUICK READY
SMART SNELL SPICY SPRIG STOUT
SWANK VIVID WIGHT YAULD YERNE
ACTUAL CLEVER DIRECT FEERIE
FEIRIE FIERCE HEARTY LIVELY
LIVING MOVING NIMBLE PROMPT
QUIVER SEMMIT SPEEDY SPRACK
SPROIL SPRUCE SPRUNT SWANKY
WIMBLE DASHING DEEDFUL DELIVER
DYNAMIC HOPPING HUMMING
KINETIC STHENIC THRODDY
YANKING ANIMATED ATHLETIC
BRAWLING DILIGENT SPIRITED
VIGOROUS
(NORMALLY —) ABOUT
ACTIVELY DOWN BUSILY DEEDILY
HEARTILY
ACTIVITY ACT ADO GOG VIR FIZZ
LIFE PLAY STIR BLAST CAPER
EVENT HEART RAJAS RALLY TRADE
VIGOR ACTION AGENCY BUSTLE
ENERGY HUSTLE SATTVA SPROIL
AGILITY CALLING BUSINESS
EXERCISE FUNCTION MOVEMENT
PARERGON STIRRING
(FUNCTIONAL —) SHOP
(MENTAL —) CONCEIT BRAINWORK
(SHARED —) COMMUNITY
(TROUBLESOME —) COIL
ACTON HOGTON HAQUETON
ACTOR HAM DOER HERO LEAD MIME
STAR AGENT COMIC DROLL EXTRA
HEAVY MIMIC PLANT SERIO SUPER
ARTIST COWBOY DISEUR FEEDER
FIDDLE MUMMER PLAYER PUPPET

STAGER TOMMER ARTISTE CABOTIN
DISEUSE HISTRIO PRIMOMO
ROSCIUS STORMER TROUPER
AISTEOIR COMEDIAN HISTRION
JUVENILE STROLLER THESPIAN
(INEPT —) HAM
(INFERIOR —) SHINE
ACTRESS DIVA STAR INGENUE
STARLET FARCEUSE THESPIAN
ACTUAL GOOD HARD REAL TRUE
VERY POSIT RIGHT BODILY FACTUAL
GENUINE CONCRETE DEFINITE
EXISTING MATERIAL POSITIVE
TANGIBLE
ACTUALITY FACT BEING VERITY
REALITY ENERGEIA REALNESS
ACTUALLY BUT DONE TRULY FAIRLY
ITSELF REALLY
ACTUATE ACT EGG RUN DRAW
MOVE URGE ENACT IMPEL ROUSE
START AROUSE COMPEL EXCITE
INCITE INDUCE AGITATE ANIMATE
ENLIVEN INSPIRE POINTED SHARPEN
MOTIVATE PERSUADE
ACUITY FINENESS
ACUMEN WIT INSIGHT CAPACITY
KEENNESS SAGACITY
ACUTE ACID FINE HIGH KEEN TART
HEAVY QUICK SHARP SMART SNACK
SNELL ARGUTE ASTUTE CRYING
SHREWD SHRILL SUBTLE TRELBE
URGENT CRUCIAL FEELING INTENSE
POINTED VIOLENT CRITICAL INCISIVE
POIGNANT
(MOST —) DIRE
(NOT —) SLOW GRAVE CHRONIC
ACUTENESS DEPTH SENSE ACUITY
ACUMEN NOSTRIL INCISION
SAGACITY SUBTLETY
(— OF SMELL) HYPEROSMIA
ACYCLIC SPIRAL ALIPHATIC
ADAD RAMMAN
ADAGE SAW DICT REDE TEXT WORD
AXIOM MAXIM MOTTO HOMILY
SAYING TRUISM WHEEZE BROMIDE
PRECEPT PROVERB APHORISM
APOTHEGM
ADAGIO ADAGE ADAGIETTO
ADAM ADE EDIE ADKIN
(GRANDSON OF —) ENOS ENOCH
(SON OF —) ABEL CAIN SETH
(TEACHER OF —) RAISEL
(WIFE OF —) EVE LILITH
ADAM-AND-EVE CRAWFOOT
ADAMANT FIRM GRIM HARD SOLID
STONY ADAMAS DIAMOND UNMOVED
OBDURATE SOLIDITY STUBBORN
ADAMANTINE FIRM BORON STONE
VAJRA ADAMANT
ADAMITE PICARD
ADAM'S APPLE GUZZLE
THROATBOLL
ADAM'S NEEDLE YUCCA
ADAPT APT FIT PLY PUT EDIT MOLD
SORT SUIT AGREE HUMOR INURE
SHAPE ADJUST CHANGE COMPLY
DERIVE DOCTOR HUMOUR TEMPER
ARRANGE CONFORM CONVERT
PREPARE QUALIFY ATTEMPER

CONTRIVE EQUALIZE REGULATE
ADAPTABILITY FLUIDITY ELASTICITY
ADAPTABLE LABILE ELASTIC
PLIABLE FLEXUOUS
ADAPTED FIT FOR FITTED SUITED
ADAPTER KIT ARRANGER
ADAXIAL SUPERIOR
ADD AD EIK EKE SAY SUM TOT CAST
FOOT GAIN JOIN LEND PLUS TOTE
AFFIX ANNEX GIVEN TOTAL UNITE
ACCRUE ADJECT APPEND ATTACH
CONFER FIGURE RECKON SUPPLY
ACCRETE AUGMENT COMBINE
COMPILE COMPUTE ENLARGE
SUBJOIN SUMMATE INCREASE
(— ALCOHOL) SPIKE
(— FUEL) BEET
(— IN WRITING) ASCRIBE
(— TO) ADORN ENRICH AUGMENT
(— UP) SUM TOT COUNT TOTAL
AMOUNT
(— WORT TO BEER) KRAUSEN
ADDA SCINK SKINK LIZARD
ADDAX PYGARG PYGARGUS
ADDED AND EKE PLUS ADJUNCT
(— SOMETHING) TILLY
ADDEND SUMMAND
ADDER ATHER KRAIT VIPER ELAPID
NADDER NEDDER ELAPOID
HAGWORM HYPNALE
ADDER'S-TONGUE LILY LILIUM
COXCOMB ROOSTERS
ADDICT FAN BUFF DOPE DOPY HYPE
USER COKEY COKIE FIEND HOPPY
HOUND JUNKY SLAVE BOTARY
DEVOTE JUNKER JUNKIE DELIVER
DEVOTEE HABITUE HOPHEAD
SNIFTER ACCUSTOM DOPEHEAD
SNOWBIRD
ADDICTED GIVEN PRONE HOOKED
BIBULOUS
ADDICTION HABIT MONKEY
BIBACITY
ADDITION AND EIK EKE ELL TAB
TOO ALSO ELSE GAIN PLUS AFFIX
RIDER ACCRUE AUGEND ENCORE
GANSEL INCOME PREFIX ADJUNCT
ADVANCE AUCTARY CODICIL
JOINING PENDANT UNITING
ADDENDUM INCREASE MANTISSA
(— TO ARTICLE) SHIRTTAIL
(— TO BEEHIVE) IMP
(— TO MASS) FARCE FARSE
(— TO PRICE) ADVANCE
(TRIVIAL —) FILIP FILLIP
ADDITIONAL NEW ELSE MORE
ADDED EXTRA FRESH OTHER
TIDDER TOTHER ANOTHER BESIDES
FURTHER
ADDITIVE CUMOL CUMENE
ADDLE EARN HOME IDLE MIRE
AMAZE FILTH RIPEN SPOIL CURDLE
MUDDLE THRIVE AGITATE CONFUSE
BEFUDDLE BEWILDER
ADDLED ASEA EMPTY PUTRID
MUDDLED UNSOUND
ADDRA DAMA NANGER
ADDRESS AIM SUE WOO BACK CALL
EASE HAIL HOME MINT PRAY TACT

TALK TULK TURN ABODE APPLY
BOARD COURT DRESS ELOGE
GREET POISE SKILL SPEAK TREAT
ACCOST ADJUST APPEAL BOUNCE
CHARGE DEVOTE DIRECT EULOGY
MANNER PARLEY SALUTE SERMON
SPEECH BEHIGHT CONDUCT
CONSIGN ENTRUST LECTURE
ORATION TUTOYER APPROACH
DEDICATE DELIVERY DISPATCH
FACILITY HARANGUE INSCRIBE
PETITION
(— FAMILIARLY) TOM TUTOYER
(— SAUCILY) CHYAK CHYACK
(METHOD OF —) TONE
(PULPIT —) KHUTBA KHUTBAH
ADDUCE BEAR CITE GIVE NAME
ALLAY ARGUE BRING INFER OFFER
QUOTE ALLEGE ASSIGN OBJECT
ADVANCE COUNTER MENTION
PRESENT
ADE SQUASH
ADEPS FAT LARD
ADEPT ACE APT ABLE HANDY
ADROIT ARTIST CRAFTY DEACON
EXPERT MASTER VERSED ANCIENT
CAPABLE DABSTER MAHATMA
DEXTROUS SKILLFUL
ADEQUATE DUE FIT ABLE FAIR FULL
GOOD MEET WELL AMPLE DIGNE
EQUAL COMMON DECENT ENOUGH
PROPER CONDIGN SUITABLE
ADHERE HEW HUG CLAG CLAM GLUE
HOLD JOIN KEEP LINK AFFIX APPLY
CLEAM CLING STICK UNITE ATTACH
CEMENT CLEAVE COHERE FREEZE
ACCRETE ANNERRE PERSIST
ADHERENCE CLING ADHESION
ARIANISM FIDELITY
ADHERENT IST ITE AIDE ALLY JAIN
SIKH ADEPT BAHAI BLACK BONPA
DEIST JAINA SIDER SPIKE STOOP
FACTOR KIRKER VOTARY APRISTA
BAHAIST CHANIST FASCIST FLACIAN
GNOSTIC NICAEAN OWENIAN
SECTARY SEQUELA THOMIST
AGATHIST BELIEVER BUDDHIST
CABALIST DISCIPLE FAITHFUL
FATALIST FOLLOWER HUMANIST
HYLICIST IMPERIAL PARTISAN
RETAINER SERVITOR SOCINIAN
UPHOLDER
(PL.) FOLD FOLLOWING
ADHESION BLOCKING STICKAGE
SYNECHIA
ADHESIVE GUM WAX BOND CLAM
GLUE SIZE TAPE DABBY DAUBY
PASTE TACKY BINDER CEMENT
CLINGY GLUTEN MASTIC PLUCKY
SMEARY STICKY HOTMELT
MUCILAGE
ADHIBIT USE ADMIT AFFIX APPLY
ATTACH
ADIANTUM MAIDENHAIR
ADIEU ADEW ADDIO ADIOS LEAVE
FAREWELL
ADIPOSE FAT HARD SUET FATTY
OBESE PURSY SQUAT TALLOW
ADIT DOOR ENTRY SOUGH STULM

ACCESS TUNNEL PASSAGE APPROACH ENTRANCE

ADJACENT NEAR NIGH CLOSE FLUSH HANDY BESIDE NEARBY MEETING VICINAL ABUTTING TOUCHING

ADJECTIVE ADNOUN DIPTOTE EPITHET MONINAL MODIFIER

ADJOIN ADD ABUT BUTT JOIN LINE TACK COAST MARCH TOUCH UNITE ACCOST APPEND ATTACH BORDER CONTACT

ADJOURN END MOVE RISE STAY ARISE CLOSE DEFER DELAY RECESS SUSPEND DISSOLVE POSTPONE PROROGUE

ADJUDGE TRY DEEM FIND GIVE HOLD RATE ALLOT AREAD AREED AWARD GRANT JUDGE ORDER ADDEEM ADDICT ASSIGN DECERN DECIDE DECREE ORDAIN REGARD BEHIGHT CONDEMN SENTENCE
(— GUILTY) DAMN
(— NOT GUILTY) ABSOLVE

ADJUDICATE ACT TRY HEAR PASS RULE JUDGE DECIDE ESTEEM RECKON REGARD SETTLE ADJUDGE CONSIDER SENTENCE

ADJUNCT AID HELP PART WORD ANNEX DEVICE PHRASE ADJOINT ANCILLA EPITHET FITTING GARNISH PERTAIN TEACHER ADDITION ADDITIVE APPANAGE APPENDIX ORNAMENT

ADJURATION OATH APPEAL SWEARING

ADJURE ASK BEG BID BIND ETHE PRAY CRAVE PLEAD SWEAR APPEAL CHARGE BESEECH COMMAND CONJURE CONTEST ENTREAT REQUEST UNSWEAR

ADJUST FIT FIX SET CAST EASE FORM FREE GEAR JUST LINE PARE RATE SIZE SORT SUIT TRAM TRIM TRUE ADAPT ADMIT ALIGN ALINE ANGLE EQUAL FRAME PATCH RANGE RIGHT SHAPE ACCORD ATTUNE HAMMER JUSTEN SETTLE SQUARE TEMPER WANGLE ADDRESS ARRANGE BALANCE CHANCER COMPOSE CONCERT CONFORM CORRECT DISPOSE JUSTIFY PREPARE RECTIFY COMPOUND REGULATE
(— A LOOM) GATE
(— SAIL) FLATTEN

ADJUSTED KEYED

ADJUSTER FIXER FITTER ASSESSOR

ADJUSTMENT FIT GEAR TRIM FITNESS FITTING CHANCERY

ADJUTANT AIDE ALLY STORK ARGALA HELPER HURGILA MARABOU OFFICER

ADJUVANT AIDE HELPER ADJUNCT HELPFUL

AD-LIB FAKE

ADMAN HUCKSTER

ADMEASURE METE

ADMETUS (WIFE OF —) ALCESTIS

ADMINISTER DO RUN DEAL DEEM DOSE GIVE MOVE RULE APPLY SERVE TREAT DIRECT GOVERN MANAGE SETTLE SUPPLY TENDER ADHIBIT CONDUCE CONDUCT CONTROL EXECUTE EXHIBIT FURNISH HUSBAND DISPENSE MINISTER
(— FORCIBLY) HAND
(— SACRAMENT) BISHOP HOUSEL

ADMINISTRATION HELM RULE SWAY POLICY TAHSIL CONDUCT DIOCESE ECONOMY RECTORY REGIMEN CARRIAGE DISPOSAL MINISTRY
(— OF OATH) JURATION
(REVENUE —) HACIENDA

ADMINISTRATOR CAID HELM QAID GABBAI MANAGER TRUSTEE DIRECTOR EXECUTOR MINISTER PROVICAR
(INCA —) CURACA
(MORMON —) APOSTLE

ADMIRABLE FINE GOOD HIGH GRAND GREAT LUMMY PROUD DIVINE AMIABLE CAPITAL ELEGANT MIRANDA RIPPING

ADMIRAL FLAG AMREL AMRELLE FLAGMAN GENERAL

ADMIRATION FUROR GLORY ESTEEM LIKING WONDER CONCEIT WORSHIP
(— FOR BIGNESS) JUMBOISM

ADMIRE DIG LIKE LOVE ADORE EXTOL HONOR PRIZE VALUE ESTEEM MARVEL REGARD REVERE WONDER ADULATE APPROVE DELIGHT IDOLIZE RESPECT VENERATE

ADMIRER FAN BEAU LOVER SWAIN AMATEUR DEVOTEE FOLLOWER IDOLATOR
(PL.) FOLLOWING

ADMISSION FEE ADIT CALL ENTRY ACCESS CHARGE ENTREE TICKET APOLOGY CONSENT INGRESS ENTRANCE
(— TO BAR) CALL

ADMIT KEN LET OWN AVER AVOW BEAR TAKE AGREE ALLOW ENTER GRANT IMMIT INLET ACCEDE ACCEPT ADJUST ASSENT AVOUCH ENROLL INCUCT PERMIT SUFFER ADHIBIT CONCEDE CONFESS INCLUDE PROFESS RECEIVE SUFFICE INITIATE
(— AS MEMBER) INDUCT
(— AS VALID) SUSTAIN

ADMITTANCE ACCESS ADMITTY ENTRANCE

ADMIX DALLOP DOLLOP

ADMIXTURE DASH ALLOY BLEND SHADE SPICE TINGE DALLOP DOLLOP FLAVOR LEAVEN STREAK MIXTURE SOUPCON COMPOUND INFUSION

ADMONISH WARN CHIDE SCOLD ADVISE ENJOIN EXHORT NOTIFY REBUKE REMIND SCHOOL CAUTION COUNSEL MONITOR REPROVE

ADMONITION ITEM ADVICE CAVEAT HOMILY CAUTION LECTURE REPROOF WARNING DOCUMENT REMINDER

ADNATE ADHERENT EPIGYNOUS
(— TO CALYX) INFERIOR

ADO DO COIL DEED FUSS ROUT STIR WORK HURRY TOUSE TOWSE BOTHER BUSTLE EFFORT FLURRY HUBBUB POTHER RUCKUS BLATHER BLETHER SPUTTER TROUBLE TURMOIL BUSINESS

ADOBE MUD CLAY DOBE DOBY SILT BRICK DOBIE TAPIA MUDCAP

ADOLESCENCE TEENS YOUTH NONAGE PUBERTY MINORITY

ADOLESCENT LAD YOUNG YOUTH IMMATURE TEENAGER

ADONIS ADON
(MOTHER OF —) MYRRH MYRRHA

ADOPT TAKE STEAL ACCEPT ASSUME ATTACH BORROW CHOOSE FATHER FOLLOW FOSTER MOTHER ACQUIRE EMBRACE ESPOUSE RECEIVE WELCOME ADVOCATE ARROGATE MAINTAIN

ADOPTION ESPOUSAL
(— OF DEBTS) ASSUMPTION

ADORABLE LOVELY LOVABLE CHARMING

ADORATION HOMAGE WORSHIP DEVOTION
(— OF GOD) LOVE

ADORE DOTE LAUD LOVE EXALT EXTOL HONOR WURTH ADMIRE ESTEEM PRAISE REVERE GLORIFY IDOLIZE WORSHIP VENERATE

ADORN DUB FIG GEM ORN SET BEAD BUSK DECK DILL DINK FOIL GAUD GILD LACE OUCH PICK PINK STUD SWAG TRIM ADORE ANORN ARRAY BEDUB BEGEM BELAY BRAVE CROWN DIGHT DRAPE DRESS FRONT GRACE HIGHT INLAY JEWEL MENSK PRANK PRICK PRIDE PRIMP PRINK ROUGE SPLAY SPRIG TRICK ATTIRE ATTRAP BECOME BEDECK BETRIM BLAZON BROOCH CLOTHE COLLAR DAMASK DIADEM EMBOSS ENAMEL ENRICH ENROBE FIGURE FINIFY FRIEZE FRINGE GRAITH INSTAL INVEST ORNIFY POUNCE QUAINT STATUE SUBORN TASSEL APPAREL BEDIGHT BEDIZEN COMMEND CORONET DEPAINT DIGNIFY EMPEARL FEATHER FOLIAGE FURNISH GARNISH GLORIFY GRATIFY IMPLUME SPANGLE VARNISH BEAUTIFY DECORATE EMBLAZON FLOURISH ORNAMENT SPLENDOR

ADORNED CLAD BESEEN DAEDAL ORNATE PICKED BRAIDED CLOTHED COLORED DAISIED FIGURED
(SHOWILY —) BEPRANKED

ADORNMENT TIRE ADORN DRESS PRIDE BEAUTY DECORE TAHALI TINSEL DECKING OUNDING

PRANKING TIREMENT
ADRIFT ASEA LOST AWAFT LIGAN
LOOSE AFLOAT DERELICT FLOATING
UNMOORED
ADROIT DEFT EASY FEAT GOOD
NEAT SLIM ADEPT HANDY READY
SMART SNACK TIGHT TRICK ARTFUL
CLEVER EXPERT HABILE NIMBLE
CUNNING DEXTROUS HANDSOME
SKILLFUL
ADROITNESS ART EASE TACT
KNACK SKILL ADDRESS FACILITY
ADSORBENT BASE EARTH SILICA
ADULATE FAWN LAUD GLOSS GLOZE
PRAISE FLATTER
ADULATION GLOSE GLOZE PRAISE
FLATTERY
ADULT MAN FULL MANLY MATURE
EPHEBIC GROWNUP THRIVEN
ADULTERANT DOPE ALMEIDINA
ADULTERATE CUT MIX CARD DASH
LOAD ABUSE ALLOY HOCUS TAINT
DEACON DEBASE DEFILE DILUTE
EXTEND MANAGE WEAKEN BASTARD
CORRUPT FALSIFY VITIATE
DENATURE IMPURIFY SPURIOUS
ADULTERATED CUT SHAM IMPURE
CORRUPT SPURIOUS
ADULTEROUS ERRING
ADULTERY AVOUTRY CUCKOLDOM
ADUMBRATE IMAGE SHADE VAGUE
OBSCURE SUGGEST INTIMATE
ADUMBRATION SHADE SHADOW
PHANTASM
ADUNCOUS BENT HOOKED
ADUST BURNT FIERY GLOOMY
SALLOW PARCHED SCORCHED
SUNBURNT
ADVANCE GO AID PAY SOP WAY
BULL CITE COME DASH GAIN HELP
INCH LAUD LEND LIFT LOAN MARK
MOVE NEAR NOSE PASS PUSH RISE
SHOW STEP WORM AVANT BOOST
BRING CREEP ENTER EXALT EXTOL
FAVOR FORGE MARCH OFFER
PLACE RAISE SERVE SPEED STAIR
STAKE THROW ADDUCE ADMOVE
ALLEGE AMOUNT ASSIGN ASSIST
AVAUNT BETTER DEGREE EXTEND
FAVOUR GROWTH HASTEN INCEDE
INROAD PREFER PREPAY SCHOOL
STRIDE STRIKE THRIVE VAUNCE
BENEFIT DEVELOP ELEVATE
ENHANCE FORTHGO FORWARD
FURTHER HEADWAY IMPREST
IMPROVE PROCEED PROCESS
PROMOTE PROMOVE PROPOSE
PROSPER PROVECT SUCCEED
ADDITION DEVELOPE HEIGHTEN
INCREASE PROGRESS
(— BY CUTTING) DRIVE
(— BY LEAPS) SALTATION
(— IN LIFE) WAY
(— LABORIOUSLY) STRIVE
(— OBLIQUELY) SIDLE
(— ONE'S POINT) TAKE
(— SLOWLY) INCH WORM CRAWL
CREEP
(— WAVERINGLY) HOBBLE

(— WITH EFFORT) DRAG
(DIFFICULT —) SLOG
(GRADUAL —) ILLAPSE
(STEADY —) SWING
(SUDDEN —) SHOOT
(VIGOROUS —) SWING
(PL.) APPROACHES
ADVANCED FAR DEEP GONE HIGH
LATE AHEAD OUTER FORWARD
IMPREST LIBERAL VANWARD
FOREMOST
(— IN AGE) DEEP ANTIQUATED
(— IN YEARS) SENIOR AGEABLE
ELDERLY
(MOST —) EXTREME FARTHEST
FOREMOST HEADMOST
(WELL —) AGED
ADVANCEMENT UP GOOD ASCENT
INCREASE
ADVANTAGE AD BOT USE VAN BEST
BOOT BOTE DRAW DROP EDGE
GAIN GOOD HANK JUMP MEND
NOTE ODDS PULL SAKE VAIL AVAIL
BULGE BUNCE FAVOR FRAME FRUIT
KINCH LAUGH SPEED START STEAD
USAGE BEHALF BEHOOF BETTER
CARROT EFFECT PROFIT ACCOUNT
BENEFIT EXPLOIT FORDEAL
FURTHER PROMOTE UTILITY
VANTAGE HANDICAP INTEREST
LEVERAGE OVERHAND OVERPLUS
(ACCIDENTAL —) FLUKE
ADVANTAGEOUS GOOD JOLI WELL
JOLIE GOLDEN PLUMMY SPEEDY
USEFUL ELIGIBLE
ADVENT COMING INCOME ARRIVAL
APPROACH PAROUSIA
ADVENTITIOUS CASUAL FOREIGN
STRANGE ACQUIRED EPISODIC
ADVENTURE GEST LARK RISK SEEK
WAGE EVENT GESTE PERIL QUEST
AUNTER AUNTRE CHANCE DANGER
HAZARD EMPRISE EMPRIZE
FORTUNE VENTURE ESCAPADE
JEOPARDY
ADVENTURER ROUTIER ARGONAUT
ADVENTURESS DEMIREP
DEMIMONDAINE
ADVENTUROUS RASH DARING
ERRANT AUNTROUS RECKLESS
ADVERSARY FOE ENEMY RIVAL
SATAN FOEMAN OPPONENT
(— OF GOD) DEVIL
ADVERSE FOE ILL EVIL CROSS
LOATH THRAW AVERSE INFEST
WITHER AWKWARD COUNTER
DIVERSE FROWARD HOSTILE
OPPOSED CONTRARY INIMICAL
OF POSING OPPOSITE OVERWART
THRAWART
ADVERSITY ILL WOE DECAY NIGHT
MISERY SORROW WITHER ILLNESS
TROUBLE CALAMITY DISTRESS
ADVERT HEED AVERT RECUR REFER
ALLUDE ATTEND RETURN REVERT
OBSERVE CONSIDER
ADVERTISE CRY BARK BILL CALL
PLUG PUFF STAR WARN BLURB
INFORM NOTIFY PARADE DECLARE

DISPLAY OBSERVE PLACARD
PUBLISH ANNOUNCE PROCLAIM
ADVERTISED AFFICHE
ADVERTISEMENT AD BILL SIGN
BLURB CHANT ADVERT CACHET
DODGER NOTICE POSTER TEASER
AFFICHE PLACARD STUFFER
CIRCULAR HANDBILL
ADVERTISING BUSH BILLING
PUFFERY
ADVICE AVIS AVYS LORE NEWS
REDE AVYSE STEER ADVISO DEVICE
NOTICE CAUTION COUNSEL OPINION
TIDINGS GUIDANCE MONITION
(PL.) INFORMATION
ADVISABLE BOOK PROPER PRUDENT
ADVISE SAY READ REDE TELL VISE
WARN WISE AREAD AREED COACH
GUIDE WEISE WEIZE ADJURE
ADVISO BEREDE CONFER DEVISE
EXHORT INFORM PONDER REVEAL
APPRISE APPRIZE COUNSEL
ACQUAINT ADMONISH CONSIDER
(— AGAINST) DISSUADE
ADVISED DELIBERATE
ADVISER AIDE TOUT COACH COMES
TUTOR DOCTOR EGERIA LAWYER
NESTOR ADVISOR MONITOR
STARETS TEACHER ATTORNEY
CROUPIER DIRECTOR FIELDMAN
PREACHER
ADVISORY URGING PRUDENT
ADVOCACY BOOM FAVOR AVOWRY
FAVOUR ARIANISM
ADVOCATE PRO ABET BACK URGE
VOGT ACTOR ADOPT FAVOR PLEAD
ASSERT AVOWRY BACKER DEFEND
IDEIST LAWYER PATRON SYNDIC
ABETTOR APOSTLE DECLAIM
ENDORSE ESPOUSE EXPOUND
FASCIST GOLDBUG PATRIOT
PLEADER PROCTOR SCHOLAR
SUPPORT ATTORNEY CHAMPION
CLUBBIST DEFENSOR HUMANIST
PARTISAN PREACHER
(— OF REVOLT) ANARCH
ADVOWSON ADVOCACY TENEMENT
ADZ AX AXE ADZE EDGE ADDIS
ADDICE EATCHE THIXLE HATCHET
AEACUS (FATHER OF —) ZEUS
(SON OF —) PELEUS TELAMON
AECIUM CAEOMA
AEETES (DAUGHTER OF —) MEDEA
AEGEAN SEA (ANCIENT PEOPLE OF
—) PSARA PSYRA SAMIAN LELEGES
SAMIOTE
(GULF OF —) SAROS
(ISLAND OF —) COS IOS KEOS NIOS
RODI SCIO CHIOS LEROS MELOS
NAXOS PAROS PATMO SAMOS
SIROS TENOS THERA ANDROS
IKARIA IMBROS LEMNOS LESBOS
RHODES SKYROS
(RIVER INTO —) STRUMA VARDAR
MARISTA
(TOWN ON —) CHIOS VATHY
MYTILENE
AEGEON (WIFE OF —) AEMILIA
AEGIR HLER GYMIR

(WIFE OF —) RAN

AEGIRITE ACMITE

AEGIS EGIS SHIELD AUSPICE
DEFENCE DEFENSE

AEGISTHUS (FATHER OF —)
THYESTES

AEGYPTUS (BROTHER OF —)
DANAUS
(FATHER OF —) BELUS

AENEAS (COMPANION OF —)
ACHATES
(FATHER OF —) ANCHISES
(GREAT-GRANDSON OF —) BRUT
(MOTHER OF —) VENUS APHRODITE
(SON OF —) IULUS ASCANIUS
(WIFE OF —) CREUSA LAVINIA

AENGUS (MOTHER OF —) BOANN

AEOLUS (DAUGHTER OF —) CANACE
ALCYONE HALCYONE
(FATHER OF —) HIPPOTES
(SON OF —) SISYPHUS

AEON AGE EON ERA AION AEVUM
CYCLE KALPA PERIOD
(PAIR OF —S) SYZYGY

AEPYTUS (FATHER OF —)
CRESPHONTES
(MOTHER OF —) MEROPE

AERATE AERIFY CHARGE INFLATE

AERIAL AERY AIRY TWIN AERIE
LOFTY UNREAL ANTENNA ETHEREAL

AERIALIST FLIER FLYER

AERIE AERY AIRE AYRE EYRY NEST
AIERY BROOD EYRIE

AERIFORM UNREAL GASEOUS

AEROBE BACTERIUM

AERODROME AIRPORT AIRFIELD

AEROEMBOLISM BENDS

AEROLITE AEROLITH

AERONAUT PILOT SKYMAN

AERONAUTICS AVIATION

AEROSE BRASSY

AEROSTAT AIRSHIP BALLOON
AIRCRAFT

AERUGO RUST PATINA

AESON (BROTHER OF —) PELIAS
(FATHER OF —) CRETHEUS
(SON OF —) JASON
(WIFE OF —) ALCIMEDA

AESTHETIC ARTISTIC ESTHETIC
TASTEFUL

AETA ITA

AETOLUS (FATHER OF —) ENDYMION
(SON OF —) CALYDON PLEURON
(WIFE OF—) PRONOE

AFAR OFF AWAY SAHO FERNE
FERREN REMOTE YFERRE DANAKIL
DANKALI DISTANT

AFARA LIMBA

AFFABLE FAIR OPEN CIVIL FRANK
SUAVE BENIGN FACILE FORTHY
GENIAL URBANE AMIABLE CORDIAL
GENERAL LIKABLE CHARMING
FAMILIAR FRIENDLY GRACIOUS
PLEASANT SOCIABLE TOWARDLY

AFFAIR DO JOB PIE BLOW CASE
DUEL GEAR PLOY BRAWL CAUSE
EVENT FIGHT LEVEE PARTY THING
ACTION BATTLE BEHALF DOMENT
EFFEIR MATTER SETOUT SHAURI

BLOWOUT CONCERN FUNERAL
HOEDOWN JOURNEY LIAISON
PALAVER SHEBANG BUSINESS
COMETHER ENDEAVOR HYPOTHEC
INTRIGUE OCCASION
(CONFUSED —) SCHEMOZZLE
(CRITICAL —) KANKEDORT
(LOVE —) LOVE AMOUR INTRIGUE
(SOCIAL —) FORMAL JUNKET
SUPPER
(STATE —S) ESTATE
(PL.) SQUARES

AFFECT AIL AIR HIT BEAR MELT
MOVE POSE RINE SHAM STIR SWAY
ALLOT ALTER ANNOY COLOR DRIVE
FANCY FEIGN HAUNT IMPEL MINCE
SHOCK TOUCH ASPIRE ASSIGN
ASSUME CHANGE DESIRE MOLEST
SOFTEN STRIKE THRILL ATTAINT
ATTINGE BEWITCH CONCERN
EMOTION FEELING IMPRESS
OPERATE PASSION PRETEND
PROFESS ALLOCATE DISPOSED
FREQUENT INTEREST SIMULATE
(— BY HANDLING) TOUCH
(— FAVORABLY) LIKE
(— INJURIOUSLY) INTERESS
(— STRONGLY) HIT HOLD SURPRISE

AFFECTATION AIR POSE SHAM
FRILL GRACE MINCE CHICHI
DISPLAY FOPPERY FROUNCE
GRIMACE PIETISM FONDNESS
PRETENSE PUPPYISM
(PL.) LUGS

AFFECTED MOY AIRY FEAT AILED
APISH MOVED POSEY CHICHI
FALLAL FEISTY FORMAL QUAINT
SEIZED FEIGNED MINIKIN MISSISH
REACHED SMITTEN STILTED
TAFFETA TAFFETY TOUCHED
INVOLVED PRECIEUX
(— BY DECAY) DOTY

AFFECTING AIRIFIED POIGNANT
TOUCHING

AFFECTION LOVE WAFF ALOHA
AMOUR FLAME HEART CHERTE
DOTAGE ESTEEM HYDROA MALADY
REGARD THRUSH AILMENT CHARITY
EMOTION FEELING SYMPTOM
CHLOASMA DEARNESS DEVOTION
FONDNESS KINDNESS MELICERA
TENDENCY
(PARENTAL —) STORGE
(PL.) HEART HEARTSTRINGS

AFFECTIONATE DEAR FOND WARM
ARDENT DOTING LOVING TENDER
AMOROUS DEVOTED EARNEST
ZEALOUS ATTACHED PARENTAL
SISTERLY

AFFECTIVE SENSIBLE

AFFERENT BEAR ESODIC SENSORY
ADVEHENT INFERENT

AFFIANCE AFFY FAITH TRUST
ASSURE ENGAGE ENSURE FIANCE
PLEDGE PLIGHT SPOUSE BETROTH
PROMISE CONTRACT RELIANCE

AFFIANCED INTENDED

AFFIANT DEPONENT AFFIDAVIT

AFFIDAVIT DAVY OATH AFFIANT

AFFIDAVY AFFYDAVY

AFFILIATE ALLY UNIT ADOPT MERGE
UNITE ATTACH BRANCH RELATE
ASCRIBE CHAPTER CONNECT
FILIATE

AFFINITY KIN TELE FAMILY LIKING
AVIDITY CHEMISM KINDRED KINSHIP
RAPPORT ALLIANCE GOSSIPRY
HOMOLOGY RELATION SYMPATHY

AFFIRM PUT AFFY AVER AVOW TAKE
POSIT STATE SWEAR TRUTH VOUCH
ALLEGE ASSERT ATTEST AVOUCH
DEPOSE RATIFY SUBMIT THREAP
THREEP VERIFY ASSEVER CONFIRM
DECLARE PROFESS PROTEST
TESTIFY MAINTAIN

AFFIRMATION SAY VOW YES AMEN
OATH WORD DIXIT PONENT THESIS
AVERRAL AVERMENT

AFFIRMATIVE AY AYE NOD YAH YEA
YEP YES AMEN ATEN YEAH
DOGMATIC POSITIVE

AFFIX ADD FIX PEN PIN SET CASE
CLIP FAST JOIN NAIL SEAL SIGN
ANNEX INFIX STAMP UNITE ANCHOR
APPEND ATTACH FASTEN SETTLE
STAPLE ADHIBIT CONNECT ENTITLE
FORMANT IMPRESS PLASTER
SUBJOIN

AFFLATUS FURY FUROR FRENZY
VISION IMPULSE

AFFLICT AIL RUE TRY VEX COMB
FIRE HOLD HURT PAIN PINE RACK
TUKE ARRAY BESET CURSE GRILL
GRIPE HARRY PINCH PRESS SEIZE
SMITE TRYST VISIT WOUND BURDEN
GRIEVE HARASS HUMBLE INFECT
MOLEST PESTER REMORD SCORCH
STRAIN STRESS STRIKE CHASTEN
INFLICT OPPRESS SCOURGE
TORMENT TROUBLE DISTRESS
LACERATE STRAITEN

AFFLICTED JOB SAD SORRY AILING
WOEFUL GRIEVED HAUNTED
SMITTEN IMPAIRED STRICKEN
TROUBLED

AFFLICTION WOE EVIL LOSS PAIN
SORE TEEN TRAY ASSAY CROSS
GRIEF PRESS SMART STOUR
BUFFET DURESS MISERY PATHOS
PLAGUE SORROW STRESS THRONG
AILMENT DISEASE ILLNESS PASSION
PURSUIT SCOURGE TORTURE
TROUBLE CALAMITY DISTRESS
HARDSHIP SEVERITY SICKNESS
VEXATION

AFFLICTIVE SAD DIRE SORE SOUR
HEAVY SEVERE

AFFLUENCE EASE AFFLUX INFLUX
PLENTY RICHES WEALTH FORTUNE
OPULENCE

AFFLUENT FAT RICH FLUSH RIVER
STEAM BRANCH SPRUIT COPIOUS
FLOWING HALCYON OPULENT
WEALTHY ABUNDANT INFLUENT

AFFORD GO BEAR GIVE LEND GRANT
INCUR OFFER STAND THOLE YIELD
CONFER ENDURE MANAGE SUPPLY
ACHIEVE FORWARD FURNISH

FURTHER PRODUCE PROVIDE MINISTER

AFFRAY FEUD FRAY RIOT ALARM BRAWL BROIL CLASH FIGHT MELEE SCARE SPURN ATTACK BATTLE COMBAT EFFRAY ENFRAI FRIGHT STRIFE TERROR TUMULT ASSAULT CONTEST QUARREL SCUFFLE STARTLE FRIGHTEN STRUGGLE

AFFRIGHT COW FEAR AGAST ALARM DAUNT DOUBT DREAD SCARE AGRISE APPALL DISMAY CONFUSE STARTLE TERRIFY FRIGHTEN

AFFRONT CUT DEFY SLAP ABUSE BEARD PEEVE HARASS INJURE INSULT NETTLE OFFEND SLIGHT STRUNT ASSAULT OFFENCE OFFENSE OUTRAGE PROVOKE CONFRONT DISGRACE ILLTREAT IRRITATE

AFFUSION POURING INFUSION

AFGHAN RUG GHAN COVER DURANI HASARA HAZARA BLANKET PAKHTON PAKHTUN PUKHTON ACHAKZAI COVERLET

AFGHAN FOX CORSAC CORSAK

AFGHANISTAN
CAPITAL: KABUL
COIN: PUL ABBASI AMANIA AFGHANI
LANGUAGE: DARI PASHTO PUSHTU BALOCHI BALUCHI
MEASURE: JERIB KAROH
MOUNTAIN: KOH SAFEO CHAGAI PAMIRS SULAIMAN HIMALAYAS
NATIVE: SISTANI
PARLIAMENT: SHURA
PROVINCE: GHOR FARAH HERAT KABUL KUNAR KUNUZ LOGAR ZABUL GHAZNI KAPISA PARWAN WARDAK
RIVER: LORA OXUS CABUL FARAH HARUT INDUS KABUL KHASH KUNAR KOKCHA KUNDUZ HELMUND MURGHAB
SEA: DARYA
TOWN: RUI JURM NANI WAMA ASMAR BALKH DOSHI KABUL KUNAR MARUF MATUN MUKUR PAHRA TULAK URGAN CHAMAN KUNDUZ NAUZAD PANJAO RUSTAK SANGAN SAROBI TUKZAR WASHIR BAGHLAN BAMIYAN DILARAM
TRIBE: SAFI TURK ULUS KAFIR TAJIK UZBEK BALOCH BALUCH HAZARA KIRGIZ PATHAN
WEIGHT: PAU PAW SER SIR KARWAR KHURDS

AFICIONADO FAN AMATEUR DEVOTEE FOLLOWER

AFIELD ABROAD ASTRAY

AFIRE ALOW ALOWE EAGER ABLAZE AFLAME ARDENT BURNING FLAMING

A-FLAT AS AIS

AFLOAT ASEA AWAFT AWASH ADRIFT BUOYED NATANT FLOODED

UNFIXED FLOATING

AFOOT ABOUT ASTIR ABROAD TOWARD WALKING

AFOREMENTIONED SAID SUCH

AFORESAID DITTO NAMED PRIOR PREVIOUS

AFORETIME ERE FORMER FORMERLY

AFRAID RAD REDE ADRAD FRAID REDDE TIMID AGHAST CRAVEN FEARED SCARED WROTHE AFEARED ALARMED ANXIOUS ASCARED FEARFUL GASTFUL COWARDLY GHASTFUL TIMOROUS

AFREET JINN AFRIT DEMON GIANT IFRIT JINNI AFRITE EFREET

AFRESH ANEW ANON OVER AGAIN NEWLY DENOVO ENCORE REPEATED

AFRICAN BOER AFRIC

AFRICAN MARIGOLD KHAKIBOS

AFRIKAANS TAAL DUTCH

AFT BACK REAR ABAFT AFTER ASTERN BEHIND
(FARTHEST —) AFTERMOST

AFTER A AB BY TO AFT EFT FOR SIN ANON NEXT PAST POST SYNE ABAFT APRES ARTER EFTER INFRA LATER SINCE ASTERN BEHIND BEYOND FOLLOW HINDER
(— MEALS) PC

AFTERBIRTH HEAM SOOTERKIN

AFTERBODY TONNEAU

AFTEREFFECT SEQUEL SEQUELA
(PL.) HANGOVER

AFTERGRASS FOG AFTERFEED

AFTERIMAGE SPECTRUM SENSATION
(KIND OF —) PURKINJE

AFTERMATH FOG ETCH LOSS ISSUE ROWEN ROWET TRAIL TRAIN ARRISH EDDISH EDGREW EDGROW EFFECT PROFIT RESULT ROWETT SEQUEL UPSHOT EAGRASS STUBBLE BACKWASH

AFTERMOST LAST HINDMOST

AFTERNOON AFTER TARDE UNDERN EVENING TEATIME

AFTERPIECE EPODE EXODE EXODIUM POSTLUDE

AFTERSONG EPODE

AFTERSWARM CAST SPEW SPUE CASTLING

AFTERTASTE FAREWELL

AFTERTHOUGHT FOOTNOTE

AFTERWARD EFT POST SITH THEN APRES LATER EFTSOON EFTSOONS

AGA AGHA LORD CHIEF
(WIFE OF —) BEGUM

AGAIN OR TO BIS EFT YET AGIN ANEW ANON AYEN AYIN BACK MORE OVER NEWLY AFRESH DENOVO ENCORE ITERUM EFTSOON FRESHLY FURTHER EFTSOONS MOREOVER
(— AND AGAIN) AND

AGAINST BY IN UP CON GIN NON AGIN ANTI GAIN INTO WITH AGAIN ANENT AYENS UNTIL ANENST AVERSE AYENST CONTRA GAINST UPTILL VERSUS FERNENT FORNENT OPPOSED ADVERSUS CONTRAIR

FORENENT FORNENST FORNINST
(— HOPE) AGLEE AGLEY

AGAL HEADROPE

AGALLOCH AGGUR ALOES GAROO GARROO GARROW TAMBAC LINALO AGALWOOD CALAMBAC

AGAMA AGA AGHA GUANA AGAMID IGUANA LIZARD AGAMIAN

AGAMEMNON (BROTHER OF —) MENELAUS
(DAUGHTER OF —) ELECTRA IPHIGENIA
(FATHER OF —) PLISTHENES
(GRANDFATHER OF —) ATREUS
(SON OF —) ORESTES
(WIFE OF —) CLYTEMNESTRA

AGAMID AGA AGHA BALETE BALITI

AGAPANTHUS TULBAGHIA LOVEFLOWER

AGAPE LOVE OPEN FEAST GAPING YAWNING

AGAR MOSS GELOSE KANTEN GELOSIN GELOSINE

AGARIC BLEWITS BLUSHER FLYBANE LEPIOTA

AGASP EAGER GASPING

AGATE TAW ONYX RUBY ACHATE GAGATE MARBLE PEBBLE QUARTZ

AGATI SESBANIA

AGAVE ALOE LILY AGAUE AMOLE DATIL SISAL LILIUM MAGUEY MESCAL PULQUE ZAPUPE CANTALA KARATTO KERATTO TEQUILA HENEQUEN HENIQUEN JINIQUEN SOAPWEED
(BROTHER OF —) POLYDORUS
(FATHER OF —) CADMUS
(HUSBAND OF —) ECHION
(MOTHER OF —) HARMONIA
(SISTER OF —) INO SEMELE AUTONOE
(SON OF —) PENTHEUS

AGE ALD BIN DAY ELD EON ERA AEON EDGE OLAM TIME YUGA AETAT CYCLE EPOCH OLDEN RIPEN SECLE WORLD YEARS MATURE MELLOW PERIOD SIECLE WITHER CENTURY DEVELOP GLACIAL OLDNESS SECULUM SENESCE VORHAND ANCIENTY DURATION ETERNITY LIFETIME MAJORITY MATURITY
(— OF 100 YEARS) CENTENARY
(— OF MOON) EPACT
(ADVANCED —) DOTAGE
(EARLY MIDDLE —) SUMMER
(GREAT —) ANTIQUITY GRANDEVITY
(OLD —) CRUTCH SENIUM VETUSTY SENILITY

AGED AE AET AGY OLD RIPE ANILE HOARY OLDEN PASSE FEEBLE INFIRM MATURE OGYIAN SENILE WINTRY YEARED ANCIENT ELDERLY WINTERED
(NOT —) GREEN
(WELL —) STALE

AGEE AJEE AWRY AGLEY ASKEW

AGELESS ETERNAL TIMELESS

AGELONG SECULAR SAECULAR

AGENCY DINT HAND CHECK FORCE

LEVER MEANS MOYEN ORGAN
PROXY ACTION BUREAU MEDIUM
OFFICE ARBITER BENEFIT BROKERY
FACULTY LIBRARY MACHINE
ACTIVITY COMPTOIR COURTESY
MINISTRY
(PUBLIC —) AUTHORITY
(RESTORATIVE —) BALM
(SUPPOSITITIOUS —) ENTELECHY
AGENDUM SLATE DOCKET RECORD
RITUAL PROGRAM
AGENOR (BROTHER OF —) BELUS
(DAUGHTER OF —) EUROPA
(FATHER —) ANTENOR NEPTUNE
(MOTHER —) LIBYA
(SON OF —) CILIX CADMUS PHOENIX
(WIFE OF —) TELEPHASSA
AGENT SPY AMIN DOER ETCH GENE
ACTOR AMEEN BUYER CAUSE
ENVOY MEANS ORGAN PROXY
REEVE RIDER VAKIL WALLA ADUROL
ASSIGN ATOPEN BROKER BURSAR
COMMIS DEALER DEPUTY ENGINE
FACTOR FITTER KEHAYA LEDGER
MEDIUM MINION MUKTAR PESKAR
SELLER SYNDIC VAKEEL WALLAH
BAILIFF BLISTER CHANNEL
COUCHER DRASTIC FACIENT
FEDERAL HUSBAND LEAGUER
MOOKTAR MOUNTAR MUKTEAR
MUTAGEN OFFICER PESHKAR
PROCTOR SCALPER APPROVER
ATTORNEY AUMILDAR CATALYST
EMISSARY EXECUTOR GOMASHTA
GOMASTAH IMPROVER INCITANT
INSTITOR MINISTER MOOKHTAR
OPERATOR PROMOTER QUAESTOR
RESIDENT SALESMAN VIRUCIDE
(— OF CROMWELL) AGITATOR
(ANTIKNOCK —) ADDITIVE
ALKYLATE
(CLEANSING —) SOAP
(CONFIDENTIAL —) AMIN AMEEN
(DESTRUCTIVE —) DEVOURER
(EMPLOYMENT —) PADRONE
(ENFORCEMENT —) LAW
(ESPIONAGE —) COURIER
(FISCAL —) STEWARD
(MEDICINAL —) DRASTIC
(NARCOTIC —) GAZER
(PRESS —) FLACK
(PUBLICITY —) BEATER
(PURCHASING —) CIRCAR SIRCAR
SIRKAR
(STIMULATING —) FILIP FILLIP
(SUBVERSIVE —) STOOGE
(SWEETENING —) DULCIN
(VOLATILE —) SPIRIT
(WETTING —) SPREADER
AGGLOMERATE HEAP LUMP MASS
PILE SELF SLAG WIND CHAOS
GATHER CLUSTER COLLECT
AGGLOMERATION HORDE
CONGERY FAVELLA CONGERIE
AGGRANDIZE LIFT BOOST EXALT
RAISE ADVANCE AUGMENT DIGNIFY
ELEVATE ENLARGE MAGNIFY
PROMOTE INCREASE
AGGRAVATE IRK NAG VEX FEED

LOAD TWIT ANGER ANNOY TAUNT
TEASE BURDEN PESTER WORSEN
AGGREGE BEDEVIL ENHANCE
ENLARGE MAGNIFY PROVOKE
AGGRIEVE HEIGHTEN INCREASE
IRRITATE
AGGRAVATED ACUTE
AGGREGATE ADD ALL SET SUM
AUGE BAND BULK CLON CLUB
COMB DEME FLOC GOUT LATH
MASS BLOCK BUNCH CLASS CLONE
COVER CROWD FIELD GROSS
SHOOT TOTAL UNITE WHOLE
AMOUNT BALLAS DOMAIN PLUREL
VOLUME ASBOLAN COLLECT
ARCULITE ASBOLANE ASBOLITE
AXIOLITE COMPOUND COVERAGE
CUMULITE ENSEMBLE MANIFOLD
MULTEITY TOTALITY
(— OF MICA) BOOK
(— OF MINERALS) EYE
(— OF ORE) KIDNEY
(— OF POINTS) CELL
(— OF STATEMENTS) AUTHORITY
(— OF TISSUES) BODY
(MATHEMATICAL —) FIELD
SEQUENCE
AGGREGATION HEAD HERD CLUMP
CUTIN FLOCK GORGE GROUP LURRY
SWARM COLONY FAMILY NATION
SYSTEM CLUSTER CONGERY
GALLERY SORITES CONGERIE
EUMERISM
AGGRESSION WAR RAID ATTACK
INJURY ASSAULT OFFENSE
INVASION
AGGRESSIVE PUSHING
AGGRESSIVENESS CRUST
BELLICOSITY
AGGRIEVE TRY HARM HURT PAIN
HARRY WRONG INJURE AFFLICT
OPPRESS TROUBLE DISTRESS
AGGRIEVED SORE OFFENDED
AGHAST AGAST AFRAID
AGILAWOOD AGALLOCH
AGALLOCHUM
AGILE DEFT FAST LISH SPRY WIRY
ADEPT ALERT BRISK CATTY ELFIN
FLEET LITHE QUICK WANLE WITHY
ACTIVE ADROIT FEERIE FEIRIE
LIMBER LISSOM LITHER LIVELY
LUTHER NIMBLE QUIVER SUPPLE
WANDLE LISSOME SALIENT SPRINGE
SPRINGY ATHLETIC
AGILITY LEVITY SPROIL SLEIGHT
ACTIVITY LEGERITY SALIENCE
AGING BINNING
(PREMATURE —) GERODERMA
GERODERMIA
AGIO BATTA DISAGIO PREMIUM
DISCOUNT EXCHANGE
AGIST TAX FEED RATE GRAZE
PASTURE
AGITATE FAN IRK JAR VEX WEY
FRET FUSS MOVE PLOT RILE ROCK
SEEK STIR TEEM ALARM ALTER
BREAK BROIL CHURN DRIVE HARRY
IMPEL QUAKE ROUSE SHAKE
AROUSE BETOSS BUSKLE DEBATE

DEVISE EXCITE FOMENT HARASS
INCITE JABBLE JOSTLE JUMBLE
JUSTLE LATHER MANAGE RATTLE
RUFFLE SEETHE ACTUATE CANVASS
COMMOVE CONCUSS DISCUSS
DISTURB PERTURB REVOLVE
TEMPEST TROUBLE ACTIVATE
CONTRIVE CONVULSE DISQUIET
DISTRACT TRANSACT
(— A LIQUID) SPARGE
AGITATED STEWED STORMY YEASTY
AGITATO ESTUOUS UNQUIET
AESTUOUS FEVERISH FLURRIED
SEETHING
AGITATION GOG JAR JOG BOIL
FEAR FRET FURY GUST HEAT ITCH
JERK JOLT ALARM DANCE HURRY
QUAKE SHAKE STORM STOUR
TWEAK YEAST BUSTLE DITHER
ENERGY FIZZLE FLIGHT FLURRY
FRENZY JABBLE MOTION PUCKER
QUIVER RIPPLE SHAKES TREMOR
TUMULT EMOTION FERMENT
FLUSTER FLUTTER MADNESS
RAMPAGE STICKLE SWITHER
TEMPEST TURMOIL DISQUIET
PAROXYSM UPHEAVAL
(— AND PROPAGANDA) AGITPROP
AGITATOR HOG TREATER
AGLAIA (FATHER OF —) JUPITER
(MOTHER OF —) EURYNOME
(SISTER OF —) THALIA
EUPHROSYNE
AGLET TAB TAG LACE STUD PLATE
AIGLET PENDANT SPANGLE
HAWTHORN STAYLACE
AGLEY AWRY AGLEE ASIDE ASKEW
WRONG
AGLYCON GENIN NONSUGAR
AGNATE AKIN ALLIED COGNATE
KINDRED
AGNEL MOUTON
AGNOETE THEMISTIAN
AGNOMEN NAME ALIAS EPITHET
SURNAME COGNOMEN NICKNAME
AGNOSTIC ATHEIST DOUBTER
SKEPTIC NESCIENT
AGO BY SIN BACK ERST GONE PAST
SENS SYNE YGOE YORE ABACK
AGONE SINCE YGONE SINSYNE
BACKWARD
(LONG —) ANCIENTLY
AGOG AVID KEEN ASTIR EAGER
LIVELY EXCITED VIGILANT
AGONIZE BEAR RACK STRAIN
WRITHE
AGONIZING GRINDING HARROWING
AGONY ACHE PAIN PANG DOLOR
GRIEF GRIPE PANIC STOUR THRAW
THROE TRIAL ACHING ANGUISH
ANXIETY EMOTION TORMENT
TORTURE TRAVAIL DISTRESS
PAROXYSM
AGOUTI CAPA CAVY PACA ACUCHI
AGOUTY ACOUCHI
AGRARIAN RURAL PASTORAL
AGREE FAY FIT GEE HIT PAN YES
GIBE GREE JIBE JUMP MEET SIDE
SORT SUIT ADMIT ALLOW ATONE

BLEND CHECK CLICK CLOSE FADGE
GRANT HITCH JUTTY LEVEL MATCH
PIECE STAND TALLY UNITE YIELD
ACCEDE ACCORD ASSENT ASSORT
COMPLY CONCUR CONDOG COTTON
ENGAGE REWARD SETTLE SQUARE
SUBMIT ARRANGE BARGAIN
COMPORT CONCEDE CONFORM
CONGREE CONGRUE CONSENT
CONSIGN DARESAY PACTION
PROMISE COINCIDE COMPOUND
CONTRACT COVENANT QUADRATE
(— MUTUALLY) STIPULATE
(— TO JOIN) ADHERE
(— TO) ACCEPT
(— UPON) TAILYE TAILZEE TAILZIE
(— WITH) SIT LIKE SIDE TAIL
ANSWER
AGREEABLE AMEN EASY FAIR FINE
GOOD KIND LIEF NICE SOFT WEME
AMENE CANNY DULCE GRATE JOLIE
JOLLY LITHE LUSTY QUEME READY
SAPID SMIRK SUANT SUAVE SUENT
SWEET COMELY COWDIE DAINTY
DULCET KINDLY LIKELY SAVORY
SMOOTH SUITED ADAPTED AMABILE
AMIABLE COUTHIE DOUCEUR
TUNABLE WELCOME WILLING
WINSOME AMENABLE CHARMING
DELICATE GRATEFUL LIKESOME
LOVESOME OBLIGING PLACABLE
PLAUSIVE PLEASANT PLEASING
PURSUANT SOCIABLE SUITABLE
THANKFUL
(NOT —) ABHORRENT
(UNPLEASANTLY —) SACCHARINE
AGREEING CONNATE CONTENT
AGREEMENT GO FIT NOD AXIS
BOND DEAL FINE LINE MISE PACT
TACK TAIL TRUE ATONE COVIN
LEASE MATCH TERMS TOUCH
TRUTH TRYST UNITY ACCORD
ACTION ASSENT CARTEL CAUTIO
COMITY COVINE DICKER LEAGUE
PACTUM PLEDGE TREATY UNISON
BARGAIN CLOSURE COMPACT
CONCERT CONSENT CONSULT
ENTENTE HARMONY ONENESS
PACTION RAPPORT CONTRACT
DIAPASON SANCTION SORTANCE
SYMPATHY
(— TO JOIN) ADHESION
(GRAMMATICAL —) ATTRACTION
(SECRET —) CAHOOT CAHOOTS
AGRICULTURAL GEOPONIC
GEOPONICAL
AGRICULTURE FARMING GAINAGE
TILLAGE AGRONOMY
(— SYSTEM) KOLKHOZ
AGRICULTURIST THO FARMER
GROWER SANTAL PLANTER
RANCHER
AGRIMONY CLIVE BORWORT
HEMPWEED
AGRITO AGARITA MAHONIA
ALGERITO ASHBERRY
AGROUND SEWED ASHORE
BEACHED STRANDED
AGRYPHA LOGION
AGRYPNIA INSOMNIA

SLEEPLESSNESS
AGUACATE AHUACA AVOCADO
AGUAMAS PINGUIN
AGUE CHILL FEVER MALARIA
SHAKING SHIVERS
AGUE TREE SASSAFRAS
AGUEWEED BONESET
AH ACH
AHARTALAV YARROW MILFOIL
AHEAD ON UP ALEE FORE AFORE
ALONG DORMY BEFORE DORMIE
ONWARD ALREADY ENDWAYS
ENDWISE FORWARD LEADING
ADELANTE ADVANCED ANTERIOR
(— OF TIME) FAST
(STRAIGHT —) FORERIGHT
AHEM HUM
AHOY AVAST
AHUEHUETE CEDAR SABINO
CYPRESS
AID KEY ABET BACK BEET HAND
HELP PONY REDE ALLAY BOOST
COACH FAVOR GRANT SERVE
SPEED TREAT ASSIST FAVOUR
FRIEND PROFIT RELIEF REMEDY
RESCUE SECOND SUCCOR SUPPLY
UPHOLD ADVANCE AIDANCE
ANCILLA BACKING BENEFIT
COMFORT ENDORSE FORWARD
FURTHER INDORSE RELIEVE
SECOURS SERVICE SUBSIDY
SUPPORT ADJUVATE AUXILIUM
BEFRIEND SUFFRAGE
(— A VESSEL) HOVEL
(— SECRETLY) SUBAID
(COMPLEXION —) FUCUS
(MORMON —) COUNSELOR
COUNSELLOR
AIDE AID BEAGLE DEPUTY SECOND
OFFICER ORDERLY ADJUTANT
GALLOPER
(BULLFIGHTER'S —) CAPEADOR
AIGRETTE EGRET HERON PLUME
SPRAY AIGRET FEATHERS
AIL ILE AILD EILE EYLE FAIL PAIN
PINE AFFECT BOTHER FALTER
SUFFER AFFLICT DECLINE TROUBLE
COMPLAIN DISTRESS
AILANTHUS SUMAC SUMACH
AILING SICK CRAZY CRONK DONCY
DONSY SOBER DONSIE SICKLY
UNWELL CRAICHY CREACHY
AILMENT AIL ILL COUGH MALADY
DISEASE ILLNESS DISORDER
SICKNESS WEAKNESS
AIM END LAY TRY BEAD BEAM BENT
BUTT FINE GLEE GOAL HEAD HOLD
LEAD MARK MINT PLAN SEEK TEMP
VIEW VIZY WINK ACIES BLANK
DRIVE ESSAY ETTLE GUESS LEVEL
POINT PRICK SCOPE SIGHT TRAIN
VISIE VIZZY ASPIRE DESIGN DIRECT
ESTEEM INTEND INTENT OBJECT
SCHEME STRIVE ADDRESS ATTEMPT
CHIMERA MEANING PRETEND
PURPOSE RESPECT STAGGER
CHIMAERA CONSIDER ENDEAVOR
ESTIMATE PRETENSE STEERING
TENTAMEN
(— A KICK) FLING

(— AT) EYE AFFECT
(— FURTIVELY) STEAL
(— INDIRECTLY) GLANCE
AIMED FAST
(— AT) AFFECTED
AIMING LEVEL GUNLAYING
AIMLESS IDLE BLIND CHANCE
RANDOM DRIFTING
AIMLESSNESS FLANERIE
AIR AER PEW SKY AERE ARIA AURA
AYRE BROW DIRT FEEL LILT LOFT
MIEN PORT POSE SONG TELL TUNE
VENT WIND ETHER FRILL OZONE
UTTER VOICE AERATE AETHER
ALLURE ASPECT BROACH CACHET
MANNER MELODY OSTENT PIAFFE
REGARD REGION STRAIN VANITY
WELKIN WITHER BEARING DISPLAY
EXHIBIT EXPRESS FANFARE
MALARIA NEPHELE PIAFFER
ATTITUDE BEHAVIOR CARRIAGE
PRESENCE
(— COOLED) WATERLESS
(— EXHALED) BLAST
(— IN MOTION) BREATH
(— PLANT) LIFELEAF
(BOASTFUL —) PARADO
(CONFIDENT —) BRAVURA
(COOL —) FRESCO
(COQUETTISH —) MINAUDERIE
(FETID —) REEK
(FOUL —) DIRT
(HAUGHTY —S) ALTITUDES
(MUSICAL —) ARIA SOLO TUNE
BRAWL MELODY ARIETTA ARIETTE
MUSETTE
(POMPOUS —) SWELL
(PUT ON —S) PROSS
(STALE —) STEAM
(STIFLING —) SMORE
(THE —) GATE
(WARM —) OAM
(PL.) LUGS FRONT
AIRCRAFT KITE ABORT BLIMP CRAFT
FLYER PLANE GLIDER AEROBUS
AERONEF AIRSHIP BALLOON
AEROBOAT AERODYNE AEROSTAT
AIRLINER AIRPLANE AUTOGIRO
AUTOGYRO GYRODYNE
(UNIDENTIFIED —) UFO BOGY
BOGEY BOGIE
AIRCRAFTSMAN ERK
AIRCREWMAN KICKER AIREDALE
AIRFIELD AERODROME SATELLITE
AIRFOIL FIN FLAP SLAT BLADE
SURFACE AEROFOIL ELEVATOR
AIRILY JAUNTILY
AIRLINE FEEDER SKYWAY
AIRMAN FLIER FLYER BIRDMAN
WARBIRD WASTEMAN
AIRPLANE BUS CUB JET MIG BAKA
GYRO KILL KITE SHIP ZERO AVION
CRATE FLIER FLYER FRITZ GOTHA
HEINE JENNY LINER PLANE SCOUT
SNOOP BOMBER CANARD CHASER
COPTER FERRET FESSEL FOKKER
GLIDER JENNIE SMOKER TANDEM
VESSEL AERONEF AVIATIK BIPLANE
CLIPPER FIGHTER FLIVVER FLYAWAY
HOTSHOT PENGUIN SNOOPER

SPOTTER TRACTOR WARBIRD
AEROSTAT ALBATROS KAMIKAZE
SEAPLANE SKYCOACH SKYCRAFT
SOCIABLE STRUTTER TRIPLANE
TURBOJET WARPLANE
(REMOTE-CONTROLLED —) DRONE
AIR PLANT LIFELEAF LIVELEAF
AIRPORT DROME AIRPARK JETPORT
SCUTTLE AIRDROME AIRFIELD
AIRSHIP (SEE ALSO AIRPLANE AND
AIRCRAFT) SHIP BLIMP GASBAG
AERONAT AEROSTAT PARSEVAL
ZEPPELIN
AIRSTREAM PEW DOWNWASH
AIRSTRIP LILY
AIRTIGHT SEALED AIRPROOF
HERMETIC
AIRWAY MONKEY RETURN SKYWAY
AIRWAVE WINDWAY WINDROAD
AIRY GAY COOL RARE THIN EMPTY
HUFFY LIGHT MERRY WINDY AERIAL
BREZZY FLUFFY JAUNTY JOCUND
LIVELY STARRY AIRLIKE AIRSOME
HAUGHTY JOCULAR SFOGATO
AFFECTED ANIMATED DEBONAIR
DELICATE ETHEREAL FLIPPANT
GRACEFUL SPARKISH TRIFLING
VOLATILE
AISLE ILE WAY YLE AILE LANE NAVE
WALK ALLEE ALLEY FEEDWAY
GANGWAY PASSAGE CORRIDOR
AIT OAT EYOT HOLM ISLE EIGHT
ISLET
AITCHBONE ICEBONE EDGEBONE
AJAR OPEN DISCORDANT
AJAX AIAS
(FATHER OF —) OILEUS TELAMON
(MOTHER OF —) ERIBOEA PERIBOEA
AJONJOLI SESAME
AJOWAN AJAVA AIWAIN
AKALI SHAHIDI
AKEAKE AKE HOPBUSH IRONWOOD
AKHA KAW
AKIMBO ANGLED AKEMBOLL
AKENBOLD
AKIN SIB LIKE NEAR NIGH ALIKE
CLOSE AGNATE ALLIED COUSIN
SIBBED TENDER COGNATE CONNATE
GERMANE RELATED SIMILAR
(— ON MALE SIDE) AGNATIC
(NOT —) UNSIB
AKRA ACCRA INKRA
AKU VICTORFISH
AL AAL AWL MULBERRY
ALA AXIL DRUM WING AXILLA
RECESS NOSEWING

ALABAMA
CAPITAL: MONTGOMERY
COUNTY: LEE BIBB CLAY DALE
PIKE COOSA HENRY LAMAR
MACON PERRY BLOUNT BUTLER
COFFEE DALLAS ELMORE
ETOWAH GENEVA GREENE
MARION MONROE MORGAN
SHELBY SUMTER WILCOX
CHILTON
MOUNTAIN: CHEAHA

NATIVE: LIZARD
RIVER: PEA COOSA CAHABA
MOBILE SIPSEY TENSAW
CONECUH SEPULGA TOMBIGBEE
STATE BIRD: YELLOWHAMMER
STATE FISH: TARPON
STATE FLOWER: CAMELLIA
STATE TREE: PINE LONGLEAF
TOWN: OPP PIPER SELMA ATHENS
CORONA LINDEN MARION
MOBILE SAMSON FLORALA
GADSDEN ANNISTON

ALABASTER GYPSUM TECALI
ONYCHITE
ALACK ALAS ALAKE
ALACRITY HASTE SPEED CELERITY
RAPIDITY
ALAMEDA MALL WALK
ALAN ALAND ALANT ALAUNT
ALANG-ALANG COGON KOGON
ALANS GHUZ OGHUZ
ALANTIN INULIN
ALAR PTERIC WINGED AXILLARY
WINGLIKE
ALARM COW DIN BELL FEAR FRAY
GAST LARM ALERT BROIL CLOCK
DAUNT FEEZE LARUM NOISE PANIC
ROUSE SCARE SIREN START STILL
UPSET AFFRAY ALARUM APPALL
AROUSE ATTACK BUZZER DISMAY
EXCITE FRIGHT OUTCRY SIGNAL
TERROR TOCSIN DISTURB GLOPNEN
GLOPPEN MOUNTEE STARTLE
TERRIFY TORPEDO WARNING
AFFRIGHT DISQUIET FRIGHTEN
SURPRISE
(FIRE —) STILL FIREBOX
ALARMED SCARY SCAREY FEARFUL
GASTFUL GHASTFUL SCAREFUL
STREAKED
ALARMER HUER
ALARMING SCARY SCAREY FEARFUL
SCAREFUL
ALAS AY ACH HEU LAS OCH VAE
WOE EHEU HECH OIME ALACK
HALAS HELAS OIMEE OCHONE
OTOTOI WAESUCK ULLAGONE
WAESUCKS WELLADAY WELLAWAY

ALASKA
CAPITAL: JUNEAU
ISLAND: ADAK ATKA ATTU UMNAK
KODIAK UNIMAK DIOMEDE
NUNIVAK
ISLAND GROUP: RAT ALEUTIAN
PRIBILOF ANDREANOF
LAKE: NAKNEK ILIAMNA
MOUNTAIN: BONA VETA SPURR
KATMAI PAVLOF FORAKER
MCKINLEY
MOUNTAIN RANGE: CRAZY
BROOKS KAIYUH CHUGACH
KILBUCK WRANGELL
NATIVE: ALEUT AHTENA ESKIMO
INGALIK KOYUKON TLINGIT
PENINSULA: KENAI SEWARD

RIVER: CHENA KOBUK YUKON
COPPER NOATAK TANANA
KOYUKUK SUSITNA CHULITNA
COLVILLE
STATE BIRD: PTARMIGAN
STATE FLOWER: FORGETMENOT
STATE TREE: SPRUCE
TOWN: EEK NOME KENAI SITKA
BARROW KODIAK NENANA
SKAGWAY KOTZEBUE
ANCHORAGE FAIRBANKS

ALASTRIM AMAAS
ALB ALBE AUBE CAMISIA CHRISOM
VESTMENT
ALBACORE TUNA TUNNY GERMAN
GERMON LONGFIN ALALONGA
ALALUNGA MACKEREL SCOMBRID

ALBANIA
ANCIENT PEOPLE: ILLYRIAN
CAPITAL: TIRANA TIRANE
COIN: LEK FRANC GUINTAR
KING: ZOG
LAKE: ULZE OHRIDSKO
MOUNTAIN: KORAB SHALA PINDUS
KORITNJK
REGION: EPIRUS
RIVER: MAT DRIN OSUM ERZEN
SEMAN VIJOSE SHKUMBI
TOWN: LIN FIER KLOS BERAT
DUKAT KORCE KRUJE PECIN
PEQIN QUKES RUBIC SPASH
VLONE VLORE ARLONA BITSAN
DARDHE DURRES PRESHE
VALONA DURAZZO KORITZA
SCUTARI SHKODER
TRIBE: GEG CHAM GHEG TOSK

ALBANIAN GEG GHEG GUEG
ARNAUT SKIPETAR
ALBATROSS GONY GOON GONEY
GOONY NELLY FABRIC GOONEY
GOONIE QUAKER SEABIRD
BLUEBIRD STINKPOT
ALBEIT ALL ALBE ALBEE ALLBE
THOUGH HOWBEIT
ALBINO LEUCAETHIOP
ALBIZZIA SIRIS
ALBUM ALBE BOOK RECORD
VOLUME REGISTER
ALBUMEN WHITE
ALBUMIN ALBUMEN PHASELIN
SYNTONIN
ALBUMINOID ELASTIN FIBROIN
KERATIN PROTEIN SERICIN
COLLAGEN GORGONIN
ALBURNUM SAP BLEA SPLINT
SAPWOOD
ALBUS BLANCO
ALCAEUS (FATHER OF —) PERSEUS
(SON OF —) AMPHITRYON
ALCAIDE CADE CAID QAID JUDGE
ALCADE
ALCESTIS (FATHER OF —) PELIAS
(HUSBAND OF —) ADMETUS
ALCHEMIST ADEPT ARTIST CHEMIC

CHEMICK CHEMIST HERMETIC
ALCHEMY ART MAGIC ALCUMY
CHYMIA SPAGYRIC
(GOD OF —) HERMES
ALCHORNEA DOVEWOOD
ALCINOUS (DAUGHTER OF —)
NAUSICAA
(FATHER OF —) NAUSITHOUS
(MOTHER OF —) PERIBOEA
(WIFE OF —) ARETE
ALCMAEON (FATHER OF —)
AMPHIARAUS
(MOTHER OF —) ERIPHYLE
(WIFE OF —) CALLIRHOE
ALPHESIBOEA
ALCMENE (FATHER OF —)
ELECTRYON
(HUSBAND OF —) AMPHITRYON
(SON OF —) HERCULES IPHICLES
ALCOHOL ALKY ETHAL ETHYL IDITE
LEDOL VINYL AMYROL ANDROL
CEDROL ELEMOL GLYCOL GUAIOL
HYDROL IDITOL LUPEOL LUTEIN
METHYL PHYTOL SPIRIT STERIN
STERNO STEROL TALITE ACRITOL
ADONITE ALDITOL ALKANOL ANISOIN
BORNEOL BUTANOL CAROTOL
DECANOL ETHANOL FENCHOL
HEPTITE HEXITOL INOSITE MENTHOL
PULEGOL QUINITE SCOPINE
SORBITE STETHAL STYRONE
TAGETOL TALITOL TROPINE XYLITOL
LINALOOL METHANOL
ALCOHOLATE SPIRIT ESSENCE
ALCOHOLIC ALKY
(NOT —) SOFT
ALCOHOLOMETER GENOMETER
VINOMETER
ALCOVE BAY NOOK BOWER NICHE
ORIEL STALL CARREL RECESS
CARRELL CUBICLE DINETTE
RETREAT SERVERY ALHACENA
SNUGGERY TABLINUM
ALDEHYDE ALDOL CITRAL ALKANAL
CHLORAL COGENER DECANAL
GLYOXAL HEXANAL ACROLEIN
CONGENER FURFURAL
ALDER ARN OLER ALNUS ELDER
OWLER SAGEROSE
ALDERMAN BAILIE SENIOR
HEADMAN
ALE MUM NOG BEER BOCK BREW
FLIP MILD NOGG PURL SCUD YELL
AUDIT CLINK DARBY JOUGH LAGER
NAPPY STOUT ALEGAR PORTER
STINGO SWANKY BITTERS
MOROCCO OCTOBER PHARAOH
HUGMATEE
**(— BREWED WITH BRACKISH
WATER)** TIPPER
(— MIXED WITH SWEETENER)
BRAGGET
(INFERIOR —) SWANKY SWANKEY
(NEW —) SWATS
(SOUR —) ALEGAR
(SPICED —) SWIG
(STRONG —) MUM HUFF BURTON
STINGO HUFFCAP
(WEAK —) TWOPENNY

ALEATORY HAZARDOUS
ALECOST COSTMARY
ALECTRYON TITOKI
ALEE AHEAD LEEWARD
ALEHOUSE PUB TAVERN BARROOM
MUGHOUSE POTHOUSE
ALEMBIC LIMBEC LIMBECK
CUCURBIT
ALERT APT GAY HEP HIP YAL YEP
FOXY GLEG KEEN LIVE PERT SNAP
WAKE WARN WARY YALD YEPE
ACUTE AGILE ALARM ALIVE AWAKE
AWARE BREME BRISK EAGER ERECT
LEERY MERRY PEART PEERT QUICK
READY SHACK SHARP SIREN SLICK
SWIFT TIGHT WAKER YAULD ACTIVE
ALARUM ARRECT BRIGHT DAPPER
LIVELY NIMBLE PROMPT SLIPPY
SPRACK SUDDEN TIPTOE TOCSIN
WACKER CAREFUL KNOWING
WAKEFUL WORKING PREPARED
THOUGHTY VIGILANT WAKERIFE
WATCHFUL
ALERTNESS NOUS SNAP APTNESS
APTITUDE
(MENTAL —) WIT
ALETTE WING ABUTMENT
ALEUT ATKA ORARIAN UNALASKA
**ALEUTIANS (ISLANDS AND ISLAND
GROUPS OF —)** FOX RAT ADAK
ATTU NEAR KISKA UMNAK KODIAK
(TOWN OF —) UNALASKA
(VOLCANO ON —) SHISHALDIN
ALEWIFE BANG ALICE ALOOFE
BUCKIE ALEWHAP HERRING
OLDWIFE POMPANO WALLEYE
GRAYBACK GREYBACK SAWBELLY
SKIPJACK
ALEXANDER ALEX PARIS SAWNY
ELLICK SAWNEY SAWNIE ISKANDER
(BIRTHPLACE OF —) PELLA
(HORSE OF —) BUCEPHALUS
ALFA HALFA ESPARTO
ALFALFA HAY MEDIC FODDER
LEGUME LUCERN LUCERNE
ALFILARIA ERODIUM FILAREE
FILARIA PINWEED
ALFORJA BAG POUCH WALLET
ALFARGA ALFORGE
ALGA NORI ALGAL BROWN FUCUS
JELLY SLAKE SLOAK SLOKE DESMID
DIATOM FUNORI NOSTOC AMANORI
GULAMAN HAITSAI OARWEED
SEAWEED ANABAENA FERNLEAF
GELIDIUM HAIRWEED ROCKWEED
SEABEARD SILKWEED SPOROGEN
WHIPCORD ZOOGLOEA
ALGARROBA CAROB CALDEN
ALGEBRA LOGISTIC
ALGEBRAIC COSSIC
ALGENIB MIRFAK

ALGERIA

BERBER: KABYLE SHAWIA TUAREG
BERBER DIALECT: ZENATA
  SENHAJA
CAPITAL: ALGIERS
CAVALRYMAN: SPAHI SPAHEE

DEPARTMENT: ORAN ALGIERS
GRASS: ESPARTO
HILL: TELL
HOLY MAN: MARABOUT
MEASURE: PIK REBIS TARRI
  TERMIN
MONASTERY: RIBAT
MOUNTAIN: AISSA ATLAS AURES
  DAHRA TAHAT CHELIA AHAGGAR
  MOUYDIR DJURJURA
NAME: ALGERIE NUMIDIA
NATIVE: BERBER KABYLE
PIRATE: CORSAIR
RIVER: SHELIF CHELIFF MEDJERDA
RULER: BEY DEY BEVLERBEY
SECT: SUNNITE
SETTLER: COLON PIEDNOIR
SHIP: XEBEC
TOWN: BONE ORAN AFLOU ARZEW
  BATNA BLIDA MEDEA SAIDA
  SETIF TENES ABADLA ANNABA
  AUMALE BARIKA BECHAR BEJAIA
  BENOUD BISKRA BOUGIE
  DELLYS DJANET DJELFA DZIOUA
  FRENDA GUELMA SKIKDA
  BOGHARI MASCARA MILIANA
  NEGRINE NEMOURS OUARGLA
  TEBESSA TLEMCEN
WEIGHT: ROTL

ALGERINE COOLOOLY KOOLOOLY
ALGID COLD COOL CHILLY CLAMMY
ALGOLOGY VERATRIN
ALGONKIAN EOZOIC
(— ROCKS) UNKAR
ALIAS ELSE OTHER AYLESS
ASSUMED EPITHET
ALIBI PLEA EXCUSE APOLOGY
PRETEXT
ALIDADE INDEX DIOPTER
ALIEN GER DEED FREMD METIC
ALAUNT ALLTUD AUBAIN CONVEY
EXOTIC INMATE REMOTE ADVERSE
DENIZEN FOREIGN FRAMMIT
INVADER OUTLAND STRANGE
DETAINEE STRANGER TRANSFER
ALIENATE PART WEAN ALIEN AVER
ANNALY CONVEY DEMISE DEVEST
FREEZE FORFEIT SUBVERT
AMORTIZE DISUNITE ESTRANGE
MORTMAIN SEPARATE STRANGER
TRANSFER WITHDRAW
ALIENATION GIFT DISTASTE
DISUNION DISUNITY DIVISION
DONATION INSANITY
ALIENIST PSYCHOPATH
PSYCHIATRIST
ALIGHT DROP LAND LEND REST
STOP LATCH LIGHT LODGE PERCH
ROOST STOOP SWOOP ARRIVE
SETTLE BURNING DESCEND
ALIGN LINE TRAM TRUE ALINE
ARRAY DRESS RANGE ADJUST
ARRANGE MARSHAL
(— PAPER) JOG
ALIGNED FAIR COLORED
ALIGNMENT KELTER KILTER
GROUPING

ALII ARIKI
ALIKE AKIN LIKE SAME EQUAL INLIKE
SQUARE YLICHE EQUALLY SIMILAR
UNIFORM
ALIMENT PAP FOOD FUEL BROMA
MANNA VIANDS ALIMONY PABULUM
RATIONS
ALIMONY ALIMENT
ALIPHATIC FATTY
ALIVE VIF BUSY KEEN SPRY VIVE
AGILE ALERT ALIFE ASTIR AWARE
BEING BRISK FRESH GREEN QUICK
VITAL AROUND EXTANT LIVING
SLIPPY ANIMATE VIBRANT ANIMATED
EXISTENT SENSIBLE SWARMING
ALKALI LYE REH BASE BRAK KALI
SALT SODA USAR BRACK CAUSTIC
ALKALOID BASE ERGOT ESERE
ARICIN BRUCIN CEVINE CODEIN
CONINE CURINE ESERIN QUINIA
QUININ ACONINE ARABINE ARICINE
ATROPIA BOGAINE BOLDINE
BRUCINE CAFFEIN COCAINE
CODEINE CONIINE EMETINE
HARMINE HYGRINE JERVINE KAIRINE
NARCEIN NEOPINE PTOMAIN
QUININE SCOPINE SINAPIN SOLANIN
SOPHORA VIOLINE PIPERINE
ALKANE PARAFFIN
ALKANET BUGLOSS REDROOT
ALKANNIN ORCANET ANCHUSIN
ORCHANET
ALKYD GLYPTAL
ALL A AL ANY SUM EACH FULL TOTE
AUGHT EVERY GROSS OMNES
OUGHT QUITE TOTAL TOTUM TUTTA
TUTTO WHOLE ENTIRE SOLELY
WHOLLY PLENARY ENTIRELY
EVERYONE TOTALITY
(— BUT ABSOLUTELY) ALMOST
(— IN) ALTOGETHER
(— TOGETHER) COLLECTEDLY
(AND —) ANA
(AT —) AVA ANYWISE ANYTHING
ANYWHERE
(OF —) AVA
ALLANITE CERINE CERITE ORTHITE
ALLAY AID LAY CALM CITE COOL
EASE HELP HUSH STAY ABATE
AGATE ALLOY CHARM CHECK
DELAY QUELL QUIET SALVE SLAKE
STILL ADDUCE LESSEN PACIFY
QUENCH REDUCE SOFTEN SOLACE
SOOTHE STANCH SUBDUE TEMPER
APPEASE ASSUAGE COMFORT
COMPOSE LIGHTEN MOLLIFY
RELIEVE REPRESS STAUNCH
MITIGATE PALLIATE
ALLAYED DEFERRED
ALLEGATION PLEA COUNT VOUCH
CHARGE ESSOIN AVERRAL FICTION
PROFERT SCANDAL SURMISE
AVERMENT SCIENTER
ALLEGE LAY SAY AVER AVOW CITE
SHOW URGE ALLAY CLAIM FEIGN
INFER LEDGE OFFER PLEAD QUOTE
STATE SWEAR VOUCH ADDUCE
AFFIRM ASSERT ASSIGN CHARGE
DEPOSE ESSOIN RECITE ADVANCE

ASCRIBE DECLARE LIGHTEN
PRESENT PROFESS PROPOSE
MAINTAIN
ALLEGED SUPPOSED SURMISED
ALLEGIANCE TIE DUTY FAITH
HONOR FEALTY HOMAGE LYANCE
LOYALTY SERVAGE SERVICE
TRIBUTE CIVILITY DEVOTION
FIDELITY LIGEANCE
ALLEGORICAL PARABOLIC
SYMBOLICAL
ALLEGORICALLY SECRETLY
ALLEGORIZE TALMUDIZE
ALLEGORY MYTH TALE FABLE
STORY EMBLEM PARABLE
APOLOGUE METAPHOR
ALLELUIA AEVIA LAUDS
ALL-EMBRACING INFINITE
SWEEPING
ALLERGEN INHALANT
ALLERGY ATOPY IDIOBLAPSIS
ALLEVIATE AID BALM CALM CURE
EASE HELP ABATE ALLAY QUIET
ALIGHT ALLEGE LENIFY LESSEN
PACIFY SOFTEN SOLACE SOOTHE
SUCCOR SUPPLE TEMPER ASSUAGE
COMPOSE CONSOLE CORRECT
LENIATE LIGHTEN MOLLIFY RELEASE
RELIEVE DIMINISH MITIGATE
MODERATE PALLIATE
ALLEVIATION ALAY SOLACE
ALLEY MIG ROW WAY CHAR LANE
LEAD MALL MEWS PASS PATH VENT
WALK WENT WIND WYND AISLE
ALLEE BLIND BYWAY CHARE ENTRY
TEWER WEENT PEEWEE TRANCE
VENNEL PASSAGE
(BLIND —) LOKE STOP POCKET
IMPASSE
ALLHALLOWTIDE HOLLANTIDE
ALLHEAL PANACEA WOUNWORT
ALLIANCE AXIS PACT UNION
ACCORD FUSION LEAGUE LYANCE
TREATY COMPACT ENTENTE
SOCIETY AFFINITY AGNATION
CACTALES COVENANT DREIBUND
FEDERACY FUNGALES LILIALES
TRIPLICE
(— IN WAR) SYMMACHY
ALLICE SHAD ALEWIFE POMPANO
ALLIED SIB AKIN AGNATE COUSIN
JOINED LINKED UNITED COGNATE
CONNATE FEDERAL GERMANE
KINDRED RELATED SIMILAR
RELATIVE
ALLIGATOR GATOR NIGER CAIMAN
CAYMAN CROTCH JACARE LIZARD
TRAVOY YACARE CRAWLER
CREEPER LAGARTO TRAVOIS
ALAGARTO LORICATE
(— PEAR) ZABOCA AVOCADO
AGUACATE
(— TURTLE) LOGGERHEAD
(MALE —) BULL
ALLIGATORING WEBBING
ALL-INCLUSIVE GLOBAL
ALLITERATION LETTER
ALLITERATIVE LITERAL
ALLIUM LILY ONION GARLIC

ALLNESS OMNEITY OMNITUDE
ALLOCATE DEAL DOLE METE RATE
ALLOT AWARD SHARE AFFECT
ASSIGN OUTPLACE
ALLOCATION DRAW DESIGNATION
ALLOT FIX SET BILL CAST DEAL
DOLE GIVE MARK METE PART RATE
SORT ALLOW AWARD CAVEL GRANT
SHARE ACCORD AFFECT ASSIGN
BESTOW DEPUTE DESIGN DIRECT
INTEND ORDAIN RATION ACCOUNT
APPOINT DESTINE PRORATE
QUARTER SPECIFY TRIBUTE
ALLOCATE
(— QUARTERS) CANTON
ALLOTMENT CUT LOT DOLE CAVEL
SHARE RATION SIZING LOTMENT
LOTTERY PORTION DIVISION
PITTANCE
ALLOW LET LOW BEAR GIVE HAVE
LEND LOAN ADMIT DEFER GRANT
LEAVE STAND THOLE YIELD ACCEPT
ACCORD ASSIGN BESTOW BETEEM
ENABLE ENDURE PERMIT SUFFER
APPROVE CONCEDE CONFESS
LICENCE LICENSE SUFFICE SUPPOSE
SUSTAIN CONSIDER DISPENSE
SANCTION TOLERATE
ALLOWABLE FREE LICIT LAWFUL
ALLOWANCE BOT FEE ICE AGIO
BOTE DOLE EASE EDGE GIFT HIRE
ODDS RATE SALT SIZE ARRAS
BATTA CLOFF GRANT LEAVE SHARE
STENT STINT BOUCHE BOUNTY
CORODY FODDER MARGIN RATING
REGAIN SALARY SEQUEL TANTUM
ALIMENT ALIMONY CORRODY
DIETARY DIOBELY LEAKAGE
LOWANCE PENSION PORTION
PREBEND SCALAGE STIPENT
TEARAGE APPENAGE APPROVAL
BREAKAGE DISCOUNT DRAFTAGE
ORDINARY QUANTITY SANCTION
SOLATIUM VIATICUM
(— FOR EXPENSES) DIET
(— FOR MAINTENANCE) ALIMENT
(— FOR THICKNESS) BOXING
(— FOR WASTE) TRET
(— FOR WEIGHT) BUG TARE DRAFT
DRAUGHT
(— OF ARROWS) SHEAF
(— OF FOOD) DIET BOUCHE
DIETARY
(— OF TIME OR DISTANCE) LAW
(— TO COMPETITOR) LAW
(CLOTHING —) INLAY
(CORRECTIVE —) SALT
(NEGATIVE —) INTERFERENCE
ALLOWED VENIAL LICENTIATE
(NOT —) ILLICIT FORBIDDEN
ALLOY LAY LOY MIX AICH ASEM
ALPAX BIDRI BIDRY BRASS CALIN
DURAL FLINT INVAR MOKUM MONEL
TERNE ALBATA ALNICO ALUMEL
BIDREE BILLON BRONZE CERMET
GARBLE ILLIUM LATTEN LEAVEN
NIELLO OCCAMY OREIDE OROIDE
PEWTER SOLDER TAMBAC TOMBAC
TOMBAK ACIERAL ALCHEMY

AMALGAM BABBITT BIDDERY ELINVAR INCONEL MIXTURE PAKTONG RHEOTAN RHODITE SEMILOR SIMILOR TAENITE TUTANIA TUTENAG ALFENIDE ARGENTON ARSEDINE AWARUITE CALAMINE CARACOLI DORALIUM ELECTRUM EUTECTIC GUNMETAL HARDENER KAMACITE METALINE ROMANIUM STELLITE

ALL-PERVADING UNIVERSAL

ALL RIGHT OK YES OKAY AGREED OKEYDOKE

ALLSEED FLAXSEED BURSTWORT

ALL SOULS' DAY SOULMASS

ALLSPICE BUBBY PIMENTO

ALLTHORN JUNCO

ALLUDE HINT IMPLY POINT REFER ADVERT GLANCE RELATE CONNOTE MENTION SUGGEST INDICATE INTIMATE

ALLURE IT AIR COY WIN WOO BAIT DRAW LEAD LURE MOVE SWAY WILE ANGLE BRIBE CHARM COURT DECOY SNARE TEMPT ALLECT ENTICE ENTRAP ILLURE INDUCE INVITE SEDUCE ATTRACT BEGUILE ENSNARE BLANDISH INESCATE INVEIGLE PERSUADE SIRENING

ALLUREMENT BAIT CORD LURE ALLURE GLAMOR GUDGEON

ALLURING GREEN TAKING SIRENIC SUGARED TAKEFUL CATCHING ENTICING FETCHING

ALLUSION HINT TWIT TOUCH GLANCE REFLEX INKLING MENTION INNUENDO INSTANCE

ALLUSIVE CANTING

ALLUVIUM WASH

ALLY PAL AIDE JOIN RANGE UNION UNITE BACKER COXCOX FRIEND HELPER LEAGUE ALLIANT CONNECT PARTNER ADHERENT CONFEDER FEDERATE (PL.) FOEDERATI

ALMANAC ORDO PADDY CALENDAR

ALMEMAR BEMA BIMA BIMAH

ALMIGHTY GOD GREAT CREATOR EXTREME JEHOVAH INFINITE POWERFUL PUISSANT

ALMOND DOE PILI BADAM CHUFA JORDAN KAMANI KANARI AMYGDAL BISCUIT TALISAY ALMANDER ALMENDRO AMYGDALA ROSACEAN VALENCIA (— BROWN) WOOD (— SHAPED OBJECT) MANDORLA

ALMONRY AMBRY

ALMOST JUST LIKE MOST MUCH NEAR NIGH ABOUT ANEAR CLOSE AMAIST FECKLY MOSTLY NEARLY NIGHLY MUCHWHAT WELLMOST WELLNEAR

ALMS DOLE GIFT ALMOIN AUMOUS AWMOUS BOUNTY CORBAN MAUNDY RELIEF ALMOIGN CHARITY HANDOUT PASSADE DEVOTION DONATION GRATUITY OFFERING PITTANCE

ALMSHOUSE POORHOUSE WORKHOUSE

ALMUCE HOOD AMICE VAGAS TIPPET VAKASS VARKAS

ALODIUM ODAL ODEL ODHAL ESTATE PROPERTY

ALOE PITA AGAVE

ALOEUS (FATHER OF —) NEPTUNE (SON OF —) OTUS EPHIALTES (WIFE OF —) IPHIMEDIA

ALOFT UP HIGH ABOVE AHIGH UPWARD AHEIGHT SKYWARD OVERHEAD

ALONE ALL ONE BARE LANE LORN ONLY SOLE SOLO ALOOF APART SOLUS SIMPLY SINGLE SOLEIN SOLELY SULLEN UNIQUE ALONELY FORLORN UNAIDED DESOLATE DETACHED ISOLATED SEPARATE SOLITARY (ALL —) LEELANE LEELONE

ALONG ON UP VIA AWAY LANG WITH YOND AHEAD LONGS BESIDE FORBYE FOREBY ONWARD ALONGST ENDLONG FORWARD PARALLEL TOGETHER (— THE MARGIN) DOWN (— WITH) AND (WELL —) ENDWAYS ENDWISE

ALONGSIDE AT BY ASIDE CLOSE ABOARD BESIDE ABREAST FORNENT SIDLINS FORNENST PARALLEL

ALONSOA MASKFLOWER

ALOOF DRY SHY COLD COOL ABACK ALONE APART PROUD ABEIGH FROSTY OTIOSE REMOTE SILENT DISTANT REMOVED RESERVED

ALOPECIA PELADE ATRICHIA BALDNESS

ALOPECURUS FOXTAIL

ALPACA PACO

ALPENGLOW AFTERGLOW

ALPENSTOCK STOCK BERGSTOCK

ALPHABET ABC CUFIC KUFIC LATIN ONMUN ORDER BISAYA BRAHMI CIPHER GLAGOL HANGUL HANKUL KAITHI NAGARI PRIMER ROMAJI SARADA SCRIPT TAGALA VISAYA ALJAMIA FUTHARK KALEKAH LETTERS PESHITO ALJAMIAH CROSSROW GUJARATI GURMUKHI (— SQUARE) TABLEAU

ALREADY EEN NOW DONE EVEN SINCE BEFORE

ALSACE-LORRAINE REICHSLAND

ALSINE ALLBONE

ALSO SO ALS AND EKE TOO YET ERST ITEM MORE PLUS ALONG DITTO BESIDES FURTHER THERETO LIKEWISE MOREOVER

ALTAR ARA BEMA BOMOS TABLE WEVED ACERRA AUTERE HAIKAL SHRINE TRIPOD VEDIKA CHANCEL CHANTRY ESCHARA SCROBIS THYMELE OMPHALOS REPOSOIR (— BACK) TABLE (— TOP) MENSA

ALTARPIECE ANCONA DIPTYCH TRIPTYCH

ALTAZIMUTH ABA

ALTER COOK DRAW EDIT GELD

MOVE RASE TURN VARY VEER WEND ADAPT AMEND BREAK ELIDE EMEND FORGE RESET SHAPE SHIFT ADJUST BUSHEL CENSOR CHANGE DEFORM IMMUTE JIGGER MODIFY MUTATE NEUTER REVISE TEMPER UNSAME CHAFFER COMMUTE CONVERT CORRECT CORRUPT DISTORT FASHION QUALIFY STRANGE ACTIVATE EXCHANGE (— APPEARANCE) WRY (— BOUNDARIES) DEACON (— DIRECTION) BREAK (— STANCE) CLOSE

ALTERATION DOWN CROSS ACTION CHANGE JANGLE DISEASE HEMIOLA MUTATION UPHEAVAL (— OF BOUNDARY) ERUB ERUV

ALTERATIVE LAPPA FUMARIA

ALTERCATE JANGLE STICKLE WRANGLE

ALTERCATION SPAT TIFF TILT BRAWL BROIL CROSS FIGHT BARNEY BICKER FRACAS JANGLE STRIFE BRABBLE CONTEST DISPUTE PASSAGE QUARREL WRANGLE SQUABBLE

ALTERED BURNT BROKEN VARIED ANOTHER FEIGNED ADJUSTED

ALTERNATE ELSE SWAY VARY OTHER RECUR SHIFT ALTERN CHANGE RINGER ROTATE SECOND SEESAW SPIRAL EXCHANGE INTERMIT TRAVERSE (— LEAPS AND DIVES) GREYHOUND

ALTERNATELY ABOUT RECIPROCALLY

ALTERNATION ADDITION

ALTERNATIVE OR FORK HORN CHOICE EITHER OPTION DISJUNCT ELECTION

ALTHAEA MALLOW (FATHER OF —) THESTIUS (HUSBAND OF —) OENEUS (SON OF —) MELEAGER

ALTHORN SAX ALTO ALTUS SAXHORN

ALTHOUGH ALL EEN SET ALBE ALIF EVEN THAT WHEN WHILE ALBEIT THOUGH WHENAS DESPITE HOWBEIT WHEREAS

ALTITUDE APEX PEAK HIGHT LEVEL PITCH HEIGHT STATURE

ALTO MEAN ALTUS ALTHORN SAXHORN

ALTOGETHER ALL NUDE QUITE SHEER STICK AGREAT BODILY FREELY WHOLLY EXACTLY TOTALLY UTTERLY ALLTHING ENTIRELY

ALTRUISM OTHERISM

ALTRUISTIC HEROIC HEROICAL

ALUDEL POT LUDEL UDELL

ALULA LOBE WING ALULET SQUAMA TEGULA LOBULUS WINGLET CALYPTER

ALULIM ALOROS

ALUM AUM ALME ALUMEN MIGITE TSCHER STYPTIC HARDENER KALINITE

(FEATHER —) ALUNOGEN
ALUMINA ARGIL ALOXITE
ALUMNUS GRAD PUPIL GRADUATE
ALUMROOT HEUCHERA
ALUR LUR LURI
ALVEARY HIVE BEEHIVE
ALVEOLA FAVEOLUS
ALVEOLAR SPUMOID GINGIVAL
ALVEOLATE FAVOSE FAVOUS PITTED
ALWAYS O AY AYE EEN EER EVER
SIMLE STILL ALWISE SEMPRE
ALGATES FOREVER EVERMORE
ALYSSUM ALISON
AM M AME HAM
(— NOT) NAM AINT AMNT
(I —) CHAM CHYM
AMA CUP AMULA CRUET DIVER
VESSEL CHALICE
AMABILE GENTLE TENDER
AMADAVAT WAXBILL TIGERBIRD
AMADOU PUNK TINDER
AMAH NURSE SERVANT
AMAIN GREATLY FORCIBLY
AMALA AMLAH
AMALGAM ALLOY MAGNESIA
AMALGAMATE MIX FUSE JOIN
ALLOY BLEND MARRY MERGE UNITE
BLUNGE MINGLE COMBINE
COALESCE COMPOUND
AMALGAMATION MERGER ADDITION
AMALGAMATOR PLATEMAN
AMANORI NORI LAVER
AMANUENSIS PENMAN SCRIBE
TYPIST RECORDER
AMARANTH JATACO FLORAMOR
(PL.) LIGHTHOUSES
AMARILLO FUSTIC
AMARYLLIS LILY AGAVE CRINUM
AMASS HEAP HILL MASS PILE SAVE
GROSS HOARD STACK STORE
GATHER COLLECT COMPILE
CONGEST ENGROSS ASSEMBLE
OVERHEAP
AMATA (DAUGHTER OF —) LAVINIA
(HUSBAND OF —) LATINUS
AMATEUR HAM TIRO TYRO NOVICE
SUNDAY VOTARY ADMIRER
DABBLER DEVOTEE FANCIER
JACKLEG PATRIOT VARMENT
VARMINT BEGINNER
AMATEURISH TYRONIC
AMATORY EROTIC LOVING TENDER
AMOROUS GALLANT
AMAZE AWE MAZE STAM STUN
ALARM FERLY ASTONY AWHAPE
WONDER ASTOUND CONFUSE
IMPRESS PERPLEX STAGGER
STUPEFY ASTONISH BEWILDER
CONFOUND DUMFOUND FRIGHTEN
SURPRISE
AMAZED AGAZED BUSHED ASTONIED
AMAZEMENT STAM AMAZE FERLY
GHAST FERLIE FRENZY WONDER
MADNESS SURPRISE
AMBARI KANAF KENAF KANAFF
AMBASSADOR AGENT ELCHI ENVOY
VAKIL DEPUTY ELCHEE LEDGER
LEGATE NUNCIO VAKEEL EMBASSY
LEAGUER CAPUCIUS DIPLOMAT
MINISTER

AMBER GRIS LIME AUMER AWMER
RESIN FUSTIC LAMMER SUCCIN
YELLOW BURMITE AMBEROID
ELECTRUM SUNSTONE
AMBERFISH JUREL CARANX KAHALA
RUNNER CARANGID CARANGIN
KINGFISH MACKEREL MEDREGAL
AMBERGRIS AMBER AMBRACAN
AMBERJACK ALMICORE CORONADO
AMBIENCE MILIEU AMBIANCE
AMBIGUITY AMBAGE PARADOX
AMBIGUOUS DARK VAGUE DOUBLE
FORKED CRYPTIC DUBIOUS
DOUBTFUL SLIPPERY SPURIOUS
(NOT —) EXPRESS
AMBIT LIMIT SCOPE SPACE BOUNDS
EXTENT SPHERE CIRCUIT COMPASS
BOUNDARY PRECINCT
AMBITION ATE GOAL HOPE WISH
GLORY DESIRE PURPOSE
AMBITIONLESS DRIFTING
AMBITIOUS AVID BOLD HIGH KEEN
EAGER ETTLE SHOWY EMULOUS
ASPIRING
AMBITUS TENOR
AMBIVALENCE BIPOLARITY
AMBIVALENT EQUIVOCAL
AMBLE FOOL GAIT MOOCH PADNAG
MEANDER SAUNTER TRIPPLE
AMBLING TOLUTATION
AMBO DESK PULPIT
AMBOCEPTOR COPULA MEDIATOR
AMBOYNA LINGOA KIABOOCA
AMBROSIA AMBROSE KINGWEED
AMBROSIAL DIVINE FRAGRANT
AMBRY SAFE CHEST NICHE AUMRIE
CLOSET PANTRY RECESS ALMONRY
ARMOIRE ARMARIUM CUPBOARD
AMBULANCE AUXILIUM
AMBULATE GAD HIKE MOVE WALK
AMBULATORY WALK ALURE
GALLERY PORTICO CLOISTER
PERAMBLE
AMBUSCADE WATCH WAYLAY
BUSHMENT
AMBUSH NAB LURE LURK TRAP
WAIT AWAIT BLIND BUSSE CATCH
COVER SHOMA SNARE STALE TRAIN
WATCH INBUSH THREAT WAYLAY
FORELAY SCUPPER DISGUISE
ENBUSSHE
AMCHOOR AMHAR
AMELIORATE EASE HELP MEND
AMEND EMEND BETTER REFORM
IMPROVE PROMOTE
AMEN YEA TRULY ASSENT SOBEIT
VERILY APPROVAL SANCTION
AMENABLE OPEN LIABLE PLIANT
SUBJECT
AMEND END BEET HEAL MEND
ALTER ATONE BEETE EMEND REDUB
BETTER CHANGE DOCTOR REFORM
REMEDY REPAIR REPEAL REVISE
CONVERT CORRECT ENLARGE
IMPROVE RECOVER RECTIFY
REDRESS RESTORE CHASTISE
AMENDING COMPENSATION
AMENDMENT RIDER AMENDS
SLEEPER

AMENDS BOOT MEND ASSETH
ASSYTH REWARD APOLOGY
REDRESS
AMENITY JOY COMITY FEATURE
SUAVITY CIVILITY COURTESY
MILDNESS
(PL.) AGREMENS FROUFROU
NICETIES
AMENT JUL CHAT IDIOT IULUS
MORON CATKIN CACHRYS CATTAIL
GOSLING IMBECILE NUCAMENT
AMERCE FINE MERCE MULCT TREAT
AFFEER PUNISH SCONCE CONDEMN
FORFEIT
AMERCEMENT MULCT UNLAW
BLOODWIT
AMERICA INDIA
AMERICAN YANK GRINGO YANKEE
YANQUI AMERICA WESTERN
JONATHAN
AMERICANISM HECKERISM
AMETHYST ONEGITE CORUNDUM
AMIABILITY DOUCEUR
AMIABLE GOOD KIND WARM SWEET
CLEVER GENIAL GENTLE LOVING
MELLOW SMOOTH TENDER AFFABLE
LOVABLE WINSOME CHARMING
ENGAGING FRIENDLY PLEASING
AMICABLE KIND FRIENDLY
AMICE AMIT AMYS CAPE COWL
HOOD EPHOD ALMUCE DOMINO
TIPPET VAKASS AMICTUS VESTMENT
AMID IN OMEL AMELL AMONG
AMIDST DURING IMELLE AMONGST
BETWEEN
AMIDE LACTAM SULTAM ANILIDE
ARYLIDE
AMINE ANILIN ANILINE
AMISS ILL MIS AWRY BIAS AGATE
AGLEY ASKEW WRONG ACROSS
AGRIEF ASTRAY FAULTY MISTAKE
IMPROPER
AMITY PEACE ACCORD CONCORD
HARMONY
AMMA ABBESS MOTHER
AMMONIA HARTSHORN
AMMONITE POLYPOD AMMONOID
BACULITE CACULOID CERATITE
SALIGRAM
AMMONIUM CARBONATE
HARTSHORN
AMMUNITION AMMO AMMU ARMS
SHOT BOMBS FODDER POWDER
SHELLS BULLETS GRENADES
MATERIAL MATERIEL ORDNANCE
SHRAPNEL
AMNESIA LAPSE FORGETFULNESS
AMNESTY COWLE PARDON OBLIVION
AMNION SAC CAUL SEROSA
INDUSIUM MEMBRANE
AMOBARBITAL AMYTAL
AMOEBA AMEBA AMEBULA AMOBULA
PROTEUS RHIZOPOD
AMOK MAD AMUCK CRAZY CRAZED
VIOLENT FRENZIED
AMOLE EMOL AMOULI AMOLILLA
MANFREDA
AMONG IN MID AMID INTO MANG
MONG OMEL WITH AMANG AMELL

MIDST AMIDST BIMONG IMELLE
WITHIN BETWEEN
(— OTHER THINGS) IA
AMOR EROS LOVE CUPID AMOROSO
AMORAL NEUTRAL NONMORAL
AMORITE CANAANITE
AMOROUS FOND GAMY SOFT WARM
CADGY JOLLY NUTTY ARDENT
COQUET EROTIC LOVELY LOVING
TENDER AMATIVE AMATORY
AMIABLE FERVENT GALLANT
JEALOUS SMICKER LOVESOME
VENEREAN
AMORPHOUS VAGUE HYALINE
DEFORMED FORMLESS RESINOUS
AMORT ALAMORT DEJECTED
LIFELESS
AMORTIZE DESTROY MORTISE
ALIENATE
AMOUNT GO GOB LOT SUM SUP TOT
ANTE BODY COME DOSE DRAW
FECK KIND LEVY MESS REAM RISE
SOUD SOWD UNIT WARE CHUNK
COUNT GROSS MOUNT PRICE
REACH STACK STORE STUFF TOTAL
WHOLE BUDGET DEGREE DOSAGE
EFFECT EXTENT FIGURE MATTER
NUMBER SUPPLY ADVANCE
FOOTING QUANTUM SCRUPLE
SIGNIFY SLATHER TODDICK
INCREASE QUANTITY SPOONFUL
SURMOUNT VALLIDOM
(— BORNE BY BEAST) SEAM
(— CARRIED AT ONE TIME) GANG
(— DUE) BILL SCORE
(— HELD) CAPACITY
(— OF BASS) BOOMINESS
(— OF CONCRETE) LIFT
(— OF DYE) STRIKE
(— OF FLOW) STRENGTH
(— OF FREIGHT) CARLOAD
(— OF GAS) BREATH
(— OF HERRINGS) CRANNAGE
(— OF LEAKAGE) SLIP
(— OF LIQUOR) SLUG
(— OF MEDICINE) DOSAGE
(— OF MONEY) BEAN BOND CASH
SCOT
(— OF OIL) ALLOWABLE
(— OF PAYMENT) FOOTAGE
(— OF POWDER) INCREMENT
(— OF SOIL) INTHROW
(— OF WATER) CATCHMENT
(— OF WORK) ASSIGNMENT
(— OWED) LIABILITY
(— PAID) COST
(— TURNED BY SPADE) GRAFT
(APPRECIABLE. —) BEANS
(COMPLETE —) FULL
(CONSIDERABLE —) MIGHT HANTLE
HATFUL
(EXACT —) NICK
(EXTRA —) BONUS
(GREAT —) MICKLE INFINITY
MOUNTAIN
(GROSS —) SLUMP
(INADEQUATE —) DEFICIENCY
(INDEFINITE —) BAIT SNAG SOME
(INFINITESIMAL —) IOTA

(INSIGNIFICANT —) SCRAT
(LARGE —) GOB LOB JUNT LUMP
MINT SNAG SWAG SIEGE SLASH
SPATE BOODLE SOMDEL BONANZA
SOMDIEL CARTLOAD MUCHNESS
SOMEDEAL
(LAVISH —) SLATHER
(LEAST POSSIBLE —) GRAIN
(LIMITED —) SPRINKLING
(MINUTE —) HAIR FLEABITE
(RENT —) GALE
(SIZABLE —) CHUNK SMART
(SLIGHT —) ADDED SNACK TILLY
(SMALL —) ACE BIT DAB DITE DOIT
DRAM DRIB FLOW HINT HOOT INCH
LICK SNAP SONG SPOT SPECK
SPURT TRACE DRAPPY PICKLE
SMIDGE TICKET CAPSULE DRAPPIE
GLIMMER KENNING SMIDGEN
SMIDGIN
(SMALLEST —) JOT STIVER
STEEVER STUIVER
(TENFOLD —) DECUPLE
(USUAL —) GRIST
(WHOLE —) ALL SUBSTANCE
(YEARLY —) ANNUITY
AMOUR DRURY DRUERY AMOURET
INTRIGUE PARAMOUR
AMPERSAND AND ALSO PLUS
AMPASSY IPSEAND
AMPHETAMINE BENZEDRINE
AMPHIBIA BATRACHIA
AMPHIBIAN EFT OLM FROG HYLA
NEWT RANA TOAD ANURA SIREN
SNAKE AMPHIB CAUDATE ERYOPID
PROTEUS TADPOLE AISTOPOD
AMPHIBOLE EDENITE ORALITE
URALITE ASBESTOS CROSSITE
AMPHICARPA FALCATA
AMPHIGASTRIUM UNDERLEAF
AMPHION (BROTHER OF —) ZETHUS
(FATHER OF —) ZEUS IASUS
JUPITER
(MOTHER OF —) ANTIOPE
(WIFE OF —) NIOBE
AMPHIPOD SHRIMP
AMPHITHEA (DAUGHTER OF —)
ANTICLEA
(HUSBAND OF —) AUTOLYCUS
AMPHITHEATER BOWL OVAL ARENA
CAVEA CIRCUS STADIUM THEATER
AMPHITRITE (FATHER OF —)
NEREUS OCEANUS
(HUSBAND OF —) NEPTUNE
POSEIDON
(MOTHER OF —) TETHYS
(SON OF —) TRITON
AMPHORA JUG URN VASE CADUS
DIOTA PELIKE
AMPLE BIG FAIR FULL GOOD MUCH
RICH SIDE WIDE BROAD GREAT
LARGE LUCKY PLUMP ROOMY
ROUND WALLY ENOUGH HEARTY
PLENTY PROLIX COPIOUS LIBERAL
OPULENT WEALTHY ABUNDANT
ADEQUATE BARONIAL GENEROUS
HANDSOME SPACIOUS
AMPLIFICATION GAIN
AMPLIFIED EXTENDED

AMPLIFIER BOOSTER REPEATER
AMPLIFY PAD FARCE FARSE SWELL
WIDEN DILATE EXPAND EXTEND
STRESS AUGMENT ENLARGE
STRETCH AMPLIATE HEIGHTEN
INCREASE LENGTHEN MULTIPLY
AMPLITUDE LATITUDE OPULENCE
AMPLY LARGE
AMPUTATE CUT LOP PRUNE SEVER
CURTAIL
AMPUTATION APOCOPE
AMRITA RASA
AMULA AMA VESSEL
AMULET GEM MET HAND JUJU MOJO
PLUM CHARM IMAGE MENAT SAFFI
SAFIE TOKEN FETISH GRIGRI
MASCOT SAPHIE SCROLL TABLET
AMALETT ICHTHUS ICHTHYS
PERIAPT GREEGREE HAGSTONE
LIGATURE ORNAMENT TALISMAN
AMULIUS (BROTHER OF —) NUMITOR
(FATHER OF —) PROCAS
(NEPHEW OF —) LAUSUS
AMURRU MARTU
AMUSE GAME LAKE ENJOY MIRTH
SHORT SPORT ABSORB DELUDE
DIVERT ENGAGE FROLIC PLEASE
POPJOY SOLACE TICKLE BEGUILE
DISPORT GRATIFY PASTIME
BEWILDER DISTRACT RECREATE
AMUSEMENT FAD FUN JEU GAME
JEST LAKE PLAY MIRTH SPORT
LAKING MUSERY PASTIME
COTTABUS LAUGHTER PLEASURE
(PL.) MIDWAY
AMUSING COMIC DROLL FUNNY
MERRY COMICAL FOOLISH KILLING
RISIBLE FARCICAL HUMOROUS
PLEASANT SPORTFUL
AMYGDALA TONSIL
AMYL AMYDON PENTYL ISOAMYL
AMYLASE PTYALIN DIASTASE
AMYMONE (FATHER OF —) DANAUS
(HUSBAND OF —) ENCELADUS
(SON OF —) NAUPLIUS
AMYTHAON (BROTHER OF —)
AESON PHERES
(FATHER OF —) CRETHEUS
(MOTHER OF —) TYRO
(SON OF —) BIAS MELAMPUS
(WIFE OF —) IDOMENE
AN ONE ARTICLE
ANA EVENTS OMNIANA SAYINGS
ANABAPTIST DIPPER ABECEDARIAN
ANABAS MARTINICO
ANABATIC DESCENDING
ANABO NABO ANABONG
ANABRANCH BRANCH TALLYWALKA
ANACHRONISM SOLECISM
ANACONDA BOA ABOLLA SUCURI
SUCURY CAMOUDIE SUCURUJU
ANACREONTIC TEIAN
ANACRUSIS UPBEAT
ANADEM CROWN DIADEM FILLET
WREATH CHAPLET CORONET
GARLAND
ANAGNOST LECTOR READER
ANAGOGICAL MYSTICAL
ANAGRAM REBUS PUZZLE
METAGRAM

(PL.) VERBARIUM
ANAGUA KNACKAWAY KNOCKAWAY
ANAL PODICAL
ANALABOS CLOAK
ANALGESIC ANTIPYRIN PHENALGIN
ANALOGICAL NORMAL
ANALOGOUS LIKE SIMILAR
ANALOGUE DFDT ANALOG
ANALOGY QIYAS
(CLOSE —) PARITY
ANALYSIS TEST INDEX STUDY
ANATOMY AUTOPSY SCANSION
SOLUTION
(ECONOMIC —) DYNAMICS
(LOGICAL —) SYLLOGISM
ANALYTIC SUBTLE REGULAR
(NOT —) SYNTHETIC SYNTHETICAL
ANALYTICAL CLINICAL DIVISIVE
ANALYZE RUN PART ASSAY BREAK
PARSE SENSE STUDY WEIGH
ASSESS DIVIDE REDUCE DISSECT
EXAMINE ITEMIZE RESOLVE TITRATE
UNPIECE APPRAISE CONSTRUE
DIAGNOSE SEPARATE
(— ACCOUNT) AGE
(— VERSE) SCAN
ANAMITE TWINE
ANANAS ANANA PINGUIN
ANANIAS LIAR SIDRACH
ANANSI NANCY
ANAPEST ANTIDACTYL
ANARCHIST RED REBEL ANARCH
NIHILIST REDSHIRT
ANARCHY RIOT CHAOS REVOLT
LICENSE MISRULE DISORDER
ANASARCA DROPSY
ANASAZI PUEBLO PLATEAU
ANASCHISTIC EUMITOTIC
ANASTOMOSIS GLOMUS
ANASTROPHE INVERSION
ANATHEMA WO BAN MUD WOE
OATH CURSE CENSURE
ANATHEMATIZE CURSE ACCURSE
EXECRATE
ANATOMIZE ANALYZE DISSECT
ANATOMY TOPOLOGY
(— OF HORSE) HIPPOTOMY
(MICROSCOPIC —) HISTOLOGY
(VEGETABLE —) PHYTOTOMY
ANAXIBIA (DAUGHTER OF —)
PELOPEA ALCESTIS PISIDICE
(FATHER OF —) BIAS
(HUSBAND OF —) PELIAS
(SON OF —) ACASTUS
ANCESTOR ION MIL ADAM EBER
HETH ROOT SIRE DORUS ELDER
STOCK APETUS ATAVUS AUTHOR
BELDAM EPONYM FATHER MANNUS
MILEDH PARENT STIPES ANCIENT
BELDAME BELSIRE EPAPHUS
FLEANCE FORBEAR IAPETUS
ISHMAEL SAKULYA DARDANUS
FOREBEAR FOREGOER MILESIUS
MYRMIDON RELATIVE
(— CULT) MANISM
(—S OF GOTLANDERS) GEAT
(MAORI —) TIKI TUPUNA
(PL.) OLDERS ANCESTRY
ANCESTRAL AVAL AVITAL AVITIC

LINEAL FAMILIAL
ANCESTRY KIN RACE SEED ATHEL
FAMILY ORIGIN PEOPLE SOURCE
STRAIN DESCENT KINDRED LINEAGE
BREEDING PEDIGREE
ANCHISES (FATHER OF —) CAPYS
(MOTHER OF —) THEMIS
(SON OF —) AENEAS
ANCHOR FIX BIND DRAG DRUG
HOOK MOOR REST SLUG SPUD
STOP AFFIX BERTH BOWER KEDGE
RIVET SHEET STOCK ATTACH
DROGUE FASTEN HERMIT KEDGER
KELLEG SECURE STREAM CHAPLET
CONNECT DEADMAN GRAPNEL
GROUSER KILLICK MUDHOOK
SUPPORT COCKBILL
(— IN PLACE) ACOCKBILL
(— RING) TORUS
(AT —) ASTAY
(BEAM —) WALL
ANCHORAGE DOCK STAY HARBOR
REFUGE RIDING MOORAGE
ABUTMENT BERTHAGE ROOTHOLD
ANCHORITE MONK HERMIT
ACHORET ASCETIC EREMITE
RECLUSE STYLITE
ANCHOVY NEHU BOCON SPRAT
HERRING SARDINE
(PL.) ALICI
ANCHUSA OXTONGUE
ANCIENT ELD OLD AGED AULD FERN
HIGH HOAR IAGO YORE EARLY
ELDER HOARY OLDEN BYGONE
ENSIGN FORMER NOETIC PISTOL
PRIMAL VETUST ANTIENT ANTIQUE
ARCHAIC ARCHEAN CLASSIC
OGYGEAN OGYGIAN HISTORIC
NOACHIAN OBSOLETE PRIMEVAL
PRISTINE
(MOST —) ELDEST
ANCIENTLY OLD HIGH
ANCILLA HELPER ADJUNCT SERVANT
ANCON ELBOW CORBEL CONSOLE
AND N U AN ET SO ANT TOO ALSO
PLUS BESIDES FURTHER MOREOVER
(— SO FORTH) ETC USW
ANDAMAN MINCOPI MINKOPI
MINCOPIE
ANDESITE BONINITE TIMAZITE
ANDIRON DOG CHENET COBIRON
FIREDOG HESSIAN HANDIRON
LANDIRON
ANDORRA (LANGUAGE OF —)
CATALAN
(NATIVE OF —) ANDOSIAN
(RIVER OF —) VALIRA
ANDRADITE APLOME GARNET
ANDROCONIUM STIGMA PLUMULE
ANDROID ROBOT AUTOMATON
ANDROMACHE (FATHER OF —)
EETION
(HUSBAND OF —) HECTOR HELENUS
(SON OF —) PIELUS ASTYANAX
MOLOSSUS PERGAMUS
ANDROMEDA (FATHER OF —)
CEPHEUS
(MOTHER OF —) CASSIOPEA
(RESCUER OF —) PERSEUS

ANDROMEDE BIELID
ANECDOTE GAG TOY JOKE TALE
YARN EVENT STORY SKETCH
HAGGADA EXEMPLUM HAGGADAH
ANECDOTAL LITERARY
ANECHOIC DEAD
ANEMIA SURRA SURRAH ANAEMIA
HYPAEMA HYPHEMA HYPHEMIA
ISCHEMIA SPANEMIA
ANEMIC LOW PALE WEAK WATERY
LIFELESS
ANEMONE LILY CRASS EMONY
OPELET BOWBELLS SNOWDROP
ANENT ON RE ABOUT ANENST
BESIDE TOWARD AGAINST OPPOSITE
ANESTHESIA BLOCK CORYL SPINAL
ANESTHETIC GAS ETHER ACOINE
OBTUSE OPIATE COCAINE DULLING
MENTHOL PARAFORM SEDATIVE
ANESTHETIZE FREEZE ETHERIZE
ANEW OVER AGAIN NEWLY AFRESH
ITERUM NEWLINS NEWLINGS
RECENTLY
ANFRACTUOUS SPIRAL BENDING
SINUOUS WINDING TORTUOUS
ANGEL MAH DEVA EBUS ANGLE
ARDOR ARIEL DAEVA DULIA NAKIR
YAKSA ABDIEL ARIOCH BACKER
BELIAL CHERUB MONKIR MUNKAR
NEKKAR SERAPH SPIRIT UZZIEL
YAKSHA ANGELET EGREGOR
ISRAFEL RAPHAEL SPONSOR
WATCHER ZADKIEL ZOPHIEL
APOLLYON GUARDIAN ITHURIEL
SUPERNAL
(— OF DEATH) AZRAEL SAMMAEL
(FALLEN —S) HELL
(GUARDIAN —) YAKSA YAKSHA
YAKSHI
(RECORDING —) SIJIL SIJILL
(PL.) HOST FRAVASHI SERAPHIM
ANGELFISH MONK MUNK ANGEL
QUOTT SQUAT MONACH FLATFISH
KINGSTON MONKFISH SQUATINA
ANGELIC SAINTLY BEATIFIC
CHERUBIC HEAVENLY SERAPHIC
ANGELICA JELLICA
ANGELIN PACAY ANGELEEN
ANGER ARR IRE IRK VEX BILE BURN
CRAB FELL FUME FURY GALL GRIM
HUFF MOOD RAGE RILE ROIL RUFF
TEEN TIFF ANNOY BIRSE GRAME
GRIPE HATEL IRISH PIQUE SPONK
SPUNK THRAW WRATH BOTHER
CHOLER DANDER ENRAGE EXCITE
GRIEVE MONKEY NETTLE OFFEND
RANCOR SPLEEN TALENT TEMPER
WARMTH BURNING DESPITE
DUDGEON EMOTION INCENSE
INFLAME PASSION PROVOKE
STOMACH ACRIMONY DISTRESS
EBENEZER IRRITATE VEXATION
ANGERED SORE AGRAMED PELTISH
INCENSED
ANGICO CURUPAY
ANGINA PRUNELLA
ANGIOSPERM HARDWOOD
METASPERM
ANGLE IN BOB DIP ELL OUT TEE

WRO CANT COIN COOK DRAW FISH FORK HADE KEEN KNEE LEAD NOOK PEAK SITE WICK ANCON ARRIS AXIAL BEVEL BIGHT CHOIL COIGN DRAFT DRIFT ELBOW FLEAM GROIN GUISE INGLE PHASE POINT QUOIN SLANT ALLURE ANGULE ASPECT CANTON CORNEL CORNER DIRECT ENGHLE EPAULE HADING LAGGEN LAGGIN OCTANT SCHEME SQUARE TORNUS ANGLIAN ANGULUS AZIMUTH BASTION DRAUGHT GIMMICK KNUCKLE PERIGON RAVELIN SALIENT ARGUMENT DECALAGE DIHEDRAL FISHHOOK INTRIGUE SHOULDER
(— OF BEVEL) FLEAM FLEEM
(— OF BOWSPRIT) STEEVE STEEVING
(— OF CLUB HEAD) LIE
(— OF EYELIDS) CANTHUS
(— OF HAT BRIM) BREAK
(— OF HIPBONE) HOOK
(— OF LEAF) AXIL
(— OF RAFTER) HEEL
(— OF TIMBER KNEE) BREECH
(DRIFT —) LEEWAY
(OBTUSE —) HEEL BULLNOSE
(ROOF —) HIP FASTIGIUM
(ROUND —) PERIGON
(SALIENT —) ARIS ARRIS
ANGLED CANTED NOOKED ANGULATE
ANGLER MONK FRIAR THIEF SLIMER LOPHLID RODSTER SPINNER WIDEGAB WIDEGAP ALLMOUTH FROGFISH MONKFISH PISCATOR TOADFISH
ANGLESMITH SLABMAN
ANGLEWORM ESS WORM FISHWORM
ANGLICAN EPISCOPAL
ANGLO CAUCASIAN

ANGOLA
CAPITAL: LUANDA
COIN: MACUTA MACUTE
DISTRICT: CABINDA
KINGDOM: BAKONGO
LANGUAGE: BANTU KIMBUNDU
MOUNTAIN: LOVITI
PLATEAU: PLANALTO
PORT: LOBITO LUANDA
RIVER: CONGO CUITO COANZA CUNENE KUNENE KWANGO KWANZA
TOWN: LOBITO LUANDA BENGUELA MOSSAMEDES
TRIBE: BANTU KIKONGO

ANGORA CAT GOAT ANGOLA RABBIT
ANGRILY ANGERLY IRATELY FUMINGLY
ANGRY MAD ASHY EVIL GRIM GRUM HIGH RILY ROID ROSY SORE WARM WAXY WILD WRAW CROOK CROSS GRAME HUFFY IRATE IROUS MOODY RATTY RILEY SNAKY STUNT VEXED WEMOD WROTH BIRSIT CHAFED

CROUSE FRENZY FUMING FUMOUS HEATED IREFUL LOADED SHIRTY SNAKEY STUFFY FRETFUL FURIOUS HOPPING IRACUND PAINFUL SNAKISH SPLEENY CHOLERIC INFLAMED RIGOROUS SPITFIRE TEMPERED VEHEMENT WREAKFUL
(BE —) STEAM
ANGRY-LOOKING THUNDERY
ANGUISH WOE ACHE HARM HURT PAIN PANG RACK TRAY AGONY ANGST ANGUS DOLOR GRIEF THROE MISERY REGRET SORROW ANGOISE ANGWICH REMORSE TORMENT TORTURE DISTRESS
ANGUISHED GRIEFFUL
ANGULAR BONE BONY EDGY LEAN SLIM THIN GAUNT SHARP ABRUPT POINTED SCRAWNY CORNERED
(NOT —) SOFT
ANGULARITY EDGINESS
ANGUS FORFAR FORFARSHIRE
ANHYDRIDE LACTAM SULTAM FULGIDE LACTIDE SULTONE GLUCOSAN MANNITAN SORBITAN
ANHYDROUS DRY DESICCATED
ANI WITCH CUCKOO JEWBIRD KEELBILL KEELBIRD TICKBIRD
ANIMADVERSION BLAME REMARK CENSURE COMMENT REPROOF WARNING MONITION REPROACH
ANIMAL (LOOK ALSO UNDER SPECIFIC HEADINGS) DEER BEAST BIPED BLACK BRUTE GRADE GROSS LUSTY STORE STRAY BRUTAL CARNAL DAPPLE DESPOT FLESHY KICKER MAMMAL RODENT SILVAN SORREL SPONGE SYLVAN BEASTIE BREEDER CARRION CRITTER SENSUAL BURROWER CREATURE EMIGRANT ORGANISM
(— COLLECTION) LARDER
(— FOR MARKET) STOCKER
(— INHABITED BY SPIRIT) GUACA HUACA
(— OF LITTLE VALUE) SCALAWAG SKALAWAG
(— RESEMBLING MAN) HOMINOID
(— SHOT) KILL
(— WITH BLACK COAT AND MARKINGS) PARSON
(— WITH DOCKED TAIL) CURTAL
(—S AS RENT) CAIN
(2-HORNED —) BICORN BICORNE
(BEEF —) BONER GRASSER
(BOVINE —) BOSS BRUTE
(BROKEN-DOWN —) CROCK
(CARNIVOROUS —) SARCOPHILE
(CASTRATED —) SEG SEGG SPAY SPADO GELDING
(COLD-BLOODED —) ECTOTHERM
(CREATED —) BARAMIN
(DOMESTIC —) DOER SCRUB BESTIAL FOLLOWER SCRUBBER
(DRAFT —) AVER AIVER
(EMACIATED —) FRAME SKELETON
(FABULOUS —) KYLIN BUNYIP DRAGON ACEPHAL GRIFFIN GRIFFON GRYPHON UNICORN SEMITAUR
(FEMALE —) HEN SHE LADY JENNY SHEDER

(FERAL —) CIMAROON CIMARRON CIMMARON
(FLEA-RIDDEN —) FLEABAG
(FOOTLESS —) APOD APODE
(FREAKISH —) FERLY FERLIE
(GRASSHOPPER-EATING —) WHANGAM
(GRAY —) GRIZZLE
(GRAZING —) HERBAGER
(GREEDY —) GORB
(HORNED —) HORN REEM
(HYPOTHETICAL —) PROAVIS
(IMAGINARY —) CATAWAMPUS
(LOWER —) BEAST CREATURE
(LUSTY OR PLUMP —) BILCH BILSH
(MALE —) HE TOM BUCK BULL JACK STAG JOHNNY BACHELOR
(MARINE —) LANCELET
(MATURE —) SENIOR
(MEAT —) CHOPPER
(MISCHIEVOUS —) ELF
(MYTHICAL —) HODAG KYLIN MOONACK
(ODD —) SPLACKNUCK
(PACK —) HUNIA SUMPTER
(PET —) CADE
(PURSUED —S) GAME
(ROASTED —) BARBECUE BARBEQUE
(SADDLE —) LOPER
(SCRAWNY —) SCRAG
(SHORN —) SHEAR
(SKINNY —) SCRAE
(SLUGGISH —) DRUMBLE
(SPOTTED —) CALICO
(STOCKY —) BLOCK
(STUNTED —) SHARGAR SHARGER
(THICKSET —) NUGGET
(TOTEM —) EPONYM
(UNBRANDED —) SLICK
(UNCASTRATED —) ENTIRE
(UNDERSIZED —) DURGAN DURGEN
(UNHOUSED —) OUTLER OUTLIER
(UNWEANED —) SUCKER
(WANDERING —) STRAY ESTRAY
(WARM-BLOODED —) ENDOTHERM HAEMATHERM
(WATER —) AQUATIC AQUATILE
(WEAK —) DRAG DOWNER
(WILD —) SAVAGE WILDLING
(WORNOUT —) KANCKER
(WORTHLESS —) CARRION
(YOUNG —) HOG BIRD HOGG JOEY SHOT STORE JUNIOR PULLUS FATLING LITTLIN KINDLING LITTLING SUCKLING YOUNGLET
(PL.) ZOA FAUNA NECTON NEKTON
ANIMALCULISM SPERMISM
ANIMALITY HOGGERY
ANIMA MUNDI WELTGEIST
ANIMATE ACT PEP FIRE MOVE PERK STIR URGE ALIVE BRISK CHEER DRIVE FLUSH IMBUE IMPEL LIGHT LIVEN QUICK ROUSE VITAL AROUSE BRIGHT ENSOUL EXCITE INCITE INDUCE INFORM KINDLE LIVING PROMPT SPIRIT VIVIFY ACTUATE COMFORT ENLIVEN INSPIRE QUICKEN ACTIVATE ENERGIZE INSPIRIT VITALIZE

(NOT —) BRUTE
ANIMATED UP GAY VIF GLAD VIVE
ALIVE ANIME BRISK QUICK VITAL
VIVID ACTIVE ARDENT BLITHE
BRISKY LIVELY LIVING SPARKY
SPUNKY BUOYANT JOCULAR
STHENIC BOUNCING LIFESOME
SPIRITED VIGOROUS
ANIME COPAL ELEMI RESIN ROSIN
ANIMATO
ANIMIKEAN LAWSON
ANIMISM NATURISM
ANIMOSITY HATE PIQUE SPITE
ANIMUS ENMITY HATRED MALICE
RANCOR DISLIKE
ANIMUS MIND ONDE WILL EFFORT
ENMITY SPIRIT TEMPER ATTITUDE
ANISE ANET DILL CUMEN UMBEL
FENNEL SIKIMI SHIKIMI
ANKH TAU
ANKLE COOT CUIT HOCK QUIT
ANCLE QUEET TALUS WRIST
TARSUS SHACKLE
(COCKED —S) KNUCKLING
ANKLEBONE TALUS ASTRAGAL
ANKLET SHOE SOCK BANGLE
FETTER SHACKLE
ANLAGE INCEPT PROTON INITIAL
BLASTEMA
ANNALIST WRITER RECORDER
ANNALS NIHONGI REGISTER
ANNAM (ALSO SEE VIETNAM)
VIETNAM
(BOAT OF —) GAYYOU GAYDIANG
(MEASURE OF —) LY GON NGU QUO
SAO TAT PHAN THAT SHITA THUOC
TRUONG
(TOWN OF —) HUE VINH TOURANE
QUANGTRI
(WEIGHT OF —) CAN BINH DONG
ANNATTO OTTER URUCU ORLEAN
SALMON ACHIOTE ACHUETE
ANNOTTO ARNATTO ORLEANS
ANNEAL BAKE FUSE HEAT SMELT
TEMPER INFLAME TOUGHEN
GRAPHITE
ANNEALER TUBER HEATER
ANNEALING LIGHTING
ANNELID NAID WORM LUGWORM
SERPULA ANNULATE SANDWORM
SERPULAN
ANNEX ADD ELL LAY JOIN AFFIX
SEIZE UNITE ADJECT ANNECT
APPEND ATTACH FASTEN ACQUIRE
CONNECT FIXTURE POSTFIX
SUBJOIN ADDITION ANNEXURE
DOCUMENT
ANNIHILATE END OUT KILL RAZE
RUIN SLAY ABATE ANNUL ERASE
WRECK DELETE DEVOUR NOUGHT
QUENCH REDUCE ABOLISH
DESTROY EXPUNGE DECIMATE
DISCREAT UNCREATE
ANNIHILATION FANA NEGATION
ANNIVERSARY FETE MASS EMBER
FEAST ANNUAL JUBILEE YEARDAY
BIRTHDAY FESTIVAL YAHRZEIT
(100TH —) CENTENNIAL
(150TH —) SESQUICENTENNIAL

(200TH —) BIMILLENARY
BIMILLENIUM
(25TH —) SEMIJUBILEE
(50TH —) JUBILEE SEMICENTENNIAL
ANNONA ATIS ATTA ATEES
ANNOTATE EDIT NOTE STET GLOSS
BENOTE NOTIFY POSTIL REMARK
APOSTIL COMMENT EXPLAIN
FOOTNOTE
ANNOTATION APOSTIL COMMENT
SCHOLION SCHOLIUM
ANNOTATOR NOTIST
ANNOUNCE BID CRY BODE CALL
DEEM MAKE SHOW SING TELL BRUIT
CLAIM KNELL STATE VOICE ASSERT
BLAZON BROACH DENOTE HERALD
INFORM PREACH REPORT REVEAL
SIGNAL SPRING STEVEN DECLARE
DIVULGE FORERUN GAZETTE
PUBLISH SIGNIFY DENOUNCE
FORETELL INTIMATE PROCLAIM
RENOUNCE SENTENCE
ANNOUNCEMENT BID CRY HAT
BILL CALL LEAD ALARM BANCO
BANNS BLURB EDICT ALARUM
DECREE DICTUM NOTICE GAZETTE
SENSING BULLETIN CIRCULAR
DECISION
ANNOUNCER NEBO PAGE CRIER
EMCEE CALLER HERALD NUNCIO
GONGMAN GRINDER SPIELER
NUNCIATE SPRUIKER
ANNOY ARR BUG DUN EAT EGG GET
GIG HOX IRE IRK NAG NOY NYE TRY
VEX BAIT BORE BURN FASH FRET
FUSS GALL GRIG HALE HARM HAZE
HUFF NARK PAIN RILE ROIL CHAFE
CHASE CHEVY CHIVY DEVIL GRAMY
GRATE HARRY PEEVE PIQUE SPITE
STURT TEASE THORN UPSET WEARY
WORRY BADGER BOTHER CADDLE
CHIVEY CHIVVY EARWIG ENRAGE
GRAVEL HAGGLE HARASS HECKLE
HECTOR INFEST INJURE MOLEST
NEEDLE NETTLE OFFEND PESTER
POTTER RATTLE REHETE RUFFLE
TICKLE BEDEVIL DISTURB HOTFOOT
JACKSON TERRIFY TROUBLE
DISTRESS IRRITATE
ANNOYANCE VEX FASH PEST WEED
CROSS GRIEF LOATH SPITE STALL
THORN INSECT PESTER DISGUST
FASHERY NOYANCE TROUBLE
UMBRAGE FASHERIE FLEABITE
NOISANCE NUISANCE PINPRICK
ANNOYED SORE INSULTED
ANNOYING TARE NOYOUS DISEASY
HATEFUL IRKSOME NOISOME
TARSOME FASHIOUS FRETSOME
SPITEFUL TIRESOME
ANNOYINGLY CONFOUNDED
CONFOUNDEDLY
ANNUAL BOOK BUGLE PLANT
FLOWER YEARLY ANNUARY
BUGSEED BUGWEED ETESIAN
GIFTBOOK PERIODIC YEARBOOK
(OLD WORLD —) WELD
ANNUITY CENSO CONSOL INCOME
PENSION TONTINE

ANNUL TOL CASS NULL TOLL UNDO
VOID ADNUL AVOID BLANK ELIDE
ERASE QUASH REMIT RETEX UNLAW
CANCEL FRIVOL NEGATE RECALL
REPEAL REVERT REVOKE UNLIVE
VACATE ABOLISH CASHIER CASSARE
CASSATE DESTROY NULLIFY
RESCIND RETRACT REVERSE
ABROGATE ARROGATE DEROGATE
DISANNUL DISSOLVE IMBECILE
OVERRULE
ANNULAR BANDED CYCLIC RINGED
ANNULATE CINGULAR CIRCULAR
ANNULARLY RINGWISE
ANNULET RING RIDGE FILLET
ANNULUS MOLDING
ANNULMENT UNDOING
ANNULUS RING ANNULE COLLAR
GYROMA INDUSIUM
ANNUNCIATION MARYMASS
ANNUNCIATOR TELLER INDICATOR
ANOA BUFFALO SAPIUTAN
ANODE PLATE ZINCOID
ANODIC ASCENDING
ANODYNE BALM ACOPON OPIATE
REMEDY EUGENOL SOOTHER
NARCOTIC SEDATIVE
ANOINT FAT OIL RUB BALM BEAT
CERE NARD ANELE ANOIL CREAM
CROWN ENOIL LATCH NUNCT
PRUNE SALVE SMEAR SMERL
CHRISM GREASE INUNCT SPREAD
THRASH MOISTEN UNGUENT
ANOINTMENT CHRISMATORY
ANOMALOUS ODD DIFFORM
STRANGE UNUSUAL ABERRANT
ABNORMAL ATYPICAL PECULIAR
ANOMALY CREEPER CYCLOPY
EPILOIA CYCLOPIA
ANON NAN ANEW ONCE SOON AGAIN
LATER AFRESH BEDEEN BEDENE
THENCE SHORTLY
ANONYMITY NOBODYNESS
ANONYMOUS UNKNOWN NAMELESS
UNAVOWED UNSIGNED
ANOPLURA PARASITA PEDICULINA
ANOTHER NEW THAT ALIAS FRESH
SECOND TIDDER TOTHER ANITHER
FURTHER
ANOXIA ASPHYXIA
ANSWER DO IT SAY SIT ECHO MEET
PLEA SUIT ATONE AVAIL COMES
COVER JAWAB REACT REPLY SERVE
LETTER REJOIN RESULT RETORT
RETURN RIPOST COUNTER DEFENCE
DEFENSE FULFILL RESPOND
SATISFY ANTIPHON COMEBACK
PLEADING REBUTTAL REPARTEE
RESPONSE SOLUTION
(— BACK) CHOP
(— FOR) FORM VANG
(— IN FUGUE) COMES
(— THE PURPOSE) DO FIT SUIT
AVAIL SERVE
(DECISIVE —) SOCKDOLAGER
SOCKDOLOGER
(LEGAL —) DUPLY
ANSWERABLE EQUAL LIABLE
FITTING ADEQUATE AMENABLE

ANSWERER USHABTI
ANT ANAI ANAY ANER ATTA GYNE
MIRE AMPTE EMMET KELEP MAXIM
MINIM NURSE SIAFU SLAVE AMAZON
DRIVER ERGATE NEUTER WORKER
BULLDOG FORAGER FORMICE
OUVRIER PISMIRE PISSANT PONERID
REPLETE SOLDIER TERMITE
ACULEATA DORYLINE FORMICID
GYNECOID HONEYPOT MICRANER
MYRMICID TAPINOMA
(— **LION**) DOODLEBUG
(— **SHRIKE**) BATARA
(— **STUDY**) MYRMECOLOGY
(— **THRUSH**) PITTA
(— **TREE**) WORMIGO
(**WORKER** —) ERGATE
ANTA PIER PARASTAS PEDESTAL
PILASTER
ANTACID SATURANT
ANTAGONISM WAR ANIMUS ENMITY
QUARREL AVERSION CONFLICT
(**IN** —) COUNTER
ANTAGONIST FOE ENEMY PARTY
RIVAL FOEMAN BATTLER WARRIOR
COPEMATE OPPONENT OPPOSITE
WRANGLER
ANTAGONISTIC ADVERSE COUNTER
HOSTILE ANTERGIC CONTRARY
INIMICAL OPPONENT OPPOSITE
(— **TO GROWTH**) ANTIBLASTIC
(**NOT** —) SYMPATHETIC
ANTAGONIZE CONTEST
ANT BEAR BEAR ERDVARK
AARDVARK ANTEATER EDENTATE
TAMANOIR
ANTE PAY STAKE
ANTEATER TAPIR NUMBAT ECHIDNA
TAMANDU AARDVARK AARDWOLF
DASYURID EDENTATE PANGOLIN
TAMANDUA TAMANOIR
ANTEBRACHIUM CUBIT CUBITAL
CUBITUS FOREARM
ANTECEDENT FORE CAUSE PRIOR
FORMER REASON WHENCE PREMISE
ANTERIOR PREVIOUS
(— **OF CANON**) GUIDA
ANTECHAMBER LIWAN
ANTEDATE PRECEDE PREDATE
FOREDATE
ANTEDATED FORETIMED
ANTELOPE GNU KID KOB RAM SUS
ASTE BISA BUCK DODA DUST GUIB
IBEX KOBA KUDU ORYX PUKU ROAN
SUNI TOPI TORA ADDAX BAIRA
BEIRA BEISA BEKRA BOHOR BONGO
BOVID BUBAL CHIRU ELAND GORAL
GUIBA IPETE LICHI NAGOR NYALA
ORIBI PEELE PERON SABLE SAIGA
SASIN SEROW TAKIN YAKIN
BAGWYN BHOKRA BUBALE CABREE
CABRET CABRIE CABRIT CHOUKA
DUIKER DUYKER DZERAN DZEREN
DZERIN DZERON GOORAL GRIMME
HEROLA IMPALA INYALA KOODOO
LECHWE LELWEL NAKONG NILGAI
NILGAU PALLAH POOKOO RHEBOK
ALGAZEL BLAUBOK BLESBOK
BUBALIS CHAMOIS CHIKARA

DEFASSA GAZELLE GEMSBOK
GERENUK GREENUK GRYSBOK
MADOQUA REDBUCK RHEEBOK
SASSABY STEMBOK AGACELLA
BLEEKBOK BLESBUCK BONTEBOK
BOSCHBOK BUSHBUCK KORRIGUM
LEUCORYX REEDBUCK STEENBOK
(**YOUNG** —) KID LAMB
ANTENNA DISH HORN LOOP PALP
TIER YAGI AERIAL DIPOLE FEELER
TACTOR DOUBLET WHISKER
PARABOLA RADIATOR
ANTENNATA INSECTA
ANTERIOR FORNE FRONT PRIOR
ATLOID BEFORE FORMER ANTICUS
PRORSAL VENTRAL ATLANTAL
INFERIOR PREVIOUS
ANTEROOM HALL FOYER LOBBY
ENTRANCE
ANTEWAR PREBELLUM
ANTHELION HALO NIMBUS ANTISUN
AUREOLE
ANTHELMINTIC CUNIC BRAYERA
EMBELIN
ANTHEM HYMN SONG AGNUS MOTET
PSALM INTROIT RESPOND
ASPERGES
(**JAPANESE** —) KIMIGAYO
ANTHER TIP CHIVE THECA
ANTHESIS BLOOM BLOSSOM
ANTHILL BANK TUMP
ANTHOCYANIN BETANIN PUNICIN
VIOLANIN
ANTHOLOGIST RHAPSODE
RHAPSODIST
ANTHOLOGY ANA POSY ALBUM
SYLVA CORPUS READER GARLAND
SYNTAGMA
ANTHOZOAN CORAL POLYP
ANEMONE GULINULA
ANTHRACONITE STINKSTONE
SWINESTONE
ANTHRAX CHARBON BLACKLEG
ANTHROPOLOGIST TOTEMIST
CULTURALIST
ANTHROPOPHAGITE CANNIBAL
ANTIAIRCRAFT ARCHIE
ANTIBALLOONER SEPARATOR
ANTIBIOTIC BIOTIC ABIOTIC
HUMULON CIRCULIN CITRININ
CLAVACIN CLAVATIN FRADICIN
HUMULONE NYSTATIN SUBTILIN
ANTIBODY REAGIN BLOCKER
GLUTININ
ANTIC TOY DIDO FOOL WILD CAPER
CLOWN COMIC DROLL MERRY
PRANK STUNT GAMBOL BUFFOON
CAPRICE GAMBADE GAMBADO
ANTICIPATE BALK BEAT HOPE JUMP
WISH ALLOT AUGUR AWAIT DREAD
SENSE STALL DIVINE EXPECT
THWART DEVANCE FORERUN
FORESEE OBVIATE PORTEND
PREPARE PREVENE PREVENT
PROPOSE RESPECT SUPPOSE
ANTEDATE FORECAST FOREFEEL
FORETAKE PROSPECT
ANTICIPATION ODIUM AUGURY
OPINION PROSPECT

ANTICLIMAX BATHOS
ANTICLINE ARCH DOME ISOCLINE
OVERFOLD
ANTICYCLONE HIGH
ANTIDOTE GUACO BEZOAR EMETIC
GALENA REMEDY THERIAC
DELETERY THERIACA
ANTIGEN N LYSOGEN BIOLOGIC
ANTIGONE (**BROTHER OF** —)
POLYNICES
(**FATHER OF** —) OEDIPUS
(**MOTHER OF** —) JOCASTA
ANTIGORITE SERPENTINE
ANTIMASK ANTIC ANTICK
ANTIMONIAL STIBIAL
ANTIMONY SB KOHL STIBIUM
ANTIMONY SULFIDE SURMA
SOORMA
ANTINOMIAN FIDUCIARY
ANTIOXIDANT SESAMOL
ANTIPATHY HATE ODIUM ENMITY
NAUSEA RANCOR DISGUST DISLIKE
AVERSION DISTASTE DYSPATHY
LOATHING
ANTIPHON GRADUAL GRADUALE
ANTIPHONALLY CHOIRWISE
ANTHEMWISE
ANTIPHONARY LEDGER
ANTIPODAL ANTARCTIC
ANTIPYRETIC SALOL MALARIN
THALLIN THALLINE
ANTIQUARY ARCHAIST ANTIQUARIAN
ANTIQUATED OLD AGED FUSTY
MOSSY PASSE FOSSIL VOIDED
ANCIENT ARCHAIC FOGYISH
NOACHIAN OBSOLETE OUTDATED
OUTMODED TIMEWORN
ANTIQUE ANTIC RELIC SIRUP SYRUP
VIRTU ANTICK NOETIC ANCIENT
NOACHIC NOACHIAN OUTMODED
ANTIQUITY ELD OLD PAST YORE
RELIC OLDNESS ANCIENCE
ANCIENCY
(**PL.**) ARCHEOLOGY ARCHAEOLOGY
ANTIRED WHITE
ANTI-SEMITISM JUDOPHOBIA
ANTISEPTIC CAVA EGOL KAVA SALT
AMIDO AMINE EUPAD EUSOL IODOL
SALOL AMADOL IATROL IODINE
KRELOS PHENOL PICROL ALCOHOL
ALUMNOL ARBUTIN ASEPTIC
COLYTIC LORETIN STERILE TACHIOL
TEUCRIN THALLIN CREOSOTE
ICHTHYOL KAVAKAVA METAPHEN
TEREBENE THALLINE
ANTISOCIAL HOSTILE ANARCHIST
ANTISPASMODIC KELLIN SAMBUL
SUMBAL SUMBUL KHELLIN
ANTISTROPHE REVERT
COUNTERTURN
ANTITHESIS AND CONTRAST
ANTITOXIN SERUM BIOLOGIC
ANTIVIVISECTIONIST BESTIARIAN
ANTLER DAG HORN KNOB RIAL TRAY
DAGUE RIGHT ROYAL SHOOT SPIKE
BOSSET SHOVEL TROCHE SPELLER
DEERHORN TROCHING
(— **POINT**) TROCHING
(**PL.**) HEAD ATTIRE

ANT LION DOODLEBUG
ANTSHRIKE BATARA
ANT THRUSH PITTA
ANT TREE HORMIGO
ANUS ASS ARSE BUNG VENT SIEGE
ANVIL BLOCK INCUS SNARL STAKE
STITH TEEST STETHY STITHY
ANFEELD BICKERN BEAKIRON
(— **SUPPORT**) STOCK
(**MINIATURE** —) STAKE STUMP
ANXIETY HOW CARE FEAR FRAY
PAIN ALARM ANGOR DOUBT DREAD
PANIC WORRY KIAUGH PUCKER
ANGUISH CAUTION CHAGRIN
CONCERN SCRUPLE TENSION
THOUGHT TROUBLE DISQUIET
SUSPENSE
ANXIOUS AGOG BUSY FOND TOEY
EAGER FIRST UPSET AFRAID
UNEASY CARKING EARNFUL
FORWARD TIDIOSE UNQUIET
DESIROUS RESTLESS THOUGHTY
WATCHFUL
ANY A AN AY AIR ALL ARY ONI ONY
AIRY EVER PART SOME WHAT
(— **WHATEVER**) ALL
ANYBODY ANY ONE ANYONE
SOMEONE
ANYHOW HOW NOWAY ALWAYS
ANYWAY
ANYTHING THAT AUGHT OUGHT
ANYONE HE MAN ANYBODY
ANYWAY NOHOW ALWAYS
ANYWHERE EINWER OWHERE
UBIQUE ANYPLACE
ANYWISE ANYHOW ANYWAY
ANYWAYS
AOUDAD ARUI UDAD AUDAD SHEEP
CHAMOIS
APACE FAST QUICK QUICKLY
RAPIDLY SPEEDILY
APACHE YUMA PADUCA CIBECUE
VAQUERO QUERECHO
APAGOGE ABDUCTION
APAP EPIPHI
APAR APARA BOLITA MATACO
APART BY OFF AWAY BOUT ELSE
ALONE ALOOF AROOM ASIDE RIVEN
SOLUS SPLIT YTWYN ABREID
ATWAIN LONELY SUNDRY ASUNDER
ENISLED REMOVED SEVERAL
SEVERED SEPARATE
(**WIDE** —) ASPAR
(**WIDELY** —) ABROAD
APARTMENT BUT WON DIGS FLAT
HALL ROOM STEW WENE WONE
WOON ABODE BOWER OECUS ORIEL
ROOMS SALON SOLAR SUITE
ANDRON CLOSET DECKER DINGLE
DUPLEX GROTTO LYCEUM SALOON
SINGLE SOLLAR SPENCE STANZA
BUTTERY CHAMBER COCKPIT
GALLERY MANSION PRIVACY
BUILDING EPHEBEUM SHOWROOM
SOLARIUM TENEMENT THALAMUS
(— **FOR IDOL**) TING
(— **IN CASTLE**) BOWER
(— **OF WARSHIP**) COCKPIT
(**OUTER** —) BUT

(**PRIVATE** —) MAHAL
(**RENTED** —) LET
(PL.) GYNAECEUM
APATHETIC CALM COLD COOL DEAD
DOWF DULL BLASE DOWFF INERT
STOIC GLASSY SUPINE TORPID
ADENOID PASSIVE UNMOVED
LISTLESS SLUGGISH
APATHY SLOTH ACEDIA CAFARD
PHLEGM TORPOR LANGUOR
DOLDRUMS DULLNESS LETHARGY
OMISSION STOICISM
APATITE IJOLITE MOROXITE
APAYAO ISNEG
APE KRA LAR PAN BOOR COPY DUPE
FOOL MAHA MIME MOCK SHAM
BEROK CLOWN MAGOT MIMIC
ORANG PONGO PYGMY APELET
BABOON GELADA GIBBON LANGUR
MARTEN MARTIN MONKEY OURANG
PARROT PONGID SIMIAN SIMIID
BUFFOON COPYCAT EMULATE
GORILLA IMITATE PORTRAY
PRIMATE SIAMANG DURUKULI
IMITATOR MANTEGAR SIMULATE
(— **STUDY**) PITHECOLOGY
APEAK VERTICAL
APEIRON MATTER
APER BOAR MIME SNOB CLOWN
MOCKER BUFFOON COPYCAT
APERCU DIGEST GLANCE PRECIS
SKETCH INSIGHT OUTLINE
APERIENT LAX OPENER
APERIODIC DEADBEAT
APERITIF WHET CONZANO
DUBONNET
APERTURE F EYE GAP OPE VUE
BOLE BORE HOLE LEAK PASS PORE
RIMA SLIT SLOT VENT BREAK
CHASM CLEFT CRACK LIGHT MOUTH
PUPIL STOMA CUTOUT HIATUS
KEYWAY LOUVER WINDOW FISSURE
KEYHOLE OPENING ORIFICE
OSTIOLE PINHOLE SWALLOW
TROMPIL APERTION FENESTRA
LOOPHOLE OVERTURE SPIRACLE
APEX EPI PIN TIP TOP ACME AUGE
CONE CUSP NOON PEAK RUFF
CREST HIGHT PITCH POINT SPIRE
APOGEE CLIMAX CRISIS CUPULA
GENION HEIGHT SUMMIT TITTLE
VERTEX ZENITH CACUMEN EVEREST
PAPILLA PUNCTUM PINNACLE
(— **OF HELMET**) CREST
APHAREUS (**FATHER OF** —)
PERIERES
(**SON OF** —) IDAS LYNCEUS
APHASIA ALALIA ALEXIA JARGON
APHEMIA
APHID APHIS LOUSE APTERA BLIGHT
COLLIER DIMERAN MIGRANS
PUCERON BLACKFLY GREENFLY
GYNOPARA HOMOPTER
APHORISM SAW ADAGE AXIOM
GNOME MAXIM MOTTO SUTRA
SUTTA DICTUM SAYING WISDOM
EPIGRAM PRECEPT PROVERB
APOTHEGM PISHOGUE
APHORISTIC GNOMIC

APHRODISIAC DEWTRY DAMIANA
VENEREAL
APHRODITE VENUS CYPRIS URANIA
ANTHEIA MYLITTA CYTHEREA
PANDEMOS
(**FATHER OF** —) JUPITER
(**HUSBAND OF** —) VULCAN
(**MOTHER OF** —) DIONE
(**SON OF** —) EROS CUPID AENEAS
APIARIST SKEPPIST
APIARY HIVE SKEP BEEYARD
BEEHOUSE
APICULTURE BEEKEEPING
APIECE UP ALL PER EACH SERIATIM
APIKORES BECORESH
APIO ARRACACH ARRACACHA
APIOS SOIA SOJA GLYCINE
APIS HAPI
APISH SILLY FOPPISH AFFECTED
APITONG BAGAC HAPITON KERUING
APIUM UMBEL
APLITE HAPLITE
APLOMB TACT NERVE POISE SURETY
COOLNESS
APOCALYPSE SHOWING
REVELATION
APOCRISIARY RESPONSAL
APOCRYPHAL SHAM FALSE UNREAL
DOUBTFUL FABULOUS FICTIOUS
APODAL FOOTLESS
APOGEE ACME APEX AUGE PEAK
CLIMAX ZENITH
APOGON AMIA CARDINAL
APOLLO SUN DELIUS AGYIEUS
APOLLON LYKEIOS PATROUS
PHOEBUS PYTHIUS CYNTHIUS
PYTHAEUS
(**FATHER OF** —) ZEUS JUPITER
(**MOTHER OF** —) LETO LATONA
(**SISTER OF** —) DIANA ARTEMIS
APOLLYON DEVIL SATAN ABADDON
APOLOGETIC SORRY
APOLOGUE MYTH FABLE STORY
APOLOGY PARABLE ALLEGORY
APOLOGY PLEA ALIBI AMENDS
EXCUSE PARDON REGRET SCRUPLE
APOLOGIA
APOPHYGE SCAPE ESCAPE
APOPLEXY ESCA SHOCK STROKE
POPLESIE
APOSTASY FALL LAPSE
APOSTATE RAT LAPSED CONVERT
HERETIC PERVERT SECEDER
DESERTER DISLOYAL RECREANT
RENEGADE TURNCOAT
APOSTLE ESCAPE TEACHER
DISCIPLE FOLLOWER PREACHER
(**BIBLICAL** —) JOHN JUDE LEVI PAUL
DENIS JAMES JUDAS PETER SIMON
ANDREW PHILIP THOMAS DIDYMUS
MATTHEW BARNABAS MATTHIAS
APOSTLE BIRD CATBIRD
APOSTROPHE TURNWAY TURNTALE
APOTHECARY CHEMIC SPICER
CHEMICK DRUGGIST
APOTHECIUM CUP PELTA TRICA
SHIELD ARDELLA LIRELLA PATELLA
APOTHEGM SAW DICT ADAGE AXIOM
GNOME MAXIM SUTRA DICTUM

SAYING SUTTAH PROVERB
APHORISM SENTENCE
POTHEOSIS DEIFICATION
CONSECRATION
POTHEOSIZE DEIFY EXALT
ELEVATE GLORIFY CANONIZE
PPALL STUN APPAL DAUNT SHOCK
DISMAY REDUCE REVOLT WEAKEN
ASTOUND DEPRESS DISGUST
DISMISS HORRIFY TERRIFY
AFFRIGHT ASTONISH ENFEEBLE
FRIGHTEN OVERCOME
PPALLING AWFUL AWESOME
FEARFUL TERRIBLE TERRIFIC
PPANAGE GRANT ADJUNCT
APANAGE
PPARATUS BOX GUN LOG SET
ADON DRAG ETNA FAKE GEAR GRIP
HECK HELM LAMP LIFT STOW TIRE
TOOL BURET GANCH HOIST HORSE
LEECH RELAY SCUBA SHEAR SIREN
SONAR STILL STOVE SWING BUDDLE
BUFFER COILER COOKER DEVICE
DINGUS ENGINE FEEDER FILTER
FOGGER GADGET GEYSER GRAITH
LADDER LIFTER MILKER ORRERY
OUTFIT REFLUX SEESAW SHEARS
SMOKER SMUDGE TACKLE TIPPLE
TREMIE TROMPE AERATOR ALEMBIC
APPAREL AUTOMAT BAGGAGE
BALANCE BASCULE BURETTE
COVEYER DERRICK ECHELON
FURNACE GASOGEN GRILLER
HOISTER INHALER ISOTRON
MACHINE MEGAFOG PINCERS
PRESSER SOXHLET SPRAYER
STIRRER TELEPIX TREMOLO
TRIMMER UTENSIL AGITATOR
AQUALUNG BLOWDOWN CALUTRON
CONVEYOR CRYOSTAT DIALYZER
DIAPHOTE DIGESTER DRENCHER
DUMBBELL EOLIPILE EQUIPAGE
ERGOSTAT GASIFIER GAZOGENE
INJECTOR ISOSCOPE JACQUARD
OSMOGENE OZONISER PULMOTOR
PURIFIER RECORDER REDUCTOR
REHEATER SCRUBBER SOFTENER
STRIPPER
(— IN STOMACH OF LOBSTER) LADY
(SEGMENTAL —) BRAINSTEM
APPAREL DECK FARE GARB GEAR
ROBE SECT TIRE WEAR WEDE
ADORN ARRAY CLOTH DRESS EQUIP
HABIT TUNIC ATTIRE CLOTHE
GRAITH OUTFIT PARURE ROBING
CLOBBER COSTUME FURNISH
GARMENT HARNESS PREPARE
RAIMENT VESTURE CLOTHING
FOOTWEAR HEADWEAR WARDROBE
(MILITARY —) WARENTMENT
(RICH —) ARRAY
APPARENT OPEN BREEM BREME
CLEAR OVERT PLAIN FORMAL
PARENT PATENT PHANIC CERTAIN
EVIDENT GLARING OBVIOUS
SEEMING SHALLOW VISIBLE
DISTINCT ILLUSORY MANIFEST
PALPABLE PROBABLE SEMBLANT
APPARITION HUE HANT SHOW

DREAM FANCY FETCH GHOST
HAUNT IMAGE LARVA PHASM SHADE
SHAPE SPOOK ASPECT DOUBLE
IDOLUM SOWLTH SPIRIT SPRITE
STOUND SWARTH TAISCH THURSE
VISION WRAITH DISPLAY EIDOLON
FANTASY FEATURE PHANTOM
SPECTER SPECTRE EPIPHANY
ILLUSION PHANTASM PRESENCE
REVENANT SPECTRUM
APPARITOR BEADLE PARURE
PARITOR SUMMONER
APPEAL ASK BEG BID CRY CALL
CASE PLEA SEEK SUIT APPLY
CHARM CLEPE REFER SPEAK
ACCUSE ADJURE AVOUCH INVOKE
PRAYER SUMMON ADDRESS
CONJURE ENTREAT IMPLORE
REQUEST SOLICIT APPROACH
ENTREATY PETITION
(— TO) APPLY AVOUCH INVOKE
ARRAIGN
(SEX —) IT
APPEALING CUTE NICE CATCHY
CLEVER CUNNING SUGARED
PLEASANT
APPEAR BID CAR EYE GET COME
DAWN FARE LOOK LOOM MAKE
MEET PEER REAR RISE SEEM WALK
ARISE ENTER ISSUE KITHE KYTHE
OCCUR SOUND THINK ARRIVE
BESEEM EMERGE INFORM REGARD
SPRING BLOSSOM COMPEAR
DEVELOP RESEMBLE
(— AND DISAPPEAR) COOK
(— BRIEFLY) GLINT
(— DIRECTLY BEFORE) AFFRONT
(— SUDDENLY) BURST
(— UNEXPECTEDLY) BLOOM IRRUPT
APPEARANCE AIR CUT HUE CAST
FARE FORM GARB IDEA LATE LEEN
LOOK MIEN SHOW VIEW BLUSH
COLOR EIDOS FAVOR FRONT GUISE
HABIT PHASE PHASM SHAPE SIGHT
SOUND SPICE ASPECT EFFECT
FACIES FAVOUR MANNER OBJECT
OSTENT REGARD VISAGE ARRIVAL
DISPLAY FARRAND FASHION
FEATURE GLIMPSE RESPECT
SHOWING SPECIES ARTEFACT
ARTIFACT EPIPHANY ILLUSION
LIKENESS PRESENCE PRETENSE
(— OF LIGHT ON HAIR) HAG
(CLOUDED —) HAZE CHILL
(CONSPICUOUS —) FIGURE
(DISTINCTIVE —) AURA
(FIRST —) DAWN DEBUT SPRING
(IMPOVERISHED —) BEGGARY
(MERE —) INTENTIONAL
(MOCK —) SIMULACRUM
(MOTTLED —) ROE DAPPLE
(MOTTLED SKY —) BLINK
(OUTWARD —) FACE SEEM SHOW
APPAREL BALLOON SEEMING
SURFACE
(PERSONAL —) PRESENCE
(STRIPED —) ROE
(SUPERNATURAL —) APPARITION
(SURFACE —) TOUR BLOOM

(UNGAINLY —) A
(VAGUE —) BLUR
APPEASE LAY PA
HUSH SATE ALLA
MEASE PEACE PE
STILL DEFRAY G
MODIFY PACIFY
SOOTHE ASSUAG
DULCIFY GRATIF
SATISFY STICKLE
MITIGATE
(— APPETITE) S
APPEASEMENT
APPELLATION N
STYLE TITLE AP
EPITHET GOODN
COGNOMEN ME
APPEND ADD PI
JOIN TACK AFFI
ATTACH FASTEN
APPENDAGE AF
TAG ARIL BARB
HORN LIMB LO
BEARD CAUDA
SCALE TROLL
CIRRUS CORON
LAGENA LIGULE
STIPEL STYLET
ADJUNCT ANTE
CODICIL EARLC
FIXTURE FURC
HOUSING MALE
STIPULE SWIMI
TRAILER ADDIT
ASCIDIUM BRA
FILAMENT GNA
PENDICLE PHY
RHABDITE SYN
(— ON MOCCA
(EAR-SHAPED
(PL.) ADNEXA
APPENDIX EKE
APPEND VERM
PENDANT ADD
EPILOGUE
APPERTAIN LI
BELONG RELA
APPETITE MA
TUCK URGE V
BLOOD GORG
TASTE TWIST
FAMINE GENII
LIKING OREXI
TALENT BULII
LONGING PAS
SWALLOW W
FONDNESS G
(— LOSS) AN
(ANIMAL —)
(CANINE —)
(EXCESSIVE —)
POLYPHAGIA
APPETIZER W
CANAPE RELI
SASHIMI APE
DUBONNET
APPETIZING
GUSTFUL GU
APPLAUD CL

CHEEF
ACCLA
ENDO
APPLA
CHEEF
HURRA
CLAPP
APPLE
JAMBC
DOUCI
KAVIKA
PUFFIN
BEAUF
FAMEL
POMEF
WAGE
AMPAL
GREEN
NONES
POMAN
REINET
(— OF
SHOOF
(BITTEF
(CRAB
POWITO
(EMU —
(GOLDE
(LIKE A
(PEELE
(SHRIVI
(SLICED
SCHNIT
(SMALL
(SMALL
(THORN
APPLEBI
APPLEJC
APPLE-P
APPLIAN
BRACE
GLODE
DEVICE
GAITER
MACHIN
UTENSI
APPLICA
USEFUL
RELATIV
(UNIVEF
(WIDELY
APPLICA
APPLICA
BLANK
ADDRES
EPITHEM
PRACTIC
(— OF
PRACTIS
(— TO
(MEDICI
FRONTII
(MENTA
APPLICA
APPLIED
APPLIQU
DESIGN
APPLY A
USE BE

EXTOL HUZZA PRAISE
APPROVE COMMENT
E HOSANNA PLAUDIT
E CLAP HAND BRAVO
ECLAT HUZZA SALVO
PRAISE ACCLAIM OVATION
G
P CRAB OHIA POME COPEI
BEEFIN BIFFIN CODLIN
ESOPUS GOLDIN KARELA
MACUPA MAKOPA PIPPIN
RENNET RUSSET BALDWIN
CODLING COSTARD
E GOLDING PEELING
Y RAMBURE RIBSTON
R WEALTHY WINESAP
YA COCCAGEE CORTLAND
IG JONATHAN MCINTOSH
CH PARADISE PEARMAIN
ER POROPORO QUEENING
E ROSACEAN WHITSOUR
ERU) JIMSON JIMPSON
Y

—) COLOCYNTH
) CRAB SCRAB WHARRE

COLANE
—) BEL BAEL
—) POMACEOUS
—) DUMPLING
ED —) CRUMPLING
DRIED —S) SNITS SNITZ

—) CODLIN CODLING
—S) GRIGGLES
—) MAD METEL
RRY DUMPLING
IN DEUSAN DEUZAN
LISH BROWNNOSE
CE GEAR GRAB IRON TOOL
LAMP DEVIL FLIER FLYER
HADE BONNET BREWER
NGINE FABRIC GADGET
UICER SPLINT CHARGER
SCRAPER STOPPER
BALANCER DEVIATOR
LE APT FIT MEET PROPER
ITTING PLIABLE APPOSITE
RELEVANT SUITABLE
ALLY —) CATHOLIC
—) BROAD
T PROSPECT
ION USE DAUB FORM
PIC APPEAL EFFORT
EPITHEM REQUEST
LENITIVE PETITION
SEDULITY
OWLEDGE) PRACTICE

RONG PURPOSE) ABUSE
AL —) PLASTER DRESSING
LENITIVE
—) INTENTION
OR COLPOSTAT
CLOSELY —) ACCUMBENT
DAG DAGGE ATTACH
RNAMENT
LAY PLY PUT RUB SET
BEND CLAP DAUB GIVE

HOLD MOVE SEEK TOIL TURN WORK
ADAPT GRIND IMPLY LABOR LIKEN
REFER SMEAR ADDICT APPEAL
APPOSE BESTOW BETAKE BUCKLE
COMPLY DEVOTE DIRECT EMPLOY
EXTEND RESORT ADHIBIT COMPARE
CONFORM IMPRESS OVERLAY
PERTAIN REQUEST SOLICIT UTILIZE
DEDICATE DISPENSE MINISTER
PETITION
(— **BRAKE**) BUR
(— **COSMETICS**) DO POP
(— **GRAPHITE**) BLACKLEAD
(— **GREASE**) ARM
(— **HOT CLOTHS**) FOMENT
(— **IMPROPERLY**) ABUSE
(— **ONESELF**) ATTEND INTEND
MUCKLE
(— **PIGMENT**) DRAG
(— **TO**) CONSULT CONTACT
APPOGGIATURA BACKFALL
ACCIACCATURA
(**DOUBLE** —) FALL
APPOINT ARM FIX SET CALL DECK
GIVE MAKE NAME ALLOT ARRAY
AWARD CREST DIGHT ELECT ENACT
EQUIP INSET PITCH PLACE POINT
SHAPE SLATE ASSIGN ASSIZE
ATTACH CREATE DECREE DEPUTE
DETAIL DEVISE DIRECT ENTAIL
ORDAIN OUTFIT SETTLE STEVEN
TAILYE ARRAIGN CONFIRM DESTINE
DISPOSE FURNISH GAZETTE
RESOLVE TAILZIE DELEGATE
DEPUTIZE INDICATE NOMINATE
ORDINATE
(— **A CLERIC**) COLLATE
(— **BEFOREHAND**) STALL
APPOINTEE PLACEMAN
APPOINTMENT SET DATE BERTH
ORDER TRYST BILLET OFFICE
STEVEN COMMAND STATION
CREATION DELEGACY POSITION
(— **OF HEIR**) INSTITUTION
APPORTION LOT DEAL DOLE MARK
METE PART RATE ALLOT AWARD
CAVEL GRANT PARAL SHARE SHIFT
WEIGH APPLOT ASSESS ASSIGN
DIVIDE PARCEL RATION TAVERN
ARRANGE BALANCE QUARTER
ALLOCATE DESCRIBE
APPORTIONMENT DIVISION
APPOSITE APT PAT COGENT TIMELY
GERMANE INCIDENT RELATIVE
RELEVANT SUITABLE
APPRAISAL APPRIZAL
APPRAISE GAGE LOVE METE RATE
ASSAY GAUGE JUDGE PRICE PRIZE
VALUE ASSESS ESTEEM EVALUE
PONDER PRAISE SURVEY ADJUDGE
ANALYZE COMMEND ESTIMATE
EVALUATE
APPRECIABLE ANY SENSIBLE
APPRECIATE DIG FEEL LOVE JUDGE
PRIZE RAISE SAVOR TASTE VALUE
ADMIRE ESTEEM SAVOUR ADVANCE
APPRIZE APPROVE CHERISH
REALIZE INCREASE TREASURE
APPRECIATION EYE GUSTO SENSE
CONCEIT

APPRECIATIVE AWAKE GRATEFUL
(— **OF BEAUTY**) ESTHETIC
AESTHETIC
APPREHEND COP GET LAG NAB SEI
FEAR HEAR KNOW NOTE SCAN
TAKE VIEW CATCH DREAD GRASP
GRIPE INTUE SEIZE ARREST BEHOL
DETAIN INTEND INTUIT BELIEVE
CAPTURE CONCEIT ENDOUTE
FORESEE IMAGINE REALIZE RECEIV
SENSATE SUPPOSE CONCEIVE
DISCOVER OVERTAKE PERCEIVE
APPREHENDED GRIPPIT
APPREHENSIBLE NOETIC SENSATE
SENSIBLE
APPREHENSION FEAR FRAY PAIN
PANG SCAN WERE ALARM DOUBT
DREAD FANCY WORRY ARREST
DISMAY NOESIS ANXIETY CAPTURE
CONCERN PRESAGE SUSPECT
DISTRUST MISTRUST SUSPENSE
APPREHENSIVE APT JUMPY FEARED
MORBID ANXIOUS FEARFUL
JEALOUS NERVOUS STREAKY
DOUBTFUL
APPRENTICE CUB BIND BOOT SNOB
TYRO CADET DEVIL BURSCH
HELPER JOCKEY NOVICE BANKMAN
GROMMET LEARNER TRAINEE
WAISTER APRENDIZ BEGINNER
JACKAROO SERVITOR TURNOVER
APPRENTICESHIP SERVITUDE
APPRISE WARN LEARN TEACH
ADVISE INFORM NOTIFY REVEAL
APPRIZE ACQUAINT DISCLOSE
INSTRUCT
APPROACH TRY ADIT BUMP BURN
CHAT COME DRAW NEAR NERE
NIGH ROAD ABORD BOARD CLOSE
COAST ESSAY STALK VERGE
ACCEDE ACCESS ACCOST ADVENT
ANIMUS APPEAL BORDER BREAST
BROACH COMING GATHER IMPEND
PROACH TRENCH ADVANCE
AGGRESS APPULSE CONTACT
SEAGATE SUCCEED CONVERGE
NEIGHBOR ONCOMING
(— **FROM WINDWARD**) BEAR
(— **GAME**) DRAW
(— **HOSTILELY**) SWAY
(— **NEAR**) TOUCH
(— **OF NIGHT**) FALL
(— **TENDENCY**) ADIENCE
APPROACHABLE COMMON
APPROACHING LIKE COMING
TOWARD ONCOMING
APPROBATION TEST FAVOR PROOF
TRIAL ASSENT FAVOUR LOANGE
PRAISE REGARD REPUTE PLAUDIT
APPLAUSE APPROVAL SANCTION
APPROPRIATE ADD APT DUE FIT
LAY PAT AKIN CRIB FEAT GOOD
GRAB GRIP HELP JUST MEET SINK
SUIT TAKE ALLOT ANNEX FITTY
HAPPY RIGHT STEAL USURP ASSELF
ASSIGN ASSUME BORROW DECENT
DEVOTE DEVOUR DIGEST GATHER
GENTIL KINDLY PILFER PIRATE
PROPER TIMELY WORTHY APPROVE

APROPOS CABBAGE CONDIGN
CONVERT FITTING GERMANE
GRABBLE GRADELY IMPOUND
PREEMPT PURLOIN RELATED
SECRETE SWALLOW ACCROACH
APPOSITE ARROGATE BECOMING
DESERVED EMBEZZLE GRACEFUL
HANDSOME IDONEOUS PROPERTY
RELEVANT RIGHTFUL SUITABLE
(— UNLAWFULLY) HEIST STEAL
(MOST —) CHOICE
APPROPRIATENESS APTNESS
DECENCY FITNESS APTITUDE
(NICE —) ELEGANCE
APPROPRIATION FUND VOTE
DEVOTION
(FRAUDULENT —) CON
EMBEZZLEMENT
APPROVAL AMEN ECLAT ASSENT
ESTEEM APPROOF CONSENT
PLAUDIT SUPPORT APPLAUSE
BLESSING SANCTION SUFFRAGE
APPROVE DO OK BUY TRY HAVE
LIKE OKAY OKEH PASS TEST VOTE
ALLOW BLESS CLEAR FAVOR PROVE
VALUE ACCEPT ADMIRE BISHOP
CONCUR RATIFY APPLAUD CERTIFY
COMMEND CONFIRM CONSENT
ENDORSE EXHIBIT INDORSE
SUPPORT ACCREDIT MANIFEST
SANCTION
APPROVED TRYE EXPERT PROBAL
ACCEPTED ORTHODOX
APPROVING HEARTY
APPROXIMATE NEAR ABOUT CIRCA
CLOSE COAST ROUGH COARSE
GENERAL APPROACH ESTIMATE
APPROXIMATELY SAY AWAY GAIN
MUCH NIGH ABOUT ALMOST
AROUND NEARLY TOWARD
CRUDELY ROUGHLY
APPROXIMATING COMPARATIVE
APPROXIMATION CIRCA
COUNTERFEIT
APPURTENANCE GEAR ANNEX
ASSIGN EFFEIR ADJUNCT COMFORT
APPANAGE PENDICLE
(PL.) ADDENDA
APRICOT COT UME ANSU MUME
BLENHEIM
(DRIED —S) MEBOS MEEBOS
A PRIORI PURE
APRON BIB CAP BASE BOOT BRAT
DICK RAMP SLOP TAYO TIER COVER
EPHOD BARVEL BISHOP CANVAS
DAIDLE DICKEY NAPRON RUNWAY
SHIELD TARMAC TOUSER BRATTLE
CANVASS DAIDLIE GREMIAL TABLIER
LAMBSKIN PINAFORE PRASKEEN
(— OF FURNITURE) PETTICOAT
(— OF SEAT) FALL
(CHILD'S —) TIER BISWOP SLIPPER
(LEATHER —) DICK DICKY BARVEL
DICKEY BARMFEL BARVELL
BARMSKIN
(MASON'S —) LAMBSKIN
(SILKEN —) GREMIAL
(PL.) ARMITAS
APROPOS APT FIT PAT MEET TIMELY

RELEVANT SUITABLE
APSE APSIS NICHE CONCHA RECESS
APSIS APSE AUGE
APT FIT PAT YAP ABLE DEFT FAIN
FEAT KEEN VAIN WONT ADEPT
ALERT HAPPY PRONE QUICK READY
ASPERT CLEVER DOCILE KITTLE
LIABLE LIKELY SUITED TOWARD
APROPOS CAPABLE FITTING
IDONEAL WILLING APPOSITE
DEXTROUS DISPOSED HANDSOME
IDONEOUS INCLINED PRACTIVE
PREPARED SKILLFUL SUITABLE
(— TO TURN) WALT
APTERYX KIWI RATITE KIVIKIVI
KIWIKIWI
APTITUDE ART BENT GIFT HEAD
TURN CRAFT FLAIR HABIT KNACK
SKILL VERVE GENIUS TALENT
ABILITY CONDUCT FACULTY FITNESS
LEANING CAPACITY INSTINCT
TENDENCY
APTNESS GIFT KNACK SKILL
APTITUDE FELICITY
APUS CYPSELUS MICROPUS
AQUARIUS SKINKER
AQUEDUCT AQUA DUCT CANAL
AQUAGE SPECUS CHANNEL
CONDUIT PASSAGE
(— OF SILVIUS) ITER
AQUEOUS HYDATOID WATERISH
ARA MACAW
ARAB AHL AUS IBAD OMAN SLEB
WAIF ARABY GAMIN NOMAD SAUDI
TATAR SEMITE SLUBBI URCHIN
ARABIAN BEDOUIN SARACEN
SOLUBBI AZZAZAME KABABISH
LARRIKIN SLOUBBIE YEMENITE

ARABIA

COIN: LARI CARAT DINAR KABIK
RIYAL
DESERT: NYD ANKAF DEHNA
NAFUD NEFUD
GODDESS: ALLAT
GARMENT: ABA HAIK CABAAN
BURNOUS
HOLY CITY: MECCA MEDINA
HOLY LAND: HEJAZ
ISLAND: SOCOTRA
JUDGE: CADI
KINGDOM: NEJD
MEASURE: DEN SAA FERK KIST
ACHIR BARID CABDA CAFIZ
COVID CUDDY MAKUK QASAB
TEMAN WOIBE ZUDDA ARTABA
ASSBAA COVIDO FEDDAN
GARIBA GHALVA CAPHITE
FARSAKH FARSANG KILADJA
MARHALE NUSFIAH
MOUNTAIN: NEBO HOREB SINAI
PORT: ADEN
RULER: AMIR EMIR AMEER EMEER
STATE: ASIR OMAN YEMEN
KUWAIT
TOWN: ABHA ADEN BEDA BERA
HAIL RIAD SANA TAIF DUBAI
HAUTA HOFUF JIDDA MECCA

MOCHA QATIF TAIZZ YENBO
ANAIZA MANAMA MATRAH
MEDINA RIVADH SALALA
SHAQRA BURAIDA HODEIDA
MUKALLA ONEIZAH SHARJAH
TRIBE: AUS ASIR IRAD TEMA
KEDAR DIENDEL SHUKRIA
WEIGHT: ROTL BAHAR CHEKI
KELLA MAUND NASCH NEVAT
OCQUE OUKIA RATEL TOMAN
VAKIA BOKARD DIRHEM MISKAL
FARSALAH

ARABIC CARSHUNI GARSHUNI
KARSHUNI THAMUDIC
(— ALPHABET) BA FA HA RA TA YA
ZA AYN DAD DAL JIM KAF KHA LAM
MIM NUN QAF SAD SIN THA WAW
ZAY ALIF DHAL SHIN GHAYN
ARABLE FERTILE PLOWABLE
TILLABLE
ARACHNID CRAB MITE TICK TAINT
ACARUS CARTER SPIDER CARTARE
OCTOPOD PEDIPALP SCORPION
SOLPUGID
ARAGONITE ALABASTER
ARAIN ARRAND
ARAKANESE MAGHI
ARAMAIC SYRIAC MANDAEAN
(— TRANSLATION) TARGUM
ARANEA EPEIRA
ARAPONGA BELLBIRD
ARAROBA ZEBRAWOOD
ARAUCANIAN AUCA PAMPA
MAPOCHE MOLUCHE PAMPERO
PICUNCHE
ARAWA AOTEA MATATUA
ARAWAK ARUA BARE URAN ARAUA
BAURE CAMPA CHANE GUANA INERI
SIUSI BAINOA BANIVA GUINAU
IGNERI GOAJIRO IPURINA CAQUETIO
CUSTENAU
ARBITER JUDGE CRITIC ODDMAN
UMPIRE ADVISER DAYSMAN
ODDSMAN OVERMAN REFEREE
DICTATOR STICKLER
ARBITRAGE SHUNTING
ARBITRARY SEVERE THETIC
WILLFUL ABSOLUTE DESPOTIC
MASTERLY
(NOT —) FREE
ARBITRATE DECIDE MEDIATE
ARBITRATION DAYMENT
ARBITRATOR REF JUDGE UMPIRE
ARBITER MUNSIFF REFEREE
MEDIATOR
ARBOR BAR AXLE BEAM ABODE
BOWER SHAFT STAFF STALK TRAIL
ARBOUR BOWERY GARDEN HERBER
PANDAL RAMADA VOIDER BERCEAU
HARBOUR MANDREL MANDRIL
ORCHARD PERGOLA RETREAT
SPINDLE TRELLIS FRESCADE
TONNELLE
ARBORVITAE AKEKI
ARBUTUS IVY
ARC BOW ARCH BEND FOIL HALO
CURVE HANCE ORBIT SPARK SWING

FOGBOW FOLIUM OCTANT RADIAN
COMPASS RAINBOW FROSTBOW
(— OF HORIZON) AZIMUTH
AMPLITUDE
(ELECTRIC —) SPARK
ARCA BOX CHEST PATEN ARCULA
ARCADE ORB AVENUE LOGGIA
STREET GALLERY PORTICO
ARCATURE CLOISTER
ARCANE HIDDEN SECRET
ARCH ARC BOW COY SET SLY BACK
BEND COPE COVE DOME HARP
HOOP IRIS LEER OGEE PASS PEND
PERT SPAN ARCUS CHIEF CURVE
FAULD GREAT HANCE HUNCH
INBOW JOWEL OGIVE PAUKY PAWKY
POKEY PRIME ROACH SAUCY
SWEEP VAULT ARCADE BRIDGE
CALCAR CAMBER CLEVER DIADEM
FOGBOW FORNIX GIRDLE IMPISH
INVERT LANCET MANTEL SPRING
SUNBOW WICKET ZYGOMA
ARCHWAY CUNNING EMINENT
GATEWAY ROGUISH SEGMENT
SQUINCH SUPPORT TESTUDO
TRIUMPH WAGGISH ALVEOLAR
FOGEATER OVERCAST
(— OF SKY) FIRMAMENT
(DENTAL —) ARCADE
(LOGGING —) SULKY
(PL.) SUBARCUATION
ARCHAEOCYTE SORITE
ARCHAEOLOGIST POTHUNTER
ARCHAIC OLD ANCIENT ANTIQUE
HISTORIC OBSOLETE
ARCHANGEL SATAN URIEL GABRIEL
MICHAEL RAPHAEL
ARCHBISHOP HATTO PRELATE
PRIMATE ORDINARY
ARCHDEMON BELFAGOR BELFAZOR
ARCHDIOCESE EPARCHY
ARCHDUKE ERZHERZOG
ARCHED ARCHY CONVEX EMBOWED
VAULTED HOOPLIKE
(— IN) CONCAVE
ARCHEGONIUM CALYPTRA
OOANGIUM
ARCHEMORUS (FATHER OF —)
LYCURGUS
(MOTHER OF —) EURYDICE
(NURSE OF —) HYPSIPYLE
ARCHER BOW CLIM CLYM BOWER
BUTTY CUPID ROVER BOWBOY
BOWMAN BOWYER SHOOTER
(EQUIPMENT OF —) TACKLE
ARCHERY TOXOLOGY ARTILLERY
(— SPACE) PETTICOAT
ARCHETYPE IDEA MODEL FIGURE
SAMPLE ESSENCE EXAMPLE
PARAGON PATTERN EXEMPLAR
FRAVASHI ORIGINAL
ARCHIL CORKE CORCIR CORKER
PERSIS CUDBEAR LECANORA
ORCHILLA ORSEILLE
ARCHING CAMBER
ARCHITECT MAKER ARTIST ARTISAN
BUILDER CREATOR PLANNER
BEZALEEL DESIGNER SURVEYOR
ARCHITECTURAL TECTONIC
OECODOMIC

ARCHITECTURE DRAVIDA
ARCHITRAVE EPISTYLE PLATBAND
ARCHIVES TABULARY TABULARIUM
ARCHIVOLT RING ARCHBAND
HEADBAND
ARCHLUTE THEORBO
ARCHON RULER DIRECTOR OFFICIAL
ARCHWAY ARCH PEND ARCUS
PAILOO PAILOU
ARC LAMP MONOPHOTE
ARCOGRAPH BOW
ARCO SALTANDO SPICCATO
ARCTIC ICY COLD COOL GELID
POLAR BOREAL CHILLY FRIGID
GALOSH NORTHERN OVERSHOE
ARCTIUM LAPPA
ARCTOID URSINE
ARDENT HOT AVID FOND KEEN LIVE
WARM EAGER FIERY GLEDY RETHE
SHARP ABLAZE FERVID FIERCE
IGNITE STRONG TORRID AMOROUS
BURNING CORDIAL DEVOTED
EARNEST FEELING FERVENT
FLAMING FORWARD GLOWING
INTENSE SHINING ZEALOUS
DESIROUS EMPRESSE FEVERISH
FLAGRANT SANGUINE SCALDING
SPORTIVE VEHEMENT
ARDOR DASH EDGE ELAN FIRE
GLOW HEAT LOVE ZEST ESTRO
FLAME GUSTO HEART TAPAS VERVE
WRATH DESIRE FERVOR FOUGUE
METTLE SPIRIT SPLEEN WARMTH
ARDENCY EARNEST ENTRAIN
PASSION DEVOTION FEROCITY
VIOLENCE VIVACITY
ARDUOUS HARD LOFTY STEEP STIFF
SEVERE TRYING ONEROUS
EXACTING TIRESOME TOILSOME
ARE MU RE AIR ARN ARUN HARE
AREA BELT SIZE TREF ZONE BASIN
COAST COURT FIELD RANGE REALM
SCENE SCOPE SPACE TRACT
ACCENT AREOLA EXTENT GROUND
LOCALE MOARIA REGION SECTOR
SPHERE SPREAD VOLUME ACREAGE
AMENITY AREAWAY CIRCUIT
COMPASS COUNTRY ENVIRON
EXPANSE KINGDOM PURLIEU
SURFACE CAPACITY DISTRICT
ENCEINTE PROVINCE
(— AT INTERSECTION) CIRCUS
(— BETWEEN FILLETS) CANALIS
(— IN CARTOON) BALLOON
(— IN HOSTILE TERRITORY)
AIRHEAD
(— OF EXPERIENCE) BOOK
(— OF FLAG) CANTON
(— OF OLDER LAND) KIPUKA
(— OF RIDGES) BILO
(— OF TIMBERLAND) CHENA
(— ON MOON) MARE WANE
(— UNIT) TAN YOKE LABOR
VIRGATE PLETHRON PLOWGANG
PLOWGATE
(BLANK —) BITE HOLE
(COMBAT —) GLACIS
(CULTURAL —) HORIZON
(CURLING —) PARISH

(DENUDED —) BURN
(DIKED —) SLUSHPIT
(ELONGATED —) BELT
(ENCLOSED —) FOLD SEPT
(FENCED —) CAGE COMPOUND
(FERTILE —) HAMMOCK
(FLOORING —) SQUARE
(FORTIFIED —) BASTION ENCIENTE
(GATHERING —) MANDAPA
(HUNTING —) SURROUND
(INFESTED —) FLYBELT
(LOW-LYING —) GLADE SWALE
COULEE COULIE GUTTER
(LUMINOUS —) AUREOLA AUREOLE
(MINE —) SQUEEZE
(NUCLEAR —) HEARTH ECUMENE
(OPEN —) COURT LAUND CAMPUS
SQUARE HAGGARD
(OVERGROWN —) COGONAL
(PASTURE —) SOUM
(PAVED —) CAUSEY
(PLOWED —) BREAK
(RESIDENTIAL —) BANLIEU
BANLIEUE
(SLUM —) STEW
(SMALL —) AREOLA
(SMOKING —) BULLPEN
(STERN —) AFTERPART
(SUBURBAN —) ADDITION
FAUBOURG
(SUNKEN —) SAG
(SWAMPY —) SLASH
(TEST —) MILACRE
(TIDAL —) CLAMFLAT
(TRANSITION —) ECOTONE
(TREELESS —) SLICK
(TUMID —) CERE
(UNCLEARED —) BUSH
(VOLCANIC —) SOLFATARA
(WASTE —) FOREST
(WOODED —) HAG BOSK BOSQUE
ARECA ARAK ARCHA BETEL
ARENA AREA LIST OVAL RING RINK
COURT FIELD SCENE SCOPE SPACE
STAGE CIRCUS REGION SPHERE
COCKPIT STADIUM TERRAIN
THEATER BULLRING
ARENACEOUS SANDY GRITTY
SABULOUS
AREOLA PIT AREA RING SPOT SPACE
ARES MARS ENYALIUS GRADIVUS
QUIRINUS
(FATHER OF —) ZEUS JUPITER
(MOTHER OF —) ENYO HERA JUNO
(SON OF —) REMUS CYENUS
ROMULUS
ARGALA STORK MARABOU
ARGALI AMMON ARKAR AOUDAD
ARGAN IRONWOOD
ARGENT LUNA MOON PEARL WHITE
BLANCH SILVER CRYSTAL SHINING
SILVERY

INDIAN: LULE GUARANI
LAKE: VIEDMA CARDIEL FAGNANO
MUSTERS
MEASURE: SINO VARA LEGUA
CUADRA FANEGA LASTRE
MANZANA
MOUNTAIN: TORO ANDES CHATO
LAUDO POTRO CONICO PISSIS
RINCON FAMATINA MURALLON
OLIVARES TRONADOR ZAPALERI
ACONCAGUA
PLAIN: PAMPA PAMPAS
PORT: ROSARIO
PROVINCE: CHACO JUJUY SALTA
CHUBUT CORDOBA FORMOSA
LARIOJA MENDOZA NEUQUEN
TUCUMAN MISIONES PATAGONIA
REGION: CHACO PATAGONIA
RIVER: SALI ATUEL CHICO COYLE
DULCE LIMAY NEGRO PLATA
TEUCO BLANCO CHUBUT
CUARTO FLORES GRANDE
PARANA QUINTO SALADO
BERMEJO DESEADO MENDOZA
TERCERO TUNUYAN SENGUERR
TOWN: AZUL GOYA ORAN PUAN
BAHIA JUNIN LANUS LUJAN
METAN SALTA PARANA RUFINO
ZARATE BOLIVAR CORDOBA
DOLORES FORMOSA LABANDA
MENDOZA POSADAS RAFAELA
ROSARIO TUCUMAN
VOLCANO: LANIN MAIPO DOMUYO
PETEROA
WEIGHT: LAST GRANO LIBRA
QUINTAL TONELADA

ARGIL CLAY ALUMINA
ARGOL TARTAR
ARGOSY SHIP GALLEON RAGUSYE
ARGOT CANT FLASH LINGO SLANG
JARGON PATOIS DIALECT
ARGUE JAW ARGY CHOP FUSS MEAN
MOOT MOVE SPAR WORD ARGIE
CAVIL ORATE PLEAD PROVE TREAT
ACCUSE ADDUCE CAFFLE DEBATE
EVINCE HASSLE REASON ARRAIGN
CONTEND CONTEST COUNTER
DISCUSS DISPUTE WRANGLE
ERGOTIZE INDICATE MAINTAIN
PERSUADE QUESTION TRAVERSE
(— **DEDUCTIVELY)** SYLLOGIZE
(— **SUBTLY)** DISTINGUISH
ARGUER JAW
ARGUMENT ROW AGON BEEF BLUE
CASE FUSS MOOT PLEA SPAR TEXT
CLASH DEBAT INDEX KNIFE LEMMA
PROOF THEME TOPIC BARNEY
COMBAT DEBATE DUSTUP ELENCH
HASSLE MATTER TUSSLE APAGOGE
CLAMPER DEFENCE DEFENSE
DILEMMA DISPUTE ESSENCE
FLUBDUB POLEMIC RHUBARB
SOPHISM SUMMARY ABSTRACT
CLINCHER COURSING EVIDENCE
SPARRING TRILEMMA
(**INVALID** —) SOPHISM
ARGUMENTATION DEBATE DISPUTE
ERGOTISM

ARGUMENTATIVE ERISTIC FRATCHY
FORENSIC
ARGUSFISH SCAT
ARHAT MONK LOHAN RAKAN SAINT
ARAHANT
ARIA AIR SOLO SONG TUNE MELODY
SORTIE ARIETTA ARIETTE SORTITA
ARIADNE (FATHER OF —) MINOS
(HUSBAND OF —) THESEUS
(MOTHER OF —) PASIPHAE
ARIAN AGNOETE AGNOITE HOMOEAN
ANOMOIAN EUSEBIAN
ARID DRY BALD BARE DULL LEAN
BARREN DESERT JEJUNE MEAGER
DROUTHY PARCHED STERILE
THIRSTY DROUGHTY WITHERED
ARIDITY DROUTH DROUGHT SICCITY
ARIKARA REE
ARIL POD ARILLUS COATING
ARILLODE
ARISE WAX COME FLOW FORM
GROW LIFT REAR RISE SOAR STEM
AWAKE BEGIN BUILD EXIST ISSUE
MOUNT RAISE SPRAY STAND START
SURGE TOWER WAKEN ACCRUE
AMOUNT APPEAR ASCEND ATTAIN
DERIVE EMERGE HAPPEN KITTLE
SPRING DEVELOP EMANATE
EXSURGE PROCEED REDOUND
SOURDRE
ARISING LEVEE EMERGENT
ARISTOCRACY CLASS ELITE
GENTRY ARISTOI SAMURAI NOBILITY
OPTIMACY
ARISTOCRAT LORD NOBLE ARISTO
GRANDEE PARVENU EUPATRID
OPTIMATE
(PL.) ARISTOI
ARISTOCRATIC HIGH TONY NOBLE
QUALITY CAVALIER
ARISTOTELIAN PERIPATETIC
ARITHMETIC SUM AUGRIM
ALGORISM
ARITHMOMETER MULTIPLIER

ARIZONA
CAPITAL: PHOENIX
COUNTY: GILA PIMA YUMA PINAL
APACHE MOHAVE NAVAJO
COCHISE COCONINO MARICOPA
INDIAN: HOPI PIMA YUMA NAVAHO
NAVAJO PAPAGO HUALAPAI
MOUNTAIN: BANGS GROOM
LEMMON TURRET PASTORA
HUALAPAI MERIDIAN
MOUNTAIN RANGE: GILA KOFA
MOHAWK GALIURO AQUARIUS
BUCKSKIN HUALAPAI
STATE BIRD: CACTUSWREN
STATE FLOWER: SAGUARO
STATE NICKNAME: OCOTILLO
STATE TREE: PALOVERDE
RIVER: GILA SALT ZUNI VERDE
PUERCO COLORADO
TOWN: AJO ELOY MESA NACO
YUMA GLOBE LEUPP TEMPE
BISBEE MCNARY SALOME
TOLTEC TUCSON CORTARO

KINGMAN MORENCI NOGALES
SAFFORD FREDONIA

ARJUN KUMBUK
ARK BIN BOX BOAT SHIP BARGE
CHEST HUTCH BASKET COFFER
REFUGE WANGAN RETREAT
SHELTER WANIGAN FLATBOAT
ARKANSAN ARKANSAWYER

ARKANSAS
CAPITAL: LITTLEROCK
COUNTY: CLAY DREW PIKE POLK
POPE YELL CROSS DESHA
IZARD SHARP STONE BAXTER
INDIAN: CADDO OSAGE QUAPAW
CHOCTAW CHEROKEE
LAKE: CONWAY NIMROD GREESON
NORFORK OUACHITA
MOUNTAIN: GAYLOR MAGAZINE
MOUNTAIN RANGE: OZARK
OUACHITA
NATIVE: TOOTHPICK
RIVER: WHITE SALINE BUFFALO
CURRENT COSSATOT OUACHITA
STATE BIRD: MOCKINGBIRD
STATE FLOWER: APPLEBLOSSOM
STATE TREE: SHORTLEAFPINE
TOWN: COY CUY KEO OLA ROE
ULM ALMA BONO CASA DELL
DIAZ MORO ENOLA PERLA
RONDO ALICIA

ARKOSE ARENITE SANDSTONE
ARM FIN OAR TOE BOOM HEEL LIMB
WING BLADE BOUGH CRANE EQUIP
FENCE FIORD FIRTH FJORD FORCE
GARDY INLET MIGHT OXTER POWER
RIFLE SNORD STOCK BRANCH
CRUTCH ENERGY FRETUM GIBBET
MEMBER OUTFIT PINION RADIAL
SLEEVE TAPPET WEAPON CATCHER
DERRICK DRAWARM FLIPPER
FOREARM FORTIFY FURNISH
GARNISH HARNESS OCKSTER
PREPARE PROTECT PROVIDE
QUILLON SUPPORT ARMORIAL
CROSSARM FOLLOWER FORELIMB
PULLDOWN SOUPBONE STRENGTH
TRANSEPT
(— **HOLDING FLINT)** HAMMER
(— **OF BARNACLE)** CIRRUS CIRRHUS
(— **OF CHAIR)** ELBOW
(— **OF CRANE)** JIB GIBBET
RAMHEAD
(— **OF GIN)** START
(— **OF PROPELLER)** BLADE
(— **OF SEA)** COVE FLOW MEER
MERE BRACE CANAL FIRTH FRITH
GRAIN FRETUM ESTUARY
(— **OF SPINNING MULE)** SICKLE
(— **OF WINDMILL)** VANE WHIP
(— **WITH GAFF)** HEEL
(**IRON** —) CRANE
(**LEVER** —) SWEEP NIGGER
(**PITCHING** —) SOUPBONE
(PL.) ARMORY ARMAMENT

ARMADA NAVY FLEET FLOTILLA
ARMADILLO APAR PEBA TATU APARA POYOU TATOU BOLITA MATACO MATICO MULITA PELUDO TATOUAY TATUASU EDENTATE KABASSOU LORICATE PANGOLIN
ARMAMENT ARMADA BATTERY
ARMATURE ARMING KEEPER LIFTER
ARMBAND BRASSARD
ARMCHAIR BERGERE FAUTEUIL
ARMED FLUTE HEELED DAGGERED WEAPONED

ARMENIA
ANCIENT CAPITAL: ANI ARTASHAT ARTAXATA
CAPITAL: ERIVAN
FORTRESS: EREBUNI
HERO: ARA ARAM HAIK ARAME VARTAN
KING: ASHOT GAGIK TRDAT ZAREH DIKRAN ARTAKIAS ARTASHES TIGRANES ZARIADES
KINGDOM: URARTU VANNIC CILICIA SOPHENE ARDSRUNI
LAKE: VAN SEVAN URMIA
MOUNTAIN: ARA ALAGEZ ARARAT TAURUS ALADAGH ARAGATS KARABAKH
NATIVE: ARMEN GOMER
RIVER: KUR ARAS KURA ARAKS CYRUS HALYS ZANGA ARAXES RAZDAN TIGRIS EUPHRATES
SAINT: SAHAK MESROP
TOWN: VAN SIVAS BITLIS EREVAN ERIVAN ERZURUM TRABZON YEREVAN

ARMENIAN ERMYN HADJI
ARMFUL LOCK YAFFLE
ARMHOLE MAIL SCYE OXTER ARMSCYE ARMSEYE ARMSIZE
ARMISTICE LULL PEACE TRUCE INDUCIAE
ARMLET TABLET TORQUE ARMHOOP
ARMOR (AND SPECIFIC PIECES THEREOF) ARMS BACK BOOT EGIS JAMB MAIL TACE WEED ACTON AMURE BARDS BRACE CUISH CULET DORON GUARD GUIGE JAMBE PIECE PLATE PROOF SCALE STEEL TAPUL TASSE TRUSS ARMLET ARMOUR BEAVER BRINIE BRUNIE BYRNIE CAMAIL CORIUM COUTER CRANET CUISSE GORGET GRAITH GREAVE JAMBER POLEYN RONDEL SECRET SHIELD TASSET THORAX TONLET TUILLE VOIDER AILETTE ARMHOOP BESAGNE BROIGNE CORSLET CUIRASS DEFENSE EPAULET HARNESS HAUBERK JAZERAN KNEELET LAMBOYS PANOPLY PAUDRON PLACATE POITREL REREDOS ROUNDEL SABATON VENTAIL RAMENTUM VAMBRACE
(— ON TREE) TROPHY
(— PLATE) TUILLE
(ELBOW —) CUBITIERE

(FOOT —) SABATON SABBATON SOLLERET
(HEAD —) CASQUE HELMET PALLET SCONCE
(HORSE —) BARB BARD BARDE CRINET CRINIERE
(LEATHER —) CORIUM
(LEG —) BOOT JAMB CUISH JAMBE CUISSE GREAVE JAMBER TUILLE JAMBEAU
(NECK —) COLLAR GORGET
(PADDED —) GAMBESON
(SUIT OF —) CAST STAND
ARMOR-BEARER SQUIRE ARMIGER CUSTREL
ARMORED PANZER
ARMORER GUNSMITH ARTIFICER
ARMORICAN BRETON
ARMORY HERALDRY
ARMPIT ALA OXTER AXILLA ARMHOLE
ARMS TACKLE
ARMY FERD HERE HOST IMPI LEVY MAIN ARRAY CROWD FORCE HERSE HORDE POWER RANKS ZOMBI COHORT HONVED LEGION NUMBER THRONG TROOPS MILITIA CHIVALRY MILITARY
(HOSTILE —) FOE
(PL.) SABAOTH
ARMYWORM GRASSWORM
AROID APII ARAD TARO APIUM KRUBI TANIA KONJAK TANIER YAUTIA PINUELA CALADIUM CUNJEVOI MOCOMOCO
AROMA NOSE ODOR NIDOR SAVOR SCENT SMELL SNUFF SPICE FLAVOR BOUQUET PERFUME
(— OF WINE) BLOOM
AROMATIC BALMY SPICY SWEET MASTIC ODOROUS PIQUANT PUNGENT FRAGRANT REDOLENT SPICEFUL
AROUND NEAR UMBE ABOUT CIRCA CIRCUM ENVIRON
AROUSAL INDUCTION
AROUSE SOW CALL CITE FIRE GAIN HEAT MOVE REAR SPUR STIR WAKE WHET ADAWE ALARM ALERT AWAKE EVOKE FLESH PIQUE RAISE RALLY ROUSE ROUST SHAKE STEER WAKEN ABRAID AWAKEN ELICIT EXCITE FOMENT INCITE INDUCE KINDLE REVIVE SUMMON THRILL ACTUATE AGITATE CONNOTE INCENSE INFLAME INSPIRE PROVOKE SUGGEST INSPIRIT
(— DISPLEASURE) AGGRAVATE
(— ENMITY) ESTRANGE
(— WRATH) SPLEEN
ARPEGGIO SWEEP ROULADE FLOURISH
(— EFFECT) RASGADO
ARRACACHA APIO ARRA
ARRACK ARAK RACK ARAKI RACKAPEE
ARRAIGN TRY CITE ARGUE PEACH ACCUSE CHARGE IMPUTE INDICT INDITE SUMMON APPOINT IMPEACH DENOUNCE

ARRANGE DO FIX LAY RAY SET CAST COMB EDIT FILE FORM PLAN PLAT RAIL RULE SIDE SIZE SORT TIER TIFT WORK ADAPT AGREE ALIGN ALINE ARRAY BESEE CURRY DRAPE DRESS ETTLE FANCY FRAME GRADE RANGE SCORE SHAPE SHIFT SPACE STALL TRICK ADJUST BRANCH CODIFY DAIKER DESIGN DEVISE FETTLE INFORM ORDAIN SETTLE SOLUTE TAILYE ADDRESS APPOINT BESPEAK CATALOG COLLATE COMPONE COMPOSE CONCERT DISPOSE ENRANGE GRADATE MARSHAL PERMUTE PREPARE REDRESS SERIATE TAILZEE TAILZIE ALPHABET CLASSIFY CONCLUDE ORGANIZE REGULATE TABULATE
(— BEFOREHAND) FORLAY FORELAY
(— FANTASTICALLY) HARLEQUINIZE
(— FASTIDIOUSLY) PREEN
(— HAIR) SET TED COIF TRUSS COIFFE
(— HARMONIOUSLY) GRADATE
(— IN FLOCKS) HIRSEL HIRSLE
(— IN FOLDS) DRAPE
(— IN LAYERS) DESS TIER
(— IN ROW) RACE
(— STRAW) HAULM
(— SYSTEMATICALLY) DIGEST
(— WITH BEST AT TOP) DEACON
ARRANGEMENT FIX FLY LAY RAY DEAL FLOW PLAT RANK TIFF ARRAY BUILD DRAPE INDEX ORDER SETUP BORDER DESIGN HOOKUP LAYOUT SCHEME SETOUT SYNTAX SYSTEM TREATY BLEEDER INTERIM POSTURE TONTINE ATTITUDE CONTRACT DISPOSAL GROUPING POSITURE SEQUENCE
(— IN LOCK) DETECTOR
(— OF BRISTLES) CHAETOTAXY
(— OF CHESS PAWNS) CHAIN
(— OF DRAPERIES) CAST
(— OF FLOWERS) CASCADE CORSAGE
(— OF GRADES) CURVE
(— OF GUNS) ARMADA
(— OF HAIRDO) FORETOP
(— OF HAIRS) SCOPA
(— OF HOOKS) GIG
(— OF LOOM BARS) GRIFF GRIFFE
(— OF ROCKS) BEDDING
(— OF TACKLE) BURTON
(— OF TIMBER) ANCHOR
(— OF TROOPS) ECHELON
(CIRCULAR —) CYCLE
(DISHONEST —) CROSS
(GEOMETRICAL —) LATTICE
(TRADITIONAL —) AKOLUTHIA AKOLOUTHIA
ARRANGING ORDONNANT
ARRANT BAD THIEF OUTLAW ROBBER VAGRANT PRECIOUS RASCALLY
ARRAS ORRIS ARISTE DRAPERY TAPESTRY
ARRASTRA TAHONA

ARRAU JURARA
ARRAY DON DUB FIG ARMY BUSK
DECK DOLL FYRD GALA GARB HOST
POMP RAIL RANK ROBE VEST
ADORN ALIGN ALINE ATOUR DRESS
EQUIP HABIT HARKA HEDGE ORDER
ADIGHT AGUISE ATTIRE ATTRAP
BEDECK CLOTHE DEVISE FETTLE
FINERY GRAITH INVEST MUSTER
PLIGHT SERIES SETOUT SHROUD
ADDRESS AFFAITE AFFLICT
APPAREL ARRANGE BATTERY
BEDIGHT COMPANY DISPLAY
DISPOSE ENVELOP FURNISH
FYRDUNG MARSHAL PANOPLY
REPAREL ACCOUTER
(— OF CHEMICALS) ARA
(— OF GUNS) BROADSIDE
(— OF TROOPS) PAREL
(— OF WEAPONS) ARMORY
(— TASTELESSLY) DAUB
(BATTLE —) ACIES HERSE BATTALIA
ARRAYED HABITED ABULYEIT
ARREAR DEBT BEHIND UNPAID
ARRIERE
(IN —S) BACK BEHIND
ARREST CAP COP FIX FOB LAG NAB
NIP VAG BALK CURB FALL GLOM
GRAB HALT HOLD JAIL KEEP NAIL
NICK PULL REST SHOP SIST STAY
STOP ARRET CATCH CHECK DELAY
PINCH REEST SEIZE STILL STUNT
ATTACH BRIDLE COLLAR DECREE
DETAIN ENGAGE FINGER HINDER
PLEDGE RETARD SLOUGH SNEEZE
THWART CAPTION CAPTURE
CUSTODY SUSPEND IMPRISON
OBSTRUCT RESTRAIN
(— OF BLEEDING) HEMOSTASIS
(— OF DEVELOPMENT) ABORTION
ARRESTER (SPARK —) BONNET
ARRESTING BOLD SEIZING
MAGNETIC PLEASING STRIKING
ARRET EDICT ARREST DECREE
DECISION JUDGMENT
ARRHA HANDGELD
ARRIS PIEN ANGLE PIEND ARRIDGE
ARRIVAL COMER IKBAL VENUE
ADVENT COMING INCOMING
REACHING
(— TIME RECORD) OS
ARRIVE GO SEY COME FALL FLOW
GAIN LAND LEND RIVE LIGHT
OCCUR REACH WORTH APPEAR
ATTAIN HAPPEN OBTAIN UPCOME
COMPASS
(— AT) GET HIT FIND GAIN HENT
MAKE BRING EDUCE FETCH GUESS
SEIZE ATTAIN DERIVE ESTIMATE
ARRIVED-IN DONE
ARROBA ROVE
ARROGANCE PRIDE SWANK TUMOR
BOWWOW HUBRIS BOBANCE
CONCEIT DISDAIN EGOTISM
HAUTEUR STOMACH BOLDNESS
SUCCUDRY SURQUIDY
ARROGANT BOLD COXY HIGH MOOD
COCKY GREAT HUFFY JOLLY LOFTY
PROUD STOUT SURLY WLONK

ASSUME FIERCE LORDLY UPPISH
UPPITY WANTON FORWARD
FROSTED HAUGHTY HAUTAIN
HUFFISH STATELY TOPPING
AFFECTED ASSUMING CAVALiER
FASTUOUS IMPUDENT SNUFFING
SUPERIOR TUMOROUS
ARROGATE GRAB TAKE CLAIM SEIZE
USURP ASSUME ADROGATE
ARROW FLO PIN ROD SEL BOLT
DART REED SELF SELL SHOT VIRE
BLUNT DEATH FLANE ROVER SHAFT
ARCHER FLIGHT GANYLE GARROT
QUARRY SPRITE TACKLE WEAPON
BOBTAIL DOGBOLT MISSILE
POINTER PROJECT QUARREL
SAGITTA SPINNER FISHTAIL
FORKHEAD
(— ARUM) TUCKAHOE
(— IN GRASS) GREEN SNAKE
(— IN LEG OF STAND) FOOT
(FIRE —) MALLEOLUS
(POISONED —) DERRID SUMPIT
(WOBBLING —) FISHTAIL
ARROWHEAD BUNT FORK HEAD
PILE FLUKE POINT NEOLITH
ARTIFACT CROWBILL FORKHEAD
SPICULUM
ARROWROOT PIA ARUM MUSA SAGU
ARARU CANNA TACCA TIKOR
ARARAO CURCUMA
ARROWWORM SAGITTA
CHAETOGNATH
ARROYO DRAW BROOK CREEK
GULCH GULLY HONDO ZANJA
RAVINE STREAM CHANNEL
BARRANCA BARRANCO
ARSENAL ARMORY SUPPLY
MAGAZINE
ARSHIN ARCHIN ALTSCHIN
(ONE-24TH OF —) PARMAK
PARMACK
ARSIS BEAT ICTUS ACCENT RHYTHM
UPBEAT DOWNBEAT
ARSON FIRE CRIME FELONY
BURNING
ARSONIST ARSONITE
ARSPHENAMINE SIX SALVARSAN
ART WILE CRAFT KNACK KUNST
MAGIC SKILL TRADE MISTER
TECHNE ARTWORK CALLING
CUNNING DESCANT DISCANT
FACULTY FINESSE MYSTERY
SCIENCE APTITUDE ARTIFICE
BUSINESS LEARNING PRACTICE
PRACTISE
(— OF APPLYING TESTS) DOCIMASY
(— OF BLAZONING) ARMORY
(— OF CALCULATING) ALGORISM
ALGORITHM
(— OF DEFENSE) SKIRMISH
(— OF HEALING) LEECHCRAFT
(— OF HORSEMANSHIP) MANEGE
(— OF SPEECH) RHETORIC
(DIABOLIC —) DEVILRY DEVILTRY
(DRAMATIC —) STAGE
(LEG —) CHEESECAKE
(MAGIC —) WITCHCRAFT
(MYSTERIOUS —) CABALA KABALA

CABBALA KABBALA QABBALA
CABBALAH KABBALAH QABBALAH
(OCCULT —) THEURGY
(SHODDY —) BONDIEUSERIE
ARTEMIS UPIS DELIA DIANA PHOEBE
CYNTHIA AMARYSIA
ARTERY WAY PATH ROAD AORTA
PULSE ROUTE COURSE DENTAL
FACIAL RADIAL STREET VESSEL
ANONYMA CAROTID COELIAC
CONDUIT HIGHWAY SCIATIC
VAGINAL CEREBRAL CERVICAL
CORONARY DORSALIS EMULGENT
PROFUNDA
ARTFUL APT FLY SLY FOXY WILY
AGILE CRATY DOWNY SUAVE
ADROIT CLEVER FACILE QUAINT
SCHEMY SHREWD SMOOTH TRICKY
CROOKED CUNNING KNOWING
PLAITED POLITIC PRACTIC SUBTILE
VULPINE DEXTROUS SCHEMING
STEALTHY
ARTFULNESS ARTIFICE SUBTLETY
ARTHRITIS GOUT CARPITIS
ARTHROPOD GOLACH GOLOCH
SPIDER CHILOPOD DIPLOPOD
ARTICHOKE BUR CANADA CYNARA
CHOROGI CROSNES KNOTROOT
ARTICLE AN YE LOT ONE THE BOOK
ITEM TERM BRIEF CHEAT ESSAY
GEANE PAPER PIECE PLANK POINT
STORY THEME THING CLAUSE
DETAIL LEADER NOTICE OBJECT
REPORT FEATURE BROCHURE
CAUSERIE DOCTRINE POSTFACE
TREATISE
(— OF CLOTHING) DUD DIDO APRON
CLOUT DICKY FANCY THING CASUAL
DICKEY GARMENT COINTISE
CREATION
(— OF FOOD) CATE KNACK
(— OF FURNITURE) STICK
(— OF LITTLE WORTH) DIDO
(— OF SILK) SQUEEZE
(— OF TRADE) PADNAG
(— OF UNUSUAL SIZE) IMPERIAL
(—S OF FAITH) CREDENDA
(—S OF MERCHANDISE) CHAFFER
(CAST-IRON —S) KENTLEDGE
(CHEAP —) CAMELOT
(DECORATIVE —) LACKER LAQUER
(FANCY —) CONCEIT
(FIVE —S) HAND
(GENUINE —) GOODS
(HANDICRAFT —) BOONDOGGLE
(INFERIOR —S) SHODDY
(METAL —S) BATTERY
(MISCELLANEOUS —S) SUNDRIES
(NONDESCRIPT —) DODAD DOODAB
DOODAD
(SECONDHAND —) JUNK
(SHOWY —) FRIPPERY
(VALUABLE —S) SWAG
(WORTHLESS —) TRANGAM
ARTICULATE BACK JOIN CLEAR
FRAME JOINT SPEAK UNITE UTTER
VOCAL ACCENT FLUENT VERBAL
EXPRESS JOINTED DISTINCT
ARTICULATED BACK BLADE DENTAL

DORSAL LABIAL JOINTED ALVEOLAR
CEREBRAL
ARTICULATION JOINT VOICE
SUTURE ARTHRON JUNCTURE
SYNTAXIS
(DEFECTIVE —) LALLATION
LAMDACISM
ARTIFACT CELT DISC DISK BATON
GUACA HUACA AMGARN BRONZE
EOLITH FABRIC GORGET REJECT
RONDEL SAGAIE SKEWER ABRADER
ARTEFAC DISCOID RACLOIR
SCRAPER ARTEFACT DATEMARK
RONDELLE TRANCHET
(PL.) CACHE CERAUNIA
ARTIFICE ART GIN JET GAUD HOAX
JOUK PLAN PLOT RUSE TURN WILE
BLIND CHEAT COVIN CRAFT CROCK
CROOK DODGE DRAFT FEINT FETCH
FRAUD GUILE SHIFT SKILL STALL
TRAIN TRICK CAUTEL DECEIT
DEVICE DOUBLE ENGINE COMPASS
CUNNING DODGERY DRAUGHT
EVASION FINESSE SHUFFLE SLEIGHT
COZENAGE DISGUISE DOUBLING
INTRIGUE MANAGERY MANEUVER
PRACTICE PRACTISE PRETENSE
STRATEGY TRICKERY WINDLASS
(PL.) CABAL CRANS
ARTIFICER WRIGHT ARTIFEX
WORKMAN DAEDALUS LAPIDARY
MECHANIC OPIFICER TVASHTAR
TVASHTRI
ARTIFICIAL CUTE SHAM BOGUS
DUMMY FAKED FALSE ARTFUL
ERSATZ FORCED FORGED UNREAL
ASSUMED BASTARD FEIGNED
AFFECTED FABULOUS FALSETTO
POSTICHE POSTIQUE SPURIOUS
(NOT —) REAL NATURAL
(OVERLY —) ALEXANDRIAN
ARTILLERY (OR PIECE THEREOF)
ARMS GUNS DRAKE SAKER CANNON
MINION HEAVIES LANTACA LANTAKA
CANNONRY ORDNANCE
(— FIRE) STONK RAFALE
ARTILLERYMAN GUN GUNNER
LASCAR REDLEG LASHKAR
ENGINEER TOPECHEE
ARTISAN FEVER SMITH ARTIST
COOPER ARTIFEX TARKHAN
WORKMAN KAMMALAN LETTERER
MECHANIC OPIFICER
ARTISANSHIP FOLKCRAFT
ARTIST DAB NABI ACTOR ADEPT
BRUSH HILDA RAPIN DANCER
ETCHER EXPERT FICTOR MASTER
SINGER WIZARD ARTISAN ARTISTE
ARTSMAN FAUVIST OPERANT
PAINTER PONTIST SCHEMER
COLORIST FUSINIST IDEALIST
LADISLAW LETTERER MAGICIAN
MUSICIAN SCULPTOR SKETCHER
STIPPLER
(— SCHOOL) LUMINISM
(SIDEWALK —) SCREEVER
(PL.) SCHOOL
ARTISTIC ARTLY DAEDAL EXPERT
ESTHETIC

(— MATERIAL) KITSCH
(— QUALITY) VERTU VIRTU
ARTISTRY FOLKCRAFT
ARTLESS NAIF OPEN FRANK NAIVE
PLAIN SEELY CANDID RUSTIC
SIMPLE GIRLISH NATURAL
INNOCENT
ARTS TRIVIUM
ARTY CHICHI
ARUM ARAD TARO AROID CALALU
DRAGON TAWKEE WAMPEE
MANDRAKE TUCKAHOE
ARVIRAGUS CADWAL
ARYAN MEDE SLAV NORDIC
(NOT —) ANARYA
AS S SO ALS FOR HOW QUA ALSO
INTO LIKE SOME THAT THUS TILL
WHEN EQUAL QUOAD SINCE WHILE
BRONZE WHENAS BECAUSE
EQUALLY SIMILAR QUATENUS
(— FAR AS) TO INTO QUATENAS
(— IT WERE) FAIRLY
(— LONG AS) SOBEIT
(— MUCH) ALSMEKILL
(— SOON) ALSOON ASTITE ALSWITH
DIRECTLY
(— TO) QUOAD
(— WELL AS) FORBY FORBYE
(— WELL) EVEN
(— YET) HITHERTO
ASAFETIDA HING LASER FERULA
ASARABACCA HAZEL FOALFOOT
ASBESTOS ABBEST XYLITE AMIANTH
ABSISTOS ALBESTON AMIANTUS
WOODROCK
ASCEND UP STY RISE SOAR STYE
UPGO ARISE CLIMB MOUNT SCALE
STAIR TOWER AMOUNT ASPIRE
BREAST CLIMAX UPRISE CLAMBER
UPCLIMB ESCALATE PROGRESS
ASCENDANCY SWAY POWER
CONTROL MASTERY SUCCESS
DOMINION OWERANCE PRESTIGE
ASCENDANT MOUNTANT
ASSURGENT
ASCENDING ANODAL ANODIC
UPHILL UPWARD ANABATIC
ASPIRANT SUBERECT
(— WITHOUT A TURN) FLYING
ASCENSION APOTHEOSIS
ASCENT STY HILL RAMP RISE RIST
UPGO CLIMB GLORY GRADE MOUNT
SCEND SLOPE STEEP STEPS STILL
UPWAY SOURCE STAIRS UPCOME
UPGANG UPHILL UPRISE UPWITH
INCLINE SCALING UPGRADE
UPSWING EMINENCE GRADIENT
ASCERTAIN GET SEE SET TRY FEEL
FIND COUNT GLEAN LEARN PITCH
PROVE ASSURE ATTAIN FIGURE
ANALYSE ANALYZE APPRISE
APPRIZE COMPUTE MEASURE
UNEARTH DISCOVER
ASCETIC NUN MONK SOFI SUFI YATI
YOGI DANDY FAKIR FRIAR SADHU
SOFEE STOIC YOGIN CHASTE
ESSENE HERMIT SADDHU SEVERE
SOOFEE STRICT ADAMITE AUSTERE
BHIKSHU DEVOTEE EREMITE

RECLUSE SRAMANA STYLITE
TAPASVI AVADHUTA MARABOUT
SANNYASI
(PL.) THERAPEUTAE
ASCIDIAN POLYP CUNGEBOI
CUNGEVOI TETHYDAN TUNICATE
ASCIDIUM PITCHER VASCULUM
ASCOCARP ASCOMA
ASCOMA CUPULE
ASCRIBABLE DUE
ASCRIBE LAY ARET EVEN GIVE
BLAME COUNT GUESS IMPLY INFER
PLACE REFER TITLE ACCUSE
ALLEGE ARETTE ASSIGN ATTACH
CHARGE CREDIT IMPUTE PREFER
RECKON RELATE ASCRIVE ENTITLE
ACCREDIT ARROGATE DEDICATE
INSCRIBE INTITULE
ASCRIPTION LAUD CREDIT ADDITION
ASCUS BAG SAC THECA ASCELLUS
ASEA LOST ADDLED ADRIFT
PUZZLED SAILING CONFUSED
ASEXUAL AGAMIC
ASH AS ALS ASE ASS FIG RON COKE
SORB ARTAR ASHEN EMBER FRAIN
ROWAN CINDER CORPSE DOTTEL
DOTTLE WICKEN CLINKER RESIDUE
DOGBERRY FRAXINUS HOOPWOOD
WINETREE
(SILKY —) CEDAR
(PL.) ASE AXAN KELP SOIL ASHEN
VAREC WASTE BREEZE CINDERS
PULVERIN
ASHAMED MEAN NACE NAIS
ABASHED HANGDOG HONTOUS
ASH-COLORED CINEREAL
CINEREOUS
ASHEN WAN GRAY GREY PALE
WAXEN WHITE PALLID GHASTLY
BLANCHED CINEREAL
ASHKOKO CONY DAMAN HYRAX
ASHLAR ASELAR RANGEWORK
ASHORE ACOST ALAND AGROUND
BEACHED STRANDED
ASHTRAY SPITKID SPITKIT
ASHWEED GOUTWEED
ASHUR FEROHER
ASIDE BY BYE OFF AWAY GONE
NEAR PAST AGLEY ALOOF APART
FORBY ASLANT ASTRAY BESIDE
BEYOND BYHAND FORBYE FORTHBY
LATERAL PRIVATE WHISPER
OVERHAND RESERVED SECRETLY
SEPARATE SIDEWISE
ASININE DULL CRASS DENSE INEPT
SILLY ABSURD ASSISH OBTUSE
SIMPLE STUPID DOLTISH FATUOUS
FOOLISH IDIOTIC
ASK BEG SPY SUE FAND PRAY QUIZ
CLAIM CRAVE EXACT FRAYN PLEAD
QUERY SPEAK SPEER SPEIR SPELL
SPERE ADJURE DEMAND DESIRE
EXAMIN EXPECT FRAIST FRAYNE
INVITE BESEECH BESPEAK CONSULT
ENTREAT IMPLORE INQUIRE
REQUEST REQUIRE SOLICIT
PETITION QUESTION
(— ALMS) CANT THIG
(— FOR) BEG BID CRY DUN LAIT

SEEK BESPEAK INQUIRE REQUEST
(— **PAYMENT**) CHARGE
ASKANCE AWRY ASKEW ASKILE
CROOKED SIDEWAYS
ASKEW CAM AGEE ALOP AWRY
AZEW AGLEY AMISS ATILT CRAZY
GLEED ASKANT ASLANT ATWIST
FLOOEY SKEWED ASQUINT
CROOKED OBLIQUE BIASWISE
COCKEYED SIDLING
ASLANT ASIDE SLOPE
ASLEEP DEAD FAST IDLE LATENT
NUMBED DORMANT NAPPING
ASOCIAL EGREGIOUS
ASP ESP ASPIC ASPIDE URAEUS
ASPARAGUS LILY GRASS SPRUE
ASPERGE SPARAGE SPERAGE
(— **GARNISH**) PRINCESS
ASPECT AIR HUE WAY AURA FACE
HAND KIND LEER LOOK MIEN SIDE
VIEW VULT ANGLE COLOR DECIL
FACET GUISE IMAGE NORMA PHASE
SIGHT STAGE TRINE VISOR VIZOR
DECILE FACIES FIGURE GLANCE
MANNER PHASIS REGARD VISAGE
APPAREL BEARING ESSENCE
FEATURE MALEFIC OUTLOOK
RESPECT SEXTILE SHOWING
SPECIES CARRIAGE CONSPECT
FOREHEAD OUTSIGHT PROSPECT
QUINTILE
(— **OF CURVE**) INSIDE
(— **OF EMOTION**) AFFECT
(— **OF MOON**) CRESCENT
(— **OF MUSICAL NUANCES**)
AGOGICS
(**BALEFUL** —) DISASTER
(**CULTURAL** —) EMANATION
(**DETERMINING** —) HEART
(**FACIAL** —) EXPRESSION
(**LANGUAGE** —) DURATIVE
(**PRIMARY** —) HIGHWAY
(**QUARTILE** —) SQUARE
(**SECONDARY** —) BYWAY
ASPEN APS ASP ALAMO NITHER
POPLAR POPPLE QUAKER QUAKING
TREMBLE
ASPER AKCHA AKCHEH OTHMANY
ASPERGILLUM HYSSOP SPRINKLE
STRINKLE
ASPERITY IRE RIGOR ACERBITY
ACRIMONY TARTNESS
ASPERSE SKIT SLUR SPOT ABUSE
DECRY LIBEL SPRAY DEFAME
DEFILE MALIGN REVILE SHOWER
APPEACH BLACKEN DETRACT
LAMPOON SLANDER TARNISH
TRADUCE BESMIRCH FORSPEAK
SPRINKLE
ASPERSION SLUR BAPTISM
CALUMNY INNUENDO
ASPHALT BREA SLIME FILLER
MANJAK BITUMEN CUTBACK
MANJACK BYERLITE UINTAITE
ASPHALTUM CONGO
ASPHODEL KNAVERY AFFODILL
ASPHYXIA APNEA APNOEA
ACROTISM
ASPIC JELLY GELATIN GELATINE
LAVENDER

ASPIRATION GOAL IDEAL DESIRE
RECOIL SIGHTS AMBITION
ASPIRE AIM STY HOPE LONG MINT
RISE SEEK SOAR WISH ETTLE
MOUNT TOWER YEARN ASCEND
ATTAIN DESIRE PRETEND
ASPIRIN FEBRIFUGE
ASPIRING ASPIRANT
ASS DOLT FOOL JADE KHUR MOKE
BURRO CHUMP CUDDY DUNCE
EQUID GUDDA HINNY CUDDIE
DAPPLE DONKEY ONAGER ASINEGO
ASSHEAD JACKASS LONGEAR
MALTESE SOLIPED IMBECILE
(**FEMALE** —) JENNY JENNET
(**MALE** —**S**) JACKSTOCK
(**WILD** —) KIANG KULAN KYANG
KIYAND KOULAN ONAGER HEMIPPE
CHIGETAI GHORKHAR
(**PL.**) JACKSTOCK
ASSAI MANICOLE
ASSAIL WOO BEAT FRAY HOOT JUMP
PELT SAIL ASSAY BESET SHOCK
STONE WHACK WHANG ACCUSE
ATTACK BATTER BICKER BULLET
HURTLE IMPUGN INFEST INSULT
INVADE MALIGN MOLEST OFFEND
RATTLE SAILYE SCATHE STRIKE
ASSAULT ATTEMPT BELABOR
BESEIGE BOMBARD CATCALL
ENFORCE ASSEMBLE TOMAHAWK
ASSAILANT ONSETTER
ASSAM (**MOUNTAIN OF** —) JAPVO
(**STATE OF** —) KHASI MANIPUR
(**TOWN OF** —) IMPHAL SADIYA
GAUHATI SHILLONG
(**TRIBE OF** —) AO AKA AOR AHOM
GARO NAGA
ASSARACUS (**FATHER OF** —) TROS
(**SON OF** —) CAPYS
ASSART SART THWAITE
ASSASSIN THAG THUG BRAVE
BRAVO FEDAI FIDAI CUTTLE FIDAWI
KILLER SLAYER RUFFIAN STABBER
TORPEDO HACKSTER MURDERER
SICARIUS
ASSASSINATE KILL SLAY MURDER
REMOVE
ASSASSINATION THUGGEE
ASSAULT BEAT BLOW COSH FRAY
RAID SLUG ABUSE ALARM ASSAY
BRUNT HARRY ONSET POISE POUND
SHOCK SMITE STORM STOUR VENUE
AFFRAY ALARUM ASSAIL ATTACK
BREACH BUFFET CHARGE ENGINE
EXTENT HOLDUP INSULT INVADE
ONFALL STOUND STOUSH THRUST
YOKING ATTEMPT BOMBARD
DESCENT LAMBAST PURSUIT
RUNNING VIOLATE INVASION
OUTBURST
ASSAY RUN SAY TRY TEST ESSAY
PROOF PROVE TOUCH TRIAL ASSAIL
ATTACK EFFORT ANALYZE ATTEMPT
EXAMINE TASTING ANALYSIS
APPRAISE ENDEAVOR ESTIMATE
HARDSHIP
ASSAYER POTDAR TESTER
ASSEMBLAGE ARMY BODY CAMP

CLOT COMA CREW HERD HOST
MASS PACK RUCK BUNCH CHOIR
CROWD DRIFT DROVE FLOCK
GROUP LEVEE POSSE QUIRE SALON
SHOCK SWARM CONVOY GALAXY
HOOKUP RESORT SPREAD SYSTEM
THRONG CIRCUIT CLUSTER
COLLEGE COMPANY COMPLEX
CONVENT CULTURE SOCIETY
STATION STATUTE TABAGIE
ASSEMBLY AUDITORY CONGRESS
MULTIPLE
(— **OF FOSSILS**) COLONY
(— **OF INTEGERS**) IDEAL
(**CONFUSED** —) FARRAGO
ASSEMBLE FIT LAY POD SAM BULK
CALL HERD HOST KNOT MASS MEET
ROUT SAMM AMASS ASAME FLOCK
PIECE RALLY TROOP UNITE COUPLE
GATHER HUDDLE MUSTER SUMMON
COLLATE COLLECT COMPILE
CONVENE CONVOKE RECRUIT
CONGRESS
(— **CARDS**) BUNCH
ASSEMBLER BONDER
ASSEMBLY HUI SUM BAUD BEVY
BOGY DIET DRUM DUMA FEIS HOEY
MALL MOOT RAAD ROUT SEJM
SEYM TING AGORA BOGEY COURT
COVEN CURIA DOUMA FORUM
GROUP JUNTA LEVEE PARTY PRESS
SABHA SETUP SOBOR SYNOD THING
TROOP AENACH AONACH ASSIZE
BOBBIN BUSING CHAPEL COETUS
COVINE GEMOTE MAJLIS PARADE
PLENUM POWWOW SEIMAS SENATE
STEVEN CHAMBER CHAPTER
COLLEGE COMITIA COMMAND
COMPANY CONCION CONSORT
CONVENT COUNCIL DIETINE
EOTATES FOLKMOT HUSTING
LANDTAG MEETING PENSION
SERVICE SESSION SOCIETY
SYNAGOG SYNAXIS TEMPEST
TYNWALD ZEMSTVO AUDIENCE
CONCLAVE CONGRESS ECCLESIA
FOLKMOOT PLACITUM PORTMOTE
PRESENCE SEDERUNT SOBRANJE
TINEWALD TRIBUNAL VOLKSTAG
WARDMOTE
(— **HOUSE**) KASHIM
(— **OF BLESSED**) HEAVEN
(— **OF CONDUCTORS**) BUS
(— **OF WITCHES**) COVEN SABBAT
SABBATH
(**AFTERNOON** —) LEVEE
(**BOY SCOUT** —) JAMBOREE
(**CLOSED** —) CONCLAVE
(**FASTENER** —) SEMS
(**GRENADE** —) BOUCHON
ASSENT AYE BOW NOD YEA YES
AMEN SEAL SENT ADMIT AGREE
GRANT YIELD ACCEDE ACCEPT
ACCORD BELIEF CHORUS COMPLY
CONCUR SUBMIT UNISON APPROVE
CONCEDE CONFESS CONFORM
CONSENT ADHESION SANCTION
SUFFRAGE
ASSERT LAY BRAG SHOW VOICE

AFFIRM ALLEGE ASSURE AVOUCH DEFEND DEPONE DEPOSE INTEND INTENT THREAP UPHOLD ADVANCE BETOKEN CONFIRM CONTEND DECLARE PROTEST SUPPORT ADVOCATE CHAMPION CONSTATE MAINTAIN OUTSTAND POSITIVE

ASSERTION VOW FACT HOTI CLAIM VOUCH AVERMENT
(BOASTFUL —) JACTATION
(DUBIOUS —) PLINYISM
ASSERTIVE BRASH DOGMATIC POSITIVE
ASSESS LAY TAX CESS DOOM LEVY MISE RATE SCOT TOLL CENSE PRICE TEIND VALUE AFFEER ASSIZE CHARGE EXTEND IMPOSE SAMPLE MEASURE APPRAISE ESTIMATE
ASSESSMENT FEE LUG TAX CESS DUTY LEVY SCOT TOLL CULET JUMMA PRICE RATAL TITHE WORTH EXTENT IMPOST PURVEY SURTAX TARIFF SCUTAGE BRIGBOTE TAXATION
ASSESSOR JUDGE MUFTI RATER CESSOR LISTER TASKER AUDITOR STENTOR TAXATOR
(PL.) FINTADORES
ASSET HONOR GETPENNY PROPERTY RESOURCE STRENGTH
ASSETS GOODS MEANS MONEY STOCK CREDIT WEALTH CAPITAL EFFECTS ACCOUNTS PROPERTY RESOURCE
ASSEVERATE SAY VOW AVER AVOW STATE SWEAR AFFIRM ALLEGE ASSERT ASSURE DECLARE PROTEST
ASSEVERATION VOW OATH
ASSIDUOUS BUSY GREAT ACTIVE DEVOTED PENIBLE STUDIED DILIGENT FREQUENT SEDULOUS STUDIOUS
ASSIGN FIX LET SET CAST CEDE DEAL DOLE DRAW GIVE METE RATE SEAL SHOW SIGN ALLOT ALLOW AWARD DIGHT ENDOW REFER SHIFT TITLE ADDUCE AFFECT ALLEGE CHARGE CONVEY DESIGN DIRECT ENTAIL ORDAIN ACCOUNT APPOINT ASCRIBE CONSIGN DISPOSE ENTITLE SPECIFY STATION TRIBUTE ALLOCATE ANTEDATE DELEGATE INSCRIBE TRANSFER
(— QUARTERS) BILLET
(— TASK) STINT
ASSIGNATION DATE MEET TRYST MEETING
ASSIGNMENT DECK DUTY TASK GRIND STENT STINT TUNCA CESSIO LESSON CESSION BUSINESS HOMEWORK
ASSIGNOR CEDOR CEDENS CEDENT
ASSIMILATE MIX ONE FUSE ADAPT ALTER BLEND LEARN MERGE ABSORB DIGEST IMBIBE COMPARE CONCOCT RESEMBLE
ASSIMILATION ECHOISM HOMEOSIS
(— OF FOOD) CONCOCTION
ASSINIBOIN HOHE

ASSIST AID ABET BACK HELP JOIN AVAIL BOOST COACH FAVOR NURSE SERVE SPEED STEAD ATTEND ESCORT PROMPT SECOND SQUIRE SUCCOR BENEFIT COMFORT FURTHER RELIEVE SUPPORT SUSTAIN ADJUVATE BEFRIEND
(— A READER) FESCUE
(— AT) STAY
ASSISTANCE AID ALMS CAST GIFT HAND HELP LIFT BOOST FAVOR HEEZE RELIEF REMEDY SUCCOR SUPPLY ADJUTOR COMFORT SECOURS SUBSIDY SUPPORT AUXILIUM EASEMENT GIFFGAFF LARGESSE
ASSISTANT CAD AIDE ALLY HAND HELP MAID MATE PUNK SOUS ZANY CLERK GROOM USHER VALET AIDANT BUMPER COMMIS CURATE DEPUTY FLUNKY HELPER LEGATE SECOND TULTUL YEOMAN ABETTOR ACOLYTE ADJOINT DOORMAN DRESSER HOGGLER PADRINO PARTNER PROVOST RUBBLER SHIFTER STRIKER SWAMPER ADJUTANT ADJUVANT FELDSHER GOMASHTA LECTURER MINISTER OFFSIDER PARASITE SERVITOR SIDESMAN SUBPRIOR
(— TO ANIMAL SHOW JUDGE) STEWARD
(AUCTIONEER'S —) SPOTTER
(DYEING —) CARRIER
(MASON'S —) GOUJAT
(MATADOR'S —) CHULO
(POLICE —) CORPORAL
(SURVEYOR'S —) CHAINMAN
(WAITER'S —) BUSBOY
ASSOCIATE MIX PAL AIDE ALLY BAND CHUM HERD JOIN LINK MATE MOOP MOUP PEER WALK WIFE YOKE BLEND BUDDY CRONY HABER MATCH TRAIN TROOP ASSORT ATTACH ATTEND CHABER COHORT COUSIN FASTEN FELLOW FRIEND HELPER HOBNOB MARROW MEDDLE MEMBER MINGLE PUISNE PUISNY RELATE SOCIUS SPOUSE TRAVEL ADJUNCT ASSOCIE BRACKET COALITE COMMUNE COMPANY COMPEER COMRADE CONNECT CONSORT HUSBAND PARTNER PEWMATE SOCIATE CONJOINT CONVERSE COPEMATE FAMILIAR FEDERATE FOLLOWER FREQUENT GADSHILL IDENTIFY INTIMATE PARTAKER
(— WITH) FRAT MOOP MOUP
(DEMON —) FLY
(PL.) ENTOURAGE
ASSOCIATION HUI BODY BOND BUND CLUB GILD HONG HUNT TONG ARTEL BOARD GUILD HANSA HANSE SANGH TRUCK UNION CARTEL CERCLE CHAPEL COMITY CONGER GRANGE LEAGUE LEGION LYCEUM PLEDGE SANGHA SCHOLA VEREIN CIRCUIT COMPANY CONSORT

CONTACT CONVENT COUNCIL SOCIETY SOROSIS SYNOECY AFFINITY ALLIANCE ASSEMBLY ATHENEUM CONVERSE HABITUDE INTIMACY SODALITY SYNOMOSY TAALBOND
(— OF FOSSILS) FAUNULA FAUNULE
(ANTAGONISTIC —) ANTIBIOSIS
(BOOK-SELLERS' —) CONGER
(CLOSE —) HARNESS INTIMACY
(EMPLOYERS' —) GREMIO
(FARMERS' —) GRANGE
(IN —) ALONG
(LABOR —) ARTEL UNION
(RELIGIOUS —) SAMAJ
(SECRET —) CABAL
(STUDENTS' —) CORPS
ASSOIL RID SOIL ATONE CLEAR SOLVE ACQUIT PARDON REFUTE ABSOLVE DELIVER EXPIATE FORGIVE RELEASE RESOLVE
ASSONANCE PUN RHYME PARAGRAM
ASSORT BOLT CULL SUIT WINNOW
(— COINS) SHROFF
ASSORTED CHOW CHOWCHOW
ASSORTER FEEDER LOOKER
ASSORTMENT BAG LOT SET OLIO BATCH GROUP SUITE MIXTURE
(— OF TYPE) BILL FONT
(COMPLETE —) STANDARD
ASSUAGE CALM EASE LIOS LISS ABATE ALLAY CHARM DELAY LISSE SALVE SLAKE STILL SWAGE LENIFY LESSEN MODIFY PACIFY QUENCH REDUCE SOFTEN SOLACE SOOTHE TEMPER APPEASE COMFORT MOLLIFY QUALIFY RELIEVE SATISFY DIMINISH MITIGATE MODERATE
ASSUASIVE MILD LENIENT LENITIVE SOOTHING
ASSUME DON PUT SAY SET BEAR DARE FANG GIVE MASK PULL SHAM SHIP TAKE ADOPT ANNEX CLOAK ELECT FEIGN GUESS INDUE INFER RAISE USURP ACCEPT AFFECT BETAKE CLOTHE FIGURE ASSUMPT BELIEVE PREMISE PRESUME PRETEND RECEIVE SUBSUME SUPPOSE SURMISE ACCROACH ARROGATE SIMULATE
(— CHARACTER) ACT AFFECT
(— FORM) ENGENDER
(— OFFICE) ACCEDE
(— PAINTING STANCE) BACK
ASSUMED ALIAS FALSE GIVEN FEIGNED AFFECTED
ASSUMING LOFTY UPPISH UPPITY AFFECTED ARROGANT SUPERIOR
ASSUMPTION DONNEE THESIS BALLOON FICTION SURMISE HOMEOSIS MARYMASS PRETENCE PRETENSE
(BASIC —) BEGINNING
(EMPTY —) IMAGINATION
ASSURANCE FACE GALL SEAL BRASS FAITH NERVE TRUST APLOMB BELIEF CAUTIO CREDIT PLEVIN SAFETY COURAGE PROMISE

WARRANT AUDACITY BOLDNESS COOLNESS FIRMANCE FOREHEAD SECURITY SUREMENT
ASSURE AVER SURE CINCH HIGHT VOUCH AFFEER ASSERT AVOUCH ENSURE INSURE PLEDGE SECURE SEKERE SICCAR SICKER WITTER BETROTH CERTIFY COMFIRM DECLARE HEARTEN PROMISE PROTEST RESOLVE WARRANT AFFIANCE CONVINCE EMBOLDEN PERSUADE
ASSURED BOLD CALM COLD FIRM SURE BOUND SIKER SLUSH FACILE PROBAL SECURE SICCAR SICKER CERTAIN
(BLUNTLY —) KNOCKDOWN
ASSUREDLY AMEN SOON INDEED REDELY SICCAR SICKER SURELY VERILY HARDILY WITTERLY
ASSYRIA ASHUR ASSUR ASSHUR
(CAPITAL OF —) CALAH NINEVEH
ASSYRIAN NESTORIAN
(— PLUM) SEBESTEN
ASTER ARNICA COCASH AMELLUS BEEWEED BONESET EUASTER ASTROFEL COMPOSIT CYTASTER MONASTER STARWORT STOKESIA
ASTERISK MARK STAR ASTER ASTERISM WINDMILL
(THREE —S) ASTERISM
ASTERN AFT BAFT HIND REAR ABAFT APOOP BEHIND OCCIPUT BACKWARD
ASTEROID EROS HEBE IRIS JUNO CERES DIONE FLORA IRENE METIS VESTA ASTREA EGERIA EUROPA HYGIEA PALLAS PLANET PSYCHE THALIA THEMIS THETIS ELECTRA EUNOMIA FORTUNA LUTETIA CALLIOPE MASSALIA STARFISH STARLIKE VICTORIA
ASTHMA PHTHISIC
ASTHMATIC POUCY PURSY POUCEY WHEEZY PANTING PUFFING
ASTIR UP AGOG ABOUT AFOOT AGATE ALERT GOING ACTIVE AROUND ASTEER MOVING ROUSED ABROACH EXCITED STIRRING VIGILANT
ASTONISH AWE DAZE STAM AMAZE KNOCK SHOCK DAMMER MARVEL STOUND ASTOUND GLOPPEN IMPRESS STARTLE AMERVEIL BEWILDER CONFOUND SURPRISE
ASTONISHING AMAZING FABULOUS
ASTONISHMENT MUSE FERLY DISMAY FARLEY MARVEL STOUND WONDER SURPRISE
ASTOUND BEAT STUN AMAZE APPAL SHOCK STOUN APPALL STOUND STAGGER STUPEFY STUPEND TERRIFY ASTONISH CONFOUND SURPRISE
ASTOUNDING STUNNING
ASTRAGAL TALUS CHAPLET CORNICE
ASTRAKHAN BOKHARA
ASTRAL REMOTE STARRY STELLAR

ASTRAEAN SIDEREAL STARLIKE
ASTRAY AWRY LOST WILL AGLEY AMISS ASIDE GLEED WRONG ABROAD AFIELD ERRANT ERRING FAULTY DEPAYSE DEVIOUS FORLORN SINNING WILSOME MISTAKEN STRAYING
ASTRIDE ATOP ABOARD ACHEVAL SPANNING
ASTRINGENCY ACERBITY ACRIMONY
ASTRINGENT ACID ALUM COTO SOUR TART ACERB HARSH SAPAN STERN CORNUS MASTIC PONTIC SEVERE TANNIN ALUMNOL AUSTERE BINDING CATECHU PUCKERY RHATANY STYPTIC GERANIUM TRILLIUM
ASTROLOGER JOTI JOSHI ARTIST JOTISI MERLIN ZADKIEL SCHEMIST
ASTROLOGY STARCRAFT MATHEMATICALS
ASTRONOMER JOTI JOSHI JOTISI
ASTRONOMICAL FAR HUGE GREAT URANIC DISTANT IMMENSE URANIAN COLOSSAL INFINITE
(— INSTRUMENT) ARMILL
ASTRONOMY WAGON WAGONER WAGGONER
ASTUTE SLY FOXY KEEN WILY ACUTE CANNY QUICK SHARP SMART CLEVER CRAFTY NASUTE SHREWD CUNNING KNOWING SKILLED
ASUNDER ATWO APART SPLIT ATWAIN SUNDER SUNDRY DIVIDED DIVORCED YSOWNDIR
ASURA VARUNA
ASYLUM ARK HOME JAIL ALTAR COVER GRITH HAVEN BEDLAM HARBOR REFUGE ALSATIA COLLEGE HOSPICE RETREAT SHELTER BUGHOUSE MADHOUSE
ASYMMETRIC PEDIAL
AT A AL AU BY IN TO ALS TIL TILL UNTO ATTEN THERE HEREAT
(— ALL) ANY AVA EER EVER HALF OUGHT SOEVER HOWEVER
ATABAL DRUM TABOR ATTABAL
ATAMAN CHIEF JUDGE HETMAN HEADMAN
ATAVISM REVERSION
ATELIER SHOP STUDIO BOTTEGA WORKSHOP
ATEO WAKEA
ATES SWEETSOP
ATHAMAS (DAUGHTER OF —) HELLE
(FATHER OF —) AEOLUS
(SON OF —) PHRIXUS LEARCHUS PALAEMON
(WIFE OF —) INO NEPHELE
ATHANOR OVEN ATHENOR FURNACE
ATHAPASKAN HAW HARE HUPA KATO KASKA AHTENA BEAVER CHETCO GILENO LASSIK SARCEE SEKANI CARRIER CHILULA KOYUKON KUTCHIN
ATHEIST ZENDIK DOUBTER INFIDEL NASTIKA AGNOSTIC APIKOROS NETHEIST
ATHENA ALEA AUGE NIKE ALERA AREIA ERGANE HIPPIA HYGIEA

ITONIA PALLAS POLIAS AIANTIS MINERVA APATURIA
ATHENIAN ATTIC CHORAGUS CHOREGUS
ATHLETE PRO BLUE KEMP STAR BOXER COLOR CRACK CUTEY CUTIE TURNER ACROBAT AMATEUR GYMNAST STICKER TUMBLER VARMINT GAMESTER REPEATER WRESTLER
ATHLETIC AGILE BURLY LUSTY VITAL BRAWNY GYMNIC ROBUST SINEWY STRONG BOARDLY BOORDLY MUSCULAR POWERFUL VIGOROUS
ATHLETICS GAMES SPORT EXERCISE
ATHWART CROSS ABOARD ACROSS ASLANT OBLIQUE SIDEWISE TRAVERSE
ATLAS BOOK LIST MAPS TOME TITAN TELAMON MAINSTAY
(DAUGHTERS OF —) ATLANTIDES
(FATHER OF —) IAPETUS
(MOTHER OF —) CLYMENE
(WIFE OF —) PLEIONE
ATLE ETHEL
ATMAN ATMA ATTA SELF
ATMOSPHERE AIR SKY AURA FEEL LIFT MOOD TONE AROMA CLIME DECOR ETHER SMELL FROWST MIASMA NIMBUS SPHERE WELKIN FEELING HYALINE QUALIFY AMBIANCE AMBIENCE
(— OF DISCOURAGEMENT) CHILL
(NOXIOUS —) MIASMA
(SECTION OF —) SOLENOID
(STALE —) FROUST FROWST
(STUFFY —) FUG
(SUFFOCATING —) STIFLE
ATMOSPHERICS STATIC SPHERICS
ATOM ACE BIT ION JOT DIAD DYAD HAET HATE IOTA MITE MOTE WHIT ATOMY HENAD LABEL MONAD SHADE SPECK TINGE ADATOM BRIDGE CARBYL HEPTAD ISOBAR TETRAD ATOMIZE BODIKIN IONOGEN ISOTOPE RADICAL SPECIES FUNCTION ISOSTERE MOLECULE PARTICLE QUANTITY
(— TOTALITY) MATTER
(PL.) SMITHERS SMITHEREENS
ATOMIC TINY MINUTE NUCLEAR
ATOMIZER SPRAY SPARGE SCENTER SPRAYER AIRBRUSH ODORATOR PERFUMER
ATONE AGREE AMEND ACCORD ANSWER ASSOIL RANSOM REDEEM REPENT APPEASE EXPIATE RESTORE SATISFY
(— FOR) ABY BYE ABYE MEND ABIDE ABEGGE
ATONEMENT MEND MICHTAM PENANCE
ATOP ACOR
ATORAI DAURI
ATRABILIOUS GLUM ADUST GLOOMY MOROSE SULLEN
ATREUS (BROTHER OF —) THYESTES
(FATHER OF —) PELOPS
(HALF-BROTHER OF —) THYESTES

(MOTHER OF —) HIPPODAMIA
(SON OF —) MENELAUS
(WIFE OF —) AEROPE
ATRIP AWEIGH
ATRIUM HALL ATRIO COURT CAVITY
AURICLE CHAMBER PASSAGE
ATROCIOUS BAD DARK RANK VILE
AWFUL BLACK CRUEL GROSS
ATROCE BRUTAL ODIOUS SAVAGE
WICKED HEINOUS UNGODLY
VIOLENT FLAGRANT GRIEVOUS
HORRIBLE TERRIBLE
ATROPHIC AUANTIC
ATROPHY RUST STUNT TABES
MACIES SHRINK STARVE SWEENY
WITHER SWINNEY WASTING
STULTIFY
ATTACH ADD FIX SET SEW TAG TIE
BIND BOLT GLUE HANG JOIN LINK
SPAN TAKE VEST WELD ADOPT
AFFIX ANNEX BEWED FOUND HINGE
HITCH LATCH PASTE SCREW SEIZE
SPEND STICK TACHE TATCH UNITE
ACCUSE ADDICT ADHERE ADJOIN
APPEND ARREST CEMENT DEVOTE
ENGAGE ENTAIL ENTIRE FASTEN
FATHER INDICT SPLINE ADHIBIT
APPOINT ASCRIBE CONNECT
ESPOUSE SUBJOIN
(— TEMPORARILY) SECOND
ATTACHED FAST FOND DOTING
ADJUNCT BIGOTED SESSILE
ADSCRIPT INSERTED
ATTACHING INCIDENT ALLIGATION
ATTACHMENT ARM GAG BAIL BALE
DRUM FLAY HEAD HECK LOVE MOTE
SHIM SHOE AMOUR CHUCK CRUSH
DOBBY DODAD FENCE GUARD STRIG
AFFAIR BEATER BINDER BUMPER
DAMSEL DOBBIE DOCTOR DOODAD
DREDGE FELLER FETICH FETISH
HEMMER HILLER LAPPET LAYBOY
MARKER PACKER PICKUP SECTOR
SHIELD SIDING ADAPTOR AFFAIRE
BIGOTRY BRAIDER CREASER
DROPPER FAGOTER FITTING
GIGBACK HEADSET HOLDING
JOINTER KNOCKUP LEVELER
SPANNER SPRAYER DEVOTION
DINGDONG FASTNESS FIXATION
FONDNESS GOVERNOR HEADREST
ATTACK FIT HIT HOP SIC BAIT BOMB
BOUT CLAW COSH DINT FANG FORK
FRAY GANG GIVE HOOK JUMP PAIL
PANG RAID RISE RUSH SAIL SICK
SLOW TACK TURN WADE YOKE
ABUSE ALARM ASSAY BEGIN BESET
BLAST BLITZ BRASH BRUNT CATCH
CHECK DRIVE FIGHT FLUSH FORAY
FORCE GLIDE HARRY ICTUS ONSET
POISE PULSE SALLY SCUFF SMITE
SOUSE SPASM SPELL STORM
ACCESS ACCUSE ACTION AFFRAY
AFFRET ASSAIL ATTAME BATTLE
BICKER CHARGE CRISIS DOUBLE
ENVAYE EXPUGN EXTENT GRUDGE
INDICT INFEST INSULT INVADE
OFFEND ONFALL ONRUSH POUNCE
RUFFLE SAVAGE SHOWER SORTIE

STOUND STRIKE STROKE TACKLE
TAKING THRUST AGGRESS ASPERSE
ASSAULT ATTEMPT BARRAGE
BELABOR BELIBEL BESEIGE
BOMBARD CENSURE CRUSADE
DESCENT OFFENSE PICKOUT
POTSHOT RUNNING SCALING
SEIZURE STACKER CAMISADO
ENDEAVOR ESCALADE PAROXYSM
SKIRMISH SURPRISE TOMAHAWK
(— IN COCKFIGHT) SHUFFLE
(— OF ILLNESS) GO DWAM DWALM
(— OF SICKNESS) WHIP SEIZURE
(— TO ROB) THUG
(— WITH SHOUTS) HUE
(— WITH WORDS) STOUSH
(— ZEALOUSLY) CRUSADE
(CHESS —) FORK
(CRITICAL —) SLATING
(FENCING —) GLIDE
(LIGHT —) TOUCH
(SLIGHT —) WAFF
(SUDDEN —) ICTUS RAPTUS
SURPRISE
(SUICIDAL —) KAMIKAZE
(SURPRISE —) ALARM ALARUM
(VERBAL —) FIRE BLUDGEON
ATTACKER AGGRESSOR OFFENDANT
ATTAIN GO GET HIT WIN BUMP
COME EARN GAIN RISE SORT ARISE
CATCH COVER CROSS FETCH
PROVE REACH TOUCH ACCEDE
AMOUNT ARRIVE ASPIRE EFFECT
OBTAIN SECURE STRIKE ACHIEVE
ACQUIRE COMPASS PROCURE
SUCCEED OVERTAKE
(— TO ACCOMPLISH) FIND FORCE
ATTAINMENT ARRIVAL ADEPTION
ENERGEIA PURCHASE
(— OF NIRVANA) MOKSHA
(SCHOLARLY —) LETTERS
ATTAR ITR OIL ATAR OTTO ATHAK
OTTAR ESSENCE PERFUME
ATTEMPT GO PUT SAY SHY TRY
BOUT BURL DARE DASH FAND FIST
FOND HACK JUMP MIND MINT MIRD
OSSE SEEK SHOT SLAP STAB WAGE
WORK ASSAY BEGIN ESSAY ETTLE
FLING FRAME OFFER ONSET PRESS
PROOF PROVE START TEMPT TRIAL
WHACK ASSAIL ATTACK EFFORT
FRAIST STRIVE ENFORCE IMITATE
PRETEND PROFFER STAGGER
VENTURE CONATION ENDEAVOR
EXERTION PURCHASE TENTAMEN
(— TO AROUSE) AGITATE
(— TO BRIBE) APPROACH
(— TO INFLUENCE) AGITATION
(ABORTIVE —) FUTILITY
ATTEND GO HO HOA HOO SEE HEAR
HEED LIST MIND OYES OYEZ STAY
TEND WAIT WALK APPLY AUDIT
AWAIT GUARD LAKEY NURSE SERVE
TREAT VISIT WATCH ASSIST
CONVEY ESCORT FOLLOW HARKEN
INTEND LISTEN SECOND SHADOW
SQUIRE CONDUCT CONSORT
ESQUIRE HEARKEN LACQUEY
PERPEND RETINUE

(— A LADY) WAIT
(— FUNERAL) FOLLOW
(— REGULARLY) KEEP
(— TO) MIND TREAT FETTLE INTEND
(— UPON) TENT CHASE CHAPERON
ATTENDANCE GATE SUIT CHAPEL
NUMBER OFFICE REGARD SERVICE
PRESENCE
ATTENDANT BOY FLY LAD JACK
MAID MUTE PAGE PEON SYCE ZANY
CADDY COMES GILLY GROOM GUIDE
JAGER USHER VALET ALEXAS
CADDIE DACTYL DAMSEL EMILIA
ESCORT FRIEND GESITH HAIDUK
HOGMAN JAEGER MINION PORTER
SQUIRE STOCAH TUBMAN VARLET
VERGER WAITER YEOMAN ALIPTES
ARMORER BULLDOG CHOBDAR
COURIER CROSSER DAMOSEL
FAMULUS FENELLA FOOTBOY
GHILLIE HALLMAN HOSTESS
JACKMAN LINKMAN MYRIDON
ORDERLY PAGEBOY PIQUEUR
PRESSER SEQUENT SERVANT
SHIPBOY SPOUTER TRABANT
TRESSEL ATTENDEE BEACHBOY
CHASSEUR CORYBANT CRUTCHER
FEWTERER FOLLOWER GATHERER
HANDMAID HENCHBOY HENCHMAN
HOUSEMAN MINISTER OBSERVER
ROSALINE SERGEANT SERJEANT
STAFFIER TIPSTAFF WATERMAN
(— OF CYBELE) CORYBANT
(CROSSING —) GATEMAN
(KNIGHT'S —) SWAIN ESQUIRE
(PROCTOR'S —) BULLDOG
(YOUNG —) BOY LAD JACK PAGE
KNIGHT
(PL.) STAFF CORTEGE RETINUE
ATTENDED FRAUGHT
ATTENTION EAR CARE GAUM HEED
HIST MARK MIND NOTE RUSH SHUN
TENT FLOOR GUARD STUDY TASTE
DETAIL FAVORS NOTICE REGARD
ACCOUNT ACHTUNG ADDRESS
EARNEST HEARING RESPECT
THOUGHT AUDIENCE
(— FROM SUPERIOR) TASHRIF
TASHREEF
(— TO PETTY ITEMS) MICROLOGY
(AMOROUS —) GALLANTRY
(FIXED —) DHARANA
(FLATTERING —) HOMAGE
(PLEASING —) INCENSE
(SPECIAL —) ACCENT
ATTENTIVE WARY ALERT AWAKE
CIVIL CLOSE SHARP TENTY ARRECT
INTENT POLITE CAREFUL GALLANT
HEEDFUL LISTFUL MINDFUL
PRESENT DILIGENT OBEDIENT
STUDIOUS THOUGHTY VIGILANT
WATCHFUL
(— TO) IMMINENT
ATTENUATE SAP DRAW FINE THIN
WATER DILUTE LESSEN RAREFY
REDUCE WEAKEN SLENDER
AVIANIZE DECREASE DIMINISH
EMACIATE ENFEEBLE TAPERING
ATTENUATED GAUNT AERIAL

DILUTED SPINDLY FINESPUN SMORZATO

ATTENUATION LOSS

ATTENUATOR PAD

ATTEST CHOP SEAL SIGN PROVE STATE SWEAR VOUCH ADJURE AFFIRM INVOKE RECORD WITTEN CERTIFY CONFESS CONFIRM CONSIGN TESTIFY WARRANT WITNESS EVIDENCE INDICATE MANIFEST

ATTESTATION DOCKET RECORD

ATTESTED SWORN CERTIFIED

ATTIC LOFT CELER SOLAR SOLER GARRET TALLET GRENIER COCKLOFT

(— **SIDE)** SKEELING

ATTIRE (ALSO SEE DRESS) BEGO SUIT TIRE ADORN ARRAY BIGAN DRESS HABIT AGUISE ENROBE PLIGHT REVEST TOILET ADDRESS APPAREL DUBBING PANOPLY ACCOUTER CLEADING EQUIPAGE FEATHERS

(**FORMAL** —) BALLDRESS

(**SHINING** —) SHEEN

ATTIRED TRICKSY

ATTITUDE AIR CUE SET BIAS MIEN MOOD POSE SIDE ANGLE FRAME HEART PHASE SHAPE SHELL SIGHT SLANT STAND ACTION ANIMUS ASPECT MANNER SPIRIT STANCE BEARING FEELING GESTURE POSTURE STATION STOMACH BEHAVIOR CARAPACE CROTCHET HABITUDE POSITION

(**PREVAILING** —) STREAM

ATTORNEY DOER AGENT PROXY VAKIL DEPUTY FACTOR FISCAL LAWYER LEGIST MUKTAR SYNDIC VAKEEL PROCTOR ADVOCATE

ATTRACT BAIT CALL DRAW LURE PULL TILL WIND BRING CATCH CHARM COURT FETCH TEMPT ALLURE ENGAGE ENLIST ENTICE GATHER INVITE SEDUCE STRIKE BEWITCH PROCURE INTEREST

(— **FISH)** CHUM

ATTRACTION BAIT CALL CARD CLOU DRAW PULL CHARM DRAFT SPELL TRACT APPEAL DESIRE MAGNET BLOWOFF COITION DRAUGHT GRAVITY INDRAFT ADHESION AFFINITY COHESION CONTRACT PENCHANT SIDESHOW WITCHERY

ATTRACTIVE BRAW CHIC CUTE FAIR GOOD BONNY FATAL JOLLY QUEME SWEET COMELY FLASHY FRUITY HEPPEN LOVELY PRETTY SAVORY SNAZZY TAKING TRICKY AMIABLE CIRCEAN CUNNING EYEABLE EYESOME GRADELY WINNING WINSOME ALLURING CHARMING ENGAGING ENTICING FEATURED FETCHING GRACEFUL GRACIOUS HANDSOME INVITING SPECIOUS VENEREAN

(**NOT** —) FOUL INCURIOUS

ATTRACTIVENESS CHARM GRACE BEAUTY GLAMOR AMENITY GLITTER AFFINITY HARLOTRY

ATTRIBUTABLE DUE

ATTRIBUTE FOX OWE GIVE MARK SIGN TYPE ALLOT BADGE BLAME CHARM PLACE POWER REFER ALLEGE ALLUDE ASSERT ASSIGN BESTOW CHARGE CREDIT IMPUTE PREFER REPUTE SYMBOL ADJUNCT ASCRIBE COUNTER ESSENCE PERTAIN QUALITY ACCREDIT GRANDITY INTITULE PROPERTY PROPRIUM STRENGTH

(— **WRONGFULLY)** FOIST

(—**S OF ROCKS)** GEOLOGY

(PL.) SARIRA SHARIRA

ATTRIBUTION ACCENT THEORY ANIMISM ETIOLOGY

ATTRITION WEAR GRIEF REGRET SORROW ANGUISH ABRASION BLASTING FRICTION

ATTUNE KEY TUNE ADAPT AGREE ACCORD ADJUST TEMPER PREPARE

ATUA AKUA DEMON SPIRIT

ATYPICAL BIZARRE GROTESQUE

AUBERGE INN ALBERGO

AUBERGINE EGGPLANT

AUBURN ABRAM BLOND CACHA CUTCH BLONDE CACHOU CATECHU GOREVAN

AU COURANT CONTEMPORARY

AUCTION CANT ROUP SALE SELL VEND COKER TRADE BARTER BRIDGE HAMMER OUTCRY VENDUE OUTROOP UNCTION DISPOSAL KNOCKOUT PORTSALE

AUCTIONEER CRIER CRYER OUTCRIER

AUDACIOUS BOLD BRASH BRAVE FRACK HARDY SAUCY AUDACE BRAZEN CHEEKY DARING FORWARD ARROGANT FEARLESS IMPUDENT INSOLENT INTREPID SPIRITED

(**NOT** —) CIVIL

AUDACITY CHEEK NERVE COURAGE BOLDNESS TEMERITY

AUDIBLE RIFE ALOUD CLEAR HEARD

AUDIENCE EAR PIT FANS AUDIT COURT FLOOR HOUSE PUBLIC GALLERY HEARING ASSEMBLY AUDITORY TRIBUNAL

AUDIT SCAN CHECK PROBE APPOSE RECKON VERIFY ACCOUNT EXAMINE INQUIRE INSPECT ESTIMATE

AUDITION HEARING

AUDITOR CENSOR HEARER APPOSER AUDIENT PITTITE COUNTOUR DISCIPLE LISTENER

AUDITORIUM HALL ROOM CAVEA FRONT ODEUM THEATER AUDITORY

AUDITORY ORAL OTIC AURAL AUDILE ACOUSTIC AUDITIVE

AUGER BIT BORE BORAL BORER GRILL BORING GIMLET NAUGER WIMBLE PIERCER TEREBRA

AUGHT ACHT EAWT AUCHT OWNED CIPHER NAUGHT WORTHY NOTHING VALIANT ANYTHING

AUGMENT ADD EKE FEED GROW HELP URGE BOOST EXALT SWELL APPEND DILATE EXPAND EXTEND AMPLIFY BALLOON ENHANCE ENLARGE IMPROVE INFLAME MAGNIFY COMPOUND HEIGHTEN INCREASE MAJORATE MULTIPLY

(— **IN STRENGTH)** INGROSS

AUGMENTATION RISE EKING SWELL GROWTH AUCTARY ADDITION

AUGMENTED SHARP EXTREME

AUGUR BODE OMEN SEER SPEAK AUSPEX DIVINE BETOKEN CONJECT FORESEE OMINATE PORTEND PREDICT PRESAGE PROMISE PROPHET SIGNIFY DENOUNCE FOREBODE FORESHOW FORETELL FOREWARN INDICATE PROPHESY

AUGURY ORE OMEN RITE SIGN SOOTH TOKEN HANSEL RITUAL HANDSEL PRESAGE CEREMONY

AUGUST AWFUL GRAND NOBLE KINGLY SERENE SOLEMN EXALTED STATELY IMPOSING MAJESTIC

(**FIRST DAY OF** —) LAMMAS LUGNAS LUGHNAS LUGNASAD

AUGUSTINIAN AUSTIN ASSUMPTIONIST

AUHUHU HOLA

AUK FALK LOOM ARRIE DIVER LEMOT MURRE NODDY SCOOT SCOUT SKOUT MARROT PUFFIN ROTCHE STARIK TINKER DOVEKEY DOVEKIE PENGUIN PYGOPOD SEAFOWL WILLOCK GAIRFOWL GAREFOWL ROCKBIRD

AULA HALL COURT EMBLIC

AUNT TIA BAWD AUNTY NAUNT TANTA TANTE AUNTIE GOSSIP

(— **SALLY)** STICKS

AURA AIR HALO ODOR AROMA SAVOR SMELL BREEZE BUZZARD ESSENCE FEELING

AUREATE GOLDEN ORNATE ROCOCO YELLOW

AUREOLE HALO CROWN GLORY LIGHT AREOLA CORONA GLORIA NIMBUS VESICA GLORIOLE MANDORLA

AUREUS (**HALF** —) SEMIS

AURICLE EAR PINNA ATRIUM EARLET TRUMPET PAVILION

AURIGA WAGONER WAGGONER

AURIST OTOLOGIST

AUROCHS TUR UROX URUS BISON WISENT BONASUS

AURORA EOS DAWN DRAPERY MORNING

AURORA BOREALIS DANCERS

AUSPICE CARE OMEN SIGN AUGURY PORTENT GUIDANCE

(PL.) EGIS AEGIS

AUSPICIOUS FAIR GOOD TWINE WHITE BRIGHT CHANCY DEXTER CHANCEY FAVORING

AUSTERE BARE COLD HARD SOUR BLEAK BUDGE GRAVE GRUFF HARSH RIGID ROUGH SHARP STERN STIFF STOUR BITTER CHASTE

FORMAL RUGGED SEVERE SIMPLE
SOMBER STRICT SULLEN TETRIC
ASCETIC EARNEST SERIOUS
GRANITIC RIGOROUS TETRICAL
AUSTERITY RIGOR CATOISM
AUSTRAL SOUTHERN

AUSTRALIA
ABORIGINE: MYALL
CAPE: HOWE
CAPITAL: CANBERRA
COIN: DUMP POUND SHILLING
DESERT: STURT GIBSON TANAMI
SIMPSON
ISLAND: CATO COCOS KOOLAN
CORINGA LACEPEDE ROTTNEST
TASMANIA
LAKE: EYRE COWAN FROME
BARLEE BULLOO AMADEUS
BLANCHE EVERARD TORRENS
GAIRDNER
LANGUAGE: YABBER
MEASURE: SAUM
MOUNTAIN: OLGA BRUCE LEGGE
CRADLE GARNET GAWLER
MAGNET STUART BONGONG
GREGORY CUTHBERT JUSGRAVE
MULLIGAN KOSCIUSKO
MOUNTAIN RANGE: DARLING
FLINDERS
NATIVE: MARA BINGE AUSSIE
DIGGER BILLIJIM KANGAROO
WARRAGAL WARRIGAL
JINDYWOROBAK
PENINSULA: EYRE
RIVER: DALY BULLO COMET ISAAC
PAROO ROPER SNOWY YARRA
BARCOO BARWON CULGOA
DAWSON DEGREY DARLING
FITZROY LACHLAN STAATEN
GEORGINA VICTORIA
SEA: CORAL TIMOR TASMAN
ARAFURA
SOLDIER: DIGGER SWADDY
BILLIJIM
STATE: TASMANIA VICTORIA
QUEENSLAND
TOWN: AYR YASS DUBBO PERTH
WAGGA ALBURY AUBURN
CAIRNS CASINO COBURG
DARWIN HOBART MACKAY
SYDNEY BENDIGO GEELONG
KOGARAH MILDURA MITCHAM
ADELAIDE BRISBANE ESSENDON
RANDWICK RINGWOOD
MELBOURNE TOOWOOMBA
VALLEY: GROSE JAMIESON
MEGALONG
WATER HOLE BILLABONG
WOMAN: LUBRA

AUSTRALIAN ANZAC AUSSIE DIGGER
AUSTRAL CURRENCY KANGAROO
WARRAGAL WARRIGAL
(— GIRL) LUBRA

AUSTRIA
ANCIENT PEOPLE: HUNS AVARS
RAETIANS SLOVENES
BAVARIANS
CAPITAL: WIEN VIENNA
CELTIC KINGDOM: NORICUM
COIN: DUCAT KRONE FLORIN
HELLER ZEHNER GROSCHEN
SCHILLING
DUCHY: STYRIA CARNIOLA
CARINTHIA
EMPEROR: CHARLES FRANCIS
FERDINAND
LAKE: ALMSEE FERTOTO
MONDSEE BODENSEE TRAUNSEE
CONSTANCE
MEASURE: FASS FUSS JOCH MASS
MUTH YOKE HALBE LINIE MEILE
METZE PFIFF PUNKT ACHTEL
BECHER SEIDEL DLAFTER
VIERTEL DREILING
MOUNTAIN: STUBAI EISENERZ
RHATIKON KITZBUHEL
NATIVE: STYRIAN TYROLEAN
NOBILITY: RITTER
PASS: LOIBL ARLBERG BRENNER
PLOCKEN
PROVINCE: TIROL TYROL STYRIA
VIENNA SALZBURG CARINTHIA
VORARLBERG
RIVER: INN MUR DRAU ENNS
KAMP LECH MURZ RAAB DONAU
MARCH SALZA THAYA TRAUN
DANUBE SALZACH
RIVER PORT: LINZ KREMS VIENNA
ROMAN PROVINCE: RAETIA
NORICUM PANNONIA
TOWN: ENNS GRAZ LECH LINZ
RIED WELS WIEN GMUND LIENZ
STEYR TRAUN LEOBEN VIENNA
BREGENZ MODLING SPITTAL
VILLACH DORNBIRN SALZBURG
INNSBRUCK
WEIGHT: MARC SAUM UNZE
DENAT KARCH PFUND STEIN
CENTNER PFENNIG VIERLING

AUTACOID HORMONE INCRETION
AUTARCHIC FREE
AUTHENTIC ECHT PURE REAL SURE
TRUE EXACT PUCCA PUCKA PUKKA
RIGHT VALID ACTUAL DINKUM
PROPER CORRECT CURRENT
GENUINE SINCERE CREDIBLE
OFFICIAL ORIGINAL RELIABLE
AUTHENTICATE SEAL PROVE
VOUCH ATTEST SIGNET VERIFY
APPROVE CONFIRM LEGALIZE
AUTHOR DOER JUDE SIRE JUDAS
MAKER RULER AUCTOR FACTOR
FORGER LOKMAN PARENT PENMAN
SCRIBE SOURCE WRITER ANCIENT
CLASSIC CREATOR ELOHIST
FOUNDER LOLLIUS ANCESTOR
BEGETTER COMPILER COMPOSER
IDEALIST IMMORTAL INVENTOR

JEHOVIST ORIGINAL PAYYETAN
PRODUCER
(PL.) SS
AUTHORITATIVE GRAVE CLASSIC
OFFICIAL ORACULAR POSITIVE
TEXTUARY
AUTHORITY LAW ROD SEE BALL
RULE SWAY ADEPT BOARD FAITH
POWER RICHE RIGHT STAMP SWING
TITLE ARTIST AUTHOR CREDIT
DANGER EMPERY EXPERT FASCES
REGENT REGIME SWINGE WEIGHT
AMITATE COMMAND CONTROL
DYNASTY FACULTY LEADING
LICENCE LICENSE SCEPTER
WARRANT DISPOSAL DOMINION
DOMINIUM HEGEMONY LORDSHIP
PRESTIGE SANCTION STRENGTH
(— OF SWITZERLAND) BUNDESRAT
(ARBITRARY —) ABOVE
(ROYAL —) SCEPTRE SOVRANTY
(SPIRITUAL —) KEYS KHILAFAT
(SUPREME —) SAY SIRCAR SIRKAR
(UNLIMITED —) AUTOCRACY
(PL.) ISNAD
AUTHORIZATION BARAT BERAT
PASSPORT SANCTION WARRANTY
AUTHORIZE LET LEAL VEST ALLOW
CLEAR CLOTHE PERMIT RATIFY
APPROVE EMPOWER ENDORSE
ENTITLE INDORSE JUSTIFY LICENSE
WARRANT ACCREDIT DELEGATE
LEGALIZE SANCTION
AUTHORIZED LEGAL OFFICIAL
AUTHORSHIP PENCRAFT PATERNITY
AUTO (ALSO SEE AUTOMOBILE)
CRATE CHUMMY LIZZIE
AUTOBIOGRAPHY VITA MEMOIR
AUTOCHTHONOUS NATIVE EDAPHIC
ENDEMIC
AUTOCLAVE DIGESTER DIGESTOR
AUTOCRACY MONARCHY
AUTOCRAT CZAR TSAR TZAR
MOGUL CAESAR DESPOT AUTARCH
MONARCH DICTATOR MONOCRAT
AUTOCRATIC ABSOLUTE
AUTO-DA-FE AUTO SERMO
AUTOGRAPH NAME SIGN MANUAL
INSCRIBE
AUTOMATIC MACHINE
AUTOMATON GOLEM ROBOT
AUTOMA ANDROID MACHINE
AUTOMOBILE BUG BUS CAR SIX
AUTO FOUR HEAP JEEP PONY TRAP
BUGGY COACH COUPE CRATE
EIGHT PONEY RACER SEDAN
BUCKET CHUMMY CUSTOM JALOPY
JUNKER SALOON AUTOCAR
COMPACT FLIVVER HACKNEY
HARDTOP MACHINE PHAETON
STEAMER TORPEDO VOITURE
CARRYALL DRAGSTER ELECTRIC
ROADSTER SQUADROL SUBURBAN
VICTORIA
(CONVERTIBLE —) DROPHEAD
(MIDGET —) DOODLEBUG
AUTONOMOUS FREE SEPARATE
AUTONOMY SOVEREIGNTY
SEPARATENESS

(— OF GOD) ASEITY ASEITAS
AUTOPSY NECROPSY
AUTUMN FALL KHARIF AUTOMPNE
FALLTIME MATURITY
AUXILIARY AID SUB AIDE ALLY
AIDING BRANCH DONKEY HELPER
ABETTER ABETTOR ADJUNCT
HELPING PARTNER ADJUTANT
(PL.) FOEDERATI
AVAIL DO AID DOW USE BOOT HELP
FADGE SERVE SKILL STEAD VALUE
MOMENT PROFIT BENEFIT BESTEAD
PREVAIL SERVICE SUCCEED SUFFICE
UTILIZE SUBSERVE
(— ONESELF) EMBRACE IMPROVE
SUBSERVE
AVAILABLE FIT FREE OPEN FLUSH
HANDY READY PATENT USABLE
PRESENT VISIBLE
AVALANCHE SLIDE LAWINE
VOLLENGE
AVANT-COURIER HERALD SCURRIER
AVANT-GARDE LITERATI
AVARICE GREED MISERY AVIDITY
CUPIDITY RAPACITY
AVARICIOUS CLOSE SLOAN GREEDY
HAVING HUNGRY SORDID STINGY
GRIPING GRIPPLE ITCHING MISERLY
COVETOUS GRASPING
AVATAR BALARAMA EPIPHANY
AVELLANEOUS HAZEL
AVENGE REPAY RIGHT VISIT WRACK
AWREAK PUNISH BEWREAK REQUITE
REVENGE SATISFY CHASTISE
AVENGER KANAIMA NEMESIS
WREAKER
AVENS GEUM BENNET BAREFOOT
AVENTURINE SUNSTONE
GOLDSTONE
AVENUE RUE WAY GATE MALL PIKE
ROAD ALLEE ALLEY DRIVE ENTRY
ACCESS ARCADE ARTERY RIDING
STREET AVENIDA OPENING
PASSAGE
AVER SAY AIVER CLAIM PROVE
STATE SWEAR AFFIRM ALLEGE
ASSERT ASSURE AVOUCH DEPOSE
VERIFY DECLARE JUSTIFY PROTEST
AVERAGE PAR SUM DUTY FAIR
MEAN NORM RULE RATIO USUAL
VALUE CHARGE MEDIAL MEDIAN
MEDIUM MIDDLE NORMAL TARIFF
ARRIAGE ESTIMATE MEDIOCRE
MIDDLING MODERATE ORDINARY
OVERHEAD QUANTITY STANDARD
(NOT —) BORDERLINE
AVERSE LOTH BALKY LOATH AFRAID
ADVERSE AGAINST OPPOSED
BACKWARD INIMICAL OPPOSITE
PERVERSE
(— TO) ABOVE
AVERSION TOY HATE DERRY ODIUM
ENMITY HATRED HORROR REGRET
DESPITE DISDAIN DISGUST DISLIKE
MISLIKE DISTASTE
(— TO FOOD) APOSITIA
(— TO WORK) ERGOPHOBIA
AVERT WRY BEND FEND MOVE SHUN
TURN WARD AVOID DETER DODGE

EVADE PARRY SHEER TWIST
DEFRAY DIVERT RETARD SHIELD
DECLINE DEFLECT EXPIATE
PREVENT ALIENATE ESTRANGE
FOREFEND WITHTURN
AVIARY CAGE HOUSE VOLARY
ORNITHON
AVIATOR ACE FLIER FLYER PILOT
AIRMAN FLYING ICARUS BIRDMAN
LOOPIST LUFBERY MANBIRD
SOLOIST
AVID AGOG KEEN WARM EAGER
ARDENT GREEDY HUNGRY JEJUNE
ANXIOUS ATHIRST CRAVING
LONGING THIRSTY DESIROUS
GRASPING
AVIDITY AVARICE CUPIDITY
AVIFAUNA BIRDS ORNIS BIRDLIFE
AVIKOM JACKS
AVOCADO COYO PEAR PALTA
AHUACA CHININ MARROW PERSEA
ZABOCA ABACATE ABBOGADA
AGUACATE ALLIGATO
AVOCET BARKER TILTER YELPER
SCOOPER
AVOID FLY SHY BALK FLEE HELP
MISS PASS QUIT SAVE SHUN VOID
WARE ABHOR ANNUL AVERT BURKE
DITCH DODGE ELUDE EVADE FEIGN
HEDGE PARRY SHIFT SHIRK SKIRT
SKULK SLACK SPAIR SPARE START
WANDE WONDE ABJURE BLENCH
BYPASS DETOUR ESCAPE ESCHEW
REFUTE REMOVE VACATE ABSTAIN
DECLINE EVITATE FORBEAR
FORSAKE REFRAIN
(— A PUNCH) SLIP
(— COMMITMENT) FUDGE
(— EXPENSE) HELP MISS SKIVE
(— OVERWORKING) FAVOR
(— RESPONSIBILITY) BLUDGE
AVOIDANCE DODGE OUTLET
EVASION ESCHEWAL
(— OF RISK) CAUTION
AVOUCH AVER ASSERT
AVOW OWN BIND WARE ADMIT
STATE AFFIRM ASSERT AVOUCH
DEPONE DEPOSE DEVOTE CONFESS
DECLARE JUSTIFY PROFESS
MAINTAIN
AVOWAL OATH WORD AVOURE
PROTEST
AVOWED FRANK SWORN STATED
DECLARED
AWAIT BIDE HEED KEEP PEND STAY
TEND WAIT ABIDE TARRY WATCH
ATTEND EXPECT IMPEND REMAIN
WAYLAY
(— PAYMENT) CARRY
AWAITING BEFORE BIDING
AWAKE DAW STIR WAKE ADAWE
ALERT ALIVE AWARE ROUSE ABRAID
ACTIVE AROUSE AWAKEN EXCITE
CAREFUL HEEDFUL STARTLE
VIGILANT
AWAKEN DAW STIR ALERT AROUSE
EXCITE KINDLE
AWAKENING REVIVAL WAKEFUL
AWARD LAW GIVE MARK MEED METE

WARD ALLOT GRANT MEDAL PRICE
PRIZE ACCORD ACTION ADDEEM
ASSIGN BESTOW BOUNTY CONFER
DECIDE MODIFY ADJUDGE APPOINT
CONSIGN CUSTODY KEEPING
ACCOLADE SENTENCE
(PL.) DESERTS
AWARE HEP RECK SURE WARE
WARY WISE ALERT ALIVE AWAKE
JERRY BEWARE KNOWING MINDFUL
APPRISED INFORMED SENSIBLE
SENTIENT VIGILANT WATCHFUL
AWARENESS EAR FEEL SENSE
FEELING INSIGHT
(— OF WORTH) APPRECIATION
AWAY BY TO AWA FRO OFF OUT VIA
WAY AFAR GONE PAST SCAT YOND
ALONG APART ASIDE FORTH HENCE
ABROAD ABSENT BEGONE ONWARD
THENCE DISTANT FROWARD
FAREWELL
(— FROM HOME) AFIELD OUTLAND
(— FROM PORT) AFLOAT
(— FROM) DOWN WITH ALONE
ALOOF APART BESIDE
(FARTHER —) BEYOND
AWE COW FEAR AMAZE DAUNT
DREAD SCARE FRIGHT HORROR
REGARD TERROR WONDER BUFFALO
RESPECT ASTONISH BEWILDER
OVERCOME RELIGION
AWE-INSPIRING GODFUL SOLEMN
AWESOME RELIGIO FEARSOME
OLYMPIAN
AWESOME EERY FELL HOLY AWFUL
EERIE WEIRD SOLEMN DREADED
GHOSTLY
AWESTRUCK SILENT
AWETO WERI
AWFUL DIRE FINE UGLY DREAD
GHAST AUGUST HORRID AWESOME
FEARFUL HIDEOUS SATANIC
DREADFUL SHOCKING TERRIBLE
AWFULLY AWFUL FIERCE
AWKWARD AWK CAR GAUM UNCO
CRANK FALSE FUDGY GAUMY
GAWKY GOATY INAPT INEPT SPLAY
STIFF UNCOW UNKED UNKID
CLUMSY GAUCHE RUSTIC STICKY
THUMBY UNEASY WOODEN
ADVERSE BOORISH CUBBISH
FROWARD HALTING LOUTISH
LUMPISH STILTED UNCANNY
UNCOUTH UNHANDY UNREADY
BUNGLING CLOWNISH FECKLESS
LUBBERLY PERVERSE UNGAINLY
UNTOWARD UNWIELDY
(— PERSON) TAWPY TUMFIE
(NOT —) FACILE
AWL BROD BROG NAIL NALL PROD
PROG BRODE ELSEN NALLE
BROACH DRIVER ELSHIN FIBULA
GIMLET BRADAWL SCRIBER
STABBER
AWN AIL EAR JAG BARB BEAK JAGG
PILE ARISTA BRISTLE
(— OF BARLEY) HORN
(— OF OATS) JAG JAGG
(PL.) BEARD

AWNING TILT BLIND SHADE VELUM CANOPY SEMIAN SHADER TIENDA TENTORY SEMIANNA SUNBLIND SUNSHADE VELARIUM

AWNLESS NOT NOTT HUMBLE HUMMEL POLLARD

AWRY CAM WRY AGEE BIAS SKEW AGLEY AMISS ASKEW GLEED GLEYD SNAFU WONKY WRONG ACROSS ASIDEN BLOOEY BLOOIE CAMMED FLOOEY ASKANCE ASQUINT ATHWART CROOKED OBLIQUE PERVERSE

AX ADZ AXE ADZE EAWT HACHE MATAX BIFACE PICKEL PIOLET POLEAX THIXLE TWIBIL BESAGUE BOUCHER BROADAX CHOPPER CLEAVER HATCHET JEDDING PULASKI TWIBILL FRANCISC

SUNDERER TOMAHAWK

(DOUBLE —) LABRYS

(HEADSMAN'S —) MANNAIA

(MASON'S —) CAVEL

(WOODEN —) MACANA

AXHAMMER CAVEL CAVIL KEVEL KNAPPER

AXIAL VENTRAL

AXIL ALA

AXILLA ALA AXIS ARMPIT SHOULDER

AXIOM SAW ADAGE MAXIM MOTTO BYWORD DICTUM SAYING TRUISM DIGNITY PRECEPT PROVERB APHORISM APOTHEGM DIGNITAS PETITION SENTENCE

AXIS AXE NUT AXLE STEM ARBOR HINGE STALK ARBOUR CAUDEX CENTER CHITRA RACHIS CAULOME

CORNCOB DENTATA POLAXIS SPINDLE SUCCULA SYMPODE TENDRIL AXLETREE MONOPODE

AXLE EX BAR COD PIN AXIS BOGY ARBOR BOGEY BOGIE EXTRE SHAFT AXTREE SLEEVE MANDREL SPINDLE SUCCULA

AYAH IYA CHAY EYAH MAID NURSE

AYE I AY EY EYE PRO YEA YES EVER ALWAYS ASSENT FOREVER

AYU AI SWEETFISH

AZALEA ERICA MINERVA CARDINAL

AZAZEL EBLIS

AZIMUTH ZN BEARING

AZTEC AZTECA MEXICA MEXICAN TENOCHCA

AZURE BICE BLUE HURT JOVE COBALT JOVIAL JUPITER CERULEAN SAPPHIRE

B SI BEE BAKER BRAVO
(— **FLAT**) ZA BEMOL
BA TRIPOS
BAA MAA MAE BLEAT
BABBAR UTU UTUO
BABBLE CHAT GASH KNAP TOVE
BABIL BLATE CLACK CLYDE GLOCK
HAVER PRATE TAVER WLAFF
CACKLE DITHER GABBLE GAGGLE
GLAVER GOSSIP JANGLE MURMUR
PALTER RABBLE TAIVER TUMULT
BLABBER BLATHER BLUSTER
CHATTER CHIPPER CLATTER
PRATTLE SMATTER TWADDLE
GLAISTER
BABBLER CACKLER BLATEROON
STIPITURE
BABEL DIN MEDLEY TUMULT
CHARIVARI CONFUSION
BABESIA APIOSOMA NUTTALIA
BABOON APE PAP PAPA DRILL
SPHINX BAVIAN CHACMA GIRRIT
PAPION BABUINA MANDRILL
HAMADRYAD
BABUL SANT SUNT ACACIA BABOOT
GARRAT GONAKE NEBNEB ATTALEH
GONAKIE
BABUSHKA SCARF KERCHIEF
BABY MOP BABA BABE CHAP DOLL
JOEY TOTO WEAN BAIRN CHILD
HUMOR SPOIL WAYNE CHRISM
CODDLE FONDLE INFANT MOPPET
PAMPER PUPPET SQUALL WEANIE
BAMBINO CHRISOM INDULGE
PAPOOSE WADDLER
BABY CARRIAGE PRAM BUGGY
WAGON GOCART STROLLER
BABYISH TIDDY PULING SIMPLE
PUERILE CHILDISH
BABYLONIAN (— **CYCLE**) SAROS
BABY'S BREATH GYP GYPSOPHILA
BACALAO MURRE SCAMP ABADEJO
CODFISH GROUPER GUILLEMOT
BACCATE BERRIED
BACCHANAL DEVOTEE REVELER
CAROUSER
BACCHANTE FROW MAENAD
BACCHUS LIBER LYAENS BROMIUS
DIONYSUS
(**AUNT OF** —) INO
(**FATHER OF** —) JUPITER
(**MOTHER OF** —) SEMELE
BACHELOR BACH SEAL BATCH
GARCON WANTER BACULERE
BENEDICT CELIBATE
BACILLUS GERM VIRUS MICROBE
BACK AID FRO TUB VAT ABET BAKE
BECK FULL HIND HINT NAPE NATA
REAR TAIL ABACK AGAIN ANGEL
BROAD CHINE DORSE NOTUM SPINE
SPLAT STERN VOUCH ASSIST
DORSUM HINDER SECOND SOOTHE
TERGUM TROUGH UPHOLD VERIFY
CISTERN ENDORSE FINANCE
RIGGING SPONSOR SUPPORT
SUSTAIN BACKWARD FULLBACK
HALFBACK MAINTAIN
(— **A ROWBOAT**) STERN
(— **OF ANIMAL**) RIG TERGUM

(— **OF ARCHERY TARGET**) BOSS
(— **OF AWNING**) RIDGEROPE
(— **OF BOOK**) DORSE SPINE
(— **OF BULL**) ROOF
(— **OF HAND**) OPISTHENAR
(— **OF HEAD**) NODDLE NIDDICK
OCCIPUT
(— **OF INSECT**) NOTUM
(— **OF NECK**) NAPE NUQUE SCRUFF
(— **OF PAGE**) FV
(— **OUT**) BEG JIB DUCK FLUNK
CRAWFISH
(— **TO BACK**) ADDORSED
(— **WATER**) STERN SHEAVE
(**SHOWING** —) TERGANT
BACKBITING DETRACTION
BACKBOARD BANK MONITOR
BACKBONE BACK GRIT GUTS CHINE
NERVE PLUCK RIDGE SPINA SPINE
LADDER METTLE SPIRIT GRISTLE
RIGBANE SPINULE STAMINA
VERTEBRA
(— **OF FISH**) GRATE
BACKCOUNTRY BUSH STICKS
BACKLAND BACKVELD BOONDOCKS
BACKDROP OLEO
BACKFIELD SECONDARY
BACKFIRE BOOMERANG
BACKFLASH GUTTER
BACKGAMMON IRISH LURCH TABLE
FAYLES GAMMON TABLES
BACKGAME TICKTACK
(— **MAN**) BLOT TABLEMAN
BACKGROUND FOND REAR GROUND
OFFING LINEAGE SETTING
BACKDROP DISTANCE EXTERIOR
OFFSCAPE TRAINING EDUCATION
(**MUSICAL** —) SUPPORT
BACKHANDED AWKWARD
BACKHOE PULLSHOVEL
BACKHOUSE PRIVY OUTHOUSE
BACKING AID EGIS AEGIS BACKUP
BEHIND LINING MUSLIN REFUSE
SUPPORT HEARTING FINANCING
(**LEGAL** —) STRENGTH
BACKLASH LASH SHAKE SLACK
BACKLOG RESERVE SURPLUS
BACKBRAND
BACKPIECE DOSSIERE
BACKPLATE REREDOS
BACKREST LAZYBACK
BACKROPE GOBLINE
BACKSEY SEY SIRLOIN
BACKSLIDE FALL LAPSE DESERT
REVERT RELAPSE
BACKSPIN DRAG UNDERCUT
UNDERSPIN
BACKSTITCH PURL PEARL
BACKSTOP BUTT
BACKWARD FRO JAY LAX YON
BACK CRAB DARK DULL LOTH
ABACK AREAR BLATE INAPT LOATH
THRAW UNAPT ARREAR ASTERN
AVERSE BYGONE POSTIC RETRAD
RETRAL STUPID BASHFUL LAGGARD
LAGGING REVERSE UPSTAGE
DILATORY IGNORANT LATEWARD
PERVERSE REARWARD TAILFIRST
BACKWARDNESS DARKNESS
BARBARISM

BACKWARDS YON AROUND
BACKWATER EBB COVE SLEW SLUE
BAYOU SHEAVE SLOUGH RETRACT
RETREAT BACKWASH BILLABONG
BACKWOODSMAN HICK WOODSY
BUCKSKIN HILLBILLY
BACKWORT COMFREY
BACON PIG BARD MEAT PORK
BARDE JAMON PRIZE SPECK FLITCH
GAMMON RUSTIC SAWNEY
GAMBONE SOWBELLY
BACOPA BRAMIA
BACTERIUM ROD COLI GERM
AEROBE CYTODE ANTHRAX
CHOLERA MICROBE PROTEUS
SARCINA VIBRION BACILLUS
LISTERIA BOTULINUS CYTOPHAGA
HEMOPHILE INFECTANT INFECTION
BAD BIG DUD ILL SAD EVIL FULL
HARD LEWD POOR PUNK QUED SICK
SOUR VILE WICK GAMMY NASTY
SORRY WEARY WORST WRONG
ARRANT FAULTY LITHER LUTHER
NOUGHT ROTTEN SEVERE SHREWD
SINFUL UNGOOD UNKIND WICKED
BALEFUL BANEFUL CORRUPT
FEARFUL HARMFUL HEINOUS
HURTFUL IMMORAL INUTILE
NAUGHTY SPOILED TAINTED
UNLUCKY UNMORAL UNSOUND
VICIOUS ANNOYING CRIMINAL
DEPRAVED DOGGEREL FIENDISH
FLAGRANT INFERIOR PRECIOUS
SINISTER UNSUITED
(— **MANNERS**) TROLLOPE
(**OUTRAGEOUSLY** —) GRIEVOUS
(**OUTSTANDINGLY** —) ARRANT
(**RATHER** —) INDIFFERENT
(**VERY** —) ALMIGHTY EXECRABLE
BADDERLOCKS MURLIN PURSES
HENWARE SEAWEED HONEYWARE
BADGE PIN MARK SIGN STAR COLOR
CREST CROSS FAVOR HONOR
ORDER PATCH TOKEN BUTTON
BUZZER COLLAR EMBLEM ENSIGN
FASCES GARTER GIGLIO PLAQUE
SHIELD SYMBOL TIPONI WEEPER
CHEVRON EPAULET FEATHER
BRASSARD INSIGNIA SCAPULAR
EPAULETTE
(**JAPANESE** —) MON KIRIMON
(**RUSSIAN** —) ZNAK
BADGER NAG PAT BAIT GRAY GREY
GRIS MELE PATE ANNOY BRACE
BROCK BRUSH CHEVY CHIVY
HURON MELES PAHMI RATED RATEL
TAXEL TAXUS TEASE WORRY
BAUSON BOTHER BRAROW CHIVVY
HAGGLE HARASS HAWKER HECKLE
KIDDER MELINE PESTER TELEDU
WOMBAT GRISARD TORMENT
BRAIREAU BULLYRAG CARCAJOU
HUCKSTER IRRITATE STINKARD
MISTONUSK
(— **STATE**) WISCONSIN
(**AUSTRALIAN** —) WOMBAT
(**COMPANY OF** —S) CETE
(**LIKE A** —) MELINE
BADINAGE FOOL JOKER BANTER

RAILLERY TRIFLING

BADLANDS MALPAIS

BADLY BAD ILL EVIL HARD ILLY SICK SADLY EVILLY HARDLY POORLY UNWELL FAULTILY WICKEDLY VICIOUSLY

BADMINTON POONA

BADNESS MALICE PRAVITY UNVALUE EVILNESS

BAD-TEMPERED FOUL ANGRY STINGY GROUCHY

BAFFLE FOX GET BALK BEAT FOIL LICK MATE POSE STOP UNDO CHEAT CHECK ELUDE EVADE FLING STICK STUMP BLENCH BOGGLE DEFEAT DELUDE FICKLE INFAMY OUTWIT PUZZLE RESIST THWART BUFFALO CONFUSE DECEIVE QUIBBLE STONKER BEWILDER CONFOUND DISGRACE JUGGLING

BAFFLING SHREWD ELUSIVE

BAG COD KIT MAT NET PAD POD POT SAC CELL DRAG GRIP LOBE MAIL POCK POKE SACK TOOT TRAP WOMB BELLY BOUGE BULSE CATCH DILLI DILLY EMERY FLOAT HUSSY PETER POUCH PURSE SCRIP SEIZE SNARE STEAL BLOUSE BUDGET CAVITY ENTRAP FOLLIS GASBAG MATAPI PAGGLE POCKET POUNCE SACHET SEABAG VALISE WALLET ALFORJA BALLOON BEANBAG BLISTER BUCKRAM CANTINA CAPCASE CAPTURE CUSHION GAMEBAG GOMUKHI HANDBAG HOLDALL RETICLE SANDBAG SARPIER SATCHEL TRAVOIS CARRYALL CORNSACK ENTRAILS ENVELOPE FOLLICLE KNAPSACK MONEYBAG OVERSLIP RETICULE RUCKSACK SUITCASE WINESKIN MULTIWALL WEEKENDER
(— BULGING) SWAG
(— FOR LETTERS) MAIL POUCH KAREETA MAILBAG POSTBAG
(— FOR TOOLS) WALLET
(— OF ANISEED) DRAG
(— WITH POCKETS) TIDE TIDY
(AUSTRALIAN —) SWAG DILLI SHIRT SHAMMY
(GAS —) CELL
(GRAB —) FISHPOND
(HAWSE —) JACKASS
(LEATHER —) JAG JAGG ASKOS BUDGE BOUGET MUSSUK
(NET —) SNOOD GARLAND
(SEWING —) HUSSY
(SLEEPING —) FUMBA FLEABAG SLEEPER
(WATER —) CHAGAL CHAGEN CHAGUL

BAGASSE BEGASS LINAGA MEGASS

BAGATELLE CANON TRUNK VERSE CANNON TRIFLE

BAGGAGE ARMS GEAR MINX SWAG CUTTY HUZZY NASTY SAMAN STUFF TENTS TRASH WENCH HARLOT REFUSE TRASHY TRUNKS CLOTHES DUNNAGE EFFECTS FARDAGE

PLUNDER RUBBISH SALMARY SUMPTER VALISES CARRIAGE HARLOTRY RUBBISHY UTENSILS

BAGGAGE CAR WAGON FOURGON

BAGGER SACKER BATCHER

BAGGING SOUTAGE

BAGGY LOOSE POCKY PURSY FLABBY PUFFED PURSIVE

BAGNIO BAIN BATH BAGNE PRISON BROTHEL HOTHOUSE

BAGPIPE MUSE PIPE PIVA DRONE TITTY BIGNOU BINIOU CHORUS GEWGAW MUSETTE SAMBUKE DULCIMER SYMPHONY ZAMPOGNA CORNAMUTE CORNEMUSE SYMPHONIA

BAGUETTE CHAPLET

BAH PO FOH PAH POH ROT RATS FAUGH PSHAW NONSENSE

BAHAMAS (CAPITAL OF —) NASSAU
(ISLAND OF —) ABACO EXUMA ANDROS BIMINI

BAHRAIN (CAPITAL OF —) MANAMA
(MONEY OF —) FILS DINAR
(TOWN OF —) RIFAA JIDHAFS

BAIL BOW DIP ANDI BALE BOND HOOP LADE LAVE RING RYND YOKE LADLE SCOOP THROW VOUCH BUCKET HANDLE PLEDGE SECURE SURETY VADIUM CUSTODY DELIVER RELEASE REPLEVY BAILSMAN BULWARKS SECURITY GUARANTEE
(— OUT) ABANDON

BAILEE LESSEE POSITOR CONDUCTOR

BAILER SPOUCHER

BAILIFF GRAB HIND AGENT REEVE SAFFO SCULT STAFF BAILIE BAILLI BEADLE DEPUTY FACTOR GRIEVE LOOKER OFFICE PORTER PREVOT SCHOUT VARLET BUMTRAP GRIPPER PROVOST PUTTOCK SHERIFF STEWARD APPROVER HUISSIER OVERSEER TIPSTAFF CONSTABLE HUNDREDER PORTREEVE SENESCHAL WAPENTAKE

BAILIWICK AREA FIELD DOMAIN OFFICE PROVINCE

BAILOR LESSOR

BAIN NEAR LITHE READY SHORT DIRECT LIMBER SUPPLE FORWARD WILLING

BAIT BAD BOB COG DAP LUG BITE CAST CHUM FEED HALT HANK LURE PLUG TAIL DECOY HOUND LEGER SHACK SLATE SQUID TEMPT TRAIN WORRY ALLURE APPAST ATTACK BADGER BERLEY ENTICE HARASS HECKLE HECTOR KILLER LEDGER REPAST SHRAPE SLIVER FULCRUM GUDGEON PROVOKE TAGTAIL TOLLING TORMENT CUNGEBOI
(— FOR BIRDS) SHRAP SHRAPE
(— FOR COD) CAPELIN
(GREASY —) ROGUE
(GROUND —) BERLEY
(MAGGOT —) GENTLE
(SCENTED —) DRAG

BAITING HANK

BAIZE BAY BAYES BAYETA DOMETT

BAKE DRY BURN COCT COOK FIRE BATCH BROIL GRILL PARCH ROAST ANNEAL HARDEN BISCUIT PISTATE SCALLOP CLAMBAKE ESCALLOP
(— EGGS) SHIRR
(— THOROUGHLY) SOAK

BAKED (— IN EARTH OVEN) KALUA
(— PRODUCT) KICHEL

BAKER OVEN FIRER BAXTER BURNER FURNER PISTOR FURNACE OVENMAN ROASTER

BAKER BIRD HORNERO

BAKING CUIT BATCH COCTION FURNAGE ASSATION

BAKONGO FIOT

BALACHONG NGAPI

BALANCE BEAM EVEN PEIS REST SWAY TRIM COVER ERASE PEISE POISE SCALE TRONE WEIGH WEIHE ADJUST AUNCEL CANCEL EMBLEM EQUATE KELTER KELVIN KILTER LAUNCE OFFSET SANITY SQUARE STRIKE DESEMER LIBRATE OVERRUN RESIDUE TRABUSH TRUTINE EQUALITY EQUALIZE EQUATION SERENITY WESTPHAL TREBUCHET
(— DUE) ARREAR
(— IN ACCOUNT) CREDIT
(— OF SAILS) ATRY
(MENTAL —) HEAD

BALANCED EVEN EQUAL LEVEL APOISE KITTLE WEIGHED COMPLETE QUADRATE

BALANCER HALTER ACROBAT GYMNAST HALTERE

BALATA ICICA BULLACE BEEFWOOD BORRACHA

BALCONY POY ORIEL PORCH STOOP CIRCLE GAZEBO PIAZZA PODIUM SOLLAR BALAGAN GALLERY MIRADOR PERGOLA TERRACE BRATTICE CANTORIA VERANDAH

BALD RAW BARE BASE BOLD CRUDE DODDY NAKED PLAIN CALLOW PALTRY PEELED PILLED SIMPLE CALVOUS EPILOSE LITERAL GLABROUS HAIRLESS
(— HEAD) PILGARLIC
(— SPOT) TONSURE

BALDACHIN CANOPY CIBORIUM

BALDER BALDR BALDUR BAELDAEG
(CHILD OF —) FORSETE FORSETI
(FATHER OF —) ODIN
(SLAYER OF —) HOTH LOKE HOTHR
(WIFE OF —) NANNA

BALDERDASH ROT GUFF TRASH DRIVEL JARGON FLUBDUB NONSENSE BALDUCTUM RIGMAROLE

BALDNESS ACOMIA CALVITY ALOPECIA ATRICHIA OPHIASIS

BALDPATE ZUISIN POACHER

BALDRIC BELT LACE GIRDLE ZODIAC BALTEUS SUPPORT NECKLACE

BALE NO GIB NOT WOE EVIL FIRE HARM PACK PYRE BLOCK CRATE DEATH FARDO SERON BALLOT BUNDLE EMBALE SEROON SORROW

PACKAGE SARPLER
BALEARIC ISLANDS (ISLAND OF —)
IBIZA CABRERA MAJORCA MINORCA
CONEJERA
(MEASURE OF —) PALMO MISURA
QUARTA QUARTIN BARCELLA
(TOWN OF —) IBIZA MAHON PALMA
(WEIGHT OF —) CARGO CORTA
QUARTANO
BALEEN WHALEBONE
BALEFUL BAD EVIL DEADLY MALIGN
SACRED SULLEN MALEFIC NOXIOUS
RUINOUS SIDERAL SINISTER
WRETCHED
BALI (DANCE OF —) ARDJA BARIS
KRISS BARONG KETJAK MONKEY
DJANGER
(MOUNTAIN OF —) AGOENG
(MUSICAL INSTRUMENT OF —)
GAMELAN
(RICE FIELD OF —) SAWAII
(STRAIT OF —) LOMBOK
(TOWN OF —) SINGARADJA
BALINGHASAY ANAM ANAN
BALK GAG HUE JUB SHY BEAM BILK
BUCK BULL COND FOIL GORM HADE
HEAP LICK LOFT MISS OMIT PROP
SHUN SKIP SLIP STAY STOP AVOID
BAULK BLOCK CHECK CLAMP
DEMUR HUNCH MOUND REBEL
REEST RIDGE STAKE STICK WAVER
BAFFLE DEFEAT FALTER HINDER
IMPEDE OUTWIT RAFTER REFUSE
STRAIN THWART BLUNDER CODLING
GALLOWS ISTHMUS MISTAKE
(— IN FISHING) HUE COND
(HALF —) FLITCH
(PL.) MIDDLES
BALKAN (— COIN) NOVCIC
(— COUNTRY) GREECE SERBIA
ALBANIA RUMANIA BULGARIA
(— INSTRUMENT) GUSLA
(— RIVER) JIU OLT IBAR JIUL SAVA
TISA OLTUL DANUBE MORAVA
(— SEA) BLACK AEGEAN IONIAN
ADRIATIC
BALKER HUER CONNER
BALKY NAPPY STICK MULISH REESTY
RESTIVE CONTRARY STUBBORN
OBSTINATE
BALL IN BAL BOB FLY HOP NOB ORB
PEA TOY BEAD BOWL CLEW CLUE
KNOB KNOP KNUR PICK PILL POME
TRAP DANCE EDGER FAULT FLOAT
GLOBE GLOME HURLY ORBIT PEARL
PUPPY SHAPE SNACK SPORT TRUCK
BULLET BUTTON HOOKER HURLEY
MOONIE MUDDLE PEELEE PELLET
PELOTA POMMEL POMPON RONDEL
RUNDLE SPHERE SQUASH BALLOON
CONFUSE FLOATER GLOBULE
INCURVE INSHOOT KNAPPAN
LEATHER MANDREL PELOTON
RIDOTTO SLITTER BASEBALL
BISCAYEN FANDANGO FOOTBALL
GROUNDER HANDBALL QUENELLE
SOFTBALL SPHEROID TRAPBALL
(— AS SHIP'S SIGNAL) SHAPE
(— FOR MUSKET) GOLI SLUG

(— OF CLAY) KNICKER
(— OF RICE OR MEAT) PINDA
(— OF THREAD) CLEW CLUE GOME
BOTTOM WHARROW
(— OF THUMB) THENAR CUSHION
(— OF WASTE IRON) COBBLE
(— USED IN SHINTY) PEG
(—S OF MEDICI FAMILY) PALLE
(BILLIARD —) SPOT IVORY
SNOOKER
(BOWLED —) TICE CURVE SKYER
BAILER BUMPER FIZZER GOOGLY
KICKER POODLE YORKER CREEPER
SNORTER SPINNER BREAKBACK
CROSSOVER INSWINGER
(BOWLING —) DODO JACK
(CRICKET —) SNICK SHOOTER
(FIVES —) SNACK
(GOLF —) PUTTY
(HARD —) SNUG
(HOCKEY —) NUN NUR ORR
(INK —) PUMPET
(SKITTLE —) CHEESE
(TENNIS —) PALM
(WOODEN —) KNUR
BALLAD JIG LAI LAY LILT MELE
POEM SONG CAROL DERRY FANCY
BALLET BYLINA CARVAL SONNET
BALLANT CANZONE CORRIDO
GWERZIOU SINGSONG
BALLAST BED CRIB LOAD TRIM
METAL POISE STONE BOTTOM
BURDEN GRAVEL WEIGHT BALANCE
LASTAGE SANDBAG DRAGROPE
KENTLEDGE SABURRATE
BALLET BALLAD MASQUE BOURREE
PANTOMIME
(— MOVEMENT) VOLE TEMPS
APLOMB OUVERT POINTE RELEVE
RETIRE ALLONGE ARRONDI
ASSEMBLE ATTITUDE ARABESQUE
BALLHOOTER BRUTTER
BALLISTA SWEEP MANGONEL
BALLOON BAG BALL BLIMP EXPAND
GASBAG AIRSHIP DISTEND DRACHEN
INFLATE SAUSAGE SKYHOOK
AEROSTAT ENVELOPE DIRIGIBLE
(TRIAL —) KITE
BALLOONING BOSOMY
BALLOON VINE FAROLITO
HEARTPEA HEARTSEED
BALLOT BALE POLL PROX VOTE
ELECT PROXY VOICE BILLET CHOICE
POLICY TICKET SUFFRAGE
BALLROOM SALOON
BALLYHOO BALLY HOOPLA
BALM OIL BEEB BITO DAUB SALVE
ANOINT BALSAM EMBALM LOTION
RELIEF SOLACE SOOTHE ANODYNE
BESMEAR COMFORT PERFUME
UNGUENT OINTMENT
(— OF GILEAD) CANADA
OPOBALSAM
BALMY MILD SOFT BLAND DAFFY
MOONY SPICY SUNNY SWEET
GENTLE INSANE SERENE HEALING
LENIENT AROMATIC BALSAMIC
DRESSING FRAGRANT SOOTHING
BALONEY BUNK HOOEY BUSHWA
BUSHWAH

BALSA RAFT FLOAT GUANO POLAK
POLACK BOBWOOD CORKWOOD
BALSAM BALM RIGA TOLU UMIRI
COPALM GURJAN GURJUN STORAX
AMPALEA COPAIBA CREEPER
AMPALAYA BDELLIUM BENJAMIN
OINTMENT
BALSAM APPLE KARELA AMARGOSA
AMPALAYA BALSAMINE
BALSAM FIR SAPIN BAUMIER
BALSAM POPLAR BAUMIER
TACAMAHAC
BALSAMROOT SUNFLOWER
BALSAMWEED MOONSHINE
FEATHERWEED
BALT YOD ESTH LETT ESTONIAN
BALTIC (— GULF) RIGA DANZIG
BOTHNIA FINLAND
(— ISLAND) DAGO FARO OSEL
ALAND ALSEN OESEL OLAND
GOTLAND HIIUMAA BORNHOLM
(— PORT) KIEL RIGA MEMEL REVAL
DANZIG GDANSK TALINN LEIPAJA
(— RIVER) ODER ODRA DVINA
VIADUA
(— TOWN) MEMEL DANZIG GDANSK
LEIPAJA
BALUCHISTAN (— CULTURE)
QUETTA
BALUSTER SPOKE COLUMEL
BANISTER COLUMELLA
BALUSTRADE BARRER PARAPET
RAILING BALCONET BANISTER
BAMBOO DHA CANE REED BATAK
GLUMAL GUADUA TONKIN BATAKAN
WANGHEE WHANGEE
(SACRED —) NANDIN
(WOVEN —) SAWALI
BAMBOOZLE DUPE HAVE CHEAT
COZEN GRILL CAJOLE HUMBUG
BUFFALO DECEIVE DEFRAUD
MYSTIFY PERPLEX
BAN BAR WOE TABU VETO BANAL
BANUS BLOCK CURSE EDICT ORDER
TABOO BANISH CENSOR ENJOIN
FORBID HINDER INVOKE NOTICE
OUTLAW CONDEMN EXCLUDE
ANATHEMA DENOUNCE EXECRATE
PROHIBIT
BANAK UCUUBA
BANAL FLAT CORNY INANE SILLY
STALE TRITE VAPID JEJUNE INSIPID
TRIVIAL
BANANA FEI FIG MUSA SABA BERRY
ENSETE FINGER SAGING LACATAN
PLATANO SAGUING SUNBEAM
PLANTAIN
BAND BAR GAD HUB TIE TUB ZON
BEAD BELT BEND BOND CAME CASH
CORD CREW CUFF FALL FERD FESS
GANG GATE GIRT HOOD HOOP
KNOT LACE LIST RING SASH SHOE
TAPE WISP ZONA ZONE AMPYX
BANDY BRAID CHOIR CLAMP CORSE
COVEY COVIN CRAPE CROWN
FEMUR FLOCK FRAME GIRTH GORGE
GUARD JATHA LABEL MEINY NOISE
PANEL PATTE PRIDE QUIRE SABOT
SNOOD STRAP STRIP STROP TAPIS

TORSE TRACK TRIBE UNITE WERED
WITHE ARMLET BENDEL BINDER
BORDER BOYANG BRIDGE BUNDLE
CIMBIA CLAVUS COHORT COLLAR
COLLET COPULA COVINE CRANCE
CRAVAT DECKLE FASCIA FETTER
FILLET FRIEZE FRINGE FUNNEL
GAMMON GARTER GASKET GIRDLE
HYPHEN LEGLET MATRIX NIPPER
NORSEL PLEDGE RADULA REGULA
ROLLER SCREED STRAKE STRING
STRIPE SWATHE TAENIA TETHER
TISSUE WEEPER BINDING BLANKET
CHAMBUL CIRCLET COMPANY
ENOMOTY FERRULE FRONTAL
GARLAND HATBAND HEADING
NECKTIE ORPHREY PALLIUM PIGTAIL
PROMISE SEQUELA SHACKLE
SHOEING SWADDLE VINCULUM
(— ACROSS SUNSPOT) BRIDGE
(— IN BRAIN) LIGULA FRENULUM
FUNICULUS
(— OF 13 WITCHES) COVEN
(— OF CLAY) COTTLE
(— OF COLOR) SOCK SLASH STRIA
LACING
(— OF CRAPE) WEED SCARF
(— OF INDIANS) SHIVWITS
(— OF PILLAGERS) SKINNERS
(— OF PURPLE) CLAVUS
(— OF STRAW) GAD SIMMON
(— TOGETHER) BANDY
(ARMED —) JATHA POSSE
(ARMOR —) TONLET
(CIRCULAR —) HOOP RING ANNULE
WREATH
(DANCE —) CHORO
(DECORATIVE —) PATTE LEGLET
CORNICE
(IRON —) FRET GATE TRUSS
FUNNEL STRAKE
(LACE —) SCALLOP
(MUSICIANS —) CONCERT
(RADIO —) CHANNEL
(RESONANCE —) FORMANT
(TRIBAL —) AIMAK
(PL.) GRIPES INTERLACERY
BANDAGE BAND BELT BIND TAPE
BLIND BRACE CLOUT DRESS GALEA
LINEN SLING SPICA SWARF SWATH
TRUSS BINDER COLLAR CRAVAT
FASCIA FETTLE FILLET LIGATE
NIPPER ROLLER SWARTH SWATHE
SWEATH REVERSE ROLLING
SWADDLE TRUSSER ACCIPTER
CAPELINE CINCTURE GAUNTLET
LIGAMENT LIGATURE SCAPULAR
STOCKING
(EYE —) MUFFLER
(FINGER —) HOVEL
(JAW —) FUNDA
(PL.) SWADDLING
BANDALORE QUIZ
BANDANNA WEB TURBAN BANDANA
PULICAT PULICATE PULLICAT
BANDEAU BAND STRIP FILLET
BRASSIERE
BANDICOOT RAT MARL BILBI BILBY
BADGER BIELBY PINKIE QUENDA

BANDIT CACA TORY BRAVO THIEF
BANISH HAIDUK HEYDUK OUTLAW
ROBBER BANDIDO BRIGAND
LADRONE TULISAN BUSHWACK
MARAUDER MIQUELET PICAROON
(PL.) MANZAS
BANDLEADER MASTER MAESTRO
CHORAGUS CONDUCTOR
BANDORE PANDURA
BANDSMAN WINDJAMMER
BANDSTAND KIOSK STAND
BANDY VIE BAND CART CHOP SWAP
TRADE LEAGUE RACKET STRIVE
CHAFFER CONTEND DISCUSS
CARRIAGE EXCHANGE
(— WORDS) REVIE GIFFGAFF
BANE BAN WOE BONE EVIL HARM
KILL PEST RUIN CURSE DEATH
VENOM INJURY MURDER POISON
SLAYER NEMESIS SCOURGE
MISCHIEF MURDERER NUISANCE
BANEBERRY COHOSH REDBERRY
TOADROOT GRAPEWORT
BANEFUL BAD ILL EVIL VILE SWART
HARMFUL HURTFUL NOXIOUS
RUINOUS VENOMOUS SINISTRAL
BANG POM RAP BAFF BEAT BLOW
BOOT DASH DOCK DRUB POUF
SCAT SLAM SWAP SWOP TANK
BLAFF CLASH CRACK DRIVE EXCEL
FORCE IMPEL POUND SLAKE SLUMP
SOUND SPANG STRAM THUMP
WHACK WHANG WHUMP BOUNCE
CUDGEL ENERGY FRINGE STRIKE
THRASH THUNGE THWACK SARDINE
SURPASS THUNDER FORELOCK
(— ON HEAD) BRAIN
BANGLADESH (CAPITAL OF —)
DACCA
(MONEY OF —) TAKA
(NATIVE OF —) BENGALI
(RIVER OF —) GANGES
BANG-UP SLAP CRACK TIPTOP
BANISH BAN FREE ABAND EJECT
EXILE EXPEL FLEME WAIVE WREAK
BANDIT DEPORT DISPEL DISTER
FORSAY OUTLAW ABANDON
CONDEMN CONFINE DISMISS
DIVORCE EXCLUDE DISPLACE
RELEGATE
BANISHED FUGITIVE
BANISHMENT EXILE BANNIMUS
OUTLAWRY XENELASY OSTRACISM
XENELASIA
BANISTER RAILING BALUSTER
BANJO BOX BANJORE BANJORINE
BANK BAR BAY COP JUG RIM ROW
BINK BRAE BREW BUTT CAJA DIKE
DUNE DYKE EDGE HEAD HILL LINK
MASS PILE RAKE RAMP RIPA RIVE
SAND SEAT SIDE TIER WEIR BANCO
BENCH BLUFF BRINK COAST DITCH
EARTH FENCE HOVER HURST LEVEE
MARGE MOUND MOUNT RIDGE
SAVER SHARE SHELF SHOAL SHORE
SLOPE STACK STAGE TRUST
BANQUE BORROW CAISSE CAUSEY
CRADGE DEGREE DEPEND DOUBLE
MARGIN RANDOM RECKON RIVAGE

STRAND ANTHILL BANKING CUSHION
DEPOSIT LOMBARD POTTERY
SANDBAG SHALLOW WINDROW
BARRANCA PLATFORM TRAVERSE
(— A FIRE) REST
(— OF CANAL) BERM BERME
HEELPATH
(— OF EARTH) COP DAM DITCH
(— OF RIVER) WHARF STRAND
(— OF SAND OR MUD) BAR SCALP
(— OF SNOW) WREATH SNOWDRIFT
(— OF TURF) SUNK
(OVERHANGING —) BREW HOVER
(RUSSIAN —) CRAPETTE
(STEEP —) HEUCH HEUGH WOUGH
BARRANCA BARRANCO
BANKER BOOK SETH SETT FACTOR
FINDER SAHKAR SHROFF SOUCAR
SOWCAR LOMBARD MARWARI
MONEYER SPONSOR TAILLEUR
BANQUETER FINANCIER
BANKNOTE CRISP FLIMSY SCREEN
BANKRUPT SAP BUNG BUST RUMP
BREAK BROKE DRAIN SMASH STRIP
BROKEN BUSTED DYVOUR QUISBY
CRACKED DEPLETE
BANKRUPTCY SMASH FAILURE
SMASHUP
BANKSMAN LANDER HILLMAN
BANLIEUE LOWY ENVIRONS
BANNER FANE FLAG JACK SIGN
COLOR ENSIGN FANNON PENNON
LABARUM LEADING PENNANT
SALIENT BANDEROL BRATTACH
FOREMOST GONFALON ORIFLAMB
STANDARD STREAMER VEXILLUM
BEAUSEANT ORIFLAMME
(FUNERAL —) BANNEROL
GUMPHEON GUMPHION
(PL.) ENSIGNRY
BANNOCK PANAK DIGGER JANNOCK
BANNS CRY BANS CRIES NOTICE
SIBRET SIBRIT SIBREDE SPURRINGS
BANQUET FETE MEAL DIFFA FEAST
DINNER JUNKET MANGER REGALE
REGALO REPAST SEUDAH SPREAD
AHAAINA CONVITO CONVIVE
NAMGERY REGALIO CAROUSAL
FESTIVAL SYMPOSIUM SYSSITION
BANQUETER CONVIVE SYMPOSIAST
BANQUETING EPULATION
TRENCHERING
BANSHEE BOW SIDHE
BANTAM COCK GRIG BANTY DANDY
SAUCY CHICKEN SEBRIGHT
COMBATIVE
BANTENG OX TSINE BANTIN
TEMADAU
BANTER COD KID RAG ROT CHIP
FOOL JEST JOKE JOSH MOCK QUIZ
RAIL RAZZ BORAK CHAFF DRAPE
JOLLY QUEER RALLY ROAST TAUNT
TRICK DELUDE DERIDE HAGGLE
SATIRE BADINER STASHIE BADINAGE
CHAFFING GIFFGAFF RAILLERY
RIDICULE
BANTU ILA BULU GOGO GUHA HEHE
YAKA ZULU DUALA KAFIR KAMBA
KIOKO KONDE KONGO LAMBA

SHONA SWAZI BANYAI BASUTO
DAMARA HERERO KAFFIR NATIVE
THONGA WAGUHA YAKALA CABINDA
MASHONA SWAHILI WACHANGA
(— **LANGUAGE**) ILA RONGA THONGA
NYANAJA NYAMWEZI
BANYAN BUR BURR BANIYA BUNNIA
JAGUEY
BAOBAB MOWANA IMBONDO TEBELDI
CALABASH
BAPTISM CLEANSING IMMERSION
PALINGENY PERFUSION
BAPTISMAL FONTAL
BAPTIST DIPPER DIDAPPER
SEPARATE TRASKITE
BAPTIZE DIP DEPE FULL NAME
HEAVE VOLOW PLUNGE PURIFY
ASPERSE CLEANSE IMMERSE
CHRISTEN SPRINKLE
BAPTIZED ILLUMINATE
BAR BAN DAM FID FOX GAD LAW LEG
RIB ROD TAP AXLE BALK BAND
BANK BAUR BEAM BOLT BOOM
BULL CAKE CHAR CORE CROW
DRAG FLAT GATE HIDE JOKE LOCK
MAKE OUST POLE RACK RAIL REEF
SAVE SETT SHUT SKID SLAB SLAT
SLIP SLOT SNIB STOP TREE YARD
ARBOR BENCH BETTY BILBO BILCO
BLOCK BLOOM BRACE CATCH
CLASP CLOSE COURT CRAMP
CREEL DEBAR DETER DOLLY EASER
EMBAR ESTOP FENCE FORCE
GEMEL HEDGE HORSE HUMET
LEVER PERCH PILOT PINCH PITCH
RATCH SHADE SHAFT SHAPE SIGHT
SLOTE SNEEK SPELL SPOON SPRAG
STAFF STANG STAVE STRAP STRIP
STRUT SWIPE TRACE YAIRD
ANCONY BARRET BATTEN BILLET
BISTRO BODEGA BROOCH BUMPER
CRUTCH DOFFER DOLLEY DOLLIE
EVENER EXCEPT EYEBAR FASTEN
FORBAR FORBID FORCER FORSET
GRILLE HEAVER HINDER LADDER
MEAGRE NORMAN PEELER RABBLE
RADIAL RETURN RIFFLE SALOON
SHADES SHANTY STOWER STRIPE
TABLET TANGLE TILLER TOGGLE
BARRACE BARRAGE BARRIER
BOBSTAY BOLSTER BUVETTE
CHANNEL CHARIOT CONFINE
COUNTER DRAWBAR EXCLUDE
GALLOWS MANDREL MANDRIL
OVERARM PREVENT SCRATCH
SIDEBAR SNIBBLE SPINDLE
STEMMER TOMBOLO TOPRAIL
TRUNDLE WIREBAR ASTRAGAL
KNIFEWAY MURDERER PESSULUS
(— **FOR TAPPING FURNACE**) LANCET
(— **IN FABRIC**) BARRE
(— **IN RIVER**) CHAR SANDBAR
(— **IN SEA**) SWASH
(— **OF CULTIVATOR**) ARCH
(— **OF DOOR**) SLOT STANG
(— **OF ELECTRIC SWITCH**) BLADE
(— **OF GATE**) SPAR LEDGE
(— **OF HARROW**) BULL
(— **OF LOOM**) EASER SWORD

BATTEN BACKSTAY
(— **OF RAYS**) SHOOT
(— **OF STEEL**) BLOOM STIRRUP
(— **OF WAGON**) SHETH
(— **ON SIDE OF BOWSPRIT**)
WHISKER
(— **ON WINDMILL**) UPLONG
(— **WITH SPIKES**) HERISSON
(**HERALDIC** —) FESS FESSE HUMET
LABEL
(**JOINTED** —) CHILL
(**MINING** —) MOIL
(**NOTCHED** —) RISP SKEY
(**PAIR OF** —S) GEMEL GEMMEL
(**REFRESHMENT** —) CANTEEN
(**SOAP FRAME** —) SESS
(**STIRRING** —) CRUTCH
(**TAMPING** —) STEMMER
(**TYPEWRITER** —) BAIL BALE
SPACER SHUTTLE
(**WEAVING** —) TEMPLE
(**WHEEL** —) AXLE SPOKE
BARANI BRANDY
BARB AWN BUR JAG MOW BURR
CLIP FILE FLUE HAIR HERL HOOK
JAGG BEARD HORSE POINT RIDGE
SHAFT SPEAR PIGEON STRAIN
TIPPET WITTER BARBARY BARBULE
BRISTLE FILAMENT KINGFISH
(— **OF ARROW**) HOOK WING BEARD
WITTER
(— **OF FEATHER**) HARL HERL
RAMUS PINNULA FILAMENT
(— **OF HARPOON**) FLUE FLUKE
BARBADOS (**CAPITAL OF** —)
BRIDGETOWN
(**MOUNTAIN OF** —) HILLABY
(**NATIVE OF** —) BIM
BARBADOS CHERRY ACEROLA
BARBAREA CAMPE
BARBARIAN HUN BOOR GOTH RUDE
WILD ALIEN BRUTE SAVAGE VANDAL
RUFFIAN FOREIGNER UNTUTORED
BARBARIC GROSS ATROCIOUS
BARBARISM CANT DATISM
SAVAGISM SOLECISM
BARBARITY FERITY CRUELTY
FELLNESS FEROCITY RUDENESS
SAVAGERY BRUTALITY
BARBAROUS FELL RUDE WILD
CRUEL BRUTAL FIERCE GOTHIC
BESTIAL FOREIGN HUNNISH
INHUMAN SLAVISH UNCIVIL
IGNORANT CUTTHROAT FEROCIOUS
PRIMITIVE
BARBARY MAGOT MAGHRIB
MOGHRIB
(— **STATE**) TUNIS ALGIERS
MOROCCO TRIPOLI
BARBASCO CUBE JOEWOOD
BARBECUE ASADO BOCAN BUCCAN
BARBEL BEARD CIRRUS WATTLE
BARBLET CYPRINID
BARBER NAI FIGARO POLLER
SHAVER TONSOR SCRAPER
TONSURE
(— **FISH**) TANG
BARBET BARBION BARMKIN
DREAMER BARBICAN PUFFBIRD

WATERRUG IRONSMITH PEARLBIRD
THICKHEAD TIGERBIRD
BARBITAL VERONAL
BARD BHAT MUSE POET SCOP SWAN
DRUID OVATE RUNER SCALD SKALD
OSSIAN SHAPER SINGER BARDING
PENBARD MINSTREL MUSICIAN
TALIESEN DEMODOCUS
BARE DRY BALD LEAN MERE NUDE
POOR ALONE CRUDE EMPTY NAKED
PLAIN PLUME STARK STRIP WASTE
BARISH BARREN CALLOW DENUDE
DIVERT DIVEST EXPOSE HISTIE
MARGIN MEAGER MEAGRE PALTRY
PILLED REVEAL SCARRY SIMPLE
DIVULGE EXPOSED UNARMED
UNCOVER DENUDATE DESOLATE
DISCLOSE STRIPPED DESTITUTE
(— **TEETH**) TUCK
(**NOT** —) COOL
BAREFACED GLARING IMPUDENT
AUDACIOUS SHAMELESS
BARELY JIMP JUST ONLY FANIT
HARDLY MERELY POORLY SIMPLY
UNEATH UNNETH NAKEDLY
UNNETHE EDGEWAYS SCANTILY
SCARCELY SLIGHTLY
BARER NAVVY DELVER FEIGHER
MUCKMAN CALLOWER
BARFISH DORAB
BARGAIN GO BUY RUG WOD COPE
DEAL HUCK KOOP MART MISE PACT
PICK RUGG SALE SELL SNIP TROG
WHIZ CHEAP FIGHT PRICE STEAL
TROKE TRUCK WHACK WHIZZ
BARTER DICKER HAGGLE HIGGLE
NIFFER PALTER CHAFFER CHEAPEN
COMPACT CONTEND CONTEST
DISPOSE PACTION TRAFFIC
CONTRACT COVENANT PENNORTH
PURCHASE STRUGGLE WANWORTH
(— **HARD**) PRIG
(— **IN MINING**) STURT
BARGAINER NIP KITE COPER
COWPER CHAFFERER
(**SHARP** —) SCREW
BARGAINING MART ACHATE
CHAFFER CHEAPING HUCKSTERY
BARGE ARK BOX BOY HOY TOW TUB
BARK BOAT FUST LUMP PRAM RAFT
SCOW TROW BARCA CASCO DUMMY
FOIST LUNGE LURCH PRAAM SCOLD
SHREW VIXEN BARQUE BERATE
BUGERO DREDGE GALLEY GYASSA
PRAHAM REBUKE STUMPY TENDER
THRUST WHERRY BALLOON BIRLING
CHALANA DROGHER GABBARD
GABBART GONDOLA LIGHTER
OMNIBUS TOWBOAT TUMBLER
TUMBRIL BUDGEROW CARRIAGE
MOORPUNKY
(**COAL** —) KEEL
BARGEMAN PUG BARGEE BARGER
HOYMAN HUFFLER
BARGHEST PADFOOT
BARITE CAUK CAWK TIFF CAULK
BARYTES BARYTINE HEPATITE
BARK AGO BAG BAY OUF RUB TAN
WAP YAP YIP BAFF BOAT BOOF

COAT COTO DITA HOWL HUSK OPEN
PEEL PELT PILL REND RIND ROSS
SKIN SNAP TAPA WAFF YAFF YAWP
YELP AABEC BALAT BARCA BARGE
COUGH MOCHA NIEPA SHELL SHOUT
SPEAK STRIP TIMBE YABBA YAMPH
YOUFF ABRADE AGAMID AVARAM
BARKEY BOWWOW CASSIA CORNUS
CORTEX GIRDLE MASSOY SINTOC
TRANKY WAFFLE YAFFLE MALAMBO
MESENNA PERIERA PHLOEUM
SOLICIT TANBARK DOUNDAKE
EUONYMUS FRANGULA GRANATUM
MEZEREUM WOODSKIN
(AROMATIC —) CANELLA
CULILAWAN
(EXTERIOR OF —) ROSS
(LAVER OF —) HAT
BARKER BUFFER DOORMAN
GRINDER SPIELER SPUDDER
SPRUIKER CHARLATAN
BARKING BAY SPUD QUEST
LATRANT LATRATION
BARLEY BIG BEAR BENT BIGG GRAIN
SPRAT LICORN HORDEUM
WHITECORN
(AWN OF —) HORN
(GROUND —) TSAMBA
(HULLED —) PTISAN
(REFUSE —) SHAG FLINTS
BARN BYRE AMBAR LATHE STALL
GRANGE STABLE SKIPPER
COWHOUSE
(— OWL) LULU MADGE
(COW —) SAUR SHIPPON
BARNACLE BRAY BREY ACORN
LEPAS CYPRIS ANATIFA BALANID
LEPADID CIRRIPED GNATHOPOD
SACCULINA
BARNBURNER SOFT
BARNSTORM TOUR
BARNYARD PIGHTLE BACKSIDE
FARMYARD STRAWYARD
BAROMETER GLASS ANEROID
OROMETER
BARON DAIMIO BARONET FREEMAN
FREIHERR
(COURT —) HALLMOOT
BARONY HAN DOMAIN
BAROQUE GOTHIC ORNATE ROCOCO
GROTESQUE IRREGULAR
BAROTO VINTA
BARRACK CAMP BOTHY CASERN
CANNABA CUARTEL
BARRACUDA CUDA KAKU SPET
BARRY PELON SNAKE SNOEK
SNOOK BECUNA PICUDA SCOOTS
SENNET VICUDA KATONKEL
SCOOTERS
BARRAGE BAR ATTACK VOLLEY
BARRIER DRUMFIRE UMBRELLA
CANNONADE FUSILLADE
BARRAMUNDA SALMON CYCLOID
DIPNOAN FLATHEAD CERATODUS
BARRED CUCKOO RIBBED STRIPED
BARREL FAT HUB KEG TUN VAT
BUTT CADE CASK DRUM KANG TREE
BOWIE QUILL SHELL STAND UNION
FESSEL GIRNAL GIRNEL HOGGET

RUMBLE RUNLET TIERCE TUMBLE
VESSEL CALAMUS CISTERN
PACKAGE RATTLER RUNDLET
TUMBLER CYLINDER HOGSHEAD
KILDERKIN
(— OF FEATHER) CALAMUS
(— OF REVOLVER) CHAMBER
(— ROW) LONGER
(— WITH CRANKS) VANGEE
(CAPSTAN —) SPOOL
(CORE —) LANTERN
(HERRING —) CADE CRAN
(SMALL —) KEG KIT CADE KNAG
RUNLET BARRICO RUNDLET
BARRELHOUSE GUTBUCKET
BARREN DRY ARID BARE BOWY
DEAD DEAF DOUR DULL EILD GAST
GELD LEAN NUDE POOR SALT SECK
YELD YELL BLEAK BLUNT BOWEY
DRAPE DUSTY EMPTY GAUNT
GHAST GUESS NAKED STARK STERN
WASTE YEILD DESERT EFFETE
FALLOW HISTIE HUNGRY JEJUNE
MEAGER STUPID SAPLESS STERILE
DESOLATE IMPOTENT TEEMLESS
TREELESS
(NOT —) FACILE FECUND
(PL.) LANDES
BARRENNESS VACANCY EMPTINESS
BARRICADE BAR STOP BLOCK
CLOSE FENCE ABATIS PRISON
BARRAGE BARRIER DEFENSE
FORTIFY OBSTRUCT RAMFORCE
ROADBLOCK
(— OF TREES) ABATIS
BARRIER ALP BAR DAM BOMA CRIB
CROY DIKE DOOR DYKE FOSS GATE
LINE LOCK PALE STOP WALL WEIR
BOUND CHAIN FENCE FOSSE GRILL
HEDGE LIMIT STILE STUMP CORDON
GLACIS GRILLE HURDLE SCREEN
TREBLE BARRAGE CEILING CURTAIN
GALLERY PARAPET RAILING
RAMPART BOUNDARY FORTRESS
FRONTIER STOCKADE STRENGTH
TRAVERSE
(— ACROSS RIVER) STILL KIDDLE
(— IN TRUCK) HEADER
(ARTIFICIAL —) FOSS FOSSE
(TRAFFIC —) SEPARATOR
(PL.) BAIL
BARRING BUT SAVE CLOSED
BARRISTER COLT BARMAN JUNIOR
LAWYER TUBMAN COUNSEL
POSTMAN TEMPLAR ADVOCATE
ATTORNEY SERJEANT
BARROOM PUB CAFE HOUSE
SALOON CANTINA DOGGERY
GROCERY TAPROOM DRAMSHOP
DRINKERY EXCHANGE GROGGERY
GROGSHOP
BARROW HOD HOG BANK BIER DUNE
GALT HILL MOTE TUMP CARRY
GRAVE GURRY HURLY MOUND
BURROW GALGAL KURGAN NAVETA
HILLOCK TROLLEY TUMULUS
MOUNTAIN PUSHCART
BARRULET VIVRE
BARTENDER MIXER BARMAN

BARMAID SKINKER TAPSTER
BARTER CHAP CHOP COPE COUP
HAWK MANG MONG SELL SWAP
TROG VEND CORSE TRADE TROKE
TRUCK DICKER NIFFER SCORSE
BARGAIN CAMBIUM CHAFFER
PERMUTE TRAFFIC TRUCKLE
COMMERCE EXCHANGE
BARTERER COPER COWPER
TRUCKER
BASAL BASIC BASILAR RADICAL
BASALT MARBLE NAVITE DIABASE
GHIZITE KULAITE POTTERY
AUGANITE BANDAITE DOLERITE
ANAMESITE ARAPAHITE MELAPHYRE
SUDBURITE
BASE BED DEN HUB LOW TUT ANIL
CLAM EVIL FOOT FOUL HUBB LEWD
MEAN POOR RELY REST ROOT
SACK STAY STEM STEP VILE BASIS
BLOCK CHEAP DIRTY FIRST FLOOR
FOUND LACHE MUDDY PETTY SNIDE
SOCLE STAND STOOL WORSE
ABJECT BOTTOM BRASSY COARSE
COMMON DEMISS GROUND GRUBBY
HARLOT HUMBLE MENIAL NOUGHT
PALTRY PATAND PATTEN PERRON
PODIUM RASCAL SECOND SHABBY
SORDID VULGAR BASTARD CAITIFF
COMICAL CURRISH DEBASED
FOOTING HANGDOG HILDING
HOUSING IGNOBLE PEASANT
ROINISH SERVILE SLAVISH STADDLE
STANDER SUBBASE SUPPORT
CHURLISH COISTREL COISTRIL
DEGRADED DRAWHEAD HARLOTRY
HOLDFAST INFAMOUS INFERIOR
MECHANIC MESCHANT PEDESTAL
PEDIMENT RASCALLY SCULLION
SHAMEFUL STANDARD STEPPING
SUBSTRAT UNWORTHY WRETCHED
NIDDERING
(— IN QUALITY) LEADEN
(— OF CANNON) SOUL
(— OF OPERATIONS) BOOK HOME
(— OF PETAL) CLAW
(— OF PLANT) CAUDEX
(— OF POLLINIUM) DISC DISK
(— OF TUBER) HEEL
(CHEMICAL —) ACRIDAN ADENINE
ANSERIN CHOLINE GUANINE
ACRIDANE ACTININE AGMATINE
ALDIMINE ALKALOID ANSERINE
CONYRINE GALEGINE KETIMINE
LEPIDINE SEMIDINE
(HIDDEN —) LAIR
(HOME —) DEN
(LEAF —) FOVEA
(LOGARITHM —) E
(SECOND —) KEYSTONE
(STALKLIKE —) CNIDOPOD
BASEBALL PILL APPLE DUSTER
FLOATER INSHOOT LEATHER
BEANBALL HARDBALL HORSEHIDE
STICKBALL
(— PLAYER) YANNIGAN
BASEBOARD GRIN SKIRT PLINTH
EASEMENT MOPBOARD SKIRTING
WASHBOARD

BASE-DEALING BROKING
BASELESS IDLE UNFOUNDED
BASEMAN SACKER
BASEMENT BASE CELLAR
TAHKHANA
BASENESS FELONY VILITY BEGGARY
SQUALOR TURPITUDE
BASH BAT LAM BEAT BLOW DENT
MASH SWAT WHAM WHOP ABASH
SLOSH SMASH BRUISE STRIKE
BASHFUL COY SHY HELO SHAN
BLATE HELOE TIMID MODEST
PUDENT ASHAMED DAUNTED
BACKWARD BLUSHING DAPHNEAN
DISMAYED LOATHFUL PUDIBUND
RETIRING SACKLESS SHAMEFUL
SHEEPISH SKITTISH VERECUND
BASHFULNESS PUDOR SHYNESS
BASIC BASE BASAL VITAL BOTTOM
BEDROCK CANONIC CENTRAL
CLASSIC ZINCOUS CARDINAL
ULTIMATE ELEMENTAL ESSENTIAL
SUBSTRATE
BASIL TULASI
BASIN DOP PAN BOWL COMB COVE
DISH DOCK EWER FLOW FONT GULF
LAKE PARK SINK SLAD TALA TANK
COMBE LAVER SLAKE STOUP
BASSON BULLAN CHAFER CIRQUE
HOLLOW LAVABO LEKANE LOUTER
MARINA VALLEY VESSEL CUVETTE
PISCINA RECEIPT URCEOLE
CESSPOOL LAVATORY RECEPTOR
VANITORY WASHBOWL GEMELLION
(MOUNTAIN —) HOYA
(ROCK —) KEEVE KIEVE
BASIS BASE FOND FOOT FORM FUND
ROOT SILL AXIOM STOCK ANLAGE
BOTTOM GROUND ACCOUNT
BEDROCK FOOTING PREMISE
SUPPORT GRAVAMEN STRENGTH
AUTHORITY CRITERION FUNDAMENT
GROUNDSEL SUBSTANCE
BASK SUN BEEK WARM ACRID BATHE
ENJOY REVEL BITTER REJOICE
APRICATE
BASKET IE ARK COB FAN HOT KIT
LUG PAD PED PEG POT TAP TOP
BUCK CAUL COBB COOP CORB
CORF CRIB FLAT GOAL HOTT IEIE
KIPE KISH KIST KITT LEAP MAND
MAUN SKEP TAPE TILL TOUR TRUG
WEEL CABAS CASSY CESTA CHEST
CRAIL CRASH CRATE CREEL DEVIL
DILLI DILLY FRAIL GRATE MAUND
MOLLY NATTE RUSKY SCULL SWILL
WILLY BEACON BOKARK CASSIE
CLEAVE COFFIN COURGE CRADLE
DORSEL DORSER DOSSER FANNER
FASCET GABION HAMPER HOBBET
HOBBIT HOPPET JICARA JUNKET
KIBSEY KIPSEY MOCOCK MOLLIE
MURLIN PANIER PEGALL PETARA
POTTLE PUNNET SEQUIN TAPPET
TEANAL TOPNET VOIDER WINDEL
WINDLE WISKET ZEQUIN CANASTA
CORBEIL CRESSET FLASKET
HANAPER PANNIER PATTARA
PITARAH PRICKLE SCUTTLE SEEDLIP

SHALLOW SKEOUGH SKIPPET
WATTAPE WHISKET CALATHUS
CANISTER CHEQUEEN ZECCHINO
(— BOTTOM) SLATH
(— FOR CRUMBS) VOIDER
(— FOR EELS) BUCK COURGE
(— FOR FIGS) TAP CABAS FRAIL
TAPNET
(— FOR FRUIT) MOLLY CALATHOS
CALA
BASKET MAKER ANASAZI
BASKETRY UPSET
BASKETWORK TEE SLEW WALE
SLATH STAKE SLATHE STROKE
SLEWING
BASQUE VASCON EUSCARA
EUSCARO IBERIAN BISCAYAN
(— DIALECT) LABOURDIN
(PL.) VASCONA VASCONES
BAS-RELIEF PLAQUETTE
BASS LOW PES CHUB DEEP DRUM
FOOT ROCK BASSO DRONE HURON
ROCHE SWEGO VOICE BORDUN
BRASSE BURDEN CHERNA GROUND
JUMPER REDEYE SINGER STRIPE
ACHIGAN BARFISH BOURDON
BROWNIE GROWLER JEWFISH
STRIPER BACHELOR BIGMOUTH
BLUEFISH CABRILLA ROCKFISH
SPOTTAIL STREAKER CONTINUO
TALLYWAG WELSHMAN LINESIDES
(— DRUM) TAMBURONE
(— PART) ALBERTI
(GROUND —) OSTINATO
(THOROUGH —) BC
BASSOON CURTAL FAGOTT
FAGOTTE FAGOTTO
BASSWOOD LIN BASS WAHOO
LINDEN WICOPY DADDYNUT
WHITEWOOD
BAST LIBER RAMIE PHLOEM
NOSEBURN
BASTARD GET SOB BASE FALSE
CANNON COWSON GALLEY HYBRID
IMPURE MAMZER BYSPELL GETLING
LOWBRED MONGREL WOSBIRD
BANTLING BASEBORN MISBEGET
NAMELESS SPURIOUS WHORESON
BASTE SEW BEAT CANE COOK DRUB
LARD TACK FLAMB SAUCE CUDGEL
JIPPER PUNISH STITCH THRASH
BASTION JETTY MOINEAU
BAT CAT HIT WAD BACK BAKE BATE
BEAT CLUB FOWL GAIT JACK LUMP
MASS SWAT TRAP WINK BANDY
BATON BRICK CHUCK FUNGO HARPY
PIECE SPREE STICK ALIPED BACKIE
BASTON BEETLE CUDGEL DRIVER
KALONG POMMEL RACKET STRIKE
STROKE WILLOW BAUCKIE FLUTTER
JAVELIN NOCTULE VAMPIRE
BLUDGEON SEROTINE REREMOUSE
BATAK (— DIALECT) TOBA
BATCH LOT BAKE BREW CAST CROP
FINE MASS MESS SORT FLOOR
GROUP BAKING CHEESE MAKING
BOILING BREWING FORMULA
MIXTURE RAISING QUANTITY
(— OF EGGS) SETTING

(— OF GRAIN) GRIST
(— OF MAIL) SEPARATION
BATCHER BAGGER
BATE BAIT BEET PUER PURE GRAIN
BATELEUR BERGHAAN
BATEMAN DRENCHER
BATFISH ANGLER DIABLO MALTHE
DEVILFISH
BATH DIP TUB BAIN BATE PERT
TOSH BATHE LAVER STEEP THERM
DOUCHE LIQUOR MIKVAH PICKLE
PLUNGE SHOWER SPONGE
BALNEUM LAVACRE ABLUTION
BALNEARY
(FOOT —) PEDILUVIUM
(HOT —) STEW SCALD STUFE
THERM STUPHE THERME
(MUD —) ILLUTATION
(PHOTOGRAPHIC —) FIXER
(SITZ —) BIDET SITZBAD SEMICUPE
INSESSION
(SPINNING —) DOPE
(STEAM —) SAUNA
(TANNING —) BATE SOAK
(TURKISH —) HUMMUM HOTHOUSE
BATHE BAY TUB BAIN BASK DOOK
LAVE STEW WASH CLEAN DOUSE
DOWSE EMBAY SOUSE STEEP
ENWRAP FOMENT SHOWER SPLASH
EMBATHE IMMERSE PERVADE
SUFFUSE PERMEATE
BATHHOUSE SEW STEW SAUNA
STUFE CABANA HAMMAM STUPHE
BALNEARY
BATHING LAVACRE LAVEMENT
(— SUIT) SLIP TOGS MAILLOT
BATHSHEBA (HUSBAND OF —)
DAVID URIAH
(SON OF —) SOLOMON
BATHTUB TUB TOSH LAVACRE
BATON ROD BEND BURN WAND
STAFF STICK BAGUET BASTON
CUDGEL BOURDON SCEPTER
SCEPTRE BAGUETTE CROSSBAR
TRUNCHEON
BATSMAN BAT BATTER HITTER
SLOGGER SLUGGER STRIKER
BATTALION WARD CONREY
BATTEN END LAY RIB SLEY CLEAT
LEDGE BATTON BEATER ENRICH
FATTEN REEPER THRIVE FERTILIZE
(PL.) SPARRING
BATTER RAM BEAT DENT MAIM
CLOUR DINGE FRUSH PASTE POUND
SMASH BALLER BRUISE BUFFET
HAMMER HATTER HITTER PUMMEL
THRING TUMBLE BATSMAN
BOMBARD CRIPPLE DESTROY
FRITTER SHATTER SLUGGER
STRIKER DEMOLISH
BATTERCAKE WAFFLE
BATTERING BLAST LACING
BATTERY PILE SINK TIRE TROOP
RADEAU EXCITER SINKBOX
SINKBOAT
(GUN —) SWINGER
BATTLE WAR CAMP DUEL FEUD
FRAY MART MEET TILT TOIL UNDO
BRUSH FIELD FIGHT JOUST STOUR

ACTION AFFRAY CAMLAN COMBAT
SHOWER STRIVE CONTEND
CONTEST HOSTING JOURNAL
JOURNEY WARFARE CONFLICT
SKIRMISH STRUGGLE ENCOUNTER
NAUMACHIA THEOMACHY
BATTLE-AX WIFLE POLEAX SPARTH
TWIBIL BROADAX HALBERD TWIBILL
WHIFFLE FAUCHARD FRANCISC
BATTLE CRY CRY ENSIGN
GERONIMO BEAUSEANT
BATTLEFIELD BLAIR CHAMP TAHUA
CHAMPAIGN
BATTLEMENT KERNEL MERION
PINION CORNELLE
BATTLESHIP MAINE CARRIER
BATTY BATS BUGGY CRAZY SILLY
BATLIKE FOOLISH
BAUBLE BOW TOY BEAD GAUD
BUTTON GEWGAW TRIFLE MAROTTE
TRINKET GIMCRACK PLAYTHING
BAWD AUNT HARE DIRTY MADAM
DEFILE MADAME PANDER COMMODE
MACKEREL PROCURER PURVEYOR
BAWDY DIRTY SCARLET
BAWL CRY HOWL ROUT YAUP YAWP
BLORE GOLLY SHOUT BELLOW
BOOHOO OUTCRY GLAISTER
(— **OUT**) JUMP CRACK SCOLD
BAY ARM COD DAM RIA VOE BANK
BARK CHOP COVE GULF HOLE HOPE
HOWL LOCH ROAN TREE WICK
YAUP YAWP BAHIA BASIN BAYOU
BERRY BIGHT COLOR CREEK FIORD
FJORD FLEET HAVEN HORSE INLET
LOUGH MOUTH ORIEL QUEST SINUS
SPEAK TRAVE BABBLE HARBOR
LAUREL RECESS SEVERY WINDOW
BADIOUS BAYGALL ENCLOSE
ESTUARY MALABAR SILANGA
ULULATE BREWSTER CHESTNUT
(— **OF BARN**) GOAF SKEELING
SKILLING SKILLION
(— **STATE**) MASSACHUSETTS
(**SWEET** —) BREWSTER
BEAVERWOOD
BAYBERRY AUSU PIMIENTA
WAXBERRY
BAYOU SLEW SLOO SLUE BROOK
CREEK INLET RIVER OUTLET
SLOUGH STREAM RIVULET
BACKWATER
BAY WINDOW ORIEL MIRADOR
BAZAAR FAIR FETE SALE AGORA
BURSE CHAWK CHOWK MARKET
CANTEEN BOOKFAIR EMPORIUM
BEZESTEEN
BDELLIUM GUGAL GUGUL GOOGUL
BE ABE ARE BES BEEN BETH BIST
LIVE ABIDE EXIST OCCUR WORTH
REMAIN BREATHE CONSIST SUBSIST
CONTINUE
BEACH AIR BANK CHIP MOOR NARD
RIPA SAND SLIP COAST PLAGE
PLAYA PRAYA SHORE GROUND
SHILLA STRAND HARDWAY SEASIDE
SHINGLE LAKESHORE
(— **RIDGE**) FULL
(**PROJECTING** —) CUSP

BEACH APPLE CANAJONG
BEACHCOMBER SEASONER
STRANDLOOPER
BEACH FLEA SCUD SCREW
SANDBOY
BEACH GRASS STAR SPIRE
MARRAM BENTSTAR
BEACON MARK PIKE SIGN BAKEN
FANAL GUIDE PHARE RACON
ENSIGN PHAROS RAMARK SIGNAL
CRESSET SEAMARK WARNING
NEEDFIRE SIGNPOST STANDARD
BEAD NIB POT DROP FOAM GAUD
AGGRI AGGRY BUGLE FILET GRAIN
KNURL PEARL QUIRK SIGHT STAFF
ARANGO BAGUET BAUBLE BICUNE
BUBBLE CORNET FILLET PELLET
PIPPER PRAYER RONDEL WAMPUM
DEWDROP GLOBULE MOLDING
SPARKLE TRINKET AVEMARIA
CABOCHON
(**ROSARY** —) GAUD PATERNOSTER
(**SHELL** —**S**) SEWAN
BEADING VEINING
(**PL.**) TASBIH
BEADLE CRIER MACER POKER
USHER BEDRAL BUMBLE HARMAN
HERALD BAILIFF NUTHOOK OFFICER
SERVITOR SUMMONER APPARITOR
MESSENGER
BEADSMAN BEGGAR HERMIT
BLUEGOWN GOWNSMAN
BEAK NEB NIB BECK BILL CLAP
NOSE PIKE PROW LORUM SNOUT
SWORD TUTEL MASTER NOZZLE
SPERON WEAPON EMBOLON
EMBOLUM FOREBOW MOLDING
ROSTRUM BEAKHEAD MANDIBLE
CAPITULUM
(— **OF SHELL**) UMBO
(— **OF SHIP**) SPERON
(— **OF SWORDFISH**) SWORD
BEAKER CUP HORN TASS BIKER
BOCAL BOUSE GLASS BARECA
BEAM BAR LEG RAY TIE BALK BEAK
BOOM EMIT GLOW PLAT SILE SILL
SKID SPAR STUD ARBOR CABER
FLASH GLEAM GLEED JOIST LIGHT
RAYON SHAPE SHINE SHOOT SMILE
SPEAR STANG STOCK TRAVE
BINDER CAMBER CHEESE COLLAR
FLITCH GIRDER GLANCE HEADER
MANTEL NEEDLE RAFTER SUMMER
TIMBER TRABES TREVIS WALKER
BALANCE BUMPKIN CHANNEL
CHEVRON DORMANT DRAWBAR
FRIJOLE MADRIER PINRAIL RADIATE
SLEEPER SUPPORT TRANSOM
TRIMMER TYNDALL AXLETREE
BROWPOST HERISSON PADSTONE
PLOWHEAD ROOFTREE STENTREL
TEMPLATE
(— **OF LIGHT**) CHINK GLEED RAYON
SHAFT SIGNAL STREAM SUNBEAM
STRICTURE
(**HIGH** —) BRIGHTS
(**LARGE** —) BALK LACE BAULK
SUMMER
(**LOW** —) DIM

(**SANIO'S** —) CRASSULA
(**WEAVER'S** —) TRAM TAVIL
(**PL.**) CRANEWAY
BEAMER SCUDDER
BEAMING GAY ROSY BRIGHT
LUCENT MASSIVE RADIANT SHINING
BEAMY BROAD BRIGHT JOYOUS
LUCENT MASSIVE RADIANT
MIRTHFUL
BEAN BON NIB URD CHAP FABA
FAVA GRAM HABA HEAD LIMA POLE
SNAP TEKE TICK BRAIN CARAT
PULSE SIEVA SKULL CACOON
CASTER COLLAR FELLOW KIDNEY
LABLAB LENTIL NIPPLE NOGGIN
RUNNER RUTTEE SEEWEE STRIKE
TEPARY THRASH TRIFLE CALABAR
FRIJOLE PHASEMY SNAPPER
WINDSOR BONAVIST BONNYVIS
TICKBEAN TORNILLO
(— **CURD**) TOFU
(**LOCUST** —) CAROB
(**MESCAL** —) SOPHORA
(**PL.**) NIBS FASELS FESELS PODDER
PODWARE
BEANIE DINK
BEAN-SHAPED FABIFORM
BEANSHOOTER TRUNK
PEASHOOTER
BEAN TREE BOGUM
BEAN TREFOIL LABURNUM
BEAR GO CUB LUG BALU BERN
BORN CAST DREE DUBB FURE GEST
GIVE HAVE HOLD LIFT TEEM TOTE
URSA WEAR ABIDE ALLOW BALOO
BEGET BHALU BREED BRING BROOK
BROWN BRUIN CARRY DREIE DRIVE
GESTE ISSUE KOALA POLAR PRESS
SPARE STAND STICK THOLE THROW
WEIGH WIELD YIELD AFFORD
BEHAVE BRUANG CONVEY ENDURE
IMPORT INFANT KADIAK KINDLE
KODIAK PIERCE RENDER SUFFER
THRUST UPHOLD URSULA WOMBAT
WOOBUT ARCTOID BROWNIE
COMPORT CONDUCT EPHRAIM
FORBEAR GRIZZLY MUSQUAW
PRODUCE STOMACH SUPPORT
SUSTAIN UNDERGO FISSIPED
(— **EXPENSES**) DEFRAY
(— **FLOWERS**) FLOURISH
(— **FRUIT**) FRUCTIFY
(— **INVESTIGATION**) WASH
(— **ON**) CONCERN
(— **OUT**) PROPORT
(— **PATIENTLY**) DIGEST
(— **UP**) CAPE ENDURE SUSTAIN
(— **WITH CREDIT**) BROOK
(— **WITNESS**) TEEM SPEAK ATTEST
DEPOSE
(— **YOUNG**) FIND CALVE CHILD
(**MALE** —) BOAR
(**SLOTH** —) ASWAIL
BEARBERRY LARB WHORTLE
BILBERRY DOGBERRY FOXBERRY
CREASHAKS
BEARD ANE AWN AVEL BARB DEFY
FACE FUZZ NECK NOSE PEAK TUFT
ZIFFS ARISTA BEAVER GOATEE

TASSEL AFFRONT BARBULE
CHARLEY CHARLIE VANDYKE
IMPERIAL STILETTO WHISKERS
(— OF GRAIN) AIL AWN
(— TREATISE) POGONOLOGY
(SMALL —) BARBET
BEARDED AWNIE HAIRY BARBED
BARBATE HIRSUTE POGONIATE
WHISKERED
BEARDLESS NOT NOTT IMBERBE
POLLARD
BEARER NEWS HAMAL MACER
BEADLE HAMMAL HOLDER PACKER
PORTER ANCIENT CARRIER JAMPANI
PINCERN CHAPRASI ESCUDERO
PORTATOR STANDARD SUPPORTER
(— OF GREAT BURDEN) ATLAS
(ARMOR —) ESQUIRE
(BURDEN —) HAMAL HAMMAL
(CROZIER —) CROCIARY
(CUP —) SAKI COPPER
(PALANQUIN —) BOY SIRDAR
MUSAHAR
(SHIELD —) SQUIRE ESCUDERO
(STANDARD —) ANCIENT
(STRETCHER —) BRANCARDIER
(SWORD —) PORTGLAVE
PORTGLAIVE
BEARING AIM AIR COD BALL DUCT
GEST MIEN ORLE PORT RUBY BIRTH
FRONT GESTE HABIT JEWEL POISE
SETUP TENUE TREND ALLURE
APPORT ASPECT BILLET CHARGE
COURSE DEPORT GERENT GIGLIO
MANNER ORIENT SADDLE THRUST
VOIDER ADDRESS AZIMUTH
CONDUCT FASHION GESTURE
MEANING POSTURE PURPORT
RHODING SUPPORT AMENANCE
ATTITUDE BEHAVIOR BIRTHING
CARRIAGE DELIVERY DEMEANOR
FOOTSTEP PEDESTAL PRESENCE
PRESSURE RELATION STANDARD
TENDENCY TOURNURE YIELDING
(— FRUIT) FRUCTED
(— OUTWARD) EFFERENT
(ARROGANT —) HUFF
(HERALDIC —) GAD DELF ENTE
GORE MARK ORLE CROWN DELFT
DELPH FUSIL LAVER PHEON BILLET
DEVICE ENSIGN GOUTTE CHAPLET
CLARION DEMIVOL PLASQUE
QUARTER ORDINARY QUENTISE
(PERSONAL —) GARB
BEARLIKE URSINE
BEAR'S-EAR AURICULA
BEAR'S-FOOT OXHEAL PEGROOTS
BEARSKIN BUSBY
BEAR STATE ARKANSAS
BEAST BETE HOOF BRUTE VACHE
ANIMAL JUMENT MONSTER
MUSIMON VENISON BLIGHTER
OPINICUS
(— OF BURDEN) JUMENT SUMPTER
(3-HORNED —) TRICORN
(CASTRATED —) SPADO
(DEAD —) MORKIN
(FABULOUS —) YALE THRIS
BAGWYN TRICORN DINGMAUL

EPIMACUS GYASCUTUS
(HORNED —) RETHER ROTHER
(STURDY —) NUGGET
(WILD —) FERIN FERINE OUTLAW
UNBEAST
(WILD —S) ZIIM
BEASTLY GROSS PRONE ANIMAL
BRUTAL WICKED BESTIAL BRUTISH
INHUMAN SWINISH OFFENSIVE
BEAT BAT BUM COB DAD FAN FIB
LAM PIP PLY PUN RUN TAN TAP
TAW TEW TIE WAX BAFF BAIT BANG
BASH BATE BELT BEST BLOW BOLT
BRAY BUFF CANE CAST CHAP CLAP
CLUB COIL COLT COMB CRAB DAUD
DING DINT DRUB DUMP DUNT FELL
FIRK FLAP FLAX FLOG FRAM FRAP
FRAT GROW HAZE KILL LACE LAMP
LASH LICK LOUK LUMP LUSH MAUL
MELL MEND MILL PAIK PALE PANT
PELT POSS PRAT ROUT SCAT SLAM
SLAT SLOG SOCK SOLE SOWL STUB
SWAP SWOP TACK TAKD TICK TRIM
TUND TWIG WALK WARP WELT WHIP
WHOP WIPE BASTE BATON BERRY
BIRCH CHURN CLINK CREAM CURRY
DOUSE DRASH DRESS DRIVE FEEZE
FIGHT FILCH FLAIL FLANK FORGE
ICTUS INLAY KNOCK LABOR NEVEL
NOINT POUND PULSE ROUND SCATT
SCOOP SCOUR SKELP STAMP
STRAP SWACK SWING TARGE
THREP THROB THUMP TREAD
TRUMP UPEND WADDY WHACK
WHANG WORST ACCENT ANOINT
BAMBOO BATTER BENSEL BETTLE
BOUNCE BUFFET COTTON CUDGEL
DEFEAT DOWSEL FEAGUE FETTLE
HAMMER HAMPER JACKET KNEVEL
LARRUP LATHER NEAVIL NODDLE
OUTRUN PUMMEL RADDLE REBUKE
REESLE RHYTHM SCUTCH SQUASH
STOUND STOUSH STRIKE STRIPE
STROKE SUGGIL SWINGE SWITCH
TANSEL TEWTAW TEWTER THRASH
THREAP THREIP THREPE THRESH
TICKLE WAGGLE WALLOP WATTLE
ASSAULT BATTUTA BELABOR
BLATTER BLISTER CADENCE
CANVASS CONQUER CONTUSE
EXHAUST FATIGUE FLYFLAP
KNUCKLE LAMBACK LAMBAST
LOBTAIL LOUNDER PULSATE
REESHIE SHELLAC SURPASS
SWABBLE SWADDLE TROLLOP
TROUNCE VIBRATE
(— ABOUT) BUSK BANGLE
(— AGAINST THE WIND) LAVEER
(— AGAINST) BLAD
(— BARLEY) PAIL WARM
(— CLOTHES) BATTLE
(— COVERT) TUFT
(— DOWN) LAY FELL FULL ABATE
FLASH
(— EGGS) CAST
(— FIBERS) BRUSH
(— HIGH) LEAP
(— IT) LAM
(— OF HEART) DUNT STROKE

(— ON BUTTOCKS) COB
(— SEVERELY) DRUB LUMP SOAK
BASTE SOUSE LATHER
(— SMALL) CHAP
(— WINGS) BATE FLAP
(— WOODS) TUSK
(MUSICAL —) BOUNCE BATTUTA
BEATEN BEAT BETE BATTU PARTY
TRITE TRADED
BEATER RAB MAUL SEAL CANER
LACER STOCK DASHER DRIVER
MALLET TRIMMER THRESHER
SCUTCHER
BEATIFIC DEIFIC ELYSIAN
BEATIFY SAINT HALLOW HEAVEN
ENCHANT GLORIFY SANCTIFY
BEATING COB COBB LICK TUND
BEANS DOUSE JESSE PULSE STICK
HAZING HIDING ROPAND TATTOO
BASHING BATTERY BELTING
CLANKER DASHING DUSTING
LICKING SKELPIN WELTING WHALING
BIRCHING DRESSING DRUBBING
RIBROAST WHIPPING JACKETING
STRAPPADO
BEATITUDE JOY BLISS BENISON
MACARISM HAPPINESS
BEAU BEW BOY CHAP BLADE DANDY
FLAME LOVER SPARK SWELL
ESCORT FELLOW GARCON STEADY
SUITOR TATTLE ADMIRER AIMWELL
BRAVERY COURTER COXCOMB
CUPIDON GALLANT SPARKER
FOLLOWER
BEAU GREGORY COCKEYE
BEAUTIFUL FAIR FINE GLAD GOOD
MEAR MEER MERE WALY BELLE
BONNY KALON LUSTY SHEEN WLITY
WLONK BLITHE BONNIE COMELY
DECORE FREELY LOVELY POETIC
PRETTY VENUST ELEGANT
FORMOSE FORMOUS TEMPEAN
TOKALON CHARMING DELICATE
ESTHETIC FAIRSOME GORGEOUS
GRACEFUL HANDSOME LUCULENT
SPECIOUS
BEAUTIFY FAIR GILD ADORN GRACE
HIGHT PREEN PRIMP PRUNE BEAUTY
BEDECK DECORE ENAMEL QUAINT
ADONIZE ENHANCE GARNISH
GLORIFY DECORATE FAIRHEAD
EMBELLISH PULCHRIFY
BEAUTY FACE FAIR FORM GLEE
BEAUT BELLE CHARM FAVOR GLORY
GRACE PRIDE WLITE FINERY
LOOKER LOVELY POLISH DECORUM
FEATURE TOKALON SPLENDOR
FORMOSITY
(— OF FORM) SYMMETRY
(— OF STYLE) ELEGANCE
BEAVER BOOMER CASTOR RODENT
PRALINE MUSHROOM SEWELLEL
STARLING
(— SKIN) PLEW
(— STATE) OREGON
(DARK —) NUTMEG
BEBEERINE CURINE
BEBEERU SWEETWOOD
GREENHEART

BECAUSE AS SO FOR THAT BEING CAUSE SINCE THERE FORWHY THROUGH INASMUCH
BECCAFICO FIGEATER FIGPECKER
BECHE-DE-MER PIDGIN TREPANG
BECK RUN VAT BECON BROOK
(— **AND CALL**) DEVOTION
BECKEN CYMBALS
BECKET SQUILGEE SQUILLGEE
BECKON BOW NOD WAG BECK WAFT WAVE CURTSY SUMMON BIDDING COMMAND CURTSEY GESTURE
BECKONING WAFTURE
BECLOUD HIDE MASK BEDIM DARKEN MUDDLE MYSTIFY OBSCURE
BECLOUDED FOGGY
BECOME GO FIT GET RAX SET SIT WAX COME FALL GROW LIKE PASS SUIT TAKE TILL WEAR ADORN BEFIT GRACE PROVE WORTH ACCORD BEFALL BESEEM BETIDE CHANGE IWORTH BEHOOVE FLATTER PROCEED
(— **A PARTY**) ACCEDE
(— **AUDIBLE**) ARISE
(— **DAMP**) EVE
(— **DAZED**) DWAM DWALM
(— **DIM**) DASWEN
(— **DROWSY**) DOW
(— **FAT**) GRAZE
(— **FLUID**) FLOW FLUX LEACH
(— **KNOWN**) GO KITHE KYTHE SPUNK
(— **MOLDY**) FUST MOUL FINEW
(— **MOROSE**) SOUR
(— **ROUND**) GLOBE
(— **SOUR**) FOX BLINK CARVE
BECOMING FIT FEAT GOOD BHAVA FITTY RIGHT COMELY DUEFUL GAINLY DECORUM FARRAND FARRANT DECOROUS HANDSOME SUITABLE WISELIKE
BECOMINGLY TALLY
BED COT HAY KIP PAD PAN TYE BAND BASE BODY BUNK DOSS DOWN FLOP FORM LAIR PLOT SACK VEIN WADI WADY BERTH BOIST COUCH FLASK FLOCK GRATE GROVE LAYER THORE BORDER BOTTOM COUCHE CRADLE GIRDLE HOTBED LIBKEN LIBKIN LITTER MATRIX OSIERY PALLET STRATA CHANNEL CHARPOY FLEABAG HAMMOCK LODGING QUARTER REPOSAL SEEDBED SETTING STRATUM SUBSOIL TRUCKLE TRUNDLE BASSINET CAPSTONE LENTICLE PLANCHER
(— **DOWN**) DOSS
(— **IN WAGON**) KATEL
(— **OF ANIMAL**) LAIR KENNEL
(— **OF COAL**) BRAT DELF SEAM
(— **OF EMBERS**) GRIESHOCH
(— **OF FURNACE**) HEARTH
(— **OF GUN-CARRIAGE**) FLASK
(— **OF HAND PRESS**) COFFIN
(— **OF REFUSE**) NITRIARY
(— **OF ROCK**) CAP PLUM

(— **OF ROSES**) ROSARY
(— **OF SEDIMENT**) WARP
(— **OF STREAM**) DRAW WASH BILLABONG STREAMWAY
(**CREEK** —) COULEE COULIE
(**DRIED LAKE** —) CHOTT SHOTT
(**FEATHER** —) TIE TYE
(**FOLDING** —) SLAWBANK
(**LOW** —) LOWBOY
(**OYSTER** —) STEW LAYER SCALP CLAIRE LAYING OYSTERAGE
(**RUBBLE** —) CALLOW
(**SEED** —) SEMINARY
(**WATER-BEARING** —) AQUAFER AQUIFER
BEDAUB CLAG CLAT DAUB SOIL SLAKE SMEAR SLAISTER
BEDBUG BUG CHINK CIMEX CHINCH CHINTZ COREID PUNESE VERMIN CIMICID PUNAISE REDCOAT CONENOSE HEMIPTER HOUSEBUG
BEDCHAMBER BEDROOM CUBICLE
BEDCLOTHES COVER BEDDING CLOTHES
BEDCOVER COMFORTER PALMAPORE
BEDDING BEDROLL DOMESTICS
BEDECK GEM BEDO LARD TRAP ADORN ARRAY DIGHT GRACE PRINK ORNAMENT EMBELLISH
BEDECKED PRINKY
BEDEVIL ABUSE ANNOY BESET WORRY HARASS MUDDLE PESTER BEWITCH CONFUSE TORMENT
BEDEW DEW SHOWER IRRORATE
BEDIZEN DAUB ADORN ARRAY DIZEN BEDAUB
BEDLAM RIOT NOISE RUDAS ASYLUM TUMULT UPROAR MADNESS MADHOUSE BETHLEHEM
BEDOUIN ABSI ARAB BEDU MOOR NOMAD BADAWI BEDAWEE SHAMMAR HOWEITAT
BEDQUILT POURPOINT
BEDRAGGLE TRACHLE
BEDRAGGLED FORLORN SHOPWORN
BEDRAIL RAVE RATHE
BEDRIDDEN ILL AILING BEDFAST
(**NOT** —) AFOOT
BEDROCK LEDGE NADIR SHELF BOTTOM HARDPAN STONEHEAD
BEDROLL BINDLE
BEDROOM FLAT BERTH CABIN BEDDER DORMER BOUDOIR CHAMBER CUBICULO WARDROBE GARDEROBE
BEDSORE DECUBITUS
BEDSPREAD ALEZE STRAIL BEDCOVER COVERLET COVERLID
BEDSTEAD BED COT CRIB HATCH STEAD STAPLE ANGAREP CHARPOY
BEDSTRAW CRUDWORT CURDWORT FLEAWEED BEDFLOWER CROSSWORT SCRAMBLER
BED TESTER SPARVER
BEDWARMER CURATE
BEE DOR FLY APIS BEVY KING RING KARBI MASON NOMIA NURSE PARTY DINGAR DRONEL DRONER FROLIC

INSECT NOTION TORQUE TSETSE WORKER ANDRENA DEBORAH KOOTCHA MELISSA RAISING SERPENT STINGER SWERVER TRIGONA ANDRENID ANGELITO HONEYBEE QUILTING SCOPIPED SHUCKING WAXMAKER GATHERING
(**QUEEN** —) KING
(**PL.**) BEEN BONE HIVE SPEW SOCIALES
BEEBREAD CERAGO AMBROSIA
BEECH BUCK BIRCH MYRTLE FLINDOSA FLINDOSY
BEECHNUT SPLITNUT
(**PL.**) BUCK MAST PANNAGE
BEEF JERK BEEVE BULLY GRIPE JERKY VIFDA VIVDA CASSON CUTTER CHARQUI TOPSIDE COMPLAIN COMPOUND PASTRAMI PIPIKAULA
(— **FOR SLAUGHTER**) MART
(**BOILED** —) BOUILLI
(**BROILED** —) CHURRASCO
(**CORN** —) BULLY
(**CUT OF** —) SEY LOIN RUMP SIDE BARON CHINE CHUCK FLANK ROAST ROUND SHANK STEAK ALOYAU CUTLET SADDLE BRISKET KNUCKLE QUARTER SIRLOIN EDGEBONE SHOULDER AITCHBONE NINEHOLES RATTLERAN
(**GROUND** —) HAMBURGER
(**INFERIOR** —) COMPOUND
(**JERKED** —) TASAJO BILTONG CHARQUE CHARQUI
(**LEAN** —) LIRE
(**SALTED** —) JUNK VIFDA
BEEF BREAD SWEETBREAD
BEEFEATER OXBIRD OXBITER OXPECKER TICKBIRD
BEEFWOOD TOA BELAH BELAR FILAO
BEEFY HEAVY HEFTY SOLID BRAWNY FLESHY
BEE GLUE PROPOLIS
BEEHIVE GUM BUTT GUME HIVE SKEP PYCHE STAND STATE STOCK SWARM APIARY HOPPET ALVEARY SWARMER BEEHOUSE PRAESEPE
(— **STATE**) UTAH
(— **TOMB**) TREASURY
BEEKEEPER HIVER BEEMAN BEEHERD APIARIST SKEPPIST
BEELZEBUB DEVIL
BEEN BE BON SEE BONE
BEE PLANT GUACO STINKWEED
BEER ALE MUM BIER BOCK BREW FARO GAIL GROG GYLE HOPS KVAS MALT MILD QUAS SCUD SUDS BELCH CHANG CHICA GROUT KVASS LAGER POMBE QUASS SCUDS STOUT WEISS CHICHA DOUBLE GATTER LIQUOR PORTER SPRUCE STINGO SWANKY SWIPES WALLOP ZYTHUM PANGASI PHARAOH PILSNER TANKARD TAPLASH TAPWORT CERVISIA
(**ADD TO** —) KRAUSEN
(**BAD** —) TACK TAPLASH

(HOT — AND GIN) PURL
(INFERIOR —) BELCH SWANKY
(SMALL —) TIFF GROUT
(SOUR —) BEEREGAR
(STRONG —) HUFF DOUBLE STINGO
(THIN —) PRITCH SWIPES
(TIBETAN —) CHANG
(WARM — AND OATMEAL) STORRY
(WEAK —) BEVERAGE
BEERHOUSE TIDDLYWINK
BEESWAX CAPPING
BEET CHARD MANGEL MANGOLD
STECHLING
(SUGAR —) BOLTER
BEETLE BAT BOB BUG JUT RAM
BEAT BUZZ FLEA FOWL GOGA
GOGO IPID MAUL MELL STAG TROX
TURK UANG AMARA ATLAS BORER
BULGE CAROB CHUCK DRIVE FIDIA
GOGGA HISPA LYCID MELOE SAGRA
TIGER CHAFER CLERID CUCOYO
CUCUYO ELATER GOLACH GOLOCH
HISTER JUTOUT KHAPRA LICTUS
MALLET MELOID PESTLE PRUNER
PTINID SAWYER SCARAB WEAVER
WEEVIL ADELOPS BRUCHID
BUZZARD CADELLE CARABID
CARABUS CUCUJID FIDDLER
FIREFLY GIRDLER GOLDBUG
LADYBUG LUCANID PAUSSID
PRIONID PROJECT SILPHID SKIPPER
SNAPPER SOLDIER TANBARK
TICKLER ATEUCHUS CALOSOMA
CETONIAN COCKTAIL CURCULIO
DYTISCID ENGRAVER EROTYLID
FIGEATER GLOWWORM HARDBACK
LADYBIRD LAMPYRID LOWERING
OVERHANG RUTELIAN SCOLYTID
SEARCHER SHARNBUD SHARNBUG
SKIPJACK SPHINDID SQUASHER
SQUEAKER SYMPHILE TOKTOKJE
WHIRLWIG DEDEMERID LONGICORN
OSTOMATID TUMBLEBUG TWIRLIGIG
WHIRLIGIG
(PL.) XYLOPHAGA
BEEWEED TONGUE
BEFALL HAP COME LIMP SORT TIDE
TIME CHEFE CHIVE OCCUR SHAPE
ASTART BECOME BETIDE HAPPEN
PERTAIN
BEFIT DOW SIT COME LONG SEEM
SORT SUIT BESET SERVE BECOME
BEHOVE BESEEM BETIDE BEHOOVE
BEFITTING FIT AFTER DECENT
PROPER WORTHY SEEMING THRIFTY
BECOMING DECOROUS SORTABLE
(PROFESSIONALLY —) ETHICAL
BEFOG GAUM CLOUD OBSANE
CONFUSE MYSTIFY
BEFOOL FON SOT BURN COLT CRAP
DOLT DUPE FODE JADE ASSOT
ELUDE FONNE DIDDLE TRIFLE
FOOLIFY
BEFORE OR TO AIR BUT ERE FOR
GIN TIL ANTE FORE SAID TILL YORE
AFORE AHEAD ANENT AVANT
CORAM FIRST FORBY FORNE FRONT
PRIOR SOPRA UNTIL FORBYE
FORMER RATHER SOONER TOFORE

WITHIN AGAINST ALREADY EARLIER
FORTHBY FORWARD
(— LONG) SOON ERELONG
(JUST —) TOWARD FORMERLY
BEFOUL FILE SLUT SOIL BERAY
DIRTY GRUFT BEMIRE DAGGLE
DARKEN DEFILE DRABBLE FEWMAND
POLLUTE SLUTTER BESQUIRT
ENTANGLE
BEFOULED SHARNY
BEFRIEND AID ABET HELP FAVOR
ASSIST BENFIT FOSTER FRIEND
SUCCOR SUPPORT SUSTAIN
BEFUDDLE BOX GAS ADDLE BESOT
MUDDLE BECLOUD CONFUSE
FLUSTER MYSTIFY STUPEFY
BEFUDDLED REE
BEG ASK BID CRY SUE WOO CANT
COAX KICK MUMP PRAY PRIG SEEK
SORN SUIT THIG TRAM CADGE
CRAVE MAUND MOOCH PLEAD
SCAFF TEASE YEARN ADJURE
BESEECH ENTREAT IMPLORE
MAUNDER REQUEST SKELDER
SOLICIT PETITION OBSECRATE
BEGET GET WIN BEAR HAVE KIND
SIRE BREED YIELD BIGATE CREATE
FATHER ACQUIRE ENGRAFF
CONCEIVE ENGENDER GENERATE
BEGETTER SIRE AUTHOR FATHER
MOTHER PARENT
BEGGAR BLOB RUIN ASKER HALFY
LAZAR RANDY ROGUE THRUM
TRAMP ARMINE BACACH BIDDER
CANTER DYVOUR MUMPER PARIAH
PAUPER SORNER WRETCH
ABRAHAM ALMSMAN BAIRAGI
BEGSTER JARKMAN LAZARUS
MAUNDER PARDHAN PROCTOR
RUFFLER SCAFFER SORNARI
STEMMER THIGGER ABRAMMAN
BADGEMAN BEADSMAN DUMMERER
GLASSMAN PALLIARD STROLLER
WHIPJACK SCHNORRER
(— DESCRIPTION) PASS
(PL.) GUEUX
BEGGARED PEELED
BEGGARLY MEAN POOR CHEAP
PETTY SORRY ABJECT PALTRY
PILLED PEGRALL BANKRUPT
INDIGENT HUNGARIAN
BEGGAR'S-LICE STICKWEED
BEGGAR-TICK CUCKOLD
(PL.) BOOTJACKS
BEGGARY THIG WANT INDIGENCE
PAUPERISM
BEGGING MAUND CRAVING
MENDICANT THOMASING
(— FOR FOOD) SCRANNING
(FRAUDULENT —) TRUANDISE
BEGHARD PICARD
BEGIN GIN GYN HIT FALL FANG
HEAD JUMP LEAD OPEN RISE TAME
YOKE ARISE ENTER FRONT START
ATTACK ATTAME INCEPT SPRING
STREAK COMMENCE INCHOATE
INITIATE
BEGINNER BOOT PUNK TIRO TYRO
ROOKY SOFTA GINNER NOVICE

ROOKIE SOPHTA AMATEUR
ENTRANT RECRUIT RUBBLER
STUDENT TRAINEE FRESHMAN
INCEPTOR NEOPHYTE NOVELIST
BEGINNING EGG DAWN EDGE GERM
HEAD RISE ROOT SEED ALPHA
BIRTH DEBUT ENTRY FIRST FRONT
ONSET START VAUNT AURORA
INCOME INSTIL ONCOME ORIGIN
OUTSET SETOUT SOURCE SPRING
CALENDS DAWNING GENESIS INCIPIT
INFANCY INITIAL INITION KALENDS
NASCENT OPENING SUNRISE
ENTRANCE EXORDIUM INCHOATE
OUTSTART RUDIMENT
(NEW —) EPOCH
(PL.) INCUNABULA
BEGONE OFF OUT VIA AWAY SCAT
SHOO SCOOT SCRAM AROINT
AVAUNT DEPART SKIDOO SKIDDOO
VAMOOSE
BEGONIA GAIETY GAYETY
BEGRIME COOM SOIL COLLY DITCH
GRIME BECOOM SMIRCH SMUDGE
BRUCKLE
BEGRIMED DIRTY GRIMY SMUDGY
CINDERY SMIRCHY
BEGRUDGE ENVY GRUDGE MALIGN
JALOUSE
BEGTI NAIR COCKUP
BEGUILE FOX COAX FODE FOIL
FOND GULL LURE VAMP WILE WISE
AMUSE CHARM CHEAT COZEN
ELUDE EVADE GUILE TRICK TROLL
TRYST WEIZE BRIGUE BUTTER
DELUDE DIVERT ENTRAP JUGGLE
VAMPEY DECEIVE ENSNARE
FLATTER FLUMMER MISLEAD
BEHALF HALF PART SAKE SIDE
FAVOR SCORE STEAD AFFAIR
MATTER PROFIT BENEFIT DEFENCE
SUPPORT INTEREST
BEHAVE DO ACT LET BEAR FARE
HAVE KEEP MAKE PLAY WALK
WORK CARRY REACT TREAT ACQUIT
DEMEAN DEPORT HANDLE COMPORT
CONDUCT CONTAIN DISPORT
GESTURE MANAGER FUNCTION
REGULATE RESTRAIN
(— AFFECTEDLY) MOP
(— AWKWARDLY) GAUM HOCKER
(— BOLDLY) GAUSTER
(— BRASHLY) HOOK
(— CHURLISHLY) CARL
(— EVASIVELY) DODGE
(— FOOLISHLY) DOLT
(— MISCHIEVOUSLY) LARK
(— NOISILY) HELL REHAYTE
(— OSTENTATIOUSLY) SWANK
(— VULGARLY) RAMP
BEHAVIOR AIR MIEN PORT RULE
THEW WALK FRONT GUISE HABIT
LATES USAGE ACTION COURSE
GOINGS MANNER ACTIONS BEARING
BIGOTRY COMPORT CONDUCT
DECORUM ERGASIA FACTION
FASHION HAVANCE HAVINGS
AMENANCE ATTITUDE BLINDISM
BREEDING BYRONICS CARRIAGE

FUNCTION MAINTAIN
(ARROGANT —) SIDE SWAGGER
(COURTEOUS —) COMITY
COURTESY
(DECENT —) CIVILITY
(FOOLISH —) SIMPLES SOTTISE
(LIVELY —) TITTUP
(LOUTISH —) BUFFOONRY
(RIOTOUS —) RAMPAGE
(SILLY —) SPOONISM
(STUDIED —) ART
BEHEAD NECK
BEHEST BID LAW HEST RULE ORDER
DEMAND BIDDING COMMAND
MANDATE
BEHIND AFT HINT PAST RUMP
ABACK ABAFF ABAFT AFTER AHIND
AREAR LATER PASSE TARDY
ARREAR ASTERN DERERE
BACKWARD DILATORY
BEHINDHAND TARDY LAGGARD
DILATORY HINDERLY
BEHOLD LA LO EYE SEE SPY ECCE
ESPY GAZE HOLD KEEP LOOK SCAN
STOP TOOT VIEW VISE WAIT HOLDE
OCULE SIGHT VOILA WATCH ASPECT
DESCRY MIRROR REGARD RETAIN
DISCERN OBSERVE SURVISE
WITNESS
BEHOLDEN OWING BOUNDEN
OBLIGED INDEBTED
BEHOOVE DOW FIT NEED SUIT THAR
BEFIT OUGHT THARF BELONG
PROPER REQUIRE
BEIGE HOP TAN ECRU HOPI GREGE
DORADO GREIGE STRING SUNBURN
BEING ENS ESSE FEAL SELF ENTIA
GNOME HUMAN SHAPE TROLL
ANIMAL ENTITY EXTANT LIVING
MORTAL PERSON SYSTEM ESSENCE
PRESENT REALITY VIVENCY
CREATURE EXISTENT ONTOLOGY
PRESENCE STANDING
(ANIMATE —) LIFE JAGAT
(CELESTIAL —) ANGEL CHERUB
SERAPH WATCHER DIVINITY
(DIMINUTIVE —) ELF GNOME
(DIVINE —) DEV DEVA DEMIGOD
(ESSENCE OF —) SAT
(ETERNAL —) EON AEON
(EVIL —) DEVIL GHOUL
(FABULOUS —) TENGU TORNIT
(HUMAN —) BODY BUCK JACK SOUL
BLADE HUMAN SLIME ANIMAL
ADAMITE CREATURE RATIONAL
CHRISTIAN
(IDEAL —) IMMORTAL
(ILL-FAVORED —) BLASTIE
(IMAGINARY —) SYLPH TERMAGANT
(INNER —) INWARD SPRITE INBEING
(INNERMOST —) HEART
(INTRINSIC —) ESSENCE
(LEGENDARY —) GIANT
(LIVING —) BLOOD WIGHT
(MATERIAL —) HYLIC
(PERFECT —) GOD
(PHYSICAL —) FLESH
(SEMIDIVINE —) SHEDU LAMASSU
(SMALL —) INCHLING

(SO —) SAEBEINS
(SUPERNATURAL —) DEV MAN AKUA
ATUA DEVA JANN ZEMI ADARO
BALAM DAEVA DEMON FAIRY TROLL
DAEMON GARUDA GODKIN SPIRIT
GODLING FOLLETTO HAMINGJA
(SUPREME —) DEITY MONAD
NYAMBE NZAMBI CREATOR
(TRUE —) OUSIA
BELABOR PLY BEAT DRUB LASH
WORK ASSAIL BOUNCE CUDGEL
HAMMER HAMPER THRASH THWACK
BELAY BESET BELAGE INVEST
WAYLAY BESEIGE
BELCH BOKE BOLK BURP GALP
RASP RIFT ERUCT FRUCT REBOKE
ERUCTATE
BELDAM HAG FURY CRONE RUDAS
ALECTO ERINYS RUDOUS VIRAGO
BELDAME JEZEBEL TISIPHONE
BELEAGUER BELAY BESET INVEST
ASSAULT BESEIGE LEAGUER
BLOCKADE SURROUND
BELEM PARA
BELEMNITE ARTIFACT KERAUNION
BELFRY SHED TOWER BEFFROY
CLOCHER CLOGHEAD BELLHOUSE

BELGIUM
CAPITAL: BRUSSELS BRUXELLES
CANAL: UNION ALBERT CAMPINE
GAUL TRIBE: REMI BELGAE NERVII
MEASURE: VAT AUNE LAST PIED
CARAT PERCHE BOISSEAU
MOUNTAIN: BOTRANGE
NAME: BELGIE BELGIQUE
PLATEAU: ARDENNES HOHEVENN
PORT: OSTEND ANTWERP
PROVINCE: LIEGE NAMUR
ANTWERP BRABANT HAINAUT
LIMBURG FLANDERS HAINAULT
RIVER: LYS DYLE LEIE MAAS
MARK YSER BOUCQ DEMER
LESSE MEUSE NETHE RUPEL
SENNE DENDER ESCAUT MANJEL
OURTHE SAMBRE SEMOIS
VESDRE WARCHE AMBLEVE
SCHELDT
TOWN: AS AAT ANS ATH HAL HUY
MOL SPA AATH AMAY ASSE
BOOM BREE DOEL GAND GEEL
GENK GENT HOEI LIER LOOZ
MONS VISE WAHA ZELE AALST
ALOST ARLON CINEY EEKLO
ESSEN EUPEN EVERE GENCK
GHENT HEIST IEPER JETTE
JUMET LIEGE NAMUR RONSE
TIELT UCCLE VORST WEZET
YNOIR YPRES AARLEN ANVERS
BERGEN BILZEN BRUGES
DEURNE IZEGEM LEUVEN LIERRE
MERXEM OPWIJK OSTEND
ANTWERP ARDOOIE BERCHEM
DOORWIK HERSTAL HOBOKEN
IXELLES LOUVAIN MECHLIN
ROULERS SERAING TOURNAI
BRUSSELS COURTRAI KORTRIJK
MOUSCRON TURNHOUT

VERVIERS WATERLOO
WEIGHT: LAST CARAT LIVRE
POUND CHARGE CHARIOT
ESTERLIN

BELIE BELONG DEFAME BESEIGE
FALSIFY PERTAIN SLANDER
TRADUCE DISGUISE STRUMPET
SURROUND
BELIEF CRY FAY ISM LEVE MIND
SECT TAKE TROW VIEW VOTE WEEN
CAUSE CREDO CREED DOGMA FAITH
OBEAH TENET TROTH TRUST
CREDIT GROUND CRIANCE FEELING
HOLDING OPINION TROWING
ARYANISM BITHEISM CREDENCE
DOCTRINE FINALISM HUMANISM
RELIANCE
(— IN DEVILS) DIABOLISM
(— IN GHOSTS) EIDOLISM
(FALSE —) DELUSION
(GROUNDLESS —) CANARD
(MORTAL —) HALL
(SHALLOW —) BALLOON
(SUPERSTITIOUS —) FREET
(TRADITIONAL —) ICON IKON EIKON
(UNFOUNDED —) FICTON
BELIEVE BUY WIS DEEM FEEL HOLD
TAKE TREW TROW WEEN CREED
FAITH FANCY GUESS JUDGE SEPAD
THINK TRUST ACCEPT CREDIT
ESTEEM EXPECT DARESAY SUPPOSE
ACCREDIT CONSIDER CREDENCE
(— ERRONEOUSLY) FEIGN
(— NAIVELY) SWALLOW
(— UNCRITICALLY) EAT
BELIEVER IST LEVER BOTARY KITABI
CREDENS ADHERENT ARMINIAN
BELITTLE DECRY DWARF SNEER
MINISH SLIGHT DETRACT DIMINUE
LIGHTLY MINIMIZE VILIPEND
DENIGRATE DISCREDIT DISPARAGE
BELITTLER ZOILUS
BELL HUB TOM CALL FAIR GONG
HUBB RING ROAR CHIME CLOAK
CLOCK CODON FLARE KNELL SWELL
TENOR BASKET BELLOW BUBBLE
CLOCHE CROTAL CURFEW PHONIC
SOCKET TAPPER TOCSIN TOLLER
TREBLE TRIPLE VESPER ANGELUS
BLOSSOM CAMPANA CAMPANE
COROLLA COWBELL JANGLER
JINGLER LOWBELL SKELLAT
SKILLET TAMBOUR TANTONY
TINKLER CASCABEL COCKBELL
DINGDONG DOORBELL HANDBELL
HAWKBELL MORTBELL PAVILLON
STARTLER TINGTANG
(ALARM —) TOCSIN
(CLOSED —) CROTAL
(EVENING —) CURFEW
(FUNERAL —) TELLER
(HAND —) CLAG
(LARGE —) SIGNUM
(LOWEST —) BORDON BOURDON
(PASSING —) KNELL
(SACRING —) SQUILLA
(SLEIGH —) GRELOT

BELLABELLA HAELTZUK HEILTSUK
BELLADONNA DWALE MANICON
BANEWORT DAFTBERRY
DWAYBERRY MYDRIATIC
BELLARMINE GRAYBEARD
GREYBEARD LONGBEARD
BELLBIRD MAKO SHRIKE COTINGA
ARAPUNGA KORIMAKO MAKOMAKO
CAMPANERO
BELLBOY BUTTONS
BELLE SPARK TOAST
(SPANISH —) MAJA
BELLEEK POTTERY CHAMPAGNE
BELLEROPHON (FATHER OF —)
GLAUCUS
(MOTHER OF —) EURYMEDE
BELLFLOWER RAMPION BELLWORT
HASKWORT IVYBELLS MILKWORT
BELLHOP BELLBOY HALLBOY
CHASSEUR
BELLICOSE MAD IRATE WARFUL
HOSTILE WARLIKE MILITANT
BELLIGERENT BRISTLY HOSTILE
WARLIKE CHOLERIC FIGHTING
JINGOIST COMBATIVE IRASCIBLE
LITIGIOUS WRANGLING
BELLOW CRY LOW MOO YAP BAWL
BEAL BELL GAPE ROAR ROME ROUT
YAUP YAWP BELVE BLART BLORE
CROON ROUST SHOUT BULLER
CLAMOR RUMMES BLUSTER
RUMMISH ULULATE
BELLOWING ROUT ROUST BELLING
BOATION MUGIENT
BELLOWS BELY LUNGS BULIES
FEEDER SANDER WINKER SYLPHON
WINDBAG EXPELLER
(SMALL —) PLUFF
(STORAGE —) RESERVOIR
BELLOWS FISH BUGLER SNIPEFISH
BELL RINGER TOLL YOUTH TOLLER
CLINKUM
BELLWETHER MASTER
BELLY BAG COD GIE GUT MAW POD
BOUK FILL KYTE MARY WAME WEAM
WOMB BINGY BOSOM BULGE FRONT
GORGE PLEON TABLE THARM
THERM TRIPE BAGGIE BINGEE
HUNGER PAUNCH VENTER ABDOMEN
BALLOON STOMACH TUMBREL
APPETITE
BELLYACHE COMPLAIN
COLLYWOBBLES
BELLYBAND WANTY
BELLYING BUNTING PREGNANT
BELONG BE GO FIT LIE BEAR FALL
RELY APPLY BELIE GROUP AFFEIR
INHERE RELATE RETAIN BEHOOVE
PERTAIN APPERTAIN SUBSCRIBE
BELONGINGS ALLS DUDS FARE
GEAR GOODS TRAPS ASSETS
DUFFEL DUFFLE ESTATE USINGS
BAGGAGE EFFECTS CHATTELS
PROPERTY PURPRISE FURNITURE
HOUSEHOLD
BELOVED DEAR IDOL LIEF AIMEE
BOSOM CHERI SWEET ADORED
CHERIE MINION DARLING PRECIOUS
(MOST —) ALDERLIEFEST

BELOW ALOW BAJO DOWN ABLOW
AFTER INFRA NEATH SOTTO UNDER
BEHIND BENEATH
BELT LAS AREA BAND BEAT BLOW
CEST FELT GIRD LACE LIST MARK
RING SASH ZONE GIRTH MITER
MITRE PATTE STRAP STRIP SWATH
TRACT WAIST WHACK ZONAR ZONIC
BODICE CESTUS CINGLE FETTLE
GIRDLE INVEST LUNGER REGION
STRAIT STRIPE SWATHE ZONNAR
ZONULE BALDRIC CIRCUIT PASSAGE
BALTHEUS CEINTURE CINCTURE
ELEVATOR ENCIRCLE MECHANIC
SURROUND
(ASTROLOGICAL —) CLIMATE
(CONVEYOR —) HAUL
(ENDLESS —) APRON CREEPER
(GREEK —) ZOSTER
(HINDU SWAMP —) TERAI
(MACHINE —) SWIFTER
(MINERAL —) RANGE
(TREE —) BERM BERME
BELTED ZONATE GIRDLED
CINCTURED
(— WITH WHITE) SHEETED
BELUGA HUSE HUSO HAUSEN
MARSOON WHITEFISH
BELVEDERE GAZEBO LOOKOUT
BEMIRE DAG SOIL JARBLE
BEMOAN MEAN MOAN SIGH MOURN
PLAIN BEWAIL LAMENT DEPLORE
BEMUSE SOT BULL DAZE AMUSE
BEMUSED DOPY DOPEY
BENCH PEW BANC BANK BENK BERM
BINK DAIS DEAS FORM MESA SEAT
SILL STEP TRAM BASIN BASON
BERME BREAK CABIN CHAIR FORME
JUDGE PLANK STALL STOOL
BANCUS BANKER SCONCE SEDILE
SETTEE SETTLE SITTER COUNTER
DRESSER REPOSAL SHAMBLE
SITTING TRESTLE TRIBUNE
ALEBENCH
(— FOR DAIRY TUBS) TRAM
(— FOR KNEADING DOUGH) BREAK
(OUTDOOR —) EXEDRA EXHEDRA
(PLAYER'S —) WOOD
(ROWER'S —) BANK THOFT ZYGON
THWART
(SHOEMAKER'S —) FORME
(WORKMAN'S —) SIEGE
BEND BOW NID NIP PLY SAG SET
WIN WRY ABOW ARCH BENT BOOL
BUCK COPE CURB DOME FAUD FLEX
FOLD GENU HOOK KINK LEAN LOUT
PLOY RUMP TURN VERT WEEP
ANGLE BATON BIGHT BREAK COUDE
COURB CRANK CRIMP CRINK CROOK
CULGE CURVE DROOP FLECT FRESE
HINGE HUNCH INBOW KNEEL PLICA
QUIRL ROUND SCRAG SKELP SLANT
STOOP TREND TWINE TWIST
BOUGHT BUCKLE CAMBER CONVEX
COTICE
BENDER BUM JAG LEG BUST DRUNK
SPREE BRIDGE WHOPPER GUZZLING
SIXPENCE BRANNIGAN INFLECTOR
BENDING BOW SAG KNEE KNOT

CROOK CURVE LITHE TWIST PLIANT
SUPPLE TWISTY ANFRACT FLEXION
HOGGING SINUOUS BUCKLING
FLECTION
(— OF ROCK) DRAG
BENDY TREE MIRO MAHOE
BENEATH ALOW ANETH BELOW
LOWER UNDER ANEATH
BENEDICITE BENISON CANTICLE
BENEDICTINE CLUNIAC
CAMALDOLESE
BENEDICTION ABOT AMEN ABOTH
NANDI AMIDAH BROCHO PRAYER
BENISON BERAKAH BLESSING
BENEFACTION ALMS BOON GIFT
PRESENT DONATION GRATUITY
BENEFACTOR AGENT ANGEL
DONOR FRIEND HELPER PATRON
SAVIOR MAECENAS PROMOTER
BENEFICE FEE FEU FEUD FIEF
FAVOR SCARF CURACY LIVING
BENEFIT PRELACY RECTORY
TOTQUOT DONATIVE KINDNESS
SINECURE VICARAGE
BENEFICENCE BOON GIFT GRACE
BOUNTY CHARITY GOODNESS
KINDNESS
BENEFICENT KINDLY AMIABLE
GRACIOUS
BENEFICIAL GOOD USEFUL
HEALTHY HELPFUL BONITARY
SALUTARY SANATIVE SINGULAR
AVAILABLE BENIGNANT DESIRABLE
ENJOYABLE HEALTHFUL LUCRATIVE
REWARDING WHOLESOME
BENEFICIARY HEIR USER DONEE
CESTUI CESTUY USUARY VASSAL
LEGATEE FEUDATORY
BENEFIT AID USE BOON BOOT GAIN
GIFT GOOD HELP PROW SAKE AVAIL
BOOST FRUIT SELTH STEAD VISIT
ASSIST BEHALF BEHOOF BETTER
FRINGE PROFIT SALUTE USANCE
ADVANCE BESPEAK CONCERT
DESERVE IMPROVE SERVICE UTILITY
BEFRIEND INTEREST
BENEVOLENCE JEN GOODNESS
GOODWILL HUMANITY
BENEVOLENT GOOD KING BENIGN
KINDLY LOVING AMIABLE LIBERAL
GENEROUS AVUNCULAR BENIGNANT
BENIGN BOON GOOD KIND MILD
BLAND SWEET GENIAL GENTLE
AFFABLE BENEDICT GRACIOUS
INNOCENT SALUTARY FAVORABLE
WHOLESOME
BENIGNANT KIND BLAND GENIAL
LIBERAL GRACIOUS MERCIFUL
BENJAMIN (FATHER OF —) JACOB
(MOTHER OF —) RACHEL
(SON OF —) ARD EHI BELA GERA
ROSH ASHBEL BECHER HUPPIM
MUPPIM NAAMAN
BENNET CLOVEWORT
BENNISEED SESAME
BENO TUBA
BENT AIM BOW SET BIAS CAST GIFT
TURN BOUND BOWED BOWLY
COUDE CRANK CRUMP FLAIR

HUMOR KNACK LURCH PRONE
SQUAT SWING TASTE TREND
AKIMBO ANLAGE BENNET BIASED
BRACED COURBE COURSE CURVED
DOGLEG ENERGH GENIUS HOOKED
INTENT LIKING NECKED SQUINT
SWAYED TALENT BUCKLED
CROOKED CURVANT EMBOWED
FLEXION FLEXURE IMPETUS INTENSE
LEANING LEVELED PRONATE
PURPOSE STOOPED TENSION
APTITUDE ARCUATED CRUMPLED
DECLINED FLECTION IMMINENT
INFLEXED PENCHANT REFLEXED
TENDENCY
(— AT THE END) HAMATE HOGGED
GRYPANIAN
(— DOWNWARD) BOWED DECURVED
INCUMBENT RECLINATE
(— IN) INCAVATE
(— OF MIND) GEME AFFECTION
(EASILY —) LITHY
(NATURAL —) SWING
BEN-TEAK NANDI NANAWOOD
BENUMB NIP DAZE DUNT NUMB
STUN DAVER DOZEN SCRAM SHRAM
CUMBER DEADEN STOUND BINOMEN
FRETISH FRETIZE STIFFEN STUPEFY
TORPEDO
BENUMBED CHILL SCRAM CLUMSE
CLUMSY FROZEN TORPID CLUMPST
SHRAMMED
BENUMBING LEADEN
BENZENE PHENE BENZIN BENZOL
PHENENE
BENZOIN BENJOIN LINDERA
BENJAMIN FIXATIVE
BEQUEATH GIVE WILL ENDOW
LEAVE OFFER BESTOW COMMIT
DEMISE DEVISE LEGATE QUETHE
BEQUEST COMMEND TRANSMIT
BEQUEST GIFT WILL LEGACY
BEQUEATH HERITAGE PITTANCE
ENDOWMENT
BERATE JAW NAG DRUB LASH RAIL
ABUSE BASTE CHIDE SCOLD SCORE
SLATE REVILE CENSURE REPROVE
UPBRAID CHASTISE
BERBER RIF RIFF KABYL SHLUH
KABYLE SHILHA HARATIN MZABITE
SHILLUH HARRATIN MOZABITE
(— CHIEF) CAID
BERCEUSE CRADLESONG
WIEGENLIED
BEREAVE ROB STRIP WIDOW DIVEST
SADDEN DEPRIVE DESPOIL
BEREAVED BEREFT VIDUOUS
WIDOWED DESOLATE
BEREAVEMENT ORBITY ORBITUDE
VIDUATION
BEREFT ORB LORN LOST POOR QUIT
WIDOW ORBATE FORLORN
FORFAIRN DESTITUTE
BERG FLOE BARROW ICEBERG
FLOEBERG
BERGAMOT BOSE BERGAMA
BURGAMOT
BERIBERI KAKKE
BERITH BRIS BRISS BRITH

BERM BERME LISIERE HEELPATH
BERRY BAY DEW HAW ALEY BEAT
CRAN POHA RASP BACCA BLACK
FRUIT GRAIN GRAPE LANSA MOUND
SALAL SAVIN BURROW LANSAT
LANSEH SABINE THRESH CURRANT
ETAERIO HILLOCK ACROSARC
ALLSPICE COWBERRY DEWBERRY
HAWEBAKE
(ACID —) CURRANT
(COFFEE —) CHERRY
(DRIED —) PASA
(JUMPER —) ABHAL
(LAUREL —) BAY
(POISONOUS —) BANEBERRY
BERTH BED JOB BUNK DOCK SLIP
SOPT CABIN PLACE UPPER BILLET
OFFICE SECURE LODGING MOORING
SLIPWAY POSITION ANCHORAGE
BERYL EMERALD AEROIDES
HELIODOR GOSHENITE
BERYLLIA GLUCINA GLUCINE
BESEECH ASK BEG BID CRY SUE
WOO PRAY CRAVE HALSE PLEAD
ADJURE APPEAL OBTEST CONJURE
ENTREAT IMPLORE SOLICIT
IMPETRATE OBSECRATE
BESET PLY SET SIT BEGO SAIL STUD
ALLOT BELAY BIGAN HARRY PRESS
SIEGE SPEND STEAD ASSAIL
ATTACK HARASS INFEST OBSESS
WAYLAY ARRANGE BESIEGE
OVERSET PERPLEX BLOCKADE
ENCUMBER ENTHRONG OBSTRUCT
SURROUND BELEAGUER
BESHOW SKIL CUDDY CUDDEN
CUDDIE BADDOCK COALFISH
SKILFISH
BESIDE BY HEAR INBY ALONG
ANENT ASIDE FORBY ABREAST
AGAINST FORNENT ADJACENT
FORNENST
(— ONE ANOTHER) ABREAST
(— ONESELF) FEY
BESIDES BY TO AND BUT TOO YET
ALSO ELSE MORE OVER THEN UNTO
WITH ABOVE AGAIN FORBY SUPRA
BESIDE BEYOND EXCEPT FORBYE
WITHAL THERETO WITHOUT
LIKEWISE MOREOVER
BESIEGE GIRD GIRT BELAY BELIE
BESET SIEGE STORM ATTACK
OBSESS OBSIDE PESTER PLAGUE
COMPASS SOLICIT SURROUND
BELEAGUER
BESMEAR RAY BALM DAUB SOIL
APPLY COVER GRIME GRUFT MUDDY
SLAKE SMEAR SULLY TAINT BEDAUB
PLATCH BESLIME SMOTHER
BESMIRCH BESLUBBER
BESMIRCH DASH SLUR SOIL SMEAR
SULLY SLURRY SMIRCH ASPERSE
BLACKEN DRAGGLE TURPIFY
DISCOLOR
BESOM COW MAP DRAB BISME
BROOM SWEEP SLOVEN HEATHER
BESOT DULL ASOTE ASSOT MUDDLE
STUPID STUPEFY BEFUDDLE
BESPANGLE DOT STAR STUD

ADORN JEWEL SPRINKLE
BESPATTER BLOT DASH JAUP SOIL
SPOT MUDDY PLASH STAIN SULLY
BEGARY SPARGE ASPERSE
SCATTER SMOTTER REPROACH
SPRINKLE
BESPEAK CITE HINT SHOW ARGUE
IMPLY ORDER SPEAK TRYST
ACCOST ATTEST ENGAGE STEVEN
ADDRESS ARRANGE BENEFIT
BETOKEN DISCUSS EXCLAIM
RESERVE FORETELL INDICATE
BESPECKLE DASH
BESPRINKLE DROP POWDER
ASPERSE BESTREW BESPRING
SPRINKLE BEQUIRTLE
BEST O ACE BEAT GOOD LACE MOST
PICK TOPS WALE ELITE EXCEL
WORST CHOICE DEFEAT FINEST
FLOWER OUTWIT SUNDAY TIPTOP
UTMOST ARISTOS CONQUER
GARLAND LARGEST OPTIMUM
DAMNDEST GREATEST KOHINOOR
OUTMATCH OUTSTRIP POSSIBLE
VANQUISH
BESTIAL LOW VILE WILD BRUTE
FERAL PRONE BRUTAL FILTHY
BEASTLY BRUTISH INHUMAN
SENSUAL BELLUINE DEPRAVED
BESTIR STIR AWAKE SHIFT STEER
AROUSE HUSTLE
(— ONESELF) LEG
BEST MAN PARANYMPH
BESTOW ADD PUT USE CAST DEAL
DOTE GIVE SEND STOW TAKE WARE
ALLOT ALLOW APPLY AWARD BESET
GRANT INFER LODGE PLACE SPEND
THOLE WREAK ACCORD BETEEM
CONFER DEMISE DEVOTE DIVIDE
DONATE DOTATE EMPLOY ENTAIL
ESTATE EXTEND IMPART IMPOSE
RENDER SHOWER COLLATE
COMMEND DISPOSE ENLARGE
EROGATE INDULGE INSTATE
PARTAKE PRESENT QUARTER
TRIBUTE BEQUEATH
(— LAVISHLY) HEAP
(— UPON) GIFT
BESTOWAL DOLE DISPOSAL
COLLATION LARGITION
(— OF PRAISE) ACCOLADE
BESTRIDE HORSE STRIDE STRADDLE
BET GO UP BAS BOX LAY SET VIE
WAD ANTE BACK BRAG CHIP GAGE
HOLD JACK NOIR PAIR PLAY PLOT
PUNT RISK WAGE BOUND CARRE
HEDGE ROUGE SAVER SPORT
STAKE WAGER GAMBLE HAZARD
IMPAIR MANQUE MILIEU PLEDGE
DERNIER PREMIER
(— AGAINST) MILK COPPER
(— AT LONG ODDS) SKINNER
(— BOLDLY) BLUFF
(— CHIP) CHECK
(FARO —) SLEEPER
(HEDGING —) SAVER
(POKER —) BLIND
BETA AND GAMMA GUARDS
BETAKE GO GET HIE MOVE TAKE

APPLY CATCH GRANT ASSUME
COMMIT REMOVE REPAIR RESORT
COMMEND JOURNEY WITHDRAW
(— **ONESELF TO MILL**) SUE
(— **ONESELF**) BUN HIT BOUN MARK
PIKE TEEM AVOID FOUND HAUNT
REFER TRUSS YIELD
BETEL IKMO ITMO SERI SIRI SIRIH
PUPULO
BETEL LEAF PAN BUYO PAUN
PAWNE
BETEL NUT BONGA BONYA BUNGA
SUPARI
BETHABARA NOIBWOOD
GREENHEART
BETHEL BETHESDA
BETHINK TAKE THINK ADVISE
DEVISE RECALL REFLECT CONSIDER
REMEMBER RECOLLECT
(— **ONE'S SELF**) MIN MINE
UMBETHINK
BETHLEHEM BEDLAM
BETHROOT TRILLIUM
BETIDE HAP TIDE BEFIT OCCUR
TRITE WORTH BECOME BEFALL
CHANCE HAPPEN BETOKEN
PRESAGE
BETIMES ANON RATH SOON EARLY
RATHE TIMEOUS SPEEDILY
FORTHWITH
BETOKEN MARK NOTE SHOW SIGN
AUGUR TOKEN ASSERT BETIDE
DENOTE EVINCE IMPORT SHADOW
BESPEAK EXPRESS OBLIQUE
PORTEND PRESAGE SIGNIFY
FOREBODE FORESHOW INDICATE
BETONY BROOMWORT
BETRAY BLAB BLOW BOIL GULL
SELL SHOP SILE SING SPOT TELL
TRAY UNDO WRAY CROSS FALSE
PEACH ROUND SPILL SPLIT SWICK
SWIKE ACCUSE BEWRAY DELUDE
DESCRY DESERT QUATCH REVEAL
SEDUCE SNITCH SQUEAL BEGUILE
DECEIVE FALSIFY MISLEAD
PROMOTE TRAITOR DISCLOSE
DISCOVER
(— **CONFIDENCES**) SPILL
BETRAYAL RAP ACCUSE TREASON
GIVEAWAY PRODITION
BETRAYER RAT JUDAS SKUNK
SEDUCER TRAITOR DERELICT
RECREANT SQUEALER
BETRAYING TELLTALE
BETROTH AFFY EARL TOKEN TROTH
TRUTH ASSURE ENGAGE ENSURE
PLEDGE PLIGHT ESPOUSE PROMISE
AFFIANCE CONTRACT DESPOUSE
HANDFAST
BETROTHED SURE VOWED ASSURED
ENGAGED HANDFAST INTENDED
COMBINATE
BETTA PLAKAT
BETTER AID TOP BEET MEND AMEND
EMEND EXCEL SAFER WISER
BIGGER EXCEED REFORM ADVANCE
CHOICER CORRECT GREATER
IMPROVE PROMOTE RECTIFY
RELIEVE SUPPORT SURPASS

EMINENCE INCREASE SUPERIOR
(— **A SCORE**) BREAK
(— **THAN ORDINARY**) EXTRA
BETTING ACTION GAMBLING
(— **SYSTEM**) PAROLI ALEMBERT
BETTOR ORALER
BETTY JENNY COTBETTY JOCRISSE
MOLLYCOT WIFECARL
BETWEEN AMID EMEL AMELL
AMONG ENTRE TWEEN YTWYN
ATWEEN ATWIXT TWEESH AVERAGE
BETWIXT
BEUDANITE CORKITE
BEVEL BLOW CANT CONE EDGE
PUSH REAM ANGLE BEARD BEZEL
MITER MITRE SLANT SLOPE SNAPE
SPLAY ASLANT CIPHER RHYMER
CHAMFER INCLINE OBLIQUE
(— **EDGES**) BEARD
(**WITHOUT** —) FLAT
BEVERAGE ADE ALE CUP NOG POP
RUM SAP TEA BEER BREW CHIA
GROG MABI MATE MEAD MILK NIPA
SODA WHIG WINE CHOCA CIDER
CLARY COCOA DRAFT DRINK JULEP
LAGER LEBAN MORAT MULSE
NEGUS PUNCH SHRUB SMASH
TREAT TWIST WATER BISHOP
COFFEE EGGNOG LIQUID LIQUOR
NECTAR PORTER SPRUCE TISWIN
BUNNELL CASSINA LIMEADE
OENOMEL POTABLE STEPONY
TULAPAI ALEBERRY COCKTAIL
LEMONADE PIQUETTE POTATION
CALIBOGUS CHOCOLATE
GINGERADE POMPERKIN SOMETHING
SWITCHELL
(— **FROM COW'S MILK**) KEFIR
KEPHIR
(— **FROM PEPPERS**) KAVA
KAVAKAVA
(— **FROM SAP**) TUBA
(— **OF BUTTERMILK AND WATER**)
BLAND
(— **OF CHAMPAGNE**) POPE
(— **OF HOT MILK**) POSSET
(— **OF PORT WINE**) BISHOP
(— **OF VINEGAR AND WATER**)
POSCA
(**ALCOHOLIC** —) DEW ARAK SAKE
SAKI ARRAK BASIG SHRUB SNAPS
STUFF ARRACK FIREWATER
STIMULANT
(**COLA** —) DOPE
(**EFFERVESCENT** —) FIZZ
(**FERMENTED** —) BASI KUMYS
KUMISS
(**FRUIT** —) BEVERAGE
(**INSIPID** —) WASH
(**MEXICAN** —) TEPACHE
(**WEAK** —) LAP
(**PL.**) WAIPIRO
BEVY HERD PACK COVEY DROVE
FLOCK GROUP SWARM FLIGHT
SCHOOL COMPANY
BEWAIL CRY RUE WEY KEEN MOAN
RAME SIGH WAIL WEEP MOURN
PLAIN BEMOAN GRIEVE LAMENT
PLAINT SORROW THROPE DEPLORE
COMPLAIN

BEWARE WAR CAVE GARE HEED
SHUN TENT WARD AVOID SPEND
ESCHEW WARNING
BEWILDER FOG FOX MAR BEAT
DAZE FOIL GAUM MAZE STUN
ABASH ADDLE AMAZE AMUSE
DEAVE DIZZY BAFFLE BEMIST
BEMUSE BOTHER DAZZLE DUDDER
MOIDER MOMBLE MUDDLE PUZZLE
WANDER WILDER BUFFALO
BUMBAZE CONFUSE FLASKER
MYSTIFY PERPLEX STAGGER
STUPEFY ASTONISH CONFOUND
DISTRACT ENTANGLE OVERMUSE
SQUATTER SURPRISE
BEWILDERED MAR ASEA LOST
MANG WILL AGAPE DAZED MAZED
BUSHED MAPPED STUPENT
WILSOME CONFUSED HELPLESS
WILLYARD PERPLEXED
BEWILDERMENT AWE FOG DAZE
MISMAZE STICKLE AMAZEMENT
CONFUSION
BEWITCH HEX WISH BLINK CHARM
MAGIC OBEAH SPELL WITCH
ENAMOR ENTICE GLAMOR GRIGRI
HOODOO STRIKE THRILL ATTRACT
BEDEVIL DELIGHT ENCHANT
GLAMOUR ENSORCEL FORSPEAK
GREEGREE OVERLOOK
BEWITCHED HAGGED
BEWITCHING SIREN
BEYOND BY FREE OVER YOND
ABOVE ASIDE AYOND FORBY ULTRA
BEHIND BEYANT YONDER BENEATH
BESIDES FORTHBY FURTHER
OUTGATE PASSING WITHOUT
OVERMORE SUPERIOR HEREAFTER
(— **DOUBT**) ASSURED
(— **ORDINARY METHODS**) AFIELD
(— **THE MARK**) GONE
(— **THE SEA**) ULTRAMARINE
(— **THIS**) STILL
BEZEL RIM TOP EDGE OUCH SEAL
BEVIL BEZIL CROWN FACET CHATON
FLANGE MARQUISE TEMPLATE
BEZIQUE PENCHANT
BEZOAR GOATSTONE HIPPOLITH
B-GIRL SITTER
BHAKTA BHAGAVATA
BHANG BANG BENG BENJ HASHISH
BHARAL TUR HALL NAHOOR
BURRHEL
BHIKSHU GELONG
BHUTAN (**ASSEMBLY OF** —)
TSONGDU
(**CAPITAL OF** —) THIMPHU
(**CURRENCY OF** —) PAISA RUPEE
(**LANGUAGE OF** —) DZONGKHA
(**RIVER OF** —) MACHU MANAS
AMOCHU
BHUTAN PINE KAIL
BIANNUAL BIYEARLY
BIAS PLY WRY AWRY BENT CANT
SWAY WARP AMISS COLOR FAVOR
POISE SLANT SLOPE SWING TWIST
BIGOTRY INCLINE OBLIQUE
SUGGEST CLINAMEN COLORING
DIAGONAL TENDENCY PREJUDICE

PROCEDURE SPECTACLE
BIASED SLANT COLORED PARTIAL
BIB SIP BRAT POUT APRON DRINK
FEEDER TIPPLE TUCKER BAVETTE
(CHILD'S —) BISHOP
(LEATHER —) DICK
BIBLE BOOK VULGATE SCRIPTURE
(— TEXT) MIKRA MIQRA
BIBLE LEAF COSTMARY
BIBULOUS DRINKING BIBACIOUS
BICKER JAR WAR BOWL SPAR TIFF
ARGUE BRAWL CAVIL FIGHT ASSAIL
ATTACK BATTLE CONTEND DISPUTE
PICKEER QUARREL WRANGLE
PETTIFOG SKIRMISH SQUABBLE
BICKERN ANVIL BEAKIRON
BICYCLE BIKE QUAD CYCLE HOBBY
MOUNT STEED WHEEL JIGGER
ORNARY SAFETY TANDEM ORDINAR
TRIPLET ORDINARY ROADSTER
BID GO BEG NAP BEDE BODE CALL
GIVE HEST HIST PRAY WISH CHEAP
CLEPE FRAGE OFFER ORDER
ADJURE CHARGE DIRECT ENJOIN
INVITE REVEAL SIMPLE SUMMON
TENDER BALANCE CHEAPEN
COMMAND DECLARE DROPVIE
ENTREAT PROFFER ANNOUNCE
PROCLAIM PROPOSAL
(— ADIEU) TEACH
(— AT AUCTION) CRY
(— IN CARDS) CUE FROG JUMP
SOLO FRAGE GRAND SHIFT BOSTON
DEFEND DEMAND DENIAL SMUDGE
BLUCHER COMMAND SHUTOUT
SUPPORT CONTRACT SCHMEISS
(SEALED —) TICKET
BIDDING AUCTION BIDDANCE
DIRECTIVE
BIDE FACE STAY WAIT ABIDE AWAIT
DWELL TARRY WATCH ENDURE
REMAIN SUFFER SOJOURN
CONTINUE TOLERATE
BIDENS CUCKOLD MANZANILLA
BIDET SITZBAD INSESSION
BIDRI VIDRY BIDDERY TUTENAG
BIER BEAR PYRE FRAME GRAVE
HANDY HORSE TABUT COFFIN
HEARSE LITTER SUPPORT
FERETORY FERETRUM
BIFURCATION WYE FORK SPLIT
BRANCH CROTCH FORKING DIVISION
DICHOTOMY
BIG FAT BARO BOLD HUGE MUCH
VAST BULKY CHIEF GAUCY GRAND
GREAT GROSS HUSKY LARGE
GAUCIE MIGHTY BIGGISH BUMPING
EMINENT HUMMING LEADING
MASSIVE POMPOUS UPRIGHT
VIOLENT BOASTFUL BOUNCING
ENORMOUS GENEROUS GIGANTIC
IMPOSING PLUMPING PREGNANT
SLAPPING SWANKING SWAPPING
THUMPING
(— WITH YOUNG) FULL GRAVID
(MARVELOUSLY —) TREMENDOUS
BIGHORN ARGAL AOUDAD ARGALI
CIMARRON
BIGHT BAY BEND BITE COIL GULF

LOOP ROVE ANGLE CURVE INLET
NOOSE CORNER HOLLOW POCKET
BIGOT CAFARD ZEALOT FANATIC
MUMPSIMUS
BIGOTED BIASED NARROW
HIDEBOUND ILLIBERAL SECTARIAN
BIGOTRY INTOLERANCE
BIGROOT MANROOT BITTERROOT
BIG SHOT MUCKAMUCK
BIG SKY COUNTRY MONTANA
BILE BOIL GALL HUMP VENOM
CHOLER GROWTH ATRABILE
BILGE PUMP SCUM BOUGE BULGE
BILLAGE THURROCK
BILIMBI CAMIAS KAMIAS CUCUMBER
BILINGUAL DIGLOT
BILIOUS GALLISH
BILIOUSNESS LIVER CHOLER
BILK DO GYP BALK HOAX CHEAT
COZEN TRICK DELUDE FLEECE
SWEDGE DECEIVE DEFRAUD
SWINDLE
BILL ACT DUN GET LAW NEB NIB TAB
BEAK CHIT CLAP GETT KITE NOTE
PECK SHOT CHECK ENTRY LIBEL
SCORE CARESS CHARGE DOCKET
INDICT LAWING PECKER PICKAX
POSTER STRIKE DERTRUM INVOICE
LAMPOON MATTOCK PLACARD
PROGRAM REMANET STATUTE
BILLHOOK DOCUMENT HEADLAND
INNOCENT PETITION TREASURY
(— OF ANCHOR) PEE PEAK
(— OF COMPLAINT) QUERELA
(— OF CREDIT) ANGEL
(— OF DIVORCE) GET GETT
(— OF EXCHANGE) SOLA HUNDI
DEVISE
(— OF FARE) MENU CARTE
(— OF PARCELS) FACTURE
(10-DOLLAR —) TEN TENNER
SAWBUCK
(100-DOLLAR —) CENTURY
(2-DOLLAR —) DEUCE
(5-DOLLAR —) FIN VEE FIVE FIVER
(COUNTERFEIT —S) STIFF
(DOLLAR —) BUCK SPOT SINGLE
FROGSKIN
(REVOLUTIONARY —) ASSIGNAT
BILLET BAR GAD HUT LAY LOG
LOOP NOTE PASS POST SPOT
BERTH ENROL HOUSE LODGE
ORDER SHIDE SPRAG STICK STRAP
BALLOT BULLET ENROLL HARBOR
LETTER LIBBET NOTICE TICKET
BEARING EPISTLE MISSIVE POLLACK
COALFISH DOCUMENT FIREWOOD
ORNAMENT POSITION QUARTERS
(— SOLDIERS) CESS
BILLET-DOUX CAPON
BILLETING LIVERY
BILLFISH GAR LONGJAWS SAILFISH
SPEARFISH
BILLHOOK BILL DHAW HOOK
PAWPAW SLASHER SNAGGER
SCIMITAR
BILLIARD BALL IVORY
BILLIARD CUE MACE MAST
(TIP OF —) LEATHER

BILLIARDS PILLS TRUCKS
(LAWN —) TROCO
BILLINGSGATE ABUSE SLAPDASH
BILLION MILLIARD
BILLON BAIOC VELLON BAJOCCO
BILLOW SEA BLOW WAVE BULGE
CLOUD FLOAT SURGE SWELL
RESACA RIPPLE ROLLER WALLOW
BREAKER UNDULATE
BILLY CAW CHAP CLUB GOAT MACE
MATE BATON FANNY NEDDY
CUDGEL FANNIE FELLOW BROTHER
COMRADE BILLIKIN BILLYCAN
BLUDGEON JACKSHAY BLACKJACK
TRUNCHEON
BIMAH ALMEMAR ALMEMOR
BIN ARK BOX CUB GUM BING BONE
CART CRIB VINA FRAME HUTCH
KENCH PUNGI STALL STORE WAGON
BASKET BUNKER GARNER HAMPER
MANGER POCKET TROUGH WITHIN
BLEACHER
(— FOR CEMENT) SILO
(— FOR FISH) KENCH
(— FOR GRAIN) ARK
BINARY HYDRIDE
BINATE DUAL DOUBLE PAIRED
COUPLED TWOFOLD GEMINATE
BINAURAL DIOTIC
BIND JAM LAP TIE WAP EARL FAST
FRAP GIRD GYVE HOLD HOOP KNIT
KNOT LASH MAIL NAIL TAPE YERK
BRACE CADGE CHAIN CINCH EDDER
GIRTH SNAKE STICK STRAP TRUSS
ATTACH BUNDLE COMMIT EMBIND
ENGAGE FETTER FREEZE GARTER
GIRDLE LIGATE OBLIGE STRAIN
SWATHE TETHER WRITHE ARTICLE
ASTRAIN BANDAGE CONFINE
EMBOUND ENCHAIN GRAPPLE
SHACKLE SWADDLE ASTRINGE
CONCLUDE FLIGHTER HANDFAST
INNODATE LIGATURE OBLIGATE
RESTRAIN
(— A FALCON) MAIL
(— BY LEASE) THIRL
(— BY PLEDGE) GAGE SWEAR
(— IN BUNDLE) KID BAVIN
(— INTO SHEAVES) GAVEL THRAVE
(— ONESELF) ADHERE
(— TO SECRECY) TILE
(— TOGETHER) LIME FAGOT SEIZE
CEMENT FAGGOT ASTRINGE
RELIGATE
(— UP) KILT BAVIN TRUSS UPBAND
ASTRICT REVOLVE
(— WITH THREAD) OOP
BINDER BEAM BOND BOND CORD
ROPE BALER COVER FRAME LEVER
FILLET FOLDER GIRDER HEADER
LIGNIN TARMAC HAYBAND
BONDSTONE BOOKMAKER
BINDING TAG BAND CORD GARD
HARD LEAR ROPE TAPE YAPP
COVER VALID CADDIS EDGING
RIBBON BOUNDEN CADDICE
GALLOON LAPPING MOUSING
WEBBING FAITHFUL LIGATIVE
LIGATORY STRINGENT

(— FAST) IRON
(— OF BOOK) FACE
(— OF GOLD) BISSET
(— ON DRESS) FENT
BINDWEED BINE WIRE CREEPER
TIEVINE BEARBIND BEARBINE
BELLBINE BINEWEED CORNBINE
HELLWEED MILKMAID WOODBINE
WITHYWIND
BINE WIRE
BINGE BAT BOW HIT BLOW BUST
SOAK BEANO PARTY SOUSE SPRAY
SPREE CRINGE BLOWOFF
CAROUSAL
BINGO KENO BEANO LOTTO BRANDY
SCREENO
BINNACLE PYX BITTACLE
BINOCULARS GLASS
BINOMIAL DIONYM BINOMEN
BIOGEOGRAPHY CHOROLOGY
BIOGRAPHER PLUTARCH
BIOGRAPHY BIO LIFE VITA MEMOIR
ACCOUNT HISTORY RECOUNT
(— OF SAINTS) HAGIOGRAPHA
HAGIOGRAPHY
BIOPHORE BIOGEN PLASOME
BIOPLAST MICELLA MICELLE
BIOTITE MICA ANOMITE MEROXENE
BIOTOPE STATION
BIPED DIPODE HINDQUARTERS
BIRCH COW BIRK CANE FLOG WHIP
ALDER ALNUS CANOE SWISH
BETULA BIRKEN TAWHAI HICKORY
BIRD ANI DAW DOG JAY NUN PIE TIT
COOT CROW DOVE FOWL IBIS JACK
KAGU KITE KNOT LARK QUIT RUFF
TERN TODY WING WREN BAKER
BRANT CHUCK CLEAR COVEY
EGRET FINCH FLIER FLYER GOOSE
HOBBY JUNCO LARID LIVER PEWEE
PEWIT RAVEN ROBIN SNIPE STILT
SWIFT TEREK TURCO TWITE VIREO
BULBUL DICKEY DIPPER DRIVER
DRONGO DUCKER DUNLIN FALCON
GROUSE GUINEA HOOPOE HOOTER
JACANA JAEGER LINNET MARTEN
MOCKER NESTER ORIOLE OSCINE
PHOEBE PLOVER SHRIKE SILVAN
SINGER SITTER SYLVAN THRUSH
TROGON TURNIX VERDIN WAYBUG
YAWPER ANTBIRD BABBLER
BLUEJAY BUNTING BUSTARD
BUZZARD CATBIRD CHIRPER
FEATHER FLAPPER FLICKER
FLIGGER FLOPPER GRACKLE
HALCYON HORNERO HURGILA
INCOMER IRRISOR JACAMAR
JACKDAW KINGLET MINIVET
MOULTER ORTOLAN PEACOCK
PERCHER QUILLER REDWING
SCRAPER SKINNER SKYLARK
SPARROW SUNBIRD SWALLOW
TANAGER TINAMOU TITLARK
TOMFOOL WARBLER WAXWING
ACCENTOR AIRPLANE AMADAVAT
ANNOTINE BLACKCAP BLACKNEB
BLUEBIRD BOATBILL BOBOLINK
BOBWHITE BUBBLING CAGELING
CARINATE COCKBIRD COCORICO

COTTINGA DREPANID FERNBIRD
FIREBIRD FIRETAIL GROSBEAK
GRUIFORM IBISBILL JUVENILE
KILLDEER KINGBIRD LOBEFOOT
OXPECKER PHEASANT PLUMIPED
POORWILL PREACHER REDSTART
SALTATOR SONGBIRD STARLING
SURFBIRD SWAMPHEN TAPACOLO
THRASHER THROSTLE TITMOUSE
TREMBLER UMBRETTE WHINCHAT
WOODCHAT WOODCOCK YEARBIRD
(— OF BRILLIANT PLUMAGE) TODY
JALAP ORIOLE TROGON JACAMAR
KIROMBO MINIVET TANAGER
(— OF INDIA) BAYA KALA SHAMA
(— OF OMEN) WAYBIRD
(— OF PREY) OWL HAWK KITE
EAGLE ELANT GLEAD GLEDE STOOP
EAGLET ELANET BUZZARD
GOSHAWK STOOPER VULTURE
(AFRICAN —) TAHA QUELEA
TOURACO UMBRETTE NAPECREST
(AUSTRALIAN —) EMU ROA LORY
ARARA LEIPOA BOOBOOK BUSTARD
FIGBIRD WAYBUNG BELLBIRD
LORIKEET LYREBIRD MANUCODE
(BIG-BEAKED —) BECARD HORNBILL
(CRESTED —) KAGU COPPY
HOATZIN TOPKNOT
(CROCODILE —) TROCHIL
(DECOY —) CALL STOOL
(DIVING —) AUK LOON GREBE
DOPPER DUCKER GRAYLING
PLUNGEON
(EUROPEAN —) ANI DAW MEW QUA
CIRL DARR KITE MALL MORO QUIS
ROOK STAG WHIM YITE AMSEL
BOONK GLEDE MAVIS MERLE OUSEL
OUZEL SACER SAKER SERIN TARIN
TEREK TERIN WHAUP AVOCET
COCKOO CUSHAT GAYLAG GODWIT
MARTEN MERLIN MISSEL REDCAP
WHEWER WINDLE WINNEL WRANNY
BITTERN BUSTARD HAYBIRD
KESTREL MOTACIL ORTOLAN
SAKERET STARNEL WHISKEY
WINNARD WITWALL BARGOOSE
CHEPSTER DOTTEREL GARGANEY
REDSTART WHEATEAR WHEYBIRD
WHIMBREL WRANNOCK YOLDRING
(EXTINCT —) MOA DODO JIBI KIWI
MAMO RUKH OFFBIRD
(FABULOUS —) ROC HALCYON
OOFBIRD
(FEMALE —) HEN JENNY
(FICTITIOUS —) JAYHAWK PHOENIX
(FISH-CATCHING —) OSPREY
CRABIER
(FLEDGLING —) SQUAB
(FLIGHTLESS —) EMU GOR MOA
DODO EYAS GORB GULL KAGU KIWI
CALLOW GORLIN APTERYX GORLING
NESTLER OSTRICH PENGUIN
BUBBLING NESTLING
(FRIGATE —) IOA IWA
(FRUIT-EATING —) COLY
(GALLOWS —) HEMPY HEMPIE
(GAME —) QUAIL SNIPE COLIMA
GROUSE INCOME FLAPPER INCOMER

(HAWAIIAN —) IO OO AVA IOA IWA
OOA IIWI JIBI KOAE MAMO MOHO
OMAO OOAA KAMAO PALILA
(HORN-HEADED —) KAMICHI
(INJURED —) CRIPPLE
(LARGEST —) LAMMERGEIER
(MADAGASCAR —) KIROMBO
(MECHANICAL —) ORTHOPTER
(MYTHICAL —) FUM ROC GANZA
SIMURG SIMURGH
(NEW ZEALAND —) KEA MOA OII
ROA HUIA KAKA KIWI KOKO KUKU
KULU PEHO RURU TITI WEKA
KAKAPO KOKAKO KUKUPA APTERYX
KORIMAKO MOREPORK NOTORNIS
(PASSERINE —) QUIT FINCH
SPARROW STARNEL SWALLOW
SYLVIID DREPANID FALCONET
FERNBIRD GRALLINA JACKBIRD
(PERTAINING TO —S) OSCINE
(RAPACIOUS —) JAEGER
(RASORIAL —) SCRATCHER
(RUNNING —) COURSER
(SAMOAN —) IAO
(SEA —) AUK ERN ERNE GONY
GULL SMEW TERN EIDER SOLAN
FULMAR GANNET HAGDON OSPREY
PETREL PUFFIN PELICAN SEAFOWL
MURRELET
(SHORE —) REE RAIL SORA SNIPE
STILT WADER AVOCET CURLEW
PLOVER WILLET WRYBILL
(SHORT-TAILED —) BREVE
(SINGING —) LARK WREN PIPIT
ROBIN VEERY VIREO CANARY
LINNET MOCKER ORIOLE OSCINE
SINGER THRUSH WARBLER
FAUVETTE REDSTART
(SMALL —) TIT TODY WREN DICKY
PEGGY PIPIT TYDIE VIREO DICKEY
LINNET SISKIN TOMTIT CREEPER
SPARROW TITLARK COCORICO
GNATSNAP STARLING WHEATEAR
(SOUTH AMERICAN —) GUAN MINA
MYNA RARA TOCA BAKER CHAJA
JOPIN TURCO BARBET BECARD
CHUNGA TOUCAN CARIAMA OILBIRD
BELLBIRD BOATBILL CARACARA
GUACHARO HOACTZIN PUFFBIRD
SCREAMER TAPACOLO TAPACULO
TERUTERO
(STYLIZED —) DISTELFINK
(TROPICAL —) ANI GUAN KOAE
TODY BOS'N BOSUN JALAP BARBET
BECARD MOTMOT TROGON
JACAMAR WIGTAIL LONGTAIL
SALTATOR
(WADING —) HERN IBIS RAIL SORA
CRANE HERON SNIPE STILT STORK
AVOCET GODWIT JACANA BOATBILL
FLAMINGO SHOEBILL SHOEBIRD
(WILD —S) GALLINAE
(YOUNG —) EYA GULL PIPER
FLAPPER NESTLER BIRDIKIN
NESTLING
(PL.) AVIFAUNA POLYMYODI
PRAECOCES
BIRD BOLT BURBOLT QUARREL
BIRD CAGE AVIARY PINJRA VOLARY

VOLERY PADDOCK
BIRDCATCHER FOWLER
BIRD CHERRY DOGWOOD
EGGBERRY HACKWOOD HAGBERRY
BIRDLIFE ORNIS
BIRDLIME GLUE LIME BELIME
VISCUM BIRDGLUE
BIRD OF PARADISE APUS
MANUCODE RIFLEBIRD
BIRD'S-FOOT FOWLFOOT
SERRADELLA
BIRD'S KNEE SUFFRAGO
BIRD'S MANTLE STRAGULUM
BIRI BIDI
BIRTH KIN BEAR FALL BLOOD
BURDEN GENTRY ORIGIN BEARING
BORNING DESCENT GENESIS
LINEAGE DELIVERY GENITURE
NASCENCY NATALITY NATIVITY
(FALSE —) SOOTERKIN
(GENTLE —) GENTILITY
(HONORABLE —) BLOOD
(OF LOW —) CRESTLESS
(OF NOBLE —) CORONETED
BIRTHMARK MOLE IMAGE NAEVE
NEVUS BLEMISH SPILOMA
SIGNATURE
BIRTHRATE NATALITY FERTILITY
BIRTHRIGHT KIND HERITAGE
BIRTHROOT BATHROOT BATHWORT
DEATHROOT DISHCLOTH
SQUAWROOT
BIRTHWORT GUACO ASARUM
BATHROOT
BISAYAN AKLAN CEBUAN AKLANON
CEBUANO
BISCUIT BUN NUT BAKE ROLL RUSK
SNAP WOOD BREAD SCONE WAFER
BISQUE COOKIE DODGER MUFFIN
SIMNEL CRACKER GALETTE PENTILE
PRETZEL RATAFIA RATIFIA
CRACKNEL HARDTACK ZWIEBACK
(BROKEN —S) DUNDERFUNK
(COLOR —) DOE PAWNEE
BISECT FORK CROSS HALVE SPLIT
CLEAVE DIVIDE MIDDLE SEPARATE
BISECTION MEDIATION
BISHOP EP ABBA EPUS LAWN PAPA
POPE ANGEL DENIS ARCHER
BUSTLE DESPOT EPARCH EXARCH
MAGPIE PRESUL PRIEST ROCHET
ROCKAT PONTIFF PRELATE PRIMATE
TULCHAN ANTISTES DIOCESAN
DIRECTOR ORDINARY OVERSEER
PONTIFEX
(— AND MARTYR) EM
(CHESS —) ALFIN ALPHYN ARCHER
BISHOP'S-WEED AMMI AMMEOS
KHELLA WILLIAM BOLEWORT
BULLWORT GOUTWEED TOOTHPICK
BISKOP BRUSHER STEENBRAS
BISMARK KRAPFE KRAPFEN
BISMUTH WISMUTH TINGLASS
BISON BUGLE BOVINE MITHAN
WISENT AUROCHS BONASUS
BUFFALO
BISTORT PATIENCE ADDERWORT
ASTROLOGE SNAKEWEED
SNAKEWORT

BISTRO BAR CAFE TAVERN
WINESHOP ESTAMINET NIGHTCLUB
BIT ACE FID FIP GAG JOT NIP ORT
PIP WEE ATOM BITE BITT CHIP
CROP CURB DITE DOIT DRIB FLAW
FOOD GRUE HAET HATE HOOT IOTA
ITEM LEVY MITE MOTE PART SLUT
SNAP SNIP SPOT TOOL WHIT AUGER
BLADE CHECK CRUMB DRILL GROAT
PATCH PEZZO PIECE POINT SCRAP
SHRED SMACK SNACK SPECK STEEK
TASTE THRUM WIGHT BITTIE BRIDLE
CANNON EATING MORSEL PELHAM
PICKLE SIPPET SMIDGE SPLICE
STITCH STIVER THOGHT TITTLE
TRIFLE BRADOON BRIDOON
CHILENO GLIMMER MORCEAU
PALLION PORTION SCATCHE
SMIDGEN SMIDGIN SMIGEON
SNAFFLE TRANEEN FISHTAIL
FRACTION FRAGMENT QUANTITY
SMITCHIN TWOPENNY
(— OF GOSSIP) HEARING
(— OF INFORMATION) GRIFF
GRIFFIN WRINKLE
(— OF KEY) WEB
(— OF LAND) CROOK
(— OF METAL) FLITTER
(— OF TOAST) SNIPPET
(— TO EAT) MUNGEY
(—S AND PIECES) GUBBINS
GUBBINGS
(—S OF COKE) BREEZE
(—S OF WRITING) EXCERPTA
(ONE-QUARTER —) GILL
(CUTTING —) CHASER
(DRILL —) CROWN
(FANCIFUL —) FLAM
(FIPPENY —) SIXPENCE
(FLORID —) FLOURISH
(HORSE'S —) KEVEL SNODE
CANNON PELHAM SCATCH SNAFFLE
BASTONET
(LEAST —) FIG JOT RAP HANG LICK
GHOST GROAT RIZZOM STITCH
(LITTLE —) PICK TOUCH BITTOCK
REMNANT SOUPCON
(SMALL —) BLEB GLIM SPUNK
(SMALL —S) SMATTER
(TINY —) SPECK DRIBBLE SCRINCH
TODDICK
(PL.) SMITHERS SMITHEREENS
BITCH DO GYP BICK LAMP SLUT
BRACH BROOD CHEAT GROUSE
COMPLAIN
BITE BIT CUT EAT JAW NIP BAIT
CHAM CHEW ETCH FOOD GASH
GNAP GNAW HOLD KNAP MEAL RIVE
SNAP TAKE CHACK CHAMM CHAMP
CHEAT GNASH PINCH SEIZE SMART
SNACK STING TOOTH TRICK
CRUNCH MORSEL NIBBLE PIERCE
SAVAGE BUGBITE CHEATER
CORRODE FORBITE IMPRESS
MORSURE MUNCHET PARTAKE
SHARPER SLANDER
(— AT) HIT
(— GREEDILY) HANCH
(— REPEATEDLY) CHAMP

BITING BIT HOT ACID HOAR KEEN
ACRID NIPPY QUICK SHARP SNELL
BITTER RODENT SEVERE SHREWD
STINGY TEETHY TWEAKY CAUSTIC
CUTTING MORDANT MORSURE
NIPPING PUNGENT SUBACID
DRILLING INCISIVE POIGNANT
SCALDING SCATHING STINGING
BITIS ECHIDNA
BITO BALM HAJILIJ
BITT BLOCK KNIGHT BOLLARD
(PL.) RANGEHEADS
BITTER AWA GAL ACID ACRE ASIM
BASK KEEN MARA RUDE SALT SORE
SOUR TART ACERB ACRID AMARA
ASPER BLEAK HARSH IRATE SHARP
BITING PICRIC SEVERE AUSTERE
CAUSTIC CRABBED CUTTING
FERVENT GALLING GALLISH PAINFUL
PUNGENT SATIRIC POIGNANT
STINGING SUBAMARE VIRULENT
BITTER APPLE COLOCYNTH
BITTER BIT SMALLPOX
BITTERBUSH SNAKEROOT
BITTER CLOVER YELLOWTOP
BITTERLY SOUR FELLY BITTER
ROUNDLY CURSEDLY
BITTERN BUMP SOCO BOONK BUTOR
HERON BITORE BUMBLE BUMMLE
BUTTAL KAKKAK BLITTER BUMMLER
ERICIUS DUNKADOO GRUIFORM
LONGNECK
(FLOCK OF —) SEDGE SIEGE
BITTERNESS RUE ACOR BILE FELL
GALL ATTER ENMITY MALICE
RANCOR AMARITY ACERBITY
ACRIDITY ACRIMONY FERVENCY
SEVERITY WORMWOOD
(EXTREME —) VIRULENCE
(WITH —) AMAREVOLE
BITTER PIT STIPPEN
BITTERROOT LEWISIA
TOBACCOROOT
BITTERS AMER
BITTER SPAR DOLOMITE
BITTERSWEET FELLEN DOGWOOD
LOBSTER SOLANUM WAXWORK
DULCAMARA FELONWOOD
FELONWORT FEVERTWIG
WITHYWIND WOLFBERRY
BITTER VETCH ERS
BITTERWEED RAGWEED
HORSEWEED
BITTERWORT FELWORT DANDELION
BITUMEN TAR CONGO PITCH SLIME
ASPHALT CARBENE ALKITRAN
ALCHITRAN ELATERITE
BIVALVE HEN CLAM SPAT PINNA
COCKLE DIATOM MUSSEL OYSTER
MOLLUSK NUCULID PANDORA
SCALLOP TOHEROA
BIVOUAC CAMP ETAPE WATCH
ENCAMP SHELTER
BIZARRE ODD ANTIC DEDAL OUTRE
QUEER QUAINT ANTICAL CURIOUS
FANCIFUL ECCENTRIC FANTASTIC
GROTESQUE
BLAB LAB CHAT BLART BLATE
CHEEP CLACK PEACH BABBLE

BETRAY GOSSIP REVEAL SQUEAL TATTLE BLABBER CHATTER CLATTER

BLACK DHU JET WAN CALO CROW DARK EBON FOUL INKY NOIR PIKY SOOT BUGLE COLLY DUSKY MURKY NEGRO NOIRE RAVEN SABLE SOOTY TARRY THICK ATROUS BRUNET DISMAL ETHIOP GLOOMY MURREY PITCHY SULLEN ABAISER AFRICAN BLACKEN DIAMOND MELANIC NEGRITO NIGRINE NIGROUS PICEOUS SWARTHY UNCLEAN MOURNFUL
(— **AND BLUE**) LIVID
(— **OUT**) CONK
(**BONE** —) SPODIUM
(**BROWNISH** —) LAVA
(**GREENISH** —) CORBEAU
(**IVORY** —) ABAISER
(**LIGHT-SKINNED** —) BROWN
(**RATHER** —) DUSKISH
(**VIOLET** —) CROW

BLACKAMOOR BLECK NEGRO MORIAN NEGRESS ETHIOPIAN

BLACK ASH HOOPWOOD

BLACKBALL PIP PILL BALLOT EXCLUDE HEEBALL OSTRACIZE

BLACK BASS HURON TROUT ACHIGAN GROWLER OCHIGAN

BLACKBERRY AGAWAM LAWTON DEWBERRY MULBERRY ROSACEAN
(— **BUSH**) MORE

BLACKBIRD ANI DAW PIE CROW AMSEL COLLY MERLE OUSEL OUZEL RAVEN BLACKY COLLEY MAIZER BLACKIE COWBIRD GRACKLE JACKDAW REDWING WOOFELL TROOPIAL

BLACKBOARD CHALKBOARD GREENBOARD

BLACKBREAM TARWHINE

BLACK-BROWED GLOOMY

BLACK BRYONY LILY LILIUM OXBERRY BINDWEED MANDRAKE

BLACK BUCK SASIN

BLACKCAP GULL JACK PEGGY HAYBIRD WARBLER MOCKBIRD TITMOUSE JACKSTRAW RASPBERRY

BLACKDAMP STYTH STYTHE CHOKEDAMP

BLACKDRINK YAPON YAUPON

BLACKEN INK TAR CHAR CORK SOIL SOOT BLECK CLOUD COLLY JAPAN SMOKE SULLY BEFOUL BLATCH DARKEN DEFAME MALIGN SMEETH SMIRCH VILIFY ASPERSE BENEGRO NIGRIFY SLANDER SMOLDER TRADUCE BESMIRCH

BLACKENED REECHY

BLACKEYE COWPEA

BLACKFELLOW BLACKBOY YAMMADJI

BLACKFIN CISCO SESIS

BLACKFISH GRIND TAUTOG BORLASE DOGFISH GRAMPUS POTHEAD HARDHEAD

BLACKFLY GNAT SIMULIID

BLACKFOOT BLOOD KAINAH PIEGAN SIKSIKA SIHASAPA

BLACK GROUPER MERO AGUAJI WARSAW GARRUPA

BLACKGUARD SHAG BLECK CATSO GAMIN GUARD SNUFF SWEEP ROTTER LADRONE VAGRANT BLAGGARD CRIMINAL LARRIKIN VAGABOND SCOUNDREL

BLACK GUILLEMOT CUTTY TYSTE SCRABE DOVEKEY DOVEKIE SCRABER PUFFINET

BLACK GUM TUPELO HORNPIPE STINKWOOD

BLACK HAW SLOE BOOTS ALISIER STAGBUSH VIBURNUM

BLACKHEAD COMEDO

BLACK HOREHOUND HENBIT ARCHANGEL

BLACK HORSE SUCKER SUCKEREL

BLACKING LINK BLECK BLATCH BLEACH ATRAMENT

BLACK IRONWOOD AXMASTER AXEMASTER

BLACKISH DUSKY MOREL SWART BLACKY

BLACKJACK OAK SAP CLUB COSH DUCK FLAG JACK BETLE BILLY JERKIN NATURAL BLUDGEON

BLACKLEG LEG FIRE SCAB SNOB ANTHRAX GAMBLER JACKLEG APOSTATE BLACKNEB BLACKNOB SWINDLER KNOBSTICK

BLACK LETTER GOTHIC

BLACKLY SABLY

BLACK MAGIC DIABLERIE

BLACKMAIL BRIBE CHOUT COERCE EXTORT TRIBUTE CHANTAGE

BLACKMAILER GHOUL BRIBER LEECHER

BLACK MANGROVE COURIDA

BLACK MEDIC HOP TREFOIL NONESUCH SHAMROCK

BLACKNESS GRIME DARKNESS NIGRITUDE

BLACK NIGHTSHADE MOREL DUSCLE SOLANUM BLUEBERRY MOONSHADE TROMPILLO

BLACK OLIVE OXHORN

BLACK PEPPER PIMENTA

BLACK PINE MATAI

BLACK POISON WALNUT

BLACK RHINOCEROS BORELE KEITLOA UPEYGAN

BLACK SALLY SALLEE MUZZLEWOOD

BLACK SANICLE LUNGWORT MASTERWORT

BLACK SHANK LANAS

BLACK SKIMMER CUTWATER SHEARBILL

BLACKSMITH GOW SMUG LOHAR SHOER SMITH PLOVER SMITHY VULCAN BROOKIE FARRIER STRIKER BURNEWIN IRONSMITH

BLACKSNAKE WHIP QUIRT RACER ELAPID RUNNER COLUBRID

BLACK SPECK DARTROSE

BLACK SPURGE FLUXWEED

BLACKTAIL DASSY DASSIE

BLACK TERN DARR STARN

BLACKTHORN HAW SLOE SNAG SCROG GRIBBLE SLOEBUSH SLOETREE SNAGBUSH

BLACK-VARNISH TREE THEETSEE

BLACK VULTURE URUBU CORBIE ZOPILOTE

BLACK WALNUT NOGAL

BLACKWATER STATE NEBRASKA

BLACK WIDOW POKOMOO

BLACK WOLF KARAKURT

BLACKWOOD BITI LIGHTWOOD

BLACKWORT COMFREY

BLADDER SAC VES VESICA AMPULLA BLATHER BLISTER INFLATE UROCYST UTRICLE VESICLE
(**AIR** —) POKE SWIM SOUND SINGALLY

BLADDER-AND-STRING BUMBASS

BLADDER CAMPION BEHN BEHEN SILENE COWBELL SNAPPER RATTLEBOX

BLADDER KETMIE MODESTY

BLADDERNUT BAGNUT

BLADDERWORT POPWEED

BLADDER WRACK CUTWEED KELPWARE

BLADE BIT FIN FOP OAR SAW WEB BLOW BONE BOWL EDGE FLAG HEAD LEAF LIMB TANG WEAK BLOOD BRAND DANDY FLUKE GRAIN GUIDE KNIFE LANCE SHEAR SPARK SPEAR SPIRE SWORD BLUNGE BUCKET BUSTER CUTTER DOCTOR FOIBLE HEDDLE LAMINA PAGINA RIPPER ROARER SCYTHE SICKLE TOLEDO BAYONET CHIPPER GALLANT POLESAW SCALPEL SCAPULA SCRAPER SPINNER MOLDBOARD PROPELLER
(— **OF FAN**) VANE
(— **OF GRASS**) PILE CHIRE SPEAR SPIRE STRAP TRANEEN
(— **OF KNIFE**) TANG GRAIN
(— **OF LEAF**) LIMB LAMINA
(— **OF MORION**) COMB
(— **OF OAR**) PALM PELL WASH
(— **OF SCISSORS**) BILL
(— **OF YOUNG GRAIN**) SORAGE
(**CULTIVATOR** —) SWEEP DUCKFOOT
(**SKATE** —) RUNNER
(**SURGICAL** —) LEUCOTOME

BLAFFERT PLAPPERT

BLAIN RUBY SORE BULLA BLISTER INFLAME PUSTULE

BLAKE MCKAY

BLAMABLE FAULTY CULPABLE

BLAME CALL CHOP HURT LACK ONUS SAKE SPOT TWIT WITE CHIDE FAULT GUILT ODIUM PINCH SHEND SNAPE SWICK SWIKE TOUCH WHITE ACCUSE ATTASK BUMBLE BURDEN CHARGE DIRDUM PLIGHT REBUKE REVILE SCANCE ASCRIBE CENSURE CONDEMN CULPATE OBLOQUY REPROOF REPROVE SLANDER UPBRAID WITHNIM REPROACH

BLAMED BLINDING BLISTERING

BLAMELESS ENTIRE PERFECT

INNOCENT SACKLESS SPOTLESS
WITELESS RIGHTEOUS
BLAMEWORTHY GUILTY CRIMINAL
CULPABLE REPROBATE
BLANCH FADE PALE BLENK CHALK
SCALD WHITE APPALL ARGENT
BIANCA BLEACH BLENCH FALLOW
WHITEN ETIOLATE
BLANCHED ASHEN ETIOLATE
BLOODLESS COLORLESS
BLANCMANGE FLUMMERY
BLAND COLD KIND MILD OILY OPEN
SOFT SLEEK SUAVE BENIGN BREEZY
GENIAL GENTLE SMOOTH URBANE
AFFABLE AMIABLE LENIENT
FAVONIAN GRACIOUS UNCTUOUS
BLANDISH COAX CHARM ALLURE
BLANCH CAJOLE FONDLE SMOOTH
FLATTER WHEEDLE HONEYFUG
BLANDLY CREAMILY
BLANK BARE BURR FLAN FORM
SHOT VOID ANNUL BLIND BREAK
CHASM CLEAN EMPTY FALSE RANGE
SPACE WASTE WHITE COUPON
VACANT ANTIQUE BRINDLE
NONPLUS UNMIXED VACUOUS
UNFILLED
BLANKED BLIND
BLANKET RUG BROT MAUD WRAP
BLUEY COTTA COVER CUMLY LAYER
MANTA PATTU QUILT SHEET SUGAN
THROW AFGHAN COOLER CUMBLY
GLOBAL KAMBAL MANTLE PALLET
PONCHO PUTTOO SERAPE SOOGAN
STIFLE STROUD TILPAH CHIRIPA
DOUBLER SMOTHER WHITTLE
COVERLET MACKINAW
(— A VESSEL) WRONG
(— WITH BOMBS) SATURATE
(BUSHMAN'S —) BLUEY
(QUILTED —) BROT
(SADDLE —) CORONA
BLANKETING DUFFEL DUFFLE
BLANKNESS VACUITY NEGATION
BLARE PEAL BLEAR BLART BLAST
NOISE BLAZON SCREAM FANFARE
TANTARA TRUMPET
BLARNEY CON BUTTER FLATTER
WHEEDLE
BLASPHEME ABUSE CURSE DEFAME
REVILE PROFANE
BLASPHEMOUS BAD RIBALD
IMPIOUS PROFANE
BLASPHEMY CALUMNY CURSING
IMPIETY ANATHEMA SWEARING
BLAST BUB NIP WAP BANG BLOW
FRAP GALE GUST RUIN RUST SHOT
TOOT WIND BLAME BLIST BLORE
SPLIT STUNT ATTACK BLIGHT
BUGGER FORBID NIDDER NITHER
REBUFF VOLLEY WITHER BLUSTER
DESPOIL EXPLODE SHATTER
SHRIVEL DYNAMITE OUTBURST
PROCLAIM WHIRLPUFF
(— OF WIND) GUST RISE PERRY
PIRRIE VENTOSITY
(— ON HORN) TOOT PRYSE
(— WITH COLD) SNEAP
(FURIOUS —) SNIFTER

BLASTED BLAME BLAMED BLIGHTED
BLINDING BLINKING
BLASTER FROSTER SHOOTER
SHOTMAN
BLASTING SHOOTING STELLATION
(— METHOD) MUDCAP
BLASTULA PLACULA PLANULA
PLANULAN
BLATANT GLIB LOUD BRASH GROSS
NOISY SILLY VOCAL COARSE
GARISH TONANT VULGAR BRAWLING
STRIDENT
BLATHER STIR BLEAT BABBLE
WAFFLE BLITHER PRATTLE
NONSENSE
BLAUBOK ETAAC BLUEBUCK
BLAZE LOW BURN FIRE GLOW HACK
LEAM LOWE MARK SHOT SPOT
FLAME FLARE FLASH GLARE GLEAM
GLORY INGLE RATCH SHINE STARE
STEAM TORCH BLAZON BLEEZE
BONFIRE PIONEER SPLENDOR
(— OUT) FLAP
BLAZING AFIRE FIERY FLAMY LIGHT
FLAMING FLARING
BLAZING STAR LIATRIS GRUBROOT
SNAKEROOT
BLAZON DECK SHOW ADORN BLARE
BLAZE BOAST DEPICT SHIELD
DECLARE DISPLAY EXHIBIT PUBLISH
EMBLAZON INSCRIBE
BLAZONED ARMED BANNERED
BLEACH SUN WASH BLEAK CHALK
CROFT POACH BLANCH BLENCH
CHLORE PURIFY WHITEN DECOLOR
LIGHTEN BLONDINE ETIOLATE
PEROXIDE
(— PULP) POTCH
BLEACHER WHITSTER
BLEACHERS SCAFFOLD
BLEAK DIM RAW BLAE BLAY COLD
DOUR GRAY PALE SPRAT STARK
SWALE ALBURN BITTER BLEACH
DISMAL DREARY FRIGID PALLID
CUTTING DESOLATE CHEERLESS
BLEAT BAA BLAT BLEA YARM BLART
BLATE BLATHER BLUSTER WHICKER
BLEATING BALANT
BLEB BLOB BULLA BUBBLE BLISTER
PUSTULE VESICLE SWELLING
BLEED FLUX MILK WEEP BLOOD
LEECH MULCT SWEAT SWINDLE
TEICHER
BLEEDER STICKER
BLEEDING BLOODY SANGLANT
BLEEDING HEART EARDROP
DICENTRA
BLEMISH MAR BLOT BLUR DENT
FLAW GALL LACK MAIM MARK MOIL
MOLE RIFT SAKE SCAR SLUR SPOT
TASH VICE WANT AMPER BLAME
BOTCH BRECK CLOUD CRACK
FAULT FLECK MULCT NAEVE SPECK
STAIN SULLY TACHE TAINT TOUCH
BLOTCH BREACH DEFAME DEFECT
IMPAIR INJURE MACULA MACULE
MAYHEM SMIRCH STIGMA BUBUKLE
CATFACE DEFAULT FAILING FISSURE
SUNSPOT

(— IN CLOTH) AMPER SULLY
(— IN PAPER) FISHEYE
BLEMISHED BAD WEMMY
BLENCH FOIL SHUN WILE AVOID
ELUDE EVADE QUAIL SHAKE SHIRK
TRICK BAFFLE BLANCH BLEACH
FLINCH RECOIL SHRINK DECEIVE
BLEND MIX RUN BLOT FADE FUSE
JOIN MELT MENG MOLD ADMIX
BLIND CREAM GRADE MERGE
MOULD SHADE SMEAR SPOIL STAIN
TINGE UNITE BLUNGE COMMIX
CRASIS DAZZLE MINGLE TEMPER
COMBINE CONFUSE CORRUPT
DECEIVE GRADATE MIXTURE
POLLUTE COALESCE CONCRETE
IMMINGLE TINCTURE
(— OF NOISES) CHARM
(— OF SHERRY) SOLERA
(— OF WINES) CUVEE
BLENDE JACK SPHALERITE
BLENDED FONDU FUSED MIXED
MERGED MINGLED CONFLATE
CONFLUENT
BLENDING FUSION HOTCHPOT
BLENNY GUNNEL SHANNY EELPOUT
JUGULAR KELPFISH SENORITA
WOLFFISH WRYMOUTH QUILLFISH
BLESBOK NUNNI BLESBUCK
BLESS KEEP SAIN WAVE ADORE
ANELE BENSH CROSS EXTOL FAVOR
GUARD THANK VISIT WOUND
CROUCH FAVOUR HALLOW PRAISE
THRASH APPROVE BEATIFY EMBLISS
GLORIFY PROTECT MACARIZE
PRESERVE SANCTIFY
BLESSED HOLY BLEST HAPPY SEELY
DIVINE JOYFUL SACRED SEELFUL
BENEDICT BHAGAVAT BLISSFUL
BLOOMING HALLOWED HEAVENLY
BLESSEDNESS BLISS FELICITY
BEATITUDE HAPPINESS
BLESSING BOON GIFT SAIN BLISS
DUKAN GRACE SORRA BARAKA
DUCHAN PRAISE BENISON DARSHAN
WORSHIP BERACHAH FELICITY
BEATITUDE
BLEU DE ROI SEVRES
BLIGHT NIP FIRE RUIN RUST SMUT
SOKA BLAST BRANT FROST SNEAP
MILDEW NITHER TAKING WITHER
DESTROY
BLIND BET POT ANTE BOMA DARK
DEAD DULL HIDE HOOD SEEL BISME
BLANK BLEND DUNCH SHADE STAKE
STALL WAGER AMBUSH BISSON
BLENDE DARKEN DAZZLE SCREEN
SECRET AIMLESS ANTIQUE
BANDAGE BATTERY BENIGHT
ECLIPSE EYELESS OBSCURE
PRETEXT RAYLESS SHUTTER
ABORTIVE ARTIFICE BAYARDLY
BLINDING EXCECATE HOODWINK
IGNORANT INVOLVED JALOUSIE
OUTSHINE PURBLIND UMBRELLA
VENETIAN
(— IN ONE EYE) PEED GLEED
GLEYD
(— MAN) MOLE

(HALF —) STARBLIND
(PL.) PERSIENNES
BLIND ALLEY LOKE STOP POCKET
IMPASSE
BLINDER FLAP HOOD BLIND BLUFF
LUNET WINKER BLINKER EYEFLAP
LUNETTE HOODWINK BLINDFOLD
BLINDFOLD MOP DARK BLINK BLUFF
SCARF MUFFLE BANDAGE BLINDER
OBSCURE ENCLOSER HEEDLESS
HOODWINK RECKLESS CONCEALED
BLINDING BISME BISSON
BLINDMAN'S BLUFF POST
HOODWINK
BLINDNESS BISSON CECITY
ABLEPSY ANOPSIA MEROPIA
ABLEPSIA DARKNESS IGNORANCE
(— TO TRUTH) AVIDYA AVIJJA
(COLOR —) ACHROBIA
(DAY —) HEMERALOPIA
(NIGHT —) NYCTALOPIA
(PARTIAL —) MEROPIA HEMIOPSIA
(RED-GREEN —) DALTONISM
(SNOW —) CHIONABLEPSIA
(STUDY OF —) TYPHLOLOGY
(TEMPORARY —) MOONBLINK
BLINDSTITCH FELL
BLINDWORM SLOW ORVET ANGUID
HAGWORM SLOWWORM
BLIND-YOUR-EYES GANGWA
ALIPATA
BLINK BAT PINK SHUN WINK BLUSH
CHEAT FLASH GLEAM SHINE TRICK
GLANCE IGNORE OBTUSE WAPPER
BLINTER CONDONE GLIMMER
GLIMPSE NEGLECT NICTATE
SPARKLE TWINKLE
BLINKER EYE BLINK BLUFF LIGHT
SIGNAL WINKER BLINDER FLASHER
GOGGLES COQUETTE HOODWINK
MACKEREL
BLINTZE BLIN BLINTZ PANCAKE
BLIP ECHO
BLISS JOY EDEN KAIF SEIL BLESS
GLORY ANANDA HEAVEN DELIGHT
ECSTASY GLADDEN RAPTURE
FELICITY GLADNESS PARADISE
PLEASURE
BLISSFUL HOLY SEELY BLITHE
BLESSED ELYSIAN UTOPIAN
BEATIFIED GLORIFIED
BLISTER BEAT BLEB BLOB BLOW
BOIL BURN LASH QUAT APTHA
BLAIN BLIBE BULGE BULLA TOPIC
VESIC APHTHA BUBBLE CUPOLA
SCORCH SOTTER TETTER BLADDER
BLUSTER SCALDER SKELLER
VESICLE VESICATE
BLITHE GAY GLAD BONNY BUXOM
HAPPY JOLLY MERRY BONNIE
JOVIAL JOYOUS LIVELY GAYSOME
JOCULAR WINSOME CHEERFUL
GLADSOME SPRIGHTLY
BLIZZARD BLOW GALE WIND BURAN
PURGA RETORT SNIFTER
SQUELCHER
(— STATE) SD SDAK
BLOAT BLOW BLAST BLOWN FLOAT
HOOVE HOVEN PUFFY SWELL

BOWDEN EXPAND TUMEFY DISTEND
FERMENT INFLATE
BLOATED FOZY BLOAT BROSY
CURED FOGGY HOVEN TUMID
GOTCHY SODDEN TURGID POMPOUS
REPLETE
BLOATER MOONEYE
BLOB LIP WEN BEAD BLEB BLOT
BOIL CLOT DAUB DROP GLOB GOUT
LUMP MARK MASS BUBBLE DALLOP
DOLLOP PIMPLE SPLASH BLEMISH
BLISTER BLOSSOM GLOBULE
PUSTULE SPLOTCH
BLOC RING BLOCK CABAL PARTY
UNION CLIQUE FACTION
BLOCK AME BAR COB COG DAM DIE
DOG FID HOB HUB JAM KEY NOG
ROW TOP VOL BALK BASE BEAR
BILK BLOC BUCK BUNT CAKE CLOG
CUBE DRUM FOIL FOUL FROG GLUT
HEAD JAMB LEAD MASK MASS
MOCK QUAR STAY STEP STOP TRIG
BAULK BRICK CHAIR CHECK CHEEK
CHUMP CLAMP CLEAT CLOSE
COVER DETER DOLLY DUMMY
EMBAR FLOAT HEART HORST
JUMBO NUDGE PARRY PATCH
SHAPE SPIKE SPOKE STOCK STUFF
STUMP ASSIZE DENTIL DOLLEY
DOMINO FIPPLE FORMER HAMPER
HINDER IMPEDE KIBOSH MONKEY
MUFFLE MUTULE OPPOSE OUTWIT
QUERRE RIPPER SADDLE SCOTCH
SNATCH SQUARE STREET STYMIE
TAPLET THWART TROLLY WAYLAY
BOLLOCK BOLSTER BUCKLER
CONDEMN DEADEYE ERRATIC
INHIBIT OUTLINE PREVENT QUADREL
RAMHEAD STONKER TRIGGER
TROLLEY BLOCKADE DEADHEAD
ELECTRET FOLLOWER KEYSTONE
MONOLITH OBSTACLE OBSTRUCT
STOPPAGE WITHSPAR
(— A WHEEL) SCOTE
(— AT SPAR END) STEEVE
(— FOR SKIDDING LOGS) BICYCLE
(— IN SPEAKING) STAMMER
(— OF COAL) JUD JUDD
(— OF EARTH'S CRUST) HORST
(— OF GRANITE) SET
(— OF ICE) SERAC
(— OF LAND) FORTY
(— OF SEATS) CUNEUS
(— OF TIMBER) BOLT JUGGLE
(— SUPPORTING MAST) STEP
(— UP) BAR DAM QUIRT CONDEMN
FORECLOSE
(— WITH HOLE IN IT) WAPP
EUPHROE
(— WITH PROJECTING CORE)
SETTLE
(—S OF STONE) DIMENSION
(ARCHITECTURAL —) DRUM STONE
DENTIL IMPOST MUTULE PLINTH
DOSSERET
(CHOPPING —) HACKLOG
(CLAY —) DRAWBAR
(FAULT —) MASSIF
(FELTED —) DAMPER

(FULCRUM —) GLUT
(FUSE —) CUTOUT
(IRON —) USE VOL BITT ANVIL
CHAIR
(LOGGING —) LEAD JUMBO
(NAUTICAL —) CHOCK HEART
STOCK SADDLE DEADEYE FAIRLEAD
(ORNAMENTAL —) BOSS
(PAVING —) SET CUBE SETT STONE
WHEELER
(PLASTER —) BATTER
(POLISHING —) BUFF FLOAT
(PRINTING —) CUT QUAD RISER
QUADRAT
(PULLEY —) CRAWL
(SANDSTONE —) SARSEN
(SQUARED —) MITCHEL
(STUMBLING —) HURTING
(TACKLE —) CALO TONGUE
(VAULTING —) BUCK HORSE
BLOCKADE DAM FERM BESET
BLOCK EMBAR SIEGE WHISKY
EMBARGO BLOCKAGE OBSTRUCT
BARRICADE BELEAGUER
BLOCKAGE LOGJAM
BLOCKER CASER BRACER
BLOCKHEAD ASS LUG OAF BUST
CLOT COOF COOT DAFF DOLT FOOL
MOME NOWT STUB BLOCK CHUMP
CUDDY GOLEM GOOSY IDIOT NINNY
DIMWIT DISARD NOODLE TURNIP
ASSHEAD DIZZARD DULBERT
JACKASS LACKWIT MUDHEAD
NOGHEAD TOMFOOL BEEFHEAD
BONEHEAD CLODPATE CODSHEAD
DULLHEAD DULLPATE DUMBHEAD
DUMMKOPF GAMPHREL HARDHEAD
JOLTHEAD LUNKHEAD
BLOCKHOUSE SPUR PUNTAL
GARRISON
BLOCKING JAM JAMB DUNNAGE
BLOCKADE CROSSING
BLOKE MAN CHAP COVE TOFF
BLOAK JOKER FELLOW
BLOLLY BEEFWOOD CORKWOOD
PORKWOOD
BLOND BAN FAIR LIGHT BLONDE
FLAXEN GOLDEN YELLOW LEUCOUS
BLONDINE
(AUTUMN —) FAWN
BLOOD KIN SAP GORE LIFE MASS
MOOD RACE SANG SANK BLADE
BLUDE BLUID CRUOR FLESH FLUID
SERUM STOCK CLARET INDRED
KAINAH SLUDGE GALLANT KINSHIP
KINSMAN LINEAGE RELATION
TROPHEMA
(CORRUPT —) YOUSTIR
(HALF —) DEMISANG
BLOODCURDLING GORY HORROR
BLOODFLOWER HIPPO REDHEAD
BLOODWEED
BLOODHOUND LYM LYAM LYME
HOUND LIMER SLOTH BANDOG
LEAMER SLEUTH TIEDOG
LYAMHOUND
BLOODIED BEBLED
BLOODLESS DEAD ANEMIC ANAEMIC
INHUMAN TURNIPY LIFELESS
UNFEELING

BLOODLETTER BLEEDER
BLOOD PHEASANT ITHAGINE
BLOODROOT PUCCOON REDROOT
BOLOROOT COONROOT CORNROOT
TURMERIC
BLOODSHED DEATH CARNAGE
VIOLENCE SLAUGHTER
BLOODSHOT RED INFLAMED
BLOODSTAINED GORY
BLOODSTONE SANGUINE
HEMACHATE
BLOODSUCKER LEECH SPONGER
VAMPIRE
BLOODTHIRSTY BLOODY CARNAL
TIGERISH FEROCIOUS MURDEROUS
BLOOD VESSEL VEIN COMES
HEMAD ARTERY CAPILLARY
BLOODWOOD AJHAR JAROOL
BLOODY GORY RUDE BLODE CRUEL
RUDDY BLUGGY CRUENT PLUCKY
CRIMSON BLEEDING DEATHFUL
HEMATOSE INFAMOUS SANGLANT
BUTCHERLY CRUENTOUS
FEROCIOUS MERCILESS
MURDEROUS
BLOODY BARK LANCEPOD
BLOOM DEW BLOW CAST HAZE
KNOT BLURT BLUSH CHILL BLOOTH
BLOWTH BLOSSOM BLOWING
ANTHESIS BLOOMING FLOREATE
FLOURISH
(— **OF WILLOW**) GULL
(— **ON SHELL**) CUTICLE
(— **ON TREE**) GOSLING
(**METAL** —**S**) HEAT
BLOOMER ERROR BLOWER
BLUNDER FAILURE
BLOOMERS KNICKERS PANTALETS
BLOOMERY FORGE HEARTH
FURNACE
BLOOMING PERT ROSY FLUSH
FRESH GREEN PRIME ABLOOM
FLORID BLOWING FLAMING
ROSEATE BLINKING
BLOOPER BLOOMER
BLOSSOM BUD BELL BLOB BLOW
CHIP SILK BLOOM LEHUA FLOWER
BLOWING BURGEON PROSPER
BOURGEON FLOURISH
(**BLIGHTED** —) BLAST
(**HERALDIC** —) FRASE FRAISE
(PL.) SET BLOSSOMRY
BLOSSOMING BLOWTH FLORAISON
FLORULENT
(— **AFTER NOON**) POMERIDIAN
BLOT MAR BLOB BLUR DAUB SOIL
SPOT BLACK BLANK BLEND BLOTE
ERASE SMEAR SPECK STAIN SULLY
BLOTCH CANCEL DAMAGE EFFACE
IMPAIR MACULA SHADOW SMIRCH
SMOUCH SMUDGE SMUTCH STIGMA
BLEMISH ECLIPSE EXPUNGE
INKBLOT OBSCURE SPLOTCH
TARNISH DISGRACE REPROACH
(— **OUT**) OUT ANNUL ERASE
CANCEL DELETE EXPUNGE
BLOTCH DAB BLOT DASH GOUT
MONK SPOT AMPER PATCH SMEAR
SPLAT STAIN MACULA MOTTLE

PLOTCH PURPLE SMIRCH SPLASH
STIGMA BLEMISH PUSTULE
SPLOTCH ERUPTION MACULATE
(PL.) BLIBE
BLOTCHED SCABBY MACULATE
SCABROUS SPLASHED
BLOTCHY SCOVY
BLOTTER BLAD
BLOUSE SHIRT SMOCK TUNIC
CAMISA GUIMPE JUMPER CASAQUE
VAREUSE CAMISOLE CASAQUIN
JIRKINET
(**BUSHMAN'S** —) BLUEY
BLOW BOB COB COP CUT DAB DAD
DUB FAN FIB HIT JAB JAR NAP ONE
PAT PEG POP RAP TAP TIP TIT WAP
ANDE BAFF BANG BASH BEAT BELT
BIFF BIRR BLAD BLAW BRAG BUFF
BULL BUMP BUTT CHAP CHOP CONK
COUP CRIG CUFF DASH DAUD DENT
DING DINT DIRD DOLE DRAW DRUB
DUNT DUSH FLAP FLEG FLIG FUFF
FUNK GALE GOWF GUST HACK HUFF
HURT JOLT KNAP KNEE LASH LEAD
LEFT LICK LOUK LUSH MINT ONER
PAIK PALT PANT PASS PICK PIRR
PLUG POLT PUCK PUFF PUSH SCUD
SLAM SLAP SLAT SLUG SOCK SPAT
STOP SWAP SWAT SWOP SWOT
THUD WELT WIND WIPE YANK BINGE
BLADE BLAST BLIZZ BLOOM BOAST
BRUNT BURST CLINK CLOUR CLOUT
CLUMP CLUNK CRUMP CRUNT
CURSE DEVEL DOUSE DOWSE
DUNCH FACER FILIP FLACK FLICK
FLIRT GOWFF ICTUS IMPEL KNOCK
OUTER PALMY PANDY PASTE PEISE
PLUNK PUNCH RIGHT SHAKE SHOCK
SKELP SKIRL SKITE SLASH SLIPE
SLOSH SMACK SMASH SMITE SNICK
SOUND SOUSE SPANK SPEND
STORM STRIP SURGE SWACK
SWEEP SWIPE THROW THUMP TRICE
WHACK WHANG WHIFF WHOOF
WHUFF BELTER BENSEL BENSIL
BETRAY BOUNCE BUFFET CONKER
DEPART DIRDUM DUNDER EXPAND
FILLIP FISTER FLOWER FROLIC
HANDER HUFFLE LARRUP REBUKE
SIFFLE STOUSH STRIPE STROKE
SWITCH THUNGE THWACK WALLOP
AFFLATE ASSAULT ATTAINT
BELLOWS BENSAIL BLOSSOM
BLOWOUT BLUSTER BOASTER
COUNTER CRUSHER DESTROY
INFLATE KNOCKER LAMBACK
LOUNDER MOUTHER PUBLISH
SHATTER SMACKER SPANKER
SQUELCH WHAMPLE WHIFFLE
WHITHER CALAMITY DISASTER
KNOCKOUT SASARARA SICKENER
(— **ABRASIVES**) BLAST
(— **CEMENT**) KIBOSH
(— **GUSTILY**) FLAW TUCK WINNOW
(— **IN PUFFS**) FAFF
(— **NOSE**) SNITE
(— **OFF STEAM**) SNIFT
(— **ON HEAD**) NOB CONK CLOUR
CONKER NOBBER TOPPER NOBBLER

(— **ON NOSE**) NOSER CANKER
NOZZLER SMELLER
(— **SMOKE**) NOSE
(— **SOFTLY**) BREATHE
(— **UP**) BOMB BLAST DYNAMITE
SUFFLATE
(— **VIOLENTLY**) STORM
(— **WITH CUDGEL**) DUB DRUB
CRUNT
(— **WITH FIST**) BOP BOX PEG BELT
HOOK CLOUT BUFFET
(— **WITH FOOT**) BOOT KICK SPURN
(**GLANCING** —) SCUFF
(**HARD** —) SLOG STOT YANK BEVEL
SWACK TWITCHER
(**HEAVY** —) DAD DONG DRUB DUNT
ONER SLAM SLUG CLOUT KNOCK
POISE SOUSE SQUAT STAVE SWASH
STOUND PLUMPER REEMISH
(**MOCK** —) FEINT
(**NOISY** —) DUNDER DUNNER
(**RESOUNDING** —) CLAP CRACK
(**SHARP** —) BAT NAP KNAP SLAP
SPAT CLICK FLICK FLEWIT STINGER
(**SLIGHT** —) SCLAFF
(**SMART** —) FLIP SKELP SKITE
YANKER
BLOWCASE EGG
BLOWER PAN DRIER DRYER WHALE
FANNER PUFFER BELLOWS
BLOOMER BOOSTER MUMBLER
BRAGGART OUTBURST
(**GLASS** —) GAFFER
BLOWGUN SUMPIT SUMPITAN
SARBACANE
BLOWHOLE BLOW GLOUP SPOUT
SPIRACLE
BLOWING ABLOW BLAST BLORE
GUSTY BLUSTER BLUSTERY
(— **AT LOW SPEED**) SLACK
(— **AT RIGHT ANGLES**) SIDE
(— **OF WHALE**) SPOUT
BLOWN STALE TIRED OPENED
WINDED BLOSSOM SWOLLEN
TAINTED BETRAYED FLYBLOWN
INFLATED
BLOWOUT BLOW FEED MEAL BURST
VALLEY FLAMEOUT
BLOWSY DOWDY BLOUSY BLOWZY
FROWZY
BLOWY DUSTY
BLUBBER CRY FAT BLUB FOAM WAIL
WEEP BIBLE MELON PIECE SPECK
SPICK SWELL THICK WHINE BUBBLE
FLITCH LIPPER LUBBER MEDUSA
NETTLE SEETHE BLABBER BLUSTER
SLOBBER SWOLLEN WHIMPER
(— **AT WHALE'S NECK**) CANT
(**REFUSE** —) FENKS FOOTING
FRITTERS
BLUDGEON BAT HIT SAP CLUB
MACE BILLY STICK TOWEL COERCE
COURSE TRUNCHEON
BLUE HAW LOW SAD SKY AQUA BICE
BLAE GLUM TEAL WOAD AZURE
BERYL LIVID NIKKO PERSE SMALL
WAGET COBALT GLOOMY INDIGO
LUPINE ORIENT PEWTER SEVERE
TRYPAN CELESTE CYANINE GENTIAN

GOBELIN HYPPISH LEARNED
LIBERTY LOBELIA MATELOT
MISTBLU MURILLO PEACOCK
QUIMPER REGATTA WATCHET
CERULEAN DEJECTED LABRADOR
LARKSPUR LITERARY MAZARINE
MIDNIGHT NATIONAL SAPPHIRE
WEDGWOOD POMPADOUR
(BLACKISH —) BLO BLOO
(DULL —) HAW
(ROYAL —) HATHOR
BLUEBELL CROWBELL HAREBELL
BLUEBERRY OHELO STONER
PALBERRY RABBITEYE VACCINIUM
BLUEBIRD (— GUIDE) LEADER
BLUE-BLACK BLO
BLUEBLOSSOM LILAC
BLUEBONNET CAP SCOT BLUECAP
BLUEBOTTLE BLUET BLAVER
BARBEAU BLAWORT BLOWFLY
BLUECAP BLUECUP BRUSHES
HARDOCK BLUEBLAW HYACINTH
CORNBINKS
BLUE CREEPER LOVE
BLUE CURLS FLEASEED FLEAWEED
BLUE-EYED GRASS PIGROOT
SATINFLOWER
BLUEFIN TUNNY
BLUEFISH ELF BASS ELFT SHAD
TUNA HORSE SAURY DARZEE
TAILER TAILOR FATBACK SKIPJACK
WEAKFISH
(YOUNG OF —) SNAPPER WHITEFISH
BLUEGILL BREAM SUNFISH
PONDFISH
BLUE GOOSE BALDHEAD
BLUEGRASS STATE KENTUCKY
BLUE GREEN VENICE
BLUE GUM FEVERGUM EUCALYPTUS
BLUE HEN STATE DELAWARE
BLUE HERON CRANE NAILROD
BLUEJACKET SAILOR DRAGMAN
BLUEJOINT REDTOP BLUETOPS
BLUE PETER ASK
BLUE PINE LIM
BLUE POINTER MAKO
BLUEPRINT MAP PLAN PLOT DRAFT
TRACE SKETCH DIAGRAM PROJECT
CYANOTYPE
BLUE RUNNER JUREL
BLUES MARE DUMPS CAFARD
DISMAL GLOOMS DISMALS
HORRORS HUMDRUM MEGRIMS
SADNESS DOLDRUMS DOLEFULS
BLUE SLATE SKAILLIE
BLUE SUCCORY CATNACHE
CUPIDONE
BLUET PISSABED EYEBRIGHT
INNOCENCE
BLUE TIT NUN STONECHAT
BLUE TITMOUSE YAUP TYDIE
TIDIFE BLUECAP
BLUETONGUE THICKHEAD
BLUE VERVAIN IRONWEED
BLUE VINNY DORSET
BLUEWEED ECHIUM IRONWEED
ADDERWORT
BLUFF ALTO BANK BRAG CURT FOOL
RUDE BLUNT BRAVE BURLY CLIFF

FRANK GRUFF SHORT SURLY WINDY
ABRUPT BOUNCE CRUSTY BLINDER
BLINKER BLUFTER BRUSQUE
DECEIVE UNCIVIL BARRANCA
BARRANCO CHURLISH HOODWINK
IMPOLITE
BLUISH-GRAY MERLE
BLUMEA PLACUS
BLUNDER ERR MIX BALK BONE
BUBU BULL DOLT FLUB GAFF ROIL
SKEW SLIP STIR BONER BOTCH
BREAK ERROR FAULT FLUFF GAFFE
LAPSE MISDO BOGGLE BUMBLE
BUNGLE ESCAPE FUMBLE GAZEBO
HOWLER MAFFLE MINGLE MUDDLE
BLOOMER BLOOPER CONFUSE
DERANGE FAILURE FLOATER
MISTAKE OVERSEE SOTTISE
STUMBLE SOLECISM
(— IN LANGUAGE) BULL
(— IN SPEECH) SOLECISM
(VERBAL —) SLIPSLAP SLIPSLOP
BLUNDERBUSS TRABU TRABUCO
TRABUCHO TROMBONE ESPINGOLE
BLUNDERER BUMBLER BUMMLER
KNOTHEAD LUMBERER
BLUNDERING AWKWARD BUMBLING
BLUNT BALD BATE BULL CURT DAMP
DULL FLAT MULL SNUB ABATE
BLATE BLUFF BRUSK DUBBY INERT
MORNE PLAIN PLUMP STUNT
CANDID CLUMSY DEADEN DIRECT
OBTUND OBTUSE REBATE RETUND
SHEATH STUBBY STUPID BRUSQUE
DISEDGE HACKNEY SHEATHE
SNUBBED SPADISH STUBBED
STUPEFY HEBETATE
BLUNTLY PLAT FLATLY CRUDELY
FRANKLY
BLUR DIM FOG HUM BLOB BLOT
FADE FUZZ MIST SLUR SOIL SPOT
BLEAR CLOUD FUDGE SHAKE
SMEAR STAIN SULLY MACKLE
MACULE SMUDGE STIGMA BLEMISH
CONFUSE FEATHER OBSCURE
TAILING
BLURB AD BOLT PUFF RAVE BRIEF
NOTICE
BLURRED FAINT FUZZY MUZZY
BLURRY SMUDGY SWIMMY WOOLLY
CLOUDED COMATIC EDGELESS
FLANNELLY
BLURT BLAT BOLT BLUNDER
EXCLAIM
BLUSH BLUE GLOW BLINK COLOR
FLUSH GLEAM PAINT ROUGE TINGE
CHANGE GLANCE MANTLE REDDEN
CRIMSON FLICKER LIKENESS
JOSEPHINE
BLUSHING RED ROSY ABLUSH
ROSEATE FLUSHING ROSACEOUS
BLUSTER BEEF BLOW DING HUFF
RAGE RANT BLAST BLEAT BLORE
BOAST BRACE BULLY NOISE STORM
SWANK BABBLE BELLOW BOUNCE
FRAPLE HECTOR HUFFLE TUMULT
WUTHER BLUBBER BRAVADO
FLUSTER GAUSTER ROISTER
SWAGGER WHITHER BOASTING

BULLYING THREATEN
BLUSTERER SWAG FLASH HECTOR
HUFFER FRAPLER HUFFCAP
TEARCAT
BLUSTERING BOG LOUD BRASH
VAPORS HUFFCAP VAPOURS
BULLYING
BOA BOM BOID BOMA ABOMA JIBOA
SCARF THROW ABOLLA ADJIGA
GIBOIA JOBOYA PYTHON ADJIGER
CAMOODI EMPEROR PEROPOD
ANACONDA CORALLUS
BOAR HOG APER SUID BRAWN SWINE
BARROW HOGGET TUSKER
BRAWNER SOUNDER SUIDIAN
VENISON WILRONE BRISTLER
SANGLIER HOGGASTER
(— CRY) FREAM
(— HEAD) HURE
(— IN 2ND YEAR) HOGGET
(— IN 3RD YEAR) HOGSTEER
HOGGASTER
(— STY) FRANK
(YOUNG —) GRISE SOUNDER
BOARD EAT LAG PAX TOE DAIL DEAL
DECK DIET EATS FARE FLIP HACK
JOIN KEEP LATH MEAT SHIP SIGN
SLAT TRAY TRIP BUIRD CHESE
CLEAR COARD COUCH COURT
ENTER FOUND HOUSE LODGE
MEALS PANEL PLANK RATCH SHIDE
STAGE STALL SWALE TABLE THEAL
ABACUS ACCOST COMMON PALLET
PLANCH RANDOM RIBBON SHIELD
SIDING TUCKER CABINET CHAMBER
COUNCIL CRIMPER DUOVIRI
ENPLANE ENTRAIN KNEELER
PALETTE PLANCHE SCRAPER
TABLING TRANSOM WHATMAN
APPROACH ASSEMBLY BOXBOARD
CUPBOARD EXCLUDER FETIALES
KEYBOARD LAPBOARD PEGBOARD
TRIBUNAL
(— FOR FALCON'S MEAT) HACK
(— OF BRIDGE) CHESS
(— OF LOOM) CARD
(— OF MILL WHEEL) AWE
(— ON CALF'S NOSE) BLAB
(— OVER) BERTH
(— WITH GROOVE) COULISSE
(— WITH HANDLE) CLAPPER
(— WITH NUMBER) SLATE
(— WITH PINS) RIDDLE
(— WITH TEETH) HACKLE RUFFER
(BLOCKHEAD —) DOLL
(CHANNEL —) PAN
(CHESS —) TABLER
(DRAWING —) COQUILLE
(EXHIBITION —) FRAME
(FLOOR —) KEY
(GAME —) HALMA
(HEART-SHAPED —) PLANCHET
(MORTAR —) HAWK
(NOTCHED —) HORSE
(OTTER —) DOOR
(POLING —) RUNNER
(PRESSED —S) FELT
(PULP-PRESSING —) COUCH
(RABBETED —S) SHIPLAP

(SHEATHING —S) SARKING
(STRIKE —) SCREED
(TANNING —) BEAM
(THIN —) SHIDE SARKING
(THIN —S) SLITWORK
(WARPING —) BARTREE
BOARDER MEALER TABLER GRAINER
PENSIONER SOJOURNER TRANSIENT
BOARDING LIVERY
BOARDINGHOUSE FONDA HOUSE
PENSION
BOARDWALK MARINA DUCKBOARD
BOARWOOD CHEWSTICK
BOAST BOG GAB JET BEEF BLAW
BLOW BRAG CROW POMP PUFF
RAVE VANT WIND WOST YELP
BLAST BRAVE CRACK CRAKE EXTOL
EXULT GLORY PRATE QUACK
ROOSE SCOLD SKITE VAPOR VAUNT
VOUST YOLPE AVAUNT BLAZON
BLEEZE BOUNCE CLAMOR FLAUNT
INSULT MENACE OUTCRY SPLORE
BLUSTER BRAVING CLAMOUR
DEVAUNT DISPLAY GLORIFY
SWAGGER FLOURISH THREATEN
VANTERIE VAUNTERY
BOASTER BLOW HUFF SKITE
CROWER GASCON PEDANT PRATER
SHAKER BOUNCER BRAGGER
BRAVADO CRACKER RUFFLER
BLOWHARD BRAGGART CACAFUGO
FANFARON GLORIOSO JINGOIST
RODOMONT TARTARIN WOUSTOUR
BOASTFUL BIG BRAG HIGH LARGE
BRAGGY PARADO JACTANT VAUNTIE
FANFARON GLORIOUS GASCONADE
THRASONIC
BOASTFULLY SIDE LARGE
BOASTFULNESS GLORY EGOTISM
WINDINESS
BOASTING BLOW HUFF YELP BOAST
CRACK PRATE ROOSE QUACKY
BOBANCE GASSING JACTANCE
JACTANCY QUACKISH VAUNTAGE
VENTOSITY
(EMPTY —) GAS
BOAT ARK BUM BUN CAT COG COT
DOW GIG MON TUB ACON BAIT
BARK BOOT BRIG CARV CHOP COCK
DHOW DINK DORY DUMP FLAT FOUZ
JUNK PAIR PLAT PRAM PUNT RAFT
SCOW SHIP SKAG TACK TODE TOPO
TROW WAKA YAWL YOLE ACCON
AVISO BANCA BARCA BARGE BARIS
BATEL BIDAR BOLIA BOYER BULLY
BUYER CANOE COBLE CRAFT DHONI
DINGY FERRY FOIST FORTY FUNNY
JOLLY KETCH LAKER LINER NADIR
OOLAK PIECE PILOT PRAAM RACER
SHELL SHOUT SIKAR SKIFF SKIFT
SMACK TOPPO UMIAK WAAPA WHIFF
XEBEC ZEBEC BAIDAK BANGKA
BATEAU BAWLEY BELLUM BILALO
BORLEY BOTTOM BOUTRE CAIQUE
CARVEL CAYUCO CHEBEC COCKLE
CRUISE CUTTER DINGHY DREDGE
DRIVER DROVER DUGOUT FLATTY
GALLEY GARVEY GAYYOU GLIDER
HOOKER JAGGER JIGGER KEELER

KICKER KUPHAR LERRET MAILER
NAGGAR NUGGAR PACKET PEAPOD
PEDULE PICARD PINKIE PLAYTE
PULWAR RANDAN ROCKER SANDAL
SCAPHE SCHOUW SCHUYT SETTEE
SINGLE SKERRY STRUSE TANKER
TENDER TIMBER TOGGER TORPID
TRANKY TROUGH VESSEL WAFTER
WHERRY ZEBECK AIRBOAT ALMADIA
ANGEYOK BALLOEN BALLOON
BAULEAH BUMBOAT CAISSON
CARRIER CATCHER CORACLE
CRUISER DOGBODY DRIFTER
DROGHER FLATTIE FLEETER
FLYBOAT FOYBOAT FRIGATE
GAIASSA GASBOAT GONDOLA
HOVELER HUFFLER KELLECK
LIGHTER MACHINE MASOOLA
NACELLE PEARLER PEDIWAK
PINNACE PIRAGUA POOKAWN
PUTELEE SCOOTER SCULLER
SHALLOP SHARPIE SHIKARA
SIKHARA SKAFFLE SKIPPET
SPONGER SPYBOAT STEAMER
TRAWLER TUCKNER TUMBREL
TUMBRIL VEDETTE WHIRREY
BALANGAY BARANGAY BILLYBOY
BOOMBOAT BULLBOAT BUMBARGE
CANALLER CHALOUPE CHEBACCO
CHELINGA CHELINGO COCKBOAT
DAHABEAH DUCKBOAT FIREBOAT
FLAGBOAT KEELBOAT LIFEBOAT
MACKINAW MONOXYLE NEWSBOAT
OYSTERER PALANDER PANCHWAY
PESSONER PESSULUS PULLBOAT
SAILBOAT SCHOKKER SCHOONER
SURFBOAT TONGKANG TRANSFER
(— OF MALTA) DGHAISA
(— WITH SAILS AND OARS)
LYMPHIAD
(3-OAR —) RANDAN
(6-OAR —) SEXERN
(8-OAR —) SHIP
(ABANDONED —) DERELICT
(CHEMICAL —) CAPSULE
(CHINESE —) JUNK SAMPAN
(CLUMSY —) HOOKER DROGHER
(DISPATCH —) AVISO PACKET
(ESKIMO —) KAMIK UMIAK OOMIAC
UMIACK
(FERRY —) BAC CUTT
(FISHING —) COG BOVO BUSS DONI
CANOA COBLE DHONI NOBBY
PYKAR SMACK VINTA BALDIE
BAWLEY DOGGER DROVER FISHER
KUPHAR NICKEY SANDAL SCAFFY
SEINER SEXERN TOSHER VOLYER
CARAVEL CRABBER DRAGGER
FOLLYER POOKAUN SHARPIE
SKAFFIE TRAWLER DRAGBOAT
GAROOKUH SHRIMPER
(FLAT-BOTTOM —) ARK BAC DORY
FLAT PLAT PRAM PUNT SCOW
BARGE COBLE DOREY FLOAT
MOSES PRAAM SHOUT BATEAU
BUGEYE GAYYOU PUTELI GONDOLA
LIGHTER FLATBOAT GUNDELOW
JOHNBOAT
(FLY —) BUSS FLUTE FLIGHT

(INCENSE —) NEF SHIP NAVICULA
(MORTAR —) PALANDER
(OPEN —) WHIFF LERRET SHALLOP
(PATROL —) SPITKID SPITKIT
(RACING —) SIX FOUR EIGHT SCULL
SHELL SINGLE TORPID SCULLER
(SHIP'S —) GIG MOSES DINGEY
DINGHY LAUNCH TENDER PINNACE
(SKIN —) BIDAR BAIDAR ANGEYOK
BIDARKA BULLBOAT
(WICKER —) KUFA GOOFA GOOFAH
CORACLE
(PL.) LIGHTERAGE
BOATBUILDING SETWORK
BOATHOOK STOWER HITCHER
BOATMAN DANDI DANDY PHAON
BARGER BOWMAN CHARON YAWLER
HOBBLER HOVELER HUFFLER
COBLEMAN VOYAGEUR WATERMAN
GONDOLIER
BOAT SEAT TAFT
BOAT SHELL YET SWEETMEAT
BOATSWAIN BOSN BOSUN SERANG
TINDAL
BOAZ (FATHER OF —) SALMA
SALMON
(SON OF —) OBED
(WIFE OF —) RUTH
BOB BAB BOW CUT DAB DIP HOD
JOG POP RAP TAP BALL BLOW
BUFF CALF CLIP CLOD COIN CORK
DUCK GRUB JEER JERK JEST KNOB
MOCK WORM BUNCH CHEAT DANCE
FILCH FLOAT FLOUT SHAKE TAUNT
TRICK BINGLE BOBBER BOBBLE
BUFFET CURTSY DELUDE HOBBLE
POMMEL POPPLE STRIKE WEIGHT
BOBSLED BOBTAIL CLUSTER
HAIRCUT PAGEBOY PENDANT
PLUMMET REFRAIN SHINGLE
SHILLING
(— UP) LOLLOP
BOBAC PAHMI TARBAGAN
BOBBER CORK DUCK FLOAT BOBFLY
BOBBIN PIN CONE CORD PIRN REEL
BRAID QUILL SPOOL BROCHE
HANGER SKREEL TAVELL WORKER
RATCHET SPINDLE TARELLE
TORCHON
(PL.) BONES
BOBBINET ILLUSION
BOBBLE ERROR
BOBOLINK DEER REED SUCKER
BUNTING MAYBIRD ORTOLAN
REEDBIRD RICEBIRD
BOBSLED BOB DRAY BOBLET
RIPPER TRAVERSE
BOBWHITE COLIN QUAIL PARTRIDGE
BOCACCIO TOMCOD
BOCCACCIO JACK TRECENTIST
BOCCARELLA NOSEHOLE
BOCE BOGUE OXEYE
BODE OMEN SIGN STOP AUGUR
OFFER HERALD MESSAGE PORTEND
PRESAGE FOREBODE FORECAST
FORESHOW FORETELL INDICATE
BODHISATTVA KWANNON MAITREYA
AVALOKITA PADMAPANI
BODICE JUPE CHOLI GILET JUMPS

WAIST BASQUE CORSET JELICK LYFKIE CORSAGE OVERBODY SLIPBODY

BODIERON BOREGAT

BODILY SOLID SOMAL ACTUAL CARNAL FLESHLY SOMATIC CORPORAL ENTIRELY EXTERNAL MATERIAL PERSONAL PHYSICAL SARKICAL VISCERAL CORPOREAL **(NOT —)** INTERIOR

BODKIN AWL PIN POINT BROACH DAGGER NEEDLE POPPER HAIRPIN PONIARD STILETTO EYELETEER

BODO CACHARI

BODY BAND BELL BOLE BOOK BOUK BUCK BULK CREW DEHA FORM HEAD LICH MASS MOLD NAVE RIND RUPA SOMA STEM ATOMY FLESH FRAME HABIT MOULD SHANK STIFF TORSO TRUNK CORPSE CORPUS CUERPO EXTENT FUSEAU LICHAM PERSON SARIRA AIRFOIL ANATOMY CADAVER CARCASS COMPANY ECONOMY QUANTUM SKINFUL SUPTION TEXTURE CORSAINT DEMARCHY EXTENSUM MAJORITY QUARROME TENEMENT **(— OF 12 MEN)** DOUZAINE **(— OF ARROW)** SHAFT STELE **(— OF BELIEVERS)** FAITH **(— OF CANONS)** CHAPTER **(— OF CARDINALS)** CONCLAVE **(— OF CHILDREN)** INFANTRY **(— OF CHRISTIANS)** KOINONIA COMMUNION **(— OF DOCTRINES)** DOGMA **(— OF ECHINODERM)** DISC DISK **(— OF EVIDENCE)** CASE CORPUS **(— OF FIBERS)** FORNIX **(— OF HELMET)** BELL **(— OF ISLAMIC CUSTOM)** SUNNA SUNNAH **(— OF KNOWLEDGE)** STUFF **(— OF LAW)** CODE SHAR HALAKA SHARIA SHARIAT HALACHAH **(— OF MANKIND)** HERD **(— OF MUSCLE)** BELLY **(— OF NOTIONS)** FOLKLORE **(— OF OFFICERS)** BUREAU **(— OF ORE)** BUNCH MANTO **(— OF PIGMENT)** EYESPOT IMPASTO **(— OF POETRY)** EPOS **(— OF ROCK)** DIKE DYKE HORSE STOCK BIOHERM MUDFLOW INTRUSION **(— OF SINGERS)** CHORUS **(— OF STUDENTS)** CLASS **(— OF TEN)** DECURY **(— OF TENANTS)** GAVEL HOMAGE **(— OF THIEVES)** SCHOOL **(— OF TRADITIONS)** HADIT HADITH **(— OF TROOPS)** FORCE AMBUSH BATTLE CONREY SCREEN SQUARE BRIGADE SUPPORT BATTALIA GARRISON **(— OF TYPE)** SHANK **(— OF VASSALS)** BAN **(— OF WATER)** BAY RIP SEA BAHR FORD HEAD LAKE LAVE POND POOL

WAVE ABYSS BAYOU DRINK FLOOD OCEAN SHARD SHERD SWASH LAGOON NYANZA STREAM FLOWAGE SWALLOW **(— OF WELLBORN MEN)** COMITATUS **(— OF WRITINGS)** SMRTI SMRITI **(— POLITIC)** ESTATE **(— RIDDLED BY BULLETS)** SIEVE **(CAROTID —)** GLOMUS **(CART —)** SIRPEA **(CELESTIAL —)** SUN BALL COMET PLANET SPHERE ELEMENT ASTEROID SATELLITE **(COMPACT —)** GLOBE **(CONDUCTING —)** GROUND **(CORPORATE —)** SOCIETY **(DEAD —)** LICH MORT CADAVER CARCASS CARRION SUBJECT **(ECCLESIASTICAL —)** CLASSIS **(ELASTIC —)** CUSHION **(EXTENDED —)** LENGTH **(FAT —)** EPIPLOON **(FRUITING —)** CONK CLAVA ASCOCARP **(GLOBULAR —)** NOB KNOB **(GOVERNING —)** KAHAL SYNOD DURBAR SENATE DECARCHY DIRECTORY **(HAT —)** HOOD **(HEAVENLY —)** SUN LAMP STAR COMET LIGHT CANDLE **(HYALINE —)** DRUSE **(IMMUNE —)** DESMON **(JUDICIAL —)** FORUM **(LEGISLATIVE —)** CHAMBER ASSEMBLY CONGRESS LAGTHING **(MAIN — OF ARMY)** BATTLE **(MATHEMATICAL —)** FILAMENT **(MORMON —)** BISHOPRIC **(MORTAL —)** KHET **(PRESBYTERIAN —)** SESSION JUDICATURY **(RELIGIOUS —)** SECT CONVENT **(REPRODUCTIVE —)** EGG GEMMA SPORE GEMMULA **(SONOROUS —)** PHONIC **(SPIRITUAL —)** SAHU **(SWELLING —)** BOSS **(WAGON —)** BED BUCK PUNT

BODYGUARD THANE ESCORT INWARD HUSCARL RETINUE TRABANT THINGMAN WARDCORS

BOER TAKHAAR AFRIKANER

BOG BUG CAR DUB FEN GOG HAG BOLD CARR CESS FLOW MIRE MOOR MOSS OOZE SINK SLEW SLUE SPEW STOG SUDS SYRT WASH LETCH MARSH MIZZY SAUCY SLADE SLOCK SWAMP MORASS MUSKEG SLOUGH CRIPPLE FORWARD PEATERY TURBARY QUAGMIRE **(PEAT —)** CESS MOSS YARPHA

BOG ASPHODEL KNAVERY

BOGEY BUG COW HAG BOGIE BOGLE DEVIL GNOME BOGGLE BOOGER GOBLIN BOGGARD BOGGART BUGABOO BUGBEAR SPECTER SPECTRE

BOGGLE JIB SHY BALK FOIL STOP

ALARM BOTCH DEMUR SCARE START STICK BAFFLE BUNGLE GOBLIN SHRINK BAUCHLE BLUNDER PERPLEX SCRUPLE STUMBLE FRIGHTEN HESITATE

BOGGY WET DEEP MIRY SOFT FENNY FOGGY GOUTY HAGGY MOSSY SNAPY SPEWY MARSHY QUAGGY SLOBBY SWAMPY WAUGHY BOGGISH QUEACHY SQUASHY

BOGIER RIDER GEARMAN

BOGLAND SLADE

BOG MANGANESE WAD LAMPADITE

BOGO ABILO ABILAO

BOGOMILE PATARIN PATARINE

BOGUS FAKE SHAM FALSE PHONY SPURIOUS

BOHEMIAN ARTY PICARD PICARO ARTISTIC **(— RIVER)** ELBE VLTAVA LUZNICE BEROUNKA **(— TOWN)** PISEK PLZEN PRAHA TABOR PILSEN PRAGUE

BOHOR REEDBUCK

BOIL FRY PET STY BILE BLOB BOLL BRAN BUCK BUMP COCT COOK COWL LEEP PLAY PUSH QUAT RAGE SEED SORE STEW STYE TEEM WALL WALM WELL BOTCH BREDE STEAM BETRAY BUBBLE BULDER BULLER BURBLE DECOCT GALLOP PIMPLE RISING SEETHE SIMMER TOTTLE WABBLE WOBBLE ANTHRAX BEALING BREEDER CATHAIR ELIXATE ESTUATE INFLAME AESTUATE EBULLATE FURUNCLE PHLEGMON **(— IN LYE)** BUCK **(— SYRUP)** PEARL **(SAND —)** BLOWOUT

BOILED SOD SODDEN **(— WITHOUT SAUCE)** ANGLAISE

BOILER YET REEF STILL COPPER KETTLE RETORT TEACHE ALEMBIC CALDRON FURNACE **(SALT —)** WELLER

BOILING WALM ABOIL FERVID COCTION FERVENT SCALDING SEETHING ELIXATION

BOISTEROUS GURL HIGH LOUD RUDE WILD BURLY GURLY NOISY ROUGH WINDY COARSE SHANDY STOCKY STORMY STRONG UNRULY FURIOUS MASSIVE ROARING VIOLENT BIGMOUTH CUMBROUS LARRIKIN STRIDENT VEHEMENT

BOLD BIG BOG YEP DERF HARD KEEN PERT RASH RUDE TALL WHAT YEPE APERT BARDY BIELD BRASH BRAVE BRENT FRACK FREAK FRECK GALLY HARDY JOLLY LARGE MANLY NERVY PAWKY PEART POKEY SAUCY STEEP STOUT WLONK ABRUPT AUDACE BRASSY BRAZEN CROUSE DARING FIERCE HEROIC PLUCKY STRONG ASSURED DASHING DEFIANT FORWARD GRIVOIS HAUGHTY MASSIVE VALIANT ARROGANT FAMILIAR

FEARLESS IMMODEST IMPUDENT
INTREPID MALAPERT POWERFUL
RESOLUTE TEMEROUS
(NOT —) GENTEEL
BOLDFACE BOLD BLACK FULLFACE
BOLDLY CRANK CROUSE HARDLY
HARDILY ROUNDLY STRONGLY
BOLDNESS BROW DARE FACE GALL
BIELD CHEEK NERVE PLUCK VIGOR
DARING BRAVERY COURAGE
FREEDOM AUDACITY TEMERITY
(— OF SPEECH) PARRHESIA
BOLDO NUTMEG
BOLE CLAY DOSE STEM BOLUS
CRYPT TRUNK RUDDLE TIMBER
BOLETUS CEPE
BOLIVIA PILE

BOLIVIA
CAPITAL: LAPAZ SUCRE
COIN: TOMIN CENTAVO
DEPARTMENT: LAPAZ ORURO
PANDO ELBENI POTOSI TARIJA
INDIAN: URO INCA ITEN MOXO
URAN ARAWAK AYMARA
CHARCA CHICHA IXIAMA
TACANA PUQUINA QUECHUA
SIRIONE TUMUPASA
LAKE: POOPO COIPASA ROGAGUA
AULLAGAS TITICACA
MEASURE: LEAGUE CELEMIN
MOUNTAIN: JARA CUSCO CUZCO
PUPUYA SAJAMA SORATA
ILLAMPU ANCOHUMA ILLIMANI
ZAPALERI
MOUNTAINS: ANDES SUNSAS
SANSIMON SANTIAGO
PANPIPE: SICU SIKU
PLATEAU: ALTIPLANO
RIVER: BENI YATA ABUNA APERE
BOOPI LAUCA ORTON BAURES
GRANDE ICHILO ITENEZ MADIDI
MAMORE MIZQUE TARIJA
YACUMA GUAPORE ITONAMA
MACHUPO BENECITO INAMBARI
PARAGUAY PARAPETI
SALT DEPOSIT: UYUNI EMPEXA
SWAMP: IZOZOG
TOWN: IVO ICLA ITAU MOJO POJO
SAYA YACO YATA YURA CLIZA
LAPAZ LLICA ORURO QUIME
SUCRE UNCIA UYUNI ZONGO
GUAQUI POTOSI TARIJA
VOLCANO: OLLAGUE
WEIGHT: LIBRA MARCO

BOLL BOW POD BULB KNOB SNAP
ONION BUBBLE CAPSULE
BOLLARD BITT KEVEL DOLPHIN
DEADHEAD
(—S AND BITTS) APOSTLES
BOLLER STRIPPER
BOLL WEEVIL PICUDO
BOLO MACHETE SUNDANG
BOLSHEVIST BOLO
BOLSHEVISM COMMUNISM
SOVIETISM
BOLSTER AID PAD JACK PILLOW
CUSHION HEADING STIFFEN

SUPPORT BACKSTOP BALUSTER
COMPRESS MAINTAIN
BOLT BAR JAG KEY LUE PEN PIN
ROD RUN BEAT BURR CRAM DART
DUMP FLEE GULP LOCK PAWL SHUT
SIFT SLOT SNIB SPAR STUD ARROW
BILBO CLOSE ELOPE FLASH FLOUR
GORGE LATCH RIVET SETUP SHAFT
STOCK ASSORT DECAMP DESERT
FASTEN FLIGHT GANYIE GARBLE
MOOTER PINTLE PURIFY QUARRY
REFINE SAFETY SEARCE SECURE
SNIBEL STREAK STRONG TOGGLE
WINNOW BAYBOLT DOGBOLT
EYEBOLT MISSILE QUARREL
SETBOLT SHACKLE SLABBER
THUNDER DRAWBOLT FASTENER
FISHBOLT FLATHEAD KINGBOLT
RINGBOLT SEPARATE STAMPEDE
(DOOR —) DRAWBOLT
(FIERY —) RESHEPH
(LIGHTNING —) SHAFT
(THUNDER —) FULMEN
BOLTER BOLT DRESSER MUGWUMP
BOMB DUD EGG ROC AZON BOOM
FRAG BLARE CRUMP RAZON SHELL
SQUIB ASHCAN SALUTE BALLOON
BOMBARD GRENADE MARMITE
FIREBALL WHIZBANG PINEAPPLE
(— RELEASE) TOGGLE
(TRENCH —) MINNIE
(PL.) STICK
BOMBARD BOMB CRUMP SHELL
ATTACK BATTER BOTTLE STRAFE
BOMBARDON TUBA NICOLO
POMMER BRUMMER
BOMBARDMENT BLITZ SIEGE
ATTACK RAFALE STRAFE BATTERY
SHELLING
BOMBAST GAS PAD PUFF RAGE
RANT RAVE STUFF TUMOR BLUSTER
FUSTIAN TYMPANY BOASTING
TURGIDITY
BOMBASTIC PUFFY TUMID VOCAL
WINDY FLUENT HEROIC MOUTHY
TURGID BOMBAST FLOWERY
FUSTIAN OROTUND POMPOUS
RANTING STILTED SWOLLEN
INFLATED SWELLING
(— STYLE) TYMPANY
BONACE TREE NOSEBURN
BONACI AGUAJI
BONA FIDE LEVEL GENUINE
AUTHENTIC
BONANZA STATE MONTANA
BONBON CANDY CREAM GOODY
DAINTY CARAMEL SNAPPER
CONFETTO
(PL.) CONFETTI
BOND BON DOG TIE VOW ANDI BAIL
BAND DUTY FIVE FOUR GLUE GYVE
HOLD KNOT LINK NOTE YOKE
BOUND CHAIN NEXUS SWATH
BINDER CEMENT CONNEX COUPLE
ENGAGE ESCROW FETTER LEAGUE
PLEDGE SOLDER SWATHE FOREIGN
HUSBAND LIAISON LIBERTY LINKAGE
MANACLE SHACKLE STATUTE
ADHESIVE CONTRACT COVENANT

LIGAMENT LIGATION LIGATURE
MORTGAGE SECURITY VADIMONY
VINCULUM
(PL.) IRON KHAKIS SHORTS
BONDAGE YOKE THRALL HELOTRY
SERFDOM SLAVERY BONDSHIP
THIRLING CAPTIVITY
BONDED CATTED ENGAGED
BONDMAN CARL ESNE PEON SERF
CHURL HELOT SLAVE STOOGE
SURETY THRALL VASSAL CHATTEL
PEASANT SERVANT VILLEIN
BONDSMAN
BONDSTONE BINDER BONDER
KEYSTONE
BONE OS DIB HIP RIB BANE ULNA
BLADE FEMUR HYOID ILIUM INCUS
JUGAL SLATE STONE TALUS TIBIA
UNION VOMER CANNON COCCYX
CONCHA COPULA CUBOID EPURAL
FIBULA NUCHAL PECTEN RADIAL
SPLINT STAPES TRIPOD UNGUIS
ZYGOMA
(ANKLE —) TALUS
(HIP —) HUGGIN
(SHIN —) CNEMIS
(THIGH —) FEMUR
BONEFISH OIO MACABI GRUBBER
BONYFISH LADYFISH
BONER BUBU FLUB ROCK ERROR
BRODIE STAYER STUMER BLOOMER
BLUNDER MISTAKE STEELER
STUMOUR
BONESET COMFREY AGUEWEED
EUPATORY HEMPWEEK
BONEYARD STOCK
BONFIRE BLAZE TANDLE TAWNIE
BALEFIRE BURNFIRE NEEDFIRE
BONGO DOR
BONING SAP
BONITO AKU ATU NICE COBIA
SARDA BONITA ROBALO ALBACORE
KATONKEL MACKEREL SCOMBRID
SKIPJACK
BONNET CAP HAT HOOD POKE POXY
SCON COVER DECOY SCONE SHAPE
TOQUE CAPOTE MOBCAP SLOUCH
CHAPEAU COMMODE CORONET
LEGHORN SOWBACK VOLUPER
BONGRACE HEADGEAR
BONNET MONKEY ZATI MUNGA
TOQUE MACACO RILAWA MACAQUE
BONNY GAY FINE MERRY PLUMP
BLITHE BONNIE PRETTY STRONG
HEALTHY BUDGEREE HANDSOME
BEAUTIFUL
BONTOK IGOROT
BONUS GIN TIP GIFT MEED AWARD
BRIBE BUNCE BUNTS PILON PRIZE
SPIFF REGALO REWARD CUMSHAW
DOUCEUR PREMIUM SUBSIDY
BOUNTITH DIVIDEND TANTIEME
LAGNIAPPE
BON VIVANT SPORT EPICURE
BON VIVEUR FLANEUR
BONY HARD LANK THIN LANKY STIFF
TOUGH OSTEAL SKINNY OSSEOUS
SCRAGGY SKELETAL
BONYFISH MENHADEN

BOOB ASS FOOL GOON GOOP DUNCE GOONY NEDDY NITWIT
BOOBOOK OWL PEHO RURU CUCKOO MOPOKE MOPEHAWK MOREPORK
BOOBY GAWK GONY SULA DUNCE IDIOT LOSER PRIZE SLEIGH STUPID CAMANAY PIQUERO GOOSECAP
BOOBYALLA DOGWOOD WATERBUSH
BOODLE SWAG CROWD GRAFT BUDDLE NOODLE PLUNDER CABOODLE
BOOGEYMAN PADFOOT TANKERABOGUS
BOOJUM SNARK
BOOK MO LIL LOG CHAP CODE FORM HEFT OPUS PAGE TEXT TOME ALBUM ALDUS BIBLE CANON CANTO CODEX DETUR DIARY DIVAN ENTER FLETA FOLIO FROST GUIDE KITAB LIBEL LIBER QUAIR QUIRE RAZEE ZOHAR ALDINE ANONYM BODONI CURSUS DOCKET HERBAL LEDGER MAHZOR MANUAL MISSAL NUMBER REBIND RECORD RITUAL SCHOOL TICKET TROPER VOLUME BLOTTER CATALOG COUCHER DIETARY DISCARD FEODARY GARLAND GRAMMAR JOURNAL LAWBOOK LEXICON MANDALA OCTAPLA OMNIBUS ORDINAL OUTBOOK PEERAGE RECITER SAMHITA SERVICE SLEEPER SPEAKER SPELLER SYNAXAR TERRIER TICKLER TRAVAIL TRIGLOT TYPICON TYPICUM VESPERA WRITING BANKBOOK BROCHURE CALCULUS CASEBOOK CASHBOOK CHAPBOOK COOKBOOK COPYBOOK DOCUMENT FESTIVAL GIFTBOOK GOSPELER HANDBOOK HARDBACK HERDBOOK JESTBOOK JUVENILE LIBRETTO PASTORAL POMANDER POSTBOOK REGISTER SONGBOOK STUDBOOK SYNAXARY TALEBOOK TRIODION TWENTYMO
(— BACK) DORSE
(— FOR HARVARD GRADUATE) DETUR
(— OF CHARTS) WAGONER
(— OF HERALDRY) ARMORY ARMORIAL
(— OF MAPS) ATLAS
(— OF PSALMS) PSALTER TEHILLIM
(— OF RULES) HOYLE
(— OF SOLUTIONS) KEY
(—S KEPT IN PRINT) BACKLIST
(CHEAP —) BLOOD
(CHINESE —) CHING
(COMMONPLACE —) ADVERSARIA
(ELEMENTARY —) PRIMER
(FOLDED —) ORIHON
(JOKE —) JOE JESTBOOK
(MEMORANDUM —) AGENDA JOTTER TICKLER
(MINIATURE —) BIBELOT
(PRAYER —) PORTAS SIDDUR PORTASS PORTHORS

(RECORD —) LIBER TICKLER
(RELIGIOUS —) KITAB KORAN QURAN GOSPEL HORARY KYRIAL PROSAR GRADUAL KYRIALE BREVIARY MEGILLAH ORDINARY SYNAXARY
(SERVICE —) COMES GRAIL TEXTUS
(SLOW-SELLING —) PLUG
(STRANGE —S) CURIOSA
(UNBOUND —) CAHIER
(PL.) SHELF STUDY EROTICA SCRIPTURE
BOOKBINDING STUB YAPP STRING
BOOKCASE DESK STAGE STALL SCRINE PLUTEUS CREDENZA
BOOK COVER LID SIDE FOREL RECTO VERSO FORREL REVERSE REVERSO
BOOKISH BOOKY ERUDITE STUDIOUS
BOOKLET FOLDER NOVELET BROCHURE
BOOKMAKER LAYER BOOKER BOOKIE
BOOKMARK MARKER TASSEL REGISTER
BOOK PALM TARA TALIERA
BOOKSHELF DESK PLUTEUS
(PL.) CLASSIS
BOOM JIB BEAM BOMB BUMP CRIB POLE ROAR SPAR BRAIL CHAIN CRANE CROON PROBE BUMPKIN CATHEAD CURTAIN RESOUND SUPPORT BOWSPRIT FLOURISH
(CRANE —) ARM GIB JIB
BOOMERANG KALIE KILEY KYLIE WANGO ATLATL BOUNCE RECOIL LEEWILL REBOUND WOMERAH WOOMERA BACKFIRE HORNERAH LEEANGLE RICOCHET TROMBASH
BOOMING HUMMING
BOOM IRON WITHE CRANCE
BOON GAY BENE GIFT GOOD KIND BOUND FAVOR GRANT MERRY ORDER BENIGN BOUNTY GOODLY JOVIAL PRAYER BENEFIT COMMAND PRESENT BLESSING INTIMATE PETITION
BOOR CAD OAF BOER BORE CARL HICK JACK KERN LOUT PILL RUNT SLOB CHUFF CHURL CLOWN KERNE SLAVE BUMKIN CARLOT CLUNCH HOBLOB JOBSON JOSKIN LUBBER LUMMOX RUSTIC BUMPKIN CAUBOGE GROBIAN PEASANT VILLAIN BOEOTIAN BOSTHOON
BOORISH ILL RUDE GAWKY ROUGH RUNTY SURLY CLUMSY RUSTIC SAVAGE SULLEN VULGAR WOOLEN AWKWARD CRABBED HIRSUTE HOBLIKE KERNISH LOUTISH PEAKISH ROISTER UNCOUTH VILLAIN WOOLLEN CARTERLY CHURLISH CLODDISH CLOWNISH LUBBERLY SWAINISH UNGAINLY
BOORISHNESS VILLAINY GROBIANISM
BOOST AID LEG ABET BACK BOOM HELP LIFT PLUG PUSH COACH EXALT HOIST HOOSH RAISE ASSIST

ADVANCE COMMEND ELEVATE ENDORSE PROMOTE INCREASE
BOOT PAC PAD USE CURE GAIN HALF HELP HOOF KICK SHOE SOCK AVAIL BOOTY EJECT JEMMY KAMIK PEWEE SPOIL BOOTEE BUDGET BUSKIN CASING CHUKKA CRAKOW ENRICH FUMBLE GAITER GALOSH INSHOE JOCKEY MUKLUK PEDULE SHEATH BENEFIT BOTTINE COTHURN COWHIDE CRUISER HESSIAN HIGHLOW SEABOOT SHOEPAC VANTAGE BALMORAL BOTTEKIN CHASSURE COVERING FINNESKO JACKBOOT LARRIGAN NAPOLEON
(— OF CARRIAGE) FOREBOOT
(— ON SADDLE) GAMBADE GAMBADO
(HALF —) PAC BUSKIN COCKER SKILTY
(HOB-NAILED —) BAT
(HORSE'S —) SCALPER
(LUMBERMAN'S —) CRUISER
(MARINE —) SKINHEAD
(RIDING —) JEMMY JIMMY JODHPUR
(SEALSKIN —) KAMIK
(STOUT —) STOGA STOGY
(TORTURE —) SQUEEZER
(PL.) OVERS HESSIANS
BOOTBLACK SHINER BLACKER SHOEBOY
BOOTED OCREATE
BOOTES WAINMAN HERDSMAN
BOOTH BOX COOP DESK LOGE SHED SHOP SOOK BOTHY CABIN CRAME HOUSE KIOSK LIWAN LODGE PITCH STALL STAND PAGODA PANDAL PAYBOX SUCCAH SUKKAH TIENDA BALAGAN COCKSHY TABERNA
BOOTLACE LACET
BOOTLEG SHY SLY ILLEGAL ILLICIT
BOOTY BOOT FANG GAIN LOOT PELF PREY SWAG BUTIN CHEAT FORAY GRAFT PRIZE CREAGH FLEECE SPOILS DESPOIL PILLAGE PLUNDER SPREATH STEALTH PURCHASE SPUILZIE STEALAGE
BOOZE BOLL BOUT BUDGE DRINK SPREE FUDDLE LIQUOR
BOOZY LIQUORY
BORAGE ANCHUSA
BORAX FLUX TINCAL
(— SOURCE) KERNITE
BORDER CUT HEM RIM TAB ABUT BRIM CURB DADO EAVE EDGE LIMB LINE LIST LOVE MARK NARK ORLE RAND ROON RUND SIDE TRIM WELL WELT BOARD BOUND BRAID BRINK CHEEK COAST COSTA DRAFT FILET FLANK FOREL FRAME FRILL GUARD LIMIT MARCH MARGE MARLI PLAIT SHORE SKIRT STRIP SWAGE TOUCH VERGE ADJOIN EDGING FILLET FORREL FRINGE IMPALE LACING LIMBUS LISERE MARGIN ORFRAY PURFLE QUADRA STRIPE TANIKO WEEPER CONFINE DRAUGHT FIMBRIA FLOROON MARGENT SELVAGE VALANCE BOUNDARY

DOUBLING FRONTIER MARCHESE
NEIGHBOR OUTSKIRT PLATBAND
SKIRTING SURROUND TERMINUS
TRESSOUR TRESSURE
(— OF EXTERNAL EAR) HELIX
(— OF LACE) PICOT
(— OF ROCK) SALBAND
(— OF SAIL) DOUBLING
(— OF SHIELD) BORDURE
(— OF STREAM) ROND
(— ON) ABUT ACCOST AFFRONT
NEIGHBOR
(FLOWERED —) FLOROON
(ORNAMENTAL —) WAGE FRAME
FRINGE MATTING TRESSURE
(RIBBON —) FRILAL
(PL.) CONFINE CONFINES
BORDERED ORLE LIMBATE
BORDERING MARGENT FRONTIER
BORE BIT CUT EAT IRK JET TAP
DRAG FLAT HOLE JUMP PALL POKE
REAM RUSH SINK SIZE TIDE TIRE
TOOL ANNOY CHINK DRILL EAGRE
ENNUI GAUGE GOUGE OUGHT
PLONK PRICK PUNCH SUGUR TEWEL
TRICK VAPOR WEARY BEFOOL
CANNON GIMLET PIERCE THRILL
THRUST TUNNEL WIMBLE BROMIDE
CALIBER CALIBRE CONCAVE
CREVICE HUMDRUM NUDNICK
OPENING AIGUILLE CAPILLUS
DIAMETER DRAWBORE GRATIANO
POROROCA
(— OF CANNON) SOUL CHASE
BOREAS AQUILO AQUILON
(DAUGHTER OF —) CLEOPATRA
(FATHER OF —) ASTRAEUS
(MOTHER OF —) AURORA
(SON OF —) ZETES CALAIS
BORED WEARY ENNUYEE TEDIOUS
SATIATED
BOREDOM YAWN ENNUI TEDIUM
BORELE KEITLOA UPEYGAN
BORER MOLE BARDEE WIMBLE
HAGFISH TANBARK TERMITE
TERRIER FLATHEAD SHIPWORM
WOODWORM
BORING DIM DRY FLAT SLOW
BROACH STODGY STUPID TIRING
LUMPISH TEDIOUS PIERCING
TIRESOME
(— TOOL) AIGUILLE
BORN N NEE NATE INNATE NASCENT
NATURAL UTERINE ORIGINAL
(PREMATURELY —) SLINK ABORTIVE
(WELL —) FREE EUGENIC
BORNE RODE NARROW CARRIED
ENDURED
(— AFFRONTEE) CABOCHED
(— LOWER THAN USUAL) ABASED
(— ON WATER) AFLOAT

BORNEO
BAY: ADANG KUMAI SAMPIT
CAPE: ARU DATU LOJAR PUTING
SAMBAR SELATAN
MOUNTAIN: RAJA SARAN NIJAAN
TEBANG

MOUNTAINS: IRAN MULLER
SCHWANER
NAME: KALIMANTAN
NATIVE: DYAK DAJAK
RIVER: ARUT IWAN BAHAU BERAU
KAJAN PADAS PAWAN BARITO
KAPUAS SEBUKU KAHAJAN
MAHAKAM MENDAWI PEMBUANG
TOWN: KUMAI SAMBAS SAMPIT
MALINAU PAGATAN SANGGAU
SINTANG TARAKAN KETAPANG
TREE: KAPOR KAPUR
WEIGHT: PARA CHAPAH

BORO MARIANA
BORON BORAX ULEXITE
BORORO COROADO
BOROUGH BURG CITY TOWN WICK
BRUSH BURGH CASTLE COUNTY
CITADEL FORTESS VILLAGE
TOWNSHIP
BORROW BOT BITE COPY HIRE KICK
LOAN SHIN TAKE THIG ADOPT
STEAL TOUCH DESUME DUPLEX
PLEDGE STRIKE SURETY CHEVISE
HOSTAGE MUTUATE TITHING
BORROWER BOT CRIB MUTUARY
BOS OX NEAT TAURUS
BOSH END ROT JOKE SHOW TALK
TOSH TRASH BUSHWA FIGURE
FLAUNT HUMBUG TRIVIA TOSHERY
GALBANUM NONSENSE POPPYCOCK
BOSKY BUSHY TIPSY WOODY
FUDDLED
**BOSNIA-HERZEGOVINA (RIVER OF
—)** BOSNA DRINA NERETVA
(TOWN OF —) TUZLA MAGLAJ
MOSTAR VISOKO SARAJEVO
BOSOM LAP BARM CLOSE DICKY
HEART SINUS BREAST CAVITY
DESIRE DICKEY RECESS BELOVED
EMBRACE GREMIAL INCLOSE
INTIMATE
(— OF DRESS) SQUARE
(FALSE —) PLUMPER
BOSS BUR HUB MOP NOB ORB PAD
POP BAAS BEAD BOCE BUHR BURR
COCK CZAR KNOB KNOP KNOT NAIL
NULL STUD TSAR BULLA BULLY
BWANA CHIEF EMPTY JEWEL KNOSP
ORDER OWNER PEARL ANCHOR
BROOCH BUCKRA BUTTON CHEESE
DIRECT HOLLOW MANAGE MASTER
OCULUS PATERA PELLET SHIELD
BULLION CACIQUE CAPATAZ
CAPTAIN CUSHION FOREMAN
HASSOCK HEADMAN HOBNAIL
MANAGER PADRONE PHALERA
SPANGLE SPONSON DIRECTOR
DOMINEER MISERERE OMPHALOS
OVERSEER UMBILICUS
(— OF LOGGING CAMP) BULLY
(— OF SHIELD) UMBO
(FIRE —) GASMAN
(LEATHER —) BUTTON
(MINE —) SHIFTER SHIFTMAN
(POLITICAL —) CACIQUE CAUDILLO
(STRAW —) BULL LEADER

BOSTONIAN HUBBITE
BOTANY HERBARISM PHYTOLOGY
BOTCH MAR MUX BOIL BOSS MEND
MESS MULL SORE BITCH BODGE
BUTCH FLUFF FUDGE SPOIL STICK
BOGGLE BOLLIX BUMBLE BUNGLE
COBBLE JUMBLE MUCKER REPAIR
TINKER BLUNDER BUTCHER
SCAMBLE SCLATCH SLUBBER
SWELLING
BOTCHER GRILSE SALMON TINKER
BUNGLER BUTCHER CLOUTER
COBBLER
BOTCHERY PATCHERY
BOTE KINBOT MAGBOTE CARTBOTE
FRITHBOT PLOWBOTE WAINBOTE
BOTFLY BOTT GADBEE GADFLY
NITTER CANOPID OESTRID TORSALO
DIPTERAN OESTRIAN
BOTH BO ALL TWO BAITH EQUALLY
BOTHER ADO AIL BUG NAG VEX
FASH FAZE FUSS JADE WORK
ANNOY DEAVE KNOCK PHASE TEASE
TRADE WORRY BADGER BUSTLE
CUMBER DITHER FLURRY GRAVEL
HARASS MEDDLE MITHER MOIDER
MOLEST MUCKLE PESTER POTHER
POTTER PUTTER PUZZLE TAMPER
CONFUSE DISTURB FASHERY
GRIZZLE PERPLEX TERRIFY
TRACHLE TROUBLE BEWILDER
DISTRESS IRRITATE NUISANCE
BOTOCUDO BORUN AIMORE
AYMORO
BOTONEE TREFLEE FLEURONE
BO TREE PIPAL

BOTSWANA
CAPITAL: GABORONE GABERONES
COIN: RAND
DESERT: KALAHARI
LAKE: DOW NGAMI
LANGUAGE: BANTU CLICK
KHOISAN SETSWANA
MOUNTAIN: TSODILO
NATIVE: BANTU TSWANA
BUSHMAN
RIVER: NATA OKWA CHOBE
NOSOB CUANDO MOLOPO
SHASHI CUBANGO LIMPOPO
OKAVANGO
TOWN: KANYE ORAPA TSANE
SEROWE LOBOTSI MOCHUDI
PALAPYE THAMAGA
GABERONES

BOTTLE JUG BOSS SKIN VIAL VIOL
AMPUL ASKOS BETTY BOCAL BUIRE
BURET CADUS COOJA CROFT
CRUET CRUSE FIFTH FLASK GIRBA
GLASS GOURD HOUSE PHIAL SPLIT
VERRE ALUDEL BACBUC BUNDLE
CARAFE CARBOY CASTER CASTOR
CHAGUL CHATTY CREWET DORUCK
DUBBER FESSEL FIASCO FLACON
FLAGON GOGLET GUTTUS JORDAN
LAGENA MAGNUM MARINE MATARA
NURSER PACKER SIPHON VESSEL
WOULFF BALLOON BIBERON

BOMBARD BOMBOLA BURETTE
CANTEEN CARAFON COSTREL
DEADMAN FLACKET FLOATER
GRENADE INKHORN BOMBONNE
BORACHIO BUILDING CALABASH
DECANTER DEMIJOHN GARDEVIN
JEROBOAM MARIOTTE PRESERVE
REHOBOAM
(— IN WICKER) CARBOY DEMIJOHN
(18 —S OF WINE) RIDDLE .
(EGYPTIAN —) DORUK DORUCK
(EMPTY —) MARINE
(HOT-WATER —) PIG
(LARGE —) KIT JEROBOAM
(LEATHER —) BOOT DUBBA BUDGET
DUBBER DUPPER MATARA BOMBARD
WHINNOCK WINESKIN
(OVERSIZED —) BALTHAZAR
(PAIR OF —S) GEMEL GEMMEL
(SMALL —) VIAL AMPUL PHIAL SPLIT
FLACON AMPOULE TICKLER
BOTTLE CAP CAPSULE
BOTTLE CARRIER FASCET
BOTTLE CASE CELLAR
BOTTLEHEAD DOEGLING
BOTTLER COOPER
BOTTOM ASS BED ARSE BASE DALE
DOUP FLAT FOND FOOT FUND HOLM
LEES ROOT ABYSS BASIS DREGS
FLOOR LAIGH NADIR BATHOS
FOUNCE FUNDUS GROUND GUTTER
LAAGTE LEEGTE BEDROCK
LOWLAND SUPPORT SURFACE
BUTTOCKS INTERVAL SEDIMENT
TETRAPOD
(— OF BENCH) TOE
(— OF CUPOLA) HEARTH
(— OF FURROW) SOLE
(— OF PAGE) TAIL
(— OF PISTOL GRIP) BUTT
(— OF POT) POTSTONE
(— OF PRINTER'S GALLEY) SLICE
(— OF PULLEY BLOCK) BREECH
(— OF SEA) GROUND BENTHOS
(— OF SOLE) NAUMK NAUMKEAG
(MARSHY —) SIKE
(ROCK —) HARDPAN
(PL.) HOLM HOLME
BOTTOM-DWELLING DEMERSAL
BOTTOMER FOOTMAN STATIONMAN
BOTTOMLAND STRATH
BOTTOMLESS ABYSMAL
BOTULISM LAMSIEKTE LAMZIEKTE
BOUDOIR ROOM CABIN BEDROOM
CABINET
BOUGH ARM LEG LIMB TWIG CHUCK
SHOOT SPRAY SPRIG BRANCH
RAMAGE SHROUD GALLOWS
PHYLLIS OFFSHOOT SHOULDER
(— ON TAVERN) BUSH
(PL.) RAMAGE DUNNAGE RAMMAGE
BOUGHT KEFT STORE ZEBINA
BOUGIE CANDLE COLLYRIE FILIFORM
BOULDER NOB KELK KNOB ROCK
STONE GIBBER BOOTHER DORNICK
ERRATIC GRAYBACK HARDHEAD
MEGALITH POTSTONE
BOULE BIRNE
BOULEVARD DRIVE PRADO AVENUE

STREET HIGHWAY TERRACE
BOULTER TRAWL SPILLER SPILLET
BOUNCE DAP HOP BANG BLOW
BRAG BUMP DING DIRD FIRE GATE
JUMP LEAP SACK STOT BOAST
BOUND BULLY CAROM CHUCK
EJECT KNOCK SCOLD THUMP VERVE
SPIRIT SPRING STRIKE ADDRESS
BLUSTER CHOUNCE DISMISS
REBOUND SWAGGER PROCLAIM
RICOCHET
BOUNCER CHUCKER SCROUGER
BOUNCING BIG BUXOM LUSTY
STOUT BOUNCY HEALTHY
(— OF TONGUE) FLAP
BOUND DAP END HOP LOP BENT
BIND BOND BONE BROW BUTT DART
GIRT JUMP LEAP LIST MERE RAMP
RISE SCUD SKIP STEM STOT SURE
TERM WALL AMBIT BOURN FIXED
GOING LIMIT READY SALLY START
STEND STING TILED VAULT VERGE
BORDER BOUNCE BOURNE BUTTAL
CAVORT CURVET DEFINE DOMAIN
FINISH GAMBOL GIRDED HURDLE
JETTED LIABLE LOLLOP OBLIGE
PRANCE SPRING BARRIER CERTAIN
CHAINED CLOSURE CONFINE
CONTAIN COSTIVE DELIMIT
DRESSED GAMBADO INCLUDE
REBOUND SALTATE SECURED
SUBSULT TERMINE TRUSSED
BOUNDARY CONFINED DESTINED
ENCLOSED FASCIATE FRONTIER
HANDFAST LANDMARK LIMITATE
OBLIGATE PINIONED PRECINCT
PREPARED RESTRICT SHACKLED
(— BY OATH) SWORN
(— BY OBLIGATION) AFFINED
(NOT —) SOLUTE
(RIGIDLY —) STATIC STATICAL
(PL.) AMBIT MOUND CLOSURE
COMPASS CONFINE PURLIEUS
BOUNDARY AHU END RIM DOLE
DOOL EDGE FINE FORM LINE LIST
MARK MEAR MEER MERE META
METE PALE SURF TERM TRIG WALL
AMBIT BOURN CLOSE FENCE FRAME
FRONT HEDGE LIMES LIMIT MARCH
MOUND SHORE VERGE BORDER
COLLET DEFINE OCTROI OCTROY
TROPIC BARRIER BOUNDER BUTTING
COMPASS FURLONG CURBLINE
FRONTIER LANDLINE LIMITARY
PRECINCT TERMINUS UMSTROKE
(PL.) ABUTTALS ENVIRONS
BOUNDLESS VAST UNTOLD
ENDLESS ETERNAL INFINITE
UNLIMITED
BOUNTEOUS BOON CROWNED
LIBERAL PLENTEOUS
BOUNTIFUL GOOD LUSH RICH
AMPLE FREELY LAVISH LIBERAL
PROFUSE ABUNDANT GENEROUS
BOUNTY BOON GIFT MEED AWARD
BONUS GRANT LARGE VALOR
WORTH BONTEE REWARD VIRTUE
LARGESS PREMIUM PRESENT
PROWESS SUBSIDY DONATIVE

GOODNESS GRATUITY KINDNESS
BOUQUET BOB AURA ODOR POSY
AROMA BLOOM CIGAR POSEY
SHEAF SPRAY BOWPOT BUSKET
SHOWER CORSAGE NOSEGAY
BOUGHPOT
(— GARNI) FAGOT FAGGOT
BOURGEOIS ORGON COMMON
STUPID BOORISH BURGHER
BOURSE BOLSA BORSE CAMBIO
BOURTREE ELDER
BOUT GO JOB BOOT FALL PULL
TURN BOOZE BRASH CRASH ESSAY
FIGHT MATCH PLUCK ROUND TRIAL
VENNY VENUE ATTACK COURSE
FRACAS YOKING ASSAULT ATTEMPT
CAROUSE CIRCUIT CONTEST
DEBAUCH OUTSIDE WITHOUT
CONFLICT
(DRINKING —) BAT BUST TIRL
BOOZE SPRAY SPREE SCREED
SPLORE CAROUSE GAEDOWN
WASSAIL POTATION
BOUTONNIERE BOUQUET
BUTTONHOLE
BOUW BAHU BAHOE
BOVATE OSKEN OXGANG OXGATE
OXLAND
(TWO —S) HUSBANDLAND
BOVINE OX BOS COW BOSS BULL
CALF DULL NEAT SLOW ZEBU
BEAST BISON STEER ANIMAL
COWISH HUMLIE HUMMEL OXLIKE
ROTHER BULLOCK TAURINE
BANGTAIL LEPTOBOS
BOW ARC LEG LUG NOD SAW TIE
YEW ARCH BAIL BECK BEND BENT
CURB DUCK FOLD FORE GORA
JOUK KNEE KNOT LATH LOUT MOVE
PROW SELF STEM SWIM TRUE TURN
WEND BINGE CLINE CONGE COQUE
COUCH CROOK CRUSH CURVE
DEFER GOURA HONOR KNEEL
NOEUD SHIKO STICK STOOP VENIE
YIELD ARCHER ASSENT BAUBLE
BUCKLE CONGEE CRINGE CROUCH
CURTSY FIDDLE FOGBOW RIBBON
SALAAM SALUTE SCRAPE SUBMIT
SWERVE TOURTE WEAPON DEPRESS
FOREBOW FORMBOW HANDBOW
INCLINE INFLECT LONGBOW
NECKTIE RAINBOW ARBALEST
COURTESY CRESCENT ENTRANCE
FOGEATER GREETING STONEBOW
TRUELOVE
(— DOWN) ALOUT HUMBLE
(— IN ONE PIECE) SELF
(— LOW) BINGE
(— OF VESSEL) HEAD PROW STEM
ENTRANCE
(— ON SCRAPER) BAIL BALE
(— ON SEA) ATRY
(— OUTWARD) CONVEX
(— SLIGHTLY) ADDRESS
(OVERHANGING —) SWIM
(VIOLIN —) STICK
BOWED ARCO BENT BANDY KNEED
ARCATE ARCATO CURVED BULGING
CURVANT SHAMBLE DOWNBENT

BOWELS GUT GUTS WOMB BELLY COLON ROPES VISCERA ENTRAILS
BOWER RUN BOOR JACK NOOK SALE ABODE ARBOR JOKER KNAVE ANCHOR BOWERY LEFSEL PANDAL BERCEAU CABINET CHAMBER COTTAGE EMBOWER ENCLOSE LEVESEL PERGOLA RETREAT SHELTER TRELLIS THALAMUS
(— FOR SNAKES) KISI
(GARDEN —) ALCOVE
BOWERBIRD CATBIRD COLLARBIRD
BOWFIN AMIA GANOID LAWYER MORGAY SAWYER CHOUPIC DOGFISH GRINDAL GRINDLE GRINNEL MUDFISH
BOWIE STATE ARKANSAS
BOWING FEATHERING
BOWL CAP CUP PAN TUN COUP ROLL TASS TRAY WOOD ARENA BASIN BOWIE DEPAS GUARD JORUM KITTY LAVER MAZER PHIAL PITCH ROGAN SCALE TANOA TAZZA TREEN TROLL BEAKER BICKER CHAWAN CLOSET COOTIE CRATER FESSEL JICARA KETTLE LEKANE MAZARD MORTAR TROUGH TUREEN VESSEL BRIMMER DITCHER DOUBLER DUGGLER SCYPHUS SKYPHOS SPILLER STADIUM TOUCHER TRINDLE TRUNDLE WHISKIN AQUARIUM BRIDECUP FISHBOWL LAVATORY MONTEITH REHOBOAM
(— ILLEGALLY) JERK
(— OF PIPE) STUMMEL
(— ON PEDESTAL) TAZZA SALVER
(— OUT) YORK
(— THAT TOUCHED JACK) TOUCHER
(— WITH TWO HANDLES) CAP DEPAS
(DRINKING —) TUN TASS
(OBLONG —) PITCHI
(PUNCH —) SNEAKER
(SHALLOW —) CAP COUPE WHISKIN
(SMALL —) JACK
(SOUP —) ECUELLE
(SUGAR —) SUGAR SUCRIER
(TOILET —) HOPPER
(WOODEN —) CAP BOWIE KITTY ROGAN BASSIE COOTIE
BOWLEG OUTKNEE
BOWLEGGED BANDY VALGUS
BOWLER POT DERBY KEGLER PINMAN SPINNER TRUNDLER
(CRICKET —S) ATTACK
BOWLINE BOWLIN FARGOOD
BOWLING BOWLS ATTACK KEGLING TENPINS
BOWLS RINK BOCCE BOCCIE
BOW-SHAPED ARCATE
BOWSTRING SERVING
BOWYER BOWER ARTILLER
BOX BED BIN CAR EAR FUR GIG KIT LOB LUG PIX PYX TYE ARCA BARK BODY BOOT CAGE CAJA CASE CIST CRIB CUFF CYST DRAB FLAT HEAD LOGE MILL PACK PUNG SCOB SEAT SLAP SLUG SPAR STOW TILL TRAY ARBOR BARGE BOIST BUXUS CADDY

CAPSA CHEST CLOUT CRATE FIGHT FRAME HUTCH LADLE POUCH PUNCH SHRUB STALL TRUNK ASCHAM BUFFET BUNKER CARTON CASKET COFFER COFFIN DRAWER GRILLE HAMPER HATBOX HAYBOX HOPPER ICEBOX MAROON MOCUCK PATRON PETARA PILLAR SAGGER SHRINE STRIKE TARBOX VANITY ARCANUM BANDBOX BATTERY BOXTREE BOXWOOD CABINET CAISSON CARRIER CASHBOX CASQUET CASSONE CONFINE COREBOX DICEBOX DREDGER DUSTBOX ENCLOSE EXHAUST FOSTELL FREEZER HANAPER JACKBOX PACKAGE PILLBOX PITARAH PRINTER SANDBOX SCATULA SHELTER TRUMMEL WHERRET BOXTHORN DOVECOTE DRAGEOIR JUNCTION LAVARIUM MATCHBOX POMANDER SHOWCASE SLIPCASE SOLANDER SWEATBOX
(— FOR CUTLERY) CANTEEN
(— FOR FISH) CAR NID
(— FOR MONEY OFFERING) ARCA LADLE
(— FOR SALT) DRAB
(— FOR SEAL) SKIPPET
(— FOR SEED) LEAP
(— FOR TOBACCO) BUTT DOSS CADDY SARATOGA
(— IN TIMEPIECE) BARREL
(— IN WHEEL HUB) FUR
(— OF BIRCHBARK) MOCUCK
(— OF FIRE CLAY) SAGGAR SAGGER
(— OF ORGAN) BOOT SWELL
(— TO SHELTER BELL) SCONCE
(— USED AS DARKROOM) TENT
(BERRY —) HALLOCK
(BREAD —) BARGE
(CANDLE —) BARK
(CIRCULAR —) THIMBLE
(COMPASS —) KETTLE BINNACLE
(FANCY —) ETUI ETWEE
(FLOATING —) CAISSON
(FOUNDRY —) FRAME
(IRON —) HANGER
(JUGGLER'S —) TRANKA
(MONEY —) CASH SAFE PIRLIE
(PIVOTING —) TOUR
(PRINTING —) TURTLE
(REFRIGERATOR —) COOLER
(SHALLOW —) FLAT BACKET HARBOR
(SNUFF —) MILL MULL
(TEA —) CADDY
(TIN —) TRUMMEL VASCULUM
BOX BRIER INDIGO INKBERRY
BOXCAR LOWRY STOCKCAR
BOX ELDER MAPLE NEGUNDO
BOXER CHAMP DARES BANTAM MILLER NOBBER TANKER WELTER BRUISER CRUISER FIGHTER SLUGGER SPARRER BUFFETER PUGILIST SOUTHPAW
BOXFISH CHAPIN COWFISH SHELLFISH TRUNKFISH
BOXING PLUG SAVATE PARINGS

SCIENCE SPARRING
(— GLOVE) MUFFLE
BOX TORTOISE COOTER
BOXWOOD KNYSNA DUDGEON
BOXY BLOCKY
BOY BO BUB FAG GUY HIM LAD PUR TAD BOYO CHAP LOON NINO PAGE PUER BILLY BUBBY BUDDY CHABO CHILD CRACK GAMIN GILPY GROOM KNAVE PUTTO ROGUE SWAIN VALET YOUTH BIRKIE BUTTON CALLAN CHOKRA GAFFER GARCON MANNIE MASTER NIPPER RASCAL SHAVER STIRRA UMFAAN URCHIN BOUCHAL CALLANT DRAWBOY GLEANER GOSSOON GRUMMET JACKBOY RUBBLER SERVANT SPADGER TRAPPER CLERGION HENCHBOY MUCHACHO SPALPEEN
(— DRESSED AS WOMAN) MALINCHE
(— OF FREE BIRTH) CAMILLUS
(ALTAR —) ACOLYTE THURIFER
(AWKWARD —) CUB CALF GRUMMET
(BOLD —) SPALPEEN
(CHOIR —) CHILD
(CLEANING —) BUSBOY
(COLLIER'S —) HODDER
(EFFEMINATE —) SISSY
(HEAD —) SENIOR CAPTAIN
(ILL-MANNERED —) CUB
(MY —) AVICK
(NATIVE —) MOWGLI
(NON-JEWISH —) SHEGETZ
(OFFICE —) DUFTRY DUFTERY
(PERT —) CRACK
(POOR —) HERO
(ROGUISH —) CRACK GAMIN URCHIN
(SAUCY —) NACKET
(SERVING —) KNAVE PEDEE CHOKRA MOUSSE FOOTBOY GOSSOON
(SILLY —) CALF
(SMALL —) BO BUDDY UMFAAN SPADGER
(SPRIGHTLY —) CRACK
(STABLE —) MAFU MAFOO MEHTAR
(TOWN —) CAD
(YOUNG —) LAD SONNY YOUTH NIPPER
(PL.) BOYHOOD
BOYCOTT MITE SHUN AVOID DEBAR BLACKBALL
BOYFRIEND BEAU STEADY
BRACE LEG MAN TIE TWO BEND BIND CASE FRAP GIRD JACK KNEE LACE MARK PAIR PROP SPUR STAY STEM STUD CLAMP CRANK DWANG GIRTH HOUND NERVE POISE RIDER SHORE STOCK STRUT ANKLET BINDER BRACHE CLENCH COLLAR COUPLE CRUTCH FASTEN FATHOM HURTER SPLINT STRING WIMBLE BOTTINE BRACKET EMBRACE REFRESH SPANNER STIFFEN SUPPORT ACCOLADE BITBRACE BITSTALK BITSTOCK BUTTRESS CROSSBAR ENCIRCLE
(— ACROSS CABLE) STUD
(— AND HALF) LEASH

(— **BETWEEN FRAMES**) TOM
(— **FOR POST**) SPUR
(— **UP**) ACCINGE SHARPEN
(PL.) BRIDGING
BRACED BENT
(— **ABACK**) ABOX
BRACELET BAND RING ARMIL CHAIN
ARMLET BANGLE GRIVNA ARMILLA
CURCLET MANACLE POIGNET
RACETTE WRISTER HANDCUFF
MUFFETEE WRISTLET
(**SHELL** —) SANKHA
BRACER TONIC SHORER BLOCKER
ARMGUARD STIFFENER STIMULANT
BRACHIAL HUMERAL
BRACHIOPOD ATREMATE ATRYPOID
SPIRIFER
BRACHIUM ARM
BRACING CRISP QUICK TONIC
DUNNAGE
BRACKEN FERN BRAKE PLAID
BRACKET BIBB COCK CONK FORK
GATE PUNK ANCON BELOW BRACE
CLASS CONCH COUCH CRANE
CRANK CROOK LEVEL SHELF STRUT
TRUSS ANCONE BECKET BRIDGE
CORBEL COUPLE GUSSET HANGER
LADDER SADDLE SCONCE BECKETT
CONSOLE DERRICK FEATHER
FIXTURE GATELEG LOOKOUT
POTENCE SPONSON SPOTTED
BRAGWORT CATEGORY CROTCHET
MISERERE SPECKLED STRADDLE
(PL.) HOOKS CROOKS
BRACKISH YAR FOIST SALTY
BRACKY SALINE BREACHY SALTISH
NAUSEOUS
BRACT HUSK LEAF GLUME LEMMA
PALEA PALET SCALE SPADIX
SPATHE BRACTLET PHYLLARY
BRAD PIN NAIL PRIG RIVET SPRIG
BRAE BANK BRAY BROW HILL CLEVE
SLOPE WOUGH CLEEVE VALLEY
BRAG JET BLAW BLOW CROW DEFY
FACE HUFF PUFF WIND WOST YELP
BLUFF BOAST CRACK FLIRD PREEN
SKITE STRUT VAUNT BLEEZE
BOUNCE INSULT SPLORE SPROSE
SQUIRT DISPLAY GAUSTER ROISTER
SWAGGER BRAGGART FLOURISH
PRETENSE THREATEN
BRAGGART BRAG PUFF BOAST
FACER BLOWER CROWER GASCON
HECTOR POTGUN SKITER THRASO
BLOWOFF BOASTER BOBADIL
CRACKER RUFFLER SHALLOW
VAPORER BANGSTER BLOWHARD
CACAFUGO FANFARON PAROLLES
PUCKFIST RENOWNER RODOMONT
SKIPJACK
BRAGGARTISM COCKALORUM
BRAGGING ROOSE JACTANCE
RODOMONT THRASONIC
BRAHMA KA SELF BRAMAH
BRAHMAN ARYAN HINDU PUNDIT
SMARTA BRAHMIN
BRAID CUE BRAY GIMP JERK LACE
PLAT TAIL TRIM BREDE FANCY
FREAK JIFFY LACET MILAN ONSET

ORRIS PLAIT PLEAT QUEUE START
TAGAL TRACE TRADE TRESS TRICK
TWINE VOMIT WEAVE BOBBIN
BORDER CORDON EDGING GALLON
LACING MOMENT PLIGHT RIBBON
SENNET SNATCH STRING BANDING
BULLION CAPRICE ENTWINE
UPBRAID BRANDISH ORNAMENT
REPROACH SOUTACHE TRIMMING
(— **FOR HATS**) SENNET SINNET
(— **OF WIG**) SNAKE
(**LINEN** —) INKLE
BRAIDER RATCHER
BRAIDING FROG BREDE
BRAIN MAD BEAN HARN MIND PATE
UTAC WITS AXION HAIRN HAURN
SKULL NODDLE PSYCHE FURIOUS
SENSORY THINKER CEREBRUM
(PL.) HARN PATE SCONCE HEADPICE
BRAINLESS SILLY STUPID FOOLISH
WITLESS
BRAINPAN PAN HARNPAN PANNICLE
BRAIN SAND SABULUM
BRAIZE BECKER
BRAKE COW BULL BURR CAGE CLOG
CURB DRAG FERN LOCK RACK SKID
SLOW STAY TARA TRAP BLOCK
CHECK COPSE DELAY DETER GRIPE
SNARE SPOKE SPRAG VOMIT BRIDLE
CONVOY HARROW HINDER REMORA
RETARD STAYER WARABI BRACKEN
DEADMAN DILEMMA SLIPPER
STOPPER THICKET TRIGGER
DRAGROPE RETARDER
BRAKEMAN GUARD SHACK SHAKE
BRAKIE NIPPER DILLIER SNAPPER
SWAMPER DILLYMAN INCLINER
TRAINMAN
BRAMBLE WHIN BRIER RHAMN THIEF
THORN BUMBLE JAGGER LAWYER
STICKER DEWBERRY MAYBERRY
NESSBERRY
BRAMBLE BUSH TUTU GRANJENO
BRAMBLING KATE SNOWHAMMER
BRAMBLY DUMAL SPINY THORNY
PRICKLY
BRAN GRIT SEED DARAK TREAT
CEREAL CHISEL POLLARD TOPPING
BEESWING
(— **AND MEAL**) SHORTS
(**CORNMEAL** —) HUSK
(**FINE** —) POLLEN
(**UNSORTED** —) RUBBLES
BRANCH ARM BOW LAP LEG LOP
RAY RUN BARB BROG BUSH CHAT
FANG FORK LIMB PALM PART RAME
RICE RISE SNAG SNUG SPUR STEM
STUD TANG TWIG YARD AXITE
BAYOU BOUGH BREAK BRIAR BRIER
CREEK DRUPA GRAIN LAYER LULOV
PLASH PRONG RAMUS REISE SCROG
SHOOT SHRAG SPRAY SPRIG STICK
TWIST VIMEN WITHE BUREAU
CLADUS DIVIDE DRUKPA EXOPOD
GERMEN GREAVE GROWTH LEADER
MEMBER OFFSET OUTLET PHYLUM
PORTIO RADDLE RAMAGE RAMIFY
RUNNER SHROUD SPRANG STOLON
STREAM TAPOUN CHAPTER DIALECT

DIVERGE ENDOPOD FURCATE
LATERAL PHYLLIS RAMULUS
TENDRIL TORRENT ANAPHYTE
BRONCHUS DISTRICT EFFLUENT
OFFSHOOT PEASTICK SCAFFOLD
SPRANGLE TRAILING
(— **OF ANTLER**) SPELLER
ADVANCER
(— **OF COLONY**) STIPE
(— **OF CRAFT**) INDUSTRY
(— **OF FAMILY**) SEPT
(— **OF FEATHER**) BARB
(— **OF HORN**) RIAL ANTLER
(— **OF IVY**) BUSH
(— **OF LEARNING**) ART STUDY
FACULTY KNOWLEDGE
(— **OF MATHEMATICS**) ALGEBRA
CALCULUS
(— **OF THALLUS**) STICHID
(— **OF TREASURY**) FISCUS
(**DEAD** —) FLAG
(**EVERGREEN** —**S**) GREENS
(**LOCAL** —) COURT
(**MINE** —) LEADER
(**PALM** —) LULAB
(**SMALL** —) RICE
(**YOUNGER** —) CADET
(PL.) LOFT RAMI SKIRT SPRAY
RAMAGE CYPRESS DEADWOOD
BRANCHED FORKY FORKED RAMATE
RAMOSE CLADOSE TROCHED
BRANCHIA GILL
BRANCHING ARMY RAMOSE
FURCATE DICHOTOMY
BRANCHIOPOD SHRIMP
BRANCHLET RAMULUS SPILLER
BRAND BIRN BLOT BURN CHOP
FLAW KIND MARK NOTE SEAR SMIT
SMOT SORT VENT WIPE BUIST
INURE LABEL SCEAR STAIN STAMP
SWORD TAINT TORCH BARREL
MARQUE STIGMA FLAMBEAU
BRANDING IRON BRAND CAUTER
SEARER CAUTERY
BRANDISH WAG DART STIR WAVE
WIND BLESS BRAID SHAKE SWING
WIELD FLAUNT HURTLE QUAVER
RUFFLE STRAIN WINNOW FLUTTER
GLITTER SWAGGER VIBRATE
FLOURISH VAMBRASH
BRANDY DOP BOOF FINE JACK
MARC BINGO MOBBY NANTS PEACH
RAKIA CINDER COGNAC GRAPPA
KIRSCH PUPELO RAKIJA VISNEY
ANISADO AQUAVIT QUETSCH
ARMAGNAC CALVADOS SLIVOVIC
BRANK MUMPS BRIDLE PILLORY
BRANLE BRAWL
BRANT ROUT ERECT PROUD QUINK
SHEER STEEP ROUGHT
BRASH GAY BOLD FACY RASH
HASTY SAUCY STORM ATTACK
RUBBLE BRITTLE FORWARD
IMPUDENT TACTLESS
BRASQUE STEEP
BRASS CASH ALLOY MONEY NERVE
BRAZEN BRONZE MASLIN ORMOLU
OFFICER ORICHALC
(— **PLAYER**) WINDJAMMER

BRASSIERE BANDEAU
BRAT BIB GET IMP BROT FILM SCUM
  APRON BAIRN BILSH BROLL CHILD
  CLOAK GAITT INFANT MANTLE
  TERROR URCHIN GARMENT
BRATTICER AIRMAN CANVASMAN
BRAVADO POMP BRAVE PRIDE
  STORM HECTOR BLUSTER BOMBAST
  BRAVERY SWAGGER VAUNTERY
  GASCONISM
BRAVE BOLD BRAW DARE DEFY
  FACE FINE GAME GOOD PROW TALL
  WILD ADORN BOAST BRAVO BULLY
  FELON HARDY JOLLY MANLY
  MOODY ORPED ROMAN STIFF
  STOUT VAUNT WIGHT BRAWLY
  BREAST DARING HEROIC MANFUL
  PLUCKY STURDY BRAVADO
  DOUGHTY GALLANT HAUTAIN
  SOLDIER SWAGGER VALIANT
  VENTURE WARRIOR CAVALIER
  DEFIANCE EMBOLDEN FEARLESS
  INTREPID LIONLIKE STALWART
  SUPERIOR VALOROUS VIRTUOUS
BRAVELY BIG FINELY
BRAVERY GRIT VALOR SPIRIT
  VIRTUE BRAVADO BRAVURA
  COURAGE HEROISM JOLLITY
  MANHEAD MANHOOD PROWESS
  BOLDNESS
BRAVO OLE RAH EUGE THUG BRAVE
  BULLY BANDIT CUTTER BRAVADO
  SHABASH VILLAIN APPLAUSE
  ASSASSIN
BRAWL DIN ROW BEEF CLEM FRAY
  RIOT BLIND BROIL CHIDE CLASH
  FIGHT MELEE REVEL SCOLD SCRAP
  AFFRAY BICKER FRACAS HABBLE
  REVILE RUFFLE RUMPUS SHINDY
  STOUSH STRIFE TUMULT UPROAR
  YATTER BOBBERY BRABBLE
  DISCORD DISPUTE QUARREL
  SCUFFLE WRANGLE COMPLAIN
  SQUABBLE STRAMASH
BRAWLER FRATCH NICKER SQUARER
  FRAMPLER NIGHTCAP OUTCRIER
BRAWLING NOISY BLATANT FLITING
  SCAMBLING
BRAWN BEEF BOAR LIRE FLESH
  FATTEN MUSCLE STRENGTH
  (MOCK —) HEADCHEESE
BRAWNY BEEFY FLESHY ROBUST
  SINEWY SQUARE STRONG STURDY
  CALLOUS MUSCULAR POWERFUL
  STALWART
BRAXY BRADSOT
BRAY CRY MIX RUB BEAT ROUT
  TOOL CRUSH GRIND NOISE POUND
  STAMP BRUISE HEEHAW OUTCRY
  PESTLE THRASH WHINNY
BRAYERA KOSO CUSSO KOSSO
BRAZEN BOLD CALM HARD PERT
  BRASS HARDY HARSH SASSY
  AENEAN BRASSY BLATANT CALLOUS
  FORWARD IMMODEST IMPUDENT
  INSOLENT METALLIC
BRAZENFACED CHEEKY
BRAZIER HEARTH HIBACHI REREDOS
  SCALDINO
BRAZIL ROSET

BRAZIL

BAY: MARAJO IGRANDE SEPETIBA
  GUANABARA
BIRD: MITU MITUA
CAPE: FRIO BLANCO BUZIOS
  GURUPY ORANGE SAOTOME
  SAOROQUE
CAPITAL: BRASILIA
COIN: JOE REIS CONTO DOBRA
  HALFJOE MILREIS CRUZEIRO
DAM: FURNAS PEIXOTO
DANCE: SAMBA MAXIXE
ESTUARY: PARA
FALLS: IGUAZU IGUASSU
INDIAN: ANTA ACROA ARARA
  ARAUA BRAVO CARIB GUANA
  ARAWAK CARAJA CARAYAN
  JAVAHAI TARIANA BOTOCUDO
  CHAMBIOA
ISLAND: MARACA MARAJO
  BANANAL CARDOSO CAVIANA
  MEXIANA COMPRIDA
LAKE: AIMA FEIA MIRIM
MEASURE: PE MOIO PIPA SACK
  VARA BRACA FANGA LEGOA
  MILHA PALMO PASSO TONEL
  CANADA COVADO CUARTA
  LEAGUE QUARTO TAREFA
  ALQUIER GARRAFA ALQUEIRE
MOUNTAIN: URUCUM BANDEIRA
  ITATIAIA
MOUNTAINS: MAR GERAL ORGAN
  PIAUI ACARAI GURUPI ORGAOS
  PARIMA AMAMBAI CARAJAS
  GRADAUS RONCADOR
  TOMBADOR
NATIVE: CABOCLO CURIBOCA
  MAMELUCO PAULISTA
PORT: RIO PARA BAHIA BELEM
  NATAL SANTOS PELOTAS
  SALVADOR
STATE: ACRE PARA AMAPA BAHIA
  CEARA GOIAS GOYAZ PIAUI
  PARANA PIAUHY ALAGOAS
  GUAPORE PARAIBA RORAIMA
  SERGIPE AMAZONAS MARANHAO
  PARAHIBA PARAHYBA RONDONIA
  SAOPAULO
RIVER: APA ICA DOCE GEIO IVAI
  JARI PARA PARU SONO TEFE
  ABUNA ANAUA APORE CAPIM
  CLARO CORUA ICANA IRIRI ITAPI
  JURUA JUTAI MANSO NEGRO
  PARDO PIAUI PRETO TIETE
  TURVO URUBU VERDE XINGU
  AJUANA AMAZON ARINOS
  BALSAS BRANCO CANUMA
  CONTAS CUIABA DEMINI GRAJAU
  GRANDE GURUPI IBICUI IGUACU
  JAPURA JAVARI MEARIM
  MORTES MUCURI PARANA
  PURPUS RONURO SANGUE
  TACUTU TIBAGI UATUMA
  UAUPES VELHAS CORUMBA
  IGUASSU MADEIRA PARAIBA
  SUCURIU TAPAJOS TAQUARI
  TEODORO URUGUAI ARAGUAIA

  PADAUIRI PARACATU PARAGUAI
  PARNAIBA SOLIMOES TARAUACA
TOWN: ACU EXU ICO IPU ITU JAU
  LUZ RIO UBA BAGE FARO IBIA
  IJUI ITAI LAPA LINS PARA PIUI
  TUPA UNAI BAHIA BAIAO BAURU
  BELEM CEARA NATAL NEVES
  CAMPOS CUIABA ILHEUS
  MACEIO MANAOS MANAUS
  OLINDA RECIFE SANTOS
  ARACAJU CARUARU CITORIA
  GOIANIA ITABUNA JUNDIAI
  NITEROI PELOTAS TAUBATE
  UBERABA ANAPOLIS BRASILIA
  CAMPINAS CURITIBA LONDRINA
  SALVADOR SOROCABA
  TERESINA
TREE: ICICA UCUUBA ARARIBA
WEIGHT: BAG ONCA LIBRA
  ARROBA OITAVA ARRATEL
  QUILATE QUINTAL TONELADA

BRAZIL NUT JUVIA CASTANA
BRAZILWOOD VERZINO HYPERNIO
  PEACHWOOD
BREACH GAP CHAP FLAW GOOL
  RENT RIFT SLAP BRACK BRECK
  BURST CHASM CLEFT CRACK PAUSE
  SPLIT WOUND BRUISE HARBOR
  HERNIA HIATUS INROAD SCHISM
  SCREED SLUICE ASSAULT BLEMISH
  DISPUTE FISSURE OPENING
  QUARREL RUPTURE BREAKING
  CREVASSE FRACTION FRACTURE
  INTERVAL OUTBREAK SOLUTION
  TRESPASS
  (— IN DIKE) GOOL
  (— IN SEAWAY) GOOL
  (— OF DUTY) BARRATRY
  (— OF ETIQUETTE) SOLECISM
  (— OF FAITH) TREASON
  (— OF MORALITY) SCAPE VAGARY
  (— OF PEACE) FRACTION
  (— OF UNITY) SOHISM
BREAD BAP BUN BODY BRAD DIET
  FARE FOOD LOAF PAIN PONE RIMA
  ROLL RUSH RUSK TOKE AZYME
  BATCH BATON BOXTY CAPER CHEAT
  KISRA LIMPA MICHE ROOTY TOMMY
  CHAPON COCKET DAMPER DODGER
  ENZYME HALLAH KANKIE MASLIN
  MATZOS PANNAM SIMNEL TAMMIE
  WASTEL YANNAM ALIMENT
  BANNOCK EULOGIA MANCHET
  POPOVER STOLLEN TOASTER
  CORNCAKE HARDTACK SOFTTACK
  ZWIEBACK
  (— AND MILK) POBS PANADA
  POBBIES
  (— BOX) PANETIERE
  (— QUALITY) PANEITY
  (BATCH OF —) CAST
  (BUTTERED —) CAPER
  (DRY —) TOKE
  (EUCHARISTIC —) BODY HOST
  AZYME
  (FANCY —) BRAID
  (MAIZE —) PIKI

(OATMEAL —) ANACK JANNOCK
(POTATO —) FADGE
(QUICK —) SCONE
(S. AFRICAN —) DIKA
(SLICE OF —) TARTINE TRENCHER
(SMALL LOAF OF —) COB
(SMALL PIECE OF —) SIPPET
MEALOCK
(SOPPED —) MISER BREWIS BROWIS
(SWEET —) BUN BROWNIE STOLLEN
(TOASTED —) SIPPET
(UNLEAVENED —) AZYM AZYME
BANNOCK CHAPATTI
(WHEAT —) CHEAT HOVIS COCKET
MANCHET
BREADBOARD PANEL
BREADED ANGLAISE
BREADFRUIT MASI RIMA RIMAS
DUGDUG NANGCA CAMANSI
CASTANA ANTIPOLO BREADNUT
CHESTNUT
BREADNUT RAM
BREADWINNING GAP BOON BUST
DASH HINT KNAP PICK PLOW REND
RENT RIFT RIVE
BREAK GO CUT JAR LOP TEN ABRA
BUST CHIP DRAG FALL FLAW PART
RUIN RUSH SLIP SNAP STEP STOP
TEAR TURN UNDO WASH WORK
ALTER BLANK BURST CHECK CHINK
CLEFT COMMA CRACK CRAZE
DAUNT FALSE FRUSH LAPSE PAUSE
PLUCK ROUGH SEVER SMASH
SOLVE SPAWN SPELT STAVE SWING
WOUND BRUISE CABBLE CHANGE
CLEAVE CRANNY CUTOUT DEFEAT
HIATUS IMPAIR LACUNA PIERCE
SALTUS SHREND SPRING TEWTAW
TEWTER BLUNDER CAESURA
CRACKLE CRANKLE CREVICE
CRUMBLE DESTROY DISABLE
DISPART DISRUPT EXHAUST
FISSURE GRITTLE INFRACT INTERIM
OPENING RESPITE RUPTURE
SHATTER TAILING VARIATE
BREATHER CREVASSE DIERESIS
DIFFRACT FRACTION FRACTURE
FRAGMENT INFRINGE INTERVAL
SEPARATE SOLUTION STRAMASH
(— APART) SUNDER DISRUPT
SHATTER
(— AWAY) BOLT ESCAPE
(— BOULDERS) BULLDOZE
(— DOWN) CONK FAIL GIVE CRAZE
CROCK TRAIK BRUISE TUMBLE
ANALYZE FOUNDER REFRACT
COLLAPSE INFRINGE
(— FORCE) BAFFLE
(— FORTH) BOIL ERUPT EVENT
FLASH EXPLODE
(— FROM ICE MASS) CALVE
(— GLASS) SHREND DRAGADE
(— IN PIECES) CHAP DICE KNAP
CRASH CRAZE SMASH SMOKE
SHIVER CRUMBLE FRITTER SMATTER
DEMOLISH DIFFRACT DISJOINT
SPLINTER STRAMASH
(— IN WAVES) JABBLE
(— IN YARN) SMASH

(— IN) ENTER
(— INTO FOAM) COMB
(— INTO) BROACH IRRUPT
(— INWARD) STAVE
(— LANCE) TAINT
(— OF CONTINUITY) SALTUS
(— OFF) NUB DROP SNAP CEASE
LRAVE ABRUPT DIREMPT
(— OFF END) SNUB
(— OPEN) BUST CHOP FORCE
(— ORE) COB SPALL SPAWL
(— OUT) ERUPT START ASSURD
STRIKE
(— RANKS) DISMISS
(— SHARPLY) KNACK
(— SILENCE) QUATCH QUETCH
(— SKIN) GALL
(— SLATE) SCULP
(— STONE) CAVIL KEVEL
(— THE BACK) CHINE
(— THROUGH SHELL) PIP
(— THROUGH) BEAT FORCE
(— UP EARTH) HACK FALLOW
(— UP SIEGE) LEVY
(— UP) BUCK FALL MELT FLOUR
SEVER SPALE SPLIT STASH INCIDE
DEGRADE DIFFUSE DISBAND
DISSECT DISTURB REFRACT
SCARIFY SCATTER CROSSCUT
DISJOINT DISPERSE DISSOLVE
DISUNIFY FRAGMENT
(— WATER) FIN
(— WINDOWS) NICK
(STEM —) BROWNING
BREAKABLE BRITTLE BRUCKLE
FRIABLE DELICATE FRANGIBLE
BREAKAGE GRIEF
BREAKAX IRONWOOD
BREAKDOWN EDGER BURNOUT
DEBACLE HOEDOWN COLLAPSE
DILUTION
(— OF RIND) ADUSTIOSIS
(ELECTRIC —) AVALANCHE
BREAKER JUMP SURF WAVE
BEAKER BILLOW COMBER ROLLER
CRACKER SLEDGER LEDGEMAN
SCRAPPER
(— OF WORD) WARLOCK
(CIRCUIT —) CUTOUT
(ROCK —) ALLIGATOR
(PL.) BREACH
BREAKFAST BRUNCH DISJUNE
DISJEUNE
BREAKING BREACH BREAKUP
FRACTION FRACTURE SOLUTION
(— FORTH) ERUPTIVE
(— OFF) CHIPPING ABRUPTION
(— UP) DEBACLE ANALYSIS
BREAKSTONE SAXIFRAGE
BREAKWATER COB DAM COBB
CROY DIKE MOLE PIER PILE QUAY
JETTY GROYNE REFUGE BULWARK
STOCKADE
BREAM TAI BRIM CARP CHAD SCUP
SHAD ZOPE BROOM ROMAN BALEEN
BARWIN BRAISE SARGUS OLDWIFE
SUNFISH WAREHOU CYPRINID
FLATFISH STEENJIE TARWHINE
BREAST DUG BUMP CROP FACE

BOOBY BOSOM BRAVE BUBBY
CHEST HEART PETTO STALL
PECTUS POMMEL THORAX BRISKET
COUNTER KNOCKER FOREBOWS
(— OF HORSE) COUNTER
(PL.) BUST
BREASTBAND HORSE
BREASTBONE BREAST STERNUM
XIPHOID
BREASTHOOK CRUTCH FOREHOOK
BREASTPIECE RABAT RABBI
BREASTPLATE EGIS URIM AEGIS
BREAST GORGET LORICA ORACLE
SHIELD THORAX CUIRASS PALETTE
POITREL PECTORAL PLASTRON
BREASTWORK FORT REDAN
SANGAR SCHANZ SCHERM SUNGAR
BRATTLE PARAPET PLUTEUS
RAMPART BRATTICE
BREATH AIR ANDE GASP HUFF LIFE
ONDE PANT PECH PUFF SIGH WAFT
WIND BLAST PAUSE SCENT SMELL
VAPOR WHIFF BREEZE FLATUS
PNEUMA HALITUS INSTANT RESPITE
SPIRACLE
(— OF WIND) SPIRIT
(BAD —) OZOSTOMIA
(DIVINE —) NEPHESH
(LIFE —) PRANA SPIRIT
BREATHE ANDE LIVE ONDE PANT
PECH PUFF SIGH VENT EXIST EXUDE
SPEAK SPIRE UTTER ASPIRE
EXHALE INHALE WHEEZE AFFLATE
EMANATE RESPIRE SUSPIRE
(— HEAVILY) FOB PECH FNESE
SOUGH THROTTLE
(— LABORIOUSLY) GASP
(— NOISILY) SOUGH SNOTTER
(— UPON) FAN
BREATHING AIR ALIVE PNEUMA
SPIRIT GASPING SPIRITUS
SPIRATION
(— HEAVILY) SUSPIRIOUS
(LABORED —) ASTHMA
(SMOOTH —) LENE LENIS
BREATHLESSNESS TIFT
BREATHY HOLLOW ADENOID
BRED (WELL --) FREE
BREECH BORE BUTT DOUP BLOCK
BRICK CULOTTE DRODDUM
BUTTOCKS CYLINDER DERRIERE
BREECHBLOCK BLOCK VENTPIECE
BREECHCLOTH HIPPEN HIPPING
BREECHES HOSE CHAPS JEANS
LEVIS SLOPS STOCK TREWS
BRACAE BRAGAS BREEKS GASKIN
SMALLS TIGHTS TROUSE BOMBARDS
BREEKUMS JODHPURS KICKSIES
KNICKERS LEATHERS TROUSERS
PANTALOON
BREED GET ILK BEAR KIND RACE
REAR SORT BEGET BROOD CASTE
CAUSE CLASS FANCY HATCH ISSUE
RAISE STOCK STORE TRAIN CREATE
GENDER STRAIN EDUCATE NOURISH
PRODUCE PROGENY SPECIES
VARIETY ENGENDER GENERATE
INSTRUCT MULTIPLY
BREEDER RANCHER AURELIAN

HERDSMAN HORSEMAN
(FISH —) MILTER
BREEDING ORIGIN DESCENT
NURTURE TUPPING BEHAVIOR
CIVILITY PREGNANT TRAINING
(GOOD —) GENTRY
BREEZE AIR AURA BLOW FLAW GALE
GUST PIRR STIR WIND BLAST
RUMOR SLANT WALTZ BREATH
DOCTOR REPORT SLATCH SPIRIT
ZEPHYR FRESHEN MUZZLER
QUARREL VIRASON WHISPER
(COOL —) DOCTOR
(GENTLE —) AIR AURA ZEPHYR
(LAND —) TERRAL
(STIFF —) STOUR TIFTER
BREEZE FLY WHAME
BREEZY AIRY BRISK FRESH WINDY
AIRISH
BRETHREN IKHWAN
BRETON ARMORICAN
BREVE NOTE WRIT BRIEF MINIM
ORDER SHORT PRECEPT
BREVIARY ORDO CURSUS DIGEST
LEDGER PORTAS COUCHER
EPITOME SUMMARY ABSTRACT
PORTESSE PORTHORS
BREVITY SYNTOMY LACONISM
UNLENGTH BRIEFNESS SHORTNESS
TERSENESS
BREW ALE MIX BEER BOIL MAKE
PLOT POUR DRINK HATCH STOUT
BROWST DEVISE DILUTE FOMENT
GATHER LIQUOR SEETHE CONCOCT
INCLINE PREPARE CONTRIVE
(HOME —) SAMOGON
BREWER TUNNER
BREWING GAIL GYLE BROWST
BRIBE BUD FEE FIX OIL ROB SOP TIP
BAIT GIFT HAVE HIRE MEED MOIL
PALM VAIL WAGE BONUS CUDDY
GRAFT OFFER STEAL SUGAR TEMPT
TOUCH EXTORT GREASE NOBBLE
PAYOLA SQUARE SUBORN CORRUPT
DOUCEUR SWEETEN TICKLER
GRATUITY VENALIZE
BRIBERY MEED
BRIC-A-BRAC CURIO VERTU VIRTU
BIBELOT TROCKERY TRUMPERY
BRICK BAT GLUT MARL PAVE TILE
BLOCK QUARL SPLIT STOCK STONE
TOOTH CUTTER FELLOW HEADER
PAMENT PAVIOR BACKING CLINKER
FLETTON GRIZZLE PERPEND
SOLDIER BURNOVER
(— WALL) NECK
(CRACKED —) CHUFF SHUFF
(FINAL HALF —) JACK
(IMPERFECT —) BURNOVER
(PILE OF —S) HACK CLAMP
(PULVERIZED —) SOORKY SOORKEE
(SECOND-RATE —) GRIZZLE
(SOFT —) CUTTER RUBBER PICKING
(SQUARE —) QUADREL
(STACK OF —) LIFT
(SUN-DRIED —) BAT ADOBE
(UNBURNT —) ADOBE
(WOODEN —) DOOK
(PL.) CLAYWARE

BRICKLAYER BRICKY MASONER
BRICKMAKER MOLDER
BRICKWORK HOB BRICKING
BRIDAL NUPTIAL BRIDALTY
BRIDE KALLAH SPOUSE SHULAMITE
BRIDE-PRICE LOBOLA LOBOLD
BRIDESMAID PARANYMPH
BRIDEWELL MILLDOLL
BRIDGE WAY BRIG LINK NOSE PONS
PONT REST SPAN WIEN CROSS
SIRAT TOWIE GANTRY ISLAND
JIGGER RUNWAY SANGAR AUCTION
BASCULE BIFROST CONNECT
CULVERT EXOSTRA PASSAGE
PASSING PINNOCK PONCEAU
PONTOON PROPONS TRAJECT
TRESTLE VIADUCT CONTRACT
TRAVERSE DUPLICATE
(— OF MUSICAL INSTRUMENT)
MAGAS CHEVALET
(ARCADED —) RIALTO
(CONTRACT —) GHOULIE PLAFOND
(FLUE —) ALTAR
(GATEWAY —) GOUT
(HOSE —) JUMPER
(IMPEDANCE —) DIPLEXER
(NATURAL —) ARCH
(ROPE SUSPENSION —) JOOLA
BRIDGEMAKER PONTIFEX
BRIDGEMAN EBBMAN
BRIDGING ASTRIDE STRUTTING
BRIDLE BIT CURB REIN RULE BRAKE
BRANK BRIDE CHECK GUARD GUIDE
STRUT DIRECT GOVERN HALTER
MASTER SIMPER SUBDUE BLINDER
CONTROL LORMERY REPRESS
SNAFFLE SWAGGER CAVESSON
RESTRAIN SUPPRESS
BRIDLE PATH SPURWAY
BRIEF FEW CURT LIST RIFE WRIT
BLURB BREVE CHARM PITHY QUICK
SHORT TERSE ABRUPT COMMON
CURTAL FLYING HOURLY LETTER
LITTLE SNIPPY SUDDEN ABRIDGE
CAPSULE COMPACT COMPOSE
CONCISE CRYPTIC INVOICE LACONIC
MANDATE OUTLINE PRECEPT
SUMMARY BREVIATE CONDENSE
FLEETING FLITTING SNATCHED
SNIPPETY SUCCINCT SYLLABUS
BRIEF CASE FOLIO TASHIE
BRIEFLY BRIEF ENFIN SHORTLY
BRIER BARB PIPE BRIAR THORN
SMILAX BRUYERE INKBERRY
BRIER TREE PIPER
BRIG RIG JAIL PRISON GEORDIE
BRIGADE TERZO CAMPOO
BRIGAND THIEF USKOK BANDIT
LATRON PIRATE ROBBER CATERAN
KETTRIN LADRONE ROUTIER
SOLDIER PICAROON
(PL.) TCHETNITSI
BRIGANDINE PLACCATE
BRIGHT APT GAY NET FINE GILD
GLAD GLEG HIGH LIVE ROSY ACUTE
AGLOW ALERT ANIME BEAMY BRAVE
CLEAR CRISP EAGLE FLARY FRESH
GEMMY JOLLY LIGHT LUCID NITID
PRINT QUICK RIANT SHARP SHEEN

SHEER SHINY SMART SMOLT STEEP
SUNNY TINNY VIVID WHITE WITTY
BERTHA CHEERY CLEVER FLASHY
FLORID GARISH LIMPID LIVELY
LUCENT ORIENT SHRILL SILVER
BEAMISH DIAMOND DILUCID
FORWARD FULGENT LAMBENT
RADIANT RINGING SHINING
ANIMATED CHEERFUL FLASHING
GLEAMING LIGHTFUL LUMINOUS
LUSTROUS SPLENDID SPLENDOR
STARLIKE SUNSHINY
(BLINDINGLY —) GLARING
(NOT —) SOFT
(OFFENSIVELY —) GARISH
(SOFTLY —) LAMBENT
BRIGHTEN GILD LAMP BLOOM
CHEER CLEAR FLAME GLOZE LIGHT
LIVEN SHINE SNUFF CANTLE ENGILD
POLISH ANIMATE BURNISH EMBRAVE
ENLIVEN FURBISH LIGHTEN
SMARTEN ILLUMINE
BRIGHTENER FLUOROL
BRIGHTLY GAY CLEAR LIGHT SHEEN
BRIGHT FRESHLY SHEENLY
BRIGHTNESS SUN BLAZE BLOOM
ECLAT FLAME GLARE GLEAM GLINT
GLORY GLOSS LIGHT NITOR SHEEN
SHINE ACUMEN BRIGHT CANDOR
FULGOR LUSTER CLARITY GLISTEN
GLITTER LAMBERT NITENCY
SPARKLE RADIANCE SPLENDOR
(— OF TOBACCO) FLASH
(— UNIT) STILB
BRILLIANCE FAME BLARE BLAZE
ECLAT FLAME GLARE GLORY SHINE
VALUE KEENNESS RADIANCE
SPLENDOR VIVACITY
BRILLIANCY FIRE BLARE ECLAT
GLORY REFLET CLARITY GLITTER
ORIENCY RADIANCE SPLENDOR
BRILLIANT GAY GOOD KEEN SAGE
WISE BREME QUICK VIVID BRIGHT
CLEVER LIVELY PURPLE SIGNAL
BRITTLE EMINENT FLAMING
GLARING LAMBENT LAMPING
LOZENGE PRISMAL RADIANT
SHINING BLINDING DAZZLING
DIZZYING GLORIOUS INSPIRED
LUCULENT LUMINOUS SLASHING
SPLENDID
(TRANSIENTLY —) METEORIC
BRIM LIP RIM RUT SEA EDGE TURF
BLUFF BRINK MARGE OCEAN VERGE
WATER BORDER MARGIN TURNUP
COPULATE STRUMPET
(— OF HAT) FLAP LEAF POKE BRINK
TARFE
BRIMFUL TIPFUL TOPFUL CROWNED
BRIMMING BIG FULL ABRIM
BRIMSTONE SULFUR VIRAGO
SULPHUR BRINSTON SPITFIRE
BRINDLED TAWNY BRANDED
FLECKED STREAKED
BRINE SEA MAIN SALT BRACK LEACH
OCEAN TEARS PICKLE MARINADE
BRINER COBBERER
BRING DO LAY TEE WIN BEAR BUCK
CALL FIRK LEAD STOP TAKE TEEM

CARRY DRIVE ENDUE FETCH INCUR
APPORT ARRIVE CONVEY DEDUCE
CONDUCE CONDUCT EXHIBIT
PROCURE PRODUCE
(— FORTH YOUNG) EAN KID YEAN
(— ABOUT CAPTURE) ACCOUNT
(— ABOUT) DO SEE BREW MAKE
STAY TEEM CAUSE DIGHT FRAME
INFER MOVEN SHAPE SWING
CREATE EFFECT INVOKE SECURE
SPIRIT COMPASS CONDUCE INSPIRE
OPERATE PRODUCE CATALYZE
OCCASION TRANSACT
(— BACK) REFER EFFECT RECALL
REDUCE REDUCT RELATE RETURN
REVIVE REVOKE PRODUCE RESTORE
OCCASION RETRIEVE TRANSACT
(— BEFORE) HAUL
(— CHARGE) APPEACH
(— DOWN STEER) HOOLIHAN
(— DOWN) LAY DROP FALL FELL
STOP ABATE COUCH SOFTEN
DECLINE DESCEND DISMOUNT
(— FORTH) CAST FOAL GIVE MAKE
TEEM EDUCE HATCH ISSUE SPAWN
THROW PROFER DELIVER TRADUCE
ENGENDER
(— FORWARD) CITE LEAD INFER
ADDUCE ALLEGE ADJOUST
ADVANCE PROPOSE
(— IN) EARN INFER USHER IMPORT
INDUCE INVECT REPORT RETURN
ADHIBIT
(— INTO BATTLE) COMMIT
(— INTO COURT) SIST
(— INTO DISGRACE) FOUL
(— LOW) AVALE DEGRADE
SUPPLANT
(— ON) INFER INDUCE
(— ONESELF) GET
(— OUT) DRAW ACCENT ELICIT
DISINTER HEIGHTEN
(— OVER) CONVERT
(— TO A HALT) STICK
(— TO AN END) DO END FIT DOCK
DRAW REDD CEASE FORDO DECIDE
EXPIRE FINISH FOREDO FULFIL
DISJOIN INCLUDE COMPLETE
CONCLUDE DISSOLVE SURCEASE
(— TO BAY) CORNER
(— TO BEAR) EXERT
(— TO HEEL) FACE
(— TO LIFE) EVOKE ANIMATE
(— TO LIGHT) GRUB REAP DREDGE
ELICIT EXPOSE REVEAL UNEARTH
DISCLOSE DISCOVER
(— TO NAUGHT) DASH FOIL UNDO
NEGATE CONFUTE DESTROY
(— TO PERFECTION) RIPEN
(— TO STOP) CURB HALT ARREST
(— TO THE GROUND) GRASS
(— TOGETHER) JOIN AMASS RAISE
UNITE ADDUCT CONFER CORRAL
ENGAGE ENLINK GATHER SUMMON
COLLATE COLLECT COMPILE
COMPORT ASSEMBLE CONFLATE
ENSEMBLE
(— UP) REAR BREED NURSE RAISE
TRAIN NURSLE UPREAR EDUCATE
NOURISH

BRINGING-UP BREEDING EDUCATION
BRINJAL EGGPLANT
BRINK END EVE LIP RIM SEA BANK
BRIM EDGE FOSS MARGE SHORE
VERGE BORDER MARGIN MARGENT
BRINY BRACK SALTY SALINE
MURIATED
BRIOCHE ROLL STICH SAVARIN
BRISE-SOLEIL BLIND SUNBREAK
SUNSHADE
BRISK GAY BRAG BUSY FAST KEEN
PERK PERT RACY RASH SPRY TRIG
VIVE YERN AGILE ALERT ALIVE
BUDGE CANTY CRISP FRESH FRISK
KEDGE NIPPY PEART PERKY QUICK
ROUND ZIPPY ACTIVE BREEZY
COCKET CROUSE DAPPER FLICKY
LIVELY NIMBLE SNAPPY SPRUNT
TROTTY VIVACE ALLEGRO HUMMING
ANIMATED BRUSHING FRISKFUL
RATTLING SMACKING SPANKING
SPIRITED
BRISKLY YERN SHARP YERNE
BUSILY CROUSE ALLEGRO ROUNDLY
BRISKNESS ALACRITY VIRITOOT
BRISTLE AWN JAG RIB BARB HAIR
JAGG SETA TELA BIRSE BRUSH
PARCH PREEN STARE STRUT STYLE
TOAST CHAETA PALPUS RUFFLE
SETULA STIVER STRIGA STYLET
GLOCHIS SMELLER STUBBLE
WHISKER ACICULUM FRENULUM
SPICULUM VIBRISSA
BRISTLED HORRENT
BRISTLE-SHAPED STYLOID
BRISTLING ROUGH HISPID HORRID
SETOSE THORNY HORRENT
SCRUBBY SPINOUS
BRISTLY BIRSY PENNY SETOSE
STUBBY SCRUBBY STICKLE
BRITISH ENGLISH BRITANNIC
WHITEHALL
BRITISH HONDURAS (BAY OF —)
CHETUMAL
(CAPITAL OF —) BELMOPAN
(FORMER CAPITAL OF —) BELIZE
(MOUNTAIN RANGE OF —) MAYA
(TOWN OF —) CAYO STANN
COROZAL
BRITOMARTIS (FATHER OF —)
JUPITER
(MOTHER OF —) CARME
BRITON CELT SCOT BRYTHON
BRITTANY (NATIVE OF —) BRETON
BRITTLE DRY FROW WEAK BRASH
CANDY CRISP CRUMP EAGER FRAIL
FROWY FRUSH SHORT SPALT
CRISPY CRUMPY FEEBLE FICKLE
FROUGH GINGER IMFIRM SLIGHT
BRICKLE BRUCKLE CRACKLY
FRAGILE FRIABLE REDSEAR
SHIVERY SMOPPLE BRITCHEL
DELICATE SNAPPISH
BRITTLEBUSH ENCELIA
BROACH AIR AWL CUT PIN ROD TAP
OPEN OUCH SHED SPIT SPUR STAB
TAME VEER VENT BEGIN DRESS
DRIFT PRICK RIMER SPOOL START
VOICE ATTAME BORING BROOCH

DRIVER FIBULA LAUNCH PIERCE
REAMER RHYMER STRIKE ENLARGE
EXPRESS PUBLISH SPINDLE
SQUARER VIOLATE WIDENER
APPROACH DEFLOWER DRIFTPIN
INCISION PORPOISE
BROAD DEEP FREE VAST WIDE
AMPLE BEAMY DORIC GROSS LARGE
LARGO PLAIN ROOMY SPLAY SQUAB·
STOUT THICK WOMAN COARSE
GLOBAL BELCHER EVIDENT
GENERAL GRIVOIS LIBERAL
OBVIOUS PLATOID SPACIOUS
TOLERANT
(— AND FLAT) PLATOID
(NOT —) STRAIT
BROADBILL GAYA RAYA GAPER
SCAUP BOATBILL SHOVELER
SWORDFISH
BROADCAST AIR SOW SEED SEND
CARRY RADIO STREW AIRING
SPREAD DECLARE DIFFUSE PUBLISH
SCATTER ANNOUNCE TELEVISE
TRANSMIT
BROADCLOTH CASTOR SUCLAT
TAUNTON
BROADEN BREDE WIDEN DILATE
EXPAND EXTEND SPREAD ENNOBLE
BROADHORN ARK
BROADNESS BIGNESS LIBERALITY
BROADSIDE BROAD GARLAND
BROADSWORD BILL KRIS GLAIVE
HANGER SPATHA CUTLASS
FERRARA CLAYMORE MONTANTO
SCIMITAR
BROBDINAGIAN HUGE
BROCADE ACCA BROCHE KINCOB
KINKHAB NISHIKI BAUDEKIN
DAMASSIN
BROCCOLI ASPARAGUS
BROCHURE TRACT BOOKLET
PAMPHLET TREATISE
BROCKET PITA STAG BROCK
SPITTER
BRODIAEA GRASSNUT
BROGAN STOGA STOGY BROGUE
STOGIE
BROIL ROW BURN CHAR FEUD FRAY
GRID HEAT TOIL ALARM BRAWL
GRILL MELEE SCRAP SWELT
AFFRAY BIRSLE BRAISE GRILLY
SPLORE SQUEAL TUMULT BRANDER
BRULYIE CARBONE CONTEST
DISCORD DISPUTE EMBROIL FRIZZLE
GARBOIL QUARREL SIMULTY
BARBECUE BLOODWIT CONFLICT
GRILLADE STRAMASH
BROILER GRILL SEARER CHICKEN
POUSSIN
BROKE HOG BUST STONY STONEY
CHICANE BANKRUPT
BROKEN DOWN RENT RUDE TORN
BLOWN BROKE BURST FRACT
GAPPY HAIRY ROMPU ROUGH
TAMED BRASHY HACKLY RUINED
SHAKEN CRACKED CRUSHED
FRACTED REDUCED SUBDUED
VICIOUS WHIPPED BANKRUPT
CONTRITE OUTLAWED RUPTURED

TATTERED WEAKENED
(— **BUT NOT TRAINED**) GREEN
(— **IN HEALTH**) CRAZY
(— **IN**) STOVEN
(— **OFF**) ABRUPT
(**EASILY** —) GINGER
BROKEN-DOWN HAYWIRE
DISJASKED DISJASKIT
BROKER AGENT CRIMP CORSER
DEALER FACTOR JOBBER BROGGER
CHANGER COURSER PEDDLER
REALTOR SCALPER HUCKSTER
INSTITOR MERCHANT
BROMATIUM KOHLRABI
BROME CHEAT
BROMEGRASS CHESS
BROMO ACID EOSIN EOSINE
BROMUS DRAWK
BRONCHITIS HUSK HOOSE HOOZE
BRONCO PONY PONEY CAYUSE
BRONCHO MUSTANG
BRONCOBUSTER BUSTER GINETE
BUCKAROO
BRONZE AES TAN BUST ALLOY
BROWN COWBOY ORMOLU STATUE
ASIATIC GUNMETAL
(— **AGE CULTURE**) UBAID
(**ANTIQUE** —) CACAO
(**GILDED** —) VERMEIL
(**MEDAL** —) CALABASH
BRONZEWING SQUATTER
BROOCH BAR PIN BOSS LACE OUCH
PRIN PROP CAMEO CLASP MORSE
PREEN SLIDE SPRAY SPRIG FIBULA
NOUCHE PLAQUE SHIELD FERMAIL
PETALON CROTCHET ORNAMENT
SUNBURST
BROOD EYE FRY NYE SET SIT MOPE
NEST NIDE RACE TEAM TRIP WEEP
AERIE BREED CLOCK COVER COVEY
FLOCK GLOOM GROUP HATCH
HOVER ISSUE SEDGE STOCK
WORRY YOUNG CLETCH CLUTCH
FAMILY KINDLE LITTER PONDER
PROGENY SPECIES COGITATE
INCUBATE KINDLING MEDITATE
(— **OF BIRDS**) AERY AERIE COVEY
EYRIE SEDGE SIEGE
(— **OF PHEASANTS**) EYE NID NYE
NIDE
BROODER HOVER MOTHER NURSERY
BROOK RUN BEAR BECK BURN GHYL
GILL LAKE RILL RUSH SIKE ABIDE
BAYOU BOURN CREEK GLIDE STAND
STELL TCHAI ARROYO CANADA
DIGEST ENDURE GUTTER RINDLE
RIVOSE RUNLET RUNNEL SICKET
STREAM SUFFER COMPORT
CONCOCT STOMACH QUEBRADA
TOLERATE
(**RIPPLING** —) PURL
(**SALT** —) LICK
BROOKLET BECK DOKE RILL RILLET
RUNNEL RILLOCK RIVULET
BROOM COW MOP FRAY SWAB
BESOM BISME BREAM BRUSH
SCRUB SPART SWEEP UALIS WHISK
GENISTA HAGWEED WHISKER
HACKWEED SPLINTER

(**DYER'S** —) GENET DYEWOOD
(**NATIVE** —) DOGWOOD
(**TOPS OF** —) SCOPARIUS
BROOMCORN HURL
BROOMCORN MILLET HIRSE PANIC
PANICLE KADIKANE
BROOMRAPE HELLROOT HERBBANE
BROOMROOT SACATON ZACATON
BROSE ATHOLE
BROTH SEW BREE BROO FOND KAIL
KALE SOUP GLAZE STOCK BREWIS
CULLIS JUSSAL JUSSEL LIQUOR
SKILLY CALDERA POTTAGE SOUCHIE
SUPPING BOUILLON CONSOMME
PISHPASH POSSODIE POWSOWDY
BROTHEL KIP CRIB STEW BAGNE
HOUSE BAGNIO BORDEL LUPANAR
BORDELLO CATHOUSE HOOKSHOP
HOTHOUSE JOYHOUSE SERAGLIO
BROTHER FR BUB FRA KIN PAL SIB
BHAI BRER EGIL FRAY MATE MONK
PEER BILLY BUBBY BUDDY CADET
FRERE FRIAR FELLOW FRAILE
FRATER GERMAN COMRADE SIBLING
FOSTERER
(**HUSBAND'S** —) LEVIR
(**LAY** —) SCOLOG
(**WIFE'S** —) AFFINE
(**YOUNGER** —) CADET
(**PL.**) FF BRETHREN CURIATII
HARLUNGEN
BROTHERHOOD GILD GUILD LODGE
ORDER PAPEY FRIARY BRATSVO
CHISHTI THIASOS THIASUS
BRODHULL SODALITY
(— **OF FREEMASONS**) CRAFT
(**LITERARY** —) FELIBRIGE
BROTHER-IN-LAW MAUGH
BROUGHAM PILLBOX CARRIAGE
BROUGHT BROCHT
(— **FROM ELSEWHERE**) DERIVED
(— **TO BAY**) CORNERED
(— **TOGETHER**) CONFLATE
(— **UP BY HAND**) CADE
BROW TOP BRAE EDGE MIEN SNAB
BOUND BRINK CREST EAVES FRONT
RIDGE SLOPE BOLDNESS FOREHEAD
BROWBEAT FACE ABASH BULLY
BOUNCE HECTOR DEPRESS
DUMBCOW OUTFACE SWAGGER
BROWBEATEN HACKED
BROWN (ALSO SEE COLOR) ART DUN
TAN ARAB COIN COOK DARK GOAT
LION SEAR ABRAM ACORN ARGUS
BRUNO DUSKY HAZEL KAFFA
MOSUL PABLO PENNY QUAIL SEDGE
SEPIA TAWNY TENNE TOAST UMBER
APACHE BEAVER BRUNET GLOOMY
MALAGA MANILA MASTIC MOHAWK
PALOMA PLOVER PONGEE RABBIT
RUSSET SENNET TANNED TURTLE
WIGWAM ASPHALT HARVEST
LIBERIA MUSCADE OAKWOOD
OXBLOOD POMPEII PRAIRIE
REDWOOD TANBARK TOBACCO
VESUVIN BRUNETTE MOCCASIN
MUSHROOM PHEASANT PERSIMMON
PYGMALION
(**CONDOR** —) TIFFIN

(**DARK** —) BURNET
(**GRAYISH** —) DUN
(**HAIR** —) ARGALI
(**LIGHT** —) ALOMA ALESAN STRING
(**OLIVE** —) BARK AUTUMN
(**REDDISH** —) BAY SORE SEPIA
AUBURN CROTAL GINGER RUSSET
SORREL AMBROSIA
(**YELLOWISH** —) AZTEC ALMOND
BAMBOO BLONDE BEESWAX
ALDERNEY
BROWNBACK DOWITCH DOWITCHER
BROWN HEART RAAN
BROWNIE ELK NIS COOKY DOBBY
NISSE URISK DOBBIE GOBLIN
URUISG
BROWNING SCALD SCORCH SUNTAN
BROWNISH UMBER BURNET
(— **BLACK**) LAVA
BROWNSTONE CHESTNUT
BROWSE BRUT CROP FEED GRAZE
FORAGE NIBBLE PASTURE
BRUISE JAM BASH BRAY BUBU DENT
DUNT HURT JAMB MAIM MAUL SORE
STUN TUND BLACK BREAK BRIZZ
CRUSH CURRY DELVE DINGE POUND
SQUAT BATTER BREACH HATTER
INJURY INTUSE MANGLE POUNCE
SHINER STOUND SUGGIL BATTERY
CONTUND CROWNER DAMMISH
DISABLE
BRUISED HURT LIVID FROISSE
BRUIT DIN FAME RALE ROAR TELL
NOISE RUMOR SOUND BLAZON
CLAMOR REPORT DECLARE
HEARSAY
BRUNEI (— **WEIGHT**) PARA CHAPAH
(**TOWN OF** —) SERIA
BRUNET DARK BLACK BROWN GIPSY
GYPSY MORENA SWARTHY
BRUNETTE MORENITA
BRUNT JAR BLOW JOLT CLASH
FORCE ONSET SHOCK ATTACK
EFFORT IMPACT STRAIN STRESS
ASSAULT OUTBURST VIOLENCE
BRUSH DIP DUB PIG TIP CARD COMB
DUST FLAP FLAT FRAY KIYI SKIM
SWAB BROOM CHAPE CLEAN COPSE
FIGHT FITCH GRAZE LINER SABLE
SCOPA SCRUB SCUFF SWEEP
SWOOP WHISK BADGER BATTLE
BRIGHT BROSSE DABBER DAUBER
DUSTER MOGOTE PALLET PENCIL
PICKUP PUTOIS RIGGER RUBBER
SPONGE STROKE TEASEL CLEANSE
FOXTAIL GRAINER GROOMER
MOTTLER STIPPLE STRIPER THICKET
SCRUBBER SIFTENER SKIRMISH
STIPPLER TARBRUSH
(— **ASIDE**) SCUFF
(— **IN DANCING**) SCUFFLE
(— **OF TWIGS**) COW
(— **TO CLEAN SHIP BOTTOM**) HOG
(**BLUNT** —) BLENDER
(**DENSE** —) BUNDOCKS BOONDOCKS
(**ELECTRIC** —) DOCTOR
(**EMPHASIZED** —) SLAP
(**FLESH** —) SCRAPER STRIGIL
(**GROWTH OF** —) SYLVAGE

(POLLEN —) SCOPA SAROTHRUM
(SMALL —) TOOL FITCH FITCHEW
BRUSHER LIMBER LIPPER
BRUSH MAKER FLIRTY FLICKER
BRUSH SHUNT PIGTAIL
BRUSHWOOD HAG RICE RONE RUSH
BRAKE BRUSH COPSE FRITH REISE
SCROG SCRUB SPRAY COPPET
GARSIL MALLEE RAMMEL SCRUNT
SHROGS TINNET TINSEL COPPICE
ROUGHIE TEENAGE THICKET
WOODRIS BUSHWOOD
BRUSQUE CURT RUDE BLUFF BLUNT
GRUFF HASTY ROUGH SHORT
ABRUPT VIOLENT CAVALIER
IMPOLITE
BRUTAL CRUEL FERAL GROSS
CARNAL COARSE SAVAGE BEASTLY
BESTIAL BRUTISH CADDISH
INHUMAN BELLUINE INHUMANE
INSOLENT RUTHLESS
BRUTE BEAST GROSS YAHOO
ANIMAL BRUTAL SAVAGE BEASTLY
BESTIAL BRUTISH GORILLA RUFFIAN
BRUTISH FELL CRUEL BRUTAL
CARNAL FIERCE SAVAGE STUPID
BESTIAL INHUMAN SENSUAL
GADARENE
BRYONY HOP NEP ALRAUN COWBIND
MANDRAKE
(— FRUIT) OXBERRY
BRYOPHYTE ANOPHYTE LIVERWORT
BRYTHONIC CYMRIC KYMRIC
BRITTONIC
BUBBLE AIR BUB BEAD BELL BLEB
BLOB BOIL BOLL DUPE FOAM GLOB
SCUM SEED CAPER CHEAT EMPTY
VAPOR BURBLE DELUDE HOTTER
POPPLE SEETHE SOTTER TRIFLE
BLISTER BLUBBER DECEIVE
GLOBULE DELUSIVE
(— IN GLASS) BOIL REAM SEED
BLISTER
(PL.) SUDS
BUBBLING GAY BURBLY BOILING
GASSING EFFUSIVE
BUBINGA KEVAZINGO
BUBO EMEROD
BUCCANEER PIRATE RIFLER
ROBBER VIKING CORSAIR MARINER
SPOILER MAROONER PICAROON
BUCHMANITE GROUPER
BUCHU BUKA DIOSMA
BUCK FOB RAM BOIL BUTT DEER
DUDE MALE PRIG REAR SOAK STAG
TOFF WASH BLOOD DANDY PITCH
SASIN STEEP BASKET DOLLAR
OPPOSE RESIST STRIVE SAWBUCK
BUCKJUMP BUCKWASH
(— IN 1ST YEAR) FAWN
(— IN 2ND YEAR) PRICKET
(— IN 3RD YEAR) SORREL
(— IN 4TH YEAR) SORE
(— STEADILY) SUNFISH
(— UP) BRACE
BUCKBEAN BOGBEAN THREEFOLD
BUCKER DOLLYMAN
BUCKET SAY TUB BAIL BOOT BOWK
CAGE GRAB MEAL PAIL SKIP BOWIE

CHEAT SCOOP SKEEL STOOP STOUP
BAILER DIPPER DRENCH HOPPET
KIBBLE SITULA SUCKER VESSEL
FERMAIL GRAPPLE SNAPPER
SWINDLE CANNIKIN HEDGEHOG
PAINTPOT
(— ON MILL WHEEL) AW AWE EIE
(— ON WHEELS) SKIP
(GLASS-MAKING —) CUVETTE
(GRAVEL —) GRAB
(HOISTING —) HUDGE
(TWO —S OF WATER) GAIT
BUCKEYE STATE OHIO
BUCKLAW HAYSTON
BUCKLE BOW BEND CURL KINK
OUCH TACH TACK WARP BRACE
CLASP MARRY STRAP TACHE TWIST
FIBULA CONTEND FERMAIL GRAPPLE
FASTENER STRUGGLE
BUCKLER CRAB BLOCK SCUTE
TARGE SHIELD TAIRGE TARGET
BUCKLUM BUCKRAM ROTELLA
ROUNDEL SHUTTER
BUCKLING KINK UPSET
BUCK RAKE SWEEP
BUCKRAM STIFFENER
BUCKTHORN COMA RHAMN SCROG
WAHOO ALATERN CASCARA
BEARWOOD FRANGULA LOTEBUSH
WAYTHORN STINKWOOD
BUCKWHEAT BUCK CRAP BRANK
WRIGHT SARRAZIN
(PL.) FAGOPYRUM
BUCOLIC IDYL LOCAL NAIVE RURAL
FARMER RUSTIC SIMPLE COWHERD
ECLOGUE AGRESTIC HERDSMAN
PASTORAL
BUD BUR EYE GEM IMP PIP BULB
BURR CION FORM GERM GIRL
GROW KNOP KNOT WORK CAPOT
CHILD CLOVE GEMMA GRAFT SCION
SHOOT SPRIT SPURT YOUTH
BUDLET BUTTON FLOWER GERMIN
OCULUS OILLET SPROUT BLOSSOM
BROTHER CABBAGE GEMMULE
PLUMULE ROSEBUD TENDRON
BOURGEON BULBILLA
(BLIGHTED —) BLAST
(BROOD —) SOREDIUM
(UNDEVELOPED —) EYE
(PL.) CAPERS
BUDDHA FO FOH BUTSU JATAKA
GAUTAMA SRAMANA DAIBUTSU
(— STORY) JATAKA
BUDDHISM DAIJO FOISM KEGON
CHANISM LAMAISM HINAYANA
(— CODE) VINAYA
BUDDHIST (— DOCTRINE) ANATTA
TRIKAYA
(— FESTIVAL) WESAK
(— PATH) VEHICLE
(— SCHOOL) RITSU
(— SECT) SHIN TENDAI
BUDDLE TYE FRAME BODDLE SLIMER
STRIPE TROUGH
BUDDY BO BOY BUD PAL JACK MATE
DIGGER BROTHER COMRADE
COMPADRE TENTMATE
BUDGE FUR JEE BOGY MOVE STIR

BOOZE BRISK MUDGE STIFF THIEF
JOCUND LIQUOR SOLEMN AUSTERE
POMPOUS MOVEMENT
BUDGET BAG BOGY BOOT PACK
PLAN ROLL BATCH BOGEY BOGIE
BUNCH STOCK STORE BOTTLE
BUNDLE PARCEL SOCKET WALLET
PROGRAM
BUFF ASH BOB FAN TAN BLOW COAT
CURT FIRM SHINE SNUFF SPARK
BUFFET POLISH STURDY STAMMER
STUTTER NAUMKEAG
(TILLEUL —) ALABASTER
BUFFALO OX ANOA ARNA ARNI BUFF
STAG ARNEE BISON BUGLE BUFFLE
HAMPER KERBAU MURRAH WUNTEE
CARIBAO CARIBOU GAZELLE
OVERAWE TIMARAU ZAMOUSE
BEWILDER SAPIUTAN SELADANG
BUFFALO CHIPS BODEWASH
BUFFALO FISH SUCKER BUFFALO
BIGMOUTH GOURDHEAD
BUFFER DOG PAD FROG RACK
BUMPER FENDER HURTER PISTOL
CUSHION
BUFFET BAR BOB BOX BEAT BLAD
BLOW BUFF CUFF GOWF PLAT SCAT
SLAP TOSS FILIP KNOCK SCUFF
SCUFT SMITE STOOL ABACUS
BATTER FILLIP FLEWIT SERVER
SETOUT STRIKE STRIVE THRASH
COLPHEG CONTEND COUNTER
HASSOCK SMACKER SQUELCH
CREDENCE CREDENZA CUPBOARD
SPANGHEW
BUFFETING DIRD SKITE DUSTING
BUFFLEHEAD DUCK FOOL CLOWN
BUFFLE DIPPER DOPPER MARIONET
WOOLHEAD MERRYWING
BUFFOON DOR WAG WIT APER FOOL
JAPE MIME MOME VICE ZANY
ACTOR ANTIC BUFFO CLOWN COMIC
DROLE DROLL HARLOT JESTER
MUMMER STOOGE ANTIQUE
BOUFFON JUGGLER PLAYBOY
TOMFOOL BALATRON GRACIOSO
HUMORIST MACAROON MERRYMAN
OWLGLASS PLEASANT RIDICULE
PANTALOON
BUFFOONERY JAPERY ZANYISM
CLOWNERY
BUG (ALSO SEE INSECT) DOR FLAW
GERM IDEA MITE BOGEY BULGE
FIEND LYGUS ROACH ARADID
BEDBUG BEETLE BUGGER CAPSID
CHINCH COREID CORUCO ELATER
INSECT SALDID SCHEME TINGID
BELLIED BOATMAN BUGBEAR
CIMICID CORSAIR FORWARD
POMPOUS STRIDER BARBEIRO
CONENOSE HEMIPTER HOBBYIST
NAUCORID VINCHUCA
(RED —) CHIGGA CHIGGER
(SOW —) SLATER
BUGABOO BOGY FEAR GOGA GOGO
OGRE TURK ALARM BOGEY BOGIE
GOGGA BODACH GOBLIN BUGBEAR
SPECTER SPECTRE WORRICOW
BUGANDA (— KING) KABAKA

BUGBANE COHOSH BUGWORT RICHWEED HELLEBORE
BUGBEAR BUG COW BOGY BOGEY BOGIE CADDY MORMO POKER BOGGLE BOGGART BUGABOO FEARBABE SCAREBUG
BUGGER SOD CHAP BOOGER FELLOW PERSON RASCAL HERETIC
BUGGY CART SHAY TRAP NUTTY CALESA CABOOSE CALESIN FOOLISH VEHICLE DEMENTED INFESTED STANHOPE
BUGLE BEAD HORN BLACK BUFFALO BULLOCK CLARION HUTCHET TRUMPET
(— CALL) WARISON
(YELLOW —) IVA
BUGLER WINDJAMMER
BUGLOSS ALKANET ANCHUSA BLUEWEED OXTONGUE
BUILD BIG SET FORM LEVY MAKE REAR TELD CREAT DRIVE EDIFY ERECT FOUND FRAME HOUSE RAISE SHAPE THROW FABRIC GRAITH TAILLE TIMBER COMPILE EXTRUCT FASHION ASSEMBLE
(— FIRE) CHUNK
(— HASTILY) CLAP
(— NEST) AERIE NIDIFY
(— UP) AGGRADE
(BODY —) HABITUS
BUILDER EPEUS MAKER EPEIUS HANGER ERECTOR ENGINEER TECTONIC
(DAM —) DAMMER
BUILDING GIN CASA CRIB DOME FLAT HALL IGLU JAIL LAND PILE SHED SHOP SLAB SPOT TELD AEDES ARENA BLOCK COURT FOLLY FRAME HOTEL HOUSE IGLOO JAWAB STORE STUDY ARMORY BIGGIN BOTTLE CASING CHAPEL FABRIC GARAGE HAMMAM INSULA PALACE SCHOOL SUCCOR BREWERY BROODER CARBARN COLLEGE DIORAMA EDIFICE FACTORY FLATTOP FOUNDRY MANSION SALTERN STATION SYNAGOG ATHENEUM BAGHOUSE BASILICA BROCETTO CHANCERY DIPTEROS DRYHOUSE DWELLING DYEHOUSE ELEVATOR EPHEBEUM FIRETRAP GASHOUSE GINHOUSE HOTHOUSE ICEHOUSE MAGAZINE NYMPHEUM PANORAMA SERAPEUM STEMMERY TAXPAYER TENEMENT VELODROME
(— FOR AIRCRAFT) DOCK
(— GROUPS) HAM
(— OF STONE) KAABA CASHEL TRUDDO TRULLO
(— ON POSTS) PATAKA
(BUDDHIST —) TOPE
(CIRCULAR —) THOLE THOLOS ROTUNDA
(CRUDE —) SHANTY
(DILAPIDATED —) ROOKERY FIRETRAP
(EXHIBITION —) MUSEUM
(FARM —) BARN STABLE HACIENDA

(FORTIFIED —) CASTLE
(GRAIN —) GARNER
(JAI ALAI —) FRONTON
(MOVABLE —) TURRET
(ORNAMENTAL —) ALCOVE
(PUBLIC —) CASINO THEATER THEATRE COLISEUM
(QUADRANGULAR —) TETRAGON
(QUARANTINE —) LAZARET
(SACRED —) CHURCH MOSQUE TEMPLE SACRARY PANTHEON SARAPEUM
(SERIES OF —S) SWEEP
(SLIGHT —) SHED
(SMALL —) HUT COOP HOCK EDICULE
(SPORTS —) CAGE
(STATELY —) DOME
(STORAGE —) BARN HORREUM
(SUBSIDIARY —) ANNEX
(TRADE —) HALL
(UNCOMFORTABLE —) ARK
(PL.) FUNDUS
BUILT SET BOUKIT STACKED TIMBERED
(COMPACTLY —) CORKY
(HEAVILY —) BLOCKY
(LOOSELY —) GANGLING
(STRONGLY —) BURLY GROSS QUARRY
(WELL —) BUIRDLY
BUKIDNON MONTES BINOKID
BULB BUD SET BLUB CORM IXIA KNOB LAMP ROOT SEED SEGO CLOVE FLOAT GLOBE ONION SWELL TUBER BULBIL BULBUS CROCUS GARLIC SCILLA BABIANA GALTONIA SPARAXIS TRITONIA
(— OF PERCUSSION) CONCHOID
(LIGHT —) HELION
(ONION —) BUTTON
(PL.) SQUILL
BULBIL CHIVE BULBLET
(PL.) SPAWN
BULBLET CHIVE CORMEL BULBULE NUCLEUS PROPAGO
BULBUL KALA BUHLBUHL GREENBUL LEAFBIRD

BULGARIA

ASSEMBLY: SOBRANJE SOBRANYE
CAPE: EMINE SABLA KURATAN
CAPITAL: SOFIA
COIN: LEV LEW STOTINKA
GULF: BURGAS
COMMUNE: SLIVEN SLIVNO SISTOVA
MEASURE: OKA OKE KRINE LEKHE
MOUNTAIN: BOTEV SAPKA MUSALA VIKHREN
MOUNTAINS: PIRIN BALKAN RHODOPE
PEOPLE: SLAV TATAR BULGAR SLAVIC
RIVER: LOM VIT ARDA OSMA ISKER MESTA DANUBE MARICA OGOSTA STRUMA YANTRA MARISTA STRYAMA TUNDZHA

TOWN: RILA RUSE AYTOS BUTAN BYCLU ELENA ISKRA STARA VARNA BLEVEN BURGAS DULOVO LEVSKY PLEUNA SHUMEN SHUMLA SLIVEN SLIVNO WIDDIN YAMBOL ZAGORA GABROVO KARLOVO PLOVDIV SISTOVA TIRNOVA RUSTCHUK
WEIGHT: OKA OKE TOVAR

BULGARIAN POMAK
BULGE BAG BUG JUT SAG BUMP CASK HUMP KNOB LUMP PANT BILGE BLOAT BOUGE FLASK POUCH START STRUT SWELL BEETLE BILLOW COCKLE EXTEND PUCKER WALLET BLISTER PROJECT OVERHANG PROTRUDE SWELLING
(— OUT) TUT BELLY BOWDEN STRUNT
(OFFENSIVE —) SALIENT
BULGING FULL BOMBE BOWED BUGGY GOUTY PUDGY TUMID BAGGED CONVEX GOOGLY TOROSE GIBBOUS GOUTISH SWOLLEN BOUFFANT
BULK BODY BOUK HEAP HEFT HOLD HULK HULL LUMP MASS MOLE PILE SIZE BURLY CARGO GROSS MIGHT POWER SLUMP STALL SWELL CORPSE EXPAND EXTENT FIGURE VOLUME BIGNESS MAJORITY QUANTITY
BULKHEAD CHECK BATTERY PARTITION
BULKY BIG MAIN BURLY GROSS LARGE PUDGY STOUT CLUMSY STODGY HULKING LUMPING MASSIVE WEIGHTY UNWIELDY
BULL COP SEG APIS BEEF BILL JEST MALE ROAN SEAL SEGG SLIP STOT TORO ZEBU BACIS BEEVE BOBBY BONER BOVID BRUTE DRINK EDICT ERROR ANIMAL BOVINE BUSHWA LETTER PEELER TAURUS BULLOCK BUSHWAH CRITTER CRUSADE NOVILLO TAURINE CAJOLERY DOCUMENT FLATTERY
(— AREA) QUERENCIA
(— KILLING) VOLAPIE
(HORNLESS —) DODDY DODDIE
(HUMAN-HEADED —) SHEDU CAMASSU
(YOUNG —) STOT BUGLE MICKY STIRK STOTT BULLOCK
(PL.) BATTERY
BULLA BLEB BULL SEAL BLAIN BLISTER VESICLE
BULL CELL TORIL
BULLDOG BULL BULLER BULLDOZE
BULLDOZE COW RAM BULLY FORCE SCOOP COERCE BROWBEAT BULLYRAG RESTRAIN
BULLET GUN BALL LEAD PILL SHOT SLUG TOWEL CONOID DUMDUM PELLET PICKET SINKER TRACER DINGBAT MISSILE PELLOCK

PROJECT SPITZER MUSHROOM WADCUTTER (PL.) BALL LEAD STUFF
BULLETIN ITEM MEMO NOTICE POSTER REPORT SERIAL PROGRAM NEWSBILL
BULLFIGHT CORRIDA NOVILLADA
BULLFIGHTER TORERO MATADOR PICADOR CAPEADOR TOREADOR
BULLFIGHTING REJONEO
BULLFINCH ALP OLP HOOP MAWP MONK NOPE OLPH POPE HEDGE TANNY TAWNY MONACH REDBIRD REDHOOP SHIRLEY BLOODALP TONYHOOP
BULLHEAD CUR POUT
BULLIMONG FARRAGE
BULLION BILLOT
BULLISH STIFF
BULLOCK HOG HOGG NEAT NOWT STOT BUGLE KNOUT STEER STIRK BOVINE
(DECOY —) COACH
BULL-ROARER BUZZ BUMMER BUZZER ROARER TUNDUN TURNDUN WHIZZER
BULL'S-EYE EYE BULL DUMP GOLD BLANK OXEYE WHITE TARGET ROUNDEL
BULL SNAKE GOPHER
BULL TROUT TRUFF
BULLY NUT BOAT BOSS FACE FINE GOOD HUFF MATE BRAVE BRAVO GREAT JOLLY SNOOL TIGER VAPOR BOUNCE CUTTER CUTTLE HARASS HECTOR HUFFER JOVIAL RUFFLE TYRANT BLUSTER BOUNCER BULLOCK DARLING DASHING GALLANT GAUSTER HUFFCAP ROISTER RUFFIAN RUFFLER SLASHER SOLDIER SWAGGER BANGSTER BARRATER BLUDGEON BROWBEAT BULLDOZE DOMINEER FRAMPLER NIGHTCAP RABIATOR
(MASTIC —) ACOMA
BULLY TREE BALATA BULLACE GAUSTER BEEFWOOD
BULRUSH REED RISP RUSH TULE SEDGE BUMBLE GLUMAL AKAAKAI CATTAIL PAPYRUS SCIRPUS TUSSOCK
BULWARK BAIL FORT WALL FENCE JETTY MANTA MOUND TOWER WARDER BASTION DEFENCE DEFENSE PARAPET PROTECT RAMPART WEREWALL
BUM BEG DIN BOMB BOOM HOBO DRINK DRONE IDLER MOOCH SHACK STIFF TRAMP FROLIC GUZZLE SPONGE SQUEEF GUZZLER VAGABOND
BUMBLEBEE DOR CLOCK BUMBEE BUMBLE CARDER BUMBLER
BUMMER SKIDDER
BUMP CRY HIP HIT NOB BANG BLOW BOOM BUNK DIRD JOLT KNOB LUMP WHAP WHOP BULGE CLASH CLOUR CLOUT DUNCH KNOCK ORGAN THUMP BOUNCE CANNON IMPACT

JOUNCE NODULE STRIKE BITTERN COLLIDE CONFLICT SWELLING
(— ON WHALE'S HEAD) HOVEL
BUMPER BOWL FINE GOOD FACER GLASS ROUSE BUFFER CASABE FENDER GOBLET HURTER KELTIE BRIMMER DINGMAN CARANGID
(— GUARD) OVERRIDER
BUMPKIN JAY YAP BEAM BOOM BOOR CHAW CLOD GAWK HICK LOUT RUBE SWAB SWAD TIKE TYKE CHURL CLOWN ROBIN YAHOO YOKEL FARMER JOSKIN LUMMOX BUCOLIC CAUBOGE HAWBUCK
BUNCH BOB SET BALE BOSS CHOU CLEW CLUB CLUE COMA KICK KNOB KNOT PACK SWAD TUFT WISP BREAK CLUMP FAGOT FLOCK KNOLL PAHIL THUMP CLUTCH GAGGLE HUDDLE
(— OF BANANAS) HAND STEM
(— OF FLAX) HEAD STRICK
(— OF FRUIT) HOG STRAP
(— OF GRASS) WHISK
(— OF GRAIN) RIP
(— OF GRAPES) RAISIN
(— OF HAIR) COB
(— OF HERBS) BOUQUET
(— OF IVY) BUSH
(— OF TOBACCO LEAVES) HAND BREAK
(— UP) SHRUG
(SMALL —) WISP
BUNCHER BINDER
BUNCHY TRUSS
BUNCOMBE HOOEY BUNKUM
BUND BAND QUAY PRAYA LEAGUE SOCIETY
BUNDLE KID LOT PAD TOD WAD WAP BALE BAND BEAT BOLT BOOK BUNG DRUG DRUM GARB HANK HAUL HEAD KNOT LOCK PACK ROLL SWAG BLUEY BULTO BUNCH FADGE FAGOT GAVEL GLEAN GROUP LITCH NICKY PETER SHEAF SKEIN TARRY TRACE TRUSS TURSE WADGE BARSOM BATTEN BINDLE BOTTLE BUDGET DRIVER DUFTER FAGGOT FARDEL FASCES FUMBLE GATHER KNITCH LOGGIN NUMBER PACKET PARCEL SCROLL THRAVE DORLACH FASCINE GARBAGE MATILDA PACKAGE FASCICLE
(— OF 60 SKINS) TURN
(— OF BOARDS) BOLT
(— OF FASCINES) ROULEAU
(— OF FIBRILS) AXONEME
(— OF FLAX) BEET HEAD
(— OF HAIR) LEECH
(— OF HAY, STRAW, ETC.) WAP WASE WISP GAVEL SHEAF BATTEN BOLTIN BOTTLE TIPPLE WINDLING
(— OF HEATH) KID
(— OF HIDES) KIP
(— OF NERVE FIBERS) TRACT COLUMN
(— OF PAPERS) SPUR DUFTER
(— OF RODS) FASCES
(— OF SACKS) BADGER

(— OF SACRED TWIGS) BARSOM
(— OF THONGS) KNOUT
(— OF TOBACCO) CARROT
(— OF TWIGS) BIRCH BROOM FAGGOT
(— OF WOOD) PIMP BAVIN FAGOT
(— OF YARN) HAUL SLIP
(BUSHMAN'S —) DRUM BLUEY
BUNG CORK PLUG SHIVE SPILE STOPPER
BUNGEY KIT
BUNGI-BUNGI STAVEWOOD
BUNGLE ERR GOOF MESS MUCK MUFF BLUNK BOTCH FAULT FLUFF FUDGE SPOIL STICK BOGGLE BOLLIX BUMBLE FOOZLE FUMBLE MOMBLE MUCKER MUDDLE TAILOR TOGGLE BAUCHLE BLUNDER BUTCHERY SHAMMOCK
BUNGLER LUMMOX PUDDLE TINKER BUMBLER BUMMLER FOOZLER DAUBSTER
BUNGLING FLUFF FUDGY INERT CLUMSY AWKWARD TINKERLY
BUNG START FLOGGER
BUNION ONION WYROCK
BUNJI-BUNJI CUDGERIE
BUNK BED CAR BLAA BLAH CASE JUNK SACK ABIDE BERTH BUNKO FRAME HOKUM HOOEY LEAVE LODGE SLEEP TRUCK BUNKUM TIMBER BALONEY BOLSTER CHICORY HEMLOCK TWADDLE BUNCOMBE NONSENSE
BUNKHOUSE BULLPEN
BUNKUM BLAH BUNK FUDGE HOKUM HOOPLA BALONEY BUNCOMBE
BUNTAL BURI BANGKOK
BUNTING EBB POP FLAG PAPE POPE CHINK DUMPY FINCH PLUMP COTTON STOCKY TOWHEE UNTIDY COWBIRD ETAMINE GARMENT OATFOWL ORTOLAN ROUNDED BELLYING BOBOLINK PRUSIANO RICEBIRD RINGBIRD SLOVENLY NONPAREIL
BUNTON DIVIDER
BUOY DAN WAFT BAKEN ELATE FLOAT LAGAN RAISE MARKER DOLPHIN SUSTAIN DEADHEAD LEVITATE MAKEFAST SONOBUOY
BUOYANCY BALON BALLON LEVITY SPRING ELATION
BUOYANT GAY CORKY HAPPY LIGHT BLITHE BOUNCY FLOATY LIVELY ELASTIC HOPEFUL JOCULAR LILTING SPRINGY ANIMATED CHEERFUL SANGUINE SPIRITED VOLATILE
BUR BUZZ TEAZEL STICKER
BURBARK AKONGE BOXBUSH BURRBARK
BURBOT COD CONY CUSK LING LOTA CONEY LOCHE LAWYER MORGAY DOGFISH EELPOUT GUDGEON BIRDBOLT
BURDEN TAX VEX BIRN CARE CARK CLAG CLOG DRAG DUTY FARE FOOT GANG LADE LOAD MUCK ONUS PORT SEAM TACK BIRTH CARGO

CROWD CRUSH DRONE HEAVY
LABOR MIDST CHARGE CUMBER
ENTAIL FARDEL HAMPER IMPOSE
LADING SADDLE THRACK WEIGHT
BALLAST BURTHEN CONVETH
FRAUGHT FREIGHT HAGRIDE
ONERATE OPPRESS REFRAIN
SUMPTER TROUBLE CAPACITY
CARRIAGE ENCUMBER ENGREGGE
HANDICAP OVERCOME QUANTITY
RUMBELOW MILLSTONE
(— OF SONG) WHEEL HOLDING
OVERTURN OVERWORD
(FINANCIAL —) EXPENSE
BURDENED HEAVY LADEN GRAVID
FRAUGHT HARASSED
BURDENER INCUBUS
BURDENSOME HEAVY IRKSOME
ONEROUS WEIGHTY CUMBROUS
GRIEVOUS GRINDING LOADSOME
BURDOCK DOCK GOBO CLITE CLOTS
DRAIN LAPPA BARDANE BURWEED
BUZZIES CADILLO CLOTBUR
HARDOCK HAREBUR CLEAVERS
HAULBACK
BUREAU DESK CHEST AGENCY
EXCISE OFFICE CENTRAL DRESSER
AGITPROP
BUREAUCRAT MANDARIN
BURFISH ATINGA
BURGEON BUD GROW ERUPT
SHOOT SPROUT
BURGESS CITIZEN FREEMAN
PORTMAN COMMONER GORGIBUS
(PL.) BURGWARE
BURG GRASS SANDBUR COCKSPUR
SANDSPUR
BURGLAR YEGG CRACK THIEF
GOPHER ROBBER RAFFLES
YEGGMAN PETERMAN PICKLOCK
BURGLARY BREAK CRACK THEFT
LARCENY ROBBERY STEALAGE
BURGUNDY POMMARD VOUGEOT
TONNERRE
BURIAL FUNERARY INTERMENT
(— MOUND) TOLA HUACA
BURIAL PLACE AHU TOMB GRAVE
BURIAL GIGUNU LAYSTOW PYRAMID
CATACOMB CEMETERY GOLGOTHA
LAYSTALL
BURIED HIDDEN HUMATE SEPULT
ABSORBED IMBEDDED
(NOT —) UNRESTED
(RECENTLY —) GREEN
BURIN GRAVER PLASTIC
BURL BURR KNAR KNOT LUMP
KNAUR PIMPLE PUSTULE
BURLAP GUNNY CROCUS BAGGING
HESSIAN SACKING WRAPPING
BURLER LECKER SPILER
BURLESQUE APE ODD COPY JEST
MIME BURLY DROLL FARCE REVUE
COMEDY OVERDO PARODY
BUFFOON JOCULAR MIMICRY
MOCKERY OVERACT DOGGEREL
RIDICULE TRAVESTY
BURLY FAT BLUFF BULKY GROSS
HEAVY HUSKY LARGE LUSTY NOBLE
OBESE STOUT THICK TRAMP

BOWERLY MASTIFF STATELY
IMPOSING

BURMA
BAY: BENGAL HUNTER HEANZAY
CAPITAL: RANGOON
GULF: MARTABAN
MEASURE: LY DHA GON LAN MAU
NGU SAO TAO TAT BYEE DAIN
PHAN SEIT TAUN TENG THAT
SALAY SHITA THUOC LAMANY
PALGAT TRUONG CHAIVAI
OKTHABAH
MONEY: KYAT
MOUNTAIN: POPA NATTAUNG
SARAMATI VICTORIA
MOUNTAINS: CHIN NAGA DAWNA
KACHIN KARENNI PEGUYOMA
NATIVE: AO VU WA LAI LAO MON
PYU TAI CHIN KADU KUKI LOLO
MIAO NAGA SEMA SHAN THAI
KAREN KHMER LHOTA BIRMAN
BURMAN KACHIN RENGMA
PALAUNG ARAKANESE
PORT: AKYAB BASSEIN HENZADA
MOULMEIN
SEA: ANDAMAN
TOWN: YE AVA PEGU AKYAB
BHAMO KATHA MINBU PAPUN
PROME TAVOY HSENWI HSIPAW
LASHIO MAYMYO MONYWA
SHWEBO BASSEIN HENZADA
PAKOKKU RANGOON MANDALAY
MOULMEIN
RIVER: HKA NMAI PEGU SALWIN
SHWELI KALADAN MALIKHA
MYITNGE SALWEEN SITTANG
CHINDWIN INDAWGYI
IRRAWADDY
WEIGHT: TA CAN MAT MOO PAI
VIS BINH DONG KYAT RUAY VISS
BAHAR BEHAR CANDY TICAL
TICUL ABUCCO PEIKTHA

BUR MARIGOLD BACLIN CUCKOLD
BURMESE KADU BIRMAN
ARAKANESE
BURN BREN BREW CHAR FIRE GLOW
PLOT RAZE RILL SEAR SERE TEND
TIND ADUST BLAZE BROIL BROOK
CENSE CHARK CLAMP FLAME FLARE
PARCH PLOUT QUICK ROAST SCALD
SCAUM SINGE SWEAL WASTE
WATER CROZLE IGNIFY NIGGER
SCORCH SIZZLE STREAM CHARPIT
COMBURE COMBUST CONSUME
CREMATE CROZZLE FLICKER
FRIZZLE INCENSE OXIDIZE RIVULET
SCOWDER SMOLDER FLAGRATE
SQUANDER
(— FEEBLY) GUTTER
(— FITFULLY) FLICKER
(— IN) INURE
(— MIDNIGHT OIL) LUCUBRATE
(— OUT) GUT
(— UP) ADUST EXUST
(— WITH LITTLE FLAME) SMUDGE
(LET —) BISHOP

BURNED ADUST
BURNER BEAK KORO BAKER PILOT
ARGAND BUNSEN CENSER
BATSWING CALCINER GASLIGHT
THURIBLE WELSBACH
BURNET SELFHEAL BLOODWORT
BURNING HOT FIRE LIVE AFIRE
ANGRY BLAZE CALID EAGER FIERY
FLAME GLEDY QUICK SCALD URENT
ABLAZE ARDENT FERVID FIRING
LIVING TORRID USTION ADURENT
CAUSTIC CAUTERY FERVENT
FLAMING GLARING GLOWING
MORDANT SCOWDER SHINING
ARDUROUS EXCITING FLAGRANT
INUSTION MUIRBURN PARCHING
SCOUTHER
(— BRIGHTLY) LIGHT
(— OF FORESTS IN INDIA) JHOOM
(MALICIOUS —) ARSON
(NO LONGER —) EXTINCT
BURNING BUSH WAHOO
BURNISH RUB GLAZE GLOSS INLAY
POLISH FURBISH
BURNISHER AGATE BUFFER GLAZER
FROTTON POLISHER
BURP BOKE BELCH BUBBLE
BURR NUT PAD RIB BARB BIRR BOSS
BUZZ HALO KNOB PILE RING ROVE
SLUG WHIR BRIAR BURGH WHARL
WHIRR BANYAN CIRCLE CORONA
TEASEL TUNNEL WASHER CORONET
STICKER PARASITE
(— IN WOOD) GNAR KNAR
(— OF ANTLER) CORONET
(— ON TYPE) RAG
BURRO ASS DONKEY
BURROW BED DEN DIG SET BURY
HEAP HOLE MINE MOLE PIPE ROOT
TUBE BERRY COUCH EARTH MOUND
FURROW ROOTLE TUNNEL CLAPPER
GALLERY PASSAGE SHELTER
EXCAVATE WORMHOLE
(— AS EEL) MUD
(— IN) MOIL
(— OF BADGER) SET
(— OF OTTER) COUCH
(FOSSIL —) SCOLITE
BURROWS TOWN
BURSA SAC SACK POUCH CAVITY
BURSULA
BURSAR BOWSER PURSER TERRAR
BOUCHER CASHIER
BURSE CASE SHOP FOREL BAZAAR
BOURSE POCKET
BURST FIT FLY POP BLOW BUST
DASH GUSH GUST LOSS REND SCAT
TILT BLAST BLOUT BREAK CRACK
ERUPT FLAFF FLASH GRAZE REAVE
SALVO SCATT SHOUT SPASM SPLIT
START STAVE BROKEN DAMAGE
INJURY SPROUT EXPLODE IMPLODE
RUPTURE SHATTER AIRBURST
OUTBREAK SUNDERED
(— ASUNDER) OUTRIVE
(— FORTH) ERUPT SALLY EXPIRE
BALLOON
(— IN) IRRUPT IMPLODE
(— INTO FRAGMENTS) FLITTER

(— INTO LAUGHTER) BUFF
(— OF ACTIVITY) BRASH SPURT
SPRINT SPLURGE
(— OF ARTILLERY) GRAZE RAFALE
(— OF CHEERS) SALVO
(— OF ENERGY) BANG
(— OF FIRING) COUGH
(— OF HARMONIOUS SOUND)
DIAPASON
(— OF LIGHT) FLASH GLORY
(— OF SPEED) KICK FLUTTER
(— OF TEARS) BLURT
(— OF TEMPER) BOUTADE
(— OF WIND) FLAW
(— OPEN) UPBRAST
(— OUT) PRORUMP
(— THE HEART) RIVE
BURSTER GALE LUGGER CRACKER
BURSTING TUMID ABURST BLOWOUT
RUPTION ERUPTING

BURUNDI
CAPITAL: BUJUMBURA
COIN: FRANC
LAKE: RUGWERO TSHOHOHA
NATIVE: HUTU BANTU PYGMY
TUTSI WATUSI
RIVER: KAGERA RUVUVU RUZIZI
AKANYARU
TOWN: NGOZI BURURI KITEGA
MUYINGA BUJUMBURA

BURY URN CAMP HIDE MOOL RAKE
TURF VEIL CLOAK COVER EARTH
GRAVE INTER INURN VAULT WHELM
ENTOMB ENWOMB HEARSE INHUME
SEPULT SHROUD BEDELVE
CONCEAL ENGROSS IMMERSE
PITHOLE REPRESS SECRETE
FUNERATE SUBMERGE
BUS CAMION JITNEY JEEPNEY
BUSBOY OMNIBUS PICCOLO
BUSH TOD BUTT BOSCH BURSE
CLUMP GROVE PLASH SCRAY
SHRUB BRANCH TAVERN BOSCAGE
BOUCHON CLUSTER OUTBACK
THICKET BUSHLAND
(— SICKNESS) TAURANGA
(BLACKBERRY —) BRAMBLE
(STUNTED —) SCROG
(PL.) RUFFMANS
BUSH CLOVER HAGI
BUSH COW ZAMOUSE
BUSHEL FOO FOU GOB LOT MET
BUCKET STRICK
(1-4TH —) PECK
(1-HALF —) TOVET
(1-HALF TO 3-4THS —) CABOT
(1.6 —) FANEGA
(3 TO 5 —S) SACK
(3-4THS —) SKIPPLE
(41.28 —) WEY
(8 —S) SEAM
BUSHER SWAMPER
BUSHGRASS WOODREED
BUSHING BUSH COAK DRILL LINER
BOUCHE COLLET LINING SLEEVE
BOUCHON FERRULE GROMMET
PADDING

(HALF —) STEP
BUSHMAN GUNG BUSHY KHUAI
ABATOA ABATWA WHALER
BUSHBOY SWAGMAN NEGRILLO
(PL.) SAN SAAN
BUSHMASTER CURUCUCU
SURUCUCU
BUSHWHACKER PAPAW PAWPAW
BUSHY BOSKY SHOCK DUMOSE
DUMOUS BUSHMAN QUEACHY
BUSILY THRANG
BUSINESS ADO ART BIZ FAT JOB
PIE CARE FEAT FIRM FUSS GAME
GEAR LINE NOTE TASK WORK
CAUSE CRAFT TRADE TRUCK
AFFAIR CUSTOM EMPLOY ERRAND
MATTER METIER NEGOCE OFFICE
PIDGIN RACKET TURKEY ACCOUNT
CALLING CONCERN JOURNEY
PALAVER TRADING TRAFFIC
ACTIVITY AGIOTAGE BESOIGNE
COMMERCE FOLLOWER INDUSTRY
INTEREST VOCATION
(COMIC —) LAZZO
(MONKEY —) JOUKERY PAWKERY
(STAGE —) BYPLAY
BUSINESSMAN TYCOON POACHER
BOURGEOIS CONVERTER
BUSKIN BOOT SHOE CALIGA
BOTTINE COTHURN BRODEKIN
BUSSU UBUSSU TROOLIE
BUST BUMP FAIL RUIN TAME BOSOM
BREAK BURST BUSTO CHEST EDGAR
FLUNK SPREE BRONZE DEMOTE
REDUCE STATUE DEGRADE DISMISS
FAILURE PROTOME
(— SHAPE) TAILLE
BUSTARD KORI OTIS WATO PAAUW
TURKEY BEBILYA HOUBARA
KORHAAN FLORICAN GOMPAAUM
BUSTIC AUSUBO CASSADA
BUSTLE ADO BUZZ FIKE FRAY FUSS
JUMP STIR WHEW WHIR FRISK
HASTE HYPER KNOCK PAVIE STEER
WHIRL WHIRR BISHOP BUMBLE
ENERGY FISSLE FISTLE FLURRY
FUSTLE HUDDLE HUSTLE POTHER
RACKET TATTER THRONG TUMULT
UNREST UPROAR CLATTER CLUTTER
CONTEND LOUSTER SCOWDER
SCUFFLE SCUFTER SPUFFLE
ACTIVITY IMPROVER SPLUTTER
STRUGGLE TOURNURE
BUSTLING ADO BUSY FUSSY
SPOFFISH STIRRING
BUSY FAST FELL APPLY BRISK QUICK
ACTIVE EIDENT EMPLOY INTENT
LIVELY OCCUPY STEERY THRONG
UNIDLE ENGAGED HOPPING
HUMMING OPEROSE TROUBLE
WORKING DILIGENT EMPLOYED
EXERCISE OCCUPIED SEDULOUS
TIRELESS UNTIRING
(— ONESELF) STRAP
(NOT —) SLACK
BUSYBODY BUSY SNOOP EARWIG
SPOFFY ARDELIO MARPLOT
MEDDLER SNOOPER FACTOTUM
QUIDNUNC PRAGMATIC

BUT AC LO MA BIT SED YEA YET
MERE ONLY SAVE ARRAH STILL
ALWAYS EXCEPT UNLESS BESIDES
HOWBEIT HOWEVER
BUTCHER KILL SLAY BUTCH SPOIL
BUNGLE KIDDER LEGGER LEMMER
MURDER VENDOR BOTCHER
BRAINER BRITTEN FLESHER
MEATMAN PORKMAN KILLCALF
PIGSTICK SLAUGHTER
BUTCHERBIRD SHRIKE MATAGASSE
BUTCHER'S-BROOM RUSCUS
BRUSCUS
BUTCHERY MURDER CARNAGE
MASSACRE SHAMBLES SLAUGHTER
BUTEO BUZZARD
BUTLER SOMLER YEOMAN BOTELER
SERVANT SPENCER STEWARD
CELLARER CONSUMAH KHANSAMA
STEPHANO MAJORDOMO
BUTT JUR JUT MOT PIT PUT RAM
RUN TOY TUP BUCK BUNT BURT
BUSH CART CASK DISH DOSS FOOL
GOAD GOAL GOAT HORN JOLT
JURR POLL PUCK PUSH STUB TANG
TOPE TURR BOUND HINGE JOINT
MOUND ROACH SCOPE STOCK
STUMP BREECH TARGET THRUST
BEEHIVE BUTTOCK PARAPET
PROJECT REVERSE STUMMEL
ARIETATE FLATFISH FLOUNDER
RIDICULE SACKBUTT
(— FOR RIDICULE) GAME SPORT
STALE COCKSHY
(— OF CIGAR) DOCK SNIPE
(— OF HORSEHIDE) SHELL
(— OF JOKE) JEST SCOGGIN
JESTWORD
(CIGARETTE —) BUMPER
(HALF —) BEND
BUTTE HILL PICACHO
BUTTER SHEA CLART COCUM
BAMBUK BEURRE CAJOLE SPREAD
BLARNEY FLATTER
(— MEASURE) SPAN
(ARTIFICIAL —) BOSH OLEO BOSCH
MARGARINE
(BROWNED IN —) NOISETTE
(SEMIFLUID —) GHI GHEE
BUTTER-AND-EGGS RANSTEAD
TOADFLAX
BUTTERBUR CLEAT CLOTE ELDIN
GALON GALLON OXWORT GILTCUP
FLEADOCK
BUTTERCUP BOLT CYME CRAZY
ANEMONE CRAISEY CROWTOE
GILTCUP GOLDCUP KINGCOB
KINGCUP CRAWFOOT CROWFOOT
FROGWORT
BUTTERFISH GUNNEL POMPANO
WHITING PALOMETA SKIPJACK
BUTTERFLY IO BLUE ARGUS ELFIN
GHOST NYMPH QUEEN SATYR SWIFT
WHITE ZEBRA ALPINE APOLLO
CALIGO COPPER DANAID HOPPER
IDALIA JUGATE MORPHO PIERID
PROGNE SULFUR THECLA URSULA
VIOLET YELLOW ADMIRAL BUCKEYE
DIURNAL DOLPHIN EMPEROR

FRENATE MONARCH PIERINE SATYRID SKIPPER SULPHUR TUSSOCK VANESSA VICEROY ARTHEMIS CECROPIA CRESCENT GRAYLING HESPERID ITHOMIID WANDERER
(— BREEDER) AURELIAN
BUTTERFLY FISH MOJARRA
FLATFISH
BUTTERFLY WEED FLUXROOT
MILKWEED WINDROOT
BUTTERMILK WHIG JOCOQUE
SOURDOOK
BUTTERSCOTCH TOFFY
BUTTERWORT BEANWEED
SHEEPWEED
BUTTERY BOTRY LARDER SPENCE
BUTLERY SPICERY
BUTTOCKS ASS BUM CAN FUD HAM
ARSE BUTT CULE DOCK DOUP DUFF
LEND POOP SEAT TAIL TOBY CROUP
FANNY NATES SLATS STERN TOUTE
BEHIND BOTTOM BREECH CURPIN
HEINIE HINDER CROUPON CRUPPER
DRODDUM HURDIES KEISTER
BACKSIDE DERRIERE NATIFORM
BUTTON BUD ZIP BOSS CHIN DOME
HOOK KNOB KNOP SPUR TUFT
BADGE CATCH GLIDE OLIVE PEARL
PRILL BAUBLE BUCKLE GLIDER
SHINER TOGGLE TROCHE DEWDROP
HORNTIP KNICKER PRESSEL
REGULUS DOORBELL FASTENER
OLIVETTE
BUTTONBUSH BUCKBRUSH
SWAMPWOOD
BUTTONHOLE EYE LOOP SLIT
BUTTON SNAKEROOT LIATRIS
SAWWORT

BUTTONWOOD COTONIER
BUTTRESS NOSE PIER PILE PROP
SPUR STAY BRACE BRICK OUTCAST
OUTSHOT SUPPORT TAMBOUR
ABUTMENT
(— MEMBER) TIRE
BUTYL TETRYL
BUXOM MILD AMPLE JOLLY PLUMP
PRONE SONSY BLITHE CRUMBY
CRUMMY FLORID FODGEL HUMBLE
PLIANT SONSIE BOWERLY
BOUNCING FLEXIBLE OBEDIENT
OBLIGING YIELDING JUNOESQUE
BUY CHAP COFF COUP GAIN HAVE
SHOP SNIP TAKE BRIBE CLAIM
TRADE ABEGGE MARKET RANSOM
REDEEM SECURE ACQUIRE CHAFFER
PURCHASE
(— BACK) REPRISE
(— OFF) APPEASE
(— UP STOCKS) COVER
BUYER CHAP AGENT CATER BEGGER
EMPTOR PATRON VENDEE CHAPMAN
SHOPPER ACHATOUR CUSTOMER
PROSPECT
(— OF CLOTH) REDUBBER
BUYING ACATE ACHATE EMPTION
(— MANIA) ONIOMANIA
BUZZ HUM BURR CALL DASH HISS
HUSS HUZZ RING WHIR FANCY
FLING PHONE RUMOR BUMBLE
NOTION WHISPER
BUZZARD AURA FOOL HAWK PERN
BUTEO GLADE GLEDE HARPY
STOOP BEETLE CURLEW PREYER
STUPID PUDDOCK PUTTOCK
VULTURE BROMVOEL
BUZZER BEE BELL ALARM HOWLER
SIGNAL WHIZZER

BY A P X AB AT OF TO AGO BYE GIN
PAR PER TIL ABUT ANON INTO
NEAR PAST TILL APART ASIDE
CLOSE FORBY BESIDE TOWARD
BESIDES THROUGH
(— AND BY) BELIVE BIMEBY
(— FAR) EASILY
(— HEART) PERQUEIR
(— HOOK OR CROOK) HABNAB
(— MEANS OF) PER MOYENANT
(— NO MEANS) NA
(— REASON OF THIS) HEREAT
(— STEALTH) STOWLINS
(— SURPRISE) ABACK
(— THE DAY) PD
(— THE ORDER OF) O
(— THE WAY) APROPOS
(— THIS TIME) ALREADY
(— WAY OF) VIA
(GONE —) AGO PAST
(NEAR —) GIN
BY-BIDDER FUNK CAPPER PUFFER
BY-CHANNEL BAYOU BRANCH
BYCOKET ABACOT ABOCOCKET
BYGONE PAST YORE OLDEN BYPAST
FORMER ANCIENT ELAPSED
BACKWARD DEPARTED FOREPAST
PRETERIT
BYPASS JUMP SHUN AVOID BURKE
EVADE SHUNT CUTOFF DETOUR
CIRCUIT OUTFLANK
BYPATH LANE BYWAY UNDERWALK
BY-PRODUCT SCRAP SHORTS
EFFLUVIUM
BYWAY LANE PATH ALLEY BYPATH
BYWALK OUTWAY SIDEWAY
BYWORD AXIOM MOTTO BYNAME
DIVERB PHRASE SAYING NAYWORD
PROVERB NICKNAME REPROACH

C DO CEE DOH COCA CHARLIE HUNDRED
CAAMA FOX ASSE SILVER
CAB FLY KAB TAXI ARABA ARANA CABIN GHARRI CRAWLER HACKNEY SHOWFUL TAXICAB COUPELET MOTORCAB
(**2-PONY** —) KOSONG
(**4-WHEELED** —) BOUNDE BOUNDER GROWLER
(**HINDU** —) JUDKA
(**LOW-HUNG** —) HERDIC
CABAL PLOT RING JUNTA PARTY BRIGUE CLIQUE SCHEME SECRET CHATTER CONSULT COUNCIL DISPUTE FACTION TALKING INTRIGUE
CABALISTIC MYSTIC
CABARET CAFE TAVERN
CABASSOU XENURUS
CABBAGE CAB CHOU CRIB KALE WORT CROUT FILCH SAVOY STEAL STOCK PECHAY PILFER TAILOR BOWKAIL OXHEART PAKCHOI PALMITO PURLOIN BORECOLE COLEWORT CRUCIFER CULTIGEN DRUMHEAD KOHLRABI KERGUELEN (**STUFFED** —) HOLISHKES (**PL.**) WORTS
CABBAGE BARK ANGELIM ANGELIN
CABBAGE SOUP SHCHI STCHI SHTCHEE
CABBAGE STALK CASTOCK
CABDRIVER HACK MUSH CABBY CABMAN COCHER MUSHER COCHERO HACKMAN
CABIN BOX CAB COT DEN HUT CAVE CELL CREW SHED TILT BOOTH CHOZA COACH CUDDY FELZE HOVEL LODGE SHACK BOHAWN CABANA CASITA LITTER REFUGE SALOON SHANTY WIGWAM BEDROOM BOUDOIR COTTAGE HUDDOCK MUDSILL
(**— ON SHIP'S DECK**) TEXAS
(**DOUBLE** —) SADDLEBAG
(**RUSS. LOG** —) IZBA
CABINET BOX BUHL CASE FILE SINK AMBRY BAHUT BOARD CABIN CHEST BAFFLE BUREAU CLOSET ICEBOX ALMIRAH BOUDOIR COMMODE CONSOLE COUNCIL ETAGERE FREEZER JUKEBOX WHATNOT CELLARET CUPBOARD MINISTRY SHOWCASE VARGUENO MONOCLEID
(**FILING** —) MORGUE
CABLE GUY TOW BOOM COAX CORD FAST JUNK LINK ROPE STAY WIRE CABLET GANGER STRAND TETHER COAXIAL GUNLINE SKYLINE CATENARY HIGHLINE TELEGRAM
(**— WITH EYE AT EACH END**) STRAP
(**— WOUND**) KECKLING
(**CHAIN** —) BOOM
(**DERRICK** —) BACKSTAY
(**SPLICED** —) SHOT
(**SUSPENDED** —) ROPEWAY
CABLE CAR TELFER TELPHER
CABLED RUDENTED

CABMAN IZVOZCHIK
CABOCHON CAB SHELL CARBUNCLE
CABOODLE KIT LOT CALABASH
CABOOSE CAB CAR VAN CRIB HACK BUGGY CRUMMY GALLEY PALACE BOUNCER COOKROOM DOGHOUSE
CABRILLA CONY GAPER GROUPER
CABSTAND HASARD HAZARD
CABUYA PITEIRA
CACAO BROMA COCOA ARRIBA COCKER CRIOLLO FORASTERO
CACHARI BODA
CACHE BURY HIDE DEPOT STASH STORE SCREEN CONCEAL DEPOSIT TREASURE
CACHET SEAL STAMP WAFER ESSENCE KONSEAL
CACIQUE BUNYAH CASSICAN HANGNEST
CACKEREL MENDOLE
CACKLE CANK CONK CLACK LAUGH BABBLE GABBLE GAGGLE GIGGLE GOSSIP KECKLE TITTER CHACKLE CHATTER SNICKER TWADDLE LAUGHTER
CACKLING GOOSE GREASER
CACOMISTLE CIVET ARCTOID RINGTAIL BASSARISK
CACOON SEGRA SEQUA
CACOPHONOUS HARSH RAUCOUS JANGLING STRIDENT
CACTUS BLEO DILDO NOPAL BAVOSO CARDON CEREUS CHAUTE CHENDE CHINOA CHOLLA COCHAL MESCAL PEYOTE PEYOTL TASAJO AIRAMPO BISAGRE BISNAGA SAGUARO ALICOCHE CHICHIPE PITAHAYA XEROPHIL
(**— FRUIT**) MUYUSA
CAD CUR BOOR CHUM HEEL CHURL MUCKER RASCAL ROTTER BOUNDER DASTARD ASSISTANT
CADASTRAL UNIT YOKE
CADAVER BODY STIFF CORPSE CARCASS SUBJECT SKELETON
CADAVEROUS PALE GAUNT LIVID PALLID GHASTLY HAGGARD
CADDIE NACKET
CADDIS FLY DUN CADEW SEDGE CADBIT
CADDISWORM PIPER
CADDO ADAI TEXAS EYEISH HAINAI KICHAI HASINAI
CADE LAMB SOCK
CADENCE BEAT FALL IAMB LILT PACE TONE CLOSE METER METRE SOUND SWING THROB DACTYL IAMBUS JINGLE RHYTHM BACCHIC ANAPAEST CLAUSULA MOVEMENT MEDIATION
CADENZA MELISMA BARIOLAGE
CADET SON DODO GOAT PLEBE YOUTH EMBRYO JUNIOR SERGEANT
CADGE BEG BOT BUM TIE BIND HAWK CARRY MOOCH PEDDLE SPONGE SCROUNGE
CADGER BOT DEALER HAWKER CARRIER PACKMAN SPONGER HUCKSTER

CADGY KEDGY MERRY WANTON AMOROUS LUSTFUL CHEERFUL MIRTHFUL
CADMUS (**DAUGHTER OF** —) INO AGAVE SEMELE AUTONOE
(**FATHER OF** —) AGENOR
(**MOTHER OF** —) TELEPHASSA
(**SISTER OF** —) EUROPA
(**SON OF** —) POLYDORUS
(**WIFE OF** —) HARMONIA
CADRE CORE FRAME
CADUCEUS WAND STAFF SCEPTER SCEPTRE KERYKEION
CAECUM TYPHLON
CAESURA REST STOP BREAK PAUSE INTERVAL DIAERESIS
CAFE BARROOM CABARET ESTAMINET
(**— AU LAIT**) ALESAN
CAFE CREME SUEDE
CAFETERIA AUTOMAT
CAFFEINE THEIN THEINE
CAGAYAN IBANAG
CAGE BOX CAR GIG MEW PEN COOP CORF CRIB GOAL BRAKE CAVEA GRATE HUTCH AVIARY BASKET BUCKET CHAPEL ENCAGE FLIGHT PRISON CHANTRY CONFINE ENCLOSE LANTERN SHELTER TUMBREL TUMBRIL CARRIAGE ELEVATOR IMPRISON LAVARIUM RETAINER SCAFFOLD STRAINER
(**— FOR HAWKS**) MEW
(**— FOR HENS**) CAVEY CAVIE
(**— OF MINE SHAFT**) GIG
(**— OF TRAM**) CABIN
(**BIRD** —) AVIARY PINJRA VOLARY BIRDCAGE
(**FIRE** —) CRESSET
(**LOBSTER** —) CORF CREEL
CAGED PENT CAPTIVE
CAGER ONSETTER
CAGEY CAGY WARY COONY
CAGMAG KEGMEG
CAGOT AGOTE
CAHITA YAQUI
CAHOT PITCHHOLE
CAIMAN CAYMAN JACARE ALLIGATOR
CAINGANG COROADO AWEIKOMA CORONADO
CAIRN MAN PIKE MOUND RAISE GALGAL CATSTONE STONEMAN
CAIRNGORM MORION SMOKESTONE
CAISSON BOX PONT CAMEL CHEST WAGON COFFER PONTON SAUCER CAMAILE CHAMBER LACUNAR PONTOON
CAITIFF BASE MEAN VILE COWARD WICKED CAPTIVE COWARDLY PRISONER WRETCHED
CAJOLE COG CON JIG COAX FLAM FLUM PALP WORD CARNY CHEAT CURRY DECOY FRAIK INGLE JOLLY TEASE CARNEY DELUDE ENTICE FRAISE HUMBUG WHILLY BEGUILE FLATTER PALAVER SOOTHER TWEEDLE WHEEDLE BLANDISH
CAJOLERY FRAIK SOOTH TAFFY

BUTTER FRAISE DAUBERY FLATTERY
CAKE BAR BUN NUT WIG BAKE BALL
FLAE FOOL LUMP MASS MOLE TART
ARVAL BATTY BLOCK BOXTY COOKY
CRUST CUPID FADGE KYAAK SCONE
SHIVE TORTE WAFER WEDGE
BARKLE CIMBAL COOKIE DAMPER
ECLAIR GATEAU HALLAH HARDEN
KICHEL KUCHEN NACKET PARKIN
PASTRY POPLIN SIMNEL TABLET
WASTEL ASHCAKE BANNOCK
BROWNIE CAKETTE CARAWAY
CROZZLE CRUMPET CUPCAKE
FAIRING GALETTE HOECAKE
MANCHET NUTCAKE OATCAKE
PANCAKE PLASTER POPADAM
CHRIMSEL CLAPCAKE KUGELHOF
MADELINE MARZIPAN SEEDCAKE
SOLIDIFY SOULCAKE TORTILLA
TURNPIKE
(— OF CLAY) PLATTEN
(— OF MEAL) DODGER
(— OF RUBBER) BISCUIT
(CREOLE RICE —) CALA
(FANCY —) SUNKET
(FLAT —) PLATE BUNUELO GALETTE
PLACENT CHRIMSEL
(FOURTH PART OF —) FARL FARLE
(FRIED —) WONDER CRULLER
DOUGHNUT
(GINGER —) BOLIVAR
(GRIDDLE —) LATKE FLIPPER
FRITTER FLAPJACK
(HOLIDAY —) SIMNEL
(HONEY —) LEKACH
(LAMB AND WHEAT —) KIBBE
KIBBEH
(LEAVENED —) BAP
(NEW YEAR'S —) HAGMENA
HOGMANAY
(OIL —) GRIT POONAC
(POTATO —) FADGE
(PRESS —) CACHAZA
(RUM —) BABA
(SEED —) WIG SEEDCAKE
(TEA —) LUNN SCONE
(THIN —) WAFER JUMBLE BANNOCK
TORTILLA
(YEAST —) KOJI
(PL.) AMSATH COLYBA
CAKED CLIT
CAKE PULLER KNOCKER
CALABA BIRMA GALBA
CALABASH GOURD CURUBA JICARA
CALABASH TREE JICARA HIGUERO
CALABOOSE JUG BRIG JAIL PRISON
CABOOSE BASTILLE
CALABUR TREE CAPULI CAPULIN
SILKWOOD
CALAMANCO MANKIE
CALAMINE CADMIA
CALAMITOUS BAD SAD DIRE EVIL
BLACK FATAL BITTER DISMAL
TRAGIC WOEFUL ADVERSE BALEFUL
DIREFUL HAPLESS RUINOUS
UNHAPPY UNLUCKY GRIEVOUS
TRAGICAL WRETCHED
CALAMITY ILL WOE BLOW DOOM
EVIL RUIN SLAP HYDRA STORM

WRACK MISERY ONCOME SORROW
EXTREME ACCIDENT DISASTER
DISTRESS FATALITY JUDGMENT
MISCHIEF
CALAMONDIN ORANGE CALAMANSI
CALAMUS PEN CANE REED QUILL
ACORUS RATTAN ROTANG
CALANGAY ABACAY COCKATOO
CALASH CALESA GALECHE
CALCANEUM FIBULARE
HYPOTARSUS
CALCAR OVEN SPUR FURNACE
CALCARIUM PREHALLUX
CALCEOLARIA FAGELIA IONIDIUM
CALCIFY CRETIFY
CALCINING BURNING
CALCINO MUSCADINE
CALCITE APHRITE CALCSPAR
ALABASTER ARGENTINE HISLOPITE
CALCIUM LIME
CALCIUM CARBONATE WHITING
DRIPSTONE
CALCULATE AIM SUM CALK CAST
PLAN RATE TELL COUNT FRAME
THINK CIPHER DESIGN EXPECT
FIGURE NUMBER RECKON ACCOUNT
AVERAGE CALLATE COMPUTE
PREPARE CONSIDER FORECAST
ESTIMATE
(— BY ASTROLOGY) ERECT
CALCULATED COLD
CALCULATING COLD WISE BRITTLE
CAUTIOUS
CALCULATION CARE SHARE
CALCUL ACCOUNT CAUTION
WORKING CALCULUS FORECAST
HINDCAST PRUDENCE
(PL.) FIGURES
CALCULATOR TABLE ABACUS
ABACIST SOROBAN CALCULER
COMPUTER ISOGRAPH
CALCULUS STONE UROLITH
ANALYSIS
CALDRON POT RED VAT LEAD
ALFET BOILER KELDER KETTLE
TRIPOD VESSEL CALDERA
CAULDRON
CALENDAR DIARY ALMANAC
CALENDS JOURNAL KALENDS
REGISTER SCHEDULE
(PL.) FASTI
CALENDER TABBY SCHREINER
CALENDERER CANROYER
SMOOTHER
CALENDS K KAL
CALF CA BOB BOX BOY LEG BUSS
DOLT VEAL VEAU BOBBY BOSSY
BUNCH DOGIE MOGGY PODDY
RANNY SOOKY YOUTH MUSCLE
VEALER WEANER BULCHIN FATLING
SLEEPER CALFLING
(LIKE A —) VITULINE
(PREMATURE —) SLINK
(UNBRANDED —) LONGEAR
SLEEPER
(YEARLING —) BUD DAIRT
(YOUNG —) DEACON
(PL.) CAURE
CALF'S-FOOT JELLY SULZE
FISNOGA

CALFSKIN COROVA VELLUM
GRASSER TULCHAN VEALSKIN
CALIBER BORE RANK DEGREE
TALENT ABILITY BREADTH COMPASS
QUALITY CAPACITY DIAMETER
(HIGH —) STATURE
CALIBRATED BRIX BEAUME BALLING
CALICHE CALCRETE TEPETATE
NITRATINE
CALICO BLAY PINTO SALLO CHINTZ
SALLOO CROYDON SPOTTED
GOLDFISH
CALICO ASTER WISEWEED
CALICOBACK STINKBUG
CALICO BASS CRAPPIE BACHELOR
CALICUT KOZHIKODE

CALIFORNIA
CAPITAL: SACRAMENTO
COLLEGE: MILLS POMONA
WHITTIER
COUNTY: INYO KERN MONO NAPA
YOLO YUBA MARIN MODOC
COLUSA LASSEN MERCED
PLACER PLUMAS SHASTA
SOLANO SONOMA SUTTER
TEHAMA TULARE ALAMEDA
VENTURA SISKIYOU CALAVERAS
INDIAN: HUPA POMO YANA YUKI
KAROK MAIDU MIWOK WAPPO
WIYOT YUROK PATWIN SHASTA
TOLOWA YOKUTS CHUMASH
LUISENO SALINAN SERRANO
DIEGUENO
LAKE: MONO SODA EAGLE OWENS
TAHOE SALTON TULARE
ALMANOR BERRYESSA
MOUNTAIN: MUIR LASSEN SHASTA
WHITNEY
NAME: ELDORADO
PARK: LASSEN SEQUOIA
YOSEMITE
PRESIDENT: NIXON
PRISON: ALCATRAZ
RIVER: EEL MAD PIT KERN OWENS
PUTAH STONY FEATHER
KLAMATH RUBICON TRINITY
SACRAMENTO
STATE BIRD: QUAIL
STATE FLOWER: POPPY
STATE NICKNAME: GOLDEN
STATE TREE: REDWOOD
TOWN: LODI AZUSA CHICO CHINO
INDIO BLYTHE CARMEL COVINA
EUREKA FRESNO LOMPOC
MERCED OXNARD POMONA
SONOMA TULARE ALAMEDA
BURBANK GARDENA NEEDLES
SALINAS VALLEJO VISALIA
ALTADENA BERKELEY
PASADENA REDLANDS
CUCAMONGA
UNIVERSITY: USC UCLA CALTECH
STANFORD

CALIPER JENNY ODDLEGS CALIPERS
CALIPH ABU ALI BEKR IMAM OMAR
CALIF OTHMAN ABBASID UMAYYAD
CALK JAG NAP COPY CORK FILL

STOP CAULK CLOSE HORSE ROUGH CAREEN CALTROP CHINTZE OCCLUDE SILENCE
CALKING OAKUM
CALL HO KA BAN BID CRY CUP DUB HOY SAY SEE CITE COOP HAIL JERK NAME NOTE PAGE PIST ROUP STOP TERM TOOT YELL BEDUB CLAIM CLEPE CLOCK ELECT HALLO HIGHT HOLLA PHONE ROUSE SHOUT SPEAK STYLE UTTER VISIT VOUCH WAKEN YODEL ACCUSE APPEAL AROUSE BECALL CHANGE DEMAND HALLOA HALLOO INVITE INVOKE MUSTER QUETHE SUMMON TEKIAH TERUAH YELPER ACCLAIM ADDRESS APPOINT BEHIGHT BETITLE COLLECT COMMAND CONVENE CONVOKE DECLARE ENTITLE IMPEACH INQUIRE INSTYLE MOUNTEE WHISTLE ANNOUNCE APPELATE ASSEMBLE NOMINATE PROCLAIM VOCATION
(— **A BET)** STAY
(— **ALOUD)** COUNT
(— **BACK)** RECALL REVOKE
(— **COARSELY)** ROOP ROUP
(— **DOWN)** BRAWL DEVOCATE IMPRECATE
(— **FOR HELP)** SOS
(— **FOR HOGS)** SOOK SOOEY
(— **FOR)** CRY TAKE CLAIM EXACT DEMAND DESIRE COLLECT SOLICIT
(— **FORTH)** STIR EVOKE ELICIT INDUCE INVOKE ATTRACT SUGGEST
(— **HOUNDS)** LIFT
(— **IN ANGER)** GREET
(— **IN CHILDRENS' GAMES)** FAN FEN FIN VENTS
(— **IN MARBLES)** DUBS
(— **INTO QUESTION)** IMPUGN
(— **LOUDLY)** CRY HAIL ACCLAIM
(— **MAN BY MAN)** ARRAY
(— **ON TELEPHONE)** BUZZ
(— **OUT)** HAIL LURE ASCRY EVOKE HALLO GOLLAR GOLLER HOLLER HULLOO
(— **TO ACCOUNT)** AREASON CONTROL
(— **TO ARMS)** ALARM ALARUM RAPPEL
(— **TO BELLBOY)** FRONT
(— **TO CAT)** CHEET
(— **TO COURT)** ARRAIGN
(— **TO COWS)** SOOK COBOSS SOOKIE
(— **TO FOOD)** SOSS
(— **TO HORSE)** HIE HUP WAY PROO
(— **TO MIND)** CITE MING RECORD BETHINK REDOLLECT
(— **TO PRAYER)** AZAN
(— **TO READINESS)** ALERT
(— **TO SPARROW)** PHIPE PHIPPE
(— **TO WITNESS)** APPEAL
(— **UPON)** ASK SEE CITE GREDE HALSE BECALL DEPOSE ENGAGE SUMMON ADDRESS BESEECH IMPLORE
(**BIRD'S** —) WEET
(**BOATSWAIN'S** —) WINDING

(**BRIDGE** —) DOUBLE
(**BUGLE** —) POST HALLALI STABLES
(**CLOSE** —) TOUCH
(**DUCK** —) SQUAWKER
(**FRIENDLY** —) CEILIDH
(**HUNTING** —) RECHATE RECHEAT
(**MORNING** —) MATIN
(**NAUTICAL** —) AHOY
(**SHEPHERD'S** —) OVEY
(**SPORTSMAN'S** —) HOICKS YOICKS HALLALI
(**SQUARE DANCE** —) GEE HAW
(**STAGE TRUMPET** —) SENNET SINNET
(**TRUMPET** —) BERLOQUE
CALLA LILY DRAGON MAYFLOWER
CALLBOY FRONT CALLER HALLBOY
CALLER FLOORMAN
CALLIGRAPHER PENMAN WRITER COPYIST ENGROSSER
CALLIGRAPHY LETTERING CHIROGRAPHY
CALLING ART JOB WAY CALL HAIL RANK TRADE CAREER METIER NAMING OUTCRY MISSION MYSTERY PURSUIT STATION SUMMONS WARNING BUSINESS FUNCTION POSITION SHOUTING VOCATION
CALLIOPE (**FATHER OF** —) JUPITER
(**MOTHER OF** —) MNEMOSYNE
(**SON OF** —) ORPHEUS
CALLIRRHOE (**FATHER OF** —) OCEANUS
(**HUSBAND OF** —) TROS ALCMAEON
(**SON OF** —) ILUS GANYMEDE ASSARACUS
CALLISTO (**FATHER OF** —) LYCAON
(**SON OF** —) ARCAS
CALLITHRIX HAPALE JACCHUS
CALLOP YELLOWBELLY
CALLOSAL TRABAL
CALLOSITY SEG CALLUS SITFAST TYLOSIS CHESTNUT
CALLOUS HARD HORNY TOUGH BRAWNY OBTUSE SEARED TORPID WAUKIT DEDOLENT OBDURATE
CALLOUSED BRAWNY
CALLOW BALD BARE CRUDE GREEN SQUAB MARSHY IMMATURE UNFORMED YOUTHFUL
CALLUS SEG POROMA TYLOMA CALLOUS
CALM LAY LEE COOL DILL EASY EVEN FAIR FLAT HUSH LOWN LULL MEES MILD REST SOFT STAY ABATE ALLAY CHARM LEVEL LITHE LOUND MEASE PEACE QUELL QUIET SMOLT SOBER STILL STOIC STREW DOCILE GENTLE GLASSY IRENIC PACIFY PLACID SEDATE SERENE SETTLE SLATCH SLIGHT SMOOTH SOOTHE STEADY APPEASE ASSUAGE CALMATO COMPOSE GLACIAL HALCYON MOLLIFY PACIFIC PATIENT PLACATE QUALIFY QUIETEN RESTFUL UNMOVED CALMNESS COMPOSED DECOROUS PEACEFUL PLACABLE RESTRAIN SERENITY TRANQUIL UNRUFFLE

(**INTERNAL** —) HARMONY
(**NOT** —) BOISTEROUS
CALMLY COOLY COOLLY STILLY
CALMNESS CALM LULL POISE PHLEGM REPOSE SERENE ATARAXY COOLNESS SERENITY STILLNESS
CALNO KULLANI
CALOMEL TURPETH
CALORIC THERMOGEN
CALORIE THERM THERME
CALQUE LOANSHIFT
CALTROP CROWTOE GALTRAP BULLHEAD CROWFOOT
CALUMNIATE BLOT SLUR TEEN BELIE LIBEL ACCUSE ATTACK BEFOUL DEFAME MALIGN REVILE VILIFY ASPERSE BLACKEN SLANDER TRADUCE
CALUMNIATION SATIRE ASPERSION
CALUMNY SLUR DEPRAVE OBLOQUY
CALVA CALOTTE SINCIPUT
CALVARIA SKULLCAP
CALVARY GOLGOTHA
CALVE FRESHEN
CALVINIST GENEVAN GOMARIAN
CALYCULUS CELL CALYX
CALYPTER ALULA SQUAMA
CALYPTRA CAP VEIL EPIGONIUM
CALYX CUP POP HULL HUSK LEAF CULOT SEPAL SHUCK
CAM COG AWRY LOBE TRIG ASKEW CATCH SNAIL WIPER LIFTER TAPPET CROOKED TRIPPET KNOCKOFF PERVERSE ROLLBACK
CAMACHILE INGA HUAMUCHIL
CAMAGON MABOLO
CAMAS LOBELIA
CAMBER SET ARCH SWEEP ROUNDUP CROSSFALL

CAMBODIA
CAPE: SAMIT
CAPITAL: PNOMPENH PHNOMPENH
COIN: RIEL PUTTAN PIASTER
GULF: SIAM
LAKE: TONLESAP
MOUNTAIN: PAN AURAL
MOUNTAINS: DANGREK CARDAMOM ELEPHANT
NAME: CAMBOJA CAMBODGE
NATIVE: CHAM KHMER
RIVER: SAN SEN BASSAC MEKONG PORONG SREPOK SEKHONG TONLESAP
RUINS: ANGKORWAT
TOWN: REAM TAKEO KAMPOT KRATIE PURSAT KOHNIEH KRACHEH ROVIENG SAMRONG PNOMPENH SISOPHON
WEIGHT: MACE TAEL

CAME BAND CALM
CAMEL COLT OONT DELOUL DROMED FENDER HAGEEN MEHARI CAISSON TYLOPOD BACTRIAN RUMINANT DROMEDARY
CAMEL GRASS SCHOENANTH
CAMELLIA JAPONICA
CAMEL LIP CHILOMA

CAMELOPARD GIRAFFE
CAMEO GEM GAMAHE CAMAIEU
CARVING PHALERA RELIEVO
ANAGLYPH
CAMERA KINO KODAK CHAMBER
MINICAM PANORAM ENLARGER
MINIATURE VERASCOPE
(— TUBE) VIDICON
CAMERAMAN LENSMAN
CAMEROON (CAPITAL OF —)
YAOUNDE
(RIVER OF —) DJA NYONG SANAGA
(TOWN OF —) POLI YOKO BAFIA
DOUALA
CAMISOLE WAISTCOAT
CAMLET MOHAIR BARRACAN
CAMOMILE OXEYE MORGAN
CAMOUFLAGE FAKE HIDE DAZZLE
MUFFLE SCREEN CONCEAL
DISGUISE
CAMOUFLET STIFLER
CAMP TAN PEST TENT DOUAR ETAPE
HORDE SIEGE TABOR CASTLE
LAAGER SUGARY BIVOUAC
HUTMENT LODGING MAHALLA
PALANKA ZAREEBA QUARTERS
(— OUT) MAROON OUTLIE
(HOBO —) JUNGLE
(LUMBER —) CHANTIER
CAMPA ANDA ANDI ANTI
CAMPAIGN BLITZ DRIVE PLAIN
WHOOP CANVASS CRUSADE
JOURNEY SERVICE SOLICIT
WARFARE
CAMPANA GUTTA
CAMPANERO COTINGA ARAPUNGA
BELLBIRD COTINGID
CAMPANILE TOWER BELFRY
CLOCHER STEEPLE CARILLON
CAMPESTRAL AGRARIAN
CAMPHOR ASARONE BORNEOL
MENTHOL
(ANISE —) ANETHOLE
CAMPHOR TREE KADUR KAPOR
CAMPING BIVOUAC
CAMPION ROBIN COWBELL
CAMPUS GATE QUAD YARD FIELD
CAN CUP JUG MAY MOW POT TIN
ABLE FIRE JAIL BILLY CADDY
COULD ESHIN OILER SHALL SKILL
BOTTLE VESSEL ABILITY BOMBARD
CANIKIN CAPABLE CREAMER
DISMISS GROWLER PIPETTE
BILLYCAN CONSERVE PRESERVE
(— FOR LIQUOR) JACK
(— ON WHEELS) DANDY
(BULGED —) SWELL FLIPPER
(DEFECTIVE —) SPRINGER
(LEAKY —) LEAKER
(MILK —) CHURN
(TIN —) DESTROYER
(TRASH —) DUSTBIN
CANAANITE ARKITE HIVITE AMORITE
HIVVITE JEBUSITE
CANACE (BROTHER OF —)
MACAREUS
(FATHER OF —) AEOLUS
(MOTHER OF —) ENARETE
(SON OF —) TRIOPAS

CANADA
BAY: JAMES HUDSON UNGAVA
GEORGIAN
CAPITAL: OTTAWA
INDIAN: CREE COMOX HAIDA
NISKA SARSI STALO MICMAC
NAHANE NOOTKA SARCEE
CARRIER NANAIMO SEKANEE
SHUSWAP SONGISH TAHLTAN
ALGONKIN COWICHON LILLOOET
MALECITE SQUAMISH TSATTINE
ISLAND: READ BANKS BYLOT
COATS DEVON SABLE BAFFIN
MANSEL VICTORIA ANTICOSTI
VANCOUVER
ISLANDS: PARRY BELCHER
BATHURST MAGDALEN
LAKE: BEAR CREE GARRY RAINY
SLAVE LOUISE SIMCOE ABITIBI
DUBAWNT NIPIGON KOOTENAY
OKANAGAN NIPISSING
MEASURE: MINOT PERCH ARPENT
CHAINON
MOUNTAIN: LOGAN ROYAL
ROBSON TREMBLANT
MOUNTAIN RANGE: SKEENA
CARIBOO STELIAS COLUMBIA
LAURENTIAN
NATIVE: CANUCK
PARK: YOHO BANFF ACADIA
JASPER
PENINSULA: GASPE BOOTHIA
MELVILLE
PROVINCE: QUEBEC ALBERTA
ONTARIO MANITOBA
NOVASCOTIA NEWFOUNDLAND
NEWBRUNSWICK SASKATCHEWAN
PROVINCIAL CAPITAL: QUEBEC
REGINA STJOHN HALIFAX
TORONTO EDMONTON VICTORIA
WINNIPEG CHARLOTTETOWN
RIVER: HAY RED BACK PEEL
PEACE SLAVE YUKON FRASER
NELSON OTTAWA SKEENA
THELON PETAWAWA SAGUENAY
MACKENZIE RICHELIEU
STRAIT: CABOT DEASE HECATE
HUDSON GEORGIA
SYMBOL: MAPLELEAF
TERRITORY: YUKON
TOWN: HULL BANFF LAVAL
GUELPH OSHAWA REGINA
SARNIA CALGARY HALIFAX
MONCTON NANAIMO SUDBURY
TORONTO WELLAND WINDSOR
KINGSTON MONTREAL VICTORIA
WINNIPEG SASKATOON
VANCOUVER
UNIVERSITY: MCGILL DALHOUSIE

CANADA BLUEBERRY SOURTOP
CANADA GOOSE HONKER BUSTARD
OUTARDE
CANADA JAY MEATBIRD MOOSEBIRD
CANADA LYNX PISHU LUCIVEE
CANADA PLUM CHENEY
CANADA VIOLET JUNEFLOWER

CANADIAN CANUCK
CANAILLE MOB FLOUR RABBLE
DOGGERY RIFFRAFF
CANAL CUT CANO DUCT LODE PIPE
SHAT TUBE BAYOU DITCH DRAIN
FOSSA GRAFF KLONG SCALA ZANJA
ESTERO GROOVE KENNEL STRAIT
TRENCH VAGINA ACEQUIA APHODUS
CHANNEL CONDUIT FOREBAY
RACEWAY SHIPWAY TOWPATH
AQUEDUCT EMISSARY IRRIGANT
MILLRACE PROSODUS VOLKMANN
(— LABORER) NAVIGATOR
(ALIMENTARY —) GUT ENTERON
INTESTINE
(ANATOMICAL —) SCALA MEATUS
(CARINAL —) LACUNA
CANARD DUCK HOAX RUMOR
GRAPEVINE
CANARY DICKY FRILL LIZARD
ROLLER CAYENNE CHOPPER
JONQUIL SQUEALER
(— HYBRID) MULE

CANARY ISLANDS
CAPITAL: SANTACRUZ
ISLAND: ROCA CLARA FERRO
LOBOS PALMA ROCCA GOMERA
HIERRO INFERNO GRACIOSA
TENERIFE LANZAROTTE
MEASURE: FANEGADA
MOUNTAIN: TEYDE LACRUZ
ELCUMBRE TENERIFE
PROVINCE: LASPALMAS
TOWN: LAGUNA ARRECIFE
VALVERDE

CANARY MOSS CORKIR
CANASTA SAMBA BOLIVIA
CANCEL BLOT DASH DELE OMIT
UNDO VENT WIPE ANNUL BELAY
CROSS ERASE QUASH REMIT SCORE
SCRUB DELETE EFFACE KILLER
RECALL REMOVE REVOKE STROKE
ABOLISH DESTROY EXPUNGE
NULLIFY RESCIND RETRACT
SCRATCH SUBLATE UNWRITE
ABROGATE
CANCELER BUMPER STAMPER
CANCELLATION GRID CANCEL
REVOKE SURRENDER
CANCER WOLF KASHYAPA
CANCERWORT FLUELLIN
CANDAREEN FAN FEN
CANDELABRUM PHAROS MENORAH
GIRANDOLE
CANDID FAIR JUST OPEN PURE
BLUNT CLEAR FRANK NAIVE PLAIN
HONEST ARTLESS JANNOCK
SINCERE EVENDOWN INNOCENT
SPLENDID STRAIGHT
CANDIDATE LEGACY ESQUIRE
NOMINEE ASPIRANT GRADUAND
PROSPECT
CANDIED GLACE
CANDLE DIP WAX GLIM SIZE SLUT
LIGHT SPERM TAPER TOLLY BOUGIE
CIERGE MORTAR PLANET SHAMUS

SLUSHY TALLOW TORTIS CANDELA
PERCHER PRICKET
(IMITATION —) JUDAS
(SQUARE —) QUARRIER
CANDLEFISH SKIL EULACHON
HOOLAKIN OOLACHAN SKILFISH
SABLEFISH
CANDLEHOLDER SPIDER
CANDLEMAKER CHANDLER
TALLOWER
CANDLEMAS TERM MARYMASS
CANDLENUT AMA LAMA BIABO
KUKUI IGUAPE KEMIRI LUMBANG
ABURAGIRI
CANDLESNUFFER DOUTER
CANDLESTAND TORCHERE
CANDLESTICK BUGIA DYKER JESSE
STICK CRUSIE LAMPAD MORTAR
SCONCE PASCHAL PRICKET
CHANDLER DICERION FLAMBEAU
STANDARD TRIKERION
CANDLEWICK MATCH SNAST
SHROUD
(CHARRED PART OF —) SNOT
SNUFF SNUFFING
CANDLEWOOD CIRIO OCOTILLO
TABANUCO
CANDOR PURITY FAIRNESS
KINDNESS INTEGRITY
CANDY DROP DUMP KISS PIPE ROCK
CREAM CRISP DULCE FUDGE GLACE
GUNDY LOLLY SPICE SQUIB SWEET
TAFFY BONBON COMFIT HUMBUG
NOGADA NOUGAT PATTIE PENIDE
BRITTLE CANDIEL CARAMEL
CONGEAL FLATTER FONDATE
GUMDROP SWEETEN SWEETIE
TORRONE ALPHENIG LOLLIPOP
STICKJAW
(PL.) CUTS CONFETTI
CANDYTUFT CRUCIFER
(PL.) IBERIS
CANE ROD BEAT CRAB DART FLOG
PIPE REED STEM TUBE WAND WHIP
BIRCH GIBBY GUNDY LANCE STAFF
STICK SWISH TOLLY WADDY
BAMBOO JAMBEE KEBBIE PUNISH
RATTAN CALAMUS HICKORY
KIPPEEN MALACCA SCOURGE
STADDLE TICKLER WHANGEE
GIBSTAFF
(BLACK —) JAPAN
(END OF —) FRAZE
(SPLIT —) CANEWORK
CANELLA WHITEWOOD
CANELO CIXO
CANESCENT HOARY
CANFIELD KLONDIKE
CANICULA SIRIUS
CANINE CUR DOG FOX PUP FISC
TUSH WOLF DOGLY DOGLIKE
LANIARY
CANING RATTAN BIRCHING
CANISTEL TIES EGGFRUIT
CANNA ACHIRA GOLDBIRD
CANNABIS BHANG GANJA GUAZA
GUNJA HEMPWORT
(— TOPS) TAKROURI
CANNEL BONE FURCULE

CANNEL COAL AMPELITE
CANNER CANMAN TINNER
CANNIBAL WINDIGO LESTRIGON
THYESTEAN
CANNON BIT EAR GUN BASE SHOT
TUBE ASPIC CRACK MOYEN PIECE
SACRE SACRI SAKER SHANK SLING
THIEF BICORN CURTAL FALCON
FOWLER JINGAL LICORN MORTAR
POTGUN BASTARD BOMBARD
BULLDOG CHAMBER HANDGUN
LOMBARD MOYENNE ROBINET
SERPENT STINGER UNICORN
BASILISK CULVERIN HOWITZER
MURDERER OERLIKON ORDNANCE
SPITFIRE ZUMBOORUK
(— OF BELL) EAR
(CARRIAGE OF —) NADRIER
(DISCHARGE OF —) TIRE
(DUMMY —) QUAKER
CANNONBALL GUN PILL BULLET
GUNSTONE
CANNON BOSS TRUNNION
CANNON PLUG TAMPION
CANNOT CANT CANNA DONNA
DOWNA UNABLE
CANNY SLY COZY SNUG WARY WILY
WISE COONY LUCKY PAWKY QUIET
CLEVER FRUGAL GENTLE SHREWD
STEADY CAREFUL CUNNING
KNOWING PRUDENT QUIETLY
THRIFTY CAUTIOUS SKILLFUL
WATCHFUL
CANOE AMA KIAK LISI PAHI PROA
WAKA AOTEA ARAWA BANCA BIRCH
BONGO BUNGO CANKA KAYAK
KOLEK PRAHU SKIFF TONEE UMIAK
VINTA WAAPA BAIDAR BALLAM
BAROTO CORIAL CUNNER DUGOUT
OOMIAK PAOPAO PITPAN PUNGEY
TAINUI TROUGH ALMADIA BIDARKA
BUCKEYE CANADER CASCARA
CORACLE CURIARA CURRANE
HOROUTA LAKATOI PIRAGUA
PIROGUE BALANGAY BARANGAY
FALTBOAT FOLDBOAT MONOXYLE
TAKITUMU THAMAKAU TSUKUPIN
WOODSKIN
CANON FEN LAW CODE FUGA HYMN
LAUD LIST RULE SONG AXIOM
GORGE GULCH MODEL NODUS
TABLE TENET ACTION DECREE
GNOMON LIBRARY PRECEPT
STATUTE DECISION STAGIARY
STANDARD
(BODY OF —S) CHAPTER
CANONICAL CANONIC ACCEPTED
ORTHODOX
(NOT —) APOCHRYPHAL
CANOPY SKY CEIL COPE DAIS HOOD
TILT CHUPA CROWN HOVEL SHADE
STATE VAULT AWNING BUBBLE
CELURE ESTATE FINIAL GABLET
HUPPAH SHADOW TESTER CEILING
HEAVENS MARQUEE SHELTER
SPARVER BASILICA CIBORIUM
COVERING OVERWOOD PAVILION
SEMIANNA
(— ABOVE THRONE) STATE

(— FOR LIVESTOCK) HOVEL
(— OF ALTAR) CIBORIUM
(— OF HEAVEN) VAULT
(— OVER BROODER) HOVER
(BED —) TESTER SPARVER
(HEARSE —) MAJESTY
CANT TIP COAX HEEL LEAN LIST
NOOK SING TILT TURN ARGOT
BEVEL CHANT DRIFT FLASH HIELD
LINGO LUSTY MERRY NICHE PITCH
SHARE SLANG SLANT SLOPE WHINE
CAREEN CASTER CORNER INTONE
JARGON LIVELY PATOIS PATTER
SNIVEL AUCTION DIALECT INCLINE
PORTION SINGING WHEEDLE
CHEERFUL PRETENSE VIGOROUS
CANTABRIGIAN CANTAB
CAMBRIDGE
CANTALA MAGUEY
CANTANKEROUS ILL CURSED
CUSSED ORNERY KICKISH
CANKERED CONTRARY PERVERSE
CANTATA SERENATA VILLANCICO
CANTEEN BAR FLASK BAZAAR
CANTINA
CANTER JOG RUN GAIT LOPE PACE
RACK AUBIN ROGUE BEGGAR
WHINER SNUFFLER VAGABOND
CANTERBURY BELL MILKWORT
CAMPANULA
CANTICLE ODE HYMN LAUD SONG
CANTO ANTHEM CANTIC HIRMOS
BRAVURA
CANTILEVER LOOKOUT SEMIBEAM
CARTOUCHE
CANTING CANT PIOUS SNUFFLING
CANTO AIR FIT BOOK DUAN PACE
SONG VERSE MELODY PASSUS
CANTON ANGLE UNION CORNER
VOLOST PORTION QUARTER
SECTION DISTRICT DIVISION
(HALF —) ESQUIRE
CANTOR HAZAN HAZZAN SINGER
CHANTER CHAZZAN SOLOIST
PSALMIST
CANVAS FLY PAT DUCK GLUT PATA
SAIL TARP TENT TEWK CLOTH
COAST SCRIM TOILE VITRY BURLAP
LINING MUSLIN PICTURE POLDAVY
SCUTAGE DRABBLER PAINTING
VANDELAS
(— FOR CONVEYING GRAIN) APRON
(OLD CONDEMNED —) RUMBOWLINE
(RUBBERIZED —) TOSH
(STUFFED —) BOLSTER
(TARRED —) COAT
CANVASBACK CAN DIVER CHEVAL
DUCKER POCHARD BULLNECK
CANVASS BEAT CASE DRUM HAWK
POLL SIFT RANDY STUDY DEBATE
PEDDLE SEARCH AGITATE DISCUSS
EXAMINE SOLICIT TROUNCE
CAMPAIGN CONSIDER
CANVASSER AGENT POLLER
ROADMAN
CANYON CAJON CHASM GORGE
GULCH ARROYO CANADA RAVINE
CAOUTCHOUC RUBBER ELATERITE
CAP CUP FEZ HAT LID PAD POT TAJ

TAM TIP TOP ACME COIF CORK COWL DINK DOME DOWD ETON GAGE HOOD HURE JOAN KEEP KEPI MATE SHOE SHOW TOPI BERET BOINA BUSBY CHIEF COVER CROWN EXCEL FANON GALEA HOUVE KULAH MATCH MUTCH OUTDO PHANO PUNCH SEIZE SHAKO TOPEE TRUMP ARREST BARRAD BARRET BEANIE BIGGIN BIRRUS BONNET CALPAC CLIMAX COCKUP CORNET GALERA HELMET HUBCAP JINNAH MOBCAP PILEUS PINNER PRIMER PUZZLE SUMMIT TABARD TURBAN ALOPEKE BIRETTA CALOTTE CAMAURO CAPITAL CEREVIS CHAPEAU CHECHIA CLOSURE COMMODE FERRULE FLATCAP FORAGER HEADCAP OVERLIE OVERTOP PERPLEX PETASOS PILLBOX PILLION SOWBACK SURPASS THIMBLE TURNCAP ACROSOME BALMORAL BEARSKIN BYCOCKET CAPELINE COONSKIN ELECTRIC FOLLOWER HEADGEAR PHRYGIUM SKEWBACK SKULLCAP SURPRISE TARBOOSH (— FOR PILEDRIVER) PUNCH (— OF FLAGSTAFF) TRUCK (— OF FOAM) HOOD (— OF PYXIDIUM) LID (— OF WATCH) DOME CROWN (BISHOP'S —) HURA HURE (HUNTER'S —) MONTERA MONTERO (ICE —) BRAE CALOTTE (JESTER'S —) COXCOMB FOOLSCAP (MILITARY —) KEPI BUSBY SHAKO (MOUNTAIN —) SCALP (PERCUSSION —) CAPSULE (PERUVIAN —) CHULLO (POPE'S —) CAMAURO (ROOT —) CALYPTRA (WOMAN'S —) CAUL DOWD JOAN KELL MUTCH COMMODE VOLUPER BIGGONET (WOOLEN —) BOINA TOQUE TUQUE
CAPABILITY STROIL ABILITY CONDUCT FACULTY POTENCY CAPACITY
CAPABLE APT CAN FIT ABLE GOOD ADEPT CAPAX FENDY TIGHT EXPERT SKILLED POWERFUL (— OF BEING DEFENDED) TENABLE (— OF BEING DRAWN OUT) DUCTILE (— OF BEING SEVERED) SEVTILE (— OF BEING THROWN) MISSILE (— OF BEING UTTERED) EFFABLE (— OF FLYING) VOLANT (— OF SUBMISSION) AMENABLE (NORMALLY —) ABOUT
CAPACIOUS FULL SIDE WIDE AMPLE BROAD LARGE ROOMY GOODLY ROOMFUL CAPTIOUS ROOMSOME SPACIOUS
CAPACITOR CONDENSER
CAPACITY BACK BENT BIND DISH GIFT GIVE SIZE TURN BLAST FLAIR FORCE KNACK MODEL POWER SKILL SPACE AGENCY BOTTOM BURDEN ENERGY ENGINE EXTENT GENIUS

MODULE SPREAD TALENT VOLUME ABILITY CALIBER CALIBRE CONTENT FACULTY FITNESS QUALITY APTITUDE INSTINCT STRENGTH INFLUENCE (— FOR EATING) STROKE (— FOR ENDURANCE) STAY (— FOR HIGHER KNOWLEDGE) INTELLECT (— OF LATHE) SWING (— OF SHIP) BURDEN (CIVIL —) CAPUT (INNATE —S) STAMINA (INTELLECTUAL —) BROW (LOAD-PULLING —) DRAFT DRAUGHT (MENTAL —S) BELFRY (SPECIAL —) KNACK (UNIT OF —) MUD MUID LAGEN KISHEN MEDIMNUS KILDERKIN (UNLIMITED —) INFINITY
CAPANEUS (FATHER OF —) HIPPONOUS BELLEROPHON (SLAYER OF —) JUPITER (WIFE OF —) EVADNE
CAPARISON DECK TRAP HOUSE COVERING TRAPPING
CAPE RAS COPE GAPE HEAD HOOK LOOK NECK NESS TANG WRIT AMICE CAPPA CLOAK FICHU ORALE POINT SAGUM STARE STOLE TALMA BERTHA BYRRUS CABAAN CHAPEL DOLMAN MANTLE SONTAG TABARD TIPPET LEATHER MANTEEL MOZETTA SALIENT TANJONG VANDYKE CIRCULAR COLLARET HEADLAND LAMBSKIN MANTILLA PELERINE SEALSKIN RAINPROOF (— OF STRAW) MINO (BULLFIGHTER'S —) CAPA (DRESSING —) TOILET (FEATHER —) AHUULA (HOODED —) HUKE DOMINO (LACE OR SILK —) VISITE (LOW —) TANG (PAPAL —) FANO FANON FANUM ORALE PHANO (RAIN —) CAPOTE
CAPE ANTEATER AARDVARK
CAPE ARMADILLO PANGOLIN
CAPE GOOSEBERRY POHA
CAPE HEN STINKER STINKPOT
CAPELIN SMELT ICEFISH
CAPE PIGEON PINTADO
CAPE POLECAT ZORIL MUISHOND
CAPER HOP JET DIDO HOIT JUMP LEAP ROMP SKIP SKIT ANTIC BRANK DANCE FLING FLISK FRISK PRANK SAUCE SHRUB CAVORT CURVET FRISCO FROLIC GAMBOL GAMOND PRANCE SPRING TITTUP VAGARY CORSAIR COURANT FRISCAL GAMBADO PRANKLE CAPRIOLE MARIGOLD (— ABOUT) FLING CAVORT (SILLY —) SHINE
CAPER SPURGE CATEPUCE
CAPE TOWN BOVENLAND
CAPHITE KIST
CAPITAL CAP CASH CITY FUND

GOOD LIMA MAIN RARE SEAT BASIC CHIEF FATAL GREAT MAJOR MONEY MUANG STOCK VITAL DEADLY HEADLY IMPOST LETTER LISBON MORTAL PRIMAL UNCIAL WEALTH CENTRAL CHATTEL DRESDEN LEADING RADICAL SERIOUS WEIGHTY CABECERA CATALLUM CHAPITER DOSSERET SWINGING (— OF HEAVEN) AMARAVATI (— OF HELL) PANDEMONIUM (GAMBLER'S —) STAKE (INADEQUATE —) SHOESTRING
CAPITATUM MAGNUM
CAPITELLUM KNOP
CAPITOL STATEHOUSE
CAPITOLINE SATURNIAN
CAPITULATION MUNICH TREATY
CAPITULUM HEAD KNOP ANTHODIUM
CAPOTE HOOD CAPPO CLOAK BONNET MANTLE TOPPER
CAPPER CORKER SEALER STEERER
CAPPY TALLOWY
CAPRICE FAD TOY KINK MOOD WHIM ANTIC BRAID CRANK FANCY FREAK HUMOR QUIRK CHANGE MAGGOT NOTION SPLEEN TEMPER VAGARY WHIMSY BOUTADE CONCEIT CROCHET IMPULSE TANTRUM WHIMSEY
CAPRICIOUS DIZZY DODDY FLUKY MOODY CHANCY FICKLE FITFUL KITTLE PLATTY WANTON COMICAL ERRATIC FLIGHTY MAGGOTY MOONISH PEEVISH VAGRANT WAYWARD EPISODAL FANCIFUL FREAKISH HUMOROUS SKITTISH UNSTEADY VARIABLE VOLATILE CROTCHETY FANTASTIC VAGARIOUS
CAPRICIOUSNESS FREAK
CAPRICORN GOAT
CAPRIPEDE SATYR
CAPRYL RUTYL DECANOYL
CAPSHEAF CAP HOOD
CAPSICUM AJI PEPPER (— SAUCE) TABASCO
CAPSID MIRID
CAPSIZE COUP KEEL PURL UPSET WRONG OVERTURN
CAPSTAN CRAB DRUM DANDY HOIST LEVER NIGGER CYLINDER WINDLASS
CAPSTONE LECH TOPSTONE
CAPSULE CAP POD URN BOLL CASE CYST PILL SEED PEARL PERLE SHELL THECA WAFER AMPULE BARROW CACHET OOCYST SHEATH AMPOULE EYEBALL OTOCYST SEEDBOX SILIQUE VANILLA PERICARP PYXIDIUM
CAPTAIN BO BOH BAAS HEAD JOAB RAIS REIS BARAK CHIEF LEADER MASTER NAAMAN SOTNIK CAPITAN FOREMAN HEADMAN MANAGER PATROON SKIPPER FLUELLEN GOVERNOR (— OF CAVALRY) RITMASTER (— OF CRICKET TEAM) SKIPPER (— OF CURLING TEAM) SKIP

(— OF PRIVATEER) CAPER
(— OF SHIP) WAFTER
(STRICT —) SUNDOWNER
CAPTION TITLE LEADER LEGEND
CUTLINE HEADING SUBHEAD
CITATION HEADLINE SUBTITLE
CAPTIOUS CRAFY TESTY CRAFTY
SEVERE CARPING CYNICAL FRETFUL
PEEVISH TETTISH ALLURING
CATCHING CAVILING CONTRARY
CRITICAL
CAPTIOUSLY TUTLY
CAPTIVATE WIN TAKE CATCH
CHARM ALLURE ENAMOR PLEASE
RAVISH SUBDUE ATTRACT BEWITCH
CAPTIVE CAPTURE ENCHANT
ENTHRALL OVERTAKE SURPRISE
CAPTIVATED EPRIS EPRISE CAPTIVE
CAPTIVATING TAKING KILLING
WINNING WINSOME CATCHING
CAPTIVE SLAVE DANIEL ENAMOR
THRALL BRISEIS CAITIFF PRISONER
CAPTIVITY BOND IRON CHAINS
DURESS BONDAGE SERFDOM
SLAVERY
CAPTOR TAKER VICTOR CATCHER
CAPTURE BAG COP FIX GET NAB
NET WIN FALL FANG GRAB HOOK
LAND PREY SNIB TAKE TRAP TREE
CARRY CATCH FORCE PRIZE PURSE
RAVEN SEIZE SWOOP ARREST
COLLAR CORRAL ENTRAP GOBBLE
OBTAIN PIRACY REDUCE TAKING
CAPTIVE LOWBELL SEIZURE
WINNING EXCHANGE SURPRISE
UNDERNIM
(— BACKGAMMON PIECE) HIT
(— BIRDS) TOODLE
(— GAME) SATCHEL
(— OF ALL PRIZES) SWEEP
(— TROUT) TICKLE
CAPUCHIN MONKEY CAY SAI
CEPID SAJOU WEEPER SAPAJOU
CAPULIN CEREZA
CAPYBARA CAVY CARPINCHO
CAR BOX BUS PIG AUTO BOGY BUNK
DOLL DRAG DUMP GRIP JEEP RATH
TRAM ZULU BOGEY COACH DINER
DUMMY GURRY HUTCH JIMMY
RATHA SEDAN STOCK TRAIN TRUCK
WRONG BASKET BOXCAR BUFFET
CHIPPY DINGEY DINGHY DUPLEX
HOPPER JIGGER JINGLE SALOON
SETOFF SMOKER TOURER
AWKWARD CARROCH CHARIOT
COMBINE FLATCAR FREEZER
GIRAFFE GONDOLA HANDCAR
SIDECAR TELPHER TRAILER
TROLLEY VEHICLE HORSECAR
OUTSIDER QUADRIGA ROADSTER
SINISTER
(— FOR TRAIN CREW) CABOOSE
(— ON RAIL) TROLLEY
(BAGGAGE —) BLIND
(COAL —) HUTCH JIMMY WAGON
WAGGON
(ELECTRIC —) TELFER TELPHER
(ELEVATOR —) CAB CAGE
(EMPTY —) EMPTY IDLER

(JAUNTING —) SIDECAR
(LOG —) BUNK
(LOW-WHEELED —) HUTCH TRUCKLE
(MINE —) SKIP LARRY BARNEY
GIRAFFE GUNBOAT
(MONORAIL —) GYROCAR
(OBSERVATION —) BUGGY
(POLICE —) CRUISER
(TROLLEY —) SHORT
(USED —) DOG
CARABAO BUFF BUFFALO
CARACAL GORKUN SYAGUSH
CARACARA HAWK CARANCHA
CHIMANGO
CARACOLE FRISK CAREER
CARADOC BALA CRADOCK
CARAFE CROFT BOTTLE
CARAGUATA CHAGUAR
CARAJURA CHICA
CARAMBOLA BLIMBING BALIMBING
CARAMEL BLACKJACK
CARAPA CRAB CRAPPO CRABWOOD
CARAPACE CRUST SHELL LORICA
SHIELD CALAPASH
CARAVAN VAN TREK TRIP FLEET
TRAIN CAFILA COFFLE CONVOY
SAFARI TRAVEL JOURNEY VEHICLE
CONDUCTA
CARAVANSARY INN CHAN KHAN
HOTEL SERAI ZAYAT HOSTEL
IMARET CHOULTRY HOSTELRY
SERAGLIO
CARAWAY CARVY UMBEL
CARBINE STEN DRAGON MUSKET
DRAGOON ESCOPET
CARBOHYDRATE SUGAR AMYLAN
GELOSE STARCH FUCOSAN GLUCIDE
CELLULIN DEXTRINE DEXTROSE
GLYCOGEN GRAMININ PENTOSAN
TRITICIN CELLULOSE
CARBON COAL COKE COPY SOOT
NORIT CRAYON DIAMOND REPLICA
CHARCOAL GRAPHITE SCHUNGITE
CARBONADO BORT BOART BOORT
CARBON
CARBONATE BURN CHAR FIZZ
AERATE ALKALI ENLIVEN ENERGIZER
CARBONATOR GASMAN
CARBONIZER PICKLER
CARBORUNDUM EMERY ABRASIVE
CARBUNCLE RUBY PYROPE
ANTHRAX CHARBOCLE
CARBURETOR CARB DIFFUSER
VAPORIZER
CARCASS BEEF BODY BOUK CASE
CULL BLOCK MUMMY CORPSE
CARRION
(— OF WHALE) CRANG KRANG
KRENG
CARD ACE MAP PAM WAG CLUB
COMB DRAW FACE FIVE FOUR JACK
KING MENU PLAN STOP BALOP
BLANK CARTE CHART CHECK DEUCE
DUMMY EIGHT ENTRY EQUAL FICHE
FLATS GREEN HEART JOKER LOSER
PIECE QUEEN SPADE STAMP STIFF
TAROT TEASE BENDER CARTEL
CONVEX FILLER KICKER KNIGHT
PIGEON READER SECOND TICKET

TOWSER BRAGGER BRISQUE
DIAMOND PROGRAM RELEASE
STARTER STOPPER TAROCCO
TRIUMPH BOOKMARK COMOQUER
DECKHEAD DRAWCARD SCHEDULE
SCRIBBLE SQUEEZER STRIPPER
TIMECARD
(— LAST IN BOX) HOCK HOCKELTY
(— WOOL) TUM ROVE
(3 —S IN SEQUENCE) TIERCE
FOURCHETTE
(3 ACE —S) CORONA
(3 FACE —S) GLEEK
(3 —S OF KIND) TRIO TRICON
PAIRIAL TRIPLET
(4 OF TRUMPS —) TIDDY
(5 FACE —S) BLAZE
(7, 8 AND 9 —S) VOIDS
(ACE OF CLUBS —) BASTA BASTO
MATADOR PUPPYFOOT
(ACE OF SPADES —) MATADOR
SPADILLE
(ACE OF TRUMPS —) TIB
(AVIATOR'S —) CARNET
(CLUB —) OAK
(COMPASS —) FLY ROSE
(DEAD —) SLEEPER
(DIAMOND —) PICK CARREAU
(DISCARDED —S) CRIB
(DRAWING —) BLOWOFF
(FARO —) SODA
(FOUR —) CATER QUATRE
(FOURTH —) CASE
(HIGHEST UNPAID —) COMMAND
(JOKER —) BRAGGER MISTIGRIS
(KING, QUEEN OR KNAVE —) COST
FACE
(KNAVE —) PAM TOM JACK BOWER
EQUES MAKER NODDY COQUIN
KNIGHT PICARO VARLET WENZEL
CUSTREL PEASANT VILLAIN
VARLETTO
(LAYOUT OF —S) TABLEAU
(LOW —) GUARD
(MARKED —) STAMP
(POSTAL —) COVER
(PULLING —S) TIRE
(QUEEN AND KNAVE —S) INTRIGO
INTRIGUE
(RUN OF —S) SEQUENCE
(SPADE —) PICK DIGGER
(STOCK —) TALON
(THIRD HIGHEST TRUMP —) BASTA
(THREE —) TREY THREE
(WILD —) FREAK
CARDAMOM KNOBWOOD
CARDBOARD CARD PALL BLANK
BOGUS CARTON BRISTOL
TAGBOARD
(TWO —S) SPHEROGRAPH
CARDER TOZER TEASER TUMMER
CARDIALGIA HEARTBURN
CARDIGAN CORGI FABRIC JACKET
WAMPUS SWEATER
CARDINAL MAIN BASIC CHIEF CLOAK
VITAL ALEPHA CLERIC DATARY
PRINCE RADICAL ALEFNULL
ALEFZERO CAMPEIUS
CARDINALATE PURPLE

CARDINAL BIRD CARNAL REDBIRD REDLEGS GROSBEAK REDSHANK
CARDINAL FISH FUCINITA ALFONCINO
CARDSHARP TRAMPOSO
CARDSHARPER GREEK SHARPER SPIELER
CARE DO DOW HOW CARK CURE DUTY FASH FRET HEED KEEP KEPE MIND PASS RECK SOIN TEND TENT WISH YEME COUNT GRIEF GUARD NURSE PAINS SORGE TRUST WORRY BURDEN CARIEN CHARGE CUMBER DESIRE GRIEVE LAMENT REGARD SORROW ANXIETY AUSPICE CAUTION CHERISH CONCERN CULTURE CUSTODY KEEPING RESPECT RUNNING SCRUPLE THOUGHT TUITION BUSINESS PERIERGY TENDMENT
(— FOR ONESELF) BACH
(— FOR) KNOW MIND RECK TEND WARD FORCE NURSE SAVOR FATHER MATTER REGARD CHERISH PROCURE
(— OF HOUSEHOLD) HUSBANDRY
(— OF LIVESTOCK) CHORE
(JUDICIOUS —) LEISURE
(WATCHFUL —) TENDANCE
CAREEN GIP CANT HEEL KEEL LIST TILT VEER LURCH SLOPE SWIFT INCLINE
CAREER RUN WAY LIFE ROAD TRADE CHARGE COURSE GALLOP CALLING PURSUIT
(MILITARY —) ARMS SERVICE
CAREFREE EASY FRANK HAPPY DEGAGE HOLIDAY DEBONAIR
CAREFUL BUSY WARY CANNY CHARY CLOSE EXACT HOOLY TENTY CHOICE DAINTY EIDENT EYEFUL FRUGAL NARROW TENDER ANXIOUS CURIOUS ENVIOUS GUARDED HEEDFUL PAINFUL PRUDENT THRIFTY ACCURATE CAUTIOUS CRITICAL DILIGENT DISCREET DREADFUL GINGERLY MOURNFUL PUNCTUAL TROUBLED VIGILANT WATCHFUL
CAREFULLY HOOLY NARROW CANNILY CHARILY TENTILY CHOICELY GINGERLY
CARELESS LAX COOL EASY LASH RASH SLACK CASUAL OVERLY RAKISH REMISS SECURE SLOPPY SUPINE UNTIDY UNWARY LANGUID SLIGHTY UNCANNY HEEDLESS LISTLESS MINDLESS RECKLESS SLATTERN SLIPSHOD SLOVENLY YEMELESS
CARELESSLY SLACK OVERLY SLACKLY SLIGHTLY
CARELESSNESS LACHES LAXITY INCAUTION
CARESS COY HUG PAT PET BILL CLAP DAUT DAWT KISS MUCH NECK INGLE NURSE CODDLE COSSET FONDLE PAMPER STROKE CHERISH EMBRACE FLATTER CANOODLE

CARETAKER KEEPER WARDER JANITOR
CARGO BULK LAST LOAD BURDEN LADING FREIGHT PACKAGE PORTAGE CARGASON PROPERTY SHIPLOAD SHIPMENT TRAFFICS
CARIAMA CHUNGA SERIEMA
CARIB GALIBI CALINAGO
CARIBBEAN (— GULF) DARIEN HONDURAS
(— ISLAND GROUP) LEEWARD ANTILLES WINDWARD
(— ISLAND) CUBA HAITI NASSAU TOBAGO CURACAO GRENADA JAMAICA DOMINICA
CARIBE PIRAI PIRANHA CHARACINE
CARIBOU STAG RANGIFER REINDEER
CARICATURE APE COPY MOCK SKIT FARCE LIBEL MIMIC SQUIB OVERDO PARODY SATIRE CARTOON TRAVESTY BURLESQUE
CARILLONNEUR CAMPANIST BELLMASTER
CARINA KEEL
CARMELITE EXTERN TERESIAN
CARMINATIVE GINGER CALAMUS CAMPHOR VALERIAN
CARMINE RED LAKE CRIMSON SCARLET
CARNAGE WAL MURDER POGROM STRAGE BUTCHERY MASSACRE BLOODSHED
CARNAL CROW LEWD GROSS ANIMAL BODILY SEXUAL BESTIAL BRUTISH EARTHLY FLESHLY SECULAR SENSUAL WORLDLY MATERILA PANDEMIC TEMPORAL
CARNATION JACK PINK FLAKE BIZARRE PICOTEE DAYBREAK DIANTHUS GRENADINE MALMAISON
CARNELIAN SARD COPPER
(BEAD OF —) ARANGO
CARNIVAL FETE SHOW CARNY CANVAS APOKREA CANVASS REVELRY FESTIVAL
CARNIVORE CAT DOG FOX BEAR COON LION LYNX MINK PUMA SEAL WOLF CIVET GENET HYENA OTTER PANDA PEKAN RATEL SABLE STOAT TIGER BADGER COUGAR ERMINE FELINE FERRET FISHER FOUSSA JACKAL JAGUAR MARTEN OCELOT POSSUM SERVAL WEASEL DASYURE GLUTTON LEOPARD MEERKAT POLECAT RACCOON TIGRESS MONGOOSE OPPOSSUM PREDACEAN ZOOPHAGAN
CAROB HUSK LOCUST ALGAROBA
CAROL LAY NOEL SING SONG DITTY YODEL WARBLE WASSAIL MADRIGAL AGUINALDO
CAROLINA ALLSPICE SHRUB
CAROLINE ISLANDS (— ISLAND GROUP) PALAU
(ISLAND OF —) YAP HALL PALU TRUK PELEW PULAP OROLUK PONAPE WOLEAI PELELIU
(TOWN OF —) LOT NIF RUNU KOROR MUTOK TOMIL PONAPE

MALAKAL GARUSUUN
CAROLINGIAN KARLING
CAROM SHOT BOUNCE CANNON GLANCE STRIKE REBOUND BILLIARD CARAMBOLE
CAROUSAL GELL LARK ORGY RIOT ROMP TOOT BINGE FEAST RANDY REVEL ROUSE SPRAY SPREE FROLIC SHINDY SPLORE BANQUET CAROUSE REVELRY WASSAIL DRINKING FESTIVAL JAMBOREE
CAROUSE JET BOUT HELL RANT TOOT BIRLE BOUSE DRINK QUAFF RANDY REVEL ROUSE SPREE TOAST COURANT JOLLIFY WASSAIL CAROUSAL
CAROUSER BACCHANAL
CAROUSING REVEL RAFFING
CARP KOI NAG BITE DRUM SING SNAG TALK YERK CAVIL PINCH PRATE SCOLD SPEAK CENSOR NIBBLE RECITE CENSURE CHATTER QUIBBLE COMPLAIN CYPRINID GOLDFISH
(CRUCIAN —) GIBEL
(LAKE —) DRUM LAKER
CARPAL ACTINOST
CARPEL CARPID COCCUS MERICARP CARPOPHYL
(PL.) CORE
CARPENTER ANT LOHAR FITTER FRAMER HOUSER JOINER PINNER WRIGHT BUILDER HOWSOUR WOODMAN INDENTER TECTONIC TIMBERER PITWRIGHT
(SHIP'S —) CHIPS
CARPENTRY WOODWORK WRIGHTRY
CARPER CRITIC
CARPET MAT RUG AGRA KALI KUBA HERAT KILIM SARUK SCOLD SUMAK TAPET TAPIS TEKKE USHAK AFGHAN FLOSSA FRIEZE KASHAN KIDDER KIRMAN LAVEHR NAMMAD RUNNER SAROUK SAXONY SELJUK SMYRNA TABRIZ VELVET WILTON DHURRIE GIORDES HAMADAN INGRAIN ISFAHAN ISPAHAN SHEMAKA TEHERAN AKHISSAR AMRITSAR BRUSSELS COVERING FOOTPACE KARABAGH MOQUETTE TAPESTRY TURCOMAN VENETIAN AXMINSTER
(HOLY —) KISWA
(PILELESS —) KILIM GELEEM
CARPETING FILLING
CARPET SHARK WOBBEGONG
CARPET SHELL EEROCK PULLET
CARPETWEED FICOID FICOIDAL
CARPING CRAB CAPTIOUS CAVILING CRITICAL
CARPSUCKER QUILLBACK
CARPUS WRIST CARPODITE
CARRAGEEN KILLEEN
CARREL STALL CUBICLE
CARRIAGE AIR CAB CAR FLY GIG RIG RUT SET VIS ARBA BIGA CART CHAR DUKE EKKA GAIT GARB HACK LOAD MIEN PORT RUTH SHAY TEAM TRAP WYNN ARABA BANDY BRAKE BREAK BRETT BUGGY CHAIR COACH

COUPE ESSED FRONT JUTKA MIDGE
PANEL POISE SADOO SETUP SULKY
TENUE TONGA TRUCK WAGON
BURDEN CALASH CHAISE CHARET
CISIUM CONVOY DENNET FIACRE
GHARRY GOCART HANSOM KOSONG
LANDAU MANNER MOTION PORTER
REMISE SADDLE SPIDER SURREY
TANDEM TELEGA TROIKA BAGGAGE
BEARING BERLINE BOUNDER
BRITSKA CALECHE CALESIN
CARAVAN CARIOLE CAROCHE
CHARIOT COACHEE CONDUCT
CROYDON DOGGART DOSADOS
DROSHKY FORECAR GESTURE
HACKMAN HACKNEY MINIBUS
PHAETON POSCHAY SHANDRY
SKYHOOK TALLYHO TARTANA
TILBURY TRANSIT TROLLEY
UNICORN VECTURE VEHICLE
VETTURA VOITURE VOLANTE
WAFTAGE BAROUCHE BEHAVIOR
BROUGHAM CARRYALL CLARENCE
CURRICLE DEARBORN DEMEANOR
DORMEUSE EQUIPAGE PORTANCE
PRESENCE ROCKAWAY SOCIABLE
STANHOPE TARANTAS TOURNURE
VICTORIA
(— OF HANDPRESS) COFFIN
(— OF HORSE) AIR
(AMMUNITION —) CAISSON
(ELEVATED —) LIFT
(INDIAN —) RUT EKKA BANDY
GHARRI GHARRY
(JAVANESE —) SADO SADOO
(LIVERY —) REMISE
(LOG —) DRAG
(PUBLIC —) FLY OMNIBUS
CARRIAGE HOUSE REMISE
CARRIER HOD BASE JEEP SHIP
TRAM BUGGY HAMAL KAHAR MACER
PLANE SABOT TAMEN TIGER BARKIS
BEARER CADGER COOLIE HAMMAL
HODMAN JAGGER PACKER PORTER
RUNNER TAILER WEASEL DRAYMAN
DROGHER FLATTOP POSTMAN
REMOVER TACULLI TROTTER
VEHICLE CARGADOR CARRYALL
PORTATOR RAILROAD TEAMSTER
SUBSTRATE
(COAL —) FLATIRON
(COLOR —) LUFIRIER
(ENDLESS —) TAILER
(FIRE —) PORTFIRE
(MAIL —) COURIER POSTMAN
(WATER —) BHISTI BHEESTY
CARRION KET VILE OFFAL CORPSE
HOODIE REFUSE ROTTEN CARCASS
CORRUPT DOGMEAT CROWBAIT
CARRION BIRD SCAVENGER
CARRION CROW DOWP HOODY
URUBU CORBIE HOODIE GERCROW
CARROT UMBEL CONIUM DAUCUS
CACHRYS SECRETE BUPLEVER
HILLTROT
(DEADLY —) DRIAS
(PERUVIAN —) ARRACACH
(PREPARED WITH —S) CRECY
CARROTING SECRETAGE

CARROUSEL RIDE WHIRLGIG
QUADRILLE
CARRY CAR HUG JAG LUG BEAR
BUCK CART DRAY FARE GEST HAVE
HOLD HUMP LEAD PACK PORT
SHOW TAKE TOTE TUMP BRING
BROOK CADGE CROSS FERRY
GESTE GUIDE POISE WALTZ WEIGH
BEHAVE CONVEY CONVOY DELATE
DEPORT DERIVE EXTEND COMPORT
CONDUCT CONTAIN ENTRAIN
PORTAGE PRODUCE SUPPORT
SUSTAIN UNDERGO BAJULATE
CONTINUE TRANSFER TRANSMIT
(— AWAY) FIRK DRAIN REAVE
SWEEP TRUSS ABLATE ASPORT
(— EFFIGY) GUY
(— FORWARD) EXTEND
(— IN OXCART) KURVEY
(— LIQUOR) BOOTLEG
(— OFF) HENT LIFE SACK FETCH
HEAVE RIFLE SCOUR SWOOP
ABDUCT ASPORT BRAZEN KIDNAP
SPIRIT
(— ON) DO RUN WAR HAVE LEAD
LEVY WAGE APPLY DRIVE ENSUE
FIGHT TRAIN CREATE DEMEAN
FOLLOW MANAGE OCCUPY
CONDUCT EXERCISE MAINTAIN
TRANSACT
(— ONESELF) HOLD
(— ONWARD) CONTINUE
(— OUT) DO ACT END GIVE LAST
HONOR AFFORD EFFECT ACHIEVE
EXECUTE FULFILL PERFORM
SATISFY
(— UPWARD) RAP ESCALATE
CARRYALL BUS CASE WAGON
CARRIAGE
CARRYING BURDEN GERENT
FRAUGHT
(— ON) GESTION
(— WEIGHT) EFFECTIVE
CART CAR POT RUT BUTT CHAR
COOP COUP DRAY HAUL JANG LEAD
LOAD PLOW PUTT RUTH TOTE WAIN
ARABA BANDY BOGEY BOGIE CADDY
CARRY DANDY DILLY DOLLY SULKY
TONGA TRUCK WAGON BARROW
CADDIE CHAISE CHARET CISIUM
CONVEY DOLLIE DUMPER GHARRI
GHARRY JIGGER JINKER KURUMA
LIMBER PLOUGH SPIDER CARRETA
CHARIOT DOGCART GUJERAT
HACKERY MORFREY SHALLOW
TROLLEY TRUNDLE TUMBLER
TUMBRIL TUMBRIL VEHICLE
DUMPCART HANDCART PUSHCART
(— WITH TANK) TUMBLER
(2-PONY —) KOSONG
(2-WHEELED —) BANDY BUGGY
SULKY CARRETA TUMBREL
(3-WHEELED —) PORTER
(BULLOCK —) BANDY HACKERY
(COSTER'S —) TROLL
(COVERED —) JINGLE CARIOLE
(FARMER'S —) PUTT GAMBO
MORPHREY
(FREIGHT —) CARRETON

(LOG —) BUNK
(LUMBER —) GILL BUMMER
(MILKMAN'S —) PRAM
(OX —) RECKLA
(PARCELS —) FLY
(TIMBER —) CUTS
(TIP —) COOP COUP COUPE
(UNDERSLUNG —) FLOAT
CARTE MAP CARD LIST MENU CHART
CHARTER DIAGRAM
CARTE BLANCHE BLANK
CARTEL CARD DEFY PACT POOL
SHIP PAPER TRUST CORNER LETTER
TREATY CONTRACT SYNDICATE
CARTER CARMAN JAGGER LEADER
DRAYMAN LADEMAN TRUCKER
HORSEMAN TEAMSTER
CARTILAGE COPULA TISSUE
CRICOID EPIURAL GRISTLE RADIALE
STERNUM TARSALE THYROID
EPIPUBIS HYPOHYAL SESAMOID
TURBINAL
CARTILAGINOUS CHONDRIC
CARTOGRAPH MAP PLAT CHART
CARTOGRAPHER CHARTIST
CARTON BOX CASE SHELL
CARTOON EPURE ANIMATION
CARTOUCHE MESA OVAL DURANGO
CARTRIDGE
CARTRIDGE BAG CASE HULL BLANK
SHELL SHORT BULLET MAGNUM
PATRON CAPSULE TORPEDO
HANDLOAD SHOTSHELL
CARTULARY COUCHER
CARTWHEEL CLOGWHEEL
CARUCATE CARVE PLOWLAND
CARUNCLE COMB STROPHIOLE
CARVE CUT ALAY SIDE BEHEW
BREAK GRAVE KIRVE MINCE SHEAR
SPLAY SPOIL THIGH INCISE QUINSE
SCULPT THWITE TRENCH UNLACE
ENCHASE ENGRAIL ENGRAVE
DISJOINT MALAHACK SCULLION
(— A BIRD) WING
(— CHICKEN) FRUSH
(— GOOSE) REAR
(— HEN) SPOIL
(— PEACOCK) DISFIGURE
(— PLOVER) MINCE
(— SWAN) LIFT
CARVED CARVEN GLYPHIC INCISED
CARVER BODGER KIRVER CROPPER
FROSTER IVORIST CICELEUR
TRENCHER
CARVING CAMEO GLYPH IVORY
ENTAIL SCRIVE GLYPTIC MASKOID
NICKING INTAGLIO TRIPTYCH
CARYA HICORIA
CARYATID TELAMON CANEPHORA
(PART OF —) GAINE
CARYOCAR SOUARI
CARYOPHYLLUS JAMBOSA
CARYOPSIS SEED
CASCABEL POMMEL POMMELION
CASCADE LIN FALL LINN FORCE
SPOUT CATARACT
CASCARA BUCKTHORN WAHOO
SHITTIM

CASCARILLA CROTON GOATWEED
SWEETWOOD
CASE BAG BOX CUP HAP LEG POD
POT PYX BIND BOOT BUNK BURR
CASK COPE DEED DESK DOCK
DOME FILE PACK PAIR ROLL SUIT
TICK BRACE BRIEF BULLA BURSE
CADDY CASUS CAUSE CHAPE
COVER CRATE EVENT FOLIO FOREL
HUSSY HUTCH PRESS PYXIS SHELL
STATE THECA THING TRIAL ACTION
AFFAIR APPEAL BARREL BINDER
BOXING CARTON CASING CELLAR
CHANCE COFFIN COUPLE LOCKET
LORICA MATTER PATRON PENNER
PETARD POPPET QUIVER RIDDLE
SHEATH SHRINE STATOR SURVEY
TASHIE TWEEZE VALISE VANITY
CABINET CAMISIA CAPCASE
CAPSULE COUNTER CUSHION
DIECASE ENCLOSE ENVELOP
EXAMPLE GEARBOX HOLDALL
HOLSTER HOUSING HUMIDOR
INCLOSE LAWSUIT LUNETTE
PACKAGE REMANET SATCHEL
SHIPPER WARDIAN ACCIDENT
ARGUMENT BOOKCASE CARRYALL
CUPBOARD ENVELOPE EQUIPAGE
EXEMPLAR GARDEVIN INSTANCE
KNAPSACK PACKSACK PORTFIRE
SHOWCASE SITUATED SOLANDER
TANTALUS
(WICKER —) HASK BARROW
HANAPER
(— CONTAINING ELEVATOR BELT)
LEG
(— ENCLOSING CLOCK DIAL) HOOD
(— FOR CARDS) SHOE
(— FOR COMPASS) BINNACLE
(— FOR EXPLOSIVES) TRUNK
(— FOR JEWELS) TYE
(— FOR MOLD) COPE CHAPE
(— FOR MUMMY) SLEDGE
(— FOR PISTOL) HOLSTER
(— FOR PULLEY) BLOCK
(— FOR RIFLE) BOOT
(— FOR SEWING ITEMS) HUSSY
(— FOR TOOLS) TROUSSE
(— FOR TWEEZERS) BUBBLEBOW
(— FOR WRITING MATERIALS)
STANDISH
(— IN WATCH) DOME BARREL
(— OF FLOUR BOLTER) HUTCH
(— OF VENETIAN BLIND) HEADBOX
(— OF) A
(— WITH COMPARTMENTS) RIDDLE
(BONY —) CARAPACE
(COSMETIC —) COMPACT
(COURT —) LAWSUIT
(EGG —) OVISAC OOTHECA
(FIREWORKS —) LANCE
(GRAMMATICAL —) DATIVE ESSIVE
LATIVE ELATIVE FACTIVE ABLATIVE
EQUATIVE ERGATIVE GENITIVE
ILLATIVE LOCATIVE VOCATIVE
(HOPELESS —) GONER
(LUGGAGE —) IMPERIAL
(ORNAMENTAL —) ETUI
(PAPER —) COFFIN

(PILLOW —) SLIP
CASED BOUND
CASEMENT SASH LUKET WINDOW
CASHIER CASS CAST BREAK DEALER
POTDAR PURSER CHECKER DISMISS
CASHIERED BROKEN DEGOMME
CASHMERE KASHMIR PRUNELL
CASH REGISTER DAMPER REGEST
GREFFIER RECORDER REGISTER
CASING BODY BOOT BUNG CASE
CURB HULL SHOE SKIN TIRE APRON
BELLY DERMA EPHOD GAINE LINER
ROUND STOCK TRUNK BOXING
COFFIN COLLET JACKET KISHKE
LINING SCROLL SHEATH VOLUTE
FEEDBOX HOUSING MANHEAD
OUTCASE STAVING THIMBLE
CACHEPOT COVERING PLOWSHOE
SHIRTING WHEELBOX
(— FOR BRAIN) HARNPAN
CASK KEG TUB TUN VAT BOSS BUTT
CADE COWL DRUM KNAG PIPE RAPE
RIER SLIP TREE WOOD ANKER
BOWIE BULGE FOIST STAND UNION
BARECA BARREL CARDEL CASQUE
DOLIUM FIRKIN FOODER LONGER
OCTAVE TIERCE WINGER BARRICO
BREAKER FOSTELL RUNDLET
SACKBUT CASSETTE HOGSHEAD
PUNCHEON QUARDEEL ROUNDLET
(BREWING —) UNION
(LOCKED —) TANTALUS
(PERFORATED —) POT
(SMALL —) KEG TUB KNAG STOOP
STOUP
(WINE —) FAT TUN BOSS BUTT PIPE
TIERCE HOGSHEAD
(PL.) COOPERAGE
CASKET BOX PIX TYE CASE CASK
CIST TILL TOMB BUIST CHEST
ACERRA CHASSE COFFER COFFIN
SHRINE FOSTELL CASSETTE
CASQUE CASK HORN GALEA HELMET
CASSABANANA CURUBA
CASSANDRA (FATHER OF —) PRIAM
(HUSBAND OF —) AGAMEMNON
(MOTHER OF —) HECUBA
CASSAREEP CAXIRI
CASSAVA AIPI AIPIM YUCCA CASIRI
CAZIBI MANIOC TAPIOCA
CASSEROLE TUREEN COCOTTE
MARMITE TERRINE TZIMMES
CASSIA KEZIA SENNA SICKLEPOD
CASSIA FISTULA AMALTAS
CASSIMERE ZEPHYR
CASSITERITE TINSTONE
CASSITES KUSHSHU
CASSOCK GOWN SLOP VEST GIPPO
PRIEST PELISSE SOUTANE ZIMARRA
CASSOWARY EMU MURUP MOORUP
RATITE
CAST MEW PUT SET BILL DART HURL
MOLD MOLT PICK SHED SLAT SLIP
SPEW SWAK TINT TOSS TREE TURN
WHAP WHOP WURP BLOCK BRAID
CHUCK DEUCE DRIVE EJECT ERECT
FLING FLIRT FOUND FUSIL HEAVE
IMAGE KEIST PITCH SHADE SHOOT
SLING STAMP THROW TINGE

COLLAR INJECT NOSING STRIKE
STRIND THRILL AGARWAL CASHIER
DEPOSIT DISCARD VIBRATE
CASTLING CONSPECT OUTSLING
POLYTYPE TINCTURE
(— A SPELL) TAKE HOODOO
BESPELL BEWITCH FORSPEAK
(— ASIDE) DICE FLING
(— ASPERSIONS) SLUR SKLENT
APPEACH
(— AWAY) DUMP SHOVE DEJECT
REJECT
(— DICE) WHIRL
(— DISCREDIT) GLANCE
(— DOWN) DASH DUMP HURL SINK
ABASE AMATE AMORT AWARP
STREW ABJECT DECAST DEJECT
DEMISS THRING ECLIPSE RUINATE
DEJECTED
(— FORTH) SPEW SPUE WARP
BELCH BRAID LAUNCH
(— GLOOM) DUSK CLOUD DARKEN
DEPRESS
(— IN A MOLD) STRIKE
(— LOTS) CAVEL
(— METAL) YET
(— OF DICE) COUP DEUCE
(— OF HERRINGS) WARP
(— OF LANGUAGE) IDIOM
(— OF NET) SHOT SHOOT
(— OFF) DAFF JILT MOLT SHED
DITCH LOSSE SHAKE SLUFF WAIVE
CASTEN DEVEST REFUSE REJECT
SLOUGH ABDICATE RENOUNCE
(— ON GROUND) TERRE
(— OUT) EGEST EJECT EXPEL
BANISH ABANDON EXTRUDE
OSTRACIZE
(— SHADOW) ADUMBRATE
(— UP) SUM LEVY UPBRAID
(FRESHLY —) GREEN
(PLASTER —) CUIRASS
CASTANET KNACKER KNOCKER
SNAPPER TCHAPAN CROTALUM
CASTAWAY WAIF TRAMP CRUSOE
REJECT OUTCAST DERELICT
STRANDED
CASTE (OR CASTE MEMBER) DOM
MEO AHIR BHAR BHAT GOLA JATI
KOLI KORI MALI MINA PASI TELI
BAGDI BANIA DHOBY GOALA IRAVA
KAHAR KUMNI KUNBI KURMI LADHA
LOHAR MAHAR PALLI PUGGI SAMAR
SANSI SINGH SONAR SUDRA TANTI
VARNA ARORAS BAIDYA BALIJA
BANIAN BHANGI CHAMAR CHETTY
CHUHRA DHANUK DHOBIE DOSADH
DURZEE HOLEVA HOLIYA ILAVAN
JAJMAN KALWAR KAMBOH KHATRI
KUMHAR KURUBA LOHANA MADIGA
NATION PALLAR PRABHU PULAYA
PULIAN PURVOE RAJPUT VAISYA
AGARWAL BRAHMAN BRAHMIN
DHANGAR GADARIA HARIJAN
KAYASTH KOMATRI KURUMBA
NISHADA VELLALA KAMMALAN
KHANDAIT PARAIYAN POVINDAH
RAJBANSI VAKKALIGA
(LOWER —S) PANCHAMA

CASTER VIAL CRUET CRUSE PHIAL
CASTOR HORRAL HURLER MASTER
ROLLER FOUNDER PITCHER
TRUCKLE TRUNDLE
(SURF —) SQUIDDER
CASTIGATE LASH EMEND SCARE
SCORE BERATE PUNISH REVISE
STRAFE SUBDUE CANVASS
CENSURE CHASTEN CORRECT
LEATHER REPROVE CHASTISE
LAMBASTE FUSTIGATE
CASTIGATION HELL LASHING
DRESSING
CASTING DIE PIG CAST FONT KEEP
MOLD TYMP BLOCK CHOCK CHUCK
FOUND MOULD BILLET BUMPER
MATRIX MISRUN SPIDER COULAGE
DARTING SEGMENT SEPARATOR
(— LOTS) SORTITION
(— OF HOROSCOPE) APOTELESM
(— OVERBOARD) JETTISON
(PL.) SPRAY FOUNDRY
CAST IRON YETLING
CASTLE BURY FORT HALL KEEP
ROCK ROOK ABODE COURT MORRO
PIECE CASBAH BASTILE BOROUGH
CHATEAU CITADEL SCHLOSS
UDOLPHO BASTILLE CASTELET
CASTILLO FASTNESS FORTRESS
STAROSTY TINTAGEL
(— IN CHESS) JUEZ ROOK TOUR
JUDGE TOWER
(SMALL —) PEEL TOWER CASTLET
CHATELET
CASTOR BEAVER LEATHER TRUCKLE
TRUNDLE BARKSTONE
(— AND POLLUX) TWINS GEMINI
DIOSCURI
CASTOR-OIL PLANT KIKI MAMONA
PALMCRIST
CASTRATE CUT FIX GIB LIB GELD
GLIB SPAY SWIG TRIM ALTER
CAPON DESEX PRUNE STEER
CHANGE EUNUCH NEUTER EVIRATE
CAPONIZE MUTILATE SATURNIZE
CASTRATED CUT GIBBED UNPAVED
CASTRATO EUNUCH EVIRATO
TENORINO
CASUAL GLIB STRAY BLITHE
BYHAND CHANCE FOLKSY RANDOM
CASALTY CURSORY LEISURE
NATURAL OFFHAND RUNNING
GLANCING INFORMAL
CASUALTY LOSS DEATH CADUAC
CHANCE HAZARD INJURY MISHAP
ACCIDENT DISASTER
CASUARINA BEEFWOOD
CASUIST JESUIT
CAT GIB RAT SOW TAB CHAT EYRA
FLOG LION LYNX MISS PARD PUMA
PUSS CHAUS CIVET FELID GATOL
KITTY MANUL MEWER MOGGY
OUNCE PUSSY SMOKE TABBY TIGER
TILER WHITE ZIBET ANGORA
COUGAR FELINE JAGUAR KITTEN
KODKOD MALKIN MARGAY MAWKIN
MIAUER MOUSER MUSION NEUTER
OCELOT PAJERO PURRER SERVAL
TIBERT TORTIE BURMESE CARACAL

CATHEAD CATLING CHEETAH
KITLING KUICHUA LEOPARD
LINSANG PANTHER PERSIAN
SIAMESE TIGRESS WILDCAT
WRAWLER BAUDRONS DASYURID
FISSIPED PUSSYCAT RINGTAIL
(— CRY) WAW
(— GROUP) CLOWDER
(FEMALE —) QUEEN WHEENCAT
(MALE —) GIB TOM TOMCAT
(ROOF-PROWLING —) TILER
CATACHRESIS ABUSION
CATACLYSM FLOOD DELUGE
DEBACLE DISASTER UPHEAVAL
CATACOMB TOMB CRYPT VAULT
CEMETERY HYPOGEUM
(PL.) ARENARIAE
CATADROMOUS SEAGOING
CATALECTIC HEMIAMB TRUNCATED
CATALEPSY TRANCE SEIZURE
CATATONY
CATALOG PIE PYE BILL BOOK LIST
ROLL ROTA BRIEF CANON FLIER
FLYER INDEX PINAX AUTHOR
RAGGER RAGMAN RECORD ROSTER
ARRANGE BEADROW DIPTYCH
BEADROLL BULLETIN CALENDAR
CLASSIFY REGISTER SCHEDULE
CATALOGUE DIDASCALY INVENTORY
CATALUFA SCAD TORO BIGEYE
CATALYST CARRIER SAUSAGE
ZIEGLER CATALYTE HOPCALITE
(NEGATIVE —) INHIBITER
CATAMARAN RAFT TROW BALSA
FLOAT GUNBOAT JANGADA
MONITOR AUNTSARY
CATAMITE INGLE GUNSEL NINGLE
PATHIC BARDASH GANYMEDE
CATAMOUNT LYNX PUMA COUGAR
CATAPLASM POULTICE
CATAPULT GUN BIBLE SLING SWEEP
THROW HURTLE LAUNCH ONAGER
TREPAN ALACRAN BRICOLE
PEDRERO TORMENT TRABUCH
WARWOLF BALLISTA CROSSBOW
DONDAINE LAUNCHER MANGONEL
MARTINET SCORPION SPRINGAL
STONEBOW
CATARACT LIN FALL LINN FALLS
FLOOD PEARL DELUGE CASCADE
NIAGARA CATADUPE OVERFALL
VICTORIA
CATARRH MUR COLD MURR POSE
RHEUM CORYZA
CATASTROPHE ACCIDENT CALAMITY
DISASTER
CATCH BAG COB COP GET GIN KEP
NAB NET DRAW FANG GLOM HASP
HAUL HAWK HENT HOLD HOOK
LAND MAKE MEET MESS NAIL PAWL
SAVE SEAR SNAG SNAP SNIB STOP
TAKE TRAP TREE VANG CLASP
CLEEK CREEL FETCH GLOVE GRASP
HITCH KETCH KNACK LASSO LATCH
PLANT SEIZE SNARE SNICK SWOOP
TRICK TROLL ARREST ATTAIN
BUTTON CLUTCH CORNER CORRAL
DETECT DETENT ENGAGE ENMESH
ENTRAP IMMESH LOCKET NOBBLE

NOODLE SNATCH SPRENT TAIGLE
TAKING TURNEL ATTRACT CAPTURE
ENSNARE GIMMICK GRAPNEL
RELEASE SPRINGE TRIGGER
CONTRACT CRANNAGE ENTANGLE
FASTNESS HOLDBACK HOLDFAST
OVERTAKE SNAPHAAN SURPRISE
(— AT PROPER TIME) NICK
(— ATTENTION) FLAG
(— BIRDS) BATFOWL BIRDLIME
(— EELS) SNIGGLE
(— FIRE) SPUNK IGNITE KINDLE
(— FISH WITH HANDS) GUDDLE
GRABBLE HANDFAST
(— FISH) JAB JIG GILL HANG
GILLNET
(— IN VOICE) FETCH
(— OF DOOR) LATCH SNECK SNICK
(— OF FISH) FARE HAUL SHOT
TACK TRIP SHACK
(— ONE'S BREATH) GASP CHINK
(— SIGHT OF) SPY ESPY SPOT
DESCRY
(RATCHET —) CLICK
(SAFETY —) CLEVIS
CATCHER TAKER BIRDER FANGER
LARKER RECEIVER
CATCHFLY SILENE FLYBANE
CATCHING CATCHY TAKING
ALLURING ARRESTING
CATCHPOLE BAILIFF PUTTOCK
CATCHWEED CLEAVERS
CATCHWORD CUE TAG MOTTO
BYWORD PHRASE SLOGAN STARTER
CATCHCRY
CATCHY CATCHING APPEALING
CATECHISM GUIDE MANUAL
CARRITCH QUESTIONS
CATECHU COTCH CUTCH KHAIR
GAMBIER
CATECHUMEN PUPIL AUDIENT
AUDITOR CONVERT BEGINNER
NEOPHYTE COMPETENT
CATEGORICAL DIRECT ABSOLUTE
EXPLICIT KNOCKDOWN
CATEGORIZE CODE HAVE
CATEGORY WAY KING RANK TALE
CLASS FIELD GENRE GENUS ORDER
STYLE FAMILY LEAGUE NUMBER
RUBRIC SERIES SPECIES DIVISION
(— OF TENSES) INFECTUM
(HIGHEST —) IDEA
(PRIMARY —) SUBSTANCE
(TAXONOMIC —) FORM FORMA
GENUS COHORT LEGION SUBCLASS
SUBGENUS SUBFAMILY
CATER CUT FEED HUMOR SERVE
TREAT PANDER PURVEY SUPPLY
PROVIDE
CATERER ACATER
CATERPILLAR CAT MUGA AWETO
ERUCA CANKER LOOPER PALMER
PORINA RISPER TAILOR WOUBIT
CUTWORM TRACTOR WEBWORM
HANGWORM HORNWORM SILKWORM
SKINWORM WORTWORM
CATERWAUL CRY WAIL MIAUL
CATFACE ARR SCAR
CATFISH MUD CUSK ELOD POUT

RAAD SHAL BAGRE DORAD RAASH
BARBER DOCMAC GLANIS GOONCH
GOUJON HASSAR MADTOM
BARBUDO CANDIRU COBBLER
FIDDLER PYGIDID SILURID WALLAGO
BULLHEAD BULLPOUT CORYDORA
FLATHEAD MATHEMEG PLOTOSID
SQUEAKER STONECAT
CATGUT THARM THAIRM CATLING
WHIPCORD
CATHARI BULGARI PATARINE
CATHARTIC ALOIN BRYONY PHYSIC
CALOMEL SCOURER EUONYMUS
EVACUANT HYDRAGOG KALADANA
LAPACTIC LAXATIVE SCAMMONY
SOLUTIVE SOLUTORY
CATHAYAN KITAN
CATHEDRA SEE
CATHEDRAL DOM SEE DUOMO
SOBOR MARTYRY MEMORIA
MINSTER BASILICA
CATHEXIS CHARGE
CATHODE K KA FILAMENT
ELECTRODE HYDROGODE
CATHOLIC BROAD GENERAL
LIBERAL TOLERANT
CATHOLICISM PAPISM POPERY
CATHOLICON PANACEA
CATKIN RAG TAG CHAT GULL AGLET
AMENT IULUS PUSSY CACHRYS
CATTAIL GOSLING
CATNIP NEP CATARIA CATMINT
CATWORT
CAT'S-CLAW LONGPOD ESCAMBRON
CAT'S CRADLE HEI
CAT'S-EAR GOSMORE CAPEWEED
FLATWEED
CAT'S EYE CHATOYANT
CAT'S-FOOT PUSSYTOE
CATTAIL DOD DODD FLAG MUSK
RUSH TULE AMENT BAYON BLECK
CLOUD RAUPO REREE WONGA
CATKIN GLADEN TOTORA BULRUSH
GLADDON MATREED BLACKCAP
CARBUNGI FLAXTAIL
CAT THYME HULWORT
CATTLE ZO BOW FEE GIR DHAN
GAUR KINE NEAT NOWT OXEN ZEBU
ZOBO DEVON STOCK ANKOLI
DURHAM GALYAK ONGOLE ROTHER
SINDHI SUSSEX BESTIAL NELLORE
REDPOLL COMPOUND OUTSIGHT
TUBICORN
(— CARRIED OFF) SPREATH
(BREED OF —) ANGUS BORAN
DEVON FJALL KERRY SANGA SANGU
ANGONI ANKOLI DEXTER DURHAM
FULANI JERSEY SUSSEX BAROTSE
BRAFORD BRAHMAN COASTER
CRIOLLA GUZERAT HARIANA
SAHIWAL ALDERNEY AYRSHIRE
CHARBRAY FRIBOURG FRIESIAN
GALLOWAY GUERNSEY HEREFORD
HOLSTEIN KANGAYAM LONGHORN
(DWARF —) NATA NIATA
(WILD YOUNG —) KANGAROO
CATTLE-BREEDER AHIR ALUR
CATTLE DEALER DROVER
CATTLEHIDE BUFF CROUPON

CATTLEMAN FAZENDEIRO
CATTLE MARKET SALEYARD
CATTLE PEN KRAAL
CATTLE RAID SPRAITH SPREAGH
CATTLE RUN STATION
CATTLE STEALER ABACTOR
ABIGEUS
CATTLE YARD CANCHA
CATTY KIN KATI
CAUCASIAN WHITE IRANIAN
EUROPEAN JAPHETIC PALEFACE
(— LANGUAGE) UDI UDIC UDIN
(PL.) MELANOI
CAUCHO ULE RUBBER
CAUDATA URODELA
CAUDEX STIPE
CAUGHT GRIPPIT ENTANGLED
CAUL HOW WEB KEEL KELL TRUG
VEIL GALEA HOUVE DORLOT
CREPINE KERCHER NETWORK
OMENTUM MEMBRANE SILLYHOW
TRESSOUR TRESSURE
CAULDRON KOHUA CALDRON
CAULICLE SCAPEL ROSTELLUM
CAULIFLOWER BROCCOLI
SNOWBALL CHOUFLEUR
CAULK CALK CORK FILL FLAG
CHINSE
CAUSAL GENETIC
CAUSE DO AIM GAR ISM KEY LET
WAY CASE CHAT FATE HOTI LEAD
MAKE MOVE ROOT SPUR SUIT
AGENT ARCHE BASIS BREED CAUSA
FRAME PARTY SKILL SLAKE WREAK
YIELD ADDICT CREATE EFFECT
ELICIT GOSSIP GROUND INDUCE
INVOKE MALADY MANNER MATTER
MOTIVE OBJECT ORIGIN PARENT
REASON RESORT SOURCE SPEECH
SPRING CHESOUN CONCERN
DISEASE LAWSUIT PROCURE
PRODUCE PROVOKE QUARREL
SUBJECT BUSINESS ENGENDER
GENERATE INSTANCE MOVEMENT
OCCASION WHEREFORE
(— A SORE) RANKLE
(— DAMAGE) DAMNIFY
(— FOR COMPLAINT) COMEBACK
(— OF RUIN) BANE
(— OF TERROR) AFFRIGHT
(— OF TROUBLE) TRACHLE
(— PAIN) URN
(— TO ARCH) ROACH
(— TO CONTRACT) PUCKER
(— TO CROUCH) COUCH
(— TO DESERT) DEFECT
(— TO END) ACHIEVE
(— TO MOVE RAPIDLY) GIG
(— TO PROJECT) JET
(— TO RESULT) ISSUE
(— TO STICK) MIRE
(— TO SWELL) BINGE EMBOSS
(— TO THICKEN) CURD
(FINAL —) END
(FORM-GIVING —) IDEA
(IMMEDIATE —) SIGNAL
(PRIMAL —) URGRUND
CAUSEWAY WAY DIKE ROAD
CHAUSSE HIGHWAY

CAUSTIC LYE ACID TART ACRID
QUICK SALTY SHARP SNELL BITING
BITTER SEVERE BURNING CAUTERY
CUTTING ERODENT MORDANT
NIPPING PUNGENT PYROTIC SATIRIC
ALKALINE DIERETIC SCATHING
SNAPPISH STINGING
CAUSTICITY ACRIMONY
CAUTERIZATION USTION INUSTION
CAUTERIZE BURN CHAR FIRE SEAR
BRAND INUST SINGE
CAUTION CARE FEAR HEED WARN
GUARD ADVICE CAUTEL CAVEAT
EXHORT ANXIETY COUNSEL
PRECEPT PROVISO WARNING
ADMONISH FORECAST FOREWARN
MONITION PRUDENCE WARINESS
CAUTIOUS SHY SAFE WARE WARY
ALERT CANNY CHARY SIKER FABIAN
HOOLIE SICKER TENDER TIPTOE
CAREFUL CURIOUS ENVIOUS
FEARFUL FERDFUL GUARDED
PRUDENT DISCREET SUSPENSE
VIGILANT
CAUTIOUSLY CANNY CANNILY
CHARILY EASYLIKE GINGERLY
TENDERLY
CAVALCADE RAID RIDE MARCH
TRAIN PARADE SAFARI COMPANY
JOURNEY PAGEANT
CAVALIER GAY CAVY CURT EASY
FINE BRAVE FRANK MOUNT RIDER
ESCORT KNIGHT BRUSQUE GALLANT
HAUGHTY OFFHAND SOLDIER
CAVALERO ROYALIST CHAMBERER
CHEVALIER COMMANDER
CAVALLA CERO JACK TORO ULUA
JUREL CARANX CARANGID
CREVALLE SCOMBRID
CAVALRY HORSE HEAVIES CHIVALRY
HORSEMEN YEOMANRY
CAVALRYMAN SOWAR SPAHI
SUWAR HUSSAR JINETE LANCER
ARGOLET COURIER DRAGOON
PLUNGER SABREUR TROOPER
GENDARME HORSEMAN STRADIOT
(PL.) FORAGERS
CAVE DEN TIP COVE HOLE LAIR MINE
REAR SINK TOSS WEEM ANTRE
CABIN CACHE CALVE CAVEA CRYPT
DELVE FOGOU SLADE SPEOS STORE
UPSET BEWARE CAVERN CAVITY
CELLAR DUGOUT GROTTO HOLLOW
LARDER LUSTER PANTRY PLUNGE
SHROUD MANSION RESERVE
SPELUNK CASTILLO COLLAPSE
OVERTURN MITHRAGUM
(— IN) COLT
CAVEAT BEWARE NOTICE CAUTION
WARNING
CAVE-DWELLER HORITE
TROGLODYTE
CAVE-DWELLING NATUFIAN
CAVEMAN NEANDERTHAL
CAVER SPELUNKER
CAVERN DEN CAVE COVE GROT
HOLE LAIR WEEM CROFT VAULT
ANTRUM CAVITY GROTTO HOLLOW
SPELUNK

CAVERNOUS ERECTILE
CAVESSON CHAIN
CAVETTO GULA GORGE
CAVIAR OVA ROE IKRA GARUM
IKARY
CAVIL CARK CARP HAFT HAGGLE
CAPTION CHICANE QUARREL
QUIBBLE PETTIFOG QUIDDITY
FORMALIZE
CAVILER CRITIC GIRDER HAFTER
ZOILUS
CAVILING CAPTIOUS CRITICAL
PICAYUNE
CAVITY BAG CUP PIT SAC ABRI AXIL
CASE CAVE CELL DALK DENT DUCT
HOLE MIND MINE VEIN VOID ABYSS
BOSOM BURSA CRYPT DRUSE
FOSSA GEODE GOUGE LUMEN
MOUTH ORBIT SCOOP SINUS
ANTRUM AREOLE ATRIUM AXILLA
BORING CAECUM CAMERA CAVERN
COELIA COELOM COTYLE CRATER
DEBLAI GROTTO HOLLOW LACUNA
POCKET SOCKET VACUUM VOMICA
ABDOMEN CHAMBER CISTERN
CYATHUS DIOCOEL KYATHOS
LOCULUS MORTISE VACUITY
VACUOLE VESICLE ALVEOLUS
BROODSAC EPICOELE FOLLICLE
WELLHOLE
(— IN BONE) LACUNA
(— IN CASTING) PIPE
(— IN HEAD OF WHALE) CASE
(— IN HILLSIDE) ABRI
(— IN MINE) BAG
(— MADE BY SEALS) IGLOO
(— OF SEA-SHELL) FLUE
(ALTAR —) TOMB
(BODY —) GUT BELLY THORAX
ABDOMEN STOMACH
(CHEST —) THORAX
(CRYSTAL-LINED —) VUGG DRUSE
GEODE
(GUN —) BORE
(NASAL —) CAVUM
CAVORT PLAY BOUND CAPER
CURVET GAMBOL PRANCE
CAVY PACA PONY AGOUTI APEREA
CAYUSE CAPYBARA
(FEMALE —) SOW
CAW KA CRY CALL CROAK QUARK
QUAWK
CAYMAN JACARE
CAYUSE CAVY PONY BRONCO
MUSTANG
CEASE HO BOW CUT DIE END LIN
BALK BLIN DROP FINE HALT HOLD
LIFT LISS QUIT REST SACE SHUT
STAY STOP STOW AVAST CLOSE
DOWSE LEAVE PAUSE PETER STINT
SWICK WAIVE DESIST DEVALL
EXPIRE FINISH FORGET ABSTAIN
OUTGIVE REFRAIN SUSPEND
INTERMIT OVERGIVE SURCEASE
(— MILKING COW) SINE
(— TEMPORARILY) LIFT
(— TO ASSERT) ABANDON
CEASELESS EVER ENDLESS
ETERNAL IMMORTAL UNENDING

CEASING CESSER CESSATION
CEBUS SAI
CECILIA SIS SISSU
CECROPS (DAUGHTER OF —) HERSE
AGLAUROS PANDROSOS
(WIFE OF —) AGLAURUS
CEDAR SUGI TOON SAVIN DEODAR
SABINA TUMION CYPRESS JUNIPER
WAXWING CALANTAS PAHAUTEA
CEDAR SWAMP GREENING
CEDAR WAXWING RECOLLET
CEDE CESS GIVE AWARD GRANT
LEAVE WAIVE YIELD ASSIGN RESIGN
SUBMIT CONCEDE RENOUNCE
TRANSFER
CEDILLA TITTLE
CEIBA KAPOK BENTANG POCHOTE
CEIL LINE SYLE OVERLAY WAINSCOT
CEILING TOP DOME LACE LOFT
CHUTT CUPOLA LINING SCREEN
SOFFIT SYLING CURTAIN LACUNAR
PLAFOND TESTUDO COVERING
DECKHAND PANELING PLANCHER
SEMIDOME
CELANDINE FICARY KILLWORT
WARTWEED WARTWORT
FELONWORT JEWELWEED
CELEBES (GULF OF —) BONE TOLO
TOMINI
(ISLAND OF —) MUNA BUTUNG
PELENG SULAWESI
(PEOPLE OF —) TORAJA
(TOWN OF —) BUOL LUWUK
MANADO MAKASAR
CELEBRATE FETE KEEP SING CHANT
DITTY EXTOL HONOR REVEL SACRE
SPEAK BESING CHAUNT EXTOLL
PRAISE ELEGIZE EXECUTE GLORIFY
MAFFICK OBSERVE EMBLAZON
EULOGIZE PROCLAIM
(— 2 MASSES) BINATE DUPLICATE
CELEBRATED KEPT FAMED NOTED
FAMOUS EMINENT FEASTED
RENOMME STORIED FABULOUS
GLORIOUS NOTIFIED OBSERVED
RENOWNED
CELEBRATION EED FETE GALA
POPE RITE FESTA REVEL COOLIN
CUSTOM DOMENT EASTER FIESTA
POWWOW RENOWN SIMHAH
BLOWOUT HOGMENA HOLIDAY
JUBILEE PASCHAL SHINDIG SIMCHAH
BINATION BIRTHDAY HOGMANAY
MAKAHIKI OLYMPIAD POTLATCH
SHIVAREE FESTIVITY HOOLAULEA
JUNKETING
CELEBRATOR JUBILIST
CELEBRITY FAME LION NAME STAR
CELEB ECLAT RENOWN REPUTE
CELERITY HASTE HURRY SPEED
DISPATCH RAPIDITY VELOCITY
SWIFTNESS
CELERY SIT ACHE STICK UMBEL
KARPAS SALARY SMALLAGE
CELESTIAL HOLY DIVINE HEAVEN
URANIC ANGELIC CHINESE ETHERED
EMPYREAL ETHEREAL HEAVENLY
OLYMPIAN
CELESTITE APOTOME

CELIBACY CHASTITY VIRGINITY
CELIBATE CLERK CHASTE SINGLE
BACHELOR SPINSTER
CELL BOX EGG BAND BOOT CAGE
CYTE DISC DISK GERM GONE HOLE
JAIL KILL CABIN CAROL CLINK
CRYPT CYTON FIBER FIBRE GHOST
GLAND GROUP OOTID TMEMA TORIL
VAULT ZOOID ANAXON CEPTOR
COCCUS COOLER CYTODE GAMETE
GONIUM INAXON PRISON SHIELD
SIPHON SYPHON WESTON ZYGOTE
AGAMETE AMEBULA APOCYTE
CELLULE CHAMBER CLOCHAN
CLOSTER COCCOID CUBICLE
DIPLOID DUNGEON ELEMENT
EPICYTE EUPLOID HAPLOID HEMATID
INITIAL LOCULUS MYOCYTE
OOBLAST PAPILLA PLASTID
RENETTE SEGMENT SPORONT
STEREID TRISOME UTRICLE VESICLE
AMACRINE BASOCYTE BASOPHIL
BIFORINE BIOPLAST CLOGHAUN
DIKARYON FAVEOLUS GLIOCYTE
GONIDIUM GONOCYTE HEMOCYTE
HOLDOVER IDIOSOME LOCELLUS
ORGANULE PROSORUS RECEPTOR
SCLEREID SPERMULE SYNERGID
TRACHEID TRIPLOID ZOOBLAST
(— OF LEADERS) CADRE
(BEE —) PIPE
(DETENTION —) BULLPEN
(PHOTOELECTRIC —) EYE
(PRISON —) BING HOLE CABIN
CLINK COOLER JIGGER
(STAB —) BAND
(THIN-WALLED —S) STOMIUM
(VOLTAIC —) BATTERY
(PL.) LAURA POTLINE SWEATBOX
CELLA NAOS
CELLAR CAVE VAULT BODEGA
PALACE FAVISSA HYPOGEE
BASEMENT HYPOGEUM MATAMORO
VAULTAGE
CELLARET TANTALUS
CELLARMAN SOMMELIER
CELLULOID XYLONITE
CELLULOSE CRUMB AMYLOID
LIGNOSE TAMIDINE
CELT GAEL GAUL KELT MANX IRISH
WELSH BRETON BRITON EOLITH
GOIDEL BRYTHON CORNISH
PALSTAFF PALSTAVE
(PL.) CYMRY KYMRY
CELTIC ERSE GAEL SCOTCH
CEMBALO DULCIMER ZIMBALON
CEMENT FIX KIT TIE GLUE HEAL
JOIN KNIT LIME LUTE SLIP GROUT
IMBED PASTE PUTTY SIMON STICK
TABBY UNITE BINDER CHUNAM
COHERE FASTEN FILLER GULGUL
KIBOSH MALTHA MASTIC MORTAR
OOGLEA SOLDER ASPHALT MIXTION
ADHESIVE ALBOLITE ALBOLITH
CEMENTUM HADIGEON SOLIDIFY
SOLUTION
CEMENTER GLUER GLUEMAN
SMEARER
CEMENT MIXER TEMPERER

CEMETERY HOWF KILL LAIR LITTEN CHARNEL BONEYARD CATACOMB GOLGOTHA URNFIELD
CENOBITE NUN MONK FRIAR ESSENE RECLUSE MONASTIC SYNODITE
CENOTAPH TOMB
CENSE THURIFY
CENSER INCENSER THURIBLE
CENSOR CRITIC SCREEN SYNDIC LAUNDER RESTRICT SUPPRESS
CENSORIOUS SEVERE BLAMING CARPING BLAMEFUL CAPTIOUS CRITICAL CULPABLE SLASHING
CENSORSHIP WRAPS ASSIZE CENSURE
CENSURABLE TAXABLE BLAMABLE CULPABLE
CENSURE BAN HIT NIP RAP TAP TAX WIG CALL CARP DEEM DRUB FLAY RATE SLAP TASK WITE BEANS BLAME CHIDE CURSE DECRY FAULT HOKER JUDGE PINCH SCOLD SLANG SLASH SLATE TAUNT TOUCH WHITE ACCUSE ATTACK BERATE CHARGE REBUFF REBUKE REFORM REMORD STRAFE TARGUE TIRADE BLISTER CHASTEN CONDEMN CONTROL DECRIAL DYSLOGY IMPEACH IMPROVE INVEIGH REPROOF REPROVE SCARIFY TRADUCE TROUNCE UPBRAID BACKBITE CHASTISE DISALLOW JUDGMENT LANGUAGE REPROACH SATIRIZE SENTENCE
CENSUS LIST POLL CENSE COUNT LUSTER LUSTRUM
CENT RED DUIT SANT BROWNIE CENTAVO STUIVER
(12 1-2 —S) LEVY
(ODD —S) BREAKAGE
CENTAUR CHIRON NESSUS HORSEMAN BUCENTAUR
CENTAURY BEHN BEHEN SABBATIA EARTHGALL
CENTENNIAL STATE COLORADO
CENTER COR EYE GIG HUB MID AXIS CORE NAVE SEAT SNAP YOLK FOCUS FOYER GLOME HEART MIDST PIVOT SPINE BOTTOM CENTRE MIDDLE PIPPER STAPLE TEMPLE CENTRUM ESSENCE LINEMAN NUCLEUS UMBILIC INCENTER OMPHALOS SNAPBACK
(— FOR SPINDLE) GIG
(— FOR TARGET) EYE PIN PINHOLE
(— OF ACTIVITY) HUB HIVE
(— OF ARCH) COOM
(— OF ASSURANCE) FORTRESS
(— OF ATTRACTION) FOCUS STAGE CYNOSURE
(— OF BASKET) SLATHER
(— OF CITY) DOWNTOWN
(— OF CULTIVATION) HOME
(— OF CULTURE) ATHENS
(— OF DIAMOND) WELL
(— OF FIGURE) CENTROID
(— OF FISHING NET) BUNT
(— OF FLOWER) EYE

(— OF HURRICANE) EYE
(— OF OPERATIONS) SHOP
(— OF POPULATION) CITY
(— OF POWER) SEE SIEGE
(— OF STAGE) LIMELIGHT
(— OF STRENGTH) GANGLION
(COLLECTION —) ENTREPOT
(COMMERCIAL —) MACHI EMPORIUM
(HARD —) KNOT
(INTIMATE —) BOSOM
(LATHE —) PIKE
(NERVOUS —) BRAIN
(NEURAL —) APPESTAT
(PROPAGANDA —) AGITPUNKT
(REHABILITATION —) HOSTEL
(TRADING —) BEACH EXCHANGE
(VITAL —) HEARTH HEARTBEAT
CENTERING COOM COOMB CENTRY FANTAIL
CENTERPIECE ROSACE DORMANT EPERGNE
CENTETES TENREC
CENTIARE LI
CENTIGRADE CELSIUS
CENTIME RAPPEN
CENTIMETER GAL
CENTIPEDE VEI VERI EARWIG GOLACH GOLOCH POLYPOD CHILOPOD MULTIPED MYRIAPOD SANTAPEE SCUTIGER
CENTRAL MID AXIAL BASIC CHIEF FOCAL MIXED PRIME MEDIAN MIDDLE CAPITAL CENTRIC LEADING NUCLEAR PIVOTAL PRIMARY CARDINAL DOMINANT

CENTRAL AFRICAN REPUBLIC
CAPITAL: BANGUI
COIN: FRANC
NATIVE: BAYA SARA BANDA BWAKA SANGO YAKOMA BANZIRI MANDJIA
RIVER: BOMU NANA CHARI KOTTO MBARI MPOKO OUAKA CHINKO LOBAYE UBANGI
TOWN: OBO IPPY BIRAO BOUAR KEMBE NDELE NGOTO PAOUA RAFAI ZEMIO BABOUA BAKALA BANGUI BOZOUM BAMBARI GRIMARI ZEMONGO

CENTRAL AMERICAN LADINO
(— TREE) TUNO TUNU
CENTRANTH SPURFLOWER
CENTRIFUGAL EFFERENT RADIATING
CENTRIFUGE CYCLONE SEPARATOR
CENTRIPETAL AFFERENT
CENTROSOME CENTRUM CENTRIOLE
CENTRUM CORE
CENTURIED SECULAR
CENTURY AGE SECLE SIECLE
CENTURY PLANT ALOE AGAVE MAGUEY CANTALA TEQUILA MONOCARP
CEPHALALGIA SODA HEADACHE
CEPHALIC CRANIAL ATLANTAL CEREBRAL

CEPHALOPOD SQUID CUTTLE INKFISH OCTOPUS SPIRULA DIBRANCH SCAPHITE
CEPHALUS (FATHER OF —) DEION
(MOTHER OF —) DIOMEDE
(WIFE OF —) PROCRIS
CERAMICS TILES POTTERY
CERATE WAX LARD SALVE UNGUENT OINTMENT
CERATOBRANCHIAL APOHYAL
CEREAL RYE BEAN BRAN CORN MUSH OATS RICE SAMP TEFF ARZUN GRAIN MAIZE SPELT WHEAT BARLEY BINDER FARINA HOMINY PABLUM OATMEAL SOYBEAN PORRIDGE
CEREAL LEAF FLAG
CEREBRAL CEPHALIC INVERTED
CEREBRATION THOUGHT
CEREBROSIDE KERASIN
CEREMENT SHROUD
CEREMONIAL FORM PRIM STIFF FORMAL RIALTY RITUAL SOLEMN PRECISE STUDIED TRIUMPH UPANAYA AVERSION SPLENDOR
CEREMONIOUS GRAND LOFTY STIFF FORMAL PROPER SOLEMN PRECISE STATELY STUDIED
CEREMONY BRIS FETE FORM GAUD HAKO ORGY POMP RITE SEAL SHOW SIGN SING BERIT DANCE STATE ACTION AUGURY BERITH BRIDAL BURIAL EXEQUY GOMBAY HOMAGE KERIAH MALKAH MAUNDY NIPTER OFFICE PARADE POWWOW REVIEW RITUAL SALUTE BAPTISM DISPLAY KIDDUSH MELAVEH OVATION PAGEANT PANAGIA PORTENT PRODIGY TAHARAH ACCOLADE APOLUSIS ASPERGES COEMPTIO CRIOBOLY ENCAENIA EXERCISE FUNCTION HABDALAH HAKAFOTH HERALDRY MARRIAGE OCCASION SKEYTING INAUGURAL INDUCTION
(HAZING —) CREELING
(MARRIAGE —) ESPOUSAL
(TEA —) CHANOYU
(PL.) DEGREE HOLIES AGENDUM FERALIA JUSTMENTS
CERES DEMETER
(DAUGHTER OF —) PROSERPINE PHERREPHATTA
(FATHER OF —) SATURN
(MOTHER OF —) VESTA
CERINTHE HONEYWORT
CERO SEARER SIERRA CAVALLA PINTADO KINGFISH
CERTAIN COLD COOL DEAD FAST FIRM FREE REAL SEAL SURE TRUE BOUND CLEAR EXACT FIXED PLAIN SIKER ACTUAL MEMORY SECURE SICKER STATED WITTER ASSURED PERFECT PRECISE SETTLED SRADDHA ABSOLUTE APPARENT CONSTANT OFFICIAL POSITIVE RELIABLE RESOLVED UNERRING CONFIDENT
CERTAINLY AY AYE WIS AMEN IWIS SOON SURE WHAT YWIS TRULY

CERTES INDEED PERDIE SICCAR SICKER SURELY VERILY HARDILY EVERMORE FORSOOTH SECURELY **(MOST —)** SO
CERTAINTY YEA CERT PIPE CINCH POLICY SURETY SURENESS CONSTANCY
(LACK OF —) SCRUPLE
CERTIFICATE BOND CHIT CHECK DEMIT JURAT LIBEL SCRIP TALON TITLE AMPARO ATTEST CEDULA COUPON INDENT PATENT POTTAH RETURN TICKET VERIFY CERTIFY CONSTAT DIPLOMA VOUCHER WARRANT WAYBILL AEGROTAT JUDGMENT KABBALAH NAVICERT REGISTER REGISTRY SECURITY TESCARIA TESTAMUR TEZKIRAH
(MARRIAGE —) LINES
(MINER'S —) LICENCE LICENSE
(PILOT'S —) BRANCH
(SERVANT'S —) CHIT
CERTIFICATION PASS STAMP APPROVAL HECHSHER CLEARANCE DISCHARGE
CERTIFIED SWORN
CERTIFY AVOW VISE SWEAR AFFIRM ASSURE ATTEST DEPOSE EVINCE VERIFY WITTER APPROVE ENDORSE LICENSE TESTIFY
CERTITUDE CERTAIN CONFIDENCE
CERULEAN BLUE AZURE COELIN CYANEAN CYANEOUS
CERUMEN WAX EARWAX
CESS BOG TAX CEDE DUTY LEVY LUCK RATE ABWAB SLOPE YIELD IMPOST MEASURE SURRENDER
(BAD —) SORRA
CESSATION HO END HOO BLIN HALT HUSH LISS LULL REST STAY STOP BREAK CEASE CLOSE DEVAL LETUP LISSE PAUSE SLACK STINT TRUCE CUTOFF DEMISE DISUSE OFFSET PERIOD RECESS CEASING CLOSURE RESPITE ABEYANCE BLACKOUT DESITION INTERVAL SHUTDOWN STOPPAGE SURCEASE SUSPENSE
(— OF HOSTILITIES) TRUCE INDUCIAE ARMISTICE
(— OF LIFE) DEATH
(— OF RESPIRATION) APNEA APNOEA
(— OF WORK) HARTAL
CESSPOOL SINK SUMP SINKER CISTERN JAWHOLE SINKHOLE SUSPIRAL
CESTRUM POISONBERRY
CESTUS CEST CESTON HURLBAT GAUNTLET WHIRLBAT
CETACEAN ORC CETE ORCA SUSU WHALE BELUGA COWFISH DOLPHIN GRAMPUS NARWHAL MUTILATE PORPOISE
CEYLON SERENDIP TAPROBANE

CEYLON
CAPITAL: COLOMBO
COIN: CENT

GULF: MANNAR
MEASURE: PARA PARAH AMUNAM PARRAH
POINT: PEDRO
STRAIT: PALK
TOWN: GALLE KANDY JAFFNA MANNAR MATARA BADULLA COLOMBO PUTTALAM
TREE: HORA PALU

CEYLONESE CEYLON BURGHER
CEYLON MOSS GULAMAN
CGS UNIT STILB STOKE
CHA TSIA CHAIS
CHACMA BAVIAN BOBBEJAAN

CHAD
CAPITAL: FORTLAMY
COIN: FRANC FRANCCFA
LAKE: CHAD
NATIVE: ARAB SARA KREDA MASSA TOUBOU KAMADJA MOUNDAN
PLATEAU: ENNEDI
RIVER: CHARI LOGONE BAHRAOUK
TOWN: ATI BOL LAI MAO FADA FAYA MONGO ARECHE BONGOR LARGEAU MOUNDOU MOUSSORO

CHADOR PHULKARI
CHAETOCHLOA SETARIA
CHAETOPOD SCALEBACK
CHAFE IRK RUB VEX FRET FRIG FROT FUME GALD GALL HEAT JOSH RAGE WARM WEAR ANGER ANNOY CHAFF GRIND SCOLD SNUFF WORRY WRING ABRADE BANTER EXCITE FRIDGE HARASS INJURY NETTLE RANKLE INCENSE INFLAME SNUFFLE FRICTION IRRITATE RAILLERY
CHAFER CRESSET
CHAFF GUY HAY PUG ROT BRAN CAFF CHIP GRIT GUFF JOSH PULU QUIZ RAZZ BORAK CHYAK DROSS GLUME HULLS HUSKS JOLLY SLACK STOUR STRAW TEASE TRASH BANTER BHOOSA REFUSE CAVINGS TAILING RAILLERY RIDICULE SHELLING
CHAFFER BANDY SIEVE WARES BUYING DICKER HAGGLE HIGGLE MARKET PALTER BARGAIN CHATTER SELLING TRAFFIC EXCHANGE
CHAFFINCH PINK CHINK SPINK TWINK ROBERD SCOBBY SHILFA SKELLY ROBINET SNABBIE WETBIRD
CHAFFY SCALY ACEROSE ACEROUS PALEATE
CHAFING GALLING IMPATIENCE
CHAGRIN ENVY SPITE VEXATION
CHAGRINED SICK ASHAMED
CHAIN FOB GUY NET ROW SET TEW TIE TOE TOW TUG TYE BIND BOND CURB FALL FAST FILE GYVE JOIN LINE LINK SEAL SOAM TEAM BRAIL CABLE GROUP GUARD LEASH

SHANK SHEET SLANG SLING SUITE TRACE TRAIN WRASE CARCAN CATENA COLLAR CORDON FASTEN FETTER GANGER HANGER HOBBLE JACKER JIGGER LINKER RACKAN SECURE SERIES STRING TETHER TOGGLE BOBSTAY CATFALL CHIGNON CONNECT EMBRACE ENSLAVE LASHING MANACLE NETWORK PAINTER PENDANT SAUTOIR SHACKLE TACKLER BACKROPE BRACELET CARCANET GLEIPNIR LINKWORK NECKLACE RECEPTOR RESTRAIN RIGWIDDY STROBILA WOOLDING
(— FOR ANCHOR) CATFALL PAINTER
(— FOR BINDING) JACKER TACKLER
(— FOR WRAPPING MAST) WOOLDING
(— OF AUTHORITIES) ISNAD
(— OF DUNES) SAIF SEIF
(— OF MOUNTAINS) RANGE
(— OF ROCKS) REEF
(— ON CONVICT'S LEG) SLANG
(— TO BIND CATTLE) SEAL
(DECORATIVE —) FESTOON
(ENDLESS —) CREEPER
(MAGIC —) GLEIPNIR
(SHORT —) SHANK
(SUSPENDED —) CATENARY
(WATCH —) FOB ALBERT
(PL.) IRONS CONVEYOR
CHAIN LINK SHUT COPULA SWIVEL
CHAINMAN CLASHY CLASHEE LINEMAN TAPEMAN
CHAIN-SHAPED CATENOID
CHAIR KEEP SEAT SHOP HORSE SEDAN STOOL ESTATE OFFICE PULPIT ROCKER SADDLE SITTER TONJON CACOLET COMMODE FANBACK GONDOLA SITTING VOYEUSE WINDSOR ARMCHAIR CARRIAGE CATHEDRA FAUTEUIL KANGAROO SGABELLO VOLTAIRE
(— OF STATE) THRONE
(— SLUNG FROM POLE) KAGO TALABON
(— WITH CANOPY) STATE
(BISHOP'S —) CATHEDRA FALDSTOOL
(EASY —) COGSWELL
(GREEK —) KLISMOS
(MINING —) DOG
(PORTABLE —) SEDAN
(SPRING —) PERCH
(THRONE —) SHINZA
CHAIRMAN HEAD CHAIR EMCEE PRESES SPEAKER CONVENER DIRECTOR
CHAISE GIG SHAY CHAIR CALESIN CARRIAGE
CHAISE LONGUE DAYBED DUCHESSE
CHALAZA TREAD TREADLE GALLATURE
CHALCEDONY ONYX OPAL SARD AGATE PRASE CATEYE JASPER QUARTZ CARNEOL ENHYROS OPALINE SARDINE SARDIUS

CHALCOPYRITE RUN
CHALDEAN KALDANI BABYLONIAN
(— **MEASURE**) CANE FOOT MAKUK
QASAB ARTABA GARIBA GHALVA
MANSION
(— **RIVER**) TIGRIS EUPHRATES
(— **TOWN**) UR
CHALICE AMA CUP BOWL CALIX
GRAIL REGAL GOBLET KRASIS
CHALK CAUK CORK PALE SCAR
TALC TICK CRETA FLOUR SCORE
BLANCH BLEACH CRAYON CREDIT
RUBBLE WHITEN ACCOUNT WHITING
(**GREEN** —) PRASINE
(**HARD** —) HURLOCK
(**RED** —) RUBRIC
(**SURVEYOR'S** —) KEEL
CHALKBOARD GREENBOARD
CHALKY CRETACIC
CHALLENGE VIE BRAG CALL DARE
DEFY FACE GAGE BANCO BLAME
BRAVE CLAIM QUERY STUMP
ACCUSE APPEAL BANTER CARTEL
CHARGE DACKER DAIKER DEMAND
DESCRY FORBID IMPUGN INFIRM
INVITE RECUSE SERDAB ARRAIGN
CENSURE IMPEACH PROVOKE
REPROVE SOLICIT SUMMONS
CHAMPION DEFIANCE GAUNTLET
QUESTION REPROACH
(— **A BULL**) CITE
CHALLENGING PIQUANT
BLOODSHOT
CHALYBEATE MARTIAL
CHAMBER ODA AGER CELL CIST
DOME FLAT FOLD HALL IWAN KIVA
ROOM SALE TOMB BOWER CAVUM
COURT GOMER HOUSE SENAT
SHAFT SOLAR SOLER STOVE
ATRIUM CAMARA CAMERA COFFER
HEADER HOLLOW MIHRAB SENADO
SENATE SOLLAR SPRING STANZA
WILSON BEDROOM CAISSON
CHALMAR CHANNEL CHAUMER
CONCAVE CUBICLE FAVISSA
FIREBOX GALLERY GEHENNA
MANSION RECEIPT CASEMATE
CYLINDER DIFFUSER FOUNTAIN
GROSSRAT SMOKEBOX SNEMOVNA
THALAMUS
(— **FOR MOLTEN GLASS**) FONT
(— **IN FURNACE**) SHAFT DOGHOUSE
(— **OF EAR**) SACCULE
(— **POT**) JORDAN JEROBOAM
(**AIR** —) SPONSON
(**BOMBPROOF** —) CASEMATE
(**FIRE** —) ARCH STOVE COCKLE
FIREBOX
(**FORTIFICATION** —) BUNKER
(**OPEN** —) LANTERN
(**ORGAN** —) SWELL
(**PRIVATE** —) CLOSET CONCLAVE
(**PUEBLO** —) KIVA ESTUFA
(**SLEEPING** —) BEDROOM
WARDROBE
(**SMALL** —) LOCULUS
(**SUPPLY** —) MAGAZINE
(**UNDERGROUND** —) CAVE CRYPT
CAVERN HYPOGEE

(**WATERTIGHT** —) CAISSON
CHAMBERLAIN EUNUCH FACTOR
SERVANT STEWARD PALATINE
POLONIUS
CHAMELEON ANOLE ANOLI LACERT
SAURIAN
CHAMFER BEVEL CHIMB CHIME
CHINE FLUTE CIPHER FURROW
GROOVE
CHAMOIS GEMS IZARD AOUDAD
SHAMMY
CHAMOMILE MAYWEED
CHAMP BITE CHAW FIRM HARD
MASH CHANK CHOMP FIELD GNASH
TRAMPLE
CHAMPAGNE AY BUBBLY SIMKIN
BELLEEK SILLERY
CHAMPION ACE AID FAN ABET BACK
BOSS DEFY HERO KEMP GHAZI
ASSERT ATTEND DEFEND KNIGHT
PATRON SQUIRE VICTOR ESPOUSE
FIGHTER PALADIN PROTECT
ADVOCATE DEFENDER PALMERIN
CHAMPIONSHIP TITLE LAURELS
ADVOCACY
CHAMPLEVE INLAID
CHANCE DIE HAP LOT CASE CAST
DINT DRAW FATE LINE LUCK ODDS
RISK SHOT SHOW TIDE BREAK
ETTLE STAKE WHACK BETIDE
CASUAL GAMBLE HAPPEN HAZARD
MISHAP RANDOM SQUEAK AIMLESS
FORTUNE STUMBLE VANTAGE
VENTURE ACCIDENT CASUALTY
EVENTUAL FORTUITY
(**ADVERSE** —) HAZARD
(**EVEN** —) TOSSUP
CHANCELLOR LOGOTHETE
CHANDELIER LUSTER PHAROS
PENDANT CHANDLER GASELIER
CHANDLER TALLOWER
CHANE OREJON
CHANGE MEW CHOP FLOP MOLT
MOVE ODDS PEAL TURN VARY VEER
WARP WEND ADAPT ALTER AMEND
BREAK COINS EMEND MOULT SHIFT
THROW ADJUST BECOME DIFFER
DIGEST IMMUTE MODIFY MUANCE
MUTATE REMOVE REVAMP REVISE
SWITCH WISSEL WRIXLE COMMUTE
CONVERT CUTOVER DEVIATE
FLUXION MORTIFY BECOMING
DENATURE EXCHANGE INNOVATE
LENITION REVISION TRANSFER
TRANSUME VARIANCE
(— **APPEARANCE**) DISGUISE
(— **COLOR**) TURN
(— **COURSE**) GYBE JIBE
(— **DIRECTION**) CUT CANT CHOP
HAUL KNEE VEER ANGLE BREAK
SHIFT
(— **FOR BETTER**) HELP
(— **FOR WORSE**) BEDEVIL
(— **FORM**) DEVELOP
(— **GAIT**) BREAK
(— **GRADUALLY**) PASS GRADUATE
(— **IN COURSE**) SHEER
(— **IN DIRECTION**) JOG KNEE STEP
(— **IN ELEVATION**) FORK

(— **IN SIZE**) ASTOGENY
(— **INTO VAPOR**) FLASH
(— **MONEY**) WISSEL
(— **OF FORM**) SET
(— **OF GEAR**) KICKDOWN
(— **OF MIND**) CAPRICE
(— **OF MOOD**) VARY
(— **OF PITCH**) MOTION INFLECT
(— **OF SEA LEVEL**) EUSTACY
(— **OF SOUND**) BREAKING
(— **OF WORD**) ANAGRAM
(— **ONE'S HEART**) REPENT
(— **POSITION**) STIR FLEET HOTCH
(— **QUICKLY**) FLY
(— **SHAPE**) DRAW CREEP DEFORM
(— **RESIDENCE**) FLIT
(**ABRUPT** —) DOGLEG SALTATION
(**ABNORMAL** —) LESION
(**GEAR** —) KICKDOWN
(**GRADUAL** —) DRIFT
(**PRESSURE** —) ALLOBAR
(**SHORT** —) FLUFF
(**SMALL** —) GROCERY
(**UNEXPECTED** —) SWITCH
(PL.) DOUBLES PLASTIQUE
CHANGEABLE EEMIS GIDDY IMMIS
LIGHT WINDY CHOPPY FICKLE
FITFUL GERFUL KETCHY LABILE
MOBILE MOTLEY MUABLE SHIFTY
BRUCKLE ERRATIC MUTABLE
PROTEAN UNSTAID VARIANT
VARIOUS VOLUBLE AMENABLE
CATCHING GLIBBERY MOVEABLE
TICKLISH UNSTABLE VARIABLE
VEERABLE VOLATILE WEATHERY
CHANGEABLENESS LEVITY
VIBRATION
CHANGED VARIED ANOTHER
CHANGEFUL FICKLE SHIFTY
MUTABLE RESTLESS
CHANGELESS CONSISTENT
CHANGELING AUF AWF OAF DOLT
FOOL CHILD DUNCE IDIOT WAVERER
IMBECILE KILLCROP RENEGADE
TURNCOAT
CHANGING FLUXIBLE ALTERNATE
(— **MONEY**) AGIO
(**CONTINUALLY** —) FLOATING
CHANK SANK CONCH
CHANNEL CUT GAT POD REE RUT
SOW CANO CAVA DEEP DIKE DUCT
DYKE FLUE GATE GOOL GOTE GOUT
GURT KILL KYLE LAKE LANE PACE
PIPE RACE SLEW SLOO VEIN WADI
WADY BAYOU CANAL CARRY CHASE
COWAL DITCH DRAIN DRILL FLUME
FLUTE GLYPH GUIDE INSET QUIRK
RIVER SINUS SLIDE STOOL STOVE
STRIA SWASH AIRWAY ALVEUS
ARROYO ARTERY BRANCH COURSE
CUTOFF ESTERO FURROW GROOVE
GULLET GUTTER HOLLOW KENNEL
KEYWAY LAGOON MEDIUM OFFLET
OILWAY RABBET RESACA RIVOSE
RUNWAY SLOUGH SLUICE SPECUS
STRAIT STRAND STREAM THROAT
TROUGH CHAMFER CONDUCT
CONDUIT CULVERT CUNETTE
EURIPUS OFFTAKE PASSAGE

RACEWAY RIVULET SHIPWAY
SILANGA STRIGIL THALWEG
TIDEWAY WASHOUT AQUEDUCT
FLOODWAY GUIDEWAY GUNKHOLE
RACELINE SCOURWAY SPILLWAY
(— FOR MOLTEN METAL) SOW GATE
RUNNER
(— IN CLOTH) FLUTE
(— IN ICE FIELD) LEAD
(— IN MOLD) SPRAY
(— OF AQUEDUCT) SPECUS
(— ON WHALE) SCARF
(ARTIFICAL —) GAT GOUT
(DRAINAGE —) GAW
(ENGLISH —) SLEEVE
(INCLINED —) SHOOT
(IRRIGATION —) AUWAI DROVE
(LYMPH —) CISTERNA
(SECONDARY —) BINNACLE
(SLOPING —) CHUTE SHUTE
CHANNELBILL RAINFOWL
CHANNELED FLUTED
CHANT CANT MELE SING SONG
TONE CAROL PSALM SOUGH
ANTHEM CANTUS INTONE LITANY
WARBLE CHORTLE INTROIT
PROSODE REQUIEM WORSHIP
ALLELUIA ANTIPHON SINGSONG
CHANTER STICK CANTOR SINGER
BAGPIPE SONGSTER CHALUMEAU
(— OF BAGPIPE) OBOE
CHANTERELLE CANTINO
CHANTING CHARM HAZANUT
ANTIPHONY CHAZZANUT
CHANTLATE SPROCKET
CHANTRY CAGE
CHAOS NU NUN PIE APSU GULF
HYLE MESS VOID ABYSS BABEL
CHASM JUMBLE MATTER TOPHET
ANARCHY MIXTURE DISORDER
SHAMBLES TAILSPIN TOHUBOHU
CHAOTIC MUDDLED CONFUSED
FORMLESS
CHAP BOY BUY DOG LAD MAN RAP
WAG BEAN BEAT BIRD BLOW CHIP
CHOP COVE DICK DUCK HIND JOHN
KIBE MASH MATE NABS SNAP BILLY
BLOKE BUCKO BULLY BUYER CHAFT
CHINK CLEFT CRACK FRUIT KNOCK
LOVER RUMMY SCOUT SPLIT SPORT
SPRAY SWIPE TRADE YOUTH
BARTER BOHUNK BREACH BUGGER
CALLAN CHOOSE CODGER CUFFIN
FELLOW FOUTER FOUTRA GAFFER
GEEZER JOSSER KIPPER SHAVER
STRIKE STROKE TURNIP BROTHER
CALLANT FISSURE HUSBAND
ROUGHEN BLIGHTER CUSTOMER
DIVISION MERCHANT
(— HANDS) RACK SPRAY
(— IN SKIN) KIN KIBE
(FINE —) BULLY
(OLD —) GEEZER
(QUEER —) GALOOT
(S.AFRICAN —) KEREL
(YOUNG —) GAFFER
(PL.) CHOPS
CHAPARRAL MONTE CHAMISAL
BUCKTHORN

CHAPARRO YAYA
CHAPBOOK CHAP GARLAND
CHAPE CRAMPET MORDANT
CHAPEL CAGE CAPE COPE COWL
HOOD CLOAK PORCH BETHEL
CHARRE CHURCH HAIKAL MORADA
SHRINE CAPELLA CHANTRY
CHARNEL CHHATRI GALILEE
MARTYRY MEETING MEMORIA
ORATORY SACRARY SERVICE
BETHESDA DEACONRY DIACONIA
FERETORY FERETRUM SACELLUM
SODALITY
(UNDERGROUND —) SHROUDS
CHAPERON HOOD ATTEND DUENNA
ESCORT MATRON GRIFFIN PROTECT
GUARDIAN TRAPPING
CHAPLAIN PADRE LEVITE CONDUCT
ALTARIST ORDINARY
CHAPLET BEAD ORLE STUD CROWN
ANADEM ANCHOR CIRCLE FILLET
JAMBER JAMMER ROSARY STAPLE
TROPHY WREATH CORONAL
CORONET GARLAND MOULDING
NECKLACE ORNAMENT
CHAPMAN CHAP BUYER DEALER
HAWKER TRADER COPEMAN
PEDDLER CUSTOMER MERCHANT
CHAPPIE JOCKEY
CHAPS FLEWS BREECHES LEGGINGS
OVERALLS
CHAPTER BODY CELL PACE POST
CAPUT COURT LODGE BRANCH
CABILDO CAPITAL CORRECT
COUNCIL MEETING SECTION
ASSEMBLY
(— OF BOOK) CAPITAL
(— OF KORAN) SURA SURAH
(— OF SOCIETY) CAMP CIRCLE
CHAR BURN CART COAL SEAR BROIL
CHARK CHORE SHARD SINGE TROUT
SCORCH BLACKEN CHARIOT
REDBELLY SAIBLING SALMONID
SANDBANK
CHARA MUSKGRASS
CHARACIN DORADO DOURADE
BLOODFIN
CHARACTER BALL BENT CARD CASE
CLAY CLEF DASH ECAD FLAT FOND
FORM HAIR KIND MAKE MARK MOLD
NOTE PART ROLE RUNE SIGN SORT
TONE TRIM TYPE BRAND COLOR
ETHIC ETHOS FIBER HABIT HEART
HUMOR INDEX SAVOR STAMP
TENOR TOKEN TRAIT WRITE
CARACT CIPHER COCKUP DAGGER
DIRECT EMBLEM FIGURE GENIUS
HANGER LETTER MANNER METTLE
NATURE REPUTE SIGLUM SPIRIT
STRIPE SYMBOL CLOTHES EDITION
ENGRAVE ESSENCE IMPRESS
QUALITY FRACTION IDENTITY
INFERIOR INSCRIBE LIGATURE
SELFHOOD SYLLABIC DESCENDER
(— IN DRAMA) CHORUS
(— IN PLAY) DAME BESSY
(— OF SOIL) LAIR
(ASSUMED —) ROLE FIGURE
INCOGNITO

(BAD —) DROLE BUDMASH
(BASIC —) BOTTOM
(CHINESE —) SHOU RADICAL
(COMMON —) COMMUNITY
(ESSENTIAL —) ALLOY
(FIRM —) BACKBONE
(GIVE — TO) TONE
(JAPANESE —S) HIBUNCI
(MENDELIAN —) ALLEL ALLELE
(PHYSICAL —) ARMENOID
(PRIME —) ESSENCE
(SHIFTLESS —) BEAT
(STOCK —) MACCUS
(TESTED —) ASSAY
(TRIED —) TOUCH
(VULGAR —S) ONMUN
(PL.) MANA
CHARACTERISTIC CAST COST
MARK MIEN ANGLE AROMA GRACE
POINT TACHE TOKEN TRAIT ACCENT
BEAUTY NATURE STIGMA STROKE
ADJUNCT AMENITY FEATURE
IMPRESS QUALITY SPECIES TYPICAL
ACTIVITY PECULIAR PROPERTY
SYMBOLIC
(— OF ANTIBODIES) AVIDITY
(ADVENTITIOUS —) ACCIDENT
(DISTINGUISHING —) SPECIES
HALLMARK BIRTHMARK
(PECULIAR —) IDIOPATHY
(PL.) CORNERS FACULTY
CHARACTERIZATION ELOGY
ELOGIUM
CHARACTERIZE MARK STYLE
DEFINE DEPICT TITULE ENGRAVE
ENTITLE IMPRINT PORTRAY
DESCRIBE INDICATE INSCRIBE
CHARADES GAME
CHARCOAL COAL CARBO CHARK
CARBON FUSAIN PENCIL BLACKEN
SPODIUM SCRIBBET
CHARGE FEE LAP LAY RAP TAX
BEEF BILL BUCK CALL CARE CARK
CAST COST CURE DUES DUTY FILL
GIBE KEEP LADE LIEN LOAD NICK
NOTE ONUS RACK RATE REST RUSH
SHOT SIZE SOAK SPAR TASK TOLL
WARD WIKE BLAME CAUSE CHALK
COUNT CRIME DEBIT EXTRA GYRON
ONSET ORDER PRICE REFER SCORE
SHOCK STICK STING THING TRUST
ACCUSE ADJURE ALLEGE APPEAL
ASSESS ATTACK BURDEN CAREER
CENSUS COURSE CREDIT DAMAGE
DEFAME DEMAND ENJOIN ENURNY
EXCESS IMPOSE IMPUTE METAGE
OFFICE PIPAGE REATUS SURMIT
SURTAX TARIFF TOWAGE WEIGHT
ACIDIZE ANNULET ARRAIGN ARTICLE
ASCRIBE ASSAULT AVERAGE
BOATAGE CARTAGE CENSURE
CHEVRON CLAMPER COMMAND
CONCERN CONJURE CORKAGE
CORNAGE CUSTODY DOCKAGE
DRAYAGE EMBASSY EXPENSE
FLOTAGE HAULAGE IGNITER
IMPEACH KEEPING MANDATE
MILEAGE MISSION MIXTURE
MOORAGE PANNAGE QUAYAGE

REPRISE SIDEAGE SLANDER
SLIDAGE SURMISE WARPAGE
BILLBACK BRASSAGE CASUALTY
CHASTISE CRESCENT DELAYAGE
DENOUNCE LEGATION ORDINARY
OVERLOAD PLANKAGE POUNDAGE
PROVINCE QUESTION SLINGING
SPENDING STANDAGE TUTORAGE
VIGORISH COMPLAINT
(— AGAINST) TILT
(— BATTERY) SOAK BOOST
(— EXCESSIVELY) FLEECE
(— FALSELY) SURMISE
(— OF FIREARM) LOAD
(— OF METAL) HEAT
(— OF ORE) POST
(— TO BE PAID) LAW
(— UPON PROPERTY) LIEN
(— WITH CRIME) ACCUSE INDICT
ARTICLE ATTAINT IMPEACH
(— WITH GAS) AERATE
(AGGREGATE —S) BOOK
(CANNON —) GRAPE
(COVER —) COUVERT
(DEPTH —) CAN
(EXPLOSIVE —) CAP BLAST SNAKE
SQUIB TULIP BOOSTER BURSTER
IGNITER
(FALSE —) CALUMNY
(HERALDIC —) DROP GIRON GYRON
LABEL DRAGON GURGES BEARING
ESQUIRE
(MAILING —) FRANKAGE
(POWDER —) GRAIN
(SHAPED —) BEEHIVE
(SPIRITUAL —) CURE
(TEMPORARY —) CARE
(WINE —) CORKAGE
CHARGED UP HOT LADEN BELAST
BILLETY BILLETTE ELECTRIC
INSTINCT
(— WITH EMOTION) SWOLLEN
CHARGEHAND CLICKER
CHARGEMAN BLASTER
CHARGER DISH HORSE MOUNT
STEED ACCUSER COURSER
PLATTER
CHARILY FRUGALLY GINGERLY
CHARIOT CAR BIGA CART CHAR
RATH WAIN BUGGY CHAIR ESSED
RATHA TRIGA WAGON CHARET
QUADRIGA
CHARIOTEER AURIGA CARTER
DRIVER IOLAUS LEADER CARTARE
WAGONER MYRTILUS AUTOMEDON
CHARITABLE KIND BENIGN HUMANE
LENIENT LIBERAL GENEROUS
CHARITY ALMS DOLE GIFT LOVE
PITY RUTH MERCY BASKET BOUNTY
CARITAS HANDOUT LARGESS
LENIENCE TZEDAKAH
CHARIVARI BABEL SHALLAL
SERENADE SHIVAREE
CHARLATAN FAKE CHEAT FAKER
FRAUD QUACK CABOTIN EMPIRIC
IMPOSTER MAGICIAN SYCOPHANT
CHARLES II DAVID
CHARLIE MCCARTHY STOOGE
CHARLOCK KRAUT RUNCH HARLOCK

KEDLOCK KERLOCK MUSTARD
SINAPIS YELLOWS CHARDOCK
CHEDLOCK SKEDLOCK SKELLOCH
CHARM IT GBO KEY OBI CALM CHIC
HAND JINX JUJU JYNX LUCK MOJO
PLAY RUNE SNOW SONG TAKE TILL
ZOGO ALLAY BRIEF CATCH FAVOR
FREET FREIT GRACE LAMIN MAGIC
OBEAH SAFFI SAFIE SPELL VENUS
WANGA WEIRD ALLURE AMULET
BEAUTY CARACT DEASIL ENAMOR
ENGAGE ENTICE FETISH GLAMOR
GRIGRI INCANT MANTRA MELODY
PLEASE SAPHIE SCARAB SOOTHE
SUBDUE SUMMON VOODOO
ABRAXAS ASSUAGE ATTRACT
BEGUILE BEWITCH CANTION
CANTRIP CONJURE CONTROL
DELIGHT ENCHANT ENTHRAL
FLATTER HEITIKI PERIAPT PHILTER
PHILTRE SINGING SORCERY
BLESSING BRELOQUE COQUETRY
ENTHRALL ENTRANCE GLAUMRIE
GREEGREE PISHOGUE PRACTICE
TALISMAN
CHARMED CAPTIVE
CHARMER SIREN EXORCIST
MAGICIAN SORCERER ENCHANTER
CHARMING LEPID SWEET GOLDEN
WIZARD AMIABLE DARLING
EYESOME TEMPEAN WINNING
WINSOME ADORABLE DELICATE
GRACEFUL LOVESOME
CHARNEL GHASTLY CEMETERY
GOLGOTHA
CHARON (FATHER OF —) EREBUS
(MOTHER OF —) NOX
CHARPOY COT
CHARQUI JERKY XARQUE
CHART MAP BILL CARD PLAN PLAT
PLOT ROSE CARTE GRAPH STILL
RECORD SCHEME DIAGRAM
EMAGRAM EXPLORE ISOTYPE
OUTLINE PROJECT DOCUMENT
DOPEBOOK MERCATOR PLATFORM
(— BOOK) WAGONER
(— FROM AIR) AEROVIEW
(— MARK) VIGIA
(— OF A COURSE) RUTTER
(MARINER'S —) ROSE
(WEATHER —) ANALOGUE
CHARTER FIX LET BOND BOOK DEED
HIRE RENT CARTE CHART FUERO
GRANT LEASE SANAD CHARTA
PERMIT SUNNUD DIPLOMA
CONTRACT GRUNDLOV HEIRLOOM
LANDBOOK MONOPOLY PANCHART
CHARWOMAN CHARER CHARLADY
PORTRESS JANITRESS
CHARY SHY DEAR WARY CHERE
SCANT SPARE DAINTY FRUGAL
PRIZED SKIMPY CAREFUL CURIOUS
SPARING CAUTIOUS HESITANT
PRECIOUS RESERVED SPAREFUL
VIGILANT
CHASE FOG SIC SUE FALL HUNT
JERL SHAG SHOO SICK ANNOY
CATCH CHEVY CHIVY DRIVE HARRY
HOUND SCORE SHACK CACCIA

CHIVVY CHOUSE EMBOSS FOLLOW
FRIEZE FURROW GALLOP GROOVE
HALLOO HARASS HOLLOW INDENT
PURSUE QUARRY SCORSE TRENCH
CHANNEL ENGRAVE HUNTING
PURSUIT ORNAMENT PURCHASE
(— GAME) COURSE
(— HARD) RATTLE
CHASER RAM DRINK HOUND
FROGGER
(WOMAN —) SHEEPBITER
CHASM GAP KIN PIT GULF RIFT
YAWN ABYSS BLANK CANON CHAOS
CLEFT GORGE BREACH CANYON
HIATUS FISSURE MEGARON
SWALLOW VACANCY APERTURE
CREVASSE INTERVAL VACATION
CHASSE SLIP GLIDE SASHAY
CHASSEUR HUNTER BELLBOY
DOORMAN FOOTMAN HUNTSMAN
CHASSIS SASH FRAME FIGURE
CHASTE CAST PURE CLEAN ZONED
DECENT HONEST MODEST PROPER
SEVERE VESTAL VIRGIN CLEANLY
PUDICAL REFINED CELIBATE
INNOCENT VIRGINLY VIRTUOUS
CHASTEN RATE ABASE SMITE
SMOTE SNEAP SOBER HUMBLE
PUNISH REFINE SUBDUE TEMPER
AFFLICT CENSURE CORRECT
NURTURE CHASTISE MODERATE
RESTRAIN
CHASTISE BEAT FIRK FLOG LASH
SLAP TRIM WHIP AMEND BLAME
FEEZE SCOLD SPANK SPILL STRAP
TAUNT ACCUSE ANOINT BERATE
CHARGE PUNISH PURIFY REBUKE
REFINE SWINGE TEMPER THRASH
TICKLE CHASTEN CORRECT
REPROVE SCOURGE SHINGLE
SUSPECT
CHASTISEMENT ROD TOCO TOKO
CENSURE PAYMENT FLOGGING
(DIVINE —) WRATH
CHASTITY HONOR PURITY VIRTUE
HONESTY MODESTY CELIBACY
GOODNESS PUDICITY INNOCENCE
CHASUBLE CASULA DEACON INFULA
PLANET PAENULA PIANETA
VESTMENT
CHAT GAS JAW MAG BIRD CHIN
CONE COZE DISH GIST TALK TELL
TOVE TWIG YARN AMENT CAUSE
COOSE CRACK DALLY PITCH POINT
PRATE PROSE PROSS SPEAK SPIKE
VISIT BABBLE BRANCH CATKIN
CONFAB COURSE DEVICE GABBLE
GIBBER GOSSIP GOSTER HOBNOB
JABBER NATTER POTATO POTTER
SAMARA CHAFFER CHATTER
CAUSERIE CHATTERY CONVERSE
SPIKELET STROBILE
CHATEAU HOUSE TOWER CASTLE
MANSION SCHLOSS CHATELET
FORTRESS
CHATON BASIL BEZEL BEZIL STONE
COATING SETTING
CHATTEL CATTLE PLEDGE FIXTURE
CATALLUM PERSONAL

(DISTRAINT OF —S) NAAM
(PL.) STUFF FARLEU FARLEY
COMODATO HOUSEHOLD
CHATTER GAB JAW MAG YAP BLAB
CARP CHAT CHIN CLAP CLAT DISH
GASH HACK KNAP RICK TALK TEAR
YIRR CABAL CLACK GARRE HAVER
PRATE SHAKE BABBLE BRUDGE
CACKLE CLAVER GABBLE GIBBER
GOSSIP JABBER JANGLE JARGON
PALTER RATTLE SHIVER TATTER
TATTLE TINKLE YAMMER YATTER
BLABBER BRABBLE CHACKLE
CHAFFER CHIPPER CHITTER
CLACKET CLATTER CLITTER
NASHGOB PALAVER PRABBLE
PRATING PRATTLE SHATTER
SMATTER TRATTLE TWATTLE
TWITTER TWITTLE WHITTER
BABBLING LOLLYGAG SCHMOOSE
VERBIAGE
CHATTERBOX JAY MAG PIET BUCCO
CLACK CRYSTE GOSSIP MAGPIE
CHATTERER JAY CHUET CHEWET
GABBER MAGPIE RATTLE HAVERER
CHATTERING PIET BABBLY CHAVISH
POPPING TWITTER BABBLING
CHATTY CHIRRUPY GARRULOUS
CHAUFFEUR DRIVER SHOVER
TESTER
CHAUVINISM JINGOISM
CHAUVINIST JINGO JINGOIST
CHAW JAW VEX CHEW ENVY MULL
GRIND PONDER
CHAYOTE CHOCHO TALLOTE
HUISQUIL MIRLITON
CHEAP LOW BASE GAIN POOR VILE
BORAX CLOSE FLASH GAUDY
GROSS KITCH LIGHT MUCKY NASTY
PRICE SNIDE TATTY TIGHT TINNY
VALUE ABJECT BRUMMY CHEESY
COMMON CRUMBY CRUMMY LEADEN
PLENTY SHODDY SORDID STINGY
TAWDRY TRASHY UNDEAR BARGAIN
CHINTZY POPULAR TINHORN
BRUMMAGE INFERIOR PENNORTH
SIXPENNY TWOPENNY
(— **ITEM**) TWOFER
CHEAPEN DOCK STALE VILIFY
SMALLEN
CHEAP SKATE STIFF
CHEAT DO BAM BOB COG CON FOB
FOP FUB GIP GUM GYP JEW JIG NIP
TOP BEAT BILK BITE BULL BURN
CLIP COLT CRIB DISH DUFF DUPE
FAKE FIRK FLAM FLUM GECK GULL
HAVE HOAX JILT JINK JOUK KNAP
LIAR MACE MUMP NAIL NICK NOSE
POOP PULL REAM ROOK SELL SHAM
SILE SKIN SLUR SNAP SWAP SWOP
TRIM WEED WIPE BITCH BLINK
BOOTY BUNCO BUNKO COZEN
CROOK CULLY DODGE FAKER FLING
FOIST FOURB FRAUD FUDGE GLEEK
GOUGE GREEK GUILE HOCUS KNAVE
LURCH MULCT PINCH PLOAT ROGUE
SCAMP SCREW SHARP SHORT
SLANG SPOIL STICK STIFF STING
SWICK SWIKE TOUCH TRICK VERSE

WELSH WRINK BAFFLE BLANCH
BUBBLE BUCKET CHIAUS CHISEL
CHOUSE CLOYNE COGGER DADDLE
DECEIT DELUDE DERIDE DIDDLE
DOODLE DUFFER EMUNGE EUCHRE
FIDDLE FLEECE GREASE HUMBUG
HUMMER HUSTLE ILLUDE JOCKEY
NIGGLE NOBBLE NUZZLE OUTWIT
RADDLE RENEGE SHAVER SHICER
SNUDGE SUCKER TWICER ABUSION
BEGUILE CHICANE DECEIVE
DEFRAUD ESCHEAT FAITOUR
FINAGLE FINESSE FOISTER
GUDGEON JUGGLER MISLEAD
PLUNDER QUIBBLE SHARPER
SHIFTER SKELDER SLICKER
SWINDLE VERNEUK ARTIFICE
BEJUGGLE CHALDESE CHISELER
DELUSION HOODWINK IMPOSTOR
INTRIGUE OUTREACH OVERTAKE
SHAMMOCK SWINDLER
CHEATED SOLD
CHEATER BITE GULL KNAVE BILKER
TOPPER SHARPER FINAGLER
TREACHER
CHEATING HOCUS BARRAT ODLING
ABUSIVE FUBBERY MICHERY
ROGUERY CHEATERY JUGGLING
TRICKERY
CHECK BIT DAM HAP LID NAB NIP
SAY SET TAB BAIL BALK BEAT BILK
BILL CHIP CHIT COOK CRIB CURB
DAMP FACE FOIL GAGE HURT ITEM
KITE PAWL REIN SKID SNEB SNIB
SNIP SNUB STAY STEM STOP STUB
TAKE TEST TICK TURN TWIT WERE
ABORT ALLAY ANNUL BLOCK BRAKE
CATCH CHIDE CHILL CHING CHOKE
CRACK CROOK DAUNT DELAY
DETER DRAFT EMBAR FACER FAULT
GAUGE LIMIT MODER PAUSE QUELL
REPEL SNAPE SPOKE STALL STILL
STUNT TALLY TAUNT THROW TOKEN
WAVER ARAYNE ARREST ATTACK
BAFFLE BOTTLE BRIDLE CHEQUE
COUPON DAMPEN DEFEAT DETAIN
DETENT DURESS GRAVEL HAFFET
HAFFIT HINDER IMPEDE OPPOSE
OUTWIT QUENCH RABBET REBATE
REBUFF REBUKE RETURN SCOTCH
STANCH STAYER STIFLE STYMIE
TICKET VERIFY ANSTOSS AWEBAND
BACKSET BECLOUD COMMAND
CONTAIN CONTROL COUNTER
CURTAIN DRAUGHT INHIBIT
MONITOR REFRAIN REPRESS
REPROOF REPROVE REPULSE
REVERSE SETBACK SNAFFLE
STAUNCH STOPPER TRAMMEL
TROUBLE BULKHEAD ENCUMBER
HOLDBACK OBSTRUCT PULLBACK
RESTRAIN WITHHOLD
(— **ENTHUSIASM**) DISMAY
(— **GRADUALLY**) CUSHION
(— **GROWTH**) BLAST STINT STUNT
(— **IN GLASS**) SPLIT
(— **IN TIMBER**) STARSHAKE
(— **MOTION**) SPRAG
(— **OF HORSE**) SACCADE

(— **PASSER**) PAPERHANGER
(— **PROGRESS**) DEFEAT
(**FORGED** —) STIFF STUMER
(**HOLD IN** —) COMPESCE
(**RESTAURANT** —) LAWING
(**WORTHLESS** —) DUD
CHECKED CHECK BEATEN CLOSED
CAPTIVE STOPPED
CHECKER DAM DICE FRET KING
CHECK FREAK FRECK PIECE WHITE
DAMPER DRAUGHT
CHECKERBERRY JINKS DRUNKARD
TEABERRY
CHECKERBOARD TABLE DAMBROD
DAMBOARD
CHECKERED PIED VAIR DICED PLAID
CHECKY MOTLEY
CHECKERS DRAFTS CHEQUERS
DRAUGHTS
CHECKERWORK TESSEL CHECKER
TESSERA
CHECKING REST BLOCK SETBACK
EBRILLADE
CHECKMATE LICK MATE STOP
UNDO BAFFLE CORNER DEFEAT
OUTWIT STYMIE THWART SUIMATE
CHECKSTONE CHUCK
CHEDDAR CHEESE
CHEEK CHAP CHOP GALL GENA
JAMB JOLE JOWL LEER SASS WANG
WANK BUCCA CHOKE CHYAK NERVE
SAUCE SHICK CHYACK HAFFET
HAFFIT OXCHEEK AUDACITY
TEMERITY
(— **OF SPUR**) SHANK
(— **OF VISE**) CHAP
CHEEKBONE MALAR ZYGOMA
CHEEP PIP YAP YIP CHIP HINT PEEP
PULE CHIRP CREAK TWEET SQUEAK
TATTLE
CHEER OLE RAH FARE FOOD MIND
ROOT VIVA YELL BRAVO CHIRK
ELATE ERECT FEAST HEART HUZZA
JOLLY MIRTH SHOUT SPORT TIGER
WHOOP CANTLE GAIETY HOORAY
HURRAH HUZZAH REHETE SOLACE
VIANDS ACCLAIM ANIMATE APPLAUD
CHERISH COMFORT CONSOLE
ENCHEER GLADDEN HEARTEN
JOLLITY LIGHTEN REFRESH REJOICE
SUPPORT UPRAISE APPLAUSE
BRIGHTEN HILARITY INSPIRIT
RECREATE VIVACITY
(**BURST OF** —S) SALVO
(**GOOD** —) WELFARE
(**JAPANESE** —) BANZAI
(**SORRY** —) PENANCE
CHEERFUL GAY CANT GLAD GLEG
GOOD HIGH ROSY CADGY CANTY
CHIRK DOUCE HAPPY JOLLY LIGHT
MERRY PEART READY SAPPY
SUNNY VAUDY BLITHE BRIGHT
CHEERY CHIRPY CROUSE GAWSIE
GENIAL HEARTY HILARY JOCUND
LIVELY BUOYANT CHERLY CHIPPER
JOCULAR WINSOME CHEERING
CHIRRUPY EUPEPTIC FRIENDLY
GLADSOME HOMELIKE SANGUINE
SUNBEAMY SUNSHINE

CHEERFULLY GLADLY CANTILY CHEERLY JOLLILY CHEERILY GENIALLY

CHEERFULNESS JOY GLEE TAIT CHEER CHERTE GAIETY GAYETY LEVITY SPIRIT JOLLITY FESTIVAL GLADNESS HILARITY

CHEERING GLAD CORDIAL CHEERFUL CHIRPING

CHEERLESS SAD BLAE COLD DIRE DRAB GLUM GRAY BLEAK DREAR ELYNG WASTE DISMAL DREARY GLOOMY WINTRY DOLEFUL FORLORN JOYLESS SUNLESS DEJECTED DESOLATE LITHLESS

CHEER PINE CHIL

CHEERY BRIGHT GAYSOME

CHEESE OKA BLUE BRIE EDAM FETA HAND JACK TRIP APPLE BRICK COLBY CREAM DAISY DERBY GOUDA GRANA KENNO SWISS WHEEL ZIEGA ZIGER ASIAGO BARRIE BONDON BRYNZA CANTAL CASSAN DUNLOP GLARUS JUNKET MYSOST SAANEN SBRINZ TILSIT ZIEGER ANGELOT CHEDDAR CHEVRET COTTAGE FONTINA FROMAGE GJEDOST GRUYERE KEBBUCK PRIMOST PROVOLA SAPSAGO STILTON TRUCKLE AMERICAN CHESHIRE EMMENTAL LONGHORN MUENSTER PARMESAN PECORINO SLIPCOAT LEICESTER MOUSETRAP WILTSHIRE (— FANCIER) TUROPHILE (INFERIOR —) DICK (LARGE —) KEBBOC

CHEESEPARING STINGY

CHEESE VAT CHESSEL CHESSART

CHEESEWOOD BONEWOOD WHITEWOOD

CHEETAH CAT YOUSE YOUZE GUEPARD

CHEF COOK SAUCIER CUISINIER

CHEFOO YENTAI

CHELA HAND MANUS PINCER

CHELATE COMPLEX

CHELICERA FALX FANG FALCER MANDIBLE

CHEMICAL (ALSO SEE SPECIFIC HEADINGS) ACID BASE SALT ALKALI BLEACH CHEMIC DODGER SAFENER ADDITIVE ALGICIDE CATALYST DEHORNER

CHEMIN-DE-FER SHIMMY

CHEMISE SHIFT SHIRT SIMAR SMOCK CAMISA SHIMMY LINGERIE

CHEMISETTE SHAM GUIMPE TUCKER PARTLET

CHEMIST ANALYST ASSAYER CHEMICK BENCHMAN COLORIST DRUGGIST

CHENDE CHINOA

CHENFISH KINGFISH

CHENILLE SNAIL

CHEQUEEN BASKET SEQUIN ZEQUIN CECCHINE ZECCHINO

CHERAW SARA

CHEREMIS MARI

CHERISH AID HUG PET BEAR DOTE HAVE HOPE LIKE LOVE SAVE ADORE BOSOM BROOD CHEER CLING COWER ENJOY NURSE PRIZE VALUE CARESS ESTEEM FADDLE FONDLE FOSTER GRUDGE HARBOR NESTLE NUZZLE PAMPER PETTLE REVERE COMFORT EMBOSOM EMBRACE INDULGE NOURISH NURTURE PROTECT SUPPORT SUSTAIN ENSHRINE INSPIRIT PRESERVE TREASURE

CHERISHED DEAR BOSOM DANDILY AFFECTED

CHEROOT TRICHI TRICHY

CHERRY BING CHOP DUKE FUJI GEAN MERRY MOREL CORNEL MAZARD BURBANK CAPULIN CHAPMAN LAMBERT MAHALEB MARASCA MAYDUKE MORELLO OXHEART PITANGA WINDSOR AMARELLE DURACINE EGGBERRY LUKEWARD NAPOLEON ROSACEAN

CHERRY-COLORED CERISE

CHERRY PLUM MYROBALAN

CHERRY STONE PAIP

CHERT BOONE WHINSTONE

CHERUB AMOR EROS ANGEL CUPID SERAPH SPIRIT AMORINO AMORETTO CHERUBIM

CHERVIL BUN KECK ARFOIL CERFOIL COWWEED HONEWORT MILKWEED RATSBANE

CHESS CHEAT SHOGI CHECKER SKITTLES (— MOVE) ZUGZWANG

CHESSBOARD CHESS TABLE CHECKER

CHESSMAN PIN KING PIECE CHECKER CHEQUER (— SET) MEINY MEINIE (ANY — BUT PAWN) OFFICER (BISHOP —) ALFIN ALPHIN ARCHER (CASTLE —) JUEZ ROOK TOUR UDGE JUDGE LEDGE TOWER (KNIGHT —) HORSE CHEVALIER (PAWN —) PON POUNE (QUEEN —) FERS FIERS PHEARSE

CHEST ARK BOX FIX KIT PIX PYX ARCA BUST CAJA CASH CIST CYST FUND KIST SAFE SCOB AMBRY BAHUT BUIST CADDY FRONT HOARD HUTCH RAZEE SISTA TRUNK ALMOIN BASKET BREAST BUNKER BUREAU CAISSE CAJETA CASKET COFFER COFFIN FORCER GIRNAL GIRNEL HAMPER JORDAN LARNAX LOCKER SCRINE SHRINE SPRUCE STRIPE THORAX WANGAN BRAZIER BRISKET CAISSON CAPCASE CASSONE COMMODE DEPOSIT DRAWERS DRESSER ENCLOSE HIGHBOY TOOLBOX WANIGAN WINDBAG CISTVAEN CUPBOARD FORCELET MANIFOLD STANDARD TREASURE TREASURY (— FOR CUTLERY) CANTEEN (— OF ORES) CAXON (FRONT OF —) BREAST

CHESTNUT JOKE LING RATA BROWN HORSE CASTOR MARRON SATIVA CRENATA DENTATA (HORSE —) CONKER (POLYNESIAN —) RATA (WATER —) LING

CHESTNUT-COLORED BAY ROAN

CHEVAL-DE-FRISE TURNPIKE

CHEVAL GLASS PSYCHE

CHEVALIER CADET NOBLE KNIGHT GALLANT CAVALIER HORSEMAN

CHEVIN CHUB CHEVESNE

CHEVRON BEAM MARK WOUND RAFTER STRIPE ZIGZAG

CHEVROTAIN MUSK NAPU DEERLET KANCHIL MEMINNA PLANDOK TRAGULE BOOMORAH PEESOREH RUMINANT

CHEW CUD EAT GUM TAW BITE CHAM CHAW GNAW QUID CHAMP CHONK GRIND MUNCH RUMEN CRUNCH MUMBLE CHUMBLE MEDITATE RUMINATE (— UP NOISILY) CHANK GROUZE

CHEWINK FINCH JOREE TOWHEE GRASSET

CHEYENNE DOG

CHIAN SCIAN

CHIANTI FLORENCE

CHIASTOLITE MACLE ANDALUSITE

CHIBCHA MUISCA

CHIC PERT POSH TRIG TRIM KIPPY NATTY NIFTY SMART CHICHI DAPPER GIGOLO MODISH ELEGANT STYLISH

CHICAGO PORKOPOLIS

CHICANE DECEPTION

CHICANERY DIRT RUSE WILE FEINT TRICK ARTIFICE INTRIGUE TRICKERY DECEPTION

CHICK BIRD GIRL PEEP TICK CHILD NATTY POULET SCREEN SEQUIN SPROUT CHICKEN CHUCKIE

CHICKADEE BLACKCAP TITMOUSE

CHICKEN HEN KIP COCK FOWL BIDDY CAPON CHICK CHILD CHOOK CHUCK DEEDY FRYER LAYER MANOC POULT SILKY CHICKY PULLET SULTAN SUSSEX TURKEN ANCOBAR BOARDER BROILER DIBBLER POUSSIN ROASTER ROOSTER SCRATCH ARAUCANA COCKEREL PHASANID SPRINGER (— SHELTER) MOTHER

CHICKEN COOP CAVY CAVIE

CHICKEN POX SOREHEAD VARICELLA

CHICK-PEA CHIT GRAM CHICH CICER COWGRAM SOWGRAM GARBANZO GARVANCE (PL.) FASELS

CHICKWEED BLINK BLINKS SPURRY ALLBONE STARWORT

CHICO SAPODILLA

CHICORY BUNK CREPIS ENDIVE SUCCORY WITLOOF BLUEWEED COMPOSIT

CHIDE FUSS RAIL RATE BLAME CHECK FLITE FLYTE SCOLD SNEAP

BERATE REBUFF REBUKE SCHOOL THREAP THREAT THREEP TONGUE CENSURE REPROVE UPBRAID WRANGLE ADMONISH LAMBASTE REPROACH

CHIEF (ALSO SEE CHIEFTAIN) BO AGA BIG BOH CAP CID COB DUX MIR MOI TOP AGHA ALII ARCH ARII BOSS CAID CHEF COCK DATO DEAN DOEG DUCE DUKE HEAD HIER HIGH INCA JARL JEFE KAID KHAN KING MAIN MICO MOST NAIK ONLY QAID RAIS RAJA REIS TYEE ALDER ALPHA ARIKI DATTO ELDER FIRST GREAT MAJOR MATAI NAYAK PRIMA PRIME PRIMO RAJAH RULER THANE TITAN VITAL ZAQUE ZIPPA ADALID CABEZA DEPUTY FLAITH HEADLY INKOSI KEHAYA KUBERA KUVERA LEADER LULUAI MASTER MIRDHA NAIQUE PENLOP PRABHU PRIMAL RECTOR SACHEM SAYYID SHAYKH SHEIKH SHERIF STAPLE SUDDER TOPMAN TURNUS CAPITAL CAPTAIN CENTRAL EMINENT FOREMAN GENERAL HEADMAN INGOMAR LEADING LEMPIRA MUGWUMP OVERMAN PADRONE PALMARY POLYGAR PRELATE PREMIER PRIMARY SHEREEF STELLAR SUPREME TOPSMAN TRIBUNE CABOCEER CAPITANO CARDINAL DECURION DIRECTOR DOMINANT ELDORADO ESPECIAL FOREMOST GOVERNOR HEADSMAN HIERARCH INTIMATE MOKADDAM SAGAMORE SUBCHIEF (— **IN INDIA**) PRABHU SIRDAR (— **OF 10 MEN**) DEAN (— **OF ADVOCATES**) BATONNIER (— **OF RELIGIOUS ORDER**) GENERAL (**CHINOOK** —) TYEE (**CLAN** —) TOISECH (**INDIAN** —) SUNCK SACHEM SUNCKE CACIQUE SAGAMORE (**MOHAMMEDAN** —) DATO DATTO SAYID SAYYID (**SCHOOL** —) DUX (**TIBETAN** —) POMBO (**TURKISH** —) AGA AGHA

CHIEFTAIN BEG CHAM EMIR HEAD JARL KHAN ASTUR CHIEF EMEER LEADER SIRDAR CAUDILLO HIAWATHA

CHIEFTAINCY STOOL CHIEFRY

CHIEFTAINESS QUEEN

CHIFFCHAFF PEGGY CHIPCHAP CHIPCHOP

CHIFFON SHEER

CHIFFONIER BUREAU CABINET COMMODE

CHIGGER BICHO PIQUE CHIGGA CHIGOE GIGGER JIGGER LEPTUS WHEELWORM

CHIGNON COB KNOT COBBE TWIST

CHIGOE SIKA BICHO NIGUA PIQUE SCREW CHIGGA ENIGUA JIGGER SANDBOY SANDWORM

CHIH FU PREFECT

CHILBLAIN KIBE MULE BLAIN MOOLS

MOULS PERNIO

CHILD BEN BOY BUD ELF GET IMP KID LAD SON SOT TAD TOT WAY BABA BABE BABY BATA BIRD BRAT CHIT CION FOOD GIRL GYTE PAGE PUSS TIKE TINY TOTO TROT TYKE WEAN BAIRN BIRTH BROLL BROWL CHICK CHIEL COOKY ELFIN GAMIN ISSUE KEIKI OLIVE POULT SCION TIDDY TRICK WAYNE WENCH WHELP CHERUB COOKIE ENFANT FILIUS FOSTER INFANT MOPPET NIPPER PLEDGE PROLES STUMPY TACKER TODDLE URCHIN BAMBINO CHOOKIE CHOPPER CHRISOM COCKNEY DICKENS GANGREL GYTLING KINCHIN KITLING LAMBKIN PAPOOSE PROGENY STICHEL SUBTEEN TIDDLER TODDLER TROTTIE WRAWLER YOUNKER BANTLING CHISELER DAUGHTER EPIGONUS JUVENILE LITTLING NURSLING PRATTLER RUNABOUT WEANLING WHIMLING (— **OF THE WORLD**) WELTKIND (— **UNDER 7 YEARS**) INFANS (**BAD-MANNERED** —) GOOP (**CHUBBY** —) CHUNK (**ELF'S** —) OAF CHANGELING (**FOSTER** —) DAULT NORRY NURRY FOSTER REARLING (**ILLEGITIMATE** —) MISHAP BASTARD (**INNOCENT** —) CHRISOM (**LAST-BORN** —) DILLING (**LOVED** —) JOY (**MERRY** —) SUNBEAM (**MISCHIEVOUS** —) IMP LIMB TIKE DICKENS (**NAKED** —) SCUDDY (**NEWBORN** —) STRANGER (**PAUPER** —) MINDER (**PLAYFUL** —) ELF WANTON (**PLUMP** —) FOB FUB (**PRECOCIOUS** —) PRODIGY (**PURE** —) DOVE (**ROWDY** —) HOODLUM (**SMALL** —) TAD TOT SPUD GAITT KIDDY TIDDY TOTUM KIDLET PEEWEE TACKER BAIRNIE (**SPOILED** —) CADE COCKNEY (**STUNTED** —) URF (**TROUBLESOME** —) STICHEL (**UNMANNERLY** —) SMATCHET (**YOUNG** —) BABY JOEY INFANT SQUIRT GANGREL NESTLER TODDLER BANTLING INNOCENT LITTLING SUCKLING (**YOUNGEST** —) WRIG DILLING

CHILDBED JIZZEN

CHILDBIRTH LABOR CRYING INLYING TRAVAIL OXYTOCIA (— **WOMAN**) PUERPERA

CHILDHOOD INFANCY CHILDAGE (**2ND** —) DOTAGE TWICHILD

CHILDISH TID WEAK DANSY NAIVE PETTY SILLY YOUNG CHITTY PULING SIMPLE WEANLY ASININE BABYISH CHILDLY FOOLISH KIDDISH PEEVISH PROGENY PUERILE UNMANLY

BAIRNISH BRATTISH IMMATURE TOOTLING

CHILDLESS ORBATE

CHILDREN ISSUE PROLES STRAIN PROGENY OFFSPRING (**NUMBER OF** —) PARITY

CHILE

BAY: COOK EYRE NENA TARN LOMAS OTWAY SARCO DARWIN INUTIL MORENO STOKES TONGOY DYNELEY INGLESA SKYRING DESOLATE
CAPE: DYER HORN CHOROS HORNOS QUILAN TABLAS DESEADO BASCUNAN CARRANZA
CAPITAL: SANTIAGO
CHANNEL: ANCHO CHEAP BEAGLE COCKBURN MORALEDA
COIN: PESO LIBRA CONDOR ESCUDO
DESERT: ATACAMA
GULF: ANCUD GUAFO PENAS ARAUCO
INDIAN: ONA AUCA INCA ONAN ARAUCA CHANGO YAHGAN MAPUCHE MOLUCHE PAMPEAN PATAGON PUEGIAN RANQUEL ALIKULUF PICUNCHE TSONECAN
ISLAND: LUZ PRAT BYRON GUAFO HOSTE MOCHA NUEVA NUNEZ VIDAL CHILOE DAWSON EASTER LENNOX PIAZZI PICTON QUILAN RIESCO STOSCH TALCAN ANGAMOS CAMPANA HANOVER REFUGIO TRANQUI CLARENCE HUAMBLIN NALCAYEC NAVARINO TRAIGUEN
ISLANDS: CHONOS HERMITE PAJAROS CHAUQUES
ISTHMUS: OFQUI
LAKE: TORO RANCO YELCHO PUYEHUE RUPANCO
MEASURE: VARA LEGUA LINEA CUADRA FANEGA
MOUNTAIN: MACA TORO CHATO MAIPO PAINE POTRO PULAR TORRE YOGAN APIWAN BURNEY CONICO JERVIS POQUIS RINCON CHALTEL COPIAPO FITZROY PALPANA VELLUDA COCHRANE TRONADOR YANTELES
MOUNTAINS: ANDES DARWIN ALMEIDA DOMEYKO
NATIVE: PATAGONIAN
PENINSULA: HARDY LACUY TAITAO TUMBES
POINT: TORO GALLO LILES LOBOS LOROS MORRO TALCA TETAS VIEJA CACHOS GALERA MOLLES ANGAMOS LAVAPIE
PORT: LOTA TOME ARICA COQUIMBA
PROVINCE: AISEN ARICA AYSEN MAULE NUBLE TALCA ARAUCO BIOBIO CAUTIN CHILOE CURICO OSORNO ATACAMA LINARES MALLECO COQUIMBO OHIGGINS

SANTIAGO TARAPACA VALDIVIA
RIVER: LOA LAJA YALI ALHUE
AZAPA BRAVO BUENO ELQUI
ITATA LAUCA LLUTA MAIPO
MAULE PUELO RAHUE RAPEL
VITOR BIOBIO CAMINA CHOAPA
CHOROS CISNES COLINA
HUASCO LIMARI MORADO
PALENA POSCUA TOLTEN
COPIAPO VALDIVIA
SHRUB: LITRE
STRAIT: NELSON MAGELLAN
TOWN: BOCO CUYA LEBU LOTA
OCOA TOCO TOME ARICA TALCA
ARAUCO CURICO GATICO
OSORNO SERENA TEMUCO
VICUNA YUMBEL YUNGAY
CALDERA CHILLAN COPIAPO
COQUIMBO RANCAGUA
SANTIAGO VALDIVIA
TREE: RAULI
VOLCANO: LANIN MAIPO ANTUCO
LLAIMA OYAHUE TACORA
PETEROA SOCOMAP
WEIGHT: GRANO LIBRA QUINTAL
WIND: SURES

CHILE-BELLS COPIHUE LAPAGERIA
CHI-LIN KYLIN UNICORN
CHILL ICE RAW AGUE COLD COOL
DAZY ALGID ALGOR DAVER GELID
RIGOR SCHEL SHAKE FRAPPE
FREEZE FRIGID FROSTY SHIVER
SNELLY DEPRESS FRETISH FRISSON
MALARIA COLDNESS
CHILLED ACOLD CHILL FROZEN
STARVEN
CHILLING ICY COLD EERY BLEAK
EERIE CHILLY WINTRY GLACIAL
SHIVERY
CHILLY RAW COLD COOL LASH
ALGID BLEAK HUNCH AGUISH AIRISH
ARCTIC CRIMMY FROSTY FROZEN
LEEPIT
CHIMAERA BELUE DRAGON CATFISH
PLACOID RATFISH RATTAIL
DOODSKOP
CHIME DIN RIM BELL EDGE PEAL
RING SUIT TING AGREE CHIMB
CHINE PRATE ACCORD CLOCHE
CYMBAL JINGLE MELODY CONCORD
HARMONY SINGSONG
(PL.) BELL
CHIMER CYMAR SIMAR CHIMAR
TABARD
CHIMERA FANCY MIRAGE MOSAIC
POMATO ILLUSION
CHIMERICAL VAIN WILD INSANE
UTOPIAN DELUSIVE FANCIFUL
ROMANTIC IMAGINARY
CHIMNEY BAG LUM TUN FLUE LUMM
PIPE TUBE VENT GULLY STACK
TEWEL CHIMLA FUNNEL LOUVER
SMOKER TUNNEL FISSURE OPENING
ORIFICE FUMIDUCT
CHIMNEY CAP TURNCAP
CHIMNEY CORNER FIRESIDE
INGLENOOK

CHIMNEY COWL COW
CHIMNEY HOOD JACK
CHIMNEY PIECE PAREL
CHIMNEY PIPE TALLBOY
CHIMNEY POST SPEER
CHIMNEY SEAT SCONCE
CHIMNEY SWEEP SWEEP CHUMMY
FLUEMAN RAMONEUR
CHIMPANZEE APE CHIMP JACKO
JOCKO PIGMY PYGMY NCHEGA
PIGMEW PYGMEAN
CHIN JAW CHAT TSIN MENTUM
CHOLLER
(— POINT) MENTON POGONION
(DOUBLE —) BUCCULA CHOLLER
CHINA WARE JAPAN LENOX SPODE
CATHAY PARIAN SEVRES CERAMIC
CHEENEY DRESDEN LIMOGES
MEISSEN POTTERY CINCHONA
CROCKERY EGGSHELL

CHINA

ABORIGINE: YAO MANS MIAO
MANTZU YAOMIN MIAOTSE
AREA UNIT: MU MOU MOW
BAY: LAICHOW HANGCHOW
BUDDHA: FO
CAPE: OLWANPI
CAPITAL: PEKING TAIPEI PEIPING
CHANNEL: BASHI
COIN: PU CASH CENT MACE TAEL
TIAO YUAN SYCEE DOLLAR
DEPRESSION: TURFAN
DESERT: GOBI ORDOS SHAMO
ALASHAN TAKLAMAKAN
DIALECT: WU MIN AMOY HAKKA
CANTON HSIANG SWATOW
FOOCHOW WENCHOW
KANHAKKA MANDARIN
DRY LAKE: LOPNOR
DYNASTY: WU HAN SHU SUI WEI
YIN CHIN CHOU HSIA HSIN MING
SUNG TANG YUAN CHING
SHANG
GULF: POHAI CHIHLI TONKIN
PECHILI LIAOTUNG
ISLAND: AMOY FLAT MACAO
MATSU NAMKI CHUSAN HAINAN
PRATAS QUEMOY TAIWAN
YUHWAN FORMOSA HUNGTOW
TUNGSHA CHOUCHAN
KULANGSU STAUNTON
ISLANDS: PENGHU TACHEN
CHUSHAN MIAOTAO
LAKE: TAI CHAO KAOYU OLING
TELLI BAMTSO BORNOR EBINOR
ERHHAI KHANKA LOPNOR
NAMTSO POYANG CHALING
HUNGTSE KARANOR KOKONOR
HULUNNOR MONTCALM
TAROKTSO TELLINOR TIENCHIH
TSINGHAI TUNGTING
MEASURE: HO HU KO LI MU PU TO
TU FAN FEN PAU TOU TUN YIN
CHIH FANG KISH PARA QUEI
SHIH TSUN CHANG CHING
SHENG SHING CHUPAK KUNGHO
KUNGLI KUNGMU KUNGFEN

KUNGYIN KUNGCHIH
MOUNTAIN: OMI OMEI SUNG
KAILAS POBEDA EVEREST
MUZTABH SUNGSHAN
MOUNTAINS: ALTAY KUNLUN
ALASHAN KUENLUN MEILING
MINSHAN NANLING NANSHAN
TANGLHA BOGDOULA HIMALAYA
TAPASHAN TAYULING TIENSHAN
WUYLISHAN
NAME: CATHAY
NATIVE: PAT
PENINSULA: LEICHU LUICHOW
LIAOTUNG
PORT: AMOY WUHU AIGUN SHASI
ANTUNG CANTON CHEFOO
DAIREN ICHANG NINGPO PAKHOI
SWATOW SZEMAO WUCHOW
YOCHOW FOOCHOW HUNCHUN
MENGTSZ NANKING SAMSHUI
SANTUAO SOOCHOW WENCHOW
CHANGSHA HANGCHOW
KIUKIANG KONGMOON
LUNGCHOW SHANGHAI
TENGYUEH TIENTSIN TSINGTAO
WANHSIEN
PROVINCE: HONAN HOPEI HUNAN
HUPEI HUPEN JEHOL KANSU
KIRIN TIBET ANHWEI FUKIEN
SHANSI SHENSI TAIWAN YUNNAN
KIANGSI KWANGSI NGANHUI
CHEKIANG KWEICHOW LIAONING
MONGOLIA SHANTUNG
SZECHWAN TSINGHAI
MANCHURIA
RELIGION: JU SHINTO TAOISM
BUDDHISM
RESERVOIR: SUNGARI
RIVER: SI HAN ILI MIN NEN PEI
WEI AMUR HUAI LOHO TUNG
YALU YUAN YUEN ARGUN
FENHO MACHU PEIHO TARIM
TUMEN WEIHO CHUMAR DRECHU
DZACHU KHOTAN KUMARA
LIAOHO MANASS MEKONG
OCHINA URUNGU YELLOW
HOANGHO HWANGHO KERULEN
KIALING SALWEEN SIKIANG
SUNGARI TSANGPO WUKIANG
YANGTZE YARKAND YUKIANG
CHERCHEN HANKIANG
HUNGSHUI MINKIANG
RULER: WANG
SEA: ECHINA SCHINA YELLOW
STRAIT: HAINAN TAIWAN
FORMOSA
TOWN: BAI NOH AHPA AMOY ANSI
ANTA AQSU FUYU GUMA HAMI
HUMA IPIN KIAN KISI LINI LOHO
LUTA MOHO MOYU MULI NIYA
NOHO NURA OMIN OWPU RIMA
SAKA SIAN TALI TAYU WUHU
WUSU WUTU YAAN CHIAI FUSIN
HOFEI ICHUN JEHOL KIRIN
KOKLU LHASA MACAO PENKI
SHASI TAIAN TALAI TUTZE
TUYUN TZEPO WUHAN WUSIH

YENKI YULIN YUMEN ANSHAN
ANTUNG CANTON DAIREN
FUCHAU FUSHUN HANKOW
HANTAN HARBIN HOIHOW
KALGAN LOYANG LUSHUN
MUKDEN NINGPO PAOTOW
PEKING PENGPU SUCHOW
SWATOW TAINAN TAIPEI TALIEN
TSINAN YUNNAN CHUNGTU
FATSHAN FOOCHOW HANYANG
HUHEHOT KAIFENG KUNMING
KWEISUI LANCHOW NANKING
PAOTING PEIPING SOOCHOW
TAIYUAN TZEKUNG URUMCHI
WUCHANG YENPING CHANGSHA
CHAOCHOW CHENGTEH
CHINCHOW HANGCHOW
KIAOCHOW KWEIYANG
NANCHANG QARAQASH
SHANGHAI SHENYANG SIANGTAN
TANGSHAN TENGCHOW TIENTSIN
TSINGTAO TUNGCHOW
CHUNGKING
WEIGHT: LI TA FAN FEN HAO KIN
SSU TAN YIN CHEE CHIN DONG
MACE SHIH TAEL CATTY CHIEN
LIANG PICUL TCHIN HAIKWAN
KUNGFEN KUNGSSU KUNGCHIN

CHINABERRY LILAC AZEDARACH
CHINABALL SOAPBERRY
CHINA BLUE NIKKO
CHINA HAT HAELTZUK HEILTSUK
CHINAMAN CHOW JOHN JOHNNY
(PL.) TANKA
CHINA ROSE MANETTI HIBISCUS
CHINA STONE PETUNSE
CHINA TREE LILAC HAGBUSH
CHINCHILLA ABROCOME VIZCACHA
CHINE BACK IKAT CHINK CRACK
CREST GORGE RIDGE SPINE CLEAVE
RAVINE SPROUT CREVICE
CHINESE PAT BABA CHOW CERAI
CHINK SERES SERIC SINIC MANZAS
MONGOL ASIATIC CATAIAN CHINOIS
PIGTAIL SANGLEY
CHINESE ARTICHOKE CROSNE
CHOROGI CROSNES STACHYS
KNOTROOT
CHINESE CABBAGE PECHAY
PAKCHOI
CHINESE DATE JUJUBE
CHING TSING
CHINGPAW KACHIN SINGPHO
YAWYINS
CHINIOFON YATREN
CHINK GAP BORE CASH CHAP COIN
JINK KINK RENT RIFT RIME SCAR
BOORE CHECK CHINE CHUNK CLEFT
CRACK GRIKE KNACK MONEY
CRANNY SPRAIN CHINKLE CREVICE
FISSURE APERTURE
CHINPIECE BARBEL
CHINQUAPIN OAK BONNET
BONNETS CANDOCK CHESTNUT
WANKAPIN YOCKERNUT
CHINTZ PINTADO SALAMPORE
CHIONE (FATHER OF —) BOREAS

(HUSBAND OF —) NEPTUNE
(MOTHER OF —) ORITHYIA
DAEDALION
(SLAYER OF —) DIANA
(SON —) EUMOLPUS AUTOLYCUS
PHILAMMON
CHIOT SCIOT
CHIP BIT CUT DIB GAG HEW NIG
BONE CHAP CLIP HACK KNAP KNOP
NICK PARE SAND SKIN SNIP SNUB
BEACH CHECK CRACK FLAKE PIECE
SCRAP SKELF SLICE SPALE SPALL
SPALT SPAWL SPELL SPOON WASTE
BORING CHISEL GALLET MARKER
NOODLE COUNTER SHAVING
CHIPPING COSSETTE FRAGMENT
SPLINTER WHITLING
(— OF SOLDER) LINK
(— OF WOOD) SPOON
(— OUT) DESEAM
(BUFFALO —S) BODEWASH
(CORN —S) FRITOS
(POTATO —) CRISP
(SUPPLY OF —S) STACK
CHIPMAN SCRAPMAN
CHIPMUNK CHIPPY GOPHER GRINNY
HACKEE GRINNIE SQUIRREL
CHIPPENDALE AFGHAN
CHIPPER GAY SPRY CHIRP PERKY
BABBLE COCKEY FIERCE HACKER
KIPPER LIVELY CHATTER CHEERFUL
CHIRRUP TWITTER
CHIPPINGS SWARF
CHIRO BONYFISH FRANCESCA
CHIROGRAPHY WRITING
CHIRON (— AS CONSTELLATION)
SAGITTARIUS
(FATHER OF —) SATURN
(MOTHER OF —) PHILYRA
CHIROPODIST PEDICURE
CORNCUTTER
CHIRP PEW PIP PEEK PEEP PIPE
TWIT WEAK CHEEP CHELP CHIRK
CHIRL CHIRM CHIRT TWEET TWINK
CHIPPER CHIRRUP CHITTER REJOICE
SHATTER TWEEDLE TWITTER
WHEETLE WHITTER
CHIRR PITTER
CHIRU SUS
CHISEL BUR CUT GAD CHIP ETCH
FORM MOIL PARE SEAT SETT TANG
TOOL BRUZZ BURIN CARVE CHEAT
DROVE GOUGE HARDY POINT
SCOOP SLICK STIFF BROACH
CHESIL FIRMER FORMER GRAVEL
HAGGLE POMMEL QUARRY REAMER
TOOLER BARGAIN BOASTER
CHIPPER ENGRAVE GRADINE
GRUBBER POINTER QUARREL
SCOOPER SCORPER SHINGLE
CROSSCUT SPLITTER
(BLACKSMITH'S —) HARDY HARDIE
(FLINT —) TRANCHET
(ICE —) SPUD
(JEWELER'S —) SCAUPER SCORPER
(PREHISTORIC —) CELT
(STONEMASON'S —) TOOL DROVE
POMMEL TOOLER SPLITTER
(TOOTHED —) GRADINE

(TRIANGULAR —) BUR BURR
(WHEELWRIGHT'S —) BRUZZ
CHISELER CHEAT CROOK COYOTE
GOUGER
CHIT DAB BILL NOTE DRAFT LETTER
VOUCHER
CHITARRONE ARCHLUTE
CHITCHAT GASH GUFF TALK
BANTER GOSSIP GOSSIPRY
BAVARDAGE
CHITINOUS SHELLY
CHITON EXOMIS DIPLOIS EXOMION
CHITTAMWOOD IRONWOOD
CHIVALROUS BRAVE CIVIL NOBLE
PREUX GENTLE POLITE GALLANT
GENTEEL VALIANT WARLIKE
KNIGHTLY
CHIVE CIVE SIVE CIVET SITHE
ALLIUM
CHIVY RUN VEX BAIT HUNT RACE
CHASE CHEVY TEASE BADGER
CHIVVY FLIGHT HARASS PURSUE
PURSUIT SCAMPER TORMENT
MANEUVER
CHLOASMA MOTH
CHLOR LEMON
CHLORIDE BUTTER CALOMEL
MURIATE ALEMBROTH
CHLORINE OXYGEN
CHLORION SPHEX
CHLORIS (FATHER OF —) AMPHION
(HUSBAND OF —) NELEUS
(MOTHER OF —) NIOBE
(SON OF —) NESTOR
CHLORITE AMESITE
CHOANA COLLAR
CHOBDAR USHER CHOPDAR
CHOCK COG PAD BLOCK BRACE
CHUCK CLEAT SPOKE SPRAG
WEDGE SCOTCH
(PL.) STOWWOOD
CHOCOLATE BUD CANDY COCOA
NORFOLK JACOLATT
CHOGAK SHOQ
CHOICE BET ODD TRY BEST FINE
FORE GOOD MIND PICK RARE WALE
WEAL WILL CREAM ELITE PRIME
VOICE CHOSEN DAINTY DESIRE
FLOWER OPTION PICKED PLUMMY
SELECT DILEMMA ELEGANT
EXCERPT PERMISS DELICATE
ELECTION EXIMIOUS UNCOMMON
VOLITION
(FAVORITE —) STANDBY
(FREE —) SWING DRUTHERS
CHOIR KERE QUIRE CHAPEL CHORUS
CHORALE CONCERT KAPELLE
PSALMODY
CHOIRBOY CLERGEON CHORISTER
CHOIR LEADER CANTOR CHORAGUS
CHORISTER PRECENTOR
CHOKE DAM GAG GOB CLOG DAMP
PLUG QUAR STOP WARP CHECK
CHOCK CLOSE GRAIN GRANE
SCRAG WORRY HINDER IMPEDE
STIFLE SWARVE CONGEST QUACKLE
QUEAZEN QUERKEN REPRESS
SILENCE SMOLDER SMOTHER
OBSTRUCT QUEASOME SCUMFISH

STOPPAGE STRANGLE SUPPRESS THROTTLE
(— OFF) BESET
(— UP) CLOY GORGE STUFF
CHOKEBERRY DOGBERRY SOAPBERRY
CHOKED FOUL WOOLY WOOLLY CLOTTED
CHOKEDAMP STYTHE BLACKDAMP
CHOKERMAN CHAINER CHAINMAN
CHOKWE KIOKO
CHOLER IRE BILE FURY RAGE ANGER WRATH SPLEEN TEMPER DISTEMPER
CHOLERIC MAD ANGRY CROSS FIERY HUFFY TESTY FUMISH IREFUL TOUCHY BILIOUS ENRAGED IRACUND PEEVISH PEPPERY WASPISH WRATHFUL IMPATIENT
CHOLIAMB SCAZON
CHONDRIOME CYTOME
CHOOSE OPT TRY CHAP CULL LIKE LIST LOVE LUST PICK TAKE VOTE WALE WEAL ADOPT ELECT PRICK ANOINT DECIDE PLEASE PREFER SELECT EMBRACE ESPOUSE EXTRACT SEPARATE
CHOOSY CHOICY FINICAL
CHOP AX AXE CUT HAG HEW JAW LOP CHAP CHIP DICE GASH HACK HASH HOWL RIVE SLIT CARVE CLEFT CRACK KNOCK MINCE NOTCH SLASH STAMP TRADE TRUCK WHANG BARTER CHANGE CLEAVE INCISE EXCHANGE
(— OFF) SNIG
(— SMALL) DEVIL MINCE
(— UP) HACKLE
(— WITH DULL AX) BUTTE
(PORK —) GRISKIN
CHOPINE CIOPPINO PANTOFLE
CHOPPED CUT CHAPPED
CHOPPER MINCER SLASHER TRANCHET
CHOPPINESS CHOP JABBLE
CHOPPING BLOCK HACKLOG
CHOPPING TOOL (— CULTURE) SOAN SOHAN
CHOPPY BUMPY LOPPY LUMPY PECKY ROUGH SHORT POPPLY
CHORAL (— SOCIETY) ORPHEON
CHORD CORD DYAD ROLL TONE CORDE NERVE TRIAD TRINE ACCORD STRING TENDON TETRAD CADENCE CONCORD HARMONY ARPEGGIO DIAMETER FILAMENT
CHORDATA VERTEBRA
CHORE JOB JOT CHAR DUTY TASK CHARE KNACK STINT ERRAND BUSINESS
CHOREA JUMP JERKS
CHOREOGRAPHY TERPSICHORE
CHORION SEROSA
CHORISTER SINGER CHANTER CHOIRBOY
CHORUS SONG CHOIR DRONE QUIRE ACCORD ASSENT BURDEN UNISON CHORALE HOLDING REFRAIN RESPONSE THYMELICI

(— IN PLAY) GREX
CHOSEN ELECT ELITE SORTED ELECTED FANCIED AFFECTED SELECTED
CHOUGH COW CHANK CHEWET CORBIE CHOCARD
CHOWRY COWTAIL
CHRISM CREAM CREME MURON MYRON
CHRIST X KING LORD TRUE JUDGE RANSOM VERITY MESSIAH SAVIOUR DRIGHTEN PARAMOUR
(INFANT —) BAMBINO
CHRISTEN NAME KIRSEN BAPTIZE
CHRISTENING GOSSIPING
CHRISTIAN XN XT XTIAN UNIATE GENTILE THOMEAN CHRISTEN GALILEAN MELCHITE NAZARENE ORIENTAL STONEITE TRADITOR COLOSSIAN
(JEWISH —) JUDAIZER
(PL.) FLOCK LAPSED ACEPHALI FAITHFUL
CHRISTIANIA CRISTY
CHRISTIANITY WAY XTY XNTY
CHRISTMAS NOEL YULE HOLIDAY NATIVITY YULETIDE MIDWINTER
CHRISTMAS ROSE BEARFOOT LUNGWORT MELAMPOD PEDELION
CHRIST'S-THORN NABK JUJUBE ZIZYPHUS
CHROMA COLOR QUALITY
CHROMATIC HUEFUL FLAMING SEMITONAL
CHROMATOPHORE ALLOPHORE LIPOPHORE UNIVALENT
CHROMOSOME DIAD DYAD HOMOLOG ALLOSOME AUTOSOME IDIOSOME KARYOMERE LEPTONEMA PLANOSOME
(PL.) GEMINI
CHROMOSPHERE SIERRA
CHRONIC FIXED SEVERE INTENSE CONSTANT STUBBORN
CHRONICLE BRUT ANNAL DIARY ENACT RECORD ACCOUNT HISTORY RECITAL CORNICLE REGISTER
(PL.) ANNALS ARCHIVE
CHRONICLER WRITER CHRONIST COMPILER RECORDER HISTORIAN
CHRONOLOGICAL TEMPORAL
CHRONOMETER DIAL HACK CLOCK TIMER WATCH
CHRYSAL FRET
CHRYSALIS KELL PUPA AURELIA
CHRYSANTHEMUM MUM KIKU SPOON BRUTUS POMPON KIKUMON KIRIMON AZALEAMUM
CHRYSIN FLAVONE
CHRYSOBERYL CATEYE CHRYSOPAL CYMOPHANE
CHRYSOLITE OLIVINE PERIDOT CHRYSOPAL
CHTHONIAN INFERNAL
CHUB DACE DOLT FOOL KIYI LOUT POLL CHOPA CHEVIN SHINER CYPRINID FALLFISH MACKEREL HORNYHEAD
CHUBBY FAT CHUFF FUBSY PLUMP

CHOATY CHUFFY PLUMPY ROTUND ROLYPOLY
CHUB MACKEREL TINK TINKER HARDHEAD SCOMBRID
CHUCK HEN LOG PIG CHUG GRUB HURL JERK LUMP TOSS CHOCK CLUCK PITCH THROW BOUNCE CHUCKY COLLET CHUCKLE DISCARD
CHUCK-A-LUCK SWEAT HAZARD BIRDCAGE
CHUCKER CROZER
CHUCK-FARTHING CHUCK KNICKER
CHUCKHOLE CAHOT CHUGHOLE
CHUCKLE CHUCK CLUCK EXULT LAUGH GIGGLE GIZZEN KECKLE SMUDGE TITTER CHORTLE
CHUD VEPS VEPSE
CHUDDAR PHULKARI
CHUFA SEDGE GLUMAL CYPRESS EARTHNUT GALANGAL TIGERNUT GROUNDNUT
CHUM CAD PAL BAIT MATE PARD TOLE TOLL BUDDY BUTTY CRONY AIKANE CHUMMY COBBER COPAIN FRIEND PARDNER ROOMMATE
(— AROUND) HOBNOB
CHUMMY GREAT PALLY FAMILIAR
CHUMP ASS DOLT HEAD BLOCK PUMPKIN ENDPIECE
CHUNCHO CHAMA
CHUNK DAB DAD FID GOB PAT WAD JUNK JUNT SLUG CHOCK CHUCK CLAUT PIECE THROW WHANG WHANK DORNICK KNUCKLE LUNCHEON
CHUNKY LUMPY PLUMP SQUAT STOUT THICK TRUSS BLOCKY CHUBBY STOCKY CHUNKED
CHURCH DOM SEE DOME FANE FOLD HIGH KILL KIRK KURK TERA ABBEY AUTEM FAITH FLOCK KOVIL SAMAJ TITLE CHAPEL CHARGE HIERON SPOUSE TEMPLE EDIFICE FANACLE IGLESIA LATERAN MEMORIA MINSTER RECTORY STATION TEMPLET BASILICA EBENEZER ECCLESIA PECULIAR
(— BOOK) TRIODION
(CHRISTIAN —) BODY ISRAEL HERITAGE
CHURCHMAN KIRKMAN
(HIGH —) PUSEYIST PRELATIST
(LOW —) SIM LOWBOY SIMEONITE
CHURCH SERVICE HEARING TENEBRAE
CHURCHWARDEN STRAW WARDEN WARNER
CHURCHYARD HAW LITTEN CEMETERY KIRKYARD
CHURL CAD MAN BOOR CARL GNOF HIND LOUT SERF CARLE CEORL CHUFF GNOFF KNAVE MISER BODACH CARLOT HARLOT LUBBER RUSTIC VASSAL YEOMAN BONDMAN FREEMAN HASKARD HUSBAND NIGGARD PEASANT VILLAIN VILLEIN
CHURLISH MEAN BLUFF GRUFF ROUGH RUNTY SURLY URSAL CRABBY RUSTIC SORDID SULLEN

VULGAR BOORISH CARLAGE CARLISH CRABBED INCIVIL PEEVISH VIOLENT

CHURN BEAT BOIL KIRN MOIL STIR DRILL SHAKE BUBBLE SEETHE AGITATE BARATTE TRUNDLE

CHUTE RUSH SLIP TUBE FLUME HURRY RAPID SHOOT SLIDE HOPPER TROUGH DECLINE DESCENT DOWNFALL STAMPEDE TELEGRAPH

(MINING —) PASS TELEGRAPH

CIBOL SYBO ONION SYBOW SHALLOT

CIBORIUM PIX PYX CANOPY CIVORY COFFER CIMBORIS

CICADA CAD CIGALE JARFLY LOCUST TETTIX LYREMAN HOMOPTER

CICATRICE FESTER

CICATRICLE TREAD GALLATURE

CICATRIX EYE MARK SCAB SCAR SEAM

CICATRIZE FESTER SCARIFY

CICELY MYRRH

CICERO TULLY

CICERONE GUIDE PILOT MENTOR ORATOR COURIER SIGHTSMAN

CICERONIAN TULLIAN

CID HERO CAMPEADOR

CIDER PERRY PERKIN SWANKY SYDDIR POMMAGE BEVERAGE COCCAGEE

(HARD —) APPLEJACK

(INFERIOR —) SWANKY

CIGAR PURO TOBY WEED BREVA CLARO SEGAR SHUCK SMOKE CONCHA CORONA HAVANA MADURA MADURO MANILA STOGIE TWOFER BOUQUET CHEROOT CULEBRA LONDRES REGALIA TRABUCO COLORADO LOCOFOCO PANATELA PERFECTO PICKWICK PURITANO

GARETTE CIG FAG BIRI BUTT KING PILL SKAG CUBEB JOINT SHUCK SMOKE GASPER REEFER CIGARITO

(— BUTT) ROACH

MARIHUANA —) STICK

GARFISH SCAD QUIAQUIA

LIUM HAIR LASH EYELASH UNCINUS BARBICEL CILIOLUM

LLOSIS LIFEBLOOD

MBALOM CEMBALON DULCIMER

MEX BEDBUG ACANTHIA

NCH BELT GIRD GRIP PIPE SNAP GIRTH GRAVY BREEZE CINCHA FASTEN PIANOLA SINECURE

NCHONA CHINA QUINA

NCINNATI PORKOPOLIS

NCTURE BAND BELT GIRD HALO LIST RING ZONE GIRTH CENTER CESTUS COLLAR FILLET GIRDLE BALDRIC COMPASS ENCIRCLE SURCINGLE

NDER ASH TAP COAL GRAY SCAR SLAG CHARK DROSS EMBER DANDER SCORIA CLINKER FOXTAIL RESIDUE

REFUSE —) BREEZE

VOLCANIC —) LAPILLUS

PL.) GLEEDS

CINEMATIZE FILMIZE

CINEMATOGRAPH KINO VERISCOPE VITAGRAPH

CINERARIA SENECIO

CINGULUM BAND RIDGE GIRDLE

CINNAMON CANEL SPICE CASSIA SANELA STACTE BARBASCO

(WILD —) BAYBERRY

CINNAMONROOT FLYBANE FLEAWORT

CINNAMON STONE GARNET ESSONITE

CINQUEFOIL FRASIER COWBERRY HARDHACK ROSACEAN QUINTFOIL

CINYRAS (DAUGHTER OF —) MYRRHA

(FATHER OF —) APOLLO

(SON OF —) ADONIS

CION BUD IMP SECT SLIP GRAFT SCION SHOOT UVULA SARMENT GRAFTING

CIPHER KEY NIL CODE NULL ZERO ALBAM AUGHT OUGHT DECODE DEVICE FIGURE LETTER NAUGHT NOUGHT NUMBER SYMBOL ATHBASH NULLITY MONOGRAM VIGENERE NOTHINGLY

CIRCASSIAN ADIGHE KABARD CHERKESS KABARDIN

CIRCE SIREN TEMPTER

(BROTHER OF —) AEETES

(FATHER OF —) SOL

(LOVER OF —) ULYSSES

(MOTHER OF —) PERSE

(SON OF —) TELEGONUS

CIRCLE DOT LAP ORB RED SET CLUE CULT DISK GYRE HALO HOOP IRIS LOOP MARU ORBE RING RINK ROLL TOUR TURN ZONE BLACK CAROL CLASS CROWN CYCLE FETCH FRAME GROUP KREIS MONDE PEARL REALM RHOMB RIGOL ROUND ROWEL SWIRL TWIRL BEZANT BROUGH CIRCUS CIRQUE CLIQUE COLLET COLURE CORDON CORONA DIADEM EQUANT GIRDLE RONDEL ROTATE RUNDLE SPIRAL SYSTEM TROPIC AZIMUTH CHUKKAR CHUKKER CIRCLET CIRCUIT COMPANY COMPASS CORONET COTERIE ENCLOSE HORIZON MONTHON REVOLVE RINGLET DEFERENT ECLIPTIC FROSTBOW SURROUND

(— AROUND ORGAN) ANNULET

(— IN BULL'S-EYE) CARTON

(— OF HELL) MALEBOLGE

(— OF MONOLITHS) CROMLECH

(— TRACED BY HORSE) VOLT

(ASTRONOMICAL —) EQUANT EPICYCLE

(DANCE —) GALLEY

(FAIRY —) RINGLET

(GREAT —) EQUATOR ECLIPTIC MERIDIAN

(IMAGINARY —) CYCLE DEFERENT

(INNER —) BOSOM

(PARHELIC —) FROSTBOW

(QUARTER —) ARC

(STONE —) CAROL HURLER GORSEDD

(TRAVERSE —) RACER

(TWO —S) CACHET

CIRCLET BAND HALO HOOP RING CROWN VERGE BANGLE CIRQUE CORONA CIRCUIT CORONET VALLARY BRACELET HEADBAND

CIRCUIT LAP AREA BOUT EYRE ITER LOOP TOUR WEND ZONE AMBIT CHAIN CYCLE ORBIT ROUND ROUTE VIRON AMBAGE BUFFER DETOUR DOUBLE SPHERE UMGANG ZODIAC ADAPTER ADDRESS COMARCA COMPASS COUNTER DIOCESE ACCEPTER DIPLEXER DISTRICT PERIPLUS PROGRESS

(BRANCH —) LEG

(ELECTRIC —) LEG LOOP DOUBLER SQUELCH SECONDARY

(ELECTRONIC —) GATE

CIRCUITOUS MAZY CURVED CROOKED DEVIOUS OBLIQUE SINUOUS TWISTED VAGRANT WINDING FLEXUOUS INDIRECT RAMBLING TORTUOUS DECEITFUL DEVIATING WANDERING

(— METHOD) WINDLASS

CIRCULAR O BILL FLIER FLYER LIBEL ORBAL ORBED ROUND DODGER FOLDER RINGED WHEELY ANNULAR COMPASS CYCLOID DISCOID DISLIKE HANDOUT PERFECT COMPLETE DOPEBOOK ENCYCLIC GLOBULAR INFINITE PAMPHLET DOPESHEET

CIRCULAR-KNIT SEAMLESS

CIRCULATE GO AIR MIX MOVE PASS RISE TURN WALK WIND TROLL CANARD ROTATE SCURRY SPHERE SPREAD WANDER CANVASS CONVECT DIFFUSE PUBLISH CONVOLVE

CIRCULATING WAIF AFLOAT CURRENT

CIRCULATION ISSUE COURSE COVERAGE CURRENCY

CIRCUMCISER MOHEL

CIRCUMCISION BRITH PERITOMY

CIRCUMFERENCE ARC AUGE AMBIT APSIS GIRTH VERGE BORDER BOUNDS CIRCLE LIMITS COMPASS BOUNDARY SURROUND

(— OF SHELL) LIMBUS

CIRCUMFERENTOR PLANCHETTE

CIRCUMFLEX DOGHOUSE

(INVERTED —) HACEK

CIRCUMLOCUTION AMBAGE CIRCUIT WINDING VERBIAGE

CIRCUMSCRIBE BOUND FENCE LIMIT DEFINE CAPTURE CONFINE ENCLOSE ENVIRON ENCIRCLE RESTRAIN RESTRICT SURROUND CONSCRIBE

CIRCUMSCRIBED NARROW INSULAR LIMITED

CIRCUMSPECT SHY WARY WISE ALERT CHARY CAREFUL GUARDED PRUDENT CAUTIOUS DISCREET

VIGILANT WATCHFUL
CIRCUMSPECTION RESPECT
PRUDENCE WARINESS
CIRCUMSTANCE GO FIX CASE FACT
ITEM NOTE EVENT PHASE POINT
START STATE THING AFFAIR DETAIL
FACTOR PICKLE CALLING ELEMENT
EPISODE INCIDENT INSTANCE
POSITION
(CRITICAL —S) EXTREMES
(EXECRABLE —) ATROCITY
(LUDICROUS —) JEST
(PL.) CIRCS STATE TERMS ESTATE
FORTUNE
CIRCUMSTANTIAL EXACT FORMAL
MINUTE PRECISE DETAILED
ITEMIZED
CIRCUMSTANTIATE SUPPORT
EVIDENCE
CIRCUMVENT BALK BEAT DUPE
FOIL CHEAT CHECK COZEN EVADE
OUTGO TRICK BAFFLE DELUDE
ENTRAP NOBBLE OUTWIT THWART
CAPTURE DECEIVE DEFRAUD
ENSNARE PREVENT SURROUND
UNDERFONG
CIRCUS RING SHOW ARENA CANVAS
CIRCLE CIRQUE CARNIVAL
(— LOT) TOBER
(— RING) TAN
CIRQUE CWM CIRC BASIN CIRCLE
CIRCUS CORRIE RECESS CIRCLET
EROSION
CIS SYN NERAL NORMAL
CISCO KIYI BLOAT BLOATER BLUEFIN
LONGJAW MOONEYE BLACKFIN
GRAYBACK TULLIBEE WHITEFIN
CISSA SIRGANG
CISSUS TREEBINE
CIST BOX KIST TOMB CHEST CISTA
QUOIT CASKET CHAMBER KISTVAEN
CISTERN BAC FAT SAC TUB URN
VAT BACK PANT SUMP TANK URNA
WELL LAVER CAVITY CAISSON
CHULTUN CUVETTE STEEPER
FEEDHEAD
CITADEL ARX FORT HALL ALAMO
BURSA BYRSA TOWER CASTLE
BOROUGH CHESTER KREMLIN
FASTNESS FORTRESS TOOTHILL
CITATION CITAL NOTICE MENTION
SUMMONS MONITION AUTHORITY
EVOCATION
CITE CALL NAME SIST TELL ALLAY
EVOKE QUOTE REFER ACCITE
ACCUSE ADDUCE ALLEGE AROUSE
AVOUCH EXCITE INVOKE NOTIFY
RECITE REPEAT SUMMON ADVANCE
ARRAIGN BESPEAK CONVENT
EXCERPT EXTRACT IMPEACH
MENTION INDICATE INSTANCE
REHEARSE
CITHARA CITHER PHORMINX
CITHERN ZITTERN
CITIZEN CIT ALLY VOTER NATIVE
BURGESS BURGHER CITOYEN
CLERUCH DENIZEN ELECTOR
FLATCAP FREEMAN OPPIDAN
SUBJECT TOWNMAN AMERICAN

CIVILIAN COMMONER CONSCIVE
DOMESTIC NATIONAL OCCUPANT
RESIDENT
(— OF SECOND CLASS) KNIGHT
HIPPEUS
(—S OF MEDINA) ANSAR
(FOREIGN-BORN —) ALIEN
(PL.) SUBJECT PERIOECI CITIZENRY
CITIZENRY COUNTRY SUBJECT
CITRAL GERANIAL
CITRON LIME CEDRA LEMON
CEDRAT ETHROG YELLOW
CITTERN LAUD CITHERN PENORCON
CITY FU WON BURG DORP TOWN
URBS WOON ZION BURGH CALNO
EKRON JEBUS LILLE MANOA PIECE
PLACE POLIS SETTE STEAD VILLE
CALNEH CENTER CIUDAD CUTHAH
GILEAD JAMNIA JEBUSI LAGADO
NAGARA PITHOM STAPLE BABYLON
CAMBALU CHESTER ELLASAR
FREEDOM JABNEEL MECHLIN
CABECERA ELDORADO MAGAZINE
PALENQUE
(— LIFE) ASHCAN
(ANCIENT —) PERGAMUM
(CHIEF —) CAPITAL CABECERA
MEGAPOLIS
(RICH —) MAGAZINE
(TREASURE —) RAAMSES
(WICKED —) BABYLON
CITY-STATE POLIS CIVITAS
CIVET CAT CIT GENET RASSE ZIBET
BONDAR FOUSSA MUSANG PAGUMA
ZIBETH CIVETTA FOSSANE LINSANG
NANDINE POLECAT ZIBETUM
ZINSANG FANALOKA MONGOOSE
TANGALUNG
CIVIC LAY CIVIL SUAVE URBAN
POLITE URBANE CIVICAL SECULAR
CIVIL FAIR HEND HENDE SUAVE
POLITE URBANE AFFABLE AMIABLE
COURTLY ELEGANT GALLANT
POLITIC REFINED SECULAR
DISCREET GRACIOUS OBLIGING
POLISHED WELLBRED
CIVILIAN CIT CIVIE CIVIL CIVVY
PEKIN MOHAIR CITIZEN TEACHER
CIVILIST GOWNSMAN
(— ENTERTAINING SOLDIER) PYKE
CIVILITY BONTE COMITY NOTICE
AMENITY COURTESY URBANITY
GENTILITY
(PL.) HONORS HONOURS
CIVILIZATION ISLAM KULTUR
POLICE CULTURE ECUMENE CIVICITY
(GREEK —) HELLENISM
CIVILIZE TAME TEACH TRAIN POLISH
REFINE EDUCATE HUMANIZE
URBANIZE
CIVILIZED CHRISTIAN
CLABBER LOP MUD MIRE CURDLE
LOPPER CLAUBER
CLACKDISH CLICKET
CLAD DREST ROBED BESEEN
CLEDDE DECKED ADORNED
ARRAYED ATTIRED CLOTHED
COVERED DRESSED SHEATHED
(— IN PURPLE) PORPORATE

(SCANTILY —) SINGLY
CLADOSE RAMOSE CLADINE
BRANCHED
CLAIM ASK DUE AVER AVOW CALL
CASE DIBS LIEN MINE NAME PLEA
COLOR DRAFT EXACT PLEAD RIGHT
SHOUT TITLE ASSERT DEMAND
DESIRE ELICIT EQUITY INTEND
RECKON ACCLAIM COLLECT
DERECHO DRAUGHT PRETEND
PRETEXT PROFESS RECLAIM
REQUIRE SOLICIT ARROGATE
INTEREST MAINTAIN PRETENCE
PRETENSE PROCLAIM SUBCLAIM
(— IN BUSINESS) CAPITAL
(— TO BE BELIEVED) AUTHORITY
(FALSE —) JACTATION
(INDIAN LEGAL —) HAK HAKH
CLAIMANT CLAIMER USURPER
PRETENDER
CLAIRE PARK
CLAIRVOYANCE INSIGHT VOYANCE
LUCIDITY SAGACITY TELOPSIS
CLAIRVOYANT FEY SEER OMENER
PROPHET SEERESS
CLAM MYA BASE CLOG DAUB GLAM
HUSH MEAN BLUNT CLAMP CRASH
GAPER GLAUM GRASP GROPE
PAHUA RAZOR SHELL SMEAR SOLE
SPOUT STICK VENUS ADHERE
CLUTCH GWEDUC QUAHOG STICKY
BIVALVE CLANGOR COQUINA
MOLLUSK STEAMER ADHESIVE
BULLNOSE SHIPWORM NANNINOSE
CLAMBAKE BAKE RALLY CLAMARC
SQUANTUM
CLAMBER CLIMB SCALE CLAVER
SCRAWM SPRAWL RAMMACK
SCRABBLE SCRAMBLE SPRACHLE
STRUGGLE
CLAMMY DAMP DANK SOFT WACK
MOIST SAMMY STICKY WAUGHY
SQUIDGY CLAMMISH
CLAMOR CRY DIN HUE BERE BUNK
GAFF RANE RERD ROAR ROUP
ROUT SONG UTAS WAIL BLARE
BOAST BRUIT CHIDE CHIRM NOISE
OUTAS RERDE RUMOR SHOUT
BELLOW BOWWOW HUBBUB
OUTCRY QUETHE RACKET TUMULT
UPROAR YATTER CLAMOUR
EXCLAIM ORATION STASHIE
NORATION PILILLOO PULLALUE
SHOUTING
(— AGAINST) DECRY
CLAMOROUS NIP LOUD NOISY
VOCAL BLATANT CLAMANT DINSOI
YELLING BRAWLING DECRYING
CLAMP DOG HOG LUG NIP PIN SET
BAIL BALE BEND BOLT BURY CLA
GLAM GRIP JACK MUTE NAIL VISE
YOKE BLOCK BRACE CLASP CRAM
GLAND GLAUM HORSE CLINCH
FASTEN MOPHEAD STIRRUP
FASTENER HOLDFAST
(— FOR BASS DRUM) SPUR
(— FOR CORK) AGRAFE AGRAFFE
(— FOR FLASK) GLAND
(STORAGE —) GRAVE

LAMSHELL CLAM GRAB SHUCK
LAN ATI HAN KIN SET SIB CULT
GENS HAPU NAME RACE SECT SEPT
SIOL UNIT AIMAK AYLLU CLASS
GENOS GROUP HORDE PARTY TRIBE
ABUSUA CLIQUE FAMILY SENAAH
ABIEZER KINDRED PHRATRY
SATSUMA SOCIETY ZADRUGA
CALPULLI DIVISION
(— **SUBDIVISION**) OBE
LANDESTINE BYE SLY FOXY
HEDGE PRIVY QUIET SNEAK COVERT
HIDDEN SECRET BOOTLEG FURTIVE
ILLICIT BACKDOOR HIDLINGS
STEALTHY
LANG DIN DING PEAL RING TONK
CLANK CLASH NOISE JANGLE
TIMBRE
LANGOR DIN CLAM ROAR CLANG
HUBBUB UPROAR
LANGOROUS BRAZEN PLANGENT
LANGULA HARELDA
LANK RING RACKLE
LAP BANG FLAP PEAL SLAP SPAT
TACK CHEER CLINK CRACK SMITE
POSTER STRIKE STROKE APPLAUD
CHATTER CLAPPER PLAUDIT
HANDCLAP
(— **OF THUNDER**) DINT
(— **ON**) CRACK
LAPBOARD KNAPPLE CLAPHOLT
LAPNET DAYNET
LAPPER CLAP CLACK RATTLE
TONGUE JINGLET KNACKER
KNOCKER
(— **OF BELL**) TONGUE
(PL.) BONES
LAPTRAP TRASH BLAGUE BUNKUM
DEVICE EYEWASH FUSTIAN
BUNCOMBE NONSENSE TRICKERY
SIMPLIFY
LARE MINORESS
LARENCE GROWLER
LARET TERSE LAFITTE BORDEAUX
BADMINTON
LARIAS HARMOOT KARMOUTH
LARIFIED PURED LAUTER
LARIFY CLAY FINE CLEAN CLEAR
PURGE SNUFF PURIFY REFINE
RENDER SERENE SETTLE CLEANSE
DESPUME EXPLAIN GLORIFY
DEFECATE DEPURATE ELIQUATE
SIMPLIFY
LARIN ACOCOTL
LARINET BEN BIN BON BEEN BONE
REED AULOS CLARY PUNGI
CLARONE LAUNEDDAS
LARION REST CLARE CLARY CLEAR
CLARINO SUFFLUE TRUMPET
LARITY GLORY SPLENDOR
STRENGTH CLEARNESS
LARY CLARRE SALVIA
LASH JAR BANG BOLT BUMP DASH
FRAY NEWS SLAM BRAWL BRUNT
CHECK CRASH FIGHT FRUSH KNOCK
OCCUR PRATE SHOCK AFFRAY
DIFFER GOSSIP HURTLE IMPACT
JOSTLE STRIFE STRIKE TATTLE
THRUST THWART COLLIDE DISCORD
SCANDAL ARGUMENT CONFLICT

CLASHING HARSH CONFLICT
FRICTION COLLISION
CLASP HUG PIN CLIP DOME FOLD
GRAB GRIP HASP HOLD HOOK HOOP
KEEP OUCH STAY TACH BRACE
CATCH CLING GRASP MORSE PREEN
SEIZE SLIDE SPANG TACHE ACCOLL
AGRAFE AMPLEX BECLIP BROOCH
BUCKLE CLENCH CLUTCH ENFOLD
ENWRAP FASTEN FIBULA GIMMER
GIMMOR INCLIP INFOLD JIMMER
STRAIN TASSEL AGRAFFE AMPLECT
EMBRACE ENTWINE FERMAIL
HOLDING MOUSING TENDRIL
BARRETTE CORSELET FASTENER
SURROUND
(— **HANDS**) SHAKE WRING
CLASS ILK BRAN CHOP FORM KIND
RACE RANK RATE SECT SORT SUIT
TYPE YEAR BREED CASTE GENRE
GENUS GROUP ORDER
RANGE TRIBE VARNA VERGE
ASSORT CIRCLE CLINIC DECURY
FAMILY GENDER LEAGUE MISTER
NATION PHYLUM RATING RECKON
REMOVE RUBRIC STRAIN STRIPE
CATALOG FACTION LECTURE
REGIMEN SEMINAR SPECIES
VARIETY CATEGORY DESCRIBE
DIVISION GENOTYPE GEOMOROI
(— **OF BARDS**) THULIR
(— **OF GOODS**) BRAND
(— **OF OUTCASTS**) ETA
(— **OF PEOPLE**) FOLK SALARIAT
(— **OF SECURITIES**) LEGAL
(— **OF SHASTRAS**) SRUTI SHRUTI
(— **OF SOUNDS**) ENDING
(— **OF TEASELS**) KINGS
(**ARISTOCRATIC** —) ARISTOI
(**CHOICEST** —) ROBUR
(**DEPRESSED** —) PANCHAMA
(**FIRST** —) GAY
(**HEREDITARY** —) CASTE
(**JAPANESE** —) HEIMIN KWAZOKU
(**LABORING** —) PARAIYAN
(**LEARNED** —) VATES CLERISY
(**LOWER** —) BELOW GENTE
(**LOWEST** —) LAG SCUM
(**PEASANT** —) JACQUERIE
(**SLAVEHOLDING** —) CHIVALRY
(**SOCIAL** —) ESTATE SHIZOKU
(**WORKING** —) TOIL
CLASSIC VINTAGE
CLASSICAL PURE ATTIC GREEK
LATIN ROMAN CHASTE CLASSIC
ACADEMIC HELLENIC MASTERLY
(**NOT** —) BASE
CLASSICALLY IDEALLY
CLASSIFICATION FILE RANK RATE
SORT CODEN GENRE GENUS GRADE
ORDER TAXIS RATING SYSTEM
ANALYSIS CATEGORY DIVISION
TAXONOMY BREAKDOWN
CLASSIFIED SECRET
CLASSIFIER COUNTER SEPARATOR
CLASSIFY CODE LIST RANK RATE
SIZE SORT SUIT TAPE TYPE BREAK
CLASS DRAFT GRADE GROUP LABEL
RANGE TRIBE ASSORT CODIFY

DIGEST DIVIDE IMPOST TICKET
ACCOUNT ARRANGE BRACKET
BRIGADE CATALOG DISPOSE
DRAUGHT GRAMMAR MARSHAL
SUBSUME REGISTER
(— **TOGETHER**) SLUMP
CLASSIS CONFERENCE
CLATHRATE LATTICED
CLATTER DIN JAR CLACK NOISE
RUMOR BABBLE GABBLE GOSSIP
HURTLE RACKLE RATTLE TATTLE
BLATTER CHATTER CLUNTER
CLUTTER PRATTLE REESHLE
SHATTER SLAMBANG
CLATTERING CLATTERY SLITHERING
CLAUSE ITEM PART CLOSE COMMA
JOKER PLANK RIDER TROPE
MEMBER PHRASE ARTICLE
COMMATA PASSAGE PROVISO
SLEEPER PETITION REDDENDO
SENTENCE TENENDAS TENENDUM
NOVODAMUS
(— **IN WRIT**) TESTE
(— **OF WILL**) DEVISE
(**ADDITIONAL** —) RIDER
CLAVACIN PATULIN
CLAVER PRATE CLOVER GOSSIP
CHATTER CLABBER CLAIVER
CLAMBER
CLAVICHORD CLAVIER MANICORD
UNICHORD CLARIGOLD MONOCHORD
CLAVICLE FURCULE COLLARBONE
CLAVIER MANUAL KLAVIER
CLAVUS CORN BUNION HELOMA
CLAW DIG PEG CLEE CRAB FANG
FAWN HAND HOOK NAIL PULL SERE
TEAR UNCE CHELA CLOOF CLUFE
COURT GRASP GRIFF ONGLE SCLAW
SEIZE TALON UNCUS CLUNCH
CLUTCH CRATCH NIPPER POUNCE
SCRAPE SINGLE UNGUAL UNGUIS
UNGULA WEAPON CRUBEEN
FALCULA FLATTER SCRATCH
SHUTTLE WHEEDLE SCRABBLE
(PL.) CLUTCH
CLAY BAT COB PUG WAD WAX BASS
BEND BODY BOLE BOTT GALT GLEY
LOAM LUTE MARL MIRE PAPA SMIT
TILL ARGIL BRICK CLOAM EARTH
GAULT LOESS OCHRE PASTE RABAT
TASCO BINDER CLEDGE CLUNCH
KAOLIN PUDDLE SAGGER DAUBING
MOULDER RASHING CAMSTANE
FIRECLAY GUMBOTIL LATERITE
LIFELESS SINOPITE
(— **FOR MELTING POTS**) TASCO
(— **IN GLASS**) TEAR
(— **IRON**) BULL
(— **LAYER**) VARVE
(**3-ARMED, HARD-FIRED** —) STILT
(**COVERED WITH** —) LUTOSE
(**HARD** —) BEND
(**HARDENED** —) METAL
(**INDURATED** —) BASS CLUNCH
(**PIECE OF FIRED** —) TILE
(**PIPE** —) CAMSTANE CAMSTONE
(**POTTER'S** —) SLIP ARGIL
(**REMOVE** —) UNLUTE
(**SURPLUS** —) SPARE

(TOUGH —) LECK
CLAYEY BOLAR HEAVY MALMY
MARLY CLEDGY LUTOSE ARGILLIC
CLAYMORE FERRARA
CLAY PIGEON BIRD CLAY
CLAYSTONE LECK
CLAYWARE GLOST
CLEADING CLOTHING
CLEAN DO FAY FEY HOE MOP NET
DRUM DUST FAIR NEAT PURE REDD
RIPE SIDE SMUG SWAB TRIM WASH
WIPE CLEAR CURRY EMPTY FEIGH
GRAVE SCOUR SCRUB SMART
SWEEP TERSE TOSHY BARREL
CHASTE CLEVER KOSHER PURIFY
SPANDY APINOID BANDBOX
CHAMOIS CLEANLY CLEANSE
CLEARLY FURBISH PERFECT
SWINGLE ABSTERGE BACKWASH
BRIGHTLY DEXTROUS ENTIRELY
RENOVATE SCAVENGE SPOTLESS
UNSOILED
(— A FUR) DRUM
(— A QUILL) DUTCH
(— BOAT) CAREEN
(— BY SCRAPING) GRAVE
(— BY SMOKE) SMEEK
(— CANNON) SCALE
(— FIREARM) WORM
(— FLAX) SWINGLE
(— IN ACID) BLANCH
(— OUT) USH SPEAR
(— SHIP'S BOTTOM) HOG BREAM
GRAVE
(— UP) DISPATCH
(RITUALLY —) KOSHER
CLEAN-CUT CRISP
CLEANED BRIGHT
CLEANER SOAP BORAX PURER
FOLDER GUMMER RAMROD
FLUEMAN SPOTTER CLEANSER
(AIR —) CAN
(GRAIN —) KICKER
CLEAN-LIMBED CLEVER
CLEAN-LINED SPRUCE
CLEANLY PURE CLEAN ADROIT
ARTFUL CHASTE FAIRLY SPANDY
CORRECT ELEGANT INNOCENT
SKILLFUL
CLEANNESS PURITY
CLEANSE FAY BRAN CARD COMB
FARM HEAL PICK SOAP WASH
BROOM BRUSH CLEAN CLEAR DIGHT
DRESS FEIGH FLAME FLUSH PURGE
RINSE SCOUR SCRUB SNUFF
BOTTOM CAREEN EMUNGE PICKLE
PURIFY REFINE SPONGE WILLOW
BAPTIZE CLARIFY DEBRIDE
DETERGE EXPIATE LAUNDER
MUNDIFY SWEETEN ABSTERGE
DEPURATE OFFSCOUR RENOVATE
SCAVENGE SPRINKLE
CLEANSER LYE SOAP CLEANER
PURIFIER DETERGENT DETERSIVE
CLEANSING BATH FLUSH ABLUENT
CLYSMIC WASHING ABLUTION
CLEANING LAVATION DETERGENT
(CEREMONIAL —) LAVABO
PURGATION

CLEANUP KILLING SWEEPUP
CLEAR HOT JAM NET RID WAY CAST
EASY FAIR FINE FLAT FREE GAIN
GRUB JUMP NEAT OPEN OVER PURE
PUTE QUIT REDD RIFE SHUT SLAM
VOID ACUTE ATRIP AZURE BREAK
BREME BRENT BROAD CHUCK
CLEAN CRISP DRIVE LIGHT LUCID
NAKED PLAIN PRINT PRUNE SCOUR
SHARP SMOLT SUNNY SUTEL
SWEEP UNTIE VIVID ACQUIT AERIAL
ASSOIL BRIGHT CANDID CLEVER
EXCUSE EXEMPT FLUTED LAUTER
LIMPID LIQUID LUCENT PATENT
PURIFY SERENE SETTLE SHRILL
SMOOTH UNSTOP ABSOLVE CAPITAL
CLARIFY CLARION CRYSTAL
DELIVER DILUCID EVIDENT EXPLAIN
EXPRESS GLARING GRAPHIC
LIGHTEN OBVIOUS PERVIAL
RELEASE SILVERY ACCREDIT
APPARENT BRIGHTEN BULLDOZE
DEFINITE DISTINCT EXPLICIT
LUCULENT LUMINOUS MANIFEST
PELLUCID REVELANT
(— AWAY) FAY FEY FEIGH BANISH
DISPEL DISCUSS
(— FROM) ALOOF
(— LAND) CURE BRUSH SLASH
DEADEN
(— OF GROUND) ATRIP AWEIGH
(— OF MUD) SLUTCH
(— OF SCUM) SKIM
(— OF TUFTS) HOB
(— OUT) BLOW HOOK SWAMP
SKIDDOO HIGHTAIL DISCHARGE
(— PATH) FRAY HACK BUSHWACK
(— THROAT) HOICK HOUGH
(— UP) SOLVE ASSOIL RESOLVE
DISSOLVE UNSHADOW
(NOT —) DULL DUSKY FOGGY
INEVIDENT
CLEARANCE CHOP ROOM RUNBY
BACKLASH ALLOWANCE
CLEAR-CUT LUCID SHARP DIRECT
CONCISE DECIDED CHISELED
DEFINITE DISTINCT INCISIVE
TRENCHANT
CLEARING FIELD FRITH GLADE
SHADE TRACT ALCOVE ASSART
RIDING RIDDING SLASHING
CLEARLY FAIR CLEAR LIGHT REDLY
FAIRLY FRANKLY WITTERLY
CLEAR-MINDEDNESS LUCIDITY
CLEARNESS CLARITY FINESSE
EVIDENCE FINENESS
CLEARWEED RICHWEED
CLEAT BITT STUD BLOCK CHOCK
KEVEL LEDGE RANGE WEDGE
BATTEN RIFFLE BOLLARD COXCOMB
GROUSER SIRMARK SUPPORT
SURMARK
CLEAVAGE RIFT CLEFT WASSIE
FISSION FISSURE WEDGING DIVISION
SCISSION
CLEAVE CUT RIP CHOP HANG HOLD
JOIN LINK PART RELY REND RIFT
RIVE SLIT TEAR BREAK CARVE
CHAWN CHINE CLAVE CLEFT CLING

CLOVE CRACK SEVER SHALE SHARI
SHEAR SLIVE SPLAT STICK ADHERI
BISECT COHERE DIVIDE FURROW
PIERCE SLEAVE SUNDER DISPART
FISSURE SEPARATE
(— OFF) SCIND
CLEAVER CLIVE CLEAVE FROWER
CHOPPER PARANGI
CLEAVERS GRIP CLOTE CLOTS
CLITHE HAIRIF HAIRUP BURHEAD
LOVEMAN PIGTAIL BIRDLIME
CLEAVING DYSTOME FISSION
DYSTOMIC
(— READILY) EUTOMOUS
CLECHE URDE URDY URDEE
CLEF KEY CLIVE CHIAVETTA
CLEFT CUT GAP CHAP CHOP FENT
FLAW GASH NOCK REFT RIFT RILL
RIMA RIVE SLIT BREAK CHASM
CHAWN CHINK CLOVE CRACK
CREEK CRENA GULCH RILLE RIVEN
SINUS SPLIT BREACH CHAPPY
CLEAVE CLOUGH CLOVEN CRANNY
CROTCH DIVIDE LISSOM PARTED
RECESS RICTUS STIGMA BLASTED
CHIMNEY CREVICE DIVIDED FISSURI
OPENING SLIFTER APERTURE
FRACTURE INCISION INCISURA
MULTIFID SCISSURA SCISSURE
(— IN HOOF) SEAM
(— IN THE POSTERIORS) NOCK
(— CF BUTTOCKS) CREASE
CLEMATIS PIPESTEM CURLYHEAD
CLEMENCY ORE PITY GRACE
MERCY LENITY QUARTER KINDNES
LENIENCY MILDNESS
CLEMENT MILD SOFT WARM GENTL
LENIENT MERCIFUL
CLENCH FIST GRIP GRIT HOLD NAII
BRACE CLASP CLENK CLINT CLOSE
GRASP CLINCH CLUTCH DOUBLE
(— FIST) GRIPE
CLEPE CLUPIEN
CLEPSYDRA GURRY GHURRY
CLERGY CLOTH CRAPE CHURCH
CLERISY MINISTRY
(BODY OF —) PULPIT
CLERGYMAN ABBA ABBE DEAN
PAPA CANON CLERK FROCK PADRI
PILOT PRIOR RABBI VICAR BISHOP
CLERIC CURATE DEACON DIVINE
DOMINE PAROCH PARSON PASTOR
PRIEST RECTOR SUPPLY CASSOCK
PRELATE CARDINAL CHAPLAIN
CLERICAL DIOCESAN EMERITUS
LECTURER MINISTER ORDINARY
PREACHER REVEREND SQUARSON
PRESBYTER
CLERIC ABBE CLERK FROCK
DEACON GALLAH LEVITE PRIEST
ACOLYTE ANAGNOST
CLERICAL BLACK CLERIC CLERKISI
PARSONIC PARSONLY
CLERK NUN BABU MONK AGENT
AWARD BABOO CLARK FILER RALF
WRITE BILLER CHASER CLERIC
COMMIS GRADER HERMIT KITMAN
LAYMAN MAPPER MASTER MUNSHI
PANDIT PENMAN PRIEST PUNDIT

RALPHO SCRIBE TELLER WRITER
YEOMAN ACOLYTE ACTUARY
BOOKMAN CARCOON COMPOSE
DOPSTER GOMASTA PIARIST
SCHOLAR SHIPPER SHOPMAN
STUFFER CLERGEON CLERGION
CLERKESS EMPLOYEE GREFFIER
MUTSUDDY PENCLERK RECORDER
SALESMAN
(— OF ST PAUL) BARNABITE
(HOTEL —) DESKMAN
CLERKLY LEARNED SCRIBAL
CLERGIAL SCHOLARLY
CLEVE BRAE CLIFF CLEEVE HILLSIDE
CLEVER APT SLY ABLE CUTE DEFT
FEAT FELL FINE FOXY GNIB GOOD
HEND KEEN SLIM SPRY AGILE
ALERT CANNY CLEAN CLEAR CUNNY
FALSE FEATY FENDY HANDY HEADY
HENDE LITHE QUICK SHARP SLICK
SMART SNACK WITTY ACTIVE
ADROIT ARTFUL ASTUTE BRIGHT
CRAFTY EXPERT HABILE HEPPEN
KITTLE KNACKY NEATLY NIMBLE
PRETTY SHREWD SPIFFY STALKY
SUBTLE AMIABLE CUNNING GNOSTIC
PARLISH PARLOUS VARMENT
VARMINT DEXTROUS HANDSOME
OBLIGING SKILLFUL TALENTED
CLEVERLY SLICK FEATLY TIDELY
SMARTLY ASTUTELY
CLEVERNESS CAN CHIC NOUS TACT
SKILL ESPRIT INDUSTRY DEXTERITY
CLEVIS COP DEE HAKE CLEVY
COPSE BRIDGE BRIDLE MUZZLE
SHACKLE PLOWHEAD
CLEW BALL CLUE HINT GLOBE
GLOME SKEIN BOTTOM HURDLE
THREAD
CLICHE COMMONPLACE
CLICK DOG DOT DASH PAWL SLAP
TICK AGREE CATCH FORGE SNECK
SNICK DETENT PALLET RATCHET
(HEEL —S) BELLS
(TELEGRAPH —) DASH
CLICK BEETLE ELATER
CLIENT CEILE JAJMAN PATRON
PATIENT CUSTOMER HENCHMAN
RETAINER
CLIENTELE PUBLIC CLIENTRY
CLIFF HOE NIP CRAG HILL KLIP
ROCK SCAR BLUFF CLEVE CLINT
HEUCH HEUGH KRANS SCARP
SHORE SLOPE STEEP CLEEVE
HEIGHT KRANTZ PISKUN CLOGWYN
HILLSIDE PALISADE TRAVERSE
(BROKEN —) CRAG
(ICE —) ICEBLINK
(LINE OF —S) PALISADE
CLIFFY SCARRY
CLIMATE SKY SUN MOOD CLIME
HEAVEN REGION TEMPER ATTITUDE
(SCIENCE OF —) PHENOLOGY
CLIMAX CAP TOP ACME APEX HEAD
NEAR PEAK SHUT CREST CROWN
MOUNT SCALE TIGHT APOGEE
ASCEND FINISH HEIGHT SHINNY
SUMMIT ZENITH BLOWOFF EVEREST
CAPSHEAF CAPSTONE EPIPLOCE

CLIMB GAD STY COON RAMP RISE
SHIN SKIN SOAR STYE CREEP
GRIMP MOUNT SCALE SKLIM SPEED
SPEEL SWARM TWINE ASCEND
ASCENT BREAST SCLIMB SCRAWM
SHINNY SWARVE SWERVE CLAMBER
SCRAMBLE TRAVERSE
(— ABOARD) HOP
(— DOWN) LIGHT UNSCALE
(— IN MOUNTAINEERING) CHIMNEY
(— OVER) SURMOUNT
CLIMBER CUBE AKALA AKELA KAIWI
RIGGER SCALER CRAMPON
CREEPER
(MOUNTAIN —) ALPINIST
CLIMBING SCANDENT
(MOUNTAIN —) ALPINISM
CLIMBING FERN NITO AGSAM
CLIMBING IRON SPUR PRICK
CRAMPET CRAMPIT CRAMPON
CREEPER PRICKER CRAMPBIT
CLIMBING PALM RATTAN
CLIMBING PEPPER BETEL
CLIMBING ROSE SCRAMBLE
CLINCH FIX GET HUG TOE BIND GRIP
LOCK NAIL SEAL CLAMP CLING
CLINK CLINT GRASP RIVET SEIZE
CLENCH CLUTCH FASTEN SECURE
SNATCH CONFIRM EMBRACE
GRAPPLE SCUFFLE COMPLETE
CONCLUDE HOLDFAST
CLING HUG BANK HANG HOLD RELY
CLASP HITCH STICK TRUST ADHERE
CLEAVE CLINCH COHERE DEPEND
FASTEN SHRINK WITHER CHERISH
EMBRACE SHRIVEL CONTRACT
CLINGER LIMPET
CLINGFISH SUCKER TESTAR TETARD
SUCKFISH
CLINGING CLUNG HUGGING
ADHAMANT ADHERENT OSCULANT
CLINK ALE JUG PUT RAP BEAT
BLOW BRIG CASH CLAP COIN JAIL
MOVE RING SLAP KLINK LATCH
MONEY RHYME SEIZE CLINCH
JINGLE LOCKUP MOMENT PRISON
STRIKE TINKLE INSTANT JINGLING
CLINKER BUR BUHR BURR SCAR
SLAG WASTE HOLLANDER
CLINKER-BUILT SHINGLED
LAPSTRAKE
CLINOMETER TRIMMER
CLINTONIA BLUEBEAD DOGBERRY
COWTONGUE
CLIP BAT BOB CUT DOD HUG LIP
LOP MOW NIG NIP BARB BEAK CHIP
COLL CROP DOCK DODD FLAG
HOLD PACE PARE POLL SNIP TRIM
BRUSH CLASP DRESS FORCE LUNET
MINCE PRUNE SHAVE SHEAR SHRIP
STEEK CLUPPE CLUTCH CRUTCH
FASTEN GADGET HINDER HOLDER
LACING CALIPER CURTAIL CURTAIN
EMBRACE HICKORY LUNETTE
SCISSOR SHORTEN DIMINISH
ENCIRCLE RETAINER
(— A COIN) SHORTEN
(— WOOL) CRUTCH
(CARTRIDGE —) CHARGER

(HAIR —) BARRETTE
(SPRING —) JACK
CLIPPED TONSURED
CLIPPER BOAT SHIP DOCKER SLICER
CHAINER CLAMMER CLEANER
GRABMAN GRIPPER SHEARER
SNAPPER
CLIPPING BOB SCROW CUTTING
SNIPPING
(—S OF METAL) SCISSEL
(PL.) BRASH SHORTS EXCERPTA
CLIQUE COT MOB SET BLOC CLAN
CLUB GANG KNOT RING CABAL
CROWD GROUP JUNTO WRITE
CIRCLE CLETCH SCHISM COTERIE
FACTION CONCLAVE SODALITY
CLITELLUM GIRDLE SADDLE
CINGULUM
CLOAK ABA HAP BRAT CAPA CAPE
COPE HIDE HUKE IZAR MANT MASK
PALL RAIL ROBE VEIL WRAP BURKA
CAPOT CHOGA COVER GREGO
GUISE JELAB MANTA MANTO SAGUM
SHUBA TILMA ABOLLA AHUULA
ASSUME BAUTTA CAMAIL CAPOTE
CASTER CHAMMA CHAPEL CHIMER
DOLMAN JOSEPH MANTLE MANTUA
PHAROS PONCHO RHASON SCREEN
SERAPE SHIELD SHROUD TABARD
VISITE ALICULA BAVAROY CASSOCK
CHLAMYS CONCEAL COURTBY
GARMENT MANTEAU PAENULA
PELISSE PELLARD PRETEXT
SHELTER SURCOAT ZIMARRA
ALBORNOZ BURNOOSE CAPUCHIN
DISGUISE INTRIGUE MANTILLA
PALLIATE
(— OF FEATHERS) MAMO AHUULA
(— WITH CROSSES) ANALABOS
(HOODED —) HUKE CAPOT BAUTTA
BIRRUS BAVAROY CARDINAL
(RED —) CAPE
(SOLDIER'S —) SAGUM
(WATERPROOF —) GOSSAMER
CLOAKED PALLIATE
CLOAKROOM VESTIARY
CLOAM DAUB CLOMB CROCKERY
CLOCHE BELL
CLOCK NEF BELL CALL DIAL GOER
GONG TIME WRAP BUNDY CLUCK
GURRY HATCH HURRY KNOCK
METER QUIRK STYLE VERGE WATCH
BEETLE CROUCH GHURRY ORLAGE
TICKER SKELPER STRIKER TATTLER
HOROLOGE INCUBATE ORNAMENT
RECORDER SOLARIUM TELLTALE
(— IN FORM OF SHIP) NEF
(— ON STOCKING) QUIRK GUSSET
GUSSET
(— WITH PENDULUM) PENDULE
(TIME —) BUNDY
(WATER —) GURRY GHURRY
SOLARIUM CLEPSYDRA
CLOCKER SIZER TIMER RAILBIRD
CLOCKWISE DEASIL DESSIL
SUNWISE POSITIVE
CLOD SOD CLAT CLOT DOLT DULL
LOUT LUMP SLOB TURF CLOUT
CLOWN DIVOT EARTH GLEBE GROSS

KNOLL YOKEL CLATCH GROUND
STUPID BUMPKIN
CLODDISH GROSS STUPID BOORISH
CLODHOPPER BOOR CLOD SHOE
RUSTIC HOBNAIL PLOWMAN
CLODIA LESBIA
CLODPATE CLOT DOLT FOOL
RAMHEAD CLODPOLE CLODPOLL
IMBECILE
CLOG FUR GUM JAM LOG BALL
CLAG CLAM CLOY CURB DRAG
GLUB LEAD LOAD LUMP SHOE SKID
STOP BLIND BLOCK CHECK CHOKE
DANCE SABOT SPOKE TRASH
ADHERE BURDEN CHOPIN COBCAB
DAGGLE ENCLOG FETTER FREEZE
GALOSH HAMPER HOBBLE IMPEDE
PATINE PATTEN REMORA SANDAL
SECQUE WEIGHT CONGEST
CREEPER ENGLEIM FETLOCK
PERPLEX SHACKLE SPANCEL
TRAMMEL TRIGGER BEDAGGLE
COALESCE ENCUMBER OBSTRUCT
OVERSHOE RESTRAIN
(— A FILE) PIN
(WOODEN —S) GETA GETAS
CLOG ALMANAC STAFF
CLOGGED FOUL FURRY PINNY
FROZEN CLOTTED BEGUMMED
CLOGGING CLOGGY FOULING
CUMBROUS
CLOGGY DULL HEAVY LUMPY
STICKY
CLOISONNE SHIPPO
CLOISTER HALL STOA ABBEY AISLE
ARCADE FRIARY IMMURE PIAZZA
PRIORY CLOSTER CONVENT
NUNNERY MONASTERY
CLOISTERED RECLUSE
CLOSE BY IN CAP END GUM HAW
HOT TYE AKIN BUNG CHOP CLAP
CLIT DAUB FAST FILL FINE FIRM
GRIP HARD HIDE LOUK MEET NEAR
NIGH QUIT SEAL SHUT SLAM SNUG
SPAR STOP TINE WINK WYND ZERO
ANEAR BLOCK BREAK CEASE CHEAP
CHIEF COAPT DENSE FENCE FINIS
FLIRT GARTH GROSS ISSUE MUGGY
SNECK SOLID STEEK STICK STIVY
THICK TIGHT BUCKLE BUTTON
CLAUSE CLENCH CLUTCH DOUBLE
EFFECT EXPIRY FINALE FINISH
INSTOP INWARD NARROW NEARBY
PERIOD SECRET SETTLE SILENT
STANCH STINGY STITCH STRAIT
STRICT STUFFY THRONG ADJOURN
BOROUGH CLOSING CLOSISH
COMPACT CONDEMN CONTEXT
COSTIVE EXTREME GRAPPLE
MISERLY OCCLUDE POCKETY
PUTHERY RAMPIRE RECLUSE
SHUTTER SIMILAR STAUNCH
STOPPER ACCURATE ADJACENT
BLOCKADE CLAUSULA COMPLETE
COMPRESS CONCLUDE ENCEINTE
ESPECIAL FAMILIAR FINALIZE
HAIRLINE IMMINENT INTIMATE
PARCLOSE PRECLUDE
(— BY) FORBY AROUND BESIDE

FOREBY HEREBY FORTHBY
SISTERING
(— EYES OF HAWK) SEEL
(— IN ON) TAKE
(— IN) BESET ENCLOSE INCLOSE
(— THE MOUTH) STOPPLE
(— TO BATSMAN) SILLY
(— TO COMMUNICATION) CORDON
(— TO QUARRY) HOT
(— TO THE HEART) DEAR
(— TO THE WIND) SHARP
(— TO) BY INBY NEAR NIGH ANEAR
INBYE ALMOST AGAINST
(— TOGETHER) COLLAPSE
(— UP) DIT CORK DITT FILL FOLD
STOP SERRY UPCLOSE
(— WITH A CLICK) SNECK
(— WITH) BIND
(PARTIALLY —) HOOD
(VERY —) CHIEF STINGY
CLOSE-COUPLED COMPACT
CLOSED DARK DOWN SHUT CLOSE
LUCKEN UNOPEN BLOCKED
COVERED
(— AT ONE END) BLIND
CLOSEFISTED MEAN NEAR FISTY
TIGHT SNIPPY STINGY MISERLY
HANDFAST
CLOSE-FITTING FIT HARD MEET
SNUG THEAT THEET TIGHT THIGHT
SUCCINCT
CLOSE-KNIT TRUSSED
CLOSE-LIPPED SILENT
CLOSELY FAST JUST NEAR WELL
SADLY ALMOST BARELY HARDLY
NARROW NEARLY JUNCTLY
STRICTLY
CLOSEMOUTHED SECRET SILENT
(NOT —) LEAKY
CLOSENESS DENSITY SECRECY
FIDELITY INTIMACY NEARNESS
PARSIMONY
CLOSER VAMPER CLOSURE
CLOSEST NEXT NEAREST
CLOSESTOOL STOLE
CLOSET ARK EWRY ROOM SAFE
AMBRY CUBBY CUDDY PRESS
LOCKER PANTRY SECRET CABINET
CONCEAL PRIVATE CONCLAVE
CUPBOARD GARDEVIN WARDROBE
CLOSING FLY SLAM SNAP CLOSURE
CLOTURE CLAUDENT BUTTONING
CLOSURE END GAG BOLT SEAL
BOUND LIMIT ATRESIA CLOTURE
FERRULE TENSION CLAUSURE
FINALITY KANGAROO
CLOT DOT GEL CLAG CLAT GOUT
JELL LUMP MASS MOLE SHED
CLART GRUME BALTER COTTER
LAPPER LOPPER CLODDER
EMBOLUS THICKEN CLODPATE
COAGULUM CONCRETE SOLIDIFY
CLOTH DAB RAG DRAB BLUE COAT DRAB
DRAP ECRU FELT FILE PALL SEAM
WARE WOOF BEIGE BLUET CABAN
CLOUT DITTO FOULE GOODS GREEN
LODEN LUNGI MOORY PRINT STUPE
TAMMY TAWNY TIBET TOILE TWEED
TWILL ALPACA AWNING BENGAL

BYSSUS CANAMO CANVAS CHADOR
CLAITH CLERGY COVERT DORSEL
DOSSAL DOSSER DRAPET DUSTER
FABRIC LIVERY LONGYI LOWELL
MELLAY MULETA NAPKIN RENGUE
REXINE SARONG SURNAP TILLOT
WITNEY ACETATE BOULTEL
CHADDAR CHRISOM COATING
CRIMSON DRAPERY DUSTRAG
FALDING GARMENT JACONET
ORLEANS PANUELO RAIMENT
SACKING SURNAPE TEXTILE
WATCHET WORSTED BATSWING
CHRISMAL COMPRESS CORPORAL
CRAMOISY DWELLING FROCKING
HOMESPUN LAMBSKIN MATERIAL
PHULKARI RADEVORE SHAATNEZ
SHEETING THICKSET TOILINET
(— OF GOLD) SONERI
(— FOR BELT) SHROUD
(— FOR WIPING TABLE) FILE
(— FOR WRAPPING FABRICS) TILLE"
(— FOR WRAPPING THE DEAD)
CEREMENT
(— HANGING FROM WAISTBAND)
LANGOOTY
(— OF SINGLE WIDTH) STRAITS
(— REMAINING AFTER CUTTING)
CABBAGE
(— WORN LIKE KILT) LAVALAVA
(ALTAR —) TOWEL PENDLE PALLIUM
VESPERAL CATASARKA
(ARABIAN —) HAIK CABAN CABAAN
(BARK —) TAPA TAPPA
(BED —) COVER SPREAD
(BLACK —) KISWA KISWAH
(COARSE —) DOZEN DUROY
CANGAN DOWLAS DOZENS FORFAR
FRIEZE HODDEN KERSEY KHARVA
KHARWA STAMIN STROUD TAPALO
CAMBAYE COTONIA DRUGGET
FORFARS RAPLOCH RUGGING
SARPLER SOUTAGE FLUSHING
RADEVORE SARCILIS
(COMMUNION —) FANON SINDON
CORPORAL
(COTTON —) JEAN TOBE ADATI
BLUET CAFFA CRASH DURRY JEANS
KHADI KHAKI SURAT BEAVER
CALICO CANGAN DOWLAS DURRIE
GANZIE HUMHUM KALMUK NANKIN
PENANG CAMBAYE FUSTIAN
GALATEA GINGHAM JACONET
KHADDAR LASTING NANKEEN
REGATTA BOGOTANA DOMESTIC
MUSLINET
(CRIMSON —) CRAMASIE CRAMOISY
(DECORATIVE —) SCARF
(EMBROIDERED —) SAMPLER
(GLASS —) DORON
(GOAT-WOOL —) SLING
(GREEN —) KENDAL
(GUNNY —) TAT
(HAIR —) ABA ABBA CILICE
(HEMP —) PINAYUSA
(HOMESPUN —) KELT KHADI PATTU
PUTTOO HEADING KHADDAR
(LAP —) GREMIAL
(LINEN —) BRIN LINE GULIX

DOWLAS FORFAR BRABANT
LOCKRAM SILESIA BLANCARD
CORPORAL GAMBROON GHENTING
LINCLOTH
(LONG —) LUNGI WHITE LUNGEE
(ORNAMENTAL —) TRAP DOSSAL
DOSSEL
(PACK —) MANTA
(PACKING —) SOUTAGE
(PIECE OF —) APRON CLOUT
GODET LANGOOTY
(RICH —) SCARLET
(SADDLE —) PANEL
(SILK —) CAFFA BENGAL PATOLA
(SOAKED —) BUCK
(SOFT —) RUGINE
(STAGE —) BACKDROP
(STARCHED —) GUIMPE
(STRIPED —) RAY
(STRONG —) CANVAS DURANCE
(TWILLED —) JANE JEAN
GAMBROON
(UNDYED —) HODDEN
(WASHING —) SHAMMY CHAMOIS
(WAX —) MUMJUMA
(WET —) DAB
(WOOL —) SAY DRAB PUKE BEIGE
BUREL DOZEN DUROY LAINE STARA
TAMIS TAMMY DOZENS DUFFEL
HODDEN KENDAL KERSEY MEDLEY
MELTON MUSTER SAXONY STAMIN
TAMINY TARTAN BASTARD BLANKET
DUNSTER FLANNEL RAPLOCH
ROPLOCH RUGGING BEARSKIN
BUCKSKIN FLORENCE SARCILIS
VENETIAN
(WORSTED —) RASH SHAG
BOMBAZET
CLOTHE DON DUB HAP LAP RIG TOG
DECK GARB GIRD GOWN ROBE VEST
ADORN ARRAY CLEAD CLEED
DRESS ENDOW ENDUE FLESH
FROCK HABIT INDUE ATTIRE
BEWRAP SHRIDE SHROUD SWATHE
ADDRESS APPAREL FEATHER
RAIMENT VESTURE ACCOUTER
ACCOUTRE
CLOTHED CLAD BECLAD HABITED
CLOTHES CASE DUDS GARB GEAR
GORE KAPA SUIT TACK TOGS WEAR
BRAWS DUCKS HABIT ATTIRE
FARDEL SHROUD TROGGS APPAREL
BAGGAGE COSTUME IRONING
RAIMENT REGALIA TOGGERY
VESTURE WEARING CLOTHING
FEATHERS FRIPPERY GARMENTS
INDUMENT
(CASTOFF —) FRIPPERY
(DRESS —) WAMPUM
(FINE —) BRAWS
(HANDSOME —) BRAVERY
(MOURNING —) DOLE
(SHOWY —) LUGS
(SOAKED —) BUCK
CLOTHES DRYER AIRER TUMBLER
CLOTHESPIN PEG
CLOTHESPRESS ARMOIRE TALLBOY
WARDROBE
CLOTH FOLDER CUTTLER

CLOTHING (ALSO SEE CLOTHES)
BACK BLUE BRAT COAT GARB GEAR
SEAM WEAR ARRAY BUREL CLOTH
DRESS GREEN HABIT JABOT STUFF
ATTIRE FARDEL ROBING VESTRY
APPAREL CLOBBER CLOTHES
CRIMSON DRAPERY OUTWALL
RAIMENT VESTURE WEEDERY
INDUMENT KNITWEAR ORNAMENT
SLOPWORK VESTIARY VESTMENT
(BLACK —) SABLE
(COARSE —) BUREL
(LOWER —) LAP
(MUSLIM —) IHRAM
(NAUTICAL —) SLOPS
(SHEER —) FLIMSIES
(SHOWY —) SHEEN FINERY
(WOMEN'S —) FRILLIES
(WORK —) FATIGUES
CLOTHING DEALER HOSIER
CLOTHWORKER FULLER
CLOTTED GORY CLOTTY CLOUTED
GARGETY GRUMOUS LIVERED
CLOTURE GAG CLOSURE
CLOUD DOG FOG NUE SKY BLUR
DAMP DARK DUST FOOL HAZE HELM
HIDE MIST REEK SMUR ARCUS
BEDIM BEFOG BLOOM DRIFT GLOOM
MUDDY NUBIA OXEYE SHADE STAIN
SULLY SWARM TAINT VAPOR
CIRRUS DAMAGE DARKEN DEEPEN
DEFAME FUNNEL MUDDLE NEBULA
NIMBUS PILEUS POTHER SCREEN
SHADOW STIGMA BLACKEN
CONFUSE CUMULUS ECLIPSE
FUMULUS GRANULE OBSCURE
POOTHER STRATUS SUNSPOT
TARNISH CLOUDCAP CLOUDLET
COCKTAIL NIGHTCAP NUBILATE
OVERCAST WOOLPACK
(— OF DUST OR VAPOR) STEW
SMOTHER
(— OF MIST) SOP
(— OVER MOUNTAIN) HELM
(HIGH —) CIRRUS
(HORIZONTAL —) STRATUS
(MASS OF HIGH —S) RACK
(MASSY —) CUMULUS
(NUCLEAR —) FIREBALL
(RAIN —) NIMBUS
(PL.) SCUD SOUP CARRY GASHES
CLOUDBERRY AKPEK MOLKA
AVERIN
(FRUIT OF —) NOOP
CLOUDED HAZY DIRTY DUSTY FILMY
JASPE MUCKY SHADY ACLOUD
GLOOMY TURBID INFUMATE
NEBULOUS
CLOUDINESS FAIR HAZE GLOOM
MUDDLE
CLOUDING DAPPLE
(— OF EYE) CATARACT
CLOUDLESS AZURE CLEAR BRIGHT
CLOUDY DIM DARK DULL HAZY
BLEAR FILMY FOGGY MISTY MURKY
SHADY GLOOMY LOWERY OPAQUE
SMURRY VEILED BLURRED CLOUDED
NEBULAR OBSCURE CONFUSED
NUBILOUS OVERCAST VAPOROUS

CLOUGH CLUF CLEFT CLOES
CLEUCH CLEUGH RAVINE VALLEY
CLOUT BAT BOX DAB HIT BEAT
BLOW BUMP CLOD CLUB CUFF JOIN
MEND NAIL SLAP SLUG SWAT
PATCH SMITE KLOWET STRIKE
TARGET THRASH WASHER BANDAGE
BOSTHOON
CLOVE GAP NAIL CHIVE CLEFT GILLY
BUTTON CLEAVE RAVINE SHERRY
GILLIVER
CLOVEN CLEFT SPLIT DIVIDED
BISULCATE
CLOVEN-FOOTED SLIT FISSIPED
CLOVE PINK GELOFER GRENADIN
CLOVER RED HAGI SEED HUBAM
LOTUS MEDIC NARDU PUSSY ALSIKE
BERSIM LADINO LEGUME LUXURY
NARDOO ALFALFA BERSEEM
BERSINE CLAIVER COMFORT
LUCERNE MELILOT SAPLING
TREFOIL TRIFOLY COWGRASS
HAREFOOT NAPOLEON PUSSYCAT
SHAMROCK SUCKLING YELLOWTOP
CLOVER DODDER AILWEED
EPITHYME HAILWEED HAIRWEED
HALEWEED
CLOWN HOB OAF PUT APER BOOR
FOOL GAUM GOFF JOEY LOUT MIME
MOME SWAD ZANY ANTIC BUFFO
CHURL COMIC FESTE IDIOT MIMER
PATCH PUNCH WAMBA ZANNI
AUGUST BODACH HOBBIL JESTER
LUBBER RUSTIC STOOGE AUGUSTE
BODDAGH BUFFOON BUMPKIN
CHARLEY COSTARD KOSHARE
LAVACHE LOBSTER MUDHEAD
PEASANT PIERROT PLAYBOY
SCOFFER TOMFOOL COVIELLO
KOYEMSHI MERRYMAN WHITEFACE
CLOWNISH RAW RUDE ZANY GAWKY
ROUGH CLUMSY COARSE RUSTIC
AWKWARD BOORISH HOBLIKE
KERNISH LOBBISH LOUTISH UNCIVIL
VILLAIN CLUBBISH SWADDISH
UNGAINLY
CLOY CLOG GLUT NAIL PALL SATE
GORGE PRICK ACCLOY PIERCE
SATIATE SATISFY SURFEIT
SATURATE
CLOYER SNAP
CLOYING GOOEY SWEET VANILLA
CLOYSOME LUSCIOUS
CLUB BAT DOG HIT HUI SET BEAT
CANE JOIN MACE MALL MAUL MERE
POLT TEAM BAFFY BANDY BATON
BILLY BUNCH CLOUT HURLY KEBBY
LODGE MASHY ORDER STAFF STICK
TOWEL UNITE YOKEL ZONTA
BULGER CERCLE CLIQUE CUDGEL
HURLEY KEBBIE LIBBET MACANA
MASHIE MENAGE MUCKLE NULLAH
PRIEST STRIKE TAIAHA VEREIN
WEAPON WHITES CAMBUCA
COLLEGE COUNCIL HETAERY
HETAIRY SOROSIS ATHENEUM
BLUDGEON CATSTICK SODALITY
SORORITY SPONTOON TERTULIA
KNOBKERRY

(— IN PLAYING CARDS) OAK
(— OF ANTENNA) CLAVUS
(BASEBALL —) FARM
(GOLF —) IRON WOOD BAFFY
CLEEK MASHY SPOON STICK
BRASSY BULGER DRIVER JIGGER
LOFTER MASHIE PUTTER BLASTER
MIDIRON NIBLICK PITCHER
(MAORI —) MERE MERAI MARREE
(POLICEMAN'S —) SAP BILLY
PANTOON SPONTON SPONTOON
(POLITICAL —) ROTA HETAERY
HETAIRY
(WAR —) WADDY
(WOMEN'S —) SOROSIS SORORITY
CLUB CARRIER CLAVIGER
CLUBFOOT TALUS VARUS TALIPES
CYLLOSIS POLTFOOT
CLUB MOSS MOSS FOFEET
LYCOPOD PILIGAN CROWFOOT
FERNWORT
CLUBROOT CLUB ANBURY HANBURY
CLUBBING CLUBFOOT
CLUB RUSH RUSH SEDGE GLUMAL
DEERHAIR
CLUCK HEN FUSS CHUCK CLACK
CLICK CLOCK CLOOK
CLUE KEY TIP BALL CLEW HINT IDEA
LEAD GUIDE TWINE BOTTOM
THREAD INNUENDO
CLUMP SOP TOD BLOW BUSH CLOT
HEAP KNOT LUMP MASS MOSS
MOTT TOPE TUFT TURB BLUFF
BUNCH CLAMP GROUP GROVE
HOUSE PATCH PLUMP STUMP
TREAD WUDGE CLUNCH DOLLOP
LUMPER CLUMPER CLUSTER
THICKET
(— OF BRIERS OR ROSES) ROAN
RONE
(— OF CELLS) SLUDGE
(— OF SHRUBS) BUSH
(— OF SPORANGIA) SORUS
(— OF TREES) BLUFF HOUSE HURST
HYRST BOSQUE
CLUMSILY SOUSE GREENLY
GAUCHELY
CLUMSY AWK FLOB LEWD NUMB
RUDE BLUNT BULKY GAUMY GAWKY
HOGGY HULKY INAPT INEPT SCRAM
SPLAY STIFF STOGY GAUCHE
LUBBER NOGGEN THUMBY
AWKWARD BOORISH CHOCKLE
CHUCKLE UNHANDY UNREADY
BENUMBED BUNGLING CLOWNISH
FOOTLESS HANDLESS LUMBERLY
TACTLESS UNGAINLY UNWIELDY
(NOT —) FINE
CLUSTER BOB BOG BUSH CLOT
COMA CONE CYME KNOT LUMP
TUFT BUNCH CLUMP DRUSE GROUP
PLUMP SHEAF CENTER COLONY
GATHER MORULA PLEIAD REGIME
BOUROCK CLUTHER DOLPHIN
ENVIRON FOLIAGE FASCICLE
NUCLEATE SURROUND
(— AS BEES) BALL KNIT
(— OF BANANAS) HAND
(— OF BRANCHES) SPRAY

(— OF CRYSTALS) DRUSE
(— OF FEATHERS) MUFF
(— OF FIBERS) NEP
(— OF FLOWERS) CYME CORYMB
ANTHEMY
(— OF HAIRS) MYSTAX
(— OF METAL BALLS) GRAPE
(— OF NODULES) GRAPES
(— OF PILES) DOLPHIN
(— OF PLANTS) BED
(— OF RAYS) AIGRETTE
(— OF SPORES) SORUS
(— OF STARS) PRAESEPE
(— OF TINES) TROCHE
(CONFUSED —) SPLATTER
(SUSPENDED —) SWAG
CLUSTER BEAN GUAR
CLUSTERED TUFTED RACEMOSE
AGGREGATE
CLUTCH HUG NAB SET CLAM CLAW
CLEM CLIP FIST GLAM GRAB GRIP
NEST BROOD CATCH CLASP CLAUT
CLEEK CLICK GLAUM GRASP GRIPE
GRISP HATCH LEVER POWER SEIZE
TALON CLEACH CLENCH CLETCH
CLINCH CUTOUT FASTEN RETAIN
SNATCH CONTROL CRAMPON
COUPLING
(— OF EGGS) SET LAWTER LAYING
SETTING SITTING LAUGHTER
CLUTCHING GRIP GRIPING
CLUTTER MESS STUFF BUSTLE
CUMBER CLATTER DISORDER
CONFUSION
CLUTTERED CLATTY CLOTTED
CLYMENE (FATHER OF —) OCEANUS
(HUSBAND OF —) IAPETUS
(MOTHER OF —) TETHYS
(SON OF —) ATLAS PHAETHON
MENOETIUS
CLYPEUS NASUS EPISTOME
PRELABRUM
CLYSTER LAVEMENT INJECTION
CLYTEMNESTRA (FATHER OF —)
TYNDAREUS
(HUSBAND OF —) AGAMEMNON
(MOTHER OF —) LEDA
(SON OF —) ORESTES
COACH BUS CAR FLY DRAG HACK
HELP ARABA BRIEF CABIN FLIER
FLYER PILOT PRIME STAGE TEACH
TRAIN TUTOR ADVISE DIRECT
FIACRE JARVEY SALOON ADVISER
CHARIOT COACHER CONCORD
GONDOLA PREPARE RATTLER
TALLYHO CARRIAGE DORMEUSE
PUPILIZE
(3-WHEELED —) TRICYCLE
(FAST —) FLIER FLYER
(HACKNEY —) FIACRE JARVEY
(HEAVY —) DRAG
(SLOW —) SLOWPOKE
COACHMAN FLY FISH JEHU WHIP
PILOT COACHY DRIVER COACHEE
COACHER YAMSHIK YEMSCHIK
COACTION EXPLOITATION
COADJUTOR PRIOR
COAGULANT CURD RENNET
STYPTIC COAGULUM GELATINE

COAGULATE GEL SET CAKE CLOD
CLOT CURD JELL QUAIL YEARN
COTTER CURDLE LAPPER LOBBER
LOPPER POSSET CLABBER CLOTTER
CONGEAL PECTIZE THICKEN
COAGULUM CONCRETE SOLIDIFY
COAGULATED CRUDY CURDY
LIVERED
COAGULATION GOUT CLOTTER
COAGULUM CLOT THROMBUS
COAL RIB BASS DUFF FUEL SWAD
BLOCK CHARK EMBER GHOST
GLEED STOKE BARING BRAZIL
BURGEE CANNEL CARBON CINDER
FIRING SPLINT BACKING BOGHEAD
BRIGHTS BYERITE COBBLES LIGNITE
RATTLER VITRAIN AMPELITE
LANDSALE
(— IN PLACE) SOLID
(— PILLAR) STOOK
(— SLAB) SKIP
(BAD —) SMUT
(DIRTY —) RASH
(FINE —) DUFF SCREENINGS
(IMPURE —) SWAD
(LARGE BLOCK OF —) JUD JUDD
(LIVE OR GLOWING —) GLEED
GLEYD
(REFUSE —) BREEZE
(SIZE OF —) EGG NUT PEA LUMP
RICE SLACK STOVE BARLEY
BROKEN CHESTNUT WALLSEND
BUCKWHEAT
(SLATY —) BASS BONE BONY
(SMALL LUMP OF —) NUBBLING
(SMALL PORTION OF UNCUT —)
PANEL
COAL BED SEAM
COALBIN BUNKER
COAL BROKER CRIMP
COAL CAR JIMMY
COAL CHUTE DOCK
COAL DUST COOM CULM SMUT
COOMB
COALESCE MIX CLOG FUSE JOIN
BLEND MERGE UNITE EMBODY
MINGLE COMBINE
COALESCENCE UNION FUSION
LEAGUE CAPTURE SYNANTHY
COALFISH SEY PARR CUDDY SEITH
BESHOW BILLET CUDDEN PODLER
SAITHE BADDOCK GLASHAN
GLASSIN PILTOCK POLLACK
(YOUNG —) PODLER PODLEY
COMAMIE POODLER SILLOCK
GRAYFISH
COALITION FRONT TRUST UNION
FUSION LEAGUE MERGER ENTENTE
ALLIANCE
COAL OIL KEROSENE
COALRAKE HOE FREGGIN FRUGGAN
SCRAPPLE
COAL WORKER GEORDIE HURRIER
COAL YARD REE
COAMING CURB LEDGE COMBING
COARSE FAT LOW RAW BASE BULL
DANK FOUL HARD HASK LEWD
LOUD RANK RUDE SOUR VILE
BAWDY BRASH BROAD CRASS

CRUDE DIRTY GREAT GROFF GROSS
HARSH HASKY HEAVY LARGE
LOOSE PLAIN RANDY ROUGH ROUTH
ROWTY STOGY STOUR THICK
UNORN BLOWSY BRAZEN BRUTAL
CALLOW COMMON DUDGEN EARTHY
IMPURE INCULT RANDIE RIBALD
ROUDAS RUDOUS RUSSET RUSTIC
SULTRY UNFELE VULGAR BLATANT
CARLAGE CARLISH FULSOME
GOATISH LOUTISH OBSCENE
RAPLOCH RAUCOUS ROINISH
SENSUAL CLOWNISH HOMESPUN
IMMODEST INDECENT PLEBEIAN
STUBBORN UNCHASTE
OARSE-FIBERED STRONG
OARSE-GRAINED DRY GRUFF
OARSELY BROADLY HARSHLY
OARSEN HACKNEY
OAST BANK LAND RIPA BEACH
CLIFF SHORE SLIDE WARTH ADJOIN
BORDER RIVAGE STRAND BOBSLED
SEASIDE APPROACH SEABOARD
SEASHORE
OASTER MAT SLED DOLLY TROUT
CRADLE CREEPER TOBOGGAN
OASTLAND MAREMMA
OAT FUR LAY PEE SAC TOG BARK
BLUE BUFF CONY DAUB FOIL FOLD
HIDE HUSK JACK JAMA JUPE PINK
RIND SACK SCAB SEAL TOGE ZINC
BENNY CLOTH CONEY COVER
CRUST FLASH FROCK GLACE GLAZE
HABIT JAMAH JEMMY LAYER OILER
PAINT PLATE QUYTE SAQUE SHELL
TERVE ALPACA BYRNIE COATEE
DUSTER ENAMEL EXTIMA GROUND
HACKLE INTIMA INVEST JACKET
JOSEPH KIRTLE LACKER MANTLE
MELOTE PARGET PELAGE RABBIT
REEFER SEALER SILVER SLOUGH
STUCCO TABARD VENEER BEESWAX
BOBTAIL CASSOCK COATING
COURTBY CRISPIN CUTAWAY
GARMENT GROGRAM INCRUST
KARAKUL LACQUER OILCOAT
OVERLAY PALETOT PELISSE
PLASTER SHELLAC SHOOTER
SPENCER STRATUM SUBCOAT
SURCOAT SURTOUT SWAGGER
TOGEMAN TOPCOAT VESTURE
BENJAMIN COURTEPY GRAPHITE
INTONACO MACKINAW MEMBRANE
ROCKELAY SEALSKIN SHERWANI
SILICATE TEGUMENT TRENCHER
(— FOOD) DREDGE
(— LENS) BLOOM
(— OF ARMS) CREST BLAZON
BEARINGS
(— OF BIRD SKINS) TEMIAK
(— OF CARIBOU SKINS) KOOLETAH
(— OF DEFENSE) JACK
(— OF EYE) CHOROID
(— OF EYEBALL) SCLERA
(— OF GRAVEL) BLOTTER
(— OF MAIL) FROCK BRINIE BYRNIE
SECRET HAUBERK
(— OF ORGAN) INTIMA
(— OF PLASTER) SET ARRICCIO

BROWNING INTONACO
(— OF SEED) BRAN
(— OF WOOL) FLEECE
(— WITH ALLOY) TERNE
(— WITH PITCH) PAY
(DEER'S WINTER —) BLUE
(FIRST — OF TIN) LIST
(HAIR —) MELOTE
(HOODED —) GREGO CAPOTE
(LONG —) JIBBA JIBBAH KAPOTE
DJIBBAH
(LOOSE —) CASSOCK PALETOT
INVERNESS
(MILITARY —) TUNIC BLOUSE
BUFFCOAT
(RIDING —) JOSEPH
(SEALSKIN —) NETCHA
(SHEEPSKIN —) ZAMARRA
ZAMARRO
(SHORT —) PEA SACK JERKIN
REEFER PEACOAT
(THREE-QUARTER LENGTH —)
ACHKAN
(WATERPROOF —) BURSATI SLICKER
(WOMAN'S —) CARACO DOLMAN
COATED GLACE BACKED FURRED
LOADED CANDIED
COAT HANGER SHOULDER
COATI NASUA TEJON NARICA PISOTE
ARCTOID
COATING (ALSO SEE COAT) FUR
GUM ARIL DOPE DRAB FILM FLOR
HAIR HOAR SKIN BLOOM FLASH
GLACE GLAZE ICING SCALE BEAVER
CHATON COVERT FINISH JACKET
PATINA VENEER BACKING DIPCOAT
FURRING GILDING LACQUER
PLATING TINNING ACIERAGE
CAMBOUIS CLADDING EMULSION
FLOODING MUCILAGE PERIDIUM
(— OF BACTERIA) SLIME
(— OF GLASS) MOILES FOLIATION
(— OF GLUE) ENAMEL
(— OF ICE) GLAZE
(— OF SEED) TESTA
(— OF TONGUE) ATTER
(CORROSION —) RUST
(POWDERY —) DOWN
(PRUINOUS —) FARINA
(WALL —) GROUT
COATTAIL LABIE LAPPET
COAX BEG COY PET CANT DUPE
FAGE FAWN LURE URGE JOLLY
TEASE BANTER CAJOLE CUITLE
CUTTER ENTICE FLEECH SEDUCE
BEGUILE CROODLE CROWDLE
CRUDDLE FLATTER IMPLORE
SOOTHER WHEEDLE BLANDISH
COLLOGUE INVEIGLE PERSUADE
COAXIAL CONCENTRIC
COB EAR LOB MEW COBB
COBBERER ROARER ROUSER
COBBLE DARN MEND PAVE BOTCH
PATCH BUNGLE COGGLE REPAIR
COBBLER PIE SNOB SHEEP SOLER
SUTOR ARTIST COZIER SOUTER
BOTCHER CATFISH CRISPIN
POMPANO SADDLER CHUCKLER
SCORPION SNOBSCAT

COBBLERFISH COBBLER SUNFISH
SHOEMAKER
COBBY STOUT HEARTY LIVELY
STOCKY COMPACT
COBLE MULE KOBIL
COBNUT COB OUABE HOGNUT
PIGNUT
COBRA ASP NAG HAJE NAGA NAJA
KRAIT VIPER ELAPID URAEUS
COBWEB NET TRAP SNARE WEVET
GOSSAMER
COCA CUCA KHOKA TRUXILLO
COCAINE COKE SNOW
(— MIXED WITH HEROIN)
SPEEDBALL
COCASH ASTER SWANWEED
COCCOID BERRYLIKE
COCCULUS CEBATHA FISHBERRY
COCHE MOCOA
COCHINEAL GRAIN BLANCO
COCCUS GRANILLA
COCHINEAL FIG NOPAL
COCHINEAL INSECT VERMIL
VERMEIL VERMILION
COCK COX TAP BANK BOOT COIL
FOWL HEAP KORA PILE RICK SPAN
COCKY COQUE FIGHT FUGIE GALLO
SHOCK STACK STRUT VALVE YOWLE
CRAVEN FAUCET HAMMER HEELER
LEADER CONTEND GORCOCK
PETCOCK ROOSTER SWAGGER
ASTROLOG COCKBIRD COCKEREL
COXBONES GAMECOCK JERMONAL
STOPCOCK
(— GUNLOCK) NAB
(— OF HAY) HIPPLE
(— OF THE WALK) KINGFISH
(— WITHOUT COURAGE) CRAVEN
(— WITHOUT SPURS) MUCKNA
(FIGHTING —) FUGIE HEELER
TURNPOKE
(TURKEY —) STAG
(WATER —) KORA
(WEATHER —) FANE VANE
COCKADE KNOT BADGE COCKARD
ROSETTE
COCKATIEL QUARRION
COCKATOO ARA ARARA COCKY
GALAH MACAW ABACAY COCKIE
PARROT CORELLA JACATOO
CALANGAY GANGGANG
COCKATOO BUSH BLUEBERRY
COCKBOAT COG COCK COGBOAT
COCKCHAFER OAKWEB BUZZARD
HUMBUZZ
COCKED HAT SCRAPER RAMILLIE
COCKER CODDLE COGGER QUIVER
SPANIEL
COCKEREL COCK SLIP BANTAM
COCKINESS SWAGGER
COCKLE COCK GALL GITH KILN
OAST BULGE KAKEL SHELL STOVE
DARNEL NUCULA PALOUR PUCKER
RIPPLE WABBLE ZIZANY CUCKOLD
WRINKLE HARDHEAD
COCKLEBUR COTS CLOTE COCKLE
BURDOCK BURWEED CADILLO
CLOTBUR CUCKOLD CLOTWEED
DITCHBUR

COCKNEY ORTHERIS LONDONESE
COCKPIT PIT RING RINK WELL
ARENA CABIN FIELD GALLERA
COCKROACH BUG DRUM ROACH
BEETLE BLATTID DRUMMER
KNOCKER
COCKSCOMB CREST COXCOMB
COCKSPUR FINGRIGO GARABATO
COCKTAIL SOUR ZOOM BRONX
CRUSTA GIBSON MARTINI SAZERAC
SIDECAR STINGER SWIZZLE
APERITIF DAIQUIRI
COCKY PERK PERT CRANK CROUSE
FARMER JAUNTY COCKING
ARROGANT
COCO KOKO BROMA COCOA COKER
YUNTIA
COCOA MAHAL PATASHTE
COCONUT COCO COCKER NARGIL
COCOANUT
COCONUT FIBER COIR KAIR KYAR
CAYAR
COCONUT MEAT COPRA
COCONUT PALM KOKO NIOG
COCOON POD CLEW CLUE KELL
SCAB SHED SHELL BOTTOM
DOUPION FOLLICLE
COCO PLUM ICACO HICACO
COCOWOOD KOKRA
COCUSWOOD KOKRA
COD BAG BIB COR KID POD AXLE
BANK CUSK FOOL GADE HOAX
HUSK POOR ROCK BELLY DROUD
GADID POUCH SCROD SHALE SHAUP
TORSK BURBOT CODGER CULTUS
ESCROD FELLOW MULVEL PILLOW
POCKET TOMCOD WACHNA
BACALAO CODFISH CODLING
CUSHION KEELING KILLING MILWELL
SCROTUM CABELIAU DOLEFISH
KABBELOW KLIPFISH
(BUFFALO —) LING
(CURED —) DUNFISH
(DRIED —) STOCK
(PILE OF DRIED —) YAFFLE
(SALTED —) COR KLIPFISH
HABERDINE
(YOUNG —) SPRAG
CODA CAUDA RONDO EPILOG FINALE
CODETTA EPILOGUE
CODDLE PET BABY CADE COOK
MUCH HUMOR NURSE SMALM SPOIL
CARESS COCKER COSSET COTTON
FONDLE PAMPER PTISAN QUADLE
PARBOIL
CODE LAW FLAG CANON CODEX
DOGMA FUERO CIPHER DIGEST
SECRET SIGNAL MULTEKA PRECEPT
DOOMBOOK
(— OF CHIVALRY) BUSHIDO
(— OF LAWS) ADA ADAT PANDECT
DOOMBOOK
(— OF RULES) VINAYA
(— OF WHAT IS FITTING) DECORUM
CODETTA CONDUIT
CODEX ALEF CODE ALEPH ANNAL
CODFISH POOR SPRAG TORSK
KEELING
CODGER COD CUFF CHURL CRANK

MISER FELLOW NIGGARD
CODICIL ANNEX LABEL SCRIPT
CODIFY INDEX DIGEST CLASSIFY
CODLING HAKE
CODOL RETINOL
COEFFICIENT CUMULANT
AUSTAUSCH
COELENTERATE POLYP MEDUSA
ACALEPH RADIATE ACALEPHE
COENOBIUM COLONY
COENOCYTE SYMPLASM SYMPLAST
SYNCYTIUM
COENZYME COFACTOR
COERCE COW CURB MAKE BULLY
CHECK DRIVE FORCE ORDER
COHERT COMPEL HIJACK CONCUSS
ENFORCE REPRESS SANDBAG
BLUDGEON BULLDOZE DISTRAIN
RESTRAIN RESTRICT
COERCION HEAT FORCE DURESS
COMMAND
COEUR D'ALENE SKITSWISH
COFFEE JO JOE RIO CAFE COHO
COHU JAVA MILD MOCHA BOGOTA
BRAZIL CAUFLE CHAOUA JAMOKE
SANTOS TRIAGE ARABICA BOURBON
MELANGE SUMATRA ESPRESSO
MAZAGRAN MEDELLIN TRILLADO
COFFEE BEAN QUAKER
COFFEEBERRY JOJOBA CASCARA
SOYBEAN PEABERRY
COFFEE CAKE KUCHEN
COFFEEHOUSE INN CAFE CAFENER
CAFENET
COFFEEMAKER SILEX
COFFEE TREE BONDUC CHICOT
VIRGILIA
COFFER ARK BOX DAM PYX CHEST
HUTCH TRUNK CASKET FORCER
FORCET SPRUCE TRENCH CAISSON
CASHBOX CASSOON COFFRET
LACUNAR LAQUEAR CIBORIUM
STANDARD
COFFIN BIER CASE CIST KIST MOLD
PALL SHELL BASKET CASING
CASKET COFFER HEARSE TROUGH
THROUGH
(LEADEN —) COPE
COG CAM LIE CAUK COCK GEAR
JEST CATCH CHEAT CHOCK CHUCK
COGUE COZEN TENON TOOTH
TRICK WEDGE WHEEL CAJOLE
COGGING DECEIVE PRODUCE
QUIBBLE WHEEDLE
COGENT GOOD PITHY VALID POTENT
STRONG TELLING FORCIBLE
POWERFUL
COGITATE MULL MUSE PLAN THINK
PONDER CONNATE MEDIATE
REFLECT CONSIDER
COGNATE KIN AKIN ALIKE ALLIED
COGENER KINDRED RELATED
SIMILAR BANDHAVA RELATIVE
APOPHONIC
COGNITION GNOSIS NOESIS
KENNING KNOWLEDGE
COGNITIVE KNOWING EPISTEMIC
COGNIZANCE KEN WIT HEED MARK
BADGE CREST EMBLEM NOTICE

BEARING COCKADE KNOWING
PRIVITY WITTING
COGNIZANT WARE WISE AWAKE
AWARE GUILTY KNOWING SENSIBLE
(BE —) DEEM
COGNOMEN NAME BYNAME
AGNOMEN SURNAME NICKNAME
PATRONYM
COGON ILLUK KUNAI LALANG
COGWOOD CERILLO
COHABIT LIVE DWELL ADHERE
OCCUPY COMPANY ACCUSTOM
COHERE FIT BOND GLUE SUIT
AGREE CLING SEIZE STICK UNITE
ADHERE CEMENT CLEAVE CONNECT
COINCIDE
COHERENCE UNION CONSENT
CONTEXT COHESION STRENGTH
COHERENT SERRIED
COHESION BOND ADHESION
HARDNESS STRENGTH
COHESIVE FATTY TENACIOUS
COHESIVENESS TENACITY
COHOBA PARICA
COHOSH SQUAWROOT
PAPOOSEROOT
COHUNE COROJO COROZO
COIF CAP HOW HOOD HOUVE
BEGGIN BURLET HAIRDO QUAIFE
ARRANGE CALOTTE BIGGONET
COIFFURE SKULLCAP
COIFFURE COIF HEAD HAIRDO
TUTULUS TRESSURE
COIL ADO WIN WIP ANSA CLEW
CURL FAKE FANK FURL FUSS HANK
LINK LOOP ROLL TUFT WIND ENRO
FLAKE HELIX QUERL QUILE ROUND
SPIRE TENSE TESLA TWINE TWIRL
TWIST WHORL WRING BOBBIN
BOTTOM BOUGHT DIMMER ENROLL
GLOMUS HEATER RENDER RUNDLE
SPIRAL TEASER TUMULT UPWIND
VOLUME WINDUP WREATH ENTRAIL
HAYCOCK INVOLVE PRIMARY
RINGLET SNAKING TICKLER
TROUBLE WREATHE COFUSION
ENCIRCLE INDUCTOR OVERCOIL
(— IN STILL) SCROLL
(— INTO BALL) WIRE
(— OF CAPILLARIES) TUFT
(— OF HAIR) BUN PUG
(— OF SNAKE) FOLD
(— OF WIRE) BOBBIN SOLENOID
(INDUCTION —) JIGGER
COILED GYRATE TORTILE WRITHEN
COILER FLARER
COILING SPIRY
COIN AS BU PU AVO BAN BIT BOO
COB DAM DIE DUB ECU FIL JOE KI
LAT LEK LEU LEV LEY ORI PUL SE
SOL TRA WEN WON ABAS ANNA
ATTE BAHT BATZ BESA CASH CEN
CHIP CHON DEMY DIME DOIT DONE
DOTT DUMP DURO FELS FILS GILL
GROS GROT HARP HOON HWAN
JACK JANE KRAN KYAT LEVY LION
MAIL MAKE MILL MINT MITE MULE
OBAN ONZA OORD PARA PAUL
PESA PESO PICE POND POUL QUA

RAND RIAL ROCK RYAL SCAD SENT
SINK SIZE SLUG TAEL TARA TARE
TARI TARO TIAO TREY TYPE UNIT
ACKEY AGNEL AKCHA ALBUS ALTIN
ALTUN AMANI ANGEL ANGLE ASPER
BAIOC BAIZA BATTE BEKAR BELGA
BETSO BEZZO BISTI BLANC BLANK
BODLE BROAD BROWN CHINK CLINK
COIGN CONTO COROA CROSS
CROWN CUNYE DARIC DINAR DISME
DOBLA DUCAT EAGLE EYRIR FANAM
FANON FODDA FRANC GAZET
GRANO GROAT GROSZ HALER
HECTE JACOB JULIO JUSTO KOBAN
KRONA KRONE KROON LIARD LIBRA
LITRA LOUIS MEDAL MEDIN MEDIO
MILAN MOHUR MOPUS NOBLE
NOMOS OBANG ORKEY ORKYN
PAISA PAOLO PARDO PENNY PERAU
PESSA PIECE PLACK PLATE POALI
POALO PROOF QUART QUINE RAPPE
REBIA RIDER RIYAL ROYAL RUBLE
RUPIA SAIGA SAPEK SCEAT SCUDO
SCUTE SEMIS SHAHI SICCA SMASH
SOLDO STAMP STYCA SUCRE TALER
TANGA TANKA TEMPO THRIP TICAL
TRIME UNCIA UNITE WHITE ABASSI
ABBASI AFGHAN AHMADI ARGENT
ASSARY AUREUS AZTECA BALBOA
BAUBEE BAWBEE BEAVER BEZANT
BIANCO BLANCO BOGACH BRONZE
CARLIN CENTAS CHAISE COBANG
CONDOR COPPER CORONA CUARTO
CUNZIE DECIME DENARY DENIER
DERHAM DINDER DIOBOL DIRHAM
DIXAIN DIZAIN DOBLON DODKIN
DOLLAR DOPPIA DOUBLE ESCUDO
FILLER FLORIN FOLLIS FORINT
GEORGE GIULIO GOURDE GRIVNA
GROSSO GUINEA GULDEN HARPER
HELLER ICHIBU ITZEBU JUSLIK
KLIPPE KOPECK KORONA KORUNA
LAUREL LEPTON MACUTA MAHBUB
MAIDEN MANCUS MEDINO MISKAL
NICKEL NORKYN OCHAVO OCTAVE
ONGARO PADUAN PAGODA PARDAO
PATACA PATART PHILIP QUEZAL
ROSARY SALUNG SALUTE SATANG
SEQUIN SESKIN SHEKEL SHIELD
SIGLOS SINKER SIXAIN SOMALO
SOVRAN STATER STELLA STIVER
TALENT TARGET TESTAO TESTER
TESTON THALER THOMAN TOSTON
TRIENS TUMAIN TUNGAH TURNER
TURNEY TURTLE UNGARO VINTEM
XERIFF YUZLIK ZECHIN ZEHNER
ZEQUIN ALFONSO ALTILIK ANGELET
ANGELOT ANGOLAR ANGSTER
BAIOCCO BAJOCCO BARBONE
BOLIVAR CARDECU CARLINE
CARLINO CAROLIN CAROLUS
CENTAVO CHALCUS CHALKOS
CORDOBA COUNTER CRUSADO
DAMPANG DRACHMA DUCATON
DUPLONE ESCALAN JACOBUS
JOANNES KASBEKE KREUZER
LEMPIRA LEONINE LEOPARD
LUIGINO MANGOUR MARENGO
MOIDORE MONARCH MUZOONA

NOUMMOS ONCETTA PAHLAVI
PARISIS PATACAO PATAGON
PATAQUE PENNING PFENNIG
PISTOLE QUADRIN QUARTER
QUATTIE QUETZAL QUINYIE
REDDOCK RUDDOCK RUSPONE
SANTIMS SCRUPLE SEXTANS
SILIQUA SIZEINE SOLIDUS SPECIES
STAMPEE STOOTER STUIVER
SULTANE TALLERO TEECALL
THRYMSA TORNESE TRIOBOL
UNICORN XERAFIN ALBERTIN
AMBROSIN AQUILINO AUGUSTAL
AUKSINAS BAETZNER BAGATINE
BECHTLER BLAFFERT BLANKEEL
BLANKILO BROCKAGE CAVALIER
CHINKERS CHUCKRAM COLONIAL
COURONNE CROCKARD CRUZEIRO
DECUSSIS DENARIUS DIDRACHM
DIOBOLON DOUBLOON EQUIPAGA
FARTHING FILIPPIC FREDERIK
GAZZETTA GENOVINO GIGLIATO
GIUSTINA GROSCHEN HARDHEAD
HYPERPER IMPERIAL ISABELLA
JOHANNES KREUTZER LUSHBURG
MACARONI MAJIDIEH MARCELLO
METALLIK MILESIMA PATACOON
PAVILION PICAYUNE PIEDFORT
PISTOLET PLAPPERT PORTAGUE
QUADRANS QUADRINE QUARTINE
QUINCUNX RESTRIKE RIGMAREE
RISDALER RIXDALER SCUDDICK
SEMUNCIA SESTERCE SHILLING
SIXPENCE SKILLING SLEEPING
SOLIDARE STERLING STOTINKA
SULTANIN TENPENNY TETROBOL
THIRTEEN TWOPENCE ZECCHINO
(— **AROUND NECK**) TALI
(— **IMPERFECTLY MINTED**)
BROCKAGE
(— **OF TRIFLING VALUE**) RAP
(**BASE** —) SHAND SHEEN SINKER
(**COUNTERFEIT** —) GRAY GREY SLIP
SHEEN SHOFUL STUMER STUMOR
(**PLUGGED** —) PLUG
(**SMALL THICK** —) DUMP
(PL.) CHANGE CHINKS SERIES
COINAGE
COINAGE FICTION GALUMPH
MINTAGE
COINCIDE FIT GEE JIBE JUMP
AGREE TALLY CONCUR
COINCIDENT EVEN TOGETHER
COINCIDING CONGRUENT
COINER MONIER MONEYER
COITION SOIL VENERY MEETING
CONGRESS
COKE ASK COAL COLK CORE DOPE
CHARK COCAINE
COL GAP HALS JOCH PASS HALSE
SWIRE SADDLE
COLANDER SIEVE STRAINER
COLCOTHAR SAFFRON TUSCANY
COLD FLU ICY MUR NIP COOL DEAD
DULL HARD HASK HOAR MURR
ROUP SOUR ACALE ACOLD ALGID
BLEAK CHILL CRISP FISHY FRORE
GELID GLACE GLARE OORIE OURIE
PARKY POOSE RHEUM SHARP

STONY VIRUS ARCTIC BITTER
BOREAL CHILLY CLAMMY CRIMMY
FREDDO FRIGID FRIGOR FROSTY
GLASSY MARBLY STECKY WAIRCH
WINTRY BRITTLE CATARRH CHILLED
COLDISH COSTIVE DISTANT
FROSTED GLACIAL INHUMAN
MORFOND SHIVERY STRANGE
FREEZING MORFOUND PIERCING
RESERVED RHIGOSIS STANDOFF
UNHEATED
(— **IN HEAD**) POSE POOSE CORYZA
CATARRH GRAVEDO SNIVELS
SNIFFLES SNIFTERS
(**BITTER** —) ARCTIC
(**VERY** —) FRIGID PEEVISH
COLD-BLOODED BRUTAL LEEPIT
COLD CUTS ASSIETTE
COLD-HEARTED COLD FROZEN
BLOODLESS
COLDLY DRILY DRYLY
COLDNESS COLD FROST STEEL
PHLEGM DISTANCE FROIDEUR
COLDONG FRIARBIRD
COLE CALE KAIL KALE COLZA
FRIGOR COLEWORT
COLEUS KOORKA
COLEWORT COLE KALE RIBE STOCK
CABBAGE
(**SPROUT OF** —) STOVEN
COLIC BATS FRET BATTS GUTTIE
BELLYACHE
COLICROOT UNICORN ALOEROOT
HUSKROOT HUSKWORT STARWORT
COLIMA TAPA IRONWOOD
COLISEUM HALL STADIUM THEATER
COLOSSEUM
COLL HUG CLIP CULL POLL PRUNE
EMBRACE
COLLABORATE AID ASSIST
COOPERATE
COLLAPSE CAVE FALL FLOP FOLD
GIVE SINK CRASH SLUMP WRECK
BUCKLE SHRINK TUMBLE CAPSIZE
CROPPER CRUMBLE CRUMPLE
DEBACLE DEFLATE FAILURE
FLUMMOX FOUNDER SMASHUP
CONTRACT DOWNFALL TAILSPIN
COLLAPSED QUAT CLUNG
COLLAPSIBLE FOLDING
COLLAPSING FAILURE COLLABENT
COLLAR CAP FUR NAB BAND ETON
FALL FANO GILL GRAB POKE RING
RUFF CHAIN DICKY FANON FANUM
FICHU PHANO RUCHE SEIZE STOCK
TRASH WHISK BERTHA CARCAN
CHOKER COLLET COLLUM DICKEY
GORGET PARRAL PARREL RABATO
REBATO SADDLE SLEEVE TACKLE
TORQUE TUCKER TURNUP BOBACHE
BOBECHE CAPTURE CHIGNON
CIRCLET PANUELO PARTLET
POTHOOK REBATER SHACKLE
STICKUP VANDYKE CARCANET
CINCTURE NECKBAND NECKLACE
RABATINE STARCHER TURNDOWN
(— **FOR HORSE**) BARGHAM
BRECHAM
(**HIGH** —) GILLS

(IRON —) JOUG JOUGS CARCAN
POTHOOKS
(LACE —) SCALLOP
(MAGISTRATE'S —) GOLILLA
(ROMAN —) RABAT
(WHEEL-SHAPED —) RUFF
(WOODEN —) CANG CANGUE
COLLAR BEAM SPANNER
SPANPIECE
COLLARBONE CLAVICLE
COLL'ARCO ARCATO
COLLARED ACCOLLE ACCOLLEE
TORQUATE
COLLAR PAD AFTERWALE
COLLATE BESTOW CONFER VERIFY
COMPARE
COLLATERAL SIDE MARGIN OBLIQUE
INDIRECT PARALLEL SECURITY
COLLATION TEA MEAL LUNCH
REPAST SERMON ADDRESS
READING DEJEUNER HOTCHPOT
TREATISE
COLLEAGUE AIDE ALLY UNITE
DEPUTY SOCIUS ADJUNCT COLLEGE
COMPEER CONSORT PARTNER
CONFRERE CONSPIRE
COLLECT JUG SAM TAX CALL CARD
CULL DRAW HEAP LEVY LIFT PICK
PILE POOL REAR SAMM SAVE
AMASS CROWD GLEAN GROUP
HOARD RAISE STORE SWEEP
ACCOIL ACCRUE CENTER CONFER
GARNER GATHER MUSTER PRAYER
SEMBLE SHEAVE UPTAKE ARCHIVE
CLUSTER COMPILE CONGEST
ENGROSS IMPOUND RAMMASS
RECUEIL SCAMBLE SYNAPTE
ASSEMBLE CONFLATE CONTRACT
CUPBOARD INGATHER RESEMBLE
SCRAMBLE SCROUNGE
(— AND DRIVE INTO ENCLOSURE)
WEAR
(— FOOD) FORAGE
(— GRAIN) GAVEL
(— INTO COVEY) JUG
(— MONEY) NOB
(— WAGES) UPLIFT
COLLECTED CALM COOL SOBER
SERENE PRESENT COMPOSED
COLLECTION ANA BAG KIT SET
BAND BEVY BOOK CLAN CROP FILE
HEAD HEAP KNOT LEVY OLIO RAFT
SORT ALBUM ANNEX BATCH BUDGE
DEPOT FLOCK GLEAN GROUP
HOARD KITTY SHEAF STORE SUITE
SWATH BUNDLE CONGER CORPUS
FARDEL MISHNA PARCEL RAGBAG
RECULE SORITE SPRING SWATHE
TUMBLE ACCOUNT COLLECT
CONGERY EXHIBIT FERNERY
FISTFUL FLUTTER GALLERY
QUOTITY RECUEIL SAMHITA
SMATTER SMYTRIE SYLLOGE
TERRIER ASSEMBLY CABOODLE
CONGERIE COSTOMAL FASCICLE
GATHERUM GLOSSARY ROMESCOT
ROMESHOT SYNTAGMA
(— AT FOX HUNT) CAP
(— OF 24 SHEETS) QUIRE

(— OF ANIMALS) ZOO HEAD
(— OF BOOKCASES) STACK
(— OF BOOKS) SET BIBLE CANON
LIBRARY
(— OF CONIFERS) PINETUM
(— OF DATA) GROUND
(— OF FORMULAS) CODEX
(— OF FOUR) TETRAD
(— OF LAWS) CODE
(— OF MAPS) ATLAS
(— OF OBJECTS) AFFAIR
(— OF OPINIONS) SYMPOSIUM
(— OF PERSONS) BOODLE
(— OF PLANTS) SERTULE
(— OF POEMS) DIVAN DIWAN SYLVA
ANTHOLOGY
(— OF PUS) HYPOPYON
(— OF REVENUES) TAMSIL TEHSIL
(— OF ROCKS) SUITE
(— OF RULES) SUTRA SUTTA
(— OF SAMPLES) SWATCH
(— OF SAYINGS) ANA
(— OF SPECIMENS) CABINET
(— OF STAFFS) SYSTEM
(— OF STORIES) LEGEND
(— OF TOOLS) LAYOUT
(— OF TREES) SERINGAL
(— OF UNWANTED ANIMALS)
LARDER
(CONFUSED —) CLUTTER
(MISCELLANEOUS —) OLIO FARDEL
SMYTRIE
(VAST —) CLOUD
COLLECTIVE GROUP AGGREGATE
COLLECTIVIST COMMUNIST
SOCIALIST
COLLECTOR COMB CAMEIST
CURIOSO DUSTMAN FURIOSO
UPTAKER ANTIQUER COUNTOUR
GATHERER STAMPMAN VIRTUOSO
ZAMINDAR
(— ITEMS) RARIORA
(— OF BUTTERFLIES) AURELIAN
(— OF HERBS) SIMPLER
(— OF REVENUE) AUMIL AUMILDAR
TALUKDAR ZAMINDAR
(CUSTOMS —) HOPPO CUSTOMER
(TAX —) CAID QAID GABBAI
TAHSILDAR
COLLECTORATE TALUK
COLLEEN GIRL LASS MISS BELLE
CAILIN DAMSEL
COLLEGE TOL HALL AGGIE HOUSE
LYCEE CAMPUS COLAGE SCHOOL
SIWASH ACADEMY MADRASA
SEMINARY
COLLEGER TUG
COLLET BAND NECK RING CHUCK
CULET CASING CIRCLE COLLAR
COLLUM FLANGE BUSHING
COLLIDE HIT RAM BUMP DASH FRAY
HURT CLASH CRASH KNOCK SHOCK
SMITE WRECK HURTLE STRIKE
THRUST
(— WITH) IMPINGE
COLLIE BEARDIE
COLLIER MINER PLOVER GEORDIE
COILYEAR FLATIRON SCUTCHER
COLLIQUATION SYNTEXIS

COLLISION HIT FOUL CLASH CRASH
SHOCK HURTLE IMPACT JOSTLE
SMASHUP CLASHING CONFLICT
COLLOCATE SET PLACE ARRANGE
COLLOID GEL
COLLOQUIAL FAMILIAR INFORMAL
COLLOQUIUM INDUCEMENT
COLLOQUY CHAT TALK PARLEY
DIALOGUE
COLLOTYPE ARTOTYPE HELIOTYPE
COLLUDE PLOT SCHEME CONNIVE
COLLOGUE CONSPIRE
COLLUM NECK
COLLUSION DECEIT CAHOOTS
SECRECY PRACTICE PRACTISE
COLLUSIVE COVINOUS COLLUSORY

COLOMBIA

CAPE: VELA AGUJA MARZO
AUGUSTA
CAPITAL: BOGOTA
CAY: VELA VIGIA RONCADOR
COIN: PESO REAL CONDOR
PESETA CENTAVO
FORMER NAME: DARIEN
NEWGRANADA
GULF: URABA CUPICA DARIEN
TIBUGA TORTUGAS
INDIAN: BORO CUNA HOKA MACU
MUZO PAEZ CARIB CATIO
CHOCO COFAN COGUI CUBEO
GUANE PIJAO SEONA ARAWAK
BETOYA CALIMA INGANO SALIVA
TAHAMI TUCANO TUNEBO
YAHUNA ACHAGUA ANDAQUI
CHIBCHA CHIMILA GUAHIBO
GUAJIRO PANCHES PUINAVE
PUITOTO QUECHUA TAIRONA
GUARAUNO MOTILONE
INLET: TUMACO
ISLAND: BARU NAIPO FUERTE
GORGONA CUSACHON
MEASURE: VARA AZUMBRE
CELEMIN
MOUNTAIN: CHITA HUILA PURACE
TOLIMA
MOUNTAINS: ABIBE ANDES BAUDO
COCUY AYAPEL PERIJA TUNAHI
CHAMUSA ORIENGAL
PLAINS: LLANOS
POINT: CRUCES LACRUZ SOLANO
CARIBANA GALLINAS
PORT: LORICA CARTAGENA
PROVINCE: META CAUCA CHOCO
HUILA VALLE ARAUCA BOYACA
CALDAS NARINO TOLIMA
VAUPES BOLIVAR CAQUETA
GUAJIRE VICHADA AMAZONAS
PUTUMAYO
RIVER: UVA BITA META MUCO
SINU TOMO UPIA YARI BAUDO
CAUCA CESAR ISANA MESAI
NECHI PATIA PAUTO SUCIO
AMAZON ARAUCA ARIARI
ATRATO CAGUAN VAUPES
YAPURA APAPOIS CAQUETA
GUAINIA INIRIDA TRUANDO
VICHADA CASANARE GUAVIARE

PUTUMAYO MAGDALENA
TOWN: TEN ANZA BUGA CALI MITU
MUZO PAEZ SIPI TADO TOLU
YARI BELLO CHINU GUAPI NEIVA
PASTO TUNJA BOGOTA CUCUTA
IBAGUE QUIBDO SANGIL
CARTAGO LETICIA PALMIRA
PEREIRA POPAYAN GIRARDOT
MEDELLIN MONTERIA
CARTAGENA
TREE: ARBOLOCO
VOLCANO: PURACE
WEIGHT: BAG SACO CARGA LIBRA
QUILATE QUINTAL

COLON CROWN POINT HEMISTICH
MESYMNION
COLONIAL OVERSEA OVERSEAS
COLONIST BOOR COLON FATHER
CUTHEAN PIONEER PLANTER
SETTLER EMIGRANT
(AUSTRALIAN —) STERLING
(PL.) DEHAITES DEHAVITES
COLONIZE ECIZE FOUND PLANT
GATHER SETTLE MIGRATE
COLONIZER OECIST OEKIST
COLONNADE ROW STOA PORCH
PARVIS PIAZZA GALLERY PERGOLA
PORTICO TERRACE CHOULTRY
COLONNETTE COLUMELLA
COLONY STATE STOCK SWARM
CENOBE CORMUS APOIKIA COLONIA
CENOBIUM GANNETRY
(— OF BEES) HIVE SKEP SWARM
(BRYOZOAN —) ESCHARA
COLOR DIP DYE HUE BLEE CAST
FAKE FLAG PUKE SUIT TINT TONE
BADGE BLUSH GLAZE GLOSS GRAIN
PAINT SHADE STAIN TAINT TASTE
TENNE TINCT TINGE BANNER
BLEACH BOTTOM BRIDGE CHROMA
ENSIGN INFECT LOCKET MANTLE
RADDLE REDDEN STREAK TEMPER
COULEUR DEPAINT DISTORT
ENGRAIN PENNANT PIGMENT
SPECKLE COLORING STANDARD
TERTIARY TINCTURE
(— IMPARTED TO HERRINGS)
GILDING
(— LOSS) POLIOSIS
(— OF BIRD) SMUT
(— OF BODY) HEAT
(— OF EYES OF FOWLS) DAW
(— OF HUMAN FLESH) CARNATION
(— OF ROCK) STONE
(BLUE —) FOG JAY SKY WAD AQUA
BICE CIEL CYAN DELF DELP DUSK
IRIS NAVY PAON SAXE WADE WOAD
ZINC AZURE BERYL BLUET CADET
CAPRI CHING COPEN DELFT DIANA
DRAKE EMAIL GRAPE METAL NIKKO
ORION PEARL ROYAL SLATE SMALT
SMOKE VANDA CANTON CENDRE
COELIN ENSIGN GROTTO HATHOR
INDIGO LUPINE MARINE MASCOT
MIGNON ORIENT PENSEE ROMANY
SEVRES VENICE ZENITH CELESTE
CERAMIC CHICORY DUSTBLU

GOBELIN HORIZON LIBERTY LOBELIA
LOGWOOD MATELOT PEACOCK
PETUNIA RAMESES SISTINE SIXTINE
ABSINTHE BLUEBIRD BLUEWOOD
BRITTANY CAESIOUS CATTLEYA
CERULEAN CERULEUM DUCKLING
ELECTRIC GENDARME HYACINTH
INFANTRY LABRADOR LARKSPUR
MASCOTTE MAZARINE MIDNIGHT
MOONBEAM NATIONAL SAPPHIRE
TWILIGHT WEDGWOOD
(BROWN —) BAY ELK FOX OAK TAN
ARAB BARK BOLE BRAN BURE CAIN
CLAY CORK CUBA DATE DEER DRAB
DUST ECRU FAON FAWN GOAT
GOLD HOPI IRON LAMA LION MAST
MESA MUSK SEAL SIAM TEAK
ACORN ADUST ALOMA AZTEC BEIGE
BISON BLOND BLUSH BOLUS BRIAR
BRICK BRIER BROWN BUNNY CACAO
CAMEL CANNA CLOVE COCOA
CONGO EAGLE FRIAR FUDGE GIPSY
GRAIN GYPSY HAZEL HENNA KAFFA
KHAKI LIVER MAHAL MALAY MECCA
MINIM MUMMY NEGRO OTTER
PABLO QUAIL SABEL SEDGE SEPIA
SIENA SIRUP SNUFF SUDAN SUEDE
SUMAC SYRUP TABAC TAFFY TENNE
TOAST TOPAZ AFGHAN ALESAN
ALMOND APACHE ARGALI AUBURN
BAMBOO BEAVER BISQUE BISTER
BISTRE BLONDE BRONCO BRONZE
BURNET COCHIN COFFEE CONDOR
COOKIE COWBOY CROTAL DORADO
ESKIMO FALLOW GINGER GRAVEL
GROUSE HAVANA ISABEL LOUTRE
MAROON MERIDA MOHAWK MUFFIN
NUTMEG ORIOLE PAWNEE PLOVER
PUEBLO RABBIT RACKET RUDDLE
RUSSET SAHARA SANTOS SHERRY
SORREL SPHINX SPONGE STRING
STUCCO SUMACH SUNTAN THRUSH
TIFFIN TURTLE ASPHALT BADIOUS
BEESWAX BITUMEN BRACKEN
BRONCHO CALDRON CATTAIL
CIGARET COCONUT COTRINE
CRACKER DOGWOOD DURANGO
FEUILLE FILBERT GAZELLE
GOREVAN HARVEST LEATHER
LIBERIA MALABAR MIRADOR
MORDORE MOROCCO MUSCADE
MUSTANG NORFOLK OAKWOOD
PERIQUE PRALINE RACQUET
ROSARIO SABELLA SUNBURN
SUNDOWN TALLYHO TANBARK
TOBACCO TUSCANY ALDERNEY
ALGERIAN AMBROSIA BISMARCK
BOBOLINK CALABASH CARTOUCH
CAULDRON CINNAMON CLAYBANK
CORDOVAN DOUBLOON ETRUSCAN
EUCHROME HAZELNUT ISABELLA
KOLINSKY LEAFMOLD MANDALAY
MOCCASIN MOLESKIN MOROCCAN
MUSHROOM NOISETTE PHEASANT
SAUTERNE SHAGBARK STARLING
TAMARACK TEAKWOOD TERRAPIN
TORTOISE WOODBARK
(DEEP —) DARK
(FAST —) GRAIN

(GREEN —) BOA FIR IVY ALOE BICE
FERN JADE LEEK MOSS NILE SAGE
ALOES CEDRE CHLOR DRAKE FAIRY
HOLLY KELLY LOVAT OLIVE SPRAY
CANNON EMPIRE HUNTER JASPER
LAUREL LIERRE LIZARD MEADOW
MOUSSE MYRTLE SPRUCE VERDET
CELADON CITRINE CORBEAU
CRESSON CYPRESS EMERALD
INGENUE JADEITE JUNIPER
MESANGE NEPTUNE OLIVINE
PERIDOT SEAFOAM SERPENT
TILLEUL VERDURE BAYBERRY
CHASSEUR COPPERAS EMERAUDE
GLAUCOUS GLOWWORM PARAKEET
PERRUCHE PISTACHE POPINJAY
SHAMROCK TARRAGON VIRIDIAN
WOODLAND
(GRIZZLED —) AGOUTI AGOUTY
(OTHER —S) OR ASH BAT DOE DUN
JET TEA CHIP CORN CROW DAWN
DOVE GRAY GREY GULL HEMP LAVA
LEAD MODE MOLE NICE NUDE PLUM
PORT ROAN RUST SAND SOOT
WOOD AMBER BEACH BLACK
CAMEO CERES CHILE CHILI COPRA
CRANE CRASH CREAM DWALE
EBONY FLESH GRAPE GREBE
GREGE MAUVE MOUSE PANSY
PHLOX PLOMB PRAWN PRUNE
PUTTY RIFLE SABLE SPICE STEEL
THYME TWINE ANATTO AURORA
AUTUMN CASTOR CINDER COLLIE
CORCIR DAHLIA DAMSON DENVER
EVEQUE FIESTA FUSTIC GAMBIA
GRIEGE KASPER MALLOW MODENA
NAVAHO NAVAJO NIMBUS NUTRIA
ONDINE ORCHID OXFORD OYSTER
PEANUT PEBBLE PIGEON QUAKER
RAISIN RESEDA ROUCOU SEASAN
SILVER TUSCAN VANITY VESTAL
VIOLET WALNUT ADMIRAL ANNOTTA
ARBUTUS ARDOISE ARNATTA
BEGONIA BERMUDA BLOSSOM
BRINDLE CARAIBE CARAMEL
COTRINE COWSLIP CRACKER
CRUISER MORELLO MURILLO
NATURAL OPHELIA PELICAN
PONTIFF POPCORN PRELATE
PUMPKIN QUIMPER REGATTA
ROSEBUD SAKKARA SANDUST
SPARROW SUNBEAM THISTLE
TUSSORE VERVAIN VIOLINE
WEIGELA WHEATEN ALUMINUM
AMETHYST BLONDINE CARMETTA
CHARCOAL CLEMATIS COCOBOLO
COQUETTE CREVETTE CYCLAMEN
EGGPLANT EMINENCE FELDGRAU
FLAMINGO GILLIVER GRAPHITE
GUNMETAL HONEYDEW IMPERIAL
JACINTHE LAVENDER MARATHON
MORILLON MULBERRY PALMETTO
ROSEWOOD SAUTERNE SQUIRREL
SUNBURST WIRELESS WISTARIA
WISTERIA CARNELIAN
(RED —) DAWN FLEA GOLF GOYA
HEBE LAKE MIST PUCE RUBY TULY
WINE AGATE BRASS BRICK CANNA
CANON CEDAR CORAL CUTCH

EMBER FLAME FLASH GULES LILAC
MELON NYMPH PEACH PEONY
POPPY ROSET SIENA SPARK TOTEM
ACAJOU ARCHIL AURORE AUTUMN
AZALEA BRAZIL CANYON CARROT
CATSUP CERISE CHERRY CHERUB
CLARET COGNAC DAMASK FRAISE
GAIETY GARNET GAYETY GRANET
JOCKEY KERMES MADDER MALAGA
MIKADO MURREY NECTAR ORCHIL
PATISE SALMON SANDIX SHRIMP
SIERRA SULTAN TITIAN TOMATO
AFRICAN ANAMITE ANEMONE
BEGONIA BISCUIT BOKHARA
CARMINE CATAWBA CATCHUP
CATECHU CRIMSON CURRANT
FIREFLY FUCHSIA FUCHSIN
GRANATE GRANITE HEATHER
INDIANA KETCHUP LACQUER
LOBSTER MAGENTA MASCARA
NACARAT OXBLOOD PAPRIKA
POMPEII PONCEAU REDWOOD
ROSETAN ROSETTE RUBELLE
SAFFLOR SARAVAN SCARLET
SINOPLE STAMMEL SULTANA
VERMEIL ALKERMES AMARANTH
ARCHILLA BISMARCK BORDEAUX
BURGUNDY CAMELLIA CARDINAL
CHAUDRON CHEROKEE CHERUBIM
CHESTNUT COCOANUT CONFETTI
DAMONICO DIANTHUS DUBONNET
EVENGLOW GERANIUM GRENADIN
GRIDELIN MAHOGANY MANDARIN
MAROCAIN NACARINE TOREADOR
(SOLID —) SOLID
(TONE —) TIMBRE
(YELLOW —) HAY RAT WAX BEAR
BUFF CLAY CORN CUIR ECRU FLAX
GOLD LARK LIME MOTH WELD
WOLD ACIER ALOMA AZTEC BEIGE
BLAKE BRASS CRASH CREAM GRAIN
HONEY IVORY LEMON MAIZE MAPLE
SHELL STRAW TAUPE WOULD
ACACIA ALMOND BANANA CANARY
CATHAY CHROME CITRON CITRUS
CROCUS DORADO FALLOW MANILA
MASTIC MIMOSA NANKIN NUGGET
OXGALL SULFUR SUNRAY SUNSET
ANTIQUE APRICOT BISCUIT CAVALRY
CHAMOIS GAMBOGE JASMINE
JONQUIL LEGHORN MEXICAN
NANKEEN PRAIRIE RHUBARB
SAFFRON SULPHUR SUNGLOW
ANTELOPE CALABASH CAPUCINE
COCKATOO DAFFODIL EGGSHELL
GENERALL GOLDMIST MARIGOLD
ORPIMENT PRIMROSE SNOWSHOE
(PL.) FLAG
COLORABLE SPECIOUS

COLORADO

CAPITAL: DENVER
COLLEGE: REGIS
COUNTY: BACA MESA YUMA
OTERO OURAY ROUTT GILPIN
CHAFFEE
MOUNTAIN: LONGS PIKES ELBERT
MOUNTAIN RANGE: ROCKY

NATIVE: ROVER
PARK: ESTES
RIVER: YAMPA DOLORES
APISHAPA ARIKAREE GUNNISON
PURGATOIRE
STATE FLOWER: COLUMBINE
STATE NICKNAME: CENTENNIAL
STATE TREE: SPRUCE
TOWN: ASPEN DELTA LAMAR
GOLDEN PUEBLO SALIDA
ALAMOSA BOULDER DURANGO
GREELEY GUNNISON LOVELAND
TRINIDAD

COLORATION BLEE PILE FLASH
CLOUDING COLORISM SCHILLER
COLORATURA GORGIA SOPRANO
COLOR-BLINDNESS DALTONISM
COLORED FAW HUED MALE BIASED
DEPAINT STAINED
(— IN RED) RUBRIC
(— LIKE PIPE BOWL) TROUSERED
(BRILLIANTLY —) SUPERB FLAMING
(HIGHLY —) CHROMATIC
(PARTI —) PIED PIEBALD
(UNIFORMLY —) HARD
COLORFUL GAY BRAVE JUICY VIVID
COLORY GOLDEN FREAKED
GORGEOUS
COLORING BLEE TINT PAINT TINGE
TINGENT BRONZING PAINTING
TINCTURE
(— MATTER) TINCTION
COLORLESS WAN DRAB DULL PALE
ASHEN BLAKE BLANK PLAIN
MOUSEY PALLID HUELESS NEUTRAL
ACHROMIC ACHROOUS BLANCHED
ETIOLATE LIFELESS
COLOSSAL BIG HUGE VAST GREAT
LARGE IMMENSE TITANIC
ENORMOUS GIGANTIC MONSTROUS
COLOSSUS GIANT TITAN STATUE
COLOSSO MONOLITH
COLOSTRUM FOREMILK AFTERINGS
COLT FOAL STAG FILLY POTRO
STAIG HOGGET POLEYN STAGGIE
EQUULEUS
COLTER LAVER COOTER COULTER
FOREIRON
COLTSFOOT DOCK CLOTE HOOFS
CLEATS FARFARA LAGWORT
SOWFOOT BULLFOOT CLAYWEED
FOALFOOT
COLUGO COBEGO
COLUMBATE NIOBATE
COLUMBIA SINKIUSE
COLUMBINE AQUILEGE BLUEBELL
CHUCKIES ROCKBELL
COLUMBITE DIANITE NIOBITE
COLUMELLA STALACE
COLUMN COG LAT ROW FILE FUST
GOAL LINE POLE POST PROP STUB
BAGUE SHAFT STELA STELE TORSO
TRUNK WURTZ ASOKAN CORNER
GNOMON PILLAR SCAPUS STAPLE
STRING TSWETT SUPPORT VIGREUX
CYLINDER PILASTER
(— IN EAR) MODIOLUS

(— OF FIGURES) SUM
(— OF FILAMENTS) SYNEMA
(BUDDHIST —) LAT
(FIGURE USED AS —) ATLAS
TELAMON
(ROCK —) HOODOO
(ROULETTE —) DERNIER
(SPINAL —) HORN SPINE BACKBONE
(STRUCTURAL —) LALLY
(TWISTED —) TORSO
COLUMNAR TERETE STELENE
COLUMNAL VERTICAL
COLUMNIST WRITER ANALYST
COLY MOUSEBIRD
COLZA SARSON
COMA TUFT BUNCH CARUS SLEEP
STUPOR SUBETH TORPOR TRANCE
SEMICOMA CHEVELURE
COMATOSE OUT DROWSY
LETHARGIC
COMB CARD GILL KAME LASH RACK
RAKE REDD REED SEEK TOZE
BREAK BRUSH CAMBE CLEAN
CREST CTENE CURRY FLISK RAVEL
TEASE HACKLE SMOOTH CUSHION
HATCHEL WRAITHE BEATILLE
CARUNCLE TORTOISE
COMBAT WAR BLOW BOUT COPE
DUEL FRAY MEEK MEET RUSH TILT
CLASH FIGHT JOUST REPEL STOUR
ACTION AFFRAY BATTLE MEDLEY
OPPOSE RESIST SHOWER STRIFE
CONTEND CONTEST COUNTER
DERAIGN DISPUTE EXPLOIT SCUFFLE
SERVICE ARGUMENT CONFLICT
STRUGGLE
(— BETWEEN KNIGHTS) JOUST
(FUTILE —) SCIAMACHY
(SINGLE —) DUOMACHY
COMBATANT DUELER BATTLER
FIGHTER CHAMPION GLADIATOR
COMBATIVE BANTAM MILITANT
BELLICOSE DEPENDENT
COMBED CRESTED
COMBER WAVE HANDER BREAKER
KEMPSTER
COMBINATION KEY BLOC GANG
PACT POOL RING CABAL COMBO
GROUP JUNTO PARTY TRUST UNION
CARTEL CLIQUE CORNER CRASIS
FUSION LEAGUE MEDLEY MERGER
AMALGAM COMBINE CONSORT
COTERIE FACTION HARMONY
JOINING MIXTURE ADDITION
ALLIANCE ENSEMBLE MONOPOLY
(— OF 10) DECUPLET
(— OF CARDS) SET BUILD FLUSH
SPREAD STRAIGHT
(— OF CIRCUMSTANCES) ACTION
(— OF COLORS) HARLEQUIN
(— OF FACES) FORM
(— OF FIRMS) TRUST
(— OF INTAGLIO FORMS) GRYLLI
(— OF NUMBERS) GIG SADDLE
(— OF TACKLES) JEERS
(— OF TONES) CHORD
(DANCE —) SEQUENCE
(HARMONIOUS —) CONCORD
(NOSE-JAW —) LAYBACK

(SCORING —) IMPERIAL

COMBINE ADD FIX MIX WED BIND BLOC CLUB JOIN NICK POOL BLEND GROUP JOINT MARRY MERGE TOTAL UNITE ABSORB CONCUR LEAGUE MEDDLE MERGER MINGLE SPLICE ACCRETE AMALGAM COMPACT CONJOIN CONJURE MACHINE COALESCE COMPOUND CONCRETE CONDENSE CONFLATE CONSTRUE CONTRACT CUMULATE FEDERATE
(— AGAINST) BOYCOTT
(— WITH GAS) AERATE
(— WITH WATER) AQUATE

COMBINED GUM BOUND FIXED JOINT UNITED CONJOINT

COMBUSTIBLE FUEL FIERY ARDENT CINDER PICEOUS BURNABLE

COMBUSTION FIRE HEAT FLAME THERM TUMULT BURNING BACKFIRE

COME BE GET LAY COOP DRAW FALL GROW HAUL PASS WHEN ARISE CHIVE FETCH ISSUE LIGHT OCCUR REACH ACCRUE ADVENE APPEAR ARRIVE BECOME BEFALL EMERGE HAPPEN OBTAIN SPRING ADVANCE DEVELOP EMANATE PROCEED APPROACH PRACTICE
(— ABOUT) ARISE CHANCE
(— AFTER) SUE FOLLOW
(— APART) FRAY SHED BREAK STAVE
(— BEFORE) FORERUN PREVENE ANTECEDE ANTEDATE
(— DOWN) SWOOP ALIGHT DESCEND SUCCEED DISMOUNT
(— FORTH) EMIT BREAK ISSUE ACCEDE FORTHGO FURNACE
(— FORWARD) ACCEDE
(— IN CONTACT) ATTINGE
(— INTO BLOOM) BURST BLOSSOM
(— INTO COLLISION) MEET CLASH COLLIDE
(— INTO EXISTENCE) FORM BEGIN ACCRUE HAPPEN SPRING
(— INTO POSSESSION) ACQUIRE INHERIT
(— OF AGE) MAJORIZE
(— OFF) HARL
(— OUT) ISSUE APPEAR EMERGE EMANATE
(— TO BELIEVE IN) ADOPT
(— TO CONCLUSION) DECIDE
(— TO DIE) DO DIE SET DROP EXPIRE FINISH SURCEASE
(— TO GRIEF) FOUNDER
(— TO HAND) OFFER
(— TO LIGHT) SPUNK DEVELOP
(— TO MIND) OCCUR STRIKE
(— TO PASS) SORT BREAK LIGHT BEFALL BETIDE HAPPEN
(— TO PERFECTION) RIPEN
(— TO TERMS) AGREE TRYST ACCORD BARGAIN COMPOSE COMPOUND
(— TO) TOUCH ADVENE STRIKE RECOVER REVERSE
(— TOGETHER) ADD HERD JOIN MEET AMASS CONCUR COUPLE

GATHER COLLECT COMBINE CONVENE ASSEMBLE
(— UNDER) SUBVENE
(— UPON) FIND CROSS INVENT STRIKE
(FULLY —) EXPIATE

COMEBACK RALLY ANSWER RETORT RETURN REBOUND HAULBACK RECOVERY REPARTEE

COMECRUDO CARRIZO

COMEDIAN WAG WIT CARD ACTOR ANTIC CLOWN COMIC GAGMAN JESTER BUFFOON FUNSTER COMOEDUS FUNMAKER FUNNYMAN PATTERER

COMEDO BLACKHEAD

COMEDOWN BATHOS DESCENT LETDOWN

COMEDY SOCK DRAMA FARCE LAZZO REVUE COMEDIA TEMACHA COMOEDIA TRAVESTY BACCHIDES SLAPSTICK
(HEROIC —) NATAKA

COMELINESS GRACE DECORUM FEATURE VENUSTY

COMELY FAIR GOOD HEND PERT TALL TIDY WEME BONNY HENDE QUEME SONCY SONSY TIGHT DECENT FORMAL GOODLY LIKELY LIKING LOVELY PRETTY PROPER SEEMLY SONSIE VENUST FARRANT FORMFUL SIGHTLY BECOMING DECOROUS FEATURED GRACEFUL HANDSOME PLEASING SUITABLE

COMET STAR METEOR XIPHIAS
(— HEAD) COMA

COMEUPPANCE REBUKE DESERTS BUSINESS

COMFIT CANDY SUCKLE CONFECT PRALINE CONSERVE PRESERVE

COMFORT AID EASE REST STAY BIELD CHEER LIGHT SOOTH VISIT ENDURE RELIEF REPOSE SOLACE SOOTHE SUCCOR ANIMATE ASSUAGE CHERISH CONFIRM CONSOLE ENLIVEN GLADDEN REFRESH RELIEVE SUPPORT SUSTAIN INSPIRIT NEPENTHE PLEASURE REASSURE

COMFORTABLE RUG BEIN BIEN COSH COSY COZY EASY FEEL FEIL LIKE SNUG TRIG CANNY COMFY COUTH CUSHY LITHE QUEME QUILT SCARF SONCY COUTHY HEPPEN PENTIT SONSIE RELAXED RESTFUL CHEERFUL DELICATE EUPHORIC HOMELIKE WRISTLET

COMFORTABLY SWEETLY

COMFORTED CONSOLATE

COMFORTER PUFF COVER EIDER NAHUM QUILT SCARF TIPPET CHEERER PACIFIER

COMFORTING TOSY TOSIE FRIENDLY

COMFORTLESS DREARY FORLORN UNCOUTH DESOLATE EITHLESS

COMFREY DAISY BONESET BACKWORT KNITBACK

COMIC DROLL FUNNY STRIP

BUFFONE COMIQUE THALIAN COMEDIAN FARCICAL

COMICAL LOW BASE BUFFO DROLL FUNNY MERRY QUEER STRIP WITTY BOUFFE AMUSING CARTOON JOCULAR RISIBLE STRANGE TRIVIAL HUMOROUS TICKLISH SPLITTING

COMING DUE COME NEXT VENUE ADVENT FUTURE TOWARD ARRIVAL FOOTING FORWARD BECOMING DESERVED PAROUSIA
(— AFTER) LATTER
(— AND GOING) FITFUL
(— INTO BEING) BIRTH GENESIS
(— NEAR) ACCESSION
(— OUT) ISSUE EGRESS
(— TO OFFICE) ACCESS
(— TO) ADIT
(— TOGETHER) SEANCE CONGRESS COUPLING GATHERING

COMMA POINT VIRGULE
(SCRATCH —) DIAGONAL

COMMAND DO BID SAW SOH BECK BODE BOON CALL COME EASY FIAT HEST HETE MAND RATE RULE SWAY WARN WILL WISH WORD BEKEN CHECK COVER EDICT EXACT FORCE HIGHT ORDER POWER SWEEP UKASE ADJURE BEHEST CHARGE COMPEL DEGREE DEMAND DEVICE DIRECT ENJOIN GOVERN HOOKUM IMPOSE MASTER ORACLE ORDAIN STEVEN SUMMON APPOINT BEHIGHT BIDDING CONCERN CONTROL DICTATE JUSSION JUSSIVE LEADING MANDATE OFFICER PRECEPT REQUIRE SKIPPER WARRANT BIDDANCE DOMINEER IMPERATE INSTRUCT RESTRAIN
(— OF ARMY) CONDUCT
(— TO HORSE) GEE HAW HUP HUPP WHOA GIDDAP HUDDUP
(— TO TURN RIGHT) GEE HUP HUPP
(MAGICIAN'S —) PRESTO

COMMANDANT GOVERNOR KILLADAR

COMMANDED IMPERATE

COMMANDEER PRESS

COMMANDER CID CIO DUX DUKE EMIR HEAD JEFE CHIEF EMEER ADALID LEADER MASTER RAMMER TARTAN ALCALDE CAPTAIN CROWNER DECARCH DEKARCH DRUNGAR EMPEROR GENERAL KHALIFA MARSHAL NAVARCH OFFICER VAIVODE HERETOGA HIPPARCH LOCHAGER LOCHAGUS MYRIARCH PHYLARCH RISALDAR SERASKER TAXIARCH TETRARCH VINTENER
(— IN CHIEF) SIRDAR TARTAN TURTAN ADMIRAL GENERAL

COMMANDING DOMINANT IMPERANT IMPERIAL IMPOSING

COMMANDMENT LAW RULE ORDER COMMAND MITZVAH PRECEPT BODEWORD
(DIVINE —) LAW
(TEN —S) DECALOG DECALOGUE

COMMANDO RAIDER RANGER
FEDAYEE
COMMELINA DEWFLOWER
COMMEMORATE FETE KEEP FEAST
REMENE EPITAPH MEMORATE
MONUMENT REMEMBER
COMMEMORATION AWARD MEDAL
COMMEM PLAQUE JUBILEE
MEMORIA MENTION SERVICE
EBENEZER MEMORIAL
COMMEMORATIVE HONORARY
COMMENCE FALL FANG FILE MOVE
OPEN ARISE BEGIN FOUND START
ARRAME EMBARK INCEPT LAUNCH
SPRING STREAK STREEK INITIATE
COMMENCEMENT ONSET ORIGIN
KICKOFF OPENING ENTRANCE
COMMENCING INITIAL NASCENT
INCIPIENT
COMMEND KEN PAT GIVE LAUD
ADORN ALOSE BEKEN BOOST
EXTOL GRACE OFFER BESTOW
BETAKE COMMIT PRAISE RESIGN
APPLAUD APPROVE BESPEAK
BETEACH DELIVER ENTRUST
INTRUST BEQUEATH
COMMENDABLE GOOD WORTHY
LOVABLE LOWABLE LAUDABLE
COMMENDATION LAUD PRAISE
CITATION
(EFFUSIVE —) SLAVER
(MARKED —) APPLAUSE
COMMENSAL EPIZOON MESSMATE
COMMENSALISM SYNOECY
SYMPHILY COMMUNISM
COMMENSURATE EVEN EQUAL
ENOUGH ADEQUATE RELEVANT
COMMENT BARB BRAG GIBE JIBE
NOTE TALK WORD ASIDE BREAK
DUNCE GLOSS GLOZE CUTTER
DILATE GAMBIT NOTATE POSTIL
REMARK SCANCE CAPTION
DESCANT DISCUSS EXPLAIN
EXPOUND ADDENDUM SCHOLION
SCHOLIUM DISPRAISE
(— DISAPPROVINGLY) HARRUMPH
(CAUSTIC —) SATIRE
COMMENTARY GLOSS GEMARA
MEMOIR SATIRE ACCOUNT
COMMENT MEKILTA POSTILS
FOOTNOTE GLOSSARY TREATISE
COMMENTATOR CRITIC GLOZER
ANALYST GLOSSIST SCHOLIAST
COMMERCE TRADE BARTER
CHANGE TRAFFIC BUSINESS
EXCHANGE MERCATURE
COMMERCIAL STORE TRADY
TRADAL MERCHANT TRADEFUL
(— ESTABLISHMENT) HONG
COMMERCIALISM HUCKSTERISM
COMMINGLE MIX FUSE JOIN BLEND
IMMIX MERGE UNITE MINGLE
COMBINE COMINGE EMBROIL
COMEDDLE
COMMINUTE MILL CRUSH GRIND
POUND POUNCE POWDER
COMMINUTED FINE
COMMISERATE PITY
COMMISERATION PITY EMPATHY
SYMPATHY

COMMISSION PLAT SEND TASK
BOARD PRESS TRUST BRANCH
BREVET CHARGE DEMAND DEPUTE
ERRAND LEGACY OFFICE ORDAIN
PERMIT COMMAND CONSIGN
DUOVIRI EMPOWER FITTAGE
GOSPLAN MANDATE MISSION
SQUEEZE WARRANT CORNETCY
DELEGATE ENCHARGE POUNDAGE
(— AS CAPTAIN) POST
COMMISSIONAIRE CADDY CADDIE
DUBASH
COMMISSIONER ENVOY TRIER
LEDGER ARRAYER OFFICER
PRISTAW DELEGATE
COMMISSURE VINCULUM
COMMIT DO GIVE PULL STOW TAKE
ALLOT ARRET HIGHT LEAVE REFER
TEACH ARETTE ASSIGN BETAKE
ENGAGE PERMIT REMAND BEHIGHT
BETEACH COMMAND COMMEND
COMMISE CONFIDE CONSIGN
DELIVER DEPOSIT ENTRUST
INTRUSE INTRUST BEQUEATH
DEDICATE DELEGATE IMPRISON
RELEGATE
(— ERROR) SNAPPER
(— MONEY) INVEST
(— TO BATTLE) LAUNCH
(— TO JAIL) JUG
(— TO MEMORY) CON LEARN
MEMORIZE
(— VIOLENCE) TOUCH
COMMITTAL COMPROMISE
COMMITTEE BODY JURY RUMP
BOARD GROUP JUNTA TABLE
BUREAU SOVIET COUNCIL
DELEGACY SYNDICATE
COMMIXTURE MIXTURE CONFUSION
IMMISSION
COMMODE CAP CHEST STOOL
TOPKNOT CUPBOARD FONTANGE
COMMODIOUS FIT AMPLE ROOMY
PROPER USEFUL SPACIOUS
SUITABLE CAVERNOUS
COMMODITY ITEM WARE GOODS
STUFF EXPORT FUTURE STAPLE
ARTICLE SHIPMENT
(— SOLD SHORT) BEAR
(UNSALABLE —) DRUG
(PL.) KIND SPOTS CHANDLERY
COMMON LAY LOW NOA TYE BASE
MEAN TOWN VILE BANAL BRIEF
CHEAP EJIDO EXIDO GREEN GRIMY
GROSS JOINT LEASE OFTEN SLACK
STALE TRITE USUAL COARSE
DEMOID FAMOUS MODERN MUTUAL
ORNERY PROPIO PUBLIC SIMPLE
VULGAR AVERAGE CURRENT
DEMOTIC GENERAL GENERIC
IGNOBLE NATURAL POPULAR
RAFFISH REGULAR TRIVIAL
UNNOBLE VILLAIN BANAUSIC
EPIDEMIC FAMILIAR FREQUENT
HABITUAL MECHANIC MEDIOCRE
ORDINARY PANDEMIC PLEBEIAN
TRIFLING
(— OF ESTOVERS) BOT BOTE
(IN —) ALIKE

(NOT —) UNTRADED
(PL.) COMMUNE
COMMONER SNOB CEORL PLEBE
SIMPLE BURGESS CITIZEN STUDENT
ROTURIER
COMMONLY VULGO FAMILIARLY
COMMONNESS IDIOTISM
COMMUNITY VULGARITY
COMMON PEOPLE VULGUS
COMMONPLACE DULL FADE WORN
BANAL DAILY PLAIN PROSE STALE
TOPIC TRIPY TRITE USUAL COMMON
GARDEN HOMELY MODERN TRUISM
FADAISE HUMDRUM INSIPID PROSAIC
TEDIOUS TRIVIAL BANALITY
EVERYDAY ORDINARY RUMTYTOO
COMMONPLACENESS BATHOS
HUMDRUM
COMMON SENSE WIT NOUS SALT
GUMPTION
COMMONWEAL WEAL REPUBLIC
COMMONWEALTH POLIS STATE
ESTATE PUBLIC WEALTH COMONTE
COUNTRY COMMONTY
(IDEAL —) UTOPIA
COMMOTION DO ADO DIN BREE
DUST FRAY FUSS HEAT RIOT STIR
TOSS WHIR ALARM FLARE FUROR
HURRY STORM STOUR WHIRL
BUSTLE CATHRO FISSLE FISTLE
FLURRY FRACAS FURORE GARRAY
HOOPLA MOTION MUTINY PHRASE
POTHER RUFFLE SHINDY SPLORE
SQUALL STEERY TUMULT UNREST
UPSTIR WELTER BLATHER BLUSTER
CATOUSE CLATTER KIPPAGE
SHINDIG TAMASHA TEMPEST
TURMOIL DISORDER ERUPTION
REMOTION STIRRAGE STRAMASH
TIRRIVEE UPHEAVAL UPRISING
COMMUNAL EJIDAL
COMMUNE AREA DEME TALK ARGUE
REALM SHARE TREAT ADVISE
CONFER DEBATE IMPORT PARLEY
REVEAL CONSULT DISCUSS DIVULGE
COMMERCE CONVERSE DISTRICT
STANITZA TOWNSHIP
COMMUNICABLE OPEN FRANK
CATCHING SOCIABLE
COMMUNICATE SAY GIVE SHOW
SIGN TELL BREAK DRILL SPEAK
YIELD BESTOW COMMON CONVEY
IMPART INFECT INFORM REVEAL
SIGNAL ADDRESS BREATHE
DECLARE DICTATE DIVULGE
CONVERSE DESCRIBE INTIMATE
(— BY ALLUSION) IMPLY
COMMUNICATION CALL NOTE
WORD CABLE FAVOR LETTER
SPEECH ADDRESS DIVULGE
GALLERY MESSAGE COMETHER
LANGUAGE TELEGRAM
COMMUNICATIVE FREE SOCIABLE
EXPANSIVE
COMMUNION CULT HOST MASS
SECT TALK CREED FAITH SHARE
UNITY CHURCH HOMILY COMMUNE
CONCORD NAGMAAL SYNAGOG
ANTIPHON COMMERCE CONVERSE

KOINONIA VIATICUM
(— SERVICE) ACTION
COMMUNISM LENINISM SOVIETISM
COMMUNIST RED COMMIE SOVIET
COMRADE
COMMUNITY MIR BODY BURG CITY
CLAN DESA MARK MURA DESSA
FIRCA STATE THORP CENOBY
CLIMAX COLONY FAMILY HAMLET
MILLET NATION POLITY PUBLIC
SOCIES ANTHILL BOHEMIA
COMMUNE COMONTE CONVENT
HERONRY KINGDOM PHALANX
SOCIETY VILLAGE ZADRUGA
AUTONOMY COMMONTY DISTRICT
LIKENESS PRIORATE PROVINCE
SODALITY SWEEPDOM TOWNSHIP
(— OF INTERESTS) KINSHIP
(— OF NATURE) RACE
(— OF ORGANISMS) GAMODEME
(— OF TURKS) KIZILBASH
(JEWISH —) JEWRY KOLEL ALJAMA
SHTETL JUDAISM SHTETEL
SYNAGOG KEHILLAH
(MAORI —) KAIK KAIKA
(PERUVIAN —) AYLLU COMUNIDAD
(PLANT —) HEATH FOREST ALTERNE
ENCLAVE
(RELIGIOUS —) CENOBY SAMGHA
SANGHA CONVENT CENOBIUM
(RUSSIAN —) MIR
(VILLAGE —) IKHWAN
COMMUTATE COMMUTE UNDIRECT
COMMUTATOR BREAK BREAKER
RHEOTROPE
COMMUTE ALTER CHANGE TRAVEL
CONVERT EXCHANGE
COMPACT BALL BOND CASE FAST
FIRM HARD KNIT PACK PACT PLOT
SNUG TRIM TRUE BRIEF CLOSE
COVIN CROWD DENSE GROSS
HARDY HORNY MATCH PITHY SOLID
SPISS TERSE THICK TIGHT BEETLE
COMART HARDEN LEAGUE SHRINK
SPISSY STOCKY VANITY BARGAIN
CONCISE CONCORD CROWDED
NUGGETY PACTION SERRIED
ALLIANCE CONDENSE CONTRACT
COVENANT FLAPJACK HEAVYSET
SOLIDIFY SUCCINCT
COMPACTED SAD CROWDED
COMPACTNESS BODY DENSITY
FASTNESS SOLIDITY INTENSITY
COMPANION PAL SOC CHUM FERE
MAKE MATE PEER TWIN WIFE BILLY
BUDDY BULLY BUTTY CHINA COMES
CRONY CULLY DARES GREEK
MATCH MATEY MAUGH RIVAL SPORT
ATTEND BILLIE BROLGA COBBER
COHORT COMATE CUMMER DUENNA
EGERIA ESCORT FELLOW FRIEND
GESITH GOSSIP KIMMER MARROW
PANION SHADOW SPOUSE STEADY
TROJAN ACHATES COMPANY
COMPEER COMRADE CONSORT
ELPENOR HUSBAND PARTNER
SOCIATE SOCIETY SPECIAL
BEAUPERE COMPADRE CORRIVAL
EPHESIAN EPHESINE FAITHFUL

FAMILIAR HELPMATE PARALLEL
PLAYFERE SYNODITE
(ARCHER'S —) BUTTY
(DRINKING —) CUPMATE
(POT —) ALEKNIGHT
(READING —) LECTRICE
(TABLE —) CONVICTOR
(PL.) SOCIETY
COMPANIONABLE FERE MATEY
SOCIAL CORDIAL FELLOWLY
GRACIOUS SOCIABLE
COMPANIONSHIP FERE SHIP HAUNT
COMPANY SOCIETY AFFINITY
COMPANY CRY MOB SET BAND
BEVY BODY CORE CREW CRUE
FARE FERE FIRM GANG GEST GING
HERD HOST MANY PUSH ROUT
SORT TEAM TURM AERIE COVEN
COVEY CROWD FLOCK FLOTE
GESTE GROUP GUEST HORDE
JATHA MEINY PARTY SQUAD SUITE
TROOP TURMA CIRCLE CLIQUE
COHORT COVINE CURNEY DECURY
LOCHUS RESORT THRONG TROUPE
TWENTY VOLLEY BATTERY COLLEGE
CONDUCT CONSORT HOLDING
JIMBANG MANIPLE SOCIETE
SOCIETY THIASOS THIASUS VISITOR
ASSEMBLY FAISCEAU FOLKMOOT
JINGBANG
(— OF BADGERS) CETE
(— OF DANCERS) COMPARSA
(— OF HERDSMEN) BOOLY BOOLEY
(— OF HORSEMEN) TROOP
(— OF MARTENS) RICHESSE
(— OF SINGERS) CHOIR QUIRE
CHORUS
(— OF THE FAITHFUL) FOLD
(— OF TRAVELERS) CAFILA
CAVALCADE
(— OF WOMEN) GAGGLE
(EXCLUSIVE —) CROWD
(FINANCIAL —) FACTOR
(FIRE —) SQUAD
(MILITARY —) WATCH DECURY
VENLIN PELOTON VEXILLUM
(RECORDING —) LABEL
(SUITABLE —) BESORT
COMPARABLE LIKE SAME SIMILAR
COMPARE VIE EVEN LIKE SIZE
APPLY EQUAL LIKEN MATCH SCALE
TALLY ALLUDE CONFER PARIFY
RELATE SEMBLE BRACKET COLLATE
EXAMINE SENIBLE SIGNIFY
ASSEMBLE CONFRONT CONTRAST
ESTIMATE RESEMBLE SIMILIZE
(— WITH) TO
COMPARISON SIMILE ANALOGY
BALANCE COMPARE PARABLE
DISIMILE LIKENESS LIKENING
METAPHOR PARALLEL
COMPARTMENT BAY BIN BOX CAB
POD CELL DECK FLUE PANE PART
SLOT WELL ABODE CABIN HATCH
HUTCH PANEL STALL VOLET
ABACUS ALCOVE BUNKER GARAGE
HOPPER MUFFLE REGION SEVERY
SMOKER ALVEOLE CABINET
CAPSULE CELLULE CHAMBER

FIREBOX HOUSING KITCHEN
MANSION ROTONDE SECTION
ALVEOLUS COALHOLE DIVISION
FOREPEAK GRINTERN LOCELLUS
STEERAGE TRAVERSE
(— FOR COAL) BUNKER
(— FOR TREATING ORE) KITCHEN
(— IN BARN) BAY
(— IN STOVE) BROILER
(— OF COACH) IMPERIAL
(— OF ROOF) SEVERY
(— OF WINDOW) LIGHT
(— ON GAMEBOARD) STORE
(— ON ROULETTE WHEEL) EAGLE
(CARGO —) HOLD
(GAS-TIGHT —) BALLONET
(GUNNER'S —) BLISTER
(REFRIGERATOR —) CHILLER
(SLEEPING —) CUBICLE
(STAGECOACH —) COUPE
(STORAGE—) BOOT
COMPASS BOW AREA DIAL GAIN
ROOM ROSE SIZE TOUR AMBIT
FIELD GAMUT RANGE REACH SCOPE
SWEEP TENOR WHEEL ARRIVE
ATTAIN BOUNDS CIRCLE DEGREE
DEVICE DIACLE EFFECT EXTENT
MERIST MODULE SPHERE SPREAD
VOLUME ACHIEVE AZIMUTH CALIBER
CIRCUIT CONFINE DIVIDER EMBRACE
ENCLOSE ENVIRON HORIZON
IMAGINE PELORUS PURVIEW
TRAMMEL BOUNDARY CINCTURE
CIRCUITY DIAPASON PRACTICE
PRACTISE SURROUND
(— IN SHIP'S CABIN) TELLTALE
(— NEEDLE END) LILY
(— OF MELODY) AMBITUS
(— OF TONES) DIAPASON
(— OF VOICE) GAMUT SCALE
(— POINT) RHUMB
(BELL-MAKING —) CROOK
COMPASS BOX KETTLE
COMPASS CARD ROSE PEDRERO
PERRIER
COMPASSION RUE PITY RUTH
GRACE HEART MERCY PIETY SORRY
KARUNA LENITY REMORSE
STOMACH CLEMENCY HUMANITY
KINDNESS SYMPATHY
COMPASSIONATE RUTH SOFT
HUMAN GENTLE TENDER CLEMENT
PIETOSO PITEOUS PITIFUL
GRACIOUS MERCIFUL
COMPASS PLANT PILOTWEED
ROSINWEED
COMPASS QUARTER PLAGE
COMPASS SIGHT VANE
COMPATIBLE AKIN CIVIL ARTISTIC
SUITABLE
COMPATRIOT NATIVE PATRIOT
SYNETHNIC
COMPEL GAR MAKE MOVE URGE
BRING CAUSE COACT DRIVE EXACT
FORCE IMPEL PRESS SHOVE
COERCE ENJOIN EXTORT INCITE
OBLIGE THREAT ACTUATE AFFORCE
ATTRACT COMMAND DRAGOON
ENFORCE NECESSE REQUIRE
VIOLENCE

(— **TO GO**) HALE
(— **TO PAY**) STICK
COMPELLED HAS FAIN MUST BOUND
FORCED ENFORCED
COMPELLING COGENT STRONG
TELLING BRUISING FORCEFUL
COMPELLINGLY BADLY
COMPENDIOUS BRIEF SHORT
DIRECT COMPACT CONCISE
SUMMARY SUCCINCT
COMPENDIUM LIST BRIEF APERCU
DIGEST PRECIS SKETCH SURVEY
CATALOG COMPEND EPITOME
LEXICON MEDULLA OUTLINE
PANDECT SUMMARY SYLLOGE
ABSTRACT BREVIARY BREVIATE
LANDSKIP SYLLABUS SYNOPSIS
COMPENSATE PAY JIBE AGREE
ATONE COVER REPAY TALLY
OFFSET RECOUP REDEEM REWARD
SQUARE COMMUTE CORRECT
PLASTER REDRESS REPRISE
REQUITE RESTORE SATISFY
COMPENSE DISPENSE EQUALIZE
COMPENSATION BOT FEE PAY UTU
HIRE MEND TOLL BONUS LOWER
WAGES AMENDS ANGILD GERSUM
OFFSET REWARD SALARY SETOFF
DAMAGES FREIGHT PAYMENT
REDRESS SALVAGE STIPEND
BREAKAGE DONATIVE EARNINGS
INTEREST OCTOGILD PITTANCE
REQUITAL SOLATIUM
(— **FOR KILLING MAN**) MANBOT
MANBOTE
(**MEAGER** —) PITTANCE
(**WORKER'S** —) COMPO
COMPENSATORILY EVEN
COMPETE PIT VIE COPE KEMP TEND
CLASH MATCH RIVAL STRIVE
CONTEND CONTEST EMULATE
CORRIVAL
(— **WITH**) BUCK
COMPETENCE SKILL ABILITY
FACULTY CAPACITY
COMPETENCY MAY CAPACITY
COMPETENT UP APT CAN FIT ABLE
GOOD HOME MEET SANE ADEPT
CAPAX SMART SWEET TIGHT INTACT
LAWFUL WORTHY CAPABLE
ENDOWED SKILLED ADEQUATE
SUITABLE
COMPETITION VIE DRAW GAME
HEAT JUMP MATCH PRIZE TRIAL
WAGER CONTEST PARAGON
RIVALRY CONCOURS CONFLICT
(— **AMONG REAPERS**) KEMP
COMPETITOR FOE ENEMY MATCH
RIVAL WAGER COUSIN PLAYER
ENTRANT CORRIVAL FAVORITE
GAMESTER OPPONENT
COMPILATION ANA BOOK CODE
CENTO DIGEST CASEBOOK
DIRECTORY GATHERING
COMPILE ADD EDIT AMASS GATHER
SELECT ARRANGE COLLECT
COMPOSE PREPARE
COMPILER AUTHOR EDITOR
GATHERER GLOSSIST SCISSORER

COMPLACENT CALM SMUG
FATUOUS PRIGGISH
COMPLACENTLY FATLY
COMPLAIN AIL YIP BEEF CARP CRIB
FRET FUSS GREX KEEN KICK KREX
MEAN MOAN MOOT MUTE RULE
WAIL YELP YIRN BITCH BRAWL
CRAKE CROAK CROON GRIPE
GROWL GRUMP GRUNT PINGE PLAIN
WHINE BEWAIL CHARGE COTTER
CREATE GRIEVE GROUSE GRUTCH
HOLLER MURMUR PEENGE REPINE
SQUAWK THREAP THROPE YAMMER
CHUNNER DEPLORE GRIZZLE
GRUMBLE INVEIGH PROTEST
COMPLAINANT ACTOR ASKER
ACCUSER PLAINER QUERENT
RELATOR
COMPLAINING PULY LATRANT
QUERENT DOLEANCE
COMPLAINT RAP BEEF FUSS HOWL
MEAN MOAN WAIL BITCH GRIPE
GROWL WHINE CHESON GROUCH
GROUSE GRUDGE GRUTCH HOLLER
LAMENT MALADY PLAINT REPINE
SQUAWK AILMENT DISEASE
GRUMBLE ILLNESS PROTEST
QUARREL QUERELE RECLAMA
TRAGEDY COMPLAIN DISORDER
DOLEANCE GRAVAMEN JEREMIAD
COMPLAISANCE AMENITY SUAVITY
FACILITY URBANITY
COMPLAISANT BON ABLE EASY
KIND BUXOM CIVIL SUAVE BONAIR
POLITE SMOOTH SUPPLE URBANE
AFFABLE AMIABLE BOWABLE
LENIENT GRACIOUS OBLIGING
PLEASING
COMPLEMENT CREW GANG FORCE
TALLY ALEXIN AMOUNT COUSIN
ADJUNCT OBVERSE
(**MILITARY** —) STRENGTH
COMPLETE DO ALL END BLUE DASH
DEAD DEEP FAIR FILL FINE FULL
JUST PASS PURE RANK CLOSE
CROWN EVERY GROSS LARGE PLAIN
PLUMB POINT PUCCA PUKKA QUITE
RIPEN ROUND SOUND TOTAL UTTER
WHOLE CHOATE DAMPEN DEADLY
EFFECT ENTIRE FINISH GLOBAL
HOLLOW INTACT MATURE PROPER
SINGLE STRICT ACHIEVE CONFIRM
EXECUTE EXPLETE FULFILL
GERMANE PERFECT PLENARY
REALIZE REPLETE SPHERAL
ABSOLUTE BLINKING CIRCULAR
CONCLUDE FINALIZE IMPLICIT
INTEGRAL OUTRIGHT OVERCOME
PRECIOUS PROFOUND THOROUGH
BODACIOUS
(— **CARELESSLY**) HUDDLE
(**REMARKABLY** —) SPLENDID
COMPLETED PAU OVER CLOSED
SUMMED COMPLETE FINISHED
(**NOT** —) DURATIVE
COMPLETELY ALL JAM BARE BUCK
FAIR FLAT GOOD SLAM SLAP SPAN
BLACK CLEAN CLOSE FULLY PLUMB
QUITE SHEER SMACK SPANG STICK

STOCK UTTER BODILY ENTIRE
GAINLY HOLLOW PURELY SPANDY
WHOLLY ALGATES BLANKLY
THROUGH CLEVERLY DIRECTLY
ENTIRELY HEARTILY OUTRIGHT
COMPLETENESS DEPTH ALLNESS
FULLNESS RIPENESS INTEGRITY
COMPLETION END FINISH
COMPLEX HARD MAZY BEING ETHOS
FIELD HYOID MIXED ADDUCT
DESERT KNOTTY SYSTEM CULTURE
NETWORK SAMKARA SINUOUS
TANGLED TWISTED COMPOUND
EQUATION EXCHANGE INVOLVED
MANIFOLD SAMSKARA SYNDROME
(— **OF DIALECTS**) HINDI
(— **OF HORMONES**) CALINE
(— **OF IDEAS**) EGO SYSTEM
(**BASEMENT** —) FLOOR
(**NOT** —) SIMPLE
COMPLEXION HUE RUD BLEE CAST
LEER LOOK RUDD TINT COLOR
HUMOR STATE TENOR TINGE
ASPECT TEMPER COLORING
(**BAD** —) DYSCHROA
COMPLEXITY SCHEME INTRIGUE
COMPLIANCE TRUE ASSENT
MUNICH CESSION CONSENT
HARMONY OBSEQUY ABIDANCE
CIVILITY FACILITY FORMALITY
COMPLIANT EASY OILY SOFT
BUXOM FACILE PLIANT SUPPLE
COMMODE DUCTILE DUTIFUL
WILLING OBEDIENT TOWARDLY
YIELDING
COMPLICATE INTORT PUZZLE
TANGLE EMBROIL INVOLVE PERPLEX
BEWILDER INTRIGUE INTRICATE
COMPLICATED HARD KNOTTY
PROLIX COMPLEX GORDIAN
SNARLED TANGLED INVOLVED
PLEXIFORM
COMPLICATION KNOT NODE PLOT
NODUS SNARL INTRIGUE
COMPLIMENT GIFT LAUD EXTOL
EULOGY PRAISE SALAAM SALUTE
ADULATE APPLAUD BOUQUET
COMMEND DOUCEUR FLATTER
TRIBUTE ENCOMIUM FLUMMERY
GRATUITY GREETING
COMPLY PLY CEDE OBEY ABIDE
ADAPT AGREE APPLY YIELD ACCEDE
ACCORD ASSENT ENFOLD SUBMIT
CONFORM EMBRACE OBSERVE
(— **WITH**) OBEY SERVE OBSERVE
SATISFY
COMPONE GOBONE GOBONY
COMPONENT KEY DRAG FORM ITEM
PART UNIT GIVEN FACTOR MEMBER
SIMPLE ELEMENT FORMANT
CONJUNCT INTEGRAL
(— **OF ARMY**) CAVALRY
(— **OF CELL WALLS**) CALLOSE
(**ELECTRIC** —**S**) CIRCUITRY
(**PRINCIPAL** —) BASIS
COMPORT ACT BEAR HAVE HOLD
JIBE KEEP SUIT AGREE BROOK
CARRY TALLY ACCORD ACQUIT
BEHAVE DEMEAN ENDURE SQUARE
CONDUCT

COMPORTMENT CONDUCT DEALING BEHAVIOR DEMEANOR
COMPOSE BAT PEN SET CALM COMP DITE FORM LULL MAKE ALLAY BREVE BRIEF CLERK CLINK COUCH DIGHT DRAFT FRAME ORDER PATCH PIECE SPELL STICK WRITE ACCORD ADJUST CREATE DESIGN GRAITH INDITE RECITE REDACT SETTLE SOOTHE STEADY ARRANGE COMPACT COMPILE COMPONE CONCOCT CONFORM DICTATE DISPOSE DRAUGHT FASHION PATIENT PRODUCE TYPESET COMPOUND COMPRISE REGULATE (— **POETRY**) SING
COMPOSED SET CALM COOL QUIET SOBER WROTE DEMURE DIGEST PLACID SEDATE SERENE COMPACT WRITTEN COMPOUND DECOROUS TRANQUIL
(— **IN METER**) FOOTED
(**ILL** —) LAME
COMPOSEDNESS SOSSIEGO
COMPOSER BARD POET LYRIC ODIST AUTHOR LYRIST PENMAN WRITER CONTEUR ELEGIST FANTAST MAESTRO COLORIST ELEGIAST IDYLLIST ILIADIST MELODIST MONODIST MUSICIAN PHANTAST TUNESMITH
COMPOSITE HYBRID ITALIC MOTLEY COMPLEX COMPOSED CONCRETE INTEGRAL
COMPOSITION ANA DITE MASS OPUS WORK CENTO DITTY DRAMA FUGUE GETUP MURKY PIECE POESY STUCK THEME ACCORD EULOGY FILLER HAIKAI LESSON MAGGOT MONODY THESIS THREAD VULGUS ARTICLE COMPOST CONSIST DISPLAY EBURINE EPISTLE MIXTURE PICTURE STOPPER WRITING ACROSTIC CAUSERIE COMPOUND DIALOGUE DIAPENTE EXERCISE FANTASIA FROTTAGE HEELBALL
(— **FOR BILLIARD BALLS**) COMPO
(— **TO BE ACTED**) PLAY DRAMA
(— **TO FILL LEATHER**) STUFF
(**AMOROUS** —) EROTIC
(**ARTISTIC** —) COLLAGE
(**BUILDING** —) STAFF
(**CHORAL** —) MOTET CANTATA ORATORIO
(**GUMMY** —) GROUND
(**HAND** —) CASEWORK
(**HUMOROUS** —) BURLA
(**INSTRUMENTAL** —) AIR GATO FANCY RONDO GROUND SKETCH SONATA TIENTO CANZONE BERCEUSE CONCERTO FANTASIA RHAPSODY SYMPHONY
(**IMPERFECT** —) SOOTERKIN
(**LITERARY** —) BOOK CENTO DEBAT ESSAY PIECE COMEDY SATIRE SKETCH THESIS TREATISE
(**MAGIC** —) HELLBROTH
(**MUSICAL** —) DUET GLEE IDYL OPUS SOLO SONG TRIO BURLA

CANON DANCE ELEGY ETUDE FUGUE GAZEL IDYLL NONET SCORE STUDY ADAGIO ARIOSO ENTREE GHAZEL HOCKET HOQUET SEPTET SEXTET BALLADE BOURREE BOUTADE BRAVURA QUARTET SCHERZO TOCCATA CAVATINA CHACONNE CLAUSULA CONCERTO INNOMINE SERENADE SINFONIA STANDARD SYMPHONY ANTIPHONY
(**NARRATIVE** —) BALLAD
(**PLASTIC** —) CEMENT
(**POETIC** —) GLOSS KAVYA
(**RAMBLING** —) SATIRE
(**RELIGIOUS** —) MOTET ANTHEM HYMNIC CANTATA ORATORIO
(**RUBBER** —) GUM
(**VEDIC** —) GAYATRI
(**VITREOUS** —) ENAMEL
(**VOCAL** —) ARIA SOLO SONG CANON ANTHEM ELEVATIO CONDUCTUS
(PL.) JUVENILIA LITERATURE
COMPOSITOR COMP TYPO ADMAN SETTER BANKMAN CASEMAN PRINTER STONEMAN
COMPOST PELF SOIL MINGLE COMPOTE MIXTURE COMPOUND DRESSING
COMPOSURE BOND MIEN QUIET UNION REPOSE TEMPER BALANCE POSTURE CALMNESS SERENITY
COMPOTATION SYMPOSIUM
COMPOTE BOWL COMPORT COMPOST
COMPOUND MIX BASE FILL JOIN MIXT SOUR ALKYL ALLOY AMIDE AMINE BLEND ESTER FURIL UNION ADJUST ALKIDE BORANE COPULA IODIDE JUMBLE KETONE MEDLEY PHENOL POLYOL PTERIN PYRONE SETTLE TEMPER URACIL URAMIL AGATHIN ALCOHOL ALLICIN ALLOXAN AMALGAM AMIDATE AMIDINE AMINATE AMMONIA COMBINE COMPLEX COMPONE COMPOSE COMPOST DVANDVA KAMPONG KHELLIN PHORBIN PREPARE SPIRANE STEROID AGLUCONE AGLYCONE ALIZARIN ALKOXIDE AMMONATE ANTIPODE APIGENIN BRAZILIN CEROMIDE COMPOSED FUCHSONE GARDENIN GENTISIN GOSSYPOL IODOFORM ISOLOGUE STYRACIN
(**ADHESIVE** —) SALVE
(**POISONOUS** —) KETENE CACODYL GLYCINE HELENIN STIBINE
(**SYNTHETIC** —) ANDROGEN SORBITAN
COMPOUNDED CONCRETE COMPOSITE
COMPOUNDER TANKER
COMPOUNDING INTIMACY
COMPREHEND GET SEE KNOW TAKE TWIG COVER GRASP IMPLY LATCH REACH SAVVY SEIZE SENSE SKILL SMOKE SPELL ATTAIN DIGEST EMBODY FATHOM FOLLOW PIERCE

UPTAKE COMPASS CONTAIN DISCERN EMBRACE ENCLOSE IMAGINE INCLUDE INVOLVE REALIZE RECEIVE SWALLOW COMPRISE CONCEIVE CONCLUDE PERCEIVE
COMPREHENSIBLE EXOTERIC INCLUDED SENSABLE SCRUTABLE
COMPREHENSION HOLD SABE GRASP SAVVY SENSE ESPRIT FATHOM NOESIS UPTAKE EPITOME INSIGHT KNOWING SUMMARY BEARINGS
COMPREHENSIVE BIG FULL WIDE BROAD GRAND LARGE GLOBAL SCOPIC CAPABLE CONCISE GENERAL GENERIC CATHOLIC ENCYCLIC SPACIOUS
COMPREHENSIVENESS SCOPE EXTENT BREADTH WIDENESS LARGENESS
COMPRESS NIP TIE BALE BIND FIRM LACE WRAP CLING CRAMP CROWD CRUSH PINCH PRESS SMASH BUNDLE DEFORM DIGEST GATHER SHRINK STRAIN THRONG ABRIDGE BOLSTER CABBAGE COMPACT CURTAIL DEFLATE EMBRACE FLATTEN REPRESS SQUEEZE SQUINCH ASTRINGE CONDENSE CONTRACT LAMINATE PEMMICAN RESTRAIN SUPPRESS
(— **WOOL**) DUMP
(**MEDICAL** —) BOLSTER PLEDGET
COMPRESSED STRICT CROWDED SUCCINCT
COMPRESSION CRUSH SQUEEZE PRESSURE THLIPSIS
COMPRESSOR PUMP ROTARY CONDENSER
COMPRISE HOLD COVER IMPLY SEIZE ATTACH CONFER EMBODY EMPLOY MUSTER COMPOSE CONTAIN EMBRACE ENCLOSE INCLUDE INVOLVE CONCEIVE PERCEIVE
COMPROMISE FINE TRIM COMMIT INTERIM COMPOUND ENDANGER PALLIATO
COMPROMISING FALSE
COMPULSION NEED URGE FORCE PRESS DURESS STRESS IMPULSE COACTION COERCION DISTRESS EXACTION PERFORCE
COMPULSORY COERCIVE FORCIBLE
COMPUNCTION QUALM REGRET SORROW REMORSE SCRUPLE
COMPURGATOR COJUROR COSWEARER
COMPUTATION COMPOT ACCOUNT COMPUTE CALCULUS COMPUTUS ESTIMATE
COMPUTE ADD SUM CAST ITEM RATE COUNT TALLY VALUE ASSESS CIPHER FIGURE NUMBER RECKON ACCOUNT BALANCE SUPPUTE ESTIMATE
COMPUTER ENIAC MANIAC
COMRADE PAL ALLY CHUM MATE PEER BILLY BUDDY CRONY HABER

HAVER TOWNY BURSCH CHABER
CHAVER COPAIN COUSIN DIGGER
ENGIDU FELLOE FRATER FRIEND
GOSSIP HEARTY BROTHER
COMPEER CONVIVE BEAUPERE
CAMARADA CAMARADE COMORADO
CONFRERE COPEMATE TOVARICH
(— **AT TABLE)** CONVIVE
(PL.) SOCE

CON DO RAP ANTI KNOW LEAD LOOK
PORE QUIN READ SCAN CHEAT
CUNNE GUIDE KNOCK LEARN STEER
STUDY DIRECT PERUSE REGARD
VERSUS AGAINST DECEIVE EXAMINE
INSPECT OPPOSED SWINDLE

CONCAVE CAVE VOID CAMUS MINUS
ARCHED DISHED HOLLOW SIMOUS
VAULTY VAULTED CRESCENT
INCURVED

CONCAVITY COVE CONCHA HOLLOW
VENTER KNEEPAN

CONCEAL MEW WRY BURY DERN
FEAL HIDE KEEP LENE MASK SCUG
SILE VEIL VEST WRAP BLIND BOSOM
CACHE CLOAK COUCH COVER FEIGN
LAYNE PLANT SHADE BURROW
CLOSET DOCTOR ELOIGN EMBOSS
HUDDLE HUGGER IMBOSK OCCULT
POCKET SCREEN SHADOW SHIELD
SHROUD STIFLE ABSCOND ENVELOP
OPPRESS PLASTER SECRETE
BESCREEN DISGUISE ENSCONCE
PALLIATE PRETENCE PRETENSE
WITHHOLD
(— **A FUGITIVE)** HARBOR
(— **A TRAIL)** TRASH
(— **INFORMATION)** LAYNE

CONCEALED DERN SCUG SNUG
BLIND PRIVY BURROW COVERT
HIDDEN LATENT OCCULT PERDUE
SECRET VEILED COVERED LARVATE
WRAPPED ABSTRUSE CRYPTOUS
HIDEAWAY
(— **BY)** BENEATH

CONCEALING DESIGNING
OBVELATION

CONCEALMENT MEW LAIN COVER
FRAUD NIGHT SECRECY CELATION
VELATION
(IN —) DOGGO

CONCEDE OWN CEDE GIVE ADMIT
AGREE ALLOW GRANT WAIVE YETTE
YIELD ACCORD ASSENT BETEEM
CONFESS OTTROYE BEGRUDGE
(— **AS ADVANTAGE)** SPOT

CONCEIT EGO TOY IDEA SIDE
CRANK FANCY KNACK PRIDE QUIRK
BABERY DEVICE NOTION VAGARY
VANITY BIGHEAD CAPRICE EGOTISM
OUTRAGE TYMPANY CONCETTO
FLIMFLAM

CONCEITED BUG BRAG COXY FESS
VAIN CHUFF COCKY FLORY HUFFY
PENSY PROUD SAUCY CLEVER
BIGGETY BIGGITY ARROGANT
DOGMATIC NOSEWISE PENSEFUL
PRIGGISH SNOBBISH

CONCEIVABLE EARTHLY POSSIBLE
CONCEIVE FORM HOLD MAKE PLAN

TEEM WEEN BEGIN BRAIN CATCH
DREAM FANCY FRAME GUESS IMAGE
THINK DESIGN DEVISE IDEATE
INTEND PONDER SETTLE GESTATE
IMAGINE REALIZE SUPPOSE
SUSPECT COMPRISE CONTRIVE
ENVISAGE

CONCENTRATE AIM FIX MASS PILE
COACT EXALT FOCUS PURSE UNIFY
ARREST ATTEND CENTER CITRIN
DECOCT DISTIL FIXATE GATHER
SINGLE COMPACT CONGEST DISTILL
ENGROSS ESSENCE EXTRACT
THICKEN ABSOLUTE APPROACH
ASSEMBLE CONDENSE CONTRACT
FOCALIZE GRADUATE
(— **ORE)** STRAKE

CONCENTRATED HARD DENSE
FIXED INTENT STRONG EXALTED
INTENSE
(**NOT** —) DIFFUSE

CONCENTRATION BRIX CENTER
BALLING SAMADHI ACTIVITY
FIXATION PELMANISM
(— **OF ARTILLERY FIRE)** STONK
(— **OF ENERGY)** EXCITON
(— **OF PLANTS)** BED

CONCEPT GUT GUTS IDEA FANCY
IMAGE BEGRIFF CONCEIT OPINION
THOUGHT ABSOLUTE CATEGORY

CONCEPTION ENS IDEA VIEW EIDOS
FANCY FETUS IMAGE BELIEF DESIGN
EMBRYO ENTITY NOTION CONCEIT
CONCEPT PROJECT PURPOSE
CATEGORY ESTHETIC NOTATION
RATIONAL
(— **OF IDEA)** HENT
(— **OF ONESELF)** BOVARISM
BOVARYSM
(**ABSTRACT** —) ARCHETYPE
(**FALSE** —) IDOL DELUSION
(**QUICKNESS OF** —) PREGNANCY

CONCEPTUAL IDEAL
CONCEPTUALISM SERMONISM
CONCERN BUG BEAR CARE FEAR
FIRM GEAR HAND PART RECK SAKE
APPLY CAUSE DRIVE EVENT GRIEF
HEART SORGE STAND TOUCH
WORRY AFFAIR AFFECT BEHOLD
CHARGE DIRECT EMPLOY FINGER
IMPORT MATTER REGARD ANXIETY
ARTICLE BOTTLER COMPANY
DISTURB FUNERAL INVOLVE
PERTAIN RESPECT SHEBANG
SOLICIT TROUBLE BUSINESS
HYPOTHEC INTEREST JEALOUSY
(— **ONESELF)** DEAL PASS TOUCH
INTERMIT
(**INDUSTRIAL** —) COLOSSUS
(**PRUDISH** —) COMSTOCKERY
(**SPECIAL** —) ACCENT
(**WORLDLY** —**S)** EARTH

CONCERNED INTENT ANXIOUS
WORRIED ATWITTER BOTHERED

CONCERNING BY OF ON RE TO FOR
TIL TILL ABOUT ANENT ANENST
APROPOS TOUCHING

CONCERT POP PLAN RECK UNITE
ACCORD DEVISE SMOKER ARRANGE

BENEFIT CONCENT CONCORD
CONSORT CONSULT HARMONY
POPULAR RECITAL

CONCERTINA ORGAN LANTUM
SQUIFFER BANDONION MELOPHONE

CONCESSION BOON FAVOR GRANT
LEASE STOOP ASSENT GAMBIT
OCTROY CESSION EPITROPE
MYNPACHT ADMISSION ALLOWANCE
PRIVILEGE

CONCESSIONAIRE GRIFTER
CONCH CONK PUNK SHELL COCKLE
MUSSEL STROMB STROMBUS

CONCIERGE PORTER SUISSE
WARDEN JANITOR

CONCILIATE GET CALM EASE GAIN
ATONE HONEY THING ADJUST
PACIFY SOFTEN ACQUIRE APPEASE
CONCILE MOLLIFY PLACATE SATISFY

CONCILIATOR ARBITRATOR
CONCILIATORY MILD SOFT GENTLE
GIVING IRENIC LENIENT PACIFIC
WINNING IRENICAL LENITIVE
TREATABLE

CONCISE CURT NEAT TRIG BRIEF
CRISP PITHY SHORT TERSE COGENT
CUTTED COMPACT LACONIC
POINTED PRECISE SERRIED
SUMMARY MUTILATE PREGNANT
SUCCINCT

CONCISELY PRESSLY ELLIPTICALLY
CONCISENESS BREVITY ECONOMY
SYNTOMY FASTNESS SYNTOMIA

CONCLAVE SOBOR CLOSET
CHAMBER MEETING AREOPAGY
ASSEMBLY

CONCLUDE BAR END FINE REST
TAKE CLOSE DRIVE ESTOP INFER
JUDGE LIMIT CLINCH DECIDE
DEDUCE EXPIRE FIGURE FINISH
GATHER INDUCE PERIOD REASON
RECKON SETTLE ACHIEVE ARRANGE
COLLECT CONFINE EMBRACE
ENCLOSE RESOLVE SUPPOSE
COMPLETE DISPATCH ESTIMATE
GRADUATE PARCLOSE RESTRAIN

CONCLUDED OVER COMPLETE
CONCLUDING LAST DESITIVE
CONCLUSION END AMEN CODA
ERGO FINE LAST TERM CLOSE
ENVOY EVENT FINIS ISSUE LOOSE
POINT ENDING FINALE FINISH
PERIOD RESULT SEQUEL THIRTY
UPSHOT CLOSURE CURTAIN FINDING
OUTCOME SEQUELA APODOSIS
DECISION EPILOGUE FINALITY
FRUITION GODSPEED ILLATION
ILLATIVE JUDGMENT PARCLOSE
SENTENCE
(— **OF ARIA)** CABALETTA
(**FINAL** —) ISSUE
(**RANDOM** —) SURMISE
(PL.) COLLATION

CONCLUSIVE LAST FINAL VALID
COGENT CERTAIN EVIDENT
EXTREME TELLING DECISIVE
DEFINITE ULTIMATE

CONCOCT MIX BREW COOK FAKE
PLAN PLOT VAMP FRAME HATCH

THINK DECOCT DEVISE DIGEST
INVENT MINGLE REFINE SCHEME
COMPOSE CONFECT PERFECT
PREPARE COMPOUND INTRIGUE
CONCOCTION PLAN PLOT MUMMY
DEVICE MUMMIA BREWING MIXTURE
SNEEZER BUSINESS COMPOUND
CONCOMITANT SEQUELA INCIDENT
ACCESSORY ASSOCIATE ATTENDANT
ATTENDING COMPANION CONJOINED
COOPERANT SATELLITE
CONCORD PART AGREE AMITY
PEACE TERMS UNION UNITY TREATY
UNISON COMPACT CONCENT
CONCERT HARMONY ONENESS
QUARTER COVENANT SYMPATHY
COMMUNITY
(— **OF SOUNDS**) SYMPHONIA
CONCORDANT UNISON TUNABLE
TUNEFUL HARMONIC UNISONAL
UNISONOUS
CONCOURSE CROWD HAUNT PLACE
POINT REPAIR RESORT THRONG
COMPANY ASSEMBLY FREQUENCE
(**INFERNAL** —) HELL
CONCRETE CLOT FIRM HARD REAL
BETON GROUT SOLID UNITE ACTUAL
CEMENT COMBINE CONGEAL
SPECIAL COALESCE COMPOUND
POSITIVE TANGIBLE AEROCRETE
CONCRETION CLOT KNOT MESS
FLINT FUSIL PEARL STONE BEZOAR
NODULE TOPHUS LITHITE OTOLITH
CALCULUS POTSTONE SEBOLITH
(— **IN BAMBOO**) TABASHIR
TABASHEER
CONCUBINAGE KARAO KAREWA
HETAERISM
CONCUBINE DASI HAGAR RIZPAH
BEDMATE ODALISK MISTRESS
CONCUPISCENCE DESIRE
CONCUPISCENT ANTSY
CONCUR HAND JIBE JOIN AGREE
CHECK CHIME UNITE ACCEDE
ACCORD ASSENT CONDOG APPROVE
COMBINE CONSENT CONVENT
COINCIDE CONSPIRE CONVERGE
(— **IN**) SUBSCRIBE
CONCURRENCE UNION ASSENT
BESTOW CONSENT CONSORT
MEETING ADHESION SYNDROME
ADMISSION
CONCURRENT COEVAL UNITED
MEETING COPIJNCTAL
CONCUSSION BUMP SHOCK IMPACT
ICEQUAKE COMMOTION
CONDEMN BAN CAST DAMN DEEM
DOOM FILE FINE HISS BLAME BLESS
DECRY JUDGE AMERCE ATTAIN
AWREAK BANISH DETEST ADJUDGE
CENSURE CONVICT DENOUNCE
FORJUDGE REPROACH SENTENCE
CONDEMNATION DOOM BLAME
CENSURE DECRIAL BRICKBAT
CONDEMNATORY SEVERE ADVERSE
CONDEMNED FATAL DAMNED
CONDENSATION BAN STORY
DIGEST CAPSULE BOILDOWN
CONDENSE CUT JIG BRIEF UNITE

DECOCT DIGEST HARDEN LESSEN
NARROW REDUCE SHRINK ABRIDGE
CAPSULE COMBINE COMPACT
DEFLATE DENSATE DISTILL
SHORTEN SQUEEZE THICKEN
COMPRESS CONTRACT DIMINISH
PEMMICAN SOLIDIFY
CONDENSED CURT BRIEF CAPSULE
COMPACT CONCISE ABSORBED
CONDENSER A! UDEL REFLUX
BALANCER CAPACITOR
CONDER HUER
CONDESCEND DEIGN FAVOR GRANT
STOOP ASSENT OBLIGE SUBMIT
CONCEDE DESCEND
CONDESCENDING AVUNCULAR
CONDESCENSION STOOP DISDAIN
COURTESY DIGNATION
CONDIGN DUE FIT FAIR JUST
SEVERE WORTHY ADEQUATE
SUITABLE
CONDIMENT SOY HERB KARI MACE
SAGE SALT CAPER CURRY DULCE
DULSE SAUCE SPICE THYME AIWAIN
AJOWAN CATSUP CLOVES GARLIC
PEPPER RELISH SAMBAL TAMARA
CANELLA CHUTNEY KETCHUP
MUSTARD OREGANO PAPRIKA
VINEGAR ALLSPICE BALACHAN
BLATJANG DRESSING SEASONER
TURMERIC
CONDITION IF AND FIG PLY WAY
CASE FORM MODE PASS RANK
ROTE TERM TIFF TRIM ANGLE BIRTH
CAUSE CLASS COLOR COVIN ESTRE
FACET JOKER PLACE POINT SHAPE
STAGE STATE THEAT WHACK
AGENCY DEGREE DONNEE ESTATE
FETTLE GENTRY MORALE MUSCLE
PLIGHT STATUS STRING ARTICLE
CALLING FEATHER FOOTING
PREMISE PROVISO STATION
SUSPEND COVENANT OCCASION
POSITION PROTASIS STANDING
(— **OF ANXIETY**) CARK
(— **OF BODY**) HEAT AFFECTION
(— **OF FATIGUE**) FRAZZLE
(— **OF FLUCTUATION**) EURIPUS
(— **STATED BEFOREHAND**) PREMISE
(**CHANCE** —) ACCIDENT
(**DEBASED** —) CACHEXY CACHEXIA
(**DEPRESSED** —) DOWNBEAT
(**DETERMINING** —) GROUND
(**DIRTY** —) CLAT
(**DISEASED** —) DIEBACK
(**DISGRACEFUL** —) IGNOMINY
(**DRUNKEN** —) BUN
(**FLOURISHING** —) HEALTH
(**GENERAL** —) VOGUE
(**HABITUAL** —) TENOR
(**MISERABLE** —) SQUALOR
(**MORBID** —) HOLDOVER
(**MOST APPROPRIATE** —) CHECKER
(**NECESSARY** —) MEAN
(**NEUROTIC** —) LATAH
(**ORDERLY** —) DECENCY
(**PAINFUL** —) CRICK
(**PERMANENT** —) HEXIS
(**PROPER** —) KILTER

(**PROTECTIVE** —) CALLUS CALLOUS
(**SCURFY** —) BUCKSKIN
(**STATIONARY** —) JIB
(**SUBLIME** —) HEAVEN
(**SURROUNDING** —) AIR
(**TRUE** —) SIZE
(**UNEQUAL** —) ODDS
(**UNPROSPEROUS** —) ILLTH
(**WEATHER** —**S**) ELEMENTS
(**PL.**) HAND TERMS STRINGS
CONDITIONAL EVENTUAL
CONNEXIVE QUALIFIED
CONDITIONED FINITE LIMITED
CONDITIONER DEGGER
CONDITIONING EDUCATION
HYPOTHESIS
CONDOLENCE PITY RUTH EMPATHY
SYMPATHY
CONDONE BLINK REMIT ACQUIT
EXCUSE FORGET IGNORE PARDON
ABSOLVE FORGIVE OVERLOOK
CONDOR TIFFIN BUZZARD VULTURE
CONDUCE GO AID HELP HIRE LEAD
TEND BRING GUIDE CONFER EFFECT
ENGAGE ADVANCE CONDUCT
FURTHER REDOUND
CONDUCT ACT CON RUN USE WIN
BEAR CALL COND CONN DEED FACT
FARE FIRK FORM GARB GEST HAND
KEEP LEAD MIEN PLAY QUIT RULE
SHOW TAKE WAGE WALK BATON
CARRY DRESS DRIVE FETCH GESTE
GUARD GUIDE HABIT MAYNE SITHE
TRADE TRAIN USAGE USHER ACTION
ATTEND BEHAVE COLORS CONVEY
CONVOY COURSE DEDUCE DEMEAN
DEPORT DIRECT ESCORT GOVERN
INDUCT MANAGE MANNER SQUIRE
ACTIONS BEARING CHANNEL
COMPERE COMPORT CONDITE
CONDUCE CONDUIT CONTAIN
CONTROL EXECUTE GALLANT
GESTION OFFICER OPERATE
WIREWAY ARRIVISM BEHAVIOR
CARRIAGE CHAPLAIN COURTESY
DEMEANOR GUIDANCE REGULATE
SHEPHERD TRANSACT
(— **ONESELF**) DO ACT ACQUIT
BEHAVE BESTOW DEMEAN DEPORT
COMPORT CONTAIN DISPORT
ENTREAT MAINTAIN
(**APPROPRIATE** —) DHARMA
(**BRASH** —) FACE
(**CONVENTIONAL** —) PRAXIS
(**DISORDERLY** —) RANDAN
(**DORMANT** —) LATENCY
(**ETHICAL** —) HONOR
(**PROPER** —) CRICKET
(**RECKLESS** —) DEVILRY DEVILTRY
(**RIGHT** —) TE TAO
(**SAFE** —) KOWL COWLE
(**SHOWY** —) BRAVADO
(**SLOPPY** —) SWASH
(**VAINGLORIOUS** —) HEROICS
(**WANTON** —) RUFF
(**WEAK** —) FOLLY
CONDUCTANCE G
(— **UNIT**) MHO
CONDUCTION COURSING

CONDUCTOR CON BOND CADE LEAD MAIN BRUSH GUARD SHUNT SPOUT TRUNK BRIDGE BUSMAN CARMAN CONVOY COPPER ESCORT FEEDER LEADER OFFSET RETURN CAPTAIN CATHODE MAESTRO MANAGER AQUEDUCT BATONIST CICERONE CONVEYOR DIRECTOR EMPLOYEE FILAMENT STICKMAN **(ELECTRIC —)** FILAMENT **(OMNIBUS —)** CAD **(PL.)** SERVICE

CONDUIT BOSS DUCT GOUT MAIN PIPE SINK TUBE WIRE CABLE CANAL CUNDY SEWER STACK HEADER SLUICE TROUGH CARRIER CHANNEL CHIMNEY CONDITE CONDUCT CULVERT CUNDITE EXHAUST FOGGARA LATERAL LAUNDER PASSAGE WIREWAY AQUEDUCT OLEODUCT PENSTOCK WASTEWAY **(PL.)** LIMBERS

CONDYLOMA SYCOMA

CONE CAP YOW CHAT KING PINA TOOT CONUS CRACK SCREW SHAPE SPIRE YOWIE BOBBIN CONOID MONTRE PASTIL CLUSTER CONELET CONIOLE FISSURE FRUSTUM PROLONG PYRAMID STROBIL THIMBLE CANNELON DUMPLING GALBULUS PASTILLE STROBILE STROBILUS **(— OF CLOTH)** VANE **(— OF FIR)** YOW YOWIE STROBIL STROBILE STROBILUS **(— OF GUNPOWDER)** PEEOY **(— OF HOP PLANT)** BUR BURR **(— OF SILVER AMALGAM)** PINA **(— ON LOG END)** CAP **(— ON SHOE)** CLEAT **(— STRUCTURE)** NURAGHE **(HALF —)** FORME NAPPE **(ICE CREAM —)** ICE CORNET **(INVERTED —)** HOPPER **(PAPER —)** SPILL COFFIN **(TOP CUT FROM —)** UNGULA **(PL.)** HOPS

CONENOSE BEDBUG BARBEIRO

CONESTOGA WAGON CARAVAN

CONEY CONY HYRAX HYRACID GUATIBERO

CONFAB CHAT TALK POWWOW CONFLAB PRATTLE

CONFECTION CHOW MOSS CANDY DULCE MEBOS SWEET BONBON COCKLE COMFIT DAINTY DRAGEE HALVAH JUNKET MAJOON NOUGAT SWEETY CARAMEL CONFECT FONDANT MIXTURE POMFRET PRALINE SEATRON SUCCADE ANGELICA CHOWCHOW CODINIAC COMPOUND CONSERVE DELICACY MARZIPAN PRESERVE SUBTLETY

CONFECTIONERY CIMBAL CONFISERIE

CONFEDERACY BUND COVIN CREEK KEDAR UNION COVINE LEAGUE COMPLOT ALLIANCE COVENANT FEDERACY ILLINOIS BLACKFOOT

CONFEDERATE AID PAL REB ALLY BAND PUFF REBEL STALL UNITE LEAGUE SANTAR ABETTER ABETTOR CONJURE FEDARIE FEDERAL FEODARY PARTNER STEERER CONSPIRE FEDERARY FEDERATE **(— SOLDIER)** CONFED JOHNNY GRAYBACK GRAYCOAT GREYBACK **(PICKPOCKET'S —)** STALL

CONFEDERATION BODY BUND UNION LEAGUE COMPACT HASINAI SOCIETY ALLIANCE COVENANT

CONFER DUB GIVE MEET TALK AWARD ENDOW FEOFF GRANT INFER SPEND TREAT ADVISE BESTOW COMMON CONFAB DONATE ENTAIL HUDDLE IMPARL IMPART INVEST PARLEY COLLATE COMMUNE COMPARE CONDUCE CONSULT CONTACT COUNSEL DISCUSS INSTATE PRESENT COLLOGUE COMPRISE CONVERGE **(— DEGREE UPON)** CAP **(— KNIGHTHOOD UPON)** DUB

CONFERENCE DIET TALK SYNOD TREAT TRUST CAUCUS CONFAB HUDDLE INDABA KORERO PARLEY PARVIS POWWOW SUMMIT CIRCUIT COUNCIL MEETING PALAVER PARLING SEMINAR COLLOQUE COLLOQUY CONCLAVE CONGRESS PRACTICE PRACTISE TUTORIAL

CONFERRING GRANT DATION

CONFESS NOW AVOW FESS KNOW SING ADMIT GRANT KITHE ACKNOW ATTEST AVOUCH BEKNOW COUTHE RENDER REVEAL SHRIFT SHRIVE SQUEAK CONCEDE DIVULGE PROFESS DISBOSOM DISCLOSE DISCOVER MANIFEST

CONFESSION ALHET CREDO CREED GRANT AVOWAL SHRIFT SHRIVE VIDDUI ASHAMNU FORMULA PECCAVI COGNOVIT **(MUTUAL —)** SHARING

CONFESSIONAL SHRIFT MALCHUS

CONFESSOR FATHER SHRIFT SHRIVER

CONFIDANT PRIVY FRIEND INWARD PRIVADO INTIMATE

CONFIDE AFFY RELY TELL TRUST COMMIT DEPEND LIPPEN BELIEVE CONSIGN ENTRUST INTRUST **(— IN)** VENTURE

CONFIDENCE FACE HARK HOPE BIELD CHEEK FAITH STOCK TRUST APLOMB BELIEF CREDIT FIANCE FIDUCE METTLE MORALE SECRET SPIRIT SURETY COUNSEL COURAGE PRIVITY AFFIANCE BOLDNESS CREDENCE RELIANCE SECURITY SURENESS

CONFIDENT BOLD SMUG SURE CRANK HARDY SIKER CROUSE SECURE SICKER TRAIST ASSURED CERTAIN HOPEFUL RELIANT CONSTANT FEARLESS FIDUCIAL IMPUDENT POSITIVE SANGUINE TRUSTFUL

CONFIDENTIAL BOSOM PRIVY CLOSET COVERT HUSHED INWARD SECRET PRIVATE ESOTERIC FAMILIAR INTIMATE

CONFIDING TRUSTY CREDENT RELIANT TRUSTFUL CONFIDENT

CONFIGURATION FORM SHAPE FIGURE BANDING CONTOUR DIAMOND GESTALT OUTLINE GEOMETRY POSITURE **(CELESTIAL —)** SYZYGY

CONFINE BAR BOX CUB DAM HEM NUN PEN PIN STY TIE BAIL BIND BOOM CAGE COOP CRIB FOLD HASP JAIL KEEP LACE LOCK PEND SEAL SHUT SPAN STEW STOP STOW BOUND CABIN CHAIN COART CRAMP CROWD DELAY FENCE HOUSE LIMIT MARCH PINCH POUND STICK STINT BORDER BOTTLE COARCT CORRAL EMBANK FETTER FORBAR HAMPER HURDLE IMMURE IMPALE IMPARK INTERN KENNEL PINION POCKET PRISON STRAIN TETHER ASTRICT CHAMBER COMPASS CONTAIN IMPOUND INCLUDE MANACLE PINFOLD POISTER RECLOSE SECLUDE SHACKLE TRAMMEL BASTILLE BOUNDARY CLOISTER CONCLUDE DISTRAIN FOCALIZE IMPRISON RESTRAIN STRAITEN

CONFINED ILL FAST PENT BOUND CAGED CLOSE CRAMP BEDRID IMPALE IMPENT PENTIT SEALED CAPTIVE CRAMPED CRIBBED LIMITED SQUEEZY IMPENDED IMPLICIT INTERNED **(— TO CERTAIN AREA)** ENDEMIC **(— TO SELECT GROUP)** ESOTERIC

CONFINEMENT MEW BOND HOLD JAIL WARD CRYING GATING DURANCE INLYING JANKERS WARDING CLAUSURE FIRMANCE GROANING SOLITARY

CONFINING NARROW

CONFIRM FIX SET FIRM SEAL PROVE VOUCH AFFEER AFFIRM ASSENT ASSURE ATTEST AVOUCH BISHOP CLINCH FASTEN HARDEN RATIFY REABLE SECOND SETTLE STABLE VERIFY APPROVE COMFORT CONSIGN ENDORSE FORTIFY JUSTIFY PROPORT SUPPORT SUSTAIN THICKEN ACCREDIT CONVINCE CORROBER ENTRENCH INSTRUCT SANCTION STRENGTH VALIDATE

CONFIRMATION PROOF SANCTION

CONFIRMED SET FIXED SWORN ARRANT STABLE CERTAIN CHRONIC HABITUAL HARDENED RATIFIED

CONFISCATE GRAB SEIZE USURP CONDEMN CONFISK PUBLISH DISTRAIN

CONFISCATION ESCHEAT INCENSION

CONFLAGRATION FIRE BLAZE FEVER BURNING INFERNO

CONFLICT JAR WAR BOUT BUMP

DUEL FRAY MEET MUSS RIFT
AGONY BROIL BRUSH CLASH FIGHT
GRIPS STOUR ACTION BATTLE
COMBAT MUTINY OPPOSE SCRAPE
SHOWER STRIFE CONTEND
CONTEST DISCORD SCUFFLE
WARFARE ANTIMONY DISAGREE
MILITATE SKIRMISH STRIVING
STRUGGLE
(DRAMATIC —) AGON
(FINAL —) ARMAGEDDON
CONFLICTING ADVERSE
ABHORRENT
CONFLUENCE FORK CROWD INFALL
CONFLUX MEETING JUNCTION
CONFORM DO GO FIT HEW LEAN
OBEY SORT SUIT ADAPT AGREE
APPLY SHAPE YIELD ACCEDE
ADJUST ASSENT COMPLY CONFER
SETTLE SQUARE SUBMIT COMPOSE
CONFIRM
(— TO) KEEP MEET ANSWER
BEHAVE SATISFY
CONFORMABLE DONE SUING
SUITED CONFORM PURSUANT
QUADRANT
CONFORMATION FORM BUILD
(MENTAL —) SAMSKARA
CONFORMING FAIR SAME COMELY
DECENT CORRECT CONGRUOUS
CONFORMIST BOY COMPLIER
CONFORMITY FIT ACCORD DHARMA
EQUITY HARMONY JUSTICE KEEPING
ACCURACY AFFINITY JUSTNESS
LIKENESS SYMMETRY FORMALITY
(— TO LAW) DECENCY LEGALITY
CONFOUND MIX BLOW DASH MATE
MAZE ROUT STAM STUN WHIP
ABASH ADDLE AMAZE BLAST FOUND
SHEND SPOIL STUMP WASTE
AWHAPE BAFFLE COMMIT DISMAY
DUDDER MINGLE MUDDLE RABBIT
RATTLE ASTOUND CONFUSE
CONFUTE CORRUPT DESTROY
FLUMMOX FORLESE PERPLEX
STUMBLE STUPEFY ASTONISH
BABELIZE BEWILDER DISTRACT
DUMFOUND SURPRISE
CONFOUNDED MATE BLAME
BLAMED DEUCED BLASTED MURRAIN
PEEVISH DUMMERED SWITCHED
CONSARNED
(BE —) ABAVE ABAWE
CONFRATERNITY BODY UNION
SOCIETY CONFRAIRY
CONFRONT DARE DEFY FACE MEET
NOSE BEARD BRACE BRAVE CROSS
FRONT STAND ACCOST ASSAIL
BREAST OPPOSE RESIST VISAGE
AFFRONT COMPARE PROPOSE
ENVISAGE THREATEN
CONFRONTING BEFORE ADVERSE
CONFRONT
CONFUSE BOX FOX MIX BALL DASH
DAZE DOIT DOZE DUST GAUM HARL
MAZE MUSS ROUT ABASH ADDLE
AMAZE BEFOG BITCH BLEND CLOUD
DEAVE DIZZY SHEND SHENT SNARL
STEER TWIST UPSET BAFFLE

BEDAZE BEMUSE BOTHER BURBLE
CADDLE COMMIT CORPSE DUDDER
DUDDLE FLURRY FUDDLE GRAVEL
JUMBLE MADDLE MAFFLE MAMMER
MASKER MIZZLE MOMBLE MUDDLE
PUZZLE RAFFLE RATTLE TWITCH
WIMPLE BECLOUD BEDEVIL
BLUNDER BUMBAZE DERANGE
DIFFUSE EMBROIL FLUSTER
GARBOIL GIDDIFY MYSTIFY
NONPLUS PERPLEX SCATTER
SHUFFLE STUPEFY UNRAVEL
BEFUDDLE BEWILDER CONFLATE
CONFOUND DISORDER DISTRACT
DUMFOUND ENTANGLE MISORDER
SQUATTER
(— AN ACTOR) CORPSE
(— BY NOISE) DUDDER
CONFUSED ASEA LOST ADDLE
DIZZY FOGGY FUZZY HEAVY MISTY
MUDDY MUZZY VAGUE WESTY
WOOLY BLOTTO CLOUDY DOILED
DOITED DRUMLY JUMBLY MEDLEY
MOPISH MUSHED SHAGGY TAVERT
WOOLLY BLURRED CHAOTIC
CLOUDED CONFUSE DIFFUSE
OBSCURE RATTLED STUPENT
COCKEYED DERANGED FLURRIED
INVOLVED
CONFUSING DIZZY MAZEFUL
BAFFLING BLINDING DIZZYING
CONFUSION PI DIN PIE COIL DUST
FUSS HARL MESS MOIL RIOT AMAZE
ATAXY BABEL CHAOS CHEVY CHIVY
DERAY FRASE HAVOC HURLY LARRY
SNAFU SNARL STROW ATAXIA
BABBLE BAFFLE BALLUP BEDLAM
CHIVVY FRAISE HABBLE HOBBLE
HUBBUB HUDDLE JABBLE JUMBLE
MASTIC MUCKER MUDDLE POTHER
RABBLE RUFFLE RUMPUS THRONG
TOPHET TUMULT UPROAR WELTER
ANARCHY BLUNDER BLUSTER
CLUTTER COBWEBS FARRAGE
FLUTTER GARBOIL HURLING
KIPPAGE LOUSTER MISRULE
MISMAZE ROOKERY RUMMAGE
SCADDLE SCOWDER TOPHETH
TURMOIL WHEMMEL WIDDRIM
BABELISM DISARRAY DISORDER
EQUIVOKE HOOROOSH SCOUTHER
SHAMBLES SPLUTTER TOHUBOHU
CONFUTATION DISPROOF
CONFUTE DENY EVICT REBUT
EVINCE EXPOSE REFUTE FALSIFY
IMPROVE SILENCE SUBVERT
CONCLUDE CONFOUND CONVINCE
DISPROVE INFRINGE OVERCOME
REDARGUE
CONGEAL GEL ICE SET GEAL JELL
CANDY COTTER CURDLE FREEZE
HARDEN STIFFEN STORKEN THICKEN
CONCRETE SOLIDIFY
(— INTO HOARFROST) RIME
CONGEALED FROZEN
CONGELATION FROST
CONGENER BEAVER DOTTREL
DOTTEREL
CONGENIAL SIB BOON HAPPY

NATAL NATIVE AMIABLE CONNATE
KINDRED
CONGENITAL INNATE CONNATE
CONNATAL GENETOUS
CONGERIES CALCULARY
COLLECTION
CONGEST STUFF IMPACT
CONGESTED INJECTED
CONGESTION JAM HEAP LAMPAS
LAMPERS CROWDING STOPPAGE
CONGLOMERATE HEAP MASS PILE
ROCK STACK BANKET PSEPHITE
NAGELFLUH
CONGLOMERATION HUDDLE
GLOMMOX IMBROGLIO
CONGO MUMMY ASPHALTUM

CONGO

CAPITAL: BRAZZAVILLE
COIN: FRANC FRANCCFA
LAKE: MWERU TUMBA UPEMBA
LEOPOLD
NATIVE: SUSA VILI MANTU PYGMY
BATEKE MBOCHI WABUMA
BAKONGO BANGALA
PLATEAU: BATEKE
RIVER: CONGO KWILU LULUA
NGOKO NIARI SANGA WAMBA
KWENGE LOANGE UBANGI
KOUILOU LUBILASH
TOWN: EWO EPENA HOLLE JACOB
OKOYO SEMBE MAKOUA
OUESSO ZANAGA DOLISIE
ENYELLE SOUANKE DJAMBALA
BRAZZAVILLE
TRIBUTARY: LOMAMI UBANGI
ARUWIMA LUALABA LUAPULA
ITIMBITI

CONGOU KEEMUN
CONGRATULATE HUG JOY LAUD
GREET SALUTE FLATTER MACARIZE
CONGRATULATION PARABIEN
(PL) GRATTERS
CONGREGATE HERD MASS MEET
PACK TEEM GROUP SWARM TROOP
GATHER MUSTER COLLECT
CONVENE ASSEMBLE
CONGREGATION PEW BODY FOLD
HERD HOCT MASS FLOCK SAMAJ
SWARM CHURCH PARISH COMPANY
MEETING SYNAXIS ASSEMBLY
BRETHREN CHAPELRY
(— OF WITCHES) COVEN
(JEWISH —) KOLEL ALJAMA
SYNAGOG
(PL.) CHARGE
CONGRESS MOD DAIL DIET SYNOD
UYEZD OBLAST OUYEZD POWWOW
COUNCIL GORSEDD MEETING
ASSEMBLY CONCLAVE
CONGRESSMAN SENATOR
DOUGHFACE
CONGRUITY ACCORD CONCORD
FITNESS HARMONY KEEPING
SYMMETRY COHERENCE
CONGRUOUS CONGRUE HARMONIC
SUITABLE ACCORDING

CONICAL CONIC TAPER COPPED COPPLED TAPERING
CONIFER FIR YEW PINE CEDAR LARCH SPRUCE SOFTWOOD EVERGREEN
CONIFERAE PINALES
CONIUM HEMLOCK
CONJECTURE AIM CAST PLOT ROVE SHOT VIEW AUGUR ETTLE FANCY GUESS OPINE THINK BELIEF DIVINE THEORY CONJECT IMAGINE OPINION PRESUME SUPPOSE SURMISE SUSPECT HINDCAST SUPPOSAL
CONJOIN JOIN KNIT ATTEND EMPALE IMPALE
CONJOINED JOINED JUGATE LINKED JUGATED CONJUNCT TOUCHING
CONJOINTLY JUNCTLY TOGETHER
CONJUGAL SPOUSAL CONNUBIAL
CONJUGATE YOKED JOINED UNITED COUPLED INFLECT
CONJUGATION SYNGAMY ZYGOSIS CYTOGAMY ENDOGAMY SYNOPSIS
CONJUNCTION AS ET IF OR AND BUT NOR TIE THAN JOINT SINCE SYNOD UNION UNITY THOUGH COITION CONSORT JOINDER CONJUNCT RATIONAL
CONJUNCTURE SEASON
CONJURATION ART CHARM MAGIC SPELL VOODOO EXORCISM
CONJURE PRAY WISH CHARM HALSE ADJURE ENJOIN INVENT INVOKE SUMMON BESEECH COMBINE ENTREAT IMAGINE CONSPIRE CONTRIVE EXORCIZE
CONJURE MAN CUNJAH CUNJER GOOFER GUFFER
CONJURER MAGE PELLAR POWWOW SHAMAN WIZARD JUGGLER ꟾ WARLOCK WIELARE JONGLEUR MAGICIAN PYTHONIC SORCERER
CONJURING JADU JADOO CONJURY VOODOOISM
CONK FAIL HEAD KONK NOSE FAINT KNOCK STALL BRACKET
CONNECT COG PUT TIE ALLY BIND BOND GEAR GLUE JOIN KNIT KNOT LINK AFFIX CHAIN MARRY NITCH UNITE ATTACH BRIDGE CEMENT COHERE COMMIT CONNEX COUPLE ENLINK FASTEN RELATE SPLICE COMBINE ENCHAIN INVOLVE APPARENT CATENATE CONTINUE DOVETAIL INTERTIE
(— TREADLE) CORD
CONNECTED ALLIED CONNEX AFFINED COUPLED HANGING
(ELECTRICALLY —) ALIVE
(NOT —) FOREIGN ASYNARTETE
(SYNTACTICALLY —) ABSOLUTE

CONNECTICUT

CAPITAL: HARTFORD
COLLEGE: TRINITY
COUNTY: TOLLAND WINDHAM
INDIAN: PEQUOT MOHEGAN
NIANTIC

STATE BIRD: ROBIN
STATE FLOWER: LAUREL
STATE NICKNAME: NUTMEG
STATE TREE: OAK
TOWN: AVON BETHEL CANAAN COSCOB DARIEN MYSTIC SHARON STORRS DANBURY MERIDEN NIANTIC NORWALK NORWICH TOLLAND WINDSOR NEWHAVEN SIMSBURY WESTPORT GREENWICH
UNIVERSITY: YALE WESLEYAN

CONNECTING BETWEEN SYNDETIC
CONNECTION Y HUB TAP TIE BOND LINK HITCH NEXUS UNION BUCKLE CLEVIS FAMILY GROUND REPORT SUTURE SWIVEL BEARING BOLSTER CONTACT DESCENT FERRULE HOLDING KINSHIP LIAISON SIAMESE SIBNESS SOCIETY AFFINITY ALLIANCE COMMERCE CONNEXUS INTIMACY JUNCTION LIGATION RELATIVE SYNDETIC
(ELECTRICAL —) GROUND
(FORKED —) BRANCH
(MECHANICAL —S) LEADOUT
CONNECTIVE IZAFAT SUTURAL JUNCTION LIGATIVE SYNDETIC VINCULAR
CONNING TOWER SAIL
CONNIVANCE CAHOOT CAHOOTS
CONNIVE ABET PLOT WINK BLINK CABAL ASSENT FOMENT INCITE COLLUDE
(— AT MEDICAL TREATMENT) COVER
CONNOISSEUR JUDGE CRITIC EXPERT CAMEIST EPICURE GOURMET CIDERIST DILETANT LAPIDARY
CONNOTATION DEPTH INTENT MEANING
CONNUBIAL MARITAL CONJUGAL DOMESTIC
CONQUER GET WIN BEAT BEST DOWN FIRK GAIN LICK ROUT TAME WHIP CRUSH DAUNT DEBEL EVICT DEBELL DEFEAT EVINCE HUMBLE IMPORT MASTER REDUCE SUBDUE VICTOR ACQUIRE PREVAIL SUBJECT SURPASS TRIUMPH OVERCOME OVERGANG SURMOUNT VANQUISH
CONQUEROR HERO VICTOR WINNER TRIUMPHER
CONQUEST MASTERY SCALING TRIUMPH VICTORY WINNING
CONSANGUINEOUS AKIN CARNAL KINDRED NATURAL RELATED
CONSANGUINITY BLOOD NASAB KINSHIP AFFINITY
CONSCIENCE WORD DAENA HEART INWIT SENSE SCRUPLE THOUGHT
CONSCIENTIOUS FAIR JUST EXACT RIGID EIDENT HONEST STRICT DUTIFUL UPRIGHT FAITHFUL
CONSCIENTIOUSNESS RELIGION
CONSCIOUS KEEN WARE ALIVE

AWAKE AWARE JERRY GUILTY FEELING KNOWING WITTING RATIONAL SENSIBLE SENTIENT CONSCIENT
CONSCIOUSNESS EGO HEART SENSE SPIRIT ANOESIS FEELING SENTIENT AWARENESS
CONSCRIPT LEVY CHOCO DRAFT ENROL ENLIST MUSTER DRAFTEE DRAUGHT RECRUIT JEANJEAN
CONSCRIPTION LEVY
CONSECRATE VOW FAIN HOLY SAIN SEAL BLESS DEIFY HEAVE SACRE ANOINT DEVOTE HALLOW ORDAIN SACRATE CONSACRE DEDICATE SANCTIFY
CONSECRATED BLEST OBLATE SACRED VOTARY VOTIVE BLESSED SACRATE HALLOWED HIERATIC
CONSECRATION IHRAM SACRE SACRY SACRING HOLINESS
CONSECUTIVELY TOGETHER
CONSECUTIVENESS SEQUENCE
CONSENT HEAR AGREE ALLOW GRANT YIELD ACCEDE ACCORD ASSENT BETEEM COMPLY CONCUR PERMIT APPROVE GOODWILL
CONSENTIENT UNANIMOUS
CONSEQUENCE AND END BORE EVENT FORCE FRUIT ISSUE SUITE WORTH BROWST CHARGE EFFECT ENTAIL FIGURE GROWTH IMPORT MOMENT REPUTE RESULT SEQUEL WEIGHT CONCERN OUTCOME PRODUCE SEQUELA SEQUENT AFTERING INTEREST MISCHIEF OCCASION
(DONE IN —) PURSUANT
(HARMFUL —) EVIL
(PL.) AFTERINGS
CONSEQUENT COMES THESIS ADJUNCT
CONSEQUENTIAL HEAVY POMPOUS COROLLARY
CONSEQUENTLY SO ERGO THEN THUS HENCE LATER PURSUANT PRESENTLY
CONSERTAL SUTURAL
CONSERVATION HUSBANDRY
CONSERVATISM BOURBONISM
CONSERVATIVE SAFE TORY FUSTY STAID FABIAN HUNKER STABLE BOURBON DIEHARD MODERATE UNIONIST
CONSERVATORY STOVE SCHOOL ACADEMY
CONSERVE CAN JAM SAVE GUARD GUMBO JELLY DEFEND SECURE SHIELD UPHOLD HUSBAND PROTECT SEATRON SUSTAIN MAINTAIN PRESERVE
(GRAPE —) UVATE
CONSIDER AIM BAT LET SEE CALL CAST DEEM GAUM GIVE HASH HEED HOLD MULL MUSE RATE SEEM TAKE TALE VIEW VISE WISE ALLOW BESEE COUNT ENTER ETTLE JUDGE PANSE POISE SPELL STUDY THINK VERSE VOLVE WEIGH ADVERT ADVISE

BEHOLD DEBATE DEVISE DIGEST
ESTEEM EXPEND FIGURE IMPUTE
PONDER REASON RECKON REGARD
REWARD SURVEY ACCOUNT BELIEVE
BETHINK CANVASS CONSULT
EXAMINE INSPECT PREPEND
REFLECT RESPECT REVOLVE
SUPPOSE COGITATE ESTIMATE
MEDITATE PERPENSE RUMINATE
(— **FAVORABLY**) CREDIT
(— **PROS AND CONS**) ARGUE
(— **SEPARATELY**) SPECIALIZE
CONSIDERABLE GAY GEY FAIR
GOOD CANNY GEYAN GREAT LARGE
SMART STARK GOODLY PRETTY
GOODISH HEALTHY INTENSE
NOTABLE SEVERAL HANDSOME
POWERFUL SENSIBLE UNLITTLE
CONSIDERABLY GAY GEY WELL
GEYAN PRETTY SMARTLY
CONSIDERATE KIND MILD NICE
GENTLE TENDER CAREFUL HEEDFUL
PRUDENT SERIOUS DELICATE
GRACIOUS
CONSIDERATENESS GRACE
(**MUTUAL** —) SHU
CONSIDERATION GUT GUTS SAKE
COUNT PRICE STUDY TOPIC ADVICE
ASPECT COMITY DEBATE ESTEEM
MOMENT MOTIVE NOTICE REASON
REFLEX REGARD SURVEY ACCOUNT
INSIGHT PREMIUM RESPECT
THOUGHT ALTRUISM COURTESY
DELICACY EMINENCE EMPHASIS
GRATUITY SANCTION
(**BASIC** —) BEDROCK
(**ETHICAL** —) SCRUPLE
(**THOUGHTFUL** —) THEORIA
CONSIDERED ADVISED DELIBERATE
CONSIDERING IF FOR SINCE SEEING
CONSIGN DOOM GIVE MAIL SEND
SHIP ALLOT AWARD CHECK DIGHT
REMIT SHIFT YIELD ASSIGN COMMIT
DESIGN DEVOTE REMAND RESIGN
ADDRESS BETEACH CONFIDE
DELIVER DEPOSIT ENTRUST
INTRUST BEQUEATH DELEGATE
RELEGATE TRANSFER
(— **FOR DESTRUCTION**) ACCURSE
(— **TO OBLIVION**) BURY EXPUNGE
(— **TO PERDITION**) DAMN CONDEMN
CONSIGNEE AGENT FACTOR
SHIPPER RECEIVER
CONSIGNMENT INVOICE FOREDOOM
SHIPMENT
(— **OF TEA**) BREAK
CONSIST LIE HOLD RELY REST
DWELL EXIST STAND INHERE RESIDE
CONTAIN EMBRACE COMPRISE
CONSISTENCY BODY UNION
DEGREE CONCENT CONCORD
HARMONY KEEPING COMPAGES
EVENNESS FIRMNESS SOLIDITY
SYMMETRY
CONSISTENT EVEN FIRM STEADY
DURABLE LOGICAL UNIFORM
COHERENT ENDURING SUITABLE
(— **WITH NATURE**) KIND KINDLY
(**BE** —) ACCORD

(**MAKE** —) CLEAR
CONSOLATION SOP FINE RELIEF
SOLACE COMFORT SPIRITING
CONSOLE CALM ALLAY ANCON
CHEER ORGAN TABLE SOLACE
SOOTHE BRACKET CABINET
COMFORT RELIEVE SUPPORT
SUSTAIN CARTOUCH
CONSOLER PARACLETE
CONSOLIDATE COG MIX KNIT MASS
POOL WELD BLEND CLOSE MERGE
UNIFY UNITE HARDEN MINGLE
SETTLE COMBINE COMPACT
ANKYLOSE COALESCE COMPRESS
CONDENSE ORGANIZE SOLIDIFY
CONSOLIDATED CONFLATE
CONSOLS GOSCHENS
CONSONANCE ACCORD UNISON
HARMONY DIAPASON DIAPENTE
SYMPATHY SYMPHONY
CONSONANT WAW MUTE STOP
DENTAL FORTIS LABIAL LETTER
LIQUID SONANT UNISON LATERAL
MUTABLE PALATAL SPIRANT UNIFIED
ALVEOLAR ASPIRATA ASPIRATE
BILABIAL EJECTIVE GEMINATE
HARMONIC SUITABLE
(**CONSECUTIVE** —**S**) CLUSTER
(**SMOOTH** —) LENE LENIS
(**TENSE AND STRONG** —) FORTIS
(**VOICELESS** —) SPIRATE
CONSORT COT AIDE ALLY JOIN
MATE WIFE YOKE GROUP UNITE
ACCORD ATTEND ESCORT MINGLE
SPOUSE COMPANY COMRADE
CONCERT DAMKINA EMPRESS
HUSBAND PARTNER ACCUSTOM
ASSEMBLY PRINCESS
CONSPECTUS LIST APERCU SURVEY
OUTLINE THEATER THEORIC
SPECTRUM SYNOPSIS
CONSPICUOUS BIG BOLD CLEAR
FAMED PLAIN STARY EXTANT
FAMOUS MARKED PATENT SIGNAL
BLATANT EMINENT GLARING
NOTABLE OBVIOUS POINTED
SALIENT SIGHTLY VISIBLE
APPARENT EMPHATIC FLAGRANT
KENSPECK MANIFEST STRIKING
CONSPIRACY COUP PLAN PLOT
RING CABAL COVIN JUNTO PARTY
COVINE SCHEME COMPACE
COMPACT COMPLOT INTRIGUE
CONSPIRATOR PACKER PLOTTER
SCHEMER
CONSPIRE ABET PACK PLOT UNITE
LEAGUE SCHEME COLLUDE
COMPLOT CONJURE CONNIVE
CONTRIVE
CONSTABLE COP BULL PEON SLOP
BEADLE BEAGLE HARMAN KAVASS
KEEPER WARDEN BAILIFF CORONER
DOZENER NUTHOOK OFFICER
STALLER SUBASHI ALGUAZIL
DOGBERRY TIPSTAFF
CONSTANCY ZEAL ARDOR FAITH
TRUTH FEALTY HONESTY LOYALTY
ONENESS DEVOTION FIDELITY
CONSTANT K SET EVEN FIRM JUST

LEAL TRUE FIXED LOYAL SOLID
STILL TIGHT TRIED ITHAND STABLE
STEADY CERTAIN CHRONIC
DURABLE FOREVER LASTING
REGULAR STAUNCH UNIFORM
DEFINITE ENDURING FAITHFUL
POSITIVE RESOLUTE SEDULOUS
STANDING
CONSTANTLY AWAY EVER ALWAYS
THRONG
CONSTELLATION ARA CUP FLY FOX
LEO APUS ARGO COLT CROW CRUX
DOVE GOAT GRUS HARE HARP LION
LYNX LYRA MAST PAVO PLOW SIGN
SWAN TAUR URSA VELA WAIN WOLF
ALTAR ARIES CAMEL CETUS CLOCK
CRANE DRACO EAGLE GROUP
HYDRA INDUS LEPUS LIBRA LUPUS
MALUS MENSA MUSCA NORMA
ORION PYXIS RAVEN TABLE VIRGO
WAGON WHALE ANTLIA AQUILA
AURIGA BOOTES CAELUM CANCER
CARINA CORVUS CRATER CYGNUS
DIPPER DORADO FORNAX GEMINI
HYDRUS INDIAN LIZARD OBELUS
OCTANS OKNARI PICTOR PISCES
PISCIS PLOUGH PUPPIS SCALES
SCUTUM TAURUS TIGRIS TOUCAN
TUCANA VOLANS ALGEBAR
CEPHEUS CLUSTER COLUMBA
COMPASS DOLPHIN FURNACE
GIRAFFE LACERTA MONARCH
OETAEUS PATTERN PEACOCK
PEGASUS PERSEUS PHOENIX
RHOMBUS SAGITTA SCORPIO
SERPENS SERPENT SEXTANS
SEXTANT XIPHIAS AQUARIUS
ASTERISM CHAMPION CIRCINUS
CYNOSURE EQUULEUS ERIDANUS
HERCULES HERDSMAN KASHYAPA
QUADRANS REINDEER RETICULE
SCORPION SCORPIUS SCULPTOR
TRIANGLE
CONSTERNATION FEAR ALARM
PANIC DISMAY FRIGHT HORROR
TERROR TREPIDITY
CONSTITUENCY BOROUGH
CONSTITUENT ATOM ITEM PART
PIECE VOTER DETAIL FACTOR
FUSAIN MATTER MEMBER SIMPLE
ELECTOR ELEMENT FEATURE
TAGMEME INTEGRAL
(— **OF BLOOD SERUM**) OPSONIN
(— **OF CLINKER**) ALITE CELITE
(— **OF COAL**) DURAIN FUSAIN
(— **OF DURAIN**) ATTRITUS
(—**S OF BEER**) EXTRACT
(**NECESSARY** —) ESSENCE
(**PL.**) MATTER BIOSESTON
CONSTITUTE BE FIX SET FORM
MAKE ENACT ERECT FORGE FOUND
SHAPE SPELL CREATE DEPUTE
GRAITH ORDAIN APPOINT COMPOSE
FASHION STATION COMPOUND
COMPRISE
CONSTITUTION LAW SET CODE
SETT BEING CANON FRAME HUMOR
SETUP STATE CHARTE CRASIS
CUSTOM DESIGN ESTATE HEALTH

NATURE TEMPER CHARTER HABITUS SYNODAL GRONDWET GRUNDLOV HABITUDE PHYSIQUE POLITEIA
(— **STATE**) CONNECTICUT
(**BODILY** —) HABIT SPIRITS
(**GERMINAL** —) HEREDITY
CONSTITUTIONAL WALK HECTIC INNATE RIKKEN EXERCISE
CONSTITUTIVE FORMAL
CONSTRAIN ART PUT TIE ARCT BEND BIND CURB DOOM FAIN HALE HOLD LEAD URGE CHAIN CHECK CLASP COART CRAMP DETER DRIVE FORCE IMPEL LIMIT PRESS COERCE COMPEL EVINCE OBLIGE RAVISH SECURE STRAIN THRAST ASTRICT CONFINE CONJURE ENFORCE OPPRESS REPRESS VIOLATE COMPRESS CONCLUDE DISTRESS PERFORCE POUNDAGE RELIGATE RESTRAIN
CONSTRAINED FAIN TIED VAIN BOUND FORCED FORMAL UNEASY COACTED
CONSTRAINING UNEASY COMPELLENT
CONSTRAINT BOND CRAMP FORCE DURESS STRESS RESERVE STRAINT COERCION DISTRESS PRESSURE
CONSTRICT TIE BIND CURB GRIP CHOKE CRAMP LIMIT STRAP HAMPER SHRINK STRAIN STRAIT ASTRICT DEFLATE SQUEEZE STIFFEN TIGHTEN ASTRINGE COMPRESS CONDENSE CONTRACT DISTRAIN RESTRICT
CONSTRICTED STRAIT STRICT ADENOID
CONSTRICTION KNOT CHOKE ISTHMUS STENOSIS
CONSTRICTOR BOA ABOMA GUAVINA
CONSTRUCT UP BIG ATOM FORM IDEA LEVY MAKE REAR BUILD CRAFT DIGHT EDIFY ERECT FRAME MODEL BURROW DEDUCE DESIGN DEVISE FABRIC ARRANGE CARPENT COMBINE COMPILE COMPOSE CONCEPT CONFECT CONTOUR EXTRUCT FASHION CONSTRUE ENGINEER PRACTISE
(— **ARCH**) TURN
CONSTRUCTED BUILT EDIFICATE
(**CAREFULLY** —) CLEVER
(**HASTILY** —) GIMCRACK JIMCRACK
CONSTRUCTION BOOM ALTAR FRAME FABRIC MONSTER SYNESIS APPROACH BUILDING DWELLING ERECTION
(— **OF NAME**) ABSTRACTION
(**ABSTRACT** —) STABILE
(**GRAMMATICAL** —) SYNESIS APPOSITION
(**POINTED** —) BEAK
CONSTRUCTIVE FACTIVE HELPFUL VIRTUAL CREATIVE IMPLICIT INFERRED
CONSTRUCTOR ENGINEER
CONSTRUE INFER PARSE STRUE

INTEND RENDER ANALYZE CONSTER DISSECT EXPLAIN EXPOUND RESOLVE
CONSUL SUFFECT
CONSULT LOOK SEEK TALK ADVISE CONFER EMPARL IMPARL COUNSEL RESOLVE
CONSULTANT EXPERT ADVISER COUNSEL
CONSULTATION ADVICE COUNCIL COUNSEL
CONSUME EAT SUP USE BOLT BURN CHEW FANG FARE FEED FRET GULP IDLE KILL RUST TAKE TUCK WEAR DALLY DRINK FLAME LURCH RAVEN SHIFT SPEND TOOTH WASTE ABSORB BEZZLE BROWSE CANKER DEVOUR ENGAGE EXPEND FINISH IMBIBE INHALE PERISH PUNISH VANISH CORRODE DESTROY DWINDLE ENGROSS EXHAUST SWALLOW CONTRIVE SQUANDER
(— **TOTALLY**) KILL
(— **VORACIOUSLY**) HOG
CONSUMED ALL PAU DOWN BURNT SPENT COMBUST OUTWORN
CONSUMING EATING SACRED BURNING FLAMING
CONSUMMATE END FINE FULL RIPE CLOSE IDEAL SHEER ARRANT EFFECT FINISH FULFIL RATIFY ACHIEVE CONSUME CROWNED FULFILL PERFECT PERFORM ABSOLUTE COMPLETE MERIDIAN THOROUGH
CONSUMMATION PERIOD UPSHOT
CONSUMPTION USE DECAY WASTE EXPENSE WASTING PHTHISIS SPENDING
CONSUMPTIVE LUNGY HECTIC PREDATORY
CONTACT ABUT JOIN KISS MEET SLED CROSS TOUCH TRUCK UNION ARRIVE IMPACT SYZYGY EPHAPSE HOLDING MEETING TACTION JUNCTION TANGENCY TOUCHING
(— **OF TELEGRAPH KEY**) ANVIL
(**3-POINT** —) OSCNODE
(**ELECTRICAL** —) HUB HUBB
(**EVIL** —) CONTAGION
(**FLEETING** —) BRUSH
(**FORCIBLE** —) IMPACT
CONTAGION POX TAINT VIRUS MIASMA POISON
CONTAGIOUS TAKING NOXIOUS SMITTLE CATCHING EPIDEMIC
CONTAIN RUN HAVE HOLD KEEP STOW TAKE CARRY CHECK CLOSE COVER HOUSE EMBODY ENFOLD ENSEAM HARBOR RETAIN COMPILE EMBRACE ENCLOSE INCLUDE INVOLVE RECEIVE SUBSUME SUSTAIN COMPRISE RESTRAIN
CONTAINED IN
CONTAINER BAG BOX CAN CUP HAT JAR JUG KEG LUG NIN PAN POD POT TIN TUB URN VAT BAIL BOMB CAGE CASE CASK CRIB DRUM EWER FILE FLAT JACK SACK SALT SILO

SINK SKIP TANK TUBE VASE ALBUM BASIN BILLY CADDY CHEST CRATE CRUET DEWAR EMPTY FLASK GLASS GOURD POUCH SCOOP SCRAY STAND STOOP STOUP BARREL BASKET BOTTLE BUCKET BUSHEL CARBOY CARTON CASTER CASTOR COOLER CRADLE DUSTER HAMPER HATBOX HOLDER INKPOT PICNIC RABBIT RIDDLE SHAKER WITJAR AEROSOL BANDBOX BLADDER CAPSULE COASTER COSTREL CRISPER FEEDBOX HANAPER HOLDALL INKWELL PACKAGE SEEDLIP SHIPPER STEEPER CANISTER DECANTER DEMIJOHN ENVELOPE HOGSHEAD HONEYPOT INHOLDER KNAPSACK PUNCHEON SLIPCASE
(— **FOR BEER**) GROWLER
(— **FOR COINS**) BANK
(— **FOR EXPLOSIVE CHARGE**) CAP
(— **FOR GOLD DUST**) SHAMMY
(— **FOR HOLY OIL**) STOCK
(— **FOR PLANTS**) BAND
(— **MADE OF HOLLOW LOG**) GUM
(**5-GALLON** —) JERICAN JERRICAN
(**COFFEE** —) INSET
(**EARTHENWARE** —) STEAN
(**FIRECLAY** —) SETTER
(**RAILROAD** —**S**) BUNKER
(**SHELVED** —) CABIN
(**SHIPPING** —) KIT
(**SNUFF** —) WEASAND
(**TOBACCO** —) SARATOGA
(**VENTILATED** —) CHIP
(**PL.**) CONVEYER CONVEYOR
CONTAMINATE FOUL HARM SLUR SMIT SOIL STAIN SULLY TAINT BEFOUL DEBASE DEFILE INFECT INJURE POISON ATTAINT CORRUPT DEBAUCH FLYBLOW POLLUTE TARNISH VITIATE DISHONOR
CONTAMINATED DIRTY DEGRADED INFECTED
CONTAMINATION INFECTION TAINTMENT
(— **IN GLASS**) STONE
CONTE TALE CRAYON
CONTEMN HATE FLOUT SCORN SPURN REJECT SLIGHT DESPISE DISDAIN CONTEMPT INDIGNIFY
CONTEMPLATE FACE MUSE PLAN SCAN VIEW DEIGN STUDY THINK WEIGH DESIGN PONDER REGARD SURVEY CHERISH PROPOSE REFLECT CONSIDER ENVISAGE ENVISION MEDITATE
CONTEMPLATION MUSE STUDY DHYANA MUSING PRAYER REGARD THEORY INSIGHT MOONING REQUEST THEORIA PETITION
CONTEMPLATIVE BROODY PENSIVE THEORIC STUDIOUS
CONTEMPORANEOUS COEVAL LIVING MODERN CURRENT EXISTING
CONTEMPORARY EQUAL COEVAL FELLOW CURRENT PRESENT YEALING EXISTENT

CONTEMPT PRUT SCORN SHAME
SNEER SLIGHT CONTEMN DESPECT
DESPITE DISDAIN HETHING
MOCKERY DEFIANCE DERISION
DESPISAL DISGRACE MISPRIZE
CONTEMPTIBLE LOW BASE MEAN
VILE BALLY CHEAP DIRTY DUSTY
LOUSY MANGY MUCKY PETTY
POCKY RUDDY SCALD SORRY
ABJECT BLOODY GRUBBY MEASLY
PALTRY SCABBY SCUMMY SCURVY
SHABBY SNOTTY SORDID YELLOW
BROKING LIGHTLY PEEVISH PITIFUL
SCALLED SCORNED SHITTEN
SLAVISH SQUALID BAUBLING
BEGGARLY FRIPPERY INFAMOUS
INFERIOR PITIABLE SNEAKING
UNWORTHY WRETCHED
CONTEMPTIBLENESS BEGGARY
CONTEMPTUOUS SLIGHT SNOOTY
HAUGHTY LIGHTLY SLIGHTY
SPITOUS ARROGANT FLOUTING
INSOLENT SCOFFING SCORNFUL
CONTEND TUG VIE WAR WIN CAMP
COCK COPE DEAL FRAB KEMP PLEA
RACE WAGE ARGUE BANDY BRAWL
CHIDE CLAIM FIGHT FLITE PRESS
ASSERT BATTLE BICKER BREAST
BUCKLE BUFFET BUSTLE COMBAT
DEBATE DIFFER JOSTLE JUSTLE
MEDDLE OPPOSE REASON STRIVE
BARGAIN COMPETE CONTEST
COUNTER DISPUTE PROPUGN
QUARREL SCUFFLE STICKLE
SUSTAIN WRESTLE CONFLICT
CONTRAST CONTRIVE MAINTAIN
MILITATE SQUABBLE STRUGGLE
CONTENT PAY CALM EASE GIST
GLAD PAID RATH APPAY HAPPY
HUMOR RATHE SERVE AMOUNT
CUBAGE PLEASE APPEASE
CONTENU GRATIFY REPLETE
SATIATE SATISFY SUFFICE WILLING
BLISSFUL CAPACITY CONTINEU
WILCWEME
(—S OF STOMACH) COOKIES
(ENERGY —) STRENGTH
(HEAT —) ENTHALPY
(SUPERFICIAL —S) AREA
(PL.) LINING
CONTENTED COZY FAIN VAIN QUIET
SATED CONTENT PLEASED
CHEERFUL
CONTENTION WAR BAIT BATE FEUD
PLEA RIOT TIFF TOIL BROIL CHEST
STRUT BICKER COMBAT DEBATE
ESTRIF JANGLE STRIFE CHIDING
CONTEKE CONTEST DISCORD
DISPUTE OPINION QUARREL
RIVALRY WRANGLE ARGUMENT
CONFLICT SQUABBLE STRUGGLE
VARIANCE
CONTENTIOUS CROSS BATEFUL
PEEVISH PERVERSE
CONTENTMENT EASE BLISS
HEAVEN PLEASURE
CONTERMINOUS NEXT ADJACENT
FRONTIER PROXIMAL
CONTEST GO IT BEE FIX RUN SUE

TRY VIE AGON BOUT CAMP COPE
DUEL FEUD FRAY GAME HOLD KEMP
LAKE MART PULL RACE SHOW SPAR
TIFF TILT TURN YOKE AGONY
ARGUE BROIL CLASH DERBY EVENT
FIGHT MATCH PLATE PRIZE ROLEO
SCRUB SPORT TRIAL WAGER
ACTION ADJURE AFFRAY BATTLE
BISLEY COMBAT DEBATE DEFEND
FLIGHT OPPOSE RESIST RUBBER
SEESAW STRIFE STRIVE TUSSLE
YOKING BARGAIN BRABBLE CLASSIC
COMPETE CONTECK CONTEND
DERAIGN DISPUTE GRAPPLE
PROTEST SHUTOUT TOURNEY
WARFARE ARGUMENT CONCOURS
CONFLICT DOGFIGHT HANDICAP
LITIGATE SKIRMISH SLUGFEST
STRIVING STRUGGLE WALKAWAY
WALKOVER
(— IN WORDS) SPAR
(— NARROWLY WON) SQUEAKER
(DRAWN —) TIE DRAW STALEMATE
(MOCK —) SCIAMACHY
(RACING —) DRAG
(REAPING —) KEMP
CONTESTANT VIER RIVAL WAGER
PLAYER AGONIST ENTRANT
SCRATCH FINALIST PROSPECT
CONTIGUOUS NEXT NIGH NEARBY
TANGENT ABUTTING ADJACENT
TOUCHING
CONTIGUITY ADJACENCY CONFINITY
IMMEDIACY
CONTINENT ASIA MASS SOBER
AFRICA CHASTE EUROPE CONTENT
CAPACITY MAINLAND MODERATE
ABSTINENT
CONTINGENCY BOOK CASE EVENT
CHANCE ADJUNCT CONTACT
VENTURE ACCIDENT CASUALTY
FORTUITY INCIDENT JUNCTURE
PROSPECT
CONTINGENT CASUAL CHANCE
DOUBTFUL EVENTUAL INCHOATE
TOUCHING
CONTINUAL STILL HOURLY ENDLESS
ETERNAL LASTING REGULAR
UNDYING UNIFORM CONSTANT
ENDURING UNBROKEN
CONTINUALLY AY AYE EVER STILL
ALWAYS EVERLY HOURLY STEADY
ENDLESS ETERNAL FOREVER
MINUTELY
CONTINUANCE STAY WHEN DELAY
LEASE SEQUEL DURANCE LASTING
ABIDANCE DURATION SURVIVAL
CONTINUANT OPEN LIQUID
DURATIVE
CONTINUATION SEQUEL DURATION
(— OF DOUBLET) BASQUE
CONTINUE BE DO ABY SUE BIDE
DURE HOLD JUMP KEEP LAST LIVE
STAY TIDE ABIDE CARRY EXIST
PERGE STICK UNITE ABEGGE
BELEVE ENDURE EXTEND PURSUE
REMAIN RESUME BELEAVE CONNECT
CONTUNE PERSIST PROCEED
PROLONG SUBSIST SURVIVE

SUSTAIN PROTRACT
(— UNALTERED) TARRY
CONTINUED STILL SERIAL CHRONIC
CONSTANT
CONTINUING DURABLE DURATIVE
(— FOR LONG TIME) CHRONIC
(— TO BE) YET
CONTINUITY TRACT SCRIPT
COHESION SCENARIO CONTINUUM
CONTINUOUS RUN EVEN ANEND
EIDENT ENTIRE EYDENT STEADY
CHRONIC ENDLESS RUNNING
UNBROKEN
CONTINUOUSLY AWAY EVER FAST
ANEND OUTRIGHT
CONTORT WRY BEND COIL CURL
TURN WARP GNARL SCREW TWIST
WREST CRINGE DEFORM WRITHE
DISTORT PERVERT SQUINCH
WREATHE OBVOLUTE
CONTORTED WRY WRIED KNOTTY
CRISPED KNOTTED SCREWED
WRITHEN OBVOLUTE
CONTORTION SCREW STITCH
WRITHE MURGEON WORKING
CONTOUR FORM LINE CURVE
GRAPH SHAPE SWEEP AMOEBA
FIGURE OUTLINE PROFILE
CARTOUCH CONTORNO MANDORLA
PLANFORM TOURNURE
(— ON SHIP) HANCE
CONTRA CONTRE AGAINST COUNTER
OPPOSED
CONTRABAND HOT GOODS ILLEGAL
ILLICIT SMUGGLED UNLAWFUL
CONTRABASS BASS OCTOBASS
CONTRACT GET BOND DRAW FARM
FORM HALE KNIT PACT SALE TACK
CATCH CLOSE COACT COUCH
CRAMP FEVER INCUR LEASE LIMIT
NEXUM PINCH SHRUG SNURP
CARTEL COCKLE COMMIT CRINGE
ENGAGE FUTURE GATHER HIRING
INDENT LESSEN MUTUUM NARROW
PLEDGE POLICY PROMPT PUCKER
REDUCE SHRIMP SHRINK SUBLET
TREATY ABRIDGE BARGAIN
BUMMERY CHARTER COMPACT
CRUMPLE CURTAIL DEFLATE
FIDUCIA MANDATE PROMISE
SCRUNCH SHORTEN SHRIVEL
SOCIETY WRINKLE ASSIENTO
BOTTOMRY CONDENSE COVENANT
HANDFAST HARDNESS LOCATION
RESTRICT STEELBOW STRAITEN
SYNGRAPH
(— BROW) FROWN
(— INTO WRINKLES) KNIT
(BRIDGE —) SOLO AUCTION
(MARRIAGE —) KETUBA AFFIANCE
HANDFAST BETROTHAL SPONSALIA
CONTRACTED BOXY CRAMP
BOOKED ASTRICT INGROWN
INSULAR SCREWED CONTRACT
CONTRACTILITY MOTILITY
CONTRACTION HM ANT NIP TIC TIS
AINT CANT ISNT KNIT MAAM WONT
CRAMP HADNT HASNT NISUS SPASM
CRASIS GATHER INTAKE MUSTNT

SHRINK TWITCH ELISION EPITOME
WOULDNT APNEUSIS TRACTION
(— OF HEART) SYSTOLE
(— OF SYLLABLES) SYNIZESIS
(PL.) TREPPE
CONTRACTOR KHOT BUTTY
BUILDER REMOVER SUPPLIER
CONTRADICT DENY BELIE CROSS
REBUT FORBID IMPUGN NEGATE
OPPOSE RECANT REFUTE COUNTER
GAINSAY REVERSE WITHSAY
CONTRARY DISPROVE DOWNFACE
NEGATIVE OUTSTAND
CONTRADICTION DENIAL PARADOX
WITHSAW ANTILOGY ANTIMONY
ANTILOQUY
CONTRADICTORY OPPOSE
ANTINOME OPPOSITE THWARTING
CONTRAPTION RIG TOOL DEVICE
GADGET JIGGER CONCERN MACHINE
CONTRARILY BACKWARD
CRISSCROSS
CONTRARIWISE CROSS CONTRA
CONTRARY
CONTRARY BALKY KICKY SNIVY
AVERSE CONTRA ORNERY SNIVEY
ADVERSE COUNTER CRABBED
FROWARD HOSTILE INVERSE
OPPOSED PEEVISH RESTIVE
REVERSE WAYWARD ABSONANT
ANTIPODE CAPTIOUS CONTRAIR
INIMICAL OPPOSITE PERVERSE
PETULANT SINGULAR
(— TO HAPPINESS) ILL
(— TO REASON) SILLY
(— TO) BESIDE AGAINST ATHWART
CONTRAST CLASH STRIFE COMPARE
CONTEND DISCORD ANTIMONY
DIVISION DYNAMICS OPPOSITE
CONTRAVENE DEFY DENY HINDER
OPPOSE THWART DISPUTE VIOLATE
INFRINGE OBSTRUCT
CONTRAVENTION SIN VICE CRIME
BREACH OFFENSE
CONTRETEMPS SLIP BONER HITCH
MISHAP SCRAPE ACCIDENT
INCIDENT
CONTRIBUTE AID ANTE FORK GIVE
HELP MAKE TEND CAUSE ENTER
GROUT SERVE ASSIST BESTOW
CONCUR CONFER DONATE PUNGLE
SUPPLY TENDER ANIMATE CONDUCE
FURNISH FURTHER PROVIDE
CONTRIBUTION BIT SUM TAX ALMS
BOON GIFT SCOT SHOT ESSAY
INPUT SHARE IMPOST SYMBOL
ARTICLE LARGESS PAYMENT
PRESENT RENEWAL WRITING
DONATION EXACTION OFFERING
ROMESHOT
CONTRITE WORN SORRY HUMBLE
RUEFUL PENITENT SORROWFUL
CONTRITION SORE SORROW
PENANCE
CONTRIVANCE (ALSO SEE DEVICE)
ART BOW FLY GIN JET JIG LEG
DROP GEAR HARP JACK KITE LURE
PLAN PLOT RASP REED TOOL
CARRY CHECK DOLLY DRAFT FLOAT

FRAME GUIDE HICKY KNACK MIXER
QUIPU SHIFT SNARE STOCK
ANCHOR DAMPER DECEIT DESIGN
DEVICE DOCTOR DOLLIE ENGINE
FABRIC FANGLE GABION GADGET
GIMBAL HANGER HARROW HEATER
HICKEY HOLDER JIGGER JINKER
MARKER MORTAR MUZZLE POLICY
RATTLE SCHEME SLUICE SPIDER
TEASEL WEIGHT WHEEZE WINDAS
WRENCH BOLSTER CLEANER
CLEARER CONCERN COUPLER
CUNNING DINGBAT DRAUGHT
FICTION FISHWAY HUMIDOR
KNOCKER MACHINE PAGEANT
PROJECT REDUCER ROASTER
SCRAPER SHEBANG SPANNER
STOPPER TOASTER TRIPPER
VOLVELL ADAPTION ARTIFICE
CROTCHET DUTCHMAN EUPYRION
FAKEMENT FORECAST GOVERNOR
INDUSTRY MOLITION OXIDATOR
REGISTER RESOURCE SCISSORS
SQUEEZER SUBTLETY WITCRAFT
CONTRIVE GET LAY BREW CAST
DRAW FIND FIRK MAKE PLAN PLOT
WORK FRAME FUDGE HATCH SHAPE
STAGE WEAVE AFFORD DESIGN
DEVISE DIVINE ENGINE FIGURE
INVENT MANAGE SCHEME WANGLE
ACHIEVE AGITATE COMMENT
COMPASS CONCOCT CONJURE
CONSULT CONTEND FASHION
IMAGINE MACHINE PROCURE
PROJECT REPAREL CONSPIRE
ENGINEER FORECAST INTRIGUE
PURCHASE
CONTRIVED SLICK STAGED
TIMBERED
CONTRIVER DAEDAL DAEDALUS
ENGINEER
CONTRIVING FASHION SCHEMERY
CONTROL BIT LAP LAW MAN POT
RUN CONN CURB EGIS GRIP HAND
HANK HAVE HOLD REDE REIN RULE
STAY SWAY WIND AEGIS BOOST
CHARM CHECK COACT DAUNT
DUMMY GRASP GUIDE LEASH
ORDER POWER STEER SWING
THEAT TREAT VERGE WIELD
BANDON BRIDLE CHARGE CLUTCH
COERCE CORNER DANGER DIRECT
EMPERY GOVERN HANDLE MANAGE
POCKET TEMPER AMENAGE
COMMAND CONDUCT CONTAIN
CUSTODY FORBEAR MASTERY
QUALIFY STRINGS COACTION
DOMINATE DOMINIUM IMPERIUM
MODERATE REGULATE SERVOTAB
(— A BULL) MANDAR
(— OF RESOURCES) HUSBANDRY
(ABSOLUTE —) BECK
(FIRE —) BLANKET
(GOVERNMENT —) SQUADRISM
(NONCLERICAL —) LAICISM LAICITY
CONTROLLED STEADY SERVILE
CONTAINED
CONTROLLER FENCER MASTER
STARTER

(SPEED —) GOVERNOR RHEOCRAT
CONTROLLING MASTER LEADING
DOMINANT HEGEMONIC
CONTROVERSIAL ERISTIC POLEMIC
CONTROVERSIALIST ERISTIC
POLEMIC DISPUTANT GLADIATOR
CONTROVERSY PLEA SPAT SUIT
CHEST FUROR BATTLE COMBAT
DEBATE FURORE HASSEL HASSLE
HOORAH HURRAH STRIFE TUSSLE
DISPUTE POLEMIC QUARREL
WRANGLE ARGUMENT TRAVERSE
(ART OF —) POLEMICS
CONTROVERT DENY FACE MOOT
ARGUE DEBATE DEFEND OPPOSE
OPPUGN REFUTE CONTEST DISPUTE
GAINSAY DISPROVE
CONTUMACIOUS UNRULY RIOTOUS
CONTUMAX INSOLENT MUTINOUS
PERVERSE STUBBORN
CONTUMELY ABUSE SCORN INSULT
CONTECK DISDAIN REPROOF
UPBRAID CONTEMPT RUDENESS
CONTUSE BEAT POUND THUMP
BRUISE INJURE SQUEEZE
CONTUSION POUND BRUISE
CONUNDRUM PUN WHIM ENIGMA
PUZZLE RIDDLE CONCEIT
CROTCHET
CONURE ARATINGA
CONVALESCE MEND GUARISH
RECOVER
CONVENANCE FORM
CONVENE SIT CALL HOLD MEET
UNITE GATHER MUSTER SUMMON
CONVENT CONVOKE ASSEMBLE
CONVERGE
CONVENIENCE GAIN URINAL
LEISURE COMMODITY
CONVENIENT FIT GAIN HEND HANDY
HENDE READY CLEVER FITTED
PROPER SUITED USEFUL ADAPTED
AVENANT COMMODE HELPFUL
BECOMING EXPEDITE SUITABLE
CONVENIENTLY HANDILY CLEVERLY
CONVENT ABBEY TEKKE TEKYA
CENOBY COVENT FRIARY PRIORY
CONVENT MEETING RECLUSE
CLOISTER LAMASERY
CONVENTION DIET FEIS FORM MISE
RULE TABU SYNOD TABOO USAGE
CARTEL CAUCUS CUSTOM TREATY
DECORUM MEETING ASSEMBLY
ASSIENTO CONCLAVE CONGRESS
CONTRACT COVENANT PRACTICE
(LONG-ESTABLISHED —) TRADITION
(STAGE —) ASIDE
(PL.) DECENCIES
CONVENTIONAL MORE NOMIC
RIGHT TRITE USUAL DECENT
FORMAL MODISH PROPER CORRECT
REGULAR ACADEMIC ACCEPTED
CUSTOMARY
CONVENTIONALITY FORM
ACADEMISM FORMALITY GRUNDYISM
CONVENTIONALIZE STYLIZE
CONVERGE JOIN MEET FOCUS
CONCUR CORNER DESCEND
APPROACH FOCALIZE

CONVERSANT ADEPT BUSIED EXPERT VERSED SKILLED FAMILIAR OCCUPIED

CONVERSATION SAY CALL CHAT CHIN RUNE TALE TALK CRACK PROSE CACKLE CONFAB DEVICE GOSSIP PARLEY POWWOW SPEECH YABBER CEILIDH COMMUNE CONDUCT PALAVER PURPOSE BACKCHAT BEHAVIOR CAUSERIE CHITCHAT COLLOGUE COLLOQUY DIALOGUE GIFFGAFF HARANGUE PARLANCE QUESTION (— **BETWEEN WHALERS**) GAM

CONVERSATIONALIST TALKER CAUSEUR

CONVERSE CHAT CHIN LIVE MOVE TALK DWELL SPEAK CACKLE CONFER DEVISE HOMILY PARLEY REASON COMMUNE CONVERT DISCUSS OBVERSE PROPOSE REVERSE COLLOQUE EXCHANGE OPPOSITE QUESTION

CONVERSION CHANGE EXCHANGE (— **INTO VAPOR**) FLASH (— **OF IRON**) FINING

CONVERT TAW TURN WEND ALTER AMEND APPLY MAULA RENEW CHANGE DECODE DETECT DIRECT MAWALI NOVICE SHAIKH SOUPER COMMUTE CONCOCT RESOLVE RESTORE REVERSE ACTIVATE CONVERSE DISCIPLE NEOPHYTE PERSUADE (— **COTTON**) LAP (— **INTO LEATHER**) TAN TAW (— **INTO LIQUID**) BREW (— **INTO SOAP**) SAPONIFY (— **INTO STEEL**) ACIERATE (— **INTO STONE**) LAPIDIFY (— **SOAP**) CLOSE (— **TO CARBON**) CHAR

CONVERTER ROTARY SELECTOR

CONVERTIBLE AUTO DROPHEAD

CONVEX BOWED ARCHED CAMBER CURVED BULGING EMBOWED GIBBOUS ROUNDED

CONVEY JAG BEAR BOOK CART CEDE DEED DUCT HAVE LEAD MEAN PASS SEND SIGN TAKE TOTE WAIN WILL BRING CARRY DRIVE FETCH GRANT GUIDE HURRY STEAL ARRIVE ASSIGN CONVOY DEDUCE DELATE DEMISE DEVISE ELOIGN GIGGIT IMPART IMPORT REMOVE YMMOTE AUCTION CHANNEL CHARIOT CHARTER CONDUCT DELIVER DERRICK DISPONE DISPOSE LIGHTER RESTORE ALIENATE BEQUEATH DESCRIBE TRANSFER TRANSMIT (— **AN ESTATE**) DEMISE (— **BY ALLUSION**) IMPLY (— **FORCIBLY**) HUSTLE (— **LEGALLY**) DEED GRANT LEASE DEMISE ELOIGN DISPONE (— **NEARER**) BRING (— **SECRETLY**) CRIM

CONVEYANCE BUS CAR AUTO CART DEED DRAG GIFT LOAD SLED TAXI TRAM GRANT SEDAN STAGE TAUGA THEFT TRAIN WAGON DEMISE JINGLE CHARTER CONDUCT COURIER MACHINE RATTLER TRAILER TRAJECT TRANSIT TROLLEY VECTURE VEHICLE WAFTAGE CARRIAGE CARRYING CONVEYAL DELATION FERRIAGE STEALING TRANSFER

CONVEYOR LIFT WORM DRAPER LADDER SHAKER CARRIER CREEPER HURRIER SCRAPER CAROUSEL CONVEYER ELEVATOR

CONVICT LAG CAST FIND STAR ARGUE EXILE FELON LIFER PROVE TAINT ATTAIN FORCAT LAGGER TERMER TRUSTY APPROVE ATTAINT CAPTIVE CONDEMN CULPRIT EXPIREE IMPEACH REPROVE CRIMINAL JAILBIRD PRISONER REDARGUE SENTENCE

CONVICT FISH MANINI HINALEA

CONVICTION CREDO CREED DOGMA FAITH SENSE TAINT TENET BELIEF CREDIT CONCERN OPINION SENTENCE

CONVINCE EVICT FETCH ASSURE EVINCE REPROVE RESOLVE SATISFY CONCLUDE (— **OF ERROR**) CONVICT

CONVINCED FIRM SOLD SURE CERTAIN ABSOLUTE POSITIVE

CONVINCING SOUND VALID COGENT POTENT EVIDENT TELLING FORCIBLE POWERFUL PREGNANT

CONVIVIAL GAY BOON FESTAL GENIAL JOVIAL SOCIAL FESTIVE HOLIDAY JOCULAR REVELING

CONVIVIALITY REVEL FESTIVAL

CONVOCATION DIET SYNOD CALLING COUNCIL MEETING SUMMONS ASSEMBLY CONGRESS VOCATION

CONVOKE CALL HOLD GATHER SUMMON CONVENE ASSEMBLE

CONVOLUTE COIL ROLL WIND TWIST TANGLE WRITHE CONTORT INVOLUTE OBVOLUTE

CONVOLUTED GYRATE

CONVOLUTION COIL CURL FOLD TURN WRAP GYRUS SWIRL TWINE TWIRL TWIST WHORL CUNEUS GYROMA VOLUME VOLUTION

CONVOLVE TURN WIND TWIST ENFOLD ENWRAP INFOLD WRITHE

CONVOLVULUS BINDWEED SCAMMONY

CONVOY LEAD WAFT CARRY GUARD GUIDE PILOT TRADE WATCH ATTEND CONVEY ESCORT MANAGE CONDUCT WAFTAGE

CONVULSE ROCK STIR SHAKE EXCITE AGITATE DISTURB

CONVULSION FIT SHRUG SPASM THROE ATTACK TUMULT UPROAR CONVULSE LAUGHTER PAROXYSM COMMOTION

CONVULSIVE FITFUL EPILEPTIC

CONY DAS HARE PIKA CONEY CUNNY DAMAN DASSY GANAM HUTIA HYRAX BURBOT CONEEN DASSIE GAZABO GAZEBO RABBIT WABBER ASHKOKO BOOMDAS HYRACID KLIPDAS HYRACOID KLIPDACH

COO CROO CURR WOOT CHIRR CHIZZ CROOD MURMUR CROODLE CRUDDLE

COOK DO FIX FRY BAKE BOIL CHEF COCT MAKE SEAR STEW BROIL CUSIE FRIZZ GRILL POACH ROAST SCALD SHIRR STEAM BRAISE CODDLE COOKIE COOPER DECOCT DIGEST PORTER SAUTEE SEETHE SIMMER ARTISTE BROILER FRIZZLE GRIDDLE PASTLER PERCOCT POTAGER PREPARE PROCESS SERVANT SMOTHER SWAMPER BAWARCHI BOBACHEE COCINERO CUSINERO GRILLADE MAGIRIST PASTERER (— **UP**) BUILD (**BULL** —) FLUNKY FLUNKEY GREASER (**SHIP'S** —) DOCTOR SLUSHY SKILLET SLUSHER

COOKED DONE FRIED BOILED (— **WITH SUGAR**) CANDIED

COOKEE FLUNKY HASHER FLUNKEY

COOKER CANNER HAYBOX DIGESTER

COOKERY CURY CUISINE KITCHEN MAGIRICS

COOKHOUSE GALLEY

COOKIE CAKE ROCK SNAP COOKY HERMIT KIPFEL BISCUIT BROWNIE OATCAKE PLACENT CRESCENT SEEDCAKE

COOL AIR FAN ICE CALM COLD KEEL AKELE ALGID ALLAY CHILL EVENT FRESH GELID NERVY QUEEL SOBER STAID WHOLE AIRISH CALLER CHILLY PLACID QUENCH SEDATE SERENE TEMPER UNWARM COOLISH REFROID UNMOVED CARELESS CAUTIOUS COMPOSED MITIGATE MODERATE TRANQUIL (— **IN WATER**) SLACK SLACKEN (— **OF EVENING**) SERENE

COOLED COLD FRAPPE

COOLER ICER JAIL KEEL OLLA SINK ICEBOX LOCKUP PRISON SINKER KEELFAT KEELYAT ALCOGENE (**WINE** —) GLACIER

COOLIE CHANGAR MADRASI MAZDOOR

COOLNESS COOL FROST NERVE SWALE APLOMB PHLEGM SERENITY

COOM CULM GAUM SMUT SOOT COOMB GRIME SLACK

COONTIE SAGO ZAMIA COMPTIE

COOP COT CUB CUP MEW PEN POT RIP CAGE COOB COTE JAIL CRAMP HUTCH BASKET CORRAL CONFINE (— **UP**) PEN IMMEW INCOUP (**HEN** —) CAVEY CAVIE BARTON

COOPER BUNGS COPER COWPER HEADER HOOPER TUBBER TUBBIE TUBMAN

COOPERATE HAND TEND AGREE COACT UNITE CONCUR COMBINE CONDUCE CONNIVE COADJUTE CONSPIRE

COOPERATION SOCIETY COURTESY TEAMWORK

COOPERATIVE COOP SOCIAL SYNERGIC

COORDINATE SINE ADAPT EQUAL ADJUST ARRANGE SYNTONY ABSCISSA CLASSIFY ENSEMBLE

COORDINATION BOND SKILL HARMONY LIAISON

COORG KADAGA

COOT CUIT DUCK RAIL QUEET SMYTH BELTIE GORHEN PELICK SCOTER HENBILL LOBIPED PULLDOO LOBEFOOT RAILBIRD SWAMPHEN

COP BAG NAB ROB BANK BLOW BULL HEAD HEAP JOHN LIFT PILE TRAP TUBE CATCH CREST FILCH MOUNT QUILL SHOCK SNARE STEAL STOCK SWIPE BOBBIN COPPIN PEELER SPIDER STRIKE CAPTURE

COPA YAYA COPITA

COPAL BOEA LOBA ANIME CONGO KAURI KAURY RESIN COWRIE CHAKAZI

COPE VIE WAR CAPE DUTY FACE LIFT MEET CAPPA CLOAK COVER DRESS EQUAL FIGHT MATCH NOTCH RIVAL VAULT WIELD BARTER CANOPY CHAPEL COMBAT MANTEL MUZZLE OPPOSE SEMBLE STRIKE STRIVE ANABATA CONTEND CONTEST GRAPPLE MANDYAS PLUVIAL COMPLETE EXCHANGE FACTABLE SEMICOPE STRUGGLE VESTMENT

COPEHAN WINTUN

COPEPOD CALANID CAYENNE DIAPTOMID

COPIAPITE MISY MISSY IHLEITE

COPIER COPIST SCRIBE JOHNSONIAN

COPING CAP COPE FLUE SKEW CORDON CAPSTONE FACTABLE

COPING STONE TABLET TABLING

COPIOUS FREE FULL GOOD LUSH RANK RICH AMPLE LARGE FLUENT LAVISH DIFFUSE FLOWING FULSOME LENGTHY PROFUSE REPLETE TEEMING UBEROUS ABUNDANT AFFLUENT FRUITFUL GENEROUS NUMEROUS

COPIOUSNESS COPY PLENTY

COPPER AES COP BULL CENT BOBBY METAL PENNY VENUS CUPRUM PEELER VELLON BLISTER CARNELIAN
(GILDED —) VERMEIL
(OF —) AEN

COPPERAS COPEROSE INKSTONE

COPPERHEAD REDEYE MOCCASIN

COPPERSMITH TINKERBIRD

COPPER SULFATE BLUESTONE

COPPER SULFIDE FERRETTO COVELLINE COVELLITE

COPPERY CUPREOUS

COPPICE COP BROW WOOD COPPY

COPSE FIRTH FRITH GROVE COVERT FOREST GROWTH SPROUT THICKET ARBUSTUM

COPSE CUT HAG HASP HEWT HOLT MOTT SHAW TRIM DROKE HURST CLEVIS SPINNY COPPICE LOWWOOD SHACKLE SPINNEY ARBUSTUM COPEWOOD

COPULA BAND LINK UNION

COPY APE CALK CAST ECHO EDIT MIME MOCK NICK DITTO DUMMY GROSS IMAGE MIMIC MODEL REVIE STICK STUFF TRACE CALQUE DOUBLE ECTYPE EFFIGY FILLER FLIMSY FOLLOW MATTER RECORD REFLEX SAMPLE SHADOW EDITION EMULATE ENGROSS ESTREAT EXTRACT IMITATE PATTERN REDRAFT REPLICA REPRINT RUBBING TRACING VIDIMUS APOGRAPH EXEMPLAR EXSCRIBE EXSCRIPT LIKENESS MANIFOLD POROTYPE PORTRAIT RESEMBLE SPECIMEN
(— EDITOR) SLOT
(— OF DOCUMENT) EXTRACT PROTOCOL
(— OF DRESS) FORD
(EXACT —) TENOR
(PRINTING —) KILL BOGUS
(UNREMUNERATIVE —) LEAN
(WORTHLESS —) BALAAM

COPYING MIMICRY INSINUATION

COPYIST COPIER SCRIBE COPYCAT SCRIVENER

COPYREAD EDIT SUBEDIT

COQUET TOY COPPY DALLY FLIRT TRIFLE BLINKER CELIMENE

COQUILLE SHELL

COQUINA DONAX

CORA NAYARIT

CORACLE SCOW CURAGH CURRANE

CORAL RED PINK AKORI BLOOD POLYP ALCYON PALULE PORITE FUNGIAN OCULINA ACROPORE ASTRAEAN CORALLUM FAVOSITE POLYPITE STAGHORN TUBIPORE ZOOPHYTE

CORAL BEAN SOPHORA FRIJOLILLO

CORAL-BELLS HEUCHERA

CORALBERRY BUCKBUSH

CORALFISH DOLLFISH

CORALROOT ORCHID CRAWLEY

CORAL SNAKE ELAPID ROLLER ELAPOID

CORAL TREE GABGAB ERYTHRINA

CORBEIL PANNIER

CORBEL KNOT ANCON CORBET TIMBER BRAGGER RESPOND CARTOUCH SPRINGER

CORBELING SQUINCH

CORBIESTEP CATSTEP CROWSTEP

CORCIR CORKE ARCHIL CORKER ORCHIL ARCHILLA

CORD AEA RIB AGAL BAND BIND BOND FILE LACE LASH LINE ROPE WELT BRAID CHORD FUNIS GUARD LEASH LIGNE MATCH NERVE OLONA TWINE TWIST BINDER BOBBIN

BRIDLE BUNGEE CATGUT CHORDA CORDON FIADOR GIRDLE LASHER LISERE RACHIS SENNET STRING TENDON TOGGLE AMENTUM BOWYANG BULLION CORDING FUNICLE LANIARD LANYARD MACRAME SEAMING SEIZING SKIRREH TIEBACK URACHUS BELLPULL CHENILLE DRAWCORD HAIRLINE SHOELACE WHIPCORD
(— AROUND BOWSTRING) SERVING
(— FOR PIPING) BOBBIN
(— OF CANDLENUT BARK) AEA
(CROCHETING —) CORDE
(ELECTRIC —) FLEX
(EMBROIDERY —) ARRASENE
(FRINGED —) LLAUTU
(HAMMOCK —S) CLEW
(MASON'S —) SKIRREH
(ORNAMENTED —) AGLET AIGLET
(PARACHUTE —) SHROUD
(SACRED —) KUSTI
(SPINAL —) EON AEON NUKE
(TWISTED —) TORSADE

CORDAGE DA COIR ERUC FERU HEMP IMBE JUTE KYAR ROPE HAMBER SENNIT RIGGING
(LENGTH OF —) CATENARY

CORDATE HEARTED

CORDED TIED JETTED REPPED RIBBED WELTED TWILLED

COR-DE-NUIT PASTORITA

CORDER RUFFER

CORDIAL REAL WARM CREAM ARDENT CASSIS DEVOUT ELIXIR GENIAL HEARTY CORDATE DIAMBER LIQUEUR PERSICO ROSOLIO SINCERE ZEALOUS ANISETTE FRIENDLY GRACIOUS PERSICOT VIGOROUS
(NOT —) DISTANT STANDOFF
(PL.) SWEETS

CORDIERITE IOLITE FAHLUNITE

CORDON BLEU BENGALEE

CORDONNET CRESCENT

CORDWOOD BODYWOOD

CORE AME COB HUB NUT BONE COKE COLK GIST KNOT NAVE PITH BLOCK FOCUS HEART NOWSE RUMPF SPOOL BARREL CENTER CENTRE HEATER KERNEL MATRIX MIDDLE NODULE POCKET STAPLE CENTRUM CHEMISE COMPANY CORNCOB ESSENCE NUCLEUS FILAMENT HEARTING
(— OF COAL) STOCK
(— OF COLUMN) BELL HEART
(— OF CRICKET BALL) QUILT
(— OF LOG) PITH
(WATER —) GLASSINESS

CORE ARBOR STALK

COREE CORANINE

CORELIGIONIST BROTHER

COREMIUM SYNEMA SYNNEMA

COREOPSIS TICKSEED TICKWEED LEPTOSYNE

CORF TUB CAGE CAWF COFF CORB SKIP CREEL BASKET DOSSER

CORGI CARDIGAN PEMBROKE

CORIUM CUTIS DERMA LAYER
DERMIS
CORK PLUG FLOAT SHIVE SUBER
BOBBER BOUCHON CRINKLE
PHELLEM SOBERIN STOPPER
STOPPLE
CORKER WHIZ RAKER WHIZZ
CUTTER HUMDINGER
CORKSCREW WORMER
CORKWOOD BALSA GUANO
HAREFOOT
CORM SET BULB SEED CORMEL
CORMUS FREESIA UINTJIE
CORMEL BULBLET
(PL.) SPAWN
CORMORANT SHAG CRANE GORMA
NORIE SCARF SCART DUIKER
DUYKER GORMAW GUANAY SCARFE
SCARTH GLUTTON SHAGLET
CORN ZEA DANA DENT SALT SAMP
GRAIN MAIZE SPIKE WYROK AGNAIL
CALLUS CLAVUS HELOMA INDIAN
KERNEL MEALIE NOCAKE NUBBIN
POWDER WYROCK FORMITY
FRUMENT FRUMENTY PRESERVE
SAUTERNE
(— SPURREY) YARR
(CROW —) COLICROOT
(CRUSHED —) STAMP
(DECORATED EAR OF —) TIPONI
(EAR OF —) ICKER
(GUINEA —) DURRA DHURRA
(INDIAN —) MAIZE INDIAN NOCAKE
(PARCHED —) ROKEE NOCAKE
YOKAGE GRADDAN ROKEAGE
YOKEAGE
(STRING OF —) TRACE
(UNRIPE EAR OF —) TUCKET
CORNAGE HORNGELD
CORN BREAD PONE KANKIE
BANNOCK
CORN COCKLE GITH COCKLE
POPPLE COCKWEED HARDHEAD
MELANTHY
CORNCRACKER STATE KENTUCKY
CORNCRAKE RAIL CORNBIRD
CORN CROWFOOT JOY GOLDWEED
HELLWEED JACKWEED
CORNEL DOGWOOD REDBRUSH
CORNEOUS HORNLIKE KERASINE
CORNER IN GET OUT WRO BEND
CANT COIN HALK HERN JAMB NOOK
POOL TRAP TREE WICK ANCON
ANGLE BIGHT CATCH COIGN ELBOW
HERNE INGLE JAMBE NICHE QUOIN
TRUST BOTTLE CANTLE CANTON
COLLAR CORNEL CRANNY RECESS
SQUARE QUINYIE TURNING
MONOPOLY
(— IN A DRIFT) ARRAGE
(— OF EYE) CANTHUS
(— OF GUNSTOCK) TOE
(— OF MOLDBOARD) SHIN
(— OF SAIL) CLEW CLUE TACK
GOOSEWING
(LOWER —) CLEW CLUE
(ROUNDED —) FILET FILLET
(SECRET —) CREEK
(TIGHT —) BOX

CORNERPIECE BUMPER CANTLE
CORNERSTONE COIN BASIS COIGN
HEADSTONE
CORNET HORN ZINK TWIST ZINKE
ZINCKE CORONET CORNETTO
CORNETFISH FLUTEMOUTH
HEMIBRANCH
CORNFIELD MOW
CORN FLAG LEVERS
CORNFLOWER BLUET BLAVER
BARBEAU BLUECAP BLUECUP
BLAEWORT
CORN GROMWELL SALFERN
CORNHUSK CAP
CORNHUSKER STATE NEBRASKA
CORNHUSKING SHUCKING
CORNICE CAP BAND DRIP EAVE
JOPY ANCON CROWN JOWPY
DETAIL GEISON PELMET ANTEFIX
MOLDING SURBASE ASTRAGAL
SWANNECK
(UNDER SIDE OF —) PLANCIER
CORNICLE SIPHON SYPHON
CORNISHMAN CELT KELT
CORN MARIGOLD GOLD GOOLS
BODDLE BOODLE BUDDLE GOWLAN
GOLDING GOLLAND
CORN MEAL MASA SAMP ATOLE
HOECAKE
CORN PARSLEY UMBEL
CORN POPPY BLAVER CANKER
COCKLE COPROSE EARACHE
PONCEAU REDWEED SOLDIER
CORN SALAD FETTICUS MILKGRASS
CORN STACK HOVEL
CORNSTALKS KARBI
CORNSTARCH BINDER
CORNU HORN THYROHYAL
CORNUCOPIA HORN CORNU COFFIN
CORNUS CORNIN REDBRUSH
CORN VIOLET SPECULARIA
CORN WOUNDWORT STACHYS
CORNY BANAL STALE TRITE MICKEY
BUCKEYE
COROADO BORORO
CORODY CONRED
COROLLA CUP BELL COROL CUPULE
LIGULE PERIANTH
COROLLARY DOGMA PORISM
RESULT TRUISM ADJUNCT THEOREM
COROMANDEL COLCOTHAR
CORONA BUR BURR CIGAR CROWN
GLORY AURORA FILLET ROSARY
WREATH AUREOLE CIRCLET
CORONET GARLAND SCYPHUS
CORONAL CRONET CORONEL
CROWNAL
CORONATION ABHISEKA
CROWNMENT
CORONER ELISOR CROWNER
EXAMINER SEARCHER
CORONET BAND BURR CROWN
TIARA ANADEM CIRCLE CRONET
DIADEM TIMBRE WREATH CHAPLET
CORONAL CROWNAL CROWNET
GARLAND CROWNLET
CORONOPUS CARARA
CORPORAL NYM FANO NAIG NAIK
FANON FANUM NAYAK PHANO

BODILY EXEMPT GUNNER NAIGUE
NAIQUE SINDON TINDAL
CORPORATE UNITED COMBINED
CORPORATION BODY CITY FIRM
POUCH TRUST SCHOLA BOROUGH
COLLEGE FREEDOM GUILDRY
SOCIETY SPONSOR
CORPOREAL REAL HYLIC SOMAL
ACTUAL BODILY CARNAL FLESHLY
SOMATIC MATERIAL PHYSICAL
TANGIBLE
CORPOSANT HERMO
CORPS CORE ORDU VELITES
SERAGLIO
(— DE BALLET) ENSEMBLE
CORPSE BIER BODY DUST LICH
MORT GHOST MUMMY RELIC STIFF
TRUCK ZOMBI CORPUS DEADER
ZOMBIE ANATOMY CADAVER
CARCASS CARRION CROAKER
DEADMAN FLOATER
(— WASHING) TAHARAH
CORPSMAN BEARER
CORPULENCE FAT FATNESS
STOUTNESS
CORPULENT FAT BULKY BURLY
FATTY GROSS HUSKY OBESE PLUMP
STOUT FLESHY GREASY PORTLY
ROTUND ADIPOSE BELLIED WEIGHTY
CORPUSCLE CELL GHOST GLOBULE
HEMATID HAEMATID HEMOCYTE
CORRAL PEN STY COOP ATAJO
POUND TAMBO CONFINE ENCLOSE
STOCKAGE SURROUND
(ELEPHANT —) KRAAL
CORRECT DUE FIT FIX TIC BEET
BOOK EDIT JUST LEAL LEAN MARK
MEND NICE OKAY SMUG TRUE
AMEND CHECK CLEAN EMEND
EXACT ORDER RIGHT SOUND SPILL
ADJUST BETTER CHANGE INFORM
PROPER PUNISH REBUKE REFORM
REMEDY REPAIR REVAMP REVISE
STRICT ADDRESS CHAPTER
CHASTEN CORRIGE ELEGANT
IMPROVE PERFECT PRECISE
RECLAIM RECTIFY REDRESS
REGULAR REPROVE SINCERE
ACCURATE CHASTISE DEFINITE
EMENDATE EQUALIZE REGULATE
RIGOROUS STRAIGHT TRUTHFUL
(GRAMMATICALLY —) CONGRUE
CORRECTABLE CORRIGIBLE
CORRECTION YARD CENSURE
FLEXURE IMPRINT REDRESS
FUGACITY
CORRECTIVE SALT REMEDY
CORRECTLY JUST RIGHT ARIGHT
RIGHTLY SOUNDLY PROPERLY
CORRECTNESS TRUTH DECORUM
FITNESS JUSTICE ACCURACY
JUSTNESS VERACITY
CORRELATE HARMONIZE
CORRELATIVE OR NOR THEN
EQUAL STILL EITHER MUTUAL
NEITHER ANALOGUE CONJOINT
REDDITIVE
CORRESPOND FIT GEE JIBE SUIT
AGREE MATCH TALLY WRITE

ACCORD ANSWER CONCUR SQUARE
COMPORT RESPOND COINCIDE
PARALLEL QUADRATE
(— IN SOUND) ASSONATE
(— TO) ENSUE
CORRESPONDENCE MAIL TALLY
ANALOGY CONSENT HARMONY
KEEPING LETTERS TRAFFIC
FUNCTION HOMOGENY HOMOLOGY
SYMMETRY SYMPATHY
(INCOMPLETE —) ASSONANCE
CORRESPONDENT QUADRATE
RELEVANT STRINGER SUITABLE
STRINGMAN
CORRESPONDING LIKE SIMILAR
CONGRUENT
CORRESPONDINGLY SORTLY
SIMILARLY
CORRIDA BULLFIGHT
CORRIDOR HALL AISLE ORIEL VISTA
ARCADE COULOIR GALLERY
PASSAGE COULISSE HALLCIST
TRESANCE
CORRIE CIRQUE
CORRIGENDUM ERRATUM
CORROBORATE PROVE SECOND
APPROVE COMFORT CONFIRM
SUPPORT SUSTAIN ROBORATE
CORRODE EAT BITE BURN ETCH
FRET GNAW RUST DECAY ERODE
EXEDE TOUCH WASTE BEGNAW
CANKER IMPAIR CONSUME
GRAPHITE
CORRODING BITE RODENT ESURINE
CORROSION EROSION EMBAYMENT
CORROSIVE ACID ACRID ARDENT
BITING CORSIE EATING CAUSTIC
EROSIVE ESURINE FRETFUL
MORDANT DIERETIC
CORRUGATE CRIMP CRISP FURROW
RUMPLE CRINKLE CRUMPLE
WRINKLE
CORRUGATED PLAITED WRINKLY
FURROWED WRINKLED
CORRUGATION BAT FOLD GILL
REED CREASE PUCKER CRINKLE
WRINKLE
CORRUPT BAD ILL LOW ROT WEM
EVIL RANK SICK SOIL VILE BLEND
BRIBE FALSE SPOIL STAIN SULLY
TAINT VENAL VENOM WEMMY
AUGEAN CANKER DEBASE DEFILE
FESTER IMPURE INFECT PALTER
POISON PUTRID RAVISH ROTTEN
SEPTIC ABUSIVE ATTAINT BEDEVIL
BEGRIME BESHREW CARRION
CORRUMP CROOKED DEBAUCH
DEFINED DEGRADE DEPRAVE
ENVENOM FALSIFY IMMORAL
PECCANT PERVERT POLLUTE
PUTREFY SUBVERT TRADING
VIOLATE VITIATE CONFOUND
DEPRAVED EMPOISON PERVERSE
POLLUTED PRACTICE PRACTISE
SINISTER VITIATED
CORRUPTED SICK
CORRUPTION DIRT SOIL VICE
DECAY SPOIL TAINT JOBBERY
PRAVITY SQUALOR ADULTERY
INFECTION

CORSAC ADIVE KARAGAN
CORSAGE WAIST BODICE BOUQUET
CANEZOU
CORSAIR BUG CAPER PIRATE
ROBBER CURSARO PICAROON
ROCKFISH
CORSELET THORAK ALLECRET
HALECRET
CORSET BELT BUSK STAY STAYS
GIRDLE SUPPORT
CORSICA (CAPITAL OF —) AJACCIO
(HARBOR OF —) BASTIA
(MOUNTAIN OF —) CINTO ROTONDO
(RIVER OF —) GOLO TARAVO
GRAVONE
(TOWERLIKE STRUCTURES OF —)
TORRI
(TOWN OF —) CALVI CORTE ALERIA
BASTIA AJACCIO SARTENE
(VEGETATION OF —) MAQUIS
CORSICAN PINE LARCH
CORTEGE POMP SUITE TRAIN
PARADE RETINUE
CORTEX BARK PEEL RIND MANTLE
PALLIUM PERIBLEM PERIDIUM
CORUNDUM RUBY SAND EMERY
ADAMAS ALUMINA ABRASIVE
AMETHYST CORINDON SAPPHIRE
BARKLYITE
(SYNTHETIC —) EMERALD
CORUSCATE BLAZE FLASH GLEAM
SHINE GLANCE GLISTEN GLITTER
RADIATE SPARKLE BRANDISH
CORVEE POLO
CORYZA COLD
COSCET COTTAR COTARIUS
COTSETLE
COSMETIC WASH CREAM FUCUS
HENNA LINER PAINT PETER ROUGE
BLANCH CERUSE CRAYON ENAMEL
POMADE POWDER MASCARA
STIBIUM LIPSTICK STIBNITE
COSMIC VAST MUNDANE ORDERLY
CATHOLIC INFINITE
COSMOLABE PANTACOSM
COSMOPOLITAN URBAN ECUMENIC
PANDEMIC AMPHIGEAN
COSMOS EARTH GLOBE ORDER
REALM WORLD FLOWER HEAVEN
HARMONY UNIVERSE
COSSACK TURK TATAR ATAMAN
HETMAN TARTAR ZAPOROGUE
COSSET MUD PET LAMB CARESS
CODDLE CUDDLE FONDLE PAMPER
TIDDLE
COSSETTE CHIP SLICE STRIP
SCHNITZEL
COST SIT GAFF LOSS PAIN SOAK
BASIS PRICE SPEND STAND VALUE
CHARGE DAMAGE OUTLAY SCATHE
EXPENSE REPRISE ESTIMATE
SPENDING

COSTA RICA

CAPE: ELENA VELAS BLANCO
CAPITAL: SANJOSE
COIN: COLON CENTIMO
DANCE: PUNTO TORITO

GULF: DULCE NICOYA PAPAGAYO
INDIAN: BORUCA GUAYMI
ISLAND: COCO
LAKE: ARENAL
MEASURE: VARA CAFIZ CAHIZ
FANEGA TERCIA CAJUELA
CANTARO MANZANA
MOUNTAIN: BLANCO CHIRRIPO
PENINSULA: OSA NICOYA
POINT: QUEPOS CAHUITA
GALONOS LLERENA
PORT: LIMON PUNTARENAS
RIVER: POAS IRAZU MATINA
SIXAOLA TENORIA TARCOLES
TOWN: CANAS LIMON VESTA
BORUCA NICOYA BAGACES
CARTAGO GOLFITO HEREDIA
LIBERIA NEGRITA ALAJUELA
COLORADO GUAPILES
VOLCANO: POAS IRAZU
WEIGHT: BAG CAJA LIBRA

COSTERMONGER COSTER HAWKER
NIPPER PEARLY PEDDLER
BARROWMAN
COSTIVE BOUND EMPLASTIC
COSTLINESS DEARTH DEARNESS
COSTLY DEAR FINE HIGH RICH SALT
DAINTY LAVISH SILVER COSTFUL
COSTLEW GORGEOUS PLATINUM
PRECIOUS PRODIGAL SPLENDID
COSTMARY TANSY ALECOST
MAUDLIN ROSEMARY
COSTREL KEG HEAD FLASK BOTTLE
COYSTREL
COSTUME RIG GARB ROBE SARI
SUIT BURKA DRESS GETUP HABIT
SHAPE TRUSS ATTIRE DOMINO
FORMAL SETOUT TOILET APPAREL
BLOOMER CLOTHES POLLERA
RAIMENT SCARLET UNIFORM
CHARSHAF CLOTHING ENSEMBLE
TOILETTE VENETIAN
(ACADEMIC —) GUISE
COSTUSROOT PACHAK
COSY FEEL FEIL
COT BED HUT MAT PEN BOAT COOP
COTE FOLD ABODE BOTHY CABIN
COUCH COVER HOUSE STALL
COTEEN CRADLE GURNEY PALLET
SHEATH TANGLE CHARPAI CHARPO
COTTAGE SHELTER BEDSTEAD
COTHOUSE DWELLING STRETCHER
COTERIE SET RING CABAL JUNTO
MONDE CIRCLE CLIQUE GALAXY
SETOUT CENACLE CIRCUIT COLLEG
PLATOON SOCIETY
COTHURNUS BOOT BUSKIN
COTHURN
COTILLION GERMAN
COTO OREJON
COTTA KATHA STOLE MANTLE
BLANKET SURPLICE VESTMENT
COTTAGE BOX COT HUT BACH BAR
COSH CRIB SHED WALK BOWER
CABIN HOUSE HOVEL LODGE SHACK
BOHAWN CABANA CHALET SHELTER
BUNGALOW COTHOUSE SHEELING

SHIELING THALTHAN
OTTAGE CHEESE SKYR
SMEARCASE
OTTER KEY MAT PIN VEX CLOT
BOWPIN COTMAN FASTEN MAILER
POTTER PUCKER SHRINK TOGGLE
WITHER CONGEAL COTTIER
PEASANT SHRIVEL VILLEIN
COTARIUS COTTAGER COTTEREL
ENTANGLE FORELOCK LINCHPIN
OTTON SAK BEAT DRAB FLOG
PIMA AGREE BAYAL BOLLY DERRY
MATTA SAKEL SURAT BROACH
CODDLE COMBER DHURRY FABRIC
MAARAD MALLOW NANKIN PEELER
STAPLE ALGODON BENDERS
BOMBACE DHURRIE GARMENT
GINNING SILESIA SUCCEED
(— SQUARE) TZUT TZUTE
(BOLL OF —) SNAP
(NAPPED —) LAMBSKIN
(PAINTED —) INDIENNE
(PIECE OF —) SPONGE
(PRINTED —) SARONG
(RAW —) LINT BAYAL
(SILK —) FLOSS
(STRIPED —) BENGAL
(TREE —) MACO
(TWILLED —) JEAN SALLO SALLOO
(WAD OF —) TAMPON
(WASTE —) GRABBOTS
OTTON GRASS CANNA CANNACH
DRAWLING
OTTON PLANT LAMB
(— FLOWER) SQUARE
OTTON TREEE SIMAL
OTYLEDON BUTTON PICHURIM
OUCH BED COT KIP LAY LIE HIDE
LAIR LURK SOFA SUNK DIVAN INLAY
LODGE PRESS SKULK SLINK SNEAK
SNOOP SQUAB SQUAT UTTER
BURROW CLOTHE DAYBED LITTER
PALLET PLINTH SETTEE CONCEAL
EXPRESS HAMMOCK OTTOMAN
OVERLAY RECLINE TRANSOM
(NUPTIAL —) THORE
OUCH GRASS CUTCH KUTCH
QUACK QUICK TWICH QUITCH
SCOTCH SCUTCH STROIL QUICKEN
WITHVINE
OUGAR CAT PUMA PAINTER
PANTHER CARCAJOU
OUGH YEX YOX BAFF BARK HACK
HOST CROUP HOAST HOOSE HOOZE
TUSSIS
OUGH DROP PASTIL TROCHE
LOZENGE PASTILLE
OUGH SYRUP LINCTUS
ULEE DRAW GORGE GULCH
COOLEY RAVINE
OULOMB WEBER
OUMA SORVA HYAHYA
OUNCIL BODY BULE DAEL DIET
OUMA FONO RAAD REDE YUAN
BOARD BOULE BUNGA CABAL
CAPUT DIVAN DIWAN DOUMA JIRGA
JUNTA JUNTO SABHA SOBOR STATE
SYNOD THING JIRGAH LUKIKO
MAJLIS POWWOW QUORUM SENATE

SOVIET TARYBA CABILDO CABINET
CHAMBER CONSULT GERUSIA
HUSTING MEETING PENSION
WHITLEY ASSEMBLY CONCLAVE
CONGRESS FOLKMOOT FOLKMOTE
HEEMRAAD HEEMRAAT MINISTRY
PLACITOM RIGSRAAD
COUNCILLOR RAT VIZIR ENDUNA
INDUNA VIZIER FAIPULE SENATOR
WISEMAN
COUNSEL RAD LORE REDE RULE
RUNE SILK WARD WARN AREED
CHIDE DEVIL GUIDE ADVICE ADVISE
CONFER LEADER ABOGADO
CAUTION COUNCIL LECTURE
ADMONISH ADVOCATE PRUDENCE
(JUNIOR LEGAL —) DEVIL
(KING'S —) SILK
(SACRED —) TORAH
COUNSELOR RAT SAGE WITE
CONSUL LAWYER MENTOR NESTOR
ADVISER ADVISOR COUNSEL
ECHEVIN GONZALO PROCTOR
STARETS ADVOCATE ATTORNEY
REDESMAN UCALEGON
COUNT ADD GAN SUM TOT BANK
CAST EARL FOOT GANO GRAF NAME
RELY RIME SIZE TALE TELL TOTE
COMES COMPT COMTE GRAVE
JUDGE RHYME SCORE TALLY WEIGH
CENSUS CONSUL COUNTY DEPEND
ESTEEM FIGURE IMPUTE NUMBER
RECKON TOTTLE ACCOUNT ARTICLE
ASCRIBE COMPUTE GANELON
ADNUMBER NUMERATE SANCTION
(— IN BILLIARDS) DOUBLE
(— OF A FIBER) GRIST
(— OF SHEEP OR CATTLE) BREAK
(— ON) LITE RELY
(— UNIT) WARP
COUNTABLE DISCRETE
COUNTENANCE AID MUG OWN RUD
ABET BROW FACE GIZZ LEER MIEN
PUSS SHOW VULT CHEER FAVOR
FRONT GRACE ASPECT ENDURE
UPHOLD VISAGE APPROVE BEARING
CONDUCT ENDORSE FEATURE
PROFFER SUPPORT BEFRIEND
DEMEANOR FOREHEAD SANCTION
COUNTER BAR DIB LOT BANK BUCK
CENT CHIP DESK DUMP EDDY FISH
JACK KIST PAWN STOP CAROM
CHECK FORCE HATCH JETON PIECE
SHELF STALL STAND TABLE TOTER
BUFFET COMBAT GEIGER ISLAND
JETTON MARKER OPPOSE SQUAIL
ADVERSE BUTTOCK CONTEND
CURRENT FANTAIL SHAMBLE
CONTRARY MAHOGANY OPPOSITE
TELLTALE
(— TO) AGAINST
(LEADEN —) DUMP
(LUNCH —) PLACE
COUNTERACT CHECK CANCEL
OPPOSE RESIST THWART BALANCE
CORRECT DESTROY NULLIFY
ANTIDOTE NEGATIVE
COUNTERACTION DEADLOCK
COUNTERACTIVE REMEDY
ADVERSE

COUNTERBALANCE COVER WEIGH
CANCEL SETOFF BALANCE
COUNTERCLOCKWISE DIRECT
DIRECTLY
COUNTERCURRENT BACKSET
COUNTEREARTH ANTICHTHON
COUNTERFEIT ACT BASE COIN
COPY DAUB DUFF FAKE IDOL MOCK
SHAM BELIE BOGUS DUMMY FALSE
FEIGN FLASH FORGE FUDGE GAMMY
MIMIC PHONY QUEER SNIDE AFFECT
ASSUME CHEMIC ERSATZ FORGED
PSEUDO TINSEL CHEMICK DUFFING
FALSIFY FASHION FEIGNED
FORGERY IMITANT IMITATE
DEFORMED POSTICHE POSTIQUE
RESEMBLE SIMILIZE SIMULATE
SPURIOUS SUPPOSED
COUNTERFEITER COINER JACKMAN
JARKMAN SCRATCHER
COUNTERFEITING COINING FICTION
POSTICHE POSTIQUE
COUNTERFOIL FOIL STUB CHECK
COUNTERFORT SCONCE BUTTRESS
COUNTERION GEGENION
COUNTERIRRITANT MOXA GINGER
IODINE PEPPER MUSTARD
CANTHARIS
COUNTERMAND STOP ANNUL
CANCEL FORBID RECALL REVOKE
ABOLISH RESCIND REVERSE
UNORDER ABROGATE PROHIBIT
COUNTERMOVE DEMARCHE
COUNTERMOVEMENT BACKFIRE
COUNTERPANE PANE LIGGER
BEDSPREAD
COUNTERPART COPY LIKE MATE
SPIT TWIN FETCH IMAGE MATCH
MORAL SHELL TALLY COUSIN
DOUBLE SHADOW BALANCE
COUNTER OBVERSE PENDANT
SIMILAR ANTIPART PARALLEL
RESCRIPT
(SPEECH —) A
COUNTERPOINT FOIL DESCANT
CONTRAST
COUNTERPOISE POISE OFFSET
BALANCE EQUALIZE
COUNTERPOISON ORVIETAN
COUNTERSIGN BACK MARK SEAL
SIGN SIGNAL CONFIRM ENDORSE
PASSWORD SANCTION
COUNTERSINK DISH REAM BEVEL
CHAMFER
COUNTERSTATEMENT ANSWER
COUNTERSUN ANTHELION
COUNTERWEIGHT TARE
COUNTERWORD ANIMAL COUNTER
COUNTESS OLIVIA COMTESSE
CONTESSA
COUNTLESS INFINITE
COUNTRIFIED JAY BUCOLIC
LOBBISH HOBNAILED
COUNTRY SOD DESH EARD HICK
HOME KITH LAND PAIS SOIL ADDLE
EARTH FAIRY FRITH MARCH PLAGE
REALM STATE TRACT WEALD
GROUND KINTRA KINTRY NATION
PEOPLE REGION STICKS UPLAND

IMAMATE KWINTRA MONKERY
MUFASAL DISTRICT DOMINION
ELDORADO LANDWARD MAGAZINE
MOFUSSIL REGALITY
(— OF ETHIOPIA) SEBA
(— OF ORIGIN) HOMELAND
(— OF PERFECTION) EUTOPIA
(— ON SEA) SEABOARD
(— STYLE) PAYSANNE
(ANCIENT —) ARAM
(CABIN —) LOBBY
(FRONTIER —) BORDER
(IMAGINARY —) LILLIPUT
(MARITIME —) MAREMMA
(MYTHICAL —) UTOPIA LEONNOYS
SVITHIOD SWITHIOD TEUTONIA
(OPEN —) BLED VELD FIELD VELDT
WEALD CAMPAIGN
(PETTY —) TOPARCHY
(ROUGH —) BOONDOCK BUNDOCKS
COUNTRYMAN HOB BOOR HIND
KERN TIKE CHURL CLOWN HODGE
KERNE SWAIN YOKEL GAFFER
GIBARO JIBARO GRANGER HAYSEED
LANDMAN PAISANO PEASANT
PLOWMAN LANDSMAN
(PL.) KITH
COUNTRYSIDE BLED BOCAGE
MOFUSSIL
COUNTY AMT LAN SEAT FYLKE
SHIRE DOMAIN PARISH BOROUGH
COMITAT NORFOLK DISTRICT
COUP BUY BLOW DEAL PLAN PLAY
COUPE FAULT SCOOP UPSET
ATTACK BARTER REFAIT STRIKE
STROKE CAPSIZE TRAFFIC
OVERTURN
COUP DE POING BOUCHER
HANDSTONE
COUPE CUT CABRIOLET LANDAULET
COUPED HUMETTY HUMETTEE
COUPLE DUO TIE TWO BOND CASE
DYAD JOIN LINK MATE PAIR SPAN
TEAM TWIN YOKE BRACE LEASH
MARRY TWAIN UNITE GEMINI SPLINE
SWINGE BRACKET CONNECT
COUPLER COUPLET DOUBLET
SHACKLE TWOSOME VOLTAIC
ACCOUPLE ASSEMBLE COPULATE
COUPLED GEMEL YOKED JOINED
WEDDED GEMELED COPULATE
GEMINATE
COUPLER LINK RING BOBBER
COPULA JANNEY LINKER SUTURE
UNITER DRAGBAR DRAWBAR
REDUCER SHACKLE SNAPPER
TIRASSE DRAGBOLT DRAWBOLT
DRAWGEAR SHACKLER
COUPLET BAIT COPLA ELEGIAC
COUPLING HUB HICKY UNION
CLUTCH HICKEY NIPPLE SHACKLE
SHACKLER
COUPON TWOFER
COURAGE BIEL FIRE GRIT GUTS
MIND MOOD PROW SAND SOUL
BIELD CREST HEART HONOR NERVE
PLUCK SPUNK VALOR DARING
DAUBER METTLE PECKER SPIRIT
VIRTUE VIRTUS BRAVERY COJONES

CORAGIO HEROISM MANHEAD
MANHOOD MANSHIP PROWESS
VENTURE AUDACITY BOLDNESS
FIRMNESS TENACITY
(— OF CONVICTION) STAMINA
(MORAL —) STRENGTH
COURAGEOUS BOLD GAME GOOD
TALL BRAVE GUTSY HARDY LUSTY
MANLY STOUT DARING HEROIC
MANFUL PLUCKY SPUNKY CORIAUS
GALLANT SPARTAN STAUNCH
VALIANT FEARLESS GENEROUS
INTREPID VALOROUS
COURAGEOUSLY BIG BRAVELY
COURANT ROMP CAPER DANCE
LETTER CORANTO CURRENT
GAZETTE RUNNING
COURBARIL JATOBA LOCUST
GUAPINOL CUAPINOLE
COURIER NEWS POST GUIDE SCOUT
KAVASS NEWING POSTER ESTAFET
ORDERLY PATAMAR POSTBOY
POSTMAN SOILAGE CICERONE
CURSITOR DRAGOMAN HORSEMAN
ORDINARY PATTAMAR
COURLAN LIMPKIN
COURONNE CROWN
COURSE FLY LAP RUN WAY BEAT
BENT FLOW GAGE GAME GANG
GATE HEAT HUNT LANE LINE LODE
MESS MODE PACE PATH RACE
RACK RAND RILL RING RINK ROAD
ROTA ROTE WENT CLASS COURS
CRUST CURRY CURVE CYCLE DRAFT
DRIFT DRIVE EMBER GAUGE GREAT
LAPSE LAYER LEDGE MARCH
MOYEN ORBIT PLATE POINT ROUTE
SENSE SITHE SPACE STEPS SWELT
SWING TENOR TRACK TRACT TRADE
TRAIL TREND WEENT ARTERY
CAREER COPING CURSUS DROMOS
FURROW GALLOP GIRDER GUTTER
HONORS MANNER METHOD MOTION
RESACA SCHOOL SERIES SPHERE
STREAM STREET SYSTEM TRIPOS
ZODIAC AZIMUTH BEELINE CHANNEL
CIRCUIT CONDUCT DIAULOS
DRAUGHT HIGHWAY LECTURE
PASSADE PASSAGE PATHWAY
PROCESS ROUTINE RUNNING
SEMINAR SERVICE STRETCH
SUBJECT SUCCESS TIDEWAY
TRAJECT TRUNDLE CURRENCY
CURRICLE DISTANCE ELECTIVE
PROGRESS RECOURSE SEQUENCE
STEERAGE TENDENCY
(— OF A ROPE) LEAD
(— OF ACTION) LARK TROD VEIN
DANCE CUSTOM ROUTINE
DEMARCHE
(— OF ACTIVITY) SIDELINE
(— OF BOAT) LEG
(— OF BRICK) BED ROWLOCK
SCINTLE CREASING
(— OF FEEDING) DIET
(— OF KNITTING) BOUT
(— OF LIFE) GOINGS
(— OF LUCK) FORTUNE
(— OF MASONRY) BAHUT STILT

COPING HEADING SKEWBACK
(— OF NATURE) TAO
(— OF PROCEDURE) RULE
(— OF PROCEEDING) FORE
(— OF PURSUIT) SCENT
(— OF ROADBED) SUBCRUST
(— OF STONES) BED PLINTH
(— OF STUDY) DEBATE COLLEGE
LECTURE SEMINAR ELECTIVE
(— OF SUN) JOURNEY
(— OF TREATMENT) CURE
(— OF WALL) CORNICE
(— WITH GREYHOUNDS) GREW
(BELL-RINGING —) HUNT
(CIRCULAR —) SWEEP CHUKKAR
CHUKKER COMPASS
(CURVING —) SWING
(CUSTOMARY —) GUISE
(DOWNWARD —) DIP DECLINE
TOBOGGAN
(EASY —) PIPE
(EXACT —) BEAM
(FIRST —) ANTEPAST
(FREE —) FORTH
(IRREGULAR —) ERROR
(LAST —) VOID
(MIDDLE —) MIDS TEMPER
(NATURAL —) RITA
(OBLIQUE —) SKEW
(OVERHANGING —) JET
(PREDETERMINED —) DESTINY
(ROUNDABOUT —) DETOUR
WINDLASS
(SETTLED —) BIAS GROOVE
(SKIING —) SCHUSS
COURSER HORSE RACER STEED
CUSSER CHARGER
COURSING CURSIVE
COURT BAR BID SEE SUE WOO AF
BAIL BODY CLAW FUSS GATE GIR
LEET QUAD ROTA SEAT SEEK SUI
TOWN WALE WARD WYND YARD
ARENA BENCH BUREO CURIA CUR
DAIRI DIVAN FAVOR FORUM FUER
GARTH JUDGE PATIO SHIRE SPAC
SPARK SPOON SWEET TEMPT THI
THINK TOURN TRAIN YAMEN
ADALAT ALLURE ATRIUM BAILEY
COUNTY DARGAH DURBAR DURGA
GEMOTE HOMAGE INVITE PALACE
PARVIS SPLUNT SUITOR TOLSEY
ADAWLUT ADDRESS ASSIZES
ATTRACT BARMOTE DUOVIRI
EPHETAE FOREIGN HELIAEA
HUSTING JUSTICE RETINUE SOLIC
TEMENOS TOURNEL AUDIENCE
BURHMOOT CHANCERY FOUJDAR
LAWCOURT MARKMOOT MARKMO
QUARANTY SERENADE SESSIONS
SWANMOTE TRIBUNAL WOODMOT
(— FAVOR) FAWN
(— OF A HUNDRED) MALL MALLU
MALLUS
(— OF CIRCUIT JUDGES) EYRE
(— OF FORTRESS) PEEL
(— OF MIKADO) DAIRI
(— ORDER) VACATUR
(— THE GREAT) LEVEE
(ECCLESIASTICAL —) ROTA CURI

SYNOD COLLOQUY AUDIENCIA
(EXERCISE —) EPHEBEUM
(FORTIFIED —) BAWN
(INNER —) PATIO
(MUSLIM —) DIVAN DIWAN
(REFORMED —) CLASIS
(SMALL —) WIND WYND
(SUPREME —) SUDDER
(TURKISH —) GATE
COURTEOUS FAIR HEND BUXOM
CIVIL GENTY SUAVE BONAIR
GENTLE POLITE SMOOTH URBANE
AFFABLE CORDIAL GALLANT
GENTEEL GENTILE REFINED
DEBONAIR FAMILIAR GRACIOUS
OBLIGING
COURTEOUSLY FAIR FAIRLY
GENTLY KINDLY AFFABLY
COURTESAN MADAM QUAIL THAIS
WHORE COURTY GEISHA LALAGE
MADAME PLOVER AMOROSA
CANIDIA PUCELLE DEVADASI
(PL.) DEMIMONDE
COURTESY MENSK COMITY EXTENT
GENTRY MANSHIP TASHRIF
CALIDORE CORTEISE ELEGANCE
GENTRICE GRATUITY URBANITY
(PL.) HONORS
COURTHOUSE CUTCHERY
COURTIER CURAN OSRIC WOOER
OSRICK COURTER IACHIMO
COURTMAN POLONIUS
COURTING SUING SPLUNT
COURTLY HEND AULIC CIVIL HENDE
POLITE AULICAL ELEGANT REFINED
STATELY POLISHED DIGNIFIED
COURT-NOUE RONCET
COURTSHIP SUIT AMOUR DRURY
SPARKING
COURTYARD AREA WYND CURIA
PATIO TRANCE CORTILE TETRAGON
COUSIN COZ KIN AKIN HERO ALLIED
NEPHEW
COVE CO BAY DEN CAVE CHAP FILE
GILL HOLE NOOK PASS SUMP BASIN
BAYOU BIGHT CREEK INLET COVING
YELLOW HOLLOW RECESS VALLEY
HOLDING CALANQUE GUNKHOLE
VENANT BIND BOND BRIS MISE
PACT TRUE AGREE BERIT BRITH
TOUCH ACCORD BERITH CARTEL
COMART CONAND ENGAGE INDENT
LEAGUE PATISE PLEDGE TREATY
BARGAIN COMPACT CONCORD
PROMISE ALLIANCE CONTRACT
DOCUMENT HANDFAST TREATISE
VENANTER HILLMAN
VER DO CAP COT HAP LAP LAY
FAD NAP TOP TUP WRY BIND CEIL
CLAD COAT COOM CURE DAUB
DECK FACE FADE FALL FURL GARB
GATE HEAD HEAL HEEL HIDE HILL
HOOD LATH LEAD LEAP LINE MASK
PAVE ROOF SILE SPAN TELD TICK
HIDE TILT VEIL APRON BATHE
BOARD CLOAK CLOUT COPSE
CROWN DRAPE DRESS FENCE
FLESH FLOOD GUISE HATCH KIVER
MOUNT RECTO SCARF SERVE

SHADE STREW STUDY THEAK THEEK
TOWEL TREAD VERSO WELME
WHALM AWNING BATTER BINDER
BLAZON CANOPY CHALON CLOTHE
DOUBLE EARLAP ENAMEL ENCASE
ENFOLD ENTIRE ENVEIL FOLDER
HACKLE IMMASK INVEST JACKET
KIRTLE MANTLE OVERGO POTLID
RUNNER SCONCE SCREEN SHADOW
SHEATH SHIELD SLEEVE SPREAD
SPRING SWATHE TOILET TOPPER
WHAUVE APPAREL ASPHALT
BANDAGE BESTREW BLANKET
CAPSULE CONCEAL CONTECT
COUVERT ELYTRON EMBRACE
ENCRUST FASCINE HEADCAP
HOUSING INCRUST KNEECAP
MANHEAD OBSCURE OMNIBUS
OVERLAY PRETEXT SHEATHE
SHELTER SHUTTER TAMPION
THIMBLE BEDCOVER COMPRISE
COVERCLE DEBRUISE ENCLOTHE
ENSCONCE HOODWINK IMMANTLE
OVERHAIL OVERSILE OVERWEND
PALLIATE PRETENCE PRETENSE
SLIPOVER SURPOOSE
(— A FIRE) DAMP
(— AROUND FLOWER) CYMBA
(— BRICKS) SCOVE
(— FOR ALEMBIC) HEAD
(— FOR CHALICE) PALL
(— FOR DIAPER) SOAKER
(— FOR ENGINE) COWLING
(— FOR FOOD) BELL
(— FOR GUN) TAMPION
(— FOR MILITARY CAPE) HAVELOCK
(— FOR PISTON) FOLLOWER
(— FOR POWDER PAN) HAMMER
(— FOR WIRES) BOOTLEG
(— GROUND) HEAT
(— HEARTH) FETTLE
(— OF BALL) CARCASS
(— OF BOILER) VOMIT
(— OF COFFIN) COOM
(— OF HAWSEHOLE) BUCKLER
(— OF MINE CAGE) BONNET
(— OF RIFLE MAGAZINE) GATE
(— OF SPORANGIUM) EPIGONE
(— OF VEGETATION) GROWTH
(— OPPRESSIVELY) SMOTHER
(— OVER) RAKE WELME WHELM
QUELME SHEUGH BECLOUD
OVERDECK WITHHELE
(— PLANTS) BAG
(— PROTECTIVELY) SHROUD
SHEATHE
(— ROAD) BLIND
(— SOIL WITH CLAY) GAULT
(— UP) HAP BELY FOLD BELIE
SALVE SLEEK HUDDLE
(— WITH ASHES) SOIL
(— WITH BACON) BARD
(— WITH CLAY) CLOAM
(— WITH COWL) MOB
(— WITH CRUMBS) BREAD
(— WITH DOTS) CRIBBLE
(— WITH DROPS) DAG
(— WITH EARTH) BURY HEAL INTER
(— WITH FILM) SKIM

(— WITH FLESH) INCARN
(— WITH FOAM) EMBOSS
(— WITH GOLD) GILD
(— WITH MEAL) MELVIE
(— WITH MUD) BEMUD BELUTE
(— WITH OAKUM) FOTHER
(— WITH PITCH) PAY
(— WITH PLASTER) PARGET
(— WITH SHEATH) GLOVE
(— WITH SOLDER) SPLASH
(— WITH STONE) ASHLAR
(— WITH STRAW) THATCH
(— WITH TIN) BLANCH
(— WITH TOPSOIL) KELLY
(— WITH WATER) DOUSE DOWSE
FLOOD WHELM
(— WITH WAX) CERE
(— WITH WEAVING) GRAFT
(— WITH WINGS) BROOD
(BED —S) HEALING
(BEEHIVE —) QUILT
(BOOK —) CASE SIDE
(GLASS —) STRIKE
(PACK —) MANTA
(POSTAL —) ENTIRE
(POT —) BRED
(SADDLE —) PILCH HOUSING
(SLIDING —) BRIDGE
(TABLE —) BAIZE
(WING — OF BEETLE) SHARD
COVERALL GOWN JUMPER
COVERED CLAD FULL SHOD TECT
BLIND MOSSY CLOSED COVERT
HIDDEN ENCASED OBTECTED
SCREENED
(— WITH CRYSTALS) DRUSY
(— WITH FEATHERS) HIRSUTE
(— WITH FOREST) HYLEAN
(— WITH HAIRS) COMATE VILLOUS
(— WITH PROTUBERANCES) HUMPY
(— WITH SCALES) SCUTATE
(— WITH SEAWEED) TANGLY
(THINLY —) BARISH
COVERED WAGON WHITETOP
BUCKWAGON
COVERER DECKER
COVERING (ALSO SEE COVER) BOX
COT FUR HAP KEX ARIL BARB BARK
BOOT CASE CAUL CUFF DECK FILM
HAME HEAD HOOD HULL HUSK KELL
MASK OVER PALL PUFF ROBE ROOF
SLIP SPAT TARP TILE TILT TRAP
VEIL APRON ARMOR BRAID BURSE
CRUST DRESS GLOBE GLOVE
HATCH QUILT SCALE SHELL SKIRT
STALL SWARD TESTA TUNIC TWEEL
WREIL ARMING AWNING BANCAL
BANKER CANOPY CANVAS COVERT
DRAPET EMBRYO ENAMEL FACING
FENDER GAITER GANOIN HACKLE
HATCAP HELMET JACKET MUZZLE
PELAGE SADDLE SCREEN SHEATH
SHROUD SINDON VERNIX BUFFONT
CAMISIA CAPSULE CEILING COATING
COWLING EARFLAP ENVELOP
EXCIPLE GRATING HAPPING
HEALING HEELCAP HOUSING
MUFFLER OVERLAY PURPORT
SARPLER SHADING SHELTER

SHOEING SLIPPER TECTURE TEGMENT VESTURE WRAPPER ARMGUARD BLAZONRY BOARDING CASEMENT CLEADING CLOTHING COMPRESS COVERLET EGGSHELL EPISPORE INDUMENT INDUSIUM MANTELET MANTLING OVERCAST PAVILION PERICARP SETATION UMBRELLA
(— **FOR BENCH)** BANKER
(— **FOR BOXERS' HANDS)** CESTUS
(— **FOR NECK)** TUCKER
(— **FOR ROOF APEX)** EPI
(— **FOR SHOULDERS)** STOLE
(— **FOR SKI)** SKIN
(— **FOR STIRRUP)** HOOD
(— **OF BED)** TIKE
(— **OF BELL ROPE)** GRIP
(— **OF BIRD)** INDUMENT
(— **OF BOW HANDLE)** ARMING
(— **OF CASH SHORTAGE)** LAPPING
(— **OF FEATHERS)** DOWN
(— **OF NUTMEG)** MACE
(— **OF ROPE)** SERVICE
(— **OF VEGETATION)** FLEECE
(**CAST** —**S)** EXUVIAE
(**CHIMNEY** —) COWL
(**CLOTH** —) TOILET
(**COARSE** —) CADDOW TILLET
(**DEFENSIVE** —) ARMOR KICKER
(**EAR** —) EARLAP EARFLAP EARMUFF OREILET
(**EYE** —**S)** GOGGLES
(**FLOOR** —) RUG TILE CRASH CARPET LINOLEUM OILCLOTH
(**FOUL** —) SCUM
(**HEAD** —) CAP HAT WIG HAIR HIVE HOOD BONNET HELMET BIRETTA CHAPEAU CHAPERON HAVELOCK HEADRAIL TROTCOZY
(**LEG** —) BOOT HOSE STOCK GAITER LEGGIN PEDULE KNEELET LEGGING STOCKING
(**LIGHT** —) GRIMING
(**LINEN** —) BARB
(**OUTER** —) BARK HIDE HULL HUSK CRUST TESTA JACKET CARAPACE
(**PROTECTIVE** —) APRON ARMOR SHELL COCOON
(**SLIGHT** —) CYMAR
(**STAGE** —) HEAVENS
(**STERILE** —) DRAPE
(**STICKY DAMP** —) GLET
(**THIN** —) FILM SCRUFF WASHING
COVERLET PANE HELER HOUSE QUILT REZAI THROW AFGHAN CADDOW CHALON COLCHA LIGGER SPREAD BLANKET BUFFALO COVERLID DAGSWAIN
COVER-SHAME SAVIN SAVINE
COVERT DEN LAY LIE SLY LAIR VERT EARTH NICHE PRIVY ASYLUM HARBOR HIDDEN LATENT MASKED MYSTIC REFUGE SECRET COVERED DEFENSE PRIVATE SHELTER TECTRIX THICKET DISGUISE INVOLVED
(PL.) CRISSUM
COVERTLY CLOSE CLOSELY

COVET ACHE ENVY PANT WANT WISH CRAVE YEARN YISSE DESIRE GRUDGE HANKER
COVETOUS AVID GAIR GARE EAGER FRUGAL GREEDY SORDID STINGY ENVIOUS GRIPPLE MISERLY DESIROUS GRASPING
COVETOUSNESS GREED MISERY AVARICE YISSING COVETISE PLEONEXIA
COVEY BEVY FALL BROOD FLOCK HATCH COVERT COMPANY
COVIN BAND CREW FRAUD COVINE COMPANY CONVENE ASSEMBLY TRICKERY
COW AWE KEY NOT BEEF BOGY BOSS COWL CUSH FAZE MOIL MULL NOTT ROAN RUNT VACA ABASH ALARM BEEVE BOSSY BROCK BULLY CUSHA DAUNT DOMPT DRAPE MOGGY QUAIL SCARE SNOOL VACHA BOVINE BULLER COLLOP CRUMMY GOBLIN HAWKEY HAWKIE HEIFER MAILIE MILKER MULLEY SUBDUE BOARDER BUGBEAR BULLOCK CRITTER CRUMMIE DEPRESS MESTENO MILCHER OVERTOP SQUELCH TERRIFY ALDERNEY AUDHUMLA BROWBEAT COWBRUTE DISPIRIT FRIGHTEN STRIPPER THREATEN
(— **ABOUT 3 FEET HIGH)** GYNEE
(— **BEFORE CALVING)** SPRINGER
(**BARREN** —) DRAPE BARRENER
(**DRY** —) KEY SEW
(**HORNLESS** —) NOT MOIL NOTT DODDY MULEY DODDIE HUMLIE MAILIE HUMBLIE POLLARD MOULLEEN
(**PREGNANT** —) CALVER INCALVER
(**WHITE-FACED** —) HAWKEY HAWKIE
(**YOUNG** —) STIRK HEIFER
(PL.) KINE DAIRY
COWARD COW COOF DAFF FUNK FUGIE LACHE PIKER CRAVEN FUNKER PIGEON CAITIFF CHICKEN COUCHER DASTARD MEACOCK NITHING PANURGE QUITTER NIDERING POLTROON RECREANT TURNBACK TURNTAIL
COWARDICE DASTARDY LASHNESS
COWARDLY SHY ARGH FAINT LACHE TIMID AFRAID COWARD COWISH CRAVEN TURPID YELLOW CAITIFF CHICKEN GUTLESS HILDING FACELESS NIDERING POLTROON RECREANT SNEAKING
COWBARN BYRE SAUR SHIPPON VACCARY
COWBIRD BECCO BUNTING CUCKOLD OXBITER COKEWOLD LAZYBIRD
COWBOY HAZER RIDER ROPER SCREW WADDI WADDY CHARRO GAUCHO GINETE HERDER JINETE COWHAND COWHERD COWPOKE GRAZIER HERDBOY LLANERO PANIOLO PUNCHER REFUGEE VAQUERO BUCKAROO DALLYMAN

JACKAROO NEATHERD NOWTHERD OUTRIDER PASTORAL RANCHERO SWINGMAN WRANGLER
COWCATCHER GUARD PILOT FENDER
COWED HANGDOG DOWNCAST
COWER HUG COUR FAWN RUCK HOVER QUAIL SHRUG SNOOL SQUA STOOP TOADY WINCE COORIE CRINGE CROUCH HURKLE SHRINK CROODLE CRUDDLE
COWFISH TORO BECCO CUCKOLD MANATEE SIRENIA
COWHAGE KIWACH
COWHAND PEELER FLANKER STOCKMAN
COWHERB COCKLE SOAPWORT
COWHERD HERDSMAN NEATHERD
COWHOUSE BYRE SHIPPEN SHIPPO
COWL CAP COW LID SOE TUB COU HOOD MONK MITER BONNET CUCULE CAPUCHE SCUTTLE CAPUCHIN
COW PARSNIP MADNEP CADWEED HOGWEED PIGWEED BEARWORT BUNDWEED
COWPEA SITAO FRIJOL FRIJOLE TOWCOCK BLACKEYE BLACKPEA
COWPEN CUPPEN CUPPIN
COWPOX PAPPOX KINEPOX VACCIN VACCINIA
COWRIE COWRY VENUS ZIMBI CYPRAEID
COWSLIP PAIGLE PRIMULA SHOOT AURICULA CYCLAMEN MARIGOLD PRIMROSE
COXA HIP HAUNCH
COXCOMB FOP NOB BUCK DUDE FOOL TOFF CLEAT DANDY HINGE PRINCOX POPINJAY PRINCOCK
COXCOMBRY FOPPERY
COY PAL SHY ARCH COAX NICE ALOOF CHARY DECOY QUIET SQU STILL ALLURE CARESS DEMURE MODEST PROPER BASHFUL DISTA PEEVISH STRANGE RESERVED SKITTISH
COYNESS SHYNESS
COYO CHININ
COYOL COROJO COROZO
COYOTE VARMINT
(— **STATE)** SOUTHDAKOTA
COYPU DEGU NUTRIA
COZEN COG CON BILK GULL POOF CHEAT TRICK CHISEL GREASE BEGUILE DECEIVE DEFRAUD SWINDLE HOODWINK
COZENER SNAP SNECKDRAW
COZENING SIMILATE
COZIER CADGER CODGER COSIER
COZY RUG BEIN BIEN COSY EASY HOMY SAFE SNUG BIELD CANNY CUSHY HOMEY CHATTY PENTIT SECURE TOASTY COVERING FAMILIAR HOMELIKE SOCIABLE
CRAB GIN UCA BOCO JUEY MAJA ZOEA ANGER ARROW AYUYU BLU MAIAN MAIID MAJID RACER SANDY THIEF WINCH BUSTER CANCER

GROUSE HARPER HERMIT KABURI
NIPPER PARTAN PEELER PUNGAR
PUNGER RACING SPRITE BUCKLER
BUCKLUM BURSTER CABOUCA
CANCRID FIDDLER GRUMBLE
INACHID OCYPODE PANFISH
POLYPOD SHEDDER SOLDIER
SPECTER SPECTRE SURIQUE
ARACHNID CRABFISH DORIPPID
GRAPSOID HORSEMAN IRRITATE
LIMULOID LITHODID OCHIDORE
OXYSTOME PORTUNID RANINIAN
TRAVELER WINDLASS
(MATING —) DOUBLER
RAB APPLE CRAB SCRAB SCROG
COLING
RABBED SOUR UGLY CABBY
CROSS SURLY TESTY BITTER
COPPED CROOSE CROUSE CRUSTY
MOROSE RUGGED SULLEN TEETHY
TRYING BOORISH CANKERY
CRABBIT CRAMPED CRONISH
CROOKED FRABBIT GNARLED
KNOTTED OBSCURE PEEVISH
CHURLISH CONTRARY CRABBISH
LIVERISH PETULANT VINEGARY
RABBEDNESS ACRIMONY
ASPERITY
RABCATCHER CRABIER
RABER VOLE AGOUARA
RABGRASS DRAWK FONIO PANIC
DARNEL PANICLE CRABWEED
ELEUSINE
RAB LOUSE CRAB MORPION
MOREPEON
RAB PLOVER DROME
RAB TREE GRIBBLE
RABWOOD ANDIROBA
POISONWOOD
RACK GAG KIN POP BANG BLOW
CHAP CHIP CHOP CLAP CONE DOKE
FENT FLAW GAIG JEST JIBE JOKE
KIBE LEAK LICK QUIP REND RIFT
RIME RIVE SCAR SLAT SNAP YERK
BRACK BREAK CHARK CHECK CHICK
CHINE CHINK CLACK CLEFT CRAKE
CRAZE FLAKE FLANK FLASH GRIKE
KNACK KNICK SCORE SHAKE SLASH
SPANG SPLIT CLEAVE CRANNY
SLITER SPIDER SPRING BLEMISH
CRACKLE CREVICE FISSURE SLIFTER
SLITHER FRACTURE HAIRLINE
STRAMASH
(— A WHIP) YERK FLANK
(— IN FLESH) KIN CHAP KIBE
(— IN FLOOR) STRAKE
(— IN INGOT) SPILL
(— IN MAST) SPRING
(— IN ROCK) GRIKE JOINT
(— IN SEA ICE) RIFTER
(— IN STEEL) CHECK SPILL
(— OPEN) SEAM
(— PETROLEUM) BURN
(— WHILE FIRING) DUNT
(PL.) CRAZE
RACKAJACK NAILER NAILING
RACKBRAINED CRAZY NUTTY
CRACKY ERRATIC
RACKED FLED NECKED CHAPPED

COMICAL TOUCHED CRACKERS
CRACKER BAKE LIAR WAFER
POPPER BISCUIT BOASTER
BREAKER BURSTER COSAQUE
REDNECK SALTINE SNAPPER
(— STATE) GEORGIA
(BOILED —S) CUSH
(BROKEN —S) DUNDERFUNK
CRACKERJACK TRUMP
CRACKING CRAZE SHIVERING
(PL.) SCRAP
CRACKLE SNAP BREAK CRACK
CRISP BRUSTLE CRINKLE SPARKLE
SPUTTER
CRACKLING CRISP GREAVE SNAPPY
CRACKEL CRACKLE CREMANT
GREAVES CRACKNEL CRITLING
(PL.) SCRAPS GRIEBEN
CRACKNEL SIMNEL CRACKLING
CRACKPOT CRACK ERRATIC
LUNATIC CRANKISH
CRACKSMAN YEGG BURGLAR
PETEMAN
CRADLE BED COT CRIB REST ROCK
WOMB CRATE FRAME CRECHE
MATRIX ROCKER TROUGH BERCEAU
SHELTER BASSINET CUNABULA
(— FOR SHIP) BED SLEE
(— FOR VATS) STILLING STILLION
(— IN ARCHERY) PURSE
(CERAMICS —) CHUM
(GRAIN —) CADAR CADER
(PL.) CHOCKS
CRADLESONG BERCEUSE
CRADLING BRACK
CRAFT ART BARK BOAT SAIL FRAUD
GUILE SKILL TRADE BARQUE
BATEAU DECEIT DROGER METIER
MISTER POLICE ROADER STRUSE
TALENT VESSEL ABILITY CUNNING
DROGHER MYSTERY PANURGY
SLEIGHT APTITUDE ARTIFICE
BASKETRY VOCATION
(ANTIQUATED OR CLUMSY —)
HOOKER
CRAFTILY FOXILY
CRAFTINESS DESIGN SLEIGHT
SLYNESS
CRAFTSMAN CARL HAND CARLE
CRAFT NAVVY ARTIST WRITER
ARTISAN TOHUNGA WORKMAN
LETTERER MECHANIC
CRAFTY SLY ARCH DEEP DERN FINE
FOXY SLIM WILY WISE ADEPT
COONY SLAPE SLEEK ADROIT
ARTFUL ASTUTE CALLID QUAINT
SHREWD SOLERT SUBTLE TRICKY
CUNNING SLEEKIT SLEIGHT SUBTILE
VAFROUS VERSUTE VULPINE
CAPTIOUS DEXTROUS ENGINOUS
FETCHING JESUITIC SLEIGHTY
CRAG TOR CRAW KNEE NECK ROCK
SCAR SPUR ARETE BRACK CLIFF
CLINT CRAIG HEUCH HEUGH
THROAT
CRAGGY ROUGH ABRUPT CLIFFY
CLIFTY KNOTTY PAMPER RUGGED
CRAGGED KNAGGED
CRAKE CROW RAIL ROOK RAVEN

CORNBIRD RAILBIRD
CRAKOW BEAKER CRACOWE
POULAINE
CRAM MUG RAM WAD BONE FILL
GLUT LADE PACK PANG PORR PURR
STOW TUCK URGE CROWD CRUSH
DRIVE FARCE FORCE FRANK GORGE
GRIND LEARN PRESS SCRAM STECH
STUDY STUFF TEACH AGROTE
CROMME PESTER STEEVE THRACK
CRAMMED PANG STODGY
CHOCKFUL
CRAMMER CRAM FEEDER
CRAMMING GAVAGE
CRAMP ART ARCT COOP CRIB KINK
PAIN TUCK CRICK CRIMP CROWD
DOWEL PINCH STUNT TRAMP
AGRAFE DOGTIE HAMPER HINDER
KNOTTY PESTER CONFINE CRAMPER
CRAMPET COMPRESS CONTRACT
RESTRAIN RESTRICT
CRAMPED CRIMP CRIMPED SQUEEZY
CRAMPFISH TORPEDO
CRAMPING UNEASY
CRAMPON CRAMP CRAMPET
CRAMPOON
CRANBERRY BERRY CRANE ERICAD
BOGWORT PEMBINA ACROSARC
BILBERRY BOGBERRY COWBERRY
FENBERRY FOXBERRY
(— BUSH) PIMBINA
CRANBERRY TREE PEMBINA
SNOWBALL VIBURNUM
CRANE JOB GRUS HOOK SWAY
CYRUS DAVIT HERON HOIST JENNY
RAISE SARUS TITAN WADER
BROLGA COOLEN JIGGER KULANG
SAHRAS COOLUNG CRAWLER
DERRICK GOLIATH KAIKARA
WHOOPER GRUIFORM TRAVELER
(— FOR FIREPLACE) COTTREL
COTTEREL
CRANE ARM GIB JIB GIBBET
RAMHEAD COTTEREL
CRANESBILL ALUMROOT DOVEFOOT
FLUXWEED
CRANIUM PAN HEAD CRANE CRANY
SKULL BRAINPAN
CRANK NUT WIT BENT SICK WALT
WEAK WHIM WIND BRACE LOOSE
ROGUE SHAKY THROW WALTY
WINCH AILING BOLDLY CRANKY
EVENER GROUCH HANDLE INFIRM
AWKWARD BRACKET FANATIC
LUSTILY
(SOMEWHAT —) TENDER
CRANKCASE SUMP
CRANKINESS ANGULARITY
CRANKY UGLY CRAZY CRONK
CROSS LUSTY SHAKY TESTY AILING
CRANNY FIFISH INFIRM SICKLY
CROOKED GROUCHY PERVERSE
TORTUOUS
CRANNY HOLE NOOK CHINK CLEFT
CRACK CORNER CRANNEL CREVICE
FISSURE
CRANTARA TARIE
CRANTS WREATH CORANCE
GARLAND

CRAPE BAND CURL FRIZ CREPE CRIMP DRAPE GAUZE SHROUD MOURNING

CRAPE MYRTLE JAPONICA ASTROMEDA

CRAPPIE BACH SHAD BATCH CALICO CROPPIE BACHELOR BACULERE NEWLIGHT SACALAIT TINMOUTH CHINKAPIN

CRAPS CRAP HAZARD

CRASH BASH FAIL FALL RACK BLAST BURST CLOTH CRUSH FRUSH PRANG SHOCK SMASH SOUND FIASCO FRAGOR HURTLE FAILURE SHATTER STENTER COLLAPSE ICEQUAKE SPLINTER STRAMASH (— OF THUNDER) CLAP

CRASHING ROPAND SMASHING

CRASH-LAND DITCH

CRASS RAW DULL LOUD RUDE CRUDE DENSE GROSS ROUGH THICK COARSE OBTUSE STUPID

CRASSNESS SQUALOR

CRATCH CRIB RACK CRITCH MANGER GRATING

CRATE BOX CAR CASE CRIB FLAT PLANE SERON BASKET CRADLE ENCASE HAMPER HURDLE CACAXTE CANASTA CARRIER PACKAGE VEHICLE (EMPTY —) EMPTY

CRATER CUP PIT CONE HOLE DINOS FOVEA NICHE CELEBE HOLLOW CALDERA (— FORMED BY STEAM) MAAR (LUNAR —) LINNE

CRAUNCH CRANCH SCRANCH

CRAVAT TIE TECK ASCOT FRONT SCARF STOCK CHOKER GRAVAT BANDAGE NECKTIE OVERLAY SOUBISE CRUMPLER

CRAVE ASK BEG GAPE ITCH LONG NEED PRAY SEEK WISH COVET GREED YEARN DESIRE HANKER HUNGER LINGER THIRST YAMMER BESEECH ENTREAT IMPLORE REQUEST REQUIRE SOLICIT APPETITE

CRAVEN AFRAID COWARD SCARED DASTARD COWARDLY DEFEATED OVERCOME POLTROON RECREANT SNEAKING

CRAVING AVID ITCH WANT LETCH DESIRE HUNGER THIRST LONGING APPETITE LIKEROUS TICKLING APPETENCE (— FOR LIQUOR) DRY (— FOR UNNATURAL FOOD) PICA (ABNORMAL —) BULIMY BULIMIA BOULIMIA

CRAW MAW CRAG CROP STOMACH

CRAWFISH KREEF

CRAWL LAG COON DRAG FAWN INCH LOOP RAMP SHUG SWIM CREEP KRAAL SLIDE SLIME SNAKE TRAIL BUSTLE CRINGE GROVEL SCRAWL SCRIDE CLAMBER SLITHER SNIGGLE TRUDGEN INCHWORM

CRAWLY CREEPY

CRAYFISH DAD CRAB YABBY YABBIE CAMARON CRAWDAD LOBSTER CAMBARUS CRABFISH CRAWFISH

CRAYON KEEL PLAN CHALK CONTE SAUCE PASTEL PENCIL SKETCH SANGUINE

CRAZE BUG FAD FLAW MAZE MODE RAGE BREAK CRACK CRUSH FEVER FUROR MANIA VOGUE DEFECT IMPAIR MADDEN MADDLE WEAKEN WHIMSY DERANGE DESTROY FASHION SHATTER WHIMSEY DISTRACT

CRAZED MAD REE AMOK LOCO WILD WOOD WOWF ZANY BALMY BATTY DAFFY DOTTY GIDDY MANIC NUTTY POTTY WACKY COOCOO DOTTLE INSANE LOONEY BERSERK FANATIC LUNATIC DATELESS DELEERIT DEMENTED DERANGED

CRAZINESS CRAZE LUNACY DEMENTIA

CRAZY (ALSO SEE CRAZED) OFF REE WET BUGS GYTE HITE LOCO WILD ZANY BATTY BEANY DAFFY DOTTY GOOFY LOONY POTTY CRANKY CUCKOO DOTTLE FRUITY INSANE LOCKET MENTAL SCATTY SCREWY CRACKED LUNATIC PEEVISH SCRANNY BUGHOUSE COCKEYED CRACKERS DERANGED HALLICET HALUCKET MESHUGGA

CREAK GIG GEIG GIRG JARG RASP YIRR CHARK CHEEP CHIRK CRAIK CRANK CROAK GRIND GROAN FRATCH SCREAK SCRIKE SCROOP SKRAIK SQUEAK COMPLAIN

CREAKING JARG SCREAK SCRIKE

CREAKY ARTHRITIC

CREAM DIP BEAT BEST FOOL HEAD REAM CREME ELITE FROTH REAME SAUCE BONBON CHOICE TRIFLE COLOGNE FATNESS EMULSION OINTMENT

CREAMING MANTLING

CREAM PUFF PUFF DUCHESSE

CREAMY RICH REAMY ACREAM SMOOTH LUSCIOUS

CREASE GAW CLAM FOLD LINE LIRK RUCK RUGA SEAM BLOCK CRESS CRIMP PLAIT PLEAT PRESS SCARF SCORE FURROW SCARPA SUTURE WREATH CRUMPLE CRUNKLE WRIMPLE WRINKLE (SERIES OF —S) BREAK (PL.) RASCETA

CREASED CRUMPLED ACCORDION

CREATE COIN CREE FORM MAKE PLAN BUILD CAUSE ERECT FORGE IMPEL RAISE SHAPE WRITE AUTHOR DESIGN IMPOSE INVENT COMPACT COMPOSE CONJURE FASHION IMAGINE PRODUCE COMPOUND GENERATE CONSTRUCT (— A DISTURBANCE) RIOT (— CONFUSION) GARBOIL

CREATION WORLD COSMOS EFFECT NATURE POETRY EDITION FACTURE FASHION POIESIS PRODUCT

SHAPING BERESHIT BUSINESS CREATURE UNIVERSE (MENTAL —) FANTASY PHANTASY (VISIONARY —) DREAM

CREATIVE FERTILE FORMFUL PLASTIC POIETIC FORGEFUL GERMINAL NATURING POMATIVE

CREATOR MAKER AUTHOR FATHER FORMER VARUNA WORKER KHEPERA TAGALOA DESIGNER INVENTOR OPERATOR PRODUCER TANGALOA

CREATURE MAN FOOD TOOL BEAST BEING DABBA JOKER SLAVE THING TRICK WIGHT ANIMAL FELLOW MINION PERSON WRETCH CRITTER GANGREL MINIKIN MINIMUS SHAPING CRAYTHUR CREATION HELLICAT (— OF LITTLE VALUE) SHOT (3 —S OF A KIND) LEASH (CANNIBALISTIC —) WENDIGO WINDIGO (DISORDERLY —) ROIT ROYT (DWARF —) FAIRY GNOME (ELFLIKE —) PERI (EVIL —) HELLICAT (FABLED —) LUNG SIREN MERMAN WIVERN ALBORAK MERMAID (LITTLE —) MITING (MANGY —) RONION RONYON (MANLIKE —) HOMINID HOMONID HOMINIAN (MEAN —) LEFT (MECHANICAL —) GOLEM (MISERABLE —) SNAKE (NONSENSE —) SNARK (SILLY —) GOOSE (SMALL —) ATOM GRIG BEASTIE (SPRY —) WHIPPET (STUNTED —) WIRL URLING WIRLINC (SUPERNATURAL —) MAN DRAGON (TINY —) ELF ATOMY (UNDERDEVELOPED —) SLINK (USELESS —) HUSHION (VICIOUS —) DEVIL (WORTHLESS —) SCULPIN SNIPJACK (WRETCHED —) ARMINE (PL.) CREATION

CRECHE CRIB PUTZ MANGER NURSERY

CREDENCE FAITH TRUST BELIEF BUFFET CREDIT CREANCE CREDENZA

CREDENTIAL VOUCHER CREDENCE

CREDENZA NICHE SHELF TABLE BUFFET SERVER CREDENCE CUPBOARD

CREDIBILITY FAITH CREDIT

CREDIBLE LIKELY CREDENT FAITHFUL PROBABLE TROWABLE

CREDIT LOAN TICK ASSET CHALK ENDOW FAITH HONOR IZZAT MENSK MERIT STRAP TENET TRUST BELIEF CHARGE ESTEEM IMPUTE RENOWN REPUTE TICKET WEIGHT ACCOUNT ASCRIBE BELIEVE CREANCE JAWBONE OPINION WORSHIP ACCREDIT CREDENCE HEADMARK (HOCKEY —) ASSIST

REDITABLE HONEST CREDIBLE
REPUTABLE
REDITOR DEBTEE SHYLOCK
TRUSTER ADJUDGER APPRIZER
CRANSIER CREANCER
(TROUBLESOME —) DUN
REDO FAITH
REDULITY EASINESS
REDULOUS FOND SIMPLE SPOONY
SPOONEY CREDIBLE GULLIBLE
REED ISM LAY CULT SECT CREDO
DOGMA FAITH TENET BELIEF KELIMA
SYMBOL CREANCE KALIMAH
TROWING DOCTRINE SYMBOLUM
REEK BAY CUT GEO GIO GUT RIA
RIO RUN VLY VOE BURN COVE
HOPE KILL PILL RILL SLEW SLUE
VLEI VLEY WASH WICK BACHE
BAYOU BIGHT BOGUE BROOK CRICK
DRAFT FLEET INLET ZANJA ARROYO
BRANCH BREACH CANADA ESTERO
SLOUGH STREAM DRAUGHT
ESTUARY RIVULET ZANJONA
MUSKOGEE
AUSTRALIAN —) COWAL
TIDE —) SLAKE
REEK SEDGE THATCH
REEL RIP CAUL CAWL HASK JACK
KELL RACK TRAP HARSK BASKET
JUNKET
— FOR BOBBINS) BANK
REELER TUBER LIGGER
REEP COON FAWN INCH RAMP
CRAWL CROPE DRIFT GLIDE PROWL
SKULK SLINK SMOOT STEAL TRAIL
CRINGE GROVEL SCRIDE SPRAWL
CRAMBLE CRAMMEL SNIGGLE
TAURANGA
— AS IVY) RIZZLE
PL.) WILLIES
REEPER IVY JITI SHOE VINE WORM
CREEP CROPE SNAKE COWAGE
CRADLE IPECAC REPENT ROMPER
TECOMA CLAMPER CLIMBER
COWHAGE COWITCH CRAWLER
REPTANT REPTILE RUNNING
TRAILER FOXGLOVE GUITGUIT
ICUCULE WOODBINE
REEPING SLOW REPTANT REPTILE
ERVILE
REEPING CROWFOOT SITFAST
CRAWFOOT
REEPING SNOWBERRY MOXA
EABERRY
EESE KRIS STAB CRESS CRISE
WORD DAGGER
EMATE BURN
ENEL LOOP CORNEL KERNEL
RENELT
EOLE PATOIS CRIOLLO DIALECT
AITIAN MESTIZO
— STATE) LOUISIANA
EON (DAUGHTER OF —) GLAUCE
FATHER OF —) MENOECEUS
SISTER OF —) JOCASTA
IPPONOME
EOSOTE BUSH LARREA
EPE CRAPE FRIZZED NACARAT
ANCAKE CHIRIMEN CRINKLED
WRINKLED

CREPITATE SNAP GRATE RATTLE
CRACKLE
CRESCENT HORN LUNE MOON ROOL
CURVE LUNAR LUNOID LUNULE
MOONED SICKLE WAXAND LUNETTE
DEMILUNE MENISCUS
(END OF —) CUSP HORN
CRESCENTLIKE BICORN
CRESCENT-SHAPED MOONY
LUNATE LUNATED
CRESOL FROTHER
CRESS EKER KERSE CUCKOO
MADWORT CRUCIFER WHITETOP
CRESSET TORCH BASKET BEACON
SIGNAL CRISSET FLAMBEAU
CREST COP TIP TOP ACME APEX
COMB EDGE HOOD KNAP PEAK
SEAL TUFT CHINE CROWN PLUME
RIDGE COPPLE CREASE CRISTA
CUMBRE FINIAL HEIGHT HELMET
SUMMIT TIMBER TIMBRE BEARING
FEATHER TOPKNOT CENTROID
CRESTING ECTOLOPH METALOPH
PINNACLE WHITECAP
(— OF BREAKER) SEEGE
(— OF HELMET) COMB
(— OF HILL) KNAP
(— OF MINERAL VEIN) APEX
(— OF MOUNTAIN RANGE) ARETE
SAWBACK
(— OF RIDGE) EDGE
(— ON BIRD) CROWN ECKLE
COPPLE
(IMPERIAL —) KIKUMON
(WAVE —) FEATHER WHITECAP
CRESTED COMBED MUFFED TAPPET
TAPPIT COPPLED CRISATE
CROWNED PILEATED
CRESTED GREBE CARGOOSE
CRESTED QUAIL COPPY
CRESTFALLEN COWED DEJECTED
CRESTING CHENEAU
CRETACEOUS CHALKY
CRETAN KEFTI MINOAN CANDIOT
CRETAN SPIKENARD PHU

CRETE

BAY: SUDA KANCA KISAMO
MESARA
CAPE: BUZA LIANO SALOME
SIDERO SPATHA STAVROS
LITHINON SIDHEROS
GULF: KHANIA MERABELLO
MOUNTAIN: IDA DIKTE JUKTAS
LASITHI THEODORE
MOUNTAINS: PHINO MADARAS
TOWN: HAG LATO CANEA KHORA
SITIA ZAKRO ANOYIA CANDIA
KHANIA KISAMO RETIMO
KASTELLI HERAKLION

CRETIN IDIOT
CREUSA GLAUCE GLAUKE
CREUSA (FATHER OF —) CREON
PRIAM
(HUSBAND OF —) AENEAS
(KILLER OF —) MEDEA
(SON OF —) ION ASCANIUS

CREVALLE JACK JUREL
CREVASSE CHASM SPLIT SCHRUND
CLEAVAGE
CREVICE KIN BORE LEAK NOOK
PEEP SEAM VEIN BREAK CHINE
CHINK CLEFT CRACK CREEK CUNNE
GRIKE CRANNY STRAKE CRANNEL
FISSURE GUNNIES KRAVERS
OPENING SLIFTER CREVASSE
PEEPHOLE
CREW LOT MEN MOB SET BAND
GANG GING HERD OARS SHIP TEAM
COVIN EIGHT HANDS MEINY PARTY
SQUAD STAFF COVINE MEINIE
SEAMEN THRONG AIRCREW
COMPANY FACULTY MANNING
MEMBERS RETINUE EQUIPAGE
(— OF SHEARERS) BOARD
CREWEL CRUEL CADDIS CADDICE
CRIB BED BIN BOX CAB COT CUB
HUT KEY BOOM CRUB CURB DIVE
JACK PONY RACK RAFT SKIN
BOOSE BOOSY CHEAT CRATE
FRAME HOVEL STALL STEAL
BUNKER CRATCH CRECHE CRITCH
MANGER PIGSTY PILFER CABBAGE
ENGLISH PURLOIN BASSINET
CORNCRIB CRIBBAGE CRIBBING
CRIBWORK
CRIBBER SHORER STUMPSUCKER
CRICK KINK CREEK HITCH SPASM
TWIST
CRICKET GRIG MOLE SNOB CHANGA
SADDLE GRYLLID TWIDDLER
(— HIT) SLOG
CRICKETER CUT COLT PLAYER
RABBIT GENTLEMAN
CRIER HUER CRYER BEADLE HERALD
WAILER BELLMAN MUEZZIN
WRAWLER OUTCRIER
CRIME ACT SIN EVIL FACT LACK
ABUSE ARSON BLAME CAPER FOLLY
LIBEL WRONG FALSUM FELONY
INCEST MURDER PIACLE FORFEIT
FORGERY MISDEED OFFENCE
OFFENSE INIQUITY SABOTAGE
VILLAINY
(ORGANIZED —) GANGLAND
CRIMINAL BAD SORE YEGG CROOK
FELON APACHE BASHER DACOIT
GUILTY GUNMAN INMATE KILLER
NOCENT SLAYER WARGUS WICKED
CONVICT CULPRIT HEINOUS
HOODLUM ILLEGAL NOXIOUS
SEVENER VAUTRIN CRIMEFUL
CULPABLE GANGSTER GAOLBIRD
HABITUAL HARDCASE JAILBIRD
SCELERAT
(PETTY —) ROUNDER
(VIOLENT —) DESPERADO
(PL.) AMALAITA
CRIMINATE IMPEACH
CRIMP BEND CURL FOLD FRIZ POKE
POTE WAVE WEAK CLAMP CRISP
FLUTE FRILL FRIZZ PINCH PLAIT
BUCKLE GOFFER RUFFLE CRIMPER
CRIMPLE CRINKLE FRIABLE
GAUFFER WRINKLE OBSTACLE
CRIMSON LAC RED PINK GRAIN

BLOODY JOCKEY MAROON MODENA
CARMINE SCARLET CRAMOISY
CRIMSON CLOVER NAPOLEON
CRINED MANED
CRINGE BOW BEND CURB CURR
DUCK FAWN JOUK BINGE COWER
CRAWL CREEP QUAIL SNEAK SNOOL
STOOP WINCE YIELD BUCKLE
CROUCH GROVEL SHRINK SUBMIT
CRINKLE DISTORT SCRINGE
TRUCKLE
CRINGING ABJECT HANGDOG
SERVILE SPANIEL
CRINKLE BEND CURL KINK TURN
WIND CREPE CRISP PUCKER RIPPLE
RUMPLE RUSTLE CRACKLE
CRANKLE FRIZZLE WRINKLE
CRINKLED CRIMP CURLY BUCKLED
ENCOMIC CRISPATE
CRINKLY CREPY CREPEY
CRINOID POLYP CRINITE CAMERATE
COMATULA
(BODY OF —) CROWN
CRINOLINE CRIN HOOP
CRIPPLE MAR CRIP GIMP HARM
HURT LAME MAIM BACACH HOBBLE
IMPAIR INJURE SCOTCH WEAKEN
CRAPPLE CRUMPET DISABLE
LAMETER LAMIGER LAMITER
HANDICAP LAMESTER MUTILATE
PARALYZE
(PL.) LAMZIEKTE
CRIPPLED GIMPY COUPLED
DISABLED
CRIPPLING MAIM MAYHEM
CRISIS FIT ACME CRUX FLAP HEAD
JUMP PASS TURN CARDO CRISE
PANIC PERIL PINCH POINT STATE
STORM TRIAL STRAIT DUNKIRK
DECISION JUNCTURE MOUNTAIN
CRISP NEW COLD CURL FRIZ FROW
HARD BRISK CLEAR CRIPS CRUMP
CURLY FRESH FRIZZ NIPPY PITHY
SHARP SHORT SPALT STIFF TERSE
BITING BRIGHT CRISPY LIVELY
SNAPPY BRACING BRITTLE CONCISE
CRACKLY CRUNCHY CUTTING
FRIABLE FRIZZLE SMOPPLE INCISIVE
CRISPED FUZZY FRIZZLY CRISPATE
CRISPNESS SNAP
CRISSCROSS AWRY CROSS
NETWORK CONFUSED
CRITERION LAW NORM RULE TEST
TYPE AXIOM CANON CHECK GAUGE
MODEL PROOF TOUCH CRISIS
METRIC INDICIA MEASURE PLUMMET
STANDARD
CRITIC MOME BOOER JUDGE MOMUS
CARPER CENSOR CORNER EXPERT
PUNDIT SLATER SYNDIC ZOILUS
STYLIST COLLATOR CRITIQUE
DEBUNKER OVERSEER REVIEWER
THONGMAN
CRITICAL EDGY HIGH ACERB ACUTE
CHILLY CRITIC SEVERE URGENT
ACERBIC ADVERSE CARPING
EXIGENT NERVOUS PARLOUS
CAPTIOUS CARDINAL CAVILING
DECISIVE EXACTING JUDICIAL

SLASHING TICKLISH
CRITICISM RAP FIRE GAFF SLAM
BLAME KNOCK SLATE CRITIC
REVIEW CENSURE COMMENT
DESCANT SLASHER SLATING
ZOILISM BLUDGEON CRITIQUE
DIATRIBE JUDGMENT
CRITICIZE HIT PAN RAP RIP CARP
CRAB FLAY FLOG SKIN SLAM SLUR
TIDE YELP BLAME BLAST CAVIL
DECRY GRIPE JUDGE KNOCK ROAST
SCORE SLASH SLATE BERATE
CRITIC REBUKE REVIEW CENSURE
COMMENT CONDEMN CRITIZE
EXAMINE CRITIQUE DENOUNCE
TOMAHAWK
(— SEVERELY) FLAY JUMP
(— SLASHINGLY) SLASH SLATE
CRITIQUE CRITIC REVIEW CRITICISM
CRO CROY PAYMENT
CROAK CAW DIE GASP KILL PORK
ROUP CREAK CRONK PLUNK QUALM
QUARK SPEAK CROAPE GRUMBLE
COMPLAIN FOREBODE
CROAKER SPOT RONCO CROCUS
RONCHO TOMCOD BUBBLER
CABEZON CORBINA CORVINA
CABEZONE HARDHEAD KINGFISH
SCIAENID
CROAKING CROAKY HOARSE
RANARIAN COAXATION
CROAT CHORWAT CHROBAT
SYRMIAN
(PL.) HRVATI HERVATI
CROCARD BRABANT SCALDING
SLEEPING
CROCHET HOOK KNIT BRAID PLAIT
WEAVE CROTCHET
CROCK JAR PIG POT SMUT SOIL
SOOT STEAN STEEN STOOL CHATTY
CRITCH GOOLAH PANMUG SMUDGE
CRAGGAN TERRINE POTSHERD
CROCKERY CHINA CLOAM DISHES
PIGGERY POTWARE CLAYWARE
CROCODILE GOA CROC GATOR
CAYMAN GAVIAL JACARE LIZARD
MUGGER YACARE CRAWLER
CREEPER DIAPSID REPTILE SAURIAN
SERPENT LORICATE
CROCODILE BIRD SICSAC TROCHIL
MESSMATE
CROCUS IRID LILY SAFFRON
CROFT FARM TORP CRAFT CRYPT
FIELD GARTH VAULT BLEACH
CAVERN PARROCK
CROMLECH QUOIT CIRCLE DOLMEN
CROMMEL GORSEDD
CROMORNA CREMONA KRUMHORN
CRONE HAG AUNT CRONY WITCH
BELDAM RIBIBE BELDAME
CRONY PAL CHUM BILLY GOSSY
NETOP GIMMER GOSSIP
CROOK BEND HOOK TURN WARP
CHEAT CHINK CLEEK CRANK CROMB
CROOM CRUMP CURVE HUNCH
NIBBY PEDUM STAFF THIEF TRICK
CRUMMY INDENT TWICER CAMBUCA
CROSIER CROZIER CRUMMIE
INCURVE POTHOOK SLICKER

ARTIFICE CHISELER CRUMMOCK
SWINDLER
(— IN BRANCH) KNEE
(— OF HEAD) HEEL
(SHEPHERD'S —) CROTCH
CROOKBACKED CROUCHIE
CROOKED CAM WRY AGEE AWRY
BENT GAME WOGH AGLEY ASKEW
BOWLY CRUMP FALSE GLEED KINK
SNIDE THRAW WRONG ACROOK
AKIMBO ARTFUL ASLANT CAMMED
CRABBY CRAFTY CRANKY CURVED
DOGLEG HURLED THRAWN TRICKY
WEEWAW WEEWOW ZIGZAG
ASKANCE ASQUINT CORRUPT
CRABBED CURVOUS OBLIQUE
TURNING TWISTED WINDING
CAMSHACH THRAWART TORTUOUS
CROOKEDNESS PRAVITY RHEBOSI
CROOKNECK CASHAW CUSHAW
CROON HUM LOW BOOM LULL SING
WAIL CHIRM CRONY WHINE LAMEN
MURMUR TEEDLE COMPLAIN
CROP BOB COW CUT MAW SET TOP
CLIP CRAP CRAW KNAP MINE REAP
SETT STOW TRAP TRIM WHIP FRUI
GRAZE PLANT QUIRT SHAVE SHEAR
SHIFT SWATH TILTH TRASH BURDE
DECERP GATHER GEBBIE SILAGE
BEARING BURTHEN CRAPPIN
CURTAIL CUTTING HARVEST
MAMMONI MASHLUM TILLAGE
GLEANING PROFICHI TRASHIFY
INGLUVIES
(— CANDLEWICK) SNUFF
(— OF A HAWK) GORGE
(— OF FRUIT) HANG
(— OF GRASS) LEA LEY SWATH
SWARTH SWATHE
(— OF OYSTERS) SET
(— OF POTATOES) GARDEN
(— OUT) BASSET
(GREEN —S) SOILAGE
(INDIAN —) RABI KHARIF
(LARGE —) HIT
(RIDING —) ROP
(SECOND-GROWTH —) ROWEN
(PL.) FEED TILLAGE
CROPPED GOTCH SHAVED GOTCH
CROPPER CARVER MUCKER PURLE
GRINDER PLUMPER
CROPPING EARMARK
CROQUET ROQUE BOMBARD
CROQUETTE CECIL OYSTER
KROMESKI KROMESKY
CROSIER BAGLE CROCE CROOK
PEDUM STAFF POTENT BACULUS
CAMBUCA CROZIER PASTORAL
CROSS GO CAM CUT MIX TAU ANK
CRUX FORD FUNK MARK PASS
ROOD SIGN SOUR SPAN TREE
WOOD ANGRY CANGY CHUFF
CORSE GAMMY GURLY SURLY
TEATY TESTY THRAW TRAVE TRIA
YAPPY BISECT CHUFFY CRABBY
CRANKY CROUCH DENIAL EMBLEN
GIBBET GROUTY GRUMPY HIPPED
OUTWIT PATCHY SIGNUM SNAGGY
SNASTY SULLEN SYMBOL TEETHY

WART TOUCHY WICKED WOOLLY
THWART BECROSS CALVARY
RABBED CROSIER CROZIER
RUSADE CRUSADO FRABOUS
RETFUL FROWARD OBLIQUE
SSAGE PATIBLE PEEVISH PETTISH
OTENCE SALTIER SALTIRE
AMSHACH CRANTARA CROCIATE
ROISADE CROSSLET CROTCHED
RUCIFIX DEBRUISE DEMISANG
AMPOLD FRATCHED FRUMPISH
CTORAL PETULANT PHRAMPEL
APPISH SWASTIKA THUNDERY
RAVERSE VEXILLUM WINDMILL
- **BY PLANE)** HOP
- **ONESELF)** SAIN
- **OVER)** SPAN TRAJECT
OUBLE —) BUSINESS
ALTESE —) FIREBALL
OSSARM WISHBONE
OSSBAR CROWN JUGUM DRIVER
RANSOM
- **IN GATE)** SWORD
- **IN SHAFT)** STEMPEL STEMPLE
- **OF BALANCE)** BEAM
- **OF WINDOW)** LOCKET
OSSBEAM BAR BUNK SPUR
AVE GIRDER BOLSTER TRANSOM
RAVERSE
OSSBEARER SPREADER
OSSBILL FINCH
OSSBOW PROD RODD BRAKE
TCH PIECE PRODD TILLER
URBOW ARBALEST BALLISTA
EELBOW STOCKBOW STONEBOW
OSSBREED HUSKY METIS SANGA
NGU HYBRID
OSS CARRIER CRUCIFER
OSSCURRENT SURGING
OSSCUT DRIFT OFFSET TUNNEL
UPURE
OSSCUT SAW BRIAR
OSSCUTTER BUCKER
OSSE STICK
OSSED ACROSS SQUINT WOOFED
UCIAL THWARTING
OSSER STICKER
OSSETTE EAR ANCON ELBOW
CONE CROSET
OSS-EYE ESOTROPIA
OSS-EYED SQUINT
OSS-FERTILIZATION ALLOGAMY
YTOGAMY
OSS FORM URDE URDY
OSS-GRAINED UGLY NURLY
ARLED HICKORY CONTRARY
OSSHEAD YOKE
OSSING XG PASS CROSS LACED
XTURE PASSAGE TRAJECT
UCIATE OPPOSING TRAVERSE
OSSOVER
OSSPATCH BEAR CRAB CRANK
OUCH
OSSPIECE BAR BAIL SPAR STEP
KE BEARD GLAND GRILL ROUND
OCK THWART TOGGEL TOGGLE
LSTER TRANSOM CROSSARM
OWFOOT FOOTRAIL HEADRAIL
AVERSE CHOPSTICK

(PL.) CROSSTREE
CROSS-QUESTION TARGE TAIRGE
CROSSROAD LEET VENT WENT
WEENT CAREFOX CARFOUR
COMPITUM CROSSWAY
(PL.) TRIVIA
CROSSRUFF SAW SEESAW
CROSS-SHAPED CRUCIAL CRUCIATE
CROSS-STAFF CROSS RADIUS
CROSIER CROZIER
CROSS STROKE BIND
CROSS-TEMPERED FRUMPISH
CROSSWISE CROSS ACROSS
ATHWART ACROSTIC DIAGONAL
OVERWART TRAVERSE WEFTWISE
CROSSWAYS
CROSSWORT MAYWORT MUGWEED
MUGWORT
CROTALUM CROTAL CYMBAL
CROTCH FORK POLE POST CLEFT
NOTCH STAKE CRATCH CRUTCH
GRAINS CROTCHET
CROTCHET FAD HOOK KINK WHIM
CRANK FANCY FREAK VAGARY
CORCHAT CRANKUM
CROTCHETY KINKY CRANKY
CROUCH HUG BEND CLAP COOK
CURB DARE DROP FAWN FORM
ROOK RUCK COWER HOVER SQUAT
STOOP COORIE CRINGE CROOCH
HUDDLE HUNKER HURKLE HURTLE
SCOOCH SCOUCH CROODLE
CROWDLE SCROOCH SCRUNCH
SQUATTER
CROUCHING SQUAT CROUCHANT
CROUD SCROUGE
CROUP CRUP HIVES CRUPPER
CROUPIER DEALER TOURNEUR
CROUTON DIABLOTIN
CROW AGA CAW CRY DAW BRAG
BRAN CRAW DOWP ROOK AYLET
BOAST CRAKE CROWD EXULT
HOODY KELLY RAVEN VAUNT
CARNAL CORBIE CORVUS HOODIE
KOKAKO GORCROW GRAPNEL
JACKDAW SWAGGER ABSAROKA
BALDHEAD BLACKNEB GAVELOCK
GRAYBACK GREYBACK
CROWBAR PRY SET CROW BETTY
JEMMY JIMMY LEVER SETUP SWAPE
FORCER GABLOCK PITCHER
GAVELOCK HANDSPEC
CROWBERRY HEATH HEATHER
CROWD FRY HUG JAM MOB SET TIP
BIKE CRAM CRUT FARE HEAP HERD
HOST JOSS MONG PACK PAVE PILE
PUSH ROCK ROTE ROUT RUCK
SERR SLUE SORT STOW SWAD
TURB WOOD BUNCH CLOUD COHUE
COVEY CRAMP CRUSH CRWTH
DROVE FLOCK GROUP HORDE
HURRY PLUMP POSSE PRESS ROTTA
SERRY SHACK SHOAL STECH STIVE
STUFF SWARM THREE GROUP
WEDGE BOODLE CHORUS CLIQUE
HUBBLE HUDDLE HUSTLE IMPACT
JOSTLE MITHER MOIDER PESTER
RABBLE RESORT SCRUZE THRAVE
THREAD THRIMP THRONG THRUST

TOURBE TYMPAN VOLLEY BOUROCK
CHROTTA COMPANY CONGEST
IMPRESS JIMBANG SCROOGE
SCROUGE SQUEEZE THICKEN
THRUTCH ENTHRONG FREQUENT
JINGBANG SANDWICH SATURATE
VARLETRY GATHERING
(— **ABOUT)** FLOCK
(— **AROUND)** BESIEGE
(— **OUT)** DISPLACE
(— **TOGETHER)** HUG HOTTER
HOWDER HUDDLE CLUTTER
CONTRUDE
(**CONFUSED** —) HURRY
(**MOVING** —) DROVE
(**NOISY** —) ROUT
CROWDED CLOSE DENSE SPISS
STIFF THICK FILLED SPISSY THRONG
BUNCHED COMPACT OPPLETE
POPULAR SERRIED STIPATE
STUFFED TEEMING NUMEROUS
POPULOUS
CROWFOOT JOY PAGLE EXOGEN
PAIGLE EELWARE GOLDCUP
GOLLAND GOWLAND BANEWORT
CRAWFOOT GOLDWEED HELLWEED
CROWING COCK
CROWN CAP TAJ TIP TOP BULL COIN
GULL HELM PATE PEAK POLL RIGO
TIAR ADORN BASIL BEZEL BEZIL
CREST MITER MITRE MURAL POLOS
REGAL ROUND ROYAL TIARA
ANADEM CANTLE CIRCLE CLIMAX
CORONA DIADEM DOLLAR FILLET
INVEST LAUREL POTONG REWARD
SUMMIT TIMBER TROPHY UPWARD
VALLAR VERTEX WREATH AUREOLE
CHAPLET CORNICE CORONAL
CORONET FORETOP GARLAND
INSTALL PSCHENT STEPHEN
TONSURE CORONATE CORONULE
ENTHRONE PINNACLE SURMOUNT
TURNPIKE
(— **OF CHICORY)** ENDIVE
(— **OF EGYPT)** ATEF PSCHENT
(— **OF HEAD)** PATE SKULL CANTLE
POMMEL FORETOP
(— **OF HILL)** KNAP
(— **OF LAUREL)** BAY
(**HALF** —) GEORGE ALDERMAN
(**PIECE OF** —) BULL
(**PLANT** —) STOOL
CROWNED CORONATE LAURELED
(— **WITH ROSES)** ROSATED
CROW SHRIKE MAGPIE SQUEAKER
CROW'S NEST LOOKOUT
CROZER CHUCKER
CRUCIAL ACUTE PIVOT NEEDLE
SEVERE TRYING PIVOTAL SUPREME
TELLING CRITICAL DECISIVE
CRUCIAN CARP GIBEL
CRUCIBLE POT DISH ETNA SHOE
TEST CRUCE FOYER CRUSET
HEARTH MONKEY RETORT FURNACE
CROSSLET
CRUCIFIX PAX ROOD CROSS
CRUCIFIXION CROSS RANSOM
CRUCIFY VEX HANG KILL HARRY
MORTIFY TORMENT TORTURE
CRUCIATE

CRUDE ILL RAW BALD BARE RUDE BRUTE CRASS GREEN GROSS HAIRY HARSH ROUGH TACKY CALLOW COARSE DOUGHY INCULT KUTCHA SAVAGE UNRIPE VULGAR ARTLESS GLARING SQUALID UNCOUTH IGNORANT IMMATURE IMPOLITE INDIGEST (NOT —) DELICATE

CRUDELY HARSHLY GAUCHELY

CRUDITY CRASSNESS GAUCHERIE ROUGHNESS

CRUEL ILL FELL GRIL GRIM HARD BLACK BREEM BREME BRUTE FELON HARSH RETHE SADIC STERN WROTH BITTER BLOODY BRUTAL DIVERS DREARY FIERCE IMMANE SAVAGE SEVERE UNJUST UNKIND UNMEEK UNMILD UNRIDE BESTIAL BOARISH BRUTISH GRIMFUL INHUMAN NERONIC SCADDLE SPITOUS WILROUN BARBARIC DIABOLIC FELONOUS FIENDISH INHUMANE PITILESS RUTHLESS SADISTIC TYRANNIC

CRUELLY FELL HARD CRUEL FELLY HARSHLY

CRUELTY RIGOR DURESS SADISM DEVILRY DEVILTRY FELLNESS SEVERITY

CRUET AMA JAR JUG VIAL BURET CRUSE BOTTLE CASTER CREVET CREWET GUTTUS AMPULLA BURETTE URCEOLE

CRUISE SAIL TRIP JUNKET STOOGE (— AS A PIRATE) BUSK

CRUISER SHIP VALUER VESSEL WARSHIP ESTIMATOR

CRULLER WONDER OLYCOOK OLYKOEK TWISTER DOUGHNUT

CRUMB BIT ORT MURL PIECE LITTLE MORSEL CRIMBLE CRUMBLE MEALOCK MURLACK REMNANT FRAGMENT (PL.) PANADA PANURE MOOLINGS

CRUMBLE ROT CRIM MURL MUSH BREAK BROCK CRUSH DECAY RAVEL SLAKE SPALL SPOIL BUCKLE MOLDER MYRTLE PERISH SLOUGH CORRADE CRIMBLE MOULDER COLLAPSE (— DOWN) GRUSH (— UNDER OVERWEIGHT) FLUSH

CRUMBLED UNDURE (EASILY —) CRIMP BRUCKLE CRUMBLY

CRUMBLING SAMEL SAMMEL

CRUMBLY MURLY CRUMBY CRUMMY FRIABLE

CRUMPET CAKE MUFFIN PIKELET

CRUMPLE FOLD MOOL MUSS ROOL WISP CRUSH SCREW BUCKLE CREASE FURROW RAFFLE RUCKLE RUMPLE CRIZZLE CRUNKLE FRUMPLE SCRUNCH WRINKLE COLLAPSE CONTRACT SCRUMPLE

CRUNCH BITE CHEW MUCH CHOMP CRASH CRUMP CRUSH GNASH GRIND PRESS RUNCH CRANCH

CRINCH GRANCH GROWSE CRAUNCH SCRUNCH

CRUPPER CROUP CURPEL CURPIN TAILBAND

CRUSADE WAR JEHAD JIHAD CROISEE CAMPAIGN CROCIATE

CRUSADER PILGRIM TEMPLAR EQUITIST REFORMER (PL.) CROISES

CRUSH BOW HUG JAM BEND BORE BRAY CASE CHEW CRAM DASH MASH MILL MULL PASH RAVE STUB BRAKE BREAK BRIZZ CHAMP CRASH CRAZE CREEM CROWD FORCE FRUSH GRIND GRUSH PRESS QUASH QUELL SMASH SMUSH SQUAB SQUAT STAMP TREAD UNMAN BRUISE BURDEN CRUNCH DEFOIL DEFOUL KNATCH KNETCH SCOTCH SCRUSH SCRUZE SQUASH SQUISS SUBDUE THRING THRONG THWACK ACCABLE BECRUSH CONQUER CRACKLE CRUMPLE DEPRESS DESTROY OPPRESS OVERRUN REPRESS SCRUNCH SCRUNGE SHATTER SQUEEZE SQUELCH SUCCUMB TRAMPLE COMPRESS FORBREAK OVERCOME SQUABASH SUPPRESS (— BEANS) NIB (— HAT) BONNET (— IN) STAVE (— ROCK) DOLLY DOLLEY DOLLIE (— SPIRIT) BREAK

CRUSHABLE QUASHY

CRUSHED TAME BROKEN ECRASE MUSHED CONTRITE

CRUSHER NIBBER

CRUSHING FIERCE BRUISING SMASHING SQUABASH

CRUST FUR CAKE HULL RIND SCAB SHELL SKULL COFFIN CRUSTA ESCHAR GRATIN HARDEN RONDLE SCRUFF ABAISSE CALICHE COATING ENCRUST INCRUST CARAPACE PELLICLE SCUTULUM WINEBALL DURICRUST (— ON WINE) ARGAL ARGOL (PIE —) HUFF COFFIN (PL.) SORDES

CRUSTA PES

CRUSTACEAN BUG APUS CRAB FLEA SCUD ZOEA ALIMA CARID LOUSE PRAWN SCREW SCROW CYPRID ENDITE ISOPOD SHRIMP SLATER SQUILL ARTEMIA COPEPOD CRAYLET DAPHNID DECAPOD GRIBBLE HAYSEED LOBSTER SQUAGGA SQUILLA BARNACLE CRAYFISH GAMMARID LERNAEAN MONOCULE SQUILLID

CRUSTADE DARIOLE

CRUSTY CURT BLUFF BLUNT RUSTY TESTY MOROSE SULLEN CRABBED PEEVISH PETTISH STARCHY SNAPPISH

CRUTCH FORK STILT CLUTCH CRATCH CROTCH POTENT SADDLE SCATCH STADDLE

CRUX NUB GIST HALF PITH CROSS POINT PUZZLE RIDDLE PROBLEM

CRUX ANSATA ANKH

CRWTH ROTA ROTE CROWD CRUT ROTTA ROTTE CROUTH CHROTTA

CRY HO BOO CAW CRI FAD HOA H OLE PIP SOB YIP BAWL BELL BUN CALL COWL CROW EVOE FALL GLAM GOWL HAIL HAWK HOOT HOWL KEEN MEWL NOTE OYES OYEZ PULE RAGE RAME RANE RE RERD SCRY SIKE TOOT WAIL WE YELL YELP BARLA BLART BLORE CHEVY CLEPE CRAKE CROUP CRUNK GREDE GREET GROAN QUEAK RUMOR SHOUT SOUND TROAT UTTER VOGUE WHEWL WHINE WHULE WRAWL BARLEY BELLOW BOOHOO CHIVVY CLAMC DEMAND ENSIGN LAMENT OUTCR QUETHE SCREAM SHRIEK SLOGAI SNIVEL SQUALL SQUAWL SQUEAL TONGUE WIMICK YAMMER EXCLA FASHION HOSHANA SCREECH SPRAICH GARDYLOO PROCLAIM SCRONACH (— ALOUD) BLART GREDE (— AT SIGHT OF WHALE) FALL (— DOWN) DOWNCRY BERATTLE (— FOR TRUCE) BARLA BARLY BARLEY (— HOARSELY) CROUP (— LIKE ELEPHANT) BARR TRUMP (— LIKE PIG) WRINE (— OF A BAT) CHIP (— OF ABORIGINES) COOEE (— OF BACCHANALS) EVOE (— OF BIRD) CAW COO PEW BOC CAWK CLANG BIRDCALL (— OF BITTERN) BILL (— OF CAT) MEW MEWL MIAOU MIAOW MIAUL MIAUW CALLING (— OF CONTEMPT) BOO (— OF DEER) BELL (— OF ENTHUSIASM) BANZAI (— OF GOOSE) HONK YANG (— OF GUINEA HEN) POTRACK (— OF HOUND) MUTE MUSIC (— OF JACKAL) PHEAL PHEALE PHEEAL (— OF MOURNING) KEEN TANGI (— OF NEWBORN CHILD) VAGITU (— OF RAVEN) QUALM (— OF SHEEP) BAA BLAT BLEAT (— OF SNIPE) SCAPE (— OF SORROW) ULLAGONE (— OF SURRENDER) KAMERAD (— OF WATCHMAN) WATCH (— OUT) BAY BAWL BRAY GALE GAPE HOOT HOWL JERK SCRY BLORE CHIRM CLAIM ESCRY SHC HALLOO HOLLER SCREAM SHRIEI THREAP THROPE BREATHE EXCL. RECLAIM DISCLAIM PROCLAIM (— TO CLEAR PASSAGE) HALL (— TO COMBATANTS) BAILE (— UP) CRACK (BATTLE —) CRY ENSIGN MONTJ(GERONIMO MONTJOYE

RINKING —) RIVO
IOARSE —) CROAK
IUNTING —) TIVY CHEVY CHIVY
HEVVY STABOY YOICKS TALLYHO
ILLILLOO
ROLONGED —) RANE
IALLYING —) SLOGAN
IAUCOUS —) CATCALL
IHRILL) SKIRL SQUEAK SQUEAL
CREECH YALLOCK
IAR —) DIN ALALA SLOGAN
VORDLESS —) KEEN ULULU
YING PIPING URGING CLAMANT
EINOUS VAGIENT PRESSING
ECREANT
- **OF HOUND)** BELLING
YPT PIT CRAFT CROFT CROWD
IULT CAVERN GROTTO RECESS
HROUD CHAMBER FOLLICLE
YPTIC DARK VAGUE HIDDEN
CCILT SECRET OBSCURE ELLIPTIC
YSTICAL SIBYLLIC
YPTOGRAM CODE CRYPT CIPHER
YPTOGRAPH GEMATRIA
YPTOGRAPHER VIGENERE
YPTORCHID RIDGLING
YSOPHANIC RHEUMIC
YSTAL XL ICE DIAL DOME HARD
IS SEED XTAL CLEAR GLASS
RAIN LUCID LUNET TABLE GLASSY
MPID MIRROR NEEDLE PEBBLE
JARTZ TABLET ACICULA DIAMOND
PLOID GLASSIE LUNETTE ORTHITE
VOLING ULEXITE YAJEINE ZOISITE
VELING FOURLING PELLUCID
RICHITE TRILLING
- **FOREIGN TO ROCK)** XENOCYST
INE —) BERYL
CE —S IN WATER)** FRAZIL
EEDLE-SHAPED —S) RAPHIDES
OCK —) BRISTOL
WIN —) TWIN MACLE TWINDLE
VOLING FOURLING
L.) DRUSE GRAIN
YSTAL GAZE SCRY
YSTAL GAZER SEER SCRYER
RYER
YSTALLINE PURE CRYSTAL
LLUCID
YSTALLITE BELONITE TRICHITE
CILLITE SCOPULITE
YSTALLIZE FIX FIRM JELL CANDY
GAR NEEDLE CONGEAL SOLIDIFY
YSTALLOGRAPHY LEPTOLOGY
HAPED SIGMATE
NIDIUM COMB
NOPHORE RIB NUDA CYDIPPID
LLYFISH
DRA MANZANA
I FRY PEN BEAR CHIT COOP
ED TOTO STALL WHELP LIONET
VICE CODLING REPORTER
SCOUT) WEBELOS

CUBA

Y: NIPE PIGS
PE: CRUZ MAISI LUCRECIA
PITAL: HAVANA

CIGAR: HAVANA
COIN: PESO CENTAVO CUARENTA
DANCE: CONGA RUMBA DANZON
  RHUMBA GUARACHA PACHANGA
FALLS: TOA AGABAMA CABURNI
GULF: MEXICO ANAMARIA
  BATABANO
INDIAN: CARIB TAINO ARAWAK
ISLAND: PINES
ISLANDS: SABANA CAMAGUEY
MEASURE: VARA BOCOY TAREA
  CORDEL FANEGA
MOUNTAIN: TURQUINO
MOUNTAINS: CRISTAL MAESTRA
  ORGANOS TRINIDAD
PROVINCE: HAVANA ORIENTE
  CAMAGUEY MATANZAS
RIVER: ZAZA CAUTO
SWAMP: ZAPATA
TOWN: COLON MANES BAYAMO
  GUINES HAVANA BARACOA
  HOLGUIN PALMIRA ARTEMISA
  CAMAGUEY GUAYABAL
  MATANZAS SANTIAGO
TREE: JIQUE JIQUI
WEIGHT: LIBRA TERCIO

CUBAN LILY SCILLA
CUBBYHOLE NOOK CUBBY
CUBE CUT DIE NOB KNOB BLOCK
  EIGHT SOLID TIMBO BABASCO
  CUBELET TESSELA TESSERA
  BARBASCO QUADRATE
  (— **OF BREAD)** CROUTON
  (MEAT —S) CABOB KABOB KEBOB
  (PL.) DICE
CUBIC SOLID CUBOID CUBICAL
CUBICALLY DIEWISE
CUBIC CENTIMETER FLUIGRAM
CUBIC METER STERE
CUBICLE BAY CELL ROOM BOOTH
  CABIN NICHE STALL ALCOVE
  CARREL CARRELL
CUBIT ELL CODO HATH COVID
  HASTA COUDEE
CUB SHARK LAMIA GALEID REQUIEM
CUCKING STOOL THEW TUMBLER
  TUMBREL TUMBRIL
CUCKOLD TUP HORN BECCO
  VULCAN WITTOL ACTAEON
  CORNUTE CORNUTO HORNIFY
  RAMHEAD COKEWOLD
CUCKOLDED FORKED UNICORN
CUCKOLDRY HORNWORK
CUCKOO ANI COWK CUCK FOOL
  GOUK GOWK KOEL KOIL CLOCK
  CRAZY KOKIL SILLY COUCAL DIDRIC
  HUNTER KOBIRD BOOBOOK
  CHATAKA DIEDRIC KOWBIRD
  SIRKEER CHOWCHOW PICARIAN
  RAINBIRD RAINFOWL
CUCKOOFLOWER HEAD PAGLE
  SPINK CUCKOO PAIGLE HEADACHE
  MILKMAID
CUCKOOPINT ARUM RAMP AARON
  BOBBIN DRAGON BUCKRAM
  OXBERRY MANDRAKE
CUCKOO SPIT WOODSERE

CUCULLATE COWLED HOODED
  COVERED
CUCUMBER CUKE PEPO GOURD
  CONGER CUCURB PEPINO PICKLE
  GHERKIN PICKLER CUCURBIT
  PEPONIDA PEPONIUM
  (BITTER —) COLOCYNTH
  (SHRIVELED —) CRUMPLING
  (WILD —) CREEPER
CUCURBIT BODY FLASK GOURD
  CUCURB ALEMBIC MATRASS
CUD CHEW QUID BOLUS QUEED
  RUMEN CUDGEL
CUDBEAR CORK PERSIO PERSIS
  CUDWEED
CUDDLE HUG LAP PET CARESS
  COSSET FONDLE HUGGLE KIDDLE
  KIUTLE NESTLE PETTLE CROODLE
  CRUDDLE EMBRACE SMUGGLE
  SNOOZLE SNUGGLE
CUDDLESOME HUGGABLE
CUDDY ASS LOUT BRIBE CABIN
  DONKEY GALLEY PANTRY CUDEIGH
CUDGEL BAT CUD BEAT CANE CLUB
  CRAB DRUB KENT MACE RACK
  RUNG TREE BASTE BATON DRIVE
  KEBBY KEVEL LINCH LINGE SHRUB
  STAFF STAVE STICK THUMP TOWEL
  ALPEEN BALLOW BASTON BILLET
  GIBBET KEBBIE LIBBET THRASH
  WASTER BELABOR BOURDON
  DRUBBER SWADDLE SWINGLE
  TROUNCE BLUDGEON SHILLALA
  THWACKER
CUDWEED ENAENA CATFOOT
CUE QU NOD TAG TIP HINT MAST
  TAIL WINK BRAID CLUFF PLAIT
  QUEUE TWIST PROMPT SIGNAL
  PIGTAIL
  (BILLIARD —) MAST STICK
  (SHUFFLEBOARD —) SHOVEL
  (TIP OF —) LEATHER
CUFF BOX BANK BLOW GOWF SLAM
  SLAP SLUG SWAT TURF CLOUT
  FIGHT GOWFF MISER SCUFF SCUFT
  SMITE SOUSE BUFFET CODGER
  FENDER MITTEN STRIKE TURNUP
  COLPHEG SCUFFLE WHERRET
  GAUNTLET HANDBLOW HANDCUFF
  TURNBACK
CUIR DORADO
CUIRASS CURACE CURATE CURIET
  LORICA THORAX
CUIRASSIER LOBSTER
CUISINE FOOD MENU TABLE
  COOKERY KITCHEN
CUITLATEC TECO
CUL-DE-SAC POCKET STRAIT
  IMPASSE
CULL OPT CAST COIL DUPE GULL
  PICK PIKE SIFT SORT ELECT GLEAN
  PLUCK ASSORT CHOOSE GARBLE
  GATHER REMOVE SELECT CULLING
  SEPARATE
CULLET SCRAP
CULM COOM HAULM SLACK COOMBE
  REFUSE DEPOSIT
  (PL.) SIRKI SIRKY
CULMINATION END ACME APEX

AUGE CULM NOON ROOF BLOOM CREST CROWN HIGHT POINT APOGEE CLIMAX CULMEN CUMBLE HEIGHT PERIOD SUMMIT VERTEX ZENITH BLOWOFF
CULPABILITY BLAME GUILT DEMERIT
CULPABLE FAULTY GUILTY LACHES SINFUL IMMORAL BLAMABLE CRIMINAL
CULPRIT FELON CONVICT CRIMINAL OFFENDER
CULT CLAN DADA SECT CREED KUKSU CHURCH CULTUS DOMNEI MANISM NUDISM RITUAL SCHOOL SHINTO AMIDISM DADAISM ICONISM MYALISM MYSTERY WORSHIP DEVILISM HUMANISM SATANISM
CULTCH CUTCH STOOL SCULCH
CULTIVATE EAR HOE CROP DISC DISK FARM GROW PLOW REAR TEND TILL WORK DRESS EARTH LABOR NURSE RAISE STUDY TRAIN AFFECT FOSTER FURROW HARROW MANAGE MANURE PLOUGH RATOON SARCLE SCHOOL ACQUIRE CHERISH CONTOUR CULTURE EDUCATE EMBRACE EXPLOIT HUSBAND IMPROVE NOURISH PREPARE SCRATCH CIVILIZE
(— **FAVOR**) BOOTLICK
CULTIVATED ABAD TAME CIVIL GROWN POLITE SATIVE TOILED POLITIC REFINED CULTURED
(**ARTIFICIALLY** —) HOTHOUSE
CULTIVATION CROP TILTH FINISH GROWTH CULTURE TILLAGE TILTURE LABORAGE MANURAGE
(— **IN MANNERS**) FINISH
(**MENTAL** —) HUMANITY
CULTIVATOR JAT KMET RYOT ILAVA SULKY FARMER GADABA HARROW ILAVAN MAMOTY MILLER RIDGER TILLER FLORIST GRUBBER HUSBAND MEADOWER ROSARIAN SCUFFLER
(— **GANG**) RIG
(**PL.**) LAETI
CULTURAL HUMANIST
CULTURE ART AGAR STAB KULLI NASCA NAZCA SHAKE SLANT SLOPE TAJIN TASTE TILTH JHUKAR KULTUR POLISH STREAK WILTON ABASHEV ANANINO AZILIAN IRANISM JHANGAR KAYENTA SOCIETY STARTER TILLAGE HUMANISM LEARNING
(**ESKIMO** —) DORSET
(**MEXICAN** —) MAZAPAN
CULTURED CIVIL LETTERED
CULVERIN SLING CULVER LANTACA PELICAN SPIROLE
CULVERT FOX GOUT DRAIN SLUIT BRIDGE CONDUIT CULBERT PINNOCK PONCEAU OVERPASS
CUMBER BURDEN CUMMER SHACKLE
CUMBERSOME GOURD HEAVY CLUMSY UNRIDE AWKWARD LUGSOME ONEROUS WEIGHTY CUMBROUS UNWIELDY
CUMMER GIRL LASS WOMAN KIMMER

CUMMERBUND BAND BELT SASH
CUMULATE HEAP GATHER COMBINE
CUMULATIVE CHAIN SUMMATIVE
CUNA CUEVA DARIEN
CUNEIFORM ULNARE WEDGED
CUNNER CANOE NIPPER WRASSE BURGALL CHOGSET GOLDNEY NIBBLER BERGGYLT BLUEFISH CORKWING GILTHEAD
CUNNING ART OLD SHY SLY WIT ARCH CUTE DEEP FAST FINE FOXY KEEN SLIM SNOD TRAP WILY WISE CANNY CRAFT DOWNY FAVEL GUILE LOOPY PAUKY PAWKY POKEY SHARP SMART ADROIT ARTFUL ASTUTE CALLID CLEVER CRAFTY DAEDAL DECEIT ENGINE FOXERY PRETTY SHREWD SUBTLE SUPPLE TRICKY WISDOM COMPASS CRAFTLY CURIOUS FINESSE KNOWING PARLISH PARLOUS POLITIC PRACTIC SLEIGHT SUBTILE VARMINT VULPINE CONTOISE DEXTROUS MANAGERY QUENTISE SKILLFUL SLEIGHTY STEALTHY YEPELEIC
CUNNINGLY YEPLY YEPELY
CUP AMA BOX CAN DOP MUG NOG POT TOT TUN TYG CELL DOPP HORN LOTA PECE SHOE SKEW TASS TOSS BOUSE CALIX CHARK COGUE COPPE CRUSE CYLIX DEPAS GLASS GODET GRAIL KITTY PHIAL SCALE STEIN STOOP STOUP TAZZA THECA BEAKER BICKER BUCKET BUMPER CAPPIE CHOANA COTYLA CRATER CUPULA DOBBIN EGGCUP EYECUP FALSIE FESSEL FINJAN GOBLET JICARA KOTYLE MAZARD NAGGIN NOGGIN OXHORN POTION RUMKIN TASSIE VESSEL BRIMMER CAPSULE CHALICE CHEERER CYATHUS GODDARD KYATHOS QUONIAM SCYPHUS SHERBET STIRRUP THIMBLE TRINKET VENTOSE BRIDECUP GRADUATE STANDARD TJANTING
(— **FOR HOLDING DIAMOND**) DOP DOPP
(— **FOR PERFUMES**) CONCH
(— **FOR YEAST**) SKEP
(— **IN SAUCER OF ALCOHOL**) ETNA
(— **OF FLOWER**) BELL
(— **OF TEA**) DISH SPEED OYSTER
(— **ON BULLET**) GASCHECK
(— **WITH COVER**) HANAP
(**ASSAYING** —) CUPEL
(**DRINKING** —) CAN MUG NUT TIG TUN TYG CANN HORN TASS TOSS GODET BEAKER GOBLET HOLMOS RUMMER CHALICE GODDARD TRINKET
(**FAIRY** —) COOLWORT
(**FILLED** —) BUMPER
(**IRON** —) CULOT MUSHROOM
(**LARGE** —) FACER
(**LEATHER** —) WELL GISPIN
(**LONG-HANDLED** —) CYATH DIPPER CYATHUS KYATHOS
(**NAUTICAL** —) THIEF

(**ORNAMENTAL** —) TAZZA
(**PAPER** —) DIXIE
(**PASTRY** —) DARIOLE
(**PRIZE** —) PEWTER
(**SACRED** —) GRAIL
(**SHALLOW** —) CYLIX TAZZA TAST CAPSULE
(**SMALL** —) DOP NOG TOT DOPP TASS DOBBIN NAGGIN NOGGIN TASSIE
(**SQUARE** —) MADDER METHER
(**STIRRUP** —) BONAILIE
(**WOODEN** —) COG COGUE CAPPE CAPPIE METHER QUAICH
(**PL.**) VALONIA
CUPBEARER HEBE SAKI CUPPER GANYMEDE
CUPBOARD CUB KAS BOLE CASE COIN SAFE AMBRY CHEST CUBBY CUDDY HUTCH PRESS ABACUS BUFFET CLOSET LARDER LOCKEF PANTRY SPENCE ARMOIRE CABIN DRESSER SKIBBET ALHACENA CREDENCE CREDENZA TROSTERA
(**ARCHERY** —) ASCHAM
CUPEL TEST
CUPFUL CUP CAROUSE
CUP HOLDER ZARF
CUPID DAN AMOR EROS LOVE PUTTO CHERUB AMORINO AMOUF
(**PL.**) PUTTI
CUPIDITY LUST GREED DESIRE AVARICE AVIDITY LONGING APPETITE RAPACITY
CUPOLA DOME KILN TYPE VAULT BELFRY TURRET CALOTTE FURNA LANTERN LOOKOUT CIMBORIO COCKLOFT
CUPOLAMAN HEATER
CUPPING GLASS VENTOSE
CUPSEED NUTSEED
CUP-SHAPED PEZIZOID SCYPHAT
CUPULE CUP BOLSTER CYATHUS THUMBMARK
CUR DOG YAP FICE FIST FYCE MU TIKE TYKE FEIST KEOUT MESSAN MESSIN BOBTAIL MONGREL WHAPPET
CURARE URARE URARI OORALI WOORALI
CURASSOW MITU COPPY HOCCO MITUA PAUXI
CURATE ABBE CURA AGENT VICA MINISTER
CURATIVE HEALING IATRICAL PHYSICAL REMEDIAL SALUTARY SANATIVE
CURATOR KEEPER STEWARD GUARDIAN OVERSEER
CURB BIT LID CRUB FOIL KERB R SKID SNIP SNUB BRAKE CHECK CRIMP CURVE GUARD LIMIT MOU ARREST BRIDLE COERCE COLLAF DECKLE GOVERN HAMPER STIFLE STRAIN SUBDUE THWART CONTR CURBING INHIBIT REFRAIN REPR SHACKLE ATTEMPER COMPESCE MODERATE RESTRAIN RESTRICT WITHHOLD

(OFFICIAL —) LID
(WELL —) PUTEAL
URCULIO TURK WEEVIL
URD CRUD DAHI CHEESE CURDLE
CASEINE CLABBER CONGEAL
COAGULUM
— IN MILK) ZIEGA
—S AND WHEY) SLIP PINJANE
BEAN —) TOFU
PL.) FLEETINGS
URDLE CAP LOP RUN SAM SET
CRIM CURD EARN LEEP QUAR SAMM
SOUR TURN WHIG YERN CARVE
QUAIL QUARL SPOIL YEARN CAILLE
LAPPER LOBBER LOPPER POSSET
QUARLE CLABBER CONGEAL
CRIDDLE CRUDDLE THICKEN
CONDENSE
URDLED CURDLY QUARRED
SHOTTEN
NOT —) UNCRUDDED
URE DIP DRY DUN FIX BEEF BOOT
CARE CORN HEAL HEED HELP JERK
MEND SALT SANE SAVE AMEND
BLOAT BOTEN LEECH REEST SMEEK
SMOKE CHARGE CURATE KIPPER
PHYSIC PRIEST RECURE REMEDY
SEASON SUCCOR TEMPER WARISH
BESMOKE RECOVER RESTORE
THERAPY TREACLE ANTIDOTE
BARBECUE CURATION GUERISON
PRESERVE REVOCERY
— BY SMOKING) GAMMON SMUDGE
— FISH) DUN ROUSE
— GRASS) HAY
— HAY) WIN
— HERRINGS) BLOAT
— IN SUN) RIZZAR
— SKINS) DRESS
COUGH —) SAPA SAPE
URE-ALL BALM AVENS ELIXIR
REMEDY PANACEA THERIAC
URED SALT BLOATED
URIOSITY CURIO INTEREST
— OF SMALL VALUE) GABION
—S OF THE CITY) LIONS
PL.) CURIOSA
URIOUS ODD NOSY RARE SELI
QUEER SELLE SELLY PRYING
QUAINT SNOOPY CUNNING STRANGE
UNUSUAL FREAKISH MEDDLING
PECULIAR SINGULAR
URL BOB BEND COIL FEAK FURL
LINK LOCK PURL ROLL WAVE WIND
CKER CANON CRIMP CRISP DILDO
RILL FRIZZ QUIRL SPIRE TRESS
WIRE TWIST BERGER BUCKLE
CANNON CRUCHE CURDLE FROWSE
MULLET RIPPLE SPIRAL WRITHE
RIDDLE CRIMPLE CRINKLE
ROCKET CRUDDLE EARLOCK
LEXURE FRIZZLE FROUNCE
RINGLET SERPENT TENDRIL
WHISKER FAVORITE LOVELOCK
QUIGGLE
— HAIR) CROOK
— OF WIG) SNAKE
— ON FOREHEAD) CRUCHE
ROUCHE

(— OVER) BREAK
(— UP) CRUMP HUNCH SNIRL
HUDDLE SHRINK SNUGGLE
(FRINGE OF —S) FRISETTE
FRIZETTE
(METAL —) CHIP
(SMALL —) CROCK
CURLED CRISP FUZZY KINKY SPIRY
CIRRATE COCKLED CRISPED
FRIZZLY SAVOYED WREATHY
CRISPATE GAUFFRED GOFFERED
HELICINE SCROLLED
CURLER GOFFER TEASER CRIMPER
FRIZZER MULLETS
CURLEW FUTE JACK SPOW KIOEA
SNIPE SPOWE WHAAP WHAUP
DIKKOP MARLIN SMOKER BANKERA
BUSTARD DOEBIRD BLUELEGS
WHIMBREL
CURLICUE ESS CAPER CURVE
CASSIS PARAPH SQUIRL FLOURISH
PURLICUE SCRIGGLE SQUIGGLE
CURLING MARK TEE
CURLING MATCH SPIEL
CURLING STONE IRON STONE
LOOFIE GRANITE
(— SPIN) RAISE
CURLY WAVY CRISP CRULL OUNDY
RIPPLED CRINKLED
(— HAIR) VEDDOID
CURMUDGEON CRAB CHURL MISER
GLEYDE GROUCH NIGGARD
CURMUDGEONLY STINGY
CURRANT PASA BERRY CASSIS
RAISIN RIZZAR RIZZLE CORINTH
(PL.) RIBES SPICE
CURRANT BUN WIG WIGG
CURRAWONG SQUEAKER STREPERA
CURRENCY CASH COIN PASS BILLS
CATER MONEY SCRIP SERIES
SPECIE PASSAGE WILDCAT
(FRACTIONAL —) SPONDULIX
(SHELL —) UHLLO
CURRENT NOW WAY EDDY FLOW
FLUX FORD RACE RIFE TIDE VEIN
WAFT ALIVE DRIFT GOING RAPID
ROUST SCOUR SWIFT TENOR TESLA
TREND USUAL ACTUAL COEVAL
COMMON COURSE DOUCHE DURANT
FLUENT LIVING MOTION MOVING
OFFSET OUTSET RECENT RULING
SLUICE STRAND STREAM TONGUE
VOLANT COUNTER DRAUGHT
FLOWING FRESHET GENERAL
INDRAFT INSTANT PASSANT
PRESENT RUNNING STICKLE
THERMAL TORRENT CURRANCE
DOWNCAST FREQUENT MILLRACE
PASSABLE TIDERACE TODAYISH
UNDERTOW
(— IN SPEECH) WAIF
(AIR —) DRAFT SHEET SPLIT
BREEZE DRAUGHT DOWNCAST
DOWNFLOW
(ELECTRIC —) STRAY
(HOT —) BACK
(JAPAN —) KUROSHIO KUROSIWO
(RAPID —) SWIFT TONGUE
(SOUND —) DISTORTION

(STRONG —) GALE ROOST ROUST
CURRENTLY ANYMORE
CURRISH BASE CYNICAL DOGGISH
IGNOBLE SNARLING
CURRY COMB DRUB KARI CLEAN
DRESS GROOM BRUISE CAJOLE
CARREE POWDER PREPARE
TARKEEAN
(— FAVOR) HUG NUT QUILL COTTON
SMOOGE SMOODGE
CURSE BAN BANE BLOW CUSS DAMN
OATH PIZE WARY BLAST BLESS
CORSE SHREW SPELL SWEAR
WEARY WINZE DETEST DEVOTE
GOOFER GUFFER MAKUTU MALIGN
MAUGER MAUGRE BESHREW
MALISON ANATHEMA EXECRATE
FORSPEAK
CURSED DASH CUSSED DAMNED
DASHED ACCURSED
CURSER WARIER
CURSING BLESSING BLASPHEMY
CURSIVE RUNNING
CURSORY FAST BRIEF HASTY QUICK
SHORT FITFUL ROVING SPEEDY
PASSANT PASSING SHALLOW
CARELESS RAMBLING
CURT BUFF RUDE TART BLUFF
BLUNT BRIEF BRUSK SHORT SQUAB
TERSE ABRUPT CURTAL CUTTED
SNIPPY BRUSQUE CONCISE CRYPTIC
LACONIC CAVALIER SNAPPISH
SNIPPETY SUCCINCT
CURTAIL CUT LOP CLIP CROP DOCK
PARE STOP ABATE ELIDE SHORT
SLASH STUNT TRUNK DECURT
LESSEN REDUCE ABRIDGE BOBTAIL
CRACKLE SHORTEN DIMINISH
MINORATE RETRENCH
CURTAILED TAIL SHORT STUNT
CURTAL BOBTAIL CONCISE
ABRIDGED
CURTAIN END BOOM DROP IRIS
MASK VEIL WALL BLIND DRAPE
SCENE SHADE SHEET VELUM
COSTER HANGER PURDAH SCREEN
SHROUD CEILING CONCEAL
CORTINE DRAPERY HANGING
VITRAGE·ASBESTOS PORTIERE
TRAVERSE
(CHURCH —) RIDDEL ENDOTYS
ENDOTHYS
(THEATRE —) SCRIM TEASER
TRAVELER TORMENTER
CURTAIN ROD TRINGLE
CURTAIN STRETCHER SCRAY
STRAINER
CURTAL CRAPE COURTAL CURTLAX
CURTSY BOB BOW DIP DOP BECK
DROP JOUK KNEE CONGE HONOR
CURCHY
CURUBA CASSA BANANA
CURVATED STUNT HOOKED
CURVATURE ARC PLY ARCH BENT
BOOL CURL CURVE SHEER SINUS
CAMBER CURVITY ADUNCITY
APOPHYGE CYRTOSIS GRYPOSIS
KYPHOSIS LORDOSIS
(— OF DECK) SHEER

(— OF LEGS) RHEBOSIS
(— OF SHOE SOLE) SWING
(— OF SPINE) KYPHOSIS SCOLIOSIS
(— OF STOMACH) FUNDUS
(— OF STRAKE) SPILING
CURVE ARC BOW CUP ESS SAG
ARCH BEND BOUT COME CURB
FADE HOOK KNEE LINE OGEE TURN
VEER WIND AMBIT BIGHT BREAK
CONIC CROOK CRUMP CUBIC HELIX
NONIC OGIVE PEDAL POLAR QUIRK
SLICE SWEEP SWIRL TARVE TREND
TWIST WITCH BOUGHT CAMBER
CIRCLE DEFLEX JORDAN SOLVUS
SPIRAL SPRING TOROID WIMPLE
ADIABAT BRACKET CAUSTIC CIRCUIT
CISSOID COMPASS CONCAVE
CONTOUR COSEISM CURVITY
CYCLOID ELLIPSE ENVELOP
FESTOON FLEXURE INCURVE
INFLECT LIMACON PHUGOID
PROFILE SCALLOP SINUATE
SOLIDUS CARDIOID CATENARY
CONCHOID DYGOGRAM ELASTICA
EXTRADOS FADEAWAY INTRADOS
INVOLUTE LIGATURE LIQUIDUS
OPHIURID PARABOLA SINUSOIS
TONOGRAM TRACTRIX
(— DESCRIBED BY GRAPH) GRAM
(— IN HANDRAIL) KNEE
(— IN PLANKING) HANG
(— OF ARCH) INTRADOS
(— OF BALL) DROP
(— OF BIT) LIBERTY
(— OF FINGERNAIL) GRYPOSIS
(— OF HORSE'S NECK) CREST
(— OF PLANK) SNY
(— OF SHIP'S BOW) FLAIR FLARE
(— OF TIMBER) CUP
(— SATISFYING EQUATION) BRANCH
(— SPACE) KNOT
(— WHEN DRAWN) COME
(BASEBALL —) SNAKE
(CRICKET —) SWERVE
(DOUBLE —) CIMA CYMA
(VERTICAL —) RAMP
CURVED BENT SOFT ADUNC CORBE
CURVE CURVY ROUND WOUND
CONVEX CURVEY GYRATE HAMATE
TURNED ARCUATE ARRONDI
CONCAVE CROOKED CURVANT
EMBOWED FALCATE SIGMOID
ADUNCOUS ANCHORAL AQUILINE
ARCIFORM CRUMPLED CYGNEOUS
DECURVED EXCURVED SCROLLED
ARCHIFORM
CURVET HOP LEAP LOPE SKIP TURN
BOUND CAPER FRISK PRANK VAULT
CAVORT CROUPE FROLIC GAMBOL
PRANCE PANNADE CORVETTA
CROUPADE
CURVING SPIRY SIMOUS TWISTY
AQUILINE DRAWDOWN
(— IN) CONCAVE
(SMOOTHLY —) FAIR
CUSH-CUSH CARA YAMPEE
CUSHION BAG COD MAT PAD PIG
BALL BANK BOSS PUFF SEAT SUNK
TRIM GADDI GADHI PANEL SQUAB

TRUSH BUFFER INSOLE JOCKEY
MUSNUD PILLOW SACHET BOLSTER
BRIOCHE COSSHEN HASSOCK
KNEELER MUFFLER PILLION
REPOSAL ROOTCAP CUTIDURE
OREILLER PULVINAR
(LACE-MAKERS —) BOTT
(PIN —) PRINCOD
(SEAT —) BANKER
(TAILOR'S —) HAM
CUSHIONING DUNNAGE
CUSHIONLIKE PULVINAR
CUSHION PLANT POLSTER
CUSHIONY PADDY
CUSHITIC NUBIAN
CUSK TUSK TORSK BURBOT CATFISH
CUSP APEX CONE HORN PEAK
ANGLE POINT STYLE TOOTH
CORNER SPINODE ENTOCONE
HYPOCONE METACONE PARACONE
CUSPIDOR GABOON CRACHOIR
SPITTOON
CUSSO KOSO KOUSOU BRAYERA
BRAZERA
CUSTARD FLAN FOOL FLAWN
DOUCET DOWCET CHARLET PARFAIT
FLUMMERY DIABLOTIN
CUSTARD APPLE ANONA ANNONA
PAWPAW CORAZON SWEETSOP
CUSTODIAN HACK GUARD BAILEE
CUSTOS KEEPER SEXTON WARDEN
WARDER CURATOR JANITOR
CERBERUS CLAVIGER GUARDIAN
CONCIERGE
CUSTODY LAP BAIL CARE HOLD
KEEP WARD TRUST ARREST
CHARGE SAFETY YEMSEL CONTROL
DURANCE KEEPING TUITION
COMMENDA CUSTODIA HANDFAST
SECURITY
CUSTOM FAD LAW MOS PAD TAX
URE USE ASAL DUTY FORM GARB
MODE MORE RITE ROTE RULE THEW
TOLL WONE WONT FUERO GUISE
HABIT HAUNT RITUS STYLE SUNNA
TRADE TREAD TRICK USAGE VOGUE
BYRLAW DASTUR DHARMA GROOVE
IMPOST MANNER MINHAG MONTEM
PRAXIS SUNNAH USANCE COSTUME
DUSTOOR DUSTOUR FASHION
FORMULA HALAKAH TRIBUTE
USAUNCE WARNOTH BUSINESS
ENDOGAMY HABITUDE PRACTICE
(BINDING —) LAW
(BUSINESS —) TRADE GOODWILL
(CHURCH —) COMITY
(CORRUPT —) ABUSE
(FESTIVAL —) HOCKING
(OUTMODED —) ARCHAISM
(PRIMITIVE —) COUVADE
(RURAL —) HEAVING
(SECRET —) SANDE
(TEMPORARY —) FAD VOGUE
(PL.) MORES MOEURS HAIKWAN
FOLKLORE
CUSTOMARILY USUALLY CUSTOMLY
CUSTOMARY PER RIFE TAME USED
NOMIC USUAL COMMON SOLEMN
VULGAR WONTED CLASSIC

GENERAL USITATE EVERYDAY
FAMILIAR HABITUAL ORTHODOX
(NOT —) INSOLENT
CUSTOMER CHAP BUYER CLIENT
PATRON SUCKER ACCOUNT
CALLANT CHAPMAN PATIENT
SHOPPER MERCHANT PROSPECT
(PRINTER'S —) AUTHOR
(TOUGH —) HARDCASE
(PL.) CUSTOM CLIENTELE
CUSTOMHOUSE ADUANA DOGANA
DOUANE
CUSTOM-MADE BESPOKE
BESPOKEN
CUSTOMS OFFICER SHARK WAITE
CUT AX ADZ AXE BOB DAG DAP DIE
HAG HEW KIT LOP MOW NIP RIT
SAW SNY TAP ADZE BANG BITE
BOLO BOLT BUZZ CHIP CHOP CLIP
CROP DADO DOCK FACE FELL FILE
GASH GIRD HACK HASH HEWN JER
KNAP LIMB MAKE MODE MUSH NIC
OCHE PARE RACE RASH RAZE REA
SIDE SKIN SLIT SLOT SMIT SNEE
SNEG SNIP SNUB STOW SUMP SWA
SWOP TAME TRIM VELL VIDE BEVE
BLOCK BREAK CANAL CANCH
CARVE CHIVE CLEFT COPSE COUP
CRIMP DRESS FLICK FRAZE FRITH
GOUGE GRAVE GRIDE GROOP
HOWEL KITTE KNIFE LANCE LATHE
MINCE NOTCH PLATE PRUNE RAZE
SABER SABRE SCALP SCARP SCIN
SCORE SEVER SHARE SHEAR SHIV
SHRED SKICE SKISE SLASH SLICE
SLICK SLISH SLIVE SNICK SPLIT
STAMP SWEEP SWIPE SWISH TOUC
TWITE VOGUE WHITE ABLATE
AJOURE BARBER BISECT BROACH
CAMBER CHISEL CLEAVE CORNER
CUTTED DIVIDE EXCISE FIGURE
FLETCH FLITCH FRENCH GROOVE
GULLET HACKLE HAGGLE IGNORE
INCIDE INCISE INDENT LESSEN
MANGLE OUTPUT RASURE REDUCE
RIPPLE SCORCH SCOTCH SCRIBE
SCYTHE SLIGHT SLIVER SNATHE
STRAIT STREAK SULLET SWINGE
TAILYE THWITE TRENCH AFFRONT
CONVERT CURTAIL CUTTING
DIACOPE DISSECT DRAWCUT
ENGRAVE FASHION FRITTER
HATCHET SCALPEL SCISSOR
SCUTTLE SECTILE TAILZEE WHITTL
DISSEVER FRACTION INCISION
INCISURE INTAGLIO LACERATE
MALAHACK RETRENCH THWITTLE
(— A THREAD) CHASE
(— AN OPENING) BREACH
(— AT ANGLE) CANT BEVEL
(— AT RANDOM) SLASH
(— AWAY) COPE SLIT UNDO ABAT
CONCISE
(— BACK) HEAD SPUR
(— BARK) CHIP
(— BEAM) KERF
(— CARS) LIFT
(— CHEESE) HARP
(— CLAY) SLING

(— **CORNERS**) SKIRT CHAMFER CHAMPHER

(— **CRUST**) CHIP

(— **DEEPLY**) DIG SHANK

(— **DIAGONALLY**) CATER SLANT

(— **DOWN**) MOW FELL STAG STUB RAZEE SCARP ABRIDGE SHORTEN RETRENCH

(— **FANCY FIGURE**) DASH

(— **FISH**) SOLAY STEAK

(— **FOR FODDER**) CHAFF

(— **FROM STACK**) DESS

(— **GEAR TEETH**) RATCH

(— **GLASS**) SPLIT

(— **GRAIN**) BAG FAG CRADLE SWINGE

(— **IN A TREE**) FACE

(— **IN BARREL STAVE**) HOWEL

(— **IN EXCAVATIONS**) GULLET

(— **IN RELIEF**) ENCHASE

(— **IN SOFT ROCK**) CAVATE

(— **IN SQUARES**) CHECK

(— **IN**) INSECT INCISED

(— **INTO SLIPS**) ZEST

(— **INTO STRIPS**) JERK FLETCH FLITCH JULIENNE

(— **INTO TREE**) BOX

(— **JAGGEDLY**) HACK SNAG

(— **LEDGES**) BENCH

(— **LOGS**) LUMBER

(— **OF FISH**) JOWL

(— **OF GEM**) STAR

(— **OF GRAIN**) MELL

(— **OF MEAT**) ARM SEY CROP HOCK SHIN SIDE CHUCK SHANK STEAK BRISKET FORESEY ICEBONE SIRLOIN EDGEBONE FORERIBS

(— **OF RIFLING**) GROOVE

(— **OFF BY BITS**) DRIB

(— **OFF END**) BUTT

(— **OFF WOOL**) DOD DODD

(— **OFF**) BOB LOP CLIP CROP DOCK KILL PARE SHUT SLIT STAG BELEE CROSS ELIDE PRUNE SCIND SEVER SHAVE SHEAR SKIVE SLIPE SPIKE COUPED DECIDE EXEMPT FORCUT RESECT SHIELD STIFLE SWATCH ABSCIND ABSCISE ABSCISS CURTAIL EXSCIND ISOLATE PRECIDE RESCIND AMPUTATE CLEIDOIC DESECATE RESECATE RETRENCH TRUNCATE

(— **OPEN**) SPLAY

(— **OUT**) DESS DINK CLICK BROACH EXCIDE EXCISE EXSECT

(— **PATH**) FRAY

(— **SALMON**) CHINE

(— **SHEEP**) TOMAHAWK

(— **SHORT**) BOB COW HOG LOP GANG CROP DOCK JIMP SNIB BOBBED HOGGED BOBTAIL CONCISE CANTLE PRESCIND

(— **TENDONS**) ENERVATE

(— **THE THROAT**) JUGULATE

(— **THE WAVES**) SNORE

(— **THINLY**) CURL

(— **TO PIECES**) CHOP DICE MINCE BRITTLE FRITTER

(— **TO SIZE**) TAIL

(— **TURF**) VELL

(— **UNDER**) KIRVE

(— **UNEVENLY**) CHATTER

(— **UP SWAN**) LIFT

(— **UP**) TUSK CARVE CHINE JOINT PRANK SPOIL TRAIN GOBBET COLLOPED

(— **WHALE BLUBBER**) LEAN

(— **WITH BACKWARD SLOP**) COOT

(— **WITH DIE**) DINK BLANK

(— **WITH SHEARS**) SHIRL

(— **WITH SICKLE**) BAG REAP

(**COLD** —**S**) ASSIETTE

(**CREW** —) BUTCH FLATTOP

(**DEEP NARROW** —) JAD

(**FENCING** —) STRAMAZON

(**LARGE** — **OF FOOD**) DODGE

(**NOT** —) UNCORVEN

(**SHORT** —) ATAJO

(**SLIGHT** —) SNICK SCOTCH

(**THIN** —) TARGET

CUT-AND-DRIED CANNED

CUTANEOUS DERMAL

CUTCH GAMBIR CATECHU GAMBIER

CUTE COY KEEN COONY DINKY DUCKY SHARP CLEVER PRETTY SHREWD CUNNING DARLING

CUTICLE DERM HIDE SKIN SHUCK THECA MEMBRANE PELLICLE

(— **OF EGGSHELL**) BLOOM

CUTLASS SWORD CURTAL DUSACK HANGER TESACK CURTAXE MACHETE SHABBLE CAMPILAN

CUTLASS FISH HIKU SAVOLA KALKVIS MACHETE HAIRTAIL

CUTLET SCHNITZEL

CUTOVER COUPE

CUTPURSE THIEF HORNTHUMB

CUTTER DIE BEEF BOAT IRON MILL PONE SLED BRAVO FACER FRAZE SLOOP SMACK BAYMAN CHERRY COLTER COTTER DOCKER EDITOR FRAZER MINCER SLEIGH SLICER CLIPPER COULTER DROMOND INCISOR RUFFIAN KNIFEMAN REVENUER SCHOKKER SHEPSTER

(— **OF STONES**) LAPIDARY

(**BRICK** —) RUBBER

(**PEAT** —) PINER

(**WIRE** —) SECATEUR

CUTTERHEAD WABBLER WOBBLER

CUTTHROAT BRAVO CUTTER RUFFIAN SWORDER

CUTTHROAT TROUT MYKISS

CUTTING CUT HAG RAW SET ACID CARF CURT KEEN KERF SETT SLIP TART TWIG ACUTE BLEAK CHECK CRISP EAGER EDGED GRIDE SCION SCRAP SCROW SHARP SMART BITING BITTER BORING ENTAIL GODOWN GORING JAGGED PHYTON PIPING SECANT SEVERE SNITHE BURNING CAUSTIC GRIBBLE INCISAL MORDANT NICKING OVERCUT PAINFUL PIQUANT POLLING SARMENT SATIRIC SECTION SLICING CHILLING CLEARING INCISIVE PIERCING POIGNANT QUICKSET SCISSION SNAPPISH WOUNDING

(— **FOR DIRT-CAR TRACK**) GULLET

(— **FOR WATER**) TAJO

(— **FROM PLANT**) SLIP SHROUD TRUNCHEON

(— **OF DEER**) SAY

(— **OF TREES**) HAG

(— **OFF**) AVULSION

(— **SHORT**) ABORTIVE

(**DRILL** —**S**) MUD

(**OBLIQUE** —) BARBING

(**SECOND** —) ROWEN

(**WASTE** —) SELVAGE SELVEDGE

CUTTLEBONE SEPIA SEPION SEPIUM GLADIUS SEPIARY

CUTTLEFISH SEPIA SHELL SQUID CUDDLE CUTTLE SCRIBE CATFISH DECAPOD INKFISH MOLLUSK OCTOPUS SCUTTLE

CUVETTE POT TUB TANK BASIN BUCKET TRENCH CISTERN

CYANIDE NITRILE CYANURET

CYANITE SAPPARE DISTHENE

CYANOGEN PRUSSIN PRUSSINE

CYBELE RHEA KYBELE AGDISTIS

(**DAUGHTER OF** —) JUNO

(**FATHER OF** —) URANUS

(**HUSBAND OF** —) SATURN

(**MOTHER OF** —) GAEA

(**SON OF** —) JUPITER NEPTUNE

CYCAD BANGA CICAD ZAMIA COONTIE CYCADITE

CYCLAMEN BACCHAR PRIMWORT SOWBREAD

CYCLE AGE EON ERA AEON BIKE EPOCH KALPA PEDAL PRIME ROUND SAROS SECLE WHEEL BAKTUN CIRCLE COURSE CYCLUS PERIOD BICYCLE CIRCUIT DICYCLE TRICYCLE

(— **OF WORK**) JOURNEY

(—**S CAUSED BY KARMA**) SAMSARA SANSARA

(**BUSINESS** —) JUGLAR KITCHIN

(**LUNAR** —) SAROS

(**ONE** — **PER SECOND**) HERTZ

(**SECONDARY** —) EPICYCLE

CYCLIC CYCLAR ANNULAR CYCLICAL

CYCLIST CYCLER WHEELER WHEELMAN

CYCLOLITH CROMLECH

CYCLOMETER ODOGRAPH

CYCLONE GALE GUST WIND BLAST STORM BAGUIO TORNADO TWISTER TYPHOON SECONDARY

CYCLOPEAN HUGE VAST STRONG MASSIVE COLOSSAL GIGANTIC

CYCLOPS ARGES BRONTES COPEPOD STEROPES

CYCLORAMA CYKE PANORAMA

CYCLOSIS STREAMING

CYCLOSTOME HAGFISH

CYLINDER CAN EKE GIG TIN BEAM BOMB BURR CAGE CANE DRUM LEAD MUFF PIPE PRIM ROLL SLUG TUBE WELL BLOCK CORER DRAIN FIBER FIBRE FUDGE SCREW SHELL SPOOL STELA STELE SWIFT BARREL BOBBIN BUTTON COLUMN COPPER DECKER DOFFER DUSTER FILTER GABION PISTON PLATEN ROLLER

SCREEN TIPITI TUMBLE URCHIN WORKER CUTCHER SLEEVER SUCCULA FOLLOWER GRADUATE NEURAXIS SPARKLET
(— AROUND MOLD) COTTLE
(— OF STEAM WHISTLE) BELL
(— OF TISSUE) CORTEX
(— OF YARN) CAKE
(— ON LOOM) BEAM
(— WITH PERFORATIONS) FLUSHER
(—S PULLED THROUGH DUCT) MANDREL
(ARMORED —) BARBETTE
(GLASS —) MUFF
(HOLLOW —) PIPE TUBE
(MARKING —) LEAD
(NAPPING —) GIG
(RELAY —) BATON
(REVOLVING —) BEATER ROLLER
(TOOTHED —) SPROCKET
CYLINDRICAL ROUND TERETE TOROSE CENTRIC TUBULAR TERETIAL
CYMA GOLA GULA OGEE DOUCINE MOLDING CYMATIUM
CYMA REVERSA HEEL
CYMBA YET
CYMBAL ZEL CHIME TARGET CROTALUM KYMBALON
(PL.) TAL BECKEN PIATTI
CYMBIUM MELO
CYME CYMULE BOSTRYX
CYMLING SIMNEL CYMBLIN SCALLOP PATTYPAN
CYMOSE DEFINITE SYMPODIAL
CYMRY KYMRI WELSH
CYNIC SATYR TIMON DOUBTER APEMANTUS

CYNICAL CYNIC SULLEN CURRISH DOGGISH DOGLIKE CAPTIOUS SARDONIC SNARLING JAQUESIAN
CYNOCEPHALUS AANI
CYNOSURE SHOW LODESTAR
CYPRESS CULL SABINO SIPERS FIREBALL AHUEHUETE BELVEDERE
CYPRESS SPURGE BALSAM NAPOLEON
CYPRIPEDIUM CYP DUCK NERVINE

CYPRUS

CAPE: GATA GRECO ANDREAS ARNAUTI ZEVGARI
CAPITAL: NICOSIA
COIN: PARA
MEASURE: OKA OKE PIK CASS DONUM KOUZA GOMARI KARTOS MEDIMNO
MOUNTAIN: TROODOS
TOWN: POLIS PAPHOS KYRENIA LARNACA MORPHOU NICOSIA LIMASSOL
WEIGHT: OKA OKE MOOSA KANTAR

CYRILLA TITI
CYRUS KORESH
CYST BAG SAC WEN POUCH CYSTUS RANULA DERMOID HYDATID HYGROMA VESICLE DACRYOPS MUCOCELE STEATOMA
CYSTOPTERIS FILIX
CYTOME SPHEROME
CYTOPLASM MASSULA OOPLASM DIASTEMA

CZAR CSAR IVAN TSAR TZAR PETER NICHOLAS
CZARDAS CSARDAS
(SECTION OF —) FRISS LASSU FRISZKA
CZECH CECH TSECH BOHUNK TSCEKH BOHEMIA

CZECHOSLOVAKIA

BEER: PILSEN
CAPITAL: PRAHA PRAGUE
CASTLE: HRADCANY
COIN: CROWN DUCAT HALER HELLER KORUNA
DANCE: POLKA REDOWA FURIANT
MEASURE: LAN SAH MIRA KOREC LATRO STOPA MERICE STRYCH
MOUNTAIN: ORE TATRA SUDETEN
PROVINCE: BOHEMIA MORAVIA SLOVAKIA
RIVER: UH MZE VAG VAH DYJE EGER ELBE GRAU HRON IPEL ISAR ISER LABE NISA ODER OHRE OLSE WAAG BECVA DUNAJ MARCH NITRA SLANA TISZA DANUBE MOLDAU MORAVA ONDAVA SAZAVA TORYSA VLTAVA LABOREC LUZNICE BEROUNKA
TOWN: AS ASCH BRNO CHEB EGER MOST BRUNN OPAVA PLZEN TABOR TUZLA AUSSIG BILINA KLADUS PILSEN PRESOV VSETIN ZVOLEN BUDWEIS JIHLAVA OSTRAVA TEPLITZ

DE DEE DOG DELTA
AB DAP DOB DOT DUB HIT PAT
BLOW CHIT DAUB LICK LUMP PECK
SPOT CLOUT DHABB DIGHT SMEAR
BLOTCH EXPERT STRIKE DABSTER
PORTION SPLOTCH FLATFISH
FLOUNDER MARYSOLE SANDLING
ABBER BALL PROD TAMPON
ABBING PICKING
ABBLE DAB DIB MESS DALLY
DIBBLE MEDDLE MUDDLE PADDLE
POTTER SOSSLE SPLASH TAMPER
TRIFLE DRABBLE MOISTEN PLOUTER
PLUTTER SMATTER SPATTER
DELIBATE SPRINKLE
— **WITH BLOOD)** ENGORE
ABBLER AMATEUR DABSTER
ABCHICK GREBE DIPPER DOBBER
DOPPER PUFFER HENBILL DIDAPPER
DOPCHICK
ACE CHUB DARE DART CYPRINID
GRAYLING
ACHSHUND DACHS BADGERER
ACOIT DAKU DAKOO ROBBER
CRIMINAL
ACTYLOPODITE POLLEX
ACTYLOZOOID PALPON
ACTYLUS DACTYL DIGITUS
AD BEAT BLOW DAUD HUNK LUMP
PAPA KNOCK THUMP FATHER
STRIKE
ADDY BABBO DEDDY
ADDY LONGLEGS SPINNER
ONGLEGS PHALANGID
ADO DIE GROOVE SOLIDUM
EDALUS (ANCESTOR OF —)
RECHTHEUS
NEPHEW OF —) TALUS
SON OF —) ICARUS
EMON (ALSO SEE DEMON) GHOST
DAIMON PYTHON EUDAEMON
MISTRESS
PL.) CURETES
FFODIL GLEN LILY DAFFY DILLY
ONQUIL ASPHODEL BELLWORT
CROWBELL
FT GAY WILD BALMY CRAZY
AFFY GIDDY LOONY POTTY SILLY
INSANE FOOLISH IDIOTIC IMBECILE
G JAG DAGG STAB SLASH DAGGLE
IERCE DAGGING DAGLOCK
PRICKET
GAME SALAMO MADRONA
LEMONWOOD
GGER DAG SAX DIRK ITAC KRIS
AEX SNEE SPUD STAB TANG CRISE
AGUE KATAR KREES POINT PRICK
KEAN STEEL ANLACE BODKIN
OUTEL CREESE DIESIS HANGER
IRPAN KUTTAR PANADE PINKER
DPPER SKHIAN STYLET BALARAO
ASLARD BAYONET COUTEAU
JDGEON HANDJAR KANDJAR
HANJAR OBELISK PONIARD
LASHER STABBER PUNCHEON
JNTILLA STILETTO
— **AS CERAMICS COVER)** HILLER
— **REFERENCE MARK)** SPIT
— **WITH WAVY BLADE)** KRIS

CREESE KREESE
(DOUBLE —) DIESIS
(SACRED —) KIRPAN
DAGOMBA DAGBANE DAGBANI
DAH DAO DOW DHAO
DAHLIA JICAMA POMPON
DAHOMEY (CAPITAL OF —)
PORTONOVO
(PEOPLE OF —) FON FONG
(RIVER OF —) NIGER OUEME
(TOWN IN —) KANDI NIKKI ABOMEY
OUIDAH COTONOU
DAILY ADAY DIARY DIURNAL
DAINCHA NARDOO
DAINTIES EST ESTE SOCK CATES
DIABLOTIN
DAINTILY CHOICELY GINGERLY
MINIONLY
DAINTINESS FLUTTER DELICACY
DAINTY CATE FINE NICE RARE TEAR
ACATE DAINT DENTY FRILL GENTY
NAISH BONBON CHOICE COSTLY
FRIAND MIGNON MINION PICKED
REGALO SCARCE SPICED SUNKET
CURIOUS ELEGANT FINICAL FINICKY
MINIKIN REGALIA TAFFETA TAFFETY
DAINTITH DAINTREL DELICACY
DELICATE ETHEREAL LIKEROUS
MIGNIARD TRYPHOSA
DAIRY TAMBO LACTARY VACCARY
CREAMERY DEYHOUSE
(— PRODUCTS) MILCHIGS
DAIRYMAID DEE DEY DEYWOMAN
MILKMAID
DAIRYMAN AHIR MILKMAN
DAIS PACE SEAT BENCH LEWAN
STAGE TABLE CANOPY ESTATE
LISSOM PODIUM PULPIT SETTLE
ESTRADE TERRACE TRIBUNE
CHABUTRA FOOTPACE HALFPACE
HATHPACE HUSTINGS PLATFORM
DAISY BULL GOLD DANDY GOWAN
OXEYE BENNET MORGAN SHASTA
BONESET BOWWORT COMFREY
DOGBLOW BACKWORT BONEWORT
COMPOSIT HEXAFOIL KNITBACK
PISSABED MOONPENNY
DAISY CUTTER GRUB
DAISY FLEABANE ERIGERON
SCABIOUS
DAKOTA SIOUX LAKOTA
DALE HAW DELL DENE GLEN VALE
SPOUT BOTTOM DINGLE TROUGH
VALLEY
DALEA PAROSELA
DALLES DELLS RAPIDS
DALLIANCE TOY CHAT PLAY TALK
SPORT GOSSIP TOUSEL TOUSLE
TRIFLE COLLING
DALLIER PINGLER
DALLY TOY CHAT DAFF FOOL IDLE
JAKE JAUK PLAY SWAN WAIT DELAY
FLIRT SPORT TARRY COQUET
DABBLE DAWDLE LINGER LOITER
TRIFLE WANTON DRINGLE SLIDDER
DALLYING COQUETRY SISSETON
DALMATIC TUNICLE
DAM BAR BAY PEN REE DAME HEAD
POND SADD SPUR STAY STEM STOP

SUDD WEIR BLOCK CAULD CHECK
CHOKE GARTH MOUND POUND
STANK ANICUT CAUSEY HINDER
MOTHER PARENT ANNICUT
BARRAGE BARRIER MILLDAM
PENHEAD RAMPIRE TAPPOON
ABOIDEAU BLOCKADE GRANDDAM
OBSTACLE OBSTRUCT RESTRAIN
DAMAGE MAR BLOT BURN COST
HARM HURT JEEL LOSS RUIN SKIN
TEEN BLITZ BURST CLOUD CRACK
HAVOC PRANG SPOIL WOUND
WRONG BATTER CHARGE DANGER
DEFACE DEFECT HINDER IMPAIR
INJURE INJURY INSULT SCATHE
SORROW AFFLICT DAMNIFY
DEGRADE DISTURB EXPENSE
FOUNDER OFFENCE OFFENSE
PAYMENT SCRATCH SCUTTLE
SHATTER ACCIDENT BUSINESS
DISSERVE FRACTURE FRETTING
MISCHIEF SABOTAGE
DAMAGED HURT CRAZY LESED
BROKEN CRACKED INJURED
DAMAGES INTEREST HAMESUCKEN
DAMAGING HARMFUL HURTFUL
DAMAN DAS CONY CONEY CUNNY
DASSY GANAM HYRAX DASSIE
WABBER ASHKOKO CHEROGRIL
DAMA PADEMELON TAMMAR
WALLABY
DAMASCENED WATERED
DAMASCENE WORK KOFTGARI
DAMASK LINEN DARNEX DORNIC
DORNICK DAMASSIN DRAWLOOM
DAME DINT LADY DAMIE WOMAN
MATRON
DAME'S VIOLET EVEWEED
DAMMARA AGATHIS
DAMN DEE DEM DOG RAT BLOW
BURN DANG DARN DASH DING DRAT
DUMB DURN BLAME BLANK BLAST
BLESS CURSE FETCH WHOOP
BEDAMN BUGGER DEMPNE DEVOTE
GODDAM CONDEMN CONSARN
DOGGONE GODDAMN GOLDARN
GOLDURN CONFOUND EXECRATE
DAMNABLE DAMNED ODIOUS
ACCURSED INFERNAL
DAMNABLY DEUCED CURSEDLY
DEUCEDLY
DAMNATION NATION PERDITION
DAMNED DEE DAMN DARN DEED
DURN LOST BALLY DOOMS BLOODY
DARNED DASHED DURNED GODDAM
GORMED TARNAL BLESSED
CONSARN DOGGONE ETERNAL
GOLDARN GOLDURN MUCKING
ACCURSED BLANKETY BLINKING
DASHEDLY INFERNAL JIGGERED
DAMP DEG FOG RAW WAK WET
CLAM DANK DEWY DULL MIST ROKY
SOFT WACK BLUNT DABBY HUMID
JUICY MALMY MOCHY MOIST
MOOTH MUGGY MUNGY MUSTY
RAFTY RAINY RAWKY SAPPY SOBBY
SOGGY THONE WAUGH WEAKY
CLAMMY DAMPEN DEADEN MUFFLE
QUENCH STUPOR BEDEWED

DAMPISH DEPRESS MOISTEN
SQUIDGY DEJECTED DISPIRIT
HUMIDIFY HUMIDITY MOISTURE
(— OF EVENING) SERENE
(CHOKE —) STYTHE
DAMPEN DEG DAMP MOIL CHILL
CRAMP FREEZE SPONGE MOISTURE
DAMPENER MULLER
DAMPER DAMP MUTE BREAD CHECK
CHECKER REGISTER
DAMPNESS DAMP HUMIDITY
DAMSEL GIRL WENCH MAIDEN
MOPPET DAMOSEL DAMOZEL
PUCELLE DONZELLA PRINCESS
DAMSELFISH PINTANO
DAMSELFLY NAIAD
DAN GI DEN
DANAKIL AFAR
DANAUS ANOSIA
DANCE BAL BOB HOP JIG MAI SON
BALL DRAG DUET DUMP FISH FOOT
FRUG HEEL HOOF HORA JAZZ JIVE
JUBA KOLO LEAP LOPE MASK MILL
MOVE PROM REEL SAIL SHAG SKIT
STEP BAILE BAMBA BONGO BRAWL
CANON CAPER CAROL CONGA
DANZA ENTRY FLING FLISK FRIKE
FRISK GOPAK LASYA MAMBO PAVAN
POLKA RINKA RUMBA SALLY SAMBA
STOMP SWING TANGO TRACE
TREAD TWIST VOLTA WALTZ
ALTHEA AREITO BALLET BALTER
BOLERO BOOGIE BOSTON BRANLE
CANARY CANCAN CEBELL CORDAX
DANZON DIDDLE DREHER FADING
FORMAL FROLIC GERMAN HORMOS
MASQUE MINUET MOBBLE MONKEY
MORRIS NRITTA PASSAY RACKET
RHUMBA SHIMMY TODDLE TRESCA
TUMBLE VALETA ANTHEMA BEGUINE
CALINDA CANTICO COURANT
CZARDAS DANSANT FADDING
FARRUCA FOOTING FOXTROT
FURLANA GAVOTTE MORISCO
PATTERN SALTATE SARDANA
SHUFFLE TEMPETE TRESCHE
TRIPPLE VOLTIZE ZIGANKA
ANGLAISE AURRESCU BAMBOUJA
BAMBOULA CACHUCHA CAKEWALK
CHACONNE COMPARSA COONJINE
COTILLON ENTRACTE ESTAMPIE
FANDANGO FANTASIA FLAMENCO
GALOPADE GUARACHA HABANERA
HEYDEGUY HORNPIPE KOLATTAM
MATELOTE
(— ART) NATYA ORCHESIS
(— ATTENDANCE) LACKEY LACQUEY
(— CLUMSILY) BALTER
(— DRAMA) NO NOH
(— FACE TO FACE) SET
(— FORM) PIVA
(— IN CIRCLE) JIGGER
(— METHOD) LABAN
(— NIMBLY) CANARY
(— RESEMBLING THE POLKA)
BERLIN
(— STEP) RIFF PICKUP
(— STYLE) ABHINAYA
(— TYPE) TANDAVA

(ACROBATIC —) ADAGIO
(AFRICAN —) SHOUT
(ARGENTINE —) CUANDO
(AUSTRIAN —) LANDLER
(BALINESE —) KEBYAR LEGONG
(BALLROOM —) SON CONGO
COTILLON
(BOHEMIAN —) REDOWA FURIANT
(CARNIVAL —) COOCH FOLIA
COOTCH
(CEREMONIAL —) AREITO CANTICO
DUTUBURI
(COQUETTISH —) PURPOSE
(COUNTRY —) HAY CONFESS
ANGLAISE
(COURTSHIP —) CUECA BATUQUE
LEZGIBKA
(DANISH —) SEXTUR
(FIESTA —S) AKRIEROS
(FLAMENCO —) ALEGRIAS
(FRENCH —) BAL BOREE BRAWL
GAVOT BRANLE BOURREE BOUTADE
BRANSLE GAVOTTE LAVOLTA
(GAY —) RANT GAILLARD GALLIARD
(GESTURE —) SIVA
(GREEK —) CORDAX KORDAX
SIKINNIS
(GYPSY —) FARRUCA
(HAITIAN —) JUBA
(HOBBYHORSE —) CALUSAR
(HOLIDAY —) PATTERN
(HUNGARIAN —) KOS
(INDIAN —) IRUSKA KATHAK
(IRISH —) FADING
(ITALIAN —) FORLANA FURLANA
(JAPANESE —) BUGAKU KAGURA
(JAVANESE —) SERIMPI
(LIVELY —) JIG REEL GALOP GIGUE
POLKA RUMBA BOLERO CANARY
RHUMBA SPRING BOURREE
FURLANA HOEDOWN GALLIARD
GALOPADE HORNPIPE
(MAORI —) HAKA
(MEXICAN —) DARABE HUAPANGO
SANDUNGA
(MOURNFUL —) DUMP
(NORWEGIAN —) HALLING
(OLD ENGLISH —) CEBELL MORRIS
ARGEERS ANGLAISE
(OLD-FASHIONED —) LOURE
(PEASANT —) JOTA DANZON
BALITAO
(PERUVIAN —) CUECA KASWA
CACHUA
(POLISH —) KUJAWIAK
(POLYNESIAN —) HULA
(PORTUGUESE —) FADO
(ROUND —) RAY BRAUL CAROL
WALTZ CAROLE MAXIXE
(RUSTIC —) HAY HEY HAYMAKER
(SPANISH —) JOTA POLO JALEO
BOLERO JARABE CHACONNE
FLAMENCO GUARACHA
(SPEAR —) BARIS
(SQUARE —) SQUARE ARGEERS
HOEDOWN LANCERS QUADRILLE
(STATELY —) PAVAN PAVANE
EMMELEIA SARABAND
(SWORD —) BACUBERT MATACHIN

(VENEZUELAN —) JOROPO
(WEDDING —) CANACUAS
DANCER PONY CLOWN PONEY
ARTIST CORNER HOOFER HOPPER
MAENAD APSARAS CLOGGER
DANSEUR DEVADAS PASCOLA
PRANCER PRANKER SAILOUR
STEPPER TODDLER BALADINE
BAYADERE DANSEUSE FIGURANT
MORRICER
(BALLET —) ETOILE SOLISTE
CORYPHEE
(EGYPTIAN —S) GHAWAZI
GHAWAZEE
(JAVANESE —) SERIMPI
(JAVANESE —S) BEDOYO
(MASKED —S) GAHE
(SQUARE —S) FLOOR
(SWORD —) MATACHIN
(ZUNI —) SHALAKO
DANCING SWING ADANCE BALLET
CHANGE FROLIC MORRIS SALTANT
SURGING STEPPING TRIPSOME
(— MANIA) TARANTISM
DANDELION BLOW BLOWER CANKE
DINDLE CHICORY HAWKBIT
BLOWBALL COMPOSIT PISSABED
DANDELION HEAD PUFF CLOCK
BUFFBALL BULLFICE BULLFIST
PUFFBALL
DANDER ANGER DUTCH SCURF
STROLL TEMPER WANDER HACKLE
PASSION SAUNTER DANDRUFF
DANDIFIED SPRUCE BUCKISH
ADONIZED
DANDIFY ADONIZE DANDYIZE
DANDLE DANCE DIDDLE FADDLE
FONDLE PAMPER
DANDRUFF SCURF DANDER FURFU
DANDY FOP JAY ADON BEAU BUCK
DAND DUDE FINE JAKE MAJO PRIG
TOFF TRIG YAWL BLOOD DILDO
JEMMY SWELL ADONIS MIZZEN
BUCKEEN CAPSTAN COXCOMB
ELEGANT FOPPISH JESSAMY
MACARONI SAILBOAT
DANDY HORSE HOBBY DRAISINE
DANDYISM BUCKISM
DANE DANSKER LOCHLIN DUBHGAL
DANEWORT EBULUS LOCHLIN
DANEBALL DANEWEED DEADWORT
WALLWORT
DANGER FEAR RISK DOUBT PERIL
WATHE HAZARD PLIGHT EXTREME
PITFALL VENTURE DISTRESS
JEOPARDY
DANGEROUS BAD HOT ILL RUM
DEAR FOUL GRAVE NASTY RISKY
FICKLE KITTLE SCATHY SHREWD
UNSURE AWKWARD FEARFUL
PARLOUS UNCANNY DOUBTFUL
INSECURE PERILOUS UNCHANCY
DANGLE LOP HANG LOLL DROOP
SWING DANDLE SHOGGLE SHOOG
SUSPEND TROLLOP
DANGLIN DANLI
DANK WET DAMP DONK HUMID
MOIST CLAMMY COARSE DAMPEN

DANKISH DRIZZLE WETNESS MOISTURE
ANSEUSE DANCER BALLERINA
ANZIG GDANSK
(— LIQUEUR) RATAFIA
APPER NEAT TRIM NATTY SPRUCE
FINICAL FOPPISH SPARKISH
APPLE COVER FLECK FRECK
APPLED BLOCKY DOTTED POMELY
FLECKED MOTTLED SPOTTED
FRECKLED
ARBHA KUSA KUSHA
ARDANUS (FATHER OF —) JUPITER
(MOTHER OF —) ELECTRA
ARE OSS DAST DEFU FACE OSSE
RISK BRAVE STUMP ASSUME
BANTER DACKER ATTEMPT
BRAVADE FASHION PRESUME
VENTURE
(— NOT) DASSNT DAURNA DASSENT
AREDEVIL MADCAP HARDYDARDY
ARING BOLD DARE DERF PERT
RASH WILD BRAVE HARDY MANLY
NERVE PREST FELONY HEROIC
COURAGE DAIROUS DAREFUL
BOLDNESS DEVILISH FEARLESS
ARIOLE MADELINE
ARK DIM DUN MUM SAD WAN BASE
BLAE DEEP DERK DERN DUSK EBON
HARD MALE MIRK MURK BLACK
BLIND BROWN CLOUD DINGY DUSKY
FAINT MIRKY MURKY SHADY SOOTY
SWART UMBER UNLIT VAGUE
CLOSED CLOUDY CYPRUS DIMPSY
DISMAL DRUMLY GLOOMY OPAQUE
SOMBER SOMBRE SWARTH WICKED
DARKISH DUSKISH MELANIC
OBSCURE PITMIRK RAYLESS
STYGIAN SUNLESS SWARTHY
THESTER UNCLEAR ABSTRUSE
DARKLING DARKSOME GLOOMFUL
GLOOMING IGNORANT LOWERING
SINISTER
ARK-COLORED SAD SWART
SOMBER SOMBRE SWARTH
SWARTHY
ARKEN DIM DUN BLUR DULL DUSK
BEDIM BLIND CLOUD GLOAM GLOOM
POCHE SHADE SULLY SWART
UMBER DEEPEN ENDARK SHADOW
BECLOUD BENIGHT BLACKEN
ECLIPSE EMBROWN OBSCURE
OPACATE PERPLEX SLUBBER
TARNISH OVERCAST
— HAIR) BLEND
ARKENED SABLE CLOUDY BLINDED
LAMPLESS
ARKENING SCURF
ARK HORSE MOREL
ARKISH DIM
ARKLY DARK CLOSE SABLY
MISTILY
ARKNESS DARK DERN DUSK MIRK
MURK BLACK GLOOM NIGHT SHADE
AMAS SHADOW DIMNESS PITMIRK
PRIVACY SECRECY TENEBRA
GLOAMING INIQUITY MIDNIGHT
TENEBRES TWILIGHT
RLING JO JOE PET CHOU CONY

DEAR DUCK LIFE LOVE NOBS PEAT
ROON AROON ARUIN BULLY CHERI
DEARY DUCKS LIEVE SWEET WHITE
CHERIE DAUTIE DAWTIE MINION
MOPPET OCHREE ACUSHLA
BUNTING CUSHLAM DILLING MINIKIN
PIGSNEY PINKENY QUERIDA
STOREEN DEARLING DUMPLING
FAVORITE LIEBCHEN LOVELING
MACUSHLA PRECIOUS SWEETING
DARLING PEA INDICO INDIGO
DARN DOG BLOW DERN DURN MEND
PATCH BUGGER REPAIR DOGGONE
DARNED BLAME BLAMED DEUCED
DURNED BLESSED BLINDING
DOWNGONE
DARNEL RAY CRAP TARE WEED
CHEAT CHESS DRANK DRAWK
DRUNK EAVER GRASS IVRAY NEELE
COCKLE EGILOPS AEGILOPS
DART JET POP BOLT BUZZ CANE
CHOP COLP FLIT JOUK LEAP LICK
PILE PLAN PLAY ROUT ARROW
BOUND FLAME FLING FLIRT GLEAM
GLINT LANCE SCAMP SCOOT SHAFT
SHOOT SKITE SKIVE SPEAR SPEED
SPRIT START ANCHOR BULTEN
DARTLE ELANCE GLANCE LANCET
LAUNCH METHOD SCHEME SPRING
SQUIRT STRIKE SUMPIT THRUST
JAVELIN MISSILE STRALET VERUTUM
BRANDISH GAVELOCK JACULATE
SPICULUM
(— ABOUT) SPRINKLE
(— OF LIGHTNING) STREAK
(— OF MOLDING) ANCHOR
(— REPEATEDLY) DARTLE
DARTER SPECK
DARTING SALLY ARROWY
DARTLIKE SPICULAR
DASH DAD DAH PEP ZIP BANG BOLT
CAST DING DIVE ELAN GIFT HINT
HURL LASH LINE LUSH PASH PELT
POSS RACE RASH RUIN RULE RUSH
SHOW SLAM SOSH TICK VEIN WHAP
WHOP ABASH ARDOR BLANK BREAK
CHAFE CLASH CRASH CRUSH DRIVE
ECLAT FLASH FLING FRUSH KNOCK
PLASH PLOUT SKITE SLASH SLOSH
SMASH SPEED SPEND SPICE SPURN
START STYLE SWASH SWELL TASTE
THROW TOUCH TRICK BEDASH
DALLOP DASHEE DOLLOP ENERGY
HURTLE HYPHEN RELISH SHIVER
SPIRIT SPLASH SPRINT STRAIN
STROKE THRUST BRAVURA
BREENGE COLLIDE DEPRESS
DISPLAY HUNDRED IMPINGE
SHATTER SPATTER SPLOTCH
TANTIVY CONFOUND GRATUITY
SPLINTER
(— ABOUT WILDLY) GAD REEL
(— AGAINST) BEAT
(— DOWN) QUELL STRAM
STRAMASH
(— IN PIECES) CRASH
(— OF SPIRITS) LACE LACING
(— OUT) QUELL
(— TOGETHER) COLLIDE

(— UP) FLURR
(— WITH WATER) JAW BLASH
SLASH
DASHBOARD DASH FACIA DASHER
FASCIA
DASHED SWITCHED
DASHER DASH BEATER PLUNGER
DASHING BOLD BULLY DASHY
DOGGY SHOWY SMART SWASH
JABBLE SPANKY SWANKY VELOCE
DOGGISH GALLOWS LARKING
STYLISH SWAGGER VARMINT
SLASHING SPANKING SPIRITED
DASTARD CAD SOT DAFF SNEAK
COWARD CRAVEN DULLARD
WITHING POLTROON
DASTARDLY FOUL VILLAIN
COWARDLY POLTROON SNEAKING
DASYLIRION SOTOL
DASYPUS TATU
DASYURE TIGER YABBI DAPPLE
DATA DOPE FACTS IMPUT INPUT
MATERIAL
DATE AGE DAY ERA DRAG FARD
FUSS DATUM EPOCH FARDH FRUIT
SAIDI CUTOFF FRIEND HALAWI
JUJUBE RECKON GALLANT
ANTEDATE ASHARASI DEADLINE
(— FIXED UPON) TERM
(— RIPENING) KIMRI RUTAB KHALAL
DATED GIVEN PASSE OUTMODED
DATE PLUM LOTUS SAPOTE ZAPOTE
DATOLITE BAKERITE HUMBOLDTITE
DATUM FACT ITEM GIVEN
DATURA DUTRA STRAMONY
TOGUACHA
DAUB DAB DOB MUD BALM BLOB
BLOT CLAG CLAM CLAT CLAY COAT
GAUM MOIL SOIL TEER CLAIK
CLART CLEAM COVER DITCH FLICK
PAINT SLAKE SLAUM SMEAR
BEDAUB CLATCH GREASE LABBER
SMUDGE SPLASH BESMEAR DRIBBLE
PLASTER SCLATCH SLUBBER
SPLATCH SPLOTCH SLAISTER
DAUBED GAUMY
DAUBING DUBBING MOILING
DAUBY BLOTTY
DAUGHTER ANAC BINT DAME GIRL
CHILD FILLE FILLY KIBEI REGAN
ALUMNA CADETTE DOCHTER
GONERIL CORDELIA
(PANTALOON'S —) COLUMBINE
DAUNT AWE COW DAW ADAW DARE
DAZE FAZE MATE STUN TAME
ABASH ACCOY AMATE BREAK
CHECK DETER DOMPT DANTON
DISMAY SUBDUE CONQUER
CONTROL OVERAWE REPRESS
STUPEFY TERRIFY DISPIRIT
OVERCOME
DAUNTLESS BOLD GOOD BRAVE
AWELESS FEARLESS INTREPID
DAVENPORT DESK SOFA COUCH
DIVAN
DAVID TAFFY DAWKIN
DAVIDIST JORIST
DAVIT CRANE
DAW DA DAWN DRAB DAUNT MAGPIE

DAWPATE JACKDAW SLATTERN SLUGGARD
DAWDLE LAG IDLE JAUK MUCK MULL POKE TOIT DALLY DELAY DRILL KNOCK DADDLE DAIDLE DIDDLE DOODLE DRETCH FADDLE LINGER LOITER MUCKER PICKLE PIDDLE PINGLE POTTER PUTTER TANTLE TRIFLE DRIDDLE FINNICK QUIDDLE SAUNTER LALLYGAG LOLLYGAG SHAMMOCK SLUMMOCK
DAWDLER DAWDLE MUSARD LOUTHER
DAWN DAW ROW EOAN MORN BREAK CREEK LIGHT PRIME SHINE SUNUP AURORA MORROW ORIENT SPRING UPRISE DAWNING GREKING MORNING SUNRISE COCKCROW DAYBREAK
DAY DA DEI ERA SUN YOM DATE DIEM DIES DIET TIME EPOCH LIGHT FRIDAY MONDAY PERIOD SUNDAY JOURNEY TUESDAY LIFETIME SATURDAY THURSDAY WEDNESDAY
(— **AND NIGHT**) KALPA
(— **BEFORE**) EVE
(— **OF JUDGMENT**) INQUEST DOOMSDAY
(— **OF ORIGIN**) BIRTHDAY
(— **OF REST**) SABBATH
(— **OF ROMAN MONTH**) IDES NONES CALENDS KALENDS
(5 NAMELESS —S) UAYEB
(60TH OF —) GHURRY
(8TH — AFTER FEAST) UTAS
(DOG —S) CANICULE
(EVERY —) ALDAY
(EVIL —S) DISMAL
(FAST —) ASHURA FASTEN
(FIRST — OF AUGUST) LAMMAS
(FIRST — OF MAY) BELTANE BEALTINE
(HOLY —) FEAST HOLIDAY
(HOT —) BROILER ROASTER
(LAST — OF FESTIVAL) APODOSIS
(MARKET —) NUNDINE TIANGUE
(NO FLESH —) MAIGRE
(PATRON SAINT'S —) PATTERN
(QUARTER —) TERM
(TWELFTH —) EPIPHANY
(WEEK —) FERIA
(WORK —) WARDAY
DAYAK DYAK IBAN BAHAU DUSUN KAYAN KENYA KENYAH KELABIT
DAYBOOK BOOK DIURNAL JOURNAL
DAYBREAK DAWN MORN SUNUP DAWNING DAYDAWN DAYLIGHT
DAYDREAM DWAM MUSE DREAM DWALM FANCY VISION FANTASY REVERIE PHANTASY
DAYFLOWER COHITRE
DAYLIGHT DAY LIGHT DAYSHINE
(BROAD —) FUIRDAYS
DAYWORKER DILKER
DAZE FOG DAMP DARE MAZE STUN DAUNT DAVER DIZZY DOZEN SWOON ASTONY BEDAZE BEMUSE BENUMB DAZZLE DEAFEN MUDDLE TRANCE CONFUSE PETRIFY

STUPEFY TORPIFY ASTONISH BEWILDER DUMFOUND PARALYZE
DAZED MAD ASEA DAMP ASSOT DIZZY DOYLT SILLY TOTTY CUCKOO DOILED GROGGY ROTTEN BEMUSED DONNERT SPOILED WITLESS ASTONIED BESOTTED DITHERED DONNERED WITHERED
DAZEDLY GROGGILY
DAZZLE DARE DAZE BLEND BLIND DROWN GLAIK SHINE FULGOR ECLIPSE BEWILDER OUTSHINE SURPRISE
DAZZLED BLINDED
DAZZLING FLARE FLASH FLASHY GARISH ADAZZLE FLARING FULGENT GLARING RADIANT DIZZYING GORGEOUS
DDT TDE DICOPHANE
DEACON ADEPT CLERIC DOCTOR LAYMAN LEVITE MASTER PHILIP MINISTER
DEACONESS WIDOW
DEAD FEY LOW AWAY BUNG COLD DEAF DOWD DULL FLAT GONE MORT NUMB POKY SURE TAME ADEAD AMORT BLIND DEEDS INERT NAPOO POKEY QUIET SLAIN STARK VAPID ASLEEP BYGONE FALLEN LAPSED NAPOOH REFUSE DEADISH DEFUNCT EXACTLY EXPIRED EXTINCT INSIPID SAINTED STERILE TEDIOUS ABSOLUTE COMPLETE DECEASED DEPARTED INACTIVE LIFELESS OBSOLETE
(— AT TOP) RAMPICK
DEAD-ARM NECROSIS
DEAD-DRUNK BLIND
DEADEN DAMP DULL DUMB KILL MULL MUTE NUMB SEAR STUN BLUNT SLAKE BENUMB DAMPEN MUFFLE OBTUND OPIATE RETARD STIFLE WEAKEN MORTIFY PETRIFY REPRESS SLUMBER SMOTHER AMORTIZE ASTONISH ENFEEBLE
(— A SCENT) FOIL
DEAD END PLACE
DEADENED DEAD DEAF SEAR SERE
DEADENING PUGGING
DEADHEAD SINK BOBBER SINKER
DEADHOUSE MORGUE MORTUARY
DEAD LETTER NIX
DEADLINE DATELINE
DEADLINESS LETHALITY
DEADLOCK TIE LOGJAM IMPASSE STANDOFF STOPPAGE
DEADLY WAN DIRE FELL MORT FATAL FERAL TUANT DEATHY LETHAL MORTAL CAPITAL DEATHLY FATEFUL RUINOUS MORTIFIC VENOMOUS VIRULENT
DEADLY CARROT DRIAS THAPSIA
DEAD NETTLE HENBIT
DEADS MULLOCK
DEAF SURD DUNCH DUNNY SORDA SORDO
DEAFEN DIN DORR DEAVE DEADEN
DEAFENING DEEVEY
DEAF-MUTE FENELLA SURDOMUTE

DEAFNESS ASONIA SURDITY ANACUSIA ANACUSIS COPHOSIS
DEAL GO END JOB DAIL DOLE LEND PART SALE TALE WHIZ ALLOT BOARD BROKE FETCH PLANK SERV SEVER SHAKE SHARE SHIFT TRADE TREAT TROKE TRUCK WIELD YIELD BATTEN BESTOW DIVIDE HANDLE MEDDLE NUMBER PARCEL BARGAIN DELIVER INFLICT PIANOLA PORTIO SCATTER TRUCKLE WRESTLE DISPENSE SEPARATE
(— CARDS) DRAW TALLY
(— CLANDESTINELY) TRINKET
(— IN A TRIFLING WAY) PIDDLE
(— IN BRIDGE) BOARD
(— IN GRAIN) SWALE
(— OF CARDS) COUP SPOIL GOULASH
(— SHREWDLY) JOCKEY
(— WITH) HAND COVER DIGHT TREAT BUCKET CUSTOM DEMEAN HANDLE ENTREAT
(GREAT —) MORT LOADS MIGHT SIGHT JUGFUL SKINFUL
(POLITICAL —) DICKER
DEALER BANK CHAP AGENT COPER BADGER BANKER BROKER CADGER EGGLER GROCER JOBBER JUNIOR MONGER SELLER TRADER BUTCHE CHAPMAN KEELMAN YOUNGER CHANDLER MERCHANT OCCUPIER OPERATOR STICKMAN TAILLEUR
(— IN CATTLE) COUPER COWPER DROVER
(— IN CHEMICALS) SALTER DRYSALTER
(— IN DRY GOODS) DRAPER
(— IN GRAIN) SWALER
(— IN OLD CLOTHES) FRIPPER
(— IN PAINTS) COLORMAN
(— IN TEXTILES) MERCER
(CARDS —) FARMER
(COAL —) COLLIER
(HORSE —) COPER COUPER COWPER CHANTER SCORSER
(SLAVE —) MANGO
(STOCK —) STAG JOBBER OUTSIDER
DEALFISH VAAGMAR VAAGMAER
DEALING DOLE PRICE TRUCK TRADING TRAFFIC EXCHANGE
(BUSINESS —S) TROKE
(JUST —) DOOM
(TRICKY —) BROKING
(PL.) DEAL TRAFFIC BUSINESS COMMERCE PRACTICE PRACTISE
DEAN DECAN DOYEN DEANER SENIOR VERGER PREFECT PROVO SUBDEAN ARCHDEAN PRAEFECT
DEAR JO GRA HON JOE PET AGRA CARA CHER CONY FAIR FOND GO HIGH LAMB LIEF LOVE NEAR NOB SALT BOSOM CHARY CHERE CHU DEARY HONEY LOVED SWEET TIG COSTLY DAUTIE DAWTIE DEARIE DEARLY POPPET SCARCE SEVERE SQUALL TENDER WORTHY BELOV DARLING LOVABLE PIGSNEY

QUERIDA SPECIAL TOOTSIE
ESPECIAL ESTEEMED GLORIOUS
PRECIOUS VALUABLE
●EARLY DEAR ALIFE DEEPLY
KEENLY RICHLY HEARTILY
●EARNESS CHERTE DEARTH
●EARTH LACK WANT CHERTE
FAMINE PAUCITY POVERTY
DEARNESS SCARCITY SOLITUDE
●EATH DEE END BALE BANE DEAD
DOOM EXIT FAIL FATE KILL MORS
MORT OBIT PASS REST WINK
ANKOU DECAY GRAVE GRUEL
LETHE NIGHT SLEEP CHAROS
CHARUS DEMISE DEPART ENDING
EXITUS EXPIRY MURDER PERIOD
REAPER WAGANG CURTAIN
DECEASE FUNERAL PARTING
PASSAGE QUIETUS SILENCE
BIOLYSIS CASUALTY FATALITY
NECROSIS RAWBONES THANATOS
(— ANGEL) AZRAEL
(— BY HANGING) HALTER
(— OF TISSUE) GANGRENE
●EATH ADDER ELAPID ELAPOID
●EATH CAMASS LOBELIA
●EATHLESS ETERNAL UNDYING
IMMORTAL
●EATHLIKE DEATHLY GHASTLY
MACABRE GHASTFUL MORIBUND
MORTUOUS
●EATHLY DEAD FATAL DEADLY
MORTAL GHASTLY STYGIAN
DEATHFUL MORTALLY
●EATH'S-HEAD SKULL
●EBAR DENY TABU CROSS ESTOP
REPEL TABOO DISBAR FORBID
HINDER REFUSE BOYCOTT DEPRIVE
EXCLUDE OUTSHUT PREVENT
SECLUDE SUSPEND PRECLUDE
●PROHIBIT
●EBARK LAND
●EBARRED FROZEN OUTSHUT
●EBASE SINK ABASE ALLOY AVILE
DIRTY LOWER STOOP BEMEAN
DEFILE DEMEAN DILUTE EMBASE
IMPAIR NIDDER NITHER REDUCE
REVILE VILIFY CORRUPT DEBAUCH
DECLINE DEGRADE DEPRAVE
PERVERT TRADUCE VILLAIN VITIATE
●EBASED BASE VILE BASTARD
CORRUPT SQUALID CANKERED
DEGRADED DEROGATE
●EBASEMENT TARNISH
●EBASING DOWNWARD
●EBATABLE MOOT DISPUTABLE
●EBATE AGON BEAT FRAY MOOT
ARGUE FIGHT PLEAD STUDY
ARGUFY HASSEL HASSLE REASON
STRIFE AGITATE CANVASS CONTEND
CONTEST DISCEPT DISCUSS
DISPUTE EXAMINE MOOTING
PALAVER QUARREL WRANGLE
ARGUMENT CONSIDER CONTRARY
MILITATE PARLANCE QUESTION
●EBATER PICADOR
●EBAUCH BOUT FILE SPREE TAINT
WHORE DEBASE DEBOSH DEFILE
GUZZLE MISUSE SEDUCE SPLORE

VILIFY CORRUPT DEBOISE DEPRAVE
MISLEAD POLLUTE VIOLATE
DISHONOR SQUANDER STRUMPET
STUPRATE
DEBAUCHED LEWD RAKELY
DEBOIST DEBOSHED RAKEHELL
DEBAUCHEE RIP RAKE ROUE
HOLOUR LECHER RAKEHELL
DEBAUCHERY RAKERY DEBAUCH
PRIAPISM
DEBENTURE SECURITY
DEBENZOLIZE STRIP
DEBILITATE SINK
DEBILITATED WEAK SEEDY FEEBLE
INFIRM SAPPED ASTHENIC
DEBILITY ATONY ASTHENY LANGUOR
ASTHENIA WEAKNESS
DEBIT DEBT LOSS CHARGE
DEBONAIR AIRY JAUNTY POLITE
CAVALIER GRACEFUL GRACIOUS
DEBOUCH FALL MOUTH
DEBOUCHMENT INFLUX INFLUXION
DEBRIS GUCK SLAG DECAY FRUSH
TRADE TRASH WASTE REFUSE
RUBBLE RUDERA CRUMBLE ELUVIUM
RUBBISH SLIDDER DETRITUS
(— IN WOOL) BUR BURR
(— OF INSECTS) FRASS
(— OF ROCKS) HEAD DRIFT TALUS
ELUVIUM
(FLUFFY —) FLUE
(FOREST —) SLASH
DEBT DUE SIN POST DEBIT FAULT
STOCK ARREARS DEBITUM
JUDGMENT TRESPASS
(PL.) OBLATA WANIGAN ARREARAGE
DEBTOR OWER SKIP DYVOUR
DEBITOR YIELDER
DEBUT OPENING ENTRANCE
DEBUTANTE BUD DEB DEBBY
INGENUE ROSEBUD
DECADENT EFFETE DECAYED
HOTHOUSE OVERRIPE
DECAHYDRATE SODA
DECALOGUE WITNESS
DECAMP GUY PUT BOLT HIKE KITE
ELOPE MOSEY SCOOT SCOUR
VAMOS DEPART ESCAPE LEVANT
MIZZLE MORRIS POWDER VAMOSE
ABSCOND DISCAMP VAMOOSE
DECAMPING GUY
DECAN DECURION
DECANT EMIT POUR UNLOAD
TRANSFER
DECANTER CARAFE CARAFON
URCEOLE GARDEVIN INGESTER
DECAPITATE BEHEAD DECOLLATE
DECAPITATION DECOLL HEADING
DECAPOD BUSTER
DECARBONIZE DECOKE
DECATING SPONGING
DECAY EBB ROT ROX BLET CONK
DOAT DOTE DOZE FADE RUIN SEED
WANE WEAR CROCK DEATH FAILL
SHANK SLOOM SLOUM SPOIL
WASTE CARIES FADING MARCOR
MILDEW MOLDER MOSKER SICKEN
WITHER CRUMBLE DECLINE FAILURE

MORTIFY PUTREFY DECREASE
FORDWINE
(— IN WOOD) CONK DOZE
(INCIPIENT —) BLET
DECAYED BAD DEAF DOZY ROXY
FRUSH SEEDY DAISED MARCID
PUTRID ROTTEN SPAKED RUINOUS
SNAGGLED
DECAYING COLD DOTY SHABBY
CARIOUS
DECEASE DIE FAIL OBIT PASS
DEATH DEMISE PASSAGE
DECEASED DEAD PARTED DEFUNCT
EXTINCT UMWHILE DEPARTED
UMQUHILE
DECEIT GAB DOLE FLUM GAFF GULL
RUSE SHAM TRAP TRAY WILE COVIN
CRAFT DOLUS FRAUD GUILE SARAB
SWICK SWIKE CAUTEL FELONY
WOIDRE CUNNING DISSAIT FAITERY
FICTION ARTIFICE FALSEDAD
INTRIGUE SPOOFERY SUBTLETY
TRICKERY TRUMPERY WILINESS
DECEITFUL BLIND BRAID FALSE
GAUDY JANUS LOOPY SLAPE
ARTFUL COVERT CRAFTY DOUBLE
FICKLE HOLLOW TRICKY CUNNING
EVASIVE FICTIVE SIRENIC SLEEKIT
SLIDDER UNWREST WINDING
COVINOUS GUILEFUL ILLUSIVE
INDIRECT SHAMMISH TORTUOUS
DECEITFULLY DOUBLE FALSELY
DECEITFULNESS SHAM DECEIT
FALSITY
DECEIVE BOB COG CON DOR FOB
FUB GAB GAS GUM KID LIE BILK
BRAG BUNK CRAP DUPE FAKE FLAM
FOOL GAFF GULL HAVE HOAX JILT
JOUK MOCK SELL SHAM SILE SNOW
TURN WILE ABUSE AMUSE BLEAR
BLEND BLENK BLIND BLINK BLUFF
CATCH CHEAT COZEN CROSS
CULLY DODGE DORRE FEINT GLEEK
GLOZE HOCUS LURCH PATCH
SPOOF SWICK SWIKE TRICK TROIL
TRUFF TRUMP TRYST BAFFLE
BEDOTE BEFLUM BEFOOL BETRAY
BLANCH BUBBLE CAJOLE CLOINE
CLOYNE DELUDE DIVERT EUCHRE
GAMMON HUMBUG ILLUDE JUGGLE
MISUSE NIGGLE SUCKER WIMPLE
BEGUILE DEFRAUD MISLEAD
OVERSEE TRAITOR BEJUGGLE
FLIMFLAM HOODWINK OUTREACH
DECEIVER ANGLE CHEAT HOCUS
COGGER FAITOR FALSER GUILER
MOCKER TRAPAN TREPAN FALSARY
ILLUSOR JUGGLER SHARPER
SPOOFER TRUMPER WARLOCK
WERNARD IMPOSTOR LOSENGER
LOTHARIO MAGICIAN
DECELERATE SLOW
DECENCY GRACE DECORUM
HONESTY MODESTY CHASTITY
DECENNIUM DECADE
DECENT FAIR CHASTE COMELY
HONEST MODEST PROPER SEEMLY
FITTING GRADELY JANNOCK
SHAPELY SIGHTLY DECOROUS

GRAITHLY WISELIKE
DECENTLY WHITE
DECEPTION BAM COG DOR GAG LIE
DOLE FLAM FLUM GAFF GULL HOAX
MAZE RIDE RUSE SELL SHAM WILE
ABUSE BLIND CHEAT COVIN CRAFT
CURVE DOLUS DORRE FAVEL FRAUD
GLEEK GUILE MAGIC SNARE SPOOF
TRICK BARRAT CAUTEL DECEIT
DUPERY HUMBUG JUGGLE ABUSION
BLAFLUM CHICANE CUNNING
EVASION FALLACY FALSERY FICTION
GULLAGE GULLERY KNAVERY
PRETEXT SLYNESS ARTIFICE
DISGUISE FALSEDAD FLIMFLAM
ILLUSION INTRIGUE PHANTASM
PRESTIGE SUBTLETY TRICKERY
TRUMPERY WILINESS
DECEPTIVE FLAM FALSE ARTFUL
SIRENIC TRICKSY DELUSIVE
DELUSORY FLIMFLAM ILLUSORY
IMPOSING SHAMMISH UNSICKER
DECEPTIVENESS FANTASTRY
DECIBEL (10 —S) BEL
DECIDE FIX CAST DEEM HOLD RULE
TELL WILL AWARD JUDGE PATCH
PITCH DECERN DECISE DECREE
FIGURE REWARD SETTLE ADJUDGE
DERAIGN RESOLVE CONCLUDE
SENTENCE
(— UPON) SET ELECT CHOOSE
TERMINE
DECIDED FIRM FLAT MAIN FORMED
SETTLED DECISIVE RESOLUTE
DECIDEDLY DIRECTLY DISTINCTLY
DECIDUA CADUCA
DECIGRAM LI
DECIMA TENTH TITHE
DECIMAL DENARY REPEATER
(— PART) MANTISSA
DECIMATE TENTH DESTROY
DECIPHER READ SOLVE CIPHER
DECODE DETECT REVEAL DECRYPT
DISCOVER INDICATE UNPUZZLE
DECIPHERING EPIGRAPHY
DECISION ACT END CALL DOOM
FIAT GRIT ARRET AWARD CANON
FAITH ISSUE PARTY PLUCK POINT
ACTION CHOICE CRISIS DECREE
DIKTAT RULING ACUERDO CONSULT
INTERIM PRACTIC VERDICT FINALITY
JUDGMENT PLACITUM SENTENCE
SUFFRAGE UMPIRAGE
(— OF COURT) HOLDING
(EXISTENTIAL —) LEAP
(FINAL —) ISSUE
DECISIVE FINAL CRISIC PAYOFF
VIRILE CRUCIAL DECIDED CRITICAL
CRUSHING DECRETAL POSITIVE
DECISIVELY FINALLY
DECK FIG TOG BANK BUSS DAUB
DINK FLAT HEAP PINK POOP PROW
TRIG ADORN ARRAY COVER DIZEN
DRESS EQUIP FLOOR HATCH PRANK
PRINK STORE AWNING BEDECK
BLAZON CLOTHE ENRICH FETTLE
FOCSLE LAUREL APPAREL BEDIGHT
BEDIZEN FEATHER FLOUNCE
GEMMATE BEAUTIFY DECORATE

EMBLAZON PLATFORM
(— OF CARDS) BOOK
(— OUT) BARB TIFF DIZEN SPICK
BEDECK FANGLE FINIFY BEDIGHT
(HIGH —) POOP
(LOWEST —) ORLOP
DECKED CLAD BESEEN ARMORIED
LAURELED
(— OUT) SPIFFED
DECKHAND BOATMAN TRIMMER
BARGEMAN
DECKHOUSE CABOOSE CAMBOOSE
DECKLE DECKEL FEATHEREDGE
DECKMAN TRIPPER LEVERMAN
DECLAIM GALE RANT RAVE ROLL
MOUTH ORATE SPEAK SPOUT
BLEEZE RECITE ELOCUTE INVEIGH
DENOUNCE DISCLAIM HARANGUE
PERORATE SINGSONG
DECLAIMER BARD SPEECHIFIER
DECLAMATION FROTHING
HARANGUE SPOUTING
DECLARATION BILL CALL DICK
NARR TALE WORD COUNT FUERO
LIBEL PAROL AVOWAL DECEIT
MISERE ORACLE PAROLE PLACET
SAYING EXPRESS PROMISE
RESOLVE MANIFEST PLATFORM
(— IN BRIDGE) MAKE AUCTION
(— OF HOSTILITIES) DEFIANCE
(OFFICIAL —) AUTHORITY
DECLARE BID KEN LAY SAY VOW
AVER AVOW DENY MAKE READ
SHOW SNUM SWAN TROW VOTE
AREAD AREED BRUIT KEETH KITHE
KYTHE POSIT SNORE SOUND SPEAK
STATE TRUTH VOUCH AFFIRM
ALLEGE ASSERT ASSURE AUTHOR
AVOUCH BLAZON COUTHE DEPONE
DESCRY EXPONE HERALD INDICT
NOTIFY PATEFY RELATE SPRING
UPGIVE ACCLAIM BEHIGHT DISCUSS
EXPRESS OUTTELL PROFESS
PROTEST PUBLISH SIGNIFY TERMINE
TESTIFY ANNOUNCE DENOUNCE
DESCRIBE INDICATE INTIMATE
MAINTAIN MANIFEST NUNCIATE
PROCLAIM RENOUNCE
(— A SAINT) CANONIZE
(— ARBITRARILY) GAVEL
(— INVALID) ANNUL
(— PUBLICLY) CRY
(— UNTRUE) DENY
(— WAR) DEFY
(SOLEMNLY —) AFFY SWEAR
DECLARED AVOWED STATED
DECLARER LAWMAN VIVANT
DECLINATION BIAS DECAY SLOPE
REGRET DECLINE DESCENT
REFUSAL SOUTHING SWERVING
DECLINE BEG DIP EBB SAG SET
BALK BEND BUST DENY DIVE DOWN
DROP FADE FAIL FALL FLAG FLOP
HELD SINK SLIP TURN VAIL WANE
WELK BAULK CHUTE DECAY DROLL
DROOP DWINE FAINT HEALD HIELD
LAPSE LOWER QUAIL REPEL SLACK
SLOPE SLUMP SPURN STOOP STRAY
TABES WAIVE DEBASE FALTER

REFUSE REJECT RENEGE SICKEN
WEAKEN ATROPHY DESCEND
DESCENT DETRECT DEVIATE
DISAVOW DWINDLE ECLIPSE
FAILURE FALLOFF FORBEAR
INFLECT LETDOWN SINKAGE
DECREASE DOWNBEAT DOWNTURN
FOREBEAR LANGUISH TOBOGGAN
WITHDRAW
(— IN MARKET PRICE) SPILL
(— IN POPULATION) CRASH
DECLINING DOWN AWANE BEARISH
FALLING WESTERN DECADENT
DECLIVITY BENT BREW FALL HANG
SIDE SKUG CLIFF COAST DEVEX
PITCH SCARP SLENT SLOPE CALAD
HANGER DECLINE DESCENT
HANGING DOWNHILL
DECLIVOUS PRONE SLOPING
DECOCT BOIL COOK SMELT EXCITE
KINDLE REFINE EXTRACT
DECOCTION BANG OOZE SAVE
BHANG APOZEM CREMOR PTISAN
TISANE APOZEMA DECOCTUM
DECOHERER TAPPER
DECOLLETE LOW
DECOMPOSE ROT FOUL FRIT DECA
ATTACK DIGEST DEGRADE DISSOLV
DECOMPOSED PUTRID
DECOMPOSITION DECAY BREAKUP
BIOLYSIS EXCHANGE
DECORATE DO BIND CHIP CITE
DECK EDGE FRET GAUD PINK RAIL
RULE TIFF TIRE TRIM ADORN DRES
FLOCK FRILL GRAIN INLAY MENSE
PANEL POKER TRAIL TRICK BEDEC
BUTTON DAIKER DAMASK DECORE
EMBOSS FLOWER FRESCO PARGET
POUNCE PURFLE SPONGE SUBORN
BECROSS CORONET ENCHASE
FESTOON FURNISH GADROON
GARNISH HISTORY IMPASTE
INWEAVE MINIATE PERFORM
BELETTER FLOURISH ORNAMENT
OVERWORK TITIVATE
DECORATED GIDDY LACED AJOURE
FLAMBE ORNATE ADORNED
DAMASSE FROGGED INCISED
WROUGHT COCKADED DISTINCT
FLORETED
DECORATING LIMNERY
DECORATION KEY BUHL FALL FUS
IKAT BOULE DECOR DODAD HONOF
MEDAL PRIDE BOULLE DECKER
DECORE DESIGN DOODAB DOODAD
FINERY FLORET FRIEZE GOTHIC
NIELLO PLAQUE SETOFF TINSEL
ARTWORK BARBOLA DECKING
EPERGNE FLUTING GARNISH
TRACERY BAYADERE DENTELLE
DIAMANTE ESCALLOP FLOURISH
FRETTING FRETWORK INTARSIA
ORNAMENT
(— IN GUEST CHAMBER) XENIUM
(— OF LEAVES) VIGNETTE
(— OF MONKEYS) SINGERIE
(— TECHNIQUE) PLANGI
(BOOK-COVER —) DENTELLE
(CUTOUT —) APPLIQUE

(FESTIVE —) GALA
(INESSENTIAL —) SPINACH
(MURAL —) TOPIA
(MUSICAL —) GRACE
(PORCELAIN —) KAKIEMON
(POTTERY —) BRODERIE
(WALL —S) TENTURE
(PL.) COLORS BUNTING GREENERY
DECORATIVE FANCY FIKIE
DECOROUS CALM DONE GOOD NICE
PRIM DOUCE GRAVE QUIET SOBER
STAID CHASTE DECENT DEMURE
MODEST POLITE PROPER SEDATE
SEEMLY SERENE STEADY BECOMED
FITTING ORDERLY REGULAR
SETTLED BECOMING COMPOSED
MANNERLY
DECOROUSLY FITLY
DECOROUSNESS CHASTITY
POLITESSE
DECORTICATE FLAY HULL HUSK
PARE PEEL PILL SKIN STRIP
DENUDE
DECORUM DECENCY DIGNITY
FITNESS MODESTY
DECOY COY BAIT CALL GOAD LURE
TOLE TOLL CRIMP DRILL PLANT
ROPER SHILL STALE STALL STOOL
TEMPT TRAIN ALLURE BUTTON
CALLER CAPPER ENTICE ENTRAP
PIGEON SEDUCE TOLLER TREPAN
BARNARD BERNARD DECOYER
INVEIGLE SQUAWKER
(— FOR GAMBLERS) CAPPER
(— FOR SWINDLERS) BARNARD
BERNARD
(AUCTIONEER'S —) BUTTON
DECREASE EBB BATE DROP FALL
LOSS SINK WANE WELK WILK ABATE
CROCK DECAY LAPSE SWAGE
TAPER WANZE WASTE CHANGE
DECESS DECREW IMPAIR LESSEN
NARROW REDUCE SHRINK ATROPHY
CUTDOWN DECLINE DWINDLE
SHORTEN SLACKEN SUBSIDE
DECIMATE DIMINISH DOWNTURN
MODERATE RETRENCH
(— IN FORCE) LAY
(— IN VOLUME) ABLATION
(— OF EFFICIENCY) FATIGUE
(— STITCHES) FASHION
DECREE ACT DIT LAW SAW SET
DOOM FIAT REDE RULE WILL WITE
AREAD AREED ARRET CANON EDICT
ENACT FIANT GRACE HATTI IRADE
JUDGE ORDER POINT SHAPE TENET
UKASE WRITE ARREST ASSIZE
DECERN DICTUM FIRMAN INDICT
MODIFY ORDAIN PLACIT RECESS
ADJUDGE APPOINT BESLUIT
COMMAND CONSULT DECREET
DICTATE DIVORCE ESCRIPT
GEZERAH MANDATE SETNESS
STATUTE WORKING DECISION
DECRETUM JUDGMENT PLACITUM
PSEPHISM RESCRIPT ROGATION
SANCTION SENTENCE
(— BEFOREHAND) DESTINE

(ECCLESIASTICAL —) CANON
SYNODICAL
(JUDICIAL —) AUTO
(MOHAMMEDAN —) IRADE
(OFFICIAL —) RESCRIPT
DECREPIT LAME WEAK UNORN
BEDRID CREAKY FEEBLE INFIRM
SENILE FAILING INVALID FORFAIRN
DECRY BOO SLUR LOWER ROGUE
DESCRY LESSEN ASPERSE BARRACK
CENSURE CONDEMN DEBAUCH
DEGRADE DETRACT BELITTLE
DEROGATE MINIMIZE
DECRYPT BREAK DECODE
DECURRENT DEFLUENT
DECUSSATION CHIASMA
DEDANS HAZARD
DEDICATE VOW VOTE DEVOW
SACRE SACRI DEVOTE DEVOVE
DIRECT HALLOW OBLATE ASCRIBE
ENTITLE CHRISTEN INSCRIBE
INTITULE SEPARATE
DEDICATED HOLY OBLATE SACRED
VOTIVE
DEDICATION CULT WAKF DEVOTION
DEDUCE PUT DRAW LEAD TAKE
BRING DRIVE FETCH GUESS INFER
TRACE DEDUCT DERIVE ELICIT
EVOLVE GATHER COLLECT EXPLAIN
EXTRACT SUBSUME CONCLUDE
DEDUCT BATE DOCK TAKE ABATE
ALLOW SHAVE DEFALK REBATE
RECOUP REDUCT REMOVE CURTAIL
SUBDUCT TRADUCE ABSTRACT
DISCOUNT SEPARATE SUBTRACT
DEDUCTION AGIO SALT CREDIT
DEDUCT REBATE BEAMAGE
DOCKAGE IMPRESS OFFTAKE
REPRISE DISCOUNT ERGOTISM
ILLATION STOPPAGE
DEDUCTIVE DOGMATIC
DEE DUANT
DEED DO ACT BILL BOOK CASE FACT
FAIT FEAT FIAT GEST HARD JEST
TURN WORK ACTUM ACTUS BROAD
CHART DOING GESTE ISSUE SANAD
THING TITLE ACTION CONVEY
ESCROW FACTUM POTTAH REMISE
SASINE SUNNUD TAILYE CHARTER
EXPLOIT FACTION TAILZIE CHIVALRY
HEIRLOOM PARERGON PRACTICE
PRACTISE TRANSFER
(BRUTAL —) ATROCITY
(CHARITABLE —S) ALMS
(GOOD —) BENEFIT MITZVAH
(HEBREW —) STARR
(PART OF —) HABENDUM
(VALIANT —) VALIANCE
(WICKED —) ILL
(PL.) DOINGS SERVICE MUNIMENTS
DEEM LET SAY SEE GIVE HOPE RECK
SEEM TELL JUDGE OPINE THINK
ESTEEM EXPECT ORDAIN RECKON
REGARD ACCOUNT ADJUDGE
BELIEVE RECOUNT RESPECT
SURMISE ANNOUNCE CONSIDER
JUDGMENT PROCLAIM
DEEMSTER DOOMSMAN
DE-ENERGIZE KILL CLEAR

DEEP LOW SAD SEA BOLD DUAT
HOLL HOWE NEAL RAPT ABYSS
BROAD DEWAT GRAVE GREAT
GRUFF HEAVY OCEAN STIFF STOOR
STOUR HOLLOW INTENT STRONG
SULLEN ABYSMAL INTENSE SERIOUS
UNMIXED ABSORBED ABSTRUSE
COMPLETE POWERFUL PROFOUND
THOROUGH
DEEP-DYED ENGRAINED
DEEPEN CLOUD DARKEN DREDGE
ENHANCE THICKEN HEIGHTEN
DEEPEST INMOST DEEPMOST
DEEPLY DEEP ADEEP DEARLY
SOUNDLY DEVOUTLY GROUNDLY
INWARDLY
DEEP-SEA DIPSY BATHYL DIPSEY
BATHYAL
DEEP-SEATED DEEP INTIMATE
PROFOUND INGRAINED
DEEP-TONED STOUR
DEER ELK RED ROE AXIS BUCK DAIM
HART HIND MILU MUSK OLEN PARA
PUDU RUSA SHOU SIKA STAG WILD
BROCK GEMUL MARAL MOOSE
SABIR SPADE STAIG CERVID CHITAL
CHITRA FALLOW GUEMAL HANGUL
HEARST HUEMUL PARRAH RASCAL
SAMBAR SAMBUR THAMIN VENADA
BROCKET BROWZER CARIBOU
CERVINE CERVOID CHEETAL
DEERLET FANTAIL GUAZUTI
KASTURA MUNTJAC PLANDOK
SAMBHAR THAMENG VENISON
BOBOLINK ELAPHURE RUMINANT
(— IN 3RD YEAR) SPAY SOREL
SPAYAD SPAYARD
(— UNDER 1 YEAR) KID
(2-YEAR OLD —) KNOBBER
(CASTRATED —) HAVIER
(FEMALE — IN 2ND YEAR) TEG
HEARST
(FEMALE —) DOE ROE HIND
(HINDQUARTERS OF —) FOUCH
FOURCHE
(MALE — IN 2ND YEAR) PRICKET
(MALE — IN 4TH YEAR) SORE
STAGGARD STAGGART
(MALE — OVER 5 YEARS) HART
STAG
(RED —) OLEN MARAL BROCKET
(RUSINE —) AXIS
(YOUNG —) KID FAWN SPITTER
DEER BUSH SOAPBUSH
DEER FERN HARDFERN
DEERFLY TABANID
DEERHAIR SEDGE BULRUSH
DEERHOUND DEERDOG BUCKHOUND
DEERSKIN BUCK DEER
DEFACE MAR FOUL RUIN SCAR
ERASE SHAME SPOIL CANCEL
DAMAGE DAMASK DEFAME DEFOIL
DEFORM DEFOUL EFFACE INJURE
INJURY DESTROY DETRACT DISTORT
SLANDER DISGRACE DISHONOR
MALAHACK MUTILATE OUTSHINE
DEFACED FOUL
DEFACING DIMINUTION
DEFALCATE DRIB DEFALK

DEFAMATION LIBEL DEFAME DEFAMY DEPRAVE SCANDAL SLANDER
DEFAME FOUL ABASE BELIE CLOUD LIBEL NOISE SMEAR ACCUSE CHARGE DEFACE DEFOIL DEFOUL FORGAB INFAME INJURE MALIGN SUGGIL VILIFY ASPERSE BLACKEN BLEMISH DEBAUCH DETRACT DIFFAME PUBLISH SCANDAL SLANDER SPATTER TRADUCE DISHONOR INFAMIZE
DEFAMER SYCOPHANT
DEFAULT FAIL FLAW LOSS MORA ERROR FAULT OFFEND BLEMISH FAILURE MISTAKE NEGLECT OFFENSE OMISSION
(— ON DEBT) LEVANT
DEFEASANCE DEFEAT UNDOING
DEFEASIBLE IMPERFECT
DEFEAT EAT PIP WIN BALK BEAT BEST BOWL CAST DING DOWN DRUB FOIL HAVE JINK KILL LACE LICK LOSS ROUT RUIN RUSH SINK SKIN STOP TOLL TOSS TRAP TRIM UNDO WHIP AVOID BREAK CHECK FACER FALSE FLING FLOOR OUTDO PASTE SKUNK SWAMP THROW WASTE WHACK WORSE WORST WRACK BAFFLE CUMBER DEROUT EUCHRE LARRUP MASTER MURDER STOUSH THWACK THWART WAGGLE WEAKEN CONQUER DEPRIVE DESTROY LICKING OVERSET PEREMPT REVERSE SCOMFIT SETBACK SHELLAC SNOOKER SUBVERT TROUNCE INFRINGE IRRITATE OVERCOME VANQUISH WATERLOO
(— COMPLETELY) SKUNK
(— DECISIVELY) EAT DRUB SACK BLAST CLEAN FLATTEN SHELLAC
(— IN BRIDGE) SET
(— IN LAWSUIT) CAST
(DECISIVE —) CLEANUP CLEANING
(INTO —) DOWN
(UTTER —) MATE ROUT DEROUT
DEFEATED DOWN LOST KAPUT BEATEN CRAVEN WHIPPED
DEFEATIST BOLO FATALIST
DEFECT BUG FLAW LACK MAIM TWIT VICE WANE WANT BOTCH CLOUD CRAZE ERROR FAULT MINUS MULCT TOUCH DAMAGE DESERT INJURY LACUNA MALADY MAYHEM PLIGHT VICETY VITIUM ABSENCE BLEMISH DEMERIT FAILING MISPICK PEELING PINHOLE COLOBOMA CRESCENT DRAWBACK WEAKNESS
(— IN CRYSTAL) HOLE
(— IN ENAMEL) SCAB SAGGING SCUMMING
(— IN FABRIC) GOUT SCOB BARRE BRACK SMASH
(— IN GLASS) KNOT TEAR STONE THREADS
(— IN IRON) SEAM
(— IN MARBLE) TERRAS TERRACE TERRASSE

(— IN METAL) SNAKE
(— IN PRINTING PLATE) HICKY HICKEY
(— IN STEEL) LAP
(— IN TIMBER) LAG SHAN COLLAPSE
(— IN YARN) SINGLING CORKSCREW
(— OF CHARACTER) HOLE SHADE HAMARTIA
(LINT —) SPOT
(SPEECH —) CLUTTERING
(TELEVISION —) FLOPOVER
DEFECTION LETDOWN DESERTION
DEFECTIVE BAD ILL EVIL FOXY LACK LAME MANK POOR SICK BAUCH BAUGH BLIND FALSE FLAWY PASUL COMMON FAULTY FLAWED MANGUE MEAGER MEAGRE RAGGED HALTING TOMFOOL VICIOUS DISGENIC DYSGENIC MUTILOUS VITIATED
DEFEND FEND HOLD KEEP SAVE WARD WARN WEAR COVER GUARD SHEND WATCH ASSERT FORBID SCREEN SECURE SHIELD UPHOLD WARISH BUCKLER CONTEST DERAIGN ESPOUSE EXPOUND FLANKER JUSTIFY PREVENT PROPUGN PROTECT SHELTER SUPPORT WARRANT ADVOCATE CHAMPION CONSERVE GARRISON MAINTAIN PRESERVE PROHIBIT
DEFENDANT REA REUS ACCUSED AVOWANT APPELLEE
DEFENDER FENDER PATRON ADVOCATE ASSERTER ASSERTOR CHAMPION GUARDIAN UPHOLDER
DEFENSE EGIS FORT WALL WEAR AEGIS ALIBI FENCE GRITH ANSWER BEHALF COVERT FRAISE SCONCE BARRACE BULWARK CONTEST DEFENCE OUTWORK RAMPART SHELTER BOUNDARY SECURITY SEPIMENT SPOLOGIA PALE ROCK WARD GUARD TOWER ABATIS BARRIER COUNTER DILATOR PARADOS WARDING WARRANT FRONTIER GALAPAGO GARRISON MUNITION
DEFENSELESS BARE COLD NAKED SILLY UNARMED HELPLESS
DEFENSIBLE TENABLE JUSTIFIABLE
DEFER BOW RISE STAY WAIT DELAY DRIVE HONOR REFER REMIT TARRY TRACK WAIVE YIELD ESTEEM HUMBLE RETARD REVERE SUBMIT ADJOURN SUSPEND CONSIDER INTERMIT POSTPONE PROROGUE PROTRACT SUSPENSE
DEFERENCE VAIL COURT HONOR CRINGE ESTEEM HOMAGE REGARD RESPECT WORSHIP CIVILITY
DEFERENT ECCENTRIC
DEFERENTIAL DUTIFUL OBEISANT
DEFERMENT STAY
DEFERVESCENCE LYSIS DECLINE
DEFIANCE DARE DEFI DEFY GAGE BRAVE DEFIAL
DEFIANT BOLD BARDY BRAVE STOUT

DARING STOCKY INSOLENT STUBBORN
DEFICIENCY FAIL LACK WANT ANOIA ERROR FAULT MINUS DEARTH DEFECT INLAIK ULLAGE ABSENCE ANOESIA BLEMISH DEFICIT FAILING FAILURE DELETION SCARCITY SHORTAGE
(— OF NERVOUS ENERGY) ANEURIA
(— OF OXYGEN) ASPHYXIA
(CARBON DIOXIDE —) ACAPNIA
(MENTAL —) IDIOCY AMENTIA
(PL.) SHORTS
DEFICIENT BAD LEAN WANE BLUNT MINUS BARREN FEEBLE MEAGER MEAGRE SCARCE SCRIMP SKIMPY BOBTAIL DISGENIC DYSGENIC INDIGENT
(— IN TURGOR) FLACCID
(MENTALLY —) SOFT
DEFICIT SHORTAGE UNDERAGE
DEFILE GUT RAY ABRA BAWD BEDO FILE FOIL FOUL GATE GOWL HALS LIME MOIL MUCK PACE PASS SLIP SLUT SMUT SOIL ABUSE BERAY CLEFT CROCK DIRTY FILTH GLACK GORGE HALSE NOTCH SMEAR STAIN SULLY TAINT BEWRAY DEBASE GULLET IMBRUE INFECT RAVISH SMOUCH SMUTCH CORRUPT DEBAUCH DEPRAVE DISTAIN PASSAGE POLLUTE PROFANE SMATTER TARNISH VIOLATE DISHONOR MACULATE
DEFILED DIRTY IMPURE SPOTTY UNCLEAN MACULATE
DEFILEMENT MOIL SOIL SULLAGE TAINTURE
DEFILING PIKY PITCHY
DEFINE END FIX SET MERE TERM BOUND LIMIT DECIDE CLARIFY DELIMIT EXPLAIN EXPOUND DESCRIBE DISCOVER
DEFINED FORMED
(SHARPLY —) HARD
DEFINITE SET FIRM HARD SURE CLEAR FINAL FIXED SHARP FINITE FORMED LIQUID STRAIT CERTAIN EXPRESS LIMITED POINTED PRECISE DISTINCT EMPHATIC EXPLICIT LIMITING POSITIVE PUNCTUAL SPECIFIC
DEFINITELY BUT WELL FAIRLY EVERMORE
DEFINITION GLOSS CLARITY
(— OF FORM) SFUMATO
DEFINITIVE LAST FINAL GRAND ORISTIC DEFINITE
DEFLATE EMPALE IMPALE CONTRACT
DEFLATED FLAT
DEFLATING SETDOWN
DEFLATION HANGOVER
DEFLECT CUT WRY BEND COCK SWAY WARP PARRY WREST WRING BAFFLE DETOUR DIVERT SWERVE DEVIATE DIVERGE INFLECT REFLECT REFRACT

EFLECTION DROOP SWEEP
WINDAGE
(— **ON METER)** KICK
EFLOWER FRAY DEFOIL DEFOUL
FORLIE RAVAGE RAVISH DEFLORE
DESPOIL VIOLATE UNMAIDEN
UNVIRGIN
EFORM MAR FLOW WARP GNARL
DEFACE BLEMISH CONTORT
DISFORM DISTORT DIFFORME
DISGUISE DISHONOR MISSHAPE
EFORMATION CREEP SPRING
STRAIN FLEXURE FLOWAGE
EFORMED GAMMY WRONG INFORM
PAULIE CROOKED HIDEOUS
MISBORN FORMLESS UNMACKLY
EFORMITY GALL VICE BLEMISH
HARELIP PRAVITY CLUBFOOT
CLUBHAND FLATFOOT WANSHAPE
EFRAUD ROB BEAT BILK FAKE
GULL NICK ROOK TRIM WIPE CHEAT
COZEN GOUGE MULCT SLICK STICK
TRICK WRONG BOODLE CHOUSE
CHOWSE DECEIVE SWINDLE
EFRAY PAY BEAR AVERT COVER
EXPEND PREPAY APPEASE REQUITE
SATISFY DISBURSE
EFT GAIN NEAT TALL TRIM AGILE
HANDY QUICK SLICK ADROIT
EXPERT HEPPEN NIMBLE SPRACK
SPRUCE DELIVER DEXTROUS
SKILLFUL
EFTEST EFTEST
EFTLY SLICKLY DELIVERLY
EFTNESS SLEIGHT
EFUNCT DEAD EXTINCT DECEASED
DEPARTED FINISHED
EFY BRAG DARE DEFI FACE MOCK
BEARD BRAVE STUMP TEMPT
CARTEL FORBID MAUGER MAUGRE
REJECT AFFRONT BRAVADE
DESPISE DISDAIN OUTDARE
OUTFACE CHAMPION DEFIANCE
OUTSCOUT RENOUNCE
GENERATE ROT SINK DEBADE
FFETE UNKIND DEGENER DEGRADE
DEPRAVE DESCEND DEGENDER
— **IN IDLENESS)** RUST
— **TOWARD BARBARISM)** WILDER
GENERATION WALLER ATROPHY
DIPOSIS
GRADATION FALL WOHL SHAME
DECLINE DESCENT ADULTERY
DEPOSURE IGNOMINY
GRADE BUST SINK ABASE BREAK
DECRY LOWER SHAME SHEND
STOOP STRIP UNMAN DEBASE
DEMEAN DEMOTE DEPOSE EMBASE
HUMBLE LESSEN REDUCE VILIFY
CORRUPT DECLINE DEPRESS
ABRUTE REGRADE VILLAIN
DIMINISH DISGRACE DISHONOR
DISMOUNT DISPLUME SUPPLANT
GRADED BASE SEAMY ABJECT
DEMISS FALLEN DEBASED DEGREED
PRIECED OUTCAST
GRADING BASE MENIAL
SHAMEFUL
GRAS MOELLON

DEGREE PEG PIP POL BANK CAST
DEAL FORM GREE HEAT PEEP POLL
RANK RATE RUNG STEP TERM TIER
CLASS GRADE GRADO GRECE GRICE
HONOR LEVEL NOTCH ORDER PITCH
PLACE POINT PRICK SHADE STAGE
STAIR EXTENT GRIECE LENGTH
MEDIUM SOEVER DESCENT DIGNITY
MEASURE SAENGER STATION
ACCURACY AEGROTAT QUANTITY
STANDING STRENGTH
(— **OF CLOSENESS)** FIT
(— **OF COMBINING POWER)**
VALENCE
(— **OF CONTRAST)** GAMMA
(— **OF DEVIATION)** LEEWAY
(— **OF ELEVATION)** ASCENT
(— **OF ENGAGEMENT)** DEPTH
(— **OF FLAWLESSNESS)** CLARITY
(— **OF FORCE)** KICK
(— **OF HEIGHT)** GRADE
(— **OF IMPORTANCE)** CALIBER
CALIBRE
(— **OF INFESTATION)** BURDEN
(— **OF INTOXICATION)** EDGE
(— **OF KNOWLEDGE)** SCIENTER
(— **OF LIGHTNESS)** VALUE
(— **OF MIXTURE)** ALLOY
(— **OF OPACITY)** DENSITY
(— **OF PLENTIFULNESS)**
ABUNDANCE
(— **OF SLOPE)** SPLAY
(— **OF STREAMLINING)** FAIRNESS
(— **OF THE SOUL)** RUACH
(— **OF WATER HARDNESS)** GRAIN
(— **OF WHITENESS)** BLEACH
(10 —**S OF LONGITUDE)** FACE
(15 —**S)** HOUR
(**EXCESSIVE** —) EXTREME
(**GREATEST** —) UTMOST
(**HIGHEST** —) PINK SUMMIT
SUPREME SUBLIMITY
(**INDEFINITE** —) SEEM
(**MINUTE** —) DROP SHADE
(**MUSICAL** —) SPACE SUBTONIC
(**RABINNICAL** —) SEMICHA SEMIKAH
CEMICHAH
(**SMALL** —) ACE HAIR INCH IOTA
SHADOW GLIMMER
(**SOME** —) BIT
(**UTMOST** —) SUM ACME HEIGHT
EXTREME EXTREMITY
DEGU OCTODONT
DEGUM STRIP
(— **SILK)** SOUPLE
DEHGAN SWAT SWATI
DEHORN SNUB DISBUD
DEHWAR DEHKAN
DEHYDRATE DRY DESICCATE
DEIANIRA (BROTHER OF —) TYDEUS
MELEAGER
(**FATHER OF** —) OENEUS
(**HUSBAND OF** —) HERCULES
(**MOTHER OF** —) ALTHAEA
DEIDAMIA HIPPODAMIA
(**FATHER OF** —) LYCOMEDES
(**LOVER OF** —) ACHILLES
(**SON OF** —) PYRRHUS
NEOPTOLEMUS

DEIFY GOD BEGOD DIVINE GODDIZE
DIVINIFY DIVINIZE
DEIGN STOOP VOUCHSAFE
DEIPHOBUS (BROTHER OF —) PARIS
HECTOR
(**FATHER OF** —) PRIAM
(**MOTHER OF** —) HECUBA
(**WIFE OF** —) HELEN
DEITY (ALSO SEE GOD AND
GODDESS) EA EL KA RA RE SU ABU
BEL GAD GOD RAN SHU SOL AKAL
AMEN AMON BAAL CAGN DEVA
FAUN FURY GWYN MIND MORS
RANA SIVA SOBK ALALA ALALU
AMIDA AMITA AMMON DAGAN
DAGON HOBAL HORUS HUBAL
INUUS JANUS MIDER MITRA MONAD
SATYR SEBEK SHIVA SIRIS SURYA
ZOMBI ASHIMA ATHTAR BATALA
BUNENE CAISSA FATHER FAUNUS
IASION MARDUK MOLOCH NIBHAZ
OANNES ORISHA ORMAZD ORMUZD
RIMMON SOMNUS SUCHOS SYLVAN
VARUNA ZOMBIE ALASTOR FORSETE
FORSETI GODDESS GODHEAD
GODLING GODSHIP HERSHEF
IAPETUS KHEPERA MANITOU
NINURTA NISROCH PHORCUS
PHORKYS RESHEPH SETEBOS
SILENUS TAGALOA TARANIS VIRBIUS
BAALPEOR BEELPEOR BELFAGOR
DEVARAJA DIVINITY ELAGABAL
GOVERNOR HACHIMAN MELKARTH
MERODACH PICUMNUS PILUMNUS
SEILENOS SILVANUS TANGALOA
TUTELARY ZEPHYRUS ZOOMORPH
(**AVENGING** —) ALASTOR
(**HEATHEN** —) IDOL
(**INFERIOR** —) GODKIN GODLING
DEMIURGE PETTYGOD
(**SHINTO** —) KAMI
(**SUPREME** —) HANSA
(**TUTELARY** —) NUMEN GENIUS
(PL.) CABIRI
DEJECT ABASE LOWER HUMBLE
LESSEN FLATTEN DISPIRIT
DOWNCAST
DEJECTA EGESTA
DEJECTED BAD LOW SAD DAMP
DOWN GLUM POOR SUNK AMORT
MUDDY WAPED ABASED DEJECT
DEMISS DROOPY GLOOMY PINING
SOMBER SOMBRE DUMPISH
HANGDOG HANGING HUMBLED
LUMPISH UNHAPPY DOWNCAST
DOWNWARD REPINING WOBEGONE
WRETCHED
DEJECTEDLY HEAVILY
DEJECTION DAMP GLOOM SLOTH
DISMAY DISMALS HUMDRUM
SADNESS
DEJEUNER LUNCH BREAKFAST
COLAZIONE COLLATION
DEL NABLA

DELAWARE
CAPITAL: DOVER

COUNTY: KENT SUSSEX
NEWCASTLE
INDIAN: LENAPE
STATE FLOWER: PEACH
STATE BIRD: BLUEHEN
STATE NICKNAME: DIAMOND
STATE TREE: HOLLY
TOWN: LEWES SMYRNA ELSMERE
CLAYMONT WILMINGTON

DELAY LAG LET BLIN BODE HOLD
HONE LENG LING LITE MORA SIST
SLOW SLUG STAY STOP WAIT ABIDE
ABODE ALLAY BLINE CHECK DALLY
DEFER DEMUR DETER DRIFT DWELL
FRIST REPRY SLOTH STALL STENT
STICK STINT TARDY TARRY TRACT
ARREST ATTEND BACKEN BELATE
DAWDLE DETAIN DILATE DILUTE
DRETCH ESSOIN FUTURE HINDER
HOLDUP IMPEDE LINGER LOITER
QUENCH REMORE RETARD TAIGLE
TARROW TEMPER WEAKEN
ADJOURN ASSUAGE BARRACE
CONFINE DRUTTLE FORSLOW
PROLONG RESPECT RESPITE
SLACKEN SOJOURN DEMURRAL
DILATION FORESLOW FOURCHER
HANGFIRE HESITATE MACERATE
MITIGATE MORATION OBSTRUCT
POSTPONE REPRIEVE STOPPAGE
(— **TRIAL**) TRAVERSE
(**LEGAL** —) DILATOR INDUCIAE
(**UNDUE** —) LACHES
DELAYED LATE TARDY LAGGED
BELATED OVERDUE
DELAYING TRAIN DILATORY
DELECTABLE TASTY DESIROUS
PLEASING BEAUTIFUL EXQUISITE
DELEGATE NAME SEND ASSIGN
COMMIT DELATE DEPUTE DEPUTY
LEGATE NUNCIO APPOINT CONSIGN
EMPOWER ENTRUST EMISSARY
RELEGATE TRANSFER
DELEGATION MISSION DELEGACY
(**ATHENIAN** —) DELIA
DELETE DELE EDIT OMIT BLACK
ERASE PURGE SLASH CANCEL
CENSOR DELATE REMOVE STRIKE
DESTROY EXPUNGE STONKER
CASTRATE
DELETERIOUS BAD PRAVE HARMFUL
HURTFUL NOXIOUS PRAVOUS
DAMAGING DELETERY
DELIBERATE COOL PORE RUNE
SLOW STUDY THINK ADVISE
CONFER DEBATE PONDER REGARD
ADVISED BALANCE BETHINK
CONSULT COUNCIL COUNSEL
DELIBER DELIVER REFLECT
RESOLVE STUDIED WILLING
CONSIDER DESIGNED MEASURED
MEDITATE PERPENSE PREPENSE
PROPENSE STUDIOUS
DELIBERATELY COOLY COOLLY
APURPOSE ADVISEDLY
DELIBERATENESS MATURITY
DELIBERATION ADVICE COUNCIL

COUNSEL LEISURE THOUGHT
VISEMENT
DELICACY BIT ROE CATE EASE NORI
TACT ACATE FRILL KNACK TASTE
CAVIAR DAINTY DELICE JUNKET
LUXURY NICETY REGALO FINESSE
REGALIA TENUITY AIRINESS
DAINTITH DAINTREL DELICATE
KICKSHAW LEGERETE NICENESS
PLEASURE SUBTLETY
(**PL.**) CATES ACATES
DELICATE SLY AIRY FINE LACY
NESH NICE SOFT TEAR ZART DELIE
DORTY ELFIN FRAIL LIGHT SILKY
TEWLY CASHIE CHOICE DAINTY
FLIMSY GENTLE GINGER INCONY
KITTLE MINION PASTEL PETITE
PULING QUEASY SILKEN SLIGHT
SUBTLE TENDER TICKLE TWIGGY
ELEGANT EPICENE FINICAL FRAGILE
MINIKIN REFINED SLIMMER SUBTILE
SUMMERY TAFFETA TAFFETY
TENUOUS TIFFANY WILLOWY
ARANEOUS CHARMING ETHEREAL
FEATHERY GOSSAMER GRACEFUL
HOTHOUSE LUSCIOUS MIGNIARD
PINDLING PLEASANT SENSIBLE
SUMMERLY TICKLISH UNLUSTIE
(— **IN APPEARANCE**) HUNGRY
DELICATELY FINE SMALLY FAIRILY
DELICATESSEN GASTRONOME
CHARCUTERIE
DELICIOUS DAINTY FRIAND
DELICATE
DELIGHT JOY GLEE GUST LITE LOVE
SEND TAKE BLISS CHARM EXULT
FEAST GRACE GUSTO MIRTH REVEL
SAVOR SMACK ADMIRE ARRIDE
DELICE DIVERT LIKING PLEASE
RAVISH REGALE RELISH DISPORT
ECSTASY ENCHANT GLADDEN
GRATIFY JOYANCE JOYANCY
LECHERY RAPTURE REJOICE
DELICATE ENTRANCE GLADNESS
PLEASURE SAVORING
(— **IN**) LOVE SAVOR
(**PL.**) DELICIAE
DELIGHTED GLAD
DELIGHTFUL NICE GREAT JAMMY
JOLLY MERRY SOOTH DREAMY
SAVORY ELYSIAN LEESOME
ADORABLE DELICATE DELITOUS
GLORIOUS GORGEOUS HEAVENLY
LUSCIOUS
DELIMER DRENCHER
DELIMIT FIX DEFINE SUBTEND
DELIMITED MERED MEERED
DELINEATE MAP DRAW ETCH LIMN
LINE CHALK CHART FENCE IMAGE
PAINT STELL TABLE TOUCH TRACE
TRICK BLAZON CIPHER DELINE
DEPICT DESIGN DEVISE SKETCH
SURVEY DEPAINT EXPRESS LINEATE
OUTLINE PICTURE PORTRAY
DECIPHER DEFIGURE DESCRIBE
TRAVERSE
DELINEATION DRAFT DESIGN
SKETCH SURVEY DRAUGHT
DELINQUENCY FAULT GUILT

FAILURE MISDEED OFFENSE
OMISSION
DELINQUENT CRIMINAL
(**PL.**) KALANG
DELIQUESCE MELT LIQUEFY
DISSOLVE
DELIRIOUS FEY MAD OFF REE GYTE
LIGHT MANIC INSANE RAVING
FLIGHTY FRANTIC LUNATIC
BRAINISH DELEERIT DELIERET
DERANGED FRENETIC FRENZIED
DELIRIUM FURY MAZE MANIA
FRENZY LUNACY RAVERY MADNESS
DELIRACY IDLENESS INSANITY
DELIRIUM TREMENS JUMP
HORRORS JIMJAMS JIMMIES
POTOMANIA
DELIVER DO HIT LAY LET RID BAIL
BORN DEAL FREE GIVE LEND REDD
SAVE SELL SEND TAKE BEKEN
BRING COUGH LIVER SERVE SPEAK
UTTER ADDICT ASSIZE ASSOIL
BETRAY COMMIT CONVEY EXEMPT
PREACH RANSOM REDEEM RENDER
RESCUE RESIGN SUCCOR UNBIND
BETEACH BITECHE COMMEND
CONSIGN DECLAIM DICTATE
OUTTAKE PRESENT RECOVER
RELEASE RELIEVE DISPATCH
EXORCISE EXORCIZE LIBERATE
(— **BALL**) BOWL
(— **BLOW**) LEND SEND
(— **BLOWS ON HEAD**) NOB
(— **CHILD**) LIGHT
(— **FORCEFULLY**) FASTEN
(— **LOGS**) STOCK
(— **MERCHANDISE**) UTTER
(— **OVER**) BETAKE CONSIGN
(— **RHETORICALLY**) DECLAIM
(— **SPEECH**) ADDRESS
DELIVERANCE BOOT ESCAPE
RESCUE SAVING DELIVERY
RIDDANCE SOLUTION VOIDANCE
SALVATION
DELIVERED LANDED
(— **FREE**) FRANCO
(**PRECISELY** —) FLUSH
DELIVERER SOTER DRAYMAN
SAOSHYANT
DELIVERY FLY BAIL FLIER FLYER
ISSUE RESCUE ADDRESS AIRDROP
BAILMENT SHIPMENT
(— **IN SPEAKING**) DICTION
(— **OF BALL**) BOWL
(— **WAGON**) FLY
(**MAIL** —) TAPPALL TAPPAUL
DELL DEN HOW DALE DEAN DENE
DILL DRAB GLEN VALE SLACK
SLADE TRULL WENCH DINGLE
RAVINE VALLEY
(**PL.**) DALLES
DELPHINIUM DAUPHIN DOLPHIN
LARKSPUR
DELUDE BOB JIG BILK DUPE FOOL
HOAX MOCK AMUSE CHEAT COZEN
ELUDE EVADE GLAIK SPOOF TRICK
BAFFLE BANTER BEFOOL BUBBLE
DIDDLE ILLUDE BEGUILE DECEIVE
ENCHANT MISLEAD OVERSEE

BEJUGGLE HOODWINK INVEIGLE OVERSILE

DELUGE SEA FLOW FLOOD SWAMP DILUVY CATARACT INUNDATE OVERFLOW SATURATE SUBMERGE

DELUNDUNG LINSANG ZINSANG VIVERRINE

DELUSION MAZE MOHA ABUSE DWALE FRAUD TRICK MIRAGE VISION CHIMERA FALLACY FANTASM PHANTOM WANHOPE ILLUSION NIHILISM PHANTASM

DELUSTER DULL

DELVE DEN DIG DIP PIT CAVE DINT MINE DITCH PLUMB BRUISE BURROW EXHUME FATHOM INDENT IMPRESS EXCAVATE INSCRIBE

DEMAGNETIZE DEPERM DEPOLARIZE

DEMAGOGUE CLEON LEADER ORATOR ROUSER DEMAGOG SPEAKER TRIBUNE JAWSMITH

DEMAND ASK CRY TAX USE CALL NEED RAME SALE CLAIM CRAVE DRAFT EXACT GAVEL ORDER QUERY SIGHT BEHEST CHARGE DESIRE ELICIT EXPECT SNATCH SUMMON ARRAIGN COMMAND CONSIST DRAUGHT INQUIRE MANDATE REQUEST REQUIRE SOLICIT INSTANCE QUESTION
(— **PAYMENT**) DUN CALL
(— **RECOGNITION**) CLAIM ASSERT
(PL.) EXIGENCE EXIGENCY

DEMANDABLE DUE EXIGIBLE

DEMANDED COMPULSORY

DEMANDING HEFTY EXIGENT
(— **ATTENTION**) ACUTE

DEMANTOID EMERALD OLIVINE

DEMARCATE DELIMIT SEPARATE

DEMARCATION CELL

DEMEAN ABASE CARRY LOWER BEHAVE DEBASE DEPORT CONTAIN DEGRADE DESCEND MALTREAT

DEMEANOR AIR GARB MIEN PORT FRONT HABIT ACTION HAVIOR BEARING CONDUCT DISPOSE FASHION CARRIAGE PORTANCE

DEMENTED MAD BUGGY CRAZY NUTTY INSANE SKEWED FATUOUS

DEMENTIA FATUITY INSANITY

DEMERIT MARK FAULT DESERT BROWNIE
(PL.) GIG

DEMESNE MANOR PLACE REALM DOMAIN ESTATE REGION DISTRICT

DEMETER CERES MISTRESS

DEMIGOD HERO YIMA ADAPA SATYR TRITON GODLING
(PL.) NEPHILIM

DEMIGODDESS URD NORN HEROINE

DEMILUNE RAVELIN

DEMISE WILL DEATH CONVEY DECEASE BEQUEATH

DEMISED LETTEN

DEMIT LOWER HUMBLE RESIGN ABDICATE

DEMOCRACY POPULACY COMMONALTY

DEMOCRAT DEMO DANITE HUNKER SNAPPER DEMOCRAW LOCOFOCO POPOCRAT
(**CONSERVATIVE** —) HARD

DEMODULATE DETECT

DEMOISELLE KULM CRANE COOLEN KAIKARA

DEMOLISH RASE RAZE RUIN ABATE BREAK ELIDE LEVEL WASTE WRECK BATTER SLIGHT DESTROY RUINATE SHATTER SUBVERT UNBUILD DOWNCAST STRAMASH

DEMOLITION END FALL

DEMON ALP DEV HAG IMP NAT OKI AITU ATUA BADB BALI BHUT DEVA DOOK OGRE OKEE PUCK RAHU SURT WADE ASURA DEVIL DHOUL FIEND GENIE GHOST JUMBY LAMIA LESHY LESIY OTKON SATAN SATYR SHEDU SURTR TAIPO WITCH ABIGOR AFREET ARIOCH BILWIS DAEMON DAIMON DAITYA GENIUS JUMBIE MAMMON PILWIZ PISACA THURSE VRITRA YAKSHA YAKSHI ASMADAI ASMODAY DEMONIO HARPIER PISACHA VILLAIN WARLOCK ALICHINO ASHMODAI ASMODEUS BAALPEOR BEELPEOR CURUPIRA EUDAEMON OBIDICUT SUCCUBUS WATERMAN
(— **OF WOODS**) LESHY LESIY LESHEY
(**ARABIC** —) AFRIT AFREET AFRITE EFREET
(**EVIL** —) SHEDU
(**FEMALE** —) HAG LAMIA PISACHI SUCCUBUS
(**NATURE** —) GENIUS
(**PETTY** —) IMP
(PL.) DASYUS

DEMONIAC DEMONIC LUNATIC SATANIC DEVILISH DIABOLIC FIENDISH INFERNAL

DEMONIACAL DEMONIAC INFERNAL

DEMONSTRATE GIVE SHOW CLEAR PROVE SPEAK CONVICT DISPLAY PORTRAY CONVINCE INSTANCE MANIFEST

DEMONSTRATION SHOW SIGN TIME PROOF APODIXIS BALLYHOO DARSHANA MANIFEST
(**OSTENTATIOUS** —) SPLURGE

DEMONSTRATIVE THAT THIS THESE THOSE EFFUSIVE EVINCIVE

DEMOPHON (**FATHER OF** —) CELEUS THESEUS
(**MOTHER OF** —) PHAEDRA METANIRA

DEMORALIZE WEAKEN CONFUSE CORRUPT DEPRAVE PERVERT

DEMORALIZING INFECTIOUS SHATTERING

DEMOTE BUMP BUST REDUCE UNRANK DEGRADE DISRATE

DEMOTIC POPULAR ENCHORIAL

DEMOTION BUMP

DEMULCENT MANNA SALEB SALEP BORAGE GINSENG EMULSION SOOTHING

DEMUR COY GIB JIB SHY BALK STAY DELAY DOUBT PAUSE STICK BOGGLE LINGER OBJECT STRAIN DEMEORE SCRUPLE STICKLE STUMBLE SUSPEND DEMURRER HESITATE SUSPENSE

DEMURE COY MIM SHY MURE PRIM GRAVE SPAKE STAID SUANT SUENT MODEST SEDATE PRENZIE PRIMSIE COMPOSED DECOROUS

DEN MEW CAVE COVE DEAN DELL DIVE GLEN HOLE HOLT HUNK LAIR LAKE NEST ROOM SHED SINK BIELD CABIN CAVEA COUCH DELVE HAUNT LODGE SLADE STUDY BURROW CAVERN COVERT GROTTO HOLLOW KENNEL RAVINE SHROUD RETREAT SPELUNK HIDEAWAY SNUGGERY WORKROOM
(— **OF BEAR**) WASH
(— **OF INIQUITY**) DOMDANIEL
(**FOUL** —) SPITAL
(**GAMBLING** —) DEADFALL

DENARIUS DENAR PENNY DINDER

DENIAL NO NAY WARN DENAY DENIER NAYSAY DEFENSE DEMENTI REFUSAL REPULSE CONTRARY TRAVERSE
(— **OF AUTHORITY**) ANARCHY
(— **OF TRUTH**) HERESY

DENIED LOST

DENIER DINERO NEGATOR DENARIUS DINHEIRO
(**HALF** —) MAIL MAILLE

DENIGRATE BEFOUL CRUCIFY

DENIM DUNGAREE

DENIZEN CITIZEN RESIDENT
(— **BY BIRTH**) NATIVE
(— **OF HELL**) HELLION

DENMARK

CAPITAL: COPENHAGEN
CHEESE: SAMSO
COIN: ORA ORE KRONE
COUNTY: AMT RIBE SORO VEJLE AARHUS MARIBO ODENSE TONDER VIBORG AALBORG RANDERS AABENRAA BORNHOLM
INLET: ISE LIM FJORD VEJLE NISSUM ODENSE HORSENS LOGSTOR MARIAGER
ISLAND: OE ALS FYN MON AARO AERO FANO FOHR MORS ROMO BAAGO FAERO FAROE LAESO SAMSO SANDO AMAGER SEJERO SUDERO FALSTER SEELAND ZEALAND
MEASURE: ELL FOD MIL POT ALEN FAVN RODE ALBUM KANDE LINJE PAEGL TOMME ACHTEL PAEGEL SKEPPE LANDMIL OLTONDE SKIEPPE VIERTEL FJERDING
PARLIAMENT: RIGSRAD FOLKETING LANDSTING
PENINSULA: JUTLAND

POSSESSION: FAROE ICELAND GREENLAND
RIVER: ASA HOLM OMME STOR GUDEN SKIVE SUSAA VARDE GELSAA STORAA VORGOD GUDENAA LILLEAA LONBORG
SETTLERS: OSTMEN
STRAIT: KATTEGAT SKAGERRAK
TOWN: ARS HOV HALS KOGE NIBE SORO VRAA FARUM HOBRO SKIVE AARHUS DRAGOR KORSOR NYBORG ODENSE SKAGEN STRUER VIBORG AALBORG HERNING HORSENS KOLDING RANDERS BALLERUP ELSINORE GENTOFTE GLOSTRUP ROSKILDE HELSINGOR COPENHAGEN
TRIBE: DANES JUTES ANGLES CIMBRI TEUTONS
TRIBUNAL: RIGSRAD RIGSRET
WEIGHT: ES LOD ORT VOG LAST MARK PUND UNZE CARAT KVINT POUND QUINT TONDE CENTNER LISPUND QUINTIN LISPOUND SKIPPUND

DENOMINATE CALL NAME STYLE TITLE DENOTE CHRISTEN INDICATE NOMINATE
DENOMINATION CULT NAME SECT CLASS FAITH TITLE VALUE CHURCH SCHOOL SOCIETY CATEGORY
DENOMINATIONAL SECTARIAN CONFESSIONAL
DENOTATION SIGN TOKEN EXTENT NOTION SPHERE AMBITUS BREADTH
DENOTE GIVE MARK MEAN NAME NOTE SHOW SOUND IMPORT NOTIFY BETOKEN CONNOTE EXPRESS SIGNIFY DENOTATE DESCRIBE INDICATE
DENOUEMENT END ENVOY ISSUE OUTCOME SOLITION
DENOUNCE BAN WRAY ASCRY BASTE BLAST DECRY TAUNT ACCUSE DELATE DESCRY DETEST MENACE SCATHE ARRAIGN CONDEMN DECLAIM DECLARE UPBRAID EXECRATE PROCLAIM THREATEN
DENOUNCEMENT DELATION
DENSE SAD FAST FIRM CLOSE CRASS DUNCH FOGGY GROSS HEAVY MASSY MURKY SILLY SOLID SOUND SPISS STIFF THEET THICK TIGHT WOOFY OBTUSE OPAQUE SPISSY STUPID THICKY THIGHT COMPACT CROWDED INTENSE SERRIED CONDENSE
(**NOT —**) TENUOUS
DENSITY FOG CANDY FASTNESS GAUSSAGE SOLIDITY
DENT BASH BURT DINT DOKE DUNT FAZE NICK CLOUR DELVE DINGE NOTCH STOVE TOOTH BATTER DUNTLE HALLOW INDENT BLEMISH DEPRESS

(**— OF REED**) SPLIT
(**PL.**) BEER
DENTAL POINT
DENTICULATE SERRATE SERRATED
DENTICULATION JAG JAGG
DENTIFRICE WASH
DENTIL DENTEL DENTELLO DENTICLE
DENTINE IVORY DENTIN
DENTIST ODONTIST OPERATOR
DENTURE PLATE BRIDGE
DENUDE BARE SCALP SHAVE STRIP DIVEST NUDATE DESPOIL DENUDATE
DENUNCIATION THREAT THUNDER ANATHEMA DIATRIBE
DENY NAY NAIT NICK NITE WARN BELIE DEBAR NITTE RENAY REPEL WERNE ABJURE DISOWN FORBID IMPUGN NEGATE REFUSE REFUTE REJECT RENEGE CONFUTE DEPRIVE DISAVOW DISPUTE FORSAKE GAINSAY PROTEST SUBLATE WITHSAY ABNEGATE DENEGATE DISALLOW DISCLAIM FORSWEAR NEGATIVE RENOUNCE TRAVERSE WITHHOLD
(**— ACCESS**) CLOSE
(**— RECOGNITION**) BLINK
DEOXIDIZE REDUCE
DEPART GO DIE MOG OFF WAG BLOW EXIT FLIT HOOK MOVE PACK PART PASS PIKE QUIT SHED STEP VADE VARY VOID WALK WEND WITE AVOID BREAK FOUND LEAVE MOSEY SEVER SHAKE SHIFT START TRUSS AVAUNT BEGONE DECAMP DECEDE DEMISE DESIST DIVIDE PERISH RECEDE REMOVE RETIRE SKIDOO SUNDER SWERVE WANDER ABSCOND DEVIATE DISCEDE FORSAKE RETREAT SKIDDOO VAMOOSE DISCOAST FAREWELL SEPARATE TRESPASS WITHDRAW
(**— FROM HARBOR**) SORTIE
(**— FROM LIFE**) DECEASE
(**— IN HASTE**) BREEZE
(**— IN HURRY**) SKIVE LAMMAS
(**— SECRETLY**) ABSCOND
(**— SUDDENLY**) FLEE DECAMP
(**— WITH SPEED**) VAMOOSE
DEPARTED DEAD BYGONE DEFUNCT DECEASED DECEDENT
DEPARTMENT END PART OKRUG REALM AGENCY BRANCH BUREAU EXCISE MEMBER OKROOG SPHERE FOUNDRY HANAPER PORTION REVENUE SPICERY AGITPROP CHANCERY DIVISION INDUSTRY NOMARCHY PROVINCE SCULLERY
(**— IN CHINA**) FU
(**NEWSPAPER —**) COLUMN FEATURE
(**TREASURY —**) CAMERA
DEPARTURE BUNK EXIT BREAK DEATH EXODE GOING LEAVE OUTGO CHANGE CONGEE DEPART EGRESS EXODUS HEGIRA SETOFF WAGANG WAYING DECEASE EASTING OUTGANG PARTING PARTURE RETREAT SAILING TRUNDLE WAYGATE DEPARTER FAREWELL

OFFGOING REMOTION
(**— FROM CORRECTNESS**) ATROCITY
(**— FROM SUBJECT**) ASIDE
(**— FROM THEME**) CADENZA
(**— OF SHIP**) SORTIE
(**EMERGENCY —**) BAILOUT
(**GEOLOGICAL —**) ANOMALY
(**SECRET —**) GUY SLIP
DEPEND BANK HANG LEAN PEND RELY REST RIDE STAY TURN COUNT FOUND HINGE TRUST CONFIDE
DEPENDABILITY SECURITY
DEPENDABLE GOOD SURE SIKER SOLID SOUND THERE SECURE SICCAR SICKER STANCH STEADY CERTAIN STAUNCH RELIABLE SILVENDY SUREFIRE
DEPENDENCE MAINSTAY RELIANCE SERVILITY
DEPENDENCY TALUK COLONY APANAGE APPANAGE
DEPENDENT CHILD CLIENT HANGBY MINION SPONGE VASSAL FEODARY FEUDARY PRONEUR RELIANT SERVILE SPONGER SUBJECT WRAPPED BEHOLDEN CLINGING CREATURE ENCLITIC EVENTUAL FOLLOWER RETAINER
(**— ON**) ILLATIVE
DEPENDING ATTENDANT
(**— ON UNCERTAIN EVENTS**) ALEATORY
DEPICT HUE DRAW ETCH LIMN PICT UNDO ENTER IMAGE PAINT SPEAK WRITE BLAZON SHADOW DEPAINT DISPLAY EXPRESS IMPAINT PICTURE PORTRAY DESCRIBE EMBLAZON RESEMBLE
DEPICTED DEPAINT
(**— AS BROKEN**) ROMPU
DEPICTION SCHEMA
DEPILATION PSILOSIS
DEPILATORY RUSMA EPILATOR PELADORE PSILATRO
DEPLETE DRAIN EMPTY PUNISH REDUCE UNLOAD EXHAUST BANKRUPT DIMINISH
DEPLETED WASTE BANKRUPT
DEPLETION DRAIN EROSION
DEPLORABLE SAD WOFUL WOEFUL DOLOROUS GRIEVOUS WAILSOME WRETCHED
DEPLORABLY SADLY
DEPLORE RUE MOAN SIGH WAIL MOURN BEMOAN BEWAIL GRIEVE LAMENT REGRET COMPLAIN
DEPLOY UNFOLD DISPLAY
DEPLOYMENT FORMATION
DEPOLYMERIZE DEGRADE
DEPONE SWEAR DEPOSE TESTIFY
DEPONENT AFFIANT DEPONER EXAMINATE
DEPOPULATE RAVAGE DESOLATE DISPEOPLE
DEPORT BEAR EXILE EXPEL BANISH BEHAVE DEMEAN BEARING CONDUCT DISPORT RELEGATE
DEPORTMENT AIR GEST MIEN POR GESTE HABIT ACTION DEPORT

HAVING MANNER ADDRESS BEARING
COMPORT CONDUCT GESTURE
HAVANCE BREEDING CARRIAGE
DEMEANOR MAINTAIN
DEPOSE AVER ABASE PRIVE SWEAR
AFFIRM ASSERT BANISH DEPONE
DIVEST REDUCE REMOVE DEGRADE
DEPOSIT DESTOOL TESTIFY
DETHRONE DISCROWN DISPLACE
DEPOSIT FUR LAY SET ADHI BANK
CAKE CAST CRUD DROP DUMP
FUND HIDE HOCK PAWN BLOOM
CHEST COUCH COVER DEPOT
LODGE PLACE SCURF STORE TOSCA
BESTOW DEPONE DEPOSE ENTOMB
ESCROW FLYSCH GARNER IMPOSE
INHUME PLEDGE REPOSE SALINE
SCORIA SCROLL SETTLE SINTER
TOPHUS ASHFALL CONSIGN
HORIZON DILUVIUM FOULNESS
SANDBANK
(— **BALLOT**) CAST
(— **DRIFT-SAND**) SUD
(— **EGGS**) BLOW SPAWN
(— **FOR COPYRIGHT**) ENTER
(— **IN CHAMPAGNE**) GRIFFE
(— **IN EARTH**) INTER INHUME
(— **IN GUN BORE**) FOULING
(— **IN WINE CASK**) CRUST TARTAR
(— **OF DEBRIS**) BRECCIA
(— **OF LOAM**) LOESS
(— **OF ORE**) BANK FLAT
(— **OF PEBBLES AND SAND**) BEACH
CASCALHO
(— **OF SALT WATER**) SOAK
(— **ON LEATHER**) BLOOM
(— **ON LEAVES**) HONEYDEW
(— **STOLEN ARTICLES**) FENCE
(— **USED AS FERTILIZER**) FALUN
(**ALLUVIAL** —) APRON DELTA
(**ARCHAEOLOGICAL** —) LENS LENSE
(**BANK** —**S**) CASH
(**BLACK** —) STUPP
(**CORNEA** —) ARCUS
(**EARTHY** —) GUHR MARL
(**GEOLOGIC** —) BLANKET HORIZON
(**GLACIAL** —) TILL DRIFT ESKAR
ESKER SHEET PLACER MORAINE
(**GRAVEL** —) LEAD
(**KIDNEY** —) GRAVEL
(**MASS OF SEDIMENTARY** —**S**) GOBI
(**MINERAL** —) FLAT LODE CARBONA
(**MUDDY** —) SLUDGE SLUMGULLION
(**SEDIMENTARY** —) SILT
(**SHOAL-WATER** —) CULM
(**SKELETAL** —) CORAL
(**TARRY** —) GUM
(**WELDING** —) TACK
EPOSITARY POSITOR SEQUESTER
EPOSITION PAD BURIAL DEPOSIT
OPINION SILTING DEPOSURE
SEDIMENT
EPOSITORY BANK DROP SAFE
ATTIC VAULT DEPOSIT OSSUARY
SENTINE DEPOSITO ESCROWEE
OSSARIUM
EPOT BANK BASE GARE AURANG
AURUNG STAPLE STATION
MAGAZINE TERMINAL TERMINUS

DEPRAVE TAINT DEBASE DEFILE
INFECT MALIGN REVILE BESHREW
CORRUPT PERVERT VITIATE
DEPRAVED BAD EVIL UGLY VILE
PRAVE ROTTEN SHREWD WICKED
BESTIAL CORRUPT IMMORAL
PRAVOUS VICIOUS
DEPRAVITY VICE ABYSS ILLNESS
PRAVITY VILLAINY
DEPRECATE PRAY INVOKE BESEECH
DEPRECIATE FALL LACK ABASE
AVILE DECRY SLUMP DEBASE
EMBASE LESSEN MINISH REDUCE
SHRINK CHEAPEN DEBAUCH
DEGRADE DEPRAVE DEPRESS
DETRACT SLANDER SMALLEN
BELITTLE DEROGATE DISCOUNT
DISPRIZE DISVALUE MINIMIZE
PEJORATE VILIPEND
DEPRECIATION AGIO DECRIAL
DISCOUNT
DEPREDATION PREY PILLAGE
DEPRESS BOW COW HIP LOW BATE
BEAR BORE DAMP DASH DENT FALL
FLAT SINK SUMP ABASE APPAL
BREAK CHILL COUCH CRUSH FAINT
LOWER SLUMP VAPOR WEIGH
APPALL DAMPEN DEBOSS DISMAY
HUMBLE INDENT LESSEN MURDER
SADDEN SETTLE SICKEN STRIKE
WEAKEN DECLINE DEGRADE
DESTROY FLATTEN OPPRESS
REPRESS BROWBEAT DIMINISH
DISPIRIT DOWNBEAR ENFEEBLE
DEPRESSANT HELLEBORE
DEPRESSED LOW SAD BLUE DAMP
DULL FLAT SICK SUNK WROTH
BROODY DISHED GLOOMY HIPPED
HOLLOW LONELY OBLATE SOMBER
TRISTE LETDOWN DEJECTED
DOWNCAST DOWNSOME
(— **AT THE POLES**) OBLATE
(**ECONOMICALLY** —) HARD
DEPRESSING SAD BLUE COLD
BLEAK CHILL DREAR DUSKY MUZZY
OURIE DREARY GLOOMY SOMBER
SOMBRE TRISTE
DEPRESSION COL DIP EYE GAT PAN
PIT BUST CROP DAMP DELK DENT
DOKE DOWN FALL FOSS GASH GLEN
HOLL HOWE SLEW SLOT SLUE WELL
ATRIO BASIN BLUES BOSOM CANON
COWAL CRYPT DELVE DINGE FOSSA
FOSSE FOVEA GLOOM GROIN NADIR
NAVEL ORBIT POLJE SALAR SCOOP
SELLA SINUS SLUMP SWALE AMPHID
BUCKLE CAFARD CANYON CAVITY
CRATER CUPULE DIMPLE DISMAY
FURROW GROOVE GULLEY GUTTER
INDENT RAVINE SAUCER SLOUGH
SPLEEN VALLEY WALLOW ALVEOLA
BLOWOUT BOGHOLE CHAGRIN
CLAYPAN CONCAVE COUNTER
FOSSULA FOSSULE FOVEOLA
JIMMIES SADNESS SALTPAN
SINKAGE SINKING VARIOLE
BOTHRIUM DOLDRUMS DOWNBEND
FAINTING FOLLICLE FOREDEEP
FOSSETTE FOSSULET PUNCTURE

SINKHOLE SOAKAWAY EPHIPPIUM
(— **BEHIND COW'S SHOULDERS**)
CROP
(— **BETWEEN BREASTS**) CLEAVAGE
(— **BETWEEN HILLS**) SWIRE
(— **IN BOARD**) SKIP
(— **IN BOTTLE BOTTOM**) KICK
(— **IN DOG'S FACE**) STOP
(— **IN FRUITS**) EYE
(— **IN GROUND**) DALK DELK SWAG
WELL SWALE CHARCO
(— **IN MILLSTONE**) BOSOM
(— **IN NILE VALLEY**) KORE
(— **IN RANGE**) PASS
(— **IN RIDGE**) COL
(— **IN SNOW**) SITZMARK
(— **IN VELD**) COMITJE KOMMETJE
(— **OF EAR**) SCAPHA
(— **OF SPIRITS**) JAWFALL
(— **PRONE**) VAPORISH
(**ARTICULAR** —) GLENE
(**OBLONG** —) CIRCUS
(**SMALL** —) DENT DIMPLE LACUNA
FOLLICLE
DEPRIVATION COST LOSS MAIM
WANT MAYHEM AMOTION MISTURE
DEPRIVAL
(— **OF SIGHT**) DARKNESS
DEPRIVE BAR ROB BATE DENY DOCK
EASE GELD TWIN ABATE BENIM
BREAK DEBAR EMPTY EXUTE PREVE
SPOIL STRIP WRONG AMERCE
DEFEAT DENUDE DEPOSE DEVEST
DISMAY DIVEST FAMISH FORBAR
HINDER HUSTLE REMOVE ABRIDGE
BEGUILE BEREAVE CASHIER
CURTAIL DECEIVE DEFORCE
DEPRAVE DESPOIL DESTROY
DISABLE EXHAUST FOREBAR
GUDGEON PRIVATE UNDRESS
BANKRUPT DENATURE DESOLATE
DISANNUL EVACUATE
(— **BY TRICKERY**) NOSE MULCT
(— **FRAUDULENTLY**) GUDGEON
(— **OF BRILLIANCE**) DEADEN
(— **OF COURAGE**) UNNERVE
(— **OF FREEDOM**) FETTER
(— **OF INDIVIDUALITY**) FORDIZE
(— **OF LIFE**) DEADEN
(— **OF OFFICE**) DEPOSE
(— **OF POSSESSIONS**) FLAY
(— **OF REASON**) DEMENT
(— **OF SENSATION**) BENUMB
(— **OF SENSE**) INEBRIATE
(— **OF SIGHT**) SEEL
(— **OF STRENGTH**) ENERVATE
(— **OF VIRGINITY**) DEFLOWER
DEPRIVED REFT SANS BANKRUPT
DESOLATE
DEPTH DIP BURY DEEP DROP MOHO
ABYSS MIDST SIDTH FATHOM
HEIGHT ALTITUDE DEEPNESS
PROFOUND SOUNDING STRENGTH
(— **OF NIGHT OR WINTER**) HOLL
HOWE
(— **OF SAIL**) HOIST
(— **OF SHIP**) GAGE GAUGE
(— **OF SIN**) SLOUGH
(— **OF SPADE**) SPIT GRAFT

(— OF WATER) DRAFT DRAUGHT
(LOWEST —) GROUND
(MORAL —) ABYSS
(PL.) MUD HEART
DEPUTATION MISSION THEORIA
LEGATION
DEPUTE SEND ALLOT ASSIGN
DEVOTE APPOINT DELEGATE
DEPUTY AIDE AGENT ENVOY NABOB
PROXY VICAR ANGELO COMMIS
CURATE DEPUTE EXARCH FACTOR
KEHAYA LEGATE MINION ADJOINT
BAILIFF ESCALUS QAMAQAM
SUBDEAN CAIMACAM DELEGATE
ORDINARY PYLAGORE TENIENTE
VICARIAN
DERAIL TOAD DERAILER THROWOFF
DERANGE TURN CRAZE UNWIT
UPSET HAMPER RUFFLE CONFUSE
DERAIGN DISEASE DISTURB
PERTURB UNSHAPE DISORDER
DISPLACE UNSETTLE
DERANGED OUT GYTE CRAZY
CRAZED FRANTIC FURIOUS
BUGHOUSE DEMENTED DETRAQUE
INFORMAL
DERANGEMENT MANIA UPSET
FRENZY LUNACY DISEASE MADNESS
PHRENSY RUMMAGE DELIRIUM
DISORDER INSANITY
DERBY POT CADY KATY RACE
BOXER CADDY DICER KELLY SHIRE
BOWLER
DERELICT STREET FAILURE
BETRAYER CASTAWAY
DERELICTION FAILURE RELICTION
DERIDE BOO GECK GIBE HOOT JAPE
JEER JIBE LOUT MOCK TWIT DRAPE
FLEER FLOUT KNACK LAUGH RALLY
SCOFF SCORN SCOUT TAUNT
EXPOSE ILLUDE IRRIDE CATCALL
LOWBELL RIDICULE
DERIDER IRRISOR
DERISION GECK JEER MOCK HOKER
SCORN SPORT MOWING ASTEISM
MOCKERY CONTEMPT IRRISION
RIDICULE
DERISIVE JEERY SNIDE MOWING
SATANIC DERISORY IRRISORY
SARDONIC SCOFFING
DERIVATION ORIGIN DESCENT
PEDIGREE
DERIVATIVE FURAN LININ SLOPE
ACOINE ACYLAL BORANE FURANE
INDOLE PHENOL RETENE ALKYLOL
ANALGEN DERIVED ENOLATE
FLAVONE FLUXION FULGIDE
FULVENE GERMANE SUCRATE
ALBUMOSE ANALGENE FLAVONOL
FORMAZAN HEMATINE INDAZOLE
STANNANE
DERIVE GET DRAW STEM TAKE
BRING CARRY DRIVE FETCH INFER
TRACE BORROW CONVEY DEDUCE
DESUME ELICIT EVOLVE GATHER
OBTAIN SPRING DESCEND EXTRACT
PROCEED RECEIVE TRADUCE
DERMA LAYER CORIUM DERMIS
KISHKE

DERMATITIS ICH ICK CASCADO
CUTITIS
DERMIS DERM CUTIS DERMA
CORIUM
DERNIER LAST FINAL DARREIN
DERNIER CRI FASHION
DEROGATE ANNUL DECRY LESSEN
REPEAL DETRACT SLANDER
RESTRICT WITHDRAW
DEROGATORY BAD
DERRICK JIB RIG LIFT SPAR CRANE
DAVIT HOIST TACKLE ERECTER
ERECTOR GALLOWS HANGING
HANGMAN STIFFLEG JINNYWINK
DERRIS TUBA DEGUELIA
DERVISH AGIB FAKIR FAKEER
SADITE SANTON DARWESH WHIRLER
CALENDER
DESALT DEIONIZE
DESATURATE SADDEN
DESCANT SING SONG COPULA
MELODY REMARK WARBLE
COMMENT QUINIBLE
DESCEND DIP SYE DIVE DROP DUCK
FALL SHED SINK SKIN VAIL AVALE
LIGHT LOWER SQUAT STOOP
SWOOP ALIGHT DERIVE DEVALL
DEVAUL SETTLE DECLINE DELAPSE
DEVOLVE SUBSIDE SUCCEED
DISMOUNT
(— INTO HELL) HARROW
DESCENDANT SON CION GHUZ HEIR
SEED SLIP CHILD GHUZZ SCION
BRANCH LINEAL DESCENT
AARONITE ASHERITE DAUGHTER
EPIGONUS
(— OF IMMIGRANTS) BRAVA
(— OF JEW) CHUETA
(— OF MOHAMMED) EMIR
(— OF NOAH) AD
(—S OF MOHAMMED) ASHRAF
(INSIGNIFICANT —) TAG
(PL.) SEED DONMEH DUNMEH
STRAIN PROGENY OFFSPRING
POSTERITY
DESCENDING FALL CADENT
DOWNWARD
(— FROM COMMON ANCESTOR)
AKIN
DESCENT JET KIN SET DIVE DOWN
DROP FALL KIND VAIL BIRTH BLOOD
CANCH CHUTE ISSUE SCARP SHUTE
SLOPE STOCK CLEUCH CLEUGH
ESCARP RAPPEL STRAIN ASSAULT
DECLINE DISSENT EXTRACT
FALLOUT INCLINE KINDRED LINEAGE
PROGENY ANCESTRY BREEDING
COMEDOWN DOWNCOME DOWNFALL
DOWNGATE DOWNHILL GLISSADE
INVASION PEDIGREE
(— IN MOUNTAINEERING) ABSEIL
(— OF AIRPLANE) LETDOWN
APPROACH
(— OF BIRD) STOOP
(— OF DEITY) AVATAR AVATARA
(— OF LIQUID) DRIBBLE
(— OF MASS) SLIDE
(— OF RIVER) LEAP
(FAMILIAR —) HAVAGE

(OVERWHELMING —) AVALANCHE
(PARACHUTE —) JUMP BAILOUT
(PLUNGING —) SPIN
DESCHAMPIA AIRA
DESCRIBE GIVE READ TELL BLAZE
IMAGE PAINT POINT STYLE WRITE
DEFINE DENOTE DEPICT DEVISE
DILATE RELATE REPORT SKETCH
TITULE DECLARE DEPAINT DISPLAY
EXPLAIN EXPRESS NARRATE
OUTLINE PICTURE PORTRAY
PRESENT RECOUNT STORIFY
DESCRIVE INSCRIBE REHEARSE
(— A LINE) CUT
(— AS) CALL
(— BRIEFLY) KODAK
(— GRAMMATICALLY) PARSE
DESCRIPTION KIN IMAGE BLAZON
SKETCH SURVEY ACCOUNT DICTION
DISPLAY PICTURE LANDSKIP
RELATION TREATISE
(— OF A COUNTRY) FACE
(— OF VISION) AISLING
(BRIEF —) LEGEND
(RUSTIC —) IDYL IDYLL
DESCRY SEE SPY ESPY MAKE SCRY
ASCRY SIGHT BEHOLD BETRAY
DETECT REVEAL DISCERN DISPLAY
DENOUNCE DESCRIBE DISCLOSE
DISCOVER PERCEIVE
DESECRATE ABUSE DEFILE
POLLUTE PROFANE VIOLATE
TEMERATE UNHALLOW
DESERT DUE ERG RAT RUN AREG
ARID BOLT FAIL FLEE MEED SAND
SERT TURN VAST GUILT LEAVE
LURCH MERIT PLANT SERIR START
WAIVE WASTE WORTH BARREN
BETRAY DEFECT EXPOSE LONELY
RENEGE REWARD SHRINK THIRST
WESTEN ABANDON ABSCOND
CHICKEN DEMERIT FORSAKE
HORNADA OVERRUN WESTERN
WASTINE DESOLATE RENOUNCE
SOLITARY SOLITUDE WASTABLE
(PL.) GUILT
DESERTED DEAD WYSTY LONELY
FORLORN DESOLATE FORSAKEN
SOLITARY
(— WOMAN) AGUNAH
DESERTER RAT BOLTER BUGOUT
APOSTATE BUSHWACK FUGITIVE
RECREANT RENEGADE TURNTAIL
DESERTION BUGOUT RATTERY
APOSTASY
DESERT LEMON KUMQUAT
DESERVE EARN MEED RATE MERIT
REPAY SERVE ASSERVE BENEFIT
DEMERIT DISSERVE PROMERIT
DESERVED JUST COMING WORTHY
CONDIGN
DESERVING WORTHY WORTHFUL
ADMIRABLE
DESICCATE DRY ARID SEAR SERE
DRAIN DEHYDRATE
DESICCATION XERANSIS
DESIDERATUM NEED DESIRE
DESIGN AIM END MAP CAST DRAW
GOAL IDEA MARK MEAN PLAN PLAT

PLOT TREE WORK ALLOT CHECK
DECAL DECOR DODAD DRAFT DRIFT
ETTLE FANCY MODEL MOTIF NOTAN
QUILT SHAPE STAMP STUDY
BOWPOT CACHET CORNER CREATE
DEVICE DEVISE DOODAD DOODLE
EMBLEM FIGURE FLORAL FLOWER
INCUSE INTEND INTENT INVENT
LAYOUT MODULE OBJECT OBTENT
PROJET SCHEME SKETCH SYSTEM
VERVER ALLOVER BOSCAGE
CARTOON CARVING CHASING
COMPOSE COUNSEL CROQUIS
DESTINE DIAGRAM DRAUGHT
ETCHING FANTASY FASHION
OUTLINE PATTERN PRETEND
PROJECT PROPOSE PURPORT
PURPOSE REVERSE SCALLOP
SLEIGHT APPLIQUE BAYADERE
BOUGHPOT CONTRIVE CYMATION
CYMATIUM ENGINEER FILIGREE
FLOCKING FORECAST GRAFFITO
GROOVING INTAGLIO PHANTASY
PLATFORM REMARQUE SINGERIE
STRIPING SUNBURST GOFFERING
(— AS TITLE PAGE) VIGNETTE
(— ON CARPET) MEDALLION
(— ON COIN) BEADING
(— ON FABRIC) BATIK BATTIK
(BOOK —) FILET FILLET
(CUP-SHAPED —) HUSK
(EMBLEMATIC —) IMPRESS
(ESSENTIAL —) BONES
(FASHION —) FORD
(OUTLINE —) KEYSTONE
(PERFORATED —) POUNCE
(STRIPED —) STRIA STRIE
(TESSELLATED —) MOSAIC
(TEXTILE —) STRIPE HAIRLINE
DESIGNATE SET HAIL MARK MEAN
NAME SHOW ELECT LABEL SPEAK
STYLE TITLE ANOINT ASSIGN
DENOTE DESIGN FINGER INTEND
SETTLE APPOINT EARMARK ENTITLE
EXPRESS SPECIFY SURNAME
ALLOCATE DESCRIBE IDENTIFY
INDICATE NOMINATE
DESIGNATION NAME STYLE TITLE
CAPTION HOMONYM ADDITION
(— OF PLACE) ADDRESS
DESIGNED PREPENSE SUPPOSED
DESIGNER FANCIER PLANNER
PLOTTER SCHEMER COLORIST
ENGINEER MEDALIST
(PL.) COUTURE
DESIGNING ARTFUL CUNNING
JESUITIC PLANNING PLOTTING
SCHEMING
DESIRABLE FAIR GOOD KEEN
WORTH PLUMMY AMIABLE GRADELY
HEALTHY OPTABLE WELCOME
WISHFUL DESIROUS ELIGIBLE
ENVIABLE PLEASING SALUTARY
DESIRE YEN ACHE CARE ENVY EROS
FAIN HAVE HOPE ITCH KAMA KEEP
LEST LIST LOAD LUST MIND NEED
PANT URGE WANT WILL WISH WIST
ARDOR BOSOM BRAME COVET
CRAVE FANCY GIMME GREED

GROAN HEART MANGE MANIA NISUS
QUEST STUDY TANHA TASTE WILNE
YEARN YISSE AFFECT APPETE
ASPIRE BEHEST DEMAND DEVICE
HANKER HUNGER OREXIS POTHOS
PREFER TALENT THIRST UTINAM
YAMMER AVARICE AVIDITY
CONATUS COURAGE CRAVING
EROTISM FANTASY HIMEROS
INKLING LONGING PASSION
STOMACH VOLUNTY WILLING
AMBITION APPETITE COVETISE
CUPIDITY PLEASING
(— FOR LIFE) TANHA
(— WITH EAGERNESS) ASPIRE
(ARDENT —) THIRST
(IRRITATING —) ITCH
(STRONG —) CUPIDITY SLAVERING
(UNCONTROLLABLE —) CACOETHES
DESIROUS AVID FAIN FOND LIEF
VAIN EAGER FRACK FRECK LUSTY
ARDENT WILFUL ANXIOUS WILLFUL
WILLING WISHING APPETENT
COVETOUS LIKEROUS SPIRITED
DESIST HO LIN EASE HALT QUIT
REST SIST STOP WHOA CEASE
LEAVE SPARE STINT SWICK SWIKE
WONDE DEPART ABANDON
FORBEAR FORFEIT RESPITE SUBSIST
SURCEASE
(— FROM) CUT LEAVE REMIT
FORBEAR
DESK PEW AMBO SCOB BOARD
DESSE TABLE BUREAU CAISSE
PULPIT CONSOLE LECTERN
PLUTEUS COPYDESK STANDISH
VARGUENO
DESMA CLON CLONE
DESMAN MOLE SQUASH MUSKRAT
ONDATRA
DESMANTHUS ACUAN
DESOLATE SAD BARE LORN RUIN
SACK SOLE VAST WILD ALONE
BLEAK DREAR GAUNT GUBAT STARK
UNKED UNKET UNKID WASTE WASTY
WYSTY BARREN DESERT DISMAL
DREARY GLOOMY GOUSTY LONELY
RAVAGE DESTROY FORLORN
GOUSTIE HOWLING LACKING
UNCOUTH WIDOWED WILSOME
DEPRIVED DESERTED FORSAKEN
SOLITARY WASTEFUL WOBEGONE
DESOLATION WOE RUIN GLOOM
GRIEF HAVOC WASTE RAVAGE
SADNESS
DESPAIR GLOOM UNHOPE WANHOPE
DESPAIRING HOPELESS
DESPERADO BRAVO BADMAN
BANDIT RUFFIAN CRIMINAL
RESOLUTE
DESPERATE MAD DIRE RASH
DESPERT EXTREME FORLORN
FRANTIC HEADLONG HOPELESS
PERILOUS RECKLESS
DESPERATELY BONE
DESPICABLE BASE MEAN ORRA VILE
CHEAP DIRTY FOUTY SCALY ABJECT
PALTRY SHABBY SORDID CAITIFF
IGNOBLE PITIFUL REPTILE PITIABLE

UNWORTHY WRETCHED
DESPICABLY DIRTILY
DESPISE DEFY HATE SCORN SCOUT
SPISE SPURN DETEST FORHOO
LOATHE SLIGHT VILIFY CONTEMN
DESPITE DISDAIN DISPRIZE
MISPRIZE VILIPEND
DESPITE BY VEX SPITE MALGRE
DESPISE
DESPOIL ROB PELF PILL POLL RAID
RAPE RUIN SKIN BOOTY HARRY
PLUME REAVE RIFLE SPOIL STRIP
STRUB TRICE DIVEST FLEECE
HESPEL HUSPEL RAVAGE RAVISH
REMOVE BEREAVE DEPRIVE
DISROBE PILLAGE PLUNDER
UNSPOIL DEFLOWER DISARRAY
SPOLIATE SPUILZIE UNCLOTHE
DESPOINA KORE PERSEPHONE
DESPONDENCY DUMP BLUES
DUMPS GLOOM ATHYMY MISERY
ATHUMIA ATHYMIA DESPAIR
DESPOND
DESPONDENT SAD BLUE GLOOMY
FORLORN DEJECTED DOWNCAST
HOPELESS
DESPOT CZAR TSAR TZAR ANARCH
SATRAP TYRANT AUTARCH
MONARCH AUTOCRAT
DESPOTIC LORDLY ABSOLUTE
DOMINANT
DESPOTISM TYRANNY SULTANISM
DESQUAMATE PEEL
DESSERT ICE PIE CAKE FOOL SKYR
SNOW VOID BETTY BOMBE COUPE
DOLCE FRUIT GLACE GRUNT JELLY
LACTO SLUMP AFTERS ECLAIR
JUNKET MOUSSE PASTRY SPONGE
SWEETS TRIFLE BAKLAVA BANQUET
PARFAIT PUDDING SHERBET
SOUFFLE SPUMONE STRUDEL
SUPREME DUMPLING FLUMMERY
FRUMENTY NAPOLEON SILLABUB
DESTINATION END GOAL PORT
BOURN BILLET BOURNE
DESTINE DOOM EURE FATE MARK
ALLOT SHAPE SLATE WEIRD DEPUTE
DESIGN DEVOTE INTEND ORDAIN
APPOINT PURPOSE SENTENCE
DESTINY LOT DOLE DOOM EURE
FATE SORT KARMA MOIRA STARS
WEIRD KHARMA KISMET DESTINE
FORTUNE PORTION FOREDOOM
DESTITUTE BARE NACE POOR SANS
VOID CLEAN EMPTY NAKED NEEDY
WASTE BEREFT DEVOID VACANT
WASTED FORLORN LACKING
NAUGHTY VIDUATE WANTING
BANKRUPT BEGGARED DEFEATED
DEPRIVED DESOLATE FORSAKEN
HELPLESS INDIGENT INNOCENT
VIDUATED
(— OF FEATHERS) DEPLUMATE
(— OF LEAVES) APHYLLOUS
(— OF LIGHT) DARK
(— OF TEETH) EDENTATE
(— OF WATER) ANHYDROUS
(— OF) BUT
DESTITUTION NEED WANT FAMINE

PENURY BEGGARY DEFAULT POVERTY

DESTROY BAG EAT END GUT RID BLOW CHEW FRAP FULL KILL NULL RASE RAZE RUIN RUSH SINK SLAY SMIT STRY TINE UNDO VOID BREAK CRACK CRAZE DECAY ELIDE ERASE ERODE FORDO HAVOC MISDO PRANG QUADE QUAIL QUELL SHEND SHOOT SMASH SMITE SPEED SPEND SPILL SPLIT SPOIL STROY SWAMP WASTY WRACK WRECK BLIGHT CANCEL CUMBER DEFACE DEFEAT DELETE DEVOID DEVOUR EFFACE FAMISH FOREDO MURDER PERISH QUENCH RANKLE RAVAGE STARVE UNMAKE UNPILE UNWORK UPROOT UPTEAR ABOLISH CONSUME CORRODE DEPRIVE DISTURB ENECATE EXPUNGE FLATTEN FORFARE FORLESE MORTIFY NULLIFY OVERRUN PEREMPT RUINATE SHAMASH SHATTER SMOTHER SUBVERT TERRIFY UNBUILD WHITTLE AMORTIZE CONFOUND DECIMATE DEMOLISH DESOLATE DESTRUCT DISANNUL DISPLANT DISSOLVE FRACTURE FRAGMENT IMMOLATE INFRINGE MUTILATE OVERTURN SABOTAGE STRAMASH
(— **BARK**) GIRDLE
(— **BY FIRE**) CONSUME
(— **FERTILITY**) EXHAUST
(— **SELF-POSSESSION**) ABASH
(— **TOTALLY**) SMASH SWEEP CUMBER SCUTTLE
DESTROYED FLAT BLOWN KAPUT KAPUTT
DESTROYER CAN HUN DEATH TINCAN UNDOER VANDAL VICTOR FLIVVER STROYER UNMAKER WARSHIP DEVOURER SABOTEUR
DESTROYING FELL
DESTRUCTIBLE FRAIL
DESTRUCTION BAR END HEW BANE DOGS DOOM FIRE LOSS RACK RUIN STRY TALA CRUSH DEATH DECAY GRAVE HAVOC STRIP STROY WASTE DEFEAT DISMAY ENDING EXPIRY WONDER ABADDON CARNAGE EROSION UNDOING COLLAPSE DELETION DISPOSAL DOWNFALL EVERSION EXCISION SHAMBLES SMASHERY
(— **OF BONES**) CARIES
(— **OF SHIP'S PAPERS**) SPOLIATION
(**CELL** —) LYSIS
(**GRADUAL** —) CORROSION
(**MALICIOUS** —) SABOTAGE
DESTRUCTIVE FELL FATAL DEADLY MORTAL BALEFUL DEATHLY EXITIAL FATEFUL HARMFUL HUMLIKE HURTFUL NOISOME NOXIOUS RUINOUS ANERETIC DEATHFUL EXITIOUS WASTEFUL WRACKFUL WREAKFUL ANAERETIC
DESUETUDE BREACH DISUSE
DESULTORY IDLE HASTY LOOSE

ROVING AIMLESS CURSORY RAMBLING UNSTEADY WAVERING IRREGULAR
DETACH CUT DRAFT LOOSE SEVER LOOSEN UNBIND UNGLUE UNWORK CRACKLE DISJOIN DRAUGHT ISOLATE UNHINGE UNRIVET UNSEIZE ABSTRACT DISSOLVE DISUNITE PRESCIND SEPARATE UNFASTEN WITHDRAW
DETACHABLE SLIP
DETACHED CUT COLD FREE ALONE ALOOF DEADPAN INSULAR PORTATO SCIOLTO ABSTRACT CLINICAL DISCRETE ISOLATED SEPARATE SPICCATO UNBIASED
DETACHMENT POSSE ATARAXY OUTPOST ATARAXIA AVULSION OUTGUARD
DETAIL CREW ITEM DODAD POINT ACCENT ASSIGN DOODAB DOODAD NICETY PARCEL RELATE RETAIL ACCOUNT APPOINT ARTICLE ITEMIZE MINUTIA NARRATE NULLING RESPECT SEVERAL SPECIFY INSTANCE REHEARSE SALIENCE
(—**S OF MAP**) CULTURE
(**CLIMACTIC** —) BEAUTY
(**PETTY** —) CHICKEN
(PL.) DOPE FROUFROU FURNITURE
DETAILED PROLIX CLOSEUP SPECIAL PUNCTUAL TIRESOME
DETAIN BAIL HOLD KEEP STAY STOP CHECK DELAY TARRY ARREST ATHOLD COLLAR HINDER RETARD TAIGLE IMPRISON RESTRAIN WITHHOLD   \
DETECT SEE SPY ESPY FIND NOSE SPOT CATCH SCENT SENSE SMOKE DESCRY DIVINE EXPOSE REVEAL DEVELOP DISCERN UNCOVER DECIPHER DISCOVER OVERTAKE
DETECTIVE EYE TEC BULL BUSY DICK TRAP PLANT SNOOP BEAGLE MOUSER RUNNER SHADOW SHAMUS SLEUTH TAILER TRACER GUMSHOE SCENTER SNOOPER SPOTTER TRAILER DETECTOR FLATFOOT HAWKSHAW HOUSEMAN OPERATOR SHERLOCK PINKERTON
DETECTOR COHERER REAGENT SFERICS SPHERICS
DETENT DOG PAL PAWL CATCH CLICK RATCH PALLET RATCHET
DETENTION DELAY ARREST CAPTURE DETINUE DETAINER STOPPAGE
DETER BAR FEAR BLOCK BLUFF CHECK DELAY DEHORT HINDER RETARD PREVENT TERRIFY DISSUADE PRECLUDE RESTRAIN
DETERGE PURGE CLEANSE MUNDIFY
DETERGENT SOAP SYNDET ABLUENT PURGING RHYPTIC SMECTIC SOLVENT CLEANSER GARDINOL
DETERIORATE GO FAIL GIVE SLIP SOUR WEAR DECAY ERODE SPILL WORST APPAIR APPERE DEBASE

IMPAIR SICKEN DECLINE PERVERT FIREFANG
DETERIORATING DECADENT
DETERIORATION DECAY IMPAIR MALADY DECLINE EROSION FAILURE DOLDRUMS
DETERMINABLE FIXED DEFINITE DEFINABLE GAUGEABLE
DETERMINANT CYTOGENE JACOBIAN CIRCULANT WRONSKIAN
DETERMINATE CERTAIN ORISTIC DEFINITE RESOLUTE RESOLVED SPECIFIC
DETERMINATION ACT HEST WILL ASSAY BLANK CAUSE ADVICE BEARING CONSULT PURPOSE RESOLVE ANALYSIS BACKBONE BIOASSAY DECISION DIVISION FIRMNESS FORECAST JUDGMENT JUDICIAL SENTENCE VOLITION
DETERMINATIVE FINAL FORMANT SHAPING LIMITING
(**MOST** —) DOMINANT
DETERMINE END FIT FIX GET RUN TEST WILL ASSAY AWARD JUDGE PITCH WIELD ADJUST ASSESS ASSIGN DECERN DECIDE DECREE DEFINE DESCRY DETECT DETERM DEVISE FIGURE GOVERN PERFIX SETTLE ACCOUNT ADJUDGE ANALYZE APPOINT ARRANGE COMPUTE DELIMIT DERAIGN DISPOSE RESOLVE TERMINE COGNOSCE CONCLUDE DISCOVER INFLUENCE
(— **FINENESS**) SET SETT
(— **RATE**) ASSESS
(— **ROOT**) EXTRACT
DETERMINED SET BENT DERN FIRM GRIM GIVEN STOUT UPSET BITTER DOGGED GRITTY INTENT MULISH STURDY DECIDED SETTLED DECISIVE FOREGONE PERVERSE RESOLUTE RESOLVED STUBBORN
DETERMINER GENE CHANCE
DETERMINIST JABARITE
DETEST DAMN HATE ABHOR CURSE LOATHE CONDEMN DESPISE DISLIKE DENOUNCE EXECRATE
DETESTABLE FOUL HORRID ODIOUS BLASTED HATABLE HATEFUL HELLISH HIDEOUS ACCURSED DAMNABLE HATEABLE INFAMOUS INFERNAL
DETESTATION ODIUM HATRED HORROR LOATHING ANTIPATHY
DETHRONE DEPOSE DIVEST UNCROWN
DETONATE FIRE BELCH BLAST SHOOT EXPLODE DETONIZE
DETONATION BLAST KNOCK AMBITUS PINGING PINKING
DETONATOR CAP FUSE FUZE FUSEE FUZEE SQUIB TORPEDO INITIATOR
DETOUR BYPASS CIRCUIT DIVERSION
DETRACT TAKE DECRY DEDUCT DEFAME DETRAY DIVERT VILIFY ASPERSE TRADUCE BELITTLE DEROGATE DIMINISH DISTRACT

MINIMIZE PROTRACT SUBTRACT
WITHDRAW
(— **FROM**) IMPEDE
DETRACTION CALUMNY SCANDAL
SLANDER ZOILISM
DETRIMENT COST HARM HURT LOSS
SORE WOUND DAMAGE DAMNUM
DENIAL INJURY BEATING EXPENSE
JACTURE DISFAVOR MISCHIEF
DETRIMENTAL ADVERSE CAPITAL
HARMFUL HURTFUL LOSSFUL
DAMAGING INVIDIOUS
DETRITUS OUTWASH SHINGLE
SHEETWASH
DEUCALION (FATHER OF —)
PROMETHEUS
(**WIFE OF** —) PYRRHA
DEUCE DIANTRE DICKENS
(**WILD** —) FREAK
DEUCEDLY BLAME BLAMED
DEUTERIUM H
DEUTEROGAMY DIGAMY
DEUTOMALA LABIUM
DEVA DEV DEWA SURA ANGEL DEITY
DEVASTATE EXILE HARRY HAVOC
WASTE DEVAST RAVAGE ATOMIZE
DESTROY PILLAGE PLUNDER
SCOURGE DEMOLISH
DEVASTATED WASTE
DEVASTATION RUIN EXILE HAVOC
WASTE HARASS RAVAGE SACCAGE
SACKAGE SACCADGE
DEVASTATING DEADLY LETHAL
SAVAGE CRUSHING FEROCIOUS
DEVELOP BUD RUN BOOM COOK
FORM GROW STEM TILL ARISE
BREAK BREED BUILD ERECT RIPEN
SHOOT APPEAR BRANCH DETECT
EVOLVE EXPAND FLOWER FULFIL
MATURE REVEAL UNFOLD UNFURL
BURGEON BURNISH EDUCATE
ENLARGE EVOLUTE EXPOUND
FULFILL UNCOVER DEVELOPE
DISCLOSE DISCOVER DISVELOP
ENGENDER GENERATE INCUBATE
MANIFEST
(— **A HEAD**) HEART
(— **BULB**) BOTTOM
(— **COLOR**) AGE
(— **CRACKS**) ALLIGATOR
(— **WELL**) COTTON
DEVELOPABLE TORSE
DEVELOPED DEEP FORWARD
(— **AFTER BIRTH**) ACQUIRED
(**FULLY** —) BOLD ADULT FLORID
FORMED SUMMED
(**GREATLY** —) ADVANCED
(**IMPERFECTLY** —) ABORTIVE
(**INCOMPLETELY** —) SEED
DEVELOPER ELON SOUP ORTOL
AMIDOL GLYCIN KACHIN BUILDER
GLYCINE RODINAL
DEVELOPMENT WAX DRIFT EVENT
HATCH ESTATE GROWTH DESCENT
GENESIS PROCESS STATURE
BREEDING INCREASE PEDIGREE
UPGROWTH UPSPRING
(— **OF SEX**) DIOECISM
(**FULL** —) BLOW MATURITY

(**HIGHEST** —) BLOOM
(**NORMAL** —) APHANISIA
(**SUBSEQUENT** —) SEQUEL
(**THEMATIC** —) CONTINUITY
(**UNEXPECTED** —) ACCIDENT
DEVI UMA KALI DURGA GAURI
CHANDI SHAKTI BHAVANI BHOWANI
HIMAVAT MAHADEVI HAIMAVATI
DEVIANT ABERRANT DIVERGENT
DEVIATE ERR RUN WRY YAW LEAN
MISS VARY VEER BEVEL BREAK
DRIFT LAPSE SHEER SPORT START
STRAY WAIVE CHANGE DEPART
DETOUR DIVERT RECEDE SQUINT
SWERVE WANDER DECLINE DEFLECT
DIGRESS DIVERGE INCLINE REFLECT
ABERRANT DEROGATE
(— **FROM VERTICAL**) HADE
DEVIATING SKEW DEVIANT DEVIOUS
ERRATIC SINUOUS ABERRANT
INDIRECT
DEVIATION BOW HELM JUMP SKEW
TURN DRIFT LAPSE QUIRK SHEER
TWIST ABRASH BATTER CHANGE
DETOUR FIGURE SPREAD ANOMALY
BRISURE LICENCE LICENSE
ACCURACY DRIFTAGE LATITUDE
SOLECISM VARIANCE
(— **OF COLOR**) ABRASH
(**STANDARD** —) SIGMA
DEVICE (ALSO SEE INSTRUMENT)
ARM ART DIE DOG DOP EYE FAN
FLY FOB GAG GIN GUN HOG JIG
KEY MOP MOT PEN SET TIP TUP
WAY WIT ARCH BELL BOND BOOM
BUFF COIN COMB COUP DARE DOPP
DRAG DRIP FAKE FIRE FLAG FORK
FROG FUSE FUZE GAGE GATE GOBO
GRAB GRIP GYRO HASP HAUL HEAD
HECK HORN IRIS IRON JACK KEEP
KITE LAMP LENS LOCK MOVE MULE
MUTE NAIL PACE PAGE PAWK PLOW
POKE PUMP REEL SEAL SHOE SHUT
SIGN SLAY SLEY SLUR SNAP SPUD
STOP STUD SUMP TOOL TRAP TRIP
VICE WEIR WHIM WHIP WIND WING
WOLF ALARM APRON BADGE BALUN
BITCH BLOCK BREAK BRUSH CHECK
CLAMP CODER COVIN CRAMP
CROSS DODGE DRIER DRIFT DRYER
DUMMY FADER FANCY FLAIL FLARE
FLASH FLIRT FLOAT GAUGE GLAND
GORGE GRIPE GUARD GUIDE GUILE
HICKY HINGE HOKUM IMAGE KAZOO
KEYER LADLE LASER LATCH LEVEL
MATCH OTTER PARER PLATE PUNKA
SCREW SHADE SHANK SHIFT SIEVE
SIGHT SIGIL SIREN SIZER SKATE
SLAVE SLICK SLIDE SLING SONDE
SPOOL SPOUT SQUIB STAMP STILL
STOOL STOVE SWEEP SWELL TABLE
TABUT TAMER THIEF TIMER TORCH
TRUER TUNER UNION VERGE
AGRAFE AIRWAY ALARUM ALINER
ANCHOR ARREST BAILER BASTER
BEACON BEATER BECKET BEDDER
BEEPER BINDER BLOWER BOBBIN
BOOMER BRIDLE BROOCH BUCKLE
BUFFER BULLEN BUMPER BUNGEE

BUNTER BURNER BUTTON CIPHER
COOKER DASHER DECEIT DERAIL
DESIGN DIMMER DOFFER DOTTER
DRIVER DROGUE DUMPER EMBLEM
ENGINE EVENER FABRIC FALLER
FEEDER FENDER FILLER FILTER
FINDAL FINDER FORMER GADGET
GLAZER GOFFER GOGGLE GRADER
GRATER GRISLY GUIDER HANGER
HEATER HICKEY HOLDER HOOTER
INVENT JIGGER JOGGER KEEPER
KICKER LAYBOY LETOFF LIFTER
LOOPER MARKER MIRROR MODULE
MORTAR MOTHER NIPPLE NONIUS
NOTION PACKER PEELER PLAYER
PLOUGH PORTER POTEYE PULLER
PUNKAH REROLL RINGER ROCKET
ROLLER ROOTER ROTULA ROUTER
SACKER SADDLE SAFETY SANDER
SCALER SCHEME SCREEN SEALER
SEEKER SENSOR SETTER SHAKER
SHIELD SIFTER SIGNAL SINKER
SIPPER SLEIGH SLICER SLIDER
SLIMER SLOPER SLUICE SOCKET
SOLION SORTER SPACER SPRING
STONER STYLUS SUCKER SWITCH
TACTIC TAGGER TAPPER TELLER
TEMPLE TESTER TILLER TRACER
TUCKER TUNNEL TURNER WARMER
WASHER WEANER WEEDER WHEEZE
WINDER WINNOW WORKER ADAPTER
ADJUNCT AERATOR AGRAFFE
ALIGNER BALANCE BECKETT
BIMETAL BIMORPH BINDING
BLEEDER BLENDER BLINKER
BLOCKER BLOWOFF BLOWOUT
BOOKEND BOOSTER BREAKER
CALTROP CHIPPER CLAPPER
COMPASS DASHPOT DISHMOP
DIVISOR DRAWOFF DRESSER
DRINKER EARPICK EDUCTOR
EJECTOR EMPRESA EXCITER
FACEBOW FASHION FETLOCK
FICELLE FICTION FITMENT FIXTURE
FLASHER FLIPPER FLUSHER
FLYFLAP FRISKET GAUFFER
GIMMICK GLASSES GRAINER
GRENADE GRIDDLE GRILLER
GRINDER GRIPPER GRIZZLY
GROMMET GROOVER GROWLER
GUDGEON GUZZLER HATCHER
HELIDON IGNITER IMAGINE IMPRESA
IMPRESS INFUSER INHALER
IRONMAN KICKOFF KNOTTER
LIGHTER MACHINE MUFFLER
OOGRAPH PIGTAIL PLOTTER
POINTER PRESSER RATCHET
RATTLER RECEDER REDUCER
RELEASE ROASTER ROSETTE
SAMPLER SCALPER SCANNER
SCOGGAN SCRAPER SCUPPER
SERVANT SETBACK SETOVER
SETWORK SHACKLE SHEDDER
SHIFTER SHIPPER SHOOFLY
SHUTTER SHUTTLE SINKBOX
SKIMMER SLAPPER SLEEVER
SLINGER SLITTER SLUDGER
SLUSHER SNAPPER SNIFFER
SNIGGLE SNORKEL SNUBBER

SNUFFER SNUGGER SONOVOX
SOUNDER SPARGER SPEEDER
SPLICER SPOTTER SPRAYER
SQUEEZE STACKER STAPLER
STARTER STEMMER STENTER
STIRRER STOPPER STRIKER
STRIPER SUCTION SWATTER
SWEEPER SYRINGE TAMBOUR
TENDRIL TENSION THEORIC
THINNER TICKLER TREADLE
TRINDLE TRIPPER TRIPPET
TUMBLER TURNOUT TWISTER
WASHOUT WRINGER ABSORBER
ADJUSTER AQUASTAT BACKSTAY
BAROSTAT BIOMETER BLOCKING
BOOTJACK BRAILLER BREATHER
BRONTEUM BUSINESS BUSYBODY
CATAPULT CATHETER CONTOISE
COUPLING CROTCHET CRYOTRON
DAMPENER DEHORNER DERAILER
DIFFUSER DIRECTOR DISPOSER
DOORSTOP DROPHEAD DUPLEXER
EARPHONE ESPRESSO EXPLODER
FAIRLEAD FAKEMENT FASTENER
FLASHGUN FLYBRUSH FUELIZER
GASCHECK GATHERER GIMCRACK
GUNSTICK GYROSTAT HALLMARK
HANDTRAP HEADGEAR HOLDBACK
IMPROVER INKSTAND IRENICON
IRISCOPE ISOLATOR KNOCKOUT
LAUNCHER LEEBOARD LOXOCOSM
LUNARIUM MNEMONIC MOLITION
NEOSTYLE ODOGRAPH OVERLIFT
PACIFIER PARAVANE PENWIPER
PINWHEEL PULSATOR PYROSTAT
QUADRANT QUENTISE REFILTER
REHEATER REPEATER RETARDER
REVERSER SCORCHER SCOTCHER
SCRAWLER SCUTCHER SELECTOR
SHRINKER SILENCER SILVERER
SINKBOAT SMOOTHER SNOWPLOW
SNOWSHOE SPLITTER SPREADER
SPROUTER SQUEEGEE SQUEEZER
STOPWORK STRAINER STRINGER
STRIPPER STROPPER SURFACER
SWEATBOX TELETYPE TELLTALE
TERMINAL THROWOFF THROWOUT
TRAVELER TRAVERSE TRIANGLE
(— FOR BENDING PIPE) HICKEY
(— FOR BORING WELLS) TIGER
(— FOR CONCENTRATING ORE)
JIGGER
(— FOR PUTTING IN GEAR) STRIKER
(— IN LOOM) FEELER TEMPLE
(— ON FLAG) UNION
(— PLACED OVER CHIMNEY) JACK
(— PROTECTING DENTIST'S HAND)
THIMBLE
(— TO RETAIN COFFEE GROUNDS)
GRECQUE
(CENTRIFUGAL —) CYCLONE
(CLEVER —) COUP KNACK
(DISTINGUISHING —) SPOT
(GAMBLING —) HOLDOUT
(GLASSBLOWER'S —) DUMMY
(HAMPERING —) HOBBLES
(HEATING —) ETNA
(HERALDIC —S) ARMS
(LITERARY —) FRAME

(MAGICIAN'S —) FAKE FEKE CRAFT
(MIXING —) CRUTCHER
(POLISHING —) WAGWAG
(PYROTECHNIC —) FOUNTAIN
(SIGHTING —) ALIDADE
(SIGNALLING —) CRICKET
(SKILLFUL —) ART
(SPEECH —) ITALICS
(THEATRICAL —) SLOAT SLOTE
(TIMEKEEPING —) HOROLOGE
(WATER-RAISING —) JANTU SWEEP
CHURRUS
(WEAVING —) BOAT
(PL.) ENGINERY
DEVIL DEL IMP BENG BHUT BOGY
DEIL HAZE MAHU NICK PUCK QUED
WOLF WOND ANNOY BOBBY BOGEY
BOGIE CHORT CLOOT DEMON
DEUCE EBLIS FIEND HARRY SATAN
SCRAT SHEDU TAIPO TEASE
AMAMON DAEMON DIABLE DIABLO
HORNIE NICKIE PESTER RAGMAN
SORROW THURSE AMAIMON
ANHANGA CLOOTIE DIANTRE
DICKENS GREMLIN LUCIFER
MAHOUND RUFFIAN SERPENT
SHAITAN TORMENT WARLOCK
WENDIGO WINDIGO APOLLYON
BAALPEOR BEELPEOR BELFAGOR
CAGNAZZO CURUPIRA DEVILING
DEVILKIN DIABOLUS MEPHISTO
MISCHIEF OBIDICUT PLOTCOCK
WORRICOW
(BLUE —S) MARE
DEVILFISH RAY MANTA
DEVILISH DARING DEUCED DEVILY
RAKISH WICKED DEMONIC EXTREME
FIENDLY HELLISH INHUMAN SATANIC
DEMONIAC DIABOLIC FIENDISH
INFERNAL SATURNINE
DEVILISHLY DEUCED DEUCEDLY
DEVIL'S CLUB FATSIA
DEVIL'S COACHHORSE DARDAOL
DEVIL'S-MILK WARTWEED
WARTWORT
DEVIL'S-TREE DITA
DEVIOUS DEEP ERRING LOUCHE
ROVING SHIFTY SUBTLE TRICKY
OBLIQUE PLAITED VAGRANT
WINDING HAVERING INDIRECT
RAMBLING SCHEMING TORTUOUS
DEVISE AIM CAST COOK FIND GIVE
PLAN PLOT WARP WILL ARRAY
FANCY FRAME FUDGE IMAGE LEAVE
SHAPE WEAVE ADVISE CONVEY
DECOCT DESIGN DEVICE DIVIDE
DIVINE INVENT SCHEME AGITATE
APPOINT ARRANGE BETHINK
COMMENT COMPASS CONCERT
CONCOCT CONSULT IMAGINE
PREPARE PROJECT BEQUEATH
CONTRIVE
DEVISER FINDER ARTIFICER
DEVISING DEVICE DEVISAL FORGERY
DEVITALIZE DULL DEADEN
DEVITALIZED DEGENERATE
DEVITRIFIED AMBITTY
DEVOID FREE VOID EMPTY BARREN

EXPERT VACANT SINCERE WANTING
DESOLATE
(— OF HELP) AIDLESS
(— OF KINDNESS) CRUEL
(— OF MERCY) BRUTAL
(— OF MIND) AMENTAL
(— OF VALUE) HOLLOW
(— OF) BOUT EMPTY
DEVOLUTION DESCENT
DEVOLVE FALL PASS RESULT
BLOSSOM SUCCEED OVERTURN
TRANSFER TRANSMIT
DEVOTE VOW ALLY AVOW DOOM
GIVE LEND TAKE TURN APPLY
DEVOW ADDICT ATTACH BESTOW
DEPUTE DESIGN DEVOVE DIRECT
EMPLOY INTEND RESIGN ADDRESS
CONSIGN DESTINE DEDICATE
VENERATE
(— TIME) BOTHER
DEVOTED MAD HIGH TRUE LIEGE
LOYAL PIOUS ARDENT DEVOUT
DOOMED ENTIRE FERVID OBLATE
VOTARY VOTIVE ADORING ARDUOUS
JEALOUS SERIOUS ZEALOUS
ADDICTED ATTACHED CONSTANT
FAITHFUL
(— TO COUNTRY) PATRIOTIC
(— TO ENJOYMENT) APOLAUSTIC
(OVERLY —) SUPERSTITIOUS
DEVOTEE CAT FAN NUN BUFF MONK
YATI ADEPT JNANI ADDICT BHAGAT
BHAKTA DEVOTO DEVOUT HEPCAT
VOTARY VOTEEN ZEALOT ADMIRER
AMATEUR BOPPIST BOPSTER
CINEAST FANATIC HEPSTER HIPSTER
SHAVIAN TARTUFE AMOURIST
BURNSIAN CABALIST DEVOTARY
FOLLOWER IBSENITE PARTISAN
PRIAPIAN SAVOYARD SIMPLIST
TARTUFFE VOTARESS VOTARIST
ALLIGATOR
DEVOTION CULT ZEAL ARDOR PIETY
BHAKTI NOVENA ANGELUS ARABISM
CULTISM LOYALTY FIDELITY
IDOLATRY JEALOUSY KAVVANAH
KAWWANAH RELIGION
(— OF ONESELF) VOW
(— TO HUMAN WELFARE)
HUMANISM
(FERVENT —) ADORATION
(PARENTAL —) PROGENITY
(PL.) HOLIES
DEVOTIONAL SOLEMN
DEVOUR EAT JAW FRET GULP SWAP
SWOP VOUR GORGE RAVEN WASTE
AFRETE ENGULF CONSUME
ENGORGE FRAUNCH SWALLOW
(— GREEDILY) SWILL
DEVOURING PREY EATING GREEDY
VORANT EDACIOUS
DEVOUT GOOD HOLY WARM FROOM
GODLY GRACY PIOUS HEARTY
INWARD SOLEMN CORDIAL DEVOTE
GODLIKE PITEOUS SAINTLY SINCERE
REVERENT PIETISTIC
(NOT —) LINK
DEVOUTNESS PIETY DEVOTION
DEW DAG RIME BLOOM FROST

MOISTEN REFRESH MOISTURE
(— **METER**) PAGOSCOPE
DEWBERRY MAYES
DEWDROP PEARL
DEWLAP JOWL GULLET JOLLOP
CHOLLER WATTLES
(— **OF MALE MOOSE**) BELL
DEWY DAMP RORY MOIST RORAL
RORIC RORID GENTLE ROSCID
DEXTERITY ART CHIC CRAFT KNACK
SKILL STROIL ABILITY ADDRESS
AGILITY APTNESS CUNNING FINESSE
SLEIGHT APTITUDE DEFTNESS
FACILITY
(— **IN ARMS**) CHIVALRY
DEXTEROUS APT FLY DEFT FEAT
HEND WISE ADEPT CANNY CLEAN
FEATY HANDY HAPPY HENDE JIMMY
QUICK READY SMART TIGHT ADROIT
ARTFUL CLEVER DRAFTY CUNNING
SLEIGHT DEXTROUS HANDSOME
SKILLFUL SLEIGHTY
DEXTEROUSLY YARELY HANDILY
DEXTRAN GLUCOSAN
DEXTROROTATORY POSITIVE
DEXTRORSE EUTROPIC
DEXTROSE AME CERELOSE
DHAK DAK PALAS PULAS
DHAVA BAKLI
DHOLE KOLSUN
DHOW BUGALA LATEEN SAMBUK
SAMBOUK LATEENER
DHYANA JHANA
DIABASE OPHITE DOLERITE
THOLEITE
DIABOLICAL CRUEL WICKED
DEMONIC HELLISH INHUMAN
SATANIC VIOLENT DEMONIAC
DEVILISH DIABOLIC FIENDISH
INFERNAL
DIABOLISM SATANISM
DIACETATE ACETIN
DIACONATE DEACONRY
DIACONICON PARABEMA
DIACRITIC HACEK TILDE UMLAUT
MODIFIER
DIAD DIGONAL TWOFOLD
DIADEM MIND CROWN TIARA
ANADEM CIRCLE EMBLEM FILLET
CORONET HEADBAND
DIAERESIS CESURA CAESURA
DIALYSIS
DIAGNOSE ANALYZE IDENTIFY
KNOWLEDGE
DIAGONAL BIAS SLANT SLASH
COUNTER SOLIDUS VIRGULE
BENDWISE DIAGONIC
DIAGONALLY BIAS BENDWAYS
BENDWISE
DIAGRAM MAP PLAN PLOT TREE
CARTE CHART EPURE GRAPH
DESIGN FIGURE SCHEMA SCHEME
SYMBOL YANTRA ISOGRAM ISOTYPE
SECTION VIAGRAM

DIAGRAMMATIC GRAPHIC

DIAGRAPH OE

DIAL NOB FACE KNOB WATCH
DIACLE JIGGER AZIMUTH CRYSTAL

DECLINER HOROLOGE INCLINER
RECLINER
DIAL BIRD DAYAL DHYAL
DIALECT (ALSO SEE LANGUAGE) HO
KA WU GEG GIZ KHA LAI SAC TWI
AMOY CANI CANT EFIK EGBA EPIC
GEEZ GHEG GONA GUEG IOWA ITZA
KORA MANX NAMA NORN OGAM
PALI SAUK SHOR SOGA TALK TCHI
TOSK TUBA ALTAI ARGOT ASURI
ATTIC CONOY DORIC FANTI GHEEZ
GHESE HAKKA IDIOM IONIC IOWAY
IRAQI KANSA KAREL KOINE LADIN
LINGO MAZUR MOPAN MUKRI
NGOKO OGHAM PARSI PUNIC SABIR
SAXON SCOTS SLANG TIGRE TSCHI
VALVE VOGUL ZMUDZ AEOLIC
AGNEAN ASANTE ATSINA AWADHI
BADAGA BROGUE CANTON CREOLE
DEBATE DUNGAN FAEROE FANTEE
FURLAN GASCON GULLAH GUTNIC
HARARI HARAYA IBANAG ISINAI
ITAVES JARGON KANSAS KHAMIR
KORANA KVITSH LADAKI LAHULI
LALLAN LIBYAN PARSEE PATOIS
PATTER PICARD SANTEE SCOTCH
SHARRA SKAGIT SPEECH SUDANI
SWATOW SYRIAC SZEKEL TAVAST
TONGUE TUSCAN YANKEE ZENAGA
ACADIAN AEOLIAN AMOYESE
ASHANTI BHOTANI BHUTANI
BUNDELI CHILULA CHUVASH
CLATSOP COCKNEY CORNISH
CUZCENO CYPRIOT FAYUMIC
FOOCHOW GEECHEE GHEGISH
GUTNISH JAIPURI KARAITE KITKSAN
KONKANI LADAKHI LALLAND
LEONESE LESBIAN MALTESE
MARSIAN MARWARI MIDLAND
MULTANI MUNDARI OLONETS
PANAYAN PRAKRIT SAHIDIC SANPOIL
SHORTZY SOKOTRI SPOKANE
SQUAXON SWABIAN SZEKLER
TIGRINA VAUDOIS ABANEEME
ACHMIMIC AKHMIMIC ALGERINE
ARCADIAN ASSYRIAN BAVARIAN
BHOJPURI BISCAYAN BOEOTIAN
BOHAIRIC CLAKAMAS COLVILLE
CORSICAN CYPRIOTE FALERIAN
FALISCAN FAROEISH FRANCIEN
FRIULIAN GARHWALI HARARESE
IZCATECO KANESIAN KARELIAN
KERMANJI KICKAPOO KINGWANA
LACANDON LANGUAGE LAWLANTS
MAGHREBI MAGHRIBI MAITHILI
MANDAEAN MANDARIN MANISIAN
MAZATECO MAZURIAN MEMPHITE
NABATEAN NEENGATU PANAYANO
PEKINESE RABBINIC SALTEAUX
SOULETIN SOUTHERN TAUNGTHU
TIGRINYA TIRHUTIA TUNISIAN
VENERIAN VIENNESE
(**STRANGE** —) GIBBERISH
(PL.) WU ANGLIAN
DIALECTIC PILPUL
DIALOGUE ION CRITO DIALOG
EPILOG PATTER PHAEDO TIMAEUS
COLLOQUY DUOLOGUE EPILOGUE
EXCHANGE PHAEDRUS

(—**S OF BUDDHA**) SUTRA SUTTA
(**COMIC** —) LAZZO
DIAMETER BORE GAGE GEAR MOOT
GAUGE WIDTH MODULE
(— **OF BULLET**) CALIBER CALIBRE
(— **OF PELVIS**) CONJUGATA
(— **OF PUPIL**) APERTURE
(— **OF WIRE**) GAGE GAUGE
DIAMOND GEM ICE BORT LASK PICK
ROCK ROSE BAHIA BOORT BORTZ
DORJE FANCY FIELD JAGER JEWEL
LOZEN MELEE POINT RHOMB RIVER
SANCY SPARK TABLE VAJRA
ADAMAS CANARY CARBON JAEGER
LASQUE ORLOFF PENCIL REGENT
RONDEL SHINER TABLET ADAMANT
BRIOLET CARREAU CRYSTAL
FISHEYE INFIELD LOZENGE PREMIER
RHOMBUS SPARKLE CORUNDUM
KOHINOOR RONDELLE SPARKLER
(— **CUT TOO THIN**) FISHEYE
(— **MOLDER**) DOP
(— **STATE**) DELAWARE
(— **USED FOR ENGRAVING**) SHARP
(**BLACK** —) CARBONADO
(**FLAT** —) LASQUE
(**GLAZIER'S** —) QUARREL
(**IMITATION** —) SCHLENTER
(**INFERIOR GRADE OF** —) FLAT
(**PERFECT** —) PARAGON
(**PURE WHITE** —) RIVER
(**SINGLE** —) SOLITAIRE
(**TRANSPARENT** —) CRYSTAL
(**YELLOW** —) CANARY
(PL.) MELANGE
DIAMOND BIRD PARDALOTE
DIAMORPHINE HEROIN
DIANA LUCINA TRIVIA ARTEMIS
(**BROTHER OF** —) APOLLO
(**FATHER OF** —) JUPITER
(**MOTHER OF** —) LATONA
DIANA MONKEY ROLOWAY
DIAPASON MONTRE DIAPASE
DIAPAUSE BLOCK
DIAPER FUR DIDY CLOUT DIDIE
NAPPY HIPPEN HIPPIN NAPKIN
NAPPIE DIAPERY
DIAPHANOUS CLEAR SHEER
FRAGILE DIAPHANE
DIAPHONY ORGANUM TRIPHONY
DIAPHORETIC BUCCO BUCHU
BUCKU BORAGE DIAPNOIC HIDROTIC
SUDATORY
DIAPHRAGM IRIS RIFF SLIT APRON
PHREN SKIRT WAFER DECKER
PLATEN MIDRIFF PHRAGMA
SKIRTING TRAVERSE TYMPANUM
DIAPHRAGMATIC PHRENIC
DIARRHEA LAX FLUX LASK GURRY
RELAX SCOUR SPRUE PURGING
SQUIRTS LIENTERY
DIARY LOG RECORD DAYBOOK
DIURNAL JOURNAL REGISTER
EPHEMERIS
DIASKEUAST EDITOR REVISER

DIASPORA GALUT GOLAH GALUTH

DIASPORE MIGRULE

DIASTASE MALT ENZYME AMYLASE

DIATOM BRITTLEWORT
ASTERIONELLA
DIATONIC ACHROMATIC
DIATRIBE SCREED HARANGUE
INVECTIVE
DIB DAP DIP DIBBLE DIBSTONE
DIBBLE DAP DIB DABBLE DIBBER
KIPPIN TRIFLE DIBBLER KIPPEEN
DIBS COCKAL
DICAST HELIAST JURYMAN
DICE CHOP CUBE DEES BONES
CRAPS FLATS LOWMEN REJECT
CHECKER IVORIES
(— GAME) SET RAPHE MUMCHANCE
(— HAVING FOUR SPOTS) QUATRE
(2, 3, OR 12 ON 1ST —) MISSOUT
(FALSE —) GOAD TATS GOURD
GRAVIERS SQUARIER STOPDICE
(HIGHEST THROW AT —) APHRODITE
(LOADED —) TOPS DOCTOR
(LOWEST THROW AT —) AMBSACE
(PAIRED NUMBERS AT —) DUPLET
DOUBLETS
DICE PLAYER THROWSTER
DICER DERBY GAMBLER GRAINER
DICERION DYKER
DICHONDRA LAWNLEAF
DICHOTOMY DUALITY
DICKENS HECK DEUCE
DICKER ICRE SWAP DAKER BARTER
HAGGLE BARGAIN CHAFFER
EXCHANGE
DICKEY POOP WEAK DICKY FRONT
GILET SHAKY DONKEY RUMBLE
VESTEE HADDOCK PLASTRON
DICKIE SHAM DICKY FRONT SQUARE
TUCKER STARCHER
DICLINOUS IMPERFECT
DICTATE SAW SAY DITE TELL UTTER
WRITE DECREE DICTUM ENJOIN
IMPOSE INDITE OCTROY ORDAIN
SCHOOL COMMAND DELIVER
REQUIRE SUGGEST WARRANT
DICTAMEN
DICTATION DICTAMEN
DICTATOR CZAR DUCE TSAR
CAESAR PENDRAGON
DICTATORIAL BOSSY LORDLY
CZARIST POMPOUS TSARIST
ARROGANT DOGMATIC ORACULAR
POSITIVE
DICTION STYLE TERMS PHRASE
IMAGERY LANGUAGE PARLANCE
VERBIAGE
(BAD —) CACOLOGY
DICTIONARY GRADUS CALEPIN
LEXICON GLOSSARY WORDBOOK
THESAURUS
DICTUN SAY ADAGE AXIOM EDICT
DECREE SAYING DICTATE EFFATUM
OPINION APOTHEGM PRINCIPLE
STATEMENT
DID D CAN DED DEDE DYDE
(— NOT) DIDNA DIDNT
DIDACTIC DRY PREACHY SERMONIC
DIDO ANTIC CAPER TRICK
(BROTHER OF —) PYGMALION
(FATHER OF —) BELUS
(HUSBAND OF —) SICHAEUS

(LOVER OF —) AENEAS
DIE GO BED DEE DOD END HOB HUB
PIP ROT SIX TAT BOSS COIN CONK
CUBE DADO DEAD DICE DROP EXIT
FADE FAIL FALL FINE FIVE FLIT KICK
MARK MOLD PART PASS PIKE PILE
SEAL TATT TINE WANE CROAK
FORCE FUDGE GHOST IVORY
NAPOO PATAY PRINT PUNCH QUAIL
SHAPE SNUFF SOUGH SPILL STALL
STAMP STOCK SWELT CHANCE
DEMISE DEPART DOCTOR EXPIRE
FAMISH FINISH FORCER FORMER
FULLAM MATRIX MULLAR PATRIX
PERISH ROLLER STARVE STRIKE
TORFEL TORFLE TRANCE VANISH
WITHER BLOCKER DECEASE
SUCCUMB TESSERA INTAGLIO
LANGUISH MISCARRY PUNCHEON
TRESPASS TRUSSELL
(— AWAY) FAIL SWOON
(— BY HANGING) SWING
(— DOWN) FLIT SINK
(— FOR DRAWING WIRE) WHIRTLE
WHORTLE
(— FOR MAKING DRAINPIPE) DOD
(— FOR MOLDING BRICK) KICK
(— FROM HUNGER) AFFAMISH
(— OF COLD) STARVE
(— WITH 4 SPOTS) QUATRE
(— WITH 6 SPOTS) CISE SICE SISE
SIZE
(COINING —) SICCA
(FRAUDULENT —) FULHAM FULLAM
FULLOM
(HOLLOW —) GOURD
(IMPROPER —) FLAT
(LOADED —) TAT DOCTOR FULHAM
HIGHMAN LANGRET
(LOWER —) BED
(REVOLVING —) DREIDEL
DIEBACK STAGHEAD EXANTHEMA
DIED DYDE WRATE
DIEHARD TORY BLIMP
DIESIS FEINT
DIET BANT FARE FAST FOOD SEIM
SEYM BOARD HOFTAG REDUCE
SEIMAS VIANDS VICTUS DIETINE
LANDTAG REGIMEN RIKSDAG
CONGRESS KREISTAG VOLKSTAG
DIETARY (— LAWS) KASHRUTH
DIETETICS SITOLOGY
DIETHER APIOL APIOLE DIOXANE
DIETING BANTING
DIFFER VARY RECEDE SQUARE
COMPARE DISCORD DISSENT
DIVERGE DISAGREE
DIFFERENCE SHED CHASM CLASH
FAVOR BREACH CHANGE DIFFER
ANOMALY BRISURE DISCORD
DISPUTE QUALITY VARIETY
DISTANCE DIVISION IMPARITY
VARIANCE
(— IN ELEVATION) HEAD
(— IN LATITUDE) SOUTHING
(— IN LONGITUDE) EASTING
(— IN PITCH) COMMA INTERVAL
(— IN PRESSURE) DRAFT DRAUGHT
(— IN WIDTH) BILGE

(— OF OPINION) DISSENT
ARGUMENT
(— OF VESSEL'S DRAFT) DRAG
(ANGULAR —) EXPLEMENT
(GRADED —) GRADIENT
(MINUTE —) SHADE
(PRICE —) BASIS
(SMALL —) HAIRLINE
DIFFERENT FAR MANY SERE FRESH
OTHER PARTY DIVERS SCREWY
SUNDRY UNLIKE ANOTHER DISTANT
DIVERSE SEVERAL STRANGE
UNALIKE UNUSUAL VARIANT
VARIOUS CONTRARY DISTINCT
MANIFOLD SEPARATE
DIFFERENTIA MARK LIMIT
DIFFERENTIAL FLUXION
DIFFERENTIATE APLITE DIFFER
DISCERN HAPLITE CONTRAST
SPECIATE
DIFFERENTIATION ANABOLY
DEVIATION DICHOTOMY
DIFFERING DIVERSE SINGULAR
DIVERGENT
DIFFICULT ILL HARD WICK CRAMP
CRANK GREAT HEAVY SPINY STIFF
AUGEAN CRABBY CRANKY KNOTTY
SEVERE STICKY STRAIT STRONG
TICKLE TRAPPY UNEASY UNEATH
UPHILL WENETH WICKED ARDUOUS
AWKWARD BRITTLE CRABBED
DIFFUSE LABORED NERVOUS
OBSCURE PAINFUL PERPLEX
PRACTIC SERIOUS STICKLE
UNNETHE ABSTRACT CUMBROUS
FIENDISH PUZZLING SCABROUS
STRUGGLE STUBBORN
(— TO BEAR) BITTER
(— TO COMPREHEND) STRANGE
(— TO FOLLOW) DIRTY
(— TO GRASP) FUGITIVE
(— TO HANDLE) SPINOUS
(— TO MANAGE) SURLY STURDY
(— TO OBTAIN) CLOSE
(— TO PLEASE) CURIOUS
(— TO RAISE) DORTY
(— TO SATISFY) CHOOSY CHOOSEY
(— TO UNDERSTAND) DEEP HIGH
SUBTLE CRABBED ABSTRACT
ABSTRUSE ESOTERIC
DIFFICULTY ADO BAR ILL JAM RUB
BUMP CLOG COIL HEAT JAMB KNOT
LOCK NODE PAIN PINE SNAG SORE
WERE CHECK DOUBT GRIEF NODUS
PRESS RIGOR STAND STOUR TRADE
APORIA BOGGLE BUNKER HABBLE
HOBBLE PLIGHT PLUNGE RUBBER
SCRAPE STRAIT TIFTER BARRIER
DICKENS GORDIAN PITFALL
PROBLEM SQUEEZE ASPERITY
HARDNESS HARDSHIP OBSTACLE
SEVERITY STRUGGLE
(UNEXPECTED —) SNAG
(WITH —) SCARCELY
DIFFIDENCE DOUBT MODESTY
RESERVE SHYNESS DISTRUST
HUMILITY TIMIDITY
DIFFIDENT SHY BLATE CHARY
MODEST BACKWARD RESERVED

RETIRING SHEEPISH

DIFFUSE FULL SHED BLEED EXUDE LARGE STREW WORDY DEFUSE DERIVE DILATE DIVIDE EXPAND EXTEND OSMOSE PROLIX SPREAD SPRING COPIOUS DIALYSE DIALYZE DIFFUND PERPLEX PERVADE PUBLISH RADIATE SCATTER SPARKLE SPRAWLY SPRENGE SUFFUSE VERBOSE CONFUSED DIFFUSED DIOSMOSE DISPERSE PATULENT PATULOUS SPRANGLE **(NOT —)** STRICT COMPACT

DIFFUSION SPREAD OSMOSIS BLEEDING DEFUSION

DIG HOE JOB NIP CLAW DIKE DYKE GIRD GORE GRUB HOWK MINE MOOT PION POKE PROD ROOT SINK SMUG SPIT SPUD SUMP SWOT DELVE DITCH DWELL GAULT GRAFT GRAVE LODGE POACH PROBE SNOUT SPADE START STOCK BURROW DREDGE EXHUME GRAVEL HOLLOW PLUNGE SHOVEL THRUST TUNNEL BEDELVE COSTEAN SPUDDLE UNEARTH EXCAVATE **(— OUT CREVICES)** FOSSICK **(— OUT)** SCOOP STUMP EXHUME **(— PEAT)** SHEUGH **(— POTATOES)** LIFT **(— TRENCHES)** GRIP COSTEAN COSTEEN **(— UP)** CAST GRUB STUB SPADE STOCK EXHUME UPGRAVE DISINTER **(— WITH NAILS)** SCRAPE **(— WITH SNOUT)** GROUT

DIGAMMA VAU

DIGEST COCT CODE DEFY ENDEW ENDUE INDUE RIPEN CODIFY DECOCT DOCKET MATURE SEETHE CONCOCT EPITOME PANDECT SUMMARY CONDENSE SYLLABUS

DIGESTION PEPSIS COCTION EUPEPSIA EUPEPSIA

DIGESTIVE PEPTIC DIGERENT

DIGGER DIG PAL PLOW MINER BANKER BILDAR DRUDGE PLOUGH COMRADE PEATMAN PIONEER PLODDER TRENCHER **(POST HOLE —)** LOY

DIGGING DIG DIKAGE DYKAGE STRIPPING

DIGHT DAB RUB DECK DINK DITE WIPE ADORN DICHT DRESS EQUIP ORDER RAISE TREAT MANAGE REPAIR WINNOW APPOINT CONSIGN PERFORM PREPARE

DIGIT TOE UNIT DOIGT POINT THUMB FIGURE FINGER HALLUX MEDIUS NUMBER DEWCLAW DIGITAL **(BINARY —)** BINIT **(EXTRA —)** PREPOLLEX

DIGITAL KEY MANUAL

DIGITATE DIGITAL FINGERED

DIGNIFIED GRAND LOFTY MANLY NOBLE STAID AUGUST LORDLY SEDATE SOLEMN COURTLY EXALTED STATELY TOGATED ELEVATED ENNOBLED MAJESTIC

DIGNIFY DUB ADORN CROWN EXALT GRACE HONOR RAISE ELEVATE ENNOBLE PROMOTE

DIGNITARY DON WIG RAJA RAJAH PRIEST SHERIF DIGNITY HUTUKTU PRELATE SHEREEF HUTUKHTU VESTIARY

DIGNITY DOG CHIC FACE RANK BENCH DINES HONOR IZZAT PRIDE STATE AFFAIR BARONY LAUREL REPOSE BARONRY BEARING DECORUM DUKEDOM EARLDOM FITNESS GRAVITY MAJESTY SHAHDOM STATION WORSHIP CHIVALRY EARLSHIP GRANDEUR NOBILITY **(— OF BISHOP)** LAWN **(ACCIDENTAL —)** JOY HAYZ **(PAPAL —)** TIARA

DIGRAPH CH OE PH RH TH RRH BIGRAM LIGATURE DIPHTHONG

DIGRESS VEER EXCUR DIVERT SWERVE WANDER DEVIATE DIVERGE EXCURSE DISGRESS DIVAGATE

DIGRESSION ASIDE VAGARY DIGRESS ECBASIS EPISODE EXCURSE PASSAGE TANGENT DISGRESS EXCURSUS SIDESLIP **(RHETORICAL —)** ECBOLE

DIKE BAR RIB BANK BUND DICE DICK DYKE POND POOL DIGUE DITCH LEVEE CAUSEY CRADGE CHANNEL DIKELET POWDIKE CAUSEWAY ESTACADE SPREADER

DIKER COWAN COWEN

DIKETONE BENZIL BIACETYL DIMEDONE

DILACTONE LACTIDE ANEMONIN

DILAPIDATE DESTROY

DILAPIDATED BAD BEATEN CREAKY RAGGED RUINED SHABBY WRECKY CRAICHY CREACHY RUINOUS DESOLATE TATTERED WOBEGONE

DILAPIDATION RUIN DECAY DECREPITY DISREPAIR

DILATATION BULB SINUS VARIX JARBOT SPREAD AMPULLA ECTASIA ECTASIS ANEURISM DILATION

DILATE DELAY PLUMP SWELL WIDEN DELATE EXPAND EXTEND SPREAD AMPLIFY BROADEN DESCANT DIFFUSE DISTEND ENLARGE INFLATE PROLONG STRETCH DISPERSE INCREASE LENGTHEN PROTRACT DISCOURSE

DILATOR DIOPTER DIOPTRA DIOPTRY DIVULSOR SPECULUM

DILATORY LATE SLOW SLACK SPARE TARDY FABIAN REMISS DILATOR LAGGARD LATREDE TEDIOUS BACKWARD DELAYING INACTIVE SLUGGISH

DILEMMA FIX FORK LOCK NODE BRIKE CHOICE PLUNGE CORNUTE SNIFTER JEOPARDY QUANDARY

DILETTANTE LOVER SUNDAY ADMIRER AMATEUR DABBLER DABSTER ESTHETE AESTHETE

DILIGENCE HIE CARE HEED DILLY

EFFORT CAUTION HORNING BUSINESS INDUSTRY ASSIDUITY

DILIGENT BUSY HARD TIDY ACTIVE EIDENT ITHAND STEADY CAREFUL EARNEST HEEDFUL OPEROSE PAINFUL WORKFUL CAUTIOUS CONSTANT LABOROUS SEDULOUS STUDIOUS

DILL ANET CALM SOYA ANISE UMBEL PICKLE SOOTHE DILLWEED

DILLYDALLY LAG TOY LOAF DELAY DILLY STALL LOITER TRIFLE

DILOGY ECHO

DILUENT CARRIER VEHICLE

DILUTE CUT BREW FUSE LEAN THIN WEAK ALLAY BLUNT DELAY WATER RAREFY REDUCE WEAKEN WHITISH DIMINISH LENGTHEN WATERISH **(— LIQUOR)** BREW SPLIT **(— WINE)** GALLIZE **(VERY —)** SMALL

DILUTED WASHY DILUTE REMISS

DIM DIP WAN BLUR DARK DULL FADE GRAY HAZY MIST PALE PALL VEIL BEDIM BLEAK BLEAR BLIND DUSKY DUSTY FAINT FOGGY MISTY STAIN BEMIST BLEARY CLOUDY DARKEN DASWEN DIMPSY GLOOMY OBTUSE SHADOW TWILIT DARKISH DISLIMN ECLIPSE OBSCURE OPACATE SHADOWY TARNISH DARKLING OVERCAST **(NOT —)** FRESH

DIME HOG HOGG DISME TENPENCE TENPENNY **(HALF —)** PICAYUNE

DIMEDON METHONE

DIMENHYDRINATE DRAMAMINE

DIMENSION BODY BULK SIZE SCOPE WIDTH ASSIZE DEGREE EXTENT HEIGHT LENGTH MOISON BREADTH **(COLOR —)** CHROMA **(TYPE —)** EM EN **(PL.)** GAGE SIZE GAUGE GIRTH EXTENT SIDING MEASURE

DIMIDIATE HALVED

DIMINISH GO CUT EBB SAP BATE BURN CHOP DAMP DROP EASE FADE FAIL FINE FRET MELT PARE PINK SINK WANE WEAR ABATE ALLAY BREAK CLOSE DRAFT DWARF ELIDE ERODE LOWER MINCE PETER SLACK SMALL TAPER DAMPEN DEBATE DECOCT DEDUCT DILUTE IMPAIR LESSEN MINISH REBATE REDUCE SLOUGH VANISH WITHER ABRIDGE ASSUAGE CORRODE CURTAIL DEGRADE DEPLETE DEPRESS DETRACT DIMINUE DRAUGHT DWINDLE FRITTER INHIBIT QUALIFY REFRACT RELIEVE TARNISH ADMINISH AMOINDER CONDENSE DECREASE DIMINUTE DISCOUNT MINORATE MITIGATE MODERATE RETRENCH **(— FRONT)** PLOY

DIMINISHED SLACK GRAYED DIMINUTE

DIMINISHING TAPER CRITICAL FLAGGING
(— IN LOUDNESS) CALANDO
DIMINUTION FALL WASTE DECREASE
DIMINUTIVE TOY WEE BABY TINY BANTY DWARF PETTY RUNTY SMALL YOUNG BANTAM LITTLE PETITE POCKET MANIKIN MIDGETY MINIKIN SHRIMPY EXIGUOUS
(— OF BAR) SCARP CLOSET SCARPE
DIMLY DULLY DARKLY FEEBLY SHADOWY
DIMMED BLEARY CLOUDY GRAYED BLEARED
DIMMING GRAYOUT
DIMNESS DIM HAZE MIST SLUR GLOOM CALIGO DARKNESS
DIMPLE DOKE AHMADI AHMEDI RIPPLE GELASIN FOSSETTE
DIM-SIGHTED PURBLIND
DIN BUM DUN RERD RIOT ALARM BABEL BRUIT CHIME CHIRM CLANG DEAVE DEEVE FRUSH NOISE RERDE ALARUM BELDER CLAMOR FRAGOR HUBBUB RACKET RATTLE STEVEN TUMULT UPROAR CLANGOR CLATTER DISCORD TURMOIL DINGDONG TINTAMAR
DINAR DENARE MARAVEDI
DINDLE RING QUIVER THRILL TINGLE TINKLE TREMOR STAGGER VIBRATE
DINE EAT SUP FARE FEAST REGALE
DINER EPICURE GOURMAND
DING DIN BEAT DANG DASH KICK PUSH RING WHIP CLANG DRIVE EXCEL FLING KNOCK PITCH POUND PUNCH THUMP STROKE THRASH THRUST
DINGE DENT DINT BATTER BRUISE TARNISH
DINGHY SKIFF DINGEY ROWBOAT SHALLOP SNOWBIRD
DINGLE DEN DALE DELL GLEN VALE DIMBLE DUMBLE HOLLOW VALLEY
DINGMAN BUMPER
DINGO WARRAGAL WARRIGAL
DINGUS GADGET DOOHICKEY
DINGY DUN DARK DIRTY DUSKY GRIMY OURIE SMOKY DINGHY SUBFUSC SMIRCHED
DINING CENATION
DINING ROOM TRICLINIUM
DINKA JANGHEY
DINNER DINE HALL KALE MEAL MEAT NOON BEANO FEAST DINING REPAST BANQUET PUCHERO FUNCTION
(CEREMONIAL —) SEDER
DINOSAUR DIAPSID SAURIAN DUCKBILL NODOSAUR SAUROPOD TROODONT
DINT BEAT BLOW DENT DUNT NICK CLOUR DELVE DINGE FORCE NOTCH ONSET POWER PRESS SHOCK ATTACK CHANCE EFFORT STRIKE STROKE IMPRINT EFFICACY STRIKING

DIOCESAN EPISCOPAL
DIOCESE SEE EPARCHY DISTRICT BISHOPRIC
DIODE KENOTRON
DIOLEFIN DIENE ALLENE HEXADIENE
DIOMEDES (FATHER OF —) MARS TYDEUS
(MOTHER OF —) CYRENE DEIPYLE
(WIFE OF —) AEGIALE
DIONYSUS BACCHUS BROMIOS BROMIUS LENAEUS LIKNITES
DIOPSIDE VIOLAN ALALITE PYROXENE
DIORITE CORSITE DIABASE ORNOITE APPINITE
DIOSCURI ALCIS ANACES ANAKES CASTORES
DIOXIDE SILICA BINOXIDE
DIP DAP DIB DOP SOP BAIL DROP DUCK DUNK LADE LAVE SINK SOAK BATHE DELVE LADLE LOWER MERSE PITCH SCOOP SLOPE SOUSE SWOOP TAINT CANDLE HOLLOW PLUNGE BAPTIZE DECLINE IMMERGE IMMERSE INCLINE MOISTEN DIPSTICK SUBMERGE
(— AND THROW) BAIL BALE
(— IN DANCING) CORTE
(— INTO) SAMPLE
(— OUT) KEACH
DIPENTENE CINENE CAJUPUTENE
DIPHTHONG BIVOCAL
DIPHTHONGIZED BROKEN
DIPLOIDIZE SPERMATIZE
DIPLOMA SANAD DEGREE SUNNUD CHARTER CODICIL
DIPLOMACY TACT POLICE TREATY
DIPLOMAT DEAN ENVOY CONSUL ATTACHE MINISTER
DIPLOMATIC SUAVE FECIAL FETIAL
DIPLOPIA POLYOBA AMBIOPIA
DIPNOAN DIPNOID MUDFISH
DIPODY METER METRE DIIAMB SYZYGY
DIPPER BAIL GAWN PIET PLOW GOURD HANDY LADLE SCOOP SPOON BUCKET DUNKER PIGGIN PLOUGH TUNKER DUNKARD PICKLER CALABASH
(ASTRONOMICAL —) WAGON WAGGON
DIPSOMANIA ENOMANIA POTOMANIA
DIPTERAN SYRPHID
DIPTERON DIPTER
DIPTEROUS BIALATE
DIRDUM BLOW BLAME DURDUM OUTCRY REBUKE TUMULT UPROAR SCOLDING
DIRE DERN EVIL FELL AWFUL FATAL DEADLY DISMAL DREARY FUNEST TRAGIC WOEFUL DIREFUL DOLEFUL DRASTIC FEARFUL DREADFUL FUNESTAL HORRIBLE TERRIBLE ULTIMATE
DIRECT AIM BID CON KEN SAY SET WIS AGYE AIRT BAIN BEAM BEND BOSS CAST DEAD EDIT EVEN FLAT FULL GAIN HEAD HELM HOLD LEAD NEAR NIGH OPEN REIN SEND SOON

SWAY TELL TURN WAFT WEND WILL WISE AIRTH APPLY AREAD AREED BLANK BOUND BURLY COACH DRESS ETTLE FLUSH FRAME FRANK GUIDA GUIDE HIGHT INDEX LEVEL ORDER PLUMP POINT REFER RIGHT SPEED STEER TEACH TRAIN UTTER WEISE WRITE ADVERT ARRECT CUSTOS DEVOTE ENJOIN ENSIGN FASTEN GOVERN GRAITH HANDLE HOMELY HONEST IMPART INDITE INFORM INTEND LINEAL MANAGE MASTER MOSTRA REFORM SQUARE STEADY STRECK TEMPER WITTER ADDRESS APPOINT COMMAND CONDUCT CONTROL CONVERT DEICTIC DESTINE EXECUTE EXPRESS FRONTAL GENERAL INSTANT MARSHAL OFFICER PRESIDE SPADISH ABSOLUTE CONVERSE DEDICATE DIRECTOR HOMESPUN IMMEDIAL INSTRUCT INTIMATE MANUDUCE MANUDUCT MINISTER OUTRIGHT REGULATE STRAIGHT
(— AGAINST) LAUNCH
(— ATTENTION) ATTEND
(— BLOW) MARK
(— DOGS) BLOW
(— FALL OF TREE) GUN
(— HELMSMAN) CON CONN
(— HORSE) HUP
(— ITSELF) TENT
(— ONE'S COURSE) HIT
(— PROCEEDINGS) PRESIDE
(— SECRETLY) STEAL
(— SIDEWAYS) SKLENT
(— TO GO) ADDRESS
(— UPWARD) MOUNT
DIRECTED FAST COMPULSORY
(— FORWARD) ANTRORSE
(— TOWARD GOAL) HORMIC
(— UPWARD) ERECT
DIRECTING AIM LEADING PRINCIPAL
DIRECTION AIM RUN WAY AIRT BENT CARE DUCT EAST EGIS GATE HAND LEFT PART ROAD RULE WEST WORD YARD AEGIS ANGLE COAST DRIFT EAVER KIBLA NORTH ORDER PARTY POINT QIBLA RANGE ROUTE SENSE SOUTH TENOR TREND ASPECT COURSE DESIGN ADDRESS BEARING BIDDING CHANNEL COMMAND CONDUCT CONTROL COUNSEL DICTATE HEADING HELMAGE MANDATE PRECEPT STRETCH BEARINGS CALENDAR DELEATUR DIAGONAL GUIDANCE STEERAGE STEERING TENDENCY
(— OF CURRENT) AXIS
(— OF FLOW) SET
(— OF ROCK CLEAVAGE) GRAIN
(— OF WIND) EYE CORNER
(— OUTWARD) BEAM
(—S FOR DELIVERY) ADDRESS
(DANCE —) CALL
(HORIZONTAL —) COURSE AZIMUTH
(OBLIQUE —) SKEW
(OPPOSITE —) EYE COUNTER
(SINGING —) GIMEL GYMEL

DIRECTIVE DICTATE CIRCULAR

DIRECTLY DUE BANG BOLT DEAD FLAT GAIN JUST MEAN PLAT PLUM SLAP SOON PLAIN PLUMB POINT ROUND SHEER SOUSE SPANG STANG ARIGHT CLEVER SIMPLY SQUARE RIGHTLY SHEERLY OUTRIGHT PROMPTLY SLAPDASH STRAIGHT

DIRECTNESS CLARITY IMMEDIACY

DIRECTOR BOSS HEAD COACH GUIDE PILOT STAFF ARCHON BISHOP LEADER MASTER RECTOR WARDEN CURATOR DESKMAN MANAGER PREFECT STARETS STERNER TRAINER ACCENTOR DISPOSER GOVERNOR PRAEFECT PRODUCER TETRARCH

DIRECTORY PIE BOOK

DIRGE KEEN SONG ELEGY KINAH LINOS LINUS QINAH TANGI HEARSE LAMENT MONODY THRENE EPICEDE REQUIEM CORONACH THRENODY ULLAGONE

DIRIGIBLE BLIMP AIRSHIP

DIRK SNEE SKEAN SWORD DAGGER SKHIAN SKIVER

DIRT FEN MUD PAY DUST GORE GUCK MUCK NAST SOIL SUMP EARTH FILTH GRIME GROUT SEUCH SEUGH TRASH GRAVEL GROUND REFUSE MULLOCK MUCKMENT

DIRTINESS GRIME JAKES

DIRTY LOW BASE CLAT DIRT FOUL MUSS SOIL WORY BAWDY BLACK CABBY DINGY FOGGY GRIMY GUSTY HORRY MUDDY NASTY POUSY SOILY SULLY BEMIRE CLARTY CLATTY DEFILE DIRTEN FILTHY FULYIE FULZIE GREASY GRUBBY IMPURE MUSSED POUCEY SCRIMY SLASHY SLURRY SMUTTY SOILED SORDID STORMY BEGRIME BROOKED BROOKIE BRUCKLE CLOUDED GRUFTED IMBROIN MUDDIED ROYNOUS SLOTTER SMUTCHY SQUALID SULLIED TARNISH UNCLEAN SLOBBERY SLOTTERY SOAPLESS

DISABLE OUT HOCK LAME MAIM BREAK CHINK CROCK GRUEL UNFIT WRECK BRUISE DISMAY UNABLE WEAKEN CRIPPLE

(— CANNON) SPIKE

(— TANK) BELLY

DISABLED LAME INVALID

DISABLING BUM

DISACCHARIDE BIOSE LACTOSE MALTOSE SUCROSE

DISACCUSTOM DISUSE

DISACKNOWLEDGE DISCLAIM

DISADVANTAGE HURT MISS RISK LURCH WORRY DAMAGE DENIAL INJURY STRIKE DICKENS PENALTY UNSELTH UNSPEED DISAVAIL DISFAVOR HANDICAP

DISADVANTAGEOUS HURTFUL INCONVENIENT

DISAFFECT DEBAUCH ESTRANGE

DISAFFECTED FALSE UNTRUE DISEASED DISLOYAL FORSWORN PERJURED RECREANT

DISAFFECTION DECEIT MUTINY DISEASE DISGUST DISLIKE DISORDER HOSTILITY

DISAFFIRM DENY ANNUL REVERSE DISCLAIM

DISAGREE VARY ARGUE DIFFER DISCEPT DISCORD DISSENT QUARREL CONFLICT

DISAGREEABLE BAD ILL ACID EVIL FOUL PERT SOUR UGLY VILE AWFUL CROSS HARSH NASTY STIFF GREASY PUTRID ROTTEN SNUFFY STICKY UNEASY UNGAIN CHRONIC COMICAL GHASTLY HATEFUL INGRATE IRKSOME NAUGHTY UNLUSTY CHISELLY KINDLESS TERRIBLE UNGENIAL UNLIKELY UNLOVELY UNSAVORY

DISAGREEABLENESS ILLNESS ASPERITY

DISAGREEABLY HARSHLY

DISAGREEING ODD DISSENTIVE

DISAGREEMENT BREE CLASH CROSS FIGHT BREACH FRATCH DISCORD DISGUST DISPUTE DISSENT FISSURE MISLIKE QUARREL WRANGLE ARGUMENT DISTANCY DIVISION FRICTION SQUABBLE VARIANCE

(IN —) APART

DISALLOW FORBID REJECT CENSURE DISCLAIM DISPROVE PROHIBIT

DISAPPEAR DIE FLY DROP FADE FALL FLEE LIFT PASS SINK WEND WHOP CLEAR FAINT LAPSE SLIDE SNUFF REMOVE RETIRE VANISH EVANISH IMMERGE DISSOLVE EVANESCE

(— GRADUALLY) ELY FADE DRAIN EVANESCE

(— SUDDENLY) COOK DUCK BURST MIZZLE

DISAPPEARANCE ECLIPSE FADEAWAY

DISAPPOINT BALK BILK FAIL FALL MOCK SOUR UNDO CHEAT SNAPE BAFFLE DEFEAT DELUDE OUTWIT THWART BEGUILE DECEIVE DESTROY FALSIFY NULLIFY DISPOINT

DISAPPOINTED OUTED THROWN SOREHEAD

DISAPPOINTING FIERCE FALLACIOUS

DISAPPOINTMENT RUE BALK SUCK BAULK LURCH DENIAL LETDOWN COMEDOWN

DISAPPROBATION ODIUM DISLIKE

DISAPPROVAL BAN BOOH HISS VETO CATCALL CENSURE DISFAVOR DISGRACE

DISAPPROVE GROAN REJECT RESENT CENSURE CONDEMN DISLIKE MISTAKE PROTEST DISALLOW DISPROVE

DISAPPROVED DISTASTED

DISAPPROVER WOWSER

DISARM SUBDUE UNSTEEL

DISARRANGE MUSS DEFORM GARBLE RUFFLE TIFFLE UNTIDY UNTUNE CLUTTER CONFUSE DERANGE DISTURB RUMMAGE SLATTER TROUBLE COCKBILL DISHEVEL DISORDER UNSETTLE

(— TYPE) SQUABBLE

DISARRANGEMENT DISARRAY

DISARRAY MESS STRIP CADDLE DISRAY FUFFLE HUDDLE DESPOIL UNDIGHT DISHEVEL DISORDER

DISARRAYED UNKEMPT

DISASSEMBLE STRIP DEMOUNT DISMOUNT

(— CASK) SHAKE

DISASSEMBLY TAKEDOWN TEARDOWN

DISASSOCIATE SEVER SEPARATE

DISASTER ILL WOE BALE BLOW EVIL FATE RUIN GRIEF MISHAP STROKE REVERSE ACCIDENT CALAMITY CASUALTY EXIGENCY FATALITY

DISASTROUS BAD ILL FATAL WEARY SINISTER

DISAVOW DENY DEVOW ABJURE DISOWN RECANT REFUSE DECLINE RETRACT ABNEGATE DISCLAIM DISVOUCH RENOUNCE

DISAVOWAL DENIAL

DISBAND BREAK REDUCE REFORM ADJOURN CASHIER DISMISS RELEASE SCATTER DISSOLVE

DISBAR EXCLUDE

DISBELIEF ATHEISM SCRUPLE

DISBELIEVE DOUBT REJECT SUSPECT DISCOUNT DISCREDIT

DISBELIEVER ATHEIST HERETIC INFIDEL

DISBURDEN RID EASE CLEAR UNLOAD DELIVER DISLOAD RELIEVE

DISBURSE SPEND DEFRAY EXPEND OUTLAY DEBURSE

DISC (ALSO SEE DISK) DIAL DISK BLANK MEDAL PATEN PLATE QUOIT COLTER RECORD RONDEL COULTER DISCOID PLATTER TROCHUS

(— FOR PRESSING HERRINGS) DAUNT

DISCANT HOCKET

DISCARD CAST DECK JILT JUNK MOLT OMIT OUST SHED CHUCK DITCH FLING SCRAP SHUCK SLUFF THROW CHANGE DECARD DISUSE DIVEST EXCUSS REJECT SLOUGH ABANDON CASHIER DISMISS EXPUNGE FORSAKE ABDICATE JETTISON

(— IN BRIDGE) ECHO

DISCARDED DORMANT

DISCARDING DISPOSAL

DISCERN KEN SEE SPY WIT DEEM ESPY KNOW READ SCAN JUDGE SIGHT BEHOLD DESCRY DETECT DEVISE NOTICE PIERCE SCERNE DIGNOSCE DISCOVER PERCEIVE

DISCERNIBLE EVIDENT VISIBLE

APPARENT MANIFEST
DISCERNING SAGE WISE SHREWD
SAPIENT
DISCERNMENT EYE DOOM GOUT
TACT FLAIR SENSE SKILL TASTE
ACUMEN INSIGHT ELECTION
JUDGMENT SAGACITY
DISCHARGE AX DO AXE CAN GUN
LET RUN BOLT BOOT CASS DUMP
EMIT FIRE FLOW FLUX FREE GIVE
KICK PASS POUR QUIT RIFF SACK
SEND SHOT VENT VOID BLAST
BLEED BRUSH CLEAR DRAIN EJECT
EMPTY EXPEL EXUDE FRUSH GLEET
GRASS ICHOR ISSUE LOOSE OZENA
PURGE RHEUM SHOOT SPEED
START VOMIT WHIFF YIELD ACQUIT
ASSOIL BOUNCE DEFRAY EFFECT
EXCERN EXEMPT EXHALE FEEDER
LOCHIA OZAENA TICKET UNLADE
UNLOAD ABSOLVE CASHIER
DEBOUCH DEFEASE DEHISCE
DELIVER DERAIGN DISBAND DISMISS
EXCRETE EXHAUST MISSION
PAYMENT PERFORM QUIETUS
RELEASE RELIEVE SATISFY SKITTER
SOLUTIO CATAPULT COMPOUND
DEFECATE DESPATCH DISGORGE
DISPATCH DISPLACE DISPLODE
EMISSION EVACUATE MITTIMUS
OUTSHOOT PERSOLVE SEPARATE
SOLUTION STREAMER
(— **ARROW**) TWANG
(— **BULLET**) DRIVE
(— **CARGO**) STRIKE
(— **DEBT**) MEET CLEAR LOOSING
(— **DUTY**) SERVE
(— **FROM HORSE'S FOOT**) FRUSH
(— **FROM RESERVOIR**) HUSHING
(— **MATTER**) WEEP
(— **OF DEBT**) SETOFF
(— **OF GAS**) FEEDER
(— **OF STREAM**) FALL SPOUT
(— **SUDDENLY**) HIKE
(**BLOODY** —) SHOW SANIES
(**CANNON** —) TIRE CANNON
(**CONCENTRATED** —) BARRAGE
(**DISHONORABLE** —) BOBTAIL
(**ELECTRIC** —) SPARK LEADER
EFFLUVE STREAMER LIGHTNING
(**ELECTRIC** —S) STATIC
(**HEAVY** —) STORM
(**SIMULTANEOUS** —) SALVO
BROADSIDE FUSILLADE
DISCHARGED SPED SATISFIED
DISCHARGER EXCITATOR
DISCHARGING LABILE
DISCIPLE SON JOHN MARK CHELA
JUDAS MURID PETER PUPIL TEACH
TRAIN ANANDA DISPLE DORCAS
HEARER PUNISH APOSTLE AUDITOR
MATTHEW OVIDIAN SCHOLAR
SECTARY SRAVAKA STUDENT
ADHERENT FOLLOWER GALENIST
SECTATOR
DISCIPLINARIAN RAMROD TRAINER
MARTINET
DISCIPLINARY STRICT
DISCIPLINE THEW WHIP BREAK

DRILL INURE TEACH TRAIN CHURCH
ETHICS FERULA FERULE GOVERN
INFORM PUNISH SEASON TAIRGE
VIRTUE CHASTEN CORRECT
CULTURE EDUCATE FURNACE
NURTURE SCOURGE DISCIPLE
DOCTRINE EXERCISE INSTRUCT
LEARNING MATHESIS PEDAGOGY
REGULATE RESTRAIN TEACHING
TRAINING TUTORING
(**MENTAL** —) YOGA
(**RELIGIOUS** —) CHURCH PENANCE
SADHANA
DISCIPLINED INURED STEADY
DISCLAIM DENY DEVOW ABJURE
DISOWN REFUSE DISAVOW
ABDICATE ABNEGATE DISALLOW
RENOUNCE
DISCLOSE OPE RIP BARE BLOW
CALL KNOW OPEN TELL BREAK
COUGH UNRIP UNWRY UTTER
BETRAY BEWRAY DESCRY DIVINE
EVOLVE EXPOSE IMPART REVEAL
SHRIVE UNBURY UNCASE UNHASP
UNHIDE UNLOCK UNROLL UNSEAL
UNSHUT UNVEIL UNWRAP CONFESS
DEVELOP DISCUSS DISPLAY
DIVULGE EXHIBIT EXPLAIN UNCLOSE
UNCOVER DISCOVER INDICATE
MANIFEST UNBUNDLE UNKENNEL
UNSECRET UNTHATCH
DISCLOSED OUT
DISCLOSURE REVEAL SHRIFT
COLORING DESCRIAL DISCLOSE
OVERTURE
DISCOLOR FOX BURN FADE SPOT
BLACK SMOKE STAIN TINGE SMIRCH
STREAK DISTAIN TARNISH
BESMIRCH
DISCOLORATION CORN BLEED
SCALD SPECK STAIN TINGE FOXING
LIVEDO MILDEW ARGYRIA BURNING
MELASMA BRONZING BROWNING
CHLOASMA CYANOSIS DYSCHROA
SCALDING
(— **OF FRUIT**) SUNBURN
(— **OF TURKEYS**) BLUEBACK
(— **ON CHOCOLATE**) BLOOM
(— **ON CURED FISH**) RUST
(**SMALL** —) FRECKLE
DISCOLORED HAW FOUL DINGY
FOXED RUSTY STAINED SCORCHED
USTULATE
(— **BY DECAY**) DOTY FOXED
DISCOMFIT MATE ROIT ABASH
ABAVE AFLEY SHEND SHENT UPSET
WORST BAFFLE DEFEAT FEAGUE
SQUASH CONFUSE CONQUER
DISTURB
DISCONCERT BASH BOWL FAZE
FUSS HACK ABASH BLANK DAUNT
FEEZE PHASE UPSET WORRY
BAFFLE BLENCH MISPUT PUZZLE
RATTLE SQUASH CONFUSE DISTURB
FLUMMOX NONPLUS PERTURB
SQUELCH BROWBEAT DISORDER
DISCONCERTED BLANK ASHAMED
RATTLED CONFUSED
DISCONNECT UNDO SEVER DIVIDE

UNYOKE DISJOIN DISSOLVE
DISUNITE SEPARATE UNCOUPLE
DISCONNECTED LOOSE ABRUPT
BROKEN CHOPPY CURSORY
DECOUSU RAMBLING STACCATO
DISCONSOLATE SAD GLOOMY
WOEFUL DOLEFUL FORLORN
UNCOUTH DEJECTED DESOLATE
DOWNCAST HOPELESS
DISCONTENT ENVY DISQUIET
SOURNESS
DISCONTENTED DUMPY
DISCONTINUANCE BREAK LAPSE
DEMISE CUTBACK DISUNION
SHUTDOWN
DISCONTINUE END DROP HALT
QUIT STOP BREAK CEASE CLOSE
LETUP DESIST DISUSE SUNDER
DISRUPT SUSPEND INTERMIT
SURCEASE
DISCONTINUITY JAR BREAK
DISCONTINUOUS BROKEN
DISJUNCT SALTATORY
DISCORD DIN JAR BROIL JANGLE
SCHISM STRIFE DISLIKE FACTION
FISSURE JARRING MISTONE
CONFLICT DISTANCE DIVISION
FRACTION MISCHIEF UNSAUGHT
VARIANCE
DISCORDANT AJAR RUDE CRONK
HARSH FROWZY HOARSE JANGLY
HIDEOUS JARRING SQUAWKY
ABSONANT CONTRARY JANGLING
DISCOUNT AGIO BATTA SHAVE
REBATE REDUCE DISCOMPT
DISCOURAGE CARP DAMP CHILL
DAUNT DETER FROST DAMPEN
DEJECT DISMAY FREEZE STIFLE
DEPRESS FLATTEN INHIBIT DISPIRIT
DISSUADE
DISCOURAGEMENT COLD DAMP
DAUNT LETDOWN PUTBACK
DISCOURAGING CHILL DREARY
DISCOURSE SAW CARP RANT READ
TALE TALK TELL WORD DROOL
FABLE ORATE PAPER SPEAK SPELL
THEME TRACT TREAT COMMON
DILATE EULOGY HOMILY PARLEY
PREACH REASON SCREED SERMON
THESIS TREATY ACCOUNT ADDRESS
COMMENT CONTEXT DECLAIM
DELIVER DESCANT DIETARY
DISCANT DISCUSS DISSERT
ENTREAT EXPOUND GRAMMAR
LECTURE NARRATE ORATION
PRATING PRELECT PURPOSE
TALKING ARGUMENT COLLOQUY
CONVERSE EXERCISE LOCUTION
LOQUENCE PARLANCE SPEAKING
SPELLING TRACTATE TREATISE
(— **OF LITTLE VALUE**) STUFF
(**LAUDATORY** —) PANEGYRIC
(**LONG** —) SCREED
(**PROLONGED** —) DIATRIBE
(**SERIOUS** —) HOMILY
(**SIMPLE** —) PAP
(**UNIMAGINATIVE** —) PROSE
(PL.) EXOTERICS
DISCOURTEOUS RUDE SCURVY

UNCIVIL UNHENDE IMPOLITE UNGENTLE

DISCOURTESY CUT SLIGHT

DISCOVER RIP SEE SPY WIT ESPY FEEL FIND PICK TWIG CATCH LEARN SPELL DEFINE DESCRY DETECT DIVINE EXPOSE IMPART INVENT LOCATE OVERGO REVEAL STRIKE UNHIDE CONFESS DESCURE DEVELOP DISCERN DISCURE DISPLAY DIVULGE EXHIBIT EXPLORE UNCOVER UNEARTH CONTRIVE DECIPHER DESCRIBE DISCUREN MANIFEST UNKENNEL

DISCOVERABLE VISIBLE

DISCOVERER SPY SCOUT COLUMBUS EXPLORER INVENTOR

DISCOVERY FIND TROVE DESCRY ESPIAL STRIKE DESCRIAL

DISCREDIT FOUL DECRY DOUBT REFEL DEFACE DEFECT ASPERSE BLEMISH DESTROY IMPEACH SCANDAL SUSPECT BELITTLE DISGRACE DISHONOR DISTRUST REPROACH UNCREDIT

DISCREDITABLE BLACK UNHONEST

DISCREET WARY WISE CIVIL HUSHED POLITE SILENT CAREFUL GUARDED POLITIC PRUDENT CAUTIOUS RESERVED RETICENT

DISCREETLY SENSIBLY

DISCREPANCY VARIANCE

DISCREPANT VARIANT CONTRARY DISSONANT

DISCRETE ETERNAL DISTINCT

DISCRETION TACT WISDOM CONDUCT RETENUE COURTESY JUDGMENT PRUDENCE

DISCRIMINATE PART SEVER SECERN DISCERN PERCEIVE SEPARATE

DISCRIMINATED DISTINCT

DISCRIMINATING GOOD NICE ACUTE SHARP ASTUTE CHOICE SELECT CHOOSEY CRITICAL EXPLICIT

DISCRIMINATINGLY CHOICE FINELY

DISCRIMINATION EYE DOOM TACT TASTE ACUMEN CHOICE FINESSE RESPECT DELICACY SAPIENCE

(SYMBOL OF —) HANSA

DISCURSIVE ROVING CURSORY RAMBLING DESULTORY

DISCURSIVELY WIDE

DISCUS DISC DISK QUOIT DISKOS DISCOID

DISCUSS AIR MOOT RUNE TALK ARGUE BANDY COVER DANDY TRACT TREAT COMMON CONFER DEBATE DICKER EMPARL EXCUSS IMPARL PARLEY AGITATE BESPEAK CANVASS COMMENT CONSULT DESCANR DESCANT DISCANT DISCEPT DISCUTE DISPUTE DISSERT EXAMINE NARRATE TRAVERSE

(— AT LENGTH) BAT

(— CASUALLY) MENTION

(— EXCITEDLY) AGITATE

(— LIGHTLY) BANDY

(— QUICKLY) SKIP

(— SECRETLY) ROUN

(— TERMS) CHAFFER

(— THOROUGHLY) EXHAUST

DISCUSSION MOOT DEBAT FORUM COMMON CONFAB DEBATE HASSEL HOMILY HUDDLE PARLEY TREATY BARGAIN CANVASS COMMENT COUNSEL DISCUSS DISPUTE MOOTING PRIBBLE ARGUMENT CAUSERIE CHINFEST COLLOQUY DIATRIBE ENTREATY EXCURSUS QUESTION

(CONTROVERSIAL —) DISPUTE

(DIDACTIC —) HARANGUE

DISDAIN TUT DAIN DEFY PRIDE SCORN SDAIN SPURN SDEIGN SLIGHT CONTEMN DESPISE CONTEMPT

DISDAINFUL COY DIGNE SAUCY TOSSY SCORNY SLIGHT SNIFFY SNUFFY DAINFUL HAUGHTY ARROGANT DEIGNOUS SCORNFUL SNIFFISH TOPLOFTY

DISDAINFULLY SMALL SNIFFILY

DISEASE BUG FLU MAL ROT BATS COTH CRUD EVIL FLAW GOUT GRIP NOMA PEST PHOS SORE AGROM BATTS BEJEL BENDS CAUSE COTHE CROUP DECAY DOLOR FEVER GRIEF LUPUS PHOSS PINTA PINTO SCALL SHAKE SPRUE SURRA AINHUM ANGINA CANCER CARATE CORYZA COURAP DENGUE GRAVEL GRIPPE HERPES MALADY MORBUS PALMUS PIEDRA POPEYE SCURVY SICKEN SURRAH UROSIS ZOOSIS AILMENT ALASTIM CHOLERA COXALGY DECLINE ENDEMIC ENTASIA LANGUOR LEPROSY MALEASE MISLIKE MYCOSIS MYIASIS PATHEMA RAPHANY SCOURGE SEQUELA SERPIGO SIBBENS SORANCE SYCOSIS XERASIA ZYMOTIC ATHEROMA BERIBERI COXALGIA CRIPPLER CYNANCHE DIAMONDS ENZOOTIC JAUNDICE LEUKEMIA PALUDISM PANDEMIC PELLAGRA RAPHANIA SCABBADO SICKNESS SMALLPOX SORRANCE STAGGERS SYPHILIS UNHEALTH XANTHOMA ZOONOSIS

(— OF ANIMALS, GENERAL) ROT CLAP CORE FIRE GOUT HUSK LICK WEED APTHA CLEFT CLING CLOSH COTHE CROOK DRUSE FARCY FLAPS NENTA NOANA PAINS SPEED SWEAT TAINT APHTHA AVIVES BROSOT CANKER CARNEY CREEPS FARCIN GARGET GRAPES LAMPAS NAGANA ROUGET SPAVIN SURRAH WOBBLE ANTHRAX BIGHEAD CALCINO CALORIS CARCEAG DOURING EARWORM EQUINIA FASHION FISTULA FOUNDER FROUNCE KETOSIS LAMPERS MURRAIN MURRINA QUITTER QUITTOR SLOBBER SOLDIER TAKOSIS BULLNOSE CRATCHES

CRIPPLES FERNSICK FOOTHALT HORSEPOX HYSTERIA MAWBOUND SLOBBERS SNUFFLES THWARTER VACCINIA EPIZOOTIC

(— OF APPLES) CORK BLOTCH

(— OF BANANAS) SIGATOKA SQUIRTER

(— OF BARLEY) STRIPE

(— OF BEES) SACBROOD

(— OF BEETS) HEARTROT

(— OF BIRDS) GOUT

(— OF BLUEBERRY) BLUESTEM

(— OF CABBAGE) CLUBROOT

(— OF CATERPILLARS) WILT FLACHERY

(— OF CATTLE) TURN BLAIN CLOSH FARCY HOOZE COWPOX GARGET GRAPES HAMMER HEAVES ANTHRAX BLACKLEG

(— OF CEREALS) ERGOT

(— OF CHICKEN) PIP CORYZA

(— OF COTTON) HYBOSIS CYRTOSIS STENOSIS

(— OF DUCKLING) KEEL

(— OF EYES) WALL GLAUCOMA SYNECHIA TRACHOMA

(— OF FIGS) SMUT

(— OF FINGERNAILS) FLAW

(— OF FLAX) BROWNING

(— OF FOWLS) PIP CRAY ROUP GAPES SOREHEAD

(— OF GRAIN) ILIAU ICTERUS

(— OF GRAPES) COLEUR ERINOSE ROUGEAU ROUGEOT SHELLING

(— OF HAWKS) RYE CRAY CROAK CROAKS FROUNCE

(— OF HORSES) HAW CLAP MOSE MULE WEED FARCY LEUMA SCALMA DOURINE SARCOID AZOTURIA GLANDERS HORSEPOX STRANGLES

(— OF LAMB) SWAYBACK

(— OF LETTUCE) STUNT

(— OF NARCISSUS) SMOLDER SMOULDER

(— OF ONION) SMUDGE

(— OF ORANGE) LEPROSIS

(— OF PALMS) KOLERUGA

(— OF PLANTS, GENERAL) POX ROT BUNT CORK DROP FIRE GOUT KNOT PULP SMUT BLAST DWARF EDEMA ERGOT FLECK FLOCK GRUBS SCALD SCALE SCURF SEREH SPIKE STUNT TUKRA TWIST AUCUBA BLIGHT BLOTCH BLUING BRAUNE CALICO CANKER COLEUR GIRDLE OEDEMA OIDIUM PETECA SMUDGE STREAK STRIPE VIROSE BLISTER BLUEING BRINDLE CRINKLE DIEBACK ERINOSE EYESPOT FROGEYE HYBOSIS MEASLES PRURIGO ROSETTE SHATTER SMOLDER STIPPEN TIPBURN TOMOSIS VIRUELA WALLOON BLUESTEM BREAKING BROWNING BUCKSKIN CLUBROOT CYRTOSIS DARTROSE EXANTHEM FLYSPECK GUMMOSIS KOLEROGA LEPROSIS MELANOSE MELAXUMA POLEBURN PSOROSIS SMOULDER

STENOSIS VIROSITY WHIPTAIL WILDFIRE
(— OF POTATO) CURL HAYWIRE
(— OF RABBITS) SNUFFLES
(— OF RICE) BLAST SPECK
(— OF SHEEP) CAW COE GID MAD ROT BANE BELT CORE HALT WIND BLAST BLOOD BRAXY GILLAR OVINIA PINING STURDY ANTHRAX BRADSOT DAISING RUBBERS SCRAPIE THWARTER WILDFIRE
(— OF SILKWORM) UJI CALCINO GATTINE PEBRINE FLACHERY
(— OF SUGARCANE) ILIAU SEREH EYESPOT
(— OF SWINE) GARGET
(— OF TOBACCO) ETCH CALICO BRINDLE FROGEYE
(— OF TOMATO) FERNLEAF GRAYWALL
(— OF TREES) KNOT
(— OF TULIPS) SHANKING
(— OF UNKNOWN ORIGIN) AINHUM ACRODYNIA
(CAISSON —) CHOKES
(FOOT-AND-MOUTH —) AFTOSA
(FUNGUS —) PECK
(KIDNEY —) RIPPLE
(LUNG —) CON
(MUSHROOM —) FLOCK
(SKIN —) ACNE SCAB FAVUS HIVES LEPRA MANGE PSORA SCALL TINEA ECZEMA LICHEN TETTER EXORMIA PORRIGO PURPURA SERPIGO VERRUGA IMPETIGO MILIARIA MYCETOMA SHINGLES VERRUGAS VITILIGO
(VENEREAL —) BURNING SYPHILIS
(WINE —) GRAISSE
DISEASED BAD EVIL SICKLY MORBOSE PECCANT VICIOUS MORBIFIC
DISEMBARK LAND ALIGHT DEBARK UNBARK UNBOAT DISBOARD
DISEMBARRASS EXTRICATE
DISEMBODIED SEPARATE DISBODIED FLESHLESS
DISEMBODIMENT SOUL SPIRIT
DISEMBOGUE MOUTH
DISEMBOWEL GUT HULK PAUNCH DEBOWEL EMBOWEL GARBAGE UNTRIPE GRALLOCH
DISEMIC DIMORIC DICHRONOUS
DISENCHANT DISMAY
DISENCHANTED SOUR
DISENCUMBER RID FREE REDD UNCUMBER
DISENGAGE FREE CLEAR EDUCE UNTIE DETACH EVOLVE LOOSEN CUTOVER DISGAGE RELEASE UNRAVEL LIBERATE UNCLUTCH
DISENTANGLE CARD COMB FREE REED TOSE TOZE CLEAR LOOSE RAVEL TEASE EVOLVE SCUTCH SLEAVE UNMAZE UNMESH RESOLVE UNRAVEL UNREAVE UNTWINE UNTWIST OUTTWINE UNTANGLE
DISENTANGLEMENT SOLUTION
DISESTEEM UMBRAGE DISVALUE

DISFAVOR DUTCH ODIUM DISLIKE OFFENCE OFFENSE UMBRAGE MALGRACE
DISFIGURE MAR BLUR FOUL MAIM SCAR DEFACE DEFEAT DEFORM INJURE MANGLE BLEMISH DISGRACE DISGUISE MUTILATE
DISFIGURED FOUL DEFET DEFEIT DEFORMED
DISFIGUREMENT SCAR BLEMISH CATFACE DEFORMITY
DISGORGE SPEW VENT EJECT EMPTY VOMIT
DISGRACE BLOT FOIL FOUL HISS LACK SLUR SMIT SOIL SPOT TASH ABASE CRIME ODIUM SCORN SHAME SHEND SPITE STAIN TAINT BAFFLE BEFOUL BISMER HUMBLE INFAMY REBUKE STIGMA VILIFY AFFRONT ATTAINT DEGRADE OBLOQUY OFFENCE OFFENSE REPROOF SCANDAL SLANDER UMBRAGE CONTEMPT DISHONOR IGNOMINY REPROACH SHENDING UNWORTHY VILLAINY
DISGRACEFUL MEAN SOUR FILTHY INDIGN IGNOBLE CRIMINAL DEFAMOUS INHONEST SHAMEFUL
DISGRUNTLED SORE PEEVISH
DISGUISE DAUB FACE HIDE LAIN LEAN MASK VEIL BELIE CLOAK COLOR COUCH COVER FEIGN GLOZE GUISE SHADE VISOR VIZOR COVERT DEFORM IMMASK MANTLE MASQUE VIZARD CONCEAL OBSCURE PRETEND PURPORT COLORING DISLIKEN MISGUISE PALLIATE PRETENCE PRETENSE TRAVESTY UMBRELLA
(— INFORMATION) LAYNE
DISGUISED COVERT FUCATE GILDED LATENT MYSTIC FEIGNED PALLIATE TRAVESTY
DISGUST IRK LOATH REPEL SHOCK STALL DEGOUT HORROR NAUSEA OFFEND REVOLT SICKEN STOMACH SURFEIT AVERSION DISTASTE KREISTLE LOATHING NAUSEATE SICKNESS
DISGUSTED IRK SICK IRKSOME
DISGUSTING FOUL PERT VILE LOUSY MUCKY NASTY FILTHY SCRIMY SICKLY BEASTLY FULSOME HATEFUL LOATHLY MAWKISH NOISOME OBSCENE SHITTEN FOULSOME LOATHFUL NAUSEOUS SHOCKING
DISH CAP CAUP CUSH DISC DISK FOOL MEAT MOLD PLAT SOLE BASIN BATEA COMAL DEVIL MOULD NAPPY PATEN PINAX PLATE SHAPE BASQUE BASSIE BICKER BLAZER BUTTER CHAFER CRITCH CUSCUS ENTREE FONDUE LUGGIE OLIVES PADDLE PANADA PATERA PATINA PHIALE RECIPE SAUCER SUNDAE TAMALE TUREEN BALANCE BOBOTEE BOBOTIE CEVICHE CHARGER COCOTTE COMPORT

COMPOTE CRESSET DORMANT DOUBLER EPERGNE PAPBOAT PATELLA PLATEAU PLATTER RAMEKIN SCUTTLE SUPREME TERRINE TIMBALE AMATORIO CIOPPINO CLAPDISH COQUILLE COUSCOUS GALATINE KEDGEREE MAZARINE POWSODDY STANDARD ENTREMETS
(— IN PYRAMID STYLE) BUISSON
(BAKING —) SCALLOP SCOLLOP
(BRAISED —) HASLET
(CHAFING —) CHAFER CHOFFER
(FANCY —) SURPRISE
(FLAT —) COMAL CHARGER
(HIGH-FLAVORED —) HOGO
(JEWISH —) CHOLENT
(PHILIPPINE —) BURO
(PIE —) COFFIN
(PILE OF —S) BUNG
(ROMAN —) LANX PATERA PATINA
(SAILOR'S —) SCOUSE
(SCOTTISH —) BROSE
(SIDE —) OUTWORK
(SWEET —) JUNKET FLUMMERY
(TASTY —) MORSEL
(WOODEN —) CUP CAUP BOWIE GOGGAN LUGGIE KICKSHAW
(PL.) GARNISH BAKEWARE FLATWARE ENTREMETS
DISHABILLE MOB DISARRAY DISORDER NEGLIGEE
DISHARMONY SCHISM ADHARMA FRACTION
DISHCLOTH DISHRAG
DISHCLOTH GOURD LOOFAH PATOLA DISHRAG
DISHEARTEN AMATE DAUNT FAINT DEJECT DEPRESS FLATTEN UNHEART UNNERVE DISHEART DISPIRIT
DISHEARTENED DULL GLOOMY DOWNCAST DEPRESSED
DISHEARTENING GLOOMY DESOLATE
DISHEVEL MUSS TOWZE RUFFLE TOUSEL TOUSLE TUMBLE TRACHLE DISARRAY DISORDER
DISHEVELED ROOKY BLOUSY BLOWZY FROWZY TUMBLED UNKEMPT FROWZLED SHEVELED SLIPSHOD TATTERED
DISHONEST FOUL LEWD CRONK FALSE LYING QUEER SNIDE TWISTY UNFAIR UNJUST CORRUPT CROOKED KNAVISH INDECENT INDIRECT SHAMEFUL SINISTER UNCHASTE UNHONEST
DISHONESTLY DOUBLY FALSELY
DISHONESTY IMPROBITY
DISHONOR FILE FOUL ABASE ABUSE ODIUM SHAME SPITE STAIN WRONG DEFAME DEFILE DEFORM INFAMY VILIFY DEGRADE DISTAIN OBLOQUY SLANDER VIOLATE DISGLORY DISGRACE DISPLUME IGNOMINY REPROACH VILLAINY
DISHONORABLE BASE FOUL MEAN BLACK NASTY SHABBY YELLOW

IGNOBLE SHAMEFUL UNHONEST UNWORTHY
DISHONORED DEFAMED
DISHPAN KEELER
DISHRACK FIDDLE
DISHWASHER SWILLER
DISILLUSION SOUR DISMAY
DISINCLINATION NILL UNLUST
UNWILL DISLIKE QUARREL
AVERSION DISTASTE
DISINCLINED LOTH LOATH AFRAID
AVERSE HESITANT
(— TO) ABOVE
DISINFECT SCRUB SEASON
CLEANSE SWEETEN
DISINFECTANT IODINE PHENOL
CREOLIN EUGENOL TACHIOL
FUMIGANT HALAZONE PARAFORM
DISINGENUOUS FALSE UNFAIR
OBLIQUE
DISINHERIT DEPRIVE DISHEIR
ABDICATE DISHERIT
DISINTEGRATE BEAT DUST MELT
BREAK DECAY ERODE GRUSH
SLAKE SPLIT MOLDER CRUMBLE
DISBAND RESOLVE SHATTER
COLLAPSE DISSOLVE SEPARATE
DISINTEGRATING SCHIZOID
DISINTEGRATION DECAY BREAKUP
EROSION BIOLYSIS COLLAPSE
HEARTROT
DISINTER EXHUME UNBURY UNTOMB
UNGRAVE
DISINTERESTED FAIR CANDID
APATHETIC IMPARTIAL
DISJOIN PART UNDO SEVER DETACH
SUNDER UNTACK UNYOKE DISSOLVE
DISUNITE SEPARATE
DISJOINED SEJOINED DIAZEUTIC
DISK (ALSO SEE DISC) EYE NOB ORB
PAN SAW WAX WEB BURR CHAD
DIAL DISC FLAN FLAT KNOB PALM
PUCK STAR TUFT CAKRA DAUNT
MEDAL PATEN PLATE ROUND SABLE
SABOT SPILL TOKEN TRUCK WAFER
WHEEL WHORL BEZANT BOTTOM
BUCKET BUMPER BUTTON CACHET
CARTON CHAKRA CONCHA CONCHO
CORONA DISCUS GHURRY HARROW
PALLET PELLET RECORD RIFFLE
RONDEL SEQUIN SHEAVE SQUAIL
WASHER WEIGHT ZEQUIN ACETATE
BLOTTER BOBECHE CHECKER
CHIPPER CLIPEUS DIOPTER DISCOID
GOGGLES KNICKER MEDALET
PHALERA ROSETTE SLITTER
SPINNER SPOTTER TONDINO
DIFFUSER EYEPIECE HOLDFAST
PLANCHET RONDELLE ROUNDLET
ZECCHINO
(— FOR BARRELING HERRING)
DAUNT
(— FOR CHEESE) FOLLOWER
(— FOR STRIKING HOURS) GHURRY
(— OF JELLYFISH) BELL
(— OF WAX) AGNUS
(— ON WOODEN ROD) SPILL
(BULL'S-EYE —) CARTON
(COIN-MAKING —) FLAN PLANCHET

(ECCENTRIC —) SHEAVE
(FLESHY —) SARCOMA
(HANDLED —) RIFFLE
(MEDICATED —) LAMELLA
(METAL —) SLUG MEDAL
(ORNAMENTAL —) BANGLE
SPANGLE
(PADDED IRON —) SPINNER
(PAPER —S) CONFETTI
(POTTER'S —) BAT
(REVOLVING —) WAFTER
(ROTATING —) SCANNER
(SOLAR —) ATEN ATON
(SUN —) CAKRA CHAKRA
(TROCHAL —) CORONA
(WINGED —) FEROHER
DISLIKE DOWN HATE LOTH MIND
DERRY LOATH SPITE DETEST
REGRET SPLEEN UNLIKE DESPISE
MISLIKE QUARREL SCUNDER
SCUNNER STOMACH AVERSION
DESPISAL DISFAVOR DISTASTE
(— OF CHILDREN) MISOPEDIA
(FOOLISH —) TOY
DISLOCATE LUX SLIP BREAK SPLAY
UNSET LUXATE DISLOCK UNWREST
DISJOINT DISPLACE
DISLOCATED SHOTTEN DISLOCATE
DISLOCATION BREAK SHIFT SLIDE
THROW
(PL.) SETTLEMENTS
DISLODGE BEAT BOLT BUCK BUMP
EXPEL SHAKE SHIFT SWOOP
REMOVE DISROOT UNHORSE
UNHOUSE UNLODGE DISHABIT
(— BY BLASTING) BRUSH
DISLODGING BULLING
DISLOYAL FALSE FELON UNTRUE
DISLEAL
DISLOYALTY SWICK SWIKE
UNLEWTY UNTRUTH
DISMAL SAD WAN DARK DIRE DOWF
DREE DULL EERY GASH GLUM GRAY
GREY BLACK BLEAK DOWFF DREAR
EERIE LURID OURIE SABLE SORRY
SURLY SWART WASTE WISHT
DREARY DREICH DREIGH GLOOMY
GOUSTY SULLEN TRISTE DIREFUL
DOLEFUL FUNERAL GASHFUL
GHASTLY GOUSTIE JOYLESS
OMINOUS POCOSIN UNCOUTH
UNHAPPY DESOLATE DOLESOME
DOLOROUS FUNEREAL GROANFUL
LONESOME NOVEMBRY WEARIFUL
DISMAL-LOOKING GASH
WOBEGONE
DISMALLY DERNLY DIRELY
DISMANTLE RASE RAZE STRIP
DIVEST STRIKE DEPRIVE DESTROY
UNCLOAK DISMOUNT
DISMAY BOWL FEAR RUIN ALARM
AMATE APPAL DAUNT DREAD FLUNK
APPALL ASTONY CHASSE FRIGHT
SUBDUE TERROR DEPRESS DEPRIVE
FOUNDER HORRIFY TERRIFY
AFFRIGHT CONFOUND
DISMAYED ASTONIED
DISMAYING HIDEOUS
DISMEMBER LIMB MAIM PART REND

SEVER MANGLE UNLIMB DISCERP
DISLIMB DISSECT QUARTER
DISJOINT MUTILATE
DISMISS AX AXE CAN PUT BOOT
BUMP BUST CASH CAST DROP
DRUM FIRE KICK OUST QUIT SACK
SEND SHAB SWAP SWOP TURN VAIK
VOID AMAND AMOVE BREAK BRUSH
CHUCK DEMIT DIMIT DITCH EJECT
EXPEL FLIRT FLUNK LOOSE SCOUT
BANISH BOUNCE CONGEE DISMIT
DISOWN REJECT REMOVE SHELVE
CASHIER DISBAND DISCARD
LICENCE LICENSE DISGRACE
DISPATCH DISPOINT RELEGATE
WITHDRAW
DISMISSAL AX BOOT SACK BRUSH
CHUCK CONGE SHAKE AVAUNT
KICKAXE REMOVAL DISPATCH
MITTIMUS
(UNCEREMONIOUS —) CONGE
CONGEE
DISMISSED DEGOMME
DISMOUNT AVALE AVOID LIGHT
ALIGHT DEVOID DESCEND FLYAWAY
UNHORSE UNMOUNT DISHORSE
UNSTRIDE
DISOBEDIENCE CONTEMPT
DISOBEDIENT BAD FORWARD
FROWARD NAUGHTY UNBUXOM
UNGODLY WAYWARD MUTINOUS
DISOBEY SIT REJECT
DISOBLIGE OFFEND REFUSE
AFFRONT NEGLECT
DISOBLIGING MEAN UNBAIN
UNBANE
DISORDER ILL MUX PIE CRUD FLAW
MESS MUSS RIOT RUFF STIR TOUT
CHAOS CRACK DERAY GRIME
HAVOC REVEL SNAFU SPLIT TOUSE
TUKRA UPSET BURBLE CHOREA
DESRAY HUDDLE JUMBLE LITTER
MALADY MASTIC MUCKER MUDDLE
RUFFLE TOUSLE TROPPO TUMULT
UNTIDY WALTER AILMENT CLUTTER
COBWEBS CONFUSE DERANGE
DISEASE DISTURB EMBROIL
FERMENT FLUTTER GARBOIL
ILLNESS MISDEED MISRULE
OUTRAGE PERTURB SHATTER
TROUBLE UNRAVEL UNSHAPE
DISARRAY DISHEVEL EPILEPSY
MISORDER ROWDYISM SICKNESS
UNSETTLE
(— OF EYES) HIPPUS
(— OF VISION) DIPLOPIA
(— OF WINES) CASSE
(COMPLETE —) CHAOS
(MENTAL —) INSANITY PARANOIA
(SPEECH —) LALOPATHY
DISORDERED ILL SICK CRAZY
GAUMY LIGHT MESSY UNRID
BLOTTO FROUZY FROWSY FROWZY
INCULT INSANE MUSSED CHAOTIC
CLOUDED FORLORN TUMBLED
UNSIDED CONFUSED DERANGED
DISEASED FEVERISH FLURRIED
INCHOATE
DISORDERING CRIMP

DISORDERLY RAND RANDY RABBLE UNRULY BUNTING LAWLESS ROARING CONFUSED FAROUCHE LARRIKIN SLIPSHOD SLOVENLY SLUTTISH

DISORGANIZE SHOCK UPSET CONFUSE CONTUSE DERANGE DISBAND DISRUPT DISORDER DISSOLVE

DISOWN DENY RENAY UNOWN REJECT DISAVOW RETRACT ABDICATE DISALLOW DISCLAIM RENOUNCE

DISPARAGE LACK SLUR ABUSE DECRY LOWER DEBASE LESSEN SLIGHT BACKCAP DEBAUCH DEGRADE DEMERIT DEPRESS DETRACT DISABLE DOWNCRY IMPEACH BELITTLE DEROGATE DIMINISH DISCOUNT DISHONOR DISPRIZE MINIMIZE MISLIKEN VILIPEND

DISPARAGEMENT DIASYRM SNIDERY WASHWAY

DISPARAGING SNIDE SLIGHTING

DISPARATE UNEQUAL SEPARATE

DISPARITY DISSENT DISTANCE IMPARITY

DISPASSIONATE CALM COOL FAIR STOIC SEDATE SERENE CLINICAL COMPOSED MODERATE

DISPATCH RID FREE KILL MAIL NOTE POST SEND SLAY WING BRIEF ENVOY FLASH HASTE HURRY SHOOT SPEED DIRECT EMPLOY HASTEN ADDRESS COMMAND DELIVER DISPEED EXPRESS HATCHET BREVIATE CELERITY CONCLUDE DESPATCH EXPEDITE TELEGRAM

DISPATCH BOAT AVISO PACKET

DISPATCHER STARTER

DISPEL FRAY SHOO CHASE BANISH DISCUSS SATISFY SCATTER DISPERSE

DISPENSATION LAW LILA GRACE LIVERY ECONOMY FACULTY QUIENAL TOTQUOT DISPOSAL

DISPENSE DEAL DOLE HELP WEIGH EFFUSE EXCUSE EXEMPT FOREGO MANAGE SPREAD ABSOLVE ARRANGE DISPEND DRIBBLE MINISTER
(— **WITH**) MISS WANT SPARE SUSPENSE

DISPENSER BOMB MANAGER STEWARD

DISPERSE DOT SOW FRAY MELT PART ROUT SHED LOOSE SCALE SEVER SKAIL STREW BAFFLE DEFEAT DILATE DISPEL SPARSE SPERSE SPREAD UNKNIT VANISH WINNOW DIFFUSE DISBAND DISJECT DISMISS DRIBBLE FRITTER SCATTER SHATTER SPARKLE SPARPLE SPERPLE DISSOLVE DISTRACT SEPARATE SQUANDER STAMPEDE

DISPERSING SCALE
(— **SHADOWS**) SCIALYTIC

DISPERSION CUT FOAM STAIN

SPREAD DEBACLE SCATTER DIASPORA EMULSOID SOLUTION STAMPEDE

DISPIRIT COW DAMP MATE MULL CHILL DAUNT DEJECT DEPRESS FLATTEN

DISPIRITED DOWY DOWIE ABATTU ABATTUE LETDOWN SHOTTEN DOWNCAST DOWNSOME SACKLESS UNHEARTY WOBEGONE

DISPIRITING COLD CHILL DISMAL

DISPLACE BUMP EDGE MOVE STIR BANISH DEPOSE MISLAY REMOVE WINKLE DERANGE SWALLOW UNHINGE UNPLACE ANTEVERT DISLODGE DISPLANT MISPLACE SUPPLACE SUPPLANT UNSETTLE
(— **LATERALLY**) HEAVE

DISPLACED ATOPIC DEPAYSE

DISPLACEMENT BUMP SLIP HEAVE SCEND SHIFT START CUBAGE UPSLIP FALLING EVECTION

DISPLAY ACT AIR BRAG DASH GAUD ORGY POMP SHOW SIGN STAR WEAR AGONY ARRAY BINGE BLAZE BOAST DERAY ECLAT EMOTE FLASH PRIDE SCENE SHINE SIGHT SPLAY SPORT STAGE VAUNT BLAZON DEPLOY DESCRY ESTATE EVINCE EXPOSE EXTEND FLAUNT MUSTER OSTENT OUTLAY PARADE REVEAL RUFFLE SETOUT SPLASH SPRANK SPREAD UNCASE APPROVE BALLOON BRAVERY ETALAGE EXHIBIT EXPRESS FANFARE FLUTTER GAUDERY PAGEANT PRESENT SHOWING SPLURGE TRADUCE UNCOVER BEEFCAKE BLAZONRY BOOKFAIR CEREMONY DISCLOSE DISCOVER EMBLAZON EQUIPAGE EVIDENCE EXERCISE EXPOSURE FLOURISH INDICATE MANIFEST PARAFFLE SPLENDOR TINSELRY
(— **EXCITEMENT**) FAUNCH
(— **OF EMOTION**) GUSH
(— **OF SKILL**) APPERTISE
(**BOASTFUL** —) JACTATION
(**EMPTY** —) GAUD EYEWASH
(**FLORAL** —) BLOW BLANKET
(**IMPRESSIVE** —) SWELL
(**OSTENTATIOUS** —) DOG GAUDERY SWAGGER
(**RADAR** —) SCAN

DISPLAYED SPLAY EXPANDED

DISPLEASE VEX MIFF ANGER ANNOY PIQUE MISPAY MISSET OFFEND DISLIKE DISSUIT MISLIKE PROVOKE IRRITATE

DISPLEASED GLUM UNEASY UNFAIN

DISPLEASING BAD DRY PUTRID IRKSOME TEDIOUS UNLOVELY

DISPLEASURE IRE ANGER MUMPS PIQUE INJURY STRUNT UNLUST UNWILL DISLIKE OFFENSE TROUBLE UMBRAGE UNTHANK DISFAVOR DISGRACE DISTASTE

DISPORT PLAY AMUSE FRISK SPORT DIVERT FROLIC GAMBOL DISPLAY

DISPOSAL SALE BANDON CLEANUP PROPINE BESTOWAL DEVOTION DISPATCH
(**QUICK** —) WASHWAY

DISPOSE APT SET BEND CAST DUMP GIVE MIND TRIM YARK ARRAY BRUSH DIGHT ORDER PLACE POSIT ADJUST ATTIRE BESTOW DIGEST SETTLE TEMPER APPOINT ARRANGE DISPONE GESTURE INCLINE PREPARE RESOLVE DISPATCH REGULATE
(— **OF**) JOB SELL SCRAP FINISH HANDLE

DISPOSED APT FIT SET SIB LIEF GIVEN PRONE READY WRAST MINDED MINDFUL SUBJECT WILLING ADDICTED PROCLIVE PROTENSE TALENTED
(— **AT INTERVALS**) ALTERNATE
(— **TO ACTION**) ACTIVE
(— **TO ASSOCIATE WITH ONE GROUP**) CLANNISH
(— **TOWARD**) AFFECTED
(**FAIRLY** —) CANDID
(**WELL** —) FAIN INCLINED

DISPOSITION BENT BIAS MAKE MIND MOOD RACE SORT TRIM TURN DRIVE ETHOS FRAME GRAIN HABIT HEART HUMOR SPITE TACHE AFFECT ANIMUS DESIGN GENIUS HEALTH KIDNEY NATURE PTYXIS SPIRIT SPRITE STRIND TALENT TEMPER CONCEPT COURAGE DISPOSE FACULTY STOMACH APTITUDE ATTITUDE DISPOSAL POSITURE
(— **OF DRAPERIES**) CAST
(— **OF PAWNS**) SKELETON
(— **TO ANGER**) CHOLER
(— **TO RESIST**) DEFIANCE
(**GENEROUS** —) HEART
(**KINDLY** —) CHARITY HUMANITY
(**NATURAL** —) KIND GRAIN TARAGE INDOLES
(**ORNAMENTAL** —) DECOR
(**ULTIMATE** —) FATE

DISPOSSESS OUST EJECT EVICT EXPEL STRIP WRONG DEPOSE DIVEST BEREAVE CASHIER DEPRIVE DISSEIZE SEPARATE

DISPOSSESSED LUMPEN

DISPRAISE BLAME CENSURE

DISPROOF ELENCH REFUTE IMPROOF REPROOF

DISPROPORTIONATE UNEQUAL

DISPROVE BREAK REBUT REFEL NEGATE REFUTE CONFUTE EXPLODE IMPROVE REPROVE DISALLOW REDARGUE

DISPUTABLE MOOT VAGUE UNSURE DUBIOUS FALLIBLE

DISPUTANT FENCER POLEMIC WRANGLER

DISPUTATION PARVIS PILPUL POLEMIC PROBLEM WRANGLE ARGUMENT COURSING DEBATING EXERCISE

DISPUTE JAR TAX CALL CHOP DENY

FEUD FRAY FUSS HOLD MOOT ODDS RIOT SAKE SPAR SPAT TILT ARGUE BRAWL BROIL CABAL CHEST FLITE FLYTE HURRY PLEAD SPUTE SQUIB ARGUFY BARNEY BICKER CAMPLE CANGLE DABBER DACKER DAIKER DEBATE DIFFER FITTER FRATCH HAGGLE HASSLE IMPUGN MATTER NAGGLE SHARRY SQUALL SQUEAL THREAP BRABBLE CONTEND CONTEST DERAIGN DISCUSS DISSERT FACTION GAINSAY PRIBBLE QUARREL WRANGLE ARGUMENT CATFIGHT CONTRARY POLEMIZE QUESTION SKIRMISH SPARRING SPLUTTER SQUABBLE
(POETICAL —) FLYTING PARTIMEN
DISQUALIFY DEBAR UNFIT OUTLAW DISABLE
DISQUIET VEX FEAR FRET PAIN TOSS UNRO EXCITE UNCALM UNEASE UNREST AGITATE ANXIETY DISREST DISTURB INQUIET SOLICIT TROUBLE TURMOIL UNPEACE UNQUIET
DISQUIETED UNEASY
DISQUIETUDE CHAGRIN WANREST WANRUFE
DISRAELI DIZZY
DISREGARD BY SIT BLOW MOCK OMIT PASS WANE BELAY FLING WAIVE FORGET HUBRIS IGNORE SLIGHT UNHEED CASHIER DESPISE FORHEED LICENCE LICENSE NEGLECT OVERSEE DISCOUNT DISFAVOR DISPENSE DISVALUE EASINESS OVERHALE OVERLOOK OVERPASS UNREGARD
DISRELISH DISLIKE DISTASTE
DISREPUTABLE LOW BASE GAMY HARD WAFF GAMEY SEAMY SHADY SHODDY RAFFISH SHAMEFUL UNHONEST
DISREPUTABLENESS BEGGARY
DISREPUTE DISFAME DISFAVOR DISHONOR REPROACH
DISRESPECT AFFRONT CONTEMPT RUDENESS
DISRESPECTFUL HARM SAUCY UNCIVIL IMPOLITE IMPUDENT INSOLENT
DISROBE STRIP CHANGE DIVEST DESPOIL UNDRESS
DISRUPT GASH REND TEAR BREAK CROSS HAMPER DISRUMP DISTRACT
DISRUPTED BROKEN DISRUPT
DISRUPTION BREACH BREAKUP DEBACLE RUPTURE SOLUTION
DISSATISFACTION PAIN DISTASTE VEXATION
DISSATISFIED UNEASY
DISSATISFY MISPAY
DISSECT BAR ANALYZE DISJOIN SCALPEL UNPIECE
DISSECTED MATURE
DISSECTION ANATOMY ANALYSIS
DISSEMBLE ACT FOX HIDE MASK CLOAK FEIGN BOGGLE SEMBLE

CONCEAL DISGUISE SIMULATE SIMULIZE
DISSEMBLER SIMULAR
DISSEMBLING SLY IRONIC FICTION AESOPIAN IRONICAL
DISSEMINATE SOW BEAR BLAZE STREW EFFUSE SPREAD DIFFUSE PUBLISH SCATTER SPARPLE DISPERSE SEMINATE
DISSENSION JAR ODDS DEBATE STRIFE DISCORD DISLIKE DISSENT FACTION MISLIKE BROILERY DISPEACE DISTANCE DISUNION DISUNITY DIVISION FRACTION FRICTION SEDITION
DISSENT VARY DIFFER HERESY CONTEND PROTEST DISAGREE
DISSENTER HERETIC SECTARY RECUSANT SEPARATE RASKOLNIK (PL.) SEPARATION
DISSEPIMENT REPLUM SEPTUM PHRAGMA
DISSERTATION ESSAY THEME TRACT DEBATE MEMOIR SCREED THESIS DESCANT LECTURE MEMOIRS EXCURSUS EXERCISE TRACTATE TREATISE
(— ON TEA) TSIOLOGY
DISSERVICE HARM DAMAGE INJURY MISCHIEF
DISSIDENT FRONDEUR
DISSIMILAR UNLIKE DIFFORM DIVERSE UNLIKEN
DISSIMILATE UNLIKEN
DISSIMULATION IRONY DECEIT
DISSIPATE BURN FRAY SPEND WASTE BANISH DISPEL EXPEND CONSUME DIFFUSE DISCUSS FRITTER RESOLVE SCATTER SHATTER SWATTLE TARNISH DISPERSE DISSOLVE EMBEZZLE EVANESCE SQUANDER
DISSIPATED FAST HIGH LOST SPORTY OUTWARD RACKETY
DISSOLUTE LAX LEWD WILD LOOSE SLACK RAKELY RAKISH SUBURB UNTIED WANTON IMMORAL LAWLESS VICIOUS DESOLATE RAKEHELL RECKLESS RESOLUTE SUBURBAN UNCURBED
DISSOLUTION END RUIN DECAY BREAKUP DECEASE DIVORCE DIALYSIS
DISSOLVE CUT END DEFY FADE FUSE MELT SOLV THAW BREAK FLEET LOOSE SOLVE UNFIX DIGEST DISTIL RELENT SOLUTE UNBIND UNGLUE UNKNIT ADJOURN DESTROY DISBAND DISJOIN DISTILL DIVORCE LIQUEFY RESOLVE DISCANDY DISUNITE SEPARATE
(— OUT) LEACH
DISSOLVED SOLUT REMISS SOLUTE RESOLUTE
DISSONANCE WOLF DISCORD DIAPHONY
DISSONANT HARSH RAGGED GRATING JARRING JANGLING
DISSUADE BLUFF DETER DEHORT

DIVERT RETIRE
DISTAFF ROCK
DISTANCE DX WAY BLUE GAIT GATE LOOK PIPE SPAN STEP DEPTH DRAFT RANGE SPACE GROUND HEIGHT LENGTH SPREAD STANCE STITCH BOWSHOT BREADTH DRAUGHT FARNESS JOURNEY MILEAGE MILEWAY RESERVE STRETCH YARDAGE COLDNESS COSECANT DIAMETER FOOTSTEP HANDSPAN INTERVAL LATITUDE OFFSCAPE OUTSTRIP
(SAFE —) BERTH
(— ALONG TRACK) LEAD
(— BETWEEN BATTENS) GAG
(— BETWEEN MASTS) INTERVAL
(— BETWEEN RAILS) GAGE GAUGE
(— BETWEEN RIVET-HEADS) GRIP
(— FOR PUTTING COAL) RENK
(— FROM BELLY TO BACK) BODY
(— FROM EQUATOR) HEIGHT
(— FROM LOCK FACE) BACKSET
(— FROM THE EYE) DEPTH
(— IN ADVANCE) START
(— OF ARCHERY RANGE) BUTT
(— OF BOW SHOT) CAST
(— OF HAUL) LEAD LEADAGE
(— OF TURNING SHIP) ADVANCE
(— OF VISION) KEN
(— ON FISHHOOK) BITE
(— ON GEAR WHEEL) ADDENDUM
(— OVER WHICH WIND BLOWS) FETCH
(ANGULAR —) ANOMALY
(AT A —) LARGE
(GREAT —) INFINITY
(INTERVENING —) GAP
(PERPENDICULAR —) DROP CAMBER ALTITUDE
(SEA —) OUTING STEAMING
(SHOOTING —) SHOOT
(SHORT — AWAY) OUTBYE
(SHORT —) INCH SPIT STEP SPELL FOOTSTEP
(SMALL —) HAIR STEP
(UNIT OF —) LI YOJAN PARASANG
DISTANT DX COY FAR OFF AFAR AWAY BACK COLD SIDE YOND ALOOF CHILL FERNE HENCE FERREN REMOTE YONDER FARAWAY FOREIGN FROSTED REMOVED STRANGE RESERVED
(— IN TIME) EARLY
(— PART) OFFSCAPE
(MORE —) YOND YONDER ULTERIOR
DISTASTE HATE DEGOUT UNLUST DISGUST DISLIKE MISLIKE AVERSION MISTASTE
DISTASTEFUL SOUR AUGEAN BITTER BEASTLY HATEFUL BRACKISH NAUSEOUS SHOCKING UNSAVORY
DISTEMPER SOAK STEEP CHOLER DILUTE GARGET GARGIL GARGLE MALADY PANTAS AILMENT DISEASE ILLNESS DISORDER DYSCRASE SICKNESS UNSETTLE
(— OF COLT) STRANGLES

DISTEND BAG BLOW FILL GROW HEFT BLOAT PLUMP STRUT SWELL WIDEN DILATE EXPAND EXTEND INTEND SPREAD BALLOON ENLARGE INFLATE STRETCH

DISTENDED FULL PENT TAUT TRIG WIDE BLOWN POOCH TUMID GRAVID BLOATED DISTENT SWOLLEN INFLATED PATULENT PATULOUS

DISTENTION BLOAT DISTENT TYMPANY

DISTHENE CYANITE KYANITE

DISTICH SLOKA PROODE COUPLET

DISTILL DROP ELIX EMIT RATE STILL DISTIL EXTILL INFUSE ALEMBIC LIMBECK TRICKLE

DISTILLATE GUNDY ROSIN BENZIN BENZINE

DISTILLATION RUN DESCENT

DISTILLER ABKAR STILLER

DISTILLERY STILL JIGGER STILLERY

DISTINCT HOT FAIR FREE VIVE BREME BRISK CLEAR PLAIN SHARP VIVID PLUCKY PROPER SECRET SUNDRY ANOTHER ASUNDER DIVERSE EVIDENT LEGIBLE OBVIOUS PRECISE SEVERAL SPECIAL APPARENT DISCRETE DIVIDUAL PALPABLE PECULIAR SEPARATE

DISTINCTION MARK NOTE RANK SHED TEST CLASS GLORY HONOR FIGURE LAUREL LUSTER LUSTRE RENOWN QUALITY QUILLET ACCESSIT DIVISION GRANDEZA SUBTLETY (ACADEMIC —) HONORS HONOURS (WITHOUT —) COMMON

DISTINCTIVE JUICY DIRECT PROPER SIGNAL PECULIAR PHONEMIC SEPARATE SPANKING TALENTED

DISTINCTIVENESS EMPHASIS

DISTINCTLY CLEAR REDLY FAIRLY CLEARLY

DISTINCTNESS PLUCK CLARITY SEVERALTY (LACKING —) SMUDGY

DISTINGUISH DEEM KNOW MARK SORT BADGE JUDGE LABEL SEVER SKILL STAMP DECERN DEFINE DESCRY DEVISE DIVIDE ENSIGN SECERN SINGLE CONCERN DISCERN DESCRIBE PERCEIVE SEPARATE

DISTINGUISHED CLEAR GREAT NOTED SWELL BANNER FAMOUS GENTLE MARKED SOLEMN EMINENT INSIGNE NOTABLE SIGNATE SPECIAL DISTINCT LAUREATE RENOWNED SPLENDID

DISTINGUISHING BETWEEN

DISTORT WRY SKEW CLOUD COLOR FUDGE SCREW TWIST WREST WRING CRINGE DEFACE DEFORM DETORT GARBLE SHEVEL WRITHE BLUBBER CONTORT FALSIFY GRIMACE PERVERT SHACHLE SHACKLE SLANDER OUTIMAGE WIREDRAW

DISTORTED WRY AWRY SKEW ASKEW CRANK SKEWED WARPED

CROOKED DISTORT GNARLED LOXOTIC WRITHEN CAMSHACH DEFORMED DEGRADED STRAINED TORTIOUS

DISTORTING CONVULSION

DISTORTION HOG SAG WOW WREST STRAIN FLUTTER GRIMACE GARBLING SKEWNESS (— IN WOOD) DIAMONDING

DISTRACT MAD AMUSE CRAZE STROY BEMUSE DETRAY DIVERT HARASS INSANE MADDEN MITHER MOIDER PUZZLE TWITCH AGITATE CONFUSE DETRACT DISTURB EMBROIL PERPLEX SCATTER BEWILDER CONFOUND

DISTRACTED GYTE CRAZY STRACT FRANTIC SCRANNY

DISTRACTION ALARM BLIND ALARUM ESCAPE FRENZY TUMULT ECSTASY

DISTRAIN NAM NAAM DRIVE POIND STRAIN STRESS DISTRESS POUNDAGE

DISTRAINT NAM NAAM POIND

DISTRAUGHT MAD CRAZED FRANTIC DERANGED DISTRACT DISTRAIT STRAUGHT

DISTRESS AIL ILL MAR BITE CARK HURT MOAN NEED PAIN PORT TEEN AGONY ANGER ANNOY DOLOR GRATE GRIEF GRILL GRIPE LABOR PINCH PRESS SMART TRYST TWEAK WORRY WOUND BARRAT DANGER DURESS GRIEVE GRUDGE HARASS HARROW LAMENT MISERY SORROW STRESS THRONG WORRIT AFFLICT ANGUISH ANXIETY CHAGRIN DAYMARE DESTROY DISEASE EXTREME HERSHIP MISEASE OPPRESS PASSION PENANCE PERPLEX STURBLE TORMENT TORTURE TROUBLE UNQUERT AGGRIEVE CALAMITY DARKNESS DISTASTE DISTRAIN FORHAILE PRESSURE SORENESS STRAITEN WANDRETH GRIEVANCE

DISTRESSED WRUNG DOWNGONE

DISTRESSFUL STRAIT

DISTRESSING BAD HOT SAD GRIM HARD SORE BLEAK CHARY CRUEL DIRTY SHARP BITTER SEVERE SHREWD THORNY CARKING FEARFUL GRIPING PAINFUL GRIEVOUS

DISTRIBUTE DOT SOW CAST DEAL DOLE GRID METE SEED SORT TAME ALLOT CLASS DIVVY ISSUE SHARE SHIFT SPEND ASSIGN ASSORT DEPART DEVISE DIGEST DIVIDE EXPEND IMPART PARCEL REPART SPARSE SPREAD ARRANGE DISPEND DISPOSE EROGATE PRORATE SCATTER ALLOCATE CLASSIFY DESCRIBE DISBURSE DISPENSE DISPERSE SEPARATE SPRINKLE (— GUNFIRE) SEARCH (— SEED) SOW SEED DRILL (— TYPE) THROW

DISTRIBUTED BALANCED DISPERSE

DISTRIBUTION DOLE SALE ARRAY DIVVY DETAIL DIVIDE PARTING DISPOSAL DIVIDEND

DISTRIBUTIVELY EACH APIECE

DISTRIBUTOR SOWER SHARER CARRIER ZANJERO

DISTRICT DO AMT GAU LAN SOC WON AREA COIL FARM HUNT LEET LIWA PALE PART SIDE SLUM SOKE TEMA WARD WENE WICK WOON AIMAK ANNEX COILA EXURB HARSH JAGIR JEWRY MAHAL OKRUG PAGUS PARTY SHIRE SOKEN TALUK TEMAN TRACT VICUS AGENCY BARRIO BOWERY CANTON CERCLE CIRCLE COUNTY FOREST JAGHIR MARKAZ MEMBER MERINA OKROOG PARAMO PARISH POLLAM REGARD REGION SIRCAR STAPLE STREET SYSSEL VINTRY ZILLAH CALABAR CIRCUIT CLASSIS COMARCA COMMUNE COUNTRY CURRAGH DEMESNE DIOCESE ENCLAVE FREEDOM LIBERTY MAHALLA MALACCA MAYFAIR MELIZKI MISSION PIMLICO PURLIEU QUARTER SEASIDE SLUMDOM THANAGE THEBAID UPRIVER CHAPELRY CIMARRON DISTRITO DIVISION FAUBOURG GILDABLE LEGATION MACASSAR MAGAZINE MONTANAS PRECINCT PROVINCE REGIMENT (— BORDERING RIVER) WATER (— OF COURT) LEET (— OF JAPAN) DO KEN (BROTHEL —) STEW (BURNED —) QUEMADO (CHINESE —) HIEN (ECCLESIASTICAL —) SYNOD CLASSIS DIOCESE (HUNTING —) WALK (ICELANDIC —) SYSSEL (JUDICIAL —) CIRCUIT (POOR —) SLUM SLUMS (POSTAL —) RAYON (RURAL —) WAYBACK (RURAL —S) STICKS (RUSSIAN —) STANITSA STANITZA (TENANT —) THIRL (TRIBAL —) GAU (TURKISH —) ORDU SANJAK (PL.) GAELTACHT

DISTRUST FEAR DOUBT DREAD STRIFE DIFFIDE SUSPECT UNFAITH UNTRUST DEFIANCE DISFAITH MISFAITH MISTRUST WANTRUST

DISTRUSTFUL SHY LEERY JEALOUS

DISTURB VEX BUSY FAZE FRET FUSS JOLT RILE ROIL STIR TOSS ALARM ANNOY BRASH DROVE FEEZE KNOCK PHASE ROUSE SHAKE STEER UPSET BOTHER HARASS JOSTLE MOLEST RUFFLE SQUEAK UNCALM UNEASE AGITATE COMMOTE COMMOVE DERANGE DISREST DRUMBLE FRAZZLE GARBOIL INQUIET MISMAKE PERTURB SCUFFLE SOLICIT STURBLE

TEMPEST TROUBLE CONVULSE
DISJOINT DISORDER DISQUIET
DISTRACT DISTRESS FRIGHTEN
(— BY HANDLING) TOUCH
(— SUDDENLY) START
(— THE PEACE) RIOT INQUIET
DISTURBANCE VEX BOIL BREE CAIN
COIL DUST RIOT ROUT STIR WIND
WORK ALARM BRAWL BROIL DERAY
FUGUE FUROR HURRY SHINE SHOCK
STEER STORM STROW STURT
TOUSE AFFRAY BOTHER BREEZE
CATHRO DESRAY FRACAS FRAISE
FURORE HUBBUB KICKUP POTHER
RUMBLE RUMPUS SHINDY SQUALL
STATIC TUMULT TURNUP UPROAR
BLUNDER BOBBERY BRULYIE
BRULZIE CHAGRIN CLATTER
CLUTTER DISTURB EMOTION
FERMENT GRINDER MADNESS
ROOKERY TROUBLE TURMOIL
BROILERY BUSINESS DISORDER
FOOFARAW INCIDENT REELRALL
STRAMASH TRAVALLY
(— OF OCEAN) SEA
(ATMOSPHERIC —) STORM GRINDER
(DIGESTIVE —) BLOAT
(MENTAL —) FRENZY PHRENSY
DELIRIUM
(SEISMIC —) SEAQUAKE
DISTURBED CRACKED INQUIET
MAKADOO TROUBLE AGITATED
FLURRIED STREAKED
DISTURBING BREAK HAUNTING
DISUNION DIVORCE
DISUNITE RIP PART SEVER UNTIE
DETACH DIVIDE SUNDER UNKNIT
UNLIME DISBAND DISJOIN DISLINK
DISSENT DIVORCE UNRAVEL
ALIENATE DISSEVER DISSOLVE
ESTRANGE SEPARATE UNSOLDER
DISUNITY DiSCORD DISUNION
DIVISION
DISUSE MISUSE OUTAGE ABANDON
DISCARD DISUSAGE MISAPPLY
DISUSED DEAD WASTE DESUETE
EXOLETE
DITCH GAW RUT SAP SOW DELF
DICK DIKE DYKE FOSS GOOL GOUT
GRIP GURT HOLL LEET MOAT SEEK
SICK SIKE SINK TRIG CANAL CLAUD
DELFT DELVE FENCE FLEAM FOSSA
FOSSE GRAFF GRAFT GRAVE GRIPE
GROOP GULLY PUDGE RHEEN RHINE
SEWER SHORE SLONK SLUIT SOUGH
STANK STELL ZANJA GUTTER
GUZZLE HOLLOW RELAIS SHEUCH
SHEUGH TRENCH ZANJON ABANDON
ACEQUIA CHANNEL GRINDLE
GRIPPLE LATERAL VANFOSS
ZANJONA WATERING
(MUDDY —) LETCH
(NARROW —) RELAIS
(OPEN —) STELL
DITCH GRASS ENALID
DITCH MILLET HUREEK PASPALUM
DITCH REED SPIRE BENNEL
DITHER SHAKE BOTHER LATHER
SHIVER TROUBLE

DITROCHEE DIPODY
DITTO SAME REPEAT LIKEWISE
DITTY DIT LAY DITE DYTE POEM
SING SONG THEME VERSE SAYING
DICTATE VINETTA
DIURETIC ZEA CAVA KAVA BUCCO
BUCHU LAPPA PICHI SABAL NASROL
DROSERA EMICTORY
DIVER AMA LOON DUCKER PEARLER
PLUNGER PLUNGEON
DIVERGE LEAVE BRANCH DIFFER
DIVIDE RAMIFY SPREAD SQUARE
SWERVE DEVIATE DIGRESS DIVERSE
DISAGREE DIVAGATE
DIVERGENCE DIP ERROR CHANGE
SPREAD VAGARY CONTRAST
DIVERGENT OFF APART REMOTE
TANGENT VARIANT
(MORE —) FARTHER
DIVERS EVIL MANY CRUEL SUNDRY
SEVERAL VARIOUS PERVERSE
DIFFERING
DIVERSE EVIL SERE MOTLEY
SUNDRY UNLIKE VARIED ADVERSE
SEVERAL VARIOUS DISTINCT
PERVERSE SEPARATE VARIETAL
DIVERSIFIED EXTENDED
DIVERSIFY DOT FRET VARY CHECK
FRECK BEGARIE VARIATE SPRINKLE
DIVERSION JEU GAME MASK PLAY
ALARM FEINT FRISK HOBBY SPORT
ATTACK DEDUIT DIVERT LAUGHS
SCHEME SOLACE DISPORT PASTIME
ESCAPISM PLEASURE SIDESHOW
VARIORUM
(— OF STREAM) CAPTURE
DIVERSITY CHANGE DISCORD
DISSENT VARIETY CONTRAST
DIVERT SWAY AMUSE BLANK RELAX
SHUNT SPORT WRING DERAIL
DERIVE DETURN SIPHON SWITCH
SYPHON TICKLE BEGUILE CELIGHT
DECEIVE DEFLECT DETRACT
DISPORT PASTIME PERVERT
REFLECT ABSTRACT DISSUADE
DISTRACT ESTRANGE RECREATE
(— ATTENTION) COVER
(— HEADWATERS) BEHEAD
(— STREAM) CAPTURE
(— WATER) FLUME
DIVERTED MERRY AMUSED
DISTRACT
DIVERTICULUM UTERUS OLEOCYST
DIVERTING DROLL AMUSING
FOOLISH PLEASANT SPORTFUL
LAUGHABLE
DIVEST BARE DOFF REFT TIRL
EMPTY EXUTE REAVE SHEAR SPOIL
STRIP DELAWN DENUDE DEPOSE
DEVEST DISMIT UNVEST BEREAVE
DEPRIVE DESPOIL DISROBE
UNCOVER UNDRESS DENATURE
DETHRONE UNCLOTHE
(— OF ARMOR) DEMAIL
(— OF VALUE) DEVALUE
(— OF) ABDICATE
DIVIDE CUT LOT CAST DEAL FORK
MERE PART RIFT SHED SLIP ZONE
BREAK CARVE CLASS CLEFT DIVVY

GAVEL JOINT SCALE SCIND SEVER
SHARE SHIFT SLICE SNACK SPACE
SPLIT SPRIT WHACK BEPART BISECT
BRANCH CANTLE CANTON CLEAVE
COTEAU DEPART DEVISE DIFFER
DOMIFY INDENT PARCEL RAMIFY
SECTOR SEJOIN SLEAVE SUNDER
ALIQUOT ANALYZE ATOMIZE
AVERAGE BRITTEN COMPART
DIFFUSE DIREMPT DISCIDE DISPART
DISSECT DIVERGE FISSURE FRITTER
PARTAKE PRORATE ALLOCATE
CLASSIFY CROSSCUT DISCRETE
DISSEVER DISTRACT DISUNITE
FRACTION FRAGMENT GRADUATE
HEMISECT MEDISECT SEPARATE
STRATIFY UNSEEDER
(— BEEF) BLOCK
(— FILAMENTS) SLEAVE
(— INTO 2 PARTS) HALVE BISECT
(— INTO 4 PARTS) QUARTER
(— INTO DISTRICTS) CANTON
(— INTO MEASURES) BAR
(— INTO PIECES) GOBBET
(— LAND) STINT
(— NATURALLY) FALL
(— SMALL) SCANTLE
DIVIDED ENTE REFT SIDE CLEFT
FORKY SPLIT ATOMIC CLOVEN
PRONGY FISSATE FOURCHE
GYRONNY PARTITE SEPTATE
AEROLATE CAMERATE DIVIDUAL
FOURCHEE
(— IN TWO) FOURCHE DIMIDIATE
(— INTO 4 PARTS) PALY
QUARTERED
(NOT —) GLOBAL
DIVIDEND BONUS SHARE
DIVIDER BUNTON MERIST SHARER
BUNTING COMPASS SEVERER
DIVIDANT
DIVI-DIVI LIBIDIBI
DIVINATION OMEN SORS SORT
AUGURY MANTIC SCRYING SORCERY
GEOMANCY TAGHAIRM
(— SCIENCE) MANTIC
DIVINE HOLY SORT SPAE TWIG
AREAD AREED DIVUS GUESS PIOUS
DEIFIC DETECT DEVISE GODFUL
HALSEN PRIEST SACRED BLESSED
FORESEE GODLIKE PORTEND
PREDICT PRESAGE ARIOLATE
CONTRIVE FOREBODE FOREKNOW
FORETELL HEAVENLY IMMORTAL
MINISTER PERCEIVE UBIQUIST
DIVINER SEER AUGUR SIBYL
ARUSPEX AUGURER PROPHET
HARUSPEX
DIVING BELL NAUTILUS
DIVING BOARD RISE
DIVING SUIT GANGAVA
DIVINING ROD TWIG DOWSER
DIVINITY (ALSO SEE GOD AND
GODDESS) JOSS LLEU LLEW TIEN
AHURA DEITY HYBLA NUADA NUADU
NYMPH POWER ATHTAR VEDUIS
GLAUCUS GODDESS GODHEAD
GODSHIP HYBLAEA TARANIS VIRBIUS
TEUTATES VEDIOVIS

(— CIRCUIT BINDING) YAPP
(PL.) ELOHIM
DIVISIBLE SECABLE DIVIDUAL
PARTIBLE
(— BY 2) AIM
DIVISION BAY BOX CUT DAG FIT LEG
CHAP CLAN DOLE FARM FAUN FORK
GELD GELT GORE HOLD LITH NEAT
PACE PANE PART RANK RAPE RIFT
CAPUT CHASM CLASS CLEFT CURIA
DIGOR DIVVY DULAN DULAT FIELD
FIGHT GENOS GRANT GROUP IJORE
MURUT PERES REALM SHARD
SHARE SUBAH TAXIS THEME TOMAN
WHEEN CANTON DECADE DECURY
DEGREE DIVIDE EOGAEA HAWIYA
IMAHAL JHURIA PORTIO SCHISM
SEASON SECTOR SUNDER VOLOST
ZILLAH BREAKUP COMARCA
CUSTODY DIOCESE DUALISM
ENOMOTY FISSURE FURLONG
HASHIYA KINGDOM KITSKAN
NATUARY PARTAGE PARTING
ROULADE SECTION SEGMENT
SUBRACE ARPEGGIO CATEGORY
CLEAVAGE DECANATE DIERESIS
DISTRICT FASCICLE MEROTOMY
PARGANNA PRECINCT SCISSION
SCISSURE SHEDDING SQUADRON
SUBCLASS
(— BETWEEN PIERS) BAY
(— BETWEEN STALLS) BAIL
(— FOR TAXATION) GELD
(— IN DENMARK) AMT
(— IN HUNGARY) COMITAT
(— IN MINING BED) CLEAVE
(— OF ANGELS) CHOIR
(— OF ARMY) BATTLE LOCHUS
(— OF BEJA) BISHARIN
(— OF BOOK) CHAPTER FASCICLE
(— OF BUILDING) STORY STOREY
(— OF CHARIOTEERS) FACTION
(— OF CONTEST) HEAT INNING
(— OF COUNTY) RAPE BARONY
HUNDRED
(— OF CROPLAND) FLAT
(— OF DISCOURSE) HEADING
(— OF DRAMA) ACT SCENE
(— OF FAMILY) BRANCH
(— OF FIELD) RIG
(— OF FOOT) SEMEION
(— OF FOREST) WARD
(— OF GEOLOGICAL TIME) EPOCH
(— OF GRASS) SPRIG
(— OF GREAT HORDE) DULAN
DULAT KANGLA KANGLI
(— OF HEADLINE) BANK DECK
(— OF LAND) LAINE KONOHIKI
(— OF LEGION) COHORT HASTATI
MANIPLE TRIARII
(— OF LOG LINE) KNOT
(— OF MANCHU ARMY) BANNER
(— OF MANKIND) RACE
(— OF MEAL) COURSE
(— OF NIGHT) WATCH
(— OF ORANGE) LITH
(— OF POEM) FIT DUAN CANTO
STANZA STROPHE
(— OF PROCESS) STAGING

(— OF ROCKS) SYSTEM
(— OF ROSARY) DECADE
(— OF SOCIETY) CASTE ATOMISM
(— OF SONG) FIT
(— OF STOPE) FLOOR
(— OF STRUCTURE) STAGE
(— OF TREF) RANDIR
(— OF UTTERANCE) COLON
(— OF WINDOW) DAY
(— OF ZODIAC) SIGN DECAN
(— OVER ISSUE) BREACH
(ADMINISTRATIVE —) FU LATHE
CHARGE CIRCLE COUNTY EYALET
CUSTODY DIOCESE TOWNSHIP
(ANTHROPOLOGICAL —) STOCK
(ARMY —) MORA
(ASTROLOGICAL —) FACE
(CELL —) AMITOSIS
(ECCLESIASTICAL —) SCHISM
SOCIETY PRECINCT
(GEOLOGICAL —) ERA LIAS MALM
LUDIAN SERIES LARAMIE ARNUSIAN
RICHMOND
(HINGED —) LEAF
(ISLE OF MAN —) SHEADING
(MUSICAL —) ALLEGRO
(NUCLEAR —) FISSION
(PHILIPPINE —) ATO
(POLICE —) TANA THANA
(POLITICAL —) ATO CITY LATHE
STATE COUNTY PARISH BOROUGH
HUNDRED SURPLUS DISTRICT
PURCHASE
(POPULATION —) STRATUM
(SOCIAL —) HORDE
(TRIBAL —) CLAN
DIVORCE GET GETT AHSAN HASAN
KHULA SEVER TALAK SUNDER
ASUNDER DISBAND DISMISS
MUBARAT UNMARRY DISSOLVE
DISUNION DISUNITE SEPARATE
DIVOT CLOD TURF
DIVULGE BARE CALL SHOW TELL
BLURT BREAK SPILL UTTER VOICE
BEWRAY EVULGE IMPART REVEAL
SPREAD UNFOLD PROPALE PUBLISH
UNCOVER DISCLOSE DISCOVER
EVULGATE PROCLAIM
DIZZINESS HILO SWIM DINUS TIEGO
MEGRIM VANITY MERLIGO SCOTOMY
VERTIGO SWIMMING WILLNESS
DIZZY DUNT CRAZY FAINT GIDDY
LIGHT TOTTY WESTY FICKLE STUPID
FOOLISH SWIMMING UNSTEADY
DO D ACT DIV FAY TRY BILK BURN
CHAR COME DEAL DOST MAKE
PASS SUIT AVAIL BITCH CHEAT
EXERT GUISE SERVE SHIFT TRICK
ANSWER COMMIT NOBBLE RENDER
ACHIEVE EXECUTE PERFORM
PRODUCE SATISFY SUFFICE
TRANSACT
(— AWAY WITH) BURK ABATE
BURKE FORDO BANISH FOREDO
ABOLISH AMOLISH CASHIER
CONSUME ABROGATE DEMOLISH
DISSOLVE IMBOLISH RETRENCH
(— BUSINESS) CHAFFER
(— CARELESSLY) SLIM

(— CASUAL WORK) GRASS
(— FOR) FIX GET JACK SINK FETCH
NAPOO DIDDLE
(— IMPERFECTLY) HUDDLE
(— IN SLOVENLY WAY) SLUBBER
(— INJURY) BANE
(— NOT) DONT DINNA
(— PENANCE) SATISFY
(— PIECEWORK) DACKER
(— SMARTLY) LINK
(— THOROUGHLY) FLOOR
(— WITHOUT) LACK SPARE
FORBEAR DISPENSE
(— WRONG) ERR SIN MISCARRY
(— YE) DEE
DOABLE AGIBLE
DOBLON ISABELLA
DOBRA JO JOE OCTAVE
DOCENT TUTOR TEACHER
LECTURER
DOCILE CALM MEEK TALL TAME
TAWIE FACILE GENTLE DOCIOUS
DUCTILE DUTIFUL BIDDABLE
TOWARDLY
DOCK BOB CUT BANG CLIP MOOR
PIER QUAY RUMP SCUT BASIN
SHORE WHARF CAMBER COFFER
DOCKEN FIDDLE HAMBLE MARINA
SORREL STRUNT BOBTAIL CURTAIL
PARELLA PARELLE SHORTEN
CANAIGRE PATIENCE SHIPSIDE
DOCKAGE BERTHAGE
DOCKMACKIE VIBURNUM
DOCKYARD ARSENAL
(— WORKMAN) MATEY
DOCTOR DOC COOK DOPE DOSE
FAKE BRUJO HAKIM LEECH SUGAR
TREAT CROCUS DEACON EXTERN
HAIKUN HEALER INTERN MAULVI
POWWOW CROAKER KORADJI
TEACHER MEDICATE
(— OF CANON LAW) JCD
(— OF LAWS) JD
(— UP) COOK FAKE EYEWASH
(PLAY —) FIXER
(QUACK —) CROCUS
(WITCH —) BOCOR BOKOR GOOFE
GUFFER WIZARD WITCHMAN
DOCTRINAIRE ISMY
DOCTRINE ISM DOXY LEAR RULE
CREDO CREED DOGMA LIGHT MAX
TABLE TENET ZOISM AHIMSA
BABISM BELIEF DHARMA EGOISM
EROTIC GOSPEL HOLISM MALISM
MONISM NOETIC THEORY ACROAM
AMIDISM ANIMISM ARTICLE ATAVIS
ATHEISM ATOMISM BAHAISM
DUALISM EGOTISM EVANGEL
KARAISM KRYPSIS MISHNAH
NEOLOGY NOETICS OPINION
PEELISM PRECEPT PROGRAM
REALISM SENSISM TRIKAYA
ACTIVISM AGATHISM ANALYTIC
ARIANISM ARYANISM BAJANISM
CHILIASM CYNICISM DARBYISM
DEVILISM DOCETISM DYNAMISM
ENERGISM FATALISM FINALISM
GOBINISM HEDONISM HYLOLOGY
IDENTISM IDEOLOGY ISLAMISM

IHILISM PAJONISM PAMNESIA
EJORISM POSITION POSOLOGY
SYCHISM REGALISM RHEMATIC
IDERISM SOLIDISM SPHERICS
YPOLOGY UBIQUITY VITALISM
BUDDHIST —) ANATTA ANATMAN
CONTRARY —) HERESY
ESOTERIC —) CABALA QABBALA
ABALISM
EVIL —) MOLOCH
PL.) ESOTERY SCOTISM CREDENDA
ONATISM LABADISM SCRIBISM
CUMENT DOC GET BILL BOND
OOK CALL DEED FORM GETT OLLA
EAL WRIT CHART DEMIT DIMIT
RIEF LEASE PAPER PROOF SCRIP
CRIT STIFF TARGE TEACH TITLE
ILLET BREVET CADJAN CAJANG
EDULA COCKET DOCKET PATENT
AGMAN SCHOOL SCRIPT SOURCE
URVEY TICKET VOLUME ARCHIVE
ONDUCT DIPLOMA ELOHIST
SCRIPT EXHIBIT INQUEST LICENSE
ISSIVE PLACARD PRECEPT
ARRANT WAYBILL WHEREAS
RITING CONTRACT COVENANT
URLOUGH INSTRUCT MORTGAGE
CHEDULE SECURITY TRANSIRE
CONDITIONAL —) SCRIP
COPY OF —) VIDIMUS
PL.) BUMF ARCHIVE ARCHIVES
ALAPALA
ODDER SCAD SCALD SHAKE
ODDLE DOTHER FIDEOS TOTTER
REMBLE FLAXDROP HAIRWEED
ALEWEED HELLWEED MULBERRY
ODDERING OLD INANE INFIRM
ENILE FOOLISH
ODDER LAUREL WOEVINE
STLETOE
ODDIE HUMLIE
DECANESE (— ISLAND) KOS
YME KASOS LEROS TELOS KHALKE
PSOS PATMOS NISYROS
ALYMNOS
OGE SHY BILK DUCK GAME JINK
OUK LURK RUSE AVOID CHEAT
LUDE EVADE FENCE FUDGE GLOSS
URCH PARRY SHIFT SHIRK SHUNT
ALL TRICK ESCAPE WHEEZE
CEIVE EVASION PROFFER
TIFICE CROTCHET GILENYIE
ALINGER SIDESTEP
OGER FLIER FLYER HAGGLER
NDBILL
RAFT —) BUSHWACK
GING JINK
E DA ROE TEG FAUN HIND NANNY
MOND BISCUIT
 IN 1ST YEAR) FAWN
LUE —) FLIER FLYER
ER ACTOR AGENT MAKER
THOR FACTOR FEASOR WORKER
CIENT MANAGER ATTORNEY
ECUTOR
 OF ODD JOBS) JACK
S S DOTH DUSE
NOT) DONT DISNA DOESNT
F OFF DAFF VAIL AVALE DOUSE

DOWSE STRIP DIVEST REMOVE
UNDRESS
DOFFER DRUM DUFFER
DOFFING CAP
DOG CUR MUT PUG PUP YAP ALAN
ALCO CHOW DANE FAUS GOER KIYI
MONG MUTT PAWL STAG TIKE TRAY
TYKE ALAND ALANT ARGOS BAWTY
BEDOG BESET BOUCH BOXER
CALEB CANID CORGI DERBY DODGE
HOUND HUSKY LIMER PELON
POOCH PUPPY RACHE RAKER
RATCH SLING SPITZ STALK WHELP
AFGHAN BANDOG BASSET BAWTIE
BEAGLE BELTON BORZOI BOSTON
BOWWOW BRIARD BUFFER CANINE
COCKER COLLIE COONER DANCER
DETENT DRIVER ESKIMO FINDER
GUNDOG HEADER HEELER HUNTER
JOWLER KELPIE KENNET MISSET
POODLE RANGER RATTER SALUKI
SEIZER SETTER SHOUGH SIRIUS
SUSSEX TALBOT TOLLER TOWSER
VIZSLA YAPPER YAUPER YELPER
BASENJI BEARDER BULLDOG
CARRIER COURSER CRAMPON
CREEPER DOGGESS DROPPER
GRIFFON HARRIER LURCHER
MALTESE MASTIFF MONGREL
OWTCHAR POINTER SCOTTIE
SKIRTER SLEUGHI SPANIEL
SPORTER STARTER TERRIER
TUMBLER WHIPPET YAPSTER
AIREDALE ALEUTANT ALSATIAN
CERBERUS CYNHYENA DEMIWOLF
DOBERMAN ELKHOUND FISSIPED
FOXHOUND KEESHOND LABRADOR
LANDSEER LONGTAIL MALEMUTE
MALINOIS PAPILLON PEKINESE
SAMOYEDE SEALYHAM SHEPHERD
SIBERIAN SPRINGER TURNSPIT
VERMINER WATCHDOG WATERRUG
(— OF LATHE) DRIVER
(— TRAINED AS DECOY) TOLLER
(BIRD —) BOLTER
(CHAINED —) BANDOG
(ESKIMO —) HUSKY SIWASH
(FARM —) KOMONDOR
(FEMALE —) GYP SLUT BITCH
DOGGESS
(FOXLIKE —) COLPEO
(HOUSE —) WAP WAPP
(HUNGARIAN —) KUVASZ
(HUNTING —) ALAN BRACH RACHE
RATCH ALAUND BASSET HUNTER
KENNET LUCERN RACCHE SALUKI
SEIZER SETTER SLOUGH COURSER
DROPPER HARRIER POINTER
STRIKER
(JAPANESE —) AKITA
(LAP —) MESSAN SHOUGH
(LARGE —) DANE TOWSER MASTIFF
KOMONDOR
(LIKE A —) CYNIC
(LONG-HAIRED —) ALCO SHOCK
(MONGREL —) CUR DEMIWOLF
(NON-BARKING —) BASENJI
(PARTI-COLORED —) PIE PYE
(PET —) MINX LAPDOG MOPPET

(PUG —) MOPS
(PUNCH'S —) TOBY
(SHAGGY —) RUG OWTCHAH
(SHEEP —) CUR COLLIE KELPIE
BEARDIE MALINOIS SHEPHERD
(SMALL —) TOY FICE FIST DOGGY
FEIST PIPER DOGGIE AMERTOY
SPANIEL PAPILLON PEKINESE
(VICIOUS —) TAEPO
(WATCH —) CUR GARM GARMR
(WILD —) ADJAG DHOLE DINGO
GUARA JACKAL AGOUARA
CIMARRON
(YELPING —) WAPPET
(PL.) DOGGERY
DOGBANE KENDIR KENDYR ECHITES
FLYTRAP ALSTONIA MILKWEED
DOGBOAT PIG
DOGCART GADDER TUMTUM
BOUNDER GADABOUT
DOG COLLAR TRASH
DOG DAYS CANICULE
DOG EAR LEATHER
DOG FENNEL HOGWEED
DOGFIGHT SCRAMBLE
DOGFISH DOG HOE HUSS TOPE
FLAKE HOUND HURSE MANGO
TOPER DAGGAR GALEID MORGAY
BONEDOG GABBACK SPURDOG
TRIAKID GRAYFISH SEAHOUND
DOGGED DOUR SULLEN DOGGISH
DOGLIKE STUBBORN
DOGGEREL NOMINY TRIVIA DIGGREL
SINGSONG
DOGGONE BLESSED DOWNGONE
DOGIE LEPPY STRAY
DOG KEEPER FEWTERER
DOGLIKE CYNIC CYNOID DOGGED
DOGMA CREED TENET DICTUM
DOCTRINE DOCUMENT
DOGMATIC POSITIVE CONFIDENT
DOGMATISM BOWWOW
DOGMATIST PHILODOX
DOG POUND GREENYARD
DOG ROSE BUCKY CANKER
BEDEGUAR DOGBERRY
DOG SALMON CHUM KETA MORGAY
DOGFISH
DOGSHORE DOG DAGGER
DOG'S MERCURY SAPWORT
DOG SNAPPER JOCU
DOGSTAIL BENT
DOGWOOD OSIER SUMAC CORNEL
CORNUS GAITER WIDBIN BARBASCO
FISHWOOD
DOILY MAT TIDE TIDY NAPKIN
DOING ACT DEED FACT STIR EVENT
ACTION FUNCTION PRACTIVE
(PL.) FARE GEAR
DOIT DODKIN
DOLE LOT ALMS DEAL DOOL GIFT
GOAL METE PART VAIL ALLOT
FRAUD GRIEF GUILE MOURN SHARE
DECEIT GRIEVE RELIEF SORROW
CHARITY DEALING DESTINY
HANDOUT PAYMENT PORTION
BOUNDARY DIMENSUM DISPENSE
DIVISION GRATUITY LANDMARK
PITTANCE

DOLEFUL SAD DOWY DOWIE DREAR HEAVY DISMAL DOOLFU DREARY FUNEST RUEFUL FLEBILE DOLESOME DOLOROUS FUNESTAL MOURNFUL TRAGICAL

DOLL TOY BABE BABY MOLL ARRAY DOLLY PUPPE DOLLIE KEWPIE MAIDEN MAUMET MOPPET MUNECA POPPET POUPEE PUPPET KACHINA KATCINA KATCHINA MISTRESS
(— UP) SWANK
(PASTEBOARD —) PANTINE

DOLLAR BALL BEAN BONE BUCK CASE DURO FISH ROCK SCAD SKIN SPOT ADOBE BERRY DALER EAGLE PLONK PLUNK WHEEL GOURDE PATACA DAALDER SMACKER FROGSKIN PATACOON SIMOLEON
(SILVER —) SINKER
(SPANISH —) COB DURO COBBE
(THOUSAND —S) GEE THOU GRAND

DOLLARFISH SHINER MOONFISH STARFISH

DOLLY DRAB HOBBY PEGGY PUNCH SWAGE MAIDEN FOLLOWER MISTRESS SLATTERN

DOLLYMAN BUCKER

DOLLYWAY DOCK

DOLMEN SENAM TOLMEN CROMMEL CROMLECH MEGALITH

DOLOMITE ANKERITE PEARLSPAR

DOLOR CALOR GRIEF SORROW ANGUISH SADNESS DISTRESS MOURNING

DOLOROUS SAD DISMAL DOLEFUL GRIEVOUS PATHETIC

DOLPHIN INIA SUSU BOUTO WHALE DORADO KILLER PALACH TURSIO BOLLARD COWFISH PELLOCK PULLOCK SNUFFER CETACEAN MAHIMAHI MUTILATE PORPOISE

DOLT ASS OAF PUT ASSE CALF CHUB CLOD COOF DULT FOOL GOFF MOKE PEAK STUB CHUMP DOBBY DUMMY DUNCE FUNGE IDIOT NUMPS PATCH THICK BEFOOL CUDDEN DOODLE DULTIE HOBBIL OXHEAD BLUNTIE DAWCOCK DULLARD JACKASS SCHNOOK BONEHEAD BOSTHOON CLODPATE DUMBBELL IMBECILE LUNKHEAD MACAROON MOONCALF NUMSKULL

DOLTISH DULL STUPID FOOLISH PEAKISH SOTTISH TOMFOOL BESOTTED BLOCKISH DOLTLIKE

DOMAIN LAND BOUND BOURN REALM SCOPE STATE WORLD BARONY BOURNE COUNTY DEMAIN EMPERY EMPIRE ESTATE SPHERE DEMESNE EARLDOM BIRTHDOM DOMINION LORDSHIP PROVINCE SEIGNORY STAROSTY
(— OF SULTAN) SOLDAN
(— OF THE UNCONSCIOUS) SHADOWLAND
(MATHEMATICAL —) FIELD
(NETHER —) HELL
(TRANSCENDENT —) HEAVEN
(WOMAN'S —) DISTAFF

DOMBEYA ASSONIA

DOME CAP CIMA TYPE CROWN VAULT COCKLE CUPOLA THOLOS CALOTTE EDIFICE CIMBORIO HEMIDOME
(— OVER TOMB) WELI
(BUDDHIST —) TOPE
(OBSERVATION —) BLISTER
(SNOW-CAPPED —) CALOTTE

DOMER CLASPER

DOMESTIC HIND HOME MAID MOZO DOMAL TABBY FAMILY HAMEIL HAMELT HEYDUC HOMELY HOMISH HOUSAL INLAND INMATE INWARD MENIAL NATIVE FAMILIC HEYDUCK SCALDER SERVANT FAMILIAR HOMEBRED HOMEMADE INTIMATE
(PL.) FOLK

DOMESTICALLY ONSHORE

DOMESTICATE TAME ENTAME AMENAGE RECLAIM CIVILIZE

DOMESTICATED TAME GENTLE INWARD DOMESTIC FAMILIAR

DOMICILE CRIB HOME SHED ABODE HOUSE MENAGE DWELLING

DOMINANCE SWAY INFLUENCE

DOMINANT BOSSY CHIEF FIFTH TENOR RULING SOVRAN CENTRAL REGNANT SUPREME DOMINULE SUPERIOR

DOMINATE TOP HAVE RULE CHARM REIGN COERCE DIRECT GOVERN VASSAL BEWITCH COMMAND CONTROL ENVELOP BESTRIDE DOMINEER OVERSWAY OVERTONE

DOMINATING SUPERIOR BREATHLESS

DOMINATION EMPIRE CONTROL STRINGS BOVARISM BOVARYSM DOMINION

DOMINEER BOSS BRAG LORD RULE BULLY FEAST REVEL TOWER COMPEL COMMAND SWAGGER DOMINATE OVERBEAR OVERLEAD OVERLORD
(— OVER) RIDE HECTOR

DOMINEERING SURLY LORDLY HAUGHTY ARROGANT DESPOTIC MASTERLY

DOMINICAN JACOBIN JACOBITE PREACHER PREDICANT

DOMINICAN REPUBLIC
BAY: OCOA YUMA NEIBA RINCON SAMANA ISABELA CALDERAS ESCOCESA
CAPE: BEATA FALSO CABRON ENGANO CAUCEDO ISABELA MACORIS
CAPITAL: SANTODOMINGO
COIN: ORO PESO
INDIAN: TAINO
ISLAND: BEATA SAONA ALTOVELO CATALINA HISPANIOLA
LOWLAND: CIBAO
MEASURE: ONA TAREA FANEGA
MOUNTAIN: TINA GALLO DUARTE

MOUNTAINS: NEIBA BAHORUCO ORIENTAL
RIVER: YUNA OZAMA
TOWN: AZUA BANI MOCA PENA POLO BONAO COTUI NAGUA NEIBA NIZAO SOSUA HIGUEY OVIEDO SANCHEZ BARAHONA SANTIAGO
VALLEY: REAL NEYBA

DOMINIE MASTER PASTOR

DOMINION RULE SWAY CROWN REALM REIGN DITION DOMAIN EMPERY EMPIRE REGNUM CONTRO DIOCESE DYNASTY KHANATE POUSTIE REGENCY CALIFATE IMPERIUM LORDSHIP SEIGNORY SIGNORIA SOVRANTY
(PL.) DUCHY

DOMINO DIE BONE CARD FIVE MAS TILE BLANK JETON STONE DOUBL JETTON MATADOR VENETIAN
(FIRST — PLAYED) SET
(PL.) BONEYARD

DOM PEDRO SNOOZER

DON WEAR ARRAY DRESS ENDUE INDUE THROW ASSUME CLOTHE INVEST ADDRESS NOBLEMAN

DONATE GIE GIFT GIVE BESTOW PRESENT

DONATION GIFT GRANT DONATIO PRESENT DONATIVE
(—S RECEIVED BY SINGERS) CARI

DONE GAR DEEN OVER BAKED ENDED GIVEN COOKED THROUGH FINISHED
(— BY WORD OF MOUTH) PAROL PAROLE
(— CARELESSLY) SCAMBLING
(— FOR) GONE SUNK KAPUT KAPUTT FINISHED
(— IN FAITH) AF
(— IN PLAIN SIGHT) BRAZEN
(— POORLY) BOTCHY
(— TOGETHER) CONCERTED
(— WITH) BY
(— WITHOUT DELIBERATION) SNA
(— WRONG WAY) AWK
(TO BE —) PASS

DONEE DONATOR HERITOR RECEIVER

DONJON KEEP ROCCA DUNGEON

DONKEY ASS BUSS DONK FUSS MOKE BURRO CHUMP CUDDY DIC EQUID GENET GUDDA HINNY HOR JENNY NEDDY CUDDLE DICKEY JENNET ONAGER ASINEGO BUSSOCK FUSSOCK JACKASS LONGEAR

DONKEY ENGINE DOCTOR DONK ROADER YARDER DOLLBEER

DONOR GIVER DONATOR

DO-NOTHING DONNOT DONOUGH FAINEANT

DONUM GIVER DEUNAM

DOODAD DODAD DOODAB DOFUN GIMCRACK JIMCRACK

DOOM KER LAW LOT DAMN FATE

RUIN CURSE DEATH JUDGE DECREE DEVOTE STEVEN CONDEMN DESTINE DESTINY FORTUNE STATUTE DECISION FOREDOOM SENTENCE

DOOMED FEY DEAD DONE FATAL DAMNED FORLORN ACCURSED FINISHED

DOOM PALM DOUM

DOOMSMAN LAWMAN

DOOR LID DROP EXIT FOLD GATE HECK SHUT TRAP ENTRY HATCH JANUA VALVE JIGGER PORTAL RADDLE WICKET BARRIER DOORWAY INGRESS OPENING OUTDOOR PASSAGE POSTERN ANTEPORT ENTRANCE FOREDOOR POSTICUM SERVIDOR STOPPING TRAVERSE

(— IN MINE) STOPPING

(— OF ASH PIT) ARCH

(— OF MASONIC LODGE) TILE

(AIRPLANE —) CLAMSHELL

(HALF —) HECK HATCH

(ROMAN —S) FORES

(SLIDING —) SHUT SHOJI FUSUMA TRAVERSE

(STORM —) DINGLE

(STRONG —) OAK

(TRAP —) SLOT SCRUTE VAMPIRE VAMPYRE

DOORFRAME BUCK

DOORHEAD DERNER

DOORKEEPER TILER TILIA USHER DURWAN PORTER WARDEN DOORMAN JANITOR OSTIARY DOORWARD HUISSIER JANITRIX PORTRESS WISKINKY

DOOR KNOCKER HAMMER RAPPER

DOOR LATCH SNECK HAGGADAY

DOORMAN FOOTMAN HALLMAN DOORWARD

DOORMAT COCOMAT

DOORPOST DURN JAMB PIER POST ALETTE POSTEL

DOORSILL SOIL

DOORSTOP BUMPER HOLDBACK

DOORWAY DOOR EXIT PORTAL OPENING

DOPATTA UPARNA DOOPUTTY

DOPE HOP BOOB DRUG GOFF GOON GOOP BOOBY OPIUM PASTE HEROIN INSIDE OPIATE LOWDOWN PREDICT STUPEFY NARCOTIC

DOPER GREASER

DOR BEE DORR JOKE MOCK BONGO CLOCK DORRE JOKER SCOFF TRICK BEETLE DRONER BUFFOON DECEIVE MOCKERY

DORADO CUIR XIPHIAS GOLDFISH

DORBEETLE DOR CLOCK DRONER BUZZARD BUMCLOCK

DORIS (BROTHER AND HUSBAND OF —) NEREUS

(FATHER OF —) OCEANUS

(MOTHER OF —) TETHYS

DORMANCY TORPOR ABEYANCE

DORMANT FIXED ASLEEP LATENT TORPID RESTING SLEEPER INACTIVE SLEEPING CONNIVENT

DORMER WINDOW LUCOMB MEMBER DORMANT EYEBROW LUCARNE LUTHERN

DORMITORY DORM HALL HOUSE DORMER DORTER HOSTEL BULLPEN COLLEGE DORTOUR CUBATORY QUARTERS

DORMOUSE LOIR DRYAD LEROT GLIRID SLEEPER

DORNICK DONEY LINEN DARNEX DONACK DONNICK

DORPER DORSIAN

DORSAL NOTAL DORSER DOSSER TERGAL ABAXIAL HANGING SUPERIOR

DORSUM BACK

DOSAGE (SCIENCE OF —) POSOLOGY

DOSE BOLE DOST SHOT BROMO DATIO DOSIS DRAFT STORE TREAT DATION DOCTOR DOSAGE DRENCH POTION BOOSTER BROMIDE CAPSULE DRAUGHT QUANTITY

(NARCOTIC —) LOCUS BINDLE LOCUST

DOSS BOW DOS KNOT TUFT BUNCH

DOSSERET PULVINO

DOT SET CLOT DOTE LUMP MOTE PECK SPOT STAR TICK COVER DOWER DOWRY POINT PRICK SPECK BULLET CENTER CENTRE DOTLET PERIOD STIGME TITTLE TOCHER PUNCTUM PUNCTUS SPECKLE SPOTTLE STIPPLE FLYSPECK PARTICLE SPRINKLE

(— IN CODE) DIT

(— ON FOREHEAD) BOTTU

(— ON PATCH OF DIFFERENT COLOR) ISLET

(BLACK —) DARTROSE

(PL.) LEADERS

DOTAGE DOTE FOLLY DRIVEL SENILITY TWICHILD

DOTARD DOTER SILLY DOTANT SENILE DOTTREL DOTTEREL IMBECILE LIRIPIPE LIRIPOOP

DOTCHIN STEELYARD

DOTE ROT DOVE DOZE FOND LIKE LOVE ADORE DECAY ENDOW BESTOW DOTAGE DOTARD DRIVEL STUPOR IMBECILE

DOTING FON FOND GAGA DOTAGE PAWING

DOTTED SEME SEMEED TICKED TOUCHY SPOTTED PUNCTATE SPECKLED STIPPLED STELLATED

(— SWISS) LAPPET

DOTTER SPOTTER

DOTTEREL DUPE GULL WIND PLOVER DOTTREL MORINEL

DOTTY TOTY CRAZY TOTTY FEEBLE SPOTTY

DOUBLE KA BOW PLY DUAL FOLD SORE TWIN CRACK DUPLE FETCH ROUND SOSIE BIFOLD BINARY BINATE DIPLO DUPLEX MIDDLE DIPLOID DOUBLET TWOFOLD BIVALENT GEMINATE

(— IMPRESSION) MACKLE

(— IN POKER) STRADDLE

(— MUSICAL NOTES) AUGMENT

(— UP) BUCK JACKKNIFE

(PHANTOM —) FETCH

DOUBLE BASSOON FAGOTTONE

DOUBLE CHIN CHOLLER

DOUBLECROSS BITCH CHEAT BETRAY DECEIVE SWINDLE BUSINESS

DOUBLE-CROSSER RAT HEEL

DOUBLED GEMEL GEMINOUS

DOUBLE DAGGER DIESIS

DOUBLE-DEALING DECEIT DUPLICITY

DOUBLE FLUTE DIAULOS

DOUBLENESS DUALITY PLENITUDE

DOUBLE-RIPPER BOBSLED BOBSLEIGH

DOUBLE-RUNNER SKATE

DOUBLET SNIFF DOUBLE DUPLET PALTOCK PLACCATE POURPOINT

DOUBLETREE EVENER SPREADER

DOUBLING LAP FOLD HEAD LOOP

(— OF THE BLIND) STRADDLE

DOUBLOON ONZA

DOUBT FEAR WEIR DEMUR DREAD DWERE QUERY WAVER BALANCE DIFFIDE DUBIATE DUBIETY SCRUPLE SKEPSIS SUSPECT SWITHER UMBRAGE DISTRUST DUBITATE HESITATE MISTRUST QUESTION STAGGERS MISLIPPEN

DOUBTER CYNIC SKEPTIC DUBITANTE

DOUBTFUL JUBUS DOUBTY UNSURE DUBIOUS FEARFUL JEALOUS PERHAPS WILSOME BOGGLISH DREADFUL JUBEROUS PERILOUS WAVERING

DOUBTING DUBIOUS DUBITANT

DOUBTLESS WITTERLY

DOUCEUR BONUS POURBOIRE

DOUCHE RINSE EYEWASH

DOUGH CASH DUFF CRUST DAIGH MONEY PASTE PUPPY CHANGE HALLAH NOODLE SPONGE BRIOCHE MANDLEN TEIGLACH

(BISCUIT —) CAKE

(BREAD —) SPONGE

(FERMENTING —) LEAVEN

(FRIED —) SPUD

(NOODLE —) FARFEL FERFEL

DOUGHNUT NUT SINK DONUT CYMBAL SINKER CRULLER FATCAKE NUTCAKE OLYCOOK OLYKOEK SIMBALL TWISTER BISMARCK FASNACHT

(SHAPED LIKE —) TOROIDAL

DOUGHTY FELL PREU TALL BRAVE VALIANT INTREPID

DOUGHY DUNCH SODDEN

DOUR DERN GLUM GRIM HARD SOUR ROUGH STERN GLOOMY MOROSE SEVERE STRONG SULLEN OMINOUS TACITURN

DOUSE BEAT BLOW DOFF DUCK QUIT STOW CEASE DOWSE RINSE SOUSE DRENCH PLUNGE SLUICE

STRIKE STROKE IMMERSE DOWNPOUR

DOUZEPER ANSEIS PALADIN

DOVE DOO DOW DOZE KUKU JONAH CULVER CUSHAT JEMIMA PIGEON COLUMBA DOVELET LAUGHER NAMAQUA SLUMBER DOVELING RINGDOVE
(— **SOUND**) CURR
(**GROUND** —) ROLA
(**RING** —) TOOZOO
(**ROCK** —) SOD
(**SCALE** —) INCA

DOVECOTE DOOCOT LOUVER DOVECOT DOWCOTE PIGEONRY

DOVEKIE AUK ALLE BULL ROTCH ROTGE DOVEKEY BULLBIRD DOVELIKE

DOVETAIL COG JAG JAGG TENON

DOWDINESS FRUMPERY

DOWDY POKY FRUMP POKEY TACKY BLOWZY SHABBY STODGY UNTIDY FRUMPISH SLOVENLY

DOWEL PEG PIN COAK STUD SPRIG JOGGLE PINTLE DULEDGE

DOWER DOS DOWRY ENDOW TOCHER DOARIUM PORTION HERITAGE MARITAGE

DOWITCHER SNIPE DRIVER SLEEPER GRAYBACK GREYBACK LONGBEAK

DOWN HUP BETE CAST DOON DOWL FELL FLIX FLUE FUZZ HILL LINT SOUR ADOWN BELOW DOWLE EIDER FLOOR FLUFF BEDOWN FRIEZE LANUGO PAPPUS HANDOUT HILLOCK PLUMAGE DOWNLAND
(— **AND OUT**) QUISBY
(— **AT THE HEEL**) SLIPSHOD
(— **THAT WAY**) DOWNBY DOWNBYE
(— **THE LINE**) ALONG
(**FAR** —) DEEP DEEPLY
(**FARTHEST** —) BOTTOMMOST
(**STRAIGHT** —) DOWNRIGHT

DOWNBEAT THESIS

DOWNCAST BAD SAD DOWN ABJECT GLOOMY HANGING DEJECTED HOPELESS

DOWNFALL PIT FALL FATE RUIN TRAP ABYSS FINISH DESCENT ECLIPSE UNDOING COLLAPSE DOWNCOME

DOWNFEED OVERHEAD

DOWNFLOW VAIL DEFLUX

DOWNFOLD SADDLE DOWNWARP

DOWNHILL DOWNDALE

DOWNPOUR POUR RAIN DOUSE DOWSE FLOOD SPILL SPOUT DELUGE TORRENT CATARACT

DOWNRIGHT FAIR FLAT PURE RANK BLANK BLUNT PLAIN PLUMB ROUND SHEER STARK ARRANT DIRECT FAIRLY STURDY ABSOLUTE EVENDOWN POSITIVE THOROUGH

DOWNSPOUT SPOUT DOWNPIPE DOWNTAKE

DOWNSTAIRS BELOW

DOWNSTROKE DOWNBEAT

DOWNSWING DOLDRUMS

DOWNWARD ADOWN BELOW LOWER

PRONE DEORSUM DOWNWITH
(— **ON ONE SIDE**) SIDEWAYS

DOWNWIND LEEWARD

DOWNY SOFT FLUEY MOSSY NAPPY PILAR PLUMY QUIET CALLOW FLEDGY FLOSSY FLUFFY PILARY PLACID COTTONY CUNNING KNOWING SOOTHING

DOWRY DOS DOT GIFT DOWER SULKA DOWAGE TALENT PORTION

DOWSE WITCH

DOXOLOGY GLORIA KADDISH

DOXY WENCH HARLOT

DOYEN DEAN DOYENNE

DOZE NAP NOD ROT DORM DOTE DOVE DECAY DOVER SLEEP SLOOM CATNAP DROWSE MUDDLE SNOOZE MEMENTO PERPLEX SLUMBER SNOOZLE STUPEFY

DOZEN DIZZEN DOSAIN
(**FIVE** —) TALLY
(**TWO** —) THRAVE

DOZING DOGSLEEP

DRAB BOX DAW FOX SAD DELL DRUG DULL BESOM BLEAK DINGY DOLLY GRAVE GRAZE HEAVY WENCH WHORE FRUMPY MALKIN POISON STODGY PROSAIC SUBFUSC DOLLYMOP EVERYDAY POMPLESS
(**CHAETURA** —) BEAR

DRABBLE DRAGGLE

DRACHM DRAM

DRACO ANGUIS DRAGON

DRAFT NIP SIP CHIT DOSE DRAG DRAM DRAW GLUT GULF GUST ITEM LEVY PLAN PLOT SUCK SWIG TOOT WORK BLAST CHECK DRINK EPURE SLOCK SWILL SWIPE TAPER WRITE DESIGN DRENCH GODOWN MINUTE POTION REDACT RETURN SCHEME SCROLL SKETCH WAUCHT WAUGHT ABBOZZO DRAUGHT DRAWING OUTLINE PATTERN PROJECT BEVERAGE POTATION PROTOCOL
(— **OF A VESSEL**) GAGE GAUGE
(— **OF AIR**) COOKE
(— **OF COMPOSITION**) SCORE
(— **OF LAW**) BILL
(— **OF PATTERN**) STRIP
(— **OFF**) SHED
(**HEAVY** —) WHITTER
(**LARGE** —) SCOUR CAROUSE
(**MIDDAY** —) NOONING
(**ORIGINAL** —) PROTOCOL
(**ROUGH** —) BROUILLON SCANTLING
(**SLEEPING** —) DORTER
(**SMALL** —) NIP SIP SUCK TIFF TIFT

DRAFTER HORSER

DRAFTSMAN DRAWER TRACER TIPPLER

DRAG DOG LAG DRUG HONE HOOK KITE SHOE SKID SLUR TOLE TOLL CREEP DEVIL DRAWL DRIFT FLOAT LURRY NOWEL PLUCK RALLY SLIDE SNAKE SWEEP TEASE TRAIL TRAIN TRAWL TRICE DAGGLE DROGUE LINGER REMORA SCHOOL TAIGLE TRAYNE DRAGBAR DRAGGLE GRAPNEL GRAPPLE SCHLEPP

SKIDPAN ARRASTRA DRAGSHOE
(— **ALONG**) LUG CRAWL SHOOL TRAYNE TRACHLE TRAUCHLE
(— **CARELESSLY**) HIKE
(— **DOWN**) DEGRADE
(— **FEET**) SLODGE
(— **FORCIBLY**) SNAKE
(— **HOME CARCASS OF GAME**) TUMP
(— **IN DEEP WATER**) CREEP
(— **JERKILY**) SNIG
(— **LOGS**) SKID
(— **OFF**) HARRY
(— **OUT**) DRAWL
(**PLANK** —) RUBBER

DRAGGING LEADEN
(— **DEAD BULL FROM RING**) ARRASTRE

DRAGGLE LAG DRAIL DAGGLE DRABBLE

DRAGNET FLUE TRAIN TRAWL DRAWNET TRAINEL

DRAGON AHI LUNG WORM DRAKE RAHAB NIDHOG VRITRA WYVERN BASILISK DRAGONET NIDHOGGR NITHHOGG
(— **WITH 7 HEADS**) HYDRA
(**SEA** —) QUAVIVER

DRAGONET FOX ILLECK FOXFISH GOWDNIE GURNARD JUGULAR SCULPIN LORICATE QUAVIVER

DRAGONFLY NAIAD SKIMMER LIBELLULA

DRAGON TREE DRACAENA

DRAGROPE DRAG GUSS

DRAIN DRY FRY GAN GAW SAP SEW TOP BUZZ COUP DAIL DALE DELF DIKE DRAG DRAW GOUT GRIP GURT LADE LODE MILK SIKE SINK SOAK SUFF SUMP TEEM TILE BLEED BUNNY CANAL DELFT DRAFT DREEN DRILL DROVE EMPTY FLEET GROOP GULLY LEECH RHINE SEUCH SEUGH SEWER SHORE SIVER STELL EMULGE FILTER FURROW GUZZLE RIGGOT SHEUCH SHEUGH SIPHON SPONGE SWOUGH SYPHON TRENCH TROGUE TROUGH ZANJON ACEQUIA ALBERCA CAROUSE CARRIER CHANNEL CULVERT DEPLETE DRAUGHT EXHAUST GRINDLE GRIPPLE SCUPPER ZANJONA CANALIZE CARRIAGE SINKHOLE SUBDRAIN THURROCK
(— **DRY**) JIB
(— **IN FEN**) LEAM
(— **IN MINE**) SOUGH
(— **IN STABLE**) GROOP
(**COVERED** —) THURROCK
(**OPEN** —) SIVER STELL
(**SMALL** —) TRONE

DRAINAGE ADIT SAUR SOCK SULLAGE SUMPAGE

DRAINAGEWAY DRAW

DRAINING SEEPAGE DRAINAGE EMULGENT

DRAINPIPE SINK SHELL WHELM LEADER QUELME

DRAKE STAG STAIG DRAKELET

191 DRAM • DREGS

DRAM GO NIP MITE SLUG TIFT DRAFT DRINK SOPIE CALKER DRACHM JIGGER CAULKER SNIFTER MERIDIAN POTATION QUANTITY
(— OF LIQUOR) TOT SLUG SNIFTER
(— OF SPIRITS) NOBBLER
DRAMA RAS AUTO MIME PLAY LEGIT OPERA COMEDY NATAKA SCENES SOAPER TRAGIC ATELLAN COMEDIA HISTORY PROVERB THEATRE TRAGEDY DUODRAMA MONODRAM OPERETTA PASTORAL
(DANCE —) KATHAKALI
(JAPANESE —) NO KABUKI
(MUSICAL —) OPERA SAYNETE OPERETTA
DRAMATIC WILD VIVID SCENIC THESPIAN
(— REPRESENTATION) WAYANG
DRAMATIST OG ACTOR IBSENITE
DRAMSHOP GROGSHOP
DRAPE HANG ADORN COVER CRAPE WEAVE CURTAIN FESTOON HANGING VALANCE
DRAPED BEHUNG
DRAPER TAILOR LINENMAN
DRAPERY SWAG BAIZE DRAPE SCENE CURTAIN REREDOS VALANCE MOURNING
(— ON BEDSTEAD) PAND
(PIECE OF —) HANGING
DRAPING BLOUSE DRAPERY
DRASTIC DIRE HARSH EXTREME RADICAL RIGOROUS
(NOT —) BLAND
DRAT RABBIT DOGGONE
DRATTED BLESSED
DRAUGHT (ALSO SEE DRAFT) SLUG OENOMEL
DRAVIDIAN GOND KOTA TODA TULU ARAVA COORG GONDI KHOND KLING MALTO ORAON TAMIL ANDHRA BADAGA BIRHOR BRAHUI KODAGU KURUKH TELEGU TELUGU COLLERY DRAVIDA TAMILIC KANARESE TAMILIAN
DRAW LUG TEE TIE TOW TUG DRAG DUCT HALE HAUL LADE LIMN LINE LURE PULL RAKE SPAN TILL TIRE TOLL TREK VENT CATCH DRAFT DRILL EDUCE ENDUE EXACT HEAVE PAINT SKINK TRACE TRAIN TRECK ALLURE BUCKET DEDUCE DEPICT DERIVE DESIGN DEVISE ELICIT ENGAGE ENTICE INDUCE INHALE SELECT SKETCH STRIKE ATTRACT BEGUILE CONTOUR DETRACT DOGFALL DRAUGHT EXTRACT INSPIRE PORTRAY SCUMBLE INSCRIBE INVEIGLE OUTBRAID STANDOFF
(— A CARD) CUT
(— AIR) BREATHE
(— ALONG) TRACK TRAIN
(— APART) REAM DIVEL DIDUCE DIVERGE
(— AT A PIPE) SHOOH SHAUGH
(— AWAY) ARACE DRAFT ABDUCT ARACHE DRAUGHT ENTRAIN

DISTRACT
(— AWKWARDLY) SCRAWL
(— BACK FROM) BLENCH FLINCH TORFEL TORFLE DETRECT
(— BACK LIPS) GRIN
(— BACK) FADE REVEL START WINCE ARREAR RETIRE REVOKE SHRINK CRINKLE RECLAIM WITHTEE
(— BOLT) SLOT
(— BY SUCTION) ASPIRATE
(— DEEP BREATH) SUSPIRE
(— DRINK) BIRL
(— EARTH AROUND) HILL
(— FORTH) EDUCE FETCH ELICIT DEPROME EXHAUST
(— ON) INDUE INDUCE SOLICIT
(— OUT) MILK SLUB EXACT SKINK TRACT ELICIT EXHALE EXTEND PRODUCE PROLONG LENGTHEN
(— TIGHT) FRAP THRAP STRAIN
(— TOGETHER) COWL LACE COART GATHER
(— UP) FORM MAKE HUCKLE INKNIT UPHALE
DRAWBACK OUT LETDOWN TAKEOFF DISCOUNT PULLBACK
DRAWBAR DRAGBAR BULLNOSE DRAWLINK SLIPRAIL
DRAWBRIDGE PONTLEVIS
DRAWEE ACCEPTER
DRAWER TILL LIMNER LOCKER TILLER ENTERER INTAKER SHUTTLE
(— OF WATER) GIBEONITE
(COAL —) PUTTER
(TYPEWRITER —) BED
DRAWER-DOWN KNOBBLER
DRAWER-IN ENTERER HEALDER HEDDLER
DRAWER-OFF RACKER
DRAWERS PANTS SHORTS LININGS PANTIES SHALWAR CALSOUNS CALZOONS SHINTYAN SHULWAURS
DRAWGATE SLACKER
DRAWING DRAW CHALK DRAFT ENVOI EPURE SEPTA TUSHE CRAYON DESIGN DETAIL FIGURE FUSAIN SKETCH CARTOON CROQUIS DIAGRAM DRAUGHT HAULING ISOTYPE PULLING TOUSCHE CHARCOAL CROSSING DOODLING FREEHAND FROTTAGE HATCHING LINEWORK SANGUINE SPECULUM STICKMAN TRACTION TRANSFER TRICKING
(— IN) INDRAFT
(— OF LOTS) BALLOT
(— OUT) BATTUE
(COMIC —) CARTOON DROLLERY
(SIDEWALK —) SCREEVE
DRAWING-IN DRAW ENTERING
DRAWKNIFE SHAVE JIGGER
DRAWL DRANT DRATE DRUNT TRAIN LOITER PROLATE
DRAWN DRAFT STREIT DRAUGHT GRAPHIC HAGGARD
(— APART) DISTRACT
(— AWAY) ABSTRACT
(— CLOSE) STRICT
(— OFF) DRAINED

(— OUT) DREE DREICH DREIGH EXTENDED
DRAWPLATE AGATE FLATTER
DRAWSHEET TYMPAN
DRAWSTRING LATCH STRING
DRAY CART LORRY SCOOT SLOOP WAGON CAMION JIGGER SLOVEN WHEERY
DREAD AWE DREE FEAR FRAY FUNK WARD WERE ANGST AWFUL DOUBT GRISE TIMOR ADREAD AGRISE DISMAY ESCHEW HORROR TERROR ANXIETY DISMISS DRIDDER REDOUBT AFFRIGHT DREDDOUR GASTNESS MISDREAD TERRIBLE
DREADED AWESOME BEDREAD
DREADFUL DIRE AWFUL CRUEL DISMAL GRISLY HORRID AWESOME CAREFUL DIREFUL DRIDDER FEARFUL GHASTLY GRIMFUL HIDEOUS UNCOUTH DOUBTFUL DOUBTOUS GHASTFUL HORRIBLE HORRIFIC PERILOUS SCAREFUL SHOCKING TERRIBLE TERRIFIC
DREADFULLY DIRELY GRISLY ABYSMALLY
DREADNOUGHT TANK DAREALL WARSHIP FEARLESS
DREAM METE MOON MUSE REVE FANCY SWEVEN VISION AISLING AVISION CHIMERA FANTASY IMAGINE NIRVANA REVERIE ROMANCE CHIMAERA DAYDREAM PHANTASM SOMNIATE
DREAMER POET METER MUSARD FANTAST IDEALIST PHANTAST
DREAMINESS LANGUOR
DREAMING ADREAM TRAUMEREI
DREAMTIME ALCHERA
DREAMY KEF SOFT MOONY VAGUE POETIC FARAWAY LANGUID ONEIRIC PENSIVE DREAMFUL FANCIFUL SOOTHING
DREAR DERN DISMAL GLOOMY DOLEFUL
DREARY SAD DIRE DOWY DREE DULL FLAT GLUM BLEAK CRUEL DOWIE DRURY OURIE WASTE WISHT DISMAL ELENGE GLOOMY GOUSTY LONELY DOLEFUL GOUSTIE HOWLING WILSOME GRIEVOUS WEARIFUL
DREDGE MOP DRAG DREG SIFT SCOOP TRAIN DEEPEN DRUDGE SCRAPE SPONGE GANGAVA SCALLOP EXCAVATE SPRINKLE
DREDGER DUSTER HEDGEHOG
DREDGING JILLING
DREGS LAG MUD CRAP FAEX LAGS LEES SCUT SILT SUDS TAIL DRAFF DREST DROSS DRUGS FECES FOOTS GROUT JAUPS MAGMA BOTTOM DRAINS DUNDER MOTHER REFUSE SORDES SORDOR ULLAGE DRIBBLE GROUNDS GRUMMEL HEELTAP OUTWALE RESIDUE RINSING GRUMMELS REMNANTS SEDIMENT SETTLING
(— OF LIQUOR) TAPLASH

(— OF MOLTEN GLASS) DRIBBLE
(— OF SOCIETY) WASH
DREIBUND TRIPLICE
DREIDEL TRENDEL
DRENCH DOSE HOSE SIND SINK
SOAK TOSH BLASH DOUSE DOWSE
DRAFT DRINK DROKE DROUK
DROWN SLOCK SLUSH SOUSE
STEEP SWILL BUCKET DELUGE
DOUCHE IMBRUE INFUSE POTION
SLUICE DRUNKEN EMBATHE
IMMERSE INDRENCH PERMEATE
SATURATE SUBMERGE
DRENCHED DRUNKEN
DRENCHER INFUSER
DRENCHING DOUSE DOWSE
DOWNPOUR
DRESS AX AXE BED DON DUB FIG
FIT HOE KIT RAG RAY RIG TOG
BARB BEGO BOWN BUSK BUSS
CLAY COAT COMB DESK DILL DINK
GALA GARB GEAR GORE GOWN
HONE HUKE KNAP MILL RAIL ROBE
SUIT TIFF TIRE TRIM TUBE TUCK
VEST WEAR ADORN ARRAY BIGAN
CLEAN CLOTH CRUMB CRUSH
CURRY DIGHT DIZEN EQUIP FLOAT
FROCK GUISE HABIT IHRAM MAGMA
PREEN PRICK PRIMP PRINK PRUNE
SHAPE THING TRICK AGUISE ATTIRE
BARBER BROACH CLOTHE ENROBE
FANGLE FETTLE FRAISE GRAITH
INVEST JELICK JUMPER KIRTLE
MAGPIE MULLET MUUMUU OUTFIT
PLIGHT REVEST SARONG SHEATH
SHROUD TOILET ADDRESS AFFAITE
APPAREL BANDAGE BEDIZEN
CHEMISE CLOTHES COSTUME
DALLACK DUBBING GARMENT
GARNISH HARNESS HATCHEL
RAIMENT TOGGERY VESTURE
ACCOUTER CLEADING CLOTHING
DECORATE FEATHERS HANDMADE
ORNAMENT SUNDRESS TAILLEUR
VESTMENT EMBELLISH
(— A SKIN) WHEEL
(— DOWN) BRACE
(— ELEGANTLY) DINK
(— FISH) CALVER
(— FLAX) TED
(— FLINT) NAP KNAP
(— FOOD) SAUCE
(— FOR FELTING) CARROT
(— HAIR) TIRE TRUSS BARBER
(— HIDES) BEAM
(— HURRIEDLY) HUDDLE
(— IN FINE CLOTHES) DIKE
(— MEAT) LARD SHROUD
(— NEGLIGENTLY) MOB
(— ORE) VAN
(— OVER) STOP
(— SHEEPSKINS) TAW
(— SMARTLY) DALLACK
(— STONE) DAB NIG DAUB DRAG
FACE GAGE HACK GAUGE NIDGE
POINT SCABBLE SCAPPLE
(— TAWDRILY) BEDIZEN
(— UNTIDILY) MAB
(— UP) BUSK DILL ADORN ARRAY

PRANK PRIMP PRINK SPICK WATER
FETTLE TOGGLE BECLOUT BEDRESS
(— VULGARLY) DAUB
(— WITH CHISEL) DROVE
(— WITH TROWEL) STRIKE
(— WORN BY MAN) DRAG
(— WOUND) PANSE BANDAGE
(COAT —) SIMAR SYMAR SIMARRE
(EVENING —) FORMAL
(FESTIVE —) GALA
(INCOMPLETE —) DISARRAY
(LOOSE —) SACK SACQUE
(MORNING —) PEIGNOIR
(PECULIAR —) LIVERY
(POPLIN —) TABINET TABBINET
(RUSSIAN NATIONAL —) SARAFAN
(STYLE OF —) GETUP
DRESSED CLAD DONE BOUND
BECLAD COATED COMBED HABITED
GOFFERED
(— GAILY) FRESH SPARKISH
(— IN WHITE) CANDIDATE
(LOOSELY —) DISCINCT
(RICHLY —) BROCADED
(ROUGHLY —) HEWN
(SHOWILY —) BEPRANKED
(STYLISHLY —) SMART
(WELL —) BRAW GASH
DRESSER ROBER TAWER BUREAU
FRAMER MODISTE CUPBOARD
(LEATHER —) LEVANTER
DRESSING CAST GRAVY BEATING
BLANKET IODOFORM RAVIGOTE
REMOLADE SCOLDING STUFFING
(— FOR WOUNDS) LINT SPONGE
(— OF STONE) SKIFFLING
(HAIR —) LACKER LACQUER
DRESSING ROOM SHIFT VESTRY
CAMARIN VESTUARY
DRESSMAKER SEWER SEAMER
MODISTE STITCHER COUTURIER
TIREWOMAN
DRESS RACK FRIPPERY
DRESSY SHARP
DRIBBLE DRIB DRIP DROP CARRY
DRIVEL DRIBLET DRIPPLE DRIZZLE
DRIBLET CLOT PIECE
(PL.) SMALLS
DRIED SEAR SERE ADUST GIZZEN
TORRID WIZENED GIZZENED
DRIFT FAN JET SAG DENE DUNE
FORD HERD PLOT SILT TIDE TILL
DRIVE DROVE FLEET FLOAT FLOCK
IOWAN SENSE SLIDE SLOOM SLOUM
TENOR TREND BROACH COURSE
DESIGN DEVICE DRIVER OFFSET
PODGER SCHEME STREAM TUNNEL
WINDLE CURRENT DIPHEAD DRIBBLE
GALLERY HEADING IMPETUS
IMPULSE LATERAL OUTWASH
PASTURE PROCESS PURPORT
SETBOLT DILUVIUM DRIFTPIN
TENDENCY
(— LANGUIDLY) SWOON
(— OF CLOUDS) CARRY
(— OF SAND OR SNOW) WREATH
(— SIDEWISE) CRAB
(— WITH ANCHOR DOWN) CLUB
(DOWNWARD —) DROOP

(GLACIAL —) CARY TILL IOWAN
(RUBBLE —) HEAD
DRIFTER DROVER
DRIFTING ADRIFT DRIFTAGE
DRIFT PLUG DUMMY
DRIFTWAY DROVE
DRIFTWOOD WAFTURE
DRILL GAD JAR JIG RIG SOW TAP
BORE CORE SPUD AUGER BORER
CHARK CHURN DECOY DREEL
PADDY THIRL TRAIN TUTOR TWIRL
WHIRL ALLURE BROACH ENTICE
FURROW JUMPER PIERCE SCHOOL
SEEDER SINKER STOPER THRILL
CHANNEL DRIFTER JANKERS
PLUGGER STARTER EXERCISE
INSTRUCT
(— SYSTEM) MARTINET
DRILLMAN STOPER
DRINK GO ADE ALE BIB BUM FIX GIN
HUM LAP MOP PEG POT RUM RYE
SIP SUP TEA TOT WET BALL BEER
BEND BENO BOLL BOSA BOZA
BREW BULL CHIA COKE COLA DRAG
DRAM FIZZ FLIP GROG HAVE HORN
JAKE LUSH MEAD NIPA NOGG PULL
PURL SHOT SIND SLUG SOAK SOMA
SOPE SPOT SWIG TIFF TOOT TOPE
WHET AIRAH BEVER BLAND BOMBO
BOOZE BOUSE BOZAH BUBUD
BUMBO CRUSH DAISY DRAFT FLOAT
GLOGG HAOMA JULEP LAGER
MORAT NEGUS PAINT POSCA PUNCH
QUAFF ROUSE SETUP SKINK SLING
SLOCK SMACH SMASH SMILE
SMOKE SNIFF SNORT SOPIE SOUSE
SWATS SWILL THING TOAST TODDY
VODKA WHIFF ZOMBI ABSORB
BEZZLE BRACER BRANDY BUMPER
CALKER CASIRI CATLAP CAUDLE
CHASER COFFEE COOPER DIBBLE
DRENCH EGGHOT EGGNOG FUDDLE
GIMLET GODOWN GUGGLE GUZZLE
HOOKER IMBIBE MESCAL POSSET
POTION PTISAN RICKEY SCREED
SHANDY SIPPLE SIRPLE SWANKY
SWINGE TACKLE TAMPOY TASTER
TIPPLE VELVET WAUCHT WAUGHT
ZOMBIE BRAGGET BRIMMER
CAROUSE CHEERER CHIRPER
COBBLER COLLINS CONSUME
CORDIAL DILUENT DRAUGHT
EXHAUST FLANNEL GUARANA
GUARAPO MORNING NOONING
PROPOMA SHERBET SIDECAR
SNEEZER SNIFTER SUCTION
SUPPAGE SWALLOW TANKARD
TRILLIL APERITIF BEVERAGE
BRIDECUP COCKTAIL HIGHBALL
LIBATION MAHOGANY POTATION
QUENCHER REFRESCO RUMBARGE
SANGAREE SPRITZER SYLLABUB
TEQUILA
(— AT DRAFT) TOP
(— EXCESSIVELY) TOPE BIBLE
SOUSE BEZZLE BIBBLE SWIZZLE
(— FROM FERMENTED MILK) AIRAN
(— GREEDILY) SLOP SWACK SWILL
GUTTLE GUZZLE

(— **HEAVILY**) TOOT SWINK
(— **INTOXICATING LIQUOR**) IRRIGATE
(— **LIQUOR**) TIP DRAM SOAK BOOZE PAINT
(— **NOISILY**) SLURP
(— **OF BEER**) BUTCHER
(— **OF IMMORTALITY**) SOMA
(— **OF INDIA**) SOMA SHRAB
(— **OF LIQUEUR**) FRAPPE
(— **OF LIQUOR**) WET DRAM SHOT SPOT WHET SETUP WHIFF CALKER JIGGER TASTER WETTING HIGHBALL NIGHTCAP
(— **OF MOLASSES**) SWITCHEL
(— **OF THE GODS**) NECTAR
(— **OF VINEGAR AND WATER**) POSCA
(— **OFF**) COUP
(— **SOCIALLY**) BIRL HOBNOB
(— **SPARINGLY**) BLEB
(— **TO LAST DROP**) BUZZ
(— **UP**) CRUSH EPOTE CAROUSE EXHAUST
(**ADDITIONAL** —) EIK EKE
(**ALCOHOLIC** —) BENO BINO NIPA BOMBO BUDGE BUMBO DRAIN JOUGH SHRAB SLING SNORT SNIFTER
(**BRAZILIAN** —) ASSAI ASSAHY
(**BUTTERMILK AND WATER** —) BLAND
(**DRUGGED** —) HOCUS
(**FARINACEOUS** —) PTISAN
(**FERMENTED** —) BOSA MEAD BALCHE MUSHLA CASSIRI GUARAPO
(**FREE** —) SHOUT
(**HALF-SIZED** —) CHOTAPEG
(**HEADY** —) HUFFCAP
(**HOT** —) COPUS SALOP TODDY BISHOP EGGHOT PLOTTY SALOOP CARDINAL
(**INCLINED TO** —) OUTWARD
(**INSIPID** —) SLUM
(**INTOXICATING** —) GROG SUCK BOOZE KUMISS SCOTCH DRAPPIE PAIWARI SWIZZLE SKOKIAAN
(**INTOXICATING** —S) SAUCE BOTTLE
(**LONG** —) SWIPE HIGHBALL
(**MEAN** —) LAP
(**MIDDAY** —) NOONING MERIDIAN
(**NON-ALCOHOLIC** —) GAZOZ COOLER
(**PARTING** —) BONAILIE
(**POISONOUS** —) DRENCH
(**RUSSIAN** —) OBARNE OBARNI
(**SACRED** —) HOMA AMRIT HAOMA AMRITA
(**SACRIFICIAL** —) HOMA SOMA
(**SMALL** —) PEG DRAM SOPIE DALLOP WETTING
(**STRONG** —) BUB HUM BENO SICER FUDDLE
(**TASTELESS** —) SLOP
(**THIN** —) SLOSH
(**WEAK** —) LAP BOOL BULL CATLAP
DRINKER SOT TANK POTER TOAST TOPER BARFLY BENDER CUPMAN LUSHER SOAKER SPONGE IMBIBER

INTAKER QUAFFER DRUNKARD
(**EXCESSIVE** — **OF TEA**) THEIC
(**WATER** —) HYDROPOT
DRINKING BEVER DRAFT DRINKY GUZZLE DRAUGHT POTTING CAROUSAL POTATION
DRIP LIP SIE SYE DROP LEAK SEGE SILE WEEP CANAL DRILL EAVES LABEL STILL DRIBBLE DRIPPLE LARMIER TRICKLE TRINKLE TRINTLE
(— **WITH TINKLING SOUND**) PINK
DRIPPING ADRIP STAXIS WEEPING
DRIPSTONE BAT DING LABEL HOODMOLD
DRIVE CA CAW COT FOG JOG AUTO BANG BEAR BEAT BUTT CALL CRAM DING DRUB DRUM FIRE FIRK FLOG GOAD HACK HERD HUNT HURL JASM JEHU KICK LASH PICK PILE POSS PUSH RIDE SEND SERR SINK SLOG SPUR STAB STUB TOOL TOUR TURN URGE BRAWL CHASE CHECK COACT CROWD DRIFT DROVE FEEZE FLAIL FORCE HORSE HURRY IMPEL INFER LODGE POACH PRESS PULSE PUNCH REPEL ROUST SHOVE SLASH SMITE SPANK SWEEP TEASE ATTACK BATTER BEETLE BENSEL CHARGE COMPEL CUDGEL DEDUCE DERIVE FERRET HAMMER HASTEN IMPACT JARVEY JOSTLE PLUNGE PROPEL BLUSTER ENFORCE IMPULSE OVERTAX SETDOWN TRAVAIL CATAPULT CONATION SHEPHERD TENDENCY
(— **A BALL**) LACE SEND
(— **A HORSE ONWARD**) WHIG
(— **AIR**) BLOW
(— **ANIMALS**) HAZE
(— **AT TOP SPEED**) CAREER
(— **AWAY**) RID FIRK HUSH SHOO BANDY EXILE FEEZE FLEME REPEL SMOKE SWEEP AROINT BANISH DEFEND DISPEL ENCHASE DISPLACE EXORCISE
(— **BACK AND FORTH**) TENNIS
(— **BACK**) RUSH REBUT REPEL CULBUT DEFEND REBATE REBUFF RETUND REPULSE REFRINGE
(— **BEFORE STRONG WIND**) SPOON
(— **BRISKLY**) JUNE
(— **CRAZY**) BUG
(— **DISTRACTED**) BEDEVIL
(— **FORTH**) ISH
(— **HARD**) SWEAT HACKNEY
(— **HURRIEDLY**) BUM BUCKET
(— **IN**) CRAM DINT PILE TAMP INJECT
(— **IN A PARK**) TOUR
(— **INTO THE GROUND**) STUB
(— **INTO WATER**) ENEW
(— **LOGS**) SPLASH
(— **OFF STAGE**) EXPLODE
(— **OFF**) KEEP LIFT EXCOCT
(— **OUT**) BOLT FIRE DEPEL DROWN EJECT EXPEL KNOCK WREAK EXTURB ABANDON DISLODGE EXORCISE PROPULSE
(— **RECKLESSLY**) COWBOY

(— **ROUGHLY**) CHOUSE
(— **SLANTINGLY**) TOE
(— **TO BAY**) EMBOSS
(— **TO MADNESS**) FRENZY
(— **VIOLENTLY**) THUD SMASH HURTLE
(— **WITH BLOWS**) SKELP COURSE
(— **WITH SHOUTS**) HOY HUE
DRIVEL DOTE DRIP DROOL SLUSH DOTAGE DRUDGE FOOTLE HUMBUG MENIAL SLAVER DRIBBLE EYEWASH SLABBER TWADDLE NONSENSE SALIVATE
DRIVELING SLAVERY FOOTLING IMBECILE SLOBBERY
DRIVEPIPE POINT
DRIVER MUG HACK JEHU MUSH WHIP DRABI URGER CABMAN CALLER COWBOY DROVER FLYMAN HAULER JARVEY JOCKEY MALLET MUSHER PONIER STAGER VANMAN WAINER CATCHER COCHERO FLANKER HACKMAN HOODLUM HURRIER JITNEUR PHAETON SPANKER SPEEDER SUMPTER TOPSMAN TRUCKER WHIPMAN BANDYMAN BULLOCKY CALESERO CAMELEER COACHMAN DRAGSMAN ENGINEER GALLOWAY GOADSMAN IMPULSOR JITNEUSE MOTORMAN OVERSEER TEAMSTER WHIPSTER
(— **OF ANIMALS**) DROVER SKINNER
(— **OF ELEPHANT**) MAHOUT
(— **OF OMNIBUS**) PIRATE
(**CAMEL** —) SARWAN CAMELEER
(**FAST** —) JEHU SPEEDER
(**FIELD** —) HAYWARD
(**PACK-HORSE** —) SUMPTER
(**SKILLFUL** —) REINSMAN
(**TOWPATH** —) HOGGY HOGGEE
DRIVEWAY DRIVE SWEEP AVENUE DRIFTWAY
DRIVING PELTING COACHING SLASHING
(— **ALONG**) SCUD
(— **OF GAME**) BATTUE
(— **OF WIND**) GUST
(— **TOGETHER**) DRIFT
(— **TOWARD**) APPULSE
DRIZZLE DEG MUG DANK DRIP DROW HAZE LING RAIN SMUR STEW DRISK MISLE SMURR MIZZLE DRISSEL SCOUTHER SPRINKLE
(— **OF RAIN**) SKEW
DRIZZLY SOFT DRIPPY
DROGUE DRAG DRUG
DROLL ODD COMIC DROLE FUNNY MERRY QUEER JESTER JOCOSE AMUSING BUFFOON COMICAL JOCULAR STRANGE WAGGISH FARCICAL HUMOROUS
DROLLERY WIT JEST FARCE HUMOR DROLERIE
DROMEDARY OONT CAMEL DELUL DELOUL HAGEEN HAGEIN HYGEEN MEHARI CAMAILE CAMELUS DROMOND
DRONE BEE BUM HUM DRUM SLUG DRANT DROLL IDLER SNAIL BUMBLE

BURDEN CHORUS DRAUNT DRONEL
DRONET LUBBER BAGPIPE
BUMBARD BUMBASS HUMMING
SHIRKER SLEEPER SOLDIER
SPEAKER LOITERER SLUGGARD
DRONE BASS FOOT
DRONING HUMMING
DRONISH SLOW INDOLENT
SLUGGISH
DRONGO FORKTAIL
DROOL FLAT DRIVEL SLAVER
DRIBBLE SLABBER SLOBBER
SALIVATE
DROOP FAG LOB LOP SAG BEND
DROP FADE FLAG HANG LAVE LOLL
PINE SINK SWAG WEEP WILT DAVER
DREEP DROWK FLACK HEALD HIELD
MOURN BANGLE BLOUSE DANGLE
DEPEND NUTATE SLOUCH CURTAIN
DECLINE FLITTER LANGUISH
DROOPING LOP DRAG FLAG LANK
LAZY LIMP GOTCH ADROOP
DROOPY FLAGGY NUTANT SLOUCH
SOPITE GOTCHED HANGING
LANGUID NODDING POPPIED
CERNUOUS TRAILING
(— **OF EARS**) LAVE
(— **OF EYELID**) PTOSIS
DROOPY DREEPY SLIMPSY
DROP DAP DIP SIE SYE BEAD BEDE
BLOB CAST DRIB DRIP DUMP FALL
GLOB GOUT OMIT SEGE SHED SILE
SINK SPOT STOP TEAR BREAK
CLOTH DROOP FLUMP GUTTA LAPSE
LOWER MINIM PEARL PLUMP PLUNK
SLUMP STILL SWOOP CANCEL
DISTIL DRAPPY EXTILL FUMBLE
GOBBET GOUTTE PLUNGE SINKER
SLOUGH SPRINK TUMBLE ABANDON
CURTAIN DESCENT DEWDROP
DISCARD DISMISS DISTILL DRAPPIE
DRIBBLE DRIBLET DROPLET
EXPUNGE FORSAKE GLOBULE
GUTTULA GUTTULE INCURVE
LETDOWN MELDROP PLUMMET
RELEASE SPATTER DECREASE
DROPLING
(— **ANCHOR**) SLIP
(— **ARGENT**) LARME
(— **AS SEEDS FROM A POD**) ROSE
(— **AWAY**) DESERT
(— **BAIT IN WATER**) DAP
(— **BY DROP**) DROPWISE GUTTATIM
(— **DOWN**) VAIL
(— **IN**) STOP HAPPEN INSTIL INSTILL
(— **OF GIN**) DAFFY
(— **OUT**) FLOUNCE
(**THEATRICAL** —) TAB SCRIM
(**UNEXPECTED** —) DOYST
(PL.) GTT GUTT
DROP-CURTAIN GREENY
DROP ELBOW PIERDROP
DROPLET GLOBULE
(PL.) DEW
DROPLIGHT PENDANT
DROPPER SINK BOBBER SINKER
PIPETTE
DROPPING FALL SCAT SKAT SHARD
COWSHARD

(— **ABRUPTLY**) BOLD
(— **SHARPLY**) ABRUPT
(PL.) SOIL SPOOR FLYINGS
DROPSICAL PUFFY EDEMIC
DROPSIED HYDROPIC
DROPSY EDEMA ANASARCA
DROPWORT HORSEBANE
DEADTONGUE
DROSS KISH LEES SCUM SLAG
CHAFF DREGS DRUSH SPRUE
WASTE GARBLE REFUSE SCORIA
SCRUFF SHRUFF SINTER CINDERS
LEAVING OFFSCUM
DROSSEL SLUT HUSSY DRAZEL
DRAZIL
DROUGHT DRYTH DROUTH THIRST
ARIDITY DRYNESS
DROVE MOB SENT ATAJO CROWD
DRIFT FLOCK MANADA BOASTER
DISTURB TROUBLE DRIFTWAY
DROVER DEALER DRIVER TOPMAN
TOPSMAN WHACKER HERDSMAN
DROWN DEAFEN DRENCH STIFLE
ADRENCH DRUNKEN INDRENCH
INUNDATE OVERTONE
DROWNED ADRENT
DROWNING NOYADE
DROWSE NOD SOG DOZE DOVER
DRONE SLEEP SNOOZE SLUMBER
DROWSINESS DULLNESS LETHARDY
DROWSING DORMANT
DROWSY DOZY DULL LOGY HEAVY
NODDY SLEEPY SNOOZY SOPITE
STUPID SUPINE SWOONY DORMANT
LULLING NODDING POPPIED
COMATOSE COMATOUS OSCITANT
SLUGGISH
DRUB TAP BANG BEAT BLOW DRUM
ARRAY CURRY STAMP THUMP
WHALE CUDGEL THRASH BELABOR
SHELLAC
DRUBBING LICKING SACKING
DRUDGE DIG FAG TUG DROY DRUG
GRUB HACK MOIL FLOD TOIL DROIL
GRIND SCRAT SCRUB SLAVE SWEAT
DIGGER DRIVEL ENDURE JACKAL
MOILER SCODGY SLAVEY SLUDGE
SUFFER GRUBBER HACKNEY
PLODDER SLAVERY SWEATER
TRACHLE
DRUDGERY FAG MOIL SLOG TOIL
WORK LABOR SWEAT SWINK
FAGGERY SLAVERY TRACHLE
TURMOIL DRUDGISM
DRUG HOP ALOE ALUM CURE DOPE
DRAB DULL HEMP LOAD NUMB SINA
HOCUS JALAP LOCUS MECON
OPIUM SALOL SENNA SPECE SULFA
TONGA TRUCK COOLER DEWTRY
FINGER HEROIN IPECAC JAMBUL
LOCUST MYOTIC NOBBLE OPIATE
PEYOTE PEYOTL PITURI POTION
SIMPLE SULPHA ANODYNE ATEBRIN
BOTANIC CUSHION DAMIANA
DILATER ECBOLIC ETHICAL HASHISH
JAMBOOL PHILTER PHILTRE
QUASSIA STUPEFY STYPTIC
SURAMIN ZEDOARY ADJUVANT
AROMATIC ASPIDIUM ATARAXIC

HYPNOTIC KOROMIKO LAXATIVE
MEDICATE MEDICINE NARCOTIC
NEPENTHE SALIVANT SEDATIVE
SPECIFIC TOXICANT ZERUMBET
ATARACTIC
(— **USER**) JOYPOPPER
(**VEGETABLE** —) FINGER
(PL.) DRUGGERY
DRUGGED POPPIED
DRUGGIST CHEMIST DRUGGER
GALLIPOT
DRUGSTORE APOTHEC PHARMACY
DRUID SARONIDE
DRUM GIN GOO BOWL CAGE DRUB
LALI ROUT SKIN SPOT TOPH TRAP
BONGO CONGA CRAWL DRONE
GUMBE GUMBY SHAPE SNARE
SWASH TABOR THRUM TOMBE
ATABAL BARREL CROCUS RIGGER
TABRET TAMBOR TIMBRE TUMBLE
TUMMER TYMPAN ANACARA
BUBBLER CROAKER FRUSTUM
GRUNTER RATTLER REDFISH
SNUBBER TABORIN TAMBOUR
TEMPEST TIMBREL TUMBLER
BAMBOULA BARBUKKA CANISTER
CYLINDER DERBUKKA DRUMFISH
HUEHUETL MOULINET TYMPANUM
(— **AS SHIP'S SIGNAL**) SHAPE
(— **FOR WINDING ROPE**) CAGE
(— **IN WINCH**) GIPSY GYPSY
(— **MADE FROM HOLLOW TREE**)
GUMBE GUMBY
(— **ON WINDLASS**) WILDCAT
(— **UP BUSINESS**) HUSTLE
(— **UP INTEREST**) BALLYHOO
(**HEATED** —) DRIER DRYER
(**IGOROT** —) GANGSA
(**REVOLVING** —) GURDY RATTLER
(**SUMERIAN** —) ALA ALAL
DRUMBEAT DUB FLAM RUFF TUCK
MARCH RUFFLE BERLOQUE
BRELOQUE
(— **SOUND**) TUCK
DRUMFISH SPOT CROCUS BUBBLER
CROAKER DRUMMER DRUMSLER
SCIAENID
DRUMLIN DRUM SOWBACK
DRUMMER DRUM TABOR STICKS
TABRET ROADMAN SWASHER
TAMBOUR TUMBLER DRUMSLER
SALESMAN
DRUM ROLL DIAN DIANA
DRUMSTICK LEG STICK BAGUET
TAMPON BAGUETTE
DRUNK CUT FOU REE WET GONE
HIGH LUSH NASE PAID RIPE SOSH
BLIND BOOZE BOSKY CLEAR DRINK
LUMPY LUSHY MALTY OILED QUEER
SHICK STIFF TIGHT TIPSY BAGGED
BLOTTO BOILED BUZZED CANNED
FLUFFY GROGGY JAGGED LOADED
LOOPED MORTAL SLOPPY SODDEN
SOSHED SOZZLY SPONGY SPRUNG
STEWED STINKO STONED TIDDLY
UPPISH UPPITY BLOTTER CROCKED
DRUNKEN JINGLED MAUDLIN
SCREWED SHICKER SLOPPED
SOZZLED SQUIFFY SWACKED

COCKEYED GLORIOUS MUCKIBUS PLEASANT SQUIFFED STINKING BLITHERED

DRUNKARD SOT SOAK BLOAT DIPSO DRUNK GULCH RUMMY SOUSE TOPER LUSHER SOAKER SPONGE DRUNKER FUDDLER POTSHOT SHICKER STEWBUM TIPPLER TOSSPOT BORACHIO HABITUAL SWILLTUB

DRUNKEN REE GONE WINY BLIND BOUSY DROWN DRUNK BLOTTO FLUFFY SODDEN DRUCKEN PICKLED SOTTISH WHIPCAT DRENCHED SATURATE SQUIFFED VINOLENT WOODSERE

DRUNKENNESS BUN IVRESSE POTSHOT

DRUPE TRYMA DRUPEL DRUPELET DRUPEOLE

DRUPELET GRAIN ACINUS

DRUPE STONE NUTLET

DRY EBB KEX SEC TED WIN ADRY ARID BAKE BLOT BRUT DULL EILD GELD HASK KEXY KILN PINE SAVE SERE SOUR WIPE AREFY CORKY DRAIN FROST GUESS HASKY JUSKY PARCH PROSY SANDY SECCO SMEEK SWEAT VAPID WIZEN BARKEN BARREN BIRSLE BORING CHIPPY ENSEAR GIZZEN HISTIE JEJUNE SCORCH STARKY AREFACT BRUSTLE INSIPID SAPLESS SICCATE SQUALID STERILE THIRSTY TORREFY XEROTIC BARBECUE DROUGHTY INFUMATE TIRESOME WOODSERE
(— HERRINGS) DEESE
(— IN SUN) RIZZAR
(— OF MILK) SEW EILD
(— PARTLY) SAMMY
(— UP) SERE WELK WITHER AREFACT FORWELK SKELLER
(— WOOD) BEATH SWEAT SEASON
(NOT —) SWEET

DRYAD DRYAS NYMPH CAISSA YAKSHA YAKSHI WOODMAID

DRYER DRIER STOVE SIROCCO

DRY GOODS DRAPERY

DRYING SICCANT

DRYING RACK CRIB

DRYNESS DROUTH ARIDITY DROUGHT SICCITY XEROSIS XEROTES HASKNESS

DUAL TWIN BINARY DOUBLE DUALIST TWOFOLD

DUALISM DVAITA

DUALITY DUAD TWINE TWONESS

DUANT DE DEE

DUB DIB RUB ADUB BLOW CALL NAME POOL ADORN ARRAY DRESS STYLE THUMP CLOTHE KNIGHT PUDDLE SMOOTH STRIKE ENTITLE BEGINNER DRUMBEAT ORNAMENT

DUBBIN DAUBING

DUBIOUS DICKY FISHY JUBUS DOUBTY BEARISH DOUBTFUL DOUBTING JUBEROUS
(NOT —) EXPRESS

DUCHY DUCATUS DUCHERY DUKEDOM PARMESAN

DUCK AIX BOB BOW CAN DIG DIP DOP MIG PET WIO CHAP COLK COOT DIVE DOGS DOGY DOKE DUKW JOUK LADY LORD PATO ROOK SMEE SMEW TEAL TEUK BOOBY BUNTY CRICK DILLY DODGE DOUSE DOWSE DUCKY EIDER HOUND MOMMY NODDY PADDY POKER ROUEN SCAUP SHIRK SOUSE SPIKE SPRIG STOOL BOBBER CALLOO CALLOW CANARD CANNET DUCKIE FELLOW GARROT PEKING PERSON PLUNGE QUANDY RUNNER SCOTER SMETHE BARWING BLACKIE BOWSSEN BUMMALO CANETTE CRACKER DABBLER DARLING DRABBET DUCKING DUCKLET DUNBIRD FIDDLER FLAPPER GADWALL GEELBEC GREASER MALLARD OLDWIFE PENTAIL PINKEYE PINTAIL POCHARD REDHEAD REDLEGS REDWING SCOOTER SLEEPER SPATTER WADDLER WIDGEON YAGUAZA BLUEBILL BLUEWING BOATBILL BULLNECK DUCKLING DUCKWING GARGANEY GRAYBACK GREYBACK HARDHEAD IRONHEAD MOONBILL MORILLON PIKETAIL REDSHANK RINGBILL RINGNECK SHOVELER SHUFFLER SQUEALER WIRETAIL
(— EGGS) PIDAN
(MALE —) DRAKE
(STUFFED —) DUMPOKE
(YOUNG —) CANETON FLAPPER FLOPPER

DUCKBILL OOTOCOID PLATYPUS TAMBREET

DUCKWEED GLIT GRAIN LEMNAD LENTIL DIGMEAT DUCKMEAT FROGFOOT

DUCT VAS MAIN PIPE TUBE CANAL ALVEUS BUSWAY DUCTUS MEATUS URETER CHANNEL CONDUIT DUCTULE DUCTURE LACTEAL LEADING PASSAGE TRACHEA AQUEDUCT CALIDUCT DOWNTAKE EFFERENT EMISSARY EXHALANT GONADUCT GUIDANCE OLEODUCT

DUCTILE SOFT DOCILE FACILE PLIANT PLASTIC PLIABLE TENSILE FLEXIBLE TRACTILE

DUD FLOP LEMON STUMER STUMOR FAILURE

DUDE FOP DANDY DUDINE JOHNNY COXCOMB JACKEEN

DUE HAK OWE BACK CENS DEBT FAIR FARM FLAT HAKH JUST MEED OWED TOLL DROIT ENDOW ENDUE FATED MERIT OWING COMING CUSTOM DESERT EXTENT LAWFUL MATURE PROPER UNPAID CONDIGN EXACTLY FALDFEE FITTING JETTAGE TALLAGE ADEQUATE DIRECTLY HEREGELD HEREZELD RIGHTFUL SUITABLE TRUNCAGE

DUEL TILT FENCE FIGHT AFFAIR

COMBAT DUELLO CONTEST MEETING CONFLICT DUELLIZE HOLMGANG

DUELIST FIGHTER SPADASSIN

DUENNA DRAGON CHAPERON

DUES TOLLS DROITS CHIEFRY INWARDS JETTAGE PAYMENT PENSION QUAYAGE ALTARAGE HAVENAGE SOUNDAGE THIRLAGE

DUET DUO TWO DUETTO TWOSOME
(BALLET —) ADAGIO

DUFF ALTER BRAND CHEAT FLOOR PUDDING

DUFFER DUB MUFF SHAM CHEAT BUFFER HAWKER SHICER PEDDLER

DUG (— UP) HOWKIT

DUGONG SEACOW YUNGAN COWFISH HALICORE MUTILATE SIRENIAN

DUGOUT ABRI BOAT BURY CAVE BANCA BONGO BUNGO CANOE DONGA DUNGA SHELL BAROTO BUNKER CAYUCA CAYUCO CORIAL TROUGH BANTING PIRAGUA PIROGUE SHELTER BLINDAGE LIPALIPA

DUIKER IPITI DUYKER BLAUBOK

DUKE DUC DUX KNEZ PEER AYMON CHIEF KNIAZ HERZOG LEADER ORSINO AUMERLE GORLOIS SOLINUS STEENIE HERETOGA PROSPERO

DUKEDOM DUCHY DUCATUS

DULCET SWEET DULCID SIRUPY SYRUPY SOOTHING

DULCIAN CURTAL

DULCIMER CANUN CITOLE SANTIR CEMBALO MAGADIS SANTOUR CYMBALOM PANTALON ZIMBALON

DULIA ADORATION

DULL DIM DOW DRY FAT LAX MAT SAD BLAH CLOD COLD DAMP DEAD DILL DOWD DOWF DOWY DRAB DREE DRUG DUMB FLAT GRAY GREY LOGY MOPE MULL POKY SLOW TAME THIN TURN BESOT BLAND BLATE BLEAR BLIND BLUNT BRUTE CRASS DENSE DINGY DOWFF DOWIE DOWLY DREAR DUBBY DUNCH DUNNY DUSTY FISHY FOGGY GLAZY GRAVE GROSS HEAVY INERT LOURD MATTE MORON MOSSY MUDDY MUSTY MUZZY NOOSE PLUMP POKEY PROSE PROSY SHADE SLACK SOGGY STARY STILL SULKY TERNE THICK UNAPT VAPID WASTE BARREN BLEARY BOVINE CLOUDY DAMPEN DARKEN DEADEN DISMAL DRAGGY DREARY DRIECH DRIEGH DROWSY EARTHY FRIGID FRUMPY GLASSY HEBETE JEJUNE LEADEN LOURDY MUFFLE OBTUND OBTUSE OPAQUE REBATE SLEEPY SLOOMY SODDEN SOMBER SOMBRE STODGY STOLID STUFFY STUPID SULLEN TIMBER TORPID TRISTE TURBID URLUCH WOODEN ADENOID BLUNTED CONFUSE DEADISH DISEDGE DOLTISH DOWFART

DRAINED DULLISH DUMPISH HUMDRUM INSIPID IRKSOME LANGUID LUMPISH MUMPISH PEAKISH PINHEAD PROSAIC SHEATHE SOTTISH STUPEFY TEDIOUS UNLUSTY VACUOUS BACKWARD BANAUSIC BEFUDDLE BLOCKISH BOEOTIAN BROMIDIC COMATOSE COMATOUS DIDACTIC DISCOLOR DULLSOME EDGELESS FRUMPISH GAUMLESS HEBETATE INFICETE LIFELESS LISTLESS LOURDISH OVERCAST PLODDING SLOTTERY SLUGGISH STAGNANT TIRESOME

(— EDGE OF) ABATE
(— IN MOTION) LOGY
(— SCENT) FOIL
(— WITH LIQUOR) SEETHE
(BECOME —) PALL RUST
(MENTALLY —) DOPY DOPEY BARREN

DULLARD DOLT DUNCE IDIOT MORON DODUNK STUPID BROMIDE DASTARD DOLDRUM DULBERT POTHEAD DULLHEAD

DULLED EMPTY HEAVY JADED BROKEN CLOUDY GRAYED SODDEN STUPID BLEARED

DULLISH DIRTY

DULLNESS DRAB HAZE YAWN TAMAS PHLEGM DIMNESS DOLDRUM DULLITY DUNCERY FATUITY LANGUOR OPACITY DUMBNESS HEBETUDE SLOWNESS VAPIDITY

DULL-SPIRITED MUZZY

DULL-WITTED FOZY WITLESS BESOTTED

(— PERSON) MOREPORK

DULLY FLATLY HEAVILY

DULSE DILLESK DILLISK SEAWEED

DULY DUE FITLY RIGHT RITELY PROPERLY

DUMB DULL MUTE STONY SILENT STONEY STUPID

DUMBBELL DUMMY DUNCE HALTER KNOTHEAD

DUMBFOUND DAZE STUN AMAZE CONFUSE CONFOUND SURPRISE

DUMBFOUNDED STUPENT

DUMBNESS APHRASIA

DUMBWAITER LIFT DUMMY

DUMMY COPY DOLT MUTE SHAM DUMBY FAGOT EFFIGY FAGGOT PONTIC SHADOW SILENT PHANTOM DUMBBELL

(SWORDSMAN'S —) PEL

DUMP SUM TIP BEAT CASH COIN COUP FALL HOLE JAIL MUSE NAIL TOOM EMPTY HOUSE SHOOT GRIEVE PLUNGE TIPPLE UNLOAD BOGHOLE COUNTER DEPOSIT REVERIE SADNESS STORAGE (PL.) SUDS MOPES SADNESS

DUMPCART DUMPER TUMBREL TUMBRIL

DUMPER TIPMAN

DUMPLING COB CRUST KNODEL KNAIDEL NOCKERL DOUGHBOY

QUENELLE
(PL.) KLOSSE GNOCCHI

DUMPY DUNCH GROSS PUDGY SQUAB SQUAT DUMPTY STOCKY SQUATTY

DUN BUM TAN FORT KICK URGE ANNOY BROWN CRAVE CROWD DINGY FAVEL MOUND SEPIA DUNNER LEADEN PESTER PLAGUE DUNNISH SWARTHY

DUNCE ASS DOLT DULT GABY GONY BOBBY BOOBY DOBBY IDIOT NINNY DULTIE HOBBIL PEDANT DULLARD SOPHIST NUMSKULL STUNPOLL TOMNODDY WISEACRE

DUNDERHEAD OAF DOLT DUNCE

DUNE BAR DENE MEAL MOUND TOWAN TWINE BARKAN BARCHAN BARKHAN

(SAND —) DRAB SAIF SEIF

DUNG MIS CACK CHIP DOLL FIME GORE MERD MUCK MUTE SOIL TATH ARGAL ARGOL FECES FILTH FUMET MIXEN SCARN SHARN BILLET CASSON FIANTS LESSES MANURE ORDURE SCUMBER SCUMMER TREDDLE COWSHARD DROPPING STALLAGE

(— AS FUEL) ARGOL CASSON CASSONS
(— OF BEAST OF PREY) LESSES
(— OF DEER) FUMET FEWMET
(COW —) UPLA COWSHARD COWSHARN
(OTTER'S —) SPRAINTS
(SHEEP —) BUTTONS TREDDLE TROTTERS

DUNGEON PIT CELL HELL HOLE LAKE VAULT CACHOT DONJON PRISON CONFINE OUBLIET REVOLVER

DUNGHILL MIXEN MIDDEN MIXHILL

DUNGON DONGON SUNDARI

DUNK DIP SOP SOAK STEEP IMMERSE MOISTEN

DUNKER DIPPER TAUFER TUNKER DUMPLER DUNKARD TUMBLER

DUNLIN STIB OXEYE PURRE STINT DORBIE OXBIRD REDBACK LEADBACK

DUODECIMO TWELVEMO

DUPE APE FOB FOP MUG BOOB COAX CONY CULL DUST FOOL GECK GULL HOAX LAMB ROOK TOOL CHEAT CHUMP COKES CONEY CULLY HEALD MOOTH MOUTH SLANG STALE TRICK BEFOOL BUBBLE CHOOSE CHOUSE COUSIN DELUDE DERIDE MONKEY PIGEON PLOVER SQUARE SUCKER VICTIM CATSPAW CHICANE DECEIVE GUDGEON MISLEAD SAPHEAD SWINDLE YOUNKER DOTTEREL HOODWINK RODERIGO

DUPERY RAMP

DUPLE BINARY DOUBLE TWOFOLD

DUPLEX DOUBLE TWOFOLD

DUPLEXITY EQUIVOKE

DUPLICATE BIS COPY DUPE ALIKE

DITTO SPARE TALLY DOUBLE FLIMSY REPEAT COUNTER ESTREAT MISLEAD REPLICA TWOFOLD LIKENESS

DUPLICATION DISOMATY

DUPLICITY ART GUILE DECEIT TRICKERY

DUPONDIUS BRONZE

DURABILITY WEAR FIBER FIBRE STEEL DURANCE STAMINA

DURABLE FIRM HARD LASTY STOUT STABLE STAPLE LASTING SERVICE CONSTANT ENDURING LIVELONG

DURABLENESS DURATION

DURAMEN HEARTWOOD

DURANCE DURANT DURESS CUSTODY

DURANGO CARTOUCH

DURATION AGE DATE LAST LIFE SPAN TERM TIME WHEN DUREE KALPA SPACE LENGTH PERIOD DURANCE LASTING INFINITE LIFETIME STANDING

(— BREEZE) SLATCH
(BOUNDLESS —) INFINITE
(INFINITE —) ETERNITY

DURESS FORCE DANGER CRUELTY DURANCE COERCION HARDNESS PRESSURE

DURGA CHAMUNDA

DURIAN JAK JACK JAKFRUIT

DURING IN ON BIN AMID OVER TIME AMONG INTRA WHILE AMIDST WHILST WITHIN AMONGST DURANTE PENDING ENDURING

DURRA DARI DURA MILO JOWAR CHOLUM DHURRA JONDLA SORGHUM FETERITA

DURSACK TESACK

DUSK DIM EVE DARK DIMPS GLOAM GLOOM DIMMET DIMPSY DIMNESS DUCKISH DARKNESS GLOAMING OWLLIGHT TWILIGHT

DUSKY DIM SAD WAN DARK DUSK ADUSK BROWN DINGY GRIMY MOORY TAWNY GLOOMY SMUTTY SOMBER SOMBRE SWARTH DARKISH DARLING OBSCURE SUBFUSC SUBFUSK SWARTHY BLACKISH

DUST ROW COOM DIRT FOGO MUCK MULL PILM SMUT BRISS CLEAN COOMB FLOUR POUCE STIVE STOUR DREDGE FILLER KITTEN POLLEN POWDER SMEECH BEFLOUR EBURINE REMAINS SAWDUST SMEDDUM TURMOIL ANTELOPE BULLDUST PUMICITE

(— IN FLOUR MILLS) STIVE
(— IN QUARTZ MILL) SLICKENS
(BLOOD —) HEMOCONIA
(COAL —) COOM CULM COOMB
(COKE —) BREEZE
(COSMIC —) STARDUST
(DIAMOND —) SEASONING
(FIBER —) FLOCK
(FLAX —) POUCE POUSE

DUST CLOUD STEW

DUST COVER WRAPPER

DUSTER DEVIL WILLOW ZEPHYR
DUSTCOAT
DUSTY ADUST MOTTY MOTTLE
POUCEY STOURY POWDERY
UNDUSTED
DUTCH (SEE NETHERLANDS) HOGEN
HOLLAND
DUTCH FOIL ORSEDE ORSEDUE
DUTCH GOLD CLINQUANT
DUTCHMAN HANS HOGEN BLANDA
DUTCHY BELANDA DUTCHER
MYNHEER BATAVIAN
DUTCHMAN'S-BREECHES
DICENTRA
DUTIFUL DOCILE LAWFUL DEBTFUL
DUTEOUS OBEDIENT OFFICIAL
REVERENT
DUTY DO END JOB LOT TAX CALL
CARE FYRD ONUS PART PROW
ROLE TAIL TASK TOLL WIKE CHORE
DEVER ERMIN LADLE OUGHT PREST
RIGHT STINT WIKEN BLANCH
BURDEN CHARGE COCKET DEVOIR
DHARMA EXCISE EXITUS HERIOT
IMPOSE IMPOST INGATE OFFICE
RIVAGE TARIFF AVERAGE BAILAGE
BOOMAGE FOSSAGE FURDUNG
GRANAGE INDULTO KEELAGE
LASTAGE PONTAGE PRIMAGE
ROYALTY SCAVAGE SERVICE
STATION TONNAGE TRIBUTE
TROWAGE TUNNAGE BALLIAGE
BUSINESS FUNCTION MALIKANA
MALTOLTE REDDENDO WEIGHAGE
(— FOR LEAD ORE) COPE
(FEUDAL —) HERIOT
(IMPORT —) ERMIN INDULTO
(MILITARY —) STABLES
(TIRING —) FATIGUE
(PL.) CUSTOMS INGATES ACTIVITY
UX CHIEF LEADER SUBJECT
HERETOGA
WARF ELF PUG URF AETA CRUT
GRIG GRUB NANA RUNT CRILE
CROWL GALAR GNOME KNURL
MIDGE PIGMY PYGMY SCRUB STUNT
TROLL ABLACH ALVISS CONJON
DROICH DURGAN DURGEN MIDGET
SHRIMP ANDVARI ANDWARI BLASTIE
CONGEON MANIKIN OVERTOP
PACOLET WRATACK ALBERICH
BELITTLE HOMUNCIO HOMUNCLE
HUCKMUCK KNURLING MENEHUNE
NANANDER
(PL.) CERCOPES NIBLUNGS
NIBELUNGS
WARF DANDELION KRIGIA
WARFED STUNTY STUNTED
WARFING BRACHYSM
WARFISH ELFIN PIGMY PYGMY
GRUBBY KNURLY NANOID RUNTISH
STUNTED
WARFISHNESS NANISM
WARFISM ATELIOSIS
WARF MALLOW CHEESE PELLAS
WARF RASPBERRY PLUMBOG
WELL BIG COT DIG SIT WIN WON
BIDE BIGG HAFT HARP LIVE STAY
TELD WINE WONT ABIDE BIELD

BOWER BROOD BUILD DELAY
HOUSE LODGE PAUSE SHACK STALL
TARRY LINGER REMAIN RESIDE
TENANT CLIMATE COHABIT INHABIT
CONVERSE
(— IN) BIG BIGG BEDWELL INHABIT
(— IRRITATINGLY) GRATE
(— ON) HARP BROOD GLOAT
DWELLER TENANT WONNER
DENIZEN PALEMAN DOWNSMAN
HABITANT OCCUPANT RESIDENT
(— BY SEA) PARALIAN
(BUSH —) HATTER
(CAVE —) CAVEMAN TROGLODYTE
(CITY —) SLICKER
(COAST —) BUFFALO ORARIAN
(LAKE —) LACUSTRIAN
(PL.) HUTHOLD
DWELLING DAR HUT INN SEE WON
CASA FARM FLAT FORT HAFT HALL
HOME NEST ROOF SLUM TENT WIKE
WONE ABODE CABIN DOMUS HOTEL
HOUSE HOVEL JOINT MANSE MOTEL
CASTLE DUGOUT DUPLEX HOMING
MALOCA SHANTY TEEPEE WIGWAM
WONING COTTAGE LODGING
MANSION SALTBOX TRAILER
TRIPLEX WONNING BUILDING
BUNGALOW DOMICILE TENEMENT
(— IN UNDERWORLD) CHTHONIC
(— PLACE) HOWF HOWFF
(— WITH ANOTHER) INMATE
(ATTRACTIVE —) BOWER
(CRUDE —) SHED SHEBANG
(LAKE —) PALAFITTE
(MEAN —) SHANTY
(MISERABLE —) BURROW
(NAVAJO —) HOGAN
(NEOLITHIC —) TERRAMARA
(ONE-ROOM —) CELL
(RAMSHACKLE —) HUMPY
(RUDE —) BOTHY BOTHIE
(SUBTERRANEAN —) WEEM
(SWISS —) CHALET
(PL.) HOUSING
DWINDLE FADE FAIL FINE MELT PINE
WANE DECAY DRAIN PETER TAPER
TRAIL WASTE MOLDER SHRINK
CONSUME DECLINE FRITTER
MOULDER DECREASE DIMINISH
FORDWINE
DWINDLING DOWN FLAGGING
DYBBUK GILGUL
DYE (ALSO SEE DYESTUFF) AAL DIP
LIT ANIL BLUE COLOR EMBUE
FUCUS IMBUE LOKAO STAIN SUDAN
TINCT VENOM ARCHIL INFECT
MADDER TINGER ENGRAIN INTINCT
LACMOID LOGWOOD ZAMBESI
AMARANTH COLORANT DYESTUFF
FUGITIVE INDIGOID TINCTURE
(— FUR) FEATHER
(— NOT FAST) FUGITIVE
(BLACK —) GUAKO
(BLUE —) RUM ROOM WOAD
CYANINE DICYANINE
(BROWN —) CACHOU
(GENERAL —S) NIL NILL AZINE
BROWN EOSIN GREEN DIANIL

EOSINE ISAMIN ORANGE PURPLE
VIOLET CYANINE FUCHSIN METANIL
PONCEAU PRIMULA ALIZARIN
AURANTIA CIBACRON DICYANIN
EURHODOL FUCHSINE HYPERNIC
INDULINE TURNSOLE VIRIDINE
SAFRANINE
(HAIR —) RASTIK
(ORANGE —) KAMALA
(PURPLE —) CASSIUS GALLEIN
(RED —) AAL AURIN EOSIN GRAIN
HENNA RUBIN AURINE CERISE
EOSINE RELBUN RUBINE CORINTH
CRIMSON MAGENTA PONCEAU
SAFFLOR ALIZARIN AMARANTH
BORDEAUX CORALLIN CROCEINE
(SCARLET —) TULY GRAIN
(VIOLET —) MAUVE ARCHIL ORCHIL
LACMOID ARCHILLA
(YELLOW —) ARUSA FLAVIN
CHRYSIN FISETIN FLAVINE LAWSONE
WONGSHY AURAMINE
DYED INGRAIN
(PERMANENTLY —) FAST
DYEING TINCTION
DYER LISTER TINGER TINTER
DYESTER FIELDER SKEINER
TAINTOR TINTIST
DYERMA ZARMA ZAREMA
DYERS' MULBERRY FUSTIC
DYERS'-WEED SOLIDAGO
DYESTUFF (ALSO SEE DYE) DYE LIT
WELD WOAD LOKAO WOULD
ANATTO LITMUS ORCEIN RELBUN
ALKANET ARNATTO CUDBEAR
DYEWARE SAFFRON
DYEWEED WOODWAX
DYEWOOD FUSTET FUSTIC
BARWOOD CAMWOOD HYPERNIC
DYING FEY DEATH MORENDO
PARTING MORIBUND
(— AWAY) CALANDO DILUENDO
MANCANDO PERDENDO SMORZATO
DYNAMIC POTENT DRIVING KINETIC
FORCEFUL
DYNAMITE BLAST DUALIN SAWDUST
RENDROCK GELIGNITE
DYNAMO EXCITER TORNADO
DYNASTY (OR MEMBER THEREOF)
KIN SUI WEI YIN CHIN CHOU HSIA
RACE SUNG TANG YUAN BUYID
CHING PIAST REALM RULER SHANG
HAFSID PRINCE SAFAVI SELJUK
ALMOHAD ARSACID ATTALID
AYUBITE AYYUBID BOUIDES FATIMID
HAFSITE IDRISID JAGELLO LAKHMID
MONARCH OMAYYAD ROMANOV
SAADIAN SAFAWID SAMANID
TULUNID AGHLABID AGLABITE
ASMONEAN BUWAIHID CAPETIAN
CHALUKYA DOMINION EDRISITE
GOVERNOR IDRISITE JAGIELLO
LORDSHIP SAFFARID SARGONID
SASANIAN SELEUCID SOFFARID
SASSANIDE
DYSENTERY FLUX SCOUR MENISON
TOXEMIA DIARRHEA
DYSPHORIA FIDGET
DYSSODIA BOEBERA

E EASY ECHO
EA HEA ENKI
EACH A EA UP ALL ILK THE UCH
ILKA UCHE EVERY APIECE EITHER
EVERYONE
EAGER HOT RAD YAN ACID AGOG
AVID EDGY FAIN FELL FOND FREE
GAIR HIGH KEEN RATH SOUR TARE
THRO VAIN WARM WAVE YARE
YERN AFIRE AGASP ANTSY BRIEF
FIRST FRACK FRECK HASTY HIGRE
ITCHY PRIME READY SHARP SNELL
YIVER ARDENT FIERCE GREEDY
HETTER INTENT STRONG TIPTOE
ANXIOUS ATHIRST BRITTLE BURNING
EXCITED FERVENT FORWARD
ITCHING PROVOKE DESIROUS
IRRITATE SPIRITED VIGOROUS
YEARNING
(— IN PURSUIT) SHARP
(WILDLY —) CRAZY
EAGERLY FAST FELL YERN HOTLY
BELIVE TIPTOE YARELY YEPELY
PRESTLY HUNGRILY INTENTLY
EAGERNESS GOG ELAN GARE ZEAL
ARDOR DESIRE FERVOR ARDENCY
AVIDITY ALACRITY CUPIDITY
DEVOTION FAINNESS FERVENCY
EAGLE AAR ERN CROW ERNE GIER
TERN HARPY AQUILA BERGUT
EAGLET FALCON FORMAL FORMEL
RAPTOR ALLERION BATALEUR
BEARCOOT BERGHAAN RINGTAIL
(SEA —) ERN ERNE PYGARG
PYGARGUS
EAGLE OWL KATOGLE
EAGLESTONE AETITES
EAGLET BIRD LAIGLON
EAGLEWOOD AGALLOCH
EAGRE BORE WAVE AEGIR HYGRE
EAR LUG NEB CLIP HEAR HEED
HOOK LIST OBEY PLOW TILL AURIS
BRACE PINNA SENSE SOUSE SOWSE
SPIKE CANNON CONCHA CROSET
EARLET LISTEN AURICLE HEARING
SENSORY AUDIENCE RECEPTOR
(— OF BELL) CANON CANNON
(— OF CORN) COB ICKER NUBBIN
CORNCOB
(— OF GRAIN) RISOM SPIKE RIZZOM
(— OF WHEAT) SPICA WHEATEAR
(—S OF GRAIN) CAPES EARHEAD
(UNRIPE — OF CORN) TUCKET
EARACHE OTALGY OTALGIA
EARCOCKLE PURPLES
EARDRUM TABOR TABOUR TYMPAN
DRUMHEAD TYMPANUM
EARFLAP LUG EARLAP EARTAB
EARMUFF
EARL EORL GRAF LORD PEER
COMES NOBLE CONSUL SIWARD
(— OF COVENTRY)
SNIPSNAPSNORUM
EARLDOM DERBY COUNTY
EARLIER ERE OLD ERST FORE
ELDER UPPER BEFORE FORMER
HITHER RATHER SOONER FIRSTER
FURTHER PIONEER PREMIER
PREVIOUS

EARLIEST ERST FIRST ELDEST
MAIDEN RATHEST FURTHEST
PRIMROSE
EAR LOBE LUG EARLAP
(— PEOPLE) OREJON
EARLY AIR ERE OLD GOOD HIGH
RARE RATH SOON FORME PRIMY
RATHE VERTY REARLY SUDDEN
TIMELY ANCIENT BETIMES ERLICHE
FORWARD YOUTHFUL
EARMARK BIT CROP SPLIT LUGMARK
OVERBIT SLEEPER ALLOCATE
OVERCROP UNDERBIT
EAR MUFF OREILET
EARN GET WIN FANG GAIN TILL
VANG ADDLE ETTLE GLEAR MERIT
GARNER HUSTLE OBTAIN ACHIEVE
ACQUIRE CHEVISE DEMERIT
DESERVE
(— BY LABOR) ADDLE SWINK
BESWINK
EARNEST ARRA DEAR DERN HARD
PAWN ARLES GRAVE SMART SOBER
STAID ARDENT ENTIRE HANSEL
HEARTY INTENT SEDATE SOLEMN
EMULOUS ENGAGED FERVENT
FORWARD HANDSEL INTENSE
SERIOUS SINCERE ZEALOUS
DILIGENT EMPHATIC STUDIOUS
(IN —) AGOOD
EARNESTLY HARD DEARLY WISHLY
EARNEST DEVOUTLY DINGDONG
ENTIRELY HEARTILY INTENTLY
INWARDLY
EARNESTNESS GLOW FERVOR
WARMTH GRAVITY DEVOTION
DILIGENCE
EARNINGS GET MAKING ADDLINS
PICKING ADDLINGS
EARPIECE BUTTON
EARPLUG STOPPLE TEMBETA
EARSPOOL
EARRING DROP GRIP EARBOB
EARLET PENDLE EARCLIP EARDROP
PENDANT EARSCREW
EAR SHELL ORMER ABALONE
EARSHOT SOUND HEARING
EARREACH
EARTH ERD ORB SET BALL BANK
BURY BYON CLAY CLOD DIRT DUST
FLAG FOLD GRIT LAND LOAM MARL
MASS MEAL MOLD MOOL MUCK
ROCK SOIL SORY STAR VALE YIRD
ADOBE CRUMB FLOSS GLEBE
GLOBE GROOT INTER LOESS MOULD
REGUR TERRA TRASS UMBER
WORLD CENTER CENTRE COARSE
GROUND YACATA KOKOWAI
MIDGARD TERRENE TIERRAS
TOPSOIL TRIPOLI MAGNESIA
MIDGARTH
(— PROVIDING OCHER) KOKOWAI
(— SUITABLE FOR CULTIVATION)
LAYER
(BLACK —) MUCK SORY KILLOW
AMPELITE
(BLUE —) KIMBERLITE
(BROWN —) UMBER
(CLAYEY —) LAME LOAM

(DRY —) MOOL GROOT
(FULLER'S —) CRETA
(GEM-BEARING —) BYON
(LOOSE —) CRUMB GEEST
(MOIST —) SLIME
(POOR —) RAMMEL
(REFUSE —) MURGEON
(RIVER-BANK —) GREWT
(SMALL —) TERRELLA
(SOAP —) SOAPROCK
(STRAW-YELLOW —) BISMITE
(SUN-DRIED —) SWISH
(VITRIFIED —) FLOSS
(VOLCANIC —) TRASS TARRASS
EARTHEN FICT DIRTEN EARTHLY
YARTHEN
EARTHENWARE POT DELF CHINA
CLOAM CROCK DELFT CLAYEN
JASPER ASTBURY BISCUIT FAIENCE
POTTERY TICKNEY BUFFWARE
CROCKERY TALAVERA
(BROKEN PIECE OF —) CROCK
EARTHINESS SALT TERREITY
EARTHKIN TERRELLA
EARTHLY LAIRY CARNAL EARTHY
MORTAL EARTHEN GLEBOUS
MUNDANE SECULAR TERRAIN
TERRENE WORLDLY SUBLUNAR
TEMPORAL
EARTHNUT ARNUT CHUFA HOGNUT
JARNUT PEANUT PIGNUT HARENUT
HAWKNUT TRUFFLE
EARTH PIG ERDVARK AARDVARK
EARTHQUAKE QUAKE SEISM SHAKE
SHOCK TEMBLOR SEAQUAKE
EARTHSTAR GEASTER
EARTHWALL TRINCHERA
EARTHWORK BANK RATH AGGER
CASTLE RAMPART TERRACE
EARTHWORM ESS MAD WORM
ANNELID DEWWORM IPOMOEA
MADDOCK ANGLEDOG BRANDLIN
EACEWORM FISHWORM RAINWORM
TWATCHEL LUMBRICID
EARTHY GROSS SALTY WORMY
VULGAR EARTHLY TERRENE
BARNYARD TERREOUS VISCERAL
EAR TICK PINOLEA
EAR TRUMPET CORNET
EARWAX CERUMEN
EARWIG GOLACH GOLOCH
TOUCHBELL
EARWORM BOLLWORM
EASE CALM COSY COZY EASY REST
ALLAY KNACK PEACE QUIET RELAX
SLAKE LOOSEN PACIFY REDUCE
RELIEF REPOSE QUIGHT SMOOTH
SOFTEN SOOTHE APPEASE
ASSUAGE COMFORT CONTENT
FACULTY FLUENCY FREEDOM
LEISURE LIBERTY LIGHTEN RELIEVE
SLACKEN SUBSIDE DIMINISH
FACILITY MITIGATE MODERATE
PALLIATE PLEASURE SECURITY
UNBURDEN
(— OF A BURDEN) LIGHT
(— OFF) FLOW CHECK START
SLOUGH
(APATHETIC —) INDOLENCE

(AT —) OTIOSE
(CAREFREE —) ABANDON
EASEL FRAME SUPPORT SCAFFOLD
EASEMENT EASE EASING RELIEF
HERBAGE TURBARY SERVITUS
WAYLEAVE
EASE-TAKING PICKTOOTH
EASIEST EFTEST
EASILY EASY EATH WELL LIGHT
EATHLY GENTLY GLIBLY HANDILY
LIGHTLY READILY SLIGHTLY
SMOOTHLY
EASINESS GRACE FACILITY
EASING DETENTE
EAST ASIA MORN LEVANT ORIENT
SUNRISE EASTWARD
(— OF) FOLLOWING
EAST AFRICA (— TREE) PODO
EASTER PT PACE PASCH EOSTRE
PASCHA PASQUE
EASTERN LEVANT ORTIVE AURORAL
ORIENTAL
EASTERNER DUDE
EAST INDIAN (— TREE) SAL TEAK
KOKAN LANSA MAHUA MOHWA
NIEPA ROHAN ROHUN SALAI SIMAL
EASTLAND ESTRICHE
EASTWARD EAST EASEL EASSEL
EASY CALM COZY CRIP EATH EITH
GAIN GLIB MILD RIFE SNAP SOFT
CUSHY JAMMY LARGE LIGHT PRONE
ROYAL SUAVE YEZZY CASUAL
COMODO FACILE FLUENT FRUITY
GENTLE GENTLY SECURE SIMPLE
SMOOTH UNHARD ARTLESS
GRADUAL LENIENT NATURAL
CAREFREE CARELESS CAVALIER
EXPEDITE FAMILIAR GRACEFUL
HOMELIKE MODERATE TRANQUIL
UNFORCED
(— IN MIND) SECURE
(— TO HANDLE) HANDSOME
(— TO USE) CLEVER
EASYGOING LAX DEGAGE
EAT FOG KAI SUP BITE CHOW DINE
FARE FEED FRET GNAW GRUB HAVE
HEYT MAKE PECK RUST TUCK
ERODE FEAST GRAZE MANGE
MUNCH SCOFF STOKE TASTE
WASTE ABSORB BEGNAW DEVOUR
INGEST NIBBLE RAVAGE CONSUME
CORRODE DESTROY SWALLOW
VICTUAL
(— A MEAL) GRUB
(— AS HOGS) SLUICE
(— AWAY) GNAW ERODE RANKLE
CORRODE
(— BIG MEAL) STOKE
(— CRUNCHINGLY) GROUZE
(— GLUTTONOUSLY) GUDGE STUFF
(— GREEDILY) GAMP GAWP SLAB
SLOP TUCK CHAUM MOOCH SCOFF
GOBBLE GOFFLE GUTTLE GUZZLE
RAUNGE GLUTTON GOURMAND
(— HEARTILY) THORN
(— IN GULPS) LAB
(— MINCINGLY) PICK PICKLE PIDDLE
(— NOISILY) SLOP GULCH SLURP
GUTTLE SLOTTER

(— OUT) EXEDE
(— RUDELY) TROUGH
(— SLOVENLY) SLUP MUMMICK
(— SPARINGLY) DIET
(— TO EXCESS) COLF BEZZLE
(— UP) DEMOLISH
(— VORACIOUSLY) CRAM WORRY
(— WITH GUSTO) SMOUSE
(— WITHOUT CHEWING) BOLT
EATABLE FOODY COOKER EDIBLE
ESCULENT
EATEN CANKERED
(HALF —) SEMESE
EATER PECKER DEVOURER
(GREEDY —) GOURMAND
EATING BIT FOOD ESURINE
(— BETWEEN MEALS) TIFFIN
(— COARSE FOOD) FOUL
(— INTO) CANKEROUS
(— OUT) EXESION
EAVES EASE EASING
EAVESDROP DARK HARKEN
HEARKEN
EAVESDROPPER EARWIG
DRAWLATCH
EAVES TROUGH CHENEAU
EBB FAIL FALL SINK WANE ABATE
DECAY RECEDE REFLOW REFLUX
RETIRE TIDING DECLINE SUBSIDE
DECREASE DIMINISH
(— AND FLOW) ESTUS AESTUS
FLUIDITY
EBBING AWANE REFLUENT
REFLUOUS
(— AND FLOWING) TIDAL
EBLIS JANN IBLIS
EBONY EBON BLACK GABON
GABOON WAMARA HEBENON
IRONWOOD
EBULLIENCE OVERFLOW ELEVATION
EBULLIENT BRASH FERVID BOILING
EBULLIOSCOPE ZEOSCOPE
EBULLITION SEETHE FERMENT
OUTBURST
ECAD ECOPHENE
ECCENTRIC ODD CARD DOER
CRANK DOTTY KINKY QUEER WIPER
CRANKY LOCOED OUTISH PSYCHO
SCREWY SHAGGY BIZARRE CURIOUS
DEVIOUS ERRATIC STRANGE
TOUCHED ABNORMAL FITIFIED
PECULIAR SINGULAR
ECCENTRICITY KINK FERLY ODDITY
CROTCHET QUIDDITY
(— OF CURVE) E
ECCLESIASTES KOHELETH
QOHELETH
ECCLESIASTIC ABBE ABBOT CLERK
VICAR ARCHON FATHER LEGATE
PRIEST KIRKMAN PRELATE SECULAR
EPISTLER SUBDEACON
ECCLESIASTICAL CHRISTIAN
SPIRITUAL
ECHEVIN SCABINE SCABINUS
ECHIDNA NODIAK ANTEATER
EDENTATE PORCUPINE
ECHINODERM CYSTID CRINOID
BLASTOID STARFISH
ECHINOPANAX FATSIA

ECHINO-SOREX GYMNURA
ECHION (FATHER OF —) MERCURY
(MOTHER OF —) ANTIANIRA
(SON OF —) PENTHEUS
(WIFE OF —) AGAVE
ECHO ECO RING SING CHORUS
REPEAT REVERB SECOND IMITATE
ITERATE RESOUND RESPEAK
RESPOND REVOICE RESPONSE
ECLAT FAME GLORY RENOWN
ACCLAIM SCANDAL APPLAUSE
FACILITY PRESTIGE SPLENDOR
ECLECTIC BROAD LIBERAL
ECLIPSE DIM BIND BLOT HIDE BLIND
CLOUD SHADE STAIN SULLY
DARKEN DAZZLE DEFECT EXCEED
OCCULT DEFAULT OBSCURE
PRODIGY TRAVAIL OUTRIVAL
ECLOGUE IDYL IDYLL BUCOLIC
ECOLOGIST BIONOMIST
ECOLOGY BIOLOGY BIONOMY
MESOLOGY
ECONOMICAL WARY CHARY FENDY
FRUGAL SAVING CAREFUL PRUDENT
SPARING THRIFTY SCREWING
ECONOMICS PLUTONOMY
ECONOMIST HUSBAND MANAGER
ECONOMIZE HAIN SAVE SKIMP
STINT SCRIMP HUSBAND UTILIZE
RETRENCH
ECONOMY SPARE SAVING SYSTEM
THRIFT MANAGERY
ECSTASY JOY BLISS POWER SWOON
TRANCE DELIGHT EMOTION
MADNESS RAPTURE
ECSTATIC HOT RAPT PYTHIAN
GLORIOUS
ECTENE IRENICON
ECTODERM EXODERM EPIBLAST
ECTOMORPHIC LINEAR ASHENIC
LEPTOSOME
ECTROPION EVERSION
ECU SCUTE SHIELD

ECUADOR	
ANCIENT NAME:	QUITO
CAPE:	ROSA PASADO PUNTILLA
CAPITAL:	QUITO
COIN:	SUCRE CONDOR CENTAVO
INDIAN:	CARA INCA PALTA
	CANELO JIVARO
ISLAND:	PUNA WOLF MOCHA
	PINTA BALTRA CHAVES DARWIN
	PINZON WENMAN ISABELA
ISLANDS:	COLON GALAPAGOS
LANGUAGE:	JIBARO QUECHUA
	SPANISH
MEASURE:	CUADRA FANEGA
MOUNTAIN:	ANDES SANGAY
	CAYAMBE ANTISANA COTOPAXI
NATIVE:	MONTUVIO
PROVINCE:	LOJA AZUAY CANAR
	COLON ELORO CARCHI GUAYAS
	MANABI BOLIVAR LOSRIOS
	COTOPAXI IMBABURA
RIVER:	COCA MIRA NAPO DAULE
	PINDO TIGRE GUAYAS TUMBES
	ZAMORA CURARAY PASTAZA

AGUARICO BOBONAZA
NARANJAL PUTUMAYO
TOWN: JAMA LOJA MERA NAPO
PUYO TENA CANAR GUANO
MANTA PAJAN PINAS PIURA
QUITO YAUPI AMBATO CUENCA
IBARRA PUJILI TULCAN ZARUMA
AZOGUES CAYAMBE GUAMOTE
MACHALA PELILEO PILLARO
SALINAS BABAHOYO GUARANDA
RIOBAMBA
WEIGHT: LIBRA

ECUMENE HEARTH
ECUMENICAL LIBERAL CATHOLIC
ECZEMA TETTER EARWORM
MALANDERS
EDACITY GREED APPETITE
VORACITY
EDDA SAGA
EDDISH ETCH ARRISH EEGRASS
EDDO TARO COCOYAM
EDDY CURL GULF PURL WASH WEEL
WELL ACKER GURGE SHIFT SWIRL
TWIRL WHIRL SWOOSH VORTEX
WIRBLE BACKSET WREATHE
EDDYING WALE
EDEMA BRAXY TUMOR DROPSY
BIGHEAD HYDROPS ANASARCA
SWELLING
EDEMATOUS BLOATED HYDROPIC
EDEN ADEN HEAVEN UTOPIA
ARCADIA ELYSIUM PARADISE
EDENTATA BRUTA
EDENTATE SLOTH ANTEATER
EDGE AGE BIT HEM JAG LIP RIM
BANK BERM BRIM BROW CURB
DRAW FACE KANT LIMB LIST RAND
SIDE TRIM WELL WHET ARRIS
BERME BEVEL BLADE BOARD BRINK
CHIMB CHIME CREST EAVES FRILL
KNIFE LABEL LEDGE MARGE PEARL
RULER SHARP SIDLE SPLAY VERGE
BORDER DECKLE FLANGE FORAGE
IMPALE LABRUM MARGIN NOSING
PLANGE MARGENT SELVAGE
SHARPEN VANDYKE BOUNDARY
EMBORDER KEENNESS MAJORITY
OUTSKIRT SELVEDGE STICKING
UMSTROKE
(— **FORWARD)** CREEP
(— **IN MINING DRIFT)** ARRAGE
(— **OF BASKET)** FOOT
(— **OF BED)** STOCK
(— **OF BIRD'S BILL)** TOMIUM
(— **OF BOOK COVER)** FLAP
(— **OF BOOK)** FERRULE BACKBONE
(— **OF BRILLIANT)** GIRDLE
(— **OF CASK)** CHIME CHINE
(— **OF COAL PILE)** RUN
(— **OF DAM)** CREST
(— **OF DUMP)** TOE
(— **OF FLAG)** HOIST
(— **OF MESA)** CEJA
(— **OF MINERAL VEIN)** APEX
(— **OF ROADWAY)** SHOULDER
(— **OF RUDDER)** BEARDING
(— **OF RUFFLE)** HEADING

(— **OF SAIL)** FOOT HEAD LEACH
LEECH
(— **OF SAW)** SAFE
(— **OF SHELL)** HINGE
(— **OF STRATUM)** BASSET
(— **OF STREAM)** HAG
(— **OF TOOL)** BEZEL BEZIL
(— **OF TOOTH)** SCALPRUM
(— **OF TROUSERS)** CREASE
(— **OF VAULT)** GROIN
(— **OF WOOD)** WOODRIME
(—**S OF COAT)** LAP
(**BEVELED —)** CHAMFER
(**CUTTING —)** SHOE
(**DOUBLE —)** FLAT
(**EMBROIDERED —)** SURFLE
SURPHUL
(**EXTERIOR —)** AMBITUS
(**FRONT — OF BOOK)** FACE
(**ORNAMENTAL —)** FRILL
(**RAGGED —)** RAG
(**ROUGH —S)** FASH
(**SHARP —)** ARRIS BEARD
(**UNPLOWED — OF FIELD)** RAND
(**UNTRIMMED —)** DECKLE
EDGED EDGY EROSE SHARP
CRENATE CUTTING
(— **BY ARCS)** INVECTED
EDGER WHETTER STRANDER
EDGING HEM CURB EDGE LACE LIST
FILET FRILL LEDGE PICOT BORDER
FILLET FRINGE BEADING BINDING
GIMPING HAMBURG COQUILLE
FRILLING PUNTILLA RICKRACK
SKIRTING SURROUND
EDGY EAGER SHARP ANGULAR
CRITICAL SNAPPISH
EDIBLE EDULE EATABLE ESCULENT
EDICT ACT BAN LAW BULL FIAT
TYPE ARRET BANDO BULLA IRADE
ORDER SANAD UKASE ASSIZE
DECREE DICTUM NOTICE COMMAND
EMBARGO PLACARD PROCESS
PROGRAM STATUTE ECTHESIS
EDIFICE DOME CHURCH TURBEH
BUILDING ERECTION TETRAGON
EDIFY GROW BUILD FAVOR TEACH
BENEFIT IMPROVE PROSPER
CONVINCE INSTRUCT ORGANIZE
EDIFYING HIGH SAVORY ELEVATED
EDIT CUT EMEND DIRECT REDACT
REVIEW REVISE ARRANGE COMPILE
CORRECT PREPARE PUBLISH
REWRITE COPYREAD
EDITION KIND EXTRA FINAL FIRST
ISSUE PRINT STAMP ALDINE DIGLOT
SOURCE AUSGABE BULLDOG
HEXAPLA OCTAPLA VERSION
PRINCEPS VARIORUM
(**FIRST —)** PRINCEPS
EDITOR AUTHOR OVERSEER
REDACTOR
EDITORIAL LEADER
EDO BENI BINI
EDUCATE REAR BREED TEACH
TRADE TRAIN EXPAND INFORM
SCHOOL DEVELOP NURTURE
INSTRUCT
EDUCATED BRED CIVIL TAUGHT

TRAINED INFORMED LETTERED
LITERATE
EDUCATION NURTURE BREEDING
LEARNING NORTELRY TRAINING
(**LIBERAL —)** HUMANITY
(**PHYSICAL —)** GYM
EDUCATOR TEACHER
EDUCE DRAW EVOKE ELICIT EVOLVE
EXTORT EXTRACT
EEL ELE GRIG LING OPAH SNIG TUNA
ELVER MORAY SIREN APODAN
CARAPO CONGER FAUSEN MOREIA
MURENE CONGRIO KWATUMA
LAMPREY MURAENA SNIGGLE
WRIGGLE CONGEREE GYMNOTID
KINGKLIP
(**25 —S)** STICK SWARM
(**YOUNG —)** ELVER OLIVER YELVER
EELGRASS DREW WRACK ENALID
EELPOUT BARD LING POUT QUAB
BURBOT CONGER GUFFER YOWLER
LYCODOID
EELSKIN (10 —S) TIMBER
EELSPEAR PILGER
EELWORM EEL NEMA
EERIE EERY SCARY TIMID WEIRD
WISHT CREEPY DISMAL GLOOMY
GOUSTY SPOOKY AWESOME
GHOSTLY GOUSTIE MACABRE
STRANGE UNCANNY ELDRITCH
GHOULISH POKERISH
EFFACE BLOT DASH DELE RASE
RAZE WEAR ERASE CANCEL DEFACE
SPONGE STRIKE DESTROY DISLIMN
EXPUNGE NULLIFY UNPAINT
EFFECT DO SEE DENT DOES FECK
HAVE PRAY PREY TEEM WORK
CAUSE CLOSE ECLAT ENACT ETTLE
EVENT FORCE FRUIT ISSUE STAMP
ENERGY GROWTH INDUCE INTENT
OBTAIN RESULT SECURE SEQUEL
STEREO UPSHOT ACHIEVE ACQUIRE
ARRANGE COMPASS CONDUCE
EMOTION EXECUTE FULFILL
IMPRESS IMPRINT OPERATE
OUTCOME PERFORM PROCURE
PRODUCE PURPORT REALIZE
CAUSATUM COMPLETE CONCLUDE
CONTRIVE FRUITAGE
(— **OF PAST EXPERIENCE)** MNEME
(**BLURRED —)** FUZZ
(**COUNTERBALANCING —)**
STANDOFF
(**DAZZLING —)** ECLAT
(**DECORATIVE —)** CHIPPING
(**ELECTRICAL —)** STRAY
(**ESTHETIC —)** ATMOSPHERE
(**FALSE —)** FACADE
(**FINAL —)** AMOUNT
(**ILL —)** EVIL
(**INTENSE —)** STRESS
(**MOTTLED —)** SPRINKLE
(**MUSICAL —)** BEND SHADING
(**PAINFUL —)** JAR
(**PAINTING —)** STIPPLE
(**PENETRATING —)** SEARCH
(**PERNICIOUS —)** BLAST
(**PERSONAL —S)** DUNNAGE
(**SHATTERING —)** BRISANCE

(THEATRICAL —) CURTAIN
(TO HAVE —) MILITATE
(TOTAL —) ENSEMBLE
(TOXIC —S) THEISM
(TREMOLO —) BEBUNG
(VISIBLE —) TOUCH
EFFECTIVE ABLE HOME REAL ALIVE
GREAT HAPPY SIKER VALID ACTIVE
ACTUAL CAUSAL DEADLY DIRECT
FRUITY POTENT SEVERE SICKER
SOVRAN CAPABLE FECKFUL
TELLING VIRTUAL ADEQUATE
FORCEFUL POWERFUL SMASHING
STRIKING VIGOROUS
EFFECTIVELY NAITLY
EFFECTIVENESS AIM BANG EDGE
VOLTAGE EFFICACY LEVERAGE
EFFECTUAL TOOTHY ADEQUATE
POWERFUL MAGISTRAL
EFFECTUATE FULFIL FULFILL
COMPLETE
EFFEMINATE NICE MILKY SAPPY
BITCHY FEMALE LYDIAN NIMINY
SILKEN TENDER WANTON WEAKLY
CITIZEN EPICENE WOMANLY
FEMINATE FEMININE LADYLIKE
OVERSOFT WOMANISH
EFFERENT EXODIC
EFFERVESCE FIZZ HUFF KNIT
BUBBLE SPARKLE
EFFERVESCENCE FRET CRACKLE
SPARKLE
EFFERVESCENT UP BRISK FIZZY
QUICK BUBBLY ELASTIC BUBBLING
EFFERVESCING BRISK
EFFETE SERE SPENT BARREN
DECADENT ETIOLATE MORIBUND
EFFICACIOUS VALID MIGHTY
POTENT FORCIBLE POWERFUL
SINGULAR VIGOROUS VIRTUOUS
EFFICACY DINT FECK DEVIL FORCE
GRACE MIGHT POWER DEGREE
VIRTUE POTENCY
EFFICIENCY POWER SKILL AGENCY
ABILITY FACULTY DISPATCH
EFFICACY
EFFICIENT ABLE GOOD SMART
VALID POTENT CAPABLE FECKFUL
POWERFUL SPEEDFUL
EFFIGY GUY IDOL POPE SIGN
DUMMY IMAGE LIKENESS
MONUMENT
EFFLORESCE GERMINATE
EFFLORESCENCE RASH BLOOM
BLOSSOM ROSEOLA ANTHESIS
ERUPTION WHITEWASH
EFFLUENCE ISSUE EFFLUX ELAPSE
EMANATE
EFFLUVIA SCENT
EFFLUVIUM AURA MIASMA FLUXION
SPECIES APORRHEA EMISSION
OUTGOING EMANATION
EFFLUX OUTGO OUTFLOW EFFUSION
EFFORT JOB TRY TUG DINT FIST
HUMP JUMP MINT SHOT TOIL ASSAY
BRUNT BURST CRACK DRIVE ESSAY
FLING LABOR NISUS PAINS POWER
REACH STUDY THROE TRIAL ANIMUS
DEVOIR FAVORS FIZZLE FUFFLE

PINGLE STRAIN STROKE THRIFT
ATTEMPT CONATUS MOLIMEN
NITENCY SPLURGE STRETCH
TENSURE TROUBLE WORKING
ENDEAVOR EXERTION GOODWILL
INDUSTRY MOLITION REACHING
STRIVING STRUGGLE
(— FOR ONESELF) FEND
(ABORTIVE —) FIZZLE
(AGONIZED —) THROE
(ARTICULATIVE —) ACCENT
(EARNEST —) STUDY
(EFFECTIVE —) LICK
(FINAL —) CHARETTE
(INITIAL —) ASSAY
(MAXIMUM —) BEST
(SALVATIONIST —) ATTACK
(SINGLE —) HEAT TRICE
(STRENUOUS —) HASSEL HASSLE
(UNSUCCESSFUL —) ATTEMPT
(UTMOST —) DEVOIR BUSINESS
(VIOLENT —) BURST STRAIN
OUTRAGE STRUGGLE
EFFORTLESS EASY
EFFORTLESSNESS EASE
EFFRONTERY BROW FACE GALL
FRONT BRONZE AUDACITY
BOLDNESS FOREHEAD TEMERITY
EFFULGENCE BLAZE GLORY
RADIANT RADIANCE SPLENDOR
EFFULGENT BRIGHT FULGENT
RADIANT SHINING
EFFUSE GUSH SHED FLING EFFUND
EMANATE DISPENSE
EFFUSION EFFLUX FOISON SPILTH
STREAM
EFFUSIVE GOOEY GUSHY LAVISH
SLOPPY GUSHING BUBBLING
EFFUSIVENESS SLOP
EFT ASK EVET NEWT LIZARD TRITON
EGAD ADAD ECOD IGAD SGAD
EGEST VOID EXCRETE ELIMINATE
EGG AI ABET GOAD GOOG OVUM
PROD SEED SPUR URGE CHECK
OVULE SPORE DARNER INCITE
OOCYTE PEEWEE ZYGOTE ACTUATE
COKENEY OOPLAST OOSPERM
PROTOVUM
(— CASE) POD
(— CLUTCH) LAUGHTER
(— OF FISH OR LOBSTER) BERRY
(— ON) HAG EDGE GOAD URGE
(— PRODUCT) ZOON
(—S OF BEES) BROOD
(—S OF SILKWORM) GRAINE
(ACID —) SLOWCASE
(CRACKED —) CHECK CRACK
LEAKER
(DRIED —S) AHUATLE
(DUCK —S) PIDAN
(FLY'S —) BLOW FLYBLOW
(FOSSIL —) OVULITE
(GOLDEN —S) SUNCUP
(GOOSE —) BLOB
(HUNT BIRDS' —S) OOLOGIZE
(INFERTILE —) CLEAR
(SMALL —) OVULE OVULUM
(PL.) OVA ROE SEED EYREN SPAWN
CLUTCH ETTING AHUATLE

EGG AND DART ECHINUS
EGGFRUIT LUCUMA CANISTEL
EGGHEAD HIGHBROW INTELLECTUAL
EGGNOG NOG ADVOCAAT
EGGPLANT BRINJAL SOLANUM
BRINGELA EGGFRUIT
EGG-SHAPED OOID OVAL OVATE
OVOID OOIDAL OBOVOID OVALOID
OVIFORM
EGGSHELL SHARD CASCARON
EGG WHITE GLAIR ALBUMEN
EGG YOLK YELLOW VITELLUS
EGO I SELF ATMAN EGOITY FYLGJA
CONCEIT SUBJECT
EGOCENTRIC INSEEING
EGOISM PRIDE ONEISM VANITY
CONCEIT EGOTISM OWNHOOD
SELFNESS
EGOTISM EGO PRIDE EGOISM
VANITY CONCEIT EGOMANIA
EGREGIOUS FINE GROSS CAPITAL
EMINENT FLAGRANT PRECIOUS
SHOCKING
EGREGIOUSLY BEASTLY
EGRESS EXIT ISSUE OUTGO OUTLET
EXITURE OUTCOME OUTGATE
PASSAGE REGRESS OUTGOING
EGRET HERON PLUME GAULIN
KOTUKU AIGRETTE GAULDING
EGYPT MIZRAIM

EGYPT
BAY: FOUL
CALENDAR: AHET APAP TYBI
PAYNI SHEMU THOTH CHOIAK
HATHOR MECHIR MESORE
PAOPHI PACHONS
CANAL: SUEZ
CAPE: BANAS RASBANAS
CAPITAL: CAIRO ELQAHIRA
CHRISTIAN: COPT COPTIC
COIN: FILS DINAR GIRSH POUND
DIRHAM GUINEA JUNAYH
PIASTER MILLIEME
DAM: ASWAN
DESERT: LIBYAN
GOVERNORATE: SUEZ CAIRO
CANAL SINAI BAHARIYA
BAHRIYAH ALEXANDRIA
GULF: AQABA
ISTHMUS: SUEZ
KING: AY IB KA ITI ITY TUT DJER
DJET HUNY PAMI PEPI SETI
TEOS TETI UNIS ARSES BEBTI
FOUAD ITETI KEBEH KHUFU
KNIAN MENES NEBKA NECHO
NEFER UDIMU ZEMTI ZOSER
CHEOPS DARIUS FAROUK
KHAFRE NARMER RANSES
SENEDJ XERXES MENKURE
PHARAOH PTOLEMY RAMESES
SALADIN CHEPHREN THUTMOSE
LAKE: EDKU IDKU MARYUT
MOERIS MANZALA BURULLUS
MAREOTIS
LAKES: BITTER
MEASURE: APT DRA HEN PIK ROB
DRAA KHET ROUB THEB ABDAT

ARDAB CUBIT FARDE KELEH
KILAH SAHME ARTABA AURURE
FEDDAN KEDDAH ROBHAH
SCHENE CHORYOS DARIBAH
MALOUAH ROUBOUH TOUMNAH
KASSABAH KHAROUBA
MOUNTAIN: SINAI GHARIB
KATHERINA
NAME: UAR
NATIVE: ARAB COPT NILOT
BERBER MUSLIM NUBIAN
OASIS: SIWA DAKHLA KHARGA
FARAFRA BAHARIYA
PENINSULA: SINAI
PORT: TOR SUEZ ATTUR DUMYAT
QUSEIR RASHID SAFAGA
SALLUM ROSETTA DAMIETTA
HURGHADA PORTSAID
ALEXANDRIA
PROVINCE: GIZA QENA QINA
ASWAN ASYUT MINYA SOHAG
DUMYAT FAIYUM SAWHAJ
TAHRIR ALJIZAH BEHEIRA
BENISUEF DAMIETTA GHARBIYA
MINUFIYA SHARQIYA
RESERVOIR: ASWAN
RIVER: NILE
RUINS: ABYDOS SPHINX THEBES
MEMPHIS PYRAMIDS
SUN GOD: RA RE TEM ATMU
ATUM
TOWN: NO MUT DUSH GIZA IDFU
ISNA QENA SAIS SIWA SUEZ
ZOAN ASWAN ASYUT BENHA
BULAQ CAIRO ELTUR FAYID
GIRGA GIZEH LUXOR NAKHL
SALUM SOHAG TAHTA TANIS
TANTA ABYDOW AKHMIN
DUMYAT ELQASR HELWAN
KARNAK RASHID THEBES
BURSAID ROSETTA ZAGAZIG
BENISUEF DAMIETTA ISMAILIA
WEIGHT: KAT KET OKA OKE HEML
KHAR OKIA ROTL ARTAL ARTEL
DEBEN KERAT MINAE MINAS
OKIEH POUND RATEL UCKIA
HAMLAH KANTAR DRACHMA
QUINTAL
WELL: BIRTABA
WIND: KAMSIN SIROCCO
KHAMSEEN

EGYPTIAN ARAB COPT GIPPY GYPPY
TASIAN PHARIAN BADARIAN
MEMPHIAN
EIDER COLK WAMP DIVER EDDER
DUCKER SHOREYER
EIDOLON ICON GHOST IMAGE
IDOLUM PHANTOM LIKENESS
EIGHT ETA ECHT AUGHT CHETH
OCTAD OCTET OCTAVE OGDOAD
OCTONARY
EIGHTH AUGHT
EIGHTH NOTE UNCA CROMA
CHROMA QUAVER
EIRE (SEE IRELAND)
EITHER ANY EDDER ITHER OTHER
WHETHER

EJACULATE BELCH BLURT EJECT
FLING EXCLAIM EMISSION
EJACULATION HOW COADS ZOWIE
BEGORRA UTTERING
(MYSTIC —) OM
EJACULATORY SPUTTERY
EJECT OUT BLOW BOOT CAST EMIT
FIRE HOOF OUST SHED SPAT SPEW
SPIT VOID WARP AVOID BELCH
CHUCK ERUCT ERUPT EVICT EXPEL
SHAKE SHOOT SPOUT SPURT VOMIT
BANISH BOUNCE SQUIRT DEFORCE
DISMISS EXCLUDE EXTRUDE
OBTRUDE DISGORGE OUTBRAID
EJECTION BLOW OUSTER OUTING
EVICTION
EJECTOR LIFTER EDUCTOR
EKE IMP ALSO YEKE AUGMENT
ENLARGE HUSBAND STRETCH
APPENDIX INCREASE LENGTHEN
LIKEWISE UNDERLAY
ELABORATE FIKIE GREAT LABOR
DELUXE DRESSY ELABOR ORNATE
QUAINT REFINE CURIOUS DEVELOP
ENLARGE LABORED PERFECT
ELABORATED WROUGHT
ELABORATELY FANCILY
ELABORATENESS FINENESS
CURIOSITY
ELAMITE SUSIAN ANZANITE
ELAN DASH ARDOR DRIVE GUSTO
VERVE SPIRIT WARMTH POTENCY
ELAND IMPOFO
ELAN VITAL ZOISM
ELAPS MICRURUS
ELAPSE GO RUN PASS ROLL SLIP
GLIDE SPEND EXPIRE
ELAPSING CURRENT
ELASTIC QUICK GARTER RUBATO
SPONGY BUOYANT SPRINGY
STRETCH CHEVEREL CHEVERIL
FLEXIBLE STRETCHY VOLATILE
ELASTICITY GIVE LIFE ELATER
SPRING STRETCH
ELATE BYOU CHEER EXALT EXULT
FLUSH LOFTY RAISE ELATED EXCITE
PLEASE THRILL ELEVATE GLADDEN
INFLATE SUBLIME SUCCESS
ELEVATED HEIGHTEN INSPIRIT
JUBILATE
ELATED RAD HIGH RADE CHUFF
ELATE HAPPY PROUD VAUDY VOGIE
WLONK CHUFFY JOVIAL UPPISH
UPPITY EXCITED EXULTED JOCULAR
SUBLIME EXULTANT GLORIOUS
INFLATED JUBILANT PRIDEFUL
UPLIFTED
ELATER BEETLE CRINULA SKIPJACK
ELATION JOY GLEE RUFF BUOYANCY
ELBOW ELL BEND ANCON JOINT
NUDGE SHOVE CROSET ELBUCK
JOSTLE JUSTLE SPRING PIERDROP
ELCAJA MAFURA
ELDER AIN IVA AINE WITE ELLER
OLDER PRIOR MAHANT SENIOR
ANCIENT NEGUNDO STAROST
TRAMMON ANCESTOR BOUNTREE
BOURTREE CARELESS DANEWORT
ELDERMAN

ELDERLY AGED GRAY ALDER
ELDERN SENILE BADGERLY
ELDEST AYNE EIGNE OLDEST
ELECAMPANE INULA CANADA
ELFWORT SCABWORT
ELECT CALL PICK VOICE ASSUME
CHOOSE CHOSEN DECIDE ISRAEL
PREFER SELECT
ELECTION PROXY CHOICE LECTION
ELECTIONEERING HUSTINGS
ELECTIVE OPTION
ELECTOR VOTER ELISOR CHOOSER
ELIGENT INTRANT ELECTANT
ELECTORATE PEOPLE COUNTRY
ELECTRA LAODICE
(BROTHER OF —) ORESTES
(DAUGHTER OF —) IRIS
(FATHER OF —) ATLAS AGAMEMNON
(HUSBAND OF —) PYLADES
(MOTHER OF —) PLEIONE
CLYTEMNESTRA
(SON OF —) DARDANUS
ELECTRICIAN GAFFER JUICER
BOARDMAN
ELECTRICITY JUICE PYROGEN
ELECTRIC GALVANISM
ELECTRIFY EXCITE THRILL STARTLE
ELECTROCUTE BURN EXECUTE
ELECTRODE DE DEE GRID ANODE
PLATE DYNODE CATHODE IGNITER
CROWFOOT REOPHORE
(PL.) ELEMENT
ELECTRODEPOSIT STRIKE
REGULINE
ELECTROLYTE STRIKE IONOGEN
ELECTROMAGNETIC (— UNIT)
OERSTED ABAMPERE
ELECTRON ION POLARON
ELECTRONIC RADIONIC
ELECTRONOGRAPHY ONSET
ELECTRON TUBE TRIODE
ELECTROPHONE MARTENOT
ELECTROPLATE SILVER
ELECTROTYPE PATCH CLICHE
WORKER ELECTRO
ELECTRUM AMBER ELECTRE
ORICHALC
ELECTRYON (DAUGHTER OF —)
ALCMENE
(FATHER OF —) PERSEUS
(MOTHER OF —) ANDROMEDA
ELECTUARY DIASCORD LECTUARY
THERIACA
ELEGANCE CHIC GARB LUXE CLASP
GRACE STYLE SWANK TASTE
FINERY GAIETY GAYETY LUXURY
NICETY POLISH COURTESY
EUPHUISM FINENESS FRIPPERY
GRANDEUR SPLENDOR
ELEGANT CHIC DINK FAIR FEAT FINE
FIXY GENT POSH CIVIL COMPT
FANCY SHARP SLEEK SWANK
CHOICE CLASSY DAINTY DELUXE
DRESSY FACETE MINION QUAINT
SUPERB SWANKY URBANE VENUST
CAPITAL CLEANLY COURTLY
FEATISH FEATOUS GENTEEL MINIKIN
REFINED SMICKER DELICATE
GINGERLY GRACEFUL GRAZIOSO

HANDSOME POLISHED TASTEFUL
ELEGANTLY FINE TALLY FAIRLY
GENTLY GINGERLY
ELEGIAC MOURNFUL EPICEDIAL
ELEGY POEM SONG DIRGE KINAH
QINAH LAMENT MONODY EPICEDE
ELEMENT AIR ATOM DIAD DYAD
RECT WOOF BEARD ETHER FIBER
FIBRE METAL MONAD PUNCT STUFF
AETHER ARTIAD COSTAL FACTOR
HEPTAD LOSSER MATTER MOMENT
SIMPLE ACTINON ADAPTER
BUNCHER CARRIER CATCHER
ESSENCE FEATURE ACTINIDE
BACKBONE CEREBRAL EQUATION
PERISSAD RUDIMENT SELECTOR
THERBLIG
(— IN GRAPH) SPIKE
(— IN WAVE) DART
(— IN WORD GROUP) KOINON
(— OF ALCHEMIST) AIR FIRE EARTH
WATER
(— OF EXISTENCE) DHARMA
(— OF MACHINE) HORN SPIDER
(— OF WEALTH) COMMODITY
(ALIEN —) ALLOY
(ARCHITECTURAL —) SLAB
(BINDING —) CEMENT
(CHEMICAL —) TIN GOLD IRON
LEAD NEON ZINC ARGON BORON
RADON XENON BARIUM CARBON
CERIUM CESIUM COBALT COPPER
CURIUM ERBIUM HELIUM INDIUM
IODINE MURIUM NICKEL OSMIUM
OXYGEN RADIUM SILVER SODIUM
SULFUR ARSENIC BISMUTH BROMINE
CADMIUM CALCIUM FERMIUM
GALLIUM HAFNIUM HOLMIUM
IRIDIUM KRYPTON LITHIUM
MERCURY NIOBIUM RHENIUM
RHODIUM SILICON TERBIUM
THORIUM THULIUM URANIUM
WOLFRAM YTTRIUM ANTIMONY
ASTATINE CHLORINE CHROMIUM
EUROPIUM FLUORINE FRANCIUM
HYDROGEN LUTETIUM MASURIUM
NITROGEN NOBELIUM PLATINUM
POLONIUM RUBIDIUM SAMARIUM
SCANDIUM SELENIUM TANTALUM
THALLIUM TITANIUM TUNGSTEN
VANADIUM
(COMMUNION —) GIFT
(CRIMINAL —) GANGLAND
(DECORATIVE —S) ART
(DOMINANT —) CAPSHEAF
(ELECTRIC —) IMPEDOR
(ESSENTIAL —) CORPUS
(EUCHARISTIC —S) HAGIA SPECIES
(FATAL —) BANE
(FUNDAMENTAL —) STAMEN
(HEATING —) CALANDRIA
(HYPOTHETICAL —) CORONIUM
(INTERFERING —) CRIMP
(LAMP —) GLOWER
(LEADING —) HEAD
(LINGUISTIC—) SERVILE INTENSIVE
(MILITARY —) SUPPORT
(MODIFYING —) LEAVENING
(MORAL —) DAENA

(MOST IMPORTANT —) CAPSTONE
(PRIMAL —) GUNA SALT ARCHE
(PRINCIPAL —) STAPLE
(SKELETAL —) SCLERE
(STRUCTURAL —) ARCUALE
(SUPPOSED —) WELSIUM VICTORIUM
(SUSTAINING —) BREAD STAPLE
(TRANSITORY —S) SKANDHAS
(UNITING —) BOND
(PL.) DETAIL ALPHABET
ELEMENTAL PURE BASIC PRIMAL
SIMPLE PRIMARY ULTIMATE
ELEMENTARY SIMPLE INITIAL
INCHOATE ULTIMATE
ELEMI ANEMI ANIME MATTI RESIN
CONIMA
ELEPHANT COW BULL CALF HINE
PUNK HATHI HATTY JUMBO ROGUE
MUCKNA TUSKER KOOMKIE
AIRAVATA LOXODONT MASTODON
OLIPHANT
ELEPHANT FISH JOSEF JOSUP
JOSEPH
ELEPHANTIASIS TYRIASIS
ELEPHANTINE HUGE ENORMOUS
ELEPHANT'S-EAR TARO
ELEPHANT SHREW JUMPER
ELEUT KALMUK KALMYK KALMUCK
ELEVATE HAIN JUMP LIFT REAR RISE
EDIFY ELATE ENSKY ERECT EXALT
EXTOL GRIMP HEAVE HOIST MOUNT
RAISE TOWER REFINE UPLIFT
ADVANCE DIGNIFY ENHANCE
ENNOBLE GLORIFY PROMOTE
SUBLIME UPRAISE HEIGHTEN
INSPIRIT
ELEVATED EL FINE HIGH GREAT
LOFTY NOBLE RISEN STEEP
AMOTUS ELATED RAISED RISING
WINGED ELEVATO EXALTED
MOUNTED STILTED MAJESTIC
UPLIFTED
(— IN CHARACTER) HIGH
(NOT —) COMICAL
ELEVATION UP ARM BAND BANK
DOME DRUM GLEE HIGH HILL HUMP
LIFT RISE SPUR TOFT TOOT UMBO
BULLA GRADE KNOLL MOUND PITCH
RAISE RIDGE SHOAL SWELL TOWER
WHEAL CONULE CRISTA HEIGHT
PAPULE UPLIFT DIGNITY FURCULA
MAJESTY UPRIGHT ALTITUDE
EMINENCE EVECTION HIGHNESS
LEVATION MOUNTAIN SWELLING
(— OF CARTILAGE) ANTHELIX
(— OF CUTICLE) BLEB
(— OF SKIN) BLISTER
(— ON TOOTH) STYLE
(— SEPARATING CREEKS) BUGOR
(GUN —) RANDOM
(TURRET —) HOOD
ELEVATOR BIN CAGE LIFT SILO
HOIST BRIDGE LIFTER TEAGLE
HOISTER STACKER UPTAKER
UPLIFTER UPRAISER
ELEVENTH ELFT
ELF FAY HAG HOB IMP OAF PUG
DROW FANE OUPH PERI PIXY
DWARF ELFIN FAIRY GNOME OUPHE

PIGMY PIXIE ELFKIN GOBLIN SPIRIT
SPRITE URCHIN BLASTIE BROWNIE
INCUBUS SUCCUBUS
ELFIN ELF FEY CHILD ELFIC ELFISH
URCHIN
ELFISH ELFIN ELVAN ELVISH IMPISH
URCHIN ELFLIKE TRICKSY
ELICIT DRAW MILK PUMP CLAIM
EDUCE EVOKE EXACT FETCH WREST
WRING DEDUCE DEMAND ENTICE
EXTORT INDUCE EXTRACT SOLICIT
ELIDE OMIT SKIP ANNUL IGNORE
DESTROY NULLIFY DEMOLISH
SUPPRESS
ELIGIBILITY FITNESS
ELIGIBLE FIT ACTIVE WORTHY
SUITABLE
ELIMINATE FAN COMB EDIT KILL
EDUCE EXPEL SCRUB DELETE
EFFACE EXCEPT IGNORE REMOVE
SCREEN WINNOW BLANKET
BRACKET DIVULGE EXCLUDE
EXCRETE RELEASE SCISSOR
SILENCE SUBLATE SEPARATE
ELIMINATION STRIP
ELISION SYNCOPE
ELITE BEST LITE PINK CIRCLE
CHOICE FLOWER GENTRY SELECT
PERFECTI
ELIXIR AMRITA SPIRIT AMREETA
ARCANUM CORDIAL CUREALL
ESSENCE PANACEA MEDICINE
ELK ALCE DEER LAMA LOSH ALAND
ALCES ELAND LOSHE MOOSE
CERVID SAMBAR WAPITI SAMBHUR
WAMPOOSE
(— HIDE) LOSH
(YOUNG —) DEACON
ELK BARK BIGBLOOM
ELL ULNA ELBOW ALNAGE ADDITION
ELLIPSE OVAL
ELLIPSIS BRING ELLIPSE
ELLIPSOGRAPH TRAMMEL
ELLIPSOID CONOID ELLIPTIC
SPHEROID
ELLIPTICAL OVAL OVATE OBLONG
ELLOBIUM AURICULA
ELM ULME ELVEN ULMUS WAHOO
MEZCAL CHEWBARK ORHAMWOOD
ELOCUTION SPEECH DICTION
ORATORY
ELOCUTIONIST READER RECITER
ELOIGN CONVEY REMOVE ABSCOND
CONCEAL
ELONGATE EXTEND REMOVE
STRETCH LENGTHEN PROTRACT
ELONGATED LANK LONG LINEAR
OBLONG PROLATE SLENDER
HAIRLIKE PRODUCED
ELOPE DECAMP ESCAPE ABSCOND
ELOQUENCE FACUND FLUENCY
ORATORY
ELOQUENT VOCAL DISERT FACUND
FERVID FLUENT SILVER RENABLE
SPEAKING

EL SALVADOR
CAPITAL: SANSALVADOR

COIN: PESO COLON CENTAVO
DANCE: PASILLO
GULF: FONSECA
INDIAN: PIPIL
LAKE: GUIJA ILOPANGO
MEASURE: VARA CAFIZ CAHIZ
 FANEGA TERCIA BOTELLA
 CAJUELA CANTARO MANZANA
POINT: REMEDIOS
PORT: CUTUCO ACAJUTLA
RIVER: JIBOA LAPAZ LEMPA
RUINS: TAZUMAL
TOWN: CUTUCO IZALCO CORINTO
 METAPAN ACAJUTLA USULUTAN
VOLCANO: IZALCO
WEIGHT: BAG CAJA LIBRA

ELSE OR ENS ENSE OTHER BESIDES
 INSTEAD
ELSEWHERE ALIBI EXCEPT THENCE
 (FROM —) ALIUNDE
ELUCIDATE CLEAR LUCID EXPLAIN
 SIMPLIFY
ELUDE BEAT FLEE FOIL MISS MOCK
 SLIP AVOID DODGE EVADE BAFFLE
 BEFOOL DELUDE DOUBLE ESCAPE
 BEGUILE DECEIVE HEDGEHOP
ELUSIVE EELY LUBRIC SHIFTY
 SUBTLE TRICKY TWISTY EVASIVE
 BAFFLING FUGITIVE SLIPPERY
ELYSIUM EDEN ANNWIN PARADISE
ELYTRON HUSK SCUTE SHARD
 SHERD SHEATH
ELYTRUM SHARD TEGMEN
EM EMMA
 (HALF —) EN
EMACIATED LEAN POOR EMPTY
 GAUNT MEAGER PEAKED SKINNY
 WASTED WASTREL SKELETAL
EMACIATING MARCID
EMACIATION NITON TABES MACIES
 ATROPHY POVERTY MARASMUS
EMANATE FLOW ARISE EMANE
 EXUDE ISSUE DERIVE EFFUSE
 EXHALE OUTRAY SPRING BREATHE
 OUTCOME PROCEED RADIATE
EMANATING EFFLUENT
EMANATION FUG AURA BEAM BLAS
 GLORY NITON AZILUT BREATH
 EFFLUX ELAPSE EIDOLON OUTCOME
 PROCESS SEPHIRA EMISSION
 (— FROM A MEDIUM) ECTOPLASM
 (PL.) SCENT
EMANCIPATE FREE MANUMIT
 RELEASE LIBERATE UNFETTER
EMANCIPATION FREEDOM RELEASE
 (FINAL —) NIRVANA
EMASCULATE GELD SOFTEN
 EVIRATE CASTRATE ENERVATE
EMBALM BALM CERE MUMMY SPICE
 BALSAM SEASON CONDITE MUMMIFY
EMBANK BUND
EMBANKMENT BAY BAND BANK
 BUND DIKE DYKE FILL QUAY ARGIN
 DIGUE LEVEE MOUND REVET
 BUNKER STAITH BACKING BANKING
 PILAPIL RAMPART RAMPIRE
 SEAWALL APPROACH STRENGTH

EMBARGO EDICT ORDER IMBARGE
 BLOCKADE STOPPAGE
EMBARK BANK SAIL SHIP ENGAGE
 ENLIST INSHIP INVEST LAUNCH
 IMBARGE
EMBARRASS SET CHAW CLOG FAZE
 HACK LAND ABASH ANNOY SHAME
 UPSET BOGGLE CUMBER GRAVEL
 HAMPER HINDER HOBBLE IMPEDE
 PLUNGE PUZZLE RATTLE CONFUSE
 ENTRIKE FLUMMOX INVOLVE
 NONPLUS BEWILDER CONFOUND
 DUMFOUND ENCUMBER ENTANGLE
 HANDICAP IMPESTER OBSTRUCT
 STRAITEN
EMBARRASSED FLURRIED SHEEPISH
EMBARRASSING HIDEOUS
EMBARRASSINGLY AWKWARDLY
EMBARRASSMENT FIX GENE LURCH
 SHAME STAND CADDLE HOBBLE
 PUZZLE
EMBASSY SAND ERRAND AMBASSY
 MESSAGE MISSION INBASSAT
 LEGATION
EMBATTLED BATTLED CRENELE
 BRETESSE CRENELEE
EMBAY BATHE DETAIN ENCLOSE
 SHELTER SUFFUSE ENCIRCLE
 SURROUND
EMBAYMENT FIORD FJORD
EMBED BED SET BOND IMBED
 STAMP CHARGE ENGAGE EMBOWEL
 IMMERSE
EMBEDDED INNATE ENGAGED
 IMMERSED
EMBELLISH GEM DECK GILD TRIM
 ADORN DRESS FUDGE GRACE
 BEDECK BLAZON EMBOSS ENRICH
 FIGURE FLOWER APPAREL BEDRAPE
 EMBLAZE GARNISH MYSTIFY
 VARNISH BEAUTIFY DECORATE
 FLOURISH ORNAMENT
EMBELLISHED FLORID GESTED
 ORNATE COLORED FUCUSED
 BROCADED SPLENDID
EMBELLISHMENT FILIP GRACE
 FILLIP RELISH AGREMEN GARNISH
 GILDING WINDING AGREMENT
 FLOURISH MOUNTING ORNAMENT
 PARERGON TRAPPING TRICKING
 PASSAGGIO
 (MUSICAL —) ARABESQUE
 (PL.) FIXINGS
EMBER ASH COAL AIZLE GLEED
 IMBER CINDER
 (RED-HOT —S) BAGA
EMBEZZLE STEAL PECULATE
 SQUANDER
EMBEZZLEMENT THEFT
EMBITTER SOUR BITTER CURDLE
 ACIDIFY ENVENOM ACERBATE
 EMPOISON VERJUICE
EMBITTERED SOURED ACERBATE
EMBLAZON LAUD ADORN EXTOL
 BLAZON DISPLAY EMBLAZE EXHIBIT
 GLORIFY
EMBLAZONED CLOUE CLOUEE
 CRINED CRESTED BRISTLED
 (— WITH ANTLERS) ATTIRED

 (— WITH BEARD) BARBED
EMBLAZONMENT HERALDRY
EMBLEM BAR ANKH ATEN MACE
 ORLE SEAL SIGN STAR TYPE
 AWARD BADGE CREST CROSS
 EAGLE FAVOR IMAGE TIARA TOKEN
 DEVICE DIADEM ENSIGN FIGURE
 KAHILI SABCAT SHIELD SIGNAL
 SYMBOL TRISUL CHARACT IMPRESA
 IMPRESE SCEPTER SCEPTRE
 ALLEGORY CADUCEUS COLOPHON
 INSIGNIA
 (— OF CUCKOLD) HORN
 (— OF IRELAND) SHAMROCK
 (— OF WALES) LEEK
 (PRINTING —) COLOPHON
 (SACRED —) HIEROGRAM
EMBLEMATIC TYPAL FIGURAL
 TYPICAL SYMBOLIC
EMBLIC AMLA AULA MYROBALAN
EMBODIMENT MAP SON SELF
 AVATAR GENIUS EPITOME IMAGERY
 BODIMENT
EMBODY BODY UNITE INBODY
 CONTAIN EXPRESS COALESCE
 ORGANIZE
EMBOLDEN BOLD BIELD BRAVE
 ERECT NERVE ASSURE BOWDEN
 ENHARDY HEARTEN STOMACH
EMBOLUS CLOT STYLE
EMBOSOM BOSOM FOSTER CHERISH
 ENCLOSE IMBOSOM SHELTER
 SURROUND
EMBOSS BOSS HIDE KNOB KNOT
 ADORN BLOCK CHASE GOFFER
 INDENT POUNCE ANTIQUE CONCEAL
 ENCLOSE EXHAUST GAUFFER
 INFLATE ORNAMENT
EMBOSSED BOSSED RAISED
 ANTIQUE CHAMPED
EMBOSSING CELATURE
EMBOUCHURE LIP CHOPS LIPPING
EMBOWER BOWER
EMBOWERED ARBORED
EMBRACE ARM HUG CLIP COLL
 FOLD LOVE NECK PLAT SIDE ZONE
 ADOPT BOSOM BRACE CHAIN CLASP
 CLING CRUSH ENARM GRASP HALCH
 HALSE INARM OXTER TWINE
 ABRAZO ACCEPT ACCOLL AMPLEX
 BECLIP CARESS CLINCH COMPLY
 CUDDLE ENFOLD FATHOM HUDDLE
 INCLIP INFOLD PLIGHT SHRINE
 AMPLECT CHERISH CONTAIN
 ENCLOSE ESPOUSE INCLUDE
 INVOLVE ACCOLADE AMPLEXUS
 COMPLECT COMPRESS COMPRISE
 CONCLUDE ENCIRCLE
EMBRACING COLLING OSCULANT
EMBRASURE LOOP PORT VENT
 CRENEL CRENELLE PORTHOLE
EMBROCATION ARNICA EMBROCHE
 LINIMENT
EMBROIDER RUN TAT DARN FRET
 LACE BROUD COUCH FAGOT PANEL
 SMOCK BEWORK EMBOSS FAGGOT
 FRIEZE PURFLE STITCH SURFLE
 TISSUE BROIDER TAMBOUR
 ORNAMENT

EMBROIDERED BRODE BRODEE BROWDEN BROCADED
EMBROIDERER SPRIGGER
EMBROIDERY KANT LACE OPUS WORK BREDE ASSISI BONNAZ CREWEL EDGING HEDEBO APPAREL CHICKEN CUTWORK ORPHREY SETWORK TAMBOUR ARRASENE BRODERIE BROIDERY FAGOTING LISTWORK PHULKARI SMOCKING TAPESTRY
EMBROIL BROIL JUMBLE INVOLVE PERPLEX TROUBLE DISORDER DISTRACT ENTANGLE
EMBRYO GERM CADET FETUS OVULE FOETUS EMBRYON NEURULA ACANTHOR BLASTULA GASTRULA PRINCIPE
EMBRYONIC GERMINAL
EMCEE HOST
EME AUNT YEME UNCLE FRIEND NEIGHBOR
EMEND (ALSO SEE AMEND) EDIT MEND ALTER AMEND BETTER REFORM REPEAL REVISE CORRECT IMPROVE RECTIFY REDRESS EMENDATE
EMERALD BERYL GREEN EMRAUD EMERANT PRASINE SMARAGD
EMERALD FISH ESMERALDA
EMERGE BOB DIP BOLT LOOM PEER RISE BREAK ERUPT EXUDE ISSUE START APPEAR BECOME PLUNGE SPRING DEBOUCH EXTRUDE
(— **FROM EGGSHELL**) HATCH ECLOSE
(— **FROM SLEEP**) AWAKE
EMERGENCE NEED BIRTH EGRESS GROWTH PRICKLE BECOMING DEBOUCHE ECLOSION EMERSION ERUPTION EXIGENCE TENTACLE
(— **FROM DARKNESS**) BREAK
EMERGENCY NEED PEND PUSH PINCH CRISIS STRAIT SUDDEN EMERGENT EXIGENCY JUNCTURE
EMERGENT RISING
EMERGING EMANANT EMERGENT
EMERITA HIPPA
EMERY EMERIL SMIRIS ABRASIVE CORUNDUM
EMETIC ALUM PICK PUKE PUKER VOMIT EVACUANT VOMITIVE VOMITORY
EMIGRANT EMIGRE EXODIST PATARIN SETTLER COLONIST PATERINE STRANGER
(— **FROM MECCA**) COMPANION
EMIGRATE MOVE REMOVE MIGRATE
EMIGRATION EXODUS HEGIRA HEJIRA SWARMING
EMINENCE DUN BALL BERG CRAG KNOT MONS MOTE NOTE POLE RANK RISE SCAR TOOT CHIEF HOYLE KNOLL PERCH STATE WHEAL WORTH ASCENT HEIGHT KRANTZ RENOWN RIDEAU ALTITUDE GRANDEUR TUBERCLE
(— **OF HAND**) SUBVOLA
EMINENT BIG ARCH HIGH CHIEF

GRAND GREAT LOFTY NOBLE NOTED FAMOUS MARKED SIGNAL EXCELSE GLORIOUS RENOWNED SINGULAR TOWERING
EMIR AMIR AMEER NOBLE RULER LEADER PRINCE ADMIRAL GOVERNOR
EMISSARY SPY AGENT SCOUT LEGATE DELEGATE
EMISSION FUME GUST VENT
EMISSIVE EMITTENT EXHALANT
EMIT RUN BARK BEAM CAST DRIP GIVE GUSH HURL LASH MOVE OOZE PASS POUR REEK SEND SHED SPIT VENT VOID WARP AVOID BELCH EJECT ERUCT EXERT EXUDE FLASH FLING ISSUE UTTER YIELD DECANT DONATE EVOLVE EXHALE EXPIRE SPREAD BREATHE DISTILL EMANATE EXHAUST OUTSEND RADIATE REFLAIR ERUCTATE TRANSMIT
(— **FOAM**) SPURGE
(— **FORCEFULLY**) FIRE
(— **IN PUFFS**) PLUFF
(— **LIGHT**) GLOW
(— **OUTCRIES**) CHUNNER CHUNTER
(— **PLAY OF COLORS**) OPALESCE
(— **RAYS**) RADIATE IRRADIATE
(— **SMOKE**) SMEECH
(— **SOUND**) BUFF MOVE
(— **SPARKS**) SNAP
(— **ODOR**) REEK STEAM
EMITTING EMISSIVE SOUNDING
EMMENAGOGUE ALOE SAFFRON GROUNDSEL
EMMER SPELTZ AMELCORN
EMMET ANT ENEMY PISMIRE FORMICID
EMOLLIATE SOFTEN
EMOLLIENT LENIENT ICHTHYOL LENITIVE MALACTIC MOLLIENT SUPPLING
EMOLUMENT FEES WAGES INCOME PROFIT SALARY BENEFIT STIPEND
EMOTION IRE LOVE ONDE STIR AGONY ANGER CHORD GRIEF HEART SHAME AFFECT EFFECT MOTION RAPTUS SNIVEL SPLEEN ECSTASY FEELING PASSION VULTURE GRAMERCY MOVEMENT SURPRISE
(**CONTROLLING** —) LEITMOTIF LEITMOTIV
(**EVIL** —) DEMON DAEMON
EMOTIONAL DRIPPY EMOTIVE
(**UNDULY** —) SPOONY SPOONEY
EMOTIONLESS COLD
EMPATHY SYMPATHY
EMPEROR I IMP CZAR INCA KING TSAR AKBAR RULER TENNO CAESAR DESPOT KAISER SULTAN BAGINDA MONARCH VIKRAMA AUGUSTUS IMPERIAL PADISHAH
EMPERY DOMAIN EMPIRE EMPIRY DOMINION
EMPHASIS ANGLE ACCENT STRESS WEIGHT EMPIRISM SALIENCE
EMPHASIZE HIT CLICK PINCH PRESS ACCENT BETONE CHARGE STRESS

EMPHATIC STRONG EARNEST MARCATO SERIOUS ENFATICO FORCIBLE MARCANDO POSITIVE
EMPHATICALLY FLATLY STRONGLY POINTEDLY
EMPHYSEMA HEAVES
EMPIRE RULE SWAY POWER REALM REIGN STATE DIADEM DOMAIN EMPERY CONTROL KINGDOM IMPERIUM
(— **STATE OF SOUTH**) GEORGIA
(— **STATE**) NEWYORK
(**SELJUK** —) RUM ROUM
EMPIRIC QUACK IMPOSTOR
EMPIRICIST VIRTUOSO
EMPLACEMENT BATTERY GALLERY PLATFORM
EMPLOY FEE PAY USE BUSK BUSY HIRE PLOY TAKE WAGE WISE ADOPT APPLY BESET IMPLY SPEND BESTOW ENGAGE ENLIST INFOLD INVOKE OCCUPY SUPPLY CONCERN CONDUCT ENCLOSE IMPROVE INVOLVE SERVICE UTILIZE PRACTICE
(— **FLATTERY**) COLLOGUE
(— **ONESELF ABOUT**) TOSS
(— **SHIFTS**) CHICANE
EMPLOYED APPLIED ENGAGED
EMPLOYEE HAND HELP BOOTS CLERK FACTOR LEADER BELLBOY BOOTBOY CALLBOY CARRIER SERVANT CHASSEUR CIVILIAN FLOORMAN IMPROVER
EMPLOYER JOSS BLOKE GAFFER ENGAGER MANAGER GOVERNOR
(**SMALL** —) CORK
EMPLOYMENT FEE JOB USE CALL HIRE NOTE TASK TOIL USER WORK CRAFT TRADE TREAD USAGE MISTER THRIFT CALLING PURPOSE SERVICE USAUNCE BUSINESS EXERCISE RETAINER VOCATION
(**CASUAL** —) GRASS
EMPORIUM MART SHOP BAZAR STORE BAZAAR EMPORY MARKET STAPLE MONOPOLE
EMPOWER POWER ENABLE ENTITLE DELEGATE DEPUTIZE
EMPRESS IMPX EMPERESS IMPERIAL KAISERIN
EMPTIED DRAINED
EMPTILY TOOMLY
EMPTINESS VAIN VOID INANE ANEMIA VACUUM VANITY ANAEMIA INANITY VACANCY VACUITY LEERNESS
(— **OF SPIRIT**) ENNUI
EMPTY DRY FAT RID TIM AIRY BARE BOSS BUZZ CANT DEAF DUMP EMPT FALL FARM FREE GLIB HOWE IDLE LEER NEAR POUR ROOM TEEM TOOM VAIN VIDE VOID ADDLE AVOID BLANK BLEED CLEAN CLEAR DRAIN EQUAL EXPEL HUSKY INANE LEERY MOUTH SCOOP SHOOT STARK START STRIP SWAMP TINNY WINDY BARREN BUBBLE CHAFFY DEVOID HOLLOW JEJUNE STRIKE SWASTY UNEMPT UNLOAD VACANT VACATE

DELIVER DEPLETE EXHAUST
EXPRESS UNTAKEN VACUATE
VACUOUS DISGORGE EVACUATE
EVANESCE NEGATION UNFILLED
(— AN EGG) BLOW
EMPTY-HEADED VAIN DOLLISH
EMPTYING EVACUANT
(ACT OF —) KENOSIS
EMPTY-SOUNDING TOOM
EMPUSA MONSTER SPECTER
SPECTRE
EMPYREAN ETHER AETHER
HEAVENS EMPYREUM
EMU EMEU RHEA RATITE
EMU APPLE COLANE
EMU BUSH BERRIGAN
EMULATE APE VIE COPY EMULE
EQUAL EXCEL RIVAL COMPETE
IMITATE
EMULATION STRIFE CONTEST
PARAGON RIVALRY
EMULATOR RIVAL
EMULOUS EMULATE ENVIOUS
EMULOUSLY AVIE
EMULSIFIABLE SOLUBLE
EMULSION PAP LATEX
EMU WREN STIPITURE
EN NUT
ENABLE ABLE EMPOWER ENTITLE
QUALIFY INHABILE
ENACT LIVE MAKE PASS ADOPT
DECREE EFFECT ORDAIN ACTUATE
APPOINT PERFORM PORTRAY
ENACTMENT LAW DOOM ENACT
NOVEL ASSIZE DECREE MEASURE
PASSAGE STATUTE ENACTION
ENACTURE
ENAMEL AMEL FLUX SLIP EMAIL
GLAZE GLOSS PAINT SLUSH AUMAIL
SHIPPO SMALTO DENTINE LIMOGES
SCHMELZ
ENAMOR LOVE CHARM SMITE
CAPTIVE
ENAMORED FOND EPRIS EPRISE
MASHED AMOROUS CHARMED
SMITTEN
(VAINLY —) FOOLISH
ENCAMP TELD TENT LODGE PITCH
INCAMP LAAGER BIVOUAC LEAGUER
ENCAMPMENT CAMP DOUAR SIEGE
LAAGER BIVOUAC CASTRUM
HUTMENT TOLDERIA
ENCASE CASE HOUSE SHELL INCASE
ENCHASE INCLOSE ENCAPSUL
SURROUND
ENCELIA INCIENSO
ENCEPHALON CEREBRUM
ENCHAIN FETTER INCHAIN
ENCHANT CHARM DELUDE GLAMOR
INCANT ATTRACT BESPELL BEWITCH
DELIGHT GLAMOUR BEDAZZLE
ENSORCEL
ENCHANTED RAPT HAGGED
CAPTIVE
ENCHANTER MAUGIS CHARMER
MAGICIAN MALAGIGI
ENCHANTING WIZARD HEAVENLY
SPELLFUL
ENCHANTMENT HEX TAKE CHARM

FAIRY MAGIC SPELL SPOKE CARACT
CHANTRY DEVILRY GRAMARY
SORCERY SORTIARY WITCHERY
ENCHANTRESS CIRCE FAIRY MEDEA
ACRASIA URGANDA
ENCHARGE ENJOIN ENTRUST
ENCHASE INFIX ENRICH ENGRAVE
ENCHIRIDION MANUAL HANDBOOK
TREATISE
ENCHORIAL NATIVE DEMOTIC
DOMESTIC
ENCIPHER CODE CIPHER ENCRYPT
ENCIRCLE ORB BAND BELT BIND
CLIP COIL GIRD GIRT HALO HOOP
PALE RING RINK STEM WIRE ZONE
BELAY BRACE CLASP CROWN
EMBAY EMBOW GIRTH HEDGE
INORB ROUND TWINE TWIST BECLIP
CIRCLE EMBALL ENGIRT ENLACE
ENRING ENWIND FATHOM GIRDLE
IMPALE SWATHE WRITHE BETREND
COMPASS EMBRACE ENCLAVE
ENCLOSE ENTWINE ENVIRON
ENWHEEL SERPENT WREATHE
CINCTURE CORSELET ENSPHERE
IMMANTLE SURROUND
ENCIRCLED GIRT CINCT BELTED
SUCCINCT
ENCIRCLEMENT EMBRACE
ENCIRCLING AROUND EMBRACE
CORONARY ENCYCLIC
ENCLAVE INLIER
ENCLOAK MANTLE
ENCLOSE IN BAY BOX CAN HEM LAP
MEW ORB PAR PEN PIN RIM BANK
BUNG CAGE CASE COOP FORT GIRD
HAIN HOOP PALE SPAR TINE WALL
WARD YARD BOSOM BOUND BOWER
BRICK CHEST CLOSE DITCH EMBAR
EMBED EMBOX FENCE FRAME GRIPE
HEDGE HOUSE IMBED INURN
BOUGHT CARTON CASTLE CAVERN
CIRCLE CORRAL EMBANK EMBOSS
EMPALE EMPARK EMPLOY ENCASE
ENCYST ENFOLD ENGULF ENLOCK
FASTEN IMMURE IMPALE IMPARK
INCASE INCLIP INHOOP INSACK
INWALL JACKET PICKET POCKET
TACKLE APPROVE CAPSULE
COMPASS CONFIDE CONTAIN
CURTAIN EMBOSOM EMBOWEL
EMBOWER EMBRACE ENCHASE
ENCLAVE ENGLOBE ENHEDGE
ENVELOP HARNESS IMBOSOM
IMMERSE IMPOUND INBOUND
INCLUDE INFIELD PARROCK PINFOLD
SHEATHE BULKHEAD COMPRISE
COMPRIZE CONCLUDE CONVOLVE
EMBORDER ENCIRCLE ENSHRINE
ENSPHERE IMPRISON LANDLOCK
PALISADE PARCLOSE SURROUND
(— IN ARMOR) EMPANOPLY
(— LOGS) CRIB
ENCLOSED BOUND CLOSED OBTECT
INGROWN INTERNAL
ENCLOSING LIMITARY
ENCLOSURE HAG HAW HOK MEW
PAR PEN REE STY TYE BAWN BOMA
BYTH CAGE CAVE CELL COOP DOCK

FOLD HAIN HOCK KILN LIST PEEL
SEPT SKIT SLOT TIGH TOWN WALL
WEIR YARD ALTIS ATAJO BASIN
BLIND BOOLY BOOTH BOSOM
CAROL CLOSE COURT CRAWL
CREEP CUBBY FENCE FRANK GARTH
GOTRA HOARD KENCH KRAAL
LOBBY MARAI PLECK POUND REEVE
STALL STELL AVIARY BOOLEY
BOXING CANCHA CARREL CORRAL
COWPEN CRUIVE DRYLOT GARDEN
HURDLE INTAKE KENNEL OUTSET
PALING PRISON SERAIL TAMBOR
TEOPAN TINING VIVARY WARREN
BELLOWS BOROUGH BULLPEN
CLOSURE COCKPIT EMBRACE
GALLERY GONDOLA HENNERY
HOUSING HUMIDOR LANTERN
PADDOCK PIGHTLE PUDDOCK
SEVERAL STUFFER TAMBOUR
AEDICULA CASEMATE CHIPYARD
CINCTURE CLAPNEST CLAUSURE
CLOISTER COMPOUND DELUBRUM
ENCHASER PARADISE POUNDAGE
PRECINCT PURPRISE SEPIMENT
SERAGLIO SKIRTING STOCKADE
VIVARIUM
(— ABOUT ALTAR) BEMA
(— FOR BOWLING) ALLEY
(— FOR COCKPIT) CANOPY
(— FOR FISH) CROY YAIR YARE
KENCH SPILLER SPILLET
(— FOR JURY) BOX
(— FOR KNIGHTLY ENCOUNTERS)
BARRACE
(— FOR LIGHT) LANTERN
(— FOR ROASTING ORE) STALL
(— OF HOUSE) BAWN
(— SURROUNDED BY DITCH) COP
(ELEPHANT —) KEDDAH
(OBLONG —) CIRCUS
(POULTRY —) HENNERY
(SACRED —) SECOS SEKOS
ENCOLPION PANAGIA
ENCOMIAST EULOGIST
ENCOMIUM ELOGE ENCOMY
EULOGY PRAISE PLAUDIT TRIBUTE
ENCOMPASS BEGO BELT CLIP GIRD
PALE RING SPAN WALL WRAP BELIE
BERUN BESET BIGAN CLOSE CROWN
ROUND BEGIRD BEGIRT CIRCLE
ENGIRD COMPASS EMBOWEL
EMBRACE ENCLOSE ENVIRON
INCLUDE SUBSUME UMBESET
ENCIRCLE ENGIRDLE PURPRISE
SURROUND
(— WITH ARMS) FATHOM
ENCOMPASSED AMID BAYED
AMIDST BEGIRT
ENCOMPASSING ROUND AMBIENT
CINCTURE PROFOUND INCLUSIVE
ENCORE BIS AGAIN ANCORA RECALL
REPEAT
ENCOUNTER BIDE BUMP COIL COPE
FACE FIND KEEP MEET MOOT RINK
BRUSH FIGHT FORCE GREET INCUR
OCCUR ONSET SHOCK STOUR
VENUE ACCOST AFFRAY ANSWER
ASSAIL ATTACK BATTLE BREAST

CAREER COMBAT JOSTLE JUSTLE
OPPOSE ADDRESS AFFRONT
CONTEST COUNTER DISPUTE
HOSTING JOINING PASSAGE
CONFLICT CONFRONT CONGRESS
REANSWER RECONTER SKIRMISH
(— HOSTILELY) CROSS
(HOSTILE —) CLOSE
(PUGILISTIC —) MILL
ENCOURAGE DAW EGG ABET BACK
FIRM URGE BOOST CHEER ERECT
FAVOR FLUSH HEART IMPEL NERVE
SERVE STEEL ADVISE ASSURE
EXHORT FOMENT FOSTER HALLOO
HARDEN INCITE INDUCE INVITE
NUZZLE REHETE SECOND SPIRIT
UPHOLD ADVANCE ANIMATE
CHERISH COMFORT CONFIRM
CONSOLE ENFORCE ENLIVEN
FLATTER FORTIFY FORWARD
HEARTEN INSPIRE PROMOTE
STOMACH UPCHEER UPRAISE
EMBOLDEN INSPIRIT REASSURE
ENCOURAGED BUCKED CONFIRMED
ENCOURAGEMENT BOOST FLUSH
HURRAH FOMENTO IMPETUS
BLESSING SANCTION
ENCOURAGING HELPFUL FAVORING
ENCRATITE TATIAN AQUARIAN
ENCROACH JET PINCH POACH
IMPOSE INVADE TRENCH IMPINGE
INTRUDE SHINGLE ENTRENCH
INFRINGE INTRENCH TRESPASS
ENCROACHING INVASIVE
ENCROACHMENT BREACH INROAD
ENCROACH INVASION
ENCRUST CAKE CANDY BARKEN
BARKLE INCRUST
ENCRUSTED SCABROUS
ENCUMBER CLOG LOAD PACK
BESET CHECK CROWD TRASH
BEMOIL BURDEN FELTER HAMPER
HINDER IMPEDE LUMBER MITHER
MOIDER RETARD SADDLE WEIGHT
BEPAPER INVOLVE OPPRESS
ACCUMBER ENTANGLE HANDICAP
OBSTRUCT OVERCOME OVERLOAD
ENCUMBERED HEAVY CONGESTED
ENCUMBRANCE CLOG LIEN LOAD
CLAIM BURDEN CHARGE CUMBER
TROUBLE MORTGAGE
ENCYCLICAL PASCENDI
ENCYCLOPEDIA TOME
(GAME —) HOYLE
ENCYSTED CYSTIC SACCATE
SACCATED
END EN AIM DAG EAR FAG TIP BUTT
DATE DOUP FACE FATE FINE FOOT
GOAL HALT HEEL LAST MAIN MARK
SAKE STOP TAIL TERM VIEW AMEND
ARTHA BLOCK BREAK CAUSE CEASE
CLOSE DEATH ENSUE EVENT FINIS
ISSUE LIMIT LOOSE NAPOO OMEGA
POINT PRICK RAISE SCOPE SCRAP
START STASH THULE DEFINE
DESIGN EFFECT EFFLUX ENDING
EXITUS EXPIRE EXPIRY FINALE
FINISH INTENT NAPOOH OBJECT
PERIOD RESULT THIRTY UPSHOT

UTMOST WINDUP ABOLISH ACHIEVE
CLOSURE CURTAIN DESTROY
FANTAIL FINANCE LINEMAN OUTGIVE
PURPOSE REMNANT BOUNDARY
COMPLETE CONCLUDE DESITION
DISSOLVE FINALITY SURCEASE
TERMINAL TERMINUS ULTIMATE
(— DEBATE) CLOTURE
(— OF ANTENNA) CLAVA
(— OF ANVIL) BICKIRON
(— OF ARCHERY PILE) STOPPING
(— OF ARROW) NOCK
(— OF BEEF LOIN) BUTT
(— OF BLANKET) DAGON
(— OF BONE) EPIPHYSIS
(— OF BOOM) JAW
(— OF BOW) EAR
(— OF BRICK) HEADING
(— OF BRISTLE) FLAG
(— OF BUILDING) GABLE
(— OF CAN) BREAST
(— OF CANE) FRAZE
(— OF CART) TIB
(— OF CRESCENT) HORN
(— OF EGG) DOUP
(— OF EXISTENCE) DEMISE
(— OF FABRIC) FENT
(— OF FISHHOOK) SPEAR
(— OF FLAG) FLY
(— OF FROG) TOE
(— OF HALTER) CAPITULUM
(— OF HAMMER) CLAW POLL
(— OF HAMMERHEAD) PEEN
(— OF HORSE-COLLAR) GULLET
(— OF INGOT) CROP
(— OF KEEL) GRIPE
(— OF LEVER) FORK
(— OF LOAF) HEEL
(— OF MINE TUNNEL) FACE
(— OF MINING LEVEL) DEAN
(— OF MUZZLE) MUFFLE
(— OF NAIL) CLENCH
(— OF ONE'S LIFE) DOOM
(— OF PIER) CUTWATER
(— OF PIPE) TAFT SPIGOT
(— OF POCKETKNIFE HANDLE)
BOLSTER
(— OF RAILROAD CAR) BEND
(— OF ROAD) ROADHEAD
(— OF ROD) FORKHEAD
(— OF SHEEP SHEARING) CUTOUT
(— OF SHIP) STERN
(— OF SPINE) ACRUMION
(— OF TENON) HAUNCH
(— OF TOOL) BUTT
(— OF UTERUS) FUNDUS
(- OF WORLD) PRALAYA
(— OF YARD) ARM YARDARM
(— ON POND) FOREBAY
(—S OF RIBBONS) FATTRELS
(—S OF SATURN'S RINGS) ANSA
(CANDLE —) DOUP SNUFF
(DOMINO —) ACE
(FAG —) RUMP
(HANGING —) DAG DAGGE
(JAGGED —) SHRAG
(NARROWED —) NEB
(NORTH — OF COMPASS NEEDLE)
LILY

(POINTED —) APEX
(POSTERIOR —) BOTTOM
(REEF —S) DEADMAN
(ROPE'S —) FEAZE PIGTAIL
FEAZINGS
(SPECIAL —) SAKE
(TAPERING —) POINT
(TATTERED —) FRAZZLE
(ULTIMATE —) SUM TELOS
(UNPLEASANT —) GRIEF
(UPPER —) HEAD
(WARP —S) ACCIDENTAL
ENDANGER DANGER HAZARD
IMPERIL
ENDANGERED BESTED BESTEAD
FRAUGHT
ENDANGERER MARPLOT
ENDEARMENT LOVE CARESS
ENDEAVOR DO AIM PUT TRY WIN
BEST MINT SEEK WORK ASSAY
ESSAY ETTLE EXERT OFFER STUDY
TEMPT TRIAL AFFAIR ASSAIL
DEVOIR EFFORT INTEND STRIFE
STRIVE AFFORCE ATTEMPT
CONATUS CULTURE EMPRISE
EMULATE IMITATE MOLIMEN
NITENCY WORKING EXERTION
PURCHASE STRUGGLE
(— TO CONCLUSION) STUDY
(BEST —) DEVOIR
(EARNESTLY —) FEND
ENDED DONE OVER PAST FINISHED
(— BY CONSONANT) CHECKED
ENDEMIC LOCAL ENDEMIAL
ENDING END CLOSE DEATH GRAVE
FINALE BREAKUP FINANCE DESITION
(NERVE —) SPINDLE
ENDIVE CHICORY WITLOOF
ESCAROLE SCARIOLE
ENDLESS ANANTA ETERNE ETERNAL
FOREVER UNDYING UNENDED
UNENDLY DATELESS FINELESS
IMMORTAL INFINITE UNENDING
ENDMOST TIPMOST FARTHEST
REMOTEST
ENDOCARP STONE PYRENA
PUTAMEN
ENDOGENOUS INNATE AUTOGENIC
ENDOMORPHIC PYCNIC PYKNIC
ENDOPITE PETASMA
ENDOPLEURA TEGMEN
ENDORSE BACK SIGN ADOPT BOOST
DOCKET ENDOSS SECOND APPROVE
CERTIFY INDORSE SUPPORT
ADVOCATE SANCTION
ENDORSEE HOLDER
ENDORSEMENT FIAT FORM VISA
RIDER BACKING APPROVAL
HECHSHER SANCTION
ENDOSPERM FARINA ALBUMEN
ENDOSPORIUM INTINE
ENDOW DOW DUE DOTE GIFT RENT
VEST BLESS CROWN DOWER ENDUE
EQUIP FOUND INDUE SEIZE STATE
STUFF ASSIGN CLOTHE DOTATE
ENABLE ENRICH ENSOUL ESTATE
INVEST CHARTER ENLARGE FURNISH
INSTATE APPANAGE BENEFICE
BEQUEATH ENTALENT
(— WITH FORCE) DYNAMIZE

ENDOWED ABLE GIFTED FAVORED
ENDOWMENT CLAY FINE GIFT WAKF
WAQF DOWER DOWRY GRACE
CORPSE GENIUS TALENT APANAGE
CHANTRY CHARISM FACULTY
APPANAGE DOTATION
(**NATURAL —S**) BUMP DOTES
TALENT
(PL.) ALTARAGE
ENDPAPER FLYLEAF
ENDPIECE BRACE CHUMP
(**— OF STETHOSCOPE**) BELL
ENDUE DUE ENDOW INDUE TEACH
CLOTHE INVEST INSTRUCT
ENDURABLE LIVABLE BEARABLE
LIVEABLE
ENDURANCE GAME LAST TACK
PLUCK BOTTOM COMFORT
DURANCE GRANITE LASTING
STAMINA BEARANCE DURATION
GAMENESS HARDSHIP PATIENCE
STRENGTH
ENDURE GO ABY SIT VIE ABYE BEAR
BIDE DREE DURE HOLD KEEP LAST
TAKE TIDE WEAR ABEAR ABIDE
ALLOW BROOK CARRY DRIVE
POUCH SPARE STAND STICK STOUT
THOLE TOUGH WIELD ABROOK
ACCEPT DRUDGE HARDEN REMAIN
SUFFER COMFORT FORBEAR
PERSIST SUPPORT SUSTAIN
SWALLOW TOUGHEN UNDERGO
WEARING CONTINUE FOREBEAR
TOLERATE
ENDURING FAST SURE STOUT
BIDING DURING STABLE STURDY
DURABLE ETERNAL LASTING
PATIENT IMMORTAL REMANENT
STUBBORN
ENDWAYS ANEND ENDWISE
ENEMA CLYSMA CLYSTER LAVEMENT
ENEMY FOE AXIS BOYG FEID DEVIL
FIEND SATAN FOEMAN HOSTILE
CONTRARY OPPONENT
(**— OF MANKIND**) DEVIL FIEND
SATAN
(**PERSONAL —**) HATER
ENERGETIC FAST FELL HARD LIVE
RASH BRISK DASHY LUSTY STOUT
TIGHT VITAL YAULD ACTIVE HEARTY
HUSTLE LIVELY SPROIL ACTIOUS
ANIMOSO ARDUOUS DASHING
DRIVING DYNAMIC ENERGIC
FURIOUS PUSHFUL PUSHING
EMPHATIC ENERGICO FORCEFUL
FORCIBLE HUSTLING VIGOROUS
(**— PERSON**) TOWSER
ENERGETICALLY MANLY
FURIOUSLY
ENERGIZE EXCITE ANIMATE
ENERGIZING KINETIC VIRTUAL
ENERGY U W GO PEP VIM ZIP BANG
BENT BIRR DASH EDGE JASM LIFE
SAKT SNAP TUCK ZING ARDOR
ECLAT FORCE INPUT NERVE POWER
STEAM VIGOR EFFORT FOISON
INTAKE ORGONE OUTPUT SPIRIT
SPRAWL SPRING SPROIL STARCH
VIRTUE POTENCY SPIRITS ACTIVITY

AMBITION DYNAMISM ENERGEIA
MOTIVITY PRAKRITI STRENGTH
VIVACITY
(**— PEAK**) NUCLEUS
(**EMOTIONAL —**) LIBIDO
(**LIBINAL —**) CATHEXIS
(**LIFE —**) JIVA SAKTI SHAKTI
(**LIGHT —**) RAD
(**MENTAL —**) DOCITY PSYCHURGY
(**POTENTIAL —**) ERGAL
(**RADIANT —**) SOUND ACTINISM
EINSTEIN
(**VITAL —**) HORME PANZOISM
ENERVATE SAP COOK FLAG MELT
SOFTEN WEAKEN MOLLIFY UNNERVE
UNSINEW ENFEEBLE
ENERVATED BEDRID EFFETE
LANGUID BEDRIDDEN
ENERVATING DREARY
ENERVATION COLLAPSE
ENFEEBLE NUMB FAINT SHAKE
APPALL DEADEN FEEBLE IMPAIR
SOFTEN WEAKEN DEPRESS
UNSINEW AFFEEBLE ENERVATE
IMBECILE UNSTRONG
ENFEEBLED FEY NUMB
ENFOLD (ALSO SEE INFOLD) LAP
FURL WRAP CLASP COVER DRAPE
ENROL IMPLY COMPLY ENLACE
ENROLL ENWIND ENWRAP INFOLD
INWIND SHADOW SWATHE WATTLE
EMBRACE ENCLOSE ENVELOP
ENVIRON INCLUDE INVOLVE
UMBELAP CONVOLVE
ENFORCE BULL LEVY EXACT FORCE
PRESS COERCE COMPEL EFFECT
FOLLOW INVOKE EXECUTE IMPLANT
ENFORCED COMPULSORY
ENFORCER EXECUTOR MUSCLEMAN
ENFRAMEMENT CARTOUCH
ENG AGMA
ENGAGE DIP WED BOOK BUSY GAGE
HAVE HIRE JOIN LIST MESH RENT
SIGN TAKE WAGE AGREE AMUSE
CATCH ENTER LEASE PITCH TRADE
TRYST ABSORB ARREST EMBARK
EMPLOY ENLIST INDUCE OBLIGE
OCCUPY PLEDGE PLIGHT BESPEAK
BETROTH CONCERN CONDUCE
CONSUME ENGROSS IMMERSE
INVOLVE PROMISE AFFIANCE
CONTRACT COVENANT ENTANGLE
INTEREST INTRIGUE PERSUADE
(**— DEEPLY**) DROWN
(**— IN ARGUMENT**) BALK BAULK
(**— IN COMBAT**) DEBATE STRIKE
(**— IN DEBATE**) STONEWALL
(**— IN DISCUSSION**) CONTEND
(**— IN PRANKS**) LARK
(**— IN TILT**) JUST JOUST
(**— IN**) GO CUT SUE HAVE JOIN
LEAD
(**— WHOLLY**) ABSORB CONSUME
IMMERSE
ENGAGED BENT BUSY FAST GONE
HIRED ACTIVE BONDED BOOKED
MESHED ASSURED BESPOKE
EARNEST ENTERED PLEDGED
TOKENED VERSANT ABSORBED

ATTACHED EMBEDDED EMPLOYED
INSERTED INTEREST INVOLVED
OCCUPIED PROMISED
(**— IN CONTROVERSY**) DISPUTANT
(**— IN**) ABOUT
(**MENTALLY —**) VERSANT
(**WARMLY —**) ZEALOUS
ENGAGEMENT AVAL DATE COWLE
SPURN ACTION AFFAIR BATTLE
COMBAT ESCROW PLIGHT STANZA
SURETY BARGAIN BOOKING
DUSTING SERVICE CONFLICT
RETAINER SKIRMISH WARRANTY
(**— TO MARRY**) TRYST
(**MILITARY —**) DO SHOW
(**SHORT —**) SNAP
(**SINGLE —**) GIG
(**THEATRICAL —**) SHOP
(**WRITTEN —**) COWLE
ENGAGING SOFT SAPID SWEET
TAKING
ENGENDER BEGET BREED CAUSE
EXCITE GENDER DEVELOP PRODUCE
GENERATE INGENDER OCCASION
ENGIDU EABANI
ENGINE GAS JET SIX FOUR GOAT
TANK EIGHT JINNY MOTOR OILER
STEAM BANKER DIESEL DOCTOR
DUDLER DUDLEY INGENE JORDAN
KICKER PUFFER RADIAL ROADER
YARDER MACHINE POACHER
POTCHER SKIDDER STEAMER
TRACTOR TURBINE BULLGINE
COMPOUND DOLLBEER EXPANDER
GASOLINE IMPULSOR
(**— FOR HAULING LOGS**) DUDLER
DUDLEY
(**— FOR THROWING MISSILES**) GIN
SPRINGAL
(**— OF TORTURE**) GIN RACK
(**— OF WAR**) RAM SWEEP HELEPOLE
(**DONKEY —**) DOCTOR
(**FIRE —**) TUB
(**JET —**) ATHODYD
(**MILITARY —**) BOAR TOWER FABRIC
TREPAN DONDINE PERRIER
TORMENT WARWOLF BALLISTA
DONDAINE MANGONEL MARTINET
SCORPION
(**RAILROAD —**) HOG GOAT YARDER
SWITCHER
ENGINEER PLAN GUIDE DRIVER
FANNER HOGGER MANAGE SAPPER
HOGHEAD PLANNER PLOTTER
CONTRIVE DESIGNER INGENIER
INVENTOR MANEUVER
ENGINEMAN HOISTER HOISTMAN
ENGINERY TIRE
ENGIRDLED CINCT
ENGLAND HOME ALBION LOGRIA
BLIGHTY BRITAIN LOEGRIA
HOMELAND

ENGLAND		
AIRFORCE: RAF		
BAY: TOR LYME WASH START		
MOUNTS BIGBURY BIDEFORD		
CARDIGAN FALMOUTH		

TREMADOC WEYMOUTH
CAPITAL: LONDON
CHANNEL: SOLENT BRISTOL
ENGLISH SPITHEAD
CHANNEL ISLAND: HERM SARK
JERSEY ALDERNEY GUERNSEY
COIN: ORA RIAL RYAL ACKEY
ANGEL CROWN GROAT NOBLE
PENCE PENNY POUND SPRAT
UNITE BAWBEE FLORIN GUINEA
SESKIN TESTON ANGELET
CAROLUS HAPENNY TUPPENY
FARTHING SHILLING SIXPENCE
TUPPENCE
CONSERVATIVE: TORY
COUNTY: KENT DEVON ESSEX
HANTS SALOP WIGHT DORSET
DURHAM LONDON SURREY
SUSSEX NORFOLK RUTLAND
SUFFOLK CHESHIRE CORNWALL
SOMERSET
DANCE: MORRIS
FIRTH: SOLWAY
FOREST: ARDEN EXMOOR
DARTMOOR SHERWOOD
HEAD: SPURN BEACHY FORMBY
LIZARD CEMMAES TREVOSE
HILLS: MENDIP BRENDON CHEVIOT
CHILTERN COTSWOLD
INVADER: DANE PICT ROMAN
SAXON NORMAN
ISLAND: MAN HOLY LUNDY WIGHT
COQUET MERSEA THANET
TRESCO WALNEY BARDSEY
HAYLING IRELAND SHEPPEY
ANGLESEA ANGLESEY
FOULNESS HOLYHEAD
ISLANDS: FARNE SCILLY CHANNEL
KING: HAL LUD BRAN BRUT CNUT
COLE KNUT LEAR HENRY JAMES
SWEYN ALFRED BLADUD
BRUTUS CANUTE EDWARD
EGBERT GEORGE ARTEGAL
ELIDURE RICHARD WILLIAM
GORBODUC
LAKE: CONISTON
LIBERAL: WHIG
MEASURE: CUT ELL LEA MIL PIN
ROD RUN TON TUN VAT ACRE
BIND BOLL BUTT CADE COMB
COOM CRAN FOOT GILL GOAD
HAND HANK HEER HIDE INCH
LAST LINE MILE NAIL PACE
PALM PECK PINT PIPE POLE
POOL ROOD ROPE SACK SEAM
SPAN TRUG TYPP WIST YARD
YOKE BODGE CABOT CHAIN
COOMB CUBIT DIGIT FLOAT
FLOOR FLUID HUTCH JUGUM
MINIM OUNCE PERCH POINT
PRIME QUART SKEIN STACK
TRUSS BARREL BOVATE BUSHEL
CRANNE FATHOM FIRKIN
GALLON HOBBET HOBBIT
LEAGUE MANENT OXGANG
POTTLE RUNLET SECOND
SQUARE STRIKE SULUNG
THREAD TIERCE AUCHLET

FURLONG KENNING QUARTER
RUNDLET SEAMILE SPINDLE
TERTIAN VIRGATE CARUCATE
CHALDRON HOGSHEAD
LANDYARD PUNCHEON
QUADRANT QUARTERN
STANDARD
MOUNTAIN: PEAK SCAFELL
SKIDDAW SNOWDON
MOUNTAINS: BLACK PENNINE
SNOWDON CAMBRIAN CUMBRIAN
NAME: ALBION BRITAIN BRITANNIA
PENINSULA: PORTLAND
POINT: NAZE LYNAS MORTE
SALES DODMAN LIZARD PRAWLE
HARTLAND LANDSEND
GIBRALTAR
POLICEMAN: BOBBY COPPER
PEELER
RACE TRACK: ASCOT
RESORT: BATH BRIGHTON
BLACKPOOL
RIVER: CAM DEE DON ESK EXE
LEA NEN URE WYE AIRE AVON
EDEN LUNE NENE NIDD OUSE
PENK TAME TEES TILL TYNE
WEAR YARE ANKER COLNE
DEBEN STOUR SWALE TAMAR
TAWAR TRENT TWEED HUMBER
KENNET MERSEY RIBBLE
ROTHER SEVERN THAMES
WENSUM WHARFE WITHAM
DERWENT PARRETT WAVENEY
WELLAND TORRIDGE
ROCKS: MANACLES
ROYAL HOUSE: YORK TUDOR
STUART HANOVER WINDSOR
LANCASTER PLANTAGENET
SCHOOL: ETON RUGBY HARROW
SEA: IRISH NORTH
SETTLER: JUTE PICT ANGLE
SAXON NORMAN
SOLDIER: TOMMY REDCOAT
FUSILEER
STRAIT: DOVER
TOWN: ELY BATH DEAL HULL
RYDE WARE YORK BLYTH
BRENT DERBY DOVER ERITH
FLINT LEEDS RIPON TRURO
WIGAN BARNET BOLTON
BOOTLE CAMDEN DURHAM
EALING EXETER HANLEY
JARROW LEYTON LONDON
OLDHAM OXFORD YEOVIL
BRISTOL BROMLEY BURNLEY
CHELSEA CROYDON ENFIELD
GRIMSBY HALIFAX HORNSEY
IPSWICH LAMBETH NEWPORT
NORWICH PRESTON SALFORD
SEAFORD WESTHAM BRADFORD
BRIGHTON CORNWALL
COVENTRY DEWSBURY
HASTINGS PLYMOUTH
ROCHDALE WALLASEY
WALLSALL GREENWICH
LIVERPOOL SHEFFIELD
BIRMINGHAM MANCHESTER
TRIBE: ICENI

UNIVERSITY: LONDON OXFORD
CAMBRIDGE
VALLEY: COOM EDEN TEES TYNE
COMBE COOMB COQUET
WEIGHT: BAG KIP TOD TON KEEL
LAST MAST MAUN BARGE
FAGOT GRAIN MAUND POUND
SCORE STAND STONE TRUSS
BUSHEL CENTAL FANGOT FIRKIN
FOTHER FOTMAL POCKET
QUARTER QUINTAL SARPLER

ENGLISH SAXON AUSTRAL BRITISH
ENGLAND SAXONISH SOUTHRON
STANDARD
(IN —) ANGLICE
ENGLISHMAN SAXON BRITON
GODDAM GRINGO JOHNNY
MACARONI SOUTHRON ENGLISHER
ENGLISHWOMAN INGLESA
ENGORGE GLUT GORGE DEVOUR
SWALLOW
ENGRAFT INSET
ENGRAM TRACE
(— PATTERN) MEANING
ENGRAVE CUT ETCH RIST CARVE
CHASE GRAVE HATCH PRINT SCULP
CHISEL INCISE SCULPT CRIBBLE
ENCHASE EXARATE IMPRESS
IMPRINT INSCULP STIPPLE INSCRIBE
ORNAMENT
ENGRAVED GRAVEN GRAPHIC
INCISED
ENGRAVER POINT CHASER ETCHER
GRAVER ARTISAN INSCULP BURINIST
MEDALIST SCULLION WRIGGLER
(— OF STONES) LAPIDARY
ENGRAVING CUT PRINT SCULP
STAMP GRAVERY GRAVING
GRAVURE WOODCUT AQUATINT
DRYPOINT HATCHING INTAGLIO
LINEWORK
ENGROSS BURY SINK SOAK AMASS
GROSS ABSORB ENGAGE ENROLL
ENWRAP OCCUPY SCROLL COLLECT
CONSUME IMMERSE INVOLVE
ENGROSSED DEEP FULL RAPT
INTENT WRAPPED ABSORBED
IMMERSED
ENGULF GULF ABYSM ABYSS SOUSE
SWAMP WHELM ABSORB DEVOUR
INVADE QUELME SLOUGH ENGORGE
SWALLOW SUBMERGE
ENHANCE FOIL LIFT BUILD ENARM
ENDOW EXALT RAISE DEEPEN
AUGMENT ELEVATE ENLARGE
EXHANCE GREATEN IMPROVE
SHARPEN HEIGHTEN INCREASE
ENHANCEMENT SAKE
ENHYDRA LATAX
ENIGMA WHY EGMA GRIPH REBUS
PUZZLE RIDDLE SPHINX GRIPHUS
MYSTERY PROBLEM PROVERB
ENIGMATIC HUMAN MYSTIC
CRYPTIC OBSCURE ELLIPTIC
MYSTICAL PUZZLING RIDDLING
ENJAMBMENT OVERFLOW
ENJOIN BID JOIN WILL ENIUN ORDER

CHARGE DECREE DIRECT FORBID
COMMAND DICTATE REQUIRE
ADMONISH PROHIBIT
ENJOY GO JOY FAIN HAVE LIKE
BROOK FANCY PROVE SAVOR
TASTE WIELD ADMIRE DEVOUR
RELISH DELIGHT
(— ONESELF) FEAST LAUGH
ENJOYABLE GOOD FRUITY AMIABLE
BLESSED CAPITAL GLORIOUS
SAVOROUS SPLENDID
ENJOYING FRUITIVE
ENJOYMENT FUN JOY USE BASK
BOOT EASE GUST KAMA PLAY ZEST
GUSTO LIKING RELISH COMFORT
DELIGHT JOLLITY JOYANCE
JOYANCY FELICITY FRUITION
PLEASURE SKITTLES
ENKINDLE WARM INCENSE INFLAME
ENLARGE ADD EKE BORE GROW
HONE HUFF OPEN REAM ROOM
BUILD FARCE LARGE SWELL WIDEN
BIGGEN BRANCH BROACH DIDUCE
DILATE EXPAND EXTEND FRAISE
GATHER LARGEN OMNIFY SPREAD
AMPLIFY AUGMENT DISTEND
ENHANCE GREATEN IMPROVE
INGREAT MAGNIFY STRETCH
AMPLIATE CUMULATE FLOURISH
INCREASE
(— COAL MINE) SNUB
ENLARGED BLOATED SWELLED
SWOLLEN AMPLIATE CAPITATE
EXPANDED EXTENDED VARICOSE
ENLARGEMENT BULB DISC DISK
KNOP CLAVA SWELL BLOWUP
BUNION GIBBER GROWTH SCYPHA
ENLARGE FOOTING SCYPHUS
STATION INCREASE SWELLING
(— IN MINE SHAFT) STATION
(— OF GLAND) GOITER GOITRE
(— OF GULLET) CROP
(— OF MOLD) RAPPAGE
(— OF NERVE FIBER) BOUTON
(— OF ORGAN) STRUMA
(BONY —) SPAVIN SPAVINE
ENLARGING EVASE SWELLING
ENLIGHTEN OPEN CLEAR EDIFY
TEACH ILLUME INFORM UNSEEL
EDUCATE LIGHTEN ENKINDLE
INSTRUCT
ENLIGHTENED WISE LUMINOUS
ENLIGHTENMENT BODHI LIGHT
SATORI WISDOM CULTURE SAMADHI
ENLIST DRUM JOIN LEVY SOUD
ENROL ENTER HITCH PREST
ENGAGE ENROLL INDUCT IMPRESS
RECRUIT REGISTER
ENLISTMENT LEVY HITCH PREST
LISTING
ENLIVEN DASH JAZZ WARM BRACE
BRISK CHEER QUICK ROUSE KITTLE
REVIVE ANIMATE COMFORT INSPIRE
REFRESH SMARTEN BRIGHTEN
INSPIRIT
ENLIVENING GENIAL LIVELY VIVIFIC
CHIRPING
ENMESH TRAP CATCH SNARL
IMMESH ENSNARE ENTANGLE

ENMITY WAR FEUD SPITE WRAKE
ANIMUS HATRED MALICE RANCOR
STRIFE FOEHOOD AVERSION
ENNOBLE LORD EXALT HONOR
NOBLE RAISE GENTLE UPLIFT
DIGNIFY ELEVATE GLORIFY
GREATEN NOBLIFY
ENNUI BORE TEDIUM BOREDOM
DOLDRUM
ENORMITY GRAVITY
ENORMOUS BIG GOB HUGE REAM
VAST ENORM GREAT HEROIC
MIGHTY UNRIDE IMMENSE
ABNORMAL COLOSSAL FLAGRANT
GIGANTIC WHAPPING WHOPPING
ENOS (FATHER OF —) SETH
(GRANDFATHER OF —) ADAM
(SON OF —) CAINAN
ENOUGH BAS ENOW WELL WHEN
AMPLE ASSAI BASTA ANEUCH
PLENTY APLENTY SUFFICE
ADEQUATE
(HARDLY —) SKIMP
ENOUNCE STATE UTTER AFFIRM
DECLARE PROCLAIM
ENRAGE RAGE ANGER GRIEVE
MADDEN INCENSE INFLAME
STOMACH
ENRAGED MAD ASHY WODE WOOD
ANGRY IRATE SAVAGE AGRAMED
BERSERK CHOLERIC INCENSED
MADDENED
ENRAPTURE RAVISH TRANCE
ECSTASY ENCHANT ENRAVISH
ENTRANCE
ENRAPTURED RAPT ENRAPT
TRANCED ECSTATIC
ENRICH FAT BOOT FEED FRET LARD
RICH ADORN CROWN ENDOW
GUANO BATTEN FATTEN INVEST
FEATHER FORTIFY FURNISH
GUANIZE INCREASE ORNAMENT
TREASURE
(— A GAS) CARBURET
(— A MINE) SALT
(— FUEL MIXTURE) CHOKE
ENRICHED FLORID
ENRICHMENT DITATION
ENROLL BEAR JOIN LIST POLL
ENROL ENTER WRITE ATTEST
BILLET ENFOLD ENLIST INDUCT
MUSTER RECORD ASCRIBE IMPANEL
INITIATE INSCRIBE REGISTER
ENROLLMENT LISTING REGISTRY
ENROOT ENRACE IMPLANT
ENSCONCE HIDE COVER SETTLE
CONCEAL SHELTER
ENSEMBLE CORPS DECOR WHOLE
COSTUME
(— OF ARMS) ARMORY
ENSHEATHE EMBOSS
ENSHRINE SAINT SHRINE ENCHASE
ENTEMPLE
ENSHROUD WRAP
ENSIFORM ENSATE XIPHOID
GLADIATE
ENSIGN FLAG IAGO SIGN BADGE
COLOR SENYE AQUILA BANNER
BEACON PENNON PISTOL SIGNAL

SYMBOL ALFEREZ ANCIENT INSIGNE
DANEBROG GONFALON ORIFLAMB
PAVILION STANDARD
(—S ARMORIAL) ARMS
(IMPERIAL —) TUT
(JAPANESE —) SUNBURST
(PL.) ENSIGNRY HERALDRY
ENSILE SILO SILAGE
ENSLAVE THEW CHAIN SLAVE THIRL
ENTHRAL NESLAVE SLAVISH
ENTHRALL
ENSLAVED SLAVE THRALL
ENSLAVEMENT DULOSIS SLAVERY
ENSNARE NET WEB GIRN LACE LIME
MESH TOIL TRAP WRAP BENET
CATCH NOOSE SNARE SNARL
ALLURE ATTRAP ENGINE ENMESH
ENTOIL ENTRAP TANGLE TREPAN
BEGUILE DECEIVE ENGLEIM SNIGGLE
SPRINGE BIRDLIME INVEIGLE
OVERTAKE SURPRISE
ENSNARL ENTANGLE
ENSPHERE INORB SPHERE
ENSUE FOLLOW RESULT SUCCEED
(— UPON) SUE
ENSUING NEXT SUING SEQUENT
ENSURE ASSURE INSURE SECURE
BETROTH ESPOUSE WARRANT
AFFIANCE
ENTADA LENS
ENTAIL TAIL INCUR IMPOSE CONTAIN
INVOLVE REQUIRE TAILZIE
ENTAILED AYNE TAIL EIGNE
ENTAMOEBA LOSCHIA
ENTANGLE ELF LAP MAT TAT WEB
CAST COLL FOUL HARL KNIT KNOT
LIME MESH MIRE TOIL WRAP BROIL
CATCH HALCH RAVEL SNAFU SNARE
SNARL TWIST BEFOUL COTTER
ENGAGE ENLACE ENMESH ENTRAP
ENWRAP FANKLE FELTER HAMPER
HANKLE HATTER INMAZE INMESH
PESTER PUZZLE RAFFLE RANGLE
TACKLE TANGLE WRAPLE CONFUSE
EMBRAKE EMBROIL ENSNARL
ENTRIKE IMBRIER INVOLVE PERPLEX
TRAMMEL BEWILDER ENCUMBER
IMPESTER INTRIGUE STRAPPLE
ENTANGLED DEEP FOUL COTTY
TANGLY COMPLEX KNOTTED
IMPLICIT
ENTANGLEMENT FOUL KNOT TWIT
HITCH BUNKER HEDGEHOG
OBSTACLE
ENTASIS SWELL
ENTENTE TREATY ALLIANCE
ENTER BOX DIP SET BEAR BOOK
JOIN POST ADMIT BEGIN BOARD
BREVE ENROL INCUR PROBE SHARE
START ACCEDE APPEAR BILLET
ENGAGE ENLIST ENROLL ENTRER
INCEPT INVADE PIERCE RECORD
SPREAD INGRESS INTRUDE
COMMENCE ENCROACH INITIATE
INSCRIBE NOMINATE REGISTER
(— BY FORCE) BREAK IRRUPT
INTRUDE
(— HASTILY) BULGE
(— IN ATTACK) FORCE

(— IN BOOKS) ACCRUE
(— INTO) JOIN INTERN
(— SLOWLY) SEEP
(— UNNOTICED) CREEP
(— UPON CAREER) INCEPT
(— UPON DUTIES) ASSUME
(— WITHOUT RIGHT) ABATE
ENTERING ENTRY INGOING INGRESS
INTRANT INCOMING
ENTEROTOXEMIA STRUCK
ENTERPRISE FIRM IRON PUSH TOGT
DRIVE ESSAY ACTION EMPIRE SPIRIT
VOYAGE ATTEMPT EMPRISE
HOLDING PROJECT VENTURE
BUSINESS CARNIVAL GUMPTION
VIRITOOT
(CRIMINAL —) JOB
(HARD —) DIFFICULTY
(REMEDIAL —) CRUSADE
(SPECULATIVE —) ADVENTURE
(UNPROFITABLE —) SINKHOLE
ENTERPRISING BOLD FORTHY
PUSHFUL PUSHING
ENTERTAIN INN BEAR BUSK EASE
FETE HAVE HOLD HOST AMUSE
ENJOY FEAST GUEST SPORT TREAT
DIVERT FROLIC GESTEN HARBOR
JUNKET RECULE REGALE RETAIN
SOLACE BEGUILE CHERISH DISPORT
KITCHEN CONSIDER INTEREST
(— WITHOUT CHARGE) DEFRAY
ENTERTAINED OUGHT
ENTERTAINER BHAT HOST ACTOR
AMUSER ARTIST BUSKER DANCER
FIDDLE HARLOT SINGER ACTRESS
ARTISTE GLEEMAN HETAERA
HOSTESS REGALER SPEAKER
BEACHBOY COMEDIAN HOSTELER
MAGICIAN MINSTREL
ENTERTAINING GOOD RICH TREAT
PRETTY AMUSING BEDSIDE
GUESTING SPORTFUL
ENTERTAINMENT BASH BILL FARE
FETE GALA GLEE PLAY SHOW
BOARD CHEER FEAST GAUDY
OPERA REVUE SPORT CIRCUS
DIVERT DOMENT GAIETY GAYETY
HOSTEL INFARE KERMIS NAUTCH
SETOUT SHIVVO WATTLE BANQUET
BENEFIT BUMMACK BUMMOCK
BURLESK CEILIDH CONCERT
COSHERY FESTINE FESTINO JOLLITY
KERMESS PASTIME RIDOTTO
CAKEWALK COMMORTH DROLLERY
EASEMENT ENTREATY ENTREMES
FUNCTION GESTNING GESTONIE
GUESTING HOGMANAY JONGLERY
MUSICALE WAYZGOOSE
(FAREWELL —) FOY
ENTHALPY H
ENTHRALL SEND CHARM THIRL
THRALL ENSLAVE ENTHRAL
ENTHRONE CROWN EXALT STALL
ENSEAT THRONE THRONIZE
ENTHUSIASM BUG ELAN FIRE FURY
ZEAL ZEST ZING ARDOR ESTRO
FEVER FLAME FUROR HEART MANIA
VERVE FERVOR HURRAH SPIRIT
WARMTH ABANDON ARDENCY

AVIDITY MADNESS MUSTARD
DEVOTION LYRICISM
(— IN BATTLE) EARNEST
(CONTAGIOUS —) FUROR FURORE
(EXCESSIVE —) MANIA
(WILD —) DELIRIUM
ENTHUSIAST BUG FAN NUT BUFF
BIGOT ROOTER VOTARY ZEALOT
DEVOTEE EUCHITE FANATIC
FANCIER FOLLOWER VOTARESS
VOTARIST
(PL.) ARDITI
ENTHUSIASTIC GAGA KEEN WARM
HAPPY NUTTY RABID ARDENT
HEARTY CRACKED FERVENT
GLOWING CRACKERS
(EXCESSIVELY —) FANATIC
(VAINLY —) FOOLISH
ENTICE COG COY PUT WIN BAIT
COAX DRAW DRIB LEAD LOCK LURE
TICE TOLE TOLL WILE CHARM
DECOY DRILL LATHE SIREN SLOCK
STEAL TEMPT TRAIN TROLL TULLE
ALLECT ALLURE ATTICE CAJOLE
ENLURE INCITE INDUCE INVITE
SEDUCE ATTRACT BEWITCH SOLICIT
SUGGEST INVEIGLE PERSUADE
ENTICEMENT BAIT CORD LURE TICE
ENTICING SIREN ALLURING
ENTIRE ALL DEAD EVEN FULL HALE
MEAR MERE SOLE CLEAN EVERY
GROSS PLAIN QUITE ROUND SOUND
STARK TOTAL TUTTO UTTER WHOLE
VERSAL PERFECT PLENARY
ABSOLUTE COMPLETE ENDURING
GLOBULAR INTEGRAL LIVELONG
OUTRIGHT TEETOTAL UNBROKEN
ENTIRELY DEAD DEIN FAIR FULL
PURE CLEAN CLEAR FULLY PLAIN
QUITE STARK WHOLE BODILY
WHOLLY EXACTLY QUITELY
THROUGH CLEVERLY
ENTIRETY WHOLE ENTIRE TOTALITY
ENTITLE DUB CALL NAME TERM
AFFIX STYLE ENABLE CAPTION
EMPOWER QUALIFY INTITULE
NOMINATE
ENTITLED APPARENT ELIGIBLE
ENTITY ENS BODY FORM UNIT BEING
HABIT OUSIA SPACE THING ENERGY
ESSENCE INTEGER TOTALITY
ENTOMB BURY TOMB INTER INURN
ENCAVE HEARSE IMMURE INHUME
SHRINE
ENTOMOLOGY BUGOLOGY
ENTOMOPHTHORA EMPUSA
ENTOTROPHI DIPLURA
ENTOURAGE TRAIN COMITES
RETINUE
ENTRACTE INTERACT INTERVAL
ENTRAIL BOWEL TRAIL INTRAIL
ENTRAILS GUT GUTS DRAFT TRIPE
FIBERS GIBLET HALLOW INWARD
JAUDIE MUGGET PAUNCH QUARRY
QUERRE UMBLES INSIDES NUMBLES
CHAWDRON GRALLOCH
ENTRANCE ADIT BOCA CUSP DOOR
GATE HALL BOCCA CHARM DEBUT
ENTER ENTRY FOYER GORGE INLET

MOUTH PORCH STULM THIRL TORAN
ACCESS ATRIUM ENTREE INFAIR
INGANG INGATE INROAD PORTAL
RAVISH TORANA TRANCE ZAGUAN
DELIGHT GATEWAY HALLWAY
INGOING INGRESS INITIAL INTRADO
INTROIT PASSAGE POSTERN
ENTRESSE FOREGATE VOMITORY
(— TO VALLEY) CHOPS
(ASTROLOGICAL —) CUSP
(CELLAR —) ROLLWAY
(FORCIBLE —) INROAD
(FORMAL —) DEBUT
(HARBOR —) BOCA
(HOSTILE —) INVASION
(HURRIED —) BOUT
(PRIVATE —) POSTERN
ENTRANCED RAPT CHARMED
TRANCED ECSTATIC
ENTRANCEMENT SPELL
ENTRANCING ORPHIC
ENTRANT INTRANT STARTER
BEGINNER
ENTRAP BAG EBB NET HOOK SNIB
TOIL TRAP CATCH CRIMP DECOY
NOOSE SNARE ALLURE AMBUSH
ATTRAP ENGAGE ENTOIL TAIGLE
TANGLE TREPAN BEGUILE ENSNARE
PITFALL ENTANGLE INVEIGLE
ENTRAPPED (— IN SEDIMENT)
CONNATE
ENTREAT ASK BEG BID SUE WOO
PRAY PRIG SEEK URGE CRAVE
HALSE PLEAD PRESS TREAT
ADJURE APPEAL DESIRE INVOKE
BESEECH CONJURE EXORATE
IMPLORE PREVAIL PROCURE
REQUEST SOLICIT PERSUADE
PETITION
ENTREATING TREAT CRAVING
ENTREATY DO CRY PLEA SUIT
APPEAL DEESIS PRAYER TREATY
BESEECH BIDDING ENTREAT
PURSUIT REQUEST URGENCY
PETITION PLEADING
ENTREE ENTRY ACCESS BOUDIN
OSTIUM ENTRADA INTRADA
SOUFFLE ENTRANCE FRICANDO
MAZARINE
ENTREMES SAINETE SAYNETE
ENTRENCH INVADE SCONCE
TRENCH ENCROACH TRESPASS
ENTRENCHMENT CLOSURE
LODGMENT
ENTROPY S
ENTRUST ARET FIDE GIVE STOW
BEKEN TRUST CHARGE COMMIT
CREDIT LIPPEN ADDRESS BEHIGHT
COMMEND CONFIDE CONSIGN
DEPOSIT INTRUST BEQUEATH
DELEGATE ENCHARGE
(— TO DEPUTY) DEVIL
ENTRY ADIT HALL ITEM STET BREAK
CLOSE DEBIT AUTHOR CREDIT
DOCKET ENTREE POSTEA RECORD
RINGER TRANCE ENTRADA INGRESS
INTRADO PASSAGE ENTRANCE
ENTRESSE ENTRYWAY NOTANDUM
REGISTER VOCATION

ENTWINE FOLD LACE WIND BRAID CLASP IMPLY PLASH TWINE TWIST WEAVE ENLACE INWIND ENTWIST INVOLVE SERPENT WREATHE
ENTWINED ACCOLLE BRAIDED INWOVEN ACCOLLEE
ENUMERATE POLL TELL COUNT SCORE DETAIL NUMBER RECITE RECKON RELATE COMPILE COMPUTE ITEMIZE RECOUNT ESTIMATE REHEARSE
ENUMERATION LIST TALE COUNT SCORE CENSUS ACCOUNT CATALOG RECITAL CITATION
ENUNCIATE SAY UTTER DECLARE DELIVER ENOUNCE ANNOUNCE PROCLAIM
ENUNCIATION DICTION DELIVERY (IMPERFECT —) LALLATION
ENVELOP BUR FOG LAP LOT POD WEB BURR CASE COMA FOLD HUSK MAIL BRACE CLOUD COVER KNIFE ROUND BEGIRD BEGIRT BEMIST BINDLE CLOTHE COCOON CORONA ENFOLD ENGIRT ENTIRE ENWRAP FARDEL FOLDER INFOLD INVEST JACKET MANTLE MUFFLE POCKET SHEATH SHROUD STIFLE SWATHE WRIXLE CALYMMA CAPSULE CHORION ENCLOSE ENVIRON INVOLVE SWADDLE SWALLOW VESTURE WRAPPER ENSPHERE ENVELOPE MANTLING PERIANTH PERIDIUM POCHETTE SURROUND WRAPPAGE
(— IN SMOKE) ENFUME
(GLASS —) BULB
(LUMINOUS —) CORONA
(NEBULOUS —) CHEVELURE
(OPEN —) JACKET
(PAY —) PACKET
(STAMPED —) ENTIRE
(VEGETABLE —) COD
ENVELOPED WOMPLIT
ENVELOPING AMBIENT
ENVENOM VENOM CORRUPT VITIATE EMBITTER EMPOISON
ENVIOUS YELLOW EMULOUS JEALOUS ENVIABLE
ENVIRON HEM BEGO GIRD BIGAN LIMIT VIRON ENVIRE GIRDLE SUBURB COMPASS ENVELOP INCLOSE INVOLVE PURLIEU DISTRICT ENCIRCLE SURROUND (PL.) SKIRT UMLAND BANLIEU SUBURBS PRECINCT
ENVIRONMENT HOTBED MEDIUM MILIEU AMBIENT CONTEXT ELEMENT HABITAT SETTING TERRAIN AMBIANCE CINCTURE PRECINCT (— OF NURTURE) LAP
(DOMESTIC —) INTERIEUR
(NORMAL —) HOME
ENVISAGE FACE CONFRONT ENVISION
ENVOY AGENT ELCHI ENVOI DEPUTY ELCHEE LEGATE LENVOY NUNCIO EMBASSY TORNADA ABLEGATE LEGATION METATRON

ENVY CHAW ONDE COVET GRUDGE EMULATE BEGRUDGE GRUDGERY JEALOUSY
ENWRAP FOLD ROLL CLASP IMPLY ENFOLD INFOLD KIRTLE ENGROSS ENVELOP OBVOLVE CONVOLVE ENVELOPE INSWATHE
ENZOOTIC RABIES
ENZU SIN
ENZYME ASE ZYM ZYMO RENIN CYTASE KINASE LIPASE LOTASE MUTASE OLEASE PAPAIN PEPSIN RENNIN UREASE ZYMASE ACYLASE ADENASE AMIDASE AMINASE AMYLASE APYRASE CASEASE DIATASE EMULSIN ENOLASE EREPSIN FERMENT GUANASE HYDRASE INULASE LACCASE LACTASE MALTASE MYROSIN OXIDASE PECTASE PEPSINE PHYTASE PRUNASE TANNASE TRYPSIN ALDOLASE ARGINASE BROMELIN CATALASE CATALYST CYTOLIST DIASTASE ELASTASE ERAPTASE ESTERASE FUMARASE INVERTIN NUCLEASE PROTEASE RACEMASE SEMINASE TRYPTASE
EOS MORNING
EPAULET KNOT SWAB SWOB WING SCALE SHELL
EPENDYTES HAPLOMA
EPHELIS FRECKLE
EPHEMERAL BRIEF VAGUE HORARY DIURNAL PASSANT PASSING EPISODAL EPISODIC FUGITIVE MUSHROOM STAYLESS
EPHEMERIS DIARY TABLE RECORD ALMANAC JOURNAL CALENDAR
EPHIPPIUM SADDLE
EPHTHALITE HAITHAL
EPI PEAK SPIRE FINIAL PINNACLE
EPIBLAST ECTODERM
EPIC EDDA EPOS SAGA GRAND ILIAD NOBLE BYLINA EPOPEE HEROIC BEOWULF EPYLLION RAMAYANA
EPICALYX CALYCLE
EPICARP HUSK RIND EXOCARP
EPICENE SEXLESS
EPICURE FRIAND FEASTER GLUTTON GOURMET GOURMAND PALATIST
EPICUREAN APICIAN SENSUOUS
EPIDEMIC FLU PLAGUE POPULAR PANDEMIA PANDEMIC
EPIDERMIS SKIN CUTICLE ECDERON VELAMEN
EPIDOTE SCORZA
EPIGLOTTIS FLAP WEEZLE
EPIGRAM POEM ENGLYN EPITAPH
EPIGRAMMATIC LACONIC POINTED
EPIGRAPH EPIGRAM IMPRINT
EPILEPTIC FITIFIED
EPILOGUE CLOSE APPENDIX
EPIMANIKION CUFF
EPINAOS POSTICUM
EPINEPHRINE ADRENINE
EPIPACTIS SERAPIAS
EPIPHANY TWELFTH
EPIPHARYNX PALATE EPIGLOTTIS
EPIPHRAGM TYMPANUM

EPIPHYTE KARO EPIPHYLL
EPIPHYTOTIC EPIDEMIC
EPIRUS (KING OF —) PYRRHUS
EPISCOPACY BISHOPRIC PRELATISM
EPISCOPAL PRELATIC
EPISODE GAG EPOCH EVENT SCENE STORY AFFAIR INCIDENT SEQUENCE (COMIC —) BURLA
(MUSICAL —) COUPLET
EPISPASTIC VESICANT
EPISPERM TESTA
EPISTAXIS NOSEBLEED
EPISTLE CANON JAMES LETTER PISTLE MISSIVE WRITING DECRETAL
EPISTLER SUBDEACON
EPISTOLOGRAPHIC DEMOTIC
EPISTROPHE EPODE ABGESANG
EPISTYLE PLATBAND
EPITHELIUM ENDODERM
EPITHET AKAL GOOD NAME TERM LABEL SMEAR TITLE BYWORD MONETA PHRASE AGNOMEN JAPHETIC MULCIBER (PL.) LANGUAGE
EPITOME MAP SUM FLETA DIGEST PRECIS SCHEME COMPEND PITOMIE SUMMULA ABSTRACT BREVIARY LANDSKIP SYLLABUS SYNOPSIS
EPITOMIZE RESUME CURTAIL ABSTRACT COMPRESS CONDENSE CONTRACT DIMINISH
EPITONIUM SCALA
EPIZOA PARASITA
EPOCH AGE ERA DATE ECCA TIME DWYKA EVENT EOCENE PERIOD CLINTON
EPONYM LIMMU ANCIENT
EQUABLE EVEN JUST EQUAL SUANT SMOOTH STEADY UNIFORM TRANQUIL
EQUAL AEQ PAR TIE COPE EGAL EVEN FERE JUST LIKE MAKE MATE MEET PEEL PEER SAME ALIKE LEVEL MATCH PARTY RIVAL TOUCH DOUBLE EQUATE EVENLY FELLOW MARROW PAREIL ABREAST BALANCE COMPEER EMULATE EQUABLE IDENTIC PAREGAL UNIFORM ADEQUATE EQUALIZE EVENHAND PATCHING TRANQUIL
(— IN MEANING) BE
(— QUANTITY) ANA
(— TO) ANOTHER
(NOT —) UNMEET UNMETE
EQUALING TO
EQUALITY PAR TIE EQUITY OWELTY PARAGE PAREIL PARITY BALANCE EGALITE EGALITY ISOTELY EQUATION EVENHAND EVENNESS FAIRNESS
(— BEFORE THE LAW) ISONOMY
(— OF ELEVATION) ISOMETRY
(— OF POWER) ISOCRACY
(— STATE) WYOMING
EQUALIZATION EQUATION DISCHARGE
EQUALIZE EVEN KNOT EQUAL LEVE EQUATE BALANCE ADEQUATE
EQUALIZER EVENER

EQUALLY AS BOTH LIKE ONCE SAME ALIKE EGALLY EVENLY JUSTLY EMFORTH

EQUANIMITY POISE PHLEGM TEMPER BALANCE EGALITY CALMNESS EVENNESS SERENITY

EQUATE EQUAL BALANCE EQUALIZE

EQUATING COMPARISON

EQUATION CUBIC IDENTITY

EQUATOR LINE GIRDLE EQUINOX (— CROSSER) POLLIWOG

EQUES KNIGHT

EQUIDISTANT CENTRAL HALFWAY

EQUILIBRIUM POISE APLOMB BALANCE STATION EQUATION EVENHAND ISOSTASY (— OF FLUID) LEVEL

EQUINE COLT FOAL MARE FILLY HORSE ZEBRA EQUOID EQUINAL HORSELY

EQUINIA MALLEUS

EQUIP ARM FIT IMP KIT RAY RIG ABLE BEAM DECK FEAT FIND GEAR GIRD GIRT HEEL REEK TRIM ARRAY DIGHT DRESS ENARM ENDOW POINT SPEED STUFF ATTIRE BUCKLE ORDAIN OUTFIT SUBORN APPAREL APPOINT BEDIGHT FORTIFY FRAUGHT FURNISH GARNISH HARNESS PLENISH PREPARE QUALIFY ACCOUTER ACCOUTRE (— FOR ACTION) ARM

EQUIPAGE RIG CREW SAMAN SUITE TRAIN SUPPLY RETINUE TURNOUT UNICORN CARRIAGE

EQUIPMENT KIT FARE GEAR TIRE STOCK STUFF ATTIRE CONREY DUFFEL DUFFLE FITOUT GRAITH OUTFIT SETOUT TACKLE APPAREL BAGGAGE FITMENT HARNESS PANOPLY ARMAMENT EQUIPAGE MATERIAL MATERIEL MOUNTING SUPELLEX (— FOR CATCHING FISH) CRAFT (— FOR JOURNEY) FARE

EQUIPOISE POISE BALANCE

EQUIPOTENTIAL LEVEL

EQUIPPED ARMED BODEN THERE EQUIPT ARMORED INSTRUCT WEAPONED (FULLY —) SUMMED (INADEQUATELY —) HAYWIRE (LIGHTLY —) EXPEDITE

EQUISETUM CANDOCK

EQUITABLE EVEN FAIR JUST EQUAL RIGHT EVENLY HONEST EQUABLE UPRIGHT BONITARY RIGHTFUL

EQUITY LAW EPIKY MARGIN EPIKEIA HONESTY JUSTICE EQUALITY EVENHAND FAIRNESS

EQUIVALENT KIND SAME EQUAL COUSIN UNISON ANALOGUE EVENHAND (— IN MONEY) CHANGE (— OF TWO BUSHELS) HUTCH

EQUIVOCAL SHADY DOUBLE FORKED DUBIOUS EVASIVE HALFWAY OBSCURE DOUBTFUL HAVERING PUZZLING SIBYLLIC

EQUIVOCATE LIE DODGE EVADE SHIFT ESCAPE PALTER TRIFLE WEASEL QUIBBLE SHUFFLE

EQUIVOCATION QUIP QUIRK EVASION SHUFFLE EQUIVOKE

EQUULEUS FOAL

ERA AGE AEON DATE TIME EPOCH STAGE PERIOD CENOZOIC (EMPEROR'S —) KIMIGAYO (HINDU —) SAMVAT (MUSLIM —) HEGIRA HEJIRA

ERADICATE DELE ROOT SLAY WEED CROSS ERASE STAMP DELETE EFFACE REMOVE UNROOT UPROOT ABOLISH DESTROY EXPUNGE OUTROOT SUPPLANT (— HAIR) EPILATE

ERADICATOR ERASER

ERAL MOINE

ERASE BLOT DASH DELE RACE RASE RASH RAZE ANNUL PLANE CANCEL DEFACE DELETE EFFACE EXCISE REMOVE SCRAPE SPONGE DESTROY EXPUNGE OUTRAZE SCRATCH UNWRITE

ERASER RASER RUBBER

ERASURE RASURE ERASION DELETION EXCISION

ERD SHREW RANNY

ERE OR AIR SOON EARLY PRIOR BEFORE EREWHILE FORMERLY

EREBUS (FATHER OF —) CHAOS (SISTER OF —) NOX (SON OF —) CHARON

ERECHTHEUS (DAUGHTER OF —) CREUSA PROCRIS CHTHONIA ORITHYIA (FATHER OF —) PANDION (SLAYER OF —) JUPITER (SON OF —) MERION CECROPS PANDORUS (WIFE OF —) PRAXITHEA

ERECT BIG SET BIGG LEVY REAR RECT STEP STEY SWAY TELD AREAR BRANT BUILD DRESS EXALT FRAME MOUNT RAISE SETUP STAND ARRECT UPLIFT UPREAR ADDRESS BRISTLE ELEVATE STATELY UPRAISE UPRIGHT UPSTART STANDING STRAIGHT VERTICAL (NOT —) LAZY COUCHED

ERECTED UPSET

ERECTION DOME HARD FABRIC CHORDEE MACHINE

ERELONG ANON SOON

EREMITE HERMIT ASCETIC RECLUSE ANCHORET

EREWHILE ERE WHILOM

ERG REG EROGON (PL.) AREG

ERGO SO ARGO ARGAL HENCE

ERGOT SPUR CLAVUS ECBOLIC (STAGE OF —) SPHACELIA

ERICHTHONIUS (FATHER OF —) VULCAN DARDANUS (MOTHER OF —) ATTHIS (SON OF —) PANDION

ERIDANUS (FATHER OF —) OCEANUS (MOTHER OF —) TETHYS

ERIE WENRO

ERIGONE (FATHER OF —) ICARIUS AEGISTHUS (MOTHER OF —) CLYTEMNESTRA

ERINYS FURY ALECTO MEGAERA (PL.) DIRAE FURIAE SEMNAE EUMENIDES

ERIOPHORUM DRAWLING

ERISTIC DIALECTIC

ERMINE VAIR VARE STOAT WEASEL ERMELIN FUTERET FUTTRAT MINIVER CLUBSTER WHITRACK WHITTRET

ERODE EAT COMB ETCH GNAW GULL WEAR CLIFF GULLY SCOUR ABRADE DENUDE CORRODE DESTROY

ERODIUM HERONBILL

EROS AMOR CUPID AENGUS POTHOS

EROSE ERODED UNEVEN

EROSION PIPING CHIMNEY NIVATION SCOURING

EROTIC LOVING AMATORY AMOROUS CURIOUS LESBIAN THERMAL

EROTICA CURIOSA FACETIAE

ERR MAR SIN FAIL MISS SLIP ABERR LAPSE MISGO STRAY BUNGLE FORVAY WANDER BLUNDER DEVIATE MISPLAY MISTAKE SCRITHE STUMBLE MISCARRY MISJUDGE

ERRAND CHORE ENVOY JOURNEY MISSION LEGATION (— BOY) LOBBYGOW

ERRANT STRAY ASTRAY ERRING DEVIOUS PRICKANT

ERRATIC WILD CRAZY HUMAN QUEER WACKY CRANKY WHACKY STRANGE TANGENT VAGRANT ACROSTIC ERRABUND FITIFIED PLANETAL PLANETIC TRAVELED VAGABOND

ERRATUM ERROR

ERRING ASTRAY ERRANT DEVIOUS

ERRINGLY FALSE

ERRONEOUS AMISS FALSE WRONG UNTRUE ERRATIC MISTAKEN STRAYING WRONGFUL

ERRONEOUSNESS FALLACY

ERROR X HOB SIN BUBU BULL FLUB HELL MUFF SLIP TRIP BEARD BEVUE BONER DEVIL FAULT FLUFF LAPSE SCAPE BOBBLE FUMBLE GARBLE HOWLER LAPSUS MISCUE NAUGHT SPHALM BLOOMER BLUNDER DEFAULT ERRATUM FALLACY FALSITY LITERAL MISPLAY MISSTEP MISTAKE OFFENSE RHUBARB SNAPPER STUMBLE DELUSION HAMARTIA MISPRINT MISSMENT SOLECISM

ERS VETCH KERSANNE

ERSE ERSCH IRISH CELTIC GAELIC SCOTTISH

ERST ONCE FORMERLY RECENTLY

ERSTWHILE ONCE FORMER FORMERLY

ERUCT RASP BELCH

ERUCTATION BELCH

ERUDITE LEARNED CLERGIAL DIDACTIC

ERUDITION WIT LORE WISDOM
  LETTERS LEARNING
ERUPT BOIL BELCH BURST EJECT
  IRRUPT
ERUPTING ACTIVE
ERUPTION ITCH RASH REEF RUSH
  AGRIA BURST RUPIA SALVO STORM
  BLOTCH HYDROA NIRLES ACTERID
  BLOWOUT ECTHYMA MORPHEA
  MORPHEW PUSTULE SAWFLOM
  SUDAMEN EMPYESIS ENANTHEM
  OUTBREAK OUTBURST
  (CUTANEOUS —) HUMOR
ERVUM LENS LENTILLA
ERYSICHTHON (FATHER OF —)
  CECROPS TRIOPAS
  (MOTHER OF —) AGRAULOS
  (SISTER OF —) IPHIMEDIA
ERYSIPELAS POX ROSE BLAST
  WILDFIRE
ERYTHROBLASTOSIS HYDROPSY
ERYX (FATHER OF —) BUTES
  (MOTHER OF —) VENUS
  (SLAYER OF —) HERCULES
ESAU EDOM
  (FATHER OF —) ISAAC
  (MOTHER OF —) REBEKAH
  (SON OF —) JEUSH KORAH REUEL
  JAALAM ELIPHAZ
  (WIFE OF —) ADAH BASHEMATH
ESCALADE SCALE SCALADE
  SCALADO ESCALADO
ESCAPADE CAPER PRANK SALLY
  SCHEME RUNAWAY
ESCAPE FLY GUY LAM RUN BAIL
  BALE BEAT BLOW BOLT FLEE GATE
  HISS JINK JUMP LEAK MISS SHUN
  SKEW SLIP VENT AVOID BREAK
  CHAPE DODGE ELOPE ELUDE EVADE
  FLANK ISSUE SCAPE SHIFT SKIRT
  SMOKE SPILL ASTERT DECAMP
  ESCHEW OUTLET POWDER SQUEAK
  ABSCOND AVOLATE BLOWOUT
  ELUSION EXHAUST GETAWAY
  LEAKAGE MISTAKE OUTFLOW
  SCRITHE SQUEEZE WILDING
  BLOWBACK ESCAPADE ESCAPAGE
  EXSHEATH OUTSCAPE OVERSLIP
  RIDDANCE WITHSLIP
  (— FROM WORK) SNIB
  (— FROM) FLY SHUN ILLUDE
  (— NOTICE) ELUDE
  (— OF FLUID) EFFUSION
  (NARROW —) SHAVE
ESCAPEMENT SCAPE CRUTCH
  ESCAPE FOLIOT VIRGULE KARRUSEL
ESCARGOT SNAIL
ESCAROLE ENDIVE SCAROLA
ESCARPMENT EDGE
ESCHAR SCAB CRUST ASCHER
ESCHAROTIC CAUSTIC
ESCHEAT FALL LAPSE REVERT
  EXCHEAT FORFEIT
ESCHEW SHUN AVOID FORGO
  ESCAPE FOREGO ABSTAIN
ESCOLAR PALU ROVET OILFISH
  ROVETTO MACKEREL
ESCORT MAN SEE SET TRY BEAR
  BEAU COND LEAD SHOW TEND WAIT

  BRING CARRY GUARD USHER
  ATTEND CONVEY CONVOY FOLLOW
  SQUIRE COLLECT CONDUCT
  CONSORT ESQUIRE GALLANT
  CAVALIER CHAPERON SHEPHERD
  (PAID —) GIGOLO
ESCRITOIRE DESK BUREAU
  LECTERN
ESCULENT EDIBLE EATABLE
ESCUTCHEON CREST SHIELD
ESKER AS OS OSE KAME ESKAR
  HOGBACK
ESKIMO ITA HUSKY INUIT INNUIT
  AGOMIUT AMERIND ANGAKOK
  KUNMIUT OKOMIUT ORARIAN
  AGLEMIUT ESQUIMAU IKOGMIUT
  KIDNELIK KINIPETU MAGEMIUT
  MALEMIUT NUGUMIUT SINIMIUT
  (— ASSEMBLY HOUSE) KASHIM
  (— CULTURE) PUNUK
  (— TENT) TUPEK TUPIK
ESOPHAGUS GULLET SWALLOW
  WEASAND
ESOTERIC INNER MYSTIC ORPHIC
  SECRET PRIVATE ABSTRUSE
ESPADON ESPADA SPADON
  SPADROON
ESPALIER CORDON LATTICE RAILING
  TRELLIS PALISADE
ESPARTO ALFA HALFA SPART STIPA
  ATOCHA
ESPAVE CARACOLI
ESPECIAL VERY CHIEF SPECIAL
  PECULIAR UNCOMMON
ESPECIALLY SUCH EXTRA RATHER
  CHIEFLY OVERALL SPECIAL
ESPIAL SPY ESPY SCOUT NOTICE
ESPINAL MONTE
ESPIONAGE SPYING
ESPLANADE WALK DRIVE MAIDAN
  MARINA
ESPOUSAL CEREMONY SPOUSAGE
  BETROTHAL
ESPOUSE WED AFFY MATE ADOPT
  MARRY DEFEND ENSURE SPOUSE
  BETROTH EMBRACE HUSBAND
  SUPPORT ADVOCATE MAINTAIN
ESPUNDIA UTA
ESPY SEE ASPY SPOT ASCRY SIGHT
  WATCH BEHOLD DESCRY DETECT
  LOCATE NOTICE DISCERN OBSERVE
  DESCRIBE DISCOVER
ESQUIRE RADMAN ARMIGER
  ESCUDERO SERGEANT
ESSAY TRY SEEK ASSAY CHRIA
  OFFER PAPER PROVE TASTE THEME
  TRACT TRAIL CASUAL EFFORT
  MEMOIR SAILYE SATIRE SCREED
  THESIS ARTICLE ATTEMPT PROFFER
  VENTURE WRITING ENDEAVOR
  EXERCISE EXERTION TRACTATE
  TREATISE TURNOVER
ESSE BEING
ESSENCE ENS NET ATAR BASE
  BONE CORE CRUX DRAW ESSE GIST
  GUTS KIND ODOR OTTO PITH QUID
  RASA SOUL YOLK ATTAR BASIC
  BASIS BEING EIDOS FIBER FIBRE
  FUMET HEART JUICE OTTAR OUSIA

  STUFF BOTTOM EFFECT ENTITY
  FLOWER INWARD MARROW NATURE
  SPRITE ALCOHOL ELEMENT
  EXTRACT FUMETTE GODHEAD
  INBEING MEDULLA PERFUME
  BERGAMOT CONCRETE ESSENTIA
  (— OF BEING) SAT
  (— OF FLOWERS) CONCRETE
  (— OF GOD) SPIRIT DIVINITY
  (— OF MEAT) BLOND
  (— OF TEA) DRAW
  (— OF VITAL MATTER) GLAME
  (INNERMOST —) ATMAN
  (UNIVERSAL —) FORM
  (VITAL —) STAMINA
ESSENE ESSEE ASCETIC
ESSENTIAL REAL BASAL BASIC
  VITAL ENTIRE FORMAL INWARD
  CENTRAL CRUCIAL NEEDFUL
  CARDINAL CRITICAL INHERENT
  MATERIAL
  (— TO LIFE) BIOGENOUS
ESSENTIALLY AUFOND
ESSONITE GARNET HYACINTH
ESTABLISH BED FIX PUT SET BASE
  FAST FIRM FOOT MAKE REAR REST
  SEAT BUILD DEFIX EDIFY ENACT
  ERECT EVICT FOUND PLANT PROVE
  RAISE SEIZE SETUP START STATE
  STELL ATTEST AVOUCH BOTTOM
  CEMENT CLINCH CREATE ENROOT
  FASTEN FICCHE GROUND INVENT
  INVEST LOCATE ORDAIN RATIFY
  SETTLE STABLE VERIFY ACCOUNT
  APPOINT APPROVE CONFIRM
  ENSTATE INSTALL INSTATE INSTORE
  POSSESS PREEMPT SUSTAIN
  COLONIZE CONSTATE CONTRACT
  ENSCONCE ENTRENCH IDENTIFY
  INITIATE INSTRUCT RADICATE
  REGULATE STABLISH VALIDATE
  (— FACT) APPROVE
  (— FIRMLY) INDURATE
  (— MORALS) ETHIZE
  (— TRUMP) PITCH
ESTABLISHED SAD FAST FIRM SURE
  LEGAL SEATED SICCAR STABLE
  STAPLE STATED STRONG CERTAIN
  SETTLED STANDING
ESTABLISHMENT HONG MILL SHOP
  STAB DAIRY FORGE JOINT PLANT
  SALON STORE AGENCY CAISSE
  CENOBY ECESIS LAYOUT MENAGE
  SALOON SCHOOL ARSENAL ATELIER
  BROTHEL COENOBY CONCERN
  DOUNSET DOWNSET FACTORY
  FISHERY FOUNDRY FUNDUCK
  SHEBANG AQUARIUM AVERMENT
  BUSINESS CHEESERY CREAMERY
  ERECTION HACIENDA
  (— IN NEW HABITAT) ECESIS
  (— OF COLONY) DEDUCTION
  (DOMESTIC —) MENAGE
  (DRINKING —) STUBE SALOON
  BARROOM SHEBEEN
  (GAMBLING —) HOUSE TRIPOT
  (HORSE-BREEDING —) HARAS
  (MONASTIC —) CLOISTER
ESTAFETTE COURIER STAFETTE

ESTATE FEE ALOD COPY FEOD FIEF
HOME LAND POMP RANK ACRES
ALLOD DAIRA DOWER DOWRY
ESTER ESTRE ETHEL FINCA FUNDO
HABIT HOUSE MANOR STATE TALUK
ABBACY DEMISE DOMAIN ENTAIL
GROUND LIVING MISTER QUINTA
TALUKA ALODIUM CHATEAU
COMMONS DEMESNE DIGNITY
DISPLAY FORTUNE HAVINGS
MAJORAT ALLODIUM BENEFICE
COPYHOLD DOMINION EXECUTRY
FREEHOLD HACIENDA JOINTURE
LIFEHOLD LONGACRE MESNALTY
POSITION PROPERTY SENASORY
STANDING
(— OF REBEL) FISC FISK
(— WITH SERFS) HAM
(HINDU —) CHAK
(PORTION OF —) LEGITIM
(REAL —) FUNDUS
(PL.) AMANI
STEEM AIM LET USE DEEM HOLD
TALE ADORE COUNT FAVOR HONOR
PRICE PRIDE STEEM THINK VALUE
WEIGH WORTH ADMIRE CREDIT
EXTIME REGARD REPUTE REVERE
TENDER WONDER ACCOUNT
CONCEIT OPINION RESPECT
SUSPECT APPRAISE CONSIDER
ESTIMATE VENERATE
STEEMED DEAR
STER BIXIN ETHER OLEIN SARIN
TABUN BORATE CAPRIN ERUCIN
HUMATE LAURIN MALATE OLEATE
ACETATE ADIPATE ANISATE
AZELATE CINERIN ELAIDIN FORMATE
FUROATE GALLATE HEPARIN
INDICAN LACTATE LACTONE
LAURATE MALEATE MELLATE
NITRATE OCTOATE OXALATE
OXAMATE PECTATE PEPSIDE
PICRATE SORBATE STEARIN
SULTONE ABIETATE ACRYLATE
ARSENATE ARSENITE ARSONATE
BEHENATE BENZOATE CAFFEATE
CONGENER DIPHENAN ESTOLIDE
FLUORIDE FUCOIDIN KETIPATE
LINOLATE LINOLEIN MALONATE
MARGARIN MYRISTIN NUCLEATE
PALMITIN PIMELATE PIPERATE
RACEMATE SEBACATE SELENATE
SILICATE SINAPATE STEARATE
SUBERATE TARTRATE
STIMABLE GOOD SOLID WORTH
GENTLE HONEST WORTHY THRIFTY
VALUABLE
STIMATE AIM SET CALL CAST
GAGE RANK RATE READ RECK
ASSAY AUDIT CARAT CENSE COUNT
GAUGE GUESS JUDGE MOUNT
PLACE PRIZE SCALE STOCK TALLY
VALUE WEIGH ASSESS BUDGET
ESTEEM RECKON REGARD SURVEY
ACCOUNT AVERAGE BALANCE
CENSURE COMPUTE MEASURE
APPRAISE CONSIDER CRITIQUE
— OF ONE'S SELF) OPINION
— TOO HIGHLY) OVERRATE

ESTIMATION AIM EYE CESS FAME
NAME ODOR PASS RATE COUNT
HONOR PRICE SIEGE VALUE CHOICE
ESTEEM REGARD REPUTE OPINION
JUDGMENT
(HIGH —) CONCEIT
(LOW —) DISREPUTE
ESTIMATOR CRUISER
ESTOC STOCK SWORD
ESTOILE STAR ETOILE

ESTONIA

CAPITAL: TALLINN
COIN: SENT KROON ESTMARK
DIALECT: TARTU
ISLAND: DAGO OESEL SAARE
  HIIUMAA
LAKE: PEIPUS
MEASURE: TUN ELLE LIIN PANG
  SUND TOLL TOOP FADEN VERST
  SAGENE VERSTA KULIMET
  VERCHOC TONNLAND
NATIVE: ESTH AESTI
PROVINCE: SAARE
RIVER: EMA NARVA
TOWN: NARVA PARNU REVAL
  TARTU TALLINN
WEIGHT: LOOD NAEL PUUD

ESTONIAN ESTH
ESTOP BAR FILL PLUG STOP DEBAR
  PREVENT
ESTRANGE PART WEAN ALIEN
  AVERT DIVERT ALIENATE DISUNITE
  STRANGER
ESTRANGEMENT STANCE DISTASTE
ESTRAY STRAY WANDER
ESTREAT COPY FINE EXACT RECORD
  STREET EXTRACT EXTREAT
ESTREPEMENT STRIP
E STRING QUINT
ESTRIOL THEELOL
ESTRONE THEELIN
ESTRUS HEAT SEASON
ESTUARY PARA WASH CREEK FIRTH
  FLEET FRITH INLET LIMAN ESTERO
ETCETERA ETC KTL
ETCH BITE FROST ENGRAVE
  AQUATINT INSCRIBE
ETCHED FROSTED
ETCHER POINT
ETCHING ETCH AQUATINT
ETEOCLES (BROTHER OF —)
  POLYNICES
  (FATHER OF —) OEDIPUS
  (MOTHER OF —) JOCASTA
ETERNAL ETERNE TARNAL AGELESS
  ENDLESS LASTING UNAGING
  ENDURING IMMORTAL TIMELESS
  UNCAUSED
ETERNALLY AKE EER EVER ALWAYS
  ETERNE FOREVER
ETERNITY AGE EON AEON OLAM
  GLORY ETERNE ETERNAL EWIGKEIT
  INFINITY
ETESIAN ANNUAL PERIODIC
ETHANE DIMETHYL
ETHER AIR SKY APIOL ESTER PINOLE

ANISOLE ASARONE EPOXIDE
ETHYLIN HARMINE SAFROLE
SESAMIN SESAMOL SOLVENT
ACACETIN ELEMICIN EMPYREAN
GUAIACOL
ETHEREAL AERY AIRY SKYEY
AERIAL SKYISH AIRLIKE ETHERIC
FRAGILE SLENDER DELICATE
HEAVENLY SUPERNAL VAPOROUS
ETHICAL ETHIC MORAL HONORABLE
ETHICS HEDONICS

ETHIOPIA

CAPITAL: ADDISABABA
COIN: BESA AMOLE GIRSH
  DOLLAR TALARI ASHRAFI
  PIASTER
DEPRESSION: DANAKIL
FALLS: TISISAT BLUENILE
ISLANDS: DAHLAK
LAKE: ABE TANA ABAYA SHOLA
  ZEWAY RUDOLF STEFANIE
LANGUAGE: GEEZ TIGRE SOMALI
  AMHARIC GALLINYA TIGRINYA
MARRIAGE: DAMOZ QURBAN
  SEMANYA
MEASURE: TAT KUBA SINJER
  SINZER FARSAKH FARSANG
MOUNTAIN: BATU GUGE GUNA
  TALO
MOUNTAINS: AHMAR CHOKE
NAME: ABYSSINIA
NATIVE: AFAR GALLA ABIGAR
  AMHARA ANNUAK HAMITE
  SEMITE SOMALI TIGRAI CUSHITE
  DANAKIL FALASHA
PORT: ASSAB MASSAWA
PRINCE: RAS
RIVER: OMO WEB BARO DAWA
  GILA ABBAI AKOBO AWASH
  FAFAN TAKKAZE
TOWN: EDD GOBA GORE THIO
  ADOLA ADUWA AKSUM ASSAB
  AWASH DIMTU HARAR JIMMA
  MOJJO ASMARA DESSYE
  DUNKUR GONDAR MAKALE
  GARDULA MASSAWA NAKAMTI
  DIREDAWA LALIBALA MUSTAHIL
VALLEY: RIFT
WEIGHT: KASM NATR OKET ALADA
  NETER WAKEA WOGIET
  FARASULA

ETHIOPIAN SIDI HAMITE HARARI
AETHIOP AFRICAN CUSHITE
FALASHA
ETHIOPIC GIZ GEEZ GHEEZ
ETHNIC (— GROUP) ACHANG
ETHOS MANNER
ETHYLENE ELAYL ETHENE ETHERIN
ETIQUETTE FORM DECORUM
MANNERS
(— OF DRINKING TEA) CHANOYU
ETRUSCAN TUSCAN RASENNA
ETRURIAN TYRRHENE
(PL.) TURSENOI TYRRHENI
ETUDE STUDY
ETUI CASE ETWEE TWEEZE TWEEZER
EQUIPAGE RETICULE

ETYMOLOGY ORIGIN DERIVATION
ETYMON RADIX
EUBOEANS ABANTES
EUCALYPT GUM YATE APPLE BIMBIL
  CARBUN JARRAH MALLEE MYRTAL
  CARBEEN CUTTAIL MESSMAN
  IRONBARK MESSMATE WHITETOP
  YERTCHUK
EUCALYPTOLE CINEOL CINEOLE
EUCALYPTUS EUCALYPT WHIPSTICK
EUCHARIST HOUSEL MAUNDY
  SUPPER MYSTERY VIATICUM
EUCHARISTIC (— ELEMENTS) HAGIA
EUCHITE SATANIST ADELPHIAN
  MESSALIAN
EUCHRE LOVE
  (— HAND) JAMBONE JAMBOREE
EUDAEMONIA HAPPINESS
EUDOCIMUS GUARA
EULALIA NETI
EULENSPIEGEL OWLGLASS
EULOGIST PRAISER LAUREATE
EULOGISTIC EULOGIC EPENETIC
  MAGNIFIC LAUDATORY
EULOGY PRAISE TONGUE ADDRESS
  ELOGIUM ORATION ENCOMIUM
  PANEGYRE
EUMOLPUS (FATHER OF —)
  NEPTUNE
  (MOTHER OF —) CHIONE
  (SON OF —) ISMARUS
EUNUCH CAPON SPORUS WETHER
  GELDING HALFMAN CASTRATE
EUPHAUSID SHRIMP
EUPHEMISM DEE FIB GEE GOR
  DASH GOSH GOLES GOLLY LAWKS
  DIANTRE DICKENS GRACIOUS
EUPHONIOUS TUNEFUL
EUPHORIA ELATION
EUPHROSYNE JOY
EUPHUISM GONGORISM
EURASIAN BURGHER FERINGI
EURO WALLAROO
EUROPE BELAIT CONTINENT
EUROPEAN FRANK SAHIB BOHUNK
  EUROPE FRINGE INDIAN FERINGI
  TOPIWALA
  (— IN INDIES) BLIJVER
  (WESTERN —) FRANK
EUROPEAN BARRACUDA SPET
EUROPEAN BASS BRASSE
EUROPEAN BISON AUROCHS
EUROPEAN CLOVER ALSIKE
EUROPEAN GULL MEW
EUROPEAN HERRING SPRAT
EUROPEAN JUNIPER CADE
EUROPEAN KITE GLEDE
EUROPEAN LAVENDER ASPIC
EUROPEAN LINDEN TEIL
EUROPEAN MINT HYSSOP
EUROPEAN OAK DURMAST
EUROPEAN PERCH RUFF RUFFE
EUROPEAN POLECAT FITCHEW
EUROPEAN PORGY BESUGO
EUROPEAN RABBIT CONY
EUROPEAN SHARK TOPE
EUROPEAN SPARROW WHITECAP
EUROPEAN STARLING STARNEL
EUROPEAN SWALLOW MARTIN

EUROPEAN THRUSH MAVIS OUZEL
EUROPEAN WIDGEON WHIM
  WHEWER
EUROPEAN WREN STAG
EURYPTERID SERAPHIM
EURYPYLUS (FATHER OF —)
  NEPTUNE TELEPHUS
  (MOTHER OF —) ASTYOCHE
  (SLAYER OF —) PYRRHUS
  HERCULES
EURYSACES (FATHER OF —) AJAX
  (MOTHER OF —) TECMESSA
EURYSTHEUS (FATHER OF —)
  STHENELUS
  (MOTHER OF —) NICIPPE
  (SLAYER OF —) HYLLUS
EUTECTIC STEADITE
EUTERPE (FATHER OF —) JUPITER
  (MOTHER OF —) MNEMOSYNE
EUXANTHONE PURRONE
EUXOA AGROTIS
EVACUATE PASS VENT VOID AVOID
  EMPTY EXPEL STOOL VACATE
  DEPRIVE EXCRETE EXHAUST
  NULLIFY VACUATE PERSPIRE
EVACUATION OFFICE DUNKIRK
EVADE BEG GEE BILK DUCK FLEE
  FOIL JOUK JUMP SHUN SLIP VOID
  AVERT AVOID BLINK DALLY DODGE
  ELUDE FENCE FLANK PARRY SHIRK
  SKIRT BAFFLE BLENCH BYPASS
  DELUDE ESCAPE ILLUDE BEGUILE
  FINESSE OUTSLIP QUIBBLE
  HEDGEHOP LEAPFROG SIDESTEP
  (— LEGAL PROCESS) ABSCOND
  (— PAYMENT) BILK
  (— WORK) JOUK
EVADNE (FATHER OF —) NEPTUNE
  (HUSBAND OF —) CAPANEUS
  (MOTHER OF —) IPHIS
  (SON OF —) IAMUS
EVALUATE RATE ASSESS PONDER
  RECKON DISSECT APPRAISE
  ESTIMATE
EVALUATION STOCK ESTIMATE
EVANDER (FATHER OF —) HERMES
  (MOTHER OF —) CARMENTA
EVANESCE FADE VANISH
EVANESCENCE ANICCA
EVANESCENT FLEET EVANID
  BRITTLE CURSORY EVASIVE
  FRAGILE DELICATE FLEETING
  FLITTING FUGITIVE STAYLESS
EVANGELICAL GOSPEL
  (— ACTIVITY) WARFARE
EVANGELIST LUKE MARK EVANGEL
  GOSPELER
EVAPORATE DRY EXHALE AVOLATE
  CONDENSE VAPORIZE
EVAPORATOR BOILER EFFECT
EVASION JINK SLIP DODGE QUIRK
  SALVE SHIFT ESCAPE SNATCH
  ELUSION OFFCOME SHUFFLE
  TWISTER ARTIFICE ESCAPISM
  VOIDANCE
EVASIVE SLY EELY DODGY SHIFTY
  TWISTY ELUSIVE ELUSORY TRICKSY
  SLIPPERY SLIPSKIN
EVE DUSK EREB EREV EVEN VIGIL

  SUNSET SUNDOWN
  (NEW YEAR'S —) HAGMENA
  HOGMANAY
EVEN ALL DEN EEN TIE YET FAIR
  HUNK JUST PAIR TILL ALINE EQUAL
  EVERY EXACT FLUSH GRADE HUNKY
  LEVEL MATCH PLAIN RIVAL STILL
  SUANT SUENT SWEET DIRECT
  ITSELF PLACID SILKEN SMOOTH
  SQUARE STEADY ABREAST
  BALANCE EQUABLE FLATTEN
  REGULAR UNIFORM UPSIDES
  EQUALIZE MODERATE PARALLEL
  (— NUMBERS) PAIR
  (— OFF) LEVEL
  (— THOUGH) IF ALTHO ALBEIT
  ALTHOUGH
  (MAKE —) WEIGH STEADY
EVENING DEN EVE EREB EVEN
  ABEND TARDE SUNSET VESPER
  EVENTIDE VESPERAL
  (AT —) TEEN
  (YESTERDAY —) STREEN
EVENING PRIMROSE SUNCUP
  SCABIOUS
EVENING STAR VENUS HESPER
  VESPER EVESTAR HESPERUS
EVENLY FAIR PLAIN FLATLY
  EQUALLY
EVENNESS EQUALITY
EVENT HAP CASE FACT FATE FEAT
  TILT CASUS DOING EPOCH FRAME
  ISSUE THING ACTION EFFECT
  FACTUM RESULT TIDING TIMING
  EPISODE FIXTURE MIRACLE
  PORTENT TRAGEDY INCIDENT
  OCCASION
  (AMUSING —) COMEDY
  (CHANCE —) ACCIDENT FORTUITY
  (EXTRAORDINARY —) MIRACLE
  (FORTUITOUS —) HAZARD
  (GRAVE —) CALAMITY
  (HAPPY —) GODSEND
  (IMPORTANT —) ACE ERA
  (PAST —S) HISTORY
  (SET OF —S) EPISODE
  (SIGNIFICANT —) CRISIS
  (SKI —) DOWNHILL
  (SOCIAL —) BENEFIT
  (SPORTING —) STAKE
  (THEATRICAL —) DRAW
  (TURNING-POINT —) LANDMARK
  (UNEXPECTED —) STUNNER
  AFTERCLAP
  (YEARLY —) ANNUAL
EVENTFUL NOTABLE
EVENTIDE VESPER EVENING
EVENTUAL LAST FINAL ULTIMATE
EVENTUALITY EVENT
EVENTUALLY YET FINALLY
EVENTUATE GO LEAD ISSUE
  RESULT SUCCEED ULTIMATE
EVENUS (DAUGHTER OF —)
  MARPESSA
  (FATHER OF —) MARS
EVER O AY SO AYE EER ONCE STIL
  ALWAYS ETERNE FOREVER
EVERGLADE STATE FLORIDA
EVERGREEN BOX FIR IVY YEW ASI

BAGO ILEX PINE TAWA BOLDO
CAROB CEDAR HEATH HOLLY
LARCH SAVIN THUYA TOYON
BAUERA COIGUE DAHOON LAUREL
MASTIC SPRUCE BANKSIA BARETTA
BEBEERU BILIMBI GOWIDDE
HEMLOCK JASMINE TARATAH
BOXTHORN CALFKILL CARAUNDA
IRONWOOD TILESEED
(PL.) CHRISTMAS
EVERLASTING ETERNE AEONIAL
AEONIAN AGELONG DURABLE
ENDLESS ETERNAL FOREVER
LASTING TEDIOUS ENDURING
IMMORTAL INFINITE TIMELESS
EVERLASTINGLY ALWAYS FOREVER
EVERSION BLOWOUT BEARINGS
EVERT UPSET EVERSE SUBVERT
OVERTURN
EVERY ALL ANY ILK THE EACH EVER
ILKA ENTIRE EVERICH COMPLETE
(— DAY) QD QUOTID
(— HOUR) QH
(— NIGHT) QN
EVERYBODY ALL EACH EVERYMAN
EVERYONE
EVERYDAY USUAL HOMELY PROSAIC
ORDINARY WORKADAY
EVERYTHING ALL ATHING
EVERYWHERE PASSIM UBIQUE
ALGATES AYWHERE OVERALL
ALLWHERE
EVICT OUST EJECT EXPEL
EVIDENCE MARK SHOW SIGN TEST
PROOF SCRIP SMOKE TOKEN TRACE
TRIAL ATTEST RECORD REVEAL
CHARTER EXHIBIT HEARSAY
SHOWING SUPPORT ARGUMENT
DISPROOF DOCUMENT EVICTION
INDICATE MANIFEST MONUMENT
MUNIMENT WARRANTY
(— OF DISEASE) SYMPTOM
(— OF FRESHNESS) BLOOM
(— OF WRONGDOING) GOODS
(POSITIVE —) CONSTAT
EVIDENT LOUD OPEN PERT APERT
BROAD CLEAR FRANK GROSS PLAIN
EXTANT LIQUID PATENT WITTER
EMINENT GLARING OBVIOUS
PROBATE VISIBLE APPARENT
DISTINCT FLAGRANT LUCULENT
MANIFEST PALPABLE
EVIL BAD DER ILL SIN BALE BASE
DIRE HARM LEWD PAPA POOR SORE
VICE VILE WICK YELL CRIME CURSE
DEVIL FELON FOLLY MALUM QUEDE
SORRY WATHE WRONG CANCEL
DIVERS INJURY MALIGN MENACE
NAUGHT ROTTEN SHREWD SINFUL
UNFEEL UNFELE UNGOOD UNWELL
WICKED WONDER ADVERSE
BALEFUL CORRUPT DISEASE
DIVERSE HEINOUS HURTFUL
IMMORAL MISDEED NOXIOUS
SATANIC UNHAPPY UNSOUND
VICIOUS CALAMITY DEPRAVED
DEVILISH DISASTER GANGRENE
IMPROPER INIQUITY MISCHIEF
QUEDSHIP SINISTER

(— BEING) MARE
(— OF MANY PHASES) HYDRA
(— SPIRIT) JUMBIE
(IMAGINARY —) WINDMILL
(IMPENDING —) MENACE IMMINENCE
(SOCIAL —) SCOURGE
(SPIRITUAL —) SCAB
EVILDOER SLASHER
EVIL EYE DROCHUIL MALOCCHIO
EVINCE SHOW ARGUE PROVE
SUBDUE BREATHE CONQUER
DISPLAY EXHIBIT EVIDENCE
INDICATE MANIFEST
EVISCERATE GUT DRAW BOWEL
PAUNCH GARBAGE
EVOCATION SADHANA
EVOKE FIT MOVE STIR EDUCE
AROUSE ELICIT SUMMON EVOCATE
SUGGEST
EVOLUTION DRIFT GROWTH
BIOGENY DIOECISM HOROTELY
MANEUVER BRADYTELY
(PL.) AEROBATICS
EVOLUTIONISM DARWINISM
EVOLVE COOK EMIT EDUCE DERIVE
UNFOLD UNROLL BLOSSOM
DEVELOP EVOLUTE CONCEIVE
UNPLIGHT
EWE KEB TEG CROCK CRONE DRAPE
SHEEP GIMMER LAMBER RACHEL
THEAVE CHILVER
(— AND LAMB) COUPLE
(OLD —) BIDDY CROCK CRONE
BIDDIE
(YOUNG —) THEAVE
EWER JUG CREW LAIR BASIN UDDER
PITCHER URCEOLE
EXACERBATE SOUR ENRAGE
FERMENT EMBITTER IRRITATE
EXACERBATION PAROXYSM
EXACT ASK DUE DEAD EVEN FINE
FLAT HAVE JUMP JUST LEVY NICE
TRUE VERY PRESS SCREW WREAK
WREST COMPEL DEMAND ELICIT
EVINCE EXTORT FORMAL GRAITH
MINUTE NARROW PROPER SEVERE
SQUARE STRAIT STRICT CAREFUL
CERTAIN COLLECT COMMAND
CORRECT ENFORCE ESTREAT
EXPRESS EXTRACT LITERAL
PARTILE PERFECT POINTED PRECISE
PRECISO REFINED REGULAR
REQUIRE ACCURATE CRITICAL
EXPLICIT FAITHFUL RIGOROUS
SPECIFIC
(— BY FINE) ESTREAT
(— SATISFACTION) AVENGE
(NOT —) PLATIC
EXACTING NICE HARSH STERN STIFF
TIGHT SCREWY SEVERE STRAIT
ARDUOUS EXIGENT FINICKY
CRITICAL IMPOSING IRONCLAD
PRESSING SCREWING
(— EXCLUSIVE DEVOTION) JEALOUS
EXACTION TAX MART GOUGE GRIPE
(— OF PROVISIONS) CESS COYNE
COIGNY
(UNDUE —) EXTORTION
EXACTLY DUE BANG DEAD EVEN

FLAT FLOP FULL JUMP JUST VERY
PLUMB QUITE RIGHT SHARP SPANG
TRULY ARIGHT EVENLY ITSELF
JUSTLY NICELY PERFECT SLAPDAB
DIRECTLY MINUTELY
EXACTNESS RIGOR TRUTH NICETY
ACCURACY DELICACY DISPATCH
FIDELITY IDENTITY JUSTNESS
SAPIENCE SEVERITY
(FUSSY —) FIKE
EXAGGERATE GAB MORE CHARGE
EXTEND OVERDO AMPLIFY ENHANCE
ENLARGE MAGNIFY OUTLASH
ROMANCE STRETCH INCREASE
OVERDRAW OVERLASH OVERTELL
(— OPENING OF MOUTH) CHINK
EXAGGERATED SLAB TALL
COLORED FUSTIAN FABULOUS
INFLATED OVERSHOT
EXAGGERATING ARROGANT
EXAGGERATION REACHER
HYPERBOLE
EXALT HAUT REAR AREAR BUILD
DEIFY ELATE ERECT EXTOL HEAVE
HEEZE HONOR MOUNT RAISE
TOWER ALTIFY ASCEND EXHALE
PREFER REFINE UPREAR WORTHY
ADVANCE AUGMENT DIGNIFY
ELEVATE ENHANCE ENNOBLE
FEATHER GLORIFY GREATEN
INSPIRE MAGNIFY PROMOTE
SUBLIME DIVINIZE ENTHRONE
GRADUATE HEIGHTEN INHEAVEN
PEDESTAL
EXALTATION LAUD AVATAR ELATION
RAPTURE ERECTION
EXALTED HAUT HIGH ELATE GRAND
LOFTY NOBLE SHEEN SKYEY SOARY
ASTRAL TIPTOE TOPFUL HAUGHTY
SUBLIME ELEVATED EXALTATE
EXALTING HUMAN
EXAMINATION EX MAY EXAM FACE
QUIZ TEST ASSAY AUDIT BOARD
CHECK FINAL GREAT POINT PROBE
STUDY TRIAL BIOPSY EXAMEN
REVIEW SCHOOL SEARCH SURVEY
TRIPOS AUTOPSY BEARING
CANVASS CHECKUP DIVVERS
EXAMINE HEARING INQUEST INQUIRY
MIDYEAR OPPOSAL TUGGERY
ANALYSIS CRITIQUE EXERCISE
NECROPSY RESEARCH SCANNING
SCRUTINY
(PL.) HOURS
EXAMINE ASK CON FAN SEE SPY
TRY BOLT CASE COMB FEEL LAIT
LINE LOOK OGLE QUIZ RIPE SCAN
SEEK SIFT TEST VIEW ASSAY AUDIT
CHECK ENTER GROPE PROBE
QUEST QUOTE SAMEN SENSE
SOUND STUDY VISIT APPOSE
BEHOLD CANDLE DEBATE PERUSE
PONDER REVIEW SCREEN SEARCH
SURVEY ANALYZE CANVASS
COLLATE DISCUSS EXPLORE
INQUIRE INSPECT OVERSEE
PALPATE RUMMAGE CONSIDER
OVERHAUL
(— BY TOUCH) PALPATE

(— **CAREFULLY**) SCAN SIFT PONDER
(— **LAND**) SOUM
EXAMINER POSER TRIER CENSOR
CONNER SABORA ANALYST
APPOSER AUDITOR CORONER
PROBATOR SEARCHER
EXAMPLE A CASE CAST COPY LEAD
NORM TYPE BEAUT BYSEN ESSAY
LIGHT MODEL PIECE EMBLEM
PRAXIS SAMPLE BOUNCER LEADING
LECTURE PATTERN PURPOSE
SAMPLER THEATER CALENDAR
ENSAMPLE EXEMPLAR EXEMPLUM
FORBYSEN FOREGOER INSTANCE
PARADIGM SPECIMEN
(**DISGRACEFUL** —) BIZEN BYSEN
BYZEN
(**EXTREME** —) CAUTION
(**INFERIOR** —) EXCUSE
(**INSTRUCTIVE** —) LESSON
(**OLDEST** —) DOYEN
(**SUPERLATIVE** —) BLINGER
EXANTHEMA DIEBACK ERUPTION
EXASPERATE IRE IRK MAD BAIT
GALL HEAT URGE ANNOY BLOOD
ENRAGE EXCITE NETTLE EXASPER
INFLAME PROVOKE ROUGHEN
ACERBATE IRRITATE
EXASPERATED SNAKY WROTH
SNAKEY SNAKISH
EXASPERATION GALL HEAT WRATH
EXCAVATE CUT DIG PIT HOLE HOWK
MINE MOLE MUCK PION SINK DELVE
DRILL DRIVE GRAVE NAVVY SCOOP
STOPE BURROW DREDGE EXCAVE
GULLET HOLLOW QUARRY
EXCAVATION CUT DIG PIT HOLE
MINE REDD SINK SUMP BERRY
DELFT DELPH DITCH GRAVE PILOT
STOPE BURROW CAVITY DUGOUT
GROOVE TRENCH BREAKUP
CUTTING PADDOCK TUTWORK
WORKING DENEHOLE SLUSHPIT
EXCAVATOR DIG BILDAR CLEOID
DIGGER DIPPER DRIFTER HATCHET
PIONEER
EXCEED COW TOP BEST PASS
EXCEL OUTDO OUTGO BETTER
OUTRUN OUTVIE OVERDO OVERGO
ECLIPSE OUTPASS OVERRUN
OVERTAX PRECEDE SURPASS
OUTRANGE OUTSTRIP OVERCOME
OVERGANG OVERSTEP OVERWEND
SURMOUNT
(— **THE RESOURCES**) BEGGAR
EXCEEDING VILE
EXCEEDINGLY ALL DONE PURE
TRES VERY AMAIN BLAME BLAMED
MASTER PURELY AWFULLY LICKING
PARLOUS PASSING HEARTILY
HEAVENLY HORRIBLE PROPERLY
EXCEL CAP COB TOP BANG BEAT
BEST DING FLOG MEND PASS
BLECK OUTDO OUTGO SHINE
BETTER EXCEED MASTER OUTRAY
OVERDO OVERGO PRECEL ECLIPSE
EMULATE OUTPEER SURPASS
OUTCLASS OUTRANGE OUTRIVAL
OUTSHINE OUTSTRIP OVERPEER
SUPERATE SURMOUNT

EXCELLENCE ARETE MERIT PRICE
VIRTU WORTH BEAUTY DESERT
HEIGHT VIRTUE DIGNITY PROWESS
GOODNESS SPLENDOR
(— **OF QUALITY**) STRIKE
(**MORAL** —) GRACE
(PL.) SANCTITIES
EXCELLENT GAY RUM BEST BRAW
COOL FINE GOOD HEND HIGH PURE
RARE RIAL SLAP TALL TRIM ATHEL
BONNY BONZA BRAVE BULLY BURLY
GREAT JOLLY PIOUS PRIME SOLID
SUPER SWELL TRIED WALLY BONNIE
BONZER BOSKER CHEESY CHOICE
CLASSY FAMOUS FREELY GENTLE
GOODLY PRETTY PROPER SELECT
SPIFFY WICKED WIZARD WORTHY
YANKEE BLIGHTY BOSHTER CAPITAL
CORKING CURIOUS ELEGANT
GALLANT IMMENSE QUALITY
SNIFTER STAVING TOPPING
CLIPPING EXIMIOUS GENEROUS
KNOCKOUT STUNNING SUPERIOR
VALUABLE VIRTUOUS WAUREGAN
YNGOODLY
(— **IN QUALITY**) FRANK
(**MOST** —) BEST
EXCELLENTLY BRAWLY CLEVER
FINELY FREELY PROUDLY DIVINELY
FAMOUSLY
EXCELLING BEST PASSANT
EXCEPT BAR BUT CEP NOT BATE
BOUT OMIT ONLY SAVE FORBY
SEVER EXEMPT FORBYE NOBBUT
SAVING SCUSIN UNLESS BESIDES
EXCLUDE OUTCEPT OUTTAKE
OUTWITH RESERVE WITHOUT
FORPRISE OUTTAKEN RESERVED
EXCEPTING BATING EXCEPT SAVING
UNLESS
EXCEPTION DEMUR SALVO SAVING
DISSENT OFFENSE DEMURRER
FALLENCY FORPRISE INSTANCE
EXCEPTIONAL RARE EXEMPT
STRANGE UNUSUAL ABERRANT
ABNORMAL ESPECIAL SINGULAR
UNCOMMON
EXCEPTIONALLY AMAZING
SPANKING
EXCERPT CITE PATCH QUOTE
SCRAP EXTRACT OFFPRINT
(— **FROM SONG**) SNATCH
EXCESS OVER PLUS RIOT FLOOD
INORD LUXUS PRIDE ACRASY
ACRASIA BALANCE DEBAUCH
EXTREME MISRULE NIMIETY
OUTRAGE OVERAGE OVERSET
PROFUSE RIOTISE SURFEIT
SURPLUS EXCEDENT GLUTTONY
INTEREST OVERLASH OVERMUCH
OVERPLUS PLETHORA PLEURISY
(— **OF LOGS**) BANK
(— **OF METAL**) FEEDHEAD
(— **OF SOLAR MONTH**) EPACT
EXCESSIVE TOO OVER RANK ENORM
FANCY STEEP STIFF UNDUE DEADLY
WOUNDY EXTREME FURIOUS
NIMIOUS SURFEIT ABNORMAL
CRIMINAL DEVILISH ENORMOUS
HORRIBLE INSOLENT OVERMUCH

TERRIBLE TERRIFIC
EXCESSIVELY TOO SUPER DEADLY
OVERLY STRONG UNDULY PARLISH
PARLOUS PASSING PLAGUEY
WOUNDLY DEVILISH PLAGUILY
EXCHANGE RAP SET CASH CAUP
CHOP CODE COPE COUP KULA
MART SELL SWAP SWOP BANDY
BOARD BOLSA CORSE SHIFT STORE
TRADE TROKE TRUCK BARTER
BOURSE CAMBIO CHANGE DICKER
EXCAMB MARKET NIFFER RESALE
RIALTO SCORSE SHOPPE TOLSEL
TOLZEY VALUTA WISSEL WRIXLE
BARROOM CAMBIUM CHAFFER
COMMUTE CONVERT DEALING
PERMUTE TRAFFIC COMMERCE
TRUCKAGE
(— **IN CHECKERS**) CUT SHOT
(— **OF BLOWS**) HANDPLAY
(— **OF PRISONERS**) CARTEL
(— **OF SYLLABLES**) ANACLASIS
(— **SMALL TALK**) CHAFFER
(— **THOUGHTS**) CONVERSE
(— **VISITS**) GAM
(**DANCE** —) CROSSOVER
(**FAIR** —) GIFFGAFF
(**FOREIGN** —) DEVISE
(**POETICAL** —) FLYTING
(**POST** —) CANTEEN
(**TELEPHONE** —) CENTRAL
EXCHEQUER FISC PURSE COFFER
KHALSA CHECKER FINANCE
TREASURY
EXCIPIENT OXYMEL
EXCISE TAX CROP DUTY GELD TOLL
SLASH EXCIDE EXSECT IMPOST
RESECT EXSCIND ALCABALA
RETRENCH
EXCISEMAN GAGER GAUGER
EXCISOR
EXCISION CUT ERASURE
EXCITABLE NERVOUS
EXCITATION LASH
EXCITE HOT CITE FIRE HEAT HYPO
SEND SPUR STIR URGE WAKE WHE
WORK YERK ALARM AMOVE ANGER
CHAFE ELATE ERECT FLAME FLUSH
IMPEL PIQUE RAISE ROUSE SCALD
SPOOK AROUSE AWAKEN BOTHER
DAZZLE DECOCT FLURRY FOMENT
IGNITE INCEND INCITE INVOKE
JANGLE KINDLE LATHER PROMPT
SALUTE TICKLE UPREAR WECCHE
AGITATE ANIMATE COMMOVE
ENCHAFE FERMENT INCENSE
INFLAME PHILTER PROVOKE
QUICKEN STARTLE WHITTLE
DISQUIET ENGENDER EXCITATE
IRRITATE
(— **MIRTH**) DIVERT
EXCITED UP GAY HOT AGOG GYTE
PINK CADGY EAGER RANTY SKEER
BLEEZY ELATED HEATED STEAMY
ATHRILL FEVERED HAYWIRE
SKEERED WAKENED AGITATED
ATWITTER ELEVATED FEVERISH
FLURRIED FRENETIC STARTLED
(**EASILY** —) KITTLE
EXCITEMENT ADO GOG BUZZ FUSS

GLOW HEAT KICK STIR TOSS UNCO
FEEZE FEVER FUROR LARRY MANIA
SETUP STOUR UNCOW FRENZY
SPLASH WARMTH FERMENT
FRISSON NERVISM TAMASHA
WIDDRIM BROUHAHA DELIRIUM
INTEREST RACKETRY
(FILLED WITH —) HECTIC
(GREAT —) FEVER
(MENTAL —) WIDDRIM
(PLEASANT —) SUSPENSE
(VIOLENT —) GARE
EXCITING HOT HIGH HECTIC
AGACANT BURNING RACKETY
ROUSING EXCITANT EXCITIVE
PATHETIC STIRRING TERRIFIC
(— HORROR) DIRE DIREFUL
EXCLAIM CRY HOWL BLURT ESCRY
SNORT CLAMOR OUTCRY BESPEAK
EXCLAMATION O AH AI AY BO EH
EY HA HI HO LA LO MY OH OW SO
ST YO AHA AIE BAH BAM BOO FEN
FIE FOH GEE GIP GRR GUP HAI HAW
HAY HEM HEP HEY HIC HOY HUH
NOW OCH OFF OHO OUF OUT PAH
PEW POH POX ROT SEE SUZ TCH
TCK TUT UGH VOW WEE WOW YAH
YOW AHEM ALAS AVOY BUFF DEAR
DRAT EGAD EVOE FAST GARN
GOOD HAIL HECH HECK HIST HOLA
HUFF HUNH HUSH HYKE OONS
OUGH PHEW PHOO PHUT PIFF PISH
POOH PRUT PUGH RATS RIVO SCAT
SIRS SOFT SOHO TCHU TUSH WALY
WEEK WEET WELL WHAM WHAT
WHEE WHEW WHIR WHIT WUGG
YOOP YULE ALACK BRAVO EWHOW
FAINS FANCY FAUGH FEIGH GLORY
GOODY HEIGH HELLO HOLLA HUFFA
HULLO HUMPH HUZZA JOSSA
OHONE PSHAW RIGHT SALVE SHISH
SKOAL SORRY SUGAR TEREU
WAUGH WELOO WHING WHISK
WHIST WHOOP WIRRA WOONS
CARAJO CLAMOR ENCORE HALLOO
HEYDAY HOOTAY HURRAH INDEED
OUTCRY PERFAY QUOTHA RATHER
RIGHTO SHUCKS STEADY WALKER
WHOOSH CARAMBA DOGGONE
GODSAKE HOSANNA JIGGERS
KERCHOO KERWHAM NICHEVO
PRITHEE RUBBISH SALAMAT
TANTIVY THUNDER WELCOME
WHOOPEE FAREWELL WAESUCKS
WELLAWAY
(— OF DISGUST) AUH FIE FOH PAH
UGH AUGH AVOY PHEW PISH POOT
PSHA PUGH FAUGH FEICH FEIGH
PSHAW WELOO
(— OF DISTRESS) AI AIE HARO
HARROW
(— OF DOUBT) HUM HUMPH
(— OF IMPATIENCE) GIP PHEW
(— OF INCREDULITY) AHEM INDEED
WALKER
(— OF REPUGNANCE) UGH
(— OF SURPRISE) HA OW GIP LAW
HEIN HUNH LACK LAND LAWK LORD
ODSO BABAI HEUGH LAWKS

CRIMINE CRIMINY HEAVENS JUCKIES
GORBLIMY GRAMERCY
(— OF TRIUMPH) AH IO GRIG
HEUCH HOOCH HURRAH
(PROFANE —) BAN
EXCLAMATION POINT BANG
SHOUT SCREAMER
EXCLUDE BAR SHUT SINK CLOSE
DEBAR EJECT EXPEL FENCE BANISH
DISBAR EXCEPT EXEMPT FORBAR
FORBID REJECT BLANKET DEFAULT
EXPUNGE FOREBAR FOREIGN
OUTTAKE OUTWALL REPULSE
SECLUDE SUSPEND
EXCLUDED EXEMPT FOREIGN
EXCLUDING BAR BUT LESS
BARRING
EXCLUSIVE ALL ONLY RARE SOLE
ALONE ELECT WHOLE NARROW
SELECT ENTIRELY
(— OF) BEFORE
EXCLUSIVELY ALL ALONE SINGLY
ENTIRELY
EXCOGITATE CONSIDER
EXCOMMUNICATE CURSE
UNCHURCH
EXCOMMUNICATION BAN CURSE
HEREM EXCISION
EX-CONVICT LAG LAGGER
EXCORIATE FLAY GALL SCORE
STRIP ABRADE SCORCH BLISTER
LAMBASTE
EXCREMENT LEE CRAP DIRT DREG
DUNG FRASS JAKES HOCKEY
ORDURE REFUSE VOIDING
CROTTELS
(— OF EARTHWORM) CAST
(— OF HARES) CROTTELS
(— OF INSECTS) FRASS
(PL.) DEJECTA
EXCRESCENCE NOB PIN WEN BURL
BURR GALL HORN KNOB KNOT
KNUR LUMP WART FUSEE FUZEE
KNURL THORN EXCESS HURTLE
MORULA NUBBLE PIMPLE BOLSTER
PUSTULE RATTAIL SPINACH
CARUNCLE EPITHEMA TUBERCLE
(— ON HORSE'S FOOT) FIG
(— ON WHALE'S HEAD) BONNET
EXCRETA EGESTA
EXCRETE EGEST SWEAT EXCERN
DEFECATE PERSPIRE
EXCRETION SORDES ECRISIS
EXCRUCIATE RACK GRIND AGONIZE
TORMENT TORTURE
EXCRUCIATING GRINDING
EXCULPATE FREE CLEAR REMIT
ACQUIT EXCUSE PARDON ABSOLVE
FORGIVE JUSTIFY RELEASE
PALLIATE
EXCULPATION EXCUSE
EXCURSION DIP HOP ROW DIET
RIDE SAIL SPIN TOUR TRIP ESSAY
JAUNT RANGE SALLY START TRAMP
CANTER CRUISE FLIGHT JUNKET
OUTING PASEAR RAMBLE SASHAY
VAGARY VOYAGE JOURNEY
OUTLOPE OUTRIDE OUTROAD
CAMPAIGN ESCAPADE

EXCURSIONIST TRIPPER
EXCUSABLE VENIAL ·
EXCUSE FAIK PLEA ALIBI COLOR
GLOSS PLANE REMIT SALVO SCUSE
ACQUIT ESSOIN EXEMPT PARDON
REFUGE SCONCE SECURE SUNYIE
ABSOLVE APARDON APOLOGY
CONDONE ESSOIGN EXCUSAL
FORGIVE OFFCOME PRETEXT
DISPENSE OCCASION OVERLOOK
PALLIATE PRETENCE
(CONSCIENTIOUSLY —) SCRUPLE
EXCUSS SHAKE DISCARD DISCUSS
EXECRABLE BAD CURST CURSED
DAMNED HEINOUS ACCURSED
DAMNABLE WRETCHED
EXECRATE BAN DAMN ABHOR
CURSE DEVOTE
EXECRATION CURSE
EXECUTE DO ACT CUT TOP BURN
DASH FILL GIVE HANG HAVE KILL
OBEY PASS PLAY SLAY FRAME
GANCH LYNCH SCRAG YIELD
DESIGN DIRECT EFFECT FINISH
FULFIL GARROT GIBBET MANAGE
CONDUCT ENFORCE FULFILL
GAROTTE PERFORM STRETCH
COMPLETE DISPATCH EXPEDITE
PRACTICE PRACTISE
(— BOW) WREATHE
(— POORLY) DUB
(— SUCCESSFULLY) COMPLETE
EXECUTED GIVEN
(— EXQUISITELY) CURIOUS
(— WITH CARE) ACCURATE
(CRUDELY —) DAUBY
EXECUTION GANCH TOUCH EFFECT
FACTURE GARROTE HANGING
TECHNIC CARRIAGE GARROTTE
PRACTICE
(— BY BURNING) STAKE
(— OF WILL) FACTUM
EXECUTIONER BURRIO HEADER
TORTOR BUTCHER HANGMAN
HEADMAN LOCKMAN CARNIFEX
EXECUTOR HEADSMAN
EXECUTIVE BOSS DEAN MAYOR
WARDEN CASHIER MANAGER
PODESTA PREMIER GOVERNOR
OFFICIAL
EXECUTOR DOER AGENT ALBACEA
SECUTOR ENFORCER MINISTER
EXEGESIS ANAGOGE ANAGOGY
MIDRASH HAGGADAH
EXEMPLAR MODEL FATHER MIRROR
MODULE EIDOLON EXAMPLE
PARABLE PATTERN
EXEMPLARY LAUDABLE
EXEMPLIFICATION SOUL EXAMPLE
EXEMPLIFY SAMPLE SATISFY
ENSAMPLE MODELIZE
EXEMPT EXON FREE EXEEM EXEME
FRANK SEVER SPARE EXPERT
FIDATE IMMUNE EXCLUDE RELEASE
DISPENSE EXCEPTED
EXEMPTION GRACE CHARTER
FREEDOM LIBERTY SWEATER
BLOODWIT IMMUNITY IMPUNITY
EXEQUATUR PLACET

EXERCISE ACT AIR DIP PLY URE USE BEAR HAVE DRILL ETUDE EXERT HALMA LATIN LONGE SWEAT AIRING BREATH CAREER EMPLOY EXERCE LESSON MANUAL PARADE PRAXIS SCHOOL AUFGABE BREATHE DISPLAY ENHAUNT PROBLEM ACTIVITY EXERTION FORENSIC PALESTRA PRACTICE PRACTISE
(— CONTROL) BOSS PRESIDE
(— HORSE) BREEZE
(ACADEMIC —) PRACTICUM
(CAVALRY —) MELEE
(MUSICAL —) ETUDE SOLFEGE VOCALISE
(STRONG —) INTENSION
(UNWARRANTED —) STRETCH
(PL.) ALLEGRO ATHLETICS
EXERT DO PLY PUT DRAW EMIT HUMP STIR DRIVE SPEND SWING EXTEND REVEAL STRAIN AFFORCE ENFORCE IMPRESS CHARETTE ENDEAVOR EXERCISE
(— A SPELL) TAKE
(— POWER) ACT BEAR
(— PRESSURE) SQUEEZE
(— TRACTION) HAUL
EXERTING (— POWER) AGENT
EXERTION HEFT BURST ESSAY LABOR TRIAL WHILE ACTION EFFORT MOTION STRESS STRIFE ATTEMPT TROUBLE ENDEAVOR EXERCISE STRUGGLE
(EXCESSIVE —) STRAIN
(STRENUOUS —) HUMP
EXFOLIATE SCALE
EXFOLIATION FURFUR
EXHALATION AURA FUME REEK STEAM BREATH EXPIRY MIASMA HALITUS MALARIA FUMOSITY MEPHITIS
EXHALE CAST EMIT REEK EXUDE STEAM WHIFF EXPIRE BREATHE FURNACE REFLAIR RESPIRE EXHALATE PERSPIRE
EXHALED SFOGATO
EXHAUST DO FAG SAP BEAT BURN COOK COWL EMIT FAIL FLAG FLOG JADE KILL MATE SOAK TIRE TUCK BLAST BREAK CLEAN DRAFT DRAIN EMPTY FORDO GRUEL LEECH PETER SHOOT SPEND SWINK WASTE WEARY ABRADE BETOIL BOTTOM BUGGER EMBOSS FINISH FOREDO HARASS HATTER OVERDO TAIGLE TUCKER BREATHE CONSUME DEPLETE DEPRIVE DRAUGHT EXTRACT FATIGUE OUTWEAR SCOURGE SURREIN DISTRESS EDUCTION EVACUATE FORSPEND FORWEARY OVERWEAR
EXHAUSTED TAM BEAT DEAD DONE DUNG GONE WEAK WORN BLOWN EMPTY JADED SPENT STANK TIRED BARREN BEATEN BUSHED EFFETE GROGGY MARCID PLAYED TOILED TRAIKY ATTAINT DRAINED EMPTIED FORDONE FORSUNG FORWORN TEDIOUS WHACKED BANKRUPT

CONSUMED FOREDONE FOREWORN FORFAIRN FORSPENT FOUGHTEN HARASSED OUTSPENT OVERWORN
(— OF AIR) HIGH
EXHAUSTING ARDUOUS IRKSOME PREYING
EXHAUSTION EXHAUST FATIGUE SELLOUT SOOREYN GONENESS
EXHAUSTIVE FULL MINUTE THOROUGH
EXHIBIT AIR PEN FAIR HAVE SHEW SHOW TURN WEAR SPORT STAGE BLAZON DEMEAN EVINCE EXPOSE OPPOSE OSTEND PARADE REVEAL APPROVE CONCENE DIORAMA DISPLAY EXPRESS MONSTER PERFORM PRESENT PRODUCE PROJECT PROPOSE TRADUCE BOOKFAIR BRANDISH CONCEIVE DISCLOSE DISCOVER EMBLAZON EVIDENCE FORTHSET MANIFEST SHOWCASE
(— ALARM) GLOFF
(— DOGS) BENCH
(— IN SNARLING) GRIN
EXHIBITION FAIR SALE SHOW DROLL ENTRY SALON SIGHT ANNUAL PARADE SALARY DISPLAY EXHIBIT PAGEANT PENSION PRESENT SHOWING STAGERY EXERCISE
(— OF DOGS) BENCH
(— ON STAGE) STAGERY
(PUBLIC —) SPECIES
(RIDING —) CAROUSEL
EXHIBITIONER SERVITOR
EXHIBITIONIST HAM HAMFATTER
EXHIBITOR SHOWER
EXHILARATE AMUSE CHEER ELATE ANIMATE ELEVATE ENLIVEN GLADDEN
EXHILARATED RAD GLAD HAPPY HEADY ELEVATED
EXHILARATION GAIETY JOLLITY GLADNESS HILARITY
EXHORT URGE WARN CHARM ADHORT ADVISE CHARGE DEHORT ENGAGE INCITE PREACH CAUTION ADMONISH DISSUADE
EXHORTATION ADVICE EXHORT HOMILY COUNSEL PROPHECY
EXHORTER HORTATOR PREACHER
EXHUME DIG DELVE UNBURY UNTOMB UNEARTH DISINTER EXHUMATE
EXIGENCY NEED WANT EXIGENT URGENCY JUNCTURE OCCASION PRESSURE
EXIGENT DIRE VITAL URGENT CRITICAL EXACTING PRESSING
EXIGUITY PAUCITY
EXILE EXUL POOR RUIN THIN EXPEL GALUT WREAK BANISH DEPORT GALUTH OUTLAW SCANTY WRETCH EXULATE GERSHOM OUTCAST PILGRIM REFUGEE SLENDER DIASPORA FUGITIVE OUTLAWRY
EXILED FOREIGN FUGITIVE
EXIST AM BE IS ARE LIE COME

GROW LIVE MOVE PASS DWELL CONSIST
(— IN FULL SUPPLY) FLOW
EXISTENCE ENS ESSE LIFE SEIN BEING DASEIN ENTITY IDEATE INESSE ESSENCE IDEATUM REALITY ENERGEIA IDENTITY SURVIVAL
(— AFTER DEATH) AFTERLIFE
(DULL —) DEATH
(ETERNAL —) SAT
(EVER-CHANGING —) SAMSARA SANSARA
(IN —) GOING AROUND EXTANT
(PERMANENT —) INHERENCE
(WAKING —) JAGRATA
EXISTENT HARD REAL ALIVE BEING ACTUAL EXTANT EXISTING
(— IN DIFFERENT FORMS) ALLOTROPIC
(CONTINUALLY —) STUBBORN
EXISTING GOING ACTUAL EXTANT EXISTENT
(— IN NAME ONLY) DUMMY
EXIT ISH DOOR GATE VENT GOING ISSUE LEAVE EGRESS EXITUS OUTLET OUTWAY EXITION OUTGATE OUTPORT PASSAGE DEBOUCHE
(HURRIED —) BOUT
EXITE BRACT
EX LIBRIS BOOKPLATE
EXOCYCLIC IRREGULAR
EXODUS EXODY EXITUS HEGIRA HEJIRA EXODIUM
EXON EXEMPT
EXONERATE FREE ALIBI CLEAR ACQUIT EXCUSE EXONER UNLOAD ABSOLVE RELIEVE
EXOPODITE EXOPOD SQUAMA
EXORABLE PRAYABLE
EXORBITANT STEEP UNDUE ABNORMAL
EXORDIUM PREFACE PRELUDE
EXOSKELETON CORSLET CORSELET
EXOSPORIUM EXINE EXTINE EXOSPERM
EXOSTOSIS POROMA SPLINT OSSELET
EXOTIC ALIEN FOREIGN STRANGE
EXOTOSPORE BLAST
EXOTROPIA WALLEYE
EXPAND OPE WAX BLOW BULK FLAN FLUE FOAM GROW HUFF OPEN FARCE FLASH RETCH SPLAY SWELL WIDEN DIDUCE DILATE EXTEND INTEND SPREAD SPROUT UNFOLD UNFURL AMPLIFY BALLOON BLOSSOM BOLSTER BROADEN BURGEON DEVELOP DIFFUSE DISPAND DISPLAY DISTEND EDUCATE ENLARGE EXPANSE EXPLAIN INFLATE STRETCH DISPREAD INCREASE LENGTHEN OUTREACH
(— AS A VESSEL) FLAN
(— FEATHERS) PRIDE
(— INTO PODS) KID
EXPANDED NOWY OPEN OVERT DILATE SPREAD DILATED SWOLLEN INFLATED PATULENT PATULOUS

EXPANDER EXTENDER
EXPANDING BOSOMY
EXPANSE AREA ROOM BURST FIELD
REACH TRACT EXTENT LENGTH
SPREAD COUNTRY STRETCH
DISTANCE EXPANSUM SEPARATE
(— OF ICE) SHEET
(— OF SEA ICE) FIELD
(BROAD —) ACRE MAIN
(IMMEASURABLE — OF TIME)
ETERNITY
(IMMENSE —) OCEAN
(INDEFINITE —) VAGUE
(VAST —) SEA
(WIDE —) BREADTH
EXPANSIBILITY ELATER
EXPANSION ALA BULB WING FLUSH
SPLAY GROWTH SPREAD ECTASIA
ECTASIS EXPANSE HASTULA
ACROCYST COQUILLE DIASTOLE
DILATION INCREASE SWELLING
(— IN SEEDS) ALA WING
(— OF RIVER) BROAD
(FOLIOSE —) LAMINA
(LITURGICAL —) EMBOLISM
EXPANSIVE FREE WIDE BROAD
GENIAL ELASTIC LIBERAL
GENEROUS SPACIOUS SWELLING
EXPATIATE DWELL DILATE EXPAND
SPREAD AMPLIFY BROADEN
DESCANT DIFFUSE ENLARGE
SATISFY
EXPATRIATE EXILE EXPEL BANISH
OUTLAW OUTCAST
EXPATRIATION EXILE
EXPECT ASK DEEM HOPE LITE LOOK
STAY TEND TROW WAIT WEEN
ABIDE AWAIT THINK ATTEND
DEMAND INTEND LIPPEN RECKON
PRESUME REQUIRE SUPPOSE
SUSPECT
EXPECTANT ATIPTOE CHARGED
HOPEFUL INCHOATE
EXPECTANTLY TIPTOE
EXPECTATION HOPE VIEW WAIT
WEEN EXPECT FUTURE ESPEIRE
OPINION SUPPOSE THOUGHT
WEENING PROSPECT
EXPECTED DUE SUPPOSED
EXPECTORANT CINEOL STORAX
CINEOLE EMETINE CREOSOTE
GUAIACOL TEREBENE
EXPECTORATE SPIT
EXPECTORATION EMPTYSIS
EXPEDIENCE ARTIFICE
EXPEDIENT FIT WISE ATAJO CRAFT
DODGE JOKER KNACK SHIFT DEVICE
RESORT STRING DODGERY POLITIC
STOPGAP ARTIFICE RESOURCE
DESIRABLE
EXPEDITATE LAW
EXPEDITATION LAWING
EXPEDITE HIE EASY FREE HURRY
SPEED EXPEDE GREASE HASTEN
QUICKEN DISPATCH
EXPEDITION CAMP FARE ROAD
TREK DRAVE HASTE HURRY RANGE
SCOUT TRADE SAFARI VOYAGE
CARAVAN CRUSADE ENTRADA

JOURNEY OUTLOPE SERVICE
WARFARE WARPATH COMMANDO
HEADHUNT PROGRESS
(FISHING —) DRAVE
(HUNTING —) SAFARI
(MILITARY —) HARKA CRUSADE
JOURNEY WARPATH
EXPEDITIOUS FAST HASTY QUICK
RAPID READY SHORT PROMPT
SPEEDY
EXPEL CAN OUT USH BLOW BOLT
DRUM DUMP FIRE OUST VOID WARP
AVOID CHASE CHECK DEPEL EJECT
ERUPT EVICT EXILE KNOCK SPURT
BANISH BOUNCE DEBOUT DEPORT
DEVOID DISBAR DISOWN OUTPUT
OUTRAY REFUSE ABANDON
EXCLUDE EXPULSE EXTRUDE
OBTRUDE SCRATCH SECLUDE
SUSPEND DISLODGE DISPLACE
EVACUATE FORJUDGE
(— AIR) COUGH
(— FROM MEMBERSHIP) HAMMER
(— GAS) BELCH
(— SUDDENLY) SLIRT
EXPEND USE LEND SPEND SPORT
WASTE WREAK DEFRAY IMPEND
OCCUPY PONDER CONSUME
DISPEND EROGATE EXHAUST
OVERUSE DISBURSE SQUANDER
EXPENDITURE COST OUTGO PENSE
CHARGE OUTLAY EXPENSE PENSION
SPENDING
(— OF ENERGY) EFFORT
EXPENSE EX COST GAFF LOSS
BATTA PRICE SUMPT CHARGE
DAMAGE GERSUM ONCOST OUTLAY
OUTSET OVERHEAD SUMPTURE
(— OF CARRYING) CARRIAGE
(— OF TREAT) SAM
(PL.) BATTA COSTS MISES
EXPENSIVE DEAR HIGH SALT STIFF
COSTLY LAVISH LIBERAL THRIFTY
EXPERIENCE SEE TRY FEEL FIND
HAVE HENT HOLD KNOW LIVE TEST
ASSAY EVENT PROOF PROVE SKILL
TASTE TRIAL USAGE BEHOLD
EXPERT FRAIST ORDEAL SAMPLE
SUFFER APPROVE CALVARY
CONTACT FEELING FURNACE
KNOWING REALIZE SUSTAIN
UNDERGO ESCAPADE
(— GOOD OR ILL FORTUNE) SPEED
(— OF INTENSE SUFFERING)
CALVARY
(— WITH BITTERNESS) BEAR
(CALAMITOUS —) ADVERSITY
(ORDINARY —) USE
(PAINFUL —) FIT
(PARTIAL —) GUST
(TRYING —) ORDEAL
EXPERIENCED HAD MET OLD USED
SALTY EXPERT SALTED TRADED
ANCIENT PRACTIC THRIVEN
VETERAN WEIGHED SEASONED
(— INTENSIVELY) ACUTE
(ACTUALLY —) SPECIOUS
EXPERIENTIAL EMPIRIC
EXPERIMENT SHY TRY TEST ASSAY

ESSAY TRIAL ATTEMPT CONTROL
EXPERIMENTAL SAMPLE
(NOT —) STANDARD
EXPERT ACE DAB DEFT FULL GOOD
PERT ADEPT FLASH READY SHARP
SWELL ADROIT ARTIST CLEVER
FACILE HABILE KAHUNA PANDIT
PERTLY QUAINT SUBTLE WIZARD
ARTISTE ATTACHE CAPABLE
DABSTER SKILLED DEXTROUS
GAINSOME SKILLFUL SPEEDFUL
VIRTUOSO
(— IN JEWISH LAW) DAYAN
(— ON DRIVING LOGS) LAKER
(BANK —) SHROFF
(GREAT —) ONER
(SCIENTIFIC —) BOFFIN
EXPERTNESS SAVVY SKILL FACILITY
HABILITY
EXPIATE ABY SKUG ATONE AVERT
ASSOIL RANSOM
EXPIATORY PIACULAR
EXPIRATION END DEATH BREATH
EFFLUX ELAPSE EXPIRE EXPIRY
(SPASMODIC —) SNEEZE
EXPIRE DIE END EMIT FALL EXPEL
GHOST LAPSE ELAPSE EXHALE
INLAIK OUTRUN PERISH
EXPIRED UP DEAD
EXPIRING DYING
EXPIRY ISH CLOSE DEATH EFFLUX
EXPLAIN OPEN RECE SAVE SCAN
UNDO WISE AREAD AREED CLEAR
GLOSS GLOZE PLANE RECHE SOLVE
SPEED TOUCH DEFINE EXPAND
EXPLAT EXPONE REMENE RIDDLE
UNFOLD ABSOLVE ACCOUNT
AMPLIFY CLARIFY COMMENT
CONTRUE DECLARE DEVELOP
DISCUSS EXHIBIT EXPOUND JUSTIFY
RESOLVE CONSTRUE DESCRIBE
MANIFEST SIMPLIFY UNPLIGHT
UNWONDER
EXPLAINER EXPONENT
EXPLAINING EXPONENT
EXPLANATION KEY NOTE GLOSS
SALVE SALVO ANSWER CAVEAT
ACCOUNT APOLOGY ADDENDUM
EXEGESIS INNUENDO NOTATION
SOLUTION
EXPLETIVE AND GEE BOSH EGAD
GOSH OATH BEGAD MODAL BEHEAR
SDEATH TUNKET DAMMISH
MORBLEU GOODYEAR GRACIOUS
EXPLICATE OPEN CLEAR EXPAND
UNFOLD ACCOUNT EXPLAIN
EXPLICATION CRIB ANALYSIS
EXPLICIT OPEN CLEAR EXACT FIXED
PLAIN EXPRESS PRECISE ABSOLUTE
DEFINITE IMPLICIT POSITIVE
PUNCTUAL SPECIFIC
EXPLICITLY DIRECT FORMALLY
EXPLODE POP BLOW FIRE BELCH
BLAST BURST CRUMP ERUPT PLUFF
SHOOT SQUIB SPRING BACKFIRE
DETONATE DISPLODE
EXPLOIT ACT DEED FEAT GEST JEST
MILK WORK GESTE GOUGE STUNT
PERFORM SUCCESS CHIVALRY

PARERGON PROPERTY
EXPLORATION SPY PROBE SEARCH
EXPLORE
EXPLORATORY FRONTIER
EXPLORE DO DIP MAP SPY DIVE
DRAG FEEL VIEW CHART COAST
DELVE RANGE SCOUT SOUND
SEARCH EXAMINE PALPATE
BOTANIZE DISCOVER
EXPLORER CAVEMAN PIONEER
COLUMBUS
EXPLOSION POP BLOW BLAST
BURST CRUMP SALVO BLOWUP
BOUNCE REPORT PLOSION INCIDENT
OUTBURST
(**FUEL** —) BACKFIRE
(**SLIGHT** —) PLUFF
EXPLOSIVE EGG TNT MINE AMVIS
AMATOL JOVITE LIMPET POWDER
TETRYL TONITE TORPEX TOUCHY
TRITON ABELITE AMMONAL AZOTINE
DUNNITE LIGNOSE LYDDITE PLOSIVE
PUDDING SHIMOSE THORITE
CHEDDITE DYNAMITE ECRASITE
ERUPTIVE GELATINE MELINITE
PYROLITE ROBURITE
(**CHARGE OF** —) TULIP RESPONDER
EXPOLIATE SCALE SPALL SPAWL
EXPONENT INDEX
EXPORT OUTCARRY
EXPORTATION EXPORT OUTPORT
EXPOSE AIR BARE GIVE OPEN RISK
SHOW STRIP BEWRAY DEBUNK
DETECT EXPONE GIBBET OBJECT
OPPOSE REVEAL UNHUSK UNMASK
DISPLAY EXHIBIT EXPOUND PILLORY
PROPINE PUBLISH SUBJECT
UNCOVER UNEARTH UNTRUSS
BRANDISH DISCLOSE DISCOVER
MUCKRAKE RIDICULE SATIRIZE
UNCLOTHE UNSHROUD
(**— FOR BLEACHING**) CROFT
(**— ORE**) HUSH
(**— PLAYING CARD**) BURN
(**— SELF TO**) WAGE
(**— SUDDENLY**) FLASH
(**— TO AIR**) AERATE
(**— TO DANGER**) JUMP COMMIT
SUBMIT
(**— TO HEAT**) AIR
(**— TO INFAMY**) GIBBET
(**— TO MOISTURE**) RET
(**— TO SCORN**) PILLORY
(**— TO SULFUR DIOXIDE**) STOVE
(**— TO SUN AND AIR**) FIELD
(**— TO SUN**) INSOLATE SOLARIZE
EXPOSED AIRY BARE OPEN BLEAK
LIABLE UNSAFE SUBJECT VEILLESS
(**— TO DANGER**) INSECURE
(**— TO**) AGAINST
EXPOSITION FAIR GECK SHOW
ZEND TRACT EXPOSE METHOD
SURVEY ACCOUNT EXPOSAL
MIDRASH ANALYSIS EXEGESIS
EXPOSURE EXTHESIS HAGGADAH
TREATISE
(**— OF FEAST**) SYNAXARY
EXPOSITORY EXEGETIC
EXPOSTULATE ARGUE DISCUSS

EXAMINE PROTEST
EXPOSTULATION PROTEST
EXPOSURE ASPECT EXPOSE
EXPOSAL FLASHING FRONTAGE
PROSPECT
(**— OF CARDS**) SPREAD
(**— OF KING**) CHECK
(**— TO AIR**) AERATE AIRING
(**BODY** —) FLASH
EXPOUND OPEN UNDO GLOZE
SENSE TREAT DEFINE EXPONE
EXPOSE DEVELOP DISCUSS EXPLAIN
EXPOSIT EXPRESS CONSTRUE
SIMPLIFY
EXPOUNDER MUFTI MULLAH
EXPRESS EXPONENT HERMETIC
EXPRESS AIR BID PUT SAY CAST
EMIT PASS POST VENT COUCH
EMOTE FRAME OPINE SPEAK STATE
UTTER VOICE WIELD BROACH
DEMEAN DENOTE DIRECT EVINCE
IMPORT PHRASE ABREACT BREATHE
DECLARE DICTATE EXPOUND
EXPREME TESTIFY DEFINITE
DESCRIBE DISPATCH EXPLICIT
INTIMATE MANIFEST
(**— APPROVAL**) AGREE ACCEDE
APPLAUD
(**— AS LANGUAGE**) LAY
(**— BY GESTURE**) BECK
(**— BY LAUGHTER**) LAUGH
(**— CONCERN**) CLUCK
(**— DISAPPROVAL**) BOO CHIDE
DECRY GROAN CATCALL
(**— DISDAIN**) TUT
(**— EFFERVESCENTLY**) CHORTLE
(**— FOLLY**) EXPAND
(**— GRATITUDE**) THANK AGGRATE
(**— GRIEF**) DEPLORE
(**— IN WORDS**) SAY DRAW SPEAK
PHRASE
(**— NUMERICALLY**) EVALUATE
(**— ONE'S FEELINGS**) FLOW
(**— SORROW**) LAMENT COMPLAIN
(**— WILLINGNESS**) CONSENT
EXPRESSION DIT HIT SAY CAST
EUGE FACE FORM POSE SHOW SIGN
TERM VULT WORD ADIEU GLIFF
IDIOM SNEER TOKEN VOICE
BYWORD DILOGY DIVERB EFFECT
FACIES ORACLE PHRASE SPEECH
SYMBOL COMMENT DESCANT
EPITHET EXPRESS GRIMACE
ALLEGORY AUSDRUCK DANICISM
FELICITY LACONISM MONOMIAL
(**— IN FEW WORDS**) BREVITY
(**— OF ANNOYANCE**) SOH
(**— OF APPROVAL**) EUGE PLACET
(**— OF ASSENT**) CONTENT
(**— OF BEAUTY**) ART
(**— OF CHOICE**) VOTE
(**— OF DISPLEASURE**) FROWN
(**— OF DISTASTE**) FACE
(**— OF HOMAGE**) OVATION
(**— OF JOY**) GREETING
(**— OF OPINION**) EDITORIAL
(**— OF RESPECT**) DUTY
(**— OF SADNESS**) SHADE
(**— OF SCORN**) GECK

(**— OF SINGLE IDEA**) RHEME
(**APT** —) FELICITY
(**CHEMICAL** —) EQUATION
(**COMMONPLACE** —) BROMIDE
(**CORRECT** —) SUMPSIMUS
(**CURT** —) LACONIC
(**FACIAL** —) GRIN CHEER SCOWL
SMILE
(**INCONGRUOUS** —) BULL
(**LOUD** —) CLAMOR
(**MATHEMATICAL** —) INDEX SERIES
BINOMIAL EQUATION FUNCTION
INTEGRAL
(**MOCKING** —) SCOFF
(**PECULIAR** —) IDIOM
(**PET** —) CANT
(**PUERILE** —) BOYISM
(**SARCASTIC** —) GIBE JIBE
(**SERIOUS** —) EARNEST
(**SINCERE** —) CANDOR
(**SYMBOLIC** —) FORMULA
(**TENDER** —) LANGUISH
(**TRITE** —) CLICHE
(**UNRESTRAINED** —) EFFUSION
(**VERBAL** —) LETTER
(**WISE** —) ORACLE
EXPRESSIONLESS STONY LEADEN
SODDEN VACANT WOODEN
TONELESS
EXPRESSIVE POETIC TONGUED
ELOQUENT EMPHATIC SPEAKING
EXPRESSIVENESS DICTION
DELICACY TOURNURE ELOQUENCE
EXPRESSLY NAMELY EXPRESS
PRESSLY FORMALLY
EXPRESSWAY FREEWAY SPEEDWAY
EXPROBATE CENSURE UPBRAID
EXPULSION EXILE BOUNCE
BANNIMUS EJECTION EXCISION
EXPUNGE BLOT DELE ERASE SLASH
CANCEL DELETE EFFACE EXCISE
SCRAPE DESTROY SCRATCH
DISPUNGE
EXPURGATE GELD PURGE
CASTRATE
EXPURGATION BOWDLERISM
EXQUISITE FOP DUDE FINE NICE
PERT PINK RARE DANDY EXACT
CHOICE DAINTY CAREFUL ELEGANT
GEMLIKE PERFECT REFINED
AFFECTED DELICATE ETHEREAL
MACARONI
EXQUISITELY CHOICELY
EXSCIND CUT SEVER EXCISE
EXTANT ALIVE BEING LIVING VISIBLE
EXISTING MANIFEST
EXTEMPORE SUDDEN OFFHAND
IMPROVISO
EXTEND GO EKE LIE RUN BEAR
BUSH COME DATE DRAW GROW
LAST OPEN PASS RISE ROLL SPAN
SPIN BREDE BULGE CARRY COVER
FARCE REACH RENEW RETCH SEIZE
SHOOT STENT VERGE WIDEN
AMOUNT DEEPEN DEPLOY DILATE
EXPAND INTEND OUTLIE SPREAD
SPRING STRAIN STREAK THRUST
TRENCH AMPLIFY BROADEN
DIFFUSE DISPLAY DISTEND ENLARGE

OVERLAP OVERRUN PORRECT
PORTEND PRODUCE PROFFER
PROJECT PROLONG PROMOTE
PROTEND RADIATE STRETCH
CONTINUE ELONGATE INCREASE
LENGTHEN OUTREACH PROROGUE
PROTRACT PROTRUDE
(— **ACTIVITIES**) BRANCH
(— **AROUND**) GIRTH
(— **IN SPACE**) DURE
(— **IRREGULARLY**) TRAIL
(— **OVER**) SPAN COVER CROSS
CONTAIN OVERLAP
(— **SAIL**) SHEET
(— **THE FRONT**) DEPLOY
(— **TO**) LINE REACH
EXTENDED FAT LONG OPEN BROAD
EXTENT SPREAD EXTENSE LENGTHY
PROLATE SPLAYED EXPANDED
INTENDED
EXTENDER INERT FILLER LIGNIN
EXTENDING BROAD
(— **OVER**) ASTRIDE
EXTENSION ARM EKE ELL AREA
CAPE SCOPE POCKET SATTVA
SPHERE SPREAD BREADTH STRETCH
ADDENDUM ADDITION DURATION
INCREASE PROTENSE
(— **OF BUILDING MATERIAL**) APRON
(— **OF CREDIT**) DATING
(— **OF MINERAL VEIN**) FLAT
(— **OF RACE TRACK**) CHUTE SHUTE
(— **OF SHELL**) LAPPET
(— **OF TIME**) RESPITE
(— **OF WAGON FRAME**) THRIPPLE
(**BALLET** —) BATTEMENT
EXTENSIVE HUGE VAST WIDE AMPLE
BROAD LARGE EXTENSE IMMENSE
EXPANDED INFINITE SWEEPING
EXTENT DUE RUN TAX AREA BODY
BULK DEAL GAGE LEVY PASS SIZE
WRIT AMBIT DEPTH FIELD GAUGE
LIMIT RANGE REACH SCOPE SPACE
STENT SWEEP TRACK AMOUNT
ASSIZE ATTACK DEGREE LENGTH
SPREAD STREEK ACREAGE ASSAULT
BREADTH COMPASS EXPANSE
SEIZURE STRETCH VARIETY
DISTANCE INCREASE LATITUDE
QUANTITY STRAIGHT
(— **OF FRONT**) FRONTAGE
(— **OF LAND**) HEIGHT CONTINENT
(— **OF SPACE**) ROOM
(**BROAD** —) SWEEP
(**SOME** —) BIT
(**UNLIMITED** —) INFINITY
(**UTMOST** —) FULL
(**VAST** —) DEEP
(**VERTICAL** —) ALTITUDE
EXTENUATE THIN GLOZE MINCE
EXCUSE LESSEN SOOTHE WEAKEN
DIMINISH PALLIATE
EXTERIOR CRUST ECTAD ECTAL
OUTER SHELL EXTERN OUTSIDE
OUTWARD SURFACE EXOTERIC
EXTERNAL OUTLYING
EXTERMINATE WIPE EXPEL UPROOT
ABOLISH DESTROY
EXTERNAL OUT OUTER EXTERN

OUTSIDE OUTWARD STRANGE
EXOTERIC EXTERIOR INCIDENT
EXTERNALITY OUTNESS
EXTERNALLY OUTWARD WITHOUT
EXTINCT DEAD BYGONE DEFUNCT
QUENCHED
(— **MAN**) KANJERA
EXTINCTION DOOM FINE DEATH
EXPIRY DELETION
EXTINGUISH OUT DAMP DOUT REDD
STUB ANNUL CHOKE CRUSH DOUSE
DOWSE DROWN QUELL REPEL
SLAKE SNUFF STAMP QUENCH
STANCH STIFLE BLANKET DESTROY
ECLIPSE EXPIATE EXTINCT OBSCURE
OPPRESS SLOCKEN STAUNCH
SUPPRESS
(— **CIGARETTE**) SNUB
EXTINGUISHED OUT DEAD EXTINCT
EXTINGUISHER DOUTER STAUNCH
BACKPACK QUENCHER STANCHER
EXTIRPATE DELE STUB ERASE
EXPEL STAMP STOCK EXCISE
EXTIRP UPROOT DESTROY EXSCIND
OUTROOT SUPPLANT
EXTIRPATION ROOTAGE EXCISION
EXTOL CRY FETE HYMN LAUD BLESS
CRACK EXALT KUDOS ROOSE
SPEAK EXTOLL PRAISE ADVANCE
APPLAUD COLLAUD COMMEND
ELEVATE ENHANCE GLORIFY
RESOUND UPRAISE EMBLAZON
EULOGIZE
EXTOLMENT PRECONY
EXTORT PEEL PILL BRIBE EDUCE
EXACT FORCE PINCH WREST WRING
COMPEL ELICIT SPONGE STRAIN
WRENCH WRITHE EXTRACT
OUTWREST
EXTORTION CHOUT GOUGE EXTORT
HOLDUP SCOTAL BRIBERY PILLAGE
CHANTAGE EXACTION RAPACITY
EXTORTIONATE HARD CRIMINAL
GRINDING
EXTORTIONER BRIBER POLLER
SHAVER VAMPIRE
EXTORTIONIST POLLER
EXTRA ODD MORE ORRA OVER PLUS
ADDED SPARE SPECIAL SURPLUS
SUPERIOR
EXTRACT DIG PRY CITE DRAW KINO
KOLA PULL SOAK ANIMA BLEED
CUTCH DRAFT EDUCE ELUTE EXACT
KUTCH KYPOO QUOTE RENES
RUSOT SCRAP STEEP WRING
CORTIN CURARE DECOCT DEDUCE
DERIVE DEWTRY DISTIL ELICIT
ELIXIR EVULSE EXTORT GOBBET
GUACIN MULIUM OVARIN REMOVE
RENDER RUSWUT TRIPOS UZARON
ABORTIN AMALTAS ARCANUM
CATECHU DESCENT DISTILL
DRAUGHT ERGOTIN ESSENCE
ESTREAT EXCERPT EXHAUST
FUMARIA INTRAIT LIMBECK MONESIA
PASSEWA SUMMARY VANILLA
ACETRACT AMBRETTE GINGERIN
HYPERNIC INFUSION LICORICE
PERICOPE SEPARATE TIKITIKI

TINCTURE WITHDRAW
(— **BY BOILING**) DECOCT ELIXATE
(— **BY DIGGING**) GRUB
(— **FORCIBLY**) EVULSE
(— **FROM ACACIA**) KATH CASHOO
CATECHU
(— **FROM BERBERIS**) RUSOT
RUSWUT
(— **OF GINGER**) JAKE JAKEY
(— **ORE**) STOPE
(**TANNING** —) AMALTAS
EXTRACTION KIN BIRTH STOCK
ORIGIN DESCENT EDITION ESSENCE
EXTRACT EXTREAT BREEDING
TINCTURE
(— **OF ROOTS**) EVOLUTION
(— **OF STEAM**) BLEEDING
EXTRACTIVE AGAR BANG BHANG
AMAROID CARAGEEN
EXTRADITE BANISH
EXTRANEOUS OUTER EXOTIC
FOREIGN OUTLYING SPURIOUS
EXTRAORDINARILY BYOUS
EXTRAORDINARY ODD FREM ONCO
RARE BYOUS ENORM SMASH
DAMNED EXEMPT MIGHTY RAGING
SIGNAL CORKING CURIOUS
HUMMING NOTABLE SPECIAL
STRANGE UNUSUAL ABNORMAL
EXIMIOUS FORINSEC SINGULAR
SMASHING UNCOMMON
EXTRARETINAL PAROPTIC
EXTRAVAGANCE FRILL PRIDE
WASTE LUXURY EXPENSE
RAMPANCY SQUANDER UNTHRIFT
WILDNESS
(**MENTAL** —) MADNESS
EXTRAVAGANT MAD HIGH WILD
FANCY FISHY FOLLE LARGE OUTRE
COSTLY GOTHIC HEROIC LAVISH
SHRILL WANTON BAROQUE BIZARRE
COSTLEW FANATIC FLAMING
FURIOUS NIMIOUS PROFUSE
RAMPANT VAGRANT INSOLENT
PRODIGAL RECKLESS ROMANTIC
UNTHRIFT WANDERER WASTEFUL
EXTRAVAGANTLY LARGE
EXTRAVAGATION VIBEX
EXTRAVASATION EFFUSION
EXTREME BLUE DEEP DIRE HIGH
LAST RANK SORE VILE ACUTE
BLACK CLOSE CRUEL DENSE DIZZY
FINAL GREAT LIMIT PITCH STEEP
ULTRA UNDUE UTTER ARDENT
ARRANT BRAZEN DEADLY FIERCE
HEROIC LENGTH MORTAL SAVAGE
SEVERE STRONG UTMOST WOUNDY
DRASTIC FEARFUL FORWARD
FRANTIC HOWLING INTENSE
OUTWARD PROFUSE RADICAL
SURFEIT VIOLENT ALMIGHTY
DEVILISH DREADFUL EGYPTIAN
ENORMOUS FABULOUS FARTHEST
GREATEST MERCIFUL SPENDFUL
TERRIBLE TERRIFIC ULTIMATE
EXQUISITE
(**NOT** —) SWEET
(**PL.**) PASO
EXTREMELY SO BIG DOG TOO WAY

BONE DEAD EVER FULL MAIN RANK
SELI THAT UNCO VERY AWFUL
BLACK BULLY BYOUS CRAZY CRUEL
EXTRA HEAPS RIGHT SELLE SOWAN
SUPER BITTER DAMNED DEADLY
DEUCED HIGHLY MIGHTY NATION
POISON SORELY SURELY UNCOLY
APLENTY AWFULLY BOILING
CRUELLY EXTREME GALLOWS
HOPPING INNERLY SOPPING
STAVING ALMIGHTY ENORMOUS
MORTALLY PRECIOUS PROPERLY
EXTREMISM JACOBINISM
EXTREMIST JACOBIN RADICAL
EXTREMITY END TIP HEAD NEED
PUSH TAIL CLOSE LIMIT SHIFT
START VERGE BORDER FINGER
EXIGENT EXTREME ACROSTIC
ALTITUDE DISASTER JUNCTURE
OUTRANCE TERMINAL
(— **OF MOON**) HORN
(— **OF TENDRIL**) HOLDFAST
(— **OF TOOTH ROOT**) APEX
(**REMOTEST** —) CORNER
EXTRICATE FREE HELP CLEAR
LOOSE RESCUE SQUIRM OUTWIND
EXPEDITE LIBERATE UNTANGLE
(— **ONESELF**) WANGLE
EXTRINSIC ALIEN EVERY FOREIGN
OUTWARD EXTERNAL OUTLYING
EXTROVERT SYNTONIC
EXTRUDE BEAR SPEW EJECT EXPEL
SHOOT PROJECT PROTRUDE
EXUBERANCE PRICE EXCESS
LUXURY PLENTY ABANDON
LAUGHTER OVERFLOW RAMPANCY
EXUBERANT BOUNCY FEISTY LAVISH
COPIOUS FERTILE GLOWING
PROFUSE RAMPANT EFFUSIVE
EXUDATE GUM SPEW SPUE MANNA
DIKAMALI GUAIACUM HONEYDEW
SARCOCOL
EXUDATION DIP GUM LAC SAP TAR

BALM COPAL PITCH RESIN ROSIN
SUDOR MASTIC SANIES GALIPOT
MOCHRAS SPEWING BLEEDING
EXUDENCE LAITANCE MOISTURE
EXUDE GUM DRIP EMIT OOZE REEK
SPEW BLEED STILL SWEAT EXTILL
STRAIN STREAM EXUDATE GUTTATE
SCREEVE SECRETE SWELTER
PERSPIRE
EXULT JOY CROW LEAP BOAST
GLOAT GLORY INSULT SPRING
REJOICE TRIUMPH
EXULTANT ELATED
EXULTATION JOY OVATION
RAPTURE
EXULTING EXULTANT JUBILANT
EYALET VILLAYET
EYAS NESTLING
EYE O EE HE ORB SPY DISC GAZE
GLIM LAMP LOOP MIEN OGLE SCAN
UVEA VIEW GLARE GLASS GLENE
NAVEL OPTIC SENSE SHANK SIGHT
TOISE WATCH BEHOLD COLLAR
EUCONE EYELET GOGGLE OCULAR
OCULUS OILLET PEEPER POPEYE
REGARD ROLLER SHINER STEMMA
VISION WINDOW WINKER BLINKER
EUCONIC EXOCONE EYEBALL
EYEHOLE OBSERVE OCELLUS
PIERCER PIGSNEY PINKANY PINKENY
SENSORY WITNESS LATCHING
NOISETTE OMMATEUM RECEPTOR
(— **AMOROUSLY**) OGLE
(— **FORMED BY ROPE**) TONGUE
(— **IN BIGHT**) COLLAR
(— **IN EGYPTIAN SYMBOLISM**) UTA
(— **OF BEAN**) HILUM
(— **OF FRUIT**) NOSE
(— **OF HINGE**) GUDGEON
(— **OF INSECT**) STEMMA
(— **OF RA**) SEKHET
(— **SORENESS**) LIPPITUDE
(**BLACK** —) SHINER

(**EVIL** —) DROCHUIL MALOCCHIO
(**METAL** —) HONDA
(PL.) EEN EES NIE YEN YES EYNE
LAMPS LIGHTS SEEING GOGGLES
KEEKERS GLAZIERS GLIMMERS
EYEBALL EYE BALL GLASS GLOBE
(— **MOVEMENT**) VERGENCE
EYEBOLT SPRIG RINGBOLT
(**INTERLOCKING** —**S**) SNIBEL
EYEBRIGHT EYEWORT EUPHRASY
EYEBROW BREE BROW EEBREE
WINBROW WRIGGLE
EYE-CATCHING BOLD
EYECUP EYEGLASS
EYEGLASS QUIZ NIPPER MONOCLE
EYEGLASSES GLIMS SPECS LENSES
GLASSES LORGNON NIPPERS
BIFOCALS
EYEHOLE EYELET EYEPIT
EYELASH BREE LASH CILIUM
WINKER EYEBREE
(**LOSS OF** —**S**) MADAROSIS
(PL.) CILIA EAVES
EYELET MAIL PINK OELET AGRAFE
OILLET POUNCE AGRAFFE CRINGLE
GROMMET PEEPHOLE
EYELID HAW LID BREE WINDOW
EYEBREE PALPEBRA
(PL.) EAVES
EYEPIECE OCULAR EYEGLASS
(— **OF TELESCOPE**) POWER
EYESHADE OPAQUE
EYESHOT RANGE REACH EYESIGHT
EYESIGHT VIEW LIGHT SIGHT
EYE SOCKET ORBIT
EYESORE DESIGHT
EYESPOT EYEDOT STIGMA EYEHOLE
OCELLUS EYEPOINT
EYESTALK STIPES
EYETOOTH CUSPID DOGTOOTH
EYEWASH COLLYRIE EYEWATER
EYOT AIT EIGHT ISLET
EYRE AIR ITER

F EF FF EFF FOX DIGAMMA FOXTROT
FABA VICIA
FABLE MYTH TALE FEIGN STORY
LEGEND TRIFLE FICTION PARABLE
POETIZE UNTRUTH ALLEGORY
APOLOGUE FABULATE FABULIZE
(— OF GOLD COAST) NANCY
(MORAL —) EMBLEM
FABRIC ACCA CORD DUCK GOLD
GROS HAIR HUCK IKAT SILK SUSI
TAPA TARS TUKE CHECK CREPE
DHOTI DOBBY DYNEL FANCY MOIRE
NINOW PRINT RUMAL SCRIM SPLIT
STUFF SUPER SURAH SURAT TABBY
TAMMY TARSE TERRY TEWKE
TWEED TWILL UNION VICHY VOILE
WEAVE AGARIC ALACHA BENGAL
BROCHE BYSSUS CAFFOY CARPET
COTTON CREPON CYPRUS DACRON
DAMASK DIAPER DOBBIE EPONGE
ESTRON FLEECE HARDEN LAPPET
LUSTER LUSTRE MARBLE MASHRU
MURREY POODLE SENNIT STRIPE
TAMINY TANJIB TARTAN TRICOT
TUSSAH VELURE VELVET WADMAL
WINCEY ZENANA ACETATE ALEPINE
ALLOVER BANDALA BANDING
BELTING BEWPERS BINDING
BUCKRAM CANILLE CHALLIS
CHEKMAK CHIFFON CYPRESS
DAMASSE DOESKIN DRABBET
EDIFICE ELASTIC EPINGLE FACONNE
FUSTIAN MIXTURE MORELLA
PAISLEY PLUMBET SAYETTE
SEGATHY SILESIA SUITING TABARET
TABINET TAFFETA TEXTILE TIFFANY
VESSETS AGABANEE BARRACAN
BOCASINE BOURETTE CAMELINE
CANNELLE CASEMENT CHAMBRAY
CRETONNE DUCHESSE HAIRLINE
HANDMADE HARATEEN JACQUARD
KNITTING LUSTRINE MATERIAL
MOLESKIN OSNABURG SHANTUNG
SHIRTING SICILIAN SKIRTING
SWANSKIN TAPESTRY TARLATAN
VALENCIA
(— CONTAINING GOLD OR SILVER
THREAD) ACCA TASH TASS
(— FOR STIFFENING) WIGAN
(— OF TWO OR MORE MATERIALS)
UNION
(— RESEMBLING TOWELING)
AGARIC
(— WITH INWOVEN SCENES) ARRAS
(ABSORBENT —) HUCK
(BROCADED —) LAME LAMPAS
(COARSE —) TAT CRASH HAIRE
DUFFEL RATINE STAMIN BAGGING
BOCKING DRABBET SACKING
STAMMEL DAGSWAIN
(CORDED —) REP DUCAPE POPLIN
OTTOMAN
(COTTON —) CREA DUCK JEAN
LENO LINO SUSI BAIZE BASIN DENIM
DRILL RUMAL SUPER SWISS VICHY
WIGAN BURRAH CALICO CANVAS
CATGUT CHILLO CHINTZ COUTIL
COVERT DIMITY MADRAS MUSLIN
PENANG SATEEN BLANKET BUSTIAN

CANTOON DAMASSE ETAMINE
FLANNEL GALATEA GINGHAM
HICKORY HOLLAND JACONET
PERCALE TICKING BUCKSKIN
COTELINE COUTILLE CRETONNE
DRILLING DUNGAREE INDIENNE
SHEETING
(DECORATED —) DIAMANTE
(DELICATE —) HUSI JUSI
(DURABLE —) SCRIM SERGE
(ELASTIC —) GORING ELASTIC
(EMBOSSED —) CLOKY CLOQUE
(EMBROIDERED —) BALDAQUIN
(FIGURED —) BROCADE BROCATEL
(FINE —) PIMA SILK SUSI LINEN
DIMITY MERINO MOHAIR PERCALE
(GAUZELIKE —) BAREGE GOSSAMER
(GLAZED —) CIRE
(GLOSSY —) SATIN GLORIA SATEEN
(GOAT'S-HAIR —) TIBET
(HEAVY —) GROS CRASH DENIM
DRILL BURLAP CATGUT FRIEZE
LINENE TOBINE WHITNEY
(JUTE —) BALINE BURLAP
(KNITTED —) SUEDE BOUCLE
JERSEY TRICOT CHIFFON
(LIGHTWEIGHT —) GLORIA BUNTING
DELAINE FORTISAN
(LINEN —) SINDON BEWPERS
BUCKRAM CAMBRIC DRABBET
HOLLAND CRETONNE
(MOTTLED —) CHINE
(MOURNING —) ALMA
(MUSLIN —) TANJIB
(OPENWORK —) LACE SKIPDENT
(ORNAMENTAL —) GIMP LACE
LAMPAS GALLOON
(PEBBLY-SURFACED —) ARMURE
(PILED —) TERRY KRIMMER
CHENILLE
(PRINTED —) BATIK CALICO
ALLOVER PERCALE TOURNAY
(RIBBED —) CORD GROS COTELE
FAILLE SOLEIL CORDUROY
MAROCAIN MOGADORE WHIPCORD
(ROUGH —) TERRY HOPSACK
HOMESPUN
(SATIN —) CAMLET ETOILE
(SHEER —) LAWN SHEER SWISS
DIMITY BATISTE SOUFFLE VALENCE
GOSSAMER
(SHORT-NAPPED —) RAS
(SILK —) ACCA ALMA FUGI FUJI
GROS IKAT MOFF ATLAS CARDE
PEKIN RAJAH RUMAL SATIN SHIKH
SURAH TIRAZ ARMORE BROCHE
CAMACA CHAPPE CREPON DIAPER
DUCAPE FAILLE KHAIKI MANTUA
SENDAL ALACHAH ALAMODE
BROCADE EPINGLE GROGRAM
SCHAPPE YESTING DUPPIONI
EOLIENNE IMPERIAL ORMUZINE
SHAGREEN SIAMOISE
(SOFT SILK —) KASHA BARATHEA
(SOFT-NAPPED —) PANNE DUVETYN
(STRIPED —) ABA STRIPE
BAYADERE MERALINE
(THIN —) CRISP GAUZE VOILE
PONGEE TAMISE HERNANI MARABOU

PERSIAN
(TWILLED —) SAY DENIM KASHA
SERGE SURAH COUTIL BOLIVIA
ESTAMIN FLANNEL ZANELLA
CAMELINE CASHMERE CORDUROY
DIAGONAL SHALLOON VENETIAN
(UNBLEACHED —) DRABBET
(UNGLAZED —) CRETONNE
(UPHOLSTERY —) FRIEZE BROCATEL
MOQUETTE
(VELVETY —) TRIPE DUVETYN
(WOOLEN —) REPP BAIZE DOILY
OSSET SERGE TWEED BUFFIN
BURNET COTTON DJERSA DUFFEL
FRISCA MANTLE MOREEN MOTLEY
PERPET SAXONY SHODDY STAMIN
TAMISE VICUNA WADMAL WITNEY
BATISTE BOCKING BOLIVIA CHEVIOT
CHEYNEY CRYSTAL DELAINE
DRUGGET FRISADO HEATHER
RATTEEN STAMMEL ALGERINE
BATSWING BURBERRY CASHMERE
CATALOON CHIVERET HARATEEN
LAMBSKIN PRUNELLA RATTINET
SHALLOON SHETLAND WOOLENET
ZIBELINE
(WORSTED —) TABBY COBURG
ESTAMIN ETAMINE SAGATHY
(WOVEN —) LENO TWEED TWILL
SOLBIL TISSUE GROGRAM TEXTURE
VALENCIA
FABRICATE COIN COOK FAKE FORM
MAKE MINT VAMP WARP BUILD
FORGE FRAME FRUMP WEAVE
DEVISE INVENT CONCOCT FASHION
IMAGINE PRODUCE CONTRIVE
(— CLOTH) DRAPE
(— PAPER) CONVERT
FABRICATION LIE WEB TRIFLE
CHIMERA FICTION FINGURE
FORGERY UNTRUTH BASKETRY
PRETENSE
(PL.) INVENTARY
FABRICATOR LIAR COINER FORGER
FABULIST LIAR AESOP FABLER
FABULOUS FEIGNED MYTHICAL
ROMANTIC
FACADE FACE FRONT FUCUS
FRONTAL FRONTLET
FACE JIB MAP MUG NEB PAN BIDE
CHIV CLAD COPE DARE DEFY DIAL
GIZZ HEAD LEER LINE MASK MEET
MOUE MUNS PHIZ PUSS SIDE ABIDE
BEARD BRAVE BRICK BRUNT CASTE
CHECK CHEER COVER FACET FAVOR
FRONT GUARD INDEX REVET STAND
STONE VISOR VIZOR BRAZEN
FACADE FACIES KISSER MAZARD
MUZZLE OPPOSE PHIZOG VENEER
VISAGE COMMAND DIGLYPH
FASHION FEATURE GRIMACE
GRUNTLE PROPOSE RESPECT
REVERSE SURFACE UPRIGHT
CONFRONT ENVISAGE EXTRADOS
FEATURES FROGFACE FRONTAGE
FRONTIER PROSPECT SEMBLANT
(— DOWN) DEFACE
(— IN DEFIANCE) AFFRONT
(— OF ANIMAL) MASK

(— OF CUBE) SQUARE
(— OF CUTTING TOOL) BEZEL BEZIL
(— OF GLACIER) SNOUT
(— OF STUMP) SCARF SCARPH
(— ONE'S DANCING PARTNER) SET
(— TO FACE) AFRONT BEFORE
FACIAL DIRECTLY
(— WITH MARBLE) PIN
(— WITH STONE) BATCH
(CLOCK —) DIAL TABLE WATCH
(CURVED —) EXTRADOS INTRADOS
(DIE —) ACE
(FANTASTIC —) ANTIC
(HALF DOMINO —) END
(HAVING SHORT BROAD —)
LATERAL
(INNER —) CONCAVE
(MADE-UP —) MOP
(MINING —) BANK BREAST
FOREHEAD LONGWALL
(MOCKING —) MOE MOWE
(ROCK —) CLIFF
(UPPER —) BROW
(WRY —) MOUTH GRIMACE
FACE-ARBOR KNIFE
FACE GUARD FRONTAL
FACEMAN HAGGER WINNER
FACEPLATE FRONT DOGPLATE
FACER BUMPER DRIFTER TANKARD
FACET PANE STAR BEZEL CULET
PHASE COLLET STEMMA FACETTE
LOZENGE TEMPLET
FACETIAE CURIOSA
FACETIOUS FUNNY MERRY SMART
WITTY FACETE JOCOSE JOCULAR
HUMOROUS POLISHED
FACILE ABLE EASY QUICK READY
EXPERT FLUENT GENTLE AFFABLE
DUCTILE LENIENT
FACILITATE AID EASE HELP FAVOR
SPEED ASSIST GREASE EXPEDITE
FACILITY ART EASE FEEL HELP
ECLAT KNACK SKILL ADDRESS
COMMAND FREEDOM EASINESS
(PL.) ADDITIONS
FACING DADO HARL FRONT HARLE
LAPEL LINER PANEL SKIRT BEFORE
TOWARD VENEER AGAINST
FORNENT SURFACE BLACKING
CAMPSHOT CONFRONT COVERING
FACEWORK FORNENST OPPOSITE
PITCHING
(— AGAINST GLACIER) STOSS
(— AHEAD) FULL
(— APEX) ACROSCOPIC
(— AUDIENCE OBLIQUELY) EFFACE
(— EACH OTHER) AFFRONTE
AFFRONTY
(— INWARD) INTRORSE
(— OUTWARDS) EXTRORSE
FACSIMILE COPY MODEL REPLICA
AUTOTYPE
FACT CASE DEED FAIT DATUM EVENT
SOOTH TRUTH DONNEE EFFECT
FACTUM COMPERT FORMULA
GENERAL INDICIA KEYNOTE
LOWDOWN REALITY
(CONCLUSIVE —) CRUSHER
(DECISIVE —) CLINCHER

(FUNDAMENTAL —) KEYNOTE
(TRUE —S) STRENGTH
(PL.) DATA FEAT
FACTION BLOC NERI PART SECT
SIDE WING CABAL JUNTO PARTY
BRIGUE CLIQUE SCHISM BIANCHI
DISPUTE PINFOLD QUARREL
INTRIGUE SPLINTER
(PARTY —) STASIS
FACTITIOUS SHAM WHIPPED
KRITRIMA
FACTOR GEN DOER GENE ITEM
AGENT ALLEL CAUSE MAKER
ALLELE AUTHOR CENTER DETAIL
BAILIFF CONTROL COUCHER
CUSHION ELEMENT ENTROPY
FACTRIX ISOLATE STEWARD
ADHERENT AUMILDAR COFACTOR
DOMINANT EQUATION GOMASHTA
INCIDENT INCITANT
(—S IN EVOLUTION) ANTICHANCE
(CYTOPLASMIC —) KAPPA
(DECISIVE —) CAPSTONE
(ECOLOGICAL —) INFLUENT
(ENVIRONMENTAL —) GEOGEN
(HEREDITY —) GENE INSTINCT
(INTELLIGENCE —) G
(PERSONALITY —) SURGENCY
(RESTRICTIVE —) BARRIER
FACTORY HONG MILL SHOP PLANT
USINE AURANG AURUNG FABRIC
SUGARY CANNERY HATTERY
HOSIERY OFICINA SOAPERY
BUILDING COMPTOIR FABRIQUE
FILATURE OFFICINA STAMPERY
WORKSHOP
FACTOTUM COMPRADOR
FACTUAL HARD REAL TRUE ACTUAL
BEDROCK EARTHLY EMPIRIC
LITERAL
(INSUFFICIENTLY —) ABSTRACT
FACTUALLY INSOOTH
FACULTY ART WIT BOOM EASE GIFT
WILL FANCY SENSE BREATH BUDDHI
GIFTIE SEEING TALENT ABILITY
COLLEGE COUNSEL HABITUS
APTITUDE CAPACITY FELICITY
(— OF EXPRESSION) LANGUAGE
(CRITICAL —) JUDGMENT
(MENTAL —) HEADPIECE
(POETIC OR CREATIVE —) IDEALITY
PRINCIPLE
(REASONING —) DISCOURSE
(PL.) INDULTS
FAD BUG FIKE RAGE WHIM CRAZE
FANCU HOBBY FOIBLE CROCHET
FASHION WRINKLE
FADE DIE DIM DOW FLY WAN BRIT
CAST FATE FLAT GIVE PALE PEAK
PINE PINK VADE WELK WILK WILT
BLANK DAVER DECAY FLEET PASSE
PETER QUAIL SWING SWOON
DARKLE PERISH VANISH WITHER
DECLINE INSIPID LIGHTEN DIMINISH
DISCOLOR DISSOLVE EVANESCE
LANGUISH
(— AWAY) DOW BREAK FLEET
WALLOW

FADED PASSE SHABBY EXOLETE
SHOPWORN
FADGE FAY FIT SUIT
FADING FUGITIVE SWINGING
FAG FLAG JADE TIRE TOIL DROOP
WEARY DRUDGE HARASS MENIAL
EXHAUST FATIGUE FRAZZLE
FAGGED TASKIT
FAGGOT BROSNA CHUMPA FAGALD
FAGOT KID BUNT PILE PIMP FADGE
NICKY NITCH FAGGOT KNITCH
GARBAGE
FAIL GO CUT EBB ERR BANK BUST
CONK FALL FLAG FLOP FOLD LACK
LOSE MISS SINK SKEW SPIN WANE
APPAL BREAK BURST CRACK FAULT
FLUFF FLUKE FLUNK PETER QUAIL
SLAKE SPILL VAILE APPALL BETRAY
DEFAIL DEFECT DESERT FALTER
FIZZLE REPINE WINDER DECLINE
DEFAULT EXHAUST FALSIFY FLICKER
FLUMMOX FOUNDER MISFARE
MISGIVE SCANTLE LANGUISH
(— AT) FLUB
(— IN DUTY) LAPSE
(— IN EARLY STAGES) ABORT
(— IN HEALTH) SINK BREAK
(— IN STUDIES) BILGE
(— ON RIFLE RANGE) BOLO
(— TO GROW) MISS
FAILING BAD ILL BLOT FAULT
FOIBLE BLEMISH FAILURE FRAILTY
ABORTIVE WEAKNESS
FAILURE DUD BALK BUST FAIL FLOP
FLUB FOIL LACK LOSS MISS MUFF
TRIP BAULK BILGE CRASH DECAY
ERROR FAULT FLUKE FLUNK FROST
GRIEF GUILT LAPSE LEMON PLUCK
SMASH BRODIE FIASCO FIZZLE
STUMER STUMOR BLOOMER
CROPPER DEBACLE DECLINE
DEFAULT FLIVVER FLUMMOX
NEGLECT STUMBLE ABORTION
COLLAPSE DISASTER FAILANCE
FLOPEROO OMISSION
(— OF DAM) BLOW
(— OF FIREARM) STOPPAGE
(— OF MILK SECRETION) AGALAXY
AGALAXIA
(— OF MUSCLE) ACHALASIA
(— OF PAVEMENT) BLOWUP
(— OF PRIMER) HANGFIRE
(— OF VITALITY) DELIQUIUM
(— TO RAISE OAR) CRAB
(FLAT —) DUD
(RIDICULOUS —) FIASCO
FAIN FOND GLAD LIEF EAGER
PLEASED WILLING DESIROUS
INCLINED
FAINEANT IDLE LAZY
FAINT GO DIM WAN WAW COLD
CONK COOL DARK PALE PALL SOFT
THIN WEAK LIGHT QUEAL QUEER
SHADY SWELT SWOON TIMID WAUF
WAUGH WERSH EVANID FEEBLE
REMISS SICKLY WAMBLY FEIGNED
FORGONE LANGUID OBSCURE
SWITHER SYNCOPE WEARISH
COWARDLY DELICATE LANGUISH

LISTLESS SLUGGISH TIMOROUS
(— **FROM HEAT**) SWELTER
(— **FROM HUNGER**) LEERY
(— **OF SCENT**) COLD WAUGH
FAINTHEARTED TIMID COWARD
CRAVEN COWARDLY UNHEARTY
FAINTHEARTEDNESS QUALM
FAINTING AFAINT SYNCOPE
DELIQUIUM
(— **SPELL**) DROW DWAM DWALM
FAINTLY DIMLY FAINT SMALL
FAINTNESS TENUITY GONENESS
WEAKNESS
FAINT-VOICED INWARD
FAIR GAY GEY MOP BEAU BELL
CALM EVEN FINE GAFF GALA GOOD
HEND JUST MART PLAY TIDE TIDY
BAZAR BLOND CLEAN CLEAR EQUAL
FERIA HENDE LARGE RIGHT ROUND
SHEER TRYST WHITE AONACH
BAZAAR BLONDE CANDID COMELY
DECENT DINKUM HONEST KERMIS
PRETTY SQUARE EXHIBIT JANNOCK
KERMESS STATUTE BOOKFAIR
DISTINCT FESTIVAL HORNFAIR
MIDDLING STRAIGHT UNBIASED
(— **AND CALM**) SETTLED
(— **AND SQUARE**) DINKUM
(**HINDU** —) MELA
(**VILLAGE** —) WALK
FAIRER SHIPWRIGHT
FAIRING SPAT SPINNER FAIRLING
FAIR-LEAD WAPP
FAIRLY WELL GAILY GAYLY GEYAN
EVENLY JUSTLY MEANLY HANDILY
PLAINLY RIGHTLY PROPERLY
SUITABLY
FAIRNESS FAIR CANDOR EQUITY
HONESTY JUSTICE EQUALITY
EVENNESS FAIRHEAD FAIRHOOD
FAIRWAY HOLE WATERWAY
FAIR-WEATHER SUNSHINE
FAIRY ELF FAY HOB IMP FAIN PERI
PIXY PUCK SHEE VILA OUPHE
PECHT PIXIE SIDHE WIGHT COURIL
FAERIE HATHOR KEWPIE SPIRIT
SPRITE YAKSHA YAKSHI ARGANTE
BANSHEE ORIANDA SHEOGUE
SYLPHID URGANDA FOLLETTO
MELUSINA
(**IRISH** —) SHEE SIDHE
(**TRICKSY** —) PUCK
(PL.) GENTRY
FAIRY BELL FOXGLOVE
FAIRYFOLK SHEE SIDHE
FAIRYLAND ANNWN ANNWFN
ELFLAND
FAITH DIN FAY FOY LAW LAY VAY
FACK FEGS SLAM TROW CERTY
CREED HAITH STOCK TOUCH TROTH
TRUST TRUTH BELIEF CERTIE
CREDIT GOSPEL FACKINS AFFIANCE
RELIANCE RELIGION
(**BAD** —) DUPLICITY
(**RELIGIOUS** —) SRADH SRADDHA
SHRADDHA
FAITHFUL FAST FEAL FIRM GOOD
JUST LEAL LIKE REAL TRIG TRUE
FALSE HEMAN LIEGE LOYAL PIOUS

SWEER TIGHT TREST TRIED ARDENT
ENTIRE FIDELE HONEST LAWFUL
PISTIC STANCH STEADY TRUSTY
DEVOTED SINCERE STAUNCH
ACCURATE CONSTANT RESOLUTE
SPEAKING
FAITHFULNESS HSIN FEALTY
VERITY LOYALTY FIDELITY
TRUENESS
FAITHLESS FALSE PUNIC FICKLE
HOLLOW UNJUST UNTRUE ATHEIST
APOSTATE DELUSIVE DISLOYAL
SHIFTING UNSTABLE
FAITHLESSNESS FALSITY PERFIDY
UNTRUTH
FAKE DUD DUFF FEKE HOAX HOKE
SHAM BOGUS CHEAT FALSE FEIGN
FLAKE FRAUD FUDGE PHONY
WANGLE DUFFING FALSIFY FURBISH
GUNDECK PRETEND SWINDLE
SIMULATE SPURIOUS
(— **OF STOWED ROPE**) FLEET
FAKER FAKIR QUACK HUMBUG
CAMELOT PEDDLER
FAKIR FAKIH FAQUIR DERVISH
FALCHION FALX
FALCON EYAS HAWK SORE BESRA
HOBBY SAKER STOOP GENTLE
JAGGER JUGGER LANNER LUGGAR
LUGGER MERLIN MUSKET PREYER
RAPTOR SHAHIN TERCEL KESTREL
SAKERET BERIGORA BOCKEREL
FALCONET PEREGRIN SOREHAWK
(— **BOARD**) HACK
(— **IN FIRST YEAR**) SORE
SOREHAWK
(**FEMALE** —) FORMAL FORMEL
LANNER
(**MALE** —) TASSEL TERCEL SAKERET
(**SMALL** —) HOBBY MERLIN KESTREL
(**WHITE** —) ICELANDER
FALCONER HAWKER OSTREGER
FALCONRY HAWKING
FALDSTOOL ORATORY
FALL GO EBB SAG SYE TIP BACK
BAND COME COUP DIVE DRIP DROP
DUNT FLOP HANG PICK PLOP RASH
RUIN RUSE SHED SILE SINK SLIP
SWAK SWAP SWAY SWOP TILT
WHAP WHOP ABATE CHUTE CLOIT
CRASH DROOP HANCE INCUR JABOT
LAPSE LIGHT LODGE PITCH PLUMB
PLUMP RAPID SAULT SHAKE SHOOT
SKITE SLIPE SLUMP SPILL SQUAB
SQUAT THROW TRACE TWINE
ALIGHT AUTUMN BRODIE DEVALL
DOUNCE DRYSNE FOOTER HAPPEN
HEADER JOUNCE PERISH PLUNGE
RECEDE SEASON SLOUGH STREEK
STRIKE TOPPLE TUMBLE CASCADE
CROPPER CROWNER DECLINE
DEGRADE DEPRESS DESCEND
DEVOLVE DRIBBLE ESCHEAT
ILLAPSE PLUMMET RELAPSE
RETREAT SQUELCH STUMBLE
SUBSIDE CATARACT COLLAPSE
COMMENCE DECREASE DOWNCOME
(— **ABRUPTLY**) DUMP
(— **APART**) BREAK SHIVER

COLLAPSE DISUNITE
(— **AWAY**) DEFECT
(— **BACK**) RECEDE RESORT
(— **BEHIND**) LAG
(— **DIZZILY**) SPIN
(— **DOWN**) CAVE FLOP SWAP SLUMP
REVERSE SWITHER
(— **DUE**) BEFALL
(— **FAST**) HOP
(— **FLAT**) PLAT FLIVVER
(— **FORWARD**) PECK PITCH
PROLAPSE
(— **FROM A HORSE**) PURL
(— **FROM UNDERMINING**) CALVE
(— **FROM VIRTUE**) LAPSE
(— **GRADUALLY**) EBB SAG
(— **HEAVILY**) DING LUMP SOSS
CLOIT CLYTE GULCH PLOUT PLUMP
SOUSE SWACK THROW
(— **ILL**) TRAIK
(— **IN DROPS**) DRIP STILL DRIBBLE
(— **IN FLURRIES**) SPIT
(— **IN FOLDS**) BLOUSE
(— **IN RIVER**) SAULT
(— **IN WITH**) INCUR
(— **IN**) CAVE FOUNDER
(— **INTO ERROR**) SLIP STUMBLE
(— **INTO FAINT**) DWAM DWALM
(— **INTO RUIN**) DECAY
(— **INTO SLUMBER**) DROWSE
(— **INTO TRAP**) DECOY
(— **INTO WATER**) DOP
(— **INTO**) STRIKE
(— **OF DEW**) SEREIN SERENE
(— **OF RAIN**) SKIFF SKIFT SHOWER
(— **OF SNOW**) SKIFF SKIFT ONCOME
SCOUTHER SNOWFALL
(— **OF WICKETS**) ROT
(— **OFF**) BATE SLIP SLACK
(— **ON BACK**) BACKER
(— **ON SUCCESSIVE DAYS**) CONCUR
(— **ON THE NOSE**) NOSER
(— **OUT**) LIGHT FORTUNE QUARREL
(— **PRONE**) GRABBLE
(— **RAPIDLY**) SKID
(— **SHORT**) DROP FAIL FAULT
(— **SLOWLY**) SETTLE
(— **SUDDENLY**) BOLT PLOP SLUMP
(— **THROWING HORSE AND RIDER**)
CRUMPLER
(— **TO NOTHING**) DISSOLVE
(— **TO PIECES**) BUCKLE CRUMBLE
(— **UPON**) WARP
(— **VIOLENTLY**) BEAT
(**BAD** —) BUSTER
(**HEAVY** —) PASH POUR SWAG
CLOIT GULCH SKELP SOUSE SQUAT
MUCKER
(**INCOMPLETE WRESTLING** —) FOIL
(**SOFT** —) SCLAFF
(**SUDDEN** —) HANCE SQUAT SQUASH
FALLACIOUS SLY WILY ABSURD
CRAFTY UNTRUE DELUSIVE
GUILEFUL ILLUSORY
FALLACY IDOL ERROR FALLAX
IDOLUM SOPHISM EQUIVOKE
ILLUSION
FALLEN DOWN FAUN FLAT SHED
LAPSED DECLASSE

(— IN) SUNKEN
FALLER GILL FLATHEAD
FALLFISH CHUB DACE CORPORAL
FALL HERRING TAILOR
FALLIBLE HUMAN ERRANT ERRABLE
FALLING SIT CADENT CAVING
PROLAPSE WINDFALL
(— BACK) ESCHEAT
(— DOWN) RUIN
(— INTO) INFALL
(— OF MINE ROOF) SIT
(— OF RAIN) SPIT
(— OFF) CADUCE LEEWAY
CADUCOUS
(— ON SOMETHING) INCIDENT
(— OUT) DIFFICULTY
(— SHORT) DEFICIT
FALLOPIAN TUBE TUBAL
FALLOVER OSTREGER
FALLOW LEA PALE HOBBY BARREN
VALEWE
FALLOW DEER DAMINE DAPPLE
FALLOWING ARDER
FALSE DEAD FAKE FLAM SHAM
BOGUS FAUSE LYING PASTE PHONY
WRONG FICKLE HOLLOW LUTHER
PSEUDO UNTRUE ASSUMED
BASTARD CROOKED FEIGNED
DISLOYAL ILLUSIVE RECREANT
SPECTRAL SPURIOUS
FALSE BEACHDROPS PINESAP
FALSE CRAWLEY PINEDROPS
FALSE FOXGLOVE FEVERWEED
FALSE HELLEBORE EARTHGALL
FALSEHOOD COG FIB LIE BUNG
CRAM FLAM TALE CRACK ERROR
FABLE STORY FALSET UNFACT
YANKER CRAMMER CRETISM
FALSAGE FALSERY FALSITY FIBBERY
FICTION LEASING PERFIDY
PHANTOM ROMANCE UNTRUTH
FALSHEDE ROORBACK STRAPPER
FALSE MERMAID FLOERKEA
LIMNANTH
FALSENESS SHAM
FALSE WINTERGREEN PYROLA
FALSEWORK CENTERING
FALSIES CHEATERS
FALSIFIER FALSER FORGER
FALSARY
FALSIFY LIE COOK FAKE WARP
ABUSE BELIE FEINT FORGE BETRAY
DOCTOR GUNDECK VIOLATE
EMBEZZLE
FALSITY LIE ERROR VANITY
UNTRUTH INVERITY
FALTER FAIL HALT PAUSE WAVER
BOGGLE FLINCH TOTTER FRIBBLE
STAMMER STUMBLE TREMBLE
HESITATE
FALTERING HINK HALTING
FALX FALCULA
FAME BAY CRY LOSE NAME STAR
WORD BRUIT ECLAT GLORY HONOR
KUDOS PRICE RUMOR VOICE
ESTEEM LAUREL RENOWN REPORT
REPUTE TONGUE HEARSAY
WORSHIP
(EVIL —) INFAMY

FAMED RIFE KNOWN NOTED
EMINENT RENOMEE RENOWNED
FAMILIAR FLY BAKA BOKO BOLD
COZY EASY FREE FULL HOMY TAME
TOSH CLOSE CONNU GREAT HOMEY
KNOWN PRIVY THICK USUAL
BEATEN CHUMMY COMMON ENTIRE
FOLKSY GERMAN HOMELY INWARD
KENNED STRAIT THRONG VERSED
AFFABLE FAMULAR FOLKSEY
POPULAR FREQUENT HABITUAL
INTIMATE SOCIABLE STANDARD
(— WITH) KNOWING
(MAKE —) POST
(PRESUMPTUOUSLY —) INSOLENT
FAMILIARITY HABIT FREEDOM
LIBERTY PRIVACY PRIVITY TRAFFIC
HABITUDE INTIMACY
FAMILIARIZE HAFT VERSE
ACCUSTOM ACQUAINT FREQUENT
FAMILIARLY HOMELY
FAMILY ILK KIN AIGA CLAN GING
KIND LINE NAME RACE TEAM TRIP
CINEL CLASS FLESH GOTRA GROUP
HOUSE MEINY STIRP STOCK CLETCH
FAIMLY PARAGE STEMMA STIRPS
STRAIN ZEGRIS DYNASTY KINDRED
LINEAGE ORLEANS PROGENY
CATEGORY FIRESIDE
(COSMOPOLITAN —) FELIDAE
FABACEAE
(FIRST —) FF
(LANGUAGE —) CHON BANTU CLICK
COCHE CUNAN KADAI STOCK
AIMARA ATALAN AYMARA CHOLON
GILIAK HUARPE LENCAN SERIAN
BOTOYAN CADDOAN CATIBAN
CHINOOK CHOLONA CHUMASH
COPEHAN ESSELAN KARTHLI
KARTVEL KERESAN SHASTAN
ATAKAPAN CHANGOAN
(LARGE —) QUIVERFUL
(ONE-PARAMETER —) PENCIL
(SUPER —) APINA APOIDEA
FAMINE LACK PINE WOLF DEARTH
HUNGER SCARCITY
FAMISH KILL STARVE DESTROY
ENFAMISH
FAMOUS MERE BREME FAMED
GRAND NOBLE NOTED FAMOSE
NAMELY EMINENT NAMABLE
NOTABLE RENOWNED
FAMULUS WAGNER SERVANT
FAN ONE RUN VAN BEAT BUFF COOL
WASH DELTA PUNKA WHIFF BASKET
BLOWER CHAMAR COLMAR FANNER
FLABEL FLIGHT PUNKAH ROOTER
SHOVEL SPREAD VENTOY WINNOW
ADMIRER DEVOTEE FLABRUM
FLYFLAP MPANGWE PAHOUIN
WHISKER EVENTAIL FOLLOWER
(— FOR BLOWER) WAFTER
(ALLUVIAL —) CONE APRON DELTA
(FOOTBALL —) GRIDDER
(WINNOWING —) SAIL LIKNON
(PL.) FOLLOWING
FANALOKA FOSSA FOUSSA
FANATIC MAD BIGOT CRAZY FIEND
RABID ULTRA ZEALOT DEVOTEE

FURIOSO PHANTIC PULAHAN
PULIJAN BABAYLAN FRENETIC
FANATICAL RABID ULTRA EXTREME
FURIOUS
FANCIED UNREAL DREAMED
AFFECTED
FANCIFUL ODD IDEAL QUEER VIEWY
DREAMY QUAINT UNREAL BIZARRE
FANCIED LAPUTAN STRANGE
WHIMSIC FANCICAL FILIGREE
ROMANTIC
FANCY BEE FAD GIG IDEA ITEM LIKE
LOVE MAZE TROW WEEN WHIM
BRAID BRAIN DREAM FREAK GUESS
HUMOR SHINE AFFECT BEGUIN
FIGURE FLOSSY IDEATE LIKING
MEGRIM NOTION ORNATE SHINDY
VAGARY VISION WHIMSY CAPRICE
CHIMERA CONCEIT CONCEPT
CROCHET FANCIED FANCIFY
FANTASY PROPOSE ROMANCE
SUSPECT WRINKLE CHIMAERA
CONCEIVE CROTCHET DAYDREAM
ILLUSION PHANTASM PHANTASY
(FOOLISH —) CHIMERA CHIMAERA
(PASSING —) FIKE
(PERVERSE —) CROTCHET
(WILD —) TOY MAZE
(PL.) DREAMERY
FANDANGO MURCIANA
FANE FLAG BANNER FANACLE
FANFARE TUSCH HOORAY HURRAH
TUCKET TANTARA FANFARON
FLOURISH
FANFARONADE BLUSTER FANFARE
SWAGGER BOASTING
FANFLOWER TACCADA
FANG FAN EARN FALX TAKE TANG
TUSK VANG BEGIN PRONG SEIZE
SNARE TOOTH ASSUME OBTAIN
PANGWE CAPTURE PAHOUIN
PROCURE
FANON CAPE ORALE PHANO FANNEL
MANIPLE
FAN PALM YARAY ERYTHEA
FANTREE TALIPOT
FAN-SHAPED ALARY
FANTAIL COMET SHAKER WAGTAIL
FAN-TAN PARLIAMENT
FANTASIA FANTASY QUODLIBET
FANTASTIC ODD ANTIC LUCIO
QUEER ABSURD GOTHIC ROCOCO
TOYISH UNREAL ANTICAL BIZARRE
WHIMSIC FANCIFUL FREAKISH
ROMANTIC SINGULAR
(— PERSON) KICKSHAW
FANTASY IDEA DREAM FANCY
DESIRE VISION CAPRICE CHIMERA
PHANTOM ROMANCE CHIMAERA
PHANTASM PHANTASY
FAR AWAY LONG MUCH ROOM SIDE
WELL WIDE CLEAN SIZES WIDEN
REMOTE DISTANT FARAWAY
ROOMWARD
(— AND AWAY) STREETS
(— OFF) OUTBYE
(— ON) ADVANCED
FARCE MIME DROLL EXODE FORCE
STUFF COMEDY GARLIC SOTTLE

EXODIUM MOCKERY TEMACHA
DROLLERY FARCETTA
(RELATING TO —) ATELLAN
FARCEUR WAG JOKER FORCER
FARCICAL BUFFO COMIC DROLL
ATELLAN
FARCTATE STUFFED
FARCY FARCIN EQUINIA FASHION
FARE DO GO EAT TRY COME DIET
FEND FOOD PATH RATE TIME WEND
CHEER CHEFE CHIVE FRAME GOING
LIGHT PRICE SPEED TABLE TOKEN
TRACK VIAND COMMON FARING
FETTLE HAPPEN TRAVEL CARFARE
JOURNEY PASSAGE PROCEED
PROSPER WAFTAGE WAYFARE
FERRYAGE PROGRESS
(— FOR FERRY) NAULUM FERRYAGE
(— WELL) SPEED
(COARSE —) HAWEBAKE
FAREWELL AVE VALE ADIEU ADIOS
ALOHA CONGE FINAL LEAVE
CHEERO BONALLY CHEERIO
GOODBYE LEAVING PARTING
FARFETCHED FARFET FORCED
DEVIOUS STRAINED EXQUISITE
FAR-FLUNG EXTENDED
FARINA MEAL FLOUR FARINE
POLLEN STARCH
FARKLEBERRY BLUET
FARL PARLY FARREL
FARM FEU CROP TACK TILL TORP
TOWN WALK CROFT DAIRY EMPTY
FIRMA HARAS MAINS MILPA PLACE
RANCH RANGE STEAD BARTON
BOWERY CHACRA ESTATE FURROW
GRANGE RANCHO TYDDEN TYDDYN
CLEANSE HENNERY KOLKHOZ
MAILING POTRERO POULTRY
SOVKHOS VACCARY ESTANCIA
HACIENDA HATCHERY LABORING
LOCATION STEADING TOWNSHIP
(— OUT) DIMIT ARRENT
(COLLECTIVE —) KIBBUTZ KOLKHOZ
(COMMUNAL —) KVUTZA KVUTZAH
(DAIRY —) WICK
(LARGE —) RANCH BARTON
(RENTED —) MAILING
(SMALL —) CHACRA
(STOCK —) ESTANCIA
(STUD —) STUD HARAS
FARMER HOB CARL FARM HOBB
KHOT KYLE RYOT TATE AILLT AUMIL
BOWER CARLE CEILE CLOWN
COLON HODGE KISAN COCKIE
GROWER HOGMAN JIBARO TILLER
YEOMAN BUCOLIC BUSHMAN
BYWONER COTTIER CROFTER
GRANGER HAYSEED HUSBAND
LANDMAN PLANTER PLOWMAN
RANCHER SCULLOG TILLMAN
TRUCKER COCKATOO PRODUCER
PUBLICAN RURALIST SELECTOR
(AUSTRALIAN —) SELECTOR
(NORWEGIAN —) BENDER
(POOR —) PIKE
(PROSPEROUS —) KULAK
(SMALL —) BOOR
(TENANT —) AILLT GEBUR SIRDAR

COLONUS SHAREMAN
FARMHAND HAND HELP
FARMHOLD CROFT
FARMHOUSE FARM TOWN ONSET
GRANGE QUINTA CASERIO ONSTEAD
STEADING
FARMING SOIL FARMERY
HUSBANDRY
(— SYSTEM) METAYAGE
FARMLAND ACREAGE
FARMSTEAD TOWN WICK STEAD
FARMERY
FARMYARD WERF CLOSE BARTON
RICKYARD
FARO MONTE STUSS TIGER
PHARAOH
(— CARD) SODA
FARO BANK TIGER
FAR-OFF DISTANT
FAR-REACHING GREAT FARGOING
FARRIER SHOER SMITH MARSHAL
FARROW PIG ROW RAKE DRAPE
LITTER
FARSIGHTED SHREWD SIGHTY
FARTHER YOND AHEAD STILL
LONGER FURTHER REMOTER
THITHER
FARTHEST ULTIMA ENDMOST
EXTREME FARMOST LONGEST
OUTMOST DOWNMOST FURTHEST
REMOTEST ULTIMATE
FARTHING RAG GRIG JACK QUAD
FADGE FERLING QUARTER
QUADRANS QUADRANT
(HALF —) CUE
(THREE —S) GILL
FARTHINGALE FERDEGEW
VERTUGAL
FASCIA BAND SASH FACIA FILLET
BANDAGE MOLDING LIGATURE
FASCICLE BUNDLE PHALANGE
FASCICULUS HEFT BUNDLE COLUMN
TRACTUS
FASCINATE DARE CHARM SEIZE
WITCH ALLURE ENAMOR ATTRACT
BEWITCH ENCHANT ENGROSS
GLAMOUR PHILTER PHILTRE
ENSORCEL ENTRANCE INTEREST
INTRIGUE SIRENIZE
FASCINATED BESOTTED
FASCINATING NUTTY SIRENIC
CHARMING FETCHING MESMERIC
FASCINATION CHARM SPELL
WITCHERY
FASCINE FAGOT FAGGOT SAUCISSE
FASCIOLA DISTOMA DISTOMUM
FASCIOLE SEMITA
FASCIST BLACK FASCISTA
FASHION GO CRY CUT FAD LAT TON
WAY CHIC FEAT FORM GARB GATE
KICK MAKE MODE MOLD RAGE RATE
SORT TURN TWIG WEAR WISE BUILD
CRAZE FEIGN FORGE FRAME GUISE
MODEL MOULD SHAPE STYLE
VOGUE WEAVE ASSIZE BUSTLE
CAMBER CREATE CUSTOM DESIGN
FANGLE INVENT MANNER METHOD
ALAMODE COMPOSE IMAGERY
PORTRAY QUALITY CONTRIVE

(LATEST —) KICK
(PREVAILING —) CRY
(SPECIAL —) TOUCH
FASHIONABLE CHIC PINK DASHY
DOGGY DOSSY SMART SWELL
SWISH VOGUE GIGOLO JAUNTY
MODISH TIMISH TONISH DASHING
GALLANT GENTEEL STYLISH
SWAGGER
(NOT —) DEMODE
FASHIONABLY SMARTLY
FASHIONED HUED CARVED SHAPED
WROUGHT FEATURED
FASHIONING FINGENT
FASHION PLATE SWELL
FASSAITE PYRGOM
FAST HOT HUT COLD FIRM HARD
LENT SOON SURE WIDE AGILE
APACE BRISK CHEAP FIXED FLASH
FLEET HASTY QUICK RAPID ROUND
SADLY STUCK SWIFT TIGHT TOSTO
CARENE ESTHER FASTLY LIVELY
SECURE SPEEDY SPORTY STABLE
STARVE ABIDING EXPRESS
HOTSHOT HURRIED PROVISO
RASPING SETTLED SIKERLY STATION
TAANITH ENDURING FAITHFUL
SPINNING SPORTING WIKIWIKI
(— DAY) ASHURA
FAST-DYED INGRAIN
FASTEN BAR DOG FAY FIX GAD GIB
KEY LAG PEN PIN SEW TAG TIE YOT
BELT BEND BIND BOLT BRAD CLIP
FRET GIRD GIRT GLUE GRIP HANG
HANK HASP HOOK HOOP HORN KILT
KNIT KNOT LACE LASH LINK LOCK
MOOR NAIL ROPE SEAL SNIB SOUD
SPAN SPAR STAY WELD WIRE AFFIX
ANNEX BELAY BIGHT BRACE CABLE
CATCH CHAIN CINCH CLAMP CLASP
CLING COPSE DEFIX GIRTH HALSH
HITCH INFIX LATCH PASTE RIVET
SCREW SEIZE SLOUR SNECK STEEK
STICK STRAP TRUSS WITHE
ANCHOR ATTACH BATTEN BUCKLE
BUTTON CEMENT CLINCH COTTER
COUPLE ENGAGE ENTAIL FATHER
GARTER HAMPER HANKLE INKNOT
PICKET SECURE SKEWER SOLDER
STAPLE STITCH STRAIN TETHER
BRACKET CONFINE CONNECT
EMBRACE GRAPPLE GROMMET
PADLOCK BARNACLE FORELOCK
INTERTIE OBLIGATE TRANSFIX
(— A SAIL) CROSS
(— ABOUT) THRAP
(— ANCHOR) SCOW
(— AS SPURS) SPEND
(— IN) EMBAR
(— TO) TAG
(— TOGETHER) COAPT SEIZE
SPLICE CONNECT
(— WINGS ON) IMP
(— WITH A GIRTH) WARRICK
(— WITH NOTCHES) GAIN
FASTENED FAST SHUT BOUND FIXED
BOUNDEN
FASTENER BAR GIB GIN NUT PIN
AGAL BOLT DOME FAST FROG HASP

LOCK NAIL SNAP TACK CATCH
CLAMP CLASP LATCH RIVET SCREW
SPIKE STRAP TATCH THONG
BUCKLE BUTTON HATPIN STAPLE
ZIPPER FIXATOR LATCHET PADLOCK
SNAPPER TENDRIL FASTNESS
STAYLACE

FASTENING TEE TIE FROG HASP
SEAL SNAP SNIB STAY TACK
BUCKLE CLINCH LACING MUZZLE
STRIKE TINGLE BINDING CLOSURE
LATCHET MOUSING PINNING SEIZING
FORELOCK KNITTING
(— FOR HAWK'S WING) BRAIL
(— ON HARPOON IRON) HITCH
(HOOK AND LOOP —) AGRAFE
AGRAFFE
(PL.) GRIPES

FASTIDIOUS FINE NICE CHARY
DONCY FEEST FUSSY NAISH NATTY
PAWKY CHOICE CHOICY CHOOSY
DAINTY DONSIE MOROSE PICKED
QUAINT QUEASY SPRUCE CHOOSEY
CURIOUS ELEGANT FINICAL FINICKY
HAUGHTY PICKING REFINED
TAFFETA TAFFETY CRITICAL
DELICATE EXACTING GINGERLY
OVERNICE PICKSOME PRECIOUS
SCORNFUL
(NOT —) GROSS
(OVERLY —) SAUCY

FASTIDIOUSNESS DAINTY NICETY
DELICACY

FASTING RAMADAN

FAST-MOVING SUDDEN

FASTNESS FORT CASTLE CITADEL
RETREAT FORTRESS

FAST-WORKING HOTSHOT

FAT GHI OIL TUB FOZY GHEE LARD
LIPA MORT RICH SAIM SUET ADEPS
BROSY CETIN CHUFF COCUM ESTER
FLECK FLICK FOGGY GROSS JUICY
KEDGE KOKUM LARDY LIPID LIPIN
LUSTY OBESE PLUMP PODGY
PORKY PUDDY PUDGY PURSY
SAAME SPICK SQUAB STOUT SUMEN
THICK WASTY AXUNGE BLOWSY
CHOATY CHUBBY CHUFFY DEGRAS
FATTED FINISH FLESHY GREASE
LIPIDE PLUFFY PORTLY PUBBLE
PUNCHY PYKNIC ROTUND STOCKY
STUFFY TALLOW UCUUBA ADIPOSE
BLOATED BLUBBER CEROTIN
FATNESS FERTILE FLESHLY
FULSOME LANOLIN OPULENT
PINGUID PURSIVE REPLETE STEARIN
EXTENDED FRUITFUL MARROWED
MURUMURU UNCTUOUS
(— AROUND WHALE'S NECK) KENT
(— MEAT) SPECK
(— OF HIPPOPOTAMUS) SPECK
(— PERSON) SQUAB
(ANIMAL —) GLOR SAIM SUET
ADEPS GLORE GREASE TALLOW
(FLOATING —) FLOT
(LARD —) FLARE FLECK FLICK
(LUMP OF —) KEECH
(NATURAL —) ESTER
(POULTRY —) SCHMALZ SCHMALTZ

(SOLID —) LARD KIKUEL STEARIN
FATAL FEY DIRE MORT FERAL VITAL
DEADLY DISMAL DOOMED FUNEST
LETHAL MORTAL CAPITAL DEATHLY
EXITIAL FATEFUL KILLING OMINOUS
RUINOUS UNSONSY BASILISK
DESTINED EXITIOUS FUNESTAL
MORTIFIC

FATALITY DOOM ACCIDENT
CALAMITY DISASTER

FAT-BELLIED GUTTY

FATE DIE END KER LOT CAST DOLE
DOOM EURE NORN RUIN SORT STAR
CAVEL EVENT GRACE KARMA MOIRA
MORTA WEIRD WHATE WRITE
ANANKE CHANCE KISMET DESTINY
FORTUNE OUTCOME PORTION
DOWNFALL FATALITY
(INEXORABLE —) HEAVEN
(ONE OF —S) NONA PARCA CLOTHO
DECUMA ATROPOS LACHESIS

FATED DUE FEY FATAL DOOMED
DECREED DESTINED

FATEFUL FATAL FATED DEADLY
DOOMFUL OMINOUS DOOMLIKE

FATHEAD REDFISH

FATHEADED FOZY

FATHEADEDNESS FOZINESS

FATHER BU DA PA ABU AMA DAD
POP TAT ABBA ABOU AMBA ANBA
ATEF BABA BAPU DADA PAPA PERE
SIRE ADOPT BABBO BEGET DADDY
FRIAR PADRE PATER VADER
PARENT PRIEST SUBORN ELKANAH
GENITOR TATINEK BEAUPERE
GENERATE GOVERNOR
(CHURCH —) APOLOGIST
(SEMIDIVINE —) PITRI
(SIDE OF —) AGNATE
(PL.) PP

FATHERLAND KITH HOMELAND

FATHER-LASHER GUNDIE SCULPIN
BULLHEAD LORICATE

FATHERLESS ORBATE SIRELESS

FATHOM BRACE BRASS DELVE
FADME PLUMB SOLVE SOUND
TOUCH BOTTOM MEASURE
PLUMMET

FATIGUE FAG HAG TEU BEAT COOK
JADE TASH TIRE TRAY SPEND
STALL TARRY THRIE TRAIK TRASH
WEARY HARASS OVERDO TAIGLE
TUCKER EXHAUST FATIGATE
VEXATION

FATIGUED BEAT GONE JADED TIRED
WEARY TASKIT OUTWORN WEARIED
FATIGATE HARASSED TUCKERED

FATIGUING HARD IRKSOME

FATLIKE LIPOID

FATNESS BLOOM GREASE

FATTEN FAT BEEF LARD SOIL
BRAWN FARCE FLESH FRANK PROVE
SMEAR STALL BATTEN ENRICH
FINISH TALLOW THRIVE PINGUEFY
SAGINATE

FATTENING FRANK BATTEL
BATTABLE

FATTY SUETY BACONY GREASY
ADIPOSE ADIPOUS FATLIKE PINGUID

SEBIFIC LIPAROID LIPAROUS
UNCTUOUS

FATUOUS DOPY DOPEY INANE SILLY
SIMPLE STUPID UNREAL FATUATE
FOOLISH IDIOTIC WITLESS
DEMENTED ILLUSORY IMBECILE

FAUCES JAWS

FAUCET BIB TAP BIBB COCK QUILL
SPOUT VALVE CUTOFF DOSSIL
DOZZLE OFFLET SPIGOT BIBCOCK
HYDRANT PETCOCK TURNCOCK
(WOODEN —) HORSE

FAUGH BAH FOH VAH

FAUJDAR PHOUSDAR

FAULT BUG RUB SIN CLAG COUP
DEBT FAIL FLAW FLUB HOLE LACK
LAST MOLE SAKE SLIP SPOT VICE
WANT WITE ABUSE AMISS BLAME
BREAK CULPA ERROR FLUFF GUILT
LAPSE SCAPE SHIFT SLIDE SWICK
TACHE BLOTCH DEFECT FOIBLE
RUNNER THRUST VICETY VITIUM
BLEMISH BLISTER BLUNDER
DEFAULT DEMERIT EYELAST FAILING
FAILURE FRAILTY MISTAKE NEGLECT
OFFENSE FAULTING PECCANCY
WEAKNESS
(— IN BADMINTON) SLING
(MINING —) COUP LEAP CHECK
HITCH
(PL.) FAULTAGE

FAULTFINDER MOMUS CARPER
CRITIC MOMIST CAPTION KNOCKER
NAGSTER

FAULTFINDING CARPING CAPTIOUS
CRITICAL

FAULTILY BADLY

FAULTLESS PURE CLEAN RIGHT
CORRECT PERFECT PRECISE
FLAWLESS

FAULTY BAD ILL SICK AMISS UNFIT
WRONG FLAWED FAULTED PECCANT
VICIOUS BLAMABLE CULPABLE
SPURIOUS

FAUN SATYR WOODMAN WOODWOSE

FAUNA FAUNULA FAUNULE ZOOLOGY
(FOSSIL —) BIOCHRON

FAUSSEBRAIE VAMURE VAUMURE

FAUX PAS GAFF SLIP BONER ERROR
GAFFE FLOATER MISSTEP MISTAKE
SNAPPER

FAVOR AID FOR ORE PRO BOON
ESTE FACE GREE HEAR HELP LIKE
MAKE BLESS BRIBE GRACE LEAVE
MENSK SERVE SPARE SPEED THANK
TREAT ASSIST ERRAND ESTEEM
FAVOUR LETTER NOTICE PENCEL
UPHOLD ADVANCE AGGRACE
ENFAVOR FEATURE FORWARD
GRATIFY INDULGE RESPECT
SUPPORT ADVOCACY BEFRIEND
COURTESY FAVORIZE GOODWILL
KINDNESS RESEMBLE SYMPATHY

FAVORABLE HOT BOON FAIR FREE
GOOD HIGH KIND ROSY TIDY CIVIL
CLEAR HAPPY LARGE MERRY TRINE
WHITE WILLY BENIGN DEXTER
GENIAL GOLDEN KINDLY TOWARD
BENEFIC EXALTED OPTIMAL

POPULAR PRESENT FRIENDLY
GRACIOUS PLEASING PROPENSE
SPEEDFUL TOWARDLY
(— **TO PURCHASER**) KEEN
(**NOT** —) INFAUST
FAVORABLY FAIR WELL HIGHLY
FAVORED WELL FAURD HAPPY
FAURED GIFTED BLESSED
FAVOURED
FAVORER FAUTOR FRIEND FAVORITE
FAVORING FAVONIAN
FAVORITE BOY PET POT PEAT
CHALK GREAT INGLE WHITE MINION
DARLING FANCIED MINIKIN POPULAR
SPECIAL GRACIOSO WHITEBOY
FAVORITISM BIAS FAVOR NEPOTISM
FAVUS WHITECOMB
FAWN COG BUCK CLAW DEER FAON
JOUK ROOT COWER CRAWL CREEP
GLOZE HONEY TOADY WHELP
CRINGE CROUCH GROVEL KOWTOW
SHRINK SLAVER ADULATE CROODLE
CRUDDLE FLATTER FLETHER
HANGDOG SERVILE SPANIEL
TOADEAT TRUCKLE WHEATEN
BOOTLICK
(— **UPON**) SUCK SMOOGE ADULATE
FAWNING SLEEK CRINGE GREASE
SLEEKY SURPLE FLETHER GLOZING
HANGDOG SERVILE SPANIEL
FLATTERY
FAWNSKIN NEBRIS
FAY ELF FEY FAIRY FEIGH
FAZE DAUNT FEEZE PHASE WORRY
FEALTY FEE FEWTE HOMAGE
LOYALTY SERVICE TREWAGE
FIDELITY
FEAR UG AWE DREE FLAY FUNK
WARD ALARM DOUBT DREAD JELLY
PANIC ALARUM DANGER DISMAY
FRIGHT HORROR PHOBIA TERROR
ANXIETY SUSPECT AFFRIGHT
DISQUIET DISTRUST EERINESS
MISDOUBT VENERATE
FEARFUL ARGH DIRE AWFUL PAVID
TIMID WINDY WROTH AFRAID
COWISH FRIGHTY GHASTLY
NERVOUS PANICKY WORRIED
CAUTIOUS DOUBTFUL DREADFUL
GREWSOME GRUESOME HORRIBLE
HORRIFIC SHOCKING SKITTISH
TERRIBLE TERRIFIC TIMOROUS
FEARLESS BOLD BRAVE DARING
HEROIC AWELESS IMPAVID INTREPID
FEASIBLE FIT LIKELY POSSIBLE
PROBABLE SUITABLE
FEAST (ALSO SEE FESTIVAL) EAT
FOY SUP DINE FARM FETE LUAU
MEAL TUCK UTAS AZYME CHEER
CHOES CITUA DIRGY FESTA FESTY
GAUDY REVEL TREAT ARTHEL
AVERIL DEVOUR DINNER DOUBLE
INFARE JUNKET MAUNDY REGALE
REPAST SIMPLE SMOUSE SPREAD
AHAAINA BANQUET BRIDALE
DELIGHT FESTINO GRATIFY
GREGORY LAMBALE LEMURIA
SHEVUOS SYNAXIS ANALEPSY
CAROUSAL DOMINEER EPIPHANY

FESTIVAL GESTNING GESTONIE
HANUKKAH KOIMESIS PASSOVER
POTLATCH SHABUOTH VESTALIA
(— **BEFORE JOURNEY**) FOY
(— **OF BOOTHS**) SUCCOS SUKKOTH
(— **OF LANTERNS**) HON
(— **OF LOTS**) PURIM
(— **OF WEEKS**) SHEVUOS
SHABUOTH `
(— **PLACE**) IDGAH
(**DRINKING** —) BANQUET
(**FUNERAL** —) ARVAL ARVEL DIRGY
DIRGIE DREDGIE
(**HARVEST** —) BUSK
(**JEWISH** —) SENDAH
(**RELIGIOUS** —) CANAO KANYAW
(**VILLAGE** —) TANSY
FEASTER CONVIVE
FEASTING FEAST CARNIVAL
FEAT ACT KIP DEED FATE GEST
WORK GESTE SPLIT STUNT TRICK
CRADDY CUTOFF EXPLOIT MASTERY
MIRACLE WORSHIP DEXTROUS
(**CRICKETER'S** —) DOUBLE
(**TUMBLING** —) SCISSORS
(PL.) DAGS
FEATHER BOO PEN TAB DECK DOWN
FLAG HERL SETA STUB VANE
ADORN AXIAL PENNA PINNA PLUMA
PLUME QUILL REMEX CLOTHE
COVERT CRINET FLEDGE FLETCH
FLIGHT HACKLE MANUAL PINION
SARCEL SICKLE TIPPET TONGUE
AXILLAR BRISTLE FLEMISH IMPLUME
PRIMARY RECTRIX REMICLE STIPULE
TERTIAL TOPPING AXILLARY
SCAPULAR STREAMER TERTIARY
(**BRISTLELIKE** —) VIBRISSA
(**HAWK'S** —S) BRAIL BRAILS
(**HORSE** —) SPEAR
(**NEW** —) STIPULE
(**OSTRICH TAIL** —) BOO
(**PINION** —) SARCEL
(**TAIL** —) SICKLE RECTRIX
(**YELLOW** —S) HULU
(PL.) GIG BOOT CAPE DOWN FLUE
MAIL BRAIL CRISSUM CUSHION
FLIGHTS PLUMAGE REMIGES
SPURIAE
FEATHER BED TYE
FEATHER CLOAK AHUULA TEMIAK
FEATHERED FLEDGE FLEDGY
PENNATE PINNATE FLIGHTED
FEATHERING STOCKING
FEATHER KEY FIN STOP SPLINE
FEATHER
FEATHER-LEGGED COOTY COOTIE
FEATHERLIKE PINNATE
FEATHERY PLUMY FLEDGY FLUFFY
PLUMOSE PLUMEOUS
FEATLY NEATLY FOOTINGLY
FEATURE WAY FACE ITEM NOTE
STAR BREAK FAVOR GRACE MOTIF
TOKEN TRACT TRAIT TREAT ASPECT
CACHET FAVOUR SPLASH AMENITY
OUTLINE HALLMARK SALIENCE
(— **OF WORD FORM**) ASPECT
(**ATTRACTIVE** —) AMENITY
(**DETERMINING** —) LIMIT

(**DISTINGUISHING** —) TRAIT STROKE
HALLMARK
(**FATAL** —) BANE
(**LINGUISTIC** —) ISOGLOSS
SURVIVAL
(**MAIN** —) CRUX
(**MOST COGENT** —) BEAUTY
(**OBJECTIONABLE** —) DISCOUNT
DRAWBACK
(**SALIENT** —) MOTIF
(**TOPOGRAPHIC** —) ARC
(**TOPOGRAPHIC** —S) LIE
(PL.) LAY FACE CONTOUR FASHION
GEOLOGY
FEAZE FRAY FAIZE ROUGHEN
FEBRIFUGE PEREIRA
FEBRILE PYRETIC FEVERISH
FECES DRAST HOCKEY ORDURE
FECKLESS WEAK FEEBLE
FECULENCE DREG
FECULENT DREGGY
FECUND FERTILE FRUITFUL PROLIFIC
FED FAT MEATED
FEDERATION BUND CROM UNION
LEAGUE NATION COUNCIL ALLIANCE
FEDERACY TRIALISM
FEE FEU DUES DUTY FEAL FEUL FIEF
FIER HIRE RATE WAGE CAULP
EXTRA HANSE PRICE RIGHT ALNAGE
AMOBER BARONY CHARGE DASTUR
EMPLOY EXCISE REWARD SALARY
SHEKEL BUOYAGE DASTURI
DUMPAGE DUSTOOR FIRNAGE
FURNAGE GAOLAGE GARNISH
GRATIFY GUIDAGE HALLAGE
HOUSAGE JAILAGE MULTURE
PAYMENT PINLOCK PREFINE
STIPEND STORAGE TALLAGE
TRIBUTE VANTAGE BOOTHAGE
BOUNTITH CHUMMAGE EXACTION
FAREWELL GRATUITY MALIKANA
POUNDAGE REREFIEF RETAINER
SHIPPAGE WHARFAGE
(— **TO LANDOWNER**) TERRAGE
(— **TO TEACHER**) MINERVAL
(**CUSTOMARY** —) DASTUR
(**CUSTOMS** —) LOT
(**ENTRANCE** —) HANSA HANSE
INCOME
(**INITIATION** —) FOOTING
(**PHYSICIAN'S** —) SOSTRUM
(**UNAUTHORIZED** —) GARNISH
(PL.) EXHIBITS
FEEBLE WAN FLUE LAME MEAN PALE
POOR PUNY SOFT WEAK DONCY
DOTTY FAINT SEELY SILLY SOBER
UNORN WANKY WASHY WONKY
CADUKE DEBILE DONSIE DOTAGE
FAINTY FLABBY FLIMSY FOIBLE
INFIRM PAULIE PUISNE SCANTY
SEMMIT SICKLY SIMPLE TANGLE
UNFIRM WANKLE WEANLY DWAIBLY
DWEEBLE FRAGILE INVALID LANGUID
QUEECHY RICKETY SAPLESS SHILPIT
SLENDER SLIMPSY UNWIELD
UNWREST DECREPIT DROGHLIN
FEATLESS IMBECILE IMPOTENT
INFERIOR MALADIVE RESOLUTE
THEWLESS THOWLESS UNSTRONG

UNWIELDY WATERISH YIELDING
FEEBLE-MINDED ANILE DOTTY
DOTTLE FOOLISH MORONIC
WANTING IMBECILE
FEEBLENESS DOTAGE FEEBLE
POVERTY CADUCITY DEBILITY
WEAKNESS
FEED EAT HAY BAIT BEET BRAN
CROP DIET DINE FILL FOOD GLUT
GRUB MEAL MEAT OATS SATE
AGIST FLESH FLUSH GORGE GRASS
GRAZE NURSE SERVE STOKE TABLE
BROWSE FODDER FOSTER INFEED
NOODLE REFETE REPAST SUCKLE
SUPPLY BLOWOUT FURNISH
GRATIFY HERBAGE INDULGE
KEEPING NOURISH NURTURE
PASTURE PROVENT SATIATE
SATISFY SUBSIST SURFEIT SUSTAIN
VICTUAL
(— **ABUNDANTLY**) STOKE
(— **ANIMAL**) SORT SERVE
(— **AT NIGHT**) SUP
(— **FOR CATTLE**) FODDER STOVER
TACKLE
(— **FORCIBLY**) CRAM
(— **GLUTTONOUSLY**) BATTEN
(— **GREEN FOOD TO CATTLE**) SOIL
(— **HIGH**) FRANK
(— **IN STUBBLE**) SHACK
(— **ON FLIES**) SMUT
(— **RAVENOUSLY**) FRAUNCH
(— **STOCK**) FOG SOIL SOILING
(— **TO REPLETION**) ENGORGE
(— **TO THE FULL**) SATIATE
(— **WELL**) BATTLE
(**GROUND** —) CHOP
(**POULTRY** —) SCRATCH
(**RED** —) HAYSEED
(**STOCK** —) BRAN
(**WHALE** —) GRIT
FEEDBOARD DECK
FEEDER HOGGER HOPPER PECKER
STOCKER
(**YARN** —) CARRIER
FEEDHEAD RISER FEEDER SINKHEAD
FEEDING RELIEF FOLDAGE PANNAGE
(— **GROUND FOR FISH**) MEADOW
(— **THROUGH TUBE**) GAVAGE
(**FREE-CHOICE** —) CAFETERIA
FEEL FIND PALP GROPE SENSE
THINK TOUCH FIMBLE FINGER
HANDLE RESENT EXAMINE EXPLORE
FEELING SENSATE PERCEIVE
(— **ACUTELY**) SUFFER
(— **AVERSION FOR**) HATE LOATHE
(— **CHILLY**) CREEM
(— **COMPASSION**) PITY YEARN
(— **DEJECTION**) REPINE
(— **FEAR**) UG GRUE UGGE TREMBLE
(— **GRIEF**) GRIEVE DEPLORE
(— **HAPPY OR BETTER**) LIGHT
(— **NAUSEA**) WAMBLE
(— **OF CLOTH**) HAND
(— **ONE'S WAY**) GROPE FUMBLE
GRAMMEL
(— **OUT**) SOUND
(— **PAIN**) URN
(— **REPUGNANCE**) ABHOR

(— **SHAME**) BLUSH
(— **WANT OF**) MISS
FEELER DRAW KITE PALP SNIFF
PALPUS TACTOR ANTENNA SMELLER
PROPOSAL TENTACLE
FEELING FEEL PITY TACT VIEW
CHEER HEART HUMOR SENSE
SORGE TOUCH AFFECT CEMENT
MORALE CONSENT EMOTION
OPINION PASSION VELUNGE
ATTITUDE SENTIENT
(— **ILL**) HOWISH
(— **MIRTH**) JOCUND
(— **OF ACCORD**) SYMPATHY
(— **OF AMUSEMENT**) CHARGE
(— **OF ANTIPATHY**) ALLERGY
(— **OF ANXIETY**) ANGST
(— **OF CONTEMPT**) DISDAIN
(— **OF DISGUST**) UG
(— **OF HORROR**) CREEP CREEPS
(— **OF HOSTILITY**) ANIMUS
(— **OF JOY**) GLOAT
(— **OF OPPOSITION**) KICK
(— **OF RESENTMENT**) GRUDGE
(— **OF ROMANCE**) STARDUST
(— **OF UNEASINESS**) MALAISE
(— **OF WEARINESS**) ENNUI
(— **OF WELL-BEING**) EUPHORIA
(**ANGERED** —) DUDGEON
(**BODILY** —) TABET
(**CONCEITED** —) SWELLING
(**ILL** —) HARDNESS
(**INTUITIVE** —) HUNCH
(**KINDLY** —) GOODWILL
(**REPRESSION OF** —) STOICISM
(**STRONG** —) STAB
(**PL.**) HEART WITHERS
FEET DOGS TONGS STAMPS
WALKERS GUNBOATS TRILBIES
(— **WASHING**) MAUNDY
(**BOARD** —) FOOTAGE
(**LARGE** —) GUFFINS
FEIGN ACT FAKE MINT MOCK SEEM
SHAM VEYN AVOID FABLE FALSE
FORGE PAINT SHAPE SHIRK AFFECT
ASSUME GAMMON INVENT POSSUM
CONCEAL FALSIFY FASHION IMAGINE
POETIZE PRETEND ROMANCE
DISGUISE SIMULATE
(— **ASSENT**) COLLOGUE
(— **IGNORANCE**) CONNIVE
(— **ILLNESS**) MALINGER
FEIGNED SHAM FALSE FEINT POETIC
PSEUDO ASSUMED COLORED
FICTIVE FICTIOUS SIMULATE
FEIGNING FICTION FORGERY
FEIJOA ANDRE
FEINT FAKE MINT RUSE APPEL FAINT
SHIFᵢ SPOOF TRICK FALSIFY
FEIGNED FEINTER FINCTURE
PRETENSE REVIRADO
FELDSPAR AMBITE GNEISS CELSIAN
SYENITE ANDESINE FELSPATH
SANIDINE
FELICIA AGATHAEA
FELICITATE HUG BLESS MACARIZE
FELICITOUS FIT HAPPY
FELICITOUSLY HAPPILY
FELICITY JOY BLISS SONSE HEAVEN

FELINE CATTISH
FELL CUR FEN HEW DOWN DROP
FALL HIDE HILL MOOR PELT RUIN
SKIN VERY CRUEL EAGER FIELD
GRASS GREAT SHARP DEADLY
FIERCE FLEECE INTENT MIGHTY
SAVAGE SHREWD TUMBLE BRUTISH
CRASHED DOUGHTY HIDEOUS
INHUMAN STRETCH TUMBLED
MOUNTAIN SPIRITED VIGOROUS
(— **A TREE**) HEW LODGE
FELLER GIDEON
FELLING FALL CUTTING
FELLOE BOD FELF FALLY
FELLOW S BO BOY COD DON EGG
FOX GUY JOE LAD MAC MAN MUN
NUT WAG WAT YOB BALL BEAN
BEAU BIRD BOZO BUFF CARL CHAL
CHAP COVE CUSS DEAN DICK DUCK
DULL GENT GILL GINK HIND HUSK
JACK JAKE JOHN LOON MATE NABS
PEER PRIG SNAP BILLY BIMBO
BLOKE BROCK BUDDY BULLY CARLE
CHIEL COVEY FRUIT GROOM GUEST
JOKER MATCH PARTY SCOUT SKATE
SLAVE SPORT SPRIG SWIPE
BEGGAR BILLIE BIRKIE BOHUNK
BOOGER BUDDIE BUFFER BUGGER
BUSTER CALLAN CHIELD CODGER
CUFFIN CUTTER FELLER FOOTER
FOUTER FOUTRA GALOOT GAZABO
HOMBRE JASPER JOCKEY JOHNNY
JOSSER KIPPER PERSON SHAVER
SINNER SIRRAH SISTER SOCIUS
TURNIP BASTARD BROTHER
CALLANT CHAPPIE COMRADE
CULLIES CULLION CUSTRON
KNOCKER PARTNER SCROYLE
SNOOZER BLIGHTER CONFRERE
DOTTEREL MERCHANT NEIGHBOR
SYNODITE
(**AWKWARD** —) OAF CLUB GAWK
CLOWN LOOBY GALOOT SLOUCH
(**BASE** —) CARL CARLE CULLION
(**BASHFUL** —) SHEEP
(**BOLD** —) HEARTY
(**BRUTAL** —) CLUBFIST
(**CLOWNISH** —) COOF BAYARD
LOBLOLLY
(**CLUMSY** —) FILE CAMEL FARMER
LUBBER
(**COMMON** —) JACK LOUT
(**CONCEITED** —) JEMMY DALTEEN
(**CONTEMPTIBLE** —) DOG SCUT
SMAIL SNAKE RABBIT SMATCH
PEASANT
(**CONTENTIOUS** —) SQUARER
(**CORPULENT** —) POMPION
(**COUNTRY** —) JAKE JASPER
(**CRUDE** —) STIFF
(**DASHING** —) BUCK BLADE
(**DASTARDLY** —) HOUND
(**DESPICABLE** —) FOUTER FOUTRA
HANGDOG SMATCHET
(**DIRTY** —) SCAB BROCK
(**DISAGREEABLE** —) GLEYDE
(**DISSOLUTE** —) RAKE ROUE
RAKEHELL
(**DROLL** —) CARD

(DROWSY —) LUNGIS
(DULL —) BUFF DRIP FOGY LUNGIS HUMDRUM
(FAT —) HIND GULCH GLUTTON
(FIERCE-LOOKING —) KILLBUCK
(FINE —) BAWCOCK
(FOOLISH —) SOP GABY GOFF ZANY GANDER JACKSON WIDGEON
(GOOD —) BRICK BULLY TRUMP HEARTY
(GOOD-FOR-NOTHING —) JACKEEN
(GREEDY —) SLOTE
(IDLE —) FANION FOOTER STOCAH LOLLARD SKULKER
(IGNORANT —) GOBBIN
(ILLBRED —) LARRIKIN
(IMPERTINENT —) JACK WHISK
(INSIGNIFICANT —) SQUIB
(JOLLY —) VAVASOR VAVASOUR
(LAZY —) BUM LUSK TOOL LENTO
(LOW —) RAG WAFF SWEEP LIMMER VARLET MECHANIC WHORESON
(MEAN —) CAD DOG BOOR BOUCH BUCKO CAVEL CHURL SCURF RASCAL CULLION COISTREL SNEAKSBY SPALPEEN STINKARD
(NIGGARDLY —) SNUDGE
(NOISY —) MOUTH
(OLD —) GLYDE GAFFER GEEZER
(OLD-FASHIONED —) FOGY
(OVERBEARING —) GRIMSIR
(PROSAIC —) PRUNE
(PUNY —) SMAIK
(QUARRELSOME —) HECTOR
(QUEER OLD —) GEEZER
(RESIDENTIAL —) DON
(ROGUISH —) DOG
(RUDE —) JACK ROUGH
(SHABBY —) SHAB SQUEEF
(SHEEPISH —) SUMPH
(SHIFTLESS —) PROG SHACK PROGGER
(SHREWD —) COLT
(SILLY —) TOT GUMP ZANY SHEEP SMAIK DOTTEREL MUSHHEAD
(SIMPLE —) DOODLE
(SLOVENLY —) SLUTE
(SLY —) FOX
(SNEAKING —) SNUDGE
(SORDID —) HUNKS
(SOUTH AFRICAN —) KEREL
(SPORTY —) PLAYBOY
(STRANGE —) CODGER
(STRAPPING —) SWANKY SWANKIE
(STUPID —) ASS CLOD COOF DAFF DOLT GUMP HASH MUFF SIMP BOOBY DUNCE MORON STIRK BAYARD FARMER FOOZLE GANDER DOWFART CODSHEAD SOCKHEAD
(SULLEN —) GLUMP
(TRICKISH —) HUMBUG
(TRICKY —) ROOK GREEK KNAVE SCAMP DODGER RASCAL
(UNCIVIL —) RUDESBY
(UNCOUTH —) JAKE KEMP TIKE
(VILE —) RAT SKUNK
(VULGAR —) TIGER
(WORTHLESS —) BUM CUR DOG HASH PROG WAFF JAVEL ROGUE

SCAMP SHOAT SNAKE BROTHEL BUDMASH PROGGER VAURIEN TARTARET
(WRETCHED —) DEVIL DOGBOLT
(YOUNG —) BILLY BUCKO CADIE CADDIE
FELLOWMAN BROTHER
FELLOWSHIP GUILD HAUNT UNION FAMILY COMPANY ALLIANCE SODALITY
(CHRISTIAN —) KOINONIA
FELLY RIM FELF FELLOE KEENLY CRUELLY BITTERLY FIERCELY SAVAGELY TERRIBLY
FELO-DE-SE SUICIDE
FELON WILD CRUEL FETLOW FIERCE WICKED CONVICT CULPRIT PANARIS VILLAIN WHITLOW PHLEGMON RUNROUND
FELONY ARSON CRIME OFFENSE
FELT JIG PLAIT FILTER SENSED SOLEIL VELOUR DOUBLER FELTING PANNOSE
(— INTENSIVELY) ACUTE
(— THROUGH SENSES) SENSATE
(DEEPLY —) CORDIAL INTENSE
(PERSONALLY —) CONSCIOUS
(PL.) CLOTHING
FELTWORK NEUROPIL
FEMALE DOE EWE HER SHE SOW DAME GIRL GYNE LADY MORT ADULT JENNY SMOCK SQUAW WOMAN WAHINE WEAKLY DISTAFF FEMINAL WOMANLY DAUGHTER FEMININE GYNAECIC LADYLIKE WOMANISH
(— ANCESTOR) TAPROOT
(IMPERFECT —) FREEMARTIN
(PARTHOGENETIC —) AMAZON
FEMININE FAIR SOFT WEAK WOMAN FEMALE TENDER WAHINE FEMINAL WOMANLY WOMANISH
FEMININITY MUSLIN FEMINITY
FEMME FATALE SIREN
FEMORAL CRURAL
FEMUR THIGH
FEN BOG CARR FAIN FELL FOWL MERE MOOR WASH BROAD FAINS MARSH SNIPE SWAMP VENTS MORASS QUAGMIRE
FENCE BAR HAW HAY BANK DIKE DUEL DYKE HAHA HAIN PALE PLAY RAIL STUB WALL WEIR WIRE BEARD DODGE FRITH GUARD HEDGE MOUND PALIS STICK STUMP DETENT FENDER GLANCE HURDLE LEADER PALING PICKET RADDLE RASPER SCHERM SCRIME TIMBER BARRIER BULWARK CYCLONE DEFENSE ENCLOSE FENCING FENSURE IMPALER PASSAGE RAILING SWAGMAN BACKSTOP ENCHASER ENCLOSER GRAFFAGE HOARDING PALISADE PALISADO SEPIMENT SKIRMISH
(— AROUND BULLRING) BARRERA
(— CLOSING DITCH) WOLF
(— OF LOCK) STUB
(— OF LOGS) GLANCE

(CATTLE —) WIPE SKERM SCHERM
(FISH —) WEIR LEADER
(METAL —) RAIL RAILING
FENCER DUELIST IMPALER PARRIER PROVOST SCRIMER SWORDER FOILSMAN BACKSWORD
FENCE RAIL DRAWBAR
FENCE SECTION PANE
FENCE-SITTER MUGWUMP
FENCING WIRE FENCE PALING ESCRIME PASSAGE SCIENCE SWORDING
FEND WARD PARRY SHIRK DEFEND FORBID RESIST SUPPORT
FENDER SKID WING CAMEL GUARD SKATE BUFFER BUMPER SHIELD DOLPHIN PUDDING BOWGRACE SPLASHER
(— FOR FIREPLACE) CURB KERB
(— NEAR HOLE) TELLTALE
FENDER SKID GLANCER
FENESTRA FORAMEN
FENGHUANG FUM PHOENIX
FENKS FRITTERS
FENMAN WEBFOOT
FENNEC ZERDA
FENNEL ANIS DILL HEMP SOYA FERULE FINKEL COWBANE HOGWEED SPINGEL FINOCHIO FLORENCE CAROSELLA
FENNER ZERDA
FENSTER WINDOW
FENUGREEK BAUMIER MELLILOT
(SEEDS OF —) HELBEH
FERAL WILD BRUTAL DEADLY FERINE SAVAGE BESTIAL UNTAMED FUNEREAL UNBROKEN
FER-DE-LANCE BONETAIL JARARACA
FERMATA HOLD PAUSE TENOR CORONA
FERMENT FRY LOB ZYM BARM FRET HEAT SOUR TURN WORK ZYME FEVER SWEAT YEAST DANDER ENZYME FLOWER FOMENT SEETHE SIMMER TUMULT UPROAR AGITATE QUICKEN TURMOIL DISORDER
FERMENTATION SWEAT CUVAGE FERMENT MOWBURN WORKING ZYMOSIS
FERMENTED SOD
(IMPROPERLY —) FOXY
FERMENTING WORKING
FERN HEII NITO PULU TARA WEKI BRAKE DUGAL EKAHA FROND NARDO PITAU PONGA ULUHI WHEKI AMAMAU DOODIA NARDOO OSMUND PTERIS ACROGEN ATERACH BOGFERN BRACKEN SYNANGE WOODSIA ADIANTUM ASPIDIUM BUCKHORN BUNGWALL CETERACH DAVALLIA DENDRITE FERNWORT FILICITE GOLDBACK HARDFERN KOLOKOLO MOONWORT MULEWORT PARAREKA PILLWORT POLYPODY SPOROGEN STAGHORN
FERN LEAF FROND CROSIER
FERNLIKE FERNY PTEROID
FEROCIOUS ILL FELL GRIM RUDE

WILD CRUEL FERAL BLOODY
BRUTAL FEROCE FIERCE GOTHIC
RAGING SAVAGE ACHARNE INHUMAN
OMINOUS VIOLENT WOLFISH
PITILESS RAVENOUS RUTHLESS
TARTARLY
FEROCITY FERITY SAVAGERY
VIOLENCE
FERRARA ANDREW
FERRET HOB MONK TAPE PADOU
MONACH WEASEL POLECAT
(— OUT) FOSSICK
(FEMALE —) GIL GILL JILL BITCH
(MALE —) HOB HOBB
FERRIAGE WAFTAGE
FERRIC OXIDE CROCUS
FERROTYPE GLAZE TINTYPE
FERROUS SIDEROUS
FERRULE CAP TIP CUFF RING SHOE
VIRL COLLET PULLEY RUNNER
VERREL VIROLE ARMGARN BUSHING
CRAMPET
FERRY FORD PASS PONT SCOW
PASSAGE TRAJECT TRANSFER
FERRYBOAT BAC PONT FERRY
FERRYMAN CHARON FERRIER
WATERMAN
FERTILE FAT GOOD RANK RICH
GLEBY BATFUL BATTLE FECUND
HEARTY STRONG TEEMING
ABUNDANT BATTABLE FRUITFUL
GENEROUS PREGNANT PROLIFIC
SPAWNING
FERTILITY HEART FATNESS
(PATRON OF —) YAKSHA
FERTILIZATION ENDOGAMY
POROGAMY
FERTILIZE FAT DUNG FISH LIME
MARL CHALK BATTEN ENRICH
FRUCTIFY
FERTILIZER FAT MARL GUANO
HUMUS ALINIT FLOATS MANURE
POLLEN POTASH CARRIER
COMPOTE KAINITE NITRATE
TANKAGE AMMONITE CINEREAL
NITROGEN
FERULA NARTHEX
FERULE ROD RULER COLLET FENNEL
FERULA PALMER
FERVENCY WARMTH CANDENCY
FERVENT HOT KEEN WARM EAGER
FIERY ARDENT BITTER FERVID
FIERCE INWARD RAGING SAVAGE
BOILING BURNING GLOWING
INTENSE PECTORAL VEHEMENT
FERVID HOT ARDENT TROPIC
BOILING BURNING FERVENT
GLOWING ZEALOUS UNCTUOUS
VEHEMENT
FERVOR FIRE HEAT RAGE SOUL
ZEAL ARDOR WARMTH PASSION
CANDENCY DEVOTION STRENGTH
VIOLENCE
(— IN PRAYER) KAVVANAH
KAWWANAH
FESCUE VESTER
FESS BAR BAND PERT DANCE HUMET
FESTAL GAY GALA GAUDY FESTIVE
FESTUAL FEASTFUL

FESTER ROT BEAL RANK SCAR
RANKLE PUSTULE PUTREFY
FESTERING FRETTY
FESTIVAL (ALSO SEE FEAST) ALE
BON PWE BUSK FAIR FEIS FETE
GALA HOLI MELA TIDE UTAS WAKE
DELIA FEAST FERIA FIESTA GAUDY
HALOA PURIM REVEL ROUSE SEDAR
BAIRAM BRIDAL CARNEA DEWALI
DIASIA DIPALA FIESTA HOHLEE
HUFFLE KERMIS LAMMAS LENAEA
OPALIA PONGOL POOJAH SUCCOS
AGONIUM AGRANIA BANQUET
BELTANE DASAHRA EQUIRIA
FESTIAL HILARIA KERMESS MATSURI
SUKKOTH THIASOS TOXCATL
UPHELYA VINALIA AGRIONIA
AIANTEIA APATURIA ATHENAEA
BEALTINE BRUMALIA CARNIVAL
COTYTTIA DASAHARA DIIPOLIA
DIONYSIA DUSSERAH ENCAENIA
FASNACHT FLORALIA HANUKKAH
HIGHTIDE KALENDAE MARYMASS
MATRALIA MITHRIAC MUHARRAM
MUNYCHIA NATIVITY NEOMENIA
POTLATCH STAMPEDE
(PL.) MOED VOTA
FESTIVE GAY GALA JOLLY FESTAL
GENIAL JOYOUS FEASTLY HOLIDAY
JOCULAR CONVIVAL FEASTFUL
MIRTHFUL SPORTIVE
FESTIVITY GALA UTAS UTIS FEAST
MIRTH RANDY REVEL GAIETY
GAYETY SPLORE HOLIDAY JOLLITY
JOYANCE PATTERN FESTIVAL
FUNCTION
FESTOON SWAG WREATH GARLAND
DECORATE
(PL.) ENCARPUS
FETCH FET FESH GASP GIVE SHAG
TACK TAKE TEEM WAIN BRING
SWEEP TRICK DOUBLE STROKE
WRAITH ACHIEVE ATTRACT ARTIFICE
FETCHING INTEREST
FETCHED FOSH
FETCHING SWEET CRAFTY CUNNING
ALLURING PLEASING SCHEMING
FETE FAIR GALA FEAST HONOR
BAZAAR FIESTA HOLIDAY
FETID OLID RANK MUSTY PUTID
ROTTEN VIROSE NOISOME
FETIDLY FOULLY
FETISH OBI IDOL JUJU OBIA ZEME
ZEMI ZOGO ANITO ASCON CHARM
GUACA HUACA OBEAH OBIAH
TOTEM FETICH GRIGRI NAGUAL
VOODOO SHINTAI SORCERY
FETISHRY GREEGREE TALISMAN
FETLOCK COOT FOOTLOCK
FETTER BAND BEND BOLT BOND
FIND GYVE IRON SPAN BASIL BEWET
BILBO CHAIN SWATH ANKLET
GARTER HALTER HAMPER HOBBLE
HOPPLE IMPEDE LANGEL RACKAN
SWATHE CLINKER CONFINE ENCHAIN
FETLOCK GARNISH MANACLE
SHACKLE SPANCEL TRAMMEL
RESTRAIN
(PL.) IRONS LINKS DARBIES

GARNISH GARTERS
FETTERBUSH PIPESTEM PIPEWOOD
FETTLE BEAT DECK FUSS MULL TIDY
VEIN DRESS GROOM WHACK YARAK
GIRDLE REPAIR SETTLE STRIKE
ARRANGE BANDAGE FEATHER
HARNESS
FETTLER BILLYER NOBBLER
FETTLING FIX FETTLE FIXING
FETUS BIRTH CHILD YOUNG AMELUS
BREECH EMBRYO FOETUS ABORTUS
CYCLOPS FEATURE AMORPHUS
FEUD FIEF FRAY BROIL AFFRAY
ENMITY FEODUM FEUDUM STRIFE
CONTEST DISPUTE QUARREL
VENDETTA
FEUDATORY FIEF VASSAL ZAMINDAR
ZEMINDAR
FEUILLE MORTE PHILAMOT
FEVER AGUE FIRE ARDOR CAUMA
DANDY LEUMA OCTAN CAUSUS
DENGUE FEBRIS HECTIC SEPTAN
SEXTAN SODOKU TYPHIA TYPHUS
AMAKEBE FERMENT FEVERET
HELODES MALARIA PINKEYE
PYREXIA QUARTAN TERTIAN
TYPHOID SYNOCHUS TERTIANA
TYPHINIA
(— OF HORSE) SCALMA
(BRAIN —) PHRENITIS
(MALARIAL —) TAP
(MARSH —) HELODES
(TEXAS —) TRISTEZA
FEVERED DISEASED
FEVERFEW MAYWEED MUGWORT
FEVERISH HOT FIERY FEVERY
HECTIC EXCITED FEBRILE FRANTIC
RESTLESS
FEVERLESS APYREXIA
FEVERROOT GENSON
FEVER TREE BITTERBARK
FEVERWEED FITWEED
FEW LIT CURN LESS SOME SCANT
THREE WHEEN WHONE CURRAN
PICKLE LIMITED EXIGUOUS
FEWER LESS
FEWNESS PAUCITY
FEY DEAD DYING ELFIN FATAL
UNLUCKY
FEZ TARBOOSH
FIADOR THEODORE
FIANCE TRUST SPOUSE FIANCEE
PROMISE AFFIANCE
FIASCO CRASH FLASK FROST FIZZLE
FAILURE DISASTER
FIAT EDICT ORDER DECREE
COMMAND DECISION SANCTION
FIB LIE YED FLAW WHID SLANT
STORY FITTEN PUMMEL SKLENT
FIBBER LIAR
FIBER TAL ADAD BASS BAST COIR
ERUC FERU FLAX HARL HEMP IMBE
JUTE LINE PITA SILK SUNN TULA
ABACA AGUST AZLON CAJUN
CAROA CHOEL ERIZO FIBRE GRAIN
HARLE ISOTE ISTLE IXTLE IZOTE
KENAF KITUL MURVA OAKUM RAMIE
RAPHE SIMAL SISAL STRAW TERAP
TOSSA TUCUM VIVER AMIRAY

BINDER BUNTAL BURITI CABUYA
CATENA DACRON EMBIRA FIBRIL
FIMBLE HINOKI KANAFF KENDIR
KOHEMP MUCUNA NYTRIL RAFFIA
SALAGO STAPLE STRAND STRING
SUTURE THREAD TUCUMA TURURI
VINYON YACHAN ZAPUPE ACETATE
ACRYLIC ANONANG ARAMINA
BASSINE CANTALA CASCARA
CHANDUL CHINGMA COQUITA
ESPARTO FILASSE GEBANGA
GRAVATA GUAXIMA GUMIHAN
HUARIZO KERATTO KITTOOL
MOCMAIN PALMITE PANGANE
PAUKPAN POCHOTE SABUTAN
CANAPINA CURRATOW FILAMENT
HARAKEKE HENEQUEN PIASSAVA
TOQUILLA TRONADOR
(— FROM PEACOCK FEATHERS)
MARL
(— OF PALM) DOH LIF ERUC COYOL
COROZO GOMUTI COQUITA
GEBANGA
(—S OF FLAX) HARE
(CLUSTER OF —S) NEP
(COARSE —) KEMP
(COCONUT —) COIR KYAR
(COTTON —) LINT STAPLE
(KNOT OF —) NOIL
(MANUFACTURED —) DYNEL
ESTRON SPANDEX
(MATTED —) SHAG
(MINERAL —) ASBESTOS
(MUSCLE —) RHABDIUM
(NERVE —) EFFERENT DEPRESSOR
(PULVERIZED —) FLOCK
(SILKY —) KAPOK KUMBI YACHAN
CASTULI
(TWISTED —S) STRAND
(WASTE —) FLY GOUT
(WASTE —S) FLOSS
(WOODY —) BAST GRAIN SCUTCH
(PL.) FUZZ KERATTO
IBRIL AXONEME DESMOSE
MYONEME MYOPHAN
IBRIN GLUTEN MYOSIN
BROCARTILAGE FABELLA
MENISCUS
IBROID DESMOID
BROMA INOMA FIBROID
BROUS FIBROSE STRINGY
INEMALINE
IBULA LACE CLASP BROOCH
BUCKLE SPLINT
ICKLE GERY DIZZY FALSE GIDDY
ILIGHT UNSAD HARLOT KITTLE
IMOBILE PUZZLE SHIFTY VOLAGE
IWANKLE WANKLY CASALTY
ICASELTY FLATTER MOVABLE
IMUTABLE VAINFUL VARIANT
IVOLUBLE GOSSAMER MOVEABLE
ISKITTISH STIRRING UNSTABLE
IUNSTEADY VARIABLE VOLATILE
IWAVERING
ICKLENESS LEVITY EASINESS
ICKLETY VARIANCE
ICO FIG FIGO TANTI
ICTION TALE FABLE FALSE NOVEL
IROMAN STORY DECEIT DEVICE

FABULA FITTEN LEGEND COINAGE
FANTASY FIGMENT FORGERY
MARCHEN NOVELRY ROMANCE
ROMANZA KAILYARD PHANTASY
FICTITIOUS BOGUS DUMMY FALSE
PHONY FABLED POETIC ASSUMED
FEIGNED FABULOUS FICTIOUS
MYTHICAL ROMANTIC SIMULATE
SPURIOUS LEGENDARY
FICUS PYRULA
FID PRICK NORMAN PRICKER
SPLICER
FIDDLE BOW BOX GIG SAW VIOL
CHEAT CROWD GEIGE GIGUE
GUDOK CHORUS FITHEL POTTER
TRIFLE URHEEN VIOLIN CHROTTA
SWINDLE HUMSTRUM
(— STRING) THAIRM
(— WITH) TWIDDLE
FIDDLER CRAB VIOLER VIOLIN
CROWDER SCRAPER SIXPENCE
FIDDLER CRAB RACER FIDDLER
OCYPODE SOLDIER
FIDDLESTICKS PSHAW FIDDLE
FIDELITY TRUE ARDOR FAITH PIETY
TROTH TRUTH FEALTY HONESTY
LOYALTY ADHESION DEVOTION
RELIGION VERACITY
FIDGET MOP FIKE FIRK FUSS ROIL
FIDGE FITCH HOTCH SHRUB SHRUG
WORRY BREVIT FIGGLE FISSLE
FISTLE FRIDGE FUSSER HIRSEL
JIFFLE JIGGET NESTLE NIBBLE
NIGGLE TIDDLE TRIFLE VIGGLE
WORRIT NERVOUS RESTLESS
TWITCHET
(— ABOUT TRIFLES) SPOFFLE
(STATE OF —) FANTAD FANTOD
(PL.) JUMPS
FIDGETY FIKIE FUSSY ITEMY FEISTY
FIGENT FLISKY KITTLE UNEASY
RESTIVE TWITCHY RESTLESS
FIDUCIARY TRUSTEE TRUSTFUL
FIE SISS FAUGH
FIEF FEE HAN FEUD FEOFF TIMAR
ZIAMET SATSUMA SUBFIEF
BENEFICE
(— HOLDER) TIMARIOT
FIELD LEA LOT ACRE AGER AREA
BENT CAMP FELL FLAT HADE INAM
LAND LIST MEAD PALE PARK RAND
TOWN WONG BRECK CAMPO CHAMP
CLOUR CROFT EARTH GLEBE INNAM
LAYER MILPA NILPA PADDY RANGE
ROWEN SAWAH TILTH VELDE
ARRISH CAMPUS CAREER CHAMPE
DOMAIN FURROW GARDEN GROUND
MACHAR MATTER MEADOW PINGLE
SHIELD SPHERE CHARMEL COMPASS
CULTURE DIAMOND FERRING
GARSTON INFIELD MOWLAND
NEWTAKE PADDOCK PARROCK
PIGHTLE PURVIEW QUILLET TERRAIN
THWAITE TILLAGE CLEARING
PROVINCE
(— ADJOINING HOUSE) CROFT
(— AT CRICKET) SCOUT
(— OF ACTIVITY) GAME ARENA
BARONY SPHERE TERRAIN

(— OF BATTLE) PLAIN
(— OF BLOODSHED) ACELDAMA
AKELDAMA
(— OF CONTROL) DOMAIN
(— OF ENDEAVOR) BUSINESS
(— OF SNOW) NEVE SNOWPACK
(— OF STUDY) GROUND
(— ON WHICH GRASS IS GROWN)
MEAD MEADOW
(— SOWN FOR TWO SUCCESSIVE
YEARS) HOOK
(ENCLOSED —) AGER TOWN CLOSE
CROFT
(FOOTBALL —) GRIDIRON
(FRUITFUL —) CHARMEL
(GRASSY —) LEA PEN GARSTON
(HOP —) HOPYARD
(LAVA —) PEDREGAL
(LITTLE-KNOWN —) BYWAY
(NEW GOLD —) RUSH
(PLOWED —) FURROW
(RICE —) SAWAH
(SMALL —) HAW CROFT PADDOCK
(STUBBLE —) HIRSH ROWEN ARRISH
GRATTEN GRATTON
(TILTING —) LISTS
(TOBACCO —) VEGA
(UNEXPLOITED —) FRONTIER
(UNPLOWED EDGE OF —) RAND
(PL.) FIELDEN
FIELD BALM SHEEPMINT
FIELD CAMOMILE OXEYE
FIELDER GLOVEMAN
(CRICKET —) SLIP COVER FIELD
GULLY SCOUT GULLEY INFIELDER
FIELDFARE FELT JACK REDLEG
FELLFARE HILLBIRD JACKBIRD
REDSHANK SNOWBIRD VELTFARE
FIELD MADDER SPURWORT
FIELD MOUSE VOLE MIGALE
FIELDPIECE GUN AMUSETTE
GALLOPER
FIELD SCABIOUS BLUECAP
FIELDWORK LUNET REDAN LUNETTE
FIEND FEN FOE PUG FEND FYND
DEMON DEVIL ENEMY SATAN TRULL
WIZARD SHAITAN SUCCUBA TITIVIL
BARBASON SUCCUBUS
FIENDISH CRUEL WICKED DEMONIC
FIENDLY SATANIC DEMONIAC
DEVILISH DIABOLIC INFERNAL
FIERCE ILL BOLD FELL GRIM KEEN
RUDE THRO ASPER BREME CRUEL
EAGER FELON HATEL ORPED RETHE
SHARP SMART STARK STERN
STOUR STOUT WROTH ARDENT
FEROCE GOTHIC HETTER IMMANE
RAGING RUGGED SAVAGE STURDY
UNMEEK UNMILD WICKED BRUTISH
FERVENT FURIOSO FURIOUS
GRIMFUL INHUMAN MANKIND
RABIOUS RAMPANT SCADDLE
VIOLENT STERNFUL TIGERISH
FIERCE-EYED WALLEYED
FIERCELY FELL HARD FELLY FIERCE
FIERCENESS FURY FEROCITY
FIERY HOT RED ADUST FIRED QUICK
SHARP ARDENT FLASHY IGNITE
BURNING FERVENT FLAMING

FURIOUS GLOWING HOTHEAD
IGNEOUS PARCHED PEPPERY
VIOLENT ADUSTIVE CHOLERIC
FEVERISH FRAMPOLD INFLAMED
PHRAMPEL SPIRITED SPITFIRE
VEHEMENT
FIESTA FETE FERIA PARTY HOLIDAY
(— **COSTUME**) POLLERA
FIFE STICK PIFERO PIFFERO
FIFTEEN FIVE
FIFTEENTH DOUBLETTE
FIFTH QUINT QUINTIN
FIFTY (— **YEAR ANNIVERSARY**)
JUBILEE
FIFTY-FIFTY EVEN
FIG RIG FICO ARRAY BREBA DRESS
ELEME ELEMI PIPAL SABRA TANTI
BALETE BALITI FOUTER FOUTRA
GINGER LOBFIG PEEPUL TRIFLE
FURBISH GONDANG SICONUS
SYCONUS WARINGIN
(— **CROP**) MAMME
FIG BASKET CABAS
FIGHT BOX MIX WAP WAR WIN BEAT
BEEF BLUE BOUT CAMP CLEM COCK
COPE COWP CRAB CUFF DUEL FLOG
FRAY LAKE MEET MELL MILL SHOW
SLUG SPAR TILT WAGE YOKE
BRAWL CLASH FIELD FLOLT HURRY
JOUST MATCH MELEE SCRAP SHINE
SPURN STOUR TOUSE AFFAIR
AFFRAY BARNEY BATTLE BICKER
COMBAT DEBATE FEUCHT FRACAS
FRAISE HASSLE IMPUGN MEDDLE
OPPOSE RELUCT REPUGN RESIST
RIPPIT RUFFLE SHOWER STOUSH
STRIFE STRIKE STRIVE TOUSEL
TURNUP BARGAIN BRABBLE
CONTEND CONTEST COUNTER
JOURNEY QUARREL RUCTION
SIMULTY TUILYIE WARFARE
CONFLICT DOGFIGHT DUOMACHY
FINISHER GUNFIGHT MILITATE
SKIRMISH SQUABBLE STRUGGLE
TIRRIVEE TIRRWIRR TRAVERSE
(— **AGAINST**) BUCK
(— **BETWEEN TWO**) DUEL
DUOMACHY
(— **FOR**) SERVE CHAMPION
(— **WITH CLUB**) TIMBER
(**FIST** —) RIPPIT TURNUP
(**SEA** —) NAUMACHY
(**STREET** —) HABBLE
FIGHTER PUG VAMP BOXER COCKER
BATTLER DUELIST SLUGGER
SOLDIER WARRIOR ANDABATA
BARRATER BARRATOR CHAMPION
GUERILLA PUGILIST SCRAPPER
(**FIRE** —) EXEMPT HOTSHOT
FIGHTING BLOW AFFRAY DEBATE
WARLIKE CONFLICT MILITANT
(— **WITH SHADOW**) SCIAMACHY
FIGHTING FISH PLAKAT
FIG MARIGOLD SAMH MESEM
FICOID FOXCHOP FICOIDAL
FIGMENT IDEA FICTION
FIGPECKER BECCAFICO
FIGURATE FLORID FIGURAL FIGURED
FIGURATO

FIGURATION FORM SHAPE DESIGN
OUTLINE
FIGURATIVE FLORID FIGURAL
FIGURED FLOWERY TYPICAL
ALLUSIVE TROPICAL
FIGURE HUE VOL BOSH DOLL FORM
IDEA SIGN STAR ANGLE ANTIC
DATUM DIGIT FLIRT FRAME IMAGE
MAGOT MOTIF SHAPE SPADE SPRIG
BABOON CHANGE CIPHER COCKUP
CUTOUT DEVICE EFFIGY EMBLEM
ENTAIL FIGGER GOOGOL INCUSE
NUMBER PERSON SCHEME SYMBOL
TAILLE TATTOO CHASSIS CHEVRON
CHIFFER CHIFFRE COMPUTE
CONTOUR DRAWING GESTALT
IMPRESS NUMERAL OUTLINE
STATURE DIHEDRAL FIGURATE
GRAFFITO HEXAGRAM LIKENESS
SEMBLANT
(— **FORMED BY INTERSECTING
LINES**) KNOT
(— **IN PRAYER**) ORANT
(— **IN WOOD GRAIN**) BURL FLAKE
(— **MADE OF 3 LINES**) TRIGRAM
TRIANGLE
(— **MADE OF CORN**) KNACK
(— **OF SPEECH**) IMAGE IRONY
TROPE APORIA CLIMAX FLOWER
SCHEME SIMILE VISION ANALOGY
IMAGERY METAPHOR METONYMY
(— **OUT**) BOTTOM
(— **UP**) ITEM
(— **USED AS COLUMN**) ATLAS
TELAMON CARYATID
(— **USED AS MAGIC SYMBOL**)
PENTACLE
(—**S OF SPEECH**) COLORS
(**ANATOMICAL** —) ECORCHE
(**ARTIFICIAL** —) GOLEM
(**BIBLICAL** —) ANGEL CHERUB
(**CARVED** —) GLYPH FIGURINE
(**CENTRAL** —) HERO
(**CIRCULAR** —) HOOP
(**COMIC** —) BILLIKEN
(**CONSPICUOUS** —) MARK
(**CRESCENT-SHAPED** —) LUNE
(**DANCE** —) SWING TRACE SQUARE
PURPOSE ASSEMBLE
(**DOMINANT** —) CAPTAIN
(**FEMALE** —) ORANTE
(**GEOMETRICAL** —) BODY CONE
CUBE LUNE PRISM RHOMB SOLID
CIRCLE GNOMON ISAGON ISOGON
OBLONG SECTOR SQUARE DIAGRAM
ELLIPSE LOZENGE PELCOID
RHOMBUS SECTION HEXAFOIL
SPHEROID
(**GREEK** —) KOUROS
(**GROTESQUE** —) MAGOT BABCON
MAXIMON
(**IDEAL** —) EIDOLON
(**IMAGINARY** —) BOGEYMAN
(**INCISED** —) INTAGLIO
(**MUMMYLIKE** —) USHABTI
(**MUSICAL** —) IDEA LICK
(**ODD** —) MAUMET
(**OVAL** —) SWASH ELLIPSE
(**PREHISTORIC** —) CHACMOL

CHACMOOL
(**QUADRILLE** —) POULE
(**QUEER** —) GIG
(**RHYTHMIC** —) SNAP
(**SHADOW** —) SKIAGRAM
(**SKATING** —) SPIRAL BRACKET
COUNTER
(**SPINDLE-SHAPED** —) FUSEE FUZEE
(**STUFFED** —) DUMMY
(**SYLLOGISTIC** —) SCHEMA
(**SYMBOLIC** —) MORAL EMBLEM
(**TRIANGULAR** —) TRIQUET
(**UNDRAPED** —) NUDE
(**WINGED** —) ANGEL EIDOLON
(PL.) SPILING
FIGURED FIGURY FACONNE
FIGUREHEAD DUMMY FRONT
SCROLL
FIGURINE TANAGRA CRIOPHORE
FIGWORT BARTSIA PILEWORT

FIJI

BAY: MBYA NATEWA NGALOA
SAVUSAVU
CAPITAL: SUVA
EASTERN GROUP: LAU
ISLAND: ELD KIA ONO AIWA KIOA
KORO MALI NGAU VIWA WAIA
AGATA MANGO MOALA NAIAU
RAMBI MAMOLO MATUKU
MBENGA MBULIA NAIRAI NAVITI
NGAMEA OVALAU TOTOYA
YASAWA YENDUA KAMBARA
LAKEMBA TAVEUNI VITILEVU
MOUNTAIN: NARARU MONAVATU
NIECE OR NEPHEW: VASU
POINT: VUYA
TOWN: MAU MBA MOMI REWA
SUVA TUVU THUVU ETUMBA
NALOTO NAMOLI NARATA
NASALA NAVOLA SAGARA

FIJIAN VITIAN
FILAGO GIFOLA
FILAMENT BRIN DOWL HAIR HARL
NEMA PILE SILK CHIVE CHORD
FIBER FIBRE FILUM TWIRE CIRRUS
ELATER HEATER MANTLE STRAND
THREAD CIRRHUS FLIMMER RHIZOI
TEXTILE PARANEMA PHACELLA
STERIGMA
(— **OF FEATHER**) DOWL DOWLE
(— **OF MINERAL**) STRINGER
(— **OF SILK**) BRIN
(—**S OF FLAX OR HEMP**) HARL
(**TWISTED** —**S**) STRAND
(PL.) HACKLE
FILAMENTOUS STRINGY HAIRLIKE
FILANDERS BACKWORM
FILARIASIS MUMU
FILBERT HAZEL COBNUT HAZELNU
(**SIEVE OF** —**S**) PRICKLE
FILCH BOB FUB NIM ROB BEAT FAF
PILK PRIG SMUG SNIP FETCH LUR
PILCH SNAKE SNEAK STEAL CLOY
PILFER SMOUCH STRIKE CABBAGE
PURLOIN
FILE BOX ROW BARB DECK LINE LI
RANK RASP RATE RISP ROLL SLIP

STUB EMERY ENTER FLOAT FOUND
GRAIL INDEX LABEL RIFLE TRACK
TRAIN ACCUSE ANSWER BEFOUL
CARLET DEFILE FILACE RASCAL
RUBBER STRING TOPPER ARCHIVE
ARRANGE CHOILER CONDEMN
DOSSIER EXHIBIT GRAILLE QUANNET
TICKLER DRAWFILE
(— DOWN SAW TEETH) JOINT
(— OF SIX SOLDIERS) ROT
(— OFF) DEFILE
(— USED BY COMBMAKERS) GRAIL
TOPPER GRAILER GRAILLE
(— WITH COURT OF LAW) BOX
(COARSE —) RAPE
(CURVED —) RIFFLER
ILE BOX SOLANDER
ILEFISH LIJA UNIE TURBOT
UNICORN BALISTIS FOOLFISH
ILIAL PIUS SONLY
ILIBUSTER FLIBUTOR STONEWALL
ILING RASION LIMATION
(PL.) LEMEL LIMAIL
ILIPENDULA ULMARIA
ILIPINO KALINGA KANKANAI
ILL EKE HIT PAD BUNG CLOY CRAM
FEED GLUT HOLD LADE LINE MEET
PANG QUAR SATE STOP TEEM
BELLY BLOAT BULGE CHOKE ESTOP
FLOCK GORGE KEDGE PITCH STORE
STUFF CHARGE FULFIL INFUSE
OCCUPY QUERRE SUPPLY AGGRADE
DISTEND ENLARGE EXECUTE
FILLING FRAUGHT FULFILL IMPLETE
INFLATE INVOLVE PERFECT
PERFORM PERVADE PLENISH
SATIATE SATISFY SUFFUSE
COMPLETE COMPOUND FREQUENT
PERMEATE
(— COMPLETELY) SATURATE
(— CUP TO BRIM) BRIM CROWN
BUMPER
(— FULL) FARCE STUFF
(— IN CHINKS) LIP
(— IN WITH RUBBLE) HEART
(— IN) NOG KILL STOP SLUSH
NFILL BALLAST
(— INTERSTICES) BLIND
(— LEATHER WITH OIL) FAT
(— OUT) BUNCH SWELL
(— TO EXCESS) CROWD FLOOD
CONGEST SURFEIT
(— TO OVERFLOWING) FLOW
(HWACK
(— UP HOLE) STIFLE
(— UP) STOP BRICK CHOKE CLOSE
ESTOP STOAK FULFIL IMPACT
STODGE PLENISH
— WITH ALE) RACK
— WITH ANXIETY) ALARM ALARUM
— WITH CARGO) STOW
— WITH CLAY) CAT
— WITH FEAR) APPAL APPALL
— WITH HORROR) ABHOR
— WITH LIGHT) GLUT
— WITH LIQUOR) TUN SKINK
— WITH METAL) BACK
— WITH MORTAR) GROUT
— WITH ODORS) EMBALM

(— WITH RUBBISH) BASH
(— WITH TERROR) AMAZE
(— WITH) SWILL
(ONE'S —) SLITHERS
FILLED BIG ALIVE FLUSH QUICK
SATED SOLID GRAVID LOADED
CROWDED HAUNTED IMPLETE
OPPLETE REPLETE SWOLLEN
FREQUENT INSTINCT POPULOUS
(— OUT) BOLD FULL
(— TO EXCESS) FLOWN
(— WITH EXCITEMENT) ABUZZ
(— WITH FEAR) AFRAID
(— WITH INTERSTICES) AREOLAR
(— WITH MOISTURE) FAT
(— WITH PRIDE) YNPRIDID
FILLER GARA BOGUS SILEX SILKA
SQUIB BALAAM LIGNIN FILLING
LOADING WRAPPER
FILLET BAND BONE GIRT LIST ORLE
ORLO SOLE TAPE AMPYX CROWN
FACET FILET GORGE LABEL LEDGE
MITER MITRE QUIRK SCROD SNOOD
STRAP STRIA TIARA VITTA ANADEM
BENDEL BINDER CIMBIA COMBLE
CORONA DIADEM FASCIA INFULA
LISTEL NORSEL POTONG QUADRA
REGULA RIBBON ROLLER TAENIA
TURBAN TURBOT ANNULET
BANDAGE BANDEAU CLOISON
CORONET EYEBROW FACETTE
FRONTAL GARLAND LAMBEAU
MOLDING TRESSON TRINGLE
BANDEL CINCTURE FRONTLET
HAIRLACE HEADBAND PLATBAND
TRESSOUR TRESSURE UNDERCUT
FILLIFORM CATENOID
FILL-IN MODESTY
FILLING GOB FILL MODE PLUG WEFT
WOOF INLAY STUFF FILLER
STOPPING STUFFING
(— OF GAPS) CONFAB
(— UP) CLOSURE RIPIENO
(BASKET —) SLEW
(DENTAL —) INLAY
(SILK —) SHIKII
FILLIP BLOW FLIP SNAP TOSS URGE
FILIP FLASH FLIRT FLISK IMPEL
BUFFET INCITE MOMENT PROJECT
FILLY COLT FOAL GIRL
FILM H BRAT HAZE HULL KELL MIST
SCUM SKIM SKIN VEIL WEFT BLEAR
COVER FLAKE GLAZE LAYER PEARL
PLATE SCALE SHOOT SHORT
BUBBLE MOTHER PATINA SCRUFF
CUTICLE FEATURE PHILOME
TAFFETA TOPICAL TRAILER
BEESWING FIRECOAT NEGATIVE
PELLICLE
(— OF OIL) SLICK
(— OF TARTAR) SCALE
(— ON COPPER) PATINA
(— ON PORRIDGE) BRAT
(— ON WINE) BEESWING
(DISCARDED —) OUTTAKE
(X-RAY —) BITEWING
FILMY FINE HAZY GAUZY MISTY
WISPY CLOUDY CLOUDED TIFFANY
FILMLIKE GOSSAMER

FILTER CLAY RAPE SIFT SILE DRAIN
SEITZ SIEVE BOUGIE CANDLE
COLATE LAUTER MEDIUM PURIFY
REFINE STRAIN BAGHOUSE
FILTRATE INFILTER STRAINER
FILTERER CLARIFIER
FILTH FEN KET DIRT DUNG GORE
MUCK NAST SLUT SOIL SUDS ADDLE
DRECK GLEAM GLEET JAKES POUCE
SWILL DEFILE FULYIE FULZIE
IMMUND ORDURE SORDES VERMIN
SLOTTER SQUALOR SULLAGE
FOULNESS MUCKMENT SNOTTERY
WORTHING
FILTHINESS MUCOR SQUALOR
SULLAGE CENOSITY
FILTHY LOW FOUL MIRY VILE DIRTY
DROVY DUNGY GROSS LAIRY
MUCKY NASTY BAWDRY CRUMBY
CRUMMY CRUSTY DIRTEN IMMUND
IMPURE SORDID BESTIAL HOGGISH
OBSCENE PIGGISH SQUALID
UNCLEAN ORDUROUS SLUTTISH
FILTRATE MALLEIN
FILTRATION BAGGING
FIN ARM RAG RIB ANAL BURR FANG
HAND KEEL SAIL FLASH PINNA
CAUDAL FINLET ACANTHA FEATHER
FLIPPER PINNULE VENTRAL
FORELIMB PECTORAL
FINAGLE CHEAT TRICK REVOKE
DECEIVE FENAGLE
FINAL LAST UTTER FINIAL LATTER
RUNOFF ULTIMA UTMOST DARREIN
DERNIER EXTREME FINALIS
OUTMOST PARTING SUPREME
ABSOLUTE DECISIVE DECRETAL
DEFINITE EVENTUAL FAREWELL
ULTIMATE
(— STANZA) ENVOI
FINALE END CODA FINIS ENDING
CLOSING
FINALITY END ERGO
FINALLY YET LAST AFINE LASTLY
FINANCE TAX BACK BANK FUND
GOODS REVENUE TAXATION
TREASURE
FINANCIAL FISCAL MONETARY
FINANCIER MONEYMAN
FINBACK WHALE FINNER GIBBAR
FINFISH RORQUAL JUBARTAS
FINCH FINK MORO PAPE JUNCO
SERIN TERIN BURION CANARY
CITRIL LINNET PALILA SISKIN
TOWHEE BUNTING CHEWINK
PEEWEEP REDHEAD REDPOLL
SENEGAL SPARROW TANAGER
WAXBILL AMADAVAT COMBASOU
FIRETAIL GOULDIAN GROSBEAK
HAWFINCH SNOWBIRD
(— FLOCK) CHARM
FIND GET RUG MEET CATCH INVENT
LOCATE STRIKE ADJUDGE FINDING
DISCOVER SCROUNGE
(— FAULT) CARP BARGE BLAME
CAVIL GRONT KNOCK PINCH SCOLD
NATTER ARRAIGN
(— GUILTY) ATTAINT CONVICT
(— OUT) AFIND CHECK ESSAY

LEARN SPELL TROVE DETECT
CONTRIVE DECIPHER DISCOVER
(— REFUGE) BIEL BIELD
(— SOLUTION) SOLVE
(— THE SUM) SUMMATE
(— TIME) EEM
FINDER SIGHT SEEKER FOUNDER
FINDING TROVER INQUEST VERDICT
FINE CRO GAY RUM TAX BEIN BIEN
BRAW CAIN CROP DIRE ERIC FAIR
GENT GOOD HUNK JAKE LEVY NICE
PURE RARE SEPT SLAP TALL TEAR
TINE TRIM ABWAB BONNY BRAVE
BULLY CHECK DAISY DANDY DELIE
DUCKY FRAIL GAUDY GRAND GREAT
HUNKY ISSUE KELTY MULCT NOBLE
RORTY SHARP SHEER SMALL SPALE
SWEET UNLAW WALLY WHITE
AMENDE AMERCE BONNIE BRAWLY
BRIGHT CHEESY CHOICE CLEVER
COSTLY CRAFTY DAINTY FACETE
FINISH FLUTED GERSUM HUNGRY
ORNATE PRETTY PROPER RANSOM
SARAAD SCONCE SERENE SILKEN
SLIGHT SPIFFY TENDER CLARIFY
CONDEMN CORKING CUNNING
ELEGANT ESTREAT FERDWIT
FINICAL FORFEIT FRAGILE GALANAS
GALLANT GALLOWS GRADELY
IMMENSE MARCHET MERCHET
MURDRUM ORFGILD PENALTY
PERFECT REFINED SCUTAGE
STAVING TENUOUS TOPPING
VALIANT ABSOLUTE BLOODWIT
BUDGEREE CAVALIER CLINKING
DELICATE DUSTLIKE FLITWITE
FOOTGELD HANDSOME LASHLITE
MARITAGE PENALIZE PESHKASH
PLEASANT SKILLFUL SPLENDID
SUPERIOR WARDWITE WIRESPUN
(— AGAINST SERVANTS) CHECK
(— FOR KILLING) BOTE
(— IN LIEU OF FLOGGING) HIDE
(BLOOD —) ERIC WITE
(OSTENTATIOUSLY —) GAUDY
(PRINTING OFFICE —) SOLACE
(VERY —) BUNKUM SPLENDID
(PL.) SILT FLOUR
FINE-DRAW RANTER
FINE-LOOKING SPICY SPIFFY
FINELY FINE GAILY GAYLY BRAGLY
RARELY SMALLY BRAVELY SMICKLY
SWEETLY
FINENESS ALLOY GRAIN TRICK
DENIER FINERY PURITY THREAD
EXILITY FINESSE DELICACY
(— AS RECKONED BY CARATS)
TITLE
(— OF FABRIC) CUT GAGE GAUGE
(— OF METAL) STANDARD
(— OF PITCH) COUNTS
FINERY GAUD WALY ARRAY BRAWS
WALLY BAUBLE BAWDRY BEAUTY
FEGARY GAIETY GAYETY TAWDRY
BRAVERY GAUDERY REGALIA
BEAUETRY ELEGANCE FINENESS
FOFARRAW FOLDEROL FOOFARAW
FRIPPERY ORNAMENT RIBANDRY
FINESPUN HAIR THIN TWITTERY

FINESSE ART CHEAT SKILL TRICK
PURITY SERENE CUNNING ARTIFICE
DELICACY SUBTLETY THINNESS
FINFOOT SUNBIRD
FINGER TOY PAUT PLAY DIGIT INDEX
PINKY DACTYL HANDLE MEDDLE
MEDIUS PILFER PINKIE POLLEX
ANNULAR DIGITAL MINIMUM
MINIMUS PURLOIN DIGITIZE
THRIMBLE
(— INFECTION) FELON
(FORE —) INDEX
(LITTLE —) PINKIE PIRLIE MINIMUS
AURICULAR
(RING —) RINGMAN ANNULARY
(PL.) HOOKS
FINGERFLOWER FOXGLOVE
FINGERING DOIGTE
FINGERLING PARR TROUTLET
FINGERNAIL DIGGER
(RELATING TO —) ONYCHOID
FINGERPRINT ARCH LOOP WHORL
LATENT
FINGERROOT FOXGLOVE
FINIAL EPI NOB TEE TOP CROP
KNOB KNOP KNOT BUNCH CREST
CROWN FINAL POPPY PRICKET
ORNAMENT PINNACLE
FINICAL NICE FUSSY CHOOSY
DAINTY DAPPER JAUNTY PRETTY
PRISSY SPRUCE CHOOSEY FINICKY
FINIKIN FOPPISH MINCING PICKING
SMICKER DELICATE
FINICALLY SMICKLY GINGERLY
FINICKY DINKY FIKEY FIKIE PRISSY
FINICAL FINIKIN
FINISH DO DIE END CHAR EDGE
FACE FINE MILL OVER PASS SINK
SNUG STOP BLOOM BOUND CEASE
CHARE CHEVE CLOSE CROWN
FEEZE GLACE GLAZE LIMIT SPEED
UPPER BOTTOM BUSHEL FULFIL
FULLDO PLISSE SETTLE WINDUP
ABSOLVE ACHIEVE DEPETER
EXECUTE FLUTING FULFILL PERFECT
SURFACE COMPLETE CONCLUDE
DEPRETER DRESSING FINALIZE
FROSTING TERMINAL
(— CAREFULLY) NEATEN
(— CLOTH) BURL CONVERT
(— OF FABRIC) CIRE HOLLAND
(— OF PAPER) STIPPLE
(— OFF) DASH CRUSH
(— STONE) COMB BOAST DROVE
(— WITH A SEAM) FELL
(— WORK) FLOOR
(CALENDERED —) CHASING
(DULL —) MAT MATTE
(GLAZED —) GLACE LACKER
LACQUER
(STUCCO —) SPATTER
(SUPERFICIAL —) BLAZONRY
FINISHED BY DID OER PAU DONE
DOWN FINE GONE OVER RIPE SHOT
ENDED EXACT KAPUT NAPOO
ROUND CLOSED NAPOOH ORNATE
PERFECT REFINED ROUNDED
STOPPED BANKRUPT CLIMAXED
GOFFERED LUSTERED POLISHED

(— IN NATURAL COLOR) FAIR
(— WITH NAP) BRUSHED
(ABSOLUTELY —) SUNK
(HIGHLY —) SUAVE
(IMPERFECTLY —) RUDE
FINISHER EYER ENDER GAFFER
BEETLER CEMENTER ENAMELER
FINISHING CRUSHING
FINITE LIMITED

FINLAND
CAPITAL: HELSINKI HELSINGFORS
COIN: PENNI MARKKA
DIVISION: IJORE VILLIPURI
GOD: TAPIO JUMALA
ISLAND: ALAND KARLO AALAND
HAILUTO VALLGRUND
ISTHMUS: KARELIA
LAKE: JUO MUO KEMI KIVI NASI
OULO PURU PYHA SIMO ENARE
HAUKI INARI KALLA LAPPA LESTI
PUULA LENTUA SAIMAA SOUNNE
SYVARI KOITERE NILAKKA
PIELIEN
LANGUAGE: AVAR LAPP UGRIC
MAGYAR OSTYAK TARAST
SAMOYED ESTONIAN
MEASURE: KANNU TUNNA VERST
FATHOM SJOMIL OTTINGER
SKALPUND TUNNLAND
MOUNTAIN: HALTIA
NAME: SUOMI
PARLIAMENT: EDUSKUNTA
PROVINCE: HAME KYMI LAPPI
VAASA
RIVER: II KALA OULU SIMO TENO
IVALO LOTTA OUNAS SIIKA
IIJOKI LAPUAN MUONIO PASVIK
TORNIO KITINEN KOKEMAKI
TOWN: ABA ABO KEM KEMI OULU
PORI VASA ENARE ESPOO
KOTKA LAHTI TURKU VAASA
IMATRA KUOPIO MIKKELI
TAMPERE HELSINKI
TRIBE: HAME VEPS VEPSE UGRIAN
KARJALAISET SUOMALAISET

FINLET PINNULE
FINN FIOUN INGER OSTIAK OSTYAK
TAVAST INGRIAN CHEREMIS
INGERMAN SWEKOMAN
(PL.) SUOMI
FIORD FJORD INLET
FIORIN KNOTGRASS
FIPPLE FLUTE RECORDER
FIR VER LARCH SAPIN BAUMIER
LASHORN PINABETE
FIR CLUB MOSS FOXFEET
FIRE CAN FEU LOW AGNI APOY BAI
BRIO BURN HEAT KILN LOWE POC
SWAP SWOP ZEAL ARDOR ARSON
BLAST BLAZE BREAK BURST EMPT
FEVER GLEED INGLE LIGHT LOGHI
LOOSE LOUGH PLUFF SERVE SHO
SQUIB STOKE AROUSE ENGHLE
EXCITE FERVOR IGNITE INCITE
KINDLE SMUDGE SPIRIT SPLEEN
VULCAN ANIMATE BONFIRE BURNI

BURNOUT CHIMNEY DISMISS
EMITTER EXPLODE FURNACE
GLIMMER INFLAME INSPIRE
SMOLDER BACKFIRE BALEFIRE
CAMPFIRE DETONATE HELLFIRE
ILLUMINE IRRITATE NEEDFIRE
SMOULDER VIVACITY
(— A REVOLVER) FAN
(— ON) AFIRE
(— THE CHARGE) HIT
(— TWO ROUNDS) DOUBLE
(— UPON) GUN SPRAY
(CROSS —) GANTLET GAUNTLET
(DAMPENED —) SMOTHER
(FOREST —) BREAK
(LITTLE —) SPONK SPUNK
(MASSED —) ARTILLERY
(PEAT —) GREESAGH
(RUNNING-OUT —) DANDY
(SIGNAL —) BALE BEACON
BALEFIRE
FIRE ALARM FIREBOX
FIREARM ARM GUN IRON SHOT
TUBE FIRER ORGAN PIECE RIFLE
JEZAIL MAGNUM MAUSER MUSKET
PISTOL POPPER BOMBARD CARBINE
CURRIER DEMIHAG HANDGUN
PINFIRE SHOOTER SPANNER
ARQUEBUS BROWNING CULVERIN
EXPELLER EXPLODER PETRONEL
REVOLVER
(PL.) HARDWARE ARTILLERY
FIRE ARROW MALLEOLUS
FIREBACK REREDOS MACARTNEY
FIRE BEETLE COCUYO CUCUYO
ELATER ELATERID
FIREBOAT PALANDER
FIREBRAND BLAZE BRAND BLEERY
BOUTEFEU
FIREBRICK QUARLE
(PL.) GROG
FIREBUG BUG ARSONIST
FIRE CARRIER PORTFIRE
FIRECLAY THILL
FIRE COVER CURFEW CURPHEW
FIRECRACKER DEVIL SQUIB PETARD
SALUTE CRACKER SNAPPER
FIREWORK WHIZBANG
FIRE-CURED DARK
FIREDAMP GAS FOULNESS WILDFIRE
FIREDART PHALARICA
FIREDOG DOG
FIRE ENGINE RIG TUB MANUAL
FIRE EXTINGUISHER SQUIRT
EXTINCTOR
FIRE FIGHTER EXEMPT HOTSHOT
FIREFLY CUCUYO FIREBUG GLOWFLY
LAMPFLY FIREWORM GLOWWORM
LAMPYRID
FIREGUARD FENDER
FIRELINE GUTTER
FIRELOCK FUSEE FUZEE SPANNER
FIREMAN VAMP FIRER FUELER
STOKER TEASER TIZEUR FIREBOY
HOSEMAN BAKEHEAD FURNACER
FIREPLACE FOCUS FOGON FORGE
FOYER GRATE INGLE TISAR HEARTH
CHIMNEY CHEMINEE
(— AND CHIMNEY) STACK

(— STONE) MANTEL
(PORTABLE —) BARBECUE
BARBEQUE
FIREPLUG PLUG HYDRANT
FIRER STOKER BLASTER
FIRESIDE SMOKE HEARTH
FIRESTAND HASTER HASTENER
FIRE THORN PYRACANTH
FIREWEED FIRETOP PILEWEED
PILEWORT
FIREWOOD FIRE LENA SLAB WOOD
CHUNK FAGOT BILLET BILLOT
ELDING FIRING TALWOOD FIREBOTE
TALLWOOD TALSHIDE
FIREWORK JET SUN GERB DEVIL
GERBE PEEOY SAXON SHELL WHEEL
FIZGIG MAROON PETARD ROCKET
SALUTE SHOWER TRACER CASCADE
SERPENT SPARKER TORPEDO
FOUNTAIN SPARKLER
(PL.) FUN FIRE
FIRE WORSHIPPER PARSI GHEBER
GHEBRE PARSEE
FIRING FIRE FUEL COUGH SALVO
BURNING DRUMFIRE
FIRKIN VESSEL
FIRM HUI BUFF FAST HARD IRON
NASH SURE TAUT TRIG TRIM CHAMP
CORKY CRISP DENSE FIRMA FIXED
HARDY HOUSE LOYAL RIGID SOLID
SOUND STARK STIFF STITH STOUT
SWITH TIGHT HARDEN HEARTY
SECURE SETTLE SICCAR SICKER
SINEWY STABLE STANCH STEADY
STEEVE STOLID STRONG STURDY
ADAMANT CERTAIN COMPACT
COMPANY CONCERN CONFIRM
CONTEXT DECIDED DURABLE
STAUNCH UNMOVED CONSTANT
FAITHFUL FIDUCIAL OBDURATE
RESOLUTE SUBSTANT UNSHAKEN
(— BUT EASILY CUT) SEMISOFT
(NOT —) FUZZY
FIRMAMENT SKY DEEP POLE CARRY
CANOPY HEAVEN EXPANSE
EMPYREAN EMPYREUM EXPANSUM
FIRMLY BUFF FAST FIRM HARD
SADLY STARK TIGHT HARDLY
SQUARE SURELY SOLIDLY
SECURELY STRONGLY
FIRMNESS BODY GRIT IRON ETHAN
PROOF FIXURE COURAGE FIRMITY
GRANITE BACKBONE DECISION
FASTNESS SECURITY SOLIDITY
STRENGTH TENACITY
FIRST ERST FUST GULE HEAD HIGH
MAIN ALPHA CHIEF FORME NIEVE
PRIMA PRIME PRIMO MAIDEN
PRIMAL PRIMUS VIRGIN FIRSTLY
HIGHEST INITIAL LEADING PRIMARY
EARLIEST FOREHAND FOREMOST
FORMERLY ORIGINAL PARAVANT
PREMIERE PRINCEPS
(— PRIZE) BLUE
(— SERGEANT) TOP
(— STATE) DELAWARE
FIRSTBORN AYNE EIGNE ELDEST
FIRST-CLASS GAY TOP BOSS FLASH
PRIME BUNKUM STUNNING

FIRST-FRUITS ANNATES
FIRSTHAND DIRECT PRIMARY
ORIGINAL
FIRST-RATE BOSS BRAG GOOD JAKE
MAIN SLAP BULLY DANDY LUMMY
PRIME SLEEK SLICK SUPER SWELL
BONSER BONZER BOSKER CHEESY
FAMOUS TIPTOP BLIGHTY BOSHTER
CAPITAL SKOOKUM STELLAR
TOPPING CHAMPION CLINKING
CLIPPING TOPNOTCH
FIRTH KYLE FRITH INLET COPPICE
ESTUARY
FISCAL BURSAL MONETARY
FISH AU ID AKU AWA AYU BIB CAT
COD DAB DAP DIB EEL FIN GAR GIG
GOO HEN IDE IHI JIG JUG ORF RAY
SAR TAI UKU BANK BARB BASS
BOCE BOGA CARP CAST CERO
CHUB CHUG CHUM CLOD CRAB
CUSK DACE DORY DRAG DRAW
DRUM ERSE FUGU GADE GHOL
GOBY GRIG HAKE HIND HUCH HUSO
JACK JUNK LINE LING LOTE MADO
MERO MOLA OPAH PEAL PEGA PIKE
POOR POUT PRIM QUAB RAIL RUDD
RUFF SCAD SCUP SEER SHAD SOLE
SPET SPIN SPOT TILE TORO TUNA
ACARA AHOLE AKULE ANGLE ATULE
BEGTI BINNY BLEAK BOLTI BOLTY
BREAM BULLY BULTI CABIO CATLA
CHIRO CISCO COBIA CONEY DANIO
DORAB DRAIL DRIFT DRIVE ELOPS
ERIZO FLOAT FLUKE FOGAS FRIAR
GADID GRUNT HILSA HUCHO JUREL
KILLY LAKER LANCE MANTA MIDGE
MINIM MORAY OTTER PERCH PIABA
PORGY POWAN POWER REINA
ROACH SAIDE SARGO SAURY SEINE
SHARK SKATE SMELT SNOEK
SNOOK SPRAT SQUID SULEA SWEEP
TENCH TRABU TROLL TROUT TUNNY
UMBRA VIUVA VORAZ WAHOO WHIFF
AIMARA ALEVIN ANABAS ANGLER
BARBEL BARBER BENNET BISKOP
BLENNY BONITO BOWFIN BUMPER
BURBOT CALLOP CANDIL CAPLIN
CARANX CARIBE COELHO COTTID
CREOLE CUCHIA CUNNER DARTER
DASSIE DENTEX FISHET GANOID
GINNEL GULPER GUNNEL HAMLET
HAPUKU HILSAH HUSSAR INANGA
KOKOPU LAUNCE LEDGER LIGGER
LOUVAR MAIGRE MARLIN MENISE
MILTER MINNOW MOLOID MULLET
NONNAT PHOEBE PLAICE POMPON
PUFFER PUNECA REDFIN REMORA
ROBALO ROUGHY RUNNER SABALO
SALELE SALEMA SALMON SAPSAP
SARDEL SAUGER SAUREL SERRAN
SHINER SIERRA SIMARA SPARID
SUCKER TAILER TAIMEN TANDAN
TARPON TAUTOG TESTAR TETARD
TINOSA TOMCOD TURBOT VENDIS
WALLER WEAVER WIRRAH WRASSE
ZINGEL ALEWIFE ALFIONA ANCHOVY
BACALAO BARBUDO BATFISH
BEARDIE BERYCID BIRCHIR BOXFISH
BRAGGLE BUFFALO CABEZON

CANDIRU CAPELIN CAPLING CATFISH
CAVALLA CAVALLY CHIMERA
CHROMID CICHLID CLUPEID CONVICT
CORVINA COWFISH CRAPPIE
CROAKER CUTLIPS CYCLOID
DRABBLE DREPANE DRUMMER
EELPOUT ESCOLAR FATHEAD
FINFISH GALJOEN GEELBEC
GEELBEK GOBIOID GOGGLER
GOLDEYE GOURAMI GRAYSBY
GROUPER GRUNTER GUAPENA
GUAVINA GUDGEON GULARIS
GURNARD GWYNIAD HADDOCK
HAGFISH HALIBUT HARMOOT
HERRING HINALEA HOGFISH
HOUTING ICEFISH ICHTHUS INCONNU
JAWFISH JEWFISH JUGULAR
LABROID LAGARTO LONGFIN
MACHETE MAHSEER MAYFISH
MOJARRA MOONEYE MORWONG
OARFISH OLDWIFE OQUASSA
PEGASUS PIGFOOT PINTADO
PIRANHA POISSON POLLACK
POMFRET POMPANO RONQUIL
SANCORD SARDINE SAUROID
SAVELHA SAWFISH SCALARE
SCAROID SCHELLY SCULPIN
SENNETT SILURUS SLEEPER
SMUTTER SNAPPER SOLDIER
SPAWNER STERLET SUNFISH
TELEOST TOMTATE TOPKNOT
TORPEDO TUBFISH UMBRANA
UNICORN VENDACE VIAJACA
WAREHOU WAUBEEN WHAPUKA
WHAPUKU WHITING ALBACORE
ALFONSIN APOGONID ARAPAIMA
ATHERINE BAITFISH BALISTID
BIGMOUTH BILLFISH BLENNOID
BLUEBACK BLUEFISH BOARFISH
BONEFISH BRISLING BROTULID
BULLHEAD CACKEREL CANCHITO
CARANGID CARANGIN CARDINAL
CATALINA CATALUFA CHANCITO
CHIMAERA CHOANATE CHROMIDE
CORACINE CROSSOPT CYPRINID
DEALFISH DIPNEUST DITREMID
DONCELLA DRAGONET DRUMFISH
DUMBFISH ECHENEID ELEOTRID
EPISCATE FALLFISH FILEFISH
FLAGFISH FLATFISH FLATHEAD
FLOUNDER FOOLFISH FROGFISH
FUNDULUS GAMBUSIA GEELBECK
GILTHEAD GOATFISH GOLDFISH
GRAINING GRAYFISH GRAYLING
GREYSKIN HAIRFISH HALFBEAK
HANDFISH HANDLINE HAPLOMID
HARDHEAD HARDTAIL HOMOCERC
HORNFISH HORSEMAN JACKFISH
JUMPROCK KABELJOU KARMOUTH
KELPFISH KINGFISH LADYFISH
LUMPFISH MACKEREL MENHADEN
MILKFISH MOONFISH PICKEREL
PILCHARD PORKFISH QUERIMAN
ROBALITO ROCKFISH ROCKLING
ROSEFISH SAILFISH SALANGID
SANDFISH SANDGOBY SCIAENID
SCOMBRID SCOTSMAN SEERFISH
SKILFISH SKIPJACK SOAPFISH
STUDFISH STURGEON TALLYWAG

TARWHINE TERAGLIN TILEFISH
TOADFISH TREEFISH TREVALLY
WARMOUTH WEAKFISH WHISTLER
WRYMOUTH
(— BY TROLLING) DRAIL
(— FOR EELS) GRIG SNIGGLE
(— FOR SALMON) SNIGGER
(— NETTED) LIFT
(— NOT UNDERSIZED) COUNT
KEEPER
(— TAPE) SNAKE
(— THROUGH ICE) CHUG
(— UNDERWATER) GOGGLE
(25 LBS. OF —) STICK
(BLIND —) PINKFISH
(CURED —) DUNFISH
(FABLED —) MAH
(FEMALE —) RAUN SPAWNER
(FIGHTING —) PLAKAT
(HAWAIIAN —) AU
(HERALDIC —) CHABOT
(INDIAN —) ROHU
(NUMBER OF —) SCHOOL
(OLD —) MOSSBACK
(QUANTITY OF —) MAZE
(RAW —) SASHIMI
(REFUSE —) CHUM SHACK
(SALTED —) COR
(SPLIT —) KLIPFISH
(THIN —) RACER
(YOUNG —) FRY ALEVIN
FISH BASKET POT CAUL CREEL
SLATH
FISH BOX TRUNK
FISH BRINER COBBERER
FISH CLEANER GILLER
FISH DRESSER IDLER
FISHER MART EELER PEKAN SABLE
SOBOL TAIRA TAYRA MARTEN
SEINER WEJACK MARTRIX TRAWLER
TROLLER
(SPONGE —) HOOKER
FISHERMAN (ALSO SEE ANGLER)
TOTY EELER ANGLER GIGMAN
GILLER KEDGER MAIMUL SEINER
WORMER ADMIRAL DORYMAN
DRAGMAN PRAWNER RODSTER
SHANKER SMELTER STRIKER
TRAWLER TROTTER TROWMAN
PETERMAN PISCATOR SEASONER
SHRIMPER
FISHERY FISHING PISCARY SEALERY
FISHGARTH WEIR
FISHHOOK FLY GIG HOOK LARI
ANGLE DRAIL KIRBY LARIN SLEEK
ANGULE SPROAT KENDALL
ABERDEEN BARBLESS CARLISLE
LIMERICK
(PL.) PULLDEVIL
FISHING PIKING ANGLING BANKING
BASSING GRAINING SNOEKING
(— TOOL) OVERSHOT
FISHING GROUNDS HAAF
FISHING ROD GAD
FISHING TACKLE TEW LEDGER
FISHLINE GIMP TROT SNELL TRAWL
DIPSEY LIGGER BOULTER GANGION
OUTLINE SETLINE TRIMMER
HAIRLINE TROTLINE

FISH LOUSE GISLER
FISHMONGER PESSONER
FISH NEST REDD
FISHNET FLUE SEINE SETNET
FISHPOND VIVER PISCINA VIVARIUM
FISHPOUND MADRAGUE
FISH SPEAR GRANES WASTER
LEISTER
FISHTAIL UROSOME
FISHWAY PASS RACEWAY
FISHY DULL FUNNY GLASSY VACANT
FISSION BREAKING CLEAVAGE
CLEAVING GAMOGENY SCISSION
FISSURE GAP CHAP CONE FLAW
GOOL GULL LEAK LOCH LODE RENT
RIFT RIMA RIME SEAM SLIT VEIN
VENT CHASM CHINE CHINK CLEFT
CRACK FLAKE PIPER PORTA SHAKE
SPLIT ZYGON CLEAVE CRANNY
DIVIDE LESION RICTUS RIMULA
SPRING SULCUS BLEMISH CREVICE
FISSURA OPENING SWALLET
APERTURE BLOWHOLE CLEAVAGE
COLOBOMA CREVASSE INCISURE
QUEBRADA SCISSURA TRAVERSE
(— IN BUILDING STONE) DRY
(— IN HEEL) GAUG
(— IN MAST) SPRING
(— IN PLATEAU) ABRA
(PL.) RHAGADES
FISSURED RIMATE CHAPPED
CLEFTED FISSATE
FIST JOB DUKE NAVE NEIF NIEF
FOIST GRASP INDEX NIEVE CLENCH
CLUTCH DADDLE EFFORT MAULER
MAULEY PINKER STRIKE ATTEMPT
CLUBFIST FISTNOTE PUFFBALL
TIGHTWAD
FISTFIGHT TURNUP
FISTICUFF BOX NEVEL FISTIFY
FISTULA EGILOPS
FISTULOUS TUBULAR
FIT GO APT FAY GEE PAN RIG SIT
ABLE AGUE FEAT FURY GOOD HARD
KINK MEET PANG RIPE SORT SUIT
TURN WELL WHIM ADAPT ADEPT
APPLY BESIT CHINK CLICK DIGNE
EXIES FADGE FANCY FITLY FRAME
FRISK FUROR HAPPY ICTUS MATCH
PITCH QUEME QUIRK READY RIGHT
SERVE SPASM SPELL START STOUR
SWOON TALLY ACCESS ADJUST
ANSWER ATTACK BECOME BEHOVE
BESORT DUEFUL FINISH FITTEN
HABILE HEPPEN LIABLE PROPER
SEASON SEEMLY SPLEEN SQUARE
STREAK STROKE STRONG SUITED
WORTHY ADAPTED BEHOOVE
CAPABLE CONDIGN CONFORM
CORRECT DESPAIR FASHION FITTING
HEALTHY PREPARE QUALIFY
SEIZURE TANTRUM WIDDRIM
ADEQUATE BECOMING DOVETAIL
ELIGIBLE GLOOMING IDONEOUS
OUTBREAK PAROXYSM PASSABLE
SUITABLE SYNCOPES
(— CLOSELY) FAY CHOCK
(— CORNER TO CORNER) BUTT
(— FOR THE GALLOWS) WIDDIFOW

(— **IN**) GO
(— **INTO SOCKET**) FANG
(— **LOOSELY**) SLOP
(— **OF ANGER**) FRAP FUME HUFF
RAGE TIFF FLING RAVERY SPLEEN
(— **OF DEPRESSION**) HUMP
(— **OF ILL HUMOR**) TIG FUNK TOUT
GRUMPS
(— **OF ILL TEMPER**) TANTRUM
(— **OF ILLNESS**) DROW TOUT FLING
(— **OF LAUGHTER**) GIRD KINK
(— **OF NERVOUSNESS**) TWITCHET
(— **OF RESENTMENT**) PIQUE SNUFF
(— **OF SHIVERING**) AGUE GROOSE
(— **OF SULKS**) GEE STRUM
(— **OF SULLENNESS**) DOD
(— **OF TEMPER**) WAX BAIT HISSY
TETCH GROUCH SPLEEN SQUALL
BRAINGE
(— **OF WEEPING**) CRY
(— **OF YAWNING**) GAPE
(— **ONE WITHIN ANOTHER**) NEST
(— **OUT**) ARM BUSK BEFIT EQUIP
ASTORE CLOTHE OUTFIT APPAREL
APPOINT FURNISH HABILLE
ACCOUTER
(— **RIFLE BARREL**) BED
(— **TIGHTLY**) STUFF
(— **TO BE DRUNK**) SORBILE
(— **TOGETHER**) MESH COAPT JOINT
COHERE ASSEMBLE
(— **UP**) RIG
(— **WITH COMPACTNESS**) BOX
(— **WITH FETTERS**) GARNISH
(**RITUALLY** —) KOSHER
(PL.) LUNES
ITCH LINER
ITFUL GERY CATCHY GERFUL
GLEAMY CURSORY FLIGHTY
RESTLESS UNSTABLE VARIABLE
ITLY FIT PAT DULY FEATLY GLADLY
MEETLY TIDELY APROPOS HAPPILY
PROPERLY SUITABLY
ITNESS FORM APTNESS DECENCY
DECORUM DIGNITY APTITUDE
CAPACITY IDONEITY JUSTNESS
PROPERTY
ITTED APT ABLE ADAPT KEYED
SUITED ADAPTED ENGAGED
ADJUSTED ASSORTED ELIGIBLE
ITTER TUBER GASMAN
ITTING TO APT CAP DUE LUG PAT
BUTT FAIR FEAT FORK HARP JUMP
JUST KIND MEET CLEAT HAPPY
QUEME WORTH BECOME CLENCH
CLEVIS LEADER PROPER SADDLE
SEEMLY WASHER ADAPTER
CONGRUE PENDANT SERVING
SHACKLE SUCTION TACTFUL
CONDULET DECOROUS GRACEFUL
RIGHTFUL SUITABLE
(— **TIGHTLY**) CLOSE
(**PIPE** —) CROSS ELBOW
(PL.) BRASS COVER REPAREL
FITMENTS
IVE CINQ FUNF CINQUE EPSILON
QUINQUE
(— **CENTS**) JITNEY NICKEL

(— **HUNDRED DOLLARS, POUNDS**)
MONKEY
(— **IN CRAPS**) PHOEBE
(— **OF TRUMPS**) PEDRO
(— **YEARS**) LUSTRUM
(**TWO** —**S**) QUINAS
FIVES BALL SNACK
FIVESTONES SNOBS
FIX BOX JAM PEG PIN SET FAST FIRM
GAFF GLUE HOLD HOLE JAMB LOCK
MEND MOOR NAIL PICK RELY SEAL
SPOT STAY AFFIX ALLOT DEFIX
FOUND GRAFT GRAVE IMBED INFIX
LIMIT PLACE PLANT POINT POSIT
SEIZE STATE STEEK STELL TRYST
ADJUST ANCHOR ARREST ASSIGN
ASSIZE ATTACH CEMENT CLINCH
DEFINE ENROOT ENTAIL FASTEN
FICCHE FIXATE FREEZE GROUND
IMPALE REPAIR REVAMP SETTLE
SQUARE TEMPER APPOINT
ARRANGE CALCIFY CONFIRM
DELIMIT DESTINE DILEMMA GRAPPLE
IMPLANT IMPRESS IMPRINT
PREPARE STATION RENOVATE
TRANSFIX
(— **AMOUNT**) AFFEER
(— **ATTENTION**) NAIL
(— **FIRMLY**) SEAL FREEZE IMPACT
INCUBE RAMPIRE
(— **PRICE**) ASSIZE CHARGE SETTLE
(— **UPON**) CHAP AFFIX
FIXATION FETICH FETISH
FIXATIVE FIXER SKATOLE AMBRETTE
EUDESMOL HYRACEUM LABDANUM
FIXED PAT PUT SAD SET SOT FAST
FIRM FLAT HARD GIVEN SIKER
STAID UPSET FINITE FROZEN INTENT
MENDED SICKER STABLE STATED
STEADY STRONG CERTAIN
DORMANT EMPIGHT HABITED
LIMITED SETTLED SITFAST STATARY
STATIVE STELLED ACCURATE
ARRANGED ATTACHED CONSTANT
DEFINITE EXPLICIT FASTENED
IMMOBILE IRONCLAD MOVELESS
RESIDENT RESOLUTE STANDING
STUBBORN
(**NOT** —) FLUID SHIFTY FUGITIVE
FIXEDLY SAD FAST FIRM FIXLY
INTENTLY
FIXEDNESS FASTNESS
FIXER PATCH
FIXTURE ANNEX EVENT GUARD
FAUCET SHIELD BRACKET CREEPER
KNOCKER THIMBLE
(**LIGHTING** —) SCONCE
(**STORE** —) GONDOLA
FIZZING FIZZY GASSING
FIZZLE FLOP FUSS BARNEY FAILURE
FLIVVER
FLABBINESS MYATONIA
FLABBY LAX FOZY LASH LIMP WEAK
BAGGY FLASH FOGGY FRUSH SAPPY
WOOZY CASHIE DOUGHY FEEBLE
FLAGGY FLAPPY LIMBER QUAGGY
WATERY FLACCID YIELDING
FLACCID LIMP WOOZY FLABBY

FLAGGY EMARCID FLACKED
YIELDING
FLAG FAG LAG SAG SOD FAIL FANE
FLAT HOOK JACK JADE LECK PINE
TURF WAFT WAIF WILT CREST
DROOP FAINT FLAKE SEDGE SLAKE
UNION VEXIL WHEFT WHIFF BANNER
BOUGEE BURGEE COLORS CORNET
EMBLEM ENSIGN FANION GUIDON
LEVERS PENCEL PENNON SIGNAL
TABARD WIMPLE ANCIENT BEEWORT
CALAMUS CURTAIN
DECLINE DRAPEAU FANACLE
LABARUM PENDANT PENNANT
SCOURGE BANDEROL BRATTACH
GONFALON HANDFLAG LANGUISH
PAVILION STANDARD STREAMER
TRICOLOR VEXILLUM WATCHMAN
(— **CORNER**) UNION
(— **OF DENMARK**) DANEBROG
(— **OF TRANSVAAL**) VIERKLEUR
(— **OF TRUCE**) KARTEL
(— **OF U.S.**) GRIDIRON
(**BLUE** — **WITH WHITE SQUARE**)
PETER
(**CAVALRY** —) STANDARD
(**KNOTTED** —) WAFT
(**PIRATE** —) ROGER
(**SERPENT-LIKE** —) DRACO ANGUIS
(**SHIP'S** —) DUSTER
(**TURKISH** —) ALEM
(**WATER** —) SAG
FLAG BEARER GUIDON ANCIENT
FLAGELLANT WHIPPER SCOURGER
(PL.) ALBI
FLAGELLATE MONAS
FLAGELLUM WHIP RUNNER
KONSEAL WHIPLASH
FLAGEOLET PIPE ZUFOLO BASAREE
LARIGOT SIBILUS ZUFFOLO
MONAULOS
FLAGGING WEAK LANGUID
FLAGITIOUS WICKED CORRUPT
HEINOUS CRIMINAL FLAGRANT
GRIEVOUS
FLAGON GUN STOUP BOTTLE
VESSEL FLACKET FLAGONET
REHOBOAM
FLAGRANT BAD RED RANK GROSS
ODIOUS STRONG WANTON WICKED
GLARING HATEFUL HEINOUS
SCARLET VIOLENT SHAMEFUL
FLAGSHIP FLAG ADMIRAL
FLAGSTONE FLAG LECK SLAB
FAVUS
FLAIL BEAT FLOG WHIP DRASH FRAIL
THRAIL THRASH THRESH SWINGLE
SWIPPLE STRICKLE
FLAIR RAY BENT NOSE ODOR SMELL
GENIUS LEANING
FLAKE CHIP FILM FLAG FLAW RACK
SNOW FLANK FLECK FLOCK LAMIN
SCALE SLATE SPALL SPAWL STRIP
APHTHA HURDLE LAMINA PALING
FLAUGHT SHAVING FLOCCULE
FRAGMENT
(— **OF METAL**) FLITTER
(— **OF SNOW**) FLAG
FLAKY SCALY SHIVERY

FLAMBE JUBILEE
FLAMBEAU TORCH
FLAMBOYANCE BLARE PANACHE
FLAMBOYANT FLORID GARISH
ORNATE BUCKEYE FLAMING
GORGEOUS
FLAME LOW FIRE GLOW LOWE
ARDOR BLAZE FLARE FLASH GLARE
GLEED INGLE LIGHT RESEPH
TONGUE BURNING FLAMELET
INKINDLE
(ACETYLENE —) CALCIUM
(SMALL —) SPUNK FLAMELET
FLAMMULE
(PL.) GLEED
FLAME TREE KURRAJONG
FLAMING LIVE AFIRE FIERY FLAMY
VIVID AFLARE ARDENT BLAZING
BURNING FLARING FLAGRANT
FLAN PLANCHET
FLANGE BEAD BOSS BEZEL COLLAR
COLLET FLANCH SHROUD FEATHER
DUCKBILL FOLLOWER
(WITHOUT —) BALD
FLANGER FLAYER GOUGER
FLANK LEER LISK SIDE WING CHEEK
SKIRT THIGH BORDER FLITCH
FLANNEL LANA DOMETT SAXONY
STAMIN WHITTLE MOLLETON
SWANSKIN
FLAP FAN LUG ROB TAB TAG TAP
WAP BATE BEAT BLOW CLAP FLIP
FLOG FLOP GILL LOBE LOMA SLAM
SLAT WAFF WELT ALARM APRON
FLACK FLAFF FLICK BALLUP
BANGLE LAPPET LIBBET STRIKE
TONGUE WAFFLE WINNOW AILERON
BLINDER CLICKET FLAPPET FLICKER
FLOUNCE FLUTTER SWINDLE
VALANCE AVENTAIL BACKFLAP
COATTAIL CODPIECE TURNOVER
(— OF BOOTEE) FLY
(— OF GARMENT) LAP
(— OF HAT OR CAP) VALANCE
(— OF HINGE) LEAF
(— ON HOLSTER) FLOUNCE
(— ON SADDLE) SKIRT JOCKEY
(— VIOLENTLY) FLOG SLAT
(CARDIAC —) CUSP
(FLESHY —) GILL
(TROUSERS' —) FALL
FLAPPER FLAP FLOPPER SNICKET
FLAPPING WAFF WHUTTER
FLARE BELL FLUE BLAZE FLAME
FLASH FLECK FUSEE LIGHT SPIRT
TORCH FLANCH SIGNAL SPREAD
FLICKER TRUMPET OUTBURST
(— ON SHIPBOARD) DUCK
(— UP) KINDLE
FLARING BELL FLUE EVASE GAUDY
AFLARE FLAMING GLARING
SWAGGER BOUFFANT DAZZLING
FLASH DOT BEAT DASH LAIT LAMP
LASH LEAM POOL SHOT STAB WINK
BLASH BLAZE BURST FLAME FLARE
FLOSH FLUFF GLADE GLAIK GLEAM
GLENT GLINT LEVIN MARSH SPARK
STEAM BOTTLE FILLIP GLANCE
QUIVER FLAUGHT FOULDRE

GLIMMER GLIMPSE GLISTEN
GLITTER INSTANT LIGHTEN QUICKEN
SHIMMER SPARKLE TWINKLE
SPLINTER SUNBURST
(— FORTH) OUTRAY
(HOT —) FLUSHING
(NEWS —) FUDGE
FLASHBACK THROWBACK
FLASHING CURB FLASH STEEP
BRIGHT FLASHY FORWARD LAMPING
SHINING CREASING METEORIC
SLASHING SNAPPING
FLASHLIGHT BUG GLIM FLASH
TORCH PENLITE
FLASHY GAY FLAT GAUD LOUD
BAVIN FIERY GAUDY SHOWY SLEEK
FLOSSY FROTHY GARISH SLANGY
SPORTY STUNTY INSIPID RAFFISH
TINHORN DAZZLING FLASHING
SPORTING TIGERISH VEHEMENT
FLASK BOX PIG BODY HEAD HELM
JACK OLPE SNAP BETTY BULGE
FRAME GIRBA GOURD BOTTLE
FIASCO FLACON GUTTUS HELMET
LAGENA AMPULLA BOMBOLA
CANTEEN FLASKET MATRASS
TICKLER WARBURG CHRISMAL
CUCURBIT
(POCKET —) TICKLER
FLAT DEAD DOWD DULL EVEN FADE
PLAT SLOB ABODE AFLAT BANAL
BLAND BLUNT DUSTY LEVEL MOLLE
MUSTY PLAIN PLANE PRONE ROOMS
SEBKA SLAKE VAPID WALSH
AGRUFE BORING DREARY FLASHY
JEJUNE LEADEN QUATCH SEBKA
SILENT SIMOUS DECIDED FLIPPER
INSIPID INSULSE PLATOID PROSAIC
SHILPIT TABULAR UNIFORM
DIRECTLY LIFELESS UNBROKEN
WATERISH
(— AND CIRCULAR) DISCOID
(— AND SHORT) CAMUS CAMUSE
(— IN MUSIC) BEMOL MOLLE
(— OF SWORD) PLAT
(MUD —) SLOB CORCASS
(NOT —) BRISK
(SALT —) SALINA
(THEATRICAL —) JOG
FLATBOAT ARK SCOW PULLBOAT
FLATCAR FLAT IDLER LORRY
(ON A —) PIGGYBACK
FLATFISH DAB RAY BUTT DACE KITE
SLIP SOLE TONG BREAM BRILL
FLUKE QUIFF WHIFF ACEDIA CARTER
PLAICE TURBOT HALIBUT SUNFISH
TORPEDO FLOUNDER MARYSOLE
FLATHEAD SALISH
FLATIRON IRON GOOSE STEEL
SADIRON
FLATNESS BATHOS SILENCE
EVENNESS KURTOSIS
(— OF NOSE) SIMITY
FLATTEN BEAT COMB DECK EVEN
PLAT CRUSH LEVEL PLUSH SPLAT
BEETLE CLINCH DEJECT SMOOTH
SPREAD SQUASH DEPRESS EXPLAIN
PANCAKE SUBSIDE SURBASE
COMPRESS DISPIRIT

FLATTENED ECRASE OBLATE
DILATED PLANATE
FLATTER BULL CLAW COAX DAUB
FAGE FUME PALP SOAP WORD
CHARM FLOAT GLOZE HONEY PAINT
ROOSE SLEEK SMALM BECOME
BUTTER CAJOLE FICKLE FLEECH
FRAISE GLAVER KITTLE PEPPER
PHRASE SAWDER SLAVER SMOOGE
SOOTHE STROKE ADULATE BEGUILE
BLARNEY FLETHER FLUTTER
INCENSE PALAVER SOOTHER
SWEETEN WHEEDLE BESLAVER
BLANDISH BOOTLICK COLLOGUE
FLATTERER FLOIT COGGER DAUBER
EARWIG GLOZER JENKINS PRONEUR
SOOTHER BOOTLICK CLAWBACK
COURTIER DAMOCLES LOSENGER
SLAVERER SMOOTHER
FLATTERING SOAPY SMARMY
SMOOTH BUTTERY CANDIED
COURTLY GLAVERING
FLATTERY BULL BUNK DAUB FLUM
MUSH SOAP FRAIK GLOZE SALVE
TAFFY BUTTER CARNEY FLEECH
GREASE PHRASE SAWDER SLAVER
BLARNEY DAUBING EYEWASH
FAWNING FLETHER INCENSE
PALAVER CAJOLERY
FLATULENCE VAPOR
FLATULENT GASSY WINDY TURGID
POMPOUS VENTOSE FLATUOUS
INFLATED
FLATWARE SILVER
FLATWORM ACOEL FLUKE PLATODE
RADIATE POLYCLAD
FLAUNT BOSH SHOW WAVE BOAST
STOUT VAUNT PARADE DISPLAY
FLUTTER TRAIPSE BRANDISH
FLOURISH
FLAUNTING GAUDY PURPLE
FLAGGERY
FLAVONE CHROMONE
FLAVOR GAMY GOUT MASK ODOR
RASA SALT TANG ZEST AROMA
ASSAI CURRY DEVIL SAPID SAPOR
SAUCE SAVOR SCENT SPICE TASTE
TINGE ASARUM ASSAHY INFUSE
RANCIO RELISH SEASON TARAGE
FLAVOUR PERFUME SUPTION
HAUTGOUT PIQUANCY
(HIGH —) HOGO
(SPECIAL —) GUST
(UNPLEASANT —) TACK
FLAVORED SPICY TINCT SPICED
FLAVORFUL SAVOROUS
FLAVORING DIP ALMOND MIREPOIS
FLAVORLESS STALE SILENT
WATERISH
FLAW BUG FIB GAP LIE MAR RUB
WEM BANE BLOT FLEE GALL HOLE
RASE RIFT SPOT WIND BOTCH
BRACK BURST CHICK CLEFT CRACK
CRAZE FAULT FLAKE PLUME SPECK
BLOTCH BREACH DEFECT FOIBLE
LACUNA LESION BLEMISH BLISTER
DEFAULT EYELAST FEATHER
FISSURE NULLIFY SUNSPOT VIOLAT
WHITLOW FRACTURE FRAGMENT

GENDARME WINDFLAW
(— IN CASTING) BUCKLE
(— IN CLOTH) BRACK
(— IN DIAMOND) GENDARME
(— IN MARBLE) TERRACE
(— IN METAL) SNAKE
(— IN PRECIOUS STONE) FEATHER
(— IN STEEL) STAR
(— IN STONE) DRY
(MORAL —) SMIRCH
LAWED CRACKED
LAWLESS CLEAN SOUND PERFECT
LAX LIN POB TOW CARD FLIX HARL
LINE LINT ROCK GRAIN HURDS
BREADS KORARI PEANUT PEBBLE
SCUTCH LINSEED FLAXWORT
HARAKEKE
(— DISEASE) PASMO
LAXEN FLAXY BLONDE
LAXWEED TOADFLAX
LAY SKIN STRIP FLEECE UNCASE
CENSURE PILLAGE REPROVE
SCARIFY
LEA LOP SCUD FLECH FLECK PULEX
TUNGA CHEGRE CHIGOE VERMIN
PULICID SANDBOY
(— INFESTED) PULICOSE
LEABANE SKEVISH SCABIOUS
WHITETOP
LEA BEETLE THRIPS
LEAM BEVEL
LEAWORT CAMMOCK FLEASEED
PSYLLIUM
LECHE SPIRELET
LECK FLAKE FREAK DAPPLE
FLEECE POUNCE STREAK STIPPLE
LEDGED FLUSH FLIGGED
LEDGLING SQUAB FLIGGER
BIRDLING
LEE FLY LAM RUN BOLT FLEG LOUP
SCUR SHUN TURN ELOPE ELUDE
SKIRR SPEED ESCAPE VANISH
ABANDON ABSCOND FORSAKE
SCAMPER LIBERATE
LEECE JIB KET TEG BUCK CAST
FELL GAFF MORT SKIN TEGG TEGS
FLICK PASHM PLOAT SHAVE SHEAR
SHEEP SWEAT PASHIM PIGEON
PUSHUM TOISON SHEARING
(— OF MEDIUM GRADE) SUPER
(POOREST PART OF —) ABB
LEEING FUGIENT HOTFOOT
RUNNING FUGITIVE
LEER GIBE JIBE LEER FLIRE FLOUT
SCOFF SNEER
LEET BAY FAST FLIT NAVY SAIL
SKIM SWIM CREEK DRAIN DRIFT
EVAND FLOAT FLOTA HASTY INLET
POWER QUICK RAPID SWIFT
ARGOSY ARMADA FLIGHT HASTEN
NIMBLE SPEEDY CARAVAN
COMPANY FLOTILLA WARCRAFT
LEETING BRIEF CADUCE FLYING
VOLAGE FLIGHTY PASSING POSTING
SHADOWY VOLATIC CADUCOUS
FUGITIVE VOLATILE
LESH KIN BEEF BODY FELL GAME
LAMB LIRE MEAT RACE WEED
SLATE STOCK FAMILY MUSCLE

SEASON CARNAGE KINDRED
MANKIND NATURAL HUMANITY
MOONLIGHT
(— ABOUT CHIN AND JAWS) GILL
(— OF CALF) SLINK
(— OF GOAT) CHEVON
(— OF KID) CABRITO
(— OF SHEEP) TRAIK
(— ON LOWER JAW) CHOLLER
(— OUT) CLOTHE
(— UNDER SKIN) FELL
(ANIMAL —) BRAWN
(DEAD —) MURRAIN
(HORSE —) JACK
(LIFELESS —) MUMMY
(PUTREFYING —) CARRION
(SUN-DRIED —) TAPA
(SUPERFLUOUS —) LUMBER
FLESHBRUSH STRIGIL
FLESH-COLORED SARCOLINE
FLESHER LINING
FLESHINESS FULLNESS
FLESHLY CARNAL FLESHY SENSUAL
SARKICAL
FLESHY FAT BEEFY LUSTY OBESE
PLUMP PULPY STOUT ANIMAL
BODILY BRAWNY CARNAL BUNTING
CARNOSE SARCOUS
FLETCH WING FLIGHT
FLEUR-DE-LIS LIS LYS LILY LUCY
FLEUR
FLEX BEND
FLEXED PENCHE
FLEXIBILITY WHIP FLUIDITY
FLEXIBLE LIMP LUSH SOFT BUXOM
LIMSY LITHE WANDY WITHY FLOPPY
LIMBER LITHER PLIANT SUPPLE
DUCTILE ELASTIC FINGENT FLEXILE
FLEXIVE LISSOME PLIABLE SPRINGY
WILLOWY WINDING WRIGGLE
BENDSOME YIELDING
FLEXURE ARCH BEND BENT CURL
FOLD CURVE TWIST SIGMOID
WINDING
FLICK FLIP CLICK FLACK FLANK
FLECK FLIRT FLISK
FLICKER FAIL FLIT LICK WINK BLINK
FLAME FLARE FLICK FLUNK WAVER
BICKER FITTER SHIVER YUCKER
BLINTER FLIMMER FLITTER FLUTTER
SKIMMER TREMBLE TWINKLE
WHIFFLE FLICHTER HIGHHOLE
FLICKERING FLICKY FLUTTER
LAMBENT FLEXUOUS UNSTEADY
FLICKERTAIL STATE
NORTHDAKOTA
FLIER ACE KIWI FLYER PILOT
AIRMAN AVIATOR
FLIGHT FLY HOP LAM BOLT LAKE
PAIR ROUT WING CHEVY FLOCK
GLIDE GRICE SCRAP VOLEE CHIVVY
EXODUS FUGACY HEGIRA HEJIRA
JOYHOP SPIRAL BOUQUET EVASION
FLAUGHT FLYOVER MIGRATE
MISSION SCAMPER STEPWAY
REGIFUGE STAMPEDE SWARMING
(— OF BALL) HOOK DRIVE SLICE
(— OF BIRDS) VOLARY VOLERY
VOLLEY

(— OF FANCY) SALLY
(— OF SNIPE) WISP
(— OF STEPS) RISE TRAP GRECE
PITCH SCALE STOOP PERRON
STAIRS STEPWAY STAIRWAY
(— OF WILD FOWL) SKEIN
(ABORTIVE —) ABORT
(HASTY —) TIFT
(HAWK'S —) CAREER
(HIGH —) TOWER
(IN —) ALOFT
(SUDDEN —) START STAMPEDE
(UNAUTHORIZED —) BUGOUT
(UPWARD —) SOAR
FLIGHTY ANILE BARMY GIDDY LIGHT
SWIFT FITFUL GARISH UNFIRM
VOLAGE WHISKY FLYAWAY FOOLISH
GIGGISH MOONISH ROCKETY
FLEETING FREAKISH
(— PERSON) TRIVVET
FLIMSINESS INANITY
FLIMSY LIMP THIN VAIN WEAK FRAIL
GAUDY JERRY FEEBLE PALTRY
SLEAZY SLIGHT SLIMSY HAYWIRE
SHALLOW TENUOUS TIFFANY
GIMCRACK GOSSAMER JIMCRACK
TWITTERY
FLINCH FUNK GAME JARG BLUNK
BUDGE FEIGN SHUNT START WINCE
WONDE BLANCH BLENCH FALTER
FLENSE RECOIL SHRINK SCRINGE
SCUNNER SQUINCH
FLINCHER VELLINCH
FLINDER FLITTER SMITHERS
FLINDERSIA SILKWOOD
FLINDOSA CUDGERIE
FLING SHY BUZZ CAST DART DASH
DING EMIT FLAP FLEG GIBE HURL
KICK LASH PECK PICK SLAT TOSS
WARP BRAID CHEAT DANCE FLIRT
LANCE PITCH SHOOT SLING SNEER
SWING THROW WHANG BAFFLE
EFFUSE HURTLE LAUNCH PLUNGE
REBUFF SPIRIT ENFORCE FLOUNCE
REPULSE SARCASM SCATTER
SWINDLE SHYLANCE SPANGHEW
(— MISSILES) CHUNK
(— UPWARD) HAUNCH
(HIGHLAND —) WALLOCH
FLINT CORE BLANK CHERT MISER
SILEX EOLITH QUARTZ REJECT
ESLABON FURISON SCRAPER
GRATTOIR GUNFLINT
FLINTINESS HEART
FLINTLOCK FUSEE FUSIL FUZEE
MUSKET SPANNER FIRELOCK
MIQUELET SNAPHAAN
FLINTWOOD WHITETOP
FLIP SKY TAP FLAP SNAP TOSS TRIP
FLANK FLICK FLIRT SLIRT SMART
FILLIP FLITCH LIMBER NIMBLE
PLIANT PROPEL
FLIPPANT AIRY FLIP GLIB FLUENT
LIMBER NIMBLE
FLIPPER ARM FIN PAW HAND SWELL
PADDLE FLAPPER SPRINGER
FLIRT TOY FIKE FLIP MASH TICK
FLICK ROVER SLIRT JILLET MASHER

TRIFLE GALLANT PICKEER TWINKLE
COQUETTE
FLIRTATION FIKE PASSADE
COQUETRY PHILANDER
FLIT DART FLOW SCUD FLECK FLEET
FLICK FLIRT FLOAT FLURR HOVER
QUICK SCOOT SKIFF SWIFT NIMBLE
FLICKER FLUTTER
FLITCH FLICK GAMMON LONGWOOD
MIDDLING
FLOAT BOB FLY KIT SEA BOOM
BUOY CORK DRAG FLOW FLUX
HAWK HONE HOVE LIVE PONT RAFT
RIDE SAIL SCOW SOAR SWIM TILT
WAFT WAVE BALSA BLADE CAMEL
DERBY DRIFT DRIVE FLEET FLOOD
FLUSH GRAIL HOVER LADLE QUILL
SHOAD SWOON BILLOW BOBBER
BUCKET BUNGEY CANNEL DOBBER
PADDLE PONTON RADEAU STREEL
TOPPER CAISSON DRINGLE FLATTER
FLOTTER FRESHEN OROPESA
PAGEANT PLANKER PLUMMET
PONTOON SLICKER LEVITATE
PICKOVER
(— AIMLESSLY) DRIFT
(— DELIGHTFULLY) COWD
(— FOR HERRING NET) BOWL
(— FOR RING BUOY) LEMON
(— LOGS) DRIVE
(— OF REEDS) KELEK LIGGER
(— PAST) GLACE
(— PROPERLY) WATCH
(CANOE —) AMA
(FISHLINE —) BOB CORK BOBBER
DOBBER
(PLASTERER'S —) DARBY
FLOATBOARD BLADE FLOAT LADLE
FLOATER STIFF
FLOATING FREE WAFT AWASH
LOOSE ADRIFT AFLOAT FLYING
NATANT BUOYANT FLYAWAY
PENDENT DRIFTING FLUITANT
SHIFTING UNFUNDED
FLOCCILATION TILMUS
FLOCK MOB POD BAND BANK BEVY
FOLD GAME GANG HERD MANY
PACK ROUT SAIL SORT TEAM TRIP
WISP BROOD BUNCH CHARM COVEY
CROWD DRIFT DROVE FLAKE FLECK
GROUP PLUMP SEDGE SHOAL
SWARM TRIBE TROOP COVERT
FLIGHT GAGGLE HIRSEL MANADA
MEINIE RAFTER SCHOOL SCURRY
VOLERY COMPANY GOOSERY
THICKEN PADDLING
(— OF BIRDS) POD BANK HERD
TEAM WISP BROWN COVEY SEDGE
SIEGE TRIBE FLIGHT VOLERY
(— OF BITTERNS) SEDGE SIEGE
(— OF FINCHES) CHARM
(— OF GEESE) GAGGLE
(— OF HERONS) SEDGE SIEGE
(— OF LARKS) EXALTATION
(— OF LIONS) PRIDE
(— OF MALLARDS) SORD SUTE
(— OF NIGHTINGALES) WATCH
(— OF PARTRIDGE) COVEY
(— OF PEACOCKS) MUSTER

(— OF PIGEONS) KIT LOFT
(— OF ROOKS) ROOKERY
(— OF SANDPIPERS) FLING
(— OF SHEEP) FOLD HIRSEL
(— OF SWANS) BANK GAME MARK
(— OF TURTLE-DOVES) DOLE
(— OF WIDGEONS) COMPANY
(— OF WILDFOWL) SKEIN
(— TOGETHER) RAFT
(SMALL —) SPRING
FLOCKING REPAIR
FLOG CAT TAN TAW BEAT CANE
CHOP HIDE LASH LICK LUMP TOCO
WALE WARM WELK WHIP YANK
BIRCH EXCEL FIGHT FLAIL HORSE
KNOUT LINGE QUILT SAUCE SKEEG
SWISH COTTON LARRUP LATHER
STRIKE SWITCH THRASH WALLOP
WATTLE BALEISE BELABOR
COWHIDE SCOURGE SJAMBOK
TROUNCE CARTWHIP CHAWBUCK
SLAISTER URTICATE VAPULATE
(— WATER) SCRINGE
FLOGGER HORSING SWISHER
FLOGGING TOCO TOKO TANNING
BIRCHING WHIPPING
FLOOD SEA BORE BUOY FLOW FLUX
POUR TIDE EAGRE FLOAT FLUSH
SPATE SWAMP SWILL WATER
DELUGE EXCESS RAVINE SLUICE
SPLASH DEBACLE FLOTTER
FRESHET NIAGARA TORRENT
ALLUVION CATARACT INUNDATE
OVERFLOW SURROUND
FLOODED AWASH AFLOAT
FLOODGATE CLOW DRAG GOLE
HATCH SLUICE STAUNCH CATARACT
PENSTOCK
FLOODING UP PROUD FLOWAGE
DILUVIAL FLOATING
FLOODLIGHT OLIVET
FLOODPLAIN BENCH DAMBO
FLOOR BECK DROP FLAT LAND PAVE
SEAT BOARD FLOAT GRASS PIANO
PIECE SOLAR STAGE STORY BELFRY
FLIGHT GROUND SOLLAR PLANCHE
BARBECUE FLOORING HALFPACE
PAVEMENT SUBFLOOR
(— OF COAL MINE) SOLE THILL
(— OF COAL SEAM) SILL
(— OF FORGE) HEARTH
(— OF GLASS FURNACE) SIEGE
(— OF OCEAN) SEABED
(— OF SPORTS RING) CANVAS
(— OF WOOLSHED) BOARD
(FOREST —) SEEDBED
(GROUND —) TERRENO BASEMENT
(OPENWORK —S) GRATINGS
(RAISED —) LEEWAN HALFPACE
(THRESHING —) MOWSTEAD
FLOORBOARD FOOTLING
FLOORING STAGE PARQUET
TERRAZZO
FLOORMAN CALLBOY
FLOP DOG SWOP WHOP SQUAB
TURKEY TRAGEDY
FLORA FLORULA
(— AND FAUNA) BIOTA
FLORAL TREE LEAF

FLORENCE FLASK BETTY
FLORENCE IRIS ORRIS TREOS
FLORID FINE HIGH BUXOM FRESH
RUDDY ORNATE ROCOCO ASIATIC
FLOWERY TAFFETA BLOOMING
FIGURATE RUBICUND SPLENDID
VIGOROUS

FLORIDA

BAY: APALCHEE BISCAYNE
  WACCASASSA
CAPITAL: TALLAHASSEE
COLLEGE: ROLLINS
COUNTY: DADE GUFF ALACHUA
  BREVARD BROWARD MANATEE
  OSCEOLA VOLUSIA PINELLAS
  SARASOTA
INDIAN: AIS OCALE UTINA CALUSA
  CHATOT POTANO TIMUCUA
  SEMINOLE
ISLANDS: KEYS
KEY: WEST LARGO BISCAYNE
LAKE: DORA APOPKA HARNEY
  JESSUP NEWNAN LEDWITH
  ARBUCKLE KISSIMMEE
  OKEECHOBEE
NATIVE: CONCH CRACKER
RIVER: BANANA INDIAN AUCILLA
  MANATEE SCAMBIA SUWANEE
  OCHLAWAHA
STATE BIRD: MOCKINGBIRD
STATE FLOWER: ORANGE
STATE NICKNAME: SUNSHINE
STATE TREE: PALMETTO
TOWN: TICE COCOA MIAMI OCALA
  TAMPA ORLANDO PALATKA
  SEBRING SARASOTA
  PENSACOLA
UNIVERSITY: STETSON
WETLANDS: GLADES

FLORIDIAN CRACKER
FLOSS FLUFF SKEIN WASTE CADDIS
SLEAVE CADDICE
FLOSSER FANNER
FLOSS-SILK TREE SAMOHU
FLOTSAM JETSAM WILSAM WAFTUP
WAVESON DRIFTAGE FLOATAGE
FLOUNCE FLAP HUFF SKIT SLAM
FLING FRILL RUCHE RIPPLE ROBIN
ROUNCE RUFFLE VOLANT FALBALA
FALBELO FROUNCE RUCHING
FLOUNDER FURBELOW STRUGGLE
FLOUNDER DAB GAD BUTT KEEL
POLE ROLL TOSS BREAM FLUKE
SLOSH WITCH WRELE GADOID
GROVEL MEGRIM MUDDLE PLAICE
TURBOT WALLOP WALLOW WARSL
BLUNDER FLASKER FLOUNCE
PLOUNCE STUMBLE SUNFISH
TOPKNOT VAAGMAR ANACANTH
FLATFISH FOOLFISH PLUNTHER
SANDLING
FLOUR AMYL ATTA DUST CONES
HOVIS BINDER CLEARS FARINA
FLOWER PATENT POLLEN SICKEN
TSAMBA WHITES BOXINGS CRIBBL
CANAILLE

(— OF MALT) SMEDDUM
(COARSE —) THIRD CHISEL
BOXINGS CRIBBLE
(FINE —) CONES SUJEE
(LOW-GRADE —) TAIL
(PARTICLE OF —) CHOP
(POTATO —) FROW
(UNSORTED —) ATTA
FLOURISH TAG WAG BOOM BRAG
FUSS GROW LICK RIOT RISE SHOW
WAVE ADORN BLOOM BOAST CHEVE
GLOSS QUIRK REIGN SHAKE SWASH
SWING TUSCH VAUNT CATTER
PARADE PARAPH QUAVER SQUIRL
THRIVE BLOSSOM BURGEON
CADENZA DISPLAY ENLARGE
FANFARE GAMBADE GAMBADO
PASSAGE PROSPER ROULADE
SUCCEED TRIUMPH ARPEGGIO
BRANDISH CURLICUE INCREASE
ORNAMENT SKIRMISH
(— OF BAGPIPE) WARBLER
(— OF TRUMPET) TUCKET
FLOURISHING FAR FRIM FRUM PERT
GREEN PALMY PEART VITAL
BLOOMY FLORID GOLDEN FLORENT
HEALTHY VERNANT THRIVING
VEGETOUS
FLOURY MEALY
FLOUT BOB GIBE JEER JERK JIBE
LOUT MOCK FLEER FLITE FRUMP
SCOFF SCOMM SCORN SCOUT
SNEER TAUNT DERIDE INSULT
BETONGUE
FLOW GO EBB ERN JET PUT RUN
SET SUE BORE COMB FLIT FLUX
USE GUSH HALE LAVA LAVE MELT
PASS POUR RAIL ROLL SEND SHED
SILE SLIP SOAK SWIG TAIL TEEM
TIDE WELL AVALE DRAIN DRIFT
EAGRE EXUDE FLEAM FLEET FLOAT
FLOOD FLUSH FRESH GLIDE ISSUE
QUELL RIVER SCOOT SLIDE SPEND
SPILL SPURT SWILL TRILL ABOUND
AFFLUX COURSE CURSUS DELUGE
GUGGLE GUTTER RECEDE RINDLE
SPRING STREAM CURRENT DEVOLVE
DISTILL DRIBBLE EMANATE
FLOWAGE FLUTTER FLUXION
LAPSE INDRAFT MEANDER
PURTLE TRINKLE TRINTLE
ALLUVION BACKWASH CURRANCE
CURRENCY DOWNFLOW EMISSION
FOUNTAIN INUNDATE
— AGAINST) LAP LAVE BATHE
— BACK) EBB
— BEYOND BANKS) DEBORD
SURROUND
— DOWN) AVALE
— IN RILLS) DRILL
— IN RIVULETS) GUTTER
— IN SPURTS) SALTATION
— IN) INFLOW INFLOOD
— INTERMITTENTLY) HEAD
— OF AIR) SIDEWASH
— OF ELECTRICITY) BOLT
— OF METAL) CREEP
— OF RADIO SIGNAL) BEAM
— OF SOUNDS) CADENCE

(— OUT) EMIT ISSUE EFFUSE
SPREAD EXHAUST RESOLVE
(— OVER) BERUN
(— SLOWLY) SEEP EXUDE GLEET
(— TOGETHER) CONCUR CONFLOW
(— WITH) FLEET
(CONTINUOUS —) LAPSE
(COPIOUS —) HALE RIVER
(RHYTHMICAL —) LILT
(TIDAL —) BORE AEGIR EAGER
EAGRE
FLOWER (ALSO SEE PLANT AND
HERB) BUD GAY BEST BLOW FLAG
IRIS IXIA PINK POLE POSY ROSE
ARROW ASTER BLOOM BREAK
DAISY ELITE FANCY FLOOR GOWAN
LILAC PANSY PHLOX TRUSS TULIP
TUTTY AZALIA CHOICE CORYMB
CROCUS CYMULE DAHLIA DATURA
FLORET MAYPOP ORCHID SCILLA
SEASON SHOWER SINGLE STEVIA
UNFOLD AMELLUS ANEMONE
ARBUTUS BLETHIA BLOSSOM
BOSTRYX DEVELOP ESSENCE
FLEURET FLOSCLE GAZANIA
GENTIAN GERBERA IPOMOEA
PETUNIA PICOTEE TORENIA
BELAMOUR CAMELLIA CYCLAMEN
DAFFODIL DIANTHUS GARDENIA
GERANIUM HEPATICA HIBISCUS
HYACINTH PRIMROSE SPARAXIS
(— STATE) FLORIDA
(— WITH 6 SEGMENTS) SEXFOIL
(COTTON —) SQUARE
(DEFORMED —) BULLHEAD
(DOUBLE —) BURSTER
(DRIED —S) BRAYERA
(IMAGINARY —) AMARANTH
(STRIPED —) BIZARRE
(UNFADING —) AMARANTH
(PL.) BOUQUET
FLOWERFLY SYRPHID
FLOWERING AFLOWER FLOWERY
ANTHESIS BLOOMING
FLOWERING GLUME LEMMA
FLOWER-OF-AN-HOUR SHOOFLY
FLOWERPOT POT CACHEPOT
FLOWERY BLOWN BLOOMY FLORID
POSIED FLORENT PRIMROSE
FLOWING FAIR FLUX LAVE SIDE
AFLOW FLOAT FLUID FLUOR QUICK
TIDAL AFFLUX DEFLUX FLUENT
FUSILE LIVING COPIOUS CURRENT
CURSIVE EMANANT FLUXING
FLUXION FLUXIVE RUNNING SLIDING
DEFLUENT DILUENDO FLUVIOSE
(— AT LOW SPEED) SLACK
(— BACK) EBB
(— IN) INFLUX INFLUENT INFLUXION
(— OF GLAZE) STREAMING
(— OF TIDE) FLOOD
(— OUT) ELAPSE EFFLUENT
FLOWOFF RUNOFF
FLUCAN SELVAGE SELVEDGE
FLUCTUATE SWAY VARY VEER
FLEET SWING WAVER BALANCE
VIBRATE WAMPISH UNDULATE
UNSTEADY

FLUCTUATING WAVY HECTIC LABILE
RUBATO ERRATIC FLUXIVE
WAYWARD UNSTABLE UNSTEADY
FLUCTUATION CYCLE FADING
JIGGLE FLICKER FLUTTER VIBRATO
FLUE NET BARB DOWN OPEN PIPE
THIN VENT FLARE FLUFF FLUKE
FUNNEL TUNNEL UPTAKE CHIMNEY
PASSAGE DOWNTAKE
FLUE-CURED BRIGHT
FLUENCY SKILL
FLUENT GASH GLIB FLUID READY
FACILE LIQUID SMOOTH STREAM
COPIOUS CURRENT FLOWING
FLUIDIC RENABLE VERBOSE
VOLUBLE ELOQUENT FLIPPANT
FLUFF LINT PUFF BEARD WHEEL
FLUFFING WHEELING
FLUFFY SOFT DOWNY DRUNK FILMY
FLUEY FUZZY LIGHT LINTEN PLUFFY
FEATHERY UNSTEADY
(NOT —) CLOSE
FLUID INK SAP MASS RASA BLOOD
FLUOR HUMOR JUICE LATEX SERUM
SPERM SWEAT WATER FLUENT
LIQUID WATERY FLOWING FLUIBLE
FLUXILE GASEOUS SYNOVIA
EMULSION FLOATING FLUXIBLE
FORESHOT
(ANIMAL —) SERUM
(EGYPTIAN PRIMEVAL —) NU NUN
(ETHEREAL —) ICHOR
(LIVER —) BILE
(LUBRICATING —) SYNOVIA
(MAMMARY —) MILK
(SOLDERING —) FAKE
(THICK VISCOUS —) GRUME
(WATERY —) LYE SANIES SEROSITY
(WORKING —) AIR
FLUIDITY LENGTH
(— UNIT) RHE
FLUKE FLUE PALM BLADE GRASP
PLAICE DISTOME PLATODE
SCRATCH FLATWORM FLOUNDER
(— OF ANCHOR) HOOK
(— OF WHALE'S TAIL) BLADE
FLUME CHUTE DITCH SHUTE SLUICE
FLUMMERY SOWENS WASHBREW
FLUNK BUST FAIL SKEW SPIN
FLICKER
FLUNKY SNOB TOADY COOKEE
JEAMES LACKEY FOOTMAN
SERVANT STEWARD
FLUORESCENCE BLOOM
FLUORINE PHTOR PHTHOR
FLUORITE CAND FLUX FLUOR
FLURRY ADO FIT FACT FRET GUST
PIRR SPIT STIR TEAR HASTE SKIFF
SKIRL BOTHER BUSTLE SCURRY
SQUALL CONFUSE FLUSKER
FLUSTER FLUTTER FOOSTER
SWITHER WHITHER SPITTING
FLUSH JET EVEN GLOW HUSH JUMP
POOL ROSE BLOOM BLUSH COLOR
ELATE FLASH FLUSK FRESH KNOCK
LEVEL RAISE ROUGE START VIGOR
AFLUSH EXCITE HECTIC LAVISH
MANTLE MORASS REDDEN RUDDLE
SLUICE SPRING THRILL ANIMATE

BOBTAIL CRIMSON SUFFUSE
ABUNDANT AFFLUENT PRODIGAL
ROSINESS
(— GAME) SERVE
(— IN SKY) SUNGLOW
(NOT —) FLAT
FLUSHED RED ROSY BEAMY FIERY
FLOWN FLORID FLUSHY HECTIC
CRIMSON
FLUSTER PAVIE SHAKE BOTHER
FLURRY FUDDLE MUDDLE POTHER
RATTLE CONFUSE FLUSKER
FOOSTER SWITHER BEFUDDLE
FLOWSTER FLUSTRUM
FLUTE NAY FIFE FUYE PIPE AULOS
CRIMP CUENA PUNGI QUENA STICK
STYKE TIBIA TWILL CANNEL DOUCET
FLAUTO GEWGAW GOFFER POOGYE
ZUFOLO CHAMFER DIAULOS
FLAMFEW FLUTING GAUFFER
HEMIOPE MAGADIS MATALAN
PICCOLO SIBILUS SIFFLOT TONETTE
TRANGAM WHISTLE ZUFFOLO
FLAUTINO MONAULOS RECORDER
(— OF A COLUMN) STRIGA
CHANNEL
(— STOP) VENTAGE
(CHINESE —) TCHE
(EAST INDIAN —) MATALAN
(EUNUCH —) KAZOO
(JAPANESE —) FUYE
(LYDIAN —) MAGADIS
(MOSLEM —) NAY
(PHOENICIAN —) GINGRAS
(PL.) NEHILOTH
FLUTED QUILLED
FLUTEMOUTH CORNETFISH
FLUTE PLAYER AULETE FLUTER
FLUTIST TIBICEN TOOTLER
AULETRIS FLAUTIST
FLUTING STRIX FULLER GADROON
STRIGIL COULISSE QUILLING
FLUTTER BAT FAN BATE BLOW BUZZ
FLAP FLIT FLOW PLAY WAFF WAVE
FLACK FLAFF FLARE FLECK FLICK
FLURR HOVER SHAKE WAVER
BANGLE FLAUNT FLURRY RUFFLE
SWIVET WAFFLE WALLOP FLACKER
FLAFFER FLASKER FLATTER
FLAUGHT FLICKER FLITTER
FLUSKER SKIMMER WAGTAIL
WHIFFLE FLICHTER SQUATTER
VOLITATE
(IN A —) PITAPAT
FLUTTERING AWING FLITTY
WHUTTER AFLUTTER FLICKERY
FLUTTER-TONGUING GROWL
FLUX FLOW FUSE LASK MELT BORAX
FLOAT FLOOD ISSUE RESIN ROSIN
SMEAR SMELT FUSION CURRENT
EURIPUS FLOWING LEAKAGE
OUTFLOW
(— UNIT) WEBER MAXWELL
FLY BEE FAG FAN GAD HOP RUN
FIRK FLEA FLEE FLEG FLIT GNAT
KITE KIVU LASH LEAP MELT RACK
RAKE SAIL SCUD SMUT SOAR SOLO
WHEW WHIR WHIZ WIND WING ZIMB
AGILE ALERT EMPID FLEET FLIER

FLOAT FLURR FLUSH FLYER GLIDE
LATCH MIDGE MUSCA OXFLY PERLA
PHORA PILOT QUICK SEDGE SHARP
SKIRL SKIRR STOUR WHAME WHIRR
ZEBUB ASILID AVIATE BANGLE
BLOWER BOTFLY BREEZE DAYFLY
ESCAPE FLIGHT FLYBOY GADFLY
GORFLY JARFLY LEPTID NIMBLE
PALMER PHORID PUNKIE RANDON
ROBBER SEPSID SEROOT SPRING
TIPULA TSETSE VANISH VERMIN
WINNOW AVIGATE AVOLATE
CANOPID CHALCID CONOPID
FORMATE GRANNOM KNOWING
ORTALID PYRALIS SCIARID TYRPHID
AIRPLANE BIBIONID BRACONID
COACHMAN DIPTERAN DROPPING
EPHYDRID EULOPHID GLOSSINA
HORSEFLY HOUSEFLY RUBYTAIL
SIMULIID TACHINID TATUKIRA
VOLITATE
(— AFTER GAME) RAKE
(— AIMLESSLY) BANGLE
(— ALOFT) SOAR TOWER
(— AWAY) CARRY
(— CLUMSILY) FLIGHTER
(— ERRATICALLY) GAD
(— INTO RAGE) FUFF RARE
(— LOW) DICE DRAG HEDGEHOP
(— OUT) EXPIRE
(— RAPIDLY) SCUR SKIRR
(— TOO HIGH) SCUD
(— WIDE) MISS
(FISHING —) BEE DUN OAK BUZZ
GNAT HARL HERL SMUT WASP ZULU
ABBEY ALDER BAKER FAIRY NYMPH
SEDGE BADGER BOBFLY CADDIS
CAHILL CANARY CLARET DOCTOR
HACKLE MILLER ORIOLE WILLOW
BABCOCK BUTCHER CADDICE
COLONEL DROPPER DUBBING
GRANNOM HUZZARD SPINNER
WATCHED WATCHET BUCKTAIL
CATSKILL COACHMAN FERGUSON
GOVERNOR STREAMER WOODRUFF
WRENTAIL
(MAY —) DUN DRAKE
(SHEEP —) FAG KED
(STONE —) SALLY
FLYBLOWN BLOWN STRUCK
FLYBOAT FLUTE FLIGHT
FLYCATCHER TODY PEWEE PEWIT
CHEBEC COBWEB MILLER PEEWEE
PHOEBE PIPIRI RAFTER TYRANT
YETAPA ELEPAIO FANTAIL GRIGNET
GRINDER PITIRRI TOMFOOL TYRANNI
BEAMBIRD FIREBALL FIREBIRD
FLYEATER FORKTAIL GERYGONE
KINGBIRD KISKADEE PITANGUA
WALLBIRD
FLYING AWING FLIGHT VOLANT
WAVING FLOTANT VOLATIC
AVIATION FLOATING
(— MANEUVER) LUFBERY
FLYING FISH SKIPPER VOLADOR
FLYING FOX KALONG PTEROPID
FLYING GURNARD ANGLER
BATFISH LATCHET LOPHIID
VOLADOR

FLYING LEMUR COBEGO COLUGO
KUBONG
FLYING MACHINE AVIATOR
AEROSTAT
FLYING PHALANGER CUSCUS
SQUIRREL
FLYING SQUIRREL TAGUAN
ASSAPAN
FLYWHEEL FLY FLIER FLYER WHOR
WHARVE
FLYMAN LOFTMAN
FLYSCH MACIGNO
FOAL CADE COLT FILLY PODDY
SLEEPER
FOAM FOB SUD BARM BEES BOIL
FUME HEAD KNIT REAM SCUD SCUM
SUDS WORK CREAM FROST FROTH
SPUME YEAST BUBBLE FLOWER
FLURRY FREATH IMBOST LATHER
SEETHE BLUBBER DESPUME
MELDROP
FOAMING AFOAM NAPPY YEASTY
SPUMOUS MANTLING
FOAMY BARMY SPUMY SUDSY
FROTHY SPUMOSE
FOB FUB SPUNG POCKET
FOCAL POINT OMPHALOS
FOCUS FIX PUT POINT PURSE TRAIN
CENTER CLIMAX DIRECT FASTEN
FIXATE HEARTH TEMPLE NUCLEUS
CONVERGE FOCALIZE GANGLION
FODDER HAY FEED FOOD SOIL VER
GOOMA MANGE FORAGE FOTHER
PODDER SILAGE STOVER FARRAGE
PODWARE ENSILAGE ROUGHAGE
FODDERCAGE TUMBREL
FODDERER FOGGER
FOE ENEMY FIEND RIVAL FOEMAN
HOSTILE OPPOSER OPPONENT
FOG FF DAG RAG DAMP DAZE HAAR
HAZE MIST MOKE MOSS MURK PRI
RACK ROKE SMOG SMUR SOUP
BEDIM BRUME CLOUD GRASS
HUMOR MUDDY SMIRR SPRAY
STOUR VAPOR MUDDLE NEBULA
SALMON STUPOR FOGGAGE
OBSCURE POGONIP SMOTHER
BEWILDER MOISTURE
(— OF THE NILE) QOBAR
(FROZEN —) BARBER
(LIGHT —) GAUZE
(SEA —) HAAR HARR
FOGBOW DOG FOGDOG SEADOG
MISTBOW FOGEATER
FOGDOG DOG STUBB FOGBOW
SEADOG FOGEATER
FOGGINESS CLOUDING
FOGGY DIM DULL HAZY MIRK MOK
MURK ROKY DENSE DIRTY GROSS
MISKY MISTY MURKY ROOKY ROU
SPEWY CLOUDY GREASY GROGGY
MARSHY MILKEN SMURRY BRUMO
MUDDLED OBSCURE CONFUSED
NUBILOUS VAPOROUS
FOGHORN SIREN TYFON RIPPER
MEGAFOG
FOGY FOGEY FOGRAM FOOZLE
STODGER MOSSBACK
FOGYISH MUSTY

FOIBLE FAULT FERLY FEEBLE FAILING FRAILTY WEAKNESS

FOIL BACK BALK EPEE FILE FOIN SOIL TAIN BLADE BLANK BLUNT CHEAT ELUDE EVADE FALSE STAIN STUMP SWORD TRACK TRAIL BAFFLE BLENCH BOGGLE CHATON DEFEAT DEFILE FLORET OFFSET OUTWIT STIGMA STOOGE THWART BEGUILE FAILURE FOILING FOLIATE LAMETTA PAILLON POLLUTE REPULSE STONKER TRAMPLE DISGRACE

(— STRIPS) WINDOW

(FENCING —) EPEE BLUNT FLORET FLEURET

(POINTED —) TANG

(TIN —) TAIN

FOIST WISH FUDGE FATHER SUBORN FOISTER SHOEHORN

FOLD BOW FLY LAP PEN PLY SET WAP BEND COTE CREW CRUE DART FAIL FALX FAUN FELD FLAP FURL HANK HOOD LOOP RUGA SWAG TUCK WRAP BREAK CLASP CRIMP CRISP CROZE DRAPE FAULD FLIPE FLOCK FLYPE FRILL GROIN LAYER PARMA PINCH PLAIT PLEAT PLICA PRANK QUILL SINUS YIELD BOUGHT BUCKLE COLLOP CREASE CRISTA CUTTLE DEWLAP DIAPIR DOUBLE ENFOLD FORNIX FRENUM FURDLE GATHER GUSSET HURDLE INFOLD LABIUM LAPPET MANTLE PIPING PLIGHT PUCKER RIMPLE RUMPLE WIMPLE CAPSIZE CRINKLE CRUMPLE EMBRACE ENVELOP FLEXION FLEXURE PINFOLD PLACATE PLICATE REVERSE ROLLING ROULEAU TURNING VALVULA CRIMPING FLECTION FLITFOLD QUILLING SCAPULET SPLENIUM SURROUND

(— DOWN) COLLAPSE

(— FOR CATTLE) BAWN

(— IN HOOD) SHOVE

(— INWARD) CRIMP

(— OF SKIN) APRON DEWLAP SHEATH FORESKIN

(— ROCKS) DEFORM

(—S OF TOGA) SINUS

(CARDIAC —) CUSP

(GEOLOGICAL —) DIAPIR CLOSURE EXOCLINE SYNCLINE

(LOOSE —) LAPPET

(RESTRAINING —) FRENUM FRAENUM

(SHEEP —) REEVE

FOLDAGE SOC SOKE

FOLDED SHUT DOUBLE FANLIKE PLICATE PLICATED REFLEXED WREATHED

(— AND WAVED) GYROSE

FOLDER KIT BOOK FILE FOLD ATLAS COVER FOLIO BINDER CLEANER HANDOUT LEAFLET STROKER PAMPHLET

FOLDING KNOT

(— PAPER) ORIGAMI

FOLIAGE HERB SHADE GREENS LEAVES SHROUD GILLERY LEAFAGE LEAFERY UMBRAGE FRONDAGE GREENERY

(CARVED —) KNOT

FOLIATED SPATHIC

FOLIATION SEXFOIL TREFOIL CINQFOIL SEPTFOIL

FOLIC ACID PGA

FOLIO CASE ATLAS FOLIUM

FOLK DAIONE PEOPLE

(FAIRY —) SHEE SIDHE

(PL.) GENTRY

FOLKSONG SON TONADA

FOLKTALE DROLL FABULA MARCHEN

FOLKSY HOMY HOMEY HOMESPUN

FOLLETTO DUSIO

FOLLICLE CRYPT LACUNA OVISAC

FOLLOW GO PAD SUE TAG COME COPY HUNT NEXT SEEK SHAG TAIL TAKE TOUT ADOPT AFTER CHASE DODGE ENSUE SNAKE SPOOR TRACE TRACK TRAIL TREAD ADHERE ATTEND FOLLER OCCUPY PURSUE RESULT SECOND SHADOW SUIVEZ TAGGLE HOTFOOT IMITATE OBSERVE PROFESS REPLACE SUCCEED VALOUWE PRACTICE SUPPLANT

(— A POINTER'S LEAD) BACK

(— IN SUCCESSION) VARY

(— INSIDIOUSLY) DOG

(— SCENT) ROAD CARRY

(— SLOWLY) DRAGGLE

(— TRACK) SLEUTH

(— UP) SUE ATTEND

(— UPON) WAIT

FOLLOWER FAN IST SON APER BEAU ZANY ADEPT CHELA GILLY BILFAR COHORT DRIVEN ENSUER GILLIE GUDGET KNIGHT LACKEY SEQUEL SUITOR SULTER VOTARY ACACIAN ACOLYTE CARRIER DEVOTEE EPIGONE FLATTER GRIFTER POLIGAR PURSUER RETINUE SECTARY SEQUENT SPANIEL SUPPOST TRAILER ADHERENT DISCIPLE FAITHFUL FAVORITE HENCHMAN MYRMIDON OBSERVER OFFSIDER PARTISAN RETAINER SECTATOR SERVITOR

(— OF ART) BOHEMIAN

(CAMP —) GUDGET

(CRANE —) SPOTTER

(SERVILE —) SLAVE LACKEY

(PL.) FOLK SECTA SEQUACES

FOLLOWING LAST NEXT SECT SUIT AFTER FIRST SUANT TRACE TRAIN BEHIND SEQUEL ENSUANT ENSUING SEQUENT AUDIENCE BUSINESS SEGUENDO TRAILING VOCATION

FOLLOW-UP FOLO

FOLLY ATE SIN RAGE LAPSE SOTIE BETISE DOTAGE LUNACY NICETY WANWIT DAFFERY DAFFING FOOLERY FOPPERY IDIOTCY MADNESS MISTAKE SOTTAGE UNSKILL FONDNESS FOOLHEAD IDLENESS LEWDNESS MOROLOGY

NONSENSE RASHNESS SURQUIDY UNTHRIFT UNWISDOM WILLNESS WOODNESS

FOMALHAUT DIFDA DIPHDA

FOMENT SOW ABET BREW SPUR ROUSE STUPE AROUSE EXCITE INCITE AGITATE FERMENT INSPIRE

FOND TID DAFT DEAR DOTE FAIN FOOL FUND KIND VAIN WEAK CRAZY SILLY STOCK STORE ARDENT BEFOOL CARESS CHOICE DEARLY DOTING FONDLE FONDLY LOVING SIMPLE TENDER AMATORY AMOROUS BEGUILE BROWDEN FONDISH FOOLISH INSIPID PARTIAL DESIROUS ENAMORED SANGUINE TRIFLING UXORIOUS

FONDLE PET BABY CLAP COAX DAUT DAWT FOND NECK TICK WALY DAUNT INGLE NURSE WALLY CARESS COCKER CODDLE COSSET CUDDLE CUTTER DANDLE GENTLE KIUTLE MUZZLE PAMPER SLAVER STROKE TANTLE TIDDLE CHERISH FLATTER SMUGGLE TWATTLE BLANDISH CANOODLE

FONDLING NINNY NURSLING

FONDLY DEAR FOND DEARLY FOOLISH

FONDNESS GRA LOVE FANCY FOLLY TASTE DOTAGE NOTION FEELING DEARNESS WEAKNESS

FONT BILL FUND PILA BASIN FOUNT SOURCE SPRING LAVACRE PISCINA DELUBRUM

FONTANEL MOLD MOULD FENESTRA

FOOD BIT KAI PAP BAIT BITE BUNK CATE CHIH CHOP CHOW CRAM DIET DISH EATS FARE FARM FUEL GEAR GRUB HASH JOCK KAIL KALE MEAT PECK PLAT PROG SALT SOCK STEW TACK TOKE TUCK BREAD BROMA CHEER CHUCK FLUFF FORAY GRILL SCAFF SCOFF SCRAN TABLE THING TREAT TRIPE APPAST BUTTER DODGER DOINGS EATING FODDER FOSTER LIVING MAIGRE MORSEL MUKTUK REFETE STOVER SUNKET TACKLE TUCKER VIANDS VIVERS WRAITH ALIMENT FAUSTER HANDOUT INGESTA KEEPING KITCHEN NURTURE PABULUM PASTURE PECKAGE PROVANT PULTURE EATABLES FLUMMERY GRUBBERY PEMMICAN PROVIANT TRENCHER VICTUALS

(— AND DRINK) BOUGE CHEER LOWANCE

(— AND LIQUOR) GEAR

(— AND LODGING) FOUND EASEMENT

(— BANNED DURING PASSOVER) HAMETZ CHAMETZ

(— EATEN AS RELISH) KITCHEN

(— EATEN BETWEEN MEALS) BAGGING

(— FOR ANIMALS) FODDER FORAGE

(— FOR CATTLE) BROWSE TACKLE

(— FROM KELP) KOMBU

(— IN SLICES) LEACH
(— IN STOCK) LARDER
(— NOT RITUALLY CLEAN) TEREPHAH
(— OF DUCK EGGS) BALUT
(— OF RUMINANTS) CUD
(— OF THE GODS) AMRITA AMREETA AMBROSIA
(— OF WHALE) KRILL
(— OF WORKMEN) TOMMY
(— ON TABLE AT ONE TIME) MESS
(BEE —) CANDY
(COOKED —) CURY BAKEMEAT
(DAILY —) TUCKER
(EXTRA —) GASH
(FILLING —) STODGE
(FLAVORLESS —) HOGWASH
(GROUND —) DUST
(HAWAIIAN —) POI
(LIQUID —) LAP SLOP SOUP GRUEL LEBAN LEBEN SUPPING
(LUXURIOUS —) CATE CATES JUNKET
(MADE OF SEVERAL —S) PANACHE
(MIRACULOUS —) MANNA
(SEMILIQUID —) SWILL
(SOFT —) PAP
(STARCHY —) AMYLOID
(TAPIOCA-LIKE —) SALEP
(WATERY —) SLIPSLOP
FOODLESS JEJUNE VICTLESS
FOODSTUFF TRADE CEREAL COOKABLE
FOOL APE ASS BAM BOB COD CON DAW DOR FOP FOX FUN GIG KID MUG NUP POT RIG SAP SOT TOY BULL BUTT CAKE CHUB COLT DOLT DUPE FOND GECK GOER GOFF GOWK GYPE HARE HAVE HOIT JAPE JEST JOKE MOME MUCK NIZY POOP RACA RACH SIMP TONY TOOT ZANY BLIND BLUFF BUFFO CHUMP CLOWN DALLY FUNGE GALAH GLAIK GOOSE GREEN HORSE IDIOT KNAVE MORON NINNY NIZEY NODDY PATCH SAMMY SCREW SILLY SNIPE SPOOF STICK STIRK TOMMY TRICK BUFFLE COUSIN CUCKOO CUDDEN DELUDE DIMWIT DISARD DOTARD DOTTLE FOLEYE FOOTER GAMMON JESTER MOTLEY MUCKER MUSARD NIDGET NIMSHI NINCOM NUPSON SAWNEY STRING TAMPER WITTOL ASINEGO BUFFOON COXCOMB DAGONET DECEIVE DIZZARD FATHEAD FOOLISH FRIBBLE GOMERAL GOMERIL HAVERAL JACKASS LACKWIT MADLING MISLEAD NATURAL OMADAWN PINHEAD PLAYBOY STOOKIE TOMFOOL WANTWIT WITLING BADINAGE DRIVELER FONDLING HOODWINK IMBECILE MONUMENT OMADHAUN TOMNODDY
(— AROUND) JIVE SKYLARK LALLYGAG
(— AWAY) FRIBBLE
(BORN —) MOONCALF
(LEARNED —) MOROSOPH

(NATURAL —) INNOCENT
(PL.) FOOLERY
FOOLERY GAME FOLLY BARNEY MOTLEY BAUBLERY
FOOLHARDY RASH BRASH FOOLATUM
FOOLISH FAT SOT BETE DAFT DUMB FOND FOOL GAGA GYPE IDLE MADE NICE RASH SOFT VAIN VOID WEAK ZANY BALMY BARMY BATTY BOGGY BUGGY DILLY DIPPY DIZZY EMPTY FONNE GAWKY GOOFY GOOSY INANE INEPT JERKY LOONY NODDY POTTY SAPPY SAWNY SCREW SEELY SILLY YAPPY ABSURD CUDDEN DOTISH DOTTLE FONDLY GLAKED GOTHAM GOWKIT HARISH INSANE MOMISH MOPISH SHANNY SIMPLE SLIGHT SOFTLY SPOONY STULTY STUPID TAWPIE UNWISE VACANT ASININE DAMFOOL DOLTISH FANGLED FATUOUS FLIGHTY FOLLIAL FOPPISH GLAIKIT GOOSISH GULLISH IDIOTIC PUERILE SOTTISH TOMFOOL UNWITTY WANTWIT WITLESS ABDERIAN FOOTLING FOPPERLY HEADLESS HEEDLESS HIGHLAND IMBECILE
FOOLISHLY IDLY FONDLY SIMPLE SIMPLY
FOOLISHNESS JAZZ FOLLY BARNEY BUNKUM FADDLE LEVITY LUNACY RUBBLE VANITY FATUITY BUNCOMBE FONDNESS INSANITY TOMMYROT
FOOT FIT PAT PAW PEG PES BASE COOT FUSS GOER HEEL HOOF PIED SOLE TAIL BASIS PIECE BOTTOM CLUTCH GAMMON PATTEN PODIUM RHYTHM TOOTSY TRILBY WALKER FOOTING GAMBONE MEASURE METREME PEDICEL FOREFOOT
(— OF ANIMAL) PAD PAW HOOF TROTTER
(— OF APE) HAND
(— OF INSECT) TARSUS
(— OF WINE GLASS) MULE
(CHINESE —) CHEK CHIH
(HALF —) SEMIPED
(LARGE AWKWARD —) CAVE
(METRIC —) IAMB BASIS DIAMB IONIC PAEAN DACTYL DIIAMB IAMBUS SYZYGY ANAPEST BACCHIC PYRRHIC SPONDEE ANAPAEST BACCHIUS CHORIAMB DOCHMIUS EPITRITE MOLOSSUS TRIBRACH TRIMACER
(STEWED OX —) COWHEEL
(TUBE —) SUCKER
FOOTAGE SETUP
FOOTBALL GRID HURLY ROUGE FOOTER HURLING LEATHER PIGSKIN KICKBALL
(KIND OF —) CAMP
FOOTBOY PAGE PEDES
FOOTBRIDGE PLANK LIGGER FOOTLOG
FOOTED FITTIT PEDATE

FOOTFALL PAD STEP TREAD FOOTSTEP
FOOTGEAR PATTEN FOOTWEAR
FOOTHOLD TIP HACK STEP FOOTING TOEHOLD
FOOTING PAR FOOT BASIS EARTH TRACK HEADING PIECING FOOTHOLD
FOOTLESS APODAL
FOOTLIGHTS FOOTS FLOATS LIGHTS
FOOTLIKE PEDATE
FOOTMAN SKIP FLUNKY JEAMES LACKEY VARLET DOORMAN FOOTPAD BOTTOMER CHASSEUR HIRCARRA WAGONMAN
FOOTPACE HALFPACE PREDELLA
FOOTPAD PAD WHYO PADDER ROBBER FOOTMAN PADFOOT LANDRAKER
FOOTPATH LANE TROD JETTY SENDA TRAIL FOOTWAY HIGHWAY PARAPET RAMPIRE SIDEWALK TROTTOIR
(— TO A PASTURE) DRUNG
FOOTPICK CASCROM
FOOTPIECE STEP
FOOTPRINT PUG STEP TROD PRICK SPOOR TRACE TRACK TRADE TREAD FOOTING ICHNITE PUGMARK FOOTMARK
FOOTREST HASSOCK STIRRUP
FOOTROPE HORSE
FOOTS SEDIMENT
FOOTSCRAPING SAND
FOOTSORENESS SURBATE
FOOTSTALK STRIG PODIUM PEDICEL PETIOLE PEDUNCLE
FOOTSTEP PAD STEP TROD CLAMP VESTIGE FOOTBEAT FORESTEP
FOOTSTOOL TUT LOVE MORA STOOL BUFFET SAMBLE CRICKET HASSOCK OTTOMAN FOOTREST
FOOT-WASHING NIPTER
FOOTWAY PATH CATWALK FOOTPATH
FOOTWEAR FEET
FOP TO ADON BUCK DUDE DUPE FOOL KNUT PRIG TOFF DANDY FLASH PUPPY MOPPET VANITY COXCOMB JESSAMY GIMCRACK MACARONI MACAROON MUSCADIN POPINJAY SKIPJACK
FOPPISH APISH DANDY FOPPY SAPPY SILLY DAPPER PRETTY SPRUCE STUPID BEAUISH BUCKISH FANGLED FINICAL FOOLISH DANDYISH SKIPJACK
FOR P IN TO PRO TIL VER TILL SINCE FORWHY BECAUSE FORNENT FAVORING
(— A LONG TIME) YORE
(— CASH) SPOT
(— EXAMPLE) EG VG
(— FEAR THAT) LEST
(— INSTANCE) AS SAY
(— THE EMERGENCY) PRN
(— THE MOST PART) FECKLY GENERALLY
(— TIME BEING) ACTUALLY
FORAGE ERS OAT RYE CORN GUAR

MAST PROG RAID FORAY BREVIT
RUSSUD ZACATE GOITCHO
BOOTHALE SCROUNGE
FORAGER OUTRIDER
FORAMEN PORE EXOSTOME
METAPORE
FORAY RAID MELEE FURROW
INROAD RAVAGE RAZZIA SORTIE
CHAPPOW HERSHIP PILLAGE
SPREAGH SPREATH
FORBEAR LET BEAR HELP HOLD
SHUN SIRE AVOID FORGO SPARE
WAIVE DEPORT DESIST ENDURE
PARENT RETAIN ABSTAIN DECLINE
REFRAIN RESPITE ANCESTOR
FOREBEAR WITHDRAW
(— **PROSECUTION**) COMPOUND
FORBEARANCE MERCY LENITY
NONACT QUARTER MILDNESS
PATIENCE
FORBEARING CLEMENT LENIENT
PATIENT MERCIFUL TOLERANT
FORBID BAN BAR DEFY DENY FEND
TABU VETO WARN DEBAR TABOO
BANISH DEFEND ENJOIN IMPEDE
OPPOSE REFUSE SHIELD FORFEND
FORWARN GAINSAY INHIBIT
WITHSAY DISALLOW FORSPEAK
PRECLUDE PROHIBIT
FORBIDDANCE BAN VETO FORBODE
FORBIDDEN TABU TABOO BANNED
DENIED VERBOTEN
FORBIDDING DOUR GRIM HARD
BLACK GAUNT STERN FIERCE
GLASSY GLOOMY GRISLY ODIOUS
STRICT FORBODE GRIZZLY
FORCE GAR GUT HAP JAM LID VIM
VIS ZIP BANG BEAR BEAT BEND
BIRR BODY CLIP CRAM DINT DOOM
DRAG EDGE FECK FOSS GRIP GUTS
HEAD JAMB JINX MAIN MAKE MANA
SOCK ABATE AGENT ARDOR BRAWL
BRING BRUSH CLAMP COACT CRAFT
CROWD CRUSH DEMON DRAFT
DRIVE EXACT EXERT FOHAT GAVEL
IMPEL KARMA MIGHT PAINT PEISE
POACH POINT POWER PRESS PRIZE
PUNCH REPEL SHEAR SHOVE SINEW
STEAM STUFF THROW WAKAN
WREST CHARGE COERCE COMPEL
CUDGEL DURESS EFFECT EFFORT
ENERGY EXTORT HIJACK HOTBED
IMPACT IMPOSE JOSTLE OBLIGE
POWDER RAVISH SHAKTI STRAIN
WRENCH ABILITY AFFORCE
BLUSTER CASCADE CONCUSS
DRAUGHT DYNAMIC IMPETUS
IMPRESS IMPULSE OPPRESS
REQUIRE SQUEEZE TORMENT
VIOLATE WAKANDA ACTIVITY
ADHESION AFFINITY BULLDOZE
COACTION COERCION DYNAMISM
EFFICACY HOTHOUSE MOMENTUM
PRESSURE STRENGTH VALIDITY
VIOLENCE VIRILITY
— **AIR UPON**) BLOW
— **AN ENTRANCE**) RANDOM
THRUST
— **APART**) SUNDER DISPART

(— **BACK**) REPEL RAMBARRE
(— **BY THREAT**) SWAGGER
(— **DOWN**) CLEW CLUE DETRUDE
DISMOUNT
(— **IN**) INJECT INTRUDE
(— **OPEN**) BURST JIMMY SPORT
RANFORCE
(— **OUT**) SPEW EJECT ERUPT EVICT
EXPEL KNOCK EXTUND EXPRESS
(— **PASSAGE**) SQUEEZE
(— **WAY**) CROWD WRING
(— **WITH LEGAL AUTHORITY**) POSSE
(**ALLEGED** —) OD
(**ARMED** —) CREW HEAD CONREY
ARMAMENT
(**CONCENTRATED** —) PITH
(**CONFINING** —) LID
(**CONSTRAINING** —) STRESS
(**COSMIC** —) EVIL
(**CREATIVE** —) NATURE
(**DRIVING** —) STEAM SWINGE
(**HYPOTHETICAL** —) FORTUNE
(**LIFE** —) SHAKTI
(**MAIN** —) BRUNT
(**MILITANT** —) SWORD
(**MILITARY** —) FYRD LEGION WERING
(**NAVAL** —) FLEET
(**PHYSICAL** —) NERVE
(**PREPONDERATING** —) SWAY
(**PROTECTIVE** —) CONVOY
(**RELIGIOUS** —) SANCTITY
(**SACRED** —) KAMI
(**SPIRITUAL** —) SOUL
(**UNRESTRAINED** —) FURY
(**UPWARD** —) BUOYANCY
(PL.) ARMY WILL COLORS
FORCED LABORED ENFORCED
FALSETTO SPURIOUS STRAINED
FORCEFUL GREAT GUTSY STIFF
STOUT MIGHTY PUNCHY STRONG
VIRILE DYNAMIC VIOLENT BRUISING
ELOQUENT EMPHATIC ENFATICO
FORCIBLE VIGOROUS
FORCEFULNESS EMPHASIS
FORCEMEAT FARCE BOUDIN
GODIVEAU QUENELLE STUFFING
FORCEPS DOG FURCA TONGS
TENAIL BULLDOG CLAMMER
PINCERS PINSONS CROWBILL
DENTAGRA PINCETTE VULSELLA
FORCIBLE VIVE STOUT VALID
COGENT MIGHTY POTENT STRONG
FORCIVE NERVOUS VIOLENT
WEIGHTY EMPHATIC FORCEFUL
POWERFUL PREGNANT PUISSANT
VIGOROUS
FORCIBLY AMAIN SADLY HARDLY
MAINLY HEAVILY STRONGLY
FORD PASS RIFT WADE WATH DRIFT
STREAM CURRENT FORDING
PASSAGE PASSING CROSSING
(**PAVED** —) STEAN STEENING
FORE VAN WAY AFORE AHEAD
FRONT PRIOR FORMER FURTHER
FOREARM CUBIT CUBITAL CUBITUS
FOREBEAR ANCESTOR
FOREBODE BODE GIVE OMEN
ABODE AUGUR CROAK BETIDE
DIVINE BETOKEN MISBODE OMINATE

PORTEND PREDICT PRESAGE
FORETELL
FOREBODING OMEN BLACK FATAL
AUGURY BODING DISMAL GLOOMY
ANXIETY BALEFUL BANEFUL
DRUTHER OMINOUS PRESAGE
BODEMENT SINISTER
FOREBODINGLY DIRELY
FOREBRAIN CEREBRUM
FORECAST BODE CAST SCHEME
CAUTION FORESEE FORESET
PREDICT FOREDEEM FOREDOOM
FORETELL PROPHESY
FORECASTLE FOCSLE ISLAND
FOREDOOM JINX DESTINY
FOREFACE CUSHION
FOREFATHER AYEL SIRE ELDER
PITRI PARENT ANCESTOR
FOREBEAR
FOREFINGER INDEX
FOREFOOT PAW PUD GRIPE
FOREFOOTING MANGANA
FOREFRONT VAN FRONT VAWARD
FOREGO FORGO WAIVE ESCHEW
ABSTAIN NEGLECT PRECEDE
REFRAIN ABNEGATE DISPENSE
RENOUNCE
FOREGOING PAST ABOVE ANTERIOR
PREVIOUS
FOREHEAD BROW FRONS FRONT
FRONTLET SINCIPUT
(— **INDENTATION**) STOP
(— **MARK**) KUMKUM
(**HIGH** —) LEPTENE
FOREHEARTH SETTLER
FOREIGN UNCO ALIEN FREMD
WELSH ALANGE EXILED EXOTIC
FRENCH REMOTE UNKIND DISTANT
ECDEMIC EPIGENE EXCLUDE
FRAMMIT HEATHEN OUTBORN
OUTLAND OUTWARD STRANGE
BARBARIC EPIGENIC EXTERIOR
EXTERNAL FORINSEC OVERSEAS
PEREGRIN STRANGER
(— **TO**) DEHORS
FOREIGNER ALIEN HAOLE ALLTUD
GRINGO PAKEHA GREENER
OUTBORN OUTLAND PARDESI
OUTSIDER PEREGRIN PORTUGEE
STRANGER MLECHCHHA
FOREKNOW DIVINE FORESEE
FOREWIT
FOREKNOWLEDGE PRESAGE
FORELOCK TOP BANG QUIFF
COTTER TOUPET FORETOP TOPPING
FOREBUSH
FOREMAN BOSS BULL CORK JOSS
LUNA PUSH CHIEF DOGGY GAFFER
GANGER LEADER RAMROD SIRDAR
TENTER CAPATAZ CAPORAL
CAPTAIN FOUNDER HEADMAN
MANAGER MANDOOR OVERMAN
SHOOFLY SKIDDER STEWARD
FOREHAND GANGSMAN OVERSEER
FOREMOST TOP HEAD HIGH MAIN
CHIEF FIRST FORME FRONT GRAND
BANNER FORMER LEADING
SUPREME VANMOST CHAMPION
(— **PART**) VAWARD

FOREORDAIN FATE SLATE DESTINE FORESAY PREDOOM FORECAST
FOREORDINATION FATE
FOREPART FRONT FOREHEAD
(— **OF FACE**) CHAP
(— **OF SHIP**) STEM FORWARD CUTWATER ENTRANCE
FOREPOLE LATH SPILE SPILING
FORERUN HERALD OUTRUN PRECEDE PRELUDE ANNOUNCE FORESHOT
FORERUNNER OMEN SIGN USHER AUGURY HERALD ANCESTOR FOREGOER FOURRIER PRODROME
FORERUNNING PRECURSE
FORESADDLE RACK
FORESEE SEE READ DIVINE PURVEY PREVISE PROVIDE ENVISAGE ENVISION FORECAST FOREKNOW PROSPECT
FORESHADOW HINT FIGURE HERALD FORERUN PATTERN PRELUDE UMBRATE FORETYPE
FORESHORE HARD SHORE HARDWAY SEASHORE
FORESHOW BODE ABODE AUGUR BETOKEN PORTEND SIGNIFY FORETELL PROPHESY
FORESIGHT FEAR VISION FOREWIT FORECAST FORELOOK PROSPECT PRUDENCE
FORESIGHTED CAGY CAGEY CANNY
FOREST BUSH GAPO MATA RUKH WOLD WOOD FIRTH GLADE GUBAT MATTA MATTO SYLVA TAIGA WASTE WEALD JUNGLE TIMBER BOSCAGE CALYDON COPPICE CAATINGA WOODLAND
(— **CITY**) PORTLAND SAVANNAH CLEVELAND
(— **FOR DEER**) FIRTH
(**IMMENSE** —) MONTANA
(**RAIN** —) SELVA
(**SIBERIAN** —) URMAN
(**STUNTED** —) CAATINGA KRUMMHOLZ
FORESTAGE APRON
FORESTALL BEAT HELP STALL DEVANCE FORERUN OBVIATE PREVENE PREVENT FORSTEAL
FORESTALLER GROSSER
FORESTAYSAIL JUMBO
FORESTER FOSTER WALKER MONTERO TINEMAN TREEMAN WOODMAN WOODSMAN
FORETASTE GUST HANSEL TEASER EARNEST HANDSEL ANTEPAST PROSPECT
FORETELL BODE ERST READ SPAE AUGUR INSEE WEIRD DIVINE HALSEN HERALD BESPEAK FORESAY PORTEND PREDICT PRESAGE ANNOUNCE FOREBODE FORECAST FORESHOW PROPHESY SOOTHSAY
FORETELLING PROPHECY
FORETHOUGHT CAUTION FORECAST PREPENSE PRUDENCE
FORETOKEN OMEN PORTEND

PROMISE FORECAST FORESHOW FORESIGN
FOREVER AY AKE AYE EVER ETERN ALWAYS ETERNE ENDLESS ETERNITY EVERMORE
FOREWARNING HINT PORTENT
FOREWING PRIMARY
FOREWORD PROEM PREFACE PREAMBLE
FORFEIT WED FINE LOSE TINE WITE CRIME DEDIT FORGO LAPSE FOREGO DEFAULT ESCHEAT FORWORK PENALTY FORFAULT
FORFEITURE FINE BLIND MULCT TINSEL ESCHEAT FORFEIT PENALTY
FORGE FOGE MINT TILT WELL CLICK FALSE FEIGN SMITH STOVE HAMMER SMITHY STEADY STITCH STITHY SWINGE CHAFERY FALSIFY FASHION BLOOMERY
FORGED BOGUS SPURIOUS
FORGER SMITH FALSER FALSARY LEVERMAN
FORGERY SHAM FALSUM FICTION BLOOMERY
FORGET LOSE OMIT WANT FLUFF BILEVE UNKNOW UNMIND NEGLECT OVERLOOK
FORGETFULNESS SWIM FLUFF LETHE AMNESIA AMNESTY OBLIVION
FORGET-ME-NOT MYOSOTE
FORGING HOOP CLICK JACKET
FORGIVE REMIT SPARE ASSOIL EXCUSE PARDON ABSOLVE CONDONE OVERLOOK
FORGIVENESS GRACE PARDON FORGIFT
FORGIVING GRACE HUMANE CLEMENT MERCIFUL
FORGOTTEN DERELICT UNMINDED
FORINT FLORIN
FORK CROC EVIL HOOK TANG TINE CLEFT CLOFF FURCA GLACK GRAIN GRAIP PRONG TWIST BISECT BRANCH CLITCH CROTCH DIVIDE FEEDER GAFFLE HACKER OFFSET TWISEL BIPRONG FOURCHE FRUGGIN HAYFORK TOASTER CROTCHET EQUULEUS GRAINING
(— **OF BODY**) SHARE
(— **OF PENNON**) FANON
(**THATCHER'S** —) GROM
(**TUNING** —) DIAPASON
FORKED BIFID FORKY FURCAL PRONGY DIVIDED FURCATE LITUATE BIFORKED BRANCHED FOURCHEE SUBBIFID
FORKING STAR
FORLORN LORN LOST REFT ALONE ABJECT FORFAIRN FORSAKEN HELPLESS HOPELESS PITIABLE WITLOSEN
FORM AME DIG FIG HEW HUE SET BLEE BODY CASE CAST CAUL DOME FLOW GARB IDEA KERN KITE MAKE MODE MOLD PLAN RITE SEAT THEW TURN BENCH BLANK BLOCK BOARD BUILD BUNCH CHART CHECK CRUSH DUMMY EIDOS ERECT FORGE

FORMA FORME FRAME GALBE GUISE IMAGE MATCH MEUSE MODEL SHAPE SPELL STAMP THROW USAGE ADJUST COUPON CREATE CUSTOM DEVISE DOCKET FIGURE FILLER HANGER INVENT MANNER REMOVE RITUAL SCHEMA SCHOOL SPONGE STRIKE SYSTEM TAILLE AGENDUM ARRANGE COMPOSE CONFECT CONTOUR DEVELOP FASHION FEATURE FORMULA GESTALT IMPANEL INVOICE LITURGY MAKEDOM OUTLINE PATTERN PORTRAY PORTURE PRODUCE PROFILE SPECIES STATURE BILLHEAD CEREMONY COMPOUND CONCEIVE CONTRIVE FORMWORK INSTRUCT LIKENESS ORGANIZE
(— **A HEAD**) POME
(— **A RING**) ENVIRON
(— **ASSUMED AFTER DEATH**) KAMARUPA
(— **BRANCHES**) BREAK
(— **BY CUTTING OFF**) ABJOINT
(— **CONNECTION**) ALLY
(— **FOR BELL FOUNDING**) SWEEP
(— **FOR CONCRETE**) BOXING
(— **FOR HOLDING BARREL**) SQUAW
(— **FOR MOLD**) JACKET
(— **FOR PRESSING VENEERS**) CAUL
(— **FRUIT**) KNIT
(— **INTO A CHAIN**) CATENATE
(— **INTO BALL**) CONGLOBE
(— **INTO RINGLETS**) CRISP
(— **LEATHER**) CRIMP
(— **MOUND**) TUMP
(— **OF GOVERNMENT**) ESTATE KINGSHIP
(— **OF PREDICATION**) CATEGORY
(— **POLITICAL SUCCESSION**) CAVE
(— **WITH PLASTER**) RUN
(— **YARN INTO THREAD**) CABLE
(**ANCESTRAL** —) BLASTAEA STEMFORM
(**CONVENTIONAL** —) AMENITY
(**DEXTROROTATORY** —) CAMPHOR
(**IMPERFECT** —) SEMIFORM
(**ISOMETRIC** —) DIPLOID
(**LINGUISTIC** —) FOSSIL GERUND
(**LITERARY** —) KNACK
(**LYRICAL** —) SESTINA
(**MUSICAL** —) SUITE
(**POINTED** —) ANGLE
(**SCHOOL** —) SHELL
(**SHOE** —) LAST FILLER
(**SONG** —) BAR
(**SPECTRAL** —) SHADOW
(**SPEECH** —) LEXEME
(**SPIRAL OR CIRCULAR** —) GYRE
(**TOP** —) GROOVE
(**VERB** —) FUTURE CONATIVE DEFINITE DURATIVE
(**VERSE** —) EPODE BALLAD SONNE KYRIELLE LIMERICK
(**VISIBLE** —) RUPA
(**WILD** —) AGRIOTYPE
(**WORD** —) ETYMON ANOMALY
FORMAL SET BOOK PRIM BUDGE CHILL COURT EXACT STIFF SOCIA

SOLEMN STOCKY BOOKISH LOGICAL
ORDERLY OUTWARD PRECISE
REGULAR SOLWARD STARCHY
STATELY STILTED ABSTRACT
ACADEMIC AFFECTED ELEVATED
FORMULAR OFFICIAL PUNCTUAL
STARCHED
FORMALDEHYDE FORMAL MONOSE
HARDENER METHANAL
FORMALIST PEDANT
FORMALISTIC COURT ACADEMIC
FORMALITY FORM SASINE STARCH
BUCKRAM DECENCY WIGGERY
CEREMONY
FORMALIZE STIFFEN
FORMALLY FORMLY STARCHLY
FORMAT SIZE GETUP SHAPE STYLE
FORMATION FORM RANK SPUR
BIOME FLIGHT GROWTH HARROW
MASSIF SPREAD POTENCE
BOTRYOID
(— ENCLOSING MINE WORKING)
GROUND
(— ENCOUNTERED IN DRILLING)
STRAY
(— OF BRANCHES) CANOPY
(— OF CRYSTAL) SHOOT
(— OF JOINT) ANKYLOSIS
(— OF PLANES) JAVELIN
(— ON TOAD) SPADE
(— RESEMBLING ICICLE) STIRIA
(BATTLE —) HERSE
(CLOUD —) NUBECULA
(DANCE —) SET
(DIAGONAL —) HARROW
(DRIPSTONE —) COLUMN
(ECOLOGICAL —) BIOME
(FLIGHT —) SQUADRON
(GEOLOGIC —) BOEL CULM CHICO
STRAY MARKER MEDINA CURTAIN
MANLIUS MATAWAN POTOMAC
TERRAIN AQUIFUGE FERNANDO
KOOTANIE KOOTENAI LOCKPORT
TOPATOPA YORKTOWN
(HABIT —) FIXATION
(INDENTED —) CLEFT
(INFANTRY —) TERTIA ECHELON
(LAND —) BOOTHEEL
(MILITARY —) SNAIL FLIGHT
(NAVAL —) SCREEN
(POINTED —) BEAK
'ORMATIVE PLASTIC DEMIURGIC
ORMED BUILT BOOKIT DECIDED
MATURED SETTLED WROUGHT
TIMBERED
(— AT BASE OF MOUNTAIN)
PIEDMONT
(— INTO STEPS) GRADY
(— ON SURFACE OF EARTH)
EPIGENE
(IMPERFECTLY —) ABORTIVE
(STURDILY —) BUXOM
ORMEE PATE PATTEE
ORMER DIE OLD ERER ERST FERN
FORE LATE ONCE PAST ELDER
FORME GAUGE GUIDE MAKER PRIOR
BYGONE RATHER WHILOM ANCIENT
ANOTHER CREATOR EARLIER
FIRSTER FURTHER ONETIME PRIDIAN

QUONDAM TEMPLET UMWHILE
PRETERIT PREVIOUS SOMETIME
STRICKLE UMQUHILE
FORMERLY ERE NEE OLD ERST
FORE ONCE THEN YORE GRAVE
WHILOM WHILST ONETIME
QUONDAM SOMETIME UMQUHILE
FORMIDABLE MEAN FEARFUL
ALARMING DREADFUL MENACING
TERRIBLE FEROCIOUS
(— PERSON) TARTAR
FORMLESS ARUPA DOUGHY ANIDIAN
CHAOTIC DEFORMED INDIGEST
FORMOSA (SEE TAIWAN)
FORMULA LAW MIX DATE FIAT FORM
RULE CANON CREED DHIKR GRAPH
INDEX LURRY KEKULE MANTRA
METHOD RECIPE THEORY RECEIPT
APOLYSIS CLAUSULE DOXOLOGY
EXORCISM
(— OF FAITH) KELIMA
(MAGICAL —) CARACT
(PL.) RAKA RAKAH
FORMULARY SYMBOL
FORMULATE PUT CAST DRAW
FRAME DEVISE CAPSULE COMPOSE
FORMULE PLATFORM
FORMULATED STATED WRITTEN
FORMULATION (— OF A TRUTH)
COUNT CREED DOGMA APHORISM
APOTHEGM DOCTRINE
FORMWORK SHUTTERING
FORNIX VAULT PSALIS
FORSAKE DENY DROP FLEE QUIT
SHUN ABAND AVOID FORGO LEAVE
WAIVE DEFECT DEPART DESERT
FOREGO FORHOO FORLET REFUSE
REJECT ABANDON DISCARD
FORLESE DESOLATE FORHOOIE
RENOUNCE WITHDRAW
FORSAKEN LORN FORLORN
DESERTED DESOLATE LASSLORN
FORSOOTH EVEN QUOTH
FORSWEAR DENY ABJURE REJECT
ABANDON PERJURE ABNEGATE
MANSWEAR RENOUNCE
FORT PA DUN LIS PAH LISS PEEL
SHEE SPUR WORK COTTA REDAN
SIDHE CASTLE SANGAR SCHERM
SCONCE STRONG BASTION
BULWARK CITADEL CLOSURE
REDOUBT BASTILLE CASTILLO
FASTHOLD FASTNESS FORTRESS
MARTELLO PRESIDIO
(FAIRY —) LIS LIOS LISS SHEE
SIDHE
(RUINS OF —) ZIMBABWE
(SMALL —) GURRY FORTIN BASTIDE
FORTLET FORCELET
FORTE FORT STARK STRONG
EMINENCY STRENGTH
FORTESCUE COBBLER SCORPION
FORTH OUT AWAY FURTH
FORTHRIGHT BURLY GUTTY CANDID
FORTHRIGHTLY FRANKLY
FORTHWITH NOW ANON AWAY
BEDENE DIRECT BETIMES FORTHON
DIRECTLY
FORTIFICATION BOMA FORT MOAT

WALL REDAN TOWER ABATIS
CASTLE GLACIS BASTION BULWARK
CITADEL DEFENCE DEFENSE
PARAPET PILLBOX RAMPART
RAVELIN REDOUBT FORTRESS
MUNITION RONDELLE STRENGTH
(LINE OF —S) TROCHA
FORTIFIED ARMED CONFIRMED
FORTIFY ARM MAN BANK FORT LINE
WALL WARD SPIKE STANK BATTLE
IMMURE MUNIFY MUNITE BULWARK
COMFORT DEFENSE GARNISH
RAMPIRE BASTILLE EMBATTLE
FORTRESS RAMFORCE STOCKADE
FORTITUDE GRIT GUTS SAND FIBER
FIBRE PLUCK METTLE BRAVERY
COURAGE HEROISM STAMINA
BACKBONE PATIENCE STRENGTH
FORTNIGHTLY BIWEEKLY
FORTRESS (ALSO SEE FORT) BURG
KEEP KASBA PIECE PLACE ROCCA
CASBAH CASTLE ALCAZAR BARRIER
BOROUGH CASTRUM CHATEAU
CITADEL KREMLIN ZWINGER
ALCAZAVA BASTILLE FASTNESS
STRENGTH
FORTUITOUS CASUAL CHANCE
RANDOM FORTUIT FORTUNEL
FORTUITY LUCK CHANCE
FORTUNATE EDI FAT HAP SRI GOOD
SHRI WELL CANNY FAUST HAPPY
LUCKY RIGHT WHITE DEXTER
EUROUS BLESSED FAVORED
WEIRDLY GRACIOUS
FORTUNATELY FAIR HAPPILY
FORTUNE DIE HAP LOT URE BAHI
DOOM FALL FARE FATE HAIL LUCK
PILE STAR EVENT GRACE ISSUE
LINES SONSE SPEED WEIRD WHATE
CHANCE ESTATE MISHAP RICHES
WEALTH DESTINY SUCCESS
THEEDOM VENTURE ACCIDENT
CASUALTY FELICITY STOCKING
(GOOD —) SELE SONSE SPEED
THRIFT FURTHER GOODHAP
BONCHIEF FELICITY
(ILL —) DOOM THRAW
FORTUNE-TELLER SEER SIBYL
SYBIL SPAEMAN SORTIARY
SPAEWIFE
(PL.) CHALDAEI
FORUM COURT PLATFORM TRIBUNAL
FORWARD ON TO AID BOG BUG GAY
ABET BAIN BOLD FORE FREE HELP
PERT SEND SHIP STEP AHEAD
ALONG BARDY BRASH CAGER
EAGER FAVOR FORTH FRACK FRECK
FRONT HASTY PAWKY READY
RELAY REMIT SAUCY SERVE SPACK
ULTRA AFFORD ARDENT AVAUNT
BEFORE BRIGHT COMING DEVANT
FORRIT FORTHY HASTEN NUZZLE
ONWARD PROMPT ROUDAS SECOND
TOWARD ADVANCE EARNEST
EXTREME FURTHER PROMOTE
PUSHING RADICAL SOLICIT
ADELANTE ARROGANT FROMWARD
IMMODEST IMPUDENT ONCOMING
PERVERSE PETULANT TELLSOME

TOWARDLY TRANSMIT
(MOST —) HEADMOST
FORWARDNESS IMMODESTY
FOSSA FOSS FOVEA GALET TRENCH
VALLIS FOSSULA FOSSETTE
FOSSE DITCH GRAFF
FOSSIL CYCAD CYSTID DOLITE
FUCOID ICHITE PINITE AMBRITE
BICHRON BLASTID CHAMITE CRINITE
ICHNITE JUNCITE LITUITE NEREITE
OVULITE TYLOPOD ZOOLITE
ZOOLITH AISTOPOD AMMONITE
ANCODONT ASTROITE BALANITE
BLASTOID BUFONITE CALAMITE
CERATITE CONCHITE CONODONT
ECHINITE EOHIPPUS FAVOSITE
FILICITE FUSULINA GEDANITE
GYROLITH MIMOSITE PEUCITES
POLYPITE SALIGRAM SCAPHITE
SERAPHIM SPONGOID SYNAPSID
TARSIOID
FOSTER REAR NURSE COCKER
HARBOR NUZZLE SUCKLE CHERISH
DEPOSIT EMBOSOM GRATIFY
INDULGE NOURISH NURTURE
BEFRIEND
FOSTERAGE NURSERY
FOSTERER NORRY
FOUL BAD BASE EVIL HORY RANK
ROIL VILE BAWDY BLACK DIRTY
DITCH FUNKY GRIMY GURRY HORRY
KETTY MUDDY MUSTY NASTY
RUSTY SULLY WEEDY CLARTY
DEFAME DIRTEN DREGGY FILTHY
GREASY IMPURE MALIGN ODIOUS
PUTRID ROTTEN SOILED SORDID
UNFAIR ABUSIVE DEFACED FULSOME
HATEFUL ILLEGAL IMBROIN
NOISOME OBSCENE PROFANE
SMEARED SQUALID TETROUS
UNCLEAN VICIOUS AMURCOUS
ENTANGLE FECULENT INDECENT
SLOTTERY STAGNANT STINKING
TRAUCHLE WRETCHED
(— UP) BOTCH
FOULMOUTHED ROUDAS ABUSIVE
OBSCENE PROFANE
FOULNESS FEDITY PRAVITY
(— OF MOUTH) SABURRA
FOUL-SMELLING FUNKY
FOUND FIX TRY YET BASE CAST
REST STAY BEGIN BOARD BUILD
ENDOW ERECT START ATTACH
BOTTOM DEPART GROUND INVENT
EQUIPPED PRACTICE PROVIDED
SUPPLIED
FOUNDATION BED BASE BODY FIRM
FUND GIST ROOT SILL SOLE BASIS
FOUND STOCK STOOL ANLAGE
BOTTOM CRADLE GROUND LEGACY
MATRIX PODIUM RIPRAP BEDDING
BEDROCK CHANTRY COLLEGE
MORTISE PINNING RADICAL
ROADBED SUBBASE WARRANT
BACKBONE DONATION MATTRESS
MIRAPOIX PEDESTAL PLATFORM
STANDARD UNDERLAY
(— FOR WIG) CAUL
(— OF BASKET) SLATH SLARTH

(FLOATING —) CRIB
(PRECARIOUS —) STILT
FOUNDED FUSILE
FOUNDER FAIL IMAM AUTHOR
CASTER DYNAST EPONYM HELLEN
YETTER AFOUNDE STUMBLE
BELLETER MISCARRY
FOUNT FONS FONT SOURCE
FOUNTAIN URN AQUA FOND HEAD
KELD PANT PILA SYKE WELL DIRCE
FOUNT GURGE QUELL SURGE
ORIGIN PHIALE PIRENE SOURCE
SPRING BUBBLER CONDUIT
SPRUDEL AGANIPPE SALMACIS
UPSPRING WELLHEAD
(INK —) DUCT
(SODA —) SPA
FOUNTAINHEAD ORIGIN SOURCE
FOUNTAIN PEN STICK STYLO
FOUR MESS CATER DELTA DALETH
FEOWER TETRAD QUARTET
QUATRAL MURNIVAL QUADRATE
(— OF ANYTHING) GUNDA
(— OF TRUMPS) TIDDY
(— TIMES A DAY) QD QID
(— YEAR PERIOD) PYTHIAD
FOURCHETTE FORGET SIDEWALL
WISHBONE
FOURFOLD FOURBLE QUATERN
FOURIERISM SOCIALISM
FOUR-O'CLOCK FRIARBIRD
FOURPENNY BIT JOE FLAG JOEY
GROAT
FOURTEENER SEPTENAR
FOURTH DELTA QUART FARDEL
FORPIT FERLING QUARTER
QUADRANT
(— HOUR) SEXT
(— OF BAHMIN EMPIRE) TARAF
(— OF CAKE) FARL FARLE
(— OF YEAR) RAITH
(AUGMENTED —) TRITONE
FOUSSA CIVET GALET
FOVEOLA VARIOLE
FOWL HEN RED COCK GAME GRIG
JAVA ROCK SLIP BIDDY CHUCK
CLUCK COPPY MALAY MANOC
MARAN SILKY ANCONA ASHURA
BANTAM BRAHMA CAMBAR COCHIN
HOUDAN LAMONA LEGBAR POLISH
REDCAP SULTAN SUSSEX BUFFBAR
CAMPINE CHICKEN CORNISH
DORKING FRIZZLE HAMBURG
LEGHORN MINORCA OKLABAR
POULTRY ROOSTER SPANISH
SUMATRA COCKEREL CUBALAYA
DELAWARE DUCKWING DUNGHILL
GAMECOCK LANGSHAN SHANGHAI
SHOWBIRD VOLAILLE
(5-TOED —) SILKY SILKIE
(AGGREGATION OF —) RAFT
(CASTRATED —) CAPETTE
(CRESTED —) TOPKNOT
(GUINEA —) KEEL COMEBACK
(MALE —) STAG
(STUFFED —) FARCI
(TAILLESS —) RUMKIN
FOWLER BIRDMAN
FOX DOG KIT PUG TOD ASSE FOOL

STAG WILD ADIVE CAAMA SWIFT
TRICK VIXEN ZORRO ARCTIC
BAGMAN CANDUC COLFOX CORSAC
FENNEC LOWRIE OUTWIT RENARD
BEGUILE CHARLEY CHARLIE
KARAGAN REYNARD STUPEFY
VULPINE CUSTOMER MUSKWAKI
OUTAGAMI PLATINUM
FOX-AND-GEESE MERELS
FOXGLOVE POPPY POPDOCK
THIMBLE FLAPDOCK POPGLOVE
FOX GRAPE ISABELLA LABRUSCA
FOXHOUND WALKER
FOX HUNTER PINK
FOXTAIL CAUDA CHAPE COUGH
KNEED TWITCH SETARIA GAMELOTE
FOXY SLY WILY COONY SHREWD
CUNNING VULPINE DEXTROUS
FOYER HALL LOBBY
FRACAS BOUT BRAWL MELEE MUSIC
BICKER RUMPUS SHINDY UPROAR
QUARREL SHINDIG FRACTION
INCIDENT
FRACTION BIT CUT PYO FLUX PART
BREAK PIECE SCRAP BREACH
LITTLE MOIETY DECIMAL GLUTOSE
WETNESS
(— OF RADIATION) ALBEDO
(NAPHTHA —) LIGROIN
FRACTIONAL ALIQUOT FRACTED
PARTIAL
FRACTIOUS MEAN UGLY CROSS
UNRULY CRABBED PEEVISH
WASPISH PERVERSE SNAPPISH
FRACTURE BUST FLAW REND BILGE
BREAK CLEFT CRACK FAULT JOINT
BREACH DEFORM HACKLE DIACOPE
FISSURE RUPTURE DIACLASE
FRACTION
FRACTURED SPLIT BROKEN
FRACTURING SLIP STRAIN FAILURE
FRAGILE FINE FROW WEAK FRAIL
FROWY LIGHT SWACK FEEBLE
FROUGH INFIRM SLIGHT TENDER
BRICKLE BRITTLE FROUGHY
SLENDER TIFFANY DELICATE
EGGSHELL ETHEREAL FRACTILE
SLATTERY
FRAGILITY DELICACY
FRAGMENT BIT ORT ATOM BLAD
CHIP DRIB FLAW GROT MOIT MOTE
PART RUMP SHED SNIP WISP ANGLE
BRACK BREAK BROKE CATCH
CHUNK CLOUT CRUMB FRUST
GIGOT PIECE RELIC SCRAP SHARD
SHERD SHIVE SHRED SPALL SPELL
SPLIT FARDEL FILING GOBBET
MORSEL REMAIN SCREED SHIVER
SIPPET SLIVER CANTLET EXCERPT
FLINDER FLITTER FRITTER FRUSTUM
MACERAL MAMMOCK REMANIE
REMNANT SEGMENT SHATTER
SHAVING CHIPPING DETRITUS
FRACTION POTSHERD SKERRICK
SPLINTER
(— CUT OFF) CANTLE
(— OF BONE) SEQUESTER
(— OF BRICK) BRICKBAT
(— OF DIAMOND) CLEAVAGE

(— OF ICE) CALF
(— OF LAVA) FAVILLA LAPILLUS
(— OF MELODY) LAY
(— OF ROCK) CRAG AUTOLITH
(— OF SAIL) HULLOCK
(— OF SOD) TAB
(— OF STONE) SCABBLING
(— OF UNFINISHED WORK) TORSO
(— OF VEIN MATERIAL) SHOAD
SHODE
(—S OF CLOUD) SCUD
(—S OF SAND) FINES
(CAST IRON —) POTLEG
(JAGGED —) BROCK
(MASS OF —S) BRASH
(PLANT —) SHIVE
(SHELL —S) SHRAPNEL
(WOODY —S FOUND IN FOOD) CHAD
(PL.) FRUSH SCRAPS CINDERS
FITTERS GUBBINS SMATTER
FLINDERS LEFTOVER SMITHERS
FRAGMENTARY HASHY SNIPPY
SCRAPPY DIVIDUAL
FRAGRANCE BALM ODOR AROMA
SCENT SMELL SWEET FLAVOR
FRAGOR BOUQUET INCENSE
PERFUME SUAVITY
FRAGRANT NOSY RICH BALMY
OLENT SPICY SWEET SAVORY
SPICED ODORANT ODOROUS
PERFUMY SCENTED AROMATIC
FLAGRANT NECTARED ODORIFIC
REDOLENT
FRAIL FINE PUNY WEAK CRAZY
REEDY SEELY SILLY BASKET
BROTEL CROCKY FLIMSY INFIRM
SICKLY SINGLE SLIGHT SLIMSY
SQUEAL TICKLE TOPNET BRITTLE
BRUCKLE FRAGILE SLENDER
UNHARDY DELICATE PINDLING
FRAILTY FAULT FOIBLE INVENT
FAILING DELICACY WEAKNESS
(HUMAN —) ADAM
FRAMBESIA PIAN YAWS BUBAS
FRAME BED BIN BOW BOX FLY GYM
MAT SET BAIL BEAM BIER BUCK
BULK BUNK CANT CASE CAUM CELL
CLAM CRIB CURB DESK DRAG FORM
FROG GATE GILL HACK HARP HECK
JACK MOLD PORT RACK SASH SLEY
SOLE STEP BANJO BLADE BLIND
BLOCK BUILD CADRE CHASE CLEAT
CRATE CROOK DRAFT EASEL FLAKE
FLASK FLEAK FLOAT GRATE HERSE
HORSE MOUNT OXBOW PERCH
SCRAY SHAPE STAND STATE STEAD
STOCK STOOL TRAIL BATTEN
BINDER BUCCAN BUCKET CASING
CHEVAL COFFIN CRADLE CRATCH
CRUTCH DECKLE DREDGE FABRIC
FENDER GANTRY GRILLE HANGER
HARROW HOTBED HURDLE PERSON
PILLAR QUADRA REDACT REEDER
SCREEN SETTLE SLEDGE SPIDER
SQUARE STAPLE TANGLE TENTER
TESTER ARMRACK BREAKER
CABINET CARRIER CASEBOX
CHASSIS COAMING COASTER
CRAMPON CRIMPER DRAUGHT

DROSSER FASHION FRAMING
FRISKET GALLOWS GARLAND
GATEWAY GIGTREE GRATING
HAYRACK HOUSING ICEBOAT
MACHINE MONTURE OXBRAKE
PORTRAY SETTING STADDLE
TRANSOM TRESTLE TRIBBLE
BARBECUE BOWGRACE CARRIAGE
CONCEIVE CONTRIVE DOORCASE
GRAFFAGE GRIDIRON GRILLAGE
HALBERDS HOGFRAME PLOWHEAD
RAILROAD RECEIVER RETAINER
SKELETON THRIPPLE TRIANGLE
TURNPIKE
(— FOR ARCH) COOM COOMB
(— FOR BEEHIVE) SECTION
(— FOR CANDLES) HEARSE
(— FOR CARRYING STRAW) KNAPE
(— FOR CASK) GANTRY STALDER
(— FOR CATCHING FISH) HATCH
(— FOR CLOTHES DRYING) AIRER
(— FOR CONFINING HORSE) TRAVE
TRAVAIL
(— FOR COW'S HEAD) BAIL
(— FOR DRYING FISH) HACK HAIK
(— FOR DRYING SKINS) HERSE
(— FOR FISHING LINE) CADAR
CADER
(— FOR GLAZING LEATHER) BUCK
(— FOR HAWKS) CADGE
(— FOR KILLING PIGS) CREEL
(— FOR LENS) BOW
(— FOR ROLLER BEARINGS) CAGE
(— FOR SMOKING MEAT) BOUCAN
BUCCAN
(— FOR STACK) HAYRACK STADDLE
(— OF A VESSEL) HULL
(— OF MIND) HAZE SPITE SPIRIT
FEELING
(— OF PIER) JETTY
(— OF SAW) HUSK
(— OF SPINNING MULE) SQUARE
(— OF STRAW) SIME
(— OF TINWORK) MARQUITO
(— ON STAGE) CEILING
(— TO CATCH STARFISH) TANGLE
(— TO CLEAN SHIP'S BOTTOM) HOG
(2-WHEELED —) GILL
(BELL —) SWEEP
(CARRIAGE —) BRAKE BREAK
(DIVING —) LUNET LUNETTE
(EMBROIDERY —) TABORET
TAMBOUR
(FISHING —) DREDGE
(GLAZIER'S —) FRAIL
(HARNESS —) HEALD
(LOOM —) SLAY SLEY SLEIGH
(MINING —) APRON
(PHOTOGRAPHY —) BUTTERFLY
(PORTABLE —) BIER CACAXTE
(PRINTING —) PRESS
(SHIP'S —) CANT
(SLUBBING —) BILLY
(STRETCHING —) TENT SLEDGE
TENTER
(TANNING —) BEAM
(WINDOW —) CHESS
(PL.) PROFILE
FRAMED NATE NATED ENGAGED

FRAMEWORK BED BENT BIER BONE
BUCK CAGE CRIB DURN GRID RACK
SASH BONES CADRE CHUTE COPSE
CREEL FLAKE SHELL STOCK BELFRY
BRIDGE BUSTLE CABANE CRADLE
DESIGN FABRIC GOCART GUARDS
HARROW HEARSE REBATO SHIELD
STROMA WATTLE CABINET CARCASS
CLIMBER COMMODE DERRICK
FRAMING FULCRUM JACKBOX
LATTICE PANNIER REBATER
RETABLE STADDLE TRESTLE
BARBECUE BEDSTEAD BULKHEAD
CARRIAGE CRADLING CRIBWORK
GRIDIRON GRILLAGE OSSATURE
SCAFFOLD SHELVING SHOWCASE
SKELETON
(— FOR PEAL OF BELLS) CAGE
(— OF REFERENCE) SCHEMA
(— TO EXPAND SKIRTS) BUSTLE
PANNIER
(EMPTY —) HUSK
(SCULPTOR'S —) ARMATURE
FRAMING CURB LEAD BELFRY
ARMATURE BEDPLATE

FRANCE

BAY: BISCAY ARACHON
CAPE: HAGUE
CAPITAL: PARIS
CHEESE: BLEU BRIE BONBEL
BOURSIN MUNSTER CAMEMBERT
MARCILLAT ROQUEFORT
COIN: ECU SOL SOU GROS AGNEL
BLANC BLANK FRANC LIARD
LIVRE LOUIS OBOLE SAIGA
SCUTE BLANCA BLANCO DENIER
DIZAIN TESTON AGNEAUX
CENTIME TESTOON CAVALIER
NAPOLEON
DANCE: GAVOT BRANLE CANARY
CANCAN BOUTADE GAVOTTE
DEPARTMENT: AIN LOT VAR AUBE
AUDE CHER EURE GARD GERS
JURA NORD OISE ORNE TARN
AISNE
DIVISION, ANCIENT: ARLES
PERCHE NEUSTRIA AQUITAINE
AQUITANIA
DYNASTY: CAPET VALOIS
BOURBON ORLEANS CAPETIAN
MEROVINGIAN
FOOD: PATE CREPE CANAPE
MOUSSE QUICHE BRIOCHE
SOUFFLE ESCARGOT PIPERADE
POTAUFEU TOURNEDO
ISLAND: RE YEU CITE CORSE
GROIX HYERE OLERON USHANT
CORSICA
KING: ODO EUDES PEPIN CLOVIS
LOTHAIR
LAKE: ANNECY CAZAUX
MEASURE: POT SAC AUNE LINE
MINE MUID PIED VELT ARPEN
CARAT LIEUE LIGNE MINOT
PERCH PINTE POINT POUCE
TOISE VELTE ARPENT HEMINE
LEAGUE QUARTE SETIER

CHOPINE HEMINEE POISSON
SEPTIER BOISSEAU QUARTAUT
ROQUILLE QUARTERON
MILITARY ACADEMY: STCYR
SAINTCYR
MOUNTAIN: PUY DORE BLANC
CINTO FOREZ PELAT COTEDOR
MOUNIER VENTOUX VIGNEMALE
CHAMBEYRON
MOUNTAIN RANGE: ALPS ECRINS
VOSGES CEVENNES PYRENEES
MARITIMES
NAME: GAUL GAULE GALLIA
NATIONAL ANTHEM: MARSEILLAISE
NATIVE: CELT GAUL FRANK
BASQUE BRETON GASCON
NORMAN PICARD CATALAN
GALLOIS LORRAIN FRANCIEN
LIGURIAN PROVENCAL
BURGUNDIAN
PORT: CAEN BREST CALAIS
TOULON LEHAVRE BORDEAUX
CHERBOURG DUNKERQUE
MARSEILLE
PROTESTANT: HUGUENOT
PROVINCE: FOIX ANJOU AUNIS
BEARN ALSACE ARTOIS COMTAT
POITOU AUVERGNE BRETAGNE
BRITTANY LIMOUSIN LORRAINE
PROVENCE TOURAINE
RACE TRACK: AUTEUIL
LONGCHAMPS
REPUBLIC CALENDAR: NIVOSE
FLOREAL VENTOSE BRUMAIRE
FERVIDOR FRIMAIRE GERMINAL
MESSIDOR PLUVIOSE PRAIRIAL
FRUCTIDOR THERMIDOR
VENDEMIAIRE
RESORT: PAU NICE CANNES
MENTON RIVIERA
RIVER: AIN LOT LUY LYS VAR
AIRE AUBE AUDE CHER DRAC
EURE GARD GERS LOIR OISE
ORNE TARN VIRE ADOUR AISNE
AULNE DROME INDRE ISERE
LOIRE MARNE MEUSE RHONE
RISLE SAONE SEINE SOMME
VIAUR YONNE ALLIER ARIEGE
ESCAUT SAMBRE SCARPE
VEZERE VIENNE DURANCE
GARONNE GIRONDE MAYENNE
MOSELLE CHARENTE
DRODOGNE
STOCK EXCHANGE: BOURSE
STRAIT: BONIFACIO
TOWN: AY EU AIX DAX GEX PAU
AGDE AGEN ALBI AUBY AUCH
BRON CAEN LAON LOOS METZ
NICE OPPY ORLY RIOM SENS
SETE STLO UZES VAUX VIMY
VIRE ARLES ARRAS BLOIS
BREST DIJON DINAN DOUAI
ERNEE LAVAL LILLE LISLE
LYONS NANCY NERAC NESLE
NIMES ORNES PARIS REIMS
ROUEN SEDAN TOURS TULLE
VICHY AMIENS ANGERS CALAIS
LEMANS LONGWY NANTES

PANTIN RENNES RHEIMS SARLAT
SENLIS SEVRES TARARE TARBES
TOULON TROYES VALOIX
VERDUN BAREGES CASTRES
LIMOGES ORLEANS ROUBAIX
VALENCE BORDEAUX CLERMONT
GRENOBLE MULHOUSE
ROCHELLE TOULOUSE
MARSEILLE STRASBOURG
TRIBE: REMI AEDUI ARVERNI
SALUVII ALLOBROGES
VERSE FORM: LAI ALBA AUBADE
RONDEL BALLADE DESCORT
RONDEAU VIRELAI VIRELAY
WEIGHT: GROS MARC ONCE
CARAT LIVRE POUND TONNE
TONNEAU ESTERLIN
WIND: MISTRAL
WINE: MACON MEDOC GRAVES
CHABLIS POMEROL BORDEAUX
BURGUNDY MUSCADET
SAUTERNE CHAMPAGNE
WINE DISTRICT: MEDOC ALSACE
BORDEAUX BURGUNDY
CHAMPAGNE

FRANCHISE SOC SOKE VOTE CHASE
FERRY HONOR INFANG CHARTER
FREEDOM LIBERTY CONTRACT
FREELAGE SUFFRAGE TENEMENT
FRANCOLIN COQUI TETUR TITAR
REDWING PHEASANT
FRANCOPHILE GALLOMAN
FRANGIPANI SHAKEWOOD
FRANK FREE OPEN RANK BLUFF
BLUNT BURLY LUSTY NAIVE PLAIN
BRAZEN CANDID DIRECT FORTHY
HONEST SALIAN ARTLESS GENUINE
LIBERAL PROFUSE SINCERE
CAREFREE CAVALIER GENEROUS
STRAIGHT VIGOROUS
FRANKINCENSE THUS OLIBAN
OLIBANUM
FRANKLY FREELY OPENLY PLAINLY
CANDIDLY
FRANKNESS CANDOR FREEDOM
OPENNESS
FRANKPLEDGE BORROW FRIBORG
FRANTIC MAD WOOD RABID INSANE
MANIAC FURIOUS LUNATIC VIOLENT
DERANGED FEVERISH FRENETIC
FRENZIED MANIACAL
FRAPPE ICE GRANITE
FRATERCULA MORMON
FRATERNAL BROTHERLY DIZYGOTIC
FRATERNITY FRAT FRARY HOUSE
ORDER FRATRY QUALITY SOCIETY
SODALITY
FRATERNIZE FRAT COTTON
FRAUD GYP DOLE FAKE GAFF GAUD
GULL JAPE JUNT LURK RUSE SHAM
SKIN WILE CHEAT COVIN CRAFT
DOLUS FAKER FAVEL GLAIK GUILE
HOCUS LURCH SHARK SHIFT SWICK
SWIKE TRICK BROGUE DECEIT
FULLAM HUMBUG INTAKE STUMER
WRENCH FLIVVER KNAVEFY
ROGUERY STUMOUR SWINDLE

BOODLING COZENAGE IMPOSTER
OPERATOR SUBTLETY TRUMPERY
FRAUDULENT SKIN WILY CRONK
COGGED CRAFTY QUACKY ABUSIVE
CROOKED CUNNING KNAVISH
CHEATING COVINOUS FRAUDFUL
GUILEFUL QUACKISH SINISTER
SPURIOUS
FRAXINELLA DITTANY RUEWORT
FRAY FRET BROIL BROOM FEAZE
MELEE RAVEL AFFRAY BUSTLE
CHAUVE FRIDGE TIFFLE CONTEST
FRAZZLE
FRAYED WORN FLAGGY RAVELED
FRAZER FINNER
FREAK FIRK FLAM WHIM FANCY
HUMOR LUSUS MOODS SCAPE
SPORT MEGRIM SPLEEN WHIMSY
CAPRICE CROTCHET ESCAPADE
FLIMFLAM WHIMWHAM
(CRAZY —S) LUNES
FREAKISH FREAKY FLIGHTY
MAGGOTY WHIMSIC CRANKISH
FRECKLE CHIT EPHELIS FRECKEN
LENTIGO SUNSPOT
FRECKLED FRECKLY FLECKLED
FREE LAX LET RID BOLD EASE LISS
OPEN REDD SHED SHUT CLEAN
CLEAR FLUID FRANK LARGE LISSE
LOOSE READY SCOUR SLAKE SPARE
ACQUIT DEGAGE DEVOID EXEMPT
FACILE FLUENT FREELY GRATIS
IMMUNE LOOSEN SOLUTE UNSLIP
VACANT VAGILE CLEANSE DELIVER
GRIVOIS INEXACT LASKING LIBERAL
MANUMIT RELEASE SCIOLTO
UNBOUND UNSLAVE UNTWIST
WILLING ABSOLUTE AUTARKIC
EASINESS EXPEDITE FACILITY
FREEHAND GRIVOISE INDIGENT
LAXATIVE LIBERATE UNBRIDLE
(— AND EASY) GLIB FAMILIAR
(— BROOK OF WEEDS) RODE
(— FROM ABIGUITY) HOMELY
DECIDED
(— FROM ACCUSATION) SACKLESS
(— FROM ACIDITY) DULCIFY
(— FROM ANXIETY) CONTENT
(— FROM ARTIFICIAL) ARTLESS
(— FROM BIAS) CANDID
(— FROM CARE) EASY CARELESS
(— FROM CHARGE) FDD PURGE
FRANCO
(— FROM CONSTRAINT) CASUAL
(— FROM DEDUCTIONS) NET
(— FROM DEFECT) HAIL HALE
SOUND
(— FROM DIRT) BRIGHT
(— FROM DOUBT) RESOLVE
(— FROM ELECTRICAL CHARGE)
DEAD
(— FROM ERROR) LEAL SOUND
CORRECT ACCURATE
(— FROM EVIL) RESCUE
(— FROM EXTREMES) EQUABLE
(— FROM FLAWS) GOOD
(— FROM FROST) FRESH
(— FROM IMPURITIES) FINE DRESS
DEFECATE DEPURATE

(— FROM KNOTS) ENODE ENODATE
(— FROM MARKS) BLANK
(— FROM MICROORGANISMS) ASEPTIC STERILE
(— FROM OBLIGATION) ACQUIT EXCUSE
(— FROM PENALTY) ABSOLVE
(— FROM STONES) CHESSOM
(— FROM) EX REDD DEVOID DISPATCH
(— OF DIFFICULTIES) AFLOAT
(— OF FAT) ENSEAM
(— OF TAR) WRECK
(— ONE'S SELF) SOLVE
(— PLUNGER) ARM
(— THROW AREA) KEYHOLE
FREEBOARD QUICKSIDE
FREEBOOTER TORY RIDER THIEF PIRATE CATERAN CORSAIR PILLAGER RAPPAREE SNAPHANCE
FREEBORN INGENUOUS
FREEDMAN LEYSING TITYRUS (PL.) LAET
FREEDOM RUN EASE FRITH LARGE ACCESS STREET APATHIA BREADTH LEISURE LIBERTY LICENCE LICENSE RELEASE AUTONOMY FREELAGE FREENESS IMMUNITY IMPUNITY LARGESSE WITHGATE
(— FROM BIAS) CANDOR
(— FROM CONSTRAINT) ABANDON
(— FROM DANGER) SECURITY
(— FROM ERROR) ACCURACY
(— FROM GUILT) SHRIVE
(— OF ACCESS) ENTREE
(— OF ACTION) SWINGE· LATITUDE
(— OF SPEECH) PARISIA
(— TO PROCEED) HEAD
FREEHOLD BARONY
FREEHOLDER SWAIN BONDER YEOMAN FRANKLIN
FREEING LIVERY ACQUITAL
FREE LANCE ROUTIER
FREELY FREE LIEF LARGE LARGELY READILY HEARTILY
FREEMAN BUR AIRE BARON CEORL HAULD BONDER FRANKLIN ROTURIER
FREEMASON FRATER MORGAN NOACHITE
(ONE NOT A —) COWAN
FREESTONE HAZEL
(— STATE) CONNECTICUT
FREETHINKER INFIDEL SKEPTIC AGNOSTIC
FREEZE ICE RIME CATCH CHILL FROST CURDLE FRAPPE HARDEN STARVE STEEVE CONGEAL GLACIATE
FREEZING COLD FREEZY FRIGID FROSTY GLACIAL GELATION
FREIGHT LOAD CARGO GOODS ASTRAY LADING FRAUGHT HOTSHOT PLUNDER PORTAGE TRUCKAGE
(— CAR) TRUCK
FREMD FRAIM FRAMMIT
FRENCH CREOLE FRANCO GALLIC GALLIAN GALLICAN
FRENCH GUIANA (CAPE OF —) ORANGE

(CAPITAL OF —) CAYENNE
(RIVER OF —) MARONI
(TOWN OF —) MANA KOUROU
FRENCH HONEYSUCKLE SULLA
FRENCH LAVENDER STECHADOS
FRENCHMAN FROG GAUL FROGGY PICARD FRENCHY MONSIEUR PARLEYVOO
FRENCH MULBERRY SOURBUSH
FRENCH REPUBLIC MARIANNA MARIANNE
FRENULUM TENDON
FRENUM BRIDLE FRAENUM FRENULUM VINCULUM
FRENZIED RABID RAMAGE BERSERK FANATIC FRANTIC FRENETIC FURIBUND
FRENZY AMOK FURY GERE MOON MUST RAGE AMUCK FUROR MANIA MUSTH FURORE MADNESS OESTRUS SWIVVET DELIRIUM INSANITY
FREQUENCY HERTZ CREBRITY
FREQUENT USE BANG KEEP HAUNT HOWFF OFTEN AFFECT COMMON HOURLY INFEST RESORT ENHAUNT OFTTIME CREBROUS FAMILIAR PRACTICE
FREQUENTLY OFT OFTEN HOURLY UNSELDOM
FRESH GAY HOT NEW WET FLIP GOOD RACY SMUG WARM BRISK CRISP GREEN MOIST QUICK RUDDY SASSY SMART SOUND SWEET VIVID CALLER CALVER FLORID LIVELY MAIDEN STRONG UNUSED VIRENT VIRGIN ANOTHER NOUVEAU UNFADED NOUVELLE ORIGINAL SPANKING YOUTHFUL
FRESHEN BRACE FRESH RENEW BREEZE CALLER REVIVE CHOUNCE PEARTEN REFRESH SWEETEN FRENCHEN
FRESHENER BRACER
FRESHET TIDE FLOOD FRESH SPATE TORNADO
FRESHMAN FOX BEJAN FROSH BEJANT GREENY FRESHER
FRESHNESS VERD NOVELTY VERDURE VIRIDITY
FRET DIK NAG ORP RUB RUX VEX CARK FASH FRAY FUSS GALL GNAW RAGE STEW YIRM CHAFE CRAKE CRISP FLISK GRATE PIQUE WORRY WREAK ABRADE CORSIE CRYSAL HARASS MUCKLE NETTLE PLAGUE REPINE RIPPLE RUFFLE CHRYSAL GRECQUE GRIZZLE MEANDER SCRUPLE SQUINNY ALIGREEK IRRITATE
FRETFUL GIRNY ORPIT TEATY TEENY TESTY FRETTY PENCEY SULLEN TATCHY TWISTY FRECKET PEEVISH PETTISH SPLEENY CAPTIOUS CRANKOUS FRETSOME FROPPISH PETULANT PINDLING
FRETTED FRETTY MAGGED
FRETTING FRET EATING
FREY FREYR YNGVI
FRIABLE CRIMP CRISP CRUMP FLAKY FRUSH MEALY SHORT CRUMBY

CRUMMY FLUFFY PUTRID CHESSOM CRUMBLY MOLDERY POWDERY RESOLUTE ROTTENLY SHATTERY
(NOT —) SAD
FRIAR FRATE FREER MINIM MINOR BHIKKU FRATER GELONG GOSAIN LISTER BHIKSHU JACOBIN LIMITER SERVITE BREVIGER CAPUCHIN JACOBITE MINORIST MINORITE PREACHER
FRIARBIRD COLDONG PIMLICO MONKBIRD
FRIAR SKATE DOCTOR
FRICANDEAU GRENADINE
FRICASSEE POTPIE
FRICATIVE BUZZ HISS OPEN YOGH DURATIVE
FRICTION BUZZ DRAG HISS CHAFE WINDAGE
FRICTIONLESS SMOOTH
FRIED FRIT SAUTE
FRIEDCAKE WONDER CRULLER FATCAKE DOUGHNUT
FRIEND AME AMI AMY BOR CAD EME PAX BHAI CHUM NABS OPPO WINE AMIGO BUDDY INGLE NETOP TROUT AIKANE BELAMY COUSIN CUMMER GOSSIP INWARD KIMMER PRINCE QUAKER ACHATES COMRADE SOCIETY COCKMATE COMPADRE DEMOPHIL FEDERATE HICKSITE INTIMADO INTIMATE TILLICUM
(—S NOT SPEAKING) CUTS
(CLOSE —) PRIVY COBBER COMPADRE
(DIVINE —) SOCIUS
(FAMILIAR —) CRONY GREMIAL SPECIAL
(GIRL —) DOXY DRAG DONEY DOXIE STEADY
(INTIMATE FEMALE —) CUMMER
(PRIVATE —) PRIVADO
(WOMAN —) GIMMER
(PL.) FOLK KITH SOCE FOLKS SOCIETY
FRIENDLESS FORLORN
FRIENDLINESS AMITY AFFINITY BONHOMIE GOODWILL
FRIENDLY COSH GOOD HOLD HOMY KIND CHIEF COUTH GREAT HOMEY THICK AMICAL CHATTY FOLKSY FORTHY HOMELY KINDLY SMOOTH AMIABLE AMICOUS COUTHIE AMICABLE HOMELIKE INTIMATE SOCIABLE
FRIENDSHIP PAX AMITY AMOUR
FRIEZE KELT FRISE CUSHION FALDING FRISADO FRIEZING
FRIGATE ZABRA
FRIGATE BIRD IOA IWA ALCATRAS
FRIGATE MACKEREL BONITO TASSARD
FRIGG FREA FRIJA
FRIGHT COW BOOF FEAR FLEG FRAY ALARM GHAST GLIFF GLOFF PANIC SCARE AFFRAY GASTER GLIFFY SCHRIK TERROR STARTLE SWITHER FRIGHTEN GASTNESS GLIFFING
FRIGHTEN AWE COW FLY SHY SOB BAZE BREE DOSS FEAR FLEG FLEY

FRAY FUNK HARE HAZE SHOO
AFEAR AFLEY ALARM APPAL BLUFF
GALLY GHOST GLIFF HAZEN SCARE
SHORE SPOOK AFFRAY ALARUM
APPALL BOGGLE BOOGER COWARD
FLAITE FLIGHT FRIGHT GALLEY
GALLOW AFFREUX FRECKEN
SCARIFY STARTLE TERRIFY
AFFRIGHT MISTRYST
(— **BIRDS**) KEEP
FRIGHTENED RAD EERY FRIT GAST
EERIE GHAST AFRAID AGHAST
SCARED SCAREY STURTIN
GHASTFUL
(**EASILY** —) TIMID SKITTISH
FRIGHTENING EERY DREAD EERIE
GOURY HAIRY FRIGHTY GHASTLY
SHIVERY DREADFUL FLEYSOME
FRIGHTFUL WAN GRIM UGLY AWFUL
FERLY HORRID UGSOME AFFREUX
DIREFUL FEARFUL GASHFUL
GHASTLY HIDEOUS ALARMING
DREADFUL ELDRITCH FEARSOME
GHASTFUL HORRIBLE HORRIFIC
TERRIBLE TERRIFIC
FRIGID DRY ICY COLD BLEAK FISHY
ARCTIC FROSTY FROZEN WINTRY
GLACIAL FREEZING SIBERIAN
FRIGIDITY GLARE
FRILL DIDO PURL JABOT RUCHE
RUFFLE ARMILLA FLOUNCE SPINACH
SPINAGE CHITLING CRIMPING
FRILLERY FURBELOW
(— **OF HAIR**) APRON
(PL.) PUFFERY FOOFARAW FRILLERY
FRILLINESS CHICHI
FRILLING SWEEPER
FRILLY CHICHI
FRINGE WLO EDGE GILL LOMA RUFF
WELT BEARD THRUM BORDER
EDGING MARGIN TASSEL BULLION
CREPINE EYELASH FEATHER
FIMBRIA SELVAGE TRAILER
VALANCE WHISKER CILIELLA
FRISETTE INDUSIUM SELVEDGE
TRIMMING
(**SOFT** —**S**) THRUM
(PL.) ZIZITH
FRINGED JUBATE
FRINGEFOOT UMA
FRINGEPOD LACEPOD
FRINGETAIL VEILTAIL
FRINGE TREE SHAVINGS
FRIPPERY FLIPPERY TRINKUMS
(PL.) GAUDERY
FRISK COLT FISK PLAY ROLL SKIP
WHID CAPER SKICE CAREER
CAVORT FRISCO FROLIC TITTUP
WANTON FRISCAL FRISKLE
FRISKY GAY PERT FRISK CROUSE
FEISTY KIPPER LIVELY COLTISH
JIGGISH PLAYFUL SPORTIVE
FRISON KNUB
FRIT FRETT CALCINE
FRITTER FOOL FRIT TEAR BOLLO
DRILL BANGLE DRIVEL LOUNGE
BEIGNET DRIBBLE FLITTER
SLATTERN
FRIVOLITY LEVITY FRIBBLE INANITY

ITEMING FUTILITY NONSENSE
NUGACITY
FRIVOLOUS GAY DAFT GIDDY INANE
LIGHT PETTY SILLY WASHY FLIMSY
FRILLY FRIVOL FROTHY FUTILE
TOYISH YEASTY FATUOUS FRIBBLE
LIGHTLY NIDGETY SHALLOW TRIVIAL
GIMCRACK JIMCRACK SKITTISH
TRIFLING
FRIVOLOUSNESS FUTILITY
FRIZZ FRIZ FRIZE FRIZZLE FROUNCE
FRIZZED CRISPY
FRIZZLY FUZZY CRIMPY FRIZZY
FRIZZY FUZZY CRIMPY FRIZZLY
FROCK DUD JAM GOWN JUMP SLIP
WRAP LAMMY SMOCK TRUSS TUNIC
CLERIC JERSEY LAMMIE MANTLE
ROCHET SUKKENYE
FROCK COAT CRISPIN
FROG PAD POD KICK FROSH FROSK
FROUD PADDO PADDY RONCO
ANURAN PEEPER TOGGLE CHARLIE
CRAWLER CREEPER CROAKER
CUSHION FRESHER FROGLET
PADDOCK PODDOCK QUILKIN
BULLFROG FERREIRO FROGGING
PLATANNA REPLACER
(— **IN LOOM**) HEATER
(— **OF HORSE'S HOOF**) FRUSH
CUSHION
FROG CRAB RANINIAN
FROGFISH SLIMER TOADFISH
FROGGER CHASER TRAILER
ZOOGLER
FROGGY RANARIAN
FROGHOPPER HOPPER CERCOPID
FROGMOUTH MOREPORK
PODARGUE
FROLIC BUM GAY RIG BLOW COLT
GAME GELL HAZE JINK LAKE LARK
ORGY PLAY PLOY RANT REEK ROMP
CAPER FREAK FRISK MERRY PRANK
RANDY ROUSE SPORT SPREE
CURVET FRATCH GAMBOL PLISKY
POWWOW PRANCE ROLLIX SHINDY
SPLORE VAGARY WANTON DISPORT
GAMMOCK MARLOCK PLISKIE
SCAMPER SKYLARK SPANIEL
STASHIE WASSAIL CAROUSAL
JAMBOREE
FROLICSOME GAY DAFT ROID ANTIC
FRISK GILPY LARKY FRISKY LIVELY
WANTON ANTICAL JOCULAR
LARKING LARKISH WAGGISH
ESPIEGLE FRISKFUL FROLICKY
GAMESOME LARKSOME PRANKISH
SPORTFUL SPORTIVE
FROLICSOMENESS HEYDAY
FROM A AB DE EX OF FAE FRA FRO
VAN VON THROM AGAINST
(— **A DISTANCE**) ALOOF
(— **BEGINNING TO END**) THROUGH
(— **ELSEWHERE**) ALIUNDE
(— **OFF**) AFFA
(— **SIDE TO SIDE**) OVER CROSS
ATHWART
(— **THIS PLACE**) HENCE
FROND FERN TRESS CROSIER
FRONDLET

FRONT BOW VAN BROW FACE FORE
HEAD PROW THIN AFORE VAUNT
BEFORE DEVANT FACADE FACING
FORMER OPPOSE SECTOR ADVANCE
FORWARD FRONTAL FURTHER
OBVERSE PREFACE RESPECT
SLENDER FOREHEAD FOREMOST
FOREPART FORESIDE FRONTAGE
(— **OF ASTROLABE**) WOMBSIDE
(— **OF BARN**) FOREBAY
(— **OF BIRD'S NECK**) GUTTUR
(— **OF BODY**) GROUF
(— **OF HEAD**) VISAGE FORETOP
(— **OF HELMET**) VENTAIL
(— **OF WATERWHEEL BUCKET**)
START
(— **UPON**) AFFRONT
FRONTAL FRONT SINDON FRONTON
METOPIC FRONTLET SUFFRONT
FRONTIER BOUND COAST FRONT
MARCH BARRIER FRONTURE
OUTLYING
(**FORTIFIED** —) LIMES
FRONTING OBVIOUS
FRONTISPIECE FRONT UNWAN
FRONTIS
FRONTLET TIARA FRONTAL
CHAMFRON
FRONTPIECE GORE
FROST ICE COLD HOAR RIME RIND
FROSTING ICING DIVINITY
FROSTWEED ROCKROSE
FROSTY ICY COLD RIMY CHILL CRISP
FRORE GELID GLARY HUNCH
BOREAL FRIGID FROREN CHILLING
INIMICAL PRUINOUS
(**NOT** —) OPEN
FROTH FOB BARM FOAM REAM
SCUM SUDS WORK CREAM SPUME
YEAST FLOWER FREATH LATHER
SPURGE
FROTHER CREOSOTE
FROTHING HUMMING MANTLING
FROTHY FOAMY REAMY SPEWY
SPUMY SUDSY FLASHY YEASTY
SPUMOSE SPUMOUS WHIPPED
FROWARD RANK CROSS AKWARD
PEEVISH WAYWARD CONTRARY
FROPPISH PERVERSE PETULANT
PROTERVE SHREWISH UNTOWARD
FROWN GLUM LOUR GLOOM GLOUT
GLUMP LOWER SCOWL GLOWER
GLUNCH FROUNCE FRONTLET
FROWNING GLUM GLUNCH
FROWZY BLOUSY BLOWSY BLOWZY
RAFFISH FROWZLED SCABROUS
SLOVENLY
FROZEN FAST FIXED FRORE FRORY
GELID GLARY FRAPPE FROREN
FRUCTOSE ACROSE
FRUGAL EASY MILD CANNY CHARY
ROMAN SCANT SPARE SAVING
SCARCE SCOTCH CAREFUL
PRUDENT SLENDER SPARING
THRIFTY
FRUGALITY SPARE THRIFT
ECONOMY PARCITY MANAGERY
FRUGALLY HARD CHARILY SAVINGL
FRUIT BEL FIG HAW UVA BAEL COYO

DATE DIKA DROP GEAN JACK LIME
NOOP PEAR PLUM POME SEED SLOE
SNAP SORB AKENE ANISE APPLE
BERRY CLING COUMA DRUPE GENIP
GOURD GRAPE GUAVA HAZEL ILAMA
LEMON LIMON MANGO MELON OLIVE
PAPAW PEACH RIPER SORVA
ACHENE ALMOND BANANA BUTTON
CEDRON CEREZA CHERRY CITRON
CITRUS COBNUT COCHAL COCONA
DAMSON DURIAN EMBLIC EMBOLO
GUARRI JUJUBE KEEPER LEGUME
LONGAN LOQUAT MARANG MAYPOP
MUYUSA ORANGE PAPAYA PAWPAW
PELLAS POMATO RESULT SAPOTA
SQUASH UVALHA WESTME ZAPOTE
APRICOT ATEMOYA AVOCADO
AZAROLE BILIMBI BLOATER
CARAWAY CHAYOTE CHECKER
CIRUELA COCONUT CURRANT
DESSERT GEEBUNG GENIPAP
GHERKIN KUMQUAT PIGFACE
PRODUCT RIPENER SERVICE
SHALLON SOURSOP TANGELO
ACHENIUM BAYBERRY BELLERIC
BILBERRY CALABASH CANISTEL
CAPSICUM CARDAMUM CITRANGE
CUCUMBER DEWBERRY DOGBERRY
EGGFRUIT FOLLICLE FRUITAGE
FRUITERY FRUITLET GOLKAKRA
INKBERRY LIMEQUAT OSOBERRY
PIEPRINT PODOCARP RAMBUTAN
SEBESTEN SEEDBALL SHADDOCK
SWEETSOP
(— OF CACTUS) SABRA
(— OF CAPER) CAPOT
(— OF CITRON) ETROG ETHROG
(— OF HEMLOCK) CONIUM
(— OF PALM) SALAK
(— OF ROSE) HEP HIP BUTTON
(— ON TREES) HANG
(—S COOKED IN SYRUP) COMPOTE
(AGGREGATE —) ETAERIO
DRUPETUM HETAERIO
(ASTRINGENT —) GAB GAUB
CHEBULE
(AVOCADO-LIKE —) ANAY
(CANDIED —) CONSERVE
(CARMINATIVE —) BADIAN
(COILED —) STROMBUS
(COLLECTIVE —) SYNCARP
(DRIED —) PASA CUBEB MUMMY
SABAL OREJON CAPSULE EMBELIA
(EARLY —) PRIMEUR HASTINGS
(FALLEN —) SHEDDER
(FIRST —S) ANNATES BIKKURIM
PRIMICES
(FLESHY —) SYCONIUM
(GOURD —) PEPO
(GRAPEFRUIT-LIKE —) SUHA
(GRAPELIKE —) WAMPEE
(HAWTHORN —) PEGGLE
(IMPERFECT —) SPECH NUBBIN
(MASHED —) FOOL
(MEDICINAL —) AIWAIN AJOWAN
EMBELIA
(ONE-SEEDED —) AKENE ACHENE
(PALMYRA —) PUNATOO
(PLUMLIKE —) CARISSA CIRUELA

(PRESERVED —) SUCCADE
CONFITURE
(PRICKLY —) HEDGEHOG
(SELF-FERTILIZED —) AUTOCARP
(SLICED DRIED —) SNITS SNITZ
SCHNITZ
(SPURGE —) TAMPOE
(SUPERIOR —) TOPPER
(UNRIPE OAK —) CAMATA
(WINGED —) SAMARA
(WOODY —) XYLOCARP
FRUIT BAT KALONG
FRUIT-BEARING FERTILE
FRUIT DOVE KUKU
FRUITFUL FAT FOODY BATTEL
FECUND FRUITY GRAVID FERTILE
TEEMFUL UBEROUS ABUNDANT
CHILDING FRUITIVE PREGNANT
PROLIFIC
FRUITFULNESS UBERTY FATNESS
FRUITGROWER FRUITIST
FRUITLESS DRY GELD VAIN ADDLE
BARREN FUTILE STERILE USELESS
ABORTIVE BOOTLESS
FRUIT PIGEON KUKU LUPE KUKUPA
MANUMA MANUTAGI
FRUIT STONE COB PYRENE
PUTAMEN
FRUSTRATE BALK BILK DASH DISH
FOIL LAME BLANK BLOCK CHECK
CROSS ELUDE SMEAR THRAW
WRECK BAFFLE BLIGHT DEFEAT
DELUDE KIBOSH OUTWIT SCOTCH
THWART ANIENTE DECEIVE FALSIFY
PREVENT CONFOUND INFRINGE
STULTIFY
FRUSTRATER MARPLOT
FRUSTRATING BOOTLESS
FRUSTRATION FOIL SUCK DEFEAT
FIASCO
FRUSTULE TESTULE HYPOTHECA
FRY SILE BROOD FRIZZ KRILL SAUTE
FRIZZLE GREYFISH
FRYER FRIER FRIZZER SPRINGER
FRYING PAN FRYPAN SPIDER
CREEPER SKILLET
FUCHSIA CORREA KONINI FUCHSIN
EARDROPS
FUCHSIN ROSEINE SOLFERINO
FUCHSINE RUBIN RUBINE MAGENTA
FUDDLE FUZZLE FLUSTER
FUDDLED FAP REE DOPY BOSKY
DOPEY SWASH TIPSY MAUDLIN
FUDGE HUNCH SNUDGE PENUCHE
DIVINITY
FUEL GAS OIL POB COAL COKE FIRE
PEAT UPLA ARGOL ACETOL ELDING
FIRING SHRUFF TIMBER COALITE
SYNTHOL FIREBOOT FIREBOTE
GASOGENE GAZOGENE
FUGITIVE HOT FLEME FLYER FUGIE
SCAMP OUTLAW FLEEING LAMSTER
REFUGEE RUNAWAY FLEETING
RUNAGATE UNSTABLE
(PL.) MANZAS
FUGUE FUGA
(— THEME) DUX
(PART OF —) STRETTA
FULA PEUL PEUHL FELLANI FELLATA

FULANI PEUL PEUHL
FULCRUM BAIT GLUT
FULFILL FILL FULL KEEP MEET
HONOR ANSWER COMPLY FULFIL
REDEEM SATISFY COMPLETE
COMPLISH
FULFILLMENT PASS EFFECT
FUNCTION
(— OF GOD'S WILL) KINGDOM
(IMAGINARY —) FANTASY
FULGURATION BLICK
FULL BAD BIG FAT FOW COOL DEEP
FAIR GOOD JUST PANG RANK TRIG
TUCK AMPLE AWASH BROAD CLEAR
FLUSH LARGE LUCKY PIENO PLAIN
PLENY ROUND SATED SOLID TIGHT
TOTAL WHOLE ENTIRE GOGGLE
HONEST STRONG BAPTIZE BRIMFUL
COPIOUS DESTROY DIFFUSE FULFILL
FULSOME LIBERAL OROTUND
PERFORM PLENARY REPLETE
TEEMING TRAMPLE WEALTHY
ABSOLUTE ADEQUATE BOUFFANT
BRIMMING CHOCKFUL COMPLETE
EXTENDED FREQUENT RESONANT
THOROUGH
(— CLOTH OR YARN) WALK
(— OF AIR) LIGHT
(— OF BLANKS) LACUNOSE
(— OF CHINKS) RIMOSE
(— OF DELAY) MOROSE
(— OF DEVILTRY) HEMPY HEMPIE
(— OF DIRT) FOUL
(— OF EGGS) GRAVID
(— OF ENERGY) STOUT SWANK
(— OF FLAWS) CRAZY
(— OF FUN) FROLIC
(— OF HAPPINESS) SUNSHINY
(— OF INTEREST) AGOG
(— OF IRON) SIDEROSE
(— OF LIFE) SPUNKY ANIMATE
(— OF LOOPS) KINKY
(— OF MATTER FOR THOUGHT)
MEATY
(— OF RUSHES) SPRITTY
(— OF SAND) ARENOSE
(— OF SLEEP) SOPOROSE
(— OF SMALL OPENINGS) POROSE
POROUS
(— OF SPIRIT) GENEROUS
(— OF VIGOR) FLUSH GREEN LUSTY
ANIMATED SPIRITED
(— OF ZEST) RACY
FULL-BLOWN JUICY
FULLBODIED FAT LOFTY HEARTY
FULL-BOSOMED BUXOM
FULLER GAG HARDY HARDIE ROLLER
TUCKER WALKER BLOCKER
CREASER THICKER CLOTHIER
FULL-FACED AFFRONTE AFFRONTY
FULL-FLAVORED BOLD RACY
FULL-FLEDGED SUMMED
FULL-GROWN RIPE GROWN MATURE
SEEDED
FULLNESS BODY FLAIR FLARE
FULTH PLENUM FULNESS PLEROMA
SATIETY
FULLY ALL DOWN EVEN INLY WELL
AMPLY LARGE ENOUGH FAIRLY

THRICE WHOLLY CLEARLY LARGELY
UTTERLY CLEVERLY ENTIRELY
INWARDLY MATURELY
FULMAR HAG NELLY NODDY
HAGDON NELLIE MALDUCK
MALMOCK STINKER
FULMINATE BLOW FULMINE
FULSOME SUAVE FOULSOME
FUMARIC BOLETIC LICHENIC
FUMBLE BOOT MUFF MULL PIRL
BOBBLE FAFFLE MUMBLE PRODDLE
MISFIELD THRUMBLE
FUMBLER STUMER STUMOUR
FUMBLING HALTING
FUME FUFF RAGE REEK EWDER
SMOKE STIFE SNUFFLE FUMIGATE
FUMID SMOKY SMOKEY
FUMIGATE SMEEK SMOKE PASTIL
CYANIDE PASTILLE
FUMIGATION GASSING
FUMIGATOR AERATOR
FUMITORY FUMARIA FUMEROOT
FUMEWORT
FUN GIG GAME GELL JEST JOKE
LAKE PLAY BORAK BOURD HUMOR
KICKS MIRTH MUSIC SPORT FROLIC
GAIETY GAYETY DAFFERY DAFFING
GAMMOCK WHOOPEE
(UNRESTRAINED —) HELL
FUNCTION ACT JOB RUN USE DUTY
FORM ROLE WORK ACTION AGENCY
MATRIX MISTER OFFICE SQUASH
CONCEPT FACULTY ISOLATE
SERVICE WORKING ACTIVITY
BUSINESS MINISTRY PROVINCE
(— EFFECTIVELY) AVAIL
(—S OF JUDGES) ERMINE
(APPARENT —) STUDY
(ESSENTIAL —) DHARMA
(MATHEMATICAL —) DEL FORM
INVERSE
(SPECIAL —) CEREMONY
FUNCTIONAL DYNAMIC
FUNCTIONARY FLUNKY CAPTAIN
FLUNKEY CHAPRASI
FUNCTIONING AFLOAT
FUNCTIONLESS OTIOSE
FUND BOX BANK FOND MASS CHEST
KITTY MOUNT SLUSH STOCK STORE
ESCROW CHALUKA JACKPOT
RESERVE HALUKKAH PECULIUM
(PL.) CAJA COFFER
FUNDAMENT NOCK TAIL BOTTOM
FUNDUS
FUNDAMENTAL BASAL BASIC
KLANG PRIME VITAL BOTTOM
SIMPLE BASILAR BEDROCK ORGANIC
PRIMARY RADICAL ABSOLUTE
ORIGINAL RUDIMENT SUBSTRAT
FUNDAMENTALLY AUFOND
FUNDUS FORNIX
FUNERAL TANGI BURIAL EXEQUY
BURYING CORTEGE FUNEBRE
FUNERARY MORTUARY
FUNERAL DIRECTOR BLACKMAN
FUNEREAL FERAL DISMAL SOLEMN
FUNEBRE FUNERAL DIRGEFUL
EXEQUIAL MOURNFUL
FUNGICIDE NABAM ZINEB FERBAM
CALOMEL BORDEAUX DICHLONE

FUNGOID MYCOID FUNGOUS
FUNGUS MOLD SMUT BRAND ERGOT
FUNGE HYPHO MOREL MOULD
PHOMA SPUNK SWARD TRUFF
VALSA VERPI AGARIC BOLETE
FUNGAL MILDEW OIDIUM AMANITA
BOLETUS CHYTRID FUNGOID
GEASTER LEPIOTA TRUFFLE
AECIDIUM CLATHRUS CORNBELL
EUMYCETE FUSARIUM HELVELLA
MUCEDINE MUSHROOM OOMYCETE
OTOMYCES PHALLOID POLYPORE
PUFFBALL SAPROGEN SPOROGEN
TREMELLA TUCKAHOE
(UNICELLULAR —) BEES EAST
YEAST
FUNK FUNG NESH
FUNNEL CAST STACK TEWEL TRUNK
FILLER FUMMEL SIPHON SYPHON
TUNNEL TUNNER TRUMPET TUNDISH
HYPONOME WINDSAIL
FUNNY ODD GOOD COMIC DROLL
MERRY QUEER COMICAL JOCULAR
RISIBLE STRANGE HUMOROUS
(VERY —) SPLITTING
FUR FOX BEAR CALF COON FLIX FOIN
GRAY GREY GRIS MINK PEAN PELF
PELL SEAL VAIR BUDGE COYPU
CROSS FITCH FLICK GENET GRISE
OTTER PAHMI SABLE SCARF SHUBA
BADGER BEAVER COUGAR DESMAN
ERMINE FISHER GALYAC JACKET
MARTIN NUTRIA PELAGE POTENT
RABBIT SPRING SUSLIK CALABER
CARACAL FITCHET FITCHEW
FURRURE MINIVER TOPCOAT
CACOMIXL ERMINOIS KOLINSKI
(— OF LAMBSKIN AND WOOL)
BUDGE
(— RESEMBLING PERSIAN LAMB)
KRIMMER
(BEAVER —) WOOM CASTOR
(GRAY —) GRAY GREY GRIS GRISE
CRIMMER LETTICE
(NUMBER OF — SKINS) TIMBER
TIMMER
(RABBIT —) CONY SCUT CONEY
FLICK LAPIN HATTER SEALINE
ERMILINE
(SQUIRREL —) CALABAR
(SQUIRREL OR MARTIN —) AMICE
POPEL
(STONE MARTEN'S —) FOIN
(PL.) PELTRY FURRIERY
FURBEARER PLATINUM
FURBELOW DIDO FALBALA
FURBISH DO FIG RUB FAKE FINE
VAMP CLEAN SCOUR FINIFY POLISH
BURNISH VARNISH RENOVATE
FURCATE FORKY BRANCH FURCAL
FURCULA SPRING FURCULUM
FURCULUM WISHBONE
FURFOOZ GRENELLE
FURIOUS MAD GRIM WOOD ANGRY
BRAIN GIDDY IRATE RABID SHARP
FIERCE FURIAL FURIED INSANE
RENISH STORMY FRANTIC HOPPING
MADDING MANKIND PELTING
RAGEOUS REDWOOD RUSHING
TEARING VIOLENT FRENZIED

VEHEMENT VESUVIAN WRATHFUL
FURIOUSLY CRAZY ANGERLY
TEARING
FURL FOLD HAND ROLL STOW WRAP
FRESE TRUSS FARDEL FURDLE
FURLED IN
FURLONG SHOT STADE
FURLOUGH LEAVE BLIGHTY
FURNACE ARC KILN OVEN TANK
BENCH CUPEL DRIER DRYER FORGE
MOUTH TISAR BURNER CALCAR
CUPOLA HEATER ATHANOR
CHAFERY CRESSET FIREPOT
PUDDLER ROASTER BESSEMER
BLOOMERY CALCINER FIREWORK
IRONCLAD LIMEKILN PRODUCER
REFINERY TRYWORKS
(— DOOR) TWEEL
(ALMOND —) ALMAN
(ARC —) HEROULT
(GLASS-HEATING —) TISAR
(PORTABLE —) DANDY CRESSET
FURNACEMAN BUSTLER DROSSER
SMELTER IMPROVER REHEATER
FURNISH ARM SOW DECK FEAT
FEED FILL FRET FRUB GIVE LEND
TRIM VEST ARRAY ENDOW EQUIP
FRAME INDUE PITCH POINT SERVE
SPEED STOCK STORE STUFF
AFFORD GRAITH INSURE INVEST
OUTFIT RENDER SUPPLY ADVANCE
APPAREL APPOINT BRACKET
GARNISH INSTORE PERFORM
PLENISH PRESENT PRODUCE
PROVIDE SUFFICE ACCOUTER
DECORATE FRUBBISH MINISTER
(— ABUNDANTLY) FREQUENT
(— ANALYSIS) ACCOUNT
(— FULLY) CHARGE
(— REFRESHMENT) EASE
(— WITH DRINK) BIRL BYRL
(— WITH MEALS) BOARD
(— WITH STEEP SLOPE) ESCARP
(— WITH STRENGTH) MAN
(— WITH WINGS) IMP
(— WITH) BESEE
FURNISHED ARMED BODEN GARNI
(COMFORTABLY —) BEIN
FURNISHING ADVANCE FITMENT
(PL.) STUFF BAGGAGE PENATES
FURNITURE ADAM TIRE SAMAN
STOOL STUFF GRAITH FITMENT
MEUBLES MOVABLE EQUIPAGE
ORNAMENT SUPELLEX TACKLING
(CHEAP —) BORAX
(SHIP'S —) HARNESS
FURORE FUROR BROUHAHA
FURRED PURED LOADED
FURRING PACKING
FURROW FUR GAP GAW RIB RUT
FURR GRIP HINT LINE PLOW RAIN
RILL ROUT RUCK SEAM SULK
CHASE DRAIN DRILL EARTH FIELD
RIGOL SCORE SEUGH STRIA
GROOVE GUTTER INDENT SULCUS
SUTURE TRENCH BREAKER
CHAMFER CHANNEL CRUMPLE
FEERING PLOWING QUILLET
SCRATCH WINDROW WRINKLE
CARRIAGE NOTAULIX THOROUGH

FURROWED SEAMED EXARATE
FURROWY SULCATE TRENCHED
FURROWING KNOT DRESS
FURRY SHAGGY
FUR SEAL URSAL
FURTHER MO AID YET HELP YOND
ADDED AGAIN FRESH SPEED SUPRA
BEYOND EXTEND SECOND ADVANCE
DEVELOP FARTHER FORWARD
PROMOTE MOREOVER REMANENT
ULTERIOR
FURTHERMORE BESIDES FURTHER
OVERMORE
FURTIVE SLY PRIVY CLAMMY
SECRET SHIFTY SNEAKY HANGDOG
MEACHING MYSTICAL SNEAKING
STEALTHY
FURTIVELY SLILY SLYLY SIDELINS
FURTIVENESS STEALTH
FURUNCLE BOIL
FURY HAG IRE WAX BURN RAGE
ANGER BRETH DREAD FUROR IRISH
RIGOR WRATH BELDAM CHOLER
FRENZY FURORE MADNESS WIDDRIM
DELIRIUM FEROCITY VIOLENCE
WOODNESS
FURZE FUN FUZZ LING ULEX WHIN
GORSE WHINCOW

FUSE RUN CAKE FLOW FLUX FRIT
FUZE MELT BLEND FOUND FUSEE
FUZEE QUILL SMELT SQUIB SWAGE
TRAIN UNITE MINGLE SPITTER
CONCRETE CONFLATE COPULATE
PORTFIRE SAUCISSE
FUSED CONNATE
FUSEE FUZEE SPINDLE VESUVIAN
VESUVIUS
FUSELAGE BODY
(— **MEMBER**) LONGERON
FUSIFORM FUSATE SPINDLE
FUSIL **(DIVIDED INTO —S)** PLUMETE
FUSION ZYG FLUX FUSURE CHIASMA
FLUXION CYTOGAMY MITAPSIS
FUSS DO ADO ROW TEW COIL FAFF
FIKE FIRK FIZZ FRET ROUT SONG
STIR TIME TOUSE TOWSE TRADE
WHAUP BOTHER CADDLE DIRDUM
FANTAD FETTLE FISSLE FISTLE
FIZZLE FRAISE FUFFLE FUSTLE
HOORAY HURRAH PHRASE POTHER
SETOUT STROTH TURNUP FOOSTER
FRIGGLE FUSSIFY NAUNTLE
POOTHER SPUFFLE SPUTTER
TAMASHA BUSINESS FOOFARAW
SCRONACH

FUSSBUDGETY SPOFFISH
FUSSINESS DAINTY FADDLE FIKERY
FOOSTER
FUSSING BOTHER
FUSSY FIKY FIXY FUDGY FIDFAD
PROSSY SPOFFY SPRUCE STICKY
FIDGETY SPOFFISH
FUSTET ZANTE FUSTIC
FUSTIAN HOLMES PILLOW BOMBAST
TWADDLE MOLESKIN
FUSTIC LIME MORA FUSTET
DYEWOOD AMARILLO
FUSTINESS FOIST
FUSTY FOIST MOLDY MUSTY FOISTY
FROWSTY
FUTILE IDLE VAIN OTIOSE USELESS
FOOTLESS FUTILOUS HELPLESS
FUTILITY VANITY NUGACITY
FUTTAH WHATA
FUTURE LATER SKULD COMING
ONWARD OPTION TOCOME TOWARD
LAVENIR FUTURITY
(— **TIME**) MANANA
FUZZ LINTERS
FUZZY LOUSY MUZZY WOOLY
WOOLLY

G GEE GOLF GEORGE
GA AKRA ACCRA INKRA
GAB GOB YAP BLAB CHINFEST
GABBLE WAB CANK CHAT CONK
JAVER BABBLE GAGGLE HABBLE
RABBLE TATTER YABBLE CLATTER
JAUNDER TWADDLE TWITTER
SLIPSLOP
GABBRO BOJITE NORITE EUCRITE
GABION KISH KEESH BASKET
WALING CORBEIL
GABLE GAVEL GOFOL DETAIL
DORMER GABLET KENNEL MEMBER
PINION AILERON PEDIMENT
GABON (CAPITAL OF —) LIBREVILLE
(LAKE OF —) ANENGUE AZINGUO
(MOUNTAIN OF —) MPELE
(NATIVE OF —) FANG ADOUMA
ECHIRA OKANDE
(RIVER OF —) OGOUE ABANGA
IVINDA NGOUNIE
(TOWN OF —) OYEM BONGO KANGO
MITZIC OMVANE MAKOKOU
GABOON OKOUME
GABRIELINO TOBIKHAR
GAD GAR RUN GAUD JAZZ RAKE
JINKET GADLING TRAIPSE
(— ABOUT) HAIK ROLL STRAM
GALLANT TROLLOP
(FATHER OF —) JACOB
GADABOUT GAD GADDER TRAIPSE
GADFLY GAD CLEG GLEG CLEGG
STOUT WHAME BOTFLY BREEZE
GADBEE OESTRID HORSEFLY
GADGET DODAD GISMO GIZMO
HICKY DINGUS DOODAD GILGUY
HICKEY JIGGER JIMJAM WIDGET
CONCERN DOFUNNY GIMMICK
BUSINESS GIMCRACK JIMCRACK
(PL.) GIBBLES GUBBINS GADGETRY
GADUS MORRHUA
GADWALL RODGE VOLANT GADWELL
REDWING SHUTTLE
GAEL CELT KELT SCOT GOIDEL
GAEDHEAL
GAELIC ERSE IRISH
GAFF CLIP SPAR SPUR YARD GAFFLE
GABLOCK GAFFLET SLASHER
GAVELOCK
(— MACKEREL) GAMBEER
GAG BOFF GEGG JOKE PONG SCOB
HEAVE KEVEL SCOBE AGUAJI
MUZZLE WHEEZE
GAGE (ALSO SEE GAUGE) LAY PAWN
WAGE GAUGE JEDGE NORMA
WAGER FEELER PLEDGE SPIDER
SCANTLE STANDARD UDOMETER
GAIETY JOY GALA JEST CHEER
MIRTH BAWDRY FROLIC GAYETY
LEVITY BAUDERY BEGONIA DAFFERY
DAFFING GAYNESS JOLLITY
JOYANCE ROLLICK FESTIVAL
HILARITY VIVACITY
GAILY GAY GAYLY BRAVELY LIGHTLY
GAIN BAG DAP GET NET POT WIN
BEAR BOOT DRAW GROW HAVE
LAND MAKE PELF SACK TILL ADDLE
BOOTY CATCH LATCH LUCRE
REACH SCORE ARRIVE ATTAIN

CHIEVE DERIVE GATHER INCOME
OBTAIN PROFIT STRAIN CAPTURE
CONQUER EMBRACE GAYMENT
GETTING HARVEST POSSESS
PROCURE REALIZE VANTAGE
WINNING CLEANING CONQUEST
PURCHASE
(— ADMISSION) ENTER
(— ADVANTAGE) GLEEK
(— ASCENDANCY) PREVAIL
(— BY EXTORTION) SQUEEZE
(— BY FORTUNE) DRAW HAZARD
(— COMMAND OF) MASTER
(— KNOWLEDGE) EDIFY LEARN
(— OVER) ENGAGE
(— UNDERSTANDING) SMOKE
(— WITHOUT DEDUCTION) CLEAR
(DISHONEST —) MEED
(ESTIMATED —) ESTEEM
(ILL-GOTTEN —) PELF
(MATERIAL —) PUDDING
(UNEXPECTED —) BUNCE
(PL.) PICKING PLUNDER GANANCIAS
GAINFUL LUCROUS GAINSOME
GAINSAY DENY FORBID IMPUGN
OPPOSE REFUTE RESIST DISPUTE
RECLAIM WITHSAY AGAINSAY
GAIT BAT JOG GANG LOPE PACE
RACK SKIP STEP TROT VOLT WALK
AMBLE AUBIN GOING STALK TRAIN
ALLURE CANTER GALLOP LOUNGE
SLOUCH SWINGE TODDLE WADDLE
WALLOW WAMBLE WOBBLE
DOGTROT HICKORY SAUNTER
SCUTTLE SHAMBLE SHUFFLE
WALKING WAUCHIE
(— OF ILL-BROKEN HORSE) CHACK
(4-BEAT —) AMBLE
(DEFECTIVE —) WINDING
(UNSTEADY —) STAGGER
GAITER SPAT VAMP STRAD BONNET
BRAGAS COCKER GASKIN GUETRE
HOGGER HUGGER LEGGIN PUTTEE
GAMBADE GAMBADO LEGGING
STARTUP BOOTIKIN CUTTIKIN
(PL.) UPPERS GASKINS GAMASHES
GRAMOCHES
GAIZE MALMSTONE
GAJO GORGIO
GALACTITE MILKSTONE
GALACTOSIDE IDEIN IDAEIN
GALAGO LEMUR LEMUROID
GALANAS GAINES
GALATEA (FATHER OF —) NEREUS
(LOVER OF —) ACIS
(MOTHER OF —) DORIS
GALAX COLTSFOOT
GALAXY NEBULA SPIRAL
GALBANUM FERULA GALBAN
ALBETAD
GALCHA PAMIR
GALE BLOW GELL HELM WIND
GAGEL PERRY STOUR BUSTER
EASTER BAYBUSH BURSTER
GALEAGE TEMPEST FLEAWOOD
GALEWORT NORWESTER
GALEA MITRA HELMET
GALGA INGUSH
GALIBI CARIBI KALINA

GALINGALE CYPRESS WANHORN
CHINAROOT
GALIPOT BARRAS GALLIPOT
TACAMAHAC
GALJOEN BLACKFISH
GALL GA GAW BAIT FELL FRET
WRING COCKLE HARASS BEDEGAR
GALLNUT KNOPPER NUTGALL
BEDEGUAR CECIDIUM FLEASEED
IRRITATE OAKBERRY SEEDGALL
SPURGALL TACAHOUT
(SAND —) SALT NATRON SANDIVER
(PL.) PURPLES
GALLANT GAY BEAU PROW BLADE
BRAVE BULLY CIVIL JOLLY LOVER
NOBLE PREUX SHOWY SPARK
SWAIN DONZEL ESCORT HEROIC
POLITE RUTTER SPARKY SQUIRE
SUITOR AMATORY AMORIST
AMOROUS CONDUCT GALANTE
GREGORY SPARKER STATELY
TOPPING YOUNKER CAVALIER
CICISBEO FEMALIST GALLIARD
HANDSOME POLISHED
GALLANTRY GAME DRURY DRUERY
BRAVERY COURAGE PROWESS
PARAMOUR
GALLBERRY INKBERRY
GALLED RAW
GALLEON CARAC CARRACK
GALLOON
GALLERY POY SAP COOP GODS
JUBE LOFT PAWN ALURE BOYAU
ORIEL PRADO ARCADE BURROW
DEDANS NARROW PIAZZA SCHOOL
SOLLAR SUBWAY TUNNEL BALCONY
GALERIE HEADWAY TERRACE
VERANDA BRATTICE CANTORIA
CORRIDOR HOARDING PARADISE
PERAMBLE SCAFFOLD TRAVERSE
VERANDAH
(— IN BAZAAR) PAWN
(— IN HOUSE OF COMMONS)
VENTILATOR
(— MADE BY INSECT) MINE
(CHURCH —) JUBE LAFT LOFT
(MINE —) BORD BROW SLOVAN
(MINSTREL'S —) ORIEL
(OPEN —) LOGGIA
(UNDERGROUND —) HYPOGEE
HYPOGEUM
GALLEY FUST CUDDY DRAKE FOIST
STICK BIREME GALIOT HEARTH
ZYGITE BASTARD CABOOSE
DROMOND GALLIOT HEXERIS
LYMPHAD TRIREME UNIREME
CAMBOOSE COOKROOM CROMSTER
GALLEASS RAMBERGE
(— BOTTOM) SLICE
(CHIEFTAIN'S —) BIRLING BIRLINN
(PHILLIPINE —) CALAN
(VIKING —) AESC DRAKE
GALLEY SLAVE FORSADO
SFORZATO
GALLFLY CYNIPID
GALLINAE RASORES
GALLINAZO VIRU VULTURE
GALLING BITTER
GALLINULE COOT KORA MOHO RAIL

GORHEN PUKEKO SKITTY MOORHEN STANKIE SULTANA DABCHICK HYACINTH MANUALII RAILBIRD RICEBIRD SWAMPHEN

GALLIVANT KITE GALLANT

GALLON GAWN CONGIUS

(— **OF ORE**) DISH

(**128** —**S**) LEAGUER

(**EIGHTH** —) OCTARIUS

GALLOON ORRIS

GALLOP FOG RUN AUBIN PRICK CANTER CAREER COURSE TITTUP WALLOP TANTIVY

GALLOWS NUB CRAP DROP FORK TREE BOUGH CHEAT FURCA WIDDY GIBBET DERRICK FORCHES JUSTICE POTENCE STIFLER WARYTREE

GALLOWS BIRD HEMPY WIDDY HEMPIE HEMPSEED WIDDIFOW CRACKROPE

GALOSH ARCTIC ZIPPER EXCLUDER OVERSHOE

GALUTH GOLUS GOLAHI

GALVANIC VOLTAIC

GALVANIZE ZINCIFY

GALVANOMETER DETECTOR REOMETER

GAMBESON WAMBAIS

GAMBIA (**CAPITAL OF** —) BANJUL

(**LANGUAGE OF** —) JOLA WOLOF FULANI MALINKE

(**MONEY OF** —) DALASI

(**NATIVE OF** —) JOLA PEUL WOLOF DIOLAS FULANI MANDINGO SERAHULI

(**TOWN OF** —) MANSA BINTANG KUNTAUR

GAMBIA POD BABLOH

GAMBIER CATECHU

GAMBIT MANEUVER

GAMBLE BET DICE GAFF GAME NICK PLAY PUNT RISK SPORT STAKE WAGER CHANCE GAMMON HAZARD PLUNGE FLUTTER

(— **AGAINST**) BUCK

GAMBLER PIKER SPORT CARROW DEALER PLAYER PUNTER HUSTLER PLAYMAN PLUNGER SLICKER THROWER BLACKLEG GAMESTER HAZARDER

GAMBLING GAMING HAZARDRY

(— **DEVICE**) PACHINKO

GAMBLING HOUSE HELL TRIPOT

GAMBO GOOSE SPURWING

GAMBOL HOP PLAY CAPER FRISK KEVEL PRANK CAREER CAVORT FROLIC GAMBADO

GAMBREL CAMMOCK SPREADER

GAME COB FUN JEU JIG GAMY LAKE MAIL PLAY DANCE GAMEY PARTY SPIEL SPORT WATHE BATTUE MORRIS QUARRY RAMSCH VENERY JENKINS KNICKER BREATHER FIGHTING FOREGAME

(— **FOR FISHERMEN**) SKISH

(— **LIKE HANDBALL**) FIVES

(— **LIKE HOCKEY**) DODDART

(— **NARROWLY WON**) SQUEAKER

(— **OF CAT**) BILLET

(— **OF FOOTBALL**) BOWL CAMP

(— **OF FORFEITS**) KEN

(— **OF HOCKEY**) BANDY SHINNY

(— **OF MARBLES**) TAW BOWL BONCE GULLY KEEPS KNUCKS MIGGLES

(— **OF MENTAL SKILL**) GO CHESS CHECKERS

(— **OF NINEPINS**) KAILS KAYLES

(— **OF PRISONER'S BASE**) CHEVY CHIVVY

(— **WITH BOOMERANG**) BRIST

(— **WITH COUNTERS**) DUMPS GOOSE

(— **WITH SHUTTLECOCK**) TAHYING

(**BACKGAMMON** —) HIT IRISH

(**BALL** —) CAT TUT SNOB CATCH RUGBY SOCCER SQUASH TENNIS CRICKET KNAPPAN BASEBALL FOOTBALL HANDBALL SLUGFEST SOFTBALL

(**CARD** —) AS HOC LOO MAW NAP PAM PIT PUT SET BRAG CENT FARO FISH FROG GRAB JASS LANT PINK POOL POPE POST RUFF SANT SKAT SLAM SNAP SOLO STUD VINT BEAST BUNCO BUNKO CARDS CARIE CHICO CINCH COMET CRIMP DECOY GILET GLEEK GRAND LEAST MONTE OMBER OMBRE PEDRO PITCH POKER PRIME RUMMY SCOPA STOPS STUSS TRUMP WHIST BASSET BIRKIE BOODLE BOSTON BRIDGE CASINO CHEMMY COMMIT ECARTE EIGHTS EUCHRE FARMER FLINCH HEARTS HOWELL LOADUM PANFIL PIQUET QUINZE RAMSCH ROUNCE SLOUGH SMUDGE SPIDER TOURNE AUCTION AUTHORS BELOTTE BEZIQUE CANASTA CASSINO CAYENNE CHICAGO COONCAN GARBAGE HUNDRED JACKPOT REVERSI RONTOON SCOPONE SETBACK TRIUMPH VINGTUN VITESSE BACCARAT BASEBALL BRISCOLA COMMERCE CONQUIAN CONTRACT CRIBBAGE FREAKPOT HANDICAP IMPERIAL NAPOLEON PATIENCE PENCHANT PENNEECH PINOCHLE SHOWDOWN SKINBALL SKINNING SLAPJACK TREDILLE TRESILLO VERQUERE VIDERUFF

(**CARNIVAL** —) HOOPLA

(**CHILDREN'S** —) TAG DIBS JACKS KICKBALL

(**CONFIDENCE** —) RAMP BIGMITT

(**COURT** —) SQUASH TENNIS HANDBALL

(**DICE** —) FARE BINGO CRAPS NOVUM RAPHE HAZARD BARBUDI ADDITION BARBOTTE CAMEROON HOOLIGAN

(**DRAWN** —) SPOIL REFAIT

(**DRINKING** —) HIJINKS

(**EGYPTIAN** —) SENT SENIT

(**GAMBLING** —) TAN FARO HAND PICO BOULE CRAPS MACAO MONTE POKER PROPS RONDO STUSS

BRELAN HAZARD RONDEAU ROULETTE

(**GENERAL** —) HEI HIT HOB TAG TIG BALL BASE BULL BUZZ CENT DIBS DUCK FARE GOLF HOLE JOWL KENO MALL POLO POOL SLAM SNOB TICK BANDY BINGO BONCE BOULE CHESS CHUBA CHUNK CLOSH DARTS DOLOS FIVES GOOSE HALMA HOUSE IRISH JACKS LOTTO LURCH NOVUM NULLO PITCH PUSSY RUGBY SALTA SALVO SCRUB TROCO WHOOP BEAVER CAROMS CHIVVY CHUNKY CLUMPS COBNUT COCKAL COOTIE CRAMBO FEEDER GOBANG GRACES HAZARD HOOPLA HUBBUB JEREED KAYLES MERELE PELOTA PLUMPS RAGMAN RINGER SEESAW SHINNY SIPPIO SKILLO STICKS TENNIS TIGTAG TIPCAT TIVOLI TRIGON TRUCKS BALLOON BEANBAG BEEBALL BOWLING COBBLER CONKERS CROQUET CURLING DIABOLO DODDART DOUBLES DREIDEL ENDBALL GOGGANS HANGMAN HURLBAT LOGGATS MAHJONG MATADOR MUGGINS NETBALL PALLONE PASSAGE PEEVERS PUSHPIN QUINTET RINGTAW SARDINE SQUAILS STATUES TENPINS TOMBOLA ANAGRAMS BALKLINE BASEBALL CHARADES CHECKERS CHOUETTE DOMINOES DOUBLETS DRAUGHTS DUCKPINS FIVEPINS FOOTBALL FORFEITS GIVEAWAY HARDHEAD KICKBALL LEAPFROG PARCHESI PEEKABOO PURPOSES PUSHBALL PYRAMIDS RINGTOSS ROULETTE ROUNDERS SCRABBLE SKITTLES STOBBALL STOWBALL TRAPBALL VERQUERE

(**GUESSING** —) LOVE MORA CANUTE

(**INDIAN** —) CHUNKY HUBBUB

(**INFERIOR** —) CHECK

(**NUMBERS** —) BUG

(**OUTDOOR** —) GOLF POLO HURLY ROQUE RUGBY SOCCER CROQUET HURLING BASEBALL FOOTBALL LACROSSE

(**PROGRESSIVE** —) DRIVE

(**REHEATED** —) SALMI SALMIS

(**SWISS** —) JASS

(**THREE BOWLING** —**S**) SERIES

(**TRAPSHOOTING** —) SCOOT

(**WAR** —) BARRIERS

(**WORD** —) GHOST ANAGRAMS

GAMECOCK STAG STAIG

GAMEKEEPER GAMIE KEEPER WALKER WARNER WARRENER

GAMESTER DICER PLAYER GAMBLER PLAYMAN SHARPER HAZARDER TABLEMAN

GAMETE SPERM OOCYTE ZYGOTE GAMETOID OOGAMETE OOSPHERE

GAMETOCYTE GAMONT CRESCENT GONOCYTE

GAMETOPHYTE GERMLING

GAMIN TAD ARAB URCHIN
GAVROCHE
GAMMA AGMA
GAMUT GAMME RANGE SCALE
SERIES COMPASS DIAGRAM
GANDER STEG STAIG GANNER
(— AND GEESE) SET
GANESA GUNPUT GANAPATI
GANG MOB SET BAND BUND CORE
CREW GING PACK PAIR PUSH TEAM
GROUP HORDE SPELL CHIURM
COFFLE GAGGLE LAYOUT MOHOCK
SCHOOL COMPANY
(— MEMBER) WHYO
(— OF FISHHOOKS) PULLDEVIL
(— OF MINERS) CORE
GANGLING GAWKY GANGLY
GANGLION TUMOR CEREBRUM
GANGPLANK BROW GANGWAY
GANGRENE CANKER GANGER
SPHACEL
GANGSTER HOOD WHYO BANDIT
COWBOY CHOPPER
GANGUE MATRIX LODESTUFF
VEINSTONE
GANGWAY ROAD SLIP LOGWAY
TUNNEL CATWALK COULOIR
GATEWAY
GANJA GUNJAH CANNABIS
GANNET BOOBY GAUNT SOLAN
PIQUERO SEAFOWL
GANTRYMAN DROPMAN
GANYMEDE (BROTHER OF —) ILUS
ASSARACUS
(FATHER OF —) TROS
(MOTHER OF —) CALLIRRHOE
GAP SAG FLAW GAPE GOWL GULF
MUSE NICK SLAP SLOP WANT
BREAK BRECK CHASM CHAUM
CHAWN CLOVE FRITH MEUSE MUSET
NOTCH SHARD SHERD VUIDE
BREACH GULLET HIATUS LACUNA
SPREAD THROAT VACUUM CLOSING
OPENING VACANCY VACUITY
APERTURE DIASTEMA ENTREFER
INTERVAL MULTIGAP QUEBRADA
(— IN BANK OF STREAM) GAT
(— IN MEMORY) AMNESIA
(— SERVING AS PASS) COL
GAPE GAN GAP GANT GAUP GAWK
GAWP GAZE GOVE GRIN YAWN
CHAUN HIATE STARE RICTUS
DEHISCE INHIATE
GAPING GALP AGAPE HIANT CHAPPY
CHASMA GAWISH MOUTHED
RINGENT
GAR HOUND SNOOK AGUJON
CHERNA GARFISH GARPIKE BILLFISH
GOREFISH GURDFISH HORNFISH
HORNKECK LONGJAWS LONGNOSE
GARAGE HANGAR LOCKUP SIDING
GARRIDGE
(ROW OF —S) MEWS
GARAVANCE CARAUNA GARBANZO
GARB (ALSO SEE APPAREL AND
DRESS) COWL GEAR TOGA VEST
DRESS GUISE HABIT APPAREL
CLOTHES COSTUME RAIMENT
GARBAGE GASH SLOP OFFAL TRASH

WASTE GIBLET REFUSE SCRAPS
GARBAGEMAN DUSTMAN
GARBLE GELD JUMBLE MANGLE
DISTORT GARBLING MUTILATE
GARDANT AFFRONTE
GARDEN HAW EDEN KNOT YARD
ARBOR GARTH CIRCLE POMACY
POMARY QUINTA SHAMBA VERGER
VIHARA ACADEMY HERBARY
OLITORY ORCHARD ROCKERY
TOPIARY CHINAMPA FLORETUM
HORTYARD KALEYARD LEIGHTON
PARADISE POTAGERE ROSARIUM
(— CITY) CHICAGO
(— STATE) NEWJERSEY
GARDENER MALI PONICA CROPPER
PLANNER BOSTANGI
GARDEN HELIOTROPE VALERIAN
GARDENIA TIARA
GARDENING TOPIARY
GARDEN ROCKET EVEWEED
GARDEN WARBLER JACK HAYBIRD
BECAFICO FAUVETTE FIGEATER
GARFISH (SEE GAR)
GARGANEY TEAL CRICK
GARGANTUAN HUGE VAST GIANT
HOMERIC TITANIC ENORMOUS
GIGANTIC HOMERIAN
GARGLE GURGLE COLLUTORY
GARGOYLE BOSS
GARIBALDI GOLDFISH
GARISH GAUDY GIDDY SHOWY
CRIANT GLARING
GARISHNESS GLARE
GARLAND BAY LEI CROWN VITTA
ANADEM CORONA CRANTS ROSARY
WREATH CHAPLET CORANCE
CORONAL FESTOON
GARLIC AJO MOLY CHIVE PORET
ALLIUM PORRET RAMSON
GARMENT DUD TOG BACK BRAT
COAT GOWN PELL PELT RAIL ROBE
SARK SHAG SILK SLIP SLOP SULU
VEST WEED ABAYA BUREL CENTO
CLOAK CLOTH COTTE CYMAR
DRESS FROCK HABIT HAORI JOSEY
JUPON KHAKI MANGA NABOB
SHAWL SHIFT SHIRT SIMAR SKIRT
STOLE WRIEL ALPACA ATTIRE
BARROW BLOUSE CAFTAN CAMLET
CAPOTE CHAMMA COTTON CYCLAS
ERMINE EXOMIS FECKET HUIPIL
JACKET JERSEY JUMPER KERSEY
KIRTLE MOHAIR MOTLEY SARONG
SHORTY SHROUD STROUD TAMEIN
ZIZITH AMICTUS BROIGNE BUNTING
CAMBLET CHIRIPA CRAWLER
CUCULLA CULOTTE DOUBLET
FALDING FLOCKET GROGRAM
PALETOT PELISSE RAIMENT
SHORTIE SURCOAT SWEATER
VESTURE WRAPPER BATHROBE
CAMELINE CAPUCHIN CHAUSSES
COLOBIUM CORSELET COVERALL
DEERSKIN EPIBLEMA GAMBESON
GUERNSEY HIMATION INDUMENT
PADUASOY SCAPULAR SEALSKIN
SLIPOVER SNOWSUIT VESTMENT
WEARABLE STROUDING

(— OF HERALD) TABARD
(— OF HIGH PRIEST) EPHOD
(— OF PATCHES) CENTO
(BABY'S —) BARROW CRAWLER
CREEPER
(BADLY-MADE —) DRECK
(BLUE —) MAZARINE
(BURIAL —) SHROUD
(COARSE —) BRAT STROUD
(DEFENSIVE —) JACK BROIGNE
GAMBESON
(ECCLESIASTICAL —) STOLE
RHASON CASSOCK
(ETHIOPIAN —) CHAMMA
(HINDU —) SARI SAREE
(INFANT'S —) DIAPER BUNTING
SLEEPER
(JAPANESE —) HAORI
(LEATHER —) BUFF
(LINEN —) LINE
(LONG —) JIBBA STOLE JIBBEH
MANDYAS PELISSE HIMATION
(MEDIEVAL —) ROCHET CHAUSSES
DALMATIC GAMBESON
(MONK'S —) SCAPULAR
(MOURNING —) SABLE
(OUTER —) BRAT COAT GOWN HAIK
HYKE SLOP WRAP FROCK HAORI
NABOB PALLA PILCH SMOCK
DOLMAN ROCHET CHEMISE GALABIA
PALETOT SURCOAT SWEATER
HIMATION OVERSLOP
(PADDED —) TRUSS
(SLEEVELESS —) ABA CAPE COWL
VEST MANTLE CUCULLA GANDURAH
(SQUARE —) KAROSS
(THIN —) GOSSAMER
(TIGHT-FITTING —) HOSE COTTE
LEOTARD
(WOMAN'S —) IZAR BURKA CYMAR
NABOB SIMAR BURKHA CHITON
JOSEPH PEPLOS PEPLUM VISITE
BURNOUS
(PL.) GEAR COSTUME GARNISH
FLANNELS
GARNER REAP STORE GATHER
IMBARN COLLECT
GARNET GRENAT PYROPE ANTHRAX
GRANATE OLIVINE VERMEIL
ESSONITE MELANITE ROSOLITE
YANOLITE
GARNISH LARD TRIM ADORN DRESS
EQUIP MENSE STICK FURNISH
TOPPING CHUMMAGE DECORATE
DUXELLES ORNAMENT
GARNISHED GARNI
GARNISHEE CHECK FACTOR
GARNISH
GARRET ATTIC SOLAR SOLLAR
MANSARD COCKLOFT
GARRISON WARD STUFF PRESIDY
WARNISON
GARRULITY POLYLOGY
GARRULOUS GABBY TALKY WORDY
BABBLY TONGUY VOLUBLE
GARTER GARTEN LEGLET ELASTIC
STRAPPLE
GARTH CORTILE OUTGARTH
GARUM LIQUAMEN

GAS DAMP XENON FLATUS GENAPP LEAVEN OXYGEN PETROL EXHAUST KRYPTON YPERITE AFTERGAS ETHERION FIREDAMP HYDROGEN STANNANE VESICANT
(— CONSTANT) R
(COLORLESS —) OXAN OXANE KETENE GERMANE STIBINE
(NERVE —) SARIN
(NONCOMBUSTIBLE —) INERT
(POISONOUS —) ARSINE CYANOGEN PHOSGENE
GASCONADE BRAG CROW BOAST BLUSTER
GASEOUS AERIFORM GASIFORM VOLATILE
GASH CUT CHOP LASH BLASH CRIMP GANCH GRIDE SCORE SLASH SLISH SCOTCH SLUICE TRENCH INCISION INCISURE
(— A FISH) RIM
GASKET LUTE CASKET GASKIN GROMMET SCISSIL
GASKIN BRAGAS
GASOLINE GAS AVGAS JUICE PETROL BENZINE NATURAL
GASP FOB BLOW GAPE KINK PANK PANT CHINK CROAK FETCH THRATCH
GASTRONOME EPICURE
GASTROPOD SLUG DRILL HARPA OLIVA SNAIL BUCKIE NERITE ABALONE MOLLUSK TOXIFER UNIVALVE VELUTINA
GATE BAB BAR JET HEAD LIFT PORT SASH SLAP YETT ENTRY HATCH JANUA SALLY SPRAY STICK TORAN ENAJIM ESCAPE FENDER FUNNEL HARROW INGATE LIGGAT PADDLE PORTAL RUNNER TIMBER TORANA WICKET ZAGUAN BARRIER CLICKET FIVEBAR GATEWAY LIDGATE POSTERN SHUTTER ABOIDEAU ANTEPORT DECUMANA ENTRANCE FOREGATE GURDWARA PENSTOCK TOLLGATE TOWNGATE TRIMTRAM TURNPIKE
(— OF CASTLE) BAR
(BACK —) POSTERN
(CUSTOMS —) BARRIER
(IRRIGATION —) CHECK TAPON TAPPOON
(LICH —) SCALLAGE TRIMTRAM
(RUNNING —) FUNNEL
(SAW —) FRAME
(SAWMILL —) SASH
(SLALOM —S) HAIRPIN
(SLUICE —) HATCH VALVE
(WATER —) SLUICE
GATEADO DIOMATE
GATEHOUSE BAR LODGE
GATEKEEPER WARDEN CERBERUS GATEWARD PORTITOR STILEMAN
GATEMAN GUARD
GATEPOST DURN HARR HEEL PIER POST SHAFT POSTEL
GATEWAY DAR DOOR GATE LOKE TORU PYLON TORAN TORII BARWAY GOPURA TORANA PROPYLON

GATHER GET LEK POD WIN BAND BREW CLAN CLOT CROP CULL FURL HERD HIVE HOST PICK REAP RELY TUCK AMASS BANGE BROOM BUNCH FLOCK GLEAN GUESS INFER LEASE PLUCK RAISE SWEEP ACCRUE COMPEL CORRAL DECERP DERIVE GARNER HUDDLE HUSTLE IMBARN MUSTER RAMASS SCRAPE CLUSTER COLLATE COLLECT COMPILE CONGEST CONVENE CONVOKE HARVEST RAMMASS RECRUIT ASSEMBLE CUMULATE SHEPHERD
(— AS ARMY) HOST
(— BY SCRAPING) SCRATCH
(— GRASS SEED) STRIP
(— HEADWAY) SET
(— HERBS) SIMPLE
(— IN A HEAP) HATTER
(— IN RAGS) TAT
(— SEWING) GAGE GAUGE
(— UP) KILT
GATHERED KILTED CUMULATE
GATHERER GEDDER TUCKER RUFFLER CHICLERO PLICATOR PUCKERER
GATHERING HUI LED LEK SUM FAIR FEST KNOT SING SIVA LEVEE SHINE TRYST INDABA MUDDLE PLISSE POWWOW RUELLE SMOKER COLLECT COMMERS COMPANY FUNFEST HARVEST HOSTING HUSKING JOLLITY KLATSCH MEETING MOOTING NYMPHAL ROCKING TURNOUT ASSEMBLY CONCLAVE FUNCTION JAMBOREE PANIONIA POTATION RECOURSE SINGSONG SOCIABLE STAMPEDE
(— OF ANIMALS) DRIVE
(— OF ARMED MEN) HOSTING
(— OF CLOTH) SHIRR SHIRRING
(— OF FILM) CISSING
(— OF SCOUTS) CAMPOREE JAMBOREE
(— PLACE) LESCHE
(FORMAL —) HALL
(RELIGIOUS —) SHOUT
(SOCIAL —) BEE FRY BAKE BALL CLUB DRUM STAG WINE BAILE BINGE BINGO DANCE MIXER SHIVOO SMOKER CANTICO KLATSCH SHINDIG SQUEEZE BARBECUE CAMPFIRE CLAMBAKE TALKFEST SYMPOSIUM
GAU BANT
GAUCHE CLUMSY AWKWARD
GAUD GAY GAUDY FANGLE VANITY TRINKET
GAUDINESS GLARE GLITTER
GAUDY GAY LOUD CHEAP FLARY SHOWY VAUDY BRAZEN FLASHY FLIMSY FLORID GARISH GAWISH SKYRIN TAWDRY TINSEL BRANKIE CHINTZY FLARING GAUDISH GLARING
GAUGE (ALSO SEE GAGE) BORE GAGE MOOT PLUG SIZE TRAM GADGE NORMA RANGE DENTIN FEELER FORMER GABARI DEPTHEN

TEMPLET TRAMMEL ESTIMATE INDICANT MEASURER STANDARD SURFACER TEMPLATE
(— FOR SLATES) SCANTLE
(RAIN —) UDOMETER
GAUGER SURVEYOR
GAUL GALLIA
(PL.) PICTONES
GAUNT BONY GRIM LANK LEAN SLIM THIN PINED SPARE THIRL BARREN HAGGED HOLLOW MEAGER MEAGRE SHELLY HAGGARD SLENDER DESOLATE RAWBONED
GAUNTLET TOP CUFF GLOVE GANTLET GAINPAIN GANTLOPE
GAUR BISON SELADANG
GAUZE LISSE MARLI MARLY UMPLE CYPRUS CYPRESS TIFFANY CARBASUS
GAUZY FILMY
GAVE GIN GUV YAF YAFE
GAVEL HAMMER GAVELAGE
GAVIAL NAKOO LIZARD GHARIAL LORICATE
GAVOTTE MUSETTE
GAWK GAWKY GAWNEY LUMPKIN RAMMACK
GAWKY GOWKIT AWKWARD GAWKISH
GAY MAD AIRY BOON DAFT GLAD GLEG HIGH RORY TRIM WILD BONNY GAUDY JOLLY LIGHT MERRY RORTY SUNNY VAUDY WLONK ALEGER BLITHE CHEERY FLASHY FRISKY FROLIC GARISH JOCUND JOVIAL JOYFUL JOYOUS KIPPER LIVELY SPORTY CHIPPER FESTIVE GALLANT GIOJOSO GLEEFUL LARKING RACKETY SMICKER TITTUPY WINSOME CAVALIER FROHLICH GAMESOME PLEASANT PRIMROSE SPARKISH SPLENDID SPORTIVE
GAY-FEATHER LIATRIS
GAYWINGS MAYWINGS
GAZE EYE PRY CAPE GAPE GOUK GOWK LEER LOOK MOON OGLE PEER PORE SCAN TOOT GLAIK GLARE GLOAT GLORE SIGHT STARE TWIRE VISIE WLITE ASPECT GLOWER REGARD
GAZELLE AHU GOA ADMI AOUL CORA DAMA MOHR ADDRA ARIEL KORIN DZEREN GROUSE ALGAZEL CHIKARA CORINNE DIBATAG TABITHA CHINKARA
GAZELLE HOUND SALUKI
GAZETTE COURANT JOURNAL
(— OF CRIMES) HUE
GE TAPUYAN
GEAN MERRY MURIE MURRY GUIGNE GASKINS
GEAR KIT SPUR TACK TRIM IDLER TOOTH FOURTH GRAITH HYPOID PINION TACKLE CLOBBER GEARING HARNESS REVERSE RIGGING SEGMENT TRILOBE HEADGEAR
(— OF DIVER) ARMOR
(CHAFING —) SCOTCHMAN
(DEFENSIVE —) ARMORY

(RUNNING —) CARRIAGE
(TRANSMISSION —) HIGH FIRST
SPEED FOURTH SECOND REVERSE
GEARED GIRT
GEARWHEEL UNILOBE WABBLER
WOBBLER
GEB KEB SEB
GECKO FANFOOT TARENTE
GEKKONID LACERTID
GEELBEC SALMON TERAGLIN
GEEPOUND SLUG
GEESE SET
GEIGER TREE ALOEWOOD
SEBESTEN
GEL JELL JELLY LIVER GELATE
ALCOGEL
GELATIN GLUE COLLIN GLUTIN
GLUTOID HAITSAI NORGINE
ISINGLASS
GELATINOUS MUCULENT JELLYLIKE
GELD LIB GELT ALTER CASTRATE
GELDING HORSE SPADE SPADO
GEM GIM JADE ONYX OPAL RUBY
AGATE BERYL CAMEO JAZEL JEWEL
PEARL SPARK STONE TOPAZ ZIMME
AMULET BAGUET CRUSTA GARNET
JASPER PEBBLE PYROPE RONDEL
ZIRCON CITRINE DIAMOND DOUBLET
EMERALD JACINTH KUNZITE
ONEGITE PERIDOT SPARKLE
ACHROITE AMATRICE AMETHYST
BAGUETTE HYACINTH INTAGLIO
MARQUISE ORIENTAL RONDELLE
SAPPHIRE SARDONYX HIDDENITE
(— CARVED IN RELIEF) CAMEO
INTAGLIO
(— ENGRAVED WITH CHARM)
ABRAXAS
(— OF IMPERFECT BRILLIANCY)
LOUPE
(— REFLECTING LIGHT IN 6 RAYS)
ASTERIA
(— STATE) IDAHO
(IMITATION —) PASTE
(UNCUT —) ROUGH CABOCHON
GEMMA BUD GEMMULE SOREDIUM
GEMMULE SPORE BROODSAC
GEMMY EMERALD
GEMSBOK ORYX KOKAMA
GEMSBUCK
GEMSTONE JADE STAR CHEVEE
SPINEL EMERALD FISHEYE
CROSSCUT HYALITHE
GENA CHEEK
GENDER SEX KIND CLASS FEMININE
GENE GEN ALLEL AMORPH FACTOR
LETHAL PRIMER CYTOGENE
MODIFIER
GENERAL MAIN MOST BROAD
GROSS COMMON VULGAR CURRENT
GENERIC MARSHAL SUMMARY
AUFIDIUS CANIDIUS CATHOLIC
ECUMENIC ENCYCLIC OVERHEAD
PANDEMIC PUFIDIUS STRATEGE
BRIGADIER
GENERALITY CREDO GENERALE
GENERALIZATION LAW AXIOM
BROMIDE
GENERALIZE WIDEN EXTEND

SPREAD BROADEN
GENERALIZED GROSS GLOBAL
GENERALLY BROADLY LARGELY
ROUNDLY MOSTWHAT
GENERATE MAKE SIRE TEEM BEGET
BREED IMPEL SPAWN STEAM
CREATE FATHER GENDER IMPOSE
KITTLE DEVELOP INBREED PRODUCE
ENGENDER
(— PUS) DIGEST
GENERATION AGE KIND TIME
WORLD STRAIN STRIND DESCENT
DIPLOID GETTING KINDRED
GAMOBIUM GENITURE SAECULUM
THEOGONY TRIPLOID UPSPRING
OFFSPRING
GENERATIVE GENIAL GAMETIC
GENESIC GENETIC SEEDFUL
PROLIFIC
GENERATOR BUZZER DYNAMO
RULING ELEMENT DIPHASER
GENERANT
GENEROSITY GRACE LARGE
BOUNTY GENTRY BREADTH
FREEDOM HONESTY COURTESY
GOODNESS KINDNESS LARGESSE
GENEROUS BIG FREE OPEN SOFT
FRANK HEFTY LARGE NOBLE
LIBERAL GRACIOUS HANDSOME
INSORDID LARGEOUS MAGNIFIC
GENEROUSLY LUCKY MANLY
KINDLY FRANKLY
GENESIS BIRTH ORIGIN BERESHIT
GENETICS
GENET BERBE CIVET DAPPLE
VIVERRINE
GENIAL BEIN BIEN WARM DOUCE
SONSY DOULCE FORTHY FURTHY
HEARTY KINDLY MELLOW MENTAL
CHEERFUL GRACIOUS PLEASANT
GENIALITY BONHOMIE
GENICULATE KNEED ELBOWED
GENIE GENIUS HATHOR SANDMAN
GENII XIN JANN
GENIN BUFAGIN
GENIP GINEP JAGUA IRONWOOD
GENIPAP GENIP JAGUA GUENEGE
GENISTA FURZE RETAMA
GENITAL SECRET
(PL.) HARNESS PRIVITY GENITURE
GENIUS FIRE GIFT HAPI KALI TURN
ANGEL BRAIN DEMON GENIO NUMEN
DAEMON INGENY INGINE TALENT
WIZARD DUSTMAN DUAMUTEF
EINSTEIN FRAVASHI SILVANUS
(— OF LANGUAGE) IDIOM
GENOA GEANE
GENOTYPE BIOTYPE LOGOTYPE
GENOUILLERE KNEELET
GENRE EPIC KIND SORT TYPE CLASS
STYLE FABLIAU SPECIES CATEGORY
GENS HOUSE
GENTEEL NICE GENTY GENTIL
JAUNTY POLITE STYLISH GRACEFUL
GENTIAN BIT FELWORT AGUEWEED
GALLWEED BALDMONEY
GENTILE GOI GOY ARIAN ARYAN
GOYISH HEATHEN
GENTILITY GENTRICE

GENTLE MOY CALM DEFT DEWY
FAIR HEND KIND MEEK MILD MURE
NESH SLOW SOFT SOOT TAME
BLAND CANNY LIGHT LITHE MILKY
QUIET SMALL SOBER SWEET
BONAIR CADISH DOCILE FACILE
MODEST PLACID REMISS SILKEN
SILVER SOFTLY TENDER AMABILE
CLEMENT GRADUAL SOAKING
SUBDUED DEBONAIR DOVELIKE
EGGSHELL LAMBLIKE LENITIVE
MAIDENLY MANSUETE MODERATE
PEACEFUL SARCENET TOWARDLY
TRANQUIL
(— AS OF THE WIND) LOOM
GENTLEFOLK GENTRY GENTILITY
GENTLEMAN NIB SIR BABU GENT
BABOO CURIO DORAY SAHIB SENOR
GEMMAN MILORD SENHOR SIGNOR
YONKER BRAVERY GALLANT
GENTMAN MYNHEER CAVALIER
MIRABELL SEIGNEUR SEIGNIOR
SQUIREEN
(— COMMONER) HAT
(— TRAINING FOR KNIGHTHOOD)
DONZEL
(COUNTRY —) SQUIRE
(GIPSY —) RYE
(MILITARY —) CADET
(WOULD-BE —) SHONEEN
(PL.) HERREN CHIVALRY
GENTLEMANLY JAUNTY
GENTLENESS FLESH LENITY
AMENITY DOUCEUR KINDNESS
GENTLY SOFT CANNY SOAVE EASILY
FAIRLY LIGHTLY EASYLIKE PRETTILY
TENDERLY
GENTRY COUNTY GENTRICE
SQUIRAGE SZLACHTA
GENUFLECTION VENIE KNEELING
GENUINE ECHT GOOD LEAL REAL
TRUE VRAI PLAIN PUKKA SOLID
ACTUAL ARRANT DINKUM DIRECT
HONEST KOSHER PISTIC CURRENT
GERMANE GRADELY SINCERE
VERIDIC GRAITHLY STERLING
(NOT —) TIN SHAM BOGUS
(SEEMINGLY —) COLORABLE
GENUINENESS VERIDITY
GENUS KIND CLASS ANALOG
GENDER GENERAL
(— OF ALGAE) DASYA FUCUS
BANGIA CHORDA CODIUM HYPNEA
NOSTOC PADINA DIATOMA LEMANEA
LIAGORA PTILOTA VALONIA
ZYGNEMA ANABAENA BRYOPSIS
CAULERPA CERAMIUM CHONDRUS
CONFERVA CUTLERIA DICTYOTA
DUMONTIA GELIDIUM GOMONTIA
HALIMEDA LERAMIUM LESSONIA
NEMALION OOCYSTIS PALMELLA
PORPHYRA STRIARIA TAONURUS
ULOTHRIX
(— OF AMOEBA) CHAOS
(— OF AMPHIBIAN) HYLA RANA
SIREN PROTEUS AMPHIUMA
NECTURUS
(— OF ANT) ATTA ECITON LASIUS
PONERA TERMES FORMICA

PHEIDOLE TAPINOMA
(— OF ANTELOPE) ORYX KOBUS
GAZELLA MADOQUA REDUNCA
ANTILOPE EGOCERUS
(— OF APE) PAN PONGO SIMIA
(— OF APHID) ADELGES CHERMES
(— OF ARACHNID) ACARUS
GALEODES
(— OF ARMADILLO) DASYPUS
XENURUS
(— OF ASCIDIAN) CIONA MOLGULA
BOLTENIA PYROSOMA
(— OF ASCLEPIAD) STAPELIA
(— OF AUK) ALCA ALLE
(— OF BABOON) PAPIO
(— OF BACTERIA) VIBRIO EIMERIA
ERWINIA GAFFKYA PROTEUS
SARCINA BACILLUS BRUCELLA
SERRATIA SHIGELLA
(— OF BADGER) MELES ARCTONYX
HELICTIS
(— OF BARNACLE) LEPAS BALANUS
ELMINIUS
(— OF BASIDIOMYCETE) BOVISTA
(— OF BAT) EUDERMA PETALIA
DESMODUS DIPHYLLA MOLOSSUS
MORMOOPS NOCTILIO NYCTERIS
PLECOTUS PTEROPUS VAMPYRUM
(— OF BEAR) URSUS EUARCTOS
MELURSUS
(— OF BEAVER) CASTOR
(— OF BEE) APIA APIS BOMBUS
ANDRENA TRIGONA COLLETES
HALICTUS MELIPONA
(— OF BEETLE) AMARA FIDIA HISPA
LAMIA LARIA LYTTA MELOE SAGRA
ALTICA ASILUS CLERUS ELATER
LYCTUS PTINUS SILPHA ACILIUS
ADELOPS AGRILUS ANOBIUM
ANOMALA BRUCHUS CARABUS
CASSIDA EPITRIX PRIONUS SAPERDA
SITARIS ADORETUS AGRIOTES
APHODIUS CALOSOMA CATORAMA
CYBISTER DERMETES DYNASTES
DYTISCUS EPICAUTA EUMOLPUS
HARPALUS LAMPYRIS MEGASOMA
PASSALUS POPILLIA SCOLYTUS
SPHINDUS TENEBRIO
(— OF BIRD) ARA ALCA APUS CRAX
CREX GYPS JYNX MIRO MITU MOHO
OTIS PICA RHEA SULA TYTO XEMA
AJAJA ANOUS ANSER ARDEA ARGUS
ASTUR BUCCO FALCO GAVIA GOURA
GUARA GYGIS IRENA JUNCO LARUS
LERWA LOXIA MIMUS MITUA MUNIA
PIPRA PITTA SITTA TODUS UPUPA
VIDUA VIREO ALAUDA ALCEDO
ANHIMA ANTHUS AQUILA BONASA
BRANTA CAPITO CIRCUS COLIUS
CORVUS DACELO ELANUS FULICA
GALLUS JACANA LANIUS LEIPOA
LIMOSA MARECA MENURA MEROPS
MILVUS MONASA NESTOR NUMIDA
PASSER PASTOR PERDIX PERNIS
PROGNE QUELEA RALLUS SAPPHO
SCOPUS SIALIA SPINUS STERNA
SYLVIA TETRAO TRERON TRINGA
TROGON TURDUS TURNIX VULTUR
ANHINGA APTERYX ARTAMUS

BUCEROS CACICUS CAPELLA
CARIAMA CERTHIA CHIONIS CICONIA
CINCLUS COLINUS COLUMBA
COLYBUS COTINGA CUCULUS
ELAENIA GALBULA GARRUPA
HALCYON HIRUNDO IBYCTER
ICTERUS KAKATOE LAGOPUS
LOPHURA LYRURUS MALURUS
MANACUS MESITES MILVAGO
MOMOTUS ORIOLUS PANDION
PAROTIA PIRANGA PITYLUS
PLAUTUS PLOCEUS PORZANA
REGULUS SEIURUS SERINUS
STURNUS TANAGRA TIMALIA
TOTANUS XENICUS ZENAIDA
ACCIPTER ACREDULA AFROPAVO
AGELAIUS AMIZILIA BOTAURUS
BUCORVUS BURHINUS CHAETURA
CORACIAS COTURNIX DELICHON
DIATRYMA DINORNIS DIOMEDEA
DREPANIS EMBERIZA EUPHONIA
EURYPYGA FULMARUS GARRULUS
GEOSPIZA GERYGONE GLAREOLA
GRALLINA GYPAETUS IONORNIS
LUSCINIA MACHETES MYCTERIA
NEOPHRON NOTORNIS NUMENIUS
OREORTYX PENELOPE PHAETHON
PITANGUS PLATALEA PLEGADIS
PODARGUS PRIONOPS PRUNELLA
PUFFINUS RUPICOLA SALTATOR
SAXICOLA SCOLOPAX SPEOTYTO
SPIZELLA STRUTHIO TRAGOPAN
TYRANNUS
(— OF BIVALVES) MYA PINNA
ANOMIA MACTRA NUCULA ETHERIA
MYTILUS PANDORA COLYMBUS
HINNITES PISIDIUM SAXICAVA
SPHAERUM TRIDACNA XYLOTRYA
(— OF BOWFIN) AMIA
(— OF BRACHIOPOD) ATRYPA
CRANIA ATHYRIS DISCINA SPIRIFER
(— OF BRYOZOAN) BUGULA
ESCHARA FLUSTRA RETEPORA
(— OF BUG) ANASA CIMEX EMESA
CORIXA TINGIS
(— OF BUTTERFLY) CALIGO COLIAS
DANAUS MORPHO PIERIS THECLA
EURYMUS JUNONIA KALLIMA
LYCAENA PAPILIO STRYMON
VANESSA ARGYNNIS HESPERIA
LEMONIAS MELITAEA SPEYERIA
(— OF CABBAGE) COS
(— OF CACTUS) CEREUS NOCALEA
OPUNTIA HARRISIA
(— OF CAT) FELIS ACINONYX
HEMIGALE
(— OF CEPHALOPOD) SEPIA
SPIRULA
(— OF CETACEAN) INIA
(— OF CHINK) LACUNA
(— OF CHIPMUNK) EUTAMIAS
(— OF CILIATE) COLPODA
CHILODON EUPLOTES
(— OF CIVET) FOSSA PAGUMA
(— OF CLAM) ENSIS GEMMA SOLEN
SPISULA
(— OF COCKLE) CHIONE
(— OF COCKROACH) BLATTA
(— OF CORAL) ASTREA FUNGIA

MAENDRA OCULINA PORITES
ACROPURA TUBIPORA
(— OF CRAB) UCA MAIA BIRGUS
CANCER GRAPSUS OCYPODE
PAGURUS LITHODES PORTUNUS
(— OF CRANE) GRUS
(— OF CRAYFISH) CAMBARUS
(— OF CRICKET) ACHETA GRYLLUS
(— OF CRUSTACEAN) APUS HIPPA
JASUS LIGIA MYSIS CYPRIS LIGYDA
SELLUS TRIOPS ARGULUS ARTEMIA
ASTACUS BOPYRUS CALAPPA
CHELURA DAPHNIA EMERITA
HOMARUS IDOTHEA LERNAEA
NEBALPA SQUILLA CAPRELLA
ESTHERIA GAMMARUS LEUCIFER
LIMNETIS LIMNORIA NEPHROPS
PHRONIMA
(— OF CTENOPHORE) BEROE
CESTUM
(— OF DEER) AXIS DAMA PUDU
RUSA CERVUS MAZAMA MOSCHUS
RUCERVUS
(— OF DIATOM) DIATOMA SYNEDRA
MERIDION NAVICULA
(— OF DODO) DIDUS
(— OF DOG) CUON CANIS LYCAON
(— OF DORMOUSE) GLIS
(— OF DRAGONFLY) AESCHNA
(— OF DUCK) AIX ANAS AYTHYA
MERGUS NYROCA NETTION
SPATULA CLANGULA FULIGULA
(— OF EAGLE) AQUILA
(— OF ECHINODERM) ASTERIAS
(— OF EDENTATE) MANIS
(— OF EEL) CONGER ECHIDNA
MURAENA ANGUILLA GYMNOTUS
MORINGUA
(— OF FERN) FILIX TODEA ANEMIA
AZOLLA DOODIA CYATHEA ISOETES
ONOCLEA OSMUNDA PELLAEA
WOODSIA ADIANTUM ASPIDIUM
ATHYRIUM BLECHNUM CETERACH
CIBOTIUM CLEMATIS DAVALLIA
LYGODIUM MARATTIA SALVINIA
SCHIZAEA VITTARIA
(— OF FIREFLY) LAMPYRIS
(— OF FISH) AMIA ESOX HURO
LOTA MOLA RAJA ZEUS ALOSA
BADIS BERYX BETTA DORAS ELOPS
GADUS GOBIO HUCHO LATES
MANTA MUGIL PERCA SALMO
SARDA SOLEA UMBRA ALBULA
ANABAS APOGON BAIGRE BARBUS
BELONE CARANX CLUPEA COTTUS
DIODON GERRES GOBIUS HIODON
KUHLIA LABRUS LATRIS MOBULA
MYXINE NOMEUS PAGRUS PSETTA
REMORA SCARUS SPARUS TRIGLA
TRUTTA TURSIO ABRAMIS ALOPHAS
ALOPIAS ARACANA ASPREDO
BROTULA CARAPUS CLARIAS
DREPANE ECHIDNA GARRUPA
GIRELLA GYMNORA LEPOMIS
LIMANDA LUCANIA LYCODES
OSMERUS PEGASUS PRISTIS
SCIAENA SCOMBER SEPIOLA
SERIOLA SIGANUS SILLAGO SILURUS
SPHYRNA SQUALUS SYNODUS

THUNNUS TORPEDO TOXOTES
TRIODON XIPHIAS ZOARCES
AMEIURUS ANABLEPS ANGUILLA
ARAPAIMA ASTYANAX ATHERINA
BALISTES BODIANUS CARANGUS
CHIMAERA CLADODUS CTENODUS
CYPRINUS DAPEDIUS DIPLODUS
DIPTERUS DOROSOMA ECHENEIS
ETRUMEUS FUNDULUS GADOPSIS
GALAXIAS GAMBUSIA GOBIESOX
HAEMULON ICOSTEUS KYPHOSUS
LEBISTES LUTIANUS MEGALOPS
MORMYRUS MUSTELUS NOTROPIS
OPHIDION PALOMETA PANTODON
PHOCAENA POLYODON PYGIDIUM
SERRANUS SQUATINA COREGONUS
MYCTOPHUM
(— OF FLAGELLATE) COCOS
GONIUM OPHION SYNURA VOLVOX
ATTALEA CARYOTA EUGLENA
GIARDIA BORASSUS CERATIUM
EUDORINA HEXAMITA HYDRURUS
(— OF FLEA) PULEX BOSMINA
(— OF FLY) DACUS MUSCA MYMAR
PERLA PHORA ASILUS CEPHUS
FANNIA PIMPLA RHYSSA SCIARA
TIPULA CALIROA CHALCIS DIOPSIS
EPHYDRA HYLEMYA MIASTOR
ORTALIS OSCINIS PANORPA
TACHINA THEREVA ACROCERA
AGROMYZA ANOMALON APHIDIUS
BORBORUS CHELONUS CHRYSOPA
CHRYSOPS GLOSSINA PSYCHODA
SCHEDIUS SIMULIUM STOMOXYS
(— OF FLYING SQUIRREL) BELOMYS
(— OF FOSSIL) AMPYX ERYON
ADAPIS ATRYPA BAIERA ERYOPS
GEIKIA HYENIA KLUKIA MAMMUT
OLENUS ORTHIS RHYNIA ANDRIAS
ANTEDON APTIANA ASAPHUS
CAYONIA DICERAS EXOGYRA
GANODUS HAMITES HYBODUS
KNORRIA LESKEYA LESLEYA
LOXOMMA MESONYX MOROPUS
MYGODON OTOZOUM PHACOPS
PHIOMIA PROAVIS PROETUS
WALCHIA AGLASPIS AGNOSTUS
AMYNODON APHELOPS ARCHELON
BIRKENIA BRONTOPS CALIPPUS
CALYMENE CERATOPS CLYMENIA
CTENODUS DAPEDIUS DEINODON
DIATRYMA DINOHYUS DIPLODUS
DIPTERUS ENCHODUS ENCRINUS
EODISCUS EOHIPPUS EOSAURUS
EUSMILUS GORDONIA GRYPHAEA
HALLOPUS HELIGMUS ILLAENUS
LANARKIA LEBACHIA LECROSIA
LEGUATIA LESTODON LITUITES
MACLUREA MARRELLA METOPIAS
OLDHAMIA PLACODUS PORTHEUS
RUTIODON SMILODON SPIRIFER
STEGODON STEGOMUS TAONURUS
THELODUS XIPHODON ZAMICRUS
CONULARIA
(— OF FOX) ALOPEX VULPES
UROCYON
(— OF FROG) RANA ANURA
HYLODES
(— OF FUNGUS) FOMES IRPEX

PHOMA TUBER VALSA VERPA
ALBUGO BREMIA CAEOMA EMPUSA
FUMAGO HYDNUM ISARIA OIDIUM
PEZIZA TORULA ZYTHIA ACRASIA
AMANITA BOLETUS CANDIDA
CHALARA CYATHUS ELSINOE
ERYSIBE FABRAEA GEASTER
LEPIOTA MONILIA NECTRIA OZONIUM
PACHYMA PYTHIUM RHIZINA
RUSSULA SIMBLUM STEREUM
STICTIS STILBUM TYPHULA XYLARIA
ACHORION AECIDIUM AGARICUS
BOTRYTIS CALVATIA CLATHRUS
CLAVARIA COLLYBIA COPRINUS
CORYNEUM CYPHELLA CYTTARIA
DAEDALEA DIPLODIA ENDOTHIA
ENTOLOMA ENTYLOMA ERYSIPHE
EXOASCUS FUSARIUM GEASTRUM
GNOMONIA GRAPHIUM HELOTIUM
HELVELLA LENZITES MERULIUS
MYCOGONE PAXILLUS PHOLIOTA
PUCCINIA RHIZOPUS RHYTISMA
SEPTORIA SORDARIA SPICARIA
TAPHRINA TERFEZIA TRAMETES
TREMELLA TROCHILA USTILAGO
USTULINA VENTURIA CORDICEPS
(— OF GALLFLY) CYNIPS
(— OF GASTROPOD) FICUS HARPA
LIMAX OLIVA EBURNA PATELLA
TENEBRA SCYLLAEA STROMBUS
(— OF GEESE) CHEN ANSER
NETTAPUS
(— OF GNAT) SCIARA
(— OF GOAT) IBEX CAPRA
OREAMNOS
(— OF GRASS) POA ZEA AIRA COIX
AVENA BRIZA ORYZA STIPA APLUDA
ARUNDO BROMUS ELYMUS HOLCUS
LOLIUM LYGEUM MELICA MILIUM
NARDUS PHLEUM SECALE UNIOLA
ZOYSIA BAMBUSA BUCHLOE
CHLORIS CYNODON FESTUCA
HILARIA HORDEUM LAGURUS
LEERSIA MELINIS MOLINIA PANICUM
SETARIA SORGHUM ZIZANIA
AEGILOPS AGROSTIS ARISTIDA
AXONOPUS BULBILIS CENCHRUS
DACTYLIS ELEUSINE GLYCERIA
GYNERIUM IMPERATA PASPALUM
PHALARIS SPARTINA SPINIFEX
TRISETUM TRITICUM
(— OF GRASSHOPPER) LOCUSTA
(— OF GULL) XEMA LARUS
(— OF HAWK) BUTEO CIRCUS
(— OF HERB) GYP IVA AMMI ARUM
BETA GEUM GLAX HEBE LENS MEUM
MUSA OLAX RUTA SIDA SIUM ADOXA
AJUGA APIOS APIUM CALLA CANNA
CAREX CARUM CICER DALEA DRABA
ERUCA ERVUM FEDIA GALAX GAURA
GILIA GLAUX HOSTA INULA LAPPA
LAVIA LAYIA LEMNA LINUM LOASA
LOTUS LUFFA MADIA MALVA NAPEA
PANAX PARIS PHACA PHLOX PILEA
RHEUM RHOEO RUBIA SEDUM
TACEA URENA VICIA VIGNA VINCA
VIOLA ZIZIA ACAENA ACNIDA
ACORUS ACTAEA ADONIS ALISMA
ALLIUM ALSINE AMOMUM ANOGRA

ARABIS ARALIA ARNICA ASARUM
ATROPA BACOPA BAERIA BASSIA
BELLIS BIDENS BLITUM BLUMEA
BORAGO CAKILE CALTHA CASSIA
CELSIA CICUTA CISTUS CLEOME
CNICUS COLEUS CONIUM COPTIS
COSMOS CRAMBE CREPIS CRINUM
CROCUS CROTON CUNILA CYNARA
DAHLIA DATURA DAUCUS DIODIA
DONDIA ECHIUM ELODES ELODIA
EMILIA EUCLEA FILAGO GALEGA
GALIUM GIFOLA GYNURA ISATIS
ISMENE KOCHIA KRIGIA KUHNIA
LAMIUM LECHEA LUZULA MALOPE
MENTHA MIMOSA MONTIA MUCUNA
MUILLA NERINE NERIUM NESLIA
ONONIS OTHAKE OXALIS PICRIS
PISTIA PYROLA RESEDA RESTIO
RHEXIA RIVINA RUPPIA SAGINA
SALVIA SCILLA SESBAN SESELI
STEVIA SUAEDA THALIA TULIPA
VIORNA ZINNIA ABRONIA ADLUMIA
AETHUSA ALEGRIA ALETRIS
ALKANNA ALPINIA ALTHAEA
ALYSSUM AMORPHA AMSONIA
ANCHUSA ANEMONE ANETHUM
ANYCHIA APHANES ARACHIS
ARCTIUM ARNEBIA ARUNCUS
BABIANA BARTSIA BEGONIA
BOEBERA BUTOMUS CACALIA
CAJANUS CALYPSO CARLINA
CELOSIA CHELONE CIRCAEA
CIRSIUM CLARKIA COMARUM
CROOMIA CURCUMA CUSCUTA
CYTINUS DATISCA DECODON
DERINGA DIASCIA DROSERA
ELATINE EOMECON EPISCIA
ERODIUM FELICIA FICARIA FRASERA
FREESIA FUMARIA GAZANIA
GERBERA GLECOMA GLYCINE
GUNNERA HALENIA HECHTIA
HEDEOMA HOMERIA HUGELIA
HYPOXIS IRESINE JASIONE KICKXIA
KNAUTIA KOELLIA LACTUCA
LAPPULA LAPSANA LEWISIA LIATRIS
LINARIA LINNAEA LOGANIA LOPEZIA
LUNARIA LUPINUS LYCHNIS
LYTHRUM MARANTA MEDEOLA
MIMULUS MITELLA MOLLUGO
MONESES MUSCARI NEMESIA
NIGELLA OTHONNA PAEONIA
PAPAVER PAVONIA PEGANUM
PETUNIA PLUCHEA PRIMULA
RORIPPA ROTALIA RUELLIA
SALSOLA SAMOLUS SCANDIX
SENECIO SESAMUM SHORTIA
SILYBUM SINAPIS SOLANUM
SONCHUS STACHYS STATICE
SUCCISA SWERTIA TAGETES
TALINUM TELLIMA THAPSIA THESIUM
THLASPI THURNIA TORENIA TORILIS
TOVARIA TRILISA URGINEA VALLOTA
VERBENA ZEBRINA ACALYPHA
ACANTHUS ACHILLEA ACONITUM
AGALINIS AGERATUM ALLIARIA
ALLIONIA ALOCASIA AMBROSIA
AMMODIUM ANDRYALA ANGELICA
ANTHEMIS ANTICLEA APOCYNUM
ARCTOTIS ARENARIA ARGEMONE

ARISAEMA ASPERULA ATRIPLEX
BAPTISIA BARBAREA BARTONIA
BERGENIA BERTEROA BETONICA
BISTORTA BOLTONIA BORRERIA
BRASSICA BRUNONIA BUCHNERA
CALATHEA CAMASSIA CAMELINA
CANNABIS CAPSICUM CERINTHE
CLEMATIS COCHARUS COLLOMIA
COLUMNEA COMANDRA COOPERIA
CRASSULA CUBELIUM DENTARIA
DIANTHUS DICENTRA DIPSACUS
DISPORUM DYSSODIA ECHINOPS
EPIFAGUS ERANTHIS EREMURUS
ERIGENIA ERIGERON ERYNGIUM
ERYSIMUM EUCHARIS EUTHANIA
FITTONIA FLAVERIA FLOERKEA
FRAGARIA GALACTIA GENTIANA
GERARDIA GESNERIA GILLENIA
GLAUCIUM GLECHOMA GLORIOSA
GLOXINIA GOODENIA GRATIOLA
GUZMANIA HELENIUM HELONIAS
HEPATICA HESPERIS HEUCHERA
HIBISCUS HIPPURIS HOSACKIA
HOTTONIA HUDSONIA HYDROLES
HYSSOPUS IONIDIUM ISNARDIA
JATROPHA JUSSIAEA JUSTICIA
KNEIFFIA KOHLERIA LAPORTEA
LAVATERA LEONOTIS LEONURUS
LEPIDIUM LEPTILON LIMONIUM
LOPHIOLA LYCOPSIS MACLEAYA
MANFREDA MANTISIA MEDICAGO
MEIBOMIA MYOSOTIS MYOSURUS
OBOLARIA OENANTHE OPOPANAX
ORONTIUM PAROSELA PHACELIA
PHORMIUM PHYMOSIA PHYSALIS
PHYSARIA PLANTAGO PLUMBAGO
POLYGALA POLYMNIA POTERIUM
PRUNELLA PSORALEA RAPHANUS
RHAGODIA SABBATIA SAMBUCUS
SANICULA SARCODES SAROTHRA
SATUREIA SCABIOSA SCOLYMUS
SESBANIA SESUVIUM SEYMERIA
SIDALCEA SILPHIUM SOLIDAGO
SPERGULA SPIGELIA SPINACIA
STOKESIA TAENIDIA THASPIUM
TIARELLA TRIBULUS TRILLIUM
TROLLIUS TUECRIUM UVULARIA
VACCARIA VALERIAN VANELLUS
VERATRUM VERNONIA VERONICA
VISCARIA WATSONIA XANTHIUM
(— **OF HERON**) ARDEA EGRETTA
(— **OF HORSE**) EQUUS CALIPPUS
EOHIPPUS
(— **OF HYDROZOAN**) DIPHYES
PHYSALIA
(— **OF HYENA**) HYAENA CROCUTA
(— **OF INSECT**) NEPA APHIS EMESA
JAPYX SIREX BOREUS CICADA
COCCUS CORIXA EMPUSA ICERYA
KERMES MANTIS PHASMA PODURA
SIALIS THRIPS CHALCIS FORMICA
FULGORA LEPISMA ORYSSUS
RANATRA STYLOPS VEDALIA
BACILLUS CAMPODEA EPHEMERA
LABIDURA LACCIFER LECANIUM
LYONETIA MACHILIS MANTISPA
NERTHRUS REDUVIUS
(— **OF ISOPOD**) IDOTEA IDOTHEA
CIROLANA

(— **OF JAY**) GARRULUS
(— **OF JELLYFISH**) CYANEA AURELIA
AEQUOREA
(— **OF JERBOA**) DIPUS
(— **OF KELP**) AGARUM
(— **OF LANGUR**) SIMIAS
(— **OF LEAFHOPPER**) AGALLIA
EMPOASCA
(— **OF LEECH**) HIRUDO HAEMOPIS
(— **OF LEMUR**) INDRI GALAGO
(— **OF LIANA**) BAUHINIA
(— **OF LICE**) APHIS PSYLLA
ARGULUS ONISCUS BOVICOLA
ERIOSOMA GONIODES LIPEURUS
(— **OF LICHEN**) CORA USNEA
STICTA EVERNIA GRAPHIS LECIDEA
LOBARIA PHYSCIA CETRARIA
CLADONIA LECANORA PARMELIA
ROCCELLA STRIGULA
(— **OF LIMPET**) ACMAEA
(— **OF LIZARD**) UTA AGAMA DRACO
GEKKO AMEIVA ANGUIS ANOLIS
IGUANA EUMECES LACERTA
PYGOPUS SCINCUS ACONTIAS
CHIROTES COLEONYX LYGOSOMA
RHINEURA
(— **OF LOCUST**) TETRIX TETTIX
(— **OF MACAW**) ARA
(— **OF MAMMAL**) BOS SUS HOMO
LAMA ALCES BISON CAPRA TAYRA
DUGONG FRISON AELURUS AILURUS
BUBALUS GALIDIA GYMNURA
LINSANG OTOCYON AUCHENIA
CYCLOPES CYNOGALE SURICATA
TRAGULUS
(— **OF MAPLE**) ACER
(— **OF MARSUPIAL**) DASYURUS
MACROPUS POTOROUS TARSIPES
(— **OF MARTEN**) MARTES MUSTELA
(— **OF MEDUSA**) SARSIA GERYONIA
(— **OF MICROSPORIDIAN**) GLUGEA
(— **OF MILDEW**) ERYSIPHE
UNCINULA
(— **OF MILLIPEDE**) JULUS
(— **OF MINT**) ICIMUM NEPETA
MELISSA PERILLA PHLOMIS
ORIGANUM
(— **OF MITE**) ACARUS ACERIA
LEPTUS DEMODEX ACARAPIS
MELIOLA
(— **OF MOLD**) MUCOR FULIGO
(— **OF MOLE**) TALPA SCALOPS
SCALOPUS
(— **OF MOLLUSK**) ARCA DOTO LEDA
LIMA CHAMA DONAX EOLIS FICUS
HARPA LIMAX MUREX OLIVA VENUS
AEOLIS ANOMIA BANKIA CASSIS
CHITON LEPTON LUCINA OSTREA
PECTEN PHOLAS PYRULA SEMELE
TEREDO TETHYS ACTAEON ASTARTE
ATLANTA CARDITA CARDIUM
CYPRAEA CYPRINA DOSINIA
ETHERIA EXOGYRA LINGULA
TELLINA BUCCINUM GRYPHAEA
HALIOTIS LIMACINA LUTRARIA
MODIOLUS NAUTILUS PINCTADA
SCYLLAEA STROMBUS
(— **OF MONGOOSE**) GALIDIA
(— **OF MONKEY**) AOTES AOTUS

CEBUS ATELES MACACA CACAJAO
COLOBUS NASALIS SAIMIRI PITHECIA
(— **OF MOOSE**) ALCES
(— **OF MOSQUITO**) AEDES CULEX
(— **OF MOSS**) BRYUM CHILO EUXOA
MNIUM SAMIA SESIA TINEA ACTIAS
ALYPIA ARCTIA BOMBYX COSSUS
DATANA HYPNUM LESKEA PLUSIA
PSYCHE SPHINX THYRIS URANIA
AGROTIS ALABAMA APATELA
ARCHIPS ATTACUS BARBULA
CRAMBUS FUNARIA GRIMMIA
PHASCUM PRONUBA PYRALIS
SESAMIA TORTRIX ZEUZERA
ZYGAENA ANDREAEA CATOCALA
DAWSONIA DIATRAEA DICRANUM
ENDROMIS EPHESTIA EUPREPIA
GALLERIA GELECHIA HEPIALUS
PLUTELLA PRODENIA PYRAUSTA
SATURNIA SPHAGNUM THUIDIUM
(— **OF MOUSE**) MUS APODEMUS
(— **OF MUSKRAT**) FIBER ONDATRA
(— **OF NARWHAL**) MONODON
(— **OF NEMATODE**) ACUARIA
ALAIMUS ANGUINA NECATOR
(— **OF NUDIBRANCH**) GLAUCUS
(— **OF OATS**) AVENA
(— **OF OPOSSUM**) MARMOSA
(— **OF ORCHID**) DISA VANDA BLETIA
LAELIA PHAJUS ACINETA AERIDES
ANGULOA BRASSIA CORDULA
EUCOSIA IBIDIUM ISOTRIA LIPARIS
LISTERA MALAXIS POGONIA VANILLA
ANGRECUM ARETHUSA BLETILLA
CALANTHA CATTLEYA CYTHEREA
FISSIPES GOODYERA MILTONIA
ONCIDIUM PERAMIUM SERAPIAS
SOBRALIA TRIPHORA
(— **OF OTTER**) LUTRA
(— **OF OWL**) BUBO NINOX STRIX
KETUPA NYCTEA AEGOLIUS
SPEOTYTO
(— **OF OXEN**) BIBOS
(— **OF PALM**) NIPA ARECA ASSAI
COCOS HOWEA SABAL ARENGA
ELAEIS INODES KENTIA RAPHIA
RHAPIS ATTALEA BACTRIS CALAMUS
CARYOTA CORYPHA ERYTHEA
EUTERPE GEONOMA LATANIA
LICUALA PHOENIX SERENOA
THRINAX BORASSUS HYPHAENE
IRIARTEA LODOICEA MAURITIA
(— **OF PARASITE**) STRIGA CUSCOTA
HYDNORA OLPIDIUM CASSYTHIA
(— **OF PARRAKEET**) ARATINGA
(— **OF PARROT**) AMAZONA KAKATOE
(— **OF PEACOCK**) PAVO
(— **OF PENGUIN**) EUDYPTES
(— **OF PHALANGER**) DROMICIA
(— **OF PIGEON**) GOURA DUCULA
COLUMBA
(— **OF PLANT**) ALOE ARUM COLA
DION FABA IRIS IXIA PUYA SOJA
ADOXA AGAVE ASTER BATIS CANNA
CHARA DIOON DRYAS INULA NAIAS
PIPER RUMEX TRAPA TYPHA XYRIS
YUCCA ZILLA ABROMA ACACIA
AIZOON ALBUCA ANANAS CACTUS
CUPHEA DATURA EXACUM FERULA

IBERIS JAMBOS JUNCUS LICHEN
LILIUM MAYACA MORAEA NUPHAR
PHRYMA RICCIA SILENE SMILAX
STRIGA URTICA VISCUM ALONSOA
ASTILBE BALLOTA CABOMBA
CUCUMIS CYPERUS DIONAEA
DROSERA ENCELIA EPACRIS
EPIGAEA EURYALE FAGELIA
GLYCINE GODETIA HELXINE
HOOKERA ISOETES ISOLOMA
KARATAS LYCOPUS MANIHOT
MONARDA NELUMBO NITELLA
RAOULIA RICINUS STEMONA
SYRINGA TRIURUS TURNERA
WOLFFIA WYETHIA ZOSTERA
ABUTILON ADIANTUM ANABASIS
ANTHYLIS BRASENIA BRODIAEA
BROMELIA CALADIUM CAPSICUM
CYCLAMEN FORCRAEA FURCRAEA
GALTONIA GASTERIA GERANIUM
LATHRAEA LATHYRUS MARSILEA
MONSTERA NYMPHAEA PANDANUS
PEDALIUM PELVETIA PERESKIA
SAURURUS SPARAXIS THEVETIA
TIGRIDIA TRITONIA VELLOZIA
VICTORIA ZINGIBER
(— **OF POLYZOAN**) LEPRALIA
LOXOSOMA
(— **OF POPLAR**) ALAMO
(— **OF PORCUPINE**) COENDU
HYSTRIX
(— **OF PORPOISE**) INIA
(— **OF PRAWN**) PALAEMON
(— **OF PROTOZOAN**) BODO HYDRA
MONAS ADELEA AMOEBA ACINETA
ARCELLA EIMERIA STENTOR
DIDINIUM EUGLYPHA ISOSPORA
UROGLENA
(— **OF RABBIT**) LEPUS
(— **OF RAT**) ANISOMYS
(— **OF RHIZOPOD**) AMOEBA GROMIA
LAGENA HATTERIA PELOMYXA
(— **OF RODENT**) MUS CAVIA DIPUS
LEPUS ZAPUS GEOMYS LEMMUS
SPALAX CYNOMYS DINOMYS
ECHIMYS LEGGADA MERINES
NESOKIA ZYZOMYS ALACTAGA
ARVICOLA CAPROMYS CITELLUS
CRICETUS HAPLODON HYDROMYS
LAGIDIUM MICROTUS MYOTALPA
ORYZOMYS
(— **OF ROTIFER**) HYDATINA
PEDALION
(— **OF RUST**) UREDO HEMILEIA
UROMYCES
(— **OF SALAMANDER**) ANDRIAS
EURYCEA STREDON TRITURUS
(— **OF SCALE**) KERMES LECANIUM
(— **OF SCALLOP**) HINNITES
(— **OF SCORPION**) BUTHUS
SCORPIO CHELIFER
(— **OF SEA ANEMONE**) MINYAS
ACTINIA
(— **OF SEA FAN**) GORGONIA
(— **OF SEA OTTER**) ENHYDRA
(— **OF SEA SLUG**) ELYSIA
(— **OF SEA URCHIN**) ARBACIA
CIDARIS DIADEMA ECHINUS
(— **OF SEAL**) PHOCA HYDRURGA

MIROUNGA ZALOPHUS
(— **OF SEAWEED**) ULVA ALARIA
(— **OF SEDGE**) FUIRENA SCIRPUS
SCLERIA SCHOENUS
(— **OF SHARK**) LAMNA GALEUS
ISURUS ACRODUS ALOPIAS
SPHYRNA SQUALUS CLADODUS
MENASPIS SQUATINA
(— **OF SHELL**) PUPA LAMBIS
EXOGYRA LATIRUS MALLEUS
TROCHUS HAMINOEA MACLUREA
OLIVELLA TRIGONIA UMBRELLA
(— **OF SHREW**) SOREX BLARINA
(— **OF SHRIMP**) CRAGO CRANGON
(— **OF SHRUB**) IVA ACER BIXA BRYA
HOYA ILEX INGA ITEA MABA OLEA
RHUS ROSA SIDA THEA ULEX ALNUS
ANONA BIOTA BUTEA BUXUS CATHA
DALEA DIRCA ERICA EURYA FICUS
HAKEA IXORA LEDUM MALUS
OCHNA PADUS RIBES RUBUS SABIA
SALIX TAXUS THUJA TREMA UNONA
URENA VITEX ABELIA ACAENA
ADELIA ALHAGI AMYRIS ANNONA
ARALIA ARONIA AUCUBA AZALEA
BAPHIA BAUERA BETULA BLUMEA
BYBLIS CANTUA CASSIA CELTIS
CERCIS CISTUS CITRUS CLEOME
CLUSIA COFFEA CORDIA COREMA
CORNUS CORREA CROTON DAPHNE
DATURA DERRIS DIOSMA DONDIA
DRIMYS ECHIUM EVODIA FATSIA
FEIJOA GARRYA GNETUM GREWIA
GUAREA KALMIA KERRIA LARREA
LIPPIA LITSEA LUCUMA LYCIUM
MIMOSA MYRCIA MYRICA MYRTUS
OCOTEA OLINIA OPILIA PENAEA
PERSEA PIERIS PROTEA PTELEA
PUNICA QUIINA RAMONA RANDIA
ROCHEA ROYENA RUSCUS SALVIA
SAPIUM SCHIMA SELAGO SESBAN
SORBUS STEVIA STYRAX SUAEDA
TECOMA AECULUS AMORPHA
ARBUTUS ARDISIA ARMERIA ASIMINA
ASSONIA BANKSIA BAROSMA
BENZOIN BORONIA BUMELIA
BURSERA CALLUNA CARISSA
CASASIA CERASUS CESTRUM
CLETHRA CNEORUM COLUTEA
CORYLUS COTINUS CUNONIA
CYRILLA CYTISUS DEUTZIA
DOMBEYA DURANTA EHRETIA
ENCELIA EPACRIS EPHEDRA
EUCHLEA EUGENIA EURSERA
FABIANA FUCHSIA GENISTA GMELINA
GYMINDA HAMELIA HOVENIA
KARATAS LAGETTA LANTANA
MAHONIA MERATIA MONUMIA
MORINDA MUTISIA MYRRHIS
NANDINA NEMESIA OLEARIA
OTHONNA PAVETTA PAVONIA
PENTZIA PIMELEA PISONIA PURSHIA
QUASSIA QUERCUS RAPANEA
REMIJIA RHAMNUS RHODORA
ROBINIA ROMNEYA RUELLIA
SALSOLA SENECIO SKIMMIA
SOLANUM SOPHORA SPIRAEA
SURIANA SYRINGA TAMARIX
TELOPEA VERNICA XIMENIA XYLOPIA

XYLOSMA ZELKOVA ACALYPHA
ALANGIUM ALSTONIA ANAGYRIS
ATRIPLEX BALOCHIA BAUHINIA
BERBERIS BORRERIA BUCKLEYA
BUDDLEIA CAMELLIA CAPPARIS
CAPSICUM CARAGANA CASSIOPE
CASTANEA CODIAEUM COLLETIA
CONDALIA CONNARUS COPROSMA
CORIARIA CRATAEVA DAVIESIA
DENDRIUM DILLENIA DODONAEA
DOVYALIS DRACAENA DUBOISIA
EMPETRUM EUONYMUS EUPTELEA
EXOSTEMA FRAXINUS GALACTIA
GOODENIA GORDONIA GUAIACUM
HIBISCUS HIRTELLA IONIDIUM
JASMINUM JATROPHA JUSTICIA
KNIGHTIA KRAMERIA LABURNUM
LAVATERA LAWSONIA LEONOTIS
MAGNOLIA MAYTENUS MENZIESA
MICHELIA MYOPORUM NOTELAEA
PALIURUS PAROSELA PHILESIA
PHOTINIA PHYMOSIA PLUMIERA
POLYGALA POTERIUM PROSOPIS
PSORALEA RHAGODIA ROLLINIA
RORIDULA RUSSELIA SAMBUCUS
SATUREIA SAURAUIA SESBANIA
SOLANDRA SORBARIA SPARTIUM
TABEBUIA TORRUBIA TRECULIA
VARRONIA VERNONIA VIBURNUM
VOCHYSIA WITHANIA ZIZYPHUS
(— **OF SILKWORM**) BOMBYX
(— **OF SKUNK**) MEPHITIS
(— **OF SLOTH**) BRADYPUS
(— **OF SLUG**) DOTO ARION DORIS
LIMAX ELYSIA GLAUCUS
(— **OF SNAIL**) HUA PILA CONUS
FUSUS GALBA HELIX MITRA OVULI
PHYSA THAIS TURBO CERION
EULIMA NATICA NERITA RISSOA
TRITON ANCYLUS BITTIUM BULINU
BUSYCON CYMBIUM LATIRUS
LITIOPA LYMNARA MELANIA
MODULUS PURPURA RANELLA
VALVATA VERTIGO VITRINA ZONIT
ACHATINA ALOCINMA ELLOBIUM
FOSSARIA GYRAULUS HELICINA
HELISOMA JANTHINA KATAYAMA
LITORINA NERITINA OLEACINA
SUCCINEA
(— **OF SNAKE**) BOA ERYX NAIA
NAJA ASPIS BITIS BOIGA ECHIS
ELAPS CAUSUS DABOIA ELAPHE
HURRIA ILYSIA LIGUUS NATRIX
PYTHON VIPERA ATHERIS BOAEDU
COLUBER ECHIDNA MEHELYA
OPHIDIA ZAMENIS BOTHROPS
BUNGARUS CERBERUS CROTALUS
DEMANSIA EUNECTES FARANCIA
LAVHESIS MICRURUS STORERIA
TYPHLOPS
(— **OF SPIDER**) ARANEA LYCOSA
MYGALE AGALENA ARGIOPE
ATTIDAE NEPHILA PHOLCUS
LINYPHIA ULOBORUS
(— **OF SPIROCHETE**) BORRELIA
(— **OF SPONGE**) SYCON GEODIA
SCYPHA ASCETTA CHALINA
GRANTIA SPONGIA SYCETTA
LEUCETTA

(— OF SPOROZOAN) NOSEMA
(— OF SQUID) LOLIGO SEPIOLA
(— OF SQUIRREL) SCIURUS
(— OF SUBSHRUB) LECHEA
ARMERIA ASCYRUM BEGONIA
FELICIA ATRIPLEX COLUMNEA
(— OF SWAN) OLOR CYGNUS
(— OF TAKIN) BUDORCAS
(— OF TAPEWORM) BERTIA LIGULA
DAVAINEA HARRISIA
(— OF TAYRA) GALERA GALICTIS
(— OF TELEDU) MYDAUS
(— OF TERN) GYGIS STERNA
(— OF THISTLE) CARDUUS
(— OF TICK) ARGAS ARGUS IXODES
HYALOMMA
(— OF TOAD) BUFO HYLA PIPA
ALYTES XENOPUS ASCAPHUS
(— OF TREE) ACER BIXA BRYA
COLA HURA ILEX INGA MABA OLAX
OLEA RHUS THEA ABIES AEGLE
ALNUS ANIBA BIOTA BUTEA BUXUS
CARYA CEIBA CYCAS DURIO EURYA
FAGUS FICUS HAKEA HEVEA HOPEA
IXORA KHAYA LARIX MALUS MELIA
MESUA MORUS NYSSA OCHNA
PADUS PICEA PINUS PYRUS SALIX
TAXUS THUJA TILIA TOONA TREMA
TSUGA ULMUS UNONA VITEX XYLIA
ACHRAS AKANIA AMOMIS AMYRIS
ANDIRA ANNONA ARALIA AZALEA
BAPHIA BETULA BOMBAX CANTUA
CARAPA CARICA CASSIA CEDRUS
CELTIS CERCIS CITRUS CLUSIA
COFFEA CORDIA CORNUS DATURA
DRIMYS EPERUA EPERVA EUCLEA
EVODIA FEIJOA GARRYA GENIPA
GINKGO GNETUM GREWIA GUAREA
IDESIA ILLIPE LAURUS LITCHI LITSEA
LUCUMA LYCIUM MAMMEA MIMOSA
MYRCIA MYRICA OCOTEA OLNEYA
OSTRYA OWENIA PAPPEA PARITI
PERSEA PRUNUS PTELEA QUIINA
RANDIA ROYENA SAPIUM SAPOTA
SCHIMA SENCIO SESBAN SHOREA
SIMABA SORBUS STYRAX TECOMA
AGATHIS ARBUTUS ARDISIA ASIMINA
ASSONIA BANKSIA BUMELIA
BURSERA CANELLA CASASIA
CATALPA CEDRELA CERASUS
CLETHRA COPAIVA CORYLUS
COTINUS CUNONIA CUPANIA
CYDONIA CYRILLA DOMBEYA
ECHINUS EHRETIA EPACRIS EUGENIA
FERONIA GMELINA GUAZUMA
GYMINDA HAGENIA HALESIA
HICORIA HOVENIA HUMIRIA ILLICUM
JUGLANS KADELIA KOKOONA
LAGETTA LICANIA LINGOUM
MACLURA MICONIA MORINDA
MORINGA MURRAYA OCHROMA
OLEARIA PANGIUM PIMENTA PISONIA
PLANERA POPULUS PROTIUM
PSIDIUM QUASSIA QUERCUS
RAPANEA REMIJIA RHAMNUS
ROBINIA SCHINUS SENECIO SEQUOIA
SLOANEA SOLANUM SOPHORA
SURIANA SYRINGA TAMARIX
TECTONA TELOPEA TORREYA

TROPHIS VATERIA XIMENIA XYLOPIA
XYLOSMA ZELKOVA AESCULUS
ALANGIUM ALBIZZIA ALSTONIA
ANTIARIS AVERRHOA BALANOPS
BALOGHIA BAUHINIA BRABEJUM
BROSIMUM BUDDLEIA CABRALEA
CAMELLIA CANANGIA CANARIUM
CAPPARIS CAROGANA CARPINUS
CARYOCAR CASEARIA CASTANEA
CASTILLA CECROPIA CINCHONA
CODIAEUM CONDALIA CYBISTAX
DILLENIA DIPTERYX DODONAEA
DOVYALIS DRACAENA DUBOISIA
EUCOMMIA EUONYMUS EUPTELEA
EXOSTEMA FITZROYA FRAXINUS
FUNTUMIA GARCINIA GARDENIA
GORDONIA GUAIACUM HIBISCUS
HIRTELLA HOMALIUM HYMENAEA
JATROPHA KANDELIA KNIGHTIA
LABURNUM LAPORTEA LAVATERA
LECYTHIS LEUCAENA LYSILOMA
MAGNOLIA MALLOTUS MAYTENUS
MESPILUS MICHELIA MIMUSOPS
MYOPORUM NOTELAEA PHOTINIA
PISCIDIA PISTACIA PLATANUS
PLUMIERA PONCIRUS PROSOPIS
QUILLAJA RAVENALA ROLLINIA
SAMADERA SAMBUCUS SANTALUM
SAPINDUS SAURAUIA SESBANIA
SIMARUBA SPONDIAS SWARTZIA
TABEBUIA TAXODIUM TORRUBIA
TRECULIA VARRONIA VERONICA
VIBURNUM VIRGILIA VOCHYSIA
(— OF TUNICATE) SALPA ASCIDIA
DOLIOLUM
(— OF TURTLE) EMYS AMYDA
CHELUS CHELYS CARETTA CHELONE
CLEMMYS TESTUDO TRIONYX
ARCHELON CHELONIA CHELYDRA
PELUSIOS
(— OF TWINER) STEMONA
(— OF UNIVALVE) DOLIUM
(— OF VINE) ROSA ABRUS ABUTA
PISUM TAMUS UNONA VIGNA VITIS
AKEBIA CISSUS COBAEA DERRIS
ENTADA HEDERA MUCUNA PETREA
POTHOS SICANA SICYOS SOLLYA
VIORNA ARAUJIA BASELLA
BOMAREA BRYONIA ECHITES
EMBELIA EPACRIS FALCATA
HUMULUS IPOMOEA MIKANIA
PISONIA SECHIUM UNCARIA
ZANONIA ANAMIRTA ATRAGENE
BIGNONIA CLEMATIS COCCULUS
DEGUELIA DOLICHOS EUONYMUS
JASMINUM KENNEDYA PANDOREA
PUERARIA SECAMONE SERJANIA
TACSONIA WISTARIA
(— OF WALRUS) ODOBENUS
(— OF WASP) SPHEX VESPA
BEMBEX CYNIPS SCOLIA TIPHIA
CHRYSIS EUMENES MASARIS
MUTILLA ANDRICUS CHLORION
ODYNERUS POLISTES POMPILUS
SPHECIUS
(— OF WEASEL) MUSTELA
(— OF WEED) CAPSELLA
(— OF WEEVIL) APION HYPERA
SITONA CLEONUS CALANDRA

CALENDRA CURCULIO
(— OF WHALE) CETE ARETA KOGIA
BALAENA ORCINUS ZIPHIUS
PHYSETER
(— OF WOLVERINE) GULO
(— OF WORM) DERO SPIO ALARIA
EUNICE KERRIA MERMIS NEREIS
SYLLIS ACHAETA ACHOLOE ASCARIS
DUGESIA EISENIA FILARIA GLYCERA
GORDIUS HESIONE LEODICE
POLYNOE SABELLA SAGITTA
SERPULA SETARIA SPIRURA TUBIFEX
ARABELLA ASCAROPS BIPALIUM
BONELLIA COOPERIA DOCHMIUS
ECHIURUS FASCIOLA GEOPLANA
PHORONIS SPADELLA SUBULURA
SYNGAMUS SYPHACIA
(— OF ZORIL) ICTONYX
GEODE DRUSE
GEOMETRIC CUBIST CUBISTIC
GEOMETRY EUCLID SPHERICS
GEOPHAGY PICA

GEORGIA

CAPITAL: ATLANTA
COLLEGE: SPELMAN MOREHOUSE
COUNTY: BIBB COBB TIFT RABUN
　TROUP DEKALB FULTON TALBOT
　LAURENS GWINNETT MUSCOGEE
INDIAN: GUALE YUCHI CHIAHA
　OCONEE YAMASEE
LAKE: LANIER MARTIN HARDING
　NOTTELY BANKHEAD HARTWELL
　SINCLAIR
MOUNTAIN: STONE KENNESAW
NATIVE: CRACKER
RIVER: PEA FLINT ETOWAH
　OCONEE PIGEON CONECUH
　SATILLA ALTAMAHA OCMULGEE
STATE BIRD: THRASHER
STATE NICKNAME: PEACH
STATE TREE: LIVEOAK
TOWN: JESUP MACON AUGUSTA
　CONYERS DECATUR VIDALIA
　MARIETTA MOULTRIE SAVANNAH
　VALDOSTA WAYCROSS
UNIVERSITY: EMORY GATECH
　MERCER

GEORGIAN ADZHAR CRACKER
GEORGIA PINE LONGLEAF
GEPHYREAN STARWORM
GER STRANGER
GERANIUM DOVEFOOT FLUXWEED
　SHAMEFACE
GERANIUM LAKE SPARK NACARAT
GERBIL JIRD
GERIANOL ISOLATE
GERM BUG CHIT SEED SPARK
　SPAWN SPERM GERMEN GERMULE
　MICROBE SEMINAL SEEDLING
　SEMINARY SEMINIUM
(— CELL) GONE
GERMAN HUN BALT HANS MUFF
　ALMAN BOCHE FRITZ HEINE JERRY
　ALMAIN DUTCHY HEINIE TEUTON
　SAUSAGE TEDESCO COTILLON
　GERMANIC TUDESQUE

GERMANDER POLY BETONY
FOXTAIL SOVENEZ SCORDIUM
GERMANE GERMAN PERTINENT
GERMANIC GOTHIC GOTHONIC
TEUTONIC
GERMAN SHEPHERD ALSATIAN

GERMANY

ANCIENT: ALMAIN ALMAINE
ANCIENT TRIBESMAN: JUTE
TEUTON VISIGOTH OSTROGOTH
CANAL: KIEL WESER LUDWIG
CAPITAL: BONN BERLIN
CHEESE: MUENSTER TILSITER
LIMBURGER
COAL REGION: RUHR SAAR SARRE
COIN: MARK KRONE TALER
GULDEN KRONEN THALER
PFENNIG GROSCHEN
DIALECT: KOLSCH KOELSCH
BALTISCH HESSISCH
DYNASTY: HOHENSTAUFEN
HOHENZOLLERN
FOOD: WURST KNODEL SPATZLE
STRUDEL MARZIPAN ROULADEN
HANSEATIC CITY: KOLN LUBECK
COLOGNE HAMBURG LUEBECK
ISLAND: USEDOM WOLLIN
FEHMARN FRISIAN
LAKE: DUMMER WURMSEE
AMMERSEE BODENSEE
CHIEMSEE MURITZEE
CONSTANCE
LANGUAGE: DEUTSCH
MEASURE: AAM IMI OHM FASS
FUSS LAST RUTE SACK STAB
CARAT EIMER KANNE KETTE
LINIE MAASS METZE RUTHE
SIMRI MASSEL MORGEN OXHOFT
SEIDEL STRICH JUCHART
KLAFTER TAGWERK SCHEFFEL
SCHOPPEN STUBCHEN VIERLING
MOUNTAIN: FELDBERG WATZMANN
MOUNTAIN RANGE: ORE ALPS
HARZ RHON HARDT HUNSRUCK
NAME: REICH ASHKENAZ
GERMANIA DEUTSCHLAND
NATIVE: GOTH SAXON TEUTON
RESORT: EMS BADEN AACHEN
TRIBAL REGION: GAU GAUE GAUS
UNIVERSITY TOWN: FREIBURG
HEIDELBERG
PORT: EMDEN BREMEN HAMBURG
ROSTOCK STETTIN
RIVER: ALZ EMS INN EDER EGER
ELBE ISAR LAHN LECH MAIN
NAAB NAHE ODER OKER REMS
RUHR SAAR SIEG ALLER DONAU
EIDER FULDA HAVEL HUNTE
ILLER LEINE LIPPE MOSEL
MULDE PEENE REGEN RHEIN
RHINE SAALE SAUER SPREE
UCKER WERRA WESER DANUBE
ELSTER KOCHER NECKAR
NEISSE RANDOW TAUBER
VECHTE WARNOW ALTMUHL
JEETZEL PEGNITZ SALZACH
UNSTRUT

STATE: BADEN LIPPE BAYERN
BREMEN HESSEN SAXONY
BAVARIA HAMBURG PRUSSIA
SAARLAND BRUNSWICK
TOWN: AUE EMS HOF ULM BONN
GERA GOCH HAAR HAMM JENA
KIEL KOLN LAHR AALEN AHLEN
EMDEN ESSEN FURTH GOTHA
HAGEN HALLE HERNE MAINZ
MOLLN NEUSS PIRNA TRIER
AACHEN ALTENA ALTONA
BARMEN BERLIN BREMEN
CASSEL DACHAU DESSAU
ERFURT KASSEL LINDEN
LUBECK MUNICH PLAUEN
TREVES BAMBERG BRESLAU
COBLENZ COLOGNE CREFELD
DRESDEN GORLITZ HAMBURG
HANOVER LEIPZIG MAYENCE
MUNCHEN MUNSTER POTSDAM
ROSTOCK SPANDAU ZWICKAU
AUGSBURG CHEMNITS
DORTMUND DUISBURG
FREIBURG LIEGNITZ MANNHAIM
NURNBERG WURSELEN
WURZBURG DARMSTADT
KARLSRUHE MAGDEBURG
NUREMBERG OSNABRUCK
STUTTGART WUPPERTAL
DUSSELDORF HEIDELBERG
OBERHAUSEN
WEIGHT: LOT GRAN LOTE LOTH
UNZE LOTHE PFUND STEIN
PRUNDE DRACHMA ZENTNER
VIERLING
WINE: MOSELLE RIESLING

GERMICIDE KRELOS
GERMINABLE PREGNANT
GERMINATE BUD HIT CHIP CHIT
GERM SHOOT SPIRE SPRIT BRAIRD
SPROUT STRIKE
GERMINATION CATCH
GESAN TAPUYAN CHAVANTE
GESTATION GOING BREEDING
GESTICULATE GESTURE
GESTURE CUT FIG BECK BERE GEST
SIGN FILIP GESTE HONOR SANNA
BECKON BREATH CUTOFF FILLIP
MOTION SALUTE SIGNAL CURTSEY
FASHION FLICKER MURGEON
ACCOLADE CEREMONY
(— **OF DERISION)** SNOOK
(**AFFECTED** —) GAATCH
(**USELESS** —) FUTILITY
GET COP GIT WIN FALL GAIN GRAB
HAVE HENT TAKE TILL AFONG
ANNEX CATCH COVER FETCH LATCH
DERIVE OBTAIN SECURE ACQUIRE
CONQUER PROCURE PRODUCE
RECEIVE PERCEIVE
(— **ABOARD)** FLIP
(— **ABOUT)** BEGO
(— **ALONG)** DO GEE FARE FEND
AGREE FADGE FODGE SPEED
FETTLE
(— **AROUND)** BYPASS COMPASS
FINESSE FLUMMER

(— **AT)** ATTAIN
(— **AWAY)** LAM RYNT SLIP EVADE
CHEESE ESCAPE
(— **BACK)** REDEEM RETIRE
RECOVER
(— **BETTER OF)** WAX BEST DING
DOWN DAUNT FLING SHEND SHENT
STICK STING JOCKEY OVERGO
RECOVER SURMOUNT
(— **BY ARTIFICE)** WIND
(— **BY ASKING)** KICK
(— **BY CUNNING)** WHIZZLE
(— **BY EXTORTION)** GRATE
(— **BY FLATTERY)** COG
(— **CLEAR OF)** STRIP
(— **DISHONESTLY)** FIRK
(— **DOWN)** ALIGHT
(— **ON WELL)** LIKE
(— **ON)** FARE BOARD CHEFE CHEV
FRAME SHIFT EXPLOIT
(— **OUT)** LEAK SCRAM CHEESE
OUTWIN VOETSAK
(— **PAST)** BEAT HURDLE
(— **POSSESSION)** CARRY
(— **READY)** GET PARE RANK BRAC
FRAME FETTLE ORDAIN APPAREL
(— **RID)** CAST DISH DUMP FREE
JUNK SHAB TOSS ERASE SHAKE
SHIFT SHOOT SLOUGH UNLOAD
DELIVER DISCARD EXTRUDE
DISPATCH DISSOLVE
(— **SURREPTITIOUSLY)** SNEAK
(— **THE POINT)** SAVVY
(— **TO BOTTOM OF)** FATHOM
(— **UNDER CONTROL)** RAIM
(— **UP)** ARISE HUDDUP UPRISE
HAIRPIN
GETA SABOT
GET-TOGETHER DO DRINK HOBNC
BAMBOCHE POTLATCH
GETUP SETOUT
GEWGAW DIE TOY WALY KNACK
WALLY BAUBLE FANGLE FEGARY
JIGGER FLAMFEW TRANGAM
TRINKET FOLDEROL GIMCRACK
JIMCRACK TRIMTRAM
GEYSER BORE JETTER

GHANA

CAPITAL: ACCRA
DAM: AKOSOMBO
LAKE: VOLTA BOSUMTWI
LANGUAGE: GA EWE TWI FANTI
HAUSA DAGBANI DAGOMBA
MONEY: NEWCEDI
MOUNTAIN: AFADJATO
NATIVE: GA EWE AHAFO BRONG
FANTI ASHANTI DAGOMBA
MAMPRUSI
RIVER: OTI PRA DAKA TANO
AFRAM VOLTA ANKOBRA
KULPAWN
TOWN: HO WA ODA AXIM FIAN
KETA TALA TEMA ACCRA
BAWKU ENCHI LAWRA LEGON
SAMPA YAPEI DUNKWA KARAGA
KPANDU KUMASI NSAWAM
OBUASI SWEDRU TAMALE

TARKWA WASIPE ANTUBIA
DAMONGO MAMPONG PRESTEA
SEKONDI SUNYANI WINNEBA
AKOSOMBO KINTAMPO
TAKORADI
WIND: HARMATTAN

GHARRY SHIGRAM
GHASTLY WAN GRIM PALE BLATE
GHAST LURID UNKET UNKID DISMAL
GOUSTY GRISLY PALLID CHARNEL
DEATHLY FEARFUL GASHFUL
GRIZZLY GRUGOUS HIDEOUS
MACABRE DREADFUL GRUESOME
HORRIBLE SHOCKING TERRIBLE
GHAWAZI BARAMIKA
GHERKIN CUCUMBER
GHETTO JEWRY JUDAISM
GHIBELLINE WAIBLING
GHOST HAG KER BHUT HANT JUBA
WAFF BUGAN CADDY DUFFY DUPPY
FETCH GAIST GUEST HAUNT JUMBY
LARVA PRETA SHADE SPOOK
UMBRA CHUREL SOWLTH SPIRIT
SPRITE TAISCH ANTAEUS ANTAIOS
BOGGART BUGGANE GYTRASH
PHANTOM SPECTER SPECTRE
VAMPIRE BARGHEST GUYTRASH
PHANTASM REVENANT
GHOSTFISH WRYMOUTH
GHOSTLY EERY EERIE GOUSTY
SHADOWY UNCANNY WEIRDLY
CHTHONIC GHASTFUL SPECTRAL
GHOST MOTH SWIFT HEPIALID
GHOST-WRITER SPOOK
GHOULISH SATANIC
GHUZ OGHUZ
GIAI NHANG
GIANT ORC ETEN HUGE OGRE OTUS
WATE YMER YMIR AFRIT BALOR
CACUS HYMIR JOTUN MIMAS MIMER
THRYM TITAN TROLL AFREET
ALBION FAFNIR GIGANT GOEMOT
PALLAS THJAZI THURSE TITYUS
WARLOW ANTAEUS CYCLOPS
GOLIATH WARLOCK ASCOPART
GBELLERUS COLBRAND GIGANTIC
GOEMAGOT GOGMAGOG MASTODON
MORGANTE ORGOGLIO TYPHOEUS
(1-EYED —) CYCLOPS
(100-HANDED —) GYGES COTTUS
BRIAREUS
(1000-ARMED —) BANA
(PL.) ANAK ANAKIM COTTUS
ALOADAE REPHAIM NEPHILIM
ZAMZUMMIM
GIANTESS NORN ARGANTE
GIANT FULMAR NELLY STINKER
STINKPOT
GIANT GRASS OTATE
GIANT HERON GOLIATH
GIANT LILY FIGUE MAGUEY
GIANT PUFFBALL FUZZ FUZZBALL
GIARDIA LAMBLIA
GIB JIB SHOE DEMUR SLIPPER
GIBBAR GIBBERT JUBARTAS
GIBBER CHAT CHATTER
GIBBERISH GREEK JABBER JARGON
CHOCTAW

GIBBET STOB TREE CROOK JEBAT
GALLOWS POTENCE EQUULEUS
GIBBON LAR WAWA UNGKA WUYEN
CAMPER HULOCK HOOLOCK
SIAMANG
GIBBOUS CONVEX HULCHY HUMPED
GIBE (ALSO SEE JIBE) BOB RUB GIRD
JAPE JEST JIBE PROG QUIB QUIP
SKIT WIPE FLEER FLING FLIRT
FRUMP GLEEK KNACK SCOFF
SCOMM SCORN SLANT SNEER
DERIDE GLANCE HECKLE BROCARD
SARCASM RIDICULE
GIBING SNASH
GID DUNT GIDDY STURDY GOGGLES
POTHERY VERTIGO
GIDDINESS LUNACY SOORAWN
GIDDY GLAKY LIGHT WESTY GIGLET
GLAKED GOWKED GOWKIT SHANNY
STURDY VOLAGE GLAIKET LARKING
HALUCKET HELLICAT
GIFT BOX FOY QUO SOP BENT BOON
DASH ENAM MEED SAND BONUS
BRIBE CAULP CUDDY DONUM
GRANT KNACK TOKEN CADEAU
DASHEE DONARY GENIUS GERSUM
GIFTIE GIVING HANSEL LEGACY
RECADO REGALO TALENT XENIUM
APTNESS BENEFIT CHARISM
CHARITY DEODATE DONATIO
DOUCEUR ETRENNE FACULTY
GIFTURE HANDSEL PRESENT
PROPINE REGALIO SUBSIDY TASHRIF
TRIBUTE AMATORIO APTITUDE
BENEFICE BESTOWAL BLESSING
COURTESY DONATION DONATIVE
GARRISON GIVEAWAY GRATUITY
MORTUARY OBLATION OFFERING
POTLATCH SPORTULA
(— FROM HUSBAND TO WIFE)
ARRAS
(— OF GOD) GRACE
(— OF MONEY) POUCH BAKSHISH
(— OF NATURE) DOWER DOWRY
(CHARITABLE —) ALMS ENAM
PITTANCE
(COMPULSORY —) SIXENIA
(LIBERAL —) LARGESSE
(NATURAL —) TALENT
(NEW YEAR'S EVE —) HAGMENA
HOGMANAY
(SPIRITUAL —) CHARISM CHARISMA
(PL.) OBLATA MISSILES
GIFTBOOK ANNUAL KEEPSAKE
GIG TUB BANDY CHAIR GIGGE
CHAISE DENNET WHISKY CALESIN
TILBURY STANHOPE
GIGANTIC HUGE GIANT MAMMOTH
TITANIC COLOSSAL ENORMOUS
GIGANTAL
GIGGER TEASELER
GIGGLE KECKLE SNICKER TWITTER
GIGLET JIG
GILD GILT BEGILD ENGILD ORFGILD
GILDED GILT AURATE INAURATE
GILDER TRACER
GILGAMESH IZDUBAR
GILL JILL QUAD GHYLL PLICA GILLIE
LAMELLA BRANCHIA QUADRANT

(—S OF BIVALVE) BEARD
(PL.) GINNERS CHOLLERS
GILLAR PITTO
GILLIE GILLY HENCHMAN
GILLYFLOWER STOCK GILVER
GELOFRE GILLIVER
GILTHEAD CONNER MELANURE
GIMBAL GEMEL JEMBLE
GIMCRACK QUIP BAUBLE GEWGAW
JIMJAM TRIFLE TRANGAM TRINKET
JIMCRACK WHIMWHAM
GIMLET SCREW WIMBLE PIERCEL
PIERCER
GIMMICK GAFF
GIMP TAR ORRIS GUIMPE GIMPING
GIN MAX CRAB GRIN LACE RUIN
TAPE CLEAN JACKY SNARE SNARL
DIDDLE GENEVA JAMBER JAMMER
SPRINGE TITTERY EYEWATER
HOLLANDS SCHIEDAM SCHNAPPS
(DROP OF —) DAFFY
GINGER PEPPER RATOON AROMATIC
ZINZIBER COLTSFOOT
GINGERBREAD SPICE PARKIN
GINGERLY GINGER WARILY CHARILY
EDGINGLY
GINGERROOT HAND RACE
(PL.) ASARUM
GINGHAM CHAMBRAY
GINKGO ICHO
GINSENG SANG FATIL PANAX
ARALIA IVYWORT REDBERRY
GIRAFFE OONT CAMEL DAPPLE
KAMEEL SERAPH CAMAILE
RUMINANT
GIRD BELT BIND GIRR GIRT HASP
YERK CLOSE SCOFF ENGIRD
FASTEN GIRDLE SECURE ACCINGE
ENVIRON CINCTURE SURROUND
GIRDER BEAM GIRD GIRT GIRTH
TABLE TRUSS BINDER SUMMER
WARREN GIRDING TWISTER
BUCKSTAY STRINGER
GIRDING CINCTURE
GIRDLE OBI ZON BARK BELT CEST
GIRD HOOP SASH ZONA ZONE
CEINT GIRTH MITER PATTE SARPE
WAIST BODICE CESTUS CINGLE
CIRCLE MOOCHA TISSUE ZODIAC
ZONULA ZOSTER BALDRIC BALTEUS
CENTRUM CENTURE COMPASS
GIRDING SHINGLE CEINTURE
CINCTURE CINGULUM SURROUND
(— FOR HELMET) TISSUE
(— OF DIATOM) HOOP
(BRIDE'S —) CEST CESTUS
(LITTLE —) ZONULE ZONELET
(ROYAL —) MALO
(SACRED —) KUSTI
GIRDLED RUNG
GIRL BIT GAL HER KIT POP SHE SIS
TIB TID TIT BABE BABY BINT BIRD
DAME DEEM DELL GILL JANE JILL
JUDY LASS MARY MOPS MORT PERI
SLUT WREN BEAST FILLY GUIDE
KITTY LUBRA QUEAN SISSY SKIRT
TIDDY TITTY TRULL BURDIE CALICO
CLINER CUMMER DALAGA DAMSEL
DEEMIE FEMALE FIZGIG GEISHA

GIRLIE LASSIE LOVELY MAGGIE
NUMBER PIGEON SHEILA SISTER
SUBDEB TOMATO CAMILLA COLLEEN
DAMOSEL MADCHEN MAUTHER
TENDREL BONNIBEL FARMETTE
FEMININE GRISETTE MUCHACHA
(AGILE —) YANKER
(AWKWARD —) HOIT
(BEATIFIED —) BEATA
(BEAUTIFUL —) BELLE
(BOLD —) HOIDEN HOYDEN
(CAMP FIRE —) ARTISAN
(CHORUS —) CHORINE CORYPHEE
(COUNTRY —) MEG JOAN
(DANCING —) DASI KISANG KISAENG
DEVADASI
(DANCING —S) GHAWAZI
(DEAR —) PEAT
(FLIGHTY —) GOOSECAP
(FLIRTATIOUS —) JADE JILLET
(FLOWER —) NYDIA
(FORWARD —) STRAP
(FROLICSOME —) GILPY
(GIDDY —) GIG GIGLET GIGLOT
JILLET
(GREEK —) HAIDEE
(GYPSY —) GITANA
(HIRED —) BIDDY BIDDIE
(IMPUDENT —) STRAP
(JAPANESE —) GEISHA
(LITTLE —) SIS COOKY SISSY
COOKIE LASSOCK
(MISCHIEVOUS —) CUTTY HUSSY
(MODEST —) BLUSHET
(NAIVE —) INGENUE
(NON-JEWISH —) SHIKSE SHICKSA
(PERT —) MINX HUSSY
(PRETTY —) PRIM CUTEY CUTIE
(ROMPING —) STAG TOMBOY
(SAUCY —) SNIP
(SERVANT —) SLUT
(SILLY —) SKIT
(SINGING —) ALMA ALMEH
(SLENDER —) SYLPH
(SMALL —) PINAFORE
(SPIRITED —) FILLY
(UNATTRACTIVE —) FRUMP
(UNMARRIED —) MOUSME TOWDIE
MUSUMEE
(WANTON —) GIG FILLOCK
(WILD —) BLOWZE
(WORKING —) ORISETTE
(WORTHLESS —) HUSSY
(YOUNG —) BUD MODER TITTY
MAIDEN MOTHER BAGGAGE
COLLEEN FLAPPER GIRLEEN
ROSEBUD
(PL.) GIRLERY GIRLHOOD
GIRT CINCT
GIRTH GIRD GIRT TAPE CINCH
GARTH GIRSE GRETH WANTY
CINGLE WARROK GIRDING SHINGLE
WEBBING
GIST JET NET NUB SUM CHAT CORE
GITE KNOT PITH GREAT HEART
JOIST SENSE BURDEN KERNEL
PURPORT SUMMARY STRENGTH
GITH MELANTHY
GIVE ADD GIE HOB TIP BEAR DEAL

DOLE HAND METE SELL TAKE WEVE
WHIP ALLOW AWARD COUGH GRANT
REFER YIELD ACCORD AFFORD
BESTOW CONFER DEMISE DOTATE
FASTEN IMPART IMPOSE IMPUTE
RENDER SUPPLY CONSIGN DELIVER
FORGIVE FURNISH PRESENT
BEQUEATH DISPENSE
(— A BOOST) BOLSTER
(— A PLACE TO) SITUATE
(— A REMEDY) MINISTER
(— ADHERENCE) ASSENT
(— ADMITTANCE) ACCEPT
(— ADVICE) READ ADVISE
(— AN ACCOUNT) TELL RELATE
REPORT
(— AND TAKE) GIFFGAFF
(— ANYTHING NAUSEOUS TO) DOSE
(— APPROVAL) CONSENT
(— AS CONCESSION) YETTE
(— AS EXPLANATION) ASSIGN
(— ASSURANCE) EFFRONT
(— ATTENTION TO) HEED
(— AUTHORITY) ENABLE EMPOWER
ACCREDIT
(— AWAY) PART
(— BACK) REFUND RETURN
RESTORE
(— BIRTH) KIT BEAR BORN DROP
FIND MAKE BEGET BREED ISSUE
WORLD FARROW KINDLE LITTER
DELIVER FRESHEN
(— BY WILL) DEVISE
(— CARE) NURSE
(— CLAIM TO) REMISE
(— COUNSEL) AREAD AREED
(— CREDIT FOR) FRIST
(— CURRENCY TO) PASS
(— EAR) HARK HARKEN LISTEN
HEARKEN
(— EXPRESSION TO) EMOTE FRAME
VOICE
(— FORM) CUT
(— FORTH) WARP YIELD AFFORD
CONCEIVE
(— GROUND) RETIRE
(— HEED) LOOK ATTEND
(— IN EXCHANGE) SWAP SWOP
(— IN MARRIAGE) BESTOW SPOUSE
(— IN) BOW COLLAPSE
(— INFORMATION) WARN
(— INSTRUCTION) LEAR
(— NAME TO) BAPTIZE
(— NOTICE TO APPEAR) GARNISH
(— NOTICE) WARN HERALD APPRISE
PUBLISH ANNOUNCE INTIMATE
(— OBLIQUE EDGE) CANT
(— OFF) EMIT SEND SHED FLING
DIVIDE EFFUSE EVOLVE EXHALE
EXPIRE EXCRETE SEPARATE
(— ONE'S SELF OVER TO) ADDICT
(— ONE'S WORD) PROMISE
(— OUT) BOOM LEAK EXUDE ISSUE
PETAL EVOLVE EMANATE OUTGIVE
(— PAIN) AGGRIEVE
(— PLACE) VAIL BACCARE
(— PLEDGE) GAGE
(— PROMINENCE TO) FEATURE
(— RELUCTANTLY) BEGRUDGE

(— SATISFACTION) ABY ABYE
ABEGGE
(— SPARINGLY) INCH
(— STRENGTH TO) NERVE
(— SUPPORT) ASSIST ANIMATE
(— TEMPORARILY) LEND
(— TIP) TOUT
(— TONGUE) CRY YEARN
(— UP) PUT BURY DROP PART
CHUCK DEMIT DEVOW FORGO
LEAVE REMIT SHOOT SPARE SPEND
ABJURE ADDICT BETRAY DESERT
DEVOTE FOREGO MIZZLE REFUSE
RELENT RENDER RESIGN VACATE
ABANDON DEPOSIT DESPAIR
FLUMMOX FORBEAR FORGIVE
REFRAIN RELEASE ABDICATE
RENOUNCE
(— VENT TO) EMIT ISSUE
DISCHARGE
(— VOICE) BOLT ACCENT
(— WARNING) ALERT
(— WAY) GO FAIL FOLD KEEL SINK
VAIL BREAK BUDGE BURST FAINT
SLAKE YIELD BUCKLE FALTER
RELENT SWERVE FOUNDER RECLAIM
SUCCUMB
(— WITNESS) DEPOSE
GIVEN APT DONEE NATHAN PROMPT
(— TO) ALL AFTER
GIVER DONOR
(— OF LIFE) APHETA
(NAME —) EPONYM
GIVING DOLE BOUNTY DATION
REMISE
(— HELP) ADJUTANT
(— MILK) FRESH
(— NO MILK) YELD YELL
(— TROUBLE) CUMBROUS
GIZZARD GIGERIUM
GIZZARD SHAD SKIPJACK
GLABROUS SMOOTH GLABRATE
LEVIGATE
GLACIATION MINDEL
(— STAGE) RISS WURM
GLACIER BRAE ICECAP STREAM
CALOTTE ICEBERG PIEDMONT
GLACIOLOGY CRYOLOGY
GLACIS ESPLANADE
GLAD GAY FAIN LIEF VAIN CANTY
HAPPY PROUD BLITHE FESTUS
GLADLY JOCUND JOYFUL JOYOUS
GLADFUL GLEEFUL JOCULAR
ANIMATED CHEERFUL CHEERING
FESTIVAL GLADSOME PLEASING
GLADDEN JOY GLAD BLISS CHEER
EXULT MIRTH BLITHE COMFORT
GLADIFY LIGHTEN REJOICE
GLADE LAWN LAUND SLADE SHRAD
SUNGLADE SUNSCALD
GLADIATOR THRAX RETIARY
SAMNITE SECUTOR ANDABATA
GLADIOLUS GLAD IRID LILY LEVER
LILIUM GLADIOLA
GLADLY GLAD LIEF FAINLY LIEFLY
LOVELY HAPPILY
GLADNESS JOY GLAD GLEE BLISS
MIRTH BLITHE FAINNESS GLADSHIP
PLEASURE

GLAGA KASA KUSA TALTHIB
GLAMORIZE POT GLORIFY
GLAMOROUS EXOTIC ALLURING CHARMING
GLANCE EYE RAY SEE BEAM CAST GLIM LEER PEEK SCRY SKEG VIEW WINK BLENK BLINK BLUSH CAROM FLASH GLEEK GLENT GLIDE GLIFF GLINT GLISK GRAZE PRINK SCREW SIGHT SKIME SLANT SQUIZ ASPECT CARROM GANDER REGARD SCANCE STRIKE VISION EYEBEAM EYESHOT EYEWINK GLIMPSE BELAMOUR GLIFFING OEILLADE
(— OFF) GLACE
(— THROUGH) SAMPLE
(MELANCHOLY —) DOWNCAST
(SHARP —) DART
(SIDELONG —) SHEW SLENT SKLENT
(SLY —) GLEG GLIME GLOAT
GLAND MILT NOIX SETA CLYER CRYPT GONAD LIVER MAMMA BREAST KERNEL THYMUS ADRENAL CRUMENA NECTARY PAROTID PAROTIS TEARPIT THYROID ENDOCRIN FOLLICLE FOLLOWER GANGLION GLANDULA GLANDULE HOOFWORM PROSTATE SCIRRHUS SPERMARY
GLANDERS FARCY MALLEUS
GLANDULAR EARTHY INNATE SEXUAL PHYSICAL
GLANS NUT GLAND
GLARE BEAT GAZE BLARE BLAZE BLOOM FLAME GLAZE STARE GLITTER ICEBLINK RADIANCE
GLARING HARD RANK GLARY AGLARE GARISH BURNING FLARING STARING FLAGRANT
GLASS CUP VER CALX FLAT FLUX FRIT JENA MOIL PONY VITA CHARK FACER FLINT GLAZE STOOP STOUP VERRE VITRE CALGON CEMENT CULLET SPECKS VITRUM ALEYARD BIFOCAL BRIMMER CHIRPER CRYSTAL PERLITE SCHMELZ TALLBOY VITRITE FROSTING OBSIDIAN SCHOPPEN
(— IN STATE OF FUSION) METAL
(— OF A MIRROR) STONE
(— OF BEER) BREW
(— OF BRANDY) SNEAKER
(— OF WHISKY) KELTY RUBDOWN
(— OF WINE) APERITIF
(— STICKING TO PUNTY) COLLET
(BEER —) SHELL SEIDEL
(BELL-SHAPED —) CUP CLOCHE
(BURNING —) SUNGLASS
(CHEVAL —) PSYCHE
(COLORED —) SMALT SMALTO TINTER SCHMELZ
(COLORED —S) GOGGLES
(CUPPING —) VENTOSE
(CURVED —) LENS
(DESSERT —) COUPE
(DRINKING —) GOBLET RUMKIN PILSNER PIMLICO SCUTTLE TUMBLER SCHOONER
(EXAMINATION —) SLIDE
(FULL —) BUMPER

(FUSIBLE —) FLUX
(HALF —) SPLIT
(ICE CREAM —) SLIDER
(LEAD —) STRASS
(LIQUEUR —) PONY PONEY
(LIQUOR —) GUN
(MAGNIFYING —) LOUPE
(MASS OF MOLTEN —) PARISON
(OPALESCENT —) OPALINE
(OPAQUE —) HYALITHE
(PIECE OF HOT —) BIT
(PULVERIZED —) FROSTING
(REFUSE —) CALX CULLET
(RUSSIAN —) CHARK
(SHERBET —) SUPREME
(SMOKED —) SHADE
(STAINED —) VITRAIL
(TALL —) RUMMER
(VOLCANIC —) PUMICE PERLITE
(WINDOW —) PANE
(PL.) SHELLS
GLASSBLOWER MUMBLER
GLASS CRAB SPECTER SPECTRE
GLASSHOUSE STOVE HOTHOUSE
GLASS-LIKE VITRIC
GLASSWARE AGATA AURENE BURMESE FAVRILE OPALINE STEUBEN VITRICS AMBERINA
GLASSWORK GLAZING GLAZIERY
GLASSWORKER GANGMAN GLAZIER SNAPPER GLASSMAN SERVITOR
GLASSWORT KALI KELPWORT SALTWORT SAMPHIRE
GLASSY GLIB FILMY GLAZY GLAZEN GLASSEN HYALINE HYALOID VITREAL VITREOUS
GLAUCE (FATHER OF —) CREON (HUSBAND OF —) JASON
GLAUCUS (FATHER OF —) MINOS SISYPHUS
(MOTHER OF —) MEROPE PASIPHAE
GLAZE DIP LEAD SIZE SLIP GLASS SLEET SMEAR ENAMEL QUARRY CELADON COPERTA EELSKIN GLASSEN GLAZING GLIDDER COUVERTE TIGEREYE
(— OF ICE) GLARE
GLAZED FILMY GLACE GLASSEN GLOSSED
GLAZED WARE GLOST
GLAZIER (TOOL OF —) SPRIG LADKIN
GLEAM RAY BEAM GLOW LEAM WAFT WINK BLENK BLINK BLUSH FLASH GLAIK GLEEN GLENT GLINT GLISK GLIST GLOSE SHINE SKIME SPUNK STARE STEEM TWIRE GLANCE SCANCE FOULDRE GLIMMER GLITTER SHIMMER
(— FAINTLY) SHIMMER
(— OF LIGHT) LEAM PINK GLAIK SCANCE
(FAINT —) SCAD
GLEAMING FAW GLOW CLEAR GLINT STEEP ABLAZE BRIGHT GLEAMY ADAZZLE SHINING GLOOMING
GLEAN CULL EARN REAP LEASE GATHER COLLECT SCRINGE
GLEANER STIBBLER
GLEANING CROP GATHERING

(LITERARY —S) ANALECTA ANALECTS
GLEBE SOD CLOD LAND SOIL TERMON KIRKTOWN
GLEE GLY JOY SONG MIRTH SPORT GAIETY DELIGHT ELATION WASSAIL HILARITY MADRIGAL
GLEEFUL GAY MERRY JOYOUS JOCULAR GLEESOME
GLEEMAN SONGMAN MINSTREL
GLEN DEN GILL GLYN GRIFF HEUCH HEUGH KLOOF SLACK SLADE TEMPE CANADA DINGLE POCKET
GLIADIN GLUTIN PROLAMIN
GLIB PAT FLIP SLICK CASUAL GLOSSY OFFHAND RENABLE SHALLOW VOLUBLE FLIPPANT
GLIDE GO SKI FLOW SAIL SILE SKIM SLIP SLUR SOAR SWIM COAST CREEP DANCE FLEET GLACE GRAZE LAPSE MERGE SCOOP SHIRL SKATE SKIFF SKIRR SLADE SLEEK SLICK SLIDE SLIPE STEAL GLANCE GLIDER SASHAY SNOOVE ILLAPSE SCRIEVE SCRITHE SKITTER SLITHER AIRPLANE GLISSADE VOLPLANE
(— AWAY) ELAPSE
(— BY) PASS FLEET
(— OFF) EXIT
GLIDER SCOOTER
GLIDING TRAIL SLIDING
(— OF THE VOICE) DRAG
(— OVER) LAMBENT
GLIMMER FIRE GLIM GLOW LEAM STIM BLINK FLASH GLEAM GLOOM STIME SIMPER BLINTER FLIMMER GLIMPSE GLITTER SHIMMER SPARKLE TWINKLE SUNBLINK
GLIMMERING GHOST AGLIMMER GLOOMING
GLIMPSE IDEA WAFF WAFT BLINK BLUSH FLASH GLIFF GLINT GLISK SIGHT STIME TINGE TRACE WHIFF GLANCE LUSTER SCANCE GLIMMER INKLING
(BRIEF —) APERCU
(FLEETING —) SHIM SNATCH
GLINT PEEP FLASH GLEAM GLENT GLANCE SPARKLE
GLIS MYOXUS
GLISSANDO GLISS SMEAR GLISSADE
GLISTEN FLASH GLISK GLISS GLIST SHINE GLISTER GLITTER SHIMMER SPANGLE SPARKLE
GLISTENING SHINY AGLISTEN
GLITTER FLASH GLARE GLEAM GLEIT GLINT GLORE SHEEN SHINE SKYRE STARE LUSTER SCANCE GLIMMER GLISTEN GLISTER SKINKLE SPANGLE SPARKLE TWINKLE BRANDISH RADIANCE
(FALSE —) GILT
GLITTERING GEMMY SHEEN SHINY STEEP FULGID SPANGLY AGLITTER GLITTERY
GLOAMING EVE DUSK GLOAM GLOOMING TWILIGHT
GLOAT GAZE GLUT TIRE EXULT
GLOBE ORB BALL BOWL CLEW CLUE POME AGGER GEOID MONDE ROUND

SPHERE COMPASS GEORAMA GLOBULE GRENADE AQUARIUM

GLOBEFISH FUGU TOBY TOADO ATINGA BOTETE PUFFER BLAASOP BURFISH OOPUHUE

GLOBEFLOWER BOLT GOLLAND GOWLAND CORCHORUS

GLOBE THISTLE ECHNOPS

GLOBOSE COCCOID COCCOUS CAPITATE GLOBULAR

GLOBULAR GLOBED GLOBATE GLOBOSE GLOBICAL

GLOBULE BEAD BLOB DROP GLOB PEARL BUBBLE BUTTON REGULUS GLOBULET SPHERULE

(— OF TAPIOCA) FISHEYE

GLOBULIN MAYSIN MYOSIN VIGNIN ARACHIN CORYCIN EDESTIN LEGUMIN TUBERIN VICILIN ANTIBODY BIOLOGIC EXCELSIN GLYCININ MUSCULIN ORYZENIN

GLOCKENSPIEL BELL LYRA CARILLON

GLOMERULE GLOME FASCICLE

GLOOM DUSK MURK CLOUD DREAR FROWN SOMBER DESPAIR DIMNESS GLOOMTH SADNESS DARKNESS MIDNIGHT

GLOOMY DUN SAD WAN BLUE COLD DARK DOUR DREE DULL EERY GLUM MURK ADUSK ADUST BLACK BROWN DOWFF DREAR DUSKY EERIE FERAL GUMLY HEAVY LURID MOODY MORNE MUDDY MUNGY MUSTY SABLE SORRY STERN SULKY SURLY SWART TRIST CLOUDY DREARY DREICH DROOPY DRUMLY GLUMMY MOROSE SOLEMN SOMBER SULLEN TETRIC THRAWN OBSCURE STYGIAN THESTER DESOLATE DOLESOME DOWNBEAT DOWNCAST FUNEREAL GLOOMING LOWERING OVERCAST

GLORIA GLORY AUREOLE

GLORIFY HERY LAUD BLESS DEIFY EXALT EXTOL HERSE HONOR PRIDE WURTH KUDIZE PRAISE CLARIFY ELEVATE MAGNIFY DIVINIZE EMBLAZON EULOGIZE STELLIFY

GLORIOUS SRI DEAR DERE MERE SHRI GRAND BRIGHT EMINENT RENOWNED

GLORY JOY ORE SUN FACE FAME GLOR HALO HORN BLAZE BOAST EXULT HONOR KUDOS PRIDE WULDER AUREOLA CLARITY GARLAND GLORIFY RADIANCE SPLENDOR WORTHING

GLOSS GILL COLOR DUNCE GLASS GLAZE GLOZE JAPAN SHEEN SHINE BLANCH LUSTER LUSTRE POSTIL REMARK VENEER BURNISH EXPOUND VARNISH FLOURISH PALLIATE POLITURE

(— OVER) FARD HUSH SALVE SLEEK SOOTHE

GLOSSA LINGUA

GLOSSARY GLOSS CLAVIS

GLOSSIPHONIA CLEPSINE

GLOSSY GLOZE NITID SHINY SILKY SLICK SATINY SMOOTH

GLOVE KID CUFF GAGE MITT COFFE BERLIN MITTEN CHEVRON DANNOCK GANTLET GOMUKHI GAUNTLET

(— FOR RUBBING SKIN) STRIGIL

(BISHOP'S —) GWANTUS

(BODY OF —) TRANK

(HEDGER'S —) DANNOCK

(HUSKING —) HUSKER

GLOVEMAKER DOMER GLOVER CLASPER FINGERER

GLOVER TRANKER

GLOW ARC LOW AURA BURN FIRE LEAM LOOM LOWE BLAZE BLOOM BLUSH FLAME FLASH FLUSH GLAZE GLEAM GLEED GLORY GLOSS GLOZE SHINE STEAM CORONA KINDLE WARMTH FLUSTER LIGHTEN

(— OF PASSION) ESTUS AESTUS

(— WITH INTENSE HEAT) IGNITE

GLOWER GAZE GLOW GLARE GLOOM GLORE

GLOWING HOT LIVE WARM AGLOW FIERY LIGHT QUICK RUDDY VIVID ABLAZE ARDENT ORIENT BURNING CANDENT FERVENT RADIANT SHINING FLAGRANT

GLOWWORM FIREFLY FIREWORM GLOWBIRD LAMPYRID

GLOZE FAWN PAINT SMOOTH FLATTERY

GLUCOSE AME GLYCOSE DEXTROSE

GLUCOSIDE GEIN APIIN RUTIN TUTIN ADONIN BINDER CORNIN DURRIN FRAXIN FUSTIN IRIDIN PICEIN UZARIN ACACIIN ARBUTIN DAPHNIN DIOSMIN ESCULIN ESTEVIN GITALIN GITONIN GITOXIN HEDERIN HELECIN INDICAN LOGANIN LOTUSIN LUPININ ONABAIN POPULIN ROBININ SALICIN TABACIN TEUCRIN ADONIDIN CARTHAME ERICOLIN GENISTIN GOSSYPIN MORINDIN NARINGIN PARIGLIN PARILLIN PRUNASIN QUINOVIN SAPONINE SCILLAIN SINIGRIN SYRINGIN THEVETIN VERNONIN VIBURNIN VICIANIN

GLUE PAD MOUNT STICK BEGLEW CEMENT FUNORE FUNORIN STICKER TAUROCOL

GLUEY GLUISH STICKY STRINGY VISCOUS ADHESIVE

GLUM CLUM DOUR GRUM SURLY GLOOMY GLUMPY MOROSE SULLEN

GLUMALES POALES

GLUME PILE FLIGHT

(FLOWERING —) LEMMA

(PL.) CHAFF

GLUSIDE SACCHARIN

GLUT CLOY FILL GULP QUAT SATE CHOKE DRAFT GORGE BATTEN ENGLUT EXCESS MARROW PAMPER PAUNCH ENGORGE GLUTTON SATIATE SURFEIT SWALLOW OVERFEED SATURATE

GLUTEAL NATAL

GLUTELIN AVENINE ORYZENIN

GLUTENIN AVENIN ZYMOME ZYMOMIN

GLUTINOUS ROPY SIZY ROPEY SLIMY TOUGH STICKY VISCID

GLUTTED QUAT GORGED SATIATED

GLUTTER VEER

GLUTTON PIG GLUT GORB GUTS GULCH MIKER GLOTUM HELLUO MACCUS EPICURE GUTLING LURCHER MOOCHER RAVENER SWILLER DRAFFMAN GOURMAND GULLYGUT

(STUPID —) GRUB

GLUTTONIZE BIZLE BEZZLE

GLUTTONOUS GREEDY GLUTTON HOGGISH GOURMAND

GLUTTONY GULE SURFEIT

GLYCERIDE BUTYRIN

GLYCINE SOJA

GLYCOL CARBOWAX

GLYCOPROTEIN MUCIN MUCOID

GLYCOSIDE APIIN CROCIN ACACIIN CYMARIN DIGOXIN GITALIN GITOXIN HEDERIN HYPERIN LOGANIN LOTUSIN SAPONIN ALDESIDE ANDROSIN ANTIARIN HOLOSIDE KETOSIDE

GNARL NOB KNOB KNUR KNARL KNURR SNIRL WARRE DEFORM

GNARLED GNARLY KNARRY KNOTTY CRABBED KNOTTED KNURLED

GNASH TUSK CHAMP CRASH GANCH GRASH GRATE KNASH

GNAT KNAW SMUT MIDGE STOUT KNATTE SCIARA SCIARID SCINIPH BLACKFLY DIPTERAN GNATLING

GNATCATCHER SYLVIID

GNATHION MENTON

GNAW EAT NAB BITE FRET TIRE CHELE GNARL MOUSE SHEAR ARRODE BEFRET BEGNAW CHAVEL NATTLE NIGGLE ROUNGE CHIMBLE CHUMBLE CORRODE

GNAWING EATING RODENT FRETFU ARROSION ROSORIAL

GNOME NIS NISSE PECHT PYGMY KOBOLD VAKSHA YAKSHI GNOMIDE GREMLIN HODEKEN ERDGEIST

GNOMON COCK INDEX STILE STYLE FESCUE STYLUS

GNOSTIC CLEVER SHREWD KNOWING PERATES EBIONITE MANDAEAN SEVERIAN SIMONIAN SIMONITE

GNU KOKOON BRINDLE

GO BE DO ACT GAE HOP ISH LAY NIM PEP TEE WAG BANG BEAR BIN BOWN BUSK DRAW FAND FARE FOND GANG HARK HAUL HUMP MOVE QUIT ROAM ROLL SEEK SHO SILE SLAP SNAP STAB STEP TAKE TEEM TOUR WADE WANE WEAR WEND WEVE WIND WISE WORK YEDE AMBLE BOUND CARRY CHEV DEMON DRESS FETCH FRAME HAUNT KNOCK LEAVE MOSEY PLUCK REACH SCRAM SHAKE SLOPE SPEED TOUCH TRACE TRAC TRENE TRINE TRUSS WHIZZ YONG BECOME BETAKE CHIEVE CRUISE DEPART EXTEND QUATCH QUETCH REPAIR RESORT RESULT RETIRE SASHAY STRAKE STRIKE TODDLE TRAVEL WEAKEN JOURNEY SCRIT DIMINISH WITHDRAW

(— **ABOUT DEJECTEDLY**) PEAK
(— **ABOUT GOSSIPING**) COURANT
(— **ABOUT**) JET BEGO BIGAN
(— **AHEAD**) HOLD
(— **AIMLESSLY**) ERR
(— **ALONG**) PATH
(— **AROUND**) SKIRT BYPASS CIRCUE
(— **ASHORE**) LAND
(— **ASTRAY**) ERR MAR WRY MANG
WILL MISGO DELIRE FORVAY
MISWEND DEROGATE MISCARRY
(— **AWAY**) AGO HOP BEAT BUNK
HIKE NASH PART SHOO VADE
CLEAR HENCE IMSHI LEAVE SCRAM
SHIFT BEGONE BUGGER DEPART
REMOVE VACATE SKIDDOO
ELONGATE
(— **BACK IN TIME**) MOUNT
(— **BAD**) SOUR
(— **BEFORE**) LEAD FOREGO
PRECEDE ANTECEDE PREAMBLE
(— **BEYOND**) SURPASS FOREPASS
(— **BRISKLY**) JUNE
(— **BROKE**) BUST
(— **COURTING**) WENCH
(— **DOWN**) SET SINK DROOP SOUND
DESCEND
(— **EASILY**) AMBLE
(— **ERRATICALLY**) KICK
(— **FAST**) HURRY SPLIT BEELINE
(— **FORTH**) AGO DEPART FORTHGO
(— **FORWARD**) HUP HUPP ADVANCE
AGGRESS PROCEED
(— **FOWLING**) AUCUPATE
(— **FURTIVELY**) SLINK SNEAK STEAL
(— **HANG**) SNICK
(— **HEAVILY**) LOB LAMPER
(— **IN HASTE**) LEN LAMMAS
(— **IN HURRY**) SCOFFLE
(— **IN PURSUIT**) SUE
(— **IN**) ENTER INGRESS
(— **INTO BUSINESS**) EMBARK
— **LAME**) FOUNDER
— **LEISURELY**) BUMMEL JIGGET
JIGGIT
— **LIGHTLY**) TIPTOE
— **MAD**) CRAZE MADDLE
— **NEAR**) APPROACH
— **NOISILY**) LARUM
— **OFF**) MOG DISCHARGE
— **ON BOARD**) BOARD EMBARK
NTRAIN
— **ON FOOT**) SHANK
— **ON TO SAY**) ADD
— **ON**) DO GARN LAST PASS
ERGE FURTHER PROCEED
— **OUT**) EXIT ISSUE SLOCK EGRESS
XEUNT QUENCH SORTIE
— **OVER AGAIN**) RENEW REVISE
RETRACE
— **OVER**) KNEE REVOLT SURPASS
OVERGANG
— **PROSPEROUSLY**) COTTON
— **QUICKLY**) GET HIE BUZZ LAMP
IKE SCAT SPEED
— **RAPIDLY**) LAMP SPLIT
— **SHARES**) SNACK
— **SLOWLY**) CRAWL CREEP
— **SLUGGISHLY**) SHACK
— **SMOOTHLY**) SLIP

(— **STEALTHILY**) SHIRK SLINK
SNEAK GUMSHOE
(— **SUDDENLY**) SCOOT
(— **SWIFTLY**) SCOOT SKISE STRIP
HIGHBALL
(— **THE ROUNDS**) PATROL
(— **THROUGH WATER**) SQUATTER
(— **THROUGH**) SUFFER
(— **THROUGHOUT**) COAST
(— **TO BED**) KIP FLOP SNUG
(— **TO EXCESS**) DEBORD
(— **TO HARBOR**) VERT
(— **TO PIECES**) SNURP
(— **TO SCHOOL**) SCOLEY
(— **TO SLEEP**) HUSHABY
(— **TO WAR**) RISE
(— **UP**) CLIMB AMOUNT ASCEND
(— **WEARILY**) HAGGLE
(— **WITH EFFORT**) HIKE
(— **WRONG**) MISS FAULT CURDLE
MISFARE
GOAD EGG GAD GIG HAG BAIT BROD
BROG DARE EDGE GAUD LASH
MOVE PROD SPUR URGE WHIP YERK
ANKUS HARRY IMPEL PIQUE PRICK
PROGG PUNGE STING VALET INCITE
OXGOAD ANKUSHA HOTFOOT
INFLAME PROVOKE IRRITATE
SLAPJACK STIMULUS
GOADMAN GADMAN GAUDSMAN
GOADSTER
GOAL BYE DEN END BASE BUTT
DOLE HAIL HALE MARK METE PORT
BOURN FINIS IDEAL SCOOP SCOPE
SCORE STING DESIGN OBJECT
SIGHTS DESTINY HORIZON
TERMINUS
(— **IN GAMES**) HUNK
(**FIELD** —) BASKET
(**REMOTE** —) THULE
(**UNATTAINABLE** —) STAR
GO-ASHORE KOHUA
GOAT TUR IBEX TAHR BEDEN BILLY
BOVID EVECK SEROW ALPINE
ANGORA AOUDAD CAPRID CHAMAL
JEMLAH MAZAME NUBIAN PASANG
SAANEN WETHER CHAMOIS
AEGAGRUS CAPRIPED MARKHOOR
(**DOMESTIC** —) HIRCUS
(**FEMALE** —) NANNY DOELING
(**MALE** —) BUCK BUCKLING
(**YOUNG** —) KID KIDDY TICCHEN
GOATLING
GOAT ANTELOPE GORAL SEROW
GOORAL
GOATEE TUFT
GOATFISH MOANO
GOATHERD DAMON
GOAT-LIKE GOATISH HIRCINE
GOAT MOTH COSSID
GOATSBEARD ROSACEAN
GOATSKIN CRUST CASTOR
CHEVRETTE
GOATSUCKER PUCK PEWKE POTOO
EVEJAR DORHAWK GRINDER
SPINNER DOORHAWK EVECHURR
NIGHTJAR PAURAQUE
GOB CLOT GOAF SWAB SWOB
WASTE GOBBET SWABBY
GOBBLE MOP BOLT SLOP GOFFLE
GORBLE

GOBBLEDYGOOK PEDAGESE
GO-BETWEEN BAWD FIXER MEANS
BROKER DEALER PANDAR CONTACT
MEDIATOR
GOBLET DINOS GLASS HANAP
POKAL SKULL STOOP STOUP
HOLMOS RUMKIN CHALICE SNIFTER
TALLBOY JEROBOAM STANDARD
STEMWARE
GOBLIN (ALSO SEE HOBGOBLIN)
COW HAG NIS BHUT BOGY MARE
BOGEY NISSE OUPHE POOKA
BODACH BOGGLE BOOGER CHUREL
FOLIOT SPRITE BOGGART BROWNIE
BUGBEAR KNOCKER PADFOOT
BARGHEST BOGEYMAN FOLLETTO
GOBY MAPO BULLY BIGHEAD
CHALACO GOBIOID GUAVINA
GUDGEON MUDFISH BULLHEAD
PINKFISH SANDGOBY
GOCART SULKY WALKER STROLLER
GOD (ALSO SEE DEITY) RA EL ER RA
VE BEL BES COG DAD DES DEV DIS
DOD EAR GAR GAW GEB GOG GOL
GOM GUM ING KEB LAR LOK MEN
MIN ODD ORO SEB SUN TEM TYR
ULL UTU VAN AITU AMEN AMON
ARES ASUR ATEO ATUA ATYS BAAL
BEER BRAN BURE CHAC COCK
DEUS DEVA DIEU ESUS FONS FREY
GAWD GOSH HAPI HOLY HOTH INTI
JOVE KANE KING LIFE LLEU LOKE
LOKI LOVE LUGH MARS MIND NABU
NEBO NUDD ODIN PTAH SHEN SOMA
SOUL TANE THOR TIKI ULLR UTUG
VAYU XIPE YAMA ZEUS ARAWN
ASHUR ASURA ATTES ATTIS COMUS
DAGDA DEITY DEOTA DUVEL DYAUS
DYLAN EBISU ELOAH FREYR GHOST
GOLES GOLLY GRAVE GUACA
HESUS HIEMS HORUS HOTHR
HUACA HYMEN INDRA JUDGE KINGU
LADON LIBER LLUDD MENTU MIDER
MOMUS NJORD NUMEN PALES SILEN
TAMUZ THOTH TINIA TRUTH TYCHE
URASH WAKEA WODIN WOTAN
ZOMBI ADITYA ADONAI ADONAY
ANSHAR ANUBIS APOLLO ASEITY
AUTHOR CHAMOS CONSUS DEVATA
DHARMA ELATHA ELOHIM FATHER
FAUNUS GANESA HEAVEN HERMES
HOENIR METZLI MILCOM MITHRA
NEREUS NERGAL OSIRIS PATRON
PENEUS PLUTUS PUSHAN SESHAT
SOCIUS SOURCE SPIRIT SUTEKH
SYLENE TAAROA TAMMUZ TARTAK
TERAPH TRITON TRIVIA VARUNA
VEDUIS VERITY VISHNU VULCAN
WISDOM YAKSHA YAKSHI ZOMBIE
ABRAXAS ADRANUS ALPHEUS
ANTEROS BELENUS CHEMOSH
DAIKOKU DELLING ETERNAL
GODHEAD HANUMAN IAPETUS
JEHOVAH JUPITER KANALOA
MERCURY MITHRAS MUTINUS
NEPTUNE NJORTHR PROTEUS
PRYDERI REMPHAN ROBIGUS
SAVITAR SERAPIS TRIGLAV VATICAN
VEJOVIS ZAGREUS ALMIGHTY
ASTRAEUS BISHAMON CAMAXTLI

DEMIURGE DEVOTION DIVINITY
GUCUMATZ INFINITE JIUROJIN
KUKULKAN MIXCOATL MORPHEUS
POSEIDON SABAZIOS SUMMANUS
TANGAROA TERMINUS TUTELARY
VEDIOVIS ZEPHYRUS
(— OF AGRICULTURE) PICUS URASH
FAUNUS AMAETHON NINGIRSU
(— OF ARTS) SIVA
(— OF ATMOSPHERE) HADAD
(— OF COMMERCE) MERCURY
(— OF CORN) CAT
(— OF DAY) HORUS
(— OF EARTH) BEL GEB KEB SEB
DAGAN
(— OF EVIL) SET FOMOR FOMORIAN
(— OF FIRE) AGNI GIRRU NUSKU
RUDRA VULCAN
(— OF FLOCKS) PAN
(— OF HAPPINESS) HOTEI JUROJIN
(— OF HEAVENS) ANU JUMALA
(— OF JUSTICE) FORSETE FORSETI
(— OF LEARNING) IMHOTEP
(— OF LOVE) AMOR ARES EROS
KAMA BHAGA CUPID AENGUS
(— OF MOON) SIN ENZU NANNAR
(— OF NATURE) MARSYAS
(— OF POETRY) BRAGE BRAGI
(— OF RAIN) PARJANYA
(— OF SEA) LER VAN AEGIR DYAUS
NEPTUNE PROTEUS PALAEMON
POSEIDON
(— OF SKY) ANU GWYDION
(— OF SLEEP) HYPNOS HYPNUS
MORPHEUS
(— OF SOUTHEAST WIND) EURUS
(— OF STORM) ZU ADAD ADDA
ADDU MARUT RUDRA TESHUP
(— OF SUN) RA RE SHU SOL TEM
TUM UTU AMON ATMU ATUM BAAL
LLEU UTUG SAMAS SEKER SURYA
APOLLO HELIOS SOKARI KHEPERA
PHOEBUS SHAMASH PHAETHON
TONATIUH
(— OF THUNDER) THOR DONAR
PERUN PERKUN PEROUN TLALOC
HURAKAN TARANIS
(— OF UNDERWORLD) DIS GWYN
YAMA HADES ORCUS PLUTO
(— OF VEGETATION) ATYS ATTIS
(— OF WAR) ER IRA ORO TIU TYR
ARES COEL IRRA MARS MENT ODIN
THOR MONTU NINIB MEXITL SKANDA
CAMULUS MEXITLI NINURTA
ENYALIUS NINGIRSU QUIRINUS
(— OF WEALTH) BHAGA KUBERA
KUVERA PLUTUS
(— OF WIND) ADAD ADDA ADDU
VAYU MARUT AEOLUS BOREAS
EECATL
(— OF WISDOM) TAT THOTH
(— WILLING) DV
(BLIND —) HOTH HOTHR
(FALSE —) BAAL IDOL MAUMET
(FEMALE —) GODDESS
(HAWAIIAN —) AUMAKUA
(PAGAN —) DEMON
(RAM-HEADED —) AMON KHNUM
KHNEMU
(TUTELARY —) LAR

(UNKNOWN —) KA
(WOOD —) SILEN SILENUS
(PL.) DI DII AESIR IGIGI SUPERI
PANTHEON TRIMURTI
GODDESS (ALSO SEE DEITY) AI NU
ANA ANU ATE AYA DEA DON NUT
OPS UNI VAC ANTA BADB BODB
CACA DANA DANU ERIS ERUA FRIA
HELA HERA JORD JUNO MAIA MEDB
NIKE NINA NONA PELE SAGA SATI
TARA UPIS ALLAT AMENT ANATH
ANTUM ARURU BAUBO CERES
CHLOE DEESS DIANA DIANE DIRGA
DOLMA DOMNU EPONA FRIGG
HYBLA IAMBE ISTAR KOTYS MAEVE
NANAI NINTU PAKHT PALES PARCA
SALUS SEDNA SKADI TANIT TYCHE
USHAS VENUS VESTA ADEONA
AESTAS ANATUM ANUKIT APHAIA
ATHENA BELILI BENDIS BOOPIS
BRIGIT CYRENE EOSTRE FRIGGA
GEFJON HELENA HESTIA HYGEIA
INNINA KISHAR LIBERA MOTHER
NINGAL PEITHO PHOBOS POMONA
PRORSA RUMINA SEKHET SEMELE
SKATHI SOTHIS TANITH TEFNUT
TRIVIA URANIA VACUNA YDGRUN
ANAHITA ANAITIS ARTEMIS ASHERAH
DEMETER DERCETO FERONIA
FJORGYN GODHEAD LARENTA
LARUNDA MAJAGGA MAJESTA
MINERVA MORNING MORRIGU
MYLITTA NEKHEBT NEMESIS
PALATUA PARBATI PARVATI SALACIA
ADRASTEA AGLAUROS ANGERONA
BELISAMA CARMENTA CENTEOTL
COCAMAMA DESPOINA DICTYNNA
GULLVEIG MORRIGAN NEPHTHYS
PARBUTTY PRAKRITI RHIANNON
SEFEKHET THOUERIS VICTORIA
(— OF AGRICULTURE) BAU OPS
DEMETER CENTEOTL
(— OF AIR) AURA
(— OF BEAUTY) VENUS LAKSHMI
(— OF BURIAL) LIBITINA
(— OF CHILDBIRTH) LEVANA LUCINA
(— OF DAWN) EOS USAS USHAS
AURORA MATUTA
(— OF DEW) HERSE
(— OF DISCORD) ATE ERIS
(— OF EARTH) GE LUA SEB ERDA
GAEA GAIA TARI ARURU DIONE
JORTH TERRA SEMELE TELLUS
THEMIS DAMKINA PERCHTA
(— OF FERTILITY) MA ISIS MAMA
NERTHUS
(— OF FLOWERS) FLORA CHLORIS
(— OF FORTUNE) TYCHE FORTUNA
(— OF GRAIN) CERES
(— OF HEALING) EIR GULA
(— OF HEALTH) DAMIA HYGEIA
VALETUDO
(— OF HEARTH) VESTA HESTIA
(— OF HISTORY) SAGA
(— OF HOPE) SPES
(— OF INFATUATION) ATE
(— OF JUSTICE) DIKE MAAT
ASTRAEA NEMESIS JUSTITIA
(— OF LEGISLATION) EUNOMIA

(— OF LOVE) ATHOR FREYA VENUS
FREYJA HATHOR
(— OF MAGIC) HECATE
(— OF MARRIAGE) HERA
(— OF MATERNITY) APET
(— OF MERCY) KWANNON
(— OF MOTHERHOOD) ISIS
(— OF NIGHT) NOX NYX
(— OF OCEAN) NINA
(— OF OVENS) FORNAX
(— OF PEACE) PAX IRENE NERTHU
(— OF PLEASURE) BES
(— OF RAINBOW) IRIS
(— OF SEASONS) DIKE HORA
(— OF THE DEAD) HEL HELA
(— OF THE HUNT) DIANA VACUNA
ARTEMIS
(— OF THE MOON) LUNA MOON
DIANA SELENA TANITH ARTEMIS
(— OF THE SEA) INO RAN DORIS
BRANWEN EURYNOME
(— OF TRUTH) MAAT
(— OF VEGETATION) OPS CERES
COTYS COTYTTO
(— OF VENGEANCE) ARA NEMESIS
(— OF VICTORY) NIKE
(— OF WAR) ENYO ANATH ANATU
ANUNIT BELLONA
(— OF WATER) ANAHITA
(— OF WEALTH) LAKSHMI
(— OF WISDOM) ATHENA MINERVA
(— OF YOUTH) HEBE JUVENTAS
(3-HEADED —) HECATE
(COW-HEADED —) ISIS
(ESKIMO —) SEDNA
(SUBORDINATE —) DEMIURGE
(THUNDER-SMITTEN —) SEMELE
KERAUNIA
(PL.) MATRIS POINAE ASYNJUR
GO-DEVIL TRAVOIS ALLIGATOR
GODFATHER GOSSIP GODPAPA
PADRINO SPONSOR GODPHERE
GODHEAD DEITY GODHOOD DIVIN
GODLESS WICKED ATHEIST IMPIO
PROFANE UNGODLY
GODLESSNESS ATHEISM
GODLIKE DEIFIC DIVINE IMMORTA
OLYMPIAN
GODLINESS SANCTITY
GODLING DEVATA GENIUS GODKI
GODLET PANISC DEMIGOD
PANISCUS
GODLY HOLY PIOUS DEVOUT
GRACIOUS
GODMOTHER CUMMER GOSSIP
SPONSOR GODMAMMA MARRAIN
GODPARENT SPONSOR
GOD'S S
GODSON FILLEUL GODCHILD
GOD TREE CEIBA
GODWIT PICK PRINE BARKER
MARLIN SCAMMEL YARWHIP
RINGTAIL SHRIEKER SPOTRUMP
YARDKEEP YARWHELP
GOFFER FULLER GAUFFER
GO-GETTER HUSTLER
GOGGLER SCAD
GOGLET COOJA SERAI MONKEY
SURAHI GURGLET SURAHEE

GOING FARE GAIT BOUND AGOING
WAYING PASSADO SLEDDING
(— **ABOUT**) AROUND
(— **BEYOND OTHERS**) ULTRA
(— **IN**) INEUNT INFARE INGOING
(— **ON**) FARE AGATE TOWARD
(— **OUT**) EGRESS
(— **UP**) ANABASIS
GOITER WEN GLANS GOITRE
STRUMA
GOITERED ANTELOPE ZENU
GOITROUS STRUMOUS
GOLD OR ORO RED SOL DORE GILT
GULL ALTUN AURUM GUILD METAL
OCHER OCHRE RIDGE SHINY
GOLDEN OBRIZE ORMOLU YELLOW
BULLION SPANKER
(— **PIECE**) TALI
(**GREENISH** —) AENEUS AENEOUS
GOLDBEATER (**TOOL OF** —) WAGON
GOLDCREST MOON TIDLEY
MUDDLER TROCHIL
GOLDEN RED DORE GOLD BLEST
DURRY GOLDY SUNNY AUREAL
BLONDE GILDEN GILTEN AUREATE
AUREOUS HALCYON AURULENT
DEAURATE
(— **STATE**) CALIFORNIA
GOLDEN CHAIN LABURNUM
GOLDEN CLUB TAWKEE TAWKIN
TUCKAHOE
GOLDEN EAGLE RINGTAIL
GOLDENEYE CUR GARROT
COBHEAD GOWDNIE BULLHEAD
IRONHEAD MORILLON WHIFFLER
WHISTLER
GOLDEN ORIOLE PIROL WITWALL
GOLDEN PLOVER KOLEA FROGSKIN
SQUEALER WHISTLER
GOLDEN RAGWORT LIFEROOT
GOLDENROD BONEWORT SOLIDAGO
JIMMYWEED
GOLDENSEAL EYEBALM EYEROOT
CEROOT PUCCOON
GOLDEN SHINER CHUB DACE
WINDFISH
GOLDFINCH JACK FINCH GOLDY
GOWDY CANARY REDCAP FLAXBIRD
GRAYPATE
GOLDFINNY GOLDNEY CORKWING
GOLDFISH FUNA MOOR COMET
CALICO FANTAIL CYPRINID VEILTAIL
GOLD-OF-PLEASURE FLAX
MADWORT OILSEED
GOLDSMITH SONAR AURIFEX
GOLFER TEER
GOMUTI EJOO IROK ARENG KITTUL
GAGWIRE SAGOWEER
GONAD GERMEN
GONCALO ALVES KINGWOOD
GONDOLA GON BARGE GUNDALOW
GONE AWAY LOST NAPOO
(— **BY**) AGO DONE PAST AGONE
PASSE BEHIND BYGONE
(— **OUT OF USE**) EXTINCT
(— **TO PIECES**) HAYWIRE
GONG BELL CLOCK GANGSA
DOORBELL
(**SERIES OF** —**S**) BONANG
GONGORISM CULTISM

GONOPHORE MEDUSOID SPOROSAC
GOOD BON GAY TOP TRY ABLE
BEAU BEIN BIEN BOON BRAW FINE
GAIN HEND NICE NOTE PROW SAKE
BONUM BRAVE BULLY CANNY
FRESH GWEED JELLY KAPAI PAKKA
PUKKA SEELY SOUND VALID BENIGN
BRAWLY BUCKRA DIVINE EXPERT
FACTOR FORBYE HONEST MABUTI
PRETTY PROFIT PROPER WEALTH
BENEFIT COPIOUS CORKING FAIRISH
FORTHBY GODLIKE GRADELY
HELPFUL LIBERAL SNIFTER STAVING
TRAINED UPRIGHT BUDGEREE
GRAITHLY INTEREST LAUDABLE
PLEASING SALUTARY SKILLFUL
SUITABLE
(**EXCEPTIONALLY** —) SLAMBANG
(**EXTREMELY** —) SLICK
(**HOLD** —) BEAR
(**INFINITELY** —) HOLY
(**MIGHTY** —) SKOOKUM
(**NO** —) NAPOO NAPOOH
(**PRETTY** —) FAIR TIDY
(**RELATIVELY** —) SMOOTH
(**SUPERLATIVELY** —) BRAG
BEAUTIFUL
(**SUPREMELY** —) IMMENSE
GORGEOUS
(**SURPASSINGLY** —) SUPERIOR
(**VERY** —) HOT TOP DANDY DICTY
GRAND NIFTY NAILING SPLENDID
SWINGING
GOOD-BYE BY BYE TATA ADIEU
ADIOS LULLABY FAREWELL
SAYONARA
GOOD-FOR-NAUGHT LOSEL
GOOD-FOR-NOTHING BUM ORRA
SLIM SLINK KEFFEL RIBALD
BRETHEL FUSTIAN SCROYLE
SHOTTEN SKEEZIX SKYBALD
WOSBIRD VAGABOND
GOOD-KING-HENRY BLITE
ALLGOOD MARKERY MERCURY
CHENOPOD
GOOD-LOOKING FAIR BONNY
GAWSY COMELY PRETTY SEEMLY
EYESOME GRADELY WINSOME
GOODLIKE HANDSOME STUNNING
GOODLY BOON PROPER GOODLIKE
GOOD-NATURED SONSY CLEVER
AMIABLE
GOODNESS BONTE BONUM MENSK
PROOF BONITY BOUNTY SATTVA
VIRTUE KINDNESS
GOODS FEE GEAR KIND PELF CARGO
STUFF TRADE WORLD WRACK
ADVANCE CAPITAL CHATTEL
EFFECTS FINANCE HAVINGS INSIGHT
TRAFFIC CHAFFERY HIGGLERY
PROPERTY
(— **BARTERED**) DICKER
(— **CAST OVERBOARD**) JETSAM
(— **SUNK IN SEA**) LAGAN LIGAN
LAGEND
(**DRY** —) DRAPERY
(**HOUSEHOLD** —) INSIGHT
(**IMPERFECT** —) FENT
(**INFERIOR** —) BRACK
(**PIECE** —) CUTTANEE

(**SECONDHAND** —) BROKERY
(**SLOW-SELLING** —) JOBS
(**STOLEN** — **THROWN AWAY**) WAIF
(**SURPLUS** —) OVERAGE
(**VALUABLE** —) SWAG
GOOD-SIZED HEFTY GAWSIE
GOOD-TASTING DAINTY
GOODWILL GREE
GOODY-GOODY PI
GOOEY CLARTY
GOOF BOOB GOOFER
GOOGLY BOSEY WRONGUN
GOON MUSCLEMAN
GOOSANDER JACKSAW RANTOCK
GOOSE ELK LAMA NENE BRANT
BRENT EMDEN HANSA HOBBY
ROMAN SOLAN WAVEY CAGMAG
CANADA EMBDEN GALOOT GANDER
GOSLET HISSER HONKER SOLAND
AFRICAN BLACKIE BUSTARD
GAGGLER GOSLING GRAYLAG
GREASER GREYLAG OUTARDE
WIDGEON BALDHEAD BARNACLE
BERGOOSE BERNICLE SPURWING
TOULOUSE
(**MYTHICAL** —) GANZA
GOOSEBERRY BLOB FABE FAPE
POHA BRAGAS GOBLIN GOZILL
GROZER DOWNING GASKINS
GROZART CARBERRY CATBERRY
DOGBERRY EATBERRY FEABERRY
GOOSEGOG HOUGHTON INDUSTRY
(**PL.**) THAPES
GOOSE EGG DUCK
GOOSEFOOT BASSIA KOCHIA
ALLSEED PIGWEED
GOOSEGIRL GOSSARD
GOOSE GRASS HERIF HARIFFE
CLEAVERS
GOOSEHERD GOZZARD GOOSEBOY
GOOSENECK ROOSTER
GOPHER TUZA GAUFFRE GEOMYID
MUNGOFA QUACHIL SALAMICH
TUCOTUCO
(— **STATE**) MINNESOTA
GOPHERMAN SWAMPER
GOPHERWOOD FUSTIC
GORE CLY CLOY GARE HIKE HIPE
HOOK HORN PICK PIKE SHOT
CRUOR GODET STICK GORING
GUSSET
GOREVAN AUBURN
GORGE GAP JAM FILL GASH GAUM
GLUT JAMB KHOR RENT BREAK
CAJON CANON CHASM CHINE CLUSE
DRAFT FARCE FLUME GULLY GURGE
KLOOF PONGO POUCH STECH STRID
STUFF TANGI CANYON DEFILE
NULLAH RAVINE STODGE STRAIT
THROAT COULOIR DATIATE
DRAUGHT ENGORGE SATIATE
SLABBER QUEBRADA
GORGED ACCOLLE
GORGEOUS VAIN GRAND SHOWY
COSTLY DAZZLING GLORIOUS
SPLENDID
GORGERIN NECK NECKING
GORGING STODGE
GORGON MEDUSA STHENO EURYALE
GORILLA APE PIGMY PYGMY

GORING CORNUPETE
GORMANDIZE STECH STEGH
GUTTLE
GORMANDIZER HELLUO GLUTTON
GORSE ULEX WHIN FURZE GORST
GORY BLOODY
GOSHAWK GOS ASTUR TERCEL
GOSLING GULL
GOSPEL SPELL DHARMA EVANGEL
KERUGMA KERYGMA SYNOPTIC
(— OF REDEMPTION) CROSS
(PL.) TEXT
GOSSAMER MOUSEWEB STARDUST
GOSSIP EME GUP PIE AUNT BUZZ
CANT CLAT CONK COZE DIRT NEWS
TALK CAUSE CLACK CLASH CLYPE
COOSE CRACK FERLY FRUMP
GOSSY SIEVE BABBLE CADDLE
CALLET CAMPER CLAVER FERLIE
JANGLE NORATE TATTLE TITTLE
CLATTER COMPERE GOSTHER
HASHGOB NASHGAB SCANDAL
TATTLER TRATTLE CHITCHAT
GOSSIPRY QUIDNUNC
GOSSIPY BUZZY
GOTH GOTHIAN SUIOGOTH VISIGOTH
GOTHIC OGIVAL
GOUGE DIG PUG BENT SCUFF
CHISEL FLUKAN GOUGER HOLLOW
SCRIBE FLOOKAN SCORPER
SELVAGE SELVEDGE STICKING
(— OUT) BULLDOZE
(V-TYPE —) VEINER
GOUGER CHISELLER
GOURD MATE PEPO LUFFA ABOBRA
JICARA PATOLA ANGURIA DISHRAG
HECHIMA CALABASH CUCURBIT
PEPONIDA PEPONIUM
GOURMAND EPICURE GLUTTON
GORMAND
GOURMET PALATE EPICURE
GOURMAND
GOUT GUT CLOT DROP SPLASH
PODAGRA PODAGRY
GOUTTE DROP ICICLE
GOUTWEED AXWEED ASHWEED
ACHEWEED AISEWEED BOLEWORT
GOATWEED GOUTWORT
GOUTY PODAGRAL PODAGRIC
GOVERN RUN WIN CURB KING LEAD
REDE REIN RULE SWAY WALD WARD
WIND YEME GUIDE JUDGE REGLE
STEER TREAT WIELD BRIDLE DIRECT
MANAGE ORDAIN POLICE POLICY
TEMPER COMMAND CONDUCT
CONTROL PRESIDE REFRAIN
DISPENSE DOMINATE IMPERATE
MODERATE OVERRULE OVERSWAY
POLICIZE REGULATE RESTRAIN
GOVERNESS ABBESS DUENNA
FRAULEIN MISTRESS
GOVERNING REGENT REGITIVE
GOVERNMENT GATE LAND RULE
KREIS POWER STATE STEER
DURBAR HAVANA POLICY RULING
CABINET CZARISM DIARCHY
DYARCHY RECTION REGENCY
REGIMEN TSARISM CIVILITY
ENDARCHY GOBIERNO HEGEMONY

ISOCRACY ISOCRYME KINGSHIP
STEERING
(— BY 10) DECARCHY
(— BY 2) DIARCHY DUARCHY
(— BY GOD) THEONOMY
(— BY WOMEN) GYNARCHY
(— OF CEYLON) DISSAVA
(— OF TURKEY) GATE PORTE
(INDIAN —) CIRCAR SIRCAR
(MALAYSIAN —) KOMPENI
(MOROCCAN —) MAGHZEN
MAKHZAN
GOVERNMENTAL ARCHICAL
GOVERNOR BAN BEY DEY EARL
KAID LORD NAIK TUTU VALI BANUS
CLEON DEWAN DIWAN HAKIM
NABOB NAZIM SHEIK SUBAH TUPAN
AUTHOR DYNAST GRIEVE LEGATE
MOODIR MYOWUN NAIGUE NAIQUE
PATESI PENLOP RECTOR REGENT
SACHEM SATRAP SHEIKH SHERIF
TUCHUN WARDEN CATAPAN
DAROGHA LEONATO PODESTA
SHEREEF TOPARCH TSUNGTU
VICEROY WIELDER AUTOCRAT
BURGRAVE ETHNARCH HOSPODAR
LANDVOGT MISTRESS RESIDENT
SUBAHDAR TETRARCH
(— OF ALGIERS) DEY DISAWA
(— OF BURMA) WUN WOON
(— OF EGYPT) MUDIR
(— OF TAMMANY) SACHEM
(BYZANTINE —) EXARCH CATAPAN
(GERMAN —) LANDVOGT
(GREEK —) ETHNARCH
(JAPANESE —) SHOGUN TYCOON
(PAPAL —) LEGATE
(ROMAN —) TETRARCH
(SELJUK —) ATABEG ATABEK
(SPARTAN —) HARMOST
(TURKISH —) BEY WALI KEHAYA
GOVERNOR-GENERAL VALI
GOWK CUCKOO
GOWN GOR SAC GITE GORE HUKE
JAMA RAIL SACK SILK TOGA BANIA
DRESS FROCK GOUND HABIT JAMAH
MANTO TABBY TOOSH BANIAN
BANIYA CAFTAN CAMISE CANDYS
CHITON JESUIT JOHNNY KIMONO
KIRTLE KITTEL LEVITE MANTUA
ARISARD CASSOCK GARMENT
JOHNNIE SULTANA SULTANE
WRAPPER GANDOURA PEIGNOIR
(HAWAIIAN —) HOLOKU
GOYA CURRANT
GOYIM GENTES
GRAB NAB NAP RAP GLAM GOPE
GLAUM SCRAB COLLAR CRATCH
DIPPER NIPPER SNATCH CRAPPLE
GRABBLE GRAPNEL GRAPPLE
NIPPERS
GRABEN TROUGH
GRACE EST ORE BEAT ESTE GARB
HELD SWAY ADORN COULE HONOR
MENSE MENSK MERCY SLIDE THANK
VENUS BEAUTY BECOME BEDECK
CHARIS POLISH RELISH THALIA
AGGRACE CHARISM COMMEND
DIGNITY FINESSE GRATIFY MELISMA
MORDENT BACKFALL BEAUTIFY

BLESSING DECORATE EASINESS
ELEGANCE FELICITY GRATUITY
LEVATION ORNAMENT
(— OF FORM) FLOW SWAY
TOURNURE
GRACEFUL AIRY FEAT GENT GENTY
GRATE COMELY FEATLY FELINE
FLUENT GAINLY QUAINT SEEMLY
SILKEN VENUST ELEGANT FITTING
GENTEEL GRACILE SYLPHID
WILLOWY CHARMING DELICATE
GRACIOUS LEGGIERO MACEVOLE
SWANLIKE SYLPHISH
GRACEFULNESS JOLLITY
ELEGANCE
GRACEFULLY FAIR FEATLY HAPPIL
LEGGIERO
GRACELESS AWKWARD
GRACES CHARITES
GRACIOUS GOOD HEND HOLD KIND
MILD CIVIL GODLY HAPPY LUCKY
SUAVE WINLY BENIGN GENIAL
GENTLE GOODLY KINDLY AFFABLE
CORDIAL WINSOME BENEDICT
DEBONAIR GENEROUS HANDSOME
MERCIFUL PLEASING SOCIABLE
GRACIOUSLY FAIR SWEETLY
GRACIOUSNESS GRACE MENSK
FACILITY GRATUITY
GRACKLE BEO JACKDAW BOATTAIL
TINKLING TROOPIAL
GRADATION HUE CLIMAX NUANCE
GEOCLINE STRENGTH
GRADE CUT BANK CHOP EVEN FOR
MARK RANK SIZE STEP GLIDE LEV
ORDER PLANE SCORE SIEGE STAG
ASCENT DEGREE RATING STAPLE
TRIAGE FAILURE INCLINE INSPECT
DEMISANG GRADIENT GRADUATE
MERIDIAN STANDARD
(— DOWN) FAULT
(— LUMBER) SURVEY
(— OF BEEF) GOOD CUTTER
(— OF LUMBER) CULL
(— OF OAK) WAINSCOT
(— OF OFFICER) CORNET
(— ROAD) IMPROVE
(ABLAUT —) GUNA
(SUPERIOR —) SUPER
(THIRD —) FAIR
GRADER PLANER CLASSER SCRAP
GRADIENT GRADE LAPSE SLOPE
ASCENT INCLINE DOWNHILL
GRADIN GRADINO PREDELLA
GRADUAL EASY FLAT SLOW GRAIL
GENTLE LENTOUS STEPWISE
GRADUALLY GENTLY EDGINGLY
GRADATIM INCHMEAL
GRADUATE GRAD GRADE ALUMNA
DIVIDE FELLOW ALUMNUS GRADA
BACHELOR
GRADUATED SCALAR MEASURED
GRADUATION CLICK
GRAFT BUD IMP CION WORK GRAF
GRAVY INEYE BOODLE INARCH
SPLICE ENGRAFT IMPLANT JOBBE
SQUEEZE TOPWORK APPROACH
BOODLING GRAFTING INSITION
GRAFTED ENTE
GRAFTER BOODLER

GRAFTING GRAFTAGE INSITION
GRAIL CUP GRAAL CHALICE
SANGRAAL
GRAIN JOT RUN RYE WAY CORN
CURN DANA KERN PILE RICE SAND
SEED WALE WOOD EMMER FIBER
FIBRE FUNDI GAVEL GLEBE GRIST
PANIC SCRAP SPARK STUFF TRACE
WHEAT ANNONA BARLEY BRAINS
CEREAL CURRAN GROATS KERNEL
FRUMENT GRANULE PANICLE
VICTUAL GRAINING PARTICLE
STRAIGHT SWEEPAGE
(— FOR MUSH) KASHA
(— FROM MASH TUN) DRAINS
(— LEFT AFTER HARVEST) GAVEL
SHACK
(— MEASURE) THRAVE
(— OF BOARD) BEAT
(— OF GOLD) PIPPIN
(— OF WOOD) BATE
(CHAFF OF —) BRAN
(COARSE —) THIRD
(COARSELY GROUND —) MEAL
GRITS KIBBLE
(DAMAGED —) SALVAGE
(EAR OF —) SPIKE RISSOM RIZZON
(GERMINATED —) MALT
(GROUND —) GRIST
(HANDFUL OF —) REAP
(HULLED —) GRITS GROUT GROATS
SHELLING
(HUSKED —) SHEALING SHILLING
(MIXED —) MASLIN
(MIXED —S) DREDGE
(PARCHED —) GRADDAN
(REFUSE —) SHAG DRAFF
(SACRIFICIAL —) ADOR
(SHOCK OF —) COP
(STACK OF —) HOVEL
(PL.) PICKLES RAGGING
GRAIN BEETLE CADELLE
GRAINER DICER BOARDER
GRAINSMAN THROWER DRAFFMAN
GRAIN SORGHUM DURRA SHALLU
GRAM KHESARI
(MILLIONTH —) GAMMA
GRAMMAR SYNTAX GRAMARY
PRISCIAN
GRAMMARIAN PRISCIAN
GRAMPUS ORC COWFISH DOLPHIN
SPRINGER
GRANARY GOLA GUNJ SILO GOLAH
GUNGE LATHE GARNER GIRNEL
GRANGE HORREUM RESERVE
CORNLOFT GRAINERY
GRAND OLD AIRY EPIC MAIN TALL
CHIEF GREAT LOFTY NOBLE PROUD
SHOWY SWELL WLONK ANDEAN
AUGUST COSMIC EPICAL FAMOUS
GLOBAL KINGLY LORDLY SIGHTY
SUPERB SWANKY EXALTER
IMMENSE STATELY SUBLIME
COSMICAL FOREMOST GLORIOUS
GORGEOUS IMPOSING MAJESTIC
SPLENDID
GRAND CANYON STATE ARIZONA
GRANDCHILD OE OY OYE
GREAT —) IEROE
GRANDDAUGHTER NIECE

GRANDEE DON GRAND OMRAH
BASHAW GRANDO MAGNATE
GRANDEUR POMP STATE ESTATE
FIGURE PARADE MAJESTY
ELEGANCE GRANDEZA HAUTESSE
SPLENDOR VASTNESS
GRANDFATHER AIEL NONO BOBBY
GRAMP ATAVUS GRAMPS BELSIRE
GRANDAD GRANDPA GRANDFER
GUIDSIRE
(GREAT —) NONO
(GREAT-GREAT-GREAT —)
QUATRAYLE
GRANDILOQUENT TALL HEROIC
TURGID BOMBAST MAGNIFIC
GRANDIOSE GRAND COSMIC TURGID
COSMICAL IMPERIAL
GRANDMOTHER GRAM GRAN
LUCKY GRANNY GUDAME LUCKIE
BELDAME NOKOMIS BABUSHKA
GRANDAME
GRANDPARENT TUTU TUPUNA
GRAND SLAM VOLE
GRANDSON NEPHEW NEPOTE
GRANITE MOYITE RUNITE GREISEN
SYENITE ALASKITE RAPAKIVI
(— STATE) NEWHAMPSHIRE
(DECOMPOSED —) GROWAN
GRANITEWARE GRAYWARE
GRANNY TUTU BABUSHKA
GRANT AID FEU BOOK BOON CEDE
ENAM GALE GIFT GIVE HEAR LEND
LOAN MISE SEND STOW YARK
ADMIT ALLOT ALLOW AWARD
BONUS CHART COWLE FLOAT
FUERO LEASE SEIZE SPARE TITHE
YETTE YIELD ACCEDE ACCORD
AFFORD ASSENT BESTOW BETAKE
BETEEM BOUNTY CONFER DESIGN
EXTEND FIRMAN IMPART JAGEER
NOVATE OCTROI PATENT PERMIT
REMISE ADJUDGE COLLATE
CONCEDE CONSENT DISPONE
INDULGE LICENSE PRESENT
PROMISE SUBSIDY TRIBUTE
APPANAGE BESTOWAL CONTRACT
DONATION EXCHANGE MONOPOLY
PITTANCE TRANSFER
(— AS PROPER) ACCORD
(— OF LAND) FEU ENAM GALE PATA
SASAN CASATE
(— PERMISSION) ALLOW DISPENSE
(— RELIEF) FORGIVE
(INDIAN —) ENAM COWLE SASAN
JAGEER JAGHIR
(PL.) PORK
GRANTING IF ALTHO REMISE
ALTHOUGH
GRANTOR LESSOR
GRANULAR OPEN GRAINY
GRANULATE CORN KERN GRAIN
SUGAR
GRANULATED CORN GRANULAR
GRANULATION SUGARING
GRANULE GRIT GRANUM LUCULE
NODULE BIOBLAST GONIDIUM
GRANULET
(ALTMANN'S —S) BIOPLAST
(ICE —S) FRAZIL
GRAPE UVA VINE BERRY GRAIN

PINOT TOKAY ACINUS AGAWAM
ISABEL MALAGA MONICA MUSCAT
RAISIN VERDEA WORDEN CATAWBA
CONCORD HAMBURG MISSION
NIAGARA SULTANA VINIFER
CABERNET DELAWARE GRAPELET
ISABELLA LABRUSCA MALVASIA
MORILLON MOUNTAIN MUSCATEL
NUCULANE RIESLING SLIPSKIN
SYLVANER THOMPSON
(PL.) RAPE
GRAPEFRUIT POMOLO POMMELO
TORONJA
GRAPE HYACINTH MUSK
GRAPE JUICE MUST SAPA STUM
GRAPENUTS TERRAPIN
GRAPEROOT BERBERIS
GRAPH CHART CURVE OGIVE TRACE
CONTOUR DIAGRAM PROFILE
ISOPLETH
GRAPHITE WAD KISH LEAD WADD
KEESH PENCIL PLUMBAGO
GRAPNEL CROW DRAG GRAB CREEP
CREEPER GRABBLE GRAPPLE
SNIGGER GRABHOOK
GRAPPLE DOG CLOSE GRASP GRIPE
LATCH BUCKLE GRABBLE GRAPNEL
GRIPPLE SNIGGER SNIGGLE
WRESTLE
(— QUARRY) BIND
GRAPPLING IRON CLIP DRAG
CLASP CRAMP CORVUS CRAMPER
CRAMPON CREEPER GRAPNEL
GRAPPLE HARPAGO
GRAPTOLITHA XYLINA
GRASP HUG NAP SEE CLAM CLAW
CLUM FAKE FANG FIST GLAM GRAB
GRIP HAND HENT HOLD SNAP SPAN
TAKE VICE CATCH CINCH CLAMP
CLASP CLAUT CLEUK GRIPE GROPE
LATCH SAVVY SEIZE SENSE SHAKE
SPEND CLINCH CLUTCH COLLAR
FATHOM GOUPEN CLAUGHT
COMPASS ENCLOSE GRAPPLE
GRIPPLE SMITTLE CONCEIVE
HANDFAST HOLDFAST
(— FULLY) SWALLOW
(— MENTALLY) ENVISAGE
(— OF REALITY) EPIPHANY
GRASPING HARD NIPPY SNACK
GRABBY GREEDY GRIPPY HAVING
TAKING BROKING PUGGING
COVETOUS HANDGRIP
GRASS BON FAG FOG POA RAY
BENT COIX DISS DOOB GAMA HERB
ICHU KANS KUSA MUNJ MUSK RAGI
TORE ANKEE BARIT BROME COGON
COUCH CROFT DRAWK DRINN
FLAWN FUNDI GARSE GIRSE GLAGA
GRAMA HARIF HAVER HICHU ILLUK
KOGON KUSHA KWEEK PANIC QUILA
REESK ROOSA SEREH SPIRE STIPA
SUDAN ZORRA BARLEY BHABAR
BHARTI DARNEL EMOLOA FESCUE
GLUMAL QUITCH RAGGEE REDTOP
RIPGUT SCUTCH TOETOE TWITCH
ZACATE AMOURET CANNACH
DOGFOOT ESPARTO EULALIA
FESTUCA FINETOP FOXTAIL
GALLETA GOLDEYE HERBAGE

HORDEUM JARAGUA MATWEED MUSCOVY PANICLE PASTURE PIGROOT SETARIA SORGHUM TIMOTHY TOCUSSO TUSSOCK VETIVER ZACATON AEGILOPS BLUESTEM BROWNTOP CALFKILL CAMALOTE CELERITY COCKSPUR DOGSTAIL DRAWLING DROPSEED EELGRASS ELEUSINE FINEBENT GAMELOTE MANGRASS MATGRASS PASPALUM SANDBURR SANDSPUR SANDSTAY SPANIARD SPARTINA SPINIFEX SWEEPAGE TEOSINTE WHITETOP

(— **AMONG GRAIN**) DRAWK
(— **FOR STOCK**) EATAGE
(— **FOR THATCHING**) BANGO
(— **ON BORDER OF FIELD**) RAND
(— **READY FOR REAPING**) SWATH
SWATHE
(**AROMATIC** —) KHUS CUSCUS
KHUSKHUS
(**BEACH** —) STAR
(**BERMUDA** —) DOOB SCUTCH
(**COARSE** —) FAG RISP TATH
COGON REESK SNIDDLE
(**COUCH** —) CUTCH KWEEK QUITCH
SCUTCH STROIL SQUITCH
(**CURED** —) HAY
(**DEAD** —) FOG FOGGAGE
(**DITCH** —) ENALID
(**GOOSE** —) CLIVERS CLEAVERS
(**MEADOW** —) POA
(**NUT** —) COCO COCOA
(**ORCHARD** —) DOGFOOT
(**PASTURE** —) TORE GRAMMA
(**POVERTY** —) HEATH
(**QUAKING** —) SHAKER
(**REED** —) CARRIZO
(**REEDLIKE** —) BENT DISS
(**SUDAN** —) GARAWI
GRASSERIE JAUNDICE
GRASSHOPPER GRIG CICADA
HOPPER QUAKER SAWYER TETTIX
ACRIDID CRICKET KATYDID SKIPPER
ACRIDIAN LANGOSTA
GRASSLAND HAM LEA RAKH VELD
VELDT BOTTOM MEADOW PATANA
LEYLAND PASTURE SAVANNA
(**TRACT OF** —) PRAIRIE
(PL.) SCHIH
GRASS PEA LANG KHESARI
GRASSQUIT QUAT QUIT CIVITE
GRASS TREE BLACKBOY
GRASSY HERBY
GRATE JAR FRET GRIT RASP CHARK
DANDY DEVIL GRIND RANGE STOVE
ABRADE CHAFER SCRAPE SCREAR
SCREEK SCROOP GRATING
MANGRATE
(**FALSE** —) DANDY
GRATEFUL KIND WELCOME
THANKFUL
GRATEFULNESS GRATUITY
GRATIFICATION GLUT GUST
LUXURY RELISH REWARD SATIETY
DELICACY GRATUITY PLEASURE
TICKLING
GRATIFIED GLAD PROUD CHARMED
CONTENT PLEASED

GRATIFY PAY BABY FEED LUST
AMUSE FEAST FLESH GRACE
HUMOR MIRTH QUEME SAVOR
SERVE STILL WREAK ARRIDE
FOSTER OBLIGE PAMPER PLEASE
SALUTE TICKLE AGGRATE CONTENT
DELIGHT FLATTER GLADDEN
INDULGE SATISFY PLEASURE
(— **THE PALATE**) SEASON
GRATIFYING GOOD COMELY
DELICATE GRATEFUL
GRATING GRID HACK HARP HECK
JACK RACK CRATE CRUDE GRILL
HARSH RANGE TRAIL BAFFLE
CRATCH GITTER GRILLE HOARSE
WICKET BAFFLER ECHELLE
ECHELON BABRACOT CATAPULT
GRIDIRON SCRANNEL STRIDENT
GRATIS FREE FREELY BUCKSHEE
GRATITUDE THANK THANKS
GRATUITY
GRATUITOUS FREE WANTON
BASELESS NEEDLESS
GRATUITY FEE TIP DASH VAIL PILON
SPIFF SPILL CUMSHAW DASTURI
DOUCEUR PRESENT PRIMAGE
BAKSHISH BONAMANO BUCKSHEE
COURTESY DUSTOORI GRATUITO
REAPDOLE
(PL.) LARGESSE
GRAVE BED DRY LOW PIT SAD URN
BALK BIER CELL CIST DEEP DELF
FOSS GRIT HIGH HOME KIST LAIR
LAKE MOLD MOOL RUDE SADE
SAGE TOMB URNA DELFT FOSSE
GRAFF GROVE HEAVY MOULD
SHEOL SOBER STAID STIFF SUANT
VAULT BURIAL DEMURE GRIEVE
HEARSE SEDATE SEVERE SOLEMN
SOMBER SOMBRE STEADY AUSTERE
EARNEST FUNERAL PITHOLE
SERIOSO SERIOUS SOBERLY
DECOROUS MATRONAL SERMONIC
GRAVECLOTHES LINEN
GRAVEDIGGER BURIER FOSSOR
PITMAN
GRAVEL GRIT ARENA GEEST GRAIL
CHESIL RANGLE SAMMEL SHILLA
BALLAST CALICHE CHANNEL
RATCHEL STANNER BLINDING
(— **AND SAND**) DOBBIN
(— **DEPOSIT**) LEAD
(— **IN KIDNEYS**) ARENA
(**LOOSE** —) SLITHER
(**SCREENED** —) HOGGINS
GRAVELLY HASKY CHISELLY
GLAREOUS
GRAVELY SADLY DEEPLY
GRAVE MOUND TUMULUS
GRAVER BURIN STYLE PLASTIC
SCORPER
GRAVESTONE BAUTA PLANK STELA
STELE STONE TABLE CIPPUS
JUMPER THROUGH
GRAVEYARD CEMETERY
GRAVID HEAVY WOMBED PREGNANT
GRAVIMETER DOODLEBUG
GRAVITATIONAL UNIT SLUG
GRAVITY WEIGHT DIGNITY EARNEST
SOBRIETY

GRAVY JUS SOP BREE FOND LEAR
BLANC BUNCE JIPPER
GRAY ASH BAT FOG ASHY BEAR
BLAE BLUE DOVE DUSK GREY GRIS
GULL HOAR IRON LEAD SALT ACIEF
CAMEL CRANE HOARY LYART
MOUSE STEEL WHITE CASTOR
CINDER DENVER FROSTY FRUSTY
GREIGE GRISLY LEADEN NICKEL
NUTRIA PEWTER QUAKER STRING
BLUNKET CRUISER GRANITE
GRIZARD GRIZZLE GRIZZLY
HUELESS MURINUS NEUTRAL
PELICAN PILGRIM SARKARA
SPARROW ALUMINUM CHARCOAL
CINEREAL CINEROUS EVENGLOW
PLATINUM PLYMOUTH
(**DARKEST** —) BLACK
(**GOOSE** —) LAMA
(**MOLE** —) TAUPE
(**MOTH** —) SHEEPSKIN
GRAYBACK DOWITCH GRAYCOAT
GREYBACK
GRAY CRANE COOLEN COOLUNG
GRAYLING PINK OMBRE UMBER
HERRING UMBRANA BLUEFISH
SALMONID
GRAY PARROT JAKO
GRAYNESS CANITIES
GRAYSBY CONY CONEY
GRAY WHALE RIPSACK GRAYBACK
HARDHEAD
GRAZE BITE CROP FEED SKIM AGIS
BRUSH GRASS GRIDE RANGE
SCAMP SCUFF SHAVE SKIFF STOCK
BROWSE CREASE FODDER GLANCE
RIPPLE SCRAPE SCRASE PASTURE
GRAZIER PASTURER SQUATTER
TREKBOER
GRAZING BIT FEED GRASS COLLOP
RASANT FOLDING PASCUAGE
GREASE COOM SAIM ADEPS BLECK
COOMB SMEAR SPICK ARMING
AXUNGE CREESH ENSEAM LIQUOR
POMATE ALEMITE SAINDOUX
(— **IN HARD CAKES**) SEAK
(**PIG'S** —) MORT
(**WOOL** —) YOK DEGRAS LANOLIN
GREASE-HEELS GRAPES
GREASER DOPER
GREASEWOOD CHICO CHEMIZO
GREASY FAT GLET OILY RICH FATT
PORKY YOLKY SMEARY TRAINY
CREESHY TALLOWY UNCTUOUS
GREAT BIG FAR FAT FIT OLD BARC
DEEP DREE FELL FINE GONE GUR
HUGE KEEN MAIN MUCH RIAL TAL
UNCO VAST VILE AMPLE BURRA
CHIEF FELON GRAND LARGE MEKI
STOUR SWEET SWELL YEDER
FIERCE GAPING HEROIC MICKLE
NATION STRONG CAPITAL EMINEN
EXTREME GALLOWS HOWLING
IMMENSE INTENSE STAVING TITAN
VIOLENT VOLUMED ALMIGHTY
CRACKING ELEVATED ENORMOUS
FAVORITE GALACTIC GALAXIAN
GIGANTIC HORRIBLE INFINITE
(— **LAND**) ALASKA
(**IMMEASURABLY** —) ABYSMAL

(VERY —) MAIN SORE AWFUL STEEP
ARDENT DEADLY IMMANE INGENT
MORTAL EXTREME FRANTIC
GHASTLY HOWLING SUBLIME
DREADFUL MOUNTAIN
GREAT AUK PENGUIN PINWING
GAREFOWL
GREAT BRITAIN (SEE ENGLAND)
GREATCOAT GREGO JEMMY JOSEPH
OVERCOAT
GREATER SUPERIOR
GREATER STITCHWORT HEAD
SNAPPER HEADACHE SNAPJACK
SNAPWORT
GREATER YELLOWLEGS YELPER
GREATEST UTMOST EXTREME
MAXIMAL
(— POSSIBLE) ALL SUPREME
GREAT-GRANDCHILD IEROE
GREAT GRANDFATHER NONO
BESAIEL GRANDSIR
GREAT LAKE ERIE HURON ONTARIO
MICHIGAN SUPERIOR
GREATLY FAR MUY FELL MUCH
AMAIN SWITH FINELY MAINLY
STRONG SWYTHE SWEETLY
WOUNDLY
GREAT MOLE RAT ZEMMI ZEMNI
GREATNESS FORCE GRANDEUR
GRANDEZA MUCHNESS
GREAT RAGWEED KINGHEAD
GREAT TITMOUSE SHARPSAW
GREAVE JAMB JAMBE JAMBEAU
(PL.) CRAP HOSE GRAVES
GREBE LEAD LOON DIVER GAUNT
WITCH DIPPER DOBBER DUCKER
FINFOOT HENBILL PYGOPOD
ARSEFOOT CARGOOSE DABCHICK
DIDAPPER GRUIFORM
GRECE GRICE DEGREE GRISSEN

GREECE

ANCIENT LOCATION: ELIS DORIS
PYLOS ACHAEA ACTIUM ATTICA
DELPHI EPIRUS HELLAS LOCRIS
PHOCIS SPARTA THEBES TIRYNS
BOEOTIA CORINTH EPEIROS
LACONIA MACEDON MEGARIS
MYCENAE PAESTUM
ARMY UNIT: TAXIS
BAY: ELEUSIS SALAMIS PHALERON
CAPE: KRIOS MALEA SPADA
AKRITAS MATAPAN SIDEROS
DREPANON GRAMBYSA
TAINARON
CAPITAL: ATHENS ATHENAI
COIN: OBOL HECTE DIOBOL
LEPTON STATER DRACHMA
DIOBOLON
COLUMN: DORIC IONIC
CORINTHIAN
DANCE: PYRRHIC ROMAIKA
DIALECT: COAN ATTIC DORIC
ELEAN EOLIC IONIC AEOLIC
MELIAN THERAN ACHAEAN
ARCADIAN
DISTRICT: ARTA ELIS CANEA
CHIOS CORFU CRETE DRAMA

EVROS KHIOS PELLA SAMOS
ZANTE ACHAEA ACHAIA ATTICA
EPIRUS EUBOEA KILKIS KNANIA
KOZANE LARISA LESBOS
LEUKAS PHOCIS PIERIA SERRAI
THRACE XANTHE AETOLIA
ARCADIA ARGOLIS BOEOTIA
CORINTH KAVALLA LACONIA
LARISSA LASETHI MTATHOS
PREVEZA RHODOPE CYCLADES
IOANNINA KARDITSA KASTORIA
MAGNESIA MESSENIA PHLORINA
RETHYMNE SALONIKA THESSALY
TRIKKALA MACEDONIA
GULF: VOLOS ATHENS MESARA
PATRAI PATRAS ARGOLIS
CORINTH KAVALLA KNANION
LACONIA MESSINI RENDINA
SARONIC STRIMON LEPANTRO
MESSENIA SALONIKA SINGITIC
THERMAIC TORONAIC
HOME OF GODS: OLYMPUS
ISLAND: DIA IOS KEA KOS NIO
CEOS KEOS MILO SYME SYRA
CHIOS CORFU CRETE DELOS
KASOS KHIOS LEROS MELOS
MILOS NAXOS PAROS PAXOI
PAXOS PSARA RODOS SAMOS
SARIA SYROS TELOS TENOS
THERA THIRA TINOS ZANTE
ANAPHE ANDROS CANDIA
CERIGO CHALKE EUBOEA
EVVOIA GAVDOS IKARIA ITHACA
ITHAKI LEMNOS LESBOS LEUKAS
LEVKAS PATMOS RHENEA
RHODES SIFNOS SKYROS
THASOS AMORGOS CIMOLUS
CYTHERA KERKYRA KIMOLOS
KYTHERA KYTHNOS LEVITHA
MYKONOS NISYROS SALAMIS
SIPHNOS KALYMNOS MYTILENE
SANTORIN SERIPHOS
ISLANDS: IONIAN CYCLADES
SPORADES DODECANESE
STROPHADES
LAKE: KARLA VOLVE COPAIS
KOPAIS PRESPA TOPOLIA
KASTORIA TACHINOS VISTONIS
LETTER: MU NU PI XI CHI ETA PHI
PSI RHO TAU BETA IOTA ZETA
ALPHA DELTA GAMMA KAPPA
OMEGA SIGMA THETA LAMBDA
EPSILON OMICRON UPSILON
MARKET PLACE: AGORA
MEASURE: PIK BEMA PIKI POUS
BARIL CADOS CHOUS CUBIT
DIGIT MARIS PEKHE PODOS
PYGON XYLON ACAENA BACHEL
BACILE BARILE COTULA DICHAS
GRAMME HEMINA KOILON
ORGYIA PALAME PECHYS
SCHENE AMPHORA CHENICA
CHOENIX CYATHOS DIAULOS
HEKTEUS METRETA STADION
STADIUM STREMMA CONDYLOS
DAKTYLOS DEKAPODE
DOLICHOS MEDIMNOS
METRETES PALAISTE PLETHRON

PLETHRUM SPITHAME
STATHMOS
MOUNTAIN: IDA IDHI OSSA ATHOS
PAROS ELIKON PARNON PELION
PILION WITSCH HELICON
OLYMPUS VURANON KRAGNOVO
SMOLIKAS TAYGETOS
PARNASSUS
MOUNTAINS: OETA OTHRYS
PINDUS RODOPI RHODOPE
HYMETTOS TAYGETUS
NAME: ELLAS HELLAS
PENINSULA: ACTE AKTE AKTI
MOREA SITHONIA PELOPONNESE
PORT: SYRA CORFU PYLOS SYROS
VOLOS MEGARA PATRAI PATRAS
KAVALLA KERKYRA PIRAEUS
SALONIKA
RIVER: IRI ARDA ARTA AURO
AXIOS DOONA EVROS LERNA
ALFIOS NESTOS PENEUS PINIOS
STRUMA VARDAR ALPHEUS
EUROTAS EVROTAS ILISSOS
PENEIOS ROUFIAS SARANTA
STRIMON ACHELOUS AKHELOOS
ALIAKMON KEPHISOS RHOUPHIA
RUINS: DELOS PELLA SAMOS
CORINTH ELEUSIS ELEVSIS
ACROPOLIS
SEA: CRETE AEGEAN IONIAN
MIRTOON
STATE: PHOCIS
TOWN: IOS KEA KOS ARTA ELIS
KYME PETA SYME YDRA ADREA
AGYIA ARGOS CANEA CHIOS
CORFU DRAMA KARYA MELOS
NAXOS NEMEA PELLA POROS
PSARI PYLOS PYRGI SAMOS
SYROS TENOS VAMOS VATHY
VOLOS VYRON ZANTE ACTIUM
ATHENS CANDIA DAPHNI DELPHI
EDESSA ITHACA JANINA KOZANE
LARISA MEGARA NIKAIA PATRAS
RHODES SERRAI SERRES
SPARTA THEBES TIRYNS
XANTHE ATHENAI CORINTH
ELEUSIS KERKYRA LARISSA
MYCENAE PIRAEUS IOANNINA
KOMOTINE MARATHON
PHARSALA SALONIKA TRIKKALA
VALLEY: NEMEA
VERNACULAR: DEMOTIC
WEIGHT: MNA OKA OKE MINA
OBOL LITRA LIVRE MANEH
POUND DIOBOL DRAMME
KANTAR OBOLOS OBOLUS
STATER TALENT CHALCON
CHALQUE DRACHMA DIOBOLON
TALANTON
WOMEN: THYIAD

GREED AVARICE AVIDITY HOGGERY
CUPIDITY
GREEDINESS AVARICE AVIDITY
GULOSITY
GREEDY AVID GAIR GORB YELP
EAGER GUTTY YIVER GRABBY
GUNDIE KITISH STINGY GLUTTON

GRIPPLE HOODOCK MISERLY PIGGISH COVETOUS ESURIENT GRASPING RAVENOUS
GREEK GREW ATTIC HADJI KOINE METIC ARGIVE IONIAN KLEPHT ACHAIAN GRECIAN GRIFFON HELLENE GRECANIC HELLENIC ITALIOTE SICELIOT
GREEN LEEK VERD VERT CRUDE FRESH CALLOW VIRENT VORENT NOUVEAU SINOPLE UNFIRED VERDANT BAYBERRY IMMATURE NOUVELLE VAGABOND VIRIDIAN WEDGWOOD WOODLAND
(**— MOUNTAIN STATE**) VERMONT
(**COOKED —S**) SALAD
(**NILE —**) BOA
(**PALE —**) ALOE ALOES
(**YELLOWISH —**) GLAUZY ABSINTHE GLAUCOUS
GREEN AMARANTH REDROOT
GREENBACK FROGSKIN
(**PL.**) GREEN LETTUCE
GREEN CORMORANT SHAG
GREENFISH BLUEFISH
GREENHEART BIBIRU BEBEERU
GREEN HERON KIALEE
GREENHORN JAY YAP JAKE IKONA GREENY SUCKER SOFTHORN
GREENHOUSE STOVE GREENERY HOTHOUSE ORANGERY COOLHOUSE

GREENLAND

AIR BASE: THULE
BAY: DISKO BAFFIN MELVILLE
CAPE: JAAL GRIVEL WALKER BISMARCK BREWSTER FAREWELL LOWENORN
CAPITAL: GODTHAAB
DISCOVERER: ERIC
MOUNTAIN: FOREL PAYER KHARDYU
STRAIT: DAVIS DENMARK
TOWN: ETAH NORD THULE UMANAK GODHAVN IVIGTUT GODTHAAB

GREENLING BOREGAT BODIERON LORICATE
GREEN MONKEY GUENON
GREENNESS VERD VERT VERDURE VERDANCY VIRIDITY
GREEN PIKE JACK
GREENROOM FOYER
GREENSHANK TATTLER
GREENSTONE POUNAMU
GREEN SUNFISH REDEYE
GREENWEED WOODWAX
GREEN WOODPECKER ECCLE SPRITE YOCKEL YUKKEL HEWHALL HEWHOLE SNAPPER SPEIGHT YAFFLER WOODHACK WOODWALL
GREET CRY JOY CROW HAIL HALSE ACCOST HERALD SALUTE ADDRESS RECEIVE WELCOME
GREETING HOW HIYA ALOHA GREET HELLO HOWDY KOMBO ACCOST CHEERO SALAAM SALUTE SHALOM ADDRESS CHEERIO COMMEND SLAINTE WELCOME

GREGARIOUS GREGAL SOCIAL
GREGE NUTRIA
GRENADE EGG TROMBE GRENADO FIREBALL PINEAPPLE
GRENADIER RATTAIL WHIPTAIL
GRENADINE FLORENCE
GREY (SEE GRAY)
GREYHOUND GREW BANJARA SAPLING WHIPPET
GRID BOOCAN BUCCAN GRIDDLE GRIDIRON
GRIDDLE COMAL GRILL GIRDLE GRILLE BRANDER
GRIDDLE CAKE AREPA LATKE CHAPATTY CORNCAKE FLAPJACK SLAPJACK
GRIDIRON GRID GRILL TRAIL BRANDER BROILER GRIDDLE
GRIEF WOE CARE DILL DOLE DOOL DREE HARM HURT MOAN MOOD PAIN RUTH SORE TEEN TINE AGONY DOLOR GRAME RUING TRIAL WRONG BARRAT DESIRE MISHAP REGRET SORROW STOUND WONDER ANGUISH CHAGRIN EMOTION FAILURE OFFENSE SADNESS THOUGHT TROUBLE WAESUCK WAYMENT DISASTER DISTRESS HARDSHIP
(**— STEM**) KELLY
(**SECRET —**) CANKER
GRIESEN ZWITTER
GRIEVANCE BEEF GRIEF BURDEN BYGONE GRAVAMEN HARDSHIP
GRIEVE CARE DOLE DUMP EARN ERME HURT PAIN PINE SIGH WAIL GRAME GRIPE MOURN SORRY WOUND YEARN ATHINK CORSIE LAMENT SORROW AFFLICT CHAGRIN CONDOLE GRIZZLE TROUBLE WAYMENT COMPLAIN DISTRESS
GRIEVED WOE GRAME SORRY
GRIEVING SORRY
GRIEVOUS SAD DEEP DERF HARD SORE CHARY DIRTY GRIEF HEAVY SORRY WEARY BITTER DREARY SEVERE SHREWD HEINOUS WEIGHTY DOLOROUS
GRIEVOUSLY FOULLY SORELY HEAVILY
GRIFFE SPUR
GRIFFIN GRIPE GRYPHON EPIMACUS
GRILL REJA BRACE BROIL DEVIL TRAIL AFFLICT BROILER GRILLADE
GRILLE FACE REJA HAZARD
GRILLROOM GROOM
GRILSE PEAL FINNAC GRAWLS BOTCHER FORKTAIL
GRIM GASH SOUR BLEAK CRUEL GAUNT STERN GRIMLY GRISLY HORRID SULLEN TORVID GHASTLY GRIZZLY HIDEOUS TORVOUS PITILESS RUTHLESS
GRIMACE MOP MUG POT FACE GIRN IRPE MOUE MUMP YIRN FLEER MOUTH SNEER SNOOT GIMBLE SHEYLE STITCH MURGEON SIMAGRE
GRIME DIRT SMUT COLLY SMOUCH SMUTCH
GRIMME COQUETOON

GRIMNESS TORVITY
GRIMY DINGY GRUBBY SCABROUS
GRIN DRAD GIRN MUMP FLEER SNEER SIMPER GRIZZLE
GRIND DIG SAP BONE BRAY CHEW FILE GRUN MILL MULL MUZZ SMUG SWOT CRUSH FLOAT FLOUR GRAT▮ GRIDE GRIST QUERN CRUNCH DRUDGE POWDER EMERIZE GRISTL▮ SWOTTER LEVIGATE
(**— COARSELY**) KIBBLE
(**— SMALL**) BRAY
(**— TEETH**) GNASH GRATE GRINT GRISBET
GRINDER CRASH MULLER BRUISER
GRINDING BREAK MOLAR ABRASIO▮
(**— OF MEAL**) BREAK GRIST
GRINDSTONE MANO PAVER STONE
GRIP BITE BURR CLIP FANG FIST HOLD HOLT TAKE VICE CHOKE CINCH CLAMP CLASP GRASP GRIP PINCH SALLY SEIZE BARREL CLIN▮ CLUTCH CRADLE FREEZE EMBRAC▮ HANDBAG HOLDING SEIZURE ADHESION FOOTLOCK HANDFAST HANDGRIP HANDHOLD
(**— OF A SWORD**) FUSEAU
(**— OF BELL ROPE**) SALLY
(**— TO A SPAR**) DOG
GRIPE FRIB BITCH CREATE HOLLE▮ NATTER SNATCH GRIZZLE COMPLAIN
GRIPER GRIZZLER
GRIPES TORMINA
GRIPING GRIPPLE PINCHING
GRIPPER KEEPER NIPPER
GRIPPING STONY STONEY
GRIQUA BASTARD BASTAARD
GRISLY GRIM GHASTLY GRIZZLY HIDEOUS GRUESOME
GRISON HURON GALICTIS
GRIST PABULUM
GRIT SAND GRIND BOTTOM BRAVE DECISION GRITROCK RUBSTONE
(**PL.**) CUTLINGS
GRITH MUND GYRTH
GRITTY SANDY SHARP GRISTY CHISELLY SABULINE SABULOUS
GRIVET TOTA WAAG GEUNON NISNAS
GRIZZLED GRISLY STREAKED
GRIZZLY BEAR (**— STATE**) CALIFORNIA
GROAN MOAN ROME GRANK GRU▮ STECH COMPLAIN
GROAT BIT FLAG GILL HARP
GROCER SPICER EPICIER PEPPER
GROCERY PULPERIA
GROG RUMBO TEMPER CHAMOTT▮
GROGGERY SHANTY GROGSHOP
GROGGY SHAKY UNSTEADY WAVERING
GROGSHOP SHANTY DOGGERY GROGGERY
GROIN LISK PIER SHARE CLITCH INGUEN GRUNZIE
GROMMET BECKET COLLAR EYE CRINGLE GARLAND
GROMWELL REDROOT GRAYMIL▮

GROOM LAD MAFU NEAT SYCE CURRY DRESS MAFOO STRAP SWIPE TIGER BARBER FETTLE FOGGER GUINEA MEHTAR OSTLER HOSTLER MARSHAL COISTREL GROOMLET STRAPPER
GROOVE RUT BEAD DADO GAIN KERF LUCE PORT RAKE SLOT CANAL CHASE CROZE FLUTE GLYPH GORGE GOUGE GUIDE JOINT QUIRK REGAL RIFLE RIGOL SCARF SCORE STRIA SWAGE CREASE CULLIS FULLER FURROW GUTTER KEYWAY RABBET RAGGLE RAGLET REBATE RIFFLE RUNNER SCROBE SULCUS THROAT TRENCH CHAMFER CHANNEL GARLAND KEYHOLE PLOWING SULCATE BOTHRIUM GROOVING PHILTRUM
(— IN AUGER) POD
(— IN COLUMN) FLUTE
(— IN MASONRY) RAGGLE
(— IN STAVES) CROZE
(— IN STONE) JAD
(— IN TIRE) SIPE
(— ON UPPER LIP) PHILTRUM
(— ON WEEVIL) SCROBE
(— ON WHALE) SCARF
(— UNDER COPING) GORGE
(—S ON ROCK) LAPIES
ROOVED FLUTED EXARATE SULCATE
ROOVER FLUTER
ROPE CLAM CLAW FEEL POKE GLAUM GRAIP FUMBLE GUDDLE GRABBLE GRAPPLE GROPPLE GRUBBLE SCRABBLE
ROSBEAK FINCH HAWFINCH
ROSGRAIN ROYALE
ROSS FAT DULL FOUL RANK CRASS FOGGY GREAT GUTTY LARGE THICK WHOLE ANIMAL COARSE EARTHY FILTHY GREASY SORDID STRONG BLOATED FULSOME CLODDISH FLAGRANT INDECENT SLUTTISH
ROSSO MATAPAN
ROTESQUE ANTIC WOOZY BIZARRE CROTESCO FANCIFUL
ROTTO CAVE GROT SPEOS CAVERN
ROUCH SULK CRANK GROUSE SOURBALL SOURPUSS
ROUND SEW SOD SUE BASE CLOD DIRT FOLD FOND GIST LAND MOLD REST ROOT SOIL STAY WOLD EARTH FIELD FIRTH FOUND MOULD PLACE SCORE TRAIN TUTOR VENUE CREASE MATTER REASON SMACKED FORELAND INITIATE
(— AT TOP OF SHAFT) BANK
(— COVERED WITH RUBBLE) TITI
(— FOR COMPLAINT) BEEF
(— OF FLAG) FIELD
(— OF LACE) FOND
(— OVERLYING TIN DEPOSIT) BURDEN
(BOGGY —) SOG SNAPE
(BROKEN —) HAG
(BURYING —) CEMETERY

(CAMPING —) AUTOCAMP
(COLLEGE —S) CAMPUS
(DUMPING —) TIP TOOM
(FALLOW —) BRISE
(FEEDING —) HAUNT
(FIRM-HOLDING —) LANDFANG
(FISHING —) HAAF
(FROZEN —) TJAELE
(GRASSY —) LAWN CLOWRE
(HARD —) HARDPAN
(HUNTING —) CHASE
(LOW —) INCH SWALE TALAO
(MIDDLE —) LIMBO
(NEW ENCLOSED —) TINING
(ORIGINAL —) URGRUND
(PASTURE —) HIRSEL
(RECREATION —) PARK
(RISING —) HURST HYRST
(SLOPING —) CLEVE
(SOLID —) HILL
(SPONGY —) BOG
(SWAMPY —) PUXY CRIPPLE
(UNCULTIVATED —) JUNGLE
(UNUSED —) AREA
(WET WASTE —) MOOR
(PL.) GROUT STOCK
GROUND HEMLOCK SHINWOOD
GROUND HOG MARMOT
GROUND IVY GILL HEWE HOVE JILL YARROW ALEHOOF CATFOOT GAGROOT MILFOIL TUNHOOF FOALFOOT
GROUNDLESS IDLE FALSE BASELESS
GROUNDLINE SETLINE
GROUNDMAN GRUNT
GROUNDMASS PASTE CEMENT MATRIX
GROUNDNUT GOBBE PEANUT PIGNUT
GROUND PINE FOXTAIL STAGHORN
GROUNDSEL SIMSON DOGBUSH SENCION SENECIO BINDWEED BIRDSEED
GROUNDSMAN CURATOR
GROUND SQUIRREL GOPHER GRINNY SUSLIK SCIURID SOUSLIK SCIURINE
GROUND THRUSH PITTA
GROUNDWORK BASE FOND FUND BASIS FUNDUS
GROUP MOB SET BAND BEVY BODY CREW DECK FOLD GANG KNOT PAIR RING SECT SORT STEW TREF ARRAY BATCH BREED CLASS CLUMP COVEY FIRCA FLOCK GENUS GLOBE PLUMP SABHA SKULK SQUAD STACK TALLY WHEEN CLUTCH COHORT FAMILY GRUPPO PARCEL RUBRIC AGGROUP BATTERY BOILING BOUROCK BRACKET COLLEGE COMPANY CONSORT FELLOWS FLUTTER QUOTITY SECTION SEVERAL SOCIETY ALLIANCE CATEGORY CLASSIFY DIVISION FAISCEAU FLOTILLA GROUPING
(— OF 10 NOTES) DECUPLET
(— OF 1000) CHILIAD
(— OF 12) DOZEN

(— OF 2 VOWELS) DIGRAM DIGRAPH
(— OF 40 THREADS) BEER BIER
(— OF 60 PIECES) SHOCK
(— OF ANGELS) FLIGHT
(— OF ARTIFACTS) CACHE
(— OF BADGERS) CETE
(— OF BUILDINGS) BLOCK
(— OF CASTINGS) SPRAY
(— OF CATS) CLOWDER
(— OF CELLS) GLAND ISLET CENTER CORONA EPITHEM SEMILUNE
(— OF DECOYS) STOOL
(— OF DEITIES) CABEIRI
(— OF DIALECTS) AEOLIC
(— OF EELS) SWARM
(— OF EIGHT) OCTAD OCTET OCTETTE
(— OF FAMILIES) FINE
(— OF FIVE) PENTAD CINQUAIN
(— OF FOUR) MESS QUARTET
(— OF FRIENDS) BUNCH
(— OF FURNISHINGS) ENSEMBLE
(— OF HAITIANS) COMBITE COUMBITE
(— OF HOUSES) BOROUGH
(— OF HUTS) BUSTI KRAAL BUSTEE
(— OF ISOGLOSSES) BUNDLE
(— OF KINDRED) SIOL
(— OF KINSMEN) AHL
(— OF LAYMEN) COFRADIA
(— OF LIONS) PRIDE
(— OF LISTENERS) AUDIENCE
(— OF MARTENS) RICHESSE
(— OF MILITARY VEHICLES) DEADLINE
(— OF MOLDINGS) DANCETTE
(— OF NUCLEONS) SHELL
(— OF OFFSPRING) CLUTCH
(— OF ORGANISMS) FORM STRAIN
(— OF PARACHUTISTS) STICK
(— OF PERSONS) BAG CLUB KNOT SWAD CROWD DROVE CIRCLE GAGGLE KENNEL
(— OF RETORTS) BENCH SETTING
(— OF SCULPTURE) MORTORIO
(— OF SEVEN) HEPTAD SEPTET HEBDOMAD
(— OF SIX) HEXAD SENARY
(— OF SLAVES) COFFLE
(— OF SOILS) LATERITE
(— OF SOLDIERS) DRAFT COHORT
(— OF STARS) ASTERISM
(— OF STRATIFIED BEDS) FACIES
(— OF STUDENTS) SEMINAR
(— OF SYLLABLES) FOOT
(— OF SYMBOLS) FORMULA
(— OF SYMPTOMS) SYNDROME
(— OF TEN) DECADE DENARY
(— OF TENTS) CAMP CANVAS
(— OF THEATERS) CIRCUIT
(— OF THREE) TRIO GLEEK TRIAD TRINE
(— OF TRAITS) COMPLEX
(— OF TROUT) HOVER
(— OF VERSES) SYSTEM
(— OF WINGS) RUFFLE
(— OF WIRES) DROP
(— OF WORDS) ACCENT GENITIVE

(— ON NINE) ENNEAD NONARY
(ASSISTANCE —) AINI
(ATOMIC —) LIGAND
(AUTHORITATIVE —) CONCLAVE
(CONFUSED —) SNARL
(CORE —) CADRE
(ECOLOGICAL —) GUILD
(ETHNIC —) LI ACHANG BALAHI
BATTAK ETHNOS CHINGPAW
(ETHNOLOGICAL —) ISLAND
(EXCLUSIVE —) ELECT
(FAMILY —) GWELY
(HARMONIOUS —) DOVECOTE
(INTIMATE —) COTERIE
(KINSHIP —) SUSU
(LIVELY —) GALA
(NON-MOSLEM —) MILLET
(PAGAN —) BATAK BATANGAN
(PHILOSOPHICAL —) CENACLE
(POLITICAL —) BLOC PARTY
COMMONS
(SEGREGATED —) GHETTO
(SOCIAL —) KITH SEPT TRIBE
FAMILY INGROUP
GROUPED AGMINATE
GROUPER GAG HIND MERO GUASA
HAMEL SCAMP AGUAJI BONACI
CHERNA GROPER HAMLET WARSAW
BACALAO GARLOPA GARRUPA
GOURAMI JEWFISH REDFISH
LAPULAPU REDBELLY ROCKFISH
SCIRENGA SERRANID
(YOUNG —) SNAPPER
GROUPING KIND ARRAY BATTERY
KINDRED DIVISION GROUPAGE
SODALITY SYNTAGMA
(— OF POTTERY) SERIES
GROUSE CRAB BITCH GANGA
GORHEN GROUCH HOOTER
ATTAGEN CHEEPER GAZELLE
GORCOCK PINTAIL COMPLAIN
MOORBIRD MOORFOWL
(YOUNG —) POULT SQUEALER
GROUT GROOT LARRY SLUSH
GROUTING
GROUTER GUNITER
GROVE CAMP HEWT HOLT MOTT
SHAW TOFT TOPE WONG ALTIS
BLUFF COPSE GLADE HURST HYRST
GARDEN GREAVE GROVET ISLAND
OLIVET SPRING ACADEMY ARBORET
BOSCAGE COPPICE THICKET
WOODING SERINGAL WODELEIE
(— OF ALDERS) CARR
(— OF MANGO TREES) TOPE
(— OF OAKS) ENCINAL
(— OF OSIERS) HOLT
(— OF SUGAR MAPLES) CAMP
(SACRED —) ALTIS SARNA
(SMALL —) SHAW
GROVEL FAWN ROLL CREEP CRINGE
TUMBLE WALLOW WELTER GRABBLE
FLOUNDER
GROVELING WORMY HANGDOG
REPTILE
GROW AGE BUD GET HIT ICH WAX
BOLL COME CROP ECHE ITCH MAKE
RISE SEED THEE THRO WEAR EDIFY
ISSUE PLANT PROVE RAISE SHOOT

SWELL ACCRUE BATTEN BECOME
DOUBLE EXPAND EXTEND GATHER
SPRING SPROUT THRIVE AUGMENT
BROADEN BURGEON DEVELOP
DISTEND ENLARGE IMPROVE
NOURISH ADOLESCE FLOURISH
HEIGHTEN INCREASE THRODDEN
(— ANGRY) STIVER
(— BETTER) IMPROVE
(— DARK) GLOAM GLOOM NIGHT
DARKEN DARKLE
(— FAINT) DIE APPAL APPALL
(— FAT) FEED BATTEN
(— IN LENGTH) ELONGATE
(— IRREGULARLY) SCRAMBLE
(— LESS) SLAKE ASSUAGE
DECREASE
(— LIGHT) DAWN
(— LUXURIANTLY) THRIVE
(— MAD) WOOD
(— MILD) GIVE
(— OLD) AGE OLD SENESCE
(— OVER) INVADE
(— PLUMP) PLIM
(— RICH) FATTEN
(— SOUND) HEAL
(— SPIRITLESS) FLAG
(— STILL) HUSH
(— STRONG) FORTIFY STORKEN
(— THIN) PEAK
(— TO HEAD) CABBAGE
(— TO STALK) SPINDLE
(— TOGETHER) KNIT ACCRETE
CONCREW COOSIFY COALESCE
(— UNDER GLASS) GLASS
(— UP) STEM ACCRUE
(— WEAK) FAINT
GROWING GROWY CRESCENT
CRESCIVE
(— ANGRY) IRASCENT
(— IN CLUSTERS) RACEMOSE
(— IN GRAIN FIELDS) SEGETAL
(— IN HEAPS) ACERVATE
(— IN MEADOW) PRATAL
(— IN PAIRS) BINATE
(— IN WATER) AQUATIC
(— ON A STEM) CAULINE
(— OUT) ENATE
(— RAPIDLY) BOOMING
(— THICKLY) HOUSY
(— VIGOROUSLY) THRIFTY
(— WILD) SAVAGE AGRARIAN
AGRESTAL
GROWL YAR GNAR GURL GURR
NARR RASE ROIN ROME WIRR YARR
YIRR GARRE GNARL GNARR GROIN
SNARL GOLLAR HABBLE GRUMBLE
MAUNDER
GROWLER CLARENCE
GROWLING GROIN SURLY
GROWN THRIVEN
(— COLD) DEAD
(— HIGH) LOGGY
(— TOGETHER) ADNATE ACCRETE
(FULL —) GREAT MATURE
(WELL —) THRODDY
GROWN-UP ADULT GROWN
GROWTH FUR WAX BUSH COAT
CORN FILM GROW JUBA RISE SPUR

SUIT DUVET FLUSH GUMMA MAQUI
STAND STOCK STOOL SWELL
BUTTON CALLUS CANCER CLAVUS
EATAGE EPULIS FRINGE FUNGUS
LANUGO SCREEN SPROUT TYLOSE
UPCOME WASTME AUXESIS
BRACKEN COPPICE ERINEUM
FUNGOID MACCHIE SARCOID
STATURE TYLOSIS BEARDING
CARUNCLE ENDOGENY INCREASE
SETATION SWELLING UPSPRING
(— IN EYE) FILM
(— OF BEARD) DOWN
(— OF HAIR) SUIT
(— OF HORN) BUTTON SPIDER
(— OF TREES) BOSQUE BOSCAGE
COPPICE SHINNERY
(— ON HORSE'S LEG) FUSEE FUZEE
(— ON VESSEL'S BOTTOM) GARR
(2ND — OF GRASS) FOG
(ABUNDANT —) FLUSH
(DENSE —) BRUSH FOREST
SHINNERY
(DOWNY —) LANUGO
(GREEN —) GREENTH
(HARD —) STONE
(LUXURIANT —) FLOURISH
(ROUGH —) STUBBLE
(RUDIMENTARY —) STUB STUMP
(SIDE —) SPRIG
(SPARSE —) SCRAGGLE
(SUPERFICIAL —) MILDEW
(TRANSPARENT —) DRUSE
(VIGOROUS —) THRIFT
(WOODY —) BURL
GRUB BOB DIG EATS HUHU MOIL
MOOT STUB WORM CHUCK GROUT
MATHE SCRAN SNOUT WROTE
ASSART ESSART GRUGRU MUZZLE
ROOTLE NEASCUS PIGROOT
FLAGWORM GRUBWORM
MUCKWORM SKINWORM
GRUBROOT STARWORT
GRUDGE DOWN ENVY DERRY PEEVE
SCORE SPITE GROUCH GRUNCH
GRUTCH SPLEEN DESPITE EYELAST
SIMULTY
GRUDGING JEALOUSY
GRUEL SLOP BLEERY BURGOO
CONGEE CROWDY SOFKEE
BROCHAN CROWDIE LOBLOLLY
WANGRACE
GRUESOME UGLY GRISLY HORRID
SORDID FEARFUL GHASTLY
HIDEOUS MACABRE
GRUFF BLUFF ROUGH CLUMSE
SULLEN AUSTERE BEARING
BRUSQUE CLUMPST
(PL.) TAILINGS
GRUIFORMES GRALLAE
GRUMBLE GIRN GREX HONE KREX
ROIN BROCK CROAK DRUNT GROIN
GROWL GRUMP GRUNT MUNGE
GROUCH GROUSE GRUDGE GRUNC
MUMBLE MUNGER MURMUR MUTTE
NOLLER PEENGE REPINE RUMBLE
SQUEAL TARROW YAMMER
CHANNER CHUNNER CHUNTER
GNATTER GRIZZLE GRUNTLE

MAUNDER MURGEON QUADDLE
SWAGGER COMPLAIN
GRUMBLER GROUCH QUADDLE
GROGNARD
GRUMBLING BITCH DRUNT GRIPE
GROIN GRUDGE MURMUR MURGEON
GRUMPY ILL CROSS GLUMPY
GLUMPISH GRUMPISH
GRUNION SMELT
GRUNT BURRO GROIN HUMPH
RONCO SARGO GRUMPH RONCHO
BURRITO CROAKER GRUNTER
GRUNTLE PIGFISH PINFISH TOMTATE
KNORHAAN KOORHAAN PORKFISH
REDMOUTH RONCADOR
GUACHARO FATBIRD OILBIRD
GUAICURU CADUVEO
GUAMA INGA PACAY
GUAN JACU ORTALIS PHEASANT
GUANA CHANE
GUANABANA SOURSOP
GUANCHE CANARIAN
GUANO OSITE
GUAPENA SERRAN SERRANA
AGUAVINA
GUARANTEE (ALSO SEE GUARANTY)
BAIL BAND SEAL CINCH COVER
AVOUCH ENGAGE ENSURE INSURE
RATIFY SECURE SURETY CAUTION
CERTIFY HOSTAGE WARRANT
AWARRANT GUARANTY PRESTATE
SECURITY WARRANTY
GUARANTEED ASSURED CERTIFIED
FOOLPROOF
GUARANTOR ENGAGER GRANTOR
GUARAND GUARANTY
GUARANTY (ALSO SEE GUARANTEE)
ANDI AVAL PAWN SEAL CAUTIO
PLEDGE WARRANT SECURITY
WARRANTY
GUARD BOW LEG NIT PAD SEE CARE
CURB HERD HOLD KEEP KNOW
LOOK REDE SAVE STOP STUB TENT
TILE WAIT WEAR WERE WITE YEME
ASKAR AWARD BLESS BLOCK
CHECK COVER FENCE FORAY
HEDGE HINGE PILOT SCREW SKIRT
TUTOR WAKEN WATCH ASKARI
BANTAY BASKET BRACER BRIDLE
BUMPER BUTTON CONVOY DEFEND
DRAGON ESCORT FENDER GHAFIR
GUNMAN JAILER KAVASS KEEPER
MIDDLE POLICE SCREEN SECURE
SENTRY SHIELD SHROUD WAITER
WARDER YEMING CHERISH
ESGUARD FRONTAL GHAFFIR
GHATWAL GUARDER KEEPING
PANDOUR PRESIDY PROTECT
SOULACK TRABANT WARDAGE
WARRANT CHAPERON GARRISON
MUDGUARD OUTGUARD PEDESTAL
PILOTMAN PRESERVE SECURITY
SENTINEL SHEPHERD SPLASHER
WARDSMAN WATCHMAN
(— ON FOIL) BUTTON
(AXLE —) HOUSING
(COACH —) SHOOTER
(CONSULAR —) KAVASS
(IMPERIAL —) BOSTANGI BOSTANJI

(KEYHOLE —) LAPPET
(MOUNTED —) SHOMER
(NECK —) CAMAIL
(ON —) AWARE
(PRISON —) HACK SCREW CHASER
JAILER
(SWORD —) BOW TSUBA
(PL.) HEAVIES
GUARDED WARY IMMUNE MANNED
GUARDEDLY GINGERLY
GUARDHOUSE BRIG CLINK BULLPEN
HOOSEGOW
GUARDIAN HERD ANGEL ARGUS
TUTOR YEMER CUSTOS KEEPER
MIMING PASTOR PATRON SHOMER
WARDEN CURATOR GARDANT
GARDEEN BARTHOLO BELLERUS
CERBERUS CREANCER DEFENDER
ECKEHART FRAVASHI GOVERNOR
GUARDANT PROTUTOR TUTELARY
(— OF HOME) SIF
(WORLD —) LOKAPALA MAHARAJA
(PL.) SELLI SELLOI
GUARDIANSHIP WARD TUTELA
CUSTODY KEEPING TUITION
WARDAGE WARDING CUSTODIA
GUARDAGE TUTELAGE WARDENRY
WARDSHIP
GUARDROOM WARDROOM
GUARDSMAN GUARDEE
GUASA MERO

GUATEMALA
CAPITAL: GUATEMALACITY
COIN: PESO CENTAVO QUETZAL
DANCE: ELSON GUARIMBA
GULF: HONDURAS
INDIAN: MAM CHOL ITZA IXIL
  MAYA XINCA CARIBE QUICHE
  POCOMAM
LAKE: DULCE GUIJA PETEN IZABAL
  ATITLAN
MEASURE: VARA CUARTA FANEGA
  TERCIA CAJUELA MANZANA
MOUNTAIN: AGUA FUEGO PACAYA
  TACANA ATITLAN TOLIMAN
  TAJAMULCO
PORT: OCOS BARRIOS LIVINGSTON
RIVER: AZUL BRAVO DULCE LAPAZ
  BELIZE CHIXOY NEGINO PASION
  SAMALA CHIAPAS MOTAGUA
  SARSTUN POLOCHIC
RUINS: TIKAL
TOWN: OCOS COBAN VIEJA
  CHAHAL CHISEC CUILCO
  FLORES IZTAPA JALAPA SALAMA
  SOLOLA TACANA TECPAN
  YALOCH ZACAPA ANTIGUA
  CUILAPA JUTIAPA SANJOSE
  PROGRESO
VOLCANO: AGUA FUEGO ATITLAN
WEIGHT: CAJA LIBRA

GUAVA ARACA MYRTAL GUAYABA
GUAYABO GOIABADA
GUAYCURU MBAYA
GUDDLE GUMP NOODLE HANDFISH
GUDGEON PIN QUAB CHALDER
TRUNNION

GUELDER-ROSE GAITER OPULUS
DOGWOOD WHITTEN DOGBERRY
SNOWBALL VIBURNUM
GUENON GRIVET NISNAS VERVET
TALAPOIN TALLAPOI MOUSTACHE
GUEREZA COLOBIN COLOBUS
GUERRILLA COWBOY GORILLA
JAYHAWK SKINNER BUSHWACK
FELLAGHA KOMITAJI
GUESS AIM CALL HARP REDE SHOT
WEEN AREAD COUNT ETTLE FANCY
INFER TWANG DEVISE DIVINE
RECKON IMAGINE SURMISE
SUSPECT
(— CORRECTLY) TOUCH
GUEST COME GOER HOST DINER
INVITEE VISITOR SYMPHILE VISITANT
(— AT RANCH) DUDE
(UNINVITED —) SHADOW
(PL.) LEVEE COMPANY
GUFA KUFA GOOFAH KUPHAR
GUFFAW GAFF HEEHAW
GUIDANCE AIM DUCT EGIS AEGIS
STEER CONDUCT GUIDAGE
HELMAGE LEADING WISSING
AUSPICES ENGINERY REGIMENT
STEERAGE
GUIDE GUY LAY PIR TIP AIRT BEAD
CURB GAGE GATE LEAD PASS REIN
RULE SWAY CARRY CHARM DRESS
FRAME GAUGE LIGHT MAHDI MOROC
PILOT STEER TEACH WEISE ADALID
BARKER BEACON BEDWAY CONVOY
DIRECT ESCORT FORMER GILLIE
GOVERN INFORM LEADER MANAGE
POPPET CONDUCE CONDUCT
COURIER GHILLIE INSPIRE MARSHAL
MERCURY PIONEER SHIKARI
STERNER TRACKER CALENDAR
CICERONE DIRECTOR DRAGOMAN
ENGINEER FAIRLEAD LODESMAN
PEDESTAL POLESTAR PRACTICO
REPEATER SHIKAREE SIGNPOST
(SPIRITUAL —) PIR GURU BISHOP
DIVINE
(TRAFFIC —) MUSHROOM
GUIDEBOOK ABC GUIDE WAYBOOK
BAEDEKER HANDBOOK ROADBOOK
GUIDELINE SLUG
GUIDEPOST GUIDE PARSON
WAYMARK WAYPOST SIGNPOST
GUIDEWAY SLAY SLEY SLEIGH
SLIDEWAY SWANNECK
GUIDING POLAR BEHIND HOMING
LEADING
GUILD HUI GILD HOEY HONG YELD
CRAFT HANSA HANSE GREMIO
GUIDRY SCHOLA BASOCHE
COLLEGE COMPANY MYSTERY
GUILE DOLE WILE CHEAT CRAFT
FRAUD TRAIN DECEIT HUMBUG
CUNNING FALLACY ARTIFICE
GUILELESS PLAIN CANDID HONEST
ARTLESS ONEFOLD IGNORANT
INNOCENT UNNOOKED
GUILLEMOT AUK COOT LARY LAVY
LOOM QUET TURR URIA ARRIE
CUTTY FROWL MURRE SCOUT TOIST
TYSTE GRYLLE LUNGIE MAGGIE

MARROT SCRABE TINKER DOVEKEY
DOVEKIE SKIDDAW TARROCK
WILLOCK PUFFINET ROCKBIRD
SCUTTOCK SPRATTER
GUILT SIN SAKE WITE BLAME CULPA
FAULT PIACLE PLIGHT NOCENCE
OFFENSE HAMARTIA INIQUITY
GUILTLESS FREE PURE CLEAN
UNSAKED INNOCENT SACKLESS
GUILTY FAULTY NOCENT WICKED
CORREAL HANGDOG NOXIOUS
BLAMEFUL CRIMINAL CULPABLE
GUILTFUL
(**— OF ERROR)** LAPSED

GUINEA

CAPE: VERGA
CAPITAL: CONAKRY
COIN: SILY FRANC
ISLAND: TOMBO TRISTAO
MEASURE: JACKTAN
MOUNTAIN: TAMGUE
MOUNTAINS: LOMA NIMBA
NATIVE: SUSU TOMA KISSI FULANI
GUERZI MALINKE KOURANKE
LANDUMAN
RIVER: NIGER BAFING FALEME
SENEGAL KONKOURE TINKISSO
TOWN: BOKE FRIA KADE LABE
BENTY BEYLA COYAH KOULE
MAMOU DABOLA DALABA
DOUAKO FABALA KANKAN
KINDIA BOFOSSO CONAKRY
FARANAH KONFARA KOUMBIA
OUASSOU SIGUIRI KEROUANE
WEIGHT: AKEY PISO UZAN BENDA
SERON QUINTO AGUIRAGE

GUINEA MEG BEAN QUID QUEED
GEORGE SHINER GEORDIE
(HALF —) SMELT
GUINEA FOWL KEEL KEET PEARL
MEBACK GALEENY PINTADO
COMEBACK GALLINEY
(SOUND OF —) POTRACK
GUINEA GRASS PANIC PANICLE
SACATON ZACATON GAMELOTE
GUINEA PEPPER PIMENTO
GUINEA PIG CAVY
(MALE —) BOAR BUCK
GUINEA RUSH ADRUE
GUISE HUE FORM GARB COLOR
COVER SHAPE MANNER PERSON
APPAREL CLOTHES GUISARD
LIKENESS
GUITAR BOX KIT PIPA JAMON KITAR
SITAR TIPLE GIMBRI KITTAR
SANCHO SATTAR CITHERN CITTERN
MACHETE UKULELE CHARANGO
CHITARRA
GUITARFISH RAY BATOID PURAQUE
GUITGUIT PITPIT
GULANCHA GILO GILOE
GULCH GULLY SLUIT CANYON
RAVINE
GULDEN FLORIN GUILDER
(100,000 —) TUN
GULES MARS RUBY TORTEAU

GULF SINE CHAOS GULPH VORAGE
VORAGO
(BOTTOMLESS —) ABYSM ABYSS
GULFWEED SARGASSO
GULL COB COX MEW COBB CONY
COOT CULL DUPE FOOL GOLL LARI
MALL PINT PIRR SELL SKUA XEME
ALLAN ALLEN ANNET BOSUN CHEAT
CHUMP COBBE COKES CROCK
CULLY HOODY JAGER LARID LARUS
PEWIT SCULL SMELT YAGER BONXIE
BUBBLE CHOUSE COUSIN JOCKEY
PIGEON SIMPLE TEASER TULIAC
VICTIM WAGGEL WHILLY CROCKER
DECEIVE MEDRICK PICKMAW
POPELER SCAURIE SEABIRD
SEAFOWL SWARBIE TARROCK
TRUMPIE BLACKCAP DIRTBIRD
DOTTEREL DUNGBIRD SEEDBIRD
(LIKE A —) LAROID
GULLET MAW GULE LANE GORGE
GARGLE PECHAN THROAT KEACORN
STOMACH SWALLOW WEASAND
GURGULIO
GULLIBLE GOOFY GREEN SIMPLE
CULLIBLE
GULLIVER GRILDRIG
GULLY BOX GUT DRAW GULL RAIK
RAKE SICK SIKE DONGA DRAFT
GOYLE GULCH SLAKE SLUIT ZANJA
ARROYO GULLET GULLEY GUTTER
NULLAH SHEUCH SHEUGH CHIMNEY
COULOIR DRAUGHT BARRANCA
GULP BOLT GAUP GLUT GULL POOP
SOPE SWIG GULCH QUILT SLOSH
SWIPE ENGLUT GLUTCH GOBBLE
GOLLOP PAUNCH SLABBER
SWALLOW SWATTLE
(— NOISILY) SLORP
GUM AMRA BLOB FILL GOOM LOAD
TUNO AMAPA BABUL CUMAY DHAVA
CHICLE KARAYA TOUART TUPELO
CARANNA CARAUNA GINGIVA
GUMWOOD BORRACHA CARABEEN
DRESSING FEVERGUM
(ACACIA —) GEDDA
(AROMATIC —) MYRRH
(ASTRINGENT —) KINO
(CHEWING —) WAX
(FRAGRANT —) BUMBO
(RED —) JARRAH
(UNGRADED —) SORTS
(WOOD —) XYLAN
(PL.) ULA
GUM ARABIC KIKAR ACACIA ACACIN
GUMBO OKRA
GUMBOIL PARULIS
GUMBO-LIMBO JOBO BIRCH
GOMART MASTIC NEGRITO
ALMACIGO ARCHIPIN
GUMDROP GUM JUJUBE
GUMMER BIDDY BIDDIE SCRAPER
SCUFFER SCUFFLER SCUPPLER
GUMMY GLUEY CLAGGY MASTIC
GUMMOUS
GUMPTION SENSE SPRAWL
GUM SUCCORY HOGBITE
GUM TREE KARI KARRI TOOART
TOUART TUPELO EUCALYPT

GUMWEED GRINDELIA SUNFLOWER
GUN GAT POP BREN HAKE PIAT
ROER TUBE BARIL FIFTY FIRER
FUSEE FUZEE RAKER REWET RIFLE
ARCHIE BERTHA CANNON CHASER
CULVER DUCKER INCHER JEZAIL
MINNIE QUAKER RANDOM SWIVEL
TUPARA CALIVER FIREARM
HACKBUT HANDGUN JINGALL
LANTACA MUZZLER AMUSETTE
ARQUEBUS CHAUCHAT CULVERIN
FIRELOCK GALLOPER SHAGBUSH
TROMBONE
(BOAT —) BASE
(LOWER-DECK —) BARKER
(MACHINE —) CHOPPER GATLING
(TOY —) SPARKLER
(PL.) FLAK CHASE ARTILLERY
GUNA RAJAS TAMAS SATTVA
GUNBOAT SKIP BARCA GONDOLA
TINCLAD
GUN CARRIAGE PANEL MADRIER
GALLOPER
GUNCREWMAN PLUGMAN
GUNFLINT STONE
GUNITE SHOTCRETE
GUNLOCK ROWET FIRELOCK
GUNMAN HOOD GUNSEL GUNSMAN
TORPEDO ENFORCER GANGSTER
GUNNEL BLENNY SWORDICK
GUNNER GUN POPPER FIREMAN
SHOOTER ENGINEER
GUNNY TAT BURLAP BAGGING
SACKING
GUNNYSACK CORNSACK
GUNPOWDER SULFUR SULPHUR
GUNSIGHT VISIE HAUSSE
GUNSTOCK BLANK TIPSTOCK
GUNSTONE OGRESS PELLET
GUNWALE GUNNEL PORTOISE
GUNZ SCANIAN
GUPPY MILLIONS BELLYFISH
GUR GOOR KHAUR JAGGERY
VOLTAIC
GURGLE GLOX QUARK SLOSH
BURBLE GOLLER GUGGLE
GURGLINGLY TRILLIL
GURJUN YANG
GURNARD CUR TUB PIPER ELLECK
ROCHET BATFISH CAPTAIN
GRUNTER LATCHET SOLDIER
TRIGLID TUBFISH VOLADOR
HARDHEAD KNORHAAN LORICATE
GURO KWENI
GUSH JET BOIL FLOW FOAM HUSH
RAIL SLOP WALM BELCH SLUSH
SMALM SMARM SPIRT SPURT STO
SWOSH BURBLE PHRASE SWOOSH
WALLOW WHOOSH SLOBBER
GUSHING SLOPPY SMARMY
EFFUSIVE
GUSSET GORE MITER MITRE QUIRK
PIECETTE
GUST BUB FLAN GALE GUSH WAFF
WAFT WIND BLAST FRESH SLANT
FLURRY HUFFLE SQUALL WILLIWA
WINDFLAW
(— OF RAIN) SKIT
(— OF WIND) FLAM FLAN FUFF

GALE GUSH PIRR SCUD TIFT BERRY
BLAST FLAFF THODE SQUALL
WINDELAW
USTATION TASTE
USTO GUST ZEST RELISH
USTY DIRTY PUFFY BLASHY
BLASTY FRETFUL GUSTFUL
SQUALLY
UT GIB BOWEL CECUM CLEAN
CAECUM CATGUT HOLLOW STRING
ELISION GRALLOCH
(FISH —) GIP GILL
(TWISTED —) THARM THERM
(PL.) BOWELS COJONES PUDDING
ENTRAILS
UTTA SOH DROP PUAN SIAK SUSU
DUJAN GERIP SANGE SUNDIK
CAMPANA JANGKAR SEMARUM
TRENAIL TRUNNEL HANGKANG
KETAPANG
UTTER GRIP SIKE GRIPE GULLY
SIVER SPOUT SWEAL BOTTOM
CANNEL CULLIS GROOVE GUZZLE
KENNEL RIGGOT STRAND TROUGH
VENNEL CHANNEL CHENEAU
GRIZZLE

(— OF STREET) KENNEL
(MINING —) BOTTOM HASSING
(ROOF —) RONE
(PL.) LIMBERS
GUTTERMAN SWAMPER
GUTTURAL GRUM BURRY HARSH
THICK
GUY BOD CAT EGG JOE NUT BIRD
BOZO GENT GINK HUSK JACK JOHN
COOKY JOKER SCOUT SPOOF
BUFFER COOKIE GAZABO GAZEBO
GAZOOK GILGUY HOMBRE JASPER
JIGGER MALKIN MAUMET MAWKIN
KNOCKER BLIGHTER
GUY ROPE STAY VANG
GUZ GAZ GEZ ZAR ZER GUDGE
GUZERAT KANKREJ
GUZZLE BUM GUM SOT TUN BEND
GULL SLOSH SWILL GOOZLE
GUDDLE SWATTLE SWIZZLE
GUZZLER BENDER
GWYNIAD SCHELLY
GYASCUTUS PROCK
GYMNASIUM GYM PALESTRA
TURNHALL

GYMNAST SOKOL BENDER TURNER
ACROBAT TUMBLER
GYMNASTIC (— SOCIETY) SOKOL
GYNOECIUM BRUSH APOCARP
GYNOPHORE PODOGYN
GYPSUM GYP GYPS YESO GESSO
LUDIAN PARGET GYPSITE SATINITE
SELENITE ALABASTER
GYPSY CALO APTAL CAIRD GIPSY
ROMNI BOSHAS GITANO ROMANY
TINKER AZUCENA CZIGANY
MOONMAN TINKLER TZIGANE
ZINGARO BOHEMIAN EGYPTIAN
FLAMENCO ZIGEUNER
(NON —) GORGIO
(SEA —) BAJAU
(PL.) ROMANESE
GYRATE GYRE SPIN TURN TWIRL
WHIRL CURVET INGYRE ROTATE
REVOLVE SQUIRREL
GYRATORY GIDDY GYRAL
GYRFALCON JERKIN
GYRON GIRON ESQUIRE

H HOW AITCH HOTEL ASPIRATE
HABERDASHERY TOGGERY
HABERGEON HAUBERK
HABILIMENT GARB HABIT APPAREL
  RAIMENT CLOTHING
  (PL.) CLOTHES EQUIPAGE
HABILITATE ENABLE
HABIT LAW PAD SET USE COAT
  GARB GATE SUIT THEW WONT
  FROCK HAUNT TACHE TRADE TRICK
  USAGE CUSTOM GROOVE MANNER
  PRAXIS TALENT CLOTHES FOLKWAY
  HABITUS WONTING CROTCHET
  HABITUDE PHYSIQUE PRACTICE
  PRACTISE
  (— OF GRINDING TEETH) BRUXISM
  (BAD —) HANK VICE MISTETCH
  (SPEECH —S) ACCENT
  (PL.) DAPS
HABITABLE BIGLY
HABITAT ECE HOME RANGE PATRIA
  STATION LOCALITY
HABITATION HOLD TELD TENT
  ABODE BIELD HABIT HOUSE WONING
  DOMICILE DWELLING PANTHEON
  TENEMENT RESIDENCE
  (— SITE) YACATA
  (QUIET —) SHADE
  (UNDERGROUND —) HOLE
HABITUAL USUAL COMMON HECTIC
  CHRONIC REGULAR FREQUENT
  ORDINARY
HABITUATE USE HOWF ENURE
  FLESH HABIT INURE ADDICT SEASON
  HACKNEY ACCUSTOM ACQUAINT
  OCCASION
HABITUATED WONT SEASONED
HABITUDE HABIT SCHESIS
HABITUE DENIZEN COURTIER
HABRONEMIASIS BURSATI
  BURSATTEE
HACEK WEDGE
HACK HAG HEW BOLO CHIP HAKE
  DEVIL HATCH DRUDGE FIACRE
  HACKLE HAGGLE HODMAN JOBBER
  MANGLE HACKNEY MATTOCK
  VETTURA MUTILATE
  (LITERARY —) GRUB DEVIL
HACKBERRY EGGBERRY HACKTREE
  HAGBERRY ONEBERRY
HACKBUT HAGBUT DEMIHAG
  HACKBUSH
HACK GHARRI SHIGRAM
HACKLE COMB RUFF HECKLE
  NAPPER RUFFER HATCHEL
  ROUGHER
HACKNEY HACK MIDGE NODDY
HACKNEY CARRIAGE MIDGE
  FIACRE JARVEY VETTURA
HACKNEYED HACK WORN HOARY
  TRITE CANNED CLICHE COMMON
  FOREWORN
HAD D HED HEDDE
  (— NOT) HADNA HADNT
HADDOCK GADE GADID SCROD
  DICKEY HADDIE
  (DRIED —) CRAIL RIZZAR SPELDING
  SPELDRIN
HADE UNDERLIE

HADES PIT HELL AIDES ORCUS
  PLUTO SHEOL SHADES TARTAR
  AIDONEUS TARTARUS
  (FATHER OF —) SATURN
  (WIFE OF —) PROSERPINA
HAECCITY THISNESS
HAFNIUM CELTIUM
HAFT HEFT HOVE HELVE DUDGEON
HAFTER HANDLER
HAG ATE MARE REBEC RUDAS
  VECKE WITCH BELDAM HECATE
  ROUDAS BELDAME HAGGARD
  HELLCAT HARRIDAN
HAGAR (SON OF —) ISHMAEL
HAGBOAT HOGGET HOGGIE
HAGFISH HAG BORER VECKE
  MYZONT SUCKER PLACOID
  MYXINOID
HAGGARD PALE THIN GAUNT WISHT
  HAGGED
HAGGLE CHOP PRIG DODGE BADGER
  BANTER BOGGLE DICKER HACKER
  HIGGLE HUCKLE NAGGLE PALTER
  SCOTCH THREEP BARGAIN CHAFFER
  HUCKSTER
HAGGLER DODGER
HAGGLING BARGAIN CHAFFER
HAGIOGRAPHA KETUBIM
HAGIOSCOPE SQUINT SQUINCH
HAIDA SKITTAGET
HAIL AVE HOY HALE GREET SALVE
  SPEAK STORM ACCOST BAYETE
  HAGGLE HALLOO HERALD SALUTE
  (SOFT —) GRESIL GRAUPEL
HAILSTONE STONE
HAINAI IONI
HAIR FAX JAG RIB WIG BARB CROP
  FLUE GLIB HEAD KEMP PELF PILE
  SETA WIRE BEARD CRIMP CRINE
  FRIZZ FRONT PILUS QUIFF ANGORA
  BRILLS BRUTUS CRINET FIBRIL
  FROWZE MERKIN SETULA THATCH
  TRAGUS CULOTTE ELFLOCK
  GLOCHIS TOPKNOT WHISKER
  CAPILLUS COLLETER PALPOCIL
  TENTACLE TRICHODE TRICHOME
  VIBRISSA
  (— BROWN) ARGALI
  (— OF ANIMALS) FUR PELF
  (— OF HORSES OR COWS) CERDA
  (— OF TERRIER) FALL
  (— ON LEAF) GLAND
  (— ON TEMPLES) HAFFET HAFFIT
  (— ON THIGHS) CULOTTE
  (— OVER EYES) BROW GLIB
  EYELASH
  (BARBED —) GLOCHIS
  (BRAID OF —) QUEUE PIGTAIL
  (BUNDLE OF —) LEECH
  (CAMEL'S —) DEER
  (COARSE —) KEMP BRISTLE
  (CURLED —) FRIZZ
  (CUTDOWN —) STUMPS
  (FALSE —) WIG JANE FRONT
  PERUKE
  (FRIZZED —) FROWZE
  (GRAY —) GRIZZLE
  (LOCK OF —) TUZ FEAK TATE
  FLOCK TRESS

  (LONG HEAVY —) MANE
  (LOOSE —) COMBINGS
  (MATTED —) SHAG ELFLOCK
  (MOP OF —) TOUSLE
  (NOSE —) VIBRISSA
  (PLANT —) COLLETER
  (ROOT —) FIBRIL
  (SNARL OF —) TANGLE
  (SOFT —) DOWN LANUGO
  (STINGING —) STING STIMULUS
  (STRAY LOCK OF —) TAG
  (TUFT OF —) PLUME KROBYLOS
  (WAVING LOCK OF —) WIMPLER
  (WHITE —) SNOW SNOWS
  (PL.) COWAGE COWHAGE HACKLES
HAIRBREADTH HERMELE WHISKER
HAIRBRUSH TOILETRY
HAIRCLOTH HAIR CILICE
HAIRCUT BOB CUT CROP BUTCH
  SHINGLE DUCKTAIL
HAIRDO FRISURE
HAIRDRESSER WAVER FRISEUR
  COIFFEUR
HAIRDRESSING FRISURE
HAIR FRAME PALISADE
HAIRINESS PILOSISM PILOSITY
HAIRLESS PELON CALLOW ATRICHIC
  DEPILOUS
HAIRLIKE TRICHOID
HAIRLINE WHISKER
HAIRPIN ACUS BODKIN SKEWER
HAIRSPLITTING FINE PILPUL
HAIRWORM GORDIID GORDIOID
HAIRY FAXED MOSEY ROUGH
  COMATE COMOUS PILARY PILINE
  CRINOSE HIRSUTE PILEOUS VILLOUS
  UNSHAVEN

HAITI	
CAPE: FOUX	
CAPITAL: PORTAUPRINCE	
CHANNEL: SUD STMARC	
COIN: GOURDE	
DEITY: LOA	
INDIAN: TAINO	
ISLAND: VACHE GONAVE TORTUE	
NAVASSA TORTUGA	
ISLAND GROUP: ANTILLES	
CAYMITES	
LAKE: SAUMATRE	
MAGIC: OBI OBEAH	
MOUNTAIN: NORD CAHOS NOIRES	
LAHOTTE LASELLE TROUDEAU	
PLAIN: NORD CAYES JACMEL	
LEOGANE ARCAHAIE CULDESAC	
GONAIVES	
PRIEST: BOCOR HOUNGAN	
RIVER: GUAYAMOUL ARTIBONITE	
SPIRIT: LOA BAKA BOKO	
TOWN: AQUIN CAYES FURCY	
LIMBE HINCHE JACMEL JEREMIE	
LEOGANE SALTROU GONAIVES	
KENSCOFF	

HAKAM CACAM HAHAM CHOCHEM
  KHAKHAM
HAKE GADE HAIK LING GADOID
  CODLING HADDOCK WHITING

ANACANTH QUODLING
HAKENKREUZLER SWASTIKA
HALBERD BILL PIKE GLAIVE GLEAVE
POLEARM PARTISAN
HALBERDIER DRABANT
HALCYON CALM ALCYON GOLDEN
HALE YELL FRACK FRECK TRAIL
ROBUST STRONG HEALTHY
VIGOROUS
HALER HELLER
HALF M ARF ELF DEMI HAUF HOVE
SEMI SIDE MEDIO HALFEN HALFLY
MOIETY MEDIETY
(— GALLON) POTTLE
(— OF DRAW) BRACKET
(— OF EM) EN
(— OF INNING) BOTTOM
(— OF MOLD) VALVE
(FRUIT —S) SLABS
HALFBEAK GAR IHI BALAO PIPER
BALLYHOO
HALF-BLOOD DEMISANG
HALF BOOT BUSKIN
HALF-BREED BREED METIF METIS
SAMBO MUSTEE RAMONA CABOCLO
MESTIZO METISSE DEMISANG
HARRATIN MIXBLOOD
HALF-CASTE TOPAZ TOPASS
HALF-CRAZY FIFISH
HALF CROWN GEORGE ALDERMAN
HALF DENIER MAILE MAILLE
HALF DOBRA PECA
HALF-EATEN SEMESE
HALF-FARTHING CUE MITE MINUTE
HALF GAINER ISANDER
HALF-GROWN HALFLIN
HALF-GUINEA SMELT
HALF HITCH ROLLING
HALF MASK LOUP DOMINO
HALF-MOON LUNETTE DEMILUNE
HALF NOTE MINIM
HALFPENCE GROCERY
HALFPENNY OB MAG MEG DUMP
GRAY GREY MAIL MAKE MEKE OBOL
SOUSE STAMP BAUBEE MAILLE
HAPENNY STUIVER
(COUNTERFEIT —) RAP GRAY
(THICK —) DUMP
HALF-PIKE SPONTON DEMIPIKE
SPONTOON
HALF-PINT CUP JACK CUPFUL
HALF REST SOSPIRO
HALF SOLE TAP
HALF STEP CHROMA
HALFTONE DROPOUT
HALF TURN DEMIVOLT
HALF-WIT DOLT DUNCE HAVEREL
TOMFOOL STAUMREL UNDERWIT
HALF-WITTED SOFT DOTTY SIMPLE
HALUCKET IMBECILE STAUMREL
HALIBUT BUT BUTT FLITCH TURBOT
FLATFISH
HALIFAX BALLYHACK
HALIOTIS ABALONE
HALIRRHOTHIUS (FATHER OF —)
NEPTUNE
(MOTHER OF —) EURYTE
(SLAYER OF —) MARS
HALL HA AULA HELL IWAN SALA

AIWAN ATREO ATRIO BALAI BURSA
CURIA DIVAN ENTRY FOYER HOUSE
OECUS SALLE SALON ATRIUM
CAMERA DURBAR GARDEN LESCHE
SALOON SCHOOL SENATE TOLSEY
TRANCE APADANA CHAMBER
DANCERY GALLERY HALLWAY
KURHAUS KURSAAL MEGARON
PASSAGE VINGOLF ANTEROOM
ARCHEION ASSEMBLY CHOULTRY
COLISEUM CORRIDOR FOREHALL
HASTROND HOSPITAL RAADZAAL
TOLBOOTH VALHALLA
(— FOR PERFORMANCES) ODEON
ODEUM
(— WITH STATUES) VALHALLA
(DINING —) COMMON
(LECTURE —) SCHOLA
(MISSION —) CITADEL
(MUSIC —) GAFF
(TOWN —) CABILDO RATHAUS
TRIBUNAL
(UNIVERSITY —) BURSA
HALLMARK CROWN SHOPMARK
HALLOO HO HOO LOO ALEW LURE
WHOOP ACCOST TALLYHO
HALLOW BLESS HALWE DEDICATE
SANCTIFY
HALLOWED HOLY SACRED BLESSED
HALLUCINATION DWALE ACOASMA
ACOUASM ACOUSMA FANTASY
PHONEME DELUSION ILLUSION
PHANTASY ZOOSCOPY
HALLUX TALON
HALLWAY ENTRY FOYER TRANCE
HALMA HOPPITY
HALMALILLE PETWOOD
HALO DOG BURR GLOR NIMB GLORY
SHINE AREOLA CIRCLE CORONA
GLORIA NIMBUS SUNDOG AREOLET
AUREOLE BOROUGH CINCTURE
HALT HO HOP ALTO BAIT BALK HOLD
LIMP SKID STAY STOP TRIP WAIT
BAULK BLOCK BREAK CEASE CHECK
HILCH HITCH STAND ARREST
BARLEY SCOTCH STANCE CONTAIN
CRIPPLE STATION STOPPAGE
(— GAME) CALL
(— TO DOGS) TOHO
HALTER EVIL SOLE BRANK TRASH
WANTY WIDDY WITHE POISER
CAUSSON CAVESON JAQUIMA
POINTEL BALANCER NECKLACE
HALTING BODE LAME ZOPPA
CRIPPLE LIMPING
HALVE DIMIDIATE
(PL.) HALVERS
HALVING HAPLOSIS
HAM PIG GAMMON JAMBON JARRET
PESTLE GAMBONE
(FATHER OF —) NOAH
(PICNIC —) CALA CALI
(SON OF —) CUSH CANAAN
HAMATUM UNCIFORM
HAMESUCKEN HAMFARE
HAMITE BORAN BORANA DANAKIL
DANKALI
HAMLET KOM DORP TOWN TREF
VILL CASAL HAMEL SITIO STEAD

THORP VICUS ALDEIA BUSTEE
THORPE CLACHAN KAMPONG
KIRKTON KIRKTOWN
HAMMER AX AXE BIT DOG PEG SET
CALL COCK DROP HORN MALL
MASH MAUL MELL SETT TILT CAVIL
KEVEL KNOCK MADGE POUND SMITE
THUMP BEETLE BUCKER CLOYER
DRIVER FALLER FULLER MALLET
MARTEL NOPPER OLIVER PLEXOR
SCUTCH SLEDGE TACKER TILTER
KNAPPER KNOCKER MALLEUS
PLESSOR STRIKER CRANDALL
MALLEATE MJOLLNIR SCUTCHER
TREMBLER
(— FOR DRESSING STONE) KEVEL
(— OF GUNLOCK) DOG COCK
DOGHEAD
(— OUT) ANVIL
(BRICKLAYER'S —) SCOTCH SCUTCH
SCUTCHER
(LEADEN —) MADGE
(MINER'S —) BULLY
(PAVING —) REEL
(PNEUMATIC —) GUN BUSTER
(STEAM —) IMPACTER IMPACTOR
(TUNING —) KEY
HAMMERED BEATEN WROUGHT
HAMMERHEAD CORNUDA
HAMMERKOP UMBER UMBRETTE
HAMMERLOCK BAR ARMLOCK
HAMMERMAN STRIKER
HAMMOCK SACK HUMMOCK
(— CARRIED BY BEARERS) DANDY
(— SLUNG ON POLE) MACHILA
(WOODEN —) KATEL KARTEL
HAMPER BIN COT MAR PED TUB
BEAT BIND CLOG CURB FLAT HURT
LOAD SLOW TUCK BLOCK CRAMP
CRATE MAUND RUSKY SERON
BASKET BURDEN FETTER HALTER
HINDER HOBBLE HOPPLE IMPEDE
BUFFALO CONFINE HANAPER
MANACLE PANNIER PERPLEX
SHACKLE TRAMMEL ENCUMBER
ENTANGLE OBSTRUCT RESTRAIN
RESTRICT STRAITEN
HAMPERING STIFLING DIFFICULT
HAMSTER CRICETID
HAMSTRING HOX HOCK LAME
HOUGH ENERVATE
HANAPER HAMPER
HAND M CAT DAB FAM FIN HAN PAW
PUD CLAW DEAL DUKE GIVE GOLL
HALF JACK LOOF MAIN MANO MITT
PART PASS SPAN CAMAY CLAUT
CLEUK FLUSH GLAUM GRASP GRIPE
INDEX MANUS MAULY NIEVE POWER
SHARE STIFF STOCK BRIDGE
CLUNCH CLUTCH DADDLE DOUBLE
FAMBLE GOWPEN HANDLE MINNIE
STAGER WORKER CLAWKER
FAMELEN FLAPPER FLIPPER
POINTER WORKMAN GRAPPLER
MORTMAIN
(— COUNTING ZERO) BACCARA
BACCARAT
(— DOWN) DEVOLVE TRADUCE
BEQUEATH TRANSMIT

(— GESTURES) MUDRA
(— IN POKER) FULL SKIP BLAZE
FLUSH SKEET TIGER BICYCLE
JACKPOT SKIPPER IMMORTAL
STRAIGHT
(— IN WHIST) MORT TENACE
(— ON) BUCK
(— OVER) GIVE REACH BETEACH
BITECHE DELIVER
(— UP STRAW) SERVE
(— WITH 5 HIGHEST TRUMPS)
JAMBOREE
(BABY'S —) SPUD
(BIG AND UNGAINLY —) MAIG
(BRIDGE —) BID DUMMY DOUBLE
LAYDOWN
(CLENCHED —) FIST
(COLD —S) SHOWDOWN
(CURSIVE —) CIVILITE
(DECK —) HAWSEMAN
(DUMMY —) BOARD
(ELDEST —) EDGE SENIOR
(EXTRA — IN LOO) MISS
(FRENCH —) COULEE
(GRASPING —) CLAUT
(GREEN —) FARMER JACKEROO
(LEFT —) SINISTRA
(LONE —) JAMBONE
(PERSIAN —) SHIKASTA
(POKER —S) BOARD
(RANCH —) COWBOY
(REEL —) SPINDLER
(RIGHT —) DEXTER
(ROUND —) RONDE
(SECTION —) SNIPE
(SKILLFUL —) DAB
(SPARE — IN CARDS) CAT
JAMBOREE
(UNSKILLED —) DABSTER
(UPPER —) BULGE EMINENCE
(WEAK CARD —) BUST
HANDBAG BAG CABA NEIF CABAS
PURSE SATCHEL ENVELOPE
GRIPSACK POCHETTE RETICULE
HANDBALL PALM
HANDBARROW BIER HANDY TRUCK
BARROW
HANDBELL SKELLAT TANTONY
HANDBILL BILL FLIER FLYER LIBEL
DODGER
HANDBOOK VADY GRADUS MANUAL
BAEDEKER
HANDBOW STONEBOW
HANDCAR DRAG
HANDCART PRAM DANDY HURLY
TRUCK GOCART TROLLY TROLLEY
HANDCUFF CUFF STAY LINKER
NIPPER STAYER MANACLE TRAMMEL
WRISTER BRACELET HANDBOLT
HANDLOCK LIGAMENT SNITCHER
WRISTLET
(PL.) IRONS SNAPS DARBIES
NIPPERS
HANDER-IN INGIVER
HANDFUL M MAN GRIP LOCK WISP
YELM CLAUT GRIPE LITCH GOUPIN
GOWPEN HANTLE YAFFLE FISTFUL
MANIPLE
(— OF GRAIN) REAP SINGLE
SONGLE

(— OF LEAVES) PATRIN
(DOUBLE —) GOWPEN
(LAST — OF HARVEST) KIRN
HANDGRIP TUFFING
HANDGUN HAKE CALIVER HANDARM
HANDICAP START BURDEN DENIAL
HAMPER HINDER IMPEDE STRIKE
ENCUMBER PENALIZE
HANDICAPPED CRIMP CRIMPED
HANDICRAFT MYSTERY MECHANIC
HANDCRAFT
HANDICRAFTSMAN ARTISAN
HANDILY HANDY GAINLY
HANDINESS YARAGE
HANDIWORK MACHINE
HANDKERCHIEF WIPE CLOUT
FOGLE HANKY STOOK WIPER
HANKIE MADRAS NAPKIN SUDARY
TIGNON BANDANA BELCHER
FOULARD KERCHER MANIPLE
SNEEZER BANDANNA KERCHIEF
MOCKETER MONTEITH MOUCHOIR
SUDARIUM VERNACLE VERONICA
HANDLE BOW EAR FAN NIB NOB PAD
PIN PLY USE ANSA BAIL BALE BOOL
BUTT CROP FEEL FIST GAUM GRIP
HAFT HALE HAND HANK HILT KILP
KNOB LIFT RAPE RUNG STOP
GRASP GRIPE GROPE HELVE MOUNT
SHAFT SPOKE STAIL STALE START
STEAL STELE STOCK SWING TREAT
WIELD BECKET FETTLE FINGER
FUSEAU HANGER LIFTER MANAGE
MANURE POMMEL ROUNCE TILLER
CONDUCT DUDGEON WOOLDER
BEERPULL BELLPULL BITSTALK
BITSTOCK DISPENSE HANDGRIP
HANDHOLD HANDLING MOPSTICK
STAGHORN
(— AWKWARDLY) FUMBLE THUMBLE
(— BADLY) ILLGUIDE
(— CLUMSILY) PAW FUMBLE
(— IMPROPERLY) GAUM
(— MODISHLY) GALLANT
(— OF AXE) HELVE
(— OF BENCH PLANE) TOAT TOTE
(— OF DAGGER) DUDGEON
(— OF KETTLE) BAIL
(— OF LADLE) SHANK
(— OF OAR) GRASP
(— OF PLOW) HALE STAFF START
STILT PLOWTAIL
(— OF PRINTING PRESS) ROUNCE
(— OF RAKE) STALE
(— OF SCYTHE) TACK SNATH
SNEAD THOLE SNATHE SNEATH
(— OF SWORD) HAFT HILT
(— OF WHIP) CROP
(— RECKLESSLY) FOOL
(— ROUGHLY) MALL MAUL TOWSE
MUZZLE GRABBLE
(— VIOLENTLY) BOUNCE
(CRANK —) WINK
(CROSSBOW —) TILLER
(CURVED —) BOOL BOUL
(DETACHABLE —) KILP
(LIFTING — OF GUN) DOLPHIN
(PUMP —) BRAKE SWIPE
(ROPE —) SHACKLE

(WOODEN —) TREE
(PL.) HALES
HANDLED (EASILY —) BANTAM
HANDLER DOCKHAND
(AIRPLANE —) AIREDALE
HANDLING USE CONTROL
(SKILLFUL —) CONDUCT
(UNSKILLFUL —) BUNGLING
HANDMAID ANCILLA
HANDOUT DOWN
HANDRAIL BAR RAIL MANROPE
BANISTER EASEMENT MOPSTICK
TOADBACK
HANDSHAKE SHAKE SHRUG
HAND-SHAPED PALMATE
HANDSOME BRAW FAIR FINE PERT
TALL BONNY FETIS FITTY FUSOM
LUSTY ADONIC BRAWLY CLEVER
FARAND GOODLY HEPPEN LIKELY
PROPER SEEMLY ADONIAN AVENAN
ELEGANT FEATISH FEATOUS
FEWSOME GALLANT LIBERAL
SMICKER GOODLIKE STUNNING
VENEREAN WEELFARD
HANDSOMELY FAIRLY HANDSOME
HANDSTONE MANO
HAND STRAP TOGGEL TOGGLE
HANDSTROKE TALLY
HANDWORK TOOLING
HANDWRITING PAW FIST HAND
WRITE DUCTUS NIGGLE SCRIPT
SCRIVE BATARDE WRITING
BACKHAND HANDWRIT
HANDY DAB DEFT GAIN WEME
JEMMY LUSTY QUEME READY TIGH
CLEVER HEPPEN KNACKY
DEXTROUS EXPEDITE HANDSOME
SKILLFUL
HANDYMAN MOZO JUMPER
GREASER SWAMPER
HANG NUB TOP CRAP DRAG FALL
HANK KILT PEND TREE TUCK DRA
DROOP HOVER KETCH NOOSE
STRAP SWING TRINE TRUSS TWIS
ANHANG APPEND GIBBET GIBBET
HALTER IMPEND SLOUCH STRING
TALTER DOGGONE HANGING
LANTERN STRETCH SUSPEND
(— ABOUT) DRING HOVER
(— AROUND) KNOCK HANKER
SLINGE
(— BACK) LAG BOGGLE
(— BEHIND) PLOD
(— CRIMINAL) STRAP TOTTER
(— DOWN) DIP LOP LAVE DROOP
DEPEND FESTOON PROPEND
(— HEAVILY) SWAG
(— LOOSELY) BAG SAG FLAG FLO
LOLL BANGLE DANGLE PAGGLE
(— ONE'S HEAD) SLINK
(— OUT) LILL
(— OVER) WAUVE IMPEND WHAU
(— PICTURE NEAR CEILING) SKY
(— SOGGILY) TROLLOP
(— WITH TAPESTRY) TAPIS
HANGAR DOCK GARAGE AIRDOCK
HANGER PASSIVE SHABBLE
WHINYARD
(— FOR CARCASSES) STANG

(COAT —) SHOULDER
(CRANK —) BRACKET
(LACE-MAKING —) WORKER
(SWORD —) CARRIAGE
HANGER-ON BUR BURR SPIV LEECH
TOADY HANGBY HEELER LACKEY
LACQUEY PENDING PARASITE
HANGING FLAG HEMP TURN ARRAS
BAGGY DRAPE SWING CELURE
DORSEL DOSSER DERRICK DRAPERY
PENDENT PENSILE ANTEPORT
HANGMENT
(— LOOSE) LOPPY BAGGED
(— LOW) SIDE
(— THREATENINGLY) IMMINENT
(LIMPLY —) FLAGGY SLIMPSY
(WALL —) CEILING TENTURE
(PL.) TAPIT TAPPET DRAPERY
PARAMENT
HANGMAN KETCH HANGER HANGIE
TOPMAN DERRICK GREGORY
TOPSMAN VERDUGO CARNIFEX
SCRAGGER
(HALTER OF —) TOW
HANGMAN'S DAY FRIDAY
HANGNAIL AGNAIL
HANGOUT JOINT SCATTER
HANGOVER HOLDOVER RESIDUUM
HANK HASP SKEIN BOBBIN
SELVAGEE
(— OF FLAX) HEAD
(— OF TWINE) RAN
(— OF YARN) SLIP
HANKER HANK LONG LINGER
HANKERING ITCH HANKER
HANKUL ENMUN ONMUN
HANSOM CAB SHOFUL SHOWFUL
HANUMAN ENTELLUS
HAP REDE CHANCE FORTUNE
HAPPING
HAPHAZARD CASUAL CHANCE
CHANCY RANDOM BUCKEYE
SCRATCH CARELESS SCRAMBLY
SLAPDASH
HAPHAZARDLY ANYHOW
HAPLESS POOR UNLUCKY
HAPLY HAPS HAPPILY
HAPPEN BE DO GO HAP COME COOK
FALL FARE GIVE LUCK PASS TIDE
TIME BREAK EVENE EVENT LIGHT
OCCUR SHAPE ARRIVE BECOME
BEFALL BETIDE CHANCE TUMBLE
FORTUNE STUMBLE SUCCEED
BECHANCE OVERCOME
(— TOGETHER) CONCUR
HAPPENING HAP FACT EVENT THING
CHANCE TIDING TIMING INCIDENT
OCCASION
(ACTUAL —) FACT
(UNEXPECTED —) ACCIDENT
HAPPILY FAIN FITLY GLADLY
JOYOUSLY
HAPPINESS JOY WIN GLEE SELE
SONS WEAL BLISS GLORY MIRTH
SOOTH FELICE WEALTH DELIGHT
ECSTASY FELICIA RAPTURE UTILITY
FELICITY GLADNESS HILARITY
HAPPY FIT COSH FAIN GLAD GLEG
SELI WELY BONNY FAUST FELIX

LIGHT LUCKY MERRY PROUD SEELY
SONSY SUNNY WHITE BONNIE
JOYFUL COMICAL GLEEFUL
HALCYON JOCULAR PERFECT
SEELFUL WEALFUL WEIRDLY
BLISSFUL CAREFREE DISPOSED
FROHLICH GRACIOUS SUNSHINE
HARA-KIRI SEPPUKU
HARANGUE ORATE CONCIO PATTER
SERMON SPEECH ADDRESS
DECLAIM EARBASH DIATRIBE
PERORATE
HARASS FAG GIG HAG HOX MAG
NAG RAG TAW VEX BAIT CARK
FRAB FRET GALL GNAW HAKE HALE
HARE HAZE HOCK JADE PAIL RIDE
SEEK TIRE TOIL TOSS WORK ANNOY
BESET BULLY CHAFE CHASE CHEVY
CHIVY CURSE FLISK GRIND GRIPE
HARRY HURRY TARGE TEASE
WEARY WORRY BADGER BOTHER
CHOUSE CUMBER FERRET HATTER
HECKLE HECTOR HESPEL HOORAY
HURRAH INFEST MOLEST MURDER
OBSESS PESTER PLAGUE POTHER
PURSUE AFFLICT AGITATE BEDEVIL
DRAGOON HAGRIDE HARRAGE
OPPRESS PERPLEX PROVOKE
TERRIFY TORMENT TRAVAIL
TROUBLE TURMOIL BULLYRAG
DISTRACT DISTRESS EXERCISE
FORHAILE IRRITATE SPURGALL
SUPPRESS
(— MENTALLY) GRUDGE
HARASSED BESTEAD HARRIED
HAUNTED
(— BY) BEFORE
HARASSING WARM
HARBINGER ANGEL USHER HERALD
FORAGER FORAYER FURRIER
PRODROME
(— OF SUMMER) SWALLOW
HARBOR REE BEAR DOCK HOLD
PIER PORT BASIN BAYOU CHUCK
CREEK HAVEN HITHE SLADE
BREACH BUNDER COTHON FOSTER
OUTPORT PORTLET SEAPORT
SHELTER CARENAGE ENHARBOR
SHIPRADE
(— A CRIMINAL) RESET
HARBOR SEAL DOTANT DOTARD
RANGER SEALCH TANGFISH
HARD DRY FIT ILL COLD DEAR DOUR
DURE FAST FIRM IRON MEAN NASH
OPEN CHAMP CLOSE CORKY HARSH
HORNY ROCKY SMART SNELL SOLID
SOUND STERN STONY STOOR
STOUT TIGHT BOARDY BRAWNY
COARSE FLINTY GLASSY KITTLE
KNOBBY KNOTTY ROBUST RUGGED
SEVERE STARKY STINGY STRICT
STRONG UNEATH UNNETH ARDUOUS
AUSTERE CALLOUS HARDWAY
ONEROUS SUBDURE CORNEOUS
DILIGENT HARDBACK HARDENED
IRONHARD OBDURATE PETROSAL
RIGOROUS SCLEROID SCLEROSE
TOILSOME
(— BY) FORBY FORTHBY

(— TO BEAR) FIERCE
(— TO MANAGE) SALTY
(— TO PLEASE) FINICKY CONCEITY
(— TO REACH) CUMBROUS
(— TO READ) BLIND
(— TO SATISFY) EXIGENT EXIGEANT
(— TO SELL) STICKY
(— TO UNDERSTAND) DIFFUSE
HARD-BILL SEEDEATER
HARD-BITTEN GNARLED
HARDEN SET TAW BAKE BEEK CAKE
FIRM HARN KERN SEAR BRAZE
ENURE FLESH INURE STEEL STONE
ENDURE FREEZE OBDURE POTASH
SEASON TEMPER CALCIFY
EMBRAWN STIFFEN THICKEN
CONCRETE ENHARDEN INDURATE
SOLIDIFY
(— QUILL) DUTCH
(CASE —) STEEL
HARDENED DRAW HARD LOST
SALTED CALLOUS CRUSTED
FIBROUS INDURATE OBDURATE
HARDENING SET POROMA
SCLEROMA
HARDHACK SPIREA IRONBUSH
WHITECAP
HARDHEAD LION BOCHE
HARDHEARTED STERN STONY
OBDURATE
HARDIHOOD PLUCK COURAGE
AUDACITY
HARDLY ILL SCANT BARELY RARELY
SCARCE UNEATH SCARCELY
HARDNESS SEG GRAIN PROOF
RIGOR STEEL DURESS DURITY
ADAMANT HARDSHIP SEVERITY
SOLIDITY
(— OF CHARACTER) HEART
HARD-OF-HEARING DULL DUNCH
DEAFISH
HARDPAN PAN CLAYPAN MOORPAN
ORSTEIN MOORBAND ORDSTEIN
HARDSHIP HARD GRIEF RIGOR
STOUR THRONG UNWEAL SQUEEZE
ASPERITY HARDNESS
(PL.) EXTREMES
HARDTACK PANTILE
(— AND MOLASSES) BURGOO
HARDWARE TRIM IRONWARE
HARDWOOD HARD BREAKAX
LEAFWOOD
HARDWORKING EIDENT
HARDY DOUR HARD WIRY LUSTY
MANLY STOUR STOUT TOUGH
GARDEN INURED RUGGED STURDY
SPARTAN STUBBED GAILLARD
GALLIARD STUBBORN
HARE PUG WAT BAWD CONY PUSS
SCUT BAWTY CUTTY LEPUS PUSSY
MALKIN MAUKIN BELGIAN LEPORID
VENISON KLIPHAAS LEPORINE
(— IN FIRST YEAR) LEVERET
(— TRACK) PRICK
(FEMALE —) DOE
(GREAT —) MANABOZHO
(LITTLE CHIEF —) CONY PIKA
(MALE —) BUCK
(SIBERIAN —) TOLAI
(PL.) FLICK

HAREBELL THIMBLE BLAEWORT
BLUEBELL
HAREBRAINED GIDDY WINDY
HARELIP LAGOSTOMA
HAREM SERAI ZENANA ANDERUN
HAREMLIK SERAGLIO
HARE'S-EAR MODESTY
HARIJAN PANCHAMA
HARL WHIRL
HARLEQUIN DUCK SQUEALER
(FEMALE —) LADY
(MALE —) LORD
HARLOT PUG DRAB SLUT HIREN
PAGAN QUEAN RAHAB STRAP
TWEAK WHORE RIBALD TOMBOY
DELILAH MERMAID WAGTAIL
MERETRIX MISWOMAN STRUMPET
HARLOTRY PUTAGE BITCHERY
HARM NEY NOY NYE WEM ARME
BALE BANE DERE HURT SORE TEEN
WERD GRAME HERME LOATH
QUALM SHEND SPOIL TOUCH
WATHE WEMMY WOUGH WOUND
WRAKE WREAK WRONG DAMAGE
DAMNUM DANGER GRIEVE INJURE
INJURY SCATHE SORROW WONDER
DESPITE DISEASE FORFEIT IMPEACH
TROUBLE UNQUERT BUSINESS
DISAVAIL DISSERVE ENDAMAGE
MISCHIEF NOCUMENT NUISANCE
(— REPUTATION) DEFAME
(DO —) ENVY
HARMFUL BAD EVIL HARM NASTY
NOXAL NOCENT NOCIVE NOYFUL
UNSELY BANEFUL HURTFUL
NOISOME NOXIOUS DAMAGING
INIMICAL SINISTER
HARMFULNESS VICE MALICE
HARMLESS SAFE SELI TAME SEELY
WHITE DOVISH FEARLESS HURTLESS
INNOCENT SACKLESS UNHARMED
HARMONIA (DAUGHTER OF —) INO
AGAVE SEMELE AUTONOE
(FATHER OF —) MARS
(HUSBAND OF —) CADMUS
(MOTHER OF —) VENUS
(SON OF —) POLYDORUS
HARMONICA HARP SYRINX AEOLINE
PANPIPE ARMONICA ZAMPOGNA
HARMONIOUS HAPPY SWEET
COSMIC SILKEN UNITED MUSICAL
SPHERAL TUNEFUL BALANCED
CHARMING HARMONIC PEACEFUL
HARMONITE RAPPIST RAPPITE
HARMONIUM ORGAN VOCALION
HARMONIZE GO FIT GEE KEY JIBE
SORT TUNE AGREE ATONE BLEND
CHORD GROUP HITCH ACCORD
ASSORT COTTON COMPORT
CONCENT CONCORD CONSORT
ORDINATE
HARMONIZING HENOTIC
HARMONY SUIT TUNE CHIME CHORD
UNITY ACCORD ATTUNE COSMOS
HEAVEN MELODY UNISON BALANCE
CONCERT CONCORD CONSENT
CONSORT KEEPING RAPPORT
DIAPASON SYMPATHY SYMPHONY
HARNESS TUG GEAR HAME LEAF

REIN BRACE CROWN DRAFT FRONT
GEARS SLING TRACE COLLAR
FETTLE GULLET INSPAN TACKLE
DRAUGHT GEARING GIGTREE
LORMERY SIMBLOT TOGGERY
DRAWGEAR ENCLOSER HEADGEAR
TACKLING TURNBACK
(— FOR LOOM) LEAF HEALD
MOUNTING
(DECORATIVE —) CAPARISON
(WEAVING —) HEADLE HEDDLE
HARNESSED ANTELOPE GUIB
GUIBA BOSCHBOK BUSHBUCK
HARNESS MAKER KNACKER
WHITTAW
HAROLD I HAREFOOT
HARP ARPA FORK VINA NABLA
NANGA HARPER SABECA CHROTTA
DECHORD SAMBUKE AUTOHARP
CLARSACH
(CELTIC —) TELYN
(FINNISH —) KANTELA KANTELE
(ICELANDIC —) LANGSPIL
(JAPANESE —) KOTO
(JEW'S —) TRUMP
(PERSIAN —) SANG
(TRIANGULAR —) TRIGON TRIGONON
HARPOON IRON FIZGIG GRAINS
FISHGIG PARPAGO STRIKER
HARPAGON
HARPOONED FAST
HARPOONER STRIKER
HARP SEAL HARP BEATER SADDLER
HARPSICHORD SPINET CEMBALO
CLAVIER CLAVECIN HASPICOL
HARPY HAG AELLO CELAENO
OCYPETE PODARGE
HARQUEBUS HAGBUT CALIVER
HACKBUT ARQUEBUS
HARQUEBUSIER CARABIN
HARRIER HAWK KAHU FALLER
MILLER PUTTOCK HARROWER
HARROW COG CHIP DISC DISK DRAG
HARO TINE BRAKE BREAK HERSE
DREDGE DRUDGE FALLOW LADDER
SPADER CUTAWAY LACERATE
OXHARROW
HARROWED HAGGARD
HARROWING TINE TINING TEARING
HARRY HAG BRACE CHIVEY CHIVVY
FERRET HARASS CRUCIFY
HARSH ILL ACID BULL DOUR FOUL
HARD HASH HASK IRON RUDE SOUR
ACERB ACRID ASPER BRUTE CRONK
CRUDE GRILL GRUFF HEAVY HUSKY
RASPY ROUND RUVID SHARP SNELL
STARK STERN STIFF STOUR STOUT
BRUTAL COARSE FLINTY GRAVEL
GRISLY HOARSE RAGGED RASPED
RUGGED SEVERE SHREWD STURDY
SULLEN TETRIC UNKIND UNRIDE
AUSTERE RASPING RAUCOUS
SQUAWKY ACERBATE ASPERATE
ASPEROUS CATONIAN CLASHING
DRACONIC GRAVELLY GRINDING
GUTTURAL JANGLING OBDURATE
RIGOROUS SCABROUS SCRANNEL
STRIDENT STROUNGE STUBBORN
TETRICAL UNGENTLE UNKINDLY

(— OF VOICE) STEER
HARSHLY HARD HARSH SHORTLY
HARSHNESS WOLF RIGOR DURESS
CATOISM CRUDITY CRUELTY
DUREZZA ACERBITY ASPERITY
FELLNESS HARDNESS HASKNESS
SEVERITY
HART SPADE VENISON
HARTEBEEST ASSE TORA TORI
BUBAL CAAMA KAAMA KONZE
LECAMA BUBALIS CONGONI
KONGONI
HART'S-TONGUE LONGLEAF
HARUSPEX ARUSPEX ARUSPICE
EXTISPEX
HARVEST IN WIN CROP HEAP RABI
REAP SLED SNAP FOISON GATHER
HAIRST RUBBEE COMBINE GRABBLE
INGATHER SHEARING
HARVEST FISH WHITING MOONFISH
STARFISH
HARVEST HOME KIRN MELL
HOCKEY HORKEY
HARVESTING SLEDDING
HARVESTMAN CARTER CARTARE
HAS S AS HATH
(— NOT) NAS AINT
HAS-BEEN WUZZER
HASH RAPE MINCE HACHIS
HASHISH HEMP ASSIS
HASID ASSIDEAN
HASKALAH (FOLLOWER OF —)
MASKIL
HASP COP HAPS COPSE SPRENT
HASSAR DORAD
HASSOCK TUT BOSS PESS TOIT
TRUSH BUFFET TUFFET
HASTE HIE POST RACE RAGE RAPE
CHASE FEVER HASTY HURRY SPEED
BUSTLE FLURRY SWIVET DISPATCH
RAPIDITY STROTHER
(HEADLONG —) SPURN
(IN —) HOTFOOT
(IN GREAT —) AMAIN
HASTEN HIE RAP RUN BUSK DUST
FIRK PELL PLAT POST RACE RAPE
RUSH SPUR URGE CATCH CHASE
DRIVE FLEET HASTE HURRY PRESS
PREST SLATE SPEED STEER EXPEDE
SCURRY STREAK SWITHE ADVANCE
FORWARD HACKNEY HOTFOOT
PREVENT QUICKEN SLITHER
SWIFTEN WITHHIE DISPATCH
EXPEDITE
(— AWAY) FLEE SHERRY SQUIRR
HASTILY HOTLY RAPELY RASHLY
FOOTHOT HOTFOOT HYINGLY
HEADLONG
HASTY FAST RAPE RASH FLEET
QUICK FLYING RAPELY CURSORY
HOTHEAD HURRIED TEARING
HASTEFUL HEADLONG SUBITANE
(TACTLESSLY —) BRASH
HAT DIP FEZ LID NAB ATTE BAKU
COIF DISC DISK FELT FLAT HIVE
HOOD KNAB MOAB SLOP TILE TOPI
BEANY BENJY BENNY BERET BOXER
CADDI CORDY DERBY DICER GIBUS
JERRY KELLY MILAN MITER MITRE

SHELL TARAI TOPEE TOQUE TRUSH
ABACOT BEANIE BEAVER BOATER
BOWLER BRETON BUMPER CASQUE
CLAQUE CLOCHE COCKUP COIFFE
FEDORA HELMET PANAMA PILEUS
RAFFIA SAILOR SHAVEL SLOUCH
TOPPER TURBAN VIGONE BANDEAU
BANGKOK BRIMMER BYCOKET
CATSKIN CAUBEEN CHAPEAU
FANTAIL HATTING HATTOCK
HOMBURG LEGHORN PETASOS
PILLBOX PLATEAU PLATTER
SALACOT SCRAPER SHALLOW
SKIMMER SMASHER BONGRACE
CAPELINE GOSSAMER HEADGEAR
JIPIJAPA MONTABYN MUSHROOM
NABCHEAT RAMILIES REHOBOAM
ROUNDLET SOMBRERO
(— BLOCKER) ROPER
(3-CORNERED —) TRICORN
(BEAVER —) CASTOR
(CLERGYMAN'S —) SHOVEL
(COCKED —) BICORNE RAMILIE
SCRAPER
(COWBOY —) STETSON
(FABRIC —) TOQUE
(FELT —) DERBY JERRY TARAI
TERAI ALPINE BOWLER TRILBY
(HIGH —) KYL TILE TOPPER
(IRON —) GOSSAN GOZZAN
(MILITARY —) BUSBY BEARSKIN
(OILSKIN —) SQUAM
(OPERA —) GIBUS CLAQUE
(PITH —) TOPI TOPEE
(SILK —) KYL BEAVER SHINER
CATSKIN
(STIFF —) TILE DERBY KELLY
BOATER BOWLER SAILOR
(STOVEPIPE —) CAROLINE
(STRAW —) BAKU FLAT HOOD KADY
KATY BENJY BENNY CADDY STRAW
BOATER PANAMA LEGHORN
(TOP —) PLUG TOPPER
(UNBLOCKED —) CONE
(WIDE-BRIMMED —) FLAT BENJY
TARAI SUNDOWN
HATBAND BAND WEED WEEPER
HAT BRIM LEAF TARFE TURNUP
HATCH HECK BROOD CLECK CLOCK
COVEY GUICHET UNSHELL
DISCLOSE INCUBATE
HATCHERY CHICKERY
HATCHET MOGO HACHE GWEEON
THIXIE FRANCISC TOMAHAWK
HATCHING CLETCH BREEDING
ECLISION
HATCHWAY HATCH SCUTTLE
HATE FIRE TEEN ABHOR SPITE
DETEST HATRED LOATHE UNLOVE
DESPITE
HATEFUL FOUL LOTH BLACK CURST
DIRTY HATEL LOATH CURSED
ODIOUS HEINOUS HIDEOUS
FLAGRANT
HATER ULYSSES
HATH MOOLUM
HAT MONEY TAMPANG
HATRED DOSA ENVY HATE HELL

ONDE HAINE ODIUM SPITE ENMITY
RANCOR AVERSION
(— OF CHILDREN) MISOPEDIA
(— OF MARRIAGE) MISOGAMY
(— OF MEN) MISANDRY
(— OF NEW IDEAS) MISCAINEA
(— OF WOMEN) MISOGYNY
HATTER GADGER HURRER
HAUBERK BYRNIE
HAUGHTILY BIGLY
HAUGHTINESS AIR PRIDE HEIGHT
MORGUE ORGUIL HAUTEUR
STOMACH HAUTESSE
HAUGHTY DAIN HIGH RANK STAY
DIGNE DORTY HUFFY LOFTY LUSTY
POTTY PROUD STOUT SURLY TAUNT
FEISTY FIERCE HAUGHT QUAINT
DISTANT HAUTAIN HONTISH
PAUGHTY STATELY SUBLIME
ARROGANT CAVALIER DEIGNOUS
FASTUOUS GLORIOUS IMPERIAL
INSOLENT ORGULOUS PRIDEFUL
SCORNFUL SNIFFISH SUPERIOR
TOPLOFTY
HAUL KEP LUG RUG TEW TOW TUG
DRAG DRAW DRAY HALE HURL
JUNK PULL SKID TAKE TOTE TRAM
BOUSE DRAVE HEAVE LIGHT ROUSE
SNAKE TRACT TRAVOY DRAUGHT
SCHLEPP CORDELLE HANDBANK
(— AFT) TALLY
(— DOWN) STRIKE
(— IN) GATHER
(— LOGS) TODE SLOOP SWAMP
SIWASH HANDBANK
(— OF FISH) TACK DRAVE
(— OF NET) LIFT
(— SAIL) BUNT CLEW CLUE
(— SHIP) SPRING
(— TO DECK) BOARD
(— UP AND FASTEN) TRICE
(— WITH TACKLE) BOUSE
HAULAGE DOOK
HAULAGEWAY GANGWAY
HAULING HALE CARTAGE
HAUNCH HIP HOOK HUCK HANCE
HUCKLE
(PL.) GRUG HUNKERS
HAUNT DEN HANT HOME HOWF KEEP
NEST WALK GHOST HOWFF SPOOK
STALK INFEST OBSESS OUTLAY
REPAIR PURLIEU FREQUENT
PRACTICE
(— OF ANIMALS) LIE HOME
(FAMILIAR —) SLAIT
HAUNTED SPOOKY
HAUNTING SPOOKY BESETTING
HAUSTELLATE GLOSSATE
HAUSTORIUM SINK SINKER SUCKER
HAUTBOY OBOE WAIT
HAUTEUR HEIGHT
HAVE A AN OF OWN HOLD BOAST
ENJOY OUGHT WIELD POSSESS
HAVEN HOPE PIER PORT HITHE
HARBOR HAVENET
HAVOC HOB HELL WASTE RAVAGE
HAW HOI HECK SLOE WIND WYND
BOOTS PEGGLE ALISIER

HAWAII

BAY: POHUE HALAWA KIHOLO
MAMALA KAMOHIO KANEOHE
WAIAGUA KAWAIHAE MAUNALUA
BEACH: WAIKIKI
CAPITAL: HONOLULU
CHANNEL: AUA KAIWI KALOHI
PAILOLO
COUNTY: MAUI KAUAI HAWAII
HONOLULU
CRATER: KILAUEA
DESERT: KAU
DISTRICT: KONA PUNA
FISH: ULUA AKULE MOANO
HARBOR: PEARL
HEAD: DIAMOND
ISLAND: MAUI OAHU KAUAI KAULA
LANAI NIIHAU MOLOKAI
MOUNTAIN: KAALA KOHALA
KAMAKOU MAUNAKEA
LANAIHALE
MOUNTAIN RANGE: KOHALA
KOOLAU WAIANAE
NATIVE: KANAKA
STATE BIRD: GOOSE
STATE FLOWER: HIBISCUS
STATE NICKNAME: ALOHA
STATE TREE: CANDLENUT
TOWN: EWA AIEA HANA HILO LAIE
PAIA KAPAA LIHUE MAILI KAILUA
KEKAHA KAHULUI KANEOHE
WAHIAWA WAIANAE WAILUKU
HONOLULU
TREE: KOA NAIO WILIWILI
VALLEY: MANOA
VOLCANO: MAUNALOA

HAWAIIAN KANAKA KAMAAINA
HAWFINCH KATE GROSBEAK
HAWK IO EYAS KITE ALLAN BATER
BUTEO CADGE EYESS HOICK HOUGH
REACH RIVER STOOP BAWREL
FALCON FOOTER HIGGLE MERLIN
MUSKET OSPREY PALLET PEDDLE
RAMAGE RAPTOR RIFLER SHIKRA
VERMIN BUZZARD GOSHAWK
HAGGARD HARRIER HERONER
LENTNER SWOOPER BRANCHER
CARACARA HARROWER LENTINER
PASSAGER ROUGHLEG SPARHAWK
TALENTER TARTARET
(— FIGHT) CRAB
(CROP OF —) GORGE
(FEMALE —) FORMAL FORMEL
(MALE —) JACK TASSEL TERCEL
(YOUNG —) EYAS NIAS BRANCHER
HAWKER CRIER CRYER BADGER
CADGER COSTER DUFFER JOWTER
PEDDER PETHER CAMELOT
CHAPMAN HIGGLER MERCURY
PEDDLER CRATEMAN GLASSMAN
HUCKSTER
HAWKEYE STATE IOWA
HAWKING FALCONRY
HAWK PARROT NIA
HAWKWEED DINDLE BUGLOSS
FIREWEED
HAWSE BAG JACKASS

HAWSER FAST WARP HEADLINE
HAWTHORN HAW MAY QUICK
THORN AIGLET MAYBUSH
COCKSPUR MAYBLOOM MAYTHORN
QUICKSET
(FRUIT OF —) HAZEL PEGGLE
HAY HEI RIP MATH RAKH RISP
FETTLE STOVER WINDLIN
SWEEPAGE
(— CUT FINE) CHAFF
(— PUT IN BARN) END
(BUNDLE OF —) TRUSS
(PILE OF —) TUMBLE
(ROW OF —) WINDROW
(SECOND-GROWTH —) EDDISH
(SMALL LOAD OF —) HURRY
(SMALL PIECE OF —) TATE
HAYCOCK MOW COIL HOVEL QUILE
SHOCK DOODLE HIPPLE LAPCOCK
HAYSHOCK
HAYFIELD PARK RAKH MOWING
HAYFORK PIKE PICKEL
HAYLOFT LOFT TALLET SCAFFOLD
HAYMAKER PICKMAN
HAYMOW GOAF HAYLOFT OVERDEN
OVERHEAD
HAYRACK HECK HAYRIG THRIPPLE
HAYSTACK COB PIKE RICK HOVEL
HAYRICK STACKAGE
HAYSUCK EYSOGE
HAY SWEEP BUCK
HAYWARD MEADSMAN
HAZAN CANTOR CHAZZAN
HAZARD DIE LAY LOT JUMP PAWN
RISK WAGE JENNY LOSER PERIL
CHANCE DANGER BALANCE IMPERIL
VENTURE ENDANGER JEOPARDY
HAZARDOUS RISKY CHANCY
QUEASY RISQUE UNSAFE UNSURE
PERILOUS
HAZARDOUSLY CHANCILY
HAZE FOG URE FILM GLIN MIST REEK
SMOG TRUB DEVIL GAUZE HAZLE
SMEETH
HAZEL AGLET AIGLET COBNUT
MUFFIN FILBERT HAZELNUT
NOISETTE
(— FOR THATCHING) SPRAYS
HAZEL HOE PULASKI
HAZELNUT NIT HAZEL FILBERT
HAZEL TREE AVELLANO
HAZILY DIMLY
HAZINESS HAZE GRAYOUT
HAZY DIM FOGGY MISTY SMOKY
THICK VAGUE CLOUDY DREAMY
OBSCURE SMUISTY NEBULOUS
HE A E HI HO HEH HEY HIM HYE SHE
ILLE THON CESTUI
(— DIED) OB
(— GAVE AND DEDICATED) DDD
(— MADE) F FEC
(— PAINTED IT) PNXT
(— READS) LEG
(— WAS NOT FOUND) NEI
HEAD BIT BUT COP DON FAT MIR
NAB NOB PEN POW TOP BEAN BOSS
CAPE COCO CONK COSP CROP
DATU DEAN DOME HELM JOLE JOWL
KAID KNOB LEAD MASK NOLL PASH

PATE POLL RAIS TURN YEAD ALDER
ATTIC BLADE BLOCK CHIEF CHUMP
CROWN DATTO MAZER ONION RISER
SCALP SHODE SKULL START TIBBY
TROPE BELFRY BLANCH CABEZA
CENTER CHAULE COBBRA COCKER
DAROGA EXARCH GARRET GATHER
HEADER KAISER MAHANT MAZARD
NAPPER NODDLE PALLET RUBRIC
SCONCE CAPITAL CAPTAIN
COCONUT COSTARD COSTREL
COXCOMB CRUMPET CUPHEAD
GENARCH HEADING HEGUMEN
NUCLEUS PRELATE TOPKNOT
CALABASH CEPHALON DECURION
DIRECTOR DUFFADAR FOUNTAIN
HEADLINE INITIATE PHYLARCH
POINTING TOPPIECE
(— IN PARTICULAR DIRECTION)
STEM
(— OF 10 MONKS) DEAN
(— OF ABBEY) ABBOT
(— OF ALEMBIC) MITER MITRE
(— OF BEAR, WOLF OR BOAR) HURE
(— OF CABBAGE) LOAF
(— OF CEREAL) EAR
(— OF CHAIR) MAKER
(— OF CLOVER) COB SUCKER
(— OF COMET) COMA
(— OF CONVENT) ABBESS
SUPERIOR
(— OF DRILL BRACE) CUSHION
(— OF FAMILY) ALDER GOODMAN
(— OF FISH) JOWL
(— OF GANG) TINDAL
(— OF GOVERNMENT) MUKHTAR
(— OF GRAIN) ICKER
(— OF HAIR) SUIT CRINE FLEECE
(— OF HARPOON) BOMB
(— OF HERRING) COB
(— OF JEWISH ACADEMY) GAON
(— OF LANCE) MORNE MOURNE
(— OF LOOM) JACQUARD
(— OF MONASTERY) HEGUMEN
(— OF MUSICAL INSTRUMENT)
SCROLL
(— OF NUNNERY) DAME
(— OF ORDER) MURSHID
(— OF RING) CHATON
(— OF RIVET) BULLHEAD FLATHEAD
SNAPHEAD
(— OF STATE) PRINCEPS
(— OF TAPEWORM) SCOLEX
(— OF TREE) COMA
(— ON) SQUARE
(— PREMATURELY) BUTTON
(— USED AS TARGET) SARACEN
(BAKED SHEEP'S —) JAMES JEMMY
(BALD —) PILGARLIC
(BARBED —) FLUKE
(DRAGON'S —) RAHU
(FLOWER —) DAISY ARNICA BUTTON
PINBALL
(FLOWER —S) CURD ANTHEMIS
(NAIL —) ROSEHEAD
(POPPY —) POST
(PRINTED —) BOXHEAD
(SEED — OF FLAX) HOPPE

(SHRUNKEN —) TSANTSA
(PL.) GEONIM
HEADACHE HEAD SODA BUSTHEAD
HEADWARK MIGRAINE
HEADBAND MITER MITRE VITTA
CARCAN DIADEM TAENIA CIRCLET
GARLAND CARCANET FOOTBAND
STEPHANE
HEADBOROUGH VERGES
HEADCAP SETHEAD
HEADDRESS FLY TOP TOY APEX
COIF FRET HEAD HORN PARE POUF
TETE TIRE TOUR AEGIS AMPYX
CROWN GABLE LAUTU PASTE
POLOS PSHEM SHAKO TIARA
TOWER VITTA ALMUCE ATTIRE
ATTOUR BONNET CASQUE CORNET
FAILLE HENNIN KENNEL KULLAH
MOBCAP PINNER TIRING TUINGA
BANDORE COMMODE FLANDAN
MORTIER PSCHENT STEEPLE
TABLITA THERESE TRESSON
TUTULUS BILIMENT BINNOGUE
BYCOCKET CAPRIOLE COIFFURE
HEADGEAR HEADTIRE KAFFIYEH
MASKETTE STEPHANE TRESSURE
(— OF DOGES) TOQUE
(— WITH LONG LAPPET) PINNER
(HIGH —) TOWER STEEPLE
(WIDOW'S —) BANDORE
HEADED KNOTTED
(— OUT) RIZZOMED
HEADER BINDER NOBBER SADDLE
KNOBBER HEADSMAN STRETMAN
HEADFAST HEADROPE
HEADFIRST HEADLONG
HEADFOREMOST TOPSAIL
HEADFRAME POPPET GALLOWS
HEADGEAR (ALSO SEE HEADDRESS)
HIVE PASTE BONNET BRIDLE
HEADWEAR
HEADHUNTER LAKHER TAIYAL
ATAIYAL QUIANGAN
HEADING END HEAD STOW PILOT
TROPE WICKET CAPTION DIPHEAD
HEADILY STENTON WITCHET
FOREHAND STENTING
HEADLAND KOP PEN RAS BILL HEA
MULL NAZE NESS NOOK PEAK
SCAW THRUM FORELAND
HEADLINE HEAD LABEL BANNER
CAPTION DROPLINE SCREAMER
STREAMER
HEADLONG FULL RANK HASTY
PRONE STEEP SUDDEN RAMSTAM
TANTIVY GADARENE HEADLING
RECKLESS
HEADMAN JARL CHIEF DATTO MALI
PATEL POMBO VIDAN ATAMAN
CABEZA HETMAN INDUNA LOWDAH
LULUAI POTAIL TOPMAN KOMARCH
ALDERMAN CABOCEER CAPITANO
HEADSMAN KONOHIKI MALGUZAR
MOKADDAM PENGHULU PRINCEPS
STAROSTA TENIENTE
HEADMASTER HEAD REGENT
HEADMOST FOREMOST
HEADNOTE SYLLABUS
HEADPIECE CAP POT BASKET

ASQUE HELMET PALLET TESTER
REMOR CASQUET CHAMFRON
ESTIERE
ADPIN KINGPIN
ADQUARTERS DEPOT YAMEN
GENCY FONDACO EXCHANGE
ATTALION
ADROPE BALK BAULK HEADLINE
ADSET PHONES
ADSHIP CHIEFTY
SPIRITUAL —) KHALIFAT
ADSPACE OUTAGE
ADSTALL HALTER BRADOON
RIDOON JAQUIMA
ADSTOCK POPPET
ADSTRONG RASH COBBY
ACKLE STOCKY UNRULY HOTSPUR
AMSTAM VIOLENT WAYWARD
ADWAITER CAPTAIN
ADWAY WAY DENT SEAWAY
AYGATE HEADROOM
ADWORD ENTRY
ADY BOLD NAPPY HUFFCAP
AL CURE HALE MEND SAIN AMEND
OVER LEECH SALVE SOUND
HOLE PHYSIC RECURE SUPPLE
EMPER WARISH CLEANSE GUARISH
ECOVER REDRESS RESTORE
EDICATE
— OVER) INCARN
ALD CAMB DUPE HAVEL
ALER CURER ALTHEA SHAMAN
OWWOWER
ALING IATRIC POWWOW
ALSAMIC CURATION IATRICAL
ANATION
ALTH SAP HAIL HEAL SONS
UART SALEW LIKING PLEDGE
ALUTE SANITY EUCRASY SLAINTE
UCRASIA TONICITY VALETUDE
OOD —) PLIGHT VERDURE
LL —) SICKNESS
ORMAL —) USUAL
ALTHFUL HEALTHY HYGIENIC
ALUTARY SALUTARY SANITARY
ALTHY FIT FIER FIRM HALE IRON
AFE SANE TIDY WELL BONNY
ODDY QUART SOUND STOUT VALID
NTIRE HEARTY ROBUST BOUNCING
AUDABLE SALUTARY SANITARY
EGETOUS VIGOROUS
AP COP CUB HOT MOW PIE SOW
ON BALE BING BULK DECK DESS
LL HOTT LEET PILE POKE POOK
EEK RUCK SESS TASS TUMP
MASS CLAMP CLUMP COUCH
ROWD SHOCK STACK WOPSE
URROW HIPPLE HOTTER ISLAND
EILER OODLES QUARRY RICKLE
UCKLE SCRAPE SORITE TOORIE
DUROCK CUMULUS ENDORSE
AYCOCK HAYRICK HURROCK
DOROCK TUMMELS WINDROW
ASURALE
— HAY) UNCOCK
— OF DEAD BODIES) CARNAGE
— OF GAME) QUARRY
— OF ORE) PANEL
— OF PRODUCE) BURY CLAMP

(— OF REFUSE) BURROW BASURAL
(— OF RUBBISH) GAGING
(— OF SILVER ORE) TORTA
(— OF STONES) AHU MAN CAIRN
SCRAE SCREE HURROCK MONTJOY
(— OF VEGETABLES) HOG
(— REPROACHES) KICK
(— TOGETHER) AGGEST HOWDER
LUMBER CUMULATE
(— UP) HILL SACK AGGEST
ACERVATE AGGERATE OVERHEAP
(COMBUSTIBLE —) PYRE
(MANURE —) HOTT MIXEN
(PROMISCUOUS —) RAFF
HEAR EAR LIST OYES OYEZ LEARN
LITHE HARKEN LISTEN HEARKEN
(— DIRECTLY) IMPINGE
HEARD AUDIBLE
(EASILY —) CLEAR
HEARER AUDIENT AUDITOR
HEARING EAR LIST OYER AUDIT
SOUND ASSIZE AUDIENCE AUDITION
HEARKEN HARK HEAR HEED LIST
TEND LITHE ATTEND HARKEN
INTEND
HEARSAY REPORT ACCOUNT
HEARSE HACK CATAFALCO
HEART AB COR CORE GIST HATI
RAAN SOUL YOLK BOSOM BOWEL
CHEER QUICK BREAST CENTER
CENTRE DEPTHS HASLET MIDDLE
TICKER VISCUS COURAGE EMOTION
ESSENCE FEELING
(— OF DIXIE) ALABAMA
(DEAR —) DILIS
HEARTACHE SORROW
HEARTBEAT STROKE
HEARTBURN PYROSIS
HEART CHERRY GASKINS
HEARTEN BIELD CHEER HEART
SPIRIT EMBOLDEN INSPIRIT
HEARTFELT DEAR DEEP REAL TRUE
INFELT INWARD CORDIAL GENUINE
SINCERE
HEARTH EARD SOLE TEST ASTRE
CUPEL EARTH FOCUS FOGON
FOYER SMOKE CHIMNEY
(— GODDESS) VESTA
HEARTILY INLY AGOOD DEARLY
FREELY WARMLY SHEERLY
DINGDONG INWARDLY STRONGLY
HEARTINESS GOODWILL
HEARTTHROB DUNT
HEARTWOOD HEART SAPAN SPINE
GUAYAB BUBINGA DURAMEN
TRUEWOOD
HEARTY REAL WARM COBBY FRECK
HEAVY STOUT DEVOUT ENTIRE
ROBUST STANCH BOBBISH CORDIAL
EARNEST HEALTHY RAFFING
SINCERE HEARTFUL VIGOROUS
HEAT HET HOT RUT SUN TAP BOIL
FIRE GLOW SALT WARM ARDOR
BROIL CALOR CAUMA CHAFE FEVER
PRIDE PROUD STECH TEPOR TRIAL
ACHAFE ANNEAL DEGREE DIGEST
FERVOR HEATEN IGNITE SCORCH
SEASON SPARGE WARMTH CALCINE
CALORIC ENCHAFE FERMENT

FLUSTER INCENSE INFERNO
PASSION SWELTER UPERIZE
CALIDITY
(— GENTLY) SOAK
(— OF BATTLE) PRESS
(— SCRAP IRON) BUSHEL
(— SWEETEN, AND SPICE) MULL
(— TOBACCO) SAP
(SCORCHING —) EWDER
HEATED WARM FIERCE STEAMY
HEATER FIRE COCKLE SMOKER
CHAFFER CHOFFER LATROBE
HEATH BENT YETH BESOM BRIAR
BRIER ERICA ERICAD COMMONS
HEATHER
HEATHEN AKKUM PAGAN ETHNIC
GENTILE PROFANE SARACEN
GENTILIC
HEATHENISM ODINISM OTHINISM
PAGANISM
HEATHER BENT GRIG LING BROOM
ERICA HEATH HADDER
HEATHERY LINGY
HEATH PEA CARMELE
HEATING BAKEOUT BURNING
HEATLESS ATHERMIC
HEAVE GAG BUNG HEFT HOVE KECK
LIFE QUAP FETCH HOIST SCEND
SURGE BUCKLE KECKLE POPPLE
ESTUATE
HEAVEN SKY HIGH ABOVE BLISS
DYAUS ETHER GLORY CANAAN
HIMMEL SVARGE SWARGA URANUS
WELKIN KINGDOM OLYMPUS
DEVALOKA EMPYREAL EMPYREAN
PARADISE SVARLOKA
(12TH PART OF —) HOUSE
(PL.) ARCH LIFT LANGI HEIGHT
REGION SPHERE ELEMENT TENGERE
EMPYREAN KAMALOKA
HEAVENLY ABOVE DIVINE ANGELIC
URANIAN ETHEREAL OLYMPIAN
HEAVENWARD ZIONWARD
HEAVER COALY DANNER HEFTER
HEAVILY SOSS CLOIT CLYTE HEAVY
SADLY SOUSE SWACK
HEAVINESS HEFT GLOOM POISE
WEIGHT GRAVITY
HEAVY FAT HOT SAD CLIT DEEP
DULL HARD BEEFY BURLY DENSE
DOWFF DUNCH GRAVE GREAT
GROSS HEFTY HOGGY STIFF THARF
THERF WROTH CHARGE CLUMSY
DOUGHY DRAGGY HEARTY LEADEN
LIVERY LOGGER SODDEN STODGY
STRONG STUPID INSIPID LABORED
LIVERED LUMPING MASSIVE
ONEROUS WEIGHTY CUMBROUS
GRIEVOUS PERSANTE PREGNANT
THUMPING
HEAVY-FOOTED SOGGY LEADEN
INFICETE
HEBDOMADARY WEEKLY
HEBE (FATHER OF —) JUPITER
(HUSBAND OF —) HERCULES
(MOTHER OF —) JUNO
HEBREW RABBINIC
HECATE TRIVIA
(FATHER OF —) PERSES

(MOTHER OF —) ASTERIA
HECKLE BAIT GIBE HACK BADGER
HARASS HECTOR HATCHEL
HECTIC ETIK SEPTIC HECTIVE
FEVERISH FRENETIC FRENZIED
HECTOLITER VAT
(5.82 —S) LEAGUER
HECTOR BAIT HUFF BULLY HARRY
WORRY HARASS HECKLE BLUSTER
BRAVADO BROWBEAT
(FATHER OF —) PRIAM
(MOTHER OF —) HECUBA
(WIFE OF —) ANDROMACHE
HECUBA (DAUGHTER OF —)
POLYXENA
(FATHER OF —) DYMAS CISSEUS
(SON OF —) PARIS HECTOR
POLYDORUS
HEDDLE CAMB DOUP HAVEL HEALD
(PL.) CAAM
HEDGE BAR HAW HAY HYE OXER
SAVE BEARD EDDER FENCE FRITH
FUDGE HOVER MOUND QUICK
COPPER FRIGHT RADDLE ENCLOSE
QUICKSET RUFFMANS SEPIMENT
SURROUND THICKSET
HEDGE BINDWEED CREEPER
HELLWEED WOODBINE
HEDGEHOG ORCHEN URCHIN
ECHINUS ERICIUS YLESPIL
HEDGEPIG HERISSON
HEDGE LAUREL TARATA
HEDGE MUSTARD BANKWEED
FLUXWEED
HEDGE NETTLE STACHYS
HEDGE PARSLEY HOGWEED
HEDGE-PRIEST PATRICO
HEDGE SPARROW DICKY DONEY
DICKEY EYSOGE PHILIP CHANTER
DUNNOCK HAYSUCK PINNOCK
TITLING ACCENTOR
HEDGEWOOD LAYER
HEED CARK COME CURE GAUM HEAR
KEEP LOOK MIND NOTE RECK TEND
TENT VISE WARE YEME AWAIT
TASTE VALUE ATTEND INTENT
NOTICE REGARD REMARK REWARD
CAUTION OBSERVE RESPECT
SUSPECT THOUGHT
HEEDFUL WARE ATTENT DILIGENT
HEEDLESS RASH BLIND DIZZY GIDDY
BLITHE REMISS UNWARY LANGUID
UNHEEDY CARELESS LISTLESS
MINDLESS RECKLESS WISTLESS
HEEDLESSLY BLIND HEADLONG
HEEL TIP BUTT CALX FROG HIELD
SPIKE TALON DOTTLE INCLINE
BOOTHEEL
(— IN) SHOUGH
(— OF GATE) HARR
(— OF HORSESHOE) SPONGE
(— OF SWORD BLADE) TALON
RICASSO
(— OVER) SEEL TILT CAREEN
HEEL BEVEL RAND
HEEL PLATE SHOD CLEAT
HEFT WEIGHT
HEFTY HEAVY
HEIFER IO QUI QUEE QUEY QUOY

BULLER STOCKER
(— IN 2ND YEAR) STIRK
(YEARLING —) BURLING
HEIGH-HO HECH
HEIGHT SUM ACME ALTO APEX FELL
HIGH LOFT MOTE PINK TUNE CREST
HICHT STATE ALTURE INCHES
SUMMIT CEILING COMMAND
HEIGHTH STATURE SUPREME
ALTITUDE EMINENCE HAUTESSE
SIDENESS VERTICAL ACROPOLIS
(— OF FASHION) GO
(— OF PROSPERITY) GLORY
(— OF ROOM) STUD STUDDING
(— OF SAIL) HOIST
(GREATEST —) SUMMIT ZENITH
(ROCKY —) KNOT
HEIGHTEN ENDOW EXALT FORCE
RAISE ACCENT BOLSTER ENHANCE
SUBLIME
(— FLAVOR) PETUNE
HEINOUS SWART CRYING WICKED
SCARLET FLAGRANT GRIEVOUS
HEIR SCION SPRIG COHEIR HERITOR
APPARENT PARCENER
(— APPARENT) ATHELING ETHELING
(FEMALE —) DISTAFF
HEIRESS BEGUM PORTIA FORTUNE
HERITRIX
HEIRLOOM(PL.) CIMELIA
HELENUS (FATHER OF —) PRIAM
(MOTHER OF —) HECUBA
(SON OF —) CESTRINUS
(WIFE OF —) ANDROMACHE
HELIANTHEMUM SUNROSE
HELICAL SPIRAL
HELICOPTER COPTER CHOPPER
WINDMILL
HELIOPOLIS ON
HELIOS HYPERION PHAETHON
(FATHER OF —) HYPERION
(MOTHER OF —) THEIA
HELIOSIS SUNBURN
HELIOTROPE HELIO BENNET
SETWALL GIRASOLE TURNSOLE
HELIPORT SKYPORT
HELIX COIL SPIRAL
HELIXIN HEDERIN
HELL PIT POT HECK PAIN ABYSS
AVICI BLAZE DEUCE HADES SHEOL
BLAZES NARAKA TARTAR TOPHET
TUNKET ABADDON GEHENNA
HELLBOX INFERNO TARTARUS
BARATHRUM
HELLBENDER TWEEG
HELLE (FATHER OF —) ATHAMAS
(MOTHER OF —) NEPHELE
(SISTER OF —) PHRIXUS
HELLEBORE POKE BUGBANE
ITCHWEED LINGWORT LUNGWORT
NOSEWORT POKEROOT VERATRUM
EARTHGALL
HELLEN (FATHER OF —) DEUCALION
(MOTHER OF —) PYRRHA
(SON OF —) DORUS AEOLUS
XUTHUS
(WIFE OF —) ORSEIS
HELLER HALER HALERZ
HELLERI SWORDTAIL

HELLGRAMMITE DOBSON SIALID
CLIPPER CRAWLER SPRAWLER
HELLISH HELLY SATANIC STYGIAN
DEVILISH INFERNAL TOPHETIC
HELLO HALLO HILLO HULLO HILLOA
HELM KEY STEER STERN TIMON
HELMET TIMBER STEERAGE
HELMET CAP POT CASK HELM HOOD
ARMET CREST GALEA MAZER
MOUND BARBEL BEAVER CASQUE
CASTLE GALERA HEAUME MORION
PALLET SALADE SALLET TESTER
BASINET CASQUET GALERUM
GALERUS AVENTAIL BURGONET
HEADGEAR KNAPSCAP SCHAPSKA
SKULLCAP TARNHELM TESTIERE
(— PART) VENTAIL
(PITH —) TOPI TOPEE
HELMET-SHAPED GALEATE
HELMSMAN PILOT STEER GLAUCUS
TIMONEER
HELP AID BOT ABET BACK BOOT
CAST LIFT STOP AVAIL FAVOR
FRITH HEEZE RESET SPEED START
STEAD YELDE ASSIST HELPER
RELIEF REMEDY SECOND SUCCOR
UPTAKE BENEFIT BESTEAD CHEVISE
COMFORT FORWARD FURTHER
HELPING IMPROVE PRESIDY
PROMOTE REDRESS RELIEVE
SUPPORT SUSTAIN ADJUMENT
BEFRIEND SUFFRAGE
(— FORWARD) FRANK FURTHER
(— ON) ADVANCE
(— ONWARD) FORWARD
(— OUT) FIRK
(HIRED —) LABOR
HELPER AID CAD FOAL HELP MATE
PAGE ANSAR AIDANT BARBOY
COOKEE DIENER FLUNKY JUMPER
NIPPER TENTER WAITER ADJOINT
ADJUTOR ANCILLA CASHBOY
GALOPIN SUMPMAN SWAMPER
HELPMATE OFFSIDER SCULLION
TROUNCER
(— IN GLASSWORKS) SNAPPER
(BLACKSMITH'S —) STRIKER
(CHIMNEY SWEEP'S —) CHUMMY
(COOK'S —) SLUSHY
(COOPER'S —) TUBBIE
(HORSESHOER'S —) FLOORMAN
(PICKPOCKET'S —) BULKER
(YOUNG —) FOAL
HELPFUL GOOD AIDANT AIDFUL
HELPLY SECOND SPEEDY USEFUL
ADJUVANT HELPSOME OBLIGING
SINGULAR
HELPING HELP AIDANT PORTION
SERVING ADJUTORY ADJUVANT
HELPLESS NUMB SILLY ABJECT
UNABLE AIDLESS FORLORN
FECKLESS HAVELESS REDELESS
HELTER-SKELTER TAGRAG
PELLMELL
HELVE HELM SHAFT
HELVE HAMMER OLIVER
HEM HUM WLO FELL SLIP WELT
HEDGE SPLAY PURFLE TURNUP
HEMMING TURNING SURROUND

(— AND HAW) HAVER
(— GLOVE) WRIST
(— IN FISH) EBB
(— IN) BOX LAP BEBAY BESET
IMPALE BESIEGE COMPASS
ENCLOSE ENVIRON STRAITEN
SURROUND
(— OF SAIL) TABLING
(— OF TROUSERS) CUFF
HEMATITE ORE OLIGIST SANGUINE
HEMICRANIA MIGRAINE
HEMIEPES ENOPLION
HEMIMORPHITE CALAMINE
HEMIOLIC SESCUPLE
HEMISTICH SECTION
HEMLOCK BUNK CASH KELK
BENNET CICUTA COWBANE DEATHIN
SHINWOOD
HEMOPHILIAC BLEEDER
HEMORRHAGE STAXIS APOPLEXY
BLEEDING HEMOPTOE PETECHIA
HEMOSTATIC ERIGERON
HEMP IFE KEF KIF TOW BANG CARL
POOA RINE SUNN ABACA BHANG
DACHA DAGGA FIQUE GANJA HURDS
MURVA SABZI SISAL AMBARY
CABUYA FIMBLE LIAMBA NALITA
SINAWA AMYROOT CABULLA
GAGROOT NIYANDA PANGANE
PITEIRA SOSQUIL BIRDSEED
CANNABIS CHUCKING LOCOWEED
NECKWEED NEPENTHE
HEMP AGRIMONY EUPATORY
HEMPWEED
HEMPEN NOGGEN
HEMP NETTLE IRONWORT
HEMPWEED BONESET DUCKBLIND
HEN FOWL BIDDY CHUCK LAYER
BROODY MABYER PULLET HOVERER
PARTLET
(— THAT HAS NOT LAID) TOWDIE
(— WITH CHICKENS) CLUCK
(— WITH SHORT LEGS) GRIG
(1-YEAR-OLD —) YEAROCK
(BROODY —) SITTER
HENBANE HEBENON CHENILLE
HENCE AWAY ERGO HYNE THUS
AVAUNT HETHEN HEREOUT
HENCEFORTH YET HENCE
HENCHMAN FELLOW SATRAP
FOLLOWER
HEN COOP CAVY CAVIE
HENGEST (BROTHER OF —) HORSA
(KINDOM FOUNDED BY —) KENT
(SON OF —) AESC
HEN HARRIER FALLER KATABELLA
(IMMATURE —) RINGTAIL
(MALE —) MILLER
HENNA MENDY ALCANNA ALHENNA
CAMPHIRE
HENNIN STEEPLE
HENRY QUAD HAWKIN SECOHM
HEINRICH QUADRANT
HEP (NOT —) ICKY
HEPATICA AI TRINITY
HEPATITIS JAUNDICE
HEPHAESTUS LEMNIAN
(FATHER OF —) ZEUS
(MOTHER OF —) HERA
(WIFE OF —) CHARIS

HER A ARE SHE HARE HERS HURE
HERA JUNO
(FATHER OF —) KRONOS
(HUSBAND OF —) ZEUS
HERALD BODE USHER BEADLE
DECLARE FORERUN PREFACE
STENTOR BLAZONER PRECURSE
PROCLAIM ROTHESAY
HERALDIC FECIAL FETIAL
HERALDRY ARMORY
HERB ANU APE PIA RUE UDO WAD
ALOE ANET ANYU ARUM COUS DILL
HEMP IRID LEEK MINT MOLY POLY
RAPE SAGE SOLA WOAD WORT
YAMP YARB AWIWI BLITE BRUSH
CREAT CROUT DAGGA DAISY DRABA
GALAX GAURA GILIA GRASS HOSTA
LOASA LUFFA MEDIC MUNGO NANCY
SEDGE SOLAH STOCK SULLA THYME
ZIZIA ALLIUM ARALIA ARNICA
AXSEED BAGPOD BAMBAN BANANA
BLINKS BORAGE CANCER CATGUT
CATNIP CENIZO CICELY CISTUS
CLOVER COCASH COLEUS CONIUM
COWISH COWPEA ELODEA ENDIVE
ERYNGO FENNEL GALAXY GINGER
HARMEL HYSSOP KOCHIA KRIGIA
KRIGLA LOOFAH LOVAGE RAMTIL
RATTLE ROBERT SESAME SESELI
SHEVRI WASABI ABRONIA ALPINIA
ALTHAEA ALYSSUM AMORPHA
AMSONIA ANCHUSA ANEMONE
ANGELON ARACHIS BABIANA
BABROOT BARTSIA BIRDEYE
BLINKER BONESET BUGSEED
BUGWEED CHICORY CUDWEED
CULVERS DEWDROP DYEWEED
EPISCIA ERODIUM FREESIA FROGBIT
FUMMORY GERBERA GINSENG
GOITCHO GOSMORE GOUAREE
GUAYULE GUNNERA HARMALA
HEDEOMA HENBANE HERBLET
IRESINE ISOLOMA JONQUIL LABIATE
LEWISIA LINNAEA MARANTA
MIMULUS MUDWEED MUDWORT
MULLEIN MUSTARD NAILROD
NEMESIA NIEVETA PAVONIA PETUNIA
PINESAP PINWEED PUCHERA
ROSELLE SAFFLOR SALSIFY
SEEDBOX SKIRRET SOWBANE
SPIGNEL STACHYS ABELMUSK
ACANTHUS ACONITUM AGERATUM
ALOCASIA ALUMROOT AMBROSIA
AMMOBIUM ANGELICA ARGEMONE
ASPHODEL BEDSTRAW CALATHEA
CAPEWEED CARELESS CENTAURY
CHENILLE COLLOMIA COSTMARY
COWWHEAT CRASSULA CROMWELL
DANEWEED DEERWEED DROPWORT
ECHINOPS EGGPLANT EREMURUS
ERIGERON EUCHARIS FEVERFEW
FLEABANE FOWLFOOT GAYWINGS
GERARDIA GESNERAD GESNERIA
GHETCHOO GLOXINIA GOATROOT
GUZMANIA HAREBELL HEPATICA
HEUCHERA HIBISCUS HOLEWORT
HONEWORT HOROKAKA HUDSONIA
IRONWEED LICORICE LOCOWEED
MANDRAKE MANFREDA MANYROOT

MARJORAM MARTYNIA MURRNONG
PHACELIA PINKROOT PLUMBAGO
SACALINE SAINFOIN SALICORN
SAMPHIRE SANDBURR SCABIOUS
SHINLEAF SMALLAGE SNOWDROP
SOAPROOT SOAPWORT STAPELIA
SUNDROPS TETRIFOL TOCALOTE
WOODRUFF
(— COUNTERACTING POISON)
CANCER
(— OTHER THAN GRASS) FORB
(AROMATIC —) MINT ANISE CLARY
CATNIP CAAPEBA CHERVIL DITTANY
(BIENNIAL —) LEEK PARSLEY
ANGELICA
(BULBOUS —) LILY CANNA ALLIUM
CRINUM GARLIC NERINE SQUILL
BABIANA SHALLOT DOGTOOTH
SLANGKOP
(FABULOUS —) MOLY PANAX
PANACE
(FLOATING —) FROGBIT
(FORAGE —) FITCHES GOITCHO
(POISONOUS —) CONIUM HEMLOCK
(PL.) POTAGERIE
HERBAGE HAY BITE GRASS GRAZE
PICHI ADONIS SACATE ZACATE
GRAZING
HERB EVE IVA IVY
HERB GRACE RUE
HERBICIDE IPE
HERB IMPIOUS DOWNWEED
HOARWORT
HERB PARIS TRUE ONEBERRY
TRUELOVE
HERB ROBERT JENNY ROBIN
ROBERT
HERCULEAN HUGE
HERCULES ERCLES ALCIDES
HERSHEF OETAEUS OVILLUS
HERAKLES
(BROTHER OF —) IPHICLES
(FATHER OF —) JUPITER
(MOTHER OF —) ALCMENA
(WIFE OF —) HEBE MEGARA
DEIANIRA
HERCULES ALLHEAL OPOPANAX
HERCULES-CLUB ARALIA IVYWORT
RUEWORT SHOTBUSH
HERD BOW GAM MOB BAND CREW
GAME GANG HEAD RACE ROUT TAIL
TEAM TRIP DROVE FLOCK HEARD
TROOP CAVIYA CHOUSE HIRSEL
HUDDLE MANADA MEINIE REMUDA
SPREAD THRAVE CREAGHT
RANGALE SHEPHERD
(— CATTLE) TAIL WRANGLE
(— OF CATTLE) FLOTE
(— OF COLTS) RAG
(— OF HORSES) RACE HARAS
HARRAS
(— OF SEALS) PATCH
(— OF WHALES) GAM
(— OF WILD SWINE) SOUNDER
HERDBOY BOUCHAL
HERDER DROVER FEEDER HERDBOY
HERDSMAN AMOS SENN GAUCHO
HERDER LOOKER PASTOR HERDBOY
LLANERO THYRSIS VAQUERO

BEASTMAN DAMOETAS GARTHMAN
NEATHERD PASTORAL PASTURER
RANCHERO SWANHERD WRANGLER
HERE READY WHERE HEREAT HITHER
PRESENT
(**— AND THERE**) ABOUT ABROAD
AROUND PASSIM SPARSIM
HEREAFTER BEYOND
HEREDITAMENT LAND
HEREDITARY INBORN INNATE
KINDLY LINEAL
HEREIN WITHIN
HERESY KETZEREI MISBELIEF
HERETIC BUGGER KETZER ZINDIQ
LOLLARD PATARIN PROFANE
SECTARY JUDAIZER
HERETICAL HERETIC HETERODOX
MISCREANT
HERETO HITHER
HERETOFORE ERST BEFORE
ERENOW EREWHILE FORMERLY
HERITAGE HEIRDOM HEIRSHIP
HERMA MERCURY
HERMAPHRODITE MOPH SCRAT
HERMAPHRODITIC BISEXED
BISEXUAL
HERMAPHRODITISM GYNANDRY
HERMAPHRODITUS (FATHER OF —)
MERCURY
(**MOTHER OF —**) VENUS
HERMES MERCURY AGORAIOS
CYLLENIUS
(**FATHER OF —**) ZEUS
(**MOTHER OF —**) MAIA
HERMIONE (FATHER OF —)
MENELAUS
(**HUSBAND OF —**) PYRRHUS
(**MOTHER OF —**) HELEN
HERMIT ARME MUNI HANIF MINIM
ANCHOR SANTON SULLEN ASCETIC
EREMITE RECLUSE TAPASVI
ANCHORET MARABOUT SOLITARY
HERMITAGE ASHRAM ASHRAMA
RECLUSE
HERNIA BURST RAMEX BREACH
RUPTURE MEROCELE
HERO KIM RAB AJAX EGIL IDAS MAUI
NALA NATA OFFA RINK YIMA ADAPA
BERNE DEBON ETANA FAUST GHAZI
HODER HOTHR IRAYA KIPPS MARKO
ORSON TASSO TIMON VOTAN
EGMONT FIGARO GIDEON GOLIAS
HEROIC IASION IOLAUS MAUGIS
MINYAS OSSIAN PELHAM PENROD
RIENZI ROLAND RUSTAM SIGURD
TARZAN USHEEN VATHEK ALCESTE
BOGATYR DEMIGOD FAUSTUS
GLUSKAP INGOMAR JAMSHID
MACBETH MANRICO MARMION
MAZEPPA ORLANDO OTHELLO
PALADIN RAFFLES TANCRED
THALABA THESUES TROILUS
ULYSSES VOLPONE WERTHER
WIDSITH WIELAND ACADEMUS
ARGONAUT FANSHAWE FERUMBAS
FRITHJOF GAEDHEAL GILGAMES
LAMMIKIN MALAGIGI MORGANTE
OROONOKO PALMERIN PARSIFAL
PERICLES RASSELAS RODOMONT

SUPERMAN TRISTRAM WAVERLEY
(**LOVER OF —**) LEANDER
(**TRIBAL —**) JUDGE
HEROIC EPIC FELL GREAT NOBLE
EPICAL FEATLY EXTREME GALLANT
VALIANT FEARLESS HEROICAL
HOMERIAN INTREPID
HEROIN JUNK HORSE
HEROINE AIDA EMMA MIMI RUTH
JULIE MEDEA NORMA SEDNA THAIS
ESTHER FEDORA GUDRUN HELENA
JUDITH JULIET MARTHA MIGNON
PAMELA PHEDRE RAMONA ROMOLA
SALOME SILVIA TRILBY UNDINE
ERMINIA EVELINA GALATEA GINEVRA
GRAINNE HEROESS MONIMIA
SHIRLEY ZENOBIA ZULEIKA
ATALANTA ISABELLA MARGARET
PATIENCE POMPILIA ROSMUNDA
SOFRONIA
HEROISM VALOR BRAVERY
COURAGE
HERON QUA POKE SOCO CRAIG
CRANE EGRET FRANK HERNE
PADDY QUAWK YABOA AIGRET
KIALEE KOTUKU QUAKER SQUAWK
BITTERN CRABIER GOLIATH
HANDSAW QUABIRD SQUACCO
BOATBILL GAULDING HERONSEW
UMBRETTE
(**— FLOCK**) SIEGE
HERON'S-BILL ERODIUM
HERPES TETTER
HERPES ZOSTER ZONA SHINGLES
HERRING ALEC BRIT CHUB SILD
BLOAT CAPON CISCO DORAB HILSA
MARAY MATIE SPRAT KIPPER
TAILOR BLOATER CLUPEID NAILROD
ROLLMOP SHADINE BLUEBACK
BRISLING BUCKLING CROPSHIN
GRAYBACK QUODDIES SCUDDAWN
STRADINE
(**— SEASON**) DRAVE
(**— UNIT**) LAST MAZE
(**2, 3 OR 4 —S**) WARP
(**FEMALE —**) RAUN
(**LAKE —**) KIYI CISCO
(**RED —**) CAPON SOLDIER
(**SMOKED —**) BLOATER
(**YOUNG —**) COB BRIT SILE SILL
SOIL WILE COBBE MATIE SPRAT
SARDINE SPERLING
HERS HERN SHISN
HERSE (FATHER OF —) CECROPS
(**SISTER OF —**) AGLAUROS
(**SON OF —**) CEPHALUS
HERSELF HI HER SELF ITSELF
HERSHEF ARSAPHES
HESHVAN BUL CHESHVAN
HESIONE (FATHER OF —)
LAOMEDON
(**HUSBAND OF —**) TELAMON
(**RESCUER OF —**) HERCULES
HESITANCY HANG
HESITANT SHY CAGY CHARY
GROPING HALTING SUSPENSE
(**NOT —**) FACILE
HESITATE COY HEM STAY STOP
CHECK CRANE DEMUR DOUBT

FORCE PAUSE STAND STICK SUSSY
WAVER BOGGLE FALTER HANKER
LINGER MAMMER RELUCT SCOTCH
TARROW TARTLE BALANCE
PROFFER SCRUPLE STAGGER
STAMMER SWITHER THRIMBLE
(**— IN SPEAKING**) HACKER
HESITATING JUBUS HALTING
BACKWARD DOUBTFUL JUBEROUS
TIMOROSO
HESITATION HANG HINK WAND
PAUSE STAND STICK SUSSY
SWITHER
HESSIAN BURLAP
HESTIA (FATHER OF —) KRONOS
(**MOTHER OF —**) RHEA
HETAERA LAIS THAIS PHRYNE
MISTRESS
HETERODOX HERETIC SINISTRAL
HETERODOXY HERESY CACODOXY
HETEROGENEOUS MIXED MOTLEY
UNLIKE DIVERSE PIEBALD
ASSORTED
HETEROMYS SACCOMYS
HETEROTROPHIC HOLOZOIC
HETEROXENOUS INDIRECT
HETEROZYGOUS CROSS SPLIT
IMPURE
HETMAN ATAMAN
HEW CUT HAG CHIP SNAG STUB
SHRED SLICE
(**— OUT**) CARVE
(**— STONE**) CHAR
HEWER JOEY GETTER GIDEON
FACEMAN
HEX WITCH VOODOO WHAMMY
HEXAGON SEXANGLE
HEXAGONAL HEX DIMETRIC
HEXAGRAM PENTACLE
HEXAMETER MIURUS
(**DACTYLIC —**) EPOS HEROIC
HEXOBARBITAL EVIPAL
HEXOSAN MANNAN GLUCOSAN
MANNOSAN
HEYDAY MAY HIGHDAY
HEZEKIAH (FATHER OF —) AHAZ
HIATUS GAP BREAK CHASM BREACH
HIATAL LACUNA
HIBERNATE SHACK WINTER
SLUMBER
HIBERNATING LATITANT
HIBERNIA JUVERNA
HIBERNIAN IRISHMAN IVERNIAN
HICCUP YEX YOX HICK HOCKET
HOQUET SINGULTUS
HICK BOOR HIND JAKE BACON
BUSHMAN CORNBALL
HICKORY NOGAL PIGNUT BULLNUT
SHAGBARK
HICKORY NUT TRYMA PIGNUT
BULLNUT KISKITOM
HICKWALL ECCLE HECKLE HICKWAY
HIDDEN HID SHY DEEP DERN LOST
TECT BLIND DUSKY PERDU PRIVY
ARCANE BURIED COVERT INNATE
LATENT MASKED MYSTIC OCCULT
SECRET VEILED BOSOMED COVERED
CRYPTIC OBSCURE RECLUSE
SUBTILE ABDITIVE ABSTRUSE

CRYPTOUS HIDEAWAY PALLIATE
SCREENED SECLUDED SNEAKING
HIDE HOD WRY BUFF BURY CASE
CROP DARK DERN FELL FELT HILL
HOOD JOUK LEAN MASK PELL PELT
SCAB SKIN SKUG SNUG STOW VEIL
WELL BELIE BELLY BLIND CACHE
CLOAK CLOUD COUCH COVER
DITCH EARTH FLANK GLOSS LAYNE
LOSHE MANSE PLANT SHADE SPOIL
STASH STEER TAPIS BURROW
BUSHEL CASATE EMBOSS ENCAVE
ENWOMB FOREST HUDDLE IMBOSK
MANENT PELAGE SCREEN SHADOW
SHIELD SHROUD CONCEAL COWHIDE
EMBOWEL OBCLUDE OVERLAY
SECLUDE SECRETE SPREADY
CARUCATE DISGUISE ENSCONCE
HIDELAND HOODWINK PALLIATE
PLOWLAND SQUIRREL SUPPRESS
(— AS AN EEL) MUD
(— IN WOODS) WOOD BUSHWACK
(— UNDER) BUSHEL
(CALF'S —) DEACON
(DRESSED —S) LEATHER
(HALF OF —) BEND
(HAVING SOFT —) MELLOW
(SHEEP'S —) SLAT
(TANNED —) CROP
(THICKEST —S) BACKS
(UNDRESSED —) KIP
(PL.) KIP JUFTI JUFTS
HIDE-AND-GO-SEEK BOGLE WHOOP
BOGGLE
HIDEAWAY MEW LAIR
HIDEBOUND BORNE NARROW
BIGOTED
HIDEOUS FELL GRIM UGLY AWFUL
TOADY DEFORM GRIMLY GRISLY
HORRID ODIOUS OGRISH GHASTLY
DEFORMED DREADFUL FIENDISH
GRUESOME HORRIBLE SHOCKING
TERRIBLE
HIDEOUSLY FOULLY
HIDING MICHING SECRECY ABDITIVE
HIDEAWAY
HIEMAL WINTRY
HIERACIUM DINALE HAWKWEED
HIERARCHY SATRAPY
HIEROGLYPH CIPHER
(PL.) SIGNARY
HIGGLE HUCK HAGGLE
HIGH UP ALT AIRY DEAR HAUT MAIN
MUCH TALL ACUTE ALOFT BRENT
CHIEF CLOSE FIRST GREAT LOFTY
MERRY NOBLE SHARP STEEP
COSTLY SHRILL EMINENT EXALTED
HAUGHTY SUBLIME TOPPING
VIOLENT ELEVATED FOREMOST
PIERCING TOWERING
(— AND MIGHTY) HOGEN
(— IN CHROMA) STRONG
(— IN PITCH) ALT ACUTE
(— IN RANK) MUCH
(— PITCH) ORTHIAN
(MOST —) SERENE
(PRETTY —) STIFFISH
(VERY —) TAUNT
HIGHBORN NOBLE GENEROUS

HIGHBOY TALLBOY
HIGHBRED SOFT REFINED
HIGHBROW EGGHEAD
HIGH-CLASS CLASSY UPSTAGE
HIGH-CLIMBER TOPPER
HIGH-COLORED BLOWSY BLOWZY
HIGHER ABOVE SENIOR SUPERIOR
HIGHEST TOP HEXT FIRST EXTREME
MAXIMAL SUPREME BUNEMOST
HIGHMOST OVERMOST
(— IN DEGREE) LAST
HIGHFALUTIN PAUGHTY
HIGH-FED BEANY
HIGH-FLAVORED GAMY
HIGH-FLOWN TALL TUMID
HIGH-HANDED CAVALIER
HIGHLAND RAND CERRO
HIGHLANDER GAEL TARTAN
NAINSEL PLAIDMAN REDSHANK
TREWSMAN UPLANDER
(PL.) TREWS TARTAN
HIGHLIGHT ADORN HEIGHTEN
SALIENCE
HIGHLY THRICE
HIGH-MINDED HAUGHT
HIGHNESS ALTESSE ALTEZZA
ALTITUDE
(— OF PRICE) DEARTH
HIGH-PITCHED PROUD PIPING
TREBLE SHRIEKY
HIGH-POWERED MAGNUM
HIGH-PRICED DEAR
HIGH-RIGGER TOPPER
HIGH-SOUNDING BIG BOMBAST
MAGNIFIC SONORANT SONOROUS
SOUNDING
HIGH-SPIRITED CRANK FIERY
FIERCE LIVELY GALLANT GINGERY
RAMPANT CAVALIER VASCULAR
HIGH-SPIRITEDNESS SPLEEN
HIGH-STRUNG TENSE NERVOUS
HIGH-TONED TONY DICTY DICKTY
HIGHWAY VIA WAY BELT ITER PATH
PIKE ROAD TOBY BOLOS ARTERY
CAUSEY COURSE RUMPAD SKYWAY
STREET BELTWAY CALZADA
FREEWAY RAMPIRE ARTERIAL
BROADWAY CAUSEWAY CHAUSSEE
HIGHROAD SPEEDWAY
(— ROBBERY) TOBY
(LOCATED OFF THE —) DEVIOUS
HIGHWAYMAN PAD RIDER SCAMP
CUTTER PADDER RODMAN FOOTPAD
LADRONE PRANCER RODSMAN
TOBYMAN BIDSTAND DAMASTES
HIGHTOBY HIJACKER LANCEMAN
OUTRIDER
HIGH-WROUGHT INTENSE
HIKE MUSH MARCH TRAMP RAMBLE
HILARIOUS MAD JOVIAL JOCULAR
CHIRPING GLORIOUS
HILARITY GIG JOY GLEE LAUGH
MIRTH GAIETY GAYETY DEVILRY
JOLLITY WHOOPEE
HILL BEN DEN HOE HOW KOP LOW
PUY VAN ALTO BANK BERG BRAE
BULT BUMP COTE DAGH DENE
DOWN DRUM FELL HIGH HONE KNAP
LOMA LUMP MESA MOOR MOTE

NOUP PAHA TOFT ZION BARGH
BUTTE CERRO CLIFF COAST HEUGH
KNOCK KNOLL KOPJE MORRO
MOUND MOUNT STILL SWELL TELLE
WATCH ASCENT BARROW BEACON
COBBLE COLLIS COPPLE CUESTA
HEIGHT HEUVEL LOMITA SPRUNT
STRONE CAELIAN CAPITOL COLLINE
DRUMLIN HILLOCK NUNATAK
PICACHO SOWBACK VIMINAL
AREOPAGY CATOCTIN DRUMLOID
FOOTHILL MONTICLE QUIRINAL
(— OF SAND) DENE DUNE
(— OF STRATIFIED DRIFT) KAME
(— UP) MOLD
(BROAD-TOPPED —) LOMA
(CONICAL —) LAW
(CRAGGY —) TOR
(FORTIFIED —) RATH
(HIGH —) BEN
(ISOLATED —) HUM TOFT BARGH
BUTTE
(LAST —) STRONE
(LOW —) HOW BAND WOLD
SOWBACK
(NIPPLELIKE —) PAP
(NORTH AFRICAN —) JEBEL DJEBEL
(RESIDUAL —) CATOCTIN
(ROUNDED —) DODD HONE
(SHARP-POINTED —) KIP KIPP
(SMALL —) KNAP KNOLL KOPJE
KOPPIE HILLOCK MOLEHILL
(STEEP —) BREW BROW STILL
(STONY —) ROACH
(SUGAR-LOAF —) SPITZKOP
(WOODED —) HOLT HURST
HILLOCK HOW LOW NOB BOSS BULT
DOWN KAME KNOB TERP TUMP
BERRY HEAVE HURST KNOCK
KNOLL KOPJE MOUND TOMAN
BURROW COPPET HILLET HUMMOCK
TUMMOCK TUMULUS MOLEHILL
HILLSIDE BENT BRAE COTE EDGE
CLEVE FALDA SLADE FELLSIDE
SIDEHILL
HILLTOP PIKE KNOLL
HILLY KNOBBY
HILT HAFT POIGNET HANDGRIP
(— OF DAGGER) DUDGEON
(PART OF —) LANGUET
HILUM EYE HILUS PORTA NUCLEUS
CICATRIX
HIM A EN HE HEM HIN MUN
HIMATION PALLION PALLIUM
HIMSELF HIM IPSE SELF HISSEL
ITSELF HERSELF HISSELF
HIND ROE CONY HINE HINT CONEY
HEARST HINDER VENISON CABRILLA
HINDER BAR DAM KEP LET MAR ROB
CLOG HELP SLOW SLUG STAY STOP
TENT WARN AFTER BLOCK CHEAT
CHECK CHOKE CRAMP DEBAR
DELAY DETER EMBAR ESTOP HEDGE
SLOTH THROW TRASH ARREST
CUMBER DETAIN FORBID FORLET
HAMPER HARASS HINNER IMPEDE
IMPEND INJURE RETARD SCOTCH
TAIGLE UNHELP ABSTAIN DEPRIVE
FORELAY IMPEACH INHIBIT PREVENT

TRACHLE ENCUMBER HANDICAP
IMPEDITE OBSTRUCT PRECLUDE
PROHIBIT
HINDERED FOUL
HINDERER LETTER
HINDERMOST LAG ACHTER
HINDQUARTER HIND HAUNCH
(HALF —) LEG
(PL.) FOUCH CRUPPER HAUNCHES
HINDRANCE BAR LET RUB BALK
CURB REIN SLUG STAY STOP
BLOCK CHECK DELAY HITCH TRASH
ARREST CUMBER DENIAL HINDER
OBJECT UNHELP UNSPEED
DISCOUNT DRAWBACK HOLDBACK
OBSTACLE PULLBACK
HINDU BABU BABOO SUDRA BABHAN
GENTOO JAJMAN KALWAR KHATRI
NAYADI SHUDRA THAKUR VAISYA
MUSAHAR VAIRAGI
(— ASCETIC) SADHU
(— ASSOCIATION) SANGH
(— CASTE) TELI VARNA
(— CUSTOM) SATI SUTTEE
(— ENERGY) SAKTI SHAKTI
(— IDOL) SWAMI
(— INTERJECTION) OM AUM
(— PHILOSOPHY) VEDANTA
(— PRACTICE) PURDAH
(— RITE) PUJA POOJA
(— SAGE) RSI RISHI
(— VARNA MEMBER) SUDRA
(— WORSHIPER) SAKTA
(— WRITINGS) SMRTI TANTRA
(TWICE-BORN —) KSATRIYA
HINDUSTANI URDU HINDI OORDOO
DAKHINI
HINGE RUN BAND BUTT FLAP HARR
TRIM TURN CARDO CROOK GEMEL
JOINT MOUNT NODUS SKELL SKEWL
TWIST DEPEND GARNET GEMMEL
GIMMER HANGLE JIMMER SNIBEL
CHARNEL COXCOMB FULCRUM
HOLDBACK
(— OF BIVALVE SHELL) CARDO
(— OF HELMET) CHARNEL
(— TOGETHER) SCISSOR
(HALF OF —) FLAP
(PHILATELIC —) STICKER
HINGED SWING
HINNY BURDON FUNNEL JENNET
HINT CUE ASTE ITEM MINT WINK
CHEEP IMPLY INFER POINT SPELL
STEER TOUCH TRACE WHIFF
ALLUDE GLANCE OFFICE SMATCH
WHEEZE INKLING LEADING
MEMENTO SUGGEST UMBRAGE
WHISPER WRINKLE ALLUSION
INDICATE INNUENDO INTIMATE
TELLTALE
HINTERLAND BLED BACKLAND
HIP HEP COXA HUCK PITCH SHOOP
HAUNCH HUCKLE HIPBERRY
(— JOINT) THURL
(— OF ROSE) BERRY CHOOP SHOOP
(— OF TARGET) SPOT
HIPBONE FINBONE EDGEBONE
SIDEBONE
HIPPEUS KNIGHT

HIPPOCAMPUS ERGOT HIPPO
HIPPOCOON (BROTHER OF —)
TYNDAREUS
(FATHER OF —) OEBALUS
(MOTHER OF —) GORGOPHONE
(SLAYER OF —) HERCULES
HIPPODAMIA (FATHER OF —)
ADRASTUS OENOMAUS
(HUSBAND OF —) PELOPS
PEIRITHOUS
(SON OF —) ATREUS TROEZEN
PITTHEUS THYESTES
HIPPOLYTUS (FATHER OF —)
THESEUS
(MOTHER OF —) HIPPOLYTE
(STEPMOTHER OF —) PHAEDRA
HIPPONACTEAN SCAZON
HIPPOPOTAMUS HIPPO ZEEKOE
BEHEMOTH BUNODONT
HIPPOTRAGUS OZANNA EGOCERUS
HIRE FEE JOB HAVE MEED RENT
SIGN WAGE PREST WAGES EMPLOY
ENGAGE RETAIN SALARY BESPEAK
CHARTER CONDUCE CONDUCT
FREIGHT STIPEND
(— CATTLE) TACK
HIRED PAID TEEKA TICCA WAGED
HIRELING HACK VENAL HACKNEY
MYRMIDON WAGELING MERCENARY
HIRSUTE HAIRY SHAGGY
HIS S AS ES IS HISN
HISPID STRIGOSE STRIGOUS
HISS BLOW FUFF HISH HIZZ QUIZ
SISS SIZZ GOOSE WHISS FISSLE
FIZZLE SIFFLE WHOOSH WHISTLE
SIBILATE
(— OF SWORD) SOUGH
HISSING BIRD SIBILANT
HISTONE GLOBIN
HISTORIAN MORONI STORIER
ANNALIST
HISTORICAL GENETIC
HISTORIOGRAPHER SCALD SKALD
HISTORY STORY ANNALS LEGEND
SURVEY ACCOUNT ANCESTRY
PROPHECY RELATION
(— OF EXPERIENCES) MEMOIRS
(— OF JAPAN) KOJIKI
(LIFE —) COURSE
HISTRIONIC ACTORY ACTORISH
ACTRESSY
HIT BAT BOP BOX DOT GET HAT JOB
PEG PIP WOW BASH BEAN BEAT
BELT BLOW BOFF BUST CHOP CONK
DONG FOUR GOLD NAIL PINK PUCK
PUNT RUFF SLAM SOCK SWAT SWIP
TAKE TANK TUNK WART WIPE
ANGLE CHECK CLOUT CLUNK
CROWN FIVER FLICK GOUFF KNOCK
POTCH PRANG PUNTA PUNTO
SCORE SLASH SLOSH SMITE SNICK
SWIPE TAINT TOUCH VENUE ATTAIN
DOUBLE FOURER HURTLE SCLAFF
STRIKE VOLLEY ATTAINT BOFFOLA
CONNECT MUZZLER SANDBAG
WHERRET BLUDGEON BOUNDARY
LENGTHER STRICKEN
(— A KEY) STRIKE
(— BALL) CUR FLY DINK DRIVE

SHOOL SNICK
(— BUNT) DRAG
(— GAME) STOP
(— GENTLY) BABY
(— GOLF BALL) CAN BLAST
EXPLODE
(— HARD) DUMP SLOG SLUG SOUSE
STOUSH STONKER
(— IN BOXING) LEADOFF
(— IN FIELD HOCKEY) CORNER
(— IN TILTING) TAINT
(— IT OFF) CLICK
(— LIGHTLY) KISS
(— ON BULL'S-EYE) GOLD
(— POORLY) DUB
(— TOGETHER) CLASH
(— UPON) FIND
(— WITH FOOT) KICK SPURN
(BASE —) BINGLE DOUBLE SAFETY
SINGLE TRIPLE SCRATCH SMOTHER
(CRICKET —) SLOG BOUNDARY
(EASILY —) SITTING
(FENCING —) HAI HAY
(SHARP —) LICK
(SMASH —) SOCKEROO
HITCH JET TUG HALT HIKE ITCH
KNOT PULL CATCH HOTCH SPELL
TRACE HIRSLE INSPAN MAGNUS
(NOSE —) BOZAL
HITCHHIKE HOP THUMB
HITCHING KNOT SHRUG
HITHER HERE
HITHERTO YET BEFORE
HIT-OR-MISS CASUAL CHANCE
HOBNOB CARELESS
HITTER SWATTER
HITTING BATTING SLOGGING
HITTITE HATTI KHATTI TABALIAN
HIVE GUM BIKE SKEP PYCHE STAND
STATE STOCK SWARM APIARY
ALVEARY BEEHIVE SWARMER
(— PLACED OVER ANOTHER) SUPER
HLORRITHI THOR THORR
HOAR GRAY RIME HOARY
HOARD HEAM POSE SAVE AMASS
HUTCH MISER STOCK COFFER
MAGPIE MUCKER STOUTH GENIZAH
HUSBAND SQUIRREL TREASURE
HOARDER MUCKER STORER
HUSBAND
HOARFROST RAG HOAR RIME RIND
HOARINESS HOAR MUCOR
HOARSE RAW FOGGY GRUFF HEAZY
HUSKY RAWKY ROKEY ROUGH
ROUPY STOUR CROAKY RASPED
ROUPIT GRATING RAUCOUS
HOARSENESS FROG ROUP QUACK
HASKNESS
HOARY GRAY GREY HOAR WHITE
FROSTY ANCIENT HOARISH
INCANOUS
HOATZIN ANNA HANA HOACTZIN
HOAX BAM COD FUN GAG HUM KID
RAG RIG BILK DUPE FAKE GAFF
GEGG GUNK QUIZ RAMP RUSE SEL
SHAM SKIT CHEAT FRAUD GREEN
SHAVE SPOOF TRICK WINDY
CANARD DIDDLE HUMBUG STRING
BLAFLUM DECEIVE FLIVVER
ARTIFICE

HOB HUB PUNCH MATRIX
HOBBER LEANER
HOBBLE GIMP LOCK SPAN BUNCH
HILCH HITCH STILT STUMP HABBLE
HIRPLE HOPPLE LANGLE LANKET
TOLTER CRAMBLE CRAMMEL
CRIPPLE SHACKLE SHAFFLE
SPANCEL STAGGER SIDELINE
HOBBLEBUSH DOGWOOD
HOBBY BUG FAD HOBBLER
AVOCATION
HOBBYHORSE HOBBY PLAYMARE
HOBBYIST BUG
HOBGOBLIN (ALSO SEE GOBLIN)
COW HAG HOB PUG BOGY PUCK
BOGEY BUCCA BUGAN POKER
SCRAT SPOOK BOODIE BOWSIE
BUGANE EMPUSA SPOORN
BUGABOO RAWHEAD BOGGLEBO
COLTPIXY POPLEMAN PUCKEREL
WORRICOW
HOBNAIL HOB HUB PUNCH TACKET
HOBNAILED TACKETY
HOBO BO BOE BUM STIFF
HOCK HAM HOX HEEL HOUGH HUXEN
SINEW SKINK JARRET GAMBREL
HOCKSHIN SUFFRAGO
HOCKEY HURLY HORKEY HURLEY
SHINNY CAMMOCK HURLBAT
HOCKEY STICK HOOKY HURLY
STICK BULGER SHINNY CAMBUCA
CAMMOCK DODDART HURLBAT
HOCUS-POCUS HUMBUG FLIMFLAM
QUACKERY
HOD TRAY
HOD CARRIER PADDY
HODGEPODGE CHOW HASH MESS
OLIO RAFF SALAD BOLLIX JUSSEL
MAGPIE MEDLEY CHIVAREE
CHOWCHOW HOTCHPOT KEDGEREE
MISHMASH PASTICHE PORRIDGE
SCRAMPUM
HOE BROD CHIP CLAT HACK HOWE
SHIM LARRY THIRD CHONTA
HACKER PAIDLE SARCLE GRUBBER
PULASKI SCRAPER SCUFFLE
GRIFFAUN
(— HANDLE) STAIL
(HORSE —) NIDGET NIGGET
HOECAKE CORNCAKE
HOG BEN SOW BOAR GALT GILT
PORK DUROC GRUNT SHOAT
BARROW HOGGET HOGGIE PORKER
PORKET YORKER BACONER
BUTCHER GRUNTER HOGLING
MONTANA BABIRUSA BENODONT
BUNODONT HEREFORD LANDRACE
VICTORIA
HOGBACK FLATIRON HOGFRAME
HOGCHOKER SOLE
HOGFISH CAPITAN LADYFISH
LORICATE SCORPION
HOGGER HUGGER HOGHEAD
HOGGISHNESS GRILL GRYLL
HOGNOSE SNAKE ADDER
FLATHEAD
HOG PLUM AMRA JOBO
HOGSHEAD CASK CARDEL
HOG'S-MEAT TOSTON HOGWEED

HOG-TIE HAMPER
HOGWASH DRAFF SWASH SWILL
PIGWASH
HOIST FID HEFT KILT LIFT SWAY
SWIG WHIM WHIP ERECT HEAVE
HEEZE HEIST HOICK HOOSH HORSE
RAISE WEIGH JAMMER LAUNCH
LIFTER TUGGER WHIMSY DERRICK
(— A LOG) CANNON
(— FISH) BRAIL
(— FLUKES) FISH FANCHER
HOISTED (— TIGHT) ATRIP
HOISTMAN CAGEMAN
HOKUM BLAA BLAH HOKE JUNK
HOLD HOD OWN BULK DEEM FEEL
FILL GAUM GIVE GRIT HANK HAVE
HELD HEND HILT HOLE HOLT HOOK
KEEP LOCK NAIL RELY STOW
AFONG AHOLD AHOLT CARRY CINCH
CLAMP CLING GRASP GRIPE LATCH
LEASE PAUSE ROCCA STORE
WOULD ADHERE ADSORB ARREST
CLUTCH DETAIN HANDLE INTERN
MANURE OCCUPY REGARD REPUTE
RETAIN ADJUDGE CAPTURE
CONFINE CONTAIN ENCLOSE
FERMATA GRAPPLE HOLDING
RECEIVE SEIZURE SUBSIST
SUSPEND COMPRISE FOOTHOLD
FOREHOLD HANDFAST HANDHOLD
HEADLOCK HOLDFAST PURCHASE
THURROCK
(— A BELIEF) SUPPOSE
(— AS PRECIOUS) TREASURE
(— AS TRUE) ACCEPT
(— AT BAY) DOMPT
(— BACK ON LEASH) TRASH
(— BACK) STOP WELL BELAY
LAYNE BOGGLE DETAIN FLINCH
HINDER RETIRE SHRINK CONTAIN
DETRACT FORBEAR INGIBIT
RECLAIM REFRAIN SLACKEN
HESITATE SUPPRESS WITHDRAW
(— CLOSELY) CRADLE CUDDLE
(— CONSULTATION) ADVISE
(— CORONER'S INQUEST) CROWN
(— DEAR) CHERISH
(— DOWN) PINION CONTAIN
(— FAST) FIX BAIL BITE CLING
SNARL CLENCH CLINCH SECURE
STABLE
(— FIRMLY) INSIST
(— FOR FOOD) COZY COSEY
(— GOOD) SERVE
(— IN CHECK) REIN GOVERN
REPRESS COMPESCE
(— IN CONTEMPT) SMILE DISPRIZE
(— IN PLACE) ANCHOR
(— OF PLASTER) KEY
(— ON COURSE) STEM FETCH
STAND
(— ON FINAL NOTE) TENOR
(— ON SHORE) LANDFAST
(— OUT) DREE LAST STAY OFFER
EXTEND PROTEND STRETCH
SUSTAIN
(— PROTECTIVELY) LAP
(— TIGHTLY) CLIP STICK
(— TOGETHER) BOND COHERE
CONSIST

(— UP BY LEADING STRINGS) DADE
(— UP TO CONTEMPT) FLEER
(— UP TO PUBLIC NOTICE) GIBBET
(— UP) BEAR HALT STAY ERECT
HEIST IMPEDE UPHOLD RUMPADE
SUPPORT SUSTAIN TRADUCE
(SHIP'S —) HOLE HOLL FISHHOLD
(WRESTLING —) CROTCH KEYLOCK
CHANCERY HEADLOCK SCISSORS
SIDEHOLD
HOLDER WYE HAVER STOCK DIPPER
SOCKET CRACKER JAGIRDAR
(— FOR CARRYING GLASS) FRAIL
(— FOR COIL) SPOOL
(— FOR CUP) ZARF
(— FOR TOOLS) TURRET
(— OF GRANT) ENAMDAR
(CANDLE —) SPIDER GIRANDOLE
(LAMP —) BODY
(PL.) GRIPPERS
HOLDFAST CLINCH HAPTERON
HOLDIKEN HADDIN
HOLDING HAL COPY COTE HOLD
TAKE GRASP HONOR HADDIN
POFFLE TENANT TENURE TENANCY
COMMENDA
(— DIFFERENT OPINIONS) APART
(— FAST) IRON
(— OF SECURITIES) CARRY
(PL.) FLOCKS PROPERTY
HOLDUP HEIST STICKUP
HOLE CAN CUP EYE GAP PIT TAP
BORE BURY LEAK MAIL MUSE PECK
PINK POCK PUKA WANT CHINK
DITCH FLOSS FOSSE MEUSE SINUS
SLACK SPRUE SQUAT TEWEL THURL
BURROW CAVITY CENTER CENTRE
CRANNY CRATER EYELET HOLLOW
LACUNA OBTAIN OILLET PIERCE
POCKET POUNCE WEEPER
BLOWOUT BOGHOLE BOTHROS
DIBHOLE EYEHOLE KEYHOLE
MORTICE MORTISE OILHOLE
OPENING PINHOLE POTHOLE
SCUTTLE SWALLET VENTAGE
ACCEPTER APERTURE BLOWHOLE
BOREHOLE COALHOLE CRABHOLE
FUMAROLE HANDHOLE KNOCKOUT
KNOTHOLE OVERTURE PEEPHOLE
POSTHOLE PUNCTURE WELLHOLE
WINDHOLE
(— CAUSED BY LEAK) GIME
(— FOR WIRE) HUB HUBB
(— IN BANK OF STREAM) GAT
(— IN GARMENT) FRACK
(— IN GUILLOTINE) LUNET LUNETTE
(— IN HEDGE) SMEUSE
(— IN KEEL) RUFFLE
(— IN KIVA) SIPAPU
(— IN STREAM BED) DUMP
(— IN WIND INSTRUMENT) LILL
(— INTO MOLD) SPRUE
(AIR —) SPIRACLE
(DEEP —) POT GOURD
(FOX —) KENNEL
(GOLF —) CUP DOGLEG
(MELON —) GILGAI
(SAND —) BUNKER
(SINK —) SOAKAWAY

(TO —) GOBBLE HAZARD
(VOLCANIC —) FUMAROLE
(WATER —) DUB CHARCO
(WELL-LIKE —) CASCAN
HOLIDAY HOL PLAY TIDE WAKE
FERIE FESTA MERRY FIESTA JOVIAL
FESTIVE HALEDAY PLAYDAY
YEARDAY SHABUOTH WAYGOOSE
(HALF —) REMEDY
(PL.) FERIA
HOLINESS PIETY HALIDOM SANCTITY
HOLLA SOLA
HOLLAND (ALSO SEE NETHERLANDS)
FROGLAND
HOLLANDAISE GULASH GOULASH
HOLLANDER DUTCHMAN
HOLLANDS GIN GENEVA
HOLLER HALLO HOLLO HALLOO
KYOODLE
HOLLO SOLA
HOLLOW DEN DIP KEX BOSS BOWL
CAVE COMB COOM COVE DALK
DELL DENT DINT DISH DOCK DOKE
FOLD GORE HOLE HOLL HOWE
KEXY SINK SLOT THIN VOID WAME
BASIN BIGHT CAVUM CHASE CLEFT
CUPPY DELVE DOWFF EMPTY
GAUNT GOYLE GULCH GULLY
HEUCH LAIGH NOTCH SCOOP SINUS
SLOCK SWAMP WOMBY BULLAN
CAVITY CORRIE DIMPLE HOLLER
INDENT KETTLE MATRIX POCKET
SOCKET SUNKEN VACANT WALLOW
BOXLIKE CONCAVE UNSOUND
VACUITY CAVITARY CHELIDON
CRUCIBLE FISTULAR FOSSETTE
NOTCHING SPECIOUS
(— AMONG HILLS) SWAG SLOCK
(— IN COIL OF CABLE) TIER
(— IN HILL) COOM CLASH COOMB
CORRIE
(— IN TILE) KEY
(— OF ARM) LEAD ARMPIT
(— OF HANDS) GOUPEN GOWPEN
(— OF HORSE'S TOOTH) MARK
(— OF KNEE) HAM
(— OUT) CUT DIG BORE HOWK
KERF CAVERN EXCISE
(LONG —) GROOVE
(NOT —) SOLID FARCTATE
(PASSING —) CRESCENT
(SECLUDED —) GLEN
(SPRINGY —) GAW
(WOODED —) GULLY
HOLLOWED HOWKIT CONCAVE
SPOUTED
HOLLOWNESS VANITY INANITY
VACUITY
HOLLY HOLM HULL ILEX MATE
DAHOON HOLLIN HULVER TOLLON
YAUPON CATBERRY INKBERRY
MILKMAID
HOLLYHOCK HOCK ALTHEA
MALLOW
HOLOTHURIAN TREPANG
HOLY SRI SHRI HUACA SAINT SANTO
DEVOUT DIVINE SACRAL SACRED
BLESSED PERFECT SAINTLY
SINLESS BLISSFUL INNOCENT
REVEREND

(— MAN) SADHU
(— OF HOLIES) ADYT ADYTUM
(ALL —) PANAGIA
HOLY BASIL TULCE TOOLSY
HOLY STONE BEAR BIBLE
HOLY WOOD LIGNUM
HOMAGE FEE COURT HONOR YMAGE
FEALTY MANRED INCENSE LOYALTY
MANRENT MANSHIP OVATION
SERVICE TREWAGE EMINENCE
(SUPREME —) LATRIA
HOME BYE DEN HAM HAME HUNK
WIKE ABODE ASTRE BEING DOMUS
FOYER HAUNT SMOKE HEARTH
BLIGHTY SHELTER DOMICILE
FIRESIDE ROOFTREE
(— FOR THE POOR) HOSPICE
(— OF THE BLESSED) GIMLE
(FUNERAL —) CHAPEL
(HARVEST —) KERN KIRN MELL
HOCKEY
(REST —) FARM HOSTEL
HOMELAND HAVAIKI
HOMELESS ROOFLESS VAGABOND
HOMELIKE HOMEY HAMEIL HAMILT
HOMISH HOMESOME
HOMELINESS YEOMANRY
HOMELY FOUL UGLY PLAIN DUDGEN
PLAINLY EVERYDAY FAMILIAR
HOMELIKE
HOME PLATE RUBBER
HOMER KOR CHOMER
HOME RUN SWAT SWOT
HOMESICKNESS HEIMWEH
NOSTALGIA
HOMESPUN KERSEY RUSSET
HOMESTEAD TOFT TREF ONSET
PLACE WORTH TYDDYN FARMERY
ONSTEAD STEADING
HOMESTEADER NESTER
HOMETHRUST HAI HAY
HOMEWORK PREP
HOMICIDE DEATH MORTH KILLING
HOMILETIC KERYSTIC
HOMILY PRONE OMELIE POSTIL
SERMON
HOMINY SAMP NASAUMP
HOMOEOMERY GERM SEED
(PL.) SPERMATA
HOMOGENEITY SAMENESS
HOMOGENEOUS LIKE SOLID
GLOBAL SIMPLE COMPACT SIMILAR
HOMOGENOUS ENTIRE
HOMOLOGUE CYANINE HOMOTYPE
HOMOPHONY MONODY
HOMORGANIC COGNATE
HOMOZYGOUS PURE ISOGENIC

HONDURAS

CAPITAL: TEGUCIGALPA
COIN: PESO CENTAVO LEMPIRA
GULF: FONSECA
INDIAN: MAYA PAYA SUMO ULVA
CARIB LENCA PIPIL TAUIRA
JICAQUE MISKITO MOSQUITO
ISLAND: ROATAN
ISLANDS: BAY BAHIA
LAKE: CRIBA YOJOA BREWER

MEASURE: VARA MILLA MECATE
TERCIA CAJUELA MANZANA
MOUNTAINS: PIJA AGALTA
CELAQUE
PORT: LACEIBA TRUJILLO
RIVER: COCO SICO ULUA AGUAN
LEMPA NEGRO TINTO WANKS
PATUCA SULACO GUAVAPE
OLANCHO SEGOVIA SANTIAGO
RUINS: TENAMPUA
TOWN: TELA YORO COPAN LAPAZ
ROATAN GRACIAS LACEIBA
TRUJILLO YUSCARAN JUTICALPA
WEIGHT: CAJA LIBRA

HONE HO STROKE
HONEST FAIR GOOD TRUE AFALD
FRANK ROUND SOUND WHITE
CANDID DEXTER DINKUM ENTIRE
PROPER RUSTIC SINGLE SQUARE
SINCERE UPRIGHT RIGHTFUL
STRAIGHT
HONESTLY TRULY DINKUM HONEST
INDEED SINGLY SQUARE SQUARELY
HONESTY FAITH HONOR SATIN
EQUITY LUNARY REALTY VERITY
JUSTICE LUNARIA PROBITY
BOLBONAC FAIRNESS FIDELITY
MOONWORT SATINPOD YEOMANRY
HONEY MEL MELL HINNY HONEYBUN
(— BEVERAGE) MULSE
HONEYBEE (ALSO SEE BEE) BEE
GYNE KING DRANE DRONE QUEEN
DINGAR DRONER EGATES CYPRIAN
DEBORAH DESERET KOOTCHA
MELISSA STINGER ACULEATE
ANGELITO
HONEY BUZZARD PERN
HONEYCOMB COMB FRAME
WAXCOMB
HONEYCREEPER IIWI MAMO PALILA
DREPANID GUITGUIT
HONEYDEW MILDEW
HONEY EATER OO IAO TUI MOHO
MINER TENUI MANUAO MAOMAO
ROSTER BELLBIRD WURRALUH
HONEYED SWEET HYBLAN SUGARY
SUGARED HYBLAEAN LUSCIOUS
HONEY GUIDE MOROC
HONEY MESQUITE ALGAROBA
HONEYPOD
HONEY PLANT HOYA HUAJILLO
HONEYSUCKLE VINE SUCKLE
WEIGELA BINDWEED SUCKLING
WOODBINE

HONG KONG

BAY: SHEKO REPULSE
CAPITAL: VICTORIA
COIN: CENT DOLLAR
DISTRICT: WANCHAI
GARDENS: TIGERBALM
ISLAND: LANTAO
MOUNTAIN: CASTLE VICTORIA
PENINSULA: KOWLOON

HONK KONK YANG CRONK

HONOR BAY ORE FAME FETE HORN
ADORE GLORY GRACE HERRY IZZAT
MENSE MENSK SPEAK TREAT
CREDIT DECORE ENHALO ESTEEM
HOMAGE HONOUR LAUREL PRAISE
REVERE SALUTE WORTHY DIGNITY
EMBLAZE GLORIFY HONESTY
MANSHIP RESPECT WORSHIP
DECORATE GRANDEZA TASHREEF
(PL.) ACES
HONORABLE DEAR FREE GOOD
DIGNE NOBLE OPIME WHITE GENTLE
HONEST HONORA LORDLY SQUARE
UPRIGHT GENEROUS HANDSOME
HONORARY
HONORABLENESS HONESTY
HONORABLY GENTLY
HONORARIUM SALARY DOUCEUR
ALTARAGE HONORARY
HONORED GOOD FAMOUS LAUREL
LAURELED
HONORIFIC MAGNIFIC
HOOD HOW COIF COWL HEAD HUDE
JACK AMICE ALMUCE BIGGIN
BONNET BURLET CALASH CAMAIL
CANOPY CAPOTE CUTOFF DOMINO
FUNNEL MANTLE RAFFIA BANGKOK
BASHLYK CALOTTE CAPUCHE
BLINDAGE CAPUTIUM CHAPERON
CUCULLUS FOOLSCAP LIRIPIPE
LIRIPOOP MAZARINE TROTCOZY
(— **AND CAPE COMBINED)**
FALDETTA
(— **OF BOILER)** VOMIT
(— **OF CARRIAGE)** HEAD
(— **OF MAIL)** COIF CAMAIL COIFFE
(— **OF VEHICLE)** TOP CAPOTE
(— **ON CUPBOARD)** TREMOR
(— **ON HORSES)** BLINKER
(LENS —) SUNSHADE
(MONK'S —) COWL
(STIRRUP —) TAPADERO
(STRAW —) JAVA
(WOMAN'S —) SURTOUT VOLUPER
HOODED COWLED GALEATE
HOODED CROW HOODIE GRAYBACK
GREYBACK
HOODED MERGANSER SMEW
SNOWL SPIKE TADPOLE TOWHEAD
MOSSHEAD
HOODED SEAL WIG HOOD
HOODCAP
HOODLUM HOOD BADDY BADDIE
SKOLLY LURCHER HOOLIGAN
LARRIKIN
HOODOO JINX
HOODWINK MOP DUPE FOOL BLEAR
BLIND BLUFF CHEAT CLOYNE
DELUDE GAMMON WIMPLE AVEUGLE
BEGUILE BLINKER DECEIVE MISLEAD
INVEIGLE
HOOEY BUSHWAH
HOOF CLOOF CLOOT COFFIN UNGUIS
UNGULA CLOOTIE HOOFLET
FOREHOOF
HOOK DOG GAB JIG PEW TUG CLIP
DRAG FLAG GAFF HAKE HUCK KILP
MEAK NOCK PRIN PUGH SETT SKID
STAY TACK CATCH CLEEK CLICK

CRAMP CROME CROOK DRAIL
HAMUS ONCIN PREEN SARPE SPOON
TACHE UNCUS BECKET DETENT
HANGLE HINGLE PINTLE TENTER
AGRAFFE GAMBREL GRUNTER
HAMULUS HITCHER HOOKLET
KNUCKLE NUTHOOK PELICAN
PENNANT PINHOOK POTHOOK
RAMHEAD SNIGGLE SPERKET
UNCINUS BOATHOOK CROTCHET
GRABHOOK PORTHOOK PULLBACK
VULSELLA WEEDHOOK
(— **FISH)** FOUL HANG SNAG DRAIL
HITCH STRIKE SNIGGLE FISHHOOK
(— **FOR BACON)** COMB
(— **FOR KETTLE)** KILP HANGLE
TRAMMEL
(— **FOR POT)** DRACKEN POTHOOK
SLOWRIE
(— **FOR TWISTING HEMP)** WHIRL
WHIRLER
(2 —**S FASTENED AT SHANKS)**
DOUBLES
(BENCH —) JACK
(BOAT —) HITCHER
(BOXING —) CROSS
(COUPLING —) JIGGER
(LONG-HANDLED —) HOCK MEAK
(MUSICAL —) FLAG PENNANT
(PRUNING —) SARPE CALABOZO
(REAPING —) HINK TWIBILL
(SAFETY —) CLEVIS
(SKIDDING —S) GRAB
HOOKAH KALIAN
HOOKED ADUNC UNCOUS FALCATE
HAMATED HAMULAR ADUNCATE
AQUILINE HAMIFORM UNCINATE
HOOKEDNESS ADUNCITY
HOOKER-OUT STICKMAN
HOOK-SHAPED ANKYROID
HOOKUP CIRCUIT
HOOKWORM STRONGYL
HOOLIGAN GOONDA
(PL.) AMALAITA
HOOP RIB BAIL BAND BOND BOOL
CLIP GIRD GIRR PASS RING TIRE
GARTH GIRTH FRETTE HOOPLE
LAGGIN WICKET CIRCLET GARLAND
TRUNDLE
(— **FOR A SPAR)** BANGLE
(— **FOR BARREL)** BAND GIRD GIRTH
(— **FOR LAMPSHADE)** HARP
(— **FOR ORE BUCKET)** CLEVIS
(— **FOR WINNOWING GRAIN)**
WEIGHT
(— **NET)** TRUNK
(— **TO STRENGTHEN GUN)** FRETTE
(HALF —) BAIL BALE
HOOPED RUNG
HOOPOE HOOP UPUPA WHOOP
IRRISOR DUNGBIRD PICARIAN
HOOPSKIRT TUBTAIL
HOOP SNAKE WAMPUM
HOOSE HUSK
HOOSIER STATE INDIANA
HOOT CURR WHOO WHOOT EXPLODE
ULULATE
HOP HIP NIP FLIP JUMP LEAP BOUND
HITCH SWINE FLIERS GAMBOL

SPRING TITTUP CROWHOP HOPBIND
HOPVINE LUPULUS SKIPPER
HOPBUSH AKE AKEAKE
HOP CLOVER SHAMROCK SUCKLING
HOPE WON DEEM SPES TROW THINK
TRUST DESIRE EXPECT PERDUE
ESPEIRE THOUGHT SPERANZA
VELLEITY
(VAIN —) PIPE WANHOPE
HOPEFUL FOND SANGUINE
WENLICHE
HOPELESS DULL ABJECT FORLORN
DOWNCAST
HOPELESSNESS DESPAIR
HOP HORNBEAM DEERWOOD
HARDHACK IRONWOOD
HOPI MOKI MOQUI
HOP-LIKE LUPULINE
HOPPER CURB JACK CLOSET
HAPPER MACARONI
HOPPLE HOBBLE PASTERN
SIDELANG
HOPS SHATTER
(— **BETWEEN 2 AND 4 YEARS)** OLDS
HOPSCOTCH POTSY HOPPERS
PALLALL PEEVERS
HOP TREE RUEWORT WINGSEED
HORDE ARMY CAMP CLAN PACK
CROWD GROUP SWARM LEGION
THRONG
(INNER —) BUKEYEF
HOREHOUND HENBIT MARVEL
WONDER MARRUBE
HORIZON LAYER COMPASS FINITOR
ORTERDE SKYLINE
HORIZONTAL LEVEL LINEAR NAIANT
ACLINAL STRAIGHT
HORIZONTALLY FLATLY BARWAYS
BARWISE ENDLONG FESSWAYS
FESSWISE
HORMIGO QUIRA
HORMONE CORTIN LUTEIN EQUILIN
ESTRIOL ESTRONE GASTRIN INSULIN
RELAXIN THEELIN THEELOL
ANDROGEN ENDOCRIN ESTROGEN
FLORIGEN GALACTIN LACTOGEN
OESTRIOL SECRETIN CORTISONE
HORN BEAK BATON BUGLE CONCH
CORNO CORNU SHOOT ANTLER
CLAXON KLAXON OXHORN TOOTER
ALPHORN ALTHORN BUFFALO
CLARONE FOGHORN HELICON
HUTCHET OUTHORN PRICKET
SHOPHAR UNICORN BEAKIRON
BUCKHORN CLAVICOR CORNICLE
OLIPHANT SLUGHORN STAGHORN
WALDHORN
(— **NOTE)** MORT
(— **OF CRESCENT MOON)** CUSP
(— **OF DILEMMA)** PIKE
(— **OF DRINK)** SLOSH
(— **OF YOUNG STAG)** BUNCH
(BUDDING —) SHOOT
(DRINKING —) RHYTON
(ENGLISH —) CA
(FRENCH —) CORNO
(GREY —) COLUMN
(HUNTER'S —) HUTCHET
(INSECT'S —) ANTENNA

(RAM'S —) SHOPHAR
(RUDIMENTARY —) SLUG
(STUNTED —) SCUR
HORNBEAM HARDBEAM HARDHACK
HORNWOOD IRONWOOD
HORNBILL TOCK CALAO TOUCAN
HOMURAI BROMVOEL PICARIAN
YEARBIRD
HORNBLENDE SIDERITE
HORNED FORKED
HORNED DACE CHUB
HORNED POUT CATFISH
HORNED SCREAMER ANHIMA
KAMACHI UNICORN
HORNED VIPER WAMPUM
CERASTES
HORNET VESPA VESPID STINGER
HORNGELD CORNAGE
HORNLESS NAT NOT MOIL POLL
DODDY MULEY POLEY DODDED
HUMBLE HUMMEL MAILIE MULLEY
POLLED ACEROUS
HORNPIPE MATELOTE
HORN POPPY SQUATMORE
HORNSTONE KERALITE
HORNTAIL SIREX ORYSSID
UROCERID WOODWORM
HORNWORT COONTAIL HORNWEED
HORNY WAUKIT CALLOUS CERATOID
CORNEOUS KERASINE KERATOID
HORNYHEAD CHUB
HOROSCOPE SCOPE THEME FIGURE
GENESIS NATIVITY
HORRIBLE DIRE GRIM UGLY GREAT
GRISLY HORRID GEARFUL GHASTLY
HIDEOUS HORRENT UNSLOGH
DREADFUL GRUESOME HORRIFIC
SHOCKING TERRIBLE
HORRID GRIM UGLY AWFUL ROUGH
RUGGED SNUFFY UGSOME WICKED
HIDEOUS DREADFUL GRUESOME
HORRIBLE SHOCKING
HORRIFIC FEARFUL
HORRIFIED AGHAST GHASTLY
HORRENT
HORRIFY DISMAY ENHORROR
HORROR FEAR DREAD TERROR
(PL.) JIMJAMS
HORS D'OEUVRE CANAPE RELISH
OUTWORK ZAKUSKA
(PL.) ASSIETTE
HORSE BAY CUT DUN GEE GRI NAG
PAD POT RIP TIT ARAB AVER BARB
DOON GOER GROG HACK HAND
HOSS JADE MARE MOKE PRAD
PROD QUAD RACK RIDE ROAN ROIL
SKIN STUD TEAM TURK WEED YAWD
ZAIN AIVER ARION ARVAK BEAST
BIDET BLACK BROCK CAPLE CAPUL
CHUNK CREAM CROCK DUMMY
EQUID FAVEL GLYDE GRANI HAIRY
HOBBY MILER MOREL PACER PINTO
PIPER POLER PUNCH RACER ROGUE
RUNSY SCREW SHIER SHIRE SKATE
SOMER STEED STIFF TACKY WALER
WIDGE ALEZAN AMBLER BANKER
BOLTER BRONCO BRUMBY BUCKER
BUSSER CABBER CALICO CASTER
CHEVAL COLLOP CURTAL CUSSER

DAPPLE DOBBIN DRIVER ENTIRE
EQUINE FENCER FILLER GANGER
GARRON GLEYDE GRULLA HUNTER
JUMPER KEFFEL LEADER MAIDEN
MORGAN NUBIAN ORLOFF OUTLAW
PELTER PLATER POSTER PULLER
ROARER ROUNCY RUNNER SAVAGE
SORREL STAGER TARPAN TRACER
TURKEY VANNER WARPER WEAVER
ALSVINN ALSVITH ARABIAN
BARBARY BELGIAN BOARDER
CABALLO CHARGER CLICKER
CLIPPER COACHER COCOTTE
COURSER CRIBBER CRIOLLA
CRITTER DRAFTER FLEMISH
GALATHE GELDING GIGSTER
GRUNTER HACKNEY KNACKER
LEEFANG MONTURE MUSTANG
NEIGHER PACOLET PALFREY
PIEBALD PRANCER PRANKER
RATTLER REESTER REFUSER
REMOUNT RUNAWAY SADDLER
SLEDDER SLEEPER SPANKER
STAGGIE STEPPER SUFFOLK
SUMPTER TRAPPER TRESTLE
TROOPER TROTTER WHEELER
ARDENNES BATHORSE BUCKSKIN
CHESTNUT CHEVALET COCKTAIL
COLICKER CREATURE CYLLAROS
DEMISANG DESTRIER EOHIPPUS
FOOTROPE FRIPPERY GALLOPER
GALLOWAY HRIMFAXI KADISCHI
MACHINER OUTSIDER RIDGLING
ROADSTER SKEWBALD STIBBLER
TRIPPLER WHISTLER YARRAMAN
(— ACT) MANAGE
(— CERTAIN NOT TO WIN) STIFF
(— ESTABLISHMENT) HARAS
(— LOSING FIXED RACE) STUMER
STUMOUR
(— OF UNIFORM DARK COLOR) ZAIN
(— RACE) WALKOVER
(—S RUNNING BEHIND) RUCK
(2-YEAR OLD —) TWINTER
(3 —S ABREAST) TROIKA
(3 —S ONE BEHIND ANOTHER)
RANDEM
(4 —S ABREAST) QUADRIGA
(ARABIAN —) ARAB KOHL ARABIAN
(BALKY —) JIBBER
(BROKEN-DOWN —) JADE CROCK
SCREW DURGAN GARRAN
(CALICO —) PINTO
(CASTRATED —) GELDING
(CLUMSY —) STAMMEL
(DECREPIT —) SKATE GLEYDE
(DRAFT —) HAIRY PUNCH SHIRE
BEETEWK BELGIAN SUFFOLK
(DROVE OF —S) ATAJO
(EASY-PACED —) PAD
(FALLOW —) FAVEL
(FAMILY —) DOBBIN
(FAST —) GANGER
(FEMALE —) MARE FILLY
(FLEMISH —) ROIL
(GRAY —) SCHIMMEL
(HIGH-SPIRITED —) STEPPER
(IMAGINARY —) AULLAY
(IMMUNIZED —) BLEEDER

(INFERIOR —) PLUG PLATER
(JUMPING —) LEPPER
(MALE —) STALLION
(NEAR —) HAND
(OLD —) JADE PROD AIVER CROCK
(PACK —) BIDET SUMPTER
(RANGE —) FANTAIL
(SHAFT —) SHAFTER THILLER
(SHAGGY —) ALTAI
(SLUGGISH —) HOG
(SMALL —) NAG TIT BIDET GENET
HOBBY JENNET GALLOWAY
(STOCKY —) COB
(TEAM —S) CARTWARE
(TEAM OF 3 —S WITH LEADER)
UNICORN
(TRICK —) SIMON
(UNBROKEN —) BRONCO
(VICIOUS —) LADINO
(WILD —) FUZZY BRUMBY KUMRAH
TARPAN JUGHEAD BANGTAIL
FUZZTAIL WARRIGAL
(WINGED —) PEGASUS
(WORN-OUT —) HACK GARRAN
KNACKER CROWBAIT
(WORTHLESS —) JADE SHACK
KEFFEL
(YOUNG —) TIT COLT FOAL STAG
STOT STAGGIE
(PL.) MANADA STABLE UNICORN
HORSE BALM KNOBWEED
KNOTROOT RICHWEED
HORSE BLANKET RUG MANTA
HORSE BOY TRACER
HORSE CHESTNUT CONKER
HORSECLOTH HOUSE HOUSING
HORSE DEALER COPER CHANTER
COURSER
HORSE-EYE JACK XUREL
HORSE FENNEL SESELI
HORSEFLESH JACK
HORSEFLY BOT GAD CLEG CLEGG
STOUT BOTFLY BREEZE GADBEE
GADFLY BULLDOG DEERFLY
TABANID
HORSEHAIR SETON
HORSELAUGH GUFFAW
HORSELEECH ALUKAH
HORSELOAD SEAM
HORSE MACKEREL TUNNY SAUREL
HORSEMAN RIDER CHARRO
COWBOY HUSSAR KNIGHT RUTTER
COURIER PICADOR PRICKER
GALLOPER
(PL.) HORSE CAVALRY
HORSEMANSHIP CAVALRY
HORSEMINT RIGNUM
HORSE MUSHROOM WHITECAP
HORSE NETTLE SOLANUM
HORSEPLAY HIJINKS
HORSEPOWER SOUP
HORSEPOX GREASE
HORSE-RADISH MAROR MOROR
REDCOLL
HORSE-RADISH TREE BEHN BEHEN
HORSESHOE TIP SHOE PLATE
HOBBER LUNETTE
HORSETAIL TAIL PRELE TOADPIPE
HORSETAIL LICHEN TREEHAIR

HORSETAIL TREE AGOHO AGOJO
HORSEWEED COCASH COWTAIL
HOGWEED FIREWEED SCABIOUS
HORTATORY EMOTIVE
HORUS SEPT SOPT SEPTI
HORMAKHU
(FATHER OF —) OSIRIS
HOSACKIA ACMISPON
HOSE LINE VAMP HOSEN GASKIN
BROGUES BULLION HOSIERY
HANDLINE HOSEPIPE
HOSIERY HOSE KNITWEAR
(— WORKER) LOOPER
HOSPICE IMARET DIACONIA
HOSPITAL
HOSPITABLE DOUCE CLEVER
DOULCE SOCIAL CORDIAL FRIENDLY
HOSPITAL BEDLAM CRECHE SPITAL
COLLEGE LAZARET
HOSPITALITY SALT MENSE
XENODOCHY
HOSPODAR VOIVOD GOSPODAR
HOST SUM ARMY FYRD WARE
CROWD JASON MAKER POWER
SWARM WERED LEGION LODGER
NATION THRONG BALEBOS
COMPANY FYRDUNG SACRING
VIANDER LANDLORD PARTICLE
(— OF INVADERS) HERE
(EUCHARISTIC —) LAMB SACRING
(PL.) SABAOTH
HOSTA NIOBE FUNKIA
HOSTAGE BORROW PLEDGE SURETY
RANSOMER
HOSTEL INN ENTRY HOSTAGE
KINGDOM HOSPITAL
HOSTESS TAUPO LANDLADY
HOSTILE FOE HARD ALIEN BLACK
ENEMY FREMT HATEL STOUT
DEADLY FRIGID INFEST ADVERSE
ASOCIAL FIENDLY OPPOSED
UNQUERT WARLIKE CONTRARY
INIMICAL OPPOSITE
HOSTILITY WAR FEID FEUD HATE
ANIMUS ENMITY HATRED RANCOR
SCHISM DAGGERS RUPTURE
(PL.) WAR ARMS ARMOR WARFARE
HOSTLER NAGMAN OSTLER
HORSEBOY
HOT WARM CALID EAGER FIERY
ARDENT ESTIVE FERVID IGNITE
SULTRY TORRID ANIMOSE ANIMOUS
BOILING BURNING FERVENT
PEPPERY THERMAL CAYENNED
FEVERISH SEETHING SIZZLING
(— WATER) SOUP
HOTBED BED HOTHOUSE
HOT-BLOODED VASCULAR
HOTBOX SMOKER STINKER
HOTEL INN SPA FLOP FONDA HOUSE
HYDRO HOSTEL HOTTLE POSADA
FLEABAG FONDACO FUNDUCK
GASTHOF HOSTELRY
HOTELKEEPER HOTELIER
HOT-HEADED BRAINISH MADBRAIN
HOTHOUSE STEW STOVE PINERY
FRUITERY
HOT ROD DRAGSTER
HOT-TEMPERED PEPPERY

CHOLERIC SPITFIRE
HOTTENTOT TOTTY HOTNOT
KOKANA WITBOOI QUAEQUAE
(PL.) BALAO BALAWU
HOUND DOG PIE BAIT HARL HUNT
MUTE BRACE BRACH ENTRY HARRY
LEASH LIMER SLATE AFGHAN
BASSET BEAGLE HUNTER LEAMER
LUCERN SLEUTH TUFTER CURTISE
ENTRADA GELLERT REDBONE
SKIRTER BARUKHZY BLUETICK
BRATCHET COURSING FOXHOUND
(BITCH —) BRACH
(CRY OF —) MUSIC
(RELAY OF —S) VANLAY
(SLEUTH —) TALBOT
(SPECTRAL —) SHUCK
(PL.) RACHES
HOUND'S-TONGUE TORYWEED
HOUR URE TIDE TIME CURFEW
GHURRY
(6 —S) QUADRANT
(CANONICAL —) NONE SEXT PRIME
MATINS TIERCE VESPERS COMPLINE
EVENSONG
(HALF —) BELL
(KILOWATT —) KELVIN
(LAST —S) DEATHBED
(STUDY —) PREP
HOURLY HORAL HORARY
HOUSE BOX KEN CASA CRIB DOME
DUMP FIRM FLET HALL HELL HOLE
HOME RACE ROOF STOW ABODE
ADOBE AERIE BAHAY BANDA COVER
DACHA DOMUS HOOSE JACAL
LODGE MEESE STAGE WHARE
BIGGIN BOTTLE CAMARA CASITA
CASTLE CHEMIS CLOTHE DUPLEX
FAMILY HEARTH MAISON PALACE
PARISH SINGLE STABLE WIGWAM
BASTIDE BIGGING CABOOSE
CASSINE EUDEMON FAZENDA
HOGGERY HOUSING MESUDGE
QUARTER SHELTER AEDICULA
BARADARI BUNGALOW DOMICILE
DOVECOTE DWELLING MEDSTEAD
MESSUAGE TENEMENT
(— AND 5 ACRES) COTE
(— AND LAND) DEMESNE
(— FOR DOGS) KENNEL
(— FOR WOMEN) HAREM
(— IN BOROUGH) HAW
(— OF A MARABOUT) KOUBA
(— OF LEGISLATURE) CHAMBER
ASSEMBLY
(— OF PARLIAMENT) COMMONS
(— OF PROSTITUTION) CRIB BAGNIO
(— OF THIEVES) KEN
(— OF WORSHIP) BETHEL CHURCH
(APARTMENT —) INSULA
(ASTROLOGICAL —) ANGLE
(AUSTRALIAN —) HUMPY
(CHANGE —) DRY
(CHAPTER —) CABILDA
(CLAY —) ADOBE TEMBE
(COACH —) REMISE
(COMMUNAL —) MORONG
(COUNTRY —) PEN DACHA CASINO
GRANGE QUINTA BASTIDE CHATEAU

(COW —) VACCARY
(DAIRY —) WICK
(EATING —) COOKSHOP
(ESKIMO —) IGLU IGLOO TOPEK
KASHGA KASHIMA
(FIJI —) BURE
(FORTIFIED —) GARRISON
(GAMBLING —) BANK HELL
(GOVERNMENT —) KONAK
(GRINDING —) HULL
(HAWAIIAN —) HALE
(LODGING —) INN KIP HOST ENTRY
HOTEL HOSTEL
(LOG —) TILT
(MANOR —) HAM HALL COURT
PLACE SCHLOSS
(PLANETARY —) TOWER
(POULTRY —) ARK HENNERY
(PUBLIC —) INN HOSTEL SNUGGERY
(RANCH —) HUT
(RELIGIOUS —) CELL CONVENT
KELLION
(RENTED —) LET
(REST —) DAK KHAN SERAI
(RETREAT —) CENACLE
(ROOMING —) DOSS FLOP FLEABAG
(ROYAL —) AERIE
(SMALL —) COT HUT BACH CELL
CABIN HOVEL SHACK CASITA
COTTAGE
(SOD —) SODDY
(STILT —) CHIKEE CHICKEE
(SUMMER —) TRELLIS
(TENEMENT —) LAND CHAWL
(THATCHED —) BANDA
(TOY —) COBHOUSE
(TURKISH —) KONAK
HOUSEBOAT BARGE HOUSER
WANGAN DAHABEAH
HOUSEBREAKER MILL JACOB
MILLKEN
HOUSEBREAKING CRACK
HOUSECARL THINGMAN
HOUSECOAT DUSTER
HOUSEFINCH BURION LINNET
REDHEAD
HOUSEHOLD HIRED HOUSE FAMILY
HOUSAL MEINIE MENAGE FIRESIDE
MAINFAST
HOUSEHOLDER ASTRER GOODMAN
GUIDMAN NAUKRAR FRANKLIN
HOUSEKEEPER HUSSY MATRON
HOUSELEEK JUBARB AYEGREEN
HOMEWORT SENGREEN SILGREEN
HOUSEMATE DOMESTIC
HOUSEWARMING INFARE
HOUSEWIFE DAME FRAU FROW
WIFE HUSSY VROUW BUSHWIFE
HAUSFRAU
(MEAN —) NIP
HOUSING BOX BASE CASE DRUM
TRAP BANJO BLIMP GLOBE HOUSE
KIOSK BARREL RADOME SHIELD
HOUSAGE SHELTER DOGHOUSE
PADCLOTH PECTORAL PEDESTAL
(HORSE'S —) BASE
(RADAR —) BLISTER
(PL.) HOLSTERS
HOVA IMERINA

HOVEL COSH CREW CRIB CRUE HELM HULK HULL CHOZA HUTCH LODGE BURROW CRUIVE PONDOK

HOVELER HOBBLER HUFFLER

HOVER BAIT FLIT HANG HOVE BROOD FLUTTER HOVERER

HOW AS FOO HOO HOWE HOWEER HOWEVER QUOMODO WHEREBY

HOWDAH TOWER AMBARI AMBAREE

HOWEVER BUT THO YET HOWSO STILL THOUGH

HOWITZER HOWITZ LICORN UNICORN

HOWITZER SHELL OBUS

HOWL WAP WOW BAWL GOWL GURL HURL WAUL WAWL YAWL YOLL YOUT YOWL TIGER WHEWL WRAWL BEHOWL STEVEN ULULATE (— **VOCIFEROUSLY**) TONGUE

HOWLER ERROR ARAGUATO

HOWLER MONKEY MONO ARABA HOWLER GUARIBA GUEREBA STENTOR ALOUATTE

HOWLING ULULANT

HOY TJALK CRUMSTER

HOYDEN MEG BLOWZE RIGSBY TOMBOY

HREIDMAR (SON OF —) REGIN FAFNER

H-SHAPED ZYGAL

HUAMUCHIL INGA

HUAVE WABI HUABI

HUB HOB BOSS NAVE STOCK CENTER CENTRE FAUCET HUBBLE SOCKET SPIDER OMPHALOS (— **AND SPOKES**) SPEECH

HUBBLE-BUBBLE CALEAN CALAHAN

HUBBUB DIN STIR CLAMOR FRAISE HUBBLE RACKET TUMULT BOBBERY CLUTTER BROUHAHA HUBBABOO ROWDYDOW SPLATTER

HUCHEN HUSO

HUCHNOM TATU

HUCKLEBERRY HURT ERICAD CRACKERS

HUCKSTER BADGER CADGER KIDDER HAGGLER KIDDIER TRUCKER OUTCRIER

HUDDLE RUCK HUNCH CRINGE FUMBLE HOWDER HURTLE SCRUMP SHRIMP SHRINK CROODLE SCRINCH SCROOCH SCRUNCH SHUFFLE

HUE RUD BLEE BLUE COND CYAN CHLOR COLOR GREEN LEMON TAINT TINCT (**DULL —**) DRAB (**SOMBER —**) DARK

HUELESS GRAY GREY

HUFF DOD BLOW RUFF DRUNT SNUFF

HUFFY FUFFY SHIRTY

HUG CLIP COLL COUL MOLD CREEM CRUSH HALSE CUDDLE HUDDLE HUGGLE STRAIN CHERISH EMBRACE SQUEEZE

HUGE BIG FELL MAIN VAST ENORM GIANT GREAT JUMBO LARGE STOUR HEROIC IMMANE BANGING BUMPING DECUMAN IMMENSE MASSIVE MONSTER TITANIC COLOSSAL ENORMOUS GALACTIC GIGANTIC MOUNTAIN PYTHONIC SLASHING SWAPPING THWACKING

HUGENESS ENORMITY

HUISACHE WABI AROMO CASSIE POPINAC OPOPANAX

HULK CHOP HULL CORSE

HULL HUD POD BODY BULK HULK HUSK PILL BURSE CASCO SWELL (— **OF COTTON BOLL**) BUR BURR (— **OF SHIP**) BODY HULK BOTTOM

HULLABALOO DIN FLAP CLAMOR HUBBUB RACKET BROUHAHA

HUM BUM BLUR BRUM BUZZ HUSS TUNE CHIRM CROON DRONE FEIGN SOUGH SOWFF HUMBLE TEEDLE FREDDON TRUMPET

HUMAN BEING MANLY FINITE FLESHY HUMANE MORTAL MANNISH HOMININE HUMANIST

HUMAN BEING MAN WIGHT MORTAL PERSON ADAMITE CREATURE RATIONAL

HUMANE CIVIL KINDLY TENDER MERCIFUL

HUMANELY MANLY

HUMANITY FLESH MENSK WORLD MANHEAD MANHOOD MANSHIP SPECIES ADAMHOOD HUMANISM KINDNESS LENITUDE

HUMBLE LOW HOWE MEAN MILD MURE POOR TAME VAIL ABASE ABATE BUXOM DEMIT DIMIT LOWER LOWLY PLAIN SILLY SMALL SOBER WORMY ATTERR DEJECT DEMISS EMBASE HONEST MASTER MODEST REDUCE SIMPLE SLIGHT UNPUFF AFFLICT DEGRADE DEPRESS FOOLISH IGNOBLE MORTIFY OBSCURE CONTRITE DISGRACE (— **ONESELF**) STOOP GROVEL

HUMBLED SMALL ABASED DEJECTED

HUMBLENESS HUMILITY

HUMBLER INFERIOR

HUMBLING SETDOWN

HUMBLY SIMPLE

HUMBUG GAS GUM HUM KID FLAM GAME GUFF JAZZ SHAM CHEAT FRAUD FUDGE GUILE JOLLY SPOOK TRICK BLAGUE GAMMON FLUMMER VERNEUK FLIMFLAM FLUMMERY HUCKMUCK IMPOSTER NONSENSE

HUMDINGER DOOZY DINGER HUMMER SNORTER

HUMDRUM IRKSOME PROSAIC

HUMERUS ARM

HUMID WET DAMP DANK MOIST SOGGY STICKY SULTRY WETTISH HUMOROUS

HUMILIATE ABASE ABASH SCALP SHAME NIDDER NITHER DEGRADE MORTIFY UNPLUME DISGRACE

HUMILIATED SMALL ASHAMED

HUMILIATION DUST COMEDOWN DISGRACE

HUMILITY MODESTY MEEKNESS MILDNESS

HUMIN MELANIN

HUMMEL FALTER

HUMMING AHUM BROOL SINGING

HUMMINGBIRD RUBY STAR MANGO SYLPH TENUI TOPAZ AMAZON COQUET HERMIT HUMMER ROSTER SAPPHO COLIBRI EMERALD HUMBIRD JACOBIN RAINBOW SNOWCAP TROCHIL WARRIOR CALLIOPE COQUETTE FIRETAIL FROUFROU MIMOTYPE PICARIAN SAPPHIRE WHITETIP

HUMMOCK HUMP CHENIER HAMMOCK TUSSOCK

HUMOR CUE PIN TID WIT BABY BILE CANT MOOD TIFF VEIN WHIM FRAME IRONY TUTOR MEGRIM PHLEGM SANIES SOOTHE SPLEEN SPRITE TEMPER FOOLING GRATIFY INDULGE VITREUM VITRINA ARCHNESS DISHUMOR DROLLERY EYEWATER FUMOSITY SANGUINE VITREOUS (**BAD —**) BATS THROW (**ILL —**) BILE DUDGEON (**QUIET —**) DRYNESS (**SLIMY —**) HIPPOMANES

HUMORIST JOKER FUNSTER FUNMAKER FUNNYMAN

HUMOROUS DROLL FUNNY QUEER JOCOSE COMICAL GIOCOSO PLAYFUL WAGGISH PLEASANT SARDONIC

HUMP BOSS HUNK BULGE BUNCH CROUP CRUMP HULCH HUNCH GIBBER GIBBUS HUMMIE GIBBOUS

HUMPBACK LORD CRUMP PUNCH

HUMPBACKED HUMPED HUMPTY GIBBOSE GIBBOUS

HUMPBACKED SALMON HADDO HOLIA

HUMPED HULCH HUMPY HUTCH HUMPTY HUNCHY

HUMUS MOR MOLD MULL HUMIN MOULD

HUNCH HUMP HUNK HULCH HUNCHET SCRUNCH

HUNCHBACK URCHIN HUMPBACK

HUNDRED RHO CENT CENTUM HUNDER HUNNER CANTRED CENTARY (— **THOUSAND**) LAC LAKH (**5 —**) D

HUNDREDFOLD CENTUPLE

HUNDREDTH (— **OF INCH**) POINT (— **OF RIGHT ANGLE**) GRAD GRADE

HUNDREDWEIGHT CENT CENTAL CENTENA CENTNER HUNDRED QUINTAL

HUNGARIAN HUN KUMAN MAGYAR

HUNGARY	
CANAL:	SIO SARVIZ
CAPITAL:	BUDAPEST
COIN:	GARA BALAS LENGO FILLER FORINT KORONA
DANCE:	CZARDAS
DYNASTY:	ARPAD ANGEVIN
FOREST:	BAKONY
GYPSY:	SZIGANE TZIGANI

KING: BELA GEZA IMRE ARPAD ISTVAN KALMAN MATTHIAS
LAKE: FERTO BALATON VELENCE BLATENSEE
MEASURE: AKO HOLD JOCH YOKE ANTAL ITCZE MAROK METZE HUVELYK MERFOLD
MOUNTAIN: KEKES BAKONY MECSEK BORZSONY KORISHEGY
MOUNTAIN RANGE: BUKK MATRA MECSEK CARPATHIAN
MUSICAL INSTRUMENT: TAROGATO
NATIVE: HUN SERB CROAT GYPSY MAGYAR SLOVAK UGRIAN
PLAIN: PUSZTA
REGIME: KADAR
RIVER: DUNA MURA RAAB RABA SAJO ZALA BODVA DRAVA DRAVE IPOLY KAPOS KOROS MAROS RABCA TARNA TISZA DANUBE HENRAD POPRAD SZAMOS THEISS ZAGYVA VISTULA BERRETYO
TOWN: ABA ACS OZD VAC BUDA EGER GYOR MAKO PAPA PECS PEST TATA ZIRC KOMLO CEGLED MOHACS SOPRON SZEGED DBRECEN MISKOLC SZENTES DEBRECEN SZEGEDIN
WEIGHT: VAMFONT VAMMAZSA
WINE: EGER TOKAJ TOKAY SZEKSZARD

HUNGER BELL CLEM WANT ACORIA DESIRE FAMINE CRAVING
HUNGRY YAP HOWE KEEN LEER EMPTY THIRL HOLLOW JEJUNE PECKISH YAPPISH ANHUNGRY ESURIENT
HUNK DAD DAUD JUNK MOUNTAIN
(— OF BREAD) TOMMY
HUNT DOG GUN JAG MOB RUN GREW JACK LARK PUMP SEAL SEEK SHOP CHASE CHEVY DRIVE HOUND REVAY TRACK TRAIL BATTUE BEAGLE BREVIT CHEVVY COURSE FALCON FERRET SEARCH SHIKAR VANLAY ENCHASE AUCUPATE PIGSTICK SCROUNGE
(— BIG GAME) GHOOM
(— DEER) FLOAT
(— DOWN) QUARRY
(— DUCKS) TOLL
(— FOX) CUB
(— WITH HAWK) FLY
(— WITH SPEAR) STICK
HUNTER GUN HUNT PINK JAGER BIRDER CHASER GUNNER JAEGER NIMROD THERON ACTAEON BUSHMAN CATCHER COURSER MONTERO SHIKARI SHOOTER SKIRTER STALKER TRAILER VENERER CEPHALUS CHASSEUR FIELDMAN HUNTSMAN TRAILMAN
(— ON SNOW) CRUSTER
(BUFFALO —) CIBOLERO

(MYTHOLOGICAL —) GWYN ORION
(RING OF —S) TINCHEL TINCHILL
HUNTING DRAG HANK AHUNT WATHE SHIKAR VENERY CUBBING GUNNING BEAGLING PURCHASE SHOOTING SURROUND VENATION
(— SIGNAL) SEEK
HUNTSMAN WHIP HUNTER JAEGER ACTAEON CATCHER COURSER MONTERO SCARLET VENATOR VENERER CHASSEUR
HURDLE TRAY FLAKE FRITH PANEL STALE STICK DOUBLE RADDLE SLEDGE WATTLE
HURDS TOW
HURDY-GURDY LIRA ROTA LANTUM VIELLE SAMBUKE HUMSTRUM SYMPHONY
HURL BUN CAST CLOD DASH DUST FIRE PASH PELT PICK SLAT SOAK SOCK DRIVE FLING HEAVE LANCE PITCH SLING SMITE SPANG SWING THIRL THROW WHIRL THRILL HURLBAT SWITHER WHITHER JACULATE
HURLY-BURLY HURL UPROAR
HURRAH HAIL HUZZA HOORAY HURRAY
HURRICANE PRESTER FURACANA FURICANE WILDWIND
HURRIED HASTY THRONG HASTEFUL SNATCHED
HURRY ADO FOG NIP RAP RUB RUN DUST HUMP PELL PLAT POST RAPE RESE RUSH STIR TIFT TROT URGE WHIR CHASE CROWD HASTE HYPER LURRY PRESS SESSA SKIRT SPEED STAVE STOUR WHIRL BUCKET BUNDLE BUSTLE HASTEN HUSTLE POWDER STROTH TATTER WHORRY HOTFOOT QUICKEN SCUDDLE SKELTER SLITHER WHITHER DISPATCH EXPEDITE SPLUTTER
(— A HORSE) SPUR
(— ABOUT) SCOUR
(— AWAY) FLEE BUNCH SCREW SKIRT
(— CLUMSILY) TAVE TEAVE
(— NOISILY) SPLUTTER
(— OFF) DUST
(— UP) BUSK
HURT CUT HOT DERE FIKE GALL HARM ABUSE BLAME GRIEF GRIPE SORRY SPITE THORN WATHE WOUND BRUISE DAMAGE GRIEVE IMPAIR INJURE INJURY LESION MIFFED MITTLE PAINED SCATHE STRAIN STROKE WINGED AFFLICT HURTING OFFENCE OFFENSE MISCHIEF NUISANCE
(— EASILY) FROISSE
(— FEELINGS) CUT TOUCH
(— REPUTATION) LIBEL
(— SEVERELY) KILL
(EASILY —) GINGER
HURTFUL BAD ILL EVIL MALIGN NOCENT NOCIVE NOUGHT SHREWD TAKING BANEFUL HARMFUL MALEFIC NOCUOUS NOXIOUS

UNQUERT GRIEVOUS HURTSOME SCATHFUL
HURTLE HURL FLING THIRL
HUSBAND EKE MAN WER BOND CHAP FERE KEEP LORD MAKE MATE SAVE SIRE BARON CHURL HOARD HUBBY MATCH STORE MANAGE MASTER MISTER SPOUSE CONSORT GOODMAN GUIDMAN HENPECK PARTNER CONSERVE
(— OF ADULTRESS) CUCKOLD
(AFFIANCED —) FUTURE
(PL.) PUNALUA
HUSBANDMAN BOND BOOR CARL CLOWN COLON TILLER ACREMAN HUSBAND PLOWMAN TILLMAN AGRICOLE
HUSBANDRY GAINER GAINOR THRIFT ECONOMY MANAGERY
HUSH SH HSH MUM PAX HESH HOOT LULL BURKE SHUSH STILL WHISH WHIST WHUSH HUDDLE HUSHABY SILENCE
HUSHED QUIET STILL GENTLE WHISHT
HUSK BUR COD HUD KEX SID BARK BURR COAT COSH HOSE HUCK HULK SEED SHIV SKIN HOOSE SCALE SHACK SHALE SHAUP SHELL SHILL SHOOD SHUCK SHUDE COLDER DEHUSK FLIGHT SLOUGH BOLSTER CARCASS CASCARA
(— NUT) SHACK BOLSTER
(— OF OATS) SHUD SHOOD FLIGHT
(CORN —) HOJA
(PL.) BHUSA CHAFF BHOOSA HULKAGE SHELLING
HUSKY HUSK CODDY FOGGY FURRED BUIRDLY HULKING BOUNCING SIBERIAN
HUSSITE TABORITE
HUSSY MINX SLUT BESOM CUTTY GIPSY GYPSY MADAM STRAP HIZZIE LIMMER DROSSEL
HUSTLE FAN HUMP JUMP BLITZ SKELP BUCKET BUNDLE BUSTLE JOSTLE RUSTLE SCUFTER
HUSTLECAP PINCH
HUSTLER HUSTLE PEELER BUSTLER FIREBALL
HUT COE COT BARI BUTT COSH COTE CREW CRIB HALE HULK HULL ISBA IZBA SHED SKEO TENT BASHA BENAB BOHIO BOTHY CABIN CHAWL CHOZA HOVEL HUMPY HUTCH JACAL KRAAL LODGE SCALE SETER SHACK SHIEL TOLDO TOPEK WHARE WURLY BOHAWN CANABA CHALET GUNYAH GUNYEH MIAMIA PONDOK RANCHO REFUGE SAETER SCONCE SHANTY SHELTY WIGWAM WIKIUP BALAGAN BARRACK BOUROCK CAMALIG COTTAGE GOONDIE HUDDOCK HUTMENT SHEBANG YAKUTAT BARABARA CHANTIER RONDAWEL SHIELING THOLTHAN TUGURIUM
(— FOR TEMPORARY USE) CORF
(— OVER MINING SHAFT) COE

(ABORIGINAL —) MIMI WURLY GUNYAH MIAMIA WURLEY GOONDIE
(FISHERMAN'S —) SKEO
(HEATED —) HOTHOUSE
(HERMIT'S —) CELL
(NAVAJO —) HOGAN
(POULTRY —) IGLOO
(SAMOYED —) CHUM
(SIBERIAN —) JURT
(SOUTH AFRICAN —) STRUIS
HUTCH ARK RABBITRY
HUTIA UTIA JUTIA PILORI
HYACINTH LILY MUSK LILIUM
CROWTOE FLOATER GREGGLE
JACINTH BLUEBELL CROWFOOT
HAREBELL JACOUNCE
HYACINTH BEAN LABLAB BONAVIST
BONNYVIS DOLICHOS
HYACINTHUS (FATHER OF —)
AMYCLAS
(MOTHER OF —) DIOMEDE
HYALOGEN NEOSSIN
HYBRID DZO ZHO MULE ZOBO
CROSS GRADE HINNY LIGER
COYDOG GALYAK MOSAIC MULISH
SPLAKE TURKEN BASTARD BIGENER
CATTALO PLUMCOT ZEBRASS
ZEBRULA ZEBURRO CARIDEER
KAFERITA LIMEQUAT ZEBRINNY
HYBRIDIZE CROSS
HYDRANT CHUCK FIREPLUG
HYDRANTH SIPHON SYPHON
HYDRATE SLAKE
HYDRAZINE DIAMIDE
HYDRAZOATE AZIDE
HYDRIA KALPIS
HYDROCARBON ARENE CUMOL
FREON GUTTA IDRYL INDAN IRENE
TOLAN XYLOL ALKANE ALKYNE
ALLENE BUTANE BUTYNE CARANE
CETANE CETENE CYMENE DOCANE
ETHANE ETHENE HEXINE INDANE
INDENE MELENE NONENE OCTANE
OCTENE OCTINE PICENE PYRENE
RETENE TOLANE TOLUOL XYLENE
AMYLENE AZULENE BENZENE
CHOLANE CYCLENE DECALIN
ETHERIN FULVENE HEPTANE
HEPTENE HEPTYNE LYCOPIN
MUCKITE MYRCENE OLEFINE
PENTINE PENTYNE PROPANE
STYRENE TETROLE TOLUENE
BIPHENYL CADALENE CADINENE
CARBURAN CEROTENE CETYLENE

CHRYSENE CORONENE CUMULENE
DECYLENE DIOLEFIN DOCOSANE
DYSODILE EICOSANE ETHYLENE
EUDALENE FLUORENE HEXYLENE
ILLIPENE ISOPRENE LYCOPENE
MENTHENE NONYLENE OCTYLENE
PARAFFIN PRISTANE PYRACENE
RUTYLENE SABINENE SQUALENE
STILBENE
HYDROCYANIC PRUSSIC
HYDRODAMALIS RHYTINA
HYDROEXTRACTOR BUZZER
WHIZZER
HYDROFLUORIC PHTHORIC
HYDROGEN HYDRO
HYDROHEMATITE TURGITE
HYDROID POLYP OBELIA ACALEPH
ZOOPHYTE
HYDROLEA NAMA
HYDROMEL ALOJA
HYDROMETER SPINDLE
HYDROPERITONEUM ASCITES
HYDROPHOBIA LYSSA RABIES
HYDROPHOBIC LYSSIC
HYDROPHYLLIUM BRACT
HYDROXIDE ALKALI HYDRATE
HYDRIDE
HYDROZINCITE CALAMINE
HYENA HINE DABUH SIMIR HYAENID
HYGIENIC SANITARY
HYGRODEIK PAGOSCOPE
HYLLUS (FATHER OF —) HERCULES
(MOTHER OF —) DEIANIRA
(SLAYER OF —) ECHEMUS
(WIFE OF —) IOLE
HYLOZOIST PHYSICIST
HYMEN CHERRY BRIDEGOD
HYMENIUM THECIUM
HYMENOCALLIS ISMENE
HYMN ODE FUGE LAUD SING DIRGE
GATHA PAEAN PSALM YASHT
YMPNE ANTHEM CARVAL CHORAL
HIMENE HIRMOS MANTRA ORPHIC
THEODY VESPER CHORALE EXULTET
HEIRMOS INTROIT CANTICLE
DOXOLOGY ENCOMIUM PSALMODY
SEQUENCE
(— COLLECTION) MENAION
(MEXICAN —) ALABADO
(PL.) HYMNODY
HYMNAL HYMNARY HYMNBOOK
HYPERCORACOID RADIAL SCAPULA
HYPERCRITICAL NICE CAPTIOUS
CRITICAL

HYPERDULIA ADORATION
HYPEREMIA RUBOR
HYPEREMIC CONGESTED
HYPERICUM TUTSAN
HYPERION (DAUGHTER OF —)
AURORA
(FATHER OF —) URANUS
(MOTHER OF —) GAEA
(WIFE OF —) THEA
HYPEROPIC FARSIGHTED
HYPERSENSITIVITY ATOPY
HYPHA STOLON
HYPHEN BAND
(PL.) LEADERS
HYPNOTIC AMYTAL BARBITAL
HYPNOTISM DEVIL BRAIDISM
HYPNOSIS MESMERISM
HYPNOTIST OPERATOR SVENGALI
HYPOBLAST ENDODERM HYPODERM
HYPOCHONDRIA HIP HYP HYPO
MEGRIM
HYPOCHONDRIAC ARGAN HIPPY
HIPPIST
HYPOCOTYL RADICLE TIGELLA
TIGELLUS
HYPOCRISY SHAM POPEHOLY
HYPOCRITE CANT BIGOT CHEAT
FACER FRAUD BLIFIL CAFARD
HUMBUG MAWWORM CHADBAND
DECEIVER TARTUFFE
HYPOCRITICAL FALSE SLAPE
DOUBLE CANTING PLASTER
POPEHOLY SPECIOUS
HYPOCYCLOID ASTROID
HYPODERMIS SKIN
HYPOPHARYNX LINGUA LABIELLA
HYPOSTASIS PERSON
HYPOSTATIZE ENTIFY
HYPOTENUSE SUBTENSE
HYPOTHESIS SYSTEM THEORY
WEGENER SUPPOSAL
HYPOTHETICAL IDEAL
HYPOTRACHELIUM GORGERIN
HYPTIS OREGANO
HYRAX DAS CONY CONEY DAMAN
WABUR DASSIE WABBER ASHKOKO
KLIPDAS HYRACOID
HYSTERIA MOTHER PIBLOKTO
TARASSIS
(PRONE TO —) VAPORISH
(RELIGIOUS —) LATA
HYSTERICAL SHRIEKY

Y HI HY ICH ISS SHE ITEM UTCH
INDIA UTCHY
(— AM) ISE CHAM ICHAM
(— HAD) CHAD
(— WILL) CHILL ICHULLE
(— WOULD) CHUD
ALEMUS (FATHER OF —) APOLLO
(MOTHER OF —) CALLIOPE
AMB IAMBIC IAMBUS
(DOUBLE —) DIIAMB
APETUS (FATHER OF —) URANUS
(MOTHER OF —) GAEA
(SON OF —) ATLAS MENOETIUS
(WIFE OF —) ASIA CLYMENE
APYGIANS MESSAPII
ATROCHEMICAL SPAGYRIC
ATROCHEMISTRY SPAGYRIC
ANAG CAGAYAN
BEX KYL TEK TUR ZAC KAIL BEDEN
EVECK IZARD JAELA EVICKE
SAKEEN
BIS GUARA GANNET HADADA JABIRU
TURKEY CICONIID IRONHEAD
CARIUS (DAUGHTER OF —) ERIGONE
PENELOPE
(FAITHFUL DOG OF —) MOERA
(FATHER OF —) OEBALUS
CE YS GEAL FROST GLACE CRYSTAL
VERGLAS
(— IN ROUGH BLOCKS) RUBBLE
(ANCHOR —) FRAZIL
(DRIFTING FRAGMENT OF —) PAN
CALF
(PATCH OF —) RONE
(PINNACLE OF —) SERAC
(RIDGE OF —) HAMMOCK HUMMOCK
(SEA —) GLACON SLUDGE
(SHORE —) FAST
(SLUSHY —) SISH
(SOFT —) SLOB LOLLY
(THIN NEW —) DISH PANCAKE
(THIN OR FLOATING —) FLOE GRUE
BRASH
(WATER —) SHERBET
EBERG BERG GROWLER
FLOEBERG
EBOAT SKEETER
E CREAM BISK CREAM GLACE
AUFAIT BISQUE NOUGAT TASTER
SPUMONI TORTONI
E CREAM CONE CORNET
ED COLD GLACE FRAPPE
EFISH SALANGID
EHOUSE (— WORKER) AIRMAN

ICELAND

BALLAD: RIMUR
CAPITAL: REIKJAVIK REYKJAVIK
COIN: AURAR EYRIR KRONA
FISH: SKYR SVIO BLOOMOR
HAROFISK
EPIC: EDDA SAGA
FIRST SETTLER: ARNARSON
GEYSER: GRYLA
GIANT: ATLI
GLACIER: HOFSJOKULL
LANGJOKULL VATNAJOKULL

HERO: BELE ERIC LEIF
SIGUROSSON
LAKE: MYVATN THORISVATN
MEASURE: SET ALIN LINA ALMUD
TURMA ALMENN ALMUDE
FERFET POTTUR FATHMUR
FERALIN FERMILA OLTUNNA
SJOMILA
MOUNTAIN: JOKUL
PARLIAMENT: ALTHING
REPUBLIC: LYOVELDIO
RIVER: HVITA JOKULSA THJORSA
TOWN: AKRANES AKUREYRI
KEFLAVIK KOPAVOGUR
VOLCANIC ISLAND: SURTSEY
VOLCANO: LAKI ASKJA HEKLA
WATERFALL: GULLFOSS
DETTIFOSS
WEIGHT: PUND POUND

ICHNEUMON URVA NYMSS VANSIRE
ICHOROUS GLEETY
ICHU HICHU STIPA
ICICLE ICARY ICKLE YOKEL TANGLE
SHOGGLE SHOOGLE COCKBELL
ICINESS GLARE
ICING ICE PIPING FROSTING
MERINGUE
ICON IKON EIKON IMAGE DEESIS
ICONOCLAST DEBUNKER
ICONOSTASIS DIASTYLE
ICTEROHEMATURIA CARCEAG
ICTONYX ZORILLA
ICTUS ACCENT DOWNBEAT
ICY GELID BOREAL FRIGID WINTRY
GLACIAL
ID ES ORF GARDON SYPHILID

IDAHO

CAPITAL: BOISE
COUNTY: ADA GEM BUTTE LATAH
POWER TETON CARNAS CASSIA
BENEWAH KOOTENAI
DAM: OXBOW BROWNLEE
INDIAN: BANNOCK KALISPEL
NEZPERCE SHOSHONI
LAKE: BEAR GRAYS PRIEST
MOUNTAIN: RYAN BORAH RHODES
TAYLOR BIGBALDY BLUENOSE
MOUNTAIN RANGE: CABINET
SELKIRK
NICKNAME: GEM
RIVER: SNAKE LOCHSA SALMON
PAYETTE
SPRINGS: SODA HOOPER
LAVAHOT
STATE BIRD: BLUEBIRD
STATE FLOWER: SYRINGA
TOWN: BUHL MALAD NAMPA
MOSCOW REXBURG POCATELLO

IDAS (BROTHER OF —) LYNCEUS
(FATHER OF —) APHAREUS
(WIFE OF —) MARPESSA
IDE ORFE
IDEA EGG GIG KINK EIDOS IMAGE
THING ANONYM DHARMA ECTYPE

FIGURE INTENT NOTICE NOTION
RECEPT THREAP THROPE BEGRIFF
CONCEIT CONCEPT GIMMICK
GLIMPSE MAROTTE OPINION
PROJECT SPECIES SURMISE
THOUGHT GIMCRACK NOTIONAL
(—S OF LITTLE VALUE) STUFF
(CENTRAL —) ARGUMENT
(CONSERVATIVE —S) FOGYISM
(DULL STUPID —S) STODGE
(FAINT —) GLIMMER
(FALSE —) FALLACY
(FANTASTIC —) VAPOR
(FAVORITE —) HORSE
(FIXED —) TICK
(FUNDAMENTAL —) KEYNOTE
(IRRATIONAL —) FOLLY
(MUSICAL —) SENTENCE
(ODD —) FREAK
(OVERWORKED —) CLICHE
(PLATONIC —) ESSENCE
(RECURRING —) BURDEN
(STALE —S) BILGE
(SUPERSTITIOUS —) FREIT
(TRANSCENDENT —) FORM
(PL.) THOUGHT
IDEAL ISM IDEA DREAM AERIAL
BEAUTY DOMNEI DREAMY MENTAL
UNREAL PATTERN PERFECT
UTOPIAN ABSTRACT FANCIFUL
IDEALITY QUADRATE
(— OF BEAUTY) KALON
IDEALISM IDEOLOGY
IDEALIST IDEIST UTOPIAN FICHTEAN
UTOPIAST
IDENTICAL LIKE SAME SELF VERY
ALIKE EQUAL EVENLY PROPER
CORRECT IDENTIC NUMERIC
SELFSAME
IDENTIFICATION IDENT DOCUMENT
EQUATION
IDENTIFIED SIGNATE
IDENTIFIER BIRDER
IDENTIFY MARK NAME RANK SPOT
IDENT TALLY FINGER DISCERN
DIAGNOSE
(— WITH) ENTER
IDENTITY UNITY IPSEITY ONENESS
EQUALITY SAMENESS
IDEOGRAPH CHARACTER
(PL.) KANJI
IDEOGRAPHIC REAL
IDEOLOGICAL MENTAL
IDIOBLAST SPHERE IDIOSOME
IDIOCY ANOIA ANOESIA FATUITY
IDIOTRY MOROSIS IDIOTISM
IDIOM CANT ARGOT JUANG DORISM
IFUGAO JARGON MEDISM SPEECH
AEOLISM ANOMALY GRECISM
TURKISM DANICISM DORICISM
IDIOTISM IONICISM LANGUAGE
LOCALISM RURALISM
IDIOMORPHIC EUHEDRAL
IDIOPHONE RATTLE
IDIOSOME SPHERE
IDIOSYNCRASY WAY IDIASM
RUMNESS
IDIOT FON OAF SOT DAFF DOLT
FOOL AMENT BOOBY DUNCE FONNE

HOBBIL NIDGET NIDIOT DULLARD
NATURAL OMADAWN PINHEAD
IMBECILE INNOCENT
IDIOTIC DAFT ZANY IDIOT FATUOUS
FOOLISH WANTWIT IMBECILE
IDLE COLD DEAD HACK HAKE HANG
HULL JAUK LAKE LAZE LAZY LUSK
MUZZ SOFT SORN TICK VAIN VOID
DALLY EMPTY SHOOL SLIVE THOKE
WASTE COOTER DANDER DREAMY
FOOTER GAMMER LOUNGY OTIANT
OTIOSE SLIMSY TEETER TIDDIE
TIFFLE TRUANT UNUSED VACANT
IDLEFUL IDLESET LOAFING SAUNTER
SHACKLE SLUMBER SLUTHER
UNLUSTY VACUOUS WHIFFLE
WORLESS BASELESS FAINEANT
INACTIVE INDOLENT SHAMMOCK
SLAISTER SLOTHFUL TRIFLING
(TO BE —) SLOTH
IDLENESS LAZE RUST SLOTH IDLETY
IDLESET IDLESSE IGNAVIA VACANCY
FLANERIE IDLEHOOD INACTION
(— PERSONIFED) LAURENCE
LAWRENCE
(LIVE IN —) MAROON
IDLER BUM GAUM HAKE JAUK KERN
DRONE BADAUD BUMBLE IDLEBY
LUBBER PLAYER QUISBY RODNEY
STALKO BLELLUM BUCKEEN
DAWDLER FAITOUR FRANION
IDLESBY LOUNGER LOUTHER
LURDANE SLOUNGE TRIFLER
DOLITTLE FAINEANT IDLESHIP
LAZARONE UNWORKER WHIFFLER
IDLE WHEEL IDLER RUNNER
IDLY TOOMLY VAGUELY
IDMON (FATHER OF —) APOLLO
(MOTHER OF —) CYRENE ASTERIA
IDOCRASE EGERAN CYPRINE
VESUVIAN
IDOL GOD BAAL ICON JOSS TIKI ZEMI
ANITO BESAN EIKON GUACA HOBAL
HUACA IMAGE STOCK SWAMI
IDOLET IDOLUM MAUMET MINION
PAGODA POPPET PUPPET TERAPH
EIDOLON MAHOMET BAPHOMET
MAUMETRY PANTHEUM
(HEATHEN —) DEVIL
IDOLATER AKKUM HEATHEN IDOLIST
IDOLATROUS PAGAN IDOLISH
IDOLATRY BAALISM IMAGERY
ADULTERY MAUMETRY
IDOLIZE GOD IDOL ADORE ADMIRE
WORSHIP
IDUMAEAN EDOMITE
IDYL IDYLL BUCOLIC ECLOGUE
IDYLLIC PASTORAL
IF AN AND GIF GIN THO GEVE IFFEN
SOBEIT THOUGH PROVIDED
(— EVER) ONCE
(— NOT) BUT ELSE NISI
IGNEOUS PLUTONIC
IGNIS FATUUS WISP SPUNKIE
WILDFIRE
IGNITE FIRE TIND FLASH LIGHT
SHOOT ILLUME KINDLE CALCINE
LIGHTEN
IGNITED LIVING BURNING

IGNITER SPARKER
IGNITION FIRE LIGHTING
IGNOBLE LOW BASE MEAN VILE
ABJECT GRUBBY SORDID CURRISH
SERVILE UNNOBLE BASEBORN
SHAMEFUL
IGNOBLY BASELY
IGNOMINIOUS BASE INFAMOUS
SHAMEFUL
IGNOMINY SHAME REBUKE SCANDAL
DISGRACE DISHONOR
IGNORAMUS IDIOT IGNARO SIMPLE
AMHAAREZ
IGNORANCE IRONY TAMAS AGNOSY
AVIDYA AVIJJA BETISE NICETY
RUDITY UNSKILL DARKNESS
IDIOTISM
(FEIGNED —) IRONY
IGNORANT LAY DARK NICE RUDE
VAIN GREEN GROSS SILLY INGRAM
SIMPLE ARTLESS SECULAR
UNAWARE UNCOUTH UNKNOWN
IMPERITE INNOCENT INSCIENT
INSCIOUS NESCIENT UNTAUGHT
IGNORANTLY SIMPLY
IGNORE BALK BLOW SINK SNUB
VAIN BAULK BLINK ELIDE BYPASS
MISKEN SLIGHT DESPISE MISKNOW
CONFOUND OVERJUMP OVERLEAP
OVERLOOK
IGOROT BONTOK NABALOI KANKANAI
IGUANA GUANA GUANO LEGUAN
IJO DJO BONI BONNY
ILAIRA (FATHER OF —) LEUCIPPUS
(SISTER OF —) PHOEBE
ILEUS MISERERE
ILIA RHEA
(FATHER OF —) NUMITOR
(SON OF —) REMUS ROMULUS
ILIONE (FATHER OF —) PRIAM
(HUSBAND OF —) POLYMNESTOR
ILK KIN
ILL BAD EVIL ILLY SICK AEGER
DONCY FUNNY WISHT GROGGY
INJURY POORLY SICKLY UNWELL
SICKISH VICIOUS MISCHIEF
PHYSICAL
(— AT EASE) ASHAMED AWKWARD
ILL-ADVISED FOOLISH
ILL-BEHAVED UNTHEWED
ILL-BEING ILLTH
ILL-BODING DIRE DISMAL
ILL-BRED HOYDEN CADDISH
CHURLISH PLEBEIAN
ILL-CHOSEN UNSORTED
ILL-CONSIDERED HASTY
ILL-DEFINED BLIND VAGUE
ILLEGAL BLACK LAWLESS
UNLAWFUL WRONGOUS
(NOT —) COLD
ILLEGALITY UNLAW
ILLEGIBLE BLIND
ILLEGITIMACY BASTARDY
ILLEGITIMATE BASE BASTARD
BOOTLEG NATURAL NOTHOUS
MISBEGOT UNLAWFUL WRONGFUL
ILL-FATED UNHAPPY UNSONCY
UNCHANCY
ILL-FAVORED UGLY UNSONCY

ILL-FORMED SCRAWLY INFORMED
ILL HUMOR TID BILE DRUNT GRUMP
THRAW FANTEE SPLEEN DUDGEON
FANTIGUE
ILL-HUMORED FOUL GLUM CROOK
DUDDY GRUMPY MOROSE STUFFY
SULLEN CROOKED FRETFUL
PEEVISH
ILLIBERAL LITTLE NARROW INSULAR
GRUDGING
ILLICIT SLY BLACK ILLEGAL
UNLAWFUL
ILLIMITABLE INFINITE

ILLINOIS
CAPITAL: SPRINGFIELD
COLLEGE: AURORA EUREKA
OLIVET QUINCY SHIMER
COUNTY: BOND CASS COOK KANE
OGLE COLES MACON BUREAU
DUPAGE GRUNDY HARDIN
MASSAL PEORIA IROQUOIS
MACOUPIN SANGAMON
FRENCH SETTLEMENT: CAHOKIA
HILLS: SHAWNEE
INDIAN: FOX SAUK
LAKE: MICHIGAN
NICKNAME: PRAIRIE
RIVER: OHIO ROCK WABASH
ELKHORN MACKINAW
SANGAMON
STATE BIRD: CARDINAL
STATE FLOWER: VIOLET
STATE TREE: OAK
TOWN: PANA ALTON FLORA
OLNEY PEKIN ALBION CANTON
HERRIN JOLIET PEORIA SKOKIE
CHICAGO DECATUR GENESCO
MENDOTA NOKOMIS ROCKFORD

ILLINOISIAN SUCKER
ILLIPE BASSIA VIDORICUM
ILLITERATE UNREAD IGNORANT
MUSELESS UNTAUGHT
ILL-MADE AWKWARD
ILL-NATURED UGLY SURLY CRABBY
SNARLY SULLEN CANKERY PEEVISH
ILLNESS DROW TOUT BRASH CHILL
TRAIK MORBUS PLUNGE DISEASE
SICKNESS
(MINOR —) HURRY
(MOMENTARY —) DROW
(SUDDEN —) WEED SWEAM
ILL-NOURISHED SHELLY
ILLOGICAL SPURIOUS
ILL-OMENED DISMAL UNLUCKY
ILL-SHAPED WEEDY
ILL-SMELLING FUSTY STINKING
ILL-TEMPERED ILL FESS MEAN
PUXY CHUFF NURLY CAMMED
CHUFFY GIRNIE SHRILL SNAGGY
RAMPANT VICIOUS CAMSHACH
LUNGEOUS SHREWISH VIXENISH
ILL-TREAT FOB HOIN MISDO
AFFRONT
ILLUMINATE FIRE LIMN CLEAR
LIGHT ENLIMN ILLUME KINDLE
BESHINE CLARIFY EMBLAZE

LIGHTEN MINIATE RADIATE
EMBRIGHT FLOURISH ILLUMINE
LUMINATE
(— FAINTLY) TWILIGHT
ILLUMINATION E GLIM GLORY
LIGHT SHINE LIGHTING LUMINARY
(— INCREASE) WOMP
(— UNIT) PHOT
ILLUMINE SUN FIRE CLEAR LUMINE
ENLIGHT
ILL-USAGE ABUSE
ILLUSION DEATH ERROR FAIRY
FANCY FLESH TRICK MATTER
CHIMERA ELUSION FALLACY FICTION
MOCKERY PHANTOM RAINBOW
ZOLLNER DELUSION PHANTASM
PRESTIGE
ILLUSORY FALSE EVANID FATUOUS
APPARENT ILLUSIVE SPECTRAL
ILLUSTRATE INSTANCE
ILLUSTRATION CUT GAY ICON IKON
SHOW SPOT INSET FIGURE
COMPARE DISIMILE EXEMPLUM
INSTANCE VIGNETTE
ILLUSTRATIVE CLASSIC
ILLUSTRIOUS GRAND NOBLE NOTED
SHEEN BRIGHT CANDID HEROIC
EMINENT EXALTED GLORIED
SHINING GLORIOUS HEROICAL
LUCULENT MAGNIFIC PRECLARE
RENOWNED SPLENDID STARLIKE
ILL WILL SPITE ENMITY GRUDGE
MALICE MAUGER MAUGRE RANCOR
DESPITE AMBITION
ILL-WISHER FOE
ILUS (FATHER OF —) TROS
(MOTHER OF —) CALLIRRHOE
(SON OF —) LAOMEDON
ILVAITE YENITE LIEVRITE
ILYSIA TORTRIX
IMAGE DAP GOD MAP FORM ICON
IDOL IKON JOSS MAKE SEAL SIGN
SPIT TIKI AGNUS DITTO EPHOD
FANCY HERMA IMAGO MEDAL
MORAL PAINT PRINT SAMMY SANTO
SHAPE SIGIL SWAMI SWAMY TOTEM
AGALMA ALRAUN EFFIGY EMBLEM
FIGURE MAUMET MODULE POPPET
RECEPT REFLEX SHRINE SPHINX
STATUE SVAMIN TERAPH VISAGE
WEEPER EIDOLON EXPRESS
FANTASY GODLING IMAGERY
KATCINA PICTURE PROPOSE
CONCEIVE DAIBUTSU OPTOGRAM
PORTRAIT SURPRINT ZOOMORPH
(— IN CHINESE COSTUME)
MANDARIN
(— OF CHRIST) SUDARIUM
(— OF DEITY) SWAMI GODKIN
SVAMIN GODLING
(— OF SAINT) BULTO SAINT SANTO
GEORGE SANTON
(— OF WOOD) XOANON
(— RECALLED BY MEMORY) IDEA
(CULT —) JOSS
(FALSE —) GHOST
(GOOD-LUCK —) ALRAUN ALRUNA
(HEAVENLY —) FRAVASHI
(LINGERING —) SHADE

(MENTAL —) FANCY IMAGO RECEPT
CONCEPT FANTASY SPECIES
PHANTASM
(RADAR —) BLIP
(REFLECTED —) SHADOW SPECIES
(SEQUENCE OF —S) REVERIE
(VAGUE —S) FRINGE
(PL.) IMAGERY TERAPHIM
IMAGERY ICONISM
IMAGINARY IDEAL AERIAL FEIGNED
FICTIVE SHADOWY CHIMERAL
CHIMERIC FANCIFUL FICTIOUS
MYTHICAL NOTIONAL QUIXOTIC
ROMANTIC SCENICAL VISIONAL
IMAGINATION CHIC BRAIN FANCY
FLAME NOTION FANTASY PROJECT
THOUGHT
(DROLL —) HUMOR
IMAGINATIVE FORMFUL CREATIVE
FANCIFUL POETICAL
IMAGINE SEE WIS REDE WEEN
DREAM FANCY FEIGN FRAME GUESS
IMAGE THINK DEVISE FIGURE
IDEATE INVENT COMPASS CONCEIT
CONJURE FANCIFY FANTASY
FEATURE PICTURE PORTRAY
PROJECT PROPOSE SUPPOSE
SURMISE SUSPECT CONCEIVE
DAYDREAM JEALOUSE
IMAGINED FANCIED SUPPOSED
IMAGINER FANCIER
IMAGINING FICTION PHANTOM
IMAM IMAUM MAHDI
IMBALANCE DRIVE DYSCRASIA
IMBECILE MAD DOTE FOOL AMENT
DAFFY IDIOT CRANKY DOTARD
DOTING DOTISH CONGEON FATUOUS
IMBECILITY FATUITY
IMBIBE DRINK SMACK ABSORB
SPONGE INHAUST SWALLOW
IRRIGATE
IMBIBING SUCTION
IMBIBITORY SPONGY
IMBRUE EMBREW INSTEEP
IMBUE SOAK STEW COLOR CROWN
EMBUE INDUE SCENT STEEP TINCT
ENSOUL IMBIBE INFUSE LEAVEN
SEASON ANIMATE INGRAIN INSENSE
INSTILL SATURATE TINCTURE
IMBUED INSTINCT REDOLENT
IMIDE LACTIM SACCHARIN
IMITATE APE COPY ECHO MIME
MOCK ZANY ENSUE FORGE IMAGE
MIMIC ANSWER FOLLOW SEMBLE
COPYCAT EMULATE PAGEANT
PASTICHE RESEMBLE SIMULATE
IMITATION COPY FAKE SHAM
DUMMY IMAGE MIMIC ALPACA
ANSWER BUMPER ECTYPE SHADOW
CAMBLET FOULARD IMITANT
MIMESIS MOCKAGE MOCKERY
CHENILLE PARROTRY PASTICHE
POSTIQUE
(— OF COIN) COUNTER
(BURLESQUE —) TRAVESTY
(EXAGGERATED —) BURLESQUE
(UNSUBSTANTIAL —) GHOST
IMITATIVE ARTY MIMIC ARTFUL
ECHOIC SHODDY MIMETIC SIMULAR

SLAVISH APATETIC EPIGONAL
IMITATOR APE MIME ZANY MIMIC
COPIER COPYIST EPIGONE
EMULATOR EPIGONUS HOMERIST
IMMACULATE CLEAN CANDID
CHASTE BLOTLESS SPOTLESS
UNSOILED
IMMANENCE INBEING
IMMATERIAL MENTAL SLIGHT
ETHEREAL FORMLESS SEPARATE
TRIFLING
IMMATURE RAW CRUDE GREEN
SAPPY SMALL VEALY YOUNG
BOYISH CALLOW JEJUNE LARVAL
NEANIC TENDER GIRLISH HALFLIN
IMPUBIC LADDISH NOUVEAU
UNBAKED JUVENILE NEPIONIC
UNWEANED
IMMATURITY NONAGE
IMMEASURABLE UNTOLD INFINITE
IMMEDIACY HERE
IMMEDIATE DIRECT MODERN
PARATE SUDDEN INSTANT PRESENT
PROXIMAL SYNECTIC
IMMEDIATELY TIT ANON AWAY FAST
JUST ONCE SOON PLUMB RIGHT
ASTITE DIRECT PRESTO SUBITO
DIRECTLY HEREUPON OUTRIGHT
STRAIGHT
IMMEDIATENESS INSTANCY
IMMEMORIAL DATELESS
IMMENSE HUGE VAST GRAND GREAT
LARGE UNMEET UNRIDE TITANIC
ENORMOUS GIGANTIC INFINITE
SLASHING WHOOPING
IMMENSELY EVER
IMMENSITY VAST IMMANE IMMENSE
ENORMITY GRANDEUR HUGENESS
IMMERSE DIP SINK SOAK COVER
DOUSE MERGE MERSE SOUSE
STEEP DRENCH PLUNGE BAPTIZE
BOWSSEN DEMERGE EMBATHE
ENSTEEP IMMERGE DISSOLVE
IMMERSED DEEP INNATE
IMMERSION DIP DUNKING MERSION
IMMERSIONIST DIPPER
IMMIGRANT LAG BALT ISSEI JIMMY
METIC POMMY GUINEA HALUTZ
CHALUTZ INCOMER PILGRIM
COMELING
IMMINENCE INSTANCY
IMMINENT TOWARD PENDING
IMMOBILE FIXED STILL FROZEN
DORMANT GLACIAL TRANCED
MOVELESS
IMMOBILIZATION FUSION FIXATION
IMMOBILIZE FREEZE SPLINT
STIFFEN
IMMOBILIZED STIFF
IMMODERATE FREE DIZZY UNDUE
LAVISH UNMETH EXTREME
IMMODERATENESS EXCESS
IMMODEST FREE BRAZEN OBSCENE
INDECENT PETULANT UNCHASTE
IMMORAL BAD ILL EVIL IDLE LOOSE
WRONG WANTON CORRUPT VICIOUS
CULPABLE DEPRAVED INDECENT
SLIPPERY
IMMORTAL DIVINE ENDLESS

ETERNAL GODLIKE UNDYING
ENDURING UNDEADLY
IMMORTALITY ATHANASY ETERNITY
IMMOVABLE PAT SET FAST FIRM
FIXED RIGID ADAMANT SITFAST
CONSTANT IMMOBILE IMMOTIVE
OBDURATE
IMMUNE FREE SALTED
IMMUNITY SOC CHARTER FREEDOM
LIBERTY WOODGELD
IMMURE MURE WALL CONFINE
CLOISTER IMPRISON
IMMUTABILITY ONENESS
IMMUTABLE ETERNAL
IMP PUG LIMB DEVILET DEVILING
DEVILKIN FOLLETTO
IMPACT HIT JAR BEAT BITE BLOW
BUMP DASH JOLT SLAM BRUNT
CLASH FEEZE PEISE POISE PULSE
SHOCK SKITE GLANCE STROKE
CONTACT IMPULSE
IMPAIR MAR BLOT HARM HURT
MANK SOUR WEAR ALLOY CLOUD
CRACK CRAZE DECAY ERODE QUAIL
SPOIL TAINT ACRAZE DAMAGE
DEADEN DEFACE HINDER INJURE
LABEFY LESSEN REDUCE SICKEN
WEAKEN WORSEN BLEMISH DISABLE
IMPEACH REFRACT SHATTER
STRETCH VITIATE DECREASE
ENFEEBLE IMBECILE IMPERISH
INFRINGE LABEFACT
(— BY INACTIVITY) RUST
(— ESSENTIALLY) RUIN
IMPAIRED HURT STALE CROCKY
FLYBLOWN
(— BY AGE) FUSTY
(— IN TONE) BREATHY
IMPAIRMENT FAULT SPOIL DOTAGE
IMPAIR INJURY LESION BEATING
DEFICIT DISEASE EROSION WEARING
AKINESIA PAIRMENT
(— OF CONSCIOUSNESS) ABSENCE
IMPALA PALLA PALLAH REDBUCK
ROODEBOK
IMPALE BAIT SPIT GANCH GANSH
SPEAR SPIKE STAKE STICK STING
SKIVER TRANSFIX
IMPALPABLE ELUSIVE
IMPART GIVE SHED TELL BREAK
DRILL SHARE YIELD BESTOW
COMMON CONFER CONVEY DIRECT
IMPUTE INSTIL PARTEN REVEAL
DELIVER DIVULGE PURPORT
DISCOVER INSTRUCT INTIMATE
(— TONE) TONE
(— ZEST) ANIMATE
IMPARTIAL EVEN FAIR JUST EQUAL
LEVEL NEUTER UNBIASED
IMPARTIALITY CANDOR EQUITY
EQUACITY EVENNESS
IMPARTIALLY FAIRLY EQUALLY
IMPASSABLE WICKED PASSLESS
IMPASSE LOGJAM DEADLOCK
IMPASSION COMMOVE
IMPASSIONED ARDENT FERVID
FERVENT FEVERISH
IMPASSIVE FROZEN STOLID PASSIVE
STOICAL

IMPASSIVENESS APATHY MORGUE
STOICISM
IMPATIENT HOT ANTSY EAGER
HASTY SHARP TESTY FRETFUL
PEEVISH TIDIOSE CHOLERIC
PETULANT
IMPATIENTLY HASTILY
IMPEACH CALL ACCUSE CHARGE
INDICT ARRAIGN CENSURE IMPLEAD
TRAVERSE
IMPECCABLE SINLESS
IMPECUNIOUS POOR
IMPEDE BOG DAM GUM JAM LET
MAR CLOG GRAB JAMB KILL SLUG
SNAG ANNOY BLOCK CHECK CHOKE
DELAY EMBAR ESTOP HITCH SLOTH
SPOKE FETTER FORBID FORSET
HAMPER HARASS HINDER HOBBLE
PESTER RETARD STYMIE IMPEACH
PREVENT SHACKLE ENCUMBER
HANDICAP OBSTRUCT PRECLUDE
IMPEDIMENT BAR RUB CLOG SNAG
STOP BLEAR BLOCK HITCH SPOKE
STICK RUBBER SCOTCH BLINDER
EMBARGO OBSTACLE OBSTANCY
(— IN SPEECH) HAAR
IMPEDIMENTA STUFF
IMPEDING CATCH HEAVY FOULING
IMPEL PAT PUT BEAR BEAT CALL
CAST GOAD HURL MOVE SEND
URGE WHIP CARRY DRIVE FEEZE
FORCE KNOCK PRICK PULSE
COMPEL EXCITE INCITE INDUCE
PROPEL DESTINE INSPIRE INSTINCT
MOTIVATE
(— TO GREATER SPEED) GATHER
IMPELLER RUNNER
IMPEND BREW HANG DEPEND
IMPENDING PENDENT PENDING
IMMINENT MENACING
IMPENETRABLE HARD DENSE
MURKY PROOF THICK AIRTIGHT
HARDENED
IMPENITENT HARDENED OBDURATE
IMPERATIVE VITAL PRESSING
IMPERCEPTIBLE OCCULT SUBTLE
IMPERFECT ILL HALF POOR AMISS
BLIND FUZZY ROUGH FAULTY
PLATIC STICKIT UNWHOLE VICIOUS
INPARFIT MUTILOUS
IMPERFECTED INCHOATE
IMPERFECTION BUG RUB WEN
FLAW KINK MOLE SLUR VICE ERROR
FAULT BLOTCH DEFECT FOIBLE
BLEMISH CRUDITY DEFAULT
DEMERIT FAILING FRAILTY
WEAKNESS
(— IN BOTTLE) HEELTAP
(— IN GLASS) STRIA STREAK
(— IN LEATHER) FRIEZE
(— IN SILK) CORKSCREW
(— IN WICK) THIEF WASTER
IMPERFECTIVE ATELIC
IMPERFECTLY ILL HALF AMISS
IMPERFORATION ATRESIA
IMPERIAL TUFT ROYAL KINGLY
PURPLE MAJESTIC
IMPERIL RISK EXPONE EMPERIL
ENDANGER JEOPARDY

IMPERIOUS SURLY LORDLY
HAUGHTY DESPOTIC IMPERIAL
MASTERLY PRESSING
IMPERISHABLE ETERNAL UNDYING
ENDURING IMMORTAL
IMPERMANENCE ANICCA
IMPERMANENT FLEETING
IMPERSONAL COLD DEADPAN
INHUMAN ABSTRACT
IMPERSONATE ACT POSE TYPIFY
PERSONIFY
IMPERSONATION GENIUS
IMPERSONATOR ACTOR CACHINA
KACHINA KATCINA
IMPERTINENCE PAWK SNASH
AUDACITY
IMPERTINENT GAY FREE RUDE
FRESH SASSY SAUCY IMPERENT
IMPUDENT
IMPERTURBABILITY ATARAXY
ATARAXIA SANGFROID
IMPERTURBABLE COOL PLACID
GLACIAL TRANQUIL
IMPERVIOUS DEAD GASTIGHT
HARDENED HERMETIC
IMPETUOSITY FURY HASTE WRATH
FOUGUE POWDER RANDOM SPLEEN
IMPETUOUS HOT RAMP RUDE
BRASH EAGER FIERY FRECK HASTY
HEADY SHARP ARDENT BROTHE
FIERCE FLASHY LAVISH RACKLE
STRONG BUCKISH FURIOUS
HOTHEAD HOTSPUR BRAINISH
EMPRESSE HEADLONG SLAPDASH
VEHEMENT
IMPETUS BIRR FARD SEND DRIFT
GRACE SWING YMPET BENSEL
IMPACT POWDER RAVINE SWINGE
SWOUGH IMPULSE MOMENTUM
IMPINGE FALL IMPACT ASSAULT
CROSSCUT
IMPINGEMENT IMPACT
IMPIOUS UNHOLY ATHEIST ATHEOUS
GODLESS UNGODLY DOWNWEED
HOARWORT NEFANDOUS
IMPISH IMPY ELFISH WARLOCK
IMPLACABLE STOUT DEADLY
IMPLACABLY FATALLY
IMPLANT FIX IMP SOW HAFT ROOT
GRAFT INFIX INLAY ENRACE
ENROOT FASTEN INFUSE INSTIL
ENFORCE IMPRESS INSPIRE
ENTRENCH INSTINCT
IMPLANTED INBORN INSITE
IMPLEMENT (ALSO SEE TOOL) AX
AXE BAT CARD DISC DISK FORK
GRAB HACK HONE HOOK LOOM
PLOW SPUD SPUR TOOL CROOK
DRILL FLINT LANCE SCRUB SHEAR
SLICK SPADE SPOON STEEL STICK
TRIER AMGARN BEAMER BLADER
BROACH COLLAR COOLER DIBBLE
DREDGE DRIVER DUSTER EOLITH
FLAKER FLUTER HACKER HARROW
INVOKE LADDER LIPPER LUNATE
MARKER MEALER PACKER PADDLE
PALLET PESTLE PLOUGH RIMMER
SCREEN SCYTHE SEATER SEEDER
SERVER SHEARS SHOVEL SICKLE

SLICER SMOOTH BREAKER
CHOPPER CLEANER CLEAVER
ENFORCE FLESHER FLYFLAP
GAROTTE GRUBBER HARPOON
HUSTLER KNAPPER MATTOCK
NUTPICK SKIMMER SLABBER
SLASHER SLEEKER SLICKER
SPATTLE SPATULA SPITTLE
SPURTLE STAMPER STICKER
SWATHER UTENSIL AGITATOR
BUSHWACK MEASURER SCUTCHER
SEARCHER SHREDDER SKETCHER
SPLITTER SPREADER STRIPPER
TERRACER THWACKER TOLLIKER
TRANCHET TWEEZERS WARKLOOM
WORKLOOM
— **FOR CUTTING CHEESE)** HARP
— **FOR HANGING POT)** HALE
— **TO PREVENT MALT FROM**
OVERFLOWING) STROM
—**S OF HUSBANDRY)** WAINAGE
ANCIENT —) POINT SLICE AMGARN
OLITH NEOLITH RACLOIR
BAKER'S —) PEEL
CLIMBING —) CREEPER
ESKIMO —) ULU
GARDENING —) HOE RAKE SEEDER
ICKLE
HEDGING —) TRAMP
IRRIGATION —) CROWDER
LOGGING —) TODE
POTTER'S —) PALLET SPATTLE
PREHISTORIC —) CELT FLAKER
SHOVEL-LIKE —) SCOOP
SOLDERING —) DOCTOR
TORTURE —) ENGINE
UPROOTING —) MAKE
WINNOWING —) FAN
PL.) GEAR CUTLERY GAINAGE
LAUGHTS
PLICATE DIP ENWRAP CONCERN
MBROIL INCLUDE INVOLVE
PLICATION CLAIM IMPLIAL
INUENDO
LICIT COVERT
LIED TACIT IMPLICIT
LORATION PETITION
LORE ASK BEG CRY PRAY
HARM CRAVE PLEAD INVOKE
ESEECH CONJURE ENTREAT
OLICIT PETITION
LY HINT ARGUE CARRY COUCH
FER EMPLOY ENTAIL IMPORT
DUCE CONNOTE CONTAIN
CLUDE INVOLVE SIGNIFY SUGGEST
JPPOSE
OLITE RUDE UNCIVIL
OLITENESS CRUDITY
ONDERABLE FRIGORIC
ORT SAY WIT BEAR BODY TOUR
RIFT FORCE IMPLY MORAL SCOPE
NSE SOUND SPELL VALOR
MOUNT CHARGE DENOTE INGATE
TENT MATTER BETOKEN MEANING
RETEND SIGNIFY CARRIAGE
DICATE
L.) INWARDS
ORTANCE BORE MARK PITH
ORCE POISE WORTH CHARGE

IMPORT MATTER MOMENT REMARK
STRESS STROKE WEIGHT ACCOUNT
ESSENCE GRAVITY VALENCY
EMPHASIS
IMPORTANT DEAR DREE HIGH MAIN
REAL GRAVE GREAT GAPING
NEEDLE STRONG URGENT VALOUR
CAPITAL CRUCIAL EMINENT
MATTERY SERIOUS EVENTFUL
MATERIAL
IMPORTER MILLINER
IMPORTUNATE URGENT INSTANT
DEVILING EXIGEANT PRESSING
IMPORTUNE BEG BEAT BONE TOUT
TEASE BESIEGE INSTANT SOLICIT
TERRIFY INSTANCE
IMPORTUNITY BRASS URGENCY
IMPOSE LAY SET TOP CLAP GIVE
LEVY MUMP POLE SORN ABUSE
APPLY INPUT STAMP TRUMP
BURDEN CHARGE ENJOIN ENTAIL
FASTEN FATHER IMPONE IMPUTE
BLAFLUM DICTATE INFLICT
IRROGATE
(— UPON) FOB GAG HUM LAY DUPE
SELL CULLY TRAIL BLUDGE DELUDE
EXCISE HUMBUG NUZZLE DECEIVE
HOODWINK
IMPOSED BOUNDEN
IMPOSING BIG EPIC BUDGE BURLY
GRAND HEFTY NOBLE PROUD
AUGUST EPICAL FEUDAL PORTLY
HAUGHTY POMPOUS STATELY
HANDSOME SONORANT SONOROUS
(— UPON) PRACTICE PRACTISE
IMPOSITION BAM COD HUM LEVY
SELL TAIL GOUGE IMPOT CHOUSE
GAMMON INTAKE TAILLE IMPOSAL
ARTIFICE IMPOSURE
(MILITARY —) CESS
IMPOSSIBLE HOPELESS
IMPOST LAY TAX CAST LEVY TAIL
TASK TOLL ABWAB ANNALE AVANIA
EXCISE GABELLE POUNAMU
TALLAGE TONNAGE TRIBUTE
CHAPTREL SPRINGER
(PL.) CUSTOMS
IMPOSTOR FOB FAKE GULL IDOL
CHEAT FAKER FRAUD GOUGE
QUACK BUNYIP FOURBE HUMBUG
MUMPER EMPIRIC FAITOUR
PROCTOR SHAMMER PHANTASM
IMPOSTURE GAG FAKE HOAX SHAM
CHEAT FRAUD TRICK DECEIT
HUMBUG JUGGLE ARTIFICE
DELUSION JUGGLERY
IMPOTENCE ACRATIA UNMIGHT
WEAKNESS
IMPOTENCY UNWELTH
IMPOTENT WEAK FRIGID PAULIE
UNABLE STERILE UNMIGHTY
IMPOUND FIND POUND INTERN
IMPOVERISH PILL CLOUD BEGGAR
IMPOOR SICKEN DEPLETE DEPRESS
EMPOWER BANKRUPT POVERISH
IMPOVERISHED POOR OBOLARY
BANKRUPT INDIGENT
IMPRACTICAL CRAZY FECKLESS
IMPRECATE WISH

IMPRECATION DASH OATH PIZE
WISH BLAME CURSE DAMME
DAMMIT CONSARN ANATHEMA
IMPREGNABILITY STRENGTH
IMPREGNABLE FAST PROOF
IMPREGNATE BIG HOP DOPE FILL
LIME MILT BREED IMBUE STOCK
STUFF TINCT AERATE CHARGE
INFORM INFUSE LEAVEN SEASON
ASPHALT ENVENOM IMPREGN
CHROMATE CONCEIVE CREOSOTE
FRICTION FRUCTIFY GRAPHITE
MEDICATE PERMEATE SATURATE
SILICATE TINCTURE
IMPREGNATED BRED COATED
IMPRESS FIX BITE COIN DING DINT
ETCH MARK AFFIX BRAND CLAMP
CRIMP DRIVE GRAVE GRILL INFIX
PRESS PRINT REACH SEIZE STAMP
STEAD WRITE AFFECT ENSEAL
FASTEN INCUSE INDENT SALUTE
STRIKE ANTIQUE ENGRAVE
ENSTAMP IMPLANT IMPREST
IMPRINT INSENSE INSCRIBE
NEGATIVE
(— DEEPLY) DELVE ENGRAVE
(— SUDDENLY) SMITE
(— WITH FEAR) AFFRIGHT
IMPRESSED BLIND ANTIQUE
INDENTED
IMPRESSIBLE WAXY
IMPRESSION CUT HIT AURA CAST
CHOP DENT DINT IDEA MARK MOLD
SEAL STEP STIR FANCY GOUGE
IMAGE MOULD STAMP STATE
ECTYPE EFFECT ENGRAM FIGURE
INCUSE OFFSET SIGNET STRIKE
EOPHYTE ETCHING FANTASY
IMPRESS MOULAGE OPINION
SEALING SQUEEZE STENCIL
TOOLING BLANKING ENGRAMMA
PRESSION PRESSURE STAMPAGE
TOOLMARK
(— ON COIN) CROSS
(— WITHOUT INK) ALBINO
(AUDITORY —) SOUND
(DOUBLE —) MACKLE MACULE
(IMMEDIATE —) APERCU
(MENTAL —) GRAVING
(STRONG —) HUNCH
(VIVID —) SPLASH
IMPRESSIONABLE SOFT WAXY
WAXEN TENDER PLASTIC PASSIBLE
IMPRESSIONIST LUMINIST
IMPRESSIVE BIG FAT EPIC AWFUL
GRAND NOBLE PROUD EPICAL
PESANTE STATELY TEARING
WEIGHTY FORCIBLE IMPOSING
SMASHING SONORANT SONOROUS
STUNNING
IMPRINT DINT ETCH SIGN STEP
PRESS STAMP CUTOFF FASTEN
STRIKE ENGRAVE ENSTAMP
IMPRESS APREYNTE EPIGRAPH
PRESSION PRESSURE STAMPAGE
(— ON CHEEK) FASTEN
IMPRISON JUG LAG NUN BOND
GAOL HULK JAIL SEAL SHOP WARD
CROWD EMBAR GRATE COMMIT

IMMURE JIGGER PRISON SLOUGH CONFINE INTOWER BASTILLE
IMPRISONED FAST
IMPRISONMENT BAND BOND ARREST CHAINS DURESS PRISON CUSTODY DURANCE
IMPROBABLE FISHY UNLIKE UNLIKELY
IMPROMPTU GLIB SUDDEN OFFHAND
IMPROPER BAD PAH PAW AMISS LARGE UNDUE UNFELE UNJUST ILLICIT INDECENT TORTIOUS UNSEEMLY WRONGOUS
IMPROPRIETY SOLECISM
IMPROVE FIX GAIN GOOD GROW HELP MEND AMEND EDIFY EMEND GRADE MOISE SMART TOUCH BETTER ENRICH PROFIT ADVANCE BENEFIT CORRECT ELEVATE PROMOTE RECTIFY UPSWING
(— APPEARANCE OF HORSE) BISHOP
(— APPEARANCE OF TEA) FACE
(— CONDUCTIVITY) AGE
IMPROVED BETTER
IMPROVEMENT AMENDS PICKUP POLICY PROFIT REDRESS UPSWING
IMPROVIDENT PRODIGAL WASTEFUL
(— PERSON) MICAWBER
IMPROVISATION THEME CALYPSO
IMPROVISE JAM COOK FAKE PONG VAMP FANTASY
IMPRUDENCE FOLLY
IMPRUDENT FESS RASH FALSE UNWARY FOOLISH RECKLESS
IMPUDENCE GALL BRASS CHEEK MOUTH SLACK BRONZE PUPPYISM
IMPUDENT BOLD COXY FACY RUDE BANTY BARDY BRASH FRESH GALLY LIPPY SASSY SAUCY BRASSY BRAZEN CHEEKY STOCKY BIGGETY CHUNKED FORWARD GALLOWS PERKING INSOLENT MALAPERT
IMPUDENTLY COOLY COOLLY FRESHLY
IMPUGN DENY FALSE DISPUTE IMPEACH
IMPULSE FIT BIAS RESE SEND URGE DRIVE SPEND START DESIRE MOTIVE SIGNAL SPLEEN YETZER CALLING CONATUS IMPETUS INSTINCT MOVEMENT STIRRING
(BLIND —) ATE
(ELECTRICAL —) KICK
(SPONTANEOUS —) ACCORD
(SUDDEN —) SPLEEN
(SUPERNATURAL —) AFFLATUS
IMPULSION SWING IMPULSE
IMPULSIVE QUICK FITFUL HEADLONG
IMPURE DRY FOUL LEWD GROSS HORRY FILTHY TURBID UNPURE UNCLEAN VICIOUS INDECENT MACULATE
IMPURITY CRUD DONOR DROSS FEDITY ACCEPTER FOULNESS
(— IN LINT) SHALE
(— IN MINERAL) GANG GANGUE
(PL.) SCUM GARBLE SLUMMAGE
IMPUTATION SCANDAL

IMPUTE LAY RET ARET EVEN WITE COUNT REFER CHARGE FASTEN IMPOSE OBJECT RECKON REPUTE ASCRIBE ENTITLE IMPEACH
IN A I N Y AT TO BAJO INBY INTO UPON ALONG INTIL
(— A FAINT) AWAY
(— A SERIES) SERIATIM
(— A STATE OF ACTION) ENERGIC
(— ACCORDANCE) AFTER
(— ADDITION) EKE TOO ALSO ABOVE AGAIN ALONG FORBY STILL BEYOND BESIDES FARTHER FURTHER MOREOVER OVERPLUS THERETIL
(— ADVANCE) AHEAD FORTH BEFORE
(— ANY CASE) EVER HOWEVER
(— BEHALF OF) PRO
(— CASE THAT) AUNTERS
(— CIRCULATION) ABROAD
(— CONNECTION WITH) FORNENT FERNINST
(— EARNEST) AGOOD
(— EXCESS OF) OVER
(— FACT) SOOTH TRULY INDEED ITSELF MERELY VERILY ACTUALLY VERAMENT
(— FAITH) IVADS EFECKS YFACKS
(— FRONT) FORE AFACE FORNE AGAINST PARAVANT
(— FULL) ALONG
(— GOOD SEASON) BETIMES
(— GOOD SPIRITS) BOBBISH
(— GRACEFUL MANNER) ADAGIO
(— JEST) AGAME
(— NO MANNER) NOWISE NAEGATES
(— ONE DIRECTION) ANON
(— ORDER) FOR ATAUNT ATAUNTO
(— PLACE OF) FOR WITH INSTEAD
(— POSSESSION) WITHIN
(— PROGRESS) AFOOT TOWARD
(— PROPER MANNER) DULY
(— RESPECT TO) ANENT
(— RETURN FOR) AGAINST
(— ROTATION) ABOUT
(— SO FAR AS) AS QUA
(— SOLE CONTROL) ABSOLUTE
(— SOOTH) PARFEY PERFAY
(— SPITE OF) FOR ALTHO MALGRE AGAINST DESPITE MALGRADO
(— SUSPENSE) PENDING
(— THE DOING OF) WITH
(— THE FIRST PLACE) IMP IMPRIMIS
(— THE FUTURE) HENCE
(— THE MORNING) MANE
(— THE REAR) AREAR ASTERN
(— THE REGIONS OF UNBELIEVERS) IPI
(— THE SAME PLACE) IBID IBIDEM
(— THE SAME WAY) AS
(— TOWARD) INOWER
(— TRUTH) MARRY SOOTH CERTES INDEED VERILY SOOTHLY FORSOOTH
(— VAIN) WASTELY
(— VIEW OF THE FACT THAT) SEEING
(— WHAT MANNER) HOW QUOMODO

INABILITY (— TO FEED) APHAGIA
(— TO MASTICATE) AMASESIS
(— TO SPEAK) ALOGIA ANEPIA DUMBNESS
(— TO WALK) ABASIA
INACCESSIBLE COY REMOTE UNGAIN WICKED SHADOWY
INACCESSIBILITY FASTNESS
INACCURATE SOUR FALSE LOOSE FAULTY UNJUST INEXACT IMPROP SLIPSHOD
INACHUS (DAUGHTER OF —) IO
(FATHER OF —) OCEANUS
(MOTHER OF —) TETHYS
(SON OF —) PHORONEUS
INACTION RUST
INACTIVATE MOTHBALL
INACTIVE LAX DEAD DRUG FLAT IDLE LAZY MESO SLOW HEAVY INERT NOBLE SLACK SULKY ASL■ SUPINE CESSANT DORMANT PASSIVE RESTIVE COMATOSE COMATOUS DEEDLESS DILATORY FAINEANT SLOTHFUL SLUGGISH
INACTIVITY SLOTH ANERGY ANERGIA ABEYANCE IDLENESS CESSATION
INADEQUACY DEFECT FRAILTY SCARCITY
INADEQUATE BAD BARE POOR T INEPT SHORT SLACK FEEBLE ST■ FOOLISH INVALID SLENDER HIGHLAND INFERIOR
INADEQUATELY BADLY SLACK SLACKLY
INADVERTENCE LAPSUS
INADVERTENT CARELESS
INAJA JAGUA
INALIENABLE INHERENT
INAMORATA AMORADO AMORET
INANE DIZZY EMPTY JERKY SILL\ VAPID JEJUNE VACANT FATUOUS FOOLISH INSIPID VACUOUS IMBE SLIPSLOP TRIFLING
INANGA MINNOW
INANIMATE DEAD DULL BRUTE INERT DEADLY STOLID STUPID LIFELESS
INANITY FATUITY VACUITY
INAPPLICABLE SPURIOUS
INAPPROPRIATE INEPT UNAPT UNDUE FOREIGN UNHAPPY
INAPT BACKWARD FOOTLESS
INARTICULATA LYOPOMA
INARTICULATE DUMB LAME TH■
INARTISTIC ARTLESS
INATTENTION ABSENCE NEGLE■ APROSEXIA
INATTENTIVE DEAF SLACK ABS■ REMISS SUPINE DREAMSY UNTE CARELESS DISTRAIT HEEDLESS MINDLESS
INAUDIBLE SECRET
INAUDIBLY INWARDLY SECRETL
INAUGURATE AUGUR BEGIN HANDSEL INITIATE
INAUSPICIOUS BAD ILL EVIL FC ADVERSE OBSCENE OMINOUS UNHAPPY UNLUCKY SINISTER

INAUTHENTIC SPURIOUS
INBORN GENIAL INBRED INNATE
NATIVE CONNATE NATURAL
HABITUAL INHERENT
INBRED INBORN INNATE
INBREED SELF
INBREEDING ENDOGAMY
INCA INGUA OREJON
INCALCULABLE UNTOLD SUMLESS
UNKNOWN
INCA MAGIC FLOWER CANTUT
CANTUTA
INCANDESCENCE GLOW
INCANDESCENT BRIGHT
INCANTATION CHARM DAWUT
SPELL CARMEN FETISH MANTRA
CANTION CHANTRY GREEGREE
INCAPABLE DEAD NUMB UNABLE
HANDLESS
INCAPACITATE NAPOO UNFIT
NOBBLE UNABLE DISABLE
INCAPACITATED FLAT DISABLED
STRICKEN
INCARCERATE IMMURE CONFINE
IMPRISON
INCARNATE BODIED EMBODY
CARNATE ENFLESH HUMANIFY
INCARNATION IMAGE ADVENT
AVATAR GENIUS MNEVIS TERTON
HUTUKTU EPIPHANY
INCAUTIOUS RASH UNWARY
UNCHARY UNTENTY CAREFREE
RECKLESS
INCENDIARY FIREBUG ARSONIST
BOUTEFEU
INCENSE CENSE INFLAME KETURAH
PROVOKE IRRITATE THYMIAMA
(— INGREDIENT) ONYCHA
(— VESSEL) SHIP
INCENSED RAW IRATE WROTH
WRATHFUL
INCENTIVE BROD GOAD SPUR PRICK
MOTIVE IMPETUS IMPULSE INCITIVE
STIMULUS
INCEPTION ORIGIN ANCESTRY
INCESSANT STEADY ENDLESS
CONSTANT
INCESSANTLY FOREVER
INCH UNCH PRIME UNCIA
(100TH OF —) POINT
(4 —S) HANDFUL
(48TH OF —) IRON
(9 —S) SPAN
(ABOUT 7 —S) FISTMELE
INCHOATE FORMLESS
INCIDENT GO EVENT LIABLE
CAUTION EPISODE PASSAGE
SUBJECT ACCIDENT CASUALTY
OCCASION
(AMUSING —) BREAK
(LITERARY —) BIT
INCIDENTAL BY BYE SIDE STRAY
CASUAL EPISODIC GLANCING
INCIDENT
INCIDENTALLY BYHAND OBITER
APROPOS
INCINERATE COMBUST CREMATE
INCINERATOR BURNER
INCIPIENCE BUD

INCIPIENT INITIAL GERMINAL
INCHOATE
INCISE CHOP RASE INCIDE CHANNEL
ENGRAVE
INCISION CUT GASH SLIT SNIP
ISSUE SCORE BROACH SCOTCH
STREAK CUTDOWN DIACOPE
APLOTOMY CECOTOMY COLOTOMY
INCISIVE ACID KEEN CRISP SHARP
BITING BRUTAL CUTTING ACULEATE
INCISOR CUTTER NIPPER GATHERER
INCITE EGG HIE HOY PUT SIC TAR
ABET BUZZ EDGE FIRE GOAD LASH
MOVE PROD SICK SNIP SPUR STIR
URGE AWAKE CHIRK IMPEL PRICK
PROKE SPARK SPURN STING TEMPT
AROUSE ENTICE EXCITE EXHORT
FOMENT HALLOO INDUCE KINDLE
NETTLE PROMPT UPSTIR ANIMATE
COMMOVE INCENSE INSPIRE
PROMOVE PROVOKE QUICKEN
SOLICIT INCITATE MOTIVATE
(— SECRETLY) SUBORN
(— TO ATTACK) SET HIRR SOOL
INCITEMENT GOAD PROD SPUR
STING MOTIVE EGGMENT STIRRING
(— OF LITIGATION) BARRATRY
INCITER FEEDER MONITOR
INCENSOR INCENTOR
INCLEMENCY RIGOR CRUELTY
TYRANNY ASPERITY HARDNESS
SEVERITY
INCLEMENT RAW HARD RUDE SOUR
GURLY STARK COARSE SEVERE
UNFINE UNKINDLY
(NOT —) OPEN CIVIL
INCLINATION DIP GEE MAW PLY
SET BENT BIAS BROO CANT CARE
DRAG DRAW EDGE FALL GUST
HANG LEAN LIKE LIST LOVE LUST
MIND SLEW TURN VEIN WILL BEVEL
BOSOM DRAFT DRIFT FANCY GRAIN
HABIT HIELD HUMOR KNACK LURCH
PITCH POISE SLANT SLOPE STUDY
SWING TASTE THEAT TREND
AFFECT ANIMUS ANLAGE ASCENT
DESIRE DEVICE GATHER GENIUS
INTENT LIKING MOTION NOTION
PONDUS RELISH SQUINT TALENT
YETZER APTNESS CONATUS
COURAGE CURRENT DESCENT
DRAUGHT FANTASY INKLING
LEANING STOMACH VERSANT
WILNING APTITUDE DEVOTION
GRADIENT PENCHANT TENDENCY
VELLEITY VERGENCY WOULDING
(— DOWNWARD) DIP DESCENT
HANGING
(— OF OARSMAN'S BODY) LAYBACK
(PREDOMINATE —) STRENGTH
INCLINE APT BOW DIP TIP WRY
BEND BIAS BREW CANT CAST DOCK
DOOK DOOR DROP GIVE HANG HEEL
HELD HILL LEAN LIKE LIST PEND
RAKE STAY SWAY TILT TURN BEVEL
CLIMB CLINE DROOP FLECT HIELD
JINNY OFFER SHAPE SLANT SLOPE
SOUND VERGE AFFECT GLACIS
INTEND SHELVE STEEVE UPBROW

DECLINE DESCEND GANGWAY
PROPEND PROCLINE PROCLIVE
(— SKI) EDGE
INCLINED APT SIB BENT CANT FAIN
RIFE VAIN ARAKE GIVEN PRONE
READY COUCHE MINDED PROMPT
SLOPED SUPINE FORWARD HANGING
OBLIQUE PRONATE STUDIED
AFFECTED DISPOSED ENCLITIC
PROPENSE SIDELING TALENTED
(— TO DRINK) BIBULOUS
INCLINING HILLY SHELVY SLOPING
CERNUOUS SIDELING
INCLUDE ADD LAP HAVE TAKE
ANNEX COUCH COVER IMPLY
EMPLOY ENSEAM RECKON BELOUKE
COLLECT CONTAIN EMBRACE
IMMERSE INVOLVE RECOUNT
SUBSUME COMPRISE CONCLUDE
(— IN LIST) ENGROSS
INCLUDING TO CUM
INCLUSIVE GRAND CAPABLE
CATHOLIC
INCLUSIVELY BROADLY
INCLUSUS RECLUSE
INCOHERENT FUZZY BROKEN
RAVING INCHOATE
INCOHERENTLY IDLY
INCOMBUSTIBLE APYROUS
ASBESTIC
INCOME GAIN PORT RENT LIVING
PEWAGE PEWING PROFIT SALARY
FACULTY INTRADO INTRATE
PRODUCE REVENUE STIPEND
INTEREST PROCEEDS
(ANNUAL —) RENTE
(UNFORESEEN —) GRAVY
INCOMMENSURATE UNEQUAL
INCOMMODE VEX ANNOY MOLEST
PLAGUE TROUBLE DISQUIET
INCOMPARABLE ALONE
INCOMPATIBILITY SOLECISM
ANTIPATHY
INCOMPETENT INEPT UNFIT
SLOUCH UNABLE UNMEET FECKLESS
HANDLESS HELPLESS SPLITTER
INCOMPLETE WANE BLIND ROUGH
BROKEN UNDONE DIVIDED LACKING
PARTIAL IMMATURE INCHOATE
INCOMPLETELY BADLY HALVES
INCOMPOSITE PRIME
INCOMPREHENSIBLE PARTIAL
COCKEYED
INCONCLUSIVE FUZZY
INCONGRUITY JAR SOLECISM
INCONGRUOUS ALIEN ABSURD
INCONNU CONY NELMA CONNIE
SHEEFISH
INCONSIDERABLE LIGHT PETTY
LITTLE
INCONSIDERATE RASH UNKIND
ASOCIAL RECKLESS
INCONSISTENCY HOLE
INCONSPICUOUS OBSCURE
INCONSTANCY CHANGE LEVITY
INCONSTANT FICKLE BRUCKLE
FLUXILE SLIDING VARIOUS FLUXIBLE
MOVEABLE VARIABLE
INCONTESTABLE SURE CLEAN
CERTAIN

INCONTINENCE ENURESIS
INCONTINENT LOOSE LAXATIVE
INCONTROVERTIBLE GRAND
INCONVENIENCE FASH BOTHER
CUMBER STRESS SQUEEZE
DISQUIET
INCONVENIENT UNKED CLUMSY
UNBANE UNGAIN AWKWARD
UNHANDY ANNOYING UNCHANCY
UNTOWARD
INCOORDINATION ASTASIA
INCORPORATE MIX FOLD FUSE JOIN
ANNEX KNEAD MERGE UNITE
ABSORB EMBODY ENGRAIN ENTRAIN
INWEAVE INCORPSE
(— IN WALL) ENGAGE
INCORPOREAL AERY BODILESS
ASOMATOUS
INCORRECT BAD ILL FALSE WRONG
PECCANT UNRIGHT UNSOUND
VICIOUS
INCORRIGIBLE HARD
INCORRUPTIBLE IMMORTAL
INCREASE UP ADD EIK EKE IMP WAX
BUMP ECHE GAIN GROW HELP HIKE
ITCH JACK JUMP MEND MORE MUCH
PLUS PUSH RISE SOAR THEE THRO
BOOST BUILD BULGE CLIMB CROWD
FLUSH FRESH HEAVE LARGE RAISE
SPURT SWELL ACCENT ACCESS
BETTER BIGGEN CHANGE CREASE
DEEPEN DOUBLE EXPAND EXTEND
EXTENT GATHER GROWTH SPREAD
SPRING ADVANCE AMPLIFY AUCTION
AUGMENT AUXESIS BALLOON
DISTEND ELEVATE ENGROSS
ENHANCE ENLARGE GREATEN
IMPROVE INFLATE MAGNIFY
STEEPEN SURCRUE ACCRESCE
ADDITION COMPOUND FLOURISH
HEIGHTEN LENGTHEN MAJORATE
MAXIMATE MAXIMIZE MULTIPLY
THRODDEN
(— AT USURY) OCKER
(— HEAT OF KILN) RUSTLE GLISTER
(— IN PAY) FOGY FOGIE
(— IN STRENGTH) FRESHEN
(— KNOWLEDGE) ENRICH
(— POWER) SOUP
(— PRICE BY BIDDING) CANT
(— SPEED) JAZZ
(— STITCHES) FASHION
(— SUDDENLY) LEAP
(PRICE —) RIST
(SHORT-TERM —) BOOMLET
INCREASING GROWING CRESCENT
CRESCIVE DILATANT SWELLING
(— RAPIDLY) BOOMING
INCREDIBLE TALL STEEP DAMNED
FABULOUS
INCREDULITY UNBELIEF
INCREDULOUS INFIDEL
INCREMENT DOSE DELTA INCREASE
INCRIMINATE ACCUSE
INCRUST FOUL
INCRUSTATION CRUD MOSS CRUST
SCALE TARTAR FOULING FURRING
INCUBATE SIT BROOD CLOCK
COVER HATCH

INCUBATOR FURNACE HATCHER
COUVEUSE ISOLETTE
INCUBUS DUSE MARE DUSIO
NIGHTMARE
INCULCATE BREED INFIX INCULK
INFUSE IMPLANT IMPRESS INSTILL
INCULCATED BRED
INCUMBENT COARB BEARER
INCUR RUN BEAR GAIN WAGE
CONTRACT
INCURABLE BOOTLESS HOPELESS
INCURRENT INHALANT
INCURSION RAID ROAD FORAY
INFALL INROAD RAZZIA DESCENT
HOSTING INBREAK INCURSE
INVASION
INCUS AMBOS ANVIL
INDEBTED DEBTFUL BEHOLDEN
INDEBTEDNESS DEBT SCORE
INDECENCY IMPURITY PRIAPISM
RIBALDRY
INDECENT PAW FOUL LEWD RANK
BAWDY GROSS NASTY SAUCY
GREASY IMPURE PAWPAW SMUTTY
GRIVOIS IMMORAL OBSCENE
IMMODEST IMPROPER SHAMEFUL
UNCOMELY
INDECISION DEMUR DOUBT MAYBE
POISE SWITHER
INDECISIVE DRAWN HALTING
INDECISIVENESS SUSPENSE
INDECOROUS RUDE COARSE
FORWARD UNCIVIL IMMODEST
IMPOLITE IMPROPER INDECENT
UNSEEMLY UNTOWARD
INDEED SO ARU WIS YEA AWAT
DEED EVEN IWIS JUST SURE QUOTH
TIENS ITSELF SURELY FAITHLY
FRANKLY FORSOOTH VERAMENT
INDEFATIGABLE TIRELESS
INDEFENSIBLE INVALID
INDEFINITE HAZY FUZZY GROSS
LOOSE VAGUE DIVERS INEXACT
AORISTIC
INDEFINITELY IN
INDELIBLE FAST FIXED
INDELICATE RAW FREE WARM
BROAD GROSS COARSE GREASY
IMPOLITE IMPROPER UNSEEMLY
INDEMNIFICATION RELIEF
INDEMNIFY PAY RECOUP SATISFY
WARRANT
INDENT JAG BRIT DENT GIMP MUSH
CHASE DELVE NOTCH STAMP
TOOTH WHEEL BRUISE ENGRAIL
GAUFFER
INDENTATION CHOP DENT DINT
DOKE FOIL KINK SCAR BOSOM
BULGE CLEFT CRENA DINGE NOTCH
SINUS DIMPLE FURROW GROOVE
INDENT IMPRESS CRENELLE
TOOTHING
(— IN BOTTLE) KICK
(— IN DOG'S FACE) STOP
(— IN SHELL) EYE
INDENTED WAVED NOTCHED
INDENTURE BIND INDENT ESCALLOP
SYNGRAPH
INDEPENDENCE AUTARKY

FREEDOM AUTARCHY
(— OF GOD) ASEITY ASEITAS
(POLITICAL —) SWARAJ
INDEPENDENT FREE PROUD
SEEKER BIGGITY DIVIDED MUGWUMP
SECTARY ABSOLUTE PECULIAR
SEPARATE
INDEPENDENTLY APART
INDESCRIBABLE TERMLESS
INEFFABLE
INDETERMINATE AORISTIC
FORMLESS INFINITE
INDEX PIE FIST HAND ARNETH
ELENCH PIGNET TONGUE POINTER
ALPHABET REGISTER

INDIA

CAPE: COMORIN
CAPITAL: NEWDELHI
CASTE: JAT MAL AHIR GOLA JATI
MALI DHOBI SANSI SUDRA
VARNA DACOIT DHANUK
LOHANA VAISYA AGARWAL
BRAHMAN DHANGAR
COAST: MALABAR
COIN: LAC PIE ANNA FELS LAKH
PICE TARA ABIDI CRORE PAISA
RUPEE
COLLEGE: TOL
DESERT: THAR
DISTRICT: SIBI NASIK PATNA
SIMLA ZILLAH MALABAR
NELLORE MOFUSSIL
GULF: KUTCH CAMBAY MANNAR
ISLAND: CHILKA
LAKE: WULAR CHILKA COLAIR
DHEBAR SAMBAHR
LANGUAGE: URDU HINDI TAMIL
TELUGU SANSKRIT
MEASURE: ADY DHA GAZ GUZ
JOW KOS LAN SER BYEE COSS
DAIN DHAN HATH JAOB KUNK
MOOT PARA RAIK RATI SEIT
TAUN TENG TOLA AMUNA BIGHA
CAHAR COVID CROSA DANDA
DRONA GARCE GIREH HASTA
PALLY PARAH RATTI SALAY
YOJAN ADHAKA ANGULA
COVIDO CUDAVA CUMBHA
GEERAH LAMANY MOOLUM
MUSHTI PALGAT PARRAH
ROPANI TIPREE UNGLEE YOJANA
ADOULIE DHANUSH GAVYUTI
KHAHOON NIRANGA PRASTHA
VITASTI OKTHABAH
MOUNTAIN: MERU GHATS KAMET
MASTUJ TANKSE KALAHOI
SIWALIK VINDHYA SULEIMAN
MOUNTAIN RANGE: SATPURA
VINDHYA ARAVALLI HIMALAYA
NATIVE: HINDU TAMIL
PROVINCE: HAR ASSAM BIHAR
ANDHRA BENGAL KERALA
MADRAS MYSORE ORISSA
PUNJAB GUJARAT HARYANA
KASHMIR MANIPUR
REGION: MALABAR
RIVER: AI DOR SON TEL KOSI KUSI

NIRA REHR SIND BETWA BHIMA
DAMOH GOGRA INDUS JAWAI
RAPTI SANKH SONAR TAPTI
TUNGA CHENAB GANGES KISTNA
PENNER SUTLEJ WARDHA
CAUVERY CHAMBAL IRAWADI
KRISHNA NARMADA NARMEDA
HEMAVATI HYDASPES MAHANADI
NERBUDDA VINDHYAS
SEAPORT: DAMAN BOMBAY
COCHIN MADRAS CALCUTTA
STRAIT: PALK
TOWN: DIU AGRA DAMA GAYA
PUNA REWA ADONI AKOLA
ALWAR ARCOT BHERA DACCA
DATIA DELHI GIROT KALPI
MYSOR PATAN PATNA POONA
SALEM SIMLA SURAT TEHRI
AJMERE AMBALA BARELI
BARODA BHOPAL BOMBAY
CHAMBA COCHIN DUMDUM
HOWRAH INDORE JAIPUR
KANPUR LAHORE MADIRA
MADRAS MADURA MEERUT
MULTAN MUSORE MUTTRA
NAGPUR RAMPUR UJJAIN
ALIGARH BENARES BIKANER
CALICUT CAWNPUR DINAPIR
GWALIOR JODHPUR KARACHI
KURNOOL LASWARI LUCKNOW
RANGOON RANGPUR AMRITSAR
BHATINDA BHATPARA CALCUTTA
DINAPORE JABALPUR KOLHAPUR
MANDALAY MIRZAPUR
PESHAWAR SHOLAPUR
SRINAGAR VARANASI
TRIBE: AO GOR BHIL BADAGA
SHERANI
WEIGHT: MOD PAI SER VIS DHAN
DRUM KONA MYAT PALA PANK
PICE RAIK RATI RUAY SEER
TANK TOLA YAVA ADPAD BAHAR
CANDY CATTY HUBBA MASHA
MAUND PALLY POUAH RATTI
RETTI RUTEE TICAL TICUL TIKAL
ABUCCO DHURRA KARSHA
CHITTAK PEIKTHA

INDIAN LO RED BUCK ROJO INJUN
TAWNY INDISH BHARATI HOSTILE
NAIKPOD REDSKIN LONGHAIR
(AMERICAN —) AIS AUK FOX HOH
KAW OTO SAC SIA UTE WEA ZIA
ADAI COOS CREE CROW DOEG ERIE
EYAK HANO HOPI HUPA IOWA KATO
KOSO MOKI MONO OTOE OTTO PIMA
PIRO SAUK TANO TAOS TEWA TIOU
TOAG UTAH WACO YUMA ZUNI
ACOMA ALSEA BANAK BIDAI CADDO
CHAUI COMOX CONOY COREE
CREEK HANIS HOOPA HUECO
HURON JEMEZ KANIA KANSA KAROK
KERES KIOWA KOROA KUSAN
LENCA LIPAN MAKAH MANSO MIAMI
MINGO MODOC MOQUI NAMBE
OMAHA OSAGE OSTIC OZARK
PECOS PINAL PIUTE PONCA SAMBO
SARSI SEWEE SIOUX SITKA SKIDI

SLAVE SNAKE SOOKE TETON TEXAS
TIGUA TONTO TWANA TYIGH UINTA
UNAMI WAPPO WASCO WASHO
WIYOT YAMEL YAZOO YUCHI YUROK
AGAWAM AHTENA APACHE ATSINA
ATUAMI AVOYEL BILOXI CALUSA
CAYUGA CAYUSE CHATOT CHERAW
CHETCO COOSUC CUPENO DAKOTA
DIGGER EYEISH FARAON GILENO
HAINAI HAISLA ISLETA KAIBAB
KAINAH KANSAS KICHAI KOSIMO
KUITSH LAGUNA LENAPE MANDAN
MAUMEE MAYEYE METOAC MICMAC
MIKMAK MOHAVE MOHAWK MUNSEE
NASHUA NATICK NAUSET NAVAHO
NAVAJO NEUTER NOOTKA OGLALA
ONEIDA OREJON OTTAWA PAIUTE
PAPAJO PATWIN PAWNEE PEORIA
PEQUOD PEQUOT PIEGAN PODUNK
PUEBLO QUAPAW QUERES RIKARI
SALISH SAMISH SANTEE SAPONI
SATSOP SENECA SHASTA SILETZ
SIOUAN SIWASH SKAGIT SOKOKI
SUMASS SUMDUM SUTAIO SYLVID
TAPOSA TENINO TOHOME TOLOWA
TONGAS TUNICA TUTELO UNPQUA
WALAPI WAPATO WATALA WAXHAW
WEANOC WIKENO WINTUN YAKIMA
YAMASI YAVAPA ZUNIAN ABENAKI
ALABAMA ALIBAMU AMERIND
ANDARKO ANDASTE ARIKARA
ATAKAPA AYAHUCA BANNOCK
CAHOKIA CAHUILA CALOOSA
CATAWBA CHILCAT CHILULA
CHINOOK CHOCTAW CHUMASH
CHUMAWI CIBECUE CLALLAM
CLATSOP COCHITI COLCINE
COWLITZ DEADOSE DHEGIHA
DWAMISH ESSELEN GOSHUTE
HELLELT HIDATSA HUCHNOM
HUICHOL INGALIK JUANENO
KANAWHA KLAMATH KOASATI
KOHUANA KOPRINO KUNESTE
KUTCHIN KUTENAI LUISENO
MASHPEE MASKOKI MOHEGAN
MOHICAN MONACAN MONSONI
MONTAUK MOUSONI NANAIMO
NASCAPI NATCHEZ NIANTIC NIMKISH
NIPMUCK OJIBWAY PACIFID
PADUCAH PAMLICO PICURUS
QUAITSO SALINAN SANETCH
SANFOIL SERRANO SHAPTAN
SHAWANO SHAWNEE SIKSIKA
SIUSLAW SONGISH SPOKANE
SQUAXON STIKINE TAMAROA
TESUQUE TIMUCUA TLINGIT
TONKAWA TUALATI TULALIP
TUTUTNI UGARONO WAILAKI
WALPAPI WAMESIT WANAPUM
WASHAKI WEWENOC WHILKUT
WICHITA WISHOSK WITUMKI
WYANDOT YANKTON YAQUINA
YOJUANE YONKALA ABSAROKA
ACHOMAWI ACHUMAWI ALGONKIN
AMERICAN AMOSKEAG APALACHI
ARIVAIPA ARKANSAS ASTAKIWI
ATFALATI ATSUGEWI CAHINNIO
CAHUILLA CANARSIE CHAWASHA
CHEHALIS CHEMAKUM CHEROKEE

CHEYENNE CHIMAKUM CHOPTANK
CHOWANOC CLACKAMA COLUMBIA
COLVILLE COMANCHE COQUILLE
COYOTERO DELAWARE DIEGUENO
ETCHIMIN FLATHEAD HITCHITI
HUNKPAPA ILLINOIS IROQUOIS
KALISPEL KAWAIISU KICKAPOO
KIKATSIK KLASKINO KLIKITAT
KONOMIHU LAMANITE MALECITE
MASKOTIN MENOMINI MIKASUKI
MINITARI MISSOURI MOGOLLON
MUSCOGEE MUSKWAKI NEHANTIC
NESPELIM NOTTOWAY OKINAGAN
ONONDAGA PAMUNKEY PANAMINT
PATUXENT PAVIOTSO PENACOOK
PISHQUOW POWHATAN PUYALLUP
QUATSINO QUERECHO QUILEUTE
QUINAULT ROCKAWAY SAHAPTIN
SAULTEUR SAVANNAH SEMINOLE
SHIVWITS SHOSHONE SIHASAPA
SINGSING SINKIUSE SINKYONE
SINTSINK SISSETON SOUHEGAN
SQUAMISH SQUEDUNK TLAKLUIT
TOBIKHAR TOPINISH TSIHALIS
TUSHEPAW TUSKEGEE UMATILLA
WABANAKI WACHUSET WAHPETON
WETUMPKA YAHUSKIN YAMACRAW
DOUSTIONI SQUAWTITS
(BRAZILIAN —) BUGRE
(CANADIAN —) DENE COMOX HAIDA
SLAVE TINNE DOGRIB HAISLA
LASSIK SARSEE BEOTHUK GOASILA
KHOTANA KOYUKON CHISEDEC
COEICHAN HEILTSUK KIMSQUIT
KWAKIUTL LILLOOET SALTEAUX
(FEMALE —) SQUAW KLOOCH
(MALE —) BUCK SANNUP
(MEXICAN —) MAM OVA CHOL CORA
JOVA MAYA MAYO ROTO SERI TECA
TECO XOVA AZTEC CHIZO CHORA
HUABI HUAVE KAMIA NAHUA OPATA
OTOMI YAQUI ZOQUE CAHITA
CHOCHO CONCHO EUDEVE KILIWI
NEVOME OTONIA PAKAWA TARASC
TOLTEC ZOTZIL ACOLHUA AKWAALA
AMISHGO CHATINO CHINCHA
CHINIPA CHONTAL COTONAM
COUHIMI GUASAVE HUASTEC
HUAXTEC MAZATEC MISTECA
MIXTECA NAYARIT SINALOA
TEGUIMA TEHUECO TEPANEC
TEPEHUA TZENTAL TZOTZIL
ZACATEC ZAPOTEC CHANABAL
CHAPANEC CHUCHONA COLOTLAN
COMANITO CONICARI GUASAPAR
HUASTECO IRRITILA JACALTEC
JANAMARE LACANDON LAGUNERO
TARUMARI TECPANEC TEXCOCAN
TEZCUCAN TOTONACO TZAPOTEC
YUCATECO
(OTHER —) GE ITE ONA URO URU
YAO AGAZ ANDE ANTA ANTI AUCA
BABU CAME CANA CARA CHUJ
COTO CUNA DENE DIAU DUIT INCA
ITEN ITZA IXIL MOJO MOXO MURA
MUSO MUZO PEBA PIRO RAMA
TAMA TAPE TATU TOBA TRIO TUPI
TUPY ULUA ULVA ACROA ARARA
ARAUA ARUAC AUETO BAURE BETOI

BRAVO BUGRE CAITE CAMPA CANCA
CARIB CHANE CHIMU CHITA CHOKO
CHOLA CHOLO CHONO COCTO
COLAN CUEVA DIRIA GUANA GUATO
HUARI JAVAH KASKA LENCA MOCOA
MOZCA OPATA OYANA PALTA
PAMPA PASSE PETEN PINTO PIOJE
PIOXE PIPIL POKAN POKOM QUITU
SENCI SIUSI SMOOS TAINO UAUPE
UMAUA VEJOZ WAURA XINCA
YAGUA YAMEO YUNCA YUNGA
AGUANO AIMARA AKAVAI AKAWAI
AMORUA ANDOKE ANTISI APANTO
APARAI APIACA ARAWAK AROACO
ATORAI AYMARA BABINE BANIVA
BETOYA BORORO BRIBRI BRUNKA
CAHETE CAIGUA CANCHI CANELO
CARAHO CARAJA CARAYA CARIRI
CAUQUI CAVINA CAYAPA CHAIMA
CHARCA CHAYMA CHICHA CHISCA
CHOCOI CHORTI COCAMA COCOMA
COCORA COFANE COLIMA COTOXO
CUCAMA CULINO CUMANA DOGROB
DORASK GALIBI GOYANA GUAIMI
GUAQUE GUAYMI HUARPE HUBABO
IGNERI INCERI IXIAMA JIVARO
JUCUNA JUMANA JURUNA KARAYA
KEKCHI KUCHIN LENGUA LUCAYO
MACUSI MAKUSI MANGUE MANIVA
MIRANA MUYSCA NAHANE NASCAN
OMAGUA OTOMAC PAPAGO
PKOMAM PURUHA QUICHE SABUJA
SACCHA SALIBA SALIVA SAMUCU
SEKANE SETIBO SIPIBO SUERRE
TACANA TAGISH TAHAMI TAMOYO
TAPAJO TAPUYA TARUMA TECUNA
TICUNA TIMOTE TOTORO TUCANO
TUNEBO UIRINA UITOTO VILELA
WAIWAI WITOTO WOOLWA YAHGAN
YAHUNA YARURO YURUNA ZAPARA
ACHAGUA ACKAWOI AKAMNIK
ANDAQUI ANGAITE APALAII APINAGE
ARECUNA ARHUACO BEOTHUK
BILQULA CACHIBO CAINGUA
CALIANA CAMACAN CARANGA
CARIBAN CARIBEE CARRIER
CASHIBO CHARRUA CHIBCHA
CHIMANE CHIMILA CHIRINO
CHONCHO CHOROTE CHUMULU
CHUNCHO CHURAPA CHUROYA
CIBONEY CJACOGO COROADO
FRENTON FUEGIAN GITKSAN
GOAHIVO GOAJIRA GUA9RAU
GUAHIVO GUARA5Y GUARANI
GUARAYO GUARUAN GUATUSO
GUETARE HUANUCO HUATUSO
ITONAMA JACUNDA JICAQUE
KALIANA KOPRINO KULIANA
LUCAYAN MAIPURE MONGOYO
MORCOTE NICARAO PAMPERO
PAYAGUA PEDRAZA PIARROA
POKOMAM PUELCHE PUQUINA
QUECHUA QUEKCHI RANQUEL
SARIGUE SATIENO SHUSWAP
SINSIGA SIRIONE TAHLTAN TALUCHE
TALUHET TAMANAC TARMANA
TARRABA TAYRONA TELEMBI
TIMBIRA TIRRIBI TSONECA UARAYCU
UCAYALE VOYAVAI WOYAWAY

YUSTAGA ZUTUHIL AGUARUNA
AHOUSAHT AKIYENIK ALACALUF
AMAHUACA APOLISTA ARAQUAJU
AWISHIRA BOTOCUDO CAINGANG
CALINAGO CANAMARY CANOEIRO
CAQUETIO CARIBISI CARIJONA
CARIPUNA CAYUBABA CHAMBOIA
CHANDALA CHAVANTE CHIQUITO
CHIRIANA COLORADO COMIAKIN
CONCHUCO CORABECA CUSTENAU
GUAYAQUI GUAYCURU JAVITERO
KANHOBAL KLASKINO LOROKOTO
MACARANI MAYORUNA MISSKITO
MOSQUITO NIQUIRAN OCHOZOMA
OROTINAN PACAVARA PALENQUE
PARUKUTU PINALENO POIGUARA
POKONCHI POPOLOCO POTYUARA
PUPULUCA QUATSINO QUERENDY
QUIMBAYA SHIRIANA SNONOWAS
SUBTIABA TADOUSAC TAPACURA
TENAKTAK TOCOBAGA TOROMONA
TSATTINE TUMUPASA UAREKENA
URUKUENA USPANTEC YURUCARE
(SPANISH-AMERICAN —) CHOLO

INDIANA

CAPITAL: INDIANAPOLIS
COLLEGE: BALL BETHEL DEPAUW
  GOSHEN MARIAN PURDUE
  WABASH
COUNTY: JAY CASS VIGO JASPER
  TIPTON DAVIESS
INDIAN: MIAMI SHAWNEE
LAKE: MONROE MANITOU
  WAWASEE MICHIGAN
NATIVE: HOOSIER
RIVER: OHIO WHITE WABASH
STATE BIRD: CARDINAL
STATE FLOWER: PEONY
STATE TREE: TULIP
TOWN: GARY PERU BRAZIL
  GOSHEN JASPER KOKOMO
  MUNCIE WABASH

INDIAN BEECH KURUNJ
INDIAN BREAD TUCKAHOE
INDIAN CORN KANGA MAIZE
  CHOLUM JAGONG MEALIES
INDIAN FIG SABRA
INDIAN FISH FLATFISH
INDIAN GOOSEBERRY EMBLIC
INDIAN HEMP KEF KIF DAGGA SABZI
  AMYROOT DOGBANE
INDIANIAN HOOSIER
INDIAN JALAP TURPETH
INDIAN LICORICE JEQUIRITY
INDIAN MADDER MUNJEET
INDIAN MALLOW SIDA DAGGA
  PIEPRINT
INDIAN MILLET JONDLA
INDIAN MULBERRY AL AAL ACH
  ALROOT
INDIAN PIPE FITROOT EYEBRIGHT
  WAXFLOWER
INDIAN SHOT ALIIPOE
INDIAN TOBACCO GAGROOT
  LOBELIA PUKEWEED SOURBUSH
INDIAN YELLOW PIOURY PURREE

INDIC (— LANGUAGE) URDU VEDIC
INDICATE RUN SAY BODY CITE HINT
  LOOK MAKE MARK READ SHOW
  ARGUE INDEX INFER POINT PROVE
  SPEAK ALLUDE ATTEST BETRAY
  DENOTE DESIGN EVINCE FINGER
  IMPORT NOTIFY REVEAL BESPEAK
  BETOKEN CONNOTE DECLARE
  DISPLAY SIGNIFY SPECIFY
  ADMONISH ANNOUNCE DECIPHER
  DISCLOSE EVIDENCE MANIFEST
  OUTPOINT REGISTER
  (— BY SOUNDING) STRIKE
  (— WILLINGNESS) AGREE
INDICATION BECK CLEW CLUE HINT
  LEAD MARK NOTE SHOW SIGN
  CURVE INDEX PROOF SCENT TOKEN
  AUGURY BEACON INDICE REMARK
  SAMPLE SIGNAL AUSPICE MENTION
  PROFFER SYMPTOM ALLUSION
  ARGUMENT EVIDENCE MONITION
  MONUMENT NOTATION SIGNANCE
  TELLTALE
  (— OF APPROVAL) CACHET
  (— OF CONTROL) COLLAR
  (— OF LIGHT) AUREOLE
  (— OF OFFICE) SEAL
  (OBSCURE —) SHADOW
  (VAGUE —) GLIMMER
  (PL.) INDICIA
INDICATOR PIN HAND SIGN FLOAT
  INDEX LITMUS SHOWER STYLUS
  TARGET LACMOID POINTER
  DETECTOR TELLTALE
  (— OF BALANCE) COCK
  (— OF HOUR) GNOMON
INDICT DITE CRIME PANEL ACCUSE
  ATTACH CHARGE INDITE ARRAIGN
  ARTICLE IMPEACH TROUNCE
  WARRANT
INDICTMENT CHARGE DITTAY
INDIFFERENCE APATHY PHLEGM
  DISDAIN COLDNESS EASINESS
  FROIDEUR
INDIFFERENT COLD COOL DEAD
  DRAM EASY SOSO ALOOF BLASE
  EQUAL SOBER CASUAL DEGAGE
  FRIGID SUPINE CALLOUS NEUTRAL
  DETACHED LISTLESS LUKEWARM
  MEDIOCRE RECKLESS SUPERIOR
  UPSITTEN
INDIFFERENTIST POLITIC
INDIFFERENTLY DRYLY HUMDRUM
INDIGENCE NEED WANT PENURY
  BEGGARY POVERTY TENUITY
INDIGENE ENDEMIC
INDIGENOUS DESI NATIVE
  DOMESTIC HOMEBORN
INDIGENT POOR BEGGARLY
INDIGESTION APEPSY APEPSIA
  DYSPEPSY
INDIGNANT ANGRY WROTH
  ANNOYED INCENSED
INDIGNATION IRE ANGER WRATH
  DESPITE DISDAIN JEALOUSY
INDIGNITY CUT SLUR SCORN INSI
  SLIGHT AFFRONT OFFENCE
INDIGO ANIL NILL SHOOFLY
INDIRECT SIDE DEVIOUS OBLIQUE

CIRCULAR GLANCING OVERHEAD OVERWART SIDELONG SIDEWAYS SIDEWISE
(— WAY) AMBAGE
▌**DIRECTION** CIRCUITY
▌**DISCREET** RASH HASTY SILLY WITLESS CARELESS HEEDLESS
▌**DISCRETION** FOLLY FREDAINE
▌**DISCRIMINATE** MIXED MINGLED SWEEPING
▌**DISCRIMINATELY** PELLMELL
▌**DISPENSABLE** NEEDFUL CRITICAL
▌**DISPOSED** ILL MEAN SICK ILLISH UNWELL
▌**DISPOSITION** AIL MALADY AILMENT SICKNESS
(— TO MOTION) INERTIA
▌**DISPUTABLE** SURE CERTAIN EVIDENT MANIFEST POSITIVE
▌**DISTINCT** DIM DARK DULL HAZY FAINT FUZZY INNER LIGHT MISTY MUDDY SHADY THICK VAGUE CLOUDY DREAMY INWARD SLURRY WOOLLY BLEARED BLURRED OBSCURE SHADOWY UNCLEAR
(— IN UTTERANCE) CHOKING
▌**DISTINCTNESS** BLUR
▌**DITE** DITE DRAW
▌**DIVIDUAL** GEE MAN ONE HEAD SORT UNIT BEING MONAD THING PROPER SINGLE SPIRIT APOMICT ATAVISM AZYGOTE BIONTIC DIPLOID EIDETIC ISOLATE MONADIC NUMERIC SEVERAL SPECIAL EVERYONE IDENTITY SEPARATE SINGULAR SOLITARY SPECIMEN
▌**COUNTRIFIED —)** HOBNAIL
▌**DESPICABLE —)** HEEL
▌**DULL —)** BOEOTIAN
▌**FOOLISH —)** SOP
▌**HAUGHTY —)** POT
▌**IMMATURE —)** ADULTOID
▌**IMPUDENT —)** BOLDFACE
▌**IRRITABLE —)** SNAPPER
▌**LEADING —)** KEY
▌**MOSAIC —)** GYNANDER
▌**MUTANT —)** SALTANT
▌**PHYSIOLOGICAL —)** BION
▌**ROUGH-LOOKING —)** BOHUNK
▌**SKILLED —)** ADEPT
▌**SLOVENLY —)** GROBIAN
▌**STUPID —)** HOBBIL
▌**TRICKY —)** BILK
▌**UNDERSIZED —)** KIT KITT
▌**WINGED —)** ALATE
▌**YOUNG —)** KID
(L.) FRY
▌**DIVIDUALITY** SEITY QUALITY ELFDOM HECCEITY IDENTITY ELFHOOD
▌**DIVIDUALIZE** ATOMIZE
▌**DIVIDUALLY** APART APIECE INGLY PROPERLY
▌**DIVIDUATION** AHANKARA
▌**DIVISIBLE** PUNCTUAL
▌**O-CHINESE** SERIFORM
▌**OCTRINATE** BRIEF INSTRUCT
▌**O-EUROPEAN** ARIAN ARYAN
▌**OLE** KETOLE

INDOLENCE SLOTH LANGUOR IDLESHIP MUSARDRY SLUGGING
(— PERSONIFIED) LAURENCE LAWRENCE
INDOLENT IDLE LAZY FAINT INERT SWEER DROWSY OTIOSE SUPINE DRONISH LABGUID WILSOME FAINEANT INACTIVE LISTLESS LOUNGING SLOTHFUL SLUGGISH PICKTOOTH
INDO-MALAYAN (— TREE) SUPA

INDONESIA

CAPITAL: DJAKARTA
COIN: RUPIAH
GULF: BONE TOLO TOMINI
ISLAND: ALOR BALI BURU JAVA CERAM IRIAN SUMBA WETAR BANGKA BAWEAN BORNEO BUTUNG FLORES KOMODO LOMBOK MADURA PELENG CELEBES SALAJAR SUMATRA SUMBAWA BILLITON SULAWESI KALIMANTAN
ISLAND GROUP: EWAB SUNDA BANJAK NATUNA ANAMBAS MOLUCCA TABELAN SABALANA
LANGUAGE: BAHASA MALAYAN
LAKE: RANAU TOWUTI
MOUNTAIN: BULU NIUT RAJA DEMPO MURJO NIAPA LEUSER SLAMET MENJAPA OGOAMAS SAMOSIR KATOPASA KERINTJI MAHAMERU RINDJANI TALAKMAU
MOUNTAINS: MULLER BARISAN QUARLES SCHWANER
RIVER: HARI MUSI DIGUL KAJAN PAWAN BARITO KAMPAR KAPUAS MAHAKAM
SEA: JAVA BANDA CERAM TIMOR FLORES ARAFURA CELEBES
STRAIT: SUNDA LOMBOK MAKASSAR
TOWN: MEDAN MALANG MANADO BANDUNG MAKASAR SEMARANG SURABAJA
VOLCANO: SLAMET
WEIGHT: CATTY OUNCE THAIL

INDONESIAN NESIOT SADANG
INDOORS WITHIN
INDRA SAKKA SAKRA
INDUBITABLE SURE EVIDENT APPARENT MANIFEST UNIVOCAL
INDUCE GET DRAW LEAD MOVE URGE WORK ARGUE BRIBE BRING CAUSE IMPEL INFER TEMPT WEIGH ADDICT ADJURE ALLURE ENGAGE ENTICE IMPORT INCITE INVITE OBTAIN REDUCE SEDUCE SUBORN PREVAIL PROCURE SOLICIT MOTIVATE PERSUADE WIREDRAW
(— BY BRIBERY) FIX
INDUCEMENT MOTIVE REASON FEATURE
INDUCT STALL INSTAL INITIATE
INDUCTANCE HENRY
INDUCTION EPAGOGE

INDULGE PET BABY CADE CANT FEED GLUT HUMOR JOLLY SPOIL TUTOR WALLY WREAK COCKER FOSTER PAMPER PETTLE DEBAUCH GRATIFY
(— IN PRIDE) PRIDE
(— TO EXCESS) PAMPER DEBAUCH SURFEIT
INDULGED CADE
INDULGENCE LAW BINGE FAVOR FOLLY MERCY SPREE EXCESS INDULT PARDON PATENT JUBILEE QUIENAL SURFEIT COURTESY DELICACY EASINESS GLUTTONY POCULARY
(SEXUAL —) LECHERY
INDULGENT FOND GOOD MEEK MILD SPOONY LENIENT TOLERANT
INDURATE HARDEN INDURE
INDURATED SCLEROID SCLEROUS
INDURATION SCLEROMA
INDUSTRIOUS BUSY DEEDY EIDENT PAINFUL DILIGENT SEDULOUS VIRTUOUS WORKSOME
INDUSTRY TOIL LABOR SCREEN VIRTUE CERAMICS SEDULITY
INDWELLING IMMANENT INHERENT
INEBRIATE SOUSE EBRIATED
INEBRIATED DRUNK DRINKY
INEFFACEABLE INBURNT INDELIBLE
INEFFECTIVE DUD WEAK CLUMSY DREEPY FLABBY FUTILE FLACCID HALTING STERILE BUMBLING
INEFFECTIVELY ILL BADLY FEEBLY
INEFFECTUAL WAN DEAD IDLE TAME VAIN VOID JERKY FUTILE SPINDLY USELESS FAINEANT FIDDLING NUGATORY
INEFFICIENT ILL LAME POOR CLUMSY DOLESS UNABLE SLOUCHY USELESS FECKLESS HANDLESS
INELEGANT RUDE HOYDEN AWKWARD
INELOQUENT WANMOL
INEPT INAPT ABSURD AWKWARD FOOTLESS
INEQUAL ROUGH
INEQUALITY ODDS CAHOT ANOMALY EVECTION IMPARITY NUTATION
INEQUITABLE HARD
INERADICABLE LASTING IDELIBLE PERMANENT
INERT DEAD DULL LAZY SLOW HEAVY NOBLE SULKY LEADEN SODDEN STUPID SUPINE TORPID PASSIVE INACTIVE INDOLENT LIFELESS SLOTHFUL SLUGGISH STAGNANT
INERTIA TAMAS
INESCAPABLE DEAD
INESTIMABLE SUMLESS PRICELESS
INEVITABILITY FINALITY
INEVITABLE DUE DIRECT CERTAIN FATEFUL
INEXACT FREE ROUGH CLOUDY
INEXHAUSTIBLE INFINITE
INEXORABLE STERN STONY STRICT RIGOROUS
INEXPEDIENCY IMPOLICY

INEXPEDIENT UNWISE
INEXPENSIVE CHEAP
INEXPERIENCED RAW PUNY CRUDE
FRESH YOUNG UNSEEN KITLING
STRANGE INEXPERT INSOLENT
PRENTICE UNTRADED
INEXPERT ILL RUDE CRUDE GREEN
SIMPLE
INEXPLICABLE FELL
INFAMOUS BASE RUDDY BLOODY
NOTOUR ODIOUS BLEEDING
FLAGRANT NIDERING SHAMEFUL
INFAMY STAIN BAFFLE DEFAME
SHONDE DISHONOR IGNOMINY
INFANCY CRADLE BABYHOOD
INFANT BABE BABY TINY WEAN
CHILD MINOR PREMIE CHRISOM
MILKSOP BALDLING BANTLING
(**NAKED** —) SCUDDY
(**NEWLY-BORN** —) NEONATUS
(**VORACIOUS** -) KILLCROP
INFANTILE BABYISH
INFANTRY FOOT FANTERIE
FOOTFOLK
INFANTRYMAN ASKAR ZOUAVE
DOGFACE DRAGOON DOUGHBOY
PIOUPIOU SOREFOOT
INFATUATE FOOL ASSOT
INFATUATED MAD FOND GONE
ASSOT CRAZY DOTTY ENGOUEE
FOOLISH BESOTTED
INFATUATION ATE RAVE CRUSH
FOLLY BEGUIN
(**TRANSIENT** —) CRAZE
INFECT SMIT TAINT CANKER DEFILE
EMPEST ENTACH INFEST POISON
CORRUPT DISEASE POLLUTE
SMITTLE
INFECTED FUNGUSED
(**NOT** —) BLAND
INFECTION COLD DOSE FELON
TAINT FUNGUS
INFECTIOUS TAKING SMITTLE
CATCHING SMITABLE SMITTING
VIRULENT
INFER DRAW PICK TAKE GUESS
JUDGE DECIDE DEDUCE DEDUCT
DERIVE DIVINE GATHER INDUCE
REASON COLLECT INCLUDE
PRESUME SURMISE CONCLUDE
CONSTRUE
INFERENCE EDUCT SEQUEL
ANALOGY SEQUELA ILLATION
SEQUENCE SEQUITUR
INFERIOR BAD BUM DOG ILL LOW
SAD EVIL LESS MEAN PUNK SLIM
SOUR WAFF BASER BAUCH BELOW
DOGGY GROSS LOWER PETTY PLAIN
SCALY SCRUB WORRY BEHIND
CAGMAG COMMON CRAPPY FEEBLE
FEMALE IMPURE LESSER MEASLY
PEDARY PUISNY ROTTEN SECOND
SHABBY WOODEN BADDISH CRIPPLE
HUMBLER NAGGISH POPULAR
SCRUBBY SUBJECT ABNORMAL
ANTERIOR DEROGATE ORDINARY
INFERIORITY LESSNESS MEANNESS
INFERNAL AVERNAL ETERNAL
HELLISH SATANIC SHEOLIC STYGIAN

CHTHONIC DAMNABLE DEVILISH
PLUTONIC
INFERTILE DEAD DEAF DOUR LEAN
POOR THIN CLEAR STERILE
INFEST COE VEX BESET INFECT
PESTER PLAGUE OVERRUN
TORMENT
INFESTATION SCALE PLAGUE
STRIKE LOAIASIS
INFESTED MITY BLOWN BROOD
BUGGY FLUKY FLUKED GRUBBY
HAUNTED FLYBLOWN
INFIDEL DEIST GIAOUR PAYNIM
ATHEIST SARACEN SKEPTIC
AGNOSTIC
INFIDELITY PERFIDY ADULTERY
TRAHISON
INFIELD INTOWN DIAMOND
INFILTRATE FILTER CRETIFY
COLONIZE
INFILTRATION SEEPAGE ADIPOSIS
INFINITE CHAOS COSMIC ENDLESS
ETERNAL IMMENSE
INFINITENESS ETERNITY
INFINITESIMAL PUNCTUAL
INFINITIVE SUPINE VERBID
INFINITY OLAM ANANTA ETERNITY
INFIRM LAME WEAK ANILE CRAZY
CRONK SHAKY CRANKY FEEBLE
SICKLY UNFIRM UNSURE CASALTY
CRAICHY DOWLESS DWAIBLE
FRAGILE INVALID SAPLESS UNFEARY
DODDERED FIRMLESS INSECURE
RESOLUTE UNSTRONG
INFIRMITY WOE CRAZE DOTAGE
FOIBLE UNHEAL DISEASE FAILING
FRAILTY UNMIGHT DEBILITY
SICKNESS WEAKNESS
INFIX INLAY INSET ENGRAVE
IMPLANT INGRAIN
INFIXED INHERENT
INFLAME BURN FIRE GOAD HEAT
STIR ANGER BLAIN FLAME SCALD
SHAME AROUSE ENAMOR EXCITE
FESTER IGNITE INCEND KINDLE
MADDEN RANKLE EMBRASE
FLUSTER INCENSE ESCHAUFE
INFLAMED RED ANGRY FIERY
ABLAZE FRETTY TORRID FLAGRANT
INFLAMMABLE FIERY ARDENT
TOUCHY PICEOUS TINDERY
INFLAMMATION FIRE ANGER FELON
GLEET SCALD SEBEL AGNAIL
BLIGHT CANKER DEFLUX GREASE
IRITIS AORITIS CATARRH CECITIS
CHAFING COLITIS COXITIS FISTULA
GONITIS ILEITIS QUITTOR SUNBURN
ADENITIS ANGIITIS BURSITIS
CHILITIS CYCLITIS CYSTITIS
SHINGLES
INFLATE HOVE HUFF KITE PLIM
BLOAT BOLNE HEAVE SWELL DILATE
EMBOSS EXPAND HUFFLE INBLOW
TUMEFY BLADDER BOMBAST
DISTEND FORBLOW OUTSWELL
SUFFLATE
INFLATED BLOWN FLOWN GASSY
PUFFY TUMID TURGID BOMBAST
FUSTIAN STILTED SWOLLEN

TURGENT BLADDERY OUTBLOWN
TUMOROUS VANITOUS
INFLATION FLATUS CADENCE
TYMPANY
INFLECT COMPARE DECLINE
INFLECTION SIGN ACCENT FLEXION
LATINISM
INFLECTIONAL FORMAL
INFLEXIBILITY ACAMPSIA
INFLEXIBLE ACID DOUR FIRM HARD
IRON EAGER SOLID STERN STIFF
STONY STOUR SEVERE STRICT
STUFFY ADAMANT RESTIVE
GRANITIC IRONCLAD OBDURATE
PREFRACT RESOLUTE RIGOROUS
STIFFISH STUBBORN
INFLICT DO ADD SET GIVE SEND
INFER YIELD IMPOSE RAMROD
STRIKE
(— **CHASTISEMENT**) WREAK
(— **HURT**) BRUISE
(— **INJURY**) AGGRIEVE
(— **PAIN**) LAY CHASTISE
INFLORESCENCE CHAT CYME
AMENT ARROW BRUSH SPIKE
UMBEL CORYMB FLOWER RACEME
SPADIX TASSEL PANICLE THYRSIS
CYATHIUM FASCICLE
INFLOW INSET INCOME INFLUX
INCOURSE
INFLUENCE IN WIN BEND BIAS COA
DRAG DRAW HANK HEFT LEAD
MOVE PULL PUSH RULE SUCK SWA
BRIBE CHARM COLOR ENACT FORC
GRACE IMPEL MOYEN POWER
REACH SPELL VAPOR VOGUE WEIG
AFFECT ALLURE CREDIT EFFECT
GOVERN IMPORT INDUCE INFLOW
INFLUX MOTIVE OBSESS PONDUS
SALUTE SHADOW STROKE WEIGHT
ATTINGE ATTRACT BEARING
BEWITCH BLARNEY BOSSDOM
CAPTURE CONCUSS CONTROL
DISPUTE ENCHANT GRAVITY
IMPRINT INCLINE INSPIRE MASTERY
TENDRIL DOMINION HEGEMONY
INTEREST LEVERAGE MEDICINE
PRESTIGE SANCTION STRENGTH
CAPTIVATE
(— **BY GIFTS**) GREASE
(— **CORRUPTLY**) BRIBE
(— **OF GODS**) MANA
(— **OF THE STARS**) BLAS
(— **UNREASONABLY**) OBSESS
(**BENIGN** —) UNCTION
(**CONTROLLING** —) SWAY
(**CORRUPTING** —) SMOUCH SMUTC
(**DEPRESSING** —) CHILL
(**DIABOLICAL** —) DEVILDOM
(**DISRUPTIVE** —) GREMLIN
(**DOMINANT** —) GENIUS STREAM
(**DULLING** —) DAMPER
(**ELEVATING** —) LIFT
(**HARMFUL** —) UPAS GRUDGE
(**INJURIOUS** —) RUST
(**MALEVOLENT** —) DISASTER
(**MALIGN** —) TAKING
(**PERNICIOUS** —) BALE BLAST
(**SINISTER** —) MALICE

(SOOTHING —) SALVE
(SURROUNDING —) AIR
INFLUENCING INFUSIVE
INFLUENTIAL GRAVE POWERFUL
INFLUENZA FLU LEUMA GRIPPE
PINKEYE
INFLUX STORM INCOME INFLOW
INRUSH ILLAPSE
(— IN A MINE) COURSE
(— OF TIDE) INSET
INFOLD WRAP IMPLY TWINE EMPLOY
INWRAP ENVELOP INVOLVE
CONVOLVE
INFORM KEN BEEF BLOW FINK NOSE
POST SHOP SHOW TELL WARN WISE
LEARN PEACH ADVISE ASSURE
DELATE DETECT NOTIFY PREACH
SNITCH WITTER APPRISE EDUCATE
IMPEACH INSENSE PARTAKE
POSSESS RESOLVE SIGNIFY
SUGGEST ACQUAINT DENOUNCE
INFORMED INSTRUCT SPARSILE
INFORMAL BREEZY CASUAL CHATTY
COMMON FOLKSY TWEEDY
INTIMATE SLIPSHOD SOCIABLE
INFORMANT AUTHOR INFORMER
SYCOPHANT
INFORMATION AIR GEN OIL WIT
CLEW CLUE DOPE INFO LORE NEWS
NOTE TALE WIRE WORD DATUM
GRIFF SCOOP SKILL ADVICE INSIDE
LIGHTS NOTICE APPRISE PEMICAN
TIDINGS WITTING BRIEFING
NOTITION PEMMICAN
(BODY OF —) DIGEST
(SECRET —) ARCANUM
INFORMED UP HEP WISE AWARE
WITTY KNOWING LEARNED
INFORMER FINK NARK NOSE PIMP
STAG RUSTY SPLIT CANARY FINGER
SETTER SNITCH TELLER DELATOR
TANQUAM APPROVER PROMOTER
SQUAWKER SQUEAKER SQUEALER
TELLTALE
INFORTUNE MARS SATURN
INFRACTION BREACH OFFENCE
TRESPASS
INFRARED ULTRARED
INFREQUENCY SELDOMCY
INFREQUENT RARE SELDOM
FUGITIVE UNCOMMON
INFRINGE IMPOSE INVADE TRENCH
IMPINGE INFRACT INTRUDE
ENCROACH REFRINGE TRESPASS
INFRINGEMENT FOUL BREACH
TRESPASS VIOLENCE
INFRINGER PIRATE
INFULA FANON LABEL LAPPET
HEADBAND
INFUNDIBULUM FUNNEL PAVILION
INFURIATE ENRAGE ENFELON
INFUSE DRAW IMBUE IMMIT SPOIL
STEEP AERATE AERIFY IMMISS
INFLOW INFORM INFUND INVEST
LEAVEN BREATHE DISTILL ENGRAIN
IMPLANT INFOUND INSPIRE INSTILL
SUFFUSE SATURATE
(— TEA) TRACK
(— WITH HATRED) TURN

INFUSED SHOT
INFUSION SHADE CARDIN INCOME
TISANE HORDEATE
(— OF MALT) WORT GROUT
INFUSORIAN LEPOCYTE
INGA GUAVA
INGATE GATE LEDGE TEDGE
INGATHERING HARVEST
INGENIOUS SLY CUTE FAST FEAT
FINE ACUTE SHARP SMART ADROIT
BRAINY CLEVER CRAFTY DAEDAL
GIFTED KNACKY PRETTY SUBTLE
CUNNING SKILLFUL
INGENUITY ART WIT ENGINE
ADDRESS COMPASS ARTIFICE
CONTOISE INDUSTRY QUENTISE
INGENUOUS FREE FRANK NAIVE
PLAIN HONEST ARTLESS SINCERE
INNOCENT
INGENUOUSNESS NAIVETE
INGEST EAT INCEPT ENGLOBE
SWALLOW
INGESTION SLURP
INGOT GAD SOW WEDGE LINGOT
NIGGOT CROPHEAD
(— OF BRASS) STRIP
(— OF SILVER) SHOE TING SCHUYT
(SILVER —S) SYCEE
(SOAKING —S) HEAT
INGRAIN GRAIN INFUSE ENFLESH
INGRAINED INWORN
INGRATE SNAKE
INGRATIATE FLATTER
INGRATIATING BLAND SILKY SLEEK
SLICK SOAPY SILKEN SMOOTH
INGRATITUDE UNTHANK
INGREDIENT FACTOR BINDING
ELEMENT ADJUVANT
(ACTIVE —) ANIMA
(FUNDAMENTAL —) BASIS
(FUSIBLE —) BOND
(MAIN —) BASE
INGRESS ENTRY ENTRANCE
INGROWTH APODEMA
INGUEN GROIN
INHABIT BIG WIN WON COVER
DWELL HABIT BEDWELL INDWELL
POSSESS
INHABITANT INMATE BURGHER
CITIZEN DENIZEN DWELLER
PEOPLER BORDERER CONFINER
DEMESMAN HABITANT INCOLANT
INHOLDER
(— OF ALASKA) SOURDOUGH
(— OF BORDER REGION) MARCHER
(— OF CITY) CIT CITIZEN
(— OF INDIA) BHARATA
(— OF JUNGLE) JUNGLI
(— OF SWISS ALPS) GRISON
(— OF TORRID ZONE) ASCIAN
(— OF VIRGINIA) COOHEE
(— OF WISCONSIN) BADGER
(PL.) SIDE WARE
INHALATION SNUFF BREATH
INHALE DRAW TAKE SMOKE SNIFF
ATTRACT BREATHE INHAUST
INSPIRE RESPIRE ASPIRATE
INHALER SNIFTER
INHARMONIOUS ABSURD

INHERE CONSIST INEXIST
INHERENCE INBEING
INHERENT KIND INBORN INNATE
INWARD NATIVE PROPER INGENIT
HABITUAL IMMANENT INTEGRAL
INTERNAL RESIDENT
INHERIT HEIR SUCCEED
INHERITANCE KIND ENTAIL
HEIRDON HEIRSHIP HEREDITY
HERITAGE LANDFALL VACANTIA
(— OF CATTLE) ERF
INHERITED INBORN INNATE
INHIBIT COOP CURB SNUB CRIMP
DETER FORBID STIFLE SUPPRESS
INHIBITED COLD
INHIBITION AKINESIS
INHIBITORY COLYTIC
INHOSPITABLE STERN DESERT
INHUMAN FELL CRUEL BRUTAL
FIERCE IMMANE SAVAGE BESTIAL
MANLESS DEVILISH KINDLESS
INHUMANE WANTON
INHUMANITY CRUELTY
INHUME BURY INTER ENTOMB
INIMICAL BAD FROSTY HOSTILE
INIQUITOUS ILL DARK WRONG
SINFUL WICKED
INIQUITY SIN EVIL VICE CRIME GUILT
DARKNESS MISCHIEF
INITIAL LETTER VIRGIN ASPIREE
(INTERWOVEN —S) CIPHER
(PL.) PERFINS
INITIATE HEAD MYST OPEN ADMIT
BEGIN BREAK ENTER EPOPT FOUND
START GROUND INDUCE INDUCT
INVENT LAUNCH MYSTES ORPHIC
BAPTIZE INSTALL INSTATE OPERATE
ORPHEAN SYMMIST COMMENCE
ESOTERIC INCHOATE
INITIATION DIKSHA OPENING
ENTRANCE
(— OF GROWTH) BUDBREAK
INITIATIVE PEP LEAD GETUP ACTION
AMBITION GUMPTION
INJECT DRIVE IMMIT
INJECTION HYPO SHOT BOOSTER
CLYSTER
INJUDICIOUS UNWISE
INJUDICIOUSNESS ACRISY
INJUNCTION HEST BEHEST CHARGE
IMPOSE BIDDING DICTATE EXPRESS
MANDATE PRECEPT
INJURE DO GAS ILL MAR BURN
CHEW ENVY GALL HARM HURT
MAUL TEEN WERD ABUSE BLAST
CRAZE DIRTY MISDO SCALD SHEND
SMITE SPOIL STEER WOUND WRONG
BRUISE DAMAGE DEFACE DEFECT
DEPAIR GRIEVE HINDER IMPAIR
INJURY MANGLE RANKLE SCATHE
SCOTCH STRAIN AFFLICT AFFRONT
CONTUSE DAMNIFY DESPITE
FORWORK MISBEDE TERRIFY
DISASTER DISSERVE IMPERISH
INTERESS MISCHIEF MISGUIDE
MUTILATE PREJUDGE SPURGALL
(— BY ASPERSION) SPATTER
(— BY FALSE REPORT) SLANDER
(— BY GLANCE OF BASILISK)
STRIKE

(— BY TREADING UPON) FITTER
(— SCENT) STAIN
(— SERIOUSLY) DO KILL SPOIL
(— SLIGHTLY) ANNOY
(— THE BACK) CHINK
INJURED HURT LESED BLASTED
INJURIOUS BAD ILL EVIL NOYANT
NOYFUL SHREWD ABUSIVE
HARMFUL HURTFUL NOXIOUS
DAMAGING GRIEVOUS SINISTER
TORTIOUS TORTUOUS WRACKFUL
WRONGFUL
INJURIOUSLY HEAVILY
INJURY ILL JAM MAR BANE BURN
EVIL HARM HURT JEEL LOSS RUIN
TEEN TORT WITE ABUSE BLAME
CHAFE CRUSH GRIEF SCALD SCORE
SPITE SPOIL TOUCH WATHE WRACK
WRONG BREACH BRUISE DAMAGE
DANGER IMPAIR LESION SCATHE
STRAIN STROKE TRAUMA BEATING
DESPITE EXPENSE OFFENSE
PAYMENT SCADDLE SCRATCH
SORANCE BUSINESS CASUALTY
CREPANCE INTEREST MISCHIEF
NUISANCE
(— OF HORSES) TREAD
(— OF PLANTS) SUNSCALD
(CHIEF —) FOCUS
(SERIOUS —) MAYHEM
INJUSTICE WRONG INJURY INJURIA
UNRIGHT HARDSHIP INEQUITY
(GROSS —) INIQUITY
INK BEAT COLOR ARNEMENT
ATRAMENT
INK-BALL DABBER PUMPET
INKER SLOSHER
INKING PAD TOMPION
INKLE SPINEL
INKLING HINT ITEM SCENT GLIMMER
GLIMPSE
INKSTAND STANDISH
INKWELL FOUNT INKSTAND
INLAID PIQUE CONTISE
(— WORK) KOFTGARI
INLAND MAUKA INMORE INWARD
MIDLAND INTERIOR
INLAY PICK PIKE COUCH HATCH
INLET PIQUE SPELL CRUSTA
ENAMEL IMPAVE INDENT NIELLO
TARSIA ENCHASE ENCRUST
INCRUST COMMESSO
INLAYING TARKASHI
INLET ARM BAY CUT GEO RIA VOE
COVE DOCK HOPE MERE SLEW
WICK BAYOU BRACE CHUCK CREEK
FIORD FJORD FLEET HAVEN LOGAN
LOUGH STOMA ESTERO HARBOR
INFALL SLOUGH DOGHOLE INDRAFT
SUCTION CALANQUE SEAPOOSE
(— OF THE SEA) EA
(MUDDY —) SUMP
(TIDAL —) GAP
INLIER WINDOW
INLYING INNERLY
INMATE FISH LODGER TENANT
BEADSMAN DOMESTIC PRISONER
INMOST SECRET RETIRED
INN PUB KHAN STOP VENT ANGEL

FONDA HOTEL MESON TAMBO
VENTA CABACK HARBOR HOSTEL
HOSTRY IMARET POSADA PUBLIC
SHANTY ALBERGE AUBERGE
BOLICHE CAFENEH CAFENET
FONDACO FONDOUK HOSTAGE
LOCANDA OSTERIA SOJOURN
SURAHEE CHOULTRY GASTHAUS
HOSTELRY ORDINARY SERAGLIO
WAYHOUSE
INNARDS GIZZARD INWARDS
STUFFING
INNATE BORN KIND INBORN INBRED
CONNATE INGRAIN NATURAL
INSTINCT
(— QUALITY) LARGESS
INNER BEN ENTAL INSIDE INWARD
INWITH MENTAL INTERIOR INTERNAL
PECTORAL
(— LIGHT) SEED
INNERMOST UPPER INMOST
INTIMATE
INNINA ISHTAR
INNING END HAND HEAD FRAME
(PL.) KNOCK
INNKEEPER HOST DUENA TAPPER
VENTER GOODMAN HOSTESS
HOSTLER PADRONE BONIFACE
(PL.) CAUPONES
INNOCENCE BLUET WHITE CANDOR
PURITY
INNOCENT SOT FREE PURE CLEAR
SEELY WHITE CHASTE DOVISH
HONEST SIMPLE CHRISOM LAMBKIN
UPRIGHT HARMLESS IGNORANT
PASTORAL PRIMROSE SACKLESS
UNGUILTY ZACCHEUS
INNOCUOUS HARMLESS INNOCENT
INNOVATE NOVELIZE
INNOVATION NOVEL NOVELTY
INNOVATOR HERETIC
INNUENDO HINT SLUR SLIPE
INNUMERABLE MYRIAD
INO (FATHER OF —) CADMUS
(HUSBAND OF —) ATHAMAS
(MOTHER OF —) HARMONIA
INOCULATE SEED PLANT INFUSE
ENGRAFT EQUINATE
INOCULUM STAB STREAK
INOFFENSIVE HARMLESS
INOPERATIVE OFF DEAD NUGATORY
INOPPORTUNE UNTIMELY
INORDINATE WILD UNDUE
ENORMOUS
INORGANIC MINERAL
INOSITOL DAMBOSE
INPOURING INFLUX
INQUEST CROWN QUEST ASSIZE
OFFICE INQUIRY
INQUIET UNEASY
INQUILINE GUEST
INQUIRE ASK AXE SEEK QUERY
SPERE DEMAND FRAYNE SEARCH
EXAMINE HEARKEN QUESTION
INQUIRER ASKER QUERENT
INQUIRY PROBE QUERY THANK
TRIAL DEMAND EXAMEN TRACER
DOCIMASY QUESTION RESEARCH
SCRUTINY SPEERING

INQUISITION CUSTOM INQUIRY
QUAESTIO
INQUISITIVE NOSY PEERY PRYING
CURIOUS MEDDLING
INROAD RAID BREACH INBREAK
INVASION
INSALUBRIOUS NOXIOUS
INSANE MAD WUD DAFT WOOD
BALMY BATTY BUGGY CRAZY DIPP⁴
QUEER WRONG CRANKY LOCOED
SCREWY FLIGHTY FRANTIC FURIOU⁴
LUNATIC WITLESS BUGHOUSE
DEMENTED DERANGED DISTRACT
INSANITY RAGE CRACK CRAZE
FOLIE MANIA FRENZY LUNACY
MADNESS VESANIA DELIRIUM
DEMENTIA WOODNESS PSYCHOSIS
INSATIABLE GREEDY
INSCRIBE DELVE ENTER WRITE
BLAZON DOCKET INDITE LEGEND
LETTER SCRIBE SCRIVE SCROLL
ASCRIBE ENDORSE ENGROSS
DEDICATE DESCRIBE EMBLAZON
ENSCROLL INTITULE
INSCRIBED INWRIT WRITTEN
DESCRIPT
INSCRIPTION HEAD ELOGY CACHE⁴
LEGEND LETTER ELOGIUM EPIGRAM
EPITAPH MENTION TITULUS WRITIN⁴
COLOPHON EPIGRAPH GRAFFITO
INSCRIPT SCRIBING
(— ON TOMBSTONE) ELOGE
ELOGIUM
(3-LETTER —) TRIGRAM
INSCRUTABLE EQUIVOCAL
INSECT ANT BEE BUG DOR DUN EL⁴
FLY NIT ANER FLEA GNAT GOGO
GYNE MOTH PELA PEST PUPA SPI⁴
WASP WETA ZIMB APHID APHIS
BICHO BORER FLYER GOGGA GUE⁴
IMAGO LOUSE MINER ROACH SCAL⁴
BEETLE BLIGHT CALLOW CICADA
CIXIID EARWIG EMBIID HAWKER
HOPPER INSTAR MANTIS NITTER
PODURA SAPPER SAWFLY THRIPS
VERMIN WALKER WEEVIL ATTACUS
BLATTID BOATMAN BUZZARD
CRAWLER CREEPER CRICKET
CYNIPID DEALATE DRUMMER
EARWORM FIREBUG FIREFLY
GALLFLY GIRDLER GRAYFLY
HEXAPOD JAPYGID KATYDID
SANDBOY SCINIPH SKIPPER
SPECTRE STAINER STYLOPS
TERMITE VAGRANT WEBWORM
ALDERFLY ALKERMES BLACKFLY
BRACONID FIREBRAT FULGORID
GLOWWORM HOMOPTER HORNTAI⁴
LACEWING LECANIUM PRONYMPH
SEMIPUPA SEXUPARA SPHECOID
STINKBUG STYLOPID SYMPHILE
INSECTICIDE DDD DDT DIP CUBE
FLIT ALDRIN DERRIS ENDRIN
CALOMEL ISODRIN LINDANE OVICI⁴
CHLORDAN CULICIDE DIELDRIN
SCHRADAN
INSECTIVORE MOONRAT ALAMIQU⁴
INSECURE DICKY EEMIS LOOSE
SHAKY INFIRM TICKLE UNFAST

UNSAFE UNSURE CASALTY
INSEMINATE BREED
INSENSATE SURD FATUOUS
INSENSIBILITY DAMP APATHY
TORPOR
INSENSIBLE DEAR DULL LOST NUMB
BRUTE DENSE SEARED DATELESS
INSENSITIVE BLUNT STONY STUPID
BOORISH
INSEPARABLE WRAPPED
INSERT SLIP SPUD STOP BOTCH
DICKY ENROL ENTER FUDGE IMMIT
INFER INFIX INLET INSET STUFF
COLLET GUSSET INWORK INWEAVE
GATEFOLD INTROMIT SANDWICH
SLASHING SUBTRUDE THROWOUT
(— **IN SHOE**) CUSHION
(— **SURREPTITIOUSLY**) FOIST
INSERTION FLOWER BEADING
INSET GODET INSERT
INSHEATHE EMBOSS
INSIDE IN BEN ATHIN INBYE INNER
INWITH KEYHOLE INTERIOR
(— **OF ANGLE BAR**) BOSOM
(— **OF OUTER EAR**) BUR BURR
INSIDIOUS SLY SNARY COVERT
SUBTLE GUILEFUL
INSIGHT KEN SIGHT APERCU
THEORY NOSTRIL
INSIGNIA ORDER SIGNS COLLAR
GEORGE CADUCEUS COMMENDA
HERALDRY OPINICUS
INSIGNIFICANT NULL POOR PUNY
DINKY FOOTY PETIT PETTY POTTY
SMALL HUMBLE NAUGHT PALTRY
PUISNE SIMPLE SLIGHT FOOLISH
NAUGHTY NIFLING PELTING PIMPING
SCRUBBY TENUOUS TRIVIAL
BAUBLING INFERIOR PEDDLING
PITIABLE SNIPPING TRIFLING
TRIPENNY
INSINCERE FALSE DOUBLE FEIGNED
INSINCERITY ARTIFICE DISGUISE
INSINUATE HINT MINT WIND CRAWL
SCREW TWIST ALLUDE GLANCE
INFUSE INSTIL WRITHE IMPLANT
INNUATE
INSINUATING SNIDE SILKEN
SMARMY
INSINUATION HINT INKLING
INSIPID DRY WAW DEAD FADE FLAT
FOND FOZY TAME BANAL BAUCH
BLAND FLASH INANE PROSY STALE
VAPID WALSH WAUGH FLASHY
FRIGID JEJUNE SWASHY THREEP
WAIRSH WALLOW EXOLETE
FATUOUS INSULSE PROSAIC
SAPLESS SHILPIT WEARISH WEERISH
LIFELESS UNSAVORY WATERISH
INSIST AVER CONSIST
(— **PEEVISHLY**) CRAIK
(— **UPON**) SOLICIT
INSISTENCE URGENCY INSTANCY
INSISTENT ADAMANT INSTANT
EMPHATIC FRENZIED IMPOSING
INSOLE CUSHION SIPSOLE
INSOLENCE CHEEK PRIDE SNASH
DISDAIN AUDACITY SURQUIDY
INSOLENT FACY PERT RUDE WISE

BARDY LUSTY LORDLY WANTON
ABUSIVE DEFIANT PAUGHTY
ARROGANT IMPUDENT PETULANT
SCORNFUL
INSOLUBLE HOPELESS
INSOMNIA AHYPNIA AGRYPNIA
INSOUCIANT CAVALIER
INSPECT SEE VET CASE ESPY LOOK
BRACK CHECK SIGHT VISIT INLOOK
PERUSE SURVEY EXAMINE OVERSEE
CONSIDER OVERLOOK OVERVIEW
(— **CASUALLY**) BROWSE
(— **COINS**) SHROFF
(— **MERCHANDISE IN BALTIC**)
BRACK
INSPECTION EYE PRY VIEW CHECK
SIGHT REVIEW SURVEY BEDIKAH
CHECKUP INSIGHT INSPECT
PERUSAL VIDIMUS OVERVIEW
SCRUTINY
INSPECTOR SAYER SNOOP BISHOP
CENSOR CONNER JUMPER LOOKER
VIEWER GRAINER MOOCHER
PERCHER SAMPLER SNOOPER
VEADORE EXAMINER SEARCHER
(— **OF COAL**) KEEKER
(— **OF COTTON LOOMS**) TACKLER
(— **OF ELECTRIC LAMPS**) AGER
INSPIRATION FIRE SIGH POESY
ANIMUS SPIRIT SPRITE IMPULSE
MADNESS AFFLATUS INFLATUS
INSPIRE FIRE MOVE CHEER ELATE
EXALT SPARK BEACON INBLOW
INCUSS INDUCE INFORM INFUSE
KINDLE PROMPT ACTUATE ANIMATE
EMBRAVE ENFORCE ENLIVEN
HEARTEN IMPLANT PREMOVE
QUICKEN SUGGEST CATALYZE
ENTALENT INSPIRIT MOTIVATE
SUFFLATE
INSPIRED AFFLATED ENTHEATE
VISIONED
INSPIRER SOUL
INSPIRING INFUSIVE STIRRING
INSPIRIT CHEER HEART ROUSE
SPIRIT ANIMATE CHERISH COMFORT
ENLIVEN HEARTEN INSPIRE QUICKEN
ALACRIFY
INSPISSATE STIFFEN THICKEN
INSPISSATED STIFF THICK
INSTABILITY SLIDDER FLUIDITY
INSTALL SEAT CHAIR STALL INDUCT
INVEST ENSTOOL POSSESS
ENTHRONE INITIATE
INSTALLATION INDUCTION
(— **OF MINISTER**) INFARE
(**MILITARY** —) GARRISON
INSTALLMENT KIST SERIAL
EARNEST CONTRACT
(— **OF WAGES**) COMPO
(— **SELLER**) TALLYMAN
(**FIRST** —) HANDSEL
(**NEXT** —) SEQUEL
INSTANCE CASE PINK SAMPLE
EXAMPLE PURPOSE ENSAMPLE
EXEMPLAR
(**EXTREME** —) CAPSHEAF
INSTANT POP HINT WHIP WINK
BLICK CLINK CRACK FLASH GLENT

GLIFF GLISK JIFFY POINT SHAKE
SOUND START TRICE WHIFF WIGHT
BREATH FLIFFY MINUTE MOMENT
SECOND PRESENT CLIFFING
(**PRECISE** —) TIME
INSTANTANEOUS PRESTO
DIRECTLY
INSTANTLY SLAP SWITH SWITHE
DIRECTLY MOMENTLY
INSTAR STAGE
INSTEAD EITHER
INSTEP WRIST TARSUS
INSTIGATE EGG ABET GOAD MOVE
SPUR URGE IMPEL ATTICE ENTICE
EXCITE FOMENT INCITE INDUCE
INVOKE PROMPT SPIRIT SUBORN
INCENSE INSTINCT
INSTIGATION MOTION MOTIVE
EGGMENT INSTANCE INSTINCT
INSTIGATOR AUTHOR MOTIVE
SOURCE MONITOR
INSTILL GRAFT INFIX IMPART INFUSE
INSTIL BREATHE IMPLANT
INSTINCT KIND FILLED CHARGED
IMPULSE CAPACITY TENDENCY
INSTINCTIVE INNATE NATURAL
INHERENT ORIGINAL
INSTITUTE BRING ERECT FOUND
RAISE STUDY INVENT KINDLE
ORDAIN ACTIVATE
(— **MEMBER**) PIARIST
INSTITUTION BANK CAMP FOLD
CLINIC FRIARY SCHOOL ACADEMY
CHARITY COLLEGE GALLERY
JUBILEE LIBRARY SHELTER STATION
VERITAS SEMINARY
(— **FOR INSANE**) ASYLUM
(**CHARITABLE** —) SPITTLE
DEACONRY HOSPITAL
(**DRUIDICAL** —) GORSEDD
INSTRUCT KEN REAR SHOW WISE
COACH DRILL EDIFY ENDUE GUIDE
TEACH TRAIN CHARGE DIRECT
GROUND INDUCE INFORM LESSON
PREACH REFORM SCHOOL
COMMAND EDUCATE INSENSE
POSSESS DOCUMENT
INSTRUCTED SCIENCED
INSTRUCTION LORE ADVICE ASSIZE
CHARGE LESSON COUNSEL
PRECEPT TUITION WISSING
COACHING DOCTRINE DOCUMENT
MONITION PEDAGOGY PROPHECY
TEACHING TUTELAGE
(**DIVINE** —) LAW
(**SACRED** —) TORAH
(**PL.**) BRIEFING
INSTRUCTIVE DOCENT DIDACTIC
INSTRUCTOR DON SOAK SCREW
TUTOR MENTOR REGENT ACHARYA
CRAMMER TEACHER BEACHBOY
CHAIRMAN ELDERMAN
INSTRUMENT (ALSO SEE MUSICAL
INSTRUMENT) DEED TOOL WRIT
AGENT SLANG THEME FACTUM
UTENSIL SYNGRAPH
(— **NOT UNDER SEAL**) PAROL
(— **OF DESTRUCTION**) SWORD
(— **OF DIVINATION**) EPHOD

(— OF TORTURE) BOOT RACK
BRAKE BRANK FURCA GADGE
WHEEL TUMBREL BARNACLE
SQUEEZER
(—S OF WAR) ENGINERY
(FINANCIAL —) ITEM
(LEGAL —) DEED GRANT FACTUM
SASINE SCRIPT CHARTER CODICIL
DUPLICATE
(NEGOTIABLE —) HUNDI HOONDEE
(OFFICIAL —) SLANG
(PREHISTORIC —) CELT
(SCIENTIFIC OR OTHER —) AWL FAN
HOE KEY MET RAX SAX BROG
COMB DIAL DRAG FILE FORK GAGE
HOOK PLOW RACK RING SPAR
ARMIL BEVEL BLADE BRACE BRAKE
CHAIN CLAMP DATER DOLLY DRILL
FLAIL FLOAT FLUKE GAUGE GLASS
INDEX KNIFE LADLE LEVER METER
PILOT RAZOR SCALE SCOPE SLATE
SLICE SLING SPADE SPEAR SPRAY
STAMP STEEL SWIFT THROW TONGS
TUNER WHISK ABACUS BEETLE
BODKIN BRIDGE CIRCLE DOUCHE
ENGINE ERASER FERULE FOLDER
GRATER LEAPER MORTAR NEEDLE
PESTLE PICKER PLOUGH PULLER
PUMPER RAMMER RASPER RATTLE
RUBBER SCALER SCORER SCRIBE
SCUTCH SCYTHE SHEARS SQUARE
SQUIRT STADIA STRAIK STROBE
STYLET STYLUS TACKLE TICKER
WIMBLE ALIDADE BELLOWS
BREAKER CADRANS CLEAVER
COMPASS DIOPTER DOLABRA
DOUBLER FISTUCA GRAFTER
GRAINER GRAPPLE HATCHEL
LAYOVER MASSEUR MEASURE
OOMETER OOSCOPE PAVIOUR
PELORUS PIERCER PINCERS
PRICKER PRINTER PYROPEN
QUADRAT SCRAPER SEXTANT
SHOCKER SHUTTLE SLITTER
SOUNDER SPLAYER SPRAYER
STRIGIL SUNDIAL SWINGLE
TRAMMEL TRIMMER WHISTLE
ANALEMMA ATOMIZER BIRDCALL
BLOWPIPE BUTTERIS CALLIPER
COALRAKE DECAPPER DETECTOR
DIAGRAPH DIPMETER DIVIDERS
EQUULEUS ERGMETER EXPLORER
FATHOMER GEOPHONE HOROLOGE
IMPINGER ISOGRAPH ISOSCOPE
JOVILABE MESOLABE MHOMETER
ODOMETER OHMMETER PHOTOMER
QUADRANT RECORDER RINGHEAD
RUMMAGER SCISSORS SEARCHER
SQUEEGEE STILETTO STRICKLE
TJANTING TRIANGLE VELLINCH
VIAGRAPH YAWMETER
(SURGICAL OR MEDICAL —) GAG
HOOK SPUD FLEAM PROBE SCOOP
SNARE SOUND STAFF STYLE BILABE
BOUGIE BROACH GORGET LANCET
SEEKER TREPAN TROCAR UNGULA
VECTIS XYSTER AIRDENT DILATER
FORCEPS HARPOON LEVATOR
LIGATOR MYOTOME PELICAN

PLUGGER RONGEUR SCALPEL
SOUNDER SYRINGE TRACTOR
TRILABE TURNKEY ANOSCOPE
AURILAVE AXOMETER BISTOURY
DIRECTOR DIVULSOR ECRASEUR
ELEVATOR EXSECTOR HEMOSTAT
KERATOME MYOGRAPH SPECULUM
TREPHINE
INSTRUMENTAL MEDIATE ORGANIC
SERVILE SERVIENT
INSTRUMENTALIST KLEZMER
SIDEMAN
INSTRUMENTALITY HAND MEANS
AGENCY MEDIUM CHANNEL COUNCIL
MINISTRY
(— FOR ACQUISITION OF
KNOWLEDGE) ORGANON
(NAVAL —S) BEACH
INSUBORDINATE FACTIOUS
MUTINOUS UNWIELDY
INSUBORDINATION MUTINY
INSUBSTANTIAL AIRY INANE
FROTHY SLENDER SPECTRAL
INSUBSTANTIALITY FRAILTY
INSUFFICIENCY PAUCITY
INSUFFICIENT POOR WANE SHORT
SCANTY
INSUFFICIENTLY BARELY FEEBLY
THINLY
INSULATE ISLE ISLAND ISOLATE
INSULATION LAGGING ISOLATION
INSULATOR NOB KNOB TAPLET
VITRITE MEGOHMIT
(PL.) STRING
INSULT CAG FIG JOEY RUMP SLAP
ABUSE CHECK FLOUT FRUMP SLANG
INJURE INJURY OFFEND OUTRAY
RUFFLE SCRAPE ABUSION AFFRONT
OFFENCE OUTRAGE BRICKBAT
DISHONOR CONTUMELY
INSULTING RUDE ARROGANT
INSOLENT
INSULTINGLY FOULLY
INSURANCE LINE CHOMAGE
COVERAGE INDEMNITY
(— AGENT) TWISTER
(UNEMPLOYMENT —) DOLE
INSURE COVER ASSURE ENSURE
FURNISH
INSURGENT REBEL RISER CHOUAN
OAKBOY TAIPING BARRABAS
CAMISARD STEELBOY
INSURRECTION RIST MUTINY
REVOLT UPROAR OUTBREAK
SEDITION UPRISING
INSURRECTO GUGU
INTACT SOUND WHOLE ENTIRE
INTAGLIO ENTAIL DIAGLYPH
(PART OF —) INCAVO
INTANGIBLE VAGUE SUBTLE
AERIFORM SLIPPERY
INTEGER SUM NORM TOTITIVE
INTEGRAL FLUX NEEDFUL
INTEGRANT ELEMENT
INTEGRATE FUSE PIECE COMBINE
FULFILL
INTEGRATED FUSED INTEGRAL
INTEGRATION BALANCE HARMONY
INTEGRITY HONOR TRUTH HONESTY

JUSTICE PROBITY CHASTITY
STRENGTH
INTEGUMENT KEX SKIN TESTA
TUNIC SWATHE CUTICLE ENVELOP
EPIDERM EXODERM PRIMINE
TUNICLE EPISPERM PERISARC
SCABBARD
INTELLECT MIND HEART INWIT
MAHAT SKILL BRAINS NOTICE
REASON SPIRITS THINKING
(HIGHEST —) NOUS
INTELLECTUAL BLUE GAON IDEAL
BOOKSY MENTAL SOPHIC BRAHMIN
EGGHEAD GNOSTIC CEREBRAL
LONGHAIR SOPHICAL DIANOETIC
INTELLIGENCE AIR CIT SAT CHIT
KNOW MIND NEWS NOTE WORD
AGIEL SENSE ADVICE BRAINS
ESPRIT INGENY NOTICE WITTING
(— IN EGYPTIAN LORE) CHU
(— OF PLANET JUPITER) JOPHIEL
(LIVELY —) WIT
INTELLIGENT APT GASH PERT
ACUTE ALERT SMART SPACK
AKAMAI BRAINY BRIGHT CLEVER
MENTAL SPRACK WITFUL KNOWING
INFORMED LUMINOUS RATIONAL
SKILLFUL
INTELLIGENTSIA CLERISY
INTELLIGIBLE CLEAR PLAIN
LUMINOUS PELLUCID PERVIOUS
REVELANT
INTELLIGIBLY SIMPLY
INTEMPERANCE ACRASY EXCESS
ACRASIA OUTRAGE
INTEMPERATE SHRILL SURFEIT
(NOT —) SWEET
INTEND GO AIM FIX CAST MEAN
MIND MINT PLAN PLOT TEND ALLOT
ALLOW ETTLE TIGHT ATTEND
DESIGN RECKON BEHIGHT DESTINE
FORELAY PRETEND PROPOSE
PURPORT PURPOSE FOREMIND
MEDITATE PRETENSE
INTENDED SUPPOSED
INTENSE HOT ACID COLD DEEP
HARD HIGH KEEN BLANK DENSE
GREAT HEAVY QUICK SHARP TENSE
VIVID ARDENT BRAZEN FIERCE
INTENT PITCHY STRONG BURNING
CHARGED CHRONIC CUTTING
EXTREME FERVENT FRANTIC
FURIOUS VIOLENT EGYPTIAN
GRIEVOUS POWERFUL SEETHING
VEHEMENT
INTENSELY STIFF HIGHLY ACUTELY
CURSEDLY FERVIDLY SHREWDLY
INTENSIFIED ACUTE
INTENSIFY RISE URGE EXALT RAISE
ACCENT DEEPEN BOLSTER
ENFORCE ENHANCE IMPROVE
INFLAME SHARPEN THICKEN
CONDENSE HEIGHTEN INCREASE
INTENSION INTENT MEANING
INTENSITY EDGE HEAT ARDOR
DEPTH DRIVE FEVER FIELD DEGREE
DOSAGE FERVOR FRENZY STRESS
CURRENT FEROCITY STRENGTH
VIOLENCE

INTENSIVE HARD HIGH EXTENDED
INTENSIVELY HARD SOLIDLY
INTENT SET DEEP DOLE FELL HENT
MIND TENT BEADY CAUSE DRIFT
ETTLE FIXED HEART PRICK SCOPE
TENOR TENSE EFFECT SPIRIT
COUNSEL INTENSE PRESENT
STUDIED WISTFUL
(CRIMINAL —) DOLE
(EVIL —) DOLUS
INTENTION AIM END GOAL HENT
MIND WILL HEART SCOPE ANIMUS
ATTENT DESIGN DEVICE EFFECT
INTENT OBJECT REGARD COUNSEL
COURAGE EARNEST FORESET
MEANING PROPOSE PURPORT
PURPOSE SUPPOSE PRETENSE
INTENTIONAL SET WILLFUL WILLING
WITTING INTENDED
INTENTLY BUSILY WISHLY EAGERLY
FIXEDLY
INTER BURY EARTH ENTER GRAVE
PLANT ENTOMB INHUME INEARTH
INTERACTION COUPLING
INTERAGENT MEDIUM MIDDLER
INTERBREED CROSS
INTERBREEDING APOGAMY
MIXTURE PANMIXY CROSSING
INTERCALATE INSERT
INTERCALATION EMBOLISM
INTERCEPT KEP HEAD KEEP STOP
CATCH NORMAL TRAMMEL
GAINCOPE INTERPEL RETRENCH
INTERCEPTION CUTOFF
INTERCESSION MOYEN DIPTYCH
PLEADING
INTERCESSOR MEANS PLEADER
ADVOCATE MEDIATOR
INTERCHANGE CHANGE ANAGRAM
COMMUTE PERMUTE COMMERCE
EXCHANGE
(— OF OPINION) COUNSEL
(— OF WORDS) SPEECH
INTERCHANGEABLE FUNGIBLE
INTERCOLUMNIATION EUSTYLE
SYSTYLE DIASTYLE
INTERCOMMUNICATION LIAISON
INTERCONNECTED SYNDETIC
INTERCONNECTION BONDING
INTERCOURSE GAM DEAL MANG
MONG TRADE TRUCK TURGY
BAWDRY HOBNOB NEGOCE COITION
DEALING MIXTURE QUARTER
SOCIETY TRAFFIC BUSINESS
COMMERCE CONVERSE RECOURSE
INTERDICT BAN TABU TABOO
FORBID UTRUBI INHIBIT PROHIBIT
SUPPRESS
INTERDICTION VETO
INTEREST BUG DIP FAD USE BENT
GOOD HAND HOLD PART CLOSE
COLOR DRIVE FAVOR FETCH GAVEL
HOBBY RIGHT STAKE STUDY USAGE
USURA USURY BEHALF ENGAGE
EQUITY ESTATE FAENUS FERVOR
FINGER INCOME USANCE ATTRACT
CONCERN RESPECT USAUNCE
CONTANGO INCREASE VIGORISH
(— OF HUSBAND) CURTESY

(— ON LAND) CLOSE
(ACTIVE —) SYMPATHY
(LEGAL —) EASEMENT
(POLITICAL —) FENCE
(SECURITY —) LIEN
(SPECIAL —) ANGLE
INTERESTED HIPPED ENGAGED
SERIOUS
INTERESTING FRUITY CURIOUS
STORIED
INTERFERE CUT MAKE ANNOY
BLOCK CHECK HITCH POACH
BAFFLE HAMPER HINDER HOBBLE
IMPEDE MEDDLE STRIKE TAMPER
INTRUDE INTROMIT
(— SLIGHTLY) BRUSH
(— WITH) AIL JOLT HECKLE
BLANKET DISTURB
INTERFERENCE BALK CHOKE
THUMP HINDER JOSTLE MEDDLE
CONFLICT FREINAGE
INTERFERING CUT
INTERFEROMETER ETALON
INTERFLUVE DOAB
INTERIM BREAK VACANCY
INTERIOR BEN BELLY BOSOM INNER
ENTIRE INLAND INWARD INWITH
MIDDLE GIZZARD ENTRAILS
INTERNAL
(— OF CUPOLA) CALOTTE
(— OF TEMPLE) CELLA
(— OF VESSEL) HOLD
(— PART) MANTLE
INTERJECT ENTER SQUIB INJECT
THRUST
INTERJECTION AW ER HA LO FIE
GEE GIP HAH HEH HEY AHEM AHOY
ALAS EGAD FORE GOSH HECH HOLA
JOVE GOODY HEIGH MAFEY SUGAR
TENEZ EUREKA HARROW OUTCRY
LACKADAY
INTERLACE LACE WARP BRAID
WEAVE ENLACE PLEACH INWEAVE
WREATHE
INTERLACED BRACED FRETTED
PLEACHED
INTERLACEMENT KNOT
INTERLACING TWINY
INTERLINING DOUBLER
INTERLOCK KNIT LOCK PITCH
ENGAGE FINGER TANGLE DOVETAIL
INTERLOPE INTRUDE
INTERLUDE JEST COMEDY VERSET
TEMACHA TRIUMPH ENTRACTE
ENTREMES RITORNEL VERSETTE
(ROMANTIC —) IDYL IDYLL
INTERMEDDLER STRANGER
INTERMEDDLING GESTION
INTERMEDIARY MEAN AGENT
MOYENER MEDIATOR TRAMPLER
INTERMEDIATE MEAN MESNE
FILLER ISATIN MEDIAL MEDIUM
MIDDLE MIDDLING
INTERMEDIATOR BROKER
INTERMENT BURIAL BURYING
DEPOSIT HUMATION
INTERMINABLE ETERNAL INFINITE
TIMELESS UNENDING
INTERMINGLE MIX BRAID IMMINGLE

INTERMIT INTERMIX
INTERMINGLED AMONG AMONGST
INTERMISSION REST WAIT BREAK
DWELL PAUSE DEVALL RECESS
NOONING RELACHE RESPITE
INTERVAL SURCEASE VACATION
(— OF PAIN) SABBATH
INTERMISSIVE CESSANT
INTERMIT CEASE DEFER DEVAUL
SUSPEND
INTERMITTENT BROKEN FITFUL
PERIODIC
INTERMIX MEDLEY MINGLE
INTERMIXTURE INTIMACY
INTERNAL INLY INNER ENTIRE
INLAND INNATE INSIDE INWARD
DOMESTIC
INTERNALLY INLY INSIDE INWARD
INWARDLY
INTERNODE ROSETTE
INTERPELLATION FLOWER
INTERPENETRATED SHOT
INTERPLAY AUSPICE
INTERPOLATE FARCE FARSE FOIST
FUDGE INSERT THRUST
INTERPOLATION GAG FARSE
INTERPOSE BAR CHOP DEMUR
OBJECT THRUST THWART MEDIATE
INTERPRET MAKE OPEN READ SCAN
TAKE AREAD AREED FANCY GLOSS
GLOZE RECHE DEFINE DIVINE
INTEND CLARIFY COMMENT
DECLARE ENGLISH EXPLAIN
EXPOUND CONSTRUE DECIPHER
SIMPLIFY
INTERPRETATION REDE GLOSS
SENSE GOSPEL STRAIN ANAGOGE
BARAITA COMMENT EPIKEIA
CABALISM EXEGESIS INNUENDO
SOLARISM SOLUTION
INTERPRETER BROKER DUBASH
UNDOER EXEGETE LATINER
MUNCHEE CABALIST DRAGOMAN
EXPONENT LINKSTER TRUCHMAN
(— OF SCRIPTURE) TROPIST
(PL.) HAHAM SELLI SELLOI
CHOCHEM HAKAMIM
INTERRELATED INTIMATE
INTERRELATIONSHIP ACCORD
LIAISON COMMERCE
INTERROGATE ASK TARGE DEBRIEF
EXAMINE INQUIRE
INTERROGATION EROTESIS
QUESTION
INTERRUPT CUT MAR NIP CHOP
STOP TAKE BREAK CHECK CRACK
EMBAR ARREST DERAIL DERANGE
DISRUPT FORBREAK INTERMIT
INTERPEL OBSTRUCT
INTERRUPTED BROKEN CHOPPY
SNATCHY
INTERRUPTER BUZZER
INTERRUPTION CESS JUMP STOP
BLOCK BREAK CHECK DWELL LAPSE
PAUSE BREACH HIATUS HOCKET
HOQUET ISLAND CAESURA CUTBACK
DIASTEM BLOCKING BREAKAGE
SOLUTION STOPOVER
(WITHOUT —) FLUSH

INTERRUPTOR TIKKER BREAKER
CHOPPER RHEOTOME
INTERSECT CUT CROSS BISECT
INCISE CROSSCUT
INTERSECTING CRUCIAL COMPITAL
INTERSECTION LEET CHINE CROSS
CURVE CHIASMA CROSSING
CROSSWAY JUNCTION
INTERSEXUAL EPICENE
INTERSEXUALITY GYNANDRY
INTERSPACE SPACE POCKET
INTERSPERSE DOT SALT SHED
MEDDLE THREAD CHECKER
INTERSOW SPRINKLE
INTERSTICE PORE SEAM CHINK
GRATE AREOLA RIFFLE CELLULE
VACUITY
(PL.) CANCELLI
INTERSTRATIFY INTERBED
INTERTWINE KNIT LACE WARP
TWINE FELTER TANGLE WAMPLE
WARPLE WRITHE ENSNARL
COMPLECT INTERTEX
INTERTWINED INWOUND
INTERVAL GAP LAG CENT GULF
REST SAND SEXT SPOT STEP BLANK
BREAK COMMA CYCLE FIFTH LAPSE
QUINT SIXTH SPACE SWING TENTH
THIRD BREACH DECIMA DEGREE
DIESIS DITONE FOURTH MERLON
SECOND SYSTEM ADVANCE
DIASTEM DISCORD HEADWAY
HEMIOLA INTERIM PASTIME RESPITE
SCHISMA SETTIMO STADIUM
TRITONE DIAPASON DIAPENTE
DISTANCE ELEVENTH ENTRACTE
FONTANEL
(— **BETWEEN FINGERS**) SUBVOLA
(— **OF BRIGHTNESS**) FLICKER
(— **OF FAIR WEATHER**) SLATCH
(— **OF HARSH WEATHER**) SNAP
(— **OF SEMITONE**) APOTOME
(**REST** —) SOB
(**SHORT** —) STREAK
(**TIME** —) HEADWAY
INTERVALE BOTTOM
INTERVENE CHOP STEP STRIKE
MEDIATE OBVIATE STICKLE
INTERCUR
INTERVENING MESNE MIDDLE
MEDIANT
INTERVIEW BUZZ CONTACT
AUDIENCE CONGRESS
INTERWEAVE MAT PLAT CRISP
PLAIT PLASH RADDLE TANGLE
WATTLE ENTWINE TEXTURE TRELLIS
COMPLECT ENTANGLE IMPLEACH
INTERTEX
INTERWEAVING BREDE CROWN
INTIMATE
INTERWOVEN INWOVEN IMPLICIT
INTIMATE
INTESTINAL INNER ENTERAL
ENTERIC
INTESTINE GUT ROPE BOWEL INNER
THARM INWARD MIDDLE
(**PORTION OF** —) JEJUNUM
(PL.) VISCUS INGANGS CHITLINS
INTHROW RIDGE

INTIMACY LIAISON PRIVACY
AFFINITY CHUMMERY GOSSIPRY
INTRIGUE
(**UNDUE** —) LIBERTY
INTIMATE SIB BOON GRIT HINT
HOME HOMY KIND NEAR NEXT PACK
TOSH BOSOM CHIEF CLOSE GREAT
PALLY PRIVY THICK ALLUDE ENTIRE
FRIEND HOMELY INTIME INWARD
NOTICE SECRET STRAIT STRICT
THRANG THRONG CHAMBER
CLOSEUP GREMIAL INNERLY
INNUATE KEYHOLE PRIVADO
PRIVATE SIGNIFY SPECIAL SUGGEST
COCKMATE ESPECIAL FAMILIAR
FREQUENT FRIENDLY INDICATE
INTIMADO
(**MOST** —) MIDMOST
(PL.) FOLKS
INTIMATELY INLY TOSH WELL
COZILY CLOSELY INWARDLY
INTIMATION CUE HINT ITEM WARN
WIND SCENT NOTICE OFFICE
GLIMMER INKLING INNUENDO
MONITION
INTIMIDATE COW HAZE ABASH
BULLY COWER DAUNT DETER
HECTOR TERRIFY BROWBEAT
BULLDOZE BULLYRAG FRIGHTEN
INTO IN INTIL WITHIN
INTOLERANCE BIGOTRY
INTOLERANT CLOSED BIGOTED
INTONATION FALL ITALICS
INTONE CANT SING TONE CHANT
CHAUNT ENTUNE MODULATE
INTOXICATE FOX TIP TOX FLAW
GOOF SOAK TODDY FUDDLE
MUDDLE SOZZLE SPRING TIPSIFY
DISGUISE OVERTAKE SPRINKLE
INTOXICATED CUT FAP LIT WET
HIGH LUSH RIPE SHOT SOSH TOFT
TOSY BOSKY BUFFY DRUNK FRESH
FRIED FUNNY HEADY LACED NAPPY
PIPED TIGHT BOILED GROGGY
LOADED MELLOW PIPPED QUAINT
SCREWY SKEWED SLEWED SLOPPY
SODDEN SOSHED SOZZLE STEWED
TANKED UPPISH UPPITY EBRIATE
EXALTED FLECKED JINGLED
POTSHOT SCREWED SLOPPED
SMASHED SPIFFED SQUIFFY
UNSOBER BESOTTED COCKEYED
DELEERIT ELEVATED OVERSEEN
OVERSHOT PLEASANT SQUIFFED
TEMULENT TOXICATE
INTOXICATING HARD HEADY STARK
HUFFCAP
INTOXICATION WINE FUDDLE
IVRESSE LOCOISM DISGUISE
EBRIOSITY
(— **OF ANIMALS**) DUNZIEKTE
INTRACTABLE BAD HARD SALTY
STACK SURLY FIERCE SULLEN
THWART UNRULY CRABBED
HAGGARD RESTIVE ROPABLE
WAYWARD CHURLISH INDOCILE
MUTINOUS OBDURATE PERVERSE
SHREWISH
INTRADOS SOFFIT

INTRANSITIVE NEUTER
INTREPID BOLD BRAVE HARDY
HEROIC PRETTY SAVAGE DOUGHTY
VALIANT RESOLUTE
INTREPIDITY GAME COURAGE
INTRICACY KNOT INTRIGUE
INTRICATE HARD MAZY BLIND
DAEDAL IMPLEX KNOBBY KNOTTY
TANGLY TRICKY COMPLEX CRABBED
CURIOUS GORDIAN PERPLEX
PUZZLED SINUOUS INVOLUTE
INVOLVED
INTRIGUE PLOT ANGLE CABAL
CLOAK STORY AFFAIR AMOUNT
BRIGUE DECEIT SCHEME CONNIVE
FACTION FINAGLE JOBBERY
TRINKET TRINKLE ARTIFICE
CHEATING COLLOGUE PRACTICE
PRACTISE STRATEGY TRIPOTER
INTRIGUER JESUIT SCHEMER
DESIGNER
INTRIGUING EXCITING SCHEMING
INTRINSIC REAL TRUE INBORN
INBRED INNATE INWARD NATIVE
GENUINE NATURAL ABSOLUTE
IMMANENT INHERENT INTERNAL
INTIMATE
INTRINSICALLY PROPERLY
INTRODUCE READ DEBUT ENTER
FRONT IMMIT INFER PLANT START
USHER BROACH HERALD INDUCE
INDUCT INFUSE INJECT INSERT
INVECT INVOKE LAUNCH PREFER
FORERUN IMPLANT INSTILL INVEIGH
PRECEDE PREFACE PRELUDE
PRESENT SHUFFLE SPONSOR
ACQUAINT INNOVATE INTROMIT
WIREDRAW
(— **AIR INTO**) AERATE
(— **AS FIRST ACT**) INITIATE
(— **FROM WITHOUT**) IMPORT
(— **SURREPTITIOUSLY**) FOIST
INTRODUCTION LASSU PROEM
PRONE INTRADA INTROIT ISAGOGE
MENTION PREFACE ENTRANCE
EXORDIUM PREAMBLE PROLOGUE
(— **INTO STOMACH**) GAVAGE
(— **OF DRAMA**) PROTASIS
(— **OF NOVELTY**) CHANGE
(**MUSICAL** —) INTRO INTRADA
INTRODUCTORY EXORDIAL
LIMINARY PROTATIC SYSTATIC
INTROIT REQUIEM
INTRORSE ANTICAL
INTROSPECTION INLOOK REFLEX
INTRUDE JET ABATE CRASH POACH
BOTHER CHISEL INGYRE INJECT
INVADE IRRUPT THRUST OBTRUDE
ENCROACH INFRINGE TRESPASS
INTRUDER INTRUS INCOMER
INVADER STRANGER
INTRUSION INVASION
INTRUSIVE FRESH SPURIOUS
INTUITION HUNCH INSTINCT
INTUITIONIST EIDETIC
INULIN ALANTIN
INUNDATE FLOW DROWN FLOOD
INUND SWAMP DELUGE OVERFLOW
SUBMERGE SURROUND

NUNDATION FLOW FLOOD WATER DELUGE ALLUVIO FRESHET ALLUVION FLOODAGE OVERFLOW

NURE URE BREAK ENURE STEEL HARDEN SCHOOL SEASON ACCUSTOM INDURATE

NVADE ASSAIL INTRUDE ENCROACH INTRENCH TRESPASS

NVADER HUN PICT

NVADING INGRUENT

NVAGINATION GULLET

NVALID BAD BUM NULL NUGATORY

NVALIDATE AVOID BREAK CANCEL INFIRM IMPROVE INVALID VITIATE

NVALUABLE COSTLY PRECIOUS

NVARIABLE STEADY UNIFORM CONSTANT

NVARIABLENESS ONENESS

NVARIABLY EVER ALWAYS

NVASION RAID INROAD DESCENT INBREAK INJURIA

NVECTIVE ABUSE HOKER RAILING DIATRIBE REPROACH

NVEIGH INVECT DECLAIM DENOUNCE

NVEIGLE COAX ROPE CHARM DECOY SNARE ALLURE ENTICE SEDUCE

NVENT COIN FIND FORM MINT VAMP FEIGN FRAME FRUMP CREATE DESIGN DEVISE IDEATE CONCOCT CONJURE CONTRIVE DISCOVER

NVENTION FANCY DEVICE FINDAL NOTION FANTASY FICTION FIGMENT FORGERY WITCRAFT

(DRAMATIC —) IBSENISM

NVENTIVE ADROIT FERTILE CREATIVE MECHANIC ORIGINAL PREGNANT

NVENTIVENESS WIT ARTIFICE

NVENTOR TALOS COINER FINDER FRAMER MINTER CREATOR MINTMAN ENGINEER

NVENTORY BILL LIST STOCK ACCOUNT INVOICE TERRIER ANAGRAPH REGISTER SCHEDULE

VERSION WALDEN CHIASMUS ENTROPION

VERT CANT TURN REVERT REVERSE

VERTASE SUCRASE

VEST DON DUB PUT BELT FUND GARB GIFT GIRD GIRT GOWN LOCK SINK VEST WRAP BELAY BLOCK ENDOW ENDUE FEOFF INDUE CLOTHE EMBODY ENROBE FORSET OCCUPY COMPASS ENFEOFF ENVELOP INSTATE OBSERVE BENEFICE BLOCKADE SURROUND

— ONESELF) COVER ASSUME

— WITH AUTHORITY) SCEPTER ACCREDIT

— WITH ENERGY) CATHECT

— WITH SOVEREIGN DIGNITY) ENTHRONE

— WITH) INFEFT

VESTED GARTERED

VESTIGATE SPY SIFT CHECK PROBE SOUND STUDY EXCUSS

FATHOM SEARCH DISCUSS EXAMINE EXPLORE INQUIRE INDAGATE SCRUTATE

(— QUICKLY) SKIP

INVESTIGATION CHECK PROBE TRIAL EXAMEN PILPUL SEARCH DELVING INQUEST INQUIRY LEGWORK ZETETIC ANALYSIS QUESTION RESEARCH SCRUTINY SOUNDING

INVESTIGATOR SNOOP TRIER SLEUTH GUMSHOE SPOTTER FIELDMAN

INVESTITURE VESTURE INDUMENT

INVESTMENT DOG FLIER CUTICLE CATHEXIS

INVETERATE BLACK SWORN ROOTED CHRONIC HARDENED

INVIDIOUS ENVIOUS HATEFUL

INVIGORATE BRACE CHEER RAISE RENEW VIGOR VIVIFY COMFORT ENFORCE ENLIVEN FORTIFY INNERVE INSINEW REFRESH INSPIRIT

INVIGORATING BRISK CRISP FRESH TONIC VITAL HEARTY BRACING CORDIAL VEGETANT

INVIOLABILITY SANCTITY

INVIOLABLE SECURE STYGIAN

INVIOLATE SACRED

INVISIBLE HID SECRET UNSEEN VIEWLESS

INVITATION BID CALL CARD INVITE BIDDING CALLING

(— TO CONTEND) DARE

INVITE ASK BID WOO BEAR CALL LURE PRAY TOLL CLEPE COURT LATHE TRYST ALLURE DESIRE ENTICE INDITE ATTRACT CONVITE PROVOKE REQUEST SOLICIT

INVITING ADORABLE HOMELIKE

INVOCATION WISH DAWUT NANDI BISMILLAH

INVOICE BILL BRIEF CHALAN FACTURE MANIFEST

INVOKE WISH CLEPE EVOKE APPEAL ATTEST OBTEST CONJURE ENTREAT PROVOKE SOLICIT INVOCATE

INVOLUCRE HULL HUSK CUPULE EPICALYX

INVOLUNTARY FORCED HELPLESS

INVOLUTE INVOLVED

INVOLUTED SCREWY

INVOLUTION ATRESIA

INVOLVE DIP LAP MIX MIRE WRAP BROIL CARRY COUCH IMPLY RAVEL DIRECT EMPLOY ENGAGE ENTAIL HANKLE INWRAP TANGLE COMPORT CONCERN CONNOTE EMBRACE EMBROIL ENSNARE ENTWINE ENVIRON IMMERSE INCLUDE ENCUMBER ENTANGLE INTEREST

(— IN DIFFICULTY) STEAD

INVOLVED IN DEEP GONE BLIND KNOTTY COMPLEX ENGAGED PLAITED IMPLICIT INVOLUTE

INWARD ENTAD INNER INWITH BENWARD INNERLY HOMEFELT

INWICK INRING

IO (BROTHER OF —) PHORONEUS

(FATHER OF —) INACHUS

(SON OF —) EPAPHUS

IOLE (FATHER OF —) EURYTUS

(HUSBAND OF —) HYLLUS

IOLITE IBERITE PELIOMA

ION ACID ADION ANION CATION ISOMER KATION LIGAND AMPHION HYDRION OXONIUM SPECIES

(— DURATION) LIFETIME

(FATHER OF —) XUTHUS

(MOTHER OF —) CREUSA

IONIZATION BURST

IOTA JOT WHIT GHOST SCRUPLE

IOU MARKER

IOWA

CAPITAL: DESMOINES
COLLEGE: COE DORDT LORAS CORNELL PARSONS GRINNELL WARTBURG
COUNTY: IDA SAC LINN TAMA ADAIR KEOKUK KOSSUTH OSCEOLA
LAKE: CLEAR STORM SPIRIT
NICKNAME: HAWKEYE
PRESIDENT: HOOVER
RIVER: CEDAR SKUNK BIGSIOUX MISSOURI
STATE BIRD: GOLDFINCH
STATE FLOWER: WILDROSE
STATE TREE: OAK
TOWN: MASON PERRY SIOUX ALGONA KEOKUK LEMARS MARION ANAMOSA OTTUMWA WATERLOO DAVENPORT

IOWAN HAWKEYE

IPECAC ITOUBOU

IPHICLUS (BROTHER OF —) HERCULES

(FATHER OF —) PHYLACUS AMPHITRYON

(MOTHER OF —) ALCMENA

IPHIGENIA (BROTHER OF —) ORESTES

(FATHER OF —) AGAMEMNON

(MOTHER OF —) CLYTEMNESTRA

(SISTER OF —) ELECTRA

IPHIS (FATHER OF —) LIGDUS

(MOTHER OF —) TELETHUSA

(WIFE OF —) IANTHE

IPHITUS (FATHER OF —) EURYTUS

(SLAYER OF —) HERCULES

IPIL VESI

IPOMOEA NIL NILL BATATAS MANROOT SCAMMONY

IPSEITY SELFHOOD

IRACUND IREFUL

IRAN

CAPE: HALILEH
CAPITAL: TEHRAN TEHERAN
COIN: PUL ASAR CRAN LARI RIAL BISTI DARIC DINAR LARIN SHAHI TOMAN STATER ASHRAFI KASBEKE PAHLAVI
DESERT: KERMAN

FORMER NAME: PERSIA
LAKE: NIRIS NIRIZ TASHT TUZLU
URMIA SAHWEH SISTAN
MAHARLU NEMEKSER URUMIYEH
LANGUAGE: ZEND PAHLAVI
MEASURE: GAZ GUZ MOV ZAR
ZER CANE FOOT GAREH JERIB
KAFIZ MAKUK QASAB ARTABA
CHARAC CHEBEL GARIBA
GHALVA OUROUB CAPICHA
CHENICA FARSAKH FARSANG
MANSION MISHARA PARASANG
PIAMANEH SABBITHA STATHMOS
MOUNTAIN: CUSH KUSH HINDU
KHOSF ARARAT HAMUNT
BINALUD KHORMUJ SABALAN
DEMAVENO
MOUNTAIN RANGE: ELBURZ
SIAHAN ZAGROS JAGATAL
PEOPLE: LUR KURD MEDE SART
KAJAR MUKRI PERSE TAJIK
HADJEMI PERSIAN
PORT: JASK BUSHIRE PAHLEVI
RIVER: MAND MUND SHUR ARAKS
JAGIN KARUN RABCH SEFID
BAMPUR GORGAN HALIRI TIGRIS
KARKHEH MASHKEL SAFIDRUD
ZAYENDEH EUPHRATES
STRAIT: HORMUZ
TOWN: FAO KOM AMOL YAZD
AHVAZ KHVOY NIRIZ RESHT
ABADAN DEZFUL GORGAN
KASVIN KERMAN MASHAD
MESHED SHIRAZ TABRIZ TAURIS
HAMADAN ISFAHAN SANANDAJ
WEIGHT: SER DRAM DUNG ROTL
SANG SEER ABBAS ARTEL
MAUND PINAR RATEL BATMAN
DIRHEM GANDUM KARWAR
MISCAL NAKHOD NIMMAN
ABBASSI TCHEIREK

IRANIAN TAT SART GALCHA SHUGNI
BACTRIAN BARTANGI
(— **SOVEREIGN**) SHAH

IRAQ
CAPITAL: BAGDAD BAGHDAD
COIN: DINAR
DISTRICT: BASRA KURDISTAN
FORMER NAME: MESOPOTAMIA
MOUNTAINS: ZARGOS KURDISTAN
OASIS: MANIYA
PEOPLE: ARAB KURD
PORT: BASRA
RIVER: ZAB TIGRIS EUPHRATES
TOWN: AMARA BASRA MOSUL
NAJAF HILLAH KIRKUK KARBALA

IRASCIBILITY BILE CHOLER
IRASCIBLE WARM ANGRY CROSS
FIERY GASSY HASTY IRATE SHARP
TECHY TESTY CRANKY IREFUL
SPUNKY TETCHY TOUCHY BILIOUS
FRETFUL IRACUND PEEVISH
WASPISH CAPTIOUS CHOLERIC

PETULANT SNAPPISH STOMACHY
IRATE ANGRY HEATED CHOLERIC
WRATHFUL
IRE FURY ANGER WRATH
IREFUL ANGRY JEALOUS

IRELAND
BAY: MAL CLEW SLIGO BANTRY
DINGLE GALWAY TRALEE
DONEGAL DUNDALK KILLALA
BLACKSOD DROGHEDA
CAPE: CLEAR
CAPITAL: TARA DUBLIN
COIN: RAP REAL
COUNTY: CORK DOWN LEIX MAYO
CAVAN CLARE KERRY LOUTH
MEATH SLIGO ANTRIM ARMAGH
CARLOW GALWAY OFFALY
TYRONE ULSTER DONEGAL
KILDARE LEITRIM WEXFORD
WICKLOW KILKENNY LIMERICK
MONAGHAN
ISLAND: ARAN TORY SALTEE
RATHLIN
LAKE: DOO KEY REE TAY CONN
DERG MASK CARRA GOWNA
LEANE RAMOR BODERG COOTER
ENNELL DROMORE OUGHTER
SHEELIN
MEASURE: MILE BANDLE
MOUNTAIN: OX CAHA ANTRIM
GALTEE KEEPER MOURNE
MULREA DONEGAL ERRIGAL
KENNEDY KIPPURE WICKLOW
LEINSTER
MOUNTAIN RANGE: GALTY
STACKS COMERAGH
OTHER NAME: EIRE ERIN BANBA
IERNE IRENA ULSTER BOGLAND
HIBERNIA INISFAIL
PEOPLE: CELT ERSE GAEL CELTIC
HIBERNIAN
PERTAINING TO: CELTIC GAELIC
POINT: CAHORE CARNSORE
PROVINCE: ULSTER MUNSTER
LEINSTER CONNAUGHT
RIVER: LEE BANN DEEL ERNE
NORE SUIR BOYNE CLARE
FEALE FLESK FOYLE LAUNE
BANDON BARROW LIFFEY
KENMARE MUNSTER SHANNON
TOWN: CORK ADARE DUBLIN
LURGAN LIMERICK TIPPERARY

IRENE (FATHER OF —) JUPITER
(**MOTHER OF** —) THEMIS
IRENIC CALM HENOTIC PEACEFUL
IRENICA AITESIS
IRIDESCENCE LUSTER LUSTRE
IRIDESCENT SHOT IRISED IRIDINE
IRISATE PAVONINE
IRIS EYE SET FLAG LILY LUCE LUCY
SEGG AZURE IREOS ORRIS SEDGE
FLAGON LEVERS LILIAL LILIUM
SHADOW SUNBOW ALCAZAR
BABIANA FLAGGER GLADDON
FLAGLEAF

(**FATHER OF** —) THAUMAS
(**MOTHER OF** —) ELECTRA
IRISH ERSE EIRANN IRISHRY
MILESIAN
(— **KING**) RIG
(**ILLITERATE** —) KEELMAN
IRISHMAN MAC PAT CELT GAEL
HARP KELT MICK SCOT GREEK
IRISH MICKY PADDY YREIS TEAGUE
GRECIAN IRISHER MILESIAN
ORANGEMAN
(**LEARNED** —) OLLAMH
IRISH MOSS SLOKE CHONDRUS
IRISHWOMAN HARP
IRK BORE ITCH ANNOY WEARY
BOTHER
IRKSOME DULL WARM WEARY
HUMDRUM OPEROSE TEDIOUS
ANNOYING TIRESOME
IROKO ODUM ODOOM MUVULE
KAMBALA
IRON BIT DOG IRE MARS WIRE
ANGLE ANVIL BASIL BRAND DRAIL
DRIFT FLOSS HORSE NEGRO SPIKE
STEEL WAVER ANCONY BEATER
CALKER CAUTER FERRUM GAGGER
GOFFER JAGGER OSMUND CAUTERY
COBIRON CRAMPER FERRITE
FURISON GAMBREL GAUFFER
PRICKER SADIRON FLATIRON
TRICOUNI
(— **FOR CLOSING STAVES**) HORSE
(— **OF MILLSTONE**) RIND RYND
(— **ORE**) LIMNITE
(— **PIECES**) POTLEG
(— **PLATE**) TRAMP
(— **SUPPORTING SPIT**) COBIRON
(— **TO SUPPORT BEAM**) TORSEL
(**8 PIGS OF CAST** —) FODDER
(**ANGLE** —) LATH STIFFENER
(**BASKETWORK** —) BEATER
(**BOOM** —) WITHE WYTHE
(**BRANDING** —) BURN
(**CAST** —) METAL YETLIN SPIEGEL
YETLING SEMISTEEL
(**CLIMBING** —) GAFF SPUR CREEPER
(**CRUDE CASTING OF** —) PIG
(**DRIVING** —) CLEEK
(**GLASSBLOWING** —) BAIT
(**GOLF** —) JIGGER
(**GRAPPLING** —) CRAMPON
CRAMPOON
(**HATTER'S** —) SLUG
(**MASS OF WROUGHT** —) BLOOM
(**METEORIC** —) SIDERITE
(**PASTY** —) SPONGE
(**PIG** —) SPIEGEL KENTLEDGE
(**PRIMING** —) DRIFT
(**RUSSIAN** —) SABLE
(**SHEET** —) TERNE
(**SOLDERING** —) COPPER
(**SPECULAR** —) HEMATITE
(**TAILOR'S** —) GOOSE
(**TAMPING** —) DRIVER
(**PL.**) GARTERS
IRONBARK MUGGA
IRON BROWN NEGRO
IRONCLAD ARMORED IRONSIDE
IRON HAT GOSSAN

IRONIC ACERB ACERBIC SATIRIC
IRONICAL CRUEL
IRON-LIKE MARTIAL
IRON MAN TALUS
IRONMONGERY HARDWARE
IRONSMITH FERRER
IRONSTONE DOGGER
IRONWEED FLATTOP VERNONIA
WINGSTEM
IRONWOOD TITI COLIMA MOPANE
MOPANI PURIRI WAMARA CYRILLA
JOEWOOD AXMASTER BURNWOOD
FIREWOOD
IRONWORKER LOHAR MOSCHI
IRONWORT SIDERITE
RONY SATIRE ASTEISM SARCASM
RIDICULE
ROQUOIS HURON MINGO CAYUGA
MENGWE
RRADIATE XRAY ENBEAM
RRATIONAL REE SURD WILD SILLY
RAVING STUPID BESTIAL FOOLISH
RREDUCIBLE BASIC
RREGULAR DUMB WILD BUMPY
EROSE FANCY MIXED WOPSY
ATYPIC CATCHY FITFUL RAGGED
RUGGED SPOTTY UNEVEN UNLIKE
WEEWAW ANAXIAL ATACTIC
BAROQUE CATERAN CRABBED
CROOKED CURSORY DEVIOUS
DIFFORM ERRATIC FRECKET
MUTABLE SCRAWLY UNEQUAL
WAYWARD ABNORMAL ATYPICAL
DOGGEREL INFORMAL PINDARIC
SCRAGGLY SCRAMBLY UNLAWFUL
UNSTABLE UNSTEADY VARIABLE
RREGULARITY SNAG DEFECT
RUFFLE ANOMALY ACCIDENT
(— IN YARN) SNICK
RREGULARLY UNDULY
RRELIGIOUS PAGAN WICKED
HEATHEN IMPIOUS PROFANE
SENSUAL
RREMEDIABLE HELPLESS
HOPELESS
RREPROACHABLE SPOTLESS
RRESISTIBLE MESMERIC
RRESISTIBLY FATALLY
RRESOLUTE FICKLE INFIRM
UNSURE WANKLE DOUBTFUL
UNSTABLE
RRESPONSIBLE WILDCAT
CAREFREE FECKLESS SKITTISH
RRESPONSIVE LEADEN
RRETRIEVABLE HOPELESS
RREVERENCE IMPIETY
RREVERENT ATHEIST AWELESS
IMPIOUS PROFANE
RREVOCABLE DEAD
RREVOCABLY FATALLY FINALLY
RRIGATE FLOAT WATER SYRINGE
RRIGATION KAREZ
RRIGATOR FLOATER
RRITABILITY ERETHISM SORENESS
VAGOTONY
RRITABLE BAD EDGY BIRSY CROOK
FIERY FUSSY HASTY HUFFY JUMPY
MUSTY NAGGY TETTY TILTY TOITY

CRANKY GROWLY NETTLY SPUNKY
STOCKY TEETHY TETCHY TOUCHY
FRATCHY FRETFUL HORNETY
HUFFISH KICKISH PECKISH PEEVISH
SPLEENY TEDIOUS TWITCHY
WASPISH PETULANT SNAPPING
SNAPPISH STOMACHY
IRRITATE BUG EAT GET IRE IRK NAG
RUB TAR TEW TRY VEX BURN CRAB
FIRE FRET GALL GOAD GRIG GRIT
ITCH NARK RILE ROIL SOUR TEEN
ANGER ANNOY CHAFE EAGER
FRUMP GRATE GRILL GRIPE PEEVE
PIQUE STING TARRY ABRADE
BOTHER FRIDGE GRAVEL HARASS
HECTOR NETTLE RUFFLE AFFRONT
INCENSE INFLAME NERVOUS
PROVOKE STOMACH ACERBATE
IRRITATED RILY SORE HUFFY
MUFFED SHIRTY EMPORTE
FRATCHED SOREHEAD
(EASILY —) TESTY
IRRITATING ACRID HARSH CORSIE
ELVISH GRAVEL FRETFUL GALLING
IRKSOME PUNGENT RASPING
ANNOYING FRETSOME GRAVELLY
NETTLING SCRATCHY SPITEFUL
STINGING TIRESOME
IRRITATION FRET TEEN BIRSE PIQUE
STEAM RUFFLE TEMPER WARMTH
ANTPRICK FLEABITE PINPRICK
VEXATION
IRRUPTION BREAK INROAD INBURST
ERUPTION INVASION
IS S YS BEES
(— NOT) NIS AINT ISNT
ISAIAH ESAY ESAIAS
ISCHEMIA ANEMIA
ISCHIAL SCIATIC
ISHPINGO CINNAMON
ISHSHAKKU PATESI
ISHTAR NINNI
ISINGLASS LEAF PIPE KANTEN
ISIS (BROTHER OF —) OSIRIS
(FATHER OF —) SATURN
(MOTHER OF —) RHEA
ISLAM ABBASID
ISLAMIC (— CUSTOM) SUNNA
ISLAND CALF CAYO HOLM INCH ISLE
JAVA POLO ENNIS MALTA MAYDA
AVALON ITHACA OGYGIA REFUGE
RIALTO CIPANGO JAMAICA MADEIRA
TOWHEAD BLEFUSCU CALAURIA
DOMINICA GUERNSEY LILLIPUT
LUGGNAGG
(— IN EVERGLADES) HAMMOCK
(— OF REIL) INSULA
(ARTIFICIAL —) CRANNOG
(CORAL —) ATOLL
(FABLED —) MERU UTOPIA
(FLOATING —) HOVER
(FLYING —) LAPUTA
(LEGENDARY —) BRAZIL OBRAZIL
(LITTLE —) AIT KAY KEY ISLET
(LOW —) KEY
(ROCKY —) SKERRY
(SANDY —) BEACH BARRIER
(SMALL —) CAY ISLE ISLET

SANDKEY
ISLANDER KANAKA ISLEMAN
INSULARY
ISLE IZLE ISLET SKERRY
ISLET OE AIT CAY KEY EYOT HAFT
HOLM ILOT MOTU ROCK ISLOT
STACK NUBBLE
ISMENE (FATHER OF —) OEDIPUS
(MOTHER OF —) JOCASTA
(SISTER OF —) ANTIGONE
ISOBAR MEIOBAR MESOBAR
PLEIOBAR
ISOLATE ISLAND DISSECT SECLUDE
COLONIZE INSULATE SEPARATE
SEQUESTER
ISOLATED POCKET UNIQUE
SOLITARY STRANDED
ISOLATION HERMITRY LONENESS
SOLITUDE
ISOMER PYRAN TOSYL XYLENE
CUMIDINE DECOSANE DODECANE
ISOMERIC ISO ALLO
ISOMETRIC CUBIC REGULAR
TESSULAR
ISOPLETH GEOTHERM
ISOPOD SLATER ASELLUS BOPYRID
GRIBBLE EPICARID
ISOTOPE IONIUM CARRIER
ISOTYPE COTYPE SYNTYPE
ISPAGHUL SPOGEL
ISPAHAN HERAT HERATI

ISRAEL
CAPITAL: JERUSALEM
COIN: POUND
COLLECTIVE FARM: KIBBUTZ
DESERT: NEGEV
FORMER NAME: CANAAN
PALESTINE
LAKE: HULEH TIBERIAS
MEASURE: CAB HIN KOR LOG
BATH EPHA EZBA OMER REED
SEAH CUBIT EPHAH HOMER
KANEH QANEH
MOUNTAIN: NAFH SAGI HARIF
MERON RAMON TABOR ATZMON
CARMEL
RIVER: FARIA MALIK SOREQ
JORDAN QISHON SARIDA
YARKON LAKHISH
SEA: DEAD GALILEE
SEAPORT: ASHDOD TELAVIV
TOWN: ACRE RAMA HAIFA HOLON
JAFFA JENIN JOPPA RAMLA
SAFAD BATYAM HEBRON
NABLUS JERICHO NATANYA
TELAVIV TULKARM NAZARETH

ISRAELI SABRA
(— STUDY CENTER) ULPAN
ISRAELITE JEW SAINT HEBREW
JACOBITE
(PL.) ZION
ISSUE END ISH COME EMIT FALL
FLOW GIVE GUSH HEAD MISE REEK
TERM VENT ARISE COUNT EVENT
FRUIT LOOSE OUTGO SETON SOURD

UTTER EFFECT EFFUSE EGRESS
EMERGE ESCAPE EXITUS MUTTON
RESULT SEQUEL SETTER SPRING
UPPING BALLOON DEBOUCH
DESCENT DRIZZLE EMANATE
ESSENCE EXSURGE OUTCOME
PROCEED PROGENY REDOUND
REFLAIR SUCCESS EXPEDITE
FONTANEL INCREASE ISSUANCE
KINDLING OUTGOING
(— AND ORDER) BID
(— SLOWLY) EXUDE
(— SPASMODICALLY) BELCH
(— SUDDENLY) SALLY
(— WITH FORCE) SPOUT
(BOND —) CONSOL
(FAVORABLE —) SPEED FORTUNE
(FINAL —) UPSHOT UTMOST
(NUMEROUS —) SPAWN
ISSUED OUT
ISSUING EMANANT JESSANT
MANATION
ISTHMUS BALK STRAIT TARBET
ISTLE PITA IXTLE JUAMAVE
GUAPILLA
IT A HE HIT MUN TAGGER
(— FOLLOWS) SEQ SEQU
(— HAS BEEN SWORN) JURAT
ITALIAN ITIE ITALIC AUSONIAN
MACARONI
ITALITE VESBITE

ITALY
CAPE: TESTA CIRCEO LICOSA
LINARO COLONNE FALCONE
PASSERO RIZZUTO SANVITO
TEULADA VATICANO
CAPITAL: ROMA ROME
CHEESE: ROMANO FONTINA
RICOTTA BELPAESE PARMESAN
TALEGGIO
COIN: LIRA LIRE TARI GRANO
PAOLI PAOLO SCUDO SOLDO
DANARO DENARO DUCATO
SEQUIN TESTONE ZECCHINO
FOOD: PASTA PIZZA SCAMPI
GNOCCHI LASAGNE POLENTA
RAVIOLI RISOTTO SPUMONI
TORTONI CAPONATA LINGUINE
MACARONI PEPERONI
FAMILY: ASTI ESTE AMATI CENCE
DORIA BORGIA MEDICI SFORZA
GULF: GAETA GENOA OROSEI
SALERNO TARANTO CAGLIARI
ORISTANO
ISLAND: ELBA LERO CAPRI LEROS
PONZA GIGLIO ISCHIA LINOSA
SALINA SICILY USTICA ALICUDI
ASINARA CAPRAIA GORGONA
LEVANZO PANAREA PIANOSA
SICILIA VULCANO FILICUDI
SARDINIA
ISLANDS: EGADI LIPARI TUSCAN
PELAGIE PONTINE TREMITI
LAKE: COMO ISEO NEMI GARDA
ALBANO LESINA LUGANO
VARANO BOLSENA PERUGIA

MAGGIORE BRACCIANO
MEASURE: PIE ORNA CANNA
PALMA PALMO PIEDE PUNTO
SALMA STAIO STERO BARILE
MIGLIE MIGLIO MOGGIO RUBBIO
TAVOLA TOMOLO BOCCALE
BRACCIO SECCHIO GIORNATA
POLONICK QUADRATO
MOUNTAIN: ROSA VISO AMARO
BLANC CORNO SOMMA CIMONE
BERNINA VESUVIUS
MOUNTAIN RANGE: ALPS ORTLES
APENNINES MARITIMES
NATIVE: ITALO LATIN OSCAN
ROMAN SABINE TIRANO TUSCAN
LOMBARD SIENESE LIGURIAN
VENETIAN
PASS: FREJUS BERNINA BRENNER
SPLUGEN
PORT: BARI POLA ZARA GENOA
TRANI ZADAR RIMINI TRIESTE
REGION: CARSO APULIA LATIUM
MARCHE MOLISE PUGLIA SICILY
UMBRIA ABRUZZI LIGURIA
TUSCANY VENETIA CALABRIA
CAMPANIA LOMBARDY
PIEMONTE SARDINIA
RESORT: LIDO SANREMO
TAORMINA
RIVER: PO ADDA AGRI ARNO LIRI
NERA RENO SELE TARO ADIGE
CRATI MANNU OGLIO PARMA
PIAVE SALSO STURA TIBER
TIRSO ANIENE BELICE MINCIO
OFANTO PANARO RAPIDO
SANGRO SIMETO TANARO
TEVERE TICINO BIFERNO
BRADANO CHIENTI METAURO
MONTONE OMBRONE PESCARA
RUBICON SECCHIA TREBBIA
VOLTURNO
SEA: IONIAN ADRIATIC LIGURIAN
STRAIT: MESSINA OTRANTO
BONIFACIO
TOWN: BRA RHO ACRI ALBA ASTI
BARI COMO DEGO ELEA ENNA
ESTE FANO GELA IESI LODI
NARO NOLA PISA POLA ROMA
ROME ACQUI ANZIO AOSTA
ASOLA AVOLA CAPUA CUNEO
EBOLI FIUME FORLI GENOA
IMOLA LECCE LUCCA MASSA
MILAN MONZA OSTIA PADUA
PARMA PAVIA TEANO TRENT
TURIN UDINE VELIA ALCAMO
AMALFI ANCONA ANDRIA
AREZZO CEFALU FAENZA
FOGGIA GENOVA MANTUA
MESTRE MILANO MODENA
NAPLES NAPOLI NOVARA RIVOLI
SPEZIA TRENTO VENICE VERONA
BERGAMO BOLOGNA BOLZANO
BRESCIA CARRARA CASERTA
CATANIA COSENZA CREMONA
FERRARA FIRENZE GORIZIA
IMPERIA LEGHORN LIVORNO
MARSALA MESSINA PALERMO

PERUGIA PISTOIA POMPEII
RAVENNA TARANTO TRIESTE
BRINDISI CAGLIARI FLORENCE
PIACENZA SORRENTO
SYRACUSE
VOLCANO: ETNA SOMMA VULCANO
VESUVIUS STROMBOLI
WATERFALL: TOCE
WEIGHT: CARAT LIBRA ONCIA
POUND CARATO DENARO
LIBBRA OTTAVA
WINE: SOAVE CHIANTI MARSALA
ORVIETO

ITALY AUSONIA HESPERIA SATURNIA
ITCH EWK EACH REEF RIFF YEUK
YEWK TICKLE ITCHING SCABIES
VANILLISM
ITCHING ITCHY YEUKY PRURIENT
PRURITIS URTICANT
ITEM ANA JOB TOT ENTRY POINT
THING DETAIL ARTICLE SEVERAL
(— IN SERIES) COURSE
(— OF PROPERTY) CHATTEL
(— OF VALUE) ASSET
(APPENDED —) ADDENDUM
(COLLECTOR'S —) SPOIL
(DECORATIVE —) CONCEIT
(LUXURY —) BOUTIQUE
(NEWS —) DISPATCH
(UNPUBLISHED —S) ANECDOTE
(VALUELESS —) BEAN
(PL.) CHECKAGE
ITEMIZE DETAIL
ITERATION PLEONASM
ITHURIEL'S-SPEAR GRASSNUT
ITINERANT ERRANT AMBULANT
ITINERARY DIET JOURNAL WAYBILL
(— OF ROYAL PROGRESS) GEST
ITINERATION EYRE
ITS HIS
ITSELF IT HERSELF
ITYS (FATHER OF —) TEREUS
(MOTHER OF —) PROCNE
ITZA PETEN
IULUS ASCANIUS
IVATAN BATAN
IVORY EBURE DENTINE ELEPHANT
(DUST OF —) EBURINE
(WALRUS —) RIBZUBA RIBAZUBA
IVORY BLACK ABAISER

IVORY COAST
CAPE: PALMAS
CAPITAL: ABIDJAN
DAM: BANDAMA
LANGUAGE: DIOULA
PEOPLE: ABE AKAN ATLE KOUA
KROU MANDE ABOURE LAGOON
MALINKE VOLTAIC
RIVER: KOMOE BANDAMA
CAVALLY SASSANDRA
TOWN: TABOU BOUAKE GAGNOA
SASSANDRA

IVORY GULL SNOWBIRD

IVORY NUT ANTA TAGUA JARINA
IVORY PALM TAGUA COROJO
COROZO
IVORY TREE PALAY
IVY TOD GILL HOVE IVIN JILL PICRY

ARALIA HEDERA HIBBIN ALEHOOF
ARALIAD IVYWORT BINDWEED
FOALFOOT
IWW WOBBLY

IXION **(FATHER OF** —) PHLEGYAS
(SISTER OF —) CORONIS
(WIFE OF —) DIA
IZMIR SMYRNA

J JAY JIG JULIETT
JAAL GOAT BEDEN JAELA
JAB GAG GIG JAG JOB POKE STAB
JABBER CHAT JAVER BURBLE
  GABBER GABBLE JOBBER YABBER
  CHATTER
JABIRU STORK CICONIID
JABOT RUFFLE
JACANA PARRA
JACARE CAIMAN CAYMAN
JACINTH LIGURE
JACK DIB FLAG JACA CRICK DICKY
  KNAVE NANCA COLORS KATHAL
  SCALET SETTER WENZEL MATADOR
  BLOCKING JACKFISH POLIGNAL
  SOURJACK TURNSPIT UPLIFTER
  (— IN BOWLS) BABY MARK KITTY
  MASTER MISTRESS
  (— IN CARDS) PAM PUR TOM
  BOWER CNAFE KITTY KNAPE KNAVE
  MAKER KNIGHT VARLET WENZEL
  VARLETTO
  (— OF CLUBS) NODDY BRAGGER
  MATADOR
  (— OF SAME SUIT) NOB
  (— OF TRUMPS) TOM JASS JASZ
  BOWER HONOR PLAYBOY
  (PIANO —) HOPPER STICKER
  (SPINNING —) BEAT
JACKAL DIEB JACK KOLA THOS
  CANID CANINE DRAGON SILVER
  THOOID SIACALLE
JACKAROO RINGNECK
JACKASS JACK
JACKASS FISH MORWONG TERAKIHI
JACK BEAN OVERLOOK
JACK CREVALLE TORO
JACKDAW DAW KAE JACK SHELL
  CADDOW CARDER CHOUGH KADDER
  CADESSE DAWCOCK DAWPATE
  GRACKLE
JACKER SLIPMAN TORCHER
JACKET SAC ETON JACK JUMP JUPE
  SACK VEST ACTON COVER DICKY
  JUPON POLKA SHRUG WAMUS
  BIETLE BLAZER BOLERO CARACO
  CORSET DOLMAN FECKET GANSEY
  JERKIN JERSEY JUMPER RAILLY
  REEFER SACQUE SADDLE SLEEVE
  SLIVER SONTAG TABARD TEMIAK
  WAMPUS WARMUS BEDGOWN
  CANEZOU LOUNGER NORFOLK
  PALETOT PALTOCK PEACOAT
  RISTORI SPENCER SURCOAT
  SWEATER CAMISOLE CARDIGAN
  CHAQUETA HANSELIN JIRKINET
  MACKINAW OVERSLOP PENELOPE
  SEALSKIN
  (— FOR TURKEY) APRON
  (— LINED WITH STEEL) PLACCATE
  (— OF INDIA) BANIAN BANIYA
  (— UNDER ARMOR) ACTON TRUSS
  (CROCHETED —) SONTAG
  (HOODED —) GREGO ANORAK
  GRIEKO
  (MALAY —) BAJU BADJU
  (UNDRESS MILITARY —) SHELL
  (WORK —) BAWNEEN
JACKFRUIT JACA KATHAL
  SOURJACK

JACKHAMMER SINKER PLUGGER
JACKKNIFE JACK PIKE BARLOW
JACKMAN SHELLMAN
JACK-OF-ALL-TRADES DOCTOR
  TINKER GIMCRACK
JACKSCREW CRICK
JACKSMELT PEIXEREY
JACKSNIPE GID JED JACK PEERT
  SCAPE SNIPE SNIGHT CHOROOK
  CREAKER JUDCOCK SQUATTER
JACKSTAY JACK HORSE PARREL
  JACKROD RAILWAY
JACKSTRAW SPILIKIN
JACK TREE NANGKA
JACOB ISRAEL
JACQUARD FACONNE
JADE YU DUN TIT HACK JAUD MINX
  PLUG SLUT TIRE HUSSY QUEAN
  TRASH BEJADE HARASS RANNEL
  AXSTONE HILDING POUNAMU
  (DIRTY —) SLAISTER
JADED FORGONE SHOPWORN
  DISJASKIT
JAEGER LARI SKUA ALLAN BOSUN
  LARID SHOOL BONXIE TEASER
  TULIAC TRUMPIE DIRTBIRD
  DUNGBIRD
JAG BUN JOG GIMP JAUG LOAD
  SOSH TOOT SKATE TOOTH INDENT
JAGGED JAGGY HACKLY RAGGED
  SCRAGGY SHAGGED SNAGGED
  INDENTED SCRAGGLY TATTERED
JAGGERY GUR GOOR GOUR KHAUR
  KHAJUR KITTUL
JAGUAR CAT OUNCE TIGER
  PANTHER UTURUNCU
JAI ALAI PELOTA
  (— COURT) FRONTON
JAIL CAN GIB JUG BOOB CAGE COOP
  CRIB DUMP GAOL HELL HOLD HOLE
  KEEP LAKE LOCK STIR WARD
  CHOKY CLINK GRATE KITTY LIMBO
  LODGE TENCH TRONK BUCKET
  CARCEL COOLER ENJAIL JIGGER
  LIMBUS LOCKUP TOLZEY FREEZER
  FURNACE GEHENNA KIDCOTE
  PINFOLD TOLLERY BASTILLE
  CALABOZO HOOSEGOW IMPRISON
  MILLDOLL TOLLHALL
  (— TERM) JOLT
JAILBIRD LAG
JAILER ADAM GAOLER KEEPER
  WARDEN TURNKEY INCLUDER
JAKE FINE HICK FELLOW
JAKES AJAX GONG
JALAP MECHOACAN
JALOPY CLUNKER
JAM DIP CRAM JAMB BLOCK CHOKE
  CROWD STICK THRONG JACKPOT
JAMAICA (CAPITAL OF —) KINGSTON
  (RIVER OF —) BLACK MINHO
JAMAICA COBNUT OUABE PIGNUT
JAMAICA DOGWOOD BABASCO
  BARBASCO FISHWOOD
JAMAICAN RAINBIRD TOMFOOL
JAMAICA VERVAIN GERVAO
JAMB DURN ALETTE HAUNCH
  REVEAL DOORPOST
JAMES JEM JIM JIMMY SEAMAS
  SHAMUS

JANGLE CLAM SQUABBLE
JANGLING HARSH JANGLY AJANGLE
JANISSARY CREOLE RABIRUBIA
JANITOR DURWAN PORTER
JANIZARY SOLAK SOLACH
JANSENIST RIGORIST
JANUS IANUS BIFRONT
JAOB JOW

JAPAN
BAY: ISE MUTSU OTARU ARIAKE
  ATSUMI SENDAI SURUGA
  TOYAMA WAKASA UCHIURA
CAPE: TOI ESAN MINO NOMA SHIO
  SOYA SUZU ERIMO KYOGA
  RURUI MUROTO NOJIMA
  TODOGA SHIRIYA ASHIZURI
  SHAKOTAN
CAPITAL: TOKIO TOKYO
COIN: BU RIN SEN YEN OBAN
  KOBAN OBANG TEMPO ICHEBU
  ITZEBU KOBANG
ISLAND: IKI SADO BONIN HONDO
  KURIL REBUN HONSHU KIUSHU
  KURILE KYUSHU RYUKYU
  CIPANGO LOOCHOO RISHIRI
  SKIKOKU HOKKAIDO IKISHIMA
  OKIGUNTO OKUSHIRI YAKUJIMA
LAKE: BIWA TOYA TOWADA
  KUTCHAWA SHIKOTSU
MEASURE: BU JO SE BOO CHO
  KEN TAN HIRO SHAKU TSUBO
MOUNTAIN: ZAO FUJI ASAHI
  ASAMA YESSO ASOSAN ENASAN
  HIUCHI KIUSIU YARIGA FUJISAN
  HAKUSAN KUJUSAN TOKACHI
  FUJIYAMA
SEA: SUO AMAKUSA
STRAIT: KII BUNGO OSUMI
  NEMURO TANEGA TOKARA
  TSUGARU TSUSHIMA
STREET: GINZA
TOWN: OME KOBE KURA MITO
  NARA OITA UEDA AKITA ATAMI
  FUKUI KIOTO KOCHI KYOTO
  NIKKO OSAKA OTARU SAKAI
  UJINA CHOSHI MATSUE NAGOYA
  SASEBO SENDAI TAKADA
  TOYAMA FUKUOKA NIIGATA
  OKAYAMA OKAZAKI SAPPORO
  HAKODATE KAMAKURA
  KANAZAWA KAWASAKI
  KUMAMOTO NAGASAKI
  YOKOHAMA YOKOSUKA
VOLCANO: ASO ASAMA ASOSAN
  HAKUSAN FUJIYAMA
WEIGHT: MO FUN KIN KON RIN SH
  KATI KWAN NIYO CARAT CATTY
  MOMME PICUL KWAMME
  HIYAKKIN

JAPAN NIPPON YAMATO CIPANGO
JAPAN CEDAR SUGI
JAPANESE JAP SKIBBY JAPONIC
JAPANESE APRICOT UME
JAPANESE CHERRY SAKURA
JAPANESE DEER SIKA
JAPANESE IRIS SHADOW

JAPANESE PERSIMMON KAKI
JAPANESE PLUM KELSEY
JAPANESE PORGIE TAI
JAPANESE QUINCE JAPONICA
JAPANESE VELVET BIRODO
JAPE GAUD JOKE
JAPONICA ASTILBE
JAR TUN CELL JANG JARG JOLT
JURR OLLA BANGA CADUS CRUSE
KADOS SHOCK DOLIUM HUSTLE
HYDRIA IMPACT JUDDER KALPIS
PANKIN PINATA PITHOS TINAJA
CANOPUS CONCUSS PSYKTER
STAMNOS TERRINE MARTABAN
STINKPOT
(2-HANDLED —) AMPHORA
(BELL —) CLOCHE
(BULGING —) OLLA
(EARTHENWARE —) CAN NAN
CROCK GAMLA PITHOS TERRINE
(POROUS —) GURGLET
(SQUAT —) KORO
(STONE —) STEEN STONE CROPPA
(WATER —) BANGA CHATTI CHATTY
GUMLAH HYDRIA
JARGON CANT JIVE RANE SLUM
JARGOT SLANG LINGUA LINSEY
PATOIS PATTER PIDGIN SHELTA
SIWASH CHINOOK CHOCTAW
DIALECT JARGOON PALAVER
BARRIKIN KEDGEREE POLYGLOT
SCHMOOZE SHOPTALK
(THIEVES' —) FLASH
JARRING JARG RUDE SOUR HARSH
ROUGH DARING
JASMINE BELA MALATI PIKAKE
JESSAMY WOODBINE
JASPER JASPIS MORLOP DIASPER
CREOLITE
JAUNDICE AURIGO GULSACH
ICTERUS JANDERS YELLOWS
JAUNDERS GRASSERIE
JAUNDICED ICTERODE
JAUNT SALLY JAUNCE VAGARY
JOURNEY
JAUNTILY AIRILY BOUNCILY
JAUNTING CAR SIDECAR OUTSIDER
JAUNTY PERK COCKY PERKY SASSY
DAPPER JANTEE SHANTY FINICAL
PERKING DEBONAIR

JAVA

ISLAND: BALI LOMBOK MADURA
MEASURE: PAAL
MOUNTAIN: GEDE MURJO RAOENG
  SLAMET SEMEROE SOEMBING
PORT: BATAVIA SURABAJA
TOWN: BOGOR DESSA KEDIRI
  MALANG BANDUNG BATAVIA
  JAKARTA SEMARANG SURABAJA
WEIGHT: POND TALI

JAVA ALMOND PILI CANARI KANARI
ALISAY
JAVA COTTON KAPOK
JAVANESE KRAMA KROMO
JAVANESE SKUNK TELEDU
JAVA PLUM DUHAT JAMBUL
JOMBOY JAMBOOL

JAVA SPARROW MUNIA PADDY
RICEBIRD
JAVELIN COLP DART PILE ACLYS
PILUM JAREED LANCET ASSAGAI
HARPOON HURLBAT JAVELOT
ACONTIUM GAVELOCK
JAW JIB BEAK CHAP CHAW CHOP
JOWL WANG ANVIL CHAFT CHEEK
CHOKE SCOLD CHAWLE FEELER
JAWBONE MAXILLA MANDIBLE
(— OF FORCEPS) BEAK
(— OF SPIDER) FANG
(— OF VISE) CHAP
(—S OF BIRD) BILL
(FALSE —) CLAMP
(RECEDING NOSE AND UNDERSHOT
—) LAYBACK
(PL.) MAW BITS THROAT
JAWBONE JOWL WANG MAXILLA
CHAWBONE
JAWBREAKING CRACKJAW
JAY JAYPIET SIRGANG BLUECOAT
MEATBIRD
JAYHAWKER KANSAN
JAZERANT GESSERON
JAZZ BOP JIVE HOTCHA
JEALOUS YELLOW EMULOUS
ENVIOUS
JEALOUSY ENVY YELLOWS
EMULATION
JEAN FROCKING
JEANPAULIA BAIERA
JEEP PEEP SEEP BANTAM
JEER BOB BOO MOB GECK GIBE
GIRD JAPE JEST JIBE MOCK SKIT
WIPE FLIRT FLOUT FLUTE FLYTE
FRUMP GLAIK LAUGH SCOFF
SCOMM SNEER TAUNT CHIACK
DERIDE BARRACK RIDICULE
JEERING BIRD FLOUT DERISIVE
JEHOVAH JAH JORD JAHVE YAHWEH
(— WITNESS) PIONEER
JEJUNE DRY ARID MEAGER INSIPID
JELL COME FIRM
JELLY GEAL JEEL JELL GELEE
CULLIS JUJUBE ALCOGEL FISNOGA
GELATIN JELLIFY FLUMMERY
HYDROGEL QUIDDANY
(CALF'S-FOOT —) SULZE
(FRUIT —) ROB
(MEAT —) ASPIC
JELLYFISH JELLY QUARL CARVEL
MEDUSA ACALEPH AURELIA
MEDUSAN SLOBBER SUNFISH
SCYPHULA SEACROSS STROBILA
JELLYLIKE SLABBY
JENNY MULE JINNY
JEOPARDIZE EXPOSE HAZARD
IMPERIL ENDANGER
JEOPARDY RISK PERIL DANGER
HAZARD
JEQUIRITY BEAN EYEN RUTTEE
JERBOA GERBIL JUMPER
JEREED TZIRID
JEREMIAD TRAGEDY
JERK GAG JET NUD TIT BOUT CANT
FIRK GIRD HIKE JERT JIRT JOLT
JOUK KICK PECK SNAP SNIG YANK
YERK BRAID CHUCK FLIRT HITCH

SCHMO SNAKE SPANG SURGE
TWEAK TWICK FILLIP JIGGER
SWITCH TWITCH WRENCH FLOUNCE
SPANGHEW
JERKED MEAT TASAJO
JERKILY HITCHILY
JERKIN JACKET
JERKY NERVY SHARP CHOPPY
ELBOIC FLICKY FLINGY HITCHY
JIGGETY CHOPPING PALMODIC
RATCHETY SACCADIC
JEROBOAM REHOBOAM
JERSEY FROCK SHIRT GANSEY
TRICOT ZEPHYR MAILLOT SINGLET
CAMISOLE GUERNSEY
JERUSALEM ARIEL SOLYMA
AHOLIBAH
JERUSALEM ARTICHOKE TUBER
CANADA GIRASOL
JERUSALEM CHERRY SOLANUM
JERUSALEM OAK AMBROSIA
JERUSALEM SAGE PHLOMIS
SAGELEAF
JERUSALEM THORN CASCOL
RETAMA
JESSAMINE JASMINE WOODBINE
JEST BOG COG FUN JOE TAX BULL
GAME GAUD GIRD JAPE JOKE JOSH
PLAY QUIP QUIZ RAIL SKIT BOURD
BREAK CHAFF CLOWN DROLL FLIRT
GESTE GLEEK SPORT THING
BANTER GLANCE JAPERY RAILLY
TRIFLE DICTERY GAMMOCK JOLLITY
WAGGERY DROLLERY RAILLERY
(— SPITEFULLY) SLENT
JESTER FOOL MIME BUFFO CLOWN
DROLL IDIOT JAPER JOKER PATCH
WAMBA DISOUR MOTLEY YORICK
BADCHAN BOURDER BUFFOON
DIZZARD DROLLER JOCULAR
JUGGLER PICADOR SCOFFER
SCOGGIN TOMTRAM MERRYMAN
OWLGLASS PLEASANT RAILLEUR
TRINCULO
JESTING DROLL JAPERY WAGGISH
JESUIT PAULIST TERTIAN IGNATIAN
LOYOLITE
JESUS GEE GIS IHC IHS JHS YHS
JESU WISDOM
(SAYINGS OF —) AGRAPHA
JET BOLT TAIL TANG BREAK DUMBY
DUMMY JETTO SALLY SPOUT SPRAY
SPURT DELUGE DOUCHE GAGATE
SQUIRT FANTAIL JETTEAU SPATTER
SPURTER FOUNTAIN SOFFIONE
UPSPRING
(— OF METAL) BREAK
(— OF VOLCANIC STEAM) STUFA
(SMALL —) SQUIB
JET-BLACK BUGLE
JETTING SALIENT
JETTISON DUMP JETSAM
JETTY JET DIKE GROIN JUTTY
BRIDGE OVERHANG
JEW SAINT ESSENE JUDEAN LITVAK
SEMITE SMOUCH TOBIAD BARABAS
GRECIAN MARRANO SMOUSER
APIKOROS CONVERSO GALICIAN
JUDAHITE LANDSMAN SEPHARDI

(—S OUT OF ISRAEL) DIASPORA
(BALKAN —) LADINE
JEWEL GEM JOY DROP OUCH BIJOU
REGAL STONE BROOCH GEORGE
TRIFLE CRAPAUD GARLAND
POUNDER
(PL.) BULSE PERRIE
JEWELER GEMMARY LAPIDARY
JEWELRY ICE JUNK OUCH PARURE
COLLARET LAPIDARY
(MOCK —) LOGIE
(PIECE OF —) GAUD
JEWELWEED CEROLINE EARJEWEL
SNAPWEED
JEWFISH MERO GUASA WARSAW
PERCOID JUNEFISH MULLOWAY
SERRANID
JEWISH JUDAIC SEMITIC
(— BODY) VAAD
(— COMMUNITY) KEHILLAH
(— QUARTER) MELLAH
(— SCHOOL) ALJAMA
JEWRY GHETTO JUDAISM
JEW'S-HARP HARP TROMP TRUMP
GEWGAW FLAMFEW TRANGAM
GUIMBARD
JEW'S MALLOW DESI
JEZEBEL GILLIVER
JIB GIB DEMUR GIGUE GIBBET
SPITFIRE
JIBE (ALSO SEE GIBE) GEE KAY GAFF
GIBE JAPE JERK MOCK SKIT AGREE
FLIRD MARCH SNACK THRUST
JIFFY JIFF BRAID FLISK WHIFF
GLIFFY GLIFFING
JIG BUCK FRISK GIGUE SQUID
GARLIC JIGGER JIGGET JITTER
LOCATOR
(— FOR WASHING ORE) HUTCH
(FISHING —) PILK
JIGGER SHOT DANDY PIQUE
DOODAD GADGET JIGMAN VATMAN
CHIGGER
JIGGLE DIDDLE JUGGLE TEETER
JILT GUNK KICK SACK BEGOWK
BEGUNK MITTEN
JIMMY BETTY JAMES JEMMY
JIMSONWEED DATURA DEWTRY
JIMSON FIREWEED STRAMONY
JINGLE CHIME CLINK DINGLE RICKLE
TINKLE CHINKLE DINGDONG
JINGLING
(MEANINGLESS —) SPORT
JINGLING SMIT JANGLE RIGADIG
TINKLING
JINGO WARRIOR WARMONGER
JINKER WHIM
JINN DJIN JANN AFRIT GENIE AFREET
DJINNI SHAITAN
(PL.) JINNI
JINNI MARID AFREET ALUKAH
GENIUS YAKSHA YAKSHI JINNIVEH
JINRIKIMAN KURUMAYA
JINRIKISHA GOCART KURUMA
RICKSHAW
JINX HEX JONAH HOODOO
JIPIJAPA CHIDRA PALMILLA
TOQUILLA
JITTERBUG TRUCKING

JITTERY JUMPY SPOOKY AJITTER
JIVARO JIBARO SHUARA XIBARO
JOAN JUG JONE
(— OF ARC) PUCELLE
JOB LAY TUT CHAR FIST SHOP TURN
BERTH CHORE FIRST BILLET
HUSTLE JOBSITE SWEATER
BUSINESS
(EASY —) BLUDGE
(SMALL —) CHORE JOBBLE
JOBBER BRAGER DEALER FLUNKY
BROGGER COURSER
JOB'S TEARS COIX ADLAI ADLAY
JOCKEY JOCK ROPER WASTER
CHANTER EQUISON TURFITE
SKIPJACK
(DISC —) DEEJAY
JOCOSE JOCO LEPID JOCULAR
JOCOTE MOMBIN
JOCOTE DE MICO BARBAS
JOCULAR GAY AIRY GLAD JOKY
DROLL FUNNY HAPPY JOLLY MERRY
WITTY BLITHE ELATED JAPISH
JOCOSE JOCUND JOKISH JOVIAL
JOYFUL JOYOUS LIVELY BUOYANT
COMICAL FESTIVE GLEEFUL
PLAYFUL WAGGISH ANIMATED
CHEERFUL DEBONAIR GLADSOME
HUMOROUS JOCATORY JOKESOME
LAUGHING MIRTHFUL
JOCULARITY FUN WAGGERY
JOCUND BUDGE JOCANT JOCULAR
JOE JO
(HALF —) JOANNES JOHANNES
JOE-PYE WEED EUPATORY
JOEWOOD JOEBUSH BARBASCO
IRONWOOD
JOG BOB HOD JAG JIG JOT MOG
KICK POKE SHOG SPUD STIR TROT
WHIG DUNCH HOTCH NUDGE TWEAK
DIDDLE JITTER JOGGLE JUNDIE
(— ALONG) FADGE FODGE
(— AWKWARDLY) DODGE
(— WITH ELBOW) DUNCH
JOGGER LAYBOY
JOGGLE HOTCH JUGGLE SHOGGLE
SHOOGLE
JOHANNES JOE PECA
JOHN IAN JEAN JOCK JONE JUAN
SEAN JOHANN SEAGHAN GIOVANNI
JOHNNYCAKE CORNCAKE
JOIN ADD COP FAY MIX PAN TAG TIE
UNY ALLY COPE FAIR FUSE GAIN
GLUE KNIT LINK MEET MELL SEAM
SOUD TAIL TEAM YOKE ANNEX
BLEND BLRND ENTER FRANK GRAFT
JOINT MERGE TENON UNITE WRING
ACCEDE ADJECT ADJOIN ASSIST
ATTACH CEMENT COCKET COMMIT
CONCUR ENGAGE INDENT JOGGLE
MARROW MINGLE PIECEN RELATE
RELIDE SPLICE STITCH STRIKE
COMBINE CONJOIN CONNECT
CONTACT INJOINT JOINING SHACKLE
ACCOUPLE COALESCE COMPOUND
COPULATE DOVETAIL JUNCTION
(— BATTLE) JOUST ENGAGE
(— BY SEWING) STITCH SUTURE
(— CLOSELY) FAY AFFY WELD
GRAFT

(— IN COMBAT) BUCKLE
(— IN MARRIAGE) WED TACK HITCH
COUPLE
(— THE PARTS OF) PIECE
(— TOGETHER) CLOSE COAPT
FRANK HITCH COUPLE ENGLUE
ENJOIN ASSEMBLE COAGMENT
COALESCE
JOINED JOINT ALLIED DIRECT
SEAMED ACCOLLE ADJUNCT
APPINED EMBOITE ADJUGATE
COMBINED CONJUNCT COPULATE
INTEGRAL
JOINER SNUG JOINTER
JOINING BAR JOIN SEAM BRIDE
CLOSE SPLICE BETWEEN JOINDER
ADDITION JUNCTION JUNCTIVE
JUNCTURE SYNECTIC
JOINT BED HAR HIP BUTT COXA FISH
HEAD HELL HOCK JOIN KNEE LITH
LOCK SEAL SEAM TUCK ANKLE
BRAZE BUILD CARDO CHASE ELBOW
MITER MITRE PLACE SCAPE SCARF
SPALD UNION UNITE WRIST BOXING
COMMON HAUNCH SCARPH SPLICE
STIFLE SUTURE TOGGLE UNITER
ARTHRON ARTICLE COGGING
DIGITAL FETLOCK FLEXURE ISCHIUM
JOINING KNUCKLE SCATTER
SHIPLAP SIAMESE CONJOINT
CONJUNCT COUPLING DIACLASE
DOVETAIL FLASHING JOINTURE
JUNCTURE SUBJOINT SUFFRAGO
TROCHOID VARIATOR
(— ABOVE HOCK) STIFLE
(— OF BIRD'S WING) FLEXURE
(— OF FLAIL) CAPEL
(— OF MEAT) BARON
(— OF SHIP) CHASE
(— OF STEM) NODE
(ANKLE —) COOT
(ELBOW —) NOOP
(FLEXIBLE —) HINGE
(GROOVED —) RABBET
(HIP —) COXA THURL
(MASONRY —) JOGGLE
(MINING —) CLEAT SLINE
(SCARF —) BOXING
(UNIVERSAL —) CARDAN
(VERTICAL —) BUILD
(WHEEL-LIKE —) TROCHITE
JOINTED ARTHROUS
JOINTED CHARLOCK KRAUT
RUNCH
JOINTER JOINER SKIMMER
JOINT FIR EPHEDRA
JOINT GRASS PASPALUM
JOIST GEEST LEDGE BRIDGE RAGLIN
SLEEPER CARRIAGE
(PL.) PIGGIN JOISTING
JOJOBA PIGNUT SHEEPNUT
JOKE BAR DOR FUN GAB GAG GIG
JOE KID ROT WIT FOOL GAFF GAME
GAUD GEGG JAPE JEST JOSH LICE
NOTE QUIP QUIZ TYPE BREAK
CRACK FLIRT GLEEK GRIND LAUGH
PRANK RALLY SPORT BANTER
JAPERY PLISKY WHEEZE JOKELET
WAGGERY CHESTNUT

(PRACTICAL —) BAR FUN GAG RIG HOAX REAK SHAVIE HOTFOOT
(STALE —) CHESTNUT
(PL.) JAPERY
JOKER BUG DOR WAG CLOWN GRIND SLAVE FARCER FOOLER GAGGER JOKIST FARCEUR GIMMICK FUNNYMAN HUMORIST JOKESTER
JOKING JOSH BANTER JOCOSE
(PRACTICAL —) GAME
JOLLIFICATION RAG RANT JOLLY
JOLLITY MIRTH GAIETY HILARITY JOLLITRY
JOLLY GAY KID BUXOM GAWSY WALLY CROUSE JOVIAL STRING JOCULAR DISPOSED
JOLLY BOAT YAWL DANDY
JOLT JET JIG JOG JOT JUT BELT BUMP DIRD DIRL HIKE JOWL JUMP KICK SHOG JAUNT HOTTER IMPACT JOGGLE JOSTLE JOUNCE JUMBLE
JOLTING JERKY BUMPITY HOTTERY
JONAH JINX JONAS HOODOO
JONQUIL JONK LILY DAFFODIL

JORDAN
CAPITAL: AMMAN
COIN: DINAR
MOUNTAIN: BUKKA DABAB ATAIBA MUBRAK
REGION: PEREA BASHAN PERAEA
RIVER: JORDAN YARMUK
TOWN: AQABA ARIHA IRBID KARAK ZARQA ZERKE NABLUS

JOSEPH JOSEY GIUSEPPE
JOSEPHINE BLUSH PHENY
JOSH GUY KID RIB JOKE CHAFF STRING
JOSHI JOTI JOTISARU
JOSHUA JESUS
JOSTLE JOG JOLT JOSS PUSH SHOG CROWD ELBOW HUNCH JUNDY SHOVE HURTLE HUSTLE JOGGLE JUNDIE JUSTLE SHOULDER
JOSTLING SCRAMBLE
JOT ACE DOT ATOM IOTA MITE TARE WHIT GRAIN MINIM POINT TWINT WIGHT TITTLE SCRUPLE SYLLABLE
(— DOWN) NICK
JOTTING TOT
JOTUNN GEIRROTH
JOUNCE HIKE JOLT JAUNT
JOURNAL TOE BOOK DIARY PAPER BLAZER SERIAL DAYBOOK DIURNAL GAZETTE GUDGEON JOURNEY CASHBOOK NOCTUARY TRUNNION
(SEA —) LOGBOOK
JOURNAL BEARING RHODING
JOURNALIST SCRIBE WRITER BYLINER DIARIAN
JOURNEY BE GO JOG RUN WAY DIET EYRE FARE FORE GAIT GANG GATE HIKE JUMP RACE RIDE ROAD STEP TOUR TREK TRIP TURN WENT BROAD COVER DRIVE JAUNT REISE SITHE TRAIK TRAIL TURUS WEENT ERRAND FLIGHT HEGIRA JUNKET TRAVEL VAGARY COMMINO

EMBASSY ENTRADA EXCURSE JORNADA JOURNAL MEANDER PASSAGE STRETCH TRAVAIL TROUNCE WALKING WAYFARE GODSPEED PROGRESS
(— BY SEA) VOYAGE
(— DOWNSTREAM) DESCEND
(DAY'S —) DIET
(DESERT —) JORNADA
(FATIGUING —) TRAIK
(LONG —) TREK
(TEDIOUS —) TRANCE
JOURNEYING CRUISE
JOURNEYMAN YEOMAN
JOUST PLAY TILT JOSTLE JUSTLE TOURNEY
JOUSTER TILTER
JOVIAL GAY BOON JOVY BULLY JOLLY MERRY GENIAL HEARTY MELLOW BACCHIC HOLIDAY JOCULAR
JOVIALITY JOLLITY ROLLICK HILARITY
JOWL CHOW CHAULE
(PL.) CHOPS
JOY JO WIN GLEE LIST PLAY BLISS DREAM EXULT MIRTH REVEL GAIETY HEYDAY DELIGHT ECSTASY ELATION JOYANCE RAPTURE REVELRY FELICITY GLADNESS HILARITY PLEASURE
JOYFUL GAY GLAD BEAMY JOLLY BLITHE FESTUS JOCUND JOVIAL JOYANT JOYOUS GAUDFUL GLADFUL GLEEFUL JOCULAR GLADSOME
JOYFULLY FAIN FAINLY GLADLY JOYOUSLY
JOYLESS DESOLATE LUSTLESS UNBLITHE
JOYOUS GAY GLAD JOLLY MERRY YOUSE BLITHE JOVIAL FESTIVE GIOJOSO GLEEFUL JOCULAR FROHLICH SUNSHINY
JOYOUSNESS HILARITY
JUBILANT ELATED JOYFUL EXULTANT
JUBILATION JOY JOYANCE JUBILEE
JUDAHITE JEW
JUDAISM JEWISM HEBRAISM
JUDAS TREE CERCIS
JUDEA JEWRY
JUDEO-SPANISH LADINO
JUDGE DAN JUS SEE WIG CAID CAZY DEEM DOOM HOLD IMAM JUEZ JURY KAZI SCAN AWARD COUNT COURT DAYAN GAUGE HAKIM INFER JUDEX MINOS OPINE PUNEE TRIER WEIGH CENSOR CRITIC DANIEL DEEMER DICAST DOOMER INTEND JUDGER JURIST OPINER PUISNE SAMSON SAMUEL SETTLE SQUIRE ACCOUNT ADJUDGE ARBITER BENCHER BRIDOYE CENSURE FLAGMAN FOUJDAR HELIAST JURYMAN JUSTICE MUNSIFF PODESTA REFEREE SCABINE SHAMGAR SUPPOSE APPRAISE CENTENAR CONCLUDE CONSIDER DEEMSTER DEMPSTER DIRECTOR DOOMSMAN

DOOMSTER ESTIMATE FOREDEEM JEPHTHAH JUDGMENT JUDICATE LINESMAN MINISTER MITTIMUS ORDINARY QUAESTOR RECORDER REGICIDE SCABINUS STRADICO
JUDGMENT ACT EYE BOOK DEEM DOME DOOM REDE VIEW ARRET AWARD FANCY JUISE SENSE SIGHT SKILL TASTE ADVICE ASSIZE DECREE ESTEEM JUWISE STEVEN ACCOUNT CENSURE CONCEIT HOLDING OPINION VERDICT WITTING ESTIMATE JUDICIAL JUDICIUM SAGACITY SENTENCE THINKING
JUDICATORY SYNOD
JUDICIOUS WISE CRITICAL JUDICIAL MODERATE SENSEFUL SENSIBLE WISELIKE
JUDO (— EXERCISES) KATA
(— PRACTICE) RANDORI
JUG CAN EWER JACK JUST ASCUS ASKOS BUIRE GAMLA GOTCH JORUM JUBBE STEAN BOGGLE CROUKE GOGLET GOMLAH HYDRIA CREAMER PITCHER CRUISKEN LECYTHUS LEKYTHOS OENOCHOE PROCHOOS
(— WITH SPOUT) BUIRE DOLLIN
(ALE —) TOBY
(BULGING —) GOTCH
(LEATHER —) JACK BOMBARD
(ONE-HANDLED —) URCEUS
(SPOUTLESS —) OLPE
JUGATED BAJOIRE
JUGGLE TRICK BAFFLE FUMBLE CONJURE SHUFFLE
JUGGLER HARLOT CONJURER JONGLEUR
JUGLONE NUCIN
JUGULARES DERIPIA
JUGUM FIBULA JUGULUM
JUICE JUS SEW BREE BROO FOND OOZE SUCK ANIMA BLOND BLOOD GRAVY HUMOR MOBBY PERRY CASIRI CREMOR JIPPER SUCCUS CAMBIUM AGUAMIEL HYPOCIST VERJUICE
(— OF COCONUT) MILK
(— OF TREE) SAP LYCIUM JELUTONG
(— OF UNRIPE FRUIT) OMPHACY
(APPLE —) CIDER
(CANE —) SLING
(CONCENTRATED —) SIRUP SYRUP
(DRIED —) ALOE KINO
(FERMENTED —) SURA GRAPE
(FRUIT —) ROB ROHOB
(GRAPE —) MUST SAPA STUM
(INTOXICATING —) SOMA
(LETTUCE —) THRIDACE
(MEAT —) BLOND
(POPPY —) CHICK
(TOBACCO —) AMBEER AMBIER
(PL.) ESSENCE HUMIDITY
JUICY FAT FRIM FRUM NAISH SAPPY FRUITY SUCCOSE WATERISH
JUJUBE BER ELB TSAO LOTEBUSH LOTEWOOD ZIZYPHUS
JUKEBOX PICCOLO

JUMBLE PIE ROG HASH MESS MUSS RAFF BOTCH BOLLIX BUMBLE FUDDLE GARBLE HUDDLE JUMPER JUNGLE MEDLEY MOMBLE MUDDLE PALTER RAFFLE WELTER WUZZLE CLUTTER CONFUSE EMBROIL GOULASH SHUFFLE DISORDER MISHMASH RHAPSODY SMACHRIE (— OF SOUNDS) LURRY
JUMBLED CRAZY HASHY JUMBLY HUDDLING
JUMP HOP LEP NIP DART JETE LEAP LUTZ SKIP SKIT STEN STOT TUMB BOUND CAPER FENCE HALMA SALTO SAULT SPANG SPEND START STOIT VAULT DOUBLE FOOTER HURDLE INSULT LAUNCH SPRING SPRUNT STARRE WALLOP CISEAUX CROWHOP SALTATE SKYLARK BALLONNE
(— ABOUT) SKIT CAPER
(— FROM AIRCRAFT) BAIL BALE
(— IN FENCING) BALESTRA
(— ON HORSEBACK) LARK
(— ON SKATES) AXEL SALCHOW (PL.) ALLEGRO
JUMPER LAMMY SWAGE BARKER LEPPER HANDYMAN
JUMPING SALIENT SALTANT
JUMPY ITCHY
JUNCO SNOWBIRD
JUNCTION HIP FROG JOIN CLOSE CROWN UNION FILLET INFALL CONTACT JOINING MEETING UNITION JUNCTURE
(— OF EARTH AND SKY) HORIZON
(— OF STREAMS) GRAINS
(— OF THREADS) FELL STOP
(— ON TOOTH) CERVIX
JUNCTURE PASS PINCH CRISIS STRAIT ARTICLE BRACKET JOINING OPHRYON EXIGENCY JOINTAGE JOINTURE OCCASION QUANDARY

JUNEBERRY SHADBLOW SHADBUSH
JUNE BUG BUZZARD DUMCLOCK
JUNGLE BUSH RUKH SHOLA BOONDOCK
JUNGLE BENDY WEENONG
JUNIOR PUNY CADET YOUNG PUISNE YOUNGER
JUNIPER CADE EZEL GORSE GORST SAVIN SABINE
JUNK CRAM GEAR GOOK TOPE DRECK REFUSE SCULCH DISCARD PLUNDER TONGKANG
(WORTHLESS —) SLUM
JUNKET TRIP KNACK JINKET SAFARI
JUNKMAN TATTER SCRAPMAN SCAVENGER
JUNO MONETA PRONUBA
JUPITER JOVE STATOR FORTUNE MUSHTARI TERMINUS
JUPITER'S BEARD JOUBARB
JUR LWO LUOH
JUREL RUNNER CREVALLE HARDTAIL
JURISDICTION SOC BAIL SOKE FUERO HONOR REALM ABBACY BANDON BEYLIK DANGER DIWANI RIDING SPHERE DEANERY DEWANEE DROSTDY EMIRATE KHANATE BAILIERY FOUJDARY LIGEANCE PASHALIC PROVINCE
(— OF BISHOP) SEE
(COERCIVE —) SWORD
(MORMON —) KEYS
JURISPRUDENCE LAW REPORTS
JURIST JUDGE MUFTI BREHON LAWYER DOTTORE
JUROR JURAT ASSIZER JURYMAN CENTUMVIR
JURY ARRAY PANEL QUEST ASSIZE JURATA COUNTRY EMPANEL INQUEST
(— COUNTY) VISNE
JURYMAN DICAST JURIST ASSIZER

JURY-RIGGED HAYWIRE
JUST ALL DUE EVEN FAIR FLOP LEAL TRUE EQUAL FIRST LEVEL NOBUT ROUND VALID ZADOC CANDID GIUSTO HONEST JUSTIN JUSTUS MERELY SQUARE EQUABLE LEESOME UPRIGHT LIEFSOME RIGHTFUL SKILLFUL UNBIASED
(— AS) AFTER
(— HOVE CLEAR) ATRIP
(— IN TIME) SONICA
(ONLY —) HARDLY SCARCELY
JUSTAUCORPS JUSTICO
JUSTICE LAW DOOM RIGHT SKILL DHARMA EQUITY REASON HONESTY SHALLOW SILENCE DEEMSTER JUDGMENT JUSTITIA JUSTNESS RECORDER
(— OF PEACE) BEAK SQUIRE
JUSTIFIABLY FAIRLY
JUSTIFICATION CALL COLOR EXCUSE APOLOGY DEFENCE WARRANT APOLOGIA
JUSTIFIED FAIR JUST
JUSTIFY AVOW CLEAR PROVE SALVE DEFEND EXCUSE HONEST EXPLAIN RECTIFY SUPPORT WARRANT MAINTAIN SANCTION UNDERPIN
JUSTLY WELL TRULY EVENLY FAIRLY EQUALLY HANDILY SQUARELY
JUSTNESS SQUARE FITNESS JUSTICE ACCURACY
JUSTUS JESUS
JUT HANG BULGE JETTY JUTTY BEETLE EXTEND IMPEND EXTRUDE
JUTE PAT DESI PAUT DAISEE ARAMINA CHINGMA
JUTTING HANGING
JUVENILE YOUNG JEJUNE PUERILE YOUTHFUL
JUXTAPOSED ADJACENT
JUXTAPOSITION BALANCE CONTACT CONTRAST NEARNESS

K KA KAY KILO KING
KAABA CAABA ALCAABA
KABAYA BADJU CABIE
KABELJOU KOB
KABISTAN KUBA
KABOB KEBOB SHASLIK
KABUKALLI CUPIUBA
KACHARI BODO
KACHIN SINGFO SINGPO CHINGPAW
KADAGA COORG
KAFFIR KATI XOSA FINGO TEMBU
CAFFRE INFIDEL TAMBUKI WAIGULI
(— BOY) UMFAAN
KAGU GRUIFORM
KAIKAWAKA CEDAR
KAINGIN SWIDDEN
KAKI TRIUMPH
KALAPOOIAN LAKMIUT
KALE COLE KAIL COLLARD SPROUTS
BORECOLE
KALMUCK ELEUT UIRAD KHOSHOT
KALUMPIT ANAGEP
KAMAHI BIRCH TOWAI
KAMALA WURRUS ROTTLERA
KAMICHI SCREAMER
KANA IROFA IROHA
KANGAROO ROO EURO BILBI FLIER
FLYER TUNGO BOOMER FOSTER
WOILIE DIDELPH POTOROO
WALLABY BETTONGA BOONGARY
FILANDER FORESTER WALLAROO
(FEMALE —) DOE GIN
(YOUNG —) JOEY
KANGAROO APPLE GUNYANG
POROPORO
KANGAROO RAT JERBOA
KANHOBAL CONOB
KANKANAI IGOROT
KANS KUSA GLAGA KUSHA GLAGAH

KANSAS
CAPITAL: TOPEKA
COLLEGE: BAKER TABOR
BETHANY STERLING WASHBURN
COUNTY: ELK GOVE NESS RENO
TREGO NEMAHA ATCHISON
FORT: RILEY SCOTT
INDIAN: KANSA KIOWA PAWNEE
WICHITA COMANCHE
LAKE: CHENEY KIRWIN NEOSHO
MILFORD
MOUNTAIN: SUNFLOWER
NATIVE: JAYHAWK
NICKNAME: SUNFLOWER
PRESIDENT: EISENHOWER
RIVER: ARKANSAS MISSOURI
STATE BIRD: MEADOWLARK
STATE FLOWER: SUNFLOWER
STATE TREE: COTTONWOOD
TOWN: HAYS IOLA COLBY DODGE
SALINA CHANUTE LIBERAL
WICHITA

ANSAN JAYHAWK
AOLIANG SORGHUM
APOK CEIBO FLOSS
ARAISM ANANISM
ARAKA KOPI
ARA KIRGHIZ BURUT BOUROUT

KARATAS PITA
KAREN SGAU SGAW
KARENNI PADAUNG
KARMA (BAD —) DEMERIT
KASKA NAHANE
KAT KHAT QUAT CAFTA
KATE KAI
KAUNAS KOVNO
KAURI COWRIE BERAIROU
KAVA AVA AWA YAQONA KAVAKAVA
YANGGONA
KAW AKHA
KAZOO BAZOO GAZOO ZARAH
HEWGAG MIRLITON
KEEL FIN BACK SEEL BARGE CARINA
CRISTA SERRULA
(— OF BIRD'S MANDIBLE) GONYS
(AFTERPART OF —) SKAG SKEG
KEEN DRY FLY GAY SHY YAP ACID
DEAR FINE GAIR GLEG HIGH PERT
TART TEEN WAIL WARM WILD
ACUTE BREME BRIEF BRISK EAGER
QUICK SHARP SMART SNELL SPICY
VIVID ASTUTE BITTER CAOINE
GREEDY LIVELY SEVERE SHREWD
SHRILL CUNNING HAWKING
MORDANT PARLISH PARLOUS
PUNGENT SERIOUS THIRSTY
KEENER HOWLER
KEENLY KEEN FELLY DEARLY
ACUTELY
KEENNESS EDGE ACUITY ACUMEN
PUNGENCY
(— OF SIGHT) ACIES
KEEN-SCENTED NOSEWISE
KEEN-SIGHTED EAGLE
KEEP HUG HAVE HOLD SALT SAVE
WAIT WITE BLESS ROCCA WITIE
COFFER DETAIN CONFINE CONTAIN
DEFORCE HUSBAND KEEPING
RESERVE CONSERVE MAINTAIN
PRESERVE RESTRAIN WITHHOLD
(— A COURSE) CAPE
(— A SMALL SHOP) CRAME
(— A WOUND OPEN) TENT
(— ABREAST) FOLLOW
(— AFLOAT) BUOY
(— AN EYE ON) STAG
(— APART) DOTTLE ISOLATE
SEPARATE
(— AT A DISTANCE) ESTRANGE
(— AWAY FROM) ABHOR AVOID
(— AWAY) ABSENT
(— BACK) HAP ROB STAY ARREAR
DETAIN RETARD RESERVE
(— COMPANY WITH) GANG MOOP
CONSORT
(— FREE) ESCHEW
(— FROM BOILING OVER) KEEL
(— FROM BURNING) REDD
(— HIDDEN) HOARD SECRETE
(— IN CIRCULATION) WIND
(— IN EXCITEMENT) ALARM ALARUM
(— IN MIND) RETAIN
(— IN ORDER) TARGE
(— IN STOCK) CARRY
(— IN THE TRACK) GATHER
(— IN) CAGE
(— OFF) FEND WEAR SHIELD

(— OUT) BAR EXPEL
(— POSSESSION) HARBOR
(— SCORELESS) BLANK
(— SECRET) HUSH WHIST
(— STRAIGHT) DIRECT
(— TABS ON) FINGER
(— TIME) GO
(— TO ONESELF) BOSOM
(— UNTIL YEAR OLD) HOG
(— UP) SUBSIST SUSTAIN CONTINUE
(— WAITING) DELAY
(— WARM) STIVE STOVE FOSTER
(— WATCH) TOUT WAIT BEWAKE
KEEPER NAB KEEP SCREW TUTOR
YEMER CUSTOS GAOLER JAILER
LIFTER LOOKER PARKER PASTOR
RAHDAR RANGER WARDEN BAILIFF
CURATOR GEARMAN PIKEMAN
PROVOST BEARWARD DEERHERD
DOLLYMAN ELDERMAN FEWTERER
GUARDANT GUARDIAN HOUNDMAN
TRAITEUR WARRENER
(— OF CATTLE) HAYWARD
(— OF DOGS) FEWTERER
(— OF ELEPHANT) MAHOUT
(— OF PRISON) GAOLER JAILER
WARDEN ALCAIDE
(DOOR —) DURWAN
KEEPING CARE WARD CHARGE
CUSTODY DETAINER
KEEPSAKE DRURY TOKEN GIFTBOOK
SOUVENIR
KEEVE TUB KIEVE
KEG CAG PIN TUB CADE CASK KNAG
WOOD ANKER BARRICO COSTREL
KELP KILP LEAG VAREC WRACK
GIRDLE SEAWEED BELLWARE
KELPIE BARB
KELT SLAT
KENAF DA GOMBO MESTA AMBARI
KANAFF PAPOULA STOKROOS
KENNEL STALL VENERY VENISON
DOGHOUSE
KENO HOUSE
KENTISH (— UNIT) YOKE

KENTUCKY
CAPITAL: FRANKFORT
COLLEGE: BEREA ASBURY
CENTRE BRESCIA URSULINE
COUNTY: ADAIR ESTIL TRIGG
FAYETTE MENIFEE MAGOFFIN
INDIAN: SHAWNEE CHEROKEE
IROQUOIS
LAKE: CUMBERLAND
RIVER: DIX OHIO SALT BARREN
STATE BIRD: CARDINAL
STATE FLOWER: GOLDENROD
STATE TREE: TULIP
TOWN: BEREA CORBIN HAZARD
GLASGOW PADUCAH DANVILLE
COVINGTON LEXINGTON

KENYA
BAY: FORMOSA
CAPITAL: NAIROBI
COIN: SHILLING

KENYA

LAKE: MAGADI RUDOLF NAIVASHA VICTORIA
LANGUAGE: LUO KIKUYU SWAHILI
MEASURE: WARI
MOUNTAIN: KENYA KULAL NYIRU MATIAN LOGONOT
PEOPLE: LUO MERU BANTU KAMBA KISII LUHYA MASAI NANDI KIKUYU OGADEN BALUHYA HAMITIC HILOTIC TURKANA KIPSIGIS
RIVER: LAK ATHI TANA TURKWELL
TOWN: MERU KITUI NAROK KIPINI KISUMU MOYALE NAKURU NAYUKI ELDORET MALINDI MOMBASA

KERCHIEF CURCH ROMAL RUMAL ANALAV CYPRUS MADRAS NAPKIN PEPLUM CYPRESS KERCHER PANUELO THERESE BABUSHKA BANDANNA HEADRAIL KAFFIYEH KINGSMAN
KERF CARF SKAFF GROOVE UNDERCUT
KERI QRI KERE
KERMANSHAH COCONUT
KERMES GRAIN
KERNEL NUT BUNT CORE KERN MEAT PITH BERRY GOODY GROAT ACINUS ALMOND CARNEL PICKLE NUCLEUS
(CORN —S) HOMINY
(UNHUSKED —S) CAPES
(PL.) NIXTAMAL
KEROGEN SAPROPEL
KEROSINE PARAFFIN
KERSENNEH ERS ERVIL
KERSEY WASHER ORDINARY
KESTREL FANNER KEELIE STANNEL STANCHEL WINDHOVER
KETCH SAIC
KETONE IRONE ACETOL ARMONE CARONE CARVOL COTOIN HEXONE IONONE QUINOL ACETOIN ACETONE ACYLOIN BAEKEOL BENZOIN CAMPHOR CARVONE DYPNONE FLAVONE JASMONE MUSCONE PHORONE SHOGAOL THUJONE ACRIDONE ANTHRONE BUTANONE BUTYRONE CHALCONE CHALKONE CHROMONE DEGUELIN EXALIONE FENCHONE MENTHONE PROPIONE PULEGONE ROTENONE STEARONE TAGETONE THIENONE VALERONE XANTHONE
KETTLE LEAD STEW DIXIE BOILER CANNER FESSEL MARMIT MASLIN TRIPOD VESSEL CALDRON SKILLET STEWPOT CALABASH FLAMBEAU
KETTLEDRUM NAKER ATABAL KETTLE TIMBAL TYMBAL TIMBALE TYMPANY
KEVEL CAVEL KNAPPER
KEY CAY KAY CLEW CLUE CRIB FLAT JACK KING NOTE PLUG PONY DITAL SCREW TASTO WREST BUTTON CHIAVE CIPHER CLAVIS COTTER

SAMARA SPLINE WINDER DIGITAL LANGUET PASSKEY SPEAKER LATCHKEY
(— FOR TUNING HARP) WREST
(— OF KEYBOARD INSTRUMENT) MANUAL
(— OF LIFE) ANKH
(— OF ORGAN) TASTO DIGITAL
(— OF PIANO) IVORY NATURAL
(— OF SPINET) CHIP
(— ON WOODWIND INSTRUMENT) LANGUET SPEAKER
(— UP) STRING
(—S OF CARILLON) CLAVECIN
(ARITHMETICAL —) ADDITIVE
(ASH —) PIGEON
(FALSE —) GLUT
(FEATHER —) FIN STOP SPLINE FEATHER
(SKELETON —) GILT TWIRLER
(TELEGRAPH —) BUG TAPPER
KEYBOARD CLAVIER PEDALIER
KEYHOLE KEY LOCKHOLE
KEYNOTE A B D E KEY TONIC FINALIS
KEYSTONE KEY QUOIN VERTEX SAGITTA VOUSSOIR
(— STATE) PENNSYLVANIA
KEYWAY SPLINE KEYSLOT
KEX KECKSY
KHA KA KHMU KACHE LAMET
KHALAT SEERPAW
KHAN CAN CHAM HAWN TACON KHAKAN
KHAS-KURA NEPALI PAHARI PARBATI GORKHALI
KHATTISH HATTIC
KHEDIVE QUITEVE
KHELLIN VISAMMIN
KHOTANA KOYUKON
KHUSKHUS CUSCUS VETIVER
KIANG CHIGETAI HEMIONUS
KIBBLE GIG KETTLE
KIBBLER CRACKER
KICK BOOT FICK FLEG FLIG FOOT FUNK HEEL HOOF LASH PORR POTE PUNT SHIN TURF YERK ANGLE BUNCH FLING KEVEL PAUSE PUNCH SKELP SPANG SPURN CHARGE CORNER FITTER KICKER KICKUP SPIRAL VOLLEY DROPOUT FOUETTE KICKOFF DROPKICK
(— ABOUT) SPARTLE
(— AS A HORSE) FLING WINCE
(— HEELS UP) SPURN
(— ON SHINS) HACK SHINNER
(BALLET —) BRUSH
(SOCCER —) CORNER
KICKER TEDDER WINCER
KID COD FUN POD TUB FAWN FOOL JIVE JOKE CHILD FAGOT HORSE JOLLY KIDDY SPOOF KIDLET SQUIRT DECEIVE EANLING FATLING TICCHEN YOUNGER CHEVEREL YEANLING
KIDDING JOKE SPOOFERY
KIDNAP STEAL PANYAR SPIRIT
KIDNAPER SPIRIT PLAGIARY SNATCHER SPIRITER
KIDNAPING SNATCH PLAGIUM PLAGIARY

KIDNEY NEAR NEER REIN NEPHRON
(PL.) REINS ROGNONS
KIDNEY BEAN FRIJOLE
(PL.) FASELS
KIER KEEVE PUFFER
KIESELGUHR DOPE GUHR
KILL DO BAG END GET OUT PIP BANE BOLO COOK COOL DOWN FELL MORT NECK SLAY TAME WING BLAST BRAIN CROAK CULLE FETCH FORDO GANCH MISDO NAPOO QUELL SABER SCRAG SHOOT SMITE SNUFF SPEED SPEND SPILL SPOIL STALL STICK SWELT SWORD CORPSE DEADEN DIDDLE FAMISH FINISH HANDLE IMPALE MARTYR MURDER POISON STARVE UNLIVE ACHIEVE BUTCHER DESTROY EXECUTE FLATTEN HATCHET KILLING MORTIFY SMOTHER STONKER SUICIDE DEATHIFY DISPATCH DISSOLVE IMMOLATE JUGULATE STILETTO
(— ANIMALS) CONTROL
(— BY STONING) LAPIDATE
(— BY SUBMERSION) STIFLE
(— CALF AFTER BIRTH) DEACON
(— CATTLE) PITH
(— EVERY TENTH) DECIMATE
(— GAME) SATCHEL
(— OFF) ENECATE
(— SMALL GAME) BARK
(— TIME) GOOF
KILLDEER KILLDEE DEERKILL
KILLED KILT WINGED SKITTLED
(FRESHLY —) GREEN
KILLER GUN GUNMAN SLAYER TORPEDO MURDERER THRESHER
KILLER WHALE ORCA DOLPHIN GRAMPUS
KILLIFISH KELLY KILLY MINNOW COBBLER GUDGEON MAYFISH MUDFISH PANCHAX FUNDULUS ROCKFISH SACALAIT STUDFISH SWAMPINE
KILLING FELL KILL MORT QUELL TUANT MURDER CLEANUP HANGING CLEANING DISPATCH FELICIDE HOMICIDE
KILLJOY NARK GLOOM LEMON SOURPUSS
KILN BING KEEL LEHR OAST CULLE DRIER GLAZE STOVE TILER COCKLE CUPOLA TILERY FURNACE CALCINER LIMEKILN
KILOMETER LI
KILT QUELT PIUPIU FILIBEG PHILIBEG PETTICOAT
KILTER SKEET
KIN SIB KATI KITH CUNNE FLESH FAMILY AFFINITY RELATION
KIND ILK KIN LOT BOON CAST FAIR FORM GOOD HAIR HEND LIKE MAKE MEEK MILD MODE MOLD NICE RATE SELY SOFT SORT SUIT TYPE WING BREED CLASS GENRE GENUS GESTE ORDER SPICE STAMP BENIGN BLITHE FACILE GENDER GENTLE GOODLY HUMANE KIDNEY KINDLY

MANNER MISTER NATURE SPEECE
STRAIN STRIPE TENDER EDITION
FASHION FEATHER FLESHLY
LENIENT QUALITY REGIMEN SPECIAL
SPECIES SPECKLE FRIENDLY
GENEROUS MANSUETE OBLIGING
INDULGENT
(— OF PEOPLE) FOLK
(— OF) A
(DIFFERENT IN —) DIVERS
(DISTINCTIVE —) BRAND
(OF EVERY —) ALKIN
KINDLE BEET FIRE LUNT MOVE TAKE
TEND TIND FLAME LIGHT QUICK
SPUNK ALIGHT DECOCT ENFIRE
EXCITE IGNITE ILLUME EMBLAZE
ESPRISE INCENSE INFLAME SOLICIT
KINDLING
KINDLINESS CANDOR
KINDLING FIRE BAVIN FAGOT
TINDER IGNITION
KINDLY FAIR GAIN KIND NESH
AGREE COUTH HENDE NAISH
BENIGN BLITHE COUTHY GENIAL
HOMELY INNERLY FAVOROUS
GENEROUS GRACIOUS QUEMEFUL
TOWARDLY
KINDNESS LOVE ALOHA FAVOR
BOUNTY CANDOR LENITY SERVICE
CLEMENCY EASINESS GOODNESS
HUMANITY LENITUDE MILDNESS
KINDRED KIN SIB KIND KITH BLOOD
FLESH FAMILY KOBONG NATION
STRIND COGNATE KINFOLK KINSMEN
SIBSHIP AFFINITY
KINE KYE COWS
KINETIC ACTUAL —
(— POTENTIAL) L
KING RI SO BAN DAM LOT LUD PUL
REX REY RIG ROY AGAG BALI BELI
BIJA BORS BRAN BRES CRAL CZAR
JEHU KRAL LEIR MARK NUDD NUMA
OMRI OTTO PHUL RAJA RIAL TSAR
TZAR WANG YIMA ARDRI BALOR
BELUS CONOR CREON DAGDA
DAHAK EGLON ETZEL GYGES HIRAM
HOGNI HOSEA IPHIS IXION JOASH
LAIUS LLUDD LYCUS MESHA MIDAS
MINOS NADAB NEGUS NORSE
NUADA PEKAH PRIAM RAJAH SAMMY
SWAMI ZIMRI ZOHAK AEOLUS
AGENOR AILILL ALBOIN ALONSO
ALOROS ARIOCH BLADUD CODRUS
DIOMED DUNCAN ELATHA FINGAL
FRODHI FROTHI GOEMOT INKOSI
KABAKA LEMUEL LYCAON MEMNON
MINYAS NESTOR NODONS OENEUS
OGYGES PELEUS PELIAS SAUGHT
SHESHA SVAMIN TEUCER URIENS
UZZIAH VASUKI AHAZIAH AMAIMON
AMYCLAS ANGEVIN ARTEGAL
ATHAMAS BAGINDA BELINUS
BUSIRIS CACIQUE CEPHEUS
CROESUS ELIBURE EPAPHUS
EPOPEUS ETHBAAL EURYTUS
GUNTHER HYGELAC INACHUS
JAMSHID JEHOASH JEHORAM
KINGLET LAERTES LATINUS
LEONTES MENAHEM MONARCH

PANDION PHINEUS POLYBUS
REGULUS ROMULUS ROYALET
SMERDIS SOLOMON VOLSUNG
ACRISIUS ADRASTUS AEGYPTUS
ALBERICH AMRAPHEL ASNAPPER
BAHMANID BRENNIUS CLAUDIUS
COPHETUA ELDORADO ETEOCLES
GILGAMES GOEMAGOT GOGMAGOG
GORBODUC HEZEKIAH HROTHGAR
JEHOAHAZ JEROBOAM KINGLING
LAOMEDON LISUARTE MANASSEH
MELIADUS MENELAUS ODYSSEUS
ORCHAMUS OSNAPPAR OVERKING
PADISHAH PEKAHIAH PENTHEUS
RAMESSID REHOBOAM RODERICK
RODOMONT ROITELET SARPEDON
SHEPHERD SISYPHUS TANTALUS
(— AND QUEEN OF TRUMPS) BELLA
(— CHANGED TO WOLF) LYCAON
(— OF ARMS) GARTER NORROY
(— OF BEASTS) LION
(— OF DWARFS) ALBERICH
(— OF FAIRIES) OBERON
(— OF TRUMPS) HONOR
(IRISH —) RI RIG ARDRI ARDRIGH
(POLYNESIAN —) ALII ARII ARIKI
KINGBIRD PIPIRI PETCHARY
KINGBOLT KING KINGPIN MAINPIN
KING CRAB LIMULID LIMULUS
PANFISH
KINGDOM WEI REALM REIGN WORLD
ESTATE MONERA MORVEN REGION
SAXONY MITANNI
KINGFISH BARB CERO HAKE HAKU
MINK TOMCOD CHENFISH SCIAENID
TOMMYCOD
KINGFISHER HALCYON PODITTI
TOROTORO
KINGLET REGULI
KINGLY REGAL ROYAL BASILIC
IMPERIAL MAJESTIC PRINCELY
KING PARAKEET WELLAT
KINGSHIP STOOL KINGDOM
ROYALTY DEVARAJA KINGHOOD
KING'S PEACE GRITH
KING'S SCHOLAR TUG
KING VULTURE PAP PAPA
KINK NIB SNICK BUCKLE DOGLEG
KINKLE
(— IN ROPE) GRIND
KINKAJOU POTTO HEYRAT
APOROSO
KINKING FLUTING
KINKY ENCOMIC KINKLED
KINO BIJA BIJASAL
KINSHIP SIB BLOOD NASAB STOOL
ENATION KINDRED SIBNESS SIBSHIP
AFFINITY AGNATION RELATION
KINSMAN KIN SIB ALLY BLOOD
AFFINE AGNATE COUSIN FRIEND
BROTHER GOTRAJA KINDRED
WINEMAY BANDHAVA RELATION
RELATIVE
KINSWOMAN SISTER KINDRED
RELATIVE
KIP SKIP GRASSER KIPSKIN UPSTART
KIRGHIZ QYRGHYZ
KIRN MELL
KISS BA LIP NEB BASS BUSS PECK

PREE MOUTH POGUE SLAKE SMACK
BEKISS CARESS SLAVER SMOOCH
SMOUCH OSCULATE
(— OF PEACE) PAX
(— WETLY) SLOBBER
(STOLEN —) SMOORICH
KISSING LIPWORK
KIT CHIT DUFFEL KITTEN POCHETTE
(LUMBERMAN'S —) TURKEY
(MESS —) CANTEEN
KITCHEN BUT GALLEY CUISINE
KITCHIE COOKROOM
KITE LAP CHIL CYTE HAWK GLEDE
CHILLA DRACHE DRAGON ELANET
FALCON PREYER SENTRY MILVINE
PUDDOCK PUTTOCK FORKTAIL
HELLKITE
KITTEN KIT KITTY KITTLE CATLING
KITLING
KITTIWAKE GULL WAEG ANNET
KITTY PICKUP TARROCK TIRRLIE
KITTY CAT BADRANS BAUDRONS
KIVA ESTUFA
KIWI APTERYX
KLAMATH WEED AMBER
GOATWEED
KLANG PHONE
KLIPSPRINGER KAINSI KLIPBOK
KLONDIKE CANFIELD SOLITAIRE
KNACK ART FEAT FEEL GATE GIFT
HANG CATCH QUIRK TRICK SLEIGHT
WRINKLE INSTINCT
KNACKER CLAPPER
(PL.) BONES
KNAPSACK WALLET MOCHILA
MUSETTE SNAPBAG SNAPSACK
KNAPWEED SWEEP BLUETOP
FLATTOP BALLWEED BELLWEED
BOLEWEED BULLWEED BUNDWEED
CENTAURY CLUBWEED CROPWEED
HARDHEAD IRONHEAD IRONWEED
KNOTWEED MATFELON
KNAVE BOY ELF LAD NOB PAM PUR
TOM JACK BOWER CHEAT MAKER
NODDY ROGUE TIGER COQUIN
HARLOT KNIGHT PICARO RASCAL
VARLET WENZEL CAMOOCH
CUSTREL PEASANT VILLAIN
SWINDLER VARLETTO
KNAVERY CATZERIE PATCHERY
KNAVISH ROGUISH SCAMPISH
KNAWEL KNOTWEED KNOTWORT
KNEAD ELT TEW MOLD POST STOCK
PETRIE MASSAGE
(— HIDES) STOCK
KNEADING (— MACHINE) BRAKE
KNEE GENU HOCK CROOK KNAPPER
SLEEPER SUFFRAGO
(— HOLLOW) HAM
(— OF COMPOSING STICK) SLIDE
KNEECAP CAP PATELLA
KNEEL SIT KNEE COUCH SHIKO
KOWTOW
KNEELER SPRINGER
KNEELING SHIKO BENDED
KNEEPAN ROTULA PATELLA
KNELL BELL RING TOLL KNOLL
STROKE
KNICKKNACK TOY KNACK TRICK

GEWGAW NOTION PRETTY
GIMCRACK
KNIFE DAH DIE PIN SAX ULU BOLO
BUCK MOON SAEX SHIM SHIV SPUD
TANG BOWIE BURIN CHIVE FACON
GULLY KNIVE KUKRI PANGA SHANK
SHAVE SKEAN SLICE BARLOW
BARONG CAMPIT CARVER COLTER
COUTEL CUTTLE DAGGER DOCTOR
JIGGER PANADE PARANG PAVADE
PORKER PULLER RIMMER SICKLE
SLICER TREVET TRIVAT WORKER
BREAKER CATLING CHOPPER
COUTEAU FIPENNY KIOTOME
MACHETE PALETTE SCALPEL
SEVERER SKINNER SLASHER
SNICKER STICKER SUNDANG
TICKLER WHITTLE BELDUQUE
BILLHOOK CALABOZO JOCTELEG
SERPETTE THWITTLE YATAGHAN
(— **FOR BREAKING FLAX**) BEATER
(— **FOR LEATHER**) PIN
(— **FOR RUBBER DOUGH**) DOCTOR
(**BURMESE** —) DAH DAO DOW
(**CURRIER'S** —) CLEANER
(**ESKIMO** —) ULU
(**MORO** —) BARONG
(**SHOEMAKER'S** —) BUTT
(**SURGICAL** —) CATLING SCALPEL
BISTOURY EXSECTOR
(**TANNER'S** —) GRAINER
KNIFE-PLEATED KILTED
KNIGHT N ELF SIR ADUB GANO TULK
EQUES EQUIS HORSE LANCE RIDER
THANE TOLKE CABALL ERRANT
PENCEL RITTER ROGERO GENILON
PALADIN YOUNKER ALMANZOR
BACHELOR BANNERET CAVALIER
COLVILLE GANELONE IRONCLAD
ISENBRAS PALMERIN RUGGIERO
(— **IN CHESS**) HORSE
(— **OF ROUND TABLE**) GAN BORS
OWEN GARETH GAWAIN MODRED
CARADOC CRADOCK GALAHAD
GANELON EGLAMORE LANCELOT
PALMERIN PERCIVAL TRISTRAM
(**CARPET** —) DAMMERET
KNIGHTHOOD CAVALRY
KNIPHOFIA TRITOMA
KNIT SET BIND KNOT PLAIT PURSE
UNITE WEAVE COMPACT CONNECT
WRINKLE CONTRACT
(— **STOCKINGS**) SHANK
KNITTED FLAT WOVEN
KNITTING LOOP STEEK
KNITTING NEEDLE WIRE
KNOB BOB BUR NOB NUB BEAD
BOSS BURR CLUB DENT HEAD HEEL
KNOP KNOT KNUB LIFT NODE PULL
SNUG STUD TORE BERRY BULLA
FORTE GEMMA KNURL NATCH
ONION PLOOK PLUKE BUTTON
CROCHE EMBOSS NOBBLE NUBBLE
PIMPLE PISTON POMMEL FERRULE
HORNTIP KNOBBLE BELLPULL
DOORKNOB DRAWSTOP OMPHALOS
(— **OF HAIR**) TOORIE
(— **OF ROCK**) BUHR BURR KNUCKLE
(— **ON BILL OF SWAN**) BERRY

(— **ON BUTT OF CANNON**) GRAPE
(— **ON CHAIR**) POMMEL
(— **ON DEER'S ANTLER**) OFFER
CROCHE
(— **ON ROPE**) MOUSE
KNOBBED NODOSE TOROSE
TUBEROUS TYLOTATE
KNOBBY GOUTY KNOTTY GOUTISH
KNOBBLY
KNOCK CON DAD HIT JOW JUT POP
PUN RAP WAP BANG BASH BEAT
BUMP CALL CHAP CHOP DASH
DAUD DING DUMP DUNT HACK JOLT
JOWL KNAP NOCK NOIT PLUG POLT
POSS PUSH ROUT SLAM SLAY SNOP
TANK TIRL WHAP WHOP CLUMP
KNOIT POUND SMITE SNOCK STAVE
STRAM THUMP BOUNCE DUNTLE
KNATCH KNETCH STOTER CANVASS
PINKING
(— **ABOUT**) RUMBLE
(— **DOWN**) DROP DUMP FELL FLOOR
GRASS LEVEL SMITE SOUSE HURTLE
RAFFLE UNPILE
(— **OFF**) SECURE
(— **ON HEAD**) MAZER MAZARD
(— **OUT**) OUT SAP CONK COOL
KAYO FLATTEN STIFFEN
(— **UNCONSCIOUS**) COLDCOCK
(— **WITH THE HORNS**) DISH
KNOCKER CROW RISP HAMMER
WHACKER
(**DOOR** —) CROW HAMMER RAPPER
KNOCK-KNEED VARUS VALGUS
KNOCKOUT KO KAYO CRUSHER
NOBBLER
(**PRETENDED** —) DIVE
KNOLL NOB HIGH KNAP KNOB KNOW
TOFT HEAVE HURST HYRST MOUND
SHOAL COPPLE BOUROCK
HUMMOCK
KNOP NOB KNOB KNOSP KNAPPE
KNOT BOB BOW BUN FAG NIB NOB
NUB PIN TIE BEND BURR CHOU
CLOD CLOT CLUB HARL KILL KNAG
KNAR KNOB NODE NOIL NURL SLUG
SNUB TRUE WAFT WALL CROWN
DUNNE GNARL GNARR HALCH
HALSH HATCH HITCH KNURL MOUSE
NODUS NOEUD SNARL SNICK SWIRL
TWIST WARRE BUTTON CLINCH
CROCHE FINIAL GRANNY MASCLE
SORTIE TANGLE BOWKNOT BOWLINE
CHIGNON COCKADE GORDIAN
MAYBIRD CICISBEO DRAWKNOT
GRAYBACK KNITTING SLIPKNOT
TRUELOVE
(— **IN CLOTH**) FAG BURL
(— **IN COTTON FIBERS**) NEP
(— **IN SIGNAL FLAG**) WAFT WEFT
WHEFT
(— **IN WOOD**) PIN BURL BURR KNAG
KNAR SNUB GNARL KNAUR KNURL
(— **IN YARN**) SLUG SNICK
(— **OF HAIR**) BUN COB PUG CLUB
KNURL CHIGNON
(**LOVE** —) AMORET
(**ORNAMENTAL** —) BOW
(**SHOULDER** —) WING

(**WALL** —) WALE
KNOTGRASS LIGNUM HOGWEED
PIGWEED BINDWEED BIRDWEED
DOORWEED KNOTWEED KNOTWORT
PINKWEED POLYGONY WIREWEED
KNOTTED KNIT NOUE TIED NOWED
NODOSE SWIRLY CRABBED
NODATED SCRAGGY
KNOTTY HARD CRAMP GOUTY
COMMON CRAGGY GNARLY KNAGGY
KNOBBY KNURRY NODOSE NODOUS
COMPLEX GNARLED GOUTISH
JOINTED KNARRED KNOTTED
SCABROUS
KNOTWEED LIGNUM ALLSEED
HOGWEED JUMPSEED POLYGONY
KNOW CAN CON KEN WIS WIT WOT
CITE HAVE SABE WEET WIST WOTH
SAVVY SKILL COGNIZE
(— **NOT**) NOOT
(—**S NOT**) NOTE
(**DID NOT** —) KENDNA
(**DO NOT** —) KENNA
KNOWABLE SENSABLE
KNOW-HOW SAVVY SKILL
KNOWING FLY HEP HIP FOXY GASH
SPRY WISE AWARE CANNY DOWNY
JERRY LEERY SPACK WITTY EXPER
SCIENT SCIOUS SHREWD WITFUL
WITTER GNOSTIC SAPIENT
(— **SUPERFICIALLY**) SCIOLOUS
KNOWINGLY CANNILY SCIENTER
SHREWDLY WITTERLY
KNOWLEDGE CAN WIT BOOK KITH
KNOW LAIR LEAR LORE INWIT
JNANA SKILL VIDYA ADVICE AVIDYA
CLERGY GNOSIS NOESIS NOTICE
WISDOM CUNNING DIANOIA HEARIN
KNOWING MEANING SCIENCE
WITTING DAYLIGHT DOCTRINE
EPISTEME LEARNING LETTRURE
NOTITION PRUDENCE SAPIENCE
SCIENTIA
(— **OF SPIRITUAL TRUTH**) GNOSIS
(**FAMILIAR** —) HANG
(**LATER** —) AFTERWIT
(**MYSTERIOUS** —) ARCANUM
(**PIECEMEAL** —) SMATTER
(**PRIVATE** —) PRIVITY
(**PUBLIC** —) LIGHT
(**SLICK** —) ANGLE
(**SLIGHT** —) INKLING
(**SUPERFICIAL** —) SCIOLISM
(**SUPREME** —) PRAJNA
(**SYSTEMATIZED** —) SCIENCE
KNOWLEDGEABLE KNOWING
SKILLED STUDIED
KNOWN EVER COUTH COMMON
(**ACTUALLY** —) SPECIOUS
(**LITTLE** —) FAMELESS
(**NOT** —) DARK SILENT
(**OTHERWISE** — **AS**) ALIAS
(**PUBLICLY** —) EXOTERIC
(**UNMISTAKABLY** —) STATED
(**WIDELY** —) COMMON
KNOW-NOTHING SAM
KNUCKLE KNUCK JARRET
KNUCKLEBONE DIB DOLOS TALUS
COCKAL SHACKLE

KNURL MILL NULL DWARF SNARL
KNURLING NULLING REEDING
  KNULLING
KOALA BEAR BAALU BALOO SLOTH
  KOOLAH WOMBAT CARBORA
  PHALANGER
KOBOLD NIS NISSE HODEKEN
  HUTCHEN
KOEL KOIL KOKIL RAINBIRD
KOHL COHOL ALCOHOL
KOHLRABI BROMATIUM
KOKAN LAMPATIA
KOKO LEBBEK
KOKUM GARCINIA
KOKUMIN BAN
KOLA COLA BICHY GOORANUT
KOMBU KOBU KAMBOU CHAKOBU
KOMMETJE WALLOW COMITJE
KONAK YALI
KOOKABURRA KOOKA JACKASS
KOPECK KAPEIKA
KORAKAN RAGI RAGGI RAGGY
KORAN KITAB QURAN ALCORAN
  (SECTION OF —) SURA SURAH

KORE DESPOINA
KOREA (SEE NORTH KOREA OR
  SOUTH KOREA)
KOREC MIRA
KORINA LIMBA
KOS COAN
KOSIN KOUSSIN TAENNIN BRAYERIN
KOSO PANAMINT
KOULAN GOUR
KOWHAI GOAI PELU LOCUST
  SOPHORA
KOWTOW KNEEL SHIKO
KOYUKON TENA KHOTANA
KRAAL CRAW MANYATTA ZIMBABWE
KRAIT ADDER KORAIT BUNGARUM
KRATER KELEBE
KRAUNHIA WISTARIA
KREIS CIRCLE
KRIS CREASE CREESE DAGGER
KRISHNA VASUDEVA
KRONE CROWN CORONA
KRU KROOBOY KROOMAN
KRUMMHORN CREMONA CROMORNE
KSHATRIYA THAKUR

KUA MAKUA MAKWA
KUBA BUSHONGO KABISTAN
KUDZU VINE KOHEMP
KUI KHONDI
KU KLUXER KLUXER KLUCKER
  KLANSMAN
KUKURUKU IKPERE
KULANAPAN POMO
KUMAN POLOUTZY
KUMBUK ARJAN ARJUN
KUMMEL ALLASCH
KUMQUAT NAGAMI
KURRAJONG CALOOL LACEBARK
KURUKH ORAON
KUSA DARBHA
KUSIMANSEL MANGUE
KUTCHIN LOUCHEUX
KUWAIT (TOWN OF —) AHMADI
  HAWALLI ABDULLAH FAHAHEEL
KVASS QUASH
KWENI GURO
KYPHOSIS HUMPBACK
KYURINISH LESGHIN LEZGHIAN

L EL LIMA FIFTY
LAAGER LEEGTE LEAGUER
LABDACUS (FATHER OF —)
POLYDORUS
(MOTHER OF —) NYCTEIS
(SON OF —) LAIUS
LABDANUM MYRRH
LABEL TAG BILL FILE FICHE STAMP
TALLY TITLE DIRECT DOCKET
TICKET ENDSEAL LAMBEAU STICKER
(— ON SUIT OF CLOTHES) ETIQUET
LABELLUM LIP LABEL
(PART OF —) HYPOCHIL
LABIAL ROUND
LABIATE HOREHOUND
LABIUM LIP LABRUM
LABOR FAG TUG WIN CARK MOIL
TASK TAVE TILL TOIL WORK BEGAR
DELVE GRAFT GRIND HEAVE PAINS
SWEAT SWINK TEAVE TREAD WHILE
YAKKA CORVEE DRUDGE EFFORT
HAMMER STRIVE BULLOCK FATIGUE
MANUARY OPIFICE PROCURE
SERVICE SLAVERY TRAVAIL
TROUBLE TURMOIL BUSINESS
DRUDGERY EXERTION GROANING
INDUSTRY LABORAGE STRUGGLE
(— ARDUOUSLY) BILDER
(— HARD) THRASH THRIPPLE
(— UNDER) SUFFER
(DAY'S —) DARG JOURNEY
(DIFFICULT —) DYSTOCIA
(EXCESSIVE —) STRAIN
(FORCED —) BEGAR
(HARD —) HARD BULLWORK
(HIRED —) TOGT
(IMPOSED —) TASKAGE
(MENTAL —) HEADWORK
(SEVERE —) AGON
(UNPAID —) CORVEE
LABORATORY LAB SHOP KITCHEN
OFFICINA WORKSHOP
LABORED HEAVY FORCED SWEATY
STRAINED
LABORER (ALSO SEE WORKER AND
WORKMAN) BOY BHAR ESNE HIND
JACK JOEY MOZO PEON TOTY
BAGDI GUASO HUNKY NAVVY PALLI
PINER STIFF BALAHI BEGARI
BOHUNK COALER COOLIE DAYMAN
DILKER DOCKER FELLAH FLUNKY
FOGGER HEAVER HOLEYA JIBARO
LUMPER RAFTER TASKER WAYMAN
WORKER BRACERO BYWONER
CREWMAN DAYSMAN DIGGORY
DIRGLER DRAINER DVORNIK
HOBBLER MANUARY MAZDOOR
PICKMAN PIONEER PIPEMAN
PLOWMAN SANDHOG SCOURER
SHIPPER SMASHER SOUGHER
SPALLER STOCKER SWINKER
TOTYMAN WORKMAN BIJWONER
CHAINMAN COTTAGER DOLLYMAN
FARMHAND FLOORMAN GANGSMAN
HOLDSMAN SPADEMAN SPALPEEN
STRAPPER TIDESMAN
(INEXPERIENCED —) GREENER
LABORIOUS HARD HEAVY STIFF
SWEATY UPHILL ARDUOUS

OPEROSE SLAVISH TOILFUL
DILIGENT LABOROUS TOILSOME
LABRADOR TEA LEDUM GOWIDDIE
LABURNUM AWBER
LABYRINTH MAZE CIRCUIT MEANDER
LABYRINTHINE TORTUOUS
LAC LACCA LACQUER
LACE BEAT BEST FOND GOTA LASH
PEAK FILET LACIS LIVEN ORRIS
POINT SCREW SPRIG WEAVE
BLONDE CORDON DEFEAT EDGING
GRILLE LACING LASHER THRASH
TUCKER VENISE ALENCON ALLOVER
BULLION CURRAGH CUTWORK
FOOTING GALLOON GUIPURE
HONITON LATCHET MACRAME
MALINES MECHLIN MELANGE
NANDUTI TAMBOUR TATTING
TORCHON TROLLEY ARGENTAN
BOBBINET BONEWORK BOOTLACE
BRUSSELS DENTELLE ILLUSION
LACEWORK LIMERICK PEARLING
STAYLACE
(— EDGING) PUNTILLA
(— IN PLACE OF COLLAR) RUCHE
(— MAKER) TWISTHAND
(— PATTERN) TOILE
(KNOTTED —) TATTING
LACEBARK LAGETTO DAGUILLA
LACEWOOD
LACE BUG TINGITID
LACERATE REND TEAR ENBORE
HARROW MANGLE SCARIFY
FRACTURE
LACERATION RIP TEAR WOUND
LACEWOOD SYCAMORE
LACEWORK DENTELLE
LACHRYMOSE SAD TEARY WEEPY
MAUDLIN
LACINARIA LIATRIS
LACING LACET LINGEL ECHELLE
LANGUET
LACK FAIL LANK LIKE LOSS MAIM
MISS NEED VOID WANE WANT
FAULT MINUS DEARTH DEFECT
INLAIK ABSENCE BLEMISH DEFAULT
FAILURE PAUCITY VACANCY
SCARCITY SOLITUDE WANTROKE
(— CONFIDENCE) DOUBT
(— FAITH) DIFFIDE
(— HARMONY) DISAGREE
(— OF APPETITE) ANOREXIA
(— OF CLARITY) DARKNESS
(— OF COORDINATION) ASYNERGY
DYSERGIA
(— OF DEVELOPMENT) AGENESIS
(— OF EARNESTNESS) ITEMING
(— OF EFFUSIVENESS) RESERVE
(— OF EMOTION) APATHY
(— OF ENERGY) ATONY ANERGY
ATONIA
(— OF FLAVOR) SILENCE
(— OF FORESIGHT) MYOPIA
(— OF HARMONY) DISCORD
DISUNITY
(— OF INTENTION) ACCIDENT
(— OF INVOLVEMENT) DISTANCE
(— OF ORDER) ATAXY ATAXIA
DISARRAY

(— OF PATRIOTISM) INCIVISM
(— OF REFINEMENT) CRUDITY
(— OF SENSE OF SMELL) ANOSMIA
(— OF SENSE) FOLLY
(— OF STEADINESS) LEVITY
(— OF SYMPATHY) DYSPATHY
(— OF VIGOR) LANGUOR
(— OF VITALITY) ANEMIA ADYNAMIA
(— OF WIND) CALM
(— OF WORTH) IMMERIT
(— STRENGTH) DROOP
LACKADAISICAL LANGUID LISTLESS
LACKEY SKIP SLAVE LACQUEY
STAFFIER
LACKING BUT SHY BARE FREE
WANT ALACK GNEDE MINUS SHORT
ABSENT BARREN DEVOID WITHIN
WANTING DESOLATE INDIGENT
LACKLUSTER DULL FISHY CLOUDY
GLASSY
LACONIC CURT SHORT CONCISE
POINTED SPARTAN SUCCINCT
LA CORUNA GROIN
LACQUER LAC DOPE DUCO JAPAN
CHATON LACKER URUSHI VARNISH
LACTATION (— PERIOD) NOTE
LACTONE CUMARIN LIMONIN
MECONIN DIKETENE
LACTOSCOPE PIOSCOPE
LACUNA GAP BREAK
LACUSTRINE LAKISH
LAD BOY BUB MAN BOYO CARL CHAP
DICK HIND JOCK LOON SNAP BILLY
BUCKO CADDY CHIEL GROOM
YOUTH BURSCH CADDIE CALLAN
FELLOW LADDIE LADKIN MANNIE
NIPPER SHAVER CALLANT
MUCHACHO SPRINGER STRIPLING
(AWKWARD —) GROMET GRUMMET
(MISCHIEVOUS —) GAMIN
(MY —) AVICK
(SERVING —) GILLIE GOSSOON
LADDER STY STEE JACOB SCALE
AERIAL BANGOR ESCAPE PULEYN
GANGWAY POLEYNE POMPIER
(FIREMAN'S —) STICK
(FISH —) FISHWAY
(JACOB'S —) CHARITY
LADDIE JOCKEY LATHIE LADDOCK
LADDIKIE
LADE BAIL LAVE LADEN TRUSS
BURDEN FRAUGHT
(— INTO COOLER) STRIKE
LADEN HEAVY BELAST LOADED
FRAUGHT FREIGHT GESTANT
LADING LOAD CARGO FREIGHT
LADINO SPANIOL
LADLE DIP JET GAWN SKEP CLATH
CYATH KEACH STOOP DIPPER
LADING CUVETTE CYATHUS
KYATHOS POTSTICK
(— OUT SOUP) SLEECH
(— WITH HANDLES) CYATH SHANK
CYATHUS KYATHOS SKIPPET
(BRINE —) LOOT
(LARGE —) SCOOP
LADRONE TULISAN LATHERIN
LADY BIBI BURD DAME RANI DONNA
HANUM BEEBEE DOMINO FEMALE

KADINE RAWNIE SAHIBA SENORA
LADYKIN MADONNA SENHORA
SINEBADA
(— OF HIGH RANK) BEGUM
(— OF HOUSE) GOODWIFE
(BEAUTIFUL —) CLEAR
(TURKISH —) KHANUM
(PL.) LADYHOOD
LADYBUG VEDALIA
LADYFISH WRASSE PUDIANO
BONEFISH BONYFISH DONCELLA
LADYLIKE FEMALE
LADYLOVE LADY DELIA MINION
MISTRESS
LADY'S-COMB NEEDLES
LADY'S-MANTLE DEWCUP PADELION
LADY'S-SLIPPER DUCK YELLOW
NERVINE YELLOWS UMBILROOT
LAERTES (FATHER OF —) ARCESIUS
(MOTHER OF —) CHALCOMEDUSA
(SON OF —) ULYSSES
(WIFE OF —) ANTICLEA
LAG DRAG DRAW SLOG DELAY TRAIL
HOCKER LAGGER LINGER LOITER
STRING DRIDDLE LAGGING
(— IN PRODUCTION) SLIPPAGE
LAGGARD SLOW TARDY LAGGER
TORTOISE
LAGGING TARDY JACKET DEADING
LAGGARD CLEADING DRAWLING
FOREPOLE
LAGNIAPPE TIP GIFT BONUS PILON
PRESENT
LAGOMORPH PIKA RABBIT
LAGOON HAFF POOL BAYOU LIMAN
LAGUNA
LAID (— ACROSS WALL) INBOND
(— DOWN) THETIC THETICAL
(— WASTE) BARE
LAIR DEN LAY FORM HOLD SHED
EARTH HAUNT LODGE MEUSE
SQUAT HARBOR KENNEL SPELUNK
(— OF FOX) KENNEL
(— OF OTTER) HOLT HOVER
(— OF WILD BOAR) SOUNDER
LAISSE TIRADE
LAITY FOLK LAYMEN PEOPLE
LAIUS (FATHER OF —) LABDACUS
(SON OF —) OEDIPUS
(WIFE OF —) JOCASTA
LAKE LAY SEA VLY BAHR JAIL JHIL
LAGO LLYN LOCH MERE MOAT
SHOR TANK TARN VLEI VLEY BAYOU
CHOTT JHEEL LERNA LIMAN LOUGH
SPARK TUBIG LAGOON NYANZA
STROND ANCYLUS CARMINE
LAKELET TURLOUGH
(CASHEW —) AUBURN
(FENNY —) BROAD
(MOUNTAIN —) TARN
(RELATING TO —S) LIMNAL
(SALT —) SHOT CHOTT SHOTT
SALINA SALINE
(SMALL —) GURGES
(TEMPORARY —) PINAG
LAKE CARP DRUM LAKER
LAKE HERRING KIYI CISCO
GRAYBACK
LAKE TROUT POGY TOGUE
LAKE WHITEFISH POLLAN

LAKSHMI SRI SHREE
LAMA ELK AUCHENIA
LAMB BUM PET PUR CADE DEAR
DUPE LOME SOCK YEAN AGNUS
PESAH PODDY AGNEAU COSSET
HIEDER LAMBIE LAMKIN PESACH
SUCKER WASTER WEANER CHILVER
EANLING FATLING HOGLING
PASCHAL PERSIAN RUFFIAN
TWAGGER BAAHLING LAMBLING
PASSOVER YEANLING
(— AND WHEAT) KIBBE
(SCYTHIAN —) BAROMETZ
LAMBASTE CREAM SQUABASH
LAMBENT BRIGHT RADIANT
LAMBREQUIN MANTLING
LAMBSKIN LAMB BAGDAD BAGHDAD
SALZFELLE
LAMB'S QUARTERS MUCKWEED
LAMB'S WOOL WASSAIL
LAME BUM GAME HALT LAHN GAMMY
GIMPY GRAVEL TINSEL CRIPPLE
CRIPPLY HALTING HIPHALT
GORGERIN SPAVINED
(— A HORSE) STUB
LAMELLA PLICA FOLIUM FORNIX
LAMENESS HALT
LAMENT CRY WEY CARE DOLE HONE
HOWL KEEN MEAN MOAN PINE SIGH
TEAR WAIL WALY WEEP CROON
DUMKA GREET KINAH MOURN PLAIN
QINAH BEHOWL BEMOAN BEWAIL
BEWEEP COMMOS KOMMOS PLAINT
REPINE SORROW SQUAWK THREAP
YAMMER BEMOURN CONDOLE
DEPLORE EJULATE ELEGIZE
GRIZZLE REGRATE THRENOS
WAYMENT COMPLAIN MOURNING
THRENODY ULLAGONE WELLAWAY
LAMENTABLE YEMER RUEFUL
DOLEFUL PITIFUL PITIABLE
PLAINFUL YAMMERLY
LAMENTATION KEEN MOAN WAIL
DOLOR LINOS RUING TANGI LAMENT
PLAINT REGRET SORROW THRENE
PLANGOR TRAGEDY WILLAWA
CORONACH MOURNING PATHETIC
WAILMENT WELLAWAY LAMENTING
LAMINA FILM LAME LAMP LEAF
OBEX BLADE FLAKE LAMIN PLATE
SCALE SHELL TABLE CAPSULE
LAMINATE LEAFY FLAGGY
LAMINATED BUILT FOLIATE
TABULAR
LAMINATION SLABBING
LAMINITIS FOUNDER
LAMMAS DAY GULE TERM
LAMMERGEIER AREND
LAMP ARC EYE SEE DAVY GLIM INKY
JACK SLUT ALDIS ARGAND ASTRAL
BULLET HELION LAMPAD TARGET
ILLUMER LAMPION LAMPLET
LANTERN LUCERNE LUCIGEN
SUNLAMP SUNSPOT AEOLIGHT
CIRCLINE GASLIGHT SIDELAMP
TORCHERE
(— FOR FIREPLACE) KYLE
(4-CORNERED —) CHILL
(CHIMNEYLESS —) TORCH

(IRON —) CRUSIE
(MAKESHIFT —) BITCH
(SAFETY —) DAVY GEORDIE
(PL.) CLUSTER
LAMPBLACK LINK
LAMPETIA (FATHER OF —) APOLLO
(MOTHER OF —) NEAERA
LAMP HOLDER HUSK
LAMPOON PIPE GESTE LIBEL SQUIB
IAMBIC BERHYME PASQUIN
COCKALAN RIDICULE SATIRIZE
LAMPOONER PASQUIL PASQUIN
LAMPREY PRIDE LAMPER MYZONT
RAMPER SAYNAY SUCKER LAMPERN
LAMP RING CRIC
LAMPSHADE GLOBE
LAMPWICK MATCH
LANATE WOOLY LANOSE WOOLLY
LANCE PIC CANE DART SHAFT
SPEAR STAFF BROACH ELANCE
GLAIVE GLEAVE LANCET ROCKET
LANCELET SPICULUM
(KING ARTHUR'S —) RON
LANCE GUARD VAMPLATE
LANCE HEAD MORNE SOCKET
LANCER LANCE SOWAR UHLAN
LANCE REST QUEUE FEWTER
LANCET FLEAM FLEEM LANCELET
LANCEWOOD YAYA CIGUA CANELA
YARIYARI
LAND ERD ERF NOD RIB AGER DIRT
FOLD GALE GISH GORE JODO MARK
SITE SOIL EARTH EJIDO ETHEL
FIELD GLEBE JUGER PLANT SHORE
SOLUM ALIGHT ASSART FUNDUS
GROUND COMMONS COUNTRY
DEMESNE ELLASAR HOLDING
LANDING LIBRATE QUILLET
TERRENE ALLODIAL BOOKLAND
COMMONTY FARMLAND FLEYLAND
FOLKLAND POMERIUM PRAEDIUM
(— A PLANE) GREASE
(— BETWEEN FURROWS) SELION
(— BETWEEN RIVERS) DOAB
(— CLEARING) KAINGIN
(— CONVERTED TO TILLAGE)
TWAITE THWAITE
(— HAVING VALUE OF POUND PER
YEAR) LIBRATE
(— IN CONACRE) MOCK
(— IN GRASS) LAYER
(— LEFT FALLOW) ARDER
(— MEASURE) RIG
(— OF BLISS) GOKURAKU
(— OF GIANTS) UTGARTHAR
(— OF MANSION) DEMESNE
(— OF OPPORTUNITY) ARKANSAS
(— OF PLENTY) GOSHEN
(— OF REGION) MOLD MOULD
(— PLOWED IN A DAY) JORNADA
(— RECOVERED FROM SEA) INTAKE
INNINGS
(— REGULARLY FLOODED) SALTING
(— SURROUNDED BY WASTE) HOPE
(— UNIT) URE KIPUKA MECATE
MORGEN MANZANA VIRGATE
(ALLUVIAL —) BATTURE
(ANCESTRAL —) ETHEL
(ARABLE —) LEA LEY LAINE

(ARID —) DESERT STEPPE
(BOTTOM —) SLASH CALLOW
STRATH
(CHURCH —) GLEBE TERMON
(CHURCH —S) CROSS
(CLEARED —) ASSART
(COMMON —) EJIDO EXIDO STRAY
(CONTINENTAL —) MAIN
(CULTIVATED —) FARM ARADA
TILTH CULTURE FEERING WAINAGE
LABORAGE METAIRIE
(ENCLOSED —) CLOSE INTAKE
(FREEHOLD —) MULK
(GRAVELLY —) GEEST GRAVES
(GRAZING —) GRASS HIRSEL HIRSLE
FEEDING
(HEATHY —) ROSLAND
(HERITABLE —) ODAL UDAL
(IMAGINARY —) FAERIE COCKAYNE
LILLIPUT
(LEASED —) TACK
(LONG STRIP OF —) SLANG SPONG
(LOW —) BOG FEN GALL INKS
CARSE BOTTOM
(LOW RICH —) CARSE
(NATIVE —) BLIGHTY BIRTHDOM
HOMELAND
(OBDURATE —) TILL
(PARCEL OF —) FEU LOT MOCK
(PASTURE —) HA ALP FEED HOGA
WALK GRASS VELDT LEASON
(PLATEAU —) HIGHVELD
(PLOWED —) ARADA FALLOW
FURROW BREAKING
(PRIVATE —) SEVERAL
(PROMISED —) CANAAN
(PURE —) JODO SUKHAVATI
(RESOWN —) HOOKLAND
(ROUGH —) BRAKE
(SAVANNAH —S) LALANG
(SCRUBBY —) SCROG SCROGS
(SMALL PARCEL OF —) SUERTE
(SWAMPY —) WOODSERE
(TIMBER —S) STICKS
(WASTE —) HEATH
(WESTERN —) HESPERIA
(WET —) SOAK SWAMP SWANG
(WOODED —S) STICKS
(PL.) ACRES SUCKEN LAENDER
NOVALIA
LANDBOOK TERRIER
LANDED PRAEDIAL
LANDFORM CUSP CUESTA
LANDHOLDER LAIRD COSCET
TALUKDAR
LANDHOLDING BARONY
LANDING BANK YARD STAITH
LANDAGE ARRIVAGE FOOTPACE
HALFPACE LANDFALL
(SMOOTH —) GREASER
LANDING PLACE GHAT HARD
SCALE PALACE ARRIVAGE
LANDING STAGE MEAR STAGE
STAIR STAITH STELLING
LANDLADY WIFE DUENA PADRONA
GOODWIFE
LANDLORD HOST GOODMAN
PADRONE ZAMINDAR
LANDSMAL MAL

LANDMARK COPA DOLE DOOL MARK
MERE BAKEN BOUND CAIRN MARCH
MEITH SENAL CIPPUS SEAMARK
LANDMASS BULGE
LANDOWNER THANE BONDER
SQUIRE CACIQUE EFFENDI FREEMAN
BHUMIDAR FRANKLIN ZAMINDAR
(PL.) GAMORI GEOMOROI
LANDSCAPE BOCAGE PAYSAGE
SCENERY LANDSKIP
LANDSLIDE SLUMP LANDFALL
LANDSLIP
LAND SPRING LAVANT
LANDVOGT BAILIFF
LANE WAY GANG LOAN LOKE PASS
RACE VEIN WIND ALLEY CHASE
DRANG DRONG ENTRY BOREEN
VENNEL LANEWAY LOANING
TWITTEN DRIFTWAY
(AIR TRAFFIC —) CORRIDOR
(NARROW —) CHAR CHARE TEWER
BOREEN
(OCEAN —) SEAWAY
LANGUAGE (ALSO SEE DIALECT) LIP
CHIB CODE LEED RUNE LEDEN
LINGO SLANG LANGUS LINGUA
SPEECH TONGUE YABBER CABLESE
DIALECT IDIOLECT LEGALESE
(SPECIFIC —) GA GE HO MO VU AIS
AKA ATA EDO EFE EPE EVE EWE
FAN FON FOX FUL GEG HET ICA IJO
ILA KAI KAU KOL KOT KRU KUI LAB
LAI LAZ MON MRU SIA TWI UDI YAO
ZIA AFAR AGAO AGAU AGNI AHOM
AINU AKAN AKIM ALUR AMBO ANDI
ANTA ARUA ARAW BARI BEJA BIAK
BODO BONI BORA BUBE BUGI BULU
CARA CHAM CHIN CHOL CHUJ COOS
CORA COTO CREE CROW CUNA
DENE DOBU DYAK EFIK EKOI ERIE
EYAK FANG FIJI FULA FUNG GARO
GHEG GOLA GOLD HARE HEHE HOPI
HOVA HULA HUPA IBAN IDJO IJAW
IXIL KADU KAFA KAMI KAVI KAWI
KELE KOCH KOMI KONO KOTA KUKI
KURI LAHU LAKH LAPP LASI LATI
LAZI LESU LETT LUBA MANX MAYA
MOLE MORO NAGA NAMA NIAS NIUE
NUBA NUPE OGOR PALA PEGU PEUL
PUME RAMA SAHO SERB SERI SGAW
SHAN SIUS SORB SULU SUMO SUMU
SUSU TAAL TIAM TIBU TINO TODA
TSHI TUPI TUPY VEPS VOTE XOSA
ZULU ALEUT ALSEA ARAUA AUETO
AZTEC BAJAU BALTI BASSA BATAK
BATTA BAURE BEMBA BHILI BICOL
BILIN BONNY CAMPA CATIB CAYUA
CHANE CHIMU CHOCO CHOPE
COFAN COIBA COMAN CUEVA
CUMAN CUNZA CZECH DAFLA
DAYAK DIERI DINKA DUALA DUTCH
DYULA EMPEO FANTI FINGO FUNJI
GAFAT GALLA GANDA GETAN GETIC
GOLDI GONDI GREBO GREEK
GUAMO GUATO GURMA GYPSY
HABAB HAIDA HAIKH HATSA HAUSA
HINDI HUABI HUARI HURON HUSKY
HYLAM IGALA ILOKO IRAYA IRISH
JAKUN JATKI JUANG JUTIC KABYL

KAMBA KAMIA KANDH KAREN
KAROK KHASI KHMER KHOND KHUZI
KIOWA KISSI KIWAI KOINE KOLIS
KONDE KONGO KORKU KORWA
KOTAR KUMUK KUMYK KUSAN
KWOMA LAMBA LAMUT LANGO
LATIN LENCA LENDU LHOKE LHOTA
LIMBA LIMBU LUIAN LUNDA MAGHI
MAHRA MAHRI MALAY MALTO
MAORI MAZUR MBUBA MEDIC MENDI▪
MIKIR MODOA MOSSI MUONG MURM▪
MURUT NAHUA NOGAI NORSE
NYORO ORAON ORIYA OROMO
OSCAN PALAU PAMIR PELEW PEUHL
PLATT PUNIC RONGA SAKAI SAMAL
SANTO SAXON SCOTS SERER SHILH
SHINA SHONA SICEL SIKEL SLAVE
SOTHO SOYOT SUOMI SWAZI TAINO
TAMIL TELEI TONGA TURKI UDISH
UIGUR URIYA UZBEK VOGUL WAYAC▪
WELSH WOLOF YAKUT YUNCA
ZERMA ABIPON ABKHAS ACAWAI
ACHOLI ADIGHE ADZHAR AFGHAN
AHTENA ALTAIC ANDAKI ANDHRA
ANDOKE ANGAMI APACHE APANTO
APIACA ARABIC ARANDA ARAONA
ARAWAK ARUNTA ATAROI AVANTI
AYMARA BAGOBO BAITSI BAKELE
BANIVA BASQUE BEAVER BHOTIA
BHUMIJ BIHARI BILAAN BILOXI
BONTOC BORORO BRAHUI BRETON
BRIBRI BUKAUA BULGAR BURIAT
CAGABA CANITA CARAJA CARIAN
CARIRI CAUQUI CAVINA CAYAPA
CAYUGA CAYUSE CEBUAN CHAGGA▪
CHAIMA CHANGO CHOCHO CHOKWI▪
COCAMA CONIBO COPTIC CREOLE
DAKOTA DANISH DOGRIB DYERMA
ESKIMO EUDEVE FRENCH FULANI
FULNIO FUTUNA GADDAN GALCHA
GALIBI GATHIC GENTOO GERMAN
GILAKI GILIAK GILYAK GOTHIC
GUAIMI GUETAR GUINAU GULLAH
GURIAN HAINAN HANTIK HARARI
HATTIC HEBREW HERERO HIBITO
IBANAG IFUGAO IGNERI
IGOROT INDIAN INDOIS INNUIT
INUPIK ISINAI ISLETA IVATAN
KABARD KACHIN KAFFIR KAIBAL
KALMUK KAMASS KANAKA KANURI
KEKCHI KHALKA KHAMTI KHARIA
KHOWAR KIKUYU KILIWA KODAGA
KODAGU KOIARI KOIBAL KOLAMI
KOREAN KORYAK KOTIAK KPEELE
KUNAMA KURNAI KURUKH KYURIN
LADINO LAGUNA LAHNDA LAHULI
LENAPE LEPCHA LIBYAN LIUKIU
LIVIAN LUSHAI LUVIAN LYCIAN
LYDIAN MAGAHI MAGYAR MANCHU▪
MANOBO MBONDO MBUNDA MEDIA▪
MEGREL MINOAN MISIMI MISIMA
MOHAWK MONTES MUYSCA MYSIA▪
NEWARI NINGPO NUBIAN NYANJA
OORIVA OSTIAK OVAMPO PAHARI
PALAIC PAPUAN PASHTO PAZAND
POLISH PUSHTO PUSHTU QUECHA▪
RASHTI REJANG ROMANY SAFINE
SAKIAN SALISH SAMOAN SANGIL
SANGIR SARCEE SASSAK SAVARA

SEDANG SEKANI SELKUP SELUNG
SEMANG SENECA SENUFO SESUTO
SHARRA SHASTA SILETZ SINDHI
SLOVAK SOMALI SONRAI SUBIYA
SURHAI SUSIAN TARTAR TAVGHI
TELEGU TELEUT TETTUM THONGA
TIPURA TUNGUS VANNIC VOTYAK
YANKEE YARURA YORUBA ZAREMA
ABENAKI ACHAGUA AEQUIAN
AKWAALA AKWAPIM ALABAMA
ALTRIAN AMANAYE AMHARIC
AMORITE AMUESHA APINAYE
ARAMAIC ARAPAHO ARAUCAN
ARECUNA ARGOBBA ARICARA
ARMORIC ASHANTI ASURINI
ATACAMA ATAKAPA AUSTRAL
AVESTAN AXUMITE BAGHELI
BAGIRMI BAINING BAKONGO
BALANTE BALUCHI BAMBARA
BANGALA BANNACK BASHKIR
BENGALI BEOTHUK BERBERI
BHOTIYA BHUTANI BOSNIAN BRITISH
BULANDA BUNDELI BUNYORO
BURMESE BUSHMAN CALIANA
CALINGA CARRIER CASHIBO
CATALAN CATAWBA CAWAHIB
CHACOBO CHARRUA CHATINO
CHEBERO CHECHEN CHIBCHA
CHIMILA CHINOOK CHIRINO
CHIWERE CHONTAL CHOROTI
CHUKCHI CHUMASH CHUROYA
CHUVASH CIBONEY CLALLAM
COCHIMI CORNISH COTONAM
COWLITZ CYMRAEG DAGBANE
DAGOMBA DANAKIL DANKALI
DARGHIN DEUTSCH DHEGIHA
DRAVIDA ENGLISH ESCURA
ESSELEN EUSKERA FINNISH FLEMISH
FOOCHOW FRIESIC FRISIAN GAULISH
GOAJIRO GUAHIBO GUARANI
GUAYAKI GURUNSI GYARUNG
HAITIAN HANUNOC HIDATSA HITTITE
HUASTEC HUCHNOM HUICHOL
HURRIAN IBERIAN ILOKANO
ILONGOT INGALIK IPURINA ITALIAN
ITELMES ITONAMA JACUNDA
JAGATAI KAKHYEN KALINGA
KAMASIN KANAUJI KANNADA
KASHUBE KASSITE KIKONGO
KIPCHAK KIRANTI KIRGHIZ KIRUNDI
KLAMATH KOASATI KONKANI
KOYUKON KUBACHI KULAMAN
KURDISH KUTCHIN KUTENAI
LAMPONG LATVIAN LESGHIN
LOATUKO LUGANDA MAGADHI
MALTESE MAPUCHE MARATHI
MASKOKI MERCIAN MEXICAN
MINAEAN MINGREL MITANNI
MOABITE MOCHICA MONUMBO
MORATTY MORISCO NAHUATL
NICOBAR OSMANLI OSSETIC
PAHLAVI PALAUNG PANJABI
PARBATE PERMIAK PERMIAN
PERSIAN PICTISH PUNJABI PUQUINA
QUERCHI SABAEAN SALINAN
SAMBALI SAMNANI SAMNITE
SAMOYED SANDAWE SANTALI
SANTANA SEMITIC SERBIAN
SHAWANO SHAWNEE SHILLUH

SHIPIBO SHUSWAP SIAMESE
SIRIONO SIUSLAW SOGDIAN
SONGHAI SONGISH SORBIAN
SPANIOL SPANISH STIKINE SUBANUN
SVANISH SWAHILI SWEDISH
TAGALOG TIBETAN TUAMOTU
TURKISH UMBRIAN UMBUNDU
VISAYAN WALLOON WENDISH
YENISEI YIDDISH ZABERMA
ZONGORA ABANEEME ACHINESE
ACHUMAWI AKKADIAN AKSUMITE
ALACALUF ALBANIAN ALFURESE
AMAHUACA AMERICAN AMMONITE
ANGOLESE ANNAMESE ANZANIAN
APALACHI ARMENIAN ASSAMESE
ASSYRIAN ATJINESE AWISHIRA
BACTRIAN BALINESE BARBACOA
BECHUANA BHOJPURI BISCAYAN
BOSNISCH BOTOCUDO CAHUILLA
CAINGANG CANARESE CANOEIRO
CAQUETIO CARELIAN CARIJONA
CAYUBABA CHALDEAN CHAMORRO
CHEHALIS CHEMAKUM CHEYENNE
CHINGPAW CHIQUITO CHITRALI
COCONUCA COLUMBIA COMANCHE
CORAVECA CROATIAN CUSTENAU
DELAWARE DIEGUENO EGYPTIAN
ELAMITIC ETHIOPIC ETRUSCAN
FALISBAN FORMOSAN FRANKISH
FULFULDE GALICIAN GALLEGAN
GEORGIAN GERMANIC GORKHALI
GUAICURU GUJARATI HADENDOA
HAWAIIAN HITCHITI ILLINOIS
ILLYRIAN IROQUOIS JAPANESE
JAVANESE KANARESE KANAWARI
KANKANAI KASHMIRI KASUBIAN
KERMANJI KIMBUNDU KOLARIAN
LANDSMAL LANUVIAN LIGURIAN
LIHYANIC LILLOOET LIVONIAN
LUSATIAN MADURESE MAHRATTI
MAKASSAR MALAGASY MANDINGA
MARSHALL MASOVIAN MAYATHAN
MAZOVIAN MONGOLIC MUSKOGEE
NUMIDIAN NYAMWEZI OSSETIAN
PAMPANGO PHRYGIAN POLABIAN
PORTUGAL PRUSSIAN RABBINIC
ROMANIAN SABELLIC SANSKRIT
SAWAIORI SCOTTISH SCYTHIAN
SEBUNDOY SEECHELT SHAMBALA
SHIRIANA SHOSHONE SICILIAN
SLAVONIC SOUTHRON SQUAMISH
SUBARIAN SUBTIABA SUMATRAN
SUMERIAN TAHITIAN TALMUDIC
TAMASHEK THRACIAN TURCOMAN
VENETIAN VOLSCIAN WOGULIAN
YUGOSLAV YUKAGHIR CANAANITE
(— THAT CONDEMNS) ABUSE
(ARTIFICIAL —) RO IDO ARULO
NOVIAL VOLAPUK ESPERANTO
(FIGURATIVE —) IMAGERY
(FLORID —) SILLABUB
(FOOLISH —) STUFF FLUMMERY
(FOUL —) SMUT ORDURE
(GYPSY —) CALO
(INCOMPREHENSIBLE —) CHOCTAW
(INTERNATIONAL —) ANGLIC
(LATIN —) GRAMMAR HUMANITY
(NONSENSICAL —) BANTER
(OBSCENE —) BAWDY BAWDRY

(ORDINARY —) PROSE
(OVERPRETENTIOUS —) BOMBAST
(PERT —) SAUCE
(PIDGIN —) SABIR CAVITENO
FANAKALO
(PLAIN —) CLEAR
(SECRET —) ARGOT
(SHOWY —) FLUBDUB
(UNCLEAN —) SEWERAGE
(UNIVERSAL —) PASILALY
(WELSH —) CYMRAEG
(PL.) BALTIC FINNIC MAHORI SEMITIC
SUDANIC ILLYRIAN
LANGUE D'OC LEMOSI LIMOSI
LANGUET LANGUID LANGUAGE
LANGUID WAN LANK DOWIE FAINT
DREAMY FEEBLE SICKLY SUPINE
TORPID CARELESS FLAGGING
HEEDLESS INDOLENT LISTLESS
SLUGGISH
LANGUISH DIE FADE FALL FLAG
PINE WILT DROOP DWINE FAINT
SWOON SICKEN WITHER DECLINE
LANGUISHING FADE SICK LANGUID
LANGUOR KEF KIF ENNUI DEBILITY
LANGUR DOUC MAHA LOTONG
LUTONG SIMPAI WANDEROO
LANK LEAN THIN GAUNT LANKY
SLANK MEAGER MEAGRE SLUNKEN
LANKY LEAN RENKY SLINK GANGLY
GANGLING
LANOLIN LANUM DEGRAS
LANSEH DUKU LANSA LANZON
LANTANA OREGANO
LANTERN (ALSO SEE LAMP) BUAT
BOUET BOWET DARKY LIGHT
CUPOLA LOUVER PHAROS SCONCE
THOLUS CIMBORIC LANTHORN
(— ON ROOF) FEMEREIL
(DARK —) DARKY ABSONSA
ABSCONCE
(ELEVATED —) PHAROS
(OPTICAL —) EPISCOPE
LANTERN FISH INIOME
LANTERN FLOUNDER MEGRIM
LANTERN FLY FULGORID
LANTERN PINION RUNDLE
TRUNDLE
LANYARD WAPP GILGUY LANIARD
BACKROPE
LAODAMIA (FATHER OF —) ACASTUS
(HUSBAND OF —) PROTESILAUS
(MOTHER OF —) HIPPOLYTE
LAODICE (FATHER OF —) PRIAM
(HUSBAND OF —) HELICAON
(MOTHER OF —) HECUBA
LAOIGHIS LEIX
LAOMEDON (SON OF —) PRIAM

LAOS

CAPITAL: VIENTIANE
COIN: KIP
MEASURE: BAK
MOUNTAIN: BIA LAI LOI SAN COPI
KHAT ATWAT KHOUNG TIUBIA
PEOPLE: LU KHA LAO MEO YAO
THAI

RIVER: NOI DONE KHONG MEKONG SEBANG
TOWN: NAPE PAKSE XIENG PAKLAY THAKHEK

LAP LEP LIP BARM FOLD GORE LICK SLAP SLOD SOSS SUCK WASH WELT LAPPER LAPPET SHOVEL INTERLAP
(— **IN STEEL**) SPILL
(— **OF STRAKES**) LAND
LAPACHOL TECOMIN
LAPBOARD PANEL
LAPDOG MESSAN MESSET SHOUGH
LAPEL LAPPET REVERE REVERS
LAPIDARY STONER GEMMARY LAPIDIST
LAPILLUS RAPILLO
(PL.) CINDER
LAPIS LAZULI AZURE
LAP-JOINTED CLINCH
LAPP LAPPISH LAPPONIC
LAPPED FOLIATED
LAPPET LAP PAN BARBE FANON LABEL CORNET INFULA PINNER
LAPSE DROP FADE FALL HALT SLIP ERROR FAULT FOLLY SPACE TRACT EFFLUX HIATUS LAPSUS DELAPSE ESCHEAT FAILURE PROCESS RELAPSE RESOLVE SLIDING ABEYANCE CADUCITY
(— **OF MEMORY**) BLACKOUT
(PL.) LACHES
LAPSED CADUCOUS
LAPSTRAKE CLINCH
LAPWING WEEP WYPE PEEWEE PLOVER TIRWIT HORNPIE PEEWEEP PIEWIPE TEUCHIT FLOPWING PEESWEEP TEEWHAAP TERUTERU
LARBOARD PORT BABURD
LARCENY THEFT FELONY ROBBERY BURGLARY STEALAGE
LARCH LARICK JUNIPER EPINETTE TAMARACK
LARD MORT SAIM ADEPS DAUBE ENARM FLARE FLECK FLICK AXUNGE ENLARD INLARD NEUTRAL SAINDOUX
LARDED PIQUE CADUCE CADUCOUS
LARDER CAVE PANTRY SPENCE BUTTERY LARDINER
LARGE BIG BULL FEAT GOOD LONG MAIN ROOM TALL AMPLE BULKY BURLY GRAND GREAT GROSS HUSKY JOLLY LARGY MACRO MAXIM RENKY ROUND SMART SPACY WALLY GAWSIE GOODLY HEROIC MAXIMA STRONG TRABAL BOWERLY CAPITAL COPIOUS FAIRISH FEARFUL HEALTHY HULKING LASKING LIBERAL MASSIVE SIZABLE CHOPPING PLUMPING SENSIBLE SWACKING
(— **AND HOLLOW**) CAVAL
(— **AND ROUND**) SIDE
(— **IN DIAMETER**) STOUT
(**APPALLINGLY** —) HIDEOUS
(**EXTREMELY** —) GIANT DECUMAN GIGANTIC

(**FAIRLY** —) SMART
(**INDEFINITELY** —) NTH INFINITE
(**MODERATELY** —) FAIR
(**UNUSUALLY** —) HEAVY SKELPIN SKELPING
(**VERY** —) HUGE ROYAL BOXCAR INGENT NATION GOLIATH INTENSE BEHEMOTH SLAPPING SWINGING WHACKING
LARGE-FOOTED MEGAPOD
LARGE-FRAMED ROOMY
LARGE-LETTERED UNCIAL
LARGELY BIG HARD BIGLY
LARGENESS MICKLE BREADTH FREEDOM GIANTISM LARGEOUR
LARGEST BEST MAXIMUS
LARIA BRUCHUS
LARIAT ROPE LASSO RIATA CABESTRO
LARK GAME FROLIC PEEWEE SCHEME LAVROCK LAYROCK SKYLARK CALANDER LAVEROCK
LARKA KOLS HO
LARKSPUR LOCOWEED
LARNITE BELITE
LARRIKIN NUT ROWDY HOODLUM
LARVA BOT BLOW BOTT CRAB GRUB HUHU SLUG TURK WOLF WORM ALIMA ASCON BARDY BRUKE ERUCA LEECH OTTER REDIA SYCON CORBIE COSSID DRAGON EPHYRA GRUGRU HOPPER LEPTUS LEUCON LOOPER MAGGOT MEASLE NIGGER PEDLAR TORCEL WABBLE WORMIL WOUBIT ATROCHA BUDWORM CADELLE CREEPER DIPORPA FIGWORM FLYBLOW GORDIAN HYPOPUS PEDDLER PLANULA PLUTEUS PREPUPA WIGGLER ACTINULA ANTIZOEA ARMYWORM BOLLWORM BOMBYCID BOOKWORM CASEWORM CERCARIA COENURUS CYRTOPIA DEUTOVUM DROPWORM EPHYRULA FIREWORM FURCILIA GEOMETER GILTTAIL GLOWWORM GNATWORM LEAFTIER LEAFWORM MUCKWORM NAUPLIUS PILIDIUM ROOTWORM SCYPHULA SEMIPUPA SILKWORM SKINWORM SPANWORM SPRAWLER STAGWORM SUBIMAGO TORNARIA VERMICLE WASPLING WIREWORM WOODGRUB WOODWORM
LARVACEA ATREMATA COPELATA
LARVAL NEPIONIC
LARYNGITIS CROUP
LASCIVIOUS LEWD NICE SALT HORNY LUBRIC WANTON BLISSOM FLESHLY GOATISH
LASCIVIOUSNESS LECHERY ASELGEIA LUXURITY
LASERWORT SILPHIUM
LASH CUT BEAT FIRK FLOG JERK LACE WELT WHIP WIRE YERK LEASE LEASH SCORE SKEEG SLASH THONG WHALE CANVAS LAINER LAUNCH STRIPE SWINGE SWITCH FLYFLAP KURBASH SCOURGE
(— **TOGETHER**) RACK
LASHER THONGMAN

LASHING YARK YERK GAMMON LISTING MOUSING SEIZING SLATING FRAPPING
(PL.) OODLES OODLINS SLITHERS
LASS TIB GILL PRIM TRULL DAMSEL KUMMER LASSIE DAMOZEL LASSIKY TENDREL MUCHACHA
LASSITUDE LANGUOR LETHARGY
LASSO LASH LAZO ROPE RIATA LARIAT CABESTRO
LAST ABY LAG DURE HOLD KEEP RIDE SAVE ABIDE FINAL SERVE ABEGGE ENDURE LATEST LATTER REMAIN ULTIMA UTMOST DARREIN DERNIER EXTREME PERDURE SUPREME CONTINUE EVENTUAL HINDMOST LATEMOST REARMOST TERMINAL ULTIMATE
(— **BUT ONE**) PENULT
(— **OUT**) SPIN STAY
(**AT** —) FINALLY
(**THE** —) OMEGA
LASTING FIXED LASTY DURANT DURING STABLE ABIDING DURABLE DUREFUL CONSTANT ENDURING LIVELONG REMANENT STANDING
(— **FOR LONG PERIOD**) AEONIC AEONIAL
(— **FOR ONE DAY**) DIARY DIURNAL
LASTINGNESS STAY DURATION
LAST SUPPER CENA COENA MAUNDY
LAT STAMBHA
LATCH FLY PIN HASP RISP CATCH CHAIR CLICK CLINK SNECK SNICK KEEPER CLICKET
LATCHET DAG TAB SANDAL LANGUET
LATCHING LASKET
LATCHKEY CLICKET PASSKEY
LATE LAG NEW DEEP RIPE SLOW TARDY TARDIVE UMWHILE ADVANCED LATEWARD SOMETIME UMQUHILE
LATELY LATE ALATE NEWLY
LA TENE MARNEAN
LATENT HIDDEN ABEYANT DORMANT LATITANT
LATER POI SIN ANON POST SYNE AFTER ELDER BEHIND FUTURE LATTER PUISNE ANOTHER INFERIOR UMQUHILE
LATERAL SIDE
LATERALLY SIDELONG
LATERITE CABOOK
LATEST LAST LATTER FARTHEST FURTHEST
LATEX GUTTA SORVA
LATH SLAT SPAIL SPALE SPELL SWALE REEPER SPLENT SPLINT STOOTH LATHING FOREPOLE LATHWORK
LATHE LAY SLEY TURN LAITH THROW BEATER WISKET
(— **FOR CYLINDERS**) BROAD
(— **OF LOOM**) LAY
(**TURNING** —) THROW
(**WATCHMAKER'S** —) TURN TURNS MANDREL

LATHER FOAM SUDS FROTH FREATH SAPPLES
LATHERED SOAPY
LATIN ROMAN HISPERIC LATINITY
(— COMPOSITION) VULGUS
LATIN-AMERICAN LATIN LADINO LATINO HISPANIC
LATINUS (DAUGHTER OF —) LAVINIA
(FATHER OF —) FAUNUS
(SON-IN-LAW OF —) AENEAS
(WIFE OF —) AMATA
LATITUDE SCOPE WIDTH EXTENT HEIGHT
(HELIOCENTRIC —) LIMIT
LATONA (DAUGHTER OF —) DIANA
(FATHER OF —) COEUS
(MOTHER OF —) PHOEBE
(SON OF —) APOLLO
LATRIA ADORATION
LATRINE PRIVY TOILET BOGGARD
LATTER LAST FINAL RECENT SECOND PRESENT
(— PORTION) AUTUMN
LATTICE GRATE HERSE TWINE PINJRA UMBREL GRATING CANCELLI
(— OF POINTS) SATIN
(MOVING —) APRON
LATTICE PLANT LACELEAF
LATTICEWORK ARBOR GRATE GRATING TUKUTUKU

LATVIA
CAPITAL: RIGA
COIN: LAT RUBLIS KAPEIKA SANTIMAS
MEASURE: STOF KANNE STOFF STOOF VERST ARSHIN KULMET SAGENE VERCHOC KROUCHKA POURVETE
PEOPLE: LETT
RIVER: AA OGRE GAUJA SALACA LIELUPE
TOWN: CESIS LIBAU DVINSK LIBAVA TUKUMS JELGAVA REZEKNE DUNABURG VALMIERA
WEIGHT: LIESPFUND

AUAN KALUNTI
AUD EXTOL PRAISE ADVANCE APPLAUD COMMEND GLORIFY MAGNIFY EMBLAZON EULOGIZE MACARIZE
AUDATION EULOGY PRAISE
AUDATORY SNEER EPENETIC PRAISING
AUGH GAFF CHUCK FLEER LEUGH RISUS ARRIDE NICKER TITTER CHORTLE GRIZZLE SNICKER SNIGGER SNIRTLE TWITTER LAUGHTER
(— CONTEMPTUOUSLY) SNORT DERIDE
(— GLEEFULLY) CHECKLE
(— HYSTERICALLY) CHECKLE
(— IN AFFECTED MANNER) GIGGLE
(— IN COARSE MANNER) FLEER GUFFAW
(— LIKE HEN) CACKLE
(— LOUDLY) GAFF GUFFAW

(— QUIETLY) GULE SMUDGE CHUCKLE SNIRTLE
(BELLY —) BOFF BOFFOLA
(LOUD —) GAUSTER
LAUGHABLE ODD RICH COMIC DROLL FUNNY MERRY QUEER WITTY AMUSING COMICAL RISIBLE STRANGE WAGGISH FARCICAL HUMOROUS LAUGHING PLEASANT SPORTIVE
LAUGHING RIANT RIDENT IRRISION
(— MATTER) MOWS
LAUGHING GULL PEWIT
LAUGHING OWL WEKAU WHEKAU
LAUGHINGSTOCK GUY BUTT JEST JOKE SONG SPORT DERISION RIDICULE
LAUGHTER JOKE MIRTH RISUS SNIRT CACKLE LAWTER SPLEEN HILARITY
LAUNCE LANT LANCE SMELT AMMODYTE SANDLING
LAUNCH PUT BURST DRIVE LANCE ELANCE STRIKE BAPTIZE PINNACE STEAMER VIBRATE CATAPULT
(— HOSTILELY) DIRECT
LAUNCHER (ROCKET —) BAZOOKA
LAUNDER TYE WASH TRUNK SLUICE STRAKE LAUNDRY
LAUNDRESS TRILBY LAVENDER
LAUNDRY WASH LAVATORY
LAUREL BAY IVY LAURY UNITE WICKY DAPHNE KALMIA MALLET MYRTLE CAJEPUT IVYWOOD WOEVINE BREWSTER CALFKILL
(GROUND —) ARBUTUS
LAUREL OAK ACAJOU
LAURIC PICHURIC
LAURUSTINE VIBURNUM
LAUSUS (FATHER OF —) NUMITOR MEZENTIUS
(SISTER OF —) ILIA
(SLAYER OF —) AMULIUS
LAUTVERSCHIEBUNG SHIFT
LAVA AA ASHES SPINE COULEE LATITE SCORIA VERITE FAVILLA LAPILLO MALPAIS ASPERITE ORENDITE PAHOEHOE
(SCORIACEOUS —) AA SLAG
(SLAGGY —) SCORIA
LAVABO LAVATORY
LAVAGE LAVATION LAVEMENT
LAVALAVA SULU
LAVAN KALUNTI
LAVATORY BASIN LAVETTE WASHROOM
LAVE LIP WASH BATHE SPLASH
LAVENDER BEHN ASPIC BEHEN SPICK SPIKE INKROOT LAVANDIN STICHADO
LAVER SION SLAKE SLOKE LOUTER PHIALE AMANORI CISTERN
LAVINIA (FATHER OF —) LATINUS
(HUSBAND OF —) AENEAS
(MOTHER OF —) AMATA
LAVISH FREE LASH LUSH FLUSH LARGE SPEND SPORT WASTE COSTLY WANTON COPIOUS OPULENT PROFUSE GENEROUS

LUCULLAN PRODIGAL SQUANDER WASTEFUL
LAVISHNESS WASTE FINERY LAVISH
LAW ACT FAS IUS JUS LAY LEX ADAT DOOM JURE RULE CANON DROIT NOMOS TORAH BYELAW BYRLAW DECREE DHARMA EQUITY DANELAW DERECHO HALACHA HALAKAH JUSTICE PRECEPT SETNESS STATUTE JUDGMENT JUDICIAL ROGATION STATEWAY TANISTRY
(—S OF MANU) SUTRA SUTTA
(BEDOUIN —) THAR
(DIETARY —S) KASHRUTH
(ISLAMIC —) ADA BAI ADAT SHERI SHARIA SHERIAT
(MARRIAGE —) LEVIRATE
(OPPOSING —) ANTINOMY
(PROPOSED —) BILL
(UNIVERSAL —) HEAVEN
(PL.) LORS
LAW-ABIDING LAWFUL
LAWBREAKER FELON HOUGHER
LAWFUL DUE LEAL TRUE VERY LEGAL LICIT LOYAL VALID KINDLY LEEFUL ENNOMIC LEESOME INNOCENT LIEFSOME RIGHTFUL
LAWGIVER MINOS MOSES SOLON LAWYER LAWMAKER
LAWLESS LEWD UNRULY ILLEGAL MOBBISH ANARCHIC
LAWLESSNESS ANOMY ANOMIE
LAWMAKER LEGIFER
LAWN ARBOR GRASS LINON SWARD UMPLE CYPRUS BATISTE QUINTIN TIFFANY
LAWSUIT LIS CASE SAKE SECTA BRABBLE
LAWYER JET PEAT AVOUE PATCH SHARK BREHON JURIST LAWMAN LEGIST SQUIRE WRITER COUNSEL TEMPLAR DEFENDER LEGISTER TRAMPLER BARRISTER
LAX DULL FREE LASH LAZY LINK SLOW SWAG WIDE LARGE LOOSE RELAX SLACK TARDY REMISS BACKWARD INACTIVE DISSOLUTE
LAXATIVE LAX LASK APERIENT HYDROMEL LAPACTIC RELAXANT SOLUTIVE
LAXITY LASCHETY LATITUDE
LAY LIE SET CLAP LAIC LEWD SLEY SONG WAGE BIGHT COUCH DITTY LATHE LEDGE QUIET STAKE STILL COMMON HAZARD IMPOSE IMPUTE APPEASE ASCRIBE LAYDOWN POPULAR SECULAR
(— ASIDE) DOFF DOWN DUMP SHUCK DEPOSE DIVEST DEPOSIT
(— AWAY) STORE
(— BARE) BARE NAKE TIRL TIRVE DENUDE DETECT OPPOSE UNCOVER DENUDATE
(— CLAIM) ASSERT BESPEAK ARROGATE
(— CROSSWISE) COB
(— DOWN) ABDICATE
(— EGGS) BLOW WARP LEDGE OVIPOSIT

(— **FLAT**) SQUAT ADPRESS
(— **HOLD OF**) FANG GRIP HENT
TAKE GRIPE LATCH ATHOLD
ATTACH COLLAR COMPRISE
(— **IN BIGHTS**) JAG
(— **IN COIL**) FLEMISH
(— **IN PLEATS**) FOLD
(— **LOW**) STREW STRIKE
(— **OF LOOM**) BEATER
(— **ON**) APPLY INFLICT
(— **OPEN**) BREAK CHINE EXPOSE
UNMASK
(— **OUT**) FRAY PLAT RANGE SPELD
SPEND BEWARE DESIGN EXTEND
SPREAD STREAK STREEK CHECKER
DEVELOP STRETCH CONTRIVE
(— **PRONE**) LEVEL
(— **RUBBLEWORK**) SNECK
(— **SIEGE**) INVEST
(— **SMOOTH**) EVEN
(— **SNARE FOR RABBITS**) HAY
(— **STONE**) PAVE
(— **STRAIGHT**) COMB
(— **TYPE**) CASE
(— **UP**) HEAP HIVE ADDLE HOARD
HUTCH STOCK TREASURE
(— **WASTE**) PEEL WEST HARRY
HAVOC HARASS RAVAGE DESTROY
DESOLATE FORWASTE
LAYBOY JOGGER
LAYDOWN LAYOUT SPREAD
LAYER BED LAY BARK CAKE COAT
DASS FACE FILM FLAP FOLD LAIR
SEAM SKIN WEFT ZONA CHESS
COUCH COVER CRUST CUTIS FLAKE
FLASH LEDGE SCALE CARPET
COURSE FASCIA FILLER FOLIUM
INTINE LAMINA LISSOM STREAK
BLANKET COATING CUTICLE
EPICARP FEATHER FLAVEDO
GANGMAN INLAYER LAMELLA
PACKING PHELLEM PROPAGO
PROVINE STRATUM SUBCOAT
SUPPORT ECTOCYST ECTOSARC
ENDOCYST ENDODERM EPIBLAST
EPIBLEMA EPISPORE EPITHECA
INTERBED MOLLISOL PERIOPLE
SUBCRUST
(— **IN FUNGI**) HYMENIUM
(— **OF BLOOD VESSEL**) EXTIMA
EXTERNA
(— **OF CELLS**) EXINE CORTEX
EXTINE CAMBIUM
(— **OF CLAY**) GLEY SELVAGE
SELVEDGE
(— **OF EARTH**) SPIT
(— **OF FAT**) LEAF FINISH
(— **OF FELT**) BAT BATT
(— **OF FIBER**) LAP
(— **OF FINE MATERIAL**) CUSHION
(— **OF FOREST GROWTH**)
SUBSTORY
(— **OF FUEL**) FIREBED
(— **OF GLASS**) CASING
(— **OF IRIS**) UVEA
(— **OF MEAT**) SPINE
(— **OF NERVE FIBERS**) ALVEUS
(— **OF ORGANIC MATTER**) FLOOR
(— **OF PLASMA**) BUFFCOAT

(— **OF ROCK**) CAP SHELF SHELL
SLATE FOLIUM SEPTUM BLISTER
SKULLCAP
(— **OF ROOTS**) SOLE
(— **OF SEDIMENT**) WARP
(— **OF SHALE**) BONE
(— **OF SHEEPSKIN**) FLESHER
(— **OF SHOE HEEL**) LIFT
(— **OF SILT**) VARVE
(— **OF SKIN**) DERM DERMA EPIDERM
(— **OF SOIL**) SOLUM CALLOW
CASING HARDPAN HORIZON
(— **OF STONES**) DASS DESS
(— **OF TANBARK**) HAT
(— **OF TISSUE**) BED DARTOS FASCIA
SEROSA ELASTICA EPIBLEMA
(— **OF TOBACCO LEAVES**) HANGER
(— **OF TURF**) FLAW
(— **OF WHITE MATTER**) CAPSULE
(— **OF WOOD**) CORE
(**BONY** —) LAMELLA CEMENTUM
(**BOTTOM** —) BEDDING
(**FLAT** —) BED FLAP FLAKE
(**GERM** —) MESODERM
(**IMPERVIOUS** —) LINING
(**OUTER** —) HUSK
LAYERING LAP GOOTEE STOOLING
LAYMAN LAIC CLERK IDIOT DEACON
SECULAR DEFENSOR EXHORTER
EXOTERIC FAMILIAR STRANGER
WORLDMAN
LAYOFF FURLOUGH
LAYOUT MISE DUMMY SETOUT
(— **OF CARDS**) TABLEAU
LAZARETTO SPITAL SPITTLE
LAZINESS LAZE SLOTH SLOUCH
OISIVITY
LAZULITE SIDERITE
LAZY ARGH IDLE LASS DOXIE DRONY
FAINT INERT LINGY LUSKY RESTY
SLOAN SLOTH CLUMSY LIMPSY
LURDAN LUTHER ORNERY SWEERT
TRAILY CLUMPST LUSKISH PEAKISH
SLIVING DROGHLIN FAINEANT
FECKLESS INDOLENT LITHERLY
OSCITANT SLOTHFUL SLUGGARD
THOWLESS TRIFLING
LEA LAY GRASS LAYER LAYLAND
LEALAND
LEACH TAP LETCH SOFTEN
LEAD GO TEE VAN WIN BEAR DADE
GIVE GROW HAVE HEAD HERD LEED
SLIP TAKE TEEM WORK BLAZE
BOUND BRING CARRY GREBE GUIDE
MAYNE PILOT PRESA SOUND START
TRAIN TREAT CONVEY DEDUCE
DIRECT ESCORT INDUCE INDUCT
LEADER SATURN BEGUILE CAPTAIN
CONDUCE CONDUCT LEADING
MARSHAL PIGTAIL PIONEER
PLUMBUM PLUMMET LEADSMAN
MANUDUCE MANUDUCT SQUIRREL
(— **A BAND**) BATON
(— **AND SUPPORT**) DADE
(— **ASIDE**) CHAR SINGLE
(— **ASTRAY**) ERR MANG TURN WARP
BEFOOL BETRAY ENTICE WANDER
WILDER DEBAUCH MISLEAD
MISWEND PERVERT SOLICIT

TRADUCE BEWILDER INVEIGLE
MISGUIDE
(— **AWAY**) CHAR ABDUCT DIVERGE
(— **BACK**) REDUCT
(— **FORCIBLY**) ESCORT
(— **IN CARD GAME**) SNEAK
(— **IN RACE**) LAP
(— **IN SINGING**) PRECENT
(— **INTO ERROR**) ABUSE DELUDE
(— **MONOXIDE**) MASSICOT
(— **ON**) TRAIL
(— **PASSIVE EXISTENCE**) VEGETATE
(— **POISONING**) PLUMBISM
(**BLACK** —) WAD WADD GRAPHITE
(**COLOR** —) PLOMB
(**DEEP-SEA** —) DIPSY DIPSEY
(**OVERLAPPING** —) DRIP
(**PLUMBING** —) BLUEY
(**SYMBOL FOR** —) PB
(**WHITE** —) KREMS CERUSE
LEAD-COLORED WAN BLAE
LEADEN HEAVY PLUMBEAN
LEADER BO BOH COB DUX HOB MIR
CAST COCK DUCE DUKE HEAD
HOBB JEFE NAIG NAIK OMDA SOUL
TYEE CHIEF DOYEN ELDER FIRST
MAHDI MOSES OMDEH PILOT SEYID
TRACE ARCHON CALIPH DESPOT
HEADER RECTOR SAYYID TYCOON
ACREMAN ADVISER CAPTAIN
CONDUCT DEMAGOG DRUNGAR
FOREMAN FUEHRER INDUCER
ACCENTOR CAUDILLO DIRECTOR
FUGLEMAN HEADSMAN HERETOGA
LODESMAN PANDARUS STRATEGE
(— **OF DACOITS**) BOH
(— **OF MUTINEERS**) ELECTO
(— **OF REVOLT**) ANARCH
(**BAND** —) BATONEER
(**CHOIR** —) CANTOR
(**CHORUS** —) CHORAGUS
(**COSSACK** —) HETMAN
(**FASCIST** —) RAS
(**INTELLECTUAL** —) BRAIN
(**MOB** —) MOBOCRAT
(**POLITICAL** —) SACHEM
(**PRAYER** —) IMAM
(**RELIGIOUS** —) AGA AGHA SHEIKH
(**SCOUT** —) AKELA SIXER
(**SPIRITUAL** —) GURU SADDIK
GUARDIAN·
LEADERSHIP LEAD AEGIS MANRED
CONDUCT IMAMATE LEADING
MANRENT CHIEFDOM GUIDANCE
HEADSHIP HEGEMONY
LEADING BIG BEST COCK DUCT
HEAD LEAD MAIN CHIEF FIRST
PREMIER STELLAR GUIDANCE
(— **OUTWARD**) EMISSARY
(— **TO NOTHING**) IDLE
LEADSMAN SOUNDER
LEADWORK PLUMBAGE PLUMBING
LEADWORT CROWTOE PLUMBAGO
LEAF PAD BACK BARB BUYO FLAG
FLAP FOIL FOLD GEAR PAGE PALM
STUB BLADE BLANK FLIER FLYER
FOLIO FROND GRASS GUARD LEAVE
SCALE SEPAL SIGHT SPILL TEPAL
BONNET CADJAN COUPON FOLIUM

FRAISE FULZIE NEEDLE PEPPER
DAMIANA FOLDOUT HARNESS
LEAFLET TREFOIL WITNESS
PHYLLADE PHYLLOME
(— FAT) FLICK
(— FROM AXIL) BRACT
(— OF BOOK) PAGE FOLIO INSET
PLATE FLYLEAF
(— OF CALYX) BARB
(— OF CORN) HUSK
(— OF COROLLA) PETAL
(— OF DOOR) VALVE
(— OF HEDDLES) GEAR
(— OF PALM) FAN OLA CHIP OLLA
FROND LATANIER
(— OF SPRING) BACK
(BETEL —) PAN
(BIBLE —) COSTMARY
(DEAD —) FLAG
(HOLLOW —) PHYLLODE
(SPRING —) WRAPPER
(STRAWBERRY —) FRAISE
(THIN —) LAMELLA
(TOBACCO —) STRIP CUTTER
WRAPPER
(WASTE GOLD —) SKEWING
LEAFAGE FOLIAGE
LEAFHOPPER HOPPER JASSID
THRIPS HOMOPTER
LEAFLET PINNA TRACT MAILER
FOLIOLE STUFFER
(PAIR OF —S) JUGUM
(PL.) SENNA CATOBA
LEAFLIKE PHYLLINE
LEAFMOLD KOLINSKY
LEAFY GREEN LEAVY FOLIATE
FOLIOSE FRONDOSE
LEAGUE BOND BUND BANDY BOARD
GUEUX HANSA PARTY UNION WHEEL
CIRCUIT ALLIANCE SYSTASIS
(— OF NATIONS) GENEVA
(BUSH —S) STICKS
LEAGUED FEDERATE
LEAK BLOW SEEP WEEP GEYZE
SPUNK INLEAK SIGGER SPRING
ZIGGER LEAKAGE MELTERS
SCREEVE
(— IN ELECTRIC CIRCUIT) FAULT
LEAKAGE ESCAPE SEEPAGE
(— OF ELECTRICITY) CREEPAGE
(— OF GAS) SLIP
(— OF WIND) RUNNING
LEAKING ALEAK DRIBBLE NAILSICK
LEAKY LEAK UNTIGHT GIZZENED
LEAL FAITHFUL
LEAN BEND BONY HANG HEEL LANK
PEND POOR PRIN RACY RELY REST
STAY SWAY THIN TOOM EMPTY
GAUNT HIELD LANKY LEANY SLANK
SOUND SPARE STOOP HOLLOW
MEAGER RECUMB SKINNY SPRING
UPLEAN ANGULAR FATLESS INCLINE
SCRAGGY SCRAWNY SLUNKEN
STRINGY MACILENT SCRAGGED
SCRANNEL
(— FOR SUPPORT) ABUT
(— FORWARD) PROCLINE
(— OVER) WHAUVE
LEANER HOBBER

LEANING DRIFT FLAIR PENCHE
HANGING ACCLINAL ENCLITIC
FROMWARD
(— BACKWARD) SUPINE
(STRONG —) GENIUS PENCHANT
LEANNESS LANK POVERTY
SPARENESS
LEAN-TO SHED LINTER OUTSHOT
SKILLION
LEAP FLY HOP POP BEND DART DIVE
FALL GIVE JUMP LOPE LOUP RAMP
RISE SKIT WIND BOUND BREAK
CAPER DANCE EXULT FLIER FLYER
FRISK LUNGE PRIME SALTO SAULT
SCOPE SCOUP SPANG STEND VAULT
BOUNCE BREACH CURVET INSULT
LAUNCH SPRENT SPRING SPRUNT
WALLOP REBOUND SALTARY
SALTATE SUBSULT BUCKJUMP
LEAPFROG SPANGHEW UPSPRING
(— BACK) RESULT SPRUNT
(— FOR JOY) EXULT
(— IN DANCING) STOT
(— LIGHTLY) SKIP
(— OF HORSE) CURVET BALOTADE
CAPRIOLE
(— OF WHALE) BREACH
(— OUT) SALLY
(— OVER) FREE OVER SKIP CLEAR
HURDLE
(— UPON) ASSAIL
(BALLET —) JETE CABRIOLE
(FROLICSOME —) CAPER
(SUICIDAL —) BRODIE
(PL.) ALLEGRO
LEAPING GAMBOL SPRING SALIENT
SALTANT
LEARCHUS (BROTHER OF —)
MELICERTA
(FATHER OF —) ATHAMAS
(MOTHER OF —) INO
LEARN DO GET SEE WIT ARAL FIND
HAVE HEAR LEAR LERE EDIFY
GLEAN STUDY RECORD REALIZE
RECEIVE DISCOVER
(— FROM EXPERIENCE) ASSAY
LEARNED BLUE SEEN LERED LORED
DUCTUS BOOKISH CLERKLY
CUNNING ERUDITE STUDIED TUITIVE
ACADEMIC CLERGIAL LETTERED
OVERSEEN POLYMATH SCIENCED
(— MAN) OLLAV
(AFFECTEDLY —) INKHORN
(SOMETHING TO BE —) LIRIPIPE
LEARNEDLY CLERKLY
LEARNER PUPIL NOVICE TRAINEE
PRENTICE
(LATE —) OPSIMATH
LEARNING ART WIT BOOK LEIR
LERE LORE CLERGY WISDOM
APPRISE CUNNING GRAMMAR
INSIGHT LETTERS WISTING
BOOKLEAR BOOKLORE DOCTRINE
HUMANISM LETTRURE MATHESIS
PEDANTRY
LEASE FEU FEW LET SET FARM HIRE
RENT TACK COWLE DIMIT FIRMA
LISSE DEMISE POTTAH RENTAL
ASSEDAT CHARTER SETTING

BACKTACK SUBLEASE
LEASEHOLDER LIVIER
LEASH LEAD LYME SLIP LEASE
COUPLE STRING SWINGE
(— OF HOUNDS) HARL
(DOG —) SLIP TRASH TIRRET
(HAWK'S —) LOYN LUNE TIRRET
CREANCE
LEASING LOCATIO
LEAST LEST MINIMAL MINIMUM
MINIMUS
(AT —) HURE
LEAST FLYCATCHER CHEBEC
LEAST SANDPIPER PEEP OXEYE
STINT
LEATHER ELK KID BEND BOCK BUFF
CALF CAPE HIDE NAPA SEAL ADUST
ALUTA BALAT FLANK NIGER RETAN
SUEDE BULGAR CASTOR CHROME
LIZARD ORIOLE OXHIDE PEBBLE
RUSSET SKIVER TURKEY BELTING
BUFFING CANEPIN CHAMOIS
COWHIDE COWSKIN DEGRAIN
DOGSKIN DONGOLA HEADCAP
HOGSKIN KIDSKIN MURRAIN
PANCAKE PECCARY PERSIAN
SAFFIAN ANTELOPE BUCKSKIN
BULLNECK CABRETTA CALFSKIN
CAPESKIN CHEVEREL COLTSKIN
CORDOBAN CORDWAIN DEERSKIN
GOATSKIN KANGAROO LAMBSKIN
SHAGREEN
(— FOR DRESSING FLAX) RIBSKIN
(— SHREDS) MOSLINGS
(— STRIP) RAND
(ARABIAN —) MOCHA
(ARTIFICIAL —) KERATOL
(BOARDED —) BOX
(CORDOVAN —) CORDOBAN
CORDWAIN
(MOROCCO —) LEVANT MAROQUIN
(PATCH OF —) CLOUT
(PRUSSIAN —) SPRUCE
(RUSSIAN —) YUFT BULGAR RUSSIA
JUCHTEN
(SHEEPSKIN —) BOCK BUCK
(SOFT —) ALUTA
(SUPERIOR —) BUFF
(WASH —) LOSH LOSHE
LEATHERBACK LUTH
LEATHERFISH LIJA FOOLFISH
LEATHERJACKET FILEFISH
ZAPATERO
LEATHERLEAF CASSANDRA
LEATHERWOOD DIRCA WICOPY
BURNWOOD FIREWOOD IRONWOOD
LEADWOOD ROPEBARK
LEATHERWORKER TAWER BEDDER
CHAMAR MADIGA FLUFFER
CHUCKLER
LEAVE GO GET LET BUNK DROP
FADE FLEE HOOK LEAF PART QUIT
VADE VOID WALK AVOID FAVOR
FORGO GRACE SHOVE WAIVE
BUGGER DEPART DESERT DEVOID
FORLET PERMIT RETIRE SECEDE
STRAND VACATE FORLEIT FORLESE
FORSAKE LARGESS LIBERTY
LICENSE FAREWELL PATIENCE
UNTENANT

(— ALONE) FORBEAR DESOLATE
(— BEHIND) LET PLANT DISTANCE
(— BRIGHT TRAIL) STREAM
(— BY WILL) BEQUEATH
(— COVER) BREAK
(— HASTILY) SCUR SKIRR
(— HURRIEDLY) CUT BLOW FLEE
JUMP SCAT SKIP
(— IN ISOLATION) MAROON
(— IN SAFEKEEPING) CHECK
(— NOTHING TO BE DESIRED)
SATISFY
(— OF ABSENCE) ABSIT LIBERTY
FURLOUGH
(— OFF) CEASE DEVAL PETER
BILEVE CHEESE DESIST SURCEASE
(— OUT) BATE OMIT SKIP SLIP
ELIDE
(— PORT) CLEAR
(— QUICKLY) SCREW
(— SECRETLY) STEAL
(— SUDDENLY) KITE
LEAVEN ZYM ZYMO RAISE YEAST
INFUSE RAISING SOURING
LEAVENING EMPTINGS
LEAVES PATRIN FOLIAGE LEAFAGE
LEAFERY
(— OF BAOBAB TREE) LALO
(— OF ORCHID) FAHAM
(— OF TOBACCO) LEAF FLYINGS
SECONDS
(— ON STEM AFTER WITHERING)
INDUVIAE
(— USED AS STYPTIC) MATICO
(BOILED — OF POTHERB) CHARD
(DRIED —) LAUHALA
(MEDICINAL —) COCA FILE BUCCO
BUCKU FARFARA FUMARIA
(PALM —) ATAP ATTAP CADJAN
CAJANG
(TEA —) SOUCHONG
(WITHERED —) PININGS
LEAVE-TAKING VALE ADIEU
CONGEE PARTING WAYGANG
FAREWELL WAYGOING
LEAVING BIT
(PL.) RAFF SNUFF REFUSE RESIDUE
RESIDUUM

LEBBEK KOKO KOKKO SIRIS
LEBKUCHEN LEKACH
LECHER GOAT LUXUR PALLIARD
LECHEROUS LEWD PRIME WANTON

BOARISH CODDING GOATISH
LUSTFUL LIKEROUS SCABROUS
SPORTIVE
LECHERY LUXURY
LECTERN DESK EAGLE LUTRIN
LATERAN LATTERIN
LECTION GOSPEL EPISTLE READING
PROPHECY
LECTIONARY LEGEND
LECTOR LISTER READER
LECTURE JOBE CREED FORUM
HOMILY LECTOR LESSON SERMON
ADDRESS EARBASH HEARING
PRELECT READING JOBATION
ORDINARY
LECTURER DOCENT LECTOR
READER DRYASDUST
LEDA (DAUGHTER OF —) HELEN
CLYTEMNESTRA
(FATHER OF —) THESTIUS
(HUSBAND OF —) TYNDAREUS
(SON OF —) CASTOR POLLUX
LEDGE BEAD BERM DESS LINE STEP
ALTAR BENCH CLINT SHELF SNOUT
BEARER OFFSET SETTLE STANCE
CHANNEL LEDGING RETABLE
LEDGEMAN BREAKER
LEDGER BOOK SLAB LIEGER
JOURNAL OVERLIER
LEDGER BOARD RIBBON
LEE LEW LEEWARD
LEECH GILL HARPY LEACH APODAN
BDELLOID HELMINTH
LEEK ALLIUM PORRET SCALLION
(— COLORED) PRASINE
LEER LEAR LOOK OGLE FLEER
LEERY SKIME SMIRK TWIRE
LEERFISH GARRICK
LEES LAGS ADDLE DRAFF DREGS
DROSS GROUT AMURCA BOTTOM
DUNDER MOTHER ULLAGE
GROUNDS EMPTINGS SEDIMENT
WINEDRAF
LEEWAN SOFA DIVAN
LEEWARD DOWNWIND
LEEWAY DRIFT
LEFT G CAR KAY GAWK NEAR OTHER
TOWARD DESERTED
(— EYE) OL OS
LEFT-HAND GAUCHE
LEFT HAND MG MS SM SIN
(— PAGE) VERSO
LEFTHANDED CAR GAUCHE
AWKWARD DUBIOUS OBLIQUE
KITHOGUE SOUTHPAW
LEFT-HANDER SOUTHPAW
LEFTOVER END REMNANT
(TOBACCO —) TOPPER
(PL.) SCRAN ANALECTS
LEG ARM GAM PEG PIN CRUS GAMB
JAMB LIMB TRAM BOUGH GAMBE
JAMBE REACH SHANK STICK STUMP
BENDER GAMBON GAMMON LEGLET
MOGGAN OVIGER PESTLE PLANTA
PROLEG WALKER FORELEG
TRESTLE FORELIMB
(— OF HAWK) ARM
(— OF LAMB) GIGOT WABBLER
WOBBLER

(— OF TABLE) BALUSTER
(— OF WHEELBARROW) STILT
(— USED FOR FOOD) PESTLE
(—S OF ARTIFICAL FLY) HACKLE
(FURNITURE —) CABRIOLE
(MILK —) WEED
(TROUSER —) SLOP
(WIRE —S) SLING
(WOODEN —) PEG STUMP TIMBER
(PL.) PROPS TONGS STAMPS STICKS
LEGACY ENTAIL LEGATE BEQUEST
HERITAGE WINDFALL
LEGAL LEAL LICIT SOUND VALID
LAWFUL SQUARE JURIDIC RIGHTFUL
LEGALISM NOMISM SCRIBISM
LEGALISTIC COURT
LEGATE ENVOY DEPUTY LEGATUS
CONSULAR LEGATARY PANDOLPH
LEGATION MISSION
LEGATO SMOOTH
LEGEND EDDA MYTH POSY SAGA
TALE FABLE STORY TITLE THREAP
CUTLINE HAGGADA
(MAP —) KEY
LEGENDARY FABLED FICTIOUS
LEGERDEMAINIST JUGGLER
LEGGING SPAT COCKER BOTTINE
GAMBADO BALATONG BOOTIKIN
CHIVARRA
(LEATHER —) STRAD
(PL.) CHAPS SHANKS BROGUES
COGGERS GAMASHES LEATHERS
OVERALLS
LEGIBLE FAIR READABLE
LEGION HOST TERZO TERZIO
LEGIONARY ANT DRIVER FORAGER
LEGISLATION DYSNOMY
LAWMAKING
LEGISLATOR SOLON LAWGIVER
LAWMAKER
LEGISLATURE DIET COURT THING
LAGTING RIKSDAG LANDRATH
RIGSRAAD
LEGITIMATE JUST TRUE VERY
LEGAL LEGIT LOYAL HONEST
KINDLY KOSHER LAWFUL REABLE
SQUARE LEGITIME
LEGITIMATELY FAIRLY MULIERLY
LEGPIECE JAMBEAU
LEGUME POD GUAR PULSE LOMENT
PODDER COCHLEA LEGUMEN
PODWARE SOYBEAN STROMBUS
LEIPOA LOWAN MEGAPOD PHEASANT
LEISHMANIASIS UTA ESPUNDIA
LEISTER SPEAR WASTER
LEISURE TIME TOOM VOID OTIUM
RESPITE VACANCY VACATION
LEISURELY SLOW SOODLY TIMELY
TOOMLY GRADUAL PICKTOOTH
LEMAN UNDERPUT
LEMMING CRICETID
LEMMUS MYODES
LEMNISCUS FILET FILLET LAQUEUS
LEMON DOG DUD CEDRA CHLOR
LEMONY CEDRATE FAILURE
KUMQUAT
LEMONADE COOLER
LEMON GRASS TANGLAD
LEMON SOLE MARYSOLE

LEMON VERBENA ALOYSIA
LEMUR MAKI VARI AVAHI INDRI
  KOKAM LORIS MACAO POTTO SIFAC
  ADAPID COBEGO COLUGO GALAGO
  KUBONG MAHOLI MONKEY SIFAKA
  NATTOCK PRIMATE SEMIAPE
  TARSIER AMPONGUE BABAKOTO
  MONGOOSE PRIMATAL TARSIOID
LEND OCKER PREST SECOND
  IMPREST
  (— **AT INTEREST**) GAVEL
  (— **ITSELF**) ALLOY
LENDING (— **AGENCY**) MOUNT
LENGTH LUG DREE TOWT PITCH
  SCOPE SIDTH COURSE EXTENT
  TOWGHT FOOTAGE DISTANCE
  LEGITUDE SIDENESS
  (— **ATHWARTSHIP**) ABURTON
  (— **OF BRIDGE**) BAY
  (— **OF CABLE**) SCOPE SHACKLE
  (— **OF CHAIN**) SHOT
  (— **OF CLOTH**) CUT
  (— **OF FIBER**) STAPLE
  (— **OF FISHING LINE**) CAST
  (— **OF GEAR TOOTH**) FACE
  (— **OF HAIR IN FISHING LINE**) IMP
  (— **OF HAIR**) KNOT
  (— **OF LINE**) LOYN
  (— **OF METAL**) SHAPE
  (— **OF MOUTH**) GAPE
  (— **OF NET**) LEAD
  (— **OF ROPE**) DRIFT SPOKE BRIDLE
  COURSE STOPPER
  (— **OF SERVICE**) STANDING
  (— **OF SHOEMAKER'S THREAD**) END
  (— **OF THREAD**) STITCH
  (— **OF TILE**) GAUGE
  (— **OF TIMBER**) BALK FLITCH
  (— **OF TRIP**) GATE
  (— **OF WINDMILL ARM**) WHIP
  (— **OF YARN**) KNOT TAPE CHASE
  SKEIN
  (**AT FULL** —) ALONG
  (**CONTINUOUS** —) STRETCH
  (**FOCAL** —) FOCUS
  (**UNIT OF** —) PIC PIK ROD FOOT
  INCH KILO PIKE REED VARA WRAP
  YARD METER SHAKU POLLEX
  FURLONG PLETHRON
  (**UTMOST** —) EXTREME
ENGTHEN EKE LONG DILATE
  EXPAND EXTEND LENGTH AMPLIFY
  DISTEND PRODUCE PROLONG
  STRETCH ELONGATE INCREASE
  PROTRACT
  (— **BY INTERPOLATION**) FARSE
ENGTHENING HOLD ECTASIS
  DIASTOLE
ENGTHWISE ALONG ALENGTH
  ENDLONG ENDWAYS ENDWISE
ENGTHY LONG LARGE PROLIX
  LONGFUL EXTENDED
ENIENCY FAVOR MERCY LENITY
  LENIENCE
ENIENT LAX EASY KIND MILD SOFT
  FACILE GENTLE HUMANE LENITIVE
ENITIVE MILD MITIGANT SEDATIVE
ENITY MERCY HUMANITY KINDNESS
  LENITUDE

LENO GAUZE
LENS EYE CROWN GLASS OPTIC
  FLASER READER APLANAT BIFOCAL
  CONCAVE CONTACT DOUBLET
  ACHROMAT EYEGLASS EYEPIECE
  HYPERGON LENTICLE LUNETTES
  MENISCUS
  (**WITHOUT** —) APHAKIA
LENT CAREME IMPREST
LENTICULAR PHACOID
LENTIGO FRECKLE
LENTIL LENS LINT TILL LENTILE
  LENTICLE
LEONTOCEBUS MIDAS
LEOPARD PARD TIGER PARDAL
  WAGATI LIBBARD PAINTER PANTHER
  PARDALE
  (**SNOW** —) IRBIS OUNCE
LEPCHA RONG RONGPA
LEPER LAZAR MESEL LAZARUS
LEPIDOMELANE ANNITE
LEPIDOPTERA GLOSSATA
LEPIDOSIS SCALING
LEPRECHAUN ELF LURACAN
LEPROSY LEPRA MESEL ALPHOS
  LAZARY MESELRY
LEPROUS MESELY MESELED
LEPTON MITE
LEPTOSPIROSIS JAUNDICE
LERP LAAP
LESBIAN EROTIC TRIBADE SAPPHIST
LESION PIT GALL HIVE SORE
  CRATER ESCHAR LEPRID ANTHRAX
  CHANCRE FISSURE LEPROMA
  BEESTING ERUPTION LEUKEMID
  TERTIARY

LESOTHO
CAPITAL: MASERU
FORMER NAME: BASUTOLAND
LANGUAGE: SOTHO SESOTHO
PEOPLE: BASOTHO
RIVER: ORANGE CALEDON
TOWN: LERIBE QUTHING
  MAFETENG

LESPEDEZA SERICEA
LESS FEW MIN MENO FEWER MINOR
  LESSER SMALLER WANTING
  (— **BY A COMMA**) MINOR
LESSEE FARMER TERMOR HUURDER
  TACKSMAN
LESSEN EBB BATE DOCK EASE FAIK
  FRET KILL LESS SINK WANE ABATE
  BREAK LOWER MINCE SMALL
  BUFFER DEJECT IMPAIR INLESS
  MINIFY MINISH NARROW REBATE
  REDUCE WEAKEN AMENUSE
  ASSUAGE CURTAIL DEPLETE
  DEPRESS ELEVATE LIGHTEN
  RELIEVE SHORTEN CONTRACT
  DECREASE DEROGATE DIMINISH
  DISCOUNT EMBEZZLE MITIGATE
  MODERATE PALLIATE
  (— **FORCE**) GELD
  (— **IN VALUE**) SHRINK CHEAPEN
  (— **SENSITIVITY**) DULL
  (— **STRENGTH**) WEAR

  (— **TENSION**) RELAX
  (— **VELOCITY**) DEADEN
LESSENING LETUP
LESSER MINUTE SMALLER INFERIOR
LESSER CELANDINE PILEWORT
LESSON TAX LEAR TASK STUDY
  EXAMPLE LECTURE PRECEPT
  READING DOCUMENT LIRIPOOP
  (**DIFFICULT** —) SOAK
  (**TORAH** —) PARASHAH
LESSOR SETTER
LEST UNLESS ANANTER ANAUNTERS
LET LAT SET HIRE ALLOW LEASE
  LEAVE LETTEN PERMIT SUFFER
  TENANT
  (— **BAIT BOB**) DIB
  (— **BECOME KNOWN**) SPILL
  (— **BURN**) BISHOP
  (— **CONTINUE**) DRILL
  (— **DOWN**) DEMIT DIMIT LOWER
  STOOP STRIKE SUBMIT
  (— **FALL**) DROP VAIL AVALE AWALE
  DEPOSE
  (— **FLY**) PEG BOLT FIRE WING
  (— **GO**) DROP FAIK QUIT DEMIT
  BILEVE DEMISE DISMIT UNHAND
  DISCARD UNSEIZE
  (— **HIM TAKE**) SUM
  (— **IN**) IMMIT INLET IMMISS ADHIBIT
  (— **IT BE REPEATED**) REPET
  (— **IT STAND**) STET
  (— **KNOW**) ACQUAINT
  (— **LAND**) GAVEL
  (— **LOOSE**) FREE SLIP LIBERATE
  (— **OUT**) TEAM WAGE BREAK SPILL
  ARRENT
  (— **SLIP**) CHECK FOREGO
LETDOWN HANGOVER
LETHAL FATAL DEADLY MORTAL
LETHARGIC INERT DROWSY SLEEPY
  DORMANT COMATOSE COMATOUS
  SLUGGISH SLUMBROUS
LETHARGY STUPOR TORPOR
  SLUMBER HEBETUDE INACTION
LETO LATONA
LETT BALT
LETTER EF EL EM EN EX HE AIN AYN
  BEE CEE CHI DEE EDH ESS ETA ETH
  GEE HET JAY KAY LIL PEE SIN TEE
  VEE YOD YOK ZED ZEE ALEF ALIF
  AYIN BETA BETH BILL BULL CHIT
  DEAD HETH IOTA KAPH SHIN SORT
  YODH YOGH AITCH ALEPH BLIND
  BREVE DELTA DEMIT FAVOR GAMMA
  GIMEL GRAPH KAPPA KNOWN
  KOPPA SIGMA STAVE STIFF ZAYIN
  ACCENT ADVICE ANSWER BILLET
  CADJAN CARTEL CHARTA COCKUP
  DALETH FAVVER ITALIC LAMBDA
  LAMEDH MEDIAL SCRIPT SIGLUM
  SUNNUD SYMBOL VERSAL CODICIL
  COLLINS CONTROL DIGAMMA
  DIPLOMA EPISTLE EPSILON
  KAREETA MISSIVE SPECIAL
  AEROGRAM ASCENDER ENCYCLIC
  MONITORY NUNDINAL PASTORAL
  (— **OF DEFIANCE**) CARTEL
  (— **OF PERMISSION**) EXEAT
  (—**S DIMISSORY**) APOSTOLI

(—S OF MARQUE) MART
(ANGLO-SAXON —) EDH ETH THORN
(AUTHORIZING —) BREVE
(BEGGING —) SCREEVE
(BLACK —) GOTHIC
(BREAD AND BUTTER —) COLLINS
(CAPITAL —) CAP UNCIAL CAPITAL
FACTOTUM
(FRIENDLY —) SCREED
(LOVE —) POULET
(OFFICIAL —) BRIEF
(PAPAL —) BULL TOME ENCYCLIC
(PRIVATE —) BOOK
(SHORT —) CHIT LINE NOTE BILLET
LETTERET
(SILENT —) MUTE
(SMUGGLED —) KITE
(SUBSCRIPT —) SUBFIX
(WORD —) LOGOGRAM
(PL.) MAIL APOSTOLI
LETTER BOX APARTADO
LETTER CARRIER CORREO
MAILMAN POSTMAN
LETTERER SKETCHER
LETTERING FAC WRITE INCUSE
LETTERPRESS TEXT CAPTION
LETTING FIRMA LOCATIO
LETTING-OUT DROPPING
LETTUCE COS GRASS SALAD
KARPAS SALLET ICEBERG ROMAINE
FIREWEED MILKWEED
LEUCIPPUS (DAUGHTER OF —)
PHOEBE HILAIRA
(FATHER OF —) OENOMAUS
(WIFE OF —) PHILODICE
LEUCITE LENAD
LEUCITITE ITALITE SPERONE
ALBANITE CECILITE
LEUCOCYTE NEOCYTE HEMAMEBA
MONOCYTE OXYPHILE
LEUCOMA WALLEYE
LEUCORRHEA WHITES
LEUKEMIA CHLOROMA LEUKOSIS
LEVANT EASTERN WORMSEED
LEVEE DIKE DYKE WALL WEIR
DURBAR STOPBANK
LEVEL BONE EVEN FAIR FLAT GLAD
LUTE PLAT RAZE SHIM EQUAL
FLUSH GRADE PLAIN PLANE POINT
SLICK SOLID CHARGE DOUBLE
EVENLY FIELDY NIVEAU SLIGHT
SMOOTH STRIKE TUNNEL FLATTEN
GALLERY GANGWAY DEMOLISH
LEVELLER SUBGRADE
(— A RAFTER) EDGE
(— AFTER PLOWING) BUSH
(— AND SCATTER) GELD
(— OF SOCIETY) STRATUM
(— OF STAGE) STUDY
(— OFF) HAMMER BULLDOZE
(— PLACE) PLANILLA
(COMMON —) PAR
(ENERGY —) SINGLET
(EYE —) EYELINE
(HIGHER —S) BRASS
(HIGHEST —) SUMMIT
(LOWEST —) FLOOR BOTTOM
HARDPAN
(MINING —) HEAD GALLERY

GANGWAY
(STRATIGRAPHIC —) HORIZON
(TOP —) HIGH CEILING
LEVELED BENT
LEVELER DIGGER
LEVELING EGALITE EGALITY
LEVER KEY PRY BEAM GAUL HOOK
HORN JACK SWAY TREE FLAIL FLIRT
HELVE PEDAL PINCH PLUTO PRIZE
SPOON STANG STANK SWIPE
THROW BINDER CLUTCH COUPER
DETENT FEELER GAFFLE HAMMER
HEAVER HOPPER LOWDER PORTER
ROCKER TAPPET TILLER BALANCE
BOOTLEG POINTER RAMHEAD
SHIPPER SWINGLE TREADLE
TRIGGER TUMBLER BACKFALL
GAVELOCK SELECTOR THROTTLE
(— ARM) NIGGER
(— FOR CROSSBOW) GAFFLE
GARROT
(— FOR TURNING RUDDER) HELM
TILLER
(— IN KNITTING MACHINE) JACK
(— LIKE CANTHOOK) PEAVY PEAVIE
(— OF GIN) START
(GEARSHIFT —) STICK
(SPINNING —) BOOTLEG
(SPOKELIKE —) SWINGLE
(THROTTLE —) GUN
(WEAVING —) LAM LAMM SWELL
BINDER TIPPLER
LEVERAGE PRY PRIZE
LEVIGATE DUST
LEVITY FOLLY HUMOR GAIETY
LEVOROTATORY LAEVO LEVOGYRE
NEGATIVE
LEVY CUT TAX CESS MISE REAR
LEVEL RAISE ASSESS EXTEND
EXTENT IMPOSE IMPOST UPTAKE
IMPRESS TRIBUTE DISTRAIN
DISTRESS SHIPPAGE
(— A TAX) GELD GELT TAIL STENT
(— DISTRESS) DRIVE
(IRISH —) MART
LEVYING EXACTION
LEWD NICE BAWDY FOLLY PRIME
RANDY HARLOT IMPURE LACHES
LUBRIC RAKISH WANTON HIRCINE
LEERING LUSTFUL OBSCENE
RAMMISH SCARLET SENSUAL
WHORISH PRURIENT SLUTTISH
UNCHASTE
LEWDNESS FOLLY RAKERY
LECHERY HARLOTRY PUTANISM
LEXICON CALEPIN WORDBOOK
LIABILITY DEBT DEBIT CHARGE
TRIBUTE
LIABLE APT ABLE OPEN GUILTY
EXPOSED OBVIOUS SUBJECT
AMENABLE INCIDENT
LIAISON BOND AFFAIR LINKING
INTIMACY INTRIGUE
LIANA CIPO BEJUCO BUSHROPE
LIANG TAEL
LIAR LEAR ANANIAS BOUNCER
CRACKER CRAMMER PROCTOR
WARLOCK WERNARD FABULIST
LIBATION AMBROSIA

LIBEL DEFAME MALIGN VILIFY
SLANDER
LIBELOUS FAMOUS
LIBERAL FAIR FREE GOOD OPEN
WHIG BROAD FRANK LARGE NOBLE
SOLUTE JANNOCK PROFUSE
ADVANCED GENEROUS HANDSOME
LARGEOUS PRODIGAL SEPARATE
(CANADIAN —) GRIT
(NOT —) CHARY SPARE
LIBERAL ARTS MUSES
LIBERALITY LARGE BOUNTY
BREADTH CHARITY FREEDOM
HONESTY LARGESS
LIBERALLY LARGE BROADLY
LIBERATE FREE QUIT FRITH REMIT
UNGYVE UNWRAP DELIVER MANUMIT
RELEASE UNSLAVE UNFETTER
UNTHRALL
LIBERATION FREEDOM RELEASE
DELIVERY KAIVALYA DISCHARGE

LIBERIA
CAPITAL: MONROVIA
CUSTOM: SANDE
HILLS: BOMI
MEASURE: KUBA
MOUNTAIN: UNI NIETE NIMBA
PEOPLE: GI KRU KWA VAI VEI
GOLA KROO KROU TOMA BASSA
GIBBI GISSI GREBO KPELLE
KROOBY KRUMAN KROOBOY
MANDINGO
RIVER: CESS LOFA MANNA MORRO
DOUOBE STJOHN CAVALLA
SANPEDRO
TOWN: GRIBO REBBO HARPER
NANAKRU BUCHANAN MARSHALL

LIBERTINE PUNKER PANURGE
STRIKER LOTHARIO STRINGER
LIBERTY MAY SOC EASE LARGE
LEAVE SCOPE ACCESS STREET
FREEDOM LARGESS LICENSE
WITHGANG
(— OF ACTION) PLAY SWING
(— OF ENTRANCE) INGRESS
(— OF GOING OUT) ISH
(— OF TURNING PIGS INTO FIELDS)
SHACK
(— TO BUY AND SELL) TOLL
(— TO HUNT) CHASE
(PARTIAL — OF HAWK) HACK
(SEXUAL —) INTIMACY
(UNDUE —) HEAD
LIBERTY CAP PILLEUS
LIBIDINIZATION EGOISM
LIBIDINOUS FLESHY FLESHLY
LIBRA AS PONDUS
LIBRARY AMBRY BIBLE MUSEUM
BHANDAR BOOKERY ATHENEUM
LIBRETTO BOOK WORD TESTO
TEXTBOOK

LIBYA
ALPHABET: TIFINAGH
CAPITAL: BENGASI BENGAZI
TRIPOLI

GULF: SIDRA SIRTE
MEASURE: SAA BOZZE DONUM JABIA TEMAN BARILE MISURA MATTARO
MOUNTAIN: BETTE
OASIS: KUFRA SEBHA TAZERBO
SEAPORT: HOMS DERNA SIDRI TOBRUK BENGAZI
TOWN: HOMS SEBHA SIDRI ZAWIA ELMARJ GARIAN MURZUQ MISURATA
WEIGHT: KELE UCKIA GORRAF TERMINO KHAROUBA

LICE CREEPERS
(FISH —) EPIZOA
LICENSE CHOP GALE HEAD EXEAT LEAVE SLANG SWING BANDON CAROON FIRMAN INDULT PATENT PERMIT READER CAROOME CERTIFY CROTTLE FACULTY FREEDOM INDULTO LIBERTY LICENCE PLACARD WARRANT ESCAMBIO IMMUNITY MORTMAIN PASSPORT TEZKIRAH
(— FOR CART) CAROOME
(— PLATE) NUMBER
(PEDDLER'S —) SLANG
LICENTIOUS GAY LAX FREE LEWD WILD FRANK LARGE LOOSE FILTHY UNRULY WANTON CYPRIAN FLESHLY IMMORAL LAWLESS LIBERAL UNYOKED
LICENTIOUSNESS DIRT LICENSE
LICHEN RAG MANNA USNEA ORCHIL CROTTAL CROTTLE CUDBEAR EVERNIA OAKMOSS PARELLA ARCHILLA CAREWEED LECANORA LUNGWORT PARMELIA ROCKHAIR TREEHAIR WARTWORT
LICIT LEGAL LAWFUL LEEFUL
LICK LAP LIKE SUCK MOUTH SLAKE CONQUER
LICKER-IN TUMBLE
LICKING GRUELING
LICORICE POMFRET SWEETROOT
LICORICE PILL CACHOU
LICYMNIUS (FATHER OF —) ELECTRYON
(SISTER OF —) ALCMENA
(SLAYER OF —) TLEPOLEMUS
LID DIP BRED DECK TYMP COVER BRIDLE EYELID POTLID CLAPPER CLICKET CLOSURE SCUTTLE SHUTTER COVERCLE
LIE FIB GAB LAY LIG LIN SIT YED CRAM FALL FLAW LIGG REST RIDE WHID DEVIL DWELL FABLE FEIGN LEASE STAND STORY FITTEN RAPPER RESIDE SPRAWL VANITY BOUNCER CONSIST CRACKER CRAMMER CRUMPER FALSITY GRABBLE LEASING PLUMPER TWISTER UNTRUTH WHACKER WHISKER WHOPPER
(— ALONGSIDE) ACCOST
(— AROUND) COMPASS
(— AT ANCHOR) HOVE

(— AT FULL LENGTH) STRETCH
(— CONCEALED) DARKLE
(— CONTIGUOUS) CONFINE
(— DETECTOR) POLYGRAPH
(— DORMANT) SLEEP
(— DOWN) LEAN COUCH CHARGE
(— FLAT ON BELLY) GROVEL
(— HEAD TO WIND) TRY
(— HIDDEN) LURK MICHE TAPPISH
(— IN AMBUSH) HUGGER
(— IN BED) KIP THOKE
(— IN WAIT) AWAIT LOWER AMBUSH FORELAY
(— IN WATER) DOUSE DROWN
(— NEXT TO) ADJOIN
(— OPPOSITE TO) SUBTEND
(— OVER) COVER
(— PRONE) GROVEL GRABBLE
(— PROSTRATE) STREEK
(— QUIET) SNUDGE
(— SNUG) CUDDLE
(— UNEVENLY) SAG
(— WITH SAILS FURLED) HULL
(IMPUDENT —) BOUNCE
(MONSTROUS —) STRAMMER

LIECHTENSTEIN
CAPITAL: VADUZ
CASTLE: VADUZ GUTEMBURG
MOUNTAIN: RHATIKON
RIVER: RHINE
ROMAN NAME: RHAETIA
TOWN: HAAG BALZER SCHAAN NENDELN
TRIBE: ALAMANNI

LIED BALLAD
LIEF DEAR LEAVE LEEVE LIEVE FREELY GLADLY BELOVED
LIEUTENANT LUFF ZANY LOUEY JAYGEE KEHAYA CAIMAKAM QAIMAQAM TENIENTE WOODVILE
LIFE IT VIE ZOE HIDE JIVA PUFF SNAP TUCK VALE ANIMA BEING BLOOD DEMON HEART LIFER QUICK SWEAT BIOSIS BREATH CANDLE COURSE ENERGY SPIRIT SPRITE LIFELET LIFEWAY VITALITY VIVACITY
(— AFTER DEATH) FUTURITY
(— IN HEAVEN) GLORY
(— IN SOCIETY) SAMSARA SANSARA
(— OF FURNACE LINING) CAMPAIGN
(— OF THE SEA) HALIBIOS
(ACADEMIC —) ACADEMIA
(ANIMAL —) FLESH
(ANIMAL AND PLANT —) BIOS BIOTA BIOLOGY EDAPHON
(CLOISTERED —) VEIL
(INTELLECTUAL —) JIVATMA
(MONASTIC —) CLOISTER
(MORAL —) DAENA
(MOSS —) BRYOLOGY
(PLANT —) FLORA BOTANY
(ROBUST —) JUICE
(SINGLE —) CELIBACY
(TERRESTRIAL —) GEOBIOS
(WITHOUT —) AZOIC
LIFE BELT SAFETY
LIFEBLOOD BLOOD SWEAT

LIFELESS ARID DEAD DULL FLAT AMORT HEAVY INERT VAPID ANEMIC TORPID SAPLESS DESOLATE GRIPLESS INACTIVE
LIFELESSLY DEADLY INERTLY
LIFELESSNESS ANEMIA
LIFELIKE VIVE QUICK EIDETIC ANIMATED SPEAKING
LIFE PRESERVER FLOAT NEDDY
LIFETIME AGE DAY WORLD LIVING LIFEDAY DURATION LIFELONG
LIFT WIN BOOM BUOY CAST COCK HEFT JACK REAR TOSS WEVE BOOST BREAK ELATE HEAVE HITCH HOICK HOIST HOOSH MOUNT PRESS RAISE SPOUT STEAL WEIGH BUCKET CLEECH SNATCH ELEVATE ENHANCE HEELTAP NAUNTLE BOOKLIFT CHAIRWAY ELEVATOR LEVITATE
(— HAT) DOFF
(— IN VEHICLE) SETDOWN
(— OF WAVE) SCEND
(— ONESELF) SOAR
(— QUICKLY) PERK
(— UP) HOVE CRANE ERECT EXALT EXTOL HORSE WEIGH ADVANCE ELEVATE NAUNTLE
(— WITH BLOCK AND TACKLE) BOUSE
LIFTED ARRECT SUBLIME
LIFTER GAGGER SERVER HOISTER HOISTMAN
LIFTING HIKE UPTAKE
LIFT VALVE POPPET
LIGAMENT BAND BOND ARTERY PAXWAX STRING ZONULE ARMILLA LIGATURE
LIGAMENTOUS DESMOID
LIGATE BAR
LIGATURE CLAM PLICA DIGRAM PNEUMA STIGMA DIGRAPH LIGAMENT LIGATION
LIGGER TRIMMER
LIGHT BUG DAY GAY HAP LAW SHY SUN AIRY EASY FAIR FALL FINE FIRE FLUX GLIM LAMP LEET LUNT MILD SLUT SOFT BAVIN BLAZE CORKY FANAL FILMY FLAME FLEET FUFFY LEGER LOUGH MERRY PITCH QUICK SHEER SPILL WHITE BEACON BRIGHT CHAFFY FLOATY FLOSSY FLUFFY FROTHY GENTLE HAPPEN ILLUME KINDLE LANCET LUSTER LUSTRE MARKER PASTEL PHAROS SIGNAL SLUSHY STINGY STRIKE SUTTLE VOLAGE BENGOLA BUOYANT CRESSET FRAGILE GLITTER LAMBENT SFOGATO SMITHER SUMMERY TORTAYS TRIVIAL UNGRAVE BACKFIRE DAYLIGHT DELICATE DIAPHANE ELECTRIC EXPEDITE FEATHERY GASLIGHT GOSSAMER LEGGIERO LUMINARY PALOUSER SUNLIGHT SUNSHINE
(— AND BRILLIANT) LAMBENT
(— AND FIRE ON HORSE'S MANE) HAG
(— AND FREE) FLYAWAY

(— AND QUICK) VOLANT
(— CANDLES) TOLLY
(— FROM NIGHT SKY) AIRGLOW
(— IN WINDOW) LANCET
(— OF MORNING) AURORA
(— ON TV SCREEN) SNOW
(— UP) FLASH GLOZE ILLUME
RELUME GLORIFY
(— UPON) STRIKE
(BRIGHT —) GLARE GLEAM
(BURST OF —) FLASH
(CIRCLE OF —) HALO NIMBUS
(FAINT —) GLIMMER SCARROW
(FEEBLE —) GLIMMER
(FITFUL —) SHIMMER
(HARBOR —) BUG
(INNER —) SEED
(NEW —) SEPARATE
(NIGHT —) MORTAR
(PARKING —S) DIMMERS
(PERSIAN GOD OF —) MITHRAS
(REFLECTED —) SKYME
(SHIP'S —) FANAL
(SMALL —) TAPER
(TRAFFIC —) BLINKER
(WAVERING —) FLICKER
LIGHT-COLORED BLONDE
LIGHTEN CLEAR LEVIN LIGHT RAISE
ALLEGE BLEACH ENCLEAR FOULDRE
MOLLIFY SWEETEN THUNDER
LEVIGATE
LIGHTENING BREAK
LIGHTER SCOW ACCON CASCO
WHERRY DROGHER GABBARD
PONTOON CHOPBOAT
LIGHTERMAN KEELER KEELMAN
LIGHT-HEADED IDLE LIGHT LIVELY
CARRIED GLAIKET
LIGHT-HEARTED GAY GLAD GIDDY
WINSOME CAREFREE DEBONAIR
VOLATILE
LIGHTHEARTEDNESS BUOYANCY
LIGHTHOUSE FANAL LIGHT BEACON
PHAROS LANTERN
LIGHTLESS APHOTIC
LIGHTLY LIGHT AIRILY FAIRILY
HOVERLY LEGGIERO SLIGHTLY
LIGHT-MINDED BLITHE
LIGHTNESS CHEER VALUE GAIETY
LEVITY AIRINESS BUOYANCY
LEGERETE LEGERITY
(— OF MOVEMENT) BALLON
LIGHTNING BOLT FIRE LAIT LEVIN
FULMEN METEOR FOULDRE
SULPHUR THUNDER FIREBALL
FIREBOLT WILDFIRE
LIGHT-O'-LOVE LEVERET
LIGHT-TEXTURED FOZY
LIGHTWOOD FATWOOD
LIGIA LIGYDA
LIGNEOUS WOODY XYLOID
LIGNIN LIGNOSE XYLOGEN
LIGNUM VITAE GUAYACAN
POCKWOOD
LIGROIN BENZINE CANADOL
LIGULA LANGUET
LIGULE STRAP LIGULA
LIKE AS DIG DOTE LIST LOVE ALIKE
ENJOY EQUAL FANCY SAVOR TASTE

ADMIRE AFFECT BELIKE LIKELY
MATTER PLEASE SEMBLE SIMILE
CONCEIT SIMILAR SEMBLANT
SUITABLE
(— A GLAND) ADEMOSE ADENOUS
(— BETTER) PREFER
(— HAIR) CRINITE
(VERY —) SIAMESE
LIKELIHOOD APTNESS
LIKELY APT FAIR LIKE READY LIABLE
PROOFY SEEMLY GRADELY SMITTLE
APPARENT FEASIBLE POSSIBLE
PROBABLE
(MOST —) BELIKE
LIKEN EVEN LIKE REMENE SEMBLE
COMPARE SMILIZE ASSEMBLE
RESEMBLE
LIKENESS DAP BLEE ICON IDOL
MAKE SECT BLUSH DUMMY GLIFF
IMAGE MORAL SHAPE EFFIGY
FIGURE STATUE KINSHIP PATTERN
PICTURE RETRAIT EQUALITY
HOMOLOGY PARALLEL PORTRAIT
(PERFECT —) SPIT
LIKEWISE EKE TOO ALSO ITEM
EITHER EQUALLY LIKEWAYS
(— NOT) NOR
LIKING GOO GRA PAY GOUT GUST
LIKE LUST FANCY FLAIR GUSTO
HEART SHINE SKILL SMACK TASTE
THEAT SWALLOW AFFINITY
APPETITE FONDNESS
(ECCENTRIC —) FOIBLE
LILAC LILAS MAUVE LAYLOCK
LILACIN SYRINGIN
LILY IXIA KELP SEGO AZTEC CALLA
CLOTE AUGUST LILIUM VALLEY
COCUISA MONOCOT LILYWORT
MARTAGON NENUPHAR
(CLIMBING —) GLORIOSA
(PALM —) TI
(SEA —) CRINOID
(WATER —) CANDOCK CAMALOTE
LILY OF THE VALLEY LILIUM
MUGGET MUGUET MUGWET
LILYWORT SHINLEAF
LIMA BEAN HABA LIMA
LIMB ARM LEG CLAW FOOT KNOT
LITH TRAM WING ARTUS BOUGH
SPALD SPAUL SWAMP BRANCH
MEMBER PODITE FEATURE FLIPPER
FORCEPS NECTOPOD
LIMBA AFARA FRAKE
LIMBER BAIN FLIP LIMP LUSH LINGY
LITHE LISSOM SEMMIT SUPPLE
SWANKY BRUSHER BRUTTER
KNOTTER LIMMOCK PLIABLE
FLEXIBLE FLIPPANT
LIME CALX LIMA CEDRA CEDRAT
CHUNAM CITRON FUSTIC
(— IN BRICK) BOND
(WILD —) COLIMA
LIMESTONE HUM CAUK LIAS LYAS
MALM POROS CLUNCH KUNKUR
PISOLITE
(— REGION) KARST
LIME TREE LIME TEIL LINDEN
LIMIT END FIX BIND BUTT FINE HOLD
LINE LIST MARK MERE TAIL BLOCK

BOUND GAUGE HEDGE STENT STINT
VERGE BORDER BOURNE DEFINE
EFFLUX EXTENT FINISH FINITE
HAMPER LENGTH MODIFY NARROW
PALING SCRIMP TROPIC UPSHOT
ASTRICT CLOSURE COMPASS
CONFINE CONTENT HORIZON
MAXIMUM MEASURE BOUNDARY
CONTRACT DEADLINE IMPRISON
LIMITARY LIMITATE OUTGOING
RESTRAIN RESTRICT SOLSTICE
TERMINUS
(— EFFECT) ALLAY
(— IN A FOREST) BAIL
(— MOTION) HOLD
(— OF VISION AT SEA) KENNING
(EXTREME —) HEIGHT
(LOWER —) FLOOR
(UPPER —) CEILING
(UTTER —) EXTREME
(PL.) AMBIT CANCELS ENVIRONS
LIMITATION TAIL FRAME STINT
DENIAL CLOTURE RESERVE
(PL.) SWADDLE
LIMITED TAIL BORNE BRIEF SHORT
SMALL FINITE NARROW STINTY
STRAIT BOUNDED SPECIAL
CONFINED DEFINITE LIMITARY
(— IN APPEAL) CHICHI
LIMITING DEFINITE ADJECTIVE
EXCLUSIVE
LIMMA DIESIS
LIMMU EPONYM
LIMONENE CINENE CARVENE
CITRENE
LIMONIUM STATICE
LIMOUSINE BERLIN SUBURBAN
LIMP HIP HOP CLOP GIMP HALT HIMP
HOIT SOFT THIN HENCH HILCH
HITCH LINGY LOOSE LOPPY SLAMP
STILT FLABBY FLIMSY HAMBLE
HIMPLE HIRPLE HOBBLE LENNOW
LIMBER LIMPSY FLACCID LIMMOCK
SHAFFLE UNSMART DRAGGLED
DROOPING
LIMPET CHINK OPIHI SHELL ACMAEA
LIMPIN FLIDDER
LIMPID PURE CLEAR LUCID BRIGHT
CRYSTAL PELLUCID
LIMPING LAME GIMPY LIMPY ZOPPA
HALTING
LIMPLY LANKLY
LINAGE SPACE
LINALOOL LICAREOL
LINCHPIN FORELOCK
LINCTUS LOOCH LOHOCH LOHOCK
LINDEN LIN LIME LYNE TEIL TILIA
TILLET LINWOOD BASSWOOD
DADDYNUT WOODLIND
LINE BAR BOX FIX RAY ROW TAW
BOFF CASE CEIL COLA CRIB DASH
FACE FILE GAME GAPE LACE LARD
LATH LEAD LING MAIN MARK RACE
RANK RULE STOP TAUM WHIP
AGONE FAINT FEINT FLEET HATCH
LIGNE LINEA METER RANGE SCORE
STRIA TOUCH TRACE TRAIL TRAIN
TWIST BINDER CABURN CEVIAN
CREASE DEGREE DOUBLE EARING

GASKET ISOBAR ISOHEL ISOPAG ISOTAC METIER NETTLE SECANT SECOND SPRING STRING STRIPE AZIMUTH BABBITT CATLINE CONTOUR CREANCE ENVELOP GUNLINE HIPLINE ISOCHOR ISOGRAM ISOHYET ISONEPH ISORITH ISOSTER ISOTOME KNITTLE MARLINE NACARAT SCRATCH WINDROW BALKLINE BISECTOR BOUNDARY BUSINESS CHAMPAIN DATELINE DEADLINE DIAGONAL DIAMETER DRAGLINE DRUMLINE FISHBACK GANTLINE GEODESIC GIRTLINE HAIRLINE HANDLINE HEXAPODY ISOGLOSS ISOGONIC ISOPHANE ISOPHENE ISOPLERE ISOTHERE ISOTHERM LANDWIRE LIFELINE MARTINET SLIPBAND STRINGER SUBCLONE SUBSTILE SUBSTYLE UPSTROKE

(— **AROUND STAMP**) FRAME
(— **AS CENTER FOR REVOLVING**) AXIS
(— **HEARTH**) FIX FETTLE
(— **IN GLASS**) STRING
(— **IN HAT**) HEADLINE
(— **MINESHAFT**) TUB
(— **OF ACTION**) LAY
(— **OF BATTLE**) FRONT
(— **OF BUSINESS**) WAY
(— **OF CELLS**) ANNULUS
(— **OF CLIFFS**) SCARP BREAKS
(— **OF COLOR**) SLASH STREAK
(— **OF DANCERS**) CHAIN
(— **OF DESCENT**) SIDE STEM STIRP STOCK STRAIN ANCESTRY
(— **OF DETERMINANT**) COLUMN
(— **OF DEVELOPMENT**) STREET
(— **OF DEVOLUTION**) ENTAIL
(— **OF FIBERS**) CHRYSAL
(— **OF FIRE HOSE**) LEAD
(— **OF FLOTATION**) BEARINGS
(— **OF FORTIFICATION**) LIMES ENCEINTE
(— **OF HAY**) WAKE WALLOW
(— **OF HEALTH**) HEPATICA
(— **OF HIGH TIDE**) LANDWASH
(— **OF HOUSES**) BLOCK
(— **OF INTERSECTION**) GROIN BUTTOCK
(— **OF JUNCTION**) MEET SEAM
(— **OF MERCURY**) HEPATICA
(— **OF PERSONS**) QUEUE CORDON STICKLE
(— **OF PORES**) HATCHING
(— **OF SOLDIERS**) RAY FILE RANK WAVE CORDON
(— **OF STITCHING**) BASTING
(— **OF TIMBERS**) BOOM STOCKADE
(— **OF TREES**) SCREEN
(— **OF TYPE**) SLUG KICKER
(— **OF UNION**) SUTURE
(— **ON A LETTER**) SERIF
(— **ON BOOK COVER**) BAND
(— **ON COAT**) GORGE
(— **ON DOLPHIN**) STOP
(— **ON HIGHWAY**) BARRIER
(— **THAT CUTS ANOTHER**) SECANT

(— **TO BIND CABLES**) CABURN
(— **TO FASTEN SAIL**) EARING GASKET
(— **TO RAISE FLAG**) LANIARD LANYARD
(— **TO START RACE**) TRIG
(— **TOUCHING ARC**) TANGENT
(— **UP**) LAY
(— **WITH BRICKS**) GINGE
(— **WITH PANELLING**) WAINSCOT
(— **WITH STONES**) STEEN STEYN
(— **WITH TIMBER**) CRIB
(**42 —S**) LENGTH
(**ANCHOR —**) RODING
(**BEARING —**) CUT
(**BOUNDARY —**) MERE FENCE BORDER ISOGLOSS
(**BOUNDING —**) SIDE BOUNDARY
(**BRIEF —**) ITEM
(**COASTAL —**) SEAMARK
(**CONNECTING —**) LIGATURE
(**CONTINUOUS —**) STRETCH
(**CURVED —**) ARC SLUR SWEEP
(**DEMARCATION —**) BOMBLINE
(**DIAGONAL —**) BIAS
(**DIVIDING —**) EDGE MIDRIB DIVISION FRONTIER
(**ELECTRIC —**) HIGHLINE
(**FACIAL —**) TRAIT
(**FINISHING —**) TAPE WIRE
(**FISHING —**) TOME TROT FLEET SNELL SNOOD LEADER LEDGER NORSEL BACKING BOULTER SPILLER SPILLET TRIMMER BLOWLINE CORKLINE FISHLINE SNAGLINE TROTLINE
(**HORIZONTAL —**) LEVEL
(**IMAGINARY —**) AGONE HINGE GROOVE ISOBAR ISOGAM ISOHEL ISOPAG HORIZON ISOBASE ISOBATH ISOGRIV ISOHYET ISOLINE ISOTACH ISOBRONT ISOCHASM ISOCHEIM ISOCHLOR ISOCHORE ISOCRYME ISOPHOTE ISOPLETH ISOSTERE ISOTHERM
(**INCLINED —**) CANT
(**LONGITUDINAL —**) MERIDIAN
(**MEDIAN —**) RAPHE
(**METRICAL —**) EIGHT STAFF STICH DIMETER SAPPHIC STICHOS
(**MUSICAL —**) ACCOLADE
(**NAUTICAL —**) EARING LACING GESWARP MARLINE RATLINE DOWNHAUL
(**ONE-TENTH OF —**) GRY
(**PLOTTED —**) ADIABAT
(**RADIATING —**) BEAM
(**RAILROAD —**) STEM STUB
(**RAISED —**) RIDGE
(**SPECTRUM —**) GHOST DOUBLET SINGLET TRIPLET
(**STARTING —**) SCRATCH
(**STRAIGHT —**) CHORD BEELINE STRAIGHT
(**SUPPLY —**) AIRLIFT
(**SURVEYING —**) WAD BASE CHAIN
(**THEATRICAL —S**) FAT
(**TOW —**) CORDELLE
(**TRANSPORTATION —**) FEEDER CARRIER

(**WAVY —**) SQUIGGLE
LINEAGE GET KIN KIND RACE TEAM BIRTH BLOOD SPACE STIRP STOCK FAMILY HAVAGE NATION PARAGE SOURCE SPRING STRAIN DESCENT KINDRED PROGENY SUCCESS ANCESTRY PEDIGREE
LINEAL DIRECT
LINEAMENT LINE TRACT TRAIT FEATURE
LINEAR RUNNING
LINECUT ZINCO
LINED MASONED
LINEMAN FORWARD WIREMAN CHAINMAN
LINEN LIN LAWN IRISH TOILE BARRAS DAMASK DIAPER RAINES SENDAL HOLLAND LOCKRAM TABLING BARANDOS OSNABURG PLATILLA
(— **CLOSET**) LOCKER
(— **FOR SHIRTS**) SARKING
(**CHINESE —**) KOMPOW
(**COARSE —**) HARN BARRAS
(**FINE —**) LAKE LAWN DAMASK DIAPER RAINES
(**HOUSEHOLD —**) NAPERY TABLING
(**SCRAPED —**) LINT
(**SPANISH —**) CREA
LINER SHIP BASKET SCRIBER STEAMER
LINEUP SHOWUP
LING BURBOT DRIZZLE STOKVIS
LINGA DILDO
LINGCOD CULTUS
LINGER LAG HANG HOVE LING STAY CLING DALLY DELAY DEMUR DWELL HAUNT HOVER PAUSE TARRY DRETCH HANKER LOITER TARROW DRINGLE
LINGERER LUNGIS LAGGARD
LINGERIE FRILLIES PRETTIES
LINGERING SLOW DELAY MOROSE TARDANT DRAGGING
LINGO BAT CANT LINGUA PATTER DIALECT
LINGUA GLOSSA TONGUE
LINGUAL GLOSSAL
LINGUISTIC GLOTTIC
LINGUISTICS GRAMMAR PHILOLOGY
LINIMENT EIK EMBROCHE OPODELDOC
LININ PLASTIN
LINING FUR BACK COAT BAIZE BRASS FACING PANNEL BABBITT BUSHING CEILING FURRING FURRURE THIMBLE TINNING TUBBING CLEADING DOUBLING DOUBLURE FIREBACK SHEETING UNDERLAY WAINSCOT
(— **FOR WELL**) STEENING STEYNING
(— **OF BEARING**) JEWEL
(— **OF FURNACE**) BASQUE FIREBACK
(— **OF HAT**) TIP
LINK JAR TIE TOW JOIN KNIT LUNT SHUT YOKE NEXUS COPULA COUPLE FASTEN FETTER TOUGHT CODETTA CONNECT COUPLER ENCHAIN

INVOLVE LIAISON SHACKLE
CATENATE IDENTIFY VINCULUM
(— ARMS) CLEEK
(— IN NETWORK) LEG
(COMPOUND —) SWIVEL
(WOODEN —) LAG
LINKAGE BOND CELL COUPLING
LINKWORK
LINKED CONNEX INTEGRAL
LINKING HOOKUP ANNECTANT
(— DEVICE) LINCHPIN
LINKMAN LINKBOY LIGHTMAN
LINNET FINCH TWITE LENARD LINTIE
REDPOLL REDFINCH
LINSANG CIVET ZINSANG
LINSEED LINGET
LINSEY-WOOLSEY WINCEY
LINT FLY FLUE FLICK CADDIS
CADDICE CHARPIE CARBASUS
(SCRAPED —) XYSTUS
LINTEL CAP CLAVY HANCE CLAVEL
DARNER SUMMER SQUINCH
TRANSOM
LION CAT LLEW MORNE SHEDU
SIMBA LIONEL LIONET LEOPARD
(MOUNTAIN —) PUMA COUGAR
LION MONKEY LEONCITO
LION-TAILED MONKEY MACACO
MACAQUE WANDEROO
LIP BLOB MASK PUSS APRON CHOPS
GROIN MOUTH SPOUT TUTEL
LABIUM LABRUM ROUTER CHILOMA
LABELLUM UNDERLIP
(— DISEASE) PERLECHE
(— OF BELL) SKIRT
(— OF COROLLA) GALEA
(— OF ORCHID) SLIPPER
(— OF PITCHER) BEAK
(—S OF MOOSE) MUFFLE
(FLAT —) APRON
(LOWER —) JIB FIPPLE
(PL.) LABRAS CUSHION
LIPASE PIALYN
LIPIDE CERIDE ADIPOID STERIDE
TETHELIN
LIPOCHROME LUTEIN
LIPOMA STEATOMA
LIPPED LABIATE
LIPPIA WRIGHT ALOYSIA
LIP PLUG LABRET TEMETA
LIPPY STIMPART
LIQUEFIED FUSILE POTATE REMISS
RESOLVED
LIQUEFY RUN FUSE MELT RELENT
LIQUATE DISSOLVE ELIQUATE
LIQUEUR EAU OUZO RAKI AURUM
CREME NOYAU CHASSE GENEPI
KUMMEL PERNOD STREGA ANESONE
CORDIAL CURACAO PERSICO
RATAFIA RATIFIA ABSINTHE
ALKERMES ANGELICA ANISETTE
MANDARIN PRUNELLE VESPETRO
(PL.) EAUX
LIQUID AQUA BLASH DRINK FLUID
LEACH MOIST ACETAL FLUENT
FURANE AEROSOL BUCKING
CINEOLE EYEWASH FLOWAGE
VINASSE BLACKING EFFLUENT
EFFUSION EXCITANT FURFURAN

LEACHATE LIBATION SOLUTION
(— IN CELL) EXCITANT
(— UNIT) TUN CHENG SHENG SHING
POTTLE MUTCHKIN PUNCHEON
(ACID-RESISTANT —) GROUND
(COLORING —) HENNA
(COOKING —) BREE BROO BROTH
STOCK
(DISTILLED —) SPIRIT
(FILTHY —) ADDLE
(INSULATING —) ASKAREL
(OILY —) ANILINE CHLORAL
PICAMAR CARDANOL CREOSOTE
(PERFUMED —) COLLEN COLOGNE
(REFUSE —) SCOURAGE
(REFUSE —S) SEWAGE
(SIZING —) GLAIK
(STERILIZED —) JOHNIN
(SYRUPY —) HONEY
(TANNING —) LIME
(THICK —) DOPE SIRUP SYRUP
(VISCOUS —) TAR SCHRADAN
(VOLATILE —) ETHER ALCOHOL
DILUENT LIGROIN
(WEAK —) BLASH SLIPSLOP
LIQUIDATE SINK SETTLE
LIQUIDATION CLEANUP
LIQUOR ALE BUB DEW GAS LAP OKE
PAD POT RUM SUP TAP WET BEER
BREE FIRE FIZZ GEAR GROG LUSH
PURL SUCK SWIG TAPE TIFF BOGUS
BUDGE CEBUR DRINK GLASS
HOOCH KEFIR MOBBY NAPPY PERRY
PISCO SAUCE SHRAB SHRUB SICER
SKINK STICK BOTTLE CASSIS
CHICHA DIDDLE DOCTOR FOGRAM
FUDDLE GATTER GENEVA GUZZLE
HYDROL KIRSCH MASTIC MESCAL
POTTLE ROTGUT SAMSHU STRUNT
TIPPLE WHISKY BITTERN BRACKET
BRAGGET GROCERY PHLEGMA
SPUNKIE SUCTION TAPLASH
TEQUILA WAIPIRO WHISKEY
ABSINTHE BRAGWORT EYEWATER
HYDROMEL MEDICINE OKOLEHAO
POTATION RUMBOOZE FIREWATER
(— CABINET) TANTALUS
(— CASE) GARDEVIN
(— FROM MUST) ARROPE
(— FROM PEARS) PERRY PERRIE
(— FROM WOOL-SCOURING) SUD
SUDS
(— MIXED WITH WINE) DOCTOR
(— SALE) ABKARI
(— TAKEN IN SODA WATER) CINDER
(ACID —) VERJUICE
(ALCOHOLIC —) GIN ARAK HOOCH
ARRACK BRANDY SAMSHU AQUAVIT
BITTERS SNOOTFUL
(ALCOHOLIC —S) ARDENT
(BITTER —) TIRE
(CHEAP —) SMOKE
(COLORLESS —) GLYCID GLYCOL
GLYCIDOL GUAIACOL
(CRAB APPLE —) WHERRY
(DISTILLED —) DEW SOTOL GRAPPA
PHLEGM SCHNAPPS
(DRUGGED —) HOCUS
(HARD —) BOOZE

(INTOXICATING —) GROG LOAD
LUSH TAPE BUDGE GUZZLE KUMISS
HASHISH
(MALT —) ALE BUB BEER STOUT
ENTIRE PORTER
(MOTHER —) HYDROL BITTERN
(RICE —) SAMSHU
(SPIRITUOUS —) DEW GROG MOBBY
STRUNT WAIPIRO KAOLIANG
(STRAIGHT —) SHORT
(STRONG —) RUG TUBA VINO
HOGAN RUMBO STINGO
(TAN —) OOZE
(TANNING —) LAYAWAY TAILING
(WEAK —) SLIPSLOP
LIRA LIRE ZWANZIGER
(ONE-TWENTIETH —) SOLDO
LIRIPIPE TIPPET
LISSOME LITHE LIMBER NIMBLE
SUPPLE FLEXIBLE
LIST TIP BILL FILE HEEL LEET NOTE
POLL ROLL ROTA SWAG BRIEF
CANON GISTS INDEX PANEL SCORE
SCRIP SCROW SLATE AGENDA
CENSUS COLUMN DETAIL DOCKET
ERRATA HUDDLE LEGEND PURREL
RAGGER RAGMAN ROSTER SCREED
SCROLL SERIES CATALOG CITATOR
COMPILE DIPTYCH ITEMIZE LISTING
NOTITIA WAYBILL CALENDAR
CINCTURE HANDLIST PLATBAND
REGISTER SCHEDULE SYNONYMY
TITULARY
(— OF BOOKS) CANON
(— OF CANDIDATES) LEET SLATE
TERNA
(— OF CONTESTANTS) DRAW
SEEDING
(— OF JURORS) TALES
(— OF MAP SYMBOLS) LEGEND
(— OF PASSERS WITHOUT HONORS)
GULF
(— OF RATES) TARIFF
(— OF THEATRICAL PARTS) CAST
(GENEALOGICAL —) BEGATS
(IMPRESSIVE —) ARRAY
(LEGAL —) TABLEAU
(PRAYER —) BEADROLL
(WINE —) CARD
(PL.) CAREER
LISTEL QUADRA
LISTEN HARK HEAR LIST TEND
TENEZ ATTEND HARKEN INTEND
WHISPER
(— TO) DIG EAR HARK HEAR CATCH
ATTEND
LISTENER AUDITOR OTACUST
LISTENING PRICK AUDIENT HEARING
LISTER SULKY RIDGER
LISTERA OPHRYS
LISTING ITEM FRAME PARADE
LASHING
(— OF JURORS) ARRAY
LISTLESS DOPY DULL DOWFF FAINT
DONSIE SUPINE LANGUID UNLISTY
UNLUSTY CARELESS INDOLENT
UNHEARTY
LISTLESSLY DAVIELY
LISTLESSNESS APATHY UNLUST

LITANY AITESIS ROGATION
LITERAL VERBAL
LITERALLY SIMPLY
LITERARY BLUE BOOKISH LITERATE
(— **MATERIAL**) KITSCH
LITERATE LETTERED
LITERATI CLERISY
LITERATURE FICTION LETTERS
CLAPTRAP
(**SACRED** —) VEDA SRUTI
(**WISDOM** —) CHOKMAH HOKHMAH
LITHE BAIN SWACK CLEVER LIMBER
SILKEN SUPPLE SVELTE WANDLE
LISSOME FLEXIBLE

LITHUANIA
CAPITAL: KOVNO KAUNAS
COIN: LIT LITAS MARKA CENTAS
   FENNIG OSTMARK AUKSINAS
   SKATIKAS
NAME: LITVA LIETUVA
PEOPLE: BALT LETT ZHMUD
   LITVAK YATVYAG
RIVER: NERIS RUSNE DUBYSA
   NEMUNAS PREGOLYA
TOWN: MEMEL VILNA JELGAVA
   VILNIUS KAPSUKAS KLAIPEDA
   SIAULIAI

LITHUANIAN BALT ZHMUD
LITIGANT SUITOR
LITIGATE LAW PLEAD CONTEST
LITIGATION LAW LIS MOOT SUIT
LAWING PLEADING PLEASHIP
LITMUS LAKMUS TURNSOLE
LITOTES MEIOSIS
LITTER DIG PIG BIER RAFF REDD
BREED CABIN CLECK DOOLY DRECK
HAULM MULCH SEDAN DOOLIE
FARROW GOCART KINDLE KITTEN
MAHMAL REFUSE CLUTTER LETTIGA
LOUSTER MAMMOCK NORIMON
RUMMAGE SCAMBLE BRANCARD
CARRIAGE KINDLING MUNCHEEL
PAVILION STRETCHER
(— **FOR LIVESTOCK**) BEDDING
(— **OF PIGS**) FAR FARE FARROW
(— **ON PACK ANIMAL**) CACOLET
(**FOREST** —) DUFF
LITTERED FOUL
LITTLE FEW LIL WEE LITE TINY VEEN
CHOTA CRUMB SMALL TASTE
WHONE BITTIE DAPPER LEETLE
MINUTE PETITE PICKLE PUSILL
KENNING MODICUM THOUGHT
FRACTION SNIPPING
(— **BY LITTLE**) EDGINGLY INCHMEAL
(— **LESS THAN**) ABOUT
(— **MUSICALLY**) POCO
(— **ONE**) BUTCHA POPPET
(**A** —) SOMEWHAT
(**INDEFINITELY** —) NTH
LITTLENESS ATOMITY
LITTORAL COAST
LITURGY FORM RITE ABODAH
MAARIB MINHAG NEILAH MINCHAH
MYSTERY HIERURGY SHAHARIT
LIVE BE USE WIN KEEP LEAD STAY

ALERT ALIVE DWELL EXIST GREEN
HABIT LEEVE QUICK SHACK VITAL
HARBOR LIVELY LIVING REMAIN
RESIDE BREATHE INHABIT SUBSIST
CONTINUE CONVERSE VIGOROUS
(— **AT ANOTHER'S EXPENSE**)
COSHER
(— **BY BEGGING**) CADGE SKELDER
(— **BY STRATAGEMS**) SHARK
(— **FROM DAY TO DAY**) EKE
(— **IN CONTINENCE**) CONTAIN
(— **IN LUXURY**) STATE
(— **IN PEACE**) COEXIST
(— **IN SAME PLACE**) STALL
(— **ON**) SURVIVE
(— **RIOTOUSLY**) JET
(— **TEMPORARILY**) CAMP
(— **THROUGH**) PASS TIDE
(— **TOGETHER**) AGREE COHABIT
LIVE-BOX CAR
LIVE-FOREVER LULANG ORPINE
LIVELIHOOD BEING BREAD LIVING
LIFEHOOD
LIVELINESS PEP FIRE FIZZ LIFE
SPUNK BOUNCE GAIETY SPIRIT
SPARKLE ACTIVITY VITALITY
VIVACITY
LIVELONG LEELANG ENDURING
LIVELY GAY TID AIRY BRAG CANT
FAST FESS GLEG KECK LIVE PERT
RACY TAIT TRIG VITE VIVE WARM
YARE AGILE ALERT ALIVE BONNY
BRISK BUXOM CANTY CHIRK COBBY
CORKY CRISP DESTO FRESH FRISK
KEDGE KINKY MERRY PAWKY PEART
PEPPY POKEY RUDDY SMART VIVID
WHICK ACTIVE BLITHE BOUNCY
CHEERY CHIRPY COCKET CROOSE
CROUSE DAPPER FIERCE FRISCH
GINGER JOCUND KIPPER LIVING
NIMBLE QUIVER SEMMIT SPARKY
SPRACK TROTTY VEGETE WHISKY
WIMBLE ALLEGRO ANIMATE
ANIMOSE BUCKISH BUOYANT
GIGGISH GIOCOSO JOCULAR
KINETIC LEBHAFT POINTED SPIRITY
SPRINGY TITTUMY WINCING
ANIMATED BOUNCING CHIRRUPY
FRISKFUL FRISKING GALLIARD
SKITTISH SMACKING SPANKING
SPIRITED SPORTIVE STEERING
STIRRING TRIPSOME VEGETOUS
VOLATILE SPARKLING
LIVEN LACE CHEER ANIMATE
LIVE OAK ENCINA
LIVER MAW FOIE HEPAR VISCUS
PUDDING
(— **ATROPHY**) LUPINOSIS
(— **OF LOBSTER**) TOMALLEY
LIVERWORT HEPATICA MOSSWORT
LIVERY SUIT CLOTH LIVRE UNIFORM
CLOTHING
LIVESTOCK FEE WARE STOCK
STORE STUFF CHATTEL BESTIALS
FATSTOCK
LIVE WIRE HUSTLER
LIVID HAW WAN BLAE BLUE
LIVING KEEP ALIVE BEING BREAD
GOING QUICK VITAL WHICK AROUND

LIVELY VIABLE ZOETIC ANIMATE
SUPPORT ANIMATED
(— **IN THE WORLD**) SECULAR
(— **IN WAVES**) LOTIC
(— **NEAR THE GROUND**) EPIGEAN
(— **ON BANKS OF STREAMS**) RIPAL
RIPARIAN
(— **THING**) QUICK
(**BARE** —) CRUST
(**ECCLESIASTICAL** —) BENEFICE
LIVRE FRANC
LIXIVIATE LEACH
LIXIVIUM LYE
LIZARD DAB EFT GOH UMA UTA
DABB GILA IBIT SEPS TEGU TEJU
URAN AGAMA ANOLE BLUEY DRACO
GECKO GUANO SKINK SNAKE SWIFT
TEIID TOKAY TWEEG VARAN AMEIVA
ANGUID ARBALO DRAGON GOANNA
HARDIM IGUANA LACERT LEGUAN
MOLOCH TEIOID WORRAL ZONURE
BUMMAJO CAUDATE CHEECHA
DIAPSID MONITOR REPTILE SAURIAN
SCINCID TUATARA TUCKTOO
BASILISK KAKARIKI MOKAMOKA
SCORPION SLOWWORM TEGUEXIN
WHIPTAIL ZONUROID CHAMELEON
LIZARD FISH ULAE INIOME
SOAPFISH SPEARING
LLAMA ALPACA VICUNA GUANACO
LLUDD NUDD
LO SEE ECCE
LOACH DOJO BEARDIE MUDFISH
LOAD LUG BUCK CARK CRAM DECK
DRAW FILL HAUL LADE LAST LUMP
PACK RAKE SEAM STEM STOW
TOTE TURN BARTH CARGO DRAFT
PITCH STACK TRUSS TURSE
BURDEN CHARGE COMBLE DEMAND
FODDER FOTHER HAMPER LADING
LOADEN THRACK WEIGHT BALLAST
CARLOAD DERRICK DRAUGHT
ENDORSE FRAUGHT FREIGHT
ONERATE OPPRESS BACKPACK
CARRIAGE ENCUMBER HEADLOAD
SHIPLOAD
(— **A DIE FOR CHEATING**) COG
(— **FABRICS**) WEIGHT
(— **OF COAL**) KEEL
(— **OF HAY OR CORN**) HURRY
(— **OF LAMBS**) DECK
(— **OF LOGS**) PEAKER BUNKLOAD
(— **OF WOOL**) TOD
(— **ON BACK**) ENDORSE INDORSE
(— **SHIP**) STEM
(— **TO CAPACITY**) SATURATE
(— **TO EXCESS**) ENCUMBER
(**ELECTRIC** —) DEMAND
(**HORSE** —) SEAM SUMAGE
(**LAST** — **OF GRAIN**) WINTER
(**SMALL** —) JAG JAGG JOBBLE
(**PL.**) BUSHEL
LOADER CHARGER
LOADING LADING MARGIN
ARRASTRE
LOADSTONE MAGNET SIDERITE
LODESTONE
LOAF BAP BUM COB HACK HAKE
HULL LAKE MIKE SLIM SORN BANGE

BREAD DRING MOUCH SHOOL SLIVE SLOSH BROGUE CADDLE DIDDLE GEORGE HALLAH RODNEY SLINGE WASTEL HOOSIER MANCHET SHACKLE SLOUNGE SOLDIER OBLATION QUARTERN SHAMMOCK
(— **AROUND**) HULL HOWFF SLOSH RODNEY
(— **OF BREAD**) COB BATON FADGE MICHE TOMMY HALLAH TAMMIE
(**BROWN** —) GEORGE
(**ROUND** —) BUN
(**SMALL** —) BAP COB
(**SUGAR** —) TITLER
LOAFER BUM BEAT GRUB STIFF BUMBLE KEELIE SLOUCH SLOVEN BLUDGER COASTER FAITOUR HOODLUM SLINKER SOLDIER COBERGER HOOLIGAN LARRIKIN SEASONER
LOAFING IDLE MIKE
LOAM RAB LAME SLIP LOESS REGUR CLEDGE
LOAMY MELLOW
LOAN DHAN LEND LENT PREST CREDIT DONATE MUTUUM FIXTURE IMPREST
LOANBLEND HYBRID
LOATH LOTH LAITH LEATH SWEER DAINTY BACKWARD
LOATHE HATE SHUN ABHOR LAITH WLATE AGRISE DETEST DESPISE SCUNDER SCUNNER NAUSEATE
LOATHING NAUSEA REVOLT DISGUST
LOATHLY LAIDLY
LOATHSOME FOUL UGLY VILE POCKY LAIDLY UNLIEF HATEFUL LOATHLY OBSCENE TETROUS WLATFUL DEFORMED NAUSEOUS WLATSOME
LOBBY HALL FOYER NARTHEX TAMBOUR ANTEROOM COULISSE
LOBBYIST PROMOTER
LOBE ALA FIN LAP AXIS LIST MALA ALULA EXITE FIBER FIBRE FLUKE GALEA LOBUS TOOTH UVULA EARLAP FILLET FOLIUM GLOSSA LAPPET LIGULE LOBING MANTLE VANNUS VERMIS AROLIUM AURICLE HEMAPOD LOBULUS EPICHILE GLABELLA LABELLUM PALPIFER PHYLLOID SQUAMULE
LOBED CUT LOMATINE
LOBSTER CRAY HOMARD DECAPOD SHEDDER CRAWFISH CRAYFISH LANGUSTA MACRURAN
(— **ENCLOSURE**) CRAWL
(— **LESS THAN 10 INCHES LONG**) JOE
(**FEMALE** —) HEN
(**SMALL** —) PAWK NANCY
(**UNDERSIZED** —) SHORT
LOBSTER POT COY CRAIL CREEL TRUNK FISHPOT
LOBULARIA KONIGA
LOCAL HOME NATIVE LIMITED VICINAL REGIONAL EPICHORIC
LOCALE SITE LOCAL PLACE SCENE

LOCALITY SPA HAND PLAT SPOT LOCUS PLACE POINT SITIO SITUS STEAD HABITAT LATITUDE POSITURE
(**BARREN** —) GALL
(**GUARDED** —) POST
LOCALIZE SITUATE POSITION
LOCATE SITE SPOT PITCH PLACE BESTOW BILLET SETTLE SITUATE
(— **AT INTERVALS**) SPOT
(— **WATER**) DIVINE
LOCATED SET FIXED SEATED SITUATED
(— **OFF THE HIGHWAY**) DEVIOUS
LOCATING SYSTEM SOFAR
LOCATION FALL HOME PLOT SEAT PLACE SITUS WHERE UBIETY AMENITY STATION HOMESITE STANDING
(**ESSENTIAL** —) EYE
(**FOREST** —) CHANCE
(**GEOGRAPHIC** —) SEAT
(**MINING** —) MYNPACHT
(**NATURAL** —) HABITAT
LOCH LOUGH LOCHAN
LOCK COT KEY FEAK FRIB HOLD TRIM YALE CLASP SASSE DUBBEH ENLOCK LUCKEN DAGLOCK EARLOCK KEYLOCK PINLOCK SPANNER DEADLOCK FORELOCK
(— **IMPROPERLY**) BIND
(— **IN RIVER**) SASSE
(— **OF HAIR**) COT TAG TUZ COTT CURL FEAK TATE FLAKE FLOCK FLUKE TRESS TANGLE COWLICK EARLOCK FRIZZLE SERPENT WIMPLER FORELOCK SIDELOCK
(— **OF WOOL**) TAG COTT FRIB FLOCK STAPLE HASLOCK
(— **UP**) JAIL STOW CABINET
(**CANAL** —) CHAMBER
(**DIRTY** —) FRIB
(**MATTED** —) COT COTT DAGLOCK
(**MUSKET** —) ROWET
(**PART OF** —) STRIKE
(**WHEEL** —) REWET
LOCKED FAST LUCKEN
LOCKER HUTCH ASCHAM
LOCKERMAN NIBBLER SCOTCHER SNIBBLER
LOCKJAW TETANUS TRISMUS
LOCKNUT JAMNUT KEEPER
LOCKOUT SHUTOUT
LOCKSMITH LOCKYER
LOCKUP JUG GAOL JAIL LOCK LOGS CHOKY CLINK TRONK COOLER HOOSEGOW
LOCOMOTION FLYING LATION
LOCOMOTIVE HOG PIG BOGY GOAT HOGG MULE SHAG TANK BOGIE DINKY DUMMY MOGUL PILOT DIESEL DOCTOR DOLLIE DONKEY ENGINE LOADER PUSHER SMOKER YARDER BOBTAIL BOOSTER SHUNTER STEAMER CALLIOPE CHOOCHOO COMPOUND DOLLBEER
(— **WITHOUT CARS**) WILDCAT
(**EXTRA** —) HELPER
LOCOMOTOR ATAXIA TABES
LOCOWEED LOCO LEGUME PEAVINE

LOCUS PLACE EVOLUTE SURFACE SYNAPSE CONCHOID ENVELOPE HOROPTER
LOCUST WETA BRUKE HONEY ACACIA CICADA QUAKER SKIPPER TETRIGID
LOCUST TREE CAROB ACACIA LOCUST ROBINIA ALGAROBA
LODE LEAD REEF VEIN LEDGE COURSE FEEDER QUARRY COUNTER
LODESTONE MAGNET
LODGE DIG HUT INN LIE BEAT CAMP HOST KEEP ROOM STAY STOW TENT BOWER CABIN COUCH COURT GROVE GUEST HOGAN HOTEL HOUSE HOWFF LAYER LOGIS STICK TARRY ALIGHT BESTOW BILLET BURROW COSHER GESTEN GRANGE HOSTEL RESIDE SETTLE BARRACK LODGING QUARTER SOJOURN EMBOLIZE HARBINGE
(— **AND EAT**) COSHER
(— **FOR SAFEKEEPING**) DEPOSIT
(— **IN COURT**) BOX
(**LOCAL** —) COURT
(**SPORTSMAN'S** —) SHEAL
LODGEPOLE PINE TAMARACK
LODGER INMATE ROOMER TENANT
LODGING BED CRIB GIST HAFT HOST NEST GEAST LOGIS HARBOR HOSTEL LIVERY HOSPICE HOUSING COUCHANT GUESTING
(— **FOR SOLDIERS**) CASERN
(— **OF MARABOUT**) KOUBA
(**PL.**) DIGS DIGGINGS
LODGINGHOUSE INN KIP GITE STOP HOTEL LOGIA LOCANDA PENSION HOSTELRY
LODICULE SQUAMULA SQUAMULE
LOESS LIMON
LOFT BALK FLAT GOLF LAFT ATTIC SOLAR GARRET SOLLAR HAYLOFT COCKLOFT SCAFFOLD TRAVERSE
(**HAY** —) TALLET TALLIT
LOFTIEST SUPREME
LOFTINESS PRIDE HEIGHT DIGNITY MAJESTY EMINENCE GRANDEUR HIGHNESS
LOFTSMAN LINESMAN
LOFTY AIRY HIGH LOFT TALL ELATE GRAND GREAT NOBLE PROUD SKEY STEEP WINGY AERIAL ANDEAN HAUGHT TOPFUL TOWERY UPWARD WINGED ANDESIC ARDUOUS EMINENT EXCELSE HAUGHTY SUBLIME ARROGANT ELEVATED GENEROUS MAJESTIC OLYMPIAN TOWERING
LOG NOG BUNK CLOG DRAG SKID CHUCK CHUNK PIECE STICK STOCK BATTEN BILLET PEAKER PEELER SADDLE SAWLOG BACKLOG DAYBOOK DEADMAN DEGRADE JOURNAL LOGBOOK DEADHEAD
(— **AS ANCHOR**) DEADMAN
(— **AS RAFTER**) VIGA
(— **BINDING A RAFT**) SWIFTER
(— **CAR**) BUNK
(— **FASTENED TO TRAP**) DRAG

(— SUPPORTING MINE ROOF) NOG
(— WITH SPIKES IN END) DEADENER
(— WITHOUT BARK) BUCKSKIN
(ENCLOSED —S) BOOM
(FLOATING —S) DRIVE
(LOAD OF —S) PEAKER
(PILE OF —S) DECK ROLLWAY
(SAWED —) BOULE
(SLABBED —) CANT
(SMALL —) LOGGET
(SPLIT —) PUNCHEON
(STRIPPED —) BATTEN
(SUNKEN —) DEADHEAD
LOGANIN MELIATIN
LOGARITHM DENSITY
(— SYMBOL) PF PH PK RH
(NEGATIVE —) PH
LOGBOOK LOG JOURNAL
LOGE BOX BOOTH LODGE STALL
LOGGER RIDER BOWMAN DECKER
FALLER GOPHER HOOKER LIMBER
MARKER SCORER CHOPPER
FROGGER GRABBER SPOTTER
CATTYMAN
LOGGIA LODGE BALCONY MIRADOR
LOGIC NYAYA LOGICS CANONIC
WITCRAFT
(— OF DISCOVERY) HEURETIC
LOGICAL SANE RAISONNE RATIONAL
LOGMAN CHASER CHOPPER
LOGOGRAM IDEOGRAM
LOGOS WORD
LOGOTYPE SIG
LOG PERCH DARTER HOGFISH
ROCKFISH
LOGROLLING BIRLING
(— TOURNAMENT) ROLEO
LOGWOOD BRAZIL ADMIRAL
DYEWOOD BLUEWOOD HYPERNIC
LOGY DROWSY GROGGY
LOHAN RAKAN
LOIN LEER LISK ALOYAU LUNYIE
(2 UNCUT —S) BARON
(PORK —) GRISKIN
(PL.) REINS FILLET SADDLE
LOINCLOTH IZAR MALO MARO
DHOTI LUNGI PAGNE PAREU
MOOCHA PANUNG DHOOTIE
LOITER LAG CLUG FOOL HAKE HANG
HAWM HAZE HOVE LOUT MIKE
MUCK SLUG COOSE DELAY DRAWL
KNOCK MOUCH SHOOL SIDLE
TARRY COOTER DAWDLE LAGGER
LINGER MUCKER STRAKE TAIGLE
PROJECT SHAFFLE LALLYGAG
LOLLYGAG SCOWBANK SLAMMOCK
SLUMMOCK
LOITERER DRONE IDLER LAGGER
LAGGARD LURCHER
LOITERING SLIMSY LAGGARD
LOKAPALA MAHARAJA
LOKI (DAUGHTER OF —) HEL
(MOTHER OF —) ANGRBODHA
(WIFE OF —) SIGYN
LOLL FUG LOUT FROWST LOLLUP
LOUNGE SOZZLE SPRAWL RECLINE
SCAMBLE SCOWBANK
LOLLIPOP LOLLY SUCKER
SUCKABOB

LOLO NOSU
LONDON SMOKE COCKAGNE
(BRIDGE IN —) TOWER ALBERT
PUTNEY CHELSEA WATERLOO
(DISTRICT OF —) SOHO ACTON
ADELPHI ALSATIA BRIXTON
CHELSEA MAYFAIR
(MONUMENT IN —) GOG MAGOG
NELSON CENOTAPH VICTORIA
(RIVER OF —) THAMES
(STREET OF —) BOND FLEET
CANNON SAVILE DOWNING
WARDOUR HAYMARKET
(SUBURB OF —) KEW FINCHLEY
LONDONER FLATCAP
LONE LANE SOLE ALONE APART
SINGLE SOLITARY
(— STAR STATE) TEXAS
LONELINESS ONENESS VACANCY
SOLITUDE
LONELY ONLY SOLE VAST ALONE
UNKET UNKID WISHT ALANGE
DEAFLY SULLEN DEAVELY FORLORN
LONEFUL SOLEYNE DESOLATE
SECLUDED SOLITARY
LONESOME ALONE DOLEY LONELY
LANESOME SOLITARY
LONG HO DIE FAR FIT YEN ACHE
DREE HANK HONE ITCH LANG SIDE
TALL WILN WISH YAWN CRAVE
DREAM GREEN LATHY LONGA
MOURN STARK WEARY YEARN
ARIGUE ASPIRE DESIRE DREICH
HANKER HUNGER LINGER LONGUS
PROLIX STOUND THIRST LENGTHY
TEDIOUS WEILANG GEMINATE
INFINITE
(— AGO) FERN LANGSYNE
(— AND SLENDER) REEDY SQUINNY
(— AND UNIFORM IN WIDTH) LINEAR
(— FOR) CARE HONE COVET CRAVE
TASTE ASPIRE DESIRE SUSPIRE
(— RESTLESSLY) ITCH
(— SINCE) YORE
LONG-BILLED CURLEW SMOKER
LONGBOAT SLOOP
LONG-BODIED RACY RANGY
LONGERON SPAR
LONGEVITY VIVACITY
(— CHARACTER) SHOU
LONGING YEN ENVY ITCH LUST PINE
WISH BRAME YEARN DESIRE
HANKER TALENT THIRST ATHIRST
CRAVING THIRSTY WILLING WISHFUL
APPETENT APPETITE CUPIDITY
HOMESICK PRURIENT
LONGITUDINALLY ENDLONG
LONG-LASTING CHRONIC
LONGLEGS STILT
LONGLINE BULTOW
LONG-LIVED LONGEVE MACROBIAN
LONGSHOREMAN DOCKER
HOBBLER WHARFIE DOCKHAND
LONG-STANDING OLD
LONG-SUFFERING MEEK PATIENT
ENDURING PATIENCE
LONG-TAILED WHIDAH REDBILL
LONG TOM SKIPPER
LONG-WINDED PROLIX PROSAIC

LOOK LA LO AIR EYE KEN SEE SPY
CAST GAWK GAZE GIVE GLOM HEED
KEEK LATE LUCK MARK POKE SEEM
SWAP VIEW WAIT ACIES BLUSH
DEKKO FAVOR FLASH GLEAM GLEER
GLIFF GLINT SCREW SIGHT SQUIZ
VIZZY WLITE APPEAR ASPECT
EYEFUL GANDER GLANCE REGARD
REWARD VISION EYESHOT EYEWINK
INSIGHT SEEMING DISCOVER
LANGUISH OEILLADE
(— ABOUT) BELOOK SPECTATE
(— AFTER) TENT ATTEND FATHER
FETTLE PROCURE
(— ASKANCE) GLIM LEER SKEW
BAGGE GLENT GLEDGE SKLENT
(— AT) DIG SEE GLOM LAMP VIEW
GLISK ADVISE BEHOLD REGARD
REWARD CONSIDER SPECTATE
(— CLOSELY) PRY ESPY SCAN
(— CROSS-EYED) SHEYLE
(— DOWN UPON) SNOB DESPISE
(— DULLY) BLEAR
(— FIXEDLY) GAZE KYKE GLORE
STARE
(— FOR) SPY FOND SEEK GROPE
EXPECT PROPOSE RESPECT
(— FORWARD) EXPECT FORESEE
ENVISAGE ENVISION
(— GLANCINGLY) BLINK
(— IN SNEAKING MANNER) SNOOP
(— INTENTLY) GLOSE VISIE GLOWER
EYEBALL
(— INTO) SOUND SEARCH
(— OBLIQUELY) GLIME GOGGLE
SQUINT
(— OF DERISION) FLEER
(— OF PLANETS) ASPECTS
(— OUT) FEND MIND CHEESE
JIGGERS OUTLOOK
(— OVER) SCAN TOISE BROWSE
SURVEY EXAMINE
(— SEARCHINGLY) PEER PORE
TOOT
(— SLYLY) PEEP GLINK
(— SOUR) GLUNCH
(— STEADFASTLY) GLOAT
(— SULKY) LUMP
(— SULLEN) LOUR LOWER
(— UPON AS) ACCOUNT
(— WILDLY) GLOP WAUL WHAWL
(— WITH FAVOR) SMILE
(AMOROUS —) SMICKER
(BRIEF —) GLIM GLINT GLIMPSE
(LOVING —) BELGARD
(QUICK —) SCRY GLENT
(SEARCHING —) SCRUTINY
(SEVERE —) FROWN
(SIDELONG —) GLEE GLIME
(SLY —) GLEG GLIME TWIRE
(SULLEN —) GLOOM GLOUT
GLUNCH
(TENDER —) LANGUISH
(WANTON —) LEER
(PL.) DAPS
LOOKER BEAUTY HERDSMAN
SEARCHER
LOOKER-ON BEHOLDER
LOOKOUT TOUT SCOUT WATCH

BANTAY CONNER TOOTER FUNERAL
OUTLOOK ATALAYAN BANTAYAN
BARTIZAN COCKATOO PROSPECT
TOWERMAN WATCHOUT
LOOM BEAM BULK HULK LEEM
DOBBY FRAME GLOOM BEETLE
DOBBIE DRAWLOOM HANDLOOM
JACQUARD OVERPICK
(— **ATTACHMENT**) LAPPET
LOOM AXLE ROCKTREE
LOOM BAR EASER DAGGER
LOOMFIXER TACKLER
LOOM HARNESS LEAF HEADLE
SIMBLOT MOUNTING
LOON DIVER IMBER WABBY COBBLE
DUCKER GUNNER WHABBY
PYGOPOD
LOOP BOW EYE LUG NOB TAB TAG
ANSA BEND COIL FAKE HANK KINK
KNOB KNOP LEAF LINK LOUP PURL
BIGHT BRIDE CHAPE COQUE GUIDE
LACET LATCH NOOSE PEARL PICOT
SHANK STRAP TERRY WITHY
BECKET BILLET BUCKLE FOLIUM
HANGER HOLDER KEEPER KINKLE
PARRAL SPIRAL STAPLE STITCH
TWITCH COCKEYE COUPURE
CRINGLE CRUPPER GROMMET
KNUCKLE LATCHET SEGMENT
ANTINODE COURONNE
(— **AND THIMBLES**) CLEW CLUE
(— **BY ICESKATER**) SPOON
(— **IN KNITTING**) STEEK
(— **IN MINER'S ROPE**) SLUG
(— **IN NEEDLEWORK**) BRIDE
(— **OF INTESTINES**) KNUCKLE
(— **OF IRON**) OOLLY
(— **OF ROPE**) FAKE BIGHT FLAKE
KINCH NOOSE ANCHOR BECKET
PARRAL SNORTER SNOTTER
(— **OF SCABBARD**) FROG
(— **OF TUBING**) SCROLL
(— **ON ARMOR**) VERVELLE
(— **ON SPINNING FRAME**) BAND
(— **ON SWORD BELT**) HANGER
(**HANGING** —) FESTOON
(**HEDDLE** —) DOUP
(**ORNAMENTAL** —) PICOT
(**SHOULDER** —) EPAULET
(**SURGICAL** —) CURET CURETTE
(**TIGHT** —) KINK KINKLE
LOOPER INCHWORM SPANWORM
LOOPHOLE LOOP CHINK MEUSE
EYELET OILLET WICKET PORTHOLE
LOOSE GAY LAX EMIT FREE GLAD
LASH LIMP OPEN SOFT UNDO WIDE
WILD BAGGY CRANK FRANK LARGE
LIGHT RELAX SLACK VAGUE WASHY
ADRIFT FLUFFY LIMBER SLOPPY
SOLUTE SPORTY SUBURB UNBIND
UNGIRT UNLASH WOBBLY CHESSOM
FLYAWAY IMMORAL MOVABLE
RELAXED SHOGGLY STRINGY
UNBOUND UNHITCH UNTIGHT
DISCINCT FLOATING INSECURE
LAXATIVE SHATTERY UNSTABLE
(— **ARROW**) BOLT
(**MORALLY** —) FRANK
LOOSE-JOINTED LANKY SHACKLY

LOOSELY SLACK LARGELY SLACKLY
LOOSEN LAX BREAK SLACK UNTIE
LAXATE LIMBER UNBEND RESOLVE
SLACKEN UNGRIPE UNLOOSE
UNSCREW DISHEVEL UNSTRING
(— **ANCHOR**) TRIP
(— **ROCK**) GAD
LOOSENESS SLACK LAXITY
LATITUDE
LOOSENING START SOLUTIVE
SOLUTORY
LOOSESTRIFE KILLWEED PEATWEED
PEATWOOD PRIMWORT
LOOT SACK SWAG BOOTY HARRY
SPOIL STEAL THEFT HERSHIP
PILLAGE PLUNDER SNAFFLE
LOOTING SACK
LOP DOD LAP CLIP DODD OCHE
SNED SNIG TRIM SHRAG SHRED
SHRUB STUMP TRASH TWINE
SHROUD SNATHE TRASHIFY
TRUNCATE
(— **OFF**) COW DOD CROP DODD
HEAD SNAG SNEP PRUNE SHRED
TRUNK DEFALK AMPUTATE
LOPE SHAG
LOPPER CLABBER
LOQUACIOUS GABBY FUTILE
LOQUACITY PRATE PRATTLE
FUTILITY
LOQUAT BIWA NISPERO
LORAL FRENAL
LORD BEL DAM DEN DON GOD HER
LOR MAR SID SIR DION DOMN EROS
HERR LAUK LOSH SIRE TUAN
ANGUS ARAWN BARON LAFEU LIEGE
LUDDY NIGEL OMRAH RABBI SAHIB
SWAMI DOMINE DUMAIN KYRIOS
PRABHU SAYYID SIGNOR TANIST
THAKUR CAMILLO CERIMON
JACQUES JEHOVAH MARCHER
OGTIERN VAVASOR BHAGAVAT
DESPOTES DRIGHTEN GRANDPRE
LORDLING MARGRAVE OVERLORD
PALATINE SEIGNEUR SEIGNIOR
SUPERIOR SUZERAIN THALIARD
(— **OF DARKNESS**) HYLE
(— **OF WORLD**) LOKINDRA
(**FEUDAL** —) DAUPHIN VAVASOR
SUZERAIN
LORD CHANCELLOR WOOLPACK
LORDLINESS PRIDE
LORDLY PROUD SUPERB ARROGANT
DESPOTIC
LORDOSIS SWAYBACK
LORDSHIP NAVY DYNASTY
ERECTION SEIGNORY SIGNORIA
LORE LEAR LORUM MASTAX
LEARNING
LORGNETTE STARER
LORICA LORIC SHEATH SHIELD
CORELLA WEROOLE
LORIS KOKAM LEMUR SLOTH
LEMUROID
LORN ALONE
LORRY RULLY ROLLEY
LORY LOORY CORELLA LORIKEET
LOSE LET TIN AMIT DROP TINE WANT

FORGO LAPSE LEASE TRAIL
GAMBLE MISLAY FORBEAR FORFEIT
FORLESE SLATTER
(— **AT CARDS**) BUST
(— **BET**) WRONG
(— **BRILLIANCE**) FAINT
(— **BY DEATH**) BURY
(— **BY GAMING**) GAME
(— **BY STUPIDITY**) BLUNDER
(— **CONTROL**) BLOW CRACK
(— **COURAGE**) DREEP TAINT
(— **FLAVOR**) FOZE APPAL APPALL
(— **FORCE**) COLLAPSE
(— **FRESHNESS**) FADE WILT WITHER
(— **HEART**) JADE FAINT QUAIL
(— **HOPE**) DESPAIR DESPOND
(— **LUSTER**) TARNISH
(— **MOISTURE**) GUTTATE
(— **NERVE**) CHICKEN
(— **OFFICE**) FALL
(— **ONE'S BREATH**) CHINK
(— **ONE'S WAY**) STRAY
(— **POWER**) FAIL DISSOLVE
(— **SELF-POSSESSION**) ABASH
(— **SPIRIT**) JADE
(— **STRENGTH**) GO FADE FAIL
WEAKEN LANGUISH
(— **VISION**) DAZZLE
(— **WARMTH**) COOL CONGEAL
(— **WEIGHT**) ENSEAM
LOSS ACE COST HARM LEAK LOST
MISS LAPSE QUALM WASTE BURIAL
DAMAGE DAMNUM DEFEAT INJURY
TINSEL AVERAGE DEBACLE DEFICIT
EXPENSE JACTURE LEAKAGE
LEESING MISTURE REPRISE
AMISSION BREAKAGE CLEANING
MISSMENT
(— **BY SIFTING**) ULLAGE
(— **IN WORKING**) SLIPPAGE
(— **OF ABILITIES**) COLLAPSE
(— **OF ACTIVITY**) AKINESIA
(— **OF APPETITE**) ANOREXIA
(— **OF CONSCIOUSNESS**) SWOON
ABSENCE APOPLEXY BLACKOUT
FAINTING
(— **OF ELASTICITY**) SET
(— **OF ELECTRICITY**) EFFLUVE
(— **OF EXPRESSION**) AMIMIA
(— **OF HAIR**) DEFLUX ALOPECIA
PTILOSIS
(— **OF HOPE**) DESPAIR
(— **OF MEMORY**) AMNESIA
(— **OF PRESTIGE**) DISHONOR
(— **OF SCENT**) CHECK
(— **OF SENSE OF SMELL**) ANOSMIA
(— **OF SIZE**) WANE
(— **OF SOUND**) APOCOPE SYNCOPE
APHERESIS
(— **OF SPEECH**) ALALIA APHASIA
APHONIA
(— **OF VOICE**) ANAUDIA APHONIA
(— **OF VOWEL**) APHESIS
(— **OF WILL POWER**) ABULIA
(**CONTRACT** —) LESION
LOST GONE LORN TINT WASTE
ASTRAY BUSHED HIDDEN NAUGHT
FORFEIT FORLORN MISSING
CONFUSED OBSCURED

OT CUT HAP PEW CHOP CROP DEAL
DOLE DOOM DRAW FALL FATE HEAP
PACK PART PILE REDE SLEW SLUE
SORS SORT BATCH BLOCK BREAK
CAVEL FIELD GRACE GRIST GROSS
LINES SHARE SHOOT SIGHT SITHE
STAND TEEMS TROOP WEIRD
AMOUNT BARREL BUNDLE CHANCE
DICKER FARDEL OODLES TICHEL
BOILING DESTINY FEEDLOT
FORTUNE PORTION SANDLOT
BACKYARD CABOODLE MOUTHFUL
RIMPTION WOODLAND
(— OF 60 PIECES) SHOCK
(— OF PERSONS) BOODLE
(— OF TEA) BREAK
(BUILDING —) ERF
(BURIAL —) LAIR
(GREAT —) SWAG
(VACANT —) COMMON COMMONS
OTION WASH EYEWASH EYEWATER
LAVATORY
OTS HEAPS TEEMS BUSHEL HODFUL
OTTERY AMBO LOTTO TERNO
RAFFLE TOMBOLA
OTTO KENO BINGO TOMBOLA
(— GAME) HOUSE
OTUS LOTE LOTOS WANKAPIN
OTUS TREE SADR ZYZYPHUS
OUCHEUX KUTCHIN
OUD HARD HIGH MAIN CRUDE
FORTE GAUDY GREAT HEAVY
SHOWY STARK STOUR WIGHT
BRASSY BRAZEN COARSE CRIANT
FLASHY HOARSE VULGAR BLATANT
CLAMANT HAUTAIN VIOLENT
BIGMOUTH FRENZIED SLAMBANG
STREPENT STRIDENT VEHEMENT
OUDLY BOST ALOUD FORTE STARK
OUDNESS STRESS SONORITY
(— UNIT) PHON SONE
OUDSPEAKER WOOFER SPEAKER
TWEETER BULLHORN SQUAWKER
OUD-SPOKEN RANDY
OUIS LUIGI LODOWIC

LOUISIANA
CAPITAL: BATONROUGE
COLLEGE: LSU TULANE DILLARD
  GRAMBLING
COUNTY: CADDO ACADIA PARISH
  TENSAS LAFOURCHE
CULTURE: TCHEFUNCTE
DIALECT: CREOLE
FESTIVAL: MARDIGRAS
INDIAN: ADAI WASHA ATAKAPA
LAKE: IATT CLEAR LARTO
  BORGNE SALINE DARBONNE
  MAUREPAS
NATIVE: CAJUN CREOLE ACADIAN
NICKNAME: PELICAN
RIVER: AMITE TENSAS OUACHITA
STATE BIRD: PELICAN
STATE FLOWER: MAGNOLIA
STATE TREE: CYPRESS
STREAM: BAYOU
TOWN: HOUMA GRETNA MINDEN
  RUSTON BASTROP BOGALUSA

LOUISIANIAN CAJUN ACADIAN
LOUNGE HAWM LOLL SORN SOSS
BANGE TRAIK FROUST FROWST
GLIDER LOLLUP LOPPET RIZZLE
SLINGE SOZZLE LAMMOCK SAUNTER
SLOUNGE
LOUNGER IDLER SLOUNGER
LOUSE BOB BUG SOW CRAB CRUMB
BOOGER BRAULA COOTIE GISLER
PALMER SISTEN VERMIN MORPION
PUCERON GRAYBACK
(FISH —) GISLER ARGULUS
(PLANT —) APHID APHIS
(WOOD —) SOW SLATER
(YOUNG —) NIT
LOUSEWORT RATTLE SNAFFLES
LOUSY SEEDY CRAPPY
LOUT HOB LOB LUG BOOR CHUB
COOF GAUM GAWK LOON NOWT
SWAB SWAD CHUMP CUDDY GNOFF
LOURD ROBIN THRUM WHAUP
YAHOO BOHUNK CLUNCH GOBBIN
HOBLOB LOURDY LUBBER LUNGIS
SLOUCH TRIPAL GROBIAN HAWBUCK
LOBCOCK LOBLOLLY
(COUNTRY —) KERN BUMPKIN
LOUTISH SWAB HULKY SLOOMY
BOORISH HULKING VILLAIN
BOEOTIAN
LOUVER SLAT LOUVRE LUFFER
DIFFUSER FEMERELL
(PL.) SHUTTER
LOVABLE AMABEL CUDDLY AMIABLE
ADORABLE DOVELIKE LOVESOME
LOVABLENESS DEARNESS
LOVAGE SMELLAGE
LOVE GRA LOO AMOR EROS KAMA
LIKE ALOHA AMOUR CUPID DRURY
FANCY HEART MINNE TENDRE
CHARITY EMBRACE FEELING
DEVOTION KINDNESS LOVEHOOD
PARAMOUR
(— IN RETURN) REDAME
(— OF MARVELOUS) TERATISM
(— TO EXCESS) IDOLIZE
(— TOWARD DEITY) BHAKTI
(CHRISTIAN —) CHARITY
(INTENSE —) FIRE
(NATURAL —) STORGE
(SELF-GIVING —) AGAPE
(UNLAWFUL —) LEMANRY
LOVED DEAR BELOVED
(MUCH —) SWEET
LOVE FEAST AGAPE
LOVE KNOT AMORET
LOVELINESS BEAUTY
LOVELOCK EARLOCK
LOVELY LOVING TENDER AMIABLE
AMOROUS ADORABLE LOVESOME
LOVEMAKING AMOUR
LOVER GRA MAN BEAU CHAP AMANT
AMOUR DRURY LEMAN ROMEO
SPARK SWAIN AMADIS AMANTE
MARROW MINION SQUIRE ADMIRER
AMORIST AMOROSO CELADON
GALLANT PATRIOT SPARKER
SPECIAL SPRUNNY BELAMOUR
CASANOVA CICISBEO PARAMOUR
STREPHON

(MODEL —) LEILAH
(SILLY —) SPOON
LOVE SEAT CAUSEUSE
LOVING DEAR FOND TENDER
AMATORY AMOROUS
LOW BAS BOO LAW MOO BASE KEEN
MEAN ORRA ROUT SLOW VILE
WEAK BLORE DIRTY GROSS LAICH
PUTID SHORT SMALL SNIDE THIRD
CALLOW EARTHY FILTHY GENTLE
GRUBBY HARLOT HUMBLE LIMMER
MENIAL RASCAL RIBALD SECRET
SILKEN TURPID VULGAR BESTIAL
IGNOBLE RAFFISH REPTILE SLAVISH
SUBMISS SOUTERLY
(— AS OF A VOWEL) OPEN
(— DOWN) SIDE
(— IN LIGHTNESS) DULL
(— IN PERCEPTION) CRUDE
(— IN PITCH) GRAVE
(— IN QUALITY) HEDGE
(— IN SATURATION) GRAYISH
(— IN SPIRITS) BLUE DOWN
GLOOMY DOWNCAST
(— IN TONE) SOFT SUBMISS
(— IN WATER) RACE
(— NUMBERS) MANQUE
(— POINT) TROUGH
(IMMEASURABLY —) ABYSMAL
LOWBORN WAFF
LOWBRED BASTARD PLEBEIAN
LOW-DOWN BUCKASS
LOWER CUT DIP LOW BASE BATE
DOWN DROP DUCK FELL SINK
ABASE ABATE ALLOY AVALE BELOW
BLAME COUCH COWER DECRY
DEMIT DOUSE FROWN GLOOM
LEVEL SCOWL STOOP BEMEAN
DEBASE DEJECT DEMEAN EMBASE
GLOWER HUMBLE JUNIOR LESSEN
MODIFY NETHER REDUCE SETTLE
STRIKE SUBDUE SUBMIT BENEATH
DECLASS DEGRADE DEPRESS
SHORTEN DIMINISH DOWNWARD
INFERIOR MODERATE
(— BANNER) VAIL
(— BY HALF STEP) FLAT
(— IN ESTEEM) CHEAPEN
DEROGATE
(— IN PITCH) FLAT SHADE
(— ONESELF) SINK BEMEAN
DESCEND
(— PRICES) BEAR
(— SAIL) AMAIN
(— THE HEAD) STOOP
LOWERING DIP DUCK DOWLY HEAVY
LAPSE BEETLE SULLEN
(— OF BODY) FONDU
(— OF LAND) ABLATION
LOWEST LAST LEAST EXTREME
LOWMOST
(— CLASS) LAG
(— POSSIBLE) KNOWDOWN
LOWING MUGIENT
LOWLAND LAICH POLDER LALLAND
DOWNLAND
(— BESIDE RIVER) INKS
(BARREN —) LANDES

LOWLANDER SAXON ZHMUD
SASSENACH
LOWLIER LESS
LOWLY LOW BASE SILLY HUMBLE
BASEBORN
LOW-LYING CALLOW LALLAN
INFERIAL SUBJECTED
LOW-MINDED BASE MEAN
LOWNESS LOWTH
(— OF SPIRITS) GLOOM SPLEEN
MEGRIMS
LOW-PITCHED GRUFF
LOW-SPIRITED HIPPED DEJECTED
LOY SLICK
LOYAL FAST FEAL FIRM HOLD LEAL
REAL TRUE LIEGE PIOUS SOUND
ARDENT HEARTY LAWFUL SECRET
STANCH FAITHFUL YEOMANLY
LOYALIST TORY
LOYALLY SURELY
LOYALTY ARDOR FAITH FEALTY
HOMAGE LEALTY REALTY SPIRIT
REALITY DEVOTION FIDELITY
LOZENGE TAB JUBE COIGN QUOIN
JUJUBE MASCLE QUARRY ROTULA
RUSTRE TABLET TABULE TROCHE
CREMULE DIAMOND TABELLA
PASTILLE ROSEDROP
(— OF CEMENT) WAFER
LOZI ROZI BAROTSE
LUBBER SWAB LOOBY SLOUCH
LOBCOCK LILBURNE
LUBBERLY AWKWARD
LUBRICANT DOPE GREASE
AQUADAG UNGUENT
LUBRICATE OIL DOPE GLIB GREASE
LUBRIFY
LUBRICATOR OILER OILCAN
LUCARNE LUCOMBE
LUCENT BRIGHT LUCIBLE
LUCERNE LEGUME ALFALFA
LUCID SANE CLEAR AERIAL BRIGHT
LIMPID CRYSTAL DILUCID LITERATE
LUCULENT LUMINOUS
LUCIDITY SANITY
LUCIFER DEVIL PHOSPHOR
LUCK HAP CESS EURE SONS SPIN
GRACE ISSUE CHANCE THRIFT
FORTUNE HANDSEL SUCCESS
VENTURE HAMINGJA
(BAD — TO YOU) YLAHAYLL
(BAD —) ACE DOLE DEUCE HOODOO
UNLUCK AMBSACE
(GOOD —) HAP FORTUNE THEEDOM
(ILL —) UNHAP DIRDUM DISGRACE
(RELATING TO —) ALEATORY
(UNEXPECTED —) BUNCE
LUCKILY HAPPILY
LUCKY HOT CANNY HAPPY SONSY
CHANCY LUCKLY LUCKFUL
GRACIOUS
LUCRATIVE FAT GOOD GAINFUL
LUCRE SWAG
LUDICROUS AWFUL COMIC DROLL
ABSURD FOOLISH HIDEOUS
FARCICAL
LUDO UCKERS
LUFFA LOOFAH SPONGE
LUG EAR HUG TUG WAG SNUG SPUD

ZULU PATCH WALTZ
LUGGAGE SWAG TRAPS HATBOX
BAGGAGE TRUSSERY
LUGGAGE CASE IMPERIAL
LUGGAR JAGGAR JUGGER LAGGAR
LUGGER CAT TOUP ZULU FIFIE
LUGUBRIOUS DOLEFUL DOLOROUS
LUGWORM LOB LUG LOBWORM
SANDWORM
LUIGINO TEMIN
LUKEWARM LEW LUKE TEPID
WLACH
LULL CALM DRUG FODE HUSH ROCK
CROON HUSHO SLACK STILL SOPITE
HUSHABY HUSHEEN
LULLABY LULL BALOO BALOW
LULLAY HUSHABY HUSHEEN
ROCKABY
LULLING DROWSY CIRCEAN
LUMBER BURR DEAL RAFF NANMU
STOCK STRIP FINISH FLITCH REFUSE
SAMCHU SHORTS TIMBER DEGRADE
DUNNAGE GUMWOOD TRUNDLE
STEPPING
(INFERIOR —) SAPS SCOOT
LUMBERING AWKWARD LUMBERLY
LUMBROUS
LUMBERJACK JACK TOPPER
TIMBERER
LUMBERMAN PINER DOGGER
SCORER CHOPPER GIRDLER
TIMBERER
LUMINANCE HELIOS
LUMINARY LIGHT CANDLE PLANET
LUMINESCENCE FLAME
LUMINOSITY FIRE GLOW LIGHT
VALUE
LUMINOUS LIGHT LUCID SHINY
BRIGHT LUMINANT
LUMMOX LOBSTER
LUMP BAT BOB COB CUB DAB DAD
FID GOB JOB NIB NOB NUB WAD
BLOB BURL CLAG CLAM CLOT COOL
COWL DUNT JUNK KNOB KNOT
PONE SWAD TOKE BLOOM CHUCK
CHUNK CLAUT CLUMP CLUNK
GLEBE HUNCH KNOLL KNURL
MOUSE SLUMP STONE WEDGE
WODGE CLUNCH DOLLOP GOBBET
HUBBLE HUDDLE LUMPET NUBBLE
NUGGET CLUMPER CLUNTER
PUMPKNOT
(— IN CLOTH) BURL
(— IN GLASS) YOLK
(— OF BLACK LEAD) SOP
(— OF BLOOD) CLOD
(— OF COAL) NUBBLING
(— OF DOUGH) DIP
(— OF FAT) KEECH
(— OF GLASS) BLOOM
(— OF IRON) OOLLY
(— OF LAVA) BOMB
(— OF LINT) SLUG
(— OF METAL) MASS SLUG
(— OF ORE) ROCK HARDHEAD
(— OF RUBBER) THIMBLE
(— OF SALT) SALTCAT
(— OF YEAST) BEE
(LARGE —) DOLL HUNK

(LITTLE —) NODULE KNOBBLE
(ROUNDED —) CLOT
LUMPFISH GROSS PADDLE SUCKER
LUMPISH STODGY CHUCKLE
LUMPY GOBBY CHUNKY CLUNCH
COBBLY
LUNACY MOON FOLLY MADNESS
DELIRIUM INSANITY
LUNARIA SATINPOD
LUNARY VOLVELLE
LUNATIC GELT LOONY BEDLAM
MADMAN MANIAC FANATIC FRANTIC
CRACKPOT MOONLING MOONSICK
LUNCH CUT BAIT CRIB TIFF BEVER
PIECE SNACK BRUNCH NACKET
TIFFIN UNDERN BAGGING ELEVENS
DEJEUNER DRINKING ELEVENER
LUNCHEON
(DAIRY —) CREMERIE
(MINER'S —) SNAP
LUNCHEON CRIB LUNCH STULL
TIFFIN DINETTE NOONMEAT
LUNCHROOM EATERY
LUNETTE OUTWORK
LUNG DRAGON LONGUE
LUNGE FOIN PASS SPAR POINT
VENUE CHARGE ALLONGE
LUNGFISH CYCLOID DIPNOAN
MUDFISH SIRENOID
LUNGS LIGHTS VISCUS BELLOWS
(PERTAINING TO —) PULMONIC
LUNKHEAD DOLT JUGHEAD
LUNULE ALBEDO
LUO DHOLUO
LUPINE SUNDIAL
LURCH JOLL STOT SWAG STOIT
CAREEN STOITER STUMBLE
SWAGGER
LURCHING DRUNKEN ROLLING
LURE CON JAY BAIT HOOK ROPE
TOLL WISE DECOY DRILL FEINT
SLOCK SNARE SPOON SQUID STAL
TEMPT TROLL ALLURE CAPPER
CLARET ENTICE ENTRAP SEDUCE
TREPAN VELURE GUDGEON INVEIG
PHANTOM PITFALL WOBBLER
BUCKTAIL INVEIGLE LUREMENT
(— INTO GAMBLING) HUSTLE
(— OF CARRION) TRAIN
(— WILDFOWL) STOOL
LURI ALUR
LURID RED PURPLE SULTRY
CRIMSON GHASTLY
LURK DARE LOUT COUCH LOWER
SKULK SLINK SNEAK AMBUSH
DARKLE
LURKING LURKY GRASSANT
LUSCIOUS FOND RICH SWEET
CREAMY DULCET DELICATE
LUSH GREEN LUSTY MOIST SAVOR
FERTILE OPULENT THRIVING
LUST HELL KAMA BLOOD PRIDE
DESIRE LIBIDO LIKING LUXURY
NICETY PASSION COVETISE
CUPIDITY
LUSTER NAIF GLASS GLINT GLOSS
SHEEN SHINE WATER LUSTRE
POLISH REFLET BURNISH GLIMPS
GLISTER LUSTRUM NITENCY

FULGENCE LUSTRATE RADIANCY
SPLENDOR
(— OF FIBER) BLOOM
(BRONZE-LIKE —) SCHILLER
LUSTERLESS WAN DEAD DULL
FISHY STARY
LUSTFUL HOT GAMY GOLE LEWD
RANK SALT CADGY LUSTY PRIME
RANDY RUTTY WANTON BEASTLY
CODDING FLESHLY FULSOME
JEALOUS RAMMISH RUTTISH
LIKEROUS
LUSTFULNESS SATYRISM
LUSTILY CRANK HOTLY
LUSTING ITCHY
LUSTRATION ABHISEKA
LUSTROUS CLEAR DOGGY NITID
BRIGHT GLOSSY ORIENT SHEENY
SILKEN SILVER SHINING SPLENDID
LUSTY BRAG CANT CRANK FLUSH
FRACK FRANK FRECK GUTSY HARDY
JUICY STIFF STOUT GAWSIE
ROBUST STURDY LUSTFUL LUSTICK
BOUNCING PHYSICAL SPORTIVE
VIGOROUS
LUTE TAR BIWA LAUD DOMRA NABIA
NABLE REBAB REBEC SAROD
CITOLE ENLUTE LORICA LUTING
SCREED ANGELOT BANDORE
DICHORD DYPHONE MANDOLA
MANDORE MINIKIN PANDORE
THEORBO VIHUELA ANGELICA
ARCHLUTE PENORCAN TAMBOURA
TEMPLATE TRICHORD
LUTER DAUBER PASTER
LUTJANID JEWFISH

LUXEMBOURG
CAPITAL: LUXEMBOURG
HIGHEST POINT: BURGPLATZ

LOWLAND: BONPAYS GUTLAND
MEASURE: FUDER
MOUNTAIN RANGE: ARDENNES
PLATEAU: ARDENNES
RIVER: OUR SURE SAUER ALZETTE
MOSELLE
TOWN: ROODT WILTZ PETANGE
VIANDEN DIEKIRCH

LUXURIANT GOLE LUSH RANK RICH
FRANK PROUD LAVISH WANTON
OPULENT PROFUSE TEEMING
PAMPERED PRODIGAL
LUXURIANTLY FATLY
LUXURIATE BASK WALLOW WANTON
LUXURIOUS HIGH LUSH NICE POSH
RANK SOFT GAUDY SWANK CAPUAN
DELUXE GILDED SILKEN SWANKY
WANTON ELEGANT LUCULLAN
PRODIGAL REGALADO SENSUOUS
TRYPHENA TRYPHOSA
LUXURIOUSLY HIGH DELUXE
LUXURY FRILL FINERY OUTRAGE
DELICACY ELEGANCE PLEASURE
RICHNESS
LUXURY-LOVING DELICATE
LYCANTHROPE WEREWOLF
LYCAON (DAUGHTER OF —)
CALLISTO
(FATHER OF —) PALASGUS
LYCEUM PLATFORM
LYCHNIS FIREBALL NONESUCH
LYCIUM RUSOT
LYCOPODIUM MOSS FOXTAIL
CROWFOOT STAGHORN
LYDIA MAEONIA
LYE LEY BOUK BUCK STRAKE
LESSIVE LIXIVIUM SOAPLEES
LYING FLAT FALSE LEASE CRETISM

LEASING MENTERY
(— APART) DISSITE
(— AT BASE OF MOUNTAINS)
PIEDMONT
(— CLOSE) QUAT
(— DOWN) DOWN LODGED
DORMANT COUCHANT
(— HID) LATITANT
(— IDLE) INACTIVE
(— ON BACK) SUPINE
(— ON FACE) PRONE
(— OVER) JACENT
(— UNDER GRASS) LEA
LYING-IN INLYING CHILDBED
GROANING
LYMPH CHYLE VIRUS
LYMPHAD GALLEY
LYMPHANGITIS WEED FILLING
LYMPHOGRANULOMA BUBO
LYMPHOMATOSIS FISHEYE
LYNCEUS (BROTHER OF —) IDAS
(FATHER OF —) AEGYPTUS
APHAREUS
(WIFE OF —) HYPERMNESTRA
LYNCH HANG DEWITT
LYNX LOSSE PISHU BOBCAT GORKUN
LUCERN CARACAL LUCIVEE
WILDCAT CARCAJOU
LYRE ASOR HARP LYRA SHELL
CHELYS KINNOR KISSAR TRIGON
CITHARA PHORMIX TESTUDO
BARBITON TRICHORD TRIGONON
LYREBIRD LYRETAIL PHEASANT
LYRIC LAY LIED HOKKU MELIC
GHAZEL TENSON CANCION
CHANSON DESCORT MADRIGAL
(LOVE —) ALBA
(PL.) SONG
LYTTA WORM

M EM EMMA MIKE METRO
(WRONG USE OF —) MYTACISM
M-1 GARAND
MA'AM MARM MISTRESS
MAARIB ARBIT ARBITH
MACA ENIMAGA
MACABRE SICK HORRIBLE
MACACA PITHECUS
MACADAMIZE METAL
MACAO (CHINESE NAME OF —)
AOMEN
(ISLAND OF —) TAIPA COLOANE
MACAQUE KRA BROH BRUH MACAC
MACHIN RHESUS
MACARIA (FATHER OF —) HERCULES
(MOTHER OF —) DEIANIRA
MACARONI DITALI
MACARONIC SKEW
MACAW ARA ARARA PARROT
MARACAN ARACANGA COCKATOO
MACE CROC MALL MAUL VERGE
MALLET SPARTH CATTAIL
(REED —) DOD DODD
(ROYAL —) SCEPTER SCEPTRE
MACE-BEARER BEADLE VERGER
MACEMAN
MACERATE SOUR STEEP
MACHAON (BROTHER OF —)
PODALIRIUS
(FATHER OF —) AESCULAPIUS
(MOTHER OF —) CORONIS
MACHETE GULOC PARANG CURTAXE
CUTLASH CUTLASS
MACHIAVELLIAN CRAFTY CUNNING
GUILEFUL
MACHINATION ARTIFICE INTRIGUE
SCHEMERY
MACHINE (ALSO SEE DEVICE AND
ENGINE) GIN HOG JIG SAW AGER
COMB GEAR JACK LIFT MULE PUMP
RASP TRAY WHIM WINK ADDER
AWNER BALER BENCH BILLY BOARD
BRAKE BREAK COPER CRANE DEVIL
EDGER FRAME FUDGE FUGAL JENNY
JERRY JOLLY LATHE LAYER METER
MIXER MOWER NAVVY RAKER
RESAW ROVER SCREW SETUP
SHEEN SIZER STAMP SULKY TRONE
VINER WILLY BARKER BEADER
BEAMER BEATER BEETLE BENDER
BILLER BINDER BOLTER BUCKLE
BUMPER BUTTER CANTER CAPPER
CARDER CONCHE COOLER CREWER
DECKER DOFFER DONKEY DRAPER
DREDGE DUSTER ENGINE FLAKER
FOLDER FOOTER FORMER GADDER
GAPPER GLAZER GRADER GRATER
GUMMER HEADER HEMMER HOBBER
HOGGER HOOPER HULLER HUSKER
IRONER JIGGER JORDAN KICKER
LEGGER LIFTER LINTER LOGGER
MAILER MANGLE MILLER MITRER
NAPPER NETTER NIBBER NIPPER
PACKER PEGGER PINNER PLATER
PUMPER RIPPER ROSSER ROTARY
ROUTER SANDER SCUTCH SEALER
SEAMER SHAKER SHAPER SHAVER
SINGER SKIVER SLICER SORTER
SPACER STOCKS STOKER TEDDER

TENTER TWINER VANNER WASHER
WELDER WILLOW ABRADER
AUTOMAT AVIATOR BACKHOE
BATCHER BELLOWS BLENDER
BOTTLER BRANNER BREAKER
CANDROY CAPSTAN CHIPPER
COMBINE CRUSHER DIBBLER
DRESSER EMULSOR ENCODER
ENROBER ERECTOR EXOSTRA
FLANGER FLOSSER FREEZER
GARNETT GLASSER GRAINER
GRINDER GROOVER GROUTER
HUMIDOR IRONMAN JOINTER
KNITTER KNOTTER MACHINA
MANGLER MATCHER MITERER
PLODDER PLUCKER POTCHER
PRINTER QUILLER REPRESS
RIVETER ROASTER SAMMIER
SCALPER SHEARER SHEETER
SIROCCO SLABBER SLASHER
SLITTER SLOTTER SLUBBER
SLUGGER SMASHER SPALLER
SPEEDER SPINNER SPONGER
SPOOLER SPRAYER STACKER
STAMPER STAPLER STEAMER
STEMMER STICKER TENONER
TEREBRA TOOTHER TRAMPER
TREATER TRIMMER TRUSSER
TWILLER TWISTER TYPOBAR
WHIPPER WHIZZER AERIFIER
AIRCRAFT BROACHER CALENDER
CANCELER CARTONER CLINCHER
COLLATOR COMPRESS DUNGBECK
ELEPHANT EXPLODER EXTRUDER
FINISHER FLYWINCH FORKLIFT
GATHERER HARDENER HAYMAKER
HERCULES HUMMELER IMPACTER
KILLIFER MORTISER MOULINET
ODOGRAPH OROGRAPH PROFILER
PULSATOR SCHIFFLI SCUTCHER
SHREDDER SOFTENER SPLITTER
SPREADER SPRIGGER SQUEEZER
STITCHER STRANDER STRIPPER
SURFACER TEMPERER THREADER
THRESHER THROSTLE TRAVELER
TRISPAST TUNNELER UPSETTER
WINNOWER ADDRESSER
MACHINE GUN STINGER CHAUCHAT
MACHINERY MINT TOPCAP SUCCULA
APPARATUS
MACHINE SHOP TURNERY
MACHINIST FRILLER THINNER
MACHINER
MACKEREL CHAD PETO TINK BLINK
OPELU SNOEK TUNNY BONITO
SAUREL TINKER BLINKER BLOATER
TASSARD HARDHEAD SCOMBRID
SEERFISH
(— ABOUT 8 OR 9 INCHES) TINK
TINKER
(PICKLED —) SCALPEEN
(POOR BONY —) SLINK SLINKER
(YOUNG —) SPIKE
MACKLE SLUR SHAKE MACULA
MACROSCOPIC GROSS
MACROSPECIES LINNEON
MAD FEY AWAY GITE GYTE HYTE
WOOD YOND ANGRY BRAIN CRAZY
DIPPY FOLLE RABID BEDLAM

FRENZY INSANE MANIAC WOODEN
BERSERK FANATIC FRANTIC
FURIOUS LUNATIC MADDING
MADDOCK MANKIND REDWOOD
WITLESS DELIRANT DEMENTED
DISTRACT INFORMAL MANIACAL
MINDLESS RAVENING
MADAGASCAR (SEE MALAGASY
REPUBLIC)
MADAM MEM MUM BAWD MAAM PAN
DONNA MADAME SENORA SENHORA
SIGNORA GOODWIFE MISTRESS
SINEBADA
MADAR YERCUM
MADDEN ENRAGE INCENSE INFLAME
DISTRACT
MADDENED ENRAGED FRENZIED
MADDER GAMENE LIZARY ALIZARI
GARANCE MUNJEET TANAGRA
GARANCIN SPURWORT WOODRUFF
MAD-DOG SKULLCAP MADWEED
HOODWORT
MADE SET BUILT COMPACT
PREPARED TIMBERED
(— FLUID BY HEAT) FUSILE
(— OF DISSIMILAR PARTS) MIXED
(— OF FLAX) LINEN
(— OF GRAIN) OATEN CEREAL
(— OF IVORY) EBURNEAN
(— OF SILVER) ARGENT
(— OF STONE) STONEN
(— OF TWIGS) VIRGAL
(— SHORT) CURTAL
(— TART) EUCHRED
(— TO ORDER) BESPOKEN
(— TRANSLUCENT) AJOURE
(— UP) ACCRETE
(— WITH CEDAR) CEDARN
MADE-BEAVER SKIN CASTOR
MADEIRA ISLANDS (ISLAND OF —
GRANDE DEZERTE
(TOWN OF —) FUNCHAL
(WINE OF —) BUAL TINTA MALMSE
SERCIAL VERDELHO
MADELON POLIXENE
MADHOUSE ASYLUM BEDLAM
MADHUCA BASSIA ILLIPE
MADLY WOOD CRAZY
MADMAN BEDLAM MANIAC FURIOS
LUNATIC WOODMAN
MADNESS MAD FURY MOON WOOI
FOLLY FUROR MANIA BEDLAM
FRENZY LUNACY DEWANEE
ECSTASY MOONERY WIDDRIM
DELIRIUM DEMENTIA PIBLOKTO
WILLNESS WOODNESS WOODSHIP
MADONNA LADY VIRGIN
MADREPORE FUNGID
MADRIGAL ENSALADA
MADRONA LAUREL MANZANITA
MADTOM TADPOLE
MADWORT BUGLOSS
MAENAD FROW BASSARID
BACCHANTE
(PL.) BACCHAE
MAFIC FEMIC
MAFURA ROKA ELCAJA
MAGANI BAGANI
MAGAZINE BOOK DRUM FLAT IGL

SLICK STORE RETORT ALMACEN JOURNAL CASSETTE

(BLACKWOOD'S —) MAGA

MAGDALEN MAUDLIN

MAGGOT MAD GRUB MAWK WORM METHE GENTLE WARBLE WORMIL MADDOCK SKIPPER MUCKWORM

MAGIC JUJU MAYA RUNE CRAFT FAIRY GOETY SPELL TURGY GOETIC TREGET VOODOO ALCHEMY CANTRIP CONJURY DEVILRY GLAMOUR GRAMARY MAGICAL SORCERY BRUJERIA HECATEAN WIZARDRY

(BLACK —) GOETY GOETIC MALEFICE

(WHITE —) TURGY

MAGICAL WIZARD WONDER HERMETIC NUMINOUS THEURGIC

MAGICIAN MAGE BOKOR MAGUS UTHER CUNJAH GOETIC GOOFER GUFFER MAGIAN MERLIN WABENO WIZARD CHARMER GWYDION KOSCHEI WIELARE WISEMAN CONJURER FETISHER SORCERER THEURGIC TROLLMAN

MAGISTERIAL LOFTY PROUD AUGUST LORDLY HAUGHTY STATELY ARROGANT DOGMATIC

MAGISTERY MASTERY

MAGISTRACY AMT PRYTANY

MAGISTRATE BEAK FOUD EPHOR JUDGE JURAT MAYOR PRIOR REEVE AMTMAN ARCHON AVOYER BAILIE CENSOR CONSUL FISCAL KOTWAL SYNDIC BAILIFF BURGESS DUUMVIR ECHEVIN EPHORUS JUSTICE NOMARCH PODESTA PRAETOR PREFECT PROVOST STEWARD SUFFETE TRIBUNE ALABARCH ALDERMAN CAPITOUL DEFENSOR DEMIURGE DICTATOR GOVERNOR MITTIMUS PHYLARCH PRYTANIS RECORDER STRADICO STRATEGE HUNDREDER

(— IN CHANNEL ISLANDS) JURAT

(— OF ANCIENT ROME) EDILE

(— OF VENICE AND GENOA) DOGE

(MOHAMMEDAN —) CADI CADY

(SCOTCH —) STEWARD

MAGMA ICHOR

MAGMATIC JUVENILE

MAGNANIMITY HEIGHT FREEDOM

MAGNANIMOUS BIG FREE GREAT LARGE LOFTY NOBLE HEROIC EXALTED GENEROUS

MAGNATE MOGUL BASHAW TYCOON

MAGNESIA PULVIL

MAGNET FIELD ADAMAS MAGNES ADAMANT SOLENOID TERRELLA

MAGNETISM IT DEVIL

MAGNETITE LOADSTONE LODESTONE

MAGNETIZE TOUCH SATURATE

MAGNETOMETER DOODLEBUG

MAGNIFICENCE GITE POMP FLARE GLORY STATE PARADE JOLLITY ROYALTY GRANDEUR SPLENDOR

MAGNIFICENT RIAL GRAND NOBLE

ROYAL AUGUST LAVISH IMMENSE STATELY SUBLIME GLORIOUS GORGEOUS MAGNIFIC PALATIAL PRINCELY SPLENDID

MAGNIFY LAUD ERECT EXALT PRAISE ADVANCE DISTEND ENLARGE GLORIFY GREATEN INCREASE MAXIMIZE MULTIPLY

MAGNIFYING GLASS LOUPE READER

MAGNILOQUENT TURGID BOMBAST

MAGNITUDE BULK MASS SIZE DATUM LEVEL SOLID EXTENT FIGURE PERIOD EXTREME CONSTANT FUNCTION INFINITE

MAGNOLIA YULAN BIGBLOOM CUCUMBER MAURICIO

(— STATE) MISSISSIPPI

MAGPIE MAG PIE PIET PYAT CISSA KOTRI MADGE NINUT MARGET NANPIE PIANET PIEMAG SIRGANG HAGISTER MARGARET PHEASANT PIENANNY

MAGPIE LARK PEEWEE GRALLINA

MAGPIE ROBIN DAYAL DHYAL

MAGUEY MESCAL CANTALA

MAGYAR SZEKEL SZEKLER

MAHATMA ARHAT

MAH-JONGG WOO

MAHOE EMAJAGUA

MAHOGANY SIPO ALMON CAOBA CEDAR ACAJOU AGUANO SAPELE THITKA ALBARCO AVODIRE BAYWOOD GUNNUNG MADEIRA RATTEEN TABASCO BANGALAY HARDTACK TANGUILE

(INDIAN —) TOON

(PHILIPPINE —) BAGTIKAN

MAHONIA ASHBERRY ODOSTEMON

MAHOUND MACON

MAHUA FULWA MOWHA MOWRA MADHUCA PHULWARA

MAHUANG EPHEDRA

MAIA (FATHER OF —) ATLAS

(MOTHER OF —) PLEIONE

(SON OF —) MERCURY

MAID AYAH GIRL MEDE SLUT CHINA WENCH WOMAN MAIDEN SLAVEY TWEENY VIRGIN ANCILLA GENERAL MAIDKIN PHYLLIS PUCELLE WENCHEL BRANGANE HANDMAID SUIVANTE TIREMAID

(— IN WAITING) DAMSEL DAMOZEL

(— OF HONOR) MARIE

(— OF-ALL-WORK) SLAVEY GENERAL

(KITCHEN —) SCOGIE

(LADY'S —) AYAH TIREMAID

(NURSE —) BONNE

(OLD —) TABBY SPINSTER

(WAITING —) ABIGAIL SUIVANTE

MAIDEN MAY BIRD DAME GIRL MAID DALAGA DAMSEL FROKIN MEISJE COLLEEN CYDIPPE DAMOZEL MADCHEN DAUGHTER

(— WITH BASKET ON HEAD) CANEPHOR

MAIDENHAIR GINGKO ADIANTUM

MAIDENLY VIRGIN GIRLISH VIRGINAL

MAIDEN PINK SPINK DIANTHUS

MAIDSERVANT LASS BIDDY BONNE ANCILLA LISETTE

MAIEUTIC HEBAMIC

MAIGRE BAR SCIAENID WEAKFISH

MAIL BAG DAK HOOD POST MATTER AIRMAIL JACKPOT MAILBAG ORDINAR POSTAGE POSTBAG SEAPOST TAPPALL ORDINARY

(IMPROPERLY ADDRESSED —) NIX NIXY

MAIN LINE MOST SHEER MIGHTY

MAILBAG BAG POUCH POSTBAG

MAILBOX POST PILLAR POSTBOX

MAILLECHORT ARGENTON

MAILLOT SWIMSUIT

MAILMAN POSTMAN BREVIGER

MAIM LAME BREAK TRUNK HAMBLE MANGLE MAYHEM CRIPPLE MUTILATE

(— AN ANIMAL) LAW MANK

MAIMED SPAVINED

MAIN HIGH CHIEF GRAND GREAT PRIME CAPITAL LEADING FOREMOST

MAINE

CAPITAL: AUGUSTA

COLLEGE: BATES COLBY BOWDOIN

COUNTY: KNOX WALDO KENNEBEC AROOSTOOK

INDIAN: ABNAKI

LAKE: SEBEC SEBAGO RANGELEY SCHOODIC MOOSEHEAD

MOUNTAIN: BIGELOW CADILLAC KATAHDIN

NATIVE: MANIAC

RIVER: SACO KENNEBEC AROOSTOOK KENNEBAGO PENOBSCOT

STATE BIRD: CHICKADEE

STATE FLOWER: PINECONE

STATE NICKNAME: PINETREE

STATE TREE: PINE

TOWN: ORONO BANGOR KITTERY BOOTHBAY OGUNQUIT PORTLAND

MAINLY BROADLY CHIEFLY

MAINSTAY KEY ATLAS SINEW STOOP PILLAR BACKBONE RELIANCE

MAINTAIN BEAR FEND FIND HOLD KEEP LAST SAVE ADOPT ARGUE CARRY CLAIM ESCOT SALVE ADHERE ALLEGE ASSERT AVOUCH DEFEND INTEND RETAIN THREAP UPHOLD UPKEEP CONFIRM CONTEND DECLARE DISPUTE JUSTIFY NOURISH SUBSIST SUPPORT SUSTAIN CONTINUE PRESERVE

(— AS TRUE) AVOUCH SOOTHE

(— POSITION) STALL

(— WITHOUT REASON) ARROGATE

MAINTAINER FOUNDER RETAINER

MAINTENANCE KEEP LIVING UPKEEP ALIMONY CUSTODY FINDING KEEPING PREBEND SERVICE

(— OF POPULATION) BALANCE

MAITHILI TIRHUTIA
MAIZE CORN GRAIN CEREAL INDIAN
JAGONG STAPLE MEALIES
DJAGOONG
(— CRUSHED WITH PESTLE) STAMP
MAJAGUA HAU BARU BOLA MAHO
MOJO BURAO GUANA MOHOE
PURAU BALIBAGO CORKWOOD
EMAJAGUA
MAJESTIC HIGH GRAND LOFTY
REGAL ROYAL AUGUST KINGLY
SUPERB STATELY SUBLIME
ELEVATED IMPERIAL MAESTOSO
SPLENDID
MAJESTY DIGNITY AUGUSTUS
GRANDEUR KINGSHIP
MAJOON BANG BHANG
MAJOR DUR DURUM SHARP CAPITAL
GREATER MAGGIORE
MAJORITY BODY BULK FECK
CORPSE SUBSTANCE
(ABSOLUTE —) QUORUM
MAKARAKA IDDIO
MAKARI KOTOKO
MAKE DO CUT GAR LET MAY FORM
GIVE LEVY BRAND BUILD CAUSE
COVER FETCH FORGE FRAME SEIZE
SHAPE STAMP AUTHOR COBBLE
CREATE GRAITH INDUCE RENDER
CONFECT FASHION IMAGERY
IWURCHE PERFORM PRODUCE
CONTRIVE GENERATE
(— A DIFFERENCE) SKILL
(— A MESS OF) PIE
(— A RUG) HOOK
(— A VISIT) COSHER
(— ACKNOWLEDGMENT) CONFESS
(— ACTIVE) ENERGIZE
(— AMENDS) ABYE ATONE ABEGGE
ANSWER REDEEM EXPIATE REDRESS
(— ANGRY) GRAMY WRATH
(— ATTRACTIVE) GILD
(— AWAY WITH) ABOLISH EMBEZZLE
(— BARE) STRIP DENUDE
(— BELIEVE) LET PRETEND
(— BETTER) AMEND HEIGHTEN
(— BLUE) HIP
(— BRIGHT) ENGILD ILLUME
CLARIFY
(— BRISK) PERK
(— BROWN) TAN
(— BY STAMPING) MINT
(— CANDLE) DIP DRAW
(— CERTAIN) ASSURE ENSURE
(— CHANNEL IN) THROAT
(— CHEERFUL) SOLACE
(— CHOICE) OPT CHOOSE SELECT
(— CLAMMY) ENGLEIM
(— CLEAR) DECLARE DEVELOP
DISCUSS EXHIBIT EXPOUND LIGHTEN
DESCRIBE
(— COLD) REFREID
(— COMPLETE) SPHERE
(— CONSPICUOUS) ENNOBLE
(— CONTENT) SATISFY
(— CULTIVABLE) EMPOLDER
(— CUT PRIOR TO LAYERING)
TONGUE
(— DESTITUTE) BEREAVE

(— DIFFERENT) ALTER CHANGE
(— DIRTY) MOIL GRIME
(— DISPLAY OF) AFFECT DISCOVER
(— DRUNK) FOX SOUSE FUDDLE
SOZZLE
(— DRY) HAZLE HAZZLE
(— EARLIER) ADVANCE
(— EFFERVESCENT) AERATE
(— EFFIGY) GUY
(— END OF) SNIB FETCH
(— ENDURING) ANNEAL
(— EQUAL) WEIGH EQUATE
(— EVEN) GLAZE LEVEL WEIGH
SQUARE
(— FACES) GIMBLE MURGEON
(— FALSE PRETENSES) SHAM
(— FAST) FIX BAIL FAST GIRD KNIT
MAKE STOP BELAY HITCH BUCKLE
FASTEN SECURE
(— FAT) BATTEN
(— FIRM) FIX BRACE FASTEN
(— FIT) APTATE STRIKE
(— FOOL OF) DOR BORE DOLT
DORRE BEGOWK DOODLE
(— FOOLISH) DAFF GREEN NUGIFY
STULTIFY.
(— FOOTSORE) SURBATE
(— FROTHY) MILL
(— FULL) FARCE FULFILL
(— FUN OF) GUY KID GAFF JEST
JOSH DROLL GLAIK SCOUT SMOKE
(— FUSS OVER NOTHING) FAFF
(— GLAD) FAIN
(— GLASS) FOUND
(— GLOSSY) SLEEK
(— GLOW) FURNACE
(— GOLDEN) ENDORE
(— GRINDING NOISE) GRINCH
(— GURGLING SOUND) CROOL
(— HAPPY) BLESS ENJOY REFORM
BEATIFY SATISFY FELICIFY
(— HARD) TAW STEEL ENDURE
HORNIFY
(— HARDY) FASTEN
(— HEADWAY) STEM WALK
ENFORCE
(— HELPLESS) STAGGER
(— HOLY) BLESS SACRE HALLOW
SANCTIFY ,
(— HORSE SEEM YOUNGER) BISHOP
(— ILL) MORBIFY
(— IMMOBILE) FREEZE
(— IMPACT) ASSAIL
(— INCURSION) HARRY
(— INSIGNIFICANT) MICRIFY
(— INTO BUNDLE) FARDEL
(— INTO LAW) ENACT
(— INVALID) DAMASK
(— JOINT) SYPHER
(— KNOWN) BID OUT GIVE WISE
AREAD BEKEN BREAK KITHE SOUND
SPEAK BEWRAY BROACH COUTHE
DENOTE DESCRY EXPOSE INFORM
REVEAL SPREAD CONFESS DECLARE
DELIVER DIVULGE PUBLISH SIGNIFY
UNCOVER ANNOUNCE DECIPHER
DISCLOSE DISCOVER INDICATE
PROCLAIM PROMULGE
(— LESS DENSE) THIN RAREFY

(— LESS SEVERE) MITIGATE
(— LIABLE) DANGER
(— LOVE) WOO COURT SPOON
GALLANT
(— LUKEWARM) WLECCHE
(— LUSTERLESS) FLATTEN
(— MANIFEST) EVINCE EXPLAIN
(— MELANCHOLY) HYP
(— MELODIOUS) ATTUNE
(— MELODY) DREAM
(— MENTION) SPEAK
(— MERRY) JET GAUD CHEER
SPORT FROLIC SHROVE DISPORT
REHAYTE
(— METALLIC SOUND) CHINK
(— MISTAKE) ERR BOOB GOOF
(— MONOTONOUS NOISE) DRONE
(— MORAL) ETHICIZE
(— MUCH OF) DAWT DANDLE
(— MURMURING NOISE) BUM
(— NEAT) FEAT SMUG TIDY GROOM
(— NEST) TIMBER
(— NONMAGNETIC) DEGAUSS
(— NUMB) DAZE ETHERIZE
(— OFF) BAG BOLT HOOK ANNEX
HEIST SPIRIT SCARPER
(— ONE'S WAY) AIRT BORE TRADE
(— ONE) UNE
(— OPEN) AIR PATEFY
(— OUT) FARE FILL GLEAN SKILL
DISCERN DECIPHER
(— OVER) TURN ALIEN CHANGE
RECOCT DELIVER REFORGE
(— PALE) CHALK
(— PLEASANT) SWEETEN
(— POIGNANT) SAUCE
(— PREGNANT) ENWOMB
(— PROGRESS) GAIN STEM GATHER
(— PROUD) WLENCH
(— PUBLIC) BLOW BLAZE BREAK
BLAZON DELATE DIVULGE FANFARE
PUBLISH BULLETIN
(— QUIET) ALLAY QUIET APPEASE
(— RATTLING NOISE) TIRL
(— READY) DO BUN GET BOWN
BUSK YARK BELAY DRESS PREST
PRIME FETTLE GRAITH ADDRESS
APPAREL DISPOSE PREPARE
(— RECORD OF) REFER
(— REFERENCE) MENTION
(— RESISTANCE) REBEL
(— RESOLUTE) STEEL
(— RETURN FOR) REQUITE
(— RICH) FREIGHT IMBURSE
(— ROSY) FLUSH
(— RUSTLING SOUND) FISSLE
FISTLE
(— RUTTING CRY) FREAM
(— SCANTY LIVING) EKE
(— SERIES OF NOTES) TINKLE
(— SHIFT) SCAMBLE
(— SIGN OF CROSS) BLESS
(— SMALL) MICRIFY BELITTLE
(— SMALLER) MINIFY COMPRESS
(— SMOOTH) SLAB GLAZE SLEEK
GENTLE HAMMER SCRAPE LEVIGAT
(— SOFT) NESH GENTLE
(— SOGGY) SOP
(— SOUR) FOX WIND

(— SPIRITLESS) MOPE
(— SPORT OF) LARK
(— SPRUCE) PERK SMARTEN
(— STRAIGHT) ADDRESS
(— STRONG) STEEL FASTEN FORTIFY
(— STUPID) MOIDER STULTIFY
(— SUITABLE) ADAPT
(— SURE) SEE INSURE
(— TIPSY) FLUSTER
(— TRANSITION TO) MODULATE
(— UP ACCOUNTS) BREVE
(— UP) UP COOK FORM SPELL INDITE SETTLE ANALYZE COMPACT COMPOSE COMPUTE CONCOCT CONFECT FASHION COMPOUND COMPRISE DISPENSE
(— USE OF) FEE BUSK APPLY AVAIL BROOK SERVE SPEND EMPLOY EXECUTE IMPROVE UTILIZE
(— VIBRANT SOUND) CHIRR
(— VOID) ABATE ANNUL
(— WAR) WARRAY
(— WET) DRAGGLE
(— WHISTLING NOISE) WHEW
(— WHITE) BLANCH BLEACH CANDIFY
(— WORSE) IMPAIR PEJORATE
MAKE-BELIEVE BORAK DUMMY ASSUMED
MAKER DOER JACK KNAVE SMITH FACTOR FORGER FORMER WORKER CREATOR DECLARER OPERATOR
(— OF ARROWS) FLETCHER
(— OF BARRELS) COOPER
(— OF POTS) POTTER
(— OF SADDLETREES) FUSTER
(— OF SONGS) BULBUL
(— OF TALLOW) CHANDLER
MAKESHIFT JURY RUDE JERRY JOUSY BEWITH KUTCHA APOLOGY BACKLEG STOPGAP
MAKEUP FACE BUILD GETUP HABIT SETUP SHAPE FACIES FORMAT ANATOMY CONSIST FEATURE TRAVESTY
MAKING FACT
MALABAR BAY
MALABAR ALMOND KAMANI ALMENDRO
MALACEAE POMACEAE PYRACEAE
MALADJUSTMENT SCAR
MALADROIT ILL AWKWARD UNHANDY BUNGLING
MALADY AMOK EVIL MORB CAUSE GRIEF ONCOME AILMENT DISEASE ILLNESS DISORDER MISCHIEF SICKNESS
MALAGASAY LEMURIAN

MALAGASY REPUBLIC
ALTERNATE NAME: MADAGASCAR
CAPITAL: TANANARIVE
ISLAND GROUP: ALDABRA
LAKE: ALAOTRA
MEASURE: GANTANG
NATIVE: HOVA SAKALAVA
PEOPLE: HOVA COTIER MARINA

RIVER: IKOPA MANIA SOFIA MANGOKY MANGORO ONYLAHY
TOWN: TULEAR MAJANGA NOSSIBE TAMATAVE ANTISIRABE

MALAPROPISM SLIPSLOP
MALAR JUGAL
MALARIA MIASMA SHAKES PALUDISM
(— PARASITE) VIVAX
MALARIAL PALUDOSE PALUDOUS

MALAWI
CAPITAL: ZOMBA
COIN: KWACHA
FORMER NAME: NYASALAND
HIGHLANDS: SHIRE
LAKE: NYASA
LANGUAGE: YAO CEWA NGONI TONGA NYANJA TUMBUKA
MOUNTAIN: MLANJE
PEOPLE: YAO BANTU CHEWA NGURU NYANJA
TOWN: MZUZU BLANTYRE LILONGWE
VALLEY: RIFT

MALAY AMOK ASIL AMUCK BAJAU ILOCO JAKUN MANOBO ILOKANO
MALAYAN (— TREE) TERAP
MALAY APPLE OHIA JAMBO KAVIKA

MALAYSIA
CAPITAL: KUALALUMPUR
COIN: TRA TRAH
ISLAND: ARU GOA KAI OBI OMA ALOR BALI GAGA JAVA MUNA MURU SULO AMBON BANDA BOHOL BUTON CERAM LUZON MISOL PANAY SANGI SUMBA TIMOR WETAR BANGKA BOEFON BOEROE BORNEO BUTUNG FLORES LOMBOK MADURA PELENG SANGIR TALAUR WAIGEU AMBOINA CELEBES JAMDENA MINDORO MOROTAI PALAWAN SALAJAR SALWATI SUMATRA SUMBAWA BELITONG DJAILOLO TANIMBAR
ISTHMUS: KRA
LANGUAGE: TAGALOG
MOUNTAIN: BULU NIUT RAJA MURJO NIAPA LEUSER SLAMET BINAIJA RINDJANI
PEOPLE: ATA BAJAU SEMANG BISAYAN TAGALOG VISAYAN
RIVER: KUTAI PERAK BARITO PAHANG
TOWN: DAVAO ILOILO KUPANG MANADO KUCHING MALACCA SANDAKAN
WEIGHT: TAEL WANG TAMPANG

MALCONTENT FRONDEUR
MALE HE DOG HIM MAN BUCK BULL COCK JACK ADULT MANLY SPEAR JOHNNY MANFUL MASCLE VIRILE LALAQUI MANKIND MANLIKE MANNISH PURUSHA
(— OF ANIMALS) TOM BUCK BULL JACK STUD STALLION
(GELDED —) GALT
(YOUNG —) GROOM
MALECITE ETCHEMIN
MALEDICTION BAN WISH CURSE MALISON ANATHEMA
MALEFACTOR BADDY FELON BADDIE CULPRIT CRIMINAL EVILDOER
MALEFIC TAKING
MALEFICENT BALEFUL
MALEO MEGAPOD
MALE ORCHIS CUCKOO CROWTOE CULLION PURPLES RAGWORT CROWFOOT
MALEVOLENCE SPITE ENMITY GRUDGE HATRED MALICE RANCOR SPLEEN
MALEVOLENT ILL EVIL FELL MALIGN HATEFUL HOSTILE SPITEFUL
MALFORMATION CURL ERROR HEMITERY
(— OF CARNATION) TWITTER
(— OF FRUIT) CATFACE
MALFORMED SHAMBLE

MALI
ANCIENT CITY: TIMBUKTU
CAPITAL: BAMAKO
LAKE: DO DEBO GAROU KORAROU
LANGUAGE: DOGON DYULA MANDE MARKA PEULH BAMBARA MALINKE SENOUFO SONGHAI
MOUNTAIN: MINA MANDING
PEOPLE: MOOR PEUL TUAREG BAMBARA MALINKE SONGHAI SENOULFO
RIVER: BANI BAGOE BAKOY NIGER BAOULE AZAOUAK SENEGAL
TOWN: GAO SAN KAYES MOPTI SEGOU SIKASSO

MALICE DOLE ENVY HAIN PIQUE SPITE VENOM VIRUS ENMITY GRUDGE RANCOR SPLEEN DESPITE AMBITION
MALICIOUS SHREW TEENY BITTER DOGGED MALIGN WANTON HATEFUL HEINOUS LEERING SPITOUS CANKERED SINISTER SPITEFUL VENOMOUS
MALIGN ILL FOUL ABUSE LIBEL WRONG BEWRAY DEFAME VILIFY ASPERSE DEPRAVE HURTFUL SLANDER
MALIGNANCY FEROCITY
MALIGNANT EVIL ATTRY FELON FERAL SWART ATTERY MALIGN ENVIOUS HATEFUL HELLISH PEEVISH REPTILE VICIOUS WARLOCK SHREWISH SPITEFUL VENOMOUS VIPEROUS VIRULENT WRATHFUL
MALIGNITY LIVER VENOM VIRUS HATRED MALICE RANCOR DESPITE
MALINGER DODGE SKULK
MALINGERER SCONCER

MALL WALK ALLEE
MALLARD TWISTER
(**FLOCK OF —S**) SORD SUTE
PADDLING
MALLEABLE MILD SOFT DUCTILE
BATTABLE
MALLEIN MORVIN
MALLEMUCK MOLLIE MALMARSH
MALLET MALL MAUL MELL GAVEL
BEATER BEETLE DRIVER HAMMER
DRESSER FLOGGER STRIKER
PLOWMELL
(**— FOR BREAKING CLODS**) BILDER
(**CURRIER'S —**) MACE
(**HATTER'S —**) BEATER
(**PAVER'S —**) TUP
MALLEUS HAMMER OSSICLE
PLECTRUM
MALLOW MAW DOCK HOCK ALTEA
KOKIO MALVA MAUVE CHEESE
ESCOBA GEMAUVE ABUTILON
PIEPRINT
MALMSEY MALVASIA
MALNUTRITION CACHEXY CACHEXIA
MALODOROUS GAMY HIGH NOSY
FETID SMELLY VIROSE VIROUS
MALT WORT
(**GROUND —**) GRIST
(**REMAINS OF —**) DRAFF
MALTASE GLUCASE
MALTHA BREA
MALTHOUSE MALTINO
MALTOSE AMYLON
MALTREAT ABUSE DIGHT DEFOUL
DEMEAN HESPIL HUSPEL MISUSE
THREAT BEDEVIL MISGUIDE
MALTREATMENT ABUSE
MALVA DOCK MALLOW
MAMAMU MU
MAMBA COBRA ELAPOID
MAMMA MA MOM MAMA WIFE
MOMMA WOMAN MOTHER
MAMMAL OX ASS BAT CAT COW
DOG FOX PIG YAK BEAR BOAR
COON DEER GOAT HARE LION LYNX
MINK MOLE PUMA SEAL ZEBU
BEAST BISON CAMEL COATI COYPU
GENET HORSE HYENA LEMUR
LLAMA MOOSE OKAPI OTTER PANDA
RATEL SABLE SHEEP SHREW SKUNK
SLOTH SWINE TAPIR TIGER WHALE
ZORIL ALPACA ANIMAL BADGER
COUGAR CULPEO DESMAN DUGONG
FISHER FOUSSA GOPHER GRISON
JAGUAR MARTEN MONKEY OCELOT
TENREC VICUNA WALRUS WOMBAT
BUFFALO CARIBOU DOLPHIN
ECHIDNA GIRAFFE GLUTTON
GUANACO HIPPOID HUANACO
MANATEE OPPOSUM PECCARY
POLECAT PRIMATE RACCOON
SUCKLER SURICAT TARSIER
TYLOPOD WILDCAT ANTELOPE
BANXRING CACOMIXL CREODONT
ELEPHANT FALANAKA HEDGEHOG
KINKAJOU MAMMIFER PANGOLIN
REINDEER SQUIRREL
MAMMALIA MASTOZOA
MAMMEE ABRICO ABRICOT

MAMMILLA PAP TEAT NIPPLE
MAMMOTH HUGE LARGE GIGANTIC
MAN BO HE BOY GEE GUY HIM LAD
TAO WAT WER BUCK CHAL CHAP
COVE DICK EARL GENT GOME
HOMO JACK JONG MALE RINK TULK
BERNE BIMBO BIPED BLOKE CHURL
COVEY FORCE FREKE GROOM
GUEST HEART HOMME HORSE
JOKER SEGGE SWAIN WIGHT
BIMANE FELLOW HOMBRE MANTZU
WEPMAN BIMANUS HOMONID
KINSMAN MANKIND
(**— AFFECTING FOREIGN WAYS**)
MACARONI
(**— DRESSED AS WOMAN**) MALINCHE
(**— IN DEBT**) DYVOUR
(**— IN PRIVATE STATION**) IDIOT
(**— IN TUG-OF-WAR**) ANCHOR
(**— LEADING 12TH NIGHT**) BEAN
(**— OF ALL WORK**) MOZO
(**— OF AUTHORITY**) AGHA SEIGNIOR
(**— OF BEAUTY**) APOLLO
(**— OF BRASS**) TALOS
(**— OF GREAT WEALTH**) NABOB
(**— OF HIGH RANK**) CHAM KHAN
THAKUR GRANDEE
(**— OF SUBSTANCE**) IDLEMAN
(**— OF THE COMMON PEOPLE**) JACK
(**— OF VIGOR**) WYE
(**— OF VIOLENCE**) RABIATOR
(**— OF WAR**) ANDREW CARAVEL
CRUISER
(**— TO MAN**) SINGLE
(**ARTIFICIAL —**) GOLEM
(**BACKGAMMON —**) BLOT BUILDER
(**BALD —**) PILGARLIC
(**BEST —**) BRIDEMAN
(**BIG —**) COB BRUISER MUGWUMP
(**BRISK —**) SPARK
(**CASTRATED —**) SPADO EUNUCH
(**CHIEF —**) FOREMAN OPTIMATE
(**CHURLISH —**) NABAL BODACH
(**CLEANING —**) BUSBOY
(**COMMON —**) CARL STREET
YEOMAN
(**COVETOUS —**) HUNKS
(**CRAFTY —**) FOX
(**CRUEL —**) OGRE BRUTE
(**DISAGREEABLE —**) GLEYDE
(**DISLIKED —**) CUT
(**DISSOLUTE —**) RAKE
(**ECCENTRIC —**) GEEZER
(**EDUCATED —**) EFFENDI
(**EFFEMINATE —**) DILDO FAIRY SISSY
COCKNEY MEACOCK MIDWIFE
MILKSOP ANDROGYN
(**END —**) BONES BRAKE
(**ENLISTED —**) GI SNIPE AIDMAN
AIRMAN KEEPER STORES ARMORER
STRIKER SONARMAN
(**ENTIRE —**) EGO
(**EXTINCT —**) TEPEXPAN
(**FAITHFUL —**) TRUEMAN
(**FANCY —**) PONCE
(**FASHIONABLE —**) TOUPET
ELEGANT FOPLING GALLANT
(**FIRST —**) ASK ADAM ASKR TIKI
FOREMAN

(**FOPPISH —**) BLOOD
(**FREE —**) LIBER
(**GRAY-HAIRED —**) GRIZZLE
(**GREAT —**) VAVASOR
(**HARDHEARTED —**) KNARK
(**HOLDUP —**) FOOTPAD
(**HOLY —**) SADHU SAINT SANNYASI
(**HONORS —**) WRANGLER
(**IDEAL —**) SUPERMAN
(**IMMORAL —**) REP
(**INEFFECTUAL —**) DUFFER
(**INSANE —**) FURIOSO
(**LADY'S —**) FOPLING DAMMARET
(**LAME —**) BACACH
(**LEARNED —**) ULEMA LAMDAN
OLLAMH PUNDIT SAVANT SOPHIST
(**LECHEROUS —**) SATYR
(**LEWD —**) BROTHEL
(**LIAISON —**) COURIER
(**LITERARY —**) GIGADIBS
(**LITTLE —**) MANNET SHRIMP
MANNIKIN
(**LUSTFUL —**) GOAT
(**MAINTENANCE —**) CAMPMAN
(**MARRIED —**) HUSBAND BENEDICT
(**MEDICINE —**) PEAI DOCTOR
SHAMAN ANGAKOK
(**MEEK —**) MOSES
(**MIGHTY —**) SAMSON
(**ODD-JOB —**) JOEY
(**OLD —**) HAG OLD BOOL CUFF GAF
CRONE DOBBY UNCLE BODACH
DUFFER FATHER GAFFER NESTOR
GERONTE STARETS ECKEHART
VELYARDE
(**OLD-CLOTHES —**) POCO
(**ONE-ARMED —**) WINGY
(**ONE-EYED —**) ARIMASP
(**OVERFASTIDIOUS —**) DUDE
(**PARTY —**) SIDESMAN
(**PRIMITIVE —**) URMENSCH
(**PRINCIPAL —**) HERO TOPARCH
(**RASH —**) HOTSPUR
(**RICH —**) DIVES CROESUS
(**RIGHT-HAND —**) HENCHMAN
(**RIGHTEOUS —**) SADDIK
(**SERVING —**) GARCON
(**SOUND-EFFECTS —**) CRAWK
(**STERN —**) GRIMSIRE
(**STRAIGHT —**) STOOGE
(**STRONG —**) KWASIND
(**STRONG-ARM —**) HOOD GORILLA
(**STUPID —**) SUBMAN
(**THICKSET —**) GRUB KNAR SPUD
(**TOUGH —**) KNAR
(**UNEMPLOYED —**) BATLAN
(**UTILITY —**) JUMPER
(**VICIOUS —**) YAHOO
(**WHITE — LIVING WITH ABORIGINE**)
COMBO
(**WHITE —**) BOSTON BUCKRA
CACHILA
(**WILD —**) WOODMAN WOODWOSE
(**WISE —**) NAB HAKAM SABIO SOLO
SOPHY NESTOR WIZARD SOLOMON
TOHUNGA
(**WIZENED —**) GNOME
(**WRETCHED —**) CAITIFF
(**YOUNG —**) BOY LAD JONG YOUTH

BOCHUR DAMSEL EPHEBE KNIGHT BOUCHAL BUCKEEN YOUNKER SPRINGAL

MANABOZHO MICHABOU WINABOJO
MAN-ABOUT-TOWN FLANEUR
MANACLE BAND BOND DARBY HAMPER TIRRET SHACKLE HANDCUFF HANDLOCK (PL.) IRONS CHAINS
MANAGE DO GET MAN RUN BEAR CURB FEND HACK HOLD KEEP LEAD MAKE RULE TEND TOOL WIND WORK BROOK CARRY DIGHT FORTH FRAME GUIDE MAYNE ORDER SHIFT SPEND STEER SWING WIELD CONVEY DEMEAN DEVISE DIRECT FETTLE GOVERN HANDLE INTEND MANURE TEMPER AGITATE CONDUCT DISPOSE EXECUTE FINAGLE HUSBAND MINSTER OFFICER OPERATE SOLICIT STEWARD CONTRIVE ENGINEER (— AWKWARDLY) FOOZLE (— CLUMSILY) KEVEL (— TO BEAR) AFFORD
MANAGEABLE EASY YARE BANTAM DOCILE WIELDY DUCTILE FLEXIBLE YIELDING
MANAGEMENT CARE HEEL WORK CHARGE CONDUCT CONTROL ECONOMY GESTION RUNNING CARRIAGE DEMEANOR ENGINERY MANAGERY MANEUVER REGIMENT STEERAGE STEERING (DOMESTIC —) MENAGE HUSBANDRY (GOOD —) EUTAXY (SKILLFUL —) PRACTICE PRACTISE
MANAGER BOSS DOER AGENT DAROGA DEPUTY PURSER SYNDIC CURATOR HUSBAND STEWARD WIELDER AUMILDAR DIRECTOR DISPOSER ENGINEER HERENACA INSTITOR — OF FARM) HIND GRIEVE (ASSISTANT —) CAPORAL (MINE —) CAPTAIN (POLITICAL —) FUGLEMAN
MANAKIN PIPRA
MAN-AT-ARMS KNIGHT
MANATEE COWFISH HOGFISH MERMAID LAMANTIN MUTILATE IRENIAN
MANBARKLAK JARANA KAKARAL
MANCALA WARI
MANCHU SHERRY
MANDAEAN SABAEAN
MANDARIN TOWKAY CHINESE
MANDARIN ORANGE SATSUMA
MANDATE BREVE ORDER BEHEST CHARGE DECREE FIRMAN BIDDING COMMAND PRECEPT PROCESS MANDAMUS MANDATUM WARRANTY — OF GOD) JUDGMENT
MANDIBLE JOWL SETA JAWBONE MAXILLA NATHITE — PART) MALA
MANDINGO MANDE WANGARA
MANDOLIN OUD MANDORA

MANDRAKE ALRAUN DUDAIM
MANDREL BALL STUD SLEEVE CHEMISE SPINDLE TRIBLET
MANDRILL MAIMON MORMON
MANE JUBA MONE CREST PITRI
MAN-EATER REQUIN REQUIEM
MANEGE TRAIN
MANEUVER PLAY TURN WISE GAMBIT JOCKEY MANURE PESADE VRILLE FINAGLE FINESSE ARTIFICE DEMARCHE ENGINEER EXERCISE STRATEGY WINDLASS (- GENTLY) EASE (AERIAL —) LOOP SPIN FISHTAIL WINGOVER (ILLEGAL —) GAME (ROCK-CLIMBING —) LAYBACK (SKIING —) SNOWPLOW (WRESTLING —) ESCAPE BUTTOCK
MANEUVERABLE YARE
MANEUVERING FINESSE FLANKING
MANGE ITCH REEF SCAB CANKER DARTARS SCABIES
MANGER BIN BUNK CRIB HECK STALL CRATCH
MANGLE MAR HACK MOUTH BRUISE GARBLE HACKLE IRONER MAGGLE MURDER MAMMOCK LACERATE MUTILATE
MANGO DIKA AMHAR AMINI BAUNO AMCHOOR CARABAO PAHUTAN (POINT OF —) NAK
MANGOSTEEN SANTOL GARCINIA
MANGROVE BACAO GORAN MANGLE MYRTAL BACAUAN CERIOPS COURIDA HANGALAI LANGARAI
MANGUE CHOLUTECA CHOROTEGA
MANGY SCABBY ROINISH SCABETIC
MANHANDLE SCRAG
MANHOOD ADAMHOOD
MANIA RAGE CRAZE FUROR FRENZY DELIRIUM HYSTERIA INSANITY
MANIAC KILLER MADMAN FANATIC LUNATIC
MANIFEST HAVE NUDE OPEN RIFE SENE SHOW APERT CLEAR FRANK GROSS KITHE NAKED OVERT PLAIN PROVE SPEAK SUTEL ATTEST COUTHE EVINCE EXTANT GRAITH LIQUID OSTEND PATENT PHANIC APPROVE CONFESS DECLARE EVIDENT EXHIBIT EXPRESS OBVIOUS SIGNIFY VISIBLE APPARENT DISCLOSE DISCOVER INDICATE PALPABLE PROCLAIM (NOT —) LATENT
MANIFESTATION ACT SON BEAM COMA GLINT AVATAR COMING EFFECT OSTENT ADVANCE DISPLAY EXPRESS SHOWING EPIPHANY MANIFEST (BARELY PERCEPTIBLE —) SCINTIL (BRIEF —) GLEAM (DIVINE —) SPIRIT SHEKINAH (HORRIBLE —) CHIMAERA (MORAL —) SOUL (VAGUE —) GLIMMER
MANIFESTLY WITTERLY
MANIFESTO PLACARD

MANIFOLD MANY TURRET VARIOUS FELEFOLD MANYFOLD MULTIPLE
MANIKIN ECORCHE PANTINE PHANTOM HOMUNCIO HOMUNCLE MANNIKIN
MANIOC CATELLA
MANIPLE FANON SUDARIUM
MANIPULATE COAX COOK DIAL FAKE HAND STIR TOOL CROOK HUMOR KNEAD SHAPE TREAT WIELD CHIVVY GOVERN HANDLE JOCKEY MANAGE SHUFFLE (— BY DECEPTIVE MEANS) RIG
MANIPULATION PASS JUGGLERY MANAGERY
MANITO ORENDA POKUNT MANITOU TAMANOAS
MANKIND MAN FLESH SHEEP WORLD SPECIES HUMANITY UNIVERSE
MANLIKE MALE MANLY MANNISH HOMINOID
MANLINESS ARETE VIRTUS MANSHIP
MANLY BOLD MALE HARDY MANNY DARING VIRILE MANLIKE
MAN-MADE CULTURAL SYNTHETIC
MANNER AIR BAT JET LAT WAY FORM GAET GARB GATE KIND MAKE MIEN MODE RATE SORT THEW TOUR WISE WONE GUISE LATES STYLE TENUE TRICK COURSE CUSTOM METHOD ADDRESS AMENITY FASHION QUALITY QUOMODO CARAPACE DEMEANOR LANGUAGE (— OF APPROACH) ABORD (— OF DOING) ACTION (— OF HANDLING) HAND (— OF MAKING ANYTHING) FACTURE (— OF SITTING) ASANA (— OF SPEAKING) SLUR SOUGH ACCENT GRAMMAR (— OF WALKING) STEP (AFFECTED —) AIR (AMUSING —) DROLLERY (ARROGANT —) BRAG HAUTEUR (FORBIDDING —) SHELL (FORMAL —) STARCH (HABITUAL —) SONG (OUTWARD —) TOUR FRONT (SMOOTH —) JAPAN (SWAGGERING —) SIDE (USUAL —) HABIT (PL.) CORNERS HAVINGS BREEDING
MANNERED CUTE MORATE THEWED
MANNERISM TRICK IDIASM (PL.) DAPS
MANNERLY CIVIL
MANNERS MORES HAVANCE HAVINGS BEAUETRY BREEDING
MANNITOL MANNITE PUNICIN
MAN-OF-WAR CARAVEL
MAN-OF-WAR FISH PASTOR
MANOR HAM BURY HALL TOWN VILL COMMOTE MANSION LORDSHIP TOWNSHIP
MANPOWER BRAWN LABOR
MANROOT IPOMOEA
MANROPE LIMMER

MANSERVANT (ALSO SEE SERVANT) LAD MOZO GROOM VALET ANDREW BUTLER TEABOY
MANSION DOME HOTEL HOUSE MANSE SIEGE TOWER CASTLE HARBOR HOSTEL CHATEAU
(— **OF THE MOON**) ALNATH
MANSLAUGHTER BLOOD FELONY HOMICIDE
MANTEL CLAVY CLAVEL
MANTELET MANTA MANTLE MANTLET GALAPAGO
MANTELPIECE BRACE PAREL CLAVEL MANTEL MANTLING
MANTICORE MONTEGRE
MANTIS CAGN RACER REARER MANTOID PROPHET
MANTIS CRAB SQUILLA
MANTLE CAPA HOSE PALL ROBE CLOAK CREAM FROCK JABUL LAMBA PALLA TUNIC CAMAIL CAPOTE KHIRKA SLAVIN TABARD CHLAMYS CHRISOM CHUDDAR FERIDJI MANTEAU PAENULA PALLIUM SLEEVES WHITTLE WRAPPER BARRACAN CHRYSOME MANTELET REGOLITH RICINIUM STOCKING
MANTLEROCK REGOLITH
MANTO (FATHER OF —) HERCULES TIRESIAS
(**SON OF** —) MOPSUS
MANTRA DHARANI GAYATRI MANTRAM SAVITRI
MANTUA MANTY SEMAR
MANTZU MIAOTZE
MANUAL VADY COACH GREAT TUTOR PORTAS CAMBIST CEMBALO DIDACHE MANUARY BOMBARDE HANDBOOK KEYBOARD ORDINARY PORTHORS SYNOPSIS
(**MAGICIAN'S** —) GRIMOIRE
(**NAVIGATION** —) BOWDITCH
MANUAO IAO
MANUBRIUM HYPOSTOME
MANUFACTURE COIN FAKE MAKE FORGE PERFORM PRODUCE WORKING BOOKWORK
(— **OF LIQUOR OR DRUGS**) ABKARI
(**ILLEGAL** —) COINING
MANUFACTURED STORE
MANUFACTURER BRAND MAKER WRIGHT DISKERY SPINNER SUPPLIER
MANUMIT FREE LIBERATE
MANURE HOT MIG DUNG LIME MUCK SAUR SOIL TATH FECES MIXEN FULZIE SEASON SLEECH COMPOST FOLDING GOODING POUDRET DRESSING WORTHING
MANURED BONED
MANUS HAND
MANUSCRIPT CODEX FLIMSY MATTER SCRIPT UNCIAL CURSIVE PANDECT PINTURA WITNESS EXEMPLAR
MANX CAT RUMPY
MANX SHEARWATER CREW PUFFIN SCRABE SCRABER

MANY TEN FELE MUCH SERE FORTY GREAT MAINT MOULT TWENTY ENDLESS JILLION SEVERAL VARIOUS MANIFOLD COUNTLESS
(**BEING** —) NUMEROUS
(**GOOD** —) HANTLE
(**GREAT** —) MORT RAFF SWITH
MANYATTA KRAAL
MANY-HANDED BRIAREAN
MANYROOT RUELLIA
MANY-SIDED VARIOUS
MAORI (— **IMAGE**) TIKI
(— **LAW**) UTU
(— **VILLAGE**) PA PAH KAINGA
(**NOT** —) PAKEMA
MAP KEY CARD DICE PLAT PLOT CARTE CENTO CHART DRAFT INSET QUART STILL DRAUGHT GRAPHIC CARTGRAM GATEFOLD PLATFORM
MAPAU MAPLE MATIPO TARATA PIRIPIRI
MAPLE MAZER DOGWOOD SYCAMORE WINGSEED
(**GROVE OF** —) SAPBUSH
MAR BLOT SCAR SNIP BLOOM BOTCH SHEND SPILL SPOIL BLOTCH DEFACE DEFEAT DEFORM IMPAIR INJURE BLEMISH DISGRACE
MARABOU STORK ARGALA MORABIT
MARANAO LANAO
MARASMUS MARCOR ATHREPSIA
MARAUD RAID DACOIT PICKEER PILLAGE
MARAUDER TORY BANDIT BUMMER LOOTIE PIRATE CATERAN LADRONE
(**PL.**) BLACKS
MARAUDING BANDITRY OUTRIDING
MARBLE MIB MIG PEA POT TAW ALLY BOOL BOWL DUCK MARL AGATE AGGIE ALLEY BONCE COMMY IMMIE IVORY LINER PUREY RANCE DOGGLE MARMOR MARVEL PARIAN PEEWEE STEELY CARRARA CIPOLIN GLASSIE GRIOTTE KNICKER PARAGON PITCHER SHOOTER BROCATEL DOLOMITE KNUCKLER
(**BLACK** —) JET
(**PL.**) TAW BOWLS PLUMPS HUNDRED
MARBLED MIRLY
MARCH FILE HIKE LIDE MARK MUSH SLOG ROUTE TRACE TRINE TROOP WALTZ DEFILE DOUBLE PARADE REVIEW DEBOUCH STRETCH FOOTSLOG PROGRESS
(— **BEHIND**) COVER
(— **IN FRONT OF**) LEAD
(— **OBLIQUELY**) INCLINE
(**PL.**) FRONTIER
MARCHING (— **UP**) ANABASIS
MARCHIONESS MARCHESA MARQUISE
MARCOT GOOTE
MARCOTTAGE GOOTEE
MARE SEA YAD YADE YAUD GILLIE GILLOT GRASNI HUNTRESS
MARE'S-TAIL HIPPURID
MARGARET MEG META MARGET MARGOT GRETCHEN
MARGATE PORGY

MARGAY TIGER
MARGIN HEM RIM VAT BANK BRIM BROW CURB EDGE FOLD INCH LIMB LIST RAND BRINK EAVES MARGE VERGE BORDER FRINGE LABRUM LACING CUSHION DRAUGHT MARGENT SELVAGE HAIRLINE
(— **OF CARAPACE**) DOUBLURE
(— **OF CIRCLE**) LIMB
(— **OF LIP**) PROLABIUM
(— **OF PAGE**) BACK
(— **OF SAFETY**) LEEWAY
(— **OF SHELL**) LABRUM LIMBUS
(— **OF SUPERIORITY**) LEAD
(— **OF WING**) TERMEN
(—**S OF HERD**) SWING
(**SEA** —) COAST
MARGOSA NIM NEEM NEEMBA
MARGRAVE RUDIGER MARKGRAF
MARIANA SILYBUM
MARIGOLD GOLD GULL SAMH AZTE BOOTS GOLDE GOOLS HELIO BACLIN BUDDLE GOLDCUP GOLDIN GOLLAND KINGCUP MARYBUD TAGETES
MARIJUANA POT WEED MOOCAH LOCOWEED
MARINE JOLLY GALOOT GULPIN GYRENE TOPMAN MARINAL HALIMOUS MARITIME NAUTICAL
MARINER MARINE SAILOR SEALER SEAMAN BUSCARLE SEAFARER WARRENER
(**PL.**) SEAFOLK
MARINHEIRO ACAJOU
MARIONETTE PUPPY POPPET PUPPET
MARITAL INTIMATE HUSBANDLY
MARITIME MARINE HALIMOUS NAUTICAL
MARK AIM END HOB HUB MOT POP BELT BLOT BUOY BUTT CHOP CLI DELE DINT FAZE FIST GOAL KEEL LINE MIND NOTE RIST SCAR SEAR SIGN SMOT SMUT SPOT TEND TEX TICK VIRE WAND WIND BADGE BOTTU BRAND BREVE CHANT CHECK CLOUD DATUM DITTO DRA FLECK FRANK GHOST GRADE HILL KNIFE LABEL MARCH MARCO MEIT NOKTA PRINT PROOF ROVER SCA SCOPE SCORE SCUFF SPOOR STAMP SWIRL TOKEN TOUCH TRA TRACK TRACT WATCH WHITE ACCENT ALPIEU BEACON BESPOT BLOTCH BUTTON CARACT DAGGE DAPPLE DENOTE DIRECT INDICE LETTER MARKER NOTICE OBJECT SMUTCH STREAK STRIKE STROKE SUCKER SYMBOL TARGET UPSHO WICKER WITTER BETOKEN CHARE COCKSHY DEMERIT DIAMOND DRAUGHT EROTEME EXCUDIT FINMARK IMPRESS IMPRINT INSIG KENMARK SCARIFY SERRATE SIGNARY SPECKLE STRIATE SYMPTOM VESTIGE WAYMARK BRACELET CROWFOOT DATEMAR DIASTOLE DISPUNCT EVIDENCE

FOOTMARK FOOTSTEP IDENTIFY IDEOGRAM MONUMENT NOTATION
(— A BIRD) BAND
(— AFTER ASSAY) TOUCH
(— AS SPURIOUS) ATHETIZE
(— BY BURNING) CHAR
(— BY CUTTING) SCRIBE
(— BY PLOWING) STRIKE
(— CROSSWISE) CRANK
(— DENOTING CORRUPT PASSAGE) OBELUS
(— DIRECTIONS) ADDRESS
(— IN ARCHERY) CLOUT HOYLE ROVER WHITE
(— IN CANON) LEAD
(— IN CURLING) TEE COCK
(— IN QUOITS) MOT
(— INDICATING CONTRACTION) CORONIS
(— INDICATING DIRECTION) ARROW
(— OF ACKNOWLEDGEMENT) ACCOLADE
— OF DISGRACE) STAIN STIGMA
— OF DISTINCTION) BELT
— OF ESTEEM) LAUREL GARLAND
— OF OFFICE) SEAL
— OF OWNERSHIP) SWANMARK
— OF PURITY) HALLMARK
— OF REFERENCE) OBELISK
— OF SIGNATURE) CROSS
— OF SUPERIORITY) BELL
— OF WEAVER) KEEL
— OFF LAND) FEER PHEER
— OFF) SUBTEND
— ON ANIMAL'S FACE) BLAZE TRIPE
— ON CHART) VIGIA
— ON EXAM) PASS
— ON FEATHER) BAR SPANGLE
— ON FOREHEAD) KUMKUM
— ON PENNSYLVANIA BARNS) EXAFOOS
— ON SHEEP) SMIT
— ON SHIP) SURMARK
— ON SKIN) PLOT CREASE
— ON STAMP) CONTROL
— OUT) CANCEL DELINE AIRMARK POINT COMPART DESCRIBE
— OVER GERMAN VOWEL) UMLAUT
— OVER LETTER N) TILDE
— OVER LONG VOWELS) MACRON
— SHEEP OR CATTLE) BASTE IST DEWLAP
— TIME) COUNT
— TO BE ATTAINED) BOGEY BOGIE
— TO GUIDE VESSELS) MYTH
— TRANSVERSELY) LADDER
— UNDER LETTER C) CEDILLA
— WITH LINES) HATCH CAMLET
— WITH POINTED ROLLER) GRILL
— WITH RIDGES) RIB
— WITH STRIPES) WALE STREAM
— WITH TAR) BASTE
CENT —) VERGE
GULAR —) HOOK
LLOT —) SCRATCH
UNDARY —) MEAR MERE TERM
E MEITH STAKE LANDMARK
DENCY —) BRISURE

(CANCELLATION —) BUMPER KILLER
(DIACRITICAL —) TIL TILDE
(DIRTY —) SMIRCH
(DISTINCTIVE —) BADGE INDICIA
(DISTINGUISHING —) ITEM COCARDE EARMARK INSIGNE
(DOUBLE-DAGGER —) DIESIS
(EASY —) YAP SMELT
(EIGHTH —) URE
(EXACT —) NICK
(EXCLAMATION —) SCREAMER
(IDENTIFICATION —) MOLE CREST SPLIT SIGNET WATTLE EARMARK KENMARK LUGMARK COLOPHON
(LOW-WATER —) DATUM
(MERIDIAN —) MIRE
(MUSICAL —) PRESA CORONA
(PARAGRAPH —) PILCROW
(PROOFREADER'S —) STET CARET
(PUNCTUATION —) DASH STOP BRACE BREVE COLON COMMA HYPHEN PERIOD BRACKET DIERESIS ELLIPSIS DIACRITIC SEMICOLON
(SECTARIAN —) BOTTU TILAKA
(SKATE —) CUSP
(SMALL ROUND —) DOT
(TRAMP'S —) MONICA MONNIKER
(WHITE —) RACHE
(PL.) POINTING
MARKED FAR GREAT SCORED SEVERE SPOTTY COLORED EMINENT MARCATO POINTED SCARRED SPECKED SPOTTED
(— BY COLORED RINGS) AREOLATE
(— BY FURROWS) RIVOSE
(— BY INTELLIGENCE) ABLE
(— BY PROSTRATION) ALGID
(— BY REFINEMENT) ELEGANT
(— BY RIDGES) SERRIED
(— BY SHREWDNESS) ADROIT
(— BY SIMILARITY) AKIN
(— BY SIMPLICITY) ATTIC
(— BY WAVY LINES) GYROSE
(— OUT) DISTINCT
(— UP) FOUL
(— WITH BANDS) ZONATE
(— WITH SMALLPOX) FRETTEN
(— WITH SPOTS OR LINES) NOTATE
(EXTREMELY —) INTENSE
MARKEDLY BYOUS
MARKER HOB HUB DOLE FLAG MARK STUMP TYPER BUTTON GUIDON HOBBLE HUBBLE TABBER DAYMARK SCRIBER
MARKET CURB GUNJ MART PORT SALE SOOK VEND VENT CHEAP CROSS GUNGE HALLE PASAR PRICE TRONE TRYST BAZAAR BOURSE OUTLET PARIAN RIALTO POULTRY CHEAPING DEBOUCHE EMPORIUM EXCHANGE MACELLUM
(CATTLE —) TRISTE
(MEAT —) SHAMBLES
MARKETABLE SUK SUQ SOUK STAPLE SALABLE VENDIBLE
MARKETPLACE SUK SUQ SOUK AGORA CHAWK CHOWK HALLE PLAZA BAZAAR EMPORIUM
MARKING EYE HOOD COLLAR

CLOUDING SCARRING SCRIBING
(— OF WOOD) CURL GRAIN
(— ON FEATHER) SPANGLE
(— ON MARS) CANAL
(—S ON STEEL) DAMASK
(ANIMAL —) SADDLE SHIELD
(CATTLE —) JINGLEBOB
(CRESCENT-SHAPED —) LUNULA LUNULE
(DROP-SHAPED —) GUTTA
(POSTAL —) INDICIA
(RINGLIKE —) ANNULUS
(STRIPED —) STRAKE
MARKKA FINMARK
MARKSMAN SHOT MARKER PLUFFER SHOOTER SHOTMAN SHOOTIST
MARL MALM MARLITE
MARLI MARIE
MARLIN AU AGUJA
MARLINESPIKE FID JAEGER PRICKER STABBER
MARMALADE CHEESE SQUISH CODINIAC
MARMALADE TREE CHICO MAMMIE SAPOTE ZAPOTE
MARMOSET MICO TITI SAGOIN JACCHUS QUIRCAL SAIMIRI TAMARIN WISTITI ORABASSU
MARMOT BOBAC PAHMI GOPHER SUSLIK SCIURID SIFFLEUR WHISTLER
MARMOTA ARCTOMYS
MAROON AZTEC PICNIC CIMARRON
MARQUEE CANOPY MARQUISE
MARQUISE NAVETTE
MARQUISETTE LENO
MARRANOS ANUSIM
MARRED CUPPY SCABBY SPECKED
MARRIAGE MUTA DAIVA HYMEN KARAO BRIDAL BUCKLE SPLICE SPOUSE EXOGAMY NUPTIAL PUNALUA SPOUSAL WEDDING WEDLOCK CONUBIUM LEVIRATE OPSIGAMY
(— AFTER DEATH OF FIRST SPOUSE) DIGAMY
(— AT ADVANCED AGE) OPSIGAMY
(— BELOW POSITION) HYPOGAMY
(— CONTRACT) KETUBAH
(— OUTSIDE FAMILY) EXOGAMY
(— PORTION) TOCHER
(— WITHIN GROUP) ENDOGAMY
MARRIAGEABLE NUBILE
MARRIED COVERT WEDDED ESPOUSED
MARROW KEEST MARIE MERCH MERGH MEDULLA
MARRY TIE WED FAST WIFE WIVE CLEEK MATCH BUCKLE CROTCH ENSURE MARROW SPLICE HUSBAND NUPTIAL WEDLOCK DESPOUSE
(— OFF) BESTOW
MARS ARES MAMERS MARMAR MAVORS MASPITER TEUTATES
(FATHER OF —) JUPITER
(MOTHER OF —) JUNO
(SON OF —) REMUS ROMULUS
MARSH BOG FEN HAG CARR DANK FELL FLAM FLAT HOPE JHIL MASH

MIRE OOZE SOIL SUDS TARN VLEI
VLEY WASH WHAM FLASH GLADE
JHEEL LIMAN SLACK SLASH SLUMP
SWAMP MORASS PALUDE PUDDLE
CIENAGA CORCASS POCOSIN
PONTINE QUAGMIRE STROTHER
TURLOUGH
(SALT —) SALT SALINA SALINE
MARSHAL ARRAY MUSTER PARADE
JERONIMO MERECHAL
(— FACTS) HASH
MARSH ELDER JACKO
MARSH FEVER HELODES
MARSH GAS METHANE
MARSH HARRIER PUDDOCK
PUTTOCK
MARSHMALLOW MALLOW WYMOTE
MARSH MARIGOLD BOOTS CAPER
CRAZY GOOLS DRAGON GAMOND
GOWLAN COWSLIP ELKSLIP
GOLDCUP KINGCOB KINGCUP
MATYBUD DRUNKARD
MARSH PENNYWORT PENNYROT
WATERCUP
MARSH PINK SABBATIA
MARSH TEA LEDUM
MARSH TREFOIL BUCKBEAN
MARSH WREN LONGBILL
MARSHY FOGGY MOORY MOSSY
PONDY SNAPY SPEWY CALLOW
PLASHY QUAGGY QUASHY SLUMPY
HELODES MOORISH QUEACHY
PALUDIAL PALUDINE WATERISH
MARSUPIAL KOALA CUSCUS
POSSUM WOMBAT DASYURE
OPOSSUM KANGAROO
MART STAPLE EMPORIUM
MARTEN FOIN SABLE SOBOL FISHER
MARTRIX MUSTELID MUSTELIN
(GROUP OF —S) RICHESSE
MARTENSITE SORBITE
MARTIAL BELLIC WARLIKE WARRIOR
BELLICAL MILITARY
MARTIN MARTLET SWALLOW
MARTINET
MARTINMAS TERM
MARTYR STEPHEN WITNESS
SUFFERER
MARTYRDOM MARTYRY PASSION
MARVEL MARL MUSE FERLY SELLY
ADMIRE WONDER MAGNALE
MIRACLE MONSTER PORTENT
PRODIGY SELCOUTH
MARVELOUS MIRIFIC STRANGE
FABULOUS WONDROUS
MARY MOLL POLL MAMIE MAURA
MOLLY MIRIAM MARILLA

MARYLAND

BATTLESITE: ANTIETAM
CAPITAL: ANNAPOLIS
COLLEGE: HOOD GOUCHER
STJOHNS
COUNTY: CECIL TALBOT
ALLEGANY SOMERSET
INDIAN: CONOY NANTICOKE
LAKE: PRETTYBOY
MOUNTAIN: BACKBONE

NATIVE: WESORT TERRAPIN
NICKNAME: OLDLINE
RIVER: CHESTER POTOMAC
CHOPTANK PATUXENT
STATE BIRD: ORIOLE
STATE TREE: OAK
TOWN: EASTON TOWSON
ABERDEEN BETHESDA
POCOMOKE BALTIMORE

MARYSOLE CARTER LEADER
CARTARE
MASAI WAKWAFI WAKWAVI
MASCOT BILLIKEN
MASCULINE MALE DOGGY VIRILE
LALAQUI MANLIKE
MASH BEER CHAP MASA MASK MESH
SLOP CHAMP CREEM SMASH SMUSH
MUDDLE STILLAGE
MASHED CHAPPED DAUPHINE
MASHER FLIRT BEETLE
MASJID MOSQUE
MASK FACE HIDE JEST LOUP SLUR
VEIL BLOCK BLOOP CLOAK COVER
GRILL GUISE LARVE POINT VIZOR
DOMINO GRILLE MUZZLE SCREEN
VEILER VIZARD BECLOUD CONCEAL
CURTAIN MASKOID ANTEMASK
DEFILADE DISGUISE MASCARON
(— OUT) CROP
(GAS —) CANARY
(HALF —) LOO LOUP DOMINO
(PL.) AREITO
MASKED LARVATED VIZARDED
MASKER GUISARD MASQUER
MASKING MUMMERY MUMMING
COLORING
MASLIN MESTLEN MASHLOCH
MUNGCORN MASSELGEM
MASON LAYER BUILDER MASONER
COMACINE KNOBBLER LAMMIKIN
SCUTCHER
MASONRY ASHLAR BACKING
BLOCAGE MOELLON NOGGING
ISODOMUM QUOINING ROCKWORK
MASQUE MASK COMUS DEVICE
ANTIMASK DISGUISE
MASQUER REX
MASQUERADE MASK GUISE DOMINO
MASQUE PARADE MASKERY
DISGUISE
MASQUERADER RAGSHAG
MASQUERADING CARNIVAL
MASS BAT BED GOB SOP WAD BODY
BULK GOUT HEAP HEFT KNOT LEAD
LUMP MOLE OBIT STOW SWAD
AMASS BATCH BLOOM CLAMP
CLASH CLUMP CROWD CRUST
DIRGE GLOBE GORGE GROSS
MATTE MISSA SLUMP SOLID SPIRE
STORE WODGE COMMON GOBBET
NUGGET PROPER VOLUME WEIGHT
BOUROCK CONGEST DENSITY
MASKINS MESKINS NYSTERY
REQUIEM SALOMON CALAPITE
CONGERIE ENDOSOME FLOCCULE
MOUNTAIN SOULMASS
(— IN THE WHITE NILE) SUDD

(— OF BACTERIA) SLIME SYMPLASM
(— OF BLOSSOMS) BLOW
(— OF BLUBBER) MELON
(— OF BRANCHES) SPRAY
(— OF BUBBLES) FOAM
(— OF BUSHES) SHAG
(— OF CARPELS) SOREMA
(— OF CELLS) COMB CANCER
CUMULUS STALACE
(— OF CLOUDS) BANK
(— OF COAL) JUD
(— OF COLORS) BLOB
(— OF COTTON) FUSSOCK
(— OF CURED RUBBER) LOAF
(— OF DEBRIS) SLIDE
(— OF DOUGH) DUMPLING
(— OF FIBERS) KAPOK
(— OF FILAMENTS) FLOCCUS
(— OF FILTH) GORE
(— OF FRAGMENTS) BRASH
(— OF HAIR) GLIB TOUPET
(— OF ICE) BERG CALF FLOE FLA
PATCH ICICLE STURIS GROWLER
ICEBERG FLOEBERG
(— OF INSECTS) CACHE
(— OF IRON) BALL BLOB CORE
BLOOM INDUCTOR
(— OF LAVA) BOMB SPINE
(— OF LEAVES) FOLIAGE
(— OF LIMESTONE) HUM
(— OF LOOSE BOULDERS) CLATTI
(— OF METAL) SOW INGOT BUTTI
(— OF MOLTEN GLASS) GOB
GATHER PARISON
(— OF MUD) CLASH
(— OF ORE) BACK SLUG BUNNY
SQUAT
(— OF PEOPLE) CROWD HORDE
(— OF POMACE) CHEESE
(— OF ROCK) DOME NECK HORS
LEDGE NAPPE SCALP SNOUT INL
SARSEN BOULDER FOOTWALL
(— OF SAND) PAAR
(— OF SOAP) CURD
(— OF SPORES) SORUS
(— OF SUGAR CRYSTALS) STRIK
(— OF SUGAR) FONDANT
(— OF TISSUE) COLLAR GANGLI
(— OF WATER) HEAD
(— OF YARN) COP BALLOON
(— OF YOLK) LATEBRA
(— OVERHANGING) CORNICE
(— TOGETHER) HUDDLE
(—S OF DRIFTWOOD) EMBARRAS
(AMORPHOUS —) JUMBLE
SYMPLASM
(BILLOWY —) CLOUD
(BUSHY —) SHOCK
(COMPACT —) BRIQUET
(CONFUSED —) COT JUMBLE
JUNGLE CLUTTER RUMMAGE
SHUFFLE
(DISORDERLY —) SCRAMBLE
(EGG —) BUNION CULTCH SPON
(FATTY —) BEAN HEADSKIN
(FECAL —) SCYBALUM
(FLATTISH —) DAB
(FLUID —) FLUOR
(GLASSY —) SLAG

(GLOBULAR —) MOORBALL
(INDISTINCT —) SMUDGE
(IRREGULAR —) CUB
(LIVING —) BLASTEMA
(MOIST —) PULP
(MOUNTAIN —) OROGEN
(NUCLEAR —) SHIELD
(OVERSPREADING —) PALL
(PEAR-SHAPED —) BOULE
(POROUS —) FILTER
(PROJECTING —) BOSS
(PULPY —) SQUELCH
(RECTANGULAR —) BRICK
(ROOT —) SOLE
(ROUNDED —) COB NOB KNOB
BOLUS KUGEL BULLET RONDLE
(SEDIMENTARY —) GOBI
(SHAPED —) PAT LOAF
(SHAPELESS —) JELLY
(SLIPPERY —) SIND SLUD SLUDDER
(SLUSHY —) POSH
(SOFT —) MASH MOXA MUMMY
(SWOLLEN —) CERE
(TANGLED — OF HAIR) MOP KNURL
(UNCTUOUS —) LANOLIN
(UPRIGHT —) COLUMN
PL.) MEINY MEINIE TRENTAL

MASSACHUSETTS
CAPE: ANN COD
CAPITAL: BOSTON
COLLEGE: SMITH AMHERST
SIMMONS WHEATON WILLIAMS
RADCLIFFE WELLESLEY
COUNTY: DUKES BERKSHIRE
NANTUCKET BARNSTABLE
INDIAN: NAUSET POCOMTUC
ISLAND: DUKES NANTUCKET
LAKE: ONOTA QUABBIN ROHUNTA
WEBSTER
MOUNTAIN: BRODIE POTTER
ALANDER EVERETT GREYLOCK
MOUNTAIN RANGE: BERKSHIRE
POND: WALDEN
RIVER: NASHUA CHARLES
CONCORD QUABOAG TAUNTON
CHICOPEE DEERFIELD
STATE BIRD: CHICKADEE
STATE FLOWER: MAYFLOWER
STATE NICKNAME: BAY
STATE TREE: ELM
TOWN: AYER LYNN OTIS ATHOL
BARRE LENOX AGAWAM
DEDHAM GROTON NAHANT
NATICK REVERE SAUGUS
WOBURN HOLYOKE IPSWICH
PEABODY TAUNTON BROCKTON
CHICOPEE COHASSET SCITUATE
UXBRODGE YARMOUTH
UNIVERSITY: CLARK TUFTS
HARVARD BRANDEIS

MASSACRE SLAY POGROM
CARNAGE SCUPPER BUTCHERY
SLAUGHTER
MASSAGE WISP KNEAD FACIAL
PETRIE SHAMPOO TRIPSIS LOMILOMI
MASSAGER MASSEUR VIBRATOR

MASSECUITE GUR FILLMASS
MASSED DENSE
MASSENA QUAIL COPPY
MASSIVE BIG BEAMY BULKY GROSS
HEAVY LUSTY MASSY SOUND STERN
STRONG HEALTHY HULKING
VOLUMED TIMBERED
MAST BUCK MAIN POLE SPAR OVEST
STICK STING DRIVER JIGGER
MIZZEN ARTEMON ASHERAH
MASTAGE SPANKER FOREMAST
MAINMAST SHIPMAST
(FALLEN —) SHACK
(SIXTH —) DRIVER
MASTAX TROPHI
MASTER DON HER JOE MAS RAB
SAB SIR ARCH BAAS BEAK BOSS
COCK FACE HERR JOSS KING LORD
MIAN SIRE TUAN BWANA MARSE
MASSA RABBI SAHIB SWAMI SWAMY
SWELL BRIDLE BUCKRA CASTER
DEACON DOMINE HUMBLE MAITRE
PATRON RECTOR RHETOR SIRCAR
WAFTER CAPTAIN CONQUER
DOMINIE DOMINUS EFFENDI
MAESTRO NAKHODA OGTIERN
PADRONE RABBANI RABBONI
AMAISTER BARGEMAN BEMASTER
KINGFISH LANDLORD MAGISTER
OVERCOME SLOOPMAN SURMOUNT
VANQUISH
(— OF CEREMONIES) EMCEE
VERGER COMPERE CHAIRMAN
(— OF CRAFT) KAHUNA
(— OF HOUSEHOLD) BALABOS
GOODMAN
(— OF REVELS) ALYTARCH
(— OF WHALER) SPOUTER
(FENCING —) LANISTA
(INFERIOR —) KNIFER
MASTER-AT-ARMS JAUNTY JAUNTIE
MASTERFUL LORDLY VIRILE
HAUGHTY ARROGANT MAGERFUL
MASTERPIECE TOPPIECE
MASTERY GREE GRIP GRIPE
COMMAND MAISTRY OVERHAND
MASTHEAD FLAG HIGHTOP
MASTICATE GUM CHAW CHEW
MASTICATORY BUYO
MASTIC BULLY JOCUM JOCUMA
MASTIC TREE ACOMA AUSUBO
COCUYO COCULLO
MASTIFF ALAN MASTY BANDOG
TIEDOG
MASTIGONEME FLIMMER
MASTITIS CLAP WEED GARGET
MAST TREE ASAK
MASTURBATE ABUSE
MASTURBATION ONANISM
FROTTAGE
MASTWOOD POON KAMANI
MAT COT RUG TOD BASS FLAT FLET
FOOT HAIR MOSS NIPA PACE RAFT
SHAG TAUT DOILY KILIM TATTY
COTTER FELTER FOOTER PAUNCH
PETATE TARGET COASTER CUSHION
DOORMAT KAITAKA MATTING
FOOTPACE FROSTING MATTRESS
SPANDREL

(— BORDER) TANIKO
(BOWLING —) FOOTER
(FIBER —) IE BASS
(PALM-LEAF —) YAPA
(PICTURE-FRAME —) FLAT
(POLYNESIAN —) LAUHALA
(SCOURING —) BEAR
(TABLECLOTH —) GARDNAP
(PL.) DUNNAGE
MATACHIN BOUFFON
MATACO CORONADO
MATADOR MAT ESPADA CAPEADOR
(— MOVEMENT) PASE
MATCH GO CAP VIE BOUT COPE
EVEN FERE LUNT MAKE MATE MEET
MILL MOTE PAIR PEEL PEER SIDE
SUIT AMATE EQUAL FIRER FUSEE
FUZEE MOUSE PARTY SPUNK TALLY
VENUE VESTA ASSORT CANCEL
COMMIT FELLOW KIPPIN MARROW
QUADER RUBBER SAMPLE SWATCH
COMPEER EXAMPLE IGNITER
ILLUMER KINDLER KIPPEEN LIGHTER
LUCIFER PARAGON PAREGAL
PATTERN PENDANT SINGLES
APPROACH BONSPIEL BREATHER
EUPYRION FOURSOME INFLAMER
LOCOFOCO PORTFIRE REANSWER
VESUVIAN VESUVIUS SEMIFINAL
(— AT DICE) MAIN
(BOXING —) SPAR FIGHT SLUGFEST
(CURLING —) SPIEL BONSPIEL
(DISHONEST —) CROSS
(GOLF —) NASSAU FOURSOME
(SHOOTING —) TIR SHOOT
(SLOW —) LUNT SMIFT SQUIB
(PL.) LIGHTS
MATCHED ASSORTED
MATCHING MARROW SUITABLE
MATCHLESS ALONE UNIQUE
NONESUCH PEERLESS
MATCHMAKER SHADCHAN
MATE CAWK FERE METE PAIR PEER
BILLY BREED BUDDY BULLY CLASP
CULLY DICKY MATCH PARTY TALLY
YERBA BUNKIE FELLOW FUTURE
MARROW PAREIL BROTHER
COMPEER COMRADE CONSORT
HUSBAND PARAGON NEIGHBOR
PIRRAURA
(BOATSWAIN'S —) BUFFER
(GUNNER'S —) LADY
(SECOND —) DICKY
MATERIAL FINE MOLD GAUZE
GOUGE HYLIC METAL MOULD PASTE
PLASS STUFF THING TRADE
BORROW CYANUS FABRIC GRAITH
HOGGIN MATTER PAPREG THINGY
APPAREL FOOTING SUBJECT
TEXTILE UNIDEAL WEIGHTY
ADDITIVE CORPORAL ECONOMIC
EQUIPAGE SENSIBLE SNOODING
TANGIBLE THINGISH
(— ELIMINATED) CULLAGE
(— FOR FERMENTING) GUILE
(— FOR OYSTER BEDS) CULCH
CULTCH
(— IN GRAIN) DOCKAGE
(— IN MAKING CEMENT) ADDITION

(— IN NEEDLEWORK) INKLE
(— OF CORDED SILK) CRYSTAL
(— OF SCREENINGS) HOGGIN
HOGGING
(— REMOVED BY SAW CUT) KERF
(— USED IN WAXING) BALL
(— WEIGHED) DRAFT DRAUGHT
(—S FOR MAKING GLASS) FRIT
(ABSORBENT —) DOPE
(ALLUVIAL —) SHINGLE
(ANCIENT —) MURRA MURRHA
(ARTISTIC —) KITSCH
(BAGGING —) HOPSACK
(BITUMINOUS —) KEROGEN
(BONY —) COSMINE
(BUILDING —) LATH ADOBE BRICK
STAFF SWISH TABBY TAPIA SILLAR
CONCRETE
(BUILDING —S) TIGNUM
(CLAY —) TAPIA
(CLAYEY —) GOUGE
(COLORING —) TINCTION
(COMBUSTIBLE —) KINDLING
(CONSTRUCTION —) BREEZE
(CORE —) NIFE
(CUSHIONING —) AIRFOAM
(DEPOSITED —) FOOTS
(DIAMOND —) BORT
(DOWNY —) FLUE
(DRESS —) FOULE VOILE PEELING
COTILLON
(DYEING —) SUMAC SUMACH
(EMROIDERY —) ARRASENE
(EXCAVATED —) SPOIL
(FACING —) ENAMEL
(FISSIONABLE —) STUFF
(FOUNDATION —) UNDERLAY
(GLUTINOUS —) GELATIN
(GRANULAR —) BASIS
(HARD —) CARBIDE
(HEAT-RESISTANT —) ALSIFILM
(ILLUSTRATIVE —) ART
(INSECTICIDAL —) SCABRIN
(INSULATING —) KERITE PECITE
BLANKET LAGGING OKONITE
MEGOTALC
(LEFTOVER —S) ARISINGS
(LOOSE —) SAND GRAVEL DETRITUS
(MINING REFUSE —) ATTLE
(MINUTE —) SESTON
(NUTRITIVE —) FUEL
(ORGANIC —) EXINITE
(PAPER-THIN —) FOIL
(PATCHING —) BOTCH
(PETRIFIED —) GEMSTONE
(POLISHING —) RABAT
(POWDERED —) FINES
(RAW —) STOCK STAPLE
(REFRACTORY —) GROG BULLDOG
CASTABLE
(RESIDUAL —) CEMENT
(RESOURCE —) SWIPE
(REVERSIBLE —) DAMASK
(SEDIMENTARY —) SILT
(SILK —) HONAN PEKIN FOULARD
SARCENET
(SLIMY —) SWARF
(SMOKING —) KEF KIF
(STIFF —) CANVAS

(STIFFENING —) BOXING
(TANNING —) SYNTAN
(TILE-STRENGTHENING —) WEB
(TRASHY —) SLUSH
(TWEEDY —) HOMESPUN
(TYPE-HIGH —) BEARER
(UNPUBLISHED —) INEDITA
(VOLCANIC —) EJECTA
(WATERPROOF —) KERATOL
(WORTHLESS —) GARBLE
(WOVEN —) LAPPET
(PL.) STOCK STUFF
MATERIALISM HYLISM SOMATISM
(DIALECTICAL —) DIAMAT
MATH MUTH MONASTERY
MATERIALISTIC SENSATE SENSUAL
BANAUSIC
MATERIALIZE REIFY DESCEND
MATER LECTIONIS GRAPHY
MATERNITY WARD NATUARY
MATGRASS NARD MATWEED
MATHEMATICIAN ALGORIST
GEOMETER
MATHEMATICS METHESIS
MATING NICK COUPLE DIALLEL
BREEDING HOMOGAMY PANMIXIA
MATRASS BOLTHEAD CUCURBIT
MATRIMONIAL MARITAL NUPTIAL
SPOUSAL CONJUGAL
MATRIMONY WEDLOCK MARRIAGE
MATRIMONY VINE JASMINE
JESSAMY BOXTHORN
MATRIX BED MAT SORT PLASM
SHELL SLIDE DYADIC MASTER
MOTHER STRIKE STROMA CALYMMA
FORMULA MATRICE PATTERN
PROPLASM
MATRON DAME
MATTE SLURRY REGULUS
MATTED COTTY FELTY PINNY
FELTED TAGGED TAUTED WAUKIT
STRINGY FELTLIKE
MATTER RES BONE CASE GEAR
HYLE ITEM RECK WHAT AMPER
FORCE PARTY SKILL STUFF THEME
AFFAIR ARGUFY BEHALF DITTAY
IMPORT ARTICLE CONCERN
MATERIA SIGNIFY SUBJECT
BUSINESS COMETHER MATERIAL
(— ADDED TO BOOK) APPENDIX
(— AROUND THE TEETH) TOPHUS
(— CONSTITUTING PERFUME)
ESSENCE
(— IN DISPUTE) ISSUE
(— OF BUSINESS) SHAURI
(— OF CONCERN) FUNERAL
(— OF INTEREST) GRIST
(— TO) CONCERN
(ALLUVIAL —) GEEST
(BRAIN —) ALBA
(CARTILAGINOUS —) GRISTLE
(COLORING —) DYE COLOR CROCK
EOSIN MORIN PIURI ALNEIN BUTEIN
FUSTIC INDIGO PIOURY CARMINE
CASTORY CUDBEAR LIGULIN
OENOLIN PIGMENT PUNICIN XANTHIN
ALGOCYAN FUSTERIC LAPACHOL
SCOPARIN TINCTION
(CORRUPT —) PUS ATTER

(DECAYED ORGANIC —) DUFF
(ESSENTIAL —) POINT
(EXPLANATORY —) HAGGADA
(FATTY —) SEBUM
(FECAL —) SIEGE
(FILTHY —) GUNK
(FOREIGN —) SOIL DROSS
(FOUL —) FILTH SORDES
(FRONT —) FOREWORD
(GELATINOUS —) BREAK SPAWN
(GRAY —) GLIOSA CINEREA
(INANIMATE —) AJIVA
(INFECTIOUS —) MIASMA
(MINERAL —) FLOAT FLOATS
(POTENTIAL —) PRAKRITI
(PRIMARY —) PRADHANA
(PRINTED —) BOX DISPLAY
(PULVERIZED —) ATTRITUS
(READING —) BODY
(SLIMY —) GLAIR
(SMALL —) MINUTIA
(SOFT —) PASH
(SUBJECT —) SCOPE CONTENT
(SUPPURATIVE —) PUS
(TRIVIAL —) JOKE
(TYPESET —) CHASE
(WASTE —) DIRT DRAFF DROSS
RAMMEL SEWAGE EXCRETA
(WORTHLESS —) SLAG GARBAGE
(WRITTEN —) SCRIVE
(PL.) HARNESS SQUARES
MATTER-OF-FACT DRY LITERAL
MATTER-OF-FACTNESS PROSE
MATTING MAT TAT BEAR BUMP
SIRKI TATTY SAWALI TATAMI
COCOMAT RABANNA
MATTOCK MAT BILL HACK MATAX
PICKAX TUBBAL TWIBIL GRUBBER
MATTRESS BED MAT TICK DIVAN
QUILT RESAI REZAI PALLET
MATRACE
MATURATE MATTER
MATURE AGE OLD BOLD FULL GR
RIPE ADULT MANCY RIPEN SHOO
ACCRUE AUTUMN DECOCT DIGES
MELLOW SEASON SEEDED
CONCOCT DEVELOP FURNISH
PERFECT PROVECT MATURATE
MATURED ADULT GROWN FORME
HEADED MELLOW SEEDED
HOMOGAMY
(SEXUALLY —) HIGH
MATURING (— EARLY) RATHRIPE
MATURITY AGE RIPENESS
MATZOTH MATZOS AFIKOMEN
MAUDLIN BEERY MOIST FUDDLEL
MAUDLINISM BATHOS
MAUL FAN TUG MALL MELL GAVE
GLAUM BEATER BEETLE BEMAUL
MUZZLE
MAUND MAO MEIN MAHAN
MAUNDER HAVER
MAUNDY NIPTER MANDATE
MAUSOLEUM MOLE TOMB TURB
BARADARI
MAUVE PURPLE MAUVINE
MAW MAA GORGE CROPPY THRO
MAWKISH CUTE SAPPY SOUPY
WALSH DRIPPY SICKLY VANILLA

MAXILLA SETA GNATHITE
CULTELLUS
AXILLIPED JAWFOOT GNATHITE
AXIM SAW SAY DICT ITEM NORM
RULE TEXT WORD ADAGE AXIOM
GNOME LARGE MOTTO DICTUM
SAYING SYMBOL BROCARD DICTATE
IMPRESA PRECEPT PROVERB
APHORISM APOTHEGM DOCTRINE
MORALISM PROTASIS SENTENCE
(PL.) LOGIA
AXIMUM FULL CREST EXTREME
OUTSIDE SUMMARY ULTIMATE
AXWELL LINE WEBER
AY CAN MUN MOWE MUST PRIME
SHALL HEYDAY HAWTHORN
SYCAMORE
(3D OF —) RUDMASDAY
AYA PRAKRITI
AYAN COCOM
— CALENDAR PERIOD) UAYEB
FINAL
— GOD) CHAC CHAAC
AYAPPLE MANDRAKE
AYBE MEBBE HAPPEN PERHAPS
POSSIBLY
AY DAY BELTANE
AYFISH ROCKFISH
AYFLOWER ARBUTUS
AYFLY DUN DOON DRAKE NAIAD
MAYFLY SPINNER EPHEMERA
AYHEM FELONY
AYONNAISE GOULASH DRESSING
AYOR MAIRE BAILIFF DEMARCH
ODESTA PROVOST PALATINE
BULGARIAN —) KMET
SPANISH —) ALCALDE
AYORSHIP CHAIR
AYPOLE SHAFT
AYPOP MAYCOCK MARACOCK
AYWEED BALDER COTULA MATHER
OGWEED COMPOSIT DILLWEED
AZE JUNGLE WARREN CONFUSE
BEWILDER LABYRINTH
COY QUILL
I MA US
AD MEATHE HYDROMEL
ADOW LEA ABEL MEAD VEGA
ISH WONG FIELD GRASS LEASE
ARSH SWALE WARTH CALLOW
ARAMO SAETER SMOOTH
OTRERO THWAITE CHINAMPA
RTIFICIAL —) CHINAMPA
ISH —) BAAN
OW —) ING INGE HAUGH CALLOW
ADOW CROWFOOT FROGWORT
ADOW GRASS POA
ADOWLAND ALP MOWING
OWLAND
ADOWLARK ACORN MEDLAR
DOW MOUSE VOLE
DOW PEA COWPEA
DOW PIPIT WEKEEN CHEEPER
TICK TITLING LINGBIRD
ITLARK
DOW SAFFRON UPSTART
DOW SAXIFRAGE SESELI
DOWSWEET SPIREA
ADWORT

MEAGER BALD BARE LANK LEAN
NICE POOR GAUNT NAKED SCANT
SILLY SKIMP SOBER SPARE JEJUNE
LEEPIT LENTEN MEAGRE NARROW
PILLED SCANTY SLIGHT SPARSE
STINGY SCRAGGY SCRANNY
SCRIMPY SCRUBBY SLENDER
SPARING STARVED STERILE
SCRATCHY
MEAGERLY BARELY SPARELY
SPARINGLY
MEAGERNESS ECONOMY EXILITY
TENUITY SPARENESS
MEAL AMYL ATTA BAKE CHOW FARM
FEED HASH KAIL MEAT MONG TUCK
COENA FLOUR MANGE SCOFF
BUFFET COMIDA DINNER FARINA
MANGER POLLEN REPAST SPREAD
SQUARE SUPPER UNDERN BLOWOUT
COOKOUT CRIBBLE NAGMAAL
NOONING SETDOWN ALMUERZO
CORNMEAL EVENMETE MEALTIDE
ORDINARY TRENCHER
(— FROM CASSAVA ROOT) FARINE
FARINHA
(— GROUND BY HAND) GRADDAN
(— OF FELLOWSHIP) AGAPE
(— STIRRED WITH MILK) STUROCH
(COARSE —) GRIT GROUT KIBBLE
GURGEONS
(COLLEGE —) HALL
(CORN —) MASA ATOLE
(ELABORATE —) FEAST BANQUET
(FIRST —) ALMUERZO
(FULL —) GORGE
(HASTY —) SNAP
(HEARTY —) AIT
(IMPROMPTU —) BITE CHECK
(LIGHT —) BAIT CHECK FOURS
(MIDDAY —) NOON
(MORNING —) BRUNCH
(PURIM —) SEUDAH
(SCANTY —) PICK
(SMALL —) SNAP MORSEL
(SOLITARY —) SULLEN
(UNSORTED —) ATTA
(PL.) TUCKER
MEALTIDE MELTITH
MEALTIME CHOW MELTETH
MEALY FLOURY FARINOSE
PERONATE
MEALYBUG COCCID
MEAN LOW BASE CLAM HARD LEAN
MIDS NICE POKY SLIM VILE AGENT
ARGUE DINGY DUSTY FOOTY GRIMY
KETTY MANGY MESNE MEZZO MIDST
MINGY MOYEN MUCKY NASTY PETIT
PETTY RATTY RUNTY SCALY SCALD
SCRUB SEEDY SILLY SMALL SNIDE
SNIVY SORRY SOUND SPELL ABJECT
BEMEAN COMMON DENOTE DESIGN
DIRTEN FEEBLE FROWZY FRUGAL
GRUBBY HUMBLE HUNGRY IMPORT
INTEND LEADEN LITTLE MEASLY
MEDIAL MEDIUM MIDDLE NARROW
PALTRY PEANUT PILLED POKING
RASCAL SCABBY SCREWY SCUMMY
SCURVY SHABBY SLIGHT SNIFTY
SNIPPY SORDID SQUALL STRAIT

TEMPER YELLOW AVERAGE CAITIFF
CHANNEL CHETIVE COMICAL
CONNOTE HACKNEY HILDING
IGNOBLE MESQUIN MISERLY
MOTETUS OBSCURE PEAKING
PELTING PIGGISH PITIFUL PORTEND
REPTILE ROINISH SCABBED
SHABBED SIGNIFY VICIOUS
BEGGARLY CHURLISH DOGGEREL
MEDIOCRE MIDDLING PICAYUNE
PITIABLE RASCALLY RIFFRAFF
SHAMEFUL SNEAKING TWOPENNY
WRETCHED
MEANDER WIND STRAY TWINE
CIRCLE WIMPLE WINDLE SERPENT
WINDING STRAGGLE
MEANING WIT HANG DRIFT SENSE
SOUND IMPORT INTENT SEMEME
PURPORT PURPOSE CARRIAGE
INNUENDO SENTENCE STRENGTH
(BASIC —) EFFECT
(DOUBLE —) WHIM EQUIVOKE
(ESSENTIAL —) CORE CONTENT
(IMPLIED —) EMPHASIS
(MANIFEST —) FACE
(REAL —) SPIRIT
(SECRET —) HEART
MEANINGFULNESS BODY
MEANINGLESS FECKLESS
(— LETTER OR CODE) NULL
MEANNESS BEGGARY
MEANS MIDS AGENT DRIVE MESNE
MOYEN PURSE THEME AGENCY
AVENUE ENGINE MATTER MIDDES
POCKET STRING WRENCH BALANCE
BENEFIT DEMESNE FACULTY
FASHION QUOMODO COURTESY
(— OF COMMUNICATION) CANAL
COMMERCE
(— OF DEFENSE) HORN HEDGE
SHIELD BULWARK
(— OF ESCAPE) CHINK SCAPE
FLIGHT
(— OF LIVING) ALIMONY
(— OF OFFENSE) ARM
(— OF PROTECTION) SAFETY
(— OF SUPPORT) HOLD ALIMENT
SUPPORT
MEANSPIRITED POOR SUPINE
CURRISH RECREANT
MEANTIME MEAN WHILE WHILES
INTERIM
MEANTONE TERTIAN
MEANWHILE WHILST INTERIM
MEANTIME
MEASLES RUBEOLA MORBILLI
(BLACK —) ESCA APOPLEXY
MEASURE (ALSO SEE UNIT AND
WEIGHT) AR BU EM EN HO KO LI
MO RI SE TU AAM ARE AUM CAB
CHO DRA ELL FAT FEN FIT FOU FUN
GAD GAZ GUZ HIN HOB IMI KAB
KAN KIP KOR KOS LEA LOG LUG
MAU MIL MOY PIK RIG RIN ROD SAA
SHO TON TUN VAT VOG WEY ACRE
ALMA AUNE BARN BATH BEKA BOLL
BOUW BUTT CADE CENT CHIH
COOM COSS DEPA DOSE DRAA
DRAM DYNE EPHI FALL FANG FOOT

FULL GAGE GERA GILL GIRT GOAD GRAM GREX HAND HATT HIDE HOOP HOUR IMMI INCH KNOT KOKU LAST MEAL METE MILE NAIL NOOK PACE PINT PIPE POLL REAM RIME ROOD ROPE ROTL SAAH SACK SALM SEAH SEAM SIZE SKEP SPAN STEP TAKT TAPE TIME TRAM TRUG TSUN VARA WIST YARD ALMUD AMBER ANKER ARDAB ARURA BEKAH BIGHA BLANK BODGE BRASS CABAN CABLE CABOT CANDY CARAT CARGA CATTY CAVAN CHAIN CHANG CHING CLOVE COOMB CRANS CUBIT CUMAL CUNIT DENUM DEPOH DIGIT DRAFT DUNAM DUNUM EPHAH GAUGE GERAH GIRTH HOMER HUTCH JUGER LABOR LAGEN LIANG LIBRA LIGNE LITER LITRE MEITH METER METRE MINIM MODEL OUNCE PEISE PERCH PLANK POUND QUIRE RASER RHYME SALMA SCALE SCORE SHAKU SHENG SHING SIEVE SLEEP STACK STERE STONE STOOP STOUP THERM TOISE TOVET TRACE VERST YOJAN APATAN ARCHIN ARPENT ARSHIN ASSIZE BARREL BATMAN BEMETE BOVATE BUNDLE BUSHEL CANADA CANTAR CHOMER CHOPIN COLLOP COUDEE COVIDO CUERDA DAVACH DAVOCH DECARE DEGREE DENIER DIPODY DIRHAM DRACHM ENGLER EXTENT FANEGA FATHOM FEDDAN FINGER FIRKIN FIRLOT FLAGON FODDER FORPET FOTHER GALLON GRAMME HALEBI HIDAGE KISHEN LEAGUE MICRON MODULE MOGGIO MORGEN NUMBER OITAVA OUROUB OXHIDE QANTAR REASON SETIER SQUARE STERAD STRIKE SULUNG TERMIN THRAVE WINDLE YOJANA ADOULIE ALQUIRE AMPHORA ANAPEST ARSHINE BATTUTA BRACCIO BREADTH CADENCE CALIPER CALORIE CENTARE CENTNER CENTRAD CHITTAK COMPASS CONGIUS CONTAIN DECIARE DIOPTER DRACHMA DRAUGHT ENTROPY FARSAKH FARSANG FRUNDEL FURLONG HECTARE HEMINEE KILIARE NOCKTAT QUARTAN QUARTER SCHEPEL SCRUPLE SECCHIO SKEPFUL SKIPPLE SPANGLE SPINDLE STADION STADIUM TERTIAN VIRGATE CAPACITY CARUCATE CENTIARE CHETVERT CRANNOCK DACTYLIC DECAGRAM DECIGRAM DESIATIN DIAPASON HOGSHEAD INNOCENT LANDYARD METEWAND PLOWGANG PLOWGATE SCHOONER SCHOPPEN STANDARD
(— **DEPTH**) SOUND
(— **FOR DRINKS**) JIGGER
(— **FOR FISH**) COT VOG CRAN LAST DRAFT HAMPER DRAUGHT
(— **FOR SHELLFISH**) WASH
(— **OF BEER**) HANDLE

(— **OF BUTTER**) SPAN
(— **OF CHAFF**) FAN
(— **OF COAL**) TEN CORF KEEL CHALDER CHALDRON
(— **OF DEVELOPMENT**) AGE
(— **OF DISCREPANCY**) LEEWAY
(— **OF EELS**) BIND STICK
(— **OF EFFICIENCY**) DUTY
(— **OF FURS**) MANTLE
(— **OF GRAIN**) MOY COOP
(— **OF LIQUOR**) FIFTH
(— **OF MERCURY**) FLASK
(— **OF MINING CLAIMS**) MERE
(— **OF PEAS**) COP
(— **OF RAISINS**) FRAIL
(— **OF ROTATION**) ANGLE
(— **OF SILK**) DRAMMAGE
(— **OF STRAW**) KEMPLE
(— **OF SUPERIORITY**) LEAD
(— **OF TIMBER**) TON STANDARD
(— **OF WAR**) BLOCKADE
(— **OF WATCHES**) LIGNE
(— **OF WATERCRESS**) HAND
(— **OF WEIGHT FOR ARROWS**) SHILLING
(— **OF WOOD**) CORD STACK
(— **OF WOOL FINENESS**) BLOOD
(— **OF WORK**) POOL
(— **OF YARN**) LEA CLEW HEER THREAD SPANGLE SPINDLE
(— **OUT**) BATCH
(**ANGULAR** —) ARC
(**COERCIVE** —) SANCTION
(**DANCE** —) TRACE
(**DUE** —) MANNER
(**FULL** —) SATIETY
(**ROAD** —) SCHENE
(**SANCTIONED** —) STANDARD
MEASURED NUMEROUS
MEASURELESS ENDLESS INFINITE
MEASUREMENT GAGE DEPTH GAUGE LEVEL MEITH METAGE DIALING MEASURE SOUNDING
(— **FOR TAXATION**) HIDE HIDAGE
(— **OF CLOTH**) ALNAGE
(— **OF FINENESS**) SET SETT
(**LUMBER** —) LAST
MEASURER METER
MEAT BEEF FISH FOOD LAMB LEAN LIFT PORK FLESH STEAK VIFDA VIVDA BUCCAN CAGMAG FLEECE MATTER NUTTON TARGET PECKAGE
(— **AND FISH**) LAULAU
(— **DRIED IN SUN**) JERKY CHARQUI PEMMICAN
(— **OF CONCH**) SCUNGILI
(— **OF KID**) CAPRETTO
(— **WITH VEGETABLES**) STEW MULLIGAN
(**BOILED** —) SOD SODDEN BOUILLI
(**BROILED** —) GRISKIN GRILLADE
(**BUFFALO** —) FLEECE
(**CANNED** —) SPAM
(**CHOPPED** —) BURGER
(**COCONUT** —) COPRA
(**CURED** —) HAM
(**CUT OF** —) ARM
(**DRIED** —) MUMMY
(**FAT** —) SPECK

(**FROZEN** —) FRIGO
(**INFERIOR** —) CAGMAG STICKING
(**JERKED** —) BILTONG CHARQUI
(**LEAN** —) MUSCLE
(**MINCED** —) CHUET JIGOTE RISSOLE SANDERS
(**POTTED** —) RILLETT
(**RABBIT** —) LAPAN
(**RAGOUT OF** —) HARICOT
(**ROAST** —) BREDE CABOB
(**ROLLED** —) BIRD
(**SALTED** —) JUNK MART
(**SIDE** —) SOWBELLY
(**SMOKED** —) BUCCAN
MEAT CURER BATHMAN
MEAT HOOK GAMBREL
MEAT JELLY ASPIC
MEATLESS PARVE LENTEN PAREVE
MEAT PIE PASTY
MEATUS BUR BURR ALVEARY
MEATY PITHY
MECATE MCCARTY
MECHANIC JOINER WRIGHT ARTIS FELTMAN SHOPMAN WORKMAN
MECHANICAL FROZEN INHUMAN METALLIC AUTOMATIC
(**NOT** —) HORMIC
MECHANICALLY BLINDLY
MECHANISM FAN BOND FEED GE KITE LIFT MOTE APRON CATCH CROWD FORCE ORGAN SHAKE SLIDE SPARK STEER ACTION BOTTOM CUTOFF INFEED MOTION SICKLE STRIKE BUILDER CHANNE CONTROL EJECTOR GIGBACK GRIPPER GUNLOCK HOLDOUT SETTING TRIPPER ACTUATOR ELEVATOR KINETICS RACKWORK SELECTOR SETWORKS SIGNALER STEERING STOPWORK THROWOU
MECHANIZE DESKILL AUTOMATE
MECONIN OPIANYL
MEDAL STAR AWARD STAMP PLA MEDALET OSCELLA
MEDALLION CAMEO TONDO PAD PATERA PANHAGIA
MEDDLE TIG FOOL MELL MESS M TOUCH DABBLE FIDDLE FINGER HECKLE POTTER PUTTER TAMPE TANGLE TINKER
MEDDLER SNOOP SNOOPER BUSYBODY KIBITZER STICKLER STIFFLER BUTTINSKY
MEDDLESOME FRESH NEBBY
MEDDLING BUSY
MEDEA (BROTHER OF —) ABSYR
(**FATHER OF** —) AEETES
(**HUSBAND OF** —) JASON AEGEU
(**MOTHER OF** —) IDYIA
(**SISTER OF** —) CHALCIOPE
MEDIA ELASTICA
MEDIAL MEDIAN MEDIUM MIDDLE AVERGAGE
MEDIAN MEDIAL MESIAL AVERAG
(— **STRIP**) MALL TERRACE
MEDIANT THIRD
MEDIATE MEAN REFEREE
MEDIATING MIDDLE MIDWAY
MEDIATOR MEANS MEDIUM

DAYSMAN MIDDLER PLACATER
STICKLER
MEDIC HOP NONESUCH
MEDICAL IATRIC PHYSIC IATRICAL
PAEONIAN
(— **WORK**) ALMONING
MEDICAMENT SMEGMA FRONTAL
MEDICINAL IATRIC PHYSIC MEDICAL
THERIAL PHYSICAL SALUTARY
THERICAL
MEDICINE DRUG MUTI PEAI DROPS
GRUEL STEEL STUFF TONIC TRADE
AMULET ECLEGM ELIXIR MAGUAL
PHYSIC POWDER REMEDY SIMPLE
ANODYNE CORDIAL HEPATIC
LUCHDOM MIXTURE PLACEBO
POROTIC PYROTIC SPLENIC
AROMATIC DIGESTER DRUGGERY
EARDROPS EMULGENT LAXATIVE
LEECHDOM LENITIVE LOBLOLLY
PECTORAL PHARMACY PULMONIC
RELAXANT SPECIFIC STOMATIC
(**CHINESE** —) SENSO
(**QUACK** —) NOSTRUM
(**SYSTEM OF** —) AYURVEDA
(**UNIVERSAL** —) PANACEA
(PL.) GALIANES
MEDICINE MAN PEAI DOCTOR
KAHUNA PIACHE POWWOW SHAMAN
SINGER ANGEKOK TOHUNGA
CONTRARY POWWOWER
MEDIEVAL OLD GOTHIC
MEDIOCRE HACK MEAN SUCH
MEDIUM AVERAGE INFERIOR
MIDDLING PASSABLE
MEDITATE CAST CHEW MUSE GLOAT
STUDY WEIGH PONDER RECORD
IMAGINE PREPEND REFLECT
REVOLVE COGITATE CONSIDER
PURPENSE RUMINATE
MEDITATION MOYEN STUDY THINK
DHYANA MUSING HIGGAION
MEDITATIVE MUSING MUSEFUL
PENSIVE RUMINANT
MEDITERRANEAN MIDLAND
MEDIUM BATH EVEN LENS MEAN
ETHER JUICE MIDST MOYEN ORGAN
BALIAN BISTER BISTRE DIGEST
MIDDLE MIDWAY ORACLE SLUDGE
TEMPER PSYCHIC VEHICLE
MEDIOCRE SHOWCASE CONTINUUM
(— **OF EXCHANGE**) CURRENCY
(— **OF TRANSMISSION**) AIR
AIRWAVE
(**CULTURE** —) AGAR STAB BROTH
HYRAX SLANT CULTURE
(**ENVELOPING** —) SWATH
MEDLAR MESPIL LAZAROLE
MEDLEY OLIO BABEL REVUE JUMBLE
CHIVARI CLANGOR FARRAGO
GOULASH MELANGE MIXTURE
BROUHAHA KEDGEREE MACARONI
MISHMASH RHAPSODY SLAMPAMP
VARIORUM
MEDOC WINE LAFITTE
MEDREGAL BONITO
MEDULLA PITH MARROW
MEDULLA OBLONGATA BULB
MEDUSA JELLY QUARL GORGON

BLUBBER GERYONID
(**FATHER OF** —) PHORCYS
(**MOTHER OF** —) CETO
(**SLAYER OF** —) PERSEUS
(PL.) BRACT
MEEK LOW DAFT MURE LOWLY
GENTLE HUMBLE PACIFIC LAMBLIKE
YIELDING
MEERSCHAUM PIPE GRAVEL
KIEFEKIL SEPIOLITE
MEET FIT KEP SEE COPE FACE FILL
HENT NOSE CLOSE CROSS FRONT
GREET INCUR OCCUR PIECE TOUCH
ANSWER BATTLE BEMEET COMBAT
CONCUR FULFIL INVENT SEMBLE
CONTACT CONVENE CONVENT
COUNCIL FULFILL SATISFY
ASSEMBLE CONFRONT CONVERGE
GAINCOPE
(— **A BET**) SEE
(— **A NEED**) SUFFICE
(— **AT END**) BUTT
(— **FACE TO FACE**) AFFRONT
(— **SQUARELY**) ENVISAGE
(— **VIOLENTLY**) CHECK HURTLE
(— **WITH**) GET SEE BUMP FIND
STRIKE
(**ATHLETIC** —) GALA GYMKHANA
MEETING MOD FEIS MOOT CLOSE
FORUM SABHA SHINE STOUR SYNOD
TRYST ACCESS AUMAGA CAUCUS
CHAPEL CLINIC HUDDLE POWWOW
SEANCE CABINET CHAPTER
COLLEGE CONTACT CONVENT
COUNCIL JOLLITY MOOTING
OCCURSE REVIVAL SEMINAR
SITTING SYNAXIS ASSEMBLY
CONGRESS DELEGACY ECCLESIA
EXERCISE JUNCTION OSCULANT
TERTULIA WARDMOTE
(— **OF NEIGHBORS**) HUSKING
(— **OF SCHOLARS**) LEVY
(— **OF WORSHIPERS**) SERVICE
(**ANGLO-SAXON** —) GEMOTE
(**GENERAL** —) PRIME
(**POLITICAL** —) CAUCUS
(**PRIVATE** —) CONCLAVE
(**SECRET** —) CABAL CONSULT
(**SOCIAL** —) CLUB JOLLY HOBNOB
(**TOWN** —) TUNMOOT
MEETINGHOUSE MORADA
MEETING PLACE AMBALAM
TINWALD
MEGAPHONE VAMPHORN
MEGAPODE MALEO LEIPOA
MEGARA (**FATHER OF** —) CREON
(**HUSBAND OF** —) HERCULES
MEGILP GUMPTION
MEHTAR BUNGY BHUNGI
MELANCHOLIA ATHYMY ATHYMIA
SADNESS
MELANCHOLIC HYPPISH
MELANCHOLY WO SAD WOE BLUE
DRAM DULL DUMP MARE BLUES
DEARN DOWIE DREAR DUSKY
GLOOM SORRY WISHT GLOOMY
SOMBER SOMBRE SORROW SPLEEN
SULLEN YELLOW CHAGRIN DOLEFUL
DUMPISH ELEGIAC SADNESS

SPLEENY THOUGHT ATRABILE
LIVERISH TRISTFUL
MELANESIAN DOBUAN KANAGA
KANAKA EFATESE
MELANGE GOMBO GUMBO
MELANISM PHAEISM
MELANTERITE INKSTONE
MELATOPE EYE
MELD SET SAMBA SPREAD BOLIVIA
DECLARE
MELEAGER (**FATHER OF** —) OENEUS
(**MOTHER OF** —) ALTHAEA
MELEE BRAWL MEDLEY DOGFIGHT
PELLMELL
MELIORATE MITIGATE
MELISMA JUBILUS
MELL KIRN
MELLIFLUOUS SUGARED HYBLAEAN
MELLOW AGE OMY HAZE LUSH
MALM PLUM RICH RIPE SOFT FRUSH
FLUTED GOLDEN MATURE
MELLOWED BEERY
MELODIOUS SOFT SOOT TUNY
SWEET TUNED ARIOSO DULCET
MELODIC MUSICAL SIRENIC
SONGFUL STRENIC TUNABLE
TUNEFUL CANOROUS CHARMING
NUMEROUS SOUNDFUL
(**EXCESSIVELY** —) SIRUPY SYRUPY
MELODRAMA HAM TANK
MELODY AIR HUM LAY ARIA NOTE
TUNE CANTO CHANT CHARM DREAD
MELOS MIRTH NIGUN CANTUS
CHORAL GHAZEL MONODY NIGGUN
STROKE CANZONA CANZONE
CHORALE DESCANT HARMONY
MEASURE MELISMA PLANXTY
ROSALIA CAVATINA DIAPASON
VOCALISE
(— **COMPASS**) AMBITUS
(**MOURNFUL** —) DUMP
(**SYNAGOGAL** —S) CHAZANUT
HAZANUTH
MELON PEPO GOURD MANGO
CASABA CITRON DUDAIM MAYCOCK
CUCURBIT HONEYDEW PEPONIDA
PEPONIUM
MELT FLY RIN RUN BLOW FADE
FLOW FLUX FUSE THAW FOUND
LEACH SMELT SWEAL SWELT
TOUCH GUTTER RELENT SOFTEN
DISTILL FORMELT RESOLVE
DISCANDY DISSOLVE ELIQUATE
(— **AWAY**) SWEAL
(— **DOWN**) RENDER
(— **IRREGULARLY**) DROZE
MELTED RUN FONDU FUSED FUSILE
MELTING SOFT FUSILE FUSION
MELTWATER OUTWASH
MEMBER LIMB LITH BRANCH
FELLOW FILLET GIRDER SOCIUS
AMANIST ERANIST FAIRING
ALBRIGHT AULARIAN BRIDLING
(— **OF ANSAR**) HELPER
(— **OF BALLET**) FIGURANT
(— **OF BAND**) SIDEMAN
(— **OF BODYGUARD**) HUSCARL
(— **OF BROTHERHOOD**) ESSENE
SENUSSI

(— OF CLAN) CHILD CALEBITE
(— OF CLERGY) DEFENSOR
(— OF COAST GUARD) SPAR
(— OF COUNCIL) CONSUL
HEEMRAAD
(— OF COURT) DICAST EPHETE
(— OF CREW) HAND IDLER LAYER
DRIVER STROKE BOWSMAN
FORETOP BRAKEMAN SHAREMAN
(— OF CULT) ANGEL AMIDIST
(— OF FACULTY) COUNSEL
LECTURER
(— OF FAMILY) FETII
(— OF FRATERNAL ORDER) ELK
SHRINER FORESTER KIWANIAN
(— OF FRATERNITY) GREEK
(— OF FRENCH ACADEMY)
IMMORTAL
(— OF GANG) HENCHMAN
(— OF GENTRY) SEIGNEUR
(— OF GIRL SCOUTS) BROWNIE
(— OF GREEK ARMY) EVZONE
(— OF GUILD) COMACINE
(— OF HOUSEHOLD) FAMILIAR
(— OF HUNTING PARTY) STANDER
(— OF INN OF COURT) ANCIENT
BENCHER
(— OF ITALIAN ARMY) ALPINO
(— OF KNOW-NOTHING PARTY) SAM
(— OF LEGISLATURE) SOLON
DEPUTY DELEGATE
(— OF LITERARY GROUP) FELIBRE
(— OF MIDDLE CLASS) BURGHER
(— OF PARLIAMENT) CONTENT
THINGMAN
(— OF PRIMROSE LEAGUE) KNIGHT
(— OF RELIGIOUS ORDER) DAME
FRIAR EUDIST FRAILE FRATER
HERMIT JESUIT SISTER ALEXIAN
BRINSER DERVISH HUSSITE
SEPARTE SERVANT CENOBITE
EXORCIST HUMANIST SALESIAN
(— OF RETINUE) SEQUEL SEQUENT
(— OF RUSSIAN ARISTOCRACY)
BOYAR BOYARD
(— OF SAME GENUS) CONGENER
(— OF SECRET ORGANIZATION)
DEMOLAY
(— OF SECRET SOCIETY) BOXER
(— OF SECT) DRUSE HASID KHOJA
AUDIAN BRAHMO CATHAR DIPPER
DOPPER IBADHI JUMPER KHLYST
SMARTA AISSAWA AJIVIKA AUDAEAN
CAINITE CHASSID DREAMER EMPIRIC
EUCHITE IBADITE ISAWIYA ISMAILI
RAPPIST SEVENER AQUARIAN
CALIXTIN EBIONITE FAMILIST
GLASSITE LABADIST SADDUCEE
SEVERIAN SIMONIAN
(— OF STAFF) ATTACHE
(— OF STATE) CITIZEN
(— OF STOCK EXCHANGE)
BOARDMAN
(— OF TEAM) SPARE BOBBER
KICKER
(— OF TRIBE) LEVITE JUDAHITE
LAMANITE
(— OF UPPER CLASS) EFFENDI
(— OF VARNA) SUDRA SHUDRA

(— OF WHITE RACE) HAOLE
(— OF WINDOW) APRON
(—S OF CLASS) FRY
(—S OF PROFESSION) FACULTY
(—S OF SECT) SKOPTSY
(—S OF TRIBUNAL) ACUERDO
(ARCHITECTURAL —) FAN ARCH
FLAT SILL SPAN GABLE SOCLE
STILE STILT CORBEL FASCIA
CONSOLE CORNICE
(CHURCH —) GREEK LATIN DANITE
DUNKER KIRKER TUNKER BAPTIST
BEGHARD BROTHER DUNKARD
KIRKMAN SECEDER ARMENIAN
BRYANITE CATHOLIC DISCIPLE
DOWIEITE JACOBITE
(CHURCH —S) FAITHFUL
(EVERY —) ALL
(FEEBLEST —) WRIG
(FULL —) GREMIAL
(OLDEST —) FATHER
(OVERHANGING —) BRACKET
(POLITICAL —) CADET ENDEK SHIRT
GUELPH HUNKER LEADER APRISTA
LEFTIST LIBERAL BUCKTAIL
DEMOCRAT HERODIAN LABORITE
(PROJECTING —) TENON
(SENIOR —) DOYEN
(TENSION —) HANGER
(TERMINAL —) TOE
MEMBERSHIP SEAT GARTER
GUILDRY
MEMBRANE RIM WEB CAUL COAT
DURA FELL HEAD TELA GALEA
HYMEN VELUM AMNION AMNIOS
EXTINE INTINE MENINX MOTHER
MUCOSA PLEURA RETINA SEPTUM
SEROSA TIMBAL TUNICA TYMPAN
BLANKET CAPSULE CHORION
CUTICLE EPICYTE HYALOID
OOLEMMA PUTAMEN STRATUM
VELAMEN ECTODERM ENDOCYST
ENVELOPE EPENDYMA EPISPORE
EXOLEMMA INDUSIUM INTEXINE
LABELLUM PATAGIUM PELLICLE
STRIFFEN
(— OF ORANGE) ZEST
(NICTITATING —) HAW
(TYMPANIC —) TYMPAN MYRINGA
DRUMHEAD DRUMSKIN
(PL.) ADNEXA ANNEXA MENINGES
MEMBRANOUS HUSKY SKINNY
HYMENOID SCARIOSE SCARIOUS
MEMENTO RELIC TOKEN MEMORY
TROPHY KEEPSAKE REMINDER
SOUVENIR
MEMINNA PEESOREH
MEMNON (FATHER OF —) TITHONUS
(MOTHER OF —) AURORA
(SLAYER OF —) ACHILLES
MEMOIR ELOGE RECORD HISTORY
MEMORIAL
MEMORABLE GRAND SIGNAL
CLASSIC NOTABLE MEMORIAL
NAMEABLE
MEMORANDA (SET OF —) TICKLER
MEMORANDUM BILL CHIT NOTE
SLIP BRIEF JURAT CIPHER DOCKET
MEMOIR MINUTE TICKET JOTTING

MEMORIAL NOTANDUM PROTOCOL
MEMORIAL AHU AGALMA CAHIER
FACTUM MEMOIR MEMORY RECORD
TROPHY DENKMAL MEMENTO
MENTION EBENEZER MONUMENT
MEMORIZE LEARN MANDATE
REMEMBER
MEMORY MIND HEART IMAGE STORE
RECALL RECORD MEMENTO
STORAGE MEMORIAL SOUVENIR
(OF POOR —) FLUFFY
(PAINFUL —) SCAR
MEN THEY ORANG INNUIT MANHEAD
MANHOOD MANKIND MENFOLK
HUMANITY
MENACE BOAST IMPEND THREAT
BOGEYMAN MINATORY THREATEN
MENACING STOUT SURLY FIERCE
TOWARD MINATORY
MEN-AT-ARMS CHIVALRY
MEND DO FIX BEET DARN HEAL
HELP STOP TINK AMEND CLOUT
EMEND GRAFT MOISE PALCH
COBBLE DOCTOR FETTLE RANTER
REFORM REPAIR SOLDER SPETCH
TINKLE IMPROVE INWEAVE REDRESS
RIGHTLE
(— BY ADDING FEATHERS) IMP
(— CLUMSILY) BOTCH
(— MEN'S CLOTHES) BUSHEL
MENDACIOUS FALSE DISHONEST
MENDACITY LYING DECEIT FALSITY
UNTRUTH
MENDER TINKER KETTLER
BEATSTER
MENDICANCY BEGGARY
MENDICANT NAGA DANDI FAKIR
FRIAR UDASI BEGGAR BHIKKU
FAKEER FRATER GOSAIN AJIVIKA
BAIRAGI EUCHITE VAIRAGI
PANDARAM SANNYASI
MENDING COBBLE
MENEL NELL
MENELAUS (BROTHER OF —)
AGAMEMNON
(FATHER OF —) PLISTHENES
(WIFE OF —) HELEN
MENHADEN POGY PORGY BUNKER
CHEBOG SHINER ALEWIFE BUGFISH
BUGHEAD CLUPEID ELLFISH
FATBACK OLDWIFE SAVELHA
SHADINE WHITING BONYFISH
HARDHEAD
MENHIR BOUTA GORSEDD PEULVAN
CATSTONE HAGIOLITH
MENIAL FAG BASE LOON PAGE
KNAVE DRIVEL HARLOT POTBOY
VARLET SERVILE SLAVISH BANAUSI
SCULLION SERVITOR
MENISCOID CRESCENT
MENNONITE HOOKER AMISHMAN
AMMANITE HUTERITE
MENOETIUS (BROTHER OF —)
ATLAS PROMETHEUS
(FATHER OF —) ACTOR
(MOTHER OF —) AEGINA
(SON OF —) PATROCLUS
MENOPAUSE CLIMAX
MENSTRUATE FLOW

MENSTRUATING SICK

MENSTRUATION FLOW CURSE
FLUOR CRAMPS PERIOD COURSES

MENSTRUUM SOLVENT

MENTAL IDEAL GENIAL INWARD
MINDLY PHRENIC PSYCHIC
CEREBRAL

MENTALITY MIND SENSE ACUMEN
REASON SPIRIT PSYCHISM

MENTHA LABIATE

MENTHANE TERPANE

MENTHOL CAMPHOR

MENTION CALL CITE HINT MIND
MING MINT NAME CHEEP CLEPE
SPEAK TOUCH MEMBER NOTICE
SPEECH MEANING SPECIFY
SUGGEST CITATION INSTANCE
MEMORATE REHEARSE REMEMBER
(— BY NAME) NEMN NEMME
NEMPNE
(— CASUALLY) DROP
(HONORABLE —) ACCESSIT

MENTOR TEACHER CICERONE

MENTUM PERULA

MENU CARD CARTE

MEPERIDINE DEMEROL

MEPHISTOPHELIAN SATANIC

MERCAPTAN THIOL

MERCEDARIAN NOLASCAN
RANSOMER

MERCENARY HACK VENAL JACKAL
HESSIAN PINDARI HIRELING
WAGELING

MERCER SILKMAN

MERCERIZE SCHREINER

MERCHANDISE CARGO CHEAP
GOODS STUFF WARES ARTWARE
CHAFFER SHIPPER TRAFFIC
CHAFFERY SALEWARE
(CHEAP SHODDY —) BORAX
(RETURNED —) COMEBACK

MERCHANT ARAB SETH SETT TELI
WALLA BADGER FACTOR KITELY
NEPMAN RETAIL TAIPAN TRADER
ANTONIO CHAPMAN GOLADAR
HANSARD HOWADJI CHANDLER
HUCKSTER MARCHAND POVINDAH
SOUDAGUR
(GRAIN —) LAMBADI
(GREAT —) TAIPAN
(WINE —) VINTNER

MERCIFUL KIND MILD HUMANE
RUEFUL TENDER CLEMENT LENIENT
MILDFUL PITIFUL SPARING
GRACIOUS QUEMEFUL

MERCILESS GRIM CRUEL SHARP
BLOODY FIERCE SAVAGE WANTON
PITILESS

MERCURY HG AZOCH AZOTH
DRAGON HERMES SPIRIT CHIBRIT
MARKERY TEUTATES
(FATHER OF —) JUPITER
(MOTHER OF —) MAIA

MERCY LAW ORE HORE PITY RUTH
GRACE GRITH BLITHE LENITY
CHARITY CLEMENCY LENIENCY

MERE BARE NUDE ONLY PURE PUTE
SOLE VERY NAKED SHEER SINGLE

MEREL PIN

MERELY BUT JUST ONLY BARELY
PURELY SIMPLY SINGLY SOLELY
ALONELY UTTERLY ENTIRELY
SCARCELY

MERETRICIOUS CHEAP GAUDY
GILDED PUNKISH

MERGANSER SMEE SMEW HARLE
SNOWL SPIKE HERALD SAWNEB
WEASER BRACKET GARBILL
JACKSAW RANTOCK SAWBILL
TADPOLE TOWHEAD TWEEZER
WHEEZER EARLDUCK MOSSHEAD

MERGE FUSE JOIN BLEND ENTER
GLIDE UNIFY MINGLE COMMERGE
CONFLATE

MERGING BLEND FUSION

MERICARP COCCUS

MERIDIAN (THOSE LIVING UNDER
SAME —) ANTOECI

MERINGUE KISS

MERINO DELAINE

MERISTEM PERIBLEM

MERIT DUE EARN MEED PUNY
BROOK THANK WORTH DESERT
VIRTUE WRIHTE DEMERIT DESERVE
PUDDING
(— CONSIDERATION) COUNT
(POSSESSING —) WORTHY

MERITED JUST
(NOT —) INDIGN

MERITORIOUS CAPITAL MERITORY
THANKFUL VALOROUS

MERL BLACKIE

MERLON COP

MERMAID NIXIE SIREN MERROW
MERWOMAN

MERMAN SEAMAN MANFISH

MEROPE (BROTHER OF —)
PHAETHON
(FATHER OF —) CRESPHONTES
(HUSBAND OF —) SISYPHUS
(MOTHER OF —) CYPSELUS

MEROPODITE FEMUR MEROS

MEROZOITE AGAMETE

MERRILY GAILY GAMELY LUSTICK
JOYOUSLY

MERRIMENT FUN JOY GALE GLEE
JEST UTAS DERAY MIRTH FROLIC
SPLEEN DAFFERY DAFFING FESTIVE
JOLLITY WAGGERY HILARITY

MERRY GAY BOON CANT GLAD GOLE
BONNY CADGY CRANK DROLL
JOLLY LIGHT LUSTY MURRY SUNNY
VOGIE VOKIE BLITHE COCKET
FROLIC JOCANT JOCUND JOVIAL
JOYOUS LIVELY FEASTLY GLEEFUL
HOLIDAY JOCULAR LUSTICK
RAFFING WINSOME CHIRPING
DISPOSED FESTIVAL GAMESOME
GLEESOME LAUGHING PLEASANT
SPANKING SPORTFUL SPORTIVE

MERRY-ANDREW AIRY ZANY ANTIC
DROLL JESTER BUFFOON

MERRY-GO-ROUND CAROUSEL
TURNABOUT

MERRYMAKING ALE MAY RAG KIRN
PLOY REVEL GAIETY RACKET
SPLORE CARNIVAL

MERRYTHOUGHT WISHBONE

MERUS PALM

MESA MESILLA CARTOUCH

MESADENIA CACALIA

MESCAL PEYOTE WOKOWI MEXICAL
CHALLOTE

MESCALERO FARAON

MESENTERY CROW RUFFLE

MESH MASK MOKE CHAIN PITCH
SHALE ACCRUE ENGAGE MASCLE
SCREEN SCREENING
(— IMPROPERLY) BUTT
(IN —) DIRECT

MESHED ENGAGED

MESOCARP FLESH

MESOMORPHIC SOMAL SOMATIC
ATHLETIC

MESOPODIUM PETIOLE

MESOPOTAMIA (TREE OF —) HOMA

MESOTONIC TERTIAN MEANTONE

MESQUITE HONEY KEAWE PACAY
CASHAW ALGAROBA HONEYPOD
IRONWOOD MOSQUITO

MESS JAG JAM MIX MUX PIE SOP
CLAT FIST HASH JAMB MUCK MULL
MUSS SLUB SOSS STEW SUSS
BOTCH CAUCH JAKES STREW SWILL
BOLLIX BUNGLE CADDLE CLATCH
JUMBLE MUCKER PICKLE PUDDLE
SOZZLE TUMBLE MAMMOCK
MULLOCK SCAMBLE SLOTTER
COUSCOUS DISORDER LOBLOLLY
SHAMBLES SLAISTER
(— AROUND) JUKE
(— OF FOOD) SAND
(GREASY —) GAUM
(SLOPPY —) SLOBBER SLAISTER

MESSAGE CHIT MODE SAND SEND
WIRE WORD RUMOR BREVET
CIPHER ERRAND GOSPEL LETTER
SCROLL BLINKER BODWORD
DEPECHE EMBASSY MISSION
SENDING TIDINGS AEROGRAM
CREDENCE DISPATCH
(— BY FLAGS) HOIST
(— FROM GOD) ANGEL
(CHRISTIAN —) EVANGEL
(CIPHER —) SCYTALE
(COMPLIMENTARY —) RECADO

MESSALIAN EUCHITE

MESSENE (FATHER OF —) TRIOPAS
(HUSBAND OF —) POLYCAON

MESSENGER BODE PEON POST
SAND SEND TOTY VAUX ANGEL
ENVOY MUMMU VISOR BEADLE
BROKER BUNENE CHIAUS HERALD
LEGATE NUNCIO PIGEON RUNNER
APOSTLE CARRIER CASHBOY
CONTACT COURANT COURIER
EXPRESS FORAGER FORAYER
MALACHI MERCURY MESSAGE
MISSIVE NAMTARU PATAMAR
TOTYMAN TROTTER TRUMPET
EMISSARY FOREGOER HIRCARRA
LOBBYGOW NUNCIATE ORDINARY
PORTATOR
(— OF APSU AND TIAMAT) MUMMU
(— OF GOD) ANGEL
(— OF SHAMASH) BUNENE

(— OF THE GODS) HERMES
MERCURY
(MOUNTED —) COSSID ESTAFET
(RELIGIOUS —) APOSTLE
(UNDERWORLD —) NAMTARU
MESSIAH CHRIST WOVOKA
MESSMATE YUBA
MESSUAGE HAW TOFT MEESE
MIDSTEAD
MESSY GOOEY SLOPPY SOZZLY
STICKY
MESTIZO CHOLO LADINO CURIBOCA
MAMELUCO
METAL ORE TIN BODY DIET GOLD
IRON LEAD ZINC BARIUM CESIUM
CHROME COBALT COPPER INDIUM
LATTIN NICKEL OSMIUM RADIUM
SILVER SODIUM BISMUTH CADMIUM
CALCIUM HAFNIUM IRIDIUM LITHIUM
MERCURY RHENIUM RHODIUM
THORIUM URANIUM YTTRIUM
ALUMINUM ANTIMONY CHROMIUM
DEADHEAD PLATINUM RUBIDIUM
SCANDIUM TANTALUM TINCTURE
TITANIUM TUNGSTEN VANADIUM
(— IN MASS) BULLION
(— IN SHEETS) LEAF PLATE
(BABBITT —) LINING
(GROUND —) BRONZING
(HEAVIEST —) OSMIUM
(IMPURE MASS OF —) REGULUS
(LIGHTEST —) LITHIUM
(LIQUID —) MERCURY
(MASS OF —) INGOT
(MOLTEN —) TAP SQUIRT
(OLD POT —) POTIN
(PERFORATED —) STENCIL
(PIECE OF CRUDE —) SLUG
(POINTED —) NAIL
(POROUS —) SPONGE
(SEMIFINISHED —) SEMIS
(SHEET —) DOUBLES KALAMEIN
(WASTE —) GATE
METALLIC HARD TINNY
METALLOPHONE SARON
METALWARE LORMERY GRAYWARE
PONTYPOOL
METALWORK ZOGAN
METALWORKER BARMAN FOONER
FORKMAN FOUNDER SUDSMAN
METAMERE SOMITE SEGMENT
MEROSOME
METAMORPHOSE TURN SHAPE
INDENIZE TRANSMEW
METAMORPHOSIS METABOLE
PETALODY PHYLLODY SEPALODY
METANIRA (HUSBAND OF —)
CELEUS
(SON OF —) DEMOPHON
TRIPTOLEMUS
METAPHOR IMAGE TROPE FIGURE
METAPHORICAL FIGURAL FIGURATE
TROPICAL
METASTOMA LABIUM
METATE QUERL
METE DEAL GIVE AWARD SERVE
METEMPSYCHOSIS SAMSARA
METEOR STAR ARGID CETID COMID
DRAKE LUPID LYRID URSID ANTLID

AUGUST BOLIDE BOOTID CORVID
CYGNID DRAGON HYDRID LIBRID
LYNCID LYRAID PHASMA PISCID
TAURID AQUARID AQUILID ARIETID
AURIGID CAMELID CANCRID CEPHEID
CORONID GEMINID MEATURE
ORIONID PEGASID PERSEID POLARID
PRODIGY COLUMBID CRATERID
DRACONID ERIDANID FIREBALL
FORNAXID HERCULID LACERTID
SAGITTID SCORPIID SHOTSTAR
TOUCANID VIRGINID
METEORITE BAETYL BOLIDE
ANDRITE ATAXITE EUCRITE
AEROLITE AEROLITH BAETULUS
BAETYLUS IREOLITE SIDERITE
SKYSTONE
METEOROLOGY AEROLOGY
METER IONIC METRE SEVEN ALCAIC
RHYTHM CADENCE GAYATRI
MEASURE SUBMETER VIAMETER
YAWMETER
(10,000 —S) GREX
(CUBIC —) STERE
(MILLIONTH OF —) MICRON
(NETHERLANDS —) ELL
(SQUARE —) CENTIARE
(VEDIC —) GAYATRI
METHADONE AMIDONE
METHANE FORMENE
METHANOL WOODINE CARBINOL
METHEGLIN MEAD
METHOD ART WAY DART FORM
GARB GATE KINK LINE MIDS MODE
REDE RULE SORT ORDER STYLE
TRACK USAGE COURSE ENGINE
MANNER STEREO SYSTEM FASHION
PROCESS TACTICS WRINKLE
ADJUVANT STANDARD
(— OF ANGLING) HARLING
(— OF APPEALING) DHARNA
DHURNA
(— OF COLORING TEA) FACING
(— OF CONSTRUCTION) JACAL
(— OF CULTIVATION) JUM JOOM
STUMPING
(— OF DIETING) BANTING
(— OF DISTILLATION) DESCENT
(— OF ELECTION) SCRUTINY
(— OF FATTENING POULTRY)
GAVAGE
(— OF INDUCTION) CANON
(— OF MILKING) NIEVLING
(— OF MURAL DECORATION) KHASI
(— OF PROCEDURE) GAME
(— OF TRACKING) DOVAP
(— OF TREATMENT) SCOPE
(CLEVER —) KINK KINKLE
(FIXED —) FORMULA
(MEDICAL —) CUSHION
(OUTMODED —) ARCHAISM
(PAINTING —) GOUACHE
(PRINTING —) AQUATONE
(SCIENTIFIC —) BACONISM
(SURVEYING —) STADIA
(USUAL —) COURSE PRACTICE
METHODICAL TRIG EXACT FORMAL
ORDERLY REGULAR ORDINARY
ORDINATE

METHODIST JUMPER WESLEYAN
SWADDLING
METHODIZE REGULATE
METHYLAL FORMAL
METICULOUS FUSSY STICKY
CAREFUL FINICAL FINICKY
METONYM SYNONYM
METRICAL MEASURED
(— QUANTITY) MATRA
METROPOLIS CITY SEAT CAPITAL
METROPOLITAN EPARCH
METTLE SAUL PRIDE SPUNK GINGER
SPIRIT COURAGE
METTLESOME FIERY PROUD SKEIGH
SPUNKY STUFFY FLIGHTY GINGERY
SPIRITED
MEW WOW MEWL MIAOU MIAOW
INTERMEW SEEDBIRD
MEWER WRAWLER
MEWL WRAWL
MEXICAN CHOLO LEPERO WETBACK
MEXICAN-AMERICAN PACHUCO
MEXICAN ELM MEZCAL
MEXICAN ONYX TECALI
MEXICAN PERSIMMON CHAPOTE
MEXICAN POPPY ARGEMONE
MEXICAN TEA BASOTE APASOTE
FISHWEED WORMSEED

MEXICO

COIN: PESO TLAC ADOBE CLACO
TLACO AZTECA CENTAVO
PIASTER
LAKE: CHAPALA
MEASURE: PIE VARA ALMUD BARIL
JARRA LABOR LEGUA LINEA
SITIO FANEGA PULGADA
MOUNTAIN: BUFA BLANCO
CUPULA PEROTE ORIZABA
PENINSULA: BAJA YUCATAN
PEOPLE: MAM CORA MAYA SERI
XOVA AZTEC NAHUA OPATA
OTOMI ZOQUE EUDEVE MIXTEC
TOLTEC NAYARIT TEPANEC
TOTONAC ZACATEC ZAPOTEC
TEZCUCAN TOTONACO
ZACATECO
RIVER: BRAVO LERMA BALSAS
GRANDE PANUCO TABASCO
GRIJALVA SANTIAGO
STATE: LEON NUEVO COLIMA
OAXACA SONORA CHIAPAS
DURANGO HIDALGO NAYARIT
SINALOA TABASCO YUCATAN
CAMPECHE QUINTANA
VERACRUZ
TOWN: LEON TEPIC ARIZPE
COLIMA JALAPA JUAREZ MERIDA
OAXACA PARRAL POTOSI
PUEBLA CANANEA DURANGO
GUAYMAS MORELIA ORIZABA
PACHUCA TAMPICO TORREON
CULIACAN MAZATLAN
MONCLOVA SALTILLO
VERACRUZ
VOLCANO: COLIMA TOLUCA
JORULLO PARICUTIN
WEIGHT: BAG ONZA CARGA LIBRA

MARCO ADARME ARROBA OCHAVA TERCIO QUINTAL

MEZZANINE ENTRESOL
MIASMA MALARIA MAREMMA
MIB MIGGLE
MICA DAZE TALC GLIST SLUDE
BIOTITE GLIMMER ALURGITE
FUCHSITE
MICE (BREEDING PLACE FOR —)
MURARIUM
MICHAEL MIKE MICKY MICHEL
MIGUEL

MICHIGAN
BAY: SAGINAW THUNDER
KEWEENAW STURGEON
CAPITAL: LANSING
COLLEGE: ALMA WAYNE ADRIAN
ALBION CALVIN OLIVET OWOSSO
OAKLAND
COUNTY: IONIA IOSCO ALCONA
GOGEBIC OSCEOLA TUSCOLA
KALKASKA
INDIAN: OTTAWA
LAKE: BURT TORCH HOUGHTON
NATIVE: WOLVERINE
NICKNAME: WOLVERINE
RIVER: CASS HURON SAGINAW
ESCANABA
STATE BIRD: ROBIN
STATE FLOWER: APPLEBLOSSOM
STRAIT: MACKINAW
TOWN: ALMA CARO FLINT ADRIAN
ALPENA BADAXE OWOSSO
DETROIT LANSING SAGINAW
ANNARBOR CADILLAC
ESCANABA MANISTEE MUNISING
MUSKEGON CHEBOYGAN
KALAMAZOO

MICONIA TAMONEA
MICROBE GERM
MICROMETER BIFILAR
(— CALIPER) MIKE
MICRON MU
MICRONESIAN KANAGA NAURUAN
(— ISLAND) NUI GUAM ROTA TRUK
MAKIN NAURU WOTHO MAJURO
MICROORGANISM BUG GERM
AZOFIER BUTYRIC BACILLUS
MICROPHONE BUG MIKE PARABOLA
MICROPYLE FORAMEN
MICROSECOND (HUNDREDTH OF —)
SHAKE
MICROSCOPE GLASS SCOPE
MICROSCOPIC SMALL MINUTE
MICROSPECIES JORDANON
MICROSPOROPHYLL STAMEN
MICROTONE SRUTI SHRUTI
MICROTUS ARVICOLA
MIDDAY NOON UNDERN MIDNOON
NOONDAY MERIDIAN NOONTIME
MIDDEN BASURAL SAMBAQUI
MIDDLE MEDIO MESNE NAVEL
CENTER MEDIAL MEDIAN CENTRAL
MEDIATE MEDILLE

(— OF SAIL) BUNT
(— OF SHIP) WAIST
(— OF WINTER) HOLL HOWE
MIDDLE-AGED MIDDLING
MIDDLE EAST (— NATIVE) WOG
MIDDLEMAN BUTTY BROKER
DEALER FOGGER JOBBER LUMPER
BUMAREE BUTTYMAN HUCKSTER
REGRATER
MIDDLER PLATEMAN
MIDDLETONE HALFTONE
MIDDLING FAIR MEAN SOSO
NEUTRAL MEDIOCRE MEETERLY
(PL.) DUNST FARINA SHARPS
SIZINGS SEMOLINA WEATINGS
MIDGE GNAT SMUT MIDGET MINGIE
PUNKIE WEEVIL
MIDNIGHT NOON NOONTIDE
MIDPOINT BASION PORION STOMION
GNATHION
MIDRIB COSTA SHAFT MIDVEIN
(— OF LEAF) PEN
MIDRIFF APRON SKIRT
MIDSHIPMAN WART MIDDY PLEBE
REEFER SNOTTY OLDSTER
MIDST DEPTH CENTER MIDDLE
MIDWARD
MIDSUMMER DAY JOHNSMAS
MIDWAY MEDIO GAYWAY HALFWAY
MIDWIFE BABA DHAI GAMP DHOLL
HOWDY LUCKY COMMER CUMMER
GRANNY HOWDIE KIMMER LUCINA
LUCKIE GRANNIE HEBAMME
MIEN AIR BROW VULT ASPECT
DEMEAN MANNER OSTENT BEARING
DEMEANOR
MIG MIB DUCK
MIGHT ARM BULK MOTE FORCE
MOUND POWER SHOULD STRENGTH
MIGHTILY HEFTILY
MIGHTINESS (HIGH —) HOGEN
MIGHTY FELL HIGH KEEN MAIN
MUCH RANK RICH VAST FELON
GREAT HEFTY STERN STOOR
POTENT STRONG VIOLENT
ENORMOUS FORCEFUL POWERFUL
PUISSANT SAMSONIC
MIGNONETTE WOLD RESEDA
LUTEOLA
MIGRAINE MEGRIM
MIGRANT MOVER
MIGRATE RUN FLIT TREK DRIFT
FLIGHT COLONIZE
MIGRATION TREK EXODUS FLIGHT
EELFARE EMOTION PASSAGE
DIASPORA
MIKADO DAIRI
MIKIR ARLENG
MILD LEW MOY CALM COLD EASY
FAIR LENT MEEK NESH PLUM SOFT
TAME WARM BALMY BUXOM GREEN
LIGHT LITHE MELCH MELSH MILKY
NAISH QUIET BENIGN FACILE GENIAL
GENTLE HUMBLE KINDLY REMISS
SMOOTH AMIABLE CLEMENT
LENIENT VELVETY BENEDICT
DOVELIKE FAVONIAN LENITIVE
MERCIFUL SOOTHING TRANQUIL
MILDEW OIDIUM

MILDLY FEEBLY GENTLY
MILDNESS MILD LENITY SUAVITY
CLEMENCY HUMILITY KINDNESS
MILE (3 —S) HOUR LEAGUE
(NAUTICAL —) KNOT KAIRI
(ONE-EIGHTH —) FURLONG
(SEA —) NAUT
MILESTONE LEAGUE
MILFOIL AHARTALAV
MILIEU CLIMATE TERRAIN AMBIENCE
MILITANT WARRISH FIGHTING
MILITARY MARTIAL WARLIKE
MILITANT SOLDIERY
(— POST) THANA
(— SCIENCE) LOGISTICS
MILITIA FYRD ARRAY MILICE
MILITIAMAN CHOCO UHLAN LUMPER
TRAINER SHIRTMAN
MILK COW LAC FUZZ LAIT PAIL SKIM
BLEED JUICE MILCH MULCT BOTTLE
ELICIT RAMMEL STROKE SUCKLE
EXPLOIT
(— DRY) STRIP
(— OUT) EMULGE
(— PAN) LEAD
(— PRODUCT) KHOA
(— SICKNESS) TIRES
(BREAST —) SUCK DIDDY
(COW'S —) MESS
(CURDLED —) SKYR TYRE TAYER
LOPPER CLABBER TATMJOLK
(FERMENTED —) KUMISS MATZOON
(NEW —) RAMMEL
(SOUR —) SKYR WHIG BONNY
BLEEZE BLINKY CLABBER JOCOQUE
(WATERY —) BLASH
MILK CART KIT PRAM BUNGEY
MILKFISH AWA BANGOS SABALO
SAVOLA BANDENG SABALOTE
MILKING (— PARLOR) BAIL
(— TIME) MEAL
MILKLESS PARVE PAREVE
MILKMAN KITTER CHALKER
MILK PAIL TRUG LEGLEN
MILK SHAKE FRAPPE
MILK SNAKE ADDER
MILKSOP SOP MOLLY COCKNEY
MILKWOOD MELKHOUT
MILKWORT SENECA CENTAURY
GAYWINGS
MILKY MILCHY LACTARY LACTEAL
OPALOID LACTEOUS
MILL FULL MILN STAR BREAK FLOUR
KNURL QUERN CHERRY FANNER
STAMPS BLOOMER MOLINET
PUGMILL SMUTTER ARRASTRA
BUHRMILL SPINNERY TRAPICHE
WALKMILL
(CHOCOLATE —) MOLINET
(FULLING —) STOCKS
(SHINGLING —) FORGE
(SUGAR —) CENTRAL TRAPICHE
MILLBOARD TARBOARD
MILLDAM WARREN WARRANT
MILLED GRAINED
MILLENARIAN CHILIAST
MILLENIUM CHILIAD
MILLER MILLMAN STOCKER
MULTURER NILLWARD

MILLER'S-THUMB BLOB CULL CABOT CHABOT COTTOID MUDDLER BULLHEAD

MILLET BUDA KODA KOUS MOHA ARZUN BAJRA CHENA CUMBU DUKHN DURRA GRAIN HIRSE KODRA MILLY PANIC PROSO TENAI WHISK BAJREE DHURRA HUREEK JONDLA JOWARI MILIUM DAGASSA PANICLE ZABURRO BIRDSEED KADIKANE

MILLHAND CROPMAN

MILLILITER MIL

MILLIMETER LI

(THOUSANDTH OF —) MICRON

MILLINER ARTISTE MODISTE

MILLING GRAINING

MILLION CONTO QUENT

(10 —) CRORE

MILLIPEDE JULID POLYPOD DIPLOPOD PILLWORM RINGWORM WIREWORM

MILLISECOND SIGMA

MILLPOND DAM MILLDAM BINNACLE MILLPOOL

MILLRACE LADE LEAD LEAT FOREBAY TAILRACE

MILLRYND INK

MILLSTONE RYND STONE BEDDER LEDGER RUNNER

(PL.) RUN

MILLSTREAM FLEAM

MILLWORKER DOGGER

MILO SORGHUM

MILPA LADANG

MILT MILK SEED SPLEEN

MILTONIST DIVORCER

MIMAS (FATHER OF —) THEANO

(MOTHER OF —) AMYCUS

(SLAYER OF —) MEZENTIUS

MIME ACTOR MIMER MIMIC

(PL.) MIMIAMBI

MIMEOGRAPH RONEO

MIMIC APE HIT COPY MIME MINT MOCK MOCKER MONKEY COPYCAT IMITATE PAGEANT

MIMICRY APERY MIMESIS MOCKAGE MOCKERY

MIMOSA AROMA CASSIE ALBIZZIA HUISACHE TURMERIC

MINCE CHOP SHEAR FINICK

MINCED HACHE

MINCEMEAT GIGOT MINCE

MINCING NIMINY FINICAL MINIKIN MIGNIARD SKIPJACK

MINCINGLY FINE GINGERLY

MIND CIT CHIT HEAD HEED MOOD NOTE NOUS RECK SOUL BESEE BRAIN SENSE SKULL WATCH ANIMUS MATTER NOTICE PSYCHE REGARD COURAGE SENSORY SUBJECT THINKER THOUGHT

(CONSCIOUS —) SENTIENT

(INFINITE —) GOD

(RIGHT FRAME OF —) TUNE

(YEAR'S —) MINNING

MINDFUL HEEDY MINDLY HEEDFUL

MINE BAL PIT DELF HOLE HUEL MEUM BARGH DELFT DELPH METAL STOPE WHEAL COYOTE GOPHER

GROOVE RESCUE BONANZA BORASCA COALPIT MINERAL OPENCUT TORPEDO GOLCONDA MYNPACHT PROSPECT

(— BY BLASTING) SHOOT

(— IRREGULARLY) GOPHER

(— PASSAGE) SLUM

(COAL —) ROB COALPIT COLLIERY

(MILITARY —) FOUGADE FOUGASSE

(OLD —) GWAG

(RICH —) GOLCONDA

(TIN —) STANNARY

(UNPRODUCTIVE —) SHICER BORASCA

MINER PECK PICK PYKE BARER DOGGY ARTIST BUCKER CUTTER DAMMER DELVER DIGGER GANGER GETTER HAGGER JUMPER MATTER PELTER REEFER SNIPER STOPER TINNER TOPMAN VANNER COLLIER CRUTTER DIRGLER FEIGHER GEORDIE GROOVER HITCHER HUTCHER LEADMAN PICKMAN PIKEMAN PIONEER PLUGMAN ROCKMAN SNUBBER ENTRYMAN HEADSMAN STRIPPER WINZEMAN

(— WHO WORKS ALONE) HATTER

MINERAL JET GEET HOST MINE SPAR BERYL BLOOM EARTH FLUOR GLEBE GUEST LENAD SQUAT TRONA ACMITE ALAITE AUGITE BARITE BARYTE BLENDE CASTOR CERITE COCKLE CURITE DAVYNE EGERAN EHLITE ERRITE GALENA GARNET GYPSUM HALITE HAUYNE HELVIN HUMITE ILLITE IOLITE LABITE MIXITE NATRON NOSEAN NOSITE PINITE RUTILE SALITE SILICA SPHENE SPINEL ADAMINE ADAMITE ADELITE ALTAITE ALUMITE ALUNITE AMOSITE APATITE ATOPITE AXINITE AZORITE AZULITE AZURITE BAUXITE BAZZITE BELLITE BISMITE BITYITE BOHMITE BOLEITE BORNITE BRUCITE CALCITE CELSIAN CYANITE DIAMOND DICKITE DUFTITE EDENITE EPIDOTE ERIKITE ERINITE EUCLASE FLOKITE GAGEITE GAHNITE GEDRITE GLADITE GOTHITE GUMMITE HELVITE HESSITE HOPEITE HOWLITE HULSITE IHLEITE ILVAITE INESITE INYOITE ISERITE JADEITE JARLITE JOSEITE KEMPITE KERNITE KOPPITE KOTOITE LANGITE LARNITE LAURITE LAUTITE LEHIITE LEIFITE LEONITE LEPTITE LEUCITE LOWEITE MARTITE MELLITE OKENITE PALAITE PENNINE PETZITE PYRITES RATHITE REALGAR RETZIAN RHAGITE RINKITE ROMEITE ROSSITE SENAITE SODDITE SVABITE SYLVITE THORITE TURGITE ULEXITE UTAHITE UVANITE VAUXITE VOGLITE VRBAITE WARBITE WIIKITE ZEOLITE ZINCITE ZOISITE ZORGITE ZUNYITE AIKINITE ALLANITE ALLUVIAL ALUNOGEN AMBONITE ANAUXITE ANCYCITE ANDORITE ANKERITE ARIEGITE ARMENITE ARTINITE ASBOLITE AUGELITE AUTUNITE AWARUITE BADENITE

BAKERITE BARARITE BARYLITE BAVENITE BETAFITE BEYERITE BILINITE BIXBYITE BLAKEITE BLOEDITE BOOTHITE BORACITE BOWENITE BRAGGITE BRAUNITE BRAVOITE BROMLITE BRONZITE BROOKITE BRUSHITE CALCSPAR CARBOCER CEROLITE CHIOLITE CHLORITE CHROMITE CIMOLITE CINNABAR COHENITE COLUSITE COOKEITE COSALITE CREEDITE CROCOITE CRYOLITE DANALITE DAPHNITE DATOLITE DELTAITE DENDRITE DIASPORE DIGENITE DIOPSIDE DIOPTASE DIXENITE DOLOMITE DYSODILE EGUEIITE ELIASITE ELPIDITE EMBOLITE ENARGITE EPSOMITE ERIONITE EUCOLITE EULYTINE EULYTITE EUXENITE EVANSITE FASSAITE FAYALITE FELDSPAR FERSMITE FIBROITE FLINKITE FLUORITE FOOTEITE FUCHSITE FUSINITE GEMSTONE GENTHITE GIBBSITE GINORITE GOETHITE GOYAZITE GRIPHITE GROTHINE GROUTITE GYROLITE HANKSITE HANUSITE HARTTITE HATCHITE HAUERITE HAUYNITE HEMATITE HOMILITE HUGELITE IDOCRASE INDERITE IODYRITE JALPAITE JAROSITE JEZEKITE KALINITE KAMACITE KASOLITE KEHOEITE KLEINITE KOKTAITE KOLSKITE KRAUSITE LAGONITE LAVENITE LAZULITE LAZURITE LEVYNITE LEWISITE LIMONITE LINARITE LOMONITE LOWIGITE MARSHITE MEIONITE MELILITE MELONITE MESITITE MESOLITE MIERSITE MIMETITE MISENITE MOLYSITE MONAZITE MONETITE MORAVITE MOSESITE NADORITE NASONITE NEPOUITE NOCERITE NOSELITE OXAMMITE PEGANITE PETALITE PIMELITE PINNOITE PISANITE PODOLITE PORODINE PRICEITE PRIORITE RINNEITE ROSELITE SAGENITE SALEEITE SALESITE SAPONITE SASSOLIN SCAWTITE SHANDITE SHARPITE SHORTITE SIDERITE SMALTITE SMITHITE SODALITE SPADAITE SPURRITE STANNITE STIBNITE STILBITE STOLZITE STRUVITE STURTITE SZMIKITE TAGILITE TANGEITE TEALLITE TENORITE TILASITE TITANITE TRIPLITE TROILITE TYROLITE TYSONITE URANOTIL VEGASITE VOLTAITE VOLTZITE WEHRLITE WEISSITE WELLSITE WILKEITE WURTZITE XENOLITE XENOTIME YENTNITE ZARATITE WILLEMITE

(BLACK —) JET GEET CERINE YENITE KNOPITE NIOBITE ALLANITE GRAPHITE HIELMITE ILMENITE ONOFRITE

(BRIGHT —) BLENDE

(BROWN —) CERINE EGERAN

GUILDITE JAROSITE
(FIBROUS —) ASBESTOS
(GRAY-WHITE —) TRONA HOPEITE
(GREEN —) AMESITE GAHNITE
ILESITE PRASINE PREHNITE
SMECTITE
(ORANGE —) SANDIX
(RADIATED —) ASTROITE
(RADIOACTIVE —) CURITE
(RARE —) CYMRITE EUCLASE
TYCHITE BARYLITE
(RED —) GARNET
(SOFT —) TALC KERMES
(TRANSPARENT —) MICA POLLUX
SODALITE
(WHITE —) BARITE HOWLITE
STILBITE
(YELLOW —) TOPAZ PYRITES
(YELLOWISH-GREEN —) EPIDOTE
ECDEMITE
MINERAL TAR MALTHA
MINERAL WATER SELTZER
MINERVA MENFRA
MINESWEEPER ALGERINE
MINGLE MIX FUSE JOIN MELL MOLD
MONG MOOL ADMIX BLEND MERGE
TWINE COMMIX FELTER HUDDLE
JUMBLE MEDDLE MEDLEY COMBINE
COALESCE CONFOUND
MINGLED FUSED MEDLEY CONFUSED
MINIATURE SMALL LITTLE POCKET
MINIKIN
MINIMAL BASAL LIMINAL
MINIMIZE DECRY MINCE LESSEN
SMOOTH SCISSOR BELITTLE
DISCOUNT
MINIMUM BARE BEDROCK
MINING WORK MINERY SPATTER
GROOVING
MINION PEAT SATAN MIGNON
DARLING MINIKIN CREATURE
MINIONETTE EMERALD
MINISTER PRIG CLERK DEWAN
ELDER ENVOY HAMAN PADRE VIZIR
ATABEG DEACON DIVINE GALLAH
PANDER PARSON PASTOR PESHWA
PRIEST VIZIER BROTHER DOMINIE
OFFICER PESHKAR PREFECT
PALATINE PREACHER
(— OF FINANCE) DEWAN
(— TO) TEND SERVE INTEND
(— WITHOUT SETTLEMENT)
STIBBLER
(PRIME —) PADRONE
MINISTRANT(PL.) SELLI SELLOI
MINISTRATION SERVICE TENDANCE
MINISTRY SERVICE
MINIUM SANDIX
MINIVER LASSET
MINK FAG HURON NORSE VISON
JACKASH KOLINSKY MUSTELIN
PLATINUM

MINNESOTA
CAPITAL: STPAUL
COLLEGE: BETHEL STOLAF
WINONA BEMIDJI HAMLINE
AUGSBURG CARLETON

COUNTY: ANOKA ISANTI ROSEAU
WASECA WABASHA HENNEPIN
INDIAN: SIOUX OJIBWA CHIPPEWA
LAKE: LEECH ITASCA BEMIDJI
SUPERIOR
MOUNTAIN: EAGLE MISQUAH
MOUNTAIN RANGE: CUYUNA
MESABI MISQUAH
NICKNAME: GOPHER NORTHSTAR
RIVER: RAINY STCROIX
STATE BIRD: LOON
STATE TREE: REDPINE
TOWN: ADA ELY MORA AUSTIN
DULUTH NEWULM WINONA
BEMIDJI FOSSTON HIBBING
MANKATO BRAINERD

MINNESOTAN GOPHER
MINNOW PINK GUPPY HITCH MINIM
MINNY BAGGIE MENNON DOGFISH
FATHEAD GULARIS PHANTOM
PINHEAD PINKEEN BONYTAIL
CYPRINID FLATHEAD GAMBUSIA
MOONFISH SATINFIN
(PL.) MENISE
MINOR FLAT LESS MOLL WARD
PETIT PETTY INFANT LESSER
SLIGHT
MINORESS CLARE CLARISSE
MINORITY FEW NONAGE INFANCY
MINOS (FATHER OF —) JUPITER
(MOTHER OF —) EUROPA
(SLAYER OF —) COCALUS
(WIFE OF —) PASIPHAE
MINSTER CHADBAND
MINSTREL BARD BADHAN HARPER
JOCKEY BADCHAN GLEEMAN
JOCULAR PARDHAN PIERROT
SONGMAN JONGLEUR
MINSTRELSY GLEE DREAM
MINT COIN NANA SAGE AJUGA BASIL
ORGAN THYME HYSSOP SAVORY
STRIKE ALLHEAL BALLOTA CAPMINT
LABIATE OLITORY OREGANO
PERILLA PHLOMIS POTHERB
STACHYS BERGAMOT CALAMINT
IRONWORT LAMPWICK LAVENDER
MARJORAM SAGELEAF SELFHEAL
MINTER MONEYER
MINUET MINAWAY
MINUS LESS WANTING
MINUTE FINE NICE TINY CLOSE
MINIM PRIME SMALL ATOMIC
MOMENT INSTANT SCRUPLE
DETAILED
(24 —S) GHURRY
MINX JADE PEAT SLUT SNIT HUSSY
HUZZY LIMMER SNICKET
MIRACLE SIGN ANOMY MARVEL
WONDER PRODIGY THEURGY
MIRACLE PLAY GUARY
MIRAGE SERAB CHIMERA FLYAWAY
LOOMING ILLUSION TOWERING
MIRE BOG DUB CLAY GLAR LAIR
MOIL SLOB SLUB SLUE SLUR ADDLE
CLART EMBOG FANGO GLAUR
SEUGH SLAKE SLUSH SQUAD STALL
SLOUGH SLUDGE SLUTCH CLABBER

GUTTERS SLUBBER WORTHING
MIRITI PALM MORICHE
MIRLITON KAZOO
MIRO TOMTIT
MIRROR FLAT BERYL GLASS IMAGE
STEEL STONE PEEPER PSYCHE
REFLEX SHINER SHOWER CONCAVE
HORIZON REFLECT DIAGONAL
SPECULUM
MIRTH GLEE CHEER DREAM SPORT
GAIETY BAUDERY DISPORT JOLLITY
HILARITY
(CONTEMPTUOUS —) SPORT
(VIOLENT —) SPLEEN
MIRTHFUL CADGY MERRY FESTIVE
GLEEFUL JOCULAR DISPOSED
LAUGHFUL
MIRY OOZY PUXY LAIRY MUCKY
SLAKY CLAGGY CLASHY LUTOSE
MIRISH SLABBY GUTTERY SLOUGHY
MISADVENTURE GRIEF ACCIDENT
CALAMITY CASUALTY DISASTER
MISANTHROPE CYNIC TIMON
MISANTHROPIC CYNICAL
MISANTHROPY TIMONISM
MISAPPLIED ABUSIVE
MISAPPLY ABUSE CROOK WREST
DISUSE MISUSE
MISAPPREHEND MISTAKE
MISAPPREHENSION ILLUSION
MISBECOME MISSIT MISSEEM
MISBEHAVE MISUSE MISBEAR
MISFARE MISHAVE MISLEAD
MISGUIDE
MISBELIEF MISCREED
MISCALCULATE DUTCH MISCAST
MISCOUNT
MISCALL BECALL MISNAME
MISCARRIAGE FAIL MISHAP FAILURE
ABORTION
MISCARRY FAIL MISGO FOUNDER
MISFARE MISGIVE BACKFIRE
MISCARRYING ABORTIVE
MISCELLANEOUS CHOW ORRA
SUNDRY ASSORTED CHOWCHOW
MISCELLANY CHOW VARIA MEDLEY
WHATNOT CHOWCHOW GIFTBOOK
MISCHANCE CALAMITY CASUALTY
DISASTER
MISCHIEF HOB ILL BANE EVIL HARM
HURT JEEL WRACK INJURY MURCHY
SORROW WONDER DEVILRY
KNAVERY SCADDLE DEVILTRY
MISCHIEF-MAKING URCHIN
MISCHIEVOUS BAD SLY ARCH IDLE
ROYT ELFIN HEMPY ROYET ELFISH
ELVISH GALLUS HEMPIE IMPISH
NOYANT SHREWD SULLEN WICKED
GALLOWS HARMFUL KNAVISH
LARKISH MOCKING NAUGHTY
PARLISH PLISKIE PUCKISH ROGUISH
SCADDLE UNHAPPY UNLUCKY
WAGGISH LITHERLY LUNGEOUS
SPORTIVE SPRITISH VENOMOUS
WANSONSY
MISCHIEVOUSNESS ROGUERY
MISCONCEPTION DELUSION
ILLUSION
MISCONDUCT CULPA DOLUS

OFFENCE OFFENSE DISORDER
MISCONSTRUCTION STRAIN
MISCONSTRUE MISJUDGE
MISCREANT KNAVE
MISDEED ILL MISS SLIP AMISS
UNWORK DEFAULT FORFEIT
OFFENCE OFFENSE DISORDER
MISDEMEANOR SIN CRIME FAULT
OFFENCE OFFENSE DISORDER
MISDIRECT MISGUIDE
MISER CUFF SKIN CHUFF CHURL
FLINT GRIPE HAYNE HUNKS NABAL
SCRAT SCRIB CODGER HUDDLE
NIPPER PELTER SCRIMP SNUDGE
WRETCH DRYFIST GOBSECK
NIGGARD SCRAPER CHINCHER
GATHERER HAPTERON HARPAGON
HOLDFAST MUCKERER MUCKWORM
PINCHGUT
MISERABLE WOE EVIL GRAY PUNK
SOUR DAWNY DEENY DUSTY MISER
WOFUL YEMER ABJECT CHETIF
CRUMBY CRUMMY ELENGE FEEBLE
PRETTY UNSELY WOEFUL FORLORN
SCRUFFY UNHAPPY WANSOME
FORSAKEN PITIABLE UNTHENDE
WRETCHED
MISERERE SUBSELLA
MISERLINESS MISERISM SNUDGERY
TENACITY
MISERLY WOE MEAN GRIPPY KNIVEY
STINGY CHINCHE WANSITH
SCRAPING SNUDGERY
MISERY WO WOE RUTH GNEDE
GRAME WREAK THREAT ANGUISH
MISEASE TRAGEDY CALAMITY
DISTRESS WANDRETH WOWENING
MISFIRE SKIP SNAP
MISFORTUNE ILL BLOW DOLE DREE
EVIL HARM TEEN CURSE HYDRA
SCATH TRAIK DAMAGE DIRDUM
MISERY MISHAP RUBBER SCATHE
SORROW UNHEAL UNLUCK WANHAP
MALHEUR MISCARE MISFALL
MISFATE MISLUCK REVERSE
TRAGEDY TROUBLE UNSELTH
UNSPEED CALAMITY DISASTER
DISGRACE DISTRESS MISCHIEF
MISGIVING DOUBT QUALM
MISGOVERN MISRULE
MISGUIDED WET
MISHANDLE BUNGLE
MISHAP SLIP GRIEF SITHE UNHAP
WANHAP FORTUNE MISTIDE
ACCIDENT CASUALTY MISCHIEF
MISHEARING OTOSIS
MISHIT DUFF
MISHMASH BOTCH GOULASH
MISINFORM MIZZLE
MISINTERPRET WARP WRITHE
MISREAD MISCOUNT
MISJUDGE MISDEEM MISWERN
MISLAY LOSE DISPLACE MISPLACE
MISLEAD COG ERR BUNK DUPE
GULL HOAX BLUFF CHEAT FALSE
BETRAY DELUDE SEDUCE WILDER
CONFUSE DEBAUCH DECEIVE
MISLEAR INVEIGLE MISGUIDE

MISLEADING BLIND FALSE CIRCEAN
TORTIOUS
MISMANAGE BLUNK BLUNDER
MISLEAD MISRULE ILLGUIDE
MISGUIDE
MISOGYNIC CYNICAL
MISPLACE MISLAY MISPUT MISSET
DISPLACE
MISPLACED MALPOSED
MISPLAY BLOW DUFF ERROR FLUFF
FUMBLE
MISPRONOUNCE MISCALL STUMBLE
MISQUOTE GIVE
MISREPRESENT SKEW ABUSE BELIE
COLOR MISUSE FALSIFY SLANDER
MISCOLOR
MISREPRESENTATION FRAUD
CALUMNY DAUBERY GARBLING
MISS ERR HIP FAIL LACK LOSE SKIP
SLIP SNAB FORGO HANUM MISSY
PANNA SKIRT DESIRE FRAULEIN
MISTRESS SENORITA
MISSEL BIRD MAVIS SHIRL DRAINE
JAYPIE MISTLE SHRITE SYCOCK
CHERCOCK
MISSHAPE DEFORM
MISSHAPEN UGLY BLOWN DEFORM
THRAWN DEFORMED UNSHAPED
MISSILE GUN BALL BIRD BOLT DART
SHOT PLUMB SHAFT STONE BULLET
SEEKER BOMBARD GRENADE
MISSIVE OUTCAST PROJECT
(DEFECTIVE —) DUD
(PL.) MITRAILLE
MISSING LACK WANT ABSENT
WANTING
(— OF CUE) FLUFF
MISSION SAND CHARGE ERRAND
SORTIE VISITA MESSAGE BUSINESS
DEVOTION LEGATION
MISSIONARY APOSTLE COLPORTER

MISSISSIPPI

CAPITAL: JACKSON
COLLEGE: RUST ALCORN
  BELHAVEN MILLSAPS TOUGALOO
COUNTY: HINDS YAZOO ATTALA
  PANOLA TIPPAH NESHOBA
  NOXUBEE ITAWAMBA
INDIAN: BILOXI TUNICA CHOCTAW
  NATCHEZ CHICKSAW
LAKE: ENID SARDIS BARNETT
  GRENADA OKATIBBEE
MOUNTAIN: WOODALL
NATIVE: MUDCAT TADPOLE
NICKNAME: MAGNOLIA
RIVER: LEAF PEARL YAZOO
  BIGBLACK
STATE BIRD: MOCKINGBIRD
STATE FLOWER: MAGNOLIA
STATE TREE: MAGNOLIA
TOWN: BILOXI HELENA LAUREL
  TUPELO WINONA BELZONI
  CORINTH GRENADA NATCHEZ
  BOGALUSA MERIDIAN
  KOSCIUSKO

MISSIVE NOTE BILLET LETTER
EPISTLE MESSAGE MISSILE

MISSOURI

CAPITAL: JEFFERSONCITY
COLLEGE: AVILA DRURY TARKIO
  LINCOLN WEBSTER STEPHENS
COUNTY: RAY IRON MACON
  TANEY PETTIS DAVIESS
INDIAN: OSAGE
LAKE: OZARKS TABLEROCK
MOUNTAIN: TAUMSAUK
NATIVE: PUKE PIKER
NICKNAME: SHOWME
PLATEAU: OZARK
PRESIDENT: TRUMAN
RIVER: OSAGE
STATE BIRD: BLUEBIRD
STATE FLOWER: HAWTHORN
STATE TREE: DOGWOOD
TOWN: ELDON HAYTI LAMAR
  MACON ROLLA BUTLER
  BETHANY BOLIVAR CAMERON
  LEBANON MOBERLY SEDALIA
  STLOUIS HANNIBAL SIKESTON

MISSTATEMENT ERRATUM
MISSTEP TRIP
MIST DAG FOG MUG URE DAMP DRIP
DROW FILM HAAR HAZE MOKE
RACK ROKE SCUD SMUR BRUME
CLOUD DRISK GAUZE STEAM
MIZZLE NEBULE SEREIN SERENE
SMEETH
(COLD —) DROW BERBER
(DRIZZLING —) SMUR DRISK SMIRR
SMURR
(SMOKY —) SMOG
(WHITE —) HAG
(PL.) SMOKES
MISTAKE ERR BALK GAFF GOOF
MISS SLIP TRIP ERROR FAULT
GAFFE LAPSE BARNEY BOBBLE
ESCAPE MISCUE SLIPUP STUMER
BLUNDER CONFUSE DEFAULT
JEOFAIL STUMOUR WRONGER
CONFOUND MISPRINT MISPRISE
(STUPID —) BUBU BONER
MISTAKEN WRONG ASTRAY
OVERSEEN OVERSHOT TORTIOUS
MISTER DON REB HERR SENOR
SENHOR SIGNOR GOODMAN
SIGNIOR GOVERNOR
MISTFLOWER EUPATORY
MISTILY FOGGILY
MISTLETOE ALLHEAL GADBUSH
MISTREAT BANG VIOLATE
MISTRESS MRS PUG TOY AMIE BIBI
DAME DOLL DOXY LADY MISS PUR
AMIGA AMOUR DOLLY DONNA
DUENA FANCY LEMAN LUCKY
MADAM NANCY WOMAN BEEBEE
MINION MISSIS NEAERA PARNEL
SAHIBA SENORA TACKLE WAHINE
BEDMATE DELILAH HERSELF
HETAERA KITTOCK LEVERET
METREZA PADRONA SENHORA
SIGNORA SULTANA CAMPASPE
DESPOINA DULCINEA FARMWIFE
GOODWIFE GUDEWIFE HAUSFRAU
LADYLOVE LANDLADY MIGNIARD

PARAMOUR PECULIAR SINEBARA TIMANDRA
(— **OF CEREMONIES**) FEMCEE
MISTRUST MISTROW SURMISE DISTRUST JEALOUSE JEALOUSY MISDOUBT
MISTY HAZY MOKY DAGGY FILMY FOGGY MISKY MOCHY MOOTH RAWKY ROKEY BLURRY CLOUDY GREASY SMURRY STEAMY BRUMOUS OBSCURE NEBULOUS NUBILOUS VAPOROUS
MISUNDERSTAND MISKNOW MISTAKE
MISUSE ABUSE ABUSION PERVERT MALTREAT
MITE BIT ATOM CENT DITE DRAM ATOMY BICHO SPECK ACARID ACARUS CHIGOE LEPTUS MINUTE SMIDGE ACARIAN BDELLID CHIGGER DEMODEX SMIDGEN ARACHNID DIBRANCH FARTHING HANDWORM ORIBATID SANDMITE
MITER MITRE TIMBER TIMBRE
MITERWORT COOLWORT
MITIGATE BALM COOL EASE ALLAY DELAY MEASE RELAX REMIT SLAKE LENIFY LESSEN MODIFY PACIFY SOFTEN SOOTHE SUCCOR TEMPER ASSUAGE CUSHION ELEVATE QUALIFY RELEASE RELIEVE SWEETEN PALLIATE
(— **PAIN**) PLASTER
MITIGATING LENITIVE
MITTEN BOOT CUFF MITT MUFF LOOFIE MUFFLE NIPPER MUFFLER
MIX BOX BEAT CARD DASH FUSE JOIN KNIT MELL MENG STIR ADMIX ALLOY BLEND BRAID IMMIX KNEAD MISCE TWINE BLUNGE COMMIX CRUTCH GARBLE JUMBLE MEDDLE MEDLEY MINGLE MUDDLE PERMIX STODGE TEMPER WUZZLE BLUNDER SHUFFLE SWIZZLE CONFOUND LEVIGATE SCRAMBLE
(— **AND STIR WHEN WET**) PUG
(— **CONFUSEDLY**) BROIL
(— **FLOCKS**) BOX
(— **LIQUORS**) BREW
(— **PLASTER**) GAGE GAUGE
(— **TEA**) BULK
(— **WINE**) PART
(— **WITH YEAST**) BARM
(— **WOOL OF DIFFERENT COLORS**) TUM
(**CONCRETE** —) SOUP
MIXABLE MISCIBLE
MIXED CHOW IMPURE MEDLEY MOTLEY PIEBALD STREAKY CHOWCHOW
(— **BLOOD**) MESTIZO
(— **CHALICE**) KRASIS
(— **UP**) HAYWIRE
(**NOT** —) SINCERE
MIXER HOG BANBURY MUDDLER PICKLER
(**CEMENT** —) BOXMAN
(**CONCRETE** —) PAVER
MIXTURE AIR MIX BODY BREW DASH

FEED HASH MANG MULL OLIO PUER SOUP STEW ALGIN ALLOY BLEND BROMO DOUGH GUMBO SALAD STUFF FOURRE GARBLE GUNITE LIGNIN MASLIN MEDLEY MELLAY MINGLE MOTLEY TEMPER AMALGAM COMPOST CUSTARD FARRAGO FILICIN FORMULA GOULASH HEADING KOGASIN MELANGE MISTION MIXTION OLLAPOD RECEIPT TIMBALE ALKYLATE BLENDURE DRAMMOCK EMULSION POSSODIE POWSOWDY SOLUTION
(— **ADDED TO WINE**) DOSAGE
(— **ATTRACTIVE TO PIGEONS**) SALTCAT
(— **FOR CAKE**) BATTER
(— **FOR DRESSING LEATHER**) DUBBIN DUBBING
(— **OF ALE AND OATMEAL**) STOORY
(— **OF ALKALOIDS**) ADONIDIN JABORINE
(— **OF BARKS**) TONGA
(— **OF CEMENT AND STONE**) BUMICKY
(— **OF CLAY AND ROCK**) BODY
(— **OF CLAY AND SAND**) LOAM
(— **OF DRUGS**) SPECIES
(— **OF ELEMENTS**) DIDYMIUM
(— **OF FEEDS**) MASH
(— **OF IMPURE ARSENIDES**) SPEISS
(— **OF OATS AND BARLEY**) DREDGE
(— **OF PRINCIPLES**) EUONYMIN
(— **OF PROTEINS**) CROTIN
(— **OF SALTS**) SOYATE
(— **OF SAND AND STONES**) CHAD
(— **OF SHALE AND SANDSTONE**) HAZLE
(— **OF SLAG AND ORE**) BROWSE
(— **OF VITAMINS**) BIOS
(— **OF WHITE AND BLACK**) GRIZZLE
(— **OF WINE, HONEY AND SPICES**) CLARY
(— **TO ADULTERATE LIQUORS**) FLASH
(— **TO WHITEN BREAD**) HARDS
(— **USED AS A FERMENT**) BUB
(— **USED AT SEDER**) HAROSET CHAROSES
(**ACUTE** —) ACUTA
(**AERIFORM** —) GAS
(**CARVER'S** —) COMPO
(**CAULKING** —) BLARE
(**CLAY** —) COB SLIP
(**COATING** —) COLOR
(**CONFUSED** —) MESS CHAOS FUDDLE SOZZLE
(**CRUMBLY** —) STREUSEL
(**EXPLOSIVE** —) FIREDAMP
(**FOOD** —) FILLING
(**FREEZING** —) CRYOGEN
(**GILDING** —) ASSIETTE
(**HYDROCARBON** —) ABIETENE
(**ITALIAN CONDIMENT** —) TAMARA
(**JUMBLED** —) BOTCH
(**MECHANICS'** —) PUTTY
(**PLASTIC CEMENT** —) CLOY
(**PRESERVATIVE** —) STUFF
(**SEASONED** —) STUFFING

(**SMOKING** —) CHARAS CHURRUS
(**TANNING** —) PURE
(**THICKENING** —) ROUX
(**UNPALATABLE** —) DRAMMOCK
(**WATERY** —) SLURRY
(**WELDING** —) THERMIT
MIZZEN DANDY
MIZZONITE DIPYRE
MKS UNIT JOULE
MNEMONIC MEMORIAL
MOAN HONE MOON REEM WAIL CROON GROAN MOURN MUNGE QUIRK SOUGH MUNGER
MOANING SOUGH DIRGEFUL
MOAT FOSS DITCH FOSSE GRAFF RUNDEL
MOB CREW HERD ROUT COHUE CROWD HURRY PLEBE PLEBS MOBILE RABBLE TUMULT VOULGE DOGGERY CANAILLE RIFFRAFF VARLETRY
MOBILE FLUID MOVEABLE
MOBSTER HOODLUM
MOCCASIN PAC CONGO TEGUA SHOEPACK
(— **WITH LEGS**) LARRIGAN
(**PL.**) SHANKS
MOCCASIN FLOWER NERVINE
MOCHA BARK
MOCHICA YUNCA
MOCHILA MACHEER KNAPSACK
MOCK BOB DOR GAB MOW COPY DEFY GECK GIBE GIRD JAPE JEER JEST JIBE PLAY QUIZ BOURD DORRE ELUDE FLEER FLIRT FLOUT FRUMP HOKER KNACK MIMIC RALLY SCOFF SCORN SCOUT SLEER SPORT TAUNT BEMOCK DELUDE DERIDE ILLUDE NIGGLE IMITATE MURGEON RIDICULE
MOCKER MOWER GIRDER BOURDER FLOUTER SCORNER RAILLEUR
MOCKERNUT BULLNUT
MOCKERY DOR MOW GLEE JEER BOURD DORRE FARCE FLOUT GLAIK SCOFF SPORT BISMER HETHING LUDIBRY MOCKADO MOCKAGE DERISION ILLUSION RIDICULE SCOFFERY
MOCKING GAB ACID SPORT TRUMPERY
MOCKINGBIRD MIMUS MOWER MOCKER
MOCK ORANGE SYRINGA
MOCOA COCHE
MODE CUT JET TON WAY FORM GATE MOOD RAGA TONE TWIG WISE FERIO FINAL GENUS MODUS STATE STYLE ACTING BAROCO CESARE COURSE DATISI FAKOFO FANGLE FESAPO MANNER METHOD BAMALIP CALEMES CAMENES DABITIS DARAPTI DIBATIS DIMARIS DIMATIS DISAMIS FAPESMO FASHION FERISON FESTINO CELARENT DOKMAROK FELAPTON FRESISON
(— **OF BEHAVIOR**) THEW HABITUDE
(— **OF BEING**) CATEGORY
(— **OF CONDUCT**) LAW

(— OF DRESS) HABIT TENUE
(— OF DRESSING HAIR) MADONNA
(— OF EXPRESSION) IRONY
(— OF MORAL ACTION) CONDUCT
(— OF PARTITIONING) CANT
(— OF PROCEDURE) ORDER
SYSTEM
(— OF RULE) REGIME
(— OF SPEECH) LATINISM
(— OF STANDING) STANCE
(— OF STRUCTURE) BUILD
(PREVAILING —) GARB
(TEMPORARY —) VOGUE
MODEL WAX COPY FORM MOLD
NORM CANON DUMMY IDEAL LIGHT
MOULD NORMA SHAPE DESIGN
FUGLER GABARI MODULE PRAXIS
SOURCE DIORAMA EXAMPLE
GABARIT MODULET PARAGON
PATTERN PICTURE SAMPLER
CALENDAR ENSAMPLE EXEMPLAR
EXEMPLUM FORMULAR FUGLEMAN
MAQUETTE MODELLER MODULIZE
PARADIGM PROPLASM SPECIMEN
TYPORAMA
(— OF HUMAN BODY) FORM
MANIKIN
(— OF STATUE) ESQUISSE
(INFERIOR —) JALOPPY
(MATHEMATICAL —) SPACE
(PRELIMINARY —) MAQUETTE
PROPLASM
MODERATE BATE COOL CURB EASE
EASY EVEN MEEK SOFT ABATE
ALLAY ALLOY LIGHT LOWER MEZZO
MODER REMIT SLACK SLAKE SOBER
SWEET ARREST BRIDLE DECENT
GENTLE LESSEN MEANLY MIDWAY
MODEST MODIFY REMISS SEASON
SOFTEN SUBMIT TEMPER CENTRAL
CONTROL SLACKEN ATTEMPER
CENTRIST MEETERLY MIDDLING
MITIGATE MODERATO ORDINATE
PALLIATE PASSABLE
(— IN BURNING) SOFT
(— OF THE WIND) LOOM
MODERATELY GEY FAIR MEAN
MEETLY PRETTY MIDWISE
MEETERLY MIDDLING
MODERATENESS CLEMENCY
MODICITY
MODERATION MEAN STAY MINCE
SPARE MANNER MEDIUM REASON
COMPASS MEDIETY MODESTY
SOBRIETY IMMODESTY
MODERATO MASSIG
MODERN NEW LATE RECENT
NEOTERIC
MODEST SHY DEFT MURE NICE
SNUG DOUCE LOWLY QUIET SMALL
CHASTE DEMURE HUMBLE PUDENT
SIMPLE VIRGIN CLERKLY PUDICAL
DISCREET MAIDENLY PUDIBUND
RESERVED RETIRING SHAMEFUL
VERECUND VIRTUOUS
MODESTY PUDOR NICETY DECENCY
PUDENCY SHYNESS CHASTITY
FOREHEAD HUMILITY PUDICITY

MODICUM DROP BREAK SPICE
PENNORTH
MODIFICATION BOB ECAD FORM
SALT CHANGE ENGRAM FACIES
SANDHI SINGLE UMLAUT ENGRAMMA
(— OF A REMEDY) TINCTION
(GLOTTAL —) STOP
MODIFIED VARIANT
MODIFY EDIT VARY ALTER AMEND
HEDGE TOUCH BUFFER CHANGE
DOCTOR MASTER TEMPER ARABIZE
COMPARE FASHION QUALIFY
ATTEMPER DENATURE GRADUATE
MODERATE FAUCALIZE
(— ARTICULATION) COLOR
(— COLOR) TONE
MODILLION ANCON MODEL TRUSS
CARTOUCH
MODISH CHIC MODY SOIGNE TIMISH
TONISH STYLISH
MODISHNESS CHIC
MODULATE SINK INFLECT QUALIFY
MODULATION ACCENT CHANGE
CADENCE BUNCHING PASSAGIO
MOGUL PADISHAH
MOHAIR MOIRE
MOHAMMED MAHOMET MAHOUND
MUDEJAR PROPHET
MOHAMMEDAN MOSLEM PAYNIM
MAHOMET
MOHAMMEDANISM TURBAN
TURKERY MAUMETRY
MOHR MHORR GAZELLE
MOHUR MOOR AHMEDI
MOIETY MEDIETY
MOIST WET DAMP DANK DEWY NESH
UVID DABBY GIVEY GREEN HUMID
JUICY MADID MOCHY SAMMY SAPPY
SLACK SOAKY SOCKY SPEWY
SWACK WEEPY CLAMMY MOISTY
STICKY WETTISH HUMOROUS
MUCULENT
MOISTEN DIP WET DAMP MOIL
BASTE BATHE BEDEW JUICE LATCH
LEACH STEEP WOKIE DABBLE
DAMPEN HUMECT IMBRUE MADEFY
SPARGE TEMPER HUMIDIFY
IRRIGATE IRRORATE
(— LEATHER) SAM SAMMY
MOISTURE DEW WET BREE DAMP
DANK ROKE HUMOR MOIST WATER
PHLEGM AQUOSITY HUMIDITY
(— DEFICIENT) XERIC
(— IN STONE) SAP
(— ON BEARD) BARBER
(CONDENSED —) BREATH
MOJARRA SHAD PATAO
MOKI MOGUEY MOKIHI
MOKSHA MUKTI
MOLAR WANG FORMAL MOLARY
GRINDER
MOLASSES DIP LICK CLAGGUM
THERIAC TREACLE LONGLICK
MOLD DIE FEN PIG PLY SOW CALM
CAST CURB FORM MULL MUST SOIL
TRAP BLOCK CHAPE CHILL FRAME
INGOT MODEL MOULD MUCOR
PLASM PRINT SHAPE SHARE STENT
STINT VALVE COFFIN GABARI

INFORM LINGET MATRIX SQUARE
BASTARD FASHION FESTOON
MATRICE RILLETT SANDBOX SKILLET
TEMPLET COQUILLE FUMAGINE
HOODMOLD PROPLASM TEMPLATE
WHISKERS
(— FOR METAL) SOW SKILLET
(— OF ASPIC) DARIOLE
(— OF SHIP) SWEEP
(— THAT ATTACKS HOPS) FEN
MOLDAVITE TEKTITE
MOLDBOARD REEST
(— SURFACE) WREST
MOLDED FICTILE
MOLDER MURL CAPPER MANGLE
MOSKER FIGURER PLASTER PLASTIC
MOLDINESS FINEW MUCOR VINEW
MOLDING BEAD COVE CYMA DADO
GULA KEEL LIST OGEE OVAL CABLE
FILET GORGE LABEL LEDGE ROVER
STAFF BANDLE BASTON CASING
COLLAR CONGEE COVING FILLET
LISTEL MULLER REGLET SQUARE
ZIGZAG ANNULET BEADING
CHAPLET DOUCINE ECHINUS
EYEBROW FINGENT HIPMOLD
LOZENGE MOULAGE NECKING
SURBASE TONDINO TRINGLE
BAGUETTE BANDELET CASEMATE
CASEMENT CYMATION CYMATIUM
DANCETTE FUSAROLE HOODMOLD
KNURLING MOULDING NAILHEAD
NECKMOLD
(CONCAVE —) GORGE CONGEE
SCOTIA CAVETTO
(CONVEX —) REED CABLE OVOLO
THUMB TORUS BASTON REEDING
ASTRAGAL FUSAROLE
(OGEE —) TALON
(OUTSIDE —) BACKBAND
(PL.) LEDGMENT
MOLDY FUSTY HOARY MUCID
MUGGY MUSTY VINNY FOISTY
MOULDY FOUGHTY
MOLE COB UNT COBB MAIL OONT
PIER PILE TAPE WANT JUTTY
MOODY NEVUS TALPA TAUPE
ANICUT MOUDIE HYDATID TALPOID
MOLDWARP MOONCALF SORICOID
STARNOSE UROPSILE ZANDMOLE
MOLE CRICKET CHANGA
MOLECULE ACID ATOM BASE
AMMINE DIPOLE HYDROL LIGAND
HYDRONE SPECIES
MOLEHILL TUMP HOYLE WANTHILL
MOLE RAT SEMNI ZEMMI ZOKOR
SLEPEZ SPALACID ZANDMOLE
MOLEST GALL HAUNT TEASE
BOTHER HARASS HECKLE INFEST
PESTER MISLEST TROUBLE
MOLLIFY HUSH RELAX ADULCE
GENTLE PACIFY RELENT SOFTEN
SOOTHE TEMPER ASSUAGE DULCIFY
SWEETEN ATTEMPER MITIGATE
UNRUFFLE
MOLLIFYING MILD SUPPLING
MOLLUSK ARK CLAM CONE PIPI
SPAT BORER CHAMA CHANK CHINK
CLAMP CONCH COWRY DORIS DRILL

MUREX PINNA SNAIL VENUS AEOLID BAILER BUBBLE CERION CHITON COCKLE COURIE DOLIUM JINGLE LEPTON LIMPET MUSSEL NERITA OYSTER PECTEN PHOLAD PURPLE SEMELE STROMB ABALONE ASTARTE BIVALVE CARDITA DECAPOD JUNONIA MOLLUSC PIDDOCK SCALLOP TOHEROA TREPANG TROPHON DUCKFOOT FIGSHELL HALIOTIS NAUTILUS PTEROPOD SAXICAVA STROMBUS UNIVALVE VERMETUS

(— TRIBE) NAIADES

(LARVAL —) VELIGER

(YOUNG —) SPAT

MOLLYCODDLE MOLLY WANTON INDULGE MILKSOP

MOLOSSUS (FATHER OF —) PYRRHUS

(MOTHER OF —) ANDROMACHE

MOLT MEW CAST MUTE SHED MOULT DISCARD EXUVIATE INTERMEW

MOLTEN FUSED

MOLTING BROKEN ECDYSIS

MOLYBDENUM (EXCESS OF —) TEART

MOMBIN JOCOTE

MOMENT MO GIRD HINT SAND TICK AVAIL BLINK BRAID CLINK CRACK GLIFF GLISK JIFFY SHAKE SNIFT SPURT STOUN TRICE VALUE FILLIP GLIFFY MINUTE PERIOD SECOND STOUND WEIGHT YAWING ARTICLE INSTANT INSTANCE MOMENTUM TWINKLING

(— FOR LEGERDEMAIN ACTION) TEMPS

(— OF STRESS) CRISE

(CRITICAL —) BIT INCH CORNER

(DECISIVE —) CRISIS

(EXACT —) BIT POINT

(OPPORTUNE —) KAIROS

(SCHEDULED —) TIME

MOMENTARY MOMENTAL TRANSIENT

MOMENTOUS FELL GRAVE EPOCHAL FATEFUL WEIGHTY EVENTFUL

MOMENTOUSNESS GRAVITY

MOMENTUM WAY FORCE SPEED IMPETUS

MON PEGUAN TALAING

MONACO

DYNASTY: GRIMALDI
LANGUAGE: FRENCH
PEOPLE: MONEGASQUES
PRINCE: LOUIS ALBERT HONORE
ANTOINE CHARLES RAINIER
FLORESTAN
RIVER: VESUBIE
SECTION: MONTECARLO
LACONDAMINE MONACOVILLE

MONAD JIVA HENAD MONAS

MONADNOCK BARABOO

MONARCH KING QUEEN DANAID

DIADEM PRINCE DANAINE EMPEROR AUTOCRAT

MONARCHIAN PRAXEAN

MONARCHICAL KINGLY

MONARCHY KINGDOM

MONASTERY WAT ABBEY BADIA LAURA RIBAT TEKKE TEKYA FRIARY MANDRA VIHARA BONZERY CERTOSA CONVENT KHANKAH MINSTER CLOISTER LAMASERY

(ALGERIAN —) RIBAT

(BUDDHIST —) TERA KYAUNG BONZERY LAMASERY

(CARTHUSIAN —) CERTOSA

(HINDU —) MATH

(MOSLEM —) TEKKE TEKYA KHANKAH

MONASTIC MONKLY MONKISH CENOBIAN MONACHAL

MONASTICISM MONKERY MONKISM

MONETARY EXPLICIT

MONEY (ALSO SEE COIN) AES BOX DIB FEE FEI GET OOF ORO SAP TIN WAD CASH COAT COIN COLE CRAP CUSH DUBS DUST FUND GATE GELT GILT GOLD HOOT JACK JAKE KALE LOUR MINT MOSS MUCK PELF ROLL SALT SAND SHAG SOAP SWAG BEANS BLUNT BRASH BRASS BREAD BUNCE BUNTS CHINK CHIPS CLINK DARBY DIMES DOUGH DUMPS FUNDS GREEN GRIGS IMPUT LUCRE MOPUS OCHER PURSE RHINO ROCKS ROWDY SCADS SHINY SMASH SPUDS STIFF STUFF SUGAR ARGENT BARATO BARREL BOODLE CHANGE CUNYIE DANARO DINERO FARLEU FARLEY FEUAGE FLIMSY FUMAGE GRAITH HANSEL KELTER MAZUMA POCKET SHEKEL SILVER SPENSE SPLOSH STAMPS STEVEN STUMPY TALENT WISSEL ADVANCE CHATTEL CHINKER COUNTER CRACKER CRUSADE DEPOSIT FALDAGE GUNNAGE OOFTISH SCRATCH SPANKER SPECIES STOCKER CRIMPAGE CURRENCY DEMIMARK INCOMING INTEREST SPENDING STERLING STOCKING XERAPHIN

(— BET) COMEBACK

(— DUE) DEVOIRS

(— FOR LIQUOR) WHIP

(— LENT) LUMBER

(— OF ACCOUNT) ORA

(— PAID TO BIND BARGAIN) ARLES

(— TAKEN IN) DRAWING

(ADDITIONAL —) BONUS

(AVAILABLE —) CAPITAL

(BAR —) BONK TANG

(BASE —) SHICE

(BRIBE —) SOAP BOODLE

(COUNTERFEIT —) BOGUS QUEER BOODLE DUFFER SHOWFUL SLITHER

(EARNEST —) ARLES ARRHA DEPOSIT HANDSEL HANDGELD HANDSALE

(EXPENSE —) DIET

(FERRY —) NAULUM

(HARD —) SPECIE

(HAT —) TAMPANG

(HAVING NO —) FLYBLOWN

(INVESTED —) STOCK

(PAPER —) GREEN CABBAGE CURRENCY FROGSKIN

(PASSAGE —) SHIPHIRE

(PRIZE —) PEWTER

(PROTECTION —) ICE

(PUSH —) SPIFF

(READY —) CASH DARBY READY STUFF STUMPY

(REFUNDED —) DRAWBACK

(SHELL —) PEAG HAWOK WAKIKI WAMPUM

(SILVER —) SYCEE

(SMALL SUM OF —) SPILL

(STANDARD BANK —) BANCO

(SUBSISTENCE —) BATTA

(TRAVELLING —) VIATICUM

(WIRE —) LARI LARIN LARREE

MONEYBAG FOLLIS

MONEY BELT ZONE

MONEY BOX TILL CHEST PIRLIE

MONEY-CHANGER SARAF SHROFF ARGENTER

MONEY DRAWER TILL SHUTTLE

MONEYED RICH WEALTHY

MONEYLENDER BANYA CHETTY USURER LOMBARD MAHAJAN MARWARI SHYLOCK

MONEYMAKING BANAUSIC

MONEYWORT MANG MYRTLE PRIMWORT

MONGOL HUN KALKA BALKAR BURIAT DAGHUR SHARRA BERBERI KALMUCK KHALKHA SILINGAL

(PL.) HU

MONGOOSE MUNG URVA CIVET MUNGO MONGOE MEERKAT VANSIRE

MONGREL CUR DOG FICE FIST CROSS FEIST LIMER SCRUB BASTARD CURRISH PIEBALD DOGGEREL

MONILIALES HYPHO

MONISM HENISM ONEISM

MONITION TUITION

MONITOR MARKER MENTOR LANTERN PREFECT

MONITOR LIZARD IBID IBIT URAN VARAN WARAL GOANNA WORRAL MONITOR

MONK BO FRA COWL LAMA MARO ARHAT BONZE CLERK FRATE FRIAR PADRE YAHAN BHIKKU CULDEE GALLAH GETSUL GOSAIN MONACH VOTARY ARAHANT CALOYER CLUNIAC GALLACH STARETS STUDITE ATHONITE MARABOUT MONASTIC SANNYASI TALAPOIN TRAPPIST

(PL.) AGAPETI ACOEMETI

MONKEY APE CAY ORA PUG SAI TUP BEGA BROH BRUH DOUC KAHA MONA MONK MONO SAKI SIME TITI TOTA WAAG ZATI ARABA CEBID DIANA JACKO JOCKO KAHAU MUNGA OATAS PATAS PUGGY SAJOU TOQUE UNGKA BANDAR

COAITA COUXIA GRISON GRIVET
GUENON HOWLER LANGUR MACACO
MARTEN MIRIKI MONACH NISNAS
OUBARI PINCHE RILAWA SAMIRI
SIMIAN SIMPAI TEETEE VERVET
WARINE WEEPER WISTIT BHUNDAR
COLOBIN GUARIBA GUEREZA
HANUMAN KALASIE LUNGOOR
MACAQUE MEERKAT MOUSTOC
OUAKARI PRIMATE ROLOWAY
SAIMIRI SAPAJOU STENTOR
TAMARIN ARAGUATO CAIARARA
CAPUCHIN DURUKULI ENTELLUS
LEONCITO MALBROUK MANGABEY
MARMOSET MARTINET MUSTACHE
ORABASSU PRIMATAL TALAPOIN
TCHINCOU WANDEROO
(LIKE A —) PUGGISH
MONKEY BREAD BAOBAB
MONKEY FLOWER MIMULUS
MONKEYPOT LECYTH KAKARALI
LECYTHIS SAPUCAIA
MONKEY PUZZLE PINON PINION
MONKEYSHINE SINGERIE
(PL.) HORSE
MONKFISH MONK SQUATINA
MONKISH CENOBIAN MONASTIC
MONK PARROT LORO
MONKSHOOD ATIS ACONITE
ACONITUM NAPELLUS MOUSEBANE
MONO MONACHI
MONOACETATE ACETIN
MONOCARPELLARY SIMPLE
MONOCHORD MAGAS MAGADIS
UNICHORD
MONOCHROME CAMAIEU MONOTINT
MONOCLE QUIZ EYEGLASS
MONOCLINOUS PERFECT
MONOECISM SYNOECY SYNOEKY
MONOGRAM IHS JHS YHS CIPHER
HERALD CHRISMON
MONOGRAPH STUDY BULLETIN
DISCOURSE
MONOLITH MENHIR PILLAR
(CIRCLE OF —S) CROMLECH
MONOLITHIC GLOBAL
MONOLOGIST DISEUSE
MONOLOGUE MONOLOGY
SOLILOQUY
MONOPHTHONGAL PURE
MONOPHTHONGIZE SMOOTH
MONOPHYSITE AGNOETE AGNOITE
JACOBITE
(PL.) ACEPHALI
MONOPLANE TAUBE PARASOL
MONOPODE SKIAPOD
MONOPOLIZE LURCH ABSORB
CONSUME ENGROSS
MONOPOLY REGIE TRUST CARTEL
APPALTO
MONOSACCHARIDE OSE DIOSE
HEXOSE MONOSE GLYCOSE
HEPTOSE
MONOTONOUS ARID DEAD DULL
FLAT WASTE DREARY SAMELY
SODDEN ADENOID HUMDRUM
INSIPID IRKSOME TEDIOUS
BORESOME DRUDGING SAMESOME
UNVARIED VEGETABLE

MONOTONY DRAB DRYNESS
DULLNESS SAMENESS
MONOXENOUS DIRECT
MONSOON VARSHA
MONSTER OGRE BILCH LARVA
MORMO RAHAB TERAS UNMAN
ELLOPS GERYON MAKARA SHRIMP
TYPHON BICORNE CHIMERA
CYCLOPS DIDYMUS DIPYGUS
ECHIDNA GRENDEL GRIFFIN
GRIFFON SLAPPER UNBEAST
WARLOCK JANICEPS LINDWORM
MOONCALF TARASQUE TYPHOEUS
UROMELUS LEVIATHAN
(— WITH 100 EYES) ARGUS
(— WITH 100 HANDS) BRIAREUS
(9-HEADED —) HYDRA
(FABULOUS —) KRAKEN TANIWHA
(FEMALE —) HARPY LAMIA SCYLLA
(HALF-BULL HALF-MAN —)
MINOTAUR
(MAN-DEVOURING —) OGRE LAMIA
(MYTHICAL —) HARPY SCYLLA
SPHINX CHIMERA WARLOCK
MINOTAUR
(SEA —) BELUE KRAKEN PISTRIX
(SUPERNATURAL —) LARVA
(TWO-BODIED —) DISOMUS
(WATER —) NICKER
MONSTRANCE SUN
MONSTROSITY FREAK DIPYGUS
MONSTER ABORTION IMMANITY
MOONCALF TERATISM
MONSTROUS VAST ENORM GIANT
FIENDLY FLAMING HIDEOUS TITANIC
BEHEMOTH COLOSSAL DEFORMED
ENORMOUS FLAGRANT GIGANTIC
PYTHONIC SLAPPING
MONTAGNARD SEKANI

MONTANA

CAPITAL: HELENA
COLLEGE: CARROLL
COUNTY: HILL TETON FERGUS
WIBAUX PONDERA MISSOULA
INDIAN: CROW ATSINA SALISH
ARAPAHO KUTENAI SIKSIKA
SHOSHONE
LAKE: HEBGEN FLATHEAD
FORTPECK MEDICINE
MOUNTAIN: AJAX BALDY COWAN
SPHINX TORREY GRANITE
HILGARD TRAPPER GALLATIN
PENTAGON SNOWSHOE
MOUNTAIN RANGE: CRAZY LEWIS
POCKY BIGBELT
NICKNAME: BIGSKY TREASURE
RIVER: MILK TONGUE KOOTENAI
MISSOURI
STATE BIRD: MEADOWLARK
STATE FLOWER: BITTERROOT
TOWN: BUTTE HAURE MALTA
HARDIN HELENA BOZEMAN
CHINOOK CHOTEAU FORSYTH
GLASGOW ROUNDUP BILLINGS
MISSOULA

MONTANIST PHRYGIAN

MONTENEGRO

COIN: PARA FLORIN PERPERA
LAKE: SCUTARI SHKODER
MOUNTAIN: DURMITOR
NAME: ZETA ILLYRIA CRNAGORA
PORT: BAR ULCINJ ANTIVARI
DULCIGNO
RIVER: ZETA MORACA
TOWN: NIKSIC CETINJE TITOGRAD
PODGORICA

MONTH AB AV BUL MAY PUS SOL
ZIF ZIW ABIB ADAR AHET APAP ASIN
ELUL IYAR JETH JULY JUNE KUAR
MAGH MOON TYBI AGHAN APRIL
ASARH CHAIT IYYAR MAIUS MARCH
NISAN PAYNI RABIA RAJAB SAFAR
SAWAN SEBAT SHVAT SIVAN SIWAN
TEBET THOTH TIZRI UINAL AUGUST
BHADON CHOIAK JUMADA JUNIUS
KARTIK KISLEV KISLEW KISLEY
MECHIR MESORE NISSAN NIVOSE
PAOPHI PHAGUN SAPHAR SHABAN
SHABAT TAMMUZ TISHRI VEADAR
ABAGHAN APRILIS BAISAKH BYSACKI
CHAITRA CHISLEV ETHANIM
FLOREAL HESHVAN JANUARY
MARTIUS OCTOBER PACHONS
PHALGUN RAMADAN SARAWAN
SHAABAN SHAWWAL THAMMUZ
VENTOSE BRUMAIRE DECEMBER
DULKAADA FEBRUARY FERVIDOR
FRIMAIRE GAMELION GERMINAL
MESSIDOR MUHARRAM NOVEMBER
PLUVIOSE POSEIDON PRAIRIAL
SEXTILIS ZULKADAH SEPTEMBER
(IN NEXT —) PROXIMO
(IN PRECEDING —) ULTIMO
(PRESENT —) INSTANT
(SIX —S) SEMESTER
MONTHLY MENSAL
MONUMENT VAT WAT LECH TOMB
CROSS STONE TABUT TITLE BILITH
DOLMEN HEARSE MEMORY RECORD
TROPHY CHAITYA CHHATRI
CHORTEN DENKMAL FUNERAL
TRILITH BILITHON CENOTAPH
MEMORIAL MONOLITH TROPAION
(— OF HEAPED STONES) CAIRN
(PILLARLIKE —) SHAFT STELA
STELE
MOO LOW
MOOCH BUM CADGE SPONGE
MOOCHER MIKER CADGER GRAFTER
MOOD CUE FIT TID MIND TIFF TIFT
TONE TUNE VEIN WHIM DEVIL
FRAME FREAK HEART HUMOR SPITE
PLIGHT SPIRIT SPLEEN SPRITE
STRAIN TALENT TEMPER CAPRICE
FANTASY FEATHER JUSSIVE
ATTITUDE
(— IN LOGIC) BARBARA
(— OF BAD TEMPER) DORTS
(— OF DEPRESSION) LETDOWN
(CROSS —) FRUMPS
(FRIVOLOUS —) JEST
(GROUCHY —) DODS
(IRRITABLE —) GRIZZLE

(SULKY —) PET
(SULLEN —) STRUNT SULLENS
MOODY SAD GLUM SULKY BROODY GLOOMY MOROSE SULLEN MOODISH PENSIVE
MOON BUAT LAMP LUNA MAHI DIANA LUNET LUCINA PHOEBE CHANDRA CYNTHIA LEWANNA LUNETTE MOONLET FOGEATER MENISCUS SATELLES
(FULL —) PLENILUNE
(NEW —) PRIME
(PART OF COURSE OF —) MANSION
(WANING —) WANIAND
MOONBLIND LUNATIC
MOONEYE HIODONT
MOONEYE CISCO BLOATER
MOON-EYED LUNATIC
MOONFISH SUNFISH JOROBADA
MOONFLOWER ACHETE
MOONLIGHT FLESH MOONGLOW
MOONRAT GYMNURE
MOONSET MOONDOWN MOONFALL
MOONSHINE MOON SHINE SHINNY BOOTLEG BLOCKADE
MOONSTRUCK LUNATIC
MOONWORT LUNARY HONESTY
MOOR FEN BENT FELL POST BEACH BERTH HOVEL TURCO COMMOTY COMONTE MARRANO MOGRABI MOORMAN MORESCO MORISCO
(INFERTILE —) LANDE
MOOR COCK GORCOCK MUIRCOCK
MOORING DOCK MOORAGE
MOORLAND OUTFIELD
MOOSE BELL ELAND CERVID ORIGNAL
MOOSEWOOD DIRCA
MOOT MUTE STIR PORTMOOT
MOP BOB SOP SWAB MALKIN MERKIN MOPPET SCOVEL
(— FOR CLEANING CANNON) MERKIN
(— OF HAIR) TOUSLE
(BAKER'S —) MALKIN MAWKIN
MOPANE IRONWOOD
MOPCAP MOB
MOPE MUMP POUT SULK BROOD GLOOM
MOPING FUSTY DUMPISH
MORA LOVE TIME LIMMA SEMEION
MORAL TAG PURE CIVIL ETHIC EPIMYTH ETHICAL UPRIGHT HONORARY
(PL.) THEW
MORALISTIC DIDACTIC
MORALITY MORALS VIRTUE
MORALIZING PI
MORASS BOG FLOW MOSS ROSS SUMP FLUSH MARSH SLACK SLOUGH QUAGMIRE
MORAY PUSI ELGIN HAMLET MURAENA
MORBID SICK MORBOSE PECCANT
MORDANT HANDLE SPIRIT CAUSTIC STRIKER SCATHING
MORE MO MAE PIU HELDER
(— OR LESS) HALFWAY
(— THAN ADEQUATE) AMPLE

(— THAN ENOUGH) TOO
(— THAN HALF) BETTER
(— THAN ONE OR TWO) SUNDRY
(— THAN ONE) SEVERAL
(— THAN SUFFICIENT) ABUNDANT
(— THAN THIS) YEA
(— THAN) BUT OVER ABOVE RISING PLUSQUAM
(LITTLE —) ADVANTAGE
MOREEN TABBY
MOREL HELVELLA MORIGLIO
MORELLO MOREL GRIOTTE MULBERRY
MOREOVER EKE TOO ALSO MORE AGAIN EITHER BESIDES FARTHER FURTHER THERETO LIKEWISE OVERMORE
MOREPORK PEHO RURU MOPOKE MOPEHAWK
MORGUE LIBRARY MORTUARY
MORION CABASSET
MORMON COHAB SAINT DANITE
(— STATE) UTAH
MORNING GAY MORN MATIN MORROW UNDERN COCKCROW MORNTIME
(IN THE —) MANE
MORNING GLORY NIL KOALI TWINER GAYBINE IPOMOEA MANROOT PILIKAI BINDWEED SCAMMONY
(— GROWING AMONG GRAIN) BEAR
MORNING STAR VENUS DAYSTAR LUCIFER MERCURY BARTONIA
MORO LUTAO SAMAL YAKAN ILLANO DOLOANO MALANAO
MOROCCO MAROQUIN

MOROCCO	
CAPE:	NUN NOUN
CAPITAL:	RABAT
COIN:	OKIA RIAL OKIEH DIRHAM MOUZOUNA
DISTRICT:	ERRIF
MEASURE:	KALA SAAH FANEGA IZENBI TOMINI
MOUNTAIN:	TOUBKAL
MOUNTAIN RANGE:	RIF ATLAS
PEOPLE:	MOOR BERBER KABYLE MOSLEM MUSLIM
PORT:	SAFI CEUTA RABAT SAFFI AGADIR TETUAN LARACHE MAZAGAN MELILLA MOGADOR TANGIER
PROVINCE:	CEUTA MELILLA
RIVER:	DRA MOULOUYA
TOWN:	FES FEZ SAFI RABAT AGADIR MEKNES TANGIER MARRAKECH
WEIGHT:	ROTL ARTAL ARTEL GERBE RATEL KINTAR QUINTAL

MORON FOOL AMENT IMBECILE
MORONITY MOROSIS
MOROSE GLUM GRUM SOUR MOODY RUSTY SURLY CRUSTY GLOOMY STINGY SULLEN CRABBED CROOKED PEEVISH STROUNGE

MOROSENESS ASPERITY
MORPHEME BASE ETYMON COGNATE
MORPHOLOGICAL FORMAL
MORRIS MILL MERELS
MORSEL BIT NIG ORT TIT BITE GNAP SNAP SCRAN BUCKONE MORCEAU NOISETTE PARTICLE SKERRICK
(— OF CHEESE) TRIP
(— OF CHOCOLATE) BUD
(— OF SEASONED MEAT) GOBBET
(CHOICE —) TIDBIT TITBIT
MORTAL BEING DYING FATAL HUMAN VITAL DEADLY FINITE LETHAL BRITTLE DEATHLY DEATHFUL
MORTALITY FLESH MURRAIN
MORTALLY DEADLY FATALLY
MORTAR DAB COMPO DAGGA GROUT LARRY ROYAL SORKI SWISH CANNON CEMENT HOLMOS MINNIE POTGUN BEDDING COEHORN DAUBING PERRIER POUNDER PUGGING SOORKEE
(— AND PESTLE) DOLLY DOLLIE
(— EXTRUDED BETWEEN LATHS) KEY
(— FOR ROCKETS) TROMBE
(— FOR SALUTES) CHAMBER
(— MADE WITH STRAW) BAUGE
(INFERIOR —) SLIME
(SMALL —) HOBIT ROYAL TINKER
(THIN —) LARRY
MORTARBOARD CATERCAP TRENCHER
MORTAR BOAT PALANDER
MORTGAGE DIP LAY BOND LIEN ENGAGE MONKEY OBLIGE WADSET WEDDEED THIRLAGE
MORTGAGOR REVERSER
MORTIFICATION ENVY SHAME SPITE CHAGRIN GANGRENE NECROSIS VEXATION
MORTIFIED ASHAMED
MORTIFY ABASE ABASH SHAME SPITE HUMBLE CHAGRIN CRUCIFY MACERATE
MORTISE GAIN COCKET
(SIDE OF —) CHEEK
MORTUARY MORGUE FUNERARY SAWLSHOT
MORWONG TARAKIHI
MOSAIC AUCUBA EMBLEM MUSIVE SCREEN FRISOLEE INTARSIA TERRAZZO
(POTATO —) CRINKLE
MOSLEM MOOR HADJI HAFIZ HANIF ISLAM MALAY SALAR TURBAN ISLAMIC MOORMAN SANGGIL SARACEN ISLAMITE SANGUILE
MOSQUE JAMI MOSCH DURGAH MASJID MESKED
MOSQUITO GNAT CULICID GAMBIAE SKEETER ANOPHELE DIPTERAN
MOSS FOG MNIUM USNEA HYPNUM MUSKEG FOXFEET GULAMAN HAIRCAP PILIGAN TORTULA CROWFOOT MOSSWORT SPHAGNUM STAGHORN
(— HANGING FROM TREE) WEEPER

MOSSBUNKER MENHADEN
MOSSI MOLE MORE
MOSSI-GURUNSI GUR
MOSS PINK PHLOX
MOSSTROOPER RIDER
MOSSY FOGGY HOARY MUSCOSE
MOST BEST MOSTLY FARTHEST
MOSTLY MOST FECKLY CHIEFLY
  MOSTDEAL
MOT JEST
MOTE ATOM ATOMY FESCUE
  MOATHILL
MOTEL COURT
MOTH GEM NUN PUG HAWK MOTE
  PAGE APPLE ATLAS EGGAR EGGER
  FLAME GAMMA IMAGO PISKY PLUME
  SAMIA SWIFT THORN USHER WITCH
  ANTLER BAGONG BURNET COSSID
  DAGGER DATANA HERALD HUMMER
  JUGATE LACKEY LAPPET MILLER
  MOODER PLUSIA QUAKER RUSTIC
  SPHINX THISBE TINEID TISSUE
  TUSSUR ARCTIAN ARCTIID
  BAGWORM BUDWORM CRAMBID
  CRININE DELTOID DRINKER
  EMERALD EMPEROR EUCLEID
  FESTOON FIGWORM FOOTMAN
  FRENATE HOOKTIP NOCTUID
  PEGASUS PSYCHID PYRALIS
  SLICKER STINGER SYLINID TINEOLA
  TORTRIX TUSSOCK URANIID
  VAPORER ZYGENID AEGERIID
  ARMYWORM BOMBYCID CATOCALA
  CECROPIA CINNABAR COCHYLIS
  FISHTAIL FORESTER GEOMETER
  GOLDTAIL GRISETTE HAWKMOTH
  HEPIALID KNOTHORN MOTHWORM
  PHYCITID PLUTELLA SPHINGID
  SPRAWLER WAINSCOT
  (— BREEDER) AURELIAN
  (VERY SMALL —) MICRO
MOTH BALL REPELLER
MOTHER INA MOM DAME MAMA
  MADRE MAMMA MAMMY MATER
  MINNY MODUR MITHER MULIER
  VENTER GENETRIX
  (— OF THE GODS) RHEA
  (DIVINE —) MATRIGAN
  (GREAT —) AGDISTIS
  (NOURISHING — OF MAN) CYBELE
  (SEVEN —S) MATRIS
  (SIDE OF —) ENATE
MOTHERLAND COUNTRY
MOTHERLY MATERNAL MATRONAL
MOTHER-OF-PEARL NACRE PEARL
MOTIF SPRIG DESIGN DEVICE MOTIVE
  SCALLOP APPLIQUE
MOTILE ZO ZOO
MOTION WAY FARD FEED GIRD
  MOVE SIGN WHID HURRY PAVIE
  APPORT MOMENT MOTIVE TRAVEL
  UNREST IMPULSE ACTIVITY
  MOVEMENT OVERTURE
  (— OF AIR) AIRFLOW
  (— OF HORSE) AIR
  (— TO) ALLATIVE
  (ABRUPT —) CHOP
  (CAM —) COULIER
  (CIRCULAR —) GYRE COMPASS

(CONFUSED —) GURGE
(DANCE —) CAPER
(DIZZY —) SWIMBEL
(EXPRESSIVE —) GESTURE
(FORWARD —) HEADWAY
(GLIDING —) SWIM SKITTER
(HEAVING —) ESTUS AESTUS
(HURRIED —) HUSTLE
(ILLEGAL —) BALK BAULK
(IRREGULAR —) SWAG
(JERKING —) BOB LIPE JIGGLE
(LATERAL —) DRIFT
(QUIVERING —) TREMOR
(RAPID —) SCOUR
(REARING —) PESADE
(RECIPROCATING —) SEESAW
(ROTARY —) SWAY BACKSPIN
  SIDESPIN
(SHOWY —) FANFARE
(SIDEWAYS —) CRAB
(SLOW —) CRAWL
(SPINNING —) ENGLISH
(SWIMMING —) FLUTTER
(UPWARD —) HEAVE
(VIGOROUS —) SKELP
(VIOLENT —) JERK RAPT BENSEL
(WAVERING —) SHAKE
(WAVING —) WAFF
(WHIRLING —) SWIRL
MOTIONLESS DEAD ASLEEP
  IMMOBILE STAGNANT STIRLESS
MOTION PICTURE CINE FILM FLICK
  MOVIE BIOPIC CINEMA TALKIE
  CHEAPIE SMELLIE FLICKERS
  (PL.) SILENTS
MOTIVATE ANIMATE INSPIRE
MOTIVATED COVERT
MOTIVE GOAD SAKE SPUR CAUSE
  MOTIF SCORE ACTUAL DESIRE
  OBJECT SPRING ATTACCO IMPULSE
  PATTERN RESPECT RINCEAU
  SUBJECT INSTANCE STIMULUS
  (ALLEGED —) PRETEXT
MOTLEY MIXED MEDLEY RAGTAG
  MOTTLED PIEBALD
MOTMOT HOUTOU SAWBILL
  PICARIAN
MOTOR AUTO TOOT MOVER ENGINE
  ROTATOR TURBINE EFFERENT
MOTORBOAT LAUNCH AUTOBOAT
  RUNABOUT
MOTORCAR MOTOR DOODLEBUG
MOTORCYCLE CYCLE MOTOR
  STEED TRICAR AUTOETTE TRICYCLE
MOTORIST AUTOIST
MOTORMAN CARMAN WATTMAN
  TROLLYMAN
MOTORTRUCK DRAY LORRY
  CAMION BOBTAIL FLATBED
MOTTLE CHECK TABBY SPONGE
MOTTLED JAZZ PINTO MOTLEY
  RUMINATE SPLASHED
MOTTO MOT WORD AXIOM CACHET
  DEVICE EUREKA LEGEND REASON
  IMPRESA EPIGRAPH
  (— IN A RING) POSY
  (— OF CALIFORNIA) EUREKA
  (— OF MAINE) DIRIGO
MOUE FACE

MOUFLON MUSIMON
MOULIN CHIMNEY
MOUND AHU COP HOW LAW LOW
  BALK BANK BOSS BUND BUTT GOAL
  HILL HUMP KNOW MOLE POME TELL
  TEPE TERP TUFT TUMP AGGER
  BERRY DHERI ESKAR ESKER KNOLL
  MONDE MOTTE MOUNT PINGO RAISE
  STUPA TOMAN BARROW CAUSEY
  MEILER RIDEAU ANTHILL BOUROCK
  HILLOCK MAMELON BACKSTOP
  BARBETTE SNOWBANK TEOCALLI
  (— ABOUT A PLANT) TUMP
  (— FOR MEMORIAL) CAIRN
  (— IN BUILDING MATERIAL) DIMPLE
  (— OF DETRITUS) WASH
  (— OF ICE) DOME
  (— OF WOOD TO BE CHARRED)
  MEILER
  (BURIAL —) LAW LOW TOR TOLA
  BERRY GUACA HUACA BARROW
  KURGAN TUMULUS
  (FORTIFIED —) DUN
  (GLACIAL —) KAME
  (MILITARY —) BARBETTE
  (PALISADED —) MOTTE
  (VOLCANIC —) HORNITO
MOUNT BEN STY BACK HEAD RIDE
  RISE SCAN ARISE BIPOD BOARD
  CLIMB HEAVE HINGE SPEEL SPIRE
  SWARM ASCEND ASPIRE MORIAH
  CHARGER COLLINE HAIRPIN
  HARNESS BESTRIDE MOUNTAIN
  MOUNTING MOUNTURE SURMOUNT
  (— A HORSE) FORK LIGHT WORTH
  (— BY STEPS) SCAN
  (— ON PIN) STICK
  (— ON WINGS) SOAR
  (STEREOTYPE —) CORE
MOUNTAIN BEN KOP BERG CIMA
  DAGH FELL KLIP KNOB MONS MONT
  NEBO PICO PIKE JEBEL MOUNT
  RANGE BARROW BUNDOC GILEAD
  GUNONG HEIGHT PISGAH HELICON
  MONTURE NUNATAK BUNDUCKS
  (— INHABITED BY SPIRIT) GUACA
  HUACA
  (— MASS) OROGEN
  (— PASS) GHAT GHAUT
  (— STATE) MONTANA
  (— TRACT) DUAR
  (AT BASE OF —) PIEDMONT
  (FABLED —) KAF MERU
  (GREEK —) OSSA PELION HELICON
  OLYMPUS MAENALUS
  (HIGH —) ALP
  (ROUND —) REEK
  (SMALL —) NOB KNOB BUTTE
  (SNOW —) JOKUL
  (SUBMARINE —) GUYOT SEAMOUNT
MOUNTAIN ASH SORB SORBUS
  DOGBERRY MOZEMIZE ROUNTREE
  WINETREE
MOUNTAIN BEAVER SEWELLEL
MOUNTAIN BINDWEED SOLDANEL
MOUNTAIN CAP SCALP
MOUNTAIN CLIMBER CRAGSMAN
MOUNTAIN CRANBERRY
  FOXBERRY

MOUNTAINEER WASIR WAZIR
HEIDUC HAYDUCK HILLMAN
ORESTES MONTESCO TIERSMAN
(PL.) GUTI GUTIANS
MOUNTAIN GOAT IBEX MAZAME
MOUNTAIN LAUREL IVY HEATH
ERICAD KALMIS LAUREL IVYWOOD
CALFKILL
(THICKET OF —) SLICK
MOUNTAIN LINNET TWITE
MOUNTAIN LION PUMA COUGAR
MOUNTAIN MAHOE EMAJAGUA
MOUNTAIN MISERY TARWEED
MOUNTAINOUS RANGY VICIOUS
MOUNTAIN PARSLEY FLUELLEN
MOUNTAIN RANGE KAF QAF TIER
SIERRA SAWBACK DINDYMUS
MOUNTAIN SICKNESS VETA
MOUNTAINSIDE FELLSIDE
MOUNTAINTOP MAN DOME
MOUNTAIN WOOD ROCKWOOD
MOUNTEBANK IMPOSTOR
OPERATOR
MOUNTED CARDED SADDLE
EASELED EQUITANT
MOUNT ETNA MONGIBEL
MOUNTING MOUNT SCAPE ASCENT
FLIGHT MONTANT SOAKING
INCABLOC MOUNTURE
(— OF GEM) CHASE
(STYLE OF —) SETTING
MOURN DOLE KEEN SIGH WAIL
PLAIN GRIEVE LAMENT SORROW
GRIZZLE
MOURNER WAILER WEEPER
(HIRED —) SAULIE
(PROFESSIONAL —) BLACK KEENER
MOURNFUL SAD BLACK SORRY
WEEPY RUEFUL DERNFUL SIGHFUL
WAILFUL DEJECTED DIRGEFUL
ELEGIOUS FUNEREAL MAESTIVE
MESTFULL YEARNFUL PLAINTIVE
MOURNING DOLOR SHIVA DISMAL
WIDOWED
(— CLOTH) RADZIMIR
MOUSE MURINE MYGALE RODENT
VERMIN ARVICOLE CRICETID
MYOMORPH
(LIKE A —) MURIFORM
(MEADOW —) VOLE
(STRIPED —) KUSU
MOUSEBIRD COLY
MOUSE DEER PLANDOK
MOUSETRAP TIPE
MOUSING KEEPER
MOUTH OS GAB GAM GOB JIB MUG
MUN NEB ORF ROW YAP BEAK BEAL
BOCA HEAD MUSS PUSS SHOP TRAP
YAWN BAZOO BOCCA BRACE CHOPS
CODON STOMA TUTEL GEBBIE
KISSER MUZZLE RABBLE RICTUS
SUCKER THROAT CLAPPER
FLUMMER OSTIOLE STOMACH
LORRIKER PAVILLON
(— AND THROAT) COPPER WHISTLE
(— OF CANYON) ABRA
(— OF GLASS FURNACE) BOCCA
(— OF HARBOR) BOCA
(— OF PERITHECIUM) OSTIOLE

(— OF RIVER) BEAL BOCA LADE
ENTRY INFLUX ESTUARY OSTIARY
(— OF SHAFT) BRACE
(— OF TRUMPET) BELL CODON
PAVILLON
(— PARTS OF ARTHROPOD) TROPHI
(KILN —) KILNEYE KILNHOLE
(SORE — OF SHEEP) ECTHYMA
(WRY —) MURGEON
(PL.) ORA
MOUTHFUL GAG GOB SUP GNAP
GOLEE GOBBET
MOUTHPART BILL
MOUTHPIECE BAR BEAK BOCAL
MOUTH FIPPLE SYRINX PROPHET
(— OF BAGPIPE) MUSE
(— OF PIPE) STEM
MOUTHWASH GARGLE
MOUTH-WATERING SALIVANT
MOVABLE FREE LOOSE MOBILE
PORTABLE REMUABLE
(PL.) MEUBLES
MOVE GO ACT FIG GEE GET WAG
BOOM BORE BUCK BUMP CALL
DRAW FIRK FLIT GOAD HEAT KNEE
MAKE PIRL ROLL SILE SPUR STEP
STIR SWAY WORK ANKLE BLITZ
BUDGE CARRY CAUSE CROWD
DRAFT HEAVE IMPEL LIGHT MARCH
MUDGE QUECH REMUE ROUSE
SHAKE SHIFT GAMBIT HANDLE
HUSTLE INCITE INDUCE KINDLE
MOTION PROMPT QUITCH REMBLE
SASHAY STRAKE ACTUATE AGITATE
ANIMATE DISTURB DRAUGHT
FLUTTER INSPIRE MIGRATE
PROVOKE AMBULATE BULLDOZE
CATAPULT DEMARCHE DISLODGE
DISPLACE MOTIVATE
(— A RESOLUTION) FIRST
(— ABOUT) WEND DISPACE
SHUFFLE CONVERSE LOCOMOTE
(— ACROSS) THWART
(— ACTIVELY) YANK
(— AIMLESSLY) BOGUE
(— ALONG) SHOG
(— APART) SPREAD
(— AS IN STUPOR) DAVER
(— ASIDE) SKEW
(— ASUNDER) SINGLE
(— AT TOP SPEED) LICK
(— AWAY) CUT MOG DECAMP
RECEDE
(— AWKWARDLY) HODGE HIRSEL
LARRUP SHAMBLE
(— BACK) FADE ARSLE RECUR
RECEDE RETIRE RETREAT
(— BACKWARD AND FORWARD) GIG
SWAY DARTLE DIDDLE SHUFFLE
SHUTTLE
(— BOOM OR SAIL) JIB
(— BRISKLY) FAN HALE STIR FRICK
FRIKE FRISK KNOCK SQUIRT
TRANCE TRAVEL WHIPPET
(— BY FITS AND STARTS) JIFFLE
(— BY JERKS) HITCH JIGGET JIGGLE
JINKLE
(— BY SMALL SHOCKS) JOG
(— BY WHEELS) ROLL TRUNDLE

(— CHESS PIECE) DEVELOP
(— CLUMSILY) HOIT JOLL PAUT
BARGE KEVEL HIRSEL LUMBER
TOLTER GALUMPH STUMBLE
(— DIAGONALLY) CATER
(— DOWN) SILE STOOP DECLINE
DESCEND
(— FORCIBLY) SHOVE
(— FORWARD) BREAK ADVANCE
PROGREDE
(— FURTIVELY) LEER GLIDE SLINK
SLIVE SNEAK STEAL
(— GRADUALLY) EDGE
(— HAPHAZARDLY) BUCKET
(— HASTILY) SCUR SKIRR
(— HAUGHTILY) SWOOP
(— HEAVILY) LUG LUMP FLUMP
LUMBER
(— IN AGITATION) SEETHE
(— IN CIRCLES) MILL PURL
(— IN MARBLES) FULK
(— IN RIPPLES) CURL
(— IN SHUFFLING MANNER) MOSEY
(— IN SMALL DEGREES) INCH
(— IN WATER) SQUELCH
(— IN WAVES) LAP CRINKLE
(— INWARDLY) ENMOVE
(— JERKILY) JAG BUCK FLIP KICK
FLIRT BUCKET TWITCH
(— LANGUIDLY) MAUNDER
(— LAZILY) HULK
(— LEISURELY) AMBLE
(— LIGHTLY) BRUSH FLUFF
(— LOOSELY) SLOP
(— NERVOUSLY) DITHER
(— NIMBLY) KILT WHIP DANCE
(— OFF) FIRK RYNT MORRIS
(— ON) MOG VAMP SUCCEED
WHIGFARE
(— OUT OF SIGHT) SINK
(— OUT) BLOW
(— QUICKLY) BOB FIG DUCK FIRK
FLAX FLIT GIRD JINK KITE WHAP
WHEW YANK FLASH GLENT SKEET
SKITE SPANK SQUIB STAVE STOUR
THROW NIDDLE STRIKE WALLOP
SKIMMER
(— QUIETLY) SLIP
(— RAPIDLY) BANG BOLT BUZZ
HEEL HURL THUD CHASE GLINT
SCOUR CAREER GIGGIT HURTLE
AGITATE CLATTER HIGHTAIL
(— RESTLESSLY) FIG FIKE ITCH
SQUIB JIFFLE KELTER
(— SHAKILY) HOTTER
(— SIDEWISE) CRAB EDGE SIDLE
SLENT
(— SLOWLY) LAG MOG INCH PANT
PAUT SLUG BOGUE CRAWL CREEP
DRAWL FUDGE SLOOM SNAIL
HAGGLE LINGER TRINTLE
(— SMOOTHLY) SLIP DRIFT FLOAT
GLIDE SLEEK GLISSADE
(— SPIRALLY) GYRATE
(— STEADILY) FORGE
(— STEALTHILY) GLIDE SLINK
SMOOT SNAKE
(— STIFFLY) CRAMBLE CRAMMEL
(— SUDDENLY) BOLT LASH YERK

GLENT START FLOUNCE STARTLE
(— SWIFTLY) CUT FLY BOOM LEAP
RAKE SCUD SPIN BREEZE COURSE
SWIFTEN
(— THROUGH AIR) FLY
(— TO AND FRO) FAN FLOP DODGE
SHAKE WIGWAG AGITATE
(— TO ANOTHER PLACE) ADJOURN
(— TO LEEWARD) DRIVE
(— UNEASILY) FIDGET
(— UNSTEADILY) BICKER BUMBLE
FALTER HOBBLE WABBLE WAMBLE
WELTER WOBBLE BLUNDER
STAGGER STUMBLE
(— UP AND DOWN) BOB HOWD
SEESAW TEETER
(— UPWARD) ARISE ASCEND
GRADUATE
(— VESSEL) KEDGE
(— VIGOROUSLY) FLOG STRAY
(— VIOLENTLY) DASH FLOG HURL
LASH LEAP SWASH AGITATE
COMMOVE
(— WAVERINGLY) FLEET
(— WEAKLY) FLAG
(— WITH BEATING MOTION) FLAP
(— WITH EFFORT) ACHE
(— WITH LEAPS) SKIP SPRING
(— WITH NOISY ACTIVITY) BUSTLE
(— WITH SHORT TURNS) ZIGZAG
(CHESS —) KEY COOK NECK PLOY
GAMBIT KEYMOVE
(SUCCESSFUL —) SCORE
(SUDDEN —) GAMBADE
MOVED MOSSO ANIMATE FRANTIC
(— BY LOVE) AMOROUS
(EASILY —) FLESHLY SKINLESS
MOVEMENT EDDY MOTO PLAY STIR
CARRY CAUSE FLICK FLISK FLOAT
FRONT GESTE MUDGE TREND UKIYO
ACTION CURSUS ENTREE MOMENT
MOTION PIAFFE SPRAWL STROKE
CURRENT FURIANT GAMBADO
GESTURE KINESIS PIAFFER UKIYOYE
BUSINESS FEMINISM FUTURISM
HASKALAH STIRRING
(— BY ORGANISMS) TAXIS
(— FOR POLITICAL UNION) ENOSIS
(— FROM POINT TO POINT)
PASSAGE
(— IN BULLFIGHT) SUERTE
(— OF AIR) SPIRIT
(— OF CHORUS) STROPHE
(— OF CLOUDS) CARRY
(— OF HORSE) LEVADE
(— OF LOOM) MOUSING
(— OF PROTOPLASM) CYCLOSIS
(— OF ROPE) SURGE
(— OF SHIP) STERNWAY
(— OF TIDE) LAKIE
(— OF TROOPS) LIFT
(— TOWARD GOAL) STRIDE
(AGITATED —) WORKING
(ART —) CUBISM
(BACKWARD —) BACKUP BACKLASH
BACKWASH
(BALLET —) FRAPPE FOUETTE
FLICFLAC
(BOBBING —) BOBBLE

(BODILY —) ACTION
(BOWEL —) LAXATION
(BOXING —) SPAR
(BRISK —) SNAP
(CIRCULAR —) CYCLING
(CLEVER —) PAW
(DANCE —) BRISE CLOSE GIGUE
GLIDE SPIRAL BATTERIE
(DARTING —) FLIRT
(DOWNWARD —) DECLINE
(DROLL —) GAMBADE GAMBADO
(ENLIGHTENMENT —) HASKALAH
(EXPANSION —) BOOM
(FENCING —) VOLT
(FLAPPING —) FLAFF
(FORWARD —) SWEEP ADVANCE
PROGRESS INCESSION
(FROLICKING —) FRISK GAMBOL
(GRADUAL —) CREEPISM
(GYMNASTIC —) KIP SWING
DISMOUNT
(HUMOROUS —) BURLA
(INDEPENDENCE —) SWADESHI
(INVOLUNTARY —) REFLEX
(JERKING —S) BALLISM
(JERKY —) SNATCH
(LATERAL —) LEEWAY
(MASS —) STAMPEDE
(MILITARY —) BOUND MANEUVRE
(MUSICAL —) AIR DUET BURLA
DUMKA LARGO ENTREE FINALE
SARABAND SYMPHONY
(OSCILLATING —) HUNT
(PAINTING —) FAUVISM
(POETRY —) IMAGISM
(POLITICAL —) LEFTISM GAULLISM
(QUICK —) PAW DART WHIP YERK
GLENT SHAKE GLANCE
(RATIONALISTIC —) DEISM
(REELING —) STAGGER
(RELIGIOUS —) JOCISM STUNDISM
(RETROGRADE —) SLIP CREEP
(RETURN —) BACKHAUL
(RHYTHMIC —) DANCE
(ROCKING —) HOWD
(ROWING —) HOICK
(SKILLED —) SUERTE
(SPASMODIC —) JUMP HICCUP
SPRUNT HICCOUGH
(SPRINGY —) LILT
(STEALTHY —) SLINK
(SUDDEN —) HITCH SPANG START
FLICKER
(SWAYING —) SWAG
(SWIFT —) SWOOSH
(THEOLOGICAL —) ARIANISM
(TUMULTUOUS —) HORROR
EMOTION
(TURNING —) CARACOLE
(UP AND DOWN —) SEESAW
(UPWARD — OF VESSEL) SCEND
(UPWARD —) BULGE SCEND
(WALKING —) AMBLE
(WATCH —) EBAUCHE BAGUETTE
(ZIGZAG —) TACK
MOVER MOTIVE
MOVIE (ALSO SEE MOTION PICTURE)
FLICK FLICKS SLEEPER
MOVING WAY HIGH ASTIR GOING

QUICK AFLOAT MOVENT ANIMATE
CURRENT AMBULANT FLITTING
POIGNANT TOUCHING
(— ABOUT) AROUND AMBULANT
(— AIMLESSLY) ERRANT
(— BACKWARDS) CRAB
(— DOWN LINE) ACTIVE
(— FORWARD) ADVANCE
(— HAPHAZARDLY) AFLOAT
(— IN MANY DIRECTIONS) DIFFUSE
(— RAPIDLY) STICKLE SKELPING
(— SLOWLY) SOFT GLACIAL
(— TO AND FRO) AGITATED
(NOT —) STICKY STABILE
MOVINGLY PATETICO
MOW CUT BARB GOAF SKIM CRADLE
SCYTHE SICKLE DESECATE
(— BEANS) THROAT
(— FOR STORING GRAIN) TOSS
(— OF CORN) CANSH
(HAY —) TASS
MOWER MEADER
(FOREMOST —) LORD
MOWING MATH MOWTH SHEAR
MOZAMBIQUE (LAKE OF —) CHUALI
NHAVARRE
(RIVER OF —) SAVE MSALU
LUGENDA ZAMBEZI
(TOWN OF —) TETE BEIRA ZUMBO
CHEMBA PAFURI
MOZZETTA CAMAIL
MR HERR SIGNOR SIGNIOR SIGNORE
MRS FRAU MISS PANI HANOUM
SENORA SENHORA SIGNORA
GOODWIFE
MUCH FAR FELE MICH REAL WELL
GREAT HEAPS MOLTO MOULT SIZES
MICKLE MUCHLY ABUNDANT
MUCHWHAT
(— CALLED FOR) LEEFTAIL
(PRETTY —) GAILY GAYLY
(SO —) ALL SUCH TANTO
INSOMUCH
(TOO —) TROP TROPPO
(VERY —) ALL BADLY GREAT HEAPS
LOADS SWITHE SWYTHE APLENTY
GEYLIES GREATLY
MUCILAGE GUM MUCUS MUCAGO
MUCILAGINOUS MALACOID
MUCK CACK SOIL
MUCOID BLENNOID
MUCUS SNOT MUCOR BUBBLE
MUCAGO PHLEGM SNIVEL PITUITE
MUD DAB FEN CLAY DIRT FANC
GLAR LAIR MIRE MOIL SAUR SIND
SLAB SLEW SLOB SLOP SLUB SLUD
SLUE SLUR SUMP CLART FANGO
GLAUR GUMBO SLAKE SLIME SLOSH
SLUSH SPOSH SQUAD WAISE
PELOID SLOUGH SLUDGE CLABBER
GUTTERS MURGEON SLOBBER
SLODDER SLUDDER SLUTHER
SULLAGE
(LACUSTRINE —) GYTTJA
MUDAR AK AKUND ASHUR MADOR
YERCUM AKMUDDAR
MUDCAP ADOBE
MUD CAT FLATHEAD
MUDCAT STATE MISSISSIPPI

MUDDLE MIX BALL DOZE HASH
MASH MESS MULL MUZZ SOSS
ADDLE SNAFU BEMUSE BURBLE
FOITER FUDDLE HUDDLE JUMBLE
MAFFLE MIZZLE MOFFLE MUCKER
POTHER PUDDLE TANGLE BECLOUD
BEDEVIL BLUNDER FLUSTER
POOTHER STUPEFY BEFUDDLE
BEWILDER CONFOUND DISORDER
FLIUNDER
MUDDLED ADDLE BEERY FOGGY
FUZZY MUSED MUZZY DRUMLY
GROGGY BESOTTED CONFUSED
MUDDY DEEP FOUL GLET OOZY SICK
DIRTY DROVY DUBBY GUMLY SLAKY
CLAGGY CLARTY CLASHY DREGGY
DROUMY DRUMLY LIMOUS PUDDLY
SALLOW SLABBY SLOBBY SLOPPY
SLUBBY SLUDGY TURBID CLATCHY
GUTTERY MUDDIFY MUDDISH
SLOUGHY CLABBERY LUTULENT
SLOBBERY
(— BY STIRRING) STUDDLE
MUDFISH BOWFIN KOMTOK
MUDFLOW LAHAR MUDSPATE
MUDGUARD WING CUTTOO
SPLASHER
MUDHOLE PULK SLOUGH LOBLOLLY
MUD MINNOW DOGFISH MUDFISH
MUD PUPPY DOGFISH
MUERMO ULMO
MUFF BLOW BOBBLE MUFFLE
SNUFFKIN
MUFFIN COB GEM SINK COBBE
HAZEL SINKER MANCHET
MUFFLE MOB MOP PAD DAMP DULL
MUTE NOSE WRAP BUMBLE DEADEN
MUZZLE SHROUD STIFLE ENVELOP
(— A BELL) CLAM
(— THE HEAD) MOBLE
MUFFLED DEAD DEAF DULL CLOSE
THICK HOLLOW INWARD WRAPPED
MUFFLER SCARF MUFFLE SILENCER
MUG TOT CANN FACE STEIN NOGGIN
PEWTER SEIDEL CANETTE GODDARD
BLACKPOT SCHOPPEN
(ALE —) TOBY
(LIQUOR —) CAN GUN
MUGGER GOA
MUGGING YOKING
MUGGINS SNIFF
MUGGY FOZZY MUNGY PUGGY
STICKY MUGGISH PUTHERY
MUGWORT BULWAND MUGWEED
MUISCA CHIBCHA
MUISHOND ZORIL ZORILLE
MULATTO PARDO GRIFFE GRIQUA
GRIFFIN TERCERON
MULBERRY AL AAL ACH AUTE KOZO
MORE WAUKE ALROOT MURREY
MORELLO SOURBUSH SYCAMINE
MULBERRY FIG SYCAMORE
MULCT FINE CHECK AMERCE
SCONCE FORFEIT PENALTY
MULE BUCKER HYBRID ACEMILA
IRONMAN JARHEAD JUGHEAD
RATTAIL SUMPTER CENCERRO
HARDTAIL QUADROON QUATERON
DROVE OF —S) ATAJO MULADA

MULE ARMADILLO MULITA
MULE DRIVER SKINNER
MULE SHOE PLANCHE
MULETEER ASSMAN ARRIERO
MULISH STUPID STUBBORN
MULL CHAW BOSOM FETTLE MULMUL
STEATIN
MULLEIN TORCH AGLEAF ICELEAF
DOVEWEED FELTWORT FOXGLOVE
HAGTAPER LUNGWORT VERBASCO
MULLER DAMPENER
MULLET BOBO LISA LIZA BOURI
GARAU KANAE MOLET HARDER
MULLOID GOATFISH MUGILOID
SPRINGER
(UNPIERCED —) STAR
MULLOWAY JEWFISH KINGFISH
SCIAENID
MULTICOLORED CALICO
MULTIFARIOUS MANIFOLD
MULTIFARIOUSNESS VARIETY
MULTIFORM DIVERSE
MULTILINGUAL POLYGLOT
MULTIPLE DECUPLE SEPTUPLE
MULTIPLICAND FACIEND
MULTIPLICATION INCREASE
DUPLATION
MULTIPLICITY MULTEITY
MULTIPLIER FACIENT COFACTOR
MULTIPLY VIE BREED LAYER
DOUBLE INVOLVE ENGENDER
INCREASE MANIFOLD
MULTITUDE ARMY CRAM HEAP HIVE
HOST ROUT RUCK CLOUD CROWD
FLOTE POWER SHOAL SWARM
HIRSEL HOTTER LEGION MAMPUS
MEINIE NATION THRONG SMOTHER
(PL.) FLOCKS
MULTITUDINOUS MYRIAD MANIFOLD
NUMEROUS
MULTIVALENT POLYAD
MULTURE THIRL THIRLAGE
MUM CLUM DARK MUMMER
MUMBLE CHEW MUMP BROCK
CHELE MOUTH CHAVEL FAFFLE
FUMBLE HOTTER HUMMER MAFFLE
MOFFLE PALTER DRUMBLE
FLUMMER GRUMBLE
MUMBLER MAFFLER
MUMBLETY-PEG KNIFE
MUMMER ACTOR GUISER GUISARD
MUMMERY MORRIS HODENING
PUPPETRY
MUMMICHOG MUDFISH
MUMMY CONGO MUMMIA SKELET
MUMMY BROWN BAY SNUFF
TAMARACK
MUMMY CASE SLEDGE
MUMPS BRANKS
MUNCH CHEW CHUMP MANGE
MUNGE
MUND GRITH
MUNDANE WORLD EARTHLY
FLESHLY SECULAR TERRENE
SUBSOLAR
MUNG BEAN MUG GRAM MONGOE
BALATONG
MUNIA MAYA PADDA
MUNICIPAL TOWN

MUNICIPALITY CITY TOWN CABILDO
MUNIFICENCE BOUNTY ROYALTY
MUNIFICENT ROYAL LIBERAL
MUNIFIC PROFUSE MAGNIFIC
PRINCELY
MUNJ MOONJA MANJEET
(CULMS OF —) SIRKI SIRKY
MUNTIACUS CERVULUS
MUNTJAC KAKAR RATWA KIDANG
MURAL TOPIA FRESCO
MURCIA (RIVER OF —) SEGURA
(TOWN OF —) MULA LORCA TOTANA
MURDER BANE KILL SLAY BLOOD
BURKE DEATH SCRAG FELONY
MURDUM KILLING MURTHER
THUGGEE HOMICIDE MASSACRE
THUGGERY THUGGISM
MURDERER BANE CAIN KILLER
ASSASSIN
MURDEROUS FELL GORY CRUEL
FELON BLOODY SAVAGE DEATHFUL
MURKINESS GLOOM
MURKY DARK BLACK DIRTY MIRKY
MUDDY CLOUDY PUDDLY
MURMUR HUM BRUM BURR CLUM
HUZZ MUSE BROOL GRANK INKLE
MOURN RUMOR SOUCH SOUGH
BABBLE GRUDGE GRUTCH HUMMER
MUTTER PIPPLE RUMBLE MURGEON
WHIMPER WHISPER WHITTER
COMPLAIN
(— AGREEABLY) CHIRM
(CONFUSED —) BABBLE
(DEEP —) BROOL
MURMURING BUZZ BRABBLE
MURGEON RUMOROUS
MURRAH SURTI
MURRAL DALAG
MURRE TINK ARRIE LUNGIE STRANY
TINKER ROCKBIRD
MURREY SANGUINE
MUSA SABA
MUSANG POWCAT POLECAT
MUSCA FLY
MUSCADINE BULLACE
MUSCAT (SEE OMAN)
MUSCLE EYE LIRE THEW FLESH
MOUSE SINEW BENDER BICEPS
CORACO FLEXOR LACERT PENNON
RECTUS SOLEUS TENSOR AGONIST
AMBIENS CANINUS DELTOID
DILATOR ERECTOR EVERTOR
FLECTOR GLUTEUS ILIACUS
LEVATOR MUSCLE NASALIS
OBLIQUE ROTATOR SCALLOP
TRICEPS VAGINAL ABDUCTOR
ADDUCTOR ADJUSTER ANCONEUS
ARRECTOR BIVENTER DIDUCTOR
EXTENSOR GEMELLUS GRACILIS
INVERTOR MASSETER MENTALIS
OBLIQUUS OMOHYOID OPPONENS
PALMARIS PATHETIC PECTORAL
PERONEUS PROCERUS PRONATOR
RETENTOR SCALENUS SERRATUS
SPINALIS SPLENIUS TEMPORAL
TIBIALIS
(HAVING LUMPY —S) LOADED
(PL.) BRAWN THEWS
MUSCLE SUGAR INOSITE INOSITOL

MUSCOVY DUCK PATO SCOVY
MUSCULAR ROPY HUSKY THEWY
BRAWNY ROBUST STRONG TOROSE
ATHLETIC
MUSCULATURE DETRUSOR
MUSE CLIO DUMP REVE AMUSE
DREAM ERATO STUDY THINK THALIA
URANIA EUTERPE REFLECT
CALLIOPE COGITATE CONSIDER
MEDITATE POLYMNIA RUMINATE
(PL.) PIERIDES
MUSEUM MUSEE
MUSH KASHA SLUSH MUSHER
SEPAWN SOFKEE POLENTA
SAGAMITE SCRAPPLE
MUSHROOM FAT CEPE FLAT DEATH
MITRA AGARIC BEAVER BUTTON
FUNGUS BLEWITS BOLETUS
BROILER LEPIOTA MUSHRUMP
WHITECAP
MUSHY SOPPY
MUSIC RAG DRAG GLEE JAZZ NOME
CANOR CHIME GIMEL GYMEL MURKY
NOISE SWING DREHER MUSICA
DESCANT FORLANA LANCERS
LANDLER MUSICAL MUSICRY
FALSETTO FANDANGO GUARACHA
(CALYPSO —) GOOMBAY
(CONCERTED —) ENSEMBLE
(EVENING —) DREAM SERENA
(IDENTIFYING —) SIG
(LIVELY —) GALOP FURLANA
(MORNING —) AUBADE
(RESOUNDING —) HIGGAION
(SAD —) MESTO
(SENTIMENTAL —) SCHMALZ
SCHMALTZ
(STACCATO —) SECCO
MUSICAL LYRIC SWEET LIQUID
LYRICAL TUNEFUL HARMONIC
NUMEROUS
MUSICAL INSTRUMENT GLY GUE
KIN TAR UKE ZEL ALTO ASOR BELL
CRUT DRUM GLEE GLEW GORA
HARP HORN LIRA LUTE LYRE OBOE
SANG SAWM TAAR TUBA VINA VIOL
ANVIL AULOS BANJO BLOCK BUGLE
CELLO CHENG CRWTH CUICA
DOMRA FLUTE GORAH GOURA
GUDOK GUIRO GUSLA GUSLE
KAZOO NABLA ORGAN REBAB
REBEC ROCTA RUANA SAROD
SHAWM SHENG TARAU TELYN
TRUMP VIOLA ZANZE ZINKE BALAFO
BONANG CABASA CITOLE CORNET
CROUTH CYMBAL DOUCET FIDDLE
GENDER GLARIN GUITAR GUSLEE
JARANA RAPPEL REBECK RIBIBE
SABECA SANTIR SPINET TABRET
TREBLE TYMPAN URHEEN VIOLET
VIOLIN ZITHER ALTHORN ANGELOT
ANKLONG ARGHOOL BAGPIPE
BANDORE BANDURA BASSOON
BAZOOKA CELESTA CHEKKER
CITHARA CLARINA CLAVIER CLAVIOL
DICHORD DOLCIAN DOLCINO
DULCIAN FISTULA FLUTINA GAMELIN
GITTERN HELICON KANTELE
MAGADIS OCARINA PANDURA

PIBCORN RACKETT SAMISEN
SARANGI SARINDA SAXHORN
SERPENT SISTRUM THEORBO
TRUMPET UKULELE URANION
ADIAPHON AKALIMBA AUTOHARP
AUTOPHON BARBITON CALLIOPE
CASTANET CLARINET CORNPIPE
CRESCENT DULCIMER DYOPHONE
EUPHONON FIDICULA FLAUTINO
HORNPIPE HUMSTRUM KRUMHORN
LAPIDEON MELODION NEGILOTH
NEHILOTH PENORCON PHONIKON
PSALTERY SCHWEGEL SERINGHI
SOURDINE SYMPHONY TAMBOURA
TAROGATO TRICHORD TROMBONE
VIRGINAL ZAMBOMBA
(PL.) BRASS FAMILY STRINGS
MUSICALITY HARMONY
MUSIC HALL GAFF MELODEON
MUSICIAN BARD WAIT ASAPH LINOS
VIOLA BOPPER MUSICO VIOLER
VIOLIN BANDMAN BOPSTER CELLIST
GAMBIST ORPHEUS TWANGER
VIOLIST KORAHITE MARIACHI
MINSTREL MUSICKER THRUMMER
TWANGLER
(PL.) ENSEMBLE WAITSMEN
MUSING PENSIVE MUSARDRY
MUSK MOOST CATTAIL AMBRETTE
FIXATIVE
MUSK DEER CERVID KASTURA
MUSKELLUNGE LONGE MUSKIE
MUSKET FUSIL FUZIL MATCH
DRAGON JINGAL ENFIELD GINGALL
BANDHOOK BISCAYEN CULVERIN
ESCOPETA SNAPHAAN TOPHAIKE
MUSKET BALL GOLI
MUSKETEER FUSILEER STRELITZ
MUSKET FORK GAFFLE
MUSKMELON MANGO ATAMON
WUNGEE SPANSPEK
MUSKOGEE CREEK SEMINOLE
MUSK OX OVIBOS
MUSKRAT SQUASH ONDATRA
MUSQUASH
MUSK SHREW SONDELI
MUSK TURTLE STINKER STINKPOT
MUSKWOOD CAOBA
MUSKY MOSCHATE
MUSLIM LAZ ALIM SIDI SWAT TURK
ARAIN HAFIZ IBADHI KAZAKH
TURBAN ABBADID AYYUBID BAGIRMI
BASHKIR IBADITE KHAKSAR
MUDEJAR SUNNITE ALAOUITE
ISLAMIST ISLAMITE QADARITE
SIFATITE
(— BEADS) TASBIH
(— BROTHERHOOD) TARIQA
(— CHIEF) RAIS REIS
(— DOCTRINE) TAWHID
(— FOUNDATION) WAKF WAQF
(— JUDGE) CAID QAID
(— MYSTIC) SUFI
(— PLAY) TAZIA
(— PRACTICE) PURDAH
(— PRINCIPLE) TAQIYA
(— SCHOLARS) ULAMA ULEMA
(— SECT) WAHHABI MURJIITE
(— TOMB) TABUT

(— TREE) TUBA
(PL.) SHIA SHIAH SUNNI
MUSLIN BAN MULL DORIA SWISS
GURRAH MULMUL SHALEE SHILLA
TANJIB BETEELA FACTORY JAMDAN
ORGANDY STENTER SEERHAND
TARLATAN
(PL.) COSSAS
MUSS FUFFLE RUMPLE GLOMMOX
UNDRESS
MUSSEL CLAM UNIO NAIAD ANODON
JINGLE LACERT MUCKET PALOUR
BIVALVE GLOCHID MYTILID UNIONID
BULLHEAD DEERHORN
MUSSELCRACKER BISKOP
MUST BIT BUD BUT MAN MAY MUN
BOOD MAUN SAPA STUM DULCE
SHALL
(— BE TAKEN) SUM
(— NOT) MAUNNA
MUSTACHE WALRUS VALANCE
WHISKER
MUSTACHE MONKEY MOUSTOC
MUSTANG PONY BRONCO SPHINX
MUSTARD CRESS SENVY SINEWY
AWLWORT CADLOCK KEDLOCK
SINAPIS AUBRIETA CHADLOCK
CHARLOCK FLIXWEED
MUSTARD GAS YPERITE
MUSTELUS GALEUS
MUSTER LEVY RAISE SPUNK GATHE
HOSTING MARSHAL RECRUIT
MUSTINESS FUST MUST
MUSTY HOAR FUNKY FUSTY HOARY
MOLDY MUCID RAFTY VINNY FOIST
FROWZY FOUGHTY FROWSTY
COBWEBBY
MUTABLE FICKLE MUTATORY
VARIABLE
MUTATE SPORT
MUTATION SHIFT SPORT CHANGE
MUANCE SILKIE ANAGRAM
(VOWEL —) UMLAUT
MUTE PAD DUMB ECHO LENE SURD
BLACK MEDIA WHIST DAMPER
MUFFLE SILENT STIFLE TENUIS
SORDINE SOURDINE
(— FOR TRUMPET) DERBY
MUTED DULL SORDO STILL
DISCREET SOURDINE
MUTENESS SILENCE DUMBNESS
MUTILATE MAR HACK MAIM BREAK
GARBLE INJURE MANGLE MARTYR
MITTLE CONCISE CASTRATE
EMBEZZLE
(— AN ANIMAL) LAW
MUTILATION STRIP
MUTINEER PANDY MUTINADO
MUTINOUS UNRULY
MUTINY REVOLT STRIFE
MUTISM ALALIA
MUTTER CROOL MOTRE HOTTER
HUMMER MUMBLE MURMUR PATTE
THROAT CHANNER CHUNNER
CHUNTER GRUMBLE MAUNDER
TOOTMOOT
MUTTERING GROWL
MUTTON BRAXY VIFDA VIVDA
MOUTON BRAXIES

(LEG OF —) CABOB WABBLER
WOBBLER
MUTTONBIRD OII
MUTTONFISH SAMA ABALONE
EELPOUT MOJARRA
MUTUAL COMMON
MUZZLE NOSE MOUTH SNOUT
FOREFACE
(— FOR FERRET) COPE
(— OF CANNON) CHOPS
MUZZLE-LOADER CAPLOCK
MUZZLER
MYALL YARRAN WARRIGAL
MYCELIUM SPAWN MYCELE
TAPESIUM
MYCTERIA TANTALUS
MY DEAR MACHREE
MYIASIS STRIKE

MYNA MINA MYNAH GRACKLE
MYOCOMMA FLAKE
MYRIAD HOST COUNTLESS
MYRIAPOD JULID POLYPOD
PAUROPOD MILLIPEDE
MYRRH STACTE
MYRTLE MYRT LILAC BALTIC
JAROOL ARRAYAN JAPONICA
RAMARAMA
MYSELF SELF MYSEN HERSELF
MYSID SHRIMP
MYSOST PRIMOST
MYSTERIOUS DIM DARK DEEP EERY
SELI EERIE SABLE WAKON ARCANE
EXOTIC MYSTIC OCCULT SECRET
CRYPTIC PUCKISH UNCANNY
UNCOUTH ABSTRUSE ESOTERIC
NUMINOUS SIBYLLIC

MYSTERIOUSLY DARKLY EERILY
HEIMLICH
MYSTERY MIST RUNE CABALA
ENIGMA SECRET ARCANUM
SECRECY
MYSTIC SUFI OCCULT ORPHIC
SECRET EPOPTIC ESOTERIC
MYSTICAL MISTY MYSTIC ANAGOGIC
TELESTIC
MYSTICALLY GHOSTLY
MYSTICISM SUFIISM
MYSTIFY BEAT BEFOG BOTHER
MUDDLE PUZZLE BECLOUD
CONFUSE BEWILDER
MYTH SAGA FABLE LEGEND MYTHOS
ALLEGORY
MYTHICAL FABLED FABULOUS
FICTIOUS

N EN NU NAN
NAASSENE OPHITE
NAB HAT NIB GRAB HEAD KNAB
CATCH SEIZE ARREST CLUTCH
COLLAR NIBBLE NOBBLE SNATCH
CAPTURE APPREHEND
NABAL (WIFE OF —) ABIGAIL
NABALOI IBALOI IGOROT
NABK NUBK NABAK NEBUK NABBUK
NEBACK NEBBUK NEBBUCK
NABOB DIVES NAWAB NOBOB
DEPUTY VICEROY GOVERNOR
PLUTOCRAT
(— DEPUTY) NAWAB
(PL.) NABOBRY
NACELLE CAR BOAT BASKET
CHASSIS COCKPIT SHELTER
NACHSCHLAG SPRINGER
AFTERNOTE
NACKET BOY CAKE LUNCH NOCKET
NACRE PEARL SHELLFISH
NADIR BATHOS BEDROCK
(OPPOSED TO —) ZENITH
NAG CUT TIT BAIT FRAB FRET FUSS
GNAW JADE PLUG PONY PROD
SNAG TWIT ANNOY COBRA HOBBY
HORSE SCOLD SKATE SNAKE STEED
TEASE BADGER BERATE BOTHER
DOBBIN GARRAN GLEYDE HAGGLE
HARASS HECKLE HECTOR KEFFEL
PADNAG PESTER PLAGUE WANTON
HACKNEY HENPECK TORMENT
DINGDONG HARANGUE IRRITATE
PARAMOUR
(AMBLING —) HOBBY
NAGA SEMA COBRA KABUI LHOTA
SNAKE
NAGKASSAR SURIGA
NAGOR TOHI ANTELOPE REEDBUCK
NAHANE KASKA
NAHOOR SHA SNA SHEEP URIAL
BHARAL OORIAL
NAHUATL AZTEC CAZCAN MEXICA
NAHUM ELKOSHITE
NAIAD NAIS NYMPH MUSSEL
HYDRIAD
NAIL CUT FIX HOB PIN TEN BOSS
BRAD BRAG BROD CLAW CLOY
DUMP HOOF PILE SLUG SPAD STUB
STUD TACK TRAP AFFIX CATCH
CLOUT DRIVE GROPE PLATE SCALE
SEIZE SPEED SPIKE SPRIG TALON
BULLEN CLENCH CLINCH COOLER
CORKER DETAIN FASTEN GARRON
HAMMER SECURE SINKER TACKET
TENTER TINGLE UNGUIS UNGULA
CAPTURE FASTENER HOLDFAST
ROSEHEAD SPARABLE SPIKELET
TENPENNY TRICOUNI
(— BITING) ONYCHOPHAGIA
(— GROWTH) ONYCHAUXIS
(HEADLESS —) SPRIG
(HOOKED —) TENTER TENTERHOOK
(INGROWN —) ONYXIS ACRONYX
(MARKING —) SPAD SPEED
(OLD HORSESHOE —) STUB
(SHOEMAKER'S —) SPARABLE
(TOED —) TOSHNAIL
NAILROD STICKWEED

NAIVE OPEN RACY FRANK GREEN
CANDID SIMPLE ARTLESS NATURAL
CHILDISH INNOCENT UNTAUGHT
CHILDLIKE GUILELESS INGENUOUS
UNTUTORED UNWORLDLY
(— GIRL) INGENUE
NAIVETE GREENNESS SIMPLICITY
NAKED BALD BARE MERE NUDE
OPEN CLEAR EXACT PLAIN STARK
BARREN CUERPO SCUDDY SIMPLE
EXPOSED LITERAL OBVIOUS
MANIFEST STRIPPED SMOCKLESS
UNADORNED UNCLOTHED
UNCOVERED
NAKED OAT PILLAS PILCORN
PILKINS
NAKEDWOOD MABI SNAKEWOOD
NAKHI MOSO MOSSO
NAMAYCUSH CREE FISH LAKER
LONGE LUNGE TOGUE TROUT
LONGUE SISCOWET
NAMBY-PAMBY INANE SILLY VAPID
CODDLE INSIPID KEEPSAKE
NAME DUB FIX NOM SET CALL CITE
FAME NAIL NOMB NOUN TERM
ALIAS CLAIM CLEPE COUNT ETHIC
NEVEN NOMEN POINT QUOTE STYLE
TITLE ADDUCE APPEAL GOSSIP
MONICA REPUTE SELECT ALLONYM
APPOINT BEHIGHT DECLARE
ENTITLE EPITHET MENTION MONIKER
SPECIFY VOCABLE CATEGORY
CHRISTEN COGNOMEN IDENTIFY
IDENTITY INDICATE ENUMERATE
(— TABLET) FACIA
(— WRITTEN BACKWARDS) ANANYM
(ADDED —) AGNAME AGNOMEN
(ALTERNATIVE —) BUNCH
(ANCESTOR'S —) EPONYM
(ANOTHER —) ALIAS
(ASSUMED —) PEN ALIAS
ONOMASTIC PSEUDONYM
SOBRIQUET
(BAD —) CACONYM
(DAY —) AHAU
(DERIVATION OF —) EPONYMY
(FIRST —) FORENAME PRAENOMEN
(GOOD —) HONOR CREDIT
(REGISTERED —) AFFIX
(TECHNICAL —) ONYM
(WELL-SUITED —) EUONYM
NAMED CITED HIGHT DUBBED
YCLEPT ONYMOUS YCLEPED
NAMELESS BAS
NAMELY FOR VIZ SCIL NOTED TOWIT
FAMOUS SCILICET
NAMEPLATE MASTHEAD
NAMESAKE EPONYM JUNIOR
HOMONYM
NANDI BANANDE MUNANDI KIPSIKIS
NANDU RHEA
NANISM DWARFISM
NANNAR SIN
NANNY GOAT NURSE
NANTICOKE TOAG
NAOMI MARA
(DAUGHTER-IN-LAW OF —) RUTH
NAOS CELLA SHRINE TEMPLE
NAP GIG NOD RAS CALK CAMP

DOWN DOZE FUZZ LINT PILE RUFF
SHAG WINK COVER DOVER FLUFF
GRASP SEIZE SLEEK SLEEP STEAL
CATNAP DROWSE SIESTA SNOOZE
EMERIZE SLUMBER
(TO RAISE —) TEASE
NAPE NOD CUFF NECK NUKE POLL
NUCHA NUQUE SCRAG SCURF
NODDLE SCRUFF TURMP NIDDICK
NAPERY LINEN DOILIES NAPKINS
NAPHTALITE ENAN AHIRA
NAPHTHA NEFTE PETROLEUM
NAPKIN CLOTH DOILY TOWEL
DIAPER NAPERY KERCHIEF
SUDATORY HANDCLOTH SERVIETTE
NAPLES BISCUIT LADYFINGER
NAPLESS HARD
NAPOLEON (— III) LOUIS
BOUSTRAPA
(BATTLE OF —) ULM ACRE JENA
WATERLOO
(BIRTHPLACE OF —) CORSICA
(BROTHER-IN-LAW OF —) MURAT
(GAME LIKE —) PAM
(ISLAND OF —) ELBA HELENA
CORSICA
(MARSHALL OF —) NEY
(MOTHER OF —) HORTENSE
(PLACE OF VICTORY FOR —) LODI
LIGNY
NAPPE DECKE
NAPPY ALE DISH DOWNY HEADY
WOOLY LIQUOR SHAGGY STRONG
WOOLLY COTTONY FOAMING
VILLOUS
NARCISSUS LILY PLANT CRINUM
EGOIST FLOWER LILIUM JONQUIL
(LOVED BY —) ECHO
(TRUMPET —) DAFFODIL
NARCOTIC KAT BANG DOPE DRUG
HEMP JUNK BHANG DAGGA ETHER
OPIUM HEROIN OPIATE ANODYNE
COCAINE CODEINE HASHISH
NARCEIN HYPNOTIC MORPHINE
TAKROURI DIACODION MARIJUANA
SOPORIFIC
(— AGENT) GAZER
(— DOSE) LOCUS
(— PLANT) DUTRA MANDRAKE
(SMALL AMOUNT OF —) SNIFTER
(PL.) JUNK STUFF
NARCOTINE OPIANE
NARD SPICE ANOINT RHIZOME
MUSKROOT SPIKENARD
NARDOO ARDOO NARDU CLOVER
NARGIL COCONUT
NARGILEH PIPE HOOKA HOOKAH
NARGHILE
NARK SPY VEX NOTE ANNOY TEAS
OBSERVE INFORMER IRRITATE
NARRA NAGA ASANA APALIT
NARRATE SPIN TELL BRUIT STATE
STORY DEPICT DETAIL DEVISE
RECITE RELATE REPORT DISCUSS
RECOUNT STORIFY DESCRIBE
REHEARSE
NARRATION TALE FABLE STORY
DETAIL ACCOUNT HAGGADA
SYNAXAR DELIVERY HAGGADAH

ARRATIVE EPIC JOKE MYTH SAGA TALE CONTE DRAMA FABLE PROSE STORY COMEDY JATAKA LEGEND ACCOUNT EPISODE HISTORY MEMOIRS MIDRASH NOVELLA PARABLE RECITAL ALLEGORY ANECDOTE APOLOGUE ARETALOGY HAGIOLOGY

(— POEM) EPIC EPOS SAGA

BRIEF —) ANECDOTE

(PL.) ACTA EXEMPLA

ARRATOR TESTO TELLER RELATOR SAGAMAN TALESMAN RACONTEUR

ARROW JERK LEAN MEAN NEAR POKY SLIT TRUE BORNE CLOSE RIGID SCANT SHARP SMALL SOUND TAPER ANGUST BIASED LINEAR LITTLE MEAGER STRAIT STRICT TWITCH BIGOTED ERICOID LIMITED PRIMARY SLENDER THRIFTY CONDENSE CONTRACT PAROCHIAL

— DOWN STAVES) BUCK

— DOWN) CONFINE

— INLET) RIA

NOT —) CATHOLIC

VERY —) HAIRBREADTH

ARROWED LISTED INSWEPT CONTRACT

ARROWING CAP CHOKE INTAKE TENOSIS

ARROWLY WIDE STRAITLY

ARROW-MINDED BORNE

ARROWNESS BIAS BIGOTRY

RSINGA TRUMPET

RTHECIUM ABAMA

RTHEX HALL STOA ENTRY FOYER OBBY PORCH PORTICO PRONAOS ESTIBULE

SAB NUSUB KINSHIP

SAL NOSY NARINE RHINAL WANGY ADENOID STRINGY

SCENCY BIRTH ORIGIN GENESIS EGINNING

SEBERRY SAPODILLA

SHGAB OAF GOSSIP

SI OFFICER PATRIARCH

SICORN RHINOCEROS

STIKA ATHEIST

STURTIUM CAPUCINE NOSEWORT ADICULA STURSHUM STURTION

STY BAD PAH FOUL MEAN UGLY RTY FILTHY HORRID ODIOUS BALD BAGGAGE DEFILED ARMFUL OBSCENE SQUALID UCLEAN INDECENT NAUSEOUS ANGEROUS MALICIOUS OFFENSIVE

**" NOT DEMON SPIRIT

AL INBORN INNATE NATIVE UTEAL CONGENIAL

AL PLUM AMATUNGULA

ANT AFLOAT FLOATING WIMMING

ATORIUM BATH POOL

CHEZ STINKER STINKARD

ION BENI FOLK GEAT HOST ND LEDE RACE VOLK AEDUI STE CLASS FANTE FANTI REALM ATE TRIBE FANTEE GEATAS OPLE WAGOGO ARVERNI

COUNTRY SOCIETY LANGUAGE COMMUNITY MULTITUDE

(— SYMBOL) FLAG CREST

(HEBREW —) JACOB

(LARGE —) COLOSSUS

NATIONAL CITIZEN FEDERAL GENTILE GENTILIC

(— DEMOCRACY) ENDEX

NATIONALISM JINGOISM PHYLETISM

NATIONALITY FLAG

NATIVE ITE RAW SON TAO BORN FREE GOOK HOME KIND LIVE NEIF WILD INNER NATAL PUNTI EPIROT GENIAL INBORN INNATE KINDLY NORMAL SIMPLE VIRGIN CITIZEN DENIZEN DZUNGAR ENDEMIC GENUINE NATURAL PAISANO POLISTA DOMESTIC GRASSCUT HABITUAL HOMEBORN HOMEMADE INHERENT LANDSMAN ORIGINAL PRIMEVAL PRISTINE RESIDENT YAMMADJI ABORIGINE CONGENIAL INGRAINED INHERITED INTRINSIC ORIGINARY TAWNYMOOR

(— BEAR) KOALA

(— BEECH) FLINDOSA

(— MINERAL) LIVE

(— OF BENGAL) KOL

(— OF CHINA) CELESTIAL

(— OF FENS) SLODGER

(— OF FLORIDA KEYS) CONK CONCH

(— OF ILLINOIS) SUCKER

(— OF IRELAND) BOGTROTTER

(— OF LONDON) COCKNEY

(— OF LOW CLASS) TAO

(— OF MADAGASCAR) HOVA

(— OF MALAYA) INFIEL

(— OF MARITIME PROVINCES) BLUENOSE

(— OF N. CAROLINA) TARHEEL

(— OF NEW GUINEA) BOONG

(— OF NEW SOUTH WALES) CORNSTALK

(— OF PHILIPPINES) GUGU

(— OF SCOTLAND) GEORDIE

(— OF SOUTHERN ILLINOIS) EGYPTIAN

(— OF W. AUSTRALIA) GROPER

(— PLANT) INDIGINE

(— WHO TEACHES) CATECHIST

(BORN AND BRED AS A —) CREOLE

(FREE —) TIMAWA

(UNCIVILIZED —) MYALL

NATIVITY BIRTH GENESIS GENITURE HOROSCOPE

NATTERJACK NEWT TOAD

NATTY CHIC NEAT POSH TIDY TRIG TRIM NIFTY SMART SPICY DAPPER JAUNTY SPRUCE FOPPISH

NATURAL RAW BORN EASY FOOL HOME KIND OPEN RACY REAL WILD NAIVE USUAL CANCEL CASUAL COMMON CONJON CRETIN DIRECT HOMELY INBORN INBRED INNATE KINDLY NATIVE NORMAL PHYSIC ARTLESS GENUINE QUADRUM REGULAR INHERENT LIFELIKE ORDINARY PHYSICAL UNCOINED

PRIMITIVE REALISTIC UNASSUMED UNFEIGNED

(— LOGARITHM) LN

(— TALENT) DOWER FLAIR

(NOT —) AFFECTED

NATURALIZE ADAPT ADOPT ACCUSTOM ACCLIMATE ENDENIZEN HABITUATE

NATURALLY SN KINDLY GENIALLY

NATURALNESS EASE NAIVETE

NATURE ILK BENT BIOS CAST CLAY FORM HAIR KIND MAKE MOOD RACE SORT TYPE COLOR OUSIA SHAPE STATE TENOR ANIMAL DHARMA FIGURE HEAVEN KIDNEY PHYSIS STRIPE ESSENCE FEATHER QUALITY SPECIES PRAKRITI UNIVERSE CHARACTER

(— DIVINITY) NYMPH

(— GOD) PAN

(— GODDESS) CYBELE ARTEMIS

(— OF GOD) DIVINITY

(— PRINT) PHYTOGRAPH

(— SPIRIT) NAT

(— WORSHIP) PHYSIOLATRY

(APPARENT —) STUDY

(CONCEALED —) LATENCY

(DIVINE —) DEITY

(EMOTIONAL —) HEART

(ESSENTIAL —) ESSE FORM GENIUS

(HUMAN —) FLESH MANHEAD MANKIND

(INHERENT —) GENIUS

(INTRINSIC —) BOTTOM

(MORAL —) ETHNOS

(OF THE SAME —) HOMOGENEOUS

(ORGANIC —) BIOS

(PERT. TO —) COSMO

(ROUGH —) SPINOSITY

(SPECIAL —) IDIOM

(SPIRITUAL —) INTERNAL

(ULTIMATE —) ESSENCE

NAUGHT NIL EVIL ZERO AUGHT NAGHT OUGHT CIPHER NOUGHT WICKED NOTHING USELESS WORTHLESS

NAUGHTY BAD PAW SAD EVIL WRONG PAWPAW SHREWD WICKED OBSCENE WAYWARD IMPROPER

NAUPATHIA SEASICKNESS

NAUSEA PALL QUALM DISGUST NAUSITY LOATHING SICKNESS ANTIPATHY DIZZINESS

NAUSEATE TURN TWIST WLATE REVOLT SICKEN DISGUST STOMACH DISTASTE

NAUSEATED ILL SICKISH QUALMISH SQUEAMISH

NAUSEATING NASTY WAUGH QUEASY BILIOUS FULSOME BRACKISH STAWSOME LOATHSOME REVOLTING SICKENING

NAUTICAL (ALSO SEE NAVIGATION) NAVAL MARINE MAUTIC MARINAL OCEANIC TARRISH MARITIME NAVIGABLE

(— FLAG) CORNET PENNON

NAUTILUS MOLLUSK ARGONAUT ARGONAUTA

(— COMMANDER) NEMO
NAVAHO DINE NAVAJO LONGHAIR
(— GROUP) OUTFIT
(— RITE) WAY
NAVAL SEA MARINE NAUTICAL
NAVIGABLE
(— DEPOT) BASE
(— FORCE) NAVY FLEET ARMADA
SQUADRON
(— JAIL) BRIG
NAVE HOB HUB NEF APSE BODY FIST
PACE AISLE NATHE NIEVE CENTER
NAVEL NOMBRIL OMPHALOS
UMBILICUS
NAVIGABLE BOATABLE PORTABLE
NAVIGATE KEEL SAIL DRIVE GUIDE
SKIFF STEER AVIATE COURSE
CRUISE DIRECT MANAGE TRAVEL
CONDUCT CONTROL JOURNEY
OPERATE TRAVERSE ASTROGATE
NAVIGATION HOMING VOYAGE
NAUTICS PASSAGE SAILING TRAFFIC
CABOTAGE SHIPPING
(— MEASURE) TON KNOT SEAM
FATHOM
(— SYSTEM) LORAN
NAVIGATOR FLYER NAVVY PILOT
AIRMAN AVIATOR COPILOT LABORER
AERONAUT SEAFARER SPACEMAN
NEPTUNIAN NEPTUNIST
NAVITE BASALT
NAVVY HAND WORKER LABORER
NAVIGATOR
NAVY FLEET SHIPFERD
(— BOARD) ADMIRALTY
(— OFFICER) CPO AIDE MATE
BOSUN CHIEF ENSIGN ADMIRAL
ARMORER CAPTAIN COMMANDER
COMMODORE
(— RADIO OPERATOR) SPARKS
(— VESSEL) PT SUB CARRIER
CRUISER FLATTOP DESTROYER
SUBMARINE TRANSPORT
NAWOB NABOB NUWAB RULER
VICEROY
NAY NO NAI NEI NOT DENY EVEN
NYET FLUTE NEVER DENIAL REFUSE
REFUSAL NEGATIVE
NAZARD STOP NASAT
NAZE NASE HEADLAND
NAZI BROWN HITLERITE
(— SYMBOL) FYLFOT SWASTIKA
NAZIM VICEROY GOVERNOR
NEANDERTHAL CAVEMAN
NEANIC IMMATURE YOUTHFUL
NEAR AD AT BY IN GIN KIN NAR AKIN
BAIN DEAR FAST GAIN HARD HEND
INBY NEXT NIGH ABOUT ANEAR
ANENT ASIDE CLOSE FORBY HANDY
HENDE JUXTA MATCH NUDGE
ROUND SHORT TOUCH ALMOST
AROUND BESIDE CLIMAX HEREBY
NARROW STINGY TOWARD WITHIN
ADVANCE AGAINST FORTHBY
SIMILAR THRIFTY VICINAL ADJACENT
APPROACH IMMINENT INTIMATE
(— AKIN) GERMANE
(— POINT) PP

(— THE BEGINNING) EARLY
FORMER
(— THE EQUATOR) LOW
(— THE MOUTH) ADORAL
(— THE SURFACE) EBB FLEET
(— THE WIND) HIGH AHOLD
(CONVENIENTLY —) HANDSOME
NEARBY AROUND GAINLY LOCALLY
ADJACENT
NEARER HITHER
(— FRANCE) CISALPINE
(— ROME) CISALPINE
(— THE REAR) AFTER
NEAREST NEXT EWEST CLOSEST
NEARMOST PROCHAIN IMMEDIATE
PROXIMATE
(— THE STERN) AFTERMOST
NEARLY GAIN JUST LIKE MOST
MUCH ABOUT ALMOST FECKLY
NEARSIGHTED MYOPIC PURBLIND
NEAT GIM NET COSH COWS DEFT
DINK FEEL FEIL GENT JIMP MACK
NICE OXEN PRIM PURE SMUG SNOD
SNUG TIDY TOSH TRIG TRIM BULLS
CLEAN CLEAR COMPT CRISP DINKY
DONCY DONSY DOUCE EXACT
FEATY FETIS JEMMY NATTY PREST
QUEME SMART SMIRK TERSE TIGHT
ADROIT BOVINE CATTLE CLEVER
DAINTY DAPPER DIMBER DONSIE
HEPPEN MINION POLITE QUAINT
SPANDY SPRUCE BANDBOX
CONCISE ORDERLY PERJINK
PRECISE REFINED SHAPELY
UNMIXED MENSEFUL SKILLFUL
STRAIGHT TASTEFUL DEXTEROUS
SHIPSHAPE UNDILUTED WHOLESOME
NEATLY SNUG DEFTLY FAIRLY
FEATLY SMARTLY SPRUCELY
NEATNESS MENSE DEFTNESS
ELEGANCE SPRUCERY
NEB EAR NIB TIP BEAK BILL NOSE
POINT SNOUT

NEBRASKA
CAPITAL: LINCOLN
COLLEGE: DANA DOANE
DUCHESNE HASTINGS
COUNTY: LOUP OTOE DEUEL
SARPY COLFAX NEMAHA
INDIAN: OTO OMAHA PONCA
PAWNEE
RIVER: LOGAN DISMAL PLATTE
ELKHORN NIOGRARA
STATE BIRD: MEADOWLARK
STATE FLOWER: GOLDENROD
STATE NICKNAME: CORNHUSKER
STATE TREE: ELM
TOWN: COZAD OMAHA GERING
UNIVERSITY: CREIGHTON

NEBRIS FAWNSKIN
NEBULA SKY CRAB SPOT VAPOR
BALAXY SPIRAL PLANETARY
NEBULIZE ATOMIZE
NEBULOUS DIM DARK HAZY FOGGY
MISTY MUDDY VAGUE CLOUDY
MYSTIC TURBID CLOUDED EVASIVE
SHADOWY UNCLEAR DREAMLIKE

NEBULA SKY CRAB SPOT VAPOR
GALAXY SPIRAL PLANETARY
NEBULIZE ATOMIZE
NEBULOUS DIM DARK HAZY FOGGY
MISTY MUDDY CLOUDY MYSTIC
TURBID CLOUDED SHADOWY
UNCLEAR
NECESSARILY NEEDS NEEDLY
PERFORCE
NECESSARY NEEDY PRIVY VITAL
FRIEND TOILET KINSMAN NEEDFUL
FORCIBLE INTEGRAL ESSENTIAL
INTRINSIC
(PL.) ALIMENT MISTERS
NECESSITATE FORCE IMPEL
COMPEL DEMAND ENTAIL OBLIGE
REQUIRE CONSTRAIN
NECESSITY USE CALL DUTY FATE
FOOD LACK MUST NEED TASK
WANT DRINK ANANKE BESOIN
MISTER MUSCLE NEEDBE URGENC
PERFORCE
(— OF MOVING) ZUGZWANG
(BY —) PRESENTLY
(PL.) BREAD
NECK COL NUB PET CAPE CRAG
CROP HALS KISS WAKE BEARD
CHOKE CRAIG HALSE SCRAG SPO
SWIRE TRAIL BEHEAD CARESS
CERVIX COLLET COLLUM FONDLE
STRAIT CHANNEL EMBRACE
ISTHMUS SQUEEZE TUBULUS
LALLYGAG
(— ARTERY) CAROTID
(— MUSCLE) SCALENUS
(— OF BOTTLE) THROTTLE
(— OF LAMB) TARGET
(— OF VOLCANO) CORE
(BACK OF —) NOD NAPE NUCH
NUQUE SCRUFF NIDDICK
(PERT. TO —) JUGULAR CERVICA
(RED —) ROOINEK
NECK AND NECK TIE EVEN CLO
NECKBAND BAND COLLAR COLLE
SHIRTBAND
NECKCLOTH BOA TIE RUFF AMIC
CHOKE SCARF STOLE CHOKER
CRAVAT BURDASH NECKTIE
PANUELO STARCHER BARCELON.
SOLITAIRE STEINKIRK
NECKERCHIEF GIMP RAIL FOGLE
BELCHER FOULARD NECKLET
KERCHIEF NECKATEE NECKCLOT
NECKENGER
NECKING COLLAR GORGERIN
NECKLACE BEE LEI TORC BEADS
CHAIN NOOSE CARCAN CHOKER
COLLAR GORGET SANKHA TAWI
TORQUE BALDRIC CHAPLET RIV
SAUTOIR LAVALIER NEGLIGEE
ESCLAVAGE
NECKLINE COWL SCOOP
NECK RUFF FRAISE QUELLIO
NECKTIE BOW TIE ASCOT SCAR
CHOKER CRAVAT GRAVAT OVER
(— PARTY) HANGING LYNCHING
NECROMANCER GOETIC MAGIC
NECROMANCY GOETY MAGIC

RAMARY SORCERY WIZARDRY
GROMANCY
CROPOLIS CEMETERY
CROPSY AUTOPSY
CTAR N HONEY AMBROSIA
CTAR BIRD EATER HONEY
JNBIRD
CTARINE NECTRON NECTARIN
CTARY SPUR GLAND NECTARIUM
DDER ADDER
DDY HORSE DONKEY
E BORN
ED ASK NUD LACK TAKE THAR
ANT CRAVE DRIVE THARF BEHOVE
ESOIN DEMAND DESIRE MISTER
TRAIT BEHOOVE NEEDHAM
OVERTY REQUIRE URGENCY
STRESS EXIGENCY MISCHIEF
MERGENCE EXTREMITY NECESSITY
EDFIRE WILDFIRE
EDFUL VITAL INTEGRAL
SSENTIAL NECESSARY REQUISITE
DLE SEW VEX YEN ACUS DARN
DAD TIER WIRE ANNOY BLUNT
DINT SHARP SPIKE STRAW STYLE
DDKIN DARNER STYLUS OBELISK
RICKER PROVOKE SPICULE
IMBLER
- HOLE) EYE
- SORTER) HANDER
OMB. FORM) ACU
NE —) SPILL
NE —S) PININGS
..) TWINKLES
DLE BUG NEPID RANATRA
DLEBUSH URY PINBUSH
DLEFISH GAR SNOOK AGUJON
LONID LONGJAW
DLE GUN RIFLE DREYSE
DLELIKE ACUATE ACERATE
EROSE ACEROUS ACIFORM
ICULAR BELONOID SPLINTERY
DLEMAN TAILOR
DLESS AMOK
DLEWORK SEWING SAMPLER
AMING TATTING KNITTING
OLWORK HEMSTITCH INSERTION
DY BARE POOR INDIGENT
EDSOME HUNGARIAN PENNILESS
P NEPE TURNIP
R-DO-WELL BUM PELF LOSEL
HLEMIEL SHIFTLESS WORTHLESS
ANDOUS IMPIOUS EXECRABLE
ARIOUS WICKED HEINOUS
IOUS FLAGRANT HORRIBLE
AMOUS ATROCIOUS
ATE DENY SUBLATE
ATION NAY NOT EMPTY DENIAL
USAL ANNULMENT NONENTITY
ATIVE NA NE NO CON NAE NAY
NIX NON NOR NOT NUL DENY
M VETO NEVER NAYWARD
MPER APOPHATIC PRIVATIVE
PREFIX) IL IM IN IR UN DIS NON
PRINCIPLE) YIN
ECT DEBT FAIL HANG OMIT
FAULT FORGO SHIRK SLOTH
VE BYPASS CESSER FOREGO
IGET IGNORE LACHES LOITER

PERMIT SLIGHT DEFAULT DISOBEY
FAILURE OVERSEE RESPECT
FORSLACK OMISSION OVERLOOK
OVERSLIP RECKLESS DISREGARD
MISLIPPEN OVERSIGHT PRETERMIT
NEGLECTED TACKY SHABBY
UNDONE DORMANT OBSOLETE
NEGLECTFUL LAX REMISS
CARELESS DERELICT HEEDLESS
RECKLESS DISSOLUTE
NEGLIGEE ROBE MANTEAU MATINEE
UNDRESS PEIGNOIR DISHABILE
NIGHTGOWN
NEGLIGENCE CULPA LACHES
DEFAULT LASCHETY DISREGARD
OVERSIGHT
NEGLIGENT LAX LASH SOFT SLACK
OVERLY REMISS CARELESS
DISCINCT SLOVENLY YEMELESS
DISSOLUTE
NEGLIGIBLE FAT
NEGOTIATE DEAL SELL BROKE
FLOAT TREAT TROKE TRUCK TRYST
ADVISE ASSIGN CONFER DICKER
DIRECT MANAGE PARLEY SETTLE
ARRANGE BARGAIN CHAFFER
CONDUCT CONSULT DISCUSS
ENTREAT CONCLUDE ENTREATY
TRANSACT TRANSFER TEMPORIZE
NEGOTIATION DEAL DICKER
PARLEY TREATY PASSAGE
ENTREATY PRACTICE
NEGRITO ATA ATI ITA AETA AKKA
BATWA BLACK KARON SEMANG
TAPIRO ABENLEN BAMBUTE
NEGRO FON JUR LUO LWO SUK
AKIM ALUR BENI BINI BONI BUCK
CROW EGBA FONG IRON MADI
MOKE NUBA NUPE SIDI BENIN
BLACK BONGO CUFFY DARKY DINKA
DJUKA FULUP FUZZY HATSA MUNGO
SAMBO SEPIA SEREC SMOKE TEMNE
GULLAH HUBSHI AKWAPIM
DAHOMAN GEECHEE QUASHIE
SANDAWE SHILLUK SWELLUH
BECHUANA ETHIOPIAN MANGBATTU
(— BLOOD) TARBRUSH
(GOLD COAST —) GA FANTI
(LIBERIAN —) KRU VAI VEI GREBO
ICROO KRUMAN KROOBOY
(MALE —) BUCK
(OLD —) UNCLE
NEIGH NIE NVE WHI HINNY NICKER
WHINNY WIGHER WHICKER
NEIGHBOR BOR ADJOIN BORDER
FELLOW NEIPER ACCOLENT
BORDERER CONFINER UCALEGON
(PL.) KITH CONFINES
NEIGHBORHOOD WAY AREA HAND
VENUE BARRIO LOCALE REGION
PURLIEU SECTION DISTRICT
ENVIRONS PROCINCT VICINAGE
VICINITY BAILIWICK COMMUNITY
PROXIMITY TERRITORY
NEIGHBORING NIGH NEARBY
CONFINE VICINAL ACCOUENT
ADJACENT
NEIGHBORLY FOLKSY FOLKSEY
AMICABLE

NEITHER NOT NATHER NITHER
NOWDER
(— RIGHT NOR WRONG)
ADIAPHOROUS
NELEUS (BROTHER OF —) PELIAS
(DAUGHTER OF —) PERO
(FATHER OF —) NEPTUNE
(MOTHER OF —) TYRO
(SON OF —) NESTOR
(WIFE OF —) CHLORIS
NELLORE ONGOLE
NEMA EELWORM FILAMENT
NEMATODE ROUNDWORM
NEMATOCYST CNIDA DESMONEME
PENETRANT
NEMESIS BANE FATE UPIS AGENT
AVENGER PENALTY
NENTSI SAMOYED SAMOYEDE
NEOPHYTE TYRO EPOPT NOVICE
AMATEUR CONVERT BEGINNER
PROSELYTE YOUNGLING
NEOPLASM TUMOR GROWTH
TUMOUR SARCOMA NEWGROWTH
NEOTERIC NEW LATE FRESH NOVEL
MODERN RECENT
NEP KNOT CATNIP CATMINT CLUSTER

NEPAL

CAPITAL: KATMANDU
COIN: MOHAR RUPEE
MOUNTAIN: EVEREST
NATIVE: AOUL LIMBU MURMI
NEWAR GURKHA GORKHALI
RIVER: KALI KOSI MUGU SETI BABAI
BHERI RAPTI SARDA GANDAK
KARNALI NARAYANI
TOWN: PATAN BIRGUNJ
BHADGAON LALITPUR
BHAKTAPUR

NEPENTHE DRUG PLANT POTION
ANODYNE
NEPHELINE LENAD MINERAL
SOMMITE ELEOLITE
NEPHEW OY OYE NEVE VASU NEFFY
NEVOY NIECE NEPOTE BENVOLIO
NEPHRITE JADE POUNAM AXSTONE
POUNAMU TREMOLITE
NEPTUNE LER PAN SEA GREEN
OCEAN PLATE SEAGOD
(BROTHER OF —) PLUTO JUPITER
(CONSORT OF —) SALACIA
(DISCOVERER OF —) GALLE
(EMBLEM OF —) TRIDENT
(FATHER OF —) SATURN
(MOTHER OF —) RHEA
(SISTER OF —) JUNO
NEREID NYMPH NEREIS THALIA
THETIS CYMODOCE
NEREIDES (FATHER OF —) NEREUS
(MOTHER OF —) DORIS
NERO TYRANT FIDDLER
(MOTHER OF —) AGRIPPINA
(SUCCESSOR TO —) GALBA
(VICTIM OF —) LUCAN SENECA
(WIFE OF —) OCTAVIA
NERVE RIB CORD GALL GRIT GUTS
LINE SAND VEIN CHEEK CHORD

CRUST PLUCK PUDIC SINEW SPUNK
STEEL TENON VAGUS VIGOR
APLOMB COSTAL DARING DENTAL
ENERGY FACIAL LUMBAR RADIAL
SACRAL STRING AXILLAR COELIAC
COURAGE SAPHENA SCIATIC
SPINDLE ABDUCENS AUDACITY
BOLDNESS CERVICAL COOLNESS
EFFERENT EMBOLDEN STRENGTH
TEMERITY AUTONOMIC ENCOURAGE
EYESTRING
(— CELL) ANAXON NEURON
DIAXONE DENDRAXON
(— CENTER) BRAIN CORTEX PLEXUS
(— FIBERS) PONS
(— NETWORK) RETIA PLEXUS
(— SLEEP) NEURO HYPNOTISM
(PL.) HORRORS JITTERS
NERVELESS DEAD WEAK BRAVE
INERT UNNERVED FOOLHARDY
POWERLESS
NERVOUS EDGY TOEY FUSSY
GOOSY JUMPY TENSE TIMID WINDY
FIDGET SINEWY SPOOKY TOUCHY
UNEASY FEARFUL FRETFUL JITTERY
RESTIVE SCADDLE NEUROTIC
TIMOROUS EXCITABLE SENSITIVE
TREMULOUS TWITTERLY
(— MALADY) APHASIA NEURITIS
(— SEIZURE) TIC ANEURIA
NERVURE RIB NERVE NEURON
CUBITAL
NERVY BOLD RASH JERKY PUSHY
BRAZEN SINEWY STRONG FORWARD
JITTERY IMPUDENT INTREPID
VIGOROUS EXCITABLE
NESS RAS CAPE SUFFIX HEADLAND
NEST BED DEN EST JUG WEB AERY
BIKE BINK DRAY DREY EYRY HOME
LAIR NIDE REDD SHED TRAP ABODE
AERIE BROOD EYRIE HAUNT HOUSE
NIDUS SWARM CLUTCH COLONY
CUDDLE HOTBED RESORT WURLEY
CABINET LODGING RETREAT
VESPIARY WITHYPOT LARVARIUM
PENDULINE RESIDENCE TERMITARY
(— OF ANIMALS) BED
(— OF ANT) FORMICARY
(— OF BOXES) INRO
(— OF EGGS) CLUTCH
NESTLE JUG LAP LIE PET NEST
SNUG NICHE SPOON BURROW
CUDDLE FIDGET NUZZLE PETTLE
SETTLE SNUDGE CHERISH SHELTER
SNUGGLE SNUZZLE
NESTLING BABY BIRD EYAS NEST
POULT SQUAB CUDDLE RETREAT
BIRDLING NIDULATE FLEDGLING
NESTOR SAGE SOLON LEADER
ADVISER ADVISOR COUNSELOR
PATRIARCH
NET BAG GIN HAY LAM POT WEB
CAUL FIKE FLAN FLEW FLUE FYKE
GAIN HAAF KELL LACE LAUN LAWN
LEAD MESH MOKE NEAT PURE RETE
SALE TOIL TRAP TRIM WEIR BRAIL
CATCH CLEAN CLEAR DRIFT GAUZE
LACIS PITCH POUND SCOOP SEIZE
SNARE SNOOD TRAWL TRINK TULLE

YIELD BAGNET BASKET BRIGHT
COBWEB ENTRAP FABRIC GROUND
LEADER MALINE MASILE PANTER
PROFIT RAFFLE SAGENE SAPIAO
TOWNET TUNNEL DRAGNET
ENSNARE FLYTAIL LAMPARA
MALINES NETWORK PROTECT
RETICLE RINSING SCRINGE SHELTER
SPILLER STALKER TRAINEL
TRAMMEL MESHWORK SALAMBAO
BUCKSTALL RETICULUM
NETHER DOWN BELOW LOWER
UNDER NEDDER DOWNWARD
INFERIOR INFERNAL

NETHERLANDS
CANAL: ORANJE JULIANA
DRENTSCH
CAPITAL: AMSTERDAM
CHEESE: EDAM GOUDA LEYDEN
COIN: CENT DOIT RYDER FLORIN
GULDEN STIVER DUCATON
ESCALIN GUILDER STOOTER
ISLAND: TEXEL AMELAND
VLIELAND
MEASURE: EL AAM AHM AUM ELL
KAN MUD VAT ZAK DUIM LOOD
MIJL ROOD ROPE VOET ANKER
CARAT ROEDE STOOP WISSE
BUNDER KOPPEN LEGGER
MAATJE MUDDLE MUTSJE
STREEP SCHEPEL MIMGELEN
OKSHOOFD STEEKKAN
NAME: HOLLAND
NATIVE: DUTCH DUTCHMAN
PROVINCE: DRENTHE LIMBURG
UTRECHT ZEELAND FRIESLAND
GRONINGEN GELDERLAND
OVERIJSSEL
RIVER: EEM LECK MAAS WAAL
YSEL DONGE HUNSE MEUSE
YSSEL DINTEL DOMMEL
KROMME SCHELDT
TOWN: EDE ASTEN BREDA HAGUE
AALTEN ARNHEM LEIDEN
HAARLEM TILBURG UTRECHT
AALSMEER ENSCHEDE
NIJMEGEN AMSTERDAM
EINDHOVEN GRONINGEN
ROTTERDAM
WEIGHT: ONS LAST LOOD POND
BAHAR GREIN KORREL WICHTJE
ESTERLIN

NETHERWORLD HADES SHADES
NETLIKE MESHY NETTY RETIARY
RETICULAR
NETTING BAR CAUL LING MESH
SCREEN DEEPING FISHNET FOOTING
BOBBINET WIREWORK
NETTLE VEX FRET LINE ANNOY
CNIDA ETTLE PEEVE PIQUE STING
HENBIT ORTIGA RUFFLE SPLICE
URTICA AFFRONT BLUBBER
BLUETOP KNITTLE PROVOKE
STINGER IRRITATE CLOWNHEAL
GLIDEWORT SMARTWEED
(— RASH) HIVES UREDO URTICARIA

(— TREE) LOTUS GYMPIE
(WHITE DEAD —) ARCHANGEL
NETWORK WEB CAUL FRET MAZE
MESH MOKE RETE CHAIN LACIS
BRIDGE COBWEB CRADLE PLEXUS
RESEAU SAGENE SYSTEM DRAGNI
DIPLEXER GRIDIRON KNITTING
WATTLING RETICULUM
(— OF CRACKS) CRACKLE
(— ON MAP) GRATICULE
NEUME PES VIRGA CLIVIS PNEUMA
PODATUS PUNCTUM VIRGULA
CLIMACUS QUILISMA SEQUENCE
TORCULUS SCANDICUS
NEURAL DORSAL NERVAL NEURIC
NEURALGIA SCIATICA COSTALGIA
NEURITE AXON AXONE
NEUROTIC DRUG NERVOUS
(— CONDITION) LATAH
NEUTRAL GRAY INERT SWEET
AMORAL MIDDLING NEGATIVE
UNBIASED COLORLESS IMPARTIA
(— IN COLOR) SOBER
(OPTICALLY —) INACTIVE
NEUTRALIZE KILL ANNUL BLUNT
ERASE CANCEL ABOLISH BALANC
CORRECT DESTROY NULLIFY
VITIATE NEGATIVE SATURATE
FRUSTRATE
NEUTRINO LEPTON

NEVADA
CAPITAL: CARSONCITY
COUNTY: NYE ELKO STOREY
WASHOE
INDIAN: WASHO PAIUTE
LAKE: MEAD RUBY TAHOE
WALKER PYRAMID
RIVER: REESE TRUCKEE
HUMBOLDT
STATE BIRD: BLUEBIRD
STATE FLOWER: SAGEBRUSH
STATE NICKNAME: SILVER
STATE TREE: PINON
TOWN: ELY ENKO RENO FALLON
NELLIS SPARKS LASVEGAS

NEVE ICE FIRN SNOW NEPHEW
GLACIER
NEVER NAY NIE NOT NARY NARR
NIVER NOWHEN
NEVER-NEVER DREAMLAND
NEVERTHELESS BUT YET STILL
ALWISE ALGATES HOWBEIT
HOWEVER WHETHER
NEVUS MOLE SPOT TUMOR NAEV
SPIDER SPILUS FRECKLE LENTIG
SPILOMA BIRTHMARK
NEW NEO NEU RAW LATE NOVA
FRESH GREEN MOIST NOVEL YO
MODERN RECENT UNUSED VIRG
ANOTHER FOREIGN STRANGE
UNTRIED UPSTART INITIATE
NEOTERIC ORIGINAL YOUTHFUL
BEGINNING
(— BUT YET OLD) NOVANTIQUE
(BRAND —) SPICK
(COMB. FORM) NEO

NEWBORN YEANLING

NEW CALEDONIA (— **BIRD**) KAGU
(**CAPITAL OF** —) NOUMEA
(**ISLAND OF** —) HUON BELEP DEPINS
LOYALTY WALPOLE
(**SEAPORT OF** —) NOUMEA

NEWCASTLE GOTHAM

NEWCOMER SETTLER COMELING
FRESHMAN MALIHINI RINGNECK
GREENHORN IMMIGRANT KIMBERLIN

NEW DEAL (— **AGENCY**) CCC NRA
NYA TVA

NEWEL POST SPINDLE

NEW ENGLAND (— **INHABITANT**)
YANK YANKEE JONATHAN
(— **SETTLER**) PILGRIM PURITAN

NEWFOUNDLAND (— **CAPE**) RACE
(— **HOUSE**) TILT
(— **INHABITANT**) OUTPORTER

NEW GUINEA

BAY: ORO MILNE
GULF: HUON PAPUA
ISLAND: BUKA MANUS MUSSAU
ISLAND GROUP: CRETIN NINIGO
SAINSON SOLOMON
MOUNTAIN: ALBERT VICTORIA
NATIVE: KARON PAPUAN
PORT: LAE DARU WEWAK MADANG
RIVER: FLY HAMU SEPIK AMBERNO
TOWN: LAE WAU DARU SORON
AITAPE KIKORI RABAUL

NEW HAMPSHIRE

CAPITAL: CONCORD
COLLEGE: DARTMOUTH
COUNTY: COOS BELKNAP
LAKE: SQUAM OSSIPEE SUNAPEE
UMBAGOG WINNIPESAUKEE
MOUNTAIN: MORIAH PAUGUS
WAUMBEK CHOCORUA
MONADNOCK
MOUNTAIN RANGE: WHITE
NOTCH: CRAWFORD FRANCONIA
PRESIDENT: PIERCE
RIVER: SACO ISRAEL BELLAMY
SOUHEGAN MERRIMACK
STATE BIRD: FINCH
STATE FLOWER: LILAC
STATE TREE: BIRCH
TOWN: KEENE EXETER NASHUA
HANOVER LACONIA

NEW HEBRIDES (**CAPITAL OF** —)
VILA
(**ISLAND OF** —) EPI TANA EFATE
MAEWO MABRIM MALEKULA

NEW JERSEY

CAPITAL: TRENTON
COLLEGE: UPSALA
COUNTY: ESSEX UNION BERGEN
CAMDEN MORRIS PASSAIC
MONMOUTH
INDIAN: DELAWARE
PRESIDENT: CLEVELAND

RIVER: DENNIS HAYNES MANTUA
RAMAPO MULLICA PASSAIC
RARITAN COHANSEY TUCKAHOE
STATE BIRD: GOLDFINCH
STATE FLOWER: VIOLET
STATE NICKNAME: GARDEN
STATE TREE: REDOAK
TOWN: LODI CAMDEN NEWARK
NUTLEY RAHWAY TOTOWA
BAYONNE HOBOKEN HOHOKUS
MATAWAN NETCONG ORADELL
PARAMUS PASSAIC TEANECK
TENAFLY WYCKOFF CARTERET
FREEHOLD METUCHEN
SECAUCUS WATCHUNG
UNIVERSITY: RUTGERS PRINCETON

NEWLY ANEW AGAIN AFRESH
LATELY FRESHLY NEWLINS
RECENTLY

NEWMARKET MICHIGAN SARATOGA
GRABOUCHE

NEW MEXICO

CAPITAL: SANTAFE
COUNTY: LUNA MORA QUAY TAOS
OTERO CATRON CHAVES
HIDALGO
CULTURE: MIMBRES
INDIAN: TEWA TIWA ZUNI JEMEZ
PECOS APACHE NAVAHO
NAVAJO PUEBLO
RIVER: UTE GILA PECOS SANJOSE
STATE BIRD: ROADRUNNER
STATE FLOWER: YUCCA
STATE TREE: PINON PINYON
TOWN: JAL BELEN RATON CLOVIS
DEMING GALLUP GRANTS
ARTESIA SOCORRO

NEWS BUZZ DOPE UNCA UNKO
WORD CLASH FERLY ADVICE
CRACKS FERLIE GOSPEL NOTICE
REPORT EVANGEL KHUBBER
TIDINGS WITTING NOUVELLE
KNOWLEDGE SPEERINGS
(— **AGENCY**) AP UP DNB INS UPI
TASS ANETA DOMEI REUTERS
(— **BEAT**) SCOOP

NEWSBOY NEWSY CAMELOT
CARRIER

NEWSMONGER GOSSIP TATTLER
NOVELANT NOVELIST QUIDNUNC
REPORTER

NEWSPAPER RAG NEWS DAILY
ORGAN PAPER PRESS SHEET TIMES
ARRIBA HERALD SERIAL SUNDAY
COURANT DIURNAL GAZETTE
JOURNAL MERCURY TABLOID
TRIBUNE NEWSPRINT
(— **USED BY PICKPOCKET**) STIFF
(PL.) PRESS

NEWSPAPERMAN PRESSMAN

NEWSSTAND BOOTH KIOSK STALL
STAND BOOKSTALL

NEWT ASK EFT ESK EVET EBBET
EFFET LIZARD TRITON AXOLOTL

CRAWLER CREEPER REPTILE
MANKEEPER

NEW YEAR'S DAY NAURUZ
NOROOSE NOWROZE

NEW YEAR'S EVE HAGMENA
HOGMANAY

NEW YORK

AVENUE: PARK FIFTH MADISON
FLATBUSH
BAY: JAMAICA PECONIC MORICHES
BOROUGH: BRONX KINGS QUEENS
BROOKLYN MANHATTAN
BUILDING: RCA PANAM CHRYSLER
FLATIRON
CANAL: ERIE GOWANUS
CAPITAL: ALBANY
COLLEGE: BARD CCNY IONA PACE
FINCH UNION HUNTER VASSAR
WAGNER ADELPHI BARNARD
CANISIUS HAMILTON SKIDMORE
COUNTY: ERIE KINGS TIOGA
YATES BROOME CAYUGA
NASSAU ONEIDA OSWEGO
OTSEGO PUTNAM QUEENS
SENECA ULSTER CHEMUNG
GENESEE NIAGARA STEUBEN
SUFFOLK CHENANGO DUTCHESS
HERKIMER ONONDAGA
RICHMOND ROCKLAND
SARATOGA SCHUYLER
INDIAN: CAYUGA MOHAWK ONEIDA
SENECA MOHICAN MONTAUK
IROQUOIS ONONDAGA
ISLAND: FIRE LONG ELLIS STATEN
FISHERS LIBERTY SHELTER
GOVERNORS MANHATTAN
LAKE: ERIE CAYUGA GEORGE
ONEIDA OTISCO OTSEGO
OWASCO PLACID SENECA
CONESUS HONEOYE ONTARIO
SARANAC SCHROON SUCCESS
SARATOGA
MOUNTAIN: BEAR MARCY
MOUNTAINS: TACONIC CATSKILL
ADIRONDACK
NICKNAME: EMPIRE GOTHAM
PRESIDENT: FILLMORE VANBUREN
ROOSEVELT
PRISON: TOMBS ATTICA SINGSING
RIVER: TIOGA HARLEM HOOSIC
HUDSON MOHAWK OSWEGO
GENESEE NIAGARA
SQUARE: TIMES UNION HERALD
MADISON
STATE BIRD: BLUEBIRD
STATE FLOWER: ROSE
STATE NICKNAME: EMPIRE
STATE TREE: SUGARMAPLE
STREET: WALL BOWERY
BROADWAY
SUBWAY: BMT IND IRT LEX
TOWN: RYE ROME ILION ISLIP
NYACK OLEAN OWEGO UTICA
ATTICA AUBURN COHOES
ELMIRA GOSHEN ITHACA ONEIDA
OSWEGO TAPPAN ARDSLEY
BABYLON BATAVIA BUFFALO
CONGERS ENDWELL GENESEO

HEWLETT MAHOPAC MASSENA
MERRICK MINEOLA MONTAUK
ONEONTA PENNYAN POTSDAM
SUFFERN SYOSSET WANTAGH
YAPHANK YONKERS BETHPAGE
CATSKILL HERKIMER KINGSTON
OSSINING SYRACUSE TUCKAHOE
ROCHESTER
UNIVERSITY: LIU NYU ADELPHI
COLGATE CORNELL FORDHAM
HOFSTRA YESHIVA COLUMBIA
WATERFALL: NIAGARA

NEW ZEALAND
BAY: OHUA HAWKE LYALL
AWARUA CLOUDY GOLDEN
FITZROY PEGASUS POVERTY
RANGAUNU
CAPE: EGMONT FAREWELL
PALLISER
CAPITAL: WELLINGTON
GULF: HAURAKI
ISLAND: OTEA STEWART
PUKETUTU
LAKE: OHAU HAWEA TAUPO
PUKAKI PUPUKE TEKAPO
WANAKA BRUNNER ROTORUA
WAKATIPU
MOUNTAIN: COOK FLAT OWEN
CHOPE LYALL MITRE OTARI
STOKES AORANGI PIHANGA
TUTAMOE TYNDALL ASPIRING
EARNSLAW
NATIVE: ATI ARAWA MAORI
RINGATU
PENINSULA: MAHIA OTAGO
RIVER: MOKAU WAIPA CLUTHA
TAMAKI WAIHOU WAIROA
WAIKATO MANAWATU
STRAIT: COOK FOVEAUX
TOWN: LEUIN ORETI OTAKI TAUPO
CLUTHA FOXTON NAPIER
OAMARU PICTON TIMARU
DUNEDIN RAETIHI ROTORUA
AUCKLAND KAWAKAWA
VOLCANO: RUAPEHU NGAURUHOE
TONGARIRO

NEXT POI NEAR SYNE THEN UNTO
WISE AFTER EWEST FIRST LATER
NEIST RIGHT BESIDE COMING
SECOND TIDDER TOTHER CLOSEST
NEAREST DIRECTLY PROCHAIN
PROCHEIN ADJOINING IMMEDIATE
(— AFTER) THEN FOLLOWING
(— IN ORDER) EKA
(— MONTH) PROXIMO
(— OF KIN) GOEL
(— TO LAST) PENULT
NEXUS TIE BOND LINK CHAIN
NGAIO KIO KAIO NAIO TREE
NHANG GIAI
NIAM-NIAM ZANDE AZANDE AZANDI
ZANDEH AZANDEH BABUNGERA
NIB NEB PEN BEAK BILL KINK TEAT
POINT PRONG SCORER

NIBBLE EAT NAB NIB NIP BITE GNAW
KNAB KNAP MOOP MOUP PECK PICK
CHAMP GNARL MOUSE PIECE SHEAR
ARRODE BROWSE CHAVEL NATTLE
PICKLE PILFER CHIMBLE GNABBLE
GNATTER KNABBLE SNAGGLE

NICARAGUA
CAPITAL: MANAGUA
COIN: PESO CENTAVO CORDOBA
ISLAND: OMETEPE
LAKE: MANAGUA
MEASURE: VARA CAHIZ MILLA
SUERTE TERCIA CAJUELA
ESTADAL MANZANA
MOUNTAIN: MADERA MOGOTON
PORT: CORINTO
RIVER: COCO TUMA WANKS
GRANDE ESCONDIDO
TOWN: LEON MASAYA GRANADA
MANAGUA JINOTEGA
MATAGALPA
WEIGHT: BAG CAJA TONELADA

NICCOLITE ARITE KUPFERNICKEL
NICE APT FIT FEAT FINE GOOD JUMP
KIND NEAT NYCE PURE CANNY
EXACT FUSSY NIECE SWEET BONITA
BONITO DAINTY GENTIL MINUTE
PEACHY QUAINT QUEASY SPICED
STRICT SUBTLE TICKLE CORRECT
ELEGANT FINICAL GENTEEL MINCING
PERJINK PICKING PRECISE PRUDISH
REFINED DECOROUS DELICATE
EXACTING PLEASANT PLEASING
TICKLISH
(TOO —) SUPERFINE
NICELY JUMP
NICETY HAIR DELICACY JUSTNESS
CRITICISM CURIOSITY PRECISION
(PL.) PERJINKITIES
NICHE BAY WRO APSE CANT COVE
NOOK SLOT HERNE HOVEL NIECE
NITCH ALCOVE ANCONA COVERT
CRANNY GROOVE MIHRAB RECESS
RINCON EDICULE HOUSING RETREAT
ROUNDEL AEDICULA CREDENCE
TOKONOMA HABITACLE
NICK CUT JAG MAR NAG NOB CHIP
DENT DINT HACK NACK SLAP SLIT
CHEAT CHICK GOUGE NITCH NOTCH
PRICK SCORE SLACK SNICK TALLY
TRICK ARREST RECORD DEFRAUD
(— OF TIME) GODSPEED
NICKEL JIT COIN JITNEY NIMBUS
(ALLOY OF —) INVAR KONEL MONEL
(CONTAINING —) NICCOLIC
(SYMBOL OF —) NI
NICKELODEON JUKEBOX
NICKER NEIGHER
NICKNAME DUB DOEG NICK ALIAS
AGNAME BYWORD HANDLE MONICA
TONAME CRACKER EKENAME
MISNAME MONIKER NICKERY
COGNOMEN MONARCHO MONICKER
TARTUFFE SOBRIQUET
NICKNAMING PROSONOMASIA
NICTATE WINK BLINK CLOSE TWINK
TWINKLE NICTITATE

NIDDICK NAPE
NIDE NID NEST BROOD LITTER
NIDGE NIG SHAKE QUIVER
NIDGET HOE FOOL IDIOT
NIDOR ODOR AROMA SAVOR SCENT
SMELL
NIECE OY OYE NEPHEW
NIELLO TULA
NIEPA NIOTA KARINGHOTA
NIEVE FIST HAND NEIF SERF NATIVE
NIFTY FINE GOOD KEEN SMART
STYLISH
NIGER JOLIBA KWORRA RAMTIL
(CAPITAL OF —) NIAMEY
(MOUTH OF —) NUN
(NATIVE OF —) PEUL HAUSA
DJERMA FULANI SONGHA TOUBOU
TUAREG
(OASIS IN —) KAOUAR
(RIVER OF —) DILLIA
(TOWN OF —) MARADI TAHOUA
ZINDER

NIGERIA
CAPITAL: LAGOS
NATIVE: ARO EBO EDO IBO IJO
VAI BENI EBOE EFIK EJAM EKOI
NUPE BENIN HAUSA FULANI
YORUBA
PORT: LAGOS CALABAR
PROVINCE: ISA OYO KANO NUPE
ONDO IJEBU OGOJA WARRI
OWERRI ADAMAWA
RIVER: OLI GANA YOBE BENUE
NIGER KADANU SOKOTO
GONGOLA KOMADUGU
TOWN: ABA ADO EDE ISA IWO JOS
BIDI BUEA KANO OFFA YOLA
LAGOS ZARIA IBADAN ILESHA
ILORIN KADUNA MUSHIN
TAKOBA CALABAR ONITSHA
OSHOGBO ABEOKUTA
TREE: AFARA

NIGGARD CHURL CLOSE MISER
NIGON PIKER SCART TIGHT NIGGE
SCRIMP SCRUNT STINGY CHINCHE
DRYFIST NITHING PUCKFIST
SCRIMPER EARTHWORM PINCHBEC
PINCHFIST PUCKFOIST SKINFLINT
NIGGARDLY MEAN CLOSE STINT
NARROW NIGHLY SCANTY SCREW
SKIMPY SORDID STINGY STRAIT
CHINCHE MISERLY
NIGGERFISH CONY HIND CONEY
GROUPER GUATIVERE
NIGH AT NEAR ANEAR ANIGH CLOS
ALMOST NEARLY ADJACENT
NIGHT PM EVE DARK NUIT DARKY
DEATH NACHT NOCHE SLEEP
DARKMANS DARKNESS
(— AND DAY) NYCHTHEMERON
(COMB. FORM) NYCTI
(DEPTH OF —) HOLL
(GODDESS OF —) NOX NYX
(LAST —) YESTREEN
(NORSE —) NATT NOTT
(PERT. TO —) NOCTURNAL

(STAY OUT ALL —) PERNOCTATE

NIGHT APE DURUKULI

NIGHT BLINDNESS NYCTALOPIA

NIGHTCAP HOW COWL DOWD HOUVE PIRNY BIGGIN PIRNIE DOREMEUSE SUNDOWNER

NIGHTCLUB CAFE CLUB SPOT BOITE BISTRO CABARET DANCERY NIGHTERY

NIGHTDRESS SLOP WILYCOAT WYLIECOAT

NIGHTFALL EEN EVE DUSK EVEN SHUTTING TWILIGHT

(OCCURRING AT —) ACRONICAL

NIGHTGOWN TOOSH BEDGOWN NIGHTIE WYLIECOAT

NIGHTHAWK PISK CUIEJO BULLBAT

NIGHTINGALE JUG BULBUL FLORENCE PHILOMEL

(— SOUND) JUG

(SWEDISH —) LIND JENNY

(PL.) WATCH

NIGHTJAR POTOO EVEJAR DERHAWK SPINNER WHEELER MOREPORK

NIGHT LAMP VEILLEUSE

NIGHTMARE ALP HAG MARA MESS DREAM FANCY FIEND VISION INCUBUS CACODEMON CAUCHEMAR EPHIALTES

(— CAUSER) MARE

NIGHTSHADE HERB DWALE MOREL HENBANE MORELLE SANDBUR SOLANUM TROMPILLO

NIHIL NIL NICHIL NOTHING

NIHILIST ANARCHIST SOCIALIST

NIL ZERO NILGAI IPOMOEA NOTHING

NILE

AS GOD: HAPI

BIRD: IBIS WRYNECK

BOAT: BARIS CANGIA NUGGAR DAHABEAH

CAPTAIN: RAIS REIS

DAM: ASWAN

FALLS: RIPON

FISH: BAGRE SAIDE BICHIB DOCMAC MORMYRID MORMYROID

ISLAND: RODA PHILAE

NATIVE: MADI NILOT

NEGRO: JUR LUO LWO SUK

PLANT: SUDD LOTUS

REGION: NUBIA

SOURCE: TSANA

TOWN: QUS ABRI ARGO IDFU ISNA QINA ASYUT CAIRO REJAF SAITE ROSETTA

TRIBUTARY: ATBARA KAGERA

VALLEY DEPRESSION: KORE

NILGAI NIL NYLGAU ANTELOPE NEELGHAW

NIMBLE FLY DEFT FLIP FLIT GLEG NESH SPRY SWAK YARE AGILE BRISK FLEET LIGHT QUICK SWACK TRICK LIGHT ACTIVE CLEVER FEIRIE LIMBER LISSOM LIVELY PROMPT QUIVER SPRACK SUPPLE VOLANT

DELIVER LISSOME SWIPPER FLIPPANT TRIPPING SENSITIVE SPRIGHTLY

NIMBLENESS HASTE SLEIGHT LEGERITY DEXTERITY LIGHTNESS

NIMBLE-WITTED VOLABLE

NIMBUS AURA HALO NIMB CLOUD GLORY SHINE VAPOR GLORIA AUREOLA AUREOLE

NIMIETY EXCESS

NINCOMPOOP ASS DOLT FOOL POOP NINNY NINCOM WITLING BLOCKHEAD SIMPLETON

NINE IX NIE NYE TEAM COMET POTHOOK

(— A.M.) UNDERN MIDMORN

(— ANGLED FIGURE) NONAGON

(— DAYS DEVOTION) NOVENA

(— FOLD) NONUPLE

(— HEADED MONSTER) HYDRA

(— HUNDRED) SAN

(— INCHES) SPAN

(— OF CLUBS OR DIAMONDS) COMET

(— OF DIAMONDS) BRAGGER

(— OF TRUMPS) DIX MENEL SANCHO

(— YEAR CYCLE) JUGLAR

(GROUP OF —) ENNEAD

(MUSIC FOR —) NONET

NINEBARK ROSACEAN SEVENBARK

NINEHOLES BUMBLEPUPPY

NINEPIN SQUAIL SKITTLE SKITTLES

(PL.) KEELS KAYLES NINEPEGS

NINETEENTH LARIGOT

NINETIETH NONAGESIMAL

NINETY KOPPA

NINEVEH (FOUNDER OF —) NINUS

NINE WORLDS HEL ASGARD ALFHEIM MIDGARD NIFLHEIM VANAHEIM JOTUNNHEIM MUSPELLSHEIM SVARTALFAHEIM

NINNI ISHTAR

NINNY DOLT FOOL LOUT DUNCE IDIOT NONNY PATCH SAMMY SPOON FONDLE NOODLE FONDLING BLOCKHEAD NIDDICOCK PEAKGOOSE SIMPLETON

NINON SHEER

NINTH (EVERY —) NONAN ENNEATIC

NIOBATE TODDITE SIPYLITE COLUMBATE

NIOBE HERB HOSTA FUNKIA

(BROTHER OF —) PELOPS

(FATHER OF —) TANTALUS

(HUSBAND OF —) AMPHION

(SISTER-IN-LAW OF —) AEDON

NIOBIUM COLUMBIUM

NIP CUT SIP VEX BITE BUMP CLIP DRAM GIVE KNIP NIPE PECK SNUB TANG TAUT TUCK BLAST CHEAT CHECK CHILL CLAMP DRAFT FROST PINCH SEIZE SEVER SNAPE SNEAP THIEF BENUMB BLIGHT CATNIP TIPPLE TWITCH WITHER SARCASM SQUEEZE WETTING COMPRESS FROSTBITE VELLICATE

NIPA PALM ATAP ATTAP DRINK

NIPPER BOY LAD CLAW CRAB GRAB

HAND BITER CHELA MISER THIEF CUNNER URCHIN GRIPPER INCISOR BRAKEMAN

NIPPERS DOG NIP BITS NIPS TONGS GRATER PLIERS TURKIS FORCEPS PINCERS OSTEOTOME

NIPPLE BUD DUG PAP TIT BEAN TEAT DIDDY DUMMY SPEAN NIBBLE PILLAR MAMILLA PAPILLA THELIUM

(— POINT) THELION

NIPPLEWORT BALLOGAN WARTWEED WARTWORT

NIPPY BOLD

NIRVANA EMPTINESS

NIS NIX NISSE GOBLIN KOBOLD BROWNIE

NISUS POWER EFFORT IMPULSE ENDEAVOR

(DAUGHTER OF —) SCYLLA

NITER NITRE PETER PETRE POTASH SALTPETER

NITHER BLAST DEBASE SHIVER TREMBLE

NITID GAY BRIGHT GLOSSY SPRUCE SHINING LUSTROUS NITIDOUS

NITO AGSAM

NITON RADON

NITRATE SALT ESTER COTTON AZOTATE

NITRIC AZOTIC

NITRIDE BORAZON

NITRITE AZOTITE

NITROGEN GAS AZOTE ALKALIGEN

NITROGLYCERIN TNT SOUP SIRUP SYRUP GLONOIN GLONOINE

NITWIT DAW DOPE DIZZARD SIMPLETON

NIX NO HARD NECK NICKER NOBODY SPIRIT SPRITE UNDINE NOTHING

NJAVE ADJAB DIAVE

NO NA NE NAE NAH NAW NAY NIT NIX NUL BAAL BAIL BALE NONE NYET NAPOO NAPOOH NOGAKU

(— ONE) NIX NEMO

(— POINTS IN TENNIS) LOVE

NOAH NOE

(DOVE OF —) COLUMBA

(FATHER OF —) LAMECH

(GRANDSON OF —) ARAM

(GREAT-GRANDSON OF —) HUL

(MEXICAN —) COXCOX

(RAVEN OF —) CORVUS

(SON OF —) HAM SEM SHEM JAPHETH

(WINE CUP OF —) CRATER

NOB NAB BLOW HEAD NAVE KNAVE SWELL HANDLE TIPTOPPER

NOBILITY RANK ELITE GRACE GENTRY STATUS DIGNITY KWAZOKU PEERAGE QUALITY STATION BARONAGE SZLACHTA ELEVATION

(MEMBER OF TATAR —) MURZA

(ROMAN —) RAMNES

NOBLE DON ALII DOGE DUKE EARL EDEL EPIC FAME FREE GENT GOOD GRAF HIGH JARL JUST KAMI KUGE LORD PEER PURE RIAL ARIKI ATHEL BARON BROAD BURLY COUNT DUCAL ERECT ETHEL FURST GRAND

GREAT HIRAM KHASS LOFTY MANLY MORAL MURZA PROUD ROYAL STATE AUGUST COUSIN EPICAL FLAITH GENTLE GESITH HAUGHT HEROIC JUNKER KINGLY LORDLY LUCUMO MANFUL SIRDAR SUPERB THAKUR WORTHY YONKER ACERBAS CACIQUE GALLANT GLAUCUS GLORIED GRANDEE HIDALGO LIBERAL MAGNATE MARQUIS PATRICK STAROST STATELY STEWARD SUBLIME VOLPONE PANGLIMA

NOBLEMAN DUKE EARL EMIR LORD PEER BARON COUNT ORLOV PARIS THANE COUSIN MILORD ORLOFF THAKUR YONKER GRANDEE HIDALGO MAGNATE MARQUIS STAROST VOLPONE YOUNKER ADELIGER ALMAVIVA BELARIUS MARCHESE MARQUESS LANDGRAVE

NOBLENESS HONOR DIGNITY
(— OF BIRTH) EUGENY

NOBLEWOMAN LADY MILADY DUCHESS PEERESS BARONESS COUNTESS

NOBODY NIX NEMO NONE NADIE NOMAN SCRUB SCARAB NOTHING JACKSTRAW

NOCENT GUILTY HARMFUL HURTFUL NOXIOUS CRIMINAL

NOCTURNAL NIGHT NOXIAL NIGHTLY NIGHTISH MOONSHINE
(— ANIMAL) COON POSSUM OPOSSUM
(— BIRD) OWL
(— CARNIVORE) RATEL
(— MAMMAL) BAT LEMUR
(— SIGNS) ZODIAC

NOCTURNE LULLABY UHTSONG PAINTING SERENADE

NOD BOB BOW ERR NAP NID NIP BECK BEND DOZE NAPE SIGN SLIP SWAY WINK DROOP LAPSE ASSENT BECKON DODDLE DROWSE NODDLE NUTATE SALUTE SIGNIFY

NODDING DROWSY NUTANT ANNUENT CERNUOUS DROOPING NUTATION

NODDY AUK FOOL JACK NOIO TERN KNAVE NINNY DROWSY FULMAR NOODLE SLEEPY HACKNEY TOMNODDY SIMPLETON

NODE BOW BUMP KNOB KNOT LUMP PLOT JOINT NODUS POINT TUMOR BULBIL NODULE DILEMMA GRANULE KNUCKLE FOLLICLE PHYTOMER SWELLING TUBERCLE
(— OF GRASS) KNOT
(— OF POEM) PLOT
(— OF STEM) JOINT

NODULE BOB AUGE BUMP KNOT LUMP MASS NODE YOLK FLINT GEODE PHYMA MILIUM BLISTER CATHEAD GRANULE LEPROMA NABLOCK SARCOID AMYGDALE AMYGDOLE TUBERCLE WHITEHEAD
(— OF FLINT) CORE
(PL.) BEADING

NOEL XMAS CAROL NOWEL NATALIS CHRISTMAS

NOGGIN ALE CUP MUG NOG PEG PIN GILL HEAD PAIL PATE DRINK GOGGAN NAGGIN NOODLE

NOIL FIBER PINION

NOISE (ALSO SEE SOUND) ADO AIR BUM DIN GIG HUM POP ROW BANG BOOM BRAY BUMP BURR HOOT KLOP MUSH PEAL RALE RASH REEL RERD ROTE ROUT SLAM ZING ALARM BABEL BLARE BLAST BLOOP BRAWL BRUIT BURLE CHANG CHIRM CLICK DREAM GRASS JERRY KNOCK LARRY LEDEN PLASH QUONK REERE RERDE RUMOR SLORP SNORE SOUND STEER SWISH CACKLE CLAMOR DUNDER GOBBLE GOSSIP HUBBUB NORATE OUTCRY RACKET RANTAN RATTLE REPORT SPLASH SQUAWK STEVEN STRIFE TUMULT UPROAR BLUSTER BRATTLE CLITTER CRACKLE ORATION SCANDAL SPATTER STREPOR STRIDOR FLICFLAC QUONKING TINTAMAR CONFUSION
(ELECTRIC —) GRASS

NOISELESS QUIET STILL SWEET TACIT SILENT APHONIC CATLIKE

NOISEMAKER BELL HORN GRAGER RATTLE CLAPPER SQUEAKER

NOISETTE HAZEL HAZELNUT

NOISOME FOUL RANK FETID NASTY PUTRID RANCID HARMFUL HURTFUL NOXIOUS NUISOME STINKING OFFENSIVE

NOISY LOUD CLASHY CREAKY BLATANT DINSOME FRANTIC MOILING RACKETY RIOTOUS ROUTOUS BRAWLING CLATTERY SONOROUS STREPENT HILARIOUS RATTLEBAG

NOLL HEAD NODDLE NOODLE

NOMA CANKER

NOMAD ARAB BEJA LURI MOOR SAKA SHUA ALANI GYPSY IGDYR JAREG ROVER SHUWA NOMADE ROAMER ROVING SEMITE SLUBBI TUAREG BAZIGAR BEDOUIN SARACEN SCENITE SHORTZY SHUKRA SOLUBBI TOUAREG KABABISH SCYTHIAN SHINWARI AMALEKITE MIGRATORY
(— PEOPLE) ALANI
(PL.) AKHLAME

NOMADIC ERRATIC VAGRANT VAGABOND FOOTLOOSE ITINERANT

NOM DE PLUME PENNAME TELONISM PSEUDONYM

NOME ELIS NOMOS MELODY NOMARCHY PROVINCE

NOMENCLATURE LIST NAME TERM ONYMY NAMING GLOSSARY REGISTER CATALOGUE

NOMINAL PAR BASIC PAPER FORMAL SLIGHT UNREAL TITULAR TRIVIAL PLATONIC TRIFLING
(— RECOGNIZANCE) DOE

NOMINATE CALL LEET NAME ELECT

NEVEN SLATE SELECT APPOINT ENTITLE PRESENT PROPOSE SPECIFY DESIGNATE POSTULATE

NOMINY SPEECH RIGMAROLE

NONAGE NEANT INFANCY MINORITY PUPILAGE

NONAGREEMENT DISSENT

NON-ALCOHOLIC SMALL

NON-ARAB SHANGALLA

NONASPIRATE LENE

NONBELIEVER PAGAN ATHEIST AGNOSTIC

NONCE NANES NONES NOANCE PRESENT PURPOSE OCCASION

NONCHALANT COOL GLIB ALOOF CASUAL JAUNTY CARELESS DEBONAIR

NON-CHRISTIAN INFIDEL

NONCITIZEN TENSOR PEREGRINUS

NONCLERIC LAY LAIC

NONCOMBUSTIBLE APYROUS

NONCOMMITTAL NEUTRAL

NONCONFORMIST REBEL NONCON BEATNIK FANATIC HERETIC SECTARY BOHEMIAN RECUSANT DISSENTER
(— IN ART) FAUVE

NONCONFORMITY HERESY ADHARMA DISSENT NEGLECT REFUSAL RECUSANCE RECUSANCY

NONCONTINUOUS DISCRETE

NONDISCLOSURE FRAUD

NONDO LOVAGE ANGELICO

NONDUALISM ADVAITA

NONE NO UN NAE NIN NANE NARY NEEN NONES

NONEGO NOTSELF

NONELASTIC BROAD

NONENTITY ZERO AUGHT CIPHER NOBODY NOUGHT NOTHING NULLI

NONESSENTIAL CASUAL FRILLY UNNEEDED EXTRINSIC
(— IN RELIGION) ADIAPHORON

NONESUCH APPLE MODEL PARAG PATTERN PARADIGM MATCHLESS NONPAREIL UNRIVALED

NONEXISTENT NULL NAPOOH NOUGHT NONBEING
(PRACTICALLY —) FAT

NONFEASANCE BREACH

NON GRATA UNWELCOME

NONGYPSY GAJO

NONINJURY AHIMSA

NON-JEW GOI GOY

NONJUROR USAGER

NON-LATIN SAXON

NONLEGATO DETACHE DETACHE

NON-MOSLEM GENTILE

NONPAREIL BEST POPE TYPE PARAGON PERFECT SUPREME UNEQUAL NONESUCH PEERLESS UNRIVALED

NONPAYMENT DISHONOR

NONPLUS SET FAZE POSE STOP BLANK FLOOR POSER STICK STU TRUMP BAFFLE GRAVEL PUZZLE RATTLE CONFUSE MYSTIFY PERPLEX STAGGER QUANDARY DULCARNON EMBARRASS

ONPLUSSED FOOLISH

ONPOISONOUS EDIBLE

ONPROFESSIONAL BUM LAY LAIC AMATEUR

ONSENSE BAH GAS GUP PAH ROT BILK BLAA BLAH BOSH BUFF BUNK COCK CRAP FLAM FLUM GOOK JUNK PISH POOH PUNK TOSH BALLS BLASH DROOL FOLLY FUDGE HAVER HOOEY SPOOF STITE STUFF TRASH TRIPE WAHOO BABBLE BUNKUM DRIVEL FADDLE FOLDER KIBOSH LINSEY NAVERS RUBBLE SQUISH TRIVIA BLARNEY BLATHER BUNCOME EYEWASH FARRAGO NANITY LOCKRAM TOSHERY TRIFLES TWADDLE CLAPTRAP DISHWASH FALDEROL FLIMFLAM FLUMMERY GALBANUM MACARONI MOROLOGY PISHTOSH SKITTLES SPLUTTER TRUMPERY ABSURDITY RIVOLITY MOONSHINE POPPYCOCK SILLINESS

— CREATURE) GOOP SHOO SNARK SHIMOO

DODLE BEAN FOOL HEAD NIZY NOLL PATE NINNY NIZEY NODDY PASTA PASTE BOODLE NODDLE NOGGIN LOKSHEN NOGHEAD NOUILLE BLOCKHEAD SIMPLETON

— DISH) PANSIT RAVIOLI REPLACH

PL.) MEIN FARFEL FERFEL LASAGNA ASAGNE LOKSHEN FETTUCINI

OK IN BAY OUT WRO CANT COVE LEN HERN HOLE NALK NUCK NUIK NGLE HALKE HERNE NEUCK NICHE LCOVE CANTLE CORNER CRANNY ECESS CREVICE NOOKERY ETREAT

ON M APEX DINE NOWN SEXT NNER MIDDAY UNDERN MIDNOON ERIDIAN

ONDAY (— REST) NAP SIESTA ERIDIAN

OSE TIE TOW BOND DULL GIRN EMP LACE LOOP ROPE TRAP GHT CATCH GRANE HITCH HONDA NCH LASSO LATCH LEASH SNARE ARL WIDDY CAUDLE CHOKER LINCH ENTRAP HALTER LARIAT PRING TETHER TIPPET TWITCH HOCKER ENSNARE EXECUTE NIARD LANYARD SPRINGE ECKLACE SQUEEZER TWITCHEL

- FOR HAULING LOG) CHOKER HOCKER

- FOR SNARING FISH) DULL

- IN A CORD) KINCH

ANGMAN'S —) SQUEEZER OTKA AHT AHOUSAHT MOATCAHT DOACHAHT

RATE NOISE RUMOR GOSSIP

RDIC ARIAN ARYAN

RI AMANORI

RITE GABBRO OLIGOSITE

RM PAR RULE TYPE CANON UGE MODEL NORMA DHARMA DIAN AVERAGE MODULUS

PATTERN STANDARD TEMPLATE

NORMA MOLD RULE GAUGE MODEL SQUARE PATTERN TEMPLET STANDARD TEMPLATE

NORMAL PAR FULL HOME JUST MEAN SANE CLEAR ERECT USUAL FORMAL NATIVE SCHOOL AVERAGE NATURAL NEUTRAL REGULAR TYPICAL ORDINARY STANDARD CUSTOMARY

NORMANDY (BEACH IN —) OMAHA (CAPITAL OF —) ROUEN (RIVER IN —) EURE ORNE SEINE

NORN FATE URTH WURD WYRD NORNA SKULD URDHR URTHR VERDHANDI VERTHANDI

NORSEL BAND LINE ORSEL FILLET NOSSEL ORSELLER

NORTH SEPTENTRION

NORTH CAROLINA

CAPE: FEAR LOOKOUT HATTERAS
CAPITAL: RALEIGH
COLLEGE: ELON CATAWBA DAVIDSON
COUNTY: ASHE DARE HOKE WAKE BERTIE BLADEN ONSLOW YADKIN YANCEY CATAWBA PAMLICO
INDIAN: ENO COREE CHERAW MORATOK PAMLICO CHOWANOC HATTERAS
MOUNTAIN: HARRIS MITCHELL
PRESIDENT: POLK JOHNSON
RIVER: HAW TAR NEUSE CHOWAN LUMBER PEEDEE YADKIN ROANOKE
SOUND: BOGUE CROATAN PAMLICO
STATE BIRD: CARDINAL
STATE FLOWER: DOGWOOD
STATE NICKNAME: TARHEEL
STATE TREE: PINE
TOWN: DURHAM LENOIR SHELBY EDENTON HICKORY ROXBORO TARBORO GASTONIA CHARLOTTE
UNIVERSITY: DUKE

NORTH DAKOTA

CAPITAL: BISMARCK
COLLEGE: JAMESTOWN
COUNTY: EDDY TRAILL PEMBINA
INDIAN: MANDAN ARIKARA HIDATSA
RIVER: RUSH CEDAR HEART JAMES SOURIS DESLACS SHEYENNE WILDRICE
STATE BIRD: MEADOWLARK
STATE FLOWER: PRAIRIEROSE
STATE NICKNAME: SIOUX FLICKERTAIL
STATE TREE: ELM
TOWN: FARGO MINOT

NORTHERN PIKE ARCTIC BOREAL NORTHEN

(— BEAR) POLAR RUSSIA

(— CONSTELLATION) URSA ANDROMEDA

NORTH KOREA

CAPITAL: PYONGYANG
COIN: WON HWAN
RIVER: NAM YALU IMJIN TUMEN TAEDONG
TOWN: HAEJU HEIJO KEIJO ANDONG ANTUNG JUSHIN POCHON WONSAN HAMHUNG HUICHON HUNGNAM KAESONG SINUIJU CHONGJIN

NORTH STAR STATE MINNESOTA

NORTH VIETNAM

CAPITAL: HANOI
COIN: DONG
COMMUNIST PARTY: VIETCONG
GULF: TONKIN TONKING
MOUNTAIN: FANSIPAN
NATIVE: HOA MAN MEO TAY KINH NUNG THAI MUONG
NEWSPAPER: NHANDAN
PORT: BENTHUY HONGGAI HAIPHONG
REGION: ANNAM TONKIN
RIVER: BO CA DA LO MA CHU GAM KOI CHAY NHIHA
TOWN: BACNINH CAOBANG DONGHOI NAMDINH VIETTRI THANHHOA HAIPHOANG

NORWAY

CAPE: NORDKAPP
CAPITAL: OSLO
COIN: ORE KRONE
COUNTY: AMT OSLO FYLKE TROMS BERGEN OPLAND TROMSO FINMARK HEDMARK OSTFOLD NORDLAND ROGALAND TELEMARK VESTFOLD
DANCE: GANGAR HALLING SPRINGAR SPRINGLEIK
INLET: IS KOB RAN ALST ANDS BOKN NORD OFOT SALT SUNN TYRI VEST FIORD FJORD FOLDA LAKSE SOGNE BJORNA HADSEL HORTENS TRONDHEIM
ISLAND: VEGA BOMLO DONNA FROYA HITRA HOPEN SENJA SMOLA ALSTEN AVEROY BOUVET HINNOY KARMOY SOLUND VANNOY GURSKOY LOFOTEN MAGEROY SEILAND JANMAYEN SVALBARD
LAKE: ALTE ISTER MJOSA SNASA FEMUND ROSTAVN TUNNSJO
MEASURE: FOT MAL POT ALEN MAAL KANDE FATHOM SKIEPPE
MOUNTAIN: SOGNE KJOLEN NUMEDAL BLODFJEL SNOHETTA TELEMARK USTETIND

PARLIAMENT: LAGTING STORTING
ODELSTING
PLATEAU: DOURE FJELD
HARDANGER
RIVER: OI ENA ALTA OTRA RANA
TANA BARDU BEGNA LAGEN
ORKLA OTTER RAUMA REISA
GLOMMA LOUGEN NAMSEN
PASVIK
TOWN: GOL NES BODO MOSS
ODDA OSLO VOSS BJORT
FLORO HAMAR MOLDE SKEIN
SKJAK BERGEN HORTEN LARVIK
NARVIK ALESUND ARENDAL
DRAMMEN SANDNES
STAVANGER
WEIGHT: LOD MARK PUND
SKAALPUND BISMERPUND

NOSE CAP NEB NIZ PRY PUG SPY
BEAK BOKO CONK NASE GROIN
LORUM NASUS SCENT SMELL SNIFF
SNOOP SNOUT TRUNK BEEZER
CYRANO DETECT GNOMON MUFFLE
MUZZLE NOZZLE PECKER SEARCH
SNITCH SOCKET ADVANCE PERFUME
SMELLER DISCOVER INFORMER
OLFACTOR PERCEIVE PROBOSCIS
SCHNOZZLE
(— A LOG) SNIPE
(— BAG) MORRAL
(— CARTILAGE) SEPTUM
(— DISEASE) OZENA OZOENA
(— DIVE) VRILLE
(— FLUTE) PUNGI POOGYE
(— INFLAMMATION) CORYZA
RHINITIS
(— MEDICINE) ERRHINE
(— OF ANIMAL) GROIN
(— OPENING) NARE
(— PARTITION) VOMER
(— PIECE) NASAL
(— RING) PIRN
(BLUNT —) SNUB
(FLAT —) PUG SNUB
NOSEBAND BOSAL MUSROL
CAVESSON
NOSEBLEED EPISTAXIS
RHINORRHAGIA
NOSEGAY BOB ODOR POSY POESY
SCENT TUTTY BOUQUET CORSAGE
PERFUME
NOSINESS CURIOSITY
NOSING CURB
NOSTALGIA LONGING YEARNING
NOSTALGIC ELEGIAC ELEGIACAL
NOSTOLOGY GERIATRICS
NOSTRADAMUS SEER PROPHET
PHYSICIAN
NOSTRIL ALA NARE THIRL THRILL
BLOWHOLE
(PERT. TO —) NARIAL NARINE
(PL.) NARES NARIS SNUFFERS
NOSU LOLO
NOSY BEAKY PRYING CURIOUS
FRAGRANT INTRUSIVE
NOT NA NE NAE NAY NOR PAS BAAL
BAIL BALE NICHT SHORN SORRA

NOUGHT POLLED SHAVEN NEITHER
HORNLESS NEGATIVE
(— ANY) NO NUL NANE NARY NONE
NAIRY NOKIN STEAD
(— AT ALL) NEVER LITTLE NOWAYS
NOWHIT NOWISE
(— FINAL) NISI
(— THE SAME) OTHER ANOTHER
DIFFERENT
(— TO BE REPEATED) NR
(— WANTED) DETROP
SUPERFLUOUS
(ALMOST —) SCARCELY
(COULD —) NOTE
(PREFIX MEANING —) IL IM IN IR UN
NON
NOTABLE VIP FINE FABLED FAMOUS
GIFTED NOTARY SIGNAL UNIQUE
EMINENT STORIED SUBLIME
DISTINCT ESPECIAL EVENTFUL
HISTORIC MEMORABLE NOTORIOUS
NOTARY NOTAR GRAFFER
NOTEBOOK OBSERVER OFFICIAL
SCRIVENER
NOTARY PUBLIC TABELLION
NOTATION HOLD MEMO NOTE
ENTRY SYSTEM MARKING
(PHONETIC —) ROMIC
NOTATOR NOTER RECORDER
NOTCH CUT DAG DAP GAP HAG JAG
JOG PEG COPE DENT DINT GAIN
GIMP KERF MUSH NICK NOCK SLAP
SLOT SNIP STEP WARD CRENA
GABEL GRADE HILUM SCORE SHARD
SHERD TALLY CROTCH DEFILE
DEGREE HOLLOW INDENT JOGGLE
RECORD SCOTCH CRENATE
GUDGEON SERRATE INCISION
UNDERCUT
(— BETWEEN HILLS) SLAP
(— ON VERTEBRAE) HYPANTRUM
(— TO FELL TREE) UNDERCUT
NOTCHED EROSE JAGGY RAGULE
RAGULY SERRATE CRENATED
NOTE BON DOG IOU JOT KEY SEE
TEN UNE BILL CARD CENT CHIT
ESPY FAME FLAT GOOD HEED MARK
MEMO NAME NOIT SIGN SOLE SONG
TONE TUNE VIEW CHECK FIVER
GLOZE LABEL PRICK SHORT SIXTH
SOUND STIFF TENTH TOKEN TRAIT
TWANG ATTEND BILLET DEGREE
EXCUSE FIGURA FLIMSY LETTER
MELODY MINUTE NOTICE POLICY
RECORD REGARD REMARK RENOWN
REPORT SECOND STRAIN TENNER
BETOKEN COMMENT DISCORD
MESSAGE MISSIVE NATURAL
OBSERVE PUNCTUS REDBACK
ANNOTATE BLUEBACK BRADBURY
BREVIATE DISPATCH EMINENCE
MARGINAL PERCEIVE POSTFACE
TREASURY GREENBACK
(— FROM TRAIN) BUTTERFLY
(— OF ASSAULT) WARISON
(— OF HUMOR) TRAIT
(— OF SCALE) DO FA LA MI RE SI
SO TI UT ARE SOL
(— OF SNIPE) SCAPE

(— OF WARNING) WATCHWORD
(— ON SHOPHAR) TEKIAH
(— TO RECALL DOG) FORLOIN
(—S ON HUNTING HORN) SEEK
(100-POUND —) CENTURY
(ALTERED —) ACCIDENTAL
(BANK —S) CABBAGE
(BASS —) DRONE
(BIRD'S —) JUG CHIRP
(EIGHTH —) UNCA QUAVER
(ESCAPE —) ECHAPPEE
(EXPLANATORY —) SCHOLIUM
ANNOTATION
(GRACE —) NACHSCHLAG
(HALF —) MINIM
(HARSH —) BLOB
(HIGH-PITCHED —) BEEP
(HIGHEST —) ELA
(LONG —) LARGE
(LOVE —) POULET
(LOWEST —) KEY GAMUT
(MARGINAL —) TOT QUOTE POSTIL
APOSTIL
(MUSICAL —) ALT MESE MIND
BREVE GAMUT SHARP ALAMIRE
MEDIANT PUNCTUS PARAMESE
(NONHARMONIC —) CAMBIATA
(POUND —) BRADBURY
(PROMISSORY —) DOG GOOD HUN
(QUARTER —) CROTCHET SEMIMIN
(SIXTEENTH —) DEMIQUAVER
SEMIQUAVER
(SIXTY-FOURTH —)
HEMIDEMISEMIQUAVER
(THIRTY-SECOND —) SUBSEMIFUS
DEMISEMIQUAVER
(TWO —S) DUPLET
(WHOLE —) SEMIBREVE
(PL.) ANA GAMUT STRAIN NUMBER
TIRALEE
NOTEBOOK LOG DIARY NOTARY
RECORD STREET JOURNAL
NOTECASE WALLET POCKETBOOK
NOTED COUTH FAMED GREAT
NAMELY EMINENT INSIGNE
RENOWNED DISTINGUE
NOTEWORTHY BIG SOLEMN
EMINENT NOTABLE SPECIAL
BODACIOUS
NOTHING NIL NIX FREE LUKE NILL
WIND ZERO AUGHT BLANK NIHIL
CIPHER NAUGHT NOBODY NOUGH
TRIFLE NULLITY SCRATCH USELE
BAGATELLE
(— BUT) ALL
(— DOING) NAPOO NAPOOH
(— MORE THAN) MERE
(— OTHER THAN) ONLY
NOTHINGNESS NOT NADA ZERO
NOUGHT VACUITY NIHILITY
NOTICE AD BAN SEE SPY CALL E
GOME HEED IDEA KEEP MARK MI
NEWS NOTE PIPE RIDE SIGN SPO
TWIG ALARM AWAIT COUNT EDIC
FLOAT NOTAM ORDER QUOTE
ADVICE ALLUDE BILLET ESPIAL
NOTION PERMIT READER REGARI
REMARK REWARD AFFICHE ARTIC
DISCERN MENTION OBSERVE

PLACARD PROGRAM WARNING BULLETIN MONITION PERCEIVE WITTERING

(— UNEXPECTEDLY) CATCH

(ADVANCE —) HERALDRY

(COMMENDATORY —) BLURB

(DEATH —) OBIT OBITUARY

(FAVORABLE —) RAVE

(LEGAL —) CAVEAT

(MARRIAGE —) BANS BANNS

(OFFICIAL —) EDICT SUMMONS BULLETIN CITATION

(PUBLIC —) BAN EDICT BULLETIN SPOTLIGHT

OTICEABLE CRUDE GROSS FLASHY SIGNAL EVIDENT NOTABLE POINTED SALIENT HANDSOME PALPABLE STRIKING PROMINENT

(UNDESIRABLY —) CONSPICUOUS

OTIFICATION DRUM NOTE NOTICE SUMMONS

PUBLIC —) SIGN

OTIFY ALL BID CRY JOG CITE PAGE TELL WARN INFORM NOTICE SIGNAL APPRISE DECLARE FRUTIFY PUBLISH ACQUAINT INTIMATE

OTION BEE GEE BUZZ IDEA IDEE KINK MAZE OMEN VIEW WHIM FANCY FREIT IMAGE SENSE THING WARES BELIEF CEMENT DESIRE GONNEE GADGET NAGGOT NOTICE THEORY VAGARY BROMIDE CONCEIT CONCEPT FANTASY INKLING MAROTTE OPINION THOUGHT WRINKLE CATEGORY FOLKLORE FHANTASY SUPPOSAL WHIMWHAM ATTENTION SENTIMENT WHIRLIGIG

(FALSE —) IDOL

(FIXED —) TICK

(FOOLISH —) VAPOR VAPOUR

(PUERILE —) BOYISM

(SUPERSTITIOUS —) FREET FREIT

(L.) SMALLS SMALLWARE

OTORIETY FAME ECLAT GLORY HONOR RUMOR RENOWN REPUTE PUBLICITY

OTORIOUS BIG KNOWN ARRANT COMMON CRYING FAMOUS NOTARY FRONG EVIDENT NOTABLE NOTOIRE APPARENT FLAGRANT FAMOUS MANIFEST EGREGIOUS

OTORNIS TAKAHE

OTWITHSTANDING BUT FOR THO CT EVEN WITH ALGATE MAUGER AUGRE AGAINST ALGATES ESPITE HOWBEIT HOWEVER THOUGH NATHLESS WHATRECK

NOUGAT NUT CANDY NUTSHELL

OUGHT BAD NIL NOT NOWT ZERO OCHT WRONG NOTHING USELESS ORTHLESS

OUMENAL ONTAL ONTIC

OUN MANE WORD THING SUPINE NOMINAL CONSTRUCT INCREASER

DEFINABLE —) APTOTE

ND OF —) COMMON PROPER PROTOTE REGULAR TRIPTOTE NOPTOTE

NOTATION —) HYPOSTASIS

(VERBAL —) GERUND

NOURISH AID FEED FOOD GROW BREED NORSH NURSE TRAIN BATTLE BREAST FOISON FOSTER NORICE REFETE SUCCOR SUCKLE SUPPLY CHERISH DEVELOP EDUCATE NURTURE NUTRIFY PROVIDE SUPPORT SUSTAIN MAINTAIN CULTIVATE STIMULATE

NOURISHING ALMA RICH ALIBLE BATTLE HEARTY STRONG NUTRIENT ALIMENTAL HEALTHFUL NUTRITIVE WHOLESOME

NOURISHMENT DIET FETE FOOD KEEP MEAT MANNA FOISON FOSTER ALIMENT PABULUM PASTURE NUTRIMENT REFECTION

NOUS MIND REASON ALERTNESS INTELLECT

NOUVEAU RICHE PARVENU UPSTART

NOVEL HOT NEW BOOK EPIC RARE FRESH PROSE RECIT ROMAN STORY DARING RECENT SERIAL THRILL FICTION ROMANCE STRANGE UNUSUAL NEOTERIC ORIGINAL THRILLER UNCOMMON NARRATIVE PAPERBACK

(BRIEF —) CONTE

NOVELTY FAD NEWEL RENEW CHANGE NEWNESS PRIMEUR WRINKLE FRESHNESS

NOVEMBER 1 SAMUIN SAMHAIN

NOVICE DUB HAM BOOT COLT PUNK PUNY TIRO TYRO CHELA GOYIN PUPIL ROOKY YOUTH DRONGO RABBIT ROOKIE TYRONE AMATEUR CONVERT LEARNER STARTER STUDENT YOUNKER BACHELOR BEGINNER FRESHMAN INEXPERT NEOPHYTE ARCHARIOS GREENHORN

NOVITIATE FUCHS NOVICERY PROBATION

NOW NOO YET ARAH HERE ARRAH NONCE SINCE TODAY EVENOO EXTANT ANYMORE CURRENT INSTANT PRESENT FORTHWITH

(— AND THEN) SOMETIMES STOUNDMEAL

(BUT —) ERSTWHILE

(JUST —) ENOW FRESH

NOWADAYS ANYMORE

NOWEL DRAG

NOX NYX

(BROTHER OF —) EREBUS

(FATHER OF —) CHAOS

NOXIOUS ILL EVIL FETID DEADLY NOCENT NOYOUS PUTRID BANEFUL DAMPISH HARMFUL HURTFUL NOCUOUS NOISOME SCADDLE TEDIOUS VICIOUS INFAMOUS VIRULENT INJURIOUS MIASMATIC OFFENSIVE PESTILENT POISONOUS

(— AIR) MALARIA

(MORALLY —) UNWHOLESOME

NOZZLE BIB JET TIP BEAK BIBB NOSE ROSE VENT GIANT SNOUT SPOUT TWEER GROVEL OUTLET MONITOR NIAGARA ORIFICE

SHUTOFF ADJUTAGE ROSEHEAD VERMOREL NOSEPIECE

(BLAST FURNACE —) TUYERE

(MINING —) GIANT

NUANCE SHADE NICETY FINESSE GRADATION VARIATION

NUB EAR HUB JAB JAG KEY NOB CORE CRUX GIST HANG KNOB KNOT KNUB LUMP NECK PITH SNAG HEART NUDGE POINT KERNEL NUBBIN EXECUTE

NUBBIN EAR STUB STUMP

NUBIA WRAP CLOUD SCARF

NUBIAN NUBA BARABRA HADENDOA

(— MUSICAL INST.) SISTRUM

NUBILOUS FOGGY MISTY VAGUE CLOUDY OBSCURE

NUCHA NAPE NECK NUKE NUCHE

NUCLEAR ELEMENTARY

NUCLEATE SEED

NUCLEOSIDE VICINE INOSINE CYTIDINE ADENOSINE

NUCLEUS HUB CELL CORE GERM KERN PITH ROOT SEED CADRE FOCUS HEART MIDST SPERM UMBRA CENTER COLONY DEUTON KARYON KERNEL MIDDLE ISOTOPE NIDULUS MEROCYTE HABENDULA MESOPLAST

(— OF CELL) KARYON

(— OF STARCH GRAIN) HILUM

(— OF SUNSPOT) UMBRA

(ATOMIC —) SPECIES

(CELL —) SYNCARYON HEMIKARYON

NUDE BARE LOOSE MODEL NAKED SEASAN STATUE UNCLAD DENUDED EXPOSED PICTURE PAINTING STRIPPED UNDRESSED

(FRENCH —) ALESAN

(NOT —) DECENT

(RUN —) STREAK

NUDGE JOG NOG NUB WAG GOAD JOLT KNUB LUMP POKE POTE PROD PUSH BLOCK CHUCK DUNCH ELBOW

NUDISM NATURISM GYMNOSOPHY

NUDIST ADAMITE NUDIFIER GYMNOSOPH

NUGATORY IDLE NULL VAIN EMPTY PETTY FUTILE HOLLOW INVALID TRIVIAL USELESS TRIFLING FRUSTRATE WORTHLESS

NUGGET EYE LOB GOLD HUNK LUMP MASS SLUG PRILL YELLOW

NUISANCE BANE BORE EVIL HARM HURT PAIN PEST STING INJURY PLAGUE TERROR VEXATION ANNOYANCE

NULL NIL VOID EMPTY INEPT IRRITE INVALID NULLIFY USELESS VACUOUS NUGATORY FRUSTRATE

NULLAH GORGE GULLY NULLA NALLAH RAVINE

NULLIFY BEAT FLAW LAME NULL UNDO VETO VOID ABATE ANNUL ELIDE ERASE LAPSE CANCEL DEFEAT NEGATE OFFSET REPEAL REVOKE ABOLISH COUNTER DESTROY ABROGATE EVACUATE STULTIFY FRUSTRATE

NUMB DEAD DRUG DULL DAZED

FUNNY STONY ASLEEP BENUMB
CLUMSY DEADEN STUPID TORPID
STUPEFY ENFEEBLE HEBETATE
HELPLESS RIGESCENT TABETLESS
NUMBER SUM BAND BODY COPY
CURN DRAW HERD HOST LOTS MAIN
MANY MESS MORT SLEW SURD
TALE TELL COUNT DATUM DIGIT
FOLIE GRIST GROUP INDEX ISSUE
SCADS SCORE STAND TOTAL
WHOLE ADDEND AMOUNT BUNDLE
CIPHER ENCORE FACTOR FIGURE
FILLER HIRSEL MYRIAD POLICY
RECKON SCALAR TICHEL CHIFFER
COMPUTE DECIMAL DIVISOR
FOLIATE SEVERAL CARDINAL
FRACTION NUMERATE QUANTITY
CALCULATE MULTITUDE
(— **OF ARROWS**) END
(— **OF ATOMS**) CHAIN
(— **OF BEASTS**) HERD
(— **OF BOMBS**) STICK
(— **OF BRICKS**) CLAMP
(— **OF CATTLE**) SOUM
(— **OF FUR SKINS**) TIMBER
(— **OF HANKS OF YARN TO POUND**)
COUNT
(— **OF HAWKS**) CAST
(— **OF HONEYBEES**) CLUSTER
(— **OF NEEDLES**) GAGE GAUGE
(— **OF POEMS**) EPOS
(— **OF SHEARERS**) BOARD
(— **OF TEA CHESTS**) BREAK
(— **OF TRICKS**) BOOK
(— **OF WORDS**) FOLIO
(—**S GAME**) BUG
(**BALLET** —) ENTREE
(**CARDINAL** —) ONE TWO ALEF
ALEPH THREE
(**COMPLEX** —) IMAGINARY
(**CONSIDERABLE** —) WHEEN HATFUL
FISTFUL
(**DESCRIBABLE** —) SCALAR
(**EXCESS** —) ADVANTAGE
(**EXCESSIVE** —) SPATE
(**EXTRA** —) ENCORE
(**GOLDEN** —) PRIME
(**GREAT** —) LAC HEAP HOST LAKH
MORT BREAK HIRST MEINY POWER
SHOAL SIGHT SWARM LEGION
MYRIAD INFINITE INFINITY
THOUSAND MULTITUDE
(**GREAT** —**S**) FLOCKS
(**GREATER** —) MO
(**INDEFINITE** —) LAC STEEN SUNDRY
THARVE JILLION SEVERAL THREAVE
UMPTEEN
(**IRRATIONAL** —) SURD
(**LARGE** —) ARMY FECK HERD HOST
LUMP PECK SLEW ARRAY CROWD
FORCE SCADS SHEAF SPATE STACK
STORE WORLD GALLON HIRSEL
HIRSLE LEGION MELDER BILLION
JILLION
(**LARGE** —**S**) STRENGTH
(**LEAF** —) FOLIO
(**LEAST WHOLE** —) UNIT
(**ODD** —**S**) IMPAIR
(**OPPOSITE** —) COUSIN

(**ORDINAL** —) FIRST THIRD SECOND
(**PUT ON SERIAL** —) FOLIO
(**SMALL** —) FEW CURN CURRAN
HANDFUL PAUCITY SPATTER
(**TOTAL** —) AMOUNT
(**VAST** —) HORDE
(**WHOLE** —) ALL DIGIT INTEGER
NUMBERED MENE
NUMBERING TALE COUNT
FOLIATION
NUMBFISH TORPEDO
NUMBING WARELESS
NUMBLES UMBLES INNARDS
NOMBLES VISCERA ENTRAILS
NUMBNESS STUPOR STUPIDITY
NUMEN DEITY GENIUS SPIRIT
VESTAL DIVINITY
NUMERAL (ALSO SEE NUMBER) SUM
WORD DIGIT CIPHER FIGURE LETTER
CHAPTER
(— **STYLE**) ROMAN ARABIC
(**CLOCK** —) CHAPTER
NUMERATIVE PEN SEGREGATIVE
NUMEROUS BIG LOTS MAIN MANY
RANK RIFE GREAT LARGE STOUR
DIVERS GALORE LEGION MYRIAD
SUNDRY UNRIDE COPIOUS
CROWDED ENDLESS FEARFUL
FERTILE PROFUSE SEVERAL
TEEMING UMPTEEN ABUNDANT
FREQUENT MANIFOLD MULTIPLE
POPULOUS THRONGED EXTENSIVE
MULTIFOLD NUMBERFUL PLENTIFUL
(— **AND POWERFUL**) MAIN
(**MODERATELY** —) FAIR
(**VERY** —) EXCESSIVE
NUMIDIA (**BIRD OF** —) DEMOISELLE
(**CITY OF** —) HIPPO
(**KING OF** —) JUGURTHA
NUMSKULL NUM DAFF DOLT FLAT
DUNCE LACKWIT BONEHEAD
BLOCKHEAD
NUN BIRD SMEW CLARE CLERK
MONIAL PIGEON SISTER TERESA
VESTAL VOWESS CONFINE DEANESS
DEVOTEE EXTERNE MINCHEN
MONKESS RECLUSE TEATINE
THEATIN CHAPLAIN CLARISSE
PRIORESS TITMOUSE URBANIST
URSULINE VISITANT VOTARESS
ANGELICAL LORETTINE PRIESTESS
RELIGEUSE
(— **BIRD**) MONASE TITMOUSE
(— **HEADDRESS**) WIMPLE
(— **HOOD**) FAILLE
(— **MOTH**) TUSSOCK
(— **ORDER**) MARIST TRAPPIST
LORETTINE OOMINICAN
(**CHIEF** —) ABBA ABBESS MOTHER
(**LATIN** —) VESTA
(**SON OF** —) JOSHUA
NUNCIATE NUNCIO ANNOUNCER
MESSENGER
NUNCIO ENVOY NUNCE LEGATE
NUNTIUS DELEGATE MESSENGER
NUNCUPATE DECLARE DEDICATE
INSCRIBE PROCLAIM DESIGNATE
PRONOUNCE

NUNCUPATIVE ORAL SPOKEN
UNWRITTEN
NUNNERY ABBEY NUNRY CONVENT
CLOISTER MINCHERY
(**HEAD OF** —) ABBESS
NUPSON FOOL SIMPLETON
NUPTIAL BRIDAL GENIAL THORAL
MARITAL WEDDING ESPOUSAL
HYMENEAL MARRIAGE
(**PL.**) SPOUSAL ESPOUSAL
HYMENEALS WIFETHING
NUQUE NAPE NECK
NURSE AMAH AYAH CARE DHAI FEE
NANA NUSS REAR SABA SUCK TEN
BONNE MAMMY NANNY NORSH
ATTEND BAYMAN CRADLE FOMENT
FOSTER GRANNY KEEPER NANNIE
NORICE NUZZLE SISTER SITTER
SUCKLE UMFAAN CHERISH FURTHE
NOURISH NURTURE PROMOTE
CULTIVATE ENCOURAGE NURSEMA
(— **A GRIEVANCE**) SULK
(— **OF HIAWATHA**) NOKOMIS
(— **OF ULYSSES**) EURYCLEA
(— **OF ZEUS**) AMALTHEA CYNOSUR
(— **SHARK**) GATA
(**GULLIVER'S** —) GLUMDALCLITCH
(**WET** —) DHAI DHOLL
NURSERY RACE CRECHE BROODER
FOSTERAGE
NURSLING BABY NORRY NURRY
FOSTER FOUNDLING
NURTURE CARE DIET FEED FOOD
REAR TEND BREED NURSE TRAIN
COCKER FOSTER NUZZLE CHERISH
EDUCATE SUPPORT BREEDING
NORTELRY TRAINING EDUCATION
ESTABLISH NUTRIMENT
NUSAIRI ANSARIE
NUT ACA BEN BUR COB GUY JOU N
TAP ANTA BURR COLA CORE DOL
FOOL FROG HEAD KOLA LORE MA
NITE PILI PITH SEED TASK ACORN
BETEL BONGA BUNGA CRANK FRU
GLANS HAZEL HICAN JUVIA PECAN
TRYMA ALMOND BONDUC BRAZIL
CASHEW FELLOW HICCAN ILLIPE
KERNEL PEANUT PIGNON PINION
PYRENE CASTANA FILBERT HICKC
PROBLEM APPLENUT BEECHNUT
BREADNUT CHESTNUT GOORANUT
LARRIKIN CAPOTASTO CHINKAPIN
ECCENTRIC MACADAMIA PHILOPE
(— **COAL**) ANTHRACITE
(— **GRASS**) SEDGE
(— **OF VIOLIN BOW**) FROG
(— **PINE**) PIGNON PINOON PIGNOI
(**CASHEW** —) SEDGE
(**CONSORT OF** —) GEB KEB
(**DAUGHTER OF** —) ISIS NEPHYTH
(**FALLEN** —**S**) SHACK
(**PALM** —) BETEL LICHI COCOANU
(**PERT. TO** —) NUCAL
(**RIPE** —) LEAMER
(**RUSH** —) CHUFA
(**SON OF** —) RA
(**PL.**) MASTAGE
NUT-BEARING NUCIFEROUS
NUTCRACKER XENOPS CRACKER

PILLORY MEATBIRD NUTCRACK
NUTHATCH NUTPECKER
NUTHATCH SITTA TOMTIT XENOPS
JARBIRD SITTINE TITMOUSE
NUTJOBBER
NUTHOOK BEADLE CONSTABLE
NUTLET NUCULE PYRENA PYRENE
GYROLITH
NUTMEG SEED TREE SPICE BEAVER
CALABASH NOTEMIGGE NOTEMUGGE
(— COVERING) MACE
(— STATE) CONNECTICUT
NUTRIA FUR COYPU GREGE NEUTRIA
RAGONDIN
NUTRIENT STARTER
(PL.) FOOD HEMOTROPHE
NUTRIMENT DIET FOOD KEEP
VIANDS ALIMENT PABULUM
SUPPORT
NUTRITION EUTROPHY TROPHISM
(IMPERFECT —) DYSTROPHY
DYSTROPHIA
NUTRITIOUS BATTLE BAITTLE
TROPHIC
NUT-SHAPED NUCIFORM
NUTSHELL SHELL INCLUDER
NUTTY GAGA NUTS RACY ZANY
BUGGY QUEER SPICY FRUITY

LOVING SPRUCE AMOROUS FOOLISH
PIQUANT ZESTFUL DEMENTED
PLEASANT ECCENTRIC FLAVORFUL
NUX VOMICA SNAKEWOOD
NUZZLE DIG PET ROOT NURSE
SNUFF BURROW CARESS FONDLE
FOSTER NESTLE NUDDLE NURTURE
SNOOZLE SNUGGLE SNUZZLE
NYE EYAS NEST NIDE BROOD FLOCK
NYMPH FLY GIRL MAIA MITE MUSE
PINK PIXY PUPA TICK AEGLE DRYAD
HOURI LARVA NAIAD NIXIE OREAD
SIREN SYLPH BYBLIS CYRENE
DAMSEL DAPHNE HELICE HESTIA
KELPIE MAIDEN NEREID SPRITE
SYRINX UNDINE CORYCIA ERYTHEA
HESPERA LIRIOPE OCEANID
CALLISTO CYNOSURA EURYDICE
MARPESSA PROSOPON BUTTERFLY
HAMADRYAD
(— BELOVED BY PAN) SYRINX
(— BELOVED OF NARCISSUS) ECHO
(— OF FOUNTAIN) EGERIA
SALMACIS
(— OF HILLS) OREAD
(— OF MEADOWS) LIMONIAD
(— OF MESSINA STRAIT) SCYLLA

(— OF MT. IDA) OENONE
(CITY —) POLIAD
(LAKE —) NAIAD LIMNIAD
(OCEAN —) SIREN GALATEA
OCEANID
(QUEEN OF —S) MAB
(RIVER —) NAIS NAIAΓ
(SEA —) MERROW NEREID CALYPSO
GALATEA MERMAID
(WATER —) NAIS EGERIA LURLEI
UNDINE APSARAS HYDRIAD
JUTURNA EPHYDRIAD
(WOOD —) DRYAD NAPEA
ARETHUSA
(PL.) HYADS THRIAI CAMENAE
NYMPHAEA CASTALY CASTALIA
NYMPHOMANIAC (BOVINE —)
BULLER
NYROCA AYTHYA
NYSSA TUPELO
NYSTAGMUS TIC WINK
NYX NOX NIGHT
(— PERSONIFIED) NIGHT
(BROTHER OF —) EREBUS
(DAUGHTER OF —) DAY ERIS LIGHT
(HUSBAND OF —) CHAOS
(SON OF —) CHARON

O HO OH OCH ZERO CIPHER OMICRON

OAF AUF BOOR DOLT FOOL LOUT CLOWN DUNCE IDIOT OUPHE YOKEL MUCKER NASHGAB PALOOKA POMPION BLOCKHEAD FOUNDLING SCHLEMIEL SIMPLETON

OAHU (— BIRD) JIBI

OAK CLUB CORK HOLM ILEX BRAVE BRIAR EMORY HOLLY ROBLE ROBUR ACAJOU BAREEN CERRIS ENCINA KERMES STRONG TOUMEY VALOMA AMBROSE BELLOTA BELLOTE DURMAST EGILOPS KELLOGG PALAYAN TURTOSA BEEFWOOD BLUEJACK CHAMPION CHAPARRO FLITTERN WAINSCOT BLACKJACK CHINKAPIN

(— BARK) CRUT

(— FRUIT) MAST ACORN CAMATA BELLOTE

(JERUSALEM —) AMBROSE

(WHITE —) ROBLE

(YOUNG —) FLITTERN

OAKUM OCCAM

OAKWOOD MESA

OAR AIR BOW PLY ROW PALM PEEL POLE ALOOF BLADE ROWER SCULL SPOON SWAPE SWEEP YULOH PADDLE PALLET PROPEL OARSMAN PROPELLER

(— BLADE) PALM PEEL WASH

(— FULCRUM) LOCK THOLE OARLOCK ROWLOCK

(BOW —) GOUGER

(HANDLE OF —) GRASP

(INBOARD PORTION OF —) LOOM

(STERN —) SCULL SKULL

OARLOCK LOCK THOLE ROWLOCK

OARSMAN OAR REMEX ROWER BOWMAN STROKE BENCHER SCULLER WATERMAN

OASIS BAR OJO SPA MERV SIWA WADI WADY SPRING

OAST HOST KILN OVEN COCKLE OASTHOUSE

OAT AIT WOT FEED FOOD PIPE POEM SKEG SONG AUCHT CHEAT GRAIN HAVER PEARL ANGORA EGILOPS

(— HUSK) SHOOD FLIGHT

(— RENT) AVENAGE

(EDIBLE PORTION OF —) GROATS

(FALSE WILD —S) FATUOID

(HUSKED —) SHEALING

(NAKED —) PILLAS PILCORN

(UNTHRASHED —) OATHAY

(WILD —S) HAVERGRASS

(PL.) CORN GRAIN HAVER GROUTS PROVENDER WHITECORN

OATCAKE CAPER HAVERCAKE SOURBREAD

OATEN AITEN

OATH OD ADS BAN DAD DOD GAD GAR GOL GOR GUM ODD SAM VOW BOND CRUM CUSS DARN DRAT ECOD EGAD EGOD GEEZ GOSH HECK JEEZ JING NIGS SANG SLID SLUD WORD BEDAD BEGAD BEGOB BLIMY CURSE DAMME DEUCE GOLLY

HOKEY MORDU PARDY SACRE SFOOT SLIFE SNIGS SWEAR YERRA ADSBUD APPEAL CRACKY CRIKEY CRIPES CRUMBS FEALTY JABERS JERNIE NEAKES PARDIE PLEDGE RAPPER SBLOOD SLIGHT STRUTH ZOUNDS BEGORRA BEGORRY BEJESUS BYRLADY CORBLEU GADSLID GEEWHIZ GEEWIZZ JEEPERS JIMMINY MORBLEU ODSFISH ODZOOKS PROMISE THUNDER ANATHEMA BEJABERS BODYKINS CRICKETY GADZOOKS JURAMENT PITIKINS SANCTION SEREMENT SNIGGERS SPLUTTER AFFIDAVIT BEJABBERS BLASPHEMY DODGASTED EXPLETIVE PROFANITY SACRAMENT SLIDIKINS SWEARWORD

OATMEAL OATS STODGE YELLOW POTTAGE DRAMMOCK PORRIDGE

(— BREAD) ANACK JANNACK

(— CAKE) PONE SCONE

OBCLUDE HIDE OCCLUDE

OBDURATE FIRM HARD BALKY HARSH INERT ROCKY ROUGH STARK STONY DOGGED INURED MULISH RUGGED SEVERE STURDY SULLEN ADAMANT CALLOUS HARDENED PERVERSE STUBBORN IMPASSIVE UNBENDING

OBEAH OBI OBIA CHARM FETISH VOODOO

OBECHE ARERE AYOUS SAMBA

OBEDIENCE ORDER FEALTY CONTROL SERVICE DOCILITY OBEISANCE

OBEDIENT RULY TALL TAME BUXOM DOCILE PLIANT DEVOTED DUTEOUS DUTIFUL HEEDFUL MINDFUL ORDERLY SUBJECT AMENABLE BIDDABLE YIELDING ATTENTIVE OBSERVING SERVIABLE TRACTABLE

(— TO THE HELM) HANDY

OBEDIENTARY PRIOR

OBEDIENT PLANT DRAGONHEAD

OBEISANCE BOW LEG JOUK BINGE CONGE HONOR SALAM CONGEE CURTSY FEALTY HOMAGE SALAAM CURTSEY DEFERENCE HUMBLESSO REFERENCE

OBELISK MARK PYLON SHAFT DAGGER GUGLIA GUGLIO NEEDLE OBELUS PILLAR AGUGLIA MONUMENT HAGIOLITH

OBERON KING POEM FAIRY OPERA SATELLITE

(WIFE OF —) TITANIA

OBESE FAT FOZY PLUMP PUDGY PUFFY PURSY STOUT FLESHY PORTLY PYKNIC ROTUND TURGID ADIPOSE PURSIVE BLUBBERY LIPAROUS CORPULENT

OBESITY FAT FATNESS LIPOSIS ADIPOSIS FOZINESS ADIPOSITY

OBEY EAR HEAR HEED MIND DEFER YIELD COMPLY FOLLOW OBEISH SUBMIT EXECUTE OBSERVE OBTEMPER

(— HELM) STEER

OBFUSCATE DIM CLOUD DARKEN MUDDLE OBFUSK CONFUSE MYSTIF OBSCURE PERPLEX STUPEFY BEWILDER

OBI OBE SASH CHARM OBEAH FETICH FETISH GIRDLE

OBIT MASS REST DEATH NOTICE OBITAL DECEASE RELEASE SERVIC■ OBITUARY NECROLOGY OBSEQUIES■

OBJECT AIM END TAP BALK BEEF CARE CARP FINE GOAL IDEA ITEM KICK MAIN MIND PASS WHAT ARGU■ CAVIL DEMUR GRIPE PINCH POINT SCOPE SIGHT TELOS THING AFFAIR■ DESIGN EMBLEM ENTITY FIGURE GADGET INTENT MATTER MOTIVE OPPOSE TARGET ARTICLE DINGBAT■ DISLIKE DISSENT MEANING PROTES■ PURPOSE QUARREL REALITY RECLAIM NOUMENON TENDENCY CHALLENGE INTENTION SPECTACLE■

(— HAVING FLAWS) SPOIL

(— OF AMBITION) MAIN

(— OF ART) VASE CURIO VIRTU ANTIQUE BIBELOT FIGURINE

(— OF CRITICISM) BUTT

(— OF DEVOTION) IDOL TOTEM FETISH

(— OF DISGUST) UG

(— OF DREAD) BOGY BOGEY BOGI■ BOGGIE BUGBEAR

(— OF KNOWLEDGE) SCIBILE

(— OF PILGRIMAGE) CAABA KAABA■

(— OF PURSUIT) SHADOW

(— OF RELIANCE) STAY

(— OF RIDICULE) FUN GAME

(— OF SCORN) GECK SCOFF BYWORD HISSING DERISION

(— OF THOUGHT) CONSTRUCT

(— OF WONDER) ADMIRATION

(— TO BE TILTED AT) QUINTAIN

(BELOVED —) MINION DARLING MISTRESS

(BULKY —) WODGE

(CONICAL —) ACORN

(CONSPICUOUS —) LANDMARK

(CONTAMINATED —S) FOMITES

(CURVED —) BELLY

(CYLINDRICAL —) BOLE

(DECORATIVE —) BIBELOT

(DESIRABLE —) GRAIL

(FACTORY-MADE —S) ARTWORK

(MINUTE —) ATOM MITE

(ROUND —) RONDEL TRINDLE TRUNDLE

(SACRED —) URIM ZOGO GUACA HUACA SHRINE CHURINGA

(SILLY —) INANITY

(SMALL —) PIRLIE

(TRANSCENDENTAL —) ENTITY

(ULTIMATE —) TELOS

(VILE —S) SCUM

(WORTHLESS —) SPLINTER

OBJECTION OB BAR BUT BEEF CRAB FUSS KICK CAVIL DEMUR DOUBT CHESON QUARREL QUIBBL■ SCRUPLE QUESTION CHALLENGE CRITICISM EXCEPTION

OBJECTIONABLE VILE AWFUL

HORRID GHASTLY UNLUSTY UNLIKELY FRIGHTFUL OBNOXIOUS OFFENSIVE

OBJECTIVE AIM END FAIR GAME GOAL HOME REAL SAKE OUTER ACTUAL AMORAL ANIMUS DESIGN MOTIVE TARGET PURPOSE DETACHED TANGIBLE UNBIASED DIRECTION INTENTION POSITIVAL QUAESITUM ULTIMATUM

OBJURGATE BAN JAW DAMN ABUSE CHIDE CURSE DECRY BERATE REBUKE REPROVE UPBRAID VITUPER EXECRATE CASTIGATE

OBLATE MONK OFFER DEDICATE MONASTIC

OBLATION CORBAN OFLETE SACRED CHARITY ANAPHORA DEVOTION OFFERING SACRIFICE

OBLIGATE COMMIT STRICT

OBLIGATED LIABLE

OBLIGATION DUE IOU TIE VOW BAIL BAND BOND CALL DEBT DUTY KNOT LOAD LOAN MUST NOD OATH ONUS SEAL CHECK OUGHT SCORE ARREAR BURDEN CHARGE CONSOL CUSTOM FEALTY PLEDGE ANNUITY BONDAGE PROMISE TRIBUTE CONTRACT HYPOTHEC SECURITY WARRANTY AGREEMENT LIABILITY (— **NOT TO MARRY**) CELIBACY (— **TO RENDER RENT**) CUSTOM (**MORAL** —) BOND DUTY (PL.) STRINGS

OBLIGATORY BINDING BOUNDEN FORCIBLE IMPOSING LIGATORY INCUMBENT MANDATORY

OBLIGE PUT HOLD PAWN DRIVE FAVOR FORCE COMPEL ENGAGE PLEASE GRATIFY REQUIRE CONCLUDE MORTGAGE CONSTRAIN

OBLIGED FAIN BOUND DEBTED BOUNDEN DEBTFUL FAVORED PLEASED PLEDGED BEHOLDEN GRATEFUL OBSTRICT BEHOLDING OBLIGATED

OBLIGING KIND BUXOM CIVIL CLEVER TOWARD AMIABLE FAVOROUS AGREEABLE COURTEOUS FAVORABLE OFFICIOUS

OBLIQUE AWRY BIAS SIDE SKEW ASKEW BEVEL CROSS SLANT ASLANT ASWASH LOUCHE SQUINT THWART ASKANCE CROOKED EMBELIF EVASIVE SCALENE SIDLING SLOPING DIAGONAL INCLINED INDIRECT SIDELONG SIDEWAYS SIDEWISE SLANTING TORTUOUS INDICULAR UNDERHAND (— **IN MINING**) CLINIC (— **STROKE**) SLASH SOLIDUS (— **WORK**) SWASHWORK

OBLIQUELY AGEE AWRY BIAS AGLEE ASIDE ASKEW AWASH SLANT SLOPE ASLANT ASWASH ASKANCE EMBELIF BIASWISE SIDELONG SIDEWAYS SIDEWISE

OBLIQUITY DIRT SWEEP DIRTINESS

OBLITERATE INK BLOT DELE RASE

RAZE WIPE ANNUL BLACK COVER ERASE SMEAR CANCEL DELETE EFFACE SPONGE ABOLISH DESTROY EXPUNGE OUTRAZE SCRATCH OVERSCORE

OBLITERATION BLOT RASURE ERASURE NEGATION SYNIZESIS

OBLIVION LETHE LIMBO PARDON AMNESTY NIRVANA SILENCE OUBLIANCE

OBLIVIOUS AMORT BLISSFUL HEEDLESS OBLIVIAL FORGETFUL

OBLONG CHITON EVELONG AVELONG EVENLONG ELONGATED (**ROUNDED** —) ELLIPSE

OBLOQUY ABUSE BLAME ODIUM INFAMY CALUMNY CENSURE REPROOF CONTEMPT DISGRACE DISHONOR OBLICQUE

OBNOXIOUS FOUL PERT VILE CURST CURSED FAULTY HORRID LIABLE ODIOUS RANCID SEPTIC HATEFUL INVIDIOUS OFFENSIVE REPUGNANT VERMINOUS

OBOE PIPE REED WAIT AULOS SHAWM SURNAI SURNAY HAUTBOY MUSETTE PIFFERO CHIRIMIA HAUTBOIS SCHALMEY SZOPELKA CHALUMEAU (— **DI CACCIA**) TENOROON FAGOTTINO (**BASS** —) RACKETT

OBOLE MAIL MAILLE

OBSCENE PAW FOUL LEWD NAST BAWDY GROSS NASTY ROCKY COARSE FILTHY IMPURE RIBALD SMUTTY VULGAR KNAVISH PROFANE IMMODEST INDECENT LOATHSOME OFFENSIVE REPULSIVE SALACIOUS (— **CULT**) AISCHROLATREIA

OBSCURATION COVER ECLIPSE

OBSCURE DIM FOG BLOT BLUR DARK DEEP HARD HART HAZY HIDE PALE SLUR BEDIM BEFOG BLANK BLIND CLOUD COVER DUSKY FAINT FOGGY GLOOM INNER LOWLY MIRKY MISTY MUDDY MURKY SHADE SMEAR STAIN VAGUE BEMIST CLOUDY DARKEN DARKLE DEADEN DELUDE GLOOMY HUMBLE MYSTIC OCCULT OPAQUE REMOTE SHADOW SOMBER SUBTLE BECLOUD BENIGHT CLOUDED CONCEAL CONFUSE CRABBED CRYPTIC ECLIPSE ENCRUST ENVELOP OBLIQUE OVERLAY OVERTOP SHADOWY SLUBBER TARNISH UNCLEAR UNKNOWN UNNOTED ABSTRUSE DARKLING DISGUISE DOUBTFUL FAMELESS MYSTICAL NAMELESS OBSTRUSE OVERSILE (**MAKE** —) BECLOUD

OBSCURED HAZY HIDDEN BLINDED CLOUDED DUSKISH DARKSOME DISGUISED INFUSCATE

OBSCURITY FOG MIST CLOUD GLOOM SHADE CALIGO SHADOW DIMNESS OPACITY PRIVACY SILENCE

DARKNESS TENEBRES BLINDNESS SECLUSION (PL.) MURLEMEWES

OBSECRATE BEG PRAY BESEECH ENTREAT PETITION

OBSEQUIES MASS OBIT PYRE WAKE RITES SERVICE FUNERALS

OBSEQUIOUS SLICK MENIAL SUPPLE COURTLY DEVOTED DUTEOUS DUTIFUL FAWNING SERVILE SLAVISH VERNILE CRINGING OBEDIENT OBEISANT TOADYING ASSIDUOUS ATTENTIVE COMPLIANT (— **PERSON**) LIMBERHAM

OBSEQUY RITE EXEQUY RITUAL FUNERAL CEREMONY

OBSERVANCE ACT FORM RITE RULE FREET HONOR CUSTOM REGARD KEEPING CEREMONY PRACTICE ADHERENCE ATTENTION DEFERENCE INDICTION SOLEMNITY (— **OF PROPRIETIES**) DECORUM BREEDING ETIQUETTE (**RELIGIOUS** —) NOVENA SACRAMENT (**SUPERSTITIOUS** —) FREET FREIT (PL.) FUNERAL CEREMONY

OBSERVANT ALERT EYEFUL CAREFUL HEEDFUL MINDFUL DILIGENT VIGILANT WATCHFUL

OBSERVATION EYE SPY HEED IDEA NOTE RAOB VIEW SIGHT ESPIAL LOGION NOTICE REGARD REMARK AUSPICE AUTOPSY COMMENT CONTACT DESCANT OPINION EYESIGHT GAZEMENT SCHOLION SCHOLIUM ASSERTION ATTENTION ESPIONAGE (**ECOLOGICAL** —**S**) ANNUATION (**PRELIMINARY** —) PROEM

OBSERVATIONISM SCHAULUST

OBSERVATORY LICK TOWER LOOKOUT PALOMAR

OBSERVE LO EYE SEE SPY ESPY HEED HOLD KEEP LOOK MAKE MARK MIND NARK NOTA NOTE OBEY SPOT TENT TOUT TWIG WAIT YEME ABIDE QUOTE SMOKE STUDY UTTER WATCH ADHERE ADVERT ATHOLD BEHOLD DETECT DEVISE FOLLOW NOTICE NOTIFY REGARD REMARK SURVEY COMMENT DISCERN EXPRESS MENTION PROFESS RESPECT WITNESS PERCEIVE PRESERVE SPECTATE ADVERTISE CELEBRATE SOLEMNIZE (— **CLOSELY**) SMOKE (— **DULLY**) BLEAR

OBSERVER O BIRDER CORNER WATCHER AUDIENCE INFORMER ONLOOKER BYSTANDER SCRUTATOR SPECTATOR

OBSESS RIDE BESET HAUNT HARASS INVEST OBSEDE BESIEGE HAGRIDE POSSESS PREOCCUPY

OBSESSED CRAZY DOTTY HAPPY HIPPED BESOTTED

OBSESSION TIC CRAZE MANIA SIEGE MAGGOT ECSTASY FIXATION

OBSIDIAN CORE LAVA IZTLE IZTLI
LAPIS
OBSOLETE OLD DEAD PAST DATED
PASSE BYGONE EFFETE ABOLETE
ANCIENT ARCHAIC CLASSIC DISUSED
EFFACED EXTINCT OUTWORN
OUTDATED OUTMODED OVERWORN
DISCARDED
OBSTACLE BAR DAM LET BOYG
BUMP DRAG JUMP OBEX SNAG
STAY STOP BLOCK CHECK CLAMP
CRIMP FENCE HITCH HYDRA SPOKE
STICK STILE ABATIS BUNKER FRAISE
HOCKET HURDLE OBJECT RETARD
ANSTOSS BARRIER CHICANE
FIVEBAR STOPPER BLOCKADE
MOLEHILL BARRICADE CONDITION
HINDRANCE ROADBLOCK
TURNAGAIN
(— TO VIRTUE) SLANDER
(GOLF —) HAZARD
(INSURMOUNTABLE —) IMPASSE
OBSTETRICIAN ACCOUCHEUR
OBSTETRICS MAIEUTICS MIDWIFERY
OBSTINATE SET SOT DOUR FIRM
SULY BALKY FIXED ROWDY RUSTY
STIFF STOUT TOUGH ASSISH
CUSSED DOGGED KNOBBY MULISH
STEEVE STUFFY STUPID STURDY
SULLEN UNRULY ASININE BULLISH
CRABBED FROWARD PEEVISH
RESTIVE WILLFUL CROTCHED
OBDURATE PERVERSE PREFRACT
RENITENT STOMACHY STUBBORN
FORERIGHT PIGHEADED STONEWALL
TENACIOUS
(NOT —) SUPPLE
OBSTREPEROUS LOUD WILD NOISY
UNRULY CLAMOROUS
OBSTRUCT BAR DAM DIT GAG JAM
CLOG COOP DITT FILL FOUL JAMB
STOP TRIP BESET BLANK BLOCK
CHAIN CHECK CHOKE CROSS DELAY
HEDGE THROW ARREST CUMBER
FORBAR HAMPER HOBBLE IMPEDE
OPPOSE PESTER RETARD STIFLE
THWART WAYLAY WINDER BARRIER
FORELAY OCCLUDE BLOCKADE
EMBOLIZE ENCUMBER FLOUNDER
OPPILATE BARRICADE EMBARRASS
INCOMMODE
OBSTRUCTION BAR DAM GAG LET
RUB BOOM BUMP SLUG SNAG STAY
STOP BLOCK CHOKE GORCE HITCH
SPOKE HAMPER TAPPEN THWART
BARRACE BARRAGE BARRIER
BLINDER CHOKAGE EMBOLISM
OBSTACLE STOPPAGE EMPHRAXIS
(— IN OILWELL) BRIDGE
(— IN RIVER) GORGE
(— IN TEAT) SPIDER
(— IN VALVE) GAG
(— OF BLOOD VESSEL) EMBOLISM
(— OF PINE LEAVES) TAPPEN
(INNER —) LOAD
OBTAIN BEG BUM BUY EKE GET WIN
EARN FANG FIND GAIN HENT REAP
ANNEX CADGE CATCH ETTLE REACH
AREACH ARECHE ARRIVE ATTAIN

BORROW DERIVE EXPEDE SECURE
SPONGE ACHIEVE ACQUIRE
CAPTURE CHEVISE COMPASS
DEMERIT EXTRACT POSSESS
PREVAIL PROCURE RECEIVE
SUCCEED PURCHASE SCROUNGE
(— BY CHANCE) DRAW
(— BY HEAT) EXCOCT
(— BY REQUEST) IMPETRATE
(— BY THREAT) EXTORT
(— CONTROL) ENGROSS
(— DISHONESTLY) CROOK SHARP
FLEECE NOBBLE SKELDER
(— MONEY FROM) BLEED
(— PERMISSION) CLEAR
OBTAINABLE GOING GETTABLE
AVAILABLE DERIVABLE SECURABLE
OBTAINED (— AT SCENE OF CRIME)
LATENT
OBTRUDE JET SORN EJECT EXPEL
GLARE FLAUNT IMPOSE MEDDLE
THRUST INTRUDE INTERFERE
OBTRUSIVE FRESH PUSHY GARISH
BLATANT FORWARD PUSHING
BUMPTIOUS INTRUSIVE
OBTUND DULL BLUNT QUELL
DEADEN
OBTURATOR MUSHROOM
OBTUSE DIM DULL BLINK BLUNT
CRASS DENSE THICK OPAQUE
STUPID BOEOTIAN HEBETATE
PURBLIND
(NOT —) ACUTE
OBVERSE FACE FRONT CONVERSE
(— OF COIN) MAN HEAD
OBVIATE PREVENT PRECLUDE
FORESTALL
OBVIOUS LOUD OPEN BROAD CLEAR
CRUDE FRANK GROSS NAKED
OVERT PLAIN SLICK STARK LIABLE
PATENT BLATANT EVIDENT EXPOSED
GLARING SHALLOW SUBJECT
VISIBLE APPARENT DISTINCT
MANIFEST PALPABLE BAREFACED
PROMINENT
(NOT —) DEEP INNER ARCANE
HIDDEN MASKED OCCULT SECRET
SUBTLE DELICATE DOUBTFUL
PROFOUND INEVIDENT
OBVOLUTE CONTORTED
OVERLAPPING
OCA OKA TUBER OXALIS SORREL
SOURSOP
OCARINA CAMOTE
OCCASION SEL BOUT CALL GIVE
HINT NEED SELE SITH TIDE TIME
TURN BREAK CASUS CAUSE CHARE
EVENT INFER NONCE RAISE SITHE
SLANT STOUR WHILE YIELD AFFAIR
AUTHOR CHANCE COURSE EXCUSE
PERIOD REASON STOUND CHASOUN
INSPIRE PRETEXT QUARREL
CEREMONY ENGENDER EXIGENCY
FUNCTION INCIDENT INSTANCE
CONDITION ENCHEASON HAPPENING
(— GRIEF) GRIEVE
(— OF EXCITEMENT) ALARM
ALARUM
(DEFINITE —) TIDE

(FAVORABLE —) ADVANTAGE
(FESTIVE —) UTAS BEANO HOLIDAY
SHINDIG BEANFEST
(HAPPY —) SIMHAH SIMCHAH
(SOCIAL —) COFFEE
(SPECIAL —) CEREMONY
OCCASIONAL ODD ORRA STRAY
ANTRIN CASUAL DAIMEN SCARCE
POPPING EPISODIC FUGITIVE
SPORADIC IRREGULAR
OCCASIONALLY EVERY BETIMES
SOMETIME SOMETIMES
OCCASIVE SETTING WESTWARD
OCCIDENTAL WEST PONENT
WESTERN HESPERIAN WESTERNER
OCCLUDE SORB CLOSE ABSORB
OBSTRUCT
OCCLUSAL MORSAL
OCCLUSION CORONARY
ARTICULATION
OCCULT MAGIC ARCANE HIDDEN
LATENT MYSTIC SECRET VOODOO
ALCHEMY CRYPTIC ECLIPSE
UNKNOWN ESOTERIC MYSTICAL
SIBYLLIC CONCEALED RECONDITE
SIBYLLINE
(— SCIENCE) ESOTERICS
OCCULTATION ECLIPSE
OCCULTISM MAGIC CABALA
MYSTERY
OCCUPANT HOLDER INMATE
RENTER TENANT CITIZEN DWELLER
RESIDENT INCUMBENT
(— OF THEATER GALLERY) GOD
OCCUPATION ART JOB LAY USE
CALL GAME LINE NOTE TOIL WORK
BERTH CRAFT GRAFT TRADE
CAREER EMPLOY METIER RACKET
SPHERE TENURE THRIFT CALLING
CONCERN CONTROL MYSTERY
PURSUIT QUALITY SERVICE ACTIVIT
BUSINESS FUNCTION INDUSTRY
INVASION VOCATION
(— OF MIND) ABSORPTION
(SUBORDINATE —) HOBBY
AVOCATION
OCCUPIED BUSY FULL HELD KEPT
RAPT TOOK ACTIVE INTENT
ENGAGED ABSORBED CAPTURED
(FULLY —) ENGROSSED
OCCUPY LIE SIT USE BUSY FILL
HAVE HOLD KEEP TAKE WARM
AMUSE BELAY BESET DWELL
ABSORB BETAKE EMPLOY ENGAGE
EXPEND FULFIL OBTAIN TENANT
COHABIT CONCERN CONTAIN
ENGROSS ENTREAT IMPROVE
INHABIT INVOLVE OVERSIT PERVAD
POSSESS SWALLOW DISSOLVE
GARRISON INTEREST POURPRISE
(— ILLEGALLY) JUMP
(— QUARTERS) CAMP
OCCUR BE GO COME COOK FALL
GIVE MAKE MEET PASS RISE SORT
ARISE BREAK CLASH EXIST INCUR
LIGHT APPEAR ARRIVE BEFALL
BETIDE CHANCE HAPPEN PROCEED
TRANSPIRE
(— AGAIN) RECUR REPEAT

(— BY CHANCE) LIGHT
(— TO) CROSS ENTER STRIKE
OCCURRENCE GO HAP CASE FACT ITEM NOTE REDE EVENT WEIRD EPISODE PASSAGE INCIDENT JUNCTURE OCCASION ENCOUNTER FREQUENCE HAPPENING
(CHANCE —) ADVENTURE CONTINGENT
(COMMON —) USE FREQUENCY
(FREQUENT —) COMMUNITY
(SIMULTANEOUS —) COINCIDENCE
(SUPERNATURAL —) MIRACLE
(UNEXPECTED —) SUDDEN BLIZZARD BOMBSHELL
(UNFORTUNATE —) CASUALTY
(UNUSUAL —) ODDITY
OCCURRING (— AT NIGHTFALL) ACRONICAL
(— AT REGULAR INTERVALS) HORAL
(— AT TWILIGHT) CREPUSCULAR
(— BY TURN) ALTERNATE
(— EVERY EIGHT DAYS) OCTAN
(— EVERY FOURTH YEAR) PENTETERIC
(— FREQUENTLY) COMMON
(— IN USUAL PLACE) ENTOPIC
OCEAN SEA BLUE BRIM DEEP MAIN POND BRINE DRINK ARCTIC INDIAN EXPANSE NEPTUNE PACIFIC ATLANTIC ANTARCTIC
(— FLOATING MATTER) ALGAE LAGAN FLOTSAM
(— ROUTE) LANE
(— SPRAY) IRONWOOD CREAMCUPS
(— SWELL) SEA
(ON THE —) ASEA
OCEANIA MALAYA AUSTRALIA MELANESIA POLYNESIA
(SACRED OBJECT OF —) ZOGO
OCEANIC NAVAL MARINE PELAGIC NAUTICAL AEQUOREAL
OCEANUS TITAN
(DAUGHTER OF —) DORIS OCEANID EURYNOME
(FATHER OF —) URANUS OURANOS
(MOTHER OF —) GAEA GAIA
(SISTER OF —) TETHYS
(SON OF —) NEREUS
(WIFE OF —) TETHYS
OCELLUS EYE EYELET STEMMA EYESPOT
OCELOT CAT TOGER LEOPARD WILDCAT
OCHER RUD SIL KEEL OAKER OCHRE TIVER ABRAUM RADDLE ALMAGRA TANGIER
(BLACK —) WAD WADD
(RED —) RUD KEEL TIVER ABRAUM REDDLE RUBRIC RUDDLE KOKOWAI
(YELLOW —) SIL SPRUCE
OCOTILLO COACHWHIP CANDLEWOOD
OCREA OCHREA SHEATH
OCTAHEDROID HYPERCUBE TESSERACT
OCTAVE UTAS UTIS EIGHT EIGHTH OTTAVA HUITAIN DIAPASON SHEMINITH

(— FLUTE) FLAUTINO
(— OF THE SEVENTH) FOURTEENTH
(— SINGING) MAGADIZE
(DIMINISHED —) SEMIDIAPASON
(TRIPLE —) TRIDIAPASON
OCTAVO EIGHTS
OCTET OCTAVE OCTUOR HUITAIN OTTETTO
OCTAVIA (BROTHER OF —) AUGUSTUS
(HUSBAND OF —) ANTONY
OCTOPUS HEE POLYP POULP PREKE SQUID CUTTLE CATFISH POLYPOD POLYPUS SCUTTLE DIBRANCH OCTOPEAN DEVILFISH
(— ARM) TENTACLE
(SECRETION OF —) INK
OCTOROON METIS MESTEE MUSTEE MESTIZO METISSE OCTAROON
OCTROI TAX GRANT PRIVILEGE
OCTUPLE EIGHTFOLD
OCUBY RUM
OCULAR OPTIC VISUAL OCULARY OPTICAL ORBITAL EYEPIECE
ODD AUK AWK OUT RUM FELL LEFT LONE ORRA RARE CRAZY DIPPY DROLL EXTRA FUNNY IMPAR OUTRE QUEER UNKET UNKID WEIRD IMPAIR QUAINT SINGLE UNEVEN UNIQUE AZYGOUS BIZARRE COMICAL CURIOUS ERRATIC STRANGE UNEQUAL UNUSUAL FANCIFUL FREAKISH PECULIAR SINGULAR UNPAIRED BURLESQUE ECCENTRIC FANTASTIC GROTESQUE LAUGHABLE SQUIRRELY UNMATCHED WHIMSICAL
(— JOBMAN) JOEY
ODDBALL SPOOK
ODDITY GIG QUIP RUMNESS QUIZZITY
(PL.) PURLICUES
ODDMAN UMPIRE ARBITER FLOATER REFEREE
ODDS BISK EDGE CHALK PRICE BISQUE DISCORD DISPUTE QUARREL HANDICAP VARIANCE ADVANTAGE DISPARITY
(— AND ENDS) ORTS BROTT REFUSE SCRAPS GIBLETS SECONDS FEWTRILS REMNANTS SHAKINGS ETCETERAS FRAGMENTS
(AT —) ACROSS
(EXTRAVAGANT —) POUNDAGE
ODE HYMN POEM SONG LYRIC PAEAN PSALM MONODY ODELET CANZONA CANZONE EPICEDE CANTICLE PALINODE PINDARIC SERENATA STASIMON EPICEDIUM EPINICION PARABASIS
ODEON HALL ODEUM GALLERY THEATER
ODIN OTHIN WODAN WODEN WOTAN
(BROTHER OF —) VE VILI
(CREATED BY —) ASK EMBLA
(DAUGHTER-IN-LAW OF —) NANNA
(DESCENDANT OF —) SCYLD
(FATHER OF —) BOR BORR
(HALL OF —) VALHALLA
(HORSE OF —) SLEIPNER

(MOTHER OF —) BESTLA
(PALACE OF —) SYN
(SON OF —) TYR THOR VALI BALDR BALDER
(SWORD OF —) GRAM
(WIFE OF —) FRIA RIND FRIGG RINDR FRIGGA
ODIOUS FOUL LOTH UGLY VILE LOATH INFAND ODIBLE HATABLE HATEFUL HEINOUS HIDEOUS DAMNABLE FLAGRANT INFAMOUS ABHORRENT INVIDIOUS OBNOXIOUS OFFENSIVE REPUGNANT
ODIUM HATRED STIGMA DISLIKE AVERSION DISFAVOR DISGRACE DISHONOR ANTIPATHY
(PUBLIC —) ENVY
ODOMETER ODOGRAPH VIAMETER WAYWISER HODOMETER PEDOMETER
ODONTALGIA TOOTHACHE
ODOR AIR FUME FUNK NOSE OLID TANG WAFF WAFT AROMA EWDER FETOR FLAIR FUMET NIDOR SCENT SMACK SMELL SNUFF SPICE STINK BREATH FLAVOR FOETOR HODURE REPUTE STENCH BOUQUET ESSENCE FUMETTE NOSEGAY PERFUME VERDURE PUNGENCE EFFLUVIUM EMPYREUMA FRAGRANCE REDOLENCE
(— FROM FLOWERS) FUME
(— OF GAME) FUMET
(— OF HAY) NOSE
(BAD —) EWDER FROWST STENCH
(DISGUSTING —) STINK
(FOUL —) FIST
(FRESH —) YMUR
(PUNGENT —) SPICE
(SPICY —) BALM
(STUDY OF —S) OSMICS
ODORIFEROUS BALMY OLENT ODOROUS FRAGRANT
ODOROUS FOUL BALMY OLENT SMELLY ODORANT AROMATIC FRAGRANT NIDOROSE NIDOROUS PERFUMED REDOLENT SCENTFUL SMELLFUL
ODYSSEUS ULYSSES
(DOG OF —) ARGOS
(FATHER OF —) LAERTES SISYPHUS
(FRIEND OF —) MENTOR
(ISLAND OF —) ITHACA
(SON OF —) TELEGONUS TELEMACHUS
(WIFE OF —) PENELOPE
OECIST OEKIST COLONIZER
OEDIPUS OEDIPAL
(BROTHER-IN-LAW OF —) CREON
(DAUGHTER OF —) ISMENE ATIGONE
(FATHER OF —) LAIUS
(FOSTER MOTHER OF —) PERIBOEA
(MOTHER OF —) JOCASTA
(SON OF —) ETEOCLES POLYNICES
(WIFE OF —) JOCASTA
OEIL-DE-BOEUF OCULUS
OEILLADE OGLE ELIAD EYLIAD GLANCE ILLIAD
OENOCHOE OLPE PROCHOOS

OENOMETER VINOMETER
OESTRID FLY
(— **LARVA**) BOT
OESTRUS RUT FURY HEAT STING
DESIRE ESTRUS FRENZY IMPULSE
STIMULUS
OEUVRE OPUS WORK
OF A O BY DE OFF VAN VON FROM
HAVE TILL WITH ABOUT
(— **AGE**) AE
(— **ALL**) AVA ALDER ALLER
(— **DEATH**) M
(— **EACH**) ANA PER SING
(— **THIS DAY**) HODIERNAL
(— **THIS MONTH**) HM
OFF BY AFF FAR ODD WET AFAR
AGEE AWAY DOFF DOWN GONE
ALONG ASIDE RIGHT WONKY
WRONG ABSENT CUCKOO DEPART
REMOTE DISTANT FURTHER
REMOVED SEAWARD TAINTED
ABNORMAL OPPOSITE
(— **GUARD**) TARDY
(— **THE PATH**) ASTRAY
(— **THE SUBJECT**) AFIELD
(— **THE WIND**) ROOM ROOMWARD
(**FAR** —) DISTANT
OFFAL GURRY WASTE REFUSE
CARRION DOGMEAT GARBAGE
LEAVING RUBBISH GRALLOCH
(— **OF FISH**) GURRY STOSH
(**MILLING** —**S**) GRIT
OFFBREAK GOOGLY
OFF-CENTER ECCENTRIC
EXCENTRIC
OFF-COLOR BLUE SUGGESTIVE
OFFEND CAG ERR PET SIN VEX GALL
HARM HUFF HURT MIFF RASP RASS
ABUSE ANGER ANNOY GRATE GRILL
PIQUE SHOCK SPITE TOUCH WRONG
AGUILT ATTACK GRIEVE INJURE
INSULT NETTLE REVOLT AFFRONT
DEFAULT DISDAIN MORTIFY
OUTRAGE PROVOKE REGRATE
STOMACH UMBRAGE VIOLATE
CONFRONT DISTASTE IRRITATE
TRESPASS DISOBLIGE DISPLEASE
OFFENDED HUFF MIFF SORE
AVERTED FROISSE INJURED
INSULTED
OFFENDER SINNER CULPRIT
MISDOER PECCANT HABITUAL
OFFENDANT
(**FIRST** —) STAR
OFFENSE PET SIN HUFF LACK SLIP
WITE ABUSE CRIME ERROR FAULT
GRIEF GUILT MALUM PIQUE SNUFF
ATTACK BIGAMY DELICT FELONY
PIACLE PRITCH REATUS STRUNT
AFFRONT DEFAULT DEMERIT
DUDGEON LARCENY MISDEED
OUTRAGE SCANDAL UMBRAGE
PECCANCY TRESPASS EXTORTION
INDECORUM INDIGNITY THEFTBOTE
(— **AGAINST LAW**) MALUM DELICT
DELICTUM
(— **AGAINST MORALITY**) EVIL CRIME
OFFENSIVE BAD ACID EVIL FOUL
HARD UGLY BILGY CRUDE DIRTY

FETID GROSS NASTY SLIMY COARSE
FROWZY GARISH HORRID RANCID
RIBALD ROTTEN ABUSIVE BEASTLY
FULSOME HATEFUL HIDEOUS
NOISOME RASPING SCARLET
DREADFUL INVADING MEPHITIC
SHOCKING STINKING UNSAVORY
LOATHSOME OBNOXIOUS
REPUGNANT REVOLTING
OFFER GO BID PUT BODE GIVE HAND
LEND PLEA SHOW TAKE TEND
DEFER HEAVE PARTY SHORE START
ADDUCE AFFORD ALLEGE DELATE
INJECT OBLATE OPPOSE PREFER
SUBMIT SUPPLY TENDER ADVANCE
BIDDING COMMEND EXHIBIT
PRESENT PROFFER PROPINE
PROPOSE SUGGEST OVERTURE
VOLUNTEER
(— **EXCUSE**) ALIBI
(— **FOR SALE**) HAWK EXPOSE
(— **IN SACRIFICE**) IMMOLATE
(— **PROOF**) APPROVE
(— **PUBLICLY**) JACTITATE
(— **TO VERIFY**) AVER
(**LAST** —) ULTIMATUM
(**SOLEMN** —) PLEDGE
(**UNACCEPTED** —) POLLICITATION
OFFERING BID ALMS BALI DALI DEAL
GIFT HOST SOMA DOLLY ENTRY
CORBAN NUZZER OFLETE PIACLE
PRESENT RETABLO TRIBUTE
ANATHEMA DEVOTION DONATION
LIBATION OBLATION PESHKASH
PIACULUM SACRIFICE
(— **TO GOD**) CORBAN DEODATE
(— **TO HOUSEHOLD DEITIES**) BALI
(**PEACE** —**S**) PACIFICS
(**RELIGIOUS** —) OBLATION
(**SACRIFICIAL** —) HOLOCAUST
(**THEATRICAL** —) FLUFF
(PL.) HIERA ALTARAGE INFERIAE
OFF-GLIDE EXIT VOCULE DETENTE
OFFHAND CURT GLIB SOON ADLIB
BLUSH HASTY ABRUPT BREEZY
CASUAL BRUSQUE READILY
CARELESS CAVALIER GLANCING
INFORMAL EXTEMPORE IMPROMPTU
UNSTUDIED
OFFICE HAT JOB SEE BOMA DUTY
NONE PART POST ROLE ROOM
SHOP TASK TOGA WIKE WORK
PLACE STINT TRUST WIKEN YAMEN
ABBACY AGENCY BUREAU CHARGE
DAFTAR DIWANI DUFTER METIER
MISTER BULLPEN CAMARIN
CENTRAL DEWANEE DROSTDY
EDILITY PYSTERY SERVICE STATION
SURGERY AEDILITY CAPACITY
CUTCHERY ENSIGNCY FUNCTION
KINGSHIP MINISTRY POSITION
PROVINCE WOOLPACK BAILIWICK
BANKSHALL SITUATION
(— **BOY**) CHOKRA
(— **CHIEF**) BOSS MANAGER
(— **OF BISHOP**) LAWN
(— **OF JUDGE**) BENCH ERMINE
(— **OF PROFESSOR**) CHAIR

(— **OF ROMAN CURIA**) DATARY
DATARIA
(— **OF RULER**) REGENCY
(— **OF THE DEAD**) DIRGE
(— **WORKER**) CLERK STENO TYPIST
SECRETARY
(**BRANCH** —) WING
(**CASHIER'S** —) CAISSE
(**CLERICAL** —) CASSOCK
(**DIVINE** —) AKOLUTHIA
(**ECCLESIASTICAL** —) FROCK
BENEFICE EXORCIST
(**HIGH** —) DIGNITY
(**LITURGICAL** —) SEXT SERVICE
(**MORNING** —) ORTHRON ORTHROS
(**NAVAL** —**S**) BEACH
(**PRIESTLY** —) SACERDOCY
(**PRINTING** —) CHAPEL IMPRIMERY
(**RECORD** —) CHANCERY
(**RESIGN AN** —) DEMIT
(**TIMEKEEPER'S** —) PENNYHOLE
OFFICEHOLDER IN WINNER
OFFICIAL PLACEMAN
OFFICER (ALSO SEE OFFICIAL) COP
TAB AIDE EXEC EXON FLAG HOLD
NASI SWAB VOGT AGENT CHIEF
CRIER DEWAN DIWAN GRAND
GRAVE GROOM JURAT SEWER
TAXOR USHER ALCADE BEADLE
BEAGLE BUTLER CENSOR DEPUTY
DIRECT ENSIGN GAILLI GEREFA
HERALD KOTWAL LAWMAN LICTOR
MANAGE ORATOR PARNAS REDTAB
SYNDIC TINDAL ALNAGER ASSIZER
BAILIFF COMMAND CONDUCT
CORONER DUUMVIR EPAULET
FEDERAL FEODARY GAVELER
GENERAL JEMADAR KLEAGLE
LOBSTER MUSTANG NAPERER
PANTLER PATROON REGIDOR
SANCTUM SCHEPEN SHERIFF
SPEAKER STEWARD WHIPPER
WOODMAN ADJUTANT ALDERMAN
ALGUACIL ANDREEVE BANNERET
CHAFFWAX COFFERER CURSITOR
DOORWARD FORESTER GOVERNOR
GRASSMAN MERESMAN MINISTER
QUESTEUR REPORTER TIPSTAFF
VISCOUNT WOODWARD CONSTABLE
DIKEGRAVE FINANCIER INTENDANT
SCHOOLMAN TAHSILDAR
(— **OF CHURCH**) ABBOT ELDER
DEACON SEXTON ANTISTES
DEFENSOR LAMPADARY SACRISTAN
(— **OF COURT**) MACER BAILIFF
FEODARY FILACER CURSITOR
DEMPSTER EXAMINER SERGEANT
ASSOCIATE BYRLAWMAN
SURROGATE
(— **OF FORESTS**) AGISTER AGISTOR
(— **OF KING'S STABLES**) AVENER
(**BARDIC** —) DRUID
(**CHIEF** —) NASI DEWAN DAROGA
PARNAS
(**CUSTOMS** —) GAGER SHARK
GAUGER JERQUER DOUANIER
SEARCHER SURVEYOR TIDESMAN
(**GREEK** —) STRATEGOS STRATEGU
(**JAPANESE** —) SHIKKEN

(MASONIC —) EAST KING DEACON STEWARD

(MILITARY —) NAIG NAIK COMES MAJOR SUBAH ENSIGN NAIQUE RANKER SARDAR SIRDAR CAPTAIN COLONEL GENERAL JEMADAR MARSHAL SUBADAR WARRANT COMMANDER RABSHAKEH SHAVETAIL

(MINOR —) CHINOVNIK

(NAVAL —) CPO EXON MATE SWAB BOSUN ENSIGN PURSER YEOMAN ADMIRAL CAPTAIN MUSTANG SPOTTER YOUNKER SUNDOWNER

(POLICE —) PIG RURAL EXEMPT JAVERT KOTWAL RUNNER SBIRRO ALYTARCH SEARCHER THANADAR DETECTIVE

(PUBLIC —) JUDGE FISCAL NOTARY PODESTA

(ROMAN —) LICTOR

(SHERIFF'S —) FANG BEAGLE BAILIFF BULLDOG HUISSIER

(STAFF —) TAB AIDE REDTAB ADJUTANT

(TURKISH —) AGA AGHA MUTE VIZIR VIZIER BINBASHI

(PL.) BRAID BRASS STAFF

FFICIAL (ALSO SEE OFFICER) AGA BEG DEY VIP AMIN BOSS KUAN KWAN TRUE AGENT AHONG AMALA AMBAN AMEEN AMLAH CLERK EDILE EPHOR GYANI HAJIB HOMER JURAT LIMMU LINER MAYOR NAZIR REEVE SAHIB AEDILE ARCHON ATABEG BASHAW CENSOR CONSUL EPARCH EPONYM FISCAL FORMAL GABBAI GRIEVE HAZZAN HERALD LAWMAN MASTER NOTARY PANDIT PREVOT RABMAG SATRAP SCRIBE SEALER SINGER TAOTAI TAOYIN TRONER VERGER WARDEN WEDANA ALMONER APOSTLE ASIARCH BURGESS CERTAIN JEMADAR LANDRAT MARSHAL MOORMAN PRISTAW REFEREE STALLAR STARTER SUBASHI APPROVED CARDINAL CELLARER CUSTOMER DOGBERRY GOVERNOR LINESMAN MANDARIN PRYTANIS VESTIARY EXECUTIVE MAJORDOMO

(— APPROVAL) VISA VISE

(— DECREE) WRIT UKASE

(BLUNDERING —) DOGBERRY

(POMPOUS —) BUMBLE

(PL.) KEYS PHAR OMLAH

FFICIATE ACT FILL SERVE SUPPLY PERFORM CELEBRATE

FFICIATOR DEICIDE

FFICIOUS BUSY COOL PERT SAUCY FORMAL FORTHY PUSHING ARROGANT IMPUDENT INFORMAL MEDDLING OFFICIAL INBEARING

FFING OFF FUTURE PICTURE

FFISH CLAMMY UPSTAGE

FSCOURINGS MUD SCURF

FF-SEASON LAYOFF

FSET SLAB STEP ALTAR CRIMP ERASE POISE CANCEL CONTRA

JOGGLE REDEEM SETOFF BALANCE COUNTER LATERAL RETREAT SETBACK PROPAGULE

(— ON BULB) SPLIT

OFFSHOOT GET PUP ROD SON LIMB SPUR BOUGH ISSUE SCION SHOOT SPRIG BRANCH FILIAL GROWTH MEMBER SPROUT ADJUNCT APOPHYSIS FILIATION OUTGROWTH

(— OF LAKE) BAYOU

OFFSHORE DEEPWATER

OFFSPRING BOY FRY IMP KID KIN SON BRAT CHIT HEIR SEED SLIP BIRTH BREED BROOD CHILD FRUIT ISSUE SCION SPAWN BEGATS DUSTEE EMBRYO FOSTER GRIQUA JUMART PROLES RESULT STRAIN STRIND MORISCO NISHADA OUTCOME PRODUCE PRODUCT PROGENY YOUNGER CHILDREN DAUGHTER DEMISANG GENITURE INCREASE KINDLING BAIRNTEAM MUSTAFINA

(— OF FAIRIES) CHANGELING

(— OF NEGRO AND MULATTO) GRIFFE

(— OF WITCH) HAGSEED HOLDIKEN

(MYTHICAL —) JUMART

(PREMATURE —) CASTLING

OFICINA WORKS OFFICE FACTORY

OFLETE WAFER OBLATION OFFERING

OFTEN OFT AFTEN OFTLY COMMON EFTSOONS FREQUENT REPEATED

(VERY —) CONTINUALLY

OGDOAD EIGHT OCTOAD OGDOAS OCTONARY

OGEE (ALSO SEE MOLDING) CYMA GULA TALON MOLDING

OGIVAL HEATER

OGLE EYE GAZE LEER LOOK MASH STARE GLANCE EXAMINE MARLOCK SMICKER OEILLADE

OGRE ORC BRUTE DEMON GHOUL GIANT HUGON TYRANT YAKSHA BUGABOO BUGBEAR MONSTER WINDIGO

OGRESS PELLET GUNSTONE

OGTIERN LORD MASTER

OGYGIAN ANCIENT PRIMEVAL

OH OU OW ACH OUCH

OHIO		
CAPITAL: COLUMBUS		
COLLEGE: KENT HIRAM KENYON XAVIER ANTIOCH OBERLIN DEFIANCE		
COUNTY: ERIE ROSS MIAMI STARK SUMMIT CUYAHOGA HAMILTON		
INDIAN TRIBE: ERIE WYANDOT		
NATIVE: BUCKEYE		
NICKNAME: BUCKEYE		
PRESIDENT: TAFT GRANT HAYES HARDING GARFIELD HARRISON MCKINLEY		
RIVER: MIAMI MAUMEE SCIOTO CUYAHOGA MUSKINGUM		
STATE BIRD: CARDINAL		
STATE FLOWER: CARNATION		
STATE TREE: BUCKEYE		

TOWN: ADA LIMA AKRON BEREA NILES XENIA CANTON DAYTON LORAIN TOLEDO COLUMBUS SANDUSKY CLEVELAND

OIL BEN FAT ILE ULE BALM CHIA DIKA FUEL ZEST BRIBE CRUDE JUICE OLEUM SMEAR STOCK TRAIN ULYIE ULZIE ACEITE ANOINT BINDER BUTTER CARDOL CHRISM EUPION GREASE LIQUOR SAFROL SMOOTH ZACHUN CEDRIUM ESSENCE LANOLIN MYRRHOL PHLOROL RETINOL VETIVER BERGAMOT COUMARAN ERIGERON GINGEROL PHTHALAN SDRAVETS TETRALIN CARVACROL LUBRICATE PETROLEUM

(— BEETLE) MELOE MELOID

(— CAKE) SEEDCAKE

(— CAN) OILER

(— CASK) RIER

(— LAMP) LUCIGEN

(— OF TURPENTINE) CAMPHENE CAMPHINE

(— PALM) OILBERRY

(— PAN) SUMP

(— PLANT) SESAME

(— ROCK) SHALE LIMESTONE

(— TREE) EBOE POON TUNG MAHWA

(— VESSEL) DRUM OLPE CRUET CRUSE TANKER CRESSET

(— WELL) DUSTER GASSER GUSHER WILDCAT

(BUTTER —) GHEE

(COAL —) PHOTOGEN

(CONSECRATED —) CHRISM

(FISH —) GURRY

(FIXED —) COCUM KOKAM KOKUM

(FLOWER —) ABSOLUTE

(FRAGRANT —) ATAR OTTO ATTAR OTTAR CAFFEOL CAFFEONE GERANIOL

(INFERIOR —) MIDDLING

(LINSEED —) CARRON LINOLEUM

(MINERAL —) NAPHTHA KEROSENE

(PINE —) FROTHER

(SOLID —) KIKUEL

(VEGETABLE —) MACASSAR

(VULCANIZED —) FACTICE

(WHALE —) SPERM

OILBIRD FATBIRD GUACHARO

OILFISH ESCOLAR

OILSEED TIL TEEL SESAME LINSEED RAPESEED

OILSKIN OIL OILER SQUAM OILCASE OILCOAT SLICKER

OILSTONE HONE SHALE WHETSTONE

OILY FAT GLIB BLAND FATTY LOEIC SOAPY SUAVE GREASY OILISH OLEOSE OLEOUS SMARMY SMOOTH SUPPLE PINGUID SERVILE SLIPPERY UNCTUOUS COMPLIANT PLAUSIBLE

OINTMENT BALM MULL NARD SALVE BALSAM CERATE CEROMA UNGUENT SPIKENARD

OILBIRD FATBIRD GUACHARO

OILFISH ESCOLAR
OILSEED TIL TEEL SESAME LINSEED RAPESEED
OILSKIN OIL OILER SQUAM OILCASE OILCOAT SLICKER
OILSTONE HONE SHALE WHETSTONE
OILY FAT GLIB BLAND FATTY OLEIC SOAPY SUAVE GREASY OILISH OLEOSE OLEOUS SMARMY SMOOTH SUPPLE PINGUID SERVILE SLIPPERY UNCTUOUS COMPLIANT PLAUSIBLE
OINTMENT UNG BALM MULL NARD PASTE SALVE SMEAR BALSAM CERATE CEROMA CHARGE CHRISM GREASE POMADE REMEDY UNGUENT EYESALVE POPULEON REMOLADE SPIKENARD WHITFIELD
(— **OF GODS**) AMBROSIA
OJIBWAY CHIPPEWA SAULTEUR CHIPPEWAY
OKA OCHA OQUE OQUI OCQUE
OKAPI GIRAFFINE
OKAY OK YES HUNK OKEH HUNKY APPROVE CORRECT SANCTION AUTHORIZE
OKIA OKET OUNCE
OKINAWA (**CAPITAL OF** —) NAHA

OKLAHOMA
CAPITAL: OKLAHOMACITY
COLLEGE: CAMERON LANGSTON PHILLIPS
COUNTY: KAY ATOKA CADDO ALFALFA OKFUSKEE OKMULGEE
INDIAN TRIBE: WACO WICHITA TAWAKONI
LAKE: EUFAULA OOLOGAH
MOUNTAINS: OZARK OUACHITA
NATIVE: OKIE SOONER
RIVER: RED GRAND WASHITA ARKANSAS CANADIAN CIMARRON
STATE BIRD: FLYCATCHER
STATE FLOWER: MISTLETOE
STATE TREE: REDBUD
TOWN: ADA ALVA ENID HUGO ALTUS MIAMI PONCA TULSA ELRENO GUYMON IDABEL LAWTON SAPULPA SHAWNEE ANADARKO FORTSILL MUSKOGEE

OKRA GOBO OKRO BAMIA BENDY GOBBO GOMBO GUBBO GUMBO OCHRA BENDEE MALLOW BANDAKA BANDICOY BANDIKAI
OLD AGY ELD AGED AULD COLD WOLD YALD ANILE HOARY STALE WOULD FORMER FOROLD INFIRM MATURE SENILE SHABBY VETUST AGEABLE ANCIENT ANTIQUE ARCHAIC ELDERLY FORWORN UMWHILE DECREPIT MEDIEVAL OBSOLETE DODDERING HACKNEYED SENESCENT VENERABLE
(— **AND MELLOW**) CRUSTY
(— **BAILEY**) GAOL JAIL PRISON
(— **CLOTHESMAN**) POCO

(— **FAITHFUL**) GEYSER
(— **HAND**) LONGTIMER
(— **MAID**) SPINSTER THORNBACK
(— **MAN**) ANTIQUITY WHITEBEARD
(— **SOD**) EIRE ERIN IRELAND
(— **SQUAW**) DIVER HOUND MOMMY CALLOO CALLOW COWEEN DUCKER QUANDY OLDWIFE SCOLDER COCKAWEE LONGTAIL SHARPTAIL SOUTHERLY
(— **WOMAN**) HAG CRONE GAMMER
(**GROWING** —) SENESCENT
(**OF** —) WHILOM ERSTWHILE
OLD BAY STATE MASSACHUSETTS
OLD DOMINION STATE VIRGINIA
OLDER MORE ALDER ELDER SENIOR ANCESTOR
OLD-FASHIONED CORNY DOWDY FUSTY PASSE FOGRAM FOGRUM QUAINT STODGY ANCIENT ANTIQUE ARCHAIC ELDERLY VINTAGE FRUMPISH OBSOLETE CRINOLINE PRIMITIVE
OLD FRANKLIN STATE TENNESSEE
OLD LINE STATE MARYLAND
OLD-WOMANISH ANILE
OLEANDER LAUREL DOGBANE ROSEBAY
OLEFIN ALKENE
OLEIC RAPIC RAPINIC
OLEORESIN GUM ANIME APIOL ELEMI TOLUS BALSAM GURJUN IRIDIN COPAIBA GALIPOT LABDANUM TACAMAHAC
OLFACTION SMELL OSMESIS SMELLING ESPHRESIS
OLIGARCHY KREMLIN
OLIGARCHIC FEUDAL
OLIGOCLASE SUNSTONE
OLIO STEW MEDLEY MELANGE MIXTURE MISHMASH PASTICCIO POTPOURRI
OLIPHANT HORN ELEPHANT
OLIPRANCE ROMP SHOW FROLIC JOLLITY
OLIVE OLEA MORON BRUNET LIERRE OLIVER OXHORN PIMOLA RESEDA BAROUNI CITRINE MISSION MORILLON OLEASTER
(— **FLY**) DACUS
(**AMERICAN** —) DEVILWOOD
(**OVERRIPE** —) DRUPE
OLIVER NOLL HAMMER HOLLIPER
OLIVET PEARL
OLLA JAR JUG OLE POT OLAY PUCHERA PUCHERO
OLLA PODRIDA HASH OLIO MEDLEY POTPOURRI
OLM PROTEUS SALAMANDER
OLOGY ISM SCIENCE
OLYMPIAN CELESTIAL
OLYNTHUS ASCULA
OMAGUA CAMBEVA
OMAN (**CAPITAL OF** —) MASQAT MUSCAT
(**LANGUAGE OF** —) ARABIC BALUCHI
(**MOUNTAIN OF** —) SHAM HAFIT HARIM NAKHL TAYIN AKHDAR

(**NATIVE OF** —) ADNAN QAHTAN BALUCHI
(**TOWN IN** —) SUR NIGWA MASQAT MATRAH SALALAH
OMASUM BOOK BOUK BIBLE FARDE MANYPLIES
OMBER SOLO UMBRE HOMBRE MEDIATOR QUADRILLE
OMEGA END LAST
OMELET AMLET AMELET FOOYUNG FOOYOUNG FRITTATA
OMEN BODE LUCK SIGN ABODE AUGUR BODER FREET FREIT GUES' TOKEN WEIRD WHATE AUGURY HANDEL HANSEL AUSPICE PORTEN▪ PRESAGE PRODIGY WARNING CEREMONY FOREBODE SOOTHSAY HARBINGER
OMENTUM WEB CAUL ZIRBUS EPIPLOON
OMINOUS DIRE DOUR GRIM FATAL BODING DISMAL SHREWD AUGURA▪ BALEFUL BANEFUL BODEFUL DIREFUL DOOMFUL FATEFUL MENACING SINISTER THUNDERY PROPHETIC
OMISSION OUT CHASM SALTUS DEFAULT FAILURE MISPICK NEGLECT SILENCE PASSOVER OVERSIGHT
(— **OF A LETTER**) APOCOPE
(— **OF SYLLABLES**) SYNCOPE
(**TACIT** —) SILENCE
OMIT CUT LET BALK BATE DROP EDIT KILL MISS PASS SKIP SLIP ABATE ELIDE OBMIT SPARE BELEV▪ CANCEL DELETE EXCEPT FORGET IGNORE DISCARD EXPUNGE NEGLECT DISCOUNT OVERLOOK OVERSKIP OVERSLIP DISREGARD
OMITTED VIDE
OMMATIDIUM FACET FACETTE
OMNIBUS BUS BUSS BARGE HERDI JOGGER PIRATE AUTOBUS MOTORBUS KITTEREEN
OMNIPOTENT GOD ABLE DEITY GREAT ARRANT MIGHTY ALMIGHTY POWERFUL UNEQUALED UNLIMITE▪
OMNISCIENT WISE LEARNED POWERFUL PANSOPHIC
OMOPLATE SCAPULA
OMPHALOS HUB BOSS KNOB NAVE CENTER UMBILICUS
ON O AN IN TO ONE SUR ATOP AWAY OVER UPON ABOUT ABOVE AHEAD ALONG ANENT WITHIN FORWARD
(— **A HATCH**) ABROOD
(— **ACCOUNT OF**) IN FOR
(— **ALL SIDES**) ABOUT AROUND
(— **AND ON**) EVER FOREVER TEDIOUS
(— **EARTH**) BELOW
(— **END**) TOGETHER
(— **FOOT**) UP AFOOT TOWARD FOOTBACK
(— **HAND**) ALONG
(— **HIGH**) ALOFT
(— **THE CONTRARY**) BUT RATHER

(— THE MOVE) AFOOT
(— THE OTHER HAND) BUT AGAIN HOWEVER ALTHOUGH
(— THE OTHER SIDE) OVER ACROSS
(— THE WAY) AWAY AGATE
(— TIME) PROMPT
(— TOP OF) ATOP ABOVE ALOFT
(— WHAT ACCOUNT) WHY
)NAGER ASS GOUR KULAN KOULAN ONAGRA ALACRAN CATAPULT SCORPION
)NCE ANE EEN ERST AINCE ONCET WHILE YANCE FORMER WHILOM QUONDAM UMWHILE FORMERLY SOMETIME UMQUHILE WHENEVER ERSTWHILE
(— MORE) YET AGAIN ENCORE ITERUM
)NDRATA FIBER
)NE J AE AN HE UN AIN ANE ANY EIN MAN OON TAE UNA UNE WON YAE YAN YEN YIN YOU SAME SOLE SOME TANE TEAN THIS TONE TOON UNAL UNIT WHON WONE ALONE ALPHA UNITY WOONE FELLOW PERSON SINGLE UNIQUE UNITED NUMERAL PRONOUN SIMPLUM UNBROKEN SINGLETON UNDIVIDED UNMARRIED
(— AFTER ANOTHER) ABOUT TANDEM SERIALLY SERIATIM
(— BORN A SERF) NEIF NEIFE
(— BY ONE) APIECE SINGLY OVERHEAD
(— CONDEMNED WRONGFULLY) CALAS
(— CURIOUS TO KNOW ALL) QUIDNUNC
(— DETESTED) WARLING
(— DEVOTED TO PARTICULAR ART) IST
(— EASILY TRICKED) CULLY
(— ENGAGED IN MARAUDING) LOOTIE
(— ENROLLED IN ARMY) DRAFTEE
(— GIVEN TO DEVILTRY) HELLION
(— INSTRUCTED IN SECRET SYSTEM) EPOPT
(— LATE) SERO
(— NOT A REGULAR MASON) COWAN
(— OF PAIR) FELLOW DOUBLET
(— OVERZEALOUS) HYPER
(— SENT FORTH) APOSTLE
(— TENTH) TITHE
(— THAT UNDERGOES CHANGE) MUTANT
(— THOUSAND) MIL
(— TWENTY-FOURTH) CARAT
(— UNKNOWN) QUIDAM
(— VERSED IN LITERATURE) SAVANT
(— WHO BRINGS MEAT TO TABLE) DAPIFER
(— WHO DISPLAYS FASTIDIOUSNESS) EPICURE
(— WHO DOCTORS SOMETHING) COOK
(— WHO EXCELS) ACE
(— WHO FABRICATES) SMITH

(— WHO FOLLOWS ARMY) SUTLER
(— WHO FORSAKES FAITH) APOSTATE
(— WHO FRUSTRATES PLAN) MARPLOT
(— WHO HAS ATTAINED PERFECTION) SIDDHA
(— WHO IS AWAY) ABSENTEE
(— WHO LOADS SHIP) BUNKER
(— WHO MAKES LIVING BY TRICKERY) CADGER
(— WHO MANAGES) GERENT
(— WHO REGULATES GUN) TRAINER
(— WHO REMOVES NUISANCE) ABATOR
(— WHO REPRESENTS NEWEST) NEO
(— WHO TESTS) CONNER
(— WHOSE MIND IS IMPAIRED BY AGE) DOTARD
(— WITH FIRST-HAND INFORMATION) INSIDER
(BLESSED —) BHAGAVAT
(EVIL —) WOND SHAITAN SHEITAN
(EXTRAORDINARY —) BUTCHA TICKANINNY
(LOVED —) MINION
(SWEET —) HONEYCOMB
(TIMELESS —) AKAL
ONEGITE AMETHYST GEMSTONE
ONENESS UNION UNITY CONCORD ONEHOOD UNICITY UNITUDE IDENTITY SAMENESS AGREEMENT
ONE-NIGHT STAND GIG
ONEROUS HARD HEAVY ARDUOUS ONEROSE WEIGHTY EXACTING GRIEVOUS LABORIOUS
ONE-SIDED ECCENTRIC UNILATERAL
ONETIME FORMER FORMERLY ERSTWHILE
ONFALL ONSET ATTACK ASSAULT
ON-GLIDE TENSION ENTRANCE
ONION BOLL CEPA LEEK LILY CIBOL PEARL ALLIUM LILIUM PORRET BERMUDA HOLLEKE PICKLER SHALLOT AYEGREEN RARERIPE SCALLION VALENCIA
(ROPE OF —S) REEVE
(SEASONED WITH —S) LYONNAISE
(STRING OF —S) TRACE
ONKOS TOPKNOT
ONLOOKER BOOK GAZER WITNESS AUDIENCE BEHOLDER OVERSEER BYSTANDER SPECTATOR
ONLY ALL BUT JUST LONE MERE ONCE SAVE SOLE AFALD ALONE ARRAH FIRST MERED NOBUT OLEPY ANERLY BARELY MERELY NOBBUT SIMPLE SINGLE SINGLY SOLELY ALLENARLY EXCEPTING
(— THIS) MERE
(BEING —) SIMPLE
ONMUN HANGUL HANKUL
ONOMATOPOEIC ECHOIC IMSONIC MIMETIC IMITATIVE
ONRUSH BIRR SHAKE ATTACK TIDEWAY
ONSET DASH DINT FALL FARD RESE RUSH BRAID BRUNT FAIRD FRUSH

START STORM STOUR VENUE ACCESS AFFRET ATTACK CHARGE COURGE IMPACT INSULT ONFALL POWDER THRUST ASSAULT BRATTLE BEGINNING ENCOUNTER ONSLAUGHT
ONSETTER CAGER HITCHER
ONSLAUGHT LASH BLAST ONSET ATTACK ASSAULT DESCENT SISERARA SALIAUNCE
ONSTEAD ONSET FARMHOUSE HOMESTEAD
ONTARIO (CANAL IN —) TRENT RIDEAU
(CAPITAL OF —) TORONTO
(LAKE IN —) SIMCOE
(TOWN IN —) GALT LONDON OTTAWA WINDSOR HAMILTON KINGSTON KITCHENER
ONTO ATOP ABOARD
ONTOGENY DEVELOPMENT
ONUS DUTY LOAD BLAME BURDEN CHARGE WEIGHT INCUBUS
ONWARD AWAY AHEAD ALONG FORTH UPWARD FORTHON FORWARD TOWARDS FORERIGHT
ONYX ONIX NICOLO TECALI ONYCHIN JASPONYX SARDONYX
(MEXICAN —) ALABASTER
OOCYTE PROGAMETE GAMETOCYTE
OODLES HEAP LOTS MANY SCADS LASHINGS SLITHERS ABUNDANCE
OOGONIUM NUCULE OOCYST OOGONE
OOLAK WOLLOCK
OOLONG TEA
OOMPH PEP VIGOR ENERGY
OOPAK TEA
OORALI CURARE
OORIAL SHA SHEEP URIAL
OOTHECA OVISAC
OOZE OZ BOG MUD SOP DRIP EMIT LEAK MIRE SEEP SLEW SLOB SLUE WEEP EXUDE GLEET MARSH SLIME SWEAT WEEZE EXHALE SICKER SLEECH SLOUGH SLUDGE SQUASH SQUDGE STRAIN SCREEVE TEICHER PERCOLATE
(— OUT) SEW SPEW SPUE
OOZING WEEPY SQUDGY SEEPAGE SPEWING WEEPING
OOZY OASY SEEPY WASHY SLEECHY ULIGINOUS
OPAH CRAVO SUNFISH KINGFISH MARIPOSA MOONFISH
OPAL GEM NOBLE RESIN FIORITE GIRASOL HYALITE ISOPYRE JASPOPAL MENILITE SEMIOPAL CACHOLONG GEYSERITE
OPALESCENT OPALED OPALINE IRISATED
OPALEYE GREENFISH
OPAQUE DIM DARK DULL DENSE MUDDY SHADY THICK VAGUE OBTUSE STUPID CLOUDED OBSCURE ABSTRUSE EYESHADE
OPEN GO DUP LAX OPE AIRY AJAR BARE FAIR FLUE FREE GIVE PERT UNDO VIDE AGAPE APERT BEGIN

BLOWN BREAK BROAD BURST
CHINK CLEAR CRACK FLARE FRANK
FRESH LANCE LOOSE MUSHY
NAKED OVERT PLAIN RELAX SPALD
SPLAT SPLAY START UNBAR UNPEG
UNTIE APPERT CANDID DIRECT
ENTAME EXPAND EXPOSE FACIAL
FORTHY GAPING HONEST LIABLE
OUVERT PATENT PUBLIC SINGLE
SPREAD UNBOLT UNFOLD UNFURL
UNGLUE UNLOCK UNROLL UNSEAL
UNSHUT UNSPAR UNSTOP UNTINE
UNWINK VACANT ARTLESS
BLOSSOM DISPART FIELDEN
OBVIOUS OUTLINE SINCERE
UNCLOSE UNHINGE APPARENT
COMMENCE DISCLOSE EXPLICIT
EXTENDED INITIATE MANIFEST
PERVIOUS RESERATE UNFASTEN
(— A VEIN) BROACH
(— AIR) ALFRESCO
(— AND CLEANSE) WILLOW
(— CLOTH) SCUTCH
(— COUNTRY) VELDT WEALD
(— EYES OR LIPS) SEVER
(— THE WAY) INVITE PIONEER
(— TO PURSUIT) FAIR
(— UP) START DEVELOP DISPART
DISCLOSE
(— VIOLENTLY) SPORT
(— WIDE) YAWN EXPAND STRETCH
(— WIDELY) GAPE
(FULLY —) WIDE AGAPE YAWNING
(HALF —) MID AJAR
(TOO —) OVERBARISH
OPENBILL OPENBEAK
OPENED APPAUME ECHAPPE
OPENER KEY KNOB LATCH SESAME
APERIENT
(— IN POKER) PAIR JACKS
(FURROW —) SHOE STUBRUNNER
(OYSTER —) HUSKER
OPENHANDED FREE LIBERAL
GENEROUS RECEPTIVE
OPENING OS CUT EYE GAP YAT
ANUS BORE DAWN DOOR DROP
FENT FLUE GATE HOLE LOOP PASS
PORE PORT PYLA RIFT RIMA SLAP
SLIT SLOT SPAN VENT VOID YAWN
YEAT BLEED BRACK BREAK CHASM
CHINK CLEFT CROSS DEBUT GRILL
HILUM INLET LIGHT MOUTH SCOOT
SINUS START THIRL WIDTH ADITUS
AVENUE BREACH CASING CHANCE
GRILLE HIATUS INTAKE LACUNA
MEATUS OILLET OUTLET PORTAL
SLUICE SPREAD CREVASS CREVICE
DISPLAY FISSURE ORIFICE OUTCAST
SWALLET APERTURE BUNGHOLE
CREVASSE ENTRANCE OVERTURE
PLUGHOLE SCISSURE TEASEHOLE
(— IN EARTH) GROTTO CHIMNEY
SWALLOW
(— BELOW PENTHOUSE) GALLERY
(— FOR ESCAPE) MUSE MEUSE
(— FROM SEA) INDRAFT
(— IN ANTHER) STOMIUM
(— IN DECK) SCUTTLE

(— IN FLOOR OR ROOF) HATCH
SKYLIGHT
(— IN GARMENT) FENT ARMHOLE
(— IN LOCK TUMBLER) GATING
(— IN MINE) EYE ADIT RAISE SHAFT
WINZE WINNING
(— IN MOLD) POUR
(— IN PICTURE FRAME) SIGHT
(— IN PILLAR OF COAL) JENKIN
JUNKING
(— IN ROCK) GRIKE
(— IN SALMON TRAP) SLAP
(— IN SEA CAVE) GLOUP
(— IN SKIRT) PLACKET
(— IN SPONGE) APOPYLE
(— IN STAGE) DIP
(— IN TENNIS COURTS) GRILLE
HAZARD GALLERY
(— IN TROUSERS) SPARE
(— IN VAULT) LUNET LUNETTE
(— IN WALL) BOLE DREAMHOLE
(— OF EAR) BUR BURR
(— OF ESOPHAGUS) CARDIA
(— OF GEYSER) CRATER
(— OF PRAIRIE) BAY
(— OF SHELL) GAPE
(— THROUGH BULWARKS)
GANGWAY GUNPORT SCUPPER
(— TO ASH PIT) GLUT
(— WIDE) DEHISCENT
(— WITH LID) SCUTTLE
(— WITHOUT TREES) BLANK
(ARCHED —) ALCOVE ARCADE
(CHECKERS —) ALMA DYKE FIFE
CROSS CENTER SOUTER BRISTOL
GLASGOW PAISLEY WHILTER
DEFIANCE SWITCHER
(CHESS —) DEBUT GAMBIT
DEFENCE DEFENSE
(EROSIONAL —) FENSTER
(FUNNELLIKE —) CHOANA
(GRILL —) GUICHET
(JAR —) PITHOIGIA
(MOUTHLIKE —) STOMA OSTIUM
(SMALL —) PORE SLOT CHINK
STOMA CRANNY EYELET LACUNA
CATHOLE CREVICE DOGHOLE
FORAMEN PINHOLE QUARREL
FENESTRA
(WINDOWLIKE —) SPLITE FENESTRA
OPENLY FREELY BROADLY FRANKLY
PUBLICE ROUNDLY STRAIGHT
OPEN-MINDED LIBERAL
OPENMOUTHED GAPING GREEDY
RAVENOUS CLAMOROUS
OPENNESS FREEDOM PATENCY
DAYLIGHT FRANKNESS ROUNDNESS
OPENWORK LATTICE TRACERY
CAGEWORK FILIGREE FRETTING
FRETWORK
OPEN-WORKED AJOURISE
OPERA AIDA FAUST LAKME MANON
NORMA THAIS TOSCA BOHEME
CARMEN DAPHNE ERNANI LOUISE
MIGNON OTELLO RIENZI SALOME
ELEKTRA FIDELIO BURLETTA
FALSTAFF IOLANTHE LOKACOLO
PARSIFAL TRAVIATA WALKYRIE
LOHENGRIN PAGLIACCI RHEINGOLD

RIGOLETTO SIEGFRIED TROVATORE
(— DIVISION) SCENA
(— GLASS) GLASS JUMELLE
LORGNET LORGNETTE
(— HAT) GIBUS CLAQUE
(— SONG) ARIA
(— STAR) DIVA
(16TH CENTURY —) PASTORALE
(COMIC —) BUFFA
(HORSE —) WESTERN
(SPANISH —) ZARZUELA
(TV OR RADIO —) SOAP
OPERANT EFFICIENT OPERATIVE
OPERATE GO ACT CUT MAN RUN
PUSH TAKE WORK DRIVE MULES
AFFECT EFFECT MANAGE CONDUCT
PROCEED FUNCTION
(— BY HAND) MANIPULATE
(— GUNS) SERVE
(— MINE) FLUSH
(— RADIO) BLOOP
OPERATIC LYRIC
OPERATING GOING
(FULLY —) AFLOAT
OPERATION DEED PLAY BLAST
AGENCY EFFECT VIRTUE PROCESS
CREATION EXERCISE FUNCTION
PRACTICE EXECUTION INFLUENCE
PROCESSUS
OPERATIVE EYE HAND ARTIST
LIVING ARTISAN MECHANIC
DETECTIVE EFFECTIVE
OPERATOR DEL DOER AGENT
BAKER DEWER NABLA PILOT QUACI
BEAMER BILLER BOLTER BUMPER
BUSMAN CAPPER DEALER DEGGER
DRIVER DUNGER DYADIC GAGGER
JOCKEY KICKER RAGGER TRADER
AVIATOR BREAKER CENTRAL
CHEESER DENTIST FACIENT
GLASSER JOGGLER MANAGER
OPERANT SURGEON IDENTITY
CONDUCTOR
(INFERIOR —) PLUG
(RADIO —) HAM SPARKS SPARKER
(TRUCK —) GIPSY GYPSY
OPERCULUM LID FLAP ONYCHA
OPERCLE APTYCHUS COVERING
EYESTONE MANDIBLE
OPERETTA ZARZUELA
OPEROSE BUSY IRKSOME DILIGENT
LABORIOUS
OPHIDIAN ASP EEL SNAKE CONGEF
REPTILE SERPENT
OPHITE CAINIAN CAINITE
OPIATE DOPE DRUG HEMP DWALE
OPIUM DEADEN ANODINE HYPNOTIC
NARCOTIC SEDATIVE DORMITARY
PAREGORIC SOPORIFIC
OPIFICER OPIFEX WORKMAN
ARTIFICER
OPINE DEEM JUDGE THINK PONDER
BELIEVE SUPPOSE OPINIATE
OPINION CRY EYE MOT BOOK DOX"
FAME IDEA MIND VIEW WEEN
DOGMA FANCY FUTWA GUESS
HEART SENSE SIGHT TENET THINK
VARDI VARDY VOICE ADVICE
ASSENT BELIEF DEVICE DICTUM

ESTEEM GROUND NOTION REPUTE
SCHISM CENSURE CONCEIT
CONCEPT CONSENT COUNSEL
DIANOIA FEELING HOLDING
MEASURE SEEMING THINKSO
THOUGHT TROWING VERDICT
DECISION DOCTRINE JUDGMENT
SUFFRAGE SENTIMENT
(COLLECTION OF —S) SYMPOSIUM
(EXAGGERATED —) BIGHEAD
(EXPRESSION OF —) VOTE
(FAVORABLE —) BROO ESTEEM
(MOHAMMEDAN —) FUTWA
(SET OF PROFESSED —S) CREDO
(UNORTHODOX —) HERESY
OPINIONATED DOGMATIC
CONCEITED OBSTINATE PRAGMATIC
OPIUM HOP MUD DRUG OPIE POST
CHANDU CHANDOO MECONIUM
TOXICANT
(— ALKALOID) CODEIN CODEINE
MORPHINE NARCOTIN NARCOTINE
PAPAVERIN
(— POPPY) NEPENTHE
OPIUMISM THEBAISM
OPOSSUM QUICA YAPOK POSSUM
YAPOCK OYAPOCK SARIGUE
VULPINE MARSUPIAL PHILANDER
TACUACINE
(— SHRIMP) MYSID MYSOID
OPPONENT FOE ANTI ENEMY PARTY
RIVAL ALOGIAN OPPOSER ASSILANT
ADVERSARY
(— OF GOV CLINTON) BUCKTAIL
(BOORISH —) BOEOTIAN
(IMAGINARY —) WINDMILL
OPPORTUNE FIT PAT HAPPY LUCKY
READY TIMELY APROPOS FITTING
TIMEFUL SUITABLE FAVORABLE
OPPORTUNELY TIMELY APROPOS
HAPPILY
OPPORTUNIST CREEPER
OPPORTUNISTIC SHUFFLING
OPPORTUNITY GO MAY OPE SEL
EASE HENT MEAN MINT ROOM SELE
SHOT TIDE TIME SIGHT SLANT
SPACE CHANCE SEASON SQUEAK
LEISURE OPENING RESPITE
VANTAGE APPROACH FACILITY
OCCASION ADVANTAGE
(— TO PROCEED) WAY
(FAVORABLE —) SHOW TIME
OPPOSE PIT VIE WAR BUCK COPE
DEFY FACE HEAD MEET NOSE STEM
WARN WEAR ARGUE BLOCK CHECK
CLASH CROSS FIGHT FRONT OCCUR
REBEL REBUT REPEL BATTLE
BREAST COMBAT DEFEND NAYSAY
OBJECT OBTEND OPPUGN REPUGN
RESIST THWART WITHER CONTEST
COUNTER GAINSAY OBVIATE
REVERSE WITHSET CONFLICT
CONFRONT CONTRAST FRONTIER
OBSTRUCT ENCOUNTER WITHSTAND
(— BY ARGUMENT) REBUT
(— ONE IN AUTHORITY) REBEL
DEFORCE
OPPOSED ANTI ALIEN AVERSE
ADVERSE AGAINST COUNTER

HOSTILE CONTRARY ANTARCTIC
REPUGNANT
(PERSISTENTLY —) RENITENT
OPPOSITE TO ANENT POLAR
ACROSS ANENST AVERSE FACING
WITHER ADVERSE COUNTER
FORNENT INVERSE OBVIOUS
REVERSE ANTIPODE CONTRARY
CONTRAST CONVERSE ANTIPODAL
REPUGNANT
(— MIDDLE OF SHIP'S SIDE) ABEAM
(— OF TRUTH) DEVIL
(— THE ALTAR) WEST
(— THE SUN) ANTISOLAR
OPPOSITION CON ATILT STOUR
THWART DISCORD CONTRAST
OBSTACLE ANIMOSITY COLLISION
HOSTILITY RENITENCY
(ELECTRICAL —) IMPEDANCE
OPPRESS SIT HOLD LADE LOAD PEIS
RACK RAPE RIDE SWAY THEW
CROWD CRUSH GRIND GRIPE HEAVY
PEISE POISE PRESS WEIGH WRONG
BETOIL BURDEN DEFOIL DEFOUL
EXTORT HARASS HARROW NIDDER
NITHER RAVISH SUBDUE THREAT
AFFLICT DEPRESS INGRATE
OVERLAY REPRESS SQUEEZE
TRAMPLE CONFRONT DISTRESS
ENCUMBER PRESSURE SUPPRESS
OVERPOWER OVERTHROW
OVERWHELM
(— WITH DREAD) HAGRIDE
(— WITH HEAT) SWELTER
OPPRESSED SERVILE
OPPRESSION GRIPE PRESS THRALL
MIZRAIM DULLNESS PRESSURE
EXTORTION GRIEVANCE LASSITUDE
OPPRESSIVE HOT DIRE DOWY HARD
CLOSE DOWIE FAINT HARSH HEAVY
BITTER LEADEN SCREWY SEVERE
SMUDGY SULTRY TORRID URGENT
WEIGHT ONEROUS SLAVISH
GRIEVOUS GRINDING RIGOROUS
OPPRESSIVELY STRAIT
OPPRESSOR CSAR CZAR NERO
TSAR TZAR EGLON TYRANT
INCUBUS
OPPROBRIUM ENVY ABUSE ODIUM
SCORN SHAME INFAMY INSULT
CALUMNY DISDAIN OFFENSE
SCANDAL DISGRACE DISHONOR
REPROACH CONTUMELY
OPS (ASSOCIATE OF —) CONSUS
(CONSORT OF —) SATURN
(DAUGHTER OF —) CERES
(FESTIVAL OF —) OPALIA
(PERSONIFICATION OF —) FAUNA
TERRA TELLUS
OPT CULL PICK WISH ELECT CHOOSE
DECIDE OPTATE SELECT
OPTIC EYE OCULAR VISUAL
OPTICAL (— APPARATUS) LENS
GLASS ALIDAD ALIDADE
OPTOMETER PERISCOPE TELESCOPE
OPTIMIST UTOPIANIST
OPTIMISTIC GLAD ROSY SUNNY
JOYOUS BULLISH HOPEFUL

ROSEATE EUPEPTIC SANGUINE
EXPECTANT
OPTION UP CALL DOWN CHOICE
SPREAD REFUSAL STRADDLE
PRIVILEGE
OPTIONAL ELECTIVE VOLUNTARY
OPULENT FAT LUSH RICH WELI
AMPLE FLUSH PLUSH SHOWY
LAVISH MONEYED PROFUSE
WEALTHY ABUNDANT AFFLUENT
LUXURIANT PLENTIFUL SUMPTUOUS
OPUS WORK ETUDE STUDY
(OVERLABORED —) LUCUBRATION
OQUASSA QUASKY
OR NE ARE AUT ERE ORE GOLD
OTHER TOPAZ EITHER YELLOW
ORACHE SALTBUSH GREASEWOOD
ORACLE SEER TRIP SIBYL TRIPOD
TRIPOS DIVINER AUTOPHONE
ORACULAR OTIC VATIC ORPHIC
DELPHIC VATICAL DELPHIAN
PYTHONIC PROPHETIC
ORAL ALOUD PAROL VOCAL BUCCAL
PAROLE SONANT SPOKEN VERBAL
UTTERED UNWRITTEN
ORALE FANON
ORANGE KING MOCK CERES CHILE
CHILI CHINO FLAME GENIP HEDGE
NAVEL OSAGE TENNE AURORA
BODOCK BRAZIL COPPER MIKADO
NAVAHO SUNTAN TEMPLE TITIAN
UVALHA COWSLIP FLORIDA
LEATHER MACLURA PAPRIKA
PONCEAU PUMPKIN RANGPUR
SEVILLE TANGELO TANGIER
BERGAMOT BIGARADE CHINOTTI
CLAYBANK FLAMINGO HONEYDEW
JACINTHE MANDARIN MARATHON
MOROCCAN POMANDER SUNBURST
VALENCIA BUCCANEER CARNELIAN
PERSIMMON TANGERINE
(— GRASS) KNITWEED PINEWEED
(— HAWKWEED) FIREWEED
HIERACIUM
(— MEMBRANE) ZEST
(— MILKWORT) CANDYWEED
(— PIECE) LITH SEGMENT
(— ROCKFISH) FLIOMA
(— SEED) PIP
(BROWNISH —) SPICE
(LARGE —) KING
(MOCK —) SERINGA
(OSAGE —) HEDGE BODOCK
(SOUR —) CURACAO BIGARADE
CHINOTTO
(SWEET —) CHINA CHINO
ORANGEBIRD TANAGER
ORANGELEAF KARAMU
ORANGEMAN MARKSMAN
ORANGEWOOD OSAGE
ORANG LAUT BAJAU
ORANGUTAN APE MIAS ORANG
PONGO SATYR SATIRE SATURY
PRIMATE SALTIER WOODMAN
WOODSMAN
ORAON KURUKH
ORATE PLEAD SPEAK SPIEL SPOUT
ADDRESS DECLAIM LECTURE
BLOVIATE HARANGUE DISCOURSE
SPEECHIFY

ORATION EULOGY HESPED SERMON ADDRESS CONCION HARANGUE SUASORIA OLYNTHIAC PANEGYRIC PHILIPPIC
(— OF CICERO) PHILIPPIC
(FUNERAL —) ELOGE ELOGY MONODY ELOGIUM ENCOMIUM
ORATOR RHETOR DEMAGOG SPEAKER STUMPER CICERONE BOANERGES DEMAGOGUE PLAINTIFF SPOKESMAN
ORATORIO ELIJAH RORATORIO
ORATORICAL ELOQUENT RHETORICAL
ORATORY CHAPEL SACRARY ORACULUM SPEAKING ELOCUTION ELOQUENCE PROSEUCHE
ORB EYE SUN BALL MOON STAR EARTH GLOBE MOUND ORBIT CIRCLE PLANET SPHERE CIRCUIT ENCLOSE ENCIRCLE SURROUND FIRMAMENT
ORBED LUNAR ROUND GLOBATE
ORBIT AUGE PATH APSIS CYCLE TRACK CIRCLE SOCKET SPHERE CIRCUIT ELLIPSE EYEHOLE ECCENTRIC
(POINT IN —) APSIS APOGEE EPIGEE SYZYGY PERIGEE
ORC OGRE ORCA GIANT WHALE GRAMPUS
ORCHARD TOPE ARBOR GROVE ARBOUR GARDEN HUERTA OLIVET VERGER ARBUSTUM FRUITERY PEACHERY POMARIUM SUGARBUSH
(— GRASS) DOGFOOT COCKSFOOT
ORCHESTRA BAND GROUP CHAPEL CAPELLE GAMELAN KAPELLE ENSEMBLE GAMELANG SYMPHONY
(— BELLS) GLOCKENSPIEL
(— CIRCLE) PARQUET PARTERRE
(SECTION OF —) BRASS WINDS WOODS STRINGS WOODWINDS PERCUSSION
ORCHESTRATE SCORE ARRANGE COMPOSE
ORCHESTRION HARMONICON APOLLONICON
ORCHID FAAM FAHAM PETAL VANDA CYMBID DUFOIL LAELIA PURPLE AERIDES ANGULOA BOATLIP CALYPSO CULLION FLYWORT LYCASTE POGONIA VANILLA ARETHUSA CALANTHE DENDROBE GYNANDER LABELLUM RAMSHEAD SATYRION CORALROOT HABENARIA TWAYBLADE
ORCHIS CROWTOE CROWFOOT CRAKEFEET
ORDAIN LAW PUT DEEM DOOM LOOK MAKE SEND WILL WITE ALLOT ENACT JAPAN ORDER SHAPE WIELD WRITE DECREE PRIEST ADJUDGE APPOINT ARRANGE BEHIGHT COMMAND DESTINE DICTATE FORTUNE INSTALL PREPARE
ORDEAL FIRE GAFF TEST TRIAL CALVARY GAUNTLET
(— TREE) AKAZGA TANGHIN TANGUIN

ORDER BAN BID RAY SAY TAX BOON CALL CASE CHIT FIAT FORM ORDO RANK RULE SAND SECT STOP SUIT TELL TIFF TRIM WILL WORD ALIGN ARRAY CHIME CLASS DIGHT EDICT GENUS GRADE GUIDE HAVOC PRESS QUIET RANGE SHIFT STATE TAXIS WHACK ASSIGN AVAUNT BILLET CEDULA CHARGE COSMOS CURFEW DECREE DEGREE DEMAND DIRECT ENJOIN FIRMAN FOLLOW GRAITH HOOKUM INDENT KILTER MANAGE METHOD NATURE ORDAIN POLICE POTENT SERIES SETTLE SYNTAX SYSTEM ADJUDGE ARRANGE BESPEAK BIDDING BOOKING COMMAND COMPOSE DISPOSE EMBARGO FLOATER MANDATE PRECEPT PROCESS SOCIETY KODASHIM
(— OF ANGELS) CHOIR QUIRE MIGHTS THRONES DOMINIONS
(— OF BELLS) CHANGE
(— OF COURT) SIST VACATUR
(— OF HOLY BEINGS) HIERARCHY
(— OF WORSHIP) AGODUM
(— OFF) TURN
(— TOBACCO LEAF) CASE
(CIVIL —) EUNOMY
(COSMIC —) TAO RITA
(GOOD —) EUTAXY
(KNIGHTHOOD —) DANNEBROG
(LACKING —) AMISS MESSY MUSSY ROUGH CHAOTIC UNKEMPT CONFUSED
(LEGAL —) SIST STET WRIT DAYWRIT SUMMONS SENTENCE SUBPOENA
(LOWER — OF MAN) ALALUS
(MINOR CHURCH —) BENET
(MONASTIC —) SAMGHA SANGHA
(TRAIN —) FLIMSY
(UNIVERSAL —) KIND
(WRITTEN —) CHECK DRAFT BILLET DRAUGHT
ORDERED BANDBOX BESPOKE REGULAR SCRAPED COHERENT
(WELL —) TRIM
ORDERLINESS METHOD SYSTEM CLARITY DECORUM
ORDERLY AIDE DULY NEAT RULY SNOD TIDY TRIM CRISP SOWAR SUWAR BATMAN BURSCH COSMIC FORMAL MODEST ORDENE GRADELY REGULAR SHAPELY DECOROUS GALLOPER GRAITHLY OBEDIENT PEACEABLE SHIPSHAPE
ORDINANCE LAW DOOM FIAT RITE BYLAW EDICT ASSIZE DECREE RECESS CONTROL MANDATE SETNESS STATUTE WORKING DECRETUM JUDICIAL REGIMENT TAKKANAH DIRECTION
ORDINANT DIHELY DIHELIOS DIHELIUM
ORDINARY LAY LOW SOS FESS LALA MEAN PALL RUCK BANAL CROSS NOMIC PLAIN PROSE USUAL COMMON FILLET MODERN NORMAL

PAIRLE SIMPLE VULGAR AVERAGE NATURAL PROSAIC SALTIRE SAUTIER TRIVIAL VULGATE EVERYDAY FAMILIAR HABITUAL MEDIOCRE MIDDLING PLEBEIAN RUMTYTOO WORKADAY QUOTIDIAN SHAKEFORK
ORDINATE ORDER ORDAIN APPOINT ORDERLY REGULAR MODERATE TEMPERATE
ORDNANCE LAW GUNS ARMOR ORGUE FALCON MINION PETARD PEDRERO RABINET SERPENT WEAPONS BASILISK PETERERO ARTILLERY
ORDO ORDER ALMANAC DIRECTORY
ORE (ALSO SEE MINERAL) TIN CHAT DISH DRAG FELL GOLD IRON LEAD MINE POST PULP ROCK CRAZE CRUDE FAVOR GLORY GRACE HONOR MANTO MERCY METAL PRILL COPPER CUPRITE FLOATER RESPECT SEAWEED SMEDDUM CLEMENCY KNOCKING CARBONATE REVERENCE
(— CRUSHER) DOLLY
(— DEPOSIT) LODE SCRIN BONANZA
(— LAYER) SEAM STOPE
(— LOADING PLATFORM) PLAT
(— MASS) SQUAT
(— NOT DRESSED) WORK
(— WITH STONE ADHERING) CHAT CHATS
(BROKEN —) DIRT
(CRUDE —) HEADS
(CUBE —) SIDERITE
(EARTHY-LOOKING —) PACO
(HORSEFLESH —) BORNITE
(IMPURE —) SPEISS HALVANS
(IRON —) OCHER OCHRE MINION IRONMAN LIMNITE MINETTE OLIGIST TURGITE HEMATITE JACUTINGA
(LEAD —) BOOZE GALENA
(LUMP OF —) HARDHEAD
(MERCURY —) GRANZA CINNABAR
(SOLID —) RIB
(TIN —) ROWS CRAZE SCOVE WHITS FLORAN TINSTUFF
(WORTHLESS —) SLAG DROSS MATTE
OREAD PERI NYMPH

OREGON
CAPITAL: SALEM
COLLEGE: REED
COUNTY: LINN WASCO CLATSOP KLAMATH MALHEUR YAMHILL UMATILLA
INDIAN: ALSEA MODOC WASCO CAYUSE CHETCO KUITSH TENINO KLAMATH TAKELMA YAQUINA
LAKE: ABERT WALDO CRATER HARNEY KLAMATH MALHEUR
MOUNTAIN: HOOD WALKER WILSON GRIZZLY JACKASS TIDBITS

MOUNTAIN RANGE: BLUE COAST CASCADE
RIVER: ROGUE IMNAHA OWYHEE POWDER UMPQUA BLITZEN KLAMATH SILVIES COLUMBIA DESCHUTES
STATE BIRD: MEADOWLARK
STATE FLOWER: GRAPE
STATE NICKNAME: BEAVER
STATE TREE: FIR
TOWN: NYSSA EUGENE ASTORIA PORTLAND CORVALLIS

ORE-PRODUCING QUICK
ORESTES (FATHER OF —) AGAMEMNON
(FRIEND OF —) PYLADES
(MOTHER OF —) CLYTEMNESTRA
(SISTER OF —) ELECTRA IPHIGENIA
(WIFE OF —) HERMIONE
ORGAN CUP GILL LIMB PART CHELA FLOAT GREAT HEART MEANS PAPER REGAL SERRA ELATER FEEDER FEELER HAPTOR MEDIUM SPLEEN SUCKER CONSOLE JOURNAL ARMATURE EFFECTOR ISOGRAFT MAGAZINE MELODICA MYCETOME EQUIPMENT HARMONIUM NEWSPAPER PORTATIVE
(— GALLERY) LOFT
(— OF HEARING) EAR
(— OF SENSE) SENSE SENSORY
(— OF SILKWORM) FILATOR
(— OF TOUCH) TACTOR TACTUS
(— PIPE) REED FLUTE SCHWEGEL
(— STOP) ECHO HARP OBOE SEXT TUBA VIOL ACUTA DOLCE FLUTE ORAGE QUINT TENTH VIOLA BIDARA CURTAL CYMBAL DECIMA DULCET FUGARA GEDACT NASARD OCTAVE SCHARF TIERCE TROMBA BASSOON BOMBARD BOURDON CELESTE CLARION CREMONA DOLCIAN DOUBLET DULCIAN FAGOTTO GEDECKT PICCOLO POSAUNE SERPENT TERTIAN TRUMPET TWELFTH VIOLINA BOMBARDE CARILLON CLARINET DIAPASON DULCIANA GEMSHORN REGISTER TENOROON TROMBONE WALDHORN DOUBLETTE HARMONICA PRINCIPAL SAXOPHONE
(— VIBRATO) TREMOLO
(BRISTLELIKE —) SETA
(CHINESE —) CHENG
(HAND —) SERINETTE
(OLFACTORY —) NOSE
(RESPIRATORY —) LUNG
(SMALL —) REGAL
(VOCAL — OF BIRDS) SYRINX
(WASTE —) KIDNEY
ORGANIC VITAL INBORN NATURAL INHERENT
ORGANISM WOG BODY ECAD GERM GUEST PLANT AEROBE ANIMAL EMBRYO SYSTEM DIPLONT DISEASE MACHINE PLANONT SUSCEPT

HEMAMEBA PATHOGEN PLANKTER MESOPHILE
(— CHARACTERISTIC) MIXIS
(COMPOUND —) STOCK
(MINUTE —) AMEBA MONAD SPORE
(MODIFIED —) ECAD
(PELAGIC —S) NEKTON
(POLITICAL —) LEVIATHAN
(SIMPLE —) MONAD
(PL.) BENTHON BENTHOS HAYSEED NEUSTON
ORGANIZATION ART BIG ITO CLUB FIRM KLAN CADRE FIDAC FORUM HOUSE MAFIA SETUP AUMAGA CHURCH OUTFIT SURVEY SYSTEM CHARITY COMPANY CONCERN DEMOLAY ECONOMY GIDEONS MENORAH SOCIETY CONGRESS PATRONAGE STRUCTURE
(— OF ACTORS) COMPANY
(— OF DEALERS) AUCTION
(— OF EXPERIENCE) SCHEMA
(— WITH MANY BRANCHES) OCTOPUS
(ARMY —) LANDSTORM
(AUXILIARY —) AID SYNODICAL
(COLLEGE —) FRAT ALUMNA ALUMNI ALUMNUS SORORITY
(JEWISH —) ITO MENORAH
(MUSICAL —) BAND COMBO CAPELLE KAPELLE ENSEMBLE ORCHESTRA
(POLICE —) GESTAPO
(POLITICAL —) PARTY VEREIN HETAERIA HETAIRIA APPARATUS
(SAMOAN —) AUMAGA
(SECRET —) WOW BPOE ELKS MOOSE MASONS MIDEWIN
(SOCIAL —) POLICE
(WAR VETERANS —) AVC DAV GAR SAR VFW FIDAC AMVETS
(WOMEN'S —) DAR WAF WRC WCTU SORORITY
ORGANIZE FORM EDIFY FOUND MODEL RALLY DESIGN EMBODY ARRANGE MODULIZE REGIMENT UNIONIZE BLUEPRINT INSTITUTE INTEGRATE STRUCTURE
ORGANIZED FORMED ORGANIC
(BADLY —) INCONDITE
ORGIASTIC SATURNALIAN
ORGY LARK RITE ROMP BINGE REVEL SPREE FROLIC SHINDY REVELRY WASSAIL CAROUSAL CEREMONY
(PL.) ORGIACS DEBAUCHERIES
ORIANA (FATHER OF —) LISUARTE
(LOVER OF —) AMADIS
ORIBI OUREBI ANTELOPE BLEEKBOK PALEBUCK
ORIEL BAY CHAPEL DORMER RECESS WINDOW BALCONY GALLERY MIRADOR PORTICO CORRIDOR
ORIENT DAWN EAST ADAPT BUILD PEARL PLACE SHEEN ADJUST LEVANT LOCATE LUSTER RISING GLOWING INCLINE RADIANT SUNRISE LUSTROUS SPARKLING
ORIENTAL ASIAN PEARL BRIGHT

INDIAN ORTIVE RISING EASTERN SHINING INDOGEAN LUSTROUS PELLUCID PRECIOUS BRILLIANT LEVANTINE
ORIENTATION ASPECT PHORIA STRIKE COLORING LOCALITY
ORIFICE BUNG HOLE PORE VENT INLET MOUTH STOMA BLOWER CAVITY OUTLET RICTUS SIPHON THROAT CHIMNEY EARHOLE FORAMEN OPENING OSCULUM OSTIOLE APERTURE FUMAROLE INTROITUS
(— IN VOLCANIC REGION) FUMAROLE
(— OF INFUNDIBULUM) LURA
(BREATHING —) SPIRACLE
(VOLCANIC —) BLOWER
ORIGANUM ORGANY MARJORAM ORGAMENT
ORIGIN NEE GERM KIND RISE ROOT SEED BIRTH CAUSE START STOCK FATHER GROWTH NATURE PARENT SOURCE SPRING EDITION GENESIS LINEAGE UPSTART NASCENCE UPSPRING BEGINNING INCEPTION OFFSPRING PARENTAGE
(— ON EARTH) EPIGENE
(FOREIGN —) ECDEMIC
ORIGINAL NEW HOME SEED FIRST FRESH NOVEL PRIME STOCK FONTAL NATIVE PRIMAL PRIMER SAMPLE PRIMARY RADICAL SEMINAL NASCENCY PRISTINE AUTHENTIC AUTOGRAPH BEGINNING INVENTIVE OFFSPRING PRIMITIVE
(NOT —) DERIVED
ORIGINALITY INGENUITY
ORIGINATE COIN COME DATE GROW HEAD MAKE MOVE OPEN REAR RISE SIRE ARISE BEGIN BIRTH BREED CAUSE ENDOW FOUND HATCH RAISE START AUTHOR CREATE DERIVE DESIGN DEVISE FATHER INVENT SPRING CAUSATE DESCEND EMANATE PROCEED PRODUCE COMMENCE CONCEIVE CONTRIVE DISCOVER GENERATE INITIATE INSTITUTE
ORIGINATION DESCENT GENESIS BREEDING ORIGINAL COSMOGONY ETYMOLOGY
ORIGINATOR AUTHOR FATHER CREATOR INVENTOR GENERATOR
ORIOLE PIROL BUNYAH LARIOT LORIOT CACIQUE FIGBIRD PEABIRD FIREBIRD GOLDBIRD HANGBIRD HANGNEST TROUPIAL
ORION RIGEL ALGEBAR
(BELT OF —) ELLWAND
(HOUND OF —) ARATUS
(SLAYER OF —) ARTEMIS
ORKNEY ISLANDS (CAPITAL OF —) KIRKWALL
(ISLAND OF —) HOY POMONA ROUSAY SANDAY STRONSAY
ORLE ORLET BORDER FILLET WREATH BEARING CHAPLET TRESSURE

ORLOP DECK ARLOUP
ORMER ABALONE
ORMOLU GILT GOLD ALLOY BRASS
VARNISH
ORNAMENT BOB DUB FLY FOB GAY
JOY PIN POT TAG TEE TOY URN
BALL BOSS CURL DICE ETCH FALL
FRET FROG GAUD GEAR HUSK
KNOP LEAF NULL OUCH RULE STAR
TOOL TRIM WALY WING ADORN
BRAID BULLA CHASE CROSS CROWN
DECOR EXORN FUSEE GRACE
GUTTA HELIX HONOR INLAY LUNET
MENSK MENSO OVOID PATCH
POPPY PRUNT SPANG SPRAY SPRIG
STALK TRAIL TRICK WALLY AMULET
ANKLET ATTIRE BEDAUB BEDECK
BILLET BRANCH BROOCH BUTTON
CIMIER COLLAR DIAPER DOODAD
EDGING EMBOSS ENRICH FINERY
FLORET FLOWER GORGET INSERT
LABRET LUNULA NIELLO OFFSET
PAMPRE PARURE PATERA ROCOCO
ROSACE RUNTEE SETOFF TABLET
TAHALI TEMPLE TIRADE AGREMEN
AKROTER AMALAKA BIBELOT
BUCRANE CIRCLET COCARDE
CORBEIL CROCKET EARPLUG
ECHINUS ENGRAVE ENHANCE
FURNISH GADROON GARNISH
NETSUKE RINCEAU SEXFOIL STRIGIL
TREFOIL TRINKET APPLIQUE
DECORATE FLOURISH GIMCRACK
LAVALIER SWASTIKA
(— FOR HEAD) MIND TARGET
(— ON SHIP) BADGE
(CHILD'S —) GAY
(CLAW-LIKE —) GRIFFE
(DRESS —) FROG LACE JABOT
SEQUIN SPANGLE
(HEAD —) TIARA TEMPLE
(HORSE COLLAR —) HOUNCE
(MUSICAL —) TURN
(PENDANT —) BOB BULLA ANADEM
BANGLE TASSEL EARRING LAVALIER
(SHOULDER —) EPAULET
(TAWDRY —) GINGERBREAD
(PL.) FIGGERY KNAVERY AGREMENS
ORNAMENTAL FANCY CHICHI FRILLY
LILYTURN BLUEBEARD
ORNAMENTATION BOSS FOIL
ACORN DECOR ADORNO BABERY
CHICHI CILERY DICING CUSPING
ECHELLE LACWORK STYLING
FROUFROU HEADWORK PURFLING
ROCAILLE STAFFAGE TRESSURE
(CHEAP —) TINSEL
(EXTRAVAGANT —) ROCOCO
(MUSICAL —) GRUPPO GRUPPETTO
ORNAMENTED FIGURY FOILED
ORNATE TAWDRY ADORNED
FLOUNCY FROSTED TREFLEE
WROUGHT GOFFERED SINNOWED
ELABORATE STELLATED
ORNATE GAY FINE FANCY FUSSY
GIDDY SHOWY DRESSY FLORID
FLOSSY PURPLE SUPERB AUREATE
BAROQUE FLOWERY TAFFETA
MANDARIN OVERRIPE SPLENDID

ELABORATE UNNATURAL
(EXTREMELY —) GIDDY
ORNERY CONTRARY
ORNITHOLOGIST AUDUBON
BIRDMAN
OROTUND FULL CLEAR SHOWY
MELLOW STRONG POMPOUS
RESONANT SONOROUS BOMBASTIC
ORP FRET WEEP
ORPHAN PIP WARD FOUNDLING
STEPCHILD
ORPHANED ORBATE
ORPHEUS (BIRTHPLACE OF —)
PIERIA
(FATHER OF —) APOLLO OEAGRUS
(MOTHER OF —) CALLIOPE
(WIFE OF —) EURYDICE
ORPHREY BAND BORDER
ORPIMENT ORPIN HARTAL SPIRIT
ARSENIC HARTAIL
ORPINE SEDUM LIVELONG
BAGLEAVES EVERGREEN
ORRA ODD IDLE ORROW WORTHLESS
ORRIS GIMP IRIS LACE BRAID
ORRICE GALLOON
ORT BIT END CRUMB SCRAP MORSEL
REFUSE TRIFLE LEAVING REMNANT
FRAGMENT LEFTOVER
ORTHODOX GOOD GREEK SOUND
USUAL PROPER CANONIC CORRECT
ACCEPTED STANDARD CUSTOMARY
ORTHODOXY TRUTH SOUNDNESS
ORTHOGRAPHY WRITING
ORTHOPTERON WALKER
ORTOLAN BIRD RAIL SORA BUNTING
BOBOLINK WHEATEAR
ORTSTEIN HARDPAN
ORYX BEISA PASANG PASENG
GAZELLE GEMSBOK ANTELOPE
LEUCORYX
OS BONE ESKAR ESKER MOUTH
OPENING ORIFICE
OSAGE ORANGE HEDGE OSAGE
BODOCK BOWWOOD
OSCILLATE LOG WAG HUNT ROCK
SWAY VARY SQUEG SWING WAVER
WEAVE SHIMMY FEATHER VIBRATE
FLUCTUATE
OSCILLATION HOWL WAVE SHOCK
SEICHE SHIMMY SQUEAL FLUTTER
LIBRATION VIBRATION
OSCULATE BUSS KISS
OSCULATORY PAX
OSIER ROD WAND EDDER SALIX
SKEIN SPLIT WITHY BASKET
SALLOW WICKER WILLOW
DOGWOOD WILGERS REDBRUSH
(— CAGE) TUMBREL
(— WILLOW) TWIGWITHY
OSIRIS HERSHEF UNNEFER
(BROTHER OF —) SET SETH
(CROWN OF —) ATEF
(FATHER OF —) GEB KEB SEB
(MOTHER OF —) NUT
(SISTER OF —) ISIS
(SON OF —) HORUS ANUBIS
(WIFE OF —) ISIS
OSMANLI TURK TURKISH
OSPREY GLED HAWK OSSI GLEDE

BALBUSARD OSSIFRAGE
OSSATURE SKELETON OSSEMENTS
OSSE DARE ATTEMPT PRESAGE
PROMISE VENTURE PROPHESY
RECOMMEND UTTERANCE
OSSEOUS BONE BONY SPINY LITHIC
OSTEAL
OSSICLE BONE INCUS ADORAL
STAPES ALVEOLE BONELET
MALLEUS SCUTELLA
OSSIFICATION OSTOSIS UROSTEON
METOSTEON SIDEBONES
OSSUARY 'URN TOMB GRAVE VAULT
OSSARIUM
OSTEND SHOW REVEAL EXHIBIT
MANIFEST
OSTENSIBLE SEEMING APPARENT
SPECIOUS
OSTENT AIR MIEN SIGN TOKEN
DISPLAY PORTENT
OSTENTATION POMP SHOW CLASS
ECLAT FLARE PRIDE STRUT SWANK
VAUNT PARADE DISPLAY FLUTTER
PAGEANT PORTENT PRESAGE
FLOURISH FRIPPERY PRETENSE
SHOWINESS SPECTACLE
OSTENTATIOUS ARTY LOUD GAUDY
SHOWY SWANK FLASHY SPORTY
SWANKY TURGID FLAUNTY GLARING
OBVIOUS POMPOUS SPLASHY
FASTUOUS ELABORATE
OSTERIA INN TAVERN
OSTIOLE PORE MOUTH STOMA
OPENING ORIFICE APERTURE
OSTRACIZE BAN BAR CUT SNUB
EXILE BANISH PUNISH REJECT
ABOLISH CENSURE EXCLUDE
BLACKBALL PROSCRIBE
OSTRACON SHELL FRAGMENT
POTSHERD
OSTRICH EMU RHEA NANDU
BREVIPEN STRUCION
(— FEATHER) BOO
(JERKED —) BILTONG
OSTYAK KHANTY
OSWEGO TEA BALM
OTAHEITE TAHITI
(— APPLE) HEVI MACUPI
OTALGIA EARACHE
OTHELLO MOOR
(FRIEND OF —) IAGO
(WIFE OF —) DESDEMONA
OTHER HE MO ELSE MORE ALTER
FORMER NOTHER SECOND TIDDER
TOTHER ALTERUM FURTHER
DISTINCT DIFFERENT
() HETERO
(PL.) LAVE REST LUTRA
OTHERNESS ALTERITY
OTHERWISE OR NOT ELSE ENSE
ALIAS SECUS ALITER EXCEPT
BESIDES ELSEHOW ELSEWAY
OTIC AURAL AUDITORY ORACULAR
AURICULAR
OTIOSE IDLE LAZY VAIN ALOOF
FUTILE OTIANT REMOTE STERILE
USELESS INACTIVE INDOLENT
REPOSING

OTOLITH SAGITTA LAPILLUS OTOSTEON

OTOLOGIST AURIST

OTTAVINO PICCOLO

OTTER DOG FUR PUP FISH NAIR PELT BITCH HURON LOUTRE SIMUNG TACKLE ANNATTO PERIQUE MAMPALON MUSTELIN PARAVANE

(— TAIL) POLE

(DEN OF — S) HOLT

(SEA —) KALAN

OTTOMAN (ALSO SEE TURKEY) POUF SEAT TURK COUCH DIVAN SQUAB STOOL FABRIC OTHMAN POUFFE SULTANE FOOTSTOOL

(— COURT) PORTE

(— GOVERNOR) PASHA

(— LEADER) OSMAN

(— PROVINCE) VILAYET

(— STANDARD) ALEM

(— SUBJECT) RAIA RAYAH

OUABE HOGNUT

OUAKARI ACARI UKARI MONKEY UAKARI

OUCH OH OW ADORN BEZEL CLASP JEWEL NOUCH BROOCH FIBULA NOUCHE BRACELET NECKLACE ORNAMENT

OUGHT BIT BUD BUT MOW BOOD BOOT MOTE MUST ZERO SHALL BELONG CIPHER NAUGHT NOUGHT SHOULD BEHOOVE

OUNCE URE OKET OKIA ONCA ONCE ONZA OKIEH UNCIA CHEETAH LEOPARD WILDCAT

(EIGHT —S) CUPFUL

(ONE-16TH OF —) DRAM

(ONE-20TH OF —) EASTERLING

(ONE-8TH OF —) DRAM

OUPHE ELF OOF OUF GOBLIN

OUR UR ORE URE WER WIR HORE NOTRE UNSER

(— LORD) NS

(— SAVIOR) NSIC

OURICURY LICURI LICURY CABECUDO

OURSELVES USSELF USSELS USSELVEN

OUSIA NATURE ESSENCE SUBSTANCE

OUST BAR BUMP FIRE SACK CHUCK EJECT EVICT EXPEL BANISH DEBOUT REMOVE CASHIER DISCARD DISMISS SUSPEND DISSEIZE FORJUDGE ELIMINATE

OUSTING AMOTION

OUT EX AWAY DOWN HORS FORTH ABSENT BEGONE ISSUED OOTWITH OUTWARD EXTERNAL PUBLISHED

— LOUD) BOST

— OF BREATH) BLOWN

— OF COMMISSION) BUNG

— OF DATE) OLD DOWDY PASSE OUTWORN TIMEWORN OVERDATED

— OF DOORS) FOREIGN THEREOUT

— OF EXISTENCE) AWAY

— OF KILTER) ALOP AWRY CRANK BROKEN

(— OF ONE'S MIND) FEY DAFT DELEERIT

(— OF ORDER) AMISS KAPUT FAULTY DEFICIENT

(— OF PLACE) AMISS INEPT

(— OF PLAY) DEAD FOUL

(— OF SIGHT) DOGGO INVISIBLE

(— OF SORTS) CROOK CROSS HUMPY NOHOW COMICAL PEEVISH

(— OF THE WAY) BY BYE ASIDE BLIND CLEAR CLOSE AFIELD REMOTE

(— OF THIS LIFE) HYNE

(— OF TUNE) FALSE SCORDATO

(— OF) EX FROM DEHORS OUTWITH

(FARTHER —) UTTER

OUTAGE VENT ULLAGE HEADSPACE

OUT-AND-OUT GROSS SHEER SWORN UTTER ARRANT DIRECT WHOLLY ABSOLUTE COMPLETE CRASHING

OUTBREAK FIT ROW RASH RIOT BURST SALLY EMEUTE PLAGUE REVOLT RUCKUS TUMULT UPROAR BOUTADE OUTCROP RUCTION BLIZZARD ERUPTION OUTBURST EXPLOSION

(— OF EMOTIONALISM) HYSTERIA

(— OF TEMPER) MOORBURN

(SUDDEN —) SPURT

OUTBUILDING BARN SHED LODGE PRIVY BARTON GARAGE HEMMEL OUTHOUSE SKEELING SKILLING BACKHOUSE

OUTBURST BOUT CROW FLAW FUME GALE GUST RAGE TIFF AGONY BLAST BLAZE BREAK BRUNT BURST FLARE FLASH GEARE SALLY SPATE START STORM ACCESS BLOWER BLOWUP ESCAPE FANTAD FANTOD GOLLER TIRADE TUMULT BLOWOUT OUTCROP PASSION TANTRUM TORRENT ERUPTION EXPLOSION

(— OF ANGER) FIT GERE GEARE TATTER

(— OF ORATORY) SQUIRT

(— OF SPEECH) STRAIN

(— OF TEMPER) FUFF TIFF BLOWOUT

(SPACE —) SUPERNOVA

OUTCAST EXILE LEPER RONIN SHREW ABJECT PARIAH AOUTLET ISHMAEL MISSILE OUTWALE CASTAWAY CHANDALA REJECTED VAGABOND DIALONIAN

(HOMELESS —) ARAB

(JAPANESE —) ETA RONIN

OUTCOME END OUT FATE TERM CLOSE EDUCT EVENT HATCH ISSUE LOOSE PROOF UPSET BROWST EFFECT EXITUS OUTLET PERIOD RESULT SEQUEL UPSHOT EMANATE PROGENY SUCCESS FATALITY AFTERMATH

OUTCROP CROP LEDGE BASSET BLOSSOM BLOWOUT OUTBREAK OUTBURST

OUTCROPPING BULT SCABROCK

OUTCRY CAW CRY HUE YIP BAWL

BRAY DITE GAFF HOWL REAM ROAR SCRY UTAS YARM YELL ALARM BOAST DITTY NOISE OUTAS SHOUT STINK WHAUP BELLOW CLAMOR HOLLER RACKET SCREAM SHRIEK STEVEN TUMULT CALLING EXCLAIM PROTEST SCREECH SHILLOO COMPLAINT PHILLILEW

(PUBLIC —) STINK

OUTDATED CRINOLINE

OUTDISTANCE DROP SKIN OUTGO SURPASS OUTSTRIP

OUTDO CAP COB COP COW POT TOP BANG BEAT BEST FLOG EXCEL OUTGO TRUMP WORSE DEFEAT EXCEED OUTACT NONPLUS SURPASS OVERCOME

OUTDOORS FORTH OUTBY OUTBYE OUTSIDE

OUTER BUT ALIEN ECTAD ECTAL UPPER UTTER FOREIGN OUTSIDE OUTWARD EXTERIOR EXTERNAL FORINSEC

OUTERMOST FINAL UTTER UTMOST EVEREST EXTREME OUTWARD FARTHEST REMOTEST

OUTFACE DEFY RESIST SUBDUE CONFRONT OVERCOME

OUTFIELDER GARDENER OUTSCOUT

OUTFIT KIT RIG GANG GARB REAR REEK SUIT TEAM UNIT DRESS EQUIP GETUP HABIT TROUP ATTIRE CONREY DUFFEL FITOUT LAYOUT CLOTHES FURNISH SHEBANG EQUIPAGE FURNITURE GRUBSTAKE

(INFANT'S —) LAYETTE

(SPARE —) CHANGE

OUTFLANK OUTWING OVERWING

OUTFLOW FLUX DRAIN ISSUE OUTGO EFFLUX ESCAPE OUTPOUR

OUTGO EXIT EXCEL ISSUE OUTDO EFFLUX EGRESS EXCEED OUTLAY OUTLET OUTRUN OUTCOME PRODUCT SURPASS OUTSTRIP

OUTGROWTH BUD JAG FOOT HAIR LEAF MOSS SPUR CLAMP FRUIT HILUM HYPHA SCALE SPINE ACULEA COCKLE CUPULE FIBRIL ENATION FEATHER ISIDIUM APPENDIX EPIDERMA HAPTERON INDUSIUM OFFSHOOT CARBUNCLE EMERGENCE

OUTHOUSE SHED SKEO BIFFY LODGE PRIVY BIGGIN LINHAY OUTHUT LATRINE SKEELING SKILLION

OUTING OUT SKIP STAY TRIP JUNKET PICNIC COOKOUT HOLIDAY CLAMBAKE VACATION WAYGOOSE EXCURSION WAYZGOOSE

OUTLANDER PARDESI

OUTLANDISH ALIEN EXOTIC REMOTE BIZARRE FOREIGN STRANGE UNCOUTH PECULIAR BARBAROUS FANTASTIC GROTESQUE UNEARTHLY

OUTLAST ELAPSE SURVIVE OVERBIDE

OUTLAW BAN BAR CACO HORN TORY EXILE EXLEX FLEME RONIN

ARRANT BADMAN BANDIT BANISH
BRUMBY COWBOY DACOIT UNLEDE
BANDIDO ISHMAEL FUGITATE
FUGITIVE PROHIBIT PROSCRIBE
PROSCRIPT
(IRISH —) WOODKERN
(JAPANESE —) RONIN
(PL.) MANZAS
OUTLAWED ILLEGAL ILLICIT
LAWLESS
OUTLAWRY EXILE UTLAGARY
OUTLAY COST OUTGO EXPENSE
PENSION
OUTLET BORE DRIP EXIT VENT
ISSUE EGRESS ESCAPE EXITUS
FUNNEL OUTAGE OPENING
FUMEDUCT OVERFLOW SINKHOLE
AVOIDANCE
(— FOR COASTAL SWAMP) BAYOU
(— OF CARBURETOR) BARREL
(— OF SPRING) EYE
(AIR —) GRILL GRILLE
OUTLIER KLIP KLIPPE
OUTLINE MAP BOSH ETCH FLOW
FORM LINE PLAN PLAT BRIEF CHALK
CHART DRAFT FRAME MODEL
SHAPE TRACE AGENDA APERCU
DESIGN DOODLE FIGURE FILLET
LAYOUT SCHEMA SCHEME SCROLL
SKETCH SURVEY CAPSULE
CONTOUR DRAUGHT ELEMENT
EXTRACT FEATURE GABARIT
ISOTYPE PROFILE SUMMARY
DESCRIBE SKELETON SYLLABUS
SYNOPSIS GUIDELINE TREATMENT
(— HASTILY) SPLASH
(— OF A SCIENCE) GRUNDRISS
(— OF ANIMAL'S BODY) UNDERLINE
(— OF PLAY) SCENARIO
(— SHARPLY) ITALICIZE
(CURVING —) SWING
(DOUBLE —) FRINGE
(SHADOWY —) GHOST
OUTLIVE OUTLAST OUTWEAR
SURVIVE OVERBIDE
OUTLOOK MIND VIEW FRONK FRONT
VISTA ASPECT CLIMATE LOOKOUT
PURVIEW FRONTAGE OUTSIGHT
PROSPECT
(BRASH —) FACE
(MEDICAL —) PROGNOSIS
(SELF-CONFIDENT —) SWAGGER
OUTMANEUVER HAVE OUTPLAY
OUTMODED COLD DATED KARUT
PASSE RUSTY BYGONE EFFETE
ANTIQUE ELDERLY OBSOLETE
OUTPLAY HAVE
OUTPOST STATION FOREPOST
OUTGUARD
OUTPOURING FLOW GALE GUSH
FLOOD RIVER EARFUL LAVISH
STREAM OUTFLOW FUSILLADE
OUTPUT CUT GET CROP MAKE
EXPEL GRIST POWER YIELD ENERGY
UPCOME TURNOUT
OUTRAGE RAPE ABUSE INSULT
OFFEND RAVISH ABUSION AFFRONT
OFFENSE VIOLATE VIOLENCE
INDIGNITY

OUTRAGEOUS ENORM DAMNED
HEINOUS OBSCENE UNGODLY
FLAGRANT INFERNAL SHAMEFUL
SHOCKING ATROCIOUS DESPERATE
MONSTROUS
OUTRANK CAMP PREFER SURPASS
OUTRE ODD BIZARRE STRANGE
ECCENTRIC
OUTREACH CHEAT EXCEED EXTEND
OUTWIT SEARCH DECEIVE SURPASS
OVERREACH
OUTRIDER HAYDUK HEIDUK
HEYDUCK
(PL.) SWING
OUTRIGGER BOOM PROA BUMKIN
RIGGER SPIDER
OUTRIGHT RUN BALD CLEAN TOTAL
WHOLE DIRECT ENTIRE OPENLY
WHOLLY ABSOLUTE COMPLETE
DIRECTLY ENTIRELY
OUTRIVAL WIN EXCEL OUTDO
DEFEAT ECLIPSE SURPASS
OUTRUN BEAT COTE NICK PASS
OUTGO EXCEED ATRENNE FORERUN
OUTFOOT PREVENT
OUTRUSH GUST
OUTSET START SETOUT BEGINNING
THRESHOLD
OUTSHINE BLIND EXCEL OUTDO
STAIN DAZZLE DEFACE DISTAIN
SURPASS OVERSHINE
OUTSIDE BUT OUT BOUT FREE
OUTBY UTTER AFIELD OUTFACE
SURFACE EXTERIOR EXTERNAL
(— BOUNDS) ALOGICAL
(— OF) BESIDE
(COMB. FORM) ECTO
OUTSIDER ALIEN OUTMAN BOUNDER
ISHMAEL EXOTERIC STRANGER
EXTRANEAN FOREIGNER PHILISTER
OUTSKIRTS SIDE SKIRTS OUTSHIFTS
OUTSMART SLICK
OUTSPOKEN BOLD FREE LOUD
APERT BLUFF BLUNT BROAD FRANK
NAKED PLAIN ROUND CANDID
DIRECT ARTLESS EXPRESS EXPLICIT
OUTSTANDING ACE BIG ARCH RARE
AMONG FAMED NOTED SMASH
BANNER FAMOUS GIFTED HEROIC
MARKED SIGNAL SNAZZY UNPAID
EMINENT PALMARY STELLAR
SUBLIME SUPREME FABULOUS
INSPIRED SEASONED SKELPING
SLAMBANG SMACKING STANDOUT
BEAUTIFUL PRINCIPAL PROMINENT
UNSETTLED
OUTSTAY TARRY
OUTSTRETCHED STENT EXPANDED
EXTENDED
OUTSTRIP CAP TOP WIN BEST COTE
LEAD LOSE PASS EXCEL OUTDO
STRIP EXCEED OUTRUN DEVANCE
SURPASS DISTANCE OVERCOME
TRANSCEND
OUTVIE SURPASS OUTSTRIP
OUTWARD ECTAD OUTER OVERT
DERMAD EXODIC EXTERN FORMAL
EXTREME VISIBLE APPARENT
EXTERIOR EXTERNAL OBSOLETE

OUTFORTH EXTRINSIC
OUTWEIGH WEIGH OUTPOISE
OVERBEAR
OUTWIT FOX POT BALK BEST FOIL
HAVE BLOCK CHECK CROSS BAFFLE
EUCHRE FICKLE JOCKEY OVERGO
THWART STONKER OUTSHARP
CROSSBITE OVERREACH
OUTWORK BRAY JETTY FLECHE
TENAIL HORNWORK HORSEHOE
TENAILLE
OUTWORN WAPPENED
OUZEL PIET AMSEL COLLY OUSEL
OWZEL DIPPER THRUSH WHISTLER
OVAL O ELLIPSE STADIUM VESICAL
VULVATE AVELONGE NUMMULAR
VULVIFORM
OVARY CORAL GONAD GERMEN
OARIUM OOPHORON
OVATION HAND APPLAUSE
OVEN OON UMU KILN LEAR LEER
LEHR OAST BAKER BENCH GLAZE
GLOOM HANGI KOHUA TANUR TILER
CALCAR MUFFLE CABOOSE
FURNACE KITCHEN
(— FORK) FRUGGAN FRUGGIN
(— MOP) SCOVEL
OVENBIRD BAKER FURNER
HORNERO TEACHER ACCENTOR
OVER BY BYE OER TOO ALSO ANEW
ATOP BACK DEAD DONE GONE
UPON ABOVE AGAIN ALOFT ATOUR
ATURN CLEAR ENDED EXTRA VAULT
ABROAD ACROSS AROUND BEYOND
DESSUS EXCESS UPWARD SURPLUS
THROUGH FINISHED
(— AGAINST) FORNENT
(— AND ABOVE) ATOP ATOUR
BESIDES
(ALL —) NAPOO NAPOOH SURTOUT
(PREFIX) SUR SUPER SUPRA
OVERABUNDANCE WASTE EXCESS
SURPLUS PLETHORA
OVERACT HAM EMOTE OUTDO
BURLESQUE
OVERALLS SLIP CHAPS JEANS
TONGS DENIMS
OVERAWE COW ABASH DAUNT
BUFFALO BROWBEAT
OVERBEARING HIGH PROUD
LORDLY OVERLY HAUGHTY
ARROGANT BULLYING INSOLENT
SNOBBISH IMPERIOUS MASTERFUL
OVERBURDEN COVER HOIST
PESTER CONGEST OVERLAY
ENCUMBER STRIPPING SURCHARGE
OVERBUSY FUSSY PRAGMATIC
OVERCAST DIM SEW BIND DARK
DULL GLUM CLOUD HEAVY SERGE
CLOUDY DARKEN GLOOMY LOWERY
CLOUDED
OVERCHARGE GYP SOAK CROWD
GOUGE STICK STING BURDEN
EXCISE OPPRESS EXTORTION
OVERCOAT MINO BENNY GREGO
SHUBA BANGUP CAPOTE RAGLAN
SLIPON TOPPER ULSTER PALETOT
SPENCER SURTOUT TOPCOAT
BENJAMIN COONSKIN TAGLIONI

COTHAMORE GREATCOAT INVERNESS

OVERCOATING DUFFEL DUFFLE

OVERCOME DO AWE GET WAR WIN BEAT BEST DING LICK LOCK MATE POOP SACK SUNK TAME WAUR CHARM CRUCH DAUNT DROUK DROWN FORDO STILL STOOP THROW APPALL BEATEN BUSHED CRAVEN DEFEAT EXCEED FOREDO HURDLE MASTER OUTRAY PLUNGE SUBDUE VICTOR CONFUTE CONQUER DEPRESS ENFORCE RECOVER SMOTHER CONVINCE OUTSTRIP SUPERATE SURMOUNT SURPRISE
(— **DIFFICULTIES**) SWIM
(— **WITH FATIGUE**) FORDO FOREDO
(— **WITH WEARINESS**) HEAVY
(**BE — BY HEAT**) SWELTER

OVERCONFIDENT SECURE POSITIVE

OVERCROWD CONGEST SURCHARGE

OVERDECORATED GARISH

OVERDEVELOPED GAUDY

OVERDO EXCEED EXHAUST FATIGUE PERCOCT OVERCOOK OVERWORK BURLESQUE

OVERDONE FUSTIAN EXUBERANT

OVERDOSE SICKENER

OVERDRESS SAC SACK DIZEN SAQUE POLONAISE

OVERDRIED SLEEPY

OVERDUE BACK LATE TARDY UNPAID ARREARS BELATED DELAYED EXCESSIVE

OVEREAGER FEVERISH FEVEROUS

OVEREAT GORGE SLOFF SATIATE GOURMAND

OVERELABORATE NIGGLE

OVEREXERT TORLE TORFEL OVERPLY

OVERFED RANK FULSOME

OVERFLOW REE COME FLUX SLOP SWIM TEEM VENT BRIME FLOAT FLOOD SPATE SPILL ABOUND DEBORD OUTLET OVERRUN REDOUND BOILOVER EXUNDATE INUNDATE OUTSWELL SUBMERGE
(— **FROM MOLD**) SPEW SPUE

OVERFLOWING FLOW AWASH FLOAT DELAVY DELUGE ALLUVIO COPIOUS FRESHET PROFUSE INUNDANT EXUBERANT LANDFLOOD SUPERFLUX

OVERGARMENT SMOCK BLOUSE DUSTER

OVERGROWN FOZY RANK GAWKY BRANCHY FULSOME SPRATTY SPRITTY

OVERHAND WHIP

OVERHANG JUT BEND EAVE RAKE BULGE JETTY BEETLE SHELVE TOPPLE FANTAIL OVERLAP PROJECT SUSPEND

OVERHANGING BEETLE SHELVY HANGING PENDENT IMMINENT OBUMBRANT PENTHOUSE

OVERHAUL EXAMINE OVERHAIL

RENOVATE FOREREACH

OVERHEAD COST ABOVE ALOFT BURDEN ONCOST UPKEEP EXPENSE OVERTOP

OVERHEAT PARBOIL

OVERLAP LAP RIDE SYPHER SHINGLE IMBRICATE INTERSECT

OVERLAPPING JUGATE RIDING EQUITANT OBVOLUTE IMBRICATE
(— **IN FUGUE**) STRETTA STRETTO

OVERLAY CAP LAP CEIL COAT APPLY COUCH COVER GLAZE PATCH PLATE CEMENT CRAVAT SPREAD STUCCO VENEER ENCRUST OPPRESS OVERLIE SMOTHER APPLIQUE TEMPLATE
(— **WITH GOLD**) BEAT GILD

OVERLOAD GLUT CHARGE ENCUMBER SURCHARGE

OVERLOADED PLETHORIC PLETHOROUS

OVERLOOK BALK MISS OMIT PASS SKIP SLIP WINK FORGO ACQUIT EXCUSE FOREGO FORGET IGNORE MANAGE OVERGO ABSOLVE COMMAND CONDONE FORGIVE INSPECT MISKNOW NEGLECT CONFOUND DOMINATE DISREGARD DISSEMBLE

OVERLOOKER GAITER

OVERLORD LIEGE DESPOT ISWARA SATRAP TYRANT ISHVARA SUZERAIN TYRANNIZE

OVERLY CAP TOO

OVERLYING BROCHANT INCUMBENT

OVERMAN CHIEF LEADER ARBITER FOREMAN REFEREE OVERSEER SUPERMAN

OVERMANTLE (— **TREATMENT**) TRUMEAU

OVERMASTER GET

OVERMATCH BEST DEFEAT EXCEED SURPASS VANQUISH

OVERMODEST PRIM PRUDISH

OVERMUCH TOO EXCESS SURPLUS EXCESSIVE

OVERNICE FEAT FUSS SAUCY DAINTY QUAINT SPRUCE FINICKY PRECISE DENTICAL PRECIOUS SQUEAMISH

OVERPLAY HAM

OVERPOWER AWE BEAT ROUT RUSH CRUSH DROWN QUELL SWAMP WHELM COMPEL DEFEAT DELUGE ENGULF MASTER OVERGO SUBDUE WRIXLE CONQUER CONTROL OPPRESS REPRESS CONVINCE OUTSCOUT SCUMFISH SURPRISE
(— **WITH HEAT**) SWELT
(— **WITH LIGHT**) DAZZLE

OVERPOWERING DIRE FIERCE KILLING DAZZLING STUNNING DESPERATE MONSTROUS

OVERPRECISE FINICKY CLERKISH PRECIEUSE

OVERREACH DO POT DUPE GRAB CHEAT COZEN CHOILE GREASE NOBBLE OUTWIT OVERGO DECEIVE

OVERREADY FORWARD

OVERREFINED QUAINT PRECIOUS

OVERRIPE FRACID SQUSHY SQUUSHY

OVERRIPENESS SEED

OVERRULE VETO GOVERN ABROGATE OVERCOME

OVERRULING GREAT PREDOMINANT

OVERRUN TEEM BESET CRUSH SWARM DELUGE EXCEED INFEST INVADE OVERGO RAVAGE SPREAD DESTROY

OVERSEE TEND WATCH DIRECT HANDLE MANAGE SURVEY EXAMINE INSPECT NEGLECT DISREGARD SUPERVISE

OVERSEER BOSS CORK JOSS EPHOR GRAVE REEVE BISHOP CENSOR DRIVER GAFFER GRIEVE KEEKER MIRDHA TINDAL WARDEN BAILIFF CAPATAZ CAPORAL CURATOR FOREMAN HEADMAN KANGANI MANAGER MANDOER MAYORAL OVERMAN PRISTAW TAPSMAN BANKSMAN CHAPRASI DECURION MARTINET SURVEYOR VILLICUS
(— **OF MACHINERY**) TENTOR
(**SPIRITUAL** —) PASTOR PRIEST

OVERSENSITIVE TICKLISH

OVERSENTIMENTAL SLOPPY

OVERSHADOW DIM CLOUD COVER DWARF SHADE TOWER DARKEN EFFACE ECLIPSE OBSCURE UMBRAGE DOMINATE OVERCAST

OVERSHOE GUM BOOT GUME ARCTIC GAITER GALOSH GOLOSH PATTEN RUBBER SANDAL FLAPPER EXCLUDER FOOTHOLD PANTOFLE

OVERSIGHT EYE CARE HOLE SLIP ERROR FAULT GAFFE LAPSE WATCH CHARGE BLUNDER CONTROL JEOFAIL MISTAKE OMISSION TUTELAGE DIRECTION
(**LEGAL** —) JEOFAIL

OVERSKIRT PEPLUM PANNIER

OVERSOFT QUASHY

OVERSPREAD FOG CAST CLOT DECK PALL BATHE BREDE CLOUD COVER SMEAR STREW CLOTHE DELUGE DOODLE INDUCE SCATTER SUFFUSE BESPREAD

OVERSTATE MAGNIFY EXAGGERATE

OVERSTEP PASS EXCEED SURPASS

OVERSUPPLIED RANK

OVERT OPEN PATENT PUBLIC OBVIOUS APPARENT MANIFEST

OVERTAKE PASS ATAKE CATCH ATTAIN DETECT ENSNARE OVERHIE FOREHENT OVERHAUL
(— **BY DARKNESS**) BENIGHT

OVERTASK DRIVE

OVERTAX HOIST EXCEED STRAIN STRESS

OVERTHROW TIP CAST DASH DOWN FALL FELL FOIL FOLD HURL RAZE ROUT RUIN RUSH WALT WEND ALLAY EVERT FLING LEVEL QUASH UPSET WORST WRACK WRECK

DEFEAT DEJECT REPUTE SLIGHT TOPPLE TUMBLE UNSEAT WRITHE AFFLICT CONQUER CONVELL DESTROY DISMISS RUINATE SUBVERT UNDOING UNHORSE CONFOUND DEMOLISH OVERCOME REVERSAL SUPPLANT VANQUISH CHECKMATE CONFUSION (— BY TRIPPING) CHIP

OVERTONE PARTIAL HARMONIC

OVERTOP COW OVERREACH

OVERTURE OFFER PROEM ADVANCE OPENING PRELUDE APERTURE PROPOSAL SINFONIA VORSPIEL (INDECENT —) ASSAULT

OVERTURN TIP CAVE COUP KEEL TILT WALT WELT TERVE THROW UPSET WELME WHALM WHELM SLIGHT TIPPLE TOPPLE WELTER CAPSIZE DESTROY PERVERT REVERSE SUBVERT

OVERWEIGHT OUTGANG

OVERWHELM BOWL BURY SINK SLAY AMAZE COVER CRUSH DROOK DROUK DROWN FLOOD SEIZE SPATE SWAMP CUMBER DEFEAT DELUGE ENGULF OBRUTE PLUNGE QUELME QUENCH ASTOUND CONFUTE CONQUER ENGROSS FLATTEN IMMERSE INFLOOD OPPRESS ASTONISH DISTRESS INUNDATE SUBMERGE AVALANCHE

OVERWORK HOIN TIRE TOIL SWEAT SURMENAGE

OVINE OVIN OVILE SHEEP SHEEPLIKE

OVOID OVATE OBOVOID

OVOLO OVAL THUMB BOLTEL

OVULE EGG NIT GERM SEED EMBRYO OVULUM GEMMULE SEEDLET

OVUM EGG OVAL SEED SPORE OOSPHERE

OWAIA TREE BOBO

OWE DUE OWN REST AUGHT OUGHT SHALL POSSESS ATTRIBUTE

OWER DEBTOR

OWL ULE BUBO LULU MOMO RURU

SURN TYTO UTUM JENNY MADGE NINOX PADGE SCOPS STRIX TAWNY WEKAU AZIOLA HOOTER HOWLET KETUPA MUCARO RAPTOR STRICH VERMIN WHEKAU BOOBOOK HARFANG KATOGLE WAPACUT WOOLERT BILLYWIX POREPORK (— CALL) HOOT (LIKE AN —) STRIGINE (YOUNG —) UTUM OWLET

OWN AIN OWE AVOW FESS HAVE HOLD HOWE MEET NAIN SELF ADMIT AUGHT OUGHT MASTER CONCEDE CONFESS POSSESS

OWNER BEL MALIK WALLA HOLDER DOMINUS HERITOR ODALLER (— OF ESTATE) ALIRD (— OF FISHING PLANT) PLANTER (— OF YACHT) AFTERGUARD (PLANTATION —) COLON (SHEEP —) NABAL

OWNERSHIP ODAL UDAL AUGHT TITLE CORNER SEIZIN SEIZURE SEVERAL TENANCY DOMINIUM PROPERTY COMMUNITY

OX YAK ANOA AVER BEEF BUFF BULL GAUR MUSK NAWT NEAT NEWT NOWT OWSE REEM RUNT STOT URUS ZEBU AIVER BISON BUGLE GAYAL SANGA STEER TOLLY TSINE BOVINE MITHAN BANTENG BUFFALO KOUPREY TWINTER SELADANG TALLOWER (CAMBODIAN —) KOUPREY KOUPROH (HORNLESS —) MOIL (SMALL —) RUNT (TAME —) COACH (WILD —) URE ANOA BUFF GAUR REEM URUS BISON BUGLE BANTIN BANTENG BUFFALO SELADANG (YEARLING —) STIRK (YOUNG —) STOT

OXBLOOD KAZAK COPTIC KAZAKH

OXEN NOWT OWSEN CATTLE

OXEYE BOCE GOLD ASTER CLOUD

DAISY GOLDE DUNLIN PLOVER TARPON

OXFORD DOWN SHOE CLOTH OXONIAN SLIPPER

OXGANG OSKEN BOVATE OXGATE OXLAND PLOWGANG

OXIDATION RUST

OXIDE EARTH FLOSS CADMIA MOILES ZAFFER CALCINE LIMONITE DJALMAITE (— OF CALCIUM) LIME (— OF IRON) RUST COLCOTHAR MAGNETITE

OXLIP PAGLE PAIGLE PRIMULA MILKMAID PRIMROSE PRIMWORT

OXSHOE CUE

OXYGEN GAS OZONE OXYGENIUM

OXYGENATE AERATE VENTILATE

OYSTER COPIS COUNT PINNA PLANT SHELL COTUIT HUITRE NATIVE REEFER BIVALVE MOLLUSK RATTLER SHARPER BLUEPOINT GREENGILL LYNNHAVEN (— BED) PARK STEW LAYER SCALP CLAIRE SCALFE OYSTERAGE (— CATCHER) OLIVE PYNOT TIRMA KROCKET PIANNET REDBILL SCOLDER SHELDER PILWILLET SKELDRAKE (— CRAB) PINNOTERE (— FOSSIL) OSTRACITE (— MEASURE) WASH (— PLANT) SALSIFY (— SHELL) HUSK TEST SHUCK (— SMALLER THAN QUARTER) BLISTER (— SOLD BY POUND) COUNT (2,3, OR 4 —S) WARP (IRISH —) POWLDOODY (ROCK —) CHAMA (VEGETABLE —) SALSIFY (YOUNG —) SET SPAT

OYSTERFISH TAUTOG TOADFISH

OZARK STATE MISSOURI

OZOCERITE MALTHA NEFTGIL

OZONE AIR

P PAPA PETER
A DAD PAW FORT PAPA DADDY
  FATHER VILLAGE STOCKADE
ABULUM FOOD FUEL PROG CEREAL
  ALIMENT SUPPORT NUTRIMENT
AC BOOT SHOE MOCCASIN
ACA CAPA CAVY LAVA LABBA
  AGOUTI RODENT
ACE FIG PAD RIP WAY BEMA CLIP
  GAIT LOPE PASS PELT RACK RATE
  STEP TEAR TROT WALK AMBLE
  BRAWL CANTO SLINK SPACE SPEED
  STEEK SWING TEMPO TRACE TREAD
  CANTER GALLOP STRAIT STRIDE
  CHANNEL CHAPTER DOGTROT
  MEASURE PASSAGE SCUTTLE
  (FAST —) ROMP
  (RAPID —) CRACKER
  (SLOW —) JOG CREEP
  (PL.) MANAGE
ACER HORSE AMBLER SPANKER
  TRIPPLER
ACHISI LUDO UCKERS PARCHESI
ACHYDERM HIPPO RHINO
  ELEPHANT
ACIFIC CALM MEEK MILD IRENE
  IRENIC PLACID SERENE PEACEFUL
  TRANQUIL PEACEABLE
  (— ISLAND PINE) IE KOU IEIE LEHUA
ACIFIER DUMMY COMFORTER
ACIFIST BOLO
ACIFY PAY CALM EASE LULL STAY
  ABATE ALLAY AMESE MEASE PEASE
  QUELL QUIET STILL PECIFY SERENE
  SETTLE SOFTEN SOOTHE APPEASE
  ASSUAGE MOLLIFY PLACATE
  QUALIFY STIEKLE MITIGATE
  ALLEVIATE RECONCILE
ACK JAM PUN WAD BALE CADE
  CRAM DECK FILL GANG JAMB LADE
  LOAD PAIR STOW SWAG TAMP TUCK
  COUCH CRAME CROWD DRESS
  FLOCK HORDE SKULK SOMER STEVE
  STORE STUFF TRUSS BARREL
  BODDLE BUDGET BUNDLE CARTON
  DUFFLE EMBALE ENCASE FARDEL
  HAMPER IMPACT THWACK TURKEY
  WALLET PANNIER PORTAGE
  RUMMAGE SUMPTER KNAPSACK
  (— ANIMAL) ASS MULE BURRO
  CAMEL HORSE LLAMA DONKEY
  PACKER
  (— BUILDER) GOBBER
  (— JURY) WATER
  (— LOOSELY) HOVER
  (— OF BEARS) SLOTH
  (— OF CARDS) STOCK
  (— OF DOGS) CRY KENNEL
  (— OF FOXES) GROUP SKULK
  (— OF HOUNDS) CRY HUNT MUTE
  (— OFF) WAG SHANK TURSE
  (— ROAD) PACKWAY
  (— TIGHTLY) STIVE
ACKAGE PAD BALE BOLT PAIR
  DUMMY TRUSS BINDLE BUNDLE
  PACKET PARCEL SAMPLE SEROON
  DORLACH
  (— OF CIGARETTES) DECK
  (— OF GOLDBEATER'S SKINS)
  SHODER

(— OF LEAF) BOOK
(— OF PEPPERS) ROBBIN
(— OF STAMPS) KILOWARE
(— OF VELLUM) KUTCH
(— OF VENEER) FLITCH
(— OF WOOL) BAG PAD BUTT
  FADGE
(YARN —) CONE CHEESE
PACKER BALER LINER ROPER
  CANNER
PACKET BOAT BOOK DECK ROLL
  SCREW BUNDLE PARCEL SACHET
  (— OF VELLUM) CUTCH KUTCH
PACKHORSE SOMER JAGGER
  PACKER SUMPTER
PACKING CUP RAGS GAUZE PAPER
  STRAW WASTE GASKET GROMMET
  STOWAGE STOPPING
  (— MATERIAL) BALINE GASKET
  (CLAY —) LUTE
PACKINGHOUSE MEATWORKS
PACKMAN HAWKER
PACKSACK KYACK
PACKSADDLE BAT BARDEL
  APAREJO
PACT CARTEL PACTUM TREATY
  BARGAIN COMPACT LOCARNO
  ALLIANCE CONTRACT COVENANT
  AGREEMENT
PAD MAT WAD WAY BLAD BOSS
  FROG LURE MUTE PATH PUFF ROAD
  ROLL SHOE WALK WASE BLOCK
  INKER PERCH PILCH QUILT STENT
  STINT STUFF TABBY TRAMP BASKET
  BUFFER BUSTLE DAUBER HOLDER
  JOCKEY NUMNAH PADDLE PADNAG
  PANNEL PILLOW SPONGE TABLET
  TRUDGE VELURE WREATH BOLSTER
  BOMBAST CUSHION FOOTPAD
  PILLION SASHOON
  (— IN CRIB) BUMPER
  (— OF STRAW) SUNK WASE
  (— ON HORSE'S FOOT) FROG
  (ETCHER'S —) DABBER
  (HAIR —) RAT MOUSE TOQUE
  (INKING —) INKER TOMPION
  (PERFUMED —) SACHET
  (SADDLE —) PANEL PILLOW PILLION
PADAUK CORAIL
PADDER MANGLE
PADDING TABBY CADDIS BOLSTER
  BOMBAST BUSHING CADDICE
  FILLING PACKING ROBBERY
  WADDING MAHOITRE STUFFING
PADDLE OAR ROW SPUD WADE
  ALOOF CANOE SLICE SPANK
  BUCKET DABBLE PETTLE PUNISH
  STRIKE TODDLE SPANKER SPURTLE
  LUMPFISH
  (— BOX) WHEELHOUSE
  (— FOR FLOUR) SLICK
  (TAILOR'S —) BEATER
PADDLEFISH GANOID DUCKBILL
  STURGEON POLYODONT SPADEFISH
  SPOONBILL
PADDOCK LOT FROG PARK CLOSE
  FIELD SLEDGE GARSTON LOANING
  BIRDCAGE
PADDYMELON QUOKKA PADMELON

PADISHAH SULTAN PADASHA
  POTSHAW
PADLOCK LOCK FASTEN SECURE
  CLOSING FASTENER HORSELOCK
  (— LINK) SHACKLE
PADRE MONK CLERIC FATHER
  PRIEST CHAPLAIN
PADRONA LANDLADY MISTRESS
PADRONE BOSS CHIEF MASTER
  PATRON LANDLORD INNKEEPER
PAEAN ODE HYMN SONG PRAISE
  OUTBURST TRIUMPHAL
PAGAN ATA BUID BATAK BUKID
  APAYAO BAGOBO BANGON BILAAN
  BONTOC ETHNIC PAYNIM SABIAN
  ALANGAN DUMAGAT GENTILE
  HEATHEN INFIDEL SARACEN
  SUBANUN UNGODLY IDOLATOR
PAGANDOM PAYNIM
PAGE BOY CALL LEAF MOTH SIDE
  CHILD FACER FOLIO GROOM SHEET
  DONZEL ERRATA SUMMON VARLET
  BUTTONS CALLBOY FUNNIES
  PAVISER SERVANT HENCHMAN
  ICHOGLAN
  (— BOTTOM) TAIL
  (BLANK —S) CANCEL
  (FACING —S) SPREAD
  (LADY'S —) ESCUDERO
  (LAST FEW —S) BACK
  (LEFTHAND —) VERSO
  (RIGHTHAND —) RECTO OUTPAGE
  (TITLE —) TITLE UNWAN RUBRIC
  (PL.) ODDMENTS
PAGEANT JEST POMP SHOW ANTIC
  PARADE RIDING TABLEAU TAMASHA
  TRIUMPH AQUACADE CAVALCADE
  SPECTACLE WATERWORK
PAGEANTRY POMP PARADE
  HERALDRY SPLENDOR
PAGODA PON TAA HOON WATT
  TEMPLE VARELLA
PAHOUIN FAN FANG
PAHUTAN PAHO
PAID EVEN RESOLUTE
  (— IN COIN) DRY
  (— IN FULL) SATISFIED
PAIL CAN COG PAN SOA SOE BEAT
  BOWK GAWN MEAL STOP TRUG
  BOWIE COGUE CRUCK DANDY ESHIN
  SKEEL STOOP BLICKY BUCKET
  COGGIE HARASS KETTLE LEGLEN
  NOGGIN PIGGIN SITULA THRASH
  COLLOCK
  (MILK —) KIT SOE TRUG ESHIN
  LEGLEN
  (ON WHEELS) DANDY
  (POTTERY —) SEAL
  (SMALL —) KIT BLICKY BLICKIE
  (WOODEN —) COG COGUE LUGGIE
  PIGGIN
PAIN ACHE AGRA BALE CARE CARK
  FRET GRUE HARM HURT PANG SITE
  SORE TEEN TINE WARK AGONY
  BEANS CRAMP DOLOR GRIEF GRIPE
  PINCH PINSE SCALD SMART STING
  STOUN THRAW THROE WOUND
  BARRAT GRIEVE MISERY SHOWER
  STITCH TWINGE AFFLICH ALGESIS

ANGUISH EARACHE HURTING
MYALGIA OFFENCE PENALTY
TORTURE TRAVAIL TROUBLE
DISTRESS FLEABITE
(— IN BACK) NOTALGIA SCIATICA
(— IN HAND) CHIRAGRA
(— IN SIDE) STEEK
(— OF MIND) AGONY
(— RELIEVER) OPIATE ANODYNE
ASPIRIN
(FILL WITH —) YEARN
(SHARP —) WRING
(STOMACH —) GRIPES GNAWING
(WRENCHING —) TORSION
(PL.) LABOR WHILE EFFORT
TROUBLE
PAINFUL BAD ILL DIRE EVIL FELL
SORE SOUR TART ANGRY CRUEL
SHARP SORRY BITTER STICKY
GRIPING HURTFUL IRKSOME
PENIBLE PUNGENT EXACTING
TERRIBLE TORTUOUS DIFFICULT
HARROWING
PAINSTAKING BUSY LOVING
CAREFUL PENIBLE DILIGENT
EXACTING ASSIDUOUS ELABORATE
PAINT BLOT COAT DAUB DRAW FARD
GAUD LIMN PENT PICT SOIL COLOR
FEIGN FUCUS GRAIN ROUGE STAIN
BEDAUB DAZZLE DEPICT ENAMEL
FRESCO OPAQUE SHADOW SKETCH
BESMEAR PORTRAY PRETEND
SCUMBLE AIRBRUSH DECORATE
DESCRIBE DISGUISE URFIRNIS
CALCIMINE
(— A PIPE) SOIL
(— FACE OR BODY) FUCUS PARGET
(— HASTILY) SQUIGGLE
(— SKETCHILY) SPLASH
(— THROUGH PATTERN) STENCIL
(— WITH COSMETICS) POP POT
FARD
PAINTBRUSH WICKAWEE
NOSEBLEED
PAINTED PINTO FUCATE PASTOSE
GOFFERED
(— BEAUTY) VANESSA
(— BUNTING) POP NONPAREIL
(— CUP) WICKAWEE PAINTBRUSH
(— WAKE-ROBIN) SARA
PAINTER FAUVE ARTIST DAUBER
PICTOR PANTHER SIGNIST SIGNMAN
WORKMAN BRUSHMAN LUMINIST
MURALIST NAZARENE STIPPLER
DECORATOR TACTILIST
(PL.) ECLECTICS
PAINTING ART OIL PAT PATA DRAFT
MURAL PIECE TABLE WATER
CANVAS CROUTE FRESCO MINERY
TITIAN BODEGON CAMAIEU
CARTOON DAUBING GRADINO
GRAPHIC HISTORY FROTTAGE
PREDELLA SEAPIECE SYMPHONY
(— EQUIPMENT) OIL BRUSH EASEL
PAINT CANVAS PALLET
(— IN COLLOIDAL MEDIUM)
TEMPERA
(— OF EVERYDAY LIFE) GENRE
(— OF FOLIAGE) BOSCAGE

(— ON PLASTER) SECCO FRESCO
(— WITH OPAQUE COLORS)
GOUACHE
(CIRCULAR —) TONDO
(RELIGIOUS —) PIETA TANKA
(SCENIC —) SCAPE
(SMALL —) TABLET
(THREE PANEL —) TRIPTYCH
(PL.) GENRE
PAIR DUO TWO ZYG CASE DIAD
DUAD DUAL MATE SIDE SPAN TEAM
TWIN YOKE BRACE MARRY MATCH
TWAIN UNITE COUPLE GEMINI
COUPLET DOUBLET JUMELLE
TWOSOME
(— OF FILMS) BIPACK
(— OF MILLSTONES) RUN
(— OF SHOTS) BRACKET
(— OF TONGS) GRAMPUS GRAPPLE
(— OF WINGS) SHEARS
(— ROYAL) PARIAL
(ONE OF —) IMPAIR NEIGHBOR
(PL.) GEMELS
PAIRED GEMEL JUGATE ZYGOUS
JUMELLE
PAISLEY PRINT SHAWL DESIGN
FABRIC
PAIUTE DIGGER
PAJAMAS SHALWAR SLEEPER

PAKISTAN

BAY: SOYMIANI
CANAL: NARA ROHRI
CAPE: FASTA JADDI JIWANI
CAPITAL: ISLAMABAD
COIN: ANNA RUPEE
DAM: TARBELA
LANGUAGE: URDU PUSHTU SINDHI
  BALUCHI BENGALI PUNJABI
MOUNTAIN: TIRICHMIR
MOUNTAIN RANGE: MAKRAN
  KIRTHAR HIMALAYA SULAIMAN
NATIVE: BENGAL PATHAN SINDHI
  BALUCHI PUNJABI
PORT: CHALNA KARACHI
RIVER: NAL BADO RAVI ZHOB
  DASHT INDUS CHENAB GANGES
  JHELUM KUNDAR PORALI
  JAMUNNA
STATE: DIR SWAT KALAT KHARAN
  CHITRAL KHAIRPUR
TOWN: DACCA CHALNA KHULNA
  LAHORE MULTAN QUETTA
  KARACHI SIALKOT LYALLPUR
  PESHAWAR SARGODHA
WEIGHT: SEER TOLA MAUND

PAKTONG TUTENAG
PAL ALLY CHUM JACK PARD BILLY
BUDDY CHINA CRONY LOUKE
COBBER COPAIN DIGGER FRIEND
COMRADE PARTNER COMPANION
PALACE SALE CHIGI COURT SERAI
STEAD CASTLE ELYSEE LOUVRE
PALAIS ALCAZAR EDIFICE LATERAN
MANSION PALAZZO TRIANON
VATICAN ZWINGER SERAGLIO
WHITEHALL

(— OF SATAN) PANDEMONIUM
(FAIRY —) SHEE SIDHE
PALADIN HERO PEER ANSEIS
ASTOLF KNIGHT CHAMPION
DOUZEPER
PALAMON (RIVAL OF —) ARCITE
(WIFE OF —) EMELYE
PALANQUIN JAUN JUAN KAGE KAGO
DANDI DOOLI DOOLY PALKI SEDAN
DOOLIE LITTER PALKEE TONJON
PALATABLE SAPID SPICY TASTY
DAINTY SAVORY MOREISH DELICATE
LUSCIOUS PLEASING SAPOROUS
AGREEABLE DELICIOUS TOOTHSOME
PALATAL SOFT FRONT VELAR
GUTTURAL
PALATE TASTE VELUM RELISH
GOURMET URANISCUS
PALATIAL LARGE ORNATE STATELY
SPLENDID
PALATINE CAPE OFFICER PALADIN
PALATIAL
PALAVER GASH SLUM TALK CAJOLE
DEBATE GLAVER JARGON PARLEY
CHATTER FLATTER WHEEDLE
CAJOLERY FLATTERY
PALE DIM WAN ASHY BLOC FADE
GREY GULL LILY PALL SICK WHEY
ASHEN BLAKE BLATE BLEAK CLOSE
FAINT FENCE GREEN LIGHT LINEN
LIVID LURID MEALY STAKE STICK
WHITE ANEMIC BLANCH CHALKY
CHANGE DOUGHY FALLOW FEEBLE
PALLID PASTEL PICKET REGION
REMISS SICKLY SILVER WATERY
WHITEN DEFENSE GHASTLY
HAGGARD INSIPID OBSCURE
WATERISH
(IN —) HAURIENT
PALEA PALET SQUAMELLA
PALENESS WAN PALLOR ACHROMA
PALESTINE (SEE ISRAEL)
PALETOT COAT JACKET OVERCOAT
GREATCOAT
PALFREY HORSE PALFRY
PALIMPSET TABLET PARCHMENT
PALING PALE FENCE FLAKE LIMIT
PALIS STAKE PICKET FENCING
BLENCHING
PALISADE HAY BOMA PALE PEEL
CLIFF FENCE RIMER STAKE HURDIS
PICKET BARRIER ENCLOSE FORTIF
HURDIES STACKET TAMBOUR
ESPALIER
(MILITARY —) CIPPUS
(PL.) BAIL BARRIER
PALL FOG BORE CLOY PALE SATE
CLOAK CLOTH FAINT QUALM STAL
WEARY MANTLE NAUSEA SHROUD
DISGUST SATIATE ANIMETTA
MORTCLOTH
PALLET BED COT PAD COUCH QUI
BLANKET MATTRESS PLANCHER
PALLIARD BEGGAR LECHER RASCA
VAGABOND
PALLIATE EASE HIDE MASK VEIL
ABATE CLOAK COLOR COVER
GLOSS GLOZE LITHE BLANCH
LESSEN REDUCE SMOOTH SOFTEN

SOOTHE CONCEAL CUSHION
SHELTER DISGUISE MITIGATE
ALLID WAN ASHY PALE PALY
BLEAK WASHY WAXEN WHITE
SALLOW GHASTLY BLOODLESS
COLORLESS INNOCUOUS
ALL-MALL MAIL
ALLOR ASH WAN PALE ASHES
PALENESS
ALM DOM ATAP BRAB BURI BUSU
COCO DATE DOUM FLAT HIDE JARA
KOKO LOOF NIOG NIPA PAWN SAGO
SLIP TARA ARCHA ARECA ARENG
ASSAI BONGA BUNGA CARRY
COCOA COYOL CURUA DATIL FOIST
HOWEA INAJA JAGUA LOULU MERUS
NIKAU RATAN SABAL SALAK TECUM
TUCUM UNAMO YAGUA YARAY
ANAHAO ASSAHY BACABA BURITI
CHONTA COHUNE CONTAR COROJO
GEBANG GOMUTI GRUGRU JAMBEE
JUPATI KENTIA KITTUL LAWYER
NIBONG PACAYA RAFFIA ROTANG
THENAR TOOROO TROPHY APRICOT
BABASSU CARANDA CONCEAL
COQUITO ERYTHEA GEONOMA
MORICHE PUPUNHA SAGWIRE
TALIPOT URUCURI JACITARA
LATANIER
(— **FERN**) PONJA
(— **FOOD**) NUT COCO DATE NIPA
SAGO SURA ASSAI TAREE TODDY
COCONUT
(— **JUICE**) SURA
(— **LEAF**) OLA OLLA CAJAN FROND
(— **LILY**) TI
(— **OF HAND**) FLAT LOOF VOLA
TABLE THENAR
(— **OFF**) COG FOB TOP SHAB FOIST
TRUMP
(— **OUT**) APPAUME
(**BETEL** —) ARECA BONGA PUGUA
PINANG
(**CLIMBING** —) RATTAN
(**FEATHER** —) HOWEA GOMUTI
URUCURI
(**SPINY** —) PEACH GRIGRI GRUGRU
ALMARY CHIEF PALMAR SUPERIOR
ALMATE FLAT BROAD LOBED
WEBBED
ALMER LOUSE FERULE STROLL
TRAVEL VOTARY WANDER FOISTER
PILGRIM
ALMETTO CABBAGE PALMITO
BIGTHATCH
(— **STATE**) SOUTHCAROLINA
ALMODIC JERKY
ALMYRA BRAB TALA LONTAR
ONIER TADMOR BASSINE
(**QUEEN OF** —) ZENOBIA
LP FEEL TOUCH CAJOLE FEELER
HANDLE PALPUS FLATTER
ENTACLE
LPABLE BALD RANK PLAIN
PATENT AUDIBLE EVIDENT OBVIOUS
TACTILE APPARENT DISTINCT
MANIFEST TANGIBLE CORPOREAL
LPATION THROB WALLOP DIPPING
TAPAT

PALPEBRA EYELID
PALPITATE PANT QUAP THROB
FLACKER FLICKER FLUTTER
PULSATE
PALPITATION BEAT DUNT PANT
FLICKER FLUTTER PULSATION
THROBBING
(— **OF HEART**) THUMB
PALSIED SHAKY SHAKING
PARALYZED TOTTERING TREMBLING
TREMULOUS
PALSY PARLESIE PARALYSIS
PALTER FIB LIE BABBLE HAGGLE
MUMBLE PARLEY TRIFLE BARGAIN
CHAFFER CHATTER QUIBBLE
SHAFFLE
PALTRY BALD BARE BASE MEAN
ORRA PUNY SCAB VILE WAFF
FOOTY MINOR PETTY SCALL SCRUB
SILLY TRASH CHETIF FLIMSY
SHABBY SLIGHT TRASHY WOEFUL
HILDING PELTING PIMPING PITIFUL
RUBBISH SCABBED SCRUBBY
TRIVIAL PICAYUNE PICKLING
PIDDLING TRIFLING
PALUDAL MARSHY
PAMPA PLAIN PRAIRIE
PAMPAS (— **CAT**) KODKOD PAJERO
(— **DEER**) MAZAME
PAMPER PET BABY CRAM DELT
GLUT POMP HUMOR SPOIL TUTOR
WALLY CARESS COCKER CODDLE
COSHER COSSET CUDDLE DANDLE
FONDLE MAUNGE POSSET TIDDLE
CHERISH COCKNEY FORWEAN
GRATIFY INDULGE SATIATE
SMOODGE SAGINATE
PAMPHLET JACK LEAD QUIRE SHEET
TRACT FOLDER BOOKLET CATALOG
LEAFLET NOVELET BROCHURE
CHAPBOOK WORKBOOK CATALOGUE
PAN FIT TAB VLY MELL PART PRIG
VLEI WASH AGREE BASIN BATEA
COVER GRAND SHEET UNITE
FRACHE LAPPET PANKIN PATINA
SPIDER VESSEL CRANIUM CREAMER
HARDPAN PORTION ROASTER
SKILLET SUBSOIL RIDICULE
(— **FOR COALS**) BRAZIER
(— **OF BALANCE**) BOWL BASIN
SCALEPAN
(— **WITH 3 FEET**) POSNET
(**EVAPORATING** —) ROOM COVER
TACHE SALTPAN
(**GOD** —) FAUNUS
(**IRON** —) YET FRACHE
(**LONG-HANDLED** —) PINGLE
(**MILK** —) LEAD
(**OIL** —) SUMP
PANACEA CURE ELIXIR REMEDY
SOLACE CUREALL HEALALL
NEPENTHE

PANAMA

CAPITAL: PANAMA
COIN: BALBOA
CROP: ABACA CACAO
GULF: DARIEN CHIRIQUI

LAKE: GATUN
MEASURE: CELEMIN
MOUNTAIN: CHICO GANDI
　COLUMAN SANTIAGO
MOUNTAIN RANGE: VERAGUA
PORT: CRISTOBAL
PROVINCE: COCLE COLON
　CHIRIQUI VERAGUAS
RIVER: CHEPO SAMBU TUIRA
　BAYANO PANUGO CHAGRES
TOWN: COLON DAVID AZUERO
　BALBOA PANAMA PENONOME
　SANTIAGO
TREE: YAYA MARIA QUIRA ALFAJE
　CATIVO

PANAMA HAT JIPIJAPA
PANAMINT KOSO
PANCAKE FLAM AREPA CREPE
FADGE FLAWN KISRA LEFSE TOURT
BLINTZ FRAISE FROISE CRUMPET
FLAPPER FLIPPER FRITTER
HOTCAKE PIKELET CORNCAKE
FLAPJACK FLIPJACK
(PL.) LEFSEN
PANCREAS BUR NUT
PAND PAWN DRAPERY
PANDA WA WAH BEARCAT
PANDAVA BHIMA
PANDECT COMPENDIUM
PANDEMONIUM DIN HELL CHAOS
NOISE TUMULT UPROAR DISORDER
CONFUSION
PANDER BAWD PIMP BULLY CATER
MICHER PURVEY RUFFIAN WHISKIN
PROCURER BAWDSTROT
PANDORA BANDORE
(**BROTHER OF** —) PROMETHEUS
(**HUSBAND OF** —) EPIMETHEUS
PANE GLASS GLAZE LOZEN PANEL
QUIRK SHEET SHOCK SLASH
QUARRY SECTION PORTLIGHT
PANEGYRIC ELOGE ELOGY EULOGY
PRAISE ORATION TRIBUTE
ENCOMIUM LAUDATION
PANEL FIN PAN JURY SKIN BOARD
GROUP LABEL TABLE ABACUS
ASSIZE COFFER HURDLE MIRROR
PADDLE PILLOW ROSACE TABLET
TYMPAN CAISSON CONSOLE
FLIPPER LACUNAR DECORATE
MANDORLA
(— **IN FENCE**) LOOP
(— **IN GARMENT**) LAP STEAK
(**3-PART** —) TRIPTYCH
(**CIRCULAR** —) ROUNDEL
(**GAUZE** —) SCRIM
(**GLAZED** —) LAYLIGHT
(**LEGAL** —) ARRAY
(**RECESSED** —) ORB COFFER
LACUNAR
(**SUNKEN** —) CAISSON CASSOON
PANFISH SCUP
PANG ACHE CRAM FILL GIRD PAIN
STAB TANG AGONY PINCH PRONG
SPASM STANG STANG STOUN STUFF THROE
SHOWER STOUND TWINGE ANGUISH
TRAVAIL

(PL.) GNAWINGS
PANGOLIN MANID MANIS ANTEATER
EDENTATE TANGILIN
PANGWE FAN FANG
PANHANDLE BEG CADGE SKELB
SKILDER
(— STATE) WV WVA
PANIC FEAR FRAY FUNK WILD
ALARM AMAZE CHAOS SCARE
FRIGHT SCHRIK TERROR SWITHER
PANICKY FUNKY
PANICLE JUBA WHISK ANTHELA
PANNIER BAG PED SERON BASKET
CAJAVA CURAGH DORSEL DORSER
DOSSAL DOSSER PANTRY CORBEIL
CURRACK KAJAWAH KEDJAVE
PANOPLY POMP ARMOR UNIFORM
PANORAMA VIEW RANGE SCENE
SWEEP VISTA NEORAMA PICTURE
SCENERY CYCLORAMA POLYORAMA
PANPIPE SICU SIKU QUILL ANTARA
SYRINX ZAMPOGNA
PANSY FANCY PENSE VIOLA KISSES
PENSEE VIOLET TRINITY FANTASQUE
HEARTEASE
PANT FAB ACHE BEAT BLOW FUFF
GAPE GASP HECH LONG PANK PECH
PEGH PINE PIPE PUFF TIFT HEAVE
QUIRK STECH SUGGE THROB YEARN
ANHELE ASPIRE FRIESE PANTLE
PULSATE
PANTAGRUEL (COMPANION OF —)
PANURGE
(FATHER OF —) GARGANTUA
(MOTHER OF —) BADEBEC
PANTALOONS PANTS TROUSERS
PANTHEIST AMALRICIAN
PANTHEON TEMPLE ROTUNDA
VALHALL VALHALLA
PANTHER CAT PARD PUMA COUGAR
JAGUAR LEOPARD PAINTER PANTILE
PANTIES SCANTIES
PANTILE TILE IMBREX BISCUIT
HARDTACK
PANTING ANHELOSE ANHELOUS
PANTOGRAPH EIDOGRAPH
POLYGRAPH
PANTOMIME PLAY PANTO
PANTRY CAVE STUE AMBRY COVEY
CUDDY CLOSET LARDER SPENCE
BUTLERY BUTTERY PANNIER
PANTLER SERVERY SPICERY
CUPBOARD
PANTS JEANS LEVIS BRIEFS SLACKS
DRAWERS JODHPUR BREECHES
BRITCHES KICKSIES KNICKERS
SNUGGIES TROUSERS
(LEATHER —) CHAPS LEDERHOSEN
PANUELO COLLAR RUFFLE
KERCHIEF NECKCLOTH
PANZER TANK
PAP DUG TIT POBS TEAT NIPPLE
EMULSION FLUMMERY
PAPA PA DAD PAP PAW POP SIN
BABA EVIL DADDY LOVER PAPPY
BABOON FATHER POTATO PRIEST
HUSBAND VULTURE
PAPAL (ALSO SEE POPE) POPAL
PAPANE POPELY APOSTOLIC

PAPAW PAPA ASIMEN PAPAIO
ASIMINA CORAZON JASMINE
PAPAYA PAPAW LECHOSA
PAPER LIL WEB BILL BOND BLANK
BROKE ESSAY STUDY THEME
ASTHMA BINDLE CARTEL PAPIER
REPORT RETREE VESSEL CHEVIOT
EXHIBIT JOURNAL WRITING YOSHINO
DOCUMENT MONOGRAPH VALENTINE
(— FOLDER) STROKER
(— MAKER) WASHERMAN
(— NAUTILUS) ARGONAUT
(— PULP) WATERLEAF
(— QUANTITY) PAGE REAM QUIRE
SHEET BUNDLE
(ABSORBENT —) BLOTTER
TOWELLING
(BUILDING —) FELT
(BUNDLE OF —S) DUFTER DOSSIER
(CHINESE —) INDIA
(DAMAGED —) BROKE CASSE SALLE
RETREE
(FOLDED —) SADDLE AIRPLANE
(GLOSS —) GILL
(HARD —) PELURE
(HEAVY —) FELT
(LINING —S) SKIPS
(NEGOTIABLE —) STIFF
(OFFICIAL —) TARGE HOOKUM
DOCUMENT
(PARCHMENT —) VELLUM
PERGAMYN
(PHOTOGRAPHIC —) SEPIA
(SIZE OF —) CAP COPY DEMI NOTE
POST POTT TOWN ATLAS CROWN
FOLIO LARGE LEGAL ROYAL SIXMO
ALBERT BILLET CASING LETTER
MEDIUM THIRDS BASTARD CABINET
EMPEROR THEOREM ELEPHANT
FOOLSCAP IMPERIAL
(STRIP OF —) TAPE
(THIN —) FLIMSY PELURE TISSUE
ONIONSKIN
(TOILET —) BUMF
(UNCUT —) BOLT
(WALL —) TENTURE
(WATERMARKED —) BATONNE
(WRAPPING —) SKIP KRAFT
SEALING SCREENING
(WRITING —) FLAT LINEN WEDDING
PAPERBARK CAJEPUT MILKWOOD
PAPERBOARD BENDER VENEER
CARDBOARD CHIPBOARD
PULPBOARD
PAPILLA CERAS DEIRID NIPPLE
PAPULA MAMMULA THELIUM
(PL.) CERATA
PAPILLOMA ANGLEBERRY
PAPIO MORMON
PAPIST TORY PAPANE CATHOLIC
POPELING
PAPPUS DOWN THISTLEDOWN
PAPPY PA DAD PAW PAPA SOFT
MUSHY PULPY FATHER SUCCULENT
PAPRIKA PIMENTO PIMIENTO
PAPUA (BAY OF —) DYKE MILNE
ACLAND HOLNICOTE
(RIVER OF —) FLY KIKORI PURARI

(TOWN OF —) BUNA DARU KIKORI
SAMARAI
PAPUAN ARAU BIAK HULA KATE
BUANG EKARI KIWAI KWOMA SIVAI
SULKA BAITSI BANARO IATMUL
KEREWA KOIARI ARAPESH BAINING
PAPULE WHELK PIMPLE
PAPYRUS REED PAPER SEDGE
BIBLOS GLUMAL SCROLL BULRUSH
(— STRIP) ORIHON
PAR BY NORM EQUAL NORMAL
AVERAGE EQUALITY
(ONE OVER —) BOGIE
(ONE UNDER —) BIRDIE
(TWO UNDER —) EAGLE
PARA FODDA PERAU PARRAH
PARABLE MYTH TALE FABLE STORY
APOLOG BYWORD MASHAL SAMPLE
BYSPELL PROVERB ALLEGORY
FORBYSEN LIKENESS
PARABOLA ARC CURVE ANTENNA
PARACHUTE SILK CHUTE BROLLY
DROGUE STREAMER
PARACHUTIST PATHFINDER
(PL.) STICK
PARACLETE AIDER HELPER
PLEADER ADVOCATE CONSOLER
COMFORTER
PARADE JET TOP POMP SHOW WAL
MARCH STRUT FLAUNT MUSTER
REVIEW STROLL CORTEGE DISPLAY
EXHIBIT MARSHAL CEREMONY
EXERCISE FLOURISH GRANDEUR
SPLENDOR PAGEANTRY
(— GROUND) MAIDAN
(UNSUBSTANTIAL —) PAGEANT
PARADED AFFICHE
PARADISE EDEN JODO BLISS JENN
AIDENN GOLOKA HEAVEN ELYSIUM
NIRVANA
(— OF INDRA) SVARGA SWARGA
(— TREE) ACEITUNA STAVEWOOD
PARADOX KOAN ANTINOMY
PARADOXURE MUSANG
PARAFFIN ALKANE
PARAGON GEM PINK TYPE IDEAL
MODEL APERSEE PATTERN
PEROPUS PHOENIX NONESUCH
NONPARIEL
PARAGRAPH ITEM SIGN CAPUT
PAUSE CLAUSE NOTICE RUBRIC
ARTICLE INITIAL PILCROW SECTION
MATERIAL PEELCROW PERSONAL
SUBLEADER
(— MARK) PILCROW

PARAGUAY

CAPITAL: ASUNCION
COIN: GUARANI
DEPARTMENT: GUAIRA ITAPUA
OLIMPO CAAZAPA BOQUERON
LAKE: VERA YPOA YPACARAI
LANGUAGE: GUARANI
MEASURE: PIE LINE LINO VARA
LEGUA LINEA CORDEL CUADRA
CUARTA FANEGA
PLAIN: CHACO

RIVER: YPANE ACARAY PARANA CONFUSO
TOWN: LUQUE PILAR CAACUPE CAAZAPA TRINIDAD CONCEPCION VILLARRICA
WEIGHT: QUINTAL

PARAKEET CONURE PARROT WELLAT ARATINGA KAKARIKI POPINJAY ROSEHILL GREENLEEK
PARALLEL EVEN LIKE ALONG EQUAL MATCH SECOND EXAMPLE FRONTAL PARAGON ANALOGUE LIKENESS MULTIPLE QUANTITY
PARALLELOGRAM RHOMB OBLONG SQUARE RHOMBUS RHOMBOID RECTANGLE
PARALYSIS CRAMP PALSY SHOCK PARESIS DIPLEGIA
PARALYZE DARE DAZE STUN PALSY SCRAM ASTONY CONGEAL IMPALSY TORPEDO
PARALYZED NUMB PALSIED CRIPPLED
PARAMOUNT ABOVE CHIEF RULER SOVRAN CAPITAL SUPREME DOMINANT SUPERIOR SUZERAIN SOVEREIGN
PARAMOUR DOLL PRIM PURE LEMAN LOVER WOMAN WOOER AMORET FRIEND MASTER MINION FRANION GALLANT HETAERA RUFFIAN SERVANT SPECIAL SULTANA STALLION BOYFRIEND
PARAPET BUTT WALL BAHUT REDAN BARBET BONNET TRENCH BULWARK PLUTEUS RAILING RAMPART ENVELOPE TRAVERSE
PARAPH RUBRIC
PARAPHERNALIA GEAR EQUIPAGE APPARATUS EQUIPMENT TRAPPINGS
PARAPHRASE FARSE REWORD TARGET TARGUM PREFACE THARGUM VERSION TRANSLATE
PARASITE BUG BUR FLY BURR MOSS SPIV TRYP CHARK DRONE LEECH SHARK TOADY VIRUS FEEDER FUNGUS GNATHO SHADOW SPONGE SUCKER BLEEDER SPONGER TAGTAIL DICYEMID ENTOZOON HANGERON SLAVERER INFESTANT POTHUNTER SACCULINA SPARGANUM TOADEATER TUBHUNTER
(— ON TROUT) SUG
(PL.) ECTOZOA ENTOZOA DRIFTWOOD
PARASITIC CYTOZOIC TRENCHER BIOPHILOUS
(— JAEGER) SHOOI DIRTBIRD
PARASOL SHADE AOGIRI SHADOW ROUNDEL TIRESOL KITTYSOL SUNSHADE UMBRELLA
(— MUSHROOM) LEPIOTA
PARAVANE OTTER
PARBOILED LEEPIT
PARCEL LOT DEAD DEAL DOLE METE PACK PART WISP BULSE BUNCH

GROUP PIECE BUNDLE DIVIDE FARDEL PACKET PASSEL CONACRE PACKAGE PORTION COMMODITY
(— OF DIAMONDS) SERIES
(— OF GROUND) LOT PICK CLOSE SOLUM SUERTE CONACRE PENDICLE
(— OF HEMP FIBER) PIG
(— OF JEWELS) BULSE
(— OUT) ALLOT
PARCH DRY FRY BURN COOK SEAR ROAST TOAST PEARCH RIZZER SCORCH BRISTLE BRUSTLE GRADDAN SHRIVEL TORREFY TORRIFY
PARCHED ARID HUSK SERE ADUST FIERY GIZZEN TORRID THIRSTY SCORCHED
PARCHING URENT
PARCHMENT LARK FOREL CHARTA MEZUAH PAPYRIN SCYTALE DRUMHEAD PALIMPSEST
(— PAPER) DOCKET PERGAMYN
(FINE —) VEL VELLUM
(PIECE OF —) MEMBRANE
(ROLL OF —) PELL SCROLL
PARD PAL CHUM TIGER FRIEND LEOPARD PANTHER PARTNER COMPANION
PARDON FREE CLEAR COVER GRACE MERCY REMIT SPARE ACQUIT ASSOIL EXCUSE SHRIVE ABSOLVE AMNESTY CONDONE FORGIVE REPRIEVE TOLERATE EXCULPATE
PARDONABLE VENIAL VENIABLE EXCUSABLE
PARDONER QUESTOR QUAESTOR
PARE CUP CHIP COPE FLAY PEEL SKIN FRIZZ SHAVE SKELP SLIPE SPADE CHISEL REDUCE REMOVE RESECT CURTAIL WHITTLE
(— LEATHER) SKIVE
(— SOD) BURNBEAT
(— STAVES) BUCK
(— STONE) BOAST
PAREGORIC ANODYNE MITIGATING
PAREL PARELL APPAREL CLOTHING ORNAMENT
PARENCHYMA AMYLOM MESOPHYL
PARENT DAD DAM MAMA PAPA SIRE DADDY ELDER MATER PATER AUTHOR FATHER MOTHER ORIGIN FORBEAR GENITOR ANCESTOR BEGETTER FILICIDE GUARDIAN
PARENTAGE KIND BIRTH BROOD FAMILY ORIGIN PROGENY ENGENDURE
PARENTHESIS HOOK ASIDE PAREN BRACKET TOENAIL INNUENDO INTERVAL INTERLUDE
(PL.) HOOKS CURVES
PAREVE NEUTRAL
PARGET COAT GYPSUM PARIET PLASTER DECORATE WHITEWASH
PARGO MUTTONFISH
PARHELION DOG SUN SUNDOG
PARIAH PAREA ISHMAEL OUTCAST
PARIAN CHINA MARBLE PORCELAIN
PARIETAL SOMAL SOMATIC
PARI-MUTUEL TOTE TOTALIZER

PARING CHIP FOIL SHRED SPECK GUBBIN PARURE PEELING
(FISH —S) GUBBINS
(PL.) BOXING
PARIS ALEXANDER
(— AIRPORT) ORLY
(FATHER OF —) PRIAM
(MOTHER OF —) HECUBA
(PALACE IN —) ELYSEE LOUVRE TUILERIES
(RIVER OF —) SEINE
(STOCK EXCHANGE IN —) BOURSE
(SUBWAY IN —) METRO
(WIFE OF —) OENONE
PARISH CURE HOUSE TITLE CHARGE SOCIETY PECULIAR OUTPARISH
(— HEAD) PASTOR PRIEST MINISTER
(— MEETING) VESTRY
PARISON BLOW GATHERING
PARITY ANALOGY EQUALITY LIKENESS GRAVIDITY
PARK HAY PEN HOLE STOP WAIT GREEN LEAVE CIRCLE DAPHNE GARDEN PRATER COMMONS DIAMOND PADDOCK TERRACE PARADISE TETRAGON
PARKA PARCA ANORAK
PARLANCE TALK IDIOM SPEECH DICTION DISCOURSE
PARLAY DOUBLE
PARLEY DODGE PARLE SPEAK TREAT UTTER CONFER INDABA PALTER PAROLI DISCUSS PALAVER
PARLING DISCOURSE TEMPORIZE
PARLIAMENT DIET RUMP TING COURT SENAT CORTES FANTAN MAJLIS SAEIMA COUNCIL ESTATES LAGTING RIKSDAG CONGRESS CONVERSE STORTING VOLKSRAAD
(SCAND. —) THING
PARLIAMENTARIAN APRONEER
PARLOR BEN BOOR HALL FOREROOM LOCUTORY SNUGGERY SOLARIUM
(COUNTRY —) SPENCE
(MILKING —) BAIL
PARLORMAID MATRON
PARLOUS KEEN RISKY CLEVER SHREWD CUNNING CRITICAL PERILOUS DANGEROUS HAZARDOUS
PARMESAN GRANA
PAROCHIAL PETTY NARROW PAROCHIAN SECTARIAN
PARODIST SPOOFER
PARODY RIB SKIT SPOOF SATIRE TRAVESTY BURLESQUE IMITATION
PAROLE FAITH PLEDGE LICENSE PROMISE
PARONOMASIA PUN AGNOMINATION
PARONYCHIA FELON PANARIS NAILWORT
PAROTITIS MUMPS
PAROXYSM FIT KINK PANG AGONY COLIC QUIRK SPASM STORM STOUR THROE ACCESS ATTACK FRENZY ORGASM RAPTUS SHOWER RAPTURE EPITASIS AGITATION
PARR PAR SAMLET SCEGGER SKEGGER BRANDLIN BRANDLING

PARROT ARA HIA KEA COPY ECHO
JAKO KAKA LORO LORY POLL VAZA
ARARA CAGIT MACAW MIMIC POLLY
AMAZON CAIQUE CONURE KAKAPO
REPEAT TIRIBA CORELLA GRASSIE
LORILET COCKATOO LORIKEET
LOVEBIRD PARAKEET PICARIAN
POPINJAY BROADTAIL COCKATEEL
PARROT FISH LORO SCAR LANIA
LAUIA SCAUR VIEJA COTORO
SCARUS LABROID MUDFISH
OLDWIFE BLUEFISH
PARRY FEND STOP WARD AVOID
BLOCK DODGE EVADE FENCE PRIME
QUART SIXTE OCTAVE PARADE
QUINTE SECOND THWART TIERCE
COUNTER DEFLECT EVASION
PARSE PACE PEARCE ANALYZE
DIAGRAM DISSECT CONSTRUE
ANATOMIZE
PARSI ZOROASTRIAN
  (— HOLY BOOK) AVESTA
  (— PRIEST) MOBED DASTUR
PARSIMONIOUS GARE MEAN NEAR
NIGH CLOSE SCANT SPARE TIGHT
FRUGAL NARROW SCARCE SCOTCH
SKIMPY SORDID STINGY STRAIT
MISERLY SCRIMPY SPARING
COVETOUS GRASPING GRUDGING
SCREWING WRETCHED MERCENARY
NIGGARDLY PENURIOUS RETENTIVE
PARSLEY ACHE CUMIN UMBEL
CICELY CONIUM ELTROT KARPAS
CHERVIL HOGWEED FLUELLIN
PARSLEY CAMPHOR APIOL APIOLE
PARSNIP TANK WYPE UMBEL
CONIUM MADNEP CADWEED
HOGWEED BUNDWEED QUEENWEED
PARSON RECTOR CROAKER PATRICO
PERSONA MINISTER PREACHER
GUIDEPOST
  (COUNTRY —) RUM
  (PL.) PARSONRY
PARSONAGE GLEBE MANSE
RECTORY PASTORATE PASTORIUM
PARSON BIRD POE TUI KOKO TUWI
POEBIRD POYBIRD
PART DEL END LOT PAN DEAL DOLE
FECK GRIN HAET HALF HAND PANE
ROLE ROVE SECT SHED SIDE SOME
TWIN PARTY PIECE QUOTA SEVER
SHARE SHODE SNACK SPLIT TWAIN
BEHALF CANTON CLEAVE DEPART
DETAIL DIVIDE FEEDER FINGER
MEMBER MINUTE MOIETY PARCEL
PORTIO QUORUM SECTOR SINGLE
SUNDER UNYOKE DISJOIN ELEMENT
FEATURE FRUSTUM PORTION
SECTION SEGMENT SEVERAL
ALIENATE DISSEVER DIVISION
ELIQUATE FRACTION LIRIPIPE
  (— HAIR) SHADE
  (— OF ANIMAL'S TAIL) DOCK
  (— OF BEEF) CHUCK SKINK
  (— OF BLAST FURNACE) BOSH
BELLY
  (— OF BOW) PEAK
  (— OF CAM WHEEL) LOBE
  (— OF CANNON) CHASE

  (— OF CHAIR) SPLAT
  (— OF COMPASS) FLY
  (— OF CONCERTO) CEMBALO
  (— OF CROSSBOW) LATH
  (— OF DIAMOND) BEZEL
  (— OF FLEECE) LEECH
  (— OF FOWL'S COMB) BLADE
  (— OF GUN SHIELD) APRON
  (— OF HARBOR) FAIRWAY
  (— OF HAWK'S BEAK) CLAP
  (— OF HIDE) RANGE
  (— OF HOOKAH) CHILLUM
  (— OF POETIC FOOT) ARSIS
  (— OF PORK LOIN) GRISKIN
  (— OF RIVER) FRESH
  (— OF SADDLE TREE) FORK
  (— OF STAIR TREAD) NOSING
  (— OF STAMEN) ANTHER
  (— OF SWORD BLADE) FOIBLE
  (— OF SWORD) FORTE
  (— OF TEMPLE) CELLA
  (— OF TONGUE) DORSUM
  (— OF TURTLE) CALIPEE
  (— OF VIOLIN BOW) BAGUET
  (— OF WHEEL) SPEECH
  (— THAT REVOLVES) ROTOR
  (— WITH) GIVE LOSE SELL LEAVE
DONATE ABANDON
  (24TH —) CARAT
  (360TH —) DEGREE
  (ACCOMPANYING —) BURDEN
OBBLIGATO
  (ASSUMED —) FIGURE
  (BAGLIKE —) SAC
  (BEST —) FAT YOLK CREAM
FLOWER MARROW
  (BRISTLELIKE —) SETA
  (BROADEST — OF PLANK) TOUCH
  (CENTRAL —) HUB BODY CORE
HEART KERNEL
  (CHOICE —) ELITE
  (CLEAR — OF LIQUID) SWIM
  (CLOSING —) HEEL
  (COARSE — OF FLAX) HURDS
  (CONICAL —) BULLET
  (CURVED —) START
  (DEPRESSED —) HOLLOW
  (DISTANT —S) FARNESS
  (DUPLICATE —) SPARE
  (EDIBLE — OF CLAM) CHEEK
  (ESSENTIAL —) PITH
  (ESSENTIAL —S) STAMINA
  (FIFTH —) QUINTUS
  (FINAL —) LAST SHANK EPILOG
  (FIRST —) FRONT PRIME INITIAL
BEGINNING
  (FOURTH —) FARDEL FERLING
  (FRONT —) VAUNT BREAST
FORESIDE
  (GREATER —) HEFT SUBSTANCE
  (HARDEST —) BRUNT
  (HIGHEST —) CROP CROWN HEIGHT
  (HUNDREDTH —) CENTESM
  (IMPAIRING —) ALLOY
  (IN —) HALVES
  (INNERMOST —) FUND
  (INSTRUMENTAL —) HAND
CONTINUO
  (INTERLACED —) TWINE

  (LARGE —) FORCE
  (LATERAL — OF HEAD) CHEEK
  (LATTER —) HEEL
  (LEAST —) STITCH
  (LOWER — OF ROBE) BASES
  (LOWER —) SECONDO
  (LOWEST —) FOOT BOTTOM
GROUND DESCENT
  (MAIN —) BODY BULK SUBSTANCE
  (MATERIAL —) GIST
  (MIDDLE — OF NIGHT) HOWE
  (MIDDLE —) DEEP CENTER
  (MINOR —) BIT COG
  (MINUTE —) PRICK TITTLE
  (MISSING —) LACUNA
  (MOST IMPORTANT —) EYE
FOREHAND
  (MOST SERIOUS —) DICKENS
  (OF HORSE'S THIGH) GASKIN
  (OVERDUE —) ARREAR
  (PRINCIPAL —) BODY MAIN GROSS
  (PRIVATE —) THING MEMBER
  (PROJECTING —) ARM JAG JET JOC
APSE LOBE SPURN
  (PROTUBERANT —) BOSS BULGE
  (REJECTED —S) CHANKINGS
  (REMAINING —) BUTT DREG HEEL
  (REMOTEST —) EXTREMITY
  (RINGLIKE —) ANNULUS
  (ROOTLIKE —) RADICLE
  (ROUNDED —) BULB
  (SAWLIKE —) SERRA
  (SECRET —) RECESS
  (SLENDER —) NECK
  (SMALL —) BIT ATOM FLOW TITHE
DETAIL MINUTE SNIPPET
  (SMALLEST —) ATOM WHIT MINIM
  (SOFT — OF BREAD) CRUMB
  (SOFT — OF VEIN) LEATH
  (SOLO —) CALL
  (STILL — OF WATER) KELD
  (SWINGING —) FLAIL
  (TELLING —) POINT
  (TENTH —) TITHE
  (THIN — OF WALL) ALLEGE
  (THIRD —) THIRDENDEAL
  (TOP —) HEADPIECE
  (TWELFTH —) INCIA POINT UNCIAL
  (UPPER —) CHIEF RIDGE
OVERPARTY
  (UPPERMOST —) TOP PEAK CHIEF
UPSIDE TOPSIDE
  (VAUDEVILLE —) OLIO
  (VITAL —) HEART
  (WINGLIKE —) ALA
  (WORST —) DEPTH
  (WORTHLESS —) DREGS
PARTAKE BITE PART SHARE DIVIDE
PARTEN
  (— OF) USE HAVE SHARE TASTE
TOUCH IMPART
PARTAN CRAB
PARTED PARTITE
PARTHAON (FATHER OF —) AGENC
  (MOTHER OF —) EPICASTE
  (SON OF —) OENEUS
  (WIFE OF —) EURYTE
PARTIAL HALF PART SEMI BIASED
UNFAIR COLORED HALFWAY

UNEQUAL HARMONIC INCLINED
PARTISAN PROPENSE SKELETON
FAVORABLE
PARTIALITY FAVOR RESPECT
AFFECTION SPECIALTY
PARTIALLY HALF HALFWAY
HALFWISE
PARTICIPANT BOOK ACTOR PARTY
MEMBER PARTNER DUETTIST
PARTABLE PARTISAN
(SUBORDINATE —) STOOGE
(PL.) FIELD
PARTICIPATE JOIN SIDE ENTER
SHARE ENGAGE ENLIST IMPART
COMPETE PARTAKE
(— IN) GO HAVE JOIN STAY STAND
TASTE COMMON STICKLE
PARTICIPATION HAND PLOT
SOCIETY INTEREST
(COMMON —) COMMUNITY
PARTICIPLE VERBID
PARTICLE ACE BIT DOT FIG GRU
JOT RAY ATOM BETA CORN CROT
DUST GRUE HAET IOTA KNIT MITE
MOTE SNIP SPOT STIM WHIT ALPHA
BOSON FLAKE FLECK GHOST GRAIN
MESON POINT SHRED SPECK STARN
STIME THRUM TWINT FILING GEIGER
LEPTON MOMENT PANGEN RIZZOM
SMIDGE SMITCH TITTLE AMICRON
FERMION GEMMULE GRANULE
NUCLEUS PSYCHON SMIDGIN
ACCEPTER SMIDGEON POSITRINO
SCINTILLA
(— IN BLOOD) EMBOLUS
(— IN INTERNAL EAR) OTOCONIUM
(— OF FIRE) SPARK
(— OF GOLD) COLOR
(— OF SOOT) ISEL IZLE SMUT AIZLE
(—S IN BEER) FLOATERS
(—S OF GRAIN) CHOP
(ATOMIC —) ION ELECTRON
(ELECTRIFIED —) ION ANION
PROTON THERMION
(FINE ICY —S) SLEET
(JAGGED —) SPLINTER
(LEAST POSSIBLE —) MINIM
(LINGUISTIC —) SERVILE
(MINUTE —) JOT ORT RAY ATOM
GRAIN SPECK RAMENT GRANULE
MOLECULE RAMENTUM
(NEGATIVE —) NOR NOT
(NUCLEAR —S) FALLOUT
(POSITIVELY-CHARGED —) CATION
KATION
(SMALL —) NIP BLEB CORN MOTE
GRAIN SPECK AMICRON GRANULE
SPRINKLE SUBMICRON
(TINY —) ATOMY
(ULTIMATE —) PSYCHON
(PL.) DUST FINES SWARF SIZINGS
CUTTINGS FURFURES
ARTI-COLORED PIED FANCY
MOTLEY PARTED PIEBALD
BUTTERFLY HARLEQUIN
ARTICULAR AND ATOM FIXY ITEM
NICE SELF FUSSY PARTY POINT
THING CHOOSY DAINTY DETAIL
MINUTE MOROSE REGARD SINGLE

STICKY ARTICLE CAREFUL CERTAIN
CORRECT FINICKY PRECISE PRIVATE
RESPECT SEVERAL SPECIAL
UNUSUAL CLERKISH CONCRETE
ESPECIAL PECULIAR PICKSOME
PRECIOUS SINGULAR SUBALTERN
(NOT —) INCURIOUS
PARTICULARLY ONLY EXTRA
SINGLY SPECIAL EXPRESSLY
SPECIALLY
PARTING DEATH GOODBYE
FAREWELL
(— AS OF HAIR) SHED
PARTISAN PIKE SIDER STAFF BIASED
FACTOR FAUTOR MARIAN ZEALOT
CALOTIN DEVOTEE GUISARD
PARTNER ADHERENT CRISTINO
ESPOUSER FAVORITE FENNOMAN
FOLLOWER JACOBITE MOSSBACK
SIDESMAN STALWART URBANIST
HIGHFLIER MAZZINIST OCHLOCRAT
OLIVERIAN SECTARIAN TERRORIST
(NOT —) CATHOLIC
(PL.) FOLLOWING
PARTITION BAR CUT DAM FIN FLAG
SEPT WALL SHOJI SPEER STAGE
WITHE BAFFLE DIVIDE PARPAL
SCONCE SCREEN SEPTUM BARRIER
ENCLOSE GRATING PINFOLD
PORTION SCANTLE BRATTICE
BULKHEAD CLEAVAGE DIVISION
STOPPING TRAVERSE DASHBOARD
DAYABHAGA ICONOSTAS
STOOTHING
(— BETWEEN STALLS) TRAVIS
TREVIS TRAVISS
(— IN CHIMNEY) WITH WITHE
(— IN COTTAGE) SPEER HALLAN
(— IN LOUDSPEAKER) BAFFLE
(— IN WATERWHEEL) WREST
(— OF ESTATE) BOEDELSCHEIDING
(— OF LATH AND PLASTER)
STOOTHING
(HORIZONTAL —) STAGE
(MINING —) SOLLAR STOPPING
(PL.) CANCELLI
PARTLET HEN WOMAN PERTELOT
PARTLY WHAT PARCEL PARTIM
HALFLINGS
PARTNER BOY PAL ALLY HALF MATE
PARD WIFE BUDDY BUTTY PARTY
FELLOW MARROW SHARER
COMRADE CONSORT HUSBAND
CAMARADA COPEMATE SIDEKICK
YOKEMATE
(— OF DUMMY) VIVANT
(DANCING —) GIGOLO CAVALIER
PARTNERSHIP HUI AXIS FIRM
HOUSE FUSION CAHOOTS COMPANY
SOCIETY SOCIETEIT
PARTRIDGE HUN BIRD KYAH YUTU
LERWA RUDGE TITAR CHUKAR
REDLEG SEESEE CHEEPER PATRICK
SHRIMPI TINAMOU BOBWHITE
FRANCOLIN FRENCHMAN TETRAONID
(— NOISE) JUCK
(SAND —) TEHOO
(YOUNG —) CHEEPER SQUEALER
PARTRIDGEBERRY BOXBERRY

COWBERRY EYEBERRY ONEBERRY
SNOWBERRY TWINBERRY
PART-TIME PARCEL
PARTURITION EUTOCIA TRAVAIL
CHILDBED DELIVERY DYSTOCIA
PARTY DO BAL BEE CRY TEA CLAN
DRUM GALA SECT SIDE BINGE
BRAWL CABAL CRUSH GROUP
LEVEE COMITE FIESTA FROLIC
FRONDE GERMAN INFARE JUNKET
PERSON SETOUT SHINDY SHOWER
BLOWOUT CANTICO COMPANY
FACTION GREGORY PATARIA
SHINDIG DRINKING FENNOMAN
POTLATCH POUNDING SOCIABLE
SQUANTUM TERTULIA CONCISION
INCLINING
(— GIVEN AT HOME) HUDDLE
(AFTERNOON —) TEA RECEPTION
(BEACH —) CLAMBAKE
(BRIDAL —) SEND SHOWER
(DANCING —) HOP GERMAN
CANTICO HOEDOWN FANDANGO
(DRINKING —) KNEIPE POTATION
SYMPOSIUM
(DRUNKEN —) BLIND
(EVENING —) BALL SOIREE
GREGORY TERTULIA
(FISHING —) HUKILAU
(HUNTING —) FAID
(INFORMAL —) SOCIABLE TERTULIA
(IRISH —) HOOLEY
(MASQUERADE —) GUISE
(MEN'S —) STAG SMOKER
(POLITICAL —) SAM SIDE WAFD
HOOKS LABOR CAUCUS FRONDE
SWARAJ ZENTRUM MINSEITO
KENSEIKAI SQUADRONE
(POPULAR —) HOOKS
(SCOUTING —) ESPIAL
(SUPPLY —) BRIGADE
(TEA —) DRUM TEMPEST
(THIRD —) STRANGER
PARULIS GUMBOIL
PARVENU SNOB ARRIVE UPSTART
ARRIVIST MUSHROOM ARRIVISTE
PASCH PACE PAQUE EASTER
PASSOVER
PASCHAL LAMB CANDLE SUPPER
PASSOVER
PAS DE DEUX DUET
PASE FAROL NATURAL VERONICA
PASEAR WALK AIRING EXCURSION
PROMENADE
PASHA DEY EMIR PASAHAW
PASHTO AFGHAN
PASIPHAE (CHILD OF —) ARIADNE
PHAEDRA
(HUSBAND OF —) MINOS
PASQUEFLOWER BADGER GOSLING
APRILFOOL
PASQUINADE PIPE SQUIB SATIRE
LAMPOON PASQUIL
PASS BY GO COL DIE END FIG GAP
SAG USE ABRA BEAL CEDE CHIT
COMP COVE DREE DROP FALL FARE
FLIT FOIN GATE GHAT GULF HAND
HAVE LANE LEAD PACE RIDE ROLL
SEEK SILE SLAP SLIP STEP WADE

WALK WEAR WEND WIND CANTO
DREIE ENACT FLEET GHAUT GORGE
HALSE HURRY KOTAL LAPSE LITHE
LUNGE NOTCH OCCUR ORDER
PAPER PUNTA REACH RELAY SHAKE
SHOOT SMITE SPEND STRIP TRADE
UTTER WASTE WHELM YODEL
BILLET CONVEY DEFILE DEMISE
ELAPSE EXCEED HAPPEN PASSUS
PERMIT SPIRAL TICKET TRAVEL
TWOFER ABSOLVE ALLONGE
APPROVE BREATHE DESCEND
DEVOLVE DIFFUSE LATERAL
OVERGET PASSAGE UNDERGO
JUNCTURE REBOLERA PURWANNAH
(— A BALL) FEED HEEL
(— ABRUPTLY) LEAP
(— ALONG) DERIVE
(— AWAY) DIE SET FLEE WING
DEPART EXPIRE PERISH FORFARE
FORTHGO OVERDRIVE
(— BACK AND FORTH) FIG
CRISSCROSS
(— BAD COIN) SMASH
(— BETWEEN HILLS) BEAL SLAP
SLACK
(— BY) COTE OMIT SKIP VADE
WEND APASS CLEAR FORGO
FOREGO IGNORE OVERGO INTERMIT
OVERHEAVE
(— GRADUALLY) FADE
(— IN BULLFIGHT) SUERTE
(— IN POKER) BREATHE
(— INTO USE) ENURE INURE
(— JUDGMENT ON) DEEM
SENTENCE
(— LIGHTLY) BRUSH SKATE SKITTER
(— OFF) SHAM FOIST
(— ON) LEAK PACE
(— ONE'S LIFE) TRADE
(— OUT) CONK DEBOUCH EXHAUST
(— OVER LIGHTLY) SKIM SWEEP
OVERSKIP
(— OVER QUICKLY) SCUD FLEET
(— OVER) DO HIP BALK FREE SKIM
SKIP SLIP COVER CROSS ELIDE
FLEET SCOUR SWEEP TRANCE
OVERHIP INTERMIT OVERLOOK
OVERPOST PROGRESS TRAVERSE
(— QUICKLY) FLIT SPIN SPEED
STRIKE
(— THROUGH A BLOCK) REEVE
(— THROUGH NARROW WAY) THRID
THREAD
(— THROUGH) CROSS REEVE TRACE
DIVIDE OVERGO PIERCE SUFFER
EXCURSE PERVADE OVERPASS
OVERRIDE PERMEATE PROGRESS
PENETRATE
(— TIME) DRIVE SPEND TRADE
(— UNHAPPILY) DREE
(— UP) REJECT DECLINE
DISREGARD
(— WITH DIFFICULTY) WADE
(— WITH VIOLENCE) RAKE
(CUSTOMS —) CARNET
(FENCING —) FOIN LUNGE PUNTA
(FORWARD —) AERIAL
(HOCKEY —) CENTER

(MOUNTAIN —) COL GAP SAG GATE
GHAT SLIP CLOVE GHAUT KLOOT
KOTAL POORT SWIRE SWIRL
BEALACH
(NARROW —) ABRA GULF SLYPE
DEFILE
(SUDDEN —) LUNGE
PASSABLE FIT FAIR SOSO TOLLOL
GENUINE ADEQUATE MEDIOCRE
MODERATE POSSIBLE TRAVELED
PERMEABLE TOLERABLE
PASSABLENESS INDIFFERENCE
PASSABLY SEEMLY
PASSAGE CUT GAT GUT ROW VIA
WAY WRO ADIT BELT BORD DOOR
EXIT FARE FLUE FORD GANG GATE
HALL ITER LANE PACE PASS PAWN
RACE RAMP SLIP SLUM VENT WELL
AISLE ALLEY ALURE BAYOU BEARD
BOGUE CANAL CHOPS CHUTE
CLOSE CREEK CRUSH DRAFT DRIFT
DRIVE ENTRY FLYBY FORTE GLADE
GOING GORGE INLET JETTY MEUSE
PATCH PORCH SHUNT SLYPE
SOUND ACCESS ADITUS APORIA
ARCADE ATRIUM AVENUE BRIDGE
BURROW BYPASS CAREER COURSE
DEFILE DROMOS EGRESS ELAPSE
FAUCES HIATUS MEATUS PARODE
RELIEF SCREEN SLUICE STRAIT
TRAJET TRANCE TRAVEL TUNNEL
VOYAGE ARCHWAY BALTEUS
CHANNEL CHAPTER CONDUIT
COULOIR DIAZOMA DOGTROT
DRAUGHT ESTUARY EXCERPT
FISTULA FRAUGHT GALLERY
GANGWAY GATEWAY ISTHMUS
JOURNEY MANHOLE OFFTAKE
OUTTAKE PARADOS PROCESS
TRANSIT APPROACH AQUEDUCT
CLOISTER COMMERCE DEBOUCHE
DELETION PARADIGM SENTENCE
SHIPPING SINUSOID SPILLWAY
(— IN BOOK) WHERE EXCERPT
(— OF THREAD) FLOAT
(— TO STOMACH) SWALLOW
(— TO TOMB) DROMOS SYRINX
(—S OF LITERATURE) BEAUTIES
(AIR —) FLUE THIRL WINDWAY
THIRLING VENTIDUCT
(CENSORED —) CAVIAR
(CONTINUOUS —) LAPSE
(COVERED —) OPE PAWN PEND
(DIFFICULT —) APORIA
(LITERARY —) TEXT QUOTE
EXCERPT SNIPPET QUOTATION
(MINE —) RUN ADIT HEAD ROOF
SLUM DRIVE LEVEL SHAFT THIRL
AIRWAY STENTON UNDERCAST
(MUSICAL —) CUE CODA LINK
BREAK FORTE STAVE ARIOSO
FUGATO LEGATO REPEAT CADENZA
CODETTA FANFARE STRETTO
FLOURISH SPICCATO STACCATO
SYMPHONY VOCALISE
(NARROW —) GUT HASS ALLEY
GORGE JETTY NOTCH SLYPE
SMOOT DEFILE NARROW STRAIT
(SECURE — OF) CARRY

(SUBTERRANEAN —) POSTERN
(SWIFT —) FLIGHT
(WATER —) TICKLE TICKLER
PASSAGE HAWK TARTARET
PASSENGER
PASSAGEWAY (ALSO SEE PASSAGE)
BORD FLUE GANG HALL LANE PACE
PASS PEND PORT RACE SHED SLIP
WENT YAWN AISLE ALLEY ALURE
CHUTE DRIFT DRONG ENTRY GOING
LUMEN RAISE SHOOT SMOOT
STULM ACCESS AIRWAY AVENUE
COURSE DINGLE FUNNEL GUTTER
INTAKE MANWAY RUNWAY TRANCE
ZAGUAN DOORWAY GALLERY
SLIPWAY TWITTEN WALKWAY
WAYGATE CALLEJON CORRIDOR
HATCHWAY
(CLEARED — IN CROWD) HALL
(COVERED —) ARCADE CLOISTER
(MINE —) BORD BOARD DRIFT
SLANT STULM WINZE
(NARROW —) SLIP AISLE SMOOT
(SLOPING —) RAMP
PASSANT PAST CURRENT CURSORY
PASSING EPHEMERAL
PASSE AGED PAST WORN FADED
BELATED OBSOLETE OUTMODED
PASSENGER FARE INSIDE
FERRYMAN TRAVELER WAYFARER
(— WHO AVOIDS PAYING FARE) NIP
STOWAWAY
(— WITHOUT TICKET) HARE
(AIRPLANE —) BIRDMAN
(UNBOOKED —) CAD
(PL.) WAYBILL
PASSEPARTOUT SPANDREL
PASSERBY PASSER PASSANT
BYPASSER SAUNTERER
PASSERINE PERCHER
PASSIFLORA TACSO
PASSING DEATH DYING ELAPSE
CURSORY PASSADO RUNNING
SLIDING ELAPSING FLEETING
ENACTMENT EPHEMERAL
WAYFARING
(— BETWEEN) INTERCURRENT
(— BY) COTE
(— INTO EACH OTHER) FONDU
(— OF HOURS) TIME
(— OF TIME) EFFLUX
(SLOWLY —) LAG
PASSAGEWAY (NARROW —) SLIP
AISLE SMOOT
PASSANT PAST CURRENT CURSOR
PASSING EPHEMERAL
PASSE AGED PAST WORN FADED
BELATED OBSOLETE OUTMODED
PASSENGER FARE INSIDE
FERRYMAN TRAVELER WAYFARER
(— WHO AVOIDS PAYING FARE) NI
STOWAWAY
(— WITHOUT TICKET) HARE
(AIRPLANE —) BIRDMAN
(UNBOOKED —) CAD
(PL.) WAYBILL
PASSEPARTOUT SPANDREL
PASSERBY PASSER PASSANT
BYPASSER SAUNTERER

PASSERINE PERCHER
PASSIFLORA TACSO
PASSING DEATH DYING ELAPSE
CURSORY PASSADO RUNNING
SLIDING ELAPSING FLEETING
ENACTMENT EPHEMERAL
WAYFARING
(— **BETWEEN**) INTERCURRENT
(— **BY**) COTE
(— **INTO EACH OTHER**) FONDU
(— **OF HOURS**) TIME
(— **OF TIME**) EFFLUX
(**SLOWLY** —) LAG
PASSION IRE FIRE FURY HEAT LOVE
LUST RAGA RAGE TEAR TIDE WILL
ZEAL ANGER ARDOR BLOOD BRAME
CHAFE DEVIL ERROR FLAME LETCH
MANIA RAJAS SPUNK WRATH
AFFECT CHOLER DESIRE FERVOR
MOTHER PELTER SATTVA SPLEEN
TALENT WARMTH EARNEST
EMOTION EROTISM FEELING
OUTRAGE VULTURE APPETITE
DISTRESS VIOLENCE PADDYWACK
(— **FOR DOING GREAT THINGS**)
MEGALOMANIA
(— **FOR MUSIC**) MELOMANIA
(**ANGRY** —) FUNK
(**ANIMAL** —) KAMA
PASSIONATE HOT FOND WARM
FIERY GUTSY QUICK WHITE ARDENT
FERVID FIERCE FUMOUS IREFUL
STORMY SULTRY TORRID AMOROUS
FLAMING PEPPERY THERMAL
CHOLERIC FRENETIC VASCULAR
VEHEMENT WRATHFUL DIONYSIAN
IRASCIBLE
PASSIONATELY HASTILY FERVIDLY
PASSIONFLOWER MAYPOP
BULLHOOF
PASSIONLESS COLD FREDDO
PASSIVE INERT STOIC PATHIC
STOLID PATIENT FEMININE INACTIVE
SIGNLESS YIELDING APATHETIC
PASSIVENESS QUIETISM
PASSOVER PESAH PHASE PASQUE
PESACH
(— **FESTIVAL**) SEDER
(**JEWISH** —) EASTER
PASSPORT CHOP PASS CONGE
CONGEE DUSTUK DUSTUCK
FURLOUGH TESCARIA TEZKIRAH
SAFEGUARD
PASSUS PACE PART PASS STEP
CANTO DIVISION
PASSWORD WORD TOKEN DUSTUK
TESSERA WATCHWORD
PAST BY AGO WAS GONE YOND
YORE AFTER AGONE APAST ASIDE
ENDED SINCE BEHIND BYGONE
FOREBY PRETER ANOTHER
OREGONE PRETERIT COMPLETED
LONG —) HIGH
TIME NOT LONG —) YESTERDAY
PASTE HIT PAP BEAT BLOW DIKA
BUFF GLUE MISO PACK PATE
CREAM DOUGH FALSE GESSO
HENNA PUNCH STICK ATTACH
BATTER FASTEN GROUND PANADA

RASTIK STRASS BUCKETY CLOBBER
COLOGNE DRAWOUT FILLING
GORACCO GUARANA STICKUM
BADIGEON BARBOTINE
(— **FOR CAULKING**) BLARE
(— **FOR LINING HEARTHS**) BRASQUE
(— **FOR SHOES** BOOTS) CLOBBER
BLACKING
(— **OF CLAY**) BATTER
(— **TO FILL HOLES IN WOOD AND
STONE**) BADIGEON
(**ALIMENTARY** —) FEDELINI
SCUNGILLI SPAGHETTI
(**AROMATIC** —) PASTILE
(**COLORING** —) HENNA
(**DRIED** —) GUARANA
(**EARTHY** —) ENGOBE
(**FISH** —) BAGOONG
(**MEDICATED** —) ELECTUARY
(**PORCELAIN** —) PATE
(**POTTER'S** —) BARBOTINE
(**TOBACCO** —) GORACCO
(**WEAVER'S** —) SOWENS BUCKETY
PASTEBOARD CARD SHAM FLIMSY
TICKET MATBOARD
PASTEDOWN LINING
PASTEL WOAD LIGHT CRAYON
PICTURE DELICATE
PASTEN HOBBLE TETHER PASTOUR
SHACKLE
PASTILLE CACHOU CANDLE
LOZENGE
PASTIME GAY TOY GAME PLOY
HOBBY SPORT GOSSIP OLEARY
SAILING AMUSEMENT DIVERSION
PASTOR HERD ANGEL RABBI
CURATE KEEPER PRIEST RECTOR
DOMINIE VICAIRE GUARDIAN
MINISTER SHEPHERD
PASTORAL POEM DRAMA RURAL
RUSTIC BUCOLIC CROSIER IDYLLIC
ROMANCE ARCADIAN
PASTORALIST SQUATTER
PASTRY PIE FLAN HUFF PUFF SOCK
TART TUCK CORNET DANISH ECLAIR
ABAISSE CARCAKE STRUDEL
NAPOLEON TALMOUSE TURNOVER
APPLEJACK
(— **COOK**) PASTLER
(— **SHELL**) BOUCHEE DARIOLE
TIMBALE TALMOUSE
(— **STRIPS**) LATTICE
(— **WHEEL**) JAGGER
(**SWEET** —) DOUCET
PASTURAGE FEED GANG GATE
STRAY COLLOP EATAGE FORAGE
HERBAGE SHEEPGATE
PASTURE ALP FOG HAG HAM ING
LEA PEN TYE BENT FEED GAET
GANG GATE GISE GIST HAFT HALF
HEAF HOGA INGE KEEP PARK AGIST
DRIFT EJIDO GRASS GRAZE LAYER
LEASE RANGE VELDT INTAKE
MEADOW OUTRUN SAETER
COWGATE FOGGAGE GRAZING
HERBAGE LEALAND POTRERO
VACCARY VICTUAL HERDWICK
OUTFIELD SHEEPWALK
(— **GRASS**) TORE GRAMA

(— **IN STUBBLE**) SHACK
(— **LAND**) RAKE TACK LEASOW
(**HILL** —) HOGA
(**MOUNTAIN** —) SETER SAETER
SHIELING
(**SHEEP** —) HEAF EWELEASE
(**SHETLAND I.** —) SETER
(**SUMMER** —) AGOSTADERO
(**WET** —) SLINK
PASTURELAND BENT SOUM
PASTURING RELIEF PANNAGE
PASTY PIE PATE PATTY DOUGHY
FRACID SAMBOUGE
PAT APT DAB DIB TAP TIG BLOW
CLAP GLIB JUMP PALP TICK CHUCK
FITLY FIXED IMPEL THROW CARESS
DABBLE SMOOGE SOOTHE STRIKE
STROKE TIMELY APROPOS CHERISH
FITTING PATAPAT READILY
SUITABLE PERTINENT
PATAGIUM TEGULA TIPPET SCAPULA
PARACHUTE PTERYGODE
PATAGONIA (**DEITY OF** —) SETEBOS
(**RODENT OF** —) CAVY MARA
(**TREE OF** —) MANIU ALERCE
ALERSE
PATAMAR COURIER PATTAMAR
MESSENGER
PATAYAN YUMAN
PATCH BIT EKE FLY BOUT LAND
MEND SKIP SPOT SWAB SWOB
VAMP BLAZE BODGE CLOUT CLUMP
COVER FRIAR FUDGE PIECE SAVER
SCRAP SPECK SPLAT BLOTCH
COBBLE DOLLOP GORGET MOUCHE
PARCEL REVAMP SOLDER SPETCH
SWATCH TINKLE CLAMPER CLOBBER
INWEAVE PELIOMA REMNANT
(— **AS ORNAMENT**) MOUCHE
(— **CLUMSILY**) BOTCH CLOUT
CLAMPER
(— **OF COLOR**) CLOUP DAPPLE
SPLASH SPECULUM
(— **OF DARK HAIR**) SMUT
(— **OF DIRT**) MIRE
(— **OF FEATHERS**) BIB CAP
(— **OF ICE**) RONE
(— **OF LAND**) RODHAM
(— **OF LEATHER**) SPECK
(— **OF LIGHT**) GLADE
(— **OF PRINT**) FUDGE
(— **OF RUFFLED WATER**) ACKER
(— **OF SALIVA**) SIXPENCE
(— **OF TIRE**) BOOT
(— **ON BOAT**) TINGLE
(— **ON PRINTED PAGE**) FRIAR
(— **ON THROAT**) GORGET
(— **TOGETHER**) CONSARCINATE
(— **UP**) HEAL MEND
(**BALD** —) AREA
(**LIVID** —) PELIOMA
(**OOZY** —) SPEW SPUE
(**OPEN** — **IN FOREST**) CAMPO
(**SHOULDER** —) FLASH
PATCHOULI PACCIOLI PATCHLEAF
PATCHWORD WASTEWORD
PATCHWORK BOTCH CENTO
CENTON JUMBLE SCRAPS
PATCHERY FRAGMENTS PASTICCIO

PATE PIE TOP HEAD BROWN PASTE
PASTY PATTY BADGER NOGGIN
NOODLE COSTARD COXCOMB
PATELLA CAP PAN DISH VASE
ROTULA KNEECAP KNEEPAN
WHIRLBONE
PATEN ARCA DISC DISH DISK PLATE
PATINA PLATEN VESSEL
PATENT ARCA BALD OPEN BERAT
BROAD OVERT PLAIN SUNNUD
EVIDENT LICENSE OBVIOUS
APPARENT ARCHIVES MANIFEST
PALPABLE PRIVILEGE
PATER FATHER PRIEST
PATERFAMILIAS MASTER
PATERNAL FATHERLY
PATERNITY FATHER ORIGIN
PATESI ISHSHAKKU
PATH ARC PAD RUN RUT TAN WAY
BERM FARE GATE LANE LEAD LINE
LODE RACE RACK ROAD TRIG TROD
WALK ALLEY BYWAY GOING JETTY
PISTE ROUTE SPACE TRACK TRACT
TRADE TRAIL BOSTAL BYPASS
CAMINO CASAUN CIRCLE COMINO
COURSE GROOVE SLEUTH SPHERE
SWATHE TRENCH CHANNEL
ERGODIC FAIRWAY FOOTWAY
HIGHWAY LANDWAY MEANDER
PASSAGE RODDING SIDEWAY
TARIQAT TOWPATH TRAFFIC
TRUNDLE WAYGATE BORSTALL
CENTRODE CROSSCUT DRIFTWAY
TRAILWAY TWITCHEL CROSSWALK
(— BETWEEN HEDGES) TWITCHEL
(— CUT IN MOWING) SWATH
SWATHE
(— FOLLOWED BY ENERGY)
ERGODIC
(— MADE BY ANIMAL) PIST PISTE
(— OF CELESTIAL BODY) ORBIT
(— OF CLOUDS) RACK
(— OF MOVING POINT) CURVE
LOCUS
(— OF RACE) STRIP
(— UP STEEP HILL) BOSTAL
BORSTAL BORSTALL
(BRIDLE —) SPURWAY
(CLOSED —) CIRCUIT
(NARROW —) BERM RACK TRIG
RODDIN TROCHA RODDING
(P. I. FOOT —) SENDA
(STONE-PAVED —) STEEN
(SUFI —) TARIQAT
(WINDING —S) AMBAGES
PATHAN TURI AFRIDI SIVATI BAJOURI
BANGASH PAYTHAN DANGARIK
PATHETIC SAD SILLY TEARY
TENDER FORLORN PITIFUL
DOLOROSO PATETICO STIRRING
TOUCHING AFFECTING
PATHIC MORBID VICTIM PASSIVE
CATAMITE DISEASED SUFFERER
SUFFERING
PATHOGEN VIRUS
PATHOS BATHOS SNIVEL
PATHWAY (ALSO SEE PATH) RUN
LANE PATH RACK COURSE RAMBLA
RAMBLE RODDIN BORSTAL RODDING

PATIENCE CALM THILD BEARANCE
STOICISM COMPOSURE ENDURANCE
FORTITUDE
PATIENT CASE CURE MEEK SOBER
BOVINE PASSIVE ENDURING
THOLEMOD SUFFERANT
(— OF ASYLUM) BEDLAM
(BE —) BEAR
(HYDROPATHIC —) WATERER
(MEDICAL —) CURE
PATIO COURT COURTYARD
PATOIS CANT GOMBO GUMBO
CREOLE JARGON DIALECT
PATRIARCH JOB ABBA ENOS LEVI
NASI NOAH PAPA POPE ALDER
ELDER JACOB PITRI DESPOT
JOSEPH NESTOR ABRAHAM ANCIENT
VETERAN VENERABLE
PATRICIAN NOBLE EMPEROR
PATRICK NOBLEMAN GENTLEMAN
PATRIMONY PORTION ANCESTRY
HERITAGE LONGACRE
PATRIOT LOVER AMATEUR
PATRIOTIC PUBLIC ENVELOPE
NATIONAL
PATROL GUARD SCOUT WATCH
STOOGE PATROLE PROTECT
PATROLMAN COP GUARD FLATFOOT
INSPECTOR
PATRON BUYER GUEST STOOP
AVOWRY CLIENT FATHER FAUTOR
JAJMAN ACCOUNT PADRONE
PATROON PROCTOR SPONSOR
ADVOCATE CHAMPION CUSTOMER
DEFENDER GUARDIAN MAECENAS
(PL.) FOLLOWING
PATRONAGE AEGIS FAVOR AVOWRY
CUSTOM FAVOUR ACCOUNT
AUSPICE FOMENTO HEARING
BUSINESS PADROADO
(— AND CARE) AUSPICE
PATRONAL TITULAR
PATRONIZE USE DEIGN FAVOR
DEFEND FATHER PROMOTE
PROTECT EMPATRON FREQUENT
PATROON TRACT CAPTAIN
SUPPORTER
PATTEE FORMY FORMEE
PATTEN BASE CLOG FOOT SHOE
SKATE STAND STILT CHOPIN
GALOSH RACKET SANDAL CREEPER
RACQUET SUPPORT CIOPPINO
SNOWSHOE
PATTER CANT TALK TIRL LINGO
HAPPER JARGON BLATHER BLATTER
CHATTER DIALECT
PATTERING PITAPAT
PATTERN CUT FUR SET BASE CAST
COMB COPY FORM GIMP IDEA LAUE
MOLD NORM PLAN SEME STAR
WAVE BISON BYSEN CHECK DECOR
DISME DRAFT EPURE GUIDE IDEAL
INLAY MODEL MOIRE MOULD NOTAN
PLAID SEMEE WATER BASKET
BURELE CANVAS CHECKS DESIGN
DIAPER ENTAIL ETOILE FABRIC
FIGURE FLORAL FORMAT FORMER
LACERY MAGPIE MATRIX MIRROR
MODULE MUSTER ONDULE PATRON

POUNCE RANDOM RECIPE SAMPLE
SQUARE STRIPE SYSTEM ALLOVER
CHEVRON EXAMPLE FACONNE
FILLING FOLKWAY GESTALT
GRIZZLE HOBNAIL MEANDER
MEANING MULLION PARAGON
PROJECT SAMPLER SLEIGHT
STENCIL TEMPLET CALENDAR
DYNAMICS FILIGREE HATCHING
ILLUSION PARADIGM PLATFORM
STRICKLE PROTOTYPE
(— IN BRAIN) GYRATION
(— OF BEHAVIOR) HABIT DISPLAY
(— OF CADENCE) CURSUS
(— OF LARGE SQUARES) DAMIER
(— OF SCARS) KELOID
(— OF SEPARATE OBJECTS) SEME
(— OF STRESS) SUPERFIX
(— OF TARTAN) SET SEET SETT
SETTE
(— ON PAPER) BURELAGE
(— ON STAMP) GRILL GRILLE
(— USED BY SILVERSMITHS) WORK
BOROON
(CROSS-BARRED —) PLAID
(FACIAL —) BLAZE
(GARMENT —) SLOPER
(HAT —) BLOCK
(KNITTING —) ARGYLE
(PORCELAIN —) FITZHUGH
(RUG —) AINALEH
(SHOE —) FORME
(SKATING —) EDGE
(SOCIAL —) FAMILISM
(SPEECH —) IDIOLECT
(STRIPED —) BARRE
(TAILOR'S —) PROTRACTOR
(TATTOO —) MOKO
(TREE —) HOM HOMA
(WEAVING —) DRAW
PATTERNED GOFFERED
PATTY TABLET BOUCHEE PRALINE
PATTYPAN VOLAUVENT
(— SHELL) DARIOLE TALMOUSE
CROUSTADE
PATULOUS OPEN SPREAD
DISTENDED
PAUCITY LACK DEARTH FEWNESS
EXIGUITY SCARCITY
PAUL PAOLO
(ASSOCIATE OF —) DEMAS SILAS
TITUS ARTEMAS BARNABAS
PAULDRON POLLET EPAULET
PALERON POLDRON POLLETTE
PAULOPOST DEUTERIC
PAULOWNIA KIRI
PAUNCH TUN BELLY PENCH RUME
ABDOMEN STOMACH GUNDYGUT
POTBELLY
PAUNCHY BLOATED
PAUPER BEGGAR INDIGENT
ROUNDSMAN
PAUPERISM BEGGARY
PAUSE HO HEM HALT HANG HOLD
LULL REST RUFE STAY STOP WAI
ABIDE BREAK CEASE CHECK COM
DELAY DEMUR DEVAL DWELL
HOVER LIMMA POISE SELAH TARR
TENOR BREACH BREATH CORONA

CUTOFF FALTER HANKER HIATUS
PERIOD STANCE CAESURA FERMATA
RESPITE VIRGULE BREATHER
INTERVAL
(— **BEFORE HURDLE)** DWELL
(SUDDEN —) CHECK
(PL.) LIMMATA CAESURAE
AUT PAW POKE POWT STAMP
FINGER
AVANE DANCE PADUAN
AVE LAY PATH STUD TILE COVER
FLOOR CAUSEY COBBLE QUARRY
SMOOTH OVERLAY PREPARE
RUDERATE
(— **WITH STONES)** STEEN CAUSEY
AVED COBBLED
AVEMENT SLAB HEARTH PAEPAE
TELFORD ASAROTUM FLAGGING
FLOORING PATHMENT PEDIMENT
PITCHING SIDEWALK TROTTOIR
WASHBOARD
AVER CUBER PAVIOR
AVID TIMID AFRAID FEARFUL
AVILION BASE FLAG TELD TENT
FOLLY KIOSK PINNA ROYAL CANOPY
ENSIGN HOWDAH LITTER PANDAL
PALLION COVERING GLORIETTE
AVILLON CHINOIS CRESCENT
AVING FLAG SETT BLOCK BRICK
DALLE PAVER STEAN STEEN STONE
COBBLE TARMAC ASPHALT
TELFORD PITCHING FLAGSTONE
(SQUARE —) MITCHEL
AVIS COVER PAVADE PAVOIS
SHIELD PROTECT
AW PAT PUD TOE CLAW FOOT
GAUM GRAB HAND MAUL PATY
PAUT PORT FLAIL PATTE TRICK
CLUTCH FUMBLE HANDLE PATTEE
GRUBEEN FLIPPER FORELEG
FOREFOOT
WKY SLY ARCH BOLD CANNY
SAUCY CRAFTY LIVELY SHREWD
CUNNING FORWARD SQUEAMISH
WL COG DOG BOLT HAND SEAR
TOP TENT TRIP CATCH CLICK
ETENT FINGER PALLET TONGUE
LAWKER RATCHET
WN DIP POP WED FINE GAGE
OCK SOAK VAMP WAGE SPOUT
WEAT ENGAGE LUMBER OBLIGE
GNUS PLEDGE WADSET COUNTER
OSTAGE PEACOCK CHESSMAN
OSKENEER
PL.) PHALANX
VNBROKER MOUNT UNCLE
ROKER LUMBERER
VNEE PANEE SKIDI WATER
MOND BISCUIT PLEDGEE
VNIE PAWN PEACOCK
VNSHOP PAWN SPOUT LOMBARD
OPSHOP
BOARD PEACE TRUCE FRIEND
BLET
DO BUY FEE TIP ANTE FOOT
RK GIVE MEET RENT SOLD WAGE
TTA CLEAR COUGH DOUSE
ANK SCREW SHEPE SOUND
AGES YIELD ANSWER BETALL

DEFRAY IMPEND REWARD SALARY
SETTLE COMMUTE DEADRAY
HALVANS IMBURSE REQUITE
SATISFY SOULDIE STIPEND TRIBUTE
(— **ATTENTION)** DIG SEE COME
GAUM HARK HEED TENT ADVERT
REGARD
(— **COURT TO)** NUT SUE GALLANT
(— **DOWN)** DOUSE
(— **FLIRTATIOUS ADVANCES)** QUEEN
(— **FOR LIQUOR)** BIRL
(— **FOR)** ABY BUY BYE COUP ABIDE
COVER STAND ABEGGE
(— **HEAVY PENALTY)** SMART
EXPIATE
(— **HOMAGE)** CHEFE CHEVE CHIVE
SALAAM ADULATE
(— **IN ADVANCE)** IMPRESS
(— **MONEY)** PINGLE
(— **OF SOLDIER)** SAWDEE
(— **OFF)** LIFT SINK ACQUIT
(— **OUT)** BLEED SPEND STUMP
EXPEND DISBURSE
(— **TAXES)** GILD
(— **UP)** ANTE QUIT SETTLE
LIQUIDATE
(— **WITH IOU)** VOWEL
(ADVANCE —) IMPREST
(DAILY —) DIET
(EXTRA —) BATTA BONUS KICKBACK
(SMALL —) SCREW
PAYABLE DUE C4RTAL
PAYEE HOLDER ENDORSER
PAYMASTER BAKSHI BUKSHI
PURSER BUKSHEE PAGADOR
PAYMENT CRO DUE FEE TAX BILL
CENS DOES DOLE DUTY ERIC FEAL
FINE GALE GILD HIRE LEVY MAIL
TACK TOLL BONUS CANON CLAIM
GAVEL MAILL MENSE PREST PRICE
YIELD ANGILD BOUNTY CHARGE
LINAGE PAYOLA PLEDGE REBATE
RETURN REWARD TARIFF ADVANCE
ALIMONY ANNUITY BENEFIT
CUSTOMS DEPOSIT FOOTAGE
GARNISH PANNAGE PENSION
PRIMAGE SOLUTIO STIPEND
SUBSIDY SUBSIST TREWAGE
TUITION CASUALTY FOREGIFT
GRATUITY KICKBACK MALIKANA
MARITAGE MONEYAGE TREASURY
WOODGELD HEADPENNY
MALGUZARI
(— **FOR INJURY)** UTU
(— **FOR LABOR)** MEED
(— **FOR OFFENSE)** ENACH
(— **FOR RELEASE)** LOOSING
(— **OF FEE)** FEAL
(— **OF MINERS)** FOOTAGE YARDAGE
(— **ON DELIVERY)** COD
(DEMAND —) DUN BILL
(EVADE —) BILK DEFAULT
(HOMICIDE'S —) KELCHIN
(PERIODICAL —) GALE GAVEL
PAYNIM PAGAN PANIME HEATHEN
INFIDEL PAGANDOM
PAYOFF FIX BRIBE CLIMAX PROFIT
REWARD DECISIVE RECKONING
PEA DAL TUR DHAL GRAM LANG

SEED ARHAR CHICK CICER GANDUL
LEGUME PIGEON PODDER CARMELE
CATJANG KHESARI POWDARE
TANGIER GARVANRO
(— **DOVE)** ZENAIDA
(— **HARVESTER)** VINER
(— **PETAL)** KEEL
(EARLY —**S)** HASTINGS
(PARCHED —**S)** CARLS CARLINS
(PL.) POIS GRAIN
PEABIRD ORIOLE WRYNECK
PEACE PAX CALM EASE FINE LIOS
LISS REST AMITY FRITH GRITH
LISSE QUIET TRUCE REPOSE
SAUGHT SHALOM CONCORD
HARMONY REQUIEM
(GODDESS OF —) IRENE
(SYMBOL OF —) DOVE TOGA OLIVE
PEACEABLE FAIR SOME CIVIL QUIET
STILL GENTLE SILVER ORDERLY
PACIFIC SOLOMON AMICABLE
SACKLESS
PEACEFUL CALM SOME SOBER
STILL IRENIC PLACID SILVER
HALCYON PACIFIC
PEACE PIPE CALUMET
PEACH BLAB PAVY CLING PAVIE
SNEAK SPLIT TRUMP ACCUSE
BETRAY CARMAN CROSBY FOSTER
INDICT INFORM OREJON PEENTO
SALWEY ELBERTA PERSIAN PIENTAO
WHITTLE CRAWFORD ISABELLA
ROSEWORT
(— **STATE)** GEORGIA
(— **STONE)** PUTAMEN
PEACHBLOW FAKIR
PEACOCK MAO PAON PAVO PAWN
POSE PEKOK STRUT PAJOCK
PAVONE POWNIE PEAFOWL
PHASIANID
(— **TAIL)** TRAIN
(CONGO —) AFROPAVO
PEACOCK BITTERN SUN
PEACOCK BUTTERFLY IO
PEACOCK FISH WRASSE
PEACOCK FLOWER FLAMBEAU
POINCIANA
PEA CRAB PINNOTERE
PEAG TAX TOLL BEADS PAAGE
PEACK PEAGE PEDAGE WAMPUM
PEAI PIAY PIACHE
PEA JACKET PEACOAT
PEAK BEN NAB NOB PAP PIC TOP
TOR ACME APEX BEAK CIMA CUSP
DENT DOLT DOME KNOB KNOT PICO
PIKE TOLT BLOOM CREST CROWN
PIQUE PITCH PITON POINT SLINK
SNEAK STEAL STUMP CLIMAX
CUPULA SHASTA SHRINK SUMMIT
ZENITH EPITOME MAXIMUM
CENTROID
(— **OF ANCHOR)** PEE
(— **OF CAP)** SCOOP
(ICE —) SERAC
(ISOLATED —) TOLT
(SHARP —) HORN
(SNOW-CAPPED —) DOME CALOTTE
PEAKED WAN PALE THIN DRAWN
PIKED SHARP COPPED SICKLY

SLIMSY POINTED SLIMPSY
PEAKEDNESS KURTOSIS
PEAL CLAP RING TOLL CHIME CRACK
GRILSE SHOVEL MINNING RESOUND
SUMMONS THUNDER CARILLON
(— **OF THUNDER**) CLAP REEL
PEANUT BUR FLAX MANI MEAN
PETTY PINDA GOOBER PINDAL
ARACHIS BEENNUT ARACHIDE
EARTHPEA GRASSNUT KATCHUNG
VALENCIA MONKEYNUT
(— **DISEASE**) TIKKA
PEA POD COB PYSE QUASH PESCOD
(**POORLY FILLED** —) POP
(**UNRIPE** —) SQUASH
PEAR BOSC DIEGO MELON SABRA
BEURRE BURREL PANINI SECKEL
WARDEN WINTER KIEFFER PRICKLY
AMBRETTE BERGAMOT TASAJILLO
(**PRICKLY** —) TUNA NOPAL OPUNTIA
PEAR HAW THORN
PEARL GEM MABE TERN GRAIN
NACRE ONION PICOT UNION
BOUTON OLIVET ORIENT BAROQUE
BDELIUM BLISTER CATARACT
MOONBEAM MARGARITE
(— **WEIGHT**) TANK
(**IMITATION** —) OLIVET
(**IRREGULAR** —) SLUG
(**PIERCED** —) WIDOW
(**SEED** —) ALIOFAR
(**SMOKED** —) MITRAILLE
PEARL BLUSH ROSETAN
PEARL MILLET KOUS CUMBU
DUCHN DUKHN KOUSE JONDLA
DAGASSA
PEARLSIDES ARGENTIN
PEARLWEED SAGINA POVERTY
SEALWORT
PEARLY NACRY NACROUS PRECIOUS
PEARLY EVERLASTING LIVELONG
MOONSHINE
PEAR-SHAPED FULL MELLOW
ROUNDED PYRIFORM
PEASANT TAO BOND BOOR HERA
HIND KERN KONO KOPI PEON RAYA
RYOT SERF BAIRU BOWER CHURL
KNAVE KULAK RAYAH SWAIN
COTMAN COTTAR FARMER FELLAH
RASCAL RUSTIC BONDMAN
LABORER PAISANO VILLAIN
CHOPSTICK
(— **CLASS**) JACQUERIE
(— **OF INDIA**) RYOT KISAN RAIYAT
(**ARABIC** —) FELLAH
(**IRISH** —) KERN KERNE
(**RUSSIAN** —) KULAK MUZHIK
MUZJIK
PEASE CROW TERN
PEASHOOTER TRUNK BLOWER
PISTOL BLOWGUN
PEAT GOR PET SOD VAG COOM FUEL
MOOR MUCK MULL TURF COOMB
LAWYER MINION YARPHA DARLING
FAVORITE
(— **BOG**) CESS YARPHA
(— **CUTTER**) PINER
(— **SPADE**) SLADE TUSKAR TWISCAR
(**DRIED — FOR FUEL**) VAG
(**LAYER OF** —) FLAW

PEA TREE KATURAI
PEATY KETTY
PEBA PEVA ARMADILLO
PEBBLE DIB FLAX JACK PLUM
CHUCK SCREE STONE BANTAM
GIBBER GRAVEL QUARTZ SHILLA
SYCITE CHUCKIE CRYSTAL STANNER
JACKSTONE
(**PL.**) BEACH DREIKANTER
PECAN NOGAL PACANE
PECCADILLO FAULT OFFENSE
MISCHIEF
PECCANT FAULTY MORBID CORRUPT
SINNING DISEASED
PECCARY JAVALI WARREE TAGASSU
TAYASSU JAVELINA TAYASSUID
PECK DAB DOT JOB NIP BEAK BILL
CARP FOOD GRUB HOLE JERK KISS
PYKE PITCH PRICK STOCK THROW
HATFUL NIBBLE PEGGLE PICKLE
PIERCE STROKE CHIMBLE
(**1-4TH OF** —) LIPPY FORPET FORPIT
LIPPIE
PECKER BILL NOSE COURAGE
SPIRITS
PECTEN COMB MARSUPIUM
PECTORAL SANDPIPER JACK PERT
PEERT BROWNY BROWNIE
CHOROOK CREAKER FATBIRD
HAYBIRD KRIEKER SQUATTER
TRIDDLER JACKSNIPE
PECULATE STEAL MISUSE
EMBEZZLE
PECULIAR ODD VERY QUEER
PROPER QUAINT UNIQUE CURIOUS
PRIVATE SEVERAL SPECIAL
STRANGE UNUSUAL SEPARATE
SINGULAR SPECIFIC
PECULIARITY KINK IDIOM QUIRK
TRAIT TRICK TWIST IDIASM ODDITY
AEOLISM FEATURE IRISHRY
CROTCHET HEADMARK
(— **IN BOWL**) BIAS
(— **OF SPEECH**) IDIOLOGISM
(**CROTCHETY** —) FIKE
PECUNIARY POCKET MONETARY
FINANCIAL
PED BASKET HAMPER PANIER
PEDAGOGUE TUTOR PEDANT
DOMINIE SQUEERS TEACHER
THWACKUM
PEDAGOGY SCHOOL DIDACTICS
EDUCATION
PEDAL LEVER SWELL TREADLE
FOOTFEED PEDALIAN THROTTLE
(— **COUPLER**) TIRASSE
(**PIANO** —) CELESTE
PEDANT PRIG DUNCE TUTOR
DORBEL PURIST TASSEL ACADEME
PEDAGOG GAMALIEL DRYASDUST
OLOFERNES
PEDANTIC STODGY BOOKISH
DONNISH ERUDITE INKHORN
TEACHING
PEDDLE HAWK SELL CADGE SHOVE
TRANT TRUCK HIGGLE MEDDLE
PIDDLE RETAIL COLPORT
PEDDLER ARAB SMOUS BADGER
CRAMER JAGGER JOWTER MUGGER

STROLL WALKER NIGGLER
ROADMAN SANDBOY SWADDER
TROGGER TRUCKER HUCKSTER
BOXWALLAH DUSTYFOOT
(— **OF DOPE**) FIXER
(— **OF DRESS PIECES**) DUDDER
(— **OF FISH**) RIPIER RIPPER
(**ITINERANT** —) SMOUS SMOUSE
SMOUSER STROLLER
(**MOHAM.** —) BORA
(**STREET** —) CAMELOT
(**WARES OF** —) TROGGAN
PEDESTAL ANTA BASE BASIS BLOC
STAND PILLAR PODIUM ROCKER
AKROTER SUPPORT PADMASANA
PEDESTRIAN PED DULL FOOT SLO
HIKER FOOTER HOOFER WALKER
FOOTMAN PROSAIC PLODDING
WINGLESS
PEDICEL RAY STEM SCAPE STALK
PEDUNCLE FOOTSTALK
PEDIGREE STEMMA DESCENT
LINEAGE ANCESTRY PETEGREU
PUREBRED
PEDIMENT FRONTAL FRONTON
FASTIGIUM
PEDIPALP(PL.) LABIUM
PEDOMETER ODOGRAPH WAYWISI
PEDRERO PERRIER PETRARY
PEDUNCLE STEM SCAPE STALK
STIPES PEDICEL EYESTALK
HYPOCARP
(**PL.**) CRURA
PEEK PEEP PIKE GLANCE GLIMPSE
PEEKABOO PEEP BOPEEP PEEPE
PEEL BARK HARL HULL HUSK PAR
RIND SKIN FLAKE FLIPE SCALE
SLIPE STAKE STRIP CORTEX
SHOVEL SPITTLE UNDRESS
BARKPEEL ORANGEADO
(— **OFF**) HARL CRAZE FLAKE SHL
(**BAKER'S** —) PALE SPITTLE
(**ORANGE OR LEMON** —) ZEST
ORANGEAT
PEELER CRAB BOBBY CORER
HUSTLER SHEDDER SPUDDER
PILLAGER
PEELING RIND SKIN PARING PARL
PEEN PIN PYNE RIVET
PEEP PRY SPY JEEP PEEK PEER
PULE SKEG STEP TOOT TOTE TO
CHEEP CHIRP DEKKO GLINT PIPI
SNOOP TWEET DEGREE GLANCE
SQUEAK SQUINNY PEEKABOO
(— **SHOW**) RAREE
PEEPER EYE TOM FROG KEEK
VOYEUR
PEEPHOLE PEEP JUDAS EYELET
CREVICE
PEEPING NOSY PRYING
PEER PRY DUKE EARL FEAR GAZ
LOOK LORD MATE PEEP TOUT
BARON EQUAL GLINT GLOZE ME
NOBLE RIVAL STARE STIME THA
TWIRE APPEAR FELLOW OLIVER
PINKER COMPERE
PEERAGE RANK DIGNITY BARON
NOBILITY TENEMENT
PEERING SQUINNY

PEERLESS SUPREME MATCHLESS NONPAREIL UNRIVALED
PEESWEEP FINCH PEWIT LAPWING PEEWEEP
PEEVE IRK ANNOY GRUDGE NETTLE IRRITATE
PEEVISH SOUR CROSS DORTY PENSY SNACK TECHY TEENY TESTY TETTY THRAW TIFFY WEMOD CRUSTY GIRNIE HIPPED SNARLY SNUFFY SULLEN TATTER TOUCHY TWARLY TWAZZY TWITTY UPPISH UPPITY VAPORY CRABBED FRATCHY FRECKET FRETFUL FROWARD GROUCHY PETTISH SPLEENY TEDIOUS TIFFISH WASPISH PHRAMPEL PINDLING SANSHACH TWANKING
PEEWEE BOOT RUNT TINY PEWEE MARBLE LAPWING
EG FIX HOB HUB NOB NOG PIN HOBB KING KNAG PLUG SCOB SHAG STEP CLEAT DOWEL DRINK NOTCH PERCH PITON PRONG SPELL SPILE SPILL STAKE THOLE THROW TOOTH WADDY DEGREE DOWEL FAUCET MARKER NORMAN PICKET REASON SPIGOT TAPOUN TIPCAT PINNING PRETEXT SCOLLOP SPERKET SUPPORT TRENAIL
(— FOR PLAYING GAME) CAT SPILIKIN
(— FOR SADDLES) SPERKET
(— OF STRINGED INSTRUMENT) CHEVILLE
(— OUT) DIE FAIL
(IRON —) PITON
(THATCH —) SCOB
EGA REMORA
EGALL BASKET PACKALL
EGASUS QUAVIVER HYPOSTOME
EG TOP PIRY PEERY PEERIE
EIGNOIR GOWN DRESS KIMONO NEGLIGEE
EISE BLOW FORCE PASSE POISE POIZE IMPACT WEIGHT BALANCE POISURE
KAN WEJACK
LAGE FUR HAIR PILAGE
LAGIC MARINE AQUATIC OCEANIC PELAGIAN
LEUS (BROTHER OF —) TELAMON
FATHER OF —) AEACUS
HALF-BROTHER OF —) PHOCUS
SON OF —) PELIDES ACHILLES
WIFE OF —) THETIS ANTIGONE
LF GAIN BOOTY LUCRE MONEY POIL TRASH PILFER PILFRE EFUSE RICHES WEALTH COMPOST
LICAN DOVE ALCATRAS NOCROTAL
- STATE) LOUISIANA
LISSE POSTIN POSTEEN
LL BEAT PELE PELT HURRY PEELE ASTEN
LLAGRA MAIDISM PELAGRA
LET BB WAD BALL CAST PILL HOT BOLUS PRILL STONE BEEBEE JLLET FECULA OGRESS PILULE

CASTING GRANULE PALLION TRATTLE BUCKSHOT GUNSTONE HAILSTONE
(SNOW —S) GRAUPEL
(PL.) SHOT
PELLICLE FILM SCUM SKIN CRUST CUTICLE EPISTASIS
PELLITORY BERTRAM BERTRUM WALLWORT
PELL-MELL RUSH MELPELL DISORDER HEADLONG
PELLOCK PALACH PORPOISE
PELLUCID CLEAR BRIGHT LIMPID ORIENT CRYSTAL
PELMA TRACK
PELMET CORNICE VALANCE PALMETTE
PELOPONNESUS (CITY OF —) SPARTA
(PEOPLE OF —) MOREOTE
(RIVER GOD OF —) ALPHEUS
PELOPS (FATHER OF —) TANTALUS
(SON OF —) ATREUS TROEZEN PITTHEUS THYESTES
(WIFE OF —) HIPPODAMIA
PELORIA EPANODY
PELT FUR KIT BEAR BEAT BLOW CAPE CAST COON DASH FELL HIDE HURL KITT PELL PUSH RACK SKIN BESET CHUNK FITCH HURRY SABLE SLASH SPEED STONE WHACK BADGER BEAVER FISHER PELTER SERVAL SPRING BETHUMP COONSKIN
(— OF SEAL, WITH BLUBBER) SCULP
(— WITH MISSILES) BUM SQUAIL
(— WITH STONES) LAPIDATE
(BEAVER —) BLANKET
PELTAST SOLDIER
PELTATE SCUTATE
PELTER SKEET
PELTING SLASHING
PELTRY FURS SKINS
PELUDO POYOU ARMADILLO
PEN COT CUB GET HOK MEW PAR PIN STY BOLT CAGE COOP CROO CROW FAUD FOLD JAIL STUB WALK YARD BUGHT CRAWL CREEP CUBBY HUTCH KRAAL POINT QUILL STYLE WRITE BOUGHT CORRAL CRUIVE FASTEN FLIGHT HURDLE INDITE RECORD STYLUS ZAREBA CONFINE WARKLOOM
(— CATTLE) STANCE
(— FOR CATTLE) CUB LOT CREW CRUE LAIR REEVE
(— FOR ELEPHANTS) KRAAL
(— FOR HOGS OR SLAVES) CRAWL
(— OF CUTTLEFISH) GLADIUS
(— POINT) NEB NIB STUB
(— UP) FRANK STIVE
(AUTHOR'S —) STYLE STYLUS
(FOUNTAIN —) STICK
(REED —) CALAMUS
PENALIZE CHECK
PENALTY BETE CAIN DOOM FINE LOSS PAIN BEAST JUISE MULCT AMENDE AMERCE SOLACE FORFEIT NEMESIS SURSIZE BLOODWIT

HARDSHIP SCAFFOLD
PENANCE TAP SORE SHRIFT SORROW REMORSE SUFFERING
PEN CASE PENNER POPPET
PENCEL FLAG PENNON STREAMER PENNONCEL
PENCHANT BENT TASTE GENIUS LIKING LEANING FONDNESS
PENCIL PEN RED WAD BLUE LEAD WADD LINER SHEAF SKETCH STYLUS POINTEL CHARCOAL KEELIVINE
(SLATE —) SKAILLIE
(PL.) STATIONERY
PENCILWOOD MORDORE
PENDANT BOB JAG DROP FLAG JAGG PEND TAIL AGLET BULLA GUTTA POINT AIGLET LUSTER PALAOA PLAYER TABARD TARGET TASSEL EARDROP LANGUET SUPPORT LAVALIER
PENDENT LOP BAGGED ICICLE HANGING PROMISS
PENDULOUS LOP SLOUCH HANGING CERNUOUS DROOPING
PENDULUM SWING PENDLE SWINGEL SWINGLE VIBRATILE
(INVERTED —) NODDY
PENELOPE (FATHER OF —) ICARIUS
(FATHER-IN-LAW OF —) LAERTES
(HUSBAND OF —) ULYSSES ODYSSEUS
(SUITOR OF —) AGELAUS
PENEPLAIN STRATH ENDRUMPF
PENETRATE CUT DIG DIP SEE BITE BORE DIVE GORE PASS PINK SINK STAB WADE BREAK DRILL DRIVE ENTER IMBUE PROBE SEIZE THIRL CLEAVE FATHOM FICCHE GIMLET INVADE PIERCE RIDDLE SEARCH STRIKE THRILL WIMBLE DISCERN PERVADE
(— MENTALLY) ENTER
(— ONE'S MIND) SOAK
PENETRATED (EASILY —) MELLOW
PENETRATING ACID KEEN ACUTE LEVEL SHARP ASTUTE DEADLY SHREWD SHRILL SUBTLE GIMLETY INGOING INTRANT KNOWING PUNGENT PERCEANT REACHING TRENCHANT
PENETRATION DEPTH ACUMEN FATHOM INROAD INGOING INSIGHT SEEPAGE INCISION INVASION SAGACITY
PENGUIN AUK DIVER GENTU ARCTIC DIPPER GENTOO JOHNNY PINWING BREVIPED MACARONI
(PL.) IMPENNES
PENINSULA CAPE MULL NECK INDIA BILAND BYLAND ISLAND PENILE
PENITENCE RUE REGRET SORROW PENANCE PENANCY REMORSE
PENITENT RUER SORRY HUMBLE WEEPER STANDER CONTRITE
(— OF 3RD STAGE) KNEELER
PENITENTIARY JUG PEN JAIL STIR TENCH PRISON PENITENT

PENMAN CLERK AUTHOR SCRIBE WRITER

PENMANSHIP HAND SCRIPT PENSHIP WRITING

PENNANT FANE FLAG WHIP COLOR ROGER BANNER CORNET PENCIL PENNON PENSIL PINION PINNET MEATBALL REPEATER STREAMER

PENNILESS POOR BROKE NEEDY BANKRUPT INDIGENT STRAPPED PLACKLESS

PENNON FLAG VANE WING ANVIL BANNER PENCIL PENOUN PINION FEATHER

PENNON SPAR PEGGYMAST

PENNSYLVANIA

CAPITAL: HARRISBURG
COLLEGE: JUNIATA URSINUS LYCOMING
COUNTY: BERKS BUCKS TIOGA CAMBRIA JUNIATA VENANGO WYOMING LYCOMING
MOUNTAIN RANGE: POCONO ALLEGHENY
NATIVE: AMISH DUTCH
PRESIDENT: BUCHANAN
RIVER: LEHIGH CLARION JUNIATA LICKING TOWANDA CALDWELL DELAWARE SCHRADER ALLEGHENY SCHUYLKILL MONONGAHELA SUSQUEHANNA
STATE BIRD: GROUSE
STATE FLOWER: LAUREL
STATE NICKNAME: KEYSTONE
STATE TREE: HEMLOCK
TOWN: ERIE ETNA PLUM YORK AVOCA EASTON EMMAUS SHARON ALTOONA EPHRATA HERSHEY READING BRYNMAWR SCRANTON SHAMOKIN BETHLEHEM CHARLEROI GETTYSBURG PITTSBURGH
UNIVERSITY: PITT DREXEL LEHIGH TEMPLE BUCKNELL DUQUESNE VILLANOVA

PENNY DY AES MEG RED SOU GILL BROON BROWN OULAP PENCE COPPER FOLLIS SALTEE STIVER BROWNIE STERLING
(— DREADFUL) HORRIBLE
(DUTCH —) STIVER
(HALF —) HALFLIN
(OLD SCOTCH —) TURNER
(PL.) PENCE FOLLES

PENNYCRESS FANWEED STINKWEED

PENNY-PINCHING STINGY

PENNYROYAL PULIOL HEDEOMA HILLWORT TICKWEED SQUAWWEED

PENNYWEIGHT DWT PENNY WEIGHT STERLING

PENSION WAGE PAYMENT STIPEND SUBSIDY TRIBUTE GRATUITY MALIKANA

PENSIVE MESTO MOODY PENSY SOBER DREAMY MUSING PENCEY WISTFUL THOUGHTY

PENT CAGED PENNED CONFINED ENCLOSED RESERVOIR

PENTACLE STAR HEXAGRAM PENTAGRAM

PENTAD QUINTAD

PENTASTICH POEM UNIT STANZA STROPHE

PENTECOST SHABUOTH WHITSUNDAY

PENTHEUS (GRANDFATHER OF —) CADMUS
(MOTHER OF —) AGAVE

PENTHOUSE PENT ROOF SHED AERIE ANNEX HANGAR LOOKUM SHADOW PLUTEUS BULKHEAD SKEELING SKILLION

PENTOSAN ARABAN

PENTOSE APIOSE RIBOSE

PENTYL AMYL

PENURIOUS MEAN POOR BARREN SCANTY STINGY MISERLY WANTING INDIGENT HIDEBOUND NIGGARDLY

PENURY WANT BEGGARY BORASCO POVERTY SCARCITY INDIGENCE PRIVATION

PEON HAND PAWN SERF SLAVE PELADO THRALL FOOTMAN LABORER PEASANT SOLDIER CONSTABLE

PEONY PINY MOUTAN

PEOPLE ARO LOG MEN PUL TAT VAI YAO AKRA ASHA BENI BUGI CHIN CHUD EMIM FOLK GENS HERD HIMA HUMA IRON LAND LEDE LUBA LURI PHUD PHUL PHUT RACE RAIS REMI SAFI SARA SEBA SERE TEMA THEY TOMA TULU USUN VITI VOLK WARE AFIFI AVARS BENIN BONGO CATTI CHAGA COURS DEMOS DUALA EDONI ELYMI FOLKS GENTE GOMER HAUSA JACKS LAITY LANAO LENDU LUREM MARSI MASAI NOGAI ORANG PUNAN QUADI RAMBO ROTSE SACAE SALAR SAURA SHAKA STOCK TAURI VOLTA WARUA WORLD ABABUA ACHUAS AFSHAR AISSOR ANGAMI ANGLES ARUNTA AVIKOM BAHIMA BAKELE BAKUBA BALUBA BELTIR BOSHAS BULLOM CIMBRI COMMON DAIONE GENTRY GILAKI GILEKI HAUSSA HERERO HERULI KANWAR KPUESI KRUMAN MANTZU MINYAE MOSCHI NATION OVAMPO PAMIRI PUBLIC RAMUSI RUTULI SAFINI SAMBAL SATRAE SEMANG SHARRA TADJIK TAGAUR TELUGU TUNGUZ TURSHA VENETI VOLCAE WACAGO WAHIMA YNDOYS YUECHI ZAMBAL ACHANGO ASTOMOI BAGANDA BAGARRA BAKALAI BANGALA BANGASH BAROTSE BUNYORO DARDANI DENIZEN DURZADA FALISCI GAETULI GENERAL GEPIDAE GUHAYNA INHABIT IRISHRY ISSEDOI ITALICI KINDRED KURANKO MAKONDE MESHECH MITANNI NABALOI PICENES PICTAVI PUKHTUN ROHILLA SAMBURU SENONES SILURES

SUKKIIM TIRURAI VESTINI WABUNGA WACHAGA WAKAMBA WANGONI
(— HAVING DISTINCT LANGUAGE) TONGUE
(— OF FASHION) FLOSS
(— OF GOOD BREEDING) GENTRY GENTILITY
(ABORIGINAL —) JAKUN KHMER KODAGU SEKHWAN
(ANCIENT —) CARA CHAM JUNG ELYMI GETAE HURRI ICENI SACAE SERES SICULI DARDANI FALISCI FIRBOLG KIPCHAK SEQUANI SILURES
(CAVE-DWELLING —) HORITE
(COMMON —) DEMOS PLEBE VULGAR VULGUS TILIKUM SNOBBERY
(EXTINCT —) KOT CHONO COFAN COREE CHANGO CHATOT GUINAU HIBITO SAPONI SHIRINO
(FOREST —) SAKAI SAORA SAURA
(HONORABLE —) HONESTY
(LOWEST CLASS OF —) CANAILLE
(MARITIME —) LAMUT
(MOUNTAIN —) HUZUL HUTZUL
(NOMADIC —) SHUA HORDE IGDYR IHLAT SHUWA HABIRU SHAGIA SARACEN SHAMMAR SHORTZY SHUKRIA
(OLD —) ANCIENTRY
(ORDINARY —) LAYFOLK
(PAGAN —) IRAYA HANUNOO SUBANUN
(PRIMITIVE —) DAFLA IRULA KADIR KURUKH CHENCHU
(WHITE —) ALBICULI
(PL.) MAKHZAN

PEOPLED ABAD SETTLED POPULAT

PEORIA MASCOUTEN

PEP GO VIM DASH VERVE VIGOR ENERGY GINGER ANIMATE QUICKE ACTIVITY

PEPLUM GOWN SKIRT TUNIC PEPLO OVERSKIRT

PEPO GOURD MELON SQUASH PUMPKIN PEPONIDA PEPONIUM

PEPPER CAVA IKMO ITMO KAVA SIF BETEL CHILI MANGO PIPER SIRIH MATICO TOPEPO CAYENNE PAPRIK PIMENTA RELIENO JALAPENO KAVAKAVA
(JAVA —) CUBEB
(RED —) LADYFINGER

PEPPER-AND-SALT JASPER

PEPPERGRASS CRESS CANARY ANOUNOU COCKWEED

PEPPERMINT MENTHE LABIATE

PEPPER TREE MOLLE HOROPITO PIMIENTO

PEPPERWORT DITTANDER

PEPPERY HOT FIERY SAUCY SPICY TOUCHY PIQUANT PUNGENT SPIRITED STINGING

PEPPY GINGERY

PEPTONE ASCARON

PER BY THE EACH THROUGH

PERADVENTURE HAP DOUBT MAYBE CHANCE MAPPEN MAYHAP HAPPILY PERHAPS POSSIBLY

ERAMBULATE WALK RAMBLE
STROLL PERAMBLE TRAVERSE
ERAMBULATION WEND
ERAMBULATOR BUGGY WAGON
BASSINET VIAMETER WAYWISER
PEDOMETER
ERATE OPHITE
ERCEIVE SEE ESPY FEEL FIND
GAUM HEAR KNOW LOOK MIND
NOTE SCAN TWIG SCENT SENSE
SMELL TASTE TOUCH BEHOLD
COTTON DESCRY DIVINE FIGURE
NOTICE REMARK SURVEY COGNIZE
DISCERN OBSERVE REALIZE
SENSATE COMPRISE DESCRIBE
UNDERNIM
ERCENTAGE CUT AGIO PART
SHARE PROFIT PORTION SCALAGE
DEFLATOR
(MINING —) LEY
ERCEPT IDEA
ERCEPTIBLE NOTABLE TACTILE
VISIBLE APPARENT PALPABLE
SENSIBLE TANGIBLE TRACTABLE
(FAINTLY —) SHADOWY
(HARDLY —) FAINT
ERCEPTION RAY BUMP GAUM
TACT SAVOR SCENT SENSE SIGHT
ACUMEN VISION CLOSURE FEELING
GLIMMER NOSTRIL BEARINGS
DELICACY OUTSIGHT COGNITION
SENSATION SENTIMENT
(DIM —) GLIMMER
(MENTAL —) TACT TOUCH
SENSATION
ERCEPTIVE QUICK SHARP SUBTLE
KNOWING SENSITIVE
ERCH BAR BAS LUG PEG ROD SIT
BASS JOUK MADO OKOW PERK PIKE
POLE POPE SEAT BARSE BEGTI
BEKTI BLOCK LIGHT REACH ROOST
RUFFE STAFF ALIGHT BUGARA
CALLOP PERCID SAUGER SETTLE
ZANDER ZINGEL ALFIONE HOGFISH
STATION ROCKFISH MARTENIKO
TRUMPETER
(2-YEAR OLD —) EGLING
ERCHANCE HAPLY MAYBE
AUNTERS FORTUNE PERHAPS
POSSIBLY
ERCHER STAKER
ERCHTA BERTHA
ERCOLATE MELT OOZE PERK SEEP
SIFT SILT SIPE SOAK WEEP DRILL
EXUDE LEACH EXHALE FILTER
STRAIN
ERCOLATION SIPING SEEPAGE
LEACHING
ERCOLATOR SIPER BIGGIN
CAFETIERE DISPLACER
ERCUSSION BLOW IMPACT
STROKE PNEUMATIC
ERDITION HELL LOSS RUIN
BOWWOWS BALLYWACK DAMNATION
EREGRINATE TOUR WALK TRAVEL
WANDER JOURNEY SOJOURN
TRAVERSE
EREGRINE ALIEN EXOTIC ROVING
PILGRIM STRANGE IMPORTED

PEREGRINE FALCON SAKER
GENTLE TASSEL TERCEL
PEREMPT QUASH DEFEAT DESTROY
PEREMPTORY FLAT FINAL UTTER
EXPRESS HAUGHTY ABSOLUTE
DECISIVE DOGMATIC POSITIVE
ESSENTIAL
PERENNIAL HERB CAREX LIANA
PEONY SEDUM BANANA CENTRO
BLUEWEED CONSTANT ENDURING
KNAPWEED TOADFLAX CONTINUAL
EVERGREEN PERPETUAL
RECURRENT
PERFECT ALL BACK CURE FILL FINE
FULL HOLY PURE SURE EXACT
FINAL FULLY IDEAL PLAIN RIGHT
RIPEN SHEER SOUND TOTAL UTTER
WHOLE ENTIRE EXPERT FINISH
REFINE SPHERE CERTAIN CONCOCT
CONTENT CORRECT CROWNED
DEVELOP GEMLIKE IMPROVE
PLENARY PRECISE SINLESS
SPHERAL TYPICAL COMPLETE
FLAWLESS INFINITE INTEGRAL
(— IN RIGHTEOUSNESS) HOLY
(— SCORE) MAX
PERFECTED EXACT SUMMED
FINISHED PERQUEIR
PERFECTION ACME PINK BLOOM
IDEAL BEAUTY FINISH PLENTY
FULNESS PARAGON FINALITY
FINENESS MATURITY RIPENESS
ERUDITION
(TYPE OF —) PARAGON
PERFECTIVE TELIC
PERFECTLY SPAN QUITE IDEALLY
PERQUEIR
PERFIDIOUS FALSE SNAKY DISLEAL
SNAKISH DISLOYAL SPITEFUL
FAITHLESS
PERFIDY DECEIT TREASON
FALSEHOOD FALSENESS
TREACHERY
PERFORATE EAT DOCK HOLE DRILL
PRICK PUNCH SIEVE THIRL PIERCE
POUNCE RIDDLE THRILL PINHOLE
PUNCTURE PENETRATE TEREBRATE
(— A STAMP) CENTER
PERFORATED OPEN CRIBROSE
PERFORATION BORE HOLE THIRL
TORET BROACH EYELET STIGMA
TRESIS FORAMEN PINHOLE SEPTULA
STENCIL DIABROSIS
PERFORM DO ACT CUT KIP CHAR
FILL FULL HAVE KEEP LAST MAKE
PLAY SHOW STEP CHARE DIGHT
ENACT EXERT FETCH ACQUIT
COMMIT EFFECT FULFIL RENDER
ACHIEVE EXECUTE EXHIBIT EXPLOIT
FUNGIFY FURNISH IWURCHE
PRESENT PRESTATE
(— AWKWARDLY) BOGGLE
(— BADLY) BOLLIX
(— BRILLIANTLY) STAR SPARKLE
(— CLUMSILY) THUMB BUNGLE
(— FULLY) END
(— HASTILY) SKIMP SCAMP,
(— HURRIEDLY) SLUR
(— IN DANCING) FIGURE

PERFORMANCE ACT JOB DEED
FEAT HAND SHOW TEST WORK
CAPER SLANG SPORT STUNT
ACTING ACTION BALLET EFFECT
HORARY MASQUE ACCOUNT
ACROAMA BENEFIT BOOKING
CONCERT EXPLOIT MATINEE
MUMMERY SHOWING FAREWELL
FUNCTION PRACTICE STERACLE
(— FOR ONE) SOLO
(— OF DUTY) FEASANCE
(— OF OBLIGATION) SOLUTIO
(— VARIATIONS) COUNTER
(— WITH SENTIMENTALITY) DROOL
(ARAB —) FANTASIA
(CHRISTMAS EVE —) GOMBAY
(CLUMSY —) BUNGLE
(DRAMATIC —) TOPENG
(FIRST —) PREMIERE
(NO —) RELACHE
(PAST —) FORM
(TRIAL —) AUDITION
(VULGAR —) BLOWOFF
PERFORMER ACT DOER GEEK MOKE
STAR ACTOR SHINE ARTIST DANCER
KINKER LEADER PLAYER WORKER
ACROAMA ARTISTE GAMBIST
HORNIST HOTSHOT SOLOIST
EXECUTOR SPARKLER HAMFATTER
HEADLINER
(— ON SEVERAL INSTRUMENTS)
MOKE
(— WITH NEGRO DIALECT)
HAMBONE
(BURLESQUE —) GRINDER
(CIRCUS —) LEAPER
(INFERIOR —) HAM SHINE
PERFUME ATAR BALM FUME MUSK
NOSE OTTO AROMA ATTAR CENSE
CIVET MYRRH SCENT SMELL SPICE
CARVOL CHYPRE EMBALM FLAVOR
IONONE CARVONE DIAPASM
ESSENCE INCENSE JASMINE
NOSEGAY ODORIZE SWEETEN
BERGAMOT MARECHAL ORANGERY
PATCHOULI
(— BASE) MUSK CIVET NEROL
NEROLI
(POWDERY —) PULVIL
PERFUNCTORY CURSORY
CARELESS APATHETIC
PERGOLA ARBOR BOWER RAMADA
BALCONY TRELLIS
PERHAPS HAPS MAYBE ABLINS
BELIKE HAPPEN MAPPEN MAYHAP
ABLINGS LIGHTLY PERCASE
POSSIBLY
PERI ELF FAIRY SPRITE
PERIAPT CHARM AMULET
PERICARP BUR BOLL BURR
BLADDER
PERICRANIUM HEAD BRAIN
PERIDOTITE PICRITE EULYSITE
JOSEFITE SAXONITE WEHRLITE
PERIGEE EPIGEUM
PERIGYNIUM UTRICLE
PERIL RISK WERE WATHE CRISIS
DANGER HAZARD MENACE SCYLLA
THREAT THRONG TRANCE

JEOPARDY CHARYBDIS
PERILOUS KITTLE DOUBTFUL
DREADFUL INFAMOUS DANGEROUS
HAZARDOUS
PERIMETER RIM OUTLINE
BOUNDARY PERIPHERY
PERIOD GO AGE DOT END EON ERA
AEON DATE LIFE RACE SPAN STOP
TERM TIDE TIME YEAR AVAIL CLOSE
CYCLE EPACT EPOCH LABOR LAPSE
PATCH POINT SPACE SPELL STAGE
CUTOFF GHURRY HEMERA MOMENT
PARODY PICTUN SEASON STOUND
ACCOUNT DICOLON FLORUIT
PASTIME SESSION STADIUM
STRETCH DURATION INDUCIAE
INSTANCE LIFETIME SENTENCE
(— **ENDING FROST)** FRESH
(— **FOR WHICH ENJOYED)** TENURE
(— **IN DEVELOPMENT)** STAGE
(— **OF 10 YEARS)** DECADE
(— **OF 100 YEARS)** AGE CENTURY
(— **OF 1000 YEARS)** CHILIAD
MILLIAD
(— **OF 14 MINUTES, 24 SECONDS)**
CENTIDAY
(— **OF 2 MONTHS)** DIMESTER
(— **OF 2 YEARS)** BIENNIUM
(— **OF 20 TUNS)** KATUN
(— **OF 20 YEARS)** KATUN
(— **OF 260 DAYS)** TONALMATL
(— **OF 5 DAYS)** PENTAD LUSTRUM
(— **OF 50 YEARS)** JUBILE JUBILEE
(— **OF 7 DAYS)** HEBDOMAD
(— **OF 7 YEARS)** SEPTENARY
(— **OF ACTION)** GO BOUT
(— **OF DECLINE)** SUNSET EVENING
(— **OF DRYNESS)** DROUTH
DROUGHT
(— **OF FESTIVITY)** WAKES
(— **OF GLOOM)** DEAD
(— **OF GRACE)** DAY
(— **OF HEAT)** CALLING
(— **OF HUMID WEATHER)** SIZZARD
(— **OF IMMATURITY)** SWADDLE
(— **OF INSTRUCTION)** LESSON
(— **OF LIFE)** AGE ELD SPAN
(— **OF MILITARY SERVICE)** HITCH
(— **OF MOTILITY)** SWARMING
(— **OF MOURNING)** SHIVA SHIBAH
(— **OF PERFORMING)** STANZA
(— **OF PLAY)** HALF CHUKKER
QUARTER
(— **OF RECREATION)** HOLIDAY
VACATION
(— **OF REMISSION)** JUBILEE
(— **OF REST)** SMOKO BREATHER
(— **OF REVOLUTION OF HEAVENLY
BODY)** ORB
(— **OF TIME)** DAY HOUR WEEK
YEAR MONTH DECADE MINUTE
SECOND
(— **OF WORK)** SHIFT SPELL STINT
(— **PRECEDING IMPORTANT EVENT)**
EVE
(**CLASS** —) HOUR
(**CULTURAL** —) HORIZON
(**DEFINITE** —) MOMENT
(**DISTINCTIVE** —) EPOCH

(**DULL** —) SLACK
(**EVOLUTIONAL** —) HEMERA
(**GEOLOGICAL** —) JURA KAROO
EOCENE ALGOMAN HORIZON
CAMBRIAN DEVONIAN JURASSIC
SILURIAN TERTIARY TRANSVAAL
(**HAPPY** —) MILLENIUM
(**HYPOTHETICAL** —) ACME
(**LONG** —) EON AEON CYCLE
(**MEETING** —) SESSION
(**MENSTRUAL** —) TERMS
(**OCCASIONAL** —) SNATCH
(**PENITENTIAL** —) LENT
(**RECURRING** —) EMBER
(**SHORT** —) BIT FIT BLINK SHAKE
SPELL SPURT SNATCH
PERIODIC ERAL ANNUAL CYCLIC
ETESIAN REGULAR FREQUENT
SEASONAL
(**NOT** —) LOOSE
PERIODICAL DAILY PAPER SHEET
ANNUAL DIGEST REVIEW ETESIAN
FANZINE JOURNAL TABLOID
DREADFUL EXCHANGE MAGAZINE
EPHEMERIS
PERIODICALLY TERMLY
PERIPATETIC ROVING RAMBLING
ITINERANT
PERIPHERAL DEEP OUTER DISTAL
DISTANT EXTERNAL MARGINAL
PERIPHERY LIP RIM BRIM DOME
EDGE AMBIT LIMIT SKIRT AREOLA
BORDER BOUNDS FRINGE AMBITUS
CONTOUR SUBURBS SURFACE
CONFINES PERIMETER
PERISCOPE ALTISCOPE HYPOSCOPE
OMNISCOPE
PERISH DIE FADE FALL RUIN TINE
TYNE QUAIL SPILL SWELT WASTE
DEPART EXPIRE STARVE DESTROY
FORFARE MISCARRY
(— **GRADUALLY)** FADE
PERISHABLE SOFT DYING CADUKE
BRITTLE FUGITIVE
PERISHED MUSHY
PERISTOME FRINGE
PERITE SKILLED
PERITHECIUM ALVEOLA
PERITONEUM RIM SIPHAC
PERIWIG FLASH GALERA PERUKE
TOUPEE GALERUM PERWICK
PERIWINKLE PERY PIRE WINK
PERRY SNAIL MYRTLE WINKLE
DOGBANE PINPATCH SENGREEN
BLUEBUTTON
PERJINK NEAT TRIM PRECISE
PERJURE FORSWEAR
PERJURED MANSWORN
PERK BRISK PERCH PREEN PRINK
FRESHEN SMARTEN
PERKY AIRY PERT COCKY JAUNTY
CHIPPER
PERMANENCE STAY STABILITY
PERMANENT FIXED STABLE ABIDING
DURABLE LASTING STATIVE
CONSTANT ENDURING REMANENT
STANDING INDELIBLE
PERMANENTLY KEEPS
PERMEABLE POROUS

PERMEATE FILL SEEP SOAK BATHE
IMBUE DRENCH INFORM INVADE
ANIMATE PERVADE DOMINATE
SATURATE PENETRATE
PERMEATED SHOT
PERMIAN DYAS DYASSIC
PERMISSIBLE FREE POSSIBLE
CONGEABLE
(**NOT** —) NEFAS
PERMISSION MAY FIAT LIEF CONGE
DARST FAVOR GRACE GRANT LEAVE
ACCESS ACCORD CONSENT LIBERTY
LICENSE SANCTION
PERMISSIVE TOLERANT
CONCESSORY
PERMIT LET CHOP GIVE LEVE PASS
ADMIT ALLOW CONGE EXEAT FAVOR
GRACE GRANT LEAVE SERVE
ACCORD BETEEM CEDULA DUSTUK
ENDURE ENTREE SUFFER CONCEDE
CONSENT DUSTUCK FACULTY
LICENSE PLACARD POMPANO
WARRANT DISPENSE
(— **NEGATIVELY)** TOLERATE
(— **TO TAKE)** SOAK
PERMITTED FREE LOOT LICIT
ALLOWED INNOCENT SUPPOSED
(— **BY LAW)** LEGAL
PERMUTATION BARTER CHANGE
EXCHANGE
PERNICIOUS BAD ILL EVIL FATAL
QUICK SWIFT DEADLY MALIGN
WICKED BALEFUL BANEFUL
HARMFUL HURTFUL NOISOME
NOXIOUS RUINOUS
PERNIO CHILBLAIN
PEROPUS PARAGON
PERORATION EPILOG PERIOD
CLOSING PURLICUE
PERPEND JUMPER PARPEN PONDER
REFLECT THROUGH
PERPENDICULAR SINE ERECT
PLUMB SHEER ABRUPT NORMAL
APOTHEM UPRIGHT BINORMAL
CATHETUS EVENDOWN VERTICAL
PERPENDICULARLY BOLT SHEER
SHEERLY
PERPENDICULARITY APLOMB
PERPETRATE DO COMMIT EFFECT
PERFORM
PERPETUAL ETERN ENDLESS
ETERNAL CONSTANT INFINITO
UNENDING CONTINUAL PERENNIAL
PERPETUALLY EVER ALWAYS
FOREVER
PERPETUATE CONTINUE ETERNIZE
MAINTAIN
PERPLEX CAP MAR SET VEX BEAT
CLOG DOIT DOZE FIKE MAZE STUN
AMAZE BESET BLAIK STUMP TWIST
BAFFLE BOGGLE BOTHER CUMBER
DARKEN FICKLE GRAVEL HAMPER
HARASS HOBBLE KITTLE MAMMER
MITHER MOIDER MUDDLE PLAGUE
POTHER POTTER PUTTER PUZZLE
RAFFLE RIDDLE TWITCH WILDER
WRIXLE BEDEVIL BUMBAZE
CONFUSE DIFFUSE EMBROIL
MYSTIFY NONPLUS PLUNDER

STAGGER STUMBLE TORMENT
BEWILDER SURPRISE WINDLASS
ERPLEXED MAZY ANXIOUS
NONPLUS PUZZLED CONFUSED
TROUBLED INTRICATE
ERPLEXING HARD MAZY CRABBY
KNOBBY KNOTTY CARKING
COMPLEX CRABBED QUISCOS
BAFFLING
ERPLEXITY FOG KNOT WERE
BRAKE FOITER HOBBLE PUCKER
TANGLE ANXIETY STICKLE TROUBLE
POSEMENT SURPRISE CONFUSION
LABYRINTH
(MENTAL —) STUDY
(RELIEVE OF —) CLEAR
ERQUISITE FEE TIP PERK VAIL
GOUPIN GOWPEN INCOME ADJUNCT
APANAGE VANTAGE CONQUEST
GRATUITY
(PL.) PICKING
ERRINIST LIBERTINE
ERRIER PEDRERO
ERSE BLUE
ERSECUTE VEX BAIT ANNOY
CHASE HARRY HOUND WRACK
WRONG HARASS PESTER PURSUE
AFFLICT CRUCIFY DRAGOON
OPPRESS TORMENT TORTURE
ERSECUTED JOB REFUGEE
ERSECUTOR TORQUEMADA
ERSEPHONE KORE DESPOINA
PRAXIDIKE
(DAUGHTER OF —) CORA KORE
(FATHER OF —) ZEUS JUPITER
(HUSBAND OF —) HADES PLUTO
(MOTHER OF —) CERES DEMETER
ERSEUS RESCUER CHAMPION
(FATHER OF —) ZEUS JUPITER
(GRANDFATHER OF —) ACRISIUS
(MOTHER OF —) DANAE
(STAR OF —) ATIK ALGOL
(VICTIM OF —) MEDUSA
(WIFE OF —) ANDROMEDA
ERSEVERANCE GRIT STAMINA
INDUSTRY PATIENCE TENACITY
CONSTANCY
ERSEVERE CANK KEEP TORE
ABIDE STICK INSIST REMAIN
PERSIST CONTINUE
ERSEVERING BUSY HARD STILL
RESOLUTE ASSIDUOUS INSISTENT
RSIA (SEE IRAN)
RSIAN PERSE GILAKI HAJEMI
RANIC DURZADA HADJEMI IRANIAN
MEMNONIAN
— RED DEER) MARAL
RSICARY REDLEG REDLEGS
REDSHANK HEARTEASE HEARTWEED
EACHWORT
RSIFLAGE BANTER RAILLERY
RSIMMON KAKI SIMON SIMMON
APOTE CHAPOTE HYAKUME
RIUMPH
— TREE) GAB GAUB LOTUS
RSIST HOLD KEEP LAST URGE
DHERE ENDURE INSIST REMAIN
UBSIST CONTINUE PERSEVERE
RSISTENCE GUTS

PERSISTENCY TENACITY
PERSISTENT SET DREE FIRM HARD
GREAT STOUT DOGGED DREECH
GRITTY HECTIC SLEUTH DURABLE
RESTANT RESTIVE CONSTANT
ENDURING HOLDFAST OBDURATE
RESOLUTE SEDULOUS STUBBORN
ASSIDUOUS OBSTINATE PRIMITIVE
PERSON CAT EGG EGO GUY MAN
ONE BABY BODY CHAL CHAP DUCK
FISH FOOD FORM GINK HOOK LEDE
LIFE NABS SELF SOUL BEING
BOSOM CHILD COOKY GHOST
HEART HUMAN PARTI PARTY PIECE
STICK THING WATCH WIGHT ANIMAL
BUGGER ENTITY FELLOW GALOOT
GAZABO JOHNNY KIPPER NUMBER
SINNER SISTER SPIRIT SPRITE
ARTICLE BLISTER WAGTAIL
SPECIMEN TILLICUM
(— ACTING FOR ANOTHER) PROXY
(— ASSOCIATED WITH WORK)
WALLAH
(— BEARING HEAVY BURDEN)
CAMEL
(— BEHIND THE TIMES) FOGY
FOGEY
(— BRINGING GOOD LUCK) MASCOT
**(— FROM WHOM FAMILY IS
DESCENDED)** STIRPS
(— NAMED) NOMINEE
(— NOT OF NOBLE BIRTH)
ROTURIER
(— OF AGE) COOT FALDWORTH
(— OF CONSEQUENCE) BIGGIE
BIGWIG TALLBOY
(— OF COURAGE) SPARTAN
(— OF INFLUENCE) CAPTAIN
HEAVYWEIGHT
(— OF MEAN BIRTH) GUTTERBLOOD
(— OF RANK) STATE MAGNATE
EMINENCE
(— RESEMBLING ANOTHER) SOSIA
(— TO SERVE WRIT) ELISOR
(— TOO STRONG FOR ASSAILANT)
TARTAR
(— WITH MENTAL TWIST) CRANK
(— WITH NERVOUS DISORDERS)
NEUROTIC
(— WITH QUEER IDEAS) ROZUM
(— WITHOUT STAMINA) JELLYFISH
(—S IN AMBASSADOR'S SUITE)
COMES
(ABJECT —) SLAVE
(ABSENT-MINDED —) MUSARD
(AFFECTED —) GIMCRACK
(AGGRESSIVE —) SHOVER HOTSHOT
(ANNOYING —) FIEND
(ARABIZED —) MOZARAB
(ARROGANT —) HUFF TENGU
(ATTRACTIVE —) CUTEY CUTIE
KNOCKOUT
(AVARICIOUS —) YISSER
(AWKWARD —) PUT GAWP HICK
RUBE SLAM STAG STEG STIFF
GUFFIN TUMFIE HOOSIER KITHOGE
LOBSTER SLOMMACK SPELDRIN
(BAD —) UNSEL

(BALD —) BALLARD BALDHEAD
SKINHEAD
(BANISHED —) WRETCH
(BAPTIZED —) MEMBER ILLUMINATO
(BASE —) CUT RASCAL CAITIFF
HILDING PUTTOCK
(BELOVED —) FLAME HEARTROOT
(BIG-BELLIED —) GORBELLY
(BLACK —) BLECK
(BOASTFUL —) BLOWER GASCON
(BOORISH —) GOOP
(CALLOW —) GORLIN SMARTY
GOSLING
(CANONIZED —) SAINT
(CARELESS —) HASH TASSEL
(CHICKENHEARTED —) HEN
(CHILDISH —) BAUBLE WHIMLING
(CHUNKY —) JUNT
(CHURLISH —) TIKE TYKE
(CIRCLE OF —S) COTERIE
(CLEVER —) BIRD WHIZ WHIZZ
MERCURY
(CLOWNISH —) BUFFOON HOBNAIL
VILLAIN
(CLUMSY —) DUB BOOB GAWK
SLOB TIKE TYKE JUMBO STAUP
STIFF DUFFER KEFFEL LUMMOX
HODMADOD
(COARSE —) COW STIRK BABOON
MUCKER
(COMBATIVE —) DRAGON
GAMECOCK
(COMMONPLACE —) MUT MUTT
BROMIDE
(CONCEITED —) IT HUFF COXCOMB
PRAGMATIC
(CONFUSED —) FOOSTERER
(CONTEMPTIBLE —) YAP HEEL PUKE
SCAB SKIN SWAB CATSO SHRUB
SKITE SKUNK SNIPE INSECT SHICER
STINKER BLIGHTER PETTITOES
(COWARDLY —) FUGIE SISSY SLINK
SQUIB
(CRAFTY —) TOD FILE SHARK
JESUIT
(CRAZED —) PSYCOPATH
(CRINGING —) SNAKE SNOOL
(CRINGING —) FLUNKY SPANIEL
(CRUEL —) LAMB FIEND MALISON
(CUNNING —) PIE
(DAINTY —) MIMMOCK
(DEAD —) DEFUNCT DECEASED
DECEDENT
(DECREPIT —) WITHERLING
(DEFORMED —) CRILE CALIBAN
HODMADOD
(DENSE —) DUFFER
(DEPRAVED —) SKATE
(DESPICABLE —) HOUND SLAVE
CAITIFF
(DESTITUTE —) PAUPER
(DIMINUTIVE —) BANTY MIDGE
BANTAM MIDGET
(DIRTY —) DRIVEL HOWLET
(DISABLED —) DUCK CRIPPLE
INVALID
(DISAGREEABLE —) GOOP PILL
QUAT SKITE RATBAG
(DISGRUNTLED —) SOREHEAD

(DISHONEST —) ROGUE ROTTER BEZONIAN
(DISLIKED —) WARLING
(DISSOLUTE —) RIBALD STRIKER
(DOLTISH —) BLOCK SWINE
(DRUNKEN —) LUSH TUMBREL TUMBRIL
(DULL —) LOB BORE DODO GOON GOOP GRUB LUMP MOME MOPE SLOB CLUNK DROUD STICK STOCK LACKWIT LOBCOCK OPACITY
(DULL-WITTED —) DOPE GUMP DUNCE
(DWARFISH —) CROWL SHURF
(DYING —) MORIBUND
(ECCENTRIC —) COON GINK TIKE TYKE GAZABO GAZEBO FANTAST
(EFFEMINATE —) SOFTY SQUAW SOFTIE BADLING SOFTLING SMOCKFACE
(ELDERLY —) SENIOR SOAKER GRAYHEAD
(EMACIATED —) FRAME WASTREL SKELETON
(EMPTY-HEADED —) NITWIT
(ENROLLED —) MEMBER
(ENTERTAINING —) COMEDIAN
(EVIL —) QUED SCUM QUEDE SHREW
(EXPERIENCED —) EXPERT SOAKER STAGER
(EXTORTIONATE —) SCREW
(EXTRAORDINARY —) ONER BUSTER
(FADED —) SHARGAR SHARGER
(FAMOUS —) DON NOTORIETY
(FANTASTIC —) KICKSHAW
(FASHIONABLE —) GIMCRACK
(FASTIDIOUS —) MIMMOCK DELICATE
(FAT —) GURK BLIMP FATSO QUILT SQUAB STOUT
(FAWNING —) COGGER SPANIEL
(FEEBLEMINDED —) FEEB IDIOT MORON IMBECILE
(FEROCIOUS —) LAMB
(FICKLE —) ROVER MOONCALF
(FINE —) WHIPPA
(FLABBY —) HUDDERON
(FLASHY —) KID FLASHER
(FOOLISH —) FOP GUMP HOIT JERK BOOBY SOFTY BAUBLE DOODLE DOTARD DRIVEL HOWLET GOSLING GUBBINS
(FRANK —) TELLTRUTH
(FUSSY —) FAD FADDLE GRANNY SPOFFY GRANNIE
(GAY —) GRIG HUZZA
(GOOD-FOR-NOTHING —) KET PELF TASSEL WASTER WANHOPE WASTREL
(GOSSIPING —) SHULER SHUILER
(GOSSIPY —) BIGMOUTH NEWSMONGER
(GRAVE —) SOBERSIDES
(GREEDY —) GORB GRASPER PUTTOCK
(GROTESQUE —) GUY GOLLIWOGG
(GRUMPY —) SOURBELLY
(GULLIBLE —) JAY BOOB GULPIN

LOBSTER FLATHEAD SHLEMIEL WOODCOCK
(GYPSY —) CHI CHAI
(HARD —) MALISON
(HATEFUL —) TOAD
(HEAVY —) STODGER
(HEAVY-SET —) LUMP
(HOT-TEMPERED —) SPARK
(HUMPBACKED —) LORD
(HUNGRY —) HUNGARIAN
(IDLE —) RAGABASH SLUGGARD
(IGNORANT —) BABE BOOB PORK IDIOT
(ILL-BRED —) BOOR CHURL CLOWN
(ILL-MANNERED —) GRUB SKUNK
(ILL-NATURED —) CRAB HUNKS
(ILL-TEMPERED —) CRAB ETTERCAP TAISTREL
(IMMATURE —) BUD SQUAB GORLIN
(IMMORAL —) PERDU IMPURITAN
(IMPERTINENT —) PAUK PAWK SNIP
(IMPORTANT —) HONOR MUGWUMP
(IMPOTENT —) SPADO
(IMPUDENT —) SAUCE SQUIRT SAUCEBOX
(INANE —) SHAUP
(INEXPERIENCED —) BABE INGENUE BEGINNER
(INFERIOR —) BATA SHRUB SHABBLE
(INSIGNIFICANT —) DAB MUT MUTT BILSH CREEP JOKER SHURF SPRAT SQUIB ABLACH PEANUT PINKEEN WHIFFET GNATLING GRILDRIG PIGWIGEON
(INTRACTABLE —) BUCKIE TARTAR HAGGARD HARDCASE
(IRASCIBLE —) TOUCHWOOD
(LAME —) VULCAN
(LANK —) TANGLE GANGEREL
(LARGE —) CHUNK WHIPPA SKELPER STODGER STRAPPER
(LASCIVIOUS —) SUCCUBUS
(LAST — IN CONTEST) MELL
(LAZY —) BUM DAW HOIT POKE IDLER TRAIL LORDAN LURDAN BLELLUM LAZYLEGS SLUGGARD
(LEAN —) RIBE SHARGER THINGUT
(LEARNED —) CLERK ERUDIT ACHARYA SCHOLAR LITERATO WISEACRE LITERATUS
(LIGHTHEADED —) BEEHEAD
(LITERATE —) SCHOLAR
(LITTLE —) SMOLT SMOUT
(LIVELY —) GRIG BIRKIE HEMPIE WHISKER
(LOUD-VOICED —) STENTOR
(LOW —) PACK SCUM RASCAL BEASTMAN
(LOW SOCIETY —) MUDSILL
(LUBBERLY —) OAF
(LUMBERING —) PUMPKIN TUMBREL TUMBRIL
(LUMPISH —) DROUD
(LUSTY —) BILCH BILSH
(MAD —) MADLING
(MARRIED —) WIFE SPOUSE HUSBAND MATRIMONY
(MEAN —) RIP SCAB CHURL HOUND

MISER SKATE SNEAK SHICER BASTARD DOGBOLT BEZONIAN HUCKSTER STINKARD EARTHWORM
(MEDDLESOME —) BREVIT HESSIAN
(MISCHIEVOUS —) IMP LIMB PEST TOOL HEMPIE HELLION WHIPSTER
(MISERABLE —) SNAKE SWELP WRETCH
(MISERLY —) SKATE SCROOGE PINCHGUT PINCHBACK
(MONSTROUS —) WAMPUS
(NAIVE —) JERK CLUCK GUNSEL INGENUE INNOCENT
(NEGLECTED —) TACKY TACKEY
(NIMBLE —) MERCURY
(NOISY —) YAP HOWLET
(OBJECTIONABLE —) CUR COYOTE FOUTER
(OBSTINATE —) DONKEY STIFFNECK
(ODD —) GIG CURE QUIZZY RATBAG
(OFFENSIVE —) TICK SKITE STINKER
(OLD-FASHIONED —) FRUMP
(PALTRY —) PELTER
(PECULIAR —) BIRD CASE
(PEEVISH —) GRIZZLER SPLENETIC
(PERT —) PIE FLIRT
(POMPOUS —) PUFFIN POMPIST
(POT-BELLIED —) GORREL
(PRIVATE —) JUDEX
(PROSAIC —) PHILISTINE
(PRYING —) POKER PEEPER SMELLER
(PUGNOSED —) CAMUS CAMUSE
(PUNY —) SCART SHILP SHRIMP TITMAN
(PURITANICAL —) WOWSER
(QUEER-LOOKING —) JIGGER
(QUERULOUS —) GRUMP JACKDAW
(QUICK-TEMPERED —) SPUNKIE WILDCAT SPITFIRE
(RAGGED —) ROTO SHAGRAG TATTERWAG
(RAPACIOUS —) SHARK CATERER
(RECKLESS —) MADCAP RAMSTAM
(RED-HAIRED —) BRIQUE
(RESTLESS —) RAMPLER RAMPLOR RANTIPOLE
(RETICENT —) CLAM
(RICH —) MONEYBAGS
(RIDICULOUS —) GOOF HARE MONIMENT MONUMENT
(RIOTOUS —) ROARER
(ROUGH —) TOWSER
(ROUGH-LOOKING —) RULLION
(RUDE —) HICK PORK RULE CHURL CLOWN GROBIAN
(RUSTIC —) COON KERN KERNE HAYSEED HOMESPUN
(SAINTLY —) SADDIK
(SAUCY —) PIET
(SCRAWNY —) SCART SCRAG
(SELF-CENTERED —) HEEL DEVIL FLANEUR
(SELF-RIGHTEOUS —) PHARISEE
(SENSUAL —) SWING CARNALIST
(SHAMEFUL —) BISMER
(SHORT —) CRILE FADGE KNURL STUMP

(SHOWY —) FLASH FLASHER HOTSHOT

(SHREWD —) FILE YEPE HARDHEAD

(SICK —) SICK MALADE PATIENT AEGROTANT

(SILENT —) MUM MUMCHANCE

(SILLY —) FOP CAKE GUMP SOFT DOBBY GOOSE SOFTY SPOON CUCKOO NIMSHI SOFTIE GOOSECAP LIRIPIPE LIRIPOOP SOFTHEAD

(SIMPLE —) DRIP LAMB IDIOT PIGWIGEON

(SKINNY —) SCRAE SCARECROW

(SLATTERNLY —) SLATE

(SLIM —) SWABBLE

(SLOTHFUL —) SLOWBELLY

(SLOVENLY —) HASH SLOB SLORP TRAIL STREEL SLOMMACK STREELER

(SLUGGISH —) LUMP DOLDRUM DRUMBLE LOBCOCK

(SLY —) COON SLYBOOTS SNECKDRAW SNICKDRAW

(SMALL —) GRIG AGATE DWARF SPRAT INSECT MORSEL POPPET SACKET GNATLING

(SOPHISTICATED —) WELTKIND

(SPIRITLESS —) MOPE STICK

(SPITEFUL —) HELLCAT ETTERCAP

(SPRUCE —) SPRUSADO

(STINGY —) CHURL HAYNE STINGY

(STOCKY —) STUMP

(STOLID —) CLAM THICKSKIN

(STRANGE —) WAMPUS

(STRAY —) WAIF

(STUBBORN —) STOUT

(STUNTED —) URF SCRUNT SHARGAR

(STUPID —) ASS DUB JAY MUT BETE BOOB DODO DOLT DOPE DRIP GAUM GAWP GOOF GUMP HASH HOIT JERK MOKE MUTT BLOCK BUCCA CLUCK CLUNK DUNCE HOBBY JUKES LOACH MORON SHEEP STIRK STOCK STUPE SUMPH SWINE THICK WAMUS BOODLE DAWKIN DIMWIT DODUNK DONKEY DUFFER GANDER GILLIE GRANNY GUNSEL LUMMOX LURDAN NITWIT NOODLE SACKET STUPEX TUMFIE TUMPHY BLUNTIE DULLARD FATHEAD FUSSOCK HOWFING JACKASS JUGHEAD MUDHEAD SAPHEAD SCHNOOK BONEHEAD BULLHEAD DOTTEREL DUMBBELL FLATHEAD GAMPHREL IRONHEAD MOLDWARP MUMPHEAD STUNPOLL THICKWIT HODMANDOD MUMCHANCE THICKHEAD

(STURDY —) LUMP CHUNK TALWART

(SULKY —) GLUMP GRUMP SUMPH GROUCH

(SURLY —) CRUST HUNKS

(TACITURN —) OYSTER

(TALKATIVE —) GASSER BLELLUM BIGMOUTH

(TALL, AWKWARD —) GAMMERSTANG

(TENDER —) LAMBKIN

(THICKSET —) NUGGET

(THIRD —) GOOSEBERRY

(THOUGHTLESS —) AIRLING SKIPPER BIRDBRAIN

(TINY —) KEEROGUE

(TIRESOME —) BROMIDE PILLBORE

(TREACHEROUS —) JUDAS SNAKE VIPER GUNSEL SERPENT

(TROUBLESOME —) COW PEST HELLION HESSIAN

(TRUSTWORTHY —) TRAIST STANDBY

(UNATTRACTIVE —) GOON GRUB SCUG CREEP

(UNBENDING —) STIFF

(UNCHASTE —) SHORTHEELS

(UNCIVILIZED —) VISIGOTH

(UNCOUTH —) APE PUT STIFF BABOON SLOMMACK

(UNDERSIZED —) DURGAN SPARROW

(UNFAITHFUL —) INFIDEL

(UNHANDY —) FOUTER

(UNHAPPY —) UNSEL

(UNIQUE —) ONER

(UNKNOWN —) INCONNU STRANGER

(UNMARRIED —) MAIDEN AGAMIST BACHELOR CELIBATE SPINSTER

(UNREASONABLE —) DUFFER

(UNSCRUPULOUS —) CATSO KNAVE

(UNSOPHISTICATED —) JAY HICK NYAS HAYSEED CORNBALL INNOCENT

(UNTHANKFUL —) INGRATE

(UNTIDY —) STREEL

(UNWIELDY —) FUSTILUGS

(USELESS —) POOP SWAB UNSEL

(VALOROUS —) HERO

(VENOMOUS —) SPITPOISON

(VIGOROUS —) SNEEZER

(VIOLENT —) DRAGON SPITFIRE

(VORACIOUS —) HUNGARIAN

(VULGAR —) MUCKER

(WANTON —) FLIRT WHIPSTER

(WEAK —) SHILP SOFTY WHIMLING

(WEAK-MINDED —) SAPHEAD TOTTYHEAD

(WELL-BORN —) FREE

(WHITE —) FAY OFAY GRIFFIN EUROPEAN PALEFACE

(WICKED —) DEVIL SATAN SHREW UNLEAD UNLEDE SATANIST

(WILD —) HELLICAT RANTIPOLE

(WILY —) PIE

(WITHERED —) RUNT

(WITLESS —) WITHAM WITTOME SLABBERER

(WITTY —) WITSHIP SPARKLER

(WORNOUT —) HUSHEL

(WORTHLESS —) YAP FILE GEAR HOIT JADE LOON SCUM TOOT CRUMB LOREL LOSEL SCOUT SHAND BAUBLE BUGGER FELLOW FOUTRA SHICER BUDMASH GULLION BLIGHTER VAGABOND PHARMAKOS

(WRETCHED —) MISER MISERY

(YOUNG —) CUB KID COLT LAMB CHILD HEMPY SMOLT SMOUT SPRIG YONKE GUNSEL HEMPIE JUNIOR CHICKEN CHOOKIE GRISTLE LAMBKIN JUVENILE STRIPLING (PL.) FRY

PERSONABLE COMELY SHAPELY HANDSOME

PERSONAGE DON DUSE NIBS BLOKE FIGURE SHOGUN TYCOON (GREAT —) SOPHI SOPHY SUFFEE

PERSONAL SELF PRIVY DIRECT PRIVATE CHATTELS CORPORAL INTIMATE (— EFFECTS) DUNNAGE

PERSONALITY EGO DRAW SELF SOUL BEING ETHOS HEART EGOITY FIGURE CONTROL FACULTY DEMIURGE PRESENCE SELFHOOD SELFNESS

PERSONATE ACT FEIGN MIMIC MASKED PERSON TYPIFY PRESENT

PERSONATION (SHAM —) IDOL

PERSONIFICATION SOUL GENIUS (— OF DIVINE VIRTUE) EON (— OF JUSTICE) THEMIS

PERSONIFY EMBODY INCARNATE PERSONIZE

PERSONNEL BLOOD STAFF KITCHEN PHYSIQUE

PERSPECTIVE OPTICS DISTANCE TELESCOPE

PERSPICACIOUS KEEN ACUTE SHREWD (MAKE —) CLEAR

PERSPICACITY WIT ACUMEN

PERSPICUOUS CLEAR LUCID PLAIN PRECISE VISIBLE MANIFEST LIGHTSOME

PERSPIRATION DEW SUDOR SUINT SWEAT HIDROSIS OLIGIDRIA SUDORESIS

PERSPIRE PUG MELT BREAN SWEAT SWELTER TRANSPIRE

PERSUADE CON GET WIN COAX GAIN RULE SNOW TICE URGE WISE ARGUE BRING EDUCE SUADE SWADE WEISE ADVISE ARGUFY ASSURE CAJOLE ENGAGE ENTICE INDUCE REMOVE SUBORN CONVERT DISPUTE ENTREAT IMPRESS PREVAIL SATISFY CANOODLE INFLUENCE

PERSUADED PLIABLE GULLIBLE RESOLVED SENSIBLE

PERSUASION KIND SORT BELIEF SUASION JUDGMENT

PERSUASIVE COGENT INDUCTIVE PROTEPTIC

PERT BOLD CHIC FESS FLIP KECK SPRY TRIM ALERT ALIVE BARDY BRISK COCKY DONSY KISKY PEART PIERT QUICK SASSY SAUCY SMART TAUNT CLEVER COCKET COMELY DAPPER FRISKY SWASHY THWART PAUGHTY INSOLENT PETULANT (— TALK) CHELP

PERTAIN BE LIE BEAR COME LONG BELIE TOUCH AFFEIR BEFALL BELIMP BELONG RELATE RETAIN

CONCERN
(— TO) RINE
PERTAINING (— **TO A BISHOP**)
LAWN
(— **TO AIR**) AURAL PNEUMATIC
(— **TO ALL NATURE**) PAMPHYSIC
(— **TO ANIMALS**) ZOIC
(— **TO ANKLE**) TARSAL
(— **TO APOLLO**) PYTHIAN PAEONIAN
(— **TO APOSTLE**) PETRINE
(— **TO ARMPIT**) AXILLAR
(— **TO ARMY**) MARTIAL STRATONIC
(— **TO ARROW**) SAGITTAL
(— **TO ATHENA**) PALLADIAN
(— **TO BACK**) DORSAL TERGAL
(— **TO BATH**) BALNEAL
(— **TO BEAM**) TRAGAL
(— **TO BEARD**) BARBAL
(— **TO BED**) THORAL
(— **TO BEES**) APIAN APIARIAN
(— **TO BELLY**) ALVIN ALVINE
VENTRAL VENTRIC
(— **TO BIBLICAL LAW**) LEVITIC
(— **TO BIRDS**) AVIAN AVINE
ORNITHIC VOLUCRINE
(— **TO BIRTH**) NATAL
(— **TO BODIES AT REST**) STATIC
(— **TO BODY**) SOMAL SOMATIC
(— **TO BONE**) OSSAL OSTEAL
(— **TO BOSOM**) GREMIAL
(— **TO BRACELET**) ARMILLARY
(— **TO BRANCHES**) RAMOUS
(— **TO BREADMAKING**) PANARY
(— **TO BREAKFAST**) ENTACULAR
(— **TO BREAST**) PECTORAL
(— **TO BREASTBONE**) STERNAL
(— **TO BRISTLES**) SETAL
(— **TO BROTHEL**) STEWISH
(— **TO BUNCH**) COMAL
(— **TO CALF OF LEG**) SURAL
(— **TO CALF**) VITULINE
(— **TO CART**) PLAUSTRAL
(— **TO CARTHAGINIANS**) PUNIC
(— **TO CARVING**) GLYPHIC
(— **TO CAVE**) SPELEAN SPELUNCAR
(— **TO CHAIN**) CATENARY
(— **TO CHAMBER**) CAMERAL
(— **TO CHARIOTEER**) AURIGAL
(— **TO CHEEK**) MALAR
(— **TO CHESS**) SCACCHIC
(— **TO CHINA**) SINIAN SINISIAN
(— **TO CITY**) CIVIC URBAN
(— **TO CLAN**) SEPTAL
(— **TO CLAY**) BOLAR
(— **TO CLOTHES**) VESTIARY
VESTURAL
(— **TO COINS**) NUMMARY
NUMISMATIC
(— **TO COLOR**) CHROMATIC
(— **TO COMB**) PECTINAL
(— **TO CONSTRUCTION**) TECTONIC
(— **TO CORK**) SUBERIC SUBEROUS
(— **TO COUGH**) TUSSAL TUSSIVE
(— **TO COURT**) AULIC JUDICIAL
JUDICIARY
(— **TO CROCKERY**) PIG
(— **TO CROWN**) CORONAL
(— **TO DANCING**) SALTATORY
TRIPUDIAL

(— **TO DAUGHTER OR SON**) FILIAL
(— **TO DAWN**) EOAN
(— **TO DEFENSE**) PHYLACTIC
(— **TO DESERTS**) EREMIC
(— **TO DIAPHRAGM**) PHRENIC
(— **TO DINNER**) CENATORY
(— **TO DOVE**) COLUMBINE
(— **TO DREAMS**) ONEIRIC ONIROTIC
(— **TO DRINKING**) BIBITORY
(— **TO EARTH**) GEAL TELLURIC
TERRANEAN
(— **TO EARTHQUAKE**) SEISMAL
SEISMIC
(— **TO EAST**) EOAN
(— **TO ESSENCE**) BASIC
(— **TO EUNUCH**) SPADONIC
(— **TO EVENING**) VESPER
(— **TO EYELIDS**) BLEPHARAL
(— **TO FACE**) PROSOPIC
(— **TO FAIR**) NUNDINAL
(— **TO FAITH**) PISTIC
(— **TO FEET**) PEDAL PEDARY
(— **TO FERMENTATION**) ZYMIC
ZYMOTIC
(— **TO FIELDS**) AGRARIAN
(— **TO FINGERS**) DIGITAL
(— **TO FISHING**) HALIEUTIC
(— **TO FLEAS**) PULICENE PULICOSE
(— **TO FLESH**) SARCOUS
(— **TO FLOCK**) GREGAL
(— **TO FLOOD**) DILUVIAL DILUVIAN
(— **TO FLOWERS**) FLORAL ANTHINE
(— **TO FOREARM**) CUBITAL
(— **TO FOREHEAD**) METOPIC
(— **TO FORM**) MORPHIC
(— **TO FOX**) VULPINE
(— **TO FRESH WATER**) LIMNETIC
(— **TO FROGS**) ANURAN RANINE
(— **TO FRUIT**) POMONAL POMONIC
(— **TO FUNERALS**) EXEQUIAL
(— **TO FUNGUS**) MYCETOID
(— **TO FURNACE**) FORNACIC
(— **TO GARDEN**) HORTULAN
(— **TO GARRISON**) PRESIDIAL
(— **TO GENTILES**) ETHNIC
(— **TO GLASS**) VITREOUS
(— **TO GOVERNMENT**) ARCHICAL
POLITICAL
(— **TO GRANDPARENTS**) AVAL
(— **TO GRINDING**) MOLINARY
(— **TO GROUND**) SOLARY
(— **TO GROVE**) NEMORAL
(— **TO GUMS**) ULETIC GINGIVAL
(— **TO HAIR**) PILAR CRINAL PILARY
(— **TO HAND**) CHIRAL MANUAL
(— **TO HEAD**) CEPHALIC
(— **TO HEAP**) ACERVAL
(— **TO HEART**) CARDIAC
(— **TO HEAT**) CALORIC THERMAL
THERMIC
(— **TO HIPS**) SCIATIC
(— **TO HOLIDAY**) FERIAL
(— **TO HORIZON**) MUNDANE
(— **TO HORSE**) EQUINE HIPPIC
CABALLINE
(— **TO HOSPITALITY**) XENIAL XENIAN
(— **TO HOUSE**) DOMAL
(— **TO HUNGER**) FAMELIC
(— **TO HUNTING**) VENATIC VENERIAL

(— **TO INTELLECT**) NOETIC
(— **TO INTESTINES**) ALVIN ALVINE
(— **TO JAW**) MALAR GNATHAL
GNATHIC
(— **TO JOURNEY**) VIATIC
(— **TO KIDNEY**) RENAL NEPHRIC
(— **TO KNOWLEDGE**) GNOSTIC
(— **TO LAP**) GREMIAL
(— **TO LAUGHING**) GELASTIC
(— **TO LAUGHTER**) RISORIAL
(— **TO LEARNING**) PALLADIAN
(— **TO LEG**) CRURAL
(— **TO LIFE**) VITAL ZOETIC
(— **TO LINE**) FILAR
(— **TO LIPS**) LABIAL
(— **TO LIVER**) HEPATIC JECORAL
(— **TO LOINS**) LUMBAR
(— **TO LOVE**) EROTIC AMATORY
(— **TO LUCK**) ALEATORY
(— **TO LUNGS**) PULMONIC
PNEUMONIC PULMONARY
(— **TO MANKIND**) COMMON
ANTHROPIC
(— **TO MARBLE**) MARMORIC
(— **TO MARKET**) NUNDINAL
(— **TO MARRIAGE**) MARITAL
HYMENEAL
(— **TO MARS**) AREAN MAMERTINE
MAVORTIAL
(— **TO MASS**) MOLAR
(— **TO MASTER**) HERILE
(— **TO MEADOWS**) PRATAL
(— **TO MECCA**) MECCAWEE
(— **TO MEMORY**) MNESTIC
MNEMONIC
(— **TO MIDDAY**) MERIDIAN
(— **TO MILK**) LACTARY LACTEAL
(— **TO MILL**) MOLINARY
(— **TO MIRROR**) SPECULAR
(— **TO MOISTURE**) HYGRIC
(— **TO MOON**) LUNAR SELENIC
SELENIAN
(— **TO MORNING**) MATIN MATINAL
(— **TO MOTION**) GESTIC KINETIC
(— **TO MOUNTAINS**) MONTANE
(— **TO MOUTH**) ORAL OSCULAR
STOMATIC
(— **TO MUSCLE**) SARCOUS
(— **TO MUSIC**) HARMONIC
(— **TO NAVEL**) OMPHALIC
(— **TO NECK**) JUGULAR
(— **TO NEPHEW**) NEPOTAL
(— **TO NIGHT**) NOCTURNAL
(— **TO NOSE**) NASAL RHINAL
(— **TO NUT**) NUCAL
(— **TO NUTRITION**) TROPHIC
(— **TO OAK**) QUERCINE ROBOREO
(— **TO OCEAN**) PELAGIC OCEANOU
THALASSIC
(— **TO OLD AGE**) SENILE GERATIC
GERONTIC
(— **TO OPEN SKY**) SUBDIAL
(— **TO PARLOR**) BEN BOOR
(— **TO PASTURES**) PASCUAL
(— **TO PAWNBROKER**) AVUNCULAI
(— **TO PEACOCK**) PAVONINE
(— **TO PERSPIRATION**) SUDORIC
(— **TO PICTURE**) ICONIC
(— **TO PIGS**) PORCINE

(— TO PINE) WARRYN
(— TO PLAGUE) LOIMIC
(— TO PLEASURE) HEDONIC
(— TO POETRY) MUSAL IAMBIC
(— TO POISON) TOXIC
(— TO POTTERY) CERAMIC
(— TO PRIESTS) SACERDOTAL
(— TO PRISON) CARCERAL
(— TO PULSE) SPHYGMIC
(— TO PUNISHMENT) PENAL PUNITIVE
(— TO QUEEN) REGINAL
(— TO RAIN) HYETAL PLUVIAL
(— TO RAINBOW) IRIDAL
(— TO REMOTE PLACE) FORANE
(— TO RESONANCE) SYNTONIC
(— TO RING) ARMILLARY
(— TO RISING) ORTIVE
(— TO RIVER BANK) RIPARIAN
(— TO RIVER) AMNIC POTAMIC RIVERINE FLUMINOSE
(— TO ROAD) VIATIC
(— TO ROCK) PETREAN SAXATILE
(— TO ROD) BACULINE
(— TO SABLES) ZIBELINE
(— TO SAIL) VELIC
(— TO SALVATION) SOTERIAL
(— TO SANDARAC) THYINE
(— TO SATURDAY) SABBATINE
(— TO SEAL) SIGILLARY SPHRAGISTIC
(— TO SEAM) SUTURAL
(— TO SEASHORE) LITTORAL
(— TO SEAWEED) ALGOUS
(— TO SENSE OF TASTE) GUSTATIVE
(— TO SHEEP) VERVECINE
(— TO SHEPHERDS) PASTORAL
(— TO SHERIFF) VICONTIEL
(— TO SHIN) CNEMIAL
(— TO SHIP) NAVICULAR
(— TO SHOPMAN) APOTHECAL
(— TO SHOULDER) ALAR SCAPULAR
(— TO SIGNS) SEMIC SEMANTIC
(— TO SILVER) ARGENTAL
(— TO SISTER) SORORAL
(— TO SKIN) DERIC DERMAL CUTICULAR
(— TO SLEEP) SOMNIAL MORPHETIC
(— TO SNAKE) ANGUINE
(— TO SOFT PALATE) VELAR
(— TO SONG) MELIC
(— TO SPECTACLE) THEORIC
(— TO SPEECH) PHEMIC
(— TO SPINAL CORD) MYELIC
(— TO SPRING) VERNAL
(— TO STARS) ASTRAL STELLAR SIDEREAL
(— TO STATE AFFAIRS) PRAGMATIC
(— TO STEPMOTHER) NOVERCAL
(— TO STOMACH) GASTRIC
(— TO STORKS) PELARGIC
(— TO SULPHUR) THIONIC
(— TO SUMMER) ESTIVAL AESTIVAL
(— TO SUN) SOLAR HELIAC
(— TO SUNDAY) DOMINICAL
(— TO SUNDIAL) SCIATHERIC
(— TO SUPPER) CENATORY
(— TO SURFACE OF ANYTHING) ACIAL

(— TO SWALLOWS) HIRUNDINE
(— TO SWEAT) SUDORIC
(— TO SWIMMING) NATATORY
(— TO SWINEHERD) SYBOTIC
(— TO TAIL) CAUDAL
(— TO TAILOR) SARTORIAL
(— TO TEARS) LACRIMAL LACHRYMAL
(— TO TEMPO) AGOGIC
(— TO THE BEAUTIFUL) ESTHETIC AESTHETIC
(— TO THIEVING) KLEPTISTIC
(— TO THIGH) CRURAL
(— TO THREAD) FILAR
(— TO THROAT) GULAR JUGULAR
(— TO TILE) TEGULAR
(— TO TIN) STANNIC
(— TO TITHES) DECIMAL
(— TO TITMICE) PARINE
(— TO TOMB) TOMBAL
(— TO TONGUE) GLOSSAL LINGUAL
(— TO TORTOISES) CHELONIAN
(— TO TOUCH) TACTILE
(— TO TOWER) TURRICAL
(— TO TREES) DENDRAL ARBOREAL
(— TO TWENTY) VICENARY
(— TO UNCLE) AVUNCULAR
(— TO VESSEL) VASAL
(— TO VIRGIN) PARTHENIAN
(— TO VOW) VOTAL
(— TO WAGON) PLAUSTRAL
(— TO WALLS) MURAL PARIETAL
(— TO WAR) POLEMICAL
(— TO WASPS) VESPAL VESPINE
(— TO WAX) CERAL
(— TO WEAVING) TEXTORIAL
(— TO WEIGHT) BARIC PONDERAL PONDERARY
(— TO WELL) PHREATIC
(— TO WHALES) CETIC
(— TO WHEAT) VULGARE
(— TO WHEELS) ROTAL
(— TO WIFE) UXORIAL
(— TO WIND) EOLIAN ONEUMATIC
(— TO WINE) VINIC VINOUS
(— TO WINE-MAKING) OENOPOETIC
(— TO WINGS) ALAR PTERIC EXRUPEAL PTEROTIC
(— TO WINTER) HIEMAL
(— TO WISDOM) PALLADIAN
(— TO WOMANKIND) MULIEBRAL
(— TO WOODPECKERS) PICINE
(— TO WOODS) SYLVAN NEMORAL
(— TO WORMS) VERMICULAR
(— TO WOUNDS) VULNERAL
(— TO WRIST) CARPAL
(— TO YESTERDAY) PRIDIAN
(— TO YEW) TAXINE

PERTINACIOUS FIRM STIFF DOGGED ADHERING STUBBORN OBSTINATE
PERTINENCY FORCE
PERTINENT APT FIT PAT HAPPY COGENT PROPER TIMELY ADAPTED APROPOS GERMANE POINTED TELLING INCIDENT MATERIAL RELATIVE RELEVANT
PERTURB BITE GRATE UPSET WORRY DISMAY AGITATE CONFUSE

CONTURB DERANGE DISTURB TROUBLE
PERTURBATION DISMAY FLIGHT POTHER POOTHER STICKLE TROUBLE TURMOIL EVECTION AGITATION
PERTURBED UNEASY
PERTUSSIS COUGH CHINCOF CHINCOUGH

PERU
CAPITAL: LIMA
COIN: SOL LIBRA DINERO CENTAVO
DEPARTMENT: ICA LIMA PUNO CUSCO CUZCO JUNIN PIURA TACNA ANCASH LORETO TUMBES
ISLAND: CHINCHA
LAKE: TITICACA
LANGUAGE: AYMARA QUECHUA
MEASURE: TOPO VARA GALON CELEMIN FANEGADA
MOUNTAIN: HUAMINA COROPUNA HUASCARAN
PERIOD: RECUAY
RIVER: NAPU RIMAC SANTA TIGRE YAGUAS YAVARI CURARAY MARANON PASTAZA UCAYALI AMAZONAS APURIMAC HUALLAGA URUBAMBA
TOWN: ICA LIMA PUNO CUZCO PAITA PISCO CALLAO IQUITOS AREQUIPA TRUJILLO
VOLCANO: MISTI YUCAMANI
WEIGHT: LIBRA QUINTAL

PERUKE WIG FLASH GALERA TOUPEE GALERUM PERIWIG WIGGERY
PERUSAL SIGHT LECTURE SCRUTINY
PERUSE CON READ SCAN STUDY HANDLE SEARCH SURVEY EXAMINE INSPECT
PERVADE FILL BATHE IMBUE DRENCH INSTIL OCCUPY INSTILL PERMEATE TRAVERSE
PERVADED STIFF
PERVERSE AUK AWK CAM CAR AWRY WOGH WRAW CROSS DONSY GAMMY THRAW WROTH CUSSED DIVERS LOUCHE THRAWN THWART WICKED WILFUL WRAIST AWKWARD DIVERSE FORWARD FROWARD OBLIQUE WAYWARD CAMSHACH CRANKISH STUBBORN
PERVERSELY AUK AWK ATHWART OVERWART
PERVERSION WREST ABUSION
(— OF TASTE) MALACIA
PERVERT WRY DRAW RACK RUIN SKEW TURN WARP ABUSE CROOK GLOSS TWIST UPSET DEBASE DETORT DIVERT GARBLE INVERT MISUSE POISON WRENCH WRITHE CONTORT CORRUPT DEGRADE DEPRAVE DEVIATE DISTORT MISTURN SUBVERT TRADUCE

VITIATE MISWREST
PERVERTED BAD WICKED ABUSIVE
CORRUPT TWISTED VICIOUS
PERVERTER WRESTER
PERVIOUS LEACHY PERVIAL
PERVADING
PES NEUME TENOR PODATUS
PESKY VERY PLAGUY ANNOYING
DEVILING EXTREMELY
PESO DURO CONANT DOLLAR
CAROLUS PATACAO
PESSIMISM WELTSCHMERZ
MISERABILISM
PESSIMIST ALARMIST JEREMIAH
WORRYWART
PESSIMISTIC GLOOMY ALARMED
BEARISH CYNICAL DOWNBEAT
PEST BANE TICK WEED MOUSE
MYZUS TRAIK INSECT PLAGUE
SCHELM SORROW VERMIN NUDNICK
SANDMITE BUTTINSKY
PESTER DUN HOX NAG RIB TIG HAKE
ANNOY DEVIL TEASE WORRY
BADGER BOTHER HARASS INFEST
MOLEST BEDEVIL TORMENT
TROUBLE OBSTRUCT
PESTHOUSE LAZARET LAZARETTO
PESTICIDE BIOCIDE FUMIGANT
PESTILENCE PEST DEATH QUALM
PLAGUE MURRAIN EPIDEMIC
MORTALITY
PESTILENT FATAL DEADLY VEXING
NOXIOUS
PESTLE MIX BRAY GRIND PESTL
PILUM STAMP BEETLE BRAYER
MULLER PISTIL CHAPPER POUNDER
STAMPER
PET TOY CADE COAX DAUT DEAR
DUCK HUFF LAMB NECK PEAT SOCK
SULK TIFF DRUNT DUCKY HUMOR
QUIET SPOIL SPOON TETCH CARESS
CODDLE COSHER COSSET CUDDLE
DANDLE DAUTIE DAWTIE FADDLE
FANTAD FANTOD FONDLE GENTLE
PAMPER PETKIN SMOOCH SQUALL
STROKE WANTON CHERISH DARLING
INDULGE PINKENY TANTRUM
TIDLING UMBRAGE WHITHER
CANOODLE FAVORITE TIDDLING
PADDYWACK
PETAL ALA HELM HOOD LEAF WING
BANNER
(— **IN PEA FLOWER**) VEXILLUM
(— **OF IRIS**) STANDARD
(**UPPER** —) HOOD BANNER
(PL.) COROLLA
PETALIA NYCTERIS
PETARD PITTARD FIREWORK
PETATE BANIG
PETECHIA STIGMA
PETER P FADE FAIL PEAK SAFE
WANE CEASE PEDRO PIERS PIERRE
SIGNAL DWINDLE
(— **OUT**) FIZZLE
PETIOLE STEM SPINE STALK STIPE
PODEON PEDUNCLE PHYLLODE
PETITE SMALL LITTLE MIGNON
MIGNONNE
PETITION ASK BEG SUE BILL BOON

PLEA PRAY SUIT VOTE WISH APPLY
ORATE PLEAD APPEAL DESIRE
INVOKE MOTION PLACIT PRAYER
STEVEN ADDRESS BESEECH
ENTREAT IMPLORE ORATION
SOLICIT ROGATION SUFFRAGE
(**MAKE** —) SUE
(PL.) PRECES
PETITIONER BEGGAR ORATOR
SUITOR BEADSMAN ENTREATER
PLAINTIFF
PETO WAHOO
PETREL BILL TITI CAHOW MITTY
NELLY PRION WITCH SPENCY
TEETEE ASSILAG GLUTTON KAEDING
SEABIRD SEAFOWL STINKER
ALLAMOTH FORKTAIL STINKPOT
ALLAMOTTI NIGHTHAWK
PETRIFY DAZE DEADEN STONIFY
STUPEFY LAPIDIFY FOSSILIZE
GORGONIZE
PETRIFYING STONY GORGON
PETROL GAS GASOLINE
PETROLATUM VASELINE
PETROLEUM OIL CRUDE PETROL
NAPHTHA
(— **INDUSTRY**) OILDOM
PE-TSAI PECHAY
PETTED CADE DANDILY
PETTICOAT BAJO GORE KILT SLIP
SOUS DICKY GREEN JUPON PAGNE
SOUSE KIRTLE LUHINGA PLACKET
WHITTLE BALMORAL BASQUINE
WILYCOAT
(— **OF TARGET**) GREEN
PETTIFOG FOG CAVIL BICKER
PETTIFOGGER FOGGER SHYSTER
LEGULEIAN
PETTINESS NAGGLE PARVINIMITY
PETTING COLLING
PETTISH HUFFY FRETFUL PEEVISH
PLAINTIVE
PETTY TIN BASE JERK MEAN ORRA
PUNY VAIN GRIMY MINOR PETIT
PUNEE SMALL MEASLY MINUTE
PALTRY PEANUT POKING PUISNE
PUSILL SNIFTY KITLING PIMPING
TRIVIAL TWATTLE CHILDISH
FIDDLING INFERIOR NIGGLING
NUGATORY PICAYUNE SNIPPETY
TRIFLING PAROCHIAL
PETULANT PERT CROSS SAUCY
SHORT TESTY TIFFY FEISTY SULLEN
WANTON WILFUL CRABBED FRETFUL
FROWARD HUFFISH PEEVISH
WASPISH PERVERSE SNAPPISH
PEUMUS BOLDU
PEW PUE BOUT DESK PFUI PUGH
SEAT SLIP BENCH BUGHT STALL
BOUGHT
PEWEE PEWIT PEEWEE
PEWTER CUP BIDRI BIDRY MONEY
PUDER BIDERY TRIFLE PEAUDER
SADWARE TUTENAG
(— **MARK**) TOUCHMARK
PEYOTE HIKULI
PFENNIG PENNING
PHAEDRA (**FATHER OF** —) MINOS
(**HUSBAND OF** —) THESEUS

PHAETON DUKE FAETON SPIDER
STANHOPE
PHAETON BUTTERFLY BALTIMORE
PHALANGER ARIEL TAPOA CUSCUS
OPOSSUM PENTAIL SQUIRREL
PHALAROPE LOBIPED COOTFOOT
LOBEFOOT WHALEBIRD
PHALERA BEAD BOSS DISK STUD
CAMEO
PHANTASM DREAM FANCY GHOST
VAPOR FIGURE SHADOW SPIRIT
FANTASY PHANTOM SPECIES
SPECTER SPECTRE
PHANTASMAL UNREAL SPECTRAL
PHANTASY FANCY FANTASY
PHANTASIA
PHANTOM IDOL BOGEY BOGLE
DUMMY GHOST IMAGE PHASM
SHADE SHAPE UMBRA BOGGLE
DOUBLE FANTOM IDOLON IDOLUM
SHADOW SPIRIT BUGBEAR EIDOLON
ELUSIVE FANTASY SPECIES
SPECTER ILLUSORY ADAMASTOR
PHARAOH ALE FARO PHARO TYRAN
BUSIRIS
PHARAOH'S HEN VULTURE
PHARISEE MUGWUMP NICODEMUS
PHARMACIST DRUGGIST DISPENSE
PHARMACY FERMACY DRUGSTORE
PHAROS CLOAK LIGHT TORCH
BEACON LANTERN
PHARYNGEAL FAUCAL
PHARYNX MASTAX PROBOSCIS
PHASE EFT END LEG FAZE SIDE
ANGLE FACET GRADE STAGE
ASPECT AVATAR BACKLASH
PASSOVER DICHOTOMY
(**INITIAL** —) BUD
(**LOWEST** —) BATHOS
(**TRANSITORY** —) STREAK
PHASM FANTOM METEOR PHASMA
PHANTOM
PHEASANT CHIR GUAN ARGUS
CHEER KALIJ MINAL MONAL
GROUSE LEIPOA MAGPIE MONAUL
MOONAL PUKRAS KALLEGE
FIREBACK ITHAGINE RINGNECK
TRAGOPAN MACARTNEY
(**BREEDING PLACE FOR** —**S**) STEW
(**BROOD OF** —**S**) NID NYE NIDE
(**YOUNG** —) POULT
PHEASANT CUCKOO COUCAL
PHEASANT DUCK PINTAIL
MERGANSER
PHEASANT FINCH WAXBILL
PHEASANT'S-EYE ROSARUBY
PHELLEM CORK SUBER
PHENOBARBITOL LUMINAL
PHENOCRYST INSET
PHENOL LACCOL THYMOL ALOESC
CREOSOL DURENOL EUGENOL
ORCINOL CHAVICOL RESORCIN
PHENOMENON FIRE ANOMY COLC
EVENT IMAGE ARTHUS EFFECT
METEOR MIRAGE SHADOW ISOTO
MIRACLE PARADOX PROCESS
SYMPTOM ASTERISM PRAKRITI
SIDERISM SUNQUAKE LANDSPOUT
PHENYLSALICYLATE SALOL

HIAL CUP FIAL VIAL BOTTLE VESSEL
HILABEG KILT FILIBEG
HILANDER FOOL WOLF DALLY FLIRT SMOCK
HILANTHROPIC HUMANE
HILANTHROPIST ALTRUIST HUMANITARIAN
HILANTHROPY CHARITY ALMSGIVING
HILIP PIP PHILP SPARROW
HILIPPIC SCREED TIRADE ABUSIVE DIATRIBE

PHILIPPINES
ARCHIPELAGO: SULU
CAPITAL: BAGUIO MANILA QUEZONCITY
COIN: PESO PESETA CENTAVO
FIBER: ERUC ABACA BUNTAL
ISLAND: CEBU BOHOL LEYTE LUZON PANAY SAMAR NEGROS MASBATE MINDORO PALAWAN MINDANAO
LAKE: TAAL LANAO
LANGUAGE: MORO BICOL IBANAG ILOCANO TAGALOG VISAYAN
MEASURE: LOAN BRAZA CABAN CAUAN CHUPA GANTA APATAN BALITA QUINON
MOUNTAIN: APO IBA MAYON PULOG BANAHAO
NATIVE: ATA ATI ITA TAO AETA ATTA ETAS MORO SULU BICOL TAGAL VICOL IGOROT TIMAUA BISAYAN TAGALOG FILIPINO
PROVINCE: ABRA ALBAY CAPIZ DAVAO LANAO RIZAL CAVITE ILOILO TARLAC SURIGAO
RIVER: ABRA AGNO MAGAT PASIG AGUSAN LAOANG CAGAYAN MINDANAO PAMPANGA
TOWN: AGOA CEBU ALBAY DAVAO LAOAG PASAY VIGAN APARRI BAGUIO CAVITE ILAGAN ILOILO MANILA BACALOD BASILAN DAGUPAN CALOOCAN
TREE: DAO IBA TUA TUI ACLE ANAM ATES BOGO DITA IPIL GUIJO LAUAN LIGAS ALUPAG ANAHAU ARANGA ANONANG APITONG TINDALO ALMACIGA AMPALAYA
VOLCANO: APO MAYO CANLAON
WEIGHT: CATTY FARDO PICUL PUNTO LACHSA QUILATE CHINANTA

HILISTINE BOOB GIGMAN MUCKER BABBITT GITTITE BOEOTIAN BARBARIAN BOURGEOIS HYPOCRITE
(PL.) PULESATI PURASATI
CAPHTORIM
HILOLOGIST LAVENGRO LINGUIST
HILOLOGY SEMITICS
HILOMACHUS MACHETES
HILOMELA STOP FILOMEL
(FATHER OF —) PANDION
(RAVISHER OF —) TEREUS

(SISTER OF —) PROCNE
(SLAIN BY —) ITYS
PHILOSOPHER WIT SAGE CYNIC STOIC ARTIST IONIAN LEGIST DOTTORE ELEATIC ERISTIC SCHOLAR SOPHIST SUMMIST THINKER ZETETIC ACADEMIC EPOCHIST MAGICIAN VIRTUOSO ACADEMIST ALCHEMIST DIALECTIC PHYSICIAN SCHOOLMAN
PHILOSOPHER'S STONE ADROP MICROCOSM
PHILOSOPHIC SAGE
PHILOSOPHY ETHICS GOSPEL SYSTEM TAOISM APRISMO COSMISM DUALISM INQUIRY MIMAMSA SCEPSIS HINDUISM HUMANISM IDENTISM IDEOLOGY LEGALISM OCCAMISM STOICISM NOUMENISM SOCRATISM VEDANTISM
(— OF LIFE) LIGHTS
PHILTER DRUG CHARM WANGA FILTER POTION AMATORY
PHLEBOTOMIZE BLEED VENESECT
PHLEBOTOMUS TATUKIRA
PHLEGM FLEM GLEET MUCUS WATER FLEUME PITUITE MOUSEWEB
PHLEGMATIC CALM COOL DULL SLOW INERT MUCOID SLEEPY WATERY VISCOUS COMPOSED SLUGGISH APATHETIC IMPASSIVE
PHLOEM BAST LEPTOME
PHLOGISTIC FIERY HEATED BURNING FLAMING
PHLOMIS SAGELEAF
PHLOX CYME FLOX ALBION BEACON COBAEA
PHOEBE FEBE FIVE MOON DIANA PEWEE ARTEMIS
(DAUGHTER OF —) LETO
(MOTHER OF —) GAEA
PHOEBUS SUN APOLLO PHOIBUS
PHOENICIA (COLONY OF —) CARTHAGE
(GODDESS OF —) TANIT BALTIS TANITH ASTARTE
(KING OF —) AGENOR
(TOWN OF —) ACRE TYRE SIDON SAREPTA
PHONEME MORPH TONEME LARYNGAL
PHONEMIC BROAD
PHONOGRAM LOGOGRAM SINOGRAM
PHONOGRAPH VIC PHONO VICTROLA
(— RECORD) DISK PLATTER
PHONY FAKE SHAM BOGUS FAKER FALSE BRUMMY BUNYIP PHONEY IMPOSTOR SPURIOUS
PHOSPHATE EHLITE FLOATS APATITE CABOCLE CACOXENE GRIPHITE
PHOSPHORESCENCE BRIMING MARFIRE
PHOSPHORESCENT PHOSPHOR NOCTILUCOUS
PHOTISM SYNOPSY
PHOTOENGRAVER ZINCOGRAPHER

PHOTOENGRAVING HALFTONE HELIOGRAPH
PHOTOGRAPH MUG FILM LENS SNAP CARTE IMAGE PHOTO SHOOT STILL CANDID GLOSSY MOSAIC RETAKE SCENIC STEREO AIRVIEW PICTURE TINTYPE LIKENESS PORTRAIT SNAPSHOT TABLETOP CYCLOGRAM
(— SIZE) PANEL
(X-RAY —) SKIAGRAM
PHOTOGRAPHER LENSMAN CAMERIST CAMERAMAN
PHOTOGRAPHY STEREO PHOTOGENY
PHOTOMETER LUCIMETER
PHOTOMONTAGE COLLAGE
PHOTON BOSON TROLAND
PHRASE CRY HIT MOT SET CRIB FUSS HAVE IDEA TERM WORD COMMA COUCH IDIOM LABEL LEMMA POINT STATE STYLE TOPIC TROPE BYWORD CLAUSE CLICHE DITTON DORISM GRUPPO HOBNOB NOTION PNEUMA PRAISE SAVING SLOGAN ATTACCO DICTION EPITHET PASSAGE CONCEIVE DIVISION DORICISM FLATTERY IDEOGRAM IRISHISM LATINISM LEITMOTIV
(— DIFFERENTLY) TURN
(— UNCTUOUSLY) DROOL
(MUSICAL —) ATTACCO SUBJECT
(PET —) SHIBBOLETH
(REDUNDANT —) CHEVILLE
(STOCK —) CANT
(TRITE —) CLICHE
(WELL-TURNED —) STROKE
PHRASEOLOGY CANT STYLE DIALECT DICTION WORDING LOCUTION PARLANCE
PHRATRY CLAN
PHRENETIC PYTHIAN FRENETIC
PHRENIC MENTAL
(PL.) PSYCHOLOGY
PHRIXOS (FATHER OF —) ATHAMUS
(MOTHER OF —) NEPHELE
(SISTER OF —) HELLE
PHRYGIA (GOD OF —) ATYS ATTIS SABAZIOS
(KING OF —) MIDAS
PHRYNIN BUFIDIN
PHTHISIS DECAY
PHYLACTERY FILACTERY
(PL.) TEFILLIN TEPHILLIN
PHYLE TRIBE
PHYLUM HOKA CLASS HOKAN NADENE BRYOZOA ANNELATA ANNELIDA CHORDATA DIVISION LIGNOSAE
PHYMA TUMOR
PHYSALIS POP POPPER TOMATILLO
PHYSETER CATODON
PHYSIC CURE HEAL FISIC PURGE TRADE REMEDY MEDICAL NATURAL RELIEVE DRUGGERY
PHYSICAL ILL LUSTY SOMAL BODILY CARNAL DISTAL NATURAL SOMATIC CORPORAL CURATIVE EXTERNAL MATERIAL CORPOREAL

(PURELY —) BRUTE
PHYSICIAN ASA DOC PILL CURER
GALEN HAKIM LEECH MEDIC QUACK
ARTIST BAIDYA DOCTOR FELLOW
HEALER INTERN MEDICO DOTTORE
EMPIRIC SURGEON ALIENIST
RESIDENT SAWBONES SUNDOWNER
PHYSICIST HYLOZOIST
PHYSIC NUT TUBA CURCAS PIGNON
TARTAGO
PHYSIOCRAT ECONOMIST
PHYSIOGNOMY MUG FACE PHIZ
PHIZZ VIZNOMY PORTRAIT
VISENOMY
PHYSIOLOGY BIONOMY ZOONOMY
PHYSIQUE BODY BUILD COOST
HABIT FIGURE STRENGTH
PHYSOCARPUS NEILLIA OPULASTER
PHYSOSTIGMINE ESERE ESERINE
PHYTOMER PHYTON PODIUM
PI JUMBLE CONFUSE PREACHY
CONFUSION
PIA PI GABI GABGAB MARMOT
PIACLE SIN CRIME GUILT OFFENSE
PIAN YAWS FRAMBESIA
PIANETTE PYNOT PIANINO
PIANIST CEMBALIST CLAVIERIST
PIANO SOFT FLOOR GRAND GRANT
STORY FLUGEL GENTLY SOFTLY
SPINET SQUARE CLAVIAL CLAVIER
GIRAFFE PIANOLA QUIETLY UPRIGHT
MELOTROPE
PIASSAVA IYO JARA BAHIA PIACABA
PIASTER KURUS
PIATTI CYMBALS
PIAZZA PORCH SQUARE BALCONY
GALLERY PORTICO VERANDA
PIAZZETTA
PIC PEAK LANCE PIQUE PICADOR
PICA M EM LINE
PICARD PYKAR
PICARO KNAVE ROGUE TRAMP
BOHEMIAN VAGABOND
PICAROON ROGUE PICARO PIRATE
CORSAIR WRECKER
PICAYUNE PIC PETTY MEASLY
PALTRY PISTAREEN
PICCADILL RABATA REBATE REBATO
PICCOLO BUSBOY JUKEBOX
FLAUTINO OTTAVINO
PICHICIAGO ARMADILLO
CHLAMYPHORE
PICK NIB BILL CULL GAFF HACK LIFT
PIKE PILK SHOT WALE ADORN
BEELE BREAK CAVIL ELECT FLANG
LEASE PILCH PLUCK PRIDE CHOICE
CHOOSE GATHER PICKAX PUDDLE
TWITCH BARGAIN CASCROM
DIAMOND DRESSER MANDREL
(— APART) TOW
(— OUT) CULL SPOT TAKE WELE
CRONE GLEAN GARBLE SELECT
(— POCKETS) FIG FILE FOIST
TOUCH
(— TOBACCO) STRIP
(FILLING —) ABB
PICKAX PIX BEDE BILL PIKE GURLET
TUBBER TWIBIL TWIBILL
PICKED PICK TRIM PIKED CHOSEN

DAINTY PEAKED SELECT ADORNED
POINTED
PICKER COD HOPPER
(BERRY —) HURTER
(PEA —) VINER
PICKEREL JACK SNAKE DUNLIN
SAUGER SLINKER WALLEYE
PICKERELWEED TULE WAMPEE
PICKER-UP FINDER
PICKET PEG PALE POST TERN
FENCE STAKE FASTEN PALING
TETHER ENCLOSE FORTIFY PICQUET
PALISADE OUTPICKET
PICKLE BOX ALEC DILL MESS PECK
ACHAR BRINE GRAIN MANGO SAUCE
SOUSE ATSARA CAPERS DAWDLE
HIGDON KERNEL KIMCHI MUDDLE
NIBBLE PIDDLE PILFER PLIGHT
TRIFLE CONDITE CONFECT TROUBLE
VITRIOL MARINADE
(FISH —) ALEC
PICKLED DRUNK MURIATED
POWDERED MARINATED
PICKLOCK LOCK PICKER
PICK-ME-UP SCREW PICKUP
PICKPOCKET DIP•FIG GUN NIP
BUNG FILE WIRE DIVER FILER FOIST
BUZZER CANNON DIPPER FIGBOY
HOOKER RATERO FOISTER
MOBSMAN CLYFAKER CUTPURSE
KNUCKLER BUZZGLOAK
(HELPER OF —) STALL BULKER
PICKUP BRUSH TRUCK ARREST
BRACER ANACRUSIS
PICNIC FRY BALL GIPSY GYPSY
BURGOO FROLIC MAROON OUTING
SHOULDER SQUANTUM SUMMERING
PICOT LOOP PEARL PERLE
PICOTAH SWEEP PACOTA
PICTOGRAPH GLYPH PICTOGRAM
PICTORIAL GRAPHIC
PICTURE GAY MAP OIL COPY DAUB
ICON IKON LIMN SIGN VIEW DECAL
FRAME IMAGE LINER PAINT PHOTO
PIECE PINAX PRINT SCENE SHAPE
STAMP STORY TABLE CACHET
CANVAS CHROMO CUTOUT DEPICT
EMBLEM MARINE PASTEL SEMBLE
SHADOW STEREO TABLET CUTAWAY
DIORAMA DIPTYCH EMBLEMA
ETCHING EXHIBIT FASHION FEATURE
GOUACHE GRAPHIC HISTORY
MIZRACH PAYSAGE PORTRAY
PORTURE RETRAIT SCENERY
TABLEAU VANDYKE AIRSCAPE
AUTOTYPE DESCRIBE DROLLERY
ENVISION IDEOGRAM KAKEMONO
LANDSKIP LIKENESS MAKIMONO
MONOTINT OVERDOOR PAINTING
PORTRAIT PROSPECT RITRATTO
SEASCAPE SINGERIE SKYSCAPE
TRIPTYCH VIGNETTE ENCAUSTIC
(— IN 3 COMPARTMENTS) TRIPTYCH
(— IN BOOK) GAY
(— MAT) SPANDREL
(— OF MONKEYS) SINGERIE
(— ON ROLLER) KAKEMONO
MAKIMONO
(— PUZZLE) REBUS JIGSAW

(—S IN BOOKS) BABY
(COMIC —) DROLLERY
(RELIGIOUS —) TANKA
(STEREOSCOPIC —) ANAGLYPH
PICTURESQUE VIVID EXOTIC QUAINT
SCENIC GRAPHIC IDYLLIC ROMANTIC
PICTORIAL
PICUL TAN PICO PIKOL
PIDDLE PICK PLAY DAWDLE PICKLE
PUTTER TRIFLE
PIDDLING JERK PALTRY TRIVIAL
USELESS FOOTLING TRIFLING
JERKWATER
PIDDOCK DACTYL PHOLAD PHOLAS
PIDGIN LANGUAGE SABIR
PIE PAI FLAM FLAN HEAP MESS PATE
PILE TART DOWDY FLAWN PASTY
PATTY TORTA TOURT AFFAIR
BRIDLE CHEWET MAGPIE PASTRY
TOURTE COBBLER SMASHER
STRUDEL BAKEMEAT CRUSTADE
FLAPJACK PANDOWDY SURPRISE
TURNOVER SMASHOVER
PIEBALD PIE PIED PIET MIXED PIETY
PINTO CALICO MOTLEY SKEWBALD
PIECE BAT BIT COB CUT DAM FIG
JOB LAB LOG MAN TUT GIRL MIND
PART PISE PLAY DAGON DRAMA
DWANG FLOOR PEZZO SCRAP
SHARD SHERD SHRED SLICE SNODE
STEEK STUCK THROW COLLOP
FARDEL FUGATO GOBBET PARCEL
STITCH CANTLET EXAMPLE FLINDER
FLITTER MORCEAU OPINION
PICTURE PORTION SEGMENT
DUOLOGUE EMBOLIUM FANDANGO
PAINTING
(— AT END) HEELPIECE
(— FOR TWO) DUET DUOLOGUE
(— IN CHECKERS) DAM
(— IN ORGAN) THUMPER
(— OF ARMOR) JAMB JAMBE
(— OF BAD LUCK) DIRDUM
(— OF BLANKET) DAGON
(— OF BLUBBER) BIBLE
(— OF DECEPTION) BEGUNK
(— OF DECORATED METAL) NIELLO
(— OF FALSE HAIR) JANE
(— OF FIBER) NOIL
(— OF FIRED CLAY) TILE
(— OF GROUND SURROUNDED BY
WASTE) HOPE
(— OF HARD WOOD) MOOT
(— OF LAND) HAM LOT BUTT GORE
LEASE SPONG SQUAT HUERTA
RINCON SECTION SOLIDATE
(— OF LIGHT ORDNANCE) ASPIC
(— OF LINEN) AMIT AMICE
(— OF LOG) SLAB
(— OF MAST) TONGUE
(— OF MATZOTH) AFIKOMEN
(— OF MEAT) EYE HEEL RAND
COLLOP EPIGRAM
(— OF METAL) JAG COIN JAGG
SPRAG
(— OF MONEY) COG SOU SHINER
(— OF NEEDLEWORK) SAMPLER
(— OF NONSENSE) FUDGE
TRIMTRAM

(— OF ORE) CHAT
(— OF SAIL) HULLOCK
(— OF SEPARATED LAND) BUTT
(— OF SKIN FOR GLOVE) TRANK
(— OF SKIN) BLYPE
(— OF SLATE) SLAT
(— OF SOAP) BALL
(— OF SOMETHING EDIBLE) STULL
(— OF TIMBER) FISH COULISSE
FOREHOOK
(— OF TOAST) SLINGER
(— OF TOBACCO) FIG
(— OF TRACK) LEAD RUNBY
(— OF TRICKERY) CROOK
(— OF TURF) FLAG DIVOT SCRAW
SHIRREL
(— OF WOOD) KIP LATH APRON
BOARD CHUMP CHUNK PLANK
SPOON WADDY BILLET COMMON
STOWER TIMBER LIPPING
(— OF WORK) JOB CHAR TURN
(— OF WRITING) SCREED SCREEVE
(— OUT) EKE
(— SPLIT OFF) SPLINT
(— TO PREVENT SLIPPING) CLEAT
(—S OF MACARONI) DITALI DITALINI
(100-REAL GOLD —) ISABELLA
(25-CENT —) CUTER
(4-DOLLAR GOLD —) STELLA
(ARTILLERY —) DRAKE SAKER
LANTACA
(BACKGAMMON —) STONE
(BROAD —) SHEET
(BROKEN —) BRACK FRACTION
(BUTTING —) HURTER
(CHESS —) PIN KING PAWN ROOK
QUEEN BISHOP CASTLE KNIGHT
OFFICER
(END — OF BUCKET) CANT
(FLAT —) FLAP FLAKE
(FUR —) PALATINE
(GOLD —) SLUG TALI
(IN —S) LIMBMEAL
(IRREGULAR —) SNAG
(LARDED — OF MEAT) DAUB
(LARGE —) HUNK MOLE STULL
DOLLOP
(LITERARY —) CAMEO
(LITTLE —) STNEKI
(LONG —) STRIP
(MOVABLE — IN VIOLIN BOW) NUT
(MUSICAL —) ITEM CHORO DANCE
ETUDE CHASER LESSON ALLEGRO
ANDANTE CONCERTO DUOLOGUE
ENTRACTE INVENTION
(NARROW —) LABEL STAVE STRIP
(ODD — OF CARPENTRY)
DUTCHMAN
(ROTATING —) CAM ROTOR
SPINDLE
(SAMPLE —) SWATCH
(SHAPELESS —) DUMP MAMMOCK
(SIDE —) RIB JAMB JAMBE
(SINGLE —) LENGTH
(SLENDER —) SPILL SLIVER
(SMALL — OF FLESH) GIGOT
(SMALL — OF WOOD) KIP
(SMALL —) BIT BOB NOB PEA CHIP
SNIP TATE CRUMB PATCH PRILL

SCRAP SPECK MORSEL SIPPET
DRIBLET FLITTER PALLION SPLINTER
(SMALL —S) MATCHWOOD
(STRENGTHENING —) DWANG
HURTER
(TAPERING —) GORE GUSSET
(THICK —) JUNK HUNCH
(THIN —) SHIM FLAKE SHIVE SLICE
(WEDGESHAPED — OF WOOD) GLUT
SHIM
(PL.) MATERIAL NOBLEMEN
PIECEWORK SETWORK TUTWORK
TASKWORK
PIECEWORKER JOBBER
PIECRUST BREAD COFFIN ABAISSE
PIED PINTO SHELD MAGPIED PIEBALD
PIED ANTELOPE BONTEBOK
PIEDFORT PATAGON
PIED WAGTAIL COB COBB PEER
PILE PILLAR WAGGIE WASHER
WATERIE SEEDBIRD WASHDISH
WASHTAIL
PIEPLANT RHUBARB RHAPONTIC
PIER COB ANTA BELT COBB DOCK
MOLE PILE QUAY TILT GROIN JETTY
JOWEL JUTTY LEVEE STILT WHARF
BRIDGE BUNDER MULLION STAGION
PIEDROIT STELLING
(— CAP) SUMMER
(HALF —) RESPONSE
PIERCE CUT DAB DAG DEG DIG JAB
RIT BARB BEAR BITE BORE BROB
BROD CLOY DART DIRL GORE HOLE
HOOK LACE LACK PASS PINK PROB
RIVE ROVE STAB STOB TAME TANG
WHIP BREAK DRILL ENTER GOUGE
GRIDE LANCE PERCH PITCH POACH
PREEN PROBE PRONG SHEAR SNICK
SPEAR SPIKE STEEK STICK STING
THIRL ATTAME BROACH CLEAVE
DAGGER EMPALE FICCHE GIMLET
IMPALE LAUNCH PRITCH RIDDLE
SEARCH SKEWER STITCH STRIKE
THRILL THRING THRUST WIMBLE
ASSAGAI JAVELIN ENTHRILL
LACERATE PUNCTURE
PIERCED AJOURE CRIBRAL PERTUSE
CRIBROSE PERFORATE
PIERCING SHY FELL HIGH KEEN
LOUD TART CLEAR EAGLE SHARP
SNELL ARROWY BITTER BORING
SHREWD SHRILL SNITHE SNITHY
CUTTING GIMLETY POINTED
PUNGENT DRILLING INCISIVE
PERCEANT POIGNANT POUNCING
STABBING STICKING
PIERHEAD MOLEHEAD
PIET PYOT DIPPER MAGPIE
PIETIST LABADIST
PIETISTIC DEVOUT
PIETY HONOR LOYALTY PIETISM
DEVOTION SANCTION GODLINESS
PIFFLE FOLDEROL
PIG (ALSO SEE HOG, SWINE) COW
FAR HAM HOG SLIP BACON BONAV
BROCK CHEAT CHUCK GRICE INGOT
PIGGY SHOAT APEREA BONHAM
COCHON FARROW GUSSIE HOGGIE
PORKET PORKIN SUCKER TITMAN

WEANER BONNIVE GLUTTON
GRUMPY HOGLING PIGLING
ROOKLER GRUNTLING
(BROOD OF —S) TEAM
(EIGHT —S) FODDER
(SMALLEST — OF LITTER) TITMAN
ANTHONY DILLING TANTANY
TANTONY
(SUCKLING —) ROASTER
(UNDERSIZED —) RUNT TITMAN
TEATMAN
(YOUNG —) ELT FAR SLIP GRICE
GURRY BONEEN BONHAM
SQUEAKER
PIG DEER BABIRUSA
PIGEON DOO NUN OWL TOY BARB
CLAY DOVE JACK KING KITE LUPE
RUFF RUNT SPOT BALDY DOWVE
FRILL HOMER KOKLA PIPER SQUAB
WONGA CULTER CULVER CUSHAT
DODLET DRAGON FEEDER HELMET
JEWING MAGPIE MANUMA MAUMET
MODENA POUTER PRIEST ROCKER
SHAKER TRERON TURBIT TURNER
WATTLE ANTWERP CARNEAU
CARRIER CROPPER FANTAIL FINIKIN
JACOBIN MALTESE PINTADO
SWALLOW TIPPLER TUMBLER
BALDHEAD CAPUCHIN FINIKING
HORSEMAN MANUTAGI RINGDOVE
SQUABBER SQUEAKER SQUEALER
FRILLBACK TOOTHBILL
(CLAY —) BIRD GYROPIGEON
(STOOL —) PIG NARK
PIGEON BLOOD GARNET
PIGEON HAWK MERLIN
PIGEONHOLE BOX SLOT LABEL
SHELVE ANALYZE CELLULE
CLASSIFY CUBBYHOLE
(PL.) STOCK
PIGEON HOUSE COT DOOKET
DOVECOT COLUMBARY
PIGEON PEA DAL TUR TARE ARHAR
DAHIL GANDUL TURNER TURNOR
CATJANG
PIGEON WOODPECKER FLICKER
PIGGERY PIGS PIGSTY HOGGERY
POTTERY SWINERY CROCKERY
PIGGIN HANDY PIPKIN
PIGHEADED WILLFUL PERVERSE
STUBBORN OBSTINATE
PIGHTLE PIKLE PICKLE PIDDLE
PIGTAIL
PIG IRON GRUNDY
PIGLET PORKLING
PIGLIKE SUIFORM SUILINE
PIGMENT (ALSO SEE DYE, COLOR)
BLUE HEME BROWN COLOR EARTH
GREEN HUMIN MORIN PAINT STAIN
TONER BRONZE CEROID CERUSE
IDAEIN LITHOL MALVIN ORANGE
PURPLE SIENNA VIOLET GOUACHE
PAINTRY PUCCOON STAINER
TURACIN ALTHAEIN COLORANT
EXTENDER GOSSYPOL PAINTURE
TINCTURE UROPHEIN
(— FOR WOODWORK) KOKOWAI
(BLACK —) ABAISER MELANIN
(BLUE —) BICE SMALT CYANIN

ALTHEIN CERULEUM MARENNIN
(BLUE-GREEN —) LEUCOCYAN
(BROWN —) MUMMY SEPIA UMBER
BISTER FUSCIN ASTERIN
(BROWNISH-YELLOW —) SIENNA
(GREEN —) VERDITER
(MADDER-ROOT —) RUBIATE
(ORANGE-RED —) REALGAR
(RED —) HAEM LAKE ARUMIN
PATISE SANDYX AMATITO KOKOWAI
PUCCOON SCARLET SINOPIA
CAPSUMIN URORUBIN URRHODIN
VERMILION
(RED-VIOLET —) TURACIN
(WHITE —) CERUSE ANATASE
LITHOPONE
(YELLOW —) FLAVIN ETIOLIN
FISETIN GAMBOGE PUCCOON
DIATOMIN GALANGIN GENTISIN
ORPIMENT UROBILIN
PIGMENTATION COLOR LENTIL
LENTIGO JAUNDICE NIGRITIES
PIGNUS PAWN PLEDGE
PIGNUT HOGNUT
PIGS' FEET CRUBEEN PETTITOES
PIGSKIN SADDLE FOOTBALL
PIGSNEY EYE DARLING
PIGSTY FRANK HOGCOTE HOGGERY
PIGGERY SWINESTY
PIGTAIL PLAIT QUEUE COLETA
PIGWASH SWILL
PIGWEED QUINOA BEETROOT
CARELESS GOOSEFOOT
PIK DRA PICKI PICKL ENDAZE
ENDASEH
PIKA CONY HAIR HARE LEPORID
LAGOMORPH
PIKE GED DORE DORY GADE GEDD
JACK LUCE TANG TOUG TUCK
HAKED LUCET SNAKE SNOOK STING
VOUGE SALMON SAUGER JAVELIN
WALLEYE BLOWFISH GLASSEYE
JACKFISH NORTHERN PARTISAN
PICKEREL POULAINE TURNPIKE
PIKELET CRUMPET
PIKEMAN PIKE WATTLEBOY
PIKE PERCH PERCID SANDER
SAUGER ZANDER
PIKER TRAMP VAGRANT TELLTALE
TIGHTWAD VAGABOND
PILASTER ANTA PIER RIDGE ALETTE
RESPOND TELAMON
PILCHARD FUMADO ALEWIFE
SARDINE MENHADEN
PILE COP FUR LOT NAP PIE TIP BALE
BANK BING BULK BUNG BURR COCK
DASS DECK DESS DOWN HACK HAIR
HEAP LEET LOAD PEEL PIER POLE
POOK PYRE REEK RUCK SESS SHAG
SPUD AMASS CANCH CLAMP
CROWD FAGOT POINT SPILE SPIRE
STACK STILT TOWER CASTLE
FAGGOT FENDER FILLER GALGAL
PILLAR RICKLE RUCKLE FORTUNE
JAVELIN PYRAMID REACTOR
SPINDLE CROWBILL INCREASE
SANDPILE
(— CROSSWISE) COB
(— CURD) CHEDDAR

(— OF BRICKS) HACK
(— OF CLOTH) LAY
(— OF HAY) RICK SHOCK DOODLE
HAYCOCK HAYRICK
(— OF ICE) HUMMOCK
(— OF LOGS) DECK
(— OF PLATES) BUNG
(— OF REFUSE) DUSTHEAP
(— OF SALT FISH) BULK
(— OF SEALSKINS) PAN
(— OF SHEAVES) SESS
(— OF SHEETS) LIFT
(— OF STONES) ISLAND STONAGE
WARLOCK
(— OF TOBACCO) BULK
(— OF WOOD) STRAND
(— TO BE BURNT) PYRE
(— UP) CORD RICK COMPILE
(— WHEAT SHOCKS) STITCH
(IRON —) SPINDLE
(LITTLE —) HOT HOTT
(LOOSE —) RICKLE
(ROCK —) HOODOO
(SMALL —) COCK CANCH
(PL.) FIG DRIFT
PILEA ADICEA
PILEATED WOODPECKER
LOGCOCK WOODCOCK
PILE DRIVER TUP FISTUCA
HERCULES IMPACTER
(— DOLLY) FOLLOWER
(— WEIGHT) RAM TUP MONKEY
PILEUS CAP MITRA PILEOLUS
PILEWORT CRAIN CRANE FICARY
FIGWORT CELANDINE
PILFER ROB CRIB HOOK PELF PICK
PILK PRIG SMUG SNIG FILCH
MOOCH PILCH PROWL SHARP
SLOCK STEAL SWIPE FINGER
MAGPIE MOOTCH NIBBLE PICKLE
SMOUCH SNITCH CABBAGE
MANAVEL PLUNDER PURLOIN
SNAFFLE UNHITCH PETTIFOG
SCROUNGE
PILFERER PRIG TAKER SLOCKER
FINGERER SLOCKSTER
PILFERING MICHING PICKING
THIEVISH
PILGRIM HAJI HADJI HAJJI PALMER
PELERIN PEREGRIN WAYFARER
PILGRIMAGE TRIP TURUS VOYAGE
JOURNEY
(— TO MECCA) HADJ
PILING SPILING STOCKADE
(PL.) STARLING
PILL PIL ROB BALL BARK GOLI PEEL
POOL CREEK CACHOU EXTORT
UNHAIR DESPOIL DIURNAL GLOBULE
GRANULE PARVULE PILLULE
PREFORM BASEBALL GOOFBALL
BLACKBALL CIGARETTE
(AROMATIC —) CACHOU
(LARGE —) BALL BOLUS
(LITTLE —) PILULA PILULE
PILLAGE LOOT PEEL PILL PREY
SACK BOOTY FORAY HARRY REAVE
RIFLE SPOIL HARROW MARAUD
PICORY RAPINE RAVAGE DESPOIL
PICKEER PLUNDER RANSACK

ROBBERY BOOTHALE EXPILATE
PURCHASE SPOLIATE DEVASTATE
PILLAGER PEELER PILLER ROBBER
SACKER SPOILER SNAPHANCE
PILLAGING EXECUTION PREDATORY
PILLAR COG HERM JAMB PACK PIER
PILE POST PROP STUD TERM JAMBI
NEWEL SHAFT STELA STELE STOCK
STONE STOOP STUMP CIPPUS
COLUMN HERMES PILLER STAPLE
BEDPOST DEADMAN TRESTLE
TRUMEAU BOUNDARY MASSEBAH
PEDESTAL RESPONSE STANCHION
(— CAPPED WITH SLAB) BILITH
(— IN LARGE DOORWAY) TRUMEAU
(— IN MINE) STOOK STUMP
(— OF COAL) SPURN STOOK STOOK
(— SUPPORTING ARCH) RESPONSE
(— SURMOUNTED BY HEAD)
HERMES
(—S OF HERCULES) ABILA CALPE
(4-SIDED —) OBELISK
(BUDDHIST —) LAT
(CHANGED TO —) OLENUS
(EARTH —) HOODOO
(SACRED —) ASHERAH
(SEMITE —) MASSEBAH
(STONE —) CIPPUS
(TEMPORARY —) DEADMAN
(PL.) CRURA
PILLARIST STYLITE
PILLAS PILCORN PILKINS
PILLBOX SCATULA
PILLBUG ISOPOD KEESLIP MILLEPEI
PILLWORM CHEESELIP
PILLED BALD SHAVEN TONSURED
PILLION PAD PILLOW SADDLE
CUSHION
PILLORY THEW JOUGS TRONE
CRUCIFY HALSFANG
PILLOW COD BOTT DAWN PEEL PIL
REST FLOAT WANGER BOLSTER
CUSHION FUSTIAN HEADING
OREILLER
PILLOWCASE BEAR PILL SHAM
PILLIVER
PILM DUST
PILON BONUS LAGNIAPPE
PILOSE HAIRY PILEOUS
PILOT ACE SPY KIWI COACH GUARI
GUIDE STEER AIRMAN ESCORT
MANAGE THAMUS AVIATOR CAPTA
CONDUCT HOBBLER LODEMAN
SHIPMAN WINGMAN AIREDALE
GOVERNOR HELMSMAN PALINURUS
WHEELSMAN
PILOT BIRD PLOVER
PILOT FISH ROMERO JACKFISH
AMBERFISH
PILOTHOUSE TEXAS CHARTHOUSE
PILUM PESTLE JAVELIN
PIMENTA MYRTAL
PIMENTO PIMINTA ALLSPICE
PIMIENTO
PIMP MACK BULLY CADET FAGOT
PONCE SNEAK MACRIO PANDER
RUFFIAN INFORMER PROCUROR
PURVEYOR SCOUNDREL
PIMPERNEL BURNET WAYWORT

EYEBRIGHT MARGELINE WINCOPIPE
PIMPLE GUM NOB PAP BURL KNOB PUSH QUAT SPOT HICKY PLOOK PLOUK PLUKE PAPULA PAPULE TETTER BUBUKLE PUSTULE PIMGENET WHEYWORM
PIN FID FIX HOB HUB LAG LEG NOG PEG PEN ACUS APEX AXLE BANK BOLT MOOD PEEN POST PRIN PROP PYNE RUNG STUD DRIFT HUMOR KAYLE POINT PREEN SPILL THOLE BOBBIN BROACH BROOCH CALIGO COTTER CURLER FASTEN HATPIN NORMAN PINNET SKEWER SPIGOT TEMPER TENPIN TOGGEL TONGUE TRIFLE BAYONET CONFINE ENCLOSE GUDGEON IMPOUND LOCKPIN PAIRPIN PUSHPIN SPINDLE TAMPION TANGENT TUMBLER FORELOCK PINNACLE
(— FOR FITTING PLANKS) SETBOLT
(— IN AXLETREE) LINCHPIN
(— IN RIFLE) TIGE
(— OF DIAL) STYLE GNOMON
(— OF LANTERN PINION) RUNDLE
(— OF WATCH) DART
(— ON CLAVICHORD KEY) TANGENT
(— TO HOLD BEDCLOTHES) BEDSTAFF
(— USED AS TARGET) HOB
(BELAYING —) CAVIL
(BOWLING —) DUCKPIN HEADPIN KINGPIN SLEEPER
(BOWLING —S) DEADWOOD
(CARPENTRY —) DOWEL
(COUPLING —) DRAWBOLT
(ENGAGING —) BAYONET
(HAIR —) BARRETTE
(HEADED —) RIVET
(JEWELED —) PROP
(OAR —) THOLE
(ORNAMENTAL —) AGLET AIGLET
(PIVOT —) PINTLE
(SMALL —) LILL MINIKIN MICROPIN
(SPLIT —) COTTER FORELOCK
(SURVEYOR'S —) ARROW
(TAPERED —) DRIFT
(TIRLING —) RISP
(WOODEN —) SPILE TRENAIL
(PL.) LEGS KAILS DEADWOOD
PINACOID BASE HEMIDOME
PINAFORE SLIP TIDE TIDY TIER
PINAFORE-YER DAIDLY SAVEALL SLIPPER GABERDINE
PINBALL MACHINE PACHINKO
PINCASE POPPET
PINCE-NEZ NIPPER LORGNON NOSEPINCH
PINCERS TEU TEW CLAM CHELA TUARN PLIERS TURKIS WYNRIS FORCEPS MULLETS NIPPERS PINCHER PINSONS TWEEZERS
PINCH NIP TOP VEX WRY BITE CLAM HURT PUSH STOP TUCK CRIMP GRIPE HINCH PUGIL SNUFF SQUAT STEAL STINT TAPER THEFT TWEAK WRING ARREST CLUTCH EXTORT HARASS NARROW SNITCH STRAIT STRESS TWINCH TWITCH SCRINCH

SQUEEZE JUNCTURE PRESSURE SHORTAGE STRAITEN VELLICATE
(— OF SNUFF) SNEESH SNEESHIN
(— WITH HUNGER) CLAM CLEM
PINCHBECK SHAM CHEAP SPURIOUS PRETENDED
PINCHED CHITTY WASTED HAGGARD PUNGLED SQUINCH
PINCHPENNY CARL MISER NIGGARD NIGGARDLY
PINDARIC ODE WILD
PINE IE ARA LIM CHIL CHIR FADE FLAG HALA HONE IEIE KAIL WANT AGGAG DROOP DWAIN GRIEF KAURI MATAI MATSU MOURN OCOTE PINON WANZE WEARY WRIST YEARN APACHE AROLLA DUSTER FAMINE GRIEVE HUNGER LAMENT PANDAN SHRINK SORROW STARVE TOATOA TORFEL WITHER CYPRESS DAISING DWINDLE FORPINE FOXTAIL JEFFREY LAUHALA TARWOOD TORMENT TORTURE AKAMATSU AUSTRIAN GALAGALA LANGUISH LOBLOLLY LONGLEAF PINASTER STAGHORN TANEKAHA VANQUISH
(— AWAY) DROOP DWINE SNURP WANZE WINDER FORPINE MACERATE
(AUSTRALIAN —) BEEFWOOD
(GROUND —) FOXTAIL
(PITCH —) THYME
PINEAPPLE BOMB NANA PINA PINO PITA ANANA ANANAS ABACAXI GRENADE
PINE FINCH SISKIN
PINE MARTEN SABLE
PINE NEEDLE SHAT SPILL PINING ALFILARIA
(PL.) TWINKLES
PINE TREE STATE MAINE
PINFEATHER PEN STUMP STIPULE
PINFISH CHUB SPOT JIMMY PORGY SARGO
PINFOLD POUND
PING KNOCK
PINGUIN MAYA ANANAS AGUAMAS PINUELA HUIPILLA
PINGUITUDE FATNESS OBESITY OILINESS
PINION NOIL WING PINON QUILL PENNON SECURE LANTERN PINACLE SHACKLE TRUNDLE FLIGHTER WALLOWER
PINION WHEEL MOBILE
PINITOL SENNITE MATEZITE
PINK JAG PIP CYME DAWN DECK FADE MICE PING STAB WINK ADORN BLINK CORAL ELITE MOVED SWELL WOUND AURORE BISQUE CHERUB FIESTA HEIGHT MINNOW POUNCE SHRIMP SILENE TATTOO ZEPHYR ANNATTO ARBUTUS BEGONIA BERMUDA BLOSSOM EXTREME PARAGON REVEREE SANDUST TUSSORE CONFETTI COQUETTE DECORATE DIANTHUS GILLIVER LIMEWORT RADIANCE RECAMIER
PINKED JAGGED

PINKIE PIRLIE
PINKROOT REDROOT WORMWEED STARBLOOM
PINNA EARFLAP PINNULE APHLEBIA AURICULA PAVILION
PINNACE BARK CROWN WOMAN BARQUE PINNAGE MISTRESS
PINNACLE IT PIN TOP ACME APEX CREST CROWN SERAC SPIRE THUMB FINIAL HEIGHT SUMMIT GENDARME
(ICE —) SERAC
(ROCKY —) TOR HOODOO AIGUILLE GENDARME
PINNATE WINGED
PINNER PINDER FLANDAN STICKER
PINOCHLE BINOCLE GOULASH AIRPLANE
(— SCORE) MELD
PINPILLOW PIMPLO
PINPOINT ISOLATE
(— OF LIGHT) GLEAM
PINT O GULL PINNET SWIGGER OCTARIUS
(9-10THS —) MUTCHKIN
(FOURTH —) GILL JACK
(HALF —) CUP NIP GILL JACK CUPFUL NIPPERKIN
PINTADO CERO PIED SIER SEARER SIERRA SPOTTED KINGFISH
PINTAIL DUCK SMEE SPIKE SPRIG GROUSE SMETHE CRACKER LADYBIRD LONGNECK PIKETAIL
PINTANO PILOT COCKEYE CHIRIVITA
PINTID EMPEINE
PINTO BEAN ROSILLO
PINWEED(PL.) LECHEA
PINWHEEL WINDMILL
PINWORM NEMA OXYURID
PIN WRENCH SPANULE
PIONEER BLAZE GUIDE MINER GROPER HALUTZ SETTLE CHALUTZ EXPLORE EARLIEST EMIGRANT ORIGINAL RAWHIDER
PIOUS PI HOLY FROOM GODLY MORAL SEELY DEVOUT DIVINE INWARD PIETIC CANTING DUTIFUL GODDARD PITEOUS SAINTED SAINTLY FAITHFUL RELIGIOUS
PIP DIE CHIP ECHO KILL PAIP PEEP SPOT SPECK DEFEAT PIPPIN BLACKBALL
PIPAL BO FIG
PIPE TD BIN GUN HUB TAP TEE CALL CANE DALE DRIP DUCT FLUE HOSE LINE MAIN MUTE PULE REED TILE TUBE WEEP WORM BLAST BRAIL BRIAR CANAL CANEL CINCH CRANE CROSS CUTTY HOOKA PROBE PUNGI QUILL RIDER RISER SPOUT STAND STRAW TEWEL TRUMP TRUNK VOICE BRANCH BURROW CALEAN CASING DUCTUS FAUCET FILLER GEWGAW HEWGAG HOGGER KINURA NIPPLE NOTICE NOZZLE OFFLET OFFSET POOGYE RANKET SLEEVE SLOUCH SLUICE SUCKER TROWEL TUBULE TUNNEL UPTAKE WEEPER CHANNEL CHANTER CHIBOUK CONDUIT

DUCTURE FISTULA HYDRANT
SERVICE SPARGER SPINDLE
SUCTION TALLBOY TWEEDLE
WHISTLE CALIDUCT DOWNTAKE
GALOUBET LAMPHOLE MIRLITON
NARGHILE NARGILEH PENSTOCK
SEMIDOLE SUSPIRAL TELLTALE
THRIBBLE
(— **AS NAVIGATION AID**) SPINDLE
(— **BENDER**) HICKEY
(— **BOWL**) STUMMEL
(— **FOR CONDUCTING WATER**)
LEADER
(— **JOINT**) TURNOUT
(— **OF ORE**) BUNNY
(— **OF PAN**) SYRINX
(— **OF QUEEN BEE**) TEET
(— **ON BAGPIPE**) DRONE CHANTER
(— **SUPPORT**) CRADLE
(— **TAB**) TACK
(— **TO MUFFLE TRUMPET**) SORDINE
(— **USED IN WELL**) STRING
(— **WITH SOCKET ENDS**) HUB
(**4 LENGTHS OF** —) FOURBLE
(**CEREMONIAL** —) CALUMET
(**CLAMMING** —) BRAIL
(**CONNECTING** —) HOGGER
(**FLUE** —) LABIAL
(**HEATING** —) CALIDUCT
(**MUSICAL** —) BODY GEWGAW
FISTULA SORDINE HORNPIPE
SCHWEGEL
(**OATEN** —) OAT
(**ORGAN** —) FLUE KINURA LABIAL
ERZAHLER SCHWEGEL TREMOLANT
(**PEACE** —) CALUMET
(**SEWER** —) SLANT
(**SHEPHERD'S** —) REED LARIGOT
(**SNAKE-CHARMER'S** —) PUNGI
(**TOBACCO** —) GUN CLAY BRIAR
BRIER CUTTY HOOKA STRAW
CALEAN DUDEEN HOOKAH BULLDOG
CHIBOUK CHILLUM CORNCOB
BILLIARD CALABASH
(**TOY** —) HEWGAG
(**VERTICAL** —) STACK LAMPHOLE
(**WATER** — **FOR ENGINE**) SLOUCH
PIPED DRUNK JETTED
PIPEFISH EARL LONGJAW
PIPELAYER YARNER
PIPESTEM STOPPEL STOPPLE
PIPETTE PIPET TASTER
PIPEWORT HATPIN WOOLWEED
PIPING HOSE SOFT VERY CRYING
ROULEAU WAILING WEEPING
TRANQUIL
PIPING CROW CASSICAN FLUTEBIRD
PIPIRI PITIRRI
PIPISTRELLE BAT NOCTULE
PIPIT PEEP TEETAN WEKEEN
CHEEPER SKYLARK TIETICK TITLARK
TITLING WAGTAIL LINGBIRD
TWITLARK
PIPPIN PIP APPLE PEPPIN RIBSTON
PIPSISSEWA EVERGREEN
WINTERGREEN
PIQUANCY SALT ZEST FLAVOR
GINGER TARTNESS
PIQUANT BOLD RACY JUICY NUTTY

SALTY SHARP SPICY TASTY ZESTY
LIVELY SEVERE CUTTING PEPPERY
PUNGENT STINGING
PIQUE FRET GOAD PEAK PICK PIKE
PYKE TICK ANNOY PRISE SNUFF
SPITE STING HARASS MALICE
NETTLE PRITCH STRUNT CHIGGER
OFFENSE PROVOKE UMBRAGE
IRRITATE MARCELLA
PIRACY CAPTURE PIRATISM
PIRAGUA CANOE DUGOUT PIROGUE
PETTIAGUA
PIRANHA PIRAI CARIBE PIRAYA
PIRARUCU PAICHE ARAPAIMA
PIRATE CAPER ROVER ROBBER
VIKING CATERAN CORSAIR PICKEER
SCUMMER ALGERINE MAROONER
PICAROON BUCCANEER SALLEEMAN
(— **FLAG**) ROGER BLACKJACK
PIRIPIRI BIRK BIRCH MAPAN
PIRL SPIN TWINE TWIST REVOLVE
PIRN QUILL BOBBIN PIRNIE SPINDLE
PIROGUE CANOE PERIOQUE
PIROPLASM BABESIA
PIROSHKI PIROGEN
PISCINA POOL TANK BASIN
SACRARY LAVATORY SACRARIUM
PISE CAJON PISAY
PISHOGUE CHARM SPELL SORCERY
WITCHERY
PISMIRE ANT EMMET
PISOLITE PEASTONE
PISTACHIO FISTIC PISTICK
PISTIL CHIVE CARPEL UMBONE
POINTEL
(**PL.**) GYNECIUM
PISTILLATE FEMALE
PISTOL DAG GAT GUN POP ROD
BULL DAGG IRON TACK FLUTE
RIFLE STICK BARKER BUFFER
BULDER BULLER CANNON DRAGON
HEATER POTGUN RIFFLE BULLDOG
DUNGEON SHOOTER TICKLER
DERINGER REPORTER REVOLVER
(**TOY** —) SPARKLER
PISTON BUCKET FORCER PALLET
SUCKER EMBOLUS PLUNGER
(— **HUB**) SPIDER
PIT PET POT PUT BURY CIST DELF
DELL DISC DISK FOSS HELL HOLE
KIST LAKE MINE PLAY PUTT SILO
SINK SUMP SWAG TURN WEEM
WELL ABYSM ABYSS CRYPT DELFT
DITCH FOSSA FOVEA FROST GRAVE
LEACH MATCH PITCH PORUS SLACK
SLUIG TREAD AREOLE BORROW
BUNKER KERNEL OPPOSE RADDLE
WALLOW ABADDON ALVEOLA
AMPULLA BOTHROS CHARPIT
FOSSULA FOXHOLE HANDLER
LATRINE MEGARON PINHOLE
VARIOLE WINNING CYPHELLA
DOWNFALL FAVEOLUS FENESTRA
POCKMARK PUNCTULE WELLHOLE
(— **FOR BAKING**) IMU UMU
(— **FOR OFFERINGS**) BOTHROS
(— **OF STOMACH**) MARK WIND
(— **OF THEATER**) GROUND

(— **ON COCKROACH HEAD**)
FENESTRA
(— **ON LICHENS**) LACUNA CYPHELLA
(— **SACRED TO DEMETER**)
MEGARON
(**BITTER** —) STIPPEN
(**BOTTOMLESS** —) ABYSS ABADDON
BARATHRUM
(**COAL** —) HEUCH HEUGH
(**FODDER** —) SILO
(**MAORI** —) RUA
(**MIRY** —) SLUIG
(**RIFLE** —) SANGAR
(**ROOFED** —) CIST KIST
(**SALT** —) VAT PEZOGRAPH
(**SAND** —) BUNKER
(**SMALL** —) AREOLE LACUNA
STAPLE
(**TANNING** —) LIME LAYER LEACH
HANDLER LAYAWAY SUSPENDER
PITA PITO YUCCA ARGHAN
PITCH DIP FIT KEY LAB MEL PIC
BUCK CANT CHAT CODE COOK DIN
FALL FORK HURL PECK PICK PLUG
RAKE TELL TONE TOSS ABODE
BOOST BUNCH FLING LABOR LURC
PLANT SLENT SLOPE SPIEL THROW
TWIRL BINDER DIRECT ENCAMP
FILLER LENGTH MALTHA MANJAK
PLUNGE SQUARE TOTTER TUMBLE
VOLLEY WICKET CURRENT NARRAT
ALKITRAN OVERHANG
(— **AT A MARK**) LAG
(— **FROM FIR TREES**) ALKITRAN
(— **OF HELIX**) JAW
(— **TENT**) TELD
(**ABOVE** —) SHARP
(**AUCTION** —) SETBACK
(**BASEBALL** —) CURVE STRIKE
CRIPPLE SPITTER FADEAWAY
KNUCKLER SPITBALL
(**BELOW** —) FLAT
(**COBBLER'S** —) CODE
(**FULL** —) VOLLEY
(**GLANCE** —) MANJAK MANJACK
(**HIGH** —) BLOOPER
(**HIGHEST** —) PRIDE
(**IDENTITY IN** —) UNISON
(**MINERAL** —) BITUMEN
PITCH APPLE COPEI CUPAY
PITCHED SET
PITCHER JUG JACK OLLA PILL PRI
BUIRE CRUET GALON GORGE
GOTCH AFTABA CROUKE GALLON
HURLER POURIE STRAIN URCEUS
CANETTE CHUCKER FLINGER
GROWLER STARTER STOPPER
TWIRLER URCEOLE AIGUIERE
ASCIDIUM OENOCHOE SOUTHPAW
MOUNDSMAN
(— **AND CATCHER**) BATTERY
(— **FOR BEER**) GROWLER
(— **SHAPED LIKE MAN**) TOBY
(— **WITH ONE HANDLE**) URCEUS
(**BULGING** —) GOTCH
(**EARTHEN** —) GEORG GORGE
(**RELIEF** —) FIREMAN
(**RELIEF** —**S**) BULLPEN
(**WIDEMOUTHED** —) EWER

PITCHER PLANT BISCUIT FLYTRAP
FEVERCUP FOXGLOVE WATERCUP
NEPENTHES SKUNKWEED
PITCHFORK EVIL PICK PIKE PICKEL
SHEPPECK PITCHPIKE
(THATCHER'S —) GROOM
(PL.) HARD
PITCHHOLE CAHOT
PITCHMAN VENDER SALESMAN
PITCH PIPE TUNER EPITONION
PITEOUS MEAN PALTRY PITIFUL
MERCIFUL MOURNFUL PIERCING
PITFALL PIT FALL TRAP SNARE
DANGER TRAPFALL
PITH JET PUT SAP CORE GIST MEAT
PULP PUTT HEART VIGOR ENERGY
KERNEL MARROW ESSENCE
EXTRACT MEDULLA NUCLEUS
PAPYRUS STRENGTH
PITH HELMET TOPI TOPEE
PITH TREE AMBATCH
PITHY CRISP MEATY SAPPY TERSE
STRONG CONCISE LACONIC
MARROWY
PITIABLE SAD SEELY WOFUL
RUEFUL WOEFUL FORLORN PITIFUL
PITIFUL MEAN MEEK RUTH SILLY
SORRY PALTRY RUEFUL TENDER
HANGDOG RUESOME RUTHFUL
MERCIFUL PATHETIC
PITILESS GRIM CRUEL STERN STONY
SAVAGE RUTHLESS UNPITIED
MERCILESS
PITTANCE BIT ALMS DOLE GIFT MITE
SONG TRIFLE BEQUEST
PITTED FOVEATE OPPOSED
ALVEOLATE
PITTER STONER
PITURI BEDGERY PITCHERY
PITY RUE MEAN MOAN PETE PITE
RUTH MERCY PIETY REIVE SCATH
PATHOS MERCIFY REMORSE
WAESUCK CLEMENCY SYMPATHY
PIVOT TOE CRUX SLEW TURN HEART
CENTER SLOUGH WORDLE
GUDGEON TRAVERSE TRUNNION
PIVOTAL POLAR CENTRAL
(— POINT) KNUCKLE
PIVOTING DISHRAG
PIVOT STAND PEDESTAL
PIXY ELF FAIRY PYGMY ROGUE
IMPISH RASCAL SPRITE PUCKISH
ROGUISH
PIXILATED DAFFY DOTTY DRUNK
PIXIE BEMUSED PUCKISH TOUCHED
CONFUSED
PIZE OATH PISE CURSE
PLACABLE WEAK QUIET PACABLE
PEACEFUL YIELDING FORGIVING
PLACARD BILL POST TITLE POSTER
TICKET AFFICHE REDLINE
STOMACHER
PLACATE CALM GENTLE PACIFY
LEASE SOOTHE APPEASE FORGIVE
PLACE L DO BIT FIX PUT SET AREA
HOLE LIEU PLAT PLOT POSE POST
RANK ROOM SEAT SITE SITU SPOT
STEP STOW TEXT VICE YARK BEING
STER ESTRE HOUSE JOINT LOCUS

PLAZA POSIT SCENE SITUS STALL
STATE STEAD STELL STOUR WHERE
BESTOW CHARGE GROUND IMPOSE
INVEST LAYOUT LOCALE LOCATE
OFFICE POSSIE ROOMTH ALLODGE
ARRANGE DEPOSIT KITCHEN
STATION ABDITORY DIGGINGS
EMPORIUM LOCATION POSITION
(— ALONE) ISOLATE
(— ALTERNATELY) STAGGER
(— APART) ENISLE
(— BEFORE) APPOSE PREFIX
(— BY FORCE) PILT
(— CROSSWISE) THWART
(— FISH IN SALTING BIN) KENCH
(— FOR CATTLE) CAMP
(— FOR DUMPING RUBBISH) SHOOT
(— FOR MORTAR AND BRICK) FROG
(— FOR PHEASANTS) STEW
(— FOR PRAYERS) IDGAH
(— FOR RABBITS) WARREN
(— FOR RECEPTION) RECEIPT
(— FOR RUBBISH DEPOSITS)
LAYSTALL
(— FOR SEETHING) STEW
(— FOR SLEEPING) BED BUNK DOSS
FLOP LAIR LIBKIN
(— FOR TRAINING HORSES) LONGE
(— FROM WHICH JURY IS TAKEN)
VENUE
(— IN COMPACT MASS) STOW
(— IN ORDER) ARRAY ENRANK
(— IN WATERFALL) LEAP
(— IN) INNEST
(— OF AMUSEMENT) GAFF
(— OF ASSEMBLY) AGORA CURIA
SYNAGOG
(— OF BURIAL) AHU KIL KILL LAIR
GRAVE LAYSTOW CATACOMB
CEMETERY GOLGOTHA LAYSTALL
(— OF BUSINESS) BANK AGENCY
KNACKERY
(— OF CONCEALMENT) DEN BOMA
BLIND STALE HIDING HIDEOUT
HIDEAWAY
(— OF CONFINEMENT) BRIG CAGE
COOP LIMBO PRISON BULLPEN
(— OF CONFUSION) BABEL
TROYTOWN
(— OF DESTRUCTION) ABADDON
(— OF DWELLING) WANE
(— OF ENTERTAINMENT) INN JOINT
DANCERY HANGOUT HOSTELRY
(— OF EXERTION) ARENA
(— OF EXILE) PATMOS
(— OF MISERY) HELL
(— OF NETHER DARKNESS) EREBUS
(— OF NOISE) BABEL
(— OF PROTECTION) PORT SCUG
(— OF REFUGE) ARK BAST HOLD
ASYLUM ADULLAM HIDEOUT
(— OF RESIDENCE) SOIL DOMICILE
(— OF RESORT) PURLIEU
(— OF RESTRAINT) LIMBO
(— OF SACRIFICE) ALTAR
(— OF SAFETY) GRITH HAVEN
WARRANT
(— OF SECURITY) GRITH ASYLUM
CORRAL HARBOR GARRISON

(— OF SHELTER) LEW HOLD JOUK
COVER
(— OF SUBMISSION) CANOSSA
(— OF TORMENT) GOLGOTHA
(— OF WORSHIP) HEIAU BETHEL
CHAPEL CHURCH DESERT SHRINE
TEMPLE GURDWARA SYNAGOGUE
(— WHERE 4 OR MORE WAYS MEET)
CARFAX
(— WHERE FOOD IS KEPT) LARDER
(— WHERE MEAT IS SMOKED)
BUCAN BUCCAN
(— WHERE OUTCASTS GATHER)
HELL
(— WHERE ROADS CROSS) LEET
(— WHERE STREAM IS RAPID)
SHARP
**(— WHERE TROOPS HALT
OVERNIGHT)** ETAPE
(BOGGY —) SLUMP
(BREEDING —) NIDUS LOOMERY
PELICANRY
(CHIEF —) HEADSHIP
(CIRCULAR —) ORBELL
(CONSECRATED —) HIERON
(DRINKING —) BOOZER MUMHOUSE
(DRY —) SEARING
(DWELLING —) BY BYE DEN SEE
HAFT HIVE HOME BEING HOUSE
HOWFF SOJOURN HABITACLE
(EATING —) CAFE GRUBBERY
(EMPTY —) BLANK SPACE
(ENCLOSED —) BIN HAY WORTH
SEVERAL
(ESSENTIAL —) EYE
(FAMILIAR —) KITH
(FAULTY — IN THREAD) TRAP
(FILTHY —) STY
(FIRST —) BLUE LEAD STRAIGHT
(FORTIFIED —) LIS LISS CASTLE
FASTNESS
(GATHERING —) SHOP AGORA
FOYER JOINT LESCHE
(HALTING —) MARAH
(HIDING —) MEW CACHE HIDEL
HOARD STASH COVERT HIDDELS
RETREAT STOWAWAY
(HIGH —) EMINENCE
(HOLLOW —) GULF HOLE HOLL
SCOOP CAVITY ALBERCA SINKHOLE
(INHABITED —) ABADI
(LANDING —) GHAT HARD LEVEE
SCALE PALACE HELIPORT
(LEVEL —) PLANILLA
(LODGING —) CAMP LOGIS BIDING
BILLET LIBKEN
(LURKING —) HOLD HOLE HOARD
HULSTER
(MARKET —) AGORA TRONE
MARKET RIALTO
(MARSHY —) SLEW SLOO SLUE
SLUMP SLOUGH
(MEETING —) CLUB COURT FORUM
GUILD TRYST TOLSEL TOLZEY
AMBALAM KLAVERN TINWALD
(MUDDY —) SOIL
(NESTING —) JUG NIDARY
(OPEN —) ENAJIM
(OTHERWORLDLY —) EMPYREAN

(RAVELED —) FRAY
(REMOTE —) JERICHO
(RESTING —) LAY CAMP FORM GIST
LAIR PARAO CRADLE
(ROCKY —) ROCHER
(SACRED —) HAREM HIERON
CHAITYA SANCTUM
(SALTING —) SALADERO
(SECRET —) LAIR CORNER CRANNY
(SHADY —) GLOOM SWALE
FRESCADE UMBRACLE
(SHELTERED —) NOOK SCUG
SUCCOR
(STOPPING —) HALT MANZIL
(STORAGE —) DEPOT HOARD
LODGE SPICERY STORAGE
STOWAGE DOCKYARD
(SWAMPY —) FLUSH SOUGH
(THIRD —) SHOW
(TIGHT —) JAM JAMB
(WATCH —) TOOTHILL
(WRETCHED —) DEN MISERY
(PL.) LOCI
PLACEBO TOADY VESPERS
PARASITE
PLACED FIXED BESTEAD
(— ON ITS SIDE) LAZY
PLACEHOLDER VARIABLE
PLACE-NAME TOPONYM
PLACENTA MAZA
PLACENTAL MAZIC
PLACID CALM COOL EVEN MEEK
MILD SOFT DOWNY QUIET SUANT
SUENT GENTLE SEDATE SERENE
SMOOTH PACIFIC TRANQUIL
THROBLESS
PLACKET FENT SPARE WOMAN
CLOSING PETTICOAT
PLAGIARISM CRIB PLAGIUM
PLAGIARIST TAKER COPYIST
PLAGIARIZE CRIB LIFT STEAL
PLAGUE DUN IMP VEX FRAB FRET
GNAW PEST TWIT BESET CURSE
DEATH DEUCE HARRY QUALM
TEASE TRAIK WEARY WORRY
WOUND BURDEN HAMPER HARASS
INFEST PESTER PESTIS SORROW
WANION DESTROY MURRAIN
PERPLEX SCOURGE TORMENT
TORTURE TROUBLE HANDICAP
OUTBREAK
PLAGUY VERY PESKY VEXING
MURRAIN PESTFUL INFERNAL
PLAICE FLUKE FLATFISH FLOUNDER
PLAID CALM FAKE MAUD PLOD
TARTAN BRACKEN BRECHAN
PLAIN DRY LOW BALD BARE CHOL
EASY EVEN FLAT OPEN PLAT RIFE
VEGA WALD WOLD BLAIR BLUNT
BROAD CAMPO CORAH FIELD FRANK
GREEN GROSS LAUND LEVEL LLANO
MOURN NAKED PAMPA PROSE
ROUND SEBKA SILLY SMALL TALAO
UNORN BEMOAN BEWAIL CHASTE
CUESTA GRAITH HOMELY HONEST
HUMBLE LENTEN MACHAR PUSZTA
RUSTIC SABANA SEVERE SIMPLE
SINGLE SMOOTH ARTLESS EVIDENT
GENUINE IDAVOLL INARTED LEGIBLE

OBVIOUS POPULAR TERRACE
APPARENT CAMPAIGN DISTINCT
EVERYDAY EXPLICIT FAMILIAR
HOMEMADE HOMESPUN ITHAVOLL
PALPABLE PIEDMONT SEMPLICE
STRAIGHT
(— AMONG TREES) LAUND
(— OF ARGENTINA) PAMPA
(— OF RUSSIA) STEPPE
(ALKALI —S) USAR
(ALLUVIAL —) APRON HAUGH
(ARCTIC —) TUNDRA
(DESOLATE —) CHOL
(LOW-LYING —) MACHAR MACHAIR
(MARSHY —) BLAIR
(SALINE —) SEBKA SEBKHA
(SALT —) SALADA
(SLOPING —) HOPE CUESTA
CONOPLAIN
(SMALL GRASSY —) CAMAS CAMASS
QUAMASH
(TREELESS —) BLED TUNDRA
SAVANNA SAVANNAH
(UNOCCUPIED —) DESERT
(PL.) VIZCACHA
PLAIN CHANT CF
PLAINCLOTHESMAN SPLIT
PLAINLY FAIR BARELY FAIRLY
FLATLY SIMPLY BROADLY FRANKLY
DIRECTLY
PLAINNESS PROSE INNOCENCE
PLAINSMAN LLANERO
PLAINSONG GROUND
PLAINT WAIL PLANT LAMENT
COMPLAINT
PLAINTEXT CLEAR
PLAINTIFF SUER ACTOR ORATOR
PURSUER QUERENT
PLAINTIVE SAD CROSS PINING
DOLENTE ELEGIAC FRETFUL
MOANFUL PEEVISH PETTISH
DOLOROSO MANGENDO PETULANT
WAILSOME SORROWFUL
PLAIT CUE PLY KNIT PAIR PLAT RUFF
TURN WALE WAND BRAID BREAD
CRIMP FETCH FITCH PEDAL PINCH
QUEUE QUILL QUIRK TRACE TRESS
WEAVE BOHDER DOUBLE GATHER
GOFFER PLEACH PLIGHT RUMPLE
TUSCAN WIMPLE WRITHE FROUNCE
PIGTAIL SCALLOM COMPLECT
(— FOR HAT) DUNSTABLE
(— OF STRAW) MILAN TRACE
(SERIES OF —S) KILTING
PLAITED PLISSE DEVIOUS PLICATE
PLAITING PLISSE LEGHORN
PLAN AIM ART LAY WAY CARD CAST
COUP DART FOOT GAME HANG IDEA
MIND MOOD PLAT PLOT REDE WENT
ALLOW BRIEF CHART DARTY DRAFT
DRIFT ETTLE FRAME HOBBY MODEL
REACH SHAPE TRACE ADVICE
AGENDA BEREDE BUDGET CIPHER
DECOCT DESIGN DEVISE ENGINE
FIGURE INTEND LAYOUT METHOD
MODULE ORDAIN PROJET SCHEMA
SCHEME SURVEY THEORY ARRANGE
CONCERT COUNSEL DRAWING
FORELAY NOSTRUM PATTERN

PROJECT PURPOSE COGITATE
CONSPIRE CONTRIVE ENGINEER
FORECAST FOREGAME LANDSKIP
MEDITATE PLATFORM PRACTICE
SCHEDULE SKELETON STRATEGY
(— AHEAD) FORECAST
(— OF FUTURE PROCEDURE)
PROGRAM
(— ON A FLOOR) EPURE
(— TOGETHER) CONCERT
(5-YEAR —) PIATILETKA
(GROUND —) TRACE GRUNDRISS
PLANARIAN PLATODE TRICLAD
FLATWORM
PLANE AXCI BEAD DADO FACE FLAT
HOLL MILL AXIAL CHUTE CROZE
FACET GLIDE HOULE HOWEL LEVEL
MESON SHOOT STICK TABLE WHISK
AEQUOR BEADER HOLLOW REEDER
ROUTER SMOKER SNIBEL COURIER
INSHAVE JOINTER SURFACE
WITCHET BULLNOSE DECLINER
LEEBOARD MERIDIAN RECLINER
SYCAMORE TRAVERSE
(— HANDLE) TOAT TOTE
(— OF CLEAVAGE) BACK
(— OF EARTH'S ORBIT) ECLIPTIC
(— OF ROCK) BED
(—S OF GUNNERY FIRE) SHEAF
(ENEMY —) BANDIT
(INCLINED —) RAMP SLIP
(MOLDING —) HOLL HOULE HOLLO'
(PERSPECTIVE —) TABLE
(RABBET —) PLOW RABAT PLOUGH
REBATE FILLETER
(SLOPING —) CUESTA
PLANER JOINTER SURFACER
PLANER TREE HORNBEAM
SYCAMORE
PLANET SUN BODY IRIS JOVE MARS
MOON STAR EARTH GLOBE HYLEG
PLUTO SHREW VENUS WORLD
SATURN SPHERE URANUS VULCAN
ALMUTEN ANARETA BENEFIC
FORTUNE JUPITER MERCURY
NEPTUNE PRIMARY CHASUBLE
LUMINARY RECEPTOR TERRELLA
WANDERER
(— IN A NATIVITY) ALMUTEN
(BENEVOLENT —) FORTUNE
(CONTROLLING —) LORD
(HYPOTHETICAL —) VULCAN
(MALEFICENT —) SHREW
(RULING —) DOMINATOR
(SMALL —) IRIS ASTEROID
TERRELLA
PLANETARIUM ORRERY
PLANETOID UNDINE ASTEROID
PLANE TREE CHINAR PLATAN
COTONIER PLANTAIN SYCAMORE
PLANET-STRICKEN SIDERATED
PLANISPHERE ASTROLABE
METEORSCOPE
PLANK CLAM HOOD PATA PLAT RA'
SOLE WAIR BOARD CLAMP PATTA
SHIDE SWALE THEAL DAGGER
FLITCH ROOFER CLAPPER CROSS
DEPOSIT MADRIER RIBBAND

STEALER FOREPOLE GARBOARD STRINGER
(— 6 FT. X 1 FT.) WARE
(— AS PROTECTION) SHOLE
(— OVER BROOK) CLAM
(—S IN BRIDGE) CHESS
(—S LESS THAN 6 FT.) DEAL
(CURVED —) SNYING
(ROUGHHEWN —) SLAB
PLANK DRAG RUBBER
PLANK END STUB
PLANKING GORE RACK HATCH SWALE CEILING LAGGING BERTHING BRATTICE GARBOARD WATERWAY
PLANKSHEER WATERWAY
PLANKTON KRILL
PLANOMILLER SLABBER
PLANT AJI BED SET SOW ACHE ALGA ARUM BURY CROP FAST HERB HIDE MORE RAPE SALT SEED SLIP TREE WORT ABACA AGAVE ARGEL CAROA CHIVE CLOTE CLOVE EARLY FANCY GRAFT HEATH INTER INULA JALAP KEIKI PITCH SHRUB YERBA ACACIA AKELEY ALASAS ANNUAL BEDDER CACOON CALALU CARROT COKERY COTTON ESCAPE FICOID FORCER GALAXY GROWTH KARREE LENTIL LIGGER MANUKA MEDICK MESCAL PEPINO SETTLE SPRING ULLUCU YARROW ABANDON ALKANET ALYSSUM BREWERY CONCEAL CUTTING DAGGERS ENCELIA HAEMONY IMPLANT JIKUNGU LETTUCE PICKERY RAMBONG SAWMILL ABUTILON AGERATUM AGRIMONY ANGLEPOD BIENNIAL BLUEBELL CONSOUND DRAWLING DYEHOUSE EMERGENT ENGINERY FUMEROOT GASWORKS GROMWELL HAWKWEED HONEWORT KNAPWEED LARKSPUR
(— 2ND CROP) ETCH
(— BY SPADING) SPIT
(— DEEPLY) HEEL
(— FIRMLY) BRACE
(— GROWING IN WATER) BILDERS HYDROPHYTE
(— IN ROWS) DRILL
(— OF MEADOWS) POOPHYTE
(— ROOTED IN GROUND) LIANA LIANE
(— SUPPORTING PARASITES) SUSCEPT
(— TREE) MOTCH
(— WITH NO DISTINCT MEMBERS) THALLUS
(— WITH THREE PISTILS) TRIGYN
(— WITH THREE STAMENS) TRIANDER
(AIR —) FLOPPERS
(ANCIENT —) CYCAD
(AQUATIC —) ALISMA NUPHAR SUGAMO TAWKEE AMBULIA AWLWORT FROGBIT DUCKWEED
(AROMATIC —) MINT NARD BASIL CUMIN TANSY THYME AMOMUM CUMMIN DITTANY ALBAHACA LAVENDER SPIKENARD

(AUSTRALIAN —) LILAC STYLO LIGNUM LANCEPOD
(BULBOUS —) GALTONIA
(CLIMBING —) VETCH LAWYER ULLUCE CORALITA
(COMPOSITE —) SUCCORY HAWKWEED
(CONSECRATED —) HAOMA
(CREATED —) BARAMIN
(CREEPING —) IPECAC KAREAO KAREAU
(CROSSBRED —) HYBRID
(CRUSHING —) BREAKER
(DWARF —) CUMIN STUNT
(DYE —) WAD ANIL WOAD WOLD WOALD MADDER
(E. INDIAN —) JATI
(ETIOLATED —) ALBINO
(FIBER —) ALOE FLAX HEMP PITA CAJUN RAMIE SISAL
(FLOWERING —) HOP ROSE DAISY HOLLY POPPY ORCHID VIOLET HAWTHORN LARKSPUR POLYGALA PRIMROSE SNOWDROP
(FORAGE —) RAPE ALFALFA DAINCHA
(GERMINATING —) SPIRE
(GRAIN —) TEFF
(HEDGE —) ESPINO
(HEMP —) FIMBLE
(IMMATURE —) KEIKI
(LEAFLESS —) ULEX DODDER RESTIAD TRIURID
(MALE —) MAS MACRANDER
(MARSH —) FERN JUNCUS CATTAIL
(MEDICINAL —) ALOE HERB ERICA ARNICA CATNEP CATNIP IPECAC SIMPLE ACONITE BONESET GENTIAN LOBELIA CAMOMILE
(NON-FLOWERING —) FERN
(NURSERY —) SEEDLING
(PEPPER —) ARA
(PISTILLATE —) FEMALE
(POISONOUS —) COWBANE DEATHIN
(POTTED —) BONSAI
(POWER —) HYDRO
(PRICKLY —) BRIAR BRIER CACTUS CARDON NETTLE TEASEL TEAZEL PRICKFOOT
(PUNGENT —) PEPPER
(RAPIDLY-GROWING —) FILLER
(REEDY —) SPRIT
(RENDERING —) KNACKERY
(SENSITIVE —) MIMOSA
(SIBERIAN —) BADAN
(SPINOUS —) KANTIARA
(STAMINATE —) HUSBAND
(SUBMERGED —) ENALID
(SUCCULENT —) ALOE HERB GASTERIA HAWORTHIA LOUSELEEK
(SWORD-LEAVED —) LEVERS
(THALLOPHYTIC —) LICHEN
(TRAILING —) ARBUTUS
(TUFTED —) DRYAS
(TWINING —) SMILAX CLIMBER BINDWEED SCAMMONY
(UNIDENTIFIED —) HORDOCK
(WATER —) LIMU LOTUS AQUATILE STARFRUIT

(WEEDY —) DOCK KNAWEL
(YOUNG —) SET SPRINGER
(PL.) FLORA
PLANTAGENET ANGEVIN
PLANTAIN COCK PALA ALISMA FINGER PISANG WABRON BENTING NETLEAF PANTANO RIBWORT SITFAST BALISIER BUCKHORN FIREWEED FLEAWORT ISPAGHUL RATSBANE ROADWEED WAYBREAD
PLANTAIN EATER TOURACO SPLITBEAK
PLANTAIN LILY FUNKIA
PLANTATION PEN HOLT WALK FINCA GROVE BOSKET BOWERY COLONY ESTATE SHAMBA SPRING YERBAL CAFETAL FAZENDA NOPALRY PINETUM THICKET ARBUSTUM HACIENDA TRAPICHE VINEYARD
(HEMP —) LATE
PLANTED LISTED
PLANTER SNAG COLON SOWER FARMER SETTLER PLANTATOR
PLANTING GROVE SATION
PLANTING STICK DIBBLE
PLANT LOUSE APHID PSYLLID PUCERON HOMOPTER
PLAQUE CHIP PINAX PLATE PLATEAU SARCOID NAMEPLATE STOMACHER
PLASH LIP DASH BLASH PLOSH PLOUT PLEACH PUDDLE SPLASH SPATTER SPECKLE
PLASMA LATEX PLASM
PLASTER CAST DAUB HARL LEEP LOCK TEER CLEAM GATCH PARGE SLICK SMALM STAFF TOPIC TREAT CHARGE CHUNAM GAGING MORTAR PARGET SPARGE STOOTH STUCCO BLISTER MALAGMA DIACULUM DIAPALMA SINAPISM VESICANT
(- WITH COW DUNG) LEEP
(— BETWEEN LATHS) CAT
(— OF PARIS) GESSO GYPSUM
(2 COATS OF —) RENDERSET
(COARSE —) GROUT
(MEDICAL —) TOPIC TREAT CHARGE SPARADRAP
(MUSTARD —) SINAPISM
PLASTERBOARD GYPSUM
PLASTERED DRUNK SOUSED SWACKED
PLASTERER DAUBER DAUBSTER PARGETER SPREADER
PLASTERING KEY SETWORK ROUGHCAST
PLASTIC FOAM RICH SIRUP LABILE PLIANT ACETATE CATALIN CRYSTAL DUCTILE ORGANIC CREATIVE FLEXIBLE LAMINATE MELAMINE TECTONIC UNCTUOUS FORMATIVE
PLASTICIZER CAMPHOR
PLASTRON DICKEY CALIPEE
PLAT BED FLAT FOOD PLAN PLOT SLAP BRAID LEVEL PLACE PLAIN PLAIT BUFFET WATTLE ARRANGE FLATTEN PLATEAU QUADRAT
PLATANIST SUSU

PLATANUS PLANE COTONIER
SYCAMORE
PLATBAND IMPOST LINTEL EPISTYLE
PLATE BAT CAP CUT DIP DOD EAR
FIN GIB WEB ANAL BACK BRIN CASE
CAST CURB DIAL DISK DROP FISH
GILL GONG GULA HOME HOOF LAME
LEAF MOLD NAIL ORAL RETE ROSE
SHOE SHUT SLAB SOLE STUD TACE
TRAY AMPYX ANODE BASAL BELLY
BLADE CHAIR CLAMP CLEAT CLOUT
FACIA FENCE FLOOR FLUKE FORCE
GLAND GUARD GULAR LAMEL
PATEN PYGAL SCALE SCUTE SHEET
SHOLE SLICE STAMP STAVE STRAP
TABLE TASSE TERNE TRAMP UNCUS
WATER ADORAL BAFFLE BRIDGE
BUCKLE CASTER CIRCLE CLICHE
COLLAR COPPER COSTAL CRUSTA
DAMPER DASHER EPIGNE FASCIA
FILLER FOLIUM FRIZEL GENIAL
GNOMON GORGET GUSSET LABIAL
LAMINA LOREAL MASCLE MATRIX
MENTAL MENTUM MOTHER PALLET
PATTEN PLATEN RADIAL SCREEN
SCUTUM SEPTUM SERVER SHEATH
SHROUD SPLINT STAPLE TARSUS
TEGMEN TURTLE TYMPAN VESSEL
BESAGNE BOLSTER BRACKET
BRACTEA BUCCULA BUCKLER
CHARGER CLYPEUS COASTER
CORNULE CORONET CRYSTAL
DOUBLER ETCHING FRIZZLE
FRONTAL GRAVURE HUMERAL
INKBLOT MORDANT MYOTOME
NEPTUNE PETALON PRIMARY
ROSTRAL ROUNDEL SPANGLE
STEALER STEELER TERGITE
TESSERA VENTRAL ASSIETTE
BEDPLATE BIQUARTZ BRACHIAL
CELLOCUT DIASCOPE DRAWBACK
ELECTRUM EPIGYNUM EPIPROCT
EPISTOME FIREBACK FLOUNDER
SKEWBACK STAPLING STRINGER
SUBPLATE SURPRINT
(— **COVERING KEYHOLE**) DROP
(— **COVERING MIDDLE EAR**)
TEGMEN
(— **IN AIRPLANE WING**) SPOILER
(— **IN BATTERY**) GRID
(— **IN ORGAN PIPE**) LANGUET
(— **IN STEAM BOILER**) SPUT
DASHER
(— **OF BALEEN**) BLADE
(— **OF CTENOPHORE**) COMB
(— **OF GELATIN**) BAT
(— **OF GLASS**) SLIDE
(— **OF JAW**) AURICLE
(— **OF PRECIOUS METAL**) BRACTEA
(— **OF SOAP FRAME**) SESS
(— **OF SUNDIAL**) GNOMON
(— **ON LANCE SHAFT**) VAMPLATE
(— **ON SADDLE**) SIDEBAR
(— **ON SATCHEL STRAP**) OLIVE
(— **ON THROAT OF FISH**) GULAR
(— **ON WATERWHEEL**) SHROUD
(—**S OF CARDING MACHINE**) ARCH
(—**S OF GUN CARRIAGE**) FLASK
(**ARMOR** —) SPLINT AILETTE

(**COMMUNION** —) PATEN
(**DEEP** —) MAZARINE
(**DORSAL** —) ALINOTUM
(**EARTHEN** —) MUFFIN
(**FASHION** —) SWELL
(**FIREPLACE** —) IRONBACK
(**FLAT** —) APRON
(**GOLD** — **ON FOREHEAD**) PATA
PATTA
(**GROOVED TRAM** —) GULLY GULLEY
(**GUARD** —) SHELL
(**HINGED** —) SHUT
(**HOME** —) DISH
(**HOT** —) GRILL GRILLE
(**IRON** —) STAVE LATTEN MARVER
LAPSTONE SKEWBACK MOLDBOARD
TURNPLATE TURNSHEET
(**LARGE** —) DOUBLER
(**LOCK** —) SELVEDGE
(**NAME** —) FACIA
(**PERFORATED** —) DOD GRID
PINNULE
(**PITCHER'S** —) SLAB MOUND
(**RIMLESS** —) COUPE
(**SIEVE** —) LATTICE
(**THIN** —) LAME LAMP LAMINA
LAMELLA
(**THIN TIN** —) TAIN TAGGERS
(**WALL** —) PAN RASEN
(**WOODEN** —) TRENCHER
PLATEAU PLAT FJELD KAROO KARST
TABLE CAUSSE HAMADA MESETA
NIVEAU PARAMO SABANA UPLAND
ANASAZI PLATFORM
PLATEHOLDER CASSETTE
PLATER VATMAN CLAIMER
COLLARMAN
PLATFORM TOP BANK BEMA DAIS
DECK DRIP DROP DUCK FLAT GHAT
KITE PACE PLAT STEP WING APRON
BENCH BLIND BLOCK CHAIN DUKAN
FLAKE FLOAT HEIAU SOLEA STAGE
STAND STOEP STOOL STOOP STULL
STUMP TOLDO ARBOUR AZOTEA
BRIDGE DESIGN GANTRY HURDLE
ISLAND MACHAN PAEPAE PALLET
PERRON PILLAR PODIUM PULPIT
RUNWAY SETTLE SLEDGE ALMEMAR
BALCONY BATTERY CATWALK
ESTRADE FORETOP GALLERY
LANDING LOGEION PADDOCK
PATTERN ROLLWAY ROSTRUM
SKIDWAY SOAPBOX TRIBUNE
FOOTPACE HUSTINGS SCAFFOLD
STALLAGE
(— **FOR ACTORS**) LOGEION
THEOLOGIUM
(— **FOR ALTAR**) PREDELLA
(— **FOR DRYING FISH**) FLAKE
(— **FOR PUBLIC SPEAKING**) BEMA
PODIUM TRIBUNE
(— **FOR STORING FOOD**) WHATA
(— **IN CHURCH**) SOLEA
(— **IN SYNAGOGUE**) ALMEMAR
(— **IN TEMPLE**) DUKAN
(— **IN TREE**) MACHAN
(— **OF GALLOWS**) DROP
(— **ON RUNNERS**) SLEDGE
(— **ON TOP OF HOUSE**) AZOTEA

(— **ON WHEELS**) SKID DOLLY FLOAT
(— **TO SUPPORT MINERS**) STULL
(**GUN** —) BARBET SPONSON
BARBETTE
(**LEADSMAN'S** —) CHAIN
(**MINE** —) STULL SOLLAR SOLLER
(**MOHAMMEDAN STONE** —)
MASTABA
(**MOUNTED** —) SKID
(**NAUTICAL** —) FORETOP MAINTOP
ROUNDTOP
(**ORE** —) BUDDLE
(**RAILROAD** —) DOCK DOCKEN
TRAINWAY
(**RAISED** —) DAIS PYAL STAND
STOEP STOOL STOOP LISSOM
PANTALAN
(**ROCK** —) STANCE
(**SLEEPING** —) KANG
(**STAIRCASE** —) HALFPACE
HATHPACE
(**WOOD** —) PLANCHER
PLATING ARMOR SKIRT
PLATINUM COSTLY PLATINA
PLATITUDE TRUISM BROMIDE
DULLNESS STALENESS TRITENESS
PLATONIST IDEIST
PLATOON SQUAD VOLLEY PELOTON
PLOTTON
PLATTER DISH DISK LANX ASHET
GRAIL PLATE RECORD CHARGER
TRENCHER
PLATY MOON MOONFISH
PLATYPUS DUCKBILL DUCKMOLE
MALLAGONG
PLAUDIT APPLAUD APPROVAL
ENCOMIUM
(PL.) PRAISE APPLAUSE
PLAUSIBILITY COLOR
PLAUSIBLE FAIR OILY SNOD GLOSSY
AFFABLE POPULAR CREDIBLE
PROBABLE PROVABLE SPECIOUS
SUITABLE
PLAY FUN JEU JIG RUN RUX TOY
AUTO BEAR COME DAFF DEAL DICE
DRAW FAIR GAME JEST LAKE MOVE
MUCK PLEE PUNT ROMP SPIN TUNE
WAKE CARRY CHARM DALLY DRAMA
ENACT FLIRT FROST HORSE SHOOT
SOTIE SOUND SPIEL SPORT STUCK
WREAK YEDDE ACTION COMEDY
COQUET DANDLE DIVIDE FILLER
FROLIC GAMBLE GAMBOL GAMING
GHOSTS MUSERY NUMBER PIDDLE
ROLLIX TRIFLE CONSORT CUTBACK
DISPORT EXECUTE EXPLOIT
GUIGNOL HISTORY HOLIDAY
MIRACLE PAGEANT PASSION
PRELUDE STAGERY VENTURE
BURLETTA MORALITY SKITTLES
(— **A DOMINO**) SET POSE
(— **A PART**) DO ACT ENTER
GAMMON GUIZARD
(— **A PIPE**) CHARM
(— **ABOUT**) SPANIEL
(— **AGAINST**) BUCK
(— **AN INSTRUMENT**) BOW BLOW
SWAY FINGER TWEEDLE
(— **AT COURTSHIP**) FLIRT

(— BAGPIPE) SKIRL DOODLE DOUDLE
(— BY STROKES) STRIKE
(— FANFARE) FLOURISH
(— FAST AND LOOSE) PALTER
(— FIRST CARD) LEAD
(— FLORIDLY) DIVIDE
(— FOR TIME) STALL
(— GOLF BALL) DRIVE
(— IMPOSTER) MUMP
(— IN MUD) MUDLARK
(— IN POOL) BURST
(— IN STREAKS) FORK
(— IN TRIGGER) CREEP
(— JAZZ) BLOW
(— LEGATO) SUSTAIN
(— LOOSELY) WAVE
(— LOUT) SWAB SLUBBER
(— MEAN TRICKS) SHAB
(— NERVOUSLY) FIDGET
(— OF COLORS) IRIS
(— OF FOAM) HOOD
(— OF LIGHT) GLORY
(— ON WORDS) PUN CLENCH CLINCH
(— THE BUFFOON) DROLL
(— THE BULLY) BLUSTER
(— THE FOOL) HOIT
(— THE HYPOCRITE) FACE
(— THE TOADY) SUPE
(— TRICKS) JAPE JINK
(— TRUANT) WAG JOUK MICHE MOOCH MOUCH PLUNK TRONE MOOTCH
(— UNSKILLFULLY) STRUM FOOZLE
(— WITH) DANDLE
(AMOROUS —) GAME
(BOISTEROUS —) ROMP
(BRIDGE —) COUP ECHO SIGNAL SQUEEZE
(END —) SHAKE
(FARCICAL —) SOTIE
(FOOTBALL —) DOWN KEEP SAFETY CUTBACK SPINNER
(IN —) ALIVE
(MASKED —) GUISE
(MIRACLE —) AUTO GUARY MIRACLE
(RAPID CHESS —) SKITTLES
(USED IN —) LUSORY
(PL.) THEATER VANGELI
LAYA BEACH SEBKA SALINA SEBKHA
LAY-BY-PLAY DETAILED
LAYER IT CAP END BACK DUCK SIDE ACTOR BLACK COLOR GUARD BANKER BUSKER FEEDER STAGER STROLL TENTER ALTOIST FIELDER FORWARD GAMBLER STRIKER TRIFLER TURQUET BUDGETER GAMESTER HORNSMAN STROLLER
(— IN CHESS) BLACK WHITE
(— IN CHOUETTE) CAPTAIN
(— OF JAZZ) CAT
(— WHO CUTS CARDS) PONE
(— WHO IS IT) HE
(— WHO SCORES ZERO) DUCK
(— WITH LOWEST SCORE) BOOBY
(BACKGAMMON —) TABLER

(BASEBALL —) SHORT SACKER CATCHER FIELDER LEADOFF PITCHER BACKSTOP
(BASKETBALL —) CAGEMAN HOOPMAN HOOPSTER
(BOWLING —) LEAD
(CARD —) EAST HAND PONE WEST BLIND DUMMY NORTH SOUTH JUNIOR SENIOR BRAGGER DECLARER
(CRICKET —) LEG BOWLER INNING
(CROQUET —) MALLET
(DICE —) SHOOTER
(FLUTE —) AULETE
(FOOTBALL —) END GUARD SLANT BUCKER CENTER TACKLE BLOCKER FLANKER GRIDDER SNAPPER FULLBACK HALFBACK SCATBACK
(LACROSSE —) HOME COVER ATTACK STICKMAN
(LEAPFROG —) BACK
(POKER —) AGE
(RUGBY —) SCRUM HOOKER
(SOCCER —) CAP INNER BOOTER
(STUPID —) HAM
(TENNIS —) SMASHER
(UNSKILLFUL —) DUB
(VOLLEYBALL —) SPIKER
(WEAK —) RABBIT
PLAYFUL ELFIN MERRY FRISKY GAMBOL JOCOSE LUSORY TOYISH WANTON COLTISH GIOCOSO JIGGISH JOCULAR TOYSOME GAMESOME HUMOROUS LARKSOME SPORTFUL SPORTIVE KITTENISH
PLAYFULNESS FUN BANTER GAMMICK GAMMOCK
PLAYGROUND OVAL CLOSE PLAYSTOW PLAYSTEAD
PLAYHOUSE HOUSE MOVIE CINEMA THEATER
PLAYING FROLIC LAKING
(— CARD) ACE JACK KING TREY DEUCE QUEEN TAROT
(— CARDS) DECK
(— LIGHTLY) LAMBENT
PLAYTHING DIE TOY HOOP KNACK PLAIK SPORT BAUBLE LAKING SUCKER TRIFLE PLAYOCK
PLAYWRIGHT AUTHOR DRAMATIST PLAYMAKER
PLAZA PLEIN SQUARE ZOCALO
(— DE TOROS) BULLRING
PLEA BAR BID PLY MOOT NOLO SUIT ALIBI CLAIM PLEAD ABATER APPEAL EXCUSE REFUGE APOLOGY CONTEND DEFENCE LAWSUIT PRETEXT QUARREL DILATORY ENTREATY PRETENSE
PLEACH PLAIT PLASH INTERLACE
PLEAD BEG SUE MOOT PLEA PRAY PRIG SHOW URGE COUNT ORATE ALLEGE APPEAL ASSERT PLAYTE PURSUE ENTREAT IMPLORE SOLICIT WRANGLE ADVOCATE LITIGATE
(— FOR) SOLICIT PETITION
PLEADER ACTOR VAKIL PATRON SUITOR VAKEEL COUNTOR ADVOCATE

PLEADING PLEA PAROL ANSWER PAROLE ADVOCACY COGNOVIT DEMURRER INTENDIT MEMORIAL
PLEASANT FUN GAY BEEN BIEN BRAW FAIR FINE GLAD GOOD HEND JOLI NEAT TRIM WEME BIGLY BONNY CANNY COUTH CUSHY DOUCE DRUNK DUCKY GREEN HAPPY HENDE HODDY JOLLY LEPID LISTY MERRY NUTTY QUEME SMIRK SUAVE SWEET TIPSY WALLY WETHE COMELY DAINTY DULCET GENIAL KINDLY SAVORY SMOOTH AFFABLE ELEGANT FARRAND JANNOCK LEESOME WINSOME DELICATE GLORIOUS GRATEFUL HEAVENLY LIEFSOME LIKESOME LOVESOME THANKFUL TOWARDLY
PLEASANTLY FAIR WINLY FAIRLY AFFABLY SWEETLY GENIALLY LIKINGLY
PLEASANTNESS GAIETY NAAMAN AMENITY SUAVITY JOCUNDITY
PLEASANTRY WIT JEST JOKE SPORT BANTER JESTING JOLLITY WAGGERY
PLEASE PAY GAME LIKE LIST LUST SUIT WANT WISH AGREE AMUSE BITTE CHARM ELATE FANCY HUMOR QUEME SAVOR TASTE ARRIDE KITTLE OBLIGE REGALE SOOTHE TICKLE CONTENT DELIGHT GLADDEN GRATIFY PLACATE REJOICE SATISFY APPLEASE
(— FORWARD) FS
PLEASED FAIN FOND GLAD APAID HAPPY PROUD BUCKED CONTENT GLADSOME
(BE —) GAME
PLEASING AMEN GLAD GOOD LIEF NICE SOFT AMENE DICTY SOOTH SWEET CLEVER DREAMY FACILE FLASHY GAINLY LIKING LUSTLY AMIABLE BLESSED CORKING DARLING LIKEFUL TUNABLE WELCOME CHARMING DELICATE FAVOROUS FETCHING GRACEFUL GRACIOUS GRATEFUL HEAVENLY INVITING LIKESOME PLACABLE PLAUSIVE SPECIOUS
(— TO EAR) HARMONIC
(— TO EYE) EESOME
(— TO HEAR) FAIR
(VERY —) SNAZZY
PLEASURABLE GOOD JOLLY ANIMAL MIRTHFUL
PLEASURE JO EST FUN JOY BANG BOOT EASE ESTE GREE KAMA LIST LUST PLAY WILL KICKS MIRTH SAVOR SOOTH TASTE DAINTY DEDUIT GAIETY GAYETY LIKING LUXURY NICETY VOLUPT COMFORT DELIGHT GRATIFY JOLLITY JOYANCE VOLUPTY DELICACY FRUITION GLADNESS HILARITY VOLUPTAS
(SELFISH —) LECHERY
(STOLEN —) STOUTH STOWTH
(PL.) DELICIAE
PLEASURE SEEKER FRANION

PLEAT SET FOLD POKE FLUTE FRILL PINCH PLAIT PRANK GUSSET SUNRAY

PLEATED SUNBURST

PLEBE PLEBS FRESHMAN

PLEBEIAN LOW BASE PLEB SNOB COMMON HOMELY VULGAR IGNOBLE LOWBORN POPULAR BASEBORN EVERYDAY HOMESPUN INFERIOR MECHANIC ORDINARY RUPTUARY

PLEBISCITE VOTE DECREE

PLECTRUM PICK SPUR QUILL UVULA MALLEUS POINTEL PLECTRON (— OF HARP) FESCUE

PLEDGE LAY VAS VOW WAD WED BAND CLAP EARL GAGE HAND HEST HOCK PASS PAWN WAGE WOID WORD FAITH SIKER SPOUT STAKE SWEAR SWEAT TOKEN TROTH TRUTH WAGER ARREST BORROW COMMIT ENGAGE IMPAWN IMPONE LUMBER PIGNUS PLEVIN PLIGHT SICCAR SICKER VADIUM WADSET BARGAIN BETROTH CAUTION EARNEST HOSTAGE PROMISE BOTTOMRY MORTGAGE SECURITY SPONSION VADIMONY (— IN DRINKING) PROPINE

PLEDGED HIGHT SWORN ASSURED ENGAGED PIGNORATE (— TO MARRY) SURE

PLEDGET DOSSIL

PLEIADES MAIA MEROPE ALCYONE CELAENO ELECTRA STEROPE TAYGETA

PLEIN-AIRIST LUMINIST

PLEISTHENES (FATHER OF —) ATREUS (MOTHER OF —) AEROPE (SON OF —) MENELAUS AGAMEMNON

PLENARY FULL ENTIRE PLENAL PERFECT ABSOLUTE COMPLETE

PLENITUDE PLENITY PLEROMA FULLNESS PLETHORA ABUNDANCE

PLENTEOUS RICH COPIOUS FERTILE AFFLUENT FRUITFUL GENEROUS ABOUNDING EXUBERANT

PLENTIFUL OLD FULL RANK RICH RIFE AMPLE HEFTY LARGE ROUTH SONSY STORE ENOUGH GALORE LAVISH SONSIE COPIOUS FERTILE LIBERAL OPULENT PROFUSE UBEROUS ABUNDANT FRUITFUL NUMEROUS EXUBERANT

PLENTIFULLY RIFE FREELY GALORE APLENTY

PLENTY WON BAIT COPY MANY RAFF SONS AMPLE CHEAP COPIA FOUTH PRICE ROUTH SONSE TEEMS FOISON SCOUTH UBERTY LASHINGS (GREAT —) LASHINGS

PLEON TELSON ABDOMEN

PLEONASM ITERATION MACROLOGY TAUTOLOGY

PLETHORA EXCESS PLURISY FULLNESS PLEURISY POLYEMIA PROFUSION REPLETION

PLETHORIC TUMID TURGID

SWOLLEN INFLATED

PLEURISY EMPYEMA

PLEURON SCAPULA

PLEXUS RETE GLOMUS NETWORK PROPLEX GENIPLEX

PLIABLE WAXY WEAK LITHY WAXEN DOCILE LIMBER PLIANT SEMMIT SUPPLE BOWABLE FICTILE FINGENT FLEXILE PLASTIC WINDING CUSHIONY FLEXIBLE COMPLIANT

PLIANCY FLEXURE FACILITY

PLIANT APT FLIP SWAK BUXOM LITHE SWACK YOUNG DOCILE LIMBER SUPPLE DUCTILE FLEXILE PLIABLE SLIPPER WILLOWY APPLIANT FLEXIBLE SUITABLE WORKABLE

PLICA FOLD TRICHOMA

PLICATE FOLD PLEAT FOLDED FANLIKE PLAITED

PLIERS BENDER FLEXOR GRATER FLECTOR PINCERS

PLIGHT PLY FOLD ARRAY BRAID DRESS PLAIT POINT STATE WOVEN ATTIRE ENGAGE PICKLE PLEDGE PLISKY TAKING BETROTH MISCHIEF

PLIGHTED ASSURATE

PLIM PLUM STOUT SWELL INFLATE PLIABLE

PLINTH ORLE ORLO BLOCK ABACUS PATAND QUADRA SUBBASE FOOTSTALL SCAMILLUS

PLOD JOG GRUB PLOT SLOG STOG TORE TROG VAMP POACH TRAMP TRASH DRUDGE SLOUCH TRUDGE PLUNTHER (— ALONG) PEG TORE (— THROUGH MUD) SLOUGH

PLODDER GRUB DIGGER SLOGGER

PLOIARIA EMESA

PLOP FLUMP PLUMP HEAVILY

PLOT BREW CAST PACK PLAN PLAT CABAL DRIFT FRAUD GLEBE GRAPH GREEN HATCH MODEL PLECK SCALD STORY STUDY WATCH ACTION BRIGUE CLIQUE DESIGN DEVISE GARDEN MALIGN MYTHOS SCHEME SHAMBA TAMPER AGITATE COLLUDE COMPACT COMPASS CONJECT CONNIVE CONTOUR DRAUGHT FEEDLOT LAZYBED MACHINE PRETEND QUADRAT QUARTER SWIDDEN ARGUMENT COGITATE CONSPIRE CONTRIVE INTRIGUE PRACTICE PROTRACT SEMINARY (— OF 1-2 ACRE) ERF (— OF GRASS) SONK (— OF LAND) ERF LOT PLAT SHOT FORTY MILPA PATCH PLECK SPLAT COMMON SCHERM SHAMBA HAGGARD LAZYBED SEVERAL (GARDEN —) BED ERF QUINTA QUARTER (UNPRODUCTIVE —) HIRST

PLOTTER PACKER HATCHER JACOBIN SCHEMER DESIGNER ENGINEER

PLOUK KNOB PIMPLE

PLOVER DROME KOLEA OXEYE PILOT SANDY STILT KILDEE QUAILY TURNIX COLLIER COURSER DOTTREL LAPWING MAYCOCK OWLHEAD PAPABOT WRYBILL BULLHEAD DULWILLY HILLBIRD KILLDEER RINGNECK SPURWING SQUEALER TOADHEAD WHISTLER WIREBIRD

PLOW EAR ERE BOUT DISK FOIL HINT MOLE PLOD RIVE ROVE SLUG STIR SULK SULL TILL BREAK FLUNK SPLIT SULKY THROW ARAIRE BUSTER DIGGER FALLOW FURROW GOPHER JUMPER LISTER PLOUGH RAFTER ROOTER RUTTER SULLOW BACKSET BREAKER HUSBAND SCOOTER SULCATE TWISTER FIREPLOW FURROWER GANGPLOW SNOWPLOW TURNPLOW (— CROSSWISE) THORTER (— HANDLE) STILT (— LIGHTLY) SKIM RIFFLE (— PART) PINHEAD (PL.) OUTSIGHT

PLOWBOY YOKEL

PLOWING ARDER EARTH ARDURE ARATION CARUAGE STIRRING

PLOWLAND CARUE CARVE TILTH CARUCATE TEAMLAND

PLOWMAN PLOWER TILLER ACREMAN

PLOWSHARE LAY SLIP SOCK LAVER REEST SHARE JUMPER (— BONE) VOMER PYGOSTYLE

PLOY BENT BOWED SPORT RAMBLE TACTIC PURSUIT ACTIVITY ESCAPADE

PLUCK GO PUG ROB TUG BOUT CROP CULL DRAG GAME GRAB PELT PICK PILL POOK PULL RACE RASE RASH SAND TUCK ARBER ARBOR BREAK DRAFT HANGE NERVE PILCH PLOAT PLUME RANCH SMITE SPUNK STEAL STRIP AVULSE DECERP EVULSE FLEECE GATHER PIGEON PLITCH PLOUGH QUARRY SNATCH SPIRIT TWINGE TWITCH COURAGE DEPLUME PLUNDER BOLDNESS DECISION DEMOLISH GAMENESS (— AS A STRING) TIRL PINCH (— FEATHERS) STUB (— LEAVES) BLADE (— OF SHEEP OR CALF) RACE GATHER (— UP COURAGE) CHEER (— WOOL BY HAND) ROO

PLUCKED PLUMED PIZZICATO

PLUCKY GAMY SANDY GRITTY SPUNKY FIGHTING

PLUG BUG FID PEG PIN TAP TOP WAD BLOW BONE BOTT BUNG FILL JADE ROOT SHOT SLOG STOP SWAT SWOT BOOST DOWEL DUMMY PILOT PUNCH SHACK SKATE SPILE STUFF SWEAT BOXING BULLET COMEDO DOSSIL DOTTLE FIDDLE SPIGOT BOUCHON BUSHING CHAMBER CHUGGER FERRULE STOPPER

STOPPLE DRIVECAP FUSEPLUG PELELITH STOPCOCK
(— FOR CANNON) TAMPION
(— IN GRENADE) BOUCHON
(— IN ORGAN PIPE) STOPPLE TAMPION
(— OF CLAY) BOTT
(— OF OAKUM) FID
(— OF VOLCANO) CORE
(— UP) CLAM STOP ESTOP RAMFORCE
(FISHING —) BUG
(NOSE —) TEMBETA TEMBETARA
(WASTE —) WASHER
(WATER —) HYDRANT
PLUG-IN JACK
PLUG-UGLY THUG ROWDY TOUGH RUFFIAN ROUGHNECK
PLUM GAGE JOBO RISE ISLAY JAMAN PRUNE SWELL BEAUTY CHENEY DAMSEL DAMSON KELSEY SAPOTE APRICOT BULLACE BURBANK FORTUNE ORLEANS PRUNELLO ROSACEAN ROSEWORT VICTORIA WINDFALL
(COCO —) ICACO
(JAVA —) DUHAT JAMBUL JAMBOOL JAMBOLAN
(WILD —) SKEG SLOE ISLAY
PLUMAGE ROBE FLUFF HACKLE SHROUD FEATHER FLOCCUS JUVENAL PENNAGE FEATHERS PARADISE PTILOSIS
(— ON HELMET) CREST PANACHE
(— ON HORSE) PLUMADE
(— ON TURBAN) CULGEE
(EGRET —) OSPREY
(MILITARY —) PANACHE
LUME NUTMEG SASSAFRAS
LUMMET LEAD FLOAT PLUMB WEIGHT
LUMMING BRONZING
LUMP FAT BOLD FAIR FLOP FULL PLOP SLAP SOSS TIDY BLUNT BONNY CLUMP FLUMP FUBBY FUBSY GROUP JOLLY PLUNK SAPPY SLEEK SMACK SQUAB STOUT THICK BONNIE CHUBBY CRUMBY CRUMMY DIRECT FATTEN FLATLY FLESHY FODGEL GAWSIE PLUNGE PUBBLE ROTUND BLUNTLY BUNTING CLUSTER DISTEND FULSOME RIBLESS THRODDY FLESHFUL
(— AND ROSY) BUXOM
(— AND ROUND) CHUBBY
UM POCKET FOOL
LUMULE FEATHER GEMMULA GEMMULE GEOBLAST ACROSPIRE

PLUNDER GUT ROB BOOT FANG JUNK LOOT PILL POLL PREY RAPE REIF RIPE RUMP SACK SWAG BOOTY CHEAT GAINS HARRY PLUCK PREDE RAVEN RENNE RIFLE SCOFF SHAVE SPOIL STRIP BEZZLE BOODLE CREACH DACOIT FLEECE FORAGE HARROW MARAUD PANYAR PROFIT RAPINE RAVAGE DESPOIL ESCHEAT FREIGHT PILFERY PILLAGE SACKAGE SPULZIE BOOTHALE FREEBOOT
PLUNDERER THIEF BANDIT BUMMER POLLER RAPTOR ROBBER VANDAL ROUTIER SPOILER MARAUDER RAPPAREE
PLUNDERING PREY SACK MARAUD RAPINE ESCHEAT PURCHASE SPECHERY SPOILFUL SPOILING PREDATORY
PLUNGE BET DIG DIP CAVE DIVE DOOK DUCK DUMP JUMP PURL PUSH RAKE RISK SINK SOSS BURST DOUSE FLING PITCH PLUMP SOUSE SWOOP FOOTER GAMBLE HEADER LAUNCH SPLASH THRUST WALLOP BRAINGE IMMERSE PLOUNCE SUBMERGE
(— INTO WATER) ENEW
(— INTO) CLAP ENGULF IMMERGE
PLUNGER RAM SWAB FORCE DUCKER POMMEL BLUNGER STRIKER
PLUNGING FLING
PLUNK DIVE PLONK PLUCK PLUMP DOLLAR SUPPORT SUDDENLY
PLUNTHER PLOD FLOUNDER
PLURALIST TOTQUOT
PLURALITY MAJORITY MORENESS TRIALITY
PLUS GAIN WITH EXTRA SURPLUS ADDITION INCREASE POSITIVE
PLUSH EASY BEAVER VELOUR SUPERIOR
PLUSHY SWANK SWANKY
PLUTEUS WAGON PARAPET
PLUTO DIS HADES ORCUS
(BROTHER OF —) JUPITER NEPTUNE
(FATHER OF —) SATURN
(WIFE OF —) PROSERPINE
PLUTOCRAT NABOB RICHARD
PLUTONIC HYPOGENE INTRUSIVE VULCANIAN
PLUTUS (ASSOCIATE OF —) TYCHE EIRENE
(FATHER OF —) IASION
(MOTHER OF —) DEMETER
PLY RUN BEAT BEND BIAS CORD CORE DRAM FOLD MOLD SAIL URGE ADAPT APPLY EXERT LAYER STEER TWIST WIELD YIELD COMPLY DOUBLE HANDLE TRAVEL EXERCISE
(— WITH DRINK) BIRL ROSIN
(— WITH DRUGS) HOCUS
(OF ONE —) SINGLE
PNEUMA NEUM SOUL NEUME BREATH SPIRIT
PNEUMATIC HAMMER GUN
PNEUMATOCYST FLOAT

PNEUMONIA PULMONITIS
POACH PUG ROB COOK DROP POKE PUSH SINK BLACK DRIVE FORCE POTCH STEAL BLEACH PLUNGE INTRUDE
POACHED EGGS MOONSHINE
POACHER BLACK POGGE SPOACH LURCHER STALKER WIDGEON BALDPATE BULLHEAD
(SALMON —) REBECCA REBEKAH
(PL.) BLACKS
POALES GLUMALES
POCHARD DUCK SMEE DIVER POKER SCAUP DUNAIR DUNKER DUNBIRD REDHEAD WHINGER GOLDHEAD WHINYARD
POCHETTE KIT VIOLIN HANDBAG
POCKET BOX CLY FOB PIT CLAY KICK POKE PRAT BASIN BURSE MEANS POUCH PURSE STEAL ACCEPT BECKET CASING CANTINA PLACKET SWALLOW TROUSER ENVELOPE ISOLATED MONETARY PROFONDE SUPPRESS CONDENSED MINIATURE
(— A WRONG) PURSE
(BILLIARD —) POT HOLE HAZARD
(MAGICIAN'S —) PROFONDE
(NOODLE —S) KREPLACH
(ORE —) CHURN BONANZA
(SMALL —) FOB
(TROUSER —) FOB PRAT BECKET
(WATER —) TINAJA ALBERCA
(PL.) KREPLACH
POCKETBOOK BAG KICK SKIN PURSE INCOME READER WALLET HANDBAG LEATHER BILLFOLD NOTECASE
POCKET GOPHER TUZA QUACHIL
POCKETING COUP
POCKETKNIFE PIGSTICKER
POCKMARK PITHOLE
POD BAG COD GAM KID POP SAC BALL BEAN BOLL HUSK POKE SWAD BURSE CAROB FLOCK POUCH QUASH SHAUP SHELL SHUCK SNAIL WHAUP LEGUME PESCOD SCHOOL HARICOT PEASCOD PEASECOD PODOCARP POTBELLY SEEDCASE TAMARIND
(— FORMING) KID
(— OF LEGUME) KID
(— OF MESQUITE) HONEYPOD
(EXPLOSIVE —) SANDBOX
(SUBTERRANEAN —) EARTHNUT
(UNRIPE —) SQUASH
(PL.) SUNT GARAD BABLAH GARRAT GONAKIE ALGAROBA
PODIUM DAIS FOOT WALL LECTERN
PODOCARP YACCA
PODWARE PODDER
POEM GEM LAI LAY ODE DUAN EPIC JOSE MELE POSY RUNE SONG DIRGE DITTY HAIKU IWEIN METER STAFF VERSE AMHRAN AUBADE BALLAD CACCIA CARMEN CYCLIC DIXAIN EPOPEE EROTIC ESTRIF HEROID MELODY MONODY PIYYUT SESTET SONNET TENSON TERCET

BUCOLIC CANTARE CANTATA
CANZONE DESCORT DIZAINE
ECLOGUE ELEGIAC FLITING
GEORGIC SOTADIC TRIOLET VIRELAI
VIRELAY VOLUSPA ACROSTIC
AMOEBEUM BRINDISI CANTICLE
DINGDONG DOGGEREL INVICTUS
LIMERICK MADRIGAL TELESTIC
THEOGONY TRISTICH TROCHAIC
VERSICLE
(— ABOUT DEBATE) ESTRIF
(— ABOUT SHEPHERDS) ECLOGUE
(— GREETING DAWN) AUBADE
(— OF 10 LINES) DIZAINE
(— OF 14 LINES) SONNET
(— OF LAMENTATION) ELEGY
(AMATORY —) EROTIC SONNET
(EPIC —) EPOS EPOPEE LUSIAD
THEBAID
(HOMELY —) DIT
(IRISH —) AMHRAN
(JAPANESE —) HAIKU
(LITURGICAL —) VIDDUI VIDDUY
SELIHOTH
(LOVE —) AMORETTO
(LYRIC —) LAI LAY ODE ALBA
EPODE GHAZEL RONDEL CANZONA
PARTIMEN
(PART OF —) PASSUS
(PASTORAL —) IDYL IDYLL BUCOLIC
(PERSIAN —) GHAZAL
(RELIGIOUS —) HYMN
(RURAL —) GEORGIC
(SACRED —) PSALM YIGDAL
(SATIRICAL —) IAMBIC KASIDA
(SHORT —) DIT DITTY EPILOG
SONNET EPIGRAM EPILOGUE
EPYLLION
(TONE —) BALLADE
(WELSH —) CYWYDD
(PL.) AZAHROT MAKINGS
POET OG RSI BARD FILE FILI FIRI
LARK MUSE SCOP SWAN ARION
LAKER LINOS LINUS LYRIC MAKAR
MAKER ODIST RISHI SAYER SCALD
SKALD FINDER GNOMIC IBYCUS
LAKIST LYRIST SHAPER SINGER
DICHTER ELEGIAC EPICIST IDYLIST
IMAGIST MUSAEUS ORPHEUS
PROPHET FERAMORZ GEORGIAN
LAUREATE LUTANIST MINSTREL
SONGSTER TROUVERE
(IRISH —) FILI
(MEDIOCRE —) RIMER RHYMER
(MINOR —) BARDIE
POETASTER BARDET BAVIAN BAVIUS
POETITO BARDLING VERSEMAN
POETIC ODIC LYRIC STILTED
PEGASEAN POEMATIC
POETRY SONG BLANK MELIC POEMS
VERSE EPOPEE POESIS SONIOU
DOGGREL KALEVALA
(FINNISH —) RUNES
(GOD OF —) BRAGI
(MUSE OF —) ERATO THALIA
EUTERPE CALLIOPE
POGROM RIOT PILLAGE MASSACRE
POGY POGIE MENHADEN
POIGNANT APT HOME KEEN ACUTE

SHARP SMART BITING BITTER
MOVING SEVERE URGENT CUTTING
POINTED PUNGENT SATIRIC INCISIVE
PIERCING PRESSING STINGING
STRIKING TOUCHING AMAREVOLE
POINCIANA DELONIX FLAMBEAU
GULMOHAR FLAMBOYER
POINSETTIA BANNER FIREFLOWER
POINT AIM DOT JOT NAK NEB NIB
NUB PEG PIN RES WAY APEX BACK
BOKE CHAT CUSP FORK GAFF GAME
GOOD HEAD HOLD ITEM KNOT LACE
LOOK NAIL PEAK PICK PILE PINT
SPOT STOP WHET BEARD CHALK
DIGIT FOCUS INDEX LEVEL MUCRO
PITCH PRICK PUNCH PUNCT PUNTA
PUNTO REFER STAND TEACH THING
TOOTH ALLUDE BROACH CRAYON
CUSPIS CUTOFF DEGREE DIRECT
FLECHE JUGALE MATTER NOSING
PERIOD THESIS TITTLE VERTEX
ZYGION APICULA ARTICLE BENEFIT
CRUNODE ESSENCE GATEWAY
PUSHPIN SHARPEN TANJONG
TRAGION ANNOUNCE PUNCTULE
STRIPPER
(— AT ISSUE) BEEF CRUX
(— AT WHICH LEAF SPRINGS) AXIL
(— BEHIND EAR) ASTERION
(— FOR PHONOGRAPH RECORD)
STYLE
(— IN CAPSTAN) STRIPPER
(— IN CONSONANT) DAGHESH
(— IN DEBATE) ISSUE
(— IN ORBIT OF PLANET) AUGE
APSIS APOGEE SYZYGY APOJOVE
PERIGEE APASTRON APHELION
(— IN QUESTION) ISSUE
(— IN SEVEN-UP) GIFT
(— IN SOME GAMES) PUNT
(— NEAREST EARTH) PERIGEE
(— OF A BORDER) VANDYKE
(— OF ANCHOR) BILL
(— OF ANTLER) PRONG
(— OF ANVIL) HORN
(— OF CELESTIAL SPHERE)
ANTAPEX
(— OF CHIN) BUTTON
(— OF CONTACT) EPHAPSE
(— OF CRESCENT MOON) CUSP
(— OF DECLINE) EBB
(— OF DIVERGENCE) AXIL
(— OF ECLIPTIC) LAGNA SOLSTICE
(— OF EPIGRAM) STING
(— OF HONOR) PUNDONOR
(— OF INTEREST) CLOU
(— OF INTERSECTION) FOOT
STAURION
(— OF JAVELIN) SAGAIE
(— OF JUNCTION) MEET BREGMA
LAMBDA
(— OF LABEL) LAMBEAU
(— OF LAND) ODD CAPE SPIT
MORRO HEADLAND
(— OF LEAF) MUCRO
(— OF LIFE) HYLEG
(— OF LIGHT) GLINT SPANGLE
(— OF LIGHTNING ROD) AIGRETTE
(— OF LIPS) CHEILION

(— OF MANGO) NAK
(— OF ONSET) BRINK
(— OF ORIGIN) HIVE SOURCE
FOUNTAIN
(— OF PEN) NEB NIB
(— OF PETAL) LACINULA
(— OF REFERENCE) STYLION
(— OF STAG'S HORN) START
(— OF STORY) KNOT
(— OF STYLUS) CUTTER
(— OF SUPPORT) BEARING
(— OF TEMPERATURE) SOLIDUS
(— OF TIME) DATE INSTANT
JUNCTURE
(— OF TOOTH) CUSP
(— OF UMBRELLA) FERRULE
(— OF VIEW) EYE ANGLE FRONT
SLANT COLORS CORNER GROUND
RESPECT FUTURISM
(— OF VIOLIN BOW) HEAD
(— OF WEAPON) BARB
(— ON AUGER OR BIT) SPUR
(— ON BACKGAMMON BOARD)
FLECHE
(— ON CURVE) TACNODE
(— ON JAW) GONION
(— ON STAG'S HORN) BROACH
(— ON SUNDIAL) NODE
(— OUT) SHOW DIGIT INFER ASSIGN
DIRECT ENSIGN FINGER MUSTER
NOTIFY REMARK PRESAGE INDICAT
(ASTROLOGICAL —) INGRESS
(BARBED —) FORK
(BLUNT —) MORNETTE
(CARBON —) CRAYON
(CARDINAL —) EAST WEST HINGE
NORTH SOUTH
(CARDINAL —S) CARDINES
(CHRONOLOGICAL —) ERA EPOCH
(COMPASS —) E N S W NE NW SE
SW ENE ESE NNE NNW SSE SSW
WNW WSW AIRT AIRTH RHUMB
COURSE
(CRITICAL —) JUMP
(CROWNING —) CAPSHEAF
CAPSTONE
(CRUCIAL —) CRUX
(CULMINATING —) HEAD COMBLE
(DOUBLE — OF CURVE) ACNODE
CRUNODE
(ESSENTIAL —) MAIN
(EXACT —) TEE
(EXCESS —S) LAP
(EXCLAMATION —) BANG
SCREAMER
(EXTREME —) END
(FARTHEST —) APOGEE SOLSTICE
(FINAL —) UPCOME
(FIXED —) ABUTMENT
(GLAZIER'S —) SPRIG
(HALFWAY — IN CRIBBAGE)
CORNER
(HIGHEST —) TIP ACME APEX AUG
NOON PEAK CREST FLOOD APOGE
CLIMAX HEIGHT PERIOD SUMMIT
VERTEX ZENITH EVEREST MAXIMU
MERIDIAN SOLSTICE
(LAST —) END
(LATERAL —) ALARE

(LOWEST — OF HULL) BILGE
(LOWEST —) NADIR BOTTOM
BEDROCK
(MAIN —) JET SUM GIST
(MEDIAN —) HORMION
(NO —S) LOVE
(ONE'S STRONG —) FORTE
(PEDAL —) DRONE
(PIVOTAL —) KNUCKLE
(PRECISE —) NICK
(PROJECTING —) CRAG PEAK
BEARD
(SHARP —) PRICK PRICKLE
(SINGLE —) ACE
(SKULL —) TYLION
(STATIONARY —) SPINODE
(STRIKING —) SALIENCE
(STRONG —) FORTE
(TAPERING —) ACUMEN
(TENNIS —) LET CHASE BISQUE
(TENTH OF —) MOMENT
(TERMINAL —) GOAL BOURN BREAK
AIRPORT
(TO THE —) COGENT
(TOP —) TUFT
(TURNING —) CARDO EPOCH CRISIS
(UNIPLANAR —) UNODE
(UTMOST —) EXTREME SUBLIME
(VANTAGE —) TOWER
(VOWEL —) SERE
(WEAK —) BLOT
OINT-BLANK BLUNT PLAIN POINT
DIRECT WHOLLY EXPRESS DIRECTLY
OINTED SET HOME ACUTE EXACT
FIXED PEAKY PIKED TANGY TERSE
FITCHE LIVELY OXEOTE PEAKED
PECKED PICKED SPIRED ANGULAR
FITCHEE LACONIC PRECISE SPICATE
ZESTFUL ACICULAR ACULEATE
CULTRATE DIACTINE PUNCTUAL
STELLATE
OINTER TIP YAD COCK HAND
WAND DUBHE INDEX POINT FESCUE
FINGER GUNDOG INDICE SILKER
STYLUS FLUSHER INDICANT
SIGNITOR
(— IN GREAT BEAR) DUBHE DUBBHE
(— ON ASTROLABE) ALMURY
(— ON GAUGE) ARM
(TEACHER'S —) FESCUE
(PL.) MEN GUARDS YADAYIM
OINTLESS DRY ILL DULL FLAT
INANE SILLY VAPID FRIGID STUPID
INSIPID WITLESS
OINTSMAN TRAPPER LATCHMAN
SWITCHMAN
OISE PEE CALM HEAD REST SWAY
TACT BRACE PEIZE APLOMB OFFSET
PONDER BALANCE BEARING DIGNITY
OPPRESS POISURE DELIVERY
EASINESS SERENITY
(— RECIPROCAL) RHE
OISED SET FACILE HOVERING
(BE —) LIBRATE
OISER HALTER
OISON FIG GAS BANE BIKH DRAB
DRUG GALL TUBA VERY ATTER
TAINT TOXIN VENOM VIRUS ANTIAR
DERRIS INFECT RANKLE TOXIFY

TOXOID BABASCO CORRUPT
ENVENOM FLYBANE PERVERT
PHALLIN TANGHIN VITIATE
ACQUETTA DELETERY RATSBANE
VENENATE
(— IN DEATH CUP) PHALLIN
(ARROW —) HAYA INEE URALI
ANTIAR ANTJAR CURARE CURARI
DERRIS
(FISH —) AKIA CUBE DERRIS HAIARI
BABASCO BARBASCO
(RAT —) ANTU
(VIRULENT —) BIKH TANGHIN
POISONED BUCKEYED TOXICATE
VENENATE VENOMOUS
POISONER SEPSIN CANIDIA VENEFIC
VENOMER
POISON HEMLOCK BUNK CICUTA
POISONING PYEMIA GASSING
JIMMIES BOTULISM MYCETISM
PLUMBISM ICHTHYISM LATHYRISM
POISON IVY CLIMATH MARKERY
MERCURY MARKWEED
POISON OAK YEARA
POISONOUS ATTRY TOXIC ATTERY
VENENE VIROSE VIROUS NOISOME
NOXIOUS DELETERY MEPHITIC
TOXICANT VENENATE VENOMOUS
VIRULENT MALIGNANT
POISON SUMAC BURTREE
DOGWOOD
POISON TOBACCO HENBANE
POISONWOOD BUMWOOD
POITREL ARMOR PECTRON
POKE BAG DAB DIG DUB HIT JAB
JOG PUG PUR TIG WAD BROD PAUT
PORR PROD PROG RAUK RUCK
SACK SOCK STAB STIR NIDGE
POACH PROKE PROTE PUNCH
ROUSE STEER STOKE COWBOY
DAWDLE INCITE PIERCE POCKET
POUNCE POUTER PUGGLE PUTTER
WALLET PRODDLE
(— ABOUT) ROKE
(— AROUND) ROOT SCROUNGE
(— LIGHTLY) POTTER PUTTER
(— WITH FOOT) SCUFF
(— WITH NOSE) SNUZZLE
POKE-IN STRANDER
POKELOKEN BOGAN LOGAN
POKER DART DRAW FLIP POIT PORR
POTE STUD BLUFF BOGIE CURATE
GOBLIN STOKER ACEPOTS
FRUGGAN LOWBALL PASSOUT
POCHARD SHOTGUN BASEBALL
COALRAKE JACKPOTS MISTIGRI
SHOWDOWN
(— CHIP) JETON JETTON
(— HAND) RUNT FLUSH SKEET
KILTER PELTER STRAIGHT
(FORM OF —) DRAW STUD
POKEWEED POKE POCAN SCOKE
COAKUM GARGET FOXGLOVE
INKBERRY REDBERRY
POKY DEAD DULL JAIL SLOW DOWDY
POKEY POKING SHABBY STODGY
STUFFY STUPID CRAMPED TEDIOUS

POLAND

CAPITAL: WARSAW
COIN: DUCAT GROSZ MARKA
ZLOTY FENNIG HALERZ KORONA
DANCE: POLKA MAZURKA
KRAKOWIAK POLONAISE
GENTRY: SZLACHTA
LAKE: GOPLO MAMRY SNIARDWY
MEASURE: CAL MILA MORG PRET
LINJA MORGA SAZEN STOPA
VLOKA WLOKA CWIERK KORZEC
KWARTA LOKIEC GARNIEC
MOUNTAIN: TATRA SUDETEN
NAME: POLONIA SARMATIA
NATIVE: SLAV MARUR SILESIAN
PARLIAMENT: SEJM SEYM SENAT
RIVER: BUG SAN BRDA GWDA
LYNA NYSA ODER STYR BIALA
BZURA DRANA DWINA NOTEC
SERET WARTA WISTA NEISSE
NIEMEN PILICA PRIPET PROSNA
STRYPA WIEPRZ VISTULA
WISTOKA DNIESTER
TITLE OF ADDRESS: PAN PANI
PANIE
TOWN: LWO KOLO LIDA LODZ
LVOV OELS BREST BYTOM
CHELM POSEN RADOM SRODA
TORUN VILNA GDANSK GDYNIA
GRODNO KRACOW KRAKOW
LUBLIN POZNAN TARNOW
WARSAW ZABRZE BEUTHEN
BRESLAU CHORZOW GAROCIN
GLIWICE LEMBERG LITOUSK
WROCLAW GLEIWITZ KATOWICE
SZCZECIN TARNOPOL
WEIGHT: LUT FUNT UNCYA
KAMIAN CENTNER SKRUPUL

POLAK BALSA POLLACK
POLAR ARCTIC EMANANT PIVOTAL
DIRECTRIX
POLARIS ALRUCABA
POLE BAR LAT LEG LUG POL POY
ROD SKY XAT BEAM BIND BROG
COPE FALL HOOK KENT MAST NEAP
PALO PERK PIKE PROP SKID SPAR
TREE UFER CABER FOCUS MASUR
MAZUR PERCH QUANT REACH
SHAFT SPEAR SPOKE STAFF STANG
STILT STING STODE SWAPE SWIPE
BEACON BORITY CROTCH FLOWER
IMPOSE JUFFER KILHIG RICKER
RISSLE RYPECK SPONGE STOWER
TONGUE BARLING HEAVENS
TOWMAST ALESTAKE FLAGPOLE
FOOTPICK POLANDER STANDARD
(— AS EMBLEM OF SOVEREIGNTY)
KAHILI
(— AS HOLDFAST FOR BOATS)
RYPECK
(— FOR BEARING COFFIN) SPOKE
(— FOR PROPELLING BOAT) POY
(— FOR TOSSING) CABER KEBAR
(— HOLDING SAIL) BOOM MAST
SPRIT
(— OF TIMBER WAGON) NIB JANKER

(— OF VEHICLE) NEAP
(— ON TWO WHEELS) JANKER
(— USED AS SIGN) ALEPOLE
ALESTAKE
(— WITH BIRD DECOY) STOOL
(BOAT —) SPRIT
(CARRIAGE —) BEAM
(COUPLING —) REACH
(FIR —) UFER UPHER JUFFER
(FISHING —) WAND
(FORKED —) CROTCH
(LOGGING —) JANKER KILHIG KILLIG
(LONG —) PEW
(MANGROVE —) BORITY
(MINE —S) LAGGING
(NEGATIVE —) CATHODE
(PUNT —) QUANT STOWER
(RANGE —) FLAG
(SACRED —) ASHERAH
(SHEPHERD'S —) KENT
(SPRINGY —) BINDER
(STABLE —) BAIL
(STOUT —) KILHIG RICKER
(WATER-RAISING —) SWEEP
POLEAX STAFF POLEARM
POLECAT FITCH SKUNK ZORIL
FERRET FICHAT WEASEL FOUMART
FOULMART PERWITSKY SARMATIER
(— PELT) FITCH
POLE FLOUNDER SOLE
POLEHEAD TADPOLE
POLESTAR STAR GUIDE POLARIS
LODESTAR
POLICE GUARD WATCH GOVERN
CONTROL JEMADAR OCHRANA
POLIZEI PROTECT TOXOTAE
OPRICHNIC
(SECRET —) CHEKA
POLICEMAN COP JOE KID NAB PIG
BULL FLIC FUZZ GRAB JACK JOHN
PEON SLOP TRAP ZARP BOBBY
BULKY BURLY GAZER PEACE RURAL
SCREW SEPOY ASKARI BADGER
BOBBIE COPPER FISCAL FLATTY
HARMAN JOHNNY PEELER REDCAP
RUNNER SHAMUS CRUSHER
FOOTMAN GHAFFIR GUMSHOE
JEMADAR OFFICER SHOOFLY
TROOPER ZAPTIAH BARGELLO
BLUECOAT DOGBERRY FLATFOOT
GENDARME MINISTER
(CLUB OF —) BILLY STAFF
SPONTOON TRUNCHEON
(PL.) FINEST
POLICE STATION THANA BARGELLO
KOTWALEE
POLICY WIT DEAL FRONT ORDER
GOVERN NUMBER TICKET WISDOM
AUTARKY COUNSEL CUNNING
FLOATER LEFTISM LOTTERY
TONTINE VOUCHER ARTIFICE
SAGACITY STATEWAY
(CHOSEN —) COURSE
(PL.) APRISMO
POLISH BOB LAP MOP RUB RUD
BUFF DUCO FILE POLE CLEAN
FRUSH GLAZE GLOSS GRACE RABAT
ROUND SHINE SLICK STONE AFFILE
BARREL LUSTER PUNISH REFINE

RUMBLE SHAMMY SLIGHT SMOOTH
STREAK BEESWAX BURNISH
CHAMOIS FURBISH LACQUER
PERFECT VARNISH ELEGANCE
LEVIGATE SIMONIZE URBANIZE
POLISHED FINE COMPT ROUND
SHINY SLICK TERSE BUFFED FACETE
GLOSSY ELEGANT GALLANT
GENTEEL POLITIC REFINED
CULTURED
(NOT —) BLIND
POLISHER BUFFER GLAZER
WAGWAG WIGWAG DOLLIER
GLOSSER LAPIDARY SMOOTHER
POLISHING SANDING FROTTAGE
LIMATION
(— MATERIAL) RABAT
POLITE NEAT TIDY TRIM CIVIL SUAVE
GENTLE SMOOTH URBANE COURTLY
GALLANT GENTEEL DISCREET
LUSTROUS COURTEOUS
POLITENESS FINISH TASHRIF
COURTESY ELEGANCE URBANITY
POLITES (FATHER OF —) PRIAM
(MOTHER OF —) HECUBA
POLITIC WARY WISE SUAVE AROFUL
CRAFTY CUNNING TACTFUL
DISCREET PROVIDENT
POLITICAL (— ASSN.) VEREIN
(— PARTY) GOP TORY WHIG LABOR
POLITICIAN BOSS STATIST
WARWICK PIPELAYER STATESMAN
POLITY SERFISM
POLL COW DOD NOT POW ROB CHUB
COLL DODD HEAD NAPE NOTT PASH
CROWN SKULL STRIP CENSUS
FLEECE PARROT CANVASS DESPOIL
PILLAGE PLUNDER POLLARD
POLLACK LOB GADE LAIT GADID
LYTHE BILLET LAITHE BADDOCK
SILLOCK WALLEYE BLUEFISH
COALFISH GRAYFISH LORICATE
MOULRUSH
POLLARD CHU COW BRAN POLL
STAG SHEEP CHEVAN DODDLE
DOTARD BOLLING LOPPARD
WOOSERE
POLLARD TREE DOTARD RUNNEL
POLLED NOT NOTT POLEY
HORNLESS
POLLEN DUST MEAL FLOUR FARINA
POWDER BEEBREAD
(— BRUSH) SCOPA
(— TUBE) SPERMARY
POLLER VOTER BARBER POLLSTER
POLLEX THUMB
POLLINATE SELF FECUNDATE
FECUNDIZE FERTILIZE
POLLINATING SIBBING
POLLIWOG TADPOLE
POLLOCK PODLER
POLLUTE FOIL FOUL SOIL BLEND
DIRTY SMEAR TAINT BEFOUL DEFILE
INFECT MUDDLE RAVISH ADULTER
DEBAUCH PROFANE VIOLATE
POLLUTED FOUL DRUNK TURBID
CORRUPT
POLLUTING FILTHY
POLLUTION STAIN SULLAGE

FOULNESS IMPURITY
POLLUX POL HERCULES
(BROTHER OF —) CASTOR
(MOTHER OF —) LEDA
POLO (PERIOD IN —) CHUKKER
POLONAISE POLACCA FACKELTANZ
POLONIUS CORAMBIS
(DAUGHTER OF —) OPHELIA
(SON OF —) LAERTES
POLT BLOW THUMP STROKE
POLTERGEIST GHOST SPIRIT
POLTROON IDLER COWARD CRAVEN
WRETCH DASTARD COWARDLY
SLUGGARD
POLYANDRIUM CEMETERY
POLYGALA GAYWINGS
POLYGON DECAGON HEXAGON
NONAGON HEPTAGON PENTAGON
CHILIAGON MULTANGLE
POLYGRAPH KEELER
POLYHEDRON BEAD
POLYMER DIMER HYDROL HEXAMER
(— UNIT) MER

POLYNESIA
CHESTNUT: RATA
IMAGE: TIKI
ISLAND: COOK LINE SAMOA
   TONGA EASTER ELLICE PHOENIX
ISLE: MOTU
KING: ALII ARII ARIKI
LANGUAGE: UVEA TAGALOG
MOUND: AHU
NATIVE: ATI MAORI KANAKA
   NIVEAN TONGAN NESOGAEAN
PRINCIPLE: TIKI
WOMAN: VAHINE

POLYNESIAN MAORI KANAKA
TONGAN FUTUNAN
POLYNICES (BROTHER OF —)
ETEOCLES
(FATHER OF —) OEDIPUS
(MOTHER OF —) JOCASTA
(WIFE OF —) ARGIA
POLYNOMIAL CUBIC
POLYP CORAL HYDRA TUMOR ZOOII
ISOPOD HYDRULA OCTOPOD
POLYPARY ZOARIUM
POLYPHONY FABURDEN
COUNTERPOINT
POLYPIDOM CORMUS
POLYSACCHARIDE LEVAN GELOSE
GLYCAN INULIN IRISIN MANNAN
AMYLOSE DEXTRAN FUCOSAN
HEXOSAN POLYOSE GALACTAN
GLYCOGEN LICHENIN SECALOSE
SINISTRIN
POLYZOAN POLYP CESTODE
RADIATE
POMACE MUST RAPE POMMY STOC
STOSH CHEESE
POMADE CIDER POMATUM LIPSTICK
OINTMENT
POMANDER POUNCET
POMATO TOPATO
POME BALL APPLE GLOBE
JUNEBERRY

POMEGRANATE GRENAT GRENADE
BALAUSTA
POMELO SHADDOCK GRAPEFRUIT
POMERANIA (CAPITAL OF —)
STETTIN
(CITY IN —) THORN TORUN ANKLAM
(ISLAND IN —) RUGEN USEDOM
(PROVINCE IN —) POMORZE
POMFRET BULLY HENFISH
POMME DE TERRE POTATO
POMMEL BOB FIB NOB BEAT HORN
KNOB PAIK PAKE TORE NEVEL
BRUISE BUFFET CRUTCH FINIAL
PLUMMET
POMP BRAG FARE WEAL BOAST
PRIDE STATE ESTATE PAMPER
PARADE RIALTY SCHEME SPRUNK
BOBANCE DISPLAY PAGEANT
PANOPLY SPLURGE CEREMONY
EQUIPAGE GRANDEUR SEMBLANT
SPLENDOR
POMPANO DART JUREL ALLICE
CARANX PERMIT ALEWIFE COBBLER
OLDWIFE CARANGID MACKEREL
(— CLAM) COQUINA
POMPOSITY TUMOR TUMOUR
BIGHEAD BIGNESS
POMPOUS BIG BUG BUDGE JELLY
LARGE SHOWY TUMID WIGGY
AUGUST TURGID BLOATED
BOMBAST FUSTIAN OROTUND
STILTED SWOLLEN TURGENT
BEWIGGED INFLATED SWELLING
IMPORTANT
PONCEAU GRANAT
PONCHO MANGA RUANA
POND (ALSO SEE POOL) LAY LUM
DELF DIKE MOAT PULK SLEW STEW
TANK VLEI VLEY CANAL DECOY
DELFT LACHE LETCH STANK WAYER
CLAIRE LAGOON LOCHAN PUDDLE
SALINA SLOUGH SPLASH STAGNE
MULLETRY
(— FOR OYSTERS) CLAIRE
(— MAN) JACKER
(ARTIFICIAL —) AQUARIUM
(DIRTY —) SOAL
(FISH —) GURGES
(FISH STORING —) STEW
(SMALL —) KHAL
(STAGNANT —) DUB
PONDER CON CAST CHAW MUSE
PORE ROLL TURN BROOD STUDY
WEIGH ADVISE EXPEND REASON
RECORD REMORD BALANCE
COMPASS EXAMINE IMAGINE
PERPEND REFLECT REVERIE
REVOLVE APPRAISE COGITATE
CONSIDER MEDITATE
PONDERABILITY WEIGHT GRAVITY
PONDEROUS DULL SLOW BULKY
GRAVE HEAVY SOGGY AWKWARD
WEIGHTY UNWIELDY IMPORTANT
PONDEROUSNESS HEFT
POND HEN COOT
PONDMAN JACKER
PONDOKKIE HUT HOVEL
PONE CAKE LUMP WRIT PAUNE
PUDDING SWELLING

PONGEE PAUNCHE SHANTUNG
PONIARD STAB BODKIN DAGGER
STYLET POINADO
PONT FERRY FLOAT BRIDGE
FERRYBOAT
PONTIC DUMMY
PONTICELLO BREAK MAGAS
PONTIFF POPE BISHOP PRIEST
PONTIFEX
PONTOON FLOAT RHINO BRIDGE
PONY CAB RAW TAT CAVY YABU
DALES GRIFF PAINT PINTO POWNY
TACKY TRICK WELCH WELSH
BASUTO BHUTIA BRONCO CAYUSE
EXMOOR GARRAN SHELTY TANGUN
TATTOO ENGLISH HACKNEY
MANIPUR MUSTANG SHELTIE
FORESTER GALLOWAY SHETLAND
(STUDENT'S —) CRIB TROT BICYCLE
(PL.) DALES
POODLE SHOCK BARBET
POOK HEAP PICK PULL PLUCK
STACK
POOKA PUCK GOBLIN SPECTER
POOL (ALSO SEE POND) CAR DIB
DUB LAY LUM PIT POL POT POW
BOOK CARR DIKE FARM JHIL LAKE
LIDO LINN LLYN LUMB MERE PANT
PEEL PLUD POLK POND PULE PULK
RING SINK SLEW SOIL SWAG TANK
TARN WEEL BAYOU BOWLY DECOY
FLASH FLUSH FRESH JHEEL KITTY
LETCH LOUGH MEARE PLASH
PLUMB SLACK STANK STELL STILL
THERM TRUNK CARTEL CHARCO
FLODGE LAGOON LASHER PLUNGE
PUDDLE SILOAM SPLASH STABLE
CARLINE CATHOLE CUSHION
JACKPOT PLASHET SNOOKER
STAGNUM INTERLOT QUINIELA
(— AT JERUSALEM) BETHESDA
(— BELOW WATERFALL) LIN LINN
LLYN
(— WITH SALMON NETS) STELL
(— WITHOUT OUTLET) STAGNUM
(ARTIFICIAL —) CUSHION
(AUCTION —) CALCUTTA
(DIRTY —) SUMP
(FISH —) TRUNK STEWPOND
(MOUNTAIN —) TARN
(MUDDY —) LETCH
(SWIMMING —) BATH LIDO
NATATORY
POON DILO PEON PUNA DOMBA
KEENA TAMANU SIRPOON
MASTWOOD
POONGHIE RAHAN PRIEST PUNGYI
PHONGHI TALAPOIN
POOP DOCK FIRE GULP TOOT CHEAT
COZEN STERN BEFOOL ISLAND
DECEIVE EXHAUST HINDDECK
OVERCOME
POOR BAD SAD BASE EVIL FOUL
LEAN LEWD PUNK SICK SOUR THIN
DINKY EXILE FOOTY GROSS JERRY
KETTY SCALY SEELY SILLY SOBER
SORRY UNORN FEEBLE HUMBLE
HUNGRY LEADEN MEAGER MEAGRE
MEASLY PILLED PORAIL PRETTY

SCANTY SHABBY STREET CODFISH
HAPLESS NAUGHTY SCRAWNY
SCRUBBY SQUALID TRIVIAL
UNLUCKY INDIGENT PRECIOUS
SCRANNEL SNEAKING UNTHENDE
(— BOY) HERO
POORHOUSE MEASONDUE
POORLY ILL BADLY SADLY BARELY
FEEBLY SIMPLY SLIGHT SHABBILY
POOR SOLDIER FRIARBIRD
POORTITH POVERTY
POP GO DOT GUN HIT TRY BLOW
DART HOCK JUMP PAWN SODA
BREAK CRACK KNOCK SHOOT
ATTACK EFFORT FATHER POPPER
STROKE THRUSH ASSAULT ATTEMPT
CONCERT EXPLODE INSTANT
REDWING BACKFIRE SUDDENLY
POPDOCK FOXGLOVE
POPE PAPA PAPE RUFF BISHOP
PUFFIN SHRIKE PONTIFEX
FISHERMAN
POPERY POPEISM PAPISTRY
POPE'S-EYE NUT NOIX
POPGUN SCOOT PENGUN POTGUN
PLUFFER
POPINJAY PARROT PAPINGO
POPLAR ABBEY ABELE ALAMO
ASPEN BAHAN LIARD BALSAM
POPPLE BAUMIER ABELTREE
WHITEBARK
POPLIN TABINET
POPOLOCA CHOCHO
POPPY HEAD BLAVER CANKER
COPROSE EARACHE PONCEAU
REDWEED ARGEMONE BALEWORT
BOCCONIA HEADACHE DANNEBROG
SQUATMORE
(CORN —S) SOLDIERS
POPPYCOCK BOSH FOLLY STUFF
HAVERS
POPPYFISH POMPANO
POPPY SEED MAW MOHNSEED
POPULACE MOB MASS CROWD
DEMOS PLEBS MASSES MOBILE
PEOPLE COUNTRY
POPULAR LAY POP COMMON
GOLDEN SIMPLE VULGAR CROWDED
DEMOTIC VULGATE APPROVED
FAVORITE PEOPLISH PLEBEIAN
POPULARITY VOGUE CLAPTRAP
POPULATE MAN BREED PLANT
WORLD PEOPLE INHABIT
POPULATION DEME COLONY
FLOTSAM KINDRED TOPODEME
UNIVERSE
POPULUS SALIX
PORBEAGLE LAMNA SHARK LAMNID
LAMNOID
PORCELAIN JU KO CHINA MURRA
SPODE MURRHA NANKIN BISCUIT
CELADON DRESDEN NANKEEN
MANDARIN STEATITE
(VARIETY OF —) CAEN KUAN ARITA
HIZEN IMARI KYOTO AMSTEL
SEVRES BUDWEIS DRESDEN
LIMOGES MEISSEN SWANSEA
HAVILAND KAKIEMON CHANTILLY
PORCH HOOD STOA LANAI STOEP

STOOP INGANG PARVIS PIAZZA
PORTAL RAMADA BALCONY GALILEE
NARTHEX PASSAGE POIKILE
PORTICO PRONAOS VERANDA
ANTENAVE GALLERIE SOLARIUM
TRANSEPT VESTIBLE
(FRONT —) ANTICUM
PORCUPINE QUILL URSON
CAWQUAW COENDOU ERECTER
ERICIUS PORKPEN HEDGEHOG
HEDGEPIG
PORCUPINE ANTEATER ECHIDNA
PORCUPINE FISH ERIZO ATINGA
BURFISH DIODONT
PORCUPINE GRASS SPINIFEX
PORE GAZE GLOSE GLOZE STARE
STUDY TRYPA PONDER ALVEOLA
CINCLIS OSTIOLE TUBULUS
BAJONADO JOLTHEAD LENTICEL
PORGY TAI SCUP PARGO PLUMA
POGGY BESUGO MAMAMU PAGRUS
SPARID MARGATE MENHADEN
SPADEFISH
PORK HAM HOG PIG LARD BACON
BRAWN MONEY SWINE BALDRIB
LARDOON MIDDLING
(CHOP) BALDRIB GRISKIN
(— AND SALMON) LAULAU
(— SHOULDER) HAND
(SALT —) BACON SPECK SOWBELLY
PORKFISH SISI CATALINETA
PORKY FAT GREASY
PORNOGRAPHIC LEWD CURIOUS
OBSCENE
PORNOGRAPHY CURIOSA
ESOTERICA
POROUS OPEN LIGHT LEACHY
CELLULAR
PORPHYRY ELVAN EURITE ELVANITE
GRORUDITE
PORPOISE WHALE PALACH PUFFER
COWFISH DOLPHIN HOGFISH
PELLOCK PULLOCK SNUFFER
CETACEAN GAIRFISH
PORRECT EXTEND TENDER PRESENT
PORRET LEEK ONION PORETT
SCALLION
PORRIDGE KHIR POBS ATOLE
BROSE GROUT GRUEL BURGOO
CROWDY SKILLY SOWENS TARTAN
BROCHAN BURGOUT OATMEAL
POBBIES POLENTA POTTAGE
FLUMMERY SAGAMITE
PORRINGER TASTER TRINKET
PORT GATE GOAL LEFT MIEN WICK
WINE CARRY CREEK HAVEN HITHE
SALLY SCALE STATE APPORT
HARBOR INPORT REFUGE AIRPORT
BEARING DIGNITY LIBERTY
OUTPORT ANTEPORT DEMEANOR
LARBOARD MALTOLTE PORTHOLE
PRESENCE
PORTABLE MOBILE MOVABLE
BEARABLE
PORTAGE PACK CARGO CARRY
TARBET FREIGHT TONNAGE
HAULOVER
PORTAL DOOR GATE PORCH
DOORWAY ENTRANCE
PORTAMENTO DRAG GLIDE SCOOP

SLIDE PORTATO GLISSADE
PORTCULLIS BAR SHUT HERSE
ORGUE CATARACT
PORTE-MONNAIE PURSE
PORTE GATE
PORTEND BODE AUGUR DIVINE
EXTEND BESPEAK BETOKEN
PREDICT PRESAGE DENOUNCE
FOREBODE FORECAST FORETELL
PORTENT AYAH LUCK SIGN SOUND
TOKEN AUGURY MARVEL OSTENT
WONDER AUSPICE PREDICT
PRESAGE PRODIGY CEREMONY
DISASTER SOOTHSAY
PORTENTOUS AWFUL GRAVID
BODEFUL DOOMFUL FATEFUL
OMINOUS POMPOUS DOOMLIKE
DREADFUL INFLATED SINISTER
PORTER BEER MOZO HAMAL STOUT
TAMEN BADGER BEARER COOLIE
DARWAN DURWAN ENTIRE KHAMAL
REDCAP SUISSE DROGHER
HUMMAUL JANITOR PITCHER
REMOVER BADGEMAN CARGADOR
CHAPRASI LODGEMAN PORTITOR
RECEIVER
(— AND STOUT) COOPER
(JAPANESE —) AKABO
(MEAT —) PITCHER
(MEXICAN —) TAMEN
PORTFOLIO BLAD
PORTIA (HUSBAND OF —) BRUTUS
(LOVER OF —) BASSANIO
(MAID OF —) NERISSA
PORTIA TREE MAHO BENDY MAHOE
PORTICO STOA WALK XYST ORIEL
PORCH XYSTA ZAYAT PARVIS
PIAZZA SCHOOL XYSTUS BALCONY
GALLERY NARTHEX PRONAOS
TERRACE VERANDA PORTICUS
POSTICUM VERANDAH
PORTION BIT CUP CUT DAB JAG LAB
LOT PAN BLAD DALE DEAL DOLE
DOSE FATE FECK JAGG PART SIZE
WHAT DOWER PIECE RATIO SHARE
SLICE SNACK WHACK CANTLE
CANTON COLLOP DETAIL GOBBET
MATTER PARCEL RASHER EXCERPT
PARTAGE SECTION SEGMENT
TODDICK TRANCHE FRACTION
FRAGMENT PITTANCE QUANTITY
SCANTLET FODDERING
(— DRUNK) DRAFT DRAUGHT
(— OF ACTOR'S PART) LENGTH
(— OF ARROW) BREAST
(— OF BIRD SONG) TOUR
(— OF BREAD OR BEER) CUE
(— OF CITRUS RIND) ALBEDA
(— OF ESTATE) LEGITIM
(— OF FARMLAND) BEREWICK
(— OF FLOODPLAIN) BANCO
(— OF FODDER) JAG
(— OF FOOD) HELP GOBBET
HELPING
(— OF HIDE) HEAD
(— OF LAND) BLOCK PATTI INTAKE
DIVISION DONATION
(— OF LIQUOR) STICK DIVIDEND
(— OF LITURGY) ANAPHORA

(— OF MAST) HOUSING HOUNDING
(— OF PASTURE) BREAK
(— OF POEM) STRAIN
(— OF RUG) GRIN
(— OF SERPENT'S BODY) TRAIN
(— OF STEM) BOON
(— OF STORY) SNATCH
(— OF STREAM) LAVADERO
(— OF TEA) DRAWING
(— OF TIME) SPAN DISTANCE
(— OF TOBACCO) CUD
(— OF TONGUE) BLADE
(ADDITIONAL —) RASHER
(ALLOTTED —) MOIRA SCANTLING
(BRIDE'S —) DOWRY
(CLOTTED — OF BLOOD) CRUOR
(COARSER —) BOLTINGS
(EARLY —) SPRING
(INHABITED — OF EARTH) ECUMENE
(LATTER —) AUTUMN EVENING
(MAIN —) CORPSE
(MARRIAGE —) DOT DOTE TOCHER
(MINUTE —) GRAIN
(MOST VALUABLE —) CHIEF
(PERCEPTIBLE —) KENNING
(REPRESENTATIVE —) SAMPLE
(SIGNIFICANT —) CHAPTER
(SIZABLE —) DUNT
(SMALL — OF LIQUOR) DOLLOP
HEELTAP
(SMALL —) BIT DAB DOT DRAM
DROP SOSH CHACK SPICE SPUNK
SHADOW MODICUM REMNANT
SCANTLE SMIDGEN SOUPCON
SCANTLET
(TRIFLING —) SMACK
PORTLY FAT FULL AMPLE STOUT
GOODLY STATELY SWELLING
PORTMANTEAU BAG HOOK VALISE
POCKMANKY
PORTRAIT BUST ICON IKON IMAGE
IMAGO MODEL PIECE STATUE
VISAGE PORTRAY RETRAIT
LIKENESS RITRATTO VERONICA
(— ON COIN) EFFIGY
PORTRAY GIVE LIMN LINE BLAZE
ENACT IMAGE PAINT CIPHER
CLOTHE DEPICT FIGURE SHADOW
FEATURE IMITATE PICTURE
DECIPHER DESCRIBE RESEMBLE

PORTUGAL

BAY: SETUBAL
CAPITAL: LISBON
CAPE: MONDEGO ESPICHEL
COIN: JOE REI PECA REAL CONTO
COROA DOBRA INDIO ESCUDO
MACUTA PATACA TESTAO
VINTEM CENTAVO CRUSADO
MOIDORE EQUIPAGA
COLONY: MACAO TIMOR ANGOLA
GUINEA PRINCIPE
ISLAND: TIMOR
ISLANDS: MADEIRA
MEASURE: PE ALMA BOTA MEIO
MOIO PIPA VARA ALMUD BRACA
FANGA GEIRA LEGOA LINHA
MILHA PALMO ALMUDE CANADA

COVADO QUARTO ALQUIER
ESTADIO FERRADO SELAMIN
ALQUEIRE TONELADA
MOUNTAIN: ACOR GEREZ MARAO
MOUSA PENEDA ESTRELA
MONCHIQUE
RIVER: SOR TUA LIMA MINO MIRA
SADO SEDA TAGO TEJO DOURO
MINHO SABAR TAGUS VOUGA
ZATAS CAVADO CHANCA
TAMEGA ZEZERE MONDEGO
GUADIANA
TOWN: FARO OVAR BRAGA EVORA
PORTO GUARDA OPORTO
COIMBRA FUNCHAL SETUBAL
BRAGANCA
UNIVERSITY: COIMBRA
WEIGHT: GRAO ONCA LIBRA
MARCO ARROBA OITAVA
ARRATEL QUINTAL
WINE: PORT

ORTULACA MOSS PURSLANE
ORWIGLE TADPOLE
OSAUNE TROMBONE
OSE SET SIT HOARD MODEL OFFER
PLANT STICK BAFFLE NONPLUS
PEACOCK POSTURE PRESENT
POSITION PRETENSE PROPOUND
QUESTION
OSEIDON NEPTUNE EARTHSHAKER
(BROTHER OF —) ZEUS
(FATHER OF —) KRONOS
(MOTHER OF —) RHEA
(WIFE OF —) AMPHITRITE
OSER FACER POSEUR PUZZLE
STAYER STICKER STUMPER
TWISTER EXAMINER STICKLER
BANDARLOG
OSH SWAGGER
OSING OPPOSAL
(— TECHNIQUE) PLASTIQUE
OSIT FIX PUT SET PLACE AFFIRM
ASSUME
OSITING PONENT
OSITION LAY LIE HANG LINE POSE
RANK SITE CENSE COIGN PLANT
POSTE SITUS STAND STATE STEAD
ASSIZE FIGURE HEIGHT OCTAVE
OFFICE STANCE UBIETY VALGUS
POSTURE STATION ATTITUDE
CAPACITY DOCTRINE VOCATION
(— OF AFFAIRS) STATUS
(— OF FEAR) GAZE
(— OF HEAVENLY BODY) HARBOR
(— OF VESSEL) GAUGE HEIGHT
(— WITH NO ESCAPE) IMPASSE
(— WITH NO RESPONSIBILITY)
SINECURE
(DISTINGUISHED —) HONOR
(EMBARRASSING —) FIX HOLE
(FENCING —) CARTE SIXTE SIXTH
QUARTE TIERCE SACCOON
SECONDE SEPTIME
(FOREMOST —) HEAD LEAD STEM
(INITIAL —) ANLAUT
(MEDIAL —) INLAUT
(RELATIVE —) RANK TERMS

BEARING FOOTING STANDING
(SOCIAL —) CASTE STATE VALOUR
(SYMBOLIC —) HASTA
POSITIONAL SITUAL
POSITIVE POS POZ COOL DOWN
FLAT PLUS SURE BASIC SHEER
UTTER ACTIVE DIRECT THETIC
GENUINE HEALTHY ABSOLUTE
CONCRETE DEFINITE DOGMATIC
EXPLICIT INHERENT RESOLUTE
SIGNLESS THETICAL
(THREE —S) KROMOGRAM
POSITIVELY BUT POS FLAT PLUS
QUITE FAIRLY INDEED STRICTLY
POSITIVISM COMTISM CERTAINTY
DOGMATISM
POSITRON LEPTON
POSSESS GET OWE OWN HAVE
HOLD WALD BOAST BROOK OUGHT
REACH WIELD MASTER OBTAIN
OCCUPY BEDEVIL ENVELOP FURNISH
INHABIT INHERIT INSTALL INSTATE
SMITTLE ACQUAINT DOMINATE
INSTRUCT
POSSESSED MAD CALM COOL
OUGHT CRAZED JERUSHA
ENTHEATE
(— BY EVIL SPIRIT) DEMONIAC
POSSESSION AVER HAND HOLD
YHTE AUGHT GRASP STATE CLUTCH
CORNER HAVIOR SASINE SEISIN
SEIZIN WEALTH CONTROL COUNTER
DEMESNE DEWANEE FINGERS
KEEPING MASTERY SEIZURE
CONQUEST DEFIANCE PROPERTY
(— OF COMMON FEATURES)
AFFINITY
(— OF KNOWLEDGE) SCIENCE
(— WITH QUIET ENJOYMENT) SEISIN
SEIZIN
(BURDENSOME —) ELEPHANT
(RELIGIOUS —) POWER
(TEMPORAL —S) WORLD
(TEMPORARY —) LEND
(PL.) ALLS STORE STUFF WRACK
DOMAIN ESTATE GRAITH PROPER
CAPITAL FORTUNE HAVINGS LIVINGS
POSSET CURDLE PAMPER
POWSOWDY BALDUCTUM
MERRYBUSH
POSSIBILITY MAY MAYBE POSSE
CHANCE
POSSIBLE ABLE RIFE MAYBE LIKELY
EARTHLY ELIGIBLE FEASIBLE
PROBABLY POTENTIAL
POSSIBLY MAPPEN LIGHTLY
PERHAPS PERCHANCE
POSSUM TAIT FEIGN PRETEND
POST DAK SET TIE BITT BOMA CAMP
DAWK DOLE FAST FORT MAIL META
POLE ROOM SPOT SPUD STOB STUD
TREE BERTH CHEEK CLOSH CRANE
NEWEL PLACE SPILE SPRAG STAKE
STAND STILT STING STOCK STODE
STOOP STULP STUMP BILLET
CIPPUS COLUMN CROTCH FENDER
GIBBET INFORM OFFICE PICKET
PILLAR SAMSON SCREEN STAPLE
STOOTH STOWER TRUNCH ASHERAH

BOLLARD COURIER GARETTA
PLACARD POSTAGE POSTBOX
QUARTER STATION STUDDLE
UPRIGHT BANISTER DEADHEAD
LEGPIECE MAKEFAST PRESIDIO
PUNCHEON QUINTAIN STRADDLE
(— AS RACE MARKER) META
(— ON PIER) FAST BOLLARD
DEADHEAD
(BOUNDARY —) TERM STOOP
TERMINUS
(CHIMNEY —) SPEER
(CUSTOMS —) CHOKEY
(DOOR OR GATE —) DURN
(ECCLESIASTIC —) BENEFICE
(FENCE —) DROPPER
(HANGING —) GIBBET
(INDIAN MILITARY —) TANA TANNA
THANA
(MILITARY —) FORT GARRISON
(MOORING —) DOLPHIN
(OBSERVATORY —) CUPOLA
(SACRED —) ASHERAH
(SIGN —) PARSON
POSTAGE POST STAMPAGE
POSTAGE-FREE FRANCO
POSTAGE STAMP DUE HEAD
STICKER
POSTBOY YAMSHIK YEMSCHIK
POSTILION
POST CHAISE JACK POCHAY
POSCHAY
POSTER BILL CLAP SNIPE CLAPPE
AFFICHE PLACARD SHOWING
STICKER STREAMER
POSTERIOR BACK REAR CAUDAL
DORSAL POSTIC RETRAL ADAXIAL
BUTTOCKS
(PL.) WHEERIKINS
POSTERIORLY RETRAD
POSTERITY SEQUEL KINDRED
FUTURITY
POSTERN SIDE CLOCKET KLICKET
PRIVATE POSTICUM
POSTHOUSE YAM MUTATION
POSTICHE WIG SHAM SWITCH
TOUPEE PRETENSE SPURIOUS
POSTIL HOMILY COMMENT
POSTILION COURIER POSTBOY
YAMSHIK
POSTLUDE SORTIE SORTITA
EPILOGUE
POSTMAN MAIL CORREO MAILBAG
MAILMAN
POST OFFICE BOMA CORREO
POSTHOUSE
POSTPONE OFF STAY WAIT DEFER
DELAY FRIST REFER REMIT WAIVE
FUTURE LINGER RELONG RETARD
ADJOURN DEGRADE OVERSET
PROLONG RESPECT SUSPEND
CONTINUE PROROGUE REPRIEVE
WITHHOLD
POSTPONED DEFERRED
POSTPONEMENT MORA STAY
DELAY RESPECT RESPITE
POSTRIDE COURIER POSTILION
POSTSCRIPT EKE ENVOY
POST SUPPORT CROWFOOT

POSTULANT NOVICE
POSTULATE AXIOM CLAIM ASSERT
ASSUME DEMAND THESIS PERHAPS
PETITION PRINCIPLE
POSTURE SET POSE SEAT SITE
ASANA FRONT HEART PLACE SHAPE
SQUAT STATE LOUNGE SLOUCH
STANCE BEARING CROWHOP
STATION STATURE ATTITUDE
CARRIAGE POSITION
(— **OF DEFENSE**) GUARD
(**DANCE** —) HOLD
(**KNEELING** —) SHIKO
POSY POESY TUTTY FLOWER
BOUQUET NOSEGAY ANTHOLOGY
POT BAG CAN COOP FOOL JUST
LEAD OLLA PINT POOL RUIN CREWE
CROCK CRUSE DIXIE KITTY SHANT
SHOOT ALUDEL CHATTY CHYTRA
JORDAN JORDEN KETTLE MARMIT
MASLIN MONKEY OUTWIT PINGLE
PIPKIN POCKET POSNET CHAMBER
CUVETTE DECEIVE POTSHOT
SEETHER SKILLET YETLING
FAVORITE JACKSHEA PRESERVE
MARIJUANA
(— **FOR CATCHING FISH**) COOP
(— **OF BRASS**) MASLIN
(— **OF DRINK**) SHANT
(— **WITH 3 FEET**) POSNET
(**12-GALLON** —) DIXY DIXIE
(**BULGING** —) OLLA
(**BUSHMAN'S** —) JACKSHAY
JACKSHEA
(**CHAMBER** —) JERRY JORDAN
JORDEN COMMODE JEROBOAM
(**CHIMNEY** —) CAN TUN
(**EARTHEN** —) OLLA CROCK CHATTY
PIPKIN
(**LEATHER** —) GISPIN
(**LOBSTER** —) COY TRUNK
(**LONG-HANDLED** —) PINGLE
(**MELTING** —) CRUCIBLE
(**PEAR-SHAPED** —) ALUDEL
(**SMALL ROUND** —) LOTAH
(**TEA** —) TRACK
POTABLE DRINK BEVERAGE
POTATORY
POTAGE SOUP BROTH
POTAMOGETON PONDWEED
PONDGRASS
POTASH KALI SALINE PEARLASH
POLVERINE
(— **FACTORY**) ASHERY
POTASSIUM K KALIUM POTASS
(— **DICHROMATE**) CHROME
POTASSIUM NITRATE GROUGH
POTATION POT DRAM DRAFT DRINK
LIBATION
POTATO PAP YAM CHAT PAPA SPUD
YAMP IDAHO RURAL TATER TUBER
BATATA CAMOTE KUMARA LUMPER
MURPHY PRATEY SKERRY BURBANK
EPICURE SOLANUM BLUENOSE
(— **BALL**) NOISETTE
(— **MASHER**) RICER CHAPPER
(— **SLICES**) LATTICE
(— **STATE**) IDAHO MAINE
(—**S AND CABBAGE**) COLCANNON

(**FRENCH FRIED** —) CHIP
(**FRENCH FRIED** —**S**) GAUFRETTES
(**JAPANESE** —) IMO
(**STEWED** —**S**) STOVIES
(**WITH** —**S**) PARMENTIER
(PL.) WARE CHUNO
POT BEARER POTIFER
POTBELLIED PODDY STOMACHY
POTBELLY PAUNCH TUNBELLY
POTBOY GANYMEDE
POTE KICK MOPE POIT POKE PUSH
NUDGE PLATE POKER SHOVE
THRUST
POTEEN POTHEEN WHISKEY
POTWHISKY
POTENCE STUD CROSS GIBBET
POTENCY FORCE POWER VIGOR
ORENDA VIRTUE EFFICACY
STRENGTH VITALITY
POTENT ABLE MAIN RICH STAY
STIFF CAUSAL COGENT CRUTCH
MIGHTY STRONG DYNAMIC SUPPORT
WARRANT FORCIBLE POWERFUL
PUISSANT VIGOROUS VIRTUOUS
VIRULENT
POTENTATE KING RULER POTENT
PRINCE DICTATOR DOMINION
SOVEREIGN
POTENTIAL EH LATENT VIRTUAL
IMPLICIT INCHOATE POSSIBLE
PREGNANT
(— **ENERGY**) ERGAL
POTENTIALITY POSSE POWER
DUNAMIS DYNAMIS CAPACITY
PREGNANCY
POTGUN PISTOL POPGUN BRAGGART
POTHER ADO VEX FUSS STEW STIR
WORRY BOTHER BUSTLE HARASS
POTTER PUTTER PUZZLE PERPLEX
TURMOIL
POTHERB WORT WERTE GREENS
OLITORY POTWORT QUELITE
SPINACH TAMPALA
POTHOLE POT KETTLE TINAJA
POTHOOK HAIK HAKE CROOK
HANGLE RACKAN SLOWRIE
TRAMMEL COTTEREL
POTHOUSE TAVERN ALEHOUSE
MUGHOUSE
POTION DOSE DRUG DRAFT DRINK
DWALE STUFF DRENCH POISON
AMATORY MIXTURE PHILTER
PHILTRE NEPENTHE
POTLATCH GIFT FEAST PARTY
POTLACH FESTIVAL
POT MARIGOLD GOLD GOLDE
SUNFLOWER
POTPOURRI OLIO STEW MASLIN
MEDLEY POTPIE RAGOUT FANTASIA
PASTICHE JAMBALAYA
POTRO COLT
POTSHERD BIT TEST CROCK SHARD
SHERD FRAGMENT OSTRACON
PANSHARD
POTTAGE SEW SOUP SOWL STEW
BROTH BRUET BREWIS BROWET
POTAGE OATMEAL PULMENT
POTTED DRUNK CANNED
(— **MEAT**) RILLETT

POTTER FAD FUSS MUCK POKE
ANNOY DAKER TRUCK BOTHER
DABBLE DACKER DIDDLE DISHER
DODDER FIDDLE FOOTLE FOTTER
JOTTER KUMHAR MUDDLE NANTLE
NIGGLE PETTLE POUTER TIDDLE
TIFFIE TIFFLE TRIFLE CLOAMER
CROCKER DISTURB FIGURER
FOSSICK HANDLER NAUNTLE
PERPLEX PLOWTER PRODDLE
THROWER TROUBLE CERAMIST
TERRAPIN
(— **OFFICIOUSLY**) TEW
(**MACHINE OF** —) JOLLY
POTTERER TWIRLER
POTTERY POT BANK CHUN DELF
GROG WARE BIZEN CROCK DELFT
GLOST ROUEN SPODE BASALT
FICTIL KASHAN MIMPEI ASTBURY
BELLEEK BOCCARO BRISTOL
DIPWARE FIGMENT JETWARE
KAMARES POTBANK POTWARE
POTWORK REDWARE SATSUMA
TICKNEY TZUCHOU BUCCHERO
CERAMICS FIGULINE GRAYWARE
SLIPWARE
(— **CIVILIZATION**) MINYAN
(— **CULTURE**) PUCARA
(— **DECOR**) MISHIMA
(— **DECORATED WITH SCRATCHING**
GRAFFITO
(**ANCIENT** —) KAMARES GRAYWAR
(**BLACK** —) BASALT
(**CHINESE** —) KUAN
(**CRUSHED** —) GROG
(**HINDU** —) UDA
(**RICHLY COLORED** —) MAJOLICA
POTTERY TREE CARAIPE
POTTINGER COOK POTYCARY
POTTO LEMUR APOSORO KINKAJOU
POTTY CRAZY FOOLISH TRIVIAL
SNOBBISH
POUCH BAG COD JAG POD SAC
BELL CYST POKE BULGE BURSA
POKKE PURSE BUDGET CAECUM
CRUMEN GIPSER PACKET POCKET
PURSET SACHET ALFARGA ALFOR.
CANTINA CRUMENA GIPSIRE MICH
OVICYST SCROTUM SPORRAN
SWALLOW BURSICLE PROTRUDE
SPEUCHAN
(— **OF FLY**) AEROSTAT
(— **ON DEER'S NECK**) BELL
(**TOBACCO** —) DOSS
POUF PUFF OTTOMAN
POULAINE PIKE CRAKOW
POULPE POULP CUTTLE OCTOPUS
POULTICE QUILT STUPA STUPE
MALAGMA EPITHEME SINAPISM
POULTRY FOWL HENS DUCKS GEE
PULLEN PEAFOWL PIGEONS
PULLERY TURKEYS CHICKENS
PULLAILE VOLAILLE
POUNAMU JADE PUNAMU NEPHRI
POUNCE NAB CHOP CLAP JUMP
POKE SWAP SWOP FLECK PRICK
PUNCH SOUSE SWOOP TALON
EMBOSS PIERCE TATTOO BOBCA
DESCEND SPRINKLE

(— UPON) TIRE STOOP

OUND L LB BUM DAD LIB PIN PUN SOV BEAT CHAP DRUB FRAM PELT PIND POON POSS PUND QUID SKIT THUD TRAP TUND CRUSH FRAME KNOCK LABOR LIVRE STAMP THUMP TRAMP WEIGH BATTER HAMMER LUMBER NICKER POUNCE PRISON THRASH CONTUND CONTUSE PINFOLD THUNDER LAMBASTE RESTRAIN

(— FINE) BRAY

(1-8TH OF —) HANDFUL

(100 —S) CENTAL CENTURY

(12 —S OF BUTTER) GAUN

(25 —S) PONY PONEY

(32, 56, OR 75 —S OF RAISINS) FRAIL

(500 —S) MONKEY

(FISH —) KEEP MADRAGUE

(ISRAELI —S) LIROTH

OUNDMASTER PINDER PINNER PONDER

OUR JAW RUN TUN YET BIRL BREW DROP EMIT FILL FLOW GOSH GUSH HELD LASH LAVE RAIN TEEM TOOM POWER SLIDE SOUSE SPILL SPOUT SWARM AFFUSE DECANT SLUICE STREAM CASCADE CHANNEL DIFFUSE SUFFUSE

(— AWAY) STAVE

(— BACK) REFUND

(— BEER OR WINE) BIRL

(— CLUMSILY) SLOSH

(— COPIOUSLY) HALE

(— DOWN) RASH SILE SHOWER DESCEND DISPUNGE

(— FORTH) SHED TIDE VENT WELL DISTILL OVERFLOW

(— FREELY) SWILL

(— FROM ONE VESSEL TO ANOTHER) DECANT JIRBLE TRANSFUSE

— IN DROP BY DROP) INSTIL INSTILL

— IN) INFUSE INFOUND INHELDE

— LIKE RAIN OR TEARS) LASH

— MELTED WAX) BASTE

— MOLTEN LEAD) YOTE

— OFF) SLUICE

— OIL UPON) ANOINT

— OUT) FILL SEND SHED SKINK TOUR UTTER EFFUSE LIBATE DIFFUND DIFFUSE

— UPON) AFFUSE

OURBOIRE TIP GRATUITY TRINKGELD

OURER TEEMER INFUSER

OURPOINT GIPON JUPON QUILT DOUBLET

OUT BIB MOP MAID MOUE PUSS OULK BOODY GROIN CATFISH ELPOUT BULLHEAD PROTRUDE

OUTERIA LUCUMA

OUTING BOUDERIE

OVERTY LACK NEED WANE WANT EARTH PENURY BEGGARY DEFAULT TENUITY DISTRESS

PUIRTITH SCARCITY WANDRETH

POVERTY PLANT HEATH HEATHER LINGWORT

POVERTY-STRICKEN POOR NAKED NEEDY SQUALID SHIRTLESS

POWDER DUST KISH MILL MULL SAND CHALK CURRY ERBIA FLOUR GRIND HEMOL KOSIN PICRA STOUR CEMENT CHARGE CHINOL DECAMP DERMOL EMPASM ESCAPE FARINA FILITE GERATE KAMALA KERMES KUMKUM MELLON PEYTON PINOLE POUNCE RACHEL SMEETH YTTRIA ALCOHOL BESTREW BROCADE LUPULIN SCATTER SMEDDUM SPACKLE SPODIUM ALGAROTH CATAPASM DYNAMITE FLUMERIN PALEGOLD

(— A SHIELD) GERATE

(— FOR BRONZING) BROCADE

(— OBTAINED BY SUBLIMATION) FLOWERS

(— TO MASK SWEAT ODOR) EMPASM EMPASMA

(— USED IN CHOCOLATE) PINOLE

(ABRASIVE —) EMERY

(ANTHELMINTIC —) KOSIN

(ANTIMONY —) KOHL

(ASTRINGENT —) BORAL

(BLEACHING —) CHEMIC

(BROWNISH —) LIGNIN

(CATHARTIC —) KAMALA

(COLORING —) HENNA

(FINE —) DUST POUNCE ALCOHOL

(FLUORESCENT —) FLUMERIN

(GOA —) ARAROBA

(GOLD —) VENTURINE

(GRAPHITIC —) KISH

(GRAY —) ANTU

(HAIR —) MUST

(MALT —) SMEDDUM

(PERFUMED —) ABIR SACHET

(PINK —) CALAMINE

(POISONOUS —) ROBIN

(REDDISH —) ABIR KUMKUM SIMMON

(ROSE-COLORED —) ERBIA

(SACHET —) PULVIL

(SILICEOUS —S) SILEX

(SMOKELESS —) FILITE PEYTON CORDITE AMBERITE INDURITE SOLENITE

(WHITE —) CHINOL YTTRIA HYPORIT SCANDIA HALAZONE LANTHANA PARAFORM

(YELLOW —) KOSIN DERMOL MELLON LUPULIN MALARIN SAMARIA TANNIGEN

POWDERED SEME SPICED PICKLED SEASONED

POWDER PUFF PLUFF

POWER ARM ART JUS ROD SAY SUN VIS BEEF BULK DINT GIFT GRIP HAND HANK HEAP HORN IRON KAMI MAIN MANA MAYA SOUP SWAY WALD WILL AGENT CROWN DEMON DEVIL FORCE GRACE HUACA HYDRO INPUT LURCH MIGHT SINEW SKILL STEAM VALUE VIGOR WAKON WIELD

YARAK APPEAL BREATH CLUTCH CREDIT DANGER DEGREE DOUGHT EFFORT ENERGY FOISON IMPACT MOLOCH SHAKTI STROIL STROKE SWINGE TALENT VIRTUE WEIGHT BALANCE BOSSDOM COMMAND CONTROL DEMESNE DESTINY DUNAMIS DYNAMIS ENTHEOS FACULTY POTENCY VALENCY VOLTAGE WAKONDA ACTIVITY AUTONOMY CAPACITY COERCION DELEGACY DEMIURGE DISPOSAL DOMINION INTEREST LEVERAGE LORDSHIP SEIGNORY STRENGTH

(— OF ACID) BASICITY

(— OF ATTRACTION) ALLURE

(— OF CHOICE) LIBERTY

(— OF DIVORCE) TAFWIZ

(— OF ENTRY) INGRESS

(— OF GIVING) PROPINE

(— OF HEARING) AUDITION

(— OF KNOWING) JNANASHAKTI

(— OF MANIFESTATION) MAYA

(— OF MOVING AT SEA) YARAGE

(— OF PERFORMING) ART

(— OF RESISTANCE) STAMINA

(— OF TRANSMUTATION) ALCHEMY

(— OF VISION) KEN

(— OF WINE) SEVE

(— TO CONVINCE) FORCE

(—S OF EVIL) HELL

(CIVIL —) CAESAR

(COERCIVE —) SWORD

(DIVINE —) MOIRA

(ELEVATING —) LIFT

(EMOTIONAL —) STOMACH

(EXTRAPHYSICAL —) MANA

(FIFTH —) SURSOLID

(FOCAL —) DIOPTRY

(GROWTH —) BATHMISM

(HYPOTHETICAL —) FORTUNE

(IMPERSONAL —) WAKAN WAKON WAKANDA

(INTELLECTUAL —) WIT

(LEGAL —) JUS

(MAGIC —) ORENDA

(MAGNETIC —) MAGNES

(MENTAL —) HABITUS

(MORMON —) KEYS

(NATURAL —) OD

(OCCULT —) MAGIC

(PERSUASIVE —) RHETORIC

(PERUVIAN —) HUACA

(POLITICAL —) DOMINION

(RATIONAL —) EYE

(REFLECTIVE —) ALBEDO

(ROYAL —) RIAL

(SACRED —) KAMI

(SECOND —) SQUARE

(SOVEREIGN —) SWAY THRONE

(SPIRITUAL —) NGAI

(STAYING —) STAMINA

(SUPERNATURAL —) CHARISMA

(SUPREME —) EMPIRE HEAVEN IMPERIUM

(THIRD —) CUBE

(VITAL —) SPIRITS

POWERBOAT SEDAN SKIFF GLIDER CRUISER STINKPOT GASOLINER

POWERFUL BIG FAT ABLE DEEP
HIGH MAIN RANK RICH VERY FORTE
HEFTY HUSKY LUSTY STARK STOUT
VALID VIVID WIGHT WILDE COGENT
HEROIC MIGHTY POTENT SEVERE
STRONG CAPABLE FECKFUL
INTENSE POLLENT RICHARD
SKOOKUM STAVING VALIANT
FORCIBLE PUISSANT VIGOROUS
POWERLESS WEAK FEEBLE UNABLE
HELPLESS IMPOTENT
POWWOW PAWAW CONFAB FROLIC
COUNCIL MEETING SESSION
CONJURER
POX ROUP CANKER PLAGUE VARIOLA
(**FOWL** —) SOREHEAD
(**SHEEP** —) OVINIA
POYOU PELUDO ARMADILLO
PRABHU LORD CHIEF WRITER
PRACTICABLE AGIBLE DOABLE
USABLE FEASIBLE POSSIBLE
PRACTICAL HARD UTILE ACTUAL
THINGY USEFUL OPERARY VIRTUAL
WORKING BANAUSIC HOMESPUN
PRACTIVE THINGISH
(— **JOKE**) WAGGERY
(**NOT** —) PROFESSORY
PRACTICALLY ALMOST NEARLY
REALLY VIRTUALLY
PRACTICE ACT ISM LAW SUE TRY
URE USE KEEP LIVE PLAN PLOT
ADOPT APPLY ASSAY DRILL FOUND
GUISE HABIT HAUNT TRADE TRAIN
TREAD USAGE CUSTOM EMPLOY
FOLLOW GROOVE OCCUPY PRAXIS
RECORD BRUSHUP ENHAUNT
KNOCKUP OPERATE PROCEED
PROFESS RANDORI USAUNCE
ACTIVISM ALARMISM EXERCISE
FREQUENT GALENISM
(— **CHEATING**) FOIST
(— **DECEPTION**) DEACON
(— **DILIGENTLY**) PLY
(— **FRAUD**) SHARK
(— **HYPOCRISY**) CANT
(— **OF AN ART**) PRAXIS
(— **OF MEDICINE**) GALENISM
(— **ROWING**) TUB
(— **WITCHCRAFT**) HEX
(**BINDING** —) LAW
(**CEREMONIAL** —) RITE
(**COMMUNAL** —) SUNNA SCHEME
SUNNAH INTRIGUE
(**CORRUPT** —) ABUSE WHORE
(**DIPLOMATIC** —) ALTERNAT
(**DISHONEST** —**S**) CROSS
(**HORTICULTURAL** —) CUTTAGE
(**MEDICAL** —) ALLERGY
(**RELIGIOUS** —) CULT CULTUS
(**SUPERSTITIOUS** —) FREET
(**UNDERHAND** —) JUGGLING
(**VICIOUS** —) MOLOCH
PRACTICED EXPERT VERSED
PRACTIC SKILLED VETERAN
HACKNEYED
PRACTICING EXERCENT
PRACTITIONER DOCTOR HEALER
LAWYER NOVICE LEARNER
EXERCENT FELDSHER HUMANIST

HERBALIST HOMEOPATH
PRAD HORSE
PRAENOMEN AULUS CAIUS GAIUS
TITUS GNAEUS LUCIUS MANIUS
MARCUS SEXTUS SERVIUS SPURIUS
MAMERCUS NUMERIUS TIBERIUS
PRAESEPE CRIB CRATCH MANGER
BEEHIVE
PRAGMATIC BUSY BUSYBODY
DOGMATIC MEDDLING OFFICIOUS
PRACTICAL
PRAIRIE BAY BLED CAMAS CAMASS
MEADOW PLATEAU QUAMASH
(— **STATE**) ILLINOIS
PRAIRIE BERRY TROMPILLO
PRAIRIE CHICKEN GROUSE
PRAIRIE DOG GOPHER MARMOT
PRAIRIE WOLF COYOTE
PRAISE CRY LOF FUME HERY LAUD
LOSE LOVE PRES ADORE ALLOW
ALOSE BLESS CAROL CHANT CRACK
DEIFY EXTOL GLORY HERSE HONOR
KUDOS PLAUD PRIZE ROOSE SALVE
VALUE WURTH ANTHEM BELAUD
EULOGY FRAISE HILLEL KUDIZE
LOANGE LOVING ORCHID SALUTE
TONGUE ACCLAIM ADULATE
APPLAUD COMMEND FLATTER
GLORIFY MAGNIFY NOSEGAY
PLAUDIT PUFFING TRIBUTE
WORSHIP APPLAUSE BLESSING
DOXOLOGY ENCOMIUM EULOGIZE
(— **BE TO GOD**) LD
(— **IN THANKSGIVING**) JOY
(— **INORDINATELY**) FUME
(— **OF ANOTHER'S FELICITY**)
MACARISM
(— **TO GOD ALWAYS**) LDS
(**EFFUSIVE** —) FUSS
(**EXCESSIVE** —) FLATTERY
ADULATION
(**INSINCERE** —) CLART DAUBING
(**PUBLIC** —) PRECONY
(**SING FALSE** —**S**) CHANT
PRAISED JUDAH JUDITH LAURELED
(**UNDULY** —) BEPUFFED
PRAISEWORTHY WORTHY AMIABLE
GLORIOUS LAUDABLE SPLENDID
EXEMPLARY
PRAJAPATI KA PITRI
PRAKRIT PALI MAGADHI
PRAM CARRIAGE HANDCART
PUSHCART STROLLER
PRANCE STIR BRANK CAPER DANCE
JAUNT PRANK CAREER CAVORT
CURVET GAMBOL JAUNCE TITTUP
TRANCE PRANKLE SWAGGER
CAKEWALK
PRANCER HORSE DANCER CAPERER
PRANK JIG RAG RIG DECK DIDO
FOLD GAME JEST LARK PRAT REAK
ADORN CAPER FREAK SHINE SKITE
TRICK VAGUE BROGUE CURVET
FEGARY FIGARY FROLIC GAMBOL
SHAVIE VAGARY MARLOCK SPANGLE
ESCAPADE PRANCOME RIGWIDDIE
(**PL.**) REX GAMES JINKS
PRANKISH TRICKSY
PRASINE LEEK

PRAT PUSH NUDGE TRICK
PRATE GAB BUCK BUKH BUKK CARC
CHAT CLAP CLAT TALK BLATE
BOAST CLASH SCOLD BABBLE
CACKLE CLAVER JANGLE SQUIRT
TONGUE BLATHER BLATTER
CHATTER CLATTER PRATTLE
TWATTLE
PRATING GAFF CHATTER
PRATIQUE CUSTOM PRODUCT
PRATTLE CHAT CLACK BABBLE
BURBLE JANNER JAUNER YATTER
BLATTER CHATTER CLATTER
JAUNDER PRITTLE TRATTLE
TWADDLE BAVARDAGE
PRATTLING CHAVISH
PRAWN CARID NIPPER PENEIC
SHRIMP SQUILLA CARIDEAN
CARIDOID CREVETTE MACRURAN
PRAWN KILLER SQUILLA
PRAXIS HABIT ACTION CUSTOM
PRACTICE
PRAY ASK BEG BID BLESS CRAVE
DAVEN SOUGH VOUCH INVITE
ENTREAT IMPLORE REQUEST
WRESTLE INVOCATE
(— **FOR**) BOON
PRAYA BUND BEACH STRAND
PRAYER ACT AHA AVE VOW BEAD
BENE BOON PLEA SUIT VOTE
AGNUS ALENU NAMAZ SALAT
ABODAH APPEAL ECTENE ERRANC
LITANY MANTRA MATINS ORISON
STEVEN VESPER YIZKOR BIDDING
COMPLIN FATIHAH GAYATRI
GEULLAH KADDISH MEMENTO
ORATION PRECULE PREFACE
TAHANUN ANAPHORA APOLYSIS
CATHISMA DEVOTION KEDUSHAH
MISERERE PETITION SUFFRAGE
TEHINNAH
(— **BEADS**) ROSARY
(— **BOOK**) MAHZOR MISSAL
SERVICE
(— **LEADER**) IMAM
(— **OF DISMISSAL**) APOLYSIS
(— **RUG**) NAMAZLIK
(— **SHAWL**) TALLITH
(— **STICK**) BAHO PAHO
(— **TOWER**) MINARET
(**CANONICAL** —**S**) BREVIARY
(**CHIEF MOHAMMEDAN** —) NAMAZ
(**HINDU** —) GAYATRI
(**INWARD** —) ACT
(**JEWISH** —) ALENU ABODAH
GEULLAH HOSHANA KADDISH
(**LAST** — **OF DAY**) COMPLIN
(**LONG** —) CATHISMA
(**MUSLIM** —) SALAH SALAT
(**OPENING** —) COLLECT
(**SHORT** —) GRACE COLLECT
(**SILENT** —) SECRET
(**PL.**) HOURS NORITO TIKKUN
CHAPLET
PRAYING ORISON IMPRECANT
PREACH EDIFY SOUGH TEACH
EXHORT GOSPEL SERMON DELIV
HOMILIZE
PREACHER KHATIB MAGGID PARS

TUBMAN DARSHAN LOLLARD
MARTEXT PROPHET ROUNDER
TEACHER TUBBIST TUBSTER
EXHORTER KOHELETH MINISTER
PARDONER PULPITER QOHELETH
SERMONER SPINTEXT SWADDLER
VARTABED
(PL.) PULPIT

REACHING SPELL PULPIT SERMON
HEARING KERUGMA KERYGMA
PROPHECY PULPITRY SPELLING

REACHY DIDACTIC

REAMBLE PREFACE WHEREAS

REARRANGED SET

REBEND CANONRY

REBENDARY PROVEND

RE-CAMBRIAN MOINE EOZOIC
ARCHEAN

RECARIOUS DICKY RISKY SHAKY
CASUAL INFIRM UNSURE DUBIOUS
CATCHING DELICATE INSECURE
PERILOUS UNSTABLE DANGEROUS
UNCERTAIN

RECAUTION CARE GUARD CAUTEL

RECEDE LEAD FOREGO HERALD
FORERUN PREFACE PREVENT
ANTECEDE PREAMBLE

RECEDENCE LEAD PRIMACY
HERALDRY PRIORITY

RIGHT OF —) PAS

SOCIAL —) LEVEL

RECEDENT LEAD SIGN MODEL
TOKEN USAGE INSTANCE ORIGINAL
SPECIMEN STANDARD AUTHORITY

RECEDING OLD FORE WEST
BEFORE FORMER LEADING
ADJACENT PREVIOUS

— **ALL OTHERS**) FIRST

RECENTOR CANTOR PSALMIST
ETTERGAE

RECEPT LAW HEST LINE RULE
LORA WRIT ADAGE AXIOM BREVE
MAXIM ORDER SUTRA SUTTA TORAH
BEHEST DICTATE MANDATE
WARRANT DOCTRINE DOCUMENT
LANDMARK

RECEPTIVE DIDACTIC MANDATORY

RECEPTOR TUTOR MASTER

RECINCT BEAT AMBIT BOUND
CLOSE DOMAIN HIERON COLLEGE
ENAEUM SOCIETY TEMENOS
DISTRICT ENVIRONS
(PL.) AMBIT

RECIOUS DEAR FINE LIEF RARE
VERY CHARY CHERE GREAT HONEY
CHOICE COSTLY DAINTY GOLDEN
DOSING SILVER TENDER PRECISE
AFFECTED ORIENTAL OVERNICE
VALUABLE WORTHFUL

RECIOUSNESS PRICE

RECIPICE LIN KHUD LINN LLYN
WALI CLIFF KRANS SCREE SHEER
STEEP KRANTZ CLOGWYN
DOWNFALL HEADWALL

RECIPITATE GEL CURD HURL
RASH HASTY HURRY SHOOT SPEED
FOR ABRUPT COAGEL HASTEN
NUDGE SUDDEN TUMBLE UNWARY
STILL LYCOPIN SUBSIDE

CATALYZE HEADLONG PROCLIVE
SETTLING
(— **DYE**) STRIKE

PRECIPITATELY HEADLING
HEADLONG SLAPDASH

PRECIPITATION HAIL MIST RAIN
SNOW HASTE SLEET VIRGA

PRECIPITOUS FULL RASH BRANT
BRENT HASTY STEEP ABRUPT
CHICHI STEEPY SUDDEN PRERUPT
HEADLONG

PRECIS JUNONIA SUMMARY
ABSTRACT

PRECISE SET FLAT HARD JUMP JUST
TIDY TRIG TRUE VERY CLEAN
CLOSE EXACT PRESS RIGID SOUND
FORMAL STARCH STRICT BUCKRAM
CAREFUL CERTAIN CLERKLY
CORRECT EXPRESS PERFECT
PERJINK STARCHY ABSOLUTE
ACCURATE DEFINITE EXPLICIT
HAIRLINE PUNCTUAL

PRECISELY BUT EVEN JUST CLEAN
SHARP FINELY JUSTLY STRAIT
EXACTLY

PRECISENESS RIGOR RIGOUR
PRIMNESS

PRECISIAN PRIG PURITAN

PRECISION NICETY CLARITY
ACCURACY DELICACY ELEGANCE
JUSTNESS

PRECISIONIST PEDANT

PRECLUDE BAR DENY STOP CLOSE
CROSS DEBAR ESTOP FORBID
HINDER IMPEDE OBVIATE PREVENT
SILENCE CONCLUDE INTERPEL

PRECOCIOUS PRECOX UNRIPE
FORWARD PREMATURE RATHERIPE

PRECONCEIVE IDEATE

PRECONDITION PRIUS

PRECURSOR USHER HERALD INITIAL
ANCESTOR PRODROME WAYMAKER
HARBINGER HEMIAUXIN

PREDACITY RAVEN RAVIN

PREDATOR COACTOR

PREDATORY HUNGRY HARMFUL
RAVENOUS

PREDECESSOR ANCESTOR
FOREGOER
(PL.) OLDERS

PREDELLA FOOTPACE

PREDESTINATION FATE DESTINY
ELECTION

PREDESTINE DOOM SLATE
FOREDOOM FOREPOINT

PREDETERMINE DESTINE FORECAST

PREDICAMENT FIX JAM SOUP SPOT
CLASS STATE STEAD PICKLE PLIGHT
SCRAPE DILEMMA IMPASSE
CATEGORY JUNCTURE QUANDARY

PREDICANT FRIAR PREACHER
DOMINICAN

PREDICATE BASE FOUND AFFIRM
ASSERT PRAISE PREACH COMMEND
DECLARE EXTREME PREDICT
PROCLAIM

PREDICT LAY BODE CALL DOPE
READ REDE AUGUR WEIRD HALSEN
FORESAY PRESAGE FOREBODE

FORECAST FORETELL PROPHESY
SOOTHSAY
(— **EVIL**) CROAK

PREDICTION DOPE WEIRD AUGURY
BODING BODWORD PORTENT
PRESAGE BODEWORD FORECAST
PROPHECY VATICINE

PREDILECTION BIAS HANG FANCY
FAVOR LIKING RELISH FONDNESS

PREDISPOSE BEND INCLINE
SUBJECT

PREDISPOSED PRONE PARTIAL
TENDING INCLINED

PREDISPOSITION ITCH DIATHESIS

PREDOMINANT GREAT RULING
CAPITAL REIGNING SUPERIOR
CULMINANT HEGEMONIC

PREDOMINATE RULE DOMINE
EXCEED GOVERN PREVAIL

PREE KISS PRIE TEST TASTE TRIAL
PRYING SAMPLE PROVING TASTING

PREEMINENT BIG TOP HIGH STAR
FIRST GRAND GREAT PALMARY
PASSING STELLAR SUPREME
FOREMOST PRECLARE SPLENDID
SUPERIOR PARAMOUNT

PREEMPT COLLAR

PREEN PIN PERK PICK TRIM DRESS
GLOAT PLUME PRINK PRUNE SWELL
TRICK BROOCH GODWIT SMOOTH
REPLUME
(— **WINGS**) WHET

PREFACE FRONT PROEM USHER
HERALD PRESAY PRECEDE
PREPOSE EXORDIUM FORETALK
FOREWORD PREAMBLE PROLOGUE

PREFATORY PROEMIAL

PREFECT WALI EPARC EPARCH
MONITOR PROVOST GOVERNOR
PRESIDENT

PREFECTURE EPARCHY
(**CHINESE** —) FU
(**JAPANESE** —) KEN
(**TIBETAN** —) JONG

PREFER LAY LIKE LOVE BRING
ELECT EXALT FAVOR OFFER
CHOOSE PROFER SELECT OUTRANK
PREFECT PRESENT PROMOTE
PROPOSE SURPASS

PREFERABLE LIEF RIGHT RATHER
ELIGIBLE

PREFERENCE GOO LIKE FAVOR
DESIRE LIKING RATHER DRUTHERS
FAVORITE PRIVILEGE PROMOTION

PREFIGURE TYPE IDEATE SHADOW
TYPIFY FORERUN FORESEE PREDICT
FORESHOW

PREFIX DUN DOON PREPOSE

PREGNANCY CYESIS TROUBLE
ACCYESIS FETATION OOCYESIS
GESTATION

PREGNANT BIG GONE OPEN GREAT
HEAVY QUICK READY BAGGED
CAUGHT COGENT GRAVID PAROUS
ENCEINT FERTILE GESTANT
TEEMING WEIGHTY CHILDING
FORCIBLE GERMINAL PRESSING

PREHALLUX CALCAR

PREHEND SEIZE

PREHISTORIC IMMEMORIAL
PREINDICATE PRESAGE FORESHOW
PREJUDICE BIAS DOWN HARM HURT
KINK TURN DERRY DAMAGE IMPAIR
INJURY SCUNDER SCUNNER
JAUNDICE PREJUDGE
PREJUDICED BIGOTED INSULAR
PARTIAL
PREJUDICIAL BIASED HURTFUL
CONTRARY DAMAGING INIMICAL
SINISTER
PRELATE CHIEF LEADER PRIEST
HIERARCH ORDINARY SUPERIOR
PRELIMINARY PRIOR PRELIM
PREFACE PRELUDE LIMINARY
PREAMBLE PREVIOUS
PRELUDE PROEM VERSET DESCANT
FORERUN INTRADA PREFACE
ANTELUDE BORSPIEL OVERTURE
RITORNEL VERSETTE VORSPIEL
PREMATURE UNRIPE IMMATURE
PREVIOUS TIMELESS UNTIMELY
PREMEDITATE FORNCAST
PURPENSE
PREMEDITATED SET STUDIED
PREPENSE
PREMIER CHIEF FIRST OLDEST
LEADING EARLIEST
PREMISE LEMMA MAJOR ASSUME
GROUND REASON SUMPTION
PREMIXED INSTANT
PREMIUM USE AGIO BACK AWARD
BONUS FANCY PRIZE SHAVE USURY
BOUNTY DEPORT REWARD
CONTANGO DONATIVE FOREGIFT
GIVEAWAY
PREMONITION OMEN HUNCH
NOTICE BODWORD PRESAGE
WARNING BODEWORD FORESCENT
PREMUNE SALTED
PREOCCUPATION HEART INSIGHT
FIXATION
PREOCCUPIED DEEP LOST RAPT
CRAZY ABSENT FILLED INTENT
CRACKED ABSORBED ENGROSSED
PREPARATION DIA FIG BALM DIBS
DOPE PREP CREAM FLASH GLAZE
JELLY READY ACETUM BLEACH
BLUING DERRIS FACIAL LOTION
MEGILP NEBULA PEPSIN SIMPLE
APPREST CLEANER DIPPING
EMANIUM ESSENCE ETHIOPS
EXTRACT FITNESS FONDANT
LINCTUS MELLITE PLACEBO
TRYPSIN VARNISH ABSTRACT
CONSERVE COSMETIC FIXATURE
GELOSINE INHALANT LAUDANUM
MEDICINE RACAHOUT TRAINING
MAKEREADY
(— CONTAINING HONEY) MELLITE
(— FOR COLORING LIQUORS) FLASH
(— OF GRAPEJUICE) DIBS
(AROMATIC —) ELIXIR
(CHEESE —) FONDU
(CHEESELIKE —) YOGURT YOGHURT
(COSMETIC —) HENNA
(ENZYME —) KOJI
(EYELID —) KOHL
(IMPURE RADIOACTIVE —) EMANIUM

(INTOXICATING —) BOZA
(MEDICAL —) STUFF
(OPIUM —) LAUDANUM
(SALINE —) LICK
(SLOPPY —) SLIBBERSAUCE
(SWEET —) DULCE
(UNCTUOUS —) CERATE
PREPARATORY PIONEER
PREPARE DO FIT FIX GET LAY ABLE
BUSK COOK GIRD MAKE PARE PLOT
PREP TILL YARK ATTLE BLEND
BRACE DIGHT DRAFT DRESS EQUIP
FRAME ORDER PREDY READY TRAIN
ADJUST DESIGN GRAITH ORDAIN
ADDRESS AFFAITE APPAREL
APPOINT CONCOCT CONFECT
DISPOSE EDUCATE PRODUCE
PROVIDE QUALIFY INSTRUCT
(— BANQUET) COVER
(— BY BOILING) BREW DECOCT
(— BY HEAT) FRIT
(— CAPON) SAUCE
(— FISH) CALVER
(— FOOD) DO COOK
(— FOR BUILDING) FRAME
(— FOR BURIAL) EMBALM
(— FOR DISPLAY) DRESS
(— FOR PUBLICATION) EDIT
(— HASTILY) RASH
(— HEMP) TAW
(— LAND) CURE
(— ONESELF) ADDRESS
(— TEASEL HEADS) CARP
PREPARED UP APT BUN FIT SET
BAAN BOON BOUN BOWN GIRT RIPE
YARE ALERT BOUND PREST READY
GRAITH CURRIED EQUIPPED
(QUICKLY —) RUNNING
PREPENSE DESIGN FORETHOUGHT
PREPONDERANCE MAJORITY
DOMINANCE
PREPONDERATE EXCEED INCLINE
SURPASS DOMINATE OUTWEIGH
PERSUADE
PREPOSSESS BIAS PREVENT
PREPOSSESSION BENT BIAS FETICH
FANTASY PREJUDICE
PREPOSTEROUS RICH INEPT
ABSURD FOOLISH LAPUTAN
GROTESQUE
PREROGATIVE GRACE HONOR
RIGHT ESNECY REGALE FACULTY
PECULIAR PRIVILEGE
PRESA LEAD
PRESAGE BODE HINT OMEN OSSE
SIGN ABODE AUGUR TOKEN
AUGURY BETIDE BETOKEN FORESEE
OMINATE PORTEND PREDICT
FOREBODE FORECAST FOREDOOM
FORETELL INDICATE PREAMBLE
PROPHESY
PRESBYTER ELDER PRIEST PRESTER
ANTISTES MINISTER
PRESBYTERIAN WHIG
PRESBYTERY SENIORY EXERCISE
PARSONAGE
PRESCIENCE PRESAGE FORESIGHT
PREVISION
PRESCIND SEVER DETACH

PRESCRIBE SET TAX ALLOT GUIDE
LIMIT ORDER ASSIGN DEFINE
DIRECT ENJOIN INDITE ORDAIN
APPOINT CONFINE CONTROL
DICTATE RESTRAIN
PRESCRIBED SET BASIC THETIC
THETICAL FORMULARY
PRESCRIPT LAW COMMAND
MANDATE PRECEPT
PRESCRIPTION RX BILL FORM
CIPHER RECIPE DICTATE FORMULA
PRESENCE EYE FACE SELF BEING
ASPECT BEARING COMPANY
ASSEMBLY INSTANCE
(DIRECT —) IMMEDIACY
PRESENT AIM BOX NOW BILL BOON
GIFT GIVE HAND HERE NEAR NIGH
SAND SHOW BEING CUDDY DOLLY
ENTER FEOFF GRANT NONCE OFFE
PLACE RAISE READY STAGE THERE
ACCUSE ACTUAL ADDUCE ALLEGE
AROUND BESTOW BOUNTY BROACH
CLOTHE CUMSHA DONATE DURANT
HANSEL KHILAT LATTER MODERN
NEARBY PREFER REGALE REGALO
XENIUM COMMEND CUMSHAW
DISPLAY DOUCEUR ETRENNE
EXHIBIT EXPOUND FAIRING FURNISH
HANDSEL INSTANT LARGESS
PERFORM PORRECT PRETEND
PROPINE RESIANT TASHRIF
BLESSING CONGIARY DONATION
GRATUITY INSTANCE LAGNAPPE
OFFERING PESHKASH RESIDENT
SOULCAKE SPORTULA
(— AS GIFT) DASH
(— FOR ACCEPTANCE) TENDER
(— FROM PUPIL TO TEACHER)
MINERVAL
(— IN DETAIL) DISCUSS
(— IN MIND) DEAR
(— ONESELF) APPEAR
(— TO SOLDIERS) CONGIARY
(— TO STRANGER) XENIUM
(— TO VIEW) YIELD
(— WITHOUT WARRANT) OBTRUDE
(ALWAYS —) CHRONIC
(BRIDEGROOM'S —) HANDSEL
(CEREMONIAL —) KHILAT
PRESENTATION BILL GALA GIFT
SHOW DROLL IMAGE DHARMA
MUSTER SCHEMA BILLING DISPLAY
EPITOME HOOKUPU PRESENT
SPECIES ANALYSIS BESTOWAL
DELIVERY DONATION EXPOSURE
CANDLEMAS
PRESENTIMENT FEELING PRESAG
BODEMENT FOREFEEL PRENOTION
PRESENTLY NOW ANON ENOW
SOON SHORTLY DIRECTLY
PRESERVATION FILING SAVING
KEEPING SERVATION
PRESERVATIVE SALT BORAX SPIC
SUGAR CONSERVE TREATMENT
PRESERVE CAN JAR CORN HAIN
HOLD KEEP SAVE BLESS GUARD
SERVE SPARE SWEET WITIE ATHC
BOTTLE COMFIT DEFEND EMBALM
FREEZE GOGGLE POWDER RETAIN

SECURE SHIELD UPHOLD CONDITE
FORFEND KYANIZE PROTECT
RAISINE RESERVE SUCCADE
SUSTAIN CHOWCHOW CONSERVE
ENSHRINE MAINTAIN MOTHBALL
PARADISE WITHSAVE
(— **BY BOILING WITH SUGAR)**
CANDY
(— **BY SALTING)** CORN CURE SALT
(— **OF GRAPES)** RAISINE
(— **WOOD)** KYANIZE
(**GAME** —) MOOR SHIKARGAH
(**HUNTING** —) WALK
(**PL.)** KONFYT
RESERVED WET CONFECT
BRANDIED POWDERED
RESIDE RULE GUIDE DIRECT
MODERATE
(— **OVER)** KEEP
RESIDENCY MADRAS PRYTANY
RESIDENT MIR FOUD PREX PROXY
REEVE DEACON RECTOR PRAESES
PREFECT
(— **OF SUPREME COURT)** LAWMAN
(— **OF TRADE)** DEACON
RESIGNIFY PRESAGE FORETOKEN
RESS FLY HUG JAM SIT BEAR BEND
CRAM DOME DROP DRUK HORN
HUSH IRON JAMB KISS PLOT SERR
THEW TUCK URGE VICE YERK
ARGUE BESET BRIZZ CHAFE CHIRT
CROWD CRUSH DRIVE EXACT
FORCE KNEAD MIDST PRIZE SCREW
SHREW SMASH STAMP STUFF TWIST
WEIGH WRING ASSAIL CHISEL
CLOSET COARCT CRUNCH GOFFER
HARASS JOBBER MANGLE NUDDLE
PREACE SQUASH STRAIN STRESS
THRAST THREAP THREAT THREEP
THRIMP THRING THRONG THRUST
AFFLICT ATTEMPT BESEECH
BESIEGE CONCISE CRUMPLE
EMBRACE ENVIRON FLATBED
IMPRESS MACHINE OPPRESS
SCROOGE SCRUNGE SQUEEZE
THRUTCH CALENDER COMPRESS
PRESSURE SCROUNGE SQUEEGEE
SURROUND
(— **AGAINST)** CONTACT
(— **CLOSE)** NUDDLE
(— **CLOSELY AND PAINFULLY)** MASH
(— **DOWN)** QUAT
(— **FOR WINE)** TORCULAR
(— **FORWARD)** DRIVE BREAST
(— **HARSHLY)** GRIND
(— **IN CHEESE VAT)** CHISEL
CHIZZEL
(— **INTO)** THRIMBLE THRUMBLE
(— **ON ANVIL)** HORN
(— **ONWARD)** STRETCH
(— **OUT)** EXTRUDE
(— **PAPER)** COUCH
(— **TOGETHER)** SERRY
(— **UPON)** ELBOW DOWNBEAR
(— **WITH HEAD OR HORNS)** BOX
(— **WITH VIOLENCE)** DRIVE
RESS AGENT FLACK
RESSED SERRIED
(— **WITH BUSINESS)** THRONG

(— **WITH LEFTHAND FOREFINGER)**
BARRED
PRESSING RASH CRYING URGENT
CLAMANT EARNEST EXIGENT
INSTANT SQUEEZE CRITICAL
PREGNANT
PRESSMAN PIG MINDER PROVER
PRINTER
PRESSURE JAM HEAD HEAT PEND
PUSH SWAY DRIVE FORCE IMAGE
PINCH STAMP DURESS STRESS
THRONG WEIGHT BEARING
MERCURY PUSHING SQUEEZE
TENSION URGENCY EXACTION
EXIGENCY FUGACITY PRESSION
(— **GROUP)** LOBBY
(— **OF 1 DYNE)** BARAD
(— **ON INSTRUMENT STRING)** STOP
(— **UNIT)** TORR MICRON
(**LIQUID** —) HEAD
(**MANUAL** —) TAXIS
(**VAPOR** —) FUGACITY
PRESSURE COOKER STEAMER
AUTOCLAVE
PRESSWORK BACKUP
PRESTIDIGITATOR PALMER
JUGGLER PYTHONIC
PRESTIGE FACE MANA CASTE IKBAL
IZZAT KUDOS CACHET STATUS
STATURE ILLUSION INFLUENCE
PRESTO QUICKLY SPEEDILY
PRESUME BEAR DARE GROW IMPLY
INFER ASSUME EXPECT DARESAY
SUPPOSE
PRESUMING ARROGANT FAMILIAR
PRESUMPTION JOLLITY OUTRAGE
PRESUME AUDACITY SUCCUDRY
SURQUIDY
PRESUMPTUOUS BOLD PERT FRESH
PROUD WICKED WILFUL FORWARD
HAUGHTY ARROGANT ASSUMING
FAMILIAR INSOLENT FOOLHARDY
PRESUPPOSE IMPLY POSIT ASSUME
EXPECT PREMISE FORETAKE
PRETA PETA
PRETEND ACT LET FAKE MAKE
MOCK SHAM CLAIM FEIGN AFFECT
ASPIRE ASSERT ASSUME GAMMON
INTEND OBTEND POSSUM RECKON
SEMBLE ATTEMPT PORTEND
PRESUME PROFESS SUPPOSE
VENTURE SIMULATE
(— **IGNORANCE)** CONNIVE
(— **TO)** FA
PRETENDED FAKE SHAM BOGUS
FALSE IRONIC UNREAL ALLEGED
ASSUMED COLORED FEIGNED
SEEMING AFFECTED IRONICAL
SIMULATE
PRETENDER FOP FAKE IDOL CHEAT
COWAN FAKER FRAUD QUACK
PSEUDO SEEMER AEOLIST
CLAIMANT IMPOSTOR INTENDER
TARTUFFE
(— **TO LEARNING)** SCIOLIST
PRETENDING FICTION
PRETENSE ACT AIR FACE GRIM
MIEN PLEA RUSE SCUG SHAM SHOW
SIGN WILE CLOAK COLOR COVER

FEINT GLOSS GLOZE STUDY
EXCUSE HUMBUG CHARADE FAITERY
FASHION FICTION GRIMACE
PRETEXT PURPOSE UMBRAGE
ARTIFICE DISGUISE POSTICHE
POSTIQUE SEMBLANT
PRETENSION PARADE VANITY
PRETEXT
PRETENTIOUS BIG BRAG HIGH SIDY
FLASH GAUDY PUFFY SHOWY
BRAGGY GEWGAW GLOSSY PUFFED
ROCOCO SHODDY TINSEL BOMBAST
POMPOUS TOPPING BRAGGART
PRETENTIOUSNESS SIDE SWANK
PRETERMIT OMIT NEGLACT
SUSPEND INTERRUPT
PRETERNATURAL GOUSTY GOUSTIE
STRANGE ABNORMAL UNCOMMON
UNEARTHLY
(— **BEING)** MARE
PRETEXT PEG FLAM MASK PLEA
CLOAK COLOR COVER GLOSS
SALVO STALL EXCUSE REFUGE
SCONCE APOLOGY UMBRAGE
OCCASION PRETENCE
PRETTIFY EYEWASH
PRETTY APT GEY PAT ABLE BRAW
CUTE DEFT FAIR FEAT FINE GAIN
GENT GOOD JOLI MILD POOR TRIM
BONNY DINKY JOLIE POOTY PURTY
QUITE SWEET BONITA DIMBER
FINELY INCONY MINION PRATTY
RATHER TRETIS CLEMENT CUNNING
DOLLISH GENTEEL BUDGEREE
PRECIOUS
(— **WELL)** GAILY GAYLY
PRETTY-PRETTY KEEPSAKE
PREVAIL WIN BEAR BEAT REIGN
WIELD INDUCE OBTAIN CONQUER
PERSIST SUCCEED TRIUMPH
DOMINATE
(— **BECAUSE BEYOND CONTROL)**
RAGE
(— **OVER)** SURMOUNT
(— **UPON)** GET FOLD LEAD ARGUFY
ENTICE INDUCE OBTAIN ENTREAT
OVERSWAY
PREVAILING RIFE GOING USUAL
CURRENT DOMINANT
PREVALENCE RUN
PREVALENT UP RIFE BRIEF
COMMON POTENT CURRENT
GENERAL POPULAR REGNANT
CATHOLIC EPIDEMIC POWERFUL
PREVARICATE LIE EVADE STRAY
WANDER QUIBBLE SHUFFLE
PREVENT BAR LET HELP KEEP NILL
SHUN STAY STOP TENT WARN
AVERT CHECK DEBAR DETER ESTOP
ARREST DEFEND FORBID FORLET
HINDER OUTRUN RETAIN REVOKE
SECURE FORFEND FORLEIT
IMPEACH INHIBIT PRECEDE RETRACT
ANTEVERT INTERPEL PRECLUDE
WITHHOLD
(— **OPPONENT FROM SCORING)**
CHICAGO
PREVENTION PREFACE ESTOPPEL
OBSTACLE PREJUDICE

PREVIEW SNEAK FUTURAMA
PREVIOUS HASTY PRIOR BEFORE
FORMER RATHER EARLIER LEADING
FOREGONE
PREVIOUSLY ERE YET ERST FORE
SUPRA BEFORE ALREADY HASTILY
PRIORLY FORMERLY HITHERTO
PREVISION FORESEE FORECAST
FORESIGHT
PREY ROB FEED GAME SOYL TIRE
BOOTY PREDE RAVEN RAVIN SPOIL
QUARRY RAVAGE RAVINE VICTIM
CAPTURE PILLAGE PLUNDER
ROBBERY SPREATH VULTURE
(— UPON) DEVOUR PICAROON
DEPREDATE
PREYER KITE
PRIAM (DAUGHTER OF —) CREUSA
POLYXENA CASSANDRA
(SLAYER OF —) PYRRHUS
(SON OF —) PARIS HECTOR
TROILUS
(WIFE OF —) HECUBA
PRIAPISM TENTIGO
PRICE LAY ANTE COST FARE FEER
FIAR FIER FOOT ODDS PRYS RATE
BRIBE CHEAP CLOSE VALUE WORTH
CHARGE FIGURE HANSEL TARIFF
AVERAGE CATALOG CRANAGE
EXPENSE FURNACE HANDSEL
PRETIUM STORAGE CARRIAGE
FERRIAGE INTEREST
(— FOR KEEPING GOODS) STORAGE
(LOW —) WANWORTH
(PROPER —) VALUE
(REDUCED —) SALE BARGAIN
(RISING —S) BOOM INFLATION
PRICELESS RARE COSTLY UNIQUE
UNSALABLE
PRICK DOT JAG BROD DROB FOIN
GOAD JAGG PECK PING PROG SPUR
STAB TANG URGE DRESS ERECT
POINT PREEN PUNCH STEEK
BROACH GALLOP INTENT LAUNCH
POUNCE PRITCH SKEWER STITCH
TARGET THRUST TWINGE POINTED
BULLSEYE
(— OUT) SPOT
(— PAINFULLY) STING
(— WITH NAIL) CLY CLOY
PRICKED PIQUE
PRICKER PROD NEEDLE STABBER
PRICKET DAG SNUFFER SPITTER
PRICKING SMART PUNGENT
RETRACT POIGNANT POINTURE
PUNCTION
PRICKLE PIKE SETA SPEAR THORN
BASKET ACANTHA ACULEUS
PRINKLE SPICULA
PRICKLY BURRY JAGGY SHARP
SPINY URCHIN SPINOSE SPINOUS
STICKLY THISTLY ECHINATE
MURICATE SCABROUS SCRATCHY
SPICULAR STICKERY STINGING
VEXATIOUS
PRICKLY ASH RUEWORT
PRICKLY PEAR TUN TUNA NOPAL
SABRA OPUNTIA PINPILLOW
PRICKLY-POINTED PUNGENT

PRICKLY POPPY COCKSCOMB
PRIDE HEAT HORN LUST POMP RUFF
ADORN CREST GLORY ORGUL
PLUME PRIME WLANK EXCESS
HUBRIS METTLE NOSISM VANITY
COMPANY CONCEIT DISDAIN
EGOTISM GLORIFY HAUTEUR
STOMACH SURQUIDY WLONKHEDE
(— ONESELF) PIQUE
(EXCESSIVE —) SWELLING
PRIDEFUL FASTUOUS
PRIEST EN CURA CURE DEAN EZRA
IMAM MAGA COHEN EPULO IMAUM
ISIAC MOBED PADRE PATER SABIO
SARIP VICAR ZADOK ABACES
AMAUTA BHIKKU BISHOP DASTUR
DIVINE FALMEN FATHER FLAMEN
GALLAH GALLUS GELONG GETSUL
GOSAIN JETHRO KAHUNA LEVITE
POWWOW SHAMAN ANANIAS
ARBACES CALCHAS CASSOCK
CHANTER DESTOUR DUSTOOR
GALLACH LAOCOON PANDITA
PAPALOI PATENER PATRICO
PHINEAS POONGEE PRESTER
STOLIST TEACHER TOHUNGA
BABAYLAN BEROSSOS CASERDOS
CHRYSEIS HANANIAH KASHYAPA
MINISTER PANDARAM PENANCER
PONTIFEX POONGHIE SEMINARY
SOGGARTH SYRIARCH TALISMAN
VARDAPET ZADOKITE
(— OF APOLLO) CALCHAS CHRYSEIS
(— OF CYBELE) CORYBANT
(— OF RAMA) KASHYAPA
(— OF RHEA) CURETE
(BABYLONIAN —) BEROSSOS
(BUDDHIST —) LAMA BHIKKU
GELONG POONGEE POONGHIE
(CHIEF — OF SHRINE) EN
(CHIEF —) SYRIARCH
(EGYPTIAN —) ARBACES
CHOACHYTE
(EUNUCH —) GALLUS
(FRENCH —) PERE SULPICIAN
(GYPSY —) PATRICO
(HIGH —) ELI SARIP DASTUR
KAHUNA DESTOUR PHINEAS
PONTIFF PRELATE CAIAPHAS
HIERARCH JEHOIADA PONTIFEX
(HINDU —) PANDARAM
(INCA —) AMAUTA
(LAMAIST —) GETSUL
(MAORI —) TOHUNGA
(MORO —) SARIP PANDITA
(MOSLEM —) TALISMAN
(PAGAN —) BABAYLAN
(PARISH —) CURA CURE PAPA POPE
PARSON PERSON SECULAR
(ROMAN —) EPULO FLAMEN
(TIBETAN —) LAMA
(VAISHNAVA —) GOSAIN
(PL.) LUPERCI
PRIEST-DOCTOR SHAMAN WABENO
PRIESTESS NUN ENTUM HORSE
MAMBO MAMBU BACBUC PYTHIA
DIOTIMA MAMALOI PHOIBAD
PHITONES
(— OF APOLLO) PYTHIA PHOEBAD

(— OF THE BOTTLE) BACBUC
(BABYLONIAN —) ENTUM
(VOODOO —) HORSE
PRIESTFISH CHERNA ROCKFISH
PRIESTHOOD SALII SACERDOCY
PRIEST-KING PATESI
PRIESTLY LEVITIC SACERDOTAL
PRIG BEG FOP BRAD BUCK NAIL
SMUG DANDY FILCH PLEAD STEAL
THIEF FELLOW HAGGLE PERSON
PILFER TINKER ENTREAT PURITAN
QUIBBLE
PRIGGER THIEF
PRIM MIM NEAT TRIG TRIM MIMZY
DEMURE FORMAL MIMSEY PRIVET
PROPER STUFFY MISSISH PRECISE
PRIMSIE
PRIMACY CHIEFTY PRIMITY
HEADSHIP
PRIMA DONNA DIVA STAR
PRIMARY CYAN BASIC CHIEF FIRST
PRIME CAUCUS DIRECT FONTAL
MANUAL MAGENTA RADICAL
ARCHICAL CARDINAL HYPOGENE
ORIGINAL PRIMEVAL
PRIMATE BISHOP GALAGO LEADER
PREMAN PRINCIPAL
PRIME MAY FANG FILL LOAD MAIN
CHIEF COACH FIRST PRIDE TONIC
YOUTH CHOICE FLOWER SPRING
CENTRAL LEADING LUSTFUL
PREPARE DOMINEER ORIGINAL
YOUTHFUL PRINCIPAL
PRIME MINISTER ATABEG PREMIE
PRIMER ABC CAP WAFER CORDER
HORNBOOK
PRIMEVAL OLD NATIVE ANCIENT
OGYGIAN PRIMARY PRISTINE
PRIMITIVE
PRIMING MORSING TWOPENNY
CLEARCOLE
PRIMING IRON DRIFT
PRIMING WIRE PICKER
PRIMITIVE DARK CRUDE EARLY
FIRST GROSS NAIVE PLAIN PRIME
FANTEE GOTHIC PRIMAL SAVAGE
SIMPLE ANCIENT ARCHAIC PRIMAF
PRISCAN BARBARIC EARLIEST
IGNORANT ORIGINAL PRISTINE
PRIMNESS PRUDERY
PRIMORDIAL CRUDE FIRST PRIMAF
ARCHICAL EARLIEST PRIMEVAL
PRIMORDIUM BUD
PRIMP PRIM ADORN PREEN PRINK
PRIMROSE GAY OXLIP SPINK
FLOWER SUNCUP COWSLIP
FLOWERY SCABISH AURICULA
PLUMROCK SCURVISH AFTERGLOW
PIMPERNEL
PRIMULA OXLIP COWSLIP PRIMWO
PRINCE MIN RAS DUKE EARL EMIR
IMAM KHAN KING KNEZ LORD NAS
RAJA RANA RIAL SAID WANG ALDE
EBLIS EMEER FURST GEBIR PWYL
RAJAH SAYID ARJUNA DESPOT
DYNAST SHERIF SOLDAN BHARAT/
ELECTOR GLAUCUS HELENUS
MONARCH TANCRED TOPARCH
ZERBINO ARCHDUKE CARDINAL

AMILIUS OROONOKO PLORIZEL
ASSELAS SARPEDON
– OF ABYSSINIA) RAS RASSELAS
– OF APOSTATE ANGELS) DEVIL
BLIS
– OF ARGO) DIOMED DIOMEDES
– OF BOHEMIA) FLORIZEL
– OF DARKNESS) DEVIL SATAN
– OF DEMONS) BEELZEBUB
– OF DYFED) PWYLL
– OF SALERNO) TANCRED
– OF SCOTLAND) ZERBINO
– SOLD INTO SLAVERY)
ROONOKO
– WITH CHARLEMAGNE) ASTOLF
STOLFO
ANGLO-SAXON —) ADELING
THELING
ARAB —) SHERIF
CHINESE —) WANG
GERMAN —) FURST ELECTOR
INDIAN —) RAJA RANA RAJAH
HARATA AHLUWALIA
LYCIAN —) GLAUCUS SARPEDON
MOHAMMEDAN —) SOLDAN
MOSLEM —) IMAM SAID SAYID
AYYID SHEIKH SOLDAN
PETTY —) SATRAP VERGOBRET
SERVIAN —) CRAL
SLAVIC —) KNEZ
TROJAN —) HELENUS
INCELY NOBLE ROYAL KINGLY
TATELY SOVEREIGN
INCE'S FEATHER LILAC
LEWORT
INCESS AIDA ELSA RANI DANAE
ALLA RANEE SARAH CREUSA
LAUKE ILDICO MADAME PSYCHE
NTIOPE CORONIS PHYLLIS
RAUPADI MAHARANI
– CHANGED INTO CROW) CORONIS
– MOTHER OF ZEUS) ANTIOPA
NTIOPE
– OF ARGOS) DANAE
– OF CORINTH) CREUSA GLAUKE
– WHO SLEW ATTILA) ILDICO
MOHAMMEDAN —) BEGUM
THRACIAN —) PHYLLIS
TYRIAN —) DIDO
INCEWOOD CYP BARIA CYPRE
ERILLO CANALETE SALMWOOD
INCIPAL ARCH BOSS HEAD HIGH
MAIN STAR CHIEF FIRST GRAND
REAT PRIME STOCK AUCTOR
ORPUS MASTER STAPLE CAPITAL
APTAIN CENTRAL CHATTEL
OMINUS PREMIER PRIMARY
ALIENT STELLAR FOREMOST
FFICIAL PRESTANT PRINCELY
– OF SCHOOL) PRECEPTOR
EADMASTER
NCIPALITY ZUPA ARZAVA
RZAWA ORANGE SATRAPY
PPANAGE DESPUTAT
NCIPLE JUS LAW RTA TAO BASE
ATE RITA RULE SEED YANG AGENT
XIOM BASIS CANON CAUSE DATUM
RANA SPARK STUFF TENET

ANIMUS CNICIN COGITO CORTIN
ELIXIR EMBRYO FAGINE GOSPEL
ARCHEUS BROCARD BUFAGIN
CLYSSUS ELEMENT FORMULA
GENERAL PRECEPT QUASSIN
RADICAL THEOREM URGRUND
DOCTRINE GOSSYPOL INTIMISM
LANDMARK NICOTINE SANCTION
SPECIFIC TINCTURE
(— ACCEPTED AS TRUE) CANON
(— FROM TOAD) BUFAGIN
(— IN BEECHNUTS) FAGINE
(— OF BLESSED THISTLE) CNICIN
(— OF COTTONSEED) GOSSYPOL
(— OF EXISTENCE) TATTVA
(— OF INDIVIDUATION) AHANKARA
(— OF KEY IN MUSIC) TONALITY
(— OF REST) ADHARMA
(COSMIC —) HEAVEN URGRUND
PRAJAPATI
(DOGMATIC —) DICTUM
(ELEMENTARY —) BROCARD
(FEMALE —) YIN
(FIRST —) ABC SEED ARCHE
(FUNDAMENTAL —) GROUNDSEL
(GERMINAL —) STAMEN
(GOVERNING —) HINGE
(GUIDING —) SQUARE
(LIFE —) SOUL GHOST PRANA
(MALE —) YANG PURUSHA
(MOHAMMEDAN THEOLOGICAL —)
IJMA
(MORAL —) SCRUPLE
(NARCOTIC —) FAGINE
(ONTOLOGICAL —) DHARMA
(PRIMAL —) APEIRON
(PROMINENT —) KEY
(RHYTHMICAL —) ACCENT
(SPIRITUAL —) SOUL
(SUMMARY OF —S) CREED
(VITAL —) JIVA SPIRIT STAMEN
ARCHAEUS
PRINK PERK PRIG WINK ADORN
PRICK PRIMP PRUNE BEDECK
SMUDGE
PRINT CUT GAY GUM DRUK MARK
TYPE FUDGE PORTY PRESS SEPIA
STAMP BANNER BORDER CARBON
CARBRO ENFACE LETTER STRIKE
BROMOIL DROPOUT DUOTYPE
ENGRAVE GRAPHIC GRAVURE
IMPRESS PUBLISH TRACING
VANDYKE VESTIGE WOODCUT
AQUATONE CALOTYPE CHLORIDE
DRYPOINT HALFTONE INSCRIBE
LEIMTYPE MONOTYPE POSITIVE
URUSHIYE
(— OTHER SIDE) BACK
(— TO RIGHT) ADSCRIPT
PRINTED FONTED
PRINTER TYPO TWICER PRESSMAN
IMPRIMENT
(AID TO —) DEVIL
(PL.) TYPOTHETAE
PRINTER'S DEVIL FLY
PRINTING TIRAGE EDITION
VIGOREUX CHARACTER IMPRIMERY
(LAST —) THIRTY
PRION PETREL

PRIONID BEETLE
PRIONODON LINSANG
PRIOR ERE OLD FORE PAST EIGNE
ELDER FORMER RATHER ALREADY
EARLIER FARTHER ANTERIOR
FOREHAND HITHERTO PREVIOUS
PRIORITY PRIVILEGE PRECEDENCE
PRIORY ABBEY NUNNERY CLOISTER
PRIORATE
PRISM BLOCK NICOL CYLINDER
SPECTRUM WERNICKE
PRISMATIC SHOWY BRILLIANT
PRISON GIB JUG BRIG COOP GAOL
HELL HOCK HOLD HOLE JAIL KEEP
LAKE QUAD QUOD SHOP STIR WARD
BAGNE CLINK FLEET GRATE KITTY
LODGE POUND RATEL TENCH
TRONK VAULT BAGNIO BAILEY
BUCKET CARCEL CARCER COOLER
JIGGER RATTLE BASTILE BOCARDO
BULLPEN COLLEGE COMPTER
CONFINE COUNTER DUNGEON
FREEZER GEHENNA KIDCOTE
LUDGATE NEWGATE DARTMOOR
HOOSEGOW TOLBOOTH TRIBUNAL
(— CAMP) OFLAG
(— IN ROME) TULLIANUM
(AUSTRALIAN —) TENCH
(UNIVERSITY —) CARCER
PRISONER CON POW MUTE LIFER
DETENU INMATE REMAND CAITIFF
CAPTIVE CONVICT GAOLBIRD
JAILBIRD LONGTIMER
PRISONER'S BASE CHEVY CHIVY
PRISSY PRIM FUSSY DAINTY FINICKY
PRUDISH PRIGGISH SISSIFIED
PRISTINE NEW PURE FIRST FRESH
ANCIENT PRIMARY ORIGINAL
PRIMEVAL PRIMITIVE UNSPOILED
PRIVACY RECESS SECRET PRIVITY
RETREAT SECRECY DARKNESS
INTIMACY INTIMITY SOLITUDE
SECLUSION
(IN —) ASIDE
(PL.) VERENDA
PRIVATE SNUG ALONE GUIDE KHASS
PRIVY SHARE CLOSET COVERT
INWARD POCKET SECRET STANCH
POSTERN SECRECY SEVERAL
SOLDIER CIVILIAN ESOTERIC
HOMEFELT INTERNAL INTIMATE
PERSONAL SINGULAR UMBRATILE
PRIVATEER CAPER PIRATE ALABAMA
CORSAIR DUNKIRK PICKEER
PRIVATELY ASIDE INWARDLY
SECRETLY
PRIVATION LOSS WANT PENURY
PERISH ABSENCE POVERTY
HARDSHIP
PRIVET PRIM HEDGE SKEDGE
IBOLIUM PRIMWORT PRIMPRINT
PRIVILEGE UP PUT SOC DOWN
HAND STAR TEAM CLAIM ENTRY
FAVOR FRANK GRACE HONOR
REGAL RIGHT THEAM EXCUSE
INDULT MUNITY OCTROI OPTION
PATENT WARREN CHARTER
FALDAGE FREEDOM LIBERTY
MITZVAH PASSAGE GRANDEZA
STANDAGE

(— TO USE THINGS) BOTE
(ACQUIRED —) EASEMENT
(POKER —) EDGE
(POOL —) STAR
PRIVILEGED CURULE EXEMPT
LICENSED
(— PLACE) WARREN
PRIVY WC GONG BIFFY DRAFT ISSUE
JAKES PETTY QUIET SIEGE CLOSET
OFFICE SECRET DRAUGHT FOREIGN
LATRINE PRIVATE DONICKER
FAMILIAR INTIMATE OUTHOUSE
PERSONAL STEALTHY WARDROBE
PRIZE CUP FEE GEM PRY BELL BEND
GAME GREE PALM PREY PRIX RATE
RISK AWARD BACON BOOTY LEVER
PLATE PLUME PRICE PURSE STAKE
VALUE WAGER ESTEEM GLAIVE
PRAISE PREMIO TROPHY BENEFIT
CAPTURE GARLAND PREMIUM
ESTIMATE LEVERAGE PURCHASE
REPRISAL TREASURE
(— FOR LAST) MELL
(FIRST —) BLUE
(LOTTERY —) LOT TERN
PRIZE CUP PEWTER
PRIZED DEAR CHARY
PRIZEFIGHT GO BOUT MILL MATCH
SCRAP
PRIZEFIGHTER BOXER BLEEDER
FIGHTER SLUGGER PUGILIST
PRIZE MONEY GUNNAGE
PRO TO FOR FAVORING
PROA PARO PRAU PROW PAROO
PRAHU CARACOA
PROBABILITY ODDS SHOW CHANCE
PROBABLE MAYBE LIKELY PROBAL
TOPICAL APPARENT FEASIBLE
POSSIBLE
PROBABLY BELIKE LIKELY
PROBATION TEST PROOF TRIAL
PAROLE EVIDENCE
PROBATIONER STIBBLER
PROBE SEEK SIFT STOG TENT ENTER
GROPE SOUND FATHOM SEARCH
SEEKER STYLET THRUST ACCOUNT
EXAMINE INQUIRY SOUNDER
GYROMELE
PROBITY HONESTY INTEGRITY
RECTITUDE
PROBLEM NUT SUM WHY BOYG
CRUX DUAL ISSE KNOT BLAIK
HYDRA POSER APORIA ENIGMA
BUGBEAR DILEMMA FUNERAL
GORDIAN GRUELER TICHLER
EXERCISE HEADACHE JEOPARDY
QUESTION STICKLER
(CHESS —) DUAL MOVER SUIMATE
MINIATURE
PROBLEMATICAL DUBIOUS
DOUBTFUL PUZZLING UNCERTAIN
UNDECIDED
PROBOSCIS NOSE SNOUT TRUMP
TRUNK ANTLIA LINGUA SIPHON
SYPHON TONGUE ROSTRUM
PROBOSCIS MONKEY KAHA KAHUA
PROCAVIA HYRAX
PROCEDURE BIAS FORM HAVE VEIN
DRAFT ORDER TENOR TRACK

AFFAIR COURSE METHOD POLITY
SYSTEM DRAUGHT PROCESS
PRODUCT ACTIVITY PROTOCOL
(PRESCRIBED —S) CEREMONY
(ROUNDABOUT —) CIRCUITY
(SECRET —) STEALTH
(UNWISE —) FOLLY
PROCEED DO GO BANG BEAR FAND
FARE FLOW FOND HAVE MAKE
MARK MOVE PASS ROAM ROLL
SEEK STEP TAKE TOOL TOUR WEAR
WEND WIND YEDE AMBLE ARISE
DRESS FOUND FRAME ISSUE MARCH
REACH BREEZE INTEND PURSUE
RESULT SPRING STRAKE STRIKE
ADVANCE AGGRESS DEVOLVE
EMANATE FORTHGO PRETEND
STRETCH CONTINUE PROGRESS
(— AIMLESSLY) CIRCLE
(— ALONE) SINGLE
(— CLUMSILY) FLOUNDER
(— OBLIQUELY) CUT
(— RAGGEDLY) HALT
(— RAPIDLY) STRETCH
(— UNSTEADILY) DRIDDLE
(— WITH DIFFICULTY) STRUGGLE
(PL.) TAKE VAIL AVAILS INCOME
PROFITS PROVENT RETURNS
PREVENUE
PROCEEDING ACT DEED FARE PLOY
STEP AFFAIR AMPARO COURSE
DOMENT ISSUANT MEASURE
ONGOING PASSANT QUIETUS
TEMANET WARRANT CONCURSO
INSTANCE PLACITUM PRACTICE
(— BY THREES) TERNARY
(— FROM GOD) DIVINE
(— FROM THE EARTH) TELLURIC
(COURT —S) TRIAL
(INDIRECT —S) AMBAGES
(PARLIAMENTARY —S) HUSTINGS
(RECORDED —S) ACTA
PROCERITY HEIGHT TALLNESS
PROCESS RUN FANG FOOT TINA
WRIT CREST FURCA HAMUS MUCRO
SPINA CALCAR CAPIAS CILIUM
COURSE FEELER HABEAS INTEND
METHOD REPORT ACCOUNT
FURCULA GOBBING HAMULUS
ISOLATE LAMELLA MANDATE
SPATULA SUMMONS ACTIVITY
APPENDIX FILAMENT FRENULUM
GRAINING INSTANCE
(— OF BONE) HORN
(— OF CHANGE) ACTION
(— OF CREATING VACUUM)
EXHAUST
(— OF DYEING) BATIK HANKING
(— OF METALPLATING) ACIERAGE
(— OF PACKING) GOBBING
(— OF REASONING) ALGEBRA
(— OF SUPPLYING WANTAGE)
ULLING
(— ON FISH'S HEAD) LACINIA
(— PAPER) CONVERT
(— TO RECOVER LAND) DADENHUDD
(ABRUPT —) MUCRO
(ALCHEMICAL —) DIPLOSIS
(ARTISTIC —) FROTTAGE

(CALENDERING —) SWISSING
(CARBON —) AUTOTYPE
(CERAMIC —) FIRING
(COATING —) BLOOMING
(CURVED —) HAMUS
(DEVELOPMENTAL —) ANCESTRY
(EARLIKE —) AURICLE
(FALCONRY —) IMPING
(FINISHING —) BRUSHING CRABBIN
(FORKED —) FURCA FURCULA
(HELMETLIKE —) CASQUE
(HOOKLIKE —) HAMULUS
(HORNSHAPED —) CORNICLE
(INTELLECTUAL —S) COGITO
(KNOBLIKE —) BOSS
(LEGAL —) BAIL SUIT CAUSE
ATTAINT INSTANCE
(MATHEMATICAL —) ADDITION
DIVISION
(MENTAL —) COMPOUND
(MINING —) STOPING
(MOVIE-MAKING —) SLATING
(NERVELIKE —) AXON AXONE
(PHOTOGRAPHIC —) CARBRO
(POINTED —) AWN SPINE STYLUS
LANGUET
(PRINTING —) GRAVURE STENCIL
INTAGLIO
(REORGANIZATION —) HEMIXIS
(SMALL POINTED —) AWN
(SPINNING —) JACKING
(TEXTILE —) DECATING
(WEAVING —) HATCHING
(WINGLIKE —) ALA FIN
PROCESSED DOWN FINISHED
PROCESSION POMP WALK CORSO
DRIVE TRACE TRAIN BRIDAL
EXEQUY LITANY PARADE STREAM
CORTEGE FUNERAL THIASOS
TRIONFO TRIUMPH ENTRANCE
PROGRESS
(BOISTEROUS —) SKIMMITY
(IRISH CIVIC —) FRINGES
PROCLAIM BID CRY BAWL DEEM
HORN OYES OYEZ SCRY SING TOO
TOUT BLARE BOAST CLAIM GREDE
KNELL SOUND SPEAK BLAZON
BOUNCE DEFAME HERALD INDICT
OUTCRY CLARION DECLARE
DIVULGE PROTEST PUBLISH
TRUMPET ANNOUNCE DENOUNCE
RENOUNCE
(— ALOUD) ROAR
(— PUBLICLY) PRECONIZE
(— WITH BIG TALK) BOUNCE
PROCLAMATION CRY HUE BANS
FIAT RERD BANDO BANNS BLAZE
EDICT UKASE PLACARD PROGRAM
PROCLIVITY BENT ANLAGE APETITI
APTNESS LEANING TENDENCY
PROCNE (FATHER OF —) PANDION
(HUSBAND OF —) TEREUS
(SISTER OF —) PHILOMENA
(SON OF —) ITYS
PROCONSUL GALLIO PROVOST
PROCRASTINATE LAG TIME DEFER
DELAY LINGER ADJOURN POSTPON
PROROGUE TEMPORIZE
PROCRASTINATION DELAY
CUNCTATION

PROCREANT FRUITFUL
PROCREATE WIN SIRE BEGET
ENGENDER GENERATE OCCASION
PROCREATION INCREASE
PROCREATOR AUTHOR
PROCTOR LIAR PROG ACTOR AGENT
PROXY BEGGAR RECTOR MONITOR
PROCUTOR
PROCUMBENT HUMIFUSE
PROSTRATE
PROCURABLE PARABLE
PROCURATOR PROXY PILATE
PROCTOR
PROCURE GET WIN FANG FIND GAIN
GIVE HALE BRING INFER TOUCH
EFFECT INDUCE OBTAIN ACHIEVE
ACQUIRE COMPARE CONQUER
CONTRIVE PURCHASE
PROCURER PIMP PROXENET
PURVEYOR
PROCURESS HACK LENA PANDER
COMMODE PINNACE
PROD DAB EGG GIG JAB JOG BROD
BROG GOAD HEEL POKE PROG
HURRY NUDGE PROBE INCITE
JOSTLE THRUST IRRITATE
PRODIGAL PROD FLUSH LARGE
COSTLY LAVISH WANTON WASTER
PROFUSE SPENDER WASTRIE
WASTRIFE
PRODIGALITY WASTE WASTRY
WASTRIFE PROFUSION
PRODIGIOUS HUGE VAST GIANT
AMAZING IMMENSE STRANGE
ABNORMAL ENORMOUS GIGANTIC
MONSTROUS
PRODIGY OMEN SIGN MARVEL
OSTENT WIZARD WONDER MONSTER
PORTENT CEREMONY
PRODITION TREASON BETRAYAL
PRODUCE DO GO ANTE BEAR FORM
GIVE GROW MAKE REAR SHOW
TEEM WAGE BEGET BIRTH BREED
BRING BROOD BUILD CARRY CAUSE
DRIVE FORGE FRAME HATCH ISSUE
RAISE SPAWN THROW TRADE YIELD
APPORT CREATE EFFECT GROWTH
INCOME INVENT INWORK SECURE
ADVANCE ANIMATE COMPOSE
DEPROME GIGNATE INSPIRE
OUTWORK PRODUCT PROLONG
PROVENT CONCEIVE CONFLATE
ENGENDER GENERATE INCREASE
LENGTHEN OFFSPRING
(— A COPY OF) TYPE
(— AN EFFECT) ACT AFFECT
(— AUDIBLE EFFECT) SOUND
(— CROPS) CARRY
(— DULL APPEARANCE) CHILL
(— FRUIT) TEEM
(— HEAT) ENRAGE
(— PAID FOR RENT) CAIN
(— SHARP NOISE) CRINK
(AGRICULTURAL —) PODWARE
(FARM —) HUSBANDRY
(MINING —) LEY
PRODUCER GASMAN BEARING
SHOWMAN DIRECTOR GAZOGENE
OUTPUTTER

PRODUCING IN PROCREANT
PRODUCT HEIR ITEM BRAND CHILD
FRUIT GROSS OUTGO SPAWN
ALCLAD EFFORT FABRIC GROWTH
RESULT UPCOME OUTTURN
PRODUCE PROGENY TURNOUT
OUTBIRTH
(— OF ROCK DECAY) LATERITE
(—S OF LAND) ESPLEES
(—S OF ORCHARD) BIKKURIM
(ADDITION —) ADDUCT
(CHEESE AND MILK —S) GERVAIS
(CHOICE —) CAVIAR
(COMPLETED —) TURNOFF
(LEGISLATIVE —) ACT
(MATHEMATICAL —) SQUARE
(MINERAL —) HUTCH
(OXIDATION —) SUBSCALE
(RESIDUAL —) LATERITE
(SECONDARY —) CONGENER
(SURPLUS —S) ARISINGS
(TRANSFORMATION —) BAINITE
(WASTE —) RESIDUENT
(WORTHLESS —) CHAFF
PRODUCTION WORK FORGE FRUIT
GROSS PIECE YIELD GROWTH
EDITION GUIGNOL PRODUCE
ARTIFICE INDUCTION OPERATION
(— OF MEDIUM) APPORT
(— OF YOUNG) INCREASE
(BEST —S) FAT
(SUCCESSFUL —) HIT
PRODUCTIVE FAT RICH LOOSE
QUICK ACTIVE BATTLE PAROUD
STRONG CAUSING FERTILE GAINFUL
HEALTHY TEEMFUL TEEMING
CHILDING CREATIVE FRUITFUL
GERMINAL
PROEM PREFACE PRELUDE PROHEIM
FOREWORD OVERTURE PREAMBLE
PROETUS (BROTHER OF —)
ACRISIUS
(FATHER OF —) ABAS
(MOTHER OF —) OCALEA
(WIFE OF —) ANTEA
PROFANATION VIOLENCE
SACRILEGE
PROFANE LAY NOA BLUE FOUL
ABUSE COARSE DEBASE DEFILE
DEFOIL DEFOUL UNHOLY VULGAR
WICKED GODLESS IMPIOUS
POLLUTE SECULAR UNGODLY
VIOLATE WORLDLY TEMPORAL
UNHALLOW
PROFANITY OATH CURSE
LANGUAGE BLASPHEMY
PROFESS OWN AVOW ADMIT CLAIM
AFFECT AFFIRM ALLEGE ASSERT
ASSUME FOLLOW PRESUME
PRETEND PURPORT PRACTICE
PROFESSION ART BAR LAW COAT
FEAT GAME WALK CRAFT FAITH
FORTE TRADE CAREER CHURCH
EMPLOY METIER CALLING FACULTY
QUALITY SERVICE ADVOCACY
BUSINESS COACHING FUNCTION
SOLDIERY VOCATION
PROFESSIONAL PRO COLT PAID
HIRED EXPERT SKILLED TRAINED
FINISHED

PROFESSOR DON PROF HANIF
LAWYER REGENT ADJOINT
ACADEMIC EMERITUS
PROFESSORSHIP CHAIR FAUTEUIL
PROFFER BID CAP GIVE TEND TENT
DEFER DODGE ESSAY OFFER
EXTEND OPPOSE PREFER PROFRE
TENDER ATTEMPT PRESENT
HESITATE
PROFICIENCY SIGHT SKILL ABILITY
APTNESS MAITRISE
PROFICIENT ADEPT EXPERT SALTED
VERSED SKILLED SKILLFUL
PROFILE FORM FLANK SKETCH
CONTOUR OUTLINE SECTION
PROFIT AID GET NET WIN BOOT
GAIN MEND NOTE SKIN VAIL AVAIL
EDIFY FRAME LUCRE SCALP SPEED
BEHOOF INCOME MAKING RETURN
ACCOUNT ADVANCE BENEFIT
CLEANUP FURTHER GETTING
IMPROVE MILEAGE PLUNDER
REVENUE VANTAGE WINNING
CLEANING INCREASE INTEREST
(— BY) BROOK
(UNDERCOVER —) SQUEEZE
(PL.) GRAVY ISSUE AVAILS JALKAR
ESPLEES
PROFITABLE FAT GOOD UTILE
GOLDEN GAINFUL HELPFUL
PAYABLE BEHOVELY ECONOMIC
PROVABLE REPAYING VAILABLE
REWARDING
PROFLIGATE DEFEAT CORRUPT
IMMORAL RIOTOUS SPENDER
VICIOUS WASTREL DEPRAVED
FLAGRANT OVERCOME RAKEHELL
WASTEFUL
PROFOUND DEEP HARD WISE ABYSS
DEPTH HEAVY OCEAN SOUND THICK
PITCHY STRONG ABYSMAL INTENSE
ABSTRUSE COMPLETE REACHING
THOROUGH
PROFUNDITY ABYSS DEPTH FATHOM
DEEPNESS
PROFUSE FREE LUSH SLAB FRANK
GALORE LAVISH COPIOUS LIBERAL
ABUNDANT GENEROUS PRODIGAL
SQUANDER WASTEFUL
PROFUSELY HEARTILY
PROFUSION WASTE EXCESS LAVISH
FLUENCY OPULENCE
PROG FOOD GOAD POKE PROD
PROWL TRAMP BEGGAR FORAGE
PROCTOR
PROGENITOR BURI MANU ROOT
SIRE PITRI STOCK PARENT
ANCESTOR
PROGENY BED GET IMP KIN CLAN
KIND SEED TEAM BROOD CHILD
FRUIT ISSUE STRAIN STRIND
INCROSS KINDRED LINEAGE
OUTCOME PRODUCT CHILDREN
FRUITAGE INCREASE OUTBIRTH
OUTCROSS OFFSPRING
(— OF WATER-BUFFALO AND YAK)
DZO
(— OF WITCH AND DEMON) HOLD
(INSECT —) SOCIETY

PROGNOSIS FORECAST PROPHASIS
PROGNOSTIC OMEN SIGN TOKEN
PRESAGE PROPHECY
PROGNOSTICATE BODE AUGUR
SPELL BETOKEN CONJECT PREDICT
PRENOTE FOREBODE FORESHOW
FORETELL PROPHESY
PROGNOSTICATION RACE
PRESAGE FOREBODE FORECAST
PROGRESS PROPHECY
PROGNOSTICATOR SEER DOOMER
PROPHET HARUSPEX
PROGRAM CARD SHOW FORUM
AGENDA DESIGN SCHEME AGENDUM
PREFACE CLAMBAKE FESTIVAL
GIVEAWAY GUIDANCE JAMBOREE
PLAYBILL SCHEDULE SEQUENCE
SYLLABUS
PROGRAMMA EDICT DECREE
PREFACE PROGRAM
PROGRESS WAY BIRL DENT FARE
GAIN GROW MOVE RACE RISE STEM
STEP TOUR WEAR WEND WENT
BUILD DRIFT FORGE GOING MARCH
SWING WEENT ASCENT BUFFET
COURSE GROWTH STREEK ADVANCE
DEVELOP FOOTING HEADWAY
IMPROVE JOURNEY ONGOING
PASSAGE PROCESS
(— **CLUMSILY**) SCRAMBLE
(— **ERRATICALLY**) FLAIL
(— **FEEBLY**) DODDER
(— **INTELLIGENTLY PLANNED**)
TELESIA TELESIS
(— **NOISILY**) CHORTLE
(— **SLOWLY**) CRAWL
(**SINGLE** —) THROUGH
PROGRESSED FAR
PROGRESSION WAY SWING COURSE
GALLOP ADVANCE PASSAGE
PROGRESS SEQUENCE
(— **OF CHORDS**) SWIPE
(**MUSICAL** —) SKIP
(**SMOOTH** —) SLIDE
PROGRESSIVE ACTIVE ONWARD
FORWARD GRADUAL LIBERAL
PROGRESSIVELY STILL
PROHIBIT BAN BAR STOP VETO
BLOCK DEBAR ESTOP DEFEND
ENJOIN FORBID HINDER OUTLAW
FORFEND FORWARN INHIBIT
PREVENT DISALLOW PRECLUDE
SUPPRESS
PROHIBITED HOT TABU TABOO
ILLEGAL ILLICIT UNLAWFUL
VERBOTEN
PROHIBITION BAN NAY NON VETO
ORDER BARRIER DEFENCE DEFENSE
EMBARGO FORBODE ESTOPPEL
PROHIBITING VETITIVE
PROHIBITIONIST DRY PUSSYFOOT
PROJECT GAB GAG JET JUT LAP
TUT BEAM CAST GAME IDEA PLAN
POKE SWIM BULGE CHART DRAFT
DRIVE IMAGE JETTY JUTTY SETUP
SHOOT STICK THROW BEETLE
DESIGN DEVICE ESTATE EXTEND
FILLIP OUTJUT PROPEL SCHEME
SCREEN SHELVE EXTRUDE GOSPLAN

IMAGINE KNUCKLE PATTERN
BUSINESS CONTRIVE OUTREACH
OUTSHOOT PROPOSAL PROTRUDE
SPANGHEW
(**UNETHICAL** —) SCHEME
(**VISIONARY** —) BABEL
PROJECTILE BALL BOLT CASE SHOT
SHAFT TRACER OUTCAST POUNDER
SHRAPNEL
(— **DESIGNED TO SET FIRE TO
HOUSES**) CARCASS
(**EXPLOSIVE** —) BOMB SHELL
(**SUBMARINE** —) TORPEDO
(PL.) LEAD SHOT SALVO STUFF
PROJECTING BEETLE SHELVY
EMINENT JUTTING OUTSHOT
SALIENT SNAGGLED
PROJECTION ARM CAM COG DOG
EAR FIN GIB JET JOG JUT NAG NUT
TOE BEAK BOSS BROW BUHR COAK
COCK CROC CUSP HEEL HORN KEEL
KICK KINK KNAG KNOB KNOP LOBE
RIDE SNUG SPUD SPUR TEAT WING
BULGE CLEAT EJECT ELBOW FENCE
FURCA JUTTY SHANK SHOOT SPIKE
TOOTH BRANCH CORBEL CROSET
FUSULA HEARTH ICICLE MENTUM
PALATE RELISH TAPPET BREAKER
DRAWING EPAULET EYEBROW
FETLOCK KNUCKLE LANGUET
ORILLON PRICKER PRICKLE
RESSAUT AJUTMENT CASCABEL
DENTICLE EMINENCE FOOTLOCK
OVERHANG SALIENCE SHOULDER
SPROCKET STERIOMA OUTTHRUST
(— **CONNECTING TIMBER**) COAK
(— **EXTENDING BACKWARD**) BARB
(— **FROM CASTING**) SPRUE
(— **FROM SHIP'S KEEL**) SPONSON
(— **IN CLOCK**) SQUARE
(— **IN ORCHIDS**) MENTUM
(— **OF FOREHEAD**) ANTINION
(— **OF JAW**) GNATHISM
(— **OF PEAT**) HAG
(— **OF RAFTER**) SALLY
(— **ON CANNON**) CASCABEL
(— **ON GUN**) CROC LUMP
(— **ON HARNESS**) HAME
(— **ON HORSE'S LEG**) FETLOCK
(— **ON HORSESHOE**) STICKER
(— **ON LOCK**) FENCE STUMP
(— **ON MAST**) STOP
(— **ON OVARY**) STIGMA
(— **ON POCKETKNIFE**) KICK
(— **ON SALMON JAW**) GIB
(— **ON WHEEL**) GUB GROUSER
GROUTER
(— **OVER AIR PORT**) EYEBROW
(**FIREPLACE** —) HOB
(**JAGGED** —) SNUG
(**SHARP** —) BARB FANG
(**SUBMERGED** —) KNOLL
(PL.) GRAIN BARLEY
PROJECTOR KINO LANTERN
PLANNER SCHEMER BIOSCOPE
EPISCOPE VITASCOPE
PROLAMIN ZEIN SEINE GLIADIN
HORDEIN KAFIRIN SECALIN

PROLAPSE PTOSIS BLOWOUT
FALLING
PROLETARIAN POPULAR
PROLETARIAT MASSES
PROLIFIC BIRTHY BREEDY BROOD`
FECUND FERTILE PROFUSE TEEMI▪
ABUNDANT FRUITFUL SPAWNING
(**BE** —) INCREASE
PROLIX LARGE WORDY DIFFUSE
LENGTHY PROSAIC TEDIOUS
VERBOSE TIRESOME WEARISOME
PROLOGUE BANS BANNS INDEX
PREFACE
PROLONG DREE LENG LONG SPIN
DEFER DELAY DRIVE ELONG TWIN
DILATE EXTEND LINGER SPREAD
DISPACE PRODUCE RESPITE
SUSTAIN CONTINUE ETERNIZE
LENGTHEN POSTPONE PROROGUE
PROTRACT
PROLONGATION BEAK AORTA
CONUS STIPE STYLE FERMATA
ACROSOME GYNOBASE LABELLUM▪
PROLONGED GREAT PROLIX
DELAYED EXTENDED SOSTENUTO
PROMENADE MAIL MALL PIER PRO
WALK CORSO FRONT PASEO PRAD
MARINA PARADE PASEAR ALAMED▪
GALLERY FRESCADE
(**CARRIAGE** —) TOUR
PROMETHEUS (**FATHER OF** —)
IAPETUS
(**MOTHER OF** —) CLYMENE
PROMINENCE BUR NOB BURR KN◄
NOOP UMBO AGGER BULLA CRES▀
GRAIN OLIVA SWELL TYLUS ACCE▪
CALCAR NODULE TRAGUS BILLING
BUTTOCK CONDYLE FASHION
HAMULUS KNUCKLE LINGULA
AMYGDALA EMINENCY EMPHASIS
GLABELLA PULVINAR SALIENCE
TUBERCLE
PROMINENT BIG BOLD BEADY
BRENT GREAT STEEP BEETLE
MARKED SIGNAL BLATANT BOLTIN
CAPITAL EMINENT JUTTING LEADI▪
NOTABLE OBVIOUS SALIENT
AQUILINE MANIFEST STRIKING
(**SOCIALLY** —) SWELL
PROMISCUOUS LIGHT CASUAL
RANDOM CARELESS
PROMISCUOUSLY TAGRAG
PROMISE VOW AVOW BAND HEST
HETE HOPE HOTE OSSE PASS PLE
SURE WORD FAITH GRANT HIGHT
TRUTH ASSURE BEHEST ENGAGE
FIANCE HALSEN INSURE PAROLE
PLEDGE PLIGHT PROMIT BEHIGHT
BETROTH WARRANT CONTRACT
COVENANT GUARANTY BETROTHA▪
(— **IN MARRIAGE**) BETROTH
ESPOUSE AFFIANCE
(— **TO PAY**) NOTE
(— **TO TAKE IN MARRIAGE**) AFFY
PROMISED VOTARY
(— **IN MARRIAGE**) SURE HIGHT
ENGAGED
PROMISING APT FAIR BRIGHT
LIKELY PROOFY TOWARD GRADEL▪
TOWARDLY

ROMISSORY NOTE IOU HUNDI
HOONDI TICKET
ROMONTORY HOE NAB BEAK BILL
HEAD MULL NAZE NESS NOOK
NOUP PEAK SCAW SKAW TOOT
ELBOW POINT REACH SNOUT
SALIENT FORELAND HEADLAND
ROMOTE AID HELP LOFT AVAIL
BOOST EXALT NURSE RAISE SERVE
SPEED ASSIST EXCITE FOMENT
FOSTER LAUNCH PREFER ADVANCE
DIGNIFY ELEVATE FORWARD
FURTHER IMPROVE PREFECT
PRODUCE PROMOVE SUCCEED
SUPPORT INCREASE SUBSERVE
ROMOTER AGENT FRIEND
BETTOR BOOSTER BUBBLER
BROACHER HUMANIST
ROMOTION LIFT REMOVE ADVANCE
PROMOVAL
ROMPT APT CUE MOVE URGE YARE
ALERT PREST QUICK READY SERVE
SWIFT WILLY YEDER EXCITE INDITE
MATURE NIMBLE SPEEDY SUDDEN
ANIMATE FORWARD PROVOKE
SUGGEST PUNCTUAL REMINDER
— TO EVIL) SUGGEST
ROMPTER CUER CALLER
MEMORIST ORDINARY SOUFFLEUR
ROMPTING CALL BEHEST BEHIND
MOTIVE
SPIRITUAL —) LEADING
ROMPTLY UP PAT TID TIT SOON
ITE PRONTO YARELY PRESTLY
QUICKLY DIRECTLY SPEEDILY
ROMPTNESS ALACRITY CELERITY
DISPATCH
ROMULGATE SPREAD DECLARE
UBLISH PROCLAIM
RONAOS ANTICUM
RONE APT BENT EASY FLAT FREE
GRUF BUXOM GIVEN GROOF JACENT
LIABLE SUPINE BEASTLY BESTIAL
DORMANT SUBJECT ADDICTED
COUCHANT DISPOSED DOWNWARD
PROPENSE
— TO TAKE UP FADS) ISMY
NATURALLY —) PROLIVE
RONG NEB NIB PEG PEW BILL
TANG FORK HOOK PUGH SPUR
FANG TENG TINE TING GRAIN
SPADE SPEAN SPRONG FOURCHE
TICKLER GRAINING
— FOR EXTRACTING BUNG)
CKLER
— FOR FISH) PEW PUGH
— OF ANTLER) KNAG TIND TINE
— OF FORK) SPEAN
RONGHORN CABREE CABRIT
AZAME BERENDO BERRENDO
RONOUN HE IT ME MY WE YE ANY
HER HIM HIS ONE OUR SHE THY
WHO YOU OURS THAT THEM THEY
THOU WHAT WHOM YOUR THINE
WHICH WHOSE ITSELF MYSELF
HERSELF HIMSELF OURSELF
WHOEVER YOURSELF OURSELVES
GENDERLESS —) THON
RONOUNCE SAY PASS ACUTE

SPEAK UTTER PREACH RECITE
TONGUE ADJUDGE BEHIGHT
CENSURE MOUILLE
(— FREE) ABSOLVE
(— GUILTY) CONDEMN
(— HOLY) BLESS
PRONOUNCED HIGH MARKED
DECIDED HOWLING INTENSE
MOVABLE
(— AS FRICATIVE) GRASSEYE
(NOT —) SOFT
PRONOUNCEMENT FIAT CURSE
DICTUM DICTAMEN
PRONTO QUICK QUICKLY PROMPTLY
PRONUNCIATION BROGUE DICTION
ETACISM LIAISON DELIVERY
ENCLISIS ORTHOEPY
(BAD —) CACOEPY LABDACISM
(BROAD —) PLATEASM
(CORRECT —) ORTHOEPY
(ROUGH —) BUR BURR
PROOF MARK SLIP TEST ESSAY
PREWE TOKEN TOUCH TRIAL
GALLEY ORDEAL REASON RESULT
REVISE ATTEMPT OUTCOME
PROBATE SHOWING UTTERLY
VOUCHER WARRANT ANALYSIS
CACOLOGY DOCUMENT EVICTION
EVIDENCE GOODNESS MONUMENT
(— SPIRIT OF WINE) SVT
(— OF WRONGDOING) GOODS
(PL.) STRING WARRANTY
PROOFREADER MARK CAP DELE
STET CARET
PROP LEG BROB POST REST SPUR
STAY STUD TRIG APPUI BRACE
PERCH PUNCH RANCE SCOTE
SHORE SHOVE SOUSE SPRAG
SPURN STAFF STELL STOOP STULL
COLUMN CROTCH CRUTCH SCOTCH
SHORER STAYER UPHOLD FULCRUM
PINNING STUDDLE SUPPORT
SUSTAIN BUTTRESS CROTCHET
DUTCHMAN UNDERLAY UNDERSET
(— AS TRAP) TEEL
(— FOR ROOF OF MINE) GIB
(— UP) CUSHION
PROPAGANDA BOLOISM AGITPROP
PROPAGATE BREED HATCH LAYER
EXTEND SPREAD STRIKE DIFFUSE
GEMMATE PRODUCE PUBLISH
ENGENDER GENERATE INCREASE
POPULATE TRANSMIT
PROPAGATION BREED BREEDING
DIVISION INCREASE LAYERAGE
OFFSPRING
PROPEL ROW CALL CAST FIRE FLIP
KENT POLE PUSH SEND URGE DRIVE
FLICK IMPEL KNOCK PRICK RANGE
SPANK THROW HURTLE LAUNCH
PROJECT
(— BALL) STROKE
(— BOAT WITH FEET) LEG
(— BOAT) OAR ROW SET KENT
POLE SCULL BUSHWACK
(— ONESELF) HAUL
(— PUCK) CARRY
PROPELLER FAN SCREW AIRSCREW
WINDMILL

PROPENSITY YEN BENT ITCH LURCH
APTNESS IMPULSE LEANING
PRONITY APPETITE FONDNESS
INTEREST TENDENCY
PROPER FIT OWN GOOD JUST MEET
TRUE WELL PREST RIGHT UTTER
COMELY DECENT HONEST LAWFUL
MODEST SEEMLY CAPITAL CORRECT
FITTING GRADELY SEEMING SKILFUL
THRIFTY ABSOLUTE BECOMING
CONGREVE DECOROUS FORMULAR
IDONEOUS PECULIAR RIGHTFUL
SORTABLE SUITABLE VIRTUOUS
(APPARENTLY —) SPECIOUS
(BE — TO) BESEEM
PROPERLY DULY WELL FITLY TRULY
FAIRLY FEATLY GLADLY MEETLY
RIGHTLY
PROPERTY AVER BONA DHAN TOOL
WAIF ASSET AUGHT GOODS GRANT
MOYEN STATE STOCK THING
WORTH APPEAL DEVISE ESTATE
HAVIOR KELTER LIVING MUSHAA
REALTY TALENT USINGS WEALTH
ACQUEST APANAGE CHATTEL
DEMESNE ESCHEAT ESSENCE
FACULTY FITNESS HARNESS
HAVINGS QUALITY WARISON
ALLODIAL CATALLUM HOLDINGS
PECULIUM
(— BELONGING TO WOMAN)
STRIDHAN
(— FROM WIFE TO HUSBAND) DOS
(— GIVEN BY WILL) DEVISE
(— OF MATTER AT REST) INERTIA
(— SECURED DISHONESTLY) HARL
(— SEIZED BY FORCE) SPOIL
(ABSOLUTE —) ALODIUM
(ENEMY —) HEREM
(LANDED —) DOMAIN ESTATE
DEMESNE PRAEDIUM
(MOVABLE —) GEAR CHATTEL
EFFECTS CATALLUM
(PERSONAL —) FEE BONA GOODS
STUFF INSIGHT PLUNDER
(PRIVATE —) SEVERAL
(RURAL —) FINCA
(STOLEN —) PELF STEALTH
(THEATRICAL —S) PROPS
(WITHOUT —) LACKLAND
PROPHECY SPAE WEIRD EXHORT
PREACH PREDICT BODEMENT
FORECAST FORESHOW SOOTHSAY
VATICINE SIBYLLISM
PROPHESY OSSE SPAE AREAD
AUGUR DIVINE EXHORT PREACH
OMINATE PORTEND PREDICT
ARIOLATE FORETELL
PROPHET GAD AMOS JOEL SEER
ANGEL AUGUR DRUID ELIAS HOSEA
JONAH MICAH MOSES NAHUM SILAS
SYRUS ARIOLE BALAAM DANIEL
ELIJAH HAGGAI ISAIAH MERLIN
MORONI NATHAN PYTHON SAMUEL
EZEKIEL MALACHI SPAEMAN
HABAKKUK JEREMIAH
(PL.) VATES NEBIIM
PROPHETESS ANNA ANNE HULDA
SIBYL PYTHIA DEBORAH PHOIBAD

SEERESS VOLUSPA DRUIDESS
SPAEWIFE CASSANDRA PYTHONESS
PROPHETIC FATAL MANTIC FATEFUL
FATIDIC DELPHIAN SIBYLLIC
VATICINAL
PROPINE TIP GIFT EXPOSE PLEDGE
PROFFER
PROPINQUITY KINSHIP AFFINITY
NEARNESS VICINITY PROXIMITY
PROPITIATE MILD ATONE PACIFY
APPEASE RECONCILE
PROPITIATORY HILASMIC
PROPITIOUS FAIR KIND HAPPY
LUCKY BENIGN DEXTER KINDLY
HELPFUL PRESENT FRIENDLY
GRACIOUS MERCIFUL FAVORABLE
PROMISING
PROPONENT BACKER ADVOCATE
SUPPORTER
PROPORTION END LOT DOSE SIZE
CHIME FRAME QUOTA RATIO SCALE
SHARE ACCORD DEGREE EXTENT
FORMAT QUOTUM ANALOGY
BALANCE COMPASS CONTENT
MEASURE EURYTHMY QUANTITY
SYMMETRY
(— **OF CATTLE TO GIVEN AREA**)
SOUM
(— **OF MALT IN BREWING**) STRAIK
(**ALLOTTED** —) STENT STINT
(**EXACT** —) SQUARE
(**SMALL** —) TITHE
PROPORTIONATENESS CONTOUR
PROPOSAL BID KITE MOVE PLAN
PLEA VOEU GRACE OFFER PARTY
DEMAND FEELER MOTION MOTIVE
PROJECT PROPOSE PURPOSE
OVERTURE SCHEDULE SENTENCE
(**TENTATIVE** —) SNIFF
PROPOSE FACE MOVE PLAN POSE
SHOW WISH OFFER ALLEGE DESIGN
INJECT INTEND MOTION ADVANCE
EXHIBIT IMAGINE PROPINE PURPOSE
SUPPOSE CONFRONT CONVERSE
PROPOUND
(— **FOR DISCUSSION**) MOOT
(— **RESOLUTION**) FIRST
(— **TENTATIVELY**) SUGGEST
PROPOSITION R FACT AXIOM
MODAL OFFER THEME AFFAIR
CONNEX MEMBER PORISM GENERAL
INVERSE PREMISS PROBLEM
THEOREM TYCHISM BUSINESS
CONTRARY EMPIREMA IDENTITY
IRENICON JUDGMENT NEGATION
OVERTURE PROPOSAL PROTASIS
SENTENCE SINGULAR SUPPOSAL
(— **IN LOGIC**) TERMAL
(— **LEADING TO CONCLUSION**)
PREMISE
(**PARTICULAR NEGATIVE** —) O
(**PRELIMINARY** —) LEMMA
(**UNIVERSAL NEGATIVE** —) E
PROPOUND POSE OFFER POSIT
START STATE INVOKE PROPOSE
PURPOSE
PROPOUNDER HYLICIST
PROPRIETOR LORD LAIRD MALIK
OWNER MASTER PATRON TANIST

YEOMAN ESQUIRE PATROON
ABSENTEE BONIFACE SQUARSON
TALUKDAR YEOWOMAN
PROPRIETY GRACE IDIOM MENSE
ESTATE NATURE REASON DECENCY
DECORUM ESSENCE FITNESS
HOLDING CIVILITY PROPERTY
ETIQUETTE
PROPROCTOR RECTOR
PROPULSION DRIFT EJECTION
PROPULSIVE ELASTIC
PRORATE ALLOT ASSESS DIVIDE
APPORTION
PROROGUE DEFER ADJOURN
PROLONG POSTPONE PROTRACT
PROSAIC DRAB DULL FLAT FOOT
PROSE PROSY PROLIX STODGY
STOLID STUPID FACTUAL HUMDRUM
INSIPID LITERAL TEDIOUS TIRESOME
WORKADAY
PROSCENIUM FRAME STAGE
PROSCRIBE BAN TABU EXILE TABOO
FORBID OUTLAW REJECT PROHIBIT
PROSCRIPTION EXILE OUTLAWRY
PROSE CHAT PROSY GOSSIP
PROSAIC TEDIOUS SEQUENCE
ELOQUENCE
PROSECUTE LAW SUE HOLD URGE
CARRY ENSUE ACCUSE CHARGE
DEDUCE FOLLOW INDICT INTEND
PURSUE IMPLEAD
PROSECUTOR DA FISCAL PURSUER
SAKEBER PROMOTER QUAESTOR
(**PUBLIC** —) ACTOR
PROSELYTE CONVERT NICOLAS
NEOPHYTE PURSUANT
(**JEWISH** —) GER
PROSER HAVERER GRATIANO
PROSODY METER METRICS
PROSPECT HOPE VIEW SCENE
SPECK VISTA CHANCE CHIEVE
FUTURE REGARD SEARCH SURVEY
COMMAND EXPLORE FOSSICK
HORIZON LOOKOUT OUTLOOK
PROJECT RESPECT LANDSKIP
OFFSCAPE
(— **FOR GOLD**) SPECK
(— **WITHOUT SYSTEM**) GOPHER
(**FORBIDDING** —) DESERT
PROSPECTING LOAMING
PROSPECTIVE VIEW WATCH
LOOKOUT EXPECTED
PROSPECTOR SNIPER FOSSICKER
SOURDOUGH
(**LONE** —) HATTER
PROSPECTUS PROGRAM
PROSPER DO DOW FAY HIE LIKE
RISE THEE CHEVE CHIVE EDIFY
FRAME LIGHT SPEED BATTEN
THRIVE BLOSSOM SUCCEED
WELFARE FLOURISH
PROSPERITY HAP GLEE GOOD SEEL
SONS WEAL IKBAL SONSE HEALTH
THRIFT FORTUNE SUCCESS
THEEDOM WELFARE FLOURISH
(**GOD OF** —) FREY
PROSPERO (**DAUGHTER OF** —)
MIRANDA
(**SERVANT OF** —) ARIEL

PROSPEROUS UP FAT BEEN BEIN
BIEN BOON GOOD FELIX FLUSH
HAPPY LUCKY PALMY SONSY
EUROUS GILDED SONSIE WELSOM
HALCYON HEALTHY THRIVEN
WEIRDLY SUNSHINE THRIVING
WEALSOME
PROSTITUTE BAG BAT CAT COW
DOG MOB AUNT BAWD DOXY DRAB
HACK MAUX MISS MUFF PUNK SLUT
STEW TRUG BROAD CRACK MAWKS
PAGAN STALE WHORE BULKER
CALLET CHIPPY DEBASE GIRLIE
HARLOT HOOKER LIMMER MUTTON
RANNEL TOMATO TRADER VIZARD
BAGGAGE BROTHEL CRUISER
CYPRIAN HACKNEY HETAERA
HUSTLER PAPHIAN PINNACE
POLECAT PUCELLE SELLARY
BERDACHE COMMONER CUSTOMER
HACKSTER MAGDALEN MERETRIX
OCCUPANT RUMBELOW SLATTERN
STRUMPET VENTURER
PROSTITUTION BORDEL SACKING
BORDELLO HARLOTRY PUTANISM
PROSTRATE LOW FELL FLAT GRUF
RASE RAZE FLING GROOF PRONE
STOOP THROW ATTERR CUMBER
FALLEN REPENT WEAKEN FLATTEN
DEJECTED HELPLESS OVERCOME
PROSTERN DEPRESSED
(— **ONESELF**) HURKLE
(**BECOME** —) FALL
PROSTRATION SHOCK KOWTOW
COLLAPSE
PROSY DRY DULL JEJUNE HUMDRU
INSIPID PROSAIC PROSISH TEDIOUS
TIRESOME
PROTAGONIST HERO ACTOR
LEADER PALADIN ADVOCATE
CHAMPION
PROTAMINE SALMINE STURINE
CLUPEINE
PROTEAN EDESTAN VARIABLE
PROTECT CAP BANK BIEL BIND DIK
FEND FORT HILL KEEP REDE SAVE
WARD WEAR BLESS CHAIN CLOUT
COURE COVER FENCE GANGE
GRATE GUARD HEDGE PAVIS SHAD
SHEND UMBER ASSERT BORROW
CHIELD DEFEND SCREEN SHADOW
WARISH BULWARK CHERISH
CUSHION FASCINE FORFEND
SECLUDE SHELTER SUPPORT
WARRANT BESTRIDE CHAMPION
DEFILADE PRESERVE
(— **AGAINST RAIN**) FLASH
(— **BY COVERING**) HILL
(— **BY WINDING WITH WIRE**) GAN
(— **FROM INTRUSION**) TILE TYLE
(— **IRON OR STEEL**) BARFF
PROTECTED SHADY IMMUNE
CLOUTED GUARDED SHEATHED
SHIELDED
PROTECTING TUTELAR TUTELARY
SECUREFUL
PROTECTION LEE EGIS HOLD WAR
AEGIS ARMOR BIELD COVER GRIT
GUARD SHADE TARGE TOWER

AMULET ASYLUM AVOWRY ESCORT
FENDER REFUGE SAFETY SCONCE
SCREEN SHADOW SHROUD AUSPICE
CUSTODY DEFENCE HOUSING
MANTLET SHELTER TUITION
UMBRAGE WARRANT BLINDAGE
COVERAGE DEFILADE PASSPORT
SECURITY TUTAMENT TUTELAGE
(— FOR SAILOR) HORSE
(— FROM LOSS) INDEMNITY
(— FROM RAIN) OMBRIFUGE
(— FROM SUN) HAVELOCK
(— FROM WEATHER) LEWTH
(— RIGHT) MUND
(VALUABLE —) EDMUND
(WISE —) RAYMOND
PROTECTIVE (— SURFACE) LAGGING
PROTECTOR BIB GUARD BRACER
FAUTOR KEEPER PATRON REGENT
WARRANT DEFENDER GUARDIAN
PECTORAL PRESIDENT
(— OF PROSTITUTE) BULLY
(— OF VINEYARDS) PRIAPUS
PROTEGE WARD PUPIL SMIKE
PROTEIN ABRIN ACTIN RICIN SOZIN
AVIDIN CASEIN FIBRIN GLOBIN
MYOGEN ALBUMIN AMANDIN
ELASTIN GELATIN GLIADIN HISTONE
HORDEIN KERATIN LIVETIN MUCEDIN
SERICIN ALEURONE COLLOGEN
FERRITIN GLOBULIN GLUTELIN
GORGONIN IPOMOEIN PROLAMIN
(RICH IN —S) NARROW
PROTEOSE ALBUMOSE ELASTOSE
GELATOSE
PROTEST AVER BEEF FUSS HOWL
KICK BROCK CROAK DEMUR AFFIRM
ASSERT BOWWOW EXCEPT HOLLER
OBJECT OBTEST PLAINT SQUAWK
SQUEAL CONTEST INVEIGH PUBLISH
RECLAIM RHUBARB SCRUPLE
TESTIFY HARRUMPH PROCLAIM
(— AGAINST INJUSTICE) HARO
PROTESTANT ALASCAN GENEVAN
GOSPELER HELVETIC HUGUENOT
SWADDLER
PROTEUS OLM AMOEBA
PROTHESIS CREDENCE PARABEMA
PROTHORAX COLLAR CORSELET
MANITRUNK
PROTOPINE FUMARINE
PROTOPLASM PLASMA PLASSON
SARCODE OVOPLASM PERIPLAST
SOLEPLATE
PROTOPLAST CELL ENERGID
PROTOTYPE IDEAL MODEL FATHER
EXAMPLE PATTERN ANTITYPE
EXEMPLAR
PROTOZOAN AMEBA FORAM MONAD
MONER AGAMETE ARCELLA BABESIA
BODONID CILIATE PROTIST RADIATE
STENTOR DIDINIUM HYPOZOAN
(PL.) MICROZOA
PROTRACT DRAG DRAW DREE PLOT
SPIN DEFER DELAY DRIVE TRACT
TRAIL TRAIN DILATE EXTEND
LINGER SPREAD DETRACT PROLONG
CONTINUE LENGTHEN
PROTRACTED DREE LONG DREICH

PROLIX LENGTHY DRAGGING
EXTENDED
PROTRUDE BUG JUT LILL LOLL
POUT BLEAR BULGE BUNCH POUCH
SHOOT START STICK STRUT SWELL
EXSERT EXTEND EXTRUDE KNUCKLE
PROJECT HERNIATE OUTPOINT
OUTREACH OUTSHOOT
PROTRUDING STEEP BUNCHY
GOGGLE BLABBER EMINENT
JUTTING
PROTRUSION LAP NOB BURR KNOB
POUT HERNIA SALIENCE SHOULDER
TYLOSOID
PROTUBERANCE BUD HUB JAG
NOB NUB WEN BEAN BOLL BOSS
BULB BUMP HEEL HUMP JAGG KNOB
KNOP KNOT LUMP NODE PUFF SCAB
SNAG STUB UMBO WART BULGE
BUNCH CAPUT GLAND GNARL
HUNCH KNURL SWELL TORUS
TUBER TUMOR CALLUS HUBBLE
PIMPLE POMMEL EXTANCY PAPILLA
EMINENCE FLANKARD NODOSITY
SWELLING
(— AT BASE OF BIRD'S BILL) CERE
SNOOD
(— BEARING SPINE) UMBO
(— FROM SWELLING) PUFF
(— IN SIDE OF DEER) FLANKARD
(— ON A CASTING) SCAB
(— ON BONE) EMINENCE
(— ON HORSE'S HOOF) BUTTRESS
(— ON MANDIBLE OF GEESE) BEAN
(— ON SADDLEBOW) POMMEL
(— ON SALAMANDER) BALANCER
(— ON TONGUE) PAPILLA
(KNOBLIKE —) CAPUT
(OCCIPITAL —) INION
(RAGGED —) JAG JAGG
(ROUGH —) HUB
(SKIN —) WEN MOLE WART PIMPLE
PROTUBERANT BULGY BUMPY
PROUD STRUT TUMID BUCKED
EXTANT GOGGLE BOTTLED BULGING
EMINENT GIBBOUS SALIENT
SWOLLEN
(REGULARLY —) CONVEX
PROUD FESS GLAD HIGH IKEY LOFT
PERK RANK SIDE VAIN BRANT
CHUFF GELLY GREAT JELLY LOFTY
NOBLE ORGUL PRIDY SAUCY STEEP
STIFF STOUT VOGIE WINDY WLONK
COPPED ELATED FIERCE LORDLY
ORGUIL PENCEY QUAINT SKEICH
SKEIGH UPPISH UPPITY VAUNTY
HAUGHTY SUBLIME SWOLLEN
TOPPING ARROGANT EXULTANT
GLORIOUS IMPOSING INSOLENT
ORGULOUS SPLENDID STOMACHY
PROUDLY HIGH
PROVE TRY FAND FOND PREE SHOW
TEST ARGUE ASSAY EVICT TAINT
TASTE TEMPT ARGUFY EVINCE
SUFFER VERIFY BALANCE CONFESS
CONFIRM CONVICT DERAIGN
IMPROVE JUSTIFY CONCLUDE
CONVINCE EVIDENCE INDICATE
INSTRUCT MANIFEST

(— FALSE) BELIE BETRAY FALSIFY
(— GUILTY) ATTAINT
(— OUT) SERVE
(— TITLE) DEDUCE
(— VALID) DEFEND
PROVED TRIED EXPERT PROBATE
PROVENCAL LANGUEDOC
ROMANESQUE
PROVENDER HAY CORN FEED FOOD
OATS STRAW PROVAND PROVIANT
PROVERB SAW SAY REDE WORD
ADAGE AXIOM CREED GNOME
SOOTH BALLAD BYWORD DITTON
DIVERB MASHAL SAYING SPEECH
SYMBOL WHEEZE BYSPELL IMPRESA
NAYWORD PARABLE APHORISM
FORBYSEN PAROEMIA SCHOLION
SCHOLIUM SENTENCE SOOTHSAY
PROVIDE DO FIT SEE FEND FILL
FIND GIRD LEND LOOK BLOCK
CATER ENDOW ENDUE EQUIP SPEED
STOCK STORE AFFORD FOISON
PURVEY SUBORN SUPPLY EXHIBIT
FORESEE FURNISH INSTORE
PREPARE ACCOUTER APPANAGE
DISPENSE PURCHASE
(— AHEAD OF TIME) ADVANCE
(— AMUSEMENT) DISTRACT
(— FOOD) GRUB CATER SCAFF
(— FOR) FEND SERVE CHEVEYS
CHEVISE PROVANT
(— STINGILY) SKINCH
(— SUPPORT) ESCOT
(— WITH DOWRY) DOT
(— WITH HIP-ROOF) COOT
(— WITH) BESEE
PROVIDED IF BODEN FIXED READY
SOBEIT PROVISO INSTRUCT
PREPARED
PROVIDENCE THRIFT ECONOMY
PRUDENCE
PROVIDENT WARY WISE FRUGAL
SAVING CAREFUL PRUDENT THRIFTY
PROVINCE LAN AREA NOME WALK
AIMAK BANAT FIELD MOUTH NATAL
NOMOS REALM SHENG SHIRE
SUBAH BANNAT EMPIRE EYALET
MALAGA MONTON REGION SIRCAR
SPHERE SYSSEL YAMATO DEMESNE
DONGOLA EPARCHY MUDIRIA
PURVIEW RECTORY VILAYET
APPANAGE DISTRICT FUNCTION
MUDIRIEH NOMARCHY
(SUBDIVISION OF EGYPTIAN —)
KISM
(PL.) OUTLAND
PROVINCIAL HICK BORNE CRUDE
NARROW RUSTIC STUFFY INSULAR
SUBURBAN
PROVISION BOARD CHECK GRIST
FODDER MATTER PURVEY STOVER
UNLESS WRAITH APPREST CAUTION
CODICIL DOWNSET KEEPING
SLEEPER VICTUAL WARNISH
WARNISON
(BOUGHT —S) ACATERY
(SUBORDINATE —) ITEM
(PL.) CHOW FOOD JOCK KEEP LOAN
BOUGE CATES SCRAN STORE

TERMS TOMMY ANNONA VIANDS
VIVRES COMMONS WARNAGE
WAYFARE VICTUALS
PROVISO SALVO CAVEAT CLAUSE
CAUTION CONDITION
PROVOCATION APPEAL INCENTIVE
PROVOCATIVE GUTTY SALTY
AGACANT PIQUANT IRRITANT
APPEALING
PROVOKE BOG EGG GIG IRE TAR
VEX BEAR DARE HUFF MOVE PICK
STIR TARR TEEN URGE WORK
ANGER ANGRY ANNOY EAGER
EVOKE FRUMP PIQUE TAUNT TEMPT
APPEAL ELICIT EVINCE EXCITE
GRIEVE HARASS INCITE KINDLE
NETTLE PROMPT SUMMON TICKLE
AFFRONT ILLICIT INCENSE INFLAME
INSPIRE VROTHER CATALYZE
IRRITATE
PROVOST JUDGE PRIOR REEVE
KEEPER WARDEN STEWARD
PROW BOW BEAK SPUR STEM
PRORE SNOUT SPERON STEVEN
DIVIDER GALLANT VALIANT
(— OF GONDOLA) FERRO
PROWESS FEAT PROW VALOR
NOBLEY BRAVERY COURAGE
PROWL OWL PROG ROAM LURCH
MOOCH MOUSE RAVEN BREVIT
RAMBLE
PROWLER WALKER SLASHER
TENEBRION
PROWLIKE PROREAN
PROWLING GRASSANT
PROXIMATE NEXT CLOSE DIRECT
CLOSEST NEAREST PROXIME
IMMINENT PROXIMAL
PROXIMITY SHADOW NEARNESS
PRESENCE VICINITY
PROXY VICE AGENT VICAR BALLOT
MANDAT PROCTOR
(PL.) ELECTION
PRUDE COMSTOCK
PRUDENCE CARE ADVICE CAUTEL
WISDOM CAUTION COUNSEL
SLEIGHT FORECAST FORELOOK
PRUDENT FIT SAGE WARE WARY
WISE CANNY DOOSE DOUCE SOLID
SYKER VERTY FRUGAL QUAINT
SEKERE SICCAR POLITIC THRIVEN
CAUTIOUS DISCREET
PRUDISH NICE PRIM MIMZY MIMSEY
PRIGGISH RUDIBUND VICTORIA
PRUDISHNESS NICETY PUDENCY
PRUNE COW LOP TOP CLIP COLL
COUL GELD PLUM SNED SPUR TAME
TRIM CLEAN DRESS KNIFE PLUMB
PREEN PRIME PURGE SHEAR SHRED
SHRUB TWIST DEHORN REFORM
SHRIDE SNATHE SWITCH AMPUTATE
CASTRATE RETRENCH
(— SEVERELY) DEHORN
(IMPERFECTLY RIPENED —) FROG
PRUNING HOOK SARPE CALABOZO
PRUNING KNIFE CALABOZO
SERPETTE
PRUNING SHEARS SECATEUR
PRURIENT ITCHY

PRURITIS ITCH
PRUSSIAN PRUTENIC
PRY GAG NOSE NOTE PEEK PEEP
PEER TEET JIMMY LEVER PRIZE
SNOOP BREVIT FERRET PIGGLE
POTTER PUTTER CROWBAR
GUMSHOE LEVERAGE
(— ABOUT) OWL MOUSE SNOOK
SCROUNGE
(— INTO AND REPEAT) RAVE
(— INTO) BREVIT
PRYING NOSY NOSEY CURIOUS
PEEPING
PSALM ODE HYMN SONG DIRGE
GATHA ANTHEM CANTATE CHORALE
INTROIT MISERERE
(100TH —) JUBILATE
(95TH —) VENITE
(98TH —) CANTATE
PSALMS HALLEL
(BOOK OF —) PSALTER
PSALTERIUM BOOK LYRA OMASUM
PSALTER PSALTERY
PSALTERY GUSLA SAUTREE
PSEUDO FAKE MOCK SHAM BOGUS
FALSE FEIGNED SPURIOUS
PSEUDOCARP HIP
PSEUDONYM ALIAS ANONYM JUNIUS
PSHAW SHA POOH SUGAR SHUCKS
PSORIASIS ALPHOS
PSYCHE MIND SELF SOUL
PSYCHIATRIST ALIENIST
PSYCHOANALYST FREUDIAN
PSYCHOLOGY HORMISM HEDONICS
ANIMASTIC FORMALISM
PSYCHOPATH MATTOID
PSYCHOSIS INSANITY SENILITY
PSYCHOTIC MAD CRAZY INSANE
PSYLLA DIMERAN
PSYLLIUM FLEAWORT
PTAH (— EMBODIED) APIS
(ASSOCIATED WITH —) SEKHET
PTARMIGAN RYPE GROUSE
LAGOPODE
PTEROCARPUS LINGOUM
PTEROSAUR DIAPSID
PTERYGIUM WEBEYE
PTERYGOID EXTERNUM
PTERYLA TRACT
PTISAN TEA TISANE
PTOLEMY SOTER
(WIFE OF —) CLEOPATRA
PTOMAINE NEURIN SEPSIN SAPRINE
GADININE
PUB BAR INN BOOZER LOUNGE
SHANTY TAVERN
PUBBLE FAT FULL PLUMP
PUB-CRAWL BARHOP
PUBESCENCE DOWN SCURF YOUTH
TOMENT
PUBESCENT HIRSUTE VILLOUS
PUBLIC KUNG OPEN TOWN CIVIC
OVERT WORLD COMMON SOCIAL
VULGAR GENERAL OMNIBUS
POPULAR EXTERNAL MATERIAL
NATIONAL
(GENERAL —) GALLERY
PUBLICAN FARMER KEEPER
ZACCHEUS CATCHPOLL

PUBLICATION BOOK ORDO BIBLE
FOLIO ISSUE SHEET ANNUAL
BLAZON DIGLOT SERIAL WEEKLY
ALMANAC BOOKLET ELZEVIR
JOURNAL MONTHLY WRITING
BIWEEKLY BULLETIN DOCUMENT
EMISSION EXCHANGE PRODROME
EPHEMERIS
PUBLIC HOUSE BAR INN PUB
BOOZER PUBLIC SALOON HOSTELR'
POTHOUSE
PUBLICIST AGENT SOLON WRITER
PUBLICITY AIR ECLAT BUILDUP
PUFFERY RECLAME BALLYHOO
BROUHAHA DAYLIGHT HERALDRY
PROMOTION
PUBLICIZE CRY BLURB BREAK
BRUIT HERALD BALLYHOO HEADLIN
PUBLIC SQUARE PLAZA PLEIN
ZOCALO
PUBLISH ASH BLOW CALL EDIT EMI'
VEND VENT CARRY ISSUE PRINT
SPEAK UTTER BLAZON BROACH
DEFAME EVULGE EXPOSE SPREAD
CENSURE DECLARE DIFFUSE
DIVULGE GAZETTE PROTEST
DENOUNCE DISCLOSE EVULGATE
PROCLAIM PROMULGE
(— BANNS OF MARRIAGE) CRY
SPUR OUTASK
(— IN CHURCH) ASK
(— WITHOUT AUTHORIZATION)
PIRATE
PUBLISHER CRIER EDITOR PRINTER
STATIONER
PUCCOON GROMYL ALKANET
GROMWELL BLOODROOT
PUCE FLEA
PUCK ELF LOB PUG BLOW BUTT
DISK POKE POOK DEMON DEVIL
FAIRY PEWKE SPORT RUBBER
SPRITE STRIKE PUCKREL
HOBGOBLIN
PUCKER DRAW FULL RUCK PURSE
REEVE TIZZY COCKLE COTTER
FURROW LUCKEN WRINKLE
CONTRACT AGITATION CONSTRICT
PUCKERED BULLATE COCKLED
WRINKLED BULLIFORM
PUCKFIST BRAGGART PUFFBALL
PUCKISH PUXY ELFIN IMPISH
WHIMSICAL
PUDDING DICK DUFF LINK SAGO
DOWDY KUGEL MERIT BURGOO
FENDER HACKIN HAGGIS HAUPIA
JAUDIE SPONGE TANSEY TARTAN
DESSERT ADEQUACY BLOODING
HEDGEHOG LIVERING PANDOWDY
WHITEPOT CHARLOTTE
(— CONTAINING KALE) TARTAN
(— OF FLOUR) DUFF
(BOILED —) HOY
(FRUIT —) HEDGEHOG
(HASTY —) MUSH SEPON SUPAWN
(HAWAIIAN —) HAUPIA
(MEAT —) ISING HACKIN HACKING
(SUET —) KUGEL
PUDDINGWIFE PUDIANO DONCELL'
GLUEFISH

PUDDLE DUB PANT PLUD POOL PULK ROIL SLAB SLOP SOSS SUMP PLANT PLASH PUDGE CHARCO FLODGE MUDDLE PUDDER SPLASH TAMPER CONFUSE PLASHET SLODDER SPUDDLE BEFUDDLE **(MUD —)** DUB SLOP LOBLOLLY
PUDDLER'S RABBLE STRIKE
PUDENCY MODESTY DELICACY
PUDGY MIRY BULKY MUDDY SQUAT CHUBBY SPUDDY
PUDU VENADA
PUEBLO ANASAZI
PUELCHE PAMPA TEHUELET
PUERILE WEAK SILLY BOYISH JEJUNE TRIVIAL CHILDISH IMMATURE YOUTHFUL

PUERTO RICO

BAY: SUCIA RINCON BOQUERON AQUADILLA
CAPITAL: SANJUAN
ISLAND: MONA CULEBRA VIEQUES
LAKE: LOIZA CARITE CAONILLAS
MEASURE: CUERDA CABALLERIA
RIVER: CAMUY CANAS YAUCO ANASCO TANAMA FAJARDO
TOWN: CAYEY COAMO PONCE DORADO MANATI ARECIBO FAJARDO GUAYAMA HUMACAO MAYAGUEZ

PUFF GUF POP BLOW BRAG DRAG FLAM FLAN GUFF GUST HUFF PANT SHOW WAFF WAFT ELATE ERUPT EXTOL FLUFF GLURB QUIFF STECH SWELL WHIFF CAPFUL EXPAND FLATUS BLUSTER EXPLODE GRATIFY INFLATE WHIFFET BRAGGART OVERRATE WINDGALL BOUILLONE
(— FROM SHELL BLAST) BURST
(— OF WIND) FLAM TIFT SCART FLATUS HUFFLE
(— OUT SMOKE) EFFUME
(— OUT) BELL BLUB VENT BLUBBER EFFLATE INFLATE
(— UP) BLOW HUFF RISE BLOAT HEAVE BLADDER
(— VIOLENTLY) BLAST
(CREAM —) DUCHESSE
(SUDDEN —) FLAN FLAW GUST
PUFFBALL FIST FUZZ PUFF SMOKE FUNGUS PUFFIN BULLFICE BULLFIST PUCKFIST SNUFFBOX
PUFFBIRD BARBET MONASE NUNLET DREAMER NUNBIRD BARBACOU
PUFFED BLUB BOLLEN BLOATED SOUFFLE SWOLLEN ARROGANT INFLATED
(— OUT) BAGGY BOUFFANT
(— UP) RANK POBBY ASTRUT BLOATED SWOLLEN TURGENT
(BE — UP) BELL
PUFFER ATINGA BALLER BLOWER SLIMER TAMBOR BURFISH EGGFISH BLOWFISH TOADFISH
PUFFIN LOOM PAPE POPE MARROT MULLET MARROCK WILLOCK

COCKANDY PARAKEET TOMNODDY TOMNORRY
(HAWAIIAN —) AO
PUFFY SOFT BLOAT FAFFY GUMMY GUSTY PURSY CHUBBY FLUFFY PURFLY PERSIVE SWOLLEN BLADDERY BOUFFANT DROPSICAL
PUG FOX IMP PET BOXER CHAFF GOUGE SPOOR TRACK TRAIL CAMOIS CAMUSE GOBLIN MONKEY MISTRESS PUGILIST FOOTPRINT
PUGILIST PUG MILLER BRUISER SLOGGER
PUG-NOSED CAMUS CAMUSE
PUISNE PUNY LATER PETTY JUNIOR YOUNGER INFERIOR
PUISSANCE ARMY FORCE POWER CONTROL POTENCY PROWESS DOMINION STRENGTH
PUJUNAN MAIDU
PUKKA GOOD REAL GENUINE LASTING COMPLETE SUPERIOR AUTHENTIC
PUKRAS PHEASANT KOKLAS
PULCHRITUDE GRACE BEAUTY
PULE CRY PEEP CHIRP COWRY WHINE SNIVEL WHIMPER
PULING PULY SPINDLY WHINING
PULL IN PU EAR LUG POO POU ROG RUG TIT TOW CLAW DRAG DRAW DUCT HALE HARL HAUL HOOK RUGG SWIG TIRE TREK TUSH TWIG YANK BOUSE BREAK BUNCH DRAFT HEAVE HITCH IMPEL PLUCK POLLE PROOF TRICE TWEAK ASSUME COMMIT GATHER OBTAIN PLITCH RUGGLE SECURE TWITCH UPROOT WRENCH ATTRACT EXTRACT
(— A BELL) SET
(— ABOUT) TEW SOOL TOSE TOZE MOUSLE
(— APART) RAVE REND TEAR DIVULSE
(— AWAY) AVEL AVELL WREST REVULSE
(— BY EARS) SOLE SOWL
(— DOWN) UNPILE DESTROY DEMOLISH
(— HERE AND THERE) TOOZLE TOUSLE
(— NOSE) SNITE
(— OF DRUM) EAR
(— OFF) CROP DRAW STRIP AVULSE
(— ON FISHING ROD) STRIKE
(— OUT) RAX EXTRACT OUTBRAID
(— QUICKLY) YANK
(— ROUGHLY) WAP TOWSE WOUSE
(— SUDDENLY) TRICE
(— THE LEG) STRING
(— TOGETHER) KNOT ATTRACT
(— TRIGGER) SQUEEZE
(— UP BY THE ROOTS) ARACE
(— UP) LOUK
(— WITH JERK) HOICK SWITCH
(ZIPPER —) SLIDER
PULLDEVIL SCROUGER SCRODGILL
PULLER KNOCKER
PULLER-IN CLICKER

PULLET HEN EAROCK EEROCK EIRACK MABYER POULARD POULAINE
PULLEY RIM CONE DRUM BLOCK FUSEE FUZEE IDLER WHEEL DRIVEN IDLEBY JOCKEY POLYVE RIGGER SHEAVE SHIVER WHARVE CAPSTAN FERRULE TIGHTER TRUCKLE WHARROW PULLISEE PURCHASE TROCHLEA
(PL.) TRISPAST JACKANAPES
PULLOVER JERSEY SWEATER
PULLULATE BUD TEEM SWARM MULTIPLY
PULMONATE LUNGED
PULP PAP PUG CHUM BROKE JELLY NERVE SLUSH STOCK STUFF MARROW SQUEEZE SQUELCH
PULPIT PEW TUB AMBO BEMA DESK WOOD CHAIR PREACH ROSTRUM TRIBUNE
(— BOARD) TYPE
(— FOR CHOIR BOOKS) ANALOGION
(MOSLEM —) MIMBAR MINBAR
(OPEN-AIR —) TENT
PULPY SOFT SPEWY FLABBY FLESHY SIDDER SIDDOW BACCATE SQUELCHY
PULSATE BEAT BRIM FLAP PANT PUMP THROB COURSE STRIKE PALPITATE
PULSATION BEAT HEARTBEAT LIFEBLOOD VIBRATION
(— OF ARTERY) ICTUS
PULSE DAL BEAT DOHL TAKT URAD WAVE POUCE STUFF THROB BATTUTA IMPULSE PULSIDGE SPHYGMUS VITALITY
PULVERIZE BUCK DRAG FINE MEAL MULL STUB CRUSH FLOUR GRIND POUND POWDER ATOMIZE DEMOLISH VANQUISH COMMINUTE
PULVERIZED FINE POWDERED
PULVERIZER MULLER
PULVERULENT DUSTY CRUMBLY POWDERY
PUMA COUGAR PAINTER PANTHER
PUME YARURA
PUMICE PUMEX PUMIE
PUMMEL FIB BEAT DRUB PAIK SLAT POUND SLATE THUMP POUNCE
PUMP GIN GUN FORK JACK COURT FORCE HEART PLUMB SLUSH DOCTOR DORSAY FORCER SINKER VOLUTE BOOSTER DOWNTON EJECTOR EVACTOR PITWORK SLUDGER SYRINGE TOEPLER BEERPULL ELEVATOR INFLATER INJECTOR PULSATOR
(— ON SHIPS) DOWNTON
(GAS —) BOWSER
(HAND —) GUN
(MINE —S) SET
(SET OF —S) LIFT
PUMP DOCTOR GRATHER
PUMPER RACKER
PUMPERNICKEL BOMBERNICKEL
PUMPKIN PEPO CHUMP GOURD PEPON QUASH CITRUL CUCURB

CUSHAW SQUASH QUASHEY
CUCURBIT PEPONIDA
PUMPKINSEED RUFF SUNNY
FLATFISH FLOUNDER REDBELLY
PUN NICK WHIM ALLUDE CLINCH
QUIBBLE EQUIVOKE PARAGRAM
CALEMBOUR
PUNCH DAB DIG HUB JAB SET BASH
BLOW BOFF BUST DING PLUG POKE
SETT SOAK SOCK TIFF DOUSE
DRIFT FORCE GLOGG PASTE PENCH
SHORT SLOSH CANCEL INCUSE
PATRIX PAUNCH SHAPER STRIKE
TRACER MATTOIR PERLOIR
STARTER EMBOSSER GROUNDER
PRITCHEL PUNCTURE SWATCHEL
THICKSET
(CHASING —) TRACER
(ETCHER'S —) MATTOIR
(HORSESHOE —) PRITCHEL
(OVAL —) PLAISHER
PUNCHBOARD PUSHCARD
PUNCH BOWL SNEAKER
PUNCHED PERTUSE
PUNCHEON CASK PULE SNAP
PUNCH
PUNCHER COWBOY SOCKER
PUNCHINELLO CLOWN BUFFOON
PUGENELLO
PUNCH PRESS BEAR DROP
PUNCHY POUNCY FORCEFUL
PUNCTILIOUS NICE EXACT STIFF
FORMAL CAREFUL POINTED
PRECISE PUNCTUAL
PUNCTUAL DUE EXACT PROMPT
CAREFUL PRECISE ACCURATE
DEFINITE DETAILED EXPLICIT
PUNCTUATE MARK STOP
EMPHASIZE
PUNCTUATION MARK DOT DASH
STOP BRACE COLON COMMA PRICK
SLASH HYPHEN PERIOD STIGME
BRACKET VIRGULE ELLIPSIS
SEMICOLON
PUNCTURE HOLE PICK PINK PROD
STAB DRILL POINT PRICK PUNCH
STICK NEEDLE PIERCE PIQURE
DEFLATE DESTROY PUNCTUM
CENTESIS
PUNDIT SVAMI SWAMI CRITIC PANDIT
TEACHER
PUNGENCY HEAT SALT SNAP
ACRIMONY KEENNESS PIQUANCY
SALTNESS
PUNGENT HOT TEZ BOLD FELL
KEEN RACY SALT TART ACRID
ACUTE BRISK QUICK SHARP SMART
SNELL SPICY BITING BITTER SHRILL
SNAPPY CAUSTIC MORDANT
PEPPERY PIQUANT POINTED
TELLING CAYENNED PIERCING
POIGNANT STABBING STINGING
PUNGI BIN
PUNIC PUNICAL FAITHLESS
PUNISH FIT FIX PAY BUCK CANE
COLT COOK CUCK FINE FLOG GATE
SORT WIPE ABUSE BIRCH CURSE
ORDER SCOUR SHEND SLATE SPILL
STOCK STRAP TWINK WREAK

AMERCE AVENGE CAMPUS FERULE
FOLLOW IMMURE LESSON REFORM
SCHOOL STRIKE CHASTEN
CONSUME CORRECT CORRIGE
DEPLETE PENANCE REQUITE
SCOURGE CARTWHIP CHASTISE
DISTRAIN
(— BY COMPENSATION) FINE
AMERCE
(— BY CONFINEMENT) GATE
(— BY FINE) MULCT
(— BY LASHING WRISTS) BUCK
PUNISHING HARD GRUELING
PUNISHMENT GIG FINE LASH PAIN
PINE RACK SACK WITE YARD BEANS
GRUEL LIBEL PANDY PEINE SMART
WRACK WREAK DESERT DIRDUM
FERULE LESSON PICKET EXAMPLE
GALLOWS GANTLET JANKERS
PAYMENT PENALTY PENANCE
PENANCY REVENGE SCOURGE
HERISSON JUDGMENT PUNITION
STOCKING SUPPLICE EXECUTION
(CAPITAL —) SCAFFOLD
(MILITARY —) JANKERS
PUNITIVE PENAL PUNITORY
PUNK BAD BOY FUNK JERK MONK
POOR PUNG CONCH SPONK SPUNK
AMADOU BUNKUM NOVICE
HOODLUM RUFFIAN BEGINNER
GANGSTER INFERIOR NONSENSE
STRUMPET TERRIBLE TOUCHWOOD
PUNKIE MIDGE MIDGET
PUNNING ALLUSIVE BIVERBAL
PUNSCH ARRACK
PUNSTER SPEED
PUNT BET HIT POY KENT KICK
QUANT GAMBLE GARVEY SKERRY
PUNTER BIDDER GAMBLER SCALPER
SERVITOR
PUNY WEAK DAWNY DEENY DWARF
FRAIL PETTY SCRAM WEARY JUNIOR
MAUGER NOVICE PUISNE RECENT
SICKLY SPROTY MANIKIN PIMPING
QUEECHY SHILPIT YOUNGER
DROGHLIN INFERIOR PINDLING
(— PERSON) TITMAN
PUP PUPPY WHELP
PUPA EGG NYMPH PUPPET TUMBLER
WIGGLER FLAXSEED WRIGGLER
CHRYSALIS
PUPIL BOY GYTE TYRO WARD BLACK
CADET CHILD ELEVE NORRY NURRY
RAPIN TUTEE ALUMNA GRADER
INFANT JUNIOR SENIOR LEARNER
PAULINE SCHOLAR SOJOURN
STUDENT ABSENTEE DISCIPLE
RUGBEIAN SCHOOLER
(— AT HEAD OF CLASS) DUX
(— IN STUDIO) RAPIN
(— OF EYE) BLACK PEARL SIGHT
(ANGLO-INDIAN —) CHELA
(BOARDED —) SOJOURN
PUPILAGE (WARDSHIP PEDANTISM
PUPPET BABY DOLL DUPE IDOL
MOTE BABBY DROLL DUMMY
MAUMET MOTION POPPIN STOOGE
WAJANG WAYANG GUIGNOL
DROLLERY MARIONET

(— PLAY) WAJANG
(— SHOW) VERTEP
PUPPIS STERN
PUPPY FOP PUP DOLL DOUGH
WHELP PUPPET
(FEMALE —) GYP
(GREYHOUND —) SAPLING
PURBLIND BISME BISSON
PURCHASABLE VENAL CORRUPT
PURCHASE BUY WIN EARN FISH
GAIN KOOP WHIP BOOTY HEDGE
PRIZE DUPLEX EFFECT EMPTIO
TACKLE ACQUIRE BARGAIN EMPTION
PILLAGE PROCURE BARRATRY
(— AND FATTEN CATTLE) HIGGLE
PURCHASER BUYER EMPTOR
VENDEE CHAPMAN POULTER
SHOPPER CUSTOMER
PURE NET CAST EVEN FAIR FINE
FREE FULL GOOD HOLY MERE NEAT
PUTE TRUE CLEAN CLEAR FRESH
MORAL NAKED SHEER STARK
SYCEE UTTER WHITE WHOLE
CANDID CHASTE ENTIRE IMMIXT
LIMPID PISTIC SIMPLE VESTAL
VIRGIN CATHARI GENUINE PERFECT
SINCERE ABSOLUTE ABSTRACT
COMPLETE DOVELIKE INNOCENT
SERAPHIC SPOTLESS VIRGINAL
VIRTUOUS
PUREE SOUP CREAM
PURGATIVE PURGE SENNA DIASENE
DRASTIC TURPETH ALOEDARY
CLEANSER EVACUANT CATHARTIC
PURGATORY PAIN SWAMP
PURGE LAX RID FIRE FLUX SOIL
CLEAR SCOUR DRENCH PHYSIC
REMOVE SEETHE SHRIVE SPURGE
CHISTKA CLEANSE DETERGE
ABSTERGE
PURIFICATION BAPTISM ELUTION
LUSTRUM VASTATION
PURIFY TRY BOLT FINE PURE WASH
CLEAN PURGE SNUFF BLEACH
DISTIL FILTER REFINE SETTLE
SPURGE WINNOW BAPTIZE CHASTEN
CLEANSE EPURATE EXPIATE
LAUNDER SUBLIME SWEETEN
DEPURATE EXORCISE FILTRATE
LUSTRATE SANCTIFY SCAVENGE
SPRINKLE
(— ORE) DILVE
PURIFYING SMECTIC DEPURANT
PURIRI TEAK BULREEDY IRONWOOD
PURITAN PRIG SAINT CANTER
CROPPY BLUENOSE CATHARAN
GOSPELER ROUNDHEAD
PURITANICAL BLUE STRICT
GENTEEL PRECISE
PURITY PURE ASSAY HONOR WHITE
CANDOR SATTVA VIRTUE FINESSE
CHASTITY FINENESS PURENESS
PURL RIB EDDY KNIT PEARL UPSET
RIPPLE TOTTLE CAPSIZE OVERTURN
PURLIEU HAUNT
(PL.) BOUNDS CONFINES ENVIRONS
PURLOIN CAB CRIB WEED BRIBE
FILCH STEAL SWIPE FINGER PILFER
PIRATE CABBAGE SURREPT
ABSTRACT

PURPLE GAY VIOL REGAL SHOWY
BLATTA BLOODY CROCUS EVEQUE
MIGNON ARDOISE FUCHSIA FUCHSIN
HEATHEN LOGWOOD PETUNIA
PONTIFF AMARANTH BURGUNDY
CAMERIER CYCLAMEN EGGPLANT
EMINENCE IMPERIAL MAUVETTE
WISTARIA
(DELICATE —) MAUVE
(VISIBLE —) RHODOPSIN
PURPLE FISH MUREX
PURPLE GALLINULE SULTAN
SULTANA HYACINTH
PURPLE LOOSESTRIFE KILLWEED
PURPLE RAGWORT JACOBY
PURPLE SANDPIPER REDLEG
REDLEGS ROCKBIRD
PURPORT FECK GIST PORT DRIFT
SENSE TENOR DESIGN EFFECT
IMPART IMPORT INTEND INTENT
BEARING MEANING PROFESS
PURPOSE COVERING DISGUISE
STRENGTH
PURPOSE GO AIM END GOAL IDEA
MAIN MEAN MIND MINT PLAN SAKE
TALK TEND WEEN WILL ARTHA
CAUSE ETTLE HEART LEVEL SCOPE
STUDY THINK DESIGN DEVICE
EFFECT INTEND INTENT OBTENT
PREFIX SCHEME COMPASS COUNSEL
DESTINE EARNEST IMAGINE
MEANING PROPOSE DEVOTION
FUNCTION PLEASURE PROPOUND
DISCOURSE
(FIXED —) HEART
(MORAL —) ETHOS
PURPOSEFUL AIMFUL POINTED
PURPOSIVE TELIC HORMIC
PURPOSELESS WASTE AIMLESS
FECKLESS
PURPURA MUREX PURPLES PELIOSIS
PURPURE GOLP GOLPE PURPLE
MERCURY
PURR MURR THRUM WHURL DUNLIN
PURSE BAG CLY JAN BUNG CLAY
CLOY KNIT POKE PUSS SKIN BULSE
BURSE DUMMY FUNDS MEANS
POUCH SPUNG COMMON FOLLIS
GIPSER POCKET PUCKER READER
SHAMMY ALMONER GIPSIRE
LEATHER SPORRAN BUCKSKIN
BURSICLE CRUMENAL
PURSE CRAB PAGURID
PURSER CLERK BURSAR BOUCHER
PINCHGUT NIPCHEESE
PURSING MIMP
(— OF MOUTH) PRIM
PURSLANE PUSSLY PIGWEED
PURSLANE TREE SPEKBOOM
PURSUANCE SUING SEQUENCE
PURSUE BAY RUN SUE HUNT SEEK
CHASE CHEVY CHIVY ENSUE HOUND
QUEST SLATE STALK TRADE
COURSE FOLLOW GALLOP TRAVEL
BEDEVIL HOTFOOT CONTINUE
PRACTICE
(— ZIGZAG COURSE) TACK
PURSUER FOLLOWER PLAINTIFF
QUESTRIST

PURSUIT FAD HUNT SUIT CAPER
CAUSE CHASE CRAFT HOBBY
COURSE SEARCH ASSAULT ACTIVITY
ENTREATY
PURSUIVANT BUTE MARCH FALCON
ORMOND ATHLONE CARRICK
ANTELOPE DINGWALL FOLLOWER
PURSY FAT OBESE PUFFY
ASTHMATIC
PURULENT PYIC ATTRY ATTERY
PURVEY PANDER SUPPLY FORESEE
PROVIDE
PURVEYOR CATER TAKER ACHUAS
PROWER CATERER ACHATOUR
MANCIPLE
PUS WARE AMPER FESTER MATTER
WORSUM QUITTER
PUSH CA DUB JAM JOG JUR PUT
BANG BIRR BOIL BOOM BORE BUNT
DING DUSH FLOG KENT PICK PILT
PING PORR POSS POTE STOP BLITZ
BOOST BRUSH BUNCH CROWD
CRUSH DRIVE DUNCH ELBOW
HUNCH NUDGE PINCH POACH
POUSE SCAUT SHOVE SKELP STICK
STOVE EXTEND HURTLE HUSTLE
JOGGLE JOSTLE POTTER PROPEL
THRING THRONG THRUST ASSAULT
IMPETUS IMPULSE OPERATE
PERPLEX SHUFFLE THRUTCH
CONTRUDE INCREASE SHOULDER
STRAITEN DISMISSAL
(— ALONG) TUSH
(— APART) SPREAD
(— ASIDE) SHOG
(— BY STICK) KENT POLE
(— FORWARD) ADVANCE
(— GENTLY) NUDGE
(— INTO) INVADE
(— MONEY) SPIFF
(— ON) BEAR YERK
(— OUT) DEBOUT LAUNCH
(— RUDELY) HORSE HUSTLE
(— TO FULL STRIDE) EXTEND
(— TOGETHER) CONTRUDE
(— UP) BOOST
(— WITH ELBOW) ELBOW HUNCH
(— WITH FEET) DIG SCAUT
(— WITH HEAD) BUNT BUTT
(STRONG —) BEVEL
PUSH BUTTON PUSH PRESSEL
PUSHCART BARROW TROLLEY
PUSHER PLUNGER TRAILER
TRAMMER WHEELER
PUSHY FORWARD AGGRESSIVE
PUSILLANIMOUS WEAK TIMID
FEEBLE COWARDLY TIMOROUS
PUSS CAT FACE HARE CHEET CHILD
MOUTH RABBIT BAUDRONS
PUSTULE NOB BEAL BURL KNOB
POCK PUSH QUAT WART ACHOR
AMPER BLAIN WHEAL WHELK
BLOTCH FESTER PIMPLE TETTER
ANTHRAX BLISTER ERUPTION
WHEYWORM
PUT DO BET LAY PIT SET BANG BUTT
FILL GIVE GROW PILT REST URGE
ADAPT APPLY DIGHT DRIVE FOCUS
PLACE STALL STATE STEAD STEEK

STELL WAGER ASSIGN BESTOW
DECAMP IMPOSE INVEST PHRASE
REPOSE SPROUT THRUST DEPOSIT
EMPLACE EXPRESS INFLICT
SUBJECT
(— AN END TO) DATE SNIB ABATE
NAPOO SNUFF SPIKE STASH STILL
STINT SOPITE STANCH ASSUAGE
EXPIATE SATISFY ABROGATE
DEMOLISH SURCEASE
(— ANOTHER IN PLACE OF) RELIEVE
(— APART) DISPART
(— ASIDE) BLOW HAIN SAVE SHUNT
SHUFFLE
(— AT REST) HUSH
(— AWAY) STOW COVER ELONG
HUTCH SHIFT RECOND DIVORCE
(— BACK INTO USE) RESTORE
(— BACK) REMIT REMISE
(— BEFORE) PROFER ANTEPONE
(— DOWN) LAY DEMIT QUELL
DEPOSE SQUASH DEPRESS
OPPRESS REPRESS SILENCE
DIMINISH SUPPRESS
(— EDGE ON) TED
(— FLAX UPON A DISTAFF) DIZEN
(— FORTH BLOSSOMS) GEM
(— FORTH) GEM CAST GIVE PUSH
EXERT LANCE PROFER STRETCH
(— GRAIN IN BARN) END
(— IN AGONY) THROE
(— IN CHARGE) COMMIT
(— IN COMPETITION) PIT
(— IN DANGER) SCUPPER
(— IN DREAD) ADRAD
(— IN MOTION) AROUSE
(— IN OPERATION) LAUNCH
(— IN ORDER) DO SET REDD SIDE
SORT TRIM DIGHT MENSE SHIFT
TRICK ADJUST DAIKER GRAITH
ORDAIN SETTLE ARRANGE CLARIFY
DISPOSE REDRESS INSTRUCT
(— IN PLACE) POSE
(— IN POSSESSION) SEISE
(— IN PRISON) WARD
(— IN) ENTER INSERT INTROMIT
(— INFORMATION INTO) ADDRESS
(— INTO BARN) END
(— INTO CASE) SHEATHE
(— INTO CIRCULATION) EMIT
SPRING
(— INTO ECSTASY) ENTRANCE
(— INTO EFFECT) EXECUTE
SANCTION
(— INTO IRONS) BOLT
(— INTO RHYTHM) METER METRE
(— LIQUOR INTO CASK) TUN
(— OFF) DOFF HAFT DEFER DELAY
DEMUR FOIST PARRY REMIT REPRY
SHIFT TARRY THROW LINGER
RETARD SHELVE ADJOURN
FORSLOW PROLONG RESPITE
POSTPONE
(— ON AIRS) PROSS FINICK REVEST
(— ON ALERT) ALARM
(— ON COVER) HACKLE
(— ON GUARD) ALERT CAUTION
(— ON HAT) COVER
(— ON PRETENSE) AFFECT

(— **ON SALE**) SHOP
(— **ON SHORT ALLOWANCE**) SCRIMP
(— **ON STRING**) ENFILE
(— **ON**) DON APPLY CRACK DRAPE
ENDUE MOUNT STAGE ASSUME
INVEST ADDRESS
(— **OUT BATSMAN**) SKITTLE
(— **OUT OF ACTION**) HAMPER
(— **OUT**) GET OUT DOUT OUST
DOWSE EVICT EXERT OUTED SLAKE
SLOCK RETIRE DISMISS EXCLUDE
EXTINCT FORJUDGE
(— **RIGHT**) AMEND
(— **ROAD METAL ON**) STEEN
(— **THROUGH A STRAINER**) TAMMY
(— **TO FLIGHT**) AFLEY FEAZE GALLY
(— **TO RIGHTS**) SORT DIGHT
(— **TO SHAME**) DASH ABASH SHEND
UPBRAID
(— **TO SLEEP**) OPIATE SOPITE
SOPORATE
(— **TO USE**) STOW APPLY BESTOW
(— **TO WORK**) HARNESS
(— **TOGETHER**) ADD JOIN BUILD
COMPILE COMPOSE CONCOCT
CONFECT ASSEMBLE COMPOUND
(— **UP HAY**) BOTTLE
(— **UP WITH**) GO BEAR BIDE HACK
BROOK ENDURE SUFFER COMPORT
STOMACH SWALLOW TOLERATE
(— **UP**) ANTE ERECT FLUSH
DISPENSE
(— **UPON**) GAMMON
(— **WITH ANOTHER**) APPOSE
PUTCHER PUTLOG PUTCHEN
PUTLOCK
PUTREFACTION ROT DECAY
PUTREFACTIVE SEPTIC
PUTREFY ROT DECAY SWEAT
FESTER POLLUTE PUTRESCE
PUTRESCENT PUTRID ROTTEN
PUTRID FOUL SOUR VILE LOUSY

ROTTEN CORRUPT DECAYED
FRIABLE VICIOUS DEPRAVED
PUTT CLOWN BORROW GOBBLE
PUTTEE PAT PATA GAITER BANDAGE
LEGGING
PUTTER FUSS MESS MUCK TRUCK
CADDLE DAWDLE MUCKER MUCKLE
PIDDLE TINKER FRIGGLE
PUTTY BEDDING
PUTTYROOT CRAWFOOT
PUTZ CRECHE
PUXY SWAMPY QUAGMIRE
PUZZLE CAP GET SET BEAT CRUX
DEAD LICK POSE BEFOG GRIPH
POSER QUEER REBUS STICK BAFFLE
BOTHER ENIGMA FICKLE FOITER
GLAIKS JIGSAW KITTLE RIDDLE
CONFUSE MYSTERY MYSTIFY
NONPLUS PERPLEX STICKER
TAISSLE TANGRAM TRANGAM
ACROSTIC BEFUDDLE BEWILDER
CONFOUND DISTRACT DUMFOUND
ENTANGLE INTRIGUE REMBLERE
CROSSWORD
PUZZLED ASEA
PUZZLING KNOTTY KNOTTED
RIDDLING DIFFICULT
PYCNANTHEMUM KOELLIA
PYCNOGONID SPIDER
PYGARG ADDAX OSPREY
PYGIDIUM PODEX
PYGMALION (FATHER OF —) BELUS
MUTGO AGENOR
(**MURDERED BY** —) SICHAEUS
(**SISTER OF** —) DIDO
(**STATUE FASHIONED BY** —)
GALATEA
PYGMY ELF AKKA AMBA DOKO
ACHUA AFIFI ATOMY BATWA DWARF
GNOME PIXIE PIGMEW WOCHUA
ACHANGO ASHANGO MANIKIN
DWARFISH NEGRILLO VAALPENS
DANDIPRAT

PYGMY GOOSE GOSLET
PYGMY RATTLESNAKE
MASSASAUGA
PYGOSTYLE VOMER
PYKNIC SQUAT STOCKY STHENIC
MUSCULAR
PYRAMID BENBEN HOPPER
TEOCALLI
(— **OF CRAYFISH**) BUISSON
(**DOUBLE** —) TWIN ZIRCONOID
(**INVERTED** —) HOPPER
PYRAMIDAL HUGE ENORMOUS
IMPOSING
PYRAMIDICAL TAPER
PYRAZINE ALDINE PIAZIN DIAZINE
PYRE BALE TOPHET BONFIRE
BALEFIRE
PYRITE BALE MUNDIC
(PL.) BRAZIL STANNITE FIRESTONE
MAGISTRAL MARCASITE
PYROLA LIMONIUM SHINLEAF
PYROMANIAC FIREBUG ARSONIST
PYRONE CUMALIN
PYROPHYLLITE PENCIL
PYROTECHNICS FIREWORKS
PYROXENE AUGITE SALITE SAHLITE
DIALLAGE DIOPSIDE
PYROXENITE ARIEGITE MARCHITE
OSTRAITE NIKLESITE
PYRRHIC DIBRACH
PYRRHULOXIA GROSBEAK
BULLFINCH
PYRROLE AZOLE
PYTHON ADJIGER PEROPOD
ANACONDA
PYTHONESS WITCH PHITONES
PYTHONIC HUGE INSPIRED
ORACULAR MONSTROUS PROPHETIC
PYX BOX CAPSA CASKET VESSEL
BINNACLE CIBORIUM
PYXIDIUM CAPSULE

Q KU CUE KUE QUEEN QUEUE QUEBEC

QUA HERON QUABIRD

QUACK PUFF WHACK SALVER SUBTLE EMPIRIC IMPOSTOR OPERATOR SANGRADO CHARLATAN

QUACKERY HUMBUG

QUADRAGESIMA LENT

QUADRANGLE QUAD CLOSE COURT TETRAGON

QUADRANT BOW RADIAL SQUARE QUARTER TETRANT ALTIMETER

QUADRATE SUIT AGREE IDEAL QUADER SQUARE PERFECT BALANCED

QUADRIC CONICOID

QUADRILATERAL TRAPEZIA TETRAGRAM (PL.) TESSARA

QUADRILLE CONTREDANSE (PL.) LANCERS

QUADROON QUATERON TERCERON

QUADRUPED BABIRUSA

QUADRUPLE FOURBLE FOURFOLD

QUADRUPLET FOURLING QUARTOLE

QUAFF QUAX TOOT DRINK QUASS WAUCHT CAROUSE TRILLIL

QUAG BOG MARSH SHAKE QUIVER

QUAGMIRE BOG FEN GOG HAG QUA SOG LAIR PUXY QUAW MARSH MIZZY SWAMP MORASS PUDDLE BOGMIRE PUCKSEY

QUAHOG CLAM COHOG VENUS BULLNOSE

QUAIL COW LOWA WEET COLIN DAUNT QUAKE SPOIL WASTE BLENCH CURDLE FLINCH SHRINK TURNIX WITHER DECLINE HEMIPOD TREMBLE BOBWHITE (YOUNG —) SQUEALER

QUAINT DRY ODD NAIVE STRANGE FANCIFUL HANDSOME

QUAKE JAR QUOG RESE CHILL QUAIL SHAKE QUIVER SHIVER FLUTTER SHUDDER TREMBLE

QUAKER ASPEN HERON FRIEND OBADIAH WHACKER HICKSITE TREMBLER BEACONITE BROADBRIM SHADBELLY (— STATE) PENNA PENNSYLVANIA

QUAKER GRAY ACIER

QUAKING ASPEN QUAKY TREPID SHAKING TREMBLING

QUAKING GRASS COWQUAKE WAGWANTS

QUALIFICATION NATURE RESERVE SHADING CAPACITY

QUALIFIED FIT ABLE MEET FITTED FITTEN LIKELY CAPABLE ELIGIBLE SUITABLE AUTHENTIC (NOT —) INAPT INHABILE

QUALIFIER MODIFIER

QUALIFY FIT DASH ADAPT ALLAY EQUIP HEDGE ENABLE MODIFY SOFTEN TEMPER ABSOLVE CERTIFY ENTITLE LICENSE PREPARE GRADUATE MODERATE RESTRAIN RESTRICT

QUALITY Y BRAN BUMP CHOP COST FEEL GUNA LEAD SORT COLOR GRACE STATE TRAIT ASSIZE BARREL FABRIC STRAIN THREAD TIMBER ADJUNCT CALIBER KINSHIP STATURE ACCIDENT MOVEMENT PROPERTY (— OF PERSONAL EMOTIONS) PATHOS (— OF PHOTOGRAPH) CONTRAST (— OF TONE) TIMBRE (— OF VOWELS) LENGTH (— PECULIAR TO ONESELF) SEITY (AESTHETIC —) TASTE (ARTISTIC —) VIRTU (ATTRACTIVE —) TAKE (BASIC —) GRAIN (BASIC —S) STUFF (COLOR —) TONE (ESSENTIAL —) ALLOY SPECIES SUCHNESS (GOOD —) THEW (HEREDITARY —) STRAIN (IMPECCABLE —) FINISH (INCISIVE —) BITE (INNATE —) LARGESS (INTELLECTUAL —) BROW (NATURAL —) TARAGE (OBJECTIONABLE —) ANILITY (OF HIGH —) FRANK (PERVASIVE —) AROMA (PHYSICAL —S) BOTTOM (PRIMAL —) GUNA (PUNGENT —) SNAP (RELATIVE —) RATE (SPRINGY —) SPINE (STRUCTURAL —) TEXTURE (SUBDUED —) SHADE (SUBTLE —) BOUQUET (SUPERIOR —) SUPER FINENESS (TRIED —) TOUCH (UNUSUAL —) SURD (WAVY — OF HAIR) FLIX

QUALM CALM DROW PALL NAUSEA SQUEAM SCRUPLE

QUALMISH TEWLY SICKISH SQUEAMISH

QUAMOCLIT MOONFLOWER

QUANDARY FIX PUXY TANGLE DILEMMA NONPLUS SWITHER DOLDRUMS JUNCTURE

QUANDONG PEACH

QUANTIC NONIC OCTIC SEPTIC SEXTIC QUADRIC QUINTIC

QUANTIFIER PREFIX

QUANTITY JAG SUM SUP BODY DEAL DISH DOSE FECK JAGG LIFT MASK SOME SOUD WARE BATCH BREAK CLASH GRIST KITTY SIEGE TROOP WHEEN ACTION ADDEND AMOUNT BAGFUL BOTTLE BUDGET DICKER EFFECT HANTLE NUMBER SPINOR THRAVE CONTENT FOOTAGE PORTION QUANTUM GLASSFUL KNIFEFUL LADLEFUL (— OF ARROWS) SHEAF (— OF BUTTER) CHURNING (— OF CLOTHES) BUCKING (— OF COTTONSEED) CRUSH (— OF CUT TREES) FALL

(— OF DRINK) HOOP DRAFT DRAUGHT (— OF ELECTRICITY) FARADAY (— OF EXPLOSIVE) CHARGE (— OF FISH OR GAME) TAKE CATCH DRAFT DRAUGHT (— OF GRAIN) GAVEL (— OF HAY) TRUSS (— OF IRRIGATION WATER) DUTY (— OF LIQUID) DROP JAUP SLASH GOBBET (— OF LIQUOR) HEELTAP (— OF LUMBER) RUN (— OF METAL) BLOW (— OF MUD) CLASH (— OF NARCOTICS) BINDLE (— OF PAPER) TOKEN (— OF PRODUCE) BURY (— OF RAISINS) FRAIL (— OF THREAD) LEASE (— OF WOOD) HAG FATHOM (ESTIMATED —) WEY (EXCESSIVE —) GLUT SPATE (FIXED —) CONSTANT (GREAT —) HOST MORT MUCH HIRST SIGHT STORE BARREL FOREST SLATHER TUMMELS (LARGE —) ACRE BOLT DEAL FECK HEAP MASS PECK SCAD SLEW FLOOD FORCE GRIST JORUM POWER SCADS SHEAF STACK STORE BUCKET BUSHEL DICKER DOLLOP GALLON MATTER MELDER CLUTHER SKINFUL HECATOMB MOUNTAIN (LEAST —) BEDROCK (MINUTE —) DRAM DROP SHADE SCRUPLE (NOTEWORTHY —) CHUNK (RELATIVE —) DEGREE (SETTLED —) SIZE (SIZABLE —) SCUMP (SMALL —) ACE BIT SUP DASH DUST HAET HAIR HARL IOTA PEAK SOSH SPOT CANCH PRILL SMACK SPICE SQUIB TOUCH JOBBLE MORSEL PICKLE SAMPLE SONGLE STIVER CAPSULE CURTSEY DRIBBLE DRIBLET EPSILON HANDFUL MODICUM SMICKET SPATTER TODDICK FARTHING MOUTHFUL PENNORTH SCANTLET (UNDIRECTED —) SCALAR (VARYING —) SKID

QUANTUM PHONON PHOTON

QUAPAW KWAPA ARKANSAS

QUARANTINE DETAIN ISOLATE SANCTION

QUARENTENE ROOD FURLONG

QUARREL JAR YED BEEF CHIP DEAL FEUD FRAY FUSS JARL JOWL MIFF NIFF ODDS PICK PLEA SPAT BRACK BRAWL BRIGE BROIL FLITE FLUSK GRUFF HURRY JOWER NOISE PIQUE SCOLD SCRAP SHINE STOUR UPSET WRALL AFFRAY BARNEY BREACH BREEZE BRIGUE DEBATE DIFFER DUSTUP FRACAS FRATCH GARROT JANGLE MATTER QUARRY RIPPET

SQUARE SQUEAL STRIFE THREAP
THREEP THWART BRABBLE DISGUST
DISPUTE FACTION OUTCAST
PRABBLE RUCTION SIMULTY
STASHIE SWAGGER TUILZIE
WRANGLE DISAGREE MOORBURN
SPLUTTER SQUABBLE TRAVERSE
(— IN WORDS) JANGLE
(NOISY —) ROW FRACAS KICKUP
(PETTY —) MIFF SPAT TIFF
QUARRELING BICKER CONTEK
CHIDING CONTECK
QUARRELSOME RIXY UGLY ROWTY
FEISTY SCRAPPY DRAWLING
FRAMPOLD FRATCHED PETULANT
PHRAMPEL FRACTIOUS
(NOT —) AMICABLE
QUARRELSOMENESS SQUARING
WARIANCE
QUARRIED (NOT —) LIVE
QUARRIER FACEMAN QUARION
QUARRY DELF GAME LODE MEAT
CHASE DELFT DELPH PLUCK
LATOMY REWARD LATOMIA
LOZENGE
(HAWK'S —) MARK
QUARRYMAN SCABBLER SCAPPLER
QUART SHANT WHART
(1-8TH —) GILL
(2 —S) FLAGON
(4 —S) GALLON
(METRIC —) LITER
(ONE-HALF —) PINT
QUARTE FOURTH
QUARTER PART STUD EAVER GRITH
TRACT BARRIO BEHALF BESTOW
CANTON COLONY FARDEL HARBOR
SECTOR CONTRADA FAUBOURG
FIERDING STANDARD POBLACION
(— IN BATTLE) GRITH
(— OF A POUND) TRIPPET
(— OF BEEF OR MUTTON) BOUT
(— OF CITY) BLOCK GHETTO
(— OF COMPASS) PLAGE
(— OF FLAG) CANTON
(— OF HOUR) POINT
(— OF HUNDRED) FIERDING
(— OF YEAR) RAITH
(— ONESELF) SORN
(— UPON) LAY
(JEWISH —) ALJAME
QUARTERING LASKING CHUMMAGE
QUARTER NOTE CROTCHET
QUARTER REST SOSPIRO
QUARTERS BOTHY BILLET BOTHIE
LIVERY MENAGE FARDELS
CHUMMERY DIGGINGS LODGMENT
(— FOR IMMIGRANTS) HOSTEL
(— OF SALVATION ARMY)
BARRACKS
(HIGH —) AERY EYRY AERIE EYRIE
(JUNIOR OFFICERS' —) GUNROOM
(MEN'S —) SELAMLIK
(MONASTERY —) FRATRY
QUARTET FOURSOME
QUARTILE SQUARE TETRAGON
QUARTO FOURS
QUARTZ IRIS ONYX SARD AGATE
FLINT PRASE TARSO TOPAZ JASPER

MORION PEBBLE PLASMA SILICA
ALENCON CITRINE CRYSTAL
RUBASSE SINOPLE AMETHYST
BASANITE SARDONYX SIDERITE
YENTNITE
QUARTZITE GANISTER SILCRETE
QUASH CASS CRUSH QUELL SPIKE
SQUAT SOPITE CASSARE PEREMPT
SUPPRESS
QUAT FOUR GLUT SQUASH SATIATE
UPSTART
QUATERNION TETRAD QUADRATE
QUATREFOIL TRESSURE
(DOUBLE —) EIGHTFOIL
QUAVER QUAP CROMA SHAKE TRILL
WAVER CHROMA FALTER QUIVER
WABBLE WOBBLE WRIBLE FREDDON
VIBRATE
QUAVERY WARBLY UNSTEADY
QUAY KEY POW QUAI LEVEE BUNDER
STRAND
QUEACH BOG FEN MARSH THICKET
QUEASINESS KECK SICKNESS
QUEASY NICE SICK SQUEEZY
DELICATE NAUSEATED SQUEAMISH
QUEBRACHO BREAKAX AXMASTER
IRONWOOD AXBREAKER
QUEBRADA BROOK GULLY RAVINE
FISSURE
QUECHUA INCAN KICHUA
QUEEN REG DAME FERS LADY MEDB
RANI AEDON BEGUM FIERS RANEE
ATOSSA REGINA ROXANA TAILTE
TAMARA ARGANTE ATHALIA
CANDACE JOCASTE OMPHALE
PHEARSE STATIRA TITANIA
BRUNHILD GERTRUDE GLORIANA
GUINEVER MAHARANI
(— AND KING OF TRUMPS) BELLA
(— CITY) CINCINNATI
(— IN CHESS) FERS LADY FIERS
(— OF CLUBS) SPADILLA
(— OF DENMARK) GERTRUDE
(— OF ETHIOPIA) CANDACE
(— OF FAIRY LAND) MEDB
GLORIANA
(— OF GEORGIA) TAMARA
(— OF GOTHS) TAMORA
(— OF HEARTS) ELIZABETH
(— OF HEAVEN) HERA
(— OF JUDAH) ATHALIA
(— OF LYDIA) OMPHALE
(— OF SHEBA) BALKIS BILKIS
(— OF SPADES) BASTA LIZZY
(— OF THE ADRIATIC) VENICE
(— OF THE ANTILLES) CUBA
(— OF THE EAST) ZENOBIA
(— OF THEBES) JOCASTA
(— OF TRUMPS) HONOR
(FAIRY —) MAB ARGANTE TITANIA
(INDIAN —) RANI SUNK MAHARANI
(MOHAMMEDAN —) BEGUM
QUEEN ANNE'S LACE UMBEL
QUEEN BEE KING
QUEEN ELIZABETH DIANA ORIANA
CYNTHIA
QUEENFISH WAHOO CROAKER
DRUMFISH
QUEENLY HAUGHTY REGINAL
MAJESTIC

QUEENROOT YAWSHRUB
QUEEN'S-DELIGHT YAWSHRUB
QUEENSLAND HEMP SIDA
JELLYLEAF
QUEER HEX ODD RUM HARM DICKY
DIPPY DROLL FAINT FUNNY GIDDY
NUTTY RUMMY COCKLE HIPPED
QUEASY QUISBY UNIQUE AMUSING
COMICAL CURIOUS DISRUPT
ERRATIC STRANGE TOUCHED
WHIMSIC FANCIFUL OBSESSED
PECULIAR
(— THING) QUOZ
QUEERNESS ODDITY
QUEEST RINGDOVE
QUELL DIE CALM FLOW HUSH KILL
QUAY SLAY ABATE ALLAY CRUSH
QUASH QUIET YIELD PACIFY PERISH
REDUCE SOOTHE SPRING STANCH
STIFLE KILLING REPRESS SQUELCH
SUPPRESS
QUEME QUIM HANDY WHEAM
COMELY PLEASE GRATIFY
PLEASANT
QUENCH COOL DAMP SIND ALLAY
CHECK CRUSH SLAKE SLOCK STILL
STANCH STIFLE ASSUAGE SLOCKEN
AUSTEMPER
QUENCHED EXTINCT
QUENCHER STANCH
QUENCHING FRITTING
QUERECHO VAQUERO
QUERELA AUDITA
QUERENT INQUIRER PLAINTIFF
QUERN KERN MILL METATE
MILLSTONE
QUERULOUS WHINY FRETFUL
PEEVISH NATTERED PETULANT
IRRITABLE
QUERY ASK DOUBT DEMAND
INQUIRE INQUIRY QUESTION
QUEST ASK BAY GAPE SEEK
DEMAND EXAMINE PURSUIT SEEKING
VENTURE
QUESTING OUTREACH
QUESTION ASK HOW SPY POSE
QUIZ TALK ARGUE DOUBT DREAD
QUERY ACCUSE CHANCE CHARGE
DEMAND LEADER MATTER PONDER
REASON SHRIVE EXAMINE INQUIRE
INQUIRY PROBLEM SCRUPLE
OVERTURE RELEVANT RESEARCH
STICKLER
(— AMBIGUOUSLY WORDED) RIDDL
(— FRETFULLY) RAME
(BAFFLING —) POSER
(PERPLEXING —) STUMPER
(UNSOLVED —) CRUX
QUESTIONABLE (NOT —) DECENT
QUESTIONER APPOSER INQUIRER
QUESTIONING DUBIOUS
QUESTIONABLE FISHY QUEER
SHAKY UNSAFE CLOUDED DUBIOUS
DOUBTFUL
QUESTION MARK QUERY QUAERE
EROTEME
QUESTIONNAIRE POLL INVENTORY
QUETCH STIR TWITCH
QUETZAL QUESAL TROGON

QUEUE CUE COLA LINE BRAID PIGTAIL CROCODILE

QUEY KOY WHY WHEY HEIFER

QUIBBLE COG PUN BALK CARP QUIB QUIP CAVIL DODGE EVADE QUIRK SALVO AMBAGE BAFFLE BICKER HAFFLE BRABBLE CAPTION CHICANE QUIBLET QUIDDIT QUILLET SHUFFLE QUILLITY CONUNDRUM

QUICA OPOSSUM SARIGUE

QUICK APT RAD YAP FAST FLIT GLEG KECK KEEN LISH LIST PERT RATH RIFE SNAP SOON WHAT WHIT WICK AGILE ALIVE APACE BRISK CHEAP FLEET HASTY MERRY PREST RAPID READY SHARP SHORT SNACK SNELL SWIFT SWITH TOSTO TRICK VISTO YARRY ACTIVE CLEVER FACILE KITTLE NIMBLE PROMPT PRONTO SNAPPY SPEEDY SUDDEN DARTING SCHNELL SHUTTLE DEXTROUS TRIPPING

(— AND NEAT) DEFT

(— AS A FLASH) WHIP

(— IN PERCEPTION) ACID

(— IN RESPONSE) GNIB

(— TO DETECT) SMOKY

(— TO FLARE UP) GASSY

(— TO LEARN) APT

(— TO MOVE) YARE

(LIGHT AND —) VOLANT

QUICKEN PEP MEND STIR WHET HURRY SPEED ACUATE AROUSE HASTEN INCITE KINDLE REVIVE VIVIFY ANIMATE ENLIVEN REFRESH SHARPEN EXPEDITE INSPIRIT

QUICKENING FLICKER REVIVAL STIRRING

QUICKLY TID TIT CITO FAST RIFE SOON TIVY WHIP YARE NEWLY RADLY RATHE SHARP SKELP SNACK SNELL SWITH TIGHT WIGHT YEPLY ASTITE BELIVE HOURLY PRESTO PRONTO RASHLY EFTSOON PRESTLY READILY SPEEDILY WIKIWIKI

(— AND WITH FORCE) SWAP

MORE —) TIDDER TITTER STRETTO

QUICKNESS HASTE SPEED AGILITY ACTIVITY CELERITY DISPATCH KEENNESS SAGACITY

MENTAL —) NOUS SLEIGHT LEGERITY

QUICKSAND FLOW SYRT SYRTIS SWALLOW

QUICK-SELLING LEEFTAIL

QUICKSILVER OREMIX MERCURY HERRAS HEAUTARIT

QUICK-SPEAKING PROMPT

QUICK-TEMPERED DONCY DONSY RASCIBLE

QUICK-WITTED APT SHARP SMART NIMBLE KNOWING

QUID FID CHEW SOVEREIGN

— OF TOBACCO) CUD FID

QUIDDANY JELLY SYRUP CODINIAC

QUIDDITY QUIBBLE WHATNESS

QUIDNUNC GOSSIP BUSYBODY

QUIESCENCE STASIS DORMANCY

QUIESCENT QUIET LATENT STATIC RESTING INACTIVE

QUIET QT ST COY LAY CALM COSH DEAD DUMB EASE EASY HUSH LOUN LOWN LULL REST ROCK SNUG SOFT WEME ACCOY CANNY CIVIL DOWNY LEVEL PEACE PEASE QUATE QUELL QUEME RESTY SALVE SHADY SILKY SLEEP SOBER SQUAT STILL SUANT WHIST DREAMY GENTLE PACIFY PLACID RETIRE SAUGHT SEDATE SERENE SETTLE SILENT SMOOTH SOFTLY SOOTHE SOPITE STEADY STILLY HUSHFUL ORDERLY REQUIEM RESTFUL SILENCE DECOROUS PEACEFUL TRANQUIL UNRUFFLE

(— DOWN) DILL

(MAKE —) ALLAY

(STEALTHILY —) SLINKY

QUIETISM MOLINISM

QUIETLY FAIR CANNY STILL WINLY EVENLY GENTLY SOFTLY TIPTOE

QUIETNESS REST REPOSE SERENITY

QUIETUDE CALM INERTION

QUIETUS REST DEATH RELEASE

QUILL COP PEN RIB PIRN FLOAT STALK BOBBIN FESCUE PINION SLEEVE CALAMOS PRIMARY TRUNDLE

(— FOR WINDING THREAD) COP

(PORCUPINE —) PEN

QUILLBACK SAILFISH SKIMBACK

QUILLWORT ISOETES FERNWORT

QUILT BEAT GULP WALT WELT WHIP DUVET REZAI CADDOW CHALON PALLET THRASH SWALLOW MATTRESS POULTICE COMFORTER

QUILTING MARCELLA

QUIMPER NICE

QUINCE COYNE ANGERS SQUINCH JAPONICA

(BENGAL —) BEL BAEL

QUINCE SEED CYDONIUM

QUININE KINA SPECIFIC

QUINK BRANT

QUINONE EMBELIN

QUINTAIN FAN

QUINTE FIFTH

QUINTESSENCE CREAM ELIXIR CLYSSUS OSMAZOME

QUINTUPLE QUINARY FIVEFOLD QUINIBLE

QUIP GIBE JEST JOKE CRACK QUIRK SALLY SCOFF TAUNT CONCEIT QUIBBLE

QUIRA CAOBA ROBLE HORMIGO VENCOLA MACAWOOD

QUIRE CHOR SEXTERN

(20 —S) REAM

(PL.) INSIDES

QUIRK BEND KINK QUIP TURN CLOCK CROOK TWIST CONCEIT QUIBBLE FLOURISH PAROXYSM MANNERISM

QUIRQUINCHO PICHI PELUDO

QUIRT WHIP ROMAL

QUIS WOODCOCK

QUIT GO DROP NASH PART QUAT AVOID BELAY CEASE DOUSE LEAVE SHIFT SHOOT STASH WHITE BEHAVE CIVITE DESERT DESIST FOREGO RESIGN SECEDE VACATE ABANDON FORSAKE RELEASE UNTENANT

QUITCH COUCH QUICK SCUTCH TWITCH

QUITCLAIM ACQUIT RELEASE DISCHARGE

QUITE SO ALL BUT GEY BRAW EVEN FAIR FREE FULL JUST PLAT WELL CLEAR CLOSE FULLY SHEER STARK CLEVER DAMNED ENOUGH JUSTLY MERELY TOTALLY

(NOT —) HARDLY

QUITRENT CANON

QUITS EVEN EVENS UPSIDES

QUITTER PUS SLAG PIKER COWARD JUMPER SHIRKER TURNBACK

QUIVER DIRL QUAG QUOG BEVER NIDGE QUAKE SHAKE TRILL WAVER WIVER BICKER COCKER DIDDER DINDLE SHEATH SHIMMY SHIVER TREMOR WAMBLE DORLACH FLUTTER FRISSON SHUDDER TREMBLE TWIDDLE TWITTER VIBRATE FLICHTER WERSLETE

QUIVERING ASPEN AGUISH DIDDER DITHER QUAGGLE QUAKING AGITATED ATREMBLE

QUIVER TREE KOKERBOOM

QUIXOTIC IMAGINARY VISIONARY

QUIZ ASK GUY HOAX MOCK CHAFF EXAMINE QUESTION RIDICULE

QUIZZICAL ODD QUEER QUIZZY CURIOUS WHIMSICAL

QUO KA

QUOD JAIL QUAD PRISON

QUOIN COIN ANGLE GOIGN CORNER LOZENGE KEYSTONE VOUSSOIR

QUOIT CIST DISC DISH DISK LINER DISCUS HOBBER CROMLECH

QUOMODO HOW WAY MEANS MANNER

QUONDAM OLD ONCE WHILE FORMER ONETIME SOMETIME

QUORATEAN KAROK

QUORUM CORAM HOUSE MINYAN MAJORITY

QUOTA PART BOGEY SHARE QUOTIENT

QUOTATION PRICE QUOTE EXTRACT SNIPPET EPIGRAPH

(— DEVELOPED INTO ESSAY) CHRIA

QUOTATION MARK GUILLEMET

QUOTE CITE COAT COTE MARK NAME NOTE ADDUCE ALLEGE RECITE REPEAT EXCERPT EXTRACT OBSERVE REHEARSE

(— SARCASTICALLY) FLOUT

QUOTH CO KO CUTH QUAD QUOD SAID SPOKE UTTERED

QUOTIDIAN DAILY TRIVIAL ORDINARY

QUOTIENT QUOTE FRACTION

QUTB POLE

R AR ROGER ROMEO
(**UVULAR** —) BURR
RA RE RAE SHU TEM ATMU BACIS
HORUS MENTU KHEPERA SOKARIS
RABBAN MASTER TEACHER
RABBET CHECK GROOVE BACKJOINT
FILLISTER
RABBI TANA AMORA CACAM HAKAM
TANNA MASTER SABORA KHAKHAM
TEACHER GAMALIEL SABORAIM
(PL.) AMORAIM TANNAIM
RABBIT BUN REX TAN BUNT CONY
JACK POLE RACK BUNNY CAPON
CREAM CUNNY DUTCH FRIER LAPIN
ANGORA ASTREX CONEEN HAVANA
OARLOP PARKER POLISH SILVER
TAPETI WOOLER BEVEREN
CONYNGE FLEMISH LEPORID
SNOWSHOE WARRENER
(— **BURROW**) CLAPPER
(— **FUR**) CONY SCUT CONEY FLICK
LAPIN FLITCH
(— **MEAT**) LAPAN
(— **SKIN**) RACK
(— **TAIL**) SCUT
(— **WARREN**) CONYGER
(**CASTRATED** —) CAPON
(**FEMALE** —) DOE
(**MALE** —) BUCK
(**YOUNG** —) KITTEN
(PL.) FLICK WARREN
RABBITFISH SPINY
RABBLE MOB TAG GING HERD ROUT
SCUM FRAPE SCAFF SCUFF TRASH
MEINIE RADDLE RAFFLE RAGTAG
RASCAL TAGRAG DOGGERY
PUDDLER RABBLER RANGALE
TRAFFIC BRAGGERY CANAILLE
RAGABASH RIFFRAFF VARLETRY
(**DISORDERLY** —) HERD
RABBLE-ROUSER DEMAGOG
RABID MAD RAGING FRANTIC
FURIOUS RABIOUS RABITIC
FRENZIED RAVENING VIRULENT
RABIES LYSSA MADNESS PIBLOKTO
RAVENING
RACCOON COON COATI GUARA
TEJON AGUARA MAPACH WASHER
AGOUARA ARCTOID RATTOON
CRABEATER
RACE CAP CUP LOG ROD RUN BENT
CONE DASH DRAG GEST HUMP KIND
LINE NAME RAIS RAZE RINK TEAM
TRAM BLOOD BREED BRUSH CASTE
CHEVY CORSO DERBY FLESH
HOUSE ISSUE PLATE PURSE RATCH
REACH ROUTE SPEED STAKE
STAMM STIRP STOCK BROOSE
CHEVVY COURSE FAMILY NATION
PEOPLE PHYLON RUNOFF SPRING
STIRPS STRAIN STRIND BIOTYPE
CENTURY CLAIMER CLASSIC
HACKNEY HUNDRED KINDRED
LINEAGE MATINEE NURSERY
PROGENY PROSAPY RACEWAY
REGATTA STADIUM FUTURITY
HANDICAP MARATHON WALKOVER
OFFSPRING
(— **A HORSE**) CAMPAIGN

(— **AT WEDDING**) BROOSE BROUZE
(— **FOR BALL-BEARINGS**) CONE
(— **OF BARLEY**) BENT
(— **OF GODS**) VANIR
(— **OF PEOPLE**) VANS AMALS VANIR
HAZARA YADAVA BAMBUTE FIRBOLG
GIANTRY NISHADA RASENNA
REPHAIM AMALINGS
(— **OF UNDERGROUND ELVES**)
DROW
(— **OF WINDMILL**) CURB
(**HORSE** —) DERBY PLATE SPRINT
MATINEE FUTURITY WALKOVER
(**HUMAN** —) MAN MANKIND SPECIES
(**IMPROMPTU** —) BRUSH
(**JUMPING** —) SCURRY
(**LENTEN** —S) TORPIDS
(**MILL** —) LADE
(**PRELIMINARY** —) HEAT
(**ROWING** —) SCULLS REGATTA
(**RUNNING** —) MILE RELAY SPRINT
HUNDRED HURDLES
(**SHORT** —) BICKER
(**SHORT-DISTANCE** —) DASH
SCURRY SPRINT
(**SKI** —) SLALOM DAUERLAUF
(PL.) FOURS
RACECOURSE LIST OVAL PIST RING
TURF EPSOM CAREER CIRCUS
STADIE STRETCH GYMKHANA
SPEEDWAY
RACEHORSE DOG PACER RACER
SLEEPER TROTTER BANGTAIL
(— **THAT HAS NEVER WON**) MAIDEN
(**2-YEAR OLD** —) JUVENILE
(**INFERIOR** —) PLATER HAYBURNER
(PL.) RUCK
RACEME STRIG
RACER CRACK SNAKE RUNNER
BICYCLIST CINDERMAN
RACETRACK DROMOS FURLONG
RACEWAY CANAL TRACK GROOVE
CHANNEL FISHWAY
RACHEL POWDER
(**HUSBAND OF** —) JACOB
(**SON OF** —) JOSEPH BENJAMIN
RACHIS SPINE SPINDLE
(— **OF HOP STROBILE**) STRIG
RACHITIS RICKETS
RACIAL GENTILE GENTILIC PHYLETIC
RACIST COLOR
RACK GIN RAK RAT TUB BINK BUCK
CASE HACK HECK SHOG TACK
AMBLE BRAKE DRIER DRYER FLAKE
FRAME POKER THROW TOUSE
TRAIN WRACK WRECK WRING
CIRCLE CRATCH CUDGEL ENGINE
NIPPER PULLEY TREBLE WRENCH
AFFLICT AGONIZE PENRACK
POTTARO TORMENT TORTURE
BARBECUE EQUULEUS PINEBANK
SAWHORSE
(— **ATTACHED TO WAGON**)
SHELVING OUTRIGGER
(— **FOR BARRELS**) JIB
(— **FOR CHINAWARE**) FIDDLE
(— **FOR DISHES**) BINK
(— **FOR FEEDING**) HACK HAYRACK
(— **FOR FODDER**) HECK CRATCH

(— **FOR PLATES**) CREEL
(— **FOR STORAGE**) FLAKE
(— **IN THRESHER**) SHAKER
(**DRYING** —) CRIB TREBLE
(**WOODEN** —) BUCAN
RACKED WRUNG TORTURED
RACKET BAT DIN GAME BANDY
MUSIC RAZOO CLAMOR CROSSE
DRIVER HUBBUB HUSTLE RAQUET
RATTLE BUSINESS REVELING
STRAMASH
(**TENNIS** —) SCUFE
RACKETEER HOOD HUSTLER
GANGSTER
RACKETT CERVALET CERVELAT
RACKING FIERCE
RACKMAN TOPMAN
RACON BEACON
RACONTEUR STORYTELLER
RACQUET GAZELLE
RACY GAMY LEAN SEXY JUICY
SALTY SMART SPICY LIVELY RISQUE
PIQUANT PUNGENT ZESTFUL
SPIRITED
RAD EAGER QUICK READY AFRAID
ELATED
RADAR (— **NAVIGATION SYSTEM**)
LANAC
(— **SYSTEM**) OBOE
RADARSCOPE PPI HSCOPE
RADDLE PIT BEAT SCAR RAVEL
RUDDLE THRASH SEPARATOR
RADIAL RAY QUADRANT
RADIANCE RAY GLOW LEAM GLARE
GLEAM GLINT GLORY LIGHT SHINE
LUSTER AUREOLA GLITTER
SPLENDOR
RADIANT BEAMY SHEEN SHINY
ABLAZE BRIGHT GOLDEN LUCENT
SHEENY AURORAL BEAMFUL
BEAMING FULGENT LAMBENT
GLORIOUS LUSTROUS RELUCENT
SPLENDID
(— **INTENSITY**) J
RADIATE RAY BEAM POUR SHED
SHINE EFFUSE SPREAD EFFULGE
EMANATE
RADIATED PENCILED STELLATE
RADIATION AURA LIGHT INFRARED
(— **DOSAGE**) REM REP
(— **UNIT**) LANGLEY
RADIATOR HEATER EMANATOR
(**SET OF** —S) STACK
RADICAL KEY SURD BASAL GROUP
RADIX ROUGE ULTRA CAPRYL
HEROIC CAPITAL CAPROYL DRASTI
EXTREME FORWARD HERETIC
JACOBIN LEFTIST LEVELER LIBERAI
PRIMARY CARDINAL LOCOFOCO
(**CHEMICAL** —) AMYL CARYL CETYI
GROUP ACETYL CAPRYL PHENYL
PHYTYL HALOGEN LINALYL
CARBAMYL QINNAMAL
RADICALISM EXTREMISM
JACOBINISM
RADICEL ROOTLET
RADICLE (— **THAT DEVELOPS IN**
GRAIN) COME
RADIENT ORIENT

RADIO AIR SET WIRELESS
(— **OPERATOR**) HAM SPARKS
(— **SYSTEM**) TBS
RADIOGRAM FLIMSY
RADIOGRAPH EXOGRAPH SKIAGRAM
RADISH RUNCH DAEKON DAIKON
RIFART CADLOCK CRADLOCK
CRUCIFER CROSSWEED
RADIUS RAYON SPOKE SWEEP
THROW ADRADIUS
RADIX BASE ROOT ETYMON RADICLE
RADON NITON THORON ACTINON
EXRADIO
RADULA RIBBON TONGUE
RAFF LOW IDLE SCUM SWEEP TRASH
COMMON JUMBLE LUMBER RABBLE
RAFFLE RAGTAG SNATCH RUBBISH
RAFFISH RAKISH TAWDRY UNKEMPT
RAFFLE MOVE RAFF JUMBLE RABBLE
REFUSE RUBBISH
RAFT COW CRIB MOKI BALSA BATCH
FLOAT TABLE DINGEY DINGHY
JANGAR MOKIHI PIPERY RADEAU
JANGADA ZATTARE CATAMARAN
(— **OF INVERTED POTS**) GHARNAO
(— **OF LOGS**) BOOM CRIB
(— **WITH CABIN**) COW
(**BAMBOO** —) RAKIT
(**FIRE** —) CATAMARAN
(**LUMBER** —) BATCH
RAFT DOG RAKER
AFTER HIP BALK BLAD FIRM SILE
SOIL SPAR SPUR VIGA BLADE
CABER RIDGE BOUGAR CARLINE
RAFFMAN SLEEPER
(— **OF TURKEYS**) FLOCK
AFTY RAW DAMP FUSTY MUSTY
RANCID
AG JAG TAT HOAX JAGG SAIL
ANNOY CLOUT PRANK SCOLD
SCRAP SHRED WIPER GIBBOL
LIBBET RAGGLE TAGRAG TATTER
FLITTER REMNANT TORMENT
RAGSTONE STRAGGLE NEWSPAPER
(— **GATHERER**) TATTER
(**PL.**) DUDS CADDIS FITTERS
RAGGERY FLITTERS
AGAMUFFIN MUFFLIN BEGGARLY
SHABROON TITMOUSE
AGE GO AWE FAD RAG WAX BAIT
BEEF FARE FOAM FRET FUFF FUME
FUNK FUNX FURY GLOW GRIM HEAT
PELT RAMP RASE RESE TAVE TEAR
WOOD ANGER BRETH CHAFE CRAZE
FUROR PADDY STORM TEAVE TEVEL
VOGUE WRATH FRENZY FURORE
PELTER TYAUVE BLUSTER FASHION
RUFFIAN MADNESS PASSION
TEMPEST INSANITY WOODNESS
PADDYWACK
BE IN A —) RANT
AGFISH ICOSTEID
GGED DUDDY HARSH FRAYED
JAGGED SCOURY UNEVEN SHAGRAG
SHREDDY TATTERY SCRAGGLY
CRATCHY TATTERED
GGED ROBIN ROBIN CUCKOO
GGEE MAND RAGI MARUA
NANDUA KORAKAN ELEUSINE

RAGGLE-TAGGLE MOTLEY
RAGING HOT GRIM WILD YOND
RABID FIERCE FURIAL FERVENT
PELTING VIOLENT FLAGRANT
FURIBUND WRATHFUL
RAGOUT GOULASH HARICOT
TERRINE SALPICON CHIPOLATA
PULPATONE
(— **OF GAME**) SALMI SALMIS
RAGPICKER BUNTER RAGMAN
TATTER
RAGWEED HAYWEED HOGWEED
AMBROSIA IRONWEED KINGHEAD
KINGWEED RICHWEED FRANSERIA
RAGWORT CUSHAG JACOBY
BENWEED CAMMOCK SEGGROM
LIFEROOT
RAID RADE ROAD TALA FORAY
HARRY PINCH REISE REIVE CREACH
FORAGE HARASS INROAD MOLEST
PANYAR RAZZIA BODRAGE
BORDRAG CHAPPOW DESCENT
JAYHAWK OUTFALL OUTRAKE
OUTRIDE OUTROAD SPREATH
COMMANDO SPOILING
(**AIR** —) BLITZ
(**CATTLE** —) SPREAGH SPREATH
(**WARLIKE** —) HERSHIP
RAIDER REDLEG BUSHWACK
RAIL BAR BULL COOT GIRD JEST
KOKO LIST MOHO RANT RAVE SKID
SORA TRAM WEKA WING CRAKE
EASER FENCE GUARD PLATE RAVEL
REILE SCOFF SCOLD SLENT STANG
STANK STEEL SWEAR BANTER
BEDWAY CALLET FENDER RUNNER
SKITTY TIKLIN BIDCOCK BILCOCK
COURLAN INVEIGH OARCOCK
RACKWAY TOPRAIL BULLHEAD
CANCELLI CORNBIRD PORTLAST
TOADBACK VIGNOLES
(— **AT**) JEST CURSE SCOFF RATTLE
REVILE
(— **OF BED**) STOCK
(— **OF RAILWAY SWITCH**) TONGUE
(— **ON GUN PLATFORM**) TRINGLE
(— **ON HAY VEHICLE**) THRIPPLE
(— **ON SHIP**) FIFE
(**ALTAR** —) SEPTUM
(**ARCHED** —) HOOPSTICK
(**CHAIR** —) LEDGE
(**FENCE** —) RIDER
(**PL.**) RAILING CANCELLI RAILROAD
RAIL CHAIR CARRIAGE
RAILING BAR SEPT GRATE RAVEL
FENDER FIDDLE GITTER VEDIKA
BARRIER GALLERY PARAPET
CANCELLI ESPALIER HANDRAIL
PARCLOSE TRAVERSE
RAILLERY GAFF HASH JEST JOKE
RAGE CHAFF RALLY SPORT BANTER
BLAGUE HOORAY HURRAH SATIRE
TRIFLE MOCKERY BADINAGE
DICACITY RABULOUS RIDICULE
RAILROAD EL ROAD YARD STEEL
COALER FEEDER GRANGER
TRAMWAY CEINTURE ELEVATED
(— **CAR**) IDLER
RAILROAD CHAIR SADDLE

RAILSPLITTER MAULER
RAILWAY ROAD TUBE COGWAY
SUBWAY COGROAD INCLINE
TRANVIA WIREWAY ASCENSOR
PLATEWAY TRAMROAD FUNICULAR
RAIMENT RAY GARB CLOTH
APPAREL CLOTHES VESTURE
CLOTHING DRESSING
(**SPLENDID** —) SHEEN
RAIN WET ISLE MIST SMUR ULAN
WEET STORM DELUGE MIZZLE
SERENE SHOWER SOAKER DRIZZLE
DOWNPOUR SPRINKLE
(— **AND SNOW**) SLEET
(— **HEAVILY**) TEEM
(— **LIGHTLY**) SMUR SPIT SPRINKLE
(— **OF SPARKS**) SHOWER
(**DRIZZLING** —) DAG
(**FINE** —) MIST SEREIN SERENE
(**GOD OF** —) PARJANYA
(**HEAVY** —) PASH SPOUT
(**LIGHT** —) WEATHER HEATDROPS
(**SHORT** —) SHOWER
(**SUDDEN** —) SKEW
(**WHIRLING** —) SKIRL
(**WIND-DRIVEN** —) SCAT
(**PL.**) VARSHA
RAINBIRD KOEL TOMFOOL
STORMBIRD
(— **OF JAMAICA**) HUNTER
RAINBOW ARC BOW ARCH IRIS
GAMUT METEOR SUNBOW ILLUSION
(**BROKEN** —) WINDDOG WINDGALL
RAINBOW FISH GUPPY MAORI
RAINBOW RUNNER SKIPJACK
SHOEMAKER
RAINBRINGER KACHINA
RAINCOAT MAC MACK PONCHO
BURSATI OILSKIN SLICKER
GOSSAMER
RAINFALL PLOUT SKIFF SKIFT
ONDING STEMPLOW
RAIN GAGE UDOMETER
RAINSPOUT RONE
RAINSTORM WET SPATE
RAIN TREE SAMAN ZAMAN GUANGO
ZAMANG ALGAROBA GENISARO
MONKEYPOD
RAINY WET KICK FRESH JUICY
RAYNE SAPPY WEETY BLASHY
DRIPPY PLUNGY SPONGY PLUVIAL
PLUVINE SHOWERY WEEPING
CLUTTERY PLUVIOUS SLATTERY
(— **SEASON**) VARSHA
RAISE END SET WIN BUMP BUOY
GROW HAIN HEFT HIGH HIKE HOVE
JACK KICK LEVY LIFT MAKE OVER
REAR ROOF STIR TELD TOSS AREAR
BLOCK BOOST BREED BUILD CAIRN
CHOCK CRANE DIGHT ELATE ENSKY
ERECT EXALT FORCE GREET HANCE
HEAVE HEEZE HEVEN HOISE HOIST
HORSE LEAVE MOUND MOUNT
PRICK RISER ROUSE VOICE ASSIST
BETTER CREATE DOUBLE EMBOSS
EXHALE GATHER LEAVEN MUSTER
NANTLE PREFER REMOVE RISING
UPHOLD UPLIFT ADDRESS ADVANCE
COLLECT ELEVATE ENHANCE

LIGHTEN NOURISH PRESENT
PROMOTE RECRUIT UPSHOOT
ANGELIZE HEIGHTEN INSPIRIT
RELEVATE
(— A BUMP) CLOUR
(— A NAP) TEASE TEASEL TEAZLE
(— ALOFT) SPHERE
(— BY ASSESSMENT) LEVY
(— BY HAND) NOB
(— CLAMOR) BRAWL
(— IN PITCH) SHARP
(— OBJECTIONS) CAVIL BOGGLE
(— ONESELF) CHIN
(— TO 3RD POWER) CUBE
(— TO HIGH DEGREE) STRAIN
(— UP) BUOY AREAR ELATE EXALT
EXTOL ELEVATE CIVILIZE
RAISED HIGH UPSET ARRECT
HOGGED EXALTED ELEVATED
MOUNTANT UPLIFTED UPRAUGHT
RAISIN FIG PASA PLUM LEXIA ZIBEB
REYSON CURRANT SULTANA
MUSCATEL
(PL.) SPICE
RAJ RULE REIGN
RAJA KING CHIEF RULER PRINCE
PANGLIMA
RAJMAHAL CREEPER JITI CHITI
JETEE JEETEE
RAJPUT SAMMA SUMRA GAHRWAL
RAZBOOCH
RAKE GO HOE RIP WAY COMB PATH
RACK RAFF RAVE REAP ROAM ROUE
ROVE RUCK BLOOD CLAUT PITCH
SCOOP SCOUR SULKY TIGER
PLUNGE RABBLE ROLLER SEARCH
RANSACK SCRATCH LOTHARIO
SCRAPPLE
(— GRAIN) GAVEL
(— UP IN ROWS) HACK
(— WITH GUNFIRE) SCOUR STRAFE
ENFILADE
(— WITHOUT TEETH) LUTE
(BUCK —) SWEEP
(CRANBERRY —) SCOOP
(HORSE-DRAWN —) GLEANER
(OYSTER —) GLEANER
RAKEHELL RASCAL IMMORAL
LIBERTINE
RAKER GUMMER ROOKER
RAKISH SLANG JAUNTY SPORTY
WANTON DASHING CARELESS
DEVILISH RANTEPOLE
RALE RATTLE SIFFLE SIBILUS
RALLENTANDO DRAG RITARD
RALLY KID DRAG JOKE MOCK RELY
STIR BULLY JOLLY QUEER BANTER
DERIDE REVIVE COLLECT CLAMBAKE
RIDICULE SPEAKING
RAM PUN TIP TUP BUCK CRAM PACK
RAME STEM TEAP TOOP ARIES
CHOKE CRASH POACH ROGER SLIDE
BEETLE CHASER RANCID ROSTRUM
BULLDOZER WETHERHOG
WETHERTEG
(— OF WAR VESSEL) SPUR
(CASTRATED —) WETHER
RAMA MELCHORA
(WIFE OF —) SITA

RAMADA ARBOR PORCH
RAMAGE WILD RAMMISH UNTAMED
RAMAGE HAWK BRANCHER
RAMBLE RAKE ROAM ROVE WALK
JAUNT PROWL RANGE TRACE
TROLL RUMBLE STROLL VAGARY
WAMBLE WANDER ENRANGE
EXCURSE SPROGUE TROUNCE
FLAGARIE SCRAMBLE SPATIATE
(— AIMLESSLY) HAZE
RAMBLING GAD CURSORY DEVIOUS
WINDING DESULTORY SCATTERED
RAMBUNCTIOUS RUDE WILD
ROUGH UNRULY UNTAMED VIOLENT
RAMBUTAN SOAPWORT
RAMENTUM PALEA PALET SCALE
SHAVING
RAMIE ORTIGA
RAMIFICATION ARM RAMUS
BRANCH OFFSHOOT OUTGROWTH
RAMIFY BRANCH SPRANGLE
RAMMAN ADAD ADDA ADDU
RAMMED EARTH PISE
RAMMEL TRASH RUMMLE RUBBISH
RAMMER HEAD BOSER PUNNER
WORMER
RAMOSE CLADOSE BRANCHED
RAMP RUN BANK EXIT RAGE RANK
SLIP STORM EASING FROLIC
FOOTPAD SLIPWAY GRADIENT
RAMPAGE RAGE ROMP BINGE
SPRAY SPREE STORM RANDAN
RAMPAGEOUS UNRULY GLARING
RAMPANT VIOLENT
RAMPANT RANK PROFUSE SALIANT
SALIENT SEGREANT
RAMPART BRAY LINE WALL AGGER
ARGIN VALLUM BULWARK DEFENSE
PARAPET RAMPIER BARBICAN
MUNITION BARRICADE
RAMPER LAMPREY
RAMPIKE SNAG RAUNPICK
ROUNSPIK
RAMROD FORMAL GUNSTICK
RAMSHACKLE RUDE UNRULY
RICKETY SHACKLY UNSTEADY
RAMSON RAMP GARLIC BUCKRAM
(PL.) RAMS
RAMSTAM RASH HEADLONG
RECKLESS
RAN ARN
RANCEL SEARCH RANSACK
RANCH RUN FARM TEAR FINCA
CHACRA OUTFIT SPREAD WRENCH
STATION ESTANCIA HACIENDA
RANCHE NATURAL
RANCHER COWMAN GRAZIER
SHEEPMAN CATTLEMAN
RANCID RAM RANK SOUR FROWY
RAFTY RASTY REEST RESTY
FROWZY ODIOUS ROTTEN
RANCOR GALL HATE SPITE ENMITY
GRUDGE HATRED MALICE
ACRIMONY
RANCOROUS ACRID VENOMOUS
MALIGNANT
(NOT —) GOOD
RAND EDGE ROON RUND BORDER
HIGHLAND

RANDAN SPREE RANTAN UPROAR
RAMPAGE
RANDOM BANK FORCE LOOSE
STRAY CASUAL CHANCE CHANCY
AIMLESS RANDALL RENDOUN
SHOTGUN UNAIMED VAGRANT
(AT —) HOBNOB
(SOMEWHAT —) LONG
RANDY LEWD RUDE SPREE BEGGAR
VIRAGO LUSTFUL RIOTOUS
CAROUSAL
RANGE KEN ROW ALLY AREA BEAT
GATE GAUT GHAT LINE RANK ROA
ROVE SCUM SHOT TOUR WALK
ALIGN BLANK CARRY FIELD GAMUT
HILLS ORBIT REACH SCOPE SHOOT
SPACE STAND START SWEEP SWIN
VERGE COURSE DANGER EXTEND
EXTENT LENGTH RADIUS RAMBLE
SCOUTH SPHERE STROLL WANDER
BOWSHOT COMPASS DEMESNE
EARSHOT GUNSHOT HABITAT
HORIZON PURVIEW CLASSIFY
DIAPASON EARREACH EYEREACH
LATITUDE PANORAMA
(— OF ARROW) FLIGHT
(— OF BRICK) COURSE
(— OF FOOD) FARE
(— OF FREQUENCIES) SPECTRUM
(— OF GOVERNANCE) DOMAIN
(— OF GUN) CARRY RANDOM
GUNSHOT
(— OF HILLS) GAUT GHAT HUMP
TIER CHAIN GHAUT RIDGE SIERRA
SAWBACK BACKBONE
(— OF ORGANISM) BIOZONE
(— OF PASTURE) GANG
(— OF PLANKS) STRING
(— OF PRINTING TYPES) SERIES
(— OF SIGHT) KEN SCAN EYESHO
KENNING
(— OF TONES) KEY SCALE
GRADATION
(— OF VISION) EYE SIGHT KENNIN
(— OF WAVELENGTH) BAND
(— OVER) SWEEP
(ARCHERY —) BUTTS GREEN
(COOKING —) KITCHENER
(SHOOTING —) MES GALLERY
(TEMPERATURE —) CONE
RANGE FINDER STADIA
MEKOMETER
RANGE POLE PICKET
RANGER ROVER ROBBER MONTE
FIREWARD
RANGOON SHERRY
RANGY OPEN ROOMY SPACIOUS
RANK RAY ROW SEE DANK FOOT
FORM FOXY GOLE GREE LINE RA
RATE ROOM SEED SOUR STEP T
CENSE CHOIR CLASS FETID FRAN
FUSTY GRADE GROSS HONOR
LEVEL MARCH ORDER QUIRE RA
ROWTY SIEGE SPACE STALL STA
STATE TCHIN TRAIN AFFAIR AGR
DEGREE ERMINE ESTEEM FIGURE
LAVISH PARAGE RATING SPHERE
STATUS STRONG CALIBER CALLI
DIGNITY DUKEDOM EARLDOM

FOOTING GLARING RAMMISH
RAMPANT STATION WORSHIP
ABSOLUTE EARLSHIP ENSIGNCY
EQUIPAGE FLAGRANT GENTRICE
LADYSHIP PALPABLE STINKING
(— AND FILE) RANGALE
(— OF GENTLEMEN) GENTRY
GENTILITY
(— OF SERGEANT-AT-LAW) COIF
COIFFE
(ACADEMIC —) AGREGE
(BOTTOMMOST —) CELLAR
(HIGH —) DIGNITY EMINENCE
(LOWEST —) SCOURING
(MILITARY —) GRADE AIRMAN
CORNET CHAOUSH
(NOBLE —) ADELAIDE
(SAME —) KIND
(SOCIAL —) CLASS ESTATE
HERALDRY POSITION
ANKLE FRET CHAFE FESTER
INJURE RANCOR DESTROY INFLAME
ANSACK RIG DRAG RAKE RIPE
SACK SEEK RIFLE DACKER RANCEL
SEARCH PLUNDER RUMMAGE
ANSOM FINE RAME REDEEM
RESCUE RESGAT EXPIATE
ANSTEAD TOADFLAX
ANT CAVE HUFF RAIL RAND MOUTH
REVEL ROUSE SCOLD SPOUT
STEVEN BOMBAST CAROUSE
DECLAIM FROTHING
— AND RAVE) FAUNCH
NTING RANTISM TEARCAT
ANTIPOLE WILD CARROT RAKISH
SEESAW ROMPING
ANULA CYST FROGTONGUE
NUNCULUS MOSS GOLLAND
CROWFOOT HEDGEHOG BUTTERCUP
OULIA HAASTIA
P BOB CON CHAP GRAB KNAP
IRL TUNK WRAP CLICK CLINK
NOCK STEAL TOUCH BARTER
ANDLE
PACIOUS CRUEL GREEDY TAKING
AVENING RAVENOUS
PACITY RAVEN RAVIN CUPIDITY
XTORTION
PE COLE ABUSE COLZA FORCE
AVET NAVEW TOUCH ATTACK
ELONY RAPEYE TURNIP ASSAULT
ESPOIL NAVETTE OPPRESS
LUNDER RAPTURE STUPRUM
OLESEED COLEWORT DISHONOR
TUPRATE SUPPRESS
PESEED COLZA RAVISON
PHUS DIDUS
PID GAY FAST CHUTE HASTY
OSSO QUICK ROUND SAULT
HARP SHUTE TOSTO WINGY RIFFLE
PEEDY WINGED SCHNELL SKELPIN
TICKLE TANTIVY SLAPPING
PEEDFUL
-S IN RIVER) SAULT DALLES
FFLE STICKLE CATARACT
IORE —) STRETTO
IDITY HASTE SPEED RADEUR
LERITY VELOCITY
IDLY APACE CHEAP FLEETLY

HASTILY SPEEDILY QUICKFOOT
RAPIER TUCK TUKE BILBO ESTOC
SHARP STOCK VERDUN TOASTER
RAPINE FORCE RAVIN PILLAGE
PLUNDER VIOLENCE
RAPPAREE ROBBER CREAGHT
VAGABOND
RAPPORT ACCORD HARMONY
RELATION AGREEMENT
RAPSCALLION ROGUE RASCAL
VILLAIN HOSEBIRD VAGABOND
RAPT LOST WRAP TENSE INTENT
RAVISH TRANCE CARRIED ENGAGED
RAPTURE ABDUCTED ABSORBED
ECSTATIC
RAPTORES RAPACES
RAPTURE JOY BLISS DELIGHT
ECSTASY PAROXYSM RHAPSODY
RARA AVIS PHENIX RARITY WONDER
PHOENIX
RARE FINE REAL SELD THIN ALONE
EARLY GREAT ANTRIN CHOICE
GEASON INCONY SCARCE SEENIL
SELDOM SINDLE SUBTLE SULLEN
UNIQUE ANTERIN CURIOUS
TENUOUS UNUSUAL CRITICAL
SELDSEEN SINGULAR UNCOMMON
RAREFACTION POROSIS
RAREFIED HIGH THIN SUBTILE
ABSTRUSE AETHERED ESOTERIC
RAREFY THIN DILUTE EXTENUATE
RARELY SELDEN SELDOM
RARENESS RARITY TENUITY
SCARCITY
RARITY SWAN CURIO RELIC RARIETY
TENUITY RARENESS
(PL.) CURIOSA
RASCAL BOY CAD DOG IMP LOW
RAP BASE DUCK FILE KITE LOON
MEAN SHAG SMAK CATSO FILTH
GANEF GIPSY KNAVE ROGUE SCAMP
SHELM SLAVE SMAIK THIEF ABLACH
BRIBER BUDZAT BUGGER COQUIN
HARLOT LIMMER RABBLE RAGGIL
RIBALD SCHELM SORROW TINKER
BLEEDER CAMOOCH GLUTTON
HESSIAN NEBULON PEASANT
RAPTRIL SHELLUM SKEEZIX
SKELLUM VILLAIN HOSEBIRD
LIDDERON PALLIARD PICAROON
RAKEWELL RUBIATOR SKALAWAG
SPALPEEN TAISTREL VAGABOND
WIDDIFOW
RASCALITY FOIST RABBLE KNAVERY
ROGUING RASCALRY
RASCALLY BASE MEAN ROOKY
GALLUS LIMMER GALLOWS KNAVISH
RAGGILY SHAGRAG WIDDIFOW
RASE PULL RAIS RAZE ERASE PLUCK
INCISE SNATCH
RASH ID CUT BRASH HARDY HASTY
HEADY SLASH SLICE DARING
SUDDEN UNWARY URGENT BULRUSH
HOTSPUR RABBISH BLIZZARD
CARELESS ERUPTION EXANTHEM
HEADLONG HEEDLESS MADBRAIN
OVERSEEN PRESSING RECKLESS
TEMEROUS

RASHER SLICE COLLOP TRIFLE
COLOPPE
RASHLY HEADILY HEADLONG
RASHNESS RAGE RESE ACRISY
TEMERITY HEADINESS
RASKOLNIK POPOVETS
RASP RUB FILE RAPE ERUCT GRATE
TOOTH RAPEYE RUBBER RIFFLER
DENTICLE
(SHOEMAKER'S —) FLOAT
RASPBERRY AKPEK BAZOO MOLKA
AVARIN RASPIS PLUMBOG
ARNBERRY BLACKCAP BOGBERRY
CUTHBERT MULBERRY RESPASSE
ROSACEAN
RASPING HARSH ROUGH STOOR
STOUR HOARSE RASION RAZZLY
GRATING RAUCOUS GUTTERAL
(PL.) SCOBS
RASPY HARSH GRATING SCREAKY
SCRABBLY
RASSE CIVET WEASEL
RAT BUCK DAMN DRAT HEEL NOKI
ROTN SCAB VOLE KIORE LOUSE
METAD RATON SELVA ZEMMI ZEMNI
CRABER MURINE RODENT ROTTAN
SLEPEZ VERMIN YUNGAS CUSHION
CONFOUND INFORMER MYOMORPH
(INDIAN —) KOK
RATAPLAN RATTAN RATTLE
RATCH RASH REND ROCH SPOT
NOTCH STREAK RATCHET STRETCH
RATCHET DOG PAWL CLICK DETENT
ROCHET
RAT CHINCHILLA ABROCOME
RATE LAY RAG SET CESS CHOP GAIT
GIVE HAND KIND RANK RATA ABUSE
CULET CURVE PRIZE RATIO REBUT
SCOLD STENT STYLE VALUE ZAKAT
ASSIZE GALLOP ACCOUNT CARTAGE
DESERVE FASHION MILLAGE
REPROVE CLASSIFY ESTIMATE
QUANTIFY
(— HIGHLY) PRICE
(— OF ASCENT) GRADE
(— OF DRAINAGE) FREENESS
(— OF EXCHANGE) BATTA
(— OF INTEREST) DISCOUNT
(— OF MOTION) BAT SPEED
(— OF MOVEMENT) PACE TEMPO
(— OF RECKONING) FOOT
(— OF SPEED) BAT AGOGE
(— OF TRANSFER) FLUX
(— OF TUITION) CULET
(— SCHEDULE) TARIFF
(AT ANY —) HURE
(BIRTH —) NATALITY
RATE BOOK STREET
RATEL BADGER BURIER
RATH CAR HILL REUT RUTH EARLY
MOUND QUICK REUTE SWIFT
BETIMES CHARIOT YOUTHFUL
RATHER Y BUT GEY LIKE SOON
LOURD QUITE ASTITE BEFORE
FAIRLY HELDER KINDLY PRETTY
RUTHER SEEMLY TIDDER TITTER
EARLIER INSTEAD MIDDLING
SOMEWHAT
(— THAN) ERE BEFORE

RATIFICATION AMEN RATE SANCTION

RATIFY AMEN PASS SEAL SIGN VISA ENSEAL FASTEN OBSIGN APPROVE CONFIRM SCEPTER CANONIZE ROBORATE SANCTION

RATING E RANK CENSE CLASS GRADE WRITER STANDING

RATIO Q PI GAIN RATE SINE SLIP INDEX RESON SETUP SHEAR ASPECT CAMBER DECADE QUOTUM REASON REYSON SECANT AVERAGE PORTION CONTRAST SOLIDITY

RATIOCINATION LOGIC THOUGHT REASONING

RATION DOLE RATIO ALLOCATE

(— OF BREAD) TOMMY

(ANIMAL —) CHOW

(EXTRA —S) BUCKSHEE

(HOG —) SWILL

(PL.) FOOD BOUCH COMMON

RATIONAL SANE SOBER LOGICAL REASONAL SENSIBLE THINKING

RATIONALIZE THOB EXPLAIN

RATITE EMU MOA KIWI RHEA OSTRICH STRUTHIAN

RAT KANGAROO TUNGO POTOROO SQUEAKER

RATOON SHOOT SPROUT SUCKER

RATTAIL MULE ARREST GRENADIER

RATTAN CANE SEGA ROTAN BEJUCO ROTANG SWITCH RATTOON

RATTLE DIN BIRL BURL RICK TIRL CLACK CROTAL GRAGER HENPEN MARACA RACKLE RICKLE RIFFLE ROTTLE RUCKLE RUTTLE CHACKLE CLACKER CLAPPER CLATTER CLICKET CREAKER GNATTER GROGGER SHATTER SISTRUM SKELLAT CAIXINHA CHOCALHO COWWHEAT

(CRIER'S —) CLAPPER

(IRON —) SKELLAT SKILLET

RATTLER LIE ROMBLE RUMBLER

RATTLESNAKE BELLTAIL CASCABEL CASCAVEL

(— PLANTAIN) NETLEAF RATSBANE

RATTLESNAKE ROOT BUGBANE JOYLEAF

RATTLETRAP GEWGAW TRIFLE RICKETY

RATTLING BRISK HUSKY SLAPPING SPLENDID CREPITANT

RATTY NASTY SHABBY UNKEMPT WORTHLESS

RATWA MUNTJAC

RAUCOUS LOUD HARSH COARSE HOARSE SQUAWKY STRIDENT

RAUN ROE ROWN SPAWN

RAUPO CATTAIL

RAVAGE EAT PREY RIOT RUIN SACK FORAY HARRY HAVOC SPOIL WASTE FORAGE DESPOIL DESTROY OVERRUN PILLAGE PLUNDER DEFLOWER DESOLATE POPULATE SPOLIATE

RAVE MAD RAGE RAND WOOD AWEDE BLURB CRUSH RATHE ROUSE STORM DELIRE WANDER

RAVEL FAG RUN FRAY FRET REYLE SNARL EVENER LADDER RADDLE RUNNER SLOUGH TANGLE CONFUSE INVOLVE PERPLEX RAILING UNWEAVE

RAVELIN RABLIN OUTWORK DEMILUNE

RAVEN RALPH CORBEL CORBIE CORBIN FORAGE RAVINE WAYBIRD

(BRIGHT —) BERTRAM

RAVENING CRUEL RABIES

RAVENOUS GREEDY LUPINE TOOTHY WOLFISH RAPACIOUS VORACIOUS

RAVINE DEN GAP GUT LIN DELL DRAW GILL GULL KHOR KHUD LINN LLYN SIKE WADI BREAK BUNNY CHASM CHINE CLOVE DONGA FLUME GHYLL GLACK GORGE GOYAL GOYLE GRIFF GRIKE GULCH GULLY HEUCH KLOOF SLADE SLAKE STRID ARROYO CLEUCH CLOUGH COULEE DIMBLE DINGLE DUMBLE GULLEY HOLLOW NULLAH RAMBLA SHEUGH STRAIT BARRANCA QUEBRADA

RAVING RAVERY DELIRANT FRENZIED DELIRIOUS

RAVISH ROB RAPE ABUSE CHARM FORCE HARRY SPOIL ABDUCT ATTACK DEFILE AFFORCE CORRUPT DELIGHT ENFORCE OPPRESS OUTRAGE OVERJOY PLUNDER POLLUTE VIOLATE DEFLOWER ENTRANCE STUPRATE SUPPRESS UNMAIDEN

RAVISHER RAPTER RAVENER

RAVISHMENT ECSTASY RAPTURE TRANSPORT

RAW RA ROW BRUT LASH RUDE BLEAK CHILL CRUDE FRESH GREEN HARSH NAKED RAFTY SHARP BITTER COARSE CUTCHA KUTCHA UNRIPE VULGAR WAIRSH NATURAL NOUVEAU UNBOUND VERDANT WEARISH WEERISH IMMATURE RAWBONED UNCOOKED UNEDITED VISCERAL

(— AND COLD) CRIMPY

RAWBONED RAW BONY LEAN GAUNT LANKY SCRAG SCRAWNY

RAWHIDE WHIP WHANG COWHIDE COWSKIN GREENHIDE PARFLECHE

RAWNESS CRUDITY

RAY BEAM BETA DORN SOIL WIRE ALPHA BRAND DRESS EQUIP FLAIR FLAKE FLATH GLEAM GLEED ORDER RAYON ROKER SKATE BATOID CHUCHO OBISPO RADIAL RADIUS RAIOID SEPHEN STREAM TRYGON VISUAL BATFISH COWFISH DEWBEAM DRILVIS FIDDLER HOMELYN PLACOID RAIMENT TORPEDO WAIREPO BRACHIUM MOONBEAM NUMBFISH PLOWFISH PYLSTERT STINGRAY

(— OF LIGHT) GLINT SPEAR GLANCE SUNRAY SUNBEAM

(— OF STARFISH) ARM

(FEMALE —) MAID

(FIN —) SPINE

RAYON BEAM RADIUS DUCHESS

RAZE CUT FLAT RUIN ARASE ERASE LEVEL STREW ARRACE EFFACE SCRAPE SLIGHT UNPILE DESTROY SCRATCH SUBVERT UNBUILD DEMOLISH

RAZOR SHIV TUSK MUSSEL RASOIR SHAVER RATTLER SLASHER CUTTHROAT

RAZORBACK STATE ARKANSAS

RAZOR-BILLED AUK FALK TINK MURRE NODDY SCOOT SCOUT SKOOT TINKER SKIMMER WILLOCK ROCKBIRD

RAZOR CLAM PIROT RASOR SOLEN SPOUT RASOIR

RAZZ CHIACK RIDICULE RASPBERRY

RAZZIA RAID FORAY INCURSION

RAZZING RAZOO

RE RAY ANENT ACTION MATTER REGARDING

REACH GO GET HIT RAX RUN WIN BEAT COME FIND GAIN HAWK HENT MAKE REEK REIK RYKE SHOT SORT SPAN SPIT TEND BRACE CROSS FETCH GRASP PERCH RANGE RETCH TOUCH ADVENE ARRIVE ATTAIN DANGER EXTEND FATHOM LENGTH OBTAIN SNATCH STREEK STRIKE ACHIEVE COMPASS CONTACT GUNSHOT OVERGET POSSESS RECOVER STRETCH

(— ACROSS) SPAN OVERSTRIDE

(— AN END) STAY

(— BY EFFORT) ATTAIN

(— BY FIGURING) STRIKE

(— FORTH) EXTEND

(— GOAL) HAIL

(— OUT) UTTER SPREAD STRETCH

(— TO) LINE

(— TOTAL) AMOUNT

(— UNDERSTANDING) AGREE

(— WITH END) ABUT

(EXTREME —) PITCH STRETCH

(TRY TO —) ASPIRE

REACHER INGIVER

REACT ACT BUCK BEHAVE RETROACT

REACTION BELT BUZZ KAHN WOHL START WIDAL FAVISM RECOIL BLOWOFF EMOTION FEELING SETBACK BACKLASH EXCHANGE GUARDING KICKBACK

(— TIME) LATENCY

(VIOLENT —) SONG

REACTIONARY WHITE BOURBON BACKWARD

REACTIVATED AWAKE ACTIVE

REACTIVATOR ACTIFIER

REACTOR CHOKER FURNACE INDUCTOR

READ GO CON KRI QRI SEE CALL KERE QERI TURN CHOKE JUDGE SOLVE WRITE PERUSE RELATE FORESEE LEARNED LECTION PREDICT ABOMASUM DECIPHER FORETELL INDICATE OVERLOOK

(— ALOUD) LINE DEACON

(— HERE AND THERE) BROWSE

(— **MECHANICALLY**) RETINIZE
(— **OF**) SEE
(— **OFF**) DICTATE
(— **PROOF**) HORSE
(— **RAPIDLY**) DIP SKIM GOBBLE
(— **SLOWLY**) SPELL
(— **SYSTEMATICALLY**) FREQUENT
(— **WITH PROFOUND ATTENTION**) PORE STUDY
READER PURSE DIPPER LECTOR LISTER MAFTIR GRANTHI PISTLER DEVOURER
(**CHILD'S** —) TENPENNY
(**CHURCH** —) LECTOR ANAGNOST
(PL.) FOLLOWING
READILY PAT YERN APTLY PREST YERNE EASILY GAINLY PROBABLY SPEEDILY
READINESS ART EASE GIFT PRESS SKILL BELIEF GRAITH ADDRESS FLUENCY FREEDOM ALACRITY FACILITY GOODWILL
(**IN** —) APOISE AGAINST
READING KRI QRE QRI KERE KERI QERI KTHIB KETHIB LESSON LECTION LECTURE PERUSAL SETTING
(PL.) PROCINCT
READING DESK AMBO LECTERN
READJUST MEND ADVANCE
READY UP APT BUN FIT RAD YAP BAAN BAIN BOON BOUN BOWN FREE GIRT GLIB GNIB RIFE RIPE TALL YARE APERT EAGER FRACK HANDY HAPPY PREDY PREST PRIME QUICK SWIFT THERE TIGHT ADROIT APPERT FACILE GRAITH HEARTY PROMPT PRESENT RENABLE WILLING CHEERFUL DEXTROUS HANDSOME PREGNANT PREPARED PROVIDED SKILLFUL
(— **FOR ACTION**) ARM EXPEDITE
(— **WITH WORDS**) FLUENT
(**NOT** —) SET BOUND GROOM FORWARD DISPOSED IMPROMPT INCLINED
READY-MADE SALE STORE BOUGHT
REAGENT ETCHANT REACTOR ALTERANT REACTIVE
REAL BODY FAIR GOOD LEAL LEVY PURE RIAL TRUE VERY VRAI PAKKA PUCKA PUKKA RIGHT ROYAL SOLID SOOTH ACTUAL ENTIRE HONEST THINGY CORDIAL GENUINE GRADELY SINCERE THINGAL CONCRETE DEFINITE EXISTENT GRAITHLY POSITIVE THINGISH
(**4-8TH** —) TLAC TLACO
(**EXTERNALLY** —) TANGIBLE
REALGAR ARSENIC ROSAKER ANDARAC
REALISM REALITY LITERALISM
REALISTIC HARD SOBER VIVID EARTHLY LIFELIKE PROBABLE
REALITY FEAT TRUE BEING SOOTH THING TRUTH ACTUAL DASEIN VERSOUL REALNESS TRUENESS
(**LIMITED** —) SOMEWHAT

(**ULTIMATE** —) GOD SOURCE DIVINITY SUBSTANCE
(PL.) REALIA
REALIZATION SENSE CRUSHER FRUITION AWAKENING
REALIZE GAIN KNOW FETCH LEARN SENSE EFFECT FULFIL ACQUIRE CONCEIVE
REALIZED BODILY
(**FULLY** —) COMPLETE
REALLY ARU WIS ARAH HALF JUST ARRAH TRULY WISHA FINELY INDEED SIMPLY SURELY ACTUALLY
(**NOT** —) ILL ALMOST
REALM LAND SOIL BOURN CLIME RANGE REIGN REWME RICHE CIRCLE DEMAIN EMPIRE HEAVEN REALTY REGION SPHERE DEMESNE GAELDOM KINGDOM NOTALIA ROYALME TERRENE CLUBLAND DEVILDOM DOMINION ELDORADO GHOSTDOM GIPSYDOM NOTOGAEA
(— **OF DARKNESS**) PO
(— **OF FABULOUS RICHNESS**) ELDORADO
(— **OF THOR**) THRUTHHEIM THRUTHVANG
(**MARINE** —) NOTALIA TROPICALIA
(**VISIONARY** —) CLOUDLAND
REALTY FEALTY REAUTE ROYALTY
REAM FOAM RIME SEED SKIM CHEAT CREAM FROTH FRAISE RHYMER STRETCH
(PL.) INSIDES OUTSIDES
REAMER BUR BURR SPUD DRIFT RIMER BROACH CHERRY FRAISE RANCER RHYMER RIMMER WIDENER
REANIMATE WAKE RENEW REVIVE RECREATE
REANIMATED AWAKE
REAP BAG CUT REP CROP RIPE GLEAN SHEAR GARNER GATHER SICKLE HARVEST
REAPER LORD COCKER TASKER WINNER CRADLER SICKLER
(**GRIM** —) DEATH
REAPING HOOK SICKLE TWIBIL CROTCHET
REAPPEARANCE RENTREE EMERSION
REAR AFT BACK HIND HINT JUMP LIFT STEN TOSS BREED BUILD CARVE ERECT JUNCH STEND ACHTER AROUSE CRADLE FOSTER NURSLE SUCKLE APPREAR ARRIERE EDUCATE ELEVATE NOURISH NURTURE UPBRING BUTTOCKS HINDMOST REARWARD
(— **CAREFULLY**) TIDDLE
(**NEARER THE** —) AFTER
(**TO THE** — **OF**) ABAFT
(**TO THE** —) BACK BEHIND
REARED (— **BY HAND**) CADE
(**DELICATELY** —) SOYLED
REARHORSE MANTIS
REARING FRESNE PESADE FORCENE RAMPANT
(— **UP**) STEND
REARRANGE DO ADJUST JIGGER

REORDER READJUST
REARRANGEMENT WAGNER DIAGENESIS
REARWARD AFT BACKWARD
REASON PEG WAY HOTI NOUS REDE SAKE TALK ARGUE CAUSE COUNT LOGOS PROOF RATIO SCORE SENSE SKILL THING THINK TOPIC EXCUSE GROUND MANNER MATTER MOTION NOESIS ACCOUNT PREMISE QUARREL SUBJECT TUITION ARGUMENT ENCHESON LOGICIZE VERNUNFT
(— **FOR PRIDE**) BOAST
(**LACKING** —) INEPT
REASONABLE FAIR JUST SOBER SKILFUL FEASIBLE MODERATE RATIONAL SENSIBLE
REASONABLENESS EPIKY EPIKIKA FITNESS FAIRNESS SOBRIETY
REASONABLY SOON
REASONER (**FALLACIOUS** —) SOPHIST
REASONING LOGIC ERGOTISM RATIONAL
(**CLUMSY** —) ARGAL
(**FALLACIOUS** —) CIRCLE SOPHISTRY
REASSEMBLE RELY
REASSUME REVOKE REPRISE
REAVE ROB REFE SEIZE SPLIT REMOVE DESPOIL PILLAGE PLUNDER UNRAVEL
REB RABBI REBEL MISTER
REBAB GUSLE
REBATE BLUNT CHECK LESSEN RIBBET DIMINISH DISCOUNT DRAWBACK KICKBACK
REBEC LYRE SAROD RIBIBE RUBIBLE
REBEKAH (**HUSBAND OF** —) ISAAC
(**SON OF** —) ESAU JACOB
REBEL REB KICK RISE TURN BRAND FAUVE ANARCH CROPPY MUTINE REVOLT FRONDEUR
(— **IN ART**) FAUVE
(PL.) REBELDOM
REBELLION MUTINY PUTSCH REVOLT MISRULE UPRISING
REBELLIOUS RUSTY ANARCHIC MUTINOUS AUDACIOUS INSURGENT
REBIRTH REVIVAL
REBOUND DAP HOP HANG KISS STOT CANON CAROM STITE BOUNCE CARROM RECOIL RESULT BRICOLE REDOUND RICOCHET SNAPBACK
(— **ERRATICALLY**) KICK
REBOUND CLIP RETAINER
REBUFF SLAP SNIB SNUB CHECK FLING REPEL DEFEAT DENIAL REBUKE REBUTE REPULSE
REBUKE NIP WIG BAWL RATE REDD SNEB SNIB SNUB TRIM BARGE BLAME CHECK CHIDE DRESS SAUCE SCOLD SNAPE SNEAP TOUCH DIRDUM GANSEL LESSON RATING RATTLE REHETE REMORD CHIDING CORRECT HOTFOOT LECTURE REPROOF REPROVE SARCASM BLESSING BUSINESS CHASTISE KEELHAUL REPROACH SCORCHER

THREAPEN UNDERNIM

REBUS BADGE ENIGMA PUZZLE
RIDDLE

REBUT REPEL RECOIL REFUTE
REPULSE RETREAT DISPROVE

RECALCITRANT UNRULY RENITENT
OBSTINATE RESISTANT

RECALL CITE BRING UNSAY REMAND
REMIND RETURN REVOKE UNLOOK
RECLAIM RETRACE RETRACT
REVIVAL UNSHOUT REMEMBER
WITHCALL WITHDRAW
(— FONDLY) CHERISH

RECANT UNSAY ABJURE REVOKE
UNSING DISAVOW RETRACT
SWALLOW PALINODE RENOUNCE

RECAPITULATE SUM UNITE RECITE
REPEAT RECOUNT REHEARSE
REITERATE SUMMARIZE

RECAPTURE RETAKE RECOVER

RECEDE DIE EBB BACK FADE STEP
VARY RECUR DEPART DIFFER
RETIRE SHRINK DECLINE DIGRESS
RETREAT CONTRACT DIMINISH
ELONGATE WITHDRAW

RECEIPT CHIT RECU RESET APOCHA
BINDER RECIPE WARRANT
(PL.) GATE TAKE SALES INCOME
ENTRADA

RECEIVE GET BEAR FALL GAIN HAVE
HOLD TAKE ADMIT AFONG CATCH
GREET GUEST LATCH RESET
ACCEPT ASSUME BORROW DERIVE
GATHER HARBOR RECULE BELIEVE
CONTAIN EMBRACE INHERIT
SUSTAIN UNDERFO PERCEIVE
(— A CRIMINAL) RESET
(— AS GUEST) FANG HOST VANG
GREET
(— AS MEMBER) INCEPT
(— AS REWARD) REAP
(— FROM LOTTERY) DRAW
(— SHEETS) FLY
(— WITH PLEASURE) GRATIFY

RECEIVER FENCE PHONE PERNOR
SINDICO CYMAPHEN DONATARY
REHEATER
(— IN BANKRUPTCY) SINDICO
(— OF INCOME) PERNOR
(— OF STOLEN GOODS) LOCK
FENCE
(TELEGRAPH —) INKER INKWRITER
(TELEPHONE —) PHONE CYMAPHEN

RECENSION REVIEW SURVEY
CENSURE CRITIQUE

RECENT HOT NEW LATE PUNY
ENDER FRESH GREEN HOURLY
LATELY LATTER MODERN CURRENT
HOLOCENE NEOTERIC
(MOST —) LAST

RECENTLY ANEW JUST LATE NEWLY
LASTLY LATELY FRESHLY LATTERLY

RECENTNESS YOUTH

RECEPTACLE ARK BIN BOX CAN
CUP DIP FAT PAN TIN TUB URN VAT
BATH BOAT BOWL CASE CELL CIST
DOVE DROP FACK FONT HELL HOLD
LOOM RACK RECU SAFE SINK TIDY
TOUR ARBOR CARRY CREEL KIOSK

KITTY RESET SCOOP STEAN STEEN
TABLE TORUS BASKET BUCKET
BUTLER CARTON CUPULE DIPPER
DRAWER HAMPER HOPPER MORTAR
PITCHI POCKET RECEIT SHRINE
TABLET TROUGH ASHTRAY CAPSULE
CARRIER CORBULA DUSTBIN
ENVELOP HEADBOX LATRINE
OMNIBUS OSSUARY PARISON
SANDBOX SETTLER SOAPBOX
STOWAGE TRAVOIS BURSICLE
CANISTER CESSPOOL FOREBOOT
GYNOBASE HONEYPOT LOCKFAST
OSSARIUM OVERFLOW PERFUMER
SPITTOON STOCKPOT SEPULCHER
(— FOR ABANDONED INFANTS)
TOUR
(— FOR BONES) OSSUARY
OSSARIUM
(— FOR BROKEN TYPE) HELL
(— FOR BUTTER) RUSKIN
(— FOR COAL) BUNKER
(— FOR CONVEYING) APRON
(— FOR DRY ARTICLES) FAT
(— FOR FOUL THINGS) SINK
(— FOR GLASS BATCH) ARBOR
(— FOR HOLY WATER) FONT
(— FOR ORE-CRUSHING) MORTAR
(— FOR POKER CHIPS) KITTY
(— FOR SACRED RELICS) TABLE
SHRINE TABLET SEPULCHRE
(— FOR SAVINGS) SOCK
(— FOR SEWING MATERIALS) TIDY
(— FOR TREASURE) HANAPER
(— FOR TYPE CASES) RACK
(— FOR VOTES) SITULA
(— IN BOTTLE-MAKING MACHINE)
PARISON
(— OF CLAY OR STONE) STEAN
STEEN
(— ON WEIGHING SCALES) PAN
(— OVER ALTAR) DOVE
(CLAY —) BOOT
(DILATED —) GYNOBASE
(ELECTRICAL —) BASEPLUG
(INCENSE —) ACERRA
(OPEN —) TRAY
(PURSELIKE —) BURSICLE
(TAILOR'S —) HELL
(WOODEN —) SEBILLA

RECEPTION TEA ROUT COURT
CRUSH DIFFA LEVEE SALON TREAT
ACCOIL DURBAR RUELLE SOIREE
SQUASH ACCUEIL COUCHEE
MATINEE OVATION PASSAGE
RECEIPT RECUEIL TEMPEST
FUNCTION GREETING PERNANCY
REACTION SOCIABLE
(— AT BEDTIME) COUCHEE
(— OF NATIVE PRINCES) DURBAR
(— OF SOUND) AUDIO
(ARABIC —) DIFFA
(CORDIAL —) WELCOME
(CROWDED —) SQUASH
(FASHIONABLE —) LEVEE SALON
(WEDDING —) INFARE

RECEPTIVE SENSORY OPENHANDED

RECEPTOR STOCK RECEIVER
DOMINATOR

RECERCELEE SARCELLY

RECESS ALA ARK BAY BOX COD
CUP PAN BOLE COVE DEEP HOLE
NOOK TRAP AMBRY BOSOM CANAL
CAVUM CLEFT CREEK HAVEN HITCH
INLET NICHE ORIEL PRESS SINUS
ALCOVE ANCONA CAVERN CENTER
CHAPEL CIRQUE CLOSET COFFER
CRANNY GROTTO INDENT LOCULE
RABBET REBATE BEDSITE CONCAV
CREVICE LOCULUS MANHOLE
RETREAT SINKING INTERVAL
LOCKHOLE OVERTURE TABLINUM
TOKONOMA TRAVERSE VACATION
(— BETWEEN CAPES) BAY
(— FOR FAMILY RECORDS)
TABLINUM
(— FOR HINGE LEAF) PAN
(— FOR PIECE OF SCULPTURE)
ANCONA
(— IN CHURCH WALL) AMBRY
(— IN COLON) HAUSTRUM
(— IN JAPANESE HOUSE)
TOKONOMA
(— IN MOUNTAIN) CIRQUE
(— IN ROCK) HITCH
(— IN SIDE OF HILL) CORRIE
(— IN SIDE OF ROOM) ALA
(— IN WALL) BOLE NICHE ALCOVE
(— ON STAGE) CANOPY
(INMOST —) BOSOM
(PL.) FLASH

RECESSED SUNK SUNKEN

RECESSION BUST RETREAT

RECESSIVE BACKWARD RECEDING
RETIRING WITHDRAWN

RECHERCHE RARE CHOICE EXOTI
CURIOUS PRECIOUS UNCOMMON
EXQUISITE

RECIDIVIST REPEATER

RECIPE RX FORM RULE FORMULA
RECEIPT

RECIPIENT HEIR DONEE ALMSMAN
DONATEE LAUREATE

RECIPROCAL CROSS COMMON
MUTUAL SECANT SEESAW
(— OF A POISE) RHE
(— OF VISCOSITY) FLUIDITY

RECIPROCATE REPAY RETURN
REQUITE RETROACT

RECIPROCITY SHU ISOPOLITY
MUTUALITY

RECITAL TALE ASHRE CITAL REC
STORY EXPOSE LITANY PARADE
REPEAT TIKKUN READING RELAT
(— OF PRAYER) GEULAH HAMOT
KEDUSHAH
(UNTRUE —) TALE

RECITATION DHIKR READING
RECITAL RHAPSODY

RECITATIVE SCENA CHANSON

RECITE SAY CARP TELL STATE
INTONE RECKON RELATE RENDE
REPEAT DECLAIM DECLINE DICT
NARRATE RECOUNT REHEARSE
(— AS ELOCUTION EXERCISE)
DECLAIM
(— IN MONOTONE) INTONE
(— METRICALLY) SCAN

(— **MONOTONOUSLY**) CHANT CHAUNT

(— **NUMBERS**) COUNT

(— **PRAYERS**) BENSH DAVEN

(— **TIRESOMELY**) THRUM

(— **WITH GREAT EASE**) RUSH

RECITER SCALD SKALD ANTERI DISEUR CONTEUR DISEUSE HOMERIST ILIADIST RHAPSODE

RECITING CHARM

RECK RAK CARE DEEM PASS MATTER REGARD CONCERN CONSIDER ESTIMATE

RECKLESS RASH WILD FOLLE PERDU MADCAP RACKLE SAVAGE GALLOWS RAMSTAM CARELESS HEADLONG HEEDLESS BLINDFOLD

RECKLESSLY FAST BLIND RAMSTAM HEADLONG HEADFIRST

RECKON RET ARET CAST DATE ITEM RATE RECK RELY TALE TELL TOTE ALLOT AUDIT CLAIM CLASS COUNT JUDGE PLACE RETTE SCORE TALLY THINK ASSIGN FIGURE IMPUTE NUMBER REPUTE TOTTLE ACCOUNT ASCRIBE COMPUTE INCLUDE PRETEND RECOUNT SUPPOSE SUPPUTE CONSIDER ESTIMATE

(— **IN**) INCLUDE

RECKONING TAB BILL NICK POST SHOT TAIL TALE COUNT SCORE TALLY COMPOT LAWING REASON TAILYE TOTTLE ACCOUNT DAYTALE TAILZEE COMPUTUS

RECLAIM IN TAME OBJECT RECALL REDEEM REFORM RESCUE SUBDUE PROTEST RECOVER RESTORE

(— **FROM SAVAGE STATE**) CIVILIZE

RECLAIMANT GOEL

RECLINE LIE LIG LEAN LOLL REST COUCH ACCUMB RECUMB UPLEAN DISCUMB

(— **LANGUIDLY**) GAULSH

RECLUSE NUN MONK CULDEE HERMIT REMOTE ASCETIC EREMITE INCLUSA INCLUSE ANCHORET INCLUSUS SECLUDED SOLITARY (PL.) SECLUSE

RECOGNITION FAME SPUR HONOR SENSE CREDIT STATUS FEELING KENNING KNOWING AGNITION SANCTION

(— **OF ACHIEVEMENT**) LAUREL

RECOGNIZE KEN SEE ESPY FACE BLINK CROWN HONOR KEETH KITHE KYTHE ACCEPT ACKNOW AGNIZE BEKNOW COUTHE REVISE CORRECT DISCERN REALIZE ACCREDIT

(— **IN ANY CAPACITY**) AGNIZE

RECOGNIZED GOOD CLEAR KNOWN CLASSIC FAMILIAR

RECOIL SHY BALK KICK TURN REBUT SHRUG SHUCK START STRAM BLENCH BOUNCE FLINCH RECULE RESILE RESULT RETORT SHRINK REBOUND REDOUND REVERSE BACKLASH REJOUNCE

(**WITHOUT** —) DEADBEAT

RECOLLECT RECALL RECORD RETAIN COMPOSE RECOVER RECOLETO REMEMBER

RECOLLECTION MIND MEMORY RECALL RECORD MINDING THOUGHT MEMORIAL SOUVENIR

RECOMMENCE RENEW REOPEN RESUME REPRISE

RECOMMEND MOVE OSSE PLUG TOUT WISH ADVISE COMMIT PRAISE PREFER COMMEND CONSIGN COUNSEL ENTRUST ADVOCATE RECOMMIT

RECOMMENDATION CHIT VOEU ADVISE COUNSEL TESTIMONY

(**PARTY** —) COUPON

(**SERVANT'S** —) CHIT

RECOMPENSE PAY MEED MEND MENSE QUITS REPAY YIELD AMENDS BOUNTY HADBOT REWARD SALARY GUERDON IMBURSE PAYMENT PREMIUM REQUITE RESTORE SATISFY SERVICE

RECONCILE GREE WEAN ADAPT AGREE ATONE ACCORD ADJUST SETTLE SHRIVE REUNITE HARMONIZE

RECONCILED FAIN VAIN SAUGHT

RECONCILIATION ATONE ACCORD SAUGHT REUNION IRENICON

RECONDITE DARK DEEP HIGH HIDDEN MYSTIC OCCULT SECRET CRYPTIC CURIOUS OBSCURE RETIRED ABSTRACT ABSTRUSE ESOTERIC

RECONNAISSANCE RECCE RECCO RECCY SURVEY

RECONNOITER SCOUT RECALL SURVEY EXAMINE PICKEER DISCOVER REMEMBER

RECONSIDER REVIEW FORTHINK

RECONSTRUCT REPAIR REEVOKE REMODEL RESTORE

RECORD CAN CUT BOOK CARD DATE DISC ITER NICK PAGE ROLL SING SLIP WICK ALBUM CHART DIARY ENACT ENTER ENTRY FASTI GRAPH JUMBO PRICK QUIPO QUIPU SIJIL SLATE STYLE TITLE ANNALS CHARGE DOCKET LEGEND MEMOIR SCROLL SPREAD WARBLE ACCOUNT CALENDS CITATOR DUBBING KALENDS LEXICON MENTION MYOGRAM SHOWING TICKLER TRACING ANAGRAPH ARCHIVES CYLINDER ENTRANCE ERGOGRAM HERDBOOK INSCROLL JUDGMENT KYMOGRAM LAUEGRAM MARIGRAM MELOGRAM MEMORIAL MONUMENT ONDOGRAM PANCHART PRESSING REGISTER REMEMBER SCHEDULE STUDBOOK

(— **BY NOTCHES**) SCORE

(— **OF CAR MOVEMENTS**) JUMBO

(— **OF DOCUMENT**) PROTOCOL

(— **OF EVENTS**) FASTI

(— **OF HUMANITY'S FATE**) SIJIL SIJILL

(— **OF JOURNEY**) JOURNAL ITINERARY

(— **OF LOAN**) CHARGE

(— **OF MUHAMMAD'S SAYINGS**) HADIT

(— **OF MUSCULAR WORK**) ERGOGRAM

(— **OF PROCEEDINGS**) ACTA ITER JOURNAL MINUTES

(**COURT** —) EYRE

(**DAILY** —) DIARY

(**FORMAL** —) ACT

(**HISTORICAL** —) STORY

(**PHONOGRAPH** —) DISC DISK SINGLE BISCUIT SHELLAC

(**SHIP'S** —) LOG

(**PL.**) LIBER ANNALS ARCHIVE

RECORDER FLUTE BOOKER FLAUTO NOTATOR GREFFIER REGISTER

RECORDING ALBUM ALIVE LABEL CUTTING

RECOUNT MING TELL COUNT DEVISE RECITE REGARD RELATE REPEAT SPREAD EXPRESS HISTORY NARRATE CONSIDER DESCRIBE REHEARSE

RECOUP DEDUCT REGAIN RECOVER INDEMNIFY

RECOUPLING HOOKUP

RECOURSE SUIT ACCESS REFUGE RESORT STRING REGRESS RESTAUR RISORSE

(**HAVE** —) RECUR

RECOVER DOW COUR COWR CURE FIRM HEAL KERE COVER REACH UPSET BOUNCE RECURE REGAIN RESCUE RESUME RETAKE RETIRE REVERT REVOKE WARISH DELIVER OVERGET OVERPUT OVERSET READEPT RECLAIM RECRUIT REPAREL REPRISE RESTORE RETRIEVE

RECOVERER DIGESTER

RECOVERY CURE RECOUR RECURE REMEDY RETURN SALVAGE COMEBACK SNAPBACK

RECREANT FALSE CRAVEN YELLOW APOSTATE COWARDLY DESERTER RECRAYED

RECREATE AMUSE EVOKE REVIVE

RECREATION PLAY SPORT SOLACE RENEWAL ACTIVITY DIVERSION PALINGENY

(**PERIOD OF** —) HOLIDAY VACATION

RECREATIVE PLAYING

RECREMENT SLAG DROSS SCORIA

RECRUIT BLEU BOOT FRESH RAISE GATHER INTAKE MUSTER RECREW REPAIR REVIVE RECOVER REFRESH RESTORE ASSEMBLE BEZONIAN CONSCRIPT

(**RAW** —) ROOKY ROOKIE

RECTANGLE BOX SQUARE CHECKER

(**COTTON** —) HUIPIL

(**CURVILINEAR** —) TESSERA

(**WOVEN** —) SINKER

RECTANGULAR SQUARE BOXLIKE EMERALD

RECTIFICATION LIMATION

RECTIFIER DIODE COLUMN DETECTOR EXCITRON
RECTIFY AMEND EMEND RIGHT ADJUST BETTER DETECT REFORM REMEDY CORRECT IMPROVE REDRESS EMENDATE REGULATE
RECTITUDE DOOM EQUITY JUSTICE PROBITY
RECTOR RULER LEADER PARSON PERSONA INCUMBENT
RECTUM SIEGE TEWEL
RECUMBENT IDLE JACENT CUMBENT LEANING RESTING INACTIVE REPOSING
RECUPERATE RALLY REFETE REGAIN RECOVER RECRUIT RETRIEVE
RECUR CYCLE REFER REPEAT RESORT RETURN REOCCUR REVOLVE REAPPEAR
(— CONSTANTLY) HAUNT
RECURRENCE RESORT RETURN ATAVISM REPRISE ITERANCE ITERANCY RECOURSE
(— OF SOUND) CADENCE
RECURRENT CYCLIC FREQUENT
RECURRING ROLLING CONTINUAL
(— ANNUALLY) ETESIAN
(— EVERY THIRD DAY) TERTIAN
(— ON NINTH DAY) NONAN NONANE
(— ON SEVENTH DAY) SEPTAN
(CONSTANTLY —) ETERNAL
(CONTINUALLY —) CONSTANT
RECURVED ERICOID
RECUTTING FRESHING
RED (ALSO SEE COLOR) GOYA GULY PINK PUCE ROJO ROSY RUBY ANGRY CANNA CORAL FIERY JUDAS ROUGE RUDDY RUFUS ARCHIL AZALEA BLOODY CERISE FLORID FULGID GARNET HECTIC NECTAR ORCHIL ORIENT RAISIN RUBRIC TITIAN TRYPAN VERMIL WANTON CARMINE GLOWING NACARAT PIMENTO RADICAL RUBELLE RUBIOUS STAMMEL VERMILY ARMENIAN AUBUSSON BORDEAUX CARDINAL CHOLERIC COLORADO FLAGRANT MANDARIN MOROCAIN RUBICUND SANGUINE ARTILLERY
(— AND INFLAMED) BLOODSHOT
(— PLANET) MARS
(ANTIQUE —) CANNA
(BRIGHT —) TULY CHERRY PUNICIAL VERMILION
(DARK —) CLARET
(EUREKA —) PUCE
(FIERY —) MINIUM
(GRAYISH —) AZALEA
(HERALDIC —) GULES
(IRON OXIDE —) AGATE TARRAGONA
(PURPLISH —) LAKE MAGENTA
(WAX —) COPPER
(YELLOWISH —) MAROON
RED ADMIRAL VANESSA
RED-BACKED SHRIKE POPE
RED BANEBERRY REDBERRY TOADROOT

RED BAY PERSEA
RED-BELLIED (— TERRAPIN) SLIDER SKILPOT
(— WOODPECKER) CHAB
RED-BREASTED BREAM FLATFISH FLOUNDER
RED-BREASTED KNOT GRAYBACK GREYBACK
REDBUD CERCIS JUNEBUD
RED CAMPION ROBIN SOLDIER
RED CEDAR SAVIN SABINA JUNIPER
RED CLOVER SAPLING TREFOIL TRIFOLY
RED CURRANT GOYA RIZZLE TIZZAR
REDD RID COMB OPEN LITTER NEATEN REFUSE RESCUE SETTLE ARRANGE DELIVER SMARTEN UNBLOCK UNRAVEL
RED DEER OLEN STAG
(FEMALE —) HIND
(MALE —) HART STAG
REDDEN RUD FIRE RUBY BLUSH FLUSH LIGHT ROUGE RUDDY BLOODY RUBIFY RUBRIC RUDDLE EMPURPLE
REDDISH REDDY RUDDY RUFUS FLUSHY RUFOUS COLORADO PYRRHOUS
RED DRUM SPOT REDFISH
REDEEM BUY WIN SAVE ALESE CLEAR REPRY BORROW OFFSET RANSOM DELIVER FULFILL JUSTIFY RECLAIM WITHBEG AGAINBUY LIBERATE
REDEEMER GOEL SAVIOR
REDEMPTION RANSOM REFORM SAFETY SALVATION
REDEYE BASS RUDD VIREO WHISKY SUNFISH
RED-EYE CATSUP CICADA WHISKY
RED-EYED VIREO REDEYE GRASSET PREACHER
RED-FACED FLUSHED SCARLET
REDFIN DACE SHINER REDHORSE YELLOWFIN
REDFISH SALMON FATHEAD ROSEFISH
RED GOOSEFOOT PIGWEED SOWBANE
RED GROUPER MERO NEGRE REDBELLY
RED GROUSE GORHEN GORCOCK LAGOPODE MOORBIRD MUIRFOWL
RED GUM JARRAH EUCALYPT
RED GURNARD CUR ELLECK ROCHET SOLDIER
REDHAIRED RUFUS
REDHEAD DIVER FINCH POCHARD KIZILBASH
RED HIND GRAYSBY GROUPER CABRILLA
REDHORSE REDFIN SUCKER
REDIA SPOROSAC
REDIRECT DISPLACE READDRESS
REDISTILL COHOBATE
REDISTRIBUTE FRESHEN REASSIGN
RED LAVER SLOKE
REDNESS RED RUD GLOW HEAT

RUDD RUBOR ERYTHEMA RUBEDITY
(— OF SKY) AURORA
REDO REDACT RESTYLE
(— UNSKILLFULLY) BOTCH
RED OCHER TIVER ABRAUM RUDDLE
REDOLENCE BALM AROMA SCENT
REDOLENT RICH ODOROUS SCENTED AROMATIC FRAGRANT SMELLING
RED OSIER WILLOW REDBRUSH
REDOUBT FEAR MASK DREAD SCHANZ SCONCE
REDOUBLE REECHO INTENSIFY
REDOUND TURN ACCRUE BILLOW CONDUCE REFLECT OVERFLOW
RED RASPBERRY CUTHBERT
REDRESS HEAL DRESS REDUB AVENGE OFFSET REFORM RELIEF REMEDE REMEDY REPAIR ADDRESS CORRECT RECTIFY REFOUND RELIEVE
RED ROCKFISH TAMBOR
RED SAGE LANTANA
RED SANDALWOOD CHANDAM
REDSHANK CLEE TEUK SHAKE GAMBET REDLEG YELPER PELLILE TATTLER
REDSKIN RED ROJO TAWNY INDIAN
REDSTART YELPER BRANTAIL FIRETAIL WHITECAP FIREFLIRT
RED STOPPER EUGENIA IRONWOOD
RED-TAILED (— HAWK) REDTAIL
(— TROPIC BIRD) KOAE
RED-TAPISM BEADLEDOM
RED-THROATED LOON WABBY
REDTOP COUCH FIORIN FINETOP FINEBENT FURZETOP BLUEJOINT
REDUCE CUT BATE DOCK DROP EASE PARE PULL THIN ABASE ABATE ALLAY APPAL BREAK DRAFT ELIDE LOWER QUELL SCANT SHAVE SLAKE SLASH SMELT DEDUCE DEFALK DEJECT DELETE DEPOSE DILUTE HUMBLE LESSEN REBATE REDUCT SHRINK SUBACT SUBDUE WEAKEN ABANDON ABRIDGE ASSUAGE ATOMIZE CHANCER CONQUER CURTAIL DEFLATE DEGRADE DEPLETE DWINDLE ECLIPSE FRITTER INHIBIT RESOLVE RETREAT SCISSOR SHORTEN SUBJECT ATTEMPER CONDENSE DECREASE DIMINISH MINIMIZE
(— ACCORDING TO FIXED RATIO) SCALE
(— ANGLE) CHAMFER
(— BULK) BLEND
(— LUMBER) SIZE
(— PROFITS) SQUEEZE
(— PURITY) ALLOY
(— STONE BLOCKS) SPALL SPAWL
(— THE VALUE) DECRY BEGGAR DEPRAVE
(— TO A MEAN) AVERAGE
(— TO ASHES) CREMATE
(— TO CARBON) CHAR
(— TO FINE PARTICLES) ATOMIZE
(— TO FLAT SURFACE) LEVEL
(— TO INSIGNIFICANCE) DROWN

(— TO LOWER GRADE) BREAK DEMOTE DEGRADE
(— TO NIL) CLOSE
(— TO NOTHING) ANNUL
(— TO PASSIVITY) CHINAFY
(— TO POWDER) GRIND PULVERIZE
REDUCED SUNK TAIL BROKEN DWARFED DEGRADED WEAKENED VESTIGIAL
REDUCTION BUST LETUP SLASH CUTBACK CUTDOWN DOCKAGE SHAVING ANALYSIS DILUTION DISCOUNT SHRINKAGE
(— IN FORCE) RIF
(— IN PITCH) DROP
(— IN PRICE) SAVING CONCESSION
REDUNDANCY EXCESS NIMIETY SURPLUS PLEONASM PLETHORA VERBIAGE TAUTOLOGY
REDUNDANT WORDY LAVISH PROFUSE SURPLUS VERBOSE SWELLING EXCESSIVE
REDWING POP THRUSH WINDLE GADWALL WINNARD
REDWOOD MAD AMBOYNA BARWOOD FURIOUS SEQUOIA MAHOGANY
RE-ECHO REWORD REBOUND RESOUND REDOUBLE
REED NAL RIE RIX SAG BENT JUNK PIPE PIRN RODE SLEY TULE ARROW DONAX SPEAR TWILL BENNEL RADDLE SAGGON CALAMUS FISTULA WHISTLE WINDING
(— FOR WARPING) WRAITHE
(— FOR WINDING THREAD) PIRN SPOOL
(— IN ORGAN) VIBRATOR
(— OF LOOM) COMB
(FOXTAIL —) DOD
(GIANT —) DONAX
(MUSICAL —) OAT
(WEAVER'S —) SLAY SLEY RADDLE SLEIGH
(PL.) SPEAR
REED BENT CARRIZO
REEDBIRD BOBOLINK
REEDBUCK BOHOR NAGOR REITBOK
REED BUNTING RINGBIRD
REED CANARY GRASS SPIRE DAGGERS
REED END TONGUE
REEDING GADROON MILLING STRIGIL GRAINING
REED MACE RAUPO CATTAIL MATREED
REED ORGAN MELODEON HARMONIUM
REED PIPE MIRLITON
REED WARBLER PITBIRD
REEDY THIN WEAK FRAIL TWILLED
REEF CAY KAY KEY CAYO LODE RYFT VEIN ATOLL LEDGE SHELF STICK BOILER REEFER SADDLE SKERRY BAGREEF BALANCE BIOHERM MAKATEA TOMBOLO
REEFER CAR COAT STICK JACKET MUGGLES
REEK FOG FUG EMIT FUME HEAP

MIST PILE RICK RISE VENT EQUIP EXUDE ISSUE NIDOR SMEEK SMOKE STEAM VAPOR EXHALE OUTFIT EMANATE
(— WITH CORRUPTION) FESTER
REEL PIRN ROCK SPIN SWAB SWIM TURN GIDDY SPOOL SWIFT TRULL WAVER WHEEL WHIRL WINCE BOBBIN RECOIL SWERVE TUMULT WAGGLE WALTER WELTER WINDER WINDLE WINNLE WINTLE BALLOON STAGGER SWABBLE TITUBATE
(— FOR DRAWING SILK) FILATURE
(— FOR WARP DRYING) BALLOON
(— FOR WINDING YARN) PIRN SWIFT
(— OFF A STORY) SCRIEVE
(— USED FOR YARN) CRIB
(DYEING —) WINCE
(FISHING —) TROW TROLL TRULL WINCH
(PL.) REVELS
REELER TWINER
REELING TURN AREEL STAGGERY WAMBLING
REEM MOAN URUS UNICORN
REEVE REE REFE THREAD BAILIFF PROVOST STEWARD OVERSEER
REFECTION MEAL RELIEF REPAST
REFECTORY FRATER FRATRY
REFER DEFER LEAVE POINT ADVERT ALLUDE APPEAL ASSIGN CHARGE COMMIT DELATE DIRECT IMPUTE PREFER RELATE SUBMIT ASCRIBE REJOURN RELEGATE
(— TO SOMETHING REPEATEDLY) HARP
(— TO) SEE CITE INTEND CONCERN CONSULT MENTION INTIMATE
REFEREE BREHON UMPIRE ARBITER AUDITOR
REFERENCE TAB FOLIO REMIT SIGIL APPEAL REGARD RENVOI MEANING RESPECT ALLUSION HANDBOOK INNUENDO RELATION
(SATIRICAL —) GLANCE
REFERENDUM POLL MANDATE
REFINE RUN TRY BOLT EDIT FILE FINE PURE CUPEL EXALT PLAIN SLICK SMELT AFFINE DECOCT EXCOCT FILTER GARBLE SMOOTH CONCOCT ELEVATE SUBLIME SWEETEN HUMANIZE URBANIZE
(— AS GOLD) TEST CARAT
(— PULP) JORDAN
(— SUGAR) CLAY
(— WINE) FORCE
REFINED FINE GENT NEAT NICE TRIE EXACT PURED TERSE CHASTE EXCOCT INLAND NIMINY POLITE QUAINT SUBTLE CLEANLY COURTLY ELEGANT GENTEEL PRECISE SCRAPED DELICATE ELEVATED HIGHBRED PRECIEUX SERAPHIC
(NOT —) CRUDE
(TOO —) FINESPUN
REFINEMENT GRACE POLISH CULTURE FINESSE DELICACY ELEGANCE POLITURE SUBTLETY URBANITY

REFINER TRIER JORDAN PURIFIER
REFINING HUMAN FINING CULTURE AFFINAGE
REFINISH ANTIQUE
REFLECT COW MUSE PORE SHOW BLAZE FLASH GLASS GLINT IMAGE SHINE STUDY THINK DAZZLE DEBATE MIRROR PONDER RECORD REFLEX RELUCE RETORT RETURN REVISE STEVEN EXPRESS REDOUND REFRACT SHIMMER COGITATE CONSIDER MEDITATE REDOUBLE RUMINATE
(— IRREGULARLY) SCATTER
(— UPON) SPECULATE
REFLECTED DERIVED MIRRORED SPECULAR
REFLECTION ECHO FOLD IDEA SKIT BLAME GHOST GLARE GNOME DEBATE MUSING PONDER REFLEX RETURN SHADOW CENSURE COUNSEL SPECIES THOUGHT EYESHINE MOONPATH THINKING
(— OF SELF IN ANOTHER'S EYES) BABY
REFLECTIVE PENSIVE THOUGHTFUL
(— POWER) ALBEDO
REFLECTOR FLAT CRITIC HASTER SHINER HORIZON DIFFUSER HASTENER SPECULUM
REFLEX COPY IMAGE TROPISM ALLUSION
(NOT —) IDEOMOTOR
REFLUX EBB EBBING REFLOW
REFOREST REBOISE
REFORM MEND AMEND EMEND PRUNE BETTER REBUKE REPAIR CENSURE CORRECT DISBAND RECLAIM RECTIFY REDRESS
REFORMATORY COLLEGE MAGDALEN
REFORMER APOSTLE UTOPIAN UTOPIAST JANSENIST
REFRACT DIVIDE REFLECT REFRINGE
REFRACTION REBATE REBOUND DIACLASIS
REFRACTORY SULLEN UNRULY WANTON ALUNDUM FROWARD RESTIVE VICIOUS WAYWARD MUTINOUS PERVERSE STUBBORN CAMSTEERY
REFRAIN BOB TAG CURB DOWN KEEP SHUN AVOID FORGO SPARE WONDE BURDEN CHORUS DESIST FOREGO LUDDEN RETAIN THRAIN ABSTAIN FORBEAR LULLABY REFREIT TORNADA FALDERAL OVERCOME OVERWORD REPETEND RESTRAIN WITHDRAW
(— FROM INDULGENCE) ABSTAIN
(— FROM TELLING) LAYNE
(— FROM USING) BOYCOTT
(— FROM) CAN HELP AVOID SPARE WAIVE FOREGO RESIGN
(— OF SONG) BOB TAG DOWN FOOT WHEEL BURDEN CHORUS FALDEROL
(MEANINGLESS —) DERRY
REFRESH FAN COOL REST CHEER

FRESH SLAKE CAUDLE REFECT
REFETE REHETE REPOSE REVIVE
UNTIRE COMFORT FORTIFY
FRESHEN QUICKEN RECRUIT
IRRIGATE RECREATE
REFRESHING DEWY BALMY FRESH
TONIC CALLER LIVING COOLING
REFRESHMENT BAIT LUNCH
CHARITY NUNCHEON REFRESCO
COLLATION
(PL.) FOURS
REFRIGERANT ICE COOLER
AMMONIA COOLING CRYOGEN
REFRIGERATE CHILL
REFRIGERATOR FRIG FRIDGE
ICEBOX FREEZER CONDENSER
(— **CAR**) REEFER
REFUGE ARK HOME PORT ROCK
SOIL BIELD GRITH HAVEN RESET
ASYLUM BILBIE COVERT HARBOR
REFUTE RESORT SPITAL SUCCOR
ALSATIA CRANNOG RESERVE
RETREAT SHELTER UMBRAGE
WARRANT CRANNOGE FORTRESS
HIDEAWAY MAGDALEN RESOURCE
SAFEHOLD
REFUGEE REFFO COWBOY FUIDHIR
FUGITIVE
REFULGENT BRIGHT SHINING
RELUCENT BRILLIANT
REFUND REPAY UPSET REFOUND
RESTORE DRAWBACK KICKBACK
REFURBISH DUST RENEW REVAMP
FRESHEN BRIGHTEN RENOVATE
REFUSAL NAY VEE WARN WONT
DENIAL MITTEN NAYSAY REPULSE
ACCISMUS DECLINAL NEGATION
(— **TO SPEAK**) APHRASIA
REFUSE NAY NIL SUD BALK COOM
DENY DUST JUNK KEMP NAIT NILL
NITE PELF PELT REDD SCUM SKIM
SOIL SUDS WARN BAVIN COOMB
CRAWN DEADS DRAST DROSS
EXPEL FLOCK NITTE OFFAL RENAY
REPEL SCRAN STENT STUFF SWASH
SWILL TRADE TRASH WAIVE WASTE
COLDER DANDER DEBRIS FORBID
LITTER LUMBER MIDDEN NAYSAY
PALTRY PELTRY RAFFLE RECUSE
REFUGE REJECT SCRUFF SCULCH
SHORTS SORDES SORDOR SPILTH
BACKING BAGGAGE BROCKLE
DECLINE DETRACT DETRECT
DISAVOW DISOBEY FORSAKE
GARBAGE GUBBINS MULLOCK
OFFSCUM OUTCAST PRUNING
SOILAGE SULLAGE WITHNAY
WITHSAY CRASSIER DENEGATE
DISALLOW DISCLAIM GARBLING
LEAVINGS RIFFRAFF SWEEPAGE
WITHHOLD
(— **ADMISSION**) CLOSE
(— **FROM CHARCOAL OR COKE**)
BREEZE
(— **FROM COFFEE BERRIES**)
TAILINGS
(— **FROM CUTTING UP WHALE**)
GURRY
(— **FROM MELTING METALS**) SLAG
DROSS SCORIA

(— **FROM SIFTING COFFEE-BEANS**)
TRIAGE
(— **FROM THRESHING**) HUSK
COLDER
(— **GREASE**) COOM COOMB
(— **OF MINE**) DEAD
(— **OF CROP**) STOVER
(— **OF FLAX**) PAB POB HARDS
HURDS
(— **OF FRUITS**) MUST
(— **OF GRAIN**) PUG
(— **OF GRAPES**) MARC
(— **OF INSECT**) FRASS
(— **OF OIL MILLS**) SHODE
(— **OF SILK**) STRASS
(— **OF SPICES**) GARBLE
(— **OF WHALE**) GURRY TWITTER
(— **OF WOOL**) BACKINGS
(— **TO APPROVE**) VETO
(— **TO GO**) JIB BALK
(— **TO RECOGNIZE**) CUT
(— **TO SUPPORT**) BOLT
(— **TO TALK**) DUMMY
(**BREWERY** —) DRAFF
(**FISH** —) CHUM GUBBINS
(**FOOD** —) SWILL
(**LEATHER** —) SPETCHES
(**PLANT** —) SCROFF
(**STREET** —) FULLAGE
REFUTATION DISPROOF ELENCHUS
HYPOBOLE
REFUTE DENY AVOID REBUT REFEL
ASSOIL CONFUTE CONVELL
CONVICT REPROVE REVINCE
CONFOUND DISPROVE INFRINGE
REDARGUE
REGAIN READEPT RECOVER
RETRIEVE
(— **SOMETHING LOST**) RECOUP
REGAL REAL ROYAL KINGLY PURPLE
RIGGAL RIGOLE STATELY IMPERIAL
MAJESTIC PRINCELY REGALIAN
SPLENDID
REGALE FETE FEAST TREAT PLEASE
DELIGHT REFRESH
REGALIA KIT ROYALTY
REGALO GIFT BONUS TREAT
REGARD CON CARE DEEM FIND
GAZE GIVE HEED HOLD LIKE LOOK
MARK MIND RATE RECK TELL YEME
ADORE COUNT FAVOR HONOR
TREAT WEIGH ADMIRE ASPECT
BEHOLD ESTEEM FIGURE GLANCE
HOMAGE IMPUTE INTEND LIKING
MOTIVE NOTICE RECKON REMARK
REWARD SURVEY ACCOUNT
ADJUDGE OBSERVE RESPECT
RESPITE CONSIDER ENVISAGE
ESTIMATE
(— **AS HOPELESS**) DEPLORE
(— **AS OBJECT OF GREAT
INTEREST**) LIONIZE
(— **AS PROPER**) ACCEPT
(— **AS**) SEE
(— **HIGHLY**) ADMIRE CONSIDER
(— **WITH PROFOUND RESPECT**)
REVERE VENERATE
(— **WITH REPUGNANCE**) ABHOR
(**ATTENTIVE** —) EYE

(**MENTAL** —) EYE
(PL.) COMPLIMENTS
REGARDED (— **WITH AFFECTION**)
DEAR AFFECTED
REGARDING ABOUT ANENT
APROPOS
REGARDLESS DEAF CARELESS
HEEDLESS RECKLESS
(— **OF THAT**) BUT
REGATTA HENLEY LIBERTY
REGENCY RULE DOMINION
REGENERATE RENEW REFORM
REVIVE RECLAIM GRACIOUS
RENOVATE
(**NOT** —) CIVIL
REGENT RULER RULING WARDEN
SHIKKEN GOVERNOR PANGERANG
(— **DIAMOND**) PITT
(— **OF NORTH**) KUBERA KUVERA
REGIME FASCISM CAFETERIA
REGIMEN CURE DIET KEEP RULE
REGIMENT
REGIMENT BUFF RULE COLOR
TERCIO GUIDANCE INFANTRY
SLASHERS
(**28TH** —) SLASHERS
(**BRITISH** —) GRAYS GREYS
(**COSSACK** —) PULK
(**FRAMEWORK OF** —) CADRE
(**INDIA** —) PULTON PULTUN
(**SPANISH** —) TERCIO
(**TURKISH** —) ALAI
REGION DO ERD EYE GAU WON
AREA BELT KITH KNOT PART SOIL
WONE WOON ZONE CLIME COAST
EARTH EXURB INDIA MARCH PAGU
PLACE PLAGE REALM SHIRE TRAC
TROAD ALKALI BORDER CENTER
DESERT DOMAIN EXTENT GILEAD
GROUND GUIANA TATARY CLIMATE
CONFINE COUNTRY DEMESNE
ENCLAVE IMAMATE KINGDOM
MALABAR STATION TARTARY
CHIEFDOM CLUBLAND DEMERARA
DISTRICT ENVIRONS EPISTOME
FLATLAND FORTRESS FRONTIER
KRATOGEN LAKELAND LATITUDE
NAPHTALI PROVINCE REGIMENT
SERICANA STANNARY
(— **ABOVE MOUTH**) EPISTOMA
EPISTOME
(— **ADJACENT TO BOUNDARY**)
MARCH
(— **BEYOND ATMOSPHERE**) SPACE
(— **BEYOND DEATH**) CANAAN
(— **BORDERING ON HELL**) LIMBO
(— **FAR AWAY**) STRAND
(— **NEAR EQUATOR**) DOLDRUMS
(— **NOTED FOR MANY CONFLICTS**)
COCKPIT
(— **OF AMPLITUDE**) ANTINODE
(— **OF COLD AND DARKNESS**)
NIFLHEL NIFLHEIM
(— **OF DEAD**) AMENTI UGTARTHA
(— **OF JAPAN**) DO
(— **OF MARS**) LIBYA
(— **OF OCEAN**) COUNTRY
(— **OF ORIGIN**) CRADLE
(— **OF PHOTOSPHERE**) FACULA

(— OF SHIFTING SAND) ERG
(— OF SIMPLE PLEASURE) ARCADY ARCADIA
,— OF SOURCE OF GOLD) OPHIR
.— OF TISSUE) FIELD
— WITHOUT LAW) ALSATIA
— WITHOUT WOODS) WOLD WEALD
CELESTIAL —S) LANGI
COASTAL —) LITTORAL
CULTIVATED —) GARDEN
DARKISH —S ON MARS) MARE
DESERT —) ERG HAMADA
DESERTED —) WASTE
DESOLATE —) PUNA
DISTANT —) THULE
E. INDIAN —) DESH
ELEVATED —) ALTITUDE
FOREST —) TAIGA
FORESTED —) MONTANA
GEOGRAPHICAL —) BOWL SIDE
HEAVENLY —) SPHERE
IDEAL —) JINNESTAN
INFERNAL —S) ABYSS TARTAR ARTARUS
LARGE —) COMPAGE
LIMESTONE —) KARST
MOUNTAINOUS —) SIERRA
OPEN —) SAVANNAH
ORIENTAL —) INDOGAEA
STAGNANT —) EDDY
SUPERIOR —) HIGH
TREELESS —) HIGHMOOR
UPPER —) HIGH LOFT
UPPER —S) ETHER
WOODED —) FOREST
(L.) DIGGINGS
GIONAL LOCAL SECTIONAL
GISTER PIE BEAR BOOK FREE
ST PILE POLL READ ROLL STOP
BUM DIARY ENROL ENTER FASTI
RILL SIJIL SLATE ANNALS BEHAVE
DGER MUSTER RECORD REGEST
CRIBE CALENDS CATALOG
UCHER INDORSE KALENDS
TITIA ROTULET ARCHIVES
DASTER CALENDAR GREFFIER
DICATE INSCRIBE MENOLOGY
DIGREE POLLBOOK TOLLBOOK ROHBASS
OF JUDGMENTS) DOCKET
WEST —) CHALUMEAU
DDLE —) CLARINO
FICIAL —) TABLEAU CADASTER
ISTRAR GUARD ACTUARY
TWARI PUTWARI GREFFIER SIDENT
ISTRY FLAG STUDBOOK
LET FILET BATTEN FILLET LET
RATER HUCKSTER
RESS EGRESS RETURN
LYSIS RECOURSE
RET REW RUE RUTH GRIEF
IRE RELENT REPENT SORROW
LORE REGRATE REMORSE
THINK REPINING
RETFUL BAD SORRY REPINING
RETTABLE DIRTY DOLOROUS
ILAR DUE SET EVEN FULL JUST

WEAK SOBER SUANT SUENT USUAL
FORMAL NORMAL SQUARE STATED
STEADY CORRECT NATURAL
ORDERED ORDERLY ORDINAL
PERFECT TYPICAL UNIFORM
COMPLETE CONSTANT DECOROUS
FORMULAR HABITUAL ORDINARY
ORDINATE TESSERAL
REGULARITY METHOD SQUARE
SYSTEM EVENNESS SYNAPHEA
(— OF NATURE) LAW
REGULARLY DULY EVEN ORDERLY
PROPERLY STATEDLY
REGULATE SET RULE WIND BOOST
FRAME GUIDE ORDER RIGHT SHAPE
ADJUST ASSIZE BEHAVE DIRECT
GOVERN MASTER RADDLE SETTLE
SQUARE TEMPER ARRANGE
CONTROL DISPOSE MEASURE
QUALIFY RECTIFY ATTEMPER
MODERATE MODULIZE
(— FOOD) DIET
(— PITCH) KEY STOP
REGULATED ORDENE ORDERED
REGULATING BEHIND
REGULATION LAW RULE BYLAW
ORDER REGLE USUAL CURFEW
ZABETA CONTROL PRECEPT
STATUTE VOICING DISPOSAL
STEERAGE
(— OF PRICE) ASSIZE
REGULATOR GUIDE DISPOSER
GOVERNOR
REGULUS MATTE SLURRY KINGLET
REHABILITATE REABLE RESTORE
REINSTATE
REHASH RECHAUFFE
REHEARSAL CALL HEARSAL
HERSALL PREVIEW CLAMBAKE
NARRATION
REHEARSE TELL TRAIN DETAIL
RECITE RELATE DECLINE NARRATE
RECOUNT DESCRIBE PRACTICE
REHEAT FLASH
REHOBOAM ROBOAM
(FATHER OF —) SOLOMON
REICHSTAG DIET
REIF PLUNDER ROBBERY
REIGN RING RULE REALM RICHE
EMPIRE GOVERN KINGDOM PREVAIL
REGIMENT
(— IN INDIA) RAJ
REIMBURSE PAY REPAY DEFRAY
RECOUP REFUND REBURSE
INDEMNIFY
REIN CURB STOP CHECK SWING
THONG GOVERN BABICHE LEATHER
PLOWLINE RESTRAIN
(PL.) LINES RIBBONS
REINDEER REIN CERVID TARAND
CARIBOU CERVINE CERVOID
REINDEER MOSS SWARD
REINFORCE BAR GUY BACK FACE
STAY BRACE FORCE INLAY STUFF
SUPER CRADLE DOUBLE GUSSET
HARDEN MUSCLE SUPPLY AFFORCE
BOLSTER BULWARK ENFORCE
GROMMET NERVATE STIFFEN
SUPPORT

(— ROAD) SKID
REINFORCED KEYED SPLICED
REINFORCEMENT CREW FUEL STAY
BRACE HURTER CUNETTE SPLICING
STRAINER
(PL.) SUCCOR SUPPLY
REINVIGORATE QUICK REVIVE
RECRUIT RENERVE
REITERATE BACK REITER REPEAT
RESUME ITERATE REHEARSE
REJECT BEG ORT CAST DICE JILT
NILL SPIN ABHOR BANDY BELIE
BRUSH EJECT SCOUT ABJECT
ABJURE DELETE DESERT IGNORE
RECUSE RESPUE CASHIER DISCARD
FORSAKE REPULSE ATHETIZE
DISCLAIM DEFY FAIL KICK CHECK
REFEL REPEL SPURN WAIVE REFUSE
RETORT ABANDON CONTEMN
DECLINE DISCARD DISMISS
FORSAKE PROJECT REPROVE
REPULSE ABNEGATE DISALLOW
FORSWEAR RENOUNCE THROWOUT
(— A STUDENT) PLUCK PLOUGH
(— COPY) SPIKE
REJECTED OFFCAST OUTCAST
CASTAWAY
REJECTION SACK BRUSH SPURN
DENIAL MITTEN REBUFF REFUSAL
REPULSE DEFIANCE TURNDOWN
(— OF DOCTRINE) HERESY
REJOICE JOY FAIN GAME CHEER
ENJOY EXULT GLORY BLITHE
PLEASE DELIGHT GLADDEN
JUBILATE
REJOICING GLEE MIRTH FESTIVITY
REJOIN TAUNT ANSWER REUNITE
REJOINDER REPLY ANSWER
COUNTER RESPONSE
REJUVENATE UNOLD
REKINDLE RELUME REVIVE
RELAPSE SINK WEED LAPSE RECIDE
RETURN BACKSET SUBSIDE
BACKCAST WITHDRAW
RELATE SAY ALLY BEAR JOIN READ
TELL PITCH REFER SPELL STATE
TOUCH ALLUDE ASSERT DELATE
DETAIL DEVISE RECITE REPORT
REPUTE COGNATE CONCERN
DECLARE INVOLVE NARRATE
PERTAIN RECOUNT CALABASH
DESCRIBE REHEARSE
(— TO) TOUCH
RELATED KIN SIB AKIN ALLIED
(— BY FATHER'S SIDE) AGNATE
(— ON MOTHER'S SIDE) ENATE
ENATIC COGNATE
RELATING (ALSO SEE PERTAINING)
(— TO A RECENT PAST) ERST
(— TO) AGAINST
RELATION KIN SIB TALE BLOOD
FETII AFFINE DATIVE REGARD
ACCOUNT BEARING HISTORY
KINSHIP KINSMAN RAPPORT
RESPECT SCHESIS TELLING
AFFINITY HABITUDE RELATIVE
TENDENCY REHEARSAL RISHTADAR
(— BETWEEN SPECIES) AFFINITY
(— OF LIKENESS) ANALOGY

(BLOOD —) KIN SIB
(FIXED —) RATIO
(FRIENDLY —S) AMITY
(SYNTACTIC —) FUNCTION
(WORKING —) GEAR
RELATIONSHIP KIN BLOOD ACTION
AGENCY AMENITY AMITATE
ANGULUS BEARING CONTACT
KINDRED KINSHIP LIAISON RESPECT
SIBNESS SIBREDE SOCIETY AFFINITY
AGNATION CONTRAST GOSSIPRY
RELATIVE SYMPATHY COGNATION
FILIATION
(BUSINESS —) ACCOUNT
(CLOSE —) BOSOM AFFIANCE
INTIMACY BELONGING
(INHARMONIOUS —) OUTS
(MARITAL —) BED
(MUTUAL —) TERMS SYMMETRY
(SEXUAL —) AFFAIR
(SOCIAL —) FOOTING
RELATIVE KIN ALLY BLOOD AFFINE
AGNATE ALLIED COUSIN GERMAN
KINDRED KINSMAN APPOSITE
COGNATUS RELATION RELEVANT
PERTINENT
(PL.) KIN SIB FOLK KINDRED
KINFOLK KINNERY KINSFOLK
RELAX LAX GIVE REST ABATE BREAK
LOOSE REMIT SLACK DIVERT
LAXATE SOFTEN UNBEND UNGIVE
UNKNIT DEBLOCK RELEASE
RESOLVE SLACKEN UNPURSE
MITIGATE UNBUCKLE UNCLENCH
RELAXATION EASE LAZE REST
CREEP LETUP RELAX SOLACE
DETENTE LETDOWN BREATHER
DIVERSION
RELAXED LAX LASH LOOSE SLACK
SONSY REMISS SONSIE INFORMAL
RESOLVED UNBENDED UNBRACED
RELAXING ANIMAL ANODYNE
DETENTE
(— POINT) SEAR
RELAY SPELL RELIEF REMUDA
AVANTLAY REPEATER
(— OF DOGS) VAUNTLAY
(— OF PALANQUIN BEARERS) DAK
RELEASE LES LET BAIL DROP EMIT
FREE LESE LIOS LISS SHED SLIP
TRIP UNDO ERUPT LEISS LOOSE
MUKTI REMIT SLAKE ASSOIL DEMISE
EXCUSE EXEMPT LAUNCH MOKSHA
REMISE SPRING UNBEND UNTACK
UNWORK ABSOLVE APATHIA
DELIVER DETENTE DISBAND
FREEDOM QUIETUS SOLUTIO
UNSTICK DELIVERY DISPENSE
DISSOLVE LIBERATE DISCHARGE
(— AS DOGS) UNLEASH
(— DANCING PARTNER) BREAK
(— EMOTION) ABREAST
(— FROM CONFINEMENT) UNMEW
UNPEN SPRING STREET
(— FROM DEBT) FREITH
(— FROM MILITARY) INVALID
(— FROM SLAVERY) MANUMIT
(— ON ONE'S WORD) PAROLE
(PRESS —) HANDOUT

RELEASED OFF FREE EXEMPT
RELEGATE DOOM EXILE BANISH
COMMIT DEMOTE REJECT DEGRADE
(— TO OBSCURITY) DOWN
RELENT COME MELT ABATE YIELD
REGRET REPENT LIQUEFY MOLLIFY
SLACKEN
RELENTLESS GRIM HARD HARSH
STERN STONY BITTER SAVAGE
STRICT AUSTERE PITILESS
RIGOROUS
RELEVANT APT VALID GERMAN
APROPOS GERMANE APPOSITE
MATERIAL PERTINENT
RELIABILITY STEEL CREDENCE
RELIABLE GOOD HARD SURE TRUE
SOLID SOUND THERE TRIED TRUST
DINKUM STEADY TRUSTY CERTAIN
FAITHFUL SOOTHFUL STRAIGHT
RELIANCE HOPE TRUST CREDIT
AFFIANCE MAINSTAY
(— ON FAITH) FIDEISM
RELIC HUACO REMAIN ANTIQUE
HALIDOM LEAVING MEMENTO
RELIQUE VESTIGE SOUVENIR
SURVIVAL
(PL.) CORPSE HALIDOM REMAINS
RELICT WIDOW REMANIE RESIDUAL
SURVIVOR EPIBIOTIC
RELIEF AID LAX SOB BOOT BOTE
EASE HELP RELAY SCRUB SPELL
SWING ESCAPE REMEDY SUCCOR
COMFORT FEEDING REDRESS
RILIEVO EASEMENT REPOUSSE
(TEMPORARY —) HITCH
RELIEVE ROB BEET EASE FREE HELP
LIOS LISS ALLAY LIGHT LISSE LITHE
RIGHT SLAKE SPARE SPELL ASSIST
LESSEN PHYSIC REMEDY REMOVE
RESCUE SOOTHE SUCCOR UNMAZE
ASSUAGE COMFORT DELIVER
DEPRIVE FRESHEN LIGHTEN
REDRESS REFRESH SUCCEED
SUPPORT SUSTAIN SWEETEN
ALIGHTEN DIMINISH MITIGATE
RELEVATE
(— A SAIL) SPILL
(— OF OFFICE) AX AXE
(— OF SIN) CONFESS
RELIGIEUSE NUN CLERGESS
RELIGION BON DIN LAW SECT
BONBO CREED DAENA FAITH OBEAH
PIETY SOPHY DHARMA SHINTO
SYSTEM TAOISM ELOHISM JAINISM
JUDAISM ORPHISM PERSISM RELIGIO
SIKHISM SYNAGOG BUDDHISM
CAODAISM HINDUISM MAZDAISM
PEYOTISM
(— OF ABRAHAM) HANIFIYA
(— OF TIBET) BON
(CHRISTIAN —) WAY
(UNORTHODOX —) CULT
RELIGIOUS HOLY EXACT GODLY
PIOUS RIGID DEVOUT DIVINE
SACRED FERVENT GHOSTLY
ZEALOUS
(— HOUSE) KELLION
RELINQUISH LAY LET CEDE DROP
QUIT DEMIT FORGO GRANT LEAVE

WAIVE YIELD CANCEL DESERT
RESIGN ABANDON FORSAKE
RELEASE ABDICATE ABNEGATE
LINQUISH RENOUNCE
RELIQUARY ARCA CASKET CHASSE
COFFER MEMORY SHRINE STEEPA
TABLET CHORTEN HALIDOM
MEMORIA FERETORY
RELISH CHOW DASH EDGE GOUT
GUST LIKE SOUL SOWL TANG ZEST
ACHAR ENJOY GUSTO RELES
SAVOR SOWLE SPICE TASTE TRACE
ATSARA DEGUST FLAVOR LIKING
SAVOUR BOTARGO OUTWORK
STOMACH APPETITE FONDNESS
(— FOR FOOD) CHAW
(INTELLECTUAL —) TASTE
(MENTAL —) PALATE
(ROMAN —) GARUM
(SALT OR ACID —) ACHAR
RELUCENT RADIANT SHINING
GLEAMING
RELUCTANCE GRUDGE AVERSION
ANTIPATHY RENITENCE
(— UNIT) REL
RELUCTANT SET SHY CAGY LOTH
NICE CHARY LOATH SWEER THRAW
AFRAID AVERSE DAINTY FORCED
SWEERT UNFAIN ASHAMED HALTIN
BACKWARD GRUDGING LOATHFUL
THRAWART
RELY AFFY BANK BASE LEAN LITE
REST STAY COUNT RALLY TRUST
DEPEND GROUND RECKON REPOSE
CONFIDE
(— ON) LIPPEN VENTURE
REMAIN LIE SIT BIDE REST STAY
STOP ABIDE CLING DWELL LEAVE
STAND TARRY THOLE BELIVE
ENDURE MANENT RESIDE SUBSIST
SURVIVE CONTINUE
(— AWAKE) VIGILATE
(— IN DEADLOCK) HANG
(— MOTIONLESS) STAGNATE
(— UNDER HEAT TREATMENT) SO
(— UNDISTURBED AFTER HEAT
TREATMENT) AGE
(— UNUSED) LIE
(— UPRIGHT) STAND
(—S IN MASH TUN) GRAINS
(—S IN PIPEBOWL) TOPPER
(—S OF CANE) BEGASS BAGASSE
(—S OF FIRE) EMBER EMBERS
(—S ON STAGE) MANET
(ANIMAL —S) SPOILS
(FOUL —S) SCURF
(PL.) CHAR DUST ASHES DECAY
DRAFF GHOST SHARD SHERD
BURIAL DEBRIS FOSSIL RELIEF
CARCASS REMNANT RESIDUE
REMAINDER HEEL LAVE REST
PLUGS ARREAR EXCESS RELIEF
BALANCE REMNANT RESIDUE
SURPLUS LEAVINGS LEFTOVER
RESIDUAL RESIDUUM
(— OF ATOM) CORE
(PL.) GARBLINGS LEFTMENTS
REMAINING BIDING REMNANT
LEFTOVER REMANENT RESIDUAL

REMARK DIG SAY SEE GIRD HEED
NOTE WORD GLOSS STATE TOKEN
EARFUL GAMBIT NOTICE REGARD
COMMENT DESCANT DISCANT
OBSERVE PERCEIVE
(— **BRIEFLY**) GLANCE
(**AMIABLE** —) DOUCEUR
(**AMUSING** —) GAG
(**BITING** —) BARB
(**CONCLUDING** —S) ENVOI
(**CUTTING** —) DIG SPINOSITY
(**EMBARRASSING** —) BREAK
(**EXPLANATORY** —) SCHOLION
SCHOLIUM
(**FOOLISH** —) INANITY
(**INSULTING** —) SLUR
(**JEERING** —) JEST SKIT
(**LAUGH-PROVOKING** —) GAG
(**SARCASTIC** —) HIT GIRD SLANT
(**SATIRICAL** —) JEST SKIT SGAFT
(**SHARP** —) GANSEL STINGER
(**SILLY** —) FADAISE
(**STALE** —S) BILGE
(**UNCOMPLIMENTARY** —) BRICKBAT
(**WITTY** —) JEST CRACK
REMARKABLE FORBY GREAT
SIGNAL STRONG NOTABLE STRANGE
UNUSUAL FABULOUS MARKABLE
SINGULAR SPANKING STRIKING
UNCOMMON BODACIOUS
(**NOT** —) INCURIOUS
REMARKABLY UNCO UNKO JOLLY
UNCOW DEUCED UNCOLY SIGNALLY
REMEDIAL RELEVANT SALUTARY
REMEDILESS BOOTLESS
REMEDY AID BOT BOOT BOTE CURE
GAIN HALE HEAL HELP REDE AZOTH
MANDS REDUB SHERE TOPIC
PHYSIC RECOUR RECURE RELIEF
REPAIR RESIDY URETIC ANTACID
CORRECT DRASTIC ICTERIC
OTALGIC PLASTER RECTIFY
REDRESS RELIEVE ANTIDOTE
MEDICINE PHARMACY RECOVERY
REMEDIAL SPECIFIC
(— **COUNTERACTING POISON**)
TREACLE ANTIDOTE
(— **FOR ALL DISEASES**) PANACEA
CATHOLICON
(— **FOR JAUNDICE**) ICTERIC
(— **TO REDUCE FEVER**) FEBRIFUGE
(**CHINESE** —) SENSO
(**EXTERNAL** —) TOPIC
(**FAVORITE** —) NOSTRUM
(**SECRET** —) ARCANUM
(**TAPEWORM** —) EMBELIA
(**UNIVERSAL** —) AZOTH
(**WITHOUT** —) BOOTLESS
REMEMBER MEM MIN MEAN MIND
MINE MING IDEATE MEMBER RECALL
RECORD REMIND RETAIN REWARD
RETHINK MENTION
(— **REMORSEFULLY**) REMORD
REMEMBRANCE MiN MIND MEMORY
RECORD MEANING MINDING MINNING
MEMORIAL REMINDER SOUVENIR
MIND JOG MIN MIND MINE MING
MIND PROMPT REMEMBER
MINDER MEMO PROD TWIT

TOUCH PROMPT MINDING MONITOR
SOUVENIR
REMINISCENCE MEMORY RECALL
ANAMNESIS
REMISE RETURN RELEASE REPLACE
CARRIAGE
REMISS LAX LAZY MILD PALE FAINT
SLACK TARDY BEHIND DILUTED
LANGUID CARELESS DERELICT
DILATORY HEEDLESS
REMISSION CURE LIOS LISS
PARDON REMISE LOOSING
REMITTAL
REMISSNESS LACHES LASHNESS
REMIT SEND COVER LOOSE RELAX
CANCEL EXCUSE PARDON REMAND
REMISS RESIGN ABSOLVE FORGIVE
RELEASE SUSPEND ABROGATE
MITIGATE MODERATE
REMNANT END TAG DREG FENT
REST RUMP RUND RELIC STUMP
TRACE REMAIN LEAVING REMAINS
SURVIVOR
(— **OF CLOTH**) FENT
(— **OF FOOD**) CRUST
(— **OF ROCK MASS**) KLIP KLIPPE
(— **OF VEIL**) ANNULUS
(—S **OF FILLETS**) SCISSEL
(—S **OF VEIL**) CORTINA
(**VESTIGIAL** —) SHADOW
(PL.) EPIPLASM
REMODEL MEND RECAST CONVERT
REMONSTRANCE PROOF ADVICE
COUNSEL PROTEST REPROOF
EVIDENCE
REMONSTRANT ARMINIAN
REMONSTRATE ARGUE PROTEST
REPROVE COMPLAIN
REMORA CLOG DRAG PEGA SUCKER
GUAICAN PEGADOR ECHENEID
LOOTSMAN STAYSHIP STOPSHIP
SUCKFISH
REMORSE HELL PITY RUTH PRICK
REGRET REMORD
(— **OF CONSCIENCE**) GRUDGE
REMORSEFUL BAD PITIFUL
CONTRITE GUILTSICK
REMOTE FAR OFF DEEP FERN HIGH
LONG ALOOF HOARY UTTER
ALENGE DISTAL ELENGE EXEMPT
OTIOSE SECRET DEVIOUS DISSITE
DISTANT EXTREME FAILING
FARAWAY FOREIGN OBSCURE
OUTSIDE ABDITIVE ARMCHAIR
INTERIOR OUTLYING OUTWORLD
SECLUDED
(— **FROM LIFE**) SCHOOLISH
(**MOST** —) ULTIMA EXTREME
HINDMOST ULTIMATE
REMOTELY CLEAN DISTANTLY
REMOTENESS AWAYNESS DISTANCE
REMOTER FARTHER ULTERIOR
REMOVABLE DATIVE REMOTIVE
REMOVAL AX AXE ERASE AMOTION
CLEANUP ERASION ABLATION
EXCISION EXERESIS OFFGOING
REMOTION
(— **OF COAL**) GETTING

(— **OF ICE FROM GLACIER**)
ATTRITION
REMOVE GET PUT RID BATE COMB
DELE DRAW FILE FLIT FREE LIFT
MOVE PARE QUIT RAZE VOID WEED
APART AUFER AVOID BLAST BRUSH
CLEAR EMITY ERASE EVOID HEAVE
HOIST LIGHT PLANE RAISE REPEL
SHIFT SHUCK SLASH SLIPE STRIP
SWEEP WAIVE BANISH CANCEL
CHANGE CONVEY DEDUCT DEGREE
DEPART DEPOSE EFFACE ELOIGN
EXEMPT EXPORT MINISH RELEVE
SPIRIT AMOLISH DEPRIVE DESCENT
DISMISS DISPOST DIVORCE
EXCERPT RESCIND RETRACT
REVERSE STRANGE SUBDUCT
SUBLATE ABSTRACT ASPIRATE
DISPLACE DISPLANT ESTRANGE
EVACUATE RETRENCH SUPPLANT
TRANSFER WITHDRAW
(— **A STITCH**) DECREASE
(— **BARK FROM LOG**) ROSS
(— **BIT BY BIT**) SCAMBLE
(— **BY CUTTING**) ABLATE
(— **BY DEATH**) SNATCH
(— **CLOTHING**) DOFF STRIP
(— **COLOR**) BLEACH
(— **COVER**) UNCAP
(— **DEFECTS**) SCARF
(— **DIRT**) BLADE GARBLE
(— **EXCESS METAL**) CUT
(— **FROM CHECKER BOARD**) HUFF
(— **FROM OFFICE**) DEPOSE RECALL
DISMISS
(— **FROM REMEMBRANCE**) COVER
(— **GILLS**) BEARD
(— **HAIR**) DEPILATE
(— **HUSKS AND CHAFF**) GELD
(— **INSIDES OF FISH**) GIB GIP
(— **JUDGE**) ADDRESS
(— **LOWER BRANCHES**) BRASH
(— **MAST**) UNSTEP
(— **ORE**) EXTRACT
(— **PARTICLES OF GOLD LEAF**)
SKEW
(— **POTATOES**) GRABBLE
(— **QUEEN BEE**) DEMAREE
(— **ROOTS**) GRUB
(— **SEED FROM FLAX**) RIBBLE
(— **SEEDS**) STONE
(— **SKIN**) HULL HUSK
(— **SPROUTS FROM**) CHIT
(— **STALK FROM**) STRIG
(— **STAMENS**) CASTRATE
(— **TABLECLOTH**) DRAW
(— **THE TOP OF**) COP
(— **TROUSERS**) DEBAG
(— **WASTE TO FIBER**) GARNETT
(— **WOOL**) BELLY
(— **WORKS OF STOLEN WATCH**)
CHURCH
REMOVED UP OFF AWAY ALIEN
ALOOF APART REMOTE DISTANT
SEMOTED ABSTRACT
REMOVER MOVER CROPMAN
KNOTTER
REMUDA CAVY CAVAYARD
CAVYYARD

REMUNERATE PAY REPAY REWARD
GRATIFY SATISFY CONSIDER
REIMBURSE
REMUNERATION PAY REWARD
SALARY PAYMENT
REMUNERATIVE GAINFUL
REWARDING
REMUS (BROTHER OF —) ROMULUS
RENAISSANCE NARA REBIRTH
REVIVAL
RENAL NEPHRIC
RENCOUNTER CLASH FIGHT
DEBATE CONTEST CONFLICT
REND PULL RENT RIVE TEAR TOIL
BREAK BURST DIVEL RATCH ROWEL
SEVER SPLIT WREST CLEAVE
SCREED WRENCH DIVULSE
RUPTURE WREATHE DISPIECE
DISTRAIN FRACTURE LACERATE
SPLINTER
(— AND DEVOUR) TIRE
RENDER DO PAY PUT TRY BEAR
DRAW ECHO EMIT MAKE RENT RIND
DEFER PRICK REPAY YIELD RECITE
REPEAT RETURN DELIVER PRECARY
REFLECT REQUITE RESTORE
SERVICE TALLAGE TRANSMIT
(— ACID) PRICK
(— AGREEABLE) DULCIFY
(— AS LARD) TRY
(— ASSISTANCE TO SHIP) FOY
(— CAPABLE) ACTIVATE
(— CLEAR) OPEN
(— FIT) ADAPT
(— GODLIKE) DEIFY
(— HEAVY WITH FOOD) STODGE
(— HOMAGE) ATTORN
(— IMMUNE) FRANK VASTATE
(— INEFFECTIVE) VITIATE
(— KNOTTY) GNARL
(— OBLIQUE) SPLAY
(— OBSCURE) DARKLE
(— OF BOON WORK) PRECARY
(— QUIET) ACCOY
(— SENSELESS) STUN ASTONISH
(— TURBID) ROIL
(— UNFIT) DENATURE
(— UNSTABLE) UNHINGE
(— VERDICT) PASS
(— VOID) CASS DEFEAT
RENDERED RENDU TRIED
RENDERING RENDU ENGLISH
VERSION RENDITION
(— OF SCENE) STUDY
RENDEZVOUS DATE HAUNT TRYST
REFUGE HANGOUT MEETING
RETREAT
(— FOR SHIPS) DOWN
RENDITION ACCOUNT CONDUCT
DELIVERY
RENEGADE DORAX PERVERT
TRAITOR APOSTATE RENEGADO
RUNAGADO RUNAGATE TURNCOAT
RENEGE BEG NIG DENY RENIG
DESERT REVOKE RETRACT
FAINAIGUE
RENEW NEW REST FRESH RECALL
REFORM RENOVE REPEAT RESUME
REVIVE INSTORE REBUILD REFRESH

REPLACE RESTORE
(— WINE) STUM
RENEWAL RENEW REVIVAL
NOVATION
RENNET LAB RUEN VELL STEEP
RENNIN RUNNET EARNING
ABOMASUM YEARNING CHEESELIP
RENOUNCE PUT CEDE DEFY DENY
QUIT DEVOW FORGO RENAY WAIVE
ABJURE DISOWN FORLET FORSAY
RECANT REFUSE REJECT RENEGE
RESIGN REVOKE ABANDON
DECLARE FORLEIT FORSAKE
RETRACT WITHSAY ABDICATE
ABNEGATE DISCLAIM FORSPEAK
FORSWEAR MANSWEAR PROCLAIM
RENOVATE DUST RENEW REVIVE
FURBISH REFRESH RESTORE
RENOVIZE
(— HAT) MOLOKER MOLOCKER
RENOWN BAY BRAG FAME ECLAT
GLORY KUDOS PRICE RUMOR
ESTEEM LUSTER RENONE REPORT
EMPRISE SWAGGER WORSHIP
PRESTIGE NOTORIETY
RENOWNED FAMED NOBLE NOTED
FAMOUS EMINENT RENOMME
GLORIOUS MAGNIFIC RENOMMEE
RENT LET SET TAX FARM GALE
GAPE HIRE MAIL RACK RIME RIVE
SLIT TEAR TOLL WAGE BREAK
CANON CENSO CUDDY ENDOW
GANCH GAVEL SPLIT BLANCH
BREACH BROKEN CENSUS CHASMA
CUSTOM GAUNCH INCOME SCHISM
SCREED STRENT CHARTER CHIEFRY
FISSURE MAILING MOLLAND
ONSTAND RENTAGE REVENUE
RUPTURE TRIBUTE CHAMPART
CHIEFERY HEADRENT STALLAGE
VECTIGAL WAYLEAVE LANDGAFOL
(— BY BOAR'S TUSK) GANCH
GAUNCH
(— IN LIEU OF SUPPER) CUDDY
(— OF LAND PAID IN KIND) CAIN
(ANNUAL —) CANON
(EARTHQUAKE —) SCARPLET
(GROUND —) CENSO CENSUS
(OATS IN LIEU OF —) AVENAGE
RENTAL PORT TONNAGE TRIBUTE
TUNNAGE
RENTED LETTEN
RENTER FARMER RANTER CHIPPER
BOXHOLDER
RENUNCIATION DENIAL APOSTASY
DEFIANCE DISAVOWAL REJECTION
SACRIFICE
REP CANNELE DROGUET POPELINE
REPAIR DO EIK EKE FIX IMP HEAL
HELP MEND TINE AMEND BOTCH
DIGHT EMEND HAUNT RALLY REDUB
RENEW STORE TRADE UPSET
ASTORE BUSHEL COBBLE COGGLE
DOCTOR FETTLE RECURE REFORM
REMEDY REPASS RESORT RETURN
UPKEEP CORRECT INFAINT REDRESS
REPAREL RESTORE SERVICE
FLOCKING RETRIEVE REVIVIFY
(— BOAT) CAREEN

(— CLUMSILY) BOTCH
(— FENCE) MOUND
(— ROAD) SKID
(— SHOE) FOX TAP
REPAIRED VAMPED
REPAIRER DOCTOR COBBLER
WOFFLER CEMENTER
(SHOE —) JACKMAN BENCHMAN
(TEXTILE —) SMASHER
REPAIRMAN FETTLER
REPARATION BOTE AMENDS
REMEDY REWARD DAMAGES
REDRESS REPAIRS REQUITAL
REPARTEE WIT KNACK REPLY
RETORT RIPOST RIPOSTE
BACKCHAT BADINAGE COMEBACK
GIFFGAFF
REPAST BAIT FEED FOOD MEAL
BEVER FEAST TREAT DRINKING
(— BETWEEN MEALS) BEVER
BRUNCH BANQUET
(HASTY —) SNACK
(LIGHT —) BAIT VOID VOIDEE
COLLATION
REPAY MEED QUIT APPAY TALLY
YIELD ACQUIT ANSWER REFUND
RETORT RETURN REWARD REQUIT
RESTORE
REPEAL ANNUL CANCEL RECALL
REVOKE ABANDON ABOLISH
RESCIND REVERSE ABROGATE
DEROGATE DISENACT RENOUNCE
REPEAT SAY ECHO GAIT RAME RA
SHOW TELL DITTO QUOTE RECUR
RENEW RESAY REVIE THRUM
ANSWER RENDER RESUME RETAIL
SECOND DECLINE DIVULGE ITERAT
PRESENT REPLICA DINGDONG
REDOUBLE REHEARSE
(— BY ROTE) PARROT
(— MONOTONOUSLY) CUCKOO
DINGDONG
(— OF PATTERN) GAIT
(— TIRESOMELY) DIN
REPEATED OFTEN CONSTANT
FREQUENT
REPEATEDLY OFT EVERY THRICE
REPEATER GUN RIFLE WATCH
PISTOL FLOATER HOLDOVER
REPEL FEND TURN WARD FENCE
REBUT DEFEND REBEAT REBUFF
REFUSE REJECT REPUGN RESIST
REVOLT DISGUST PELLATE REPU
PROPULSE
REPELLENT DOPE GRIM HARSH
CAMPHOR HATEFUL SQUALID
REPELLING HARD SICKLY
REPENT REW RUE MOURN GRIEV
REGRET REPTANT CREEPING
FORTHINK
REPENTANCE REW RUE PITY RU
RUING REGRET SORROW PENAN
REMORSE
REPERCUSSION ECHO TENOR
RECOIL REPULSE BACKWASH
REPERTORY REP BOOK LIST IND
ARSENAL CATALOG
REPETITION BIS REP COPY ECH
PLOCE REVIE TROLL DILOGY

REPEAT MENTION RECITAL REPRISE
IDENTITY ITERANCE ITERANCY
NEMBUTSU PALILOGY PARROTRY
RECOVERY REDOUBLE REHEARSAL
(— IN REVERSE ORDER) EPANODOS
(— OF HOMOLOGOUS PARTS)
MERISM
(— OF SPEECH FORMS) ROTE
(— OF WORD) ANAPHORA
(UNINSPIRED —) STENCIL
REPHAIM EMIM
REPINE FRET PINE WEAKEN
COMPLAIN
REPINING MURMUR REGRET
PLAINTIVE
REPLACE SWAP SWOP RENEW
REPAY SHIFT STEAD CHANGE
FOLLOW REFUND REMISE REPONE
SUPPLY FRESHEN RESTORE
SUCCEED DISPLACE SUPPLANT
REPLACEMENT CUT ERSATZ
(— FOR HAND) HOOK
(— OF CONSONANT) LENITION
REPLENISH CHUNK REFIT RENEW
SUPPLY NOURISH PERFECT PLENISH
REPLETE RESTORE SUFFICE
REPLETE FAT FULL RIFE SATED
STOUT STUFF FILLED GORGED
IMPLETE COMPLETE HONEYPOT
REPLETION FULTH FULNESS
SURFEIT FULLNESS PLETHORA
SATURITY
REPLICA BIS PUP COPY IDEA CHARM
IMAGE REVIE FACSIMILE
REPLICATION ECHO REPLY ANSWER
REJOINDER
REPLY CAP JAWAB KNACK RESAY
ANSWER REJOIN RETORT RETURN
REPLIAL RESOUND RESPOND
REPARTEE REPLIQUE RESPONSE
SIMILITER
REPORT CRY POP FAME ITEM NOTE
TELL VENT VOTE WORD AUDIT
BRUIT COVER CRACK NOISE REFER
ROUND RUMOR SCALE STATE
STORY VOICE BREEZE CAHIER
CREDIT DELATE DETAIL FINGER
GOSSIP RAPORT RECITE RELATE
RENOWN REPUTE RETURN RUMBLE
SPEECH STEVEN SURVEY THREAP
ACCOUNT HANSARD HEARING
HEARSAY INKLING KHUBBER
NARRATE OPINION PROCESS
RECITAL ADVISORY DECISION
DESCRIBE HEMOGRAM VERBATIM
GRAPEVINE
(— NEWS) COVER
(— OF GUN) CLAP
(— OF INFRACTION) GIG
(— OF PROCEEDINGS) CAHIER
(— OF TIMBER SURVEYOR) CRUISE
(ABSURD —) CANARD
(BELIEVED —) CREDIT
(CASUAL —) FABLE
(COMMON —) CRY FAME SPEECH
(FALSE —) SHAVE CANARD FURPHY
SLANDER
(FLYING —) SOUGH
(HONORABLE —) TONGUE

(LAW —) CASE
(MILITARY —) STATE SITREP
(NEWS —) FLASH SCOOP
(NOISY —) RUMBLE
(OFFICIAL —) HANSARD
(POPULAR —) RUMOR RUMOUR
(PUBLIC —) FAME
(UNFAVORABLE —) SKIN
(UNVERIFIED —) VOICE GRAPEVINE
(VAGUE —) BREEZE
REPORTER LEGMAN PISTOL
CREEPER PRESSMAN STRINGER
(YOUNG —) CUB
REPORTING BEAT COVERAGE
REPOSE RO BED LIE CALM EASE
RELY REST PEACE PLACE POISE
QUIET SLEEP REPAST RECLINE
EASINESS QUIETUDE SERENITY
(— LAZILY) FROWST
REPOSITORY ARK AMBRY CAPSA
DEPOT HOARD VAULT ARMORY
CASKET MUSEUM VESTRY ARCHIVE
CABINET CAPSULE GENIZAH
GRANARY HANAPER SPICERY
MAGAZINE TREASURY SEPULCHER
REPOSOIR REPOSE
REPOSSESS PULL RECOVER
REPREHEND WARN BLAME CHIDE
REBUKE CENSURE REPRISE
REPROVE CRITICIZE
REPREHENSIBLE ILL AMISS
BLAMABLE CRIMINAL CULPABLE
SCABROUS
REPREHENSION BLAME REBUKE
CENSURE OBLOQUY REPROOF
REPRESENT GIVE LIKE LIMN SHOW
TYPE SHADE DEPICT SEMBLE
TYPIFY DISPLAY EXHIBIT FASHION
PICTURE PORTRAY PROTEST
TRADUCE DEFIGURE DESCRIBE
RESEMBLE
(— CONCRETELY) THING
(— IN LANGUAGE) ACT BODY DRAW
ENACT IMAGE SPEAK BLAZON
CLOTHE EMBODY FIGURE SAMPLE
BETOKEN EXPRESS DECIPHER
(— ON STAGE) ACT
REPRESENTATION SUN BUST FORM
ICON IDEA IDOL IKON SHOW SWAG
ANGLE DRAFT FANCY IMAGE INSET
LABEL MEDAL TABUT AVOWAL
BUDDHA EFFIGY FIGURE FLEECE
MODULE OBJECT SCHEMA SCHEME
SKETCH SUNRAY WAYANG
ANATOMY DIORAMA DRAUGHT
DRAWING EPITOME EXPRESS
EXTRACT FOLIAGE MAJESTY
SCENERY TABLEAU BESTIARY
BLAZONRY CREATION EPIPHANY
EXTERIOR IDIOGRAM LIKENESS
TYPORAMA
(— OF SERPENT) BASIL DRAGON
BASILISK
(— OF SHRINE OF HUSAIN) TABUT
(— OF VISION) AISLING
(DIPLOMATIC —) DEMARCHE
(FACSIMILE —) TYPORAMA
(FAINT —) SHADOW
(FUNERAL —) CADAVER

(GRAPHIC —) CHART BISECT
(HERALDIC —) LEOPARD LIONCEL
(MENTAL —) FANCY IMAGE
(MINIATURE —) MODEL
(SYMBOLIC —) ALLEGORY
REPRESENTATIVE REP FAIR TYPE
AGENT ENVOY VAKIL ASSIGN
COMMON DEPUTY EMBLEM LEDGER
SAMPLE VAKEEL BURGESS GRIEVER
TRIBUNE TYPICAL DECURION
DELEGATE EMISSARY EXPONENT
FIELDMAN GASTALDO INTIMATE
OBSERVER SALESMAN SPECIMEN
(— OF ATMOSPHERE) AERIAL
(MANUFACTURER'S —) BLOCKMAN
(PL.) COMMONS
REPRESS CURB HUSH BLUNT BRIDE
CHAIN CHECK CHOKE CRUSH DAUNT
DROWN QUELL SQUAT COERCE
DEADEN REBUKE STIFLE CONTROL
DEPRESS INHIBIT REPRIME SILENCE
SWALLOW COMPRESS RESTRAIN
RESTRICT RETRENCH REVOCATE
STRANGLE SUPPRESS WITHHOLD
REPRESSED SULLEN STIFLED
REPRIEVE DELAY GRACE ESCAPE
REPRISE RESPITE SUSPEND
POSTPONE
REPRIMAND WIG BAWL CALL CHEW
JACK SKIN SLAP SLON SNEB SNIB
TASK CHECK CREED SLATE SLOAN
SPANK TARGE CARPET EARFUL
REBUKE CENSURE CHAPTER
LECTURE REPROOF REPROVE
DRESSING
REPRINT COPY DEPRINT OFFPRINT
REIMPOSE TAUCHNITZ
REPRISAL PRIZE REPRISE REQUITAL
RECAPTION
REPROACH ILL TAX BLOT GIBE JIBE
LACK NOSE NOTE SLUR SPOT TEEN
TWIT WITE ABUSE BLAME BRAID
CHIDE SCOLD SHEND TAUNT WHITE
BISMER INFAMY REBUKE REVILE
UPCAST VILIFY CENSURE CONDEMN
REPROOF REPROVE SLANDER
UMBRAID UPBRAID WITHNIM
DISHONOR REDARGUE REVILING
REPROACHFUL BITTER ABUSIVE
SHAMEFUL
REPROBATE HARD LOST SCAMP
DISOWN RASCAL REJECT SINNER
ABANDON CENSURE CORRUPT
EXCLUDE REPROVE DEPRAVED
DISALLOW HARDENED SCALAWAG
SKALAWAG
REPRODUCE BUD HIT COPY BREED
SPORE RECITE REPEAT PORTRAY
MULTIPLY REFIGURE REMEMBER
REPRODUCTION CAST COPY REVI
IMAGE ECTYPE RECALL STEREO
EDITION ELECTRO EXOGAMY
FISSION REPLICA REVIVAL APOMIXIS
BLOCKOUT GAMOGAMY HOMOGAMY
LIKENESS
(— OF SOUND) AUDIO
REPROOF PROD RATE BLAME
CHECK LESSON REBUKE CHIDING
LECTURE SETDOWN JOBATION

REPROACH REPROVAL SCOLDING TAXATION JAWBATION

REPROVE TAP BAWL FLAY FRIE JOBE RATE SNIB TRIM BLAME CHECK CHIDE CRAWL SCOLD SHEND SHENT SNEAP BERATE CHASTE REBUKE REFORM SCHOOL THREAT CENSURE CONDEMN CORRECT IMPROVE LECTURE UPBRAID WITHNIM ADMONISH CHASTISE REDARGUE REPROACH UNDERNIM WITHTAKE

REPTILE LOW MEAN WORM GUANA SNAKE GAVIAL LIZARD MOLOCH TURTLE CRAWLER CREEPER DIAPSID GHARIAL PROTEUS SAURIAN SERPENT TUATARA BASILISK CREEPING CYNODONT DINOSAUR GALESAUR MESOSAUR MOSASAUR PLIOSAUR STEGOMUS SYNAPSID TORTOISE ALLIGATOR CROCODILE

REPTILIAN HERPETIC

REPUBLIC STATE SOVIET POBLACHT
(FRENCH —) MARIANNE
(IDEAL —) ICARIA
(IMAGINARY —) OCEANA

REPUBLICAN RED QUID STALWART SANSCULOT

REPUDIATE DEFY ABJURE DISOWN RECANT REJECT DECLINE DISAVOW DISCARD DIVORCE RETRACT DISCLAIM DISVOUCH RENOUNCE

REPUDIATING NAKIR

REPUGNANCE ENMITY HATRED HORROR DISGUST DISLIKE DISTASTE LOATHING

REPUGNANT ALIEN DIRTY ADVERSE HATEFUL OPPOSED INIMICAL OPPOSITE REPULSIVE

REPULSE FOIL ROUT RUSH CHECK FLING REBUT REFEL REPEL SMEAR DEFEAT DENIAL REBUFF REBUTE REFUSE REJECT

REPULSIVE COLD DAIN EVIL LOTH UGLY VILE LOATH GREASY LAIDLY FULSOME HATEFUL LOATHLY SQUALID SCABROUS UNHONEST

REPULSION UG DISLIKE AVERSION

REPUTABLE GOOD HONEST WORTHY CREDIBLE ESTIMABLE

REPUTATION REP FAME LOSE NAME NOTE PASS GLORY HONOR IZZAT NOISE RUMOR SAVOR VOICE CREDIT ESTEEM RECORD RENOWN SHADOW LAURELS OPINION RESPECT WORSHIP STANDING
(EVIL —) INFAMY
(GOOD —) STANDING

REPUTE FAME ODOR RANK WORD NOISE SAVOR THINK RECKON REGARD STATUS OPINION RESPECT WORSHIP ESTIMATE JUDGMENT POSITION
(ILL —) SLANDER

REPUTED DIT PUTATIVE

REQUEST ASK BEG CALL PLEA PRAY SEEK SUIT TELL WISH CLAIM LIBEL QUEST YEARN APPEAL BEHEST

DEMAND DESIRE DIRECT ENCORE INVITE MOTION BESPEAK COMMAND ENTREAT INQUIRY REQUIRE SOLICIT ENTREATY INSTANCE PETITION ROGATION
(— FOR HELP) SOS
(STRONG —) DUN DEMAND

REQUIEM HYMN MASS REST DIRGE PEACE QUIET REPOSE REQUIN

REQUIN SHARK TOMMY

REQUIRE ASK HAVE LACK NEED TAKE WANT CLAIM CRAVE EXACT FORCE GAVEL COMPEL DEMAND DEPEND DESIRE ENJOIN ENTAIL EXPECT GOVERN MISTER OBLIGE BEHOOVE DICTATE INVOLVE SOLICIT

REQUIRED DUE SET SUPPOSED

REQUIREMENT CALL NEED LEGAL ORDER BEHEST DEMAND NECESSITY
(PL.) EXIGENCE EXIGENCY

REQUISITE DUE NEED NEEDY VITAL NEEDFUL ESSENTIAL NECESSARY

REQUISITION ORDER DEMAND INDENT EMBARGO REQUEST

REQUITAL WAR APPAY MERIT REPAY SERVE TALLY YIELD ACQUIT DEFRAY REWARD GRATIFY PAYMENT REVENGE CONSIDER FORYIELD REPRISAL

RERAILER DIAMOND

REREAD DOUBLE

RERECORD DUB

REREDOS SCREEN BRAZIER DRAPERY RETABLO FIREBACK REARDOSS

REREMOUSE BAT

RES POINT THING MATTER SUBJECT

RESCIND LIFT ANNUL CANCEL REMOVE REPEAL REVOKE ABOLISH RETRACT RETREAT ABROGATE

RESCRIPT EDICT ORDER DECREE LETTER EPISTLE

RESCUE RID FREE HELP REDD SAVE BORROW RANSOM REDEEM RESKEW SUCCOR WARISH DELIVER RECLAIM RECOVER RELEASE SALVAGE DELIVERY LIBERATE RECOURSE

RESEARCH ARBEIT SEARCH ENQUIRY INQUIRY

RESECT EXCISE

RESEDA LEEK MENNUET

RESEMBLANCE SWAP SIMILE ANALOGY AFFINITY LIKENESS PARALLEL VICINITY
(DIM HAZY —) BLY
(SLIGHT —) BLUSH

RESEMBLE AGREE BRAID FAVOR IMAGE LIKEN APPEAR DEPICT FIGURE SEMBLE COMPARE IMITATE PORTRAY ASSEMBLE SIMULATE

RESEMBLING LIKE SAME SEMBLE SIMILAR SEMBLANT
(— AN EGG) OVULARIAN
(— COMB) PECTINAL
(— GOOSE) ANSERINE
(— HORSE) EQUOID
(— IVORY) EBURNEAN EBURNOUS EBURNEOID
(— SALT) HALOID

(— STAR) STELLATE
(— WALL) MURAL

RESENT HATE MEAN INDIGN MALIGN STOMACH SUGGEST

RESENTFUL HARD HURT BITTER ENVIOUS JEALOUS STOMACHY

RESENTMENT HURT DEPIT PIQUE SNUFF SPITE CHOLER ENMITY GRUDGE HATRED MALICE RANCOR DISDAIN DUDGEON OFFENCE OFFENSE STOMACH UMBRAGE JEALOUSY HEARTBURN

RESERVATION DIBS SALVO SPACE SAVING UNLESS BOOKING CAUTION KEEPING PROVISO RESERVE FORPRISE RESERVAL
(MENTAL —) SALVO SCRUPLE

RESERVE BOOK CAVE FUND HOJU HOLD KEEP SALT SAVE SPARE BACKUP NICETY SEPONE SEPOSE TRIARY BACKLOG CAUTION CONTROL DIGNITY SEPOSIT SHYNESS TENENUE COLDNESS DISTANCE FALLBACK FORPRISE IMMODEST WITHHOLD STOCKPILE
(HOME —S) LANDSTURM
(MILITARY —) HOJU YOBI TRIARY TRIARII
(MONETARY —) CUSHION
(PL.) FAT KOKUMIN STRENGTH

RESERVED COY DRY SHY COLD UNCO ALOOF CHARY SAVED BOOKED DEMURE MODEST SILENT STANCH COSTIVE DISTANT RETIRED STRANGE RETICENT RETIRING STANDOFF WITHHELD
(— FOR ROYAL USE) KHASS
(NOT —) COMMON

RESERVOIR DAM BOSS FONT KEEP LAKE PENT SUMP TANK BASIN FOUNT STANK STORE CENOTE SIPHON SOURCE SYPHON CISTERN CLEARER FAVISSA FOREBAY IMPOUND PISCINA RECEIPT AFTERBAY DEPOSITO FOUNTAIN MAGAZINE STANDAGE
(— OF WEATHERGLASS) STAGNUM

RESET HELP ABODE ALTER RECEPT RESORT SUCCOR RECEIPT REPLAN SHARPEN WELCOME

RESIDE BIG WIN BIGG HOME LIVE STAY TELD WONT ABIDE DWELL LODGE REMAIN CONSIST SOJOURN HABITATE
(— TEMPORARILY) LIE STOP

RESIDENCE DUN WON DOON HALL HOME SEAT SEMI STAY WENE WON ABODE COURT DAIRI DEMUR HOUS MAHAL MANSE YAMUN BIDING DUKERY ELYSEE HOSTEL MANOIR TENSER DEANERY DROSTDY EMBASSY SOJOURN CURATAGE DOMICILE DWELLING LEGATION RESIANCE RESIANCY RESIDUUM SEDIMENT SETTLING
(— FOR STUDENTS) INN
(— OF ARCHBISHOP) PALACE
(— OF CHIEF OF VILLAGE) TATA
(— OF ECCLESIASTIC) MANSE DEANERY CURATAGE

(— OF FRENCH PRESIDENTS) ELYSEE

(— OF MANDARIN) YAMEN YAMUN

(— OF MIKADO) DAIRI

(— OF PRIEST) CONVENTO

(— OF SOVEREIGN) PALACE

(— OF SULTAN) SERAGLIO

(FORTIFIED —) DUN

(HILL —) RATH

(OFFICIAL TURKISH —) KONAK

(RURAL —) SEAT FARMSTEAD

(SUMMER —) MAHAL

(TEMPORARY —) STAY

RESIDENT GER FIXED LEGER LIVER INMATE LEDGER STABLE CITIZEN DENIZEN DWELLER PRESENT RESIANT RESIDER RESTING HABITANT INHERENT KAMAAINA MINISTER

(— AT A UNIVERSITY) GREMIALE

(— OF HAWAII) KAMAAINA

(— OF WEST. AUSTRALIA) GROPER

(ALIEN —) GER METIC

(CHINESE — OF TIBET) AMBAN

(FOREIGN-BORN —) ALIEN

(OLD —) STANDARD

RESIDUAL RELICT REMANIE REMANENT

RESIDUE ASH DREG FOOT GUNK HEEL LAFE LAVE LEES REST SILT SLAG UNIT MAZUT SHARD SHERD BEGASS BORING BOTTOM GRUFFS RELICS BAGASSE CINDERS REMAINS HARDHEAD LEAVINGS LEFTOVER REMANENT RESIDUUM SEMICOKE TAILINGS

(— FROM FAT) CRAP

(— FROM OLIVES) SANZA

(— FROM REFINING TIN) HARDHEAD

(— IN STILL) BOTTOM BOTTOMS

(— OF COAL) COKE SEMICOKE

(— OF COKE) BREEZE

(— OF COMBUSTION) ASH

(— OF HONEYCOMB) SLUMGUM

(— OF PETROLEUM) MAZUT

(— OF SHINGLES) SPALT

(FRIABLE —) CALX

(INSOLUBLE —) MARC

(PL.) TANKAGE

RESIDUUM TAIL BOTTOM DEPOSIT RESIDUE SEDIMENT

RESIGN QUIT DEMIT FORGO REMIT YIELD PERMIT SUBMIT ABANDON COMMEND DELIVER FORGIVE ABDICATE RENOUNCE

RESIGNATION PATIENCE DEMISSION SURRENDER

RESILIENCE GIVE LIFE BOUNCE RECOIL SPRING REBOUND BUOYANCY

RESILIENT BOUNCY SUPPLE WHIPPY ELASTIC SPRINGY FLEXIBLE

RESIN ALK LAC BALM BATU BREA ALKYD AMBER ANIME COPAL CUMAR ELEMI EPOXY GUGAL GUGUL KAURI PITCH ROSEL ROSET SIRUP SYRUP ANTIAR BINDER CHARAS DAMMAR GOOGUL GUACIN MARTIN MASTIC STORAX TAMANU

ACOUCHI ACRYLIC AMBRITE BENZOIN BISABOL DERRIDE FLUAVIL GAMBOGE SAGAPEN SHELLAC ALKITRAN ALMACIGA BAKELITE BDELLIUM CACHIBOU CANNABIN COLOPHAN EUOSMITE FORMVAIL GALAGALA GALLIPOT GEDANITE GUAIACUM MALAPAHO MELAMINE OPOPANAX SANDARAC SCAMMONY

(— DRAWN FROM TREES) CHIP

(— FROM HEMP) CHARAS

(— FROM NORWAY SPRUCE) THUS

(— OF FIR TREE) BLOB

(FOSSIL —) AMBER AMBRITE HARTITE GEDANITE GLESSITE RETINITE

(GRADE OF —) SORTS

(GUM —) GUGUL LASER MYRRH ANTIAR BISABOL GAMBOGE BDELLIUM

(NARCOTIC —) CHARAS CHURUS

(TURPENTINE —) ALK GALIPOT

RESINOID ALNUIN HELONIN LOBELIN ASCLEPIN CERASEIN CHELONIN TRILLIIN

RESINOUS ROSETY ROSETTY

RESIST BUCK FACE STAY REPEL STAND DEFEND IMPUGN OPPOSE REPUGN WITHER CONTEST DISPUTE GAINSAY KNUCKLE RESERVE WITHSET OUTSTAND

(— AUTHORITY) REBEL DEFORCE

(— SEPARATION) ATTRACT

RESISTANCE DRAG LOAD OHMAGE REBUFF WITHER BALLAST ANTITYPY BLOCKAGE FASTNESS FRICTION HARDNESS OBSTACLE SEDITION

(— OF COTTON FIBERS) DRAG

(— OF KEYS) ACTION

(— THAT EXPLOSIVE MUST OVERCOME) BURDEN BURTHEN

(— TO ATTACK) DEFENCE DEFENSE

(— TO CHANGE) INERTIA

(— TO COLOR CHANGE) FASTNESS

(— TO SLIPPING) BOND

RESISTANT HARD STOUT STABILE STUBBORN

(— TO CHANGE) FAST STICKY

RESISTING OBSTANT RELUCTANT

RESISTOR BLEEDER REOSTAT DIVERTOR RHEOSTAT

RESOLUTE BOLD FIRM GRIM BRAVE FIXED HARDY MANLY STERN STIFF STOUT GRITTY MANFUL PLUCKY STANCH STEADY STUFFY STURDY ANIMOSE ANIMOUS DECIDED CONSTANT FAITHFUL INTREPID POSITIVE STALWART STUBBORN UNSHAKEN

RESOLUTELY TALLY FIRMLY STOUTLY

RESOLUTION VOW SAND THEW NERVE PARTY PLUCK POINT STARCH ACUERDO BESLUIT CENSURE COURAGE MANHEAD MANHOOD PURPOSE RESOLVE ANALYSIS DECISION DIERESIS ENACTURE STRENGTH

RESOLVE ACT BEND MELT SOIL UNDO LAPSE RELAX SALVE SOLVE SOYLE UNTIE VOUCH ADJUST ADVICE ASSOIL DECIDE DECREE FACTOR INCIDE REDUCE SETTLE STEVEN ABSOLVE ANALYZE APPOINT BETHINK CONSULT PURPOSE CONCLUDE DISSOLVE UNRIDDLE UNTANGLE

(— GRAMMATICALLY) PARSE

(— INTO ELEMENTS) ANALYSE ANALYZE

RESOLVED BENT BOUND INTENT INTENSE RESOLUTE

(HALF —) GOOD

RESONANCE BODY EMPATHY RAPPORT RESOUND SYNTONY TYMPANY SONORITY VIBRANCY

RESONANT BIG BRASS RINGY OROTUND RINGING SILVERY VIBRANT PLANGENT SONORANT SONOROUS SOUNDFUL SOUNDING

RESORT GO RUN SPA BEAT DOME HOWF LIDO SEEK TEEM TOUR TURN CAUSE FRAME HAUNT HOWFF JOINT RECUR RESET VISIT ESCORT FINISH REPAIR RETURN REVERT THRONG COMPANY PIMLICO RECOURSE RESOURCE TEETOTUM

(— TO DEVIOUS METHODS) FINAGLE

(— TO) SEEK

(DISREPUTABLE —) KEN DIVE

(LOW —) KEN DIVE STEW SPITAL

(MEANS OF —) REFUGE

(WORKINGMEN'S —) TEETOTUM

RESOUND DIN DUN ECHO PEAL RING SOUND REECHO EXPLODE REBOUND RESPEAK

RESOUNDING BRASS REVERB EMPHATIC FORCEFUL RESONANT RUMOROUS

(— WITH TALK) ABUZZ

RESOURCE WON BOOT FUND WONE MEANS SHIFT REFUGE RESORT STOPGAP PURCHASE

(PL.) EASE FOND GAIN FUNDS MEANS SINEW FACULTY FOISONS PURCHASE STRENGTH

RESOURCEFUL APT FENDY SHARP SMART CLEVER FACILE SHIFTY PLANFUL

RESOURCEFULNESS SENSE SHIFT AGILITY

RESPECT ORE WAY DUTY FACE HEED HORE LOOK MARK DEFER DULIA FRONT HONOR IZZAT PARTY VALUE ASPECT BEHALF DETAIL ESTEEM HALLOW HOMAGE NOTICE REGARD CONCERN OBSERVE RESPITE SUSPECT TASHRIF WORSHIP CONSIDER HABITUDE RELATION VENERATE

(PL.) DEVOIR

RESPECTABLE GOOD SMUG DOUCE DECENT PROPER FRUSANT CULOTTIC

RESPECTFUL AWFUL CIVIL CAREFUL DUTEOUS DUTIFUL HEEDFUL REVERENT

RESPIRATION SIGH EUPNEA
ANAPNEA DYSPNEA EUPNOEA
ROARING GRUNTING
RESPIRATOR MUZZLE CUIRASS
RESPIRE BLOW LIVE REST EXHALE
REVIVE BREATHE SNUFFLE SUSPIRE
RESPITE SOB REST STAY TRUE
DELAY PAUSE BARLEY BREATH
LAYOFF REGARD REMISE LEISURE
RESPECT INTERVAL REPRIEVE
SURCEASE
RESPLENDENCE GLORY FULGENCE
FULGENCY SPLENDOR
RESPLENDENT LUCID SHEEN
BRIGHT GILDED ORIENT SILVER
AUREATE SHINING GLORIOUS
GORGEOUS LUSTROUS SPLENDID
SUNSHINY
RESPOND REACT REPLY ANSWER
RETURN TRISAGION
(— TO LURE) STOOL
RESPONDENT ANSWERER APPELLEE
RESPONSE AMEN ECHO CHORD
REPLY SNAFF ANSWER EARFUL
VOLLEY INTROIT RESPOND
ANTIPHON BEHAVIOR INSTINCT
REACTION REANSWER
(— OF KEYS) ACTION
(— OF SHIP) STEERING
RESPONSIBILITY BALL CARE DUTY
ONUS WITE BLAME GUILT CHARGE
RESPONSIBLE GOOD SOLID DIRECT
LIABLE AMENABLE
RESPONSION REPLY ANSWER
(PL.) SMALLS
RESPONSIVE OPEN SOFT WARM
GUILTY MUTUAL SUPPLE TENDER
MEETING AMENABLE SENSIBLE
(— TO BEAUTY) ESTHETIC
(NOT —) IMMUNE
RESPONSIVENESS TOUCH FEELING
RESPONSORY ANTHEM LIBERA
GRADUAL RESPOND
REST BED LAY LIE SET SIT SOB
BASE BLOW CALM CAMP EASE
HANG HEEL LAIR LAVE LEAN LIOS
LISS PROP RELY RIDE RUST STAY
STOP COUCH FOUND LEATH PAUSE
PEACE POISE QUIET RENEW ROOST
SLEEP SPELL STAND TRUST WREST
ANCHOR BOTTOM FAUCRE FEWTER
GROUND INSIST REMAIN REPOSE
SETTLE SIESTA STEADY UNTIRE
ADHARMA BALANCE BREATHE
CAESURA CLARION COMFORT
GALLOWS NOONING RECLINE
REFRESH REMNANT REQUIEM
RESIDUE RESPITE SILENCE
SLUMBER SOJOURN SUFFLUE
SUPPORT SURPLUS AKINESIS
INTERVAL QUIETUDE STANDOFF
VACATION
(— FOR SPEAR OR LANCE) QUEUE
FAUCRE FEWTER
(— FOR SUPPORT) ABUT
(— FOR TYMPAN) GALLOWS
(— HORSE) WIND
(— IDLY) SLUG
(— LAZILY) FROWST

(— ON PLANER) SIDEHEAD
(— ON SUPPORT) BOTTOM
(— UPRIGHT) STAND
(HALF —) MINIM SOSPIRO
(LATHE —) STEADY
(LEG — ON SADDLE) CRUTCH
(MUSKET —) GAFFLE
(NOONDAY —) NAP SIESTA
(QUARTER —) SOSPIRO
RESTATE REHASH
RESTATEMENT HASH SUMMARY
RESTAURANT CAFE DINER GRILL
HOUSE PLACE BISTRO BUFFET
EATERY AUTOMAT BEANERY
CABARET CANTEEN OSTERIA
TEAROOM HIDEAWAY BRASSERIE
CHOPHOUSE TRATTORIA
(— KEEPER) BISTRO TRAITEUR
RESTFUL COOL SOFT QUIET PLACID
EASEFUL RELAXED SOOTHFUL
TRANQUIL
RESTHARROW WHIN CAMMOCK
SITFAST LANDWHIN
RESTHOUSE KHAN SERAI AMBALAM
CHHATRI KHANKAH
RESTING DORMANT
RESTING PLACE (ALSO SEE
RESTHOUSE) FORM GIST GITE
STAGE CHHATRI DHARMSALA
RESTITUTION AMENDS RETURN
RECOVERY
RESTIVE BALKY FUDGY ITCHY
RESTY RUSTY FIDGETY UNRESTY
UNWAYED CONTRARY INACTIVE
RESTLESS SKITTISH SLUGGISH
STUBBORN UNWIELDY
RESTLESS ANTSY FIKIE FUDGY
ITCHY FITFUL HAUNTY HECTIC
ROVING UNEASY AGITATO ERETHIC
FIDGETY FLIGHTY FRETFUL INQUIET
RAMPLER RAMPLOR RESTIVE
TEWSOME TOSSING UNQUIET
UNRESTY VARIANT WAKEFUL
FEVERISH FEVEROUS STEERING
(— FLYCATCHER) GRINDER
RESTLESSNESS STIR FIDGET
UNREST DISQUIET JACTATION
RESTORATION REPAIR RETURN
RENEWAL RESTORE REVIVAL
EXCHANGE RECOVERY REMITTER
RESTORAL
RESTORATIVE ACOPON BALSAMIC
SALUTARY SANATIVE ANALEPTIC
RESTORE FIX CURE HEAL AMEND
BLOCK COVER REDUB REFER
RENEW REPAY STORE YIELD
ASTORE DOCTOR RECALL REDEEM
REFORM REFUND RELATE RENDER
REVERT REVIVE CONVERT ENSTORE
INPAINT REBUILD RECLAIM
RECOVER RECRUIT REFOUND
REFRESH REPLACE REVOLVE
DECOHERE REANSWER RESTITUE
RETRIEVE
(— CONFIDENCE) REASSURE
(— TO CIVIL RIGHTS) INLAW
(— TO HEALTH) CURE HEAL MEND
(— TO ORDER) STILL
RESTRAIN DAM BATE BIND BOLT

BUCK COOP CRIB CURB DAMP GRAB
GYVE HEAD HEFT KEEP REIN SHUT
SINK SNEB SNIB SNUB STAY STEM
STOP STOW CHAIN CHECK COART
CRAMP DETER GUARD LEASH MINCE
REPEL SHUNT SOBER STILL STINT
TRASH ARREST BOTTLE BRIDLE
CHASTE COERCE DETAIN ENJOIN
FETTER FORBID GOVERN HALTER
HAMPER HINDER KENNEL OBLIGE
REBUKE RETAIN RETIRE REVOKE
STIFLE STRAIN TEMPER ABRIDGE
CHASTEN COHIBIT CONFINE
CONTAIN CONTROL ENCHAIN
EXCLUDE INHIBIT INJUNCT QUALIFY
RECLAIM REFRAIN REPRESS
RETRACT SHACKLE SNAFFLE
SWADDLE BULLDOZE COMPESCE
COMPRESS HANDCUFF IMPRISON
RESTRICT SIDELINE WITHDRAW
WITHHOLD
(— BY FEAR) OVERAWE
(— HAWK'S WING) BRAIL
(— MOTION) SNUB
RESTRAINED SOBER CHASTE
SEVERE ASHAMED DISCREET
RESERVED
RESTRAINT BIT BEND CLOG CURB
HEFT STAY STOP CHECK CRAMP
FORCE LEASH SPARE STENT STINT
ARREST BRIDLE DURESS FETTER
STAYER AWEBAND BONDAGE
CONTROL DURANCE EMBARGO
MANACLE RESERVE SNAFFLE
TRAMMEL SOBRIETY
(— OF GOODS) HOCK
RESTRICT TIE CURB HOLD BOUND
CHAIN COART FENCE HEDGE STINT
THIRL COARCT COERCE CORRAL
CORSET ENTAIL HAMPER NARROW
ASTRICT COHIBIT QUALIFY REPRESS
SCANTLE SWADDLE CONTRACT
DEROGATE DIMINISH RESTRAIN
STRAITEN
(— MEANING) MODIFY
RESTRICTED CLOSE LOCAL CLOSED
FINITE NARROW STRAIT STRICT
OBLIGATE
RESTRICTION STENT STINT BURDEN
DENIAL BARRIER CONFINE RESERVE
BLACKOUT CABOTAGE
(PL.) BARS SWADDLE
RESTRICTIVE SEVERE BINDING
STYPTIC COACTIVE LIMITARY
LIMITING CONFINING
RESTY LAZY RESTIVE INACTIVE
INDOLENT SLUGGISH
RESULT GO END OUT ECHO FALL
FAVE GROW RISE TAKE BACON
BRING CHILD ENSUE EVENT FRUIT
FUDGE ISSUE PROOF EFFECT
EFFORT ENDING FINISH FOLLOW
GROWTH RECOIL REVERT SEQUEL
SPRING UPCOME UPSHOT ENTRAIN
FINDING OUTCOME PROCEED
REBOUND REDOUND SUCCEED
SUCCESS FRUITAGE SEQUENCE
(— FAVORABLY) SUCCEED
(— FROM) SUE

(ALGEBRAIC —) DUAL EXPANSION
(AS A —) AGAIN
(INCONCLUSIVE —) DOGFALL
(INEVITABLE —) NEMESIS
(PATHOLOGICAL —S) ALCOHOLISM
(REWARDING —) HAY
(SECONDARY —) SEQUELA
(PL.) AFTERINGS
RESULTANT CONCEPT OUTCOME
PROGENY
RESUME RENEW REOPEN RECOVER
SUMMARY CONTINUE PURLICUE
REASSUME RENOVATE REOCCUPY
(PL.) EXCERPTA
RESURRECTION RISE RIST UPRIST
REBIRTH REVIVAL
RESURRECTION PLANT FERNWORT
RESUSCITATE REVIVE QUICKEN
SUSCITE REVIVIFY
RESUSCITATION KATSU RENEWAL
REVIVAL
RET RAIT RATE SOAK DEWROT
RETAIL REGRATE HUCKSTER
(— STORE) WAREHOUSE
RETAILER DEALER CLOTHIER
HUCKSTER
RETAIN HAVE HOLD KEEP SAVE
CATCH ATHOLD CONTAIN RESERVE
CONTINUE MAINTAIN PRESERVE
(— MOMENTUM) DRIFT
RETAINER FOOL HEWE LACKEY
MENIAL RIBALD SEQUEL YEOMAN
HOBBLER HUSCARL JACKMAN
LACQUEY PANDOUR SERVANT
TRAVERS EMPLOYEE FOLLOWER
HENCHMAN MYRMIDON BURKUNDAZ
(JAPANESE —) SAMURAI
(PL.) FOLK
RETALIATE REPAY AVENGE RETORT
REQUITE
RETALIATION QUITS MARQUE
TALION REPRISAL REQUITAL
(MAKE —) TURN
(VINDICTIVE —) REVENGE
RETALIATORY COUNTER
RETARD LAG CHOP DAMP DRAG
SLOW STEM BRAKE DEFER DELAY
ELONG TARDY TARRY THROW
TRASH BACKEN BELATE DEADEN
DETAIN HINDER INHIBIT SLACKEN
ENCUMBER OBSTRUCT PROTRACT
RESTRAIN
RETARDANT (FIRE —) BORAX
RETARDATION LAG DRAG DELAY
RETARDED DARK BEHIND LAGGED
SIMPLE OVERAGE
RETARDING LENTANDO
RETCH GAG BOKE KECK HEAVE
REACH VOMIT KECKLE RECCHE
STRAIN
RETEM JUNIPER
RETENTION MEMORY RETAIN
HOLDING KEEPING RETINUE
ETIARIUS RETIARY GLADIATOR
ETICENCE RESERVE SECRECY
RESTRAINT
ETICENT DARK SNUG SECRET
SILENT MIMMOUD SPARING
ETICENTLY HEIMLICH

RETICULATE MESHED NETTED
RETICULE BAG CABAS SACHET
WORKBAG CARRYALL RIDICULE
RETICULUM NET MITOME NETWORK
MATTULLA
RETINOL CODOL
RETINOPHORE VITRELLA
RETINUE CREW GING PORT ROUT
SUIT TAIL MEINY SUITE TIRED TRAIN
FAMILY REPAIR RETAIN COMPANY
CORTEGE SOWARRY EQUIPAGE
TENDANCE BODYGUARD
(— OF CAVALRY) SOWARRY
(VILLAINOUS —) BLACKGUARD
RETIRE GO GET DRAW GIVE AVOID
LEAVE MICHE REBUT DEPART
LOCATE RECALL RECEDE RECESS
RECOIL SHRINK SURVEY PENSION
REGRADE RETRACT RETREAT
WITHDRAW
(— IGNOMINIOUSLY) SLINK
RETIRED QUIET SECRET DEVIOUS
OBSCURE OUTGONE PRIVATE
SECLUSE SHADOWY ABSTRUSE
EMERITUS
(— FROM PLAY) DOWN
RETIREMENT SHADE RECESS
SECESS PRIVACY PRIVATE RETREAT
FIRESIDE SOLITUDE
RETIRING SHY NESH TIMID DEMURE
MODEST FUGIENT RESERVED
UMBRATIC
(— ROOM) RECAMERA
RETORT MOT QUIP RISE SNAP VENY
QUIRK REPAY REPLY ANSWER
REGEST RETURN RIPOST BOMBOLA
CORNUTE CRUSHER PELICAN
REFLECT SQUELCH BACKWORD
BLIZZARD COMEBACK MAGAZINE
RECEIVER REPARTEE
(CURT —) SNAPHANCE
(GROUP OF —S) SETTING
(WITTY —) KNACK
RETRACE RECALL FLYBACK
RETREAT UNTREAD BACKTRACK
RETRACT BACK UNSAY ABJURE
DISOWN RECALL RECANT RECEDE
REVOKE SHRINK UNLOCK RESCIND
RETREAT SWALLOW PALINODE
RENOUNCE WITHDRAW
RETRACTED INNER
RETRACTION PALINODE PALINODY
RETREAT DEN DOME DROP FADE
GIVE NEST ROUT ARBOR AVOID
BOWER NICHE QUAIL QUIET SHADE
START ASHRAM ASYLUM BACKUP
CASTLE RECEDE RECESS REFUGE
RETIRE REVOLT CABINET DESCEND
PRIVACY RETIRAL RETRACT
SHELTER ANABASIS CRAWFISH
DISMARCH FALLBACK FASTNESS
NESTLING RECOURSE RECULADE
SOLITUDE STAMPEDE WITHDRAW
CREEPHOLE KATABASIS
(— FOR FISH) HOD
(RELIGIOUS —) ASRAM ASHRAM
(SECURE —) STRENGTH
RETRENCH OMIT EXCISE LESSEN

REDUCE ABRIDGE CURTAIL
SHORTEN
RETRENCHMENT CUT RAMPART
EXCISION RETIRADE LESSENING
RETRIBUTION PAY RETURN
REWARD WISSEL MANNAIA PENALTY
REVENGE REQUITAL
RETRIEVE SHACK RECALL RECURE
REGAIN REPAIR RESCUE REVIVE
CORRECT RECOVER RESTORE
SALVAGE
RETRIEVER FINDER GUNDOG
LABRADOR WATERRUG
RETROFLEX DEMAL CORONAL
CEREBRAL INVERTED REFLEXED
RETROGRADE RECEDE RETRAL
DECLINE INVERSE OPPOSED
REGREDE RETREAT BACKWARD
DECADENT REARWARD WITHDRAW
RETROGRESS SINK REGRESS
BACKSLIDE
RETROGRESSION SINK REGRESS
RETREAT FALLBACK
RETUND DULL TURN BLUNT REFUTE
RETURN EBB GET COME TURN VAIL
RECUR REFER REPAY REPLY VISIT
YIELD AIRWAY ANSWER HOMING
REMISE RENDER REPAIR REPASS
REPORT RESORT RETIRE RETORT
RETOUR REVERT CLEANUP
PAYMENT REBOUND REDOUND
REFLECT REPRISE REQUITE
RESTORE REVENUE ATTOURNE
DIVIDEND ELECTION EPANODOS
FEEDBACK REACCESS REANSWER
RECOURSE RECOVERY REDITION
(— FROM DEATH) ARISE
(— OF MERCHANDISE) COMEBACK
(— TO ZERO) FLYBACK
(GROUNDED —) BOND
(TENNIS —) GET BOAST
RETURNING REDIENT REMEANT
REDITION
REUNION COLLEGE HERENIGING
(— WITH BRAHMA) NIRVANA
REUNITE RALLY REUNE REJOIN
RECONCILE
REVEAL BID BARE BLAB HINT JAMB
KNOW OPEN SHOW TELL WRAY
BREAK EXERT SPEAK SPLIT UNRIP
UNTOP UTTER YIELD ACCUSE
APPEAR BETRAY BEWRAY DESCRY
DETECT EVINCE IMPART OSTEND
PATEFY SPRING UNHELE UNLOCK
UNMASK UNVEIL UNWRAP BESPEAK
CLARIFY CONFESS DEVELOP
DISPLAY DIVULGE UNCLOAK
UNCOVER UNSHALE UNTRUSS
DECIPHER DISCLOSE DISCOVER
INDICATE MANIFEST UNBURDEN
UNSHADOW UNSHROUD
(— BY SIGNS) EXHIBIT
(— SECRETS) BABBLE
(— UNINTENTIONALLY) BETRAY
REVEILLE LEVET ROUSE SIGNAL
TRAVALLY
REVEL JOY MASK RANT RIOT BIZLE
FEAST GLOAT GLORY WATCH
BEZZLE FROLIC GAVALL SPLORE

TRESCA WALLOW WANTON
CAROUSE DELIGHT ROISTER
TRESCHE CAROUSAL DOMINEER
FESTIVAL WITHDRAW
(PL.) REVELRY
REVELATION TORA TORAH EXPOSE
ORACLE REVEAL BATHKOL
BATHQOL SHOWING GIVEAWAY
OVERTURE
(— OF GOD'S WILL) LAW
(SUDDEN —) KICK
REVELER GREEK RANTER RIOTER
FRANION PIERROT ROISTER
BACCHANT CAROUSER
REVELRY JOY ORGY RIOT RIOTISE
WASSAIL CARNIVAL CAROUSAL
FESTIVAL
REVENANT GHOST WRAITH SPECTER
REVENGE HELL WREAK WROIK
AVENGE ULTION REQUITE REQUITAL
REVANCHE
REVENGED EVEN
REVENUE RENT JAGIR MANSE YIELD
INCOME ENTRADA FINANCE PROFITS
HACIENDA INCOMING
(— FROM WATER RIGHTS) JALKAR
(— REVENUE PAID TO POPE) ANNAT
(STATE —) HACIENDA
REVERBERATE DIRL ECHO RING
REPEL RETORT REVERB REBOUND
REDOUND REFLECT RESOUND
REVERBERATING REBOANT
RESONANT SOUNDING
REVERBERATION ECHO REDOUND
REBOATION
REVERE ADORE HONOR ADMIRE
ESTEEM HALLOW RESPECT
WORSHIP VENERATE
REVERENCE AWE ORE CULT FEAR
DREAD HONOR MENSK PIETY
WURTH HOMAGE REGARD WORSHIP
DEVOTION VENERANT VENERATE
WORTHING
(— FOR ANIMALS) ZOISM
(IRRATIONAL —) FETICH FETISH
REVEREND SRI SHRI SHREE SVAMI
SWAMI POTENT STRONG
REVERENT DEVOUT STRONG
AWESOME DUTIFUL
REVERENTIAL PIOUS SOLEMN
REVERIE DUMP DWAM DREAM
DWALM STUDY PONDER MEMENTO
MOONING DAYDREAM TRAUMEREI
REVERSAL KNOCK CHANGE DOUBLE
SWITCH BACKCAST BACKFLIP
OVERTURN THROWBACK
TURNABOUT
REVERSE BACK DOWN FACE FLOP
JOLT ANNUL CHECK UPSET VERSO
CHANGE DEFEAT INVERT REPEAL
RETURN REVERT REVOKE BACKSET
COUNTER INVERSE PUTBACK
RETREAT REVERSO SETBACK
SNIFTER SUBVERT BACKCAST
CONTRARY CONVERSE OPPOSITE
OVERTURN RAMVERSE TRAVERSE
WATERLOO
(— OARS) SHEAVE
(— OF COIN) PILE TAIL WOMAN

(— OF NOTE) BACK
(— PAGE OF BOOK) VERSO
REVERSO
REVERSED INVERSE REVERTED
ROVESCIO
(NOT —) DIRECT
REVERSI QUINOLAS
REVERSION SCRAPS ATAVISM
ESCHEAT REMNANT FEEDBACK
REVERTAL REVERTER THROWBACK
REVERT ANNUL ADVERT RESORT
RESULT RETOUR RETURN REVOKE
ESCHEAT RESTORE RECOURSE
BACKSLIDE
(— TO A SUPERIOR) FALL
REVETMENT SODWORK
REVIEW HASH VIEW REVIE NOTICE
REVISE SURVEY BRUSHUP RECENSE
REJUDGE CRITIQUE REVIEWAL
REVISION
REVILE CALL RAIL ABUSE BLEIR
BRAWL REBUT SCOLD SHEND
SHENT MISUSE VILIFY MISCALL
MISNAME BACKBITE DISGRACE
EXECRATE REPROACH
REVILING ABUSION BLASPHEMY
REVISE EDIT ALTER REDACT
REFORM REVIEW CORRECT
RECENSE REFLECT REVISIT
REVISER REDACTOR REFORMER
REVIEWER
REVISION REVIEW SURVEY REVISAL
REVIEWAL EPANAGOGE
REVITALIZER BRACER
REVIVAL IMAGE REBIRTH WAKENING
REVIVE DAW EBB WAKE FETCH
QUICK RALLY RENEW ROUSE
EXHUME GINGER RECALL RELIVE
REVERT REVOKE EKPHORE ENLIVEN
FRESHEN FURBISH QUICKEN
REFRESH RESPIRE RESTORE
REDIVIVE REKINDLE RENOVATE
RETRIEVE
(— FIRE) CHUNK
REVOCATION REPEAL REVERSAL
ADEMPTION
REVOICE ECHO
REVOKE LIFT ADEEM ANNUL RENIG
CANCEL RECALL RECANT RENEGE
REPEAL REVERT ABOLISH COMMUTE
FINAGLE RECLAIM RESCIND
RETREAT REVERSE ABROGATE
REVOCATE
(— A LEGACY) ADEEM
REVOLT REBEL REPEL START
MUTINY OFFEND RELUCT UPROAR
MUTATION SEDITION UPRISING
JACQUERIE
REVOLTING GARISH HORRID
BILIOUS FEARFUL HATEFUL
HIDEOUS DREADFUL
REVOLUTION GYRE RIOT TOUR
TURN CYCLE WHEEL CHANGE
ANARCHY CIRCUIT REVOLVE
GYRATION MUTATION NOVATION
ROTATION SEDITION
REVOLUTIONARY RED RADICAL
ROTATING BOLSHEVIK
REVOLUTIONIST REDSHIRT

REVOLVE BIRL GYRE PIRL ROLL
SPIN TIRL TURN WELT PIVOT
THROW TREND TROLL TWINE VERSE
WHEEL WHIRL CENTER CIRCLE
GYRATE PONDER ROTATE SPHERE
SWINGE WAMBLE AGITATE VERSATE
CONSIDER OVERTURN REVOLUTE
(CAUSE TO —) TRUNDLE
REVOLVER GAT GUN ROD RIFLE
STICK CANNON CUTTER HOGLEG
PISTOL RIFFLE BULLDOG DUNGEON
REVOLVING ORBY VOLUBLE
GYRATORY VOLUTION
REVUE SHOW REVIEW FOLLIES
REVULSION FEAR REACTION
REWARD FEE PAY UTU GREE MEED
RENT SPUR WAGE AMEED BOOTY
BRIBE CROWN LOWER MERIT PLUM
SHEPE YIELD BOUNTY DESERT
GERSUM SALARY TROPHY WEDFEE
AUREOLE GUERDON PREMIUM
RENTAGE STIPEND WARISON
DIVIDEND EXACTION REMEMBER
REQUITAL
(— FOR INFORMATION ON CATTLE
THIEVES) TASCAL
(— OF VICTORY) CROWN
(— TO HOUNDS) HALLOW
(ILLUSORY —) CARROT
(UNEXPECTED —) JACKPOT
REWARDED APAID BOUNTIED
REWARDING FAT PREMIANT
(FINANCIALLY —) JUICY
REWRITTEN PALIMPSEST
REZAI ROSEI COVERLET MATTRESS
RHABDUS SCOPULA
RHADAMANTHUS (FATHER OF —)
JUPITER
(MOTHER OF —) EUROPA
RHAPSODIC CONFUSED EFFUSIVE
RAPTUROUS
RHAPSODY JUMBLE MEDLEY
BOMBAST ECSTASY RAPTURE
(— SECTION) LASSU
RHATANY LEGUME
RHEA EMU EMEU NANDU NANDOW
RATITE OSTRICH AGDISTIS
AVESTRUZ
(DAUGHTER OF —) JUNO CERES
VESTA
(FATHER OF —) URANUS
(HUSBAND OF —) SATURN
(MOTHER OF —) GAEA
(SON OF —) PLUTO NEPTUNE
RHEBOK PEELE REHBOC
RHENIUM BOHEMIUM
RHEOMETER STROMUHR
RHEOSTAT DIMMER
RHESUS BANDAR BUNDAR MONKEY
BHUNDER MACAQUE
RHETORIC SPEECH BOMBAST
PROSAIC ELOQUENCE
RHETORICAL FLORID FORENSIC
SWELLING
RHETORICIAN ORATOR RHETOR
RHEUM GORE TEARS CHOLER
SPLEEN
RHINARIUM MUFFLE
RHINE DITCH RUNNEL

RHINESTONE DEWDROP (PL.) GLITTER

RHINO CASH MONEY PONTOON

RHINOCEROS FOW ABADA BADAK RHINO BORELE KEITLOA UNICORN UPEYGAN NASICORN

RHINOCEROS BEETLE UANG SCARABAEID

RHINOCEROS HORNBILL TOPAU

RHIPIDION FLABELLUM

RHIZOID RHIZINA ROOTLET

RHIZOME KAVA NARD ARUKE CAAPI STOCK ARALIA ARNICA ASARUM GINGER IPECAC STOLON BERBERY CALAMUS CULVERS GENTIAN SCOPOLA ZEDOARY ASPIDIUM BARBERRY BERBERIS HELONIAS KAVAKAVA TRILLIUM TRITICUM VERATRUM (PL.) INULA GERANIUM

RHODE ISLAND
CAPITAL: PROVIDENCE
COLLEGE: BROWN BRYANT
INDIAN: NIANTIC
MOTTO: HOPE
NATIVE: GUNFLINT
RIVER: PAWTUXET
STATE FLOWER: VIOLET
STATE TREE: MAPLE
TOWN: BRISTOL NEWPORT
  CRANSTON KINGSTON

RHODE ISLAND BENT FURZETOP
RHODE ISLANDER GUNFLINT

RHODESIA
CAPITAL: SALISBURY
LANGUAGE: ILA BANTU
PEOPLE: BANTU MASHOMA
  MATABELE BALOKWAKWA
RIVER: SABI LIMPOPO ZAMBEZI
RUINS: ZIMBABWE
TOWN: GWELO UMTALI BULAWAYO

RHODODENDRON ROSEBAY SPOONHUTCH

RHOMB LOZEN WHEEL CIRCLE LOZENGE

RHOMBUS DIAMOND LOZENGE

RHUBARB ROW HASSEL CITRINE DISPUTE YAWWEED PIEPLANT

RHYME CHIME CLINK VERSE CRAMBO POETRY RHYTHM TINKLE MEASURE
(— ROYAL) TROILUS
(PL.) RIMUR

RHYTHM BEAT STOT TIME CHIME METER PULSE SWING CADENCE RAGTIME MOVEMENT SEQUENCE

RHYTHMICAL CADENCED MEASURED NUMEROUS

RIA CREEK INLET

RIAL COIN RYEL ROYAL KINGLY SPLENDID

RIALTO MART BRIDGE EXCHANGE

RIANT GAY RIDENT LAUGHING MIRTHFUL

RIATA LASSO LARIAT

RIB FIN KID BULB CORD DIKE JOKE PURL SLAT WALE WIFE CORSE COSTA GROIN NERVE OGIVE PEARL RIDGE VARIX VITTA WHELP BRANCH LIERNE PARODY RIPPLE SCROLL TIMBER TONGUE BRISTLE FEATHER NERVURE PLEURAL STRATUM FORMERET SIDEBONE
(— IN GROINED ROOF) SPRINGER
(— OF INSECT WING) VEIN
(— OF SHIP) WRONG
(— OF VIOLIN) BOUT
(—S OF UMBRELLA) FRAME
(SHORT —S) CROP
(STRENGTHENING —) FEATHER
(PL.) SLATS

RIBALD ROGUE COARSE RASCAL VULGAR

RIBALDRY HASH HARLOTRY

RIBAND RIBBON SCROLL

RIBBED RIBBY CORDED

RIBBING SPOOFERY

RIBBON BAR BOW FOB PAN BEND COST PADS BRAID CORSE FILET LABEL PADOU PIECE RUBAN SHRED TASTE BENDEL CADDIS CORDON FERRET FILLET LISERE RADULA RECORD RIBAND SHOWER STRING TAWDRY TISSUE TONGUE BANDING SAUTOIR TORSADE BANDEROL BOOKMARK FRAGMENT TRESSURE
(— AS BADGE OF HONOR) CORDON
(— AS HEADDRESS) TRESSOUR TRESSURE
(— FOR BORDER) LISERE
(— HANGING FROM CROWN) JESS
(— USED FOR GARTERS) CADDIS CADDICE
(COLORED —S) DIVISA
(END OF —S) FATTRELS
(FLOATING —) PAN
(KNOT OF —S) SORTIE
(LINGUAL —) TONGUE
(SILK —) CORSE PADOU TASTE
(WATERED —) PADS
(PL.) REINS

RIBBON FERN PTERIS

RIBBONFISH GARFISH GUAPENA AGUAVINA BANDFISH DEALFISH

RIBBONLIKE TAENFORM TAENIATE TAENIOID

RIBBON TREE AKAROA HOIHERE HOUHERE LACEBARK

RIBGRASS WINDLES BUCKHORN HARDHEAD PLANTAIN

RIBWORT KLOPS HEADMAN RATTAIL SOLDIER WINDLES HARDHEAD HEADSMAN PLANTAGO

RICE AUS AMAN BORO PADI PAGA RISE SELA TWIG ARROZ BATTY BIGAS CANIN CHITS GRAIN MACAN PADDY PALAY PATNA BRANCH CEREAL CONGEE SIDDHA ANGKHAK MANOMIN RISOTTO
(— BOILED WITH MEAT) PILAF PILAU PILAW

(— COOKED WITH MEAT) RISOTTO JAMBALAYA
(— FIELD) SAWAH
(— IN HUSK) PALAY
(— OF 2ND OR 3RD GRADE) CHITS
(— POLISHINGS) DARAC
(BOILED —) CANIN KANIN
(HUSKED —) CHAL
(INFERIOR —) PAGA
(LONG-STEMMED —) AMAN
(MOUNTAIN —) SMILO
(SHORT-STEMMED —) AUS
(SPRING —) BORO
(UNCOOKED —) BIGAS
(UNMILLED —) PADI PADDY
(WILD —) MANOMIN

RICEBIRD BUNTING CACIQUE SPARROW BOBOLINK

RICE FLOWER PIMELEA

RICEGRASS BARIT SACATE ZACATE

RICH FAT ABLE DEEP FAIR HIGH LUSH OOFY WARM GLEBY OPIME PLUMP ROUND TINNY VIVID BATFUL COSTLY DAEDAL FRUITY HEARTY PLUMMY PLUSHY PODDED SUPERB ULRICA AMUSING BAITTLE COPIOUS FERTILE MONEYED OPULENT PINGUID PLASTIC WEALTHY ABUNDANT AFFLUENT GENEROUS HUMOROUS
(— IN FAME) RODERICK
(— IN GIFTS) PREMIOUS
(— IN INTEREST) JUICY
(— IN MALT) HEAVY
(— IN SILICA) ACID
(— IN TIMBRE) GOLDEN
(— MAN) DIVES
(— OF SOIL) PINGUID

RICHARD DICCON

RICHES GOLD PELF WEAL LUCRE WORTH MAMMON TALENT WEALTH FORTUNE OPULENCE RICHESSE TREASURE

RICHLY HIGH AMPLY FATLY FULLY DEARLY

RICHNESS BODY SUMEN LUXURY ELEGANCE FECUNDITY

RICHWEED RAGWEED COOLWEED

RICK GOAF GOFE REKE CANCH RICKLE SPRAIN WRENCH CORNRICK

RICKETY SHAKY SHACKY SHACKLY UNSOUND RACHITIC SHATTERY UNSTABLE TOTTERING

RICKMATIC CONCERN BUSINESS

RICOCHET SKIP SKITE GLANCE REBOUND

RICTUS GRIN GRIMACE

RID FREE QUIT SHED SHUT CLEAR EGEST REDDE SCOUR SHIFT ACQUIT REMOVE DELIVER
(— OF INSECTS) BUG
(— OF WEEDS) CLEAN
(— ONESELF OF) DOFF DEPOSIT DISPATCH

RIDDANCE SHUT RELIEF DISPATCH

RIDDER SIFT SIEVE RIDDLE

RIDDLE SIFT BLAIK GRIPH REBUS DEBASE ENIGMA FOITER PUZZLE RUDDLE SCREEN CORRUPT EXPLAIN

GRIDDLE GRIPHUS MYSTIFY
PERPLEX PROBLEM CRATEMAN
PERMEATE
(— AS GRAIN) REE
(PL.) MURLEMEWES
RIDDLER CRATEMAN
RIDE GO RIB BAIT DOSA HACK HURL
LAST LIFT PRIG SAIL TOOL CROSS
DRIVE TEASE BANTER CANTER
DEPEND DODGEM GALLOP JUMBLE
NOTICE SADDLE HAYRIDE JOYRIDE
OVERLAP SURVIVE TANTIVY
BESTRIDE
(— FAST) PRICK POWDER
(— HARD) POUND BUCKET
(— IN HIRED VEHICLE) JOB
(— ON HORSE) BOOT LARK BURST
JOCKEY SCHOOL
(— TO HOUNDS) GO
(AMUSEMENT PARK —) SWING
RIDER TACK ANNEX CROSS HAZER
LABEL COWBOY JOCKEY SITTER
ALLONGE CODICIL NAGSMAN
PRICKER CAVALIER DESULTOR
HORSEMAN
(DUKEY —) BRAKEMAN
(DUMMY —) CROSS
RIDGE AAS ARM FIN RIB RIG RYG
BALK BAND BANK BARB BROW BULT
BURR BUTT COMB DRUM FRET FULL
HACK HILL KEEL LINK LIST PAHA
PUFF RAIN REAN ROLL SHIN SPUR
WAVE WELT BARGH CHINE COSTA
CREST EARTH EAVES GONYS
GYRUS JUGUM KNURL LEDGE RINGE
RUDGE SCOUT SHANK SPINE TORUS
VARIX WHELP BRIDGE CARINA
COLLOP CREASE CRISTA CUESTA
CULMEN DIVIDE DORSUM FRENUM
RAFTER RIDEAU SADDLE SELION
SUMMIT ANNULET APODEMA
BREAKER BUCCULA COLLINE
COSTULA EYEBROW EYELINE
HOGBACK HUMMOCK INTHROW
PROPONS RIGGING SOWBACK
WINDROW WITHERS WRINKLE
YARDANG CATOCTIN CINGULUM
FOREDUNE HEADLAND RESTBALK
SHOULDER
(— BETWEEN FURROWS) STITCH
RESTBALK
(— IN BREASTPLATE) TAPUL
(— IN COAL SEAM) HORSEBACK
(— IN HORSE'S MOUTH) EAR
(— MADE BY PLOWING) HACK
SELION
(— MADE BY TOOL) BUR BARB
BURR
(— OF BIRD'S BILL) CULM CULMEN
(— OF BRAIN CORAL) COLLINE
(— OF BREASTBONE) KEEL
(— OF CLAY) DOWLE
(— OF EARTH) BALK
(— OF FLESH) COLLOP
(— OF HORSE'S NECK) CREST
(— OF LAND) BULT RAIN SELION
STITCH HOGBACK
(— OF SAND IN WATER) REEF
SANDBAR

(— OF SCAPULA) SPINE
(— OF SNOW) SASTRUGA
ZASTRUGA
(— OF UNPLOWED LAND) LINCH
LINCHET
(— OF WAVE) CREST
(— ON BOOK) HUB
(— ON CLOTH) WALE
(— ON CROWN OF TOOTH)
CINGULUM
(— ON FINGERBOARD OF GUITAR)
FRET
(— ON FISH SCALE) CIRCULUS
(— ON FRUITS OF CARROT FAMILY)
JUGUM
(— ON GLUMES) CARINA
(— ON MOLLUSK SHELL) COSTULA
(— ON SEA FLOOR) SWELL
(— ON SEASHORE) STANNER
(— ON SHEET METAL) BEAD
(— ON SIDE OF SADDLE) PUFF
(— ON SKIN) WALE
(— ON VIOLIN) NUT
(— PROTECTING CAMP) RIDEAU
(— WITH SHARP SUMMIT) HOGBACK
(—S ON ROCK) LAPIES
(ANATOMICAL —) CARINA
(BEACH —) FULL
(CHEWING —) ENDITE
(CONNECTING —) HAUSE
(CONVOLUTED —) GYRUS
(DRAINAGE —) BREAKER
(GLACIAL —) OS KAME PAHA ESKAR
ESKER ESCHAR
(HAIRLIKE —) LIRA
(ICE —) SERAC
(ISOLATED —) BARGH
(LONG STONY —) RAND
(MOUNTAIN —) COMB SIERRA
BACKBONE
(NARROW —) DRUM RAZORBACK
(PROJECTING —) SCOUT
(RESIDUAL —) CATOCTIN
(SAND —) DUNE WAVEMARK
(SHARP-CRESTED —) ARETE
(SLIGHT —) PROPONS
(UNPLOWED —) BALK BAULK
(WOODED —) CHENIER
(PL.) KNURLING
RIDGED RIDGY SHARP CARINATE
RIDGELING RIG REGALD RIDGIL
RIGGOT RIGINAL
RIDGEPOLE ROOFTREE
RIDICULE FUN GUY MOB PAN RIG
TAX GAME GIBE JEER JEST JIBE
JOEY MOCK PLAY QUIZ RAZZ SKIT
TROT TWIT BORAK CHAFF CLOWN
HORSE IRONY MIMIC MOMUS QUEER
RALLY SCOFF SMOKE SNEER TAUNT
BANTER DERIDE EXPOSE RAILLY
SATIRE BUFFOON LAMPOON
MOCKERY SARCASM DERISION
RAILLERY SATIRIZE SPOOFERY
RIDICULOUS DOTTY DROLL FUNNY
SILLY ABSURD INSANE COMICAL
FOOLISH MOCKING DERISIVE
DERISORY FARCICAL INDECENT
RIDING AWHEEL LIVELY OVERLAP
PRICKANT SHIVAREE TRITHING
CHEVACHIE

(— ACADEMY) MANAGE MANEGE
(— CROP) ROD
(— WHIP) CROP QUIRT
RIDOTTO BALL REDOUTE
RIEM RHEIM RIMPI STRAP THONG
RIFE EASY FULL RANK QUICK READY
ACTIVE FILLED NIMBLE STRONG
CURRENT REPLETE ABUNDANT
INCLINED MANIFEST NUMEROUS
RIFFLE RIFF WAVE RAPID RIPPLE
SHUFFLE WATERFALL
RIFFRAFF MOB RAFF SCAFF TRASH
RABBLE REFUSE RUBBISH CANAILLE
POPULACE RAGABASH
RIFLE RIG ROB KRAG RIPE PIECE
YAGER CARBIN JEZAIL JUZAIL
RIFFLE SNIDER ARISAKA BULLPUP
BUNDOCK BUNDOOK CARABIN
CARBINE DESPOIL ENFIELD
ESCOPET MARTINI PILLAGE
PLUNDER RANSACK SPORTER
BANDHOOK BUNDHOOK REPEATER
SPLITTER STRICKLE TAKEDOWN
CHASSEPOT
(— BALL CASING) THIMBLE
(— PIN) TIGE
RIFLEMAN JAGER JAEGER
(PL.) RIFLERY
RIFT RIVE BELCH CHASM CRACK
SPLIT CLEAVE DIVIDE BLEMISH
FISSURE CREVASSE
(— IN TIMBER) LAG
RIG RI FIG REG HOAX JEST JOKE
REEK WIND DRESS EQUIP GETUP
PRANK RIDGE SPORT STORM TRICK
BANTER CLOTHE GUNTER ROTARY
SADDLE SCHEME MARCONI
SPUDDER SWINDLE BACKSTAY
RIDICULE
(TRUCKING —) SEMI
RIGADOON DANCE RIGODON
RIGEL REGEL ALGEBAR
RIGGED (FULLY —) ATAUNT
RIGGER CLIMBER SLINGER
SCAFFOLD
RIGGING NET GEAR ROOF RIDGE
TACKLE CLOTHING JACKSTAY
TACKLING
RIGHT DUE FEE FIT IUS OFF REE
SAY SOC BANG DUTY FAIR FLOP
GALE GOOD HAND ITER JUST LIEN
REAL RECT REET SANE SLAP SOKE
TEAM TRUE WELL CLAIM DRESS
DROIT ENTRY EXACT FAVOR FERRY
LEGAL RICHT SOUND STRAY TECH
TITLE ACTION ACTUAL BALLOT
DEMAND DEXTER EATAGE EQUITY
PROPER PUTURE ANNUITY APANAG
AUBAINE CORRECT DERECHO
DESIRED FACULTY FALDAGE FITTIN
FOLDAGE FREEDOM GENUINE
HAYBOTE LIBERTY LICENSE
PRENDER RECTIFY RELIEVE
SLAPDAB UPRIGHT WARRANT
BANALITY BLOODWIT FIREBOOT
FORESTRY HEIRSHIP INTEREST
LIFERENT SEIGNORY SLAPDASH
STALLAGE STRAIGHT SUFFRAGE
SUITABLE THIRLAGE

(— AND LEFT) HAY HEY
(— AS COMMAND TO HORSES) REE
(— EYE) OD
(— HAND) MD OPENBAND
(— IN A THING) INTEREST
(— IN WIFE'S INHERITED PROPERTY) CURTESY
(— OF CHOICE) OPTION
(— OF EXIT) ISH
(— OF FREE QUARTERS) CORODY
(— OF HOLDING COURT) TEAM
(— OF INQUIRY) SOKEN
(— OF OWNERSHIP) TITLE COMMONTY
(— OF PASTURAGE) FEED STINT EATAGE COWGATE COMMONAGE HORSEGATE
(— OF PRECEDENCE) PAS
(— OF PROTECTION) MUND
(— OF USING ANOTHER'S PROPERTY) EASEMENT
(— OF USING GRASSLAND) EATAGE
(— SIDE) OFFSIDE
(— TIME) TID
(— TO COLLECT REVENUE) DIWANI DEWANEE DEWANNY
(— TO COMMAND) IMPERIUM
(— TO CUT WOOD) VERT GREENHEW
(— TO DRAW WATER) HAUSTUS
(— TO DRIVE BEAST) ACTUS
(— TO PASS OVER LAND) ITER
(— TO SEIZE PROPERTY) ANGARY
(— TO SHOOT FIRST) CAST
(— TO WORK IN MINE) BEN
(ALL —) HUNK JAKE HUNKY
(FEUDAL —) THIRL THIRLAGE
(INDIAN LEGAL —) HAK HAKH
(LEGAL —) IUS JUS JURE DROIT ACCESS APPEAL COMMON FISHERY HYPOTHEC
(LEGAL —S) JURA
(MINING —) GALE
(NOT —) ACUTE
(PROPERTY —) DOMINIUM
(WIDOW'S —) TERCE TIERCE
(PL.) DIBS JURA
RIGHT ANGLE RECTANGLE
(HUNDREDTH OF —) GRAD GRADE
RIGHTEOUS GOOD JUST GODLY MORAL ZADOC ZADOK DEVOUT FITTING PERFECT SKILFUL UPRIGHT INNOCENT VIRTUOUS
RIGHTEOUSNESS DOOM DHARMA EQUITY JUSTICE HOLINESS JUDGMENT JUSTNESS MORALITY RECTITUDE
RIGHTFUL DUE JUST TRUE LEGAL KINDLY LAWFUL PROPER FITTING
RIGHTFULNESS JUSTICE
RIGHT-HANDED DEXTRAL SKILLED DEXTROUS CLOCKWISE
RIGHT-HANDWISE DEASIL DESSIL DEISEAL CLOCKWISE
RIGHTLY RITE FITLY ARIGHT FAIRLY JUSTLY HANDILY PERQUEER SUITABLY
RIGHT WHALE BOWHEAD BALAENID MYSTICETE NORDCAPER

RIGID SET ACID CARK FIRM HARD HIGH FIXED SOLID STARK STERN STIFF STONY STOUT TENSE TOUGH FORMAL FROZEN MARBLY SEVERE STARCH STICKY STRICT AUSTERE IRONCLAD RIGOROUS STRAIGHT INELASTIC STRINGENT
(— IN SELF-DENIAL) ASCETIC
RIGIDITY FROST RIGOR RIGOUR BUCKRAM SETNESS HARDNESS STIFFNESS
RIGMAREE COIN TRIFLE
RIGMAROLE RANE NOMINY RABBLE SLAMPAMP SLAMPANT AMPHIGORY
RIGOR TYRANNY ASPERITY HARDNESS SEVERITY
RIGOROUS FIRM HARD CLOSE CRUEL EXACT HARSH HEFTY RIGID STERN STIFF BITTER FLINTY SEVERE STRICT STRONG AUSTERE DRASTIC PRECISE DISTRICT DRACONIC EXACTING IRONCLAD STRAIGHT
(MORALLY —) PURITANIC
(NOT —) INEXACT
(UNDULY —) HARSH
RILE VEX ROIL ANGER IRRITATE
RILL PURL SIKE CLEFT DRILL PRILL GROOVE RILLOCK RIVULET BROOKLET RIVELING TRICKLET ARROYUELO WATERSHUT
RILLSTONE VENTIFACT
RIM HEM LIP BEAD BRIM CURB EDGE SHOE BEZEL BRINK CHIME EAVES FELLY FRAME HELIX SKIRT BORDER CALKER CHOANA FILLET FLANGE MARGIN EXCIPLE
(— HOLDING WATCH CRYSTAL) BEZEL BEZIL
(— OF BASKET) HOOP
(— OF COROLLA) ANNULUS
(— OF CRATER) SOMMA
(— OF EAR) HELIX
(— OF HORSESHOE) WEB
(— OF INSECT'S WING) TERMEN
(— OF SANIO) CRASSULA
(— OF TIN) LIST
(— OF WHEEL) FELLY FELLOE
(— ON CASK) CHIMB CHIME CHINE
(— ON CLOG) CALKER
(— SURROUNDING FLAGELLUM) CHOANA
(EXTERNAL —) FLANGE
(PROTECTIVE —) BANK
(RAISED —) BOSS
RIMA CHINK CLEFT RIMULA FISSURE
RIME RIM HOAR RIND RUNG CRACK CRUST FROST ROUND CRANREUCH
RIMPLE FOLD RIPPLE WRINKLE
RIND BARK PEEL PILL RYND SKIN CRUST FROST SWARD CITRON SWARTH
(— OF HAM) SKIN
(— OF MEAT) SPINE
(— OF POMEGRANATE) GRANATUM
(— OF ROASTED PORK) CRACKLING
RING GO BEE BOW BUR CUP DEE DIE EKE FAM JOW ORB PIT RIM AMBO BAIL BAND BELL BONG BURR CRIC CURB DING DIRL ECHO GYRE HOOP

JING LOOP MAIL PASS PEAL RACE RINK RUSH SHUT SING TANG TOLL VIRL WISP AMBON ANLET ARENA BAGUE CAROL CHIME CLANG CYCLE GRAIN GROUP GUARD GUIDE JEWEL KNELL LUNET PISTE RIGOL ROUND ROWEL TORUS VERGE WAFER WITHE BECKET BROUGH BUTTON CIRCLE CIRCUS CLIQUE COLLAR COLLET DINDLE EYELET FAMBLE GIMMER GIRDLE HARROW KEEPER LARIGO LEGLET RINGLE RUNDLE RUNNER SIGNET TORQUE TURRET VIROLE WASHER ANNULUS ARMILLA CIRCUIT CLAPPER COMPASS COUPLER CRINGLE DIAMOND FAMELEN FERRULE GALLERY GARLAND GROMMET GUDGEON MANILLA NUCLEUS PACKING RESOUND ROWLOCK SHACKLE STIRRUP THIMBLE BRACELET BULLRING CINCTURE CORONULE DINGDONG DRAUPNIR DUSTBAND ENCIRCLE FAIRLEAD PACIFIER SONORITY SURROUND TRAVELER
(— A TREE) FRILL
(— AROUND ARTICULAR CAVITY) AMBON
(— AROUND MOON) BROCH
(— AROUND NIPPLE) AREOLA
(— AT EACH END OF CINCH) LARIGO
(— ATTACHED TO JIB) HANK
(— BELLS) FIRE
(— FOR CARRYING SHOT) LADLE
(— FOR SECURING BIRD) VERVEL
(— FOR TRAINING HORSES) LONGE
(— FORMING HANDLE OF KEY) BOW
(— OF ANNULATED COLUMN) BAGUE
(— OF BOILER) STRAKE
(— OF COLOR) STOCKING
(— OF DOTS AROUND EDGE OF COIN) GRAINING
(— OF LIGHT) GLORY
(— OF ODIN) DRAUPNIR
(— OF RIDING SCHOOL) PISTE
(— OF ROPE) HANK BECKET GARLAND GROMMET SNORTER SNOTTER
(— OF SPINES) CORONULE
(— OF STANDING STONES) CAROL
(— OF TWO HOOPS) GEMEL GEMMEL
(— ON BATTLEAX) BUR BURR
(— ON BIRD'S TIBIA) ARMILLA
(— ON DECK) CRANCE
(— ON GUN CARRIAGE) LUNET LUNETTE
(— ON HINGE) GUDGEON
(— ON LAMP) CRIC
(— ON LANCE) BURR
(— ON UMBRELLA ROD) RUNNER
(— SUPPORTING LAMPSHADE) GALLERY
(— SURROUNDING BUGLE) VIROLE
(— SUSPENDING COMPASS) GIMBAL
(— TO ENCLOSE DEER) TINCHEL TINCHILL

(— UNDER BEEHIVE) EKE
(— USED AS MONEY) MANILLA
(— USED AS VALVE) WAFER
(— WITH GROOVED OUTER EDGE) THIMBLE
(— WITH VIBRATION) DIRL
(BRIGHT —) HALATION
(CERVICAL —) TORQUE
(CURTAIN —) EYE
(FINGER —) HOOP
(FLESHY —) ANNULUS
(HARNESS —) DEE BUTTON LARIGO TERRET TORRET TURRET
(INTERLINKED METAL —S) MAIL
(JOINED —) GIMMER GIMMOR
(LITTLE —) ANNULET
(LUMINOUS —) BROUGH
(NOSE —) PIRN
(OIL —) WIPER
(PACKING —) LUTE
(PLAITED —) RUSH WISP
(SURGICAL —) CURETTE
(TAPERING SHANK —) BELCHER
(TARGET —) SOUS SOUSE
(TOOTHED IRON —) HARROW
(TOP OF —) BEZEL BEZIL
RINGDOVE QUIST CUSHAT CUSHIE QUEEST TOOZOO ZOOZOO COWSHOT COWSHUT
RINGED GYRATE ZONATE ANNULAR
RINGED SNAKE COLUBRID
RINGER CHEER YOUTH COWBOY CROWBAR STOCKMAN
RINGHALS COBRA
RINGING BELL BRIGHT FERVID JANGLE CLANGOR OROTUND SINGING DECISIVE RESONANT SONORANT SONOROUS TINNIENT
(CHANGE —) CINQUES SINGLES
RINGLET CURL LOCK TENDRIL
(— ON FOREHEAD) FAVORITE
RING-NECKED TORQUATE
RING-NECKED DUCK DOGY SCAUP MOONBILL RINGBILL BLACKJACK
RING OUZEL AMSEL THRUSH WHISTLER
RING PLOVER SANDY COLLIER DULWILLY RINGNECK
RING-SHAPED ANNULAR ANNULARY ANNULATE CIRCULAR
RINGWORM TINEA KERION TETTER SERPIGO
RINGWORM BUSH SENNA
RINK GLACIARIUM
RINSE NET SIND WASH RANGE RENCH RENSH RINGE SCIND SWILL BLUING DOUCHE CLEANSE
RINSING NET SIND FLUSH RESIDUE
RIOT DIN HURL BRAWL REVEL WORRY ATTACK CLAMOR EXCESS JUMBLE MEDLEY RANTAN SPLORE TUMULT ANARCHY CONFUSE DESPOIL REVELRY BLOODWIT CAROUSAL
RIOTOUS ROID ROYD WILD NOISY RANDY RANTY HEMPIE RANDIE STORMY WANTON BACCHIC PROFUSE ROARING ABUNDANT BACCHIAN

RIP RIT COOP REAT TEAR BREAK SHARK SHRED SLITE UNSEW BASKET RIPPLE UNSEAM
RIPE FIT BOLD LATE DRUNK READY MATURE MELLOW SIDDER SIDDOW DIGESTED FINISHED SEASHORE SUITABLE
(EARLY —) HASTY RARERIPE
RIPEN AGE ADDLE AUGUST DIGEST MELLOW CONCOCT CRIMSON DEVELOP PERFECT COMPLETE MATURATE
RIPENESS MATURITY
RIPOSTE REPLY RETORT THRUST REPARTEE
RIPPER RIPSAW BOBSLED HUMDINGER
RIPPET FUSS TUMULT UPROAR DISPUTE QUARREL
RIPPING FINE GRAND SWELL CAPITAL TIPPING SPLENDID
RIPPLE FRET RIFF SEED WAVE ACKER CRISP TWINE COCKLE DIMPLE JABBLE LIPPER RIMPLE RUFFLE RUMBLE WIMPLE CRINKLE WAVELET WRINKLE
(— ALONG) DADE
RIPPLING BREAK BULGE JABBLE ARIPPLE
(— ON SURFACE) HORROR
RIPSAW RIPPER SPLITSAW
RIPSNORTER SNIFTER HUMDINGER
RISE COME DRAW FLOW GROW HEAD HIGH HIKE HOLT HOVE LIFT PLUM SOAR ARISE BEGIN CANCH CHEER CLIMB ERECT HEAVE HOIST MOUNT OCCUR PITCH PLUFF RAISE ROUSE SCEND SOURD STAND START SURGE SWELL TOWER YEAST ASCEND ASCENT ASPIRE AURORA BILLOW EMERGE GROWTH HAPPEN HEIGHT ORIGIN RESULT RETORT SOURCE SPRING THRIVE UPDIVE UPREAR ADVANCE APPLAUD HUMMOCK REDOUND UPHEAVE UPSHOOT EMINENCE FLOURISH HEIGHTEN INCREASE LEVITATE SCENSION UPSPRING
(— ABOVE) SURMOUNT
(— ABRUPTLY) SKYROCKET
(— AGAIN) RESURGE
(— AND FALL) LOOM HEAVE WELTER
(— AS PRICE) MEND
(— GRADUALLY) LOOM
(— IN BLISTERS) YAW
(— IN CLOUDS) STOOR
(— IN MINE FLOOR) HOGBACK
(— IN PRICES) BULGE
(— IN VALUE) IMPROVE
(— OF CURVE) CAMBER
(— OF HAWK AFTER PREY) MOUNTY
(— OF SHIP'S LINES) FLIGHT
(— OF WATER) FLOOD
(— PRECIPITOUSLY) SKY
(— RAPIDLY) KITE
(— SHARPLY) BREAK
(— SUDDENLY) BOOM SPRING
(— SWIFTLY) BOIL

(— TO BAIT) TAKE
(— TO GREAT HEIGHT) TOWER
(— TO PEAK) SWELL
(— UP) FUME REAR ASCEND INSURRECT
(SHARP —) HOGBACK
RISER HEAD RAISE FEEDHEAD INSURGENT
RISHI RSI POET SAGE SAINT DEVARSHI KASHYAPA MAHARSHI
RISIBLE FUNNY GELASTIC LAUGHABLE
RISING BOIL BULL RIST ARISE ARIST ORIENT SOURCE STRAKE UPREST UPWITH MONTANT PUSTULE SURGENT EMERGENT INCREASE MOUNTANT EXCEEDING
(— ABRUPTLY) BOLD
(— AND FALLING) TIDAL
(— AS OF HAWK) SOURCE
(— BY DEGREES) GRADIENT
(— GRADUALLY) SOFT
(— HIGH) AERIAL
(— SHARPLY) ABRUPT
(— STEEPLY) BLUFF
RISK GO RUN SET GAGE JUMP LUCK PAWN PERIL RISCO STAKE STAND THROW WAGER WATHE CHANCE DANGER GAMBLE HAZARD PLIGHT THREAT BALANCE IMPERIL VENTURE ENDANGER EXPOSURE
RISKY BOLD CHANCY DARING KITTLE RISQUE PARLISH PARLOUS TECHOUS TICKLISH
RISP BUSH RASP STEM TWIG STALK BRANCH SCRATCH
RISQUE BLUE RACY BROAD DARING SCABROUS
RISS-WURM NEUDECKIAN
RIT CUT RIP RUT REND SLIT TEAR SCRATCH
RITE KEX ASAL BORA BRIS FORM HAKO SOMA BRITH HONOR RIGHT SRADH ABDEST AUGURY EXEQUY FETISH OFFICE PANSIL PIACLE POOJAH RITUAL BAPTISM FUNERAL KATCINA LITURGY MYSTERY OBSEQUY SRADDHA TASHLIK CEREMONY HIERURGY HUSKANAW MORTUARY PIACULUM
(PL.) CULT SACRA SERVICE
RITUAL FORM RITE SOLEMN AGENDUM HAGGADA LITURGY OBSEQUY SERVICE CEREMONY VISPARAD VISPERED
RITZY HAUGHTY SNOBBISH
RIVAGE BANK RIVE COAST SHORE
RIVAL VIE EVEN PEER SIDE MATCH COMPETE CORRIVE EMULATE CORRIVAL EMULATOR OPPONENT
RIVALRY VIE GAME PARAGON JEALOUSY STRIVING EMULATION
RIVE RIP PLOW REND STAB TEAR CRACK REAVE SEVER SPLIT WEDGE CLEAVE SUNDER THRUST SHATTER FRACTURE
RIVER EA LE LEE REE RIO TJI ALPH BAHR GEON ILOG KILL WADI WADY BAYOU FLOOD GANGA GIHON GJOL

GLIDE HABOR INLET KIANG TCHAI
BARCOO GUTTER KHUBUR NYANZA
STRAIT STREAM CHANNEL COCYTUS
ESTUARY FROEMAN ILISSUS
PHARPAR RUBICON SENEGAL
AFFLUENT ERIDANUS PACTOLUS
STAIRCASE
(— CHANNEL) ALVEUS
(— NEAR GATE OF HEL'S ABODE)
GJOLL
(— OF ATTICA) ILISSUS
(— OF DAMASCUS) PHARPAR
(— OF LYDIA) PACTOLUS
(— OF PARADISE) GEON GIHON
(— OF QUEENSLAND) BARCOO
(— OF UNDERWORLD) STYX LETHE
ACHERON COCYTUS FLEGETON
(AFRICAN —) NYANZA SENEGAL
(CHINESE —) HO KIANG
(EGYPTIAN —) BAHR NILE
(FULL —) BANKER
(JAVANESE —) TJI
(MINOR —) BAYOU
(SACRED —) ALPH GANGA
(SMALL —) BACHE TCHAI
IVERBANK RIPA RIPE
IVERBED LAAGTE BATTURE
(DRY —) WADI WADY
IVERBOAT COG BARGE FOIST
PULWAR
IVER DUCK TEAL MALLARD
WIDGEON GREENWING
IVERINE (— FISH) HUCHO
IVERWEED WATERWEED
IVET STUD ROOVE PANHEAD
FLATHEAD
(— ATTENTION) GRIP
(— HEAD) CUPHEAD
IVULET RUN BURN GILL LAKE
MOTH RILL BACHE BATCH BAYOU
BOURN BROOK GHYLL RITHE
RINDLE RUNLET RUNNEL STREAM
STRIPE STRYPE CHANNEL RIVERET
BROOKLET
XY TERN
ZZAR DRY PARCH RASOUR
RAZOUR CURRANT HADDOCK
ZZOM BIT EAR RISOM STALK
STRAW RISSOM
ACH HOG BUTT ROCK SPOT
BRAISE BLATTID SUNFISH
DAD LEG PAD TAO WAY BELT
BORD CASH DRAG DRUN FARE
GAET GANG GATE LINE LODE LOKE
PASS PATH PAVE PIKE RADE RAID
RIDE RODE ROTE ROUT SLAB SPUR
WENT BARGH BLAZE BYWAY CLOSE
DRIFT DRIVE DROVE FORAY GAITE
GOING METAL PRAYA ROUTE TRACE
TRACK BYROAD CAMINO CAREER
CAUSEY CHEMIN COURSE DUGWAY
FEEDER RIDING ROUGHT RUNWAY
SLOUGH STREET TARMAC TRAJET
CALZADA CARTWAY ESTRADA
GANGWAY HIGHWAY LANDWAY
OUTGANG PACKWAY PASSAGE
RAILWAY RAMPIRE ROADWAY
ROLLWAY SKIDWAY TELFORD
AUTOBAHN BEALLACH BLACKTOP

BROADWAY CHAUSSEE CORDUROY
FOOTRILL HORSEWAY OVERPASS
RIDGEWAY SPEEDWAY TRACKWAY
TRAMROAD TRAVERSE TURNPIKE
WAGONWAY
(— BORDERING SHORE) PRAYA
(— FOR LOGGING) SKIDWAY
CROSSHAUL
(— IN COAL MINE) BORD BOARD
FOOTRILL
(— ON CLIFF) CORNICHE
(— SCRAPER) HARL HARLE
(— SURFACE) TELFORD
(CEMENT OR CONCRETE —) SLAB
(COUNTRY —) BOREEN DRIFTWAY
(DESCENDING —) BAHADA BAJADA
(IMPASSABLE —) SLOUGH IMPASSE
(IMPROVISED —) CASH
(MILITARY OR PUBLIC —) AGGER
(NARROW —) DRANG DRUNG
RODDIN
(PAVED —) CALZADA CHAUSSEE
(PRINCIPAL —) ARTERY
(PRIVATE —) LOKE DRIVE DRIVEWAY
(RAISED —) AGGER RAMPIRE
CAUSEWAY
(ROMAN —) ITER CAUSEY
(SIDE —) BRANCH SHUNPIKE
(STEEP —) BRAE PATH BARGH
SPRUNT
(TEMPORARY —) SHOOFLY
(UNIMPROVED —) DROVE
(ZIGZAG —) SWITCHBACK
ROADBED BALLAST BITUMEN
ROADBOOK MAP ITINERARY
ROAD DONKEY ROADER
ROADMAN PEDDLER SALESMAN
CANVASSER
ROADMASTER OVERSEER
ROAD RUNNER CUCKOO PAISANO
ROADSIDE HEDGE
ROADSTEAD RAID DOWNS
ROADSTER BUGGY TRAMP DRIVER
BICYCLE RUNABOUT RACEABOUT
SPEEDSTER
ROADWAY DECK EXIT STREET
MACADAM SLIPWAY TRUCKWAY
ROAM GO ERR RUN WAG RAKE
RAME RAVE ROIL ROLL ROVE WALK
GIPSY GYPSY KNOCK RANGE SCAMP
SPACE STRAY TAVER VAGUE
WAVER BANGLE RAMBLE STROLL
SWERVE TAIVER VAGARY WANDER
GALLANT PROCEED SQUANDER
VAGABOND
(— FURTIVELY) PROWL
ROAMING ERROR ROAMAGE
FUGITIVE
ROAN HORSE GRIZZLE
ROANOKE WAMPUM
ROAR CRY BAWL BEAL BELL BERE
BOOM BRAY HOWL HURL RAIR
RARE RERD ROIN ROME ROUT YELL
BROOL CRACK RERDE ROUST
SHOUT SNORE BELLOW BULDER
BULLER CLAMOR GOLLAR GOLLER
RUMMES SCREAM SHRIEK STEVEN
BLUSTER RUMMISH ULULATE

(— AS BOAR) FREAM
(— LIKE WIND) HURL
(— OF SURF) ROTE
(LOW —) BROOL
ROARING RUT LOUD AROAR BRISK
ROUST BELLOW BOOMING RIOTOUS
THRIVING
ROARING BOY TWIBIL TWIBILL
ROARING GAME CURLING
ROARING MEG CANNON
ROAST RAZZ ROTI SOAK BREDE
PARCH ASSATE CODDLE REMOVE
TORREFY TORRIFY BARBECUE
RIDICULE
(STUFFED —) FARCI
ROASTED ASADO
(NOT —) GREEN
ROASTER BURNER SCORCHER
ROASTING ASSATION
ROASTING JACK TURNSPIT
ROB COP EASE FAKE FLAP NICK
PEEL PELF PICK PILL POLL PREY
PULL RAMP RIPE ROLL TOBY BENIM
BRIBE FLIMP HARRY HEAVE HEIST
LURCH PINCH PLUCK PLUME PROWL
REAVE RIFLE ROIST SHAKE SPOIL
SPUNG STEAL STRUB TOUCH
HARROW HIJACK HUSTLE PILFER
RAVISH STRIKE THIEVE DEPRIVE
DESPOIL PLUNDER RUMPADE
SNAFFLE UNPURSE DEFLOWER
SPOLIATE
(— HOUSE) MILL
(— OF CHASTITY) DEFILE
(— OF FORCE) COOL
(— OF JOY) DESOLATE
(— OF VIGOR) ETIOLATE
(— WITH VIOLENCE) RAMP
ROBALO SNOOK SNOWK SERGEANT
ROBBED RUBATO
(NOT —) UNPILLED
ROBBER PAD FOMOR LARON THIEF
BANDIT BRIBER DACOIT FORMOR
HOLDUP LATRON RIFLER BRIGAND
FOOTPAD HEISTER LADRONE
MOONMAN PRANCER RAVENER
ROUTIER SPOILER TOBYMAN
BARRABAS FOMORIAN PILLAGER
RABIATOR
(— ON HIGH SEAS) PIRATE
(— WHO USES VIOLENCE)
RABIATOR
(GRAVE —) GOUL GHOUL
(HIGHWAY —) PAD FOOTPAD
TOBYMAN
(INDIAN MURDEROUS —) DACOIT
(IRISH —) WOODKERN
(MOUNTAIN —) CHOAR
(NIGHT —) MOONMAN
(SEA —) FOMOR FORMOR
FOMORIAN
(WANDERING —) ROUTIER
ROBBERY JOB JUMP REIF RIFE
HEIST SCREW STALE FELONY
HOLDUP STOWTH BRIBERY DACOITY
LARCENY PILLAGE PLUNDER
REAVERY STICKUP THUGGEE
PURCHASE
(— ON HIGH SEAS) PIRACY

(HIGHWAY —) TOBY
ROBE GOWN VEST KANZU STOLA
CHIMER KIMONO KITTEL MANTLE
REVEST ARISAID BUFFALO GALABIA
SURCOAT VESTURE WOLFSKIN
(— FOR THE DEAD) HABIT
(— OF MONARCH) PLUVIAL
(— PRESENTED BY DIGNITARY)
KHALAT KHILAT
(— REACHING TO ANKLES) TALAR
(ACTOR'S —) SYRMA
(BAPTISMAL —) CHRISOM
(BISHOP'S —) CHIMER CHIMERE
(CIRCULAR —) CYCLAS
(CORONATION —) COLOBIUM
DALMATIC
(DERVISH'S —) KHIRKA KHIRKAH
(EMPEROR'S —) PURPLE
(FUNERAL —) SABLE
(JEWISH —) KITTEL
(KING'S —) DALMATIC
(LOOSE —) MANT CAMIS CAMUS
CYMAR SIMAR SYMAR MANTUA
MANTEAU
(MASQUERADE —) VENETIAN
(MEXICAN —) MANGA
(MONK'S —) HAPLOMA
(OUTER —) JAMA
(TARTAN —) ARISAID
(TURKISH —) DOLMAN
(WHITE —) CHRISOM
ROBERT DOB POP RAB DOBBIN
POPKIN
ROBERT OF LINCOLN BOBOLINK
ROBIN PINFISH REDDOCK RUDDOCK
TOOTLER WINGFISH REDBREAST
ROBIN GOODFELLOW ELF PUCK
FAIRY SPRITE HOBGOBLIN
ROBINIA LOCUST
ROBIN SANDPIPER KNOT
DOWITCHER
ROBORANT TONIC
ROBOT GELEM GOLEM AUTOMAT
TELEVOX
ROBUST ABLE FIRM HAIL HALE HARD
IRON RUDE HARDY HUSKY LUSTY
RENKY SOUND STARK STIFF STOUR
STOUT TOUGH VALID WALLY
HEARTY RUGGED SINEWY STRONG
STURDY HEALTHY VALIANT
MUSCULAR PITHSOME SWACKING
VIGOROUS STRAPPING
(NOT —) SLENDER
ROBUSTNESS VALIDITY
ROC BIRD BOMB RUKH ROQUE
SIMURG SIMURGH
ROCHET CLOAK SMOCK CAMISIA
ROCK CAP JOW LOG PAY RAG DAZE
HOST KLIP REEL RUKH SIAL SIMA
SWAY SWIG TOSS BRACK CLIFF
FLOOR GREET GRUSS HORSE
LEDGE ROACH ROQUE SHAKE
SHOWD SKARN STONE TRILL FACIES
GROUND TOTTER COUNTRY FOLIATE
(— AROUND DRILL HOLE) COLLAR
(— CHUNK) KNUCKLE
(— IN ANOTHER ROCK) XENOLITH
(— IN MINE) CAPPING
(— IN SEA) STACK

(— SURFACE) KARREN
(— VIOLENTLY) STAGGER
(ARTIFICIAL —) GRANOLITH
(BANDED —) BAR
(BARE —) SCARTH
(CAP —) COVER
(COMPACT —) BASEMENT
(COUNTRY —) RIDER
(CRUSHED —) GREET
(CRYSTALLINE —) SCHIST DIORITE
GREISEN
(DECAY OF —S) GEEST LATERITE
(DECOMPOSED —) GOSSAN GOZZAN
(DENSE —) ADINOLE
(EXTRUSIVE —) DACITE SPILITE
ANDESITE CIMINITE
(FISSILE —) SHALE SHAUL
(FLUID —) LAVA
(FRAGMENTAL —) PSEPHITE
(GRANULAR —) GABBRO OOLITE
DIORITE IJOLITE KOSWITE
(GRANULATED —) GRUSS
(HARD —) WHIN
(HIGH —) SCOUT
(IGNEOUS —) BOSS SIAL SIMA TRAP
BASALT DUNITE GABBRO URTITE
FELSITE GRANITE MINETTE SYENITE
ESSEXITE TONALITE
(IMPURE —) CHERT
(INSULAR —) SKERRY
(INSULATED —) SKERRY
(INTRUSIVE —) HORTITE MAENAITE
(IRON-BEARING —) GAL
(ISOLATED —) SCAR SCARR SCAUR
(JUTTING POINT OF —) KIP
(METAMORPHIC —) SKARN GNEISS
SCHIST BUCHITE GONDITE LEPTITE
ECLOGITE HORNFELS LIMURITE
(MICA-BEARING —) DOMITE
(MOLTEN —) MAGMA
(PLUTONIC —) TAWITE HOLLAITE
TURJAITE
(POROUS —) TUFA TUFF ARSOITE
(PROJECTING —) CLINT
(PULVERIZED —) FLOUR
(RARE —) ALNOITE
(ROUGH —) CRAG KNAR SCARTH
(ROUNDED —) ROGNON SHEEPBACK
(SEDIMENTARY —) CRAG
IRONSTONE SANDSTONE
(SLATY —) PLATE SCHALSTEIN
(SOLID —) GIBBER
(STUDY OF —S) LITHOLOGY
(SUBMERGED —) SHELF
(UNDERLYING —) FLOOR
(VOLCANIC —) TUFA TUFF BASALT
DOMITE LATITE TAXITE ASHSTONE
RHYOLITE TEPHRITE TRACHYTE
(WORTHLESS —) GANG GANGUE
(PL.) ROCHER
ROCKAWAY CARRIAGE
ROCK BADGER CONY HYRAX
ROCK BASS REDEYE CABRILLA
ROCKBRUSH ROSILLA
ROCK CEDAR SABINO
ROCK CRESS SICKLEPOD
ROCK DEBRIS TALUS
ROCK DOVE SOD
ROCKER CRADLE SHOOFLY

ROCKET DRAKE REBUKE STREAK
YELLOW CONGREVE SKYLIGHT
STARSHIP FIREDRAKE
(DYER'S —) WELD WOLD WOALD
WOULD
ROCKET SALAD ROQUETTE
ROCKFISH JACK RENA REINA VIUVA
FLIOMA GOPHER RASHER TAMBOR
CORSAIR GARRUPA GROUPER
BOCACCIO CHINAFISH GREENLING
ROCK HARE KLIPHAAS
ROCK HIND MERO AGAUJI
ROCK HOPPER MACARONI
ROCKLING BAUD GADE ROKER
SORGHE WHISTLER
ROCK NATIVE SNAPPER
ROCK PIPIT TIETICK
ROCK RABBIT PIKA HYRAX
HYRACOID
ROCKROSE CISTUS HUDSONIA
ROCKCIST SAGEROSE DAYFLOWER
SUNFLOWER
ROCK SALT EMOL AMOLE HALITE
(BLOCK OF —) PIG
ROCK SANDWORT CYME
ROCKSHAFT SHAFT ROCKER
WEIGHBAR
ROCK TROUT BOREGAT GREENLING
ROCKWEED TANG FUCUS FUCOID
SEATANG SEAWEED
ROCK WHITING KELPFISH
STRANGER
ROCKY DAFT HARD STONY CLINTY
OBSCENE PETREAN PETROUS
UNCOUTH OBDURATE UNSTABLE
DIFFICULT RUPELLARY
ROCKY MOUNTAIN (— GOAT)
MAZAME
ROCOCO ORNATE QUAINT BAROCCO
BAROQUE OUTMODED
ROD BAR BOW CUE GAD GUY LUG
PIN TIE BOLT CALM CAME CANE
CORE FALL FORK GOAD GONG LINK
MACE POLE RAVE SCOB SNAP STEM
STUD WAND WHIP YARD ARBOR
BIRCH CATCH DOWEL LYTTA OSIER
PERCH POWER PUNCH REACH
ROUND SETUP SHOOT SPELK SPILL
SPOKE SPRAG STAFF STEEL STICK
STING TEYNE TOMMY TRACE VERGE
WIPER BALEYS BROACH CANARY
CARBON CENTER CRUTCH ETALON
FERULA FINGER GLOWER HANGER
PISTOL PITMAN PODGER RADDLE
RAMMER SKEWER SPRING STADIA
SWITCH TOGGLE WATTLE WICKER
BACULUS CROPPIE DRAWROD
ELLWAND FEATHER FESTUCA
PLUNGER POINTER POTHOOK
PRICKER PROBANG PROLONG
SCALLOM SCEPTER SPINDLE
STADIUM STICKER TYRANNY
VIRGULA WHISKER WINDING
AXOSTYLE BACKSTAY BILBERRY
BODSTICK BOWSTAVE DIPSTICK
JACKSTAY KINGBOLT REVOLVER
STRAINER TRAVELER WEEDHOOK
(— AS SYMBOL OF OFFICE) VERGE
(— BEARING TRAFFIC SIGNAL)
STANCHION

(— FOR ALIGNING HOLES) PODGER
(— FOR CARRYING GLASS) FORK
(— FOR DISCIPLINE) YARD FERULA
FERULE
(— FOR FASTENING THATCH) SPELK
SPRINGLE
(— FOR FIREARM BORE) WIPER
(— FOR GLASS-MAKING) PUNTY
FASCET PONTEE PONTIL CROPPIE
(— FOR HOLDING MEAT) SPIT
(— FOR TRANSMITTING MOTION)
TRACE
(— IN ARC LAMP) CARBON
(— IN CRICKET) STUMP
(— IN INTERFEROMETER) ETALON
(— IN MINE PUMP) SPEAR
(— IN NERNST LAMP) GLOWER
(— IN SPINNING WHEEL) SPINDLE
(— OF FOUNDRY MOLD) LANCE
(— OF LOOM) SHAFT
(— OF WOOD) SCOB
(— ON LOGGING TRUCK) RAVE
(— POINTED AT BOTH ENDS)
SKEWER
(— SYMBOLIZING AUTHORITY)
BACULUS
(— TO BIND A CONTRACT) FESTUCA
(— TO FASTEN SAILS) JACKSTAY
(— TO IMMERSE SHEEP) CRUTCH
(— TO URGE BEAST) GOAD PROD
(— UPSET AT ONE END) SETUP
(— USED AS KEY) TOMMY
(— WITH ENDS AT RIGHT ANGLES)
STRAINER
(— WITH SPONGE ON END)
PROBANG
(— WITH T-HEAD) TOGGLE
(AXIAL —) VIRGULA AXOSTYLE
(BASKETRY —) OSIER
(BUNDLE OF —S) DRIVER
(CARTILAGINOUS —) LYTTA
COLUMELLA
(CLAMMING —) BRAIL
(CONNECTING —) PITMAN
(CURTAIN —) TRINGLE
(DANCER'S —) CROTALUM
(DIVINING —) TWIG DOWSER
(FISHING —) GAD CALCUTTA
(FLEXIBLE —) RADDLE WATTLE
(FORKED —) CRUTCH
(GEM-CUTTING —) SETTER
(GRADUATED —) STADIA STADIUM
(IRON —) SNAP
(KNITTING —) NEEDLE
(LEAD —) CAME
(LOGGING —) CANARY
(MEASURING —) JUDGE SPILE
STADIA ELLWAND METEWAND
METEYARD
(PLIABLE —) WINDING
(SMALL —) LANCE
(STRENGTHENING —) RIB
(SUPPLE —) SWABBLE
(TETHERING —) STAKE
(THIN —) TEYNE SCALLOM
(TIE —) ANCHOR
(UMBRELLA —) STRETCHER
(WITHE —) BILBERRY
ODENT RAT CONY DEGU HARE

MARA MOCO MOLE PACA PIKA UTIA
VOLE CONEY COYPU GUNDI HUTIA
JUTIA LEROT MOUSE TUCAN ZOKOR
AGOUTI BEAVER BITING CURURO
GERBIL GLIRID GNAWER GOPHER
JERBOA MARMOT MURINE MUROID
RABBIT SOKHER BLESMOL CHINCHA
DIPODID GEOMYID GNAWING
HAMSTER LEMMING LEVERET
MUSKRAT ABROCOME CAPIBARA
DORMOUSE LEPORIDE OCTODONT
SEWELLEL SPALACID SQUIRREL
TUCOTUCO VISCACHA VIZCACHA
RODEO ROUNDUP
RODLIKE VIRGATE
RODMAN CLASHY CLASHEE
CHAINMAN
RODOMONTADE BRAG RANT BOAST
BLUSTER BOMBAST BRAGGART
ROD-SHAPED RHABDOID VIRGULATE
ROE RA DOE FRY PEA RAA RAE HIND
KELK RAUN ROUN ROWN CORAL
TRUBU CAVIAR
ROEBUCK GIRL CHEVREUIL
ROGER RAM HODGE ROGUE
ROGUE BOY GUE IMP NYM KEMP
KITE ROAG CATSO CRACK CRANK
GIPSY GREEK GYPSY HEMPY KNAVE
SCAMP SHELM BEGGAR BORGER
BUGGER CANTER COQUIN CURTAL
HARLOT LIMMER PICARA PICARO
RASCAL SORROW TINKER BLEEDER
ERRATIC FOISTER HALLION
LADRONE PANURGE SHARPER
SKELLUM SWINGER VILLAIN
COMROGUE HEMPSEED PICAROON
SWINDLER WHIPJACK
ROGUERY ROPERY KNAVERY
LOONERY WAGGERY PATCHERY
PRIGGISM TRICKERY TRUANTRY
ROGUISH SLY ARCH ROGUY WICKED
KNAVISH TRICKSY VAGRANT
WAGGISH ESPIEGLE SCAMPISH
DISHONEST
ROGUISHNESS KNAVERY ARCHNESS
ROIL VEX FOUL RILE ANNOY
BLUNDER DISTURB STUDDLE
BEWILDER DISORDER IRRITATE
ROILED TURBID
ROISTER REVEL ROIST SCOUR
CAROUSE GALRAVAGE
ROISTERER MUN GREEK HUZZA
HECTOR RIOTER SCOURER TWIBILL
EPHESIAN
ROISTERING HOYDEN
ROKE FOG DAMP MIST REEK ROWK
STIR FOGGY SMOKE STEAM VAPOR
ROKELAY ROCOLO
ROLE BIT JOB LEAD PART ROTE
HEAVY FIGURE CLOTHES BUSINESS
FUNCTION LIRIPIPE
ROLL BAP BUN ROW WEB BOLT COIL
CURL FILE FLOW FURL LIST MILL
PASS REEL ROAM ROTA SWAG
WELT WIND WRAP BAGEL BREAD
BUILD DANDY DICKY ENROL FLUTE
ROYLE SPLIT TRILL TROLL WHELM
BILLOW BUNDLE CIRCLE ELAPSE
ENFOLD GOGGLE GROVEL KIPFEL

LEGEND MUSTER PONDER ROSTER
ROTATE SCROLL UPWIND VOLUME
WAMBLE WANDER WHELVE WINTLE
WREATH BISCUIT BRIOCHE
CROCKET ENVELOP MANCHET
REVOLVE ROTULET ROTULUS
STRETCH TERRIER TRUNDLE
TWISTER BROTCHEN CANNELON
CONSIDER CRESCENT JACKROLL
LAMINATE PORTEOUS REGISTER
SEDERUNT SPREADER VOLUTATE
(— A BALL) BOWL
(— ABOUT) WALTER SCAMBLE
(— AS A SHIP) SEEL LURCH
(— AS STONE) REEL
(— BY) WALK
(— CLOSELY) FURL
(— EYES) WALL WAUL WHAWL
GOGGLE
(— GLASS) MARVER
(— INTO A BALL) CLEW CLUE
(— OF BREAD) BAP SEMMEL
TAMMIE
(— OF CLOTH) BOLT WREATH
(— OF COINS) ROULEAU
(— OF DOUGH) TWIST
(— OF DRIED BARK) QUILL
(— OF DRUM) HURRY
(— OF DUST) KITTEN
(— OF HAIR) ROACH ROWEL
CROCKET
(— OF HAY) WAKE
(— OF LINT OR LINEN) TENT DOSSIL
(— OF LUGGAGE) SWAG
(— OF MINCED MEAT) RISSOLE
(— OF OFFENDERS) PORTEOUS
(— OF PAPER) SPILL STOMP STUMP
(— OF PARCHMENT) BOOK PELL
(— OF ROULETTE WHEEL) COUP
(— OF SPUN YARN) PRICK
(— OF TOBACCO) CAROT CIGAR
PRICK SEGAR CAROTTE
(— OF WALLPAPER) BOLT
(— OF WHEAT BREAD) MANCHET
(— OF WOOL) ROVE ROVING
CARDING
(— ON LITTLE WHEELS) TRUNDLE
(— ONWARD) DEVOLVE
(— OVER) COMB JOLL WELTER
(— TO RUB DOWN DRAWING)
STUMP
(— TOGETHER) CONVOLVE
(— UP SLEEVES) REEVE
(— UP) FURL STOW COLLAR
(BLANKET —) BINDLE SHIRALEE
(DANDY —) DANCER
(HOLLOW —) CANNELON
(LONG —) FLUTE
(PADDED —) BURLET
(PENNY —) TOMMY
(TWISTED — OF WOOL) SLUB
(WHIP —) BACKREST
ROLLED (— IN SUGAR) SANDED
ROLLER FLY BOWL BRAY DRUM
JACK LEAD MILL PUCK RUBY BREAK
DANDY FINER GODET INKER RIDER
SHELL WAVER WINCH BRAYER
BREAST DOFFER DUCTOR FASCIA
MANGLE ROWLET RUNNER CARRIER

CLEARER MOIETER TRUCKLE
HEDGEHOG SQUEEGEE STRIPPER
TROUPAND
(— FOR MASSAGER) ROULETTE
(— IN HORSE'S BIT) CRICKET
(— IN ORGAN) TRUNDLE
(— IN STEELWORKS) COGGER
(— TO CLEAR FABRIC) MOIETER
(CARDING —) BREAST WORKER
SQUIRREL STRIPPER
(CHINESE —) SIRGANG
(DREDGING —) HEDGEHOG
(DROP —) DUCTOR
(GRINDING —) BREAK
(INKING —) BRAYER
(PRINTING —) DANDY SHELL
BRAYER DAMPENER
(STONE —) MAMMY TOTER
(SURGICAL —) FASCIA
(TOOTHED —) PRICK PRICKER
ROLLER COASTER SWITCHBACK
ROLLERMAN BRAKER JACKMAN
LEVERMAN
ROLLER SKATE PEDOMOTOR
ROLLICK PLAY ROMP FROLIC ROLLIX
ROLLICKING GAY WILD MERRY
JOVIAL LIVELY
ROLLING CURL GOGGLE WHEELY
SWAYING TRILLED LURCHING
VOLUTION
(— OF SCROLL) GELILAH
(— OF SHIP) LABOR
ROLLTOP TAMBOUR
ROLY-POLY ROTUND PUDDING
TUMBLER SALTWORT
ROM RO GYPSY ROMANY
ROMAN BRAVE LATIN NOBLE PAPAL
ANTIQUA UPRIGHT GOWNSMAN
(— COLLAR) RABAT
ROMAN CATHOLIC ROME ROMAN
PAPIST ROMIST BABYLONIC
ROMANCE WOO GEST ANTAR FANCY
FEIGN GESTE KATHA NOVEL STORY
ANTARA UTOPIA FANTASY FICTION
ROMANZA
(— LANGUAGE) FRENCH ITALIAN
SPANISH
ROMAN-FLEUVE SAGA

ROMANIA
CANAL: BEGA
CAPITAL: BUCHAREST
COIN: BAN LEI LEU LEY
DISTRICT: ALBA BANAT BIHOR
DOBRUJA DOBROGEA
MARAMURES
LAKE: SINOE
MOUNTAIN: BIHOR NEGOI CODRUL
RODNEI CALIMAN PIETROSU
OLD NAME: DACIA
PASS: ROSUL
PROVINCE: ARDEAL MOLDAVIA
WALACHIA
RIVER: ALT JIU OLT PRUT ALUTA
ARGES BUZDU MOROS MURES
OLTUL SCHYL SIRET VEDEA
CRASNA DANUBE ARGESUL
BISTRITA IALOMITA

RIVER PORT: BRAILA GALATI
GALATZ
TOWN: ARAD CLUJ IASI BACAV
CERNA JASSY NEAMT SIBIU
TURNU BRAILA BRASOV GALATI
GALATZ LVPENI CRAIOVA
FOCSANI PLOESTI SEVERIN
CERNAVTI KISHENEF KOLSOVAR
TEMESVAR

ROMANIST MISSARY
ROMANIZATION LATINXUA
ROMANSH LADIN
ROMANTIC AIRY WILD IDEAL
ADRENT DREAMY GOTHIC POETIC
UNREAL FERVENT FABULOUS
FANCIFUL
ROMANY RO ROM GIPSY GYPSY
ROMAN
ROME (CHAPEL IN —) SISTINE
(FOUNDER OF —) ROMULUS
(HILL IN —) CAELIAN VIMINAL
AVENTINE PALATINE QUIRINAL
(RIVER IN —) TIBER
ROMP REG RIG LARK PLAY ROIL
FRISK SHIRL SPORT TRAIN FROLIC
GAMBOL HOORAY HOYDEN HURRAH
RIPPET COURANT GAMMOCK
RAMMACK RUNAWAY
ROMPERS JUMPER JUMPERS
ROMPING ROYT ROYET
RONCADOR GRUNT CROAKER
SCIAENID
RONE BUSH BRAKE GUTTER THICKET
RONG LEPCHA
RONGA THONGA
RONSDORFER ZIONITE ELLERIAN
ROOD RUD REED ROPE CROSS
SPAWN STANG CRUCIFIX
ROODLES RANGDOODLES
ROOF TOP ATAP BACK DECK DOME
FLAT ATTAP COVER HOUSE RAISE
RISER SHELL THACK AZOTEA
BONNET CUPOLA SUMMIT TECTUM
CHOPPER CRICKET GAMBREL
MANSARD RIGGING TECTURE
BULKHEAD HOUSETOP SAWTOOTH
SEMIDOME
(— MEMBER) PURLIN
(— OF CARRIAGE) IMPERIAL
(— OF CAVERN) DOME
(— OF MINING CAGE) BONNET
(— OF MOUTH) PALATE
(— OF NASOPHARYNX) VAULT
(— OF RAILWAY CAR) DECK
(— OVER STAGE) SHADOW
(— PORTION) MONITOR
(CLOTH —) CHUTT
(FALSE —) CRICKET
(FLAT —) LEADS AZOTEA TERRACE
(STEEPLY TAPERING —) SPIRE
(THATCHED —) ATAP ATTAP
CHOPPER
(VAULTED —) DOME
ROOFING HEALING SHINDLE
PANTILING
ROOK ROC CROW DUPE RUKH
CHEAT CRAKE JUDGE TOWER

BLACKY CASTLE DEFRAUD
CASTILLO SWINDLER
ROOKERY ROOST RUMPUS BUILDING
ROOKIE COLT DRONGO NOVICE
RECRUIT BEGINNER
ROOM WON AULA CAFE CRIB FARM
HALL KILN LIEU PLAY SALA SEAT
SLUM WAME WENE WONE ATTIC
BERTH CUDDY DIVAN EWERY HOUSE
LODGE OECUS PLACE SALLE SCOPE
SHACK SOLAR SPACE STALL STOVE
STUDY BELFRY BREAST CAMERA
CASINO CHAPEL ESTUFA EXEDRA
HAMMAM LEEWAY MARGIN PARVIS
SCOUTH SINGLE SMOKER SOLLAR
STANCE STANZA STUDIO CABINET
CAMARIN CHALMER CHAMBER
EPINAOS FREEZER GALLERY
HOLDING HYPOGEE KITCHEN
LAUNDRY LIBRARY SEMINAR
SERVERY SMOKERY SURGERY
AEDICULA ASSEMBLY BASEMENT
DRYHOUSE HOTHOUSE HYPOGEUM
LAVATORY NYMPHEUM SCULLERY
SWEATBOX TABLINUM THALAMUS
(— BEHIND FACADE) ATTIC
(— BETWEEN KITCHEN AND DINING
ROOM) SERVERY
(— CONTAINING FOUNTAIN)
NYMPHEUM
(— DUG IN CLIFF) HYPOGEE
HYPOGEUM
(— FOR ACTION) LEEWAY
(— FOR BATHING) HAMMAM
(— FOR CONVERSATION) EXEDRA
(— FOR FAMILY RECORDS)
TABLINUM
(— FOR KEEPING FOOD) LARDER
PANTRY
(— FOR PAINTINGS) GALLERY
(— FOR PRIVATE DEVOTIONS)
ORATORY
(— FOR PUBLIC AMUSEMENTS)
CASINO THEATER
(— FOR STOWAGE) LASTAGE
(— FOR TABLE LINEN) EWERY
(— IN COAL MINE) BREAST
(— IN HAREM) ODA
(— IN KEEP) DUNGEON
(— IN PREHISTORIC BUILDING) CEL
(— IN REAR OF TEMPLE) EPINAOS
(— IN SIDE OF LARGER ROOM) ALA
(— IN TOWER) BELFRY
(— OF STUDENTS' SOCIETY) HALL
(— ON SHIP) CABIN STOKEHOLD
(— OVER CHURCH PORCH) PARVIS
(— OVER STAGE) SHADOW
(— TOGETHER) CHUM
(— UNDER BUILDING) CELLAR
(CHILDREN'S —) NURSERY
(DINING —) CENACLE DINETTE
REFECTORY
(DRAWING —) SALON SALOON
(DRESSING —) SHIFT BOUDOIR
CAMARIN VESTUARY WARDROBE
TIREHOUSE
(ESKIMO ASSEMBLY —) KASHGA
(EXHIBITION —) THEATER
(GRINDING —) HULL

(HEATED —) STEW
(HIGH —) AERY EYRY AERIE EYRIE
(INNER —) BEN INBY INBYE SPENCE
(INSULATED —) FREEZER
(LIVING —) HOUSE LANAI SALON SERDAB SOLARIUM VOORHUIS
(MONASTERY —) CELL LAVABO
(NARROW —) CRIB
(OCTAGONAL —) TRIBUNA
(PRIVATE —) SNUG SCHOLA
(PUEBLO ASSEMBLY —) ESTUFA
(READING —) ATHENEUM
(RECEPTION —) DIVAN PARLOR MANDARAH
(REFRIGERATED —) COOLER
(RETIRING —) RECAMERA
(ROMAN —) ATRIUM AEDICULA FUMARIUM
(ROUND —) ROTUNDA
(SEA —) BERTH
(SECLUDED —) DEN
(SERIES OF —S) SWEEP
(SITTING —) SITTER BOUDOIR
(SLEEPING —) DORMER BEDROOM DORMITORY
(SMALL —) ALA CELL SNUG STEW CUBBY CUDDY LOBBY CLOSET CUBICLE SNUGGERY
(SMOKING —) DIVAN DIWAN TABAGIE
(SORTING —) SALLE
(STEAM —) STOVE
(STORAGE —) CAMARIN MAGAZINE THALAMUS
(SWEATING —) SUDARIUM SUDATORY LACONICUM
(THRONE —) AIWAN
(TOP —) GARRET IMPERIAL
(UPPER —) SOLAR
ΟOMMATE CHUM ROOMY ROOMIE
ΟOMY WIDE LARGE RANGY SPACY ROOMSOME SPACIOUS
ΟOSE RUSE EXTOL PRAISE FLATTER BOASTING BRAGGING
ΟOST EVE SIT BAUK JOUK TIDE PERCH GARRET HARBOR LODGING ROOKERY SHELTER
ΟOSTER COCK GAME GALLO MANOC GAMECOCK
ΟOT DIG PRY ROI TAP BASE BULB CHAY CHOY GRUB MOOR MOOT MORE RACE SPUR TAIL CHEER FIBER FRUIT GROOT GROUT HEART IREOS LAPPA RADIX STOCK ALRAUN BOTTOM CARROT CATGUT GROUND MUZZLE ORIGIN SENEGA SETTLE SUMBAL SUMBUL ACONITE ALKANET AZAFRAN BIACURU BONIATA CALUMBA CHICORY COLUMBO CRAMPON GINSENG IMPLANT POMOEA NUNNARI PARIERA RADICAL RUMMAGE TURPETH DEDENDUM EARTHNUT
(— BRANCH) TAPOUN
(— CONTAINING STARCH) KOONTI
(— DEEPLY) SCREW
(— OF GINGER) RACE
(— OF ORCHID) CULLIONS
(— OF TOOTH) FANG

(— OF TREE) TANG SPURN
(— OF WORD) THEME
(— OUT) GRUB STUB STOCK EVULSE DISPLANT SUPPLANT
(— TUBERCLE) CLOG
(— WORD) ETYMON
(— YIELDING RED DYE) CHAY CHOY CHAYA
(—S FOR SEWING CANOES) WATAP WATAPEH
(—S OF ACONITE) BIKH NABEE
(CANDIED —) ERYNGO
(DRIED —) JALAP ALTHEA SENECA BRYONIA KRAMERIA LICORICE SCAMMONY
(DRIED —S) INULA IPECAC KRAMERIA VERATRUM
(EDIBLE —) YAM BEET EDDO RADISH TURNIP WASABI PARSNIP RUTABAGA TUBERCLE
(FERN —) ROI
(FINE —) STRING
(FRAGRANT —S) VETIVER
(MASS OF FIBROUS —S) SPONGE
(MEDICINAL —) JALAP LAPPA GINSENG
(PROJECTING —) SPUR
(ROASTED BEET —) BONKA
(STUMP AND —) MOCK
(PL.) CULVERS
ROOTCAP CALYPTRA SPONGIOLE
ROOTED FIXED CHRONIC
(DEEPLY —) BESETTING
ROOTER FAN PLUGGER
ROOTLET CRAMPON RADICEL RADICLE
(PL.) COME CULMS
ROOTSTOCK PIP ROI TARO ORRIS CASAVA DANNUM GINGER ORIGIN PANNUM STOLON BISCUIT TURMERIC
ROPE GAD GUY TIE TOW TUG CEEL COLT CORD FALL FAST GUSS HEMP JEFF JUNK LIFT LINE ROOD SEAL SOAM SPAN STAY TACK TAIL TAUM TOME VANG WARP BRACE BRAIL CABLE CABUL CHECK CHORD LASSO LONGE SHANK STRAP STROP SWEEP TRACE TWIST WANTY WIDDY WITHE CABLET HALTER INHAUL LARIAT LISSOM LIZARD MECATE PINION RAPEYE RUNNER SHROUD SLATCH STRAND STRING TETHER WARROK AWEBAND BEDCORD BOBSTAY CATFALL CRINGLE ENTRAIL HALYARD LASHING LEEFANG OUTHAUL PAINTER PAZAREE PENDANT PIGTAIL SEAMING SERPENT SERVICE STIRRUP SWIFTER BACKBONE BACKSTAY BUNTLINE CABESTRO CORDELLE DOWNHAUL DRAGLINE FOREFOOT FORETACK HALLIARD HAULYARD INHAULER JACKSTAY LIFELINE NECKLACE PASSAREE PROLONGE ROUNDING SEQUENCE THRAMMLE BREECHING
(— A STEER) HEEL
(— COLLAR) PARRAL PARREL

(— COVERING) QUILTING
(— FOR FASTENING GATE) CRINGLE
(— FOR FISH) STRINGER
(— FOR TRAINING HORSE) LONGE
(— FOR TYING CATTLE) CEEL SEAL AWEBAND
(— HANDLE) FETTLE SHACKLE
(— HOLDING RAFT TOGETHER) BRAIL
(— JOINT) TUCK
(— OF 10 OR MORE INCHES) CABLE
(— OF HAIR) CABESTRO
(— OF ONIONS) REEVE
(— OF STRAW) GAD SIME VINE SIMON SUGAN FETTLE SIMMON SOOGAN
(— ON DERRICK) TELEGRAF
(— ON FISHING NET) PINION SEAMING
(— ORNAMENTATION) TORSADE
(— PASSING AROUND DEADEYE) STRAP STROP
(— STOLEN FROM DOCKYARD) RUMBO
(— WITH HOOK AND TOGGLE) PROLONGE
(— WITH SWIVEL AND LOOP) TOGGEL TOGGLE
(— WOUND AROUND CABLE) KECKLING
(—S IN RIGGING) CORDAGE
(ANCHOR —) RODE VIOL VOYAL
(BELL —) TYALL HANGER
(CIRCUS —) JEFF
(DRAFT —) SOAM
(DRAG —) GUSS
(FLAG-RAISING —) HALYARD
(FOOT —) HORSE
(GRASS —) SOGA
(GUIDE —) DRAGLINE
(HANDLE —) FETTLE
(HANGMAN'S —) HEMP TIPPET
(HARNESS —) TRACE HALTER
(HARPOON —) FOREGOER
(NAUTICAL —) TIE TYE COLT FANG LIFT STAY VANG BRACE BRAIL SHEET SLING STRAP STROP GILGUY HAWSER INHAUL LACING RATLIN SHROUD BOBSTAY BOWLINE CATFALL GESWARP LANYARD LEEFANG OUTHAUL PAINTER PAZAREE PENDANT PENNANT PIGTAIL RATLINE SNORTER SNOTTER STIRRUP STOPPER SWIFTER BACKBONE BACKSTAY BUNTLINE DOWNHAUL FORETACK JACKSTAY PASSAREE ROUNDING SELVAGEE WOOLDING
(PART OF —) SLATCH
(SHORT —) SHANK
(SHORT CART —) WANTY
(SMALL HANDMADE —) FOX
(SMUGGLER'S —) LINGTOW
(TALLOWED —) GASKET
(TOW —) CORDELLE
(WIRE —) HAULBACK JACKSTAY
(WORN OR POOR —) JUNK
(PL.) CORDAGE
ROPEBAND RABAND

ROPEMAKER FOLLOWER RATLINER
ROPEWALKER FUNAMBULO
ROPEWAY TRAMWAY WIREWAY
CABLEWAY
ROPY SINEWY STRINGY VISCOUS
MUSCULAR GLUTINOUS
ROQUE CROQUET
ROQUELAURE CLOAK ROCOLO
ROCKLAY
RORIPA RADICULA
RORQUAL SEI FINBACK
ROSARY BEADS CORONA TASBIH
BEADING BEADROLL
(— BEAD) GAUD GAUDY
(MOHAMMEDAN —) COMBOLOIO
ROSE ASH GUL KNOT MOSS ROIS
BRIAR BRIDE BUCKY FLUSH RHODA
CANKER POMPON BOURBON
BURBANK GLAIEUL HUGONIS
LOZENGE MANETTI MONTHLY
OPHELIA RAMBLER AGRIMONY
COLUMBIA DOGBERRY LOKELANI
PEDELION
(COTTON —) CUDWEED
ROSE ACACIA ROBINIA
ROSE APPLE JAMBO JAMBOS
JAMBOSA
ROSEATE SPOONBILL AJAJA
ROSE-BREASTED (— COCKATOO)
GALAH
ROSEBUSH ROSER BALWARRA
ROSE CAMPION LYCHNIS
ROSE-COLORED OPTIMISTIC
(— STARLING) PASTOR TILYER
ROSEFISH BRIM BREAM BERGYLT
REDFISH
(YOUNG —) SNAPPER
ROSE HIP CHOOP CHOUP
ROSELLE SORREL SABDARIFFA
ROSEMARY COSTMARY MOORWORT
ROSMARINE
ROSE MOSS PURSLANE PORTULACA
ROSET BRAZIL
ROSETTE CHOU KNOT COCKADE
ROSEWOOD BUBINGA MOLOMPI
JACARANDA
ROSIN FLUX COLOPHONY
(— SPIRIT) PINOLIN
ROSS SCALP
ROSSER BARKER PEELER SCALPER
SLIPPER
ROSTER LIST ROTA SCROLL
REGISTER
ROSTRATE BEAKED
ROSTRUM PEW AMBE BEAK GUARD
SNOUT PULPIT ACROTER TRIBUNE
ROSY ROSEN BLUSHY AURORAL
HEALTHY AUROREAN BLOOMING
BLUSHFUL
ROT COE RET DOTE DOZE DROP
FOUL JOKE LEAK POKE SOUR WROX
DECAY SPOIL TEASE BLUING
FESTER ROTTEN CORRUPT
HOOFRUT PUTREFY NONSENSE
STAGNATE
(— BY EXPOSURE) RET
(— OF GRAPES) SLIPSKIN
(APPLE —) FROGEYE
(FOOT —) FOUL

(FRUIT —) LEAK
(LIVER —) COE
ROTA LIST ROLL ROSTER ROTULA
ROTARY CIRCLE GYRATORY
ROTATE RUN BIRL GYRE ROLL SPIN
TURN PIVOT SCREW WHEEL GYRATE
REVOLVE TRUNDLE ROTIFORM
ALTERNATE
(— HIPS) GRIND
ROTATING VOLUBLE
ROTATION SPIN TURN ROUND TWIRL
GYRATION SPINNING WHIRLING
(— ON BALL) STUFF
ROTCHE BULL RATCH ROTGE
DOVEKEY DOVEKIE BULLBIRD
ROTE CRWTH HEART ROTTA REPEAT
ROTIFER POLYP LIPOPOD LORICATE
PLOIMATE
ROTL RATTEL WEIGHT ROTTOLO
(PL.) ARTAL ARTEL
ROTOGRAVURE ROTO COLOROTO
ROTOR IMPELLER
ROTTED PECKY
ROTTEN BAD FOUL ROXY SOUR
ADDLE DAZED MOSEY PUTID
AMPERY FRACID MOOSEY PUTRID
DECAYED SPOILED DEPRAVED
UNSTABLE
(HALF —) DOTED DOATED
(PARTIALLY —) DRUXY
ROTTING SLEEPY CARIOUS
ROTTLERA KAMALA
ROTULA ROUND TROCHE KNEEPAN
PATELLA
ROTUND FAT PLUMP ROUND STOUT
CHUBBY SUBROUND
ROTURIER PEASANT PLEBEIAN
RUPTUARY
ROUE RAKE DEBAUCHEE
ROUGE RED FARD BLUSH PAINT
FUCATE REDDEN RUDDLE CLINKER
SCRIMMAGE
(ANIMAL —) CARMINE
ROUGH RU ROW RUF BEAT FOUL
GURL HARD HASK LAMB ROID ROYD
RUDE THUG WILD ACRID BLUFF
BLUNT BRUTE CHURL CRUDE DIRTY
GOBBY GROFF GURLY HAIRY HARSH
HEFTY JAGGY LUMPY REWCH
ROUCH ROWDY RUGGY RUVID
STARK STEER STERN STOUR TOUGH
TOUSY WIGHT BORREL BROKEN
BRUSHY BURRED CHOPPY COARSE
COBBLY CRABBY CRAGGY ELBOIC
ENEVEN HACKLY HISPID HOARSE
HOBBLY HORRID HUBBLY INCULT
JAGGED KNAGGY KNOTTY NOGGEN
RAGGED RAMAGE RASPED ROBUST
RUFFLE RUGGED RUMBLY RUSTIS
SEVERE SHAGGY SKETCH TOOSIE
TRYING UNFEEL UNFELE UNFINE
UNKIND UNMILD UNRIDE ABUSIVE
AUSTERE BOORISH CRABBED
HIRSUTE INEQUAL INEXACT JARRING
RABBISH RAMMAGE RAPLOCH
RUFFLED SCABRID STICKLE STICKLY
UNCOUTH UNKEMPT VICIOUS
ASPERATE CHURLISH DEPOLISH
IMPOLITE LARRIKIN OBDURATE

SCABROUS SCRAGGED STUBBORN
UNGENTLE UNTENDER MANHANDLE
(— EDGES) FASH
(— IT) SIWASH
(— UP ARROW FEATHERS)
SPRANGLE
(MAKE —) SHAG
ROUGHAGE FODDER AVERAGE
BALLAST CELLULOSE
ROUGH-AND-READY BURLY TOWSY
TOWZIE MAKESHIFT
ROUGHCAST PARGET SPARGE
ROUGHHEW SLAPDASH
ROUGHEN FRET GAIG HACK EMERY
FEAZE FLOCK FROST TOOTH
ABRADE CRISLE STIVER CRIZZLE
ENGRAIL SCRATCH UNSMOOTH
(— BRICK WALL) STAB
ROUGHER BULLDOGGER
(PONY —) STRANDER
ROUGH-HOB GASH
ROUGH-MILL GASH
ROUGHNECK ROWDY TOUGH
MUCKER UNCOUTH BANGSTER
ROUGHNESS GAFF GRAIN SCUFF
TOOTH RUFFLE CRIZZLE CRUDITY
ACRIMONY ASPERITY
(— OF SEA) LIPPER
(— OF SKIN) GOOSESKIN
GOOSEFLESH
(— OF WALL) KEY
ROUGHOMETER VIAGRAPH
ROULADE VOLATA ARPEGGIO
ROULETTE FILET FILLET TROCHOID
(1-18 IN —) MANQUE
(13-24 IN —) MILIEU
(HIGH — NUMBERS) PASSE
ROUNCEVAL GIANT LARGE
MONSTER GIGANTIC
ROUND BALL BEAT BEND BOLD
BOUT FAST FULL GIRO HEAD RICH
ROON ROTA TOUR TRIM WALK
ABOUT AMPLE BEADY BRISK CATCH
DANCE GLOBE HAMBO HARSH
LARGE MOONY ORBED PLAIN
ROMAN RONDO SPOKE TROLL
TUBBY CIRCLE COURSE ENTIRE
MELLOW NEARLY ROTUND ROUNDY
RUBBER RUNDLE SPHERY SPIRAL
STOWER STREAK ZODIAC ANNULAR
CIRCUIT SHAPELY CIRCULAR
COMPLETE CROSSBAR ENCIRCLE
GLOBULAR SONOROUS LABIALIZE
(— EDGES OF TIMBER) BEARD
(— END OF LOG) SNIPE
(— FREQUENTLY GONE OVER) BEA
(— IN BOWLING) FRAME
(— IN CARDS) GRAND
(— OF ACTIVITIES) SWING
(— OF APPLAUSE) HAND JOLLY
PLAUDIT
(— OF CHAIR) BALUSTER
(— OF KNITTING) BOUT
(— OF LADDER) STAVE
(— OF PLAY) LAP
(— OFF) TOP CROWN FILLET
(— OUT) ORB BELLY INTEGRATE
(— UP) CORRAL WRANGLE
SCROUNGE

(PLUMP AND —) CHUBBY
(SWEDISH —) HAMBO
ROUNDABOUT PLUMP DETOUR
ROTARY CURVING DEVIOUS
CIRCULAR INDIRECT TORTUOUS
(— MOVEMENT) WINDLASS
ROUNDED FULL BOMBE BOWLY
CONVEX MELLOW ROTUND TERETE
ARRONDI BUNTING CONCAVE
GIBBOUS SHAPELY COMPLETE
FINISHED HOOPLIKE SONOROUS
(— OUT) PLUM
ROUNDEL HEURT PLATE POMME
PELLET FOUNTAIN
(— AZURE) HURT
(— GULES) TORTEAU TORTEAUX
(— OR) BEZANT BYZANT
(— PURPURE) GOLP GOLPE
(— SABLE) GUNSTONE
(— SANGUINE) GUZE
(— VERT) POMEY
OUNDER SOAKER WASTREL
INFORMER
OUNDERS TUT PATBALL TUTBALL
ROUNDHEAD SWEDE CROPPY
WEAKFISH
ROUND HERRING SHADINE
STRADINE
ROUNDHOUSE BARN POOP LOCKUP
ROUNDNESS ROTUND SPHERICITY
(— OF RIBS) SPRING
ROUND POMPANO PERMIT
PALOMETA
ROUND ROBIN ANGLER SERIES
PANCAKE SEQUENCE
ROUNDSMAN VANMAN SWINGMAN
WATCHMAN
ROUNDUP RODEO CAMBER GATHER
ROUNDWORM NEMA ASCARID
EELWORM GORDIAN HELMINTH
NEMATODE STRONGYL
OUP ROLP ROOP CROAK CLAMOR
AUCTION SHOUTING
OUSE DAW GIG HOP JOG BAIT
CALL DRAW FIRK GOAD MOVE RANT
RAVE STIR WAKE WHET AMOVE
ERECT MOUNT RAISE START STEER
UPSET WAKEN AROUSE BESTIR
EXCITE FOMENT KINDLE NETTLE
RATTLE REVIVE RUFFLE WECCHE
AGITATE ANIMATE DISTURB
EKPHORE ENLIVEN HEARTEN
INFLAME STARTLE INSPIRIT
IRRITATE
(— TO ACTION) HIE ALARM ALARUM
BESTIR ALACRIFY
OUSTABOUT FLOORMAN
RAZORBACK
OUT MOB DRUM FUSS HERD BRANT
CHASE COHUE CROWD EJECT
FLOCK LURCH SMEAR SNORE
CLAMOR DEFEAT FLIGHT NUMBER
RABBLE SOIREE THRONG UPROAR
CONFUSE CONQUER DEBACLE
SCATTER SPARPLE TEMPEST
ASSEMBLY CONFOUND DISTRESS
VANQUISH
OUTE WAY BELT GATE GEST LINE
PASS PATH SEND TRACE TRACK

AIRWAY CAREER COURSE CUTOFF
SKYWAY TRAJET CHANNEL CIRCUIT
LANDWAY SHUTTLE CORRIDOR
DISTANCE LIFELINE SHORTCUT
TRAVERSE
(— MARKED OUT) ITER
(— TO DEFEAT) SKIDS
(CIRCUITOUS —) DETOUR
(MIGRATION —) FLYWAY
(OCEAN —) LANE
ROUTH PLENTY ABUNDANT
ROUTINE RUT GRIND ROUTE TROLL
GROOVE HARNESS EVERYDAY
(DOMESTIC —) HOMELIFE
(WEARISOME —) TREADMILL
ROVE RUN RAKE RAVE ROAM GUESS
KNOCK RANGE ROWAN SPACE
STRAY FORAGE MARAUD RAMBLE
STROLL WANDER SPATIATE
STRAGGLE TRANSCUR
(— ON THE WING) FLIT
ROVER FLIRT HOYLE STAKE STRAY
MASHER RANGER VIKING GANGREL
SCUMMER MARAUDER SLIVERER
TRAVELER WANDERER COLORADAN
ROVING END SLUB NOMAD ARRANT
ERRANT DEVIOUS NOMADIC
RAMPLER VAGRANT GADABOUT
RAMBLING RESTLESS SLUBBING
(— IN SEARCH OF KNIGHTLY
ADVENTURE) ERRANTRY
ROW LAY OAR RIG SET DUST FILE
LINE MUSS PULL RULE TIER ALLEY
BRAWL CHESS FIGHT MOUTH NOISE
ORDER RANGE RINGE SCOLD
SWATH TRAIN BARNEY BERATE
COURSE DUSTUP GARRAY KICKUP
LISSOM PADDLE POTHER RACKET
RUCKUS SHINDY STREET STROKE
BOBBERY BRULYIE QUARREL
SHINDIG CATEGORY OUTBURST
REMIGATE SQUABBLE
(— BACKWARD) STERN
(— OF BENCHES) STACK
(— OF CASKS) LONGER
(— OF CORN, BARLEY, ETC.) RIG
(— OF DRY HAY) STADDLE
(— OF GRAIN) SWATH SWATHE
(— OF GRASS) HACK SWATH
(— OF GUNS) TIRE
(— OF HOUSES) CRESCENT
(— OF SEATS) BARRERA
(— OF SEED) DRILL
(— OF VEGETABLES) RINGE
(PL.) EPEIRA
ROWAN RAN RODDIN
ROWAN TREE CARE SORB WICKY
WITCH RODDEN RODDIN WICKEN
WIGGEN QUICKEN RANTREE
WHITTEN WITCHEN ROUNTREE
ROWBOAT GIG OAR BARK OARS
PLAT BARIS COBLE DINGY FUNNY
KOBIL SCULL SKIFF BARQUE CAIQUE
DINGHY LURKER WHERRY SCULLER
(— SEAT) TAFT
(CLINKER-BUILT —) FUNNY
(FLAT-BOTTOMED —) DORY
(SMALL —) COG
ROWDY TOU BHOY CASH MONEY

ROUGH TOUGH TOMBOY UNRULY
VULGAR HOODLUM RAFFISH
BARRATER LARRIKIN STUBBORN
ROWDYISM YAHOOISM
ROWEN EDGROW RAWING
AFTERMATH ROUGHINGS
ROWER URGER GALIOT STROKE
OARSMAN STERNMAN CAIQUEJEE
(— ON UPPER SEATS) THRANITE
(OUTERMOST —) THALAMITE
(SECOND LEVEL —) ZYGITE
ROWING CREW
ROWLOCK LOCK CRUTCH OARLOCK
RULLOCK
ROYAL EASY REAL RIAL ELITE
REGAL SMALT AUGUST KINGLY
REGIUS SOVRAN SUPERB BASILIC
GLORIOUS IMPERIAL IMPOSING
MAJESTIC PAVILION
(— MACE) SCEPTER SCEPTRE
ROYAL ANTELOPE MADOQUA
KLEENEBOC
ROYAL FERN OSMOND OSMUND
ROYALIST TORY ULTRA REGIAN
TANTIVY CAVALIER MUSCADIN
ROYALLY PURPLEY
ROYAL PALM COYAL
ROYALTY LOT ALII GALE BONUS
REGAL REALTY MAJESTY PENALTY
LORDSHIP NOBILITY REGALITY
ROYET WILD HARSH UNRULY
ROMPING
RUB DUB BARK BILL FILE FRAY FRET
FRIG FROT RISP WIPE CHAFE DIGHT
FEEZE FRUSH GRATE GRAZE GRIDE
LABOR SCOUR SCRUB SMEAR
STONE FRIDGE RUBBER STREAK
BEESWAX FRICACE FURBISH
MASSAGE
(— AS A ROPE) SNUG
(— AS ANIMALS) SHAB
(— AWAY) ERODE ABRADE
(— BOOT) BONE
(— DOWN) WIPE STRAP
(— ELBOWS) JOSTLE JUSTLE
(— GENTLY) STRIKE STROKE
(— HARD) SCOUR SCRUB
(— HARSHLY) GRIND
(— LIGHTLY) GRAZE
(— OFF) CROCK ABRADE ABRASE
(— OUT) ERASE EFFACE EXPUNGE
(— ROUGHLY) GRATE
(— SNUFF) DIP
(— THE SKIN OFF) SHAW
(— TOGETHER) FIDDLE
(— VELVET FROM ANTLERS)
BURNISH
(— WITH GREASE) DUB
(— WITH OIL) ANOINT
RUBBED TERSE
RUBBER BUNA FOAM PARA BUTYL
CREPE RASER ALASKA BISUIT
CAUCHO DAPICO ERASER NIGGER
RUNNER BURUCHA EBONITE
ELASTIC GUAYULE RAMBONG
BORRACHA FRICTION NEOPRENE
SERNAMBY SERWAMBY SOVPRENE
(— CITY) AKRON
(HARD —) EBONITE

(RECLAIMED —) SHODDY
(PL.) SHAB
RUBBERIZE FRICTION
RUBBER TREE ULE MILKER
RAMBONG
RUBBING CHAFE CARESS ABRASION
FRICTION FROTTAGE FRICATION
RUBBISH KET CRAB FLAM FLUM
GEAR GWAG MULL PELF PELT RAFF
ROSS TRAG BRASH CRAWM CULCH
OFFAL SCOWL SLUSH STENT STUFF
TRADE TRASH TRUCK WASTE
COLDER DEBRIS GARBLE KELTER
LITTER PALTRY RAFFLE REFUSE
RUBBLE SCULCH SHRUFF SPILTH
BAGGAGE BEGGARY MULLOCK
RUMMAGE SLITHER TAFFIKE
TRAFFIC FIRETRAP NONSENSE
RIFFRAFF TRASHERY TRUMPERY
(VEGETABLE —) WRACK
RUBBISHY POUCY PALTRY TRASHY
BAGGAGE RUMMAGY
RUBBLE BRASH STENT TALUS
BACKING SLITHER
RUBE JAY BOOR HICK JAKE JASPER
BUMPKIN BUSHMAN HAYSEED
CORNBALL
RUBELLA ROTELN
RUBICUND RED ROSY RUDDY
FLORID FLUSHED
RUBIGINOUS RUSTY
RUBLE RO RUBLIS
(ONE-HALF —) POLTINIK
RUBRIC RED NAME CANON CLASS
TITLE CONCEPT CATEGORY
RUBRICATE MINIATE
RUBY AGATE RUBIN PYROPE
ANTHRAX SPARKLE VERMEIL
RUBY SPINEL BALAS ALMANDINE
RUCHING COQUILLE
RUCK RUT HEAP PILE RICK CROWD
SQUAT STACK TRASH CREASE
FURROW HUDDLE PUCKER RUBBISH
WRINKLE
RUCKUS ADO ROW FIGHT FRACAS
ROOKUS
RUCTION HURRY RUCKUS QUARREL
RUPTION FRACTION
RUDD REDEYE
RUDDER HELM STEER STERN TIMON
HELLIM RUTHER STEERER
STEERAGE GOVERNAIL
(— BACK) TALON
(— EDGE) BEARDING
(— OF WINDMILL) TAIL
(DIVING —) HYDROVANE
(PART OF —) STOCK
RUDDERFISH CHOPA OPALEYE
RUDDINESS RUBEDITY
RUDDLE RED BOLE KEEL SMIT
ROUGE
RUDDY RED RODE RUDE FRESH
VIVID BLOWSY BLOWZY FLORID
LIVELY GLOWING RUDDISH
BLUSHFUL RUBICUND SANGUINE
RUDDY DUCK ROOK BOOBY NODDY
PADDY SPRIG BOBBER DUNBIRD
GREASER PINTAIL SLEEPER
SPATTER BLUEBILL BULLNECK

HARDHEAD WIRETAIL
RUDE ILL RAW BOLD IRON LEWD
WILD BLUFF BLUNT GREEN GROSS
PLUMP ROUGH STOUR SURLY
UNORN ABRUPT BITTER BORREL
CALLOW CLUMSY COARSE DUDGEN
GOTHIC HOMELY HOYDEN INCULT
RIBALD ROBUST RUGGED RUSTIC
SAVAGE SHAGGY SIMPLE STORMY
UNFEEL UPLAND VULGAR ARTLESS
BOORISH CARLAGE CARLISH INCIVIL
LOUTISH LOWBRED NATURAL
UNCOUTH UNHENDE CHURLISH
CLUBBISH HOMESPUN IMPOLITE
INSOLENT MECHANIC PORTERLY
STUBBORN SYLVATIC UNGENTLE
UNPOLITE YOKELISH
(— AND BOLD) HOIDEN HOYDEN
RUDENESS GAFF
RUDIMENT GERM ANLAGE VESTIGE
BEGINNING
(PL.) ABC ALPHABET ELEMENTS
GRAMMATES
RUDIMENTARY BASIC GERMING
ABORTIVE ABECEDARY ELEMENTAL
EMBRYONIC
(MOST —) FIRST
RUE RU REWE MOURN CATGUT
REGRET REPENT SORROW BORONIA
TENTWORT
RUEFUL SAD RUELY WOEFUL
DOLEFUL PITIABLE
RUFF SET APEX FURY PAPE POPE
CREST PRIDE REEVE TEASE TEAZE
TRUMP COLLAR RABATO RUFFLE
TIPPET ZENITH ELATION PASSION
QUELLIO REBATER ROTONDE
PICKADILL
RUFFED BUSTARD HOUBARA
RUFFED LEMUR VARI
RUFFIAN MUN LAMB PIMP THUG
TORY BULLY DEVIL ROUGH ROWDY
TIGER APACHE BRUTAL COARSE
CUTTER CUTTLE MOHAWK MOHOCK
PANDER TOWSER HOODLUM
SWEATER TUMBLER HACKSTER
HOOLIGAN
RUFFLE VEX BAIT FRET HOOP ROOL
RUFF BULLY FRILL GRAZE JABOT
PLEAT ROUSE SHIRR ABRADE
ATTACK GATHER NETTLE RIPPLE
BLUSTER BRISTLE DERANGE
FLOUNCE FLUTTER PANUELO
STIFFEN SWAGGER TROUBLE
DISHEVEL DISORDER DISTRACT
FURBELOW IRRITATE QUILLING
SKIRMISH
(— THE TEMPER) ROIL
RUFFLED ROUGH UNKEMPT
RUFFLING (— ON THE SURFACE OF
WATER) HORROR
RUG TUG BAKU COZY HAUL MAUD
PULL SNUG TEAR WRAP BIJAR
HERAT HEREZ JURUK KAZAK KHILA
KONIA KULAH KUMEH LADIK MECCA
MELAS MOSUL NAMDA SENNA
TEKKE TUZLA USHAK YURUK ZOFRA
AFSHAR BALUCH KANARA KAROSS
KASHAN KIRMAN MOGHAN NAMMAD

PERGAM RUNNER SHIRAZ SMYRNA
TABRIZ TILPAH TOUPEE WILTON
BALUCHI BERGAMA BOKHARA
BUFFALO DERBEND DRUGGET
FERAHAN GIORDES GOREVAN
HAMADAN ISPAHAN SHEERAZ
SHIRVAN YARKAND AUBUSSON
DOMESTIC FOOTPACE PANDERMA
SARABAND SEDJADEH SERABEND
WOLFSKIN
(— OF SKINS) KAROSS WOLFSKIN
(PLAID —) MAUD
(PRAYER —) GHIORDES NAMAZLIK
(REVERSIBLE —) KILIM
RUGA FOLD CREASE WRINKLE
RUGBY FOOTER RUGGER FOOTBALL
(— PLAY) SCRUM
RUGGED RUDE WILD HAIRY HARDY
ROUGH STIFF COARSE CRAGGY
HORRID JAGGED KNAGGY KNOTTY
ROBUST SAVAGE STRONG STURDY
UNEVEN CRABBED GNARLED
OBDURATE SCRAGGED VIGOROUS
RUIN DO MAR POT BANE BANG
COOK CRAB DAMN DASH DOOM
FALL FATE FELL HELL JACK KILL
LOSS RASE RAZE SINK TALA BLAST
BOTCH BREAK CRUSH DECAY EXILE
GUBAT HUACA LEESE LEISS SHEND
SHOOT SMASH SPEED SPILL SPLIT
SPOIL SWAMP WRACK WRAKE
WRECK BEDASH BLIGHT CANCEL
COOPER DAMAGE DEFACE DEFEAT
DIDDLE DISMAY FOREDO INJURY
RAVAGE UNMAKE BOWWOWS
CORRUPT DESTROY FLATTEN
FORLESE FORWORK LEESING
PERVERT SHATTER SUBVERT
TORPEDO UNDOING BANKRUPT
COLLAPSE DEMOLISH DESOLATE
DISASTER DOWNFALL
(— AT GAMBLING) SHRUB
(SPIRITUAL —) FALL
(PL.) ASHES DEBRIS RELICS RUDERA
ZIMBABWE
RUINATION DOGS
RUINED FLAT GONE LORN KAPUT
BROKEN FALLEN NAUGHT NOUGHT
FORLORN BANKRUPT DESOLATE
RUINER MARPLOT
RUINOUS DEADLY BANEFUL
DECAYED SHENDFUL WASTEFUL
CUTTHROAT
RULE LAW MAN RAJ WIN DASH KING
NORM SWAY WALD WARD YARD
AXIOM CANON GUIDE JUDGE MAXIM
NORMA ORDER REGLE REIGN RICHE
RIGHT RULER SPILE STAFF SUTRA
SUTTA WIELD ALIDAD CUTOFF
DECIDE DECREE DITION DOMINE
EMPIRE ENTAIL GNOMON GOVERN
MANAGE MASTER METHOD REGNUM
SQUARE VASSAL BROCARD
COMMAND CONTROL COUNSEL
DICTATE DIETARY FORMULA
PLUMMET PRECEPT PRESIDE
REGENCY REGIMEN THEOREM
DICTAMEN DOCTRINE DOMINATE
FUNCTION LEGALISM MODERATE

ORDINARY OVERLEAD PERSUADE
REGIMENT REGNANCY STANDARD
TYRANNIS
(— OUT) EXCLUDE
(— TYRANNICALLY) HORSE
(—S OF CONDUCT) ETIQUETTE
(—S OF DUELING) DUELLO
(ABSOLUTE —) AUTARCHY
(OPPOSING —) ANTINOMY
RULER DEY GOG JAM MIN OBA AMIR
CZAR DAME DUKE EMIR INCA KING
LORD OBBA RULE TSAR TZAR
ALDER AMEER DECAN EMEER HAKIM
MPRET MWAMI NAGID NAWAB
SCALE SOPHI STEER SUBAH ZUPAN
APHETA ARCHON AUTHOR CAESAR
DESPOT DUARCH DYNAST EPARCH
FERULE HERSIR ISWARA KABAKA
KAISER MASTER NIMROD PATESI
PENLOP RECTOR REGENT SAWBWA
SHERIF SOLDAN SUFFEE SULTAN
TYRANT ADMIRAL ALIDADE
BOURBON DEMARCH FAIPULE
ISHVARA KHEDIVE MONARCH
MORMAER PTOLEMY RECTRIX
REGULUS REIGNER TOPARCH
TRIARCH WIELDER AUGUSTUS
BASILEUS DRIGHTEN EXILARCH
GOVERNOR HEPTARCH INTERREX
OLIGARCH PADISHAH PENTARCH
PHYLARCH REGINALD TARAFDAR
WHIPKING
(— IN A NATIVITY) APHETA
(— OF ENCLOSURE) HENRY
(CURVED —) SWEEP
(ELF —) AUBREY
(INCA —) CURACA
(JEWISH —) EXILARCH
(MONGOLIAN —) HUTUKTU
(MOSLEM —) SOLDAN
(STRONG —) REGINALD
(TATAR OR MOGUL —) CHAM
RULING CALL CHIEF REGENT
SOVRAN CURRENT HOLDING
REGITIVE HEGEMONIC
RUM ODD ROME OCUBY QUEER
RUMBO TAFIA TAFFIA BACARDI
CACHACA JAMAICA PECULIAR
SWITCHEL EXCELLENT
RUMBLE CROWL DICKY GROWL
RUMOR SNORE BUMBLE HOTTER
HUMBLE LUMBER WAMBLE
GRUMBLE QUARREL
RUMBO RUM GROG LIQUOR
RUMEN CUD PAUNCH STOMACH
RUMINANT OX COW YAK BULL DEER
GOAT CAMEL LLAMA MOOSE SHEEP
STEER TAKIN ALPACA MAZAME
VICUNA GIRAFFE QUIDDER
ANTELOPE TUBICORN
RUMINATE CHAW CHEW MULL MUSE
CONCOCT REFLECT SAUNTER
CONSIDER
RUMINATION MERYCISM
RUMKIN RUMMER
RUMMAGE GRUB ROUT SEEK
BUSTLE FORAGE TOUSLE UPROAR
FOSSICK RANSACK ROMMACK
DISORDER SKIRMISH UPHEAVAL

(— ABOUT FOR A PROFIT) FOSSICK
(— SALE) JUMBLE
RUMMY GIN RUM TUNK QUEER
CANASTA COONCAN DRUNKARD
OKLAHOMA
RUMOR CRY SAW BUZZ FAMA FAME
TALK WORD BRUIT MUDGE NOISE
SOUGH SOUND STORY VOGUE
VOICE BREEZE FURPHY GOSSIP
MURMUR POTGUN RENOWN REPORT
RUMBLE CLATTER HEARING
HEARSAY INKLING OPINION
WHISPER NORATION GRAPEVINE
RUMORED AFLOAT
RUMP ASS FUD ARSE BEAM CULE
DOCK DOUP CROUP NATCH PODEX
STERN BOTTOM CURPIN CROUPON
CRUPPER HURDIES PLUNDER
BANKRUPT BUTTOCKS DERRIERE
RUMPF CORE
RUMPLE FOLD MUSS WISP TOUSE
TOWSE MOUSLE ROMBLE CRUMPLE
SCRUNCH WRINKLE
RUMPUS RAG ROW BRAWL SHINE
CLAMOR FRACAS HUBBUB RUCKUS
TOWROW UPROAR ROOKERY
ROWDYDOW
RUMSHOP BAR SALOON TAVERN
BARROOM TAPROOM DRUNKERY
RUN GO BYE ERN FLY FOG GAD HOP
JOG LAM LEG PLY RIN RUB URN
BUNK CALL FLEE FLOW FUSE HARE
HEAT HEEL HUNT IRNE KITE LEAD
LEAP MELT PASS PLAY RACE RAKE
RINN ROAM ROVE TEND TRIG TRIP
TROT TURN WALK WEEP WORK
ASSAY BLEND BREAK CHASE COAST
EXTRA GOING HURRY NOTCH POINT
SCOUP SPEED SPEND STAND TABLE
TRACE BICKER CAREER COURSE
ELAPSE ESCAPE EXTEND GALLOP
HASTEN LADDER MANAGE RESORT
ROTATE SPRENT SPRINT STREAM
TUMBLE VOLATA ACCURRE
CONDUCT CONTAIN FLUTTER
LIQUEFY OPERATE PASSAGE
RETREAT SKELTER STRETCH
FUNCTION TRANSCUR
(— ABOUT) TIG FISK DISCURRE
(— ACROSS) STRIKE
(— AGAINST) JOSTLE
(— AGROUND) BEACH GRAVEL
HURTLE STRAND STRIKE
(— ALONG EDGE OF) SKIRT
(— AS STOCKING) LADDER
(— AT HIGH SPEED) SCORCH
(— AT THE NOSE) SNIVEL
(— AT TOP SPEED) SPRINT
(— AWAY FROM DEBTS) LEVANT
(— AWAY IN PANIC) STAMPEDE
(— AWAY) FLY GUY FLEE HIKE JINK
JUMP SMUG ELOPE SCRAM SMOKE
DECAMP SCAMPER SCARPER
FUGITATE SKEDADDLE
(— BEFORE A GALE) SCUD
(— BEFORE A JUMP) FEAZE FEEZE
(— BETWEEN) INTERCUR
(— BLINDLY) SKITTLE
(— CLUMSILY) LOPPET TUMBLE

(— COUNTER) BELY BELIE CROSS
(— DOWN) SLUR OVERRUN
(— HARD) DIG
(— HIGH) FLOOD
(— IN CRICKET) BYE WIDE EXTRA
NOTCH
(— IN DROPS) WEEP
(— INTO) INCUR
(— ITS COURSE) LAPSE
(— OBLIQUELY) SQUINT
(— OF CLAPBOARDING) STRAKE
(— OF MULE CARRIAGE) DRAW
(— OF SHAD) SPURT
(— OF STAIRS) GOING
(— OFF) BOLT SCADDLE
(— ON SKIS) SCHUSS
(— OUT) EXCUR ISSUE PETER
(— OVER) HEAT TRAMP OVERFLOW
(— RAPIDLY) KITE RAKE SCUR
SCOUR SKIRR SPLIT CAREER
(— SOAP) FRAME
(— SPEEDILY) CHASE CAREER
(— SWIFTLY) HARE LEAP SCUD
CHEVY CHIVY
(— THROUGH) PIERCE DISCURRE
(— TO EXERCISE HORSE) HEAT
(— TO) ACCURRE
(— TOGETHER) HERD MUDDY
CLUTTER
(— TRAINS) BLOCK
(— WILD) GAD ESCAPE STARTLE
(— WILDLY) STARTLE
(— WITH AFFECTED PRECIPITATION)
SCUTTLE
(— WITH SKIPS) SCOUP
(— WITH VELOCITY) DART
(BRIEF —) STREAK FLUTTER
(END —) SWEEP
(GLASS FURNACE —) BLAST
(OBSTACLE —) GYMKHANA
(RAPID MUSICAL —) TIRADE VOLATA
(SAILING —) STRETCH
(SHEEP —) SLAIT STATION
(SHORT —) FAIL BICKER SCURRY
FLUTTER RAMRACE SCUTTLE
RUNAGATE APOSTATE FUGITIVE
RENEGADE RUNABOUT VAGABOND
WANDERER
RUNAWAY ROMP RUNNER DECISIVE
DESERTER FUGITIVE RUNAGATE
RUNDI HUTU
RUNDLE DRUM RUNG ORBIT CIRCLE
SPHERE WINDLASS
RUNDLET KEG BARREL
RUN-DOWN BAD SHODDY SQUALID
DERELICT
RUNE WEN WYN WYNN CHARM
OGHAM SPELL SECRET MYSTERY
RUNG RIM GREE RIME STEP ROUND
SCALE SPELL SPOKE STAFF STAIR
STALE STAVE STEAL TREAD WRUNG
DEGREE RUNDLE STOWER STREAK
CROSSBAR TRAVERSE
(— OF CHAIR) SPELL
(— OF LADDER) RIME STEP RANGE
SPOKE STALE RONDLE STREAK
(— OF ROPE WALK) STAKE
(PL.) STILE

RUNIC ALPHABET FUTHARK
FUTHORC
RUNIC LETTER THORN
RUNLET RUSH RINDLE RUNNEL
STREAM RIVELING
RUNNEL RILL BROOK RHINE RINDLE
RUNLET POLLARD RIVULET
STREAMLET
RUNNER SOW GOER POST SCUD
SHOE SKID BLADE COBIA FLOAT
RACER SCARF SKATE SLIDE SPRAY
TEDGE CURSOR HEELER KANARA
RENNER STOLON TOUTER CHANNEL
COURIER HARRIER SARMENT
CURSITOR SKIPJACK TRAILING
(— **FOR GRINDING STONE**) MARTIN
(**BLUE** —) HARDTAIL
(**FLUME** —) HERDER
(**PAIR OF** —S) SLOOP
(**RACE** —) SCUTTLER
(**SLED** —S) BOB
(**SLEDGE** —S) SLIPES
RUNNING RUN CARE EASY RACE
FLUID QUICK COURSE LIVING
COURANT CURRENT CURSIVE
FLOWING HOTFOOT SCUTTER
SLIDING FUGITIVE
(— **ABOUT**) COURANT CURSORY
(— **ACROSS**) DIAGONAL
(— **OF SHIPS TOGETHER**) ALLISION
(— **TOWARD**) APPULSE
(— **VERTICALLY**) DOWN
(**FIRST** —S) HEAD
(**NOT** —) DEAD
RUNNING GEAR MOBILE
RUNT BOOR SCRUB SLINK STEER
STUMP STUNT HEIFER PEEWEE
SCRUMP TITMAN URLING BULLOCK
SHARGAR SHARGER SLINKER
RECKLING
RUNTY MEAN SURLY SCRUBBY
SCRUNTY STUNTED DWARFISH
RUNWAY RUN TIP DUCT TRAIL
TARMAC SLIPWAY AIRSTRIP
DOLLYWAY
(— **OF HARE**) FILE
RUPEE DIB CHIP SICCA ROUPIE
(**100,000** —S) LAC LAKH
(**ONE-SIXTEENTH** —) ANNA
(**TENS OF** —S) RX
RUPERT'S DROP TEAR
RUPIA RUPEE ERUPTION
(**HALF** —) PARDO PARDAO
RUPTURE BLOW REND RENT BREAK
BURST CRACK SPLIT BREACH
HERNIA RHEXIS DISRUPT RUPTION
FRACTION FRACTURE HERNIATE
RUPTURED BROKEN
RURAL RUSTIC BUCOLIC COUNTRY
AGRESTIC ARCADIAN LANDWARD
PASTORAL VILLATIC
RUSE HOAX ROSE SHIFT STALL
TRICK WREST ARTIFICE TRICKERY
RUSH FLY FOG RIP RIX RUB SAG
BANG BENT CLAP DASH DUSH FALL
GIRD HURL HUSH JUNK LASH LEAP
LUSH PASH RACE RACK RASH RESE
RISH ROUT SCUD SHOT SLUR SPUR
SWIP TEAR TILT WHIP WIND ADRUE

CARRY CHASE CHUTE DRASH DRIVE
FEEZE FLASH FLUSH FRAIL FRUSH
HURRY ONSET PIPES PREEL SCOUR
SEAVE SHOOT SPART SPATE SPRAT
SPRIT SPROT START STAVE STORM
WHIRL CHARGE DELUGE FESCUE
HURTLE JUNCUS POWDER RAMACK
RANDOM RAVINE STREAK THRESH
ASSAULT BRATTLE BULRUSH
DAILIES DEBACLE JUNCITE RAMMISH
RAMRACE SKELTER SMOTHER
SWITHER TANTIVY TORNADO
WHITHER CATARACT DEERHAIR
SALTWEED SPLATTER VANQUISH
(— **ABROAD**) FLUSH
(— **AGAINST**) CHARGE
(— **AWAY**) BOLT FLEE
(— **DOWN**) TRACE
(— **FOR WEAVING**) FRAIL
(— **HEADLONG**) BOIL RUIN SPURN
STAMPEDE
(— **OF LIQUID**) HEAD FLUSH
(— **OF WATER**) FRESH SHOOT
SPOUT SWASH
(— **OF WORDS**) SPATE
(— **OUT**) SALLY
(**CLUMP OF** —S) RASHBUSS
(**COMMON** —) FLOSS
(**DOWNWARD** —) HURL
(**FLAT** —) SHALDER
(**FORCEFUL** —) JET
(**NOISY** —) SCUTTER
(**ONWARD** —) BIRR SURGE
(**PL.**) REXEN
RUSHING HURL SCUD FURIOUS
HUDDLING IMPETUOUS
(— **OF WIND**) GUST
RUSHLIGHT SEAVE
RUSH NUT CHUFA
RUSK ZWIEBACK
RUSSELL'S VIPER DABOIA DABOYA
JESSUR KATUKA

RUSSIA

CAPITAL: MOSCOW
COIN: KOPEK RUBLE GRIVNA
KOPECK
COLLECTIVE FARM: KOLHOZ
KOLKHOZ
DISTRICT: KARELIA
FORTRESS: KREMLIN
LAKE: ARAL NEVA SEGO CHANY
ELTON ILMEN ONEGA BAYKAL
SELETY TAYMYR TENGIZ
ZAYSAN BALKHASH
MEASURE: FUT LOF DUIM FASS
LOOF STOF FOUTE KOREC
LIGNE OSMIN PAJAK STOFF
VEDRO VERST ARSHIN CHARKA
LINIYA PALETZ SAGENE TCHAST
BOTCHKA CHKALIK GARNETZ
VERCHOC BOUTYLKA CHETVERT
KROUSHKA
MOUNTAIN: POBEDY BELUKHA
MOUNTAIN RANGE: ALAI URAL
CAUCASUS
NAME: USSR SOVIET MUSCOVY

PENINSULA: KOLA CRIMEA
KARELIA KAMCHATKA
PORT: EISK ANAPA ODESSA
RIVER: IK OB DON ILI KET NER
OKA ROS TAZ TYM USA AMGA
AMUR KARA LENA NEVA OREL
SURA SVIR URAL LOVAT MEZEN
NADYM ONEGA TEREK TOBOL
VOLGA ABAKAN DONETS IRTYSH
DNIEPER PECHORA
SEA: ARAL AZOV KARA BLACK
BAIKAL OKHOTSK
TOWN: KIEV OMSK OREL PERM
GOMEL KASAN KAZAN KYZYL
MINSK PENSA PSKOV TOMSK
IGARKA KERTCH KURGAN NIZHN
ODESSA ROSTOV SARTOV
URALSK ALMAATA BATAISK
DONETSK IRKUTSK IVANOVO
KALININ RYBINSK KOSTROMA
ORENBURG SMOLENSK
TAGANROG TASHKENT VLADIMIR
VORONEZH YAROSLAV

RUSSIAN IVAN RUSS SLAV VELIKA
(— **BRAID**) SOUTACHE
(— **HEMP**) RINE
(— **POOL**) CARLINE
(**LITTLE** —) RUSSENE RUTHENE
UKRAINIAN
RUSSIAN BANK CRAPETTE
RUSSIAN CALF FUDGE
RUSSIAN THISTLE SALTWORT
TUMBLEWEED
RUSSIAN TURNIP RUTABAGA
RUSSIAN WOLFHOUND BORZOI
RUST CLOWN DROSS ROOST ROUS
UREDO AERUGO CANKER CORROD
FERRUGO OXIDIZE
(— **OF PLANTS**) HEMIFORM
LEPTOFORM
(**KNOT OF** —) TUBERCULE
RUSTIC HOB JAY PUT BOOR CARL
CHAW HICK HIND JAKE JOCK RUD
BACON BUSHY CARLE CHUFF
CHURL COLIN DAMON DORIC HOD
ROUGH RURAL RURIC SILLY YOKE
AGREST BUMKIN COARSE FARMER
GAFFER HONEST JOBSON RUSSET
SAVAGE SCOLOC SCOLOG STURD
SYLVAN UPLAND ARTLESS BOORIS
BUCOLIC BUMPKIN BUSHMAN
COUNTRY DAPHNIS FIELDEN
GEORGIC HAYSEED HOBNAIL
HOOSIER LANDMAN PAISANO
PEASANT PLOWMAN THYRSIS
WAYBACK AGRESTIC DAMOETAS
GEOPONIC LANDWARD MOSSBACK
CHAWBACON
(**NOT** —) CIVIL
(**UNCOUTH** —) JAKE
(**YOUTHFUL** —) SWAIN
(**PL.**) COUNTRYFOLK
RUSTLE FISLE STEAL FISSLE FISTL
HIRSEL REESLE BRUSSEL BRUSTL
CRINKLE REESTLE SKITTER WHIST
(— **OF SILK**) SCROOP
(— **UP**) SNAVVLE

USTLER THIEF WADDY DUFFER
WADDIE HUSTLER
USTLING ARUSTLE CRINKLY
FROUFROU SOUGHING FRICATION
SUSURROUS
USTY HOARY MOROSE ROOSTY
SULLEN CANKERY OUTMODED
UT RAT BRIM RACK RAIK RUCK
TRACK TREAD CREASE FURROW
GROOVE STRAKE UPROAR CHANNEL
DESTRUS WRINKLE
— IN PATH) GAY
UTABAGA BAGA SWEDE TURNIP
UTH PITY MERCY MISERY REGRET
SORROW CRUELTY REMORSE
SADNESS SYMPATHY
HUSBAND OF —) BOAZ

(MOTHER-IN-LAW OF —) NAOMI
(SON OF —) OBED JESSE
RUTHENIAN RUSSENE RUSSNIAK
UKRAINIAN
RUTHLESS GRIM CRUEL BRUTAL
PITILESS CUTTHROAT
RUTILE NIGRINE SAGENITE
RUTTER PLOW DRAGOON GALLANT
TROOPER
RUTTISH RANK LUSTFUL

RWANDA
CAPITAL: KIGALI
LAKE: KIVU
LANGUAGE: KIRUNDI SWAHILI
MOUNTAIN: KARISIMBI

MOUNTAIN RANGE: MITUMBA
PEOPLE: TWA HUTU TUTSI
RIVER: KAGERA AKANYARU
LUVIRONZA
TRIBE: BATWA BAHUTU WATUSI
BATUTSI

RYE RAY RIE ERAY REYE SPELT
WHISKY GENTLEMAN
RYEGRASS RAY EAVER DARNEL
RYMANDRA KNIGHTIA
RYND BAIL RHIND MILRIND
RYOT RAYAT FARMER RAIYAT
TENANT TILLER PEASANT

S ESS SUGAR SIERRA
SABBATH SUNDAY SABAOTH
SHABBAT SHABBOS
SABER KUKRI SABRE BANCAL
BASKET TULWAR TUWAUR ATAGHAN
CIMETER YATAGAN ACINACES
SCIMITAR
SABICU JIQUE JIQUI
SABLE DWALE SAPLE OGRESS
SATURN DIAMOND ZIBELINE
(ROUNDEL —) PELLET
SABLEFISH SKIL BESHOW COALFISH
SKILFISH
SABOTAGE MASTIC DESTROY
SAC BAG GUT POD CYST SACK
ASCUS BURSA FLOAT POUCH THECA
VOLVA ACINUS AMNION SACCUS
AMPULLA BLADDER CAPSULE
CISTERN HYGROMA UTRICLE
VESICLE BROODSAC FOLLICLE
SACCULUS SPERMARY
SACCHARIN SWEET STICKY SUGARY
GLUCOSE GLUSIDE
SACCHAROSE SUCROSE
SACERDOTAL HIERATIC PRIESTLY
SACHEM SAGAMORE
SACK BAG BED MAT SAC LOOT
POCK POKE BAYON GOOSE HARRY
POUCH SPOIL BUDGET POCKET
RAVAGE SACKET SACQUE DISMISS
PILLAGE PLUNDER RANSACK
SACKAGE SACKBAG DESOLATE
PACKSACK PEIGNOIR
(— OF PALM LEAVES) BAYONG
(MAIL —) BUM
(PACK —) KYACK
(SAD —) BOLO
SACKBUT SAMBUKE TROMBONE
SACKING SACK GUNNY CROCUS
SACKEN HESSIAN POLDAVY
SOUTAGE
SACRAMENT BAPTISM MYSTERY
PENANCE
SACRED HOLY TABU HUACA SACRE
SAINT SANCT SANTO TABOO DIVINE
SACRAL HALLOWED HEAVENLY
NUMINOUS REVEREND
SACRED FIG PIPAL
SACRED FISH KANNUME
SACREDNESS CHURINGA SANCTITY
TJURUNGA
SACRIFICE GIVE HOST LOSS OFFER
SPEND YAJNA CORBAN FOREGO
VICTIM EXPENSE CHILIOMB
IMMOLATE KAPPARAH LITATION
OBLATION OFFERING PASSOVER
SPHAGION
(— OF 100 OXEN) HECATOMB
(— OF 1000 OXEN) CHILIOMB
(— OF CARGO) JETTISON
(PL.) HAGIGAH CHAGIGAH
SACRIFICIAL PIACULAR
SACRILEGIOUS IMPIOUS
SACRISTAN SEXTON SACRIST
SACRISTY SEXTRY SACRARY
VERGERY PARATORY
SACROSANCT SACRED
SAD WAN DARK DOWY DRAM BLACK
DREAR DUSKY MESTO MOODY

SABLE SOBER SORRY WEARY
YEMER DREARY SOLEMN SULLEN
TRISTE WOEFUL DOLEFUL DUMPISH
FORLORN FUNEBRE LUCTUAL
MOANFUL SOBERLY UNHAPPY
DEJECTED GROANFUL MOURNFUL
MOURNING PITIABLE SUBTRIST
TRISTIVE UNBLITHE
SADDEN SAD DUMP GLOOM GRIEVE
ATTRIST CONTRIST DISTRESS
SADDENED BROKEN
SADDENING LUCTUAL
SADDLE PAD RIG SAG TAG LOAD
SUNK CHINE PANEL PILCH SELLE
STICK BURDEN HEADER RECADO
PIGSKIN PILLION
(— COVER) MOCHILA
(— FOR ONE-LEGGED RIDER)
SOMERSET
(— STUFFED WITH STRAW) SODS
(— WITH) STICK
(— WORKER) LORIMER
(LIGHT —) PILCH PILLION
(MOTORCYCLE —) PILLION
(PACK —) BAT
(STRAW —) SUNK SUGGAN
(WITHOUT A —) ASELLATE
SADDLEBACK JACK JACKBIRD
SADDLEBAG ALFORJA CANTINA
SUMPTER TEETSOOK
(PL.) JAGS JAGGS
SADDLE BLANKET CORONA
SADDLEBOW BOW ARSON
SADDLECLOTH HOUSE NAMDA
HOUSING PADCLOTH SHABRACK
SADDLEMAKER FUSTER KNACKER
SADDLE MAT FLET
SADDLEPAD PANEL PILLOW
SADDLER CODDER KNACKER
LORIMER WHITTAW
SADISTIC SICK CRUEL SADIC
SADLY SAD UNWINLY
SADNESS DUMP RUTH DREAR
DUMPS GLOOM GRIEF UNWIN
SORROW
SAD SACK BOLO
SAFAWID SUFI
SAFE RUG CRIB PETE SURE WELL
SALVA SIKER SOUND SECURE
SICCAR HEALTHY SYKERLY
COCKSURE SILVENDY
(— FOR MEAT) KEEP
(— TO DEAL WITH) CANNY
SAFEBLOWER PETEMAN
SAFEBREAKER YEGG YEGGMAN
SAFE-CONDUCT COWLE GRITH
CONDUCT PASSPORT
SAFECRACKER BOXMAN PETEMAN
PETERMAN TORCHMAN
SAFEGUARD SAVE WARD GUARD
HEDGE SALVE DEFEND SAFETY
SECURE BASTION BULWARK
WARRANT FREEWARD
SAFEKEEPING CUSTODY STORAGE
SAFELY SAFE SICCAR SICKER
SURELY SECURELY
SAFETY SALUTE SURETY WARRANT
SECURITY

SAFETY ZONE ISLET ISLAND
REFUGE
SAFFLOWER KUSUM ALAZOR
SAFFRON
SAFFRON CROCUS AZAFRAN
CROCEUS
SAFROLE SHIKIMOL
SAG BAG DIP TIE SWAG CREEP
DROOP PLANK SLUMP SAGGON
CURTAIN DEFLATE
SAGA EDDA EPIC MYTH TALE RIMUR
LEGEND NJALSAGA
SAGACIOUS DEEP CANNY SHARP
ARGUTE SHREWD CORDATE
SAPIENT
SAGACITY POLICY WISDOM
YEPHEDE SAPIENCE
SAGE RSI WARE WISE WITE CLARY
IMLAC KATHA RISHI SABIO SOLON
SOPHY ABARIS DHARMA SALVIA
SAULGE SHREWD WIZARD EYESEED
MAHATMA SAPIENT SOPHIST
TOHUNGA WISEMAN DEVARSHI
MAHARSHI WISEACRE
SAGEBRUSH SAGE HYSSOP
SAGEWOOD
SAGENESS SAPIENCE
SAGGER COFFIN SETTER CASSETTE
SAGGING DRAG SWAG PTOSIS
SAGITTA ARROW
SAGITTARIUS ARCHER
SAGO PALM CYCAD
SAGRADA CASCARA
SAGUARO SUAHARO SUWARRO
PITAHAYA
SAHIDIC THEBAIC
SAIBLING TORGOCH
SAID DIT QUOTH STATED RELATED
SAIL JIB LUG RAG BEAT GALE HAUL
MAIN SCUN SLAT SWAN SWIM WING
DANDY FLEET FLIER FLOAT FLYER
JUMBO RAFFE SCALE SHEET
ACCOST CANVAS COURSE CRUISE
DRIVER JIGGER LATEEN MIZZEN
MUSLIN SINGLE ARTEMON LUGSAIL
SKYSAIL SPANKER SPENCER
TRYSAIL BACKWIND FORESAIL
GAFFSAIL HEADSAIL MAINSAIL
MOONSAIL NAVIGATE RINGSAIL
STAYSAIL STUNSAIL
(— ALONG COAST) COAST ACCOST
(— AROUND) TURN DOUBLE
(— BRISKLY) SPANK
(— BY THE WIND) STRETCH
(— CLOSE TO WIND) PINCH
(— DOWN) AVALE AWALE
(— FASTER) FOOT
(— IN SPECIFIED DIRECTION) STAND
(— OF WINDMILL) ARM AWE EIE
FAN VAN EIGHE FLIER FLYER
SWEEP SWIFT
(— ON COURSE) HAUL WORK
(— QUIETLY) GHOST
(— RAPIDLY) SCUR SKIRR
(— SWIFTLY) RAMP
(— TO WINDWARD) THRASH
(— WITH WIND ABEAM) LASK
(3-CORNERED —) JIB TRINKET
(FRAGMENT OF —) HULLOCK

(LIGHT —) SHADOW
(LOWEST —) COURSE
(PART OF —) SLAB
(SMALL —) ROYAL
(TRIANGULAR —) RAFFE LATEEN BENTINCK
(WIND —) BADGIR
(PL.) VELA KITES LINENS SAILAGE CLOTHING
SAILBOAT SAIL SCOW BULLY DANDY NABBY SAPIT SCOUT SHARP SKIFF SLOOP SNIPE CANGIA DINGHY QUODDY SAILER SATTIE CATBOAT SCOOTER SHALLOP SHARPIE KEELBOAT SAILSHIP SKIPJACK
(WITCH'S —) SIEVE
SAILFISH BOHO WOOHOO GUEBUCU LONGJAW VOILIER VOLADOR BILLFISH
SAILOR GOB TAR JACK TOTY GUARD KLOSH LAKER LIMEY CALASH CLASHY DAYMAN DECKIE HEARTY MARINE MATLOW SEAMAN TARPOT TIERER TOPMAN MARINAL MARINER MATELOT SHIPMAN SWABBER WARRIOR YARDMAN CANOTIER COXSWAIN DECKHAND FLATFOOT GALIONJI GUNLAYER LANDSMAN LITHSMAN MASTHEAD SHIPMATE WATERDOG WATERMAN WATERRUG YARDSMAN
(EAST INDIAN —) LASCAR
(OLD —) SALT
(SCANDINAVIAN —) KLOSH
SAILORLIKE TARRISH
SAILOR'S-CHOICE BREAM PIGFISH PINFISH WHITING
SAIL YARD RAE
SAINFOIN ESPARCET
SAINT PIR RSI DADU HOLY QUTB WALI ALVAR ARHAT RISHI SANTO BHAGAT HALLOW PATRON SANTON CANONIZE MARABOUT
(CHINESE —) IMMORTAL
(PATRON —) AVOWRY
(PILLAR —) STYLITE
(PL.) SS
SAINT ELMO'S FIRE HERMO CASTOR FUROLE HELENA
ST-JOHN'S-BREAD CAROB
ST-JOHN'S-WORT AMBER TUTSAN CAMMOCK
SAINTLINESS HOLINESS SANCTITY
SAINTLY DEVOUT ANGELIC SAINTED BEATIFIC SAINTISH
(— PERSON) ZADDIK
REGIS RANERE
J SAIN
KE SAKI SCORE
KI BISA MONK COUXIA MONKEY ARKEE
LABLE VENAL SELLING SELLABLE ENDIBLE
LACIOUS LEWD SALT RUTTISH CARLET SCABROUS
LAD SALLET COLESLAW
CORN —) FETTICUS
LADA SALINA
LAL SHALLON

SALAMANDER OLM SOW BEAR NEWT TWEEG GOPHER LIZARD TRITON AXOLOTL CRAWLER CREEPER DOGFISH MECODONT SALAMICH SHADRACH
SAL AMMONIAC SPIRIT SALMIAC
SALARY PAY HIRE SCREW WAGES INCOME PACKET PENSION STIPEND
SALE FAIR VENT BREAK HEDGE TOUCH BOURSE VENDUE AUCTION MOHATRA SELLING HANDSALE KNOCKOUT PORTSALE
(— BY AUCTION) CANT BLOCK
(— BY OUTCRY) ROUP ROWP HAMMER
(— OF OFFICE) BARRATRY
(— OF TOBACCO) BREAK
(PUBLIC —) AUCTION
(RUMMAGE —) JUMBLE
SALESMAN CLERK BAGMAN RUNNER SELLER BOOKMAN DRUMMER OUTRIDER
SALESMANSHIP SELLING
SALESPERSON CLERK
SALESWOMAN WINSTER SHOPGIRL VENDEUSE
SALIENT SPUR BULGE CHIEF ARGINE BASTION SALTANT
SALIENTIA ANURA ANOURA ECAUDATA
SALINA SHOR SALINE
SALINE SALT SALAR SALTY MARINAL
SALIVA SPIT DROOL WATER DRIVEL SLAVER SPUTUM SPITTLE
(— FLOW) PTYALISM
SALIVARY SIALIC
SALIVATION PTYALISM SLOBBERS
SALLET SALADE
SALLOW WAN SICK ADUST LURID MUDDY SALIX SAUCH SAUGH PALLID YELLOW
SALLY GRIP JERK PASS QUIP SAIL QUICK START ESCAPE GAMBIT SORTIE GAMBADE OUTFALL OUTLEAP DEMARCHE
SALMON DOG LAX LOX SAM KETA MASU PINK AMOUT COHOE COUNT HADDO HOLIA SMOLT SMOOT SPROD TECON ALEVIN BAGGIT KIPPER LAUREL MYKISS SAMLET SAUQUI SILVER TAIMEN ANADROM ANNATTO BLUECAP BOTCHER CHINOOK DOGFISH GILLING KAHAWAI KOKANEE NEWFISH REDFISH RUNFISH SAWMONT SHEDDER SOCKEYE BLUEBACK BRANDLIN GOLDFISH HUMPBACK LASPRING SALMONID SPRINGER
(— AFTER SPAWNING) KELT SHEDDER
(— BEFORE SPAWNING) GILLING GIRLING
(— ENCLOSURE) YAIR
(— IN 2ND OR 3D YEAR) SMOLT
(— IN 2ND YEAR) SPROD HEPPER GILLING
(— IN 3D YEAR) PUG MORT
(— ON FIRST RETURN FROM SEA) GRILSE

(BLUEBACK —) NERKA SAUQUI SOCKEYE
(CURED —) KIPPER
(DOG —) CHUM KETA
(FEMALE —) RAUN BAGGIT
(HUMPBACK —) HADDO HOLIA
(MALE —) GIB BUCK COCK
(MILTER —) EKE
(NEWLY HATCHED —) PINK ALEVIN
(SMALL —) PEAL SKIRLING
(SPENT —) JUDY SLAT RUNFISH
(YOUNG —) FOG PARR PEAL GRILSE HEPPER JERKIN SAMLET BOTCHER ESSLING SKEGGER LASPRING
SALMONELLOSIS KEEL
SALON HALL SALOON GALLERY
SALOON CAFE CUDDY DIVAN SALON SHADE BARROOM CANTINA RUMSHOP SCATTER DEADFALL DRINKERY DRUNKERY EXCHANGE
SALPA SALP THALIA
SALSIFY GOATBEARD
SALT SAL CORN KERN SAWT BRINY ZIRAM AMIDOL AURATE GAMMON HALITE MALATE OLEATE OSMATE POWDER SALINE URANIN KAINITE LACTATE MALEATE NIOBATE PHYTATE TROPATE ABIETATE BRACKISH HALINOUS PIMELATE PLUMBITE
(— OUT) CUT GRAIN
(DOUBLE —) ALUM
(HAIR —) ALUNOGEN
(LUMP OF —) SALTCAT
(METAL —) SILICATE
(MIXTURE OF —S) REH
(ROCK —) PIG HALITE
SALTATE JUMP
SALT BOILER WELLER
SALTBUSH BLUEBUSH
SALTCELLAR SALT CELLAR SELLER SHAKER SALTFAT SALTFOOT
SALTED SALEE
SALTICID ATTID
SALT PAN PLAYA
SALTPETER NITER NITRE PETER ANATRON PRUNELLA
SALT PIT VAT WICH WYCH
SALT PORK SOWBELLY
SALTWORKS SALINA SALTERN SALTERY SALTPANS
SALTWORT KALI BARILLA SALSOLA KELPWORT
SALTY SALT BRINY SALINE HALINOUS
SALUBRIOUS HEALTHY SALUTARY
SALUTARY GOOD BENIGN HEALTHY HELPFUL BENEDICT
SALUTATION AVE HAIL ALOHA SALUS MIZPAH SALAAM SALUTE REGREET SLAINTE WELCOME DIEUGARD GREETING HAEREMAI
(DRINKING —) SKOAL PROSIT PROFACE
SALUTE CAP HAIL HEIL KISS MOVE YULE CHEER DRINK GREET HALCH HONOR SALUE SALVO COLORS EMBRACE CONGREET
SALVADOR BAHIA

SALVAGE SAVE SALVE RECOVERY SCROUNGE

SALVAGER SALVOR

SALVATION BODAI MOKSHA SAFETY NIRVANA KAIVALYA SAVEMENT SOULHEAL

(— **APPROACH**) MARGA

SALVE SAW TAR SALVO SAUVE NERVAL SUPPLE PLASTER UNGUENT OINTMENT

SALVER TRAY SERVER WAITER PLATEAU

SALVIA CHIA SAGE CLARY MEJORANA MINTWEED

SALVO SALUTE SPREAD PROVISO TRIBUTE STRADDLE

(PL.) LADDER

SAMARA KEY CHAT

SAMARIA AHOLAH

SAMARITAN CUTHEAN CUTHITE

SAMBA CARIOCA

SAMBAR ELK MAHA RUSA

SAME A ID EAD ILK ONE IDEM LIKE SELF VERY DITTO EQUAL SAMEN IDENTIC SELFSAME

(— **AS**) IQ

(— **PLACE**) IB

(**THAT** —) THILK THICKE

SAMENESS ONENESS EQUALITY IDENTITY MONOTONY

SAMNITES SABELLI

SAMOA (CAPITAL OF —) APIA PAGOPAGO

(**COIN OF** —) TALA

(**ISLAND OF** —) OFU TAU ROSE MANUA UPOLU SAVAII OLOSEGA TUTUILA

(**MOUNTAIN OF** —) FITO SAVAII MATAFAO

SAMOGITIAN ZHMUD

SAMOYED TUBA KOIBA YURAK BELTIR KAIBAL NENTSI KAMASSIN

SAMPHIRE SALTWEED

SAMPLE DIP CAST PREE CHECK ESSAY TASTE TRIAL CHANCE COUPON FLOWER MUSTER SWATCH TASTER EXAMPLE EXCERPT PATTERN SAMPLER TASTING INSTANCE PULLDOWN SPECIMEN

(— **OF METAL**) DIET

SAMPLING SOUNDING

SAMURAI BUSHI RONIN

SAN SAMPI

SANAD SUNNUD

SANBENITO SAMARRA

SAN BLAS TULE

SAN CARLOS ARIVAIPA

SANCTIFICATION HOLINESS

SANCTIFY SACRE SACRI DEDICATE

SANCTIMONIOUS DEVOUT

SANCTION AMEN FIAT ALLOW PIETY ASSENT BISHOP RATIFY APPROVE ENDORSE JUSTIFY PASSAGE SUPPORT ACCREDIT APPROVAL CANONIZE COURTESY SUFFRAGE

SANCTIONED CANONICAL

SANCTITY SANTY HALIDOME HOLINESS

SANCTUARY ADYT BAST BEMA FANE HOLY SOIL ABBEY ALTAR BAMAH GIRTH GRITH SECOS SEKOS TOWER ADYTON ADYTUM ASYLUM CHAPEL HAIKAL REFUGE SENTRY SHRINE SACRARY SHELTER CABIRION DELUBRUM HALIDOME HOLINESS

(— **FOR LAWBREAKERS**) ALSATIA

SANCTUM ADYT ADYTON ADYTUM

SAND DIRT GRIT ARENA GRAIL SONDE GRAVEL ISERINE ISERITE PARTING ASBESTIC BLINDING

(— **FOR STREWING ON FLOORS**) BREEZE

(— **HILL**) DENE DUNE

(— **IN KIDNEYS**) ARENA

(— **MIXED WITH GRAVEL**) GARD DOBBIN

(— **ON SEA BOTTOM**) PAAR

(**BRAIN** —) SABULUM ACERVULUS

(**COLORED** —) SMALT

(**DEAUVILLE** —) STUCCO

SANDAL TIP BAXA FLAT SOCK TEGUA CALIGA CHARUK PATTEN TATBEB RULLION SCUFFER FOOTHOLD GUARACHE HUARACHO

SANDAL TREE SANTOL

SANDALWOOD NAIO ALGUM ALMUG MAIRE CHANDAM SAUNDERS

SANDALWOOD TREE ILIAHI

SANDARAC TREE ARAR LIGNUM

SANDBAG SANDCLUB

SAND BANK AIR CHAR MEAL SAND BATCH HURST HYRST KNOCK SHELF SHOAL

SANDBAR BALK LOOP SAND BARRA SHOAL TOWHEAD

SANDBLASTER FROSTER BLASTMAN

SAND BORER SMELT

SANDBOX TREE ASSACU

SAND COLIC SABURRA

SAND DARTER SPECK

SAND DUNE TOWAN BARCHAN

SAND EEL GRIG SANDFISH

SANDEMANIAN GLASSITE

SANDERLING OXBIRD

SAND FLEA SCREW SCROW SANDBOY

SAND-FLY BUSH TURMERIC

SAND GROUSE GANGA ROCKER ATTAGEN PINTAIL

SAND HOLE BUNKER

SANDIVER NATRON

SAND LAUNCE LANT SMELT WRIGGLE AMMODYTE SANDLING SCRIGGLE

SAND LILY SOAPROOT

SANDMAN DUSTMAN

SANDPAPER TREE CHAPARRO

SANDPIPER JACK KNOT PEEP RUFF STIB WEET OXEYE SNIPE STINT TEREK TIPUP WADER DUNLIN GAMBET OXBIRD PLOVER REDLEG TEETER TILTER TILTUP TRINGA BROWNIE CHOROOK CREEKER FATBIRD FIDDLER HAYBIRD KRIEKER MONGLER MONGREL REDBACK TATTLER TIPTAIL GRAYBACK LEADBACK PEETWEET ROCKBIRD SANDPEEP SHADBIRD SQUATTER SWEESWEE TELLTALE TRIDDLER

(**FEMALE** —) REEVE

(**FLOCK OF** —**S**) FLING

SAND PIT BUNKER

SAND ROCKET FLIXWEED

SAND SHARK BONEDOG

SANDSTONE FAKE FLAG GRES GRI SAND GAIZE HAZEL ARCOSE ARKOSE ARENITE CARSTONE COCONINO GANISTER PSAMMITE RUBSTONE SANDROCK

(**BLOCK OF** —) SARSEN

SANDSTORM BURAN HABOOB TEBBAD

SANDUST VANITY

SANDWICH BURGER GRINDER WESTERN

SANDWORT LONGROOT SANDWEE

SANDY DEEP GRISTY SANDED ARENOSE PSAMMOUS SABULINE SABULOUS

SANE SAFE WISE LUCID RIGHT FORMAL HEALTHY RATIONAL SENSIBLE

SANGA-SANGA ESSANG

SANGUINARY GORY CRUEL BLOO CRIMSON SANGUINE

SANGUINE FOND GUZE MURREY HEMATIC HOPEFUL SARDONYX

SANHEDRIN GEROUSIA

SANICLE ALLHEAL SELFHEAL

SANIOUS ICHOROUS

SANITARY HYGIENIC

SANITY SENSE REASON BALANCE LUCIDITY SANENESS

SAN MARINO (CHURCH OF —) PII

(**DISTRICTS OF** —) CASTELLI

(**MOUNTAIN OF** —) TITANO

(**SUBURB IN** —) BORGO

SANNUP SQUAW

SANSKRIT HINDU

(— **SOUND OR SIGN**) VISARGA

(— **WORK**) VEDANGA

SANS SERIF DORIC GOTHIC

SANTA MARIA TREE BIRMA GAL CALABA

SANTONICA WORMSEED

SAP GOON MINE OOZE RASA SEV HUMBO KEEST LYMPH SAPPER WEAKEN ALVELOZ FLUXURE SAPHEAD

(— **COURAGE**) DAUNT

(**PALM** —) TODY TODDY

(**POISONOUS** —) UPAS

(**SUGAR MAPLE** —) HUMBO

SAPAJOU SAJOU WARINE

SAPANWOOD BOKOM SIBUCAO

SAPEK DONG

SAPID SIPID FLAVORY

SAPIENT WISE SHREWD KNOWIN

SAPLING SCOB PLANT SAPLE SP RUNNEL SPRING TILLER STADDL ASHPLANT SEEDLING SHILLALA SPRINGER

(— **AMONG FELLED TREES**) WA

SAPODILLA GUM CHICA CHICO DILLY ACHRAS MAMMEE SAPOT SAPOTE ZAPOTE NISPERO NISBERRY

APONIFYING KILLING
APONIN GITONIN SENEGIN
CYCLAMIN STRUTHIN
APONITE PIOTINE
APOTA MATASANO
APPHIRE SAFIR TOPAZ ADAMAS
ASTRION HYACINTH
APPHIRINE GURNARD TUB
APPY FRIM FRUM SAPFUL
APSAP PEPEREK
APUCAIA COCO COCOA KAKARAL
APWOOD SAP BLEA SPLENT SPLINT
GUAYABI LISTING ALBURNUM
ARA (— WOMAN) UBANGI
ARABAITES REMOBOTH
ARACEN CORSAIR
ARAH ATOSSA
ARAKOLLE WAKORE
ARASVATI VAC VACH BENTEN
ARCASM RUB GIBE WIPE FLING
IRONY TAUNT RUBBER SATIRE
BROCARD RIDICULE SCORCHER
ARCASTIC ACID WITTY BITING
IRONIC ACERBIC CUTTING MORDANT
INCISIVE SARDONIC SATIRICAL
ARCASTICALLY DRILY DRYLY
ACIDLY
ARCOCARP FLESH
ARCOPHAGUS TOMB COFFIN
ARCOPSYLLA TUNGA
ARDINE BANG LOUR SARD SILD
CLUPEID PILCHARD SARDELLE

SARDINIA
CHEESE: ROMANO PECORINO
COIN: CARLINE
GREEK COLONY: OLBIA
GULF: OROSEI ASINARA CAGLIARI
　ORISTANO
MOUNTAIN: RASU FERRY LINAS
　GALLURA LIMBARA SERPEDDI
　VITTORIA
NAME: SARDEGNA
PROVINCE: NUORO SASSARI
　CAGLIARI
RIVER: MANNU TIRSO LASCIA
　COGHINAS
TOWN: NUORO SASSARI THATARI
　CAGLIARI IGLESIAS

ARGASSUM GULFWEED
ARGO ZEBRA
ARI PATOLA TAMEIN
ARONG PAU KAIN COMBOY KIKEPA
ARSAPARILLA NUNNARI SHOTBUSH
ASH BAR BELT BENN FAJA GATE
OBE SCARF TAPIS TOWEL FASCIA
IRDLE BURDASH CHASSIS
UBBECK CASEMENT CORSELET
(JAPANESE —) OBI
(WINDOW —) CHESS
ASHAY CHASSE
ASH BAR MUNTIN ASTRAGAL
ASSABY TSESSEBE
ASSAFRAS FILE SALOP SALOOP
AXIFRAX
ASSY KICKY
ATAN ANGEL DEVIL EBLIS FIEND

SHREW BELIAL LUCIFER SATANAS
DIABOLUS SATANAEL
SATANIC SABLE INFERNAL
SATCHEL HANDBAG KEESTER
SATE GLUT SATIATE SATISFY
SATURATE
SATED SAD BLASE
SATEEN VENETIAN
SATELLITE MOON ARIEL LUNET
DEIMOS MOONET OBERON PHOBOS
ACOLYTE ACOLYTH LUNETTE
ORBITER SPUTNIK TRABANT
UMBRIEL COURTIER FOLLOWER
(— OF JUPITER) IO EUROPA
CALLISTO GANYMEDE
(— OF SATURN) RHEA DIONE MIMAS
TITAN PHOEBE TETHYS IAPETUS
JAPETUS HYPERION
SATIATE CLOY FILL GLUT PALL
QUAT SADE SATE FLESH GORGE
SERVE STALL ENGLUT STODGE
RASSASY SATISFY SURFEIT
SATURATE
SATIATED SICK JADED SATED
SATIATING STODGY FULSOME
SATIETY FULNESS SURFEIT
CLOYMENT
SATIN SAY ATLAS CYPRUS MUSHRU
COOTHAY CYPRESS SATINET
(SILK —) DUCHESS
SATINFLOWER SAFFRON
SATINPOD HONESTY LUNARIA
SATINWOOD HAREWOOD
SATIRE WIT GRIND IRONY IAMBIC
LAMPOON SARCASM SOTADIC
RIDICULE
SATIRIC BITTER IRONIC ABUSIVE
CAUSTIC CUTTING POIGNANT
SLASHING
SATIRIST GRIND SATIRE JUVENAL
PASQUIN
SATIRIZE SKIN SKIT GRIND EXPOSE
IAMBIZE LAMPOON PASQUIN
SATISFACTION CRO FIN PAY UTU
EASE GREE BELLY ENACH TREAT
AMENDS ASSETH REASON COMFORT
CONTENT DELIGHT GLADNESS
PLEASURE
SATISFACTORILY SPROWSY
CLEVERLY
SATISFACTORY FAIR GOOD WELL
DUCKY HUNKY CLEVER DECENT
ADEQUATE LAUDABLE
SATISFIED SAD FAIN FULL GLAD
PAID VAIN APAID CHUFF PROUD
ASSURED CONTENT GRUNTLED
SENSIBLE WILCWEME
SATISFY PAY EVEN FEED FILL MEET
SAIR SATE SUIT ADEEM APPAY
QUEME SERVE SLAKE SPEED
ANSWER DEFRAY PLEASE STODGE
SUPPLY ASSUAGE CONTENT
EXPLETE FULFILL GRATIFY GRUNTLE
RESPOND SATIATE STAUNCH
SUFFICE SATURATE
(— APPETITE) STAY
(— BY PROOF) CONVINCE
(— NEEDS) DO ADJUST
SATISFYING DUE AMPLE SQUARE
PERFECT

SATURATE SOG GLUT SATE SOAK
DRAWK IMBUE SOUSE STEEP
DRENCH IMBIBE SEETHE SODDEN
DRUNKEN INGRAIN SATIATE
SLOCKEN
(— WITH SYRUP) CANDY
SATURATED SOBBY SOGGY SOPPY
SODDEN SPONGY DRUNKEN
SATURATION CHROMA PURITY
SATURITY
SATURN: (FATHER OF —) URANUS
(MOTHER OF —) GAEA
(SATELLITE OF —) RHEA DIONE
MIMAS TITAN TETHYS JAPETUS
HYPERION ENCELADUS
(SON OF —) JUPITER
SATURNINE SULLEN SATANIC
SATYAGRAHA GANDHISM
SATYR FAUN SAUMON SALTIER
WOODMAN WOODWOSE
SATYRIASIS TENTIGO
SAUCE MOLE SASS SOWL BERCY
CHILE CHILI CREAM CREME CURRY
GRAVY PESTO CATSUP GANSEL
MORNAY ROBERT KETCHUP
MARENGO SOUBISE SUPREME
TABASCO VELOUTE BECHAMEL
CHAWDRON DRESSING DUXELLES
MATELOTE POIVRADE RAVIGOTE
REMOLADE
(CURRY —) SAMBAL
(FISH —) ALEC BAGOONG
(SALAD —) DRESSING
(SAVORY —) DIP
(THICK —) LEAR
SAUCEDISH SAUCER BIRDBATH
SAUCEPAN GOBLET POSNET
SKILLET STEWPAN
SAUCER BIRD PATERA PHIALE
CAPSULE
SAUCINESS SAUCE DICACITY
SAUCY BOG ARCH BOLD COXY
BRASH DONSY DORTY FRESH LIPPY
PAWKY POKEY SASSY SMART
BANTAM COCKET COPPED CROUSE
THWART FORWARD PAUGHTY
MALAPERT PETULANT SANSHACH
SAUDI ARABIA: (CAPITAL OF —)
JIDDAH RIYADH
(COIN OF —) RIYAL
(DESERT REGION OF —) NEFUD
DAHANA ALNAFUD
(PLATEAU OF —) NEJD
(TOWN OF —) HAIL MECCA MEDINA
ALHOFUF
(WEIGHT OF —) OKE
SAUNTER IDLE ROAM ROVE TOIT
AMBLE RANGE SHOOL SIDLE STRAY
TRAIK BUMMEL DACKER DANDER
FAFFLE LINGER LOITER LOUNGE
POTTER PUTTER RAMBLE SOODLE
STREEL STROLL TODDLE WANDER
SNAFFLE STAIVER STRAVAGE
SAURA MAGA
SAUREL SCAD XUREL GASCON
BLUEFISH SKIPJACK
SAURY LONGJAW SKIPPER BILLFISH
GOWDNOOK SKIPJACK
SAUSAGE POT LINK COPPA GIGOT

BOUDIN POLONY SALAMI BOLOGNA
BOLONEY CHORIZO PUDDING
SAVELOY BLACKPOT CERVELAT
DRISHEEN KIELBASA LIVERING
ROLLICHE
(KIND OF —) METT
SAUTE PANFRY
SAUTERNE YQUEM
SAVAGE ILL FELL GRIM RUDE WILD
BRUTE CRUEL EAGER FELON FERAL
STERN FIERCE GOTHIC BRUTISH
FERVENT HOWLING INHUMAN
MANKEEN MANKIND ROPABLE
UNCIVIL VIOLENT WILROUN
CANNIBAL PITILESS THEREOID
WARRAGAL
SAVAGELY FELLY UNMANLY
SAVAGERY FURY FEROCITY
SAVANNA CAMPO SABANA
(— LANDS) LALANG
SAVANT ARTIST VIRTUOSO
SAVE BAR WIN HAIN HELP KEEP
SAFE STOP SALVE SPARE SPELL
DEFEND EXCEPT RESCUE SAVING
SCRIMP DELIVER HUSBAND
SALVAGE WARRANT CONSERVE
PRESERVE
SAVIN HEATH SABINE JUNIPER
SAVING FRUGAL THRIFT ECONOMY
SPARING THRIFTY
SAVINGS FAT ADDLINGS
(— CLUB) MENAGE
SAVIOR LORD SAVER SOTER
REDEEMER
SAVOR EDGE SALT SAPOR SMACK
TASTE DEGUST FLAVOR RELISH
RESENT SAVOUR SEASON TASTEN
SAPIDITY
SAVORLESS FOND INSIPID
SAVORY GUSTY MERRY SAPID
TASTY DAINTY SMERVY GUSTFUL
GUSTABLE TASTEFUL
SAVVY SABE
SAW SAG SEY WEB BUCK REDE
ADAGE FREIT GNOME SCEAR SPOKE
JIGSAW PITSAW RIPSAW SAYING
SCRIBE BACKSAW BUCKSAW
CONVERT DRAGSAW FRETSAW
HACKSAW HANDSAW HEADRIG
HEADSAW PROVERB SLABBER
WHIPSAW CROSSCUT SENTENCE
(— INTO LOGS) BUCK
(— LENGTHWISE OF GRAIN) RIP
(— OF SAWFISH) SERRA
(— WITH TWO BLADES) STADDA
(CIRCULAR —) BUR BURR EDGER
DAPPER TRIMMER
(CROSSCUT —) BRIAR
(CYLINDER —) CROWN TREPAN
TREPHINE
SAWAN SRABAN SHRAVAN
SAWDUST COOM COOMB SAWINGS
SAW FERN DYGAL BUNGWALL
HARDFERN
SAWFISH RAY BATOID COMBFISH
SAWFLY CEPHID
SAW GATE FRAME
SAWHORSE BUCK JACK SETTER
SAWBUCK TRESTLE

SAW KERF SKAFF
SAWMILL RASPER
(— DEVICE) KICKER
(— WORKER) PONDMAN LEVERMAN
SAWYER WETA SAWER PITMAN
TOPMAN KNOTTER
SAXHORN ALTO TUBA ALTHORN
SAXTUBA BARITONE BARYTONE
SAXIFRAGE BAUERA BENNET SESELI
ASTILBE ROCKFOIL SELFHEAL
SENGREEN
SAXONIAN MINDEL
SAXOPHONE SAX ALTO TENOR
SOPRANINO
SAY DEED MEAN MOVE TAKE TELL
SPEAK SPELL AUTHOR QUETHE
RELATE REMARK SAYING REHEARSE
(— A BLESSING) BENSH
(— FOOLISHLY) BLABBER
(— FURTHER) ADD
(— GLIBLY) SCREED
(— NO TO) NAIT NICK
(— OVER AGAIN) REPEAT
(— SPITEFUL THINGS) BACKBITE
(— TOO MUCH) OVERSAY
(— UNDER OATH) DEPOSE
SAYING DIT SAW SAY DICT ITEM
REDE TEXT WORD ADAGE AXIOM
CHRIA DITTY FREIT MAXIM SPEAK
BALLAD BYWORD DICTUM DIVERB
LOGION DICTION PROVERB
APOTHEGM SENTENCE SPEAKING
(— LITTLE) DUMB
(—S OF JESUS) AGRAPHA
(—S OF RELIGIOUS TEACHER)
LOGIA
(CLEVER —) QUIP
(CURRENT —) DICTUM
(OBSCURE —) ENIGMA
(QUICK —) JERK
(TERSE —) EPIGRAM
(TRUE —) SOOTHSAW
(WISE —) SCHOLIUM
(WITTY —) MOT SALLY DICTERY
WITNESS
(WITTY —S) FACETIAE
SCAB RAT ROIN SHAB SNOB CRUST
CANKER ESCHAR RATTER GREENER
RUBBERS BLACKLEG BLACKNEB
SCABBARD CHAPE SHEATH PILCHER
SCABBARD FISH HIKU
SCABBLE SCAB SCALP
SCABBY MANGY SCALD ROINISH
SCABIOUS
SCABIES ITCH SCAB PSORA
SCABIOSA KNAUTIA
SCABIOUS SCABIA BLUECAP
BUNDWEED PREMORSE
SCABROUS SULTRY ASPEROUS
SCAD AKULE XUREL GOGGLER
QUIAQUIA
SCAFFOLD CAGE PEGMA STAGE
BRIDGE CATASTA HAYLOFT
STAGING HOARDING
SCAFFOLDING DOCK STAGING
SCALD BURN LEEP PLOT SCAD
BLAST PLOUT SCAUD BLANCH
SCALDER
SCALE LEAF PELA STEP TAPE CLIMB

FLAKE GAMUT GENUS GULAR PALEA
PELOG PELOK PELTA POISE SCUTE
SHALE SHARD SHELL SHERD SHIVE
TRUNK ASCEND CAUDAL CINDER
COCCID FORNIX GUNTER IMBREX
KELVIN LABIAL LADDER LAMINA
LIGULE LOREAL MENTAL OCULAR
PERULE RAMENT RONDLE RUSTRE
SHIELD SQUAMA STRIGA BALANCE
CLINKER ELYTRON FRONTAL
FULCRUM HUMERAL LATERAL
NUCHALE REAUMUR ROSTRUM
VENTRAL VERNIER ANALEMMA
BRACHIAL LECANIUM LODICULE
MEALYBUG ODOPHONE RAMENTUM
SCRAMBLE SQUAMULE TEMPORAL
UROSTEGE
(— DOWN) DEGRADE
(— OF 7 TONES) SEPTAVE
(— OF CORNSTALK) SHIVE
(— USED BY TAILORS) LOG
(GRADUATED —) RETE
(GREAT —) GAMUT
(SHAD —) CENIZO
(PL.) CHAFF DANDER
SCALEBOARD SCABBARD
SCALEPAN BASIN
SCALER CULLER SOOTER
SCALES TRON TRONE BALANCE
SCALETAIL SQUIRREL
SCALLION PORRET
SCALLOP CRENA QUEEN SQUIN
PECTEN COQUILLE DOUGHBOY
ESCALLOP PECTINID
SCALLOPED INVECTED
SCALP SCAUP SKELP ATTIRE
SCALPER PUNTER
SCALY SCABBY SQUAMY LEPROSE
PALEATE LEPIDOTE SCABROUS
SQUAMOSE
SCAMP LAD RIP LIMB SLIM ROGUE
SKEMP SKIMP THIEF BOOGER
BUGGER NICKUM SINNER SORREL
SORROW HALLION HESSIAN
PEASANT RAMMACK SCUBBER
SKELLUM SNOOZER SCALAWAG
SLYBOOTS SPALPEEN VAGABOND
WIDDIFOW
SCAMPER CHEVY SCOUP CHIVVY
BRATTLE SKITHER SKITTER
SCAN PIPE GLASS METER DEVISE
SURVEY EXAMINE
SCANDAL GUP CLASH CRACK ECL.
SHAME CALUMNY SCANMAG
SLANDER
SCANDALIZE SHOCK
SCANDALMONGER CLAT
SCANDALOUS UNHOLY SHAMEFUL
SCANDINAVIAN DANE LAPP NORS
SWEDE VIKING LOCHLIN NORSEMA
NORTHMAN SCANDIAN VARANGIAN
(PL.) OSTMEN
SCANT SHY JIMP LEAN MEET POO
SCAMP SHORT SKIMP SPLAY
BARISH GEASON LITTLE SCANTY
SKINNY STINGY STINTY SLENDER
SCRATCHY
SCANTILY BARELY FEEBLY SMALL
SCANTLY SPARSELY

SCANTINESS PENURY PARCITY EXIGUITY SPARSITY

SCANTLING STUD FILET JOIST FILLET BOLSTER RIBBAND STUDDING

SCANTY BARE JIMP LANK LEAN POOR SLIM EXILE GNEDE SCANT SHORT SILLY SKIMP SPARE FRUGAL MEAGER SCRIMP SKIMPY SLIGHT SPARSE SCRANNY SCRIMPY SLENDER SPARING EXIGUOUS

SCAPOLITE DIPYRE

SCAPULA BLADE OMOPLATE

SCAPULAR CUCULLA

SCAR ARR EYE WEM SEAM SEAR CHALK FESTER KELOID RADDLE STIGMA TRENCH CHELOID SCARIFY CICATRIX SMALLPOX CICATRICE

(— ON SAWED STONE) STUN

(— ON SEED) HILUM

(— ON TREE) CATFACE

SCARAB ATEUCHES

SCARCE DEAR RARE THIN SLACK DAINTY GEASON CLASSIC UNCOMMON

SCARCELY ILL VIX JIMP SCANT BARELY HARDLY MERELY ONETHE SCARCE SCRIMP WENETH SCANTLY UNEATHS UNNETHE

SCARCITY LACK WANT FAULT SCANT DEARTH FAMINE RARITY PAUCITY

SCARE COW BOOF BREE FAZE FEAR FLEG FLIG FRAY GAST HUSH SHOO ALARM GLIFF GLOFF SPOOK AFFRAY FRIGHT GASTER SCARIFY STARTLE TERRIFY AFFRIGHT FRIGHTEN

(— BIRDS) KEEP

SCARECROW BOGLE BUCCA MOGGY BOGGLE DUDMAN MALKIN MAUMET MAWKIN SCARER SHEWEL BOGGART BUGABOO DEADMAN HODMADOD SHAWFOWL

SCARED SCART SCARY AFRAID GOOSEY STREAKED

SCAREMONGER ALARMIST

SCARF BARB HOOD SASH ABNET ASCOT BARBE CLOUD CYMAR FICHU LUNGI NUBIA SHADE STOCK STOLE TABLE THROW CRAVAT REBOZO SCREEN SQUARE TAPALO TIPPET UPARNA BURDASH DOPATTA FOULARD MUFFLER NECKTIE OVERLAY PUGGREE SAUTOIR TALLITH CLAUDENT COINTISE LIRIPIPE LIRIPOOP MANTILLA MUFFETEE SLENDANG

— ON KNIGHT'S HELMET) COINTISE

ARABIAN —) CABAAN

FEATHER —) BOA

PRAYER —) TALLIS TALLITH

SCARFING GRAFTING

SCARIFY LIFT

SCARLET LAC RED PINK TULY GRAIN KERMES

SCARLET HAW HAWTHORN

SCARLET IBIS GUARA

SCARLET LYCHNIS FIREBALL ONESUCH

SCARLET TANAGER REDBIRD FIREBIRD

SCARLIKE ULOID

SCARP CLIFF SCARF ESCARP SCARPLET

SCATHING MORDANT SCALDING

SCATHINGLY ROUNDLY

SCATOLOGICAL BARNYARD

SCATTER DAD SOW TED FLEE SALT SCAT SEED SHED SPEW VOID FLING SCALE SCHAL SEVER SHAKE SPRAY STREW STROW DISPEL SHOWER SKIVER SPARSE SPREAD SPRENG WINNOW DIFFUSE DISBAND DISJECT FRITTER RESOLVE SCAMBLE SHATTER SKINKLE SKITTER SLATTER SPARKLE SPARPLE SPATTER SWATTER DISPERSE INTERSOW SEPARATE SPLUTTER SPRINKLE SQUANDER SQUATTER

(— BAIT FOR FISH) TOLE TOLL

(— OVER) BESTREW

(— WATER) SPLASH

SCATTERED LAX OPEN STRAY DAIMEN SPARSE DIFFUSE SPOTTED FUGITIVE SPARSILE

SCATTERING SOWING DIASPORA SCATTERY

SCAUP DUCK DOGS DIVER DUCKER DUNBIRD POCHARD BLUEBILL GRAYBACK SHUFFLER

SCAVAGE SCEWING

SCAVENGE CLEANSE GARBAGE

SCAVENGER BUNGY BHANGI BHUNGI MEHTAR REMOVER SCAFFIE CORYDORA HALALCOR

SCAZON CHOLIAMB

SCEAT SKEAT STYCA

SCENE JOG SET CODA CYKE FLAT SITE VIEW ARENA STAGE BRIDGE VISION EPISODE PAGEANT COULISSE EXTERIOR INTERIOR PROSPECT TABLETOP

(— IN OPERA) SCENA

(— OF ACTION) STAGE

(— OF ACTIVITY) BEEHIVE

(— OF CONFUSION) BABEL BEDLAM

(CLOSING —) FINALE

(FINAL —) CURTAIN EPILOGUE

SCENERY DROP FLAT DECOR CUTOUT IMAGERY PROFILE

(PIECE OF —) MASKING

SCENESHIFTER GRIP

SCENT AIR DRAG NOSE ODOR VENT WIND CIVET FAULT FLAIR RELES SAVOR SMACK SMELL SNIFF SNUFF SPOOR TASTE ESSENCE INCENSE NOSEGAY ODORIZE VERDURE FUMIGATE MARECHAL PASTILLE

(— OF ANIMAL FOLLOWED BY HOUNDS) FEUTE

(— OF COOKING) NIDOR

(— OF FOX) DRAG

(FALSE —) RIOT

(LOST —) FAULT

SCENTED OLENT ODORATE PERFUMY ESSENCED

SCAPTER ROD WAND VERGE BAUBLE CEPTER FERULA WARDER

SCHEDULE BOOK CARD HOLD LIST SKED TIME PANEL SCRIP SCROW SETUP SLATE TABLE SCROLL CATALOG TABLEAU CALENDAR REGISTER

(— OF DUTIES) TARIFF

(— OF GAMES) SEASON

SCHEDULED DUE

SCHEELITE TUNGSTEN

SCHEMA FORM

SCHEME AIM GIN LAY WAY WEB CAST DART GAME PLAN PLAT PLOT REDE SWIM ANGLE BABEL CADRE DODGE DRAFT DRIFT KNACK PINAX REACH SCALE SETUP SHIFT TABLE THINK TRAIN BRIGUE BUBBLE CIPHER DESIGN DEVICE DEVISE FIGURE HOOKUP POLICY SCHEMA SYSTEM TAMPER THEORY UTOPIA COUNSEL DRAUGHT GIMMICK IMAGINE KNAVERY NOSTRUM PROJECT PURPOSE CONTRIVE FORECAST GIMCRACK IDEOLOGY INTRIGUE MANEUVER PLATFORM PRACTICE TRIPOTER WINDMILL

(— OF RANK) LADDER

(BETTING —) SYSTEM

(DECEITFUL —) SHIFT

(DELUSIVE —) BUBBLE

(DIAGRAMMATIC —) PINAX

(FANCIFUL —) WINDMILL

(FAVORITE —) NOSTRUM

(VISIONARY —) BABEL

SCHEMER ARTIST DESIGNER ENGINEER SCHEMIST SLEEVEEN

SCHEMING SCHEMY PLANFUL SPIDERY FETCHING PRACTICE

SCHISM RENT SCISSION SCISSURE

SCHISMATIC HERETIC

SCHIST RAG AMPELITE MICACITE MYLONITE OLLENITE PHYLLITE

SCHIZONT MONONT AGAMONT

SCHIZOPHRENIA CATATONY

SCHNAPPER WOLLOMAI

SCHOLAR TUG DEMY GAON IMAM CLERK PUPIL DIVINE DOCTOR FELLOW JURIST LAMDEN MASTER PANDIT SABORA SAVANT SCOLOG SHEIKH BIBLIST BOOKMAN DANTIST LATINER LEARNER MAULANA STUDENT DISCIPLE HEBRAEAN HUMANIST ISLAMIST MASORITE TABERDAR THAUMASTE

SCHOLARLY CLERKLY ACADEMIC

SCHOLARSHIP ART BOOK BURSE BURSARY DEMYSHIP LEARNING

SCHOOL GAM TOL EDDY PREP AGGIE BOOKS ECOLE HEDER MYAYA SAKHA TEACH TRADE TRAIN TUTOR ALJAMA CAMPUS CHEDER CHURCH KUTTAB KYAUNG MADHAB MALIKI RABFAK SCHOLA SCHULE SQUEEL TRIPOS ACADEME ACADEMY CRAMMER MADRASA PENSION STUDIUM YESHIVA AUDITORY DOCUMENT EXERCISE EXTERNAT PEDAGOGY SEMINARY

(— FOR SINGERS) MAITRISE

(— OF BLACKFISH) GRIND

(— OF BUDDHISM) CHAN DHYANA SANRON
(— OF FISH) HERD SCALE
(— OF HINDU PHILOSOPHY) NYAYA
(— OF PAINTING) GENRE
(— OF PHILOSOPHY) SECT ACADEMY AUDITORY
(— OF VEDA) SAKHA SHAKHA
(— OF WHALES) GAM POD
(ART —) LUMINISM
(AZTEC —) CALMECAC
(COMPARATIVE —) FOLKLORE
(DAY —) EXTERNAT
(ELEMENTARY —) GRADES
(HIGH —) HIGH ACADEMY COLLEGE
(MOSLEM —) HANAFI KUTTAB SHAFII HANBALI
(REFORM —) BORSTAL
(RELIGIOUS —) ALJAMA YESHIVA
(RIDING —) MANEGE
(SANSKRIT —) TOL
(SCOTCH —) SQUEEL
(SECONDARY —) LYCEE LYCEUM COLEGIO
(WRESTLING —) PALESTRA
SCHOOLBOOK COCKER
SCHOOLBOY SCUG PETTY CLERGION
SCHOOLHOUSE PORTABLE
SCHOOLING LEARNING
SCHOOLMASTER CAJI CAXI AKHUN KHOJA KHODJA MASTER PEDANT AKHOOND DOMINIE PEDAGOG ORBILIUS
SCHOOLROOM HOMEROOM
SCHOOL SHARK TOPE TOPER
SCHOOLWORK BOOKWORK
SCHOONER JACK TERN QUART QUINT WUINT PUNGEY BALLAHOO
SCHORL COCKLE
SCHRADAN OMPA
SCHROTHER SHREDDER
SCHUYT SHOE SCOUT EELBOAT
SCIATICA BONESHAW
SCIENCE ART OLOGY SOPHY MATHESIS SCIENTIA
(— OF ALGAE) ALGOLOGY
(— OF ANIMALS) ZOOLOGY
(— OF AQUEOUS VAPOR) ATMOLOGY
(— OF ATOMS) ATOMICS
(— OF BEING OR REALITY) ONTOLOGY
(— OF BIOLOGICAL STATISTICS) BIOMETRY
(— OF BREEDING) GENETICS
(— OF CAUSES) ETIOLOGY
(— OF CHARACTER) ETHOLOGY
(— OF CLASSIFICATION OF DISEASES) NOSOLOGY
(— OF DOSES) DOSOLOGY POSOLOGY
(— OF EARTH'S FORMATION) GEOGONY
(— OF EXCHANGE) CAMBISTRY
(— OF FERMENTATION) ZYMOLOGY
(— OF FORMS OF SPEECH) GRAMMAR
(— OF FRUIT GROWING) POMOLOGY

(— OF FUNDS MANAGEMENT) FINANCE
(— OF GEMS) GEMMARY GEMOLOGY
(— OF GOD) DIVINITY
(— OF GOVERNMENT) POLITICS
(— OF HEALTH MAINTENANCE) HYGIENE
(— OF HEAT) PYROLOGY
(— OF HISTORY OF EARTH) GEOLOGY
(— OF IDEAS) IDEOLOGY
(— OF LAW) NOMOLOGY
(— OF LIFE INFLUENCES) EUGENICS
(— OF LIFE OF TREES) SILVICS
(— OF LIFE) BIOLOGY
(— OF LIGHT) OPTICS
(— OF MEASURING TIME) HOROLOGY
(— OF MEDIEVAL CHEMISTRY) ALCHEMY
(— OF MIDWIFERY) TOKOLOGY
(— OF MORAL DUTY) ETHICS
(— OF MOSSES) BRYOLOGY
(— OF MOUNTAINS) OROLOGY
(— OF MUSCLES) MYOLOGY
(— OF NUMBERS COMBINATIONS) ALGEBRA
(— OF PERSUADING A GOD) THEURGY
(— OF PLANTS) BOTANY
(— OF RACIAL IMPROVEMENT) EUGENICS
(— OF REASONING) LOGIC
(— OF RECORDING GENEALOGIES) HERALDRY
(— OF REFRIGERATION) CRYOLOGY
(— OF REMEDIES) ACOLOGY
(— OF SERUMS) SEROLOGY
(— OF SOUND) PHONICS ACOUSTICS
(— OF SPATIAL MAGNITUDES) GEOMETRY
(— OF STRUCTURE OF ANIMALS) ANATOMY
(— OF THE EAR) OTOLOGY
(— OF TIDES) TIDOLOGY
(— OF VERSIFICATION) PROSODY
(— OF VIRTUE) ARETAICS
(— OF WEIGHT OR GRAVITY) BAROLOGY
(— OF WINES) ENOLOGY OENOLOGY
(LEGAL —) LAW
(MILITARY —) STRATEGY
(NATURAL —) STINKS PHYSICS
(RELIGIOUS —) THEOLOGY
SCIMITAR SAX SEAX TURK KHEPESH TULWAUR
SCINDAPSUS POTHOS
SCINTILLATE SNAP FLASH GLEAM GLANCE GLITTER SPARKLE TWINKLE
SCINTILLATION SPARKLE SPARKLET
SCION IMP ROD CION CYON ROOT SLIP GRAFT SPRIG BRANCH SPROUT SARMENT SETLING
SCISSORS SHEARS CLIPPER SECATEUR
SCLERITE TORMA LABIUM PLANTA PLAGULA AXILLARY EPIMERON

SCLERODERMA MORPHEA
SCLEROPROTEIN SPONGIN
SCLEROTIUM ERGOT SCLEROTE TUCKAHOE
SCOFF DOR GAB GALL GIBE GIRD JEER JIBE MOCK RAIL CURSE FLEE FLOUT GLEEK SCORN SCOUT SNEI TAUNT DERIDE REPROVE RIDICULE
SCOFFER MOCKER ABDERITE
SCOLD JAW MAG MOB NAG RAG ROW WIG YAP BAWL CALL CAMP CANT DING FRAB FUSS HAZE JACI JOBE JOWL JUMP RAIL RANT RATE REDD RICK SHAW SNAG SNUB TUC YAFF ABUSE BARGE BASTE BOAST CHIDE DRESS FLIRT FLITE PRATE SCALD SCORE SHORE SHREW SLANG TARGE VIXEN BERATE BOUNCE CALLET CAMPLE CARPET HAMMER HOORAY HURRAH MAGPI RATTLE REHETE REVILE TATTER THREAP TONGUE YAFFLE CHANNE REPROVE TRIMMER TROUNCE BALLYRAG BERATTLE CHASTISE CIDESTER DINGDONG LIPBRAID RIXATRIX
SCOLDING JAW HURL JESSE SCOI DIRDUM JAWING RAKING RATTLE SISERA FLITING HEARING LECTUR RAGGING WIGGING BLESSING CARRITCH JOBATION
SCOLEX HEAD
SCOLYTUS IPS
SCONCE SWAPE APPLIQUE
SCONE FARL FARLE
SCOOP BAIL DRAG ROUT DIDLE GOUGE KEACH SHAUL SKEET BUCKET DIPPER DISHER SHOVEL WIMBLE SCRAPER SKIMMER SKIPPET SCOOPFUL
(— FOR CANNON) LADLE
(— FOR DAMPENING CANVAS) SKEET
(— FOR GRAIN) WECHT
(— UP) LAP LAVE GATHER
(CHEESE —) PALE
(JAI ALAI —) CHISTERA
(LONG-HANDLED —) DIDLE
(SURGICAL —) CURET CURETTE
SCOOT SCOUT SKEET SKYHOOT
SCOPE AREA AMBIT RANGE REAC SCOOP SWEEP VERGE SCOUTH SPHERE TETHER BREADTH CIRCL OPERAND PURVIEW CONFINES DIAPASON LATITUDE
(— OF VISION) COMMAND
(FREE —) SWING
SCOPOLINE OSCIN OSCINE
SCORCH BURN CHAR PLOT SCAM SEAR ADURE ADUST PARCH PLAI REESE SCALD SCAUM SINGE SWI SWELT BIRSLE BISHOP DEGREE SMITCH SOTTER SPARCH SWINGE SWITHE BLISTER BRISTLE FRIZZL SCORKLE SCOWDER SWITHEN SWITHER TORRIFY FIREFANG SCOWTHER
SCORCHED ADUST LEEPIT
SCORCHER SIZZLER

ORCHING BAKING FIRING
.DURENT SCALDING
ORE ACE CUT RUN CARD DROP
.AME GOAL HOLE MAKE MARK NICK
OST RIDE SLOG CHASE CORGE
OUNT EXTRA NOTCH OPERA TALLY
OOREE FURROW SAFETY SCOTCH
CRIVE SPADES STRING TARGET
ICKET TWENTY CONVERT SCORING
CRATCH SQUEEZE GAMEBALL
ARTITUR
- FOR ALE) ALESHOT
- IN BRIDGE) BOARD BONUS
WING
- IN CRIBBAGE) GO PEG FIFTEEN
- IN CRICKET) BLOB CENTURY
- OF NOTHING) DUCK
PTITUDE —) STANINE
ASKETBALL —) HOOP
OWLING —) PINFALL
OLF —) DEUCE EAGLE BIRDIE
JZZARD
INOCHLE —) LAST
ENNIS —) CALL FIVE LOVE DEUCE
ORTY FIFTEEN
IE —) HALVE DEADLOCK
L.) MUSIC
ORED SULCATE SULCATED
OREKEEPER SCORER TALLIER
LLYMAN
ORER NIB MARKER NOTCHER
ORIA SCUM SLAG CINDER
ILLAGE
ORIFIER CAPSULE
ORIFY SMELT
ORN GECK LOUT HOKER SCARN
URN BISMER SLIGHT CONTEMN
SPISE DESPITE DISDAIN
ONTEMPT DERISION MISPRIZE
ORNFUL SAUCY SCORNY SNIFFY
IFTY HAUGHTY FRUMPISH
OLENT
ORNFULLY ASKEW ASWASH
ORPION NEPA ALACRAN STINGER
OPYGI ARACHNID PEDIPALP
IPTAIL
ORPION FISH LAPON SERRAN
GFISH SCULPIN LORICATE
SCACIO
RPION FLY PANORPID
T (ALSO SEE SCOTSMAN) CELT
CK KELT SAXON SCOTTY
JECAP SCOTSMAN
.) SAWNY SAWNEY LALLANS
TCH TRIG SCOTS SCOTTISH
TCHMAN MAC GAUL SANDY
RTAN SCOTCHY SCOTTIE
OTSMAN
TER COOT FILK DIVER SCOUT
ILK BASQUE DUCKER SURFER
HAUG SCOOTER SKUNKTOP
TIA MOUTH
TIST DUNCE

SCOTLAND

V: SCAPA
PITAL: EDINBURGH

COIN: DEMY BODLE GROAT PLACK
RIDER BAWBEE
COUNTY: AYR BUTE FIFE ROSS
ANGUS BANFF MORAY NAIRN
PERTH ARGYLL LANARK
ORKNEY BERWICK KINROSS
PEEBLES RENFREW SELKIRK
WIGTOWN ABERDEEN AYRSHIRE
CROMARTY DUMFRIES
ROXBURGH SHETLAND
STERLING
FIRTH: LORN CLYDE FORTH
MORAY SOLWAY PENTLAND
ISLAND: JURA LONA MULL RHUM
SKYE ARRAN BARRA ISLAY
LEWIS HARRIS ORKNEY
SHETLAND
ISLANDS: ORKNEY HEBRIDES
SHETLAND
LAKE: TAY NESS MORAR LAGGAN
LINNHE LOMOND KATRINE
RANNOCH
LANGUAGE: ERSE LALLAN
LALLAND
MEASURE: COP BOLL CRAN FALL
MILE PECK PINT ROOD ROPE
SPAN CRANE LIPPY FIRLOT
AUCHLET CHALDER CHOPPIN
MUTCHKIN STIMPART
MOUNTAIN: HOPE ATTOW DEARG
NEVIS TINTO WYVIS CHEVIOT
MACDHUI
NATIVE: GAEL PICT SCOT
ORDER: THISTLE
RESORT: OBAN
RIVER: AYR DEE DON ESK TAY
DOON GLEN NITH NORN SPEY
AFTON ANNAN FORTH GARRY
TWEED YTHAN AFFRIC TEVIOT
TUMMEL DEVERON FINDHORN
SEAPORT: ALLOA LEITH DUNDEE
ABERDEEN
TOWN: AYR DUNS OBAN ALLOA
BRORA CUPAR ELLON LEITH
PERTH SALEN TROON DUNDEE
GIRVAN HAWICK DUNKELD
GLASGOW PAISLEY ABERDEEN
DUMFRIES GREENOCK KIRKWALL
STIRLING
WEIGHT: BOLL DROP TRONE
BUSHEL

SCOTLAND ALBANY ALBION SCOTIA
ALBAINN ALBANIA
(NORTHERN —) PICTLAND
SCOTSMAN SANDY SAWNY
SCOTTISH SCOTCH SCOTLAND
SCOTTISH TERRIER DIEHARD
SCOTTIE VERMINER
SCOUNDREL RAP PIMP SCAB VILE
WARY BLECK FILTH KNAVE SHREW
SMAIK SWEEP THIEF WHAUP BRIBER
LIMMER SLOVEN VARLET CATAIAN
GLUTTON HALLION NITHING
SCROYLE SKELLUM VILIACO VILLAIN
WARLOCK BEZONIAN LIDDERON
MASCHANT
SCOUNDRELLY VILLAIN

SCOUR ASH BEAT RAKE SCUM SEEK
SCOOR SCRUB SKIRR SWEEP
DRENCH SCURRY SLUICE DEGRADE
FURBISH BACKWASH STONEFILE
(PL.) SKIT
SCOURER BLOOMER DOLLIER
PICKLER
SCOURGE EEL TAW LASH CURSE
FLAIL KNOUT SLASH SWING BALEYS
PLAGUE SWINGE SCORPION
SCOURGER WHIPSTER
SCOURING BEAT SCOUR HUSHING
SCRUBBING
SCOUT SPY BEAR LION SKIP ROVER
SPIAL VISOR ESPIAL GAYCAT
DESPISE MARINER PICKEER
PIONEER SCOURER WATCHER
EMISSARY OUTRIDER OUTSCOUT
SCURRIER SKIRMISH
(BOY —) CUB BOBCAT SCOUTER
WEBELOS EXPLORER
SCOW ACCON FLOAT GARVEY
SCOWL LOUR FROWN GLARE GLOOM
GLOUT LOWER SKIME GLOWER
VENNER GLOOMING
SCOWLING FROWNY GLARING
SCRAGGY WEEDY
SCRAM HOP LAM BUNK BUGGER
SCRAMBLE MUSS SPURL SCRAWM
SPRAWL CLAMBER LOUSTER
SCRABBLE SCRAFFLE SCRATTLE
SPRACHLE
SCRAP BIT END JAG PIP CRAP ITEM
JAGG JUNK PICK SNAP BRAWL
GRAIN PATCH SCRAN SHRED THRUM
WASTE DISCARD MAMMOCK
REMNANT FRACTION SCRAPPET
SKERRICK SNATTOCK
(— FOR PATCHING) SPETCH
(— OF PAPER) SCRIP
(— OF SONG) CATCH
(— OF WRITING) SCRAPE
(LITERARY —S) ANA
(RAGGED —) SCART
(PL.) ORTS SCRAN RELICS SCROFF
GARBAGE GUBBINGS
SCRAPE LEG RUB CLAW COMB RAZE
CLAUT CURET ERADE ERODE GRATE
GRAZE GRIDE SCALP SCART SCUFF
SHAVE ABRADE RUGINE SCREED
SCROOP CORRADE CURETTE
JACKPOT SCRATCH SCRABBLE
(— ALONG) HARL HARLE SHOOL
(— GOLF CLUB ON GROUND)
SCLAFF
(— OFF) SPUD
(— OUT) ERASE HOLLOW
(— SKINS) MOON SCUD FLESH
HARASS
(— TOGETHER) RAKE GLEAN
MUCKER SCAMBLE
(— WITH FEET) SCAUT
SCRAPED BRIGHT
SCRAPER PAN HARL SLIP CURET
GLOVE HARLE QUIRL RASER SPOON
DOCTOR FRESNO GRADER GRATER
CURETTE FLANGER LEVELER
SLUSHER STRIGIL GRATTOIR
SCRAPPLE TERRACER UNHAIRER

SCRAPING GRIDE RASURE
(CRACKER —S) CUSH
(METAL —S) DIET
(PL.) RAMENTA
SCRAPMAN CHIPMAN
SCRAPPER BREAKER FIGHTER
SCRAPPLE PANHAS PONHAWS
SCRAPPY BITTY
SCRATCH RAT RIT CLAW CRAB
RACE RAIN RAKE RAPE RASE RAUK
RAZE RISP RIST SLUG STUN CHALK
CLAUT CLAWK FRUSH GRAZE
RANCH SCART SCLUM SCORE
SCRAB SCRAT SCROB SCRUB
SHRUB SKELP TEASE TOUCH
BRUISE CANCEL CRATCH RASURE
RIPPLE SCORCH SCOTCH SCRAPE
SCRAWK SCRAWL SCRAWM SCRAZE
SCRIVE TORACE DECLARE EMERIZE
EXPUNGE SCARIFY SCRABBLE
SCRATTLE SCRIBBLE
SCRATCHER RASER
SCRAWL SCRAWM SPRAWL
SCRATCH SCRABBLE SCRIBBLE
SQUIGGLE
SCRAWNY BONY LEAN SLINK
SCRANK SCRAGGY SCRANKY
SCRANNY SCRAGGED
(— PERSON OR ANIMAL) RIBE
SCREAM CRY YAW REME WEAK
YARM YAUP YAWL YAWP YOWT
SKIRL SHRAME SHRIEK SHRILL
SQUALL SQUAWL YAMMER
SCREECH YELLOCH SKELLOCH
SCREAMER CHAJA ANHIMA
SCREECH QUAWK QUOCK SCREAM
SCREEK SCRITCH SKREIGH
SKELLOCH
SCREECH OWL STRICH
SCREED TIRADE
SCREEN TRY CAGE GOBO HARP
HIDE LAWN MASK PICK REJA SCUG
SEPT SIFT TENT ARRAS BLIND
CHEEK CHICK CLOAK CLOSE COVER
FIGHT GAUZE GRATE HOARD SHADE
SHOJI SIEVE SPEER SPIER TATTY
BAFFLE BASKET CANVAS DEFEND
ESCORT MEDIUM PURDAH RESEAU
SCHERM SCONCE SHAKER SHIELD
SHROUD THREAD VOIDER CEILING
CONCEAL CURTAIN FLYWIRE
GOGGLES GRIZZLY REREDOS
SECLUDE SHELTER SHUTTER
TESTUDO TROMMEL BACKSTOP
BESCREEN BLINDAGE COVERING
DIFFUSER ECLIPSER EXCLUDER
HOARDING OCCULTER PARAVENT
PARCLOSE PAVISADE SCREENER
SPLASHER STRAINER TRAVERSE
UMBRELLA
(— ALONGSIDE SHIP) PAVISADE
(— BEHIND ALTAR) REREDOS
(— FOR BATTING PRACTICE) CAGE
(— FOR SHIP'S COMBATANTS)
FIGHT
(— FOR SIZING ORE) GRATE
TROMMEL
(— FOR THEATER LIGHT) JELLY
MEDIUM

(— OF BAMBOO SLIPS) CHEEK
CHICK
(— OF BRUSHWOOD) SCHERM
(— OF FIRE) BARRAGE
(— OF SHIELDS FOR TROOPS)
TESTUDO
(— OF TAPESTRY) ARRAS CEILING
(— ON AUTOMOBILE) GRILL GRILLE
(— TO PROTECT LOOKOUTS)
DODGER
(— USED BY ARCHERS) PANNIER
(BULLETPROOF —) MANTA MANTEL
MANTELET
(CHANCEL —) JUBE
(FIRE —) FENDER
(MECHANICALLY ACTUATED —)
GRIZZLY
(PAPER —) SHOJI
(PL.) CANCELLI
SCREENED BLIND SECLUDED
SCREENINGS CULM SLACK SLECK
SCREENPLAY SCENARIO
SCREW HOB VISE WORM CRICK
FEEZE SCROW TEMPER TOGGLE
COCHLEA AIRSCREW FLATHEAD
SETSCREW THUMBKIN WINDMILL
(KIND OF —) ALLEN MEANTIME
SCREW BEAN MESQUITE
SCREWPOD TORNILLA
SCREWED SQUINCH
SCREWER WORMER
SCREWMAN JACKMAN
SCREW PINE IE ARA HALA IEIE
AGGAG PALMA VACOA VACONA
LAUHALA PANDANUS
SCREW TREE TWISTY
SCRIBBLE SQUIB DOODLE SCRAWL
SCRATCH SCRABBLE SQUIGGLE
SCRIBE EZRA CLERK THOTH
BOOKER SCRIVE SOPHER WRITER
GRAFFER MASORET SCRIVAN
NOVERINT PENCLERK SCRIPTOR
SCRIVANO
(PL.) SOPHERIM
SCRIMMAGE BULLY ROUGE BICKER
SPLORE SKIRMISH
SCRIMP HINCH SCREW SKIMP
SCRIPT BOOK NEUM RONDE SERTA
SERTO NASKHI NESKHI SCRITE
SOOLOOS THULUTH BASTARDA
GURMUKHI HIRAGANA KANARESE
MAGHRIBI MAITHILI MEROITIC
NASTALIQ SCENARIO
SCRIPTURE WRIT AGAMA CHING
SUTRA SUTTA
(PL.) BIBLE GRANTH GRUNTH
TANACH TENACH SHASTRA
SCRIVENER PENMAN WRITER
GRAFFER SCRIVER NOVERINT
SCROFULA EVIL CRUELS
SCROLL BEND ROLL LABEL SCRIT
AMULET ESCROL LEGEND SCRAWL
STEMMA VOLUME VOLUTE EVOLUTE
PAPYRUS RINCEAU BANDEROL
CARTOUCH
SCROLL-LIKE TURBINAL
SCROPHULARIA FIGWORT
SCROTUM BAG COD PURSE

SCRUB FILE SCROG COPPET
SCODGY CLEANSE SCRUBBER
YANNIGAN
SCRUBBY SHRUBBY
SCRUBLAND GARIGUE GARRIGUE
SCRUFF CUFF SCUFF SCROFF
SCRUPLE PASS DEMUR DOUBT
FORCE POINT QUALM STAND STICK
BOGGLE SCOTCH STRAIN STICKLE
STUMBLE
SCRUPULOUS NICE SPICED TENDER
CAREFUL FINICKY PRECISE
DELICATE
SCRUTINIZE PRY SEE SPY SCAN
AUDIT PROBE SIGHT SOUND VISIT
SURVEY EXAMINE INSPECT
ENSEARCH
SCRUTINIZING NARROW SCANNING
SCRUTINY EYE SEARCH CANVASS
EXAMINE HAWKEYE PERUSAL
SCRYER SEER
SCUD RACK RAMP SKID SKIM SCOOT
SCUDO FILIPPO
SCUFF SLARE SLIDE SCLAFF
SCUFFER SCUFFLE SHUFFLE
SCUFFLE CUFF BUSTLE CLINCH
TUSSLE WISTER BRULYIE SHAMBLE
SHUFFLE SCRUFFLE
SCULL FUNNY SKULL
SCULLERY SINKROOM
SCULLION GIPPO SCULL SLUSH
GALOPIN SWILLER CUSTROON
QUISTRON
SCULPIN COTTID GRUBBY JOHNNY
BIGHEAD DRUMMER BULLHEAD
BULLPOUT CABEZONE HARDHEAD
LORICATE SCALAWAG
SCULPTOR GRAVER IMAGER
MARBLER PLASTIC
SCULPTURE CAMEO DRAFT GRAVE
SCULP BRONZE ENTAIL GISANT
SCULPT CARVING DRAUGHT
ENGRAVE GRADINO IMAGERY
INSCULP STABILE MORTORIO
NATIVITY PORTRAIT PREDELLA
SCULLION
SCULPTURED GRAVEN GLYPHIC
SCUM BRAT FOAM GALL HEAD REAM
SCUD SILT SKIM SKIN DROSS FROTH
SCURF SLOAK SLOKE SPUME
FLURRY REFUSE RIDDAM SCRUFF
BLANKET CACHAZA OFFSCUM
LAITANCE SANDIVER SCOURING
SCUMMING
SCUP BREAM PORGY SPARID
SCUPPAUG
SCURF SCALD DANDER FURFUR
SCRUFF DANDRUFF
SCURFY SCALD SCURVY LEPROSE
SCRUFFY SCABROUS
SCURRILITY ABUSE REPROACH
SCURRILOUS LOW FOUL VILE DIRT
GROSS RIBALD VULGAR ABUSIVE
SCURRIL INDECENT
SCURRY BELT CRAB SKIN CURRY
HURRY SKICE SKURRY SCUFFLE
SCUTTER SCUTTLE SKELTER
SKITTER
SCURRYING SKITTER

CURVY SCALD SCUMMY SHABBY
ROYNOUS SCORBUCH SCORBUTE
UNLIKING
CUTAGE ESCUAGE
CUTATE CLYPEATE
CUTCH SCOTCH SWINGLE
CUTE PLATE SCUTUM SCUTELLA
CUTELLATION SCALING
CUTIFORM PELTATE
CUTTLE HOD CRAB SKEP BEETLE
MANHOLE SCUDDLE SCUTTER
CYLLA (FATHER OF —) NISUS
TYPHON
CYLLITOL INOSITOL
CYPHUS PYXIS
CYTHE SY LEA HOOK MEAK
CRADLE
CYTHIAN LAMB BAROMETZ
A ZEE BAHR BLUE BRIM FOAM
FRET GULF HOLM LAVE MAIN RACE
TIDE WAVE BRINE BRINY FLOAT
FLOOD LOUGH OCEAN AEQUOR
PONTUS SEALET STRAND TETHYS
HANNEL HYALINE NEPTUNE
BOSPORUS DEEPNESS SEAFLOOD
THALASSA
— DIVINITY) TRITON
— GOD) PROTEUS
— LETTER) PASSPORT
HEAVY —) POPPLE
MODERATE —) SEAWAY
A ANEMONE POLYP DAHLIA
PELET ACTINIA VESTLET ACTINIAN
DANTHID
A BASS HANAHILL HUMPBACK
ERRANID TALLYWAG
A BEAR OTARIOID
A BIRD HAGDON
A BISCUIT BREAD GALETTE
ANTILE
A BOARD COAST
, BREAD HARDTACK
A BREAM CARP CHAD PORGY
OMAN BRAISE SARGUS SPARID
RWHINE
COAST BANK SEABOARD
ASHORE
COW SIREN DUGONG RHYTINA
RENIAN
CUCUMBER BALATE TREPANG
ICUMBER SYNAPTID TEATFISH
DOG FOGBOW
DRAGON PEGASID QUAVIVER
DUCK DIVER EIDER DIPPER
CKER SCOTER
EAGLE ERN ERNE PYGARG
GARGUS
FARER SEAGOER
FOX THRASHER
GIRDLE CUVY CUTWEED
GULL COB GOR MEW COBB
NET COBBE POPELER
GYPSY SELUNG
HOLLY ERYNGO ERYNGIUM
KALE COLE
. CAN FIX FOB GUM BULL CHOP
RK HARP HOOD JARK LUTE
NK BULLA CLOSE EAGLE PHOCA
L STAMP SWILE THONG UGRUG

URSUK WAFER ASSEAL BEATER
CACHET COCKET DOTARD ENSEAL
ENSIGN FASTEN GASKET MAKLUK
MATKAH OBSIGN PHOCID RANGER
SEALCH SECURE SIGNET CONFIRM
CONSIGN COWROID ENGLUTE
HOODCAP IMPRESS QUITTER
SADDLER SEALING SEALKIE
SIGNARY WEDDELL ADHESIVE
BACHELOR BEDLAMER BRELOQUE
CYLINDER MANDORLA PINNIPED
SECRETUM SEECATCH SIGILLUM
SIGNACLE TANGFISH VALIDATE
(— FOR WATCH CHAIN) ONION
BRELOQUE
(— OFF) CAP
(— OVER CORK) CAPSULE
(3-YEAR OLD —) TURNER
(BEARDED —) URSUK MAKLUK
(EARED —) OTARY
(FEMALE —) MATKA
(GOLD —) BEZEL
(HARBOR —) DOTARD RANGER
TANGFISH
(HERD OF —S) PATCH
(IMMATURE —) BEDLAMER
(MALE —) WIG SADDLER BACHELOR
SEECATCH
(NEWFOUNDLAND —) SWILE
RANGER
(PAPAL —) BULL BULLA
(SHETLAND —) SILKIE
(YEARLING —) HOPPER
(YOUNG —) PUP BEATER JACKET
BLUEBACK
SEA LACE WHIPLASH
SEA LAVENDER INKROOT STATICE
SEALED CLOSE
SEALER CAPPER GASKET
SEA LETTUCE LAVER SLAKE SLOKE
SEAWEED
SEALSKIN SKIN SCULP MATARA
SEALSKIN COAT NETCHA
SEALYHAM TERRIER
SEAM DRY BAND DART FASH FELL
PURL REND DEVIL PEARL SPILL
FAGGOT INSEAM STREAK SUTURE
SEAMLET JUNCTURE OVERSEAM
(— IN INGOT) SPILL
(— IN SHIP'S HULL) DEVIL
(— OF COAL) RIDER SPLIT STREAK
(IRREGULAR —) FASH
SEAMAN SALT JACKY ARTIST
CALASH LUBBER SAILOR MARINER
MASTMAN SHIPMAN SHIPPER
SMASHER WAISTER YOUNKER
DESERTER SEASONER
SEAMARK MEITH
SEAMED SEAMY RUGGED
SEA MILE NAUT
SEAMOUNT GUYOT
SEAMSTER TAILOR SEMPSTER
SEAMSTRESS SEAMER SEWSTER
SEANCE SITTING
SEA NETTLE BLUBBER
SEA ONION SCILLA
SEA OTTER KID KALAN
SEA OXEYE SALTWEED SAMPHIRE
SEA PINK THRIFT SABBATIA

SEAPLANE HYDRO AIRBOAT
AEROBOAT
SEA PLANTAIN GIBBALS
SEA POACHER BULLHEAD
SEAPORT PARA PORT GROIN NATAL
HARBOR MACASSAR
SEA PUSS OFFSET
SEAR BURN FIRE SERE FLAME FRIZZ
ENSEAR SCORCH SIZZLE FRIZZLE
SEA RAVEN SCULPIN
SEARCH FAN SPY BEAT COMB DRAG
DRAW FAND FOND GAPE HUNT LAIT
RAKE RIPE ROUT SEEK SIFT WAIT
FRISK PROBE QUEST SNOOP VISIT
DACKER DREDGE FERRET FUMBLE
RANCEL SLEUTH ENQUIRE EXPLORE
FOSSICK INQUEST INQUIRE INSPECT
RANSACK SCRINGE ZETETIC
FINECOMB OUTREACH SCRABBLE
SCROUNGE
(— ABOUT) GRUB PROG GROPE
(— BY FEELING) GROPE
(— DEEPLY) TENT
(— EVERYWHERE) BUSK
(— FOR FOX'S TRAIL) CIPHER
(— FOR GAME) DRAW GHOOM
QUEST
(— FOR GOLD) FOSSICK
(— FOR KNOWLEDGE) OUTREACH
(— FOR PROVISIONS) FORAGE
(— FOR SMUGGLED GOODS)
DACKER JERQUE
(— FOR WEAPONS) FRISK
(— FOR) FORK HUNT LAIT REQUIRE
(— GROPINGLY) GLAMP
(— INTO) EXQUIRE INDAGATE
(— OUT) FERRET INVENT EXQUIRE
(— SHIP) RUMMAGE
(— SYSTEMATICALLY) COMB
(— THROUGH) TURN
(— UNDERWATER) FISH
(SYSTEMATIC —) SWEEP
SEARCHER FINDER
SEARCHING HARD SHREWD
CURIOUS GROPING
SEARED ADUST
SEARING CAUTERY
SEA ROBIN GURNARD WINGFISH
SEA ROVER VIKING SCUMMER
SEASAN NUDE
SEASCAPE SEAPIECE
SEA SCORPION COBBLER
SEA SERPENT ELOPS
SEASHELL PROP
SEASHORE SEA RIPE CLEVE COAST
MARINE SEASIDE SEABEACH
SEABOARD SEACOAST
SEASICKNESS HILO NAUPATHIA
SEA SNAIL LIPARIAN
SEA SNAKE CHITAL KERRIL
SEASON BEEK CORN DASH FALL
PERT SALT SEEL TIDE TIME GRASS
SAUCE SAVOR SHEMU SPICE
AUTUMN EASTER FLOWER HARDEN
HAYING MASTER SPRING STEVEN
STOUND SUMMER WINTER BUDTIME
FLYTIME HARVEST KITCHEN
OATSEED SEEDTIME
(— FOR HERRING FISHING) DRAVE

(— HIGHLY) DEVIL
(— IN THE SUN) HAZE
(— OF JOY) JUBILEE
(— OF MERRYMAKING) CARNIVAL
(CLOSED —) SHUTOFF
(DULL —) SLACK
(EGYPTIAN —) AHET PERT SHEMU
(HAYING —) HAYING HAYSEL
(LENTEN —) CAREME
(RAINLESS —) DRY
(RAINY —) KHARIF VARSHA
(REGULARLY RECURRING —) EMBER
(SPRING —) WARE APRIL GRASS
(THE RIGHT —) TID
SEASONABLE PAT TIDY TIMELY
TIDEFUL TIMEFUL VETERAN
TOWARDLY
SEASONABLY TIMELY APROPOS
BETIMES
SEASONED SAGY SALT SALTED
INDIENNE POWDERED
(MILDLY —) SWEET
SEASONER SURFACER
SEASONING SALT SPICE SEASON
SPICING
SEA SQUIRT ASCIDIAN
SEA SWALLOW TERN
SEAT BOX CAN SEE SET BANK BOSS
COSY DAIS FLOP FORM FROG ROOM
SILL SLIP SUNK TOIT ASANA BENCH
CELLE CHAIR DICKY SELLA SELLE
SETTE SIEGE SLIDE STALL STOOL
BOUGHT DODONA EXEDRA HUMPTY
INSIDE RUMBLE SADDLE SEATER
SEGGIO SETTEE SETTLE THWART
BUTTOCK CUSHION GRADINE
GRADINO INSTALL OTTOMAN
SEATING TABORET TRANSOM
BLEACHER ENTHRONE PULVINAR
SEGGIOLA SUBSELLA WOOLPACK
(— AT PUBLIC SPECTACLE)
PULVINAR
(— FOR CLERGY) SEDILE
(— FOR GRINDER) HORSING
(— FOR PLANE IRON) FROG
(— OF BIRTH) SIDE
(— OF EMOTIONS) CHEST SPLEEN
(— OF FEELINGS) STOMACH
(— OF HARE) FORM
(— OF INTELLECT) HEAD
(— OF KNOWLEDGE) RUACH
(— OF ORACLE) DODONA
(— OF PITY) BOWEL
(— OF POWER) SEE
(— OF REAL LIFE) SOUL
(— OF RESPONSIBILITY) SHOULDER
(— OF RULE) OGDOAD
(— OF TURF) SUNK
(— OF UNDERSTANDING) SKULL
(— ON ELEPHANT'S BACK) TOWER
CASTLE HOWDAH
(— ONESELF) LEAN PITCH
(— SLUNG ON POLES) HORSE
(— WITH BRAZIER BELOW)
TENDOUR
(— WITHIN WINDOW OPENING)
CAROL
(AIRPLANE —) DORMETTE
(BACKLESS —) STOOL HASSOCK

(BISHOP'S —) APSE BISHOPRIC
(CANOPIED —) COSY COZY
(CARRIAGE —) DICKY
(CHIMNEY —) SCONCE
(CHURCH —) PEW DESK STALL
SEDILE
(COACH —) BOOT POOP
(COUNTRY —) TOWER GRANGE
QUINTA
(DRAPED —) MUSNUD
(DRIVER'S —) BOX DICKY FORETOP
(ELEVATED —) PERCH
(FIXED —) DAIS
(KEY —) KEYWAY
(LONG —) BANK FORM BENCH
(NIPPLE —) LUMP
(OARSMAN'S —) TAFT
(PORCH —) GLIDER
(RECLINING —) DORMEUSE
(ROWER'S —) THWART
(ROYAL —) SIEGE STEAD THRONE
(STAGECOACH —S) BASKET
(STRAW —) BOSS
(TIER OF —S) TENDIDO
(UNRESERVED —S) BLUES
SEA TANGLE FURBELOW
SEA TROUT SEWEN SMELT KIPPER
HERLING HIRLING BODIERON
(— AFTER SPAWNING) KELT
(YOUNG —) PEAL
SEA TURTLE CHELONID
SEA URCHIN WANA REPKIE ARBACIA
CIDARID ECHINID ECHINUS RADIATE
(FOSSIL —) ECHINITE
SEAWALL BULWARK
SEAWARD OFF MAKAI
SEAWEED ORE AGAR ALGA KELP
LIMU MOSS NORI OOZE REEK REIT
TANG WARE DRIFT DULSE KOMBU
LAVER SLAKE SLOKE VAREC VRAIC
WRACK DELISK FUCOID FUNORI
TANGLE HAITSAI OARWEED
OREWEED OREWOOD REDWARE
SEATANG SEAWARE CARAGEEN
CORALINE GULFWEED HEMPWEED
ROCKWEED SARGASSO SEABEARD
WHIPCORD WHIPLASH
(PL.) LUMUT
SEBESTEN MYXA
SECANT SEC CHORD
SECCO FRESCO
SECEDE SPLINTER
SECESSIONIST SECESH SEPARATE
SECLUDE TACKLE ENCLOSE ISOLATE
RECLUSE CLOISTER
SECLUDED COY SHY DEEP CLOSE
QUIET HIDDEN REMOTE SECRET
PRIVATE RETIRED RECLUSE
HIDEAWAY MONASTIC SEPARATE
UMBRATIC
SECLUSION RECESS SHADOW
PRIVACY PRIVITY RETREAT
SECRECY SEQUEST SOLITUDE
SECOND AID SEC ABET BACK BETA
TICK OTHER VOUCH ASSIST LATTER
MOMENT TARTAN TIDDER TOTHER
ANOTHER INSTANT SUPPORT
SUSTAIN STICKLER
(— BASE) KEYSTONE

(— IN COMMAND) DEPUTY
(— PERSON USE) TUISM
(1000TH OF A —) SIGMA
(60TH OF A —) THIRD
SECONDARY BY BYE SUB SLACK
DONKEY SECOND CUBITAL DERIVE
INFERIOR
(PL.) FLAGS
SECONDHAND USED
SECOND-RATE COMMON INFERIOR
SECOND-RATER PIKER
SECRECY DERN HUSH HIDING
SECRET PRIVACY PRIVITY SILENCE
DARKNESS SCUGGERY VELATION
SECRET SLY DARK DERN BLIND
CABAL CLOSE PRIVY QUIET ARCA
CLOSET COVERT HIDDEN INWARD
POCKET STOLEN ARCANUM
COUNSEL CRYPTIC EOPTIC
FURTIVE MYSTERY PRIVACY
PRIVATE PRIVITY RECLUSE RESER
RETIRED SECRETA UNKNOWN
ESOTERIC HIDLINGS MYSTICAL
SNEAKING STEALTHY
SECRETARY CLERK COPPY BARU
MUNSHI RAPTOR SCRIBE FAMULU
MUNSHEE MOONSHEE
SECRETE HIDE NICHE RESET
SECERN SECRET CONCEAL
SECLUDE SALIVATE SEPARATE
(— MILK) LACTATE
(— ONESELF) HIVE
(— SALIVA) DROOL
SECRETION INK LAC GOWL LAAP
LERP MILT SPIT WOOL HUMOR
LAARP MUCUS SEPIA SLIME SPAC
CEMENT SALIVA SMEGMA CERUM
CHALONE FLOCOON HORMONE
SPITTLE ENDOCRIN
(THICKENED —) GUM
(WAXY —) LERP LAARP
SECRETIVE SLY DARK SNUG
COVERT SECRET SILENT INVOLVE
SECRETIVENESS SECRECY
SLYNESS
SECRETLY CLOSE DARKLY DERN
SECRET CLOSELY HIDLINGS
INWARDLY
SECT SET ZEN BABI CULT JODO
KIND SHIN ALOGI BHORA ISAWA
PANTH BOHORA DONMEH HERES
SCHISM SCHOOL DHUNDIA DOCE
HASIDIM ISAWIYA KHALSAH
RINGATU SECTARY SEQUELA
SHAIKHI SHINGON SIVAISM SUBS
AGNOETAE AHMADIYA AISSAOUA
MURJIITE NAASSENE SECTUARY
SHAKTISM
(MEMBER OF —) KHLYSI OPHITE
YEZIDI MOLOKAN NUSAIRI LINGA
SECTARIAN CULTIST HERETIC
MAZHABI SECTARY SECTIST
SECTARY JESUIT HERETIC SECTI
SECTUARY SEPARATE
SECTION CUT END AREA PACE P
SECT UNIT CAPUT FRUST SHARE
TMEMA BILLET BRANCH BRIDGE
CANTON LENGTH MEMBER SECT
ARTICLE CUTTING HEADING

SEGMENT TRANCHE ADDENDUM
DIVISION FRACTION
(— AROUND HOP KILN) CURB
(— OF A BODY) LAMINA
(— OF AVICENNA'S WORK) FEN
(— OF BLOOM) STAMP
(— OF BUILDING) ENTRY
(— OF FENCE) FLAKE
(— OF FILM) EXPOSURE
(— OF FILTER) LEAF
(— OF FISHING TACKLE) TRACE
(— OF GARMENT) GORE
(— OF GLASS) SHAWL
(— OF HIGH GROUND) DIVIDE
(— OF KORAN) SURA
(— OF LADDER) FLY
(— OF LOG) BOLT FLITCH
(— OF LOOM) LAY
(— OF NET) DEEPING
(— OF NEWSPAPER) LEAD
(— OF PARLIAMENT) LAGTHING
(— OF PSALTER) CATHISMA
(— OF RHAPSODY) LASSU
(— OF ROOF) SEVERY
(— OF ROOTSTOCK) BIT
(— OF SHIP) STEERAGE
(— OF SONG) STOLLEN
(— OF THREE SHEETS) TERNION
(— OF TRENCH) BAY
(— OF VIOLIN) BOUT
(— OF WOOD) HAG
(— OF YARN) SLUB
(—S OF SCENERY) BOOK
(4-PAGE —) OUTSERT
(CONCLUDING —) ABGESANG
(CONIC —) PARABOLA
(DULL —) LONGUEUR
(LOWEST —) BOTTOM
(MINE —) BORASQUE BORRASCA
(MUSICAL —) CODA EPILOG FINALE
(NARROW —) STRIPE
(NATIVE —) KASBA CASBAH
(ONE-SIXTEENTH OF —) FORTY
(PERCUSSION —) BATTERY
SECTIONALISM LOCALISM
SECTOR AREA HOUSE
SECULAR LAIC COMMON EARTHLY
PROFANE WORLDLY TEMPORAL
SECURE FID GET GIB KEY POT SEW
WIN BAIL BOLT BOND CAUK COCK
HOLD EASY FAST FIND FIRM FRAP
GAIN GIRD HOOK LAND MOOR NAIL
SAFE SEAL SHOT SNUG STAY SURE
WARM BELAY BLOCK CINCH CLEAT
FLOUR SOUND STRAP TRUST
ANCHOR ASSURE BECKET BUTTON
CLINCH DEFEND ENSURE FASTEN
OBTAIN PLEDGE SETTLE SICCAR
WICKER STABLE STAPLE TRAIST
BULWARK CONFINE DUNNAGE
FORFEND FORTIFY RAMPIRE
WARRANT GARRISON PRESERVE
(— A SAIL) TRICE
(— AGAINST INTRUSION) TILE
(— AID OF) ENLIST
(— BAIT) EBB
(— FROM LEAKING) COFFER
(— WITH BARS) GRATE
(SECURED BOUND SETTLED

SECURELY FAST SAFE SICCAR
SICKER STRAIT SURELY SOLIDLY
SOUNDLY
SECURITY PUP BAIL BAND EASE
GAGE SEAL WAGE FRITH GRITH
GUARD QUIET STOCK BORROW
CEDULA EQUITY PLEDGE SAFETY
SCREEN SEVERE SURETY VADIUM
CAUTION DEFENSE DEPOSIT
FLOATER HOSTAGE SHELTER
SLEEPER WARRANT COLONIAL
COVENANT FASTNESS GUARANTY
HYPOTHEC STRENGTH VADIMONY
(PL.) PERCENTS
SEDAN SEDIA JAMPAN SALOON
TONJON TOMJOHN BROUGHAM
SEDATE CALM COOL DOUCE QUIET
SOBER STAID SERENE EARNEST
SERIOUS SETTLED DECOROUS
SEDATENESS SOBRIETY
SEDATIVE AMYTAL CALMANT
LENITIVE QUIETIVE SOOTHING
SEDENTARY STILL SESSILE
INACTIVE
SEDGE SAG LING RAIT REIT STAR
CAREX CHUFA TIKUG BHABAR
EHUAWA GLUMAL THATCH TOETOE
TOITOI BULRUSH MONOCOT
PAPYRUS SNIDDLE TUSSOCK
GALANGAL JIMSEDGE
SEDGE FLY GRANAM GRANNOM
SEDGE WARBLER WREN MOCKBIRD
REEDBIRD
SEDGY SAGGY SEGGY TWILLED
SEDIMENT CARR DREG FAEX FOOT
GOBI LEES MULM SILT WARP DRAST
DREGS FECES FOOTS MAGMA
BOTTOM SIMMON SLUDGE DREWITE
GROUNDS GRUMMEL SAPROPEL
SETTLING
(— OF BEER OR ALE) CRAP
(IRON —) CAR CARR
(REDDISH —) SIMMON
SEDITION REVOLT TREASON
SEDITIOUS RIOTOUS FACTIOUS
MUTINOUS
SEDUCE DRAW JAPE LOCK DECOY
TEMPT WRONG ALLURE BETRAY
ENTICE DEBAUCH ENSNARE
MISLEAD SUGGEST TRADUCE
INVEIGLE
(— WITH THE EYE) LEER
SEDUCER UNDOER LOTHARIO
SEDUCTION LURE BRIBE CHARM
SEDULOUS BUSY INTENT STUDIED
DILIGENT UNTIRING
SEDULOUSNESS INDUSTRY
SEDUM MOSS ORPINE SENGREEN
SEE LO EYE KEN SPY VID ESPY
LOOK MIND NOTE PIPE SEAT SEGE
SPOT VIDE VIEW BESEE CATCH
CHAIR SIEGE SIGHT STOOL TENEZ
WATCH ATTEND BEHOLD DESCRY
NOTICE QUAERE REMARK SURVEY
ARCHSEE DISCERN GLIMPSE
OBSERVE WITNESS CATHEDRA
CONCEIVE PERCEIVE
(— ABOVE) VS
(— BELOW) VI

(— FIT) CHOOSE
(— INTO) INSEE
(— TO) FIX
(— VISIONS) SCRY
SEED BEN MAW NIB PIP BEAN BOIL
CHAT CORN DIKA GERM KOLA LIMA
MOTE SETH TARE BEHEN BERRY
CACAO CARAT GRAIN SEMEN
SPAWN SPERM STONE ABILLA
ACHENE ACINUS CARNEL FENNEL
KERNEL LEGUME LENTIL NICKER
NUTLET PIGNON PIPPIN TILLEY
ACHIOTE ACHUETE ALPISTE
ANISEED BUCKEYE CALINUT FRIJOLE
HARICOT HAYSEED SEEDKIN
SEEDLET SEMINAL AMBRETTE
COKERNUT CYDONIUM DILLSEED
FLAXSEED FLEASEED HEMPSEED
PIGNOLIA PRINCIPE SEEDLING
SEEDNESS
(AROMATIC —S) ANISE
(EDIBLE —) PEA BEAN
(FENUGREEK —) HELBEH
(GRAPE —) ACINUS
(IMMATURE —) OVULE
(MUSTARD —) SENVY SINEWY
(NUTLIKE —) PEANUT
(OILY —) ABILLA
(PALM —) COROZO
(POPPY —) MAW MOHNSEED
(SESAME —) JINJILI GINGELLY
(PL.) ANISE COFFEE SESAME ZERAIM
IGNATIA LARKSPUR
SEEDCAKE WIG WIGG
SEEDCASE TEST TESTA THECA
SEED COAT TESTA SPIRICLE
SEEDED ARABLE
SEEDER SEEDMAN
SEEDLING FREE LINER
SEEDY MANGY SCUFFY
SEEING SIGHT SIGHTED
(— THAT) SITH SINCE
SEEK ASK BEG SIC WOO FAND FEEL
FISH FOND FORK HUNT LAIT LOOK
SICK SIFT COURT DELVE ESSAY
FETCH SCOUR APPETE BOTTOM
FERRET FOLLOW FRAIST PURSUE
SEARCH FORSEEK INQUIRE
RANSACK REQUIRE RUMMAGE
SOLICIT ENDEAVOR
(— AFTER) SUE SUIT ENSUE
EXPLORE
(— AIMLESSLY) PROG
(— FAVOR) WISH
(— FOR) APPETE EXPLORE
(— IN MARRIAGE) WOO PRETEND
(— OUT) COMB ENSEARCH
(— TO ATTAIN) ASPIRE
SEEKER TRACER PETITOR ZETETIC
SEARCHER
(— AFTER FACTS) GRADGRIND
(— OF KNOWLEDGE) PHILONIST
(JOB —) CHANCER
(PLEASURE —) FRANION
SEEKING SOKE SOKEN ZETETIC
SEEM BID EYE SEE FARE LOOK PEER
SOUND APPEAR BESEEM REGARD
(— TO BE) LIKE
(IT —S) SEMBLE

SEEMING GUISE QUASI LIKELY
SEEMLY APPARENT SEMBLANT
SEEMINGLY QUASI SEEMLY
SEEMING
SEEMLINESS GRACE DECENCY
DECORUM
SEEMLY FIT TALL CIVIL COMELY
DECENT LIKELY MODEST BECOMING
DECOROUS GRACEFUL
SEEP LEAK OOZE SIPE EXUDE
SEEPAGE SEEP SIPAGE SPRING
SEEPY WEEPY
SEER SIR SWAMI MOPSUS SCRYER
PROPHET CHALDEAN MELAMPUS
SEERBAND TURBAN
SEERESS SAGA SIBYL VOLVA
ALRUNE ALBRUNA PHOIBAD
SEESAW PUMP TILT DANDLE TEETER
TIDDLE TILTER TITTER TOTTER
SEETHE FRY JUG BOIL CREE ITCH
STEW WALL WALM BULLER HOTTER
SIMMER BLUBBER ELIXATE
FERMENT
SEETHING ASEETHE BOILING
HUMMING ITCHING SCALDING
SEGMENT CUT LAP FALL HAND LITH
MERE PART BLANK CHORD ELITE
FEMUR FURCA SHARE SLICE TMEMA
CANTLE GLOSSA LENGTH SAMPLE
SYZYGY ARTICLE DIGITUS EXERGUE
FESTOON ISOMERE MYOMERE
MYOTOME SECTION SETIGER
ANTIMERE BRACHIUM COLUMNAL
DACTYLUS DIVISION GONOTOME
HYPOMERE INTERVAL MESOMERE
METAMERE MYOCOMMA NARICORN
(— OF CASK) CANT
(— OF CAULIFLOWER) FLOWERET
(— OF CIRCLE) SECTION
(— OF COMMUNITY) FACIES
(— OF EARTH'S CRUST) GRABEN
(— OF FIBER) BAND
(— OF IRIS) FALL
(— OF LEAF) LACINIA
(— OF MAXILLA) STIPES SUBGALEA
(— OF RATTLESNAKE'S RATTLE)
BUTTON
(— OF SPEECH) DOMAIN
(HERALDIC —) FLANCH FLANCHE
(INSTRUCTIONAL —) LESSON
(MERE —) SNAPSHOT
(PEASANT —) HERA
SEGMENTATION CLEAVAGE
SEGMENTED INSECTED
SEGNO SIGN
SEGREGATE SHED SEVER INTERN
ISOLATE CLASSIFY INSULATE
SEPARATE
SEIGNORAGE ROYALTY
SEIGNORY LORDSHIP
SEINE NET FARE TUCK TRAIN
POCKET SAGENE SPILLER
MADRAGUE
SEISIN VESTURE
SEIZE BAG CAP CLY GET HAP NAB
NAP BEAK BONE CLAW CLUM FANG
GALL GLOM GRAB GRIP GRUP HAND
HENT HOOK JUMP KEEP LEVY NAIL
RAMP SMUG SNAP SPAN TAKE TIRE

YOKE CATCH CESSE CLASP CLEEK
CLICK DRIVE GRASP GRIPE LATCH
PINCH RAVEN RAVIN REACH REAVE
SNACK ARREST ASSUME ATTACH
CLUTCH COLLAR EXTEND FASTEN
FREEZE GOBBLE NOBBLE QUARRY
SECURE SNATCH ASSEIZE CAPTURE
ENCLASP ENCLOSE GRABBLE
GRAPPLE IMPOUND POSSESS
PREHEND SCAMBLE SWALLOW
ARROGATE COMPRISE DISTRAIN
SPUILZIE SURPRISE UNDERNIM
(— AND HOLD FIRMLY) TRUSS
(— BAIT) STRIKE
(— BY NECK) SCRAG COLLAR
SCRUFF
(— PREY) CHOP
(— SUDDENLY) NAB NIP SWOOP
SNATCH
(— UPON) ATTACK INFECT
(— WITH CLAWS) STRAIN
(— WITH TEETH) BITE
(— WITH WHOLE HAND) GLAUM
(— WITHOUT RIGHT) USURP
SEIZIN SASINE VESTURE
SEIZING FANG GRIP MARQUE
CAPTION SEIZURE
SEIZURE PIT BITE HOLD GRIPE
ICTUS SPELL ARREST EXTENT
PRISAL RAPTUS TAKING ANGARIA
CAPTION CONCEIT TELLACH
DISTRESS STOPPAGE
SELDOM RARE SELD RARELY
UNOFTEN
SELDOM-SEEN ANTRIN ANTERIN
SELECT ORT TAP TRY CULL PICK
SIFT SORT TAKE WALE DRAFT
ELECT ELITE PITCH TRIED ASSIGN
BALLOT CHOICE CHOOSE CLUBBY
DECIDE DESUME EXEMPT PREFER
SINGLE WINNOW DRAUGHT
EXCERPT EXTRACT OUTLOOK
EXIMIOUS HANDPICK SELECTED
(— BY LOT) DRAW
(— BY PATTERN) SWATCH
(— JURY) STRIKE
SELECTED DRAFT ELECT FANCY
DRAUGHT
SELECTING DRAFT GARBLING
SELECTION BLAD CHAP CULL ITEM
PICK CHOICE CHOOSE EXCERPT
EXTRACT ELECTION HAFTARAH
PERICOPE
(— OF PSALMS) HALLEL
(VERSE —) SINGSONG
SELECTIVE CHOOSY ECLECTIC
SELF EGO SEL SEN JIVA SELL SOUL
DAENA NATURE PERSON PSYCHE
(INNER —) ANIMA
(OWN —) AINSELL NAINSEL
(SUPREME UNIVERSAL —) ATMAN
SELF-ACCUSATION GUILT
SELF-AGGRANDIZING IMPERIAL
SELF-ASSERTIVE BRASH PERKY
CHESTY BLUSTERY
SELF-ASSURANCE CHEEK APLOMB
COOLNESS
SELF-ASSURED CALM CONFIDENT
SELF-CENTERED SELFISH

SELF-CENTEREDNESS EGOTISM
SELFHOOD
SELF-COMMAND NERVE
SELF-CONCEIT NOSISM
SELF-CONCEITED COXY PENSY
COCKSY PENCEY
SELF-CONFIDENCE CREST HUBRIS
JOLLITY OPINION
SELF-CONFIDENT FLUSH CHESTY
SELF-CONSCIOUS GAWKY BASHFUL
SELF-CONTAINED ABSOLUTE
SELF-CONTAINMENT CLOSURE
SELF-CONTRADICTORY ABSURD
SELF-CONTROL STAY WILL
ENCRATY MODESTY RETENUE
PATIENCE
SELF-DECEPTION FLATTERY
SELF-DENIAL DENIAL
SELF-DENYING ASCETIC
SELF-DESTRUCTION SUICIDE
SELF-DESTRUCTIVE SUICIDAL
SELF-DETERMINATION FREEDOM
AUTONOMY
SELF-DISCIPLINE ASCESIS
SELF-ENRICHMENT GROWTH
SELF-ESTEEM EGO PRIDE CONCEIT
SELFNESS
SELF-EVIDENT MANIFEST
SELF-EXALTATION NOSISM ELATIO
SELF-EXISTENT BEER INCREATE
UNCAUSED
SELF-FERTILIZATION AUTOGAMY
SELF-FULFILLMENT FREEDOM
SAMADHI
SELF-GENERATION AUTOGENY
SELF-GLORIFICATION VANITY
SELF-GOVERNMENT SWARAJ
SELF-HEAL ALLHEAL HOOKHEAL
HOOKWEED
SELFHOOD SEITY EGOITY IPSEITY
OWNHOOD PROPRIUM SELFNESS
SELF-IDENTITY IPSEITY
SELF-IMPORTANT PURDY CHESTY
BIGGETY POMPOUS
SELF-INDULGENCE NICETY
PLEASURE
SELFISH PIGGISH SELFFUL
DISSOCIAL
SELFISHNESS EGO SELF EGOTISM
SUICISM PHILAUTY SELFHOOD
SELFNESS
SELF-LOVE CONCEIT PHILAUTY
SELF-POLLUTION ONANISM
SELF-POSSESSED COOL ASSURED
COMPOSED
SELF-POSSESSION APLOMB
COOLNESS
SELF-REALIZATION FREEDOM
ENERGISM
SELF-RELIANT BOLD FREE
SELF-REPROACH GUILT REGRET
SELF-RESTRAINT HO HOO ASCESIS
CONTROL RESERVE RETENUE
HAVLAGAH
SELF-RIGHTEOUS STUFFY
SELF-SACRIFICING HEROIC
GALLANT
SELFSAME SAME SELFSAID
IDENTICAL

SELFSAMENESS IDENTITY
SELF-SATISFIED SMUG STODGY
ASSURED
SELF-SUFFICIENCY ASEITY ASEITAS
AUTARCHY
SELF-SUFFICIENT ABSOLUTE
SELF-WILLED SET SENSUAL
WAYWARD CONTRARY
SELION BUTT
SELL DO GIVE VEND CHEAP PITCH
SHAVE TRADE UTTER AFFORD
BARTER MARKET AUCTION BARGAIN
(— **AT LOW PRICE)** DUMP
(— **BELOW COST)** FOOTBALL
(— **BY AUCTION)** CANT ROUP
(— **FOR)** BRING FETCH
(— **IN SMALL QUANTITIES)** RETAIL
(BUY AND —) CHOP
SELLER BOOMER BUSKER CADGER
VENDOR CHANTER FLESHER
CHANDLER
(WINE —) ABKAR
SELLING (SPECULATIVE —)
AGIOTAGE
SELSYN SYNCHRO
SELVAGE LIST GOUGE FORREL
LISTING STICKING
SEMANTEME RHEME
SEMANTICS SEMOLOGY
SEMAPHORE FISHTAIL
SEMBLANCE FACE SHOW SIGN
COLOR GHOST GLOSS GUISE IMAGE
SCHEME VISAGE PRETEXT SEEMING
UMBRAGE LIKENESS SEMBLANT
SKERRICK
(— **OF DIGNITY)** FACE
(— **OF REALITY)** DREAM
(FALSE —) COLORING
SEME SEMY GUTTY HURTY FLEURY
GOUTTE GUTTEE BEZANTE
SEME-DE-LIS FLORETTY
SEMELE (BROTHER OF —)
POLYDORUS
(FATHER OF —) CADMUS
(MOTHER OF —) HARMONIA
(SISTER OF —) INO AGAVE
AUTONOE
(SON OF —) BACCHUS
SEMEN SEED SPERM
SEMESTER HALF
SEMIDARKNESS DUSK
SEMIDIAMETER RADIUS
SEMIDOME CONCHA
SEMIFLUID SOFT HUMOR
SEMIGLOSS EGGSHELL
SEMINARY YESHIVA JUVENATE
SEMIOPAQUE HORNY
SEMIPORCELAIN GOMBROON
SEMIRAMIS (HUSBAND OF —) NINUS
(MOTHER OF —) DERCETO
SEMITE JEW ARAB HARARI SYRIAN
SEMITIC SHEMITE ARAMAEAN
ASSYRIAN CHALDEAN
SEMITIC JEWISH
(— **LANGUAGE)** GAFAT
SEMITONE FEINT LIMMA DEMITONE
HEMITONE
SEMOLINA SUJI SEMOLA
SENATE BOULE SENATO COUNCIL

SENATUS GEROUSIA SENATORY
(— **AND PEOPLE OF ROME)** SPQR
(— **DIVISION)** PRYTANY
SENATOR SOLON CONSUL FATHER
LAWMAKER
SENATORSHIP TOGA
SEND MIT FAST PACK SHIP ENVOY
SCEND THROW ADDRESS CHANNEL
COMMAND CONSIGN DELIVER
FORWARD DISPATCH TRANSMIT
(— **ABOUT)** TROLL
(— **ALOFT)** CROSS
(— **AWAY)** MAND SHIP AMAND
BANISH DISBAND DISMISS RELEGATE
(— **BACK)** ECHO TURN WISE REMIT
REMAND REMISE RENVOY RESEND
RETURN REFRACT
(— **BY MAIL)** DROP
(— **DOWN)** DEMIT DIMIT STRIKE
(— **FOR)** SUMMON
(— **FORTH IN RAYS)** RADIATE
(— **FORTH)** BEAR CAST EMIT MAND
DIMIT FLING EFFUSE OUTSEND
(— **IN)** IMMIT IMMISS INTROMIT
(— **MESSAGE)** BLINKER
(— **OFF UNCEREMONIOUSLY)** SHANK
(— **OFF)** WING
(— **OFFICIALLY)** ISSUE
(— **OUT)** BEAM EMIT AMAND SHOOT
SPEED DEDUCE DEPORT LAUNCH
DIFFUSE EXPEDITE
(— **TO JAIL)** LAG MITTIMUS
(— **TO PERDITION)** CONFOUND
SENDING SAND
(— **OUT)** EMISSIVE

SENEGAL

CAPITAL: DAKAR
MOUNTAIN: GOUNOU
NATIVE: PEUL SOCE DIOLA FOULA
LAOBE SERER WOLOF FULANI
SERERE BAMBARA MALINKE
TUKULER MANDINGO
RIVER: FALEME GAMBIA SALOUM
SENEGAL
TOWN: THIES KAOLACK RUFISQUE

SENILE DOLD DOTARD
SENILITY DOTAGE CADUCITY
PROGERIA
SENIOR AINE DEAN SIRE DOYEN
ELDER ANCIENT SUPERIOR
SENIORITY AGE ANCIENTY
SIGNEURY
SENNET SPET SIGNET
SENOR DON
SENORITA MISS SRTA SRITA
SENSATION FEEL ITCH SOUR SENSE
TABET TASTE TIBBIT VEDANA
FEELING ESTHESIS
(— **OF COLD)** RHIGOSIS
(— **OF FRIGHT)** FRISSON
(— **OF HEAT)** HOTNESS
(ANTICIPATORY —) FOREFEEL
(BURNING —) ARDOR
(DARTING —) SHOOT
(STRONG —) CREEP
(SUBJECTIVE —) AURA

(TASTE —) GUST BITTER
(TINGLING —) DIRL
(VIBRATING —) FREMITUS
(VISUAL —) PHOSE PHOTOMA
SENSATIONAL GORY YELLOW
SAFFRON SPLASHY THRILLY
STUNNING
SENSATIONALISM BLARE SENSISM
SENSE WIT FEEL SALT SMELL
LETTER MATTER REASON SCONCE
WISDOM FEELING HEARING
MARBLES MEANING SMEDDUM
CARRIAGE GUMPTION JUDGMENT
(— **OF APPREHENSION)** ANXIETY
(— **OF HEARING)** EAR
(— **OF HUMOR)** MUSIC
(— **OF ONENESS)** KINSHIP
(— **OF OUTRAGE)** SHOCK
(— **OF PANIC)** JITTERS
(— **OF RIGHT)** GRACE
(— **OF SIGHT)** VISION
(— **OF SMELL)** SCENT
(— **OF SUPERIORITY)** EGOTISM
(— **OF TOUCH)** FEEL TASTE
(— **ON ONE'S WORTH)** PRIDE
(COMMON —) SALT BALANCE
GUMPTION
(DISCRIMINATING —) FLAIR
(LACKING —) INEPT
(PLAIN —) ENGLISH
(SOUND —) MATTER
SENSE-DATUM SENSUM
SENSELESS MAD COLD DUMB
FRIGID STUPID UNWISE FOOLISH
IDIOTIC PEEVISH SOTTISH UNIDEAED
SENSIBILITY HEART SENSE FEELING
DELICACY ESTHESIA JUDGMENT
(PL.) FEELINGS
SENSIBLE SANE WISE AWARE PRIVY
ACTUAL FEELABLE MATERIAL
PASSIBLE RATIONAL SENSICAL
SENTIENT WISELIKE
SENSITIVE FINE KEEN SORE ALIVE
QUICK LIABLE NIMBLE TENDER
TETCHY FEELING NERVOUS PRICKLY
ALLERGIC DELICATE EROGENIC
SENSIBLE SENTIENT SKINLESS
TOUCHOUS
(— **TO PAIN)** TART
(NERVOUSLY —) TOUCHY
SENSITIVENESS SENSE TOUCH
ALGESIA DELICACY
SENSITIVE PEA HONEYCUP
SENSITIVE PLANT MIMOSA
SENSITIVITY FLESH DELICACY
FINENESS
SENSORY SENSUAL AFFERENT
SENSUAL LEWD BRUTE MUDDY
CARNAL FLESHY SULTRY WANTON
BESTIAL BRUTISH FLESHLY LESBIAN
SWINISH PANDEMIC SENSUOUS
SENSUALITY FLESH LIKING LUXURY
SENSUOUS SOFT SATINY SENSAL
FLESHLY SENSUAL LUSCIOUS
SENSIBLE
SENTENCE DIT RAP SAW DAMN
DOOM TIME AWARD FUTWA JUISE
TENER TROPE ARREST COMMIT
DECREE DEPORT JUWISE REASON

ADJUDGE CENSURE CONDEMN
FLOATER IMPRESA LAGGING
FOREDOOM JUDGMENT VERSICLE
(— INDICATING CHARACTER)
MOTTO
(CONCISE —S) LACONICS
(IMPRISONMENT —) LAG RAP LIFE
LAGGING STRETCH
(MUSICAL —) PERIOD
(SHORT —) CLAUSE
(WITTY —) ATTICISM
SENTENTIOUS CONCISE LACONIC
SENTIENCE SENSE
SENTIENT FEELING SENSILE
SENSIVE SENSEFUL SENSIBLE
SENTIMENT MIND POSY ETHNOS
GENIUS HOBNOB PLEDGE FEELING
(SLOPPY —) DRIP
SENTIMENTAL SLAB SOFT CORNY
GOOEY GUSHY MUSHY SAPPY
SOBBY SOPPY SOUPY FRUITY
SLUSHY SPOONY SUGARY SYRUPY
INSIPID MAUDLIN MAWKISH
ROMANTIC SCHMALZY SNIVELLY
SENTIMENTALISM BATHOS
SCHMALZ SCHMALTZ
SENTIMENTALIST SOFTHEAD
SENTIMENTALITY GOO HAM MUSH
SIRUP SYRUP BATHOS
SENTINEL WAIT DEINO GUARD
WATCH BANTAY PICKET SENTRY
PICQUET COCKATOO PEPHEDRO
WATCHMAN
(MOUNTED —) VEDET VEDETTE
(PL.) GRAEAE GRAIAE
SENTINEL BOX STATION
SENTRY KITE WATCH SENTINEL
SEPAL LEAF HELMET LEAFLET
SEPARATE CUT TOM COMB CULL
CURD DEAL FALL FRAY FREE HAZE
PART REDD SERE SIFT SORT TWIN
BLEED BREAK CALVE ELONG FENCE
FLAKE HEDGE PARTY SCALE SEVER
SIEVE SKILL SPLIT TWAIN TWIST
ABDUCT ABRUPT ASSORT AVULSE
BISECT CLEAVE DECIDE DEPART
DETACH DIGEST DIVIDE DIVISI
PROPER REMOTE SCREEN SECERN
SECRET SEJOIN SETTLE SINGLE
SOLUTE SPREAD SUNDER SUNDRY
SWATCH UNLUTE WINNOW ABSCISE
ABSCISS BRACKET CONCERN
DIALYZE DISJOIN DISLINK DISPAIR
DISPART DIVERSE EXPANSE FISSION
ISOLATE SCATTER SECTION
SEJUNCT SEVERAL SWINGLE
ABSTRACT BULKHEAD DETACHED
DIFFRACT DISCRETE DISJOINT
DISSEVER DISSOLVE DISTINCT
DISTRACT DISUNITE DIVIDANT
DIVIDUAL FRACTION LAMINATE
LEVIGATE LIBERATE PECULIAR
SEVERATE SPORADIC UNMINGLE
UNSOLDER UNSTRING
(— BY BEATING) SCUTCH
(— BY CROSSWALL) ABJOINT
(— BY PICKING) LEASE LEAZE
(— COINS) JOURNEY
(— COMBATANTS) STICKLE

(— FIBERS) HACKLE
(— FROM HERD) IMPRIME
(— GRAIN FROM CHAFF) FAN CAVE
WINNOW
(— HAIR) BLOCK
(— INTO COMPONENTS) STRIP
(— INTO FLOCKS) DRAFT DRAUGHT
(— INTO SHREDS) TEASE
(— ONESELF) ABDICATE
(— ORE) JIG SMELT DILLUE
(— SHEEP) DRAW
(— THREADS) SLEY SLEAVE
SEPARATED FREE ALONE BROKEN
DISTANT DIVIDED ABSTRACT
ISOLATED RESOLVED
(— BY INTERVAL) OPEN
SEPARATELY APART SINGLY
SUNDRY SEVERAL SUNDERLY
SEPARATING BETWEEN
SEPARATION GAP GULF PART SHED
CHASM SPLIT SCHISM BARRIER
DIVORCE ELUTION PARTING
ANALYSIS AUTOTOMY AVULSION
CREAMING DECISION DIALYSIS
DISTANCE DISUNION DIVISION
INCISION SHEDDING TWINNING
(— OF LEAF) CHORISIS
(— OF MAN AND WIFE) ZIHAR
DIVORCE
(— OF METALS) DEPART
(— OF PIGMENT) FLOATING
(— OF WORD PARTS) TMESIS
(— OF YEAST IN BEER) BREAK
SEPARATIST ZOARITE BIMMELER
SEPARATOR RAVEL PARTER
CREAMER SETTLER SEVERER
SUBSIDER
SEPARATRIX SLASH DIAGONAL
SEPIA COCONUT SEPIARY
SEPOY TELINGA
SEPT KIN
SEPTET SEPTUOR
SEPTIVALENT HEPTAD
SEPTUAGINT LXX
SEPTUM VITTA TABULA MYOTOME
PHRAGMA MYOCOMMA
SEPULCHER BIER GRAVE TITLE
MONUMENT MORTUARY
SEPULCHRAL HOLLOW CHARNEL
TUMULARY
SEQUEL SUITE EFFECT SEQUENT
BACKWASH SEQUENCE
SEQUENCE ROPE SUIT TRACT TRAIN
DOCKET ENTAIL SEQUEL SERIES
STRING CADENCE CORONET
SEQUENT SUCCESS SPECTRUM
STRAIGHT
(— OF BEHAVIOR) ACT
(— OF BILLIARD SHOTS) BREAK
(— OF CARDS) STRINGER
(— OF CHESS MOVES) DEFENCE
DEFENSE
(— OF EVENTS) CYCLE
(— OF MELODRAMA) CHASE
(— OF ROCK UNITS) SECTION
(— OF SOUNDS) AFFIX
(ACTING —) EXTERIOR
(CUSTOMARY —) COURSE
(FILM —) INTERCUT

(LITURGICAL —) CANON
SEQUENT ENSUANT SEQUITUR
SEQUESTER SINGLE ISOLATE
RECLUDE
SEQUESTERED LONELY PRIVATE
RECLUSE RETIRED SECLUDED
SOLITARY
SEQUIN CHICK SPANG VENTIN
ZEQUIN CHEQUIN CHEQUEEN
VENETIAN ZECCHINO
(PL.) GLITTER
SERAGLIO HAREM SERAI ZENANA
SERAPHIC BEATIFIC
SERBOCROATIAN ILLYRIAN
SERE SEAR SERULE UNGREEN
HALOSERE
SERENADE AUBADE HORNING
ALBORADA NOCTURNE SERENATA
(MOCK —) SHIVAREE
SERENADER WAIT
SERENE CALM EVEN CLEAR LITHE
SEDATE SMOOTH HALCYON
DECOROUS
SERENITY CALM PEACE REPOSE
SERF BOND THEW CHURL HELOT
SLAVE THEOW PENEST SERVUS
THRALL BONDMAN COLONUS
PEASANT ADSCRIPT PRAEDIAL
YANACONA
SERFDOM BONDAGE HELOTRY
SERFAGE SERVAGE HELOTISM
SERFHOOD SERFSHIP
SERGE SAGATHY
SERGEANT TOP SARGE CHIAUS
DESKMAN SERVANT TOPKICK
SERIAUNT
SERGEANT-AT-LAW COUNTOR
COUNTOUR
SERGEANT FISH LING CABIO COBI
SNOOK BONITO CUBBYYEW
SERGEANT MAJOR PINTANO
SERIALLY SERIATIM
SERIEMA CARIAMA GRUIFORM
SCREAMER
SERIES RUN SET ECCA RANK SUIT
TIRE CHAIN DRIFT DWYKA ORDER
SUITE TALLY TRACE COURSE
EOCENE SEQUEL STRING SYSTEM
BATTERY CASCADE CATALOG
BEADROLL SEQUENCE
(— GATHERED TOGETHER) SORITE
(— OF ABSTRACTS) SYLLABUS
(— OF ARCHES) ARCADE
(— OF BALLET TURNS) CHAINE
(— OF BOAT RACES) REGATTA
(— OF CELLS) FILAMENT
(— OF CHARACTERS) CLINE
(— OF CHESS MOVES) COOK
(— OF CLASHES) CLATTER
(— OF COMMUNITIES) SERE
(— OF DANCE MOVEMENTS) ADAGI
(— OF DRAIN TILES) FIELD
(— OF EVENTS) EPOS ACTION
(— OF EXTRACTS) CATENA
(— OF FORTIFICATIONS) CEINTURE
(— OF IMAGES) DREAM
(— OF LEGENDS) SAGA
(— OF LIPS) GILL
(— OF MEETINGS) SESSION

(— OF METAL DISKS) PILE
(— OF MILITARY OPERATIONS)
CAMPAIGN
(— OF MOVEMENTS) DANCE
(— OF NEIGHBORING LOTS) COTE
(— OF NOTES) GAMUT GLISSADE
(— OF PASSES) FAENA
(— OF PILES) DRIFT
(— OF POEMS) DIVAN DIWAN
(— OF PRAYERS) COURSE SYNAPTE
(— OF RACES) CIRCUIT
(— OF REASONS) ARGUMENT
(— OF RINGS) COIL GIMMAL
(— OF ROOMS) SWEEP
(— OF SHOTS) BURST
(— OF SIMILAR STRUCTURES)
STROBILA
(— OF SLALOM GATES) FLUSH
(— OF SLIPS) DOCK
(— OF SOILS) CECIL
(— OF STAIRS) FLIGHT
(— OF STAMPS) SET
(— OF STITCHES) STAY
(— OF STRAPS) LADDER
(— OF TANKS) SOAPER
(— OF THREADS) BINDER STUFFER
(— OF TONES) SCALE
(— OF TRAVELS) ODYSSEY
(— OF VERSES) ANTIPHON
(— OF WORDS) ACROSTIC
ALPHABET
(CARD —) CORONET
(CONNECTED —) CATENA
(CONSECUTIVE —) STREAK
(DANCE —) DOUBLE
(GEOLOGICAL —) ECCA DWYKA
KENAI EOCENE KEEWATIN
(IMPRESSIVE —) ARRAY
(RADIOACTIVE —) FAMILY
ERIOUS RUM SAD DEEP HIGH
ACUTE GRAVE HEAVY SOBER SOLID
STAID DEMURE SEDATE SEVERE
SOLEMN SOMBER SOMBRE SULLEN
AUSTERE CAPITAL EARNEST
SERIOSO WEIGHTY GRIEVOUS
ERIOUSLY BAD ILL DOWN SADLY
DEEPLY GRAVELY SOLIDLY
ERIOUSNESS EARNEST GRAVITY
SADNESS
ERMON SPELL HOMILY ADDRESS
FUNERAL SEREMENT SERMONET
ERMONIZING MORALITY
EROPURULENT SANIOUS
EROUS ICHOROUS
EROW JAGLA SERAU
ERPENT (ALSO SEE SNAKE) AHI
SEPS WORM ABOMA ADDER APEPI
ATHER OPHIS SIREN SNAKE TRAIN
CHITAL DIPSAS DRAGON GERARD
HYDRUS PYTHON APOPHIS PRESTER
SCYTALE JARARACA
(— WORSHIPER) NAASSENE
(FEATHERED —) GUCUMATZ
KUKULKAN
(NORSE —) GOIN
(SACRED —) AVANYU AWANYU
(SKY —) AHI
ERPENTINE SNAKY SPIRY OPHITE
SNAKISH BOWENITE METAXITE
SCROLLED

SERPENT STAR OPHIURAN
SERRANO PERCOID GITANEMUK
SERRATE SAWED ARGUTE RAFFLE
NOTCHED SERRIED
SERRATION SERRA DENTILE
SERUM WHEY FLUID BIOLOGIC
SERVANT BOY FAG KID MAN PUG
TAG AMAH BATA COOK DASI DAVY
HELP HIND JACK LUCE MATY MOZO
ALILA BAGOT BOOTS BOULT DAVUS
GILLY GROOM HAMAL MAMMY
SEWER SLAVE SOSIA SPEED USHER
ABDIEL ANDREW BATMAN BEARER
BILDAR BUTLER CHAKAR CLASHY
DORINE EWERER FEEDER FERASH
FLUNKY GILLIE GRUMIO HAIDUK
HARLOT KHAMAL MENIAL PAMELA
SIRCAR SLAVEY TEABOY TEAGUE
TRANIO VARLET VASSAL VOIDER
ANCILLA BOOTBOY BOUCHAL
COURIER DUFTERY FAMULUS
FEODARY FERRASH FLUNKEY
FOOTMAN GENERAL GHILLIE
MALCHUS PANDOUR PANTLER
PAPELON PIQUEUR PISANIO
WASHPOT ASSIGNEE CHAPRASI
CROMWELL DOMESTIC FOLLOWER
GRASSCUT HENCHMAN HOUSEBOY
MANCIPLE MINISTER OUTRIDER
PANTHINO PHILOTUS PINDARUS
SERGEANT SERVITOR STANDARD
TRENCHER VADELECT WARDMAID
KITCHENER
(— IN CHARGE OF BREAD) PANTLER
(— IN CHARGE OF DAIRY) DEY
(— IN OFFICE) DUFTERY
(— OF SCHOLAR OR MAGICIAN)
FAMULUS
(— WHO CARVES) TRENCHER
(— WHO CLEARS TABLE) VOIDER
(— WHO RUNS BEFORE CARRIAGE)
PIQUEUR
(— WHO SERVES TABLE) SEWER
(ARMED —) PANDOUR
(ARMY —) BATMAN LASCAR
(BENGAL —) MEHTAR SIRCAR
(BODY —) VALET SIRDAR
(BOY —) BOY KNAVE CHOKRA
BOUCHAL
(CAMP —) BILDAR
(CLOWNISH —) SPEED LAUNCE
(COLLEGE —) GYP SKIP SCOUT
(FEMALE —) AMA NAN AMAH DASI
GIRL LASS MAID MAMMY NURSE
WENCH PAMELA SKIVVY ANCILLA
HANDMAID MUCHACHA WARDMAID
(GENERAL —) FACTOTUM
(HEAD —) BUTLER TINDAL
(HIGH PRIEST'S —) MALCHUS
(HINDU —) DAS DASI
(HOUSE —) COOK HEWE SEWER
DOMESTIC MATRANEE SCULLION
(KITCHEN —) COOK WASHPOT
(LORD OR KING'S —) THANE
(LYING —) FAG
(MAID —) NAN BONNE
(MAN —) BOY JACK MOZO SWAIN
VALET ANDREW GILLIE KNIGHT

GHILLIE KHANSAMA MUCHACHO
SERVITOR
(MISCHIEVOUS —) TEAGUE
(PETULANT —) DORINE
(PHILIPPINE —) BATA ALILA
(SCOTTISH —) JURR
(SOLDIER'S —) PAGE
(TRUSTY —) TROUT
(PL.) FOLK VOLK STAFF FAMILIA
NETHINIM
SERVE DO KA ACT AID HOP GIVE
HELP LEAP SHEW SLAP STAY TEND
TOSS WAIT COVER FRAME HORSE
SARRA STAND ANSWER ASSIST
FRIEND INTEND SAIRVE SARROW
SETTLE SPREAD SUCCOR ADVANCE
ASSERVE BESTEAD CONVENT
FORWARD FURTHER SERVICE
FUNCTION
(— A DISH) MESS
(— AS ESCORT) SQUIRE
(— AS HOST) GIVE
(— AS SUBSTITUTE) PASS
(— AS WELL AS) AVAIL
(— DRINK) SKINK
(— FOOD) HASH KITCHEN
(— FOR PASTURE) GRAZE
(— OBSEQUIOUSLY) LACKEY
LACQUEY
SERVER SALVER ACOLYTE MINISTER
SERVICE AID FEE CENS DUTY HELP
RITE TIDE YOKE FAVOR MUSAF
STEAD DEVOIR EMPLOY ERRAND
FACTOR OFFICE YIZKOR BENEFIT
BONDAGE CHAKARI CORNAGE
FUNERAL LITURGY OBSEQUY
RETINUE SERVAGE SERVING
BREEDING EQUIPAGE FUNCTION
HEADWARD KINDNESS MINISTRY
ROUNDING SERVITUM TENDANCE
(ASSIGNED —) MYSTERY
(BODYGUARD —) INWARD
(BREAKFAST —) DEJEUNER
(CHORAL —) MATIN
(CHURCH —) LAUDS CHAPEL
CHURCH HEARING STATION SYNAXIS
EVENSONG
(COFFEE —) CABARET
(COMPULSORY —) ANGARIA
(DOMESTIC —) CHAKARI
(FEUDAL —) BOON AVERA SEAWARD
HEADWARD
(MILITARY —) ARMS CAMP DUTY
ESCUAGE
(MILITIA —) COMMANDO
(RELIGIOUS —) AHA SEDER
COMMON
(SECRET —) OGPU
(TENNIS —) ACE LET
SERVICEABLE USEFUL DURABLE
THRIFTY FRIENDLY VAILABLE
SERVICE TREE SORB SORBUS
CHECKER
SERVILE BASE BOND ABJECT
MENIAL SUPINE VASSAL CAITIFF
SLAVISH VERNILE COISTREL
CRAWLING CRINGING SERVIENT
THEWLIKE
SERVILITY CRINGE

SERVING OBED SMACK DISHFUL
HELPING SERVIENT WHIPPING
SERVITOR FAG GROOM PUNTER
SERVANT PUNTSMAN
SERVITUDE USE VIA YOKE BONDAGE
SERVICE SLAVERY SERVITUS
THEOWDOM THIRLAGE
SERVOMECHANISM SERVO
BOOSTER
SERVOMOTOR RELAY SERVO
SESAME TIL TEEL BENNE BENNI
SEMSEM VANGLO OILSEED
WANGALA AJONJOLI BENISEED
SERGELIM
SESBANIA AGATI
SESQUITERPENE CEDROL CLOVENE
COPAENE HUMULENE
SESSION DAY BOUT DIET HOUR
SEAT COURT CLINIC SCHOOL
SEANCE ACUERDO HEARING
SEMINAR SITTING CONGRESS
SEDERUNT SEMESTER
(JAM —) CLAMBAKE
(PL.) ASSIZES
SESTERTIUS BRONZE
SESTINA SEXTAIN
SET DO DIP FIX GEL KIT LAY MOB
PUT SIC SIT SOT CASE CREW CUBE
GAGE GANG GIVE JELL KNIT KNOT
NEST PAIR PICK PILT POSE REST
SETT SORT STEP STOW BATCH
CLASS CLOCK CROWD FIXED GAUGE
GLADE GROUP INFIX PAVER PLACE
POSIT STACK STAID STAND STEAD
STEEK STICK SUITE ADJUST CIRCLE
DEFINE FASTEN FINALE FORMAL
GLAZED GROUND HARDEN IMPOSE
SERIES SETTLE SPREAD SQUARE
STATED BATTERY COMPANY
COMPOSE CONFIRM COTERIE
DEPOSIT DISPOSE ENCHASE
FACTION IMPLANT INSTATE
PLATOON SERVICE STATION
STIFFEN STRATUM EQUIPAGE
PANTALON SEQUENCE SOLIDIFY
STANDARD
(— A PERIOD) DATE
(— A PRICE) ASK
(— ABOUT) FALL FANG GANG BEGIN
ADDRESS
(— AFLOAT) LAUNCH
(— APART) SHED DESIGN DEVOTE
EXEMPT SACRED SEPONE SEPOSE
APPOINT ISOLATE RESERVE
ALLOCATE DEDICATE INSULATE
SEPARATE
(— ARROWS IN ORDER) FRUSH
(— AS ONE'S SHARE) ALLOT
(— ASIDE) BAR DISH DROP HAIN
SIDE SINK SLIP BURKE KAPUT
SEPOSE BRACKET EARMARK
PURLOIN RESERVE SUSPEND
ABROGATE DISPENSE OVERRIDE
OVERRULE REVERSED
(— AT DEFIANCE) BEARD
(— AT LIBERTY) FREE RELEASE
LIBERATE
(— BACK TO BACK) ADDORSED
ADDOSSED

(— CLOSE TOGETHER) PAVEED
(— DOG ON) SIC SLATE
(— DOWN UNDER NAME) TITLE
(— DOWN) JOT LAY GIVE LAND
SCORE EXPONE DEPOSIT
(— EDGEWISE) SURBED
(— ERECT) COCK
(— FIRMLY) FIRM STEM PLANT
POSIT
(— FORTH) DRAW ETCH SHOW
GIVEN STATE DEPART EXPOSE
SPREAD ARTICLE DISPLAY ENOUNCE
EXHIBIT EXPOUND PRESENT
PROPONE PROPOSE PURPOSE
PROPOUND
(— FORWARD) PREFER ADVANCE
(— FREE) BAIL EASE REMIT SKILL
SOLVE ACQUIT ASSOIL ABSOLVE
DELIVER ENLARGE UNLOOSE
WINFREE DISPLACE DISSOLVE
EXPEDITE UNVASSAL
(— GOING) INITIATE
(— IN EARTH) STRIKE
(— IN FROM MARGINS) INDENT
(— IN MOTION) SOW
(— IN OPERATION) DRIVE
(— IN OPPOSITION) PIT
(— IN ORDER) ARRAY FRUSH
ADIGHT DAIKER FETTLE INFORM
ADDRESS
(— INTO A GROOVE) DADO
(— INTO) INLAY
(— LIMITS TO) SPAN BOUND
(— OF 3 ANIMALS) LEASH
(— OF ACTORS) CAST
(— OF ARMS) CONVEYER
(— OF BARS) CONCAVE
(— OF BELLS) RING CHIME
CARILLON
(— OF BOOKS) PLENARY
(— OF CARS) DRAG
(— OF CHIMES) DOORBELL
(— OF CIRCUMSTANCES) CASE EGIS
FRAME
(— OF CORDS) SIMPLE
(— OF DISHES) GARNISH SERVICE
CUPBOARD
(— OF EIGHT) OGDOAD
(— OF EXERCISES) KATA
(— OF FACTS) BOOK
(— OF FISH NETS) DRIFT
(— OF FOLDED SHEETS) QUIRE
(— OF FOUR) WARP
(— OF FURNITURE) SUITE DINETTE
(— OF GARMENTS) SUIT
(— OF GEARS) GEARSET
(— OF HIDES) KIP
(— OF HOUNDS) VANLAY VAUNTLAY
(— OF IDEAS) SYSTEM
(— OF JEWELLED ORNAMENTS)
PARURE
(— OF LEAVES) COROLLA
(— OF LETTERS) ALPHABET
(— OF MUSICAL INSTRUMENTS)
CONSORT
(— OF OPINIONS) CREDO
(— OF ORGAN PIPES) STOP
(— OF PINS) KAILS KNOCKOUT
(— OF POINTS) INTERVAL

(— OF PUMPS) LIFT
(— OF QUADRILLES) LANCERS
(— OF RADIATORS) STACK
(— OF ROOMS) STORY
(— OF RULES) CODE EQUITY
DECALOG
(— OF SAILS) CANVAS
(— OF SHELVES) STAGE BUFFET
DRESSER WHATNOT
(— OF SKI FASTENINGS) BINDING
(— OF STAVES) SHOOK
(— OF STEPS) LADDER
(— OF SYMBOLS) KATAKANA
(— OF TABLES) COMPUTUS
(— OF TEETH) DENTURE
(— OF TEN) DECADE
(— OF THREE) BALE
(— OF TOOLS) STRING
(— OF TRAMS) JOURNEY
(— OF TYPEFACES) FAMILY
(— OF VALUES) CURRENCY
(— OF VATS) SOLERA
(— OF VERSES) STAVE
(— OF VOWELS) SERIES
(— OF WARP THREADS) LEA
(— OFF TO ADVANTAGE) ADORN
COMMEND
(— OFF) FOIL SEVER SHOOT
ACCENT BUNDLE BALANCE
EMBLAZE CONTRAST DECORATE
EMBLAZON
(— ON END) UPEND
(— ON FIRE) SPIT TIND LIGHT
ACCEND IGNIFY IGNITE KINDLE
ENFLAME INFLAME ENKINDLE
(— ONESELF) GO
(— OUT) FOUND SALLY START
INTEND STARTLE
(— OVER) COUCH
(— RIGHT) REDD ADJUST SCHOOL
SQUARE CORRECT REDRESS
(— SNARE) TAIL TILL
(— SOLIDLY) EMBED
(— STRAIGHT) DRESS
(— THICKLY) STUD
(— TO MUSIC) AIR DITTY
(— TRAP) TELD
(— TYPE) KEYBOARD
(— UP IN COLUMNS) TABULAR
(— UP) AREAR ERECT RAISE
INSTALL UPDRESS ACTIVATE
(— UPON) BESET ATTACK AGGRESS
BROWDEN
(— UPRIGHT) ERECT STAND
(— VALUE) APPRAISE
(— WITH BRISTLES) STRIGOSE
(— WITH GEMS) CHASE
(ANTIGEN —) SEROTYPE
(BECOME —) STRIKE
(CHESS —) MEINY MEINIE
(CHROMOSOME —) GENOME
COMPLEX
(COMPLETE —) STAND
(INFINITE —) FAMILY
(MINIATURE —) DIORAMA
(RADIO —) BLOOPER
(SMART —) TON
(STAGE —) SCENE

(UNALTERABLY —) STOUT
(PL.) DECOR
SETA STALK WHISK CHAETA SETULA
SETULE CROTCHET PODETIUM
SETBACK DASH JOLT KNOCK LURCH
BACKSET LICKING PUTBACK
BUSINESS COMEDOWN HAYMAKER
SETLINE GEAR TRAWL BULTOW
OUTLINE TROTLINE
SETTEE SETTLE WINDSOR
SETTER SOFA GUNDOG DROPPER
FLUSHER SETTLER
SETTERWORT PIGROOTS
SETTING SET FALL PAVE CHASE
MIDST SETUP CHATON MILIEU
FERMAIL MONTURE SITTING
INTERIOR MARQUISE MOUNTING
SHOWCASE
(— APART) BETWEEN
(— FREE) SOLUTION
(— OF GEM) FOIL OUCH CHASE
GALLERY
(— OF REED) CAAMING
(— OF WHEELS) CAMBER
(CAMERA —) BULB
(FAMILIAR —) HOME
(MUSICAL —) CREDO BALLAD
BALLADE
(SHUTTER —) TIME
(STAGE —) SCENE
SETTLE BED FIT FIX PAY SAG SET
SIT TAX BANK BIND CALM DAIS
DEAS FAST FIRM HAFT LEND NEST
REST ROOT SEAT SINK SNUG TOIT
AGREE CLEAR COUCH ISSUE LIGHT
LODGE ORDER PITCH PLACE PLANT
QUIET SQUAT STATE STILL ADJUST
ASSIGN CLINCH DECIDE DECREE
ENCAMP LOCATE NESTLE PURIFY
RESIDE SCREEN SECURE SOOTHE
SOPITE SQUARE ACCOUNT APPEASE
APPOINT ARRANGE BALANCE
CLARIFY COMPONE COMPOSE
CONCERT CONFIRM DEPOSIT
DERAIGN INHABIT RESOLVE SUBSIDE
COLONIZE REGULATE SQUATTLE
(— AMICABLY) COMPOUND
(— DOWN) CAMP SLUMP STEADY
DESCEND
(— ITSELF) INVEST
(— LANDS ON A PERSON) ENTAIL
(— ON) POINT
(— UPON) AFFIX AGREE TIGHT
(— VERTICALLY) SQUASH
SETTLED SAD SET FIRM FIXED QUIET
STAID FORMED RANGED SEATED
SEDATE SQUARE STAPLE STATED
CERTAIN DECIDED EMPIGHT
STATARY DECOROUS RESOLVED
STANDING
(NOT —) FARROW
SETTLEMENT AUL DEAL FINE FORK
POST BARRIO COLONY DIKTAT
MOSHAV WINDUP ACCOUNT
BIVOUAC FINANCE MAABARA
OUTPOST STATION CLERUCHY
DECISION DISPATCH JOINTURE
KEVUTZAH PRESIDIO SETTLING
SHOWDOWN TOWNSHIP

(— OF MONKS) SCETE SKETE
(COLLECTIVE —) KVUTZA KIBBUTZ
(MARRIAGE —) MAHR ARRAS
DOWNSET
(NEW ZEALAND —) PA PAH
(RAPID —) BOOM
SETTLER METIC SAHIB LIVYER
NESTER GRUELER PEOPLER
PILGRIM PIONEER TRIMMER
FINISHER GACHUPIN HABITANT
SHAGROON SIBERSKI SIBERYAK
(— IN AUSTRALIA) GROPER
SETTLING SIT
(— OF ESTATE) ENTAIL
(PL.) LEES SEDIMENT
SET-TO BOUT TURN PLUCK FETTLE
TURNUP BRANGLE
SETUP SET SITTER
SEVEN SEPT ZETA ZAYIN HEPTAD
SEPTET HEBDOMAD SEPTETTE
(— OF DIAMONDS) POPE
(— OF TRUMPS) MANILLA
(GROUP OF —) PLEIAD
SEVENFOLD SEPTUPLE
SEVEN-UP SLEDGE
SEVER AX AXE CUT BITE DEAL HACK
REND SLIT TWIN SHEAR SHRED
CLEAVE DEPART DETACH DIVIDE
SUNDER DISALLY DISCERP DISCIDE
DISJOIN OUTRIVE DISSEVER
PRESCIND SEPARATE SEVERIZE
SEVERAL ODD TEN SERE WHEEN
DIVERS SUNDRY DIVERSE VARIOUS
DISTINCT MULTIPLE
SEVERALLY APIECE SEVERAL
SEVERANCE SUNDER SOLUTION
(— OF RELATIONSHIPS) AIR
SEVERE BAD DRY ACID BLUE DEAR
DOUR DURE FIRM HARD IRON KEEN
ROID RUDE SALT SIDE SORE TART
TAUT ACUTE BREME CRUEL EAGER
GRUFF HARSH RETHE RIGID ROUGH
SHARP SMART SNELL SOBER
SOUND STARK STEER STERN STIFF
STOUR BITING BITTER BRUTAL
CHASTE COARSE FROSTY HETTER
SIMPLE SOLEMN STRICT TORVID
UNKIND UNMILD ACERBIC ASCETIC
AUSTERE CHRONIC CONDIGN
CRUCIAL CUTTING DRASTIC
SERIOUS SPARTAN TORVOUS
UNCANNY VIOLENT WEIGHTY
ACULEATE EXACTING GRIEVOUS
GRINDING HORRIBLE IRONCLAD
IRONHARD RIGOROUS SCATHING
STALWART STRAIGHT
(MOST —) EXTREME
SEVERELY BAD HARD BADLY STARK
STIFF HARDLY SORELY STRONG
HEAVILY ROUGHLY SMARTLY
SOUNDLY STITHLY SHREWDLY
SEVERIAN AGNOETE AGNOITE
SEVERITY FROST RIGOR CRUELTY
TORVITY TYRANNY ACRIMONY
ASPERITY FERVENCY HARDNESS
RIGIDITY SORENESS VIOLENCE
SEW SUE FELL SEAM SLIP PREEN
STEEK NEEDLE STITCH OVERSEW
THIMBLE OVERHAND

(— A CORPSE) SOCK
(— LOOSELY) BASTE
(— TO REINFORCE) BAR
(— WAVED PATTERN) DICE
SEWAGE SOIL WASTE SOILAGE
SULLAGE AFFLUENT DRAINAGE
SEWERAGE
SEWELLEL BEAVER BOOMER
SEWER SINK SIRE DRAFT DRAIN
FLEET ISSUE MAKER SHORE
CLOACA KILTER TACKER VENNEL
BELTMAN COPYIST CULVERT
DRAUGHT GULLION JAWHOLE
SHIRRER PIQUIERE
SEWING TACK SUTURE SEMPSTRY
SEX KIND SECT GENDER
(FEMALE —) SMOCK
(MALE —) WEPMANKIN
SEXLESS NEUTER EPICENE
SEXT MIDDAY
SEXTET SESTET SEXTUOR SESTETTO
SEXTON SAXON SHAMUS WARDEN
SACRIST SHAMASH VESTURER
SEXTUPLE SENARY
SEXTUPLET SESTOLE SEXTOLE
SESTOLET SEXTOLET
SEXUAL GAMIC INTIMATE
SEXY FREUDIAN
SHA YASHIRO
SHAB RUBBERS
SHABBINESS WAFFNESS
SHABBY BASE MEAN POKY WORN
DINGY DOWDY MANGY RATTY
SCALD SEEDY TACKY CHEESY
FROWZY GRUBBY SCABBY SCOFFY
SCOURY SCURVY SHODDY SHROVY
SLEAZY TAGRAG BUNTING MESQUIN
SCALLED SCRUBBY SCRUFFY
SCUFFED SHABBED SQUALID
PALTERLY SLIPSHOD WAFFLIKE
SHACK COE HUT CRIB SHAG HUMPY
HUTCH SHANTY
SHACKLE COP TIE BAND BIND BOLT
BOND GYVE LOCK STAY BASIL
BILBO CLAMP COPSE CRAMP CRANK
HUMPY TRASH TRAVE FETTER
GARTER HAMPER PINION SHANGY
STAYER SWATHE COTTAGE
COUPLER FETLOCK MANACLE
PASTERN SNACKLE TRAMMEL
RESTRAIN
(PL.) IRONS
SHACKLER SLOTTER
SHAD BUCK CHAD ALLIS ALOSE
TRABU ALLICE TWAITE ALEWIFE
ANADROM CLUPEID FLATFISH
SAWBELLY
SHADBUSH DOGWOOD SERVICE
SHADDOCK LUCBAN POMELO
POMPION
SHADE EYE CAST DULL SCUG SHED
TONE VEIL BLEND COLOR ENNUE
GHOST GLIDE GLOOM GRAIN SCAUM
SWALE SWILL TASTE TINCT TINGE
TRACE UMBER UMBRA DEGREE
FRESCO SHADOW SHIELD SHROUD
SPRITE STRAIN STRIPE TONING
CURTAIN ECLIPSE GRADATE
HACHURE PROTECT SECTION

SHADING UMBRAGE HALFTONE
UMBRELLA
(— OF COLOR) EYE TONE
(— OF DIFFERENCE) NUANCE
(— OFF) GRADUATE
(EYE —) UGLY
(OVERHANGING —) CANOPY
(WINDOW —) STORE
SHADED OMBRE SHADY DRUMLY
SOMBER SOMBRE DARKLING
SHADINESS GLOOM
SHADING FLUTING LAYERING
SHADOW FOX BLOT SCUG TAIL
CLOUD SHADE UMBER UMBRA
CLEEKS DARKEN FINGER SHROUD
TAILER ISOGYRE PHANTOM
SCARROW SUGGEST UMBRAGE
UMBRATE PENUMBRA PHANTASM
SHEPHERD
SHADOWED DARKLING
SHADOWINESS GLOOM
SHADOWLESS ASCIAN WHITEOUT
SHADOWY MISTY VAGUE GLOOMY
GHOSTLY OBSCURE
SHADRACH ANANIAS HANANIAH
SHADY DARK CLOUDY SHADOW
SHADOWY UMBROSE ADUMBRAL
SHAFT BAR NIB ROD BALK BOLT
DART FUST HOLE PILE POLE TRAM
WELL ARBOR HEUGH QUILL REACH
SCAPE SHANK SHOOT SNEAD
SPRAG STAFF STALE STAVE STEAL
STILT STING THILL TRUNK BOLTEL
CANNON COLUMN GNOMON SCAPUS
STAPLE TILLER UPRISE VAGINA
BOWTELL CHIMNEY INCLINE
MANDREL SPINDLE CAMSHAFT
DOWNCAST ESCONSON HOISTWAY
LAMPHOLE SHAFTWAY STANDARD
WEIGHBAR WELLHOLE
(— CONNECTING WHEELS) AXLE
(— IN GLACIER) MOULIN
(— IN WATCH) STEM
(— OF CANDLESTICK) BALUSTER
(— OF CARRIAGE) FILL SILL THILL
(— OF CART) ROD TRAM SHARP
STANG
(— OF CAVERN) DOME
(— OF CHARIOT) BEAM
(— OF CLUSTERED PIER) BOLTEL
(— OF COLUMN) FUST TIGE SCAPE
(— OF FEATHER) SCAPE SCAPUS
(— OF MINE) PIT WORK GRUFF
HEUCH HEUGH SLOPE GROOVE
STAPLE INCLINE WINNING
(— OF PADDLE) ROUND
(— OF SPEAR OR LANCE) TREE
STALE
(— OF WAGON) STAVE THILL
LIMBER
(HARNESS —) HEALD
(HOLLOW —) CANNON
(MAIN —) ARBOR
(ORNAMENTAL —) VERGE
(SCYTHE —) SNEAD
(STAIRWAY —) VICE
(TWISTED —) TORSO
(VENTILATION —) UPCAST UPTAKE
WINDHOLE

SHAG PILE
SHAGGY SHAG SWAG HARSH NAPPY
ROUGH SHOCK TATTY TOUSY
BRUSHY COMATE RAGGED TOOSIE
HIRSUTE SHAGRAG SQUALID
SWAGGED THRUMMY VILLOUS
TATTERED
SHAGREEN GALUCHAT
SHAGROON PILGRIM
SHAKE BOB DAD JAR JOG ROG WAG
JOLT JOWL PLUM QUAG RESE ROCK
SHOG STIR SWAY TOZE WEVE
WHAP WHOP HOTCH JAUNT KNOCK
NIDGE QUASH SHOCK SWING TRILL
DIDDER DITHER DODDER DODDLE
EXCUSS GOGGLE HOTTER HUSTLE
JOGGLE JOUNCE JUMBLE QUATCH
QUAVER QUITCH QUIVER ROGGLE
RUFFLE SHIMMY SHIVER TOTTER
WAMBLE WANGLE WARBLE WEAKEN
WOBBLE AGITATE BRANDLE
CHOUNCE CONCUSS SHUDDER
STAGGER SUCCUSS TREMBLE
TWITTER WHIFFLE WHITHER
BRANDISH CONVULSE ENFEEBLE
(— HERRING) SCUD
(— LIGHTLY) LIFT
(— OFF) ARISE EXCUSS
(— TO SEPARATE) HOTCH
(— UP) JABBLE JUMBLE RATTLE
(WIND —) ANEMOSIS
SHAKER DUSTER SIFTER DREDGER
JUMBLER POUNCET SANDBOX
SHAKING ASHAKE TREMOR JARRING
AGITATED
(— OF AIRPLANE) BUFFET
SHAKTI TARA PRAKRITI
SHAKTIS MATRIS
SHAKY CRANK DICKY QUAKY ROCKY
TOTTY WONKY WOOZY AGUISH
CRANKY GROGGY INFIRM WAMBLY
CASALTY DWAIBLE DWEEBLE
PALSIED RICKETY SHOGGLY
TITTUPY TOTTERY COGGLEDY
INSECURE
SHALE BAT BASS BONE CLOD FLAG
KOLM METAL PLATE XALLE KILLAS
SHILLET MUDSTONE SLIGGEEN
SHALL SE MAY MUN MUST SALL
(— NOT) SANNA SHANT SHANNA
SHALLOON CUBICA
SHALLOT CIBOL ALLIUM ESCHALOT
SCALLION
SHALLOW EBB BANK FLAN FLAT
FLUE GLIB FLEET INANE SHOAL
SILLY SMALL FLIMSY FROTHY
LITTLE RIFFLE SLIGHT UNDEEP
CRIPPLE CURSORY TRIVIAL
MAGAZINY
(PL.) FORD
SHALLOWNESS INANITY
SHAM BAM FOB FOX GIG FAKE HOAX
MOCK PUFF BLUFF BOGUS CHEAT
DUMMY FALSE FEIGN FRAUD LETON
QUEER ASSUME BRUMMY BUNYIP
CHOUSE DECEIT DUFFER HUMBUG
PSEUDO STUMER FALSITY FORGERY
GRIMACE MOCKISH PLASTER

PRETEND STUMOUR PRETENSE
SPURIOUS
SHAMAN PEAI CURER MACHI
KAHUNA WABENO ANGEKOK
TOHUNGA CONTRARY WITCHMAN
SHAMBLE SHALE SHOOL SCAMBLE
SHACHLE SHACKLE SKEMMEL
ABATTOIR SHAMMOCK
(PL.) BUTCHERY
SHAMBLING SHACKLY
SHAME SISS ABASH AIDOS SPITE
ASHAME BISMER REBUKE MORTIFY
SCANDAL SLANDER CONTEMPT
DISGRACE DISHONOR REPROACH
SHENDING VERGOYNE VITUPERY
(— BY CENSURE) TOUCH
SHAMEFACED SHY
SHAMEFACEDNESS PUDENCY
SHAMEFUL BASE FOUL MEAN
GROSS HONTOUS IGNOBLE
FLAGRANT IMPROPER INFAMOUS
SHAMELESS HARD BRASH ARRANT
BRAZEN BASHLESS BROWLESS
IMMODEST IMPUDENT
SHAMELESSNESS BRASS
SHAMPOO TRIPSIS
SHAMROCK SEAMROG SHAMROOT
SHANK BODY CRUS GAMB JAMB
TANG FENUR GAMBE CANNON
NIBBLE TARSUS KNUCKLE
(THREAD —) STEM
SHANNY BULLY
SHANTY BOIST HUMPY HUTCH
SHACK CHANTIER DOGHOUSE
SHAPE AX ADZ AXE CUT DIE HUE
ADZE BEAT BEND CAST COLE COPE
DRAW FACE FAIR FORM HACK MOLD
NICK BEVEL BLOCK BOAST BUILT
COLOR DRAPE DRESS FEIGN FORGE
FRAME GUISE HORSE JOLLY LATHE
MODEL MOULD SWAGE BROACH
CHISEL CUTOUT EFFORM FIGURE
FORMER FRAISE HAMMER JIGGER
SQUARE CHANNEL CONFORM
CONTOUR FASHION GESTALT
INCLINE PATTERN TONNEAU
CONTRIVE LIKENESS
(— BY HAMMERING) SMITH
(— DIAMOND) BRUTE
(— GARMENTS) BOARD
(— METAL) SWAGE EXTRUDE
(— OF BUST) TAILLE
(— OF ENVELOPE FLAP) KNIFE
(— ON POTTER'S WHEEL) THROW
(— ONE'S COURSE) ETTLE
(— RIGHTLY) FIT
(— ROUGHLY WITH CHISEL) BOAST
(— ROUGHLY) BOAST SCABBLE
SCAPPLE
(— STONE) BROACH SCABBLE
(CLAY —) FLOATER
(CONICAL —) BEEHIVE
(GEM —) BAGUET BAGUETTE
(GLOVE —) TRANK
(SPIRALLING —) SWIRL
(SURFACE —) GEOMETRY
(UNBLOCKED —) HOOD
SHAPED BUILT FITTED BLOCKED
FEATURED

(— **LIKE BEAN**) FABIFORM
(— **LIKE BOAT**) SCAPHOID
(— **LIKE BUCKLER**) SCUTATE
(— **LIKE CLUB**) CLAVATE CLUBBED
(— **LIKE CONE**) CONIFORM
(— **LIKE CUP**) SCYPHATE
(— **LIKE DOME**) DOMAL
(— **LIKE EAR**) AURIFORM
(— **LIKE HALBERD**) HASTATE
(— **LIKE HEART**) CORDATE
(— **LIKE HOOK**) ANKYROID
(— **LIKE KEEL**) CARINATE
(— **LIKE LEAF**) FOLIATE
(— **LIKE LENS**) LENTOID
(— **LIKE NEEDLE**) ACUATE
(— **LIKE RING**) ANNULAR
(— **LIKE ROD**) BACILLAR
(— **LIKE S**) SIGMATE
(— **LIKE SHIELD**) ASPIDATE
CLYPEATE
(— **LIKE SICKLE**) FALCULAR
(— **LIKE SPINDLE**) FUSOID
FUSIFORM
(— **LIKE SPUR**) CALCARINE
(— **LIKE STAR**) ASTROID
(— **LIKE STRAP**) LIGULATE
(— **LIKE SWORD**) GLADIATE
(— **LIKE THREAD**) FILIFORM
(— **LIKE WEDGE**) CUNEAL CUNEATE
(— **LIKE X**) SALTIRE
(— **WITH AX**) HEWN
SHAPELESS DUMPY DEFORM
DUMPTY INFORM FORMLESS
UNSHAPED
SHAPELINESS DELICACY
SHAPELY GENT TRIM CLEAN TIGHT
DECENT FORMAL GAINLY FORMFUL
SHAPABLE
SHAPING DESCENT
SHARD SCAUR SHERD SHRED
(PL.) PITCHER
SHARE CUT END LOT CANT DALE
DEAL DOLE HAND PART PLOT RENT
SCOT SNIP DIVVY ENTER PARTY
QUOTA RATIO SHEAR SHIFT SLICE
SNACK SNICK SNUCK SPLIT WHACK
COMMON COPART DEPART DIVIDE
FINGER IMPART RATION SHOVEL
PARTAGE PARTAKE PORTION
DIVIDEND DIVISION INTEREST
PURPARTY
(— **A BED**) BUNK
(— **EQUALLY**) HALVE
(— **OF EXPENSES**) LAW CLUB
(— **OF LAND**) DAIL DALE FREEDOM
(— **OF PROFIT**) LAY
(— **OF STOCK**) STOCK ACTION
(— **QUARTERS**) CHUM
(— **SECRETS**) CONFIDE
(**ALLOTED** —) DOLE
(**ANCESTRAL** —) PATTI
(**FULL** —) SKINFUL
(**GREATER** —) FECK
(**LEGAL** —) HAK
(**ONE'S** —) AFFERE
(**PROPORTIONAL** —) QUOTA
SHARECROPPER BYWONER
CROPPER
SHARED JOINT BETWEEN

SHARING (— **OF EXPENSE**) CLUB
(— **VICARIOUSLY**) ARMCHAIR
SHARK FOX GATA HAYE KULP MAKO
MANO TOPE GUMMY HOMER HOUND
LAMIA TIGER TOPER DAGGAR
GALEID PALOMA REQUIN WHALER
ACRODUS BONEDOG DOGFISH
FOXFISH HUNFYSH PLACOID
REQUIEM SLEEPER SOUPFIN
SQUALID SUNFISH TIBERON
TIGRONE TUBARON BULLHEAD
HYBODONT ROUSETTE SAILFISH
SEAHOUND SKAAMOOG SPEAREYE
SQUATINA THRASHER
(**YOUNG** —) CUB SHARKLET
SHARP DRY SHY ACID ACRE CUTE
EDGY FELL FINE GAIR GASH GLEG
GNIB HARD HIGH KEEN PERT SALT
TART ACERB ACRID ACUTE ALERT
BRASH BREME BRISK CRISP DOWNY
EAGER EDGED FALSE HARSH NEBBY
PEERY QUICK SMART SNELL SQUAB
STEEP STIFF VIVID YAULD ARGUTE
ASTUTE BITING BITTER BRIGHT
CRISPY DIESIS GLASSY JAGGED
PLUCKY SEVERE SHREWD SHRILL
SNELLY SNITHE STINGY TOOTHY
TWEAKY UNRIDE ANGULAR
AUSTERE BRITTLE CAUSTIC
CUTTING GINGERY PIQUANT
POINTED PUNGENT SHARPEN
SLICING SPINOUS VARMINT VIOLENT
HATCHETY INCISIVE POIGNANT
SHARP-EDGED CULTRATE
SHARPEN EDGE FILE FINE HONE
KEEN WHET BRISK FROST GRIND
POINT RAISE SHARP SLYPE STONE
STROP ACCENT AFFILE STROKE
ENHANCE QUICKEN SMARTEN
EXACUATE HEIGHTEN
SHARPENED ACUATE
SHARPENER SHARPER STROPPER
(**SCYTHE** —) RIP RIFLE
SHARPER GUE GYP BITE KITE ROOK
SKIN SNAP BITER CHEAT CROOK
GREEK ROGUE SHARK SHARP
BESTER COGGER NICKUM PICARO
ROOKER SHARPY BARNARD
CATATAN GAMBLER SHARKER
SPIELER BLACKLEG DECEIVER
PIGEONER SWINDLER
SHARPLY DAB SHARP SNACK ACIDLY
ROUNDLY SHEERLY SMARTLY
STEEPLY
SHARPNESS WIT EDGE SALT WHET
PLUCK ACRITY ACUITY ACIDITY
ACERBITY ACRIDITY ACRIMONY
EDGINESS PUNGENCY
SHARP-POINTED ACUATE
ACULEATE
SHARPSHOOTER VOLTIGEUR
SHARP-SIGHTED SIGHTY LYNCEAN
SHARP-TAILED GROUSE PINTAIL
SHARP-WITTED CANNY SNELL
SHREWD
SHASTRA PURANA SASTRA
(— **CLASS**) SRUTI
SHATTER BLOW DASH DICE BLAST
BREAK BURST CRASH CRAZE

CREEM FRUSH SMASH SMOKE SPLIT
WRECK SHIVER SPIDER BEGUILE
CHATTER CONVEIL EXPLODE
SMATTER TORPEDO DEMOLISH
DYNAMITE SPLINTER
(— **CLAY TARGET**) KILL
SHATTERED BROKEN BROOZLED
DODDERED
SHAVE BARB BITE DRAW PARE RAZE
GLACE GRAZE SKIVE SCHAWE
SCRAPE FLATTEN UPRIGHT
SHAVED POLLED SHAVEN
SHAVEN NOT NOTT PILLED
TONSURED
SHAVING SHAVE SHRED SPALE
SPELL RAMENT RAMENTUM
(PL.) COOM COOMB SCOBS
MOSLINGS
SHAWL MAUD LAMBA MANTA MANTO
NUBIA PATTU TOZIE AFGHAN
ANGORA KAMBAL PEPLOS PEPLUM
PEPLUS PUTTOO SERAPE TAPALO
TOILET ZEPHYR AMLIKAR PAISLEY
WHITTLE WRAPPER CASHMERE
EPIBLEMA SLENDANG TURNOVER
(**COARSE** —) KAMBAL
(**COTTON** —) FARDA
(**PLAID** —) MAUD
(**TASSELED** —) TALLITH
SHAWM WAIT SHALM BOMBARD
SCHALMEI
SHE A HE HEO HER SHU HAEC SCHO
SHEAF TIE BEAT BUNG GAIT GERB
OMER FLASH GAVEL GERBE GLEAN
BATTEN THRAVE HATTOCK
CAPSHEAF CORNBOLE
(— **LEVIED AS TAX**) CORNBOLE
(— **OF ARROWS**) FLASH
(— **OF FLAX OR HEMP**) BEAT BEET
GLEAN
(— **OF GRAIN**) GAIT GARB HOSE
GARBACE
(**LAST** — **OF CORN**) NECK
(**LAST** — **OF HARVEST**) KIRN
(**PROTECTING** —) HATTOCK
(**UNBOUND** —) REAP GAVEL
SHEAR COW CUT DOD LIP NOT CLIP
CROP NOTT TRIM BREAK FORCE
SHARE SHEER SHIRL SLIDE STRIP
FLEECE STRESS
SHEARABLE TONSILE
SHEARER SNAGGER
SHEARLING SHEARHOG
(PL.) ALPACA
SHEARS LEWIS SNIPS FORFEX
SHEARER SNOUTER SECATEUR
SHEARWATER HAG CREW COHOW
HAGDON HAGLET PETREL PUFFIN
SCRABE PIMLICO SCRABER SEABIRD
HACKBOLT
SHEATFISH WELS DORAD WALLER
CATFISH SILURID
SHEATH COT HOT BOOT CASE CYST
HOSE HOTT ARMOR CHAPE FOREL
GAINE SHADE SHEAF SPILL THECA
CONDOM FORREL MYELIN OCHREA
QUIVER SLOUGH VAGINA AXILEMMA
EPILEMMA SCABBARD STANDARD
VAGINULA

(— FOR BOOK) FOREL FORRIL
(— FOR FINGER) STALL
(— FOR GAMECOCK'S SPUR) HOT
HOTT
(— OF CIGARETTE) SPILL
(— OF PLOW) STANDARD
(MEDULLARY —) CORONA
SHEATHBILL PADDY
SHEATHE CLAD COPPER MUZZLE
IMPLATE
SHEATHING SKIN ARMOR COPPER
FACING SHEATH INLAYER SHIPLAP
SLITWORK
SHEA TREE KARITE KARITI
SHEAVE SHEAF SHIVER HATTOCK
TRUCKLE
(24 —S OF GRAIN) THRAVE
THREAVE
SHED BOX CUB SOW ABRI CAST
COTE DROP HELM HULL KILN MOLT
POUR SHUD SKEO SLIP HIELD
HOVEL MOULT SCALE SHADE SPILL
THROW VINEA ZAYAT BELFRY
BROACH DINGLE EFFUSE GARAGE
HANGAR HEMMEL INFUSE LINHAY
MISTAL PANDAL SLOUGH COTTAGE
DIFFUSE DISCARD MUSCULE
RADIATE SKIPPER EXUVIATE
SKEELING SKILLION WOODSHED
(— BLOOD) BROACH
(— DROPS) DRIZZLE
(— FEATHERS OR HORNS) MEW
(— FOR LIVESTOCK) SHIPPEN
(— FOR SHEEP) SHEALING
(— OVER MINE SHAFT) COE
(— TEARS) GIVE
(— TO PROTECT SOLDIERS)
TESTUDO
(CATTLE —) CUB HELM LAIR
BELFRY
(MOVABLE —) SOW BAIL MUSCULE
(TEMPORARY —) PANDAL
(WEATHER —) DINGLE
SHEDDING FALL SPILTH ECDYSIS
APOLYSIS
SHE-DEMON LAMIA
SHEEN GLAZE SHINE LUSTER
LUSTRE SHIMMER
SHEEP SNA TEG DOWN LAMB LONK
MUGS SHIP SOAY URIN ZENU
ANCON BOVID DUMBA HEDER HUNIA
MUGGS OVINE SAIGA SHORN TAGGE
AOUDAD ARGALI BARHAL BHARAL
BIDENT CHURRO DECCAN DORPER
DORSET EXMOOR HIRSEL MARKER
MASHAM MERINO MUTTON NAYAUR
OXFORD PANAMA PAULER ROMNEY
WETHER WOOLIE WOOLLY BIGHORN
BLEATER BRAXIES CHEVIOT
CRIOLLA DELAINE DISHLEY FREEZER
FRONTER JUMBUCK KARAKUL
LINCOLN POLLARD SUFFOLK
TARGHEE TWINTER VERMONT
BIKANERI COMEBACK COTSWOLD
DARTMOOR HERDWICK LONGWOOL
LUGHDOAN RUMINANT SHEARHOG
SHEARING TALLOWER THRINTER
(— DIFFICULT TO HANDLE)
COBBLER

(— IN 2ND YEAR) HOB TAG TEG
TAGGE TWINTER
(— THAT HAS SHED PORTION OF
WOOL) ROSELLA
(— TO BE SHEARED) BOARD
(3-YEAR-OLD —) THRINTER
(DEAD —) BRAXY
(FEMALE —) EWE GIMMER SHEDER
(HORNLESS —) NOT NOTT
(LOST —) WAIF
(MALE —) RAM TUP BUCK HEDER
(MOUNTAIN —) IBEX
(OLD —) GUMMER
(THICK-WOOLED —) MUG
(UNSHORN —) HOG TEG
(WILD —) SHA ARGAL RASSE URIAL
AOUDAD ARGALI BHARAL SHAPOO
BURRHEL MOUFLON
(YOUNG —) HOG HOGG HOGGEREL
SHEEPBERRY ALISIER VIBURNUM
SHEEPCOTE SHEPPEY
SHEEPDOG KELPIE SHELTY BOBTAIL
MALINOIS SHETLAND
SHEEP FLY FAG
SHEEPFOLD REE FANK KRAAL
REEVE STELL BOUGHT BARKARY
SHEPPEY SHEEPCOT
SHEEPHERDER SNOOZER
STOCKMAN
SHEEPISH SHY
SHEEP LAUREL IVY HEATH WICKY
KALMIA LAUREL CALFKILL LAMBKILL
SHEEPLIKE OVINE
SHEEPMAN HOBBER
SHEEP PLANT RAOULIA
SHEEP ROT CAW
SHEEP RUN STATION
SHEEPSHEAD JAMES JEMMY JIMMY
PARGO PORGY TAUTOG FATHEAD
PERCOID SPAROID
SHEEPSHEARER GUN
SHEEPSKIN ROAN SLAT MOUTON
SOLDIER CAPESKIN LAMBSKIN
WOOLFELL WOOLSKIN
(— TANNED WITH BARK) BASAN
BASIL
(— THAT SWEATS UNEVENLY)
SOLDIER
(— WITHOUT WOOL) SLAT
(ROUGH-TANNED —) CRUST
SHEEP SORREL SOURWEED
SHEEP TICK FAG KEB KED KADE
SHEEPWALK SLAIT
SHEER BOLD FINE MAIN MERE PURE
BLANK BRANT CRUDE FRANK STARK
STEEP SIMPLE CLOTTED GAZETTE
EVENDOWN
(MADE OF — FABRIC) PEEKABOO
SHEET FIN CARD FILM FINE FLAT
FOIL LEAF SILL BLANK FLONG
FOLIO NAPPE CANVAS CIRCLE
DOUBLE FASCIA FENDER FLIMSY
SHROUD SINDON BLANKET
CHUDDER FLOGGER FRISKET
LEAFLET PALLIUM PAPYRUS
WRAPPER AIRSHEET EIGHTEEN
FOLLOWER HANDBILL INTERLAY
SHEETLET
(— ADDED TO DEED) FOLLOWER

(— ATTACHED TO INVOICE) APRON
(— FOR BRIDGE SCORES) FLOGGER
(— OF CELLULOID) CEL CELL
(— OF CLOUDS) PALLIUM
(— OF DOUGH) STRUDEL
(— OF FIBER) BAT LAP BATT
(— OF ICE) GLARE GLAZE
(— OF IRON) CRAMPET CRAMPIT
(— OF LAVA) COULEE
(— OF LEAD) SOAKER
(— OF LEATHER) BUFFING
(— OF MICA) FILM
(— OF PAPER) FLAT FOLIO FRISKET
LEAFLET HANDBILL
(— OF PARCHMENT) SKIN
FOLLOWER
(— OF RUBBER) DAM
(— OF STRAW) YELM
(— OF SUGAR) SLAB
(— OF TISSUE) FASCIA
(— OF TOBACCO) BINDER
(— OF WATER) NAPPE
(— USED FOR MATRIX) FLONG
(HEATED —) CAUL
(METAL —S) LATTENS
(NEWS —) GAZETTE
(ORGANIZATION —) BILL
(PERFORATED —) SIEVE
(PROTECTIVE —) CURTAIN
(THEATRICAL —) SIDE
(THIN —S OF IRON) DOUBLES
(TRANSPARENT —) GELATINE
(WINDING —) SINDON SUDARY
SHEETING DOMESTIC AMERIKANI
SHEKINAH GLORY
SHELDRAKE SHELDER BARGOOSE
SHELF BANK BERM BINK DECK DESS
STEP TACK BENCH LEDGE SKELF
STAGE STOOL MANTEL SCONCE
SETTLE SHELVE BACKBAR BRACKET
COUNTER PLATEAU CREDENCE
CUPBOARD
(— BEFORE STOVE) HEARTH
(— BEHIND ALTAR) GRADINE
GRADINO RETABLE
(— IN MINE) BUNNING
(— OF ROCK) CAR LENCH
LENCHEON
(ALTAR —) BUTSUDAN
(CONTINENTAL —) PLATFORM
(FIREWORKS —) BALLOON
(RAISED —) SETTLE
SHELL ARD HUD PEN POD BAND
CASK CHOU CONE HARD HOOF
HULL HUSK MAIL OBUS PELL PILL
PIPI PUPA SKIN SWAD UMBO UNIO
BALAT CHANK CHINK CONCH COPIS
CRUMP CRUST DRILL FRITZ GOURD
MITER MITRA MUREX ORMER SCAUP
SHALE SHARD SHEAL SHERD SHOCK
SHUCK TESTA TIARA TROCA TURBO
VALVE VENUS ANOMIA BUCKIE
BULLET BURGAU CERION COCKLE
CONKER COWRIE CRUSTA DENTAL
DOLIUM ECLAIR JINGLE LORICA
MAROON NOUGAT NUCULA PULLET
PURPLE SANKHA SINGLE SLOUGH
STROMB TERBRA TRITON TURBAN
VANNET VENTER VOLUTE WINKLE

BALLOON CARACOL CARCASS COCONUT DARIOLE DISCINA GLADIUS LIMACEL MARINER PAPBOAT PHILINE PROJECT SCALLOP SPICULE SPINDLE SPONDYL THIMBLE TOHEROA TORPEDO TOXIFER TROCHID TRUMPET UNICORN BACULITE BACULOID CARAPACE CONCHITE COQUILLE CYLINDER DUCKFOOT EGGSHELL ENVELOPE ESCALLOP FIGSHELL FOCALOID FRUSTULE HELICINA MERINGUE OLIVELLA PUPARIUM SEASHELL SOLARIUM STROMBUS UNIVALVE VELUTINA VERMETID VERMETUS WARRENER WHIZBANG WOODCOCK **(— CONTAINING MEDICINE)** CAPSULE **(— OF DIATOM)** FRUSTULE **(— OF OYSTER)** HUSK SHUCK **(— OF SHIP)** HULK SKIN **(— OF SLUG)** LIMACEL **(— SYSTEMATICALLY)** COMB **(—S FROM GUN)** STUFF **(ANTIAIRCRAFT —)** FLAK **(CARTRIDGE —S)** BRASS **(CAST —S)** EXUVIAE **(CUSTARD-FILLED —)** ECLAIR DARIOLE **(FOSSIL —)** DOLITE AMMONITE BACULITE BALANITE CONCHITE **(HOWITZER —)** OBUS **(MATHEMATICAL —)** HOMEOID **(OYSTER —S)** CULCH CULTCH **(PASTRY —)** CORNET DARIOLE TIMBALE TALMOUSE **(SNAIL —)** CONKER HODMADOD **(SPIRAL —)** CHANK **(TORTOISE —)** HOOF **(VEGETABLE —)** DOLMA **SHELLED** VINED **SHELLFISH** COCK NACRE PIROT LIMPET WIGGLE MOLLUSK PERIWIG **SHELLING** RATTLES **SHELL-LESS** OON **SHELL MONEY** UHLLO WAKIKI **SHELTER** CAB HUT LEE LOO ABRI BURY EAVE GIDE GITE HERD HIDE HIVE JOKE JOUK ROOF SCOG SCUG BARTH BENAB BERRY BIELD BOIST BOTHY BOWER CABIN CLEAD CLOAK COVER EMBAY HAVEN HOARD HOUSE HOVEL HOVER HOWFF HUTCH LEWTH LITHE RESET SHADE SHEAL ASYLUM AWNING BELFRY BILBIE BOOLEY BOUGHT BURROW COVERT CRADLE DEFEND DUGOUT GABION GUNYAH HANGAR HARBOR HOSTEL PANDAL REFUGE SCONCE SCREEN SHADOW SHIELD SHROUD SUKKAH BOROUGH CABINET CARPORT CHAMBER DEFENSE EMBOSOM EMBOWER HOUSING NACELLE QUARTER RETREAT ROOFING TABERNA UMBRAGE WANIGAN WICKIUP BESCREEN DOGHOUSE ENSCONCE LODGMENT PALLIATE SECURITY SNOWSHED WAYHOUSE

(— FOR CATTLE) HELM BOOLY STELL HEMMEL **(— FOR CROP WATCHERS)** KISI **(— FOR DANCES)** ENRAMADA **(— FOR SENTRY)** GUERITE **(— FROM WEATHER)** LEWTH **(— OVER BEEHIVE)** HOOD **(BULLETPROOF —)** MANTLET MANTELET **(CONCRETE-AND-STEEL —)** PILLBOX **(CRAMPED —)** HUTCH **(FISH —)** CROY **(LEAFY —)** LEVESEL **(MINING —)** TALPA **(PORTABLE —)** MANTA CABANA **(ROCK —)** KRAPINA **(ROUGH —)** JACAL **(TEEPEELIKE —)** CHUM **(TEMPORARY —)** HALE HOLD CABIN BIVOUAC **SHELTERED** LEE LEW LOWN BIELD LITHE SHADY COVERT **(— SPACE)** KILLOGIE **SHELTERING** BIELDY SHADING **SHELTERLESS** HOMELESS ROOFLESS **SHELVE** DISH BURKE SHELF **SHELVES** STAGE ETAGERE **SHENG** SANG CHENG SHING **(ONE-HUNDREDTH —)** CHAO **SHEOL** HELL **SHEPHERD** HERD SHEP COLIN CORIN GADDI GYGES SWAIN FEEDER PASTOR TARBOX CORYDON DAPHNIS DRAFTER GADARIA KURUMBA THYRSIS TITYRIS MELIBEUS MENALCAS PASTORAL SHEEPMAN STREPHON **(GERMAN —)** ALSATIAN **SHEPHERDESS** DELIA MOPSA PHEBE DORCAS BERGERE GALATEA PASTORA PERDITA **SHEPHERD'S-PURSE** TOYWORT CASEWEED COCOWORT **SHERBET** ICE GLACE SORBET GRANITA SOUFFLE **SHERD** SCARTH **SHERIFF** FOUD FOWD SCULT XERIF DEPUTY GRIEVE SCHOUT SHIRRA BAILIFF SHREEVE SHRIEVE ALGUACIL HUISSIER SHIREMAN VISCOUNT **SHERRY** FINO CLOVE JEREZ XERES DOCTOR MANCHU SOLERA OLOROSO RANGOON SHERRIS MONTILLA **SHEVRI** SESBAN **SHICER** DUFFER **SHIELD** ECU EGIS HIDE PELT AEGIS APRON BIELD BOARD CLOAK COVER FENCE GUARD GULAR MULGA PATCH PAVIS PELTA PYGAL SCUTE SHEND TARGE YELDE ANCILE ANGARA BLAZON CASQUE DEFEND FENDER GUNTUB GYROMA LINDEN MENTAL OCULAR PAUNCH RONDEL SCREEN SCUTUM SECURE TARGET BUCKLER CLIPEUS CONCEAL PANNIER PAVISSE PRIDWIN

PROTECT ROSTRAL ROTELLA ROUNDEL SHELTER SUPPORT TESTUDO CARTOUCH CUCULLUS HIELAMEN INSULATE MARGINAL PRESERVE RONDACHE STERNITE SUNSHADE BREASTING **(— BELOW A DAM)** APRON **(— FOR ARCHERS)** PANNIER **(— FOR HORSE)** BIB **(— FOR LAMP)** BONNET CHIMNEY **(— OF A STIRRUP)** HOOD **(— OF ABORIGINES)** MULGA HIELAMEN **(— OF CONTINENT)** CORE **(— OF HIDE)** SKILDFEL **(— OF SOMITE)** STERNITE **(— OF TRILOBITE)** CEPHALON **(— ON MAST)** PAUNCH **(— ON THROAT OF FISH)** GULAR **(— OVER BASE OF FAN)** CANOPY **(BONY —)** CARAPACE **(BULLETPROOF —)** MANTA MANTLET MANTELET **(HERALDIC —)** BLAZON **(KING ARTHUR'S —)** PRIWEN PRIDWIN **(LEATHER —)** CHAFE **(SACRED —)** ANCILE **(SIBERIAN —)** ANGARA **(WICKERWORK —)** SCIATH **SHIELDBEARER** SQUIRE ESQUIRE PELTAST ESCUDERO SCUTIFER **SHIELD BUG** STINKBUG **SHIELD FERN** FERNGALE **SHIELDMAKER** TYCHIOS **SHIELD-SHAPED** PELTATE SCUTATE THYROID **SHIFT** JIB BACK CHOP FEND FLIT HAUL MOVE RUSE SHIP TACK TOUR TURN VARY VEER WEND BREAK BUDGE CREEP CYMAR DRIFT HOTCH QUIRK SHIRK SHUNT SIMAR SKIFT SLIDE SMOCK SPELL TRICK BAFFLE CHANGE DENIAL DEVICE DOUBLE PALTER SKYFTE SWERVE SWITCH CUTBACK EVASION FRESHEN SHUFFLE SLEIGHT WHIFFLE ARTIFICE DISLODGE DISPLACE DOGWATCH DOUBLING MUTATION REVIRADO TRANSFER TRAVERSE TURNOVER WINDLASS **(— ABOUT AS THE WIND)** LARGE **(— ABRUPTLY)** JUMP **(— IN DANCING)** BALANCE **(— IN TACKING)** JIB **(— ORDER OF BELLS)** HUNT **(— RAILROAD EQUIPMENT)** DRILL **(— SUDDENLY)** FLY CHOP GYBE JIBE **(— WEIGHT)** WING **(MINING —)** CORE **SHIFTING** FLUID QUICK CHOPPING DRIFTING FLOATING SLIPPAGE VARIABLE VEERABLE **SHIFTLESS** DRIFTY SOZZLY DRIFTING FECKLESS HAVELESS **SHIFTLESSNESS** SLOUCH **SHIFTY** GREASY DEVIOUS EVASIVE HANGDOG SLIDING SLIPPERY

SHIITE SHIAH SECTARY SHAIKHI
TWELVER
SHILHA SHLU CHLEUH
SHILL STICK BONNET CAPPER
BOOSTER
SHILLING BOB HOG CHIP HOGG
LEVY DEENER HARPER TESTON
TEVISS THIRTEEN
(20 —S) POUND
(21 —S) GUINEA
(5 —S) CROWN DECUS
SHILLY-SHALLY BACK BOGGLE
SHIM GLUT LINER SHIMMER
SHIMMER FLASH GLIMMER SHIMPER
SKIMMER
SHIN SHANK SKINK SWARM CNEMIS
SHINNY
SHINDIG SHINDY SHIVOO
SHINE RAY SUN BEAM BUFF GLOW
LAMP LEAM LINK STAR BLARE
BLICK BLINK BLOOM EXCEL GLAIK
GLARE GLEAM GLEIT GLENT GLINT
GLISS GLORE GLORY GLOSS GLOZE
SHEEN SKYRE STARE BEACON
DAZZLE GLANCE LUSTER LUSTRE
SCANCE EFFULGE GLIMMER
GLISTEN GLITTER RADIATE REFLECT
SHIMMER SPARKLE RUTILATE
(— BRIGHTLY) BEEK FLAME LIGHT
(— FAINTLY) SCARROW
(— UPON) SUN SMITE
SHINER CHUB DACE BREAM REDFIN
CYPRINID WINDFISH
SHINER-UP PATCHER
SHINGLE SHIM BEACH SHAKE SLATE
CHESIL KNOBBLE STARTER
SHINGLER NOBBLER
SHINGLES ZONA ZOSTER
SHININESS GLARE GLAZE GLOSS
SHINING GLAD NEAT CLEAR GLARY
LIGHT LUCID SHEER WHITE ARDENT
ARGENT ASHINE BRIGHT FULGID
GLOSSY GOLDEN LUCENT NITENT
ORIENT SERENE SHEENY SPUNKY
STARRY ADAZZLE BURNING
FULGENT GLARING GLIMMER
LAMPING FLASHING GLEAMING
LUCULENT LUSTRANT LUSTROUS
NITIDOUS RELUCENT RUTILANT
SPLENDID STARLIKE SUNBEAMY
SUNSHINY
SHINLEAF PYROLA
SHINNY PEG SHINTY
SHINTO (— SECT) RYOBU
SHIP (ALSO SEE BOAT AND VESSEL)
ARK CAT COG HOY NAO BARK
BOAT BOOM GRAB HAND HULK
KEEL LADE NAVY PAHI PINE PINK
SAIL SEND SNOW TREE WOOD ZULU
CHECK LAKER OILER PINTA PRORE
RAZEE SCOUT SCREW SKIFF WHELP
ANDREW ARGOSY BARKEY BARQUE
BOTTOM CARTEL CASTLE CHASER
COALER CODMAN DECKER DIESEL
GALIOT GALLEY HOLCAD HOPPER
LANCHA LATEEN LORCHA MASTER
MISTIC MOTHER PACKET PUFFER
RUNNER SAILER SALVOR SEALER
SMOKER TONNER TRAVEL VESSEL

ADMIRAL CARRACK CLIPPER
COLLIER FACTORY FELUCCA
FOREIGN FRIGATE FRUITER
GABBARD GALLEON GUNBOAT
INVOICE MACHINE MULETTA
ONERARY PATAMAR PINNACE
POLACRE SHALLOP SHIPLET SPITKIT
STEAMER BALANDRA BALINGER
BILANDER CAPITANA DRUMBLER
FLAGSHIP GALLEASS GAYDIANG
INDIAMAN JAPANNER LANCHARA
MAGAZINE PESSONER PIPPINER
REPEATER SAILSHIP SCHOONER
SMUGGLER SPANIARD
(— BUILT FROM NAILS OF DEAD)
NAGLFAR
(— OF ARGONAUTS) ARGO
(— OF NORSEMEN) KEEL
(CLUMSY —) HULK
(DEPOT —) TENDER
(ESCORT —) CORVETTE
(FLEET OF —S) ARMADA
(JAPANESE —) MARU
(MALAY —) COUGNAR
(NOVA SCOTIAN —) BLUENOSE
(OBJECT SHAPED LIKE A —) NEF
(PIRATE —) GALLIVAT
(PRIZE —) CAPTURE
(QUARANTINE —) LAZARET
(RECEIVING —) GUARDO
(REMOTE-CONTROLLED —) DRONE
(SLOW —) BUCKET
(STORE —) FLUTER
(SUPPLY —) COPER COOPER
(UNTRIM —) BALLAHOO
(VIKING —) DRAKE
(PL.) NAVY MARINE SEACRAFT
SHIPPING
SHIPFITTER FITTER ERECTOR
SHIPMENT CARLOT RAILING
DISPATCH SHIPPAGE
SHIPSHAPE NEAT TIDY TRIM CIVIL
ATAUNT ORDERLY
SHIP SWEEPER TOPASS TOPIWALA
SHIPWAY BERTH
SHIPWORM ARTER BORER COBRA
TEREDO PILEWORM WOODWORM
SHIPWRECK WRACK NAUFRAGE
SHIPWRIGHT WAYMAN BUILDER
SHIRE DERBY SHEER COUNTY
SHIRK FUNK GOOF MIKE BLINK
BUDGE DODGE FEIGN FUDGE SKULK
SLACK RODNEY FINAGLE SHACKLE
SHAFFLE SOLDIER SHAMMOCK
SHIRKER FUNK PIKER FUNKER
ROTTER BLUDGER SLACKER
SLINKER SUGARER COBERGER
EMBUSQUE SCOWBANK
SHIRR SMOCK
SHIRT TOB JUPE SARK TOBE BLUEY
HAIRE JUPON KAMIS SHIFT BANIAN
BANIYA CAMISA CAMISE PALAKA
UNDERGO VAREUSE KAMLEIKA
(HAIR —) HAIRE CILICE
(SLEEVELESS —) FECKET
(WORKMAN'S —) FROCK
(WORNOUT —) DICKY
SHIRTING CHEVIOT HARVARD
HOLLAND SARKING

SHIRTWAIST BLOUSE GARIBALDI
SHITTIMWOOD BOXWOOD
SHIVAREE BELLING CHIVARI
HORNING SERENADE
SHIVER JAR GIRL GRUE BEVER
BREAK CHILL CREEM CREEP FRILL
GROWS QUAKE SHRUG SLICE
CHIVER DITHER DUDDER GROOSE
HOTTER NIDDER NITHER QUIVER
SHRIMP SPLINT CHITTER FLICKER
FRISSON SHATTER SHITHER
SHUDDER TREMBLE KAMLEIKA
SPLINTER
SHIVERING CHILL OURIE TREMOR
ASHIVER
SHOAL BAJO BANK FLAT REEF SPIT
BARRA DRAVE FLOTE SCULL SHELF
SCHOOL SHALLOW TOWHEAD
SHOAT GURRY SHOOT SHOTT
SHOCK COP JAR BLOW BUMP DINT
JOLT RACK SHOG STUN TURN
APPAL BRUNT GAVEL GLIFF GLOFF
SHAKE STOOK STOUR DISMAY
FRIGHT IMPACT JOSTLE JUMBLE
REJOLT RICKLE ROLLER STRIKE
ASTOUND CANVASS DISGUST
HATTOCK HORRIFY STAGGER
STARTLE STUPEFY TERRIFY
DISEDIFY GLIFFING SURPRISE
(— OF CORN) STOOK STOUT STITCH
(MENTAL —) TRAUMA
SHOCK ABSORBER SHOCK BUFFER
DASHPOT SNUBBER
SHOCKED AGHAST
SHOCKER RICKER STOOKER
SHOCKING GRIM AWFUL HORRID
UNHOLY BURNING FEARFUL
FEARING GHASTLY HIDEOUS
DREADFUL ENORMOUS HORRIBLE
SHOD CALCED
SHODDY SOFT CHEAP FOOTY SOFTS
SLEAZY
SHOE BAL CUE PAN BOOT BROG
CLOG DRAG FLAT HALF SKID SOCK
TURN BLAKE DERBY KLOMP MOYLE
ROMEO SABOT SCRAE SLING SPIKE
STOGA STOGY STRAP ANKLET
BEAKER BROGAN BROGUE BUSKIN
CALIGA CALIGO CHOPIN COBCAB
COCKER CRAKOW CREOLE DORSAY
GAITER GALOSH KILTIE MULLER
PATTEN PINSON POLISH SADDLE
SANDAL SECQUE BAUCHLE
BLUCHER CALCEUS CHOPINE
COWHIDE FLIPPER RULLION
SHOEPAC SLIPPER SNEAKER
BALMORAL BRODEKIN COLONIAL
PLIMSOLL SABOTINE SANDSHOE
SKEWBACK SLIPSLOP SOLLERET
(— FOR GRINDING) MULLER
(— FOR MULE) PLANCHE
(— IN TRUSS OR FRAME)
SKEWBACK
(— NOT FASTENED ON) PUMP
(— OF A SLEDGE) HOB
(— OF AN OX) CUE
(— OF COMIC ACTOR) BAXA
(— OF SUBWAY CAR) PAN
(— REPAIRER) JACKMAN

(— TO CHECK WHEEL) DRAG SKID
(— USED AS BRAKE) SKATE
(— WORN ON EITHER FOOT) STRAIGHT
(—S AND STOCKINGS) FEET
(BABY'S —) CACK
(HOBNAILED —) TACKET
(LARGE —S) GUNBOATS
(LOW-CUT —) SOCK GILLY ANKLET
BUSKIN SLIPPER COLONIAL
(MILITARY —) CALIGA
(OLD —) BAUCHLE
(PIKED —) BEAKER
(RAWHIDE —) HIMMING
(SPORTS —S) GILLIES
(STEEL —) SOLLERET
(THIN —) PINSON SCLAFF
(WINGED —S) TALARIA
(WOODEN —) KLOMP SABOT
PATTEN RACKET RACQUET
(WORN —) SCRAE
(PL.) SHEEN SHOON SHUNE SCHONE
FOOTGEAR
SHOEMAKER SNOB FOXER SOLER
ARCHER CHAMAR CODGER COZIER
FUDGER GOUGER SOOTER SOUTER
VAMPER COBBLER CRISPIN
CROWNER SHOEMAN SNOBBER
UPPERER CORVISER SNOBSCAT
SHOEMAKING SNOBBING
SHOGUN TYCOON
SHOO HOOSH DISPEL
SHOOK PACK BLANK SHAKE
SHOOT DAG GUN IMP PAY POT PUT
ROD BANG BOLT BROD CANE CHIT
CION DRAW LEAF PLUG SLIP WEFT
BLAST BLAZE BROWN DRILL DRIVE
EXPEL FLUSH FROND GEMMA
GLEAM LANCE LAYER PLUFF SCION
SHEET SOBOL SPEAR SPRAY SPRIG
SPRIT SPURT SQUIB STICK STOOL
TUBER TURIO VIMEN BRANCH
FLIGHT FLOWER GERMEN GROWTH
HEADER HURTLE LAUNCH LEADER
OFFSET RATOON SALLOW SOBOLE
SPRING SPROUT STOLON STOVEN
STRIKE SUCKER TILLER TURION
BUDLING CHIMNEY DROPPER
SCOURGE SPIRING TENDRIL
TENDRON THALLUS ANAPHYTE
APOBLAST CATAPULT TRAILING
(— A MARBLE) LAG TAW KNUCKLE
(— A WHALE) STRIKE
(— ASIDE FROM MARK) DRIB
(— AT LONG RANGE) SNIPE
(— DOWN) SPLASH
(— DUCKS) SKAG
(— FORTH) JET GLEAM SPIRE
(— FROM DEER'S ANTLER) SPELLER
(— INDISCRIMINATELY) BROWN
(— MOOSE OR DEER) YARD
(— OF A TREE) STOW WHIP LANCE
BRANCH
(— OUT) JUT CHIT DART
(— SEAL) SWATCH
(— UP) SPIRE SPURT
(—S USED AS FODDER) BROWSE
(FIRST —S) BRAIRD
(FLEXIBLE —) BINE

(LATERAL —) ARM
(ORE —) BONANZA
(PAWNBROKER'S —) SPOUT
(SUGARCANE —) LALO
(TENDER —) FLUSH
(WILLOW —) SALLOW
SHOOTER SCOOT BLASTER
GUNSTER PLUFFER SHOTMAN
SKEETER
SHOOTING COCKING GUNNING
GUNPLAY HUNTING POTTING
SHOOTING STAR METEOR COWSLIP
SHOOTER PRIMWORT
SHOP CRIB TOKO BURSE STORE
KOSHER SHOPPE TIENDA WINKEL
ALMACEN APOTHEC BOTTEGA
CABARET MERCERY SPICERY
TABERNA TURNERY BOUTIQUE
COOKSHOP CREMERIE EMPORIUM
ESPRESSO EXCHANGE MAGAZINE
SHOWSHOP SLOPSHOP TENDEJON
WAREROOM
(BARBER —) BARBERY
(BLACKSMITH —) SMITHY
(LIQUOR —) SALOON
(OLD CLOTHES —) FLIPPERY
(PAWNBROKER'S —) LUMBER
SPROUT
(REPAIR —) GARAGE
(SUTLER'S —) CANTEEN
SHOPKEEPER CIT ARAB BAKAL
CHETTY SOUDAGUR
SHOPLIFT BOOST
SHOPLIFTER BOOSTER
SHORE GIB TOM BANK RIPE RIVE
SAND SIDE BEACH BENCH CLIFF
COAST RAKER RANCE SHOAR
WARTH RIVAGE STRAND BUTTRESS
DOCKSIDE LANDFALL LANDSIDE
SEACOAST
SHOREBIRD TATTLER WRYBILL
SURFBIRD
SHORE CRAB OCHIDORE
SHOREFISH OPALEYE
SHORER BRACER CRIBBER
SHORN NOT NOTT POLLED
TONSURED
SHORT AIM LAG LOW SHY BAIN
CURT NEAR NIGH SOON BLUFF
BRIEF BUNTY CLOSE CRISP CUTTY
FUBBY FUBSY PUNCH SQUAB
UNDER CRISPY SCARCE STUGGY
STUNTY SUDDEN ULLAGE BOBTAIL
BRUSQUE CURTATE LACONIC
SQUIDGY STUBBED SUMMARY
SNAPPISH SUCCINCT
(— AND FLAT) CAMUS
(— AND THICK) CHUNKY STOCKY
STUBBY STUMPY TRUNCH
TRUNCHED
(— AND THICKSET) NUGGETY
(— AS OF WOOL) FRIBBY
(— PERSON OR ANIMAL) PUNCH
(STOUT AND —) BUNTY CHUFFY
PLUGGY THICKSET
(PL.) BERMUDAS
SHORTAGE FAMINE DROUGHT
WANTAGE UNDERAGE
SHORTCHANGE FLUFF SHORT

SHORTCOMING SIN DEFECT FOIBLE
SHORT-COUPLED CHUFFY
SHORTCUT CUTOFF
SHORT-EARED OWL MOMO
SHORTEN CUT CLIP STAG ELIDE
SLASH REDUCE ABRIDGE CURTAIL
EXCERPT CONTRACT DIMINISH
RETRENCH
(— AND THICKEN IRON) JUMP
(— GRIP) CHOKE
SHORTENED CURTED BOBTAIL
CURTATE ABRIDGED
SHORTENING (— OF SYLLABLE)
SYSTOLE
SHORTEST LEAST
SHORTHORN DURHAM
SHORT-LIVED FRAGILE
SHORTLY DUMPILY DIRECTLY
SHORT-NAPPED RAS
SHORTNESS BREVITY CURTNESS
UNLENGTH
SHORT-RANGE TACTICAL
SHORT-SIGHTED SANDED PURBLIND
SHORTSIGHTEDNESS MYOPIA
SHORT-TEMPERED SNIPPY SNUFFY
SHORT-TERM FLOATING
SHORT-WINDED PURSY PURFLY
PURFLED PURSIVE
SHOT POP SET BLUE CASE JOLT
OVER SETT SLUG BLANK FLIER
FLING FLUFF FLYER OUTER PLUFF
SHOOT TOWEL WHITE CARTON
CENTER CENTRE FOLLOW MUDCAP
REBOTE ALIIPOE BOMBARD
CUTAWAY DEADEYE GUNSHOT
LANGREL PELICAN SIGHTER
BLIZZARD BUCKSHOT HAILSHOT
LANGRAGE MARKSHOT SCORCHER
(— BEYOND TARGET) OVER
(— FOR CULVERIN) PELICAN
(— IN FIFTH CIRCLE) WHITE
(— IN FOURTH CIRCLE) BLACK
(— IN THIRD CIRCLE) BLUE
(— OF NARCOTIC) FIX
(— STRIKING BULL'S-EYE) CARTON
(ARCHERY —) GREEN
(BADMINTON —) CLEAR
(BILLIARD —) DRAG STAB CAROM
MASSE SCREW FOLLOW SAFETY
SPREAD BRICOLE SCRATCH
(BOW —) DRAFT
(CAMERA —) INTERCUT
(CROQUET —) SPLIT FOLLOW
(CURLING —) INWICK OUTWICK
(FINAL —) UPSHOT
(GOOD —) SCREAMER
(PISTOL —) BARK
(POOL —) BREAK
(SIZE OF —) F T BB FF TT BBB
DUST BUCKSHOT
(TENNIS —) ACE LOB DINK SERVE
SMASH
(VOLLEY OF —S) BLIZZARD
SHOTGUN DOUBLE TUPARA
PEPPERER
SHOULD MOW SUD WANT OUGHT
(— NOT) SHUDNA SHOULDNA
SHOULDNT
SHOULDER DOD AXLE CLOD DODD

GAIN HUMP SHIP STEP SULD BOUGH
PITCH SPALL SPULE VERGE AXILLA
EPAULE RELISH SPAULD KNUCKLE
RIMBASE SHOUTHER
(— AROUND TENON) RELISH
(— OF BOLT) NAB
(— OF FIREARM STOCK) RIMBASE
(— OF FLY) CHEEK
(— OF PORK) HAND PICNIC
CUSHION
(— OF RABBIT OR HARE) WING
(— OF ROAD) BERM BERME
HAUNCH QUARTER
(— PAIN) OMODYNIA
(BEVELED —) GAIN
(PL.) FOREBOWS
SHOULDER BLADE SPALD SPEAL
SCAPULA
SHOUT BAY BOO CRY HOY HUE
BAWL CALL CROW GAPE HAIL HOCH
HOOP HOOT REME ROOT ROUP
ROUT SCRY TOOT YELL BRAWL
CHEER CLAIM CLEPE CRACK GREDE
HAVOC HOLLO HUZZA REERE
WHEWT WHOOP ABRAID BOOHOO
CLAMOR GOLLAR GOLLER HALLOO
HOLLER HURRAH STEVEN YAMMER
ACCLAIM SHILLOO GARDYLOO
LULLILOO SCRONACH
(— AS CHILDREN) BELDER
(— DERISIVELY) BARRACK
(— OF APPROVAL) BRAVO
(— OF ENCOURAGEMENT) HARK
(— OF JOY) IO
(HUNTING —) CHEVY
SHOUTING HUE GLAM ROUP ROUT
HOLLO CLAMOR HOLLOA JUBILEE
SHOVE JUT PUT BUNT DUSH FEND
MUCK PICK POTE PUSH SHOG SHUN
BOOST CROWD DUNCH ELBOW
HUNCH SHIVE SHUNT HUSTLE
JOSTLE JUSTLE MUSCLE THRUST
SCAMBLE
(— IN MARBLES) FULK
SHOVEL FAN VAN CAST PEEL SPUD
SCOOP SHOOL SPADE SPOON
SCOPPIT SCUPPIT SLUDGER
DUCKBILL DUCKFOOT STROCKLE
(— FOR COIN) MAIN
(— FOR DRESSING ORE) VAN
(BRICKMAKING —) CUCKHOLD
(CASTING —) SCUTTLE
(CHARCOAL BURNER'S —) RABBLE
(FIRE —) PEEL SLICE
(GRATED —) HARP
(MINER'S —) BANJO
(PERFORATED —) SKIMMER
SHOVELER SCOOPER WHINGER
BLUEWING SHOULERD WHINYARD
SHOW DO SAY SEE WIS BOSH CALL
DASH HAVE ITEM LEAD MARK MIEN
SCAW SEEM SHEW TENT VIEW
WEAR WISE ARGUE ASSAY EXERT
FLASH GLOSS GLOZE KITHE PRIDE
PROVE SHINE SIGHT SLANG SPORT
TEACH ACCUSE ASSIGN BETRAY
BLAZON CHICHI COUTHE DENOTE
DETECT DEVICE DIRECT ENSIGN
ESCORT EVINCE EXPOSE FIGURE

FLAUNT GAIETY GAYETY LAYOUT
MUSTER OBJECT PARADE REVEAL
SCHEME SPREAD SPRUNK ADVANCE
ANALYZE BALLOON BESPEAK
BETOKEN BRAVURA BREATHE
DECLARE DISPLAY DIVULGE EXHIBIT
EXPRESS FASHION MONSTER
PRESAGE PRODUCE PROPOSE
SELLOUT SHOWING SIGNIFY
TRIUMPH COLORING CONCLUDE
EVIDENCE FLOURISH FORESHOW
INDICATE MANIFEST PRETENCE
SEMBLANT SIDESHOW
(— APPROVAL) CLAP APPLAUD
(— CONTEMPT) SCOFF
(— DISCONTENT) GROUCH
(— DISPLEASURE) POUT
(— ENTHUSIASM) DROOL
(— FORTH) BLAZE CIPHER
(— IN PUBLIC CELEBRATION)
PAGEANT
(— ITSELF) APPEAR
(— MERCY) SPARE
(— OF LEARNING) SCIOLISM
(— OF LIGHT) BLINK
(— OF REASON) COLOR
(— OF VANITY) AIR
(— OFF) FLASH SPORT SWANK
PARADE
(— ONESELF) BE
(— POSITION OF) MEITH
(— PROMISE) FRAME SHAPE
(— RESPECT FOR) REGARD
(— REVERSE TREND) REACT
(— SIGNS OF GIVING WAY) WAVER
(— SIGNS OF ILLNESS) GRUDGE
(— THE BOTTOM) KEEL
(— THE SIGHTS) LIONIZE
(— THE TEETH) GIRN GRIN
(— THE WAY) LEAD CONDUCT
(— TO BE FALSE) BELIE DISPROVE
(— UNKINDNESS) WAIT
(— WITHOUT SUBSTANCE) FORM
(ARTFUL —) GRIMACE
(FALSE —) FUCUS BUBBLE TINSEL
ILLUSION
(FLOOR —) CABARET
(GAUDY —) HOOPLA BRAVERY
(MERE —) PHANTOM
(MOMENTARY —) FLASH
(ORNATE —) FLUBDUB
(OSTENTATIOUS —) SPRUNK
DISPLAY
(OUTSIDE —) VARNISH
(OUTWARD —) FUCUS VISAGE
(PUPPET —) DROLL MOTION
WAJANG WAYANG GUIGNOL
(RIDICULOUS —) FARCE
(RUDIMENTARY —) SATURA
(SPECIOUS —) GLOZE
(SUPERFICIAL —) GLOSS VENEER
(TRAVELLING —) SLANG
SHOWCASE ISLAND VITRINE
SHOWER WET HAIL RAIN SCAT SUMP
AUGER BLASH SKITE SOUSE
FLURRY PELTER SHEWER DRIBBLE
SHATTER WEATHER COMMORTH
SCOUTHER
(CONCENTRATED —) BARRAGE

(HEAVY —) SUMP
(RAIN —) RASH
(SUDDEN —) SCUD SKIT BRASH
PLUMP
SHOWERY BRASHY CLASHY SCATTY
SHOWILY GAILY BRAVELY GAUDILY
SHOWINESS DASH GLARE GLITTER
FLOURISH GEWGAWRY SPLENDOR
SHOWING SPRANK SPARKLE
(— SAME NATURE) AKIN
(SUPERFICIAL —) FACE
SHOW-ME STATE MISSOURI
SHOW-OFF CUTUP
SHOWY GAY FINE LOUD NICE RORY
DASHY FLARY FLASH FRESH GAUDY
GIDDY GRAND SPICY TOPPY VAUDY
VIEWY BRANKY BRAZEN BRUMMY
CHICHI DRESSY FLASHY FLOSSY
GARISH GEWGAW GLOSSY JAUNTY
PURPLE SHANTY SPANKY SPORTY
TAWDRY DASHING FLAUNTY
GALLANT GAUDFUL HOTSHOT
POMPOUS SHOWFUL SHOWISH
SPLASHY CLAPTRAP FASTUOUS
GIMCRACK GORGEOUS ORGULOUS
SPARKISH SPECIOUS SPLENDID
TRUMPERY
(NOT —) CIVIL LENTEN DISCREET
SHRED DAG HOG JAG RAG ROND
ROON SNIP WISP BLYPE CLOUT
SHRAG SHRIP CULPON SCREED
SLIVER TARGET FRITTER SHATTER
FILAMENT
(— FISH) SCROD
(— OF CLOTHES) TACK
(— OF FLESH) TAG
(— OF HAIR) TAIT
(PL.) TAVERS CADDICE TAIVERS
SHREDDED CUT
SHREDDER DEVIL
SHREW JES TANA PRESS RANNY
SOREX VIXEN CALLET JUMPER
MIGALE TARGER TARTAR TUPAIA
VIRAGO BLARINA HELLCAT
MUSKRAT PENTAIL SCYTALE
TUPAIID SINSRING SORICINE
SORICOID UROPSILE
(TREE —) BANXRING
SHREWD DRY SLY ACID CUTE FELL
GASH SAGE TIDY WARE WISE
ACUTE CAGEY CANNY HEADY
PAWKY POKEY SHARP SMART
SWACK ARGUTE ARTFUL ASTUTE
CLEVER CRAFTY SPRACK SUBTLE
CUNNING GNOSTIC KNOWING
PARLISH PARLOUS PRACTIC
SAPIENT
(— PERSON) FILE
SHREWDLY SLILY CANNILY
ASTUTELY
SHREWDNESS SAVVY ACUMEN
POLICY SLYNESS GUMPTION
SAGACITY CALLIDITY
SHREWISH CURST CURSED SHREWD
VIXENISH
SHREWMOUSE MYGALE SCYTALE
SHRIEK CRY YIP YARM YELL CHIRK
SKIRL SCREAM SCRIKE SHRIKE
SKRIKE SPRAICH

SHRIKE POPE BATARA BOUBOU
BRUBRU FISCAL FLASHER FLUSHER
LOGHEAD MIGRANT MINIVET
TRILLER BELLBIRD FALCONET
PUFFBACK WOODCHAT
SHRILL HIGH KEEN ACUTE PIPEY
SHARP SHILL SHIRL ARGUTE
BRASSY GLASSY PIPING SQUEAK
TREBLE HAUTAIN MINIKIN SCREAKY
STRIDENT
(MAKE — NOISE) POTRACK
SHRIMP GRIT APANG CARID MYSID
PARVA PRAWN NIPPER PANDLE
ARTEMIA BROWNIE CAMARON
DECAPOD POLYPOD REDTAIL
SPECTER SPECTRE CARIDEAN
CRAWFISH CREVETTE MACRURAN
SHRINE ADYT NAOS GUACA HUACA
ISEUM MAZAR STUPA ZIARA
ADYTON ADYTUM CHASSE DAGABA
DAGOBA DURGAH HALLOW HIERON
MEMORY SAMADH ZIARAT CHAITYA
CHORTEN EDICULE FANACLE
MARTYRY MEMORIA SACRARY
TEMENOS THESEUM AEDICULA
DELUBRUM FERETORY FERETRUM
GURDWARA LARARIUM MARABOUT
PANTHEON VALHALLA
(— STUDY) NAOLOGY
SHRINK COY SHY DUCK FULL FUNK
GIVE PEAK ABHOR ARGHE CLING
COWER CRINE QUAIL RELAX RIVEL
SHRAM SHRUG SHUCK START
WINCE BLANCH BLENCH BOGGLE
COTTER CRINGE FLINCH LESSEN
RECOIL SCRUMP SETTLE SHRIMP
WEAZEN CRIMPLE DWINDLE
SCUNNER SHRIVEL COLLAPSE
CONTRACT
(— FROM DRYNESS) GIZZEN
SHRINKAGE SETTLE SHRINK
SINKAGE
(— OF TYPE) SQUEEZE
SHRINKING COY SHY TIMID BLETHE
DASTARD FULLING LOATHFUL
TIMOROUS
SHRIVE SHRIFT CONFESS SHRIEVE
SHRIVEL SEAR BLAST CLING CRINE
PARCH RIVEL SHRAM SNERP WIZEN
COTTER GIZZEN SCORCH SCRUMP
SHRINK WEAZEN WITHER CROZZLE
SHRIVELED WEDE CLUNG CORKY
THIRL GIZZEN STARKY PUNGLED
SHIRPIT WIZENED WRITHEN
SHRAMMED WRIZZLED
SHROPSHIRE SALOP
SHROUD HIDE SARK CLOAK CRAPE
DRAPE HABIT SHEET SWIFT EMBOSK
HEARSE KITTEL MUFFLE SCREEN
SHADOW SINDON SUDARY BENIGHT
CONCEAL CURTAIN INVOLVE
SWIFTER CEREMENT
(PL.) PUTTOCK
SHROVETIDE SHROVE GUTTIDE
CARNIVAL
SHROVE TUESDAY FASTENS
GUTTIDE
SHRUB TI BAY HAW KAT MAY QAT
TOD AKIA ALEM BUSH COCA HOYA

INGA ITEA KARO KEUR KHAT MUSK
ULEX AKALA AKELA ALDER ALISO
ARUSA BOCCA BROOM CEIBO
CUMAY ELDER GOOMA GOUMI
HAZEL HENNA IXORA LEDUM LEMON
LILAC MAQUI MARIA MUDAR RETEM
SALAL SHROG SUMAC TOYON ZILLA
ABELIA AGRITO AKONGE AMULLA
ANAGUA ANILAO ARALIA ARUSHA
AUCUBA AUPAKA AZALEA BLOLLY
CENIZO CHEKAN CHERRY CISTUS
CORREA DAPHNE DHAURI DRIMYS
FEIJOA FRUTEX JACATE JOJOBA
KARAMU KOWHAI LABRUM LARREA
LAUREL MATICO MYRTLE NARRAS
PENAEA PITURI RAETEM SAVINE
STORAX STYRAX AFERNAN AGARITA
AMORPHA ARBORET ARRAYAN
ARRIMBY AZAROLE BANKSIA
BORONIA BUCKEYE CANTUTA
CHACATE CHAMISE CHANCHE
DEUTZIA EHRETIA ENCELIA EPACRID
EPHEDRA FUCHSIA GUMWOOD
GUTWORT HOPBUSH HOPSAGE
JASMINE JETBEAD JEWBUSH
JOEWOOD KUMQUAT LANTANA
MAHONIA NUNNARI PAVONIA
PEABUSH PIMELEA RHODORA
SPIRAEA TARBUSH THEEZAN
ABELMOSK ALLTHORN BARBERRY
CAMELLIA CARAGANA COMEBACK
COPALCHE DRACAENA GOATBUSH
GOWIDDIE GRAVILEA HARDHACK
HARDTACK HAWTHORN HIBISCUS
IRONWOOD KEURBOOM KOROMIKO
MOORWORT NINEBARK OCOTILLO
OLEASTER OSOBERRY PIPEWOOD
PONDBUSH ROSEMARY SANDSTAY
SANDWOOD SASANQUA SHRUBLET
SNOWBALL SNOWBELL SNOWBUSH
SOAPBARK STANDARD
(AROMATIC —) THYME CLUSIA
BORONIA HOGBUSH ALLSPICE
(AUSTRALIAN —) GOOMA BUDDAH
DRIMYS GEEBUNG MILKBUSH
SANDSTAY
(CHINESE —) KERRIA
(CLIMBING —) CATCLAWS
SOLANDRA
(DESERT —) AFERNAN
(EVERGREEN —) BOX BAGO ILEX
TITI BOLDO ERICA FURZE HEATH
HOLLY KOSAM PYXIE SALAL SAVIN
TOYON BAUERA DAHOON KALMIA
LAUREL PEPINO RUSCUS SAKAKI
ARDISIA BARETTA JASMINE JUNIPER
MADRONA CALFKILL CARAUNDA
EVONYMUS OLEANDER SASANQUA
(FRAGRANT —) JASMINE HUISACHE
MEJORANA MEZEREON ROSEMARY
(HAWAIIAN —) AKALA AKELA ILIMA
KOKIO OLONA
(LOW —) AYAPANA
(MEXICAN —) BLUEBUSH
(NEW ZEALAND —) KARO KAWA
TUTU KARAMU KIEKIE KAWAKAWA
KOROMIKO
(PASTURE —) COWBERRY
(PHILIPPINE —) IPILIPIL

(POISONOUS —) GIF CUBE LITHI
SUMAC GIFBLAAR LABURNUM
(PRICKLY —) CAPER COLIMA
BRAMBLE CATCLAWS
(SPINY —) ULEX AROMA GORSE
JUNCO ESPINO BUMELIA CARISSA
CYTISUS GENISTA GOATBUSH
GRANJENO GUAJILLO HUAJILLO
(STRONG-SMELLING —) SALTWORT
(STUNTED —) SCRAB SCROG SCRUB
(THORNY —) CHANAR HAWTHORN
(TREELIKE —) ARBUSCLE
(TROPICAL —) INGA MAJO HENNA
CAMARA DERRIS MOMBIN OLACAD
PERSEA HAMELIA JEWBUSH
LANTANA SOAPBARK
(WEST INDIAN —) ANIL RATWOOD
MILKWOOD
(XEROPHYTIC —) SAXAUL
SHRUBBERY MOGOTE ARBORET
SHRUG SHUG HURKLE SHRINK
SHRUNKEN LANK CLUNG PUNGLED
SLUNKEN WIZENED CONTRACT
(— HEAD) TSANTSA
SHUCK HULL SHACK SHELL SHOCK
SHUDDER GRUE CREEP HIRCH
QUAKE SHRUG AGRISE GROOSE
HIRTCH HOTTER HURKLE SHIVER
FRISSON TREMBLE
SHUDDERING RIGOR
SHUFFLE JANK MAKE MILK SLUR
SCUFF SHALE SHIFT SHOOL JUGGLE
RIFFLE RUFFLE SCLAFF SHOVEL
DRAGGLE QUIBBLE SHACKLE
SHAFFLE SHAMBLE SLIPPER
SLUTHER
SHUN FIN SHY BALK FLEE TABU
VOID WARE AVOID EVADE EVITE
SHUNT TABOO ASTART DEVOID
ESCAPE ESCHEW REFUSE SHRINK
DECLINE FORBEAR FORSAKE
SHUNT AYRTON BRIDGE BYPASS
SWITCH
SHUSH HUSH WHISH SUPPRESS
SHUSWAP ATNAH
SHUT FAST HASP MAKE SEAL SHOT
SLAM SLOT SPAR TAKE TEEN TINE
CLOSE LATCH STEEK STICK CLOSED
CABINET OCCLUSE UPCLOSE
(— EYES) WINK
(— IN) BAR LAP CAGE COPSE
EMBAR EMBAY FORBAR PENTIT
TACKLE BELOUKE ENCLAVE
(— OFF) SCREEN SECLUDE
(— OUT) BAR DEBAR REPEL SKUNK
HINDER DEPRIVE EXCLUDE
OCCLUDE OUTSHUT PRECLUDE
(— TOGETHER) CLASP
(— UP) BAR CUB MEW PENT STOP
CHOKE FRANK STIVE STOVE
CLOSET EMBOSS ENJAIL IMMURE
IMPARK CONDEMN CONFINE
DUNGEON ENCLOSE IMPOUND
INCLUDE OCCLUDE OPPRESS
PARROCK RECLUSE SECLUDE
CONCLUDE PRECLUDE
(HALF —) PINK
SHUTDOWN LAYOFF
SHUTOUT SKUNK

SHUTTER LID DROP SHUT BLIND
SHADE CUTOFF DOUSER AUTOMAT
BUCKLER SHUTTLE JALOUSIE
(— **IN ORGAN**) SHADE
(— **OF TRIPTYCH**) VOLET
SHUTTING CLAUDENT
SHUTTLE FLY FLUTE SHUNT BROCHE
LOOPER SWIVEL SHITTLE
SHUTTLECOCK BIRD PETECA
VOLANT
SHY COY JIB MIM SCAR SHAN SHUN
SKIT UNKO WILD BLATE CAGEY
CHARY DEMUR FLING SCARE SHUNT
SQUAB TIMID UNCOW BOGGLE
BOOGER DEMURE MODEST SHANNY
SKIEGH TARTLE BASHFUL GAWKISH
RABBITY STRANGE TREMBLY
UPSTAGE BACKWARD DAPHNEAN
FAROUCHE RETIRING SHEEPISH
SKITTISH SWAIMOUS WILLYARD
SHYNESS COYNESS MODESTY
RESERVE TIMIDITY
SIALAGOGUE SALIVANT
SIAM (SEE THAILAND)
SIAMANG UNGKA GIBBON
SIB SEPT AYLLU SIBLING SIBSHIP
CALPULLI
SIBERIA (**GULF IN** —) OB
(**MOUNTAIN RANGE IN** —) URAL
ALTAI
(**NATIVE IN** —) YAKU SAGAI TATAR
KIRGIZ TARTAR KIRGHIZ YUKAGIR
(**RIVER IN** —) OB ILI KET PUR TAZ
TYM AMGA AMUR LENA MAYA ONON
UCUR ALDAN ISHIM NADYM SOBOL
TOBOL ANGARA IRTYSH OLEKMA
VILYUY
(**TOWN IN** —) OMSK CHITA KYZYL
TOMSK IGARKA KURGAN BARNAUL
IRKUTSK LENINSK YAKUTSK
SIBERIAN SQUILL SCILLA
SIBYL SYBIL SIBYLLA VOLUSPA
AMALTHEA
SIC SOOL

SICILY

CAPE: BOEO FARO PASSARO
CAPITAL: PALERMO
CATHEDRAL: MONREALE
COIN: LITRA UNCIA
GULF: NOTO CATANIA
ISLAND: EGADI LIPARI USTICA
MEASURE: SALMA CAFFISO
MOUNTAIN: EREI ETNA MORO
SORI IBREI NEBRODI
NATIVE: ELYMI SICEL SICANI
SICULI
OLD NAME: TRINACRIA TRIQUETRA
PROVINCE: ENNA RAGUSA
CATANIA MESSINA PALERMO
TRAPANI SIRACUSA
RIVER: SALSO TORTO BELICE
SIMETO PLATANI
SEAPORT: ACI CATANIA MARSALA
MESSINA PALERMO TRAPANI
TOWN: ENNA NOTO RAGUSA
CATANIA MARSALA MESSINA

TRAPANI SYRACUSE
VOLCANO: ETNA AETNA

SICK BAD ILL BADLY CRONK CROOK
MORBID MAWKISH SEASICK
UNWHOLE CROPSICK MALADIVE
PHYSICAL STREAKED
SICKEN TIRE TURN WEARY SUNDER
SUNNER WEAKEN DISGUST SURFEIT
NAUSEATE
SICKENING FELL SICKLY FULSOME
SICKISH NAUSEOUS
SICKISH DAUNCY
SICKLE HOOK CROOK
SICKLY WAN FLUE FOND PALE PUKY
SICK DAWNY DONCY FAINT GREEN
PEAKY SILLY TEWLY WEARY WISHT
AMPERY CLAMMY CRANKY FEEBLE
INFIRM PUKISH PULING WANKLY
WEAKLY INVALID LANGUID MAWKISH
PEAKING PEAKISH PIMPING
QUEECHY SICKISH WEARISH
WEERISH DELICATE DISEASED
MALADIVE PINDLING
SICKNESS (ALSO SEE DISEASE) SICK
SORE TAKING AILMENT DISEASE
ILLNESS SURFEIT DISORDER
(**MILK** —) SLOWS TIRES
(**MOTION** —) KINETOSIS
(**MOUNTAIN** —) SOROCHE
SIDA ILIMA ESCOBA
SIDE COST EDGE FACE HALF HAND
KANT LEAF PART BOARD CHEEK
FLANK LATUS PARTY SITHE BEHALF
PTERON ENGLISH PENDANT
FORESIDE SIDELONG
(— **BY SIDE**) ACCOLE ACCOSTED
PARALLEL
(— **OF ATTIC**) SKEELING SKILLING
SKILLION
(— **OF BOOM JAW**) HORN
(— **OF BOW**) BELLY
(— **OF CAVITY**) WALL
(— **OF DECK**) GANGWAY
(— **OF DITCH**) SCARP
(— **OF DIVIDERS**) LEG
(— **OF FACE**) CHEEK
(— **OF GATE**) FOLD
(— **OF GEM**) BEZEL
(— **OF HEARTH**) BREAST
(— **OF HILL**) SCUG
(— **OF HOG**) FLITCH
(— **OF HORSESHOE**) BRANCH
(— **OF LACE**) FOOTING
(— **OF LOG**) RIDE
(— **OF NAVE**) AISLE
(— **OF OPENING**) JAW JAMB
(— **OF PIG**) BACON
(— **OF QUADRANGLE**) PANE
(— **OF RABBET**) LEDGE
(— **OF RACECOURSE**) STRETCH
(— **OF RECTANGLE**) SQUARE
(— **OF ROOF**) CATSLIDE
(— **OF SHIP**) BEAM WALE BOARD
BULWARK LARBOARD SEABOARD
(— **OF TENNIS RACKET**) ROUGH
SMOOTH
(— **OF TRIANGLE**) LEG

(— **OF TYPE**) BACK
(— **OF VALLEY**) COTEAU
(— **PIECE**) RAVE
(— **SHELTERED FROM WIND**) LEE
LEW LEEWARD
(— **WITH**) SUFFRAGE
(—**S OF GALLERY**) SLIPS
(**BACK** —) REAR BEHIND BACKSIDE
(**DRESSED** —) FACE
(**FOR EACH** —) ALL
(**MOUNTAIN** —) PUNA VETA
SOROCHE
(**OUTER** — **OF SKIN**) GRAIN
(**RIGHT** — **OF SWORD**) INSIDE
(**RIGHT** —) FACE
(**UNDERNEATH** —) BOTTOM
SIDEBAR HOUND
SIDEBOARD ABACUS BUFFET
SERVER DRESSER CELLARET
CREDENCE CREDENZA
SIDE DISH OUTWORK
SIDEPIECE BAR BOW JAMB WING
CHEEK GUSSET EARPIECE LANDSIDE
SIDESLIP SKID SLIP DRIFT DRILL
SIDESMAN HOGGLER QUESTMAN
SIDESTEP BEG AVOID DODGE
SIDEWALK WALKWAY TROTTOIR
SIDEWISE ASIDE ASIDEN
SIDING CURB SPUR GARAGE
SIDLE EDGE SLIVE SAUNTER
SIDRA PARASHAH
SIEGE BOUT SEDGE ASSIEGE
JOURNEY LEAGUER
(— **ENGINE**) WARWOLF
SIERRA CERO SERRA SAWBACK
KINGFISH

SIERRA LEONE

CAPITAL: FREETOWN
COIN: LEONE
LANGUAGE: KRIO MENDE TEMNE
MEASURE: LOAD KETTLE
MOUNTAIN: LOMA
NATIVE: VAI KONO LOKO SUSU
KISSI LIMBA MENDE TEMNE
FULANI GALLINA SHERBRO
MANDINGO
RIVER: MOA JONG SEWA ROKKEL
SCARCY
SEAPORT: HEPEL BONTHE SULIMA
TOWN: BO KISSI KENEMA

SIESTA NAP MERIDIAN
SIEVE FRY TRY BOLT BUNT DRUM
HARP LAWN PREE SCRY SHOE SIFT
SILE SIZE TEMS GRATE RANGE
SCALP TAMIS TAMMY TEMSE
BOLTER RANGER RIDDER RIDDLE
SEARCE SEARCH SEMMET SIFTER
WEIGHT BOULTEL CHAFFER CRIBBLE
DILLUER PRICKLE TIFFANY
SEARCHER STRAINER
SIFT REE TRY BOLT DUST SCRY
RANGE SCALP SIEVE TEMSE
DREDGE GARBLE RIDDER RIDDLE
SCREEN SEARCE WINNOW CANVASS
CRIBBLE DRIBBLE SIFTAGE
CRIBRATE

(— FLOUR) DRESS
(— IN MINING) LUE
(— IN) INFILTER
(— MEAL) BUNT
(— SHOT) TABLE
(— WHEAT) SCALP
IFTER SIEVE BOLTER CASTER
SIEVER
IFTING DRIFT GARBLING
(PL.) BOLTING FANNINGS SIEVINGS
IGH SOB PECH SIFE SOCK WIND
MOURN SIGHT SITHE SOUGH TWANK
BEMOAN BEWAIL SORROW SUTHER
DEPLORE SINGULT SUSPIRE
IGHT EYE KEN RAY BONE ESPY
FACE GAZE PEEP SEET VIEW FERLY
RAISE SCENE SCOPE SICHT TRACK
VISIE VIZZY BEHOLD DESCRY
OBJECT TICKET VISION DISCERN
DISPLAY EYESHOT GLIMPSE
MONSTER CONSPECT DISCOVER
EYESIGHT GUNSIGHT
(— FOR GUN) LEAF PEEP SCOPE
VISIE VIZZY HAUSSE GUNSIGHT
(— OF COMPASS) VANE
(— ON SURVEYOR'S STAFF) TARGET
(— TO SEE IF LEVEL) BONE
(—S OF CITY) LIONS
(AMAZING —) STOUND
(IMAGINARY —) VISION
(PITIFUL —) RUTH
(SORRY —) BYSEN
(STRANGE —) FERLY FERLIE
GHTER ALINER ALIGNER
GHTING LANDFALL
(— DEVICE) ALIDADE
GHTLY VIEWLY EYEABLE
GLOS DARIC
GN INK AYAH DASH FIRM HINT
HIRE MARK NOTE OMEN TYPE
BADGE COLON FRANK GHOST
GUIDA HAMZA INDEX SIGIL SINGE
SPOOR STAMP TOKEN TRACE
ASSIGN AUGURY CARACT EFFECT
EMBLEM ENGAGE ENSIGN FUGLER
INDICE MOTION NOTICE PARAPH
REMARK SIGLUM SIGNAL SIGNET
SIGNUM SYMBOL TITTLE WITTER
ALEBUSH AUSPICE CHECKER
CHEQUER CONSIGN EARMARK
ENDORSE INDICIA INSIGNE KNOWING
PORTENT PRESAGE PRODIGY
PROFFER SHINGLE SHOWING
SIGNARY SURMISE SYMPTOM
VESTIGE WARNING CEREMONY
INDICANT INSTANCE MONUMENT
PROCLAIM SIGNACLE SYLLABIC
TELLTALE
— DOCUMENT) FIRM
— FOR KEYNOTE) ISON
— OF ALEHOUSE) LATTICE
— OF AN IDEA) EMBLEM
— OF APPROVAL) CACHET
— OF CONTEMPT) FIG
— OF DANGER) SEAMARK
— OF GLOTTAL STOP) HAMZA
HAMZAH
— OF MULTIPLICATION) DOT
— OF ZODIAC) LEO RAM BULL

CRAB GOAT LION ARIES HOUSE
LIBRA TWINS VIRGO ARCHER
CANCER FISHES GEMINI PISCES
TAURUS VIRGIN BALANCE SCORPIO
AQUARIUS SCORPION
(— ON MAP) ICON
(ASTROLOGICAL —) CIPHER
(MATHEMATICAL —) NAME
FUNCTOR
(MUSICAL —) GUIDA SEGNO SWELL
SIMILE FERMATA
(OUTWARD —) EVIDENCE
(SANSKRIT —) ANUSVARA
(SLIGHT —) SURMISE
(SUBSCRIPT —) SUBFIX
(SUPERSTITIOUS —) GUEST
(TAVERN —) BUSH ALEBUSH
ALEPOLE CHECKER CHEQUER
ALESTAKE
(TRAMP'S —) MONICA MONIKER
(VOWEL —) SEGOL SEGHOL
(PL.) INDICIA INSIGNIA
SIGNAL OS CUE GUN PST WAG BALK
BECK BELL BUZZ CALL COND FLAG
GATE HASH SIGN WAFT WAVE WINK
ALARM ALERT BLINK FLARE FUSEE
FUZEE LIGHT SHAPE SHORT SPEAK
TOKEN WHIFF ALARUM BANNER
BEACON BECKON BUZZER ENSIGN
HERALD MARKER OFFICE RECALL
SIGNET TARGET WAVING WIGWAG
BLINKER CHAMADE EMINENT
NOTABLE RETREAT TURNOUT
CRANTARA DIAPHONE FLAGFALL
LOGOGRAM STANDARD STRIKING
(— FISHERMEN) BALK
(— FOR A PARLEY) CHAMADE
(— FOR WHALERS) WAIF
(— IN WHIST) ECHO PETER
(— OF DISTRESS) SOS
(— ON HORN) SEEK BLAST STRAKE
(— TO ATTACK) CHARGE
(— TO BEGIN ACTION) CUE
(— WITH FLAGS) WIGWAG
(AUDIO —) HUM
(BOAT'S —) WAFF WAFT
(DEATH —) KNELL
(FOG —) FOGHORN TORPEDO
DIAPHONE
(HUNTER'S —) SEEK PRIZE GIBBET
STRAKE
(MILITARY —) FLARE TURNOUT
ASSEMBLY
(NAVAL —) SECURE
(RADIO —) BEAM
(RAILROAD —) BANJO BOARD
FUSEE FUZEE TARGET HIGHBALL
(WARNING —) ALARM KLAXON
TOCSIN
SIGNALLING TICKTACK
SIGNALMAN FLAGS BELLBOY
BELLMAN
SIGNATE SENNET
SIGNATORY SIGNEE SIGNER
SIGNATURE BOLT FIRM HAND VISA
FRANK SHEET SIGIL THEME SIGNUM
TUGHRA SECTION HANDWRIT
SIGNATOR
SIGNBOARD SIGN SHINGLE

SIGNET SIGIL
SIGNIFICANCE WIT BODY SOUND
AMOUNT IMPORT INTENT LETTER
STRESS WEIGHT BEARING CONTENT
GRAVITY MEANING SENTENCE
STRENGTH
(DEVOID OF —) JEJUNE
(HIDDEN —) HYPONOIA
(LACKING —) INANE
SIGNIFICANT REAL GREAT
AUGURAL EPOCHAL OMINOUS
POINTED SERIOUS SENSEFUL
SPEAKING
SIGNIFICANTLY SENSIBLY
SIGNIFICATION SENSE VALOR
VALUE ETYMON IMPORT MOMENT
NOTION MEANING CARRIAGE
SIGNIFIE
SIGNIFICS SENSIFICS
SIGNIFY BE SAY BEAR GIVE MAKE
MEAN NOTE SIGN WAVE AUGUR
IMPLY SKILL SOUND SPEAK SPELL
TOKEN UTTER AMOUNT ARGUFY
ASSERT BEMEAN DENOTE EMPLOY
IMPORT INTEND MATTER SIGNAL
BESPEAK BETOKEN CONNOTE
DECLARE EXPRESS PORTEND
PRETEND DESCRIBE INDICATE
INTIMATE MANIFEST
SIGNPOST GUIDE MERCURY
WAYMARK HANDPOST
SIGURD (HORSE OF —) GRANI
(SLAIN BY —) FAFNIR
(SLAYER OF —) HOGNI
(WIFE OF —) GUDRUN
SIKH AKALI SINGH UDASI MAZHABI
SIKKIM (CAPITAL OF —) GANGTOK
(NATIVE OF —) RONG BHOTIA
LEPCHA
(RIVER OF —) TISTA
SIKSIKA SIHASAPA
SILENCE GAG MUM CALK CLUM
HUSH REST CHOKE FLOOR QUIET
SHUSH SQUAT STILL CLAMOR
MUFFLE SETTLE STIFLE WHISHT
CONFUTE SQUELCH DUMBNESS
PRECLUDE SUPPRESS
SILENCED STILL
SILENCER SOURDINE
SILENT MUM CLUM HUSH HUST
MUET MUTE SNUG CLOSE STILL
TACIT WHIST MUETTE SULLEN
TIPTOE WHISHT APHONIC UNWORDY
ASPIRATE RESERVED RETICENT
TACITURN
SILHOUETTE SHADE ISOTYPE
SILICA FLINT SILEX TRIPOLI
SILICATE MICA ALVITE CERITE
EUCLASE ILVAITE LOTRITE ZEOLITE
CALAMINE ERIONITE WELLSITE
SILICEOUS SHELLY
SILICLE POUCH SILICULE
SILICOSIS CON
SILK SAY SOY CRIN ERIA LOVE
MUGA FLOSS GREGE HONAN JAPAN
TABBY BLATTA CRACKS CULGEE
DUCAPE FRISON MANTUA RADIUM
SENDAL SHALEE SHILLA SOUPLE
TUSSAH ALAMODE CHIFFON

HABUTAI PERSIAN SQUEEZE TSATLEE TUSSORE YAMAMAI ARMOZEEN ARMOZINE LUSTRINE MILANESE

(— FOR LININGS) SARSNET SARCENET

(HEAVY —) CRIN ARMOZINE

(RAW —) GREIGE MARABOU TAYSAAM TSATLEE MARABOUT

(REFUSE —) BUR BURR

(TWILLED —) SURAH TOBINE FOULARD LOUSINE

(UNDYED —) CORAH

(UNTWISTED —) SLEAVE

(UPHOLSTERY —) TABARET

(WASTE —) KNUB NOIL FRISON

SILK COTTON KAPOK

SILK-COTTON TREE BULAK SEMUL SIMAL YAXCHE BENTANG MUNGUBA POCHOTE

SILKEN SILL SERIC SILKY SUAVE SEREAN

SILK GRASS KARATAS

SILK GUM SERICIN

SILK OAK LACEWOOD

SILKSMAN SCALPER

SILK TREE SIRIS

SILKWORM ERI ERIA SINA TUSSAH TUSSORE YAMAMAI BOMBYCID

SILKY GLOSSY SILKEN

SILKY CORNEL REDBRUSH

SILKY TAMARIN MARIKINA

SILL GIRD SOLE PLATE PATAND PATTEN SADDLE MUDSILL DOORSILL

SILLINESS BOSH FOLLY BETISE GOOSERY INANITY SIMPLES IDLENESS NONSENSE

SILLY TID BETE DAFT FOND FOOL NICE VAIN APISH BALMY BUGGY CAKEY DENSE DILLY DIZZY GOOFY INANE SAPPY SEELY BLASHY CRANKY CUCKOO DAWISH DOTARD DOTTLE FOOTLE FRUITY GUCKED PAULIE SAWNEY SHANNY SIMPLE SINGLE SKIVIE SLIGHT SPOONY VACANT ASININE FATUOUS FOOLISH FOPPISH FRIBBLE GLAIKET PEEVISH SCRANNY SHALLOW UNWITTY ANSERINE FEATLESS FOOTLING FOPPERLY

(BE —) DRIVEL

SILOXANE SILICON

SILT DREGS SLEECH DEPOSIT RESIDUE SULLAGE BULLDUST

SILVER LUNA MOON PINA DIANA PLATE SYCEE WEDGE WHITE ALBATA ARGENT SILLER BULLION VERMEIL ARGENTUM STERLING ARGENTINE

(— STATE) NEVADA

(DEBASED —) VELLON

(GILDED —) VERMEIL

SILVER BELL HALESIA BELLWOOD COWLICKS

SILVERFISH SHINER SLICKER FISHTAIL WOODFISH

SILVERING BACKING

SILVERSIDES IAO BRIT TINK BRITT FRIAR SMELT TAILOR TINKER

GRUNION ATHERINE PEIXEREY PEJERREY SKIPJACK

SILVERSMITH SONAR

SILVER TREE IRONWOOD

SILVER TREE FERN PITAU

SILVERVINE CATVINE

SILVERWEED TANSY

SILVERWING CINDER

SILVERY WHITE ARGENT SILVER SILVERN

SILYBUM MARIANA

SIMAR CYMAR SYMAR ZIMARRA

SIMILAR LIKE SUCH ALIKE EVENLY LIKELY SIMILE COGNATE KINDRED SEEMABLE SELFLIKE SUCHLIKE SUITABLE

SIMILARITY SIMILE ANALOGY HOMOLOGY HOMOTAXY LIKENESS PARALLEL SAMENESS

SIMILARLY EQUALLY LIKEWISE

SIMILE ICON IKON IMAGE FIGURE SUIVEZ COMPARE

SIMILITUDE IMAGE FIGURE ANALOGY PARABLE PORTRAIT

SIMMER FRY CREE SILE STEW SIMPER SOTTER TOTTLE

SIMON ZELOTES

SIMONY BARRATRY

SIMOOM SAMUM SAMIEL

SIMPER MINCE SMIRK BRIDLE

SIMPLE LOW BALD BARE EASY FOND MERE NICE ONLY PURE RUDE SNAP VERY WEAK AFALD BLEAK DIZZY GREEN NAIVE NAKED PLAIN SEELY SILLY SMALL SOBER CHASTE GLOBAL HOMELY HONEST HUMBLE NATIVE OAFISH RUSTIC SEMPLE SEVERE SINGLE STUPID VIRGIN ARTLESS ASININE AUSTERE BABYISH FATUOUS FOOLISH ONEFOLD POPULAR SIMPLEX SPECIES EXPLICIT HOMEMADE INNOCENT SACKLESS SEMPLICE SOLITARY

SIMPLE-MINDED SEELY SILLY INNOCENT

SIMPLETON AUF AWF COX DAW FON NUP OAF SAP SOT BOOB CAKE COOT CULL FLAT FOOL GABY GAUP GAWP GOFF GOUK GOWK GOWP GUFF PEAK SIMP SOFT TONY TOOT ZANY COKES GALAH GOOSE IDIOT IKONA JACOB LOACH NINNY NODDY PRUNE SAMMY SMELT SPOON TOMMY BADAUD DAUKIN FONDLE GANDER GAUPUS GAWNEY GOTHAM GREENY GULPIN JOSSER NINCUM NOODLE NUPSON SAWNEY SIMKIN SIMPLE DAWPATE GOMERAL GUBBINS JUGGINS MAFFLIN MUGGINS WIDGEON ABDERITE FLATHEAD FONDLING INNOCENT JEANJEAN JOCRISSE KNOTHEAD MOONCALF MOONLING OMADHAUN PEAGOOSE SILLYTON SOFTHEAD WISEACRE WOODCOCK

SIMPLICITY NICETY PURITY MODESTY NAIVETE ELEGANCE

SIMPLIFY CLARIFY EXPOUND

SIMPLY JUST ALONE FONDLY MERELY PLATLY CRUDELY QUIETI NATIVELY

SIMULATE ACT FAKE MOCK FEIGN MIMIC AFFECT ASSUME SEMBLE SIMULE SKETCH

SIMULATED FAINT FAKED ERSATZ FICTIOUS

SIMULATION ACTING ANALOGUE PRETENSE

SIMULTANEOUS CONJOINT CONJUGATE

SIMULTANEOUSLY ONCE TOGETHER

SIN ERR CULP DEBT ENZU EVIL HI PAPA VICE BLAME CRIME ERROR FAULT FOLLY GUILT SLOTH WATI WRONG AGUILT COMMIT FELONY NANNAR OFFEND PIACLE PLIGHT VENIAL FRAILTY OFFENSE HAMARTIA INIQUITY PECCANCY QUEDSHIP TRESPASS

(DEADLY —) ACEDIA

(ORIGINAL —) ADAM

SINCALINE CHOLINE

SINCE AS AGO FOR FRO NOW GO SETH SITH SYNE BEING WHERE FORWHY BECAUSE SITHENS WHEREAS INASMUCH SITHENCE

SINCERE GOOD REAL TRUE AFAL FRANK DEVOUT ENTIRE HEARTY HONEST SIMPLE SINGLE CORDIAL EARNEST GENUINE ONEFOLD UPRIGHT FAITHFUL

SINCERELY TRULY SIMPLY SINGL DEVOUTLY ENTIRELY HEARTILY

SINCERITY FAITH HEART HONEST REALITY

SINDON CORPORAL

SINEW THEW FIBER FIBRE NERVE LEADER SINNER TENDON

SINEWY WIRY NERVY THEWY ROBUST FIBROSE FIBROUS STRIF TENDINAL

SINFONIA SYMPHONY

SINFUL BAD EVIL VILE NEFAS WRONG WICKED UNGODLY VICIOI PIACULAR

SING HUM JIG LIP CANT CARP GA HYMN LILT TUNE CAROL CARRY CHANT CHIRL CROON DIRGE DIT DRING FEIGN LYRIC RAISE TOUCI YEDDE CHAUNT CHORUS DIVIDE INTONE MELODY RECORD RELISI STRAIN WARBLE CHORTLE COUNTER DESCANT GRIDDLE SINGING TWEEDLE CHERUBIM FALDERAL MODULATE SINGSONG VOCALIZE

(— ABOUT) BESING

(— ABOVE TRUE PITCH) SHARP

(— AS A BEGGAR) GRIDDLE

(— BRISKLY) KNACK

(— CHEERFULLY) LILT

(— FLORIDLY) DIVIDE

(— HARSHLY) SCREAM

(— IN A CRACKED VOICE) CRAKI

(— IN CHORUS) CHOIR

(— IN LOW VOICE) CROON

— IN SWISS MANNER) YODEL
— LOUDLY) BELT TROLL TROLLOL
— PRAISES) LAUD
— ROMANCES) GEST GESTE
— SECOND PART) SURCENT
— SOFTLY) SOWF SOWTH
— WITH FLOURISHES) ROULADE
‌GAPORE (RIVER IN —) SUNGEI
‌ELETAR
‌STRAIT OF —) JOHORE SEMBILAN
‌GE GAS BURN SWEAL GENAPP
‌CORCH SWINGE SCOWDER
‌WITHEN FIREFANG
‌GER ALTO BARD LARK SWAN
‌ASSO BUFFA BUFFO SKALD VOICE
‌ULBUL BUSKER CANARY CANTOR
‌YRIST SONGER BASSIST CHANTER
‌ROONER PRIMOMO SOLOIST
‌ONGMAN SOPRANO TROLLER
‌ARBLER BAYADERE CANTADOR
‌ASTRATO CHANTEUR FALSETTO
‌RIDDLER MELODIST MONODIST
‌HAMYRIS VOCALIST
— OF FOLK SONGS) CANTADOR
— OF THE GODS) GANDHARVA
‌EMALE —) SONGBIRD
‌MENDICANT —) BUSKER
‌RINCIPAL —) PRIMOMO
‌ROVENCAL —) MUSAR
‌GING CANT SCAT CHANT LYRIC
‌YMNODY JONGLERY
— CAROLS) PLYGAIN HODENING
‌ANTORIAL —) HAZANUTH
‌AZZANUT
‌IMULTANEOUS —) CHORUS
‌GLE ODD ONE LAST ONLY SOLE
‌NAL AFALD SIMPLE SOLEIN
‌JLLEN UNIQUE VERSAL ALONELY
‌ZYGOUS ONEFOLD SEVERAL
‌MPLEX TWOSOME PECULIAR
‌EPARATE SINGULAR SOLITARY
‌PORADIC
— OUT) CUT SPOT ISOLATE
‌EPARATE
‌GLE-FOOT RACK
‌GLEHANDEDLY SINGLY
‌GLENESS UNITY ONENESS
‌GLETON (— LEAD) SNEAK
‌GLY SINGLE SOLELY SLONELY
‌GPHO CHINGPAW
‌GSONG SOUGH CHANTING
‌GULAR ODD RARE QUEER SEENIL
‌NGLE STRANGE PECULIAR
‌GULARISM HENISM
‌GULARITY DOUBLET ONENESS
‌NLINESS
‌STER AWK CAR KAY DARK DIRE
‌LL GRIM DISMAL LOUCHE
‌BLIQUE OMINOUS
‌STRAL REVERSED
‌K DIP DOP EBB LUM SAG SET
‌'E BORE DRAU DRAW DROP FADE
‌JIL FALL GOWT HELD KILL LUMB
‌LE SWAG AVALE DRAFT DRAIN
‌IOOP DROWN HIELD LAPSE
‌)WER MERGE POACH SQUAT
‌OOP SWAMP VERGE DOLINA
‌LINE DRENCH GUTTER PLUNGE
‌DDLE RESIDE SETTLE COMMODE

DECLINE DESCEND DRAUGHT
FOUNDER GULLION IMMERSE
RELAPSE SCUTTLE SUBSIDE
SWALLOW DECREASE SINKHOLE
SOAKAWAY
(— A WELL) DRILL
(— AND FALL) TWINE
(— AS IN MUD) LAIR
(— DOWN) BOG AVALE STOOP
DECLINE
(— FANGS INTO) STRIKE
(— INTO OOZE) WASEL
(— NAILHEAD) SET
(— SUDDENLY) SLUMP
(— UNDER TRIAL) QUAIL
SINKBOX BOX SINK BATTERY
SINKER BUR BURR SINK DIPSY
PLUMB BULLET
SINKHOLE SINK PONOR UVALA
CENOTE COLLECT
SINKING GONE SINKAGE
(— DOWN) FONDU
SINKIUSE COLUMBIA
SINLESS INNOCENT
SINLESSNESS HOLINESS
SINNER DEBTOR PECCANT
SINNING PECCANT
SINUATE GYROSE
SINUOSITY WRIGGLE
SINUOUS WAVY SNAKEY SINUATE
SNAKISH TORTILE WINDING
INDENTED SWANLIKE
SINUS BOSOM RECESS LOCULUS
TEARPIT
SINUSITIS ROUP
SIOUAN ABANIC DAKOTA SANTEE
SAPONI CATAWBA DACOTAH
SIOUX (— FORCE) WAKAN WAKON
SIP BIB NIP SUP BLEB SEEP SLUP
SUCK TIFF KEACH SNACK WHIFF
TIPPLE TICKLER DELIBATE
SIPHON CRANE THIEF VALINCH
FLINCHER
SIPPING LIBANT
SIPUNCULOIDEA ACHAETA INERMIA
SIR PO DAN DEN DON PAN AZAM
HERR MIAN STIR TUAN SAHIB
SENOR SEYID SIEUR MESSER
SAYYID SIGNOR SIRREE DOMINUS
EFFENDI MESSIRE SIGNIOR SIGNORE
GOSPODIN GOVERNOR
(PL.) LORDINGS
SIRCAR BANIAN
SIRE BEGET THROW FATHER GETTER
SIREN HOOTER LIGEIA LIGYDA
LORELEI MERMAID SIRENIAN
SIRENIAN COWFISH MUTILATE
SIRENOMELUS SYMPUS SYMMELUS
SIRICID UROCERID
SIRIS KOKO LEBBEK
SIRIUS SOTHIS TISHIVA CANICULA
SIRLOIN SEY BACKSEY
SIRMUELLERA BANKSIA
SIRUP WAX LICK GOLDY SYRUP
GOWDIE GREENS LIQUER ORGEAT
RUNOFF CLAIRCE ECLEGMA
MOLASSES QUIDDANY
SIRWASH SIDELINE
SISAL CABUYA SISALANA

SISKIN TARIN
SISSIFIED PRISSY
SISSOO TALI SHISHAM
SISSY SIS CISSIE SISTER CHICKEN
SISTER NUN SIB SIS GIRL NURSE
SISSY TITTY WOMAN EXTERN
PERSON
(YOUNGER —) CADETTE
(PL.) SISTERN SISTREN
SISTERHOOD SORORITY
SISTERLY SORORAL
SISYPHUS (FATHER OF —) AEOLUS
(WIFE OF —) MEROPE
SIT SET LEAN SEAT BENCH PRESS
ROOST SQUAT WEIGH BESTRIDE
(— ABRUPTLY) CLAP
(— ASTRIDE) CROSS HORSE
STRADDLE
(— ERECT LIKE A DOG) BEG
(— FORCIBLY) DOSS
(— IN JUDGMENT) DEEM
(— ON) BROOD COVER
(— OVER EGGS) RUCK BROOD
SITATUNGA NAKONG
SITE AREA PLOT SEAT SITU SOLE
SPOT TOFT FIELD PLACE SITUS
STAND STANCE BIVOUAC DAMSITE
HABITAT STEADING
(— OF BIRD SEXUAL DISPLAY) LEK
(— OF HUNT) DRIVE
(— OF SMELTER) BOLE
(EXCAVATION —) DIC
(THRESHING —) SETTING
SITTER DOLLY DOLLIE INSESSOR
SITTING DIET SEAT ASSIS SEANCE
SEDENT SEJANT SESSION
CONGRESS SEDERUNT
SITUATE PLACE POSITION
SITUATED SET SEATED STATURED
(— OPPOSITE) COUNTER
SITUATION JOB LIE CASE PASS
PLOT POST SEAT SITE SPOT BERTH
SIEGE SITUS STATE STEAD ASSIZE
CHANCE ESTATE OFFICE PLIGHT
STATUS EPISODE PICTURE PORTENT
POSTURE STATION INCIDENT
INSTANCE POSITURE STANDING
UBIQUITY
(— BESET BY DIFFICULTIES)
SCRAPE
(— IN CRIBBAGE) GO
(— IN FARO) CATHOP
(— OF PERPLEXITY) HOBBLE STRAIT
(AMUSING —) BAR
(AWKWARD —) SCRAPE
(CRITICAL —) CLUTCH
(DIFFICULT —) BOX PUXY BOGGLE
NINEHOLES
(DISTRESSING —) STYMIE
(EXECRABLE —) ATROCITY
(FAVORABLE —) BREAK
(FINAL — OF ACT) CURTAIN
(HOPELESSLY DOOMED —)
RATTRAP
(NECESSITOUS —) BREACH
(PAINFUL —) DISTRESS
(RELATIVE —) BEARING
(UNSATISFACTORY —) DILEMMA
(VEXATIOUS —) HEADACHE

(VILE —) DUNGHILL
(ZODIACAL —) HAYZ
SITZ BATH SITZBAD SEMICUPE
SITZMARK BATHTUB
SIVA RUDRA SHIVA ISVARA SHAMBU
BHAIRAVA MAHADEVA NATARAJA
SIX VAU WAW SICE SISE HEXAD
HEXADE SENARY SEXTET STIGMA
DIGAMMA SIXSOME
SIXFOLD SEXTUPLE
SIX-FOOTED HEXAPOD
SIXMO SEXTO
SIXPENCE HOG PIG BEND KICK
SIMON SPRAT TIZZY BENDER
FIDDLE TANNER TESTON CRIPPLE
FIDDLER TESTRIL
SIXTEENTH ANA ANNA
SIXTIETH (— PART OF DAY) GHURRY
SIXTY SAMECH SAMEKH
SIZABLE SNUG LARGE HANDSOME
SIZE WAX AREA BIND BULK MARK
MASS DRESS GIRTH MOUND PLANK
SCALE EXTENT FORMAT GROWTH
MICKLE MOISON PICNIC SIZING
BIGNESS CONTENT CORSAGE
FITTING THIRTEEN TWELVEMO
(— OF **BOOK**) FOLIO
(— OF **CARDS**) TOWN LADIES
(— OF **HOLE**) BORE
(— OF **HOSIERY**) POPE
(— OF **PAPERBOARD**) LARGE
(— OF **PARTICLE**) GRIND
(— OF **ROPE**) GRIST
(— OF **TYPE**) GEM PICA RUBY
AGATE CANON ELITE PEARL MINION
PRIMER BREVIER DIAMOND
EMERALD ENGLISH PARAGON
(— **YARN**) SLASH
(**CLOTHING** —) LONG SHORT STOUT
JUNIOR PETITE
(**EXTRA LARGE** —) SUPER
(**RELATIVE** —) SCALE
(**UNUSUAL** —) OUTSIZE
SIZING DRESSING SLASHING
(— **LIQUID**) GLAIR
SIZZLE FRIZZ
SKAT CAT NULL TOURNEE
SKATE BOB RAY TUB RAJA RINK
SKIT TINK TUBE FLAIR SCULL
BATOID DOCTOR FLATHE PATENT
PATTEN ROCKER ROLLER RUNNER
SKETCH TINKER CHOPINE FLAPPER
PLACOID SKETCHER
(— **MARK**) CUSP
(**FEMALE** —) MAID
SKATER PATTENER SKETCHER
SKEDADDLE BUNK
SKEET KELTER KILTER PELTER
SKEIN RAP HANK HASP SCAN
BOTTOM SLEAVE SELVAGE
SKEINER RANDER SLIPPER
SKELETIN SPONGIN
SKELETON CUP CAGE MORT RAME
ATOMY BONES FRAME LOOFAH
SICULA SKELET ANATOMY CARCASS
RAWBONE ARMATURE CORALLUM
MANDIBLE OSSATURE
SKELETON KEY GILT SCREW
TWIRLER

SKEPTIC DOUBTER INFIDEL ZETETIC
APIKOROS APORETIC
SKEPTICAL APOREIC DOUBTFUL
SKEPTICISM HUMISM UNBELIEF
SKETCH BIT DASH DRAW LIMN PLAN
VIEW VITA DRAFT ENTER PAINT
TRACE APERCU DESIGN DOODLE
SCHEME SPLASH CROQUIS
DRAUGHT DRAWING ETCHING
OUTLINE SCHIZZO MONOGRAM
PROSPECT VIGNETTE
(— **BEFOREHAND**) INDICATE
(**AUTOBIOGRAPHICAL** —) VITA
(**BIOGRAPHICAL** —) ELOGY ELOGIUM
(**FIRST** —) ESQUISSE
(**HERALDIC** —) TRICK
(**OUTDOORS** —) LANDSKIP
(**PRELIMINARY** —) DRAFT ABBOZZO
MAQUETTE
(**ROUGH** —) NOTE POCHADE
ESQUISSE
(**SATIRICAL** —) SKIT
SKEW ASKEW GAUCHE
SKEWBACK SPRINGER
SKEWER PROD PROG SPIT PRICK
TRUSS SKIVER TASTER
SKEWERER TUBER
SKI SKEE SNOWSHOE
(— **DOWN SLOPE**) SCHUSS
(— **METHOD**) PASSGANG
(— **MOVEMENT**) RUADE
(— **POSITION**) VORLAGE
(— **RACING**) LANGLAUF
(— **TURN**) TELEMARK
(PL.) BOARDS
SKID DOG DRAG SLEW SLUE TRIG
DRIFT DRILL SLOUGH SKIDPAN
SLIPPER TRIGGER SIDESLIP
(— **LOGS**) SNAKE TWICH TRAVOY
TWITCH
(— **ON RAIL**) SKATE
(**FENDER** —) GLANCER
SKIDDER SNAKER
SKIDI LOUP
SKIDWAY PIT
SKIER KANONE SNOWBIRD
SKIFF SKIFT CAIQUE DINGHY
SAMPAN CURRANE SKIPPET
SKIING TOURING
SKIL BESHOW SKILFISH
SKILL ART CAN WIT FEAT FEEL HAND
PATE TACT CRAFT DRAFT HAUNT
KNACK TRICK ENGINE TECHNE
ABILITY ADDRESS APTNESS
CUNNING FINESSE MASTERY
MYSTERY SCIENCE SLEIGHT
ARTIFICE CAPACITY CHIVALRY
DEFTNESS FACILITY INDUSTRY
LEARNING
(**LACK OF** —) INERTIA
(**NAVIGATION** —) SEACRAFT
SKILLED OLD WISE ADEPT ASTUTE
PERITE SCIENT SKILLY VERSED
HOTSHOT PRACTIC EDUCATED
SKILLFUL
SKILLET PRIG SPIDER
SKILLFUL APT SLY ABLE DEFT FEAT
FILE FINE GOOD PERT TIDY WISE
ADEPT CANNY FITTY HANDY HENDE

READY SLICK SWEET ADROIT
ARTFUL CLEVER CRAFTY DAEDAL
EXPERT HABILE SCIENT SKILLY
SOLERT SUBTLE CUNNING SKILLEC
DEXTROUS PRACTIVE SLEIGHTY
TACTICAL
SKILLFULLY DEFTLY CRAFTILY
SKILLFULNESS CRAFT
SKIM TOP RIFF SCUD SCUM SCUN
SCUR SILE SKIP FLEET GRAZE
SCALE SKIFF SKIRR SKIVE BROWS
RABBLE SAMPLE DESPUME SKITTE
(— **ON WATER**) SCHOON
SKIMMED FLAT FLET
SKIMMER FALK LARI SKEP SCOOP
LINGEL SCUMMER CUTWATER
SKIMMINGS SCRUFF
SKIMP JIMP SLUR SCAMP SKINCH
SKIMPY JIMP CHARY SPARE SCANT
STINGY
SKIN KIP KIT BACK BARK CASE CAS
DERM FELL FLAY FLEA HIDE HILD
KITT MORT PEAU PEEL PELT RIND
BALAT BLYPE BRAWN FLOAT GENE
SLUFF STRIP SWARD PELTRY
SWARTH UNCASE CUTICLE DOESK
ENDERON KIDSKIN LEATHER
PELLAGE SKIMMER BUCKSKIN
DRUMHEAD LAMBSKIN PARADERM
PELLICLE SEALSKIN TEGUMENT
VITILIGO WOOLFELL
(— **FOR BOOKBINDING**) BASAN
(— **OF BACON**) SWARD
(— **OF BOARDS**) CARPET
(— **OF FRUIT**) PEEL
(— **OF GOOSE**) APRON
(— **OF INSECT**) CAST
(— **OF POTATO**) JACKET
(— **OF POULTRY NECK**) HELZEL
(— **OF RABBIT**) RACK CONEY
(— **OF SEAL**) SCULP
(— **OF THE HEAD**) SCALP
(— **OF WALNUT**) ZEST
(— **OF YOUNG CALF**) SLINK DEAC
(— **WITH WOOL REMAINING ON IT**)
WOOLFELL
(60 —**S**) TURN
(**BARE** —) BUFF
(**BEAVER** —) PLEW
(**BOAR'S** —) SHIELD
(**CAST** —) SPOIL SLOUGH EXUVIAE
(**CHAFED OR SORE** —) IRE
(**CHAMOIS** —) FURWA
(**DEEP LAYER OF THE** —) CUTIS
(**FAWN** —) NEBRIS
(**INNER PART OF THE** —) DERMA
(**LAMB — PREPARED LIKE FUR**)
BUDGE
(**OUTER** —) HUSK
(**PENDULOUS FOLD OF** —) DEWLA
(**ROUGHTANNED** —) CRUST
(**SHARK** —) SHAGREEN
(**SHEEP** —) BASIL
(**SQUIRREL** —) VAIR
(**THICKENED** —) BRAWN
(**THIN** —) FILM PELLICLE STRIFFE
SKINFLINT SKIN FLINT SCREW
HUDDLE PELTER SCRAPER SKEEZ
SKINK ADDA SCINCID SCORPION

KINNY BONY LEAN THIN SLINK
KIP DAP HIP BALK BOUT FOOT
JUMP LEAP SLIP TRIP BOUND
CAPER DANCE FRISK SALTO SCOON
SCOPE SCOUP SKITE SMOKE VAULT
GAMBOL GLANCE LAUNCH SPRING
GUNBOAT SKIPPER SKITTER
TRIPPLE PORPOISE
(— SCHOOL) TIB
KIPJACK SKIP BONITO SKIPPER
KIPPER IHI SKIP LAODAH LOWDAH
SERANG SHIPPER
KIRMISH FRAY BRUSH CLASH
MELEE SKIRM BICKER HASSLE
PICKEER RUNNING
KIRMISHER HUSSAR
KIRMISHING SPARRING
KIRT CUT LAP BANK BASE COAT
ENGI JUPE SAYA TUBE COAST
JUPON LABIE PAREU PASIN STRIP
TREND TWIST BASQUE DIRNDL
HOBBLE JUMPER KIRTLE PEPLUM
SARONG TAMEIN QUARTER
BASQUINE PULLBACK SKIRTING
(ARMOR —) TASSES LAMBOYS
(DIVIDED —) CULOTTE
(HOOPED —) TUBTAIL
(TARTAN —) KILT ARISAID
PL.) DOCK DOCKEN
KIRTING SKIRT PLINTH
PL.) BROKES
KIT BLACKOUT
KITTAGETAN HAIDA
KITTISH SHY CORKY GOOSY WINDY
FLISKY KITTLE SKEIGH SPOOKY
FLIGHTY SCADDLE SKADDLE
STARTLY BOGGLISH SKITTERY
STARTFUL
KITTLES KAYLES KITTLES SQUAILS
KUA BONXIE JAEGER TEASER
TULIAC STINKPOT WHIPTAIL
KULDUGGERY JOUKERY PAWKERY
KULK DERN JOUK LURK LUSK
MOOCH SCOUT
KULL BEAN POLL CRANY MOOCH
SCALP SCAUP VAULT COBBRA
PALLET SCONCE CRANIUM HARNPAN
HEADMOLD PANNICLE
— BONE) VOMER
— POINT) TYLION
BACK OF —) OCCIPUT
INCOMPLETE —) CALVARIA
UPPER HALF OF —) SINCIPUT
KULLCAP COIF PIXY PIXIE SKULL
VAULT BEANIE COIFFE CALOTTE
CAPELINE HOODWORT
ARABIAN —) CHECHIA
JEWISH —) YAMILKE YARMULKE
STEEL —) SECRET
KUNK ANNA PUSS HURON SKINK
SNIPE ZORIL CHINCHA POLECAT
EECAWK SMELLER CONEPATE
CONEPATL MUSTELID PHOBYCAT
FORRILLO
JAVANESE —) TELEDU
KUNK CABBAGE COLLARD
OCKWEED
Y BLUE HIGH LIFT LOFT POLE TIEN
AZURE CARRY DYAUS ETHER LANGI

VAULT CAELUS CANOPY HEAVEN
REGION WELKIN ELEMENT HEAVENS
OLYMPUS TENGERE WEATHER
(ICE —) ICEBLINK
SKYLARK LARK YERK
SLAB BAT CANT CLAM LECH PARE
SLAT BLADE DALLE LINER PANEL
PLANK SLATE STELA STELE TABLE
WADGE ABACUS FLITCH MARVER
MIHRAB PAVIOR RUNNER FLAPPET
PLANCHE PORPHYRY PUNCHEON
SLABWOOD
(— OF CLAY) BAT
(— OF COAL) SKIP SLIP
(— OF LIMESTONE) BALATTE
(— OF MARBLE) DALLE
(— OF PEAT) SCAD
(— OF SANDSTONE) COMAL
(— OVER BROOK) CLAM
(MEMORIAL —) LEDGER
(PAINTER'S —) SLANT
(STONE —) PLANK STELA STELE
INKSTONE
SLACK DRY LAX CULM DUFF NESH
SLOW SOFT CHECK FLOWN LOOSE
SLAKE TARDY ABATED FLABBY
FLAPPY REMISS UNGIRT BACKING
MAKINGS RELAXED SLACKEN
SMEDDUM CARELESS DILATORY
INACTIVE SLOBBERY
(— IN TRIGGER) CREEP
(— SHEET OF SAIL) FLOW
(COAL —) COOM COOMB
(PL.) BAGS
SLACKEN LAG PAY EASE FLAG
SLOW DELAY DOWSE LOOSE RELAX
SLACK SLAKE START SURGE
EXOLVE RELENT UNBEND
(— SPEED) HANG
SLACKENING HANG LETUP DETENTE
LETDOWN SLACKAGE
SLACKER SPIV ROTTER COUCHER
SLINKER EMBUSQUE
SLACKNESS LACHES LASHNESS
SLADE SOLE
SLAG SCAR DROSS CINDER DANDER
SCORIA SLAKIN THOMAS QUITTER
SLACKEN
SLAIN FALLEN
SLAKE ABATE SLACK LESSEN
QUENCH REFRESH SATISFY
SLAKING FAT
SLAM CLAP DASH FLUB SLOG SLOT
VOLE CLASH GRAND PLANK SLOSH
STRAM CHELEM FLOUNCE
SLANDER CANT BELIE LIBEL NOISE
BEFOUL DEFAME INJURE MALIGN
MISSAY ASPERSE CALUMNY
OBTRECT SCANDAL TRUMPET
BACKBITE DEROGATE STRUMPET
SLANDERER JUROR
SLANDEROUS FAMOUS VILIPEND
SLANG CANT ARGOT FLASH DIALECT
SLANT TIP CANT FLUE SKEW TILT
BEVEL DRAFT SLOPE SPLAY STOOP
FLANCH SKLENT DRAUGHT
COLORING DIAGONAL
SLANTED CANTED COLORED
COCKEYED

SLANTING BIAS CANT SKEW SLOPE
ASLANT ASLOPE SKLENT SQUINT
LOXOTIC OBLIQUE SLOPING
AVELONGE COLORING OVERWART
SIDELONG
SLANTINGLY AHOO ASWASH
SLANTLY
SLANT LINE VIRGULA VIRGULE
SLAP BOX DAB BLIP BLOW CLAP
CUFF FLAP LICK PLAT SCUD SLAT
SNUB SPAT TACK BLIBE CLINK
CRACK POTCH SKEEG SKELP
SMACK SPANK TWANG TWANK
BLEEZE BUFFET SCLAFF SLIGHT
STRIKE TINGLER WHERRET
BACKSLAP
(— HARD) BLAD
(RANDOM —) FLAY
SLAPDASH BUCKEYE
SLASH CAG CUT JAG COUP GASH
HASH PANE RACE RASH SLIT TOPS
KNIFE MINCE SCORE SKICE SLISH
RAMMEL SCORCH STREAK SLITTER
DIAGONAL SLASHING
SLASHED JAGGED DECOPED
TATTERED
SLASHING ABATIS
SLAT BOW LAG FLAT PALE SLOT
WAND BLADE SCLAT STAVE SPLINE
EUPHROE BEDSTAFF
SLATE RAG SLAT FRAME KILLAS
TABLET TICKET SHALDER SHINDLE
SLATING
(— IN SMALL IRREGULAR PIECES)
SCANTLE
(BLUE —) SHIVER SKAILLIE
(EXPOSED PART OF ROOFING —)
BARI
(SURFACE —) BONE
SLATER HELER HELLIER SLATTER
SKIMMITY
(TOOL OF —) STAKE
SLATTERN DAB DAW MAB FROW
MAUX SLUT TRUB DOLLY FAGOT
MAWKS MOGGY MOPSY BLOUSE
CLATCH DOLLOP MALKIN STREEL
TRAPES LADRONE TROLLOP
HUCKMUCK SLUMMOCK
SLATTERNLY DOWDY BLOWSY
DAWISH FROWZY SORDID TRAPISH
SLATTERN SLOVENLY
SLAUGHTER WAL FELL KILL SLAM
SLAY BUTCH HALAL QUELL BATTUE
MURDER STRAGE BUTCHER
CARNAGE KILLING SHAMBLE
BUTCHERY MASSACRE OCCISION
SHECHITA
(— ACCORDING TO MOSLEM LAW)
HALAL
(— OF LARGE NUMBER) HECATOMB
(WHOLESALE —) QUELL
SLAUGHTERER KILLER SHOHET
SHOCHET
SLAUGHTERHOUSE ABBATOIR
BUTCHERY MATADERO SHAMBLES
(— WORKER) LIMEMAN
SLAUGHTERING SHEHITA SHECHITA
SLAV VEND WEND CZECH HUNKS

HUNKY SLAVE USKOK CROATIAN
MORAVIAN
SLAVE DAS ARDU BOND DASI DUPE
ESNE SERF DAVUS HELOT SWINK
THEOW ALIPIN ALLTUD CUMHAL
FORSAR GUINEA HIEROS MAMLUK
SLAVEY THRALL VASSAL BONDMAN
CAPTIVE CHATTEL FORSADO
HACKNEY PEDAGOG SERVANT
SLAVISH BONDMAID LORARIUS
MAMELUKE MANCIPLE MORGIANA
PRAEDIAL SLAVELET THEOWMAN
(— **IN TEMPLE**) HIEROS
(— **WHO WHIPS OTHERS**) LORARIUS
(**DEFORMED** —) CALIBAN
(**FREED** —) CLIENT
(**FUGITIVE** —) MAROON CIMMARON
(**GALLEY** —) FORSAR FORSADO
SFORZATO
(**HAREM** —) ODALISK
(**HINDU** —) DAS DASI
(PL.) CHIURM COFFLE HELOTRY
TOXOTAE
SLAVER DROOL FROTH DRIVEL
DRIBBLE SLABBER SLOBBER
SALIVATE
SLAVERY YOKE THRALL BONDAGE
HELOTRY MIZRAIM THRALDOM
SLAVEY DRUDGE
SLAVISH MEAN MENIAL
SLAVONIC (— **BEING**) VILA
SLAY KILL SMITE SPILL MURDER
STRIKE BUTCHER EXECUTE
STRANGLE
SLAYER BANE HOGNI KILLER
MURDERER
SLEAZY FLIMSY
SLED LUGE TODE JUMBO SCOOT
SLIDE SLIPE SLOOP HURDLE
JUMPER SLEDGE SLEIGH BOBSLED
CLIPPER COASTER DOGBOAT
DOGSLED MONOSKI POINTER
SLIPPER TRAILER TRAVOIS
HANDSLED SKELETON TOBOGGAN
SLEDGE DAN DRAG DRAY PULK
SLED GURRY PULKA SLIDE SLIPE
TRAIL TRAIN TROLL TRUNK SLEIGH
KOMATIK PADDOCK TROLLEY
TRAINEAU
(— **FOR CRIMINALS**) HURDLE
(— **FOR STRAIGHTENING RAILS**)
GAG
(**LOG** —) SLOOP TIEBOY
(**MINER'S** —) MALLET
SLEDGEHAMMER SMASHER
SLEEK SNOD CLOSE JOLLY SILKY
SLICK TRICK SILKEN SLEEKY SLIGHT
SMARMY SMOOTH SVELTE SLEEKIT
SOIGNEE SLIPPERY
SLEEKNESS GLOSS
SLEEP BED KIP LIB LIE NAP CALK
CAMP DORM DOSS DOZE HALE
REST WINK BALMY DORSE ROOST
SWOON DROWSE SIESTA SNOOZE
SOMNUS SWEVEN SLUMBER
WINKING
(— **BROKEN BY SNORING**) GRUFF
(— **ON A PERCH**) JOUK
(**DEEP** —) SWOON

(**LIGHT** —) SLOOM
(**PRETENDED** —) DOGSLEEP
(**PROFOUND** —) SOPOR
(**SHORT** —) NAP SIESTA SNOOZE
SLEEPER TIE FENDER DORMANT
DORMEUSE ELEOTRID STRINGER
SLEEPING BED ASLEEP DORMANT
SLEEPLESS LIDLESS WAKEFUL
RESTLESS WATCHFUL
SLEEPLESSNESS WATCH INSOMNIA
SLEEPY DOZY HEAVY NODDY PEEPY
DROWSY GROGGY MORPHIC
SLEEPISH SLUMBERY SOMNIFIC
SLEET STORM
SLEEVE ARM BAND POKE ARMLET
MANCHE MOGGAN BUSHING
CATHEAD CUBITAL HOUSING
THIMBLE
(— **ON A SHAFT**) CANNON
(— **ON GUN**) BAND
(**HANGING** —) TAB
(**LEG-OF-MUTTON** —) GIGOT
(**LONG** —) POKE
(**TAPERED** —) SKEIN
SLEIGH SLO PUNG SLED BOOBY
SLIPE TRAIN BERLIN CUTTER
SLEDGE CARIOLE TRAINEAU
SLEIGHT ARTIFICE
SLENDER FINE HAIR JIMP LANK
LEAN PRIN SLIM THIN DELIE EXILE
FAINT LATHY REEDY SLANK SLEEK
SMALL SPIRY SWAMP WISPY FILATE
SEMMIT SLIGHT SPINNY SPIRED
STALKY SVELTE TENDER GRACILE
LISSOME SLIVERY SPIRLIE SQUINNY
TENUOUS THREADY WASPISH
ACICULAR ETHEREAL HAIRLIKE
SPINDLED
SLENDERNESS EXILITY TENUITY
SLEW LOT RAFT SLUE STROKE
SLICE CUT BITE CHOP FLAG FLAP
JERK DASH STOW CANCH CAPER
GIGOT LEACH SHARE SHAVE SHIVE
SKELB SLIPE SLIVE CANTLE COLLOP
CORNET CULPON SHIVER SLIVER
TARGET THIBLE TRENCH SECTION
SHAVING TRANCHE COSSETTE
TURNOVER
(— **CUT IN PLOWING**) FLAG
(— **OF BACON**) BARD BARDE
LARDON RASHER
(— **OF BREAD**) BUTTY WHANG
CROUTE TRENCHER
(— **OF CHEESE**) KEBBOC
(— **OF COAL**) SKIP
(— **OF FISH**) COBBIN
(— **OF MEAT**) STEAK COLLOP
CUTLET SCALLOP TAILZIE
(— **OF SMOKED SALMON**) CORNET
(— **REMOVED FROM ROADWAY**)
CANCH
(— **WITH MOTIONS**) SAW
(—**S OF APPLES**) CHOPS
(**LARGE** —) BLAD DODGE
(**THICK** —) SLAB
(**THIN** —) CHIP SECTION
SLICED CUT
SLICK LOY GLIB SNUG SLEEK

CLASSY GLOSSY SMOOTHY
SLIDDERY
SLICKER FLOAT SLICK SMOOTH
SLEEKER SMOOTHER
SLIDE SCLY SKID SLEW SLIP SLUR
BALOP CHUTE COAST COULE CRE
GLIDE HURRY MOUNT SCOOT SHI
SLADE FINDER SLOUGH SLIDDER
SLITHER SLUTHER FADEAWAY
GLISSADE SLIDEWAY
(— **A DIE**) SLUR
(— **CARDS**) SKIN
(— **DOWN**) RUSE SLUMP
(— **FOR LOWERING CASKS**)
POLEYNE
(— **ON DRUMHEAD**) BRACE
(— **SIDEWISE**) SKID
(**TENT** —) EUPHROE
SLIDER REGISTER
SLIDEWAY PULLEY
SLIDING COULE
SLIGHT CUT OFF EASY FINE HURT
POOR SLAP SLIM SLUR SNUB TH
WEAK FILMY GAUZY LIGHT MINOF
SCANT SMALL SOBER FLIMSY
FORGET LACHES LITTLE MINUTE
REMOTE TWIGGY FRAGILE GRACI
NEGLECT NOMINAL SHALLOW
SKETCHY SLENDER SLIGHTY
THREADY VILLAIN DELICATE
MISPRIZE OVERLOOK SCRANNEL
VILIPEND
SLIGHTER LESS
SLIGHTEST FIRST LEAST
SLIGHTINGLY LIGHTLY
SLIGHTLY FAINTLY SOMEWHAT
SLIGHTNESS DELICACY GRACILIT
SLIM THIN GAUNT WANDY SLIGHT
SLENDER TENUOUS
SLIME GLIT GORE OOZE SLAB SL
SLUM GLEET SLAKE SLOAK SLOK
SLEECH SLUDGE SCHLICH SLUBB
SLUTHER
SLIMY OOZY SLAB MUCID GLAIRY
GLEETY GLETTY LIMOUS MUCOUS
SNOTTY SLEECHY MUCULENT
SLINE JOINT
SLING DUST LOOP FLING HONDA
SLUNG BRIDGE BRIDLE HALTER
SLACKIE
(— **FOR HAULING GAME**) TUMPLI
(— **OF BRAIDED FIBERS**) MA
SLINGER FUNDITOR
SLINGSHOT SLING SLAPPY
TWEAKER CATAPULT SHANGHAI
SLINK SLY CAST HINT LEER LOOP
LURK PEAK SHIRK SLING SLUNK
SNEAK SLINKY
(— **AWAY**) SHAG SLOKE FLINCH
MIZZLE SHRINK
SLIP DIP IMP NOD SLY BALK CARE
CHIT DOCK FALL JINK LOOP RUS
SKEW SKID SLEW SLUR SPEW
BEWET BEWIT BONER CHECK
DAGGE ERROR FLIER FLYER GLI
LABEL LAPSE SCAPE SHIFT SHIR
SKATE SKITE SLICK SLIDE SLIPE
SLIVE SLUMP STALK SURGE
COUPON ENGOBE LAPSUS MISCU

SLOUGH SLURRY TICKET UNSLIP
DELAPSE FOUNDER ILLAPSE
MISSTEP MORTISE SLIDDER
SLUTHER SNAPPER STUMBLE
BOOKMARK GERTRUDE GLISSADE
HEADBAND QUICKSET SCHEDULE
SIDESLIP SLIPPAGE SLIPPING
— **AWAY)** GO BILK SKIN WISE
VADE ELAPSE
— **BY)** ELAPSE
— **FROM A PLANT)** STALLON
— **OF FISH)** RAND
— **OF PAPER)** ALLONGE
— **OF WOOD)** SPILL
— **OFF COURSE)** SLEW SLOUGH
— **ON CARELESSLY)** SLIVE
— **OUT)** TIB
— **SECRETLY)** CREEM
— **SMOOTHLY)** SWIM
CERAMICS —) SLOP ENGOBE
INFANT'S —) GERTRUDE
PILLOW —) BIER
SLIPCASE CASE FOREL FORREL
SLIPKNOT BOW SNITTLE DRAWKNOT
SLIPMAN JACKER
SLIPOVER OVERSLIP
SLIPPER FLAT MULE NEAP PUMP
OCK TURN GLAVE MOYLE ROMEO
CUFF BALLET BOOTEE DORSAY
JULIET PANTON PINSON SANDAL
CLAFF SCLIFF BAUCHLE CHINELA
RAKOWE EVERETT SCUFFER
ABOUCHE FEWTERER PANTOFLE
CLAFFER SLIPSHOE
SLIPPERINESS SLIDDER
SLIPPERY GLEG GLIB SLID GLARY
LINT SLAPE SLEEK SLICK SOAPY
WACK CRAFTY GLINSE GREASY
LUBRIC SHIFTY SLIPPY ELUSIVE
VASIVE GLIDDER SHUTTLE SLIDDRY
LIDING SLITHER GLIBBERY
LABBERY SLICKERY SLIDDERY
LITHERY
SLIPPERY DICK DONCELLA
SLIPSHOD JERRY SLOPPY UNKEMPT
LAPDASH SLOVENLY
SLIPSTREAM RACE
SLIT CUT EYE JAG KIN NAG RIT FENT
ATE PORT RACE RENT SCAR SLOT
ENT CRACK SPARE BOUCHE
CRANNY OSTIUM STRENT FISSURE
PLACKET SLITTED SLOTTEN
WINDWAY APERTURE BOTHRIUM
— **HIND LEG)** HARL
— **IN EDGE OF SHIELD)** BOUCHE
— **IN STONE)** GRIKE
— **MADE BY CUT)** KERF
ORNAMENTAL —) SLASH
SLITHER SLIDE HIRSEL SLIDDER
LUTHER
SLIVER TOP SHAVE SKELF SLICE
PELK SPELL SHIVER DELIVERY
PLINTER
— **OF WOOL)** ROLL ROVE
SPINNING —) END RIBBON
DELIVERY
SLOB JOKER SLUDGE SLOBBER
LOMMACK
SLOBBER SLOP SLUP SMALM

SMARM SLAVER SLABBER SLATHER
SLIVVER BESLAVER
SLOBBERY SLOBBY SMARMY
SLAVERY
SLOE SLA SNAG SLONE
SLOG SLOSH STRIKE
SLOGAN CRY CACHET PHRASE
CATCHCRY SLUGHORN WARDWORD
SLOOP STAR BOYER COMET SMACK
SCHUIT HOOGAARS
SLOP SLAP SOSS SQUAB SWILL
SOSSLE SOZZLE HOGWASH
SLATTER
(— **AROUND)** SLAISTER
(PL.) SLIVERS SLIPSLOP SLOPPAGE
SLOPE UP DIP LIE BAND BANK BENT
BRAE CANT CAST CURB DROP FALL
HANG HILL LEAN PALI RAKE RAMP
RISE SIDE SINK TILT BEVEL CLIFF
COAST GAMMA HIELD PINCH SCARP
SLANT SLENT SLOOP SPLAY STEEP
TALUS VERGE YUNGA ASCENT
BAJADA BATTER BROACH GLACIS
HADING SHELVE TUMBLE UPBROW
UPRISE CUTBANK DESCENT
DOWNSET FORESET HANDING
INCLINE LEANING PENDANT
UPGRADE VERSANT WEATHER
BANKSIDE DRIPPING GLISSADE
GRADIENT SHOULDER SIDELING
SNOWBANK
(— **BACK)** BATTER
(— **DOWN)** SHED
(— **OF CUESTA)** INFACE
(— **OF ROOF)** CURB
(— **OF STERNPOST)** RAKE
(— **UPWARD)** CLIMB ASCEND
BATTER
(**DOWNWARD** —) HANG DEVALL
DECLINE DESCENT HANGING
DOWNHILL
(**GENTLE** —) GLACIS
(**MARGINAL** —) CESS
(**MOUNTAIN** —) ADRET
(**STEEP** —) BROW HEADWALL
SLOPING CANT DEVEX SLANT SLOPE
SLOPY ASLOPE SHELVY DECLIVE
DOWNHILL SIDELING
(— **ABRUPTLY)** BOLD
(— **BACKWARD)** SUPINE
SLOPPY JUICY SOPPY SLABBY
SOZZLY SPLOSHY SLABBERY
SLAPDASH SLATTERN SLATTERY
SLIPSHOD WATERISH
SLOSH DOWSE SLASH SLUSH SOUSE
SQUDGE SPLODGE
SLOT COVE DROP SCROLL SPLINE
KEYHOLE GUIDEWAY
SLOTH AI UNAU TARDO ACEDIA
IGNAVY ACCIDIE IGNAVIA BRADYPOD
EDENTATE PIGRITIA SLUGGING
SLOTH BEAR BHALU ASWAIL
SLOTHFUL FAT ARGH IDLE LAZY
INERT LITHER THOKISH UNLUSTY
DELICATE INDOLENT SLUGGISH
SLOUCH LOUCH LARRUP LOLLOP
LOUNGE SLIDDER TROLLOP
SHAMMOCK SLOUCHER
SLOUCH HAT SMASHER

SLOUGH CORE SHED SLEW SLUE
BAYOU RAVEL SHUCK SLONK SLUFF
SPOIL SWAMP ESCHAR DISCARD
LAMMOCK
SLOVEN BESOM CLART SLUSH
TROLLY HALLION TRACHLE
HUDDROUN
SLOVENLY DOWDY GAUMY MESSY
BLOWZY CLATTY FROWZY GRUBBY
SHABBY SLOPPY SLOVEN TRAILY
UNTIDY BUNTING SLIVING SLOUCHY
UNSONCY CARELESS HUDDROUN
SLIPSHOD SLOBBERY SLUBBERY
SLUTTISH TROLLOPY
SLOW BOG LAG LAX LEK WET ARGH
DREE DULL LATE LAZY LENT SKID
SLUG SULK BLUNT DUNCH DUNNY
HEAVY HOOLY INERT POKEY SLACK
SLOTH SWEER TARDE TARDO
TARDY UNAPT ARREST BEHIND
DRIECH DUMMEL HINDER RETARD
SLOOMY SOODLY TRAILY COSTIVE
DRONISH HALTING LAGGARD
LANGUID SLACKEN SOAKING
STRANGE TARDANT TEDIOUS
UNREADY DILATORY INACTIVE
LATESOME SLUGGISH
(— **DOWN)** SEIZE
(— **IN BURNING)** SOFT
(— **IN MOVEMENT)** GRAVE INERT
SULKY
(— **OF MIND)** STUPID
(— **TO LEARN)** BACKWARD
(— **TO RESPOND)** GROSS
(— **UP)** SLACK SLACKEN
(**MODERATELY** —) ANDANTE
(**MUSICALLY** —) LENTO
(**PLEASANTLY** —) SOFT
(**VERY** —) LARGO
SLOW-BURNING PUNKY
SLOWED STIFF
SLOWER LATTER
SLOW LORIS KOKAN
SLOWLY SLOW DULLY GRAVE
HOOLY LENTO ADAGIO GENTLY
HEAVILY
SLOW-MOVING SLEEPY DORMANT
DRAWLING SLUGGISH
SLOWNESS LAG SLOTH LENTOR
TARDITY LATENESS
SLOW-WITTED FAT DENSE STUPID
SLOWWORM HAGWORM
SLUDGE GUNK SLOB
SLUE SLEW SWAMP SLOUGH
SLUG BUST LINE MILL PLOW SHOT
SNAG STEW ARION CLUMP LIMAX
SNAIL RATTLE STRIKE SNIFTER
TREPANG GEEPOUND
SLUGGARD DAW SLOW SLUG
DRONE CAYNARD LUGGARD
SWINGER SLOWBACK SLUGABED
SLUGGISH LAG DOZY DULL FOUL
LATE LAZY SLOW BROSY DOPEY
DRONY FAINT HEAVY INERT LOURD
RESTY SULKY BOVINE DRAGGY
DROWSY LEADEN SLEEPY SLOOMY
SLUGGY SUPINE TORPID COSTIVE
DORMANT DRONISH LAGGARD
LANGUID LENTOUS LUMPISH

RESTIVE DILATORY INACTIVE
INDOLENT LOURDISH SLOTHFUL
SLOTTERY SLUGGARD
SLUGGISHNESS LEAD SLOTH
APATHY LENTOR PHLEGM INERTIA
LANGUOR
SLUICE CLOW GOOL GOTE GOUT
SASSE SLUSH TRUNK CLOUGH
FENDER LAUNDER PENSTOCK
WASTWEIR
SLUICEWAY FLASH
SLUM BUSTI BUSTEE WARREN
SLUMBER DORM DOVE DOZE JOUK
REST ROUT SLEEP SLOOM DROWSE
SLUMP FALL FLOP SOSS SLOUCH
LETDOWN TROLLOP
SLUR BIND SLIM COULE GLIDE SLIME
SCRUFF SLIGHT SLUBBER LIGATURE
(— IN PRINTING) SHAKE
SLURRY SLIP
SLUSH MIRE POSH SIND SLOP FLUSH
SLOSH SPOSH STUFF SWASH
SWOSH LOPPER SLUTCH SLOBBER
SLODDER
SLUSHY SLASHY SLOPPY SLOSHY
SLUDGY STICKY SPLASHY
SLOBBERY
SLUT MAUX BITCH FILTH QUEAN
DOLLOP DRAZIL DROSSEL
SLATTERN
SLUTTISH SLUTTY SORDID
SLY ARCH FOXY SLEE SLID SLIM
CANNY COONY LOOPY PAWKY
POKEY SLOAN SNAKY ARTFUL
CRAFTY FELINE SUBTLE SUPPLE
CUNNING EVASIVE FURTIVE LEERING
SUBTILE UNFRANK GUILEFUL
SLEIGHTY SNEAKING STEALTHY
THIEVISH
SLYNESS CUNNING PAWKERY
STEALTH ARCHNESS
SMACK BANG BARK BUSS KISS SALT
SCAT SLAP TANG TROW VEIN
BAWLY GOUFF SAVOR SNACK
TASTE BARQUE FLAVOR SMATCH
SMACKEE SPANKER BRAGOZZO
SLAPDASH TINCTURE
(— OF) RELISH
SMACKING SKELPING
SMALL BIT SMA WEE BABY MEAN
PINK SEED SLIM TINY WEAK BIJOU
BITTY DAWNY DEENY DINKY ELFIN
PETIT PETTY PINKY POKEY TEENY
WEENY BANTAM FRIBBY GRUBBY
LITTLE MINUTE NARROW PEANUT
PETITE SLIGHT SMALLY CAPSULE
NAGGISH NANITIC PICCOLO
QUEECHY SCRIMPY SLENDER
THRIFTY PILULOUS SNIPPETY
(— AND NUMEROUS) MILIARY
(— AND THICK) DUMPY DUMPTY
(— BUT TANGIBLE) CERTAIN
(— PORTION) MODICUM
(DAINTILY —) MIGNON
(EXCESSIVELY —) BOXY
(NOT —) GOOD
(VERY —) WEE FINE TINY DWARF
PUSIL PYGMY TEENY MINUTE
MiNIKIN TIDDLEY DWARFISH

SMALLAGE MARCH
SMALLCLOTHES SHORTS SMALLS
SMALL CRANBERRY FENBERRY
SMALLER LESS MINOR LESSER
SMALLEST FIRST LEAST MINIM
TITMAN MINIMUS
SMALLHOLDER TOFTMAN
SMALL-MINDED PETTY
SMALLNESS EXILITY FEWNESS
PAUCITY EXIGUITY SCARCITY
SMALLPOX POX VARIOLA ALASTRIM
SMALT ROYAL ESCHEL SMALTZ
ZAFFER ASMALTE
SMART YEP BRAW FESS FLIP FOXY
GNIB NICE PINK RACY SNAP SPRY
TRIG ACUTE BRISK CLEAN DINKY
FLASH HEADY JIMMY KIPPY NIFTY
NOBBY NUTTY PEERT PRANK PRIDY
SASSY SAUCY SHARP SLEEK SLICK
SMIRK SMOKE SMUSH SPICY SPRIG
STING SWANK SWISH TIGHT TIPPY
TOFFY TRICK AKAMAI BRAWLY
CHEESY CLEVER DAPPER GIGOLO
JAUNTY KITTLE PERTLY SHREWD
SPANKY SPIFFY SPRINK SPRUCE
STOUND SWANKY SWIDGE TIDDLY
KNOWING PUNGENT SWAGGER
TOFFISH VOGUISH BRUSHING
(— IN APPEARANCE) POSH
(— IN DRESS) GALLANT
SMART ALECK FLIP SMARTY
SMARTEN FINE PUSS SMUG SLICK
TITIVATE
SMARTLY SMART SNACK YEPLY
TIDELY
SMARTNESS TON SNAP SMART
SWISH
SMARTWEED CULERAGE REDKNEES
SMASH BASH BUMP CAVE DASH
PASH RUSH SCAT TRAP BREAK
CRACK CRASH CRAZE SOCKO
STAVE WRECK CRACKER SHATTER
SMASHUP DEBRUISE DEMOLISH
OVERHEAD STRAMASH
(— A GAP) BREACH
SMASHED BUNG STOVEN BROOZLED
SMASHING CRACKING
SMASHUP STRAMASH
SMATTERING SMACK SMATCH
SMATTER
SMEAR RUB BLOT BLUR CLAM DAUB
DOPE GAUM GLOB GORM MOIL
CLEAM DITCH GLAIR SLAKE SLARE
SMALM SMARM SULLY BEDAUB
BESLAB DEFILE PLATCH SLAVER
SLURRY SMIRCH SMOOCH SMUDGE
SPREAD STREAK STRIKE BEPAINT
BESMEAR PLASTER POLLUTE
SPLOTCH SLAISTER
(— OVER) ENGLUTE
(— WITH BLOOD) GILD
(— WITH EGG WHITE) GLAIR
(— WITH MUD) CLART SLIME
(— WITH SOMETHING STICKY)
GAUM GORM LIME
(— WITH TAR) PAY
(— WITH WAX) CERE
SMEAR DAB FLATFISH MARYSOLE
SMEARED FOUL BROSY MUSSY

SCOVY BLOODY SMUDGY BLURREI
BEGUMMED
SMEARY DAUBY GAUMY
SMEDDUM SMITHUM
SMELL FUNK FUST GUSH NOSE
ODOR VENT AROMA FETOR FLAIR
SAVOR SCENT SMACK SNIFF SNOC
SNUFF STIFE TASTE OLFACT
RESENT SMEECH BREATHE
PERFUME REFLAIR VERDURE
(— AFTER PREY) BREVIT
(— OFFENSIVELY) REEK
(DAMP FUSTY —) RAFT
(DISAGREEABLE —) GOO STENCH
(HAVING PLEASANT —) SNIFTY
(MUSTY —) FUST
(OFFENSIVE —) FUNK FETOR STIN
MEPHITIS
(STRONG —) HOGO
(SWEET —) SWEET
SMELLY FUGGY WHIFFY SMELLFUL
SMELT DECOCT INANGA EPERLAN
ICEFISH ELIQUATE SALMONID
SPARLING SPERLING
(FRY OF —) PRIM
SMEW NUN PIED SMEE DIVER
SMETHE
SMILAX LILY SARSA LILIUM
SMILE BEAM GRIN FLASH FLEER
SMEER ARRIDE SMUDGE SMIRKLE
(— AMOROUSLY) SMICKER
(AFFECTED —) SMIRK
(SELF-CONSCIOUS —) SIMPER
SMILING GOOD RIANT SMILY SMIRI
TWINKLY SMILEFUL
SMIRCH SMIT SOIL SMEAR SULLY
SLURRY SOILURE TARNISH
SMIRCHED DINGY
SMIRK DRAD YIRN SIMPER SMICKE
SMIRKLE SMURTLE
SMITE DUNT FRAP GIRD SLAY FLIN
SKITE STRIKE
(— WITH LIGHTNING) LEVEN
SMITH MIMIR REGIN BOSSER
FORGER SMITHY FARRIER GLUTTE
SMITHER STEELER WAYLAND
FLOORMAN FORGEMAN PANSMITH
SMITHSONITE CALAMINE
SMITHY FORGE SMIDDY STITHY
STUDDIE FARRIERY
SMITTEN EPRISE STRICKEN
SMOCK BRAT SLOP KAMIS SMOKE
JIBBAH JUMPER CHEMISE SMOCE
SMOKE PEW USE FLAN FOGO FUFF
FUME FUNK HAVE LUNT NAVE PIP
REEK ROKE TOVE DRINK REECH
SMEEK SMORE SMUSH STIVE VAPO
WHIFF BREATH BUCCAN POTHER
SMEECH SMUDGE INCENSE
SMOLDER SMOTHER BACONIZE
(— MARIJUANA) BLAST
(FROST —) BARBER
(OFFENSIVE —) FUNK
(TOBACCO —) BLAST
SMOKEHOUSE FUMATORY
SMOKEJACK STACKMAN
SMOKER FUNKER
SMOKESTACK STACK FUNNEL
TUNNEL CHIMNEY

SMOKE TREE ZANTE FUSTET FUSTIC SCOTINO

SMOKING ROOM DIVAN TABAGIE

SMOKY HAZY ROKY DINGY FUMID FUMISH FUMOSE SMUDGY SMUISTY

SMOLDER SMUSH SMOTHER SMOLDERING PUNKY

SMOLT SMELT SMOUT SPROD

SMOOCH LALLYGAG LOLLYGAG

SMOOTH DUB FAT LAP NOT BOSS COMB DRAG EASE EASY EVEN FACE FAIR FILE FLAT GLAD GLEG GLIB HONE IRON LENE NOTT REET SLID SNOD SOFT BLAND BRENT CLEAR COUTH DARBY DIGHT DOLCE DRESS EMERY FLOAT FRAZE GLARE GOOSE HOWEL LEVEL LITHE PLAIN PLANE PRESS QUIET SCARF SILKY SLAPE SLEEK SLICK SMOLT SNUFF SOAPY SUANT SUAVE SUENT TERSE ABRASE BUFFED CREAMY EQUATE EVENLY FETTLE FLUENT GLOSSY GREASE GREASY LEGATO LIMBER MANGLE POLITE SCREED SILKEN SLIGHT STREAK STRIKE STROKE SVELTE UNFRET BOULDER ERUGATE FLATTEN SLEEKIT EXPLICIT GLABRATE GLABROUS GLIBBERY GRAZIOSO LEVIGATE SARSENET GLIDDERY SQUEEGEE STRICKLE UNRUFFLE
— **BY BREAKING LUMPS)** BILDER
— **MARBLE)** GRIT
— **ONESELF UP)** PREEN
— **OVER)** GLOZE PLASTER
— **TYPE)** KERN

HYPOCRITICALLY —) SLEEK

PHONETICALLY —) LENE LENIS

SMOOTHER GLAZER

SMOOTHLY SLICK EASILY EVENLY GLIBLY SMOOTH SPROWSY SWEETLY POLITELY

SMOOTHNESS EASE FLUENCY

SMOOTH-RUNNING SWEET

SMOOTH WINTERBERRY CANHOOP

SMOTHER BURKE CHOKE SMEAR SMOKE SMORE MOIDER QUEZEN MUDGE STIFLE FLASKER OPPRESS QUEASON SMOLDER SMUDDER

SMOTHERED ETOUFFE STIFLED

SMUDGE GAUM SLUR SMUT SOIL SOOT CROCK SMEAR SMOKE MOOCH SMUTCH SMOLDER SMOTHER SOILURE

SMUDGED SMUTCHY

SMUG SMUSH SUAVE SMUDGE

SMUGGLE RUN STEAL BOOTLEG SHUFFLE

SMUGGLER OWLER RUNNER SPOTSMAN

SMUGGLING OWLING

SMUGLY FATLY

SMUT BUNT COOM BLACK BLECK SOLLY COOMB CROCK GRIME SMOOT SMITCH SMUTCH SMATTER SOLBRAND

SMUTCH BLOT SMIRCH SMITCH SMOUCH SMUDGE

SMUT GRASS TUSSOCK

SMUTTY BAWDY DIRTY SOOTY SULTRY BARNYARD FREUDIAN

SMYRNA USHAK

SNACK BIT CUT BAIT BITE SNAP TAPA CHACK CHECK SHARE SNICK TASTE GOUTER MUNGEY SNATCH NUNCHEON

SNAFFLE GAG

SNAG KNAG SNUG STUB POINT PLANTER SNAGGLE
(PL.) EMBARRAS

SNAIL HUA PILA SNAG CHINK DRILL HELIX OLIVA PHYSA SHELL THAIS TURBO WHELK CERION CONKER DODMAN NATICA PHYSID PURPLE TRITON WINKLE RISSOID UNICORN VERTIGO ZONITID CASSIDID ESCARGOT HODMADOD JANTHINA LYMNAEID MELANIAN NERITOID RAMSHORN SOLARIUM

SNAILFLOWER CARACOL

SNAKE (ALSO SEE SERPENT AND REPTILE) ASP BOA BOM NAG BOBA BOID BOMA JUBO NAGA NAJA SNIG ABOMA ASPIC COBRA CONGO CRIBO DRILL JIBOA KRAIT MAMBA PTYAS RACER SNECK TIGER VIPER BOIGID BONGAR CANTIL CHITAL DABOIA ELAPID GOPHER HISSER JESSUR KERRIL PYTHON ROLLER RUNNER TAIPAN WENONA ADJIGER ANILIID BOKADAM CAMOODI CRAWLER CREEPER CULEBRA DIAPSID HAGWORM LABARIA LANGAHA PRESTER RATTLER REGULUS REPTILE SERPENT SPITTER WALPAPI ANACONDA BONETAIL BUNGARUM CASCAVEL CERASTES CROTALID EGGEATER FLATHEAD HAIRWORM JARARACA KEELBACK MOCCASIN OPHIDIAN RINGHALS SNAKELET VIPERINE

SNAKEBARK IRONBARK

SNAKEBIRD DARTER PLOTUS ANHINGA DUCKLAR

SNAKEHEAD MURRAL

SNAKELIKE ANGUINE

SNAKEMOUTH POGONIA

SNAKEPIECE POINTER

SNAKEROOT STEVIA BABROOT BUGBANE SANGREL SANICLE SAWWORT POOLWORT RICHWEED WHITETOP

SNAKESKIN SPOIL HACKLE SLOUGH
(CASTOFF —S) EXUVIAE

SNAP SET ZIP BARK BITE CHOP GNAP HUFF JERK KNAP LIRP SETT BREAK CLACK FILIP FLICK GANCH KNACK KNICK SMACK SNACK BLUDGE SNAPPY SNATCH FASTENER PUSHOVER SNAPHEAD
(— **AT)** HANCH
(— **LIGHTLY)** KNICK
(— **OFF)** SNIP
(— **TOGETHER)** CRASH
(— **UP)** SNUP SNAFFLE
(— **WITH FINGER)** LIRP FILIP THRIP FILLIP

SNAPBACK PASSBACK

SNAPDRAGON BULL SNAPS BULLER BULLDOG DOGMOUTH

SNAPE FLINCH

SNAPPER UKU BRIM JOCU SESI BREAM PARGO VORAZ CUBERA HUSSAR JENOAR LAWYER NATIVE TAMURE ULAULA COCKNEY CRACKER BIAJAIBA CACHUCHO FLAMENCO GNATSNAP LUTIANID WILLOMAI SCHNAPPER

SNAPPING DOGGISH

SNAPPING BEETLE ELATER SKIPPER SNAPPER ELATERID SKIPJACK

SNAPPING TURTLE LOGHEAD SHAGTAIL

SNAPPISH CRUP EDGY PUXY CROSS SNACK TESTY WASPY CUTTED SNAGGY SNAPPY SNIPPY DOGGISH PEEVISH

SNAPPY CRISP JEMMY ZIPPY

SNARE GIN HAY NET PIT SET BUKE FANG GIRN GRIN HOOK LACE LIME TOIL TRAP WAIT WIRE BRAKE CATCH FRAUD GNARE LATCH LEASH SINEW SNARL SNIRL STALE SWEEK TRAIN COBWEB GILDER PANTER SNATCH SPRINT TREPAN TUNNEL ENSNARE OVERNET PITFALL SETTING SNICKLE SPRINGE BIRDLIME INVEIGLE LIMEBUSH SPRINGLE TENDICLE
(— **DEER)** WITHE
(— **FOR ELEPHANTS)** KEDDAH

SNARL ARR BITE CARL GIRN GNAR GURR HARL HURR NARR TWIT WAFF YARR GNARL GNARR GRILL KNURL RAVEL SNIRL TWINE BOWWOW BUMBLE GAUNCH MUCKER TANGLE VENNER GRIZZLE GRUMBLE

SNARLED SNAFU

SNARLER CYNIC

SNARLING LATRANT

SNATCH HAP NAB NIP GRAB HINT RACE RASE SNAP SNIP WHIP WRAP YERK YUCK BRAID CATCH CLAWK CLICK EREPT GANCH GRASP GRIPE PLUCK SNACK STRIP SWIPE SWOOP TWEAK WREST SNITCH STRIKE TWITCH WRENCH CLAUGHT GRABBLE SCAMBLE VULTURE

SNEAK GRUB LEER LOOP LOUT LURK PEAK PIMP SHUG SNIG LURCH MEECH SCOUT SHIRK SKULK SLIDE SLINK SLIPE SLIVE SLOKE SNEAP SNICK SNOOK BLIFIL MICHER WEASEL SLOUNGE SNIGGLE SNEAKSBY
(— **AWAY)** SLIPE
(— **OFF)** MAG SHAB
(**PRYING —)** SNOOP

SNEAKER CREEPER GUMSHOE

SNEAKING HANGDOG PEAKING SLIVING

SNEAKY FURTIVE MEECHING

SNEER SHY FLON GIBE GIRD GIRN GULE JEER JERK JIBE MOCK FLEER FLING FLOUT GLEEK JAUNT SCOFF SLARE SLEER SNIRT GIZZEN

SNEEST WRINKLE RIDICULE
SNEERING FRUMPERY
SNEEZE NEESE NEEZE ARREST
(— AT) CONDEMN DESPISE
SNEEZEWEED ALANT ROSILLA
HELENIUM
SNEEZEWOOD NIESHOUT
SNEEZEWORT HARDHEAD
PTARMICA
SNEEZING PTARMIC
SNELL SNOOD TIPPET GANGING
SNICK TIP SNECK
SNICKER TITTER SMIRKLE SNIGGER
SNIGGLE
SNIFF NOSE TIFT VENT WIND SMELL
SNAFF SNIFT SNUFF SNIVEL
SNAFFLE SNIFFLE SNOTTER
SNIFTER SLUG BALLOON INHALER
SNIGGER WHICKER
SNIGGLE BRAGGLE
SNIP CUT CLIP CROP SHRED SNICK
SNIPE JACK NICK WISP SCAPE SNITE
WADER WILLET BLEATER BLITTER
DOWITCH HUMILITY LONGBILL
SHADBIRD
SNIPER TEASER BUSHWACK
SNIVEL BUBBLE SNIFFLE SNIFTER
SNOTTER SNUFFLE
SNOB SNAB SNOOT FLUNKY
SHONEEN SNOBBER
SNOBBISH DICKTY SNOBBY SNOOTY
UPSTAGE
SNOOK SNOOT ROBALO
SNOOP PRY PEEK PEEP SNEAK
BREVIT PIROOT GUMSHOE
SNOOPER CREEP BUSYBODY
SNOOPY CURIOUS
SNOOZE SLEEP SNOOZLE
SNORE ROUT SNARK SNORK SNORT
SNOCKER SNOTTER
SNORING STERTOR RHONCHUS
SNORT BLOW ROUT SNUR TOOT
VENT FNESE SNARK SNEER SNORE
SNORK WHOOF EXCLAIM SNIFTER
SNOCKER SNORKEL SNORTLE
SNOTTER
SNOUT NEB SAW BILL NOSE WROT
GROIN SNOOT MUFFLE MUZZLE
NOZZLE GRUNTLE ROSTRUM
SNOUT BEETLE CURCULIO
SNOUT MITE BDELLID
SNOW CORN DRIP GRUE COVER
SPOSH STORM SUGAR WHITE
POWDER COCAINE GRAUPEL
RAMPART WEATHER SCOUTHER
WINDSLAB
(— PELLETS) GRAUPEL
(— SLIGHTLY) SPIT
(DISSOLVING —) FLUSH
(DRIFTED —) WINDLE
(GLACIER —) FIRN NEVE BLIZZ
(HEAVY FALL OF —) PASH
(MUSHY —) SLOB
(NEW-FALLEN —) MANNA
(PARTLY MELTED —) SLUSH
(WHIRLING —) SKIRL
SNOWBERRY MOXA WAXBERRY
SNOWBIRD JUNCO
SNOW BUNTING OATFOWL

SNOWBIRD SNOWFOWL
SNOW COCK JERMONAL
SNOWDRIFT YOWDEN
SNOWDROP TREE BELLWOOD
COWLICKS TISSWOOD
SNOWFALL PASH SKIFF SKIFT
FLURRY ONDING
SNOWFLAKE FLAG FLAUCHT
SNOW FLEA PODURAN PODURID
SNOW GOOSE WAVY
SNOWINESS NIVOSITY
SNOW LEOPARD IRBIS
SNOWLESS GREEN
SNOWMAN YETI
SNOW MOUNTAIN JOKUL
SNOWSHOE WEB PATIN PATTEN
RACKET RACQUET
SNOWSTORM PURGA DRIFTER
BLIZZARD
SNOWY NIVAL WHITE NIVEOUS
SNUB AIR RITZ SLAP SNIB FRUMP
SNEAP SWANK REBUFF REBUTE
SIMOUS SLIGHT SNOUCH SNUBBY
SETDOWN
SNUBBING MAIL
SNUBBY PUGGISH
SNUB-NOSED SIMOUS
SNUFF TOP VENT MUSTY SNIFF
SNUSH TABAC COHOBA PULVIL
RAPPEE SNEESH STIFLE SNUFFLE
BERGAMOT MACCABOY ORANGERY
SMUTCHIN
SNUFFBOX MILL
SNUFFBOX BEAN CACOON
SNUFFER PRICK DOUTER TOPPER
PRICKER
SNUFFLE SNIVEL SNAFFLE SNIFFLE
SNIFTER
SNUG LEW RUG BIEN COSH COZY
NEAT TAUT TEAT TOSH TOSY
CANNY CLOSE COUTH POVIE QUEME
TIGHT PENTIT COUTHIE SNUGGERY
SNUGGISH
SNUGGLE SNUG BURROW CUDDLE
SNUDGE CROODLE SNUZZLE
SNUGLY SHORT COSILY
SO SAE SUCH THAT THIS THUS
THISSEN INSOMUCH SUCHWISE
THUSWISE
(— AM I) LIKEWISE
(— BE IT) AMEN
(— FAR AS) QUOAD
(— TO SPEAK) FAIRLY
(NOT —) SECUS
(QUITE —) EXACTLY
SOAK RET SOB SOD SOG SOP WET
BOWK BUCK SIPE BINGE DROUK
DROWN SOUSE STEEP TOAST
DRENCH EMBAIN IMBIBE IMBRUE
SEETHE SODDEN SPONGE INSTEEP
MICKERY SWELTER SATURATE
(— A CASK) GROG
(— FLAX) RET RATE
(— IN) SOP FEATHER
SOAKED SOGGY SOPPY SOBBED
SODDEN WATERY DRUNKEN
SOBBING DRAGGLED
SOAKING BATH SUING SOGGING
INFUSION

SOAP SAPO SUDS CHIPS STOCK
NIGGER CASTILE TALLATE WINDS(
SANDSOAP
(CAKE OF —) TABLET TABULATE
(LIQUID —) FIT
SOAPBARK QUILLAI SOAPWOOD
SOAPFISH JABON
SOAP PLANT AMOLE PALMILLO
SOAPROOT SOAPWEED
SOAPSTONE ALBERENE STEATITE
SOAPSTONER TALCER
SOAPWORT BORITH COWHERB
SAPONARY SOAPROOT SOAPWEEI
SOAR FLY STY KITE FLOAT MOUNT
PLANE SPIRE TOWER ASPIRE
AIRPLANE
SOARING FLIGHT ICARIAN SPIRING
ESSORANT
SOB YEX SIKE SNOB SNUB SOUGH
BLUBBER SINGULT
SOBBING GREET
SOBER SAD CALM COOL SAGE CIV
FRESH GRAVE QUIET STAID DOUL
SEDATE SEVERE SOLEMN SOMBEI
STEADY EARNEST PENSIVE
REGULAR SERIOUS UNFOXED
DECOROUS MODERATE
SOBRIETY DRYNESS GRAVITY
SOBRIQUET BYNAME HAWKEYE
SO-CALLED ALLEGED
SOCCER FOOTER FOOTBALL
SOCIABLE COSY CHUMMY CLUBB
FOLKSY SOCIAL AFFABLE AMIABL
INNERLY CLUBABLE FAMILIAR
FELLOWLY INFORMAL
SOCIAL DISTAL SUPPER SOCIABLE
SOCIETAL
(— WORKER) ALMONER
SOCIALISM ETATISM MARXISM
GUESDISM
SOCIALIST FABIAN NIHILIST
SOCIALIZE CIVILIZE
SOCIETY BUND HALL HERD SANG
GUILD MONDE SABHA SAMAJ SAⁿ
SOKOL MENAGE NANIGO PARISH
SYSTEM VEREIN ACADEMY COLLE
COLORUM COMPANY COUNCIL
KINGDOM SOCIETE THIASOS
EXCHANGE HETAERIA PRECINCT
SOCIETAS SODALITY SORORITY
(— OF RELIGIOUS FANATICS)
COLORUM
(CHORAL —) CHOIR
(CLOWN —) KOSHARE KOYEMSHⁿ
(CRAFT —) ARTEL
(DEBATING —) POP
(GYMNASTIC —) SOKOL
(HIGH —) SWELLDOM
(LITERARY —) HALL
(RELIGIOUS —) CHURCH
(SECRET —) HUI EGBO HOEY POⁿ
TONG LODGE OGBONI PURRAH
(UTOPIAN —) ANARCHY
SOCINIAN RACOVIAN
SOCIOLOGY DEMOTICS
SOCK BOP ONE BIFF BUST HOSE
VAMP ANKLET ARGYLE VAMPEY
STOCKING
(— OF GOAT'S HAIR) UDO

(INFANT'S —) BOOTEE BOOTIE
(JAPANESE —) TABI
)CKET BOX CUP PAD POD BUSH
CELL HOSE LEAD NOSE SHOE CHAIR
POINT SHANK BUCKET BUDGET
COLLET EYEPIT NOZZLE POCKET
SAUCER SCONCE ALVEOLE
COCKEYE FERRULE FUTCHEL
GUDGEON THIMBLE TORULUS
ALVEOLUS DRAWHEAD
(— FOR LANCE) PORT
(— FOR LENS) CELL
(— FOR MOUTHPIECE) BIRN
(— IN GOLF CLUB HEAD) HOSE
HOSEL
(— OF BONE) POT
(— OF HINGE) PAN
(— OF MILLSTONE) INK COCKEYE
(— OF WATER PIPE) BELL
(BIT —) POD
)CLE ZOCCO
)CRATES (— METHOD) MAIEUTIC
)D HUB BEAT DELF FAIL FLAG
SCAD SONK TURF DELPH GAZON
GLEBE SCRAW SWARD CLOWER
TERRON SODDING
)DA BARILLA
)DA POP TONIC
)DDEN SAMMY SAPPY SOGGY
POACHY DRAGGLED
)DIUM NA SODA NATRIUM
)DIUM BICARBONATE SODA
BICARB
)DIUM BORATE BORAX
)DIUM CARBONATE SODA TRONA
ANATRON BARILLA SALSODA
)DIUM CHLORIDE SALT HALITE
)DIUM THIOSULFATE HYPO
)DOMITE DOG BUGGER SPINTRY
BOUGERON
)EVER SOME
)FA BOIST COUCH DIVAN SQUAB
CANAPE LOUNGE SETTEE
CAUSEUSE SOCIABLE
)FFIT GATHER PLANCIER
)FT COY TID FEIL LASH LIMP LUSH
MILD MURE NASH PLUM SART TOSY
WAXY WEAK BALMY BLAND CUSHY
DABBY DOLCE DOWNY FAINT GIVEY
HOOLY LENIS LIGHT MALMY MELCH
MUSHY PADDY PAPPY PIANO PLIFF
SILKY SLACK SMALL SOAPY SOOTH
SWASH SWEET WAXEN WETHE
YAPPY CASHIE CREAMY EFFETE
LAGGY FLOSSY FLUFFY GENTLE
LYDIAN MELLOW PIPING PLACID
SAMMEL SIDDER SILKEN SLOPPY
SOFTLY SPONGY SPOONY TENDER
INDURE CLEMENT COTTONY
DUCTILE FLESHLY LENIENT
SQUASHY CUSHIONY FEMININE
LEXIBLE HOTHOUSE LADYLIKE
ARCENET SQUELCHY TRANQUIL
(— AND FLEXIBLE) FLOPPY
(— AND LIFELESS) DOUGHY
(— IN TEXTURE) SUPPLE
VERY —) SQUASHY
FT-COVER PAPERBACK
)FTEN CUT CREE MELT SOAK

SOFT TAME ALLAY BATCH BREAK
FRIZZ LITHE MALAX TOUCH WOKIE
DIGEST GENTLE LENIFY PACIFY
RELENT SOOTHE SUBDUE SUBMIT
TEMPER WEAKEN APPEASE
ASSUAGE CUSHION LENIATE
MOLLIFY QUALIFY SWEETEN
UNSTEEL AMOLLISH ATTEMPER
ENFEEBLE HUMANIZE MITIGATE
MODULATE PALLIATE PRETTIFY
(— BY BOILING) CREE
(— BY KNEADING) MALAX
(— BY STEEPING) MACERATE
(— COLOR) CUT SCUMBLE
(— FIBERS) BREAK
(— GRADUALLY) SQUAT
(— JUTE) BATCH
(— LEATHER) BREY FRIZ FRIZZ
(— METAL) ALLAY
(— TONE) SURD
SOFTENED ROXY ANODYNE
FLEXUOUS
SOFTENING LENIENT MALACIA
BLETTING
SOFTER MANCANDO
SOFTHEARTED TENDER
SOFTLY BAJO SOFT FAIRLY GENTLY
SWEETLY CREAMILY TENDERLY
SOFTNESS SOFT MOLLITIES
(— IN COAL SEAM) LUM LUMB
SOFT-SHELLED TURTLE FLAPPER
FLIPPER FLAPJACK
SOFT-SOAP CON
SOFT-SPOKEN MEALY
SOGGY SAD DUNCH SOBBY SODDEN
SPONGY WATERY
SOIL DAG DUB MUD RAY SOD BLOT
BLUR CLAY CLOD DAUB DIRT DUST
FOIL FOUL GRIT LAND MIRK MOOL
MOSS MUCK MURK MUSS SAUR SILE
SLUR SMUT SOOT TASH BULLI
CROCK EARTH GLEBE GRIME
GUMBO LAYER MUCKY ROSEL
SLUSH SMEAR SOLUM SOULE
SPARK STAIN SULLY BARING
BEDAUB BEMIRE BEMOIL GROUND
PODZOL SLURRY SMIRCH SMOOCH
SMUDGE SPLASH SUDDLE BEGRIME
BENASTY BESMEAR BESMOKE
BETHUMB FEWMAND POLLUTE
REGOSOL SEEDBED TARNISH
TRACHLE AGROTYPE ALLUVIAL
BEDABBLE BESMIRCH BUCKSHOT
FLYSPECK LATERITE RENDZINA
WOODCOCK
(— ABOVE CLAY) KELLY
(— DEPOSITED BY WIND) ELUVIUM
(— FORMED BY DECAY) GEEST
(— INTERMEDIATE BETWEEN SAND
AND CLAY) ROSEL
(— PREPARED FOR SOWING) TILTH
(— REMOVED FROM ORE) BARING
(— WITH GREASE) LARD
(AGGREGATE —) PED
(ALKALINE —) SOLONETZ
(ASHLIKE —) PODSOL PODZOL
(CLAYEY —) GALT MALM MAUM
ADOBE SOLOD SOLOTH
(DRY —) GROOT

(FRIABLE —) CRUMB
(GRAVELLY —) ROACH GROWAN
(HARD —) RAMMEL
(INFERTILE —) GALL
(LEACHED —S) LATOSOL
(PLUMBER'S —) SMUDGE
(POROUS —) SPONGE
(POTTING —) COMPOST
(PRAIRIE —) BRUNIZEM
(SILTY —) GUMBO
(SPRINGY —) WOODSERE
(ZONAL —) SEROZEM SIEROZEM
SOILAGE SOIL SMUDGE SOILING
SOILED FOUL BLACK DINGY DIRTY
MUSSY SOOTY TARRY SMUDGY
SMUTTY SNUFFY THUMBED
DRAGGLED SHOPWORN
SOIL-EXPOSING EROSIVE
SOIREE EVENING
SOJOURN LIE BIDE STAY STOP
ABIDE ABODE TARRY RESIDE
ALLODGE MANSION STATION
SOJOURNER PILGRIM
SOKOL FALCON
SOL SOH SOU ALCOSOL EMULSOID
HYDROSOL SOLUTION
SOLA SHOLA PAUKPAN
SOLACE CHEER CHEERER COMFORT
SWEETEN SOLUTION
SOLAR SOLLER SOLARIUM
(— SYSTEM APPARATUS) ORRERY
SOLAR DISK ATEN ATON
(CENTER OF —) CAZIMI
SOLD SELT BOOKED
(ILLICITLY —) BOOTLEG
SOLDER PALE BRAZE FLOAT
SOWDER SPELTER
SOLDERER BROGUER
SOLDERING IRON COPPER DOCTOR
SOLDIER SON TAP BLEU BOLO
GOUM GUGU KERN LEVY SHOT
SWAD TULK WART BERNE CROAT
FRITZ GUARD GUFFY KHAKI LANCE
LIMEY LINER MINER NIZAM PERDU
PIKER PIVOT POILU SAMMY SWEAT
TOLKE TOMMY TOPAS ASKARI
BONAGH BUMMER DARTER DIGGER
EXPERT GALOOT GUNNER GURKHA
HAIDUK HEINIE HOSTER LANCER
MARKER PIETON REITER SENTRY
SKIEUR SOLDAT SWADDY THRASO
WEAPON ZOUAVE BILLJIM BLIGHTY
BRIGAND CARABIN CATERAN
CORSLET DARTMAN DOGFACE
DRAGOON FEDERAL FEEDMAN
FIGHTER GENETOR GOUMIER
HOBBLER INVALID MATROSS
ORDERLY PALIKAR PANDOUR
PAVISOR PIKEMAN POLTAST
PRIVATE REDCOAT REGULAR
REISTER SCARLET SLINGER
SOLDADO STRIKER TROOPER
VETERAN WARRIOR ARQUEBUS
BEZONIAN BLUECOAT BUCKSKIN
BUFFCOAT CAMELEER CAVALIER
DESERTER FENCIBLE FUGLEMAN
FUSILIER GALLOPER GENDARME
GRAYBACK GRAYCOAT IRONSIDE
JANIZARY KHANDAIT LANCEMAN

LINESMAN MILITANT MIQUELET MUSTACHE PIOUPIOU RAPPAREE SENTINEL SERVITOR SILLADAR SPEARMAN SWORDMAN TOLPATCH TRANSFER TRIARIAN WARFARER WHIFFLER YARDBIRD
(— OF MUSCOVITE GUARD) STRELITZ
(— WITH SIDE WHISKERS) BADGER
(ALBANIAN —) PALIKAR
(ALGERIAN —) ARBI
(ANT —) MAXIM
(AUSTRALIAN —) ANZAC DIGGER BILLJIM
(BOMBAY —S) DUCKS
(BRITISH —) LIMEY TOMMY BLIGHTY LOBSTER REDCOAT
(BRUTAL —) PANDOUR
(COWARDLY —) CAPITANO
(FILE OF 6 —S) ROT
(FILIPINO —) GUGU
(FOOT —) KERN PAGE PEON PIETON FOOTMAN TOLPATCH
(GERMAN —) HUN FRITZ HEINE KRAUT HEINIE
(GREEK —) EVZONE HOPLITE
(INCOMPETENT —) BOLL
(INDIAN —) SEPOY GURKHA
(INVALID —) FOGY FOGEY
(IRREGULAR —) CATERAN JAYHAWK MIQUELET SILLADAR
(MOROCCAN —) ASKARI
(MOUNTED —) LANCER DRAGOON GENETOR LOBSTER TROOPER VEDETTE CAVALIER
(OLD —) GROGNARD
(PROFESSIONAL —) SAMURAI
(REVOLUTIONARY —) REDCOAT BUCKSKIN
(ROMAN —S OF THIRD LINE) TRIARY TRIARII
(RUSSIAN —) IVAN
(SCOTTISH —) JOCK
(TURKISH —) NIZAM REDIF
(PL.) FOOT ELITE TERZO TROOP TERTIA CATERVA ENOMOTY MILITIA VELITES FORAGERS INFANTRY SOLDIERY
SOLDIERLY WARLIKE
SOLDIERY HORSE MILITIA SEBUNDY MILITARY SIBBENDY
SOLE CORK FACE GADE MERE ONLY SLIP SOCK SPUR AFALD ALONE CLUMP OLEPI PELMA WHOLE GADOID INSOLE ONLEPY PLANTA SINGLE SOLEYN SULLEN THENAR TONGUE UNIQUE ANACANTH FLATFISH HOGCHOKE MARYSOLE SINGULAR SOLITARY
(— A SHOE) SPECK
(— FOR WALKING OVER SAND) BACKSTER
(— OF BIRD'S FOOT) PTERNA
(— OF FOOT) PLAT VOLA PELMA PLANT
(— OF PLANE) FACE
(— OF PLOW) SLADE
(HALF —) SHOULDER
(TOWARD THE —) PLANTAD

SOLELY SOLE ALONE SIMPLY SINGLY WHOLLY SHEERLY ENTIRELY
SOLEMN DEEP SAGE BUDGE SOBER DEVOUT FORMAL RITUAL EARNEST SERIOUS WEIGHTY FUNEREAL
SOLEMNITY OBIT RITE SACRE GRAVITY SEVERITY
SOLEMNIZE KEEP SEAL
SOLEMNLY GRAVE HIGHLY
SOLENODONT AGOUTA ALMIQUE
SOLEPIECE SOLE GIRDER
SOL-FA SOLMIZATE
SOLICIT ASK BEG SUE WOO DRUM MOVE SEEK TOUT URGE APPLY COURT CRAVE TREAT ACCOST HUSTLE INVITE INVOKE BESEECH CANVASS ENTREAT IMPLORE INSTANT PROCURE REQUEST APPROACH PETITION
SOLICITATION SUIT QUEST CANVASS INSTANT SOLICIT ENTREATY INSTANCE
SOLICITOR LAWYER WRITER ADVOCATE TRAMPLER
SOLICITOUS URGENT CAREFUL CURIOUS JEALOUS DESIROUS CONCERNED
SOLICITUDE CARE FEAR HEED PAIN YEME HEART WORRY ANXIETY CONCERN BUSINESS JEALOUSY
SOLID DRY SAD CONE CUBE FAST FIRM FULL HARD CHAMP LEVEL MASSY MEATY SOUND STIFF STOUT THICK TIGHT SECURE STABLE STRONG STURDY COMPACT CUPRENE UNIFORM CONSTANT GROUNDLY MATERIAL STERLING
(GEOMETRICAL —) CONE CUBE PRISM CONOID CUPROID FRUSTUM (PL.) POCHE
SOLIDARITY CIVILITY
SOLIDIFIED SOLID HARDENED
SOLIDIFY DRY SET JELL SHOOT HARDEN COMPACT STIFFEN CONCRETE
SOLIDITY SADNESS FASTNESS FIRMNESS HARDNESS
SOLIDLY FIRMLY SQUARE STOUTLY GROUNDLY
SOLIDUS BEZANT NOMISMA DIAGONAL HYPERPER
(HALF —) SEMIS
SOLIPSISM EGOISM
SOLITAIRE CLARINO CANFIELD KLONDIKE NAPOLEON PATIENCE SOLITARY
SOLITARY ODD WAF LONE SOLE ALONE ELYNG LONELY ONLEPY SAVAGE SINGLE SOLEYN SULLEN EREMITE PRIVATE RECLUSE UNCOUTH WIDOWED DESOLATE EREMITIC ISOLATED LONESOME SECLUDED SEPARATE
SOLITUDE PRIVACY RETREAT SOLITARY
SOLLERET SABBATON
SOLO ARIA CALL ARIOSO CAVATINA SPADILLA

SOLOMON ISLANDS (CAPITAL OF —) HONIARA
(ISLAND OF —) BUKA TULAGI MALAITA CHOISEUL
SOLOMON'S SEAL LILY SEALWORT
SOLOMON SAM KOHELETH
SOLON SAGE GNOMIC GNOMIST SENATOR LAWMAKER
SOLSTICE SUNSTAY SUNSTEAD
SOLUBLE FRIM FRUM FIXED SOLUTE SOLVABLE
SOLUTION IT LYE AQUA EUSOL STAIN TINCT ACETUM ANSWER ASSOIL DOCTOR ERASER SALINE EXTRACT EYEWASH LACQUER RESOLVE SOLUTIO WORKING ANALYSIS LEACHATE TINCTURE
(— ADDED FOR GOOD MEASURE) INCAST
(— OF CHESS PROBLEM) COOK
(— OF FERMENTED BRAN) DRENCH
(— OF GUM TRAGACANTH) BED
(ALCOHOLIC —) ESSENCE
(PICKLING —) SOUSE
(PRESERVING —) BOLIN
(SALINE —) BRINE
(SOAP —) NIGRE
(STERILE —) JOHNIN
(VISCOUS —) GLUE
(WATERY —) EAU SAF
SOLVE DO FIX READ UNDO WORK BREAK CRACK LOOSE SALVE ANSWER ASSOIL CIPHER FIGURE REDUCE RIDDLE SOLUTE RESOLVE UNRAVEL DECIPHER DISSOLVE
SOLVENT ETHER ELUENT SPIRIT ACETONE ALCOHOL BENZINE COUPLER DILUENT REMOVER SPOTTER CARBITOL SOLVABLE STRIPPER TETRALIN
(UNIVERSAL —) ALKAHEST
SOMALI SOMAL SHUHALI
(PL.) ASHA
SOMALIA (COIN OF —) BESA
(DIVISION OF —) HAWIYA
(MEASURE OF —) TOP CABA CHEL DARAT TABLA CUBITO
(MOUNTAIN RANGE OF —) GUBAN
(NATIVE OF —) GALLA HAWIYA ISBAAK SOMALI DANAKIL
(RIVER OF —) JUBA NOGAL SCEBE
(TOWN OF —) MERCA BERBERA HARGEISA KISIMAYU
(WEIGHT OF —) PARSALAH
SOMATIC SOMAL BODILY
SOMBER SAD DERN DULL GRAVE SOBER GLOOMY LENTEN SOLEMN SOMBRE SULLEN AUSTERE SERIOU DARKSOME SOMBROUS
SOME ANY ODD THIS CERTAIN
SOMEBODY QUIDAM SOMEONE
SOMEDAY ONCE
SOMEHOW HOW ONEHOW SOMEW/ SOMEGATE
SOMEONE SUCH
SOMERSAULT FLIP TOPPLE FLIFFU SPOTTER TWISTER BACKFLIP SOMERSET
SOMETHING WHAT ALIQUID

WHATNOT SOMEWHAT
(— ABNORMAL) FREAK
(— ADDED) IMP EXTRA DOCTOR
(— ATTRACTIVE) DUCK
(— BELIEVED) CREDIT
(— BIG) BOUNCER
(— BRIGHT RED) CORAL
(— CHERISHED) APPLE
(— COMMONPLACE) DROSS
(— CONSECRATED) SACRUM
(— CONTRARY TO LOGIC) ALOGISM
(— CORRUPT) CARRION
(— COUNTERFEIT) DUFFER
(— DIFFICULT) STINKER
(— DISLIKED) DOGMEAT
(— DONE) GERENDUM
(— ELABORATE) DEVICE
(— ELUSIVE) FUGITIVE
(— EXCELLENT) DANDY
(— EXCESSIVE) LUXUS
(— EXTRAORDINARY) SNORTER
(— FALSE) HOOEY
(— FAMILIAR) KNOWN
(— FIRST-RATE) CHEESE
(— FLAWED) CRIPPLE
(— FOOLISH) IDIOCY FATUITY
(— FORGOTTEN) CORPSE
(— FORKED) CORNUTE
(— FRAUDULENT) CROSS
(— HORRIFYING) SHOCKER
(— IDENTICAL) ISOMORPH
(— ILL-DEFINED) BLOB
(— IN ADDITION TO ORDINARY)
BONUS
(— INCOMPLETE) END
(— INFERIOR) DOG CULL LESS
CAGMAG
(— INJURIOUS) ENEMY
(— INSIGNIFICANT) STRAW
FEATHER SNICKET FRAGMENT
(— INTRICATE) KNOT
(— LARGE) GIANT SMASHER
(— MADE UP) FIGMENT
(— NOT ESSENTIAL) FRILL
(— NOT EXPLAINED) MYSTERY
(— NOTABLE) DEUCE
(— OF GREAT VALUE) EYETOOTH
(— OF LITTLE VALUE) SHUCK
FOUTER FOUTRA
(— OF NO VALUE) HAW DAMN
BAUBEE DOCKEN
(— OFFERED FOR LOAN) PREMIUM
(— OR OTHER) ANYTHING
(— OUTSTANDING) BROTH DOYEN
GASSER STANDOUT
(— PAINFUL) GAFF
(— PATCHED UP) VAMP
(— POOR) FLUMMERY
(— PRECIOUS) DUMPLING
(— PREJUDICIAL) FOE
(— PROVOKING) DEVIL
(— REPELLENT) SPINACH
(— RISKED) HAZARD
(— SHAPELESS) DUMP
(— SHOWY) FLOSS
(— SHRIVELED) SCRUMP
(— SMALL) DOT SNIP
(— SPECTACULAR) DILLY
(— STICKY) CAB

(— STOLEN) CRIB
(— STRANGE) FANTASIA
(— SUPERLATIVE) DARB
(— TAUGHT) DOCUMENT
(— THAT IS LIGHT) SKIFF SKIFT
(— THAT WHIRLS) GIG
(— TO BIND BARGAIN) EARNEST
(— TRIVIAL) CHIP FLUFF
(— UNDECIDED) ACRISY
(— UNINTELLIGIBLE) GREEK
(— UNPLEASANT) GUCK SOUR
(— UNSPECIFIED) ITEM
(— UNSUBSTANTIAL) FROTH
(— UNTRUE) HOKUM
(— USELESS) CRAP BLANK
(— VILE) DUNG
(— WORTHLESS) BOTH DUST
HOKUM DUFFER AMBSACE
(— WRITTEN) SCRIPT
SOMETIME FORMER SOMDEL
WHILOM ANCIENT QUONDAM
SOMEDEAL SOMEPART SOMEWHEN
SOMETIMES NOW TOO WHILE
WHILES UMQUHILE
SOMEWHAT BIT SOME RATHER
SLIGHT SUMMAT ALIQUID
SOMEDEAL
SOMEWHERE SOMERS SOMEGATE
SOMITE ZONITE SEGMENT TERGITE
GONOTOME MEROSOME MESOMERE
SOMATOME
SOMNIFEROUS OPIATE SOMNIFIC
SOMNUS HYPNUS
SON BEN BOY LAD ANAC FILS FITZ
ZONE CHILD KIBEI MOPSY FILIUS
JUNIOR REUBEN EPAPHUS
EPIGONUS MONSIEUR
(— OF CHIEF) OGTIERN
(— OF KING OF FRANCE) DAUPHIN
(— OF NISEI) SANSEI
(— OF PEER) MASTER
(— OF SUDRA) CHANDALA
(DAVID'S FAVORITE —) ABSALOM
(FOURTH —) MARTLET
(ILLEGITIMATE —) NEPHEW
(YOUNG —) MOPSY
(YOUNGER —) CADET
SONAR ASDIC
SONCHUS DINDLE
SONG AIR DIT JIG LAY UTA CANT
DUAN FOLK GATO GLEE LEED MELE
NOTE RANT RUNE SANG TUNE
BLUES CANSO CAROL CHANT
CROON DILDO DITTY MELOS MOLPE
VOCAL BALLAD BRANLE BUBBLE
CANTIC CANZON CARMEN CHANTY
CHORUS HIMENE JINGLE MELODY
ORPHIC SHANTY STRAIN VINATA
WAIATA WARBLE BACCHIC BALLATA
CANCION CHANSON COMIQUE
DESCANT MELISMA MELODIA
REQUIEM REVERDI ROMANCE
SCOLION SONGLET THRENOS
BIRDSONG BRINDISI CANTICLE
CANZONET COONJINE FLAMENCO
JUBILATE PALINODE RHAPSODY
SERVENTE SINGSONG ZORTZICO
(— ACCOMPANYING TOAST)
BRINDISI

(— FOR TWO VOICES) GYMEL
(— OF BASQUES) ZORTZICO
(— OF BIRD) LAY KOLLER
(— OF JOY) CAROL PAEAN
JUBILATE
(— OF MINSTREL) YEDDING
(— OF OCEANIA) HIMENE
(— OF PRAISE) HYMN CAROL
ANTHEM CHORALE
(— UNACCOMPANIED) GLEE
(— WITH MONOTONOUS RHYME)
VIRELAI VIRELAY
(—S OF BIRDS) RAMAGE
(ANDALUSIAN —) SAETA
(ART —) LIED
(BOAT —) JORRAM
(CEREMONIAL —S) AREITO
(CRADLE —) HUSHO
(CUBAN —) GUAJIRA COMPARSA
(DANCE —) BALLAD BAMBUCO
(DRINKING —) BACCHIC WASSAIL
(EVENING —) SERENA EVENSONG
SERENATA
(FOLK —) SON FADO FOLK BLUES
DOINA BYLINA CANTIGA JUBILEE
(FUNERAL —) DIRGE MONODY
EPICEDE THRENODY
(FUNEREAL —) ELEGY
(GAY —) LILT
(GERMAN —) LIED
(HAWAIIAN —) MELE
(HEBREW —) HATIKVAH
(IMPROMPTU —) SCOLION
(JAPANESE —) UTA
(LOVE —) CANSO CANZO FANCY
AMORET AUBADE SERENA
SERENATA
(MELISMATIC —) DIVISION
(MOCKING —) JIG
(MORNING —) MATIN AUBADE
(MOURNFUL —) DUMP PLAINT
ENDECHA
(NEW ZEALAND —) WAIATA
(NIGHT —) COMPLIN
(NO —S) UTAI
(NUPTIAL —) HYMEN
(PART —) CHACE TROLL CACCIA
CANZONET FROTTOLA MADRIGAL
(PASTORAL —) OAT
(PLAIN —) GROUND
(PORTUGUESE —) FADO
(RELIGIOUS —) HYMN CAROL
PSALM SHOUT ANTHEM POLYMNY
SIRVENT
(SAILOR'S —) CHANTY SHANTY
(SANSKRIT —) GITA
(STUPID —) STROWD
(VINTAGE —) VINATA
(WORK —) HOLLER
(PL.) ZEMMI AREITO
SONGBIRD CHAT IORA LARK WREN
MAVIS ROBIN SABIA SIREN VEERY
VIREO BULBUL CANARY LINNET
MOCKER ORIOLE SINGER THRUSH
CATBIRD GRASSET WARBLER
BENGALEE BLUEBIRD BOBOLINK
CARDINAL SONGSTER
SONGSTER SINGER WARBLER
SONG THRUSH MAVIE MAVIS

SON-IN-LAW GENER MAUGH
SONOROUS SHILL TONOUS
OROTUND VIBRANT RESONANT
SOUNDFUL SOUNDING
SONOROUSLY DEEPLY
SONSHIP FILIETY
SOOLOOS THULUTH
SOON ERE ANON CITO TITE EARLY
NEWLY RADLY RATHE BELIVE
SUDDEN TIMELY BETIMES ERELONG
PRESTLY SHORTLY DIRECTLY
SPEEDILY
SOONER ERE ERER ERST FIRST
BEFORE TITTER
(— **STATE**) OKLAHOMA
(— **THAN**) OR ERE
SOONEST ERST RATHEST
SOOT COOM IZLE SMUT STUP SUMI
BLECK BROOK COLLY COOMB
CROCK GRIME SOTIK FULIGO
SMOUCH SMUTCH SPODIUM
(— **ON GRATE BAR**) STRANGER
SOOTHE COY DEW BALM CALM DILL
EASE HUSH LULL ACCOY ALLAY
CHARM DULCE HUMOR QUELL
SALVE STILL BECALM PACIFY
SETTLE SMOOTH SOLACE STROKE
SUPPLE ADDULCE ASSUAGE
COMPOSE CONSOLE DEMULCE
FLATTER GRUNTLE LULLABY
PLASTER QUALIFY ATTEMPER
MITIGATE UNRUFFLE
SOOTHER ANODYNE
SOOTHING MILD BALMY BLAND
DOWNY DULCE STILL SWEET
ANIMAL DREAMY DULCET GENTLE
SMOOTH ANODYNE BALSAMIC
SEDATIVE
SOOTHSAY SORT
SOOTHSAYER SEER AUGUR WEIRD
ARIOLE DIVINE ARUSPEX DIVINER
CHALDEAN HARUSPEX TIRESIAS
SOOTY COLLY SMUTTY BROOKIE
COLLIED
SOOTY ALBATROSS NELLIE
QUAKER STINKER BLUEBIRD
STINKPOT
SOOTY SHEARWATER TITI
SOP SPONGE SUGARSOP SWEETSOP
SOPHER SCRIBE
SOPHISM FETCH ELENCH FALLACY
SOPHEME
SOPHIST SOPH DUNCE
SOPHISTICATE GARBLE MONDAINE
SOPHISTICATED WISE BLASE CIVIL
SALTY SVELTE WORLDLY
SOPHISTICATION CHIC
SOPHISTRY DECEIT FALLACY
SOPHISM
SOPORIFIC DWALE DROWSY OPIATE
SLEEPY HYPNOTIC NARCOTIC
SOMNIFIC
SOPPY JUICY SOAKY
SOPRANO CANARY TREBLE
DESCANT CASTRATO
SORB LUSATIAN
SORBIAN WENDISH
SORBOSE ACROSE
SORCERER MAGE BOYLA BRUJO

WITCH BOOLYA NAGUAL VOODOO
WIZARD KORADJI WARLOCK
WIELARE FETISHER MAGICIAN
WITCHMAN
(PL.) GOETAE
SORCERESS BRUJA CIRCE LAMIA
WITCH ARMIDA HECATE BABAJAGA
KORRIGAN WALKYRIE
SORCERY OBI MAGIC SPELL
MAKUTU PISHOGUE PRESTIGE
SORTIARY WIGELING WITCHERY
WITCHING
(**VOODOO** —) WANGA OUANGA
SORDES SABURRA
SORDID RAW BASE GAMY MEAN VILE
DIRTY DUSTY MUCKY CHETIF
GRUBBY SODDEN MESQUIN SQUALID
CHURLISH
SORE BUM FOX PET BUBA CHAP
DEAR GALL KIBE KYLE OUCH BLAIN
BOTCH GAMMY AGNAIL BITTER
BOUBAS CANKER FESTER MELLIT
MORMAL RANKLE TAKING CATHAIR
CHANCRE SORANCE SCALDING
(— **ON HORSE'S FOOT**) MELLIT
(**ARTIFICIAL** —) FOX
(**SUMMER** —**S**) CALORIS LEECHES
SORENESS FROG
SORGHUM CANE CUSH MILO BATAD
DARSO DURRA SORGO CHOLAM
HEGARI IMPHEE KAFFIR SHALLU
FETERITA KAOLIANG
SOROCHE PUNA
SORREL OCA OKA SORE CUCKOO
HEARTS OXALIS RUBICAN SOUROCK
ALLELUIA STABWORT
SORREL TREE TITI ELKWOOD
SOURWOOD
SORROW WO RUE WOE BALE CARE
DOLE HARM MOAN RUTH SORE
TEEN DOLOR GRAME GRIEF MOURN
RUING SARRA UNWIN GRIEVE
LAMENT MISERY REGRET STOUND
UNLUST ANGUISH CONDOLE
DEPLORE PENANCE REGRATE
REMORSE THOUGHT TROUBLE
WOEFARE CALAMITY DISTRESS
DOLEANCE DREARING EGRIMONY
MOURNING
SORROWFUL BAD SAD WAN CHARY
DREAR TRIST WOFUL DISMAL
DOLENT DREARY RUEFUL DOLEFUL
LUCTUAL RUESOME UNHAPPY
WAILFUL CONTRITE DESOLATE
DOLESOME DOLOROSO GRIEFFUL
MOURNFUL PITIABLE
SORROWFULLY SADLY WRATH
HEAVILY
SORRY BAD SAD WOE HURT VEXED
UNFAIN PITIFUL CONTRITE
WRETCHED
SORT KIN LOT BRAN COMB GERE
HUMP KIND RANK SUIT WING WORK
BRACK BREED GENUS GRADE
SAVOR SPICE ASSORT BARREL
DILLUE GARBLE GENDER KIDNEY
MANNER MISTER NATURE STRAIN
STRIPE FASHION SPECIES SPECKLE
VARIETY CLASSIFY SEPARATE

(— **COTTON BY STAPLE**) STAPLE
(— **MAIL**) CASE
(— **MERCHANDISE**) BRACK
(— **OF PERSON**) LIKE
SORTER SHALEMAN
SORTIE ISSUE SALLY ATTACK
OUTFALL
SORTILEGE LOT
SORTING GARBLING
(— **ROOM**) SALLE
SORVA BORRACHA
SOT LUSH SOAK DRUNK LOURD
TOPER LOURDY BLOTTER DASTAR*
TOSSPOT DRUNKARD
SOTHO SUTO SESUTO
SOTIK SOOT
SOUFFLE FONDU FONDINE
SOUGHT QUESITED
SOUL BA EGO ALMA ANIMA ATMAN*
GHOST HEART SHADE BUDDHI
DIBBUK NATURE PNEUMA PSYCHE
SPIRIT SPRITE NEPHESH PURUSHA*
INTERNAL
(—**S OF THE DEAD**) LEMURES
(**ANIMAL** — **IN MAN**) NEPHESH
(**DISEMBODIED** —) KER
(**EGYPTIAN IMMORTAL** —) BA
(**INDIVIDUAL** —) JIVA
(**LIBERATED** —) KEVALIN
(**UNIVERSAL** —) HANSA
(**WANDERING** —) DIBBUK DYBBUK
SOULFULLY GEISTLICH
SOULLESS TURNIPY
SOU MARQUE STAMPEE
SOUND GO CRY FIT BLOW DING
DRIP FAST FERE FIRM FLOG GLU(
GOOD HAIL HALE KYLE NOTE RIN*
SAFE SANE TEST TONE TRIG WIS*
AFFIX BLAST BUGLE CHEEP FLICK*
FRESH GLIFF GLUCK GRIND GROF*
HODDY NOISE PLANG PLUMB PRO*
RIGHT SLUSH SOLID SPANG SPAN*
SPEAK SWASH VALID WHOLE
BICKER BIRDIE DORSAL ENDING
ENTIRE FATHOM FAUCAL HEARTY*
INTACT LAGOON ROBUST SIGNAL
SINGLE SONANT SPLASH STABLE
STURDY HEALTHY HEARING
HURLING PERFECT PHONEME
PLUMMET SCRATCH SONANCE
VOCABLE FLAWLESS FOOTFALL
GRINDING GROUNDLY LAUGHTER
RELIABLE SEARCHER SYLLABIC
WAKELESS
(— **A BAGPIPE**) DOODLE
(— **BELL**) PEAL RING KNELL KNO*
(— **DRUM OR TRUMPET**) TUCK
(— **FORTH**) BOOM
(— **IN GREEK AND LATIN**) AGMA
(— **IN MIND**) FORMAL
(— **INDEPENDENTLY OF THE**
PLAYER) CIPHER
(— **LESS LOUD**) FALL
(— **LIKE THUNDER**) BRONTIDE
(— **LOUDLY**) TANG LARUM
(— **MELODIOUSLY**) CHARM
(— **OF BAGPIPE**) DRONE
(— **OF BEATING**) RATAPLAN
(— **OF BELL**) DING PEAL RING

KNELL STROKE DINGDONG
TINGTANG
(— OF BIRD) JUG
(— OF BULLET) ZIP
(— OF CONTEMPT) HUMPH
(— OF CORK) CLOOP CLUNK
(— OF DISAPPROVAL) BOO HOOT
BAZOO
(— OF DOG) BOOK
(— OF DYING PERSON'S VOICE)
TAISCH
(— OF ENGINE) CHUG
(— OF EXPLOSION) BOUNCE
(— OF F) DIGAMMA
(— OF FLUTE) TOOTLE
(— OF GLOTTAL STOP) HAMZA
HAMZAH
(— OF HEN) CLUCK
(— OF HOG) GRUNT
(— OF HOOF) CLOP
(— OF HORN) BEEP TOOT
(— OF HORSE) BLOWING
(— OF PLUCKED STRING) TUM
(— OF POURING LIQUID) GLUG
GLUGGLUG
(— OF RAIN) SPAT
(— OF RENDING) SCAT
(— OF SHEEP) BAA BLEAT
(— OF STEAM ENGINE) CHUFF
(— OF STRAW OR LEAVES) RUSTLE
(— OF TRUMPET) CLARION
(— OF WIND IN TREES) WOOSH
(— OUT) FEEL
(—S HAVING RHYTHM) MUSIC
ABNORMAL —) BRUIT
ADVENTITIOUS —) RALE
BLOWING —) SOUFFLE
BRAWLING —) CHIDE
BUBBLING —) BLATHER
BUZZING —) Z WHIR WHIRR
CLICKING —) SNECK
CONSONANT —) ALVEOLAR
COOING —) CHIRR TURTUR
CRACKLING —) RISK
CRISP —) BLIP
CRUNCHING —) CRUMP SCRUNCH
DELICATE —) TINK TINKLE
DISCORDANT —) JAR BRAY JANGLE
DISTINCTIVE —) SONG
DULL —) CLONK FLUMP SQUELCH
EXPLOSIVE —) POP BARK CHUG
PUFF SNORT REPORT
FAINT —) PEEP GLIFF WHISHT
INKLING
FINAL —) AUSLAUT
GULPING —) GLUCK
GUTTURAL —) GROWL
HARSH —) JAR BRAY BLARE CLASH
CRANK TWANG SCROOP DISCORD
STRIDOR
HEAVY —) DUMP
HIGH-PITCHED —) TING
HISSING —) FIZZ SIZZ SWISH
SIZZLE
HOLLOW —) CHOCK THUNGE
HUMMING —) HUM BURR SUUM
DRONE SINGING
INDISTINCT —) BLUR SURD
INITIAL — OF WORDS) ANLAUT

(JINGLING —) SMIT
(LAPPING —) SLOOSH
(LIGHT REPEATED —) PITAPAT
(LOUD —) PEAL BLARE CLANG
CRASH CLANGOR
(LOW-PITCHED —) BASS
(MEANINGLESS —S) GABBLE
(MEDIAL —) INLAUT
(MENTALLY —) SANE WISE
(MOANING —) SUUM SOUGH
(MOURNFUL —) GROAN
(MUSICAL —) CHIME
(NASAL —) ANUSVARA
(NON-SIGNIFICANT —) GLIDE
(NONVIBRATORY —) FRICTION
(PLEASING —) EUPHONY EUPHONIA
(RASPING —) BUZZ SKIRR SCROOP
(REPEATED —) ECHO
(RESONANT —) BONG
(REVERBERATING —) PLANG
(RINGING —) CLANG CLANK CLING
TWANG RINGLE DINGDONG
(ROARING —) BEAL
(RUSHING —) SWOOSH HURLING
(RUSTLING —) FISSLE FISTLE
(SCRAPING —) GRIDE
(SHARP —) POP PING SNAP CHINK
CRAKE KNACK SPANG SQUIRK
(SHRILL —) CHEEP KNACK SKIRL
SCREED SQUEAK STRIDOR
(SHUFFLING —) SCUFFLE
(SIBILANT —) HISS SHISH SHUSH
(SLIGHT —) SWISH
(SNORING —) SNORK
(SOBBING —) YOOP
(SPEECH —) SURD DOMAL TENUE
VOWEL APICAL PHONEME
CEREBRAL
(SPLASHING —) LAP CHUNK FLURR
SPLAT SWASH
(SPOKEN —) BREATH
(SQUEAKY —) CREAK
(SQUELCHING —) SQUASH
(STRANGLED —) GLUB GLUG
(SWISHING —) SCHLOOP
(TELEPHONE —) SIDETONE
(TRAMPING —) STUMP
(TRILLING —) CHIRR CHIZZ
HIRRIENT
(TUNEFUL —) HARMONY
(UNPLEASANT —) BLOOP
(WARNING —) ALARM SIREN
ALARUM TOCSIN
(WHIRRING —) BIRR FLURR SKIRR
(WHISPERING —) SUSURRUS
(WHISTLING —) STRIDOR
SOUND-ABSORBENT ACOUSTIC
SOUNDBOARD BELLY
SOUNDER TICKER LEADMAN
SOUNDING RAWIN SONANT INKLING
SONDAGE SONATION
(— HARSH) BRAZEN
(— OF BELL) CURFEW
(— OF ORGAN PIPE) CIPHER
(— WITH REVERBERATIONS)
PLANGENT
SOUNDLY FAST TIGHT FIRMLY
SOUNDNESS SANITY FITNESS
SOBRIETY STRENGTH

SOUP BREE KAIL KALE BROTH
GUMBO POSOL BISQUE BORSCH
BURGOO JOUTES POZOLE BORSCHT
GARBURE MARMITE CONSOMME
GAZPACHO MINESTRA MORTREUX
(— UP) SUPE
(BARLEY —) SMIGGINS
(BEEFSKIN —) SKINK
(CABBAGE —) SHCHI STCHI
(CLEAR —) CONSOMME JULIENNE
(JELLIED —) GAZPACHO
(LARGE QUANTITY OF —) SLASH
(THICK —) BISK GUMBO HOOSH
PUREE BISQUE BURGOO CHOWDER
GARBURE POTTAGE HOTCHPOT
MORTREWES
(THIN —) BROTH
SOUR AWA DRY YAR ACID ASIM
CRAB DOUR FOXY GRIM GRUM
HARD TART TURN ACERB ACRID
AIGRE EAGER GOURY GRUFF MUSTY
TEART BITTER CRUETY CURDLE
PONTIC RUGGED SULLEN TORVID
ACETOSE ACIDIFY AUSTERE
SUBACID ACERBATE VINEGARY
(SLIGHTLY —) BLINK BLINKY
ACESCENT
SOURCE FONS FONT HAND HEAD
HIVE MINE RISE RIST ROOT SEED
FOUNT SPAWN SURGE AUCTOR
AUTHOR BOTTOM CENTER FATHER
FONTAL ORIGIN PARENT RESORT
STAPLE EDITION FOUNTAIN
WELLHEAD
(— OF AID) RECOURSE
(— OF ANCESTRAL LINE) STOCK
(— OF ANNOYANCE) BOGY BOGIE
HARROW BUGBEAR
(— OF ASSURANCE) FORTRESS
(— OF CONCERN) BUGABOO
(— OF CONFIDENCE) ANCHOR
(— OF DISPLEASURE) DISGUST
(— OF ENERGY) TAPAS
(— OF HAPPINESS) SUNSHINE
(— OF HARM) CURSE
(— OF HONOR) CREDIT
(— OF INCOME) TITLE REVENUE
(— OF INFORMATION) CHECK
(— OF INSPIRATION) CASTALIA
CASTALIE
(— OF LAUGHTER) SPLEEN
(— OF LIGHT) LAMP
(— OF NOURISHMENT) BREAST
(— OF POWER) STRENGTH
(— OF REGRET) SCATH SCATHE
(— OF STREAM OR RIVER) FILL
(— OF STRENGTH) HORN
(— OF SUPPLY) SHOP FEEDER
ARSENAL
(— OF TROUBLE) HEADACHE
(— OF WATER) BRON SPRING
(— OF WEALTH) GOLCONDA
KLONDIKE
(ENCLOSED —) FLOW
(FROM ANOTHER —) ALIUNDE
(MALIGNANT —) CANCER
(PHYSICAL —) MOTHER
(PRIMARY —) RADIX
SOURDOUGH LEAVEN

SOURED FOXY QUARRED
SOURNESS ACIDITY ACERBITY
ACRIMONY ASPERITY TARTNESS
VERJUICE
SOURSOP CORRESOL GUANABANA
SOURWOOD TITI ELKWOOD
SOUSE DIP DUCK TOSH STOOP
PLUNGE SOZZLE
SOUTANE SIMAR ZIMARRA
SOUTH MIDI AUSTER MIDDAY
MERIDIAN
(FARTHER —) BELOW

SOUTH AFRICA
BAY: ALGOA FALSE
CAPE: AGULHAS
CAPITAL: CAPETOWN PRETORIA
COIN: CENT RAND POUND FLORIN
LANGUAGE: BANTU HINDI TAMIL
TELUGU BUJARATI
MOUNTAIN: AUX KOP KATHKIN
INJASUTI
NATIVE: YOSA BANTU NAMAS
PONDO DAMARA SWAHILI
BECHUANA HOTTENTOT
PROVINCE: TRANSVAAL
RIVER: MODDER MOLOPO ORANGE
KURUMAM LIMPOPO OLIFANTS
TOWN: AUS MARA STAD BENONI
DURBAN SEVERN UMTATA
KOKSTAD MAFEKING

SOUTH CAROLINA
CAPITAL: COLUMBIA
COLLEGE: COKER FURMAN
LANDER CITADEL CLAFFIN
CLEMSON ERSKINE WOFFORD
COUNTY: AIKEN HORRY DILLON
JASPER OCONEE SALUDA
FORT: SUMTER
INDIAN: PEDEE SEWEE CUSABO
SANTEE WAXHAW CATAWBA
SUGEREE WATEREE CONGAREE
LAKE: MARION MURRAY CATAWBA
WATEREE HARTWELL MOULTRIE
MOUNTAIN: SASSAFRAS
NATIVE: WEASEL PALMETTO
PLATEAU: PIEDMONT
PRESIDENT: JACKSON
RIVER: BROAD EDISTO PEEDEE
SALUDA SANTEE ASHEPOO
SAVANNAH
STATE BIRD: WREN
STATE FLOWER: JESSAMINE
STATE TREE: PALMETTO
TOWN: AIKEN GREER UNION
BELTON CAMDEN CHERAW
CONWAY DILLON SENECA
SUMTER BAMBERG LAURENS
MANNING BEAUFORT FLORENCE
NEWBERRY WALHALLA

SOUTH CAROLINIAN WEASEL
PALMETTO

SOUTH DAKOTA
BUTTE: MUD CROW SULLY FINGER
SADDLE THUNDER DEERSEARS

CAPITAL: PIERRE
COLLEGE: HURON YANKTON
COUNTY: DAY BRULE MOODY
SPINK CUSTER JERAULD
YANKTON MELLETTE
INDIAN: BRULE SIOUX DAKOTA
CHEYENNE
LAKE: OAHE BIGSTONE TRAVERSE
MONUMENT: RUSHMORE
MOUNTAIN: BEAR SHEEP TABLE
CROOKS HARNEY MOREAU
NICKNAME: COYOTE
RIVER: JAMES MOREAU CHEYENNE
MISSOURI
STATE BIRD: PHEASANT
STATE FLOWER: PASQUE
STATE TREE: SPRUCE
TOWN: LEAD HURON CUSTER
EUREKA LEMMON MILLER
WINNER STURGIS WEBSTER
YANKTON ABERDEEN
DEADWOOD SISSETON

SOUTHERLY AUSTRINE
SOUTHERN SUDIC AUSTRAL
MERIDIAN SOUTHRON
SOUTHERN CROSS CRUX CROSS
CROSIER
SOUTHERNER CAVALIER SOUTHRON
SOUTHERN FRANCE MIDI
SOUTHERN ILLINOIS EGYPT
SOUTHERN INDIA DRAVIDA

SOUTH KOREA
BAY: KANGHWA
CAPITAL: SEOUL
COIN: WON HWAN
MOUNTAIN: CHIRI
RIVER: HAN KUM PUKHAN SOMJIN
NAKTONG YONGSAN
TOWN: MASAN MOKPO PUSAN
SUWON TAEGU CHINJU CHONJU
INCHON KUNSAN TAEJON
KWANGJU CHUNCHON

SOUTHLAND AUSTER
SOUTH SEA ISLANDER KANAKA

SOUTH VIETNAM
CAPITAL: SAIGON
LANGUAGE: CHAM KHMER RHADE
MEASURE: GANG PHAN THON
MOUNTAIN: BADINH NINHHOA
KNONTRAN NGOKLINH
TCHEPONE
NATIVE: CHAM MALAY
PORT: DANANG SAIGON QUINHON
NHATRANG
REGION: ANNAM COCHIN
RIVER: BA MEKONG DONGNAI
TOWN: HUE HOIAN ANNHON
DANANG QUINHON SONGCAN
TAYNINH PHANRANG QUANGTRI
VINHLOI
WEIGHT: CAN YET UYEN

SOUTHWESTER SQUAM

SOUVENIR RELIC TOKEN FAIRING
NICKNACK
SOVEREIGN BEY SIR SOV BEAN
CHAM CHIP FREE KHAN QUID SHAH
SKIV JAMES NEGUS NIZAM QUEED
CHAGAN COUTER GUINEA KAISER
KINGLY MASTER PRINCE SAMORY
SHINER SOLDAN SOVRAN SULTAN
CROWNED MONARCH ZAMORIN
DOMINANT IMPERIAL SUFFRAIN
SUZERAIN
(DIVINELY —) THEARCHIC
(FELLOW —) COUSIN
(HEAVENLY —) TENNO HEAVEN
(MOSLEM —) SOLDAN
SOVEREIGNTY SWAY CROWN REIGN
DIADEM EMPERY EMPIRE THRONE
DEMESNE DYNASTY KINGDOM
MAJESTY SCEPTER SCEPTRE
AUTARCHY DOMINION IMPERIUM
MONARCHY REGALITY REGNANCY
SOVRANTY
(— OF REASON) AUTONOMY
(JOINT —) SYNARCHY
SOVIET (ALSO SEE RUSSIA) VOLOST
COUNCIL GUBERNIA
SOW HOG GILT SEED SHED YILT
DRILL PLANT PLUMP STREW
CHANNEL GRUMPHY IMPLANT
OVERSOW SCATTER ENGENDER
INTERSOW SEMINATE
SOW BUG ISOPOD SLATER
ISOPODAN
SOWENS SONS SWEENS FLUMMERY
WASHBREW
SOWER SEEDER SEEDMAN
SEEDSTER SEMINARY
SOWING SATION SEMENCE
SEEDNESS
SOWN SEME SATIVE SEEDED
SEMEED
SOW THISTLE DINDLE GUTWEED
HOGWEED MILKWEED
SOY SHOYA SHOYU
SOYBEAN SOJA SOYA
SPA BATH CURE HYDRO
SPACE AREA BLUE CORD COSO
DENT FACE LUNG PALE RANK ROOM
SIDE VOID ABYSS BLOCK CHINK
CLEFT FIELD PLACE RANGE HIATUS
INDENT MATTER ROOMTH ARRANGE
FOREIGN GUNNIES LEGROOM
ROOMAGE SPACING SPATIUM
DIASTEMA DISTANCE EXOCOELE
INTERVAL
(— ABOVE EARTH) AIRSPACE
(— AMONG MUSCLES) SINUS
(— AROUND HOUSE) AMBIT
(— AT WHARF) BERTHAGE
(— BEHIND ALTAR) FERETORY
(— BETWEEN BED AND WALL)
RUELLE
(— BETWEEN BRIDGE PIERS) LOCK
(— BETWEEN CONCENTRIC
CIRCLES) ANNULUS
(— BETWEEN DECKS) LAZARET
(— BETWEEN EYE AND BILL) LORE
(— BETWEEN FEATHERS) APTERYLA

(— **BETWEEN FLUTINGS**) FILET FILLET GORGERIN
(— **BETWEEN FURROWS**) RIG
(— **BETWEEN PAGES**) GUTTER
(— **BETWEEN RAILROAD TIES**) CRIB
(— **BETWEEN SAW TEETH**) GULLET
(— **BETWEEN SHIP'S BOWS AND ANCHOR**) HAWSE
(— **BETWEEN STRANDS**) CANTLINE
(— **BETWEEN TEETH**) DIASTEMA
(— **BETWEEN THUMB AND LITTLE FINGER**) SPAN
(— **BETWEEN TIMBERS**) SPIRKET
(— **BETWEEN TWO WIRES**) DENT
(— **BETWEEN VEINS OF LEAVES**) AREOLA
(— **DEVOID OF MATTER**) VACUUM VACUITY
(— **FOR SECRETION**) BAG
(— **IN CHURCH**) KNEELING
(— **IN COIL OF CABLE**) TIER
(— **IN FOREST**) GLADE
(— **IN MINE**) GOB
(— **IN THEATER**) BOX
(— **IN TYPE**) CORE
(— **OCCUPIED**) VOLUME
(— **OF TIME**) DAY PULL STEAD GHURRY STITCH INTERVAL
(— **ON BILLIARD TABLE**) BALK BAULK
(— **ON COIN**) EXERGUE
(— **OVER STAGE**) FLIES
(— **OVERHEAD**) HIGH
(— **UNDER STAGE**) DOCK
(— **USED AS LIVING-ROOM**) LANAI
(— **WITHIN LIMITS**) CONTENT
(**AIR** —) CENTRUM
(**ARCHITECTURAL** —) METOPE PEDIMENT SACELLUM
(**BARE** — **ON BIRD**) APTERIUM
(**BLANK** —) ALLEY LACUNA
(**BOUNDLESS** —) INFINITE
(**CLEAR** —) FAIRWAY HEADWAY DAYLIGHT
(**COUNTER** —) BACKBAR
(**CRAMPED** —) CUBBY
(**EMPTY** —) AIR BLANK CAPACITY
(**ENCLOSED** —) AREA BOWL HATCH VERGE CHAMBER CIRCUIT CLOSURE COMPASS PTEROMA CLOISTER CONFINES
(**EUCLIDEAN** —) FLAT
(**FLAT** —) HOMALOID
(**LEVEL** —) PLATEA PARTERRE
(**NARROW** —) SLOT STRAIT
(**OPEN** — **OF WATER**) WAKE
(**OPEN** —) OUT LAWN ALLEY COURT LAUND TAHUA MAIDAN AREAWAY FAIRWAY LOANING APERTURE DAYLIGHT KNEEHOLE
(**OVERHANGING** —) DOME
(**POPLITEAL** —) HAM HOCK
(**ROOF** —) CELL
(**SEATING** —) CAVEA
(**SHELTERED** —) KILLOGIE
(**STORAGE** —) ATTIC
(**TRIANGULAR** —) SPANDREL
(**UNFILLED** —) GAP GAPE CAVITY HOLLOW BREAKAGE

(**VAULTED** —) ALCOVE
(**VERTICAL** —) HEADROOM
(**WORKING** —) COUNTER
SPACED MEATIC
SPACIOUS ROOM SIDE WIDE AMPLE BROAD RANGY ROOMY GOLDEN BARONIAL SCOPIOUS
SPADE DIG LOY FECK LILY PEEL PICK SPIT SPUD DELVE DIDLE GRAFF SLADE SLANE TRAMP DIGGER PADDLE SERVER SHOVEL TUSKAR GRAFTER SCAFFLE SCUPPIT SPADDLE SPITTER TWISCAR
(**LONG NARROW** —) LOY
(**PEAT** —) SLADE SLANE TUSKAR
(**PLASTERER'S** —) SERVER
(**TRIANGULAR** —) DIDLE
SPADEFISH POGY PORGY MOONFISH
SPADEFUL SPIT SPITFUL
SPAGHETTI PASTA SLEEVING
SPAGNUOLO LADINO

SPAIN

CAPE: AJO NAO GATA CREUS MORAS PALOS PENAS PRIOR DARTUCH ORTEGAL SALINAS TORTOSA ESPICHEL MARROQUI SACRATIF
CAPITAL: MADRID
COIN: COB DURO PESO REAL DOBLA CUARTO DINERO DOBLON ESCUDO PESETA ALFONSO CENTIMO PISTOLE REALDOR DOUBLOON
DIALECT: BASQUE CATALAN GALICIAN
ISLAND: IBIZA PALMA GOMERA HIERRO ALBORAN MAJORCA MINORCA MALLORCA TAGOMAGO TENERIFE
ISLANDS: CANARY BALEARIC
MEASURE: PIE CODO COPA DEDO MOYO PASO VARA BRAZA CAFIZ CAHIZ CARGA LEGUA LINEA MEDIO MILLA PALMO SESMA ARROBA CORDEL CUARTA ESTADO FANEGA RACION YUGADA AZUMBRE CANTARA CELEMIN ESTADEL PULGADA ARANZADA FANEGADA
MOUNTAIN: GATA ANETO ROUCH TEIDE ESTATS NETHOU TELENO BANUELO CERREDO PERDIDO ALMANZOR MONTSENY MULHACEN PENALARA
MOUNTAIN RANGE: CUENCA GREDOS MORENA TOLEDO ALCARAZ DEMANDA MONCAYO MALADETA MONEGROS PYRENEES
NAME: ESPANA IBERIA HISPANIA
NATIVE: CATALAN IBERIAN
PORT: ADRA NOYA VIGO CADIZ GADES GADIR GIJON PALOS ABDERA CORUNA MALAGA ALMERIA ALICANTE BARCELONA
PROVINCE: JAEN LEON LUBO ALAVA AVILA CADIZ SORIA

BURGOS CORUNA CUENCA GERONA HUELVA HUESCA LERIDA MADRID MALAGA MURCIA ORENSE OVIEDO TERUEL TOLEDO ZAMORA ALMERIA BADAJOZ CACERES CORDOBA GRANADA LOGRONO NAVARRA SEGOVIA SEVILLA VIZCAYA ALBACETE ALICANTE BALEARES PALENCIA VALENCIA ZARAGOZA
REGION: LEON ARAGON BASQUE MURCIA CASTILE GALICIA NAVARRE ASTURIAS CASTILLA VALENCIA
RIVER: SIL TER CEGA EBRO ESLA LIMA MINO TAJO ULLA ADAJA CINCA DOURO DUERO GENIL JALON JUCAR NAVIA ODIEL RIAZA SEGRE TAGUS TINTO TURIA ALAGON ARAGON ERESMA HUERVA JARAMA ORBIGO SEGURA TOROTE ALMERIA ALMONTE ARLANZA BARBATE CABRIEL DURATON GALLEGO HENARES MIJARES PERALES GUADIANA
TOWN: ASPE BAZA ELDA HARO IRUN JAEN LEON LUGO OLOT REUS ROTA SAMA VIGO BAENA BEJAR CADIZ CIEZA CUETA ECIJA EIBAR ELCHE GIJON IBIZA JEREZ JODAR LORCA OLIVA PALMA RONDA SIERO UBEDA XERES YECLA ZAFRA AVILES AZUAGA BILBAO BURGOS DUENCA GANDIA GERONA GETAFE GUADIX HELLIN HUELVA HUESCA JATIVA LERIDA LUCENA MADRID MALAGA MATARO MERIDA MURCIA ORENSE OVIEDO TERMEL TOLEDO UTRERA ZAMORA BADAJOS CORDOBA DAIMIEL GRANADA JUMILLA LINARES LOGRONO MANRESA SEGOVIA SEVILLA TARRASA VITORIA BADALONA FIGUERAS PAMPLONA SABADELL SANTIAGO TORRENTE VALENCIA ZARAGOZA
WEIGHT: ONZA FRAIL GRANO LIBRA MARCO TOMIN ADARME ARROBA DINERO DRACMA OCHAVA ARIENZO QUILATE QUINTAL CARACTER TONELADA
WINE: RIOJA SHERRY

SPALL SCALE SPAWL GALLET
SPAN ARCH BEAM PAIR CHORD SPANG SWING BRIDGE EXTEND SPREAD OPENING QUARTER BESTRIDE
(— **WITH FINGERS**) SPEND
(**UNSUPPORTED** —) BEARING
SPANDREL GROIN ALLEGE SPANDLE
SPANGLE AGLET PRANK SPANG SEQUIN CHEQUEEN SPANGLET ZECCHINO

SPANGLED POWDERED SPANKLED
SPANIARD DON DIEGO MULADI
SPANIEL TRASY COCKER SUSSEX
PAPILLON SPRINGER WATERRUG
SPANISH ALJAMIA
SPANISH-AMERICAN CHINO
SPANISH BAYONET IZOTE YUCCA
SPANISH HOGFISH LADYFISH
SPANISH JACINTH SCILLA
SPANISH JASMINE MALATI
SPANISH MACKEREL SIERRA
SPANISH PLUM SIRUELAS
SPANISH STOPPER IRONWOOD
SPANK PRAT SCUD SKELP SLIPPER
SPANKER DRIVER
SPANKING SMACKING
SPANNER KEY WRENCH
SPANNING ASTRIDE
SPAR BEAM BOOM CAUK CLUB GAFF
MAST RAFT SPUR YARD CABER
SPAAD SPATH SPELK SPRIT STODE
BOUGAR STEEVE BASTITE DERRICK
DOLPHIN JIBBOOM RIBBAND
BOWSPRIT LAZULITE
(BITTER —) DOLOMITE
(HEAVY —) CAUK BARITE BARYTE
SPARE BONY FAIK HAIN LEAN NICE
SAVE SLIM THIN FAVOR LANKY
SPELL LENTEN SKIMPY RESERVE
SLENDER PRESERVE
SPARGE PIPE WEEPER
SPARING CHARY GNEDE SCANT
SPARE DAINTY FRUGAL STINGY
ENVIOUS ECONOMIC SPAREFUL
(— OF WORDS) CURT
(NOT —) HANDSOME
SPARINGNESS PARCITY SCARCITY
SPARK FUNK IZLE AIZLE GRAIN
LIGHT PURSE SPERK SPUNK
FLANKER SPARKLE SPUNKIE
SPARKLET
(VITAL —) GHOST LIGHT
SPARKER IGNITER
SPARKLE FUNK SNAP WINK BLINK
FLASH GLENT GLINT SHINE SPARK
GLANCE KINDLE SIMPER CRACKLE
FLANKER GLIMMER GLISTEN
GLISTER GLITTER RADIATE SHIMMER
SKINKLE SPANGLE TWINKLE
SPRINKLE
SPARKLER TWINKLER
SPARKLING DEWY CRISP QUICK
SUNNY SPUNKY STARRY CREMANT
DIAMOND SHINING TWINKLY
MOUSSEUX SMIRKING SPERLING
(MAKE —) AERATE
SPARLING SMELT
SPARROW SPUG DICKY DONEY
FINCH HEMPY ISAAC PADDA PADDY
SPRIG SPRUG CHIPPY PHILIP
SPRONG TOWHEE CHANTER CHIPPIE
DUNNOCK FIELDIE HAYSUCK
PINNOCK SPADGER SPURDIE
TITLENE TITLING TITTLIN ACCENTOR
FIRETAIL HAIRBIRD WHITECAP
SPARROW HAWK MUSKET
SPARHAWK
SPARSE BALD THIN MEAGER SCANTY
THRIFTY

SPARTAN LACONIC
SPASM QUALM TONUS ENTASIA
FLUTTER RAPTURE SPASMUS
MYOTONIA PAROXYSM
(— OF PAIN) GRIP
(—S OF WHALE) FLURRY
(TONIC —) HOLOTONY
SPASMODIC FITFUL SNATCHY
SPASMIC SPASTIC SPURTIVE
SPAT SEED BROOD JOWER GAITER
LEGGING BOOTHOSE BOOTIKIN
SPATE SLUICE
SPATHE CYMBA SHEATH
SPATHIC SPARRY SPATHOSE
SPATIAL STERIC
SPATTER DASH JAUP BERAY SKIRP
SLART SPARK SPURT DABBLE
SPLASH SQUIRT BESPAWL BESPETE
SHATTER SMATTER SPATTLE
SPIRTLE SPLATTER SPRINKLE
(— WITH FOAM) EMBOSS
(— WITH MUD) JAP BEMUD SPARK
SPATTERDASH SPAT BONNET
GAITER CUTIKIN LEGGING
BOOTHOSE BOOTIKIN
SPATTERDOCK DUCK CLOTE TUCKY
WOKAS NUPHAR BONNETS
CANDOCK
SPATULA SPAT SLICE THIBLE THIVEL
CESTRUM SPATTLE SPLATTER
SPAVIN JACK SPAVIE VARISSE
SPAWN RUD RAUN REDD RUDD SILE
SPORE TODDER
SPAWNEATER SHINER
SPAWNING SICK MILKY SEEDING
SPAY FIX GELD ALTER DESEX SPADE
CHANGE SPEAVE CASTRATE
SPEAK ASK CUT SAY CANT CARP
MEAN MOOT MOVE TALE TALK TELL
WORD BREAK MOUTH NEVEN ORATE
PARLE SOUND SPELL SPIEL UTTER
ACCENT PARLEY PATTER QUETHE
SERMON SPEECH SQUEAK TONGUE
ADDRESS BESPEAK DECLAIM
DELIVER EXCLAIM PARRALL
CONVERSE REHEARSE
(— ABUSIVELY) JAW
(— AFFECTEDLY) MIMP KNACK
(— AGAINST) ACCUSE GAINSAY
FORSPEAK
(— ANGRILY) ROUSE CAMPLE
(— AT LENGTH) DISSERT ENLARGE
(— BROKENLY) FALTER
(— CAJOLINGLY) COLLOGUE
(— CONFUSEDLY) HATTER CLUTTER
SPLATHER
(— CONTEMPTUOUSLY) SCOFF
(— CRITICALLY) LAUNCH
(— CURTLY) BIRK SNAP
(— EVIL) BLACKEN
(— FALSELY) ABUSE
(— FAMILIARLY) HOBNOB
(— FIRST TO) ACCOST
(— FOOLISHLY) PRATE GIBBER
(— HALTINGLY) HACK HAMMER
STAMMER
(— HOARSELY) CROAK CROUP
(— ILL OF) KNOCK DEPRAVE
DETRACT

(— IMPERFECTLY) LISP
(— IMPUDENTLY) CHEEK
(— IMPULSIVELY) BLURT
(— IN DRAWL) DRANT DRAUNT
(— IN JEST) FOOL
(— IN ONE'S EAR) HARK
(— IN POINTLESS MANNER) DROOL
(— IN STUMBLING WAY) STUTTER
(— IN UNDERTONE) WHISPER
(— IN WHINING VOICE) CANT
(— INDISTINCTLY) FUMBLE JABBER
MUFFLE MAUNDER SPLUTTER
(— INEPTLY) BUMBLE
(— INSOLENTLY) SNASH
(— LOUDLY) TANG
(— MINCINGLY) NAB MIMP
(— MONOTONOUSLY) DROLL
(— OF) CALL NEVEN MENTION
(— OUT) LEVEL SHOOT
(— PLAYFULLY) BANTER
(— POMPOUSLY) CRACK
(— PROFUSELY) PALAVER
(— QUERULOUSLY) CREAK
(— RAPIDLY) TROLL GIBBER JABBER
SQUIRT CHATTER
(— RESENTFULLY) HUFF
(— RHETORICALLY) DECLAIM
(— SARCASTICALLY) GIRD
(— SHORTLY) JERK
(— SLIGHTINGLY OF) BELITTLE
(— SLOWLY) DRAWL
(— THROUGH THE NOSE) SNAFFLE
(— TRUTH) SOOTHSAY
(— WITH EMPHASIS) DWELL
(— WITH LIPS CLOSED) MUMBLE
SPEAKEASY SHEBEEN
SPEAKER VOICE BRYTHON LOCUTOR
MOUTHER STYLIST EPILOGUE
SPEECHER
(ORATORICAL —) SPOUTER
(PUBLIC —) ORATOR STUMPER
SPEAKING STEVEN LOQUENT
SPELLING
(— ARTICULATELY) MEROP
MEROPIC
(— MANY LANGUAGES) POLYGLOT
(EVIL —) PRATING
SPEAR GAD DART FRAM GAFF PIKE
GRAIN LANCE REJON SHAFT STAFF
VALET AMGARN BORDUN BROACH
FIZGIG FRAMEA GIDJEE GLAIVE
WASTER ASSEGAI BOURDON
HARPOON IMPALER JAVELIN
TRIDENT VERUTUM EELSPEAR
GAVELOCK LANCEGAY STANDARD
WALSPERE
(EEL —) ELGER PILGER
(FISH —) GIG GAFF TREN POACH
FIZGIG GRAINS FISHGIG LEISTER
SNIGGER
(SALMON —) WASTER
SPEARFISH AGUJA GOGGLE MARLIN
BILLFISH LONGJAWS
SPEAR GRASS SPANIARD
SPEARHEAD BUNT GAFF SPUD
CORONAL
SPEARMINT MENTHE LABIATE
SPEAR-SHAPED HASTATE
SPEAR THROWER ATLATL

WOMMALA WOOMERAH
SPEARWORT BANEWORT
SPECIAL VERY EXTRA KHASS
CONCRETE ESPECIAL PECULIAR
SPECIFIC
SPECIALIST SWELL EXPERT HERALD
LEGIST ALTAIST ARABIST FAUNIST
FEUDIST GRECIAN OLOGIST
SURGEON AQUINIST ARBORIST
BANTUIST BOTANIST ETHICIST
GEMARIST GEOGNOST GEOMETER
HEBRAIST HOMERIST LATINIST
URBANIST
SPECIES FOLK FORM KIND SORT
BROOD CLASS EIDOS GENRE
ESPECE MANNER MISTER APOMICT
FEATHER SPECIAL ANALOGUE
GENOTYPE INDIGENE
(ATOMIC —) DAUGHTER
SPECIFIC EXPRESS SPECIAL TRIVIAL
CONCRETE ESPECIAL
SPECIFICALLY NAMELY
SPECIFICATION MENTION
SPECIFICITY HECCEITY
SPECIFIED SET GIVEN
SPECIFY DESIGN DETAIL ARTICLE
EXPRESS MENTION INDICATE
NOMINATE
SPECIMEN CAST TEST ESSAY
FACER MODEL SPICE CHANCE
SAMPLE SWATCH EXAMPLE ICOTYPE
ISOTYPE PATTERN SAMPLER
ALLOTYPE EXEMPLAR HOLOTYPE
HYPOTYPE IDEOTYPE INSTANCE
(ADDITIONAL —) COTYPE
(EXTRAORDINARY —) BENDER
(FEMALE —) GYNETYPE
(FINEST —) PEARL
(LARGE —) ELEPHANT
(SMALL —) SPRIG
SPECIOUS GAY FAIR FALSE WHITE
FACILE GLOSSY HOLLOW TINSEL
PAGEANT PLAUSIVE PROBABLE
SPURIOUS
SPECIOUSNESS DISGUISE
SPECK DOT PIN PIP MOTE SPOT
TICK WHIT BLACK GLEBE PLECK
APHTHA SPECKLE FLYSPECK
NUBECULA
(— IN LINEN) SPRIT
(— ON FINGERNAIL) GIFT
(BLACK —) DARTROSE
SPECKLE FLECK GARLE SPECK
MIZZLE PECKLE STIPPLE
SPECKLED SHELD FIGGED MAILED
MENALD SANDED BLOBBED
BRACKET PECKLED SPECKED
SPECKLY FRECKLED IRONSHOT
IRRORATE JASPERED STIPPLED
SPECTACLE POMP SHOW SPEC
BYSEN SIGHT CIRCUS DEVICE
OBJECT EYEMARK PAGEANT
SPECIES TAMASHA MONUMENT
NAUMACHY STERACLE
(ODD —) TRACK
(SORRY —) BIZEN BYSEN
(WATER —) AQUACADE
SPECTACLES PAIR SPECS BRILLS
LUNETS PEEPER SIGHTS GLASSES

GOGGLES WINKERS CHEATERS
SPECTACULAR VIEWY PAGEANT
SPECTATOR FAN VIEWER WITNESS
BEHOLDER OBSERVER OVERSEER
RAILBIRD VIEWSTER
(PL.) DEDANS
SPECTER BUG BOGY MARE BOGIE
BOGLE GHOST LARVA POOKA
SPOOK TAIPO BOGGLE EMPUSA
PHOOKA REDCAP SHADOW SPIRIT
SPOORN WRAITH BOGGART
BUGBEAR PHANTOM RAWHEAD
REDCOWL SPECTRE GUYTRASH
PHANTASM PRESENCE REVENANT
SPECTRUM
SPECTRAL SPOOKY GHOSTLY
SHADOWY
SPECULATE JOB STAG GAMBLE
PONDER CONSIDER RUMINATE
THEORIZE
SPECULATION THEORY THEORIC
VENTURE GAMBLING IDEOLOGY
(DISHONEST —) BUBBLE
SPECULATIVE ACADEMIC
SPECULATOR PIKER GAMBLER
PLUNGER SCALPER BUMMAREE
OPERATOR
SPECULUM METAL MIRROR DILATER
DIOPTER DIOPTRIC
SPEECH GOB LIP SAW SAY TAT TOY
COAX LEED REDE RUNE TALE
DUALA FRUMP GLOZE LEDEN LINGO
SERMO SPEAK SPELL SPOKE SQUIB
VOICE BREATH DILOGY EPILOG
GAELIC GASCON GILAKI JARGON
LEMOSI ORISON REASON SALUTE
STEVEN TONGUE ADDRESS
BROCARD EASTERN MEITHEI
ORATION VULGATE EPILOGUE
GALICIAN HARANGUE LANGUAGE
LOCUTION LOQUENCE MORAVIAN
QUESTION SONORITY SPEAKING
(— FORM) LEXEME
(— IN GREEK DRAMA) RHESIS
(— IN PLAY) SIDE
(— REDUCER) VOCODER
(AFFECTED —) CANT
(BITTER —) DIATRIBE
(BOASTFUL —) BLUSTER
(BOMBASTIC —) SQUIRT HARANGUE
(COARSE —) HARLOTRY
(CONFUSED —) SPUTTER
(CONTEMPTUOUS —) FRUMP
(IRRITABLE —) SNAP
(JAVANESE —) KRAMA
(LONG —) MONOLOG
(LONG-DRAWN —) TIRADE
(MOCKING —) TRIFLE
(OBSCURE —) ENIGMA
(OFFENSIVE —) INJURY
(PRETENTIOUS —) FUSTIAN
(ROUNDABOUT —) CIRCUIT
(SANCTIMONIOUS —) SNUFFLE
(SINGSONG —) CANT
(SLANDEROUS —) EVIL
(VAPID —) WASH
SPEECHIFIER SPOUTER
SPEECHLESS DUMB MUTE SILENT
SPEECHMAKING SPOUTING

(— TO GAIN APPLAUSE) BUNKUM
BUNCOMBE
SPEED BAT HIE RIP RUN FLEE FOOT
GAIT HIGH PACE PELT PIRR POST
TILT BLAST HASTE HURRY SMOKE
WHIRL ASSIST CAREER FOURTH
HASTEN STREAK QUICKEN WHIZZLE
AIRSPEED CELERITY DISPATCH
EXPEDITE FASTNESS MOMENTUM
RAPIDITY VELOCITY
(— OF NAUTICAL MILE) KNOT
(— OF PITCH) STUFF
(— UP) HASTEN CATALYZE
EXPEDITE
(AT FULL —) AMAIN
(AUTOMOTIVE —) LOW HIGH DRIVE
FIRST THIRD FOURTH SECOND
REVERSE
(DRIVING —) SWING
(GOOD —) BONALLY
SPEEDILY CITO SOON APACE RATHE
BELIVE BETIMES HYINGLY QUICKLY
TANTIVY
SPEEDING HURTLING
SPEEDWELL CATEYE HENBIT
FLUELLEN NECKWEED NICKWELL
SPEEDY FAST SOON HASTY QUICK
RATHE SWIFT RAKING SUDDEN
POSTING TANTIVY EXPEDITE
SPEEDFUL SPINNING
SPELEOLOGIST CAVEMAN
SPELL GO FIT HEX JAG HACK JINX
MOJO PULL RUNE TACK TAKE TIFF
TIME TOUR TURN BRIEF CHARM
CRAFT CRASH MAGIC PATCH SPACE
WANGA WEIRD WHEEL ACCESS
GLAMOR GOOFER GRIGRI GUFFER
MAKUTU MANTRA PERIOD SNATCH
STREAK CANTRIP SORCERY
SPELDER CANTRAIP EXORCISM
GREEGREE MALEFICE PISHOGUE
(— OF ACTIVITY) BOUT
(— OF EXERCISE) BREATHER
(— OF LISTLESSNESS) DOLDRUMS
(— OF SHIVERING) AGUE
(— OF WEATHER) SNAP SLANT
SEASON
(BREATHING —) BLOW
(BRIEF —) SNATCH
(DRINKING —) FUDDLE
(EVIL —) JINX
(FAINTING —) DROW DWALM
(NIPPING —) SNAPE
(STORMY —) FLAW
(VOODOOISTIC —) WANGA
SPELLBIND ENCHANT
SPELLBINDING BASILISK
SPELLING GRAPH WRITING
SPELT FAR EMMER FITCH SPELTZ
SPELTZ EMMER
SPEND COST DREE DROP LEAD
PASS STOW WARE WEAR DALLY
DREIE SERVE SHOOT TRADE
BESTOW BEWARE EXPEND LAVISH
OUTRUN CONSUME DISPEND
EXHAUST UNPURSE CONFOUND
CONTRIVE DISBURSE
(— FRUITLESSLY) DAWDLE
(— IN IDLENESS) DRONE

(— **LAVISHLY**) BLUE SPORT DEBAUCH
(— **MONEY**) MELT
(— **RECKLESSLY**) BLOW LASH
(— **SUMMER**) ESTIVATE
(— **TIME TEDIOUSLY**) DRANT
(— **TIME**) DREE FOOL DREIE
(— **WASTEFULLY**) SPILL SQUANDER
SPENDTHRIFT WASTER PANURGE ROUNDER SPENDER WASTREL PRODIGAL
SPENSER IMMERITO
SPENT DONE WEARY EFFETE OVERWORN
SPERM SEED SEMINIUM
SPERMACETI SPERM CETACEUM
SPERMOGONIUM PYCNIUM
SPERMOPHILE MARMOT SUSLIK
SPERM WHALE CACHALOT
SPET SIGNET SINNET
SPEW PUKE SPUE VOMIT
SPHAERIUM CYCLAS
SPHAGION HIERA
SPHAGNUM MUSKEG
SPHALERITE JACK BLENDE
SPHENODON HATTERIA
SPHERE ORB AREA BALL BOWL LOKA SHOT FIELD GLOBE RANGE SCOPE CIRCLE CROTAL DOMAIN HEAVEN REGION RUNDLE COUNTRY ELEMENT GLOBOID KINGDOM ORBICLE EARTHKIN EMPYREAL EMPYREAN MOVEABLE PROVINCE
(— **OF ACTION**) AMBIT ARENA WORLD DOMAIN
(— **OF ACTIVITY**) FIELD FRONT
(— **OF AUTHORITY**) DIOCESE
(— **OF INFLUENCE**) DOMAIN SATRAPY
(— **OF LIFE**) EARTH WORLD STATION
(— **OF OPERATION**) THEATER THEATRE
(— **OF WORK**) TITLE
(**CELESTIAL** —) CYCLE ELEMENT
(**ENCOMPASSING** —) AMBIENT
(**MAGNETIZED** —) EARTHKIN TERRELLA
(**METAL** —) HAMMER
(**SMALL** —) ORBICLE SPHERULE
(**TINKLING** —) CROTAL
SPHERICAL ORBIC GLOBAL ROTUND GLOBATE GLOBOSE ORBICAL SPHERIC GLOBULAR
SPHERULE GLOBULE VARIOLE
SPHINX MUSTANG COLOSSUS HAWKMOTH
SPICA AZIMECH
SPICCATO PIQUE
SPICE MACE VEIN AROMA CLOVE EPICE TASTE GINGER NUTMEG PEPPER SEASON STACTE SPICERY SPICING ALLSPICE CINNAMON SEASONER
SPICEBUSH BENZOIN SNAPWOOD
SPICED SPICY POWDERED
SPICKNEL MEW SCLERE BEARWORT
SPICULE OXEA TOXA ASTER CHELA CYMBA DESMA DIACT SIGMA SPINE

STYLE ACTINE ANCHOR MONACT SCLERE STYLUS TRIACT TRIPOD TYLOTE CALTROP DIACTIN EUASTER HEXAXON MONAXON PINULUS SPERULA SPICKLE TETRACT TORNOTE TRIAENE TRIAXON TYLOTUS HEXASTER ISOCHELA OXYASTER POLYAXON SCLERITE SPHERULA SPICULUM STRONGYL TETRAXON TRICHITE TYLASTER
SPICY RACY SEXY GAMEY NUTTY SWEET SPICED GINGERY FRAGRANT SPICEFUL
SPIDER BUG COB ARAIN ATTID COBBE COPPE LOPPE NANCY TAINT ANANSI ARRAND EPEIRA HUNTER KATIPO WEAVER ARANEID CREEPER DRASSID JAYHAWK KNOPPIE POKOMOO RETIARY SERPENT SKILLET SOLDIER SPINNER ARACHNID ATTERCOP CTENIZID DICTYNID ETTERCAP KARAKURT ORBITELE PHALANGY PHOLCOID SALTICID SOLPUGID TELARIAN ULOBORID VENANTES WANDERER TARANTULA
SPIDER CRAB MAIAN MAIID
SPIDERFLOWER QUARESMA
SPIDER MONKEY SAJOU COAITA SAPAJOU
SPIDERWORT TRINITY
SPIELER BARKER
SPIGOT TAP SPILE DOSSIL DOZZLE STOPCOCK
SPIKE GAD BROB PICK PIKE PILE SPUR TINE PITON ROUGH SPEAR MOOTER PRITCH SPADIX SPIKER TENTER ALICOLE GADLING PRICKER PRICKET TRENAIL TURNPIN SPIKELET STROBILE WHEATEAR
(— **OF CEREAL**) EAR
(**BRACTED** —) AMENT
(**DRIED** —**S**) CANNABIS
SPIKED SPICATE SPINDLED
SPIKELET CHAT ALICOLE LOCUSTA SPICULE
SPIKENARD PHU NARD ARALIA SUMBUL ARALIAD IVYWORT SPIGNET SPIGNUT
SPILE TAP SPILL FOREPOLE
SPILL LET DRIP SHED SLOP FLOSH SCALE SPILE SQUAB STAVE JIRBLE PURLER SLATTER SLOBBER TURNOVER
(— **FOR LIGHTING PIPES**) FIDIBUS
SPIN CUT BIRL DRAW GYRE HURL PIRL PURL SCREW SPONE TWIST WEAVE WHIRL FOLLOW GYRATE VRILLE WAMBLE TWIZZLE TEETOTUM
(— **AND MAKE HUM**) BUM
(— **AROUND**) SWING
(— **ON BASEBALL**) STUFF
(— **ON BILLIARD BALL**) SIDE
(— **OUT**) SHOOT
(— **SILK**) THROW
(— **SMOOTHLY**) SLEEP
(— **UNEVENLY**) TWITTER
SPINACH SAVOY EPINARD OLITORY POTHERB

SPINAL CORD AXION NUCHA MYELON
(**WHITE MATTER OF** —) ALBA NUKE
SPINDLE PIN AXLE HASP SPIT STEM STUD ARBOR FLOAT QUILL SPIKE SPILL VERGE BOBBIN BROACH CANNON FUSEAU BOLSTER MANDREL SPINNEL TRENDLE WHARROW
(**AXLE** —) ARM
(**FOURTH OF** —) HASP
(**ONE 24TH OF** —) HEER
SPINDLE TREE GAITER DOGWOOD PEGWOOD EUONYMUS
SPINDLING SPEARY SPINDLY SPIRLIE
SPINDLY LEGGY PULING
SPINE HORN PIKE PILE SETA SPUR CHINE PRICK QUILL SPEAR SPIKE SPINA THORN ACUMEN CHAETA RACHIS ACANTHA ACICULA FULCRUM GLOCHIS PAXILLA PRICKER PRICKLE ROSTRUM SPINULE ACICULUM BACKBONE ILLICIUM PAXILLUS PELELITH SPICULUM SPINELET
(— **OF SURGEON FISH**) TUCK
(**CURVATURE OF** —) LORDOSIS
SPINEL BALAS CANDITE ESPINEL VERMEIL PICOTITE SPINELLE
SPINELESS SLAVISH
SPINET ESPINET GIRAFFE OCTAVINA SOURDINE VIRGINAL
SPINNERET GALEA MAMMULA SPINNER
SPINNING LANIFICE
(— **WEB**) TELARIAN
SPINNING JENNY MULE JENNY
SPINNING MULE IRONMAN
SPINNING WHEEL TURN CHARKHA CHURRUCK
SPINSTER TABBY VIRGIN
SPINULE(PL.) CTENII
SPINY PICKED THORNY
SPINY OYSTER SPONDYLE
SPINY RAT OCTODONT
SPIRACLE STOMA STIGMA BLOWHOLE
SPIRAEA MAY ROSACEAN
SPIRAL COIL CURL GYRE SPIN SCREW SNARE SPIRE BUTTON GURGES LITUUS SCREWY SCROLL SPIRED TWIRLY VOLUTE HELICAL ROLLING SPIROID STROPHE WINDING WREATHY GYROIDAL HELICINE HELICOID
SPIRANT VAU WAW HISS OPEN DURATIVE
SPIRANTHES IBIDIUM
SPIRE SHAFT SIKAR SPEAR TAPER TOLLY BROACH FLECHE PRICKET SHIKARA SIKHARA SPIRALE SPIRELET
SPIRE-BEARER SPIRIFER
SPIREME SKEAN SKEIN
SPIRIT GO FLY NAG VIM AITU AKUA ALMA ATUA BRIO DASH DOOK ELAN FIRE GALL GIMP HYLE JINN LIFE MARC MARE MIND MOOD SOUL

TONE ZEMI ZING AGIEL ARDOR
ARIEL ASURA AZOTH CHEER DEMON
DHOUL DJINN DOBBY ETHOS FLING
GEIST GHOST GORIC GUACA HAUNT
HEART HOLDA HUACA JINNI LARVA
NUMEN PLUCK POWER PRETA
RALPH SAINT SHADE SHRAB SPOOK
SPUNK VERVE ASTRAL ASUANG
BOTTOM BREATH CHULPA COURIL
DAEMON ESPRIT FAINTS FYLGJA
GENIUS GINGER INWARD KOBOLD
LESHEY METTLE MORALE ORISHA
PNEUMA PYTHON SPRAWL SPRITE
TAFFIA WRAITH ALCOHOL BRAVERY
CONTROL CORDIAL COURAGE
ENTRAIN EUDEMON KNOCKER
MANITOU PISACHI PURUSHA
RAPPIST SMEDDUM STOMACH
CALVADOS ERDGEIST FAMILIAR
FOLLETTO PHANTASM SPIRACLE
SPIRITUS
(— DWELLING IN JEWEL) AZOTH
(— DWELLING IN MINES) KNOCKER
(— HAUNTING PRINTING HOUSES)
RALPH
(— OF DEAD) CHINDI CHINDEE
(— OF DEATH) CHULPA
(— OF DECEASED) AKH
(— OF FERTILITY) YAKSA YAKSHA
YAKSHI
(— OF HOSTILITY) ANIMUS
(— OF LOYALTY) PIETAS
(— OF MAN) AKH
(— OF ONE WHO HAS MET VIOLENT
DEATH) PISACHI
(— OF PHYSICAL HEART) AB
(— OF TRAGEDY) COTHURN
(— OF UNBAPTIZED BABE) TARAN
(— WHICH ACTUATES CUSTOMS)
ETHOS
(—S OF LOWER WORLD) INFERI
(—S OF THE DEAD) MANES
(ANCESTRAL —) ANITO KATCHINA
(ARDENT —) RAK RACK ARRACK
(ASTRAL —) AGIEL ASTRAL JOPHIEL
UUCHATON
(AVENGING —) FURY ALECTO
ALASTOR MEGAERA
(COMBATIVE —) SWORD
(DISEMBODIED —) KUEI KWEI SOUL
GHOST LARVA SHADE ASUANG
SPECTER SPECTRE
(DIVINE —) ISVARA ISHVARA
(EARTH —) ERDGEIST
(EFFULGENT —S) ARDORS
(EMANCIPATED —) MUKTATMA
(EVIL —) DEV HAG IMP OKI BAKA
BENG BOKO BOLL DEVA DUSE
MARA OKEE ASURA BUGAN DAEVA
DEMON DEVIL JUMBY OTKON
DAITYA DIBBUK DYBBUK LILITH
AHRIMAN BUGGANE CASZIEL
INCUBUS KANAIMA SHAITAN
SHEITAN SKOOKUM WINDIGO
ASMODEUS BAALPEOR BEELPEOR
HOBOMOCO
(FAMILIAR —) FLY GENIUS HARPIER
(FEMALE —) DUFFY DUPPY DUSIO
HOLDA UNDINE BANSHEE ATAENSIC

BABAJAGA BELFAGOR BELFAZOR
(FIGHTING —) DEVIL
(FOREST —) MIMING
(FULL OF —) CRANK
(FULL OF —S) BRAG
(GOOD —) EUDEMON
(GOVERNING —) ANIMUS
(GUARDIAN —) ANGEL TOTEM
FYLGJA NAGUAL
(HIGH —) GINGER COURAGE
(HIGH —S) CREST GAIETY HEYDAY
ELATION
(HOSTILE —S) LEMURES
(HOUSEHOLD —S) LARES PENATES
(HUMAN —) JIVATMA
(IMPISH —) PO
(IMPURE —) FAINTS
(IN VIGOROUS —S) FIERCE
(LOW —S) DUMP BLUES DISMALS
(MALEVOLENT —) BHUT GORIC
LARVA
(MALICIOUS —) DOBBY
(MALIGNANT —) IMP KER GYRE
DEMON
(MANLY —) SPLEEN
(MISCHIEVOUS —) KOBOLD
TIKOLOSH
(MOUNTAIN —) RUBEZAHL
(MOVING —) SOUL
(MUSICAL —) BRIO
(NATURE —) NAT
(PARTY —) FACTION
(REFINED —) ELIXIR
(RESOLUTE —) SPRAWL
(SEA —) TANGIE
(SOOTHSAYING —) PYTHON
(SUPERNATURAL —) FAMILIAR
(SYLVAN —) LESHY SYLVAN
(TRICKSY —) ARIEL
(TUTELARY —S) DIS LARES
(VITAL —) TUCK
(VOLATILE —) ESSENCE
(WATER —) ARIEL KELPY UNDINE
(WICKED —) IMP THURSE
(PL.) IGIGI DAUBER
SPIRITED BRAG FELL RACY TALL
BEANY BIRKY CRANK EAGER FIERY
FLUSH KEDGE KINKY LIFEY SASSY
SEEDY SMART SPICY VIVID AUDACE
FIERCE GINGER LIVELY METTLE
PLUCKY SKEIGH SPRUCE SPUNKY
VIVACE ANIMATO DASHING
FORWARD HUMMING NERVOUS
PEPPERY SPIRITY DESIROUS
FRAMPOLD GENEROUS PHRAMPEL
SLASHING STOMACHY VASCULAR
SPIRITEDLY GAMELY
SPIRITLESS DEAD MEAN MEEK TAME
AMORT FAINT MILKY MUSTY SEEDY
SOGGY VAPID DREEPY FLASHY
LEADEN SODDEN SOFTLY WOODEN
INSIPID LANGUID FECKLESS
FLAGGING LISTLESS THEWLESS
SPIRITLESSLY DAVIELY
SPIRITLIKE ETHEREAL
SPIRITS LACE RAKI HOOCH MANES
FETTLE PECKER FEATHER LEMURES
WAIPIRO
SPIRITUAL ABOVE DEVOUT INWARD

MISTLY GHOSTLY CHURCHLY
INTERNAL NUMINOUS SUPERIOR
(— LEADER) ZADDIK
SPIRITUALISM SPOOKISM
SPIRITUALITY HEAVEN
SPIRITUALIZE REFINE
SPIRITUOUS HARD
SPIROCHETE BORRELIA
SPIT FUFF RACK FROTH REACH
SPAWL BROACH SPITTLE SANDSPIT
SPITTING
SPITE ENVY ONDE DEPIT LIVOR
PIQUE VENOM MALICE MAUGRE
RANCOR SPLEEN DESPITE AMBITION
SPITEFUL CATTY NEBBY SNAKY
ELVISH SULLEN WANTON CATTISH
ENVIOUS PEEVISH SNAKISH VICIOUS
WASPISH CANKERED KNAPPISH
VENOMOUS
SPITFIRE PEPPERBOX
SPITTING SNAKE RINGHALS
SPITTLE SPIT SPAWL SPUTUM
SLOBBER
SPITTOON GABOON PIGDAN
SPITBOX CRACHOIR CUSPIDOR
SPLANCHNIC VISCERAL
SPLASH JAW LAP DASH GLOB GOUT
JAUP LOSH LUSH SKIT SOSS SPAT
WASH BLASH FLASH FLICK FLOOD
FLOSH PLASH PLOUT QUASH SKIRP
SLART SLASH SLOSH SLUSH SQUAT
SWILK BEDASH DABBLE DOLLOP
JABBLE LABBER PLATCH SLUNGE
SOZZLE SPLOSH SPRENT SQUIRT
SPATTER SPIRTLE SPLODGE
SPLURGE SWATTER SPLAIRGE
SPLATHER SPLATTER SPLOTHER
SPLUTHER SPLUTTER
(— OF COLOR) GOUT
(SLIGHT —) GILP
SPLASHBOARD FENDER SPLASHER
SPLASHING SWASH FLASHY JABBLE
DASHING SPATTER SPLUTTER
SWASHING
SPLASHY BLASHY SLOPPY SPRAWLY
SPLATTER DASH BLASH SPLAIRGE
SPLAY FLAN
SPLAYFOOT FLATFOOT
SPLEEN BILE LIEN MELT MILT
STOMACH
SPLEENY PEEVISH
SPLENDID GAY BRAW FINE RIAL
BRAVE GRAND JOLLY NOBLE
PROUD REGAL ROYAL SHEEN
SHOWY STOUT WALLY WLONK
CANDID COSTLY SIGHTY SOLEMN
SPIFFY SUPERB ELEGANT GALLANT
SHINING SUBLIME TEARING
BARONIAL CHAMPION CLINKING
GLORIOUS GORGEOUS MAJESTIC
ORGULOUS RATTLING SLASHING
STUNNING
(CHEAPLY —) TINNY
SPLENDIDLY FINE FINELY SPROWSY
SPLENDOR SUN UMA GITE LUXE
POMP BLAZE GLARE GLEAM GLORY
SHEEN SHINE FULGOR LUSTER
LUSTRE PARADE RUFFLE CLARITY
DISPLAY JOLLITY GRANDEUR

RADIANCE SUMPTURE
SPLENETIC SULLEN VAPORY
PEEVISH
SPLENIC LIENAL
SPLICE FOOT JOIN SCAB PIECE
SCARE SKELB CROTCH PIECEN
SPLICING
SPLICER STRAPPER
SPLINE FIN FEATHER
SPLINT SCOB FANON MATCH SPELK
SPELL TASSE SPLENT THOMAS
CALIPER SPLINTER
(— **FOR FRACTURE**) JUNK
SPLINTER BROOM BURST PURSE
SHAKE SHIDE SHIVE SKELB SLICE
SPAIL SPALE SPALT SPEEL SPELK
SPELL SPILE SPILL SPLIT SPOON
SLIVER SPLEET SPLINT FLINDER
SHATTER SLITHER SPLITTER
SPLINTERY SKELVY
SPLINTWOOD ALBURNUM
SPLIT AX AXE CUT RIT BUCK CHAP
CONE DUNT GAIG MALL MAUL REND
RENT RIFT RIVE SKAG SLAT TEAR
BREAK CHECK CHINE SHAKE SHEAR
SLENT SLIVE SMASH SPALD SPLAT
CLEAVE CLOVEN CREASE DIVIDE
FLAGGY FLERRY SCHISM SPRING
SUNDER BIVALVE SHATTER SLITHER
CREVASSE SCISSION SCISSURE
SPLINTER
(— **FISH**) SCROD
(— **IN BOWLING**) BEDPOSTS
(— **OFF**) SPALL SPAWL SCREEVED
(— **TICKET**) SCRATCH
SPLITTERMAN BOLTER
SPLITTING FLAGGY FISSION
SCISSION
(PL.) FILMS
SPLOTCH DAB BLOB DASH HALO
SPOT FLICK SMUDGE SPECKLE
SPLATCH SPLURGE
SPLURGE BINGE SPRAY SPREE
SPLASH
SPLUTTER FUFF GLUTTER SPATTER
SPUTTER SPLOTHER
SPODOPTERA LAPHYGMA
SPODUMENE KUNZITE TRIPHANE
SPOIL MAR ROT BLOT BOOT COOK
DAZE FANG FOIL FRAB GAIN KILL
MANK PELF PREY ADDLE BITCH
BLEND BOOTY BOTCH CROSS
DECAY QUAIL QUEER SHEND SPILL
STAIN STRIP TOUCH WALLY
COOPER CORPSE CURDLE DEFACE
DEFORM FORAGE INJURE MANGLE
RAVAGE TIDDLE BEDEVIL BLEMISH
CONNACH CORRUMP CORRUPT
ESTREPE INDULGE MULLOCK
PILLAGE PLUNDER SPOLIUM
TARNISH VIOLATE BANKRUPT
CONFOUND DISGRACE MISGUIDE
SPOLIATE
SPOILED BAD BLOWN DAZED MUSTY
CADISH STICKIT BRATTISH
(**EASILY** —) GINGER
SPOILER HARROWER
SPOILFIVE MAW
SPOILS BAG LOOT SKIN SWAG

BOOTY FORAY SPOLIA PILLAGE
PLUNDER
SPOILSPORT NARK LETGAME
SPOILT MARDY
SPOKE RUNG QUOTH SPACK SPAKE
LOWDER SPONDIL SPONDYL
SPOKEN ORAL SAID VERBAL
SPOKESMAN MOUTH HERALD
PROPHET SPEAKER TRUMPET
SPOLIATION SPOIL RAPINE PILLAGE
PLUNDER SPOILING
SPONGE BOT FORM MUMP POLE
SILK SORN SWAB ASCON CADGE
GRASS LUFFA SCAFF SHARK SHIRK
SYCON ASCULA COSHER LEUCON
LOOFAH MALKIN MOPPET RHAGON
ROLLER YELLOW BADIAGA BLEEDER
GELFOAM RADIATE SCOURER
SCRUNGE SYCONID ZIMOCCA
DEADBEAT HARDHEAD HEDGEHOG
MANDRUKA OLYNTHUS REDBEARD
SILICEAN SPHERIDA SUBERITE
ZOOPHYTE
(**YOUNG** —) SEEDLING
SPONGER BOT TRAMP SPONGE
SCAMBLER SMOOTHER
SPONGINESS FOZINESS
SPONGING TRENCHER
SPONGY FOZY FUZZY QUAGGY
SPONSOR COACH GOSSIP SURETY
WITNESS
(— **AT BAPTISM**) HEAVE
SPONSORSHIP EGIS AEGIS
SPONTANEOUS FREE CARELESS
FREEWILL UNTAUGHT
SPONTANEOUSLY KINDLY SELFLY
SPOOK GYRE GHOST HAUNT SCARE
SPOOL COB COP REEL QUILL SPILL
SPULE TWEEL TWILL BOBBIN
BROACH CHEESE COPPIN CARRIER
(— **FOR NETS**) GURDY
SPOON HORN CUTTY LABIS SHELL
COCHLEA JUMBLER MUDDLER
SKIMMER SPINNER STIRRER
BARSPOON COCHLEAR GOBSTICK
(**EUCHARISTIC** —) LABIS
(**FISHING** —) TROLL
(**LONG-HANDLED** —) LADLE
(**SKIMMING** —) LINGEL SKIMMER
(**SNUFF** —) PEN
SPOONBILL AJAJA SPOONY
POPELER CICONIID
SPOON-SHAPED COCHLEAR
SPATULAR
SPOOR SIGN SPUR PISTE
SPORADIC POPPING ISOLATED
SPORANGIUM THECA OOTHECA
SPORE CYST SEED SPORID AGAMETE
AKINETE BISPORE ISOLATE
SPORULE SWARMER CONIDIUM
GONIDIUM
SPOROCYST ZOOCYST SPOROSAC
SPORT FUN GIG KID MUM RIE RUX
SEE TOY ALSO GAME GAUD GLEE
JEST JOKE LAKE LARK PLAY PLOY
RAGE TAIT BREAK DALLY DROLL
FREAK MIRTH FROLIC LAUGHS
POPJOY RACING SHIKAR SKIING
BOATING CAMOGIE DISPORT

DUCKING FOWLING MARLOCK
PASTIME ROLLICK ROUNDER
SAILING SPANIEL FALCONRY
PLEASURE
(— **OF HAWKING**) RIVER
(**BOISTEROUS** —) HIJINKS
(**JAPANESE** —) KENDO
(**ROUGH** —) ROMP
(**WATER** —**S**) NAUTICS AQUATICS
SPORTING VARMINT SPORTIVE
SPORTIVE GAY TAIT LARKY MERRY
FRISKY JOCUND LIVELY LUSORY
TOYFUL TOYING WANTON COLTISH
FESTIVE GAMEFUL JESTING
JOCULAR PLAYFUL TOYSOME
TRICKSY WAGGISH FROLICKY
GAMESOME PLAYSOME PLEASANT
SPORTFUL
SPORTIVENESS HELL KNAVERY
SPORTSMAN SPORT ATHLETE
SHIKARI
SPORTSMANLIKE CLEAN SPORTY
SPORTY FLASH RORTY FLASHY
RAKISH
SPORULE GRANULE
SPOT BIT DAB PIP WEM BLOT CHUB
DIRT DRAB FLAW GALL MOIL MOLE
PLOT SCAM SITE SKIP SLUR SMUT
SOIL SPAT TICK AMPER BLACK
CLOUD FLECK GARLE GOODY
GUTTA HATCH JIMMY MACLE PATCH
PLACE PLECK POINT ROACH SMEAR
SPLAT STAIN SULLY TACHE TAINT
WHERE BLANCH BLOTCH DAPPLE
FOGDOG GERATE MACULE MAZUCA
MOTTLE SMUDGE SMUTCH SPLECK
STIGMA BLEMISH CHARBON
CHECKER FLECKER FRECKLE
GUTTULA MASOOKA OCELLUS
OLDWIFE SMATTER SMITTER
SPATTER SPECKLE SPLOTCH
SPOTTLE STATION STIPPLE TERRAIN
FENESTRA LOCALITY MACULATE
PUNCTULE SPARKLET SPRINKLE
(— **A SHIELD**) GERATE
(— **IN CLOTH**) YAW
(— **IN MINERAL**) MACLE
(— **IN PAPER**) SHINER
(— **IN SAW BLADE**) BLOB
(— **IN STEEL**) STAR
(— **IN WOOD**) WEM
(— **IN YARN**) MOTE
(— **OF INK**) MONK
(— **OF PAINT**) DAUB
(— **OF QUICKSAND**) SUCKHOLE
(— **ON CAT'S FACE**) LAVALIER
(— **ON CAT**) BUTTON
(— **ON EGG**) EYE
(— **ON FINGERNAIL**) GIFT
(— **ON FOREHEAD**) TILAK TILAKA
(— **ON HAWK**) GOUT
(— **ON HORSE**) RACE SNIP STAR
RACHE
(— **ON HORSES'S TOOTH**) CHARBON
(— **ON INSECT WINGS**) BULLA
(— **ON MOTH'S WINGS**) FENESTRA
(— **ON PLAYING CARD**) PIP
(— **ON SUN**) FACULA GRANULE
SUNSPOT

(—S IN BOOKS) FOXING
(BARREN —) GALL
(BLIND —) SCOTOMA SCOTISIS
(BROWN —) SPRAIN SPRAING
(CRUSTY —) SCAB
(ESSENTIAL —) EYE
(FERTILE —) OASIS
(FIRM — IN BOG) HAG
(GREEN — IN VALLEY) HAW
(INFLAMED —) AMPER
(LEAF —) TIKKA BLACKARM
(LIVER —S) CHLOASMA
(LIVID —) TOKEN
(LOW —) DIP SWAMP HOLLOW
(RED —) FLEABITE
(RETIRED —) SHADE
(ROUGH — IN WOVEN GOODS) FAG
(SCABBY —) SCALD
(SKIN —) MOLE BLISTER FRECKLE
LENTIGO
(SMALL —) DOT PLECK STIGMA
LUNULET SPARKLET
(SOILED —) SLOP
(SORE —) BUBU BOTCH
(SWAMPY —) FLAM
(TIGHT —) JAM JACKPOT
(WEAK —) GALL HOLE CHINK NERVE
(WORN —) FRAY FRET
(PL.) MOONING
SPOTLESS FAIR PURE WEMLESS
INNOCENT
SPOTLIGHT ARC SPOT DEUCE
SPOTTED MARLY SCOVY SHELD
CALICO FIGGED HAWKED MACLED
MAILED MARLED MIRLED SPOTTY
TICKED BRACKET BROOKED
FINCHED MOTTLED PARDINE
SPARKED SPECKED SPECKLY
TIGROID FRECKLED LITURATE
MACULOSE SPECKLED STIPPLED
SPOTTED EAGLE RAY MILLER
OBISPO
SPOTTED FLYCATCHER COBWEB
RAFTER WALLBIRD
SPOTTED GUM EUCALYPT
SPOTTED JEWFISH GUASA
SPOTTED SANDPIPER TIPUP
TILTUP CREEKER TIPTAIL
SPOTTED SPURGE DOVEWEED
SPOTTED WINTERGREEN
RATSBANE
SPOTTED WOODPECKER WITWALL
SPOTTER DOTTER
SPOTTY MEALY PATCHY PLATTY
SCABBY SPOTTED
SPOUSE EX MAKE WIFE BRIDE
MATCH PARTY FELLOW MARROW
CONSORT ESPOUSE HUSBAND
SPOUT JET LIP BEAK DALE GEAT
GUSH NOSE SHOE SPILE SPUME
SPURT NOZZLE STRONE RIGGOT SPLOIT
SPROUT STRONE STROUP BUBBLER
FOUNTAIN GARGOYLE
(RAIN —) RONE
SPOUTER VAPORER
SPOUTING BLOW SALIENT
SPRAG TRAILER
SPRAGGER SCOTCHER
SPRAIN RICK CHINK STAVE THRAW

THROW WRAMP WREST WRICK
STRAIN WRENCH STREMMA
SPRAT SMY SPRET SPRIT GARVIE
ALFIONE GARVOCK
(—S CAUGHT EARLY IN SEASON)
DROVE
SPRAWL LOLL TAVE SPURL SCRAWL
GRABBLE SCAMBLE SPARTLE
SPELDER SCRAMBLE SPRADDLE
SPRANGLE STRADDLE
SPRAWLING SPRANGLY
SPRAY FOG HOSE SCUD SPRY STEW
SPREE STOUR SWISH TRAIL TWIST
SHOWER SPARGE SPLASH SPRANG
SPRITZ CURTAIN SPAIRGE SYRINGE
INHALANT SPRANGLE
(— FROM SMALL WAVES) LIPPER
(— MASH) SPARGE
(— OF GEMS) AIGRETTE
(REDUCE TO —) NEBULIZE
SPREAD BED FAN LAY RUN COAT
DRAW FLUE SPAN TELD TUCK VEIN
WALK APPLY CLEAM CREEP FLARE
KILIM PASTE SCALE SLICE SPEND
SPLAT SPLAY STALK STREW WIDEN
BUTTER EXTEND FLANGE LARDER
LAYOUT MANTLE SETOUT THRUST
UNFOLD UNFURL BROADEN
CANVASS DIFFUSE DISPLAY DISTEND
EXPANSE EXPLAIN FEATHER
OPENING SCATTER STRETCH
DIASPORA DISPENSE DISPERSE
HUMIFUSE INCREASE MULTIPLY
SPLATHER STRAGGLE
(— ABROAD) TOOT DELATE SPRING
DIVULGE EMANATE
(— APART) GAPE
(— AS GOSSIP) BUZZ
(— BY REPORT) BLOW NOISE
NORATE
(— DEFAMATION) LIBEL
(— FOR DRYING) TED
(— INTO) INVADE
(— LIKE GRAIN) FLOOR
(— NEWS) HORN
(— ON THICK) COUCH SLATHER
(— OUT) FAN FLOW OPEN SPAN
ASPAR BREDE SPLAT SPLAY SPRAY
EXPAND FLANGE FRINGE MANTLE
OUTLAY SPRAWL UNLOCK DIFFUSE
DISPAND DISTENT EXPLAIN FEATHER
DIFFUSED SPRADDLE SPRANGLE
STRAGGLY
(— OUTWARD) FLARE
(— OVER) LAP DASH COVER
SUFFUSE
(— PAINT) KNIFE
(— THINLY) BRAY DRIVE TOUCH
SCANTY
(— TO THE WIND) SET
(— TO) CATCH
(EVENLY —) SUANT
(TAPESTRY-WOVEN —) KILIM
SPREADER PLOW PLOUGH SANDER
SPREADING FLAN BUSHY FLANGE
PATENT ASPREAD DIFFUSE FLARING
SPRAYEY PATULENT PATULOUS
SPRANGLY
(— OF LIGHT) HALATION

(— RAPIDLY) RUNNING
(NOT —) ERECT
(SLOW —) CREEPAGE
SPREE BAT BUM JAG BLOW BUST
GELL RANT SOAK TEAR TIME TOOT
BEANO BINGE BOOZE BURST DRINK
DRUNK SOUSE SPRAY BENDER
BUSTER HOORAY HURRAH RANDAN
RANTAN BLOWOFF JAMBOREE
WINGDING
SPRIG POINT
(—S FOR MOURNING) CYPRESS
SPRIGGER STRIPPER
SPRIGHTLINESS GAIETY AIRINESS
ALACRITY BUOYANCY VIVACITY
SPRIGHTLY GAY TID AIRY GNIB
PERT WARM ALIVE BRISK CANTY
CRISP DESTO MERRY QUICK
ALEGER JAUNTY LIVELY SPANKY
WIMBLE CHIPPER DELIVER JOCULAR
SPARKLY LIFESOME PLEASANT
SPRING EN AIN BUG EYE FLY HOP
JET OJO URN VER WAX BATH BOLT
BOUT BUCK DART FLOW FONT
GEON HAIR HEAD JUMP KELD LEAP
PERT RISE SEEP SKIP SOAK STEM
URNA WALM WARE WELL WIND
ARISE BOUND DANCE FLIRT FOUNT
FRESH GIHON GLENT GRASS ISSUE
LYMPH PRIME QUELL SALLY SOURD
SPEND SPOUT START STEND SURGE
THROW VAULT BOUNCE CHARCO
DERIVE GAMBOL GEYSER JUMPER
LOCKET ORIGIN PIRENE RESORT
RESULT SILOAM SOURCE SPRINT
VENERO BUDTIME EMANATE
ESTUARY FLOUNCE GAMBADO
PROCEED REBOUND WRAPPER
BACKSTAY BANDUSIA CASTALIA
FOUNTAIN SPANGHEW
(— AWKWARDLY) KEVEL
(— BACK) RECOIL RESULT RETORT
REBOUND
(— DOWN) ALIGHT
(— FORWARD) LAUNCH
(— FROM) DESCEND
(— OF THE YEAR) VER VOAR
(— ON SHEARS) BACKSTAY
(— SEASON) APRIL GRASS BUDTIME
(— SUDDENLY) FLY BOUNCE
(— TO FASTEN NECKLACE) LOCKET
(— UP) ARISE SHOOT SPROUT
BURGEON UPSPRING
(BOILING —) TUBIG
(CARRIAGE —) ROBBIN
(ERUPTIVE —) WALM GEYSER
(GUSHING —) CHARCO
(HOT —) SPRUDEL
(INTERMITTENT —S) GIPSIES
GYPSIES
(LAND —) LAVANT
(MECHANICAL —) RESORT RESSORT
(MINERAL —) SPA
(SALT —) LICK SALINE
(WARM —S) THERMAE
(WATCH —) SLEEVE
SPRING BEAUTY LETTUCE
SPRINGBOARD BATULE TREMPLIN
SPRINGBOK GAZELLE SPRINGER

SPRING CHAPLET JAMMER
SPRINGILY BOUNCILY SPONGILY
SPRINGINESS GIVE LIFE
SPRINGING LAUNCH SALIENT
(**— BACK**) RESULT ELASTIC
(**— FROM STEPS**) GRADY
SPRINGLIKE VERNAL
SPRING ORANGE STYRAX
SPRINGTAIL PODURA FURCULA
PODURID SKIPTAIL
SPRINGTIME VER GERMINAL
SPRINGY WHIPPY ELASTIC FLEXIBLE
SPRINKLE ASH DAG DEG BLOW
DAMP SHED SPIT FLASH SHAKE
SPURT WATER BEDROP DABBLE
POUNCE SPARGE SPRENT SPRINK
SQUIRT ARROUSE ASPERGE
ASPERSE DRIZZLE RANTIZE
SCATTER SKINKLE SKITTER SPAIRGE
SPARKLE SPARPLE SPATTER
SPATTLE SPERPLE SPURTLE
DISPUNGE INTERSOW SPITTING
SPRINGLE STRINKLE
(**— IN BAPTISM**) RANTIZE
(**— OF RAIN**) SPIT
(**— SEED**) SPRAIN
(**— TOBACCO**) BLOW
(**— WITH FLOUR**) DREDGE
(**— WITH POWDER**) DUST
(**— WITH SALT**) CORN
(**— WITH SAND**) SAND
SPRINKLED SEEDED SPRENT
(**— OVER**) BESPRENT
SPRINKLER SPARGER SPRAYER
WATERER DAMPENER STRINKLE
SPRINKLING SEME LACING SPARGE
STRANK RANTISM STIPPLE
STOURING
(**— OF PEOPLE**) SALT
SPRINT BICKER SPRENT SPRUNT
SPRITE AND ELF HOB PUG SEE ALSO
PIXY PUCK BUCCA DOBBY FAIRY
HOLDA PIXIE GOBLIN PILWIZ SPIRIT
SPOORN UMBRIEL COLTPIXY
GLAISTIG WATERMAN
(**WATER —**) NIX NECK NIXIE NICKER
SPRITELY WIMBLE
SPROCKET WHELP
SPROUT BUD PUT BROD CHIT CHUN
CION DRAW TOOT CATCH CHICK
SCUTE SHOOT SPEAR SPIRE SPRIT
SPURT BRAIRD GERMEN RATOON
SIRING STOVEN TELLER TILLER
BURGEON COPPICE SPURTER
TENDRON
(**— OF BARLEY**) TAIL
(**FIRST —S**) BREER BRAIRD BREIRD
(**STUMP —**) TILLER
SPRUCE GIM DEFT JIMP NEAT POSH
SMUG SPRY TRIG TRIM BRISK
COMPT CRISP DINKY FRESH JEMMY
JIMMY NATTY SLICK SMART SMIRK
SPIFF SPRIG DAPPER PICKED
SPONGE SPRUNT SPRUSH FINICAL
FOPPISH SMARTEN SMICKER
SPRUNNY EPINETTE TITIVATE
SPRUE RUNNER PSILOSIS
SPRUER GATER
SPRY AGILE BRISK QUICK NIMBLE

SPUD BARKER PADDLE SPUDDER
SPUME EST BEES FOAM FROTH
YEAST
SPUNK GETUP SPRAWL SMEDDUM
SPUR ARM GAD GIG EDGE GAFF
GOAD KNAG MOVE STUD TANG
DRIVE PRICK PRONG ROWEL SPURN
BROACH CALCAR DIGGER EXCITE
FOMENT GAFFLE GRIFFE INCITE
MOTIVE OFFSET RIPPON SICKLE
SPERON WEAPON BICYCLE
GABLOCK INCITER LORMERY
SCRATCH COCKSPUR GAVELOCK
(**— OF COCK**) HEEL
(**— ON HORSESHOE**) CALK
(**—S OF COCK**) WEAPON
SPURGE BALSAM INTISY SUNWEED
CATEPUCE DOVEWEED FLUXWEED
MILKBUSH MILKWEED TITHYMAL
WARTWEED WARTWORT
SPURIOUS DOG FAKE SHAM BOGUS
FUNNY QUEER SHICE SNIDE NOTHAL
PSEUDO BASTARD NOTHOUS
SYNDIETIC
SPURN FOOT TACK SCORN REJECT
CONSPUE CONTEMN DECLINE
DESPISE DISDAIN
SPURRY YARR FRANK COWQUAKE
SANDWEED
SPURT JET GILP GIRD GOUT JAUP
SPAR SPIN BURST CHIRT FLASH
PULSE SALLY SPOUT GEYSER
RANDOM SPLURT SPRING SPROUT
SQUIRT SPATTER
SPUTTER SPIT FIZZLE SOTTER
SPATTER SPLUTTER
SPUTUM SPIT
SPY FLY PRY ESPY NARK NOSE STAG
TOOT TOUT WAIT WORM LOWER
PERDU PLANT SCOUT SNEAP SPIAL
SPION WATCH BEAGLE BEHOLD
DESCRY GAYCAT MOUTON PEEPER
PERDUE SEARCH SHADOW SPIRAL
TOUTER WAITER EXAMINE LURCHER
OTACUST SMELLER SPOTTER
WATCHER DISCOVER EMISSARY
HIRCARRA MOUCHARD
(**— ON RACEHORSES**) TOUT
(**— UPON**) LAY
(**PLANTED —**) STOOGE
(**POLICE —**) SETTER
SPYBOAT VEDET VEDETTE
SQUAB PIPER SQUABBY SQUEAKER
SQUEALER SQUILGEE
SQUABBLE MUSS BRAWL SCRAP
BICKER JANGLE SQUALL BOBBERY
BRABBLE BRANGLE CONTEND
PRABBLE QUARREL SWABBLE
SQUAD CREW DECURY TWENTY
PLATOON
(**— OF DETECTIVES**) HOMICIDE
SQUADRON SOTNIA SQUADER
SQUALID DINGY DIRTY MANGY
SEEDY FILTHY FROWZY SCABROUS
SQUALL DROW FRET GUST MEWL
WAUL BARAT FRESH PERRY SKELP
BAYAMO FLURRY SQUAWK
BORASCA SUMATRA TORNADO
BORASQUE CHUBASCO

SQUALOR DIRT
SQUAMA ALULA TEGULA
SQUANDER SOT BLOW BLUE BURN
GAME LASH WARE SPEND SPILL
SPORT WASTE LAVISH MAFFLE
MUDDLE PADDLE PALTER PERISH
TIPPLE CONSUME DEBAUCH
DEBOISE DISPEND PROFUSE
SCATTER SKITTLE SLATHER
SWATTER EMBEZZLE MISSPEND
SQUATTER
SQUANDERER PRODIGAL
SQUANDERING WASTEFUL
SQUARE FIX EDGE EVEN FOUR FULL
POST QUAD SUIT AGREE CHECK
CROSS FRAME HUNKY PLACE PLAIN
PLAZA SUPER BLOCKY DINKUM
ISAGON PIAZZA QUARRY ZENZIC
ZOCALO CARREAU CHECKER
COMMONS EMERALD UPRIGHT
QUADRANT QUADRATE SQUADRON
TETRAGON
(**— A STONE**) PITCH
(**— FOR BOWLING SCORE**) FRAME
(**— OF CANVAS**) SKATE
(**— OF CLOTH**) PANE
(**— OF DOUGH**) KNISH
(**— OF FRAMING**) PAN
(**— OF GLASS**) QUARREL
(**— OF TURF**) DIVOT QUADREL
(**— OFF**) BUTT
(**— ON BILLIARD TABLE**) CROTCH
(**— ON CHESSBOARD**) HOUSE POINT
(**BUILDINGS FORMING —**) INSULA
(**CARPENTER'S —**) NORMA
(**LINEN —**) SUDARIUM
(**PATTERN OF —S**) DAMIER
(**WOVEN —**) SINKER
SQUARED HEWN QUARTO SQUARE
SQUARE DANCE TUCKER
SQUARE-DEALING WHITE
SQUARELY BUNG FAIR FULL FLUSH
SPANG FAIRLY DIRECTLY
(**— AND SHARPLY**) SMACK
SQUARISH BOXY
SQUASH PEPO QUAT GOURD SQUAB
CASHAW CUCURB CUSHAW
MARROW SIMNEL SQUISH SQUUSH
TURBAN HUBBARD PUMPKIN
CUCURBIT CYMBLING PEPONIUM
ZUCCHINI
SQUASH BUG STINKBUG
SQUASHY SWASHY SQUUSHY
SQUAT QUAT RUCK STUB SWAT
SWOT COWER DUMPY FUBSY
HUNCH PUDGY SQUAB FODGEL
HUNKER HURKLE QUATCH STOCKY
STUBBY SQUATTY TAPPISH
SQUATTLE THICKSET
SQUATINA RHINA
SQUATTER NESTER BYWONER
SQUAW JACK WEBB HOUND WENCH
MAHALA SQUARK
SQUAWBUSH SHOVAL
SQUAWFISH CHUB BOXHEAD
BIGMOUTH CHAPPAUL
SQUAWK SCRAWK SQUALL SQUARK
SQUAWL COMPLAIN
SQUAWROOT CLAPWORT ELOTILLO

SQUEAK GIKE PEEP WEAK CHEEP QUEAK SCRAWK SCROOP SQUEAL
SQUEAKY CREAKY
SQUEAL PIP FINK HOWL SWEEL SCREAK WHISTLE
SQUEALER FINK CANARY
SQUEAMISH HELO NICE NAISH PAWKY PENSY DAINTY DAUNCH PENCEY QUAINT QUEASY SPICED TICKLE WAIRCH WAMBLY FINICAL MAWKISH WEARISH NAUSEOUS OVERNICE
SQUEAMISHNESS NICETY DISGUST DELICACY
SQUEEZE EKE HUG JAM NIP CLAM MULL MURE VISE ZEST BUNCH CHIRT CREEM CROWD CRUSH PRESS SQUAB SQUAT WRING GRUDGE QUEASE SCRUMP SCRUZE SQUASH STRAIN THRIMP THRING THRONG TWEEZE TWITCH SCRINGE SCROOGE SCROUGE SCRUNCH SCRUNGE SQUEEGE SQUINCH COMPRESS CONTRACT PRESSURE SHOEHORN THRIMBLE THRUMBLE
(— FROM) SPONGE
(— IN) FUDGE
(— INTO) THRIMBLE
(— OUT) PINCH STRAIN
SQUEEZED STRETTA STRETTO
SQUEEZER REAMER ALLIGATOR
SQUELCH QUELCH SQUASH SQUISH SQUIDGE
SQUELCHER BLIZZARD
SQUETEAGUE DRUM DRUMMER SQUETEE BLUEFISH CHICKWIT WEAKFISH
SQUIB MOTE FILLER EXPLODER
SQUID PLUG
SQUIGGLE SCRIGGLE
SQUILL SCILLA SLANGKOP
SQUINT GLEE GLEG SKEN SKEW BAGGE GLENT GLEDGE GOGGLE SHEYLE SKELLY SQUINCH SQUINNY
SQUINT-EYED GLEE GLEED
SQUINTING LOUCHE
SQUIRE SWAIN DONZEL TIMIAS ARMIGER ESQUIRE SQUIRET YOUNKER HENCHMAN SCUTIGER SERVITOR SQUIREEN
SQUIRM CURL WIND TWINE WRING WRITHE WRESTLE WRIGGLE SCRIGGLE SQUIGGLE
SQUIRREL BUN CON BUNT LEAD SCUG BUNNY XERUS BOOMER CHIPPY GOPHER RODENT TAGUAN ARDILLA SCHILLU SCIURID CHIPMUNK EGGEATER GRAYBACK JELERANG RATATOSK
(— SKIN) VAIR
(FLYING —) ASAPAN
SQUIRRELFISH ALAIKI MARIAN MOJARRA SERRANO SOLDIER SANDFISH WELSHMAN
SQUIRREL SHREW TANA TUPAIA PENTAIL
SQUIRT CHIRT SCOOT SKITE SLIRT SPIRT SPOUT SPURT SQUIB SQUIT SPLOIT SPRENT SPRITZ SCOOTER SQUITTER

STAB DAB DAG JAB JAG JOB DIRK GORE PINK PROB SHIV STOB STOG STUG YERK CHIVE KNIFE POACH PRICK PRONG STICK STOKE BROACH DAGGER PIERCE POUNCE SLIVER STITCH THRUST BAYONET STAGGER PRICKADO STILETTO STOCCADO STOCCATA
(— IN MIDBREAST) SLOT
STABBING THORNY JABBING PUNGENT STICKING
STABILITY POISE BALANCE SADNESS FIRMNESS SECURITY
STABILIZE FIX SET EVEN TRIM POISE SCHOOL STEADY BALANCE BALLAST STIFFEN
STABILIZER ACARDITE
STABLE BYRE FAST FIRM SURE HARAS HEMEL SOLID SOUND STALL STIFF STOUT TAMBO LINTER LIVERY SECURE SICKER STATIC STEADY STRONG STURDY DURABLE EQUERRY LASTING OXHOUSE SETTLED SHIPPEN STABILE IMMOBILE RESIDENT STANDING
(ROYAL —S) MEWS
STABLEBOY LAD JACKBOY
STABLEMAN OSTLER HOSTLER
STACCATO TUT SECCO DETACHE SALTATO RICOCHET SALTANDO
(NOT —) TENUTO
STACK COB MOW SOW BIKE DESS LEET PACK PILE POKE RICK CANCH CLAMP GOAVE POAKE SCROO SHOCK STAKE STALK STOCK COLUMN FUNNEL RICKLE CALENDER STACKAGE
(— BRICKS) SCINTLE
(— IN KILN) BOX
(— LUMBER) STICK
(— OF ARMS) PILE
(— OF BRICK) LIFT
(— OF CERAMICS) BUNG
(— OF CORN) SHOCK
(— OF FISH) BULK
(— OF GRAIN) RICK
(— OF HIDES) BED
(— OF PANS) SWEATER
(— OF SHEETS) BOOK
(HAY OR CORN —) HOVEL
(SMALL —) COB CANCH RICKLE
(TILE —) WELL
STACKER CROWDER PITCHER STACKMAN
STACKYARD MOWIE MOWHAY HAGGARD
STADIUM BOWL STADE STAGE FURLONG STADION COLISEUM
STAFF PIN ROD TAU TAW CANE CLUB KENT LIMB MACE MALL MAUL PIKE POLE RUNG TREE VARE YARD BATON CROOK CROSS KEVEL NIBBY PEDUM PERCH STAVE STICK SUITE VERGE BASTON CADUCE CEPTER CLEEKY CROCHE CRUTCH FAMILY FERULE GROUND LITUUS MULETA POTENT PRITCH RADIUS RISSLE TAIAHA THYRSE WARDER BACULUS BOURDON CAMBUCA CROSIER

CRUMMIE DISTAFF FESTUCA PALSTER SCEPTER SCEPTRE STADDLE THYRSUS CADUCEUS CRUMMOCK PARTISAN PASTORAL PLOWFOOT TIPSTAFF
(— AT END OF NET) BRAIL
(— OF AUTHORITY) VARE VERGE
(— WITH CROSSPIECE) POTENT
(BISHOP'S —) BAGLE BACULUS CROSIER CROZIER PASTORAL
(FIELD MARSHAL'S —) BATON
(FORKED —) LINSTOCK
(GRADUATED —) LIMB
(HOTTENTOT —) KIRVI
(MAGICIAN'S —) RHABDOS
(NEWSPAPER —) DAYSIDE
(NUBIAN —) KUERR
(PLASTERER'S —) BEATER
(SHEPHERD'S —) KENT CROOK
(TEACHING —) FACULTY
(THIEVES' —) FILCH
STAG HART ROYAL SPADE STAIG WAPITI BULLOCK KNOBBER POINTER KNOBBLER
(— OF 8 YEARS OR MORE) ROYAL
(— OF THE 3D YEAR) SPIRE
(— THAT HAS CAST HIS ANTLERS) POLLARD
(3-YEAR OLD —) SPADE
(DEAD —) MORT
(HORNLESS —) HUMMEL
(TURNED TO —) ACTAEON
STAG BEETLE LUCANID
STAGE LEG BANK GEST POST STEP TREK DUMMY ETAGE FLAKE GRADE PEGME PHASE POINT SCENE STAIR STATE BOARDS DEGREE HEMMEL PERIOD STRIDE CATASTA MANSION ROSTRUM STADIUM INSTANCE PLATFORM SCAFFOLD
(— FOR DRYING FISH) FLAKE
(— FOR HAY) HEMMEL
(— IN DELIRIUM) TILMUS
(— IN FEVER) FLUSH
(— IN PORCELAIN FURNACE) HOWELL
(— IN TRAVELING) GEST
(— MANAGER) REGISSEUR
(— OF CUPOLA) LANTERN
(— OF DEVELOPMENT) ERA BLOSSOM
(— OF GLACIATION) ACHEN MINDEL
(— OF INSECT) INSTAR
(— OF LIFE) AGE ASRAMA ASHRAMA
(— OF PERSONALITY) LATENCY
(— OF ROCKET) BOOSTER
(— OF THEATER) SCAENA THEATRON
(— WHERE SLAVES WERE SOLD) CATASTA
(BOTTOMMOST —) CELLAR
(COMIC —) SOCK
(FINAL —) CLOSE FINISH STRETCH
(FIRST —) YOUTH SPRING
(FLOATING —) DUMMY
(FLOOD —) CREST
(GEOLOGICAL —) GUNZ GLACIAL
(INITIAL —) INFANCY

(LANDING —) STAIR BRIDGE STAITH STELLING
(MOVING —) PEGMA PEGME
(RADIO —) STEP
(THIRD —) AUTUMN
STAGECOACH DILLY STAGE
STAGEHAND DAYMAN
STAGER SOAKER
STAGGER REEL ROLL STOT DAVER DODGE HODGE STITE STOIT DACKER FALTER GOGGLE STIVER SWAVER WALTER WAMBLE WELTER WIGGLE WINTLE MEGRIMS STACHER STACKER STAMMER STOITER STOTTER STUMBLE SWAGGER VANDYKE WAUCHLE TITUBATE
STAGGERBUSH LAMBKILL
STAGGERED STURTAN STURTIN
STAGGERS DUNT GOGGLES STAVERS VERTIGO
STAGHEAD SPIKETOP
STAGING STAGE CRIPPLE DERRICK HURRIES
STAGNANCY STASIS
STAGNANT DEAD DULL INERT STILL STATIC COBWEBBY SLUGGISH STAGNATE STANDING
STAGNATION STASIS TORPOR LANGUOR
STAID SET CIVIL GRAVE SOBER DEMURE STEADY EARNEST SERIOUS DECOROUS
STAIN DYE LIT WEM BLOT BLUR BUFF DIRT DRAB FILE FOIL HURT MEAL MOLE RUST SCAM SLUR SMAD SMIT SMUT SOIL SPOT TASH BLACK BLEND CLOUD DIRTY HATCH PAINT PLECK SMEAR SPECK SULLY TACHE TAINT TINGE WEMMY BREATH GIEMSA IMBRUE INFAMY INFECT MACULA SMIRCH SMUDGE SMUTCH SPLASH STIGMA SUDDLE ATTAINT BESTAIN BLEMISH DEPAINT DISTAIN SLUBBER SOILURE SPATTER SPLOTCH STADDLE TARNISH BESMIRCH CARMALUM DISCOLOR DISGRACE DISHONOR FLYSPECK MACULATE TAINTURE
(— BLACK) EBONIZE
(— IN LINEN) MELL
(— ON BRICK) SCUMMING
(— WITH BLOOD) ENGORE
STAINED FOXY RUSTY SMUDGY SMUTCHY
(— BY DECAY) DOATY
(— WITH BLOOD) BLOODY IMBRUED
STAINED GLASS VITRAIL
STAINER TRACER
STAINLESS CHASTE INNOCENT
STAIR STY GREE RUNG STEP DEGREE COCHLEA ESCALIER
(MINING —) LOB
(PL.) PAIR PITCH FLIGHT DANCERS ESCALIER
STAIRCASE SCALE ESCALIER
(SPIRAL —) SPIRAL CARACOLE
STAIRWAY STOOP GREESE PERRON DESCENT ESCALIER
(— ON RIVER BANK) GHAT

(CURVED —) SWEEP
(SHIP'S —) LADDER
(WINDING —) VICE TURNPIKE
STAKE BET HOB LAY SET TAW VIE WAD WED ANTE BENT GAGE MAIN PALE PAWN PEEL POOL RISK STAB STOB TREE WAGE PITCH SPILE SPOKE SPRAG STOCK STOOP STOUR WAGER BAIKIE CAULIS CHANCE CORNER CROTCH ENGAGE GAMBLE HAZARD IMPONE LOGGAT LOGGET PALING STOWER TRUNCH WEDFEE STOATER STUCKEN VENTURE INTEREST PALISADE PEASTICK STUCKING
(CART —) RUNG
(COMPULSORY — IN POKER) BLIND
(POINTED —) SOULE SOWEL PICKET
(SURVEYORS' —) HUB
(TETHERING —) PUTTO
(TINSMITH'S —) TEEST
STAKE-SHAPED SUDIFORM
STALACE COLUMELLA
STALE OLD COLD HOAR PALL SICK WORN BLOWN DUSTY FROWY HOARY MOLDY MUSTY RAFTY SANDY TRITE FROWZY MOULDY STUFFY EXOLETE FROUGHY INSIPID OVERWORN STAGNANT
(DAMP AND —) WAUGH
STALEMATE PATT STALE
STALK BUN RAY CORN MOTE POLE RISP STAM STEG STEM TIGE QUILL SCAPE SHANK SPEAR SPIRE STAKE STALE STEAL STIPE STUMP WRIDE COULIS RATOON STIPES CASTOCK PEDICEL PETIOLE SPINDLE FILAMENT PEDUNCLE PODETIUM STALKLET STERIGMA
(— OF BUCKWHEAT) STRAW
(— OF CRINOID) COLUMN
(— OF GRAIN) RESSOM RIZZOM
(— OF GRASS) BENT SPEAR
(— OF HAY) RISP
(— OF PLANT) SPINDLE TENACLE
(— OF SPOROGONIUM) SETA
(— OF STAMEN) FILAMENT
(— OF SUGAR CANE) RATOON
(— OF UMBEL) RAY
(—S OF GRAIN) KARBI STRAW
(CABBAGE —) CASTOCK
(CROSSBOW —) TILLER
(DRY —) KEX KECK
(FLOWER —) SCAPE
(HOLLOW —) BUN KEX
(PL.) HAULM STRAW WRIDE IWAIWA
STALL BIN BOX CUB PEW BULK CRIB SPAR STAW BOOSE BOOSY BOOTH CRAME PITCH STAND STASH CARCER CARREL TRAVIS WICKET BALAGAN CABINET SHAMBLE BUTCHERY STANDING TRAVERSE
(— FOR TIME) HAVER STRETCH
(— IN CLOISTER) CAROL
(— IN COAL MINE) BREAST WICKET
(— IN MUD) STOG
(— IN ROMAN CIRCUS) CARCER
(CHURCH —) PEW
(THEATER —) LOGE FAUTEUIL

STALLED STOODED
STALLION SIRE STAG STUD ENTRE HORSE COOSER ENTIRE STALLAND
STALWART RUDE STARK STIFF WIGHT STRONG STURDY BUIRDLY VALIANT
STAMEN TAMIN STAMMEL
STAMINA GUTS SAND BOTTOM
STAMMER FAM HACK MANT STOT STUT GANCH WLAFF FAFFLE FALTER FAMBLE HACKER HAFFLE HAMMER HOCKER HOTTER MAFFLE MAMMER YAMMER FRIBBLE STUMBLE STUTTER HESITATE SPLUTTER TITUBATE
STAMMERING HACK TRAULISM
STAMP CHOP COIL DRUB FAKE MARK NIXY PAUT POSS RUFF SEAL SNAP TYPE APPEL BLOCK DOLLY ERROR FRANK LABEL LOCAL NIXIE PRINT PUNCH STOCK STOMP STUNT TENOR TOUCH WRITE ACCENT CACHET CLICHE DOCKER FULLER INCUSE INCUTE INDENT LOCKUP PASTER POUNCE SCRIBE SHAPER SIGNET STRAMP STRIKE CARRIER CHARACT EDITION IMPRESS IMPRINT MINTAGE POUNDER REPRINT SEEBECK SPECIAL SQUELCH STICKER TAXPAID WRAPPER HALLMARK ORIGINAL PRESSURE PUNCHEON
(— AFTER ASSAY) TOUCH
(— BOOK COVER) BLIND
(— FOR CUTTING DOUGH) DOCKER
(— HERRING BARREL) DUNT
(— HIDES) STOCK
(— HOLES) STOACH
(— OUT) SCOTCH
(— WITH DIE) DINK
(BOOKBINDING —) BLOCK FILLET
(CANCELLING —) KILLER
(HALF OF —) BISECT
(HAND —) CANCELER
(OFFICIAL —) CHOP
(POSTAGE —) AIR DUE CAPE FAKE HEAD ERROR LABEL LOCAL BUREAU INVERT AIRMAIL BICOLOR CHARITY CLASSIC REPRINT STICKER ADHESIVE COLONIAL ORIGINAL SPECIMEN
(REVENUE —) FISCAL TAXPAID
(SMART —) APPEL
(PL.) MIXTURE KILOWARE
STAMPEDE RUSH BLITZ CHUTE DEBACLE STAMPEDO
STAMPER FANCIER STOMPER
STAMPING TITLING
STANCE STATION STANDING
(— OF GOLFER) ADDRESS
(— OF HORSE) GATHER
STANCH FIRM STEM STIFF STOUT HEARTY TRUSTY STAUNCH FAITHFUL RESOLUTE
STANCHION BAIL PITON CROTCH CRUTCH STENCIL STANCHEL STANCHER
STAND GO JIB SET BANK BEAR BIER DESK HALT RACK RANK REST STAY

ZARF BLOCK ERECT FRAME FRONT KIOSK NIPOD STALL STICK STONE STOOL CASTER COLORS ENDURE HASTER INSIST PATTEN PILLAR SMOKER STANZA STOUND STRIKE TEAPOY TRIPOD TRIVET CONSIST DIOPTER EPERGNE FOURBLE LECTERN STATION TABORET TRESTLE TROLLEY ATTITUDE BLEACHER COATRACK CROWFOOT FRIPPERY GUERIDON HASTENER INKSTAND POSITION SCAFFOLD STALLAGE STANDING STANDISH STILLAGE STILLING STILLION
(— AS SPONSOR) FANG HEAVE CHRISTEN
(— AT AN ANGLE) CATER
(— AT ATTENTION) BACK
(— BACK) BACCARE BACKARE
(— BEFORE A FIRE) FOOTMAN
(— BEHIND) COVER
(— BY) SERVE
(— CLOSE) CROWD ENVIRON
(— FASTENED TO MESS TABLE) CROWFOOT
(— FIRM) STAY
(— FOR AUCTIONING) BLOCK
(— FOR BARRELS) JIB THRALL
(— FOR COFFIN) BIER
(— FOR COMPASS) BINNACLE
(— FOR CONFINING HEAT) HASTER HASTENER
(— FOR DRESSES) FRIPPERY
(— FOR DRILL PIPE) FOURBLE
(— FOR FINJAN) ZARF
(— FOR TILES) CRISS
(— FOR WRITING MATERIALS) STANDISH
(— FOR) DENOTE
(— GUARD) COVER
(— IN AWE) FEAR
(— OF FOREST) GROWTH
(— OF PLANTS) STOOL
(— OFF) AROINT
(— ON AND OFF SHORE) BUSK
(— ON END) STARE UPEND
(— ON TWO FEET) BIPOD DUOPOD
(— OUT) CUT TOOT FLAUNT
(— READY) ABIDE
(— STILL) HO HOO HALT STAY
(— TO SHOOT) ADDRESS
(— TREAT) MUG SHOUT
(— UNSTEADILY) STAGGER
(— UP STIFF) STIVER
(— UP TO) CONFRONT
(— WITH LEGS APART) STRIDE
(CONCESSION —) JOINT
(FIRECLAY —) CRANK
(ONE-NIGHT —) GIG
(PRINTER'S —) BANK FRAME
(PULPIT-LIKE —) AMBO
(RAISED —) PERGOLA
(SCULPTOR'S —) CHASSIS
(SHOOTING —) BUTT
(THREE-LEGGED —) TRIVET
STANDARD ALEM DICK FIAR FLAG GAGE IDEA MARK NORM SIGN TEST TOUG ALLOY BOGEY CANON CHECK DOLLY DRAKE EAGLE GAUGE IDEAL

JEDGE MODEL NORMA SCALE STAND STOOL AQUILA ASSIZE BANNER CORNET DOLLIE FILLER SOCKET SQUARE STAPLE TIPONI TRIPOD VIOLLE ANCIENT CLASSIC DECORUM DRAPEAU LABARUM MODULUS STANDER BRATTACH GONFALON MOUNTING ORIFLAMB ORTHODOX VEXILLUM
(— IN GATE) STRIKE
(— OF CONDUCT) LINE GNOMON
(— OF PERFECTION) IDEAL
(— OF PERFORMANCE) BOGY BOGEY BOGIE
(— OF PITCH) DIAPASON
(— OF QUALITY) GRADE
(—S OF BEHAVIOR) ETHICS
(LIGHT —) CARCEL
(TURKISH —) ALEM TOUG
(PL.) LIGHTS HOLSTERS
STANDARD-BEARER ENSIGN ALFEREZ ANCIENT STALLER SIGNIFER STANDARD
STANDARDIZE FORDIZE MACHINE CALIBRATE
STANDEL STORER
STANDING BEING ERECT STATE CREDIT ESTEEM RESPECT STAGNANT
(— ALONE) SEPARATE
(— BY ITSELF) ABSOLUTE DETACHED
(— ERECT) HORRENT
(— INCOORDINATION) ASTASIA
(— ON STEPS) DEGRADED
(— OUT CLEARLY) EMINENT
(— OUT) BOLD EXTANT SALIENT
(— POSITION) OFFHAND
(MODE OF —) STANCE
(SOCIAL —) LEVEL ESTATE FASHION STATION
STANDPATTISM TORYISM
STANDPOINT STANCE
STANDSTILL JIB SET HALT REST STAY STAND STANCE
STANZA CALL RANN ENVOI ENVOY STAFF STAND STAVE VERSE BASTON DIXAIN DIZAIN OCTAVE SEPTET SESTET SEXTET SIXAIN STANCE STANZO HUITAIN SEXTAIN STROPHE TRIOLET TROILUS CINQUAIN OCTONARY QUATRAIN QUINTAIN RISPETTO SETTAINE TRISTICH
STAPES STIRRUP
STAPLE LOOP FLOSS STITCH STEEPLE VERVELLE
STAR COR SUN BEID FIRE LAMP ASTER COMES DWARF GIANT MOLET RISHI SHINE STARN ALNATH ASTRAL BINARY COUPLE DOUBLE ETOILE LUCIDA MULLET NITHAM SHINER SPHERE STELLA BENEFIC DINGBAT ESTOILE GEMINID STARLET STARNIE ASTERISK ASTEROID HEXAGRAM MALEFICE PENTACLE SUBDWARF SUBGIANT VARIABLE
(7 —S OF GREAT BEAR) CAR
(COMPANION —) COMES

(DOG —) SEPT SOPT SEPTI SIRIUS
(EVENING —) VENUS HESPER VESPER EVESTAR HESPERUS
(FEATHER —) COMATULA
(GUIDING —) LOADSTAR LODESTAR
(MORNING —) VENUS DAYSTAR PHOSPHOR
(NEW —) NOVA
(OFFICER'S —) PIP
(PULSATING —) CEPHEID
(SHOOTING —) METEOR SHOOTER
(SPECIFIC —) YED ADIB ALYA ATIK CAPH ENIF ENIR IZAR KIED MAIA NAOS PHAD SADR VEGA WEGA ACRAB ACRUX AGENA ALCOR ALGOL ALKES ANCHA ARNEB CHARA DABIH DELTA DENEB DUBHE GIEDI GUIAM GUYAM HAMAL HAMUL JUGUM MERAK MIZAR NIBAL NIHAI PHAET PHARD RIGEL SAIPH SPICA TEJAT WASAT WEZEN ZOZMA ADHARA ALHENA ALIOTH ALKAID ALMACH ALTAIR ALUDRA APOLLO ARIDED CASTOR CELENO CHELEB DIPHDA ELNATH ETAMIN GIENAH HYADES KOCHAB LESUTH MAASYM MARKAB MARKEB MARSIC MEGREZ MENKAB MENKAR MERACH MEROPE MIRFAK MIRZAM NEKKAR PHECDA POLLUX PROPUS RANICH SCHEAT SHEDIR SIRIUS THABIT THUBAN ACUBENS ALBIREO ALCHIBA ALCYONE ALGENIB ALGIEBA ALGORAH ALMAACK ALNILAM ALNITAH ALPHARD ALPHIRK ALSHAIN ANTARES AZIMECH BUNGULA CANOPUS CAPELLA DENEBOLA ELECTRA GIANSAR GOMELZA GRUMIUM MEBUSTA MELUCTA MENCHIB MINTAKA MUFRIDE POLARIS PROCYON REGULUS ROTANIM RUCHBAR SCHEDAR SEGINUS SHELLAK STEROPE TARAZED TAYGETA TEGMINE THEENIM ACHERNAR ALPHECCA ARCTURUS ASTERION DENEBOLA GRAFFIAS HERCULES MULIPHEN PRAESEPE SCALOOIN SCHEMALI SHERATAN
(THREE —S) KIDS ELLWAND TRIANGLE
STAR APPLE CAIMITO
STARCH AMYL ARUM SAGO STIFF TIKOR AMYDON AMYLUM FARINA FECULA CASSAVA CURCUMA FAECULA MARANTA TALIPOT AMIDULIN DRESSING FIXATURE GLUCOSAN
(ANIMAL —) GLYCOGEN
STARCHED FORMAL
STARE EYE BORE DARE GAPE GAUM GAUP GAWK GAWP GAZE GOVE GYPE KIKE LOOK PORE GLARE GLORE GLOWER GOGGLE EYEBALL
(— IDLY) GOVE GOAVE
(— VACANTLY) GOWK
(COLD —) FISHEYE
STARFISH PAD STAR RADIATE ASTEROID OPHIURAN

STARING STEEP ASTARE GOGGLE
GOOGLY HAGGARD
STAR JELLY STARSHOT
STARK BUCK CARK FAIR HARD
CRUDE HARSH STIFF STARCH
DESOLATE METALLIC
STARLIKE ASTRAL SPHERY
STARLING SALI STARE BEAVER
PASTOR TILYER SPREEUW STARNEL
STAYNIL CHEPSTER CUTWATER
SHEPSTER
STARRED LIZARD HARDIM
STARRING FEATURED
STARRY ASTRAL STARNY STELLED
SIDEREAL
STAR SAPPHIRE ASTERIA ASTRION
ASTROITE
STAR-SHAPED ASTROID
START DIG SET BOLT BOUN DART
DASH HEAD JERK JUMP OPEN TURN
WHIP BEGIN BIRTH BRAID BREAK
BUDGE ENTER FLIRT GLENT ONSET
RAISE ROUSE THROW BOGGLE
BROACH FLINCH INTEND OFFSET
SETOFF SETOUT STRIKE TWITCH
GETAWAY OPENING STARTLE
SUNRISE COMMENCE CONCEIVE
INCHOATE OUTSTART
(— A HORSE) WINCE
(— ASIDE) SHY SKIT DODGE
(— BURNING) SPIT KINDLE
(— FERMENTATION) PITCH
(— OF BIRD'S FLIGHT) SOUSE
(— OUT) FRAME INTEND
(— UP) JUMP ASTART ASTERT
(SUDDEN —) SHY SQUIRT
STARTER KOJI
(BUNG —) FLOGGER
STAR THISTLE CALTROP CALTHROP
STARTING INCOMING
STARTLE SOHO ALARM SCARE
SHOCK START STURT AFFRAY
BOGGLE BOOGER FRIGHT FRIGHTEN
SURPRISE
STARTLING ALARMING SHOCKING
STARVATION LACK FAMINE
STARVE CLEM FAST FAMINE FAMISH
AFFAMISH
STARVED MEAGER MEAGRE
STARVEN
STARVED-LOOKING SLINK
STARVELING SHARGAR SHARGER
STARVING CLUNG
STARWORT ASTROFEL
STATE WU LAY PUT SAY CASE MODE
NAME POMP PORT TERM TIFF COVIN
ESTER ESTRE POLIS SPEAK STADE
TERMS TUATH WHACK AFFIRM
AGENCY ASSERT ASSURE CAESAR
EFFEIR EMPIRE ESTATE IMPORT
NATION PLIGHT POLICY POLITY
RENDER RIALTY SOVIET STATUS
STEVEN CIVITAS DECLARE DESERET
DUKEDOM ENOUNCE EXPOUND
EXPRESS KINSHIP PROPOSE
SPECIFY STATION TERMINE
DEVACHAN DOMINION FRANKLIN
HEGEMONY INDICATE KINGSHIP
REPUBLIC STATELET

(— EXPLICITLY) DEFINE
(— FORMALLY) ENOUNCE
(— IN NORTH CAROLINA) FRANKLIN
(— OF AFFAIRS) CASE ARRAY
STATUS
(— OF ALARM) GAST FEEZE SCARE
(— OF AMAZEMENT) STOUND
(— OF ANGER) FUME
(— OF APATHY) STUPOR
(— OF BEING CUT) SCISSION
(— OF BEING DRAWN) TRACTION
(— OF BEING OVERFULL) PLETHORA
(— OF BEING POISONOUS) TOXICITY
(— OF BEING WORSE) PEJORITY
(— OF CONCENTRATION) DHARANA
DHAYANA SAMADHI
(— OF CONFUSION) FOG FLAP HACK
MUSS CHAOS SWIRL HASSLE
HUBBUB FLUMMOX TROYTOWN
(— OF CONSECRATION) IHRAM
(— OF COOPERATION) HOOKUP
(— OF DISASTER) SMASH
(— OF DISORDER) HELL MUSS
FANTAD ANARCHY
(— OF DISSENSION) SCISSION
(— OF DISTURBANCE) GARBOIL
(— OF DOUBT) MIST
(— OF EAGERNESS) HURRY
(— OF ECSTASY) SWOON
(— OF ENCHANTMENT) SPELL
(— OF ENLIGHTENMENT) BODHI
(— OF EXALTATION) FURY ECSTASY
(— OF EXCITATION) FOMENT
(— OF EXCITEMENT) FRY FLAP
GALE HIGH SNIT STEW FEEZE
HOIGH DITHER DOODAH HUBBUB
FANTEEG FLUSTER KIPPAGE
SWELTER FANTIGUE
(— OF EXHAUSTION) GONENESS
(— OF FEAR) FUNK JELLY SCARE
(— OF HAPPINESS) ELYSIUM
PARADISE
(— OF HEALTH) EUCRASIA
(— OF HUMILIATION) DUST
(— OF IDEAL PERFECTION) UTOPIA
(— OF IMPERFECTION) SCARCITY
(— OF INACTION) DEADLOCK
(— OF INCIPIENCE) EMBRYO
(— OF INTENSITY) BUILD
(— OF IRRITABILITY) FUME GALL
FANTAD
(— OF JOY) JUBILEE
(— OF MELANCHOLY) GLOOM
(— OF MENTAL INACTIVITY)
TORPOR
(— OF MENTAL READINESS)
ATTITUDE
(— OF MIND) CUE HIP CASE MOOD
HUMOR FETTLE CARAPACE
(— OF MISERY) HELL GEHENNA
(— OF NEGLECT) LIMBO
(— OF OPPOSITION) DEFIANCE
(— OF OSTRACISM) COVENTRY
(— OF PERTURBATION) CRISE
(— OF PREOCCUPATION) CARE
(— OF READINESS) GUARD
(— OF REALITY) ACT
(— OF REJECTION) GATE
(— OF REPOSE) CALM

(— OF RETIREMENT) GRASS
(— OF REVERIE) DUMP
(— OF SENSITIVITY) NERVES
(— OF SLUGGISHNESS) COMA
(— OF SUSPENSE) TRANCE
(— OF TENSION) FANTEEG STRETCH
FANTIGUE
(— OF THE SOUL) BARDO
(— OF THINGS) FARE PASS
(— OF TRANQUILLITY) KEF KIF
PEACE
(— OF UNCERTAINTY) FOG FLUX
(— OF UNREST) FERMENT
(— OF WEATHER) FREEZE
(— OF WORRY) TEW SWEAT FANTAD
(— POSITIVELY) AFFIRM
(— UNDER OATH) ALLEGE
(AGITATED —) FUSS SNIT STIR
CHURN STORM LATHER SWIVET
(BUFFER —) GLACIS
(CHINESE —) WU SHU WEI
(DAZED —) DAMP
(DEPRESSED —) GLOOM WALLOW
(DISTURBED —) STIR STORM
UNREST
(DOMINANT —) SUZERAIN
(DROWSY —) DOVER
(EMOTIONAL —) FEVER FEELING
(FEUDAL —) WEI
(FICTITIOUS —) FABLE
(FILTHY —) DIRT
(FREE —) SAORSTAT
(GLOOMY —) DUMP
(HIGHEST —) SUPREME
(HORIZONTAL —) LEVEL
(INDONESIAN —) NEGARA
(IRISH —) TUATH
(LIQUID —) FLUOR FLUIDITY
(MARRIED —) SPOUSAL
(MENTAL —) EARNEST DELUSION
(MORBID —) HIP IODISM
(MORMON —) DESERET
(NEUTRAL —) BUFFER
(PECUNIARY —) FACULTY
(PERTURBED —) DEVIL
(PROFOUND —) DEPTH
(SWISS —) CANTON
(ULTIMATE —) END
(UNFAVORABLE —) FOULNESS
(VERIFIED —) FACT
STATED GIVEN CERTAIN
(DIRECTLY —) EXPRESS
STATEHOUSE CAPITOL
STATELINESS STATE DIGNITY
MAJESTY GRANDEUR
STATELY DATE BURLY GRAND
LARGO LOFTY NOBLE REGAL STATE
STOUT AUGUST COUPON PORTLY
SOLEMN SUPERB TOGATE GALLANT
BARONIAL IMPOSING MAESTOSO
MAJESTIC STATEFUL
STATEMENT SAY BILL VOTE WORD
AXIOM BRIEF COUNT DIXIT LIBEL
STATE STORY BELIEF DICTUM
DOCKET EXPOSE FACTUM RETURN
SAYING SPEECH ACCOUNT ADDRESS
ANALOGY DISSENT EPITAPH
EPITOME FORMULA INVOICE
MENTION SHOWING ABSTRACT

ANTINOMY ARGUMENT AVERMENT
BULLETIN DELIVERY EQUATION
EXPLICIT JUDGMENT PROPOSAL
SCHEDULE SENTENCE SPEAKING
SYNGRAPH SYNOPSIS
(— AS PRECEDENT) AUTHORITY
(— OF OPINION) CHANT
(— OF RELATIONS) THEOREM
(— ON DRUG LABEL) LEGEND
(AUTHORITATIVE —) DICTUM
(CASUAL —) REMARK
(CONCISE —) SCHEME APHORISM
(CONDENSED —) RESUME SYNOPSIS
(DEFAMATORY —) LIBEL
(EXAGGERATED —) STRETCH
(FABRICATED —) CANARD
(FINAL — OF ACCOUNT) AUDIT
(FINANCIAL —) BUDGET
(FOOLISH —) INANITY
(FORMAL —) CITATION
(IRRATIONAL —) ALOGISM
(OBSCURE —) ENIGMA
(PLAINTIFF'S —) BODY
(POMPOUS —) BRAG
(SELF-CONTRADICTORY —)
PARADOX
(SOOTHING —) SALVE
(UNTRUE —) LIE
STATER COLT TURTLE PEGASUS
CYZICENE
STATEROOM BIBBY CABIN
STATESMAN GENRO SOLON FATHER
STATIST WARWICK JACOBEAN
WEALSMAN
STATICE ARMERIA LIMONIUM
STATION BY BYE FIX ORB RUN SET
GARE POST RANK ROOM STOP
BEING CHOKY DEPOT PLACE POSTE
SIEGE STAGE STALL STAND STATE
DEGREE LOCATE STANCE CONTROL
CUARTEL DIGNITY HABITAT
OUTPOST GARRISON PILTDOWN
POSITION STANDING TERMINAL
TERMINUS TRANSFER
(— IN BASEBALL) BASE
(— IN LIFE) BEING CALLING
(— OF HERON) SEDGE SIEGE
(CONCEALED —) AMBUSH
(CUSTOMS —) CHOKEY
(EXALTED —) PURPLE
(POLICE —) TANA TANNA THANAH
KOTWALEE
(POST —) DAK
(RADIO —S) CHAIN NETWORK
(RAILWAY —) GARE CABIN
(SIGNALLING —) BANTAY BEACON
(SURVEYING —) STADIA
(TRADING —) FACTORY
(WAY —) TAMBO
STATIONARY SET FAST FIXED STILL
LEDGER STATIC DORMANT SITFAST
STABLE STATARY IMMOBILE
STATISTICIAN ANALYST STATIST
STATOBLAST SPORE
STATUARY IMAGERY
STATUE HERM ICON IDOL IKON
TERM BUSTO HERMA IMAGE MOSES
AGALMA BRONZE HERMES MEMNON
STATUA WEEPER XOANON ILISSUS

PASQUIN PICTURE STATURE
STATUTE ACROLITH CARYATID
MARFORIO MONUMENT PANTHEUM
PORTRAIT VICTORIA
(— ENDOWED WITH LIFE) GALATEA
(— OF GIGANTIC SIZE) COLOSSUS
(COLOSSAL —) GOG MAGOG
STATUETTE WAX EMMY OSCAR
WINNIE TANAGRA FIGULINE
FIGURINE SIGILLUM
STATURE PITCH GROWTH HEIGHT
INCHES WASTME CAPACITY
STATUS RANK SEAT PLACE STATE
ASPECT FOOTING STATURE
STANDING
(— OF YOUNGER SON) CADENCY
(HIGH —) CACHET
(LEGAL —) CAPUT
(SECONDARY —) BACKSEAT
STATUTE ACT LAW LEX DOOM EDICT
ASSIZE DECREE SETNESS SITTING
STATUTUM TANZIMAT
(— FAIR) MOP
STATUTORY LEGAL
STAUNCH FAST STOUT FAITHFUL
STAVE LAG SLAT STAP SHAKE STAFF
STOVE VERSE BASTON STANZA
WATTLE
(— IN) BILGE BULGE
(SET OF —S) SHOOK
(PL.) LAGGEN LAGGIN STICKS
STAVING
STAY DAY GET LIE BASE HOLD LEND
PROP REST SIST STOP WAIT ABIDE
ABODE APPUI DEFER DELAY DEMUR
DWELL LEAVE STINT TARRY THOLE
ARREST ATTEND BIDING DETAIN
EXPECT GUSSET POTENT REMAIN
TIMBER UPHOLD EMBASSY JIBSTAY
LAYOVER MANSION SOJOURN
SUSPEND BACKSTAY CONTINUE
FORESTAY HORNSTAY MAINSTAY
(— AWAY) SKIP
(— BEHIND) LAG
(— CLEAR) AVOID
(— FOR) AWAIT
(— THE NIGHT) BUNK HOSTLE
(— WITH) STICK
(PRIEST'S —) STATION
(TAILORING —) BRIDLE
(PL.) JUMPS JUPES BODICE
STAY-AT-HOME HOMEBODY
HOMESTER
STAYER BONER
STAYLACE AGLET AIGLET
STAYSAIL JUMBO
STEAD LIEU ROOM VICE PLACE
BEHALF
STEADFAST SAD FAST FIRM SURE
TRUE ROCKY STAID STEER STABLE
STANCH STEADY CERTAIN EXPRESS
SETTLED STAUNCH VALIANT
CONSTANT FAITHFUL RESOLUTE
STEADFASTLY FIRM FIRMLY
INTENTLY
STEADILY SAD FAST STEADY
STEADINESS NERVE BALANCE
STEADING ONSET ONSTEAD
STEADY GUY SAD BEAU EVEN FIRM

SURE TRIG TRUE CANNY FRANK
LEVEL SOBER STUDY SUANT TIGHT
STABLE STANCH BALLAST EQUABLE
STABILE STATARY STAUNCH
CONSTANT DECOROUS DILIGENT
FAITHFUL RESOLUTE TRANQUIL
UNSHAKEN
(— AT ANCHOR) HOLSOM
STEAK BROIL SHELL FLITCH TUCKET
GRISKIN
STEAL BAG CAB CLY COP FOX GYP
LAG NAP NIM NIP RAP RIG BONE
CHOR COON CRIB FAKE GLOM
HOOK LIFT LURK MAGG MAKE MILL
NAIL NICK PEAK PICK PRIG SLIP
SMUG ANNEX BOOST BRIBE CLOUT
CREEP FETCH FILCH FLIMP FRISK
GLIDE HARRY HEIST HOIST LURCH
MOOCH MOUCH PINCH PLUCK
POACH SCOFF SHAKE SHARP SHAVE
SLIDE SNAKE SNARE SNEAK STALK
SWIPE TOUCH TRUFF COLLAR
CONVEY FINGER HIJACK MOOTCH
NOBBLE PILFER SNITCH STRIKE
THIEVE BESTEAL CABBAGE
PLUNDER PURLOIN SCHLEPP
SKYUGLE SNABBLE SNAFFLE
SURREPT ABSTRACT CRIBBAGE
EMBEZZLE LIBERATE MANARVEL
PECULATE SCROUNGE SHOPLIFT
(— A GLANCE) GLIME
(— A WATCH) FLIMP
(— ALONG) SLIME SLINK
(— AWAY) LOOP SLINK
(— BY ALTERING BRANDS) DUFF
(— CALVES) NUGGET
(— CATTLE) DUFF RUSTLE
(— COPPER FROM VESSEL'S
BOTTOM) TOSH
(— OFF) RUN
(— SLYLY) SCROUNGE
STEALER (CATTLE —) DUFFER
ABACTOR
STEALTHILY SIDLINS THIEFLY
SIDELINS
STEALTHY CATTY PRIVY ARTFUL
FELINE TIPTOE CATLIKE FURTIVE
SNEAKING THIEVISH
STEAM OAM ROKE STEM BLAST
SMOKE SWEAT VAPOR BREATH
POTHER CUSHION
STEAMBOAT KICKUP STEAMER
STEAMER CLAM LINER TENDER
STEAMER CUNARDER
STEAMER DUCK RACER LOGHEAD
STEAMSHIP SCREW STEAM
STEAMER SEATRAIN SHOWBOAT
STEAM SHOVEL NAVVY NAVVIE
STEATIN MULL
STEATITE LARDITE POTSTONE
SOAPROCK
STEATOPYGOUS RUMPY
STEED ROIL STEAD PEGASUS
SLEIPNER
STEEL RAIL BLOOM BRACE FUSIL
TERNE WEAPON WHITTLE FLEERISH
(— FOR STRIKING FIRE) ESLABON
(— FOR USE WITH FLINT) FUSIL
FURISON FLEERISH

(— INLAID WITH GOLD) KOFT
KOFTGARI
(DAMASCUS —) DAMASK
(INDIAN —) WOOTZ
(MOLTEN —) HEAT
STEELER BONER
STEELING ACIERAGE
STEELWORKER HOOKER STICKMAN
STRANDER STRANNER
STEELYARD BISMER DESEMER
DOTCHIN STATERA
STEENBRAS BISKOP
STEEP SOP BATE BOLD BOWK BUCK
DRAW DUNG ELIX LIME MASH SOAK
STAY STEW STEY BRANT BRENT
HATCH HEAVY HILLY QUICK SHARP
SHEER SOUSE STIFF ABRUPT
BLUFFY CLIFFY CLIFTY DECOCT
IMBIBE INFUSE SPRUNT STEEPY
ARDUOUS BRASQUE CLIVOSE
INSTEEP PRERUPT STICKLE
HEADLONG MACETATE SATURATE
SIDELING STIFFISH STRAIGHT
STEEPED SODDEN
STEEPING SOUSE INFUSION
STEEPLE SPEAR SPIRE
STEEPLECHASE CHASE GRIND
STEER COX PLY BEEF BULL HELM
LEAD STEM STOT GUIDE SPADE
SPADO STERN TOLLY CANNER
RUDDER BULLOCK STOCKER
COWBRUTE MOSSHORN NAVIGATE
(— VEHICLE) DRIVE
(FAT —) BEAST
(HORNLESS —) NOT NOTT
(VICIOUS —) LADINO
(WILD —) YAW YEW COWBRUTE
(YOUNG —) STOT STOTT
STEERAGE STERN
STEERER CAPPER
STEERSMAN PILOT WHEEL PATRON
SLEWER CANOPUS SHIPMAN
STEERER COXSWAIN HELMSMAN
SEACUNNY STERNMAN WHEELMAN
STEIN SHANT
STELE SHAFT EUSTELE
STELLAR STARRY
STELLATE STARRY ASTROSE
STEM BUN BASE BEAM BINE BIRN
CANE CULM NOSE PIPE PROW RISP
ROOT RUNT STUD DTRAW FILUM
HAULM SCAPE SCREW SHANT
SHANK SHOOT STALE STALK STEAL
STICK STIPE STOCK THEME TRUNK
TUBER BRANCH CAUDEX CAULIS
DERIVE SCAPUS SPRING CAULOME
CONTAIN FULCRUM HOPBINE
HOPVINE PEDICEL PETIOLE PLASHER
SPINDLE STEMLET TIGELLA
CAULICLE ENGENDER FORESTEM
PEDUNCLE PIPESTEM TIGELLUM
(— OF ARROW) SHAFT
(— OF BANANAS) COUNT
(— OF GLASS) BALUSTER
(— OF GRAPES) RAPE
(— OF HOOKAH) SNAKE
(— OF MATCH) SHAFT
(— OF MUSHROOM) STIPE
(— OF MUSICAL NOTE) TAIL FILUM
VIRGULA

(— OF PIPE) STAPPLE
(— OF PLANT) AXIS RUNT CAULIS
(— OF SHIP) PROW STEMPOST
(— OF TREE) BOLE
(—S OF CULTIVATED PLANTS)
HAULM
(BULBLIKE —) CORM
(DRY WITHERED —) BIRN
(EDIBLE —) EDDO
(GRIEF —) KELLY
(MAIN — OF DEER'S ANTLERS)
BEAM
(ORNAMENTAL —) STAVE
(PITHY JOINTED —) CANE
(THORNY —) LAWYER
(TWINING —) BINE
STEMLESS ACAULINE
STEMMA OCELLUS OCELLANA
PEDIGREE
STEMMER STRIPPER
STENCH FOGO HOGO FETOR SMELL
STINK WHIFF FOETOR MEPHITIS
STENCIL (— PROCESS) POCHOIR
STENCILED GOFFERED
STENOSIS SMALLING
STEP CUT FIT JOG PEG PIP BEMA
DESS FOOT GREE LINK PACE PEEP
RUNG STAP BRASS CORTE DODGE
FLIER FLYER GRECE NOTCH POINT
STAGE STAIR TOOTH TRACE TREAD
DEGREE GRADIN RUNDLE STRIDE
WINDER CURTAIL DESCENT
FOOTING GRADINE GRADING
COONJINE DEMARCHE DOORSTEP
FOOTPACE FOOTSTEP FORESTEP
PREDELLA STRATLIN
(— ASIDE) DIGRESS
(— BACKWARD) DODGE
(— BY STEP) GRADATIM
(— DOWNWARD) DESCENT
(— FOR GEM MOUNTING) KITE
(— FORWARD) ADVANCE
(— IN A BEARING) BRASS
(— IN BELL RINGING) DODGE
(— IN DOCK) ALTAR
(— IN SELF-ESTEEM) PEG
(— IN SOCIAL SCALE) CUT
(— LIVELY) SKELP
(— OF LADDER) RIME RUNG ROUND
RUNDLE
(— OF TUSK) TOOTH
(— SUPPORTING MILLSTONE)
TRAMPOT
(—S OF BOWLER) APPROACH
(ALTAR —S) GRADUAL
(BALLET —) SISSONE SISSONNE
(BALLET —S) ALLEGRO
(BOUNDING —) SKIP
(CLUMSY —) STAUP
(DANCE —) DIP PAS SET BUZZ
DRAG DRAW FLAT SHAG SKIP
BRAWL CHASS COULE GLIDE IRISH
STOMP BRANLE CANTER CHASSE
DOUBLE INTURN STRIDE BRANSLE
BUFFALO FISHTAIL GLISSADE
(FALSE —) HOB SLIP SPHALM
SNAPPER SPHALMA STUMBLE
(FIRST —) STARTER RUDIMENT
(FLIGHT OF —S) GRECE GRICE

PERRON GEMONIES
(HALF —) HALFTONE SEMITONE
(MINING —) LOB STEMPEL STEMPLE
(POMPOUS —) STRUT
(PRIM —) MINCE
(SET OF —S) STILE
(STATELY —) STALK
(PL.) STY STILE LADDER
STEPFATHER FATHER STEPSIRE
STEPLADDER TRAP STEPS
STEPMOTHER MOTHER HANGNAIL
STEPDAME
(RELATING TO —) NOVERCAL
STEPPE PUSZTA
STEPPED STOPEN
STEREOISOMER ANOMER EPIMER
STEREOTYPE CAST CLICHE STEREO
STEREOTYPED CHAIN STAGE TRITE
USUAL STEREO
STERILE DRY DEAD DEAF GELD
POOR AXENIC BARREN GALLED
MEAGER MULISH OTIOSE ASEPTIC
ACARPOUS BANKRUPT IMPOTENT
STERILITY ATOCIA APHORIA
STERILIZE INSULATE
STERILIZING BURNING
STERLING SOUND
(100,000 POUNDS —) PLUM
STERN GRIL GRIM HARD POOP
ASPER CRUEL GRUFF HARSH RIGID
ROUGH ROUND STARK STOUR
FLINTY GLOOMY GRIMLY SHREWD
STRICT SULLEN TORVID UNKIND
WICKED AUSTERE TORVOUS
STEERAGE STERNFUL STRAIGHT
(— OF SHIP) DOCK APLUSTRE
STERNFAST PROVISO
STERNNESS RIGOR TORVITY
SEVERITY
STERNPOST POST STEM MAINPOST
STERNUTATIVE ERRHINE PTARMIC
STERNUTATOR ERRHINE
STEROL AMYRIN STERIN AMBRAIN
STEVEDORE STOWER TRIMMER
WHARFIE CARGADOR DOCKHAND
STEVENSON, R.L. TUSITALA
STEW JUG FRET ITCH SLUM SNIT
BREDI CIVET CURRY DAUBE STIVE
STOVE SWEAT BURGOO HODDLE
MUDDLE PAELLA SEETHE SIMMER
BROTHEL CALDERA GOULASH
HARICOT NAVARIN PUCHERO
STOVIES FRIJOADA HOTCHPOT
MORTREUX MULLIGAN STEWPOND
STUFFATA
(— A HARE) JUG
(— IN A SAUCE) DAUBE
(— MADE IN FORECASTLE) HODDLE
(— OF TRAMPS) MULLIGAN
(FISH —) STODGE CHOWDER
(IRISH —) STOVIES
(MUTTON —) NAVARIN
STEWARD HIND VOGT DEWAN DIWAN
GRAFF GRAVE FACTOR FARMER
GRIEVE LOOKER SIRCAR SIRDAR
CURATOR DAPIFER FLUNKEY
GRANGER HUSBAND MAORMOR
MORMAOR PESHKAR PROCTOR
PROVOST SPENCER SPENDER

VILLCUS APPROVER BHANDARI
CELLARER CONSUMAH GASTALDO
HERENACH KHANSAMA LARDINER
MALVOLIO MANCIPLE PROVISOR
STEADMAN
(JOCKEY CLUB —) STIPE
STEWED SODDEN
STEWING ITCHING
STEWPAN STEW COCOTTE SKILLET
STHENELUS (FATHER OF —)
PERSEUS CAPANEUS ANDROGEOS
(MOTHER OF —) EVADNE
ANDROMEDA
(SON OF —) EURYSTHEUS
(WIFE OF —) NICIPPE
STHENOBOEA (FATHER OF —)
IOBATES
(HUSBAND OF —) PROETUS
STIBNITE SURMA STIBIUM ANTIMONY
STIBOPHEN FUADIN
STICHIC SERIAL
STICK CAT CLA DIP GAD HEW WAN
BROG BUFF CHOP CLAG CLAM CLUB
CRAB GLUE HANG HURL PALO PICK
POLE POTE RICE RUNG STAY TREE
YARD BATON BRAIL CAMAN CLAME
CLAVE CLEAM CLING CROME
DEMUR HURLY PRICK SPELK STAFF
STAKE STANG STAVE STEND STING
STOCK STOKE VALET VERGE
WADDY ADHERE ATLATL BALLOW
BATLER BATLET BATTLE BILLET
BROACH BULGER CEMENT CLEAVE
CLEEKY COHERE CUDGEL FESCUE
HOCKEY INHERE KIPPIN LIBBET
MALLET RADDLE RAMMER RISSLE
STRIKE STRING THIVEL TWITCH
BACKSET BATLING CAMMOCK
CUMMOCK GAMBREL HURLBAT
KILNRIB KIPPEEN MOLINET NOBBLER
SHANGAN SPURTLE WOOLDER
ASHPLANT BLUDGEON BRINGSEL
BRINSELL CATPIECE CATSTICK
DIPSTICK DUTCHMAN GIBSTAFF
GOBSTICK KILNTREE POTSTICK
SPREADER
(— AS ARCHERY MARK) WAND
(— FAST) JAM JAMB SEIZE FITCHER
(— FASTENED TO DOG'S TAIL)
SHANGAN
(— FOR ADMITTING TENANTS)
VERGE
(— FOR KILLING FISH) NOBBLER
(— FOR MAKING FENCE) RADDLE
(— FOR MIXING CHOCOLATE)
MOLINET
(— FOR SNUFF) DIP
(— FOR THATCHING) SPAR GROOM
SPELK SPRINGLE
(— IN MUD) STODGE
(— IN OPERATION) FREEZE
(— IT OUT) LAST
(— OF A FAN) BRIN
(— OF CANDY) GIBBY
(— OF CHALK) CRAYON
(— OF ORCHESTRA LEADER) BATON
(— OUT) BUG POKE BULGE SHOOT
EXTEND EXXERT EXTRUDE
(— REGULATING SLUICEWAY)
CATPIECE

(— SEPARATING LUMBER PILES)
STICKER
(— TO BEAT CLOTHES) BATLER
BATLET
(— TO DISTEND CARCASS) STEND
BACKSET
(— TO HOLD BOW) TILLER
(— TO HOLD LOG LOAD) DUTCHMAN
(— TO KEEP ANIMAL QUIET)
TWITCH
(— TO MARK CROSSING) BROG
(— TO POKE WITH) POTE
(— TO REMOVE HOOK FROM FISH)
GOBSTICK
(— TO STRETCH NET) BRAIL
(— TO STUFF DOLLS) RAMMER
(— TO THROW AT BIRDS) SQUAIL
(— TO TIGHTEN KNOT) WOOLDER
(— TOGETHER) CLOT BLOCK CLING
BALTER CEMENT COHERE
COAGMENT
(— UP) COCK
(— USED AS POINTER) FESCUE
(BAMBOO —) LATHI LATHEE
(BASKETRY —) LEAGUE
(BENT —) RIFLE
(FIELD HOCKEY —) BULGER
CAMMOCK
(FISHING —) GAD
(FORKED —) GROM GROOM
(HOCKEY —) CAMAN HURLY
HOCKEY HURLEY SHINNY CAMMOCK
CUMMOCK DODDART
(IRON-POINTED —) VALET
(KNOBBED —) BILLET
(LACROSSE —) CROSSE
(LARGE —) MOCK
(MARKING —) LEAD
(ODD —) JAY
(POLISHING —) BUFF
(PRAYER —) PAHO
(PRINTER'S —) SHOOTER
(RANGE-FINDING —) STADIA
(ROUND —) DOWEL SPINDLE
(STIRRING —) MUNDLE POOLER
SPURTLE POTSTICK SWIZZLER
(STOUT —) BAT LOWDER
(TALLY —) TAIL
(THROWING —) ATLATL HORNERAH
(TOBACCO —) LATH
(WALKING —) CANE KEBBY WADDY
JAMBEE JOCKEY KEBBIE WHANGEE
ASHPLANT GIBSTAFF
STICKER HINGE LABEL STRIP WAFER
HOPPER PASTER BLEEDER
CROSSER MOPSTICK STICKLER
STICK-IN STRANDER
STICKINESS TACK
STICKING ADHERENT ADHESION
COHESION COHESIVE
STICKLE DEMUR BOGGLE HAGGLE
HIGGLE
STICKLEBACK BAGGIE BANDIE
HACKLE GHOSTER PINFISH
STICKLER (— FOR FORMALITY)
TAPIST
STICKMAN DEALER
STICKY CAB CLAM CLIT ICKY DABBY
FATTY GAUMY GLUEY GOOEY

GUMMY JAMMY MALMY PUGGY
SHORT TACKY TOUGH CLAGGY
CLAMMY CLARTY CLOGGY PLUCKY
VISCID VISCOUS ADHESIVE
STIFF BUM SAD CARK HARD NASH
TRIG BUDGE CLUNG RIGID SOLID
STARK STEER STITH STOUR THARF
TOUGH BOARDY CLEDGY CLUMSY
CLUNCH FORMAL FROZEN PLUGGY
STARKY STEEVE STICKY STILTY
STOCKY STURDY UNEASY WOODEN
ANGULAR COSTIVE STARCHY
STILTED RAMRODDY RIGOROUS
STAFFISH
(SOMEWHAT —) CARKLED
STIFFEN GUM SET SIZE BRACE
STARK STIFF STRUT TRUSS HARDEN
STARCH STOVER STARKEN
(— PRICE) HARDEN
STIFFENED FUSED CARKLED
STIFFENER KNEE COUNTER
STIFFENING PUFF DRESS
STIFFNESS KINK RIGOR STARCH
BUCKRAM PRIMNESS RIGIDITY
SEVERITY
STIFLE DAMP SLAY CHOKE CRUSH
STIVE STUFF MUFFLE QUENCH
FLASKER QUERKEN SMOTHER
STRANGLE SUPPRESS THROTTLE
STIFLED DEAF ETOUFFE
STIFLING STUVY SMUDGY POTHERY
SMOTHERY
STIGMA BLOT FOIL NOTE SLUR
SPOT BRAND ODIUM STAIN TAINT
BLOTCH BLEMISH
STIGMATIZE BLOT BRAND
DENOUNCE
STILBITE DESMINE
STILE STY STICK TIMBER
STILETTO BODKIN STYLET PIERCER
POINTEL
STILL BUT COY LAY YET BODY CALM
COSH HUSH LOWN LULL WORM
CHECK QUIET WHIST HOWEER
HUSHED PACIFY QUENCH SETTLE
SILENT SOOTHE SUBDUE WITHAL
ALEMBIC CORNUTE HOWEVER
PELICAN SILENCE CUCURBIT
RECEIVER RESTRAIN STAGNANT
STILLERY SUPPRESS
(— PART) KELD
STILLAGE SLOP STILLING STILLION
STILL-HUNT STALK
STILLNESS CALM HUSH REST PEACE
SILENCE STATION
STILT KAKI POGO TILT LAWYER
PATTEN SCATCH YEGUITA
LONGLEGS STILTIFY TRIANGLE
STILTED LOFTY STIFF FORMAL
POETIC STILTY POMPOUS
STIMULANT STIM INULA BRACER
FILLIP GINGER HARMAL PHYTIN
CAMPHOR REVIVER ADONIDIN
AMMONIAC EXCITANT STIMULUS
STIMULATE FAN HOP PEP FUEL
GOAD HYPO MOVE SEED SPUR STIR
URGE WHET FILIP IMPEL ROUSE
SPARK STING AROUSE EXCITE
FILLIP INCITE SPIRIT TICKLE UPSTIR

ANIMATE ENLIVEN INNERVE INSPIRE
QUICKEN ACTIVATE FARADIZE
IRRITATE MOTIVATE
STIMULATING SEXY BRISK
PUNGENT EROGENIC EXCITING
GENEROUS INCITANT STIRRING
(**— ANGER)** ADRENAL
STIMULATION IMPETUS
(**MENTAL —)** SPRITE
STIMULUS CUE AURA BROD EDGE
GOAD HYPO SPUR STIM STING
FILLIP MOTIVE SOURCE BAHNUNG
IMPETUS OESTRUS
STING NIP BITE BURN FOIN GOAD
TANG ATTER DEVIL PIQUE PRICK
STANG TOUCH NETTLE ACULEUS
BUGBITE PIERCER IRRITATE
STIMULUS
STINGILY STRAIT SCARCELY
STINGING KEEN SMART PEPPERY
PIQUANT POINTED PRICKLY
PUNGENT ACULEATE NETTLING
SCALDING URTICANT
STINGING ANT KELEP
STINGRAY ANGLER OBISPO TRYGON
BATFISH LOPHIID STEPHEN STINGER
WAIREPO
STINGY DRY DREE GAIN GAIR HARD
MEAN NEAR NIGH CLOSE MINGY
SCALY TIGHT DRIECH GRIPPY
HUNGRY NARROW SCABBY SCARCE
SCRIMY SKIMPY SKINNY SNIPPY
STRAIT CHINCHY CHINTZY MISERLY
NIGGARD
STINK FOGO GOAD STEW SMELL
SMEECH STENCH
STINKBIRD HOACIN HOATZIN
STINKING FOUL HIGH FETID PUTID
STINKY
STINKWOOD DOGWOOD
STINT TASK GRIST PINCH SCANT
SNAPE SKINCH STINGY TANTUM
SCANTLE
(**SHORT —)** SNATCH
(**WITHOUT —)** FREELY
STIPE STEM STALK
STIPEND ANN HIRE ANNAT WAGES
SALARY PENSION PREBEND
PROVEND COMMENDA
STIPENDIARY BEAK
STIPPLE SPONGE
STIPPLED DOTTED
STIPULATE ARTICLE PROTEST
COVENANT
STIPULATION IF ANNEX CLAUSE
ARTICLE PREMISE PROVISO
COVENANT
(**PL.)** TERMS
STIPULE SPINE SHEATH STIPEL
STIPULA TENDRIL
STIR DO ADO FAN GOG PUG WAG
BEET BUZZ CARD FUSS MOVE PEAL
RAUK ROKE WAKE AMOVE BUDGE
CHURN CREEP ERECT FUROR
HURRY MUDGE POACH RAISE
ROUST SLICE SPARK STING STOOR
STURT TEASE TOUCH AROUSE
AWAKEN BUBBLE BUSTLE CRUTCH
EXCITE FLURRY GINGER HUBBUB

JUMBLE KIAUGH MUDDLE POUTER
QUINCH QUITCH REMBLE REMOVE
ROUNCE STODGE SUMMON TATTER
ACTUATE ANIMATE BLATHER
FLUTTER PROVOKE STARKLE
SWIZZLE TROUBLE
(**— ABOUT)** KNOCK
(**— CALICO COLORS)** TEER
(**— DRINK)** MUDDLE SWIZZLE
(**— LIQUID)** ROG
(**— SOIL)** CHISEL
(**— UP WITH YEAST)** BARM
(**— UP)** FAN MIX BUZZ DRUM FUSS
MOVE PROG ROIL TOSS AMOVE
AREAR AWAKE ERECT QUICK ROUSE
SNURL SPOOK STOKE TARRY
BESTIR BOTHER CHOUSE EXCITE
INCITE JOSTLE KINDLE PUDDLE
RUMBLE TICKLE UPSTIR AGITATE
ANIMATE COMMOVE DISTURB
PRODDLE PROVOKE STUDDLE
TORMENT UNQUEME DISTRACT
STIRRER HOG DOLLY ROUSER
RUMMAGER
STIRRING RACY ASTIR DEEDFUL
THRILLY EXCITING PATHETIC
STIRRUP IRON CHAPELET STEELBOW
STITCH BAR RUN SEW KNIT LOOP
PURL WHIP CABLE CLOSE POINT
PREEN PUNTO STEEK ACCRUE
FESTON SUTURE TRICOT CROCHET
POPCORN FAGOTING
(**— OF CLOTHES)** TACK
(**PL.)** JOURS FILLING
STITCHBIRD IHI
STITCHDOWN SEWROUND
STITCHER WHIPPER
STITCHING SERGING FAGOTING
STOATING WHIPPING
STITCHWORT PAIGLE ALLBONE
SNAPPER HEADACHE SNAPJACK
SNAPWORT
STITHY STUDY SMITHY STIDDY
STUDDY
STOAT VAIR ERMINE WEASEL
CLUBSTER FUTTERET WHITRACK
STOCK COP DOG KIN ROD CANT
CROP FILL FOND FUND SEED SELL
STEM TRIP BLOND BLOOD BROTH
CASTE CREAM FLESH HOARD ISSUE
STALE STIRP STORE STUFF TALON
BUDGET CHOKER COMMON FUTURE
KAFFIR SHARES STOVEN STRAIN
SUPPLY CAPITAL DESCENT PILLORY
PROSAPY PROVIDE REPLETE
RESERVE BONEYARD CROSSBAR
DIESTOCK GILLIVER GUNSTOCK
MAGAZINE MERCHANT ORDINARY
SECURITY
(**— OF ANCHOR)** CROSS
(**— OF BREEDING MARES)** STRUDE
(**— OF FOOD)** FARE
(**— OF GRAIN)** COP
(**— OF MORPHEMES)** LEXICON
(**— OF WEAPONS)** ARSENAL
(**— OF WHIP)** CROP
(**— OF WINE)** CELLAR
(**— SOLD SHORT)** BEAR
(**FARM —)** BOW

(**LANGUAGE —)** SALISH SIOUAN
BOROTUKE
(**MEAT —)** BLOND BOUILLON
(**PLASTIC —)** BISCUIT
(**RAILROAD —)** GRANGER
(**PL.)** FOODS CIPPUS HARMAN
TIMBER CATASTA KAFFIRS
STOCKADE BOMA PEEL ETAPE
ZAREBA BARRIER TAMBOUR
STOCKADO
STOCK EXCHANGE BOURSE
COULISSE
STOCKFISH STOCK LUTFISK TITLING
SPELDING SPELDRON
STOCKING HOSE SOCK SHANK
STOCK CALIGA MOGGAN SCOGGER
SHINNER
(**FOOTLESS —)** HOGGER HUSHION
(**SOLELESS —)** TRAHEEN
(**PL.)** HOSE BUSKINS BOOTHOSE
STOCKJOBBING AGIOTAGE
STOCKWORK CARBONA
STOCKY FAT COBBY DUMPY GROSS
SQUAT STOUT CHUMPY CHUNKY
DUMPTY STUBBY STUGGY STUNTY
BUNTING COMPACT HEAVYSET
STOCKISH THICKSET
STODGY STUFFY STUGGY
STOIC IMPASSIVE
STOKEHOLD FIREROOM
STOKER FIREMAN BLOCKMAN
STOLE STAW ARMIL ORARY ARMILLA
ORARION
STOLEN HOT INOME STOUN FURTIVE
(**— GOODS)** MAINOUR
STOLID BEEFY CLUMSE STUPID
WOODEN CLUMPST DEADPAN
PASSIVE
STOLIDITY MORGUE
STOLON WIRE SOBOL SOBOLE
SOLENIUM
STOMACH MAW CROP GUTS KYTE
MARY POKE READ TANK WAME
WOMB BINGY BROOK GORGE
GROUF HEART TUMMY BINGEE
BINGEY BONNET CROPPY GEBBIE
PECHAN CONCOCT CRAPPIN
GIZZARD ABOMASUM
(**— OF ANIMAL)** CRAW
(**— OF CALF)** VELL
(**— OF RUMINANT)** READ RUMEN
BONNET OMASUM PAUNCH
ABOMASUM MANIFOLD RODDIKIN
(**PIG'S —)** JAUDIE
STOMACHACHE FANTAD GULLION
STOMACHER GIMP TRUSS ECHELLE
PLACARD POITREL FOREPART
STOMACHIC COTO CORNUS
GENTIAN ANTHEMIS
STONE DAM GEM BOND DUCK FLAG
HERD KLIP KNAR MARK ROCK STEN
TRIG BAUTA CAPEL DRAKE GUARD
LAPIS PAVER PITCH SCRAE SCREE
SNECK STANE ASHLAR BEDDER
BENBEN CEPHAS CHATON CLOSER
COBBLE GAMAHE GIBBER HEADER
JUMPER LEDGER MARVER METATE
MULLER NUTLET PEEVER PINNER
RUNNER SUMMER TORSEL ANGRITE

CALLAIS DINGBAT DONNOCK
DORNICK GLIDDER KNEELER
KNICKER PERPEND PITCHER
PUTAMEN RATCHEL STANNER
SURFACE THROUGH BAETULUS
CABOCHON DENDRITE EBENEZER
HAGSTONE LAPIDATE LAPILLUS
LAPSTONE MACEHEAD MONOLITH
NAKHLITE SKEWBACK TOPSTONE
(— ADHERING TO LEAD ORE) KEVEL
(— AS AMULET) HAGSTONE
(— AS IT COMES FROM QUARRY)
RUBBLE
(— AS ROAD MARKER) LEAGUE
(— AT DOOR) RYBAT
(— BLOCK) ASSIZE
(— FOR GLASS-ROLLING) MARVER
(— FORMING CAP OF PIER)
SUMMER CUSHION
(— HARD TO MOVE) SITFAST
(— HEAP) MAN
(— IN BLAST FURNACE) DAM
(— IN MEMORY OF DEAD)
MONUMENT
(— IN SMALL FRAGMENTS)
RATCHEL
(— OF FRUIT) COB PIT PAIP COBBE
NUTLET PYRENE PUTAMEN
(— OF PYRAMID SHAPE) BENBEN
(— PROVIDING CHANGE OF
DIRECTION) KNEELER
(— SET IN RING) CHATON
(— SHOT FROM STONE-BOW) JALET
(— TO DEATH) LAPIDATE
(— USED AS MONUMENT) MEGALITH
(— USED IN GAME) DUCK DRAKE
(— WITH INTERNAL CAVITY) GEODE
(—S FROM CRUSHER) TAILINGS
(—S IN WATER) STANNERS
(ARTIFICIAL —) ALBOLITE
(BINDING —) PERPEND THROUGH
PIERPONT
(BOND —) GIRDER KEYSTONE
(BOUNDARY —) TERM TERMINUS
(BROKEN — USED FOR ROADS)
BALLAST MACADAM
(BUILDING —) SUMMER MITCHEL
SPERONE
(CARVED —) CAMEO CUVETTE
(CASTING —) TYMP
(CHINA —) PETUNSE
(CLAY —) LECH
(COPING —) SKEW TABLET TABLING
CAPSTONE
(CURLING —) HOG HERD GUARD
LOOFIE POTLID
(DESERT —) GIBBER
(DRUID —) SARSEN
(DRYING —) STILLAGE
(EDGING —) SETTER
(FLAT —) PLAT DRAKE LEDGER
(FOUNDATION —) BEDDER
(GLITTERING —) DAZE
(GRAVE —) BAUTA STELE
(GREEN —) CALLAIS
(GRINDING —) METATE MULLER
(HOLY —) BEAR
(HOPSCOTCH —) PEEVER PALLALL
(IMAGINARY —) ADAMANT

(KIDNEY —) NEPHRITE
(LAST — IN COURSE) CLOSER
(LOOSE —) GLIDDER
(MEMORIAL —) BAUTA EBENEZER
(METEORIC —) ANGRITE NAKHLITE
(MIDDLE —) HONEY
(MONUMENTAL —) LECH
(PAVING —) PAVER PITCHER
(PHILOSOPHER'S —) ADROP
(PRECIOUS —) GEM OPAL RUBY
EWAGE JEWEL TOPAZ ADAMAS
LIGURE SHAMIR ASTERIA ASTRION
CRAPAUD CUVETTE DIAMOND
DIONISE EMERALD GELATIA JACINTH
OLIVINE SARDIUS AMETHYST
ASTROITE HYACINTH PANTARBE
SAPPHIRE YDRIADES
(PRECIOUS —S) PERRIE
(REFUSE —) ROACH
(SACRED —) BAETYL BAETULUS
(SEMIPRECIOUS —) ONYX SARD
MURRA GARNET CITRINE TIGEREYE
(SHARPENING —) HONE WHET
(SHOEMAKER'S —) LAPSTONE
(SMALL ROUND —) JACK
(SOFTENED —) SAP
(STEPPING —) GOAT
(STRATIFIED —) FLAG SLAB
(TALISMANIC —) GAMAHE
(UNSQUARED —) BACKING
(UPRIGHT —) BAUTA MENHIR
MASSEBAH
(PL.) LAPIDES LAPILLI
STONEBASS BAFARO WHAPUKU
STONEBOAT DRAY
STONEBOW RODD
STONECHAT CHAT SMICH
WHEATEAR
STONECROP SEDUM ORPINE
PRICKET WALLWORT
STONE CURLEW BUSTARD
STONECUTTER JADDER LAPICIDE
SCABBLER SCAPPLER SQUAREMAN
STONEFLY NAIAD
STONEHAND LOCKUP
STONELIKE LITHOID
STONEMAN IMPOSER
STONE MARTEN FOIN
STONEMASON DORBIE
STONE PARSLEY HONEWORT
STONE PINE PINON
STONE ROLLER MAMMY MOMMY
TOTER
STONE TOTER CUTLIPS
STONEWALLER STICKER
STONEWARE GRES BASALT JASPER
BASALTES CANEWARE
STONINESS LAPIDITY PETREITY
STONY RIGID COBBLY PETROUS
LAPIDOSE PETROSAL
STOOL FORM MORA SEAT STAB
COPPY CROCK HORSE STOLE
TREST BUFFET CREEPY CURRIE
TRIPOD TUFFET COMMODE CREEPIE
KNEELER SHAMBLE TABORET
TRESTLE TUMBREL BARSTOOL
STILLAGE
(3-LEGGED —) THRESTLE
(CLOSE —) TOM

(CUCKING —) THEW
(LOW —) COPPY SUNKIE CREEPIE
STOOLBALL TUTBALL
STOOL PIGEON NARK SNITCH
STOOGE STOOLIE
STOOP BOW BEND LEAN LOUT SINK
COUCH DEIGN STOPE STULP
COORIE CROUCH HUCKLE BALCONY
DECLINE DESCEND RUCKSEY
SUCCUMB
(— OF HAWK) SOUSE
STOOPING DUCK ASTOOP DESCENT
STOP HO BAS COG CUT DAM DIE
DOG END HOO LIN MAR SET BALK
BODE BUNG CALK CALL COOL DROP
EASE HALT HELP HOLD HOOK KILL
QUIT REED REST SIST SNUB STAP
STAY STEM STOW TEAT TENT TOHO
TRIG VIOL WEAR WHOA ABIDE
AVAST BASTA BELAY BLOCK BRAKE
BREAK CAULK CEASE CHECK
CHOKE CLAMP CLOSE DELAY
EMBAR HITCH LEAVE MEDIA PEACE
POINT QUINT SCOTE SLAKE SPARE
SPRAG STAND STASH STEEK STICK
STINT VIOLA AEOLIN ANCHOR
ARREST ASTINT BIFARA BOGGLE
BORROW CHEESE CLAMOR COLLAR
DESIST DETAIN GRAVEL INSTOP
MONTRE NASARD PERIOD SCOTCH
SQUASH STANCE STANCH STIFLE
TENUIS TROMBA BASSOON
CAESURA MELODIA MUSETTE
OPPRESS SOJOURN STATION
TERTIAN TWELFTH ASPIRATA
BACKSTOP BOMBARDE PRECLUDE
RECORDER STOPOVER STOPPAGE
SUPPRESS SURCEASE TENOROON
WALDHORN WITHSPAR
(— AS IF FRIGHTENED) BOGGLE
(— BLAST) DAMP
(— FLOW) BAFFLE STANCH
(— FOR FOOD) BAIT
(— FOR HORSE) BLOW
(— FROM FERMENTING) STUM
(— GROWTH) BLAST
(— GUN BREECH) OBTURATE
(— IN EARLY STAGES) ABORT
(— IN SPEAKING) HAW
(— LEAK) CALK CAULK FOTHER
(— ROWING) EASY
(— SHORT) JIB
(— SWINGING) SET
(— UNDESIREDLY) STALL
(— UP) DAM CALK CLOG CLOY FILL
PLUG CHINK ESTOP STUFF STANCH
STAUNCH OPPILATE
(— USING) SINK
(— WITH CLAY) PUG
(— WORK) SECURE
(BRIEF —) CALL
(GLOTTAL —) STOD CATCH STOSS
STOSSTON
(HARPSICHORD —) LUTE
(ROUGH —) ASPIRATA
(SUCTION —) CLICK
(TEMPORARY —) PAUSE SUSPEND
(VOICELESS —) TENUIS
(PL.) REEDWORK

STOPCOCK BIB BIBB BIBCOCK
TURNCOCK
STOPLIGHT IMPEDER
STOPOVER LAYOVER
STOPPAGE JAM ALLAY CHECK
HITCH LEATH STICK STINT ARREST
DEVALL STASIS EMBARGO GASLOCK
REFUSAL SHUTOFF STOPPLE
SHUTDOWN STOPWORK
(— OF DEVELOPMENT) ATROPHY
(WORK —) LOWSIN STRIKE
STOPPED PILEATA
(— WITH HAND) BOUCHE
STOPPER WAD BUNG CORK STOP
VICE CHECK FIPPLE STANCH
BOUCHON CLOSURE SHUTOFF
STOPGAP STOPPLE TAMPION
STOPCOCK
STOPPING STAY HOLDUP STOPPAGE
STORAGE STORE STOWAGE
BESTOWAL
STORAX COPALM STACTE STYRAX
LORDWOOD
STORE CAVE CRIB DECK FOND FUND
HOLD KEEP MASS SAVE SHOP
STOW TOKO CACHE DEPOT HOUSE
HUTCH STASH STOCK UPLAY
BAZAAR GARNER GIRNEL RECOND
STEEVE SUPPLY TIENDA WINKEL
ARSENAL BHANDAR BOOTERY
GROCERY HARVEST HUSBAND
IMBURSE REPOSIT RESTORE
BOUTIQUE EMPORIUM EXCHANGE
GARRISON MAGAZINE TENDEJON
WAREROOM WARNISON
(— BEER) AGE LAGER
(— CROP) BARN
(— FODDER) ENSILE
(— IN A MOW) GOVE
(— IN LUMBER CAMP) VAN
(— KEPT BY CHINESE) TOKO
(— OF FOOD) LARDER
(— OF WEALTH) FORTUNE
(— UP) FUND POWDER IMBURSE
SQUIRREL
(ABUNDANT —) MINE
(HIDDEN —) BIKE
(LARGE —) RAFF
(LIQUOR —) GROGGERY
(RESERVE —) SLUICE
(RICH —) ARGOSY
(SMALL —S) SLOPS
(PL.) SAMAN SUPPLY
STOREHOUSE BIKE GOLA CACHE
DEPOT ETAPE STORE ARGOSY
ARMORY BODEGA GODOWN PALACE
PANARY STAPLE VINTRY ARSENAL
BHANDAR CAMALIG CAMARIN
GRANARY STORAGE MAGAZINE
SADDLERY TREASURE
(— FOR BREAD) PANARY
(RAISED —) WHATA FUTTAH PATAKA
(UNDERGROUND —) PALACE
STOREKEEPER MERCHANT
STOREMAN
STOREROOM CAVE GOLA WARD
GOLAH BODEGA CELLAR DINGLE
BOXROOM BUTTERY GENIZAH
LAZARET POULTRY THALAMUS

(PAWNBROKER'S —) LUMBER
STORESHIP FLUTE
STORK WADER ARGALA JABIRU
SIMBIL HURGILA MAGUARI MARABOU
ADJUTANT CICONIID MARABOUT
OPENBEAK OPENBILL
STORKLIKE PELARGIC
STORKSBILL ERODIUM
STORM RIG WAP BLOW HAIL HUFF
RAGE RAMP RAND RAVE WIND
BLIZZ BLOUT BRASH DEVIL DRIFT
FORCE ORAGE STOUR ATTACK
BARBER EASTER EXPUGN WESTER
BLUSTER BRAVADO CYCLONE
DUSTING EQUINOX GAUSTER
PISACHI SHAITAN SNIFTER TEMPEST
TORMENT WEATHER BLOWDOWN
CALAMITY ERUPTION UPHEAVAL
WILLIWAW
(— OF BLOWS) STOUR
(DUST —) DEVIL DUSTER HABOOB
KHAMSIN PEESASH SHAITAN
(FURIOUS —) TEMPEST
(HAWAIIAN —) KONA
(SEVERE —) PEELER SNIFTER
(VIOLENT —) FLAW TUFAN CYCLONE
SNORTER
STORM DOOR DINGLE
STORMY FOUL GURL RUDE WILD
DIRTY DUSTY GURLY GUSTY STARK
WINDY COARSE RUGGED UNFINE
WINTRY FURIOUS NIMBOSE RIOTOUS
SQUALLY TROUBLE VIOLENT
AGITATED BLUSTERY CLUTTERY
ORAGIOUS TEMPESTY
STORMY PETREL MITTY WITCH
SPENCY
STORY GAG SAW DECK DIDO FLAT
LORE REDE TALE TEXT YARN ATTIC
CRACK ETAGE FABLE FLOOR KATHA
PITCH PROSE RECIT SOLAR SPELL
SPIEL STAGE STORE CUFFER
FABULA FLIGHT PISTLE SCREED
SOLLAR ADVANCE HAGGADA
HISTORY MANSARD MARCHEN
PROCESS RECITAL ANECDOTE
DREADFUL ENTRESOL
(— FROM THE PAST) LEGEND
(— OF BEEHIVE) SUPER
(— OF BUILDING) DECK FLAT ATTIC
CHESS ETAGE FLOOR PIANO SOLAR
STAGE FLIGHT SOLLAR MANSARD
ENTRESOL
(— OF HEROES) SAGA
(ABSURD —) CANARD
(ADVENTURE —) YARN
(AMUSING —) DROLLERY
(BIRTH —) JATAKA
(DOLEFUL —) JEREMIAD
(EERIE —) CHILLER
(FAKE —) STRING
(FALSE —) SHAVE CANARD
WHOPPER
(MADE-UP —) FUDGE
(MONSTROUS —) BANGER
(MORBIDLY SENSATIONAL —)
DREADFUL
(MYSTERY —) WHODUNIT
(NEWS —) SIDEBAR

(NEWSPAPER —) LEAD FEATURE
(OLD —) DIDO
(POMPOUS —) BRAG
(PREPOSTEROUS —) CUFFER
(RIBALD —) HARLOTRY
(SATIRICAL —) SKIT
(SHORT —) CONTE NOVELLA
(STALE —) CHESTNUT
(UPPER —) ATTIC GARRET
HYPEROON
(PL.) LEGENDA
STORY BOOK TALEBOOK
STORYTELLER CONTEUR DISCOU▮
DISSOUR
STOUP STOOP BENITIER
STOUT FAT SAD FIRM STUT TRIM
BROSY BULKY BUNTY BURLY
COBBY FRACK FRECK GREAT
HARDY KEDGE OBESE PLUMP
PODDY PUNCH STARK STERN
FLESHY PORTER PORTLY PRETTY
PYKNIC ROTUND SQUARE STRON▮
STUFFY STURDY BOWERLY REPLE▮
FORCIBLE POWERFUL ROBOREAN▮
STALWART THICKSET
(— PERSON) GURK
STOUTHEARTED GOOD VALIANT
STOUTLY FAST HARDILY
STOUTNESS STRENGTH
STOVE HOD STOW BOGEY CHULA
PEACH PLATE CHULHA COCKLE
COOKER HEATER PRIMUS BRASE▮
CHAUFFER FRANKLIN POTBELLY
(— FOR DRYING GUNPOWDER)
GLOOM
(— ON SHIP) GALLEY
(RUSSIAN —) PEACH
(WARMING —) KANGRI
STOVER OVENSMAN
STOW BIN BOX SET CRAM LADE
MASS CROWD DOUSE STORE
BESTOW COOPER STEEVE DUNNA▮
RUMMAGE
STOWAGE BURTON
STOWED IN
STOWER TOPPER
STOWING BINNING GOBBING
STRABISMUS CAST CROSS SQUIN▮
TROPIA ANOPSIA COCKEYE
WALLEYE
STRADDLE SADDLE SPREAD STRI▮
BESTRIDE SPRADDLE STRIDDLE
STRAGGLE ROVE RANGLE SPRAW▮
STREEL TAGGLE WANDER DRAGG▮
MEANDER SCRAMBLE SPRANGLE
STRAGGLER STRAY
STRAGGLING RAGGED RAGGLED
SPRAYEY SCRATCHY VAGULOUS
STRAIGHT BOLT FAIR FULL GAIN
BRANT CLEAN DOGGY FLUSH RIG▮
SHORT SPANG ARIGHT DIRECT
HONEST STRAIT STRICT BOBTAIL
UPRIGHT DIRECTLY SEQUENCE
(— AHEAD) ANON PLUMP OUTRIG▮
(— UP AND DOWN) SHEER CLEVE▮
EVENDOWN
(NOT —) CRAZY
STRAIGHTEDGE RULER STRICKL▮
STRAIGHTEN GAG ORDER STENT

XTEND SQUARE UNKINK COMPOSE
ECTIFY STRETCH
— BY HEATING) SET
— NEEDLE) RUB
— RAILS) GAG
RAIGHT-FIBERED BROAD
RAIGHTFORWARD EVEN PLAT
PERT FRANK LEVEL NAKED ROUND
ANDID DEXTER DIRECT HONEST
IMPLE SQUARE JANNOCK SINCERE
VENDOWN HOMESPUN OUTRIGHT
TRAIGHT
NOT —) CROOKED PLAITED
RAIGHTFORWARDLY SINGLY
QUARE STRAIGHT
RAIGHT-THINKING CLEAR
RAIGHTWAY ANON AWAY RIGHT
RIGHT BEDEEN BEDENE DIRECTLY
RAIN FIT LAG RAX SIE TAX TRY
UG ACHE BEND CALL DASH DRAG
EAT HEFT LAWN NOTE PULL RANN
ILE SINE SOLO SONG VEIN WORK
RUNT CHAFE DEMUR DRAIN FORCE
EAVE PRESS RETCH SHADE SHEAR
TOCK SURGE TAMMY TOUCH
REST WRICK CLENCH EFFORT
XTEND EXTORT FILTER INTEND
PRAIN SPRING STREAK STRESS
TRIND THRONG DESCANT DISCANT
UPLOID FATIGUE STRAINT
TRETCH STROPHE TENSION
ORMENT DIAPASON DIATRIBE
IHYBRID SUBBREED
— MILK) SIE SYE
— OF AN ARCH) THRUST
— OF CHICKENS) ANCOBAR
— OF RAILING LANGUAGE)
IATRIBE
— ON BUGLE) MOT
— ON HORN) MOT RECHASE
ECHEAT
— THROUGH COLANDER) COIL
CONCLUDING —) CADENCE
MUSICAL —) FIT SOLO POINT
MUSICAL —S) TOUCH
MUTANT —) SALTANT
RAINED PENT TENSE INTENSE
ABORED INTENDED
RAINER CAGE ROSE SILE RENGE
EVE STRUM TAMIS TAMMY THEAD
EARCE SEARCH CRIBBLE
OLATORY COLATURE SEARCHER
— OF TWIGS) HUCKMUCK
COFFEE —) GRECQUE
MILK —) SAY MILSEY MILSIE
WICKER —) THEAD THEDE
RAINING CUTE COILED ASTRAIN
TENSE COLATURE
RAIT CUT GUT BAND BELT FRET
YLE NECK PACE BRAKE CANAL
HARE PINCH SHARD ANGUST
RETUM NARROW PLUNGE CHANNEL
URIPUS BOSPORUS JUNCTURE
N —S) SET
EWFOUNDLAND —) TICKLER
L.) CHOPS PRESS EXTREMES
RAITEN PINCH SCANT STRAIT
RAITENED CRIMP NARROW
RIMPED

STRAITJACKET CAMISOLE
STRAITLACED STIFF BLUENOSED
STRAKE SHEER COURSE RISING
STREAK COAMING SAXBOARD
(PL.) TIRE
STRAMONIUM DEWTRY
STRAND PLY TOP BANK CORE FLAT
TOWT BEACH BRAID CLIFF PRAYA
READY SHORE LISSOM SINGLE
SLIVER STRAIN STRIKE SUTURE
HAIRLINE
(— OF HAIR) LICK SWITCH
(— OF PROTOPLASM) BRIDGE
STRANDED ISOLATED
STRANDER EDGER
STRANGE ODD EERY FELL FREM
NICE RARE UNCO ALIEN EERIE
FREMT FUNNY NOVEL QUEER UNKET
UNKID WOOZY ALANGE FERLIE
QUAINT UNIQUE UNKENT UNKIND
CURIOUS ERRATIC HEATHEN
UNHEARD UNKNOWN UNUSUAL
FANCIFUL INSOLENT INSOLITE
PECULIAR SELCOUTH SINGULAR
UNCOLIKE UNCOMMON UNKENNED
UNKINDLY
STRANGER COME UNCO UNKO
ALIEN GUEST FRENNE GANGER
INCOME INMATE FUIDHIR INCOMER
UNCOUTH MALIHINI OUTCOMER
PEREGRIN
STRANGLE CHOKE GRAIN GRANE
SNARL WORRY STIFLE GARROTE
QUACKLE GARROTTE JUGULATE
THROTTLE
STRANGLEHOLD CHANCERY
STRANGUL
STRAP BAR TUG BAND CLIP CURB
GIRD HASP RIDE RIEM BRACE
CHEEK GIRTH GUIGE PATTE RIDER
RISER SABOT SLING STROP THONG
TRACE ANKLET BACKER RILLET
COLLAR ENARME GARTER HALTER
HANGER LAINER LATIGO SANDAL
TOGGLE WARROK BABICHE
BOWYANG CRIBBER DOLPHIN
LANYARD LATCHET LEATHER
RIEMPIE STIRRUP TICKLER WEBBING
BACKSTAY BRETELLE SQUILGEE
TURNBACK WRISTLET
(— AROUND HORSE'S THROAT)
CRIBBER
(— AROUND MAST) DOLPHIN
(— FOR SHIELD) GUIGE ENARME
BRETELLE
(— IN FLAIL) TAPLING
(— OF BRIDLE) REIN
(— OF SENNIT) BACKER
(— ON HAWK'S LEAD) JESS JESSE
SENDAL
(— WITH SLIT END) TAWS TAWSE
(ANKLE —) BRACELET
(DOOR —) HASP
(MINER'S —) BYARD
(SHOE —) BAR
(STIRRUP —S) CHAPELET
(TIE —) SHANK
(U-SHAPED —) STIRRUP
(PL.) LADDER

STRAP FERN LONGLEAF
STRAPHANGER COMMUTER
STRAPPER SPLICER
STRAPPING SWANK CHOPPING
SLAPPING SWANKING
STRAP-SHAPED LORATE LIGULAR
LIGULATE
STRATA TERRANE UNDERAIR
(— OF COAL) MEASURES
STRATAGEM JIG COUP LOCK RUSE
TRAM TURN WILE ANGLE DRAFT
FETCH FRAUD GUILE JOKER KNACK
TRAIN TRICK WREST BLENCH
DECEIT DEVICE HUMBUG POLICY
TRAPAN TREPAN WOIDRE WRENCH
FINESSE SLEIGHT ARTIFICE
CONTOISE FARFETCH INTRIGUE
LIRIPIPE LIRIPOOP PRACTICE
PRACTISE QUENTISE STRATEGY
STRATEGY GAME FINESSE
STRATIFICATION BEDDING
STRATIFIED BEDDED VARVED
STRATUM BED CAP CUT LAY RIB
FAST LAIN SEAM COUCH ELITE
FLOOR LAYER LEDGE SHELF TABLE
COUCHE GIRDLE GRAVEL LAYING
LISSOM PINNEL AQUAFER AQUIFER
ENTIRIS FISHBED SUBSOIL UPRIGHT
AQUIFUGE FAHLBAND SUBGRADE
(— OF COAL) BENCH
(— OF FIRECLAY) THILL
(— OF PALE COLOR) FAHLBAND
(— OF SANDSTONE) PINNEL
(— OF SOIL) SOD
(— OF STONE) GIRDLE
(SOCIAL —) CUT
(THIN —) SEAM LENTIL
STRAW BAKU GLOY MOTE REED
RUSH TOYO WASE HAULM PEDAL
SHILF STALK STREW YEDDA FESCUE
FETTLE PANAMA RIZZOM SIPPER
TUSCAN BANGKOK SABUTAN
STUBBLE WINDLIN STRAMMEL
(— CUT FINE) CHAFF
(— FOR MAKING HATS) SENNIT
BANGKOK LEGHORN SABUTAN
(— FOR THATCHING) YELM
(— MEASURE) KEMPLE
(— TO PROTECT PLANTS) MULCH
(BROKEN —) BHUSA BHOOSA
(COOKERY —S) PAILLES
(PLAITED —) SENNIT
(WAXED —) STRASS
STRAWBERRY BERRY DUNLAP
FRAISE RUNNER HAUTBOY FRUTILLA
HAUTBOIS KLONDIKE ROSACEAN
STRAWBERRY BUSH WAHOO
EUONYMUS EVONYMUS FISHWOOD
STRAWBERRY FINCH AMADAVAT
AVADAVAT
STRAWBERRY SHRUB BUBBY
COWBERRY
STRAWBERRY TOMATO PHYSALIS
STRAY ERR ODD FALL RAVE ROVE
WAFF WAIF WALK DRIFT RANGE
TRAIK VAGUE WAVER ESTRAY
RANGLE SWERVE VAGARY WANDER
WILDER DEVIATE FORLORN

STRAYER DIVAGATE MAVERICK
STRAGGLE
STRAYING ASTRAY ERRANT
ABERRANT VAGATION
STREAK PAY RAY BAND SEAM VEIN
WALE FLAKE FLECK FLICK FREAK
GARLE GLADE SLASH FACULA
SMUDGE STRAIN STRAKE STREAM
STRIPE FLECKER SPRAING STIPPLE
DISCOLOR TRAVERSE
(— IN FABRIC) CRACK SHINER
(— IN GLASS) SKIM
(— IN HAIR) BLAZE
(— IN SKY) ICEBLINK
(— IN WOOD) ROE
(— OF BLUBBER) BLANKET
(— OF LIGHT) STREAM
(— ON SURFACE OF SUN) FACULA
(— WITH FINE STRIPES) LACE
(—S FROM PLANE) CONTRAIL
(BACTERIOLOGICAL —) STROKE
(LOSING —) SLUMP
(THEATRICAL —) HAM
(WHITE —) SHIM
STREAKED ROWY LACED BRINDLE
BROCKED BROOKED FINCHED
SPARKED STRIPED WHIPPED
BRINDLED IRONSHOT PINROWED
STREAKY ROWY SCOVY STREAKED
STREAM EA PUP RIO RUN BECK
BURN FLOW FLUX FORD GILL GOTE
KHAL KILL LAKE PUIT PURL RILL
SICK SIKE SILE SPIN TIDE BACHE
BATCH BAYOU BOGUE BROOK
CREEK DRILL DRINK FLARE FLASH
FLEAM FLOOD FLOSS FLUOR FRESH
GHYLL NYMPH PRILL RITHE RIVER
SWAMP TCHAI TRAIN ARROYO
BANKER BOURNE BRANCH BURNIE
CANADA COULEE FILLER FLUENT
GUZZLE OUTLET PIRATE RANDOM
RUNDLE RUNNEL SLUICE SPRUIT
STRAND STRONE CHANNEL
CURRENT DRIBBLE FLUENCE
FRESHET RIVULET TRICKLE
AFFLUENT INFLUENT
(— ALONG) SLIDE
(— FULL TO TOP) BANKER
(— OF AIR OR SMOKE) PEW
(— OF ELECTRODES) BEAM
(— OF LAVA) COULEE
(— OF SIRUP) THREAD
(— OF SPEECH) STRAIN
(— OUT) BREAK
(FLOWING —) NYMPH
(HIGH-SPEED —) JET
(MYTHOLOGICAL —S) ELIVAGAR
(SLOW —) OOZE
(SLUGGISH —) LANE
(SMALL —) BECK LAKE SIKE DRAFT
RITHE COULEE SICKET SQUIRT
STRIPE DRAUGHT GRINDLE
(THIN —) TRICKLE TRICKLET
(TIDAL —) COVE SEAPOOSE
(TRANSIENT —) RILL
(TRICKLING —) DRILL
(TURBID —) DRUVE
(UNDERGROUND —) AAR SWALLET
(VIOLENT —) TORRENT

(WEAK —) DRIP
STREAMER FLAG VANE GARTER
GUIDON LAPPET PENCEL PENNON
SCROLL SIMPLE WIMPLE BANDEROL
FILAMENT
(— OF MOSS) WEEPER
(PAPER —S) CONFETTI
STREAMING SLUICY ASTREAM
CYCLOSIS DOWNPOUR
STREAMLET RILL RILLET RUNDLE
RUNLET RUNNEL RIVULET
STREAMLINE SIMPLIFY
(— FLOW) LAMINAR
STREAMLINED CLEAN SLEEK
STREET ROW RUE WAY CHAR DRUM
GATE PAVE STEM TOBY BLOCK
BORGO CALLE CANON CHAWK
CORSO DRIVE AVENUE BOWERY
CANYON CAUSEY RAMBLA CHAUSEE
POULTRY TERRACE THROUGH
ARTERIAL BROADWAY BYSTREET
CONTRADA PROSPECT
(— IN BARCELONA) RAMBLA
(— IN FLORENCE) BORGO
(MAIN —) CHAWK CHOWK
TOWNGATE
(NARROW —) CHAR ALLEY CHARE
(PRINCIPAL —) ARTERY
(SIDE —) HUTUNG
STREETCAR TRAMCAR ELECTRIC
STREET CLEANER ORDERLY
CLEANSER
STREET CLEANING SLOPPING
STREETWALKER CRUISER
STRENGTH EL ARM VIR BEEF DRAW
GRIP GUTS HEAD HORN IRON MAIN
THEW BRAWN CRAFT ETHAN FIBER
FIBRE FORCE HEART JUICE MIGHT
NERVE POWER SINEW VIGOR
ENERGY FOISON MAUGHT STARCH
VIRTUE COURAGE STAMINA STHENIA
CAPACITY FIRMNESS VALIDITY
(— OF ACID OR BASE) AVIDITY
(— OF ALE) STRIKE
(— OF CARD HAND) BODY
(— OF CHARACTER) GRISTLE
(— OF CURRENT) AMPERAGE
(— OF SOLUTION) TIRE TITER
(— OF SPIRITS) PROOF
(— OF TEA) DRAW
(— OF WILL) BACKBONE
(— OF WINE) SEVE
STRENGTHEN IMP ABLE BACK BIND
FIRM FRAP HELP PROP SOUD STAY
BRACE CLEAT FORCE SINEW STEEL
THRAP TONIC TRUSS ANNEAL
ASSURE DEEPEN ENDURE ENFIRM
ENFORT GABION HARDEN INTEND
MUNIFY MUNITE NEEDLE SETTLE
STRING STRONG AFFORCE
BUCKRAM COMFORT CONFIRM
ENFORCE FASCINE FORTIFY
NERVATE QUICKEN RAMPIRE
SUPPORT THICKEN BUTTRESS
ENERGIZE ENTRENCH HEIGHTEN
ROBORATE
STRENGTHENED BULLED
STRENGTHENING ROBORANT
STRENGTHLESS DOWLESS

STRENUOUS HARD EAGER
ARDUOUS WILLING VIGOROUS
STREPSIPTERON STYLOPS
STRESS HIT BRUNT ICTUS PINCH
SHEAR ACCENT STRAIN THRONG
CENTROID DOWNBEAT EMPHASIS
(— OF SOUND) LENGTH
STRESSED TONIC STRONG
STRETCH EKE LAG LIE RAX RUN
BEAT DRAW LAST MAIN PASS RAC
REAM ROLL SPAN TEND BOARD
BURST FETCH RATCH RETCH SIGH
SPELL SWAGE VERGE EXTEND
LENGTH SMOOTH STRAIN STRAKE
STREEK DISPLAY DISTEND EXPANS
SPELDER ELONGATE STRAIGHT
LENGTHEN
(— CLOTH) TENTER
(— INJURIOUSLY) SPRAIN
(— IRREGULARLY) TRAIL
(— LEATHER) DRAFT STAKE
DRAUGHT
(— METAL) FORM
(— OF ARMS) FATHOM
(— OF GROUND) BRECK
(— OF INTERVAL) CARSE
(— OF LAND) SWALE COMMON
GALLOP COMMONS
(— OF ROAD) SIGHT
(— OF SEA) CHOP
(— OF TIME) TIFF
(— OF WALL) CURTAIN
(— OF WATER) GLIDE LEVEL LOGI
FAIRWAY
(— OUT) GROW SPIN REACH STEN
STRUT TWINE INTEND OUTLIE
SPRAWL SPREAD SPRING DISTEND
OUTSPAN PORTEND ELONGATE
(— THE NECK) CRANE
(GRASSY —) DRINN
(LEVEL —) LAWN
STRETCHED (— OUT) PORRECT
PROJECT PROLATE ELONGATE
EXTENDED
(TENSELY —) TAUT TORT STIFF
STRETCHER COT GURNEY LITTER
ANGAREP TROLLEY ANGAREEB
STRAINER
STREW BED SOW CLOT DUST LARI
SPEW BESET STRAW STRAY STRO
LITTER SPREAD BESTREW SCATTE
SKINKLE SPARKLE
(— WITH BULLETS) SPRAY
STREWING SEME
STREWN DOTTED BESPRENT
STRIA CORD STRIOLA DRAGLINE
STRIOLET
STRIATE VEIN
STRIATION STREAK STRIGA
STRICKEN STREAKED
STRICKER TIPPLER
STRICKLE SWEEP STRIKER
STRICT HARD TAUT TRUE CLOSE
EXACT HARSH RIGID STARK STER
GIUSTO SEVERE STRAIT STRONG
ASCETIC AUSTERE PRECISE
DISTRICT RESTRICT RIGOROUS
(NOT —) LAX SCIOLTO

RICTLY NARROW STRAIT CLOSELY
PROPERLY
RICTNESS RIGOR RIGIDITY
RIGORISM SEVERITY
RIDE SAIL STEP FLOAT SKELP
SPANG STEND STRUT LAMPER
STROAM STROKE STROME
BESTRIDE POINTING STRIDDLE
— LOFTILY) STALK
— PURPOSEFULLY) SLING
RIDENT HARD HARSH BRASSY
GLASSY SHRILL RAUCOUS YELLING
GRINDING
RIDULATE PITTER
RIFE TUG WAR WIN BATE FEUD
HOLD PLEA BRIGE CHEST FLITE
JEHAD JIHAD NOISE STOUR STROW
STRUT STURT BARRAT DEBATE
ESTRIF MUTINY STRIVE CONTEST
DISCORD DISPUTE HURLING
QUARREL CONFLICT CONTRAST
DISPEACE STRUGGLE
CIVIL —) STASIS
RIGIL COMB SCRAPER
RIKE GO BAT BOB BOP BOX BUM
COB CUE DAD DUB GET HAB HIT
JOB JOW LAM LAY PUG RAP ABRE
BAFF BEAK BEAT BELT BILL BLAD
BLIP BUFF BUMP CHAP CLUB COIN
COPE COSH CUFF DING DINT DONG
DUNT FALL FANG FIRK FLAP FLOG
RAP GIRD GOWF HACK HURT JOWL
KILL KNEE LASH LILT LUSH MARK
MAIL PAIK PLAT PUCK ROUT SLAM
SLAP SLAT SLAY SLOG SLUG SOCK
SPAR SPAT SWAP SWAT SWIP TAKE
WHOP WIPE ANGLE BATON CATCH
CHECK CHIME CHINK CLOUT CLUNK
CRACK CRUNT DEVEL DOUSE
DOWSE DRIVE DUNCH FETCH FILCH
FILP FLAIL KNOCK PANDY PASTE
POKER POTCH SABER SKELP SKITE
SLOSH SMACK SMITE SNICK SOUND
SPANK SQUAP STAMP STEEK
SWACK SWEEP SWIPE SWISH
THROW WHALE WHANG ACOUPE
AFFECT AFFRAP ATTAIN BATTER
BOUNCE BUFFET COURSE DUNDER
KETTLE FILLIP HAMMER INCUSE
INCUTE KEEPER SLOUGH STOUSH
STRICK STRIPE SWITCH THRASH
WALLOP BEARING FLYFLAP IMPINGE
KNUCKLE PERCUSS STRIKER
BURNOUT WHAMPLE WILDCAT
TOPPAGE STOPWORK STRICKLE
— A WICKET) BREAK
— ABOUT) FLOP
— AGAINST) RAM BANG STUMP
ASSAULT COLLIDE
— AND REBOUND) CAROM
— CRICKET BALL) EDGE
— DOWN) LAY FALL SLAY WEND
LASH FLOOR AFFLICT SIDERATE
— DUMB) DUMFOUND
— FEET TOGETHER) HITCH
— FORCIBLY) GET CLOUT DEVEL
LASH
— GENTLY) PAT
— GOLF BALL) HOOK DRIVE
CLAFF

(— HEAVILY) BASH DUNT FLOP
SLUG CLUMP SLOUGH
(— IN CURLING) WICK
(— LIGHTLY) BOB DAB SPAT FLICK
(— OF LOCK) KEEPER STRIKER
(— ON HEAD) COP NOBBLE
(— OUT) FAN TAKE CROSS ELIDE
CANCEL EXPUNGE OUTLASH
EXCUDATE
(— REPEATEDLY) DRUM LICK
(— SHARPLY) CUT SNICK
(— SMARTLY) NAP RAP KNAP
(— TEETH TOGETHER) GNASH
(— TOGETHER) CLASH KNACK
(— UP) LILT YERK RAISE
(— VIOLENTLY) RIP BASH DING
SOUSE BENSEL
(— WITH AMAZEMENT) CONFOUND
(— WITH BAT) DRIVE
(— WITH FEAR) ALARM ASTONISH
(— WITH FIST) PLUG NODDLE
(— WITH FOOT) KICK BUNCH SPURN
STAMP
(— WITH HAMMER) CHAP JOWL
MELL
(— WITH HORNS) BUNT BUTT HOOK
(— WITH SPEAR) STICK
(— WITH STICK) SQUAIL
(— WITH WHIP) JERK LASH QUIRK
(— WITH WONDER) SURPRISE
(BOWLING —S) DOUBLE
(HUNGER —) ENDURA
(LABOR —) STEEK STICK TURNOUT
WALKOUT
(MINING —) TREND
(THREE —S) TURKEY
STRIKEBREAKER FINK BLACKLEG
STRIKER BATMAN DRUMMER
TURNOUT PULSATOR
STRIKER-OUT SETTER
STRIKING FITTY FRESH SHOWY
VIVID DARING SIGNAL STRONG
SALIENT SKELPIN COLORFUL
CONFLICT DRAMATIC KNOCKOUT
SENSIBLE SPEAKING
STRING LAG BAND CORD FILE LACE
MEAN PAIR SLIP TAPE TAUM BRAID
BRIDE CHORD POINT SINEW SNEAD
STRAP CORDON STRAND TREBLE
MINIKIN LIGATURE RHAPSODY
(— OF BEADS) ROSARY CHAPLET
NECKLACE
(— OF CASH) QUAN TIAO
(— OF DRUM) SNARE
(— OF FIDDLE) THARM
(— OF FLAGS) HOIST
(— OF LOCK) KEEPER
(— OF LYRE) TRITE
(— OF MUSICAL INSTRUMENT) WIRE
CHORD DRONE CATLING MINIKIN
(— OF ONIONS) REEVE TRACE
(— OF RAILWAY CARS) SET
(— OF SUGAR CRYSTALS) COB
(— OF VEGETABLES) STRAP
(— OF VIOL) MEAN
(— TOBACCO) SEW
(BONNET —) BRIDE
(E —) QUINT
(LEADING —) BAND

(ORNAMENTAL —) CORDON
(SURGICAL —) LIGATURE
(VIOLIN —) THAIRM VIBRATOR
(WEAVING —) LEASH
STRING BEAN SNAP HARICOT
SNAPPER
STRINGCOURSE LEDGE TABLE
CORDON STRING
STRINGENT HARD RIGID SEVERE
STRICT EXTREME
STRINGER BALK BAULK
STRINGHALTED CRAMPY
STRINGY ROPY WOOLY SINEWY
THONGY WOOLLY GARGETY
SINEWED
STRIP BAR LAG TAG BAND BARE
BEAD BELT BEND BUSK DRIP FUSE
GAGE GAIR HILD HUSK LIST MALL
NAKE NUDE PEEL RAND ROLL SACK
SHIM SKIN TIRR WELT CLEAN DRIVE
EXUTE FILET FLAKE GAUGE GLEAN
GUARD HARRY LABEL LINER LYNCH
PANEL PLUME REEVE SHEAR SHRED
SKELP SLIPE SPEEL SPOIL STRAP
STROP STRUB SWATH UNGUM
UNRIG BORDER BOXING BRIDGE
COLLAR CULPON DENUDE DEVEST
DIVEST FEELER FILLET FLEECE
LIBBET MATRIX PANUNG SCROLL
SPLINE STREAK STRIPE TARGET
UNBARE UNBARK UNCASE BANDAGE
BEREAVE CHANNEL DEPLUME
DEPRIVE DESPOIL DISROBE
FEATHER FLOUNCE LAMBEAU
LANGUET NAILROD PINRAIL
PLUNDER UNCLOAK UNCOVER
UNDRESS BOOKMARK COSSETTE
DISARRAY DISENDOW DISTRUSS
FOOTBAND SEPARATE
(— A PLANT) SPRIG
(— BARK) PILL
(— BINDING STALKS TO WALL)
TACK
(— BLUBBER FROM WHALE) FLENSE
(— EAR OF CORN) SILK
(— FOR DRAWING CURVED LINES)
SPLINE
(— FOR GUIDING PLASTER) BEAD
(— FOR MAKING TUBE) SKELP
(— HANGING AROUND SKIRT)
FLOUNCE
(— IN BASKETMAKING) INSIDES
(— IN BEEHIVE) STARTER
(— IN CANING) SPLENT SPLINT
(— IN TYPEWRITER) DRAWBAND
(— OF CANVAS) FOOTBAND
(— OF CLOTH) LIST PATA RIND
GUARD BANNER DUTCHMAN
(— OF CORK) SPREADER
(— OF FABRIC) FLIPPER
(— OF FAT) FATBACK LARDOON
(— OF FIELD HOCKEY AREA) ALLEY
(— OF FUR) GROTZEN
(— OF GRASS) VERGE
(— OF HIDE) SPECK DEWLAP
(— OF LAND) BUTT LAND RAIK RAIN
RAKE TANG BREAK CREEK SLANG
SLIPE SPONG SCREED SELION
STRAKE STRIPE FURLONG ISTHMUS

CORRIDOR SIDELING
(— OF LEATHER) LAY RAND WELT
APRON RANGE THONG BACKSTAY
(— OF LEAVES) TWIST
(— OF LINEN) SETON
(— OF MASONRY) ARCHBAND
(— OF OFFICE) BREAK
(— OF OSIER) SKEIN
(— OF PALM LEAF) CADJAN CAJANG
(— OF PASTRY) STRAW
(— OF PLANKING) APRON
(— OF PRAIRIE) COVE
(— OF PROVISIONS) FORAGE
(— OF RANK) DEGRADE
(— OF ROADWAY) LANE
(— OF RUBBER) CUSHION
(— OF TURF) PARKING
(— OF UNPLOWED LAND) GAIR
HADE HEADLAND
(— OF WATER) INLET
(— OF WOOD) LAG LAT LATH LIST
SHAW SLAT WELT CHINK CLEAT
STAVE BATTEN INWALE REEPER
REGLET FOOTING FURRING STICKER
TRACKER FOOTLING
(— OFF SKIN) CASE FLAY
(— OFF) TIRL FLIPE FLYPE SLIPE
(— ON FOLDING DOORS) ASTRAGAL
(— ON PRINTER'S GALLEY) LEDGE
(— ON SQUASH COURT) TELLTALE
(— ON TIRE) CHAFER
(— SEPARATING LINES OF TYPE)
LEAD REGLET
(CAMOUFLAGING —) GARLAND
(COMIC —) FUNNY
(CONSTRUCTION —S) LAGGING
(CORSET —) BUSK
(DEPENDENT —) LAMBEAU
(DIVIDING —) CLOISON
(HORSESHOE-SHAPED —) BAIL BALE
(IRON IN —S) NAILROD
(NARROW —) SEAM SLAT SLIP TAPE
REEVE STRAKE
(PAPER —) ORIHON
(PROJECTING —) FEATHER
(RAISED —) RIDGE
(STRENGTHENING —) BEND
(THATCHING —) LEDGER
STRIPE BAR RAY BAND BEND LIST
PALE SLAT WALE WEAL WELT ZONE
FLECK PLAGA STRIA STRIP SWATH
VITTA WHEAL BORDER CLAVUS
COTICE FRENUM LADDER RIBBON
STRAKE STREAK STREAM COTTISE
SPRAING MUSTACHE TRAVERSE
(— OF CHEVRON) ARC
(— OF COLOR ON CHEEK) FRENUM
FRAENUM
(— ON ANIMAL'S FACE) SNIP BLAZE
(— ON FABRIC) CROSSBAR
(— ON MILITARY SLEEVE) SLASH
(ENCIRCLING —) ZONE
(PURPLE —) CLAVUS
(SET OF —S) BAR
STRIPED BANDY PALED PIRNY
RAWED RAYED ROWED WALED
ZONED BARRED CORDED LISTED
PIRNED BROCKED TIGROID VITTATE
FASCIATE STRIPPED

STRIPED BASS ROCKFISH SERRANID
STRIPED MAPLE DOGWOOD
STRIPING HAIRLINE
STRIPLIGHT BORDER
STRIPLING LAD SLIP STIRRA
YONKER SPAUGHT YOUNKER
SKIPJACK SPRINGAL
STRIPPED BARE NUDE NAKED
HUSKED PICKED PLUMED UNPEELED
STRIPPER STEMMER SPRIGGER
STRIPPING STROKINGS
(PL.) JIBBINGS
STRIPTEASER STRIPPER ECDYSIAST
STRIVE AIM HIE TEW TRY TUG DEAL
FEND PAIN TOIL WORK BANDY
DRIVE EXERT FIGHT FORCE LABOR
PRESS BUCKLE BUFFET DEBATE
INTEND PINGLE STRAIN STRIKE
AGONIZE CONTEND CONTEST
DISPUTE ENFORCE SCUFFLE
CONTRAST ENDEAVOR PURCHASE
STRUGGLE
(— AFTER) SEEK FOLLOW CANVASS
(— FOR SUPERIORITY) VIE
(— IN OPPOSITION) RIVAL CONTEND
(— TO EQUAL) EMULATE
(— TO OVERTAKE) ENSUE
STRIVING NISUS HORMIC STRIFT
CONATUS CONATION
STRIX SYRNIUM
STROBILE BUR BELL BURR CHAT
CONE BRUSH
STROKE BAT COY CUT DAB FIT JOW
ODD PAT PET POP RUB BAFF BEAT
BLOW CHAP CHOP CLAP COUP
DASH DENT DING DINT DIRD DRAW
DUNT EDGE FIRK FLAP FLEG FLIP
FLOP FUNG GOWF HURT JERK JOWL
KERF LASH LICK NACK PAIK PEAL
PECK SHOT SMIT SWAP TILT TIRE
TUCK WELT WHAP WIPE BRUSH
CHASE DOUSE DOWSE DRAFT
FLACK FLICK FORCE HATCH ICTUS
MINIM PANDY PULSE SHOCK SLASH
SLING SLIVE SLOSH STRIP SWEEP
SWING SWIPE THROW TRAIT TRICE
WHACK CARESS CENTER FONDLE
FOOZLE GENTLE GLANCE PLAGUE
PLUNGE SMOOTH STRAIK STRAKE
STRIKE STRIPE DRAUGHT OUTLASH
SOLIDUS VIRGULE APOPLEXY
DRUMBEAT FOREHAND INSTROKE
SCORCHER
(— IN PAINTING) HAND
(— IN PENMANSHIP) MINIM
(— IN TENNIS) LET LOB BOAST
CHASE SMASH BRICOLE BACKHAND
FOREHAND
(— OF A LETTER) DUCT STEM SERIF
CROSSBAR
(— OF BAD FORTUNE) CLAP
(— OF BELL) JOW BELL JOWL
KNELL TELLER
(— OF FORTUNE) CAST BREAK
FELICITY
(— OF LUCK) HIT FLUKE STRIKE
TURNUP CAPTION
(— OF SCYTHE) SWATH SWATHE
(— OF SHEARS) SNIP

(— OF WIT) FLIRT
(— OF WORK) BAT CHAR
(— ON THE PALM) LOOFIE
(BILLIARDS —) SPOT STUN FLUK
FORCE MASSE HAZARD
(CONNECTING —) LIGATURE
(CRICKET —) CUT GLANCE
(CUTTING —) GIRD
(DOUBLE SPINNING —) DRAW
(DRUM —) DRAG
(GOLF —) ODD BAFF BISK HOOK
LIKE SLICE BISQUE FOOZLE SCL
APPROACH
(HOCKEY —) JOB SCOOP
(JERKY —) STAB
(LIGHTNING —) BOLT
(MEDICAL —) ICTUS APOPLEXY
(ORNAMENTAL —) FLOURISH
(QUICK —) FLIP
(SKATING —) EDGE MOHAWK
CHOCTAW
(SMART —) FIRK
(SOOTHING —) COY
(SWIMMING —) CRAWL
(SWINGING —) HEW
(SWORD —) MONTANTO
STROLL JET IDLE ROAM ROVE
ANTER JAUNT RANGE STRAY TR
BUMMEL DACKER DANDER GANC
LOUNGE PALMER RAMBLE SOOD
STROAM STROME WANDER
SAUNTER TURNOUT SPATIATE
STRAVAGE
STROLLER SULKY TRAMP SHULE
SHUILER VAGRANT BOHEMIAN
STROLLING FLANERIE FUGITIVE
STROMA ECOID OECOID
STRONG FAT FIT HOT FELL FERE
FIRM FORT HALE HANG HARD HI
IRON KEEN RANK SURE TRIG TR
ACRID BONNY FORCY FRECK FR
HARDY HEAVY HOGEN HUSKY JC
LUSTY NAPPY NERVY ORPED PIT
SHARP SMART SOLID SOUND ST
STEER STERN STIFF STOUR STO
SWITH THEWY VALID VIVID WIGH
YAULD ARDENT BRAWNY BUCKR
BUNKUM FEIRIE FIERCE MIGHTY
POTENT PRETTY ROBUST RUGGI
SECURE SEVERE SINEWY STABL
STANCH STARCH STURDY WIELD
BOARDLY BUIRDLY DOUGHTY
DURABLE EXALTED FECKFUL
HUFFCAP HUMMING INTENSE
LUSTFUL NERVOUS SKOOKUM
STHENIC ATHLETIC BIDDABLE
MUSCULAR REVERENT ROBOREA
SPANKING STALWART STIFFISH
VIGOROUS
STRONGBOX PETE COFFER
DEEDBOX
STRONGEST EXTREME
STRONGHOLD HOLD KEEP PIECI
PLACE TOWER CASTLE WARDER
CITADEL KREMLIN FASTHOLD
FASTNESS FORTRESS FRONTIER
STRENGTH
STRONGLY BUT SAD BADLY SWI
FIRMLY STRONG DURABLY FRES

EFTILY SOLIDLY STITHLY STOUTLY
EARTILY
RONG-SCENTED HIGH RANK
RONG-SMELLING FOXY
ROP RIP STRAP
ROPHE ALCAIC LAISSE STANZA
APPHIC
ROPHIUS (FATHER OF —)
RISSUS
SON OF —) PYLADES
RUCK (— SHARPLY) SMITTEN
- WITH AMAZEMENT) AGHAST
RUCTURAL ANATOMIC TECTONIC
- UNIT) IDANT
RUCTURE CAGE FALX FORM
AKE ANNEX BOOTH CABIN FLOAT
RAME GETUP HOUSE KIOSK PEGMA
ETUP SHAPE STOCK BRIDGE
AGEOT FABRIC GANTRY GIRDER
OGEN KELSON TIMBER COTTAGE
DIFICE FAIRING FEATURE GATEWAY
ESTALT KEELSON MANSION
URAGHE OUTCAST PAGEANT
RADIUM TURNOUT ZEUGITE
EDICULA AIRCRAFT AIRFRAME
JILDING BUTTRESS CRIBWORK
OMATIUM ENDOCONE ESCORIAL
EADWORK MOUNTURE NEOMORPH
KELETON STANDARD
- BUILT IN WATER) PIER
- CONTAINING KILN) HOVEL
- EXTENDED INTO SEA) JETTY
- FOR PIGEONS) COTE
- FRAMING SHIP) KEELSON
- OF CARTRIDGE) ANVIL
- OF PRETENSION) PERRON
- ON ROOF) CUPOLA FEMERELL
- ON SHIP) BLISTER
- ON STEAMER) TEXAS
- PRODUCING SMOOTH OUTLINE)
IRING
- SHELTERING INSECTS)
OMATIUM
- SUPPORTING AIRSHIP
OPELLER) PYLON
- WITHIN SHELL) ENDOCONE
NATOMICAL —) BUD APRON
ARINA CRESCENT
NTICLINAL —) SWELL
RCHED —) FORNIX
ODILY —) FRAME PHYSIQUE
RICK —) KANG HOVEL
RISTLIKE —) ARISTA
RONZE AGE —) HENGE
ABINLIKE —) CABANA
LIMBING —) LADDER
OMPLEX —) EMBOLUS
ONELIKE —) PYRAMID
ONICAL —) BULLET
ROWNLIKE —) CORONA
YLINDRICAL —) SILO
EADENING —) BAFFLE
EFENSIVE —) CAT
ORTIFIED —) CAVALIER
ENERAL —) GETUP
EOLOGICAL —) CAMBER
IGH —) TOWER
OLLOW —) SHELL
NEE-LIKE —) GENU

(LENS-SHAPED —) LENTOID
(LOFTY —) BABEL STEEPLE
(LOGICAL —) EIDOS
(ORGANIZED —) BULK
(ORIENTAL STORIED —) PAGODA
(ORNAMENTAL —) KIOSK
(PLANT —) DISC DISK
(POINTED —) BEAK
(PUEBLO —) KIVA
(RAISED —) CIMBORIO
(RAMSHACKLE —) COOP
(RINGLIKE —) ANNULUS
(RUDE STONE —S) SPECCHIE
(SACRIFICIAL —) ALTAR
(SENTENCE —) SYNTAX
(SHELTERING —) COT
(SICKLE-SHAPED —) FALX
(SLENDER —) HAIR
(STONE —) TAULA
(TEMPORARY —) HUT
(THEATER —) SKENE
(UNDERLYING —) BOTTOM
(UNSTABLE —) COBHOUSE
(WATERTIGHT —) CAMEL
(WHITE —) ALBEDO
STRUGGLE IT TEW TUG VIE WIN
AGON COPE DEAL FEND FICK FRAB
GAME PULL TAVE TOIL FIGHT FLING
HEAVE LABOR STRAY SWORD
TEAVE TWEIL WORRY WRELE
BATTLE BUCKLE BUFFET BUSTLE
COMBAT EFFORT HASSLE JOSTLE
JUSTLE PINGLE RELUCT SEESAW
SPRAWL SPRUNT STIVER STRIFE
STRIVE TERVEE TUSSLE WARSLE
WIDDLE AGONIZE CLAMBER
CONTEND CONTEST DISPUTE
FLOUNCE GRAPPLE SCUFFLE
TUILYIE WARFARE WAUCHLE
WRESTLE CONFLICT ENDEAVOR
FLOUNDER SCRAFFLE SCRAMBLE
SLUGFEST SPRANGLE SPRATTLE
(— ALONG) HOBBLE
(— CONVULSIVELY) SPRAWL
(— FOR LARGESS) SCAMBLE
(— FORTH) ELUCTATE
(— TO GAIN FOOTING) SCRABBLE
SPROTTLE
(AGONIZED —) THROE
(CONFUSED —) MUSS
(DEATH —) AGONY
(HAND-TO-HAND —) GRAPPLE
(HAPHAZARD —) SCUFFLE
(SPIRITUAL —) PENIEL
(UNCEREMONIOUS —) SCRAMBLE
STRUGGLER LAOCOON
STRUM THRUM
STRUMA GOITER GOITRE
STRUMPET BRIM PUNK TRULL
WENCH WHORE BLOWEN BULKER
STIVER TOMBOY TOMRIG COCOTTE
SUCCUBA DOLLYMOP PUNKLING
SUCCUBUS VENTURER
(WORN-OUT —) HARRIDAN
STRUT JET BRAG COCK POMP SPUR
CORSO MAJOR PRINK SWANK
SASHAY STROKE STROOT STRUNT
NAUNTLE PEACOCK STEMPLE
SWAGGER TRANSOM

STRUTTER HAM
STRUTTING COCKING
STUB BUTT SNAG SPUD STOB STUD
CHECK ERGOT GUARD HINGE
STUMP SPRUNT
STUBBLE BUN ETCH MANE SHACK
ARRISH EDDISH STOVER STUMPS
EEGRASS GRATTEN STIBBLE
STUBBORN SOT ROWDY RUSTY
STIFF STOUT STUNT THRAW TOUGH
MULISH STURDY THWART BULLDOG
PEEVISH PIGGISH RESTIVE
WAYWARD WILLFUL OBDURATE
PERVERSE STUNKARD THRAWART
STUBBORNNESS STOMACH
ADAMANCY
STUBBY STUB CUTTY SQUAT
STOCKY STUMPY STUBBED
STUCCO ALBARIUM
STUCK FAST MASHED STICKIT
STOODED
STUCK-UP BUG FROSTED
STUD SET BOLT BOSS KNOP KNOT
LNOB NAIL RACE SLUG SPOT BESET
BULLA CLOUT HARAS JOIST WRIST
ASHLAR ENSTAR INSTAR STOOTH
STRING CONTACT POTENCE
QUARTER STUDDLE PUNCHEON
STANDARD STUDDERY
(— FARM) HARAS
(— IN BOOT SOLE) SLUG
(— IN WATCH) POTENCE
(— SHOES) HOBNAIL
(— WITH NAILS) CLOUT
(INTERMEDIATE —) PUNCHEON
(ORNAMENTED —) AGLET AIGLET
STUDDED BOSSY BILLETY STELLED
BILLETTE
STUDDLE POST ROIL
STUDENT BOY DIG WIT COED PLUG
PREP SMUG SOPH AGGIE BAHUR
FUCHS GRIND MEDIC PUPIL SIZAR
SPOON BOCHER BURSAR BURSCH
INTERN JUNIOR JURIST MEDICO
OPTIME PRIMAR PRIMER PUISNE
SCOLOG SENIOR ADVISEE CLASSIC
DANTEAN EDUCAND ETONIAN
FAILURE GOLIARD GRECIAN
INTERNE INTRANT LEARNER
MOOTMAN OPPIDAN PASSMAN
PHARMIC PLUGGER SCHOLAR
STUDIER TEMPLAR THEOLOG
BOTANIST CABALIST COLLEGER
DEMOTIST DISCIPLE EDUCATOR
FEMINIST HOMERIST HOSTELER
ISLAMIST PREMEDIC REPEATER
SECONDAR SUBSIZAR TRANSFER
(— IN TALMUDIC ACADEMY) BAHUR
(— LAST IN CLASS) SPOON
(— OF LOW RANK) TERNAR TERNER
(— WHO LIVES IN TOWN) OPPIDAN
(1ST-YEAR —) FUCHS
(3RD-YEAR —) JUNIOR TERTIAN
(ABNORMALLY ABSORBED —) SAP
(DAY —) EXTERN EXTERNE
(DIVINITY —) STIBBLER
(DRUDGING —) PLUG
(ENGLISH SCHOOL —) BLUE SWOT
ETONIAN SWOTTER

(GRADUATE —) FELLOW
(LAW —) PUNEE JURIST LEGIST
PUISNE TEMPLAR STAGIARY
(MILITARY —) CADET
(NON-COLLEGIATE —) TOSHER
(PLODDING —) DIG SMUG
(WANDERING —) GOLIARD
(PL.) GOWN CLASS HOUSE SEMINAR
STUDIED COOL STUDIOUS
STUDIO LOT SHOT ATELIER
BOTTEGA GALLERY
STUDIOUS BOOKY BOOKISH
CLERKLY DILIGENT SEDULOUS
STUDY CON BEAT BONE BOOK CASE
MUZZ SIFT STUD GRIND ESTUDY
EXAMEN LESSON MUSEUM SCOLEY
SURVEY ABBOZZO ACCOUNT
ANALYZE CANVASS CROQUIS
POCHADE REVOLVE SANCTUM
ANALYSIS BOOKWORK CONSIDER
EXERCISE MEDITATE SCRUTINY
TYPOLOGY
(— HARD) DIG MUG BONE SMUG
STEW SWOT
(— OF PUNISHMENT) PENOLOGY
(— OF SACRED EDIFICES) NAOLOGY
(— OF SNOW AND ICE) CRYOLOGY
(— UNDER PRESSURE) CRAM
(ART —) ABBOZZO CROQUIS
POCHADE
(CLAY —) BOZZETTO
(MUSICAL —) ETUDE
(PRELIMINARY —) SKETCH
(UNINTERESTING —) GRIND
STUFF PAD RAM WAD CRAM GAUM
GEAR PANG STOP TACK TUCK
WHAT CROWD DUROY FARCE
FORCE KEDGE METAL PASTE SQUAB
TRADE FABRIC GRAITH KIBOSH
MATTER PAUNCH STEEVE STODGE
TACKLE TIMBER BOMBARD
BOMBAST DRUGGET ELEMENT
ENFARCE DIAPHANE MARINATE
MATERIAL SPLUTTER WHIPPING
(— AND NONSENSE) HAVERS
PICKLE PIFFLE
(— FILLET OF VEAL) BOMBARD
(— FULL) STODGE
(— OF POOR QUALITY SILK) RASH
(— ONESELF) MAST
(— POULTRY) FARCE MARINATE
(— WITH DRESSING) QUILT
(COTTON —) CALICO
(HOUSEHOLD —) GEAR
(INFERIOR —) MOCKADO
(SILKEN —) TARS TARSE DIAPHANE
(STICKY —) GOOK
(THIN —) CRAPE
(THIN SILK —) LOVE
(WISHY-WASHY —) BLASH
(WOOLEN —) DUROY TWILLY
DRUGGET
(WORTHLESS —) GEAR HOGWASH
STUFFED PANG TRIG BLOAT FARCI
STODGY BLOATED BOMBAST
STUFFING PAD TAR FARCE STECH
STUFF BOMBAST FARCING SAWDUST
STUFFAGE
(— FOR MATTRESS) PULU

STUFFY CLOSE FUBBY FUBSY FUGGY
STIVY WOOLY WOOLLY FROUSTY
STULTIFY SOT PUPPIFY
STUMBLE CHIP FALL HAMP PECK
STOT TRIP HAMEL LURCH SPURN
STOIT STUMP BUMBLE CHANCE
FALTER HALPER HAMBLE HAPPEN
LUMPER OFFEND STEVEL TUMBLE
WAGGER BLUNDER FOUNDER
SCAMBLE SNAPPER STAMMER
STAMPLE STOITER STOTTER
STUMMER FLOUNDER THRUMBLE
STUMBLING HACK HURTING
OFFENCE OFFENSE
STUMP CAG JOB SET BUTT DOCK
GRUB LUMP MORE RUNT SNAG
STAB STAM STOB STUB STUD
CHUNK SCRAB STICK STOCK STOMP
STOOL STOOP STOWL DOTARD
NUBBIN SCRUNT SPRONG STOVEN
WICKET DODDARD RAMPICK
RAMPIKE SLEEPER STUMMEL
BALDHEAD HUSTINGS STUBBLES
(— AND ROOT) MOCK
(— OF TAIL) STRUNT
(CIGAR —) TOPPER
(CRICKET —) STICKS
(DEAD —) RUNT
(TREE —) MOCK STOW STOCK
STOOP ZUCHE DOTARD NUBBIN
STOVEN DODDARD
(WALNUT —) BUTT
STUMPY SNUB BUNTY SNUBBED
STUN DIN BOWL DAZE DAUNT DAVER
DEAVE DOVER DOZEN DROWN
STONY ASTONY BEDAZE BENUMB
DEADEN DEAFEN NOBBLE STOUND
WITHER ASTOUND DAMMISH
SANDBAG SILENCE STUPEFY
STUPEND ASTONISH
(— BY A SHOT) CREASE
STUNNED SILLY STUPENT ASTONIED
STUNNER KNOCKER THUMPER
TRIMMER
STUNNING CRASHING SHOCKING
STUNT GAG KIP BLAST CANOE
CROWL DWARF STINT STOCK
BARANI BARONI CRADDY DOLPHIN
BACKBONE CATALINA CRUCIFIX
PORPOISE SUPPRESS
(SWIMMING —) SHARK SPIRAL
STUNTED URLED GRUBBY RUNTISH
SCROGGY SCRUBBY SCRUFFY
SCRUNTY
STUPA TOPE CHORTEN
STUPEFACTION STOUND STUPOR
STUPEFIED MAD DAMP DAZED
MAZED SILLY BEMAZED DONNERT
DOZENED DOZZLED STUPENT
BESOTTED DATELESS MINDLESS
STUPEFIER OPIUM
STUPEFY FOX BAZE DAMP DAZE
DOZE DRUG DULL GOOF MAZE
STUN BESOT DAUNT DAVER DEAVE
DIZZY DOZEN SHEND SMOKE STONY
ASTONE ASWEVE BENUMB DUDDLE
FUDDLE MUDDLE STOUND ASTOUND
CONFUSE FORDULL SLUMBER
SMNIATE STUPEND ASTONISH

BEFUDDLE BEWILDER CONFOUND
MORPHINE SOPORATE
STUPEFYING STONY
STUPENDOUS GREAT IMMENSE
ENORMOUS
STUPID FAT BETE DOWF DULL DU[
DUNT FOOL HAZY LEWD NICE NU[
SLOW BLUNT BRUTE CRASS DEN[
DUNNY GLAKY GOOSY GROSS
HEAVY INERT MOSSY MUZZY SILL
THICK ASSISH BARREN CUCKOO
DAWKIN DOITED DROWSY DUMME[
HEBETE LOGGER OBTUSE OPAQU[
SIMPLE STOLID STULTY STURDY
SUMPHY URLUCH WOODEN ASINI[
BRUTISH CHUCKLE DOLTISH
DOWFART DUFFING DUMPISH
FATUOUS FOOLISH FOPPISH
GAWKISH GLAIKIT GULLISH INSUL[
LUMPISH LURDANE PEAKISH
PINHEAD PROSAIC SOTTISH TAIVE[
TOMFOOL VACUOUS WITLESS
ANSERINE BAYARDLY BESOTTED
BLOCKISH BOEOTIAN CLODDISH
DONNERED DUNCICAL FOOTLESS
GAUMLESS HEADLESS IMBECILE
STOCKISH
(— PERSON) HOIT JUKES SUMPH
LUMMOX TUMFIE KALLIKAK
STUPIDITY BETISE BOBBERY
DENSITY DUNCERY FATUITY
DULLNESS DUMBNESS HEBETUDE[
STUPOR FOG SOG DAMP DOTE
SOPOR SWARF STOUND TRANCE
NARCOMA LETHARGY NARCOSIS
STURDILY BUFF TOUGH
STURDY GID BUFF DUNT RUDE TA[
THRO BURLY CRANK FELON HAR[
HUSKY LUSTY SOLID SOUND STA[
STERN STIFF STOUT VAUDY WAL[
FEERIE PLUGGY ROBUST RUGGE[
RUSTIC SQUARE STABLE STEADY
STEEVE STOCKY STRONG STUGG
VIRILE FECKFUL UPRIGHT VALIAN[
STALWART STUBBORN VIGOROUS[
YEOMANLY
STURGEON HUSO ELOPS BELUGA[
GANOID MAMMOSE STERLET
STUTTER FAM BUFF HACK MANT
STOT STUT GANCH FAMBLE HAB[
HABBLE STAMMER
STUTTERER RATTLER
STUTTERING TRAULISM
STY PEN QUAT STYE WEST FRANK[
PIGPEN STITHE HORDEOLUM
STYLE AIR CUT DUB PEN SAY TO[
WAY CHIC FACE FORM GARB KIN[
MODE MOLD NAME PILE RATE TV[
VEIN GENRE GETUP GUISE SHAPE
STATE SWANK TASTE FESCUE
FORMAT GNOMON GOTHIC PHRAS[
STEELE STYLUS UMBONE COSTU[
DIALECT DICTION FASHION INSTY[
QUALITY EQUIPAGE LANGUAGE
MARINISM NARRANTE PULLBACK
(— OF ARCHITECTURE) ORDER
DRAVIDA GEORGIAN
(— OF COOKING) CUISINE
(— OF DRESS) GUISE

'— **OF GEM SETTING**) BOX
— **OF HANDWRITING**) CHANCERY
SCRIPTION
— **OF HAT**) BLOCK
'— **OF MOUNTING**) SETTING
— **OF MUSIC**) BOOGIE
— **OF PAINTING**) GENRE
— **OF PENMANSHIP**) HAND
— **OF SPEAKING**) ADDRESS
AFFECTED —) EUPHUISM
ARTISTIC —) GUSTO GOTHIC
ARTIFICE DANDYISM
BOOKBINDING —) ALDINE MAIOLI
MAJOLI FANFARE GROLIER
ETRUSCAN HARLEIAN ROXBURGH
CUSTOMARY —) GATE
DISTINCTIVE —) CLOTHES
FAVORED —) GROOVE
HAIR —) CROP TETE
INFLATED —) FUSTIAN
LATEST —) KICK
PRETENTIOUS —) BOMBAST
PROPER —) WEAR
THEATRICAL —) LYCEUM
YLET SPEAR STILET STYLUS
TROCAR MANDRIN STILETTE
YLIDIUM CANDOLEA
YLISH CHIC DOSS DOGGY NIFTY
NOBBY SASSY SHARP SMART
SWELL TIPPY TOPPY CHEESY
CLASSY DAPPER FLOSSY JAUNTY
SWANKY TONISH DASHING DOGGISH
GENTEEL KNOWING SWAGGER
TOFFISH
YLOID BELONOID
YLUS GAD PEN STYLE CUTTER
GREFFE TRACER HARPAGO POINTEL
PYROPEN
YPTIC ALUM AMADOU MATICO
AROMETZ STANCHER
YRENE STYROL CINNAMOL
YX (FATHER OF —) OCEANUS
HUSBAND OF —) PALLAS
MOTHER OF —) TETHYS
AEDA DONDIA
AN PAN SOROBAN
AVE OILY SMUG SOFT BLAND
SOAPY SVELT GLOSSY SILKEN
SMOOTH FULSOME UNCTUOUS
AVELY CREAMILY
AVITY URBANITY
'**B** GRASS
BALTERN WART
BBASE PLINTH
BCINCTORIUM BALTEUS
ALTHEUS
BCLASS GENDER BRYALES
ESTODA CYCLIAE DIGENEA
SPECIES AMOEBAEA ANAPSIDA
ESTODES COPEPODA GANOIDEI
ELACHII
BCUTANEOUS DEEP
BDEACON MINISTER
BDIVIDE CARVE MINCE
BDIVISION DEN OBE SEX BEAT
AZA DHER HAPU ITEM TASU
UNDA CORPS CURIA DEKAN DHERI
ERAE FORTY HSIEN IOWAN NAHIE
KRUG PHYLE SITIO STAGE TALUK

TARAF TURMA UINTA ALBIAN
ARENIG BANNER BUREAU CERCLE
CIRCLE COHORT COLUMN DAKOTA
DANIAN DOGGER FACIES GUELPH
HEMERA IMBREX LENGTH LUDLOW
MARKAZ NAHIYE OBLAST ONEIDA
SANJAK SECTOR SERIAL SHIRAZ
STRAIN SUBAGE TAHSIL TASSOO
TEHSIL BUKEYEI CENTURY
CHEMUNG CHIRIPA COCHITI
COMARCA ECOTYPE ELEMENT
EPARCHY EPISODE GENESEE
MONTANA PHRATRY RONDOUT
SASTEAN SECTION SEEDBED
SUBAREA SUBLINE SUBPLAT
SUBPLOT SUBRACE SUBZONE
SUPPORT TRENTON TRINITY
WASATCH WASHITA WENLOCK
WICHITA BANOVINA DISTRICT
DIVISION DJAGATAY ENDBRAIN
FLOTILLA GUBERNIA LOCATION
MONTEREY NAUCRARY PRECINCT
STOCKTON SUBCASTE SUBORDER
SUBSTAGE SUBTRIBE TOWNSHIP
(— **OF SCOUTS**) CREW
(EGYPTIAN —) KISM
SUBDOMINANT FOURTH
SUBDUE ADAW BEAT BEND QUAY
TAME ACCOY ALLAY AMATE CHARM
CRUSH DAUNT DOMPT QUAIL
QUASH QUELL SOBER STILL
ADAUNT BRIDLE CHASTE DEBELL
DISMAY EVINCE GENTLE MASTER
QUENCH REDUCE SUBACT SUBMIT
UNWILD ABANDON AFFAITE
CAPTURE CHASTEN CONQUER
REPRESS REPRIME SUCCUMB
CONVINCE OVERCOME SUPPEDIT
SUPPRESS SURMOUNT VANQUISH
SUBDUED MAK SOFT TAME SOBER
STILL UNDER BROKEN CHASTE
GENTLE ASHAMED SUBMISS
SOURDINE
SUBFAMILY KHOISAN CUSHITIC
ACRAEINAE
SUBGROUP BAND FAMILY
SUBHEAD BOXHEAD SIDEHEAD
SUBIMAGO DUN
SUBINDEX SUFFIX
SUBIRRIGATE SUB SUBWATER
SUBIRRIGATION SUBBING
SUBJECT DUX PUT ABLE ALLY BODY
BONE ITEM TEXT HOBBY PLACE
STOOP STUDY TESTO THEMA
THEME TOPIC GROUND IMPOSE
LIABLE PATHIC REDUCE SACOPE
SUBDIT SUBMIT THRALL VASSAL
CITIZEN FEODARY FEUDARY
OBVIOUS SERVILE ELECTIVE
INCIDENT INFERIOR OBEDIENT
OCCASION SENTENCE SUBJUGAL
(— **OF DISCOURSE**) NOUN
(— **OF FUGUE**) GUIDA
(— **OF PROPOSITION**) EXTREME
(— **TO ABUSE**) REVILE
(— **TO ARGUMENT**) MOOT
(— **TO BAD TEMPER**) MOODY
(— **TO CHANGE**) MUTABLE FUGITIVE
(— **TO CRITICISM**) SCOURGE

(— **TO FATE**) FIE
(— **TO PERCOLATION**) DISPLACE
(— **TO SOME ACTION**) TREAT
(CONTROVERTED —) ISSUE
(LOYAL —) LIEGE
(PL.) FOLK
SUBJECTION SLAVERY SERVITUS
THIRLING
SUBJECTIVE IMMANENT INSEEING
INTERNAL PECTORAL EPISTEMIC
SUBJUGATION BONDAGE
SERVITUDE
SUBKINGDOM PHYLUM ANNULOSA
CHORDATA
SUBLEADER HEADMAN
SUBLEASE FARMOUT SUBTACK
SUBLET JOB SUBSET CONACRE
SUBLEASE
SUBLIME FUME GRAND LOFTY
NOBLE REFINE SOLEMN WINGED
ELEVATO EXALTED EMPYREAL
EMPYREAN MAGNIFIC MAJESTIC
SERAPHIC SPLENDID
(— **IN STYLE**) MILTONIC
SUBLIMITY GRANDEUR
SUBLUNARY EARTHLY
SUBMARINE SUB BOAT DIVER FRITZ
GUPPY SUBSEA PIGBOAT TIDDLER
SUBMEDIANT SIXTH
SUBMERGE BOG DIP BURY DIVE
DUNK HIDE SINK SOAK TAKE
DROWN SOUSE SWAMP WHELM
DELUGE DRENCH ENGULF DEMERGE
IMPLUNGE INUNDATE SUBMERSE
SURROUND
SUBMERGENCE ONLAP
SUBMISSION VAIL PATIENCE
SUBMISSIVE MEEK BUXOM DEMISS
DOCILE DUTIFUL PASSIVE SERVILE
SLAVISH SUBJECT SUBMISS
UNERECT OBEDIENT RESIGNED
YIELDING
(— **TO WIFE**) UXORIOUS
SUBMISSIVENESS SLAVERY
SUBMIT BOW EAT ABOW BEND CAVE
LEAN OBEY TAKE VAIL AVALE
DEFER HIELD STAND STOOP YIELD
ASSENT DELATE RESIGN CONSIGN
KNUCKLE SUBJECT SUBMUSE
SUCCUMB TRUCKLE
(— **FOR CONSIDERATION**) REMIT
(— **TAMELY**) EAT
(— **TO**) ABIDE STAND SUFFER
SUBNORMAL SICK ABNORMAL
SUBORDER LARI ALCAE APODA
APODI GALLI GRUES ARDEAE
COHORT CUCULI SAURIA AGLOSSA
ANSERES ARCACEA ASCONES
CORACII COSTATA SARCURA
SYCONES ACRASIDA ADEPHAGA
BATOIDEI COLUMBAE CORACIAE
CURSORIA ENOPLINA EUSUCHIA
FALCONES FREGATAE SELACHII
SUBORDINARY ENDORSE ROUNDEL
SUBORDINATE SUB SINK PETTY
SCRUB UNDER EXEMPT MINION
PUISNE SECOND YEOMAN SERVANT
SERVILE SUBJECT HENCHMAN
INFERIOR MYRMIDON PARERGAL

POSTPONE SERVIENT
SUBORN HAVE BRIBE
SUBOVAL PETALOID
SUBPHYLUM EUCHORDA
SUBPOENA SUMMONS
SUBRACE STOCK
SUBSCRIBE SIGN ASSENT ASCRIBE
CONSIGN SUBSIGN
SUBSCRIBER RAILBIRD
SUBSCRIPT INFERIOR
SUBSEQUENT AFTER LATER
FUTURE PUISNE ENSUING POSTNATE
SUBSEQUENTLY SO LATER SINCE
SUBSERVIENT OILY VASSAL
DUTEOUS SERVILE SLAVISH
OFFICIAL
SUBSHRUB STOCK GUAYULE
COLUMNEA
SUBSIDE DIE EBB LAY LIE CALM
FALL LULL SILE SINK VAIL ABATE
ALLAY LAPSE RESIDE SETTLE
ASSUAGE RELAPSE UNSWELL
WITHDRAW
SUBSIDENCE FALL SETTLING
SUBSIDIARY CHILD DONKEY
SUBSIDY
SUBSIDIZE BONUS
SUBSIDY AID BONUS BOUNTY
POUNDAGE
SUBSILICIC BASIC
SUBSIST BE LIVE RELY
SUBSISTENCE BEING LIVING
SUBSISTENT ENTITY
SUBSOIL PAN LECK SOLE SHRAVE
RATCHEL
SUBSTAGE CARY GUNZ IOWAN
MANKATO STADIAL TAZEWELL
SUBSTANCE FAT SUM BODY CORE
GIST GITE TACK WHAT ADROP
AGENT ALLOY ARCHE FOMES
GREAT KEEST METAL MOYEN OUSIA
PROOF SENSE STUFF THING
BOTTOM GADUIN GETTER IMPORT
MATTER STAPLE WEALTH AEROSOL
AGAROID ANTIGEN COLICIN
COLLOID CONTENT ELEIDIN
EMANIUM ERGUSIA ESSENCE
HYALINE MEANING PURPORT
REAGENT SUBJECT SUPTION
ACCEPTOR ADDITIVE ADHESIVE
ALLERGEN AMBEROID ANTIFOAM
BASSORIN HARDNESS MATERIAL
(— CAPABLE OF EXPANSION)
DILATANT
(— FORMED IN VINEGAR) MOTHER
(— FROM CRUSHED APPLES)
POMACE
(— IN BLOOD) ALEXINE ABLASTIN
(— IN LIGHT BULBS) GETTER
(— IN WOODY TISSUE) LIGNIN
(— OF DENTINE) IVORY
(— OF EXTREME HARDNESS)
ADAMANT DIAMOND
**(— PRODUCING POISONOUS
ATMOSPHERE)** GAS
**(— SURROUNDED BY FOREIGN
TISSUE)** ENCLAVE
(— TO ADD STABILITY) BALLAST
(— TRANSPORTING GERMS) FOMES

(— USED AS HYPNOTIC) URAL
(— USED IN DETECTING OTHERS)
REAGENT
(— WITH MOLDY ODOR) CHARACIN
(ADHESIVE —) GLUE GLOEA PASTE
CEMENT STICKER
(AMORPHOUS —) GLASS RESIN
LIGNIN PECTIN FERRITE SAPONIN
(AROMATIC —) BALSAM
(ASTRINGENT —) ALUM CATECHU
(BITTER —) ALOIN LININ ILICIN
(BLACK —) SOOT BLECK
(CLEANSING —) LYE
(COLLOIDAL —) ALGIN EXPANDER
(COMBUSTIBLE —) COAL
(CORROSIVE —) CAUSTIC
(CRYSTALLINE —) LAURIN ALANINE
HELENIN ELATERIN
(DARK —) ATRAMENT
(DISSOLVED —) SOLUTE
(ETERNAL —) DHARMA ADHARMA
(FATLIKE —) DEGRAS LIPOID
ERGUSIA
(FATTY —) SMEAR SUBERIN
(FERMENTATION —) LEAVEN
(FIBROUS —) COTTON
(FILAMENTOUS —) HARL
(FILMY —) GOSSAMER
(FIRST —) YLEM
(GRINDING —) ABRASIVE
(GUMMY —) GUM GURRY AMYLOID
GLACTAN
(HARD ANIMAL —) BONE ENAMEL
(HORNY —) BALEEN CHITIN
CHONDRIN
(HYPOTHETICAL —) FLUID INOGEN
PROTYL
(IDEAL —) CONTINUUM
(INFLAMMABLE —) BITUMEN
(INSOLUBLE —) CARRIER HYALOGEN
(LIVERLIKE —) HEPAR
(NARCOTIC —) DRUG
(NITROGENOUS —) LACTENIN
(POISONOUS —) ARSENIC PHRYNIN
EXOTOXIN
(POWDER OF ANY —) FLOUR
(POWDERY —) STOUR
(PREDOMINATING —) BASE
(RESINOUS —) LAC COPAL
COPALINE COPALITE
(SELF-DEFENSIVE —) ACRAEIN
(SEMISOLID —) GEL
(SOUR —) ACID
(STICKY —) GOO GOOP SIZE STICK
GLUTEN BIRDLIME
(SUBTLE —) SPIRIT
(SWEET —) SUGAR
(SYNTHETIC —) HORMONE
(TRANSLUCENT —) HYALINE
(UNBREAKABLE —) ADAMANT
(UNCREATED —) ADHARMA
(VISCOUS —) GLAIR GREASE
SLUBBER
(VITAL —) KEEST
(WAXY —) CERIN PARAFFIN
SUBERINE
SUBSTANDARD BAD BAUCH
SUBSTANTIAL FAT FIRM MEATY
PUKKA STOUT ACTUAL BODILY

HEARTY SQUARE STABLE STANCI
STUFFY STURDY MASSIVE MATEF
SUBSTANT TANGIBLE
SUBSTANTIATE BACK CONFIRM
SUPPORT VALIDATE
SUBSTANTIVE DIRECT
SUBSTITUTE SUB VICE AKORI
EXTRA PROXY VICAR BEWITH
CHANGE DEPUTY DOUBLE ERSAT
COMMUTE REPLACE RESERVE
STANDBY STOPGAP SUBDEAN
SUFFECT SUPPOSE DISPLACE
EMERGENT
(— FOR TEA) TIA FAHAM
(NOT —) FULL
(POOR —) APOLOGY
SUBSTITUTION SHIFT CHANGE
ERSATZ ENALLAGE EXCHANGE
NOVATION
(— OF SOUNDS) LALLATION
SUBSTRATUM SUB GROUND
SUBBING SUBJECT
SUBSTREAM MATTER
SUBSTRUCTURE PODIUM FOOTII
SUBSUME COVER EXPLAIN INCLL
SUBSUMING GENERIC
SUBTENANT VAVASOUR
SUBTERFUGE MASK BLIND CROC
QUIRK SHIFT TRICK WRINK CHIC
ARTIFICE PRETENCE TRAVERSE
VOIDANCE
SUBTILE SUBTLE TENUOUS
SUBTITLE TITLE LEADER CAPTIO
SUBTLE SLY FINE NICE WILY WIS
ACUTE ARGUTE CRAFTY FRAGIL
SUBTILE CLERGIAL
(TOO —) FINESPUN
SUBTLETY FRAUD DECEIT EXILIT
FINESSE DELICACY FINENESS
QUIDDITY QUOLIBET
SUBTLY FINE SLILY SLYLY
SUBTRACT BATE PULL TAKE SH
DEDUCE DEDUCT DETRACT
SUBDUCE SUBDUCT SUBTRAY
DIMINISH
SUBTRIBE HAPU SENAAH SEMNC
SUBURB ANNEX BORGO BARRIO
PETTAH BANLIEU ENDSHIP
FAUBOURG
(PL) SKIRTS ENVIRONS OUTPAR
SUBURBIA
SUBURBIA VILLADOM
SUBVERSION FALL SABOTAGE
SUBVERSIVE RUINOUS
SUBVERT SAP KILL RAZE RUIN
EVERT UPSET GAINSAY OVERSE
REVERSE RUINATE OVERTURN
SUBVERTED LOST
SUBWAY DIVE METRO
SUCCEED GO FAY HIT FARE RIS
WORK CLICK ENSUE FADGE PRC
SPEED COTTON FOLLOW SECOI
THRIVE ACHIEVE PROSPER
THROUGH FLOURISH SUPPLANT
(— TO THRONE) ACCEDE ASCEI
SUCCEEDING VICE AFTER CHAI
ULTERIOR
SUCCESS DO GO HIT MAX WIN
BANG CESS LUCK SMASH SPEE

RIFT EXPLOIT FORTUNE FURTHER
FEEDOM FELICITY GODSPEED
- **IN A MATCH)** GAME
RILLIANT —) ECLAT
UDDEN —) KILLING
NEXPECTED —) JACKPOT
VORLDLY —) ARTHA
CCESSFUL HOT SOCK LUCKY
PEEDFUL THRIVING
CCESSFULLY GREAT HAPPILY
ROUDLY
CCESSION RUN SUIT ROUND
UITE TRACK ASSISE COURSE
EQUEL SERIES STREAM STRING
EIRDOM SUCCESS ANCESTRY
ADOCHE MUTATION SEQUENCE
- **OF CHANGES)** FLUX
- **OF CHORDS)** CADENCE
- **OF CRUSTS)** CALICHE
- **OF STAGES)** CASCADE
- **OF WAVES)** CRIMP
- **RULERS)** DYNASTY
CCESSIVELY AROW
CCESSOR HEIR CALIF HERES
ALIPH HAERES EPIGONUS
- **OF CHIEFTAIN)** TANIST
- **OF MUHAMMAD)** CALIF CALIPH
L.) DIADOCHI
CCINCT BRIEF SHORT TERSE
ONCISE LACONIC SUMMARY
CCINIC DIACETIC
CCOR AID HELP RESET SERVE
PEED ASSIST RELIEF RESCUE
UPPLY UPTAKE COMFORT DELIVER
RESIDY RELIEVE SECOURS
USTAIN BEFRIEND
CCULENT FRIM FRUM LUSH
UICY LUSHY PAPPY PULPY SAPPY
OUNG CASHIE FLESHY TENDER
ATERISH
CCUMB BREAK QUAIL STOOP
RAIK YIELD
CH SIC SICK THAT SWICH
CHNESS TATHATA
CK SOUK SWIG SWOOP SUCKLE
- **DRY)** SOAK
- **UP)** DRINK ABSORB TIPPLE
CKEN THIRL
CKER CHUB FISH GULL SOBOL
HIEF CHUPON CUPULE MULLET
ATOON REDFIN SOBOLE SPROUT
QUARE SUPPER TILLER CUTLIPS
ONOTYL LOCULUS OSCULUM
COURGE BOTHRIUM HUMPBACK
SHOVER REDHORSE SURCULUS
CKLE FEED MILK SUCK LACTATE
OURISH
CKLING SUCKER LACTANT
UCKLER TEATLING
CTION INTAKE
CTORIA ACINETAE

SUDAN

APITAL: KHARTOUM
ESERT: NUBIAN
ANGUAGE: GA EWE IBO KRU EFIK
MOLE TSHI YORUBA MANDINGO
EASURE: UD

MOUNTAIN: KINYETI
NATIVE: DAZA GOLO NUER SERE
  DINKA FULAH HAUSA MOSSI
  NUBIYIN
REGION: DARFUR KASSALA
  KORDOFAN
RIVER: NILE
TOWN: KOSTI MEROE ATBARA
  ALUBAYD MALAKAL OMDURMAN
WEIGHT: HABBA

SUDANESE FULA FULAH
SUDAN GRASS GARAVA GARAWI
SUDDEN FERLY HASTY ICTIC SWIFT
  ABRUPT FIERCE SNAPPY SPEEDY
  PRERUPT HEADLONG SPURTIVE
  SUBITANY SUBITOUS
SUDDENLY BOB POP BOLT FLOP
  SLAP AMAIN SHORT SKELP SOUSE
  ASTART BOUNCE PRESTO SUBITO
  ASUDDEN UNAWARES
SUDDENNESS ATTACK SUDDENTY
SUDORIFIC SWEAT SWEATER
  HIDROTIC SUDATORY
SUDRA VELLALA
SUDS BUCK FOAM SAPPLES
  SOAPSUDS
SUE LAW WOO SUIT IMPLEAD
  TROUNCE
SUET TALLOW
SUFFER BYE GET LET BEAR DREE
  FIND GAIN HURT PAIN PINE ALLOW
  DREIE LABOR PROVE SMART SMOKE
  STAND THOLE ABEGGE ENDURE
  PERMIT AGONIZE SUPPORT SUSTAIN
  UNDERGO TOLERATE
  (— **AGONY)** THROE
  (— **AT STAKE)** SMOKE
  (— **DEFEAT)** BOW
  (— **FOR)** ABY ABYE ABIDE
  (— **FROM TIME)** AGE
  (— **GREAT AFFLICTION)** GROAN
  (— **HUNGER)** CLEM STARVE
  AFFAMISH
  (— **LOSS OF)** GIVE
  (— **PAIN)** STOUND ANGUISH
  (— **PENALTY)** SWEAT
  (— **REMORSE)** RUE
  (— **RUIN)** WRECK
  (— **SYNCOPE)** FAINT
  (— **THROUGH)** PASS
  (— **TO ENTER)** ADMIT
SUFFERABLE PATIBLE
SUFFERANCE PAIN MISERY
  PATIENCE THOLANCE
SUFFERER MARTYR AMNESIC
  DOORMAT PATIENT
SUFFERING BALE COST DREE HURT
  PAIN PINE RACK DOLOR GRIEF
  SMART WRAKE PATHIC PATHOS
  THRALL INVALID LANGUOR PASSION
  PASSIVE TRAVAIL DISTRESS
  HARDSHIP
  (— **FROM HANGOVER)** CHIPPY
  (— **FROM ILL HEALTH)** DOWN
  (— **OF MIND)** CARE
  (—**S OF CHRIST)** AGONY

SUFFICE DO LAST REACH SERVE
  SATISFY
SUFFICIENCY ENOUGH ADEQUACY
SUFFICIENT DUE FAIR GOOD AMPLE
  DECENT ENOUGH BASTANT
  ADEQUATE RELEVANT COMPETENT
  (**BARELY** —) SCANT SKIMP SCRIMPY
  (**BE** — **FOR)** COVER
SUFFICIENTLY DULY WELL ENOUGH
SUFFIX POSTFIX
SUFFOCATE CHOKE DROWN SMOOR
  STIVE STUFF SWELT SLOKEN STIFLE
  OVERLIE QUACKLE SMOLDER
  SMOTHER SCUMFISH STRANGLE
  THROTTLE
SUFFRAGE VOTE VOICE TONGUE
  VERSICLE
SUFFUSE FILL BATHE EMBAY INFUSE
SUFFUSION COLOR
SUGAR CANDY DIOSE IDOSE MELIS
  PIECE SUCRE THIRD ACROSE
  ALDOSE ALLOSE FUCOSE GULOSE
  HEXOSE INVERT KETOSE LYXOSE
  OCTOSE PANELA TALOSE TRIOSE
  XYLOSE AGAVOSE ALTROSE
  BASTARD CHITOSE GLUCOSE
  GLUTOSE GLYCOSE LACTOSE
  MALTOSE PAPELON PENOCHI
  PENTOSE PENUCHE SORBOSE
  SUCROSE SWEETEN TETROSE
  THREOSE BROWNING CONCRETE
  CYMAROSE DEXTROSE FRUCTOSE
  FURANOSE LEVULOSE PYRANOSE
  RHAMNOSE RHODEOSE SECALOSE
  TURANOSE
  (**BROWN** —) CARAIBE JAGGARY
  JAGGHERY
  (**COARSE** —) RAAB
  (**CRUDE** —) GUR HEAD MELADA
  CONCRETE
  (**INFERIOR** —) BASTARD
SUGARCANE CANE GRAIN GLUMAL
  RATOON MATTRESS
  (— **SAP)** LIQUOR
SUGARHOUSE (PART OF —)
  PURGERY
SUGARLESS DRY
SUGARPLUM KISS
SUGARY FAT SUGAR SWEET
  OVERRIPE
SUGGEST JOG BEAR GIVE HINT MINT
  IMPLY OFFER SPEAK ALLUDE INDITE
  INFUSE MOTION PROMPT RESENT
  SUBMIT CONNOTE DICTATE INSPIRE
  INDICATE INTIMATE
  (— **DRINKING)** PROPOSE
  (— **INSIDIOUSLY)** INFUSE
  (— **STRONGLY)** ARGUE
SUGGESTIBLE SOFT
SUGGESTION CUE CAST HINT TANG
  GLIFF ADVICE BREATH MOTION
  SMATCH INKLING LEADING PROFFER
  REMNANT SOUPCON WRINKLE
  INNUENDO INSTANCE PROPOSAL
SUGGESTIVE ANICONIC PREGNANT
  (— **OF MELODY)** CANOROUS
SUICIDAL KAMIKAZE
SUIT DO GO APT DOW FIT GEE HIT
  SET SIT ACTO LIKE LIST PAIR SORT

ADAPT AGREE APPLY BEFIT BESIT
CLUBS COLOR DRAPE DRESS
FADGE FANCY FRAME HABIT LEVEL
MATCH PLEAD QUEME SAVOR
SERVE SHAPE STAND SUING TALLY
AFFEIR ANSWER BECOME COHERE
COMPLY DITTOS HEARTS PRAYER
SPADES SPEECH SQUARE BEHOOVE
COMPORT COSTUME COULEUR
PURSUIT REQUEST SEERPAW
DIAMONDS INSTANCE QUADRATE
SKELETON STANDARD TAILLEUR
TROPICAL
(— AT LAW) ACTO CASE LAWSUIT
(SWIMMING —) BATHER BIKINI
SUITABILITY (MUTUAL —) DECENCY
IDONEITY SYMPATHY
SUITABLE APT FIT PAT ABLE FEAT
GAIN GOOD JUMP JUST MEET TALL
WELL WEME DIGNE EQUAL FITTY
QUEME RIGHT SUITY COMELY
FITTEN GAINLY GIUSTO HABILE
HONEST LIABLE LIKELY PROPER
SUITLY AVENANT COMMODE
CONDIGN CONGRUE FITTING
IDONEAL PLIABLE SEEMING
BECOMING ELIGIBLE FEASIBLE
HANDSOME IDONEOUS SORTABLE
(— FOR STAGE PERFORMANCE)
ACTING
SUITABLENESS APTNESS HONESTY
APTITUDE PROPERTY
SUITABLY FITLY MEETLY TIDELY
APROPOS GRADELY
SUITCASE BAG CAP GRIP CAPCASE
DORLACH KEESTER
SUITE SET SUIT SWEEP SWEET
SERIES PARTITA RETINUE
ENSEMBLE EQUIPAGE
(— OF MOLDINGS) LEDGMENT
(— OF ROOMS) FLAT CHAMBER
SUITED FIT ADAPT SEEMLY ADAPTED
ASSORTED
(POORLY —) CROOK
SUITING COVERT CHEVIOT
SUITOR MAN SUER SWAIN WOOER
GALLANT SERVANT
SUKU WASUKUMA
SULFIDE GLANCE CUBANITE
SULFURET
SULFUR BRIMSTONE
SULK DOD PET CHAW CRAB DORT
GLUM SULL BOODY FRUMP GLUMP
GROUT GRUMP GROUCH SNUDGE
THURMUS
(PL.) GEE HUMP MUMPS FRUMPS
SULLENS BOUDERIE
SULKER MUMPER
SULKINESS DORT GRUMP
SULKY CART CHUFF DODDY DORTY
GOURY HUFFY HUMPY CHUFFY
GLUMPY GROUTY JINKER SNUFFY
STUFFY SULLEN SUMPHY DOGGISH
HUFFISH MUMPISH
(NOT —) GOOD
SULLEN DOUR FOUL GLUM GRIM
SOUR BLACK CHUFF CROSS DUMPY
FELON GRUFF HARSH MOODY
RUSTY STERN SULKY SURLY

WEMOD CRUSTY DOGGED GLOOMY
GLUMMY GLUMPY GLUNCH GROUTY
MOROSE MULISH SOMBER SOMBRE
STUFFY AUSTERE CRABBED
CYNICAL FRETFUL LOURING
MUMPISH PEEVISH CHUMPISH
CHURLISH LOWERING PETULANT
SPITEFUL STUNKARD
SULLENNESS GEE DORT GLUM
MUMPS STOMACH
SULLIED DIRTY SPOTTED
SULLY BLOT BLUR DASH FOUL SLUR
SMIT SMUT SOIL CLOUD DIRTY
GRIME SMEAR SMOKE STAIN TAINT
DARKEN DEFILE SMIRCH SMUTCH
ATTAINT BEGRIME BESMEAR
BLEMISH CORRUPT DISTAIN ECLIPSE
POLLUTE SLUBBER TARNISH
BESMIRCH
SULPHATE ALUM BARITE ILESITE
LOWEITE SULFATE VITRIOL
KRAUSITE
SULPHIDE HEPAR GLANCE ZARNEC
SULFIDE ZARNICH CUBANITE
(PL.) MATTE
SULPHUR ORE SPIRIT SULFUR
YELLOW QUEBRITH BRIMSTONE
SULPHURIC ACID VITRIOL
SULTAN SOLDAN
SULTANATE SULTANY ZANZIBAR
SULTANESS SOWDONES
SULTRY CLOSE FLUSH FAINTY
SMUDGY POTHERY PUTHERY
SWELTRY FEVERISH
SUM ALL GOB CASH DRAB DUMP
FARM FINE FOOT FUND MASS TALE
DEDIT GROSS KITTY SUMMA TOTAL
WHOLE AMOUNT DEMAND DYADIC
FIGURE NUMBER DECUPLE INGOING
MANBOTE SUBSIDY SUMMARY
SUMMATE ENTIRETY OCTONION
QUANTITY MOUNTANCE
(— AND SUBSTANCE) TOUR SHORT
UPSHOT
(— AS COMPENSATION FOR
KILLING) MANBOTE
(— FOR REENLISTMENT) GRATUITY
(— FOR SCHOLARSHIP) BURSARY
(— IN BASSET) SEPTLEVA
(— OF 25 POUNDS) PONY PONEY
(— OF 3 FARTHINGS) GILL
(— OF 500 POUNDS) MONKEY
(— OF DETERMINANTS) STIRP
(— OF EXPONENTS) DEGREE
(— OF FACTORS) COMPLEX
(— OF GOOD QUALITIES) ARETE
(— OF MONEY) POT BANK COVER
STOCK BUNDLE ACCOUNT STIPEND
(— OF) SIGMA
(— PAYABLE AT FIXED INTERVALS)
FARM
(— RISKED) STAKE
(— UP) ADD TOT FOOT RECKON
SUBSUME SUMMATE COMPRISE
CONCLUDE PERORATE
(ENTIRE —) SOLIDUM
(EXCESS —) BONUS
(FORFEITED —) DEDIT
(GREAT —) PLUNK SIGHT MICKLE

(LARGE —) GOB SCREAMER
(PETTY —) CENT DIME DRAB
(SMALL — OF MONEY) SPILL
DRIBBLE DRIBLET
(TRIFLING —) HAY
(UNEXPENDED —S) SAVINGS
(VECTOR —) GRADIENT
SUMAC KAREE SUMACH ANACARD
BURTREE SCOTINO SHOEMAKE
SUMATRA (LANGUAGE IN —) NIAS
(MEASURE OF —) PAAL
(MOUNTAIN IN —) LEUSER KERINT
(RIVER IN —) HARI MUSI ROKAN
DJAMBI
(TOWN IN —) ACHIN KUALA MEDA
NATAL SOLOK DJAMBI LANGSA
PADANG RENGAT BONKULIN
SUMBUL SAMBUL MUSKROOT
SUMERIAN ACCADIAN AKKADIAN
SUMMARIZE PRECIS RESUME
ABSTRACT
SUMMARY SUM LEAD BRIEF CHAR
SCORE SHORT SUMMA TOTAL
PRECIS RESUME SUMMAR CHAPTE
CONCISE EPITOME EXTRACT
MEDULLA VIDIMUS ABSTRACT
ARGUMENT BREVIARY BREVIATE
DRUMHEAD HEADNOTE SUCCINCT
SYNOPSIS
(— OF FAITH) SYMBOL
(— OF PRINCIPLES) CREED
SUMMATION SUM DIGEST SUMMA
SUMMER SHEMU SOMER AESTAS
SIMMER DORMANT
(OF —) ESTIVAL
SUMMER CYPRESS KOCHIA
SUMMER FLOUNDER PLAICE
SUMMERHOUSE FOLLY KIOSK
MAHAL TUPEK ALCOVE CASINO
GAZEBO PAGODA CABINET
SUMMER HYACINTH GALTONIA
SUMMER TANAGER REDBIRD
SUMMERWOOD LATEWOOD
SUMMIT DOD SUM TIP TOP VAN
ACME APEX BALD CRAP DODD
HELM KNAP KNOT PEAK ROOF
CREST CROWN SPIRE COMBLE
HEIGHT VERTEX ZENITH CALOTTE
SUMMARY SUMMITY PINNACLE
(— OF TUBE) MOUTH
(— WITHOUT FOREST) BALD
(ROCKY —) KNOT
(ROUND —) DOD DODD
(SNOW-CAPPED —) CALOTTE
SUMMON BAN CRY BUZZ CALL CI
DRUM HAIL SIST BUGLE CHARM
CLEPE EVOKE HIGHT KNELL SOUI
VOUCH ACCITE ADVOKE BECALL
COMPEL DEMAND SOMPNE VOCAT
ACCERSE COMMAND CONJURE
CONVENE CONVENT CONVOKE
PROVOKE SUMMONS WHISTLE
ASSUMMON EXORCISE
(— FOR HIRING) YARD
(— INTO COURT) DEMAND
(— TOGETHER) BAND MUSTER
ASSEMBLE
(— UP) FIND GATHER COLLECT
SUMMONER SUMNER LOCKMAN

;OMPNER OUTRIDER
IMMONING CALL ARRAY
— OF KING'S VASSALS) BAN
IMMONS BAN CRY CALL BIDDING
:ALLING STICKER WARNING
VARRANT CITATION VOCATION
FALCONER'S —) WO
IMP SINK STANDAGE
IMPTUOUS RICH GRAND SHOWY
/LONK COSTLY DELUXE SOLEMN
:UPERB COSTLEW ELEGANT
iPLENDID
IMPTUOUSNESS DAINTY
iUMPTURE
IN SOL ATEN ATON INTI LAMP
iTAR SENGE SURYA TITAN SUNLET
)AYSTAR IOSKEHA PHOEBUS
iAVITAR JOUSKEHA
— MOON AND STARS) HOST
RISING —) HERAKHTI
NAPEE TROUT SAIBLING
NBEAM BANANA
N BEAR BRUANG
NBIRD MAMO CADET
N BITTERN CARLE CAURALE
,UNBIRD
N BLIND UMRELLA
NBONNET TILT UGLY CRESIE
APPIE SHAKER
NBURN GREENING HELIOSIS
NBURNT ADUST TANNED
NBURST SUNRAY SUNBREAK
UNSHINE
NDAE GEDUNK
NDAY EXAUDI JUDICA GAUDETE
RINITY
THIRD — AFTER EASTER) JUBILATE
NDER PART TWIN BREAK SEVER
WAIN TWINE DEPART DIVIDE
INDER ASUNDER DISALLY DISJOIN
IVORCE DISSEVER SEJUGATE
EPARATE UNSOLDER
NDEW DROSERA EYEBRIGHT
NDIAL DIAL GHURRY HOROLOGE
:APHION SOLARIUM
N DISK ATEN ATON CAKRA
HAKRA
NDOG WINDGALL
NDOWNER WHALER TUSSOCKER
N-DRIED TILED
NDROPS SCABISH
NDRY DIVERS DIVERSE SEVERAL
NFISH SUN HURO MOLA RUFF
REAM FLIER FLYER ROACH SUNNY
IVVER MOLOID REDEAR REDEYE
RAPPIE CROPPIE PERCOID
LUEGILL FLATFISH FLOUNDER
EADFISH MOONFISH PONDFISH
'ARMOUTH
NFLOWER GOLD HELIO CANADA
OLDEN SUNFOIL GIRASOLE
JRNSOLE
— STATE) KANSAS
N-GREBE FINFOOT SUNBIRD
'RUIFORM
NK SUNKEN
— TO LOW STATE) ABJECT
NKEN SUNK HOLLOW
NLESS BLAE

SUNLIGHT GLARE
SUNN SAN SANN DAGGA SANAI
JANAPA MADRAS JANAPAN
SANNHEMP
SUNNITE IHLAT SUNNI SUNNIAH
SUNNY GOOD SUNSHINE
SUN PARLOR SOLARIUM
SUNRISE ARIST SUNUP ORIENT
SUNSET SUNFALL
(— STATE) OREGON ARIZONA
SUNSHADE PARASOL ROUNDEL
TIRESOL SOMBRERO
SUNSHINE SUN SHINE SUNLIGHT
(— STATE) FLORIDA
SUNSPOT SPOT FACULA MACULA
SUNSPURGE SUNWEED TURNSOLE
WARTWEED WARTWORT
SUNSTROKE HELIOSIS SIRIASIS
SUNTAN MERIDA
SUN TREE HINOKI
SUNWISE DEASIL DESSIL
SUNYATA VOID
SUP EAT DINE SOWP FEAST
CONSUME SWALLOW
SUPAWN MUSH
SUPERABOUND OVERFLOW
SUPERABUNDANCE FLOOD EXCESS
CATARACT PLETHORA PLEURISY
SUPERABUNDANT RANK LAVISH
PROFUSE
SUPERALTAR PREDELLA
SUPERANNUATE OVERYEAR
SUPERB GRAND GOLDEN GORGEOUS
SPLENDID
SUPERCARGO MERCHANT
SUPERCILIOUS GRAND POTTY
PROUD OVERLY SNIFFY SNIPPY
SNOOTY SNOTTY SNUFFY HAUGHTY
ARROGANT CAVALIER SNIFFISH
SUPERIOR
SUPERCLASS AGNATHA
SUPERCONSCIOUSNESS SAMADHI
SUPERCOOL SUBCOOL SURFUSE
SUPERFAMILY APINA APOIDEA
BOVOIDEA
SUPERFICIAL GLIB ECTAL SUPER
FACIAL FACILE FLIMSY FORMAL
FROTHY GLASSY OVERLY SLIGHT
OUTSIDE OUTWARD SHALLOW
SKETCHY SLIGHTY SURFACE
SURFACY EXTERNAL MAGAZINY
SMATTERY DEPTHLESS
SUPERFICIALLY FLEET
SUPERFICIES TERM EXTENT
SUPERFLUITY FAT FRILL LUXUS
EXCESS OVERSET SURFEIT
(CONFUSING —) FLUTHER
SUPERFLUOUS SPARE USELESS
NEEDLESS
SUPERFRONTAL FRONTLET
SUPERHEATED GASEOUS
SUPERHUMAN DEMON DAEMON
DIVINE INHUMAN UNHUMAN
SUPERIMPOSE LAY OVERLAY
SURPRINT
SUPERIMPOSING DISSOLVE
SUPERINTEND CON CONN GUIDE
OVERSEE PRESIDE
SUPERINTENDENCE CARE

CONTROL EPISCOPY GUIDANCE
SUPERINTENDENCY EDILITY
AEDILITY
SUPERINTENDENT BOSS SUPE
EPHOR SUPER EDITOR VENEUR
VIEWER CAPTAIN EPHORUS
MANAGER DIRECTOR OVERSEER
SURVEYOR SWINGMAN
SUPERIOR JOE AYNE COOL FINE
MORE OVER TRIE ABBOT ABOVE
CHIEF CREAM EIGNE ELDER ELITE
EXTRA FANCY FRANK GREAT LIEGE
PRIOR UPPER ABBESS BETTER
COCKUP CUSTOS DOMINA FATHER
FORBYE MAHANT SELECT SENIOR
STRONG FORTHBY PALMARY
RANKING ABNORMAL DOMINANT
GUARDIAN SINGULAR SPLENDID
SUPERIAL
(— OF CONVENT) HEGUMEN
(— TO) BEFORE
SUPERIORITY DROP GREE PRICE
HEIGHT MASTERY PROWESS
EMINENCE PRIORITY
(MENTAL —) GENIUS
SUPERLATIVE RAVING CURIOUS
CRASHING OLYMPIAN PEERLESS
SWINGING
(ABSOLUTE —) ELATIVE
SUPERLATIVELY CRACKING
SWINGING
SUPERMAN OVERMAN
SUPERNATURAL DIVINE NUMINOUS
SUPERIOR
(— FORCE) WAKANDA
SUPERSTITION FREIT IDOLATRY
SUPERORDER GLIRES
SUPERPOSE APPLY
SUPERSCRIBE DIRECT
SUPERSCRIPT SUPERIOR
SUPERSEDE REPLACE OVERRIDE
SUPPLANT
SUPERSTITIOUS FREITY
SUPERTONIC SECOND
SUPERVENE FOLLOW
SUPERVISE GUIDE DIRECT GOVERN
HANDLE SURVEY FOREMAN
OVERSEE ENGINEER OVERLOOK
CHAPERONE
SUPERVISION EYE CARE DUTY
HAND CHECK CHARGE
SUPERVISOR BULL EPHOR GUIDE
SUPER CENSOR GASMAN RUNMAN
SOURER WARDEN DESKMAN
ALYTARCH CHAIRMAN FLOORMAN
FOREHAND KNIFEMAN LEACHMAN
MASHGIAH OVERSEER
SUPINE INERT DROWSY LANGUID
SERVILE UPRIGHT CARELESS
INACTIVE INDOLENT LISTLESS
SLUGGISH
SUPPER MEAL CUDDY HOCKEY
PASCHAL
(HARVEST-HOME —) HOCKEY
(LAST —) MAUNDY
SUPPING CENATION
SUPPLANT FOLLOW REMOVE
REPLACE DISPLACE DISPLANT
SUPPLE BAIN FLIP OILY SOFT LINGY

LITHE SLAMP SWACK AJOINT
LIMBER LITHER LUTHER SUMPLE
SWANKY WANDLE LISSOME PLIABLE
SPRINGE FLEXIBLE
SUPPLEJACK SOAPWORT
SUPPLEMENT ARM EKE MEND TACK
ANNEX SUPPLY BOLSTER CODICIL
ADDENDUM APPENDIX BOUNTITH
(PL.) FIXINGS
SUPPLEMENTAL SPECIAL
SUPPLEMENTARY ADDED RIPIENO
REMANENT
SUPPLENESS WHIP
SUPPLIANT ASKER PLEADING
SUPPLICATE BEG PRAY CRAVE
PLEAD INVOKE OBTEST SUPPLY
BESEECH ENTREAT IMPLORE
REQUEST SOLICIT PETITION
SUPPLICATION CRY VOW BEAD BILL
LIBEL VENIE LITANY PRAYER
CRAVING SYNAPTE ENTREATY
PETITION PLEADING ROGATION
ROGATIVE SUFFRAGE
SUPPLICATORY EUCTICAL
SUPPLIED (— WITH FOOD) THORN
(AMPLY —) ABUNDANT
(SCANTILY —) BARE
SUPPLIER SOURCE
SUPPLIES STOCK STUFF DUFFEL
STORES VICTUAL ESTOVERS
ORDNANCE
SUPPLY FEED FILL FIND FRET FUND
GIVE HEEL LEND LINE ARRAY
CATER ENDUE EQUIP INDUE OFFER
SERVE STOCK STORE STUFF YIELD
BUDGET DONATE EMPLOY FOISON
LAYOUT POCKET SUBMIT ADVANCE
FORTIFY FRAUGHT FURNISH
LISSOME PROVIDE
(— ABUNDANTLY) SWILL
(— ARRANGED BEFOREHAND)
RELAY
(— FOR AN OCCASION) GRIST
(— OF MONEY) BANKROLL
(— OF POTENTIAL JURORS) TALES
(— OF TIN) SERVING
(— PROVISIONS) PURVEY
(— THE NEED) FOR
(— WITH CLOTHES) INFIT
(— WITH FUEL) STOKE
(— WITH MONEY) GILD
(— WITH OXYGEN) AERATE
(— WITH WATER) FANG
(CACHED —) CAVE
(CONSTANT —) STREAM
(EXTRA —) RESERVE
(FRESH —) RECRUIT
(HIDDEN —) HOARD
(INADEQUATE —) DEARTH
(OVERABUNDANT —) SURFEIT
(PLENTIFUL —) CHOICE
(RESERVE —) CUSHION
(RICH —) ARGOSY
(SCANTY —) SCANT
SUPPORT AID ARM BAY BED BOW
KAI LEG PEG RIB TIE TOM ABET
ABUT AXIS BACK BASE BEAM BEAR
BUOY CRIB DADE FEND FIND FIRM
FORK FUEL HAVE HELP HOLD KEEP

KILP LIFT POST PROP RACK REST
ROCK SALT SIDE STAY STEM STUD
TRIG ADOPT ANGEL APPUI ATLAS
BIPOD BLOCK BRACE CARRY CHAIR
CHEER CHOCK CLEAT CRANK
FAVOR FLOAT FRAME OXTER PLUNK
RANCE SALVE SHORE SPURN STAFF
STAKE STEAD STELL STIPE STOCK
STRUT STULL TOWER VOUCH WEIGH
ANCHOR ASSERT ASSIST BARROW
BEHALF CHEVAL COLUMN CORSET
CRADLE CRUTCH DEFEND DONKEY
DUOPOD GARTER PATTEN PILLAR
POTENT PULPIT PUTLOG SADDLE
SECOND SHIELD SOCKET SPLINT
STAYER STEADY SUFFER TASSEL
TIMBER TINGLE TORSEL UPHAND
UPHOLD UPKEEP UPTAKE WHIMSY
ARMREST BACKING BOLSTER
COMFORT CONFIRM CRIPPLE
DEADMAN ENDORSE FINDING
FULCRUM GROMMET HOUSING
JACKLEG JUSTIFY KEEPING
KNUCKLE NOURISH NURTURE
PABULUM PROTECT RADICAL
SPIRALE SQUINCH STADDLE
STANDER STIFFEN STIRRUP SUBSIST
SUSTAIN THICKEN TRESTLE
ADJUMENT ADVOCATE BALUSTER
BEFRIEND BESTRIDE BOOKREST
BUTTRESS CAPSHORE FAIRLEAD
FOOTREST FORESTAY FORTRESS
HANDREST HOLDFAST JACKSTAY
KEYSTONE MAINSTAY MAINTAIN
MOUNTING NEEDLING OVERCAST
PEDESTAL PEDIMENT STANDARD
STILLAGE STOCKING STRENGTH
SYMPATHY UNDERLIE UNDERPIN
UNDERSET
(— FOR ANVIL) STOCK
(— FOR BELL CLAPPER) BALDRIC
(— FOR CATALYST) CARRIER
(— FOR HEAVY MACHINERY)
BUNTING
(— FOR LEVER) BAIT
(— FOR LIFE-CAR) BAIL
(— FOR MILL) LOWDER
(— FOR MINE PASSAGE) OVERCAST
(— FOR PLATFORM) STEMPEL
STEMPLE
(— IN A LATHE) DOCTOR
(— IN PAPERMAKING TUB) DONKEY
(— OF COPING) KNEELER
(— OF MOLD CORE) ARBOR
ARBOUR
(— OF RAIL) CHAIR BALUSTER
(— THROUGH BIT AND BRIDLE)
APPUI
(CRUTCHLIKE —) DEADMAN
(ELBOW-SHAPED —) CRANK
(EMBEDDED —) SPURN
(FIREPLACE —) ANDIRON
(GIVE —) FEED
(INCLINED —) RIDER
(MINING —) CAP FRAME
(PORTABLE —) STOOL
(PRINCIPAL —) BACKBONE
(TEMPORARY —) NEEDLING
(UPRIGHT —) POPPET BANISTER

(WHEELED —) CARRIAGE
(PL.) SHIPWAY
SUPPORTED BASED BLOCKED
ACCOSTED SUCCINCT
(— BY EVIDENCE) PROBABLE
SUPPORTER ALLY JOCK ATLAS
STOOP COHORT DRAGON SATRA
BOOSTER DEVOTEE FAVORER
FOUNDER LAUDIAN PATROON
PROPPER SUPPORT ADHERENT
ASSERTER ERASTIAN ESPOUSER
FAVORITE HENCHMAN UPHOLDER
CHURCHITE
(ATHLETIC —) CUP JOCK
(CHIEF —) STOOP
(PL.) SECOND
SUPPORTING BEHIND BEARING
SUPPOSE SAY SEE SET WIS WIT
DEEM POSE READ TAKE TROW
WEEN ALLOW COUNT ETTLE FAN
GUESS JUDGE OPINE SEPAD THIN
ASSUME DEVISE DIVINE EXPECT
RECKON BELIEVE CONCEIT
DARESAY IMAGINE PRESUME
PROPOSE SUPPONE SURMISE
CONCEIVE CONCLUDE CONSIDER
OPINIATE
SUPPOSED ALLEGED ASSUMED
PUTATIVE
SUPPOSING IF
SUPPOSITION IF IDEA FICTION
SURMISE WEENING
SUPPOSITORY BOUGIE CANDLE
PESSARY
SUPPRESS LAY DOWN GULP HID
HUSH SINK SLAY SNUB STOP BL
BURKE CHOKE CRUSH ELIDE QU
QUELL SHUSH SMORE SPIKE STI
QUENCH SQUASH STIFLE CONTA
CUSHION INHIBIT OPPRESS
REPRESS SILENCE SMOLDER
SMOTHER SQUELCH RESTRAIN
STRANGLE SUPPRIME VANQUISH
SUPPRESSED BLIND CENSORED
SUPPRESSION ABEYANCE AMEIC
BLACKOUT
(— OF VOWEL) ELISION
(— OF WORD SOUNDS) SYNCOP
ECLIPSIS
SUPPURATE RUN BEAL WHEAL
DIGEST MATTER QUITTER
MATURATE
SUPPURATION PYOSIS BEALING
COCTION
SUPPURATIVE DIGERENT
SUPRACLAVICLE SCAPULA
SUPREMACY PALM PRIMACY
DOMINION OVERRULE
SUPREME HIGH LAST CHIEF VITA
SUBLIME SUMMARY TOPLESS
FOREMOST GREATEST PEERLES
SURA FATIHA FATIHAH
SURCHARGE PACK
SURCINGLE WANTY ROLLER
SURCOAT JUPON CYCLAS KABA
SURD SHARP ATONIC FLATED
SURE COLD BOUND SECURE SICK
STEADY WITTER ASSURED CERT

RFECT COCKSURE POSITIVE
ERRING
ELY WIS FINE SURE PARDY
OLY ATWEEL PARDIE
ENESS SURETY SECURITY
ETY VAS ANDI BAIL BAND
RROW CAUTION ENGAGER
VERTY SPONSOR BAILSMAN
CURITY
ETYSHIP SPONSION
F BREACH KALEMA
NOISE) RUT ROTE
FACE DAY AREA FACE ORLO
AT RYME SIDE BOSOM FLOOR
ONE SWARF CHROME FINISH
OUND SCRUFF ASPHALT
ANKET COUNTER ENVELOP
TFACE OUTSIDE STRETCH
HEREND CONCRETE EXTERIOR
ATFORM
BETWEEN FLUTES OF SHAFT)
LO
BETWEEN TRIGLYPH CHANNELS)
ROS
IN BEATER) BACKFALL
OF BEAM) BACK
OF BODY) FLESH HABIT
OF COAL) BUTT
OF CRICKET FIELD) CARPET
OF DIAMOND) SPREAD
OF EARTH) DUST GROUND
RRENE
OF ESCUTCHEON) FIELD
OF GROUND OVER MINE) DAY
OF PARACHUTE) CANOPY
OF RIFLE BARREL) LAND
OF SAWED LUMBER) FUR
OF TOOTH) TRITOR
OF VAULT) GROIN
OF WATER) RYME SCRUFF
WITHIN EARTH) GEOID
NCAVE —) LAP
RVED —) BELLY
LL —) MAT MATTING
AT —) BED FLAT AEQUOR
GINA
OOR —) BOWL
OMETRIC —) TORE CONOID
HERE CONICOID CYLINDER
LICOID
OSSY —) GLAZE
OOVED —) DROVE
IRY —) NAP
RIZONTAL —) LEVEL
CLINED —) CANT DESCENT
NERAL —) DRUSE
VED —) FOOTWALK
LE —) FRIEZE
ANE —) AREA FACET
INCIPAL —) FACE
INTING —) CUT
OTECTIVE —) LAGGING
AD —) MACADAM CORDUROY
UGH —) KEY CRIZZLE STUBBLE
UGHENED —) MAT FOOTGRIP
IPPERY —) GLARE
OPING —) SHELVING
RIKING —) BLADE
DER — OF SKI) PALM

(UNGLOSSY PAINT —) FLAT
(UPPER —) NOTAEUM
(UPRIGHT —) JAMB
SURFACER SEASONER
SURF DUCK COOT SCOTER
SURFEIT CLOY FILL GLUT SATE
STAW STALL STUFF AGROTE
ENGLUT SICKEN SATIATE SATIETY
SURCLOY SATURATE
SURFEITED SAD SICK BLASE JADED
WEARY REPLETE SATIATED
SURF FISH PERCH ALFIONA
SURF SCOTER COOT SCOTER
SURFER PISHAUG SKUNKTOP
SURF SHINER SPARADA
SURGE GUST TIDE WASH DRIVE
GURGE LUNGE SPURT SWELL
BILLOW BREACH COURSE WALLOW
WALTER ESTUATE REDOUND
AESTUATE UNDULATE
(SHOREWARD —) SUFF
SURGEON (ALSO SEE PHYSICIAN
AND DOCTOR) LEECH ARTIST
INTERN MEDICO OPERATOR
SAWBONES
(TREE —) TREEMAN
SURGEONFISH TANG TANGE
DOCTOR MEDICO BARBERO
SURGEON SAWBONES
SURGERY KNIFE
SURGING WALE ESTURE ESTUOUS
SURICATE ZENICK MEERKAT
SURINAM TOAD PIPA PIPAL
SURINAMINE ANDIRANE ANGELINE
SURLINESS MOROSITY
SURLY BAD ILL GRUM LUNT BLUFF
CHUFF GRUFF GURLY PURDY
ROUGH RUNTY RUSTY CHUFFY
CRUSTY GRUFFY GRUMPY MOROSE
RUGGED SNARLY SULLEN CHURLISH
SURMISE DEEM REDE GUESS INFER
TWANG SURMIT JALOUSE SUSPECT
WEENING MISTRUST
SURMOUNT TOP BEAT TIDE CROWN
ENSIGN HURDLE MASTER OUTTOP
OVERGO SUBDUE CONQUER
SURPASS OVERCOME SUPERATE
(— DIFFICULTIES) SWIM
SURMOUNTING BROCHANT
SURNAME BYNAME SURNOUN
COGNOMEN OVERNAME SURSTYLE
SURPASS CAP COB TOP WAR BANG
BEAT CAMP COTE DING FLOG FOIL
HEAD PASS SHED WHAP EXCEL
OUTDO OUTGO ATREDE BETTER
EXCEED OUTRAY OUTVIE OUTWIT
OVERDO PRECEL ECLIPSE FORPASS
OUTPEER OVERTOP PARAGON
PRECEDE ANTECEDE DISTANCE
DOMINATE OUTCLASS OUTMATCH
OUTRANGE OUTREACH OUTSTRIP
OUTWRITE SURMOUNT
SURPASSING BEST FINE ABOVE
PASSANT PASSING DOMINANT
TOWERING
SURPLICE COTTA EPHOD CHRISOM
(PL.) WHITES
SURPLUS OVER PLUS REST EXCESS
LUMBER VELVET OVERAGE

OVERRUN OVERSUM ARISINGS
LEFTOVER OVERCOME OVERMUCH
OVERPLUS
SURPRISE CAP SHED SWAN YACH
AMAZE SHOCK SNEAK FERLIE
WAYLAY WONDER ASTOUND
GLOPPEN PERPLEX STARTLE
ASTONISH BEWILDER CONFOUND
DUMFOUND
(BY —) ABACK
(EXCLAMATION OF —) QUOTHA
(EXPRESS —) MIRATE
(SUDDEN —) KICK
SURPRISING FERLIE STRIKING
SURRA MBORI
SURREJOINDER TRIPLY
SURRENDER HEM LET PUT CEDE
CESS DING FALL QUIT TAKE REMIT
YIELD ADDICT REMISE RENDER
RESIGN SUBMIT ABANDON CONCEDE
DELIVER FORSAKE KAMERAD
ABDICATE ABNEGATE DEDITION
DELIVERY RENOUNCE UNDERLIE
(— BY DEED) REMISE
SURREPTITIOUS SECRET BOOTLEG
FURTIVE SNEAKING
SURROUND HEM LAP ORB BELT
DIKE DYKE FOLD GIRD GIRT HOOP
WRAP BESET BRACE CLASP EMBAY
EMBED FENCE HEDGE IMBED INARM
ROUND BECLIP BEGIRD BEGIRT
CIRCLE COLLET CORRAL ENFOLD
ENWRAP FORSET GIRDLE IMPALE
INCASE INVEST SPHERE SWATHE
ARROUND BESEIGE BESTAND
COMPASS EMBOSOM ENCLAVE
ENCLOSE ENROUND ENVELOP
ENVIRON INVOLVE WREATHE
CLOISTER ENCIRCLE ENTRENCH
STOCKADE
(— WITH BOOM) CRIB
(— WITH CORD) GIRT
(— WITH MORTAR) GROUT
SURROUNDED AMID AMONG AMIDST
AMONGST BETWEEN
SURROUNDING MIDST ROUND
CIRCUM AMBIENT
(PL.) SCENE HARNESS ENVIRONS
SURVEILLANCE SCRUTINY
STAKEOUT
SURVEY SEE DIAL SCAN VIEW AVIEW
STOCK STUDY PERUSE REGARD
REVIEW SEARCH CANVASS CAPSULE
OVERSEE SURVIEW THEORIC
EPISCOPY LUSTRATE OVERLOOK
OVERVIEW PROSPECT SURVEYAL
TRAVERSE
(— RAPIDLY) GLANCE
(— TIMBER) SKYLOOK
(BRIEF —) APERCU
SURVEYING GEODESY GROMATICS
(MINE —) LATCHING
SURVEYOR BOLO ARTIST DIALER
DIALLER NOTEMAN CHAINMAN
GROMATIC LEVELMAN
SURVIVAL ECHO RELIC RELICT
(ANACHRONISTIC —) LEFTOVER
(USELESS —) SNUFF

SURVIVE LAST BILEVE OUTLAST
OUTLIVE
SURVIVOR RELICT
SUSCEPTIBILITY CAVIL SENSE
EMOTION FEELING FRAILTY
(— **TO ILL-HEALTH**) DELICACY
SUSCEPTIBLE EASY SOFT LIABLE
FEELING PATIENT SENSIBLE
TOLERANT
(— **TO CHANGE**) CASALTY
SUSIAN ELAMITE
SUSLIK SISEL ZIZEL MARMOT
SUSPECT FEAR DOUBT FANCY
GUESS SMOKE THINK BELIEVE
ENDOUTE JALOUSE MISDEEM
SUPPOSE DISTRUST JEALOUSE
MISDOUBT MISTRUST
(**NOT** —) COLD
SUSPECTED SPOTTED SUSPECT
SUSPEND CALL HALT HANG OUST
SHUT SIST STAY BREAK CLOSE
DEBAR DEFER DEMUR EXPEL POISE
REMIT SLING SWING APPEND
DANGLE ADJOURN EXCLUDE
FLUIDIZE INTERMIT OVERHANG
REPRIEVE SCAFFOLD SUSPENSE
(— **ANCHOR**) COCKBILL
SUSPENDED SWING AFLOAT LATENT
HANGING PENDANT PENDENT
PENSILE HOVERING SUSPENSE
SUSPENDER GALLUS GARTER
BRETELLE
(PL.) BRACES GALLOWS GALLUSES
SUSPENSE DEMUR POISE
SUSPENSION FOG BREI FUME SIST
STAY STOP DELAY DOUBT MAGMA
SMOKE BREACH CUTOFF SLURRY
AEROSOL FAILURE RESPITE
ABEYANCE BACTERIN EMULSION
INFUSION SHUTDOWN SUSPENSE
WISHBONE
(— **OF JUDGMENT**) EPOCHE
(— **OF NOISE**) HUSH
(— **OF RESPIRATION**) SYNCOPE
SUSPENSIVENESS DRIVE
SUSPENSORY SUPPORT
SUSPICION HINT DOUBT SOUPCON
SURMISE SUSPECT UMBRAGE
DISTRUST JEALOUSY MISDOUBT
MISTRUST TINCTURE
SUSPICIOUS SHY FISHY LEERY
PEERY QUEER SMOKY JEALOUS
SUSPECT DOUBTFUL WAFFLIKE
SUSPICIOUSLY ASKANCE
SUSQUEHANNA CONESTOGA
SUSTAIN ABET BACK BEAR BUOY
DURE HELP HOLD LAST PROP STAY
ABIDE CARRY FAVOR SPRAG STAND
ASSIST CONVEY ENDURE FOSTER
SECOND SUCCOR SUFFER UPHOLD
UPSTAY CONTAIN NOURISH
OUTBEAR PROLONG SUPPORT
UNDERFO BEFRIEND BUTTRESS
CONTINUE MAINTAIN PRESERVE
SUSTAINED SOUTENU
SUSTENANCE GEAR SALT BREAD
FOISON LIVING RELIEF ALIMENT
PABULUM TABLING
SUSU GERIP SOOSOO DOLPHIN

SUSURRUS WHISPER
SUTLER PROVANT VIVANDIE
SUTTEE SATI
SUTURE SEAM RAPHE SETON
HARMONY PTERION
SVANTOVIT TRIGLAV
SWAB GOB MOP SWOB PATCH
DOSSIL SPONGE EPAULET SWABBER
SQUILGEE
SWADDLE SWEEL SWATHE
SWAG DRUM GAME LOOT BOOTY
LUCRE MONEY BOODLE FESTOON
MATILDA
SWAGE BOSS MOUTH UPSET FULLER
JUMPER SHAPER SWAGER SWEDGE
FLATTER
(PL.) OLIVER
SWAGGER JET ROY BRAG COCK
FACE ROLL BOAST BRAVE NUTTY
STRUT SWANK SWASH BOUNCE
GOSTER HECTOR PARADO PRANCE
RENOWN RUFFLE SPROSE BLUSTER
BRAVADO GAUSTER PANACHE
ROISTER SOLDIER DOMINEER
TIGERISM
SWAGGERER HUFF SWAG FACER
TIGER CUTTLE JETTER PISTOL
BRAVADO HUFFCAP RUFFLER
FANFARON
SWAGGERING HUFFY FACING
GASCON HUFFCAP TEARCAT
BLUSTERY TIGERISH
SWAGMAN WHALER DRUMMER
TRAVELER
SWAIN COLIN CUDDY STREPHON
SWAINSONA INDIGO
SWALE SLASH
SWALLOW OFF SUP BOLT DOWN
GAUP GAWP GLUT GULP SINK TAKE
CLUNK DRINK GORGE GURGE
POUCH QUILT SLOCK SWOOP
ABSORB ENGLUT ENGULF GLUTCH
GOBBET GOBBLE GODOWN GUZZLE
IMBIBE INGEST MARTIN POCKET
PROGNE SWELLY CONSUME
ENGORGE ARUNDELL WITCHUCK
(— **GREEDILY**) BEND SLUP GORGE
GULCH SWILL WORRY INHALE
(— **HASTILY**) SWAP SWOP GLOUP
(— **IN AGAIN**) RESORB
(— **UP**) GULF SWAMP ABSORB
DEVOUR
(— **WITH GREEDINESS**) ENGORGE
(**LOSS OF ABILITY TO** —) APHAGIA
(**NOISY** —) SLURP
(**WOMAN TURNED INTO** —) PROCNE
SWALLOWTAIL TROILUS
SWAMP BOG FEN FLAT FLOW MIRE
MOSS SLEW SLUE SOAK SUMP VLEI
VLEY WHAM WHIN FLUSH LERNA
LETCH MARSH SWALE SWANG
URMAN DELUGE DISMAL ENGULF
MORASS SLOUGH CIENAGA
POCOSIN GREENING INUNDATE
QUAGMIRE
SWAMP COTTONWOOD LIAR
SWAMPER BUSHER GOPHER
SWAMPHEN COOT

SWAMP LOOSESTRIFE PEATWEE
PEATWOOD
SWAMP MAHOGANY GUNNUNG
SWAMP MILKWEED DAGGA
SWAMPY PUXY BOGGY POOLY
CALLOW POACHY QUASHY QUEAS
SLUMPY MOORISH
SWAMPY CREE MASKEGON
SWAN COB ELK PEN OLOR CYGNE
HOOPER SWANNET WHOOPER
(**FLOCK OF** —**S**) GAME MARK
SWANFLOWER SWANWORT
SWANK CHIC
SWANKY SWASH
SWAP CHOP SWOP TRADE TRUCK
DICKER EXCHANGE
SWARD SOD TURF SPINE SWARF
SWATH SWARTH
SWARM FRY SNY BIKE CAST FARE
HOST KNIT NEST SORT SWIM
CLOUD CROWD FLOCK FLUSH
FRACK HORDE SNARL FLIGHT
HOTTER RABBLE SWARVE THRON
SUBCAST
(— **IN**) FILL
(— **OF BEES**) BIKE HIVE
(— **OF INSECTS**) BAND FLIGHT
(— **OF PEOPLE**) BIKE DRIFT
(**THIRD** — **OF BEES**) COLT
SWARMING ALIVE ASWARM SWAR
SWARTBACK SWARBIE
SWARTHY DUN DARK BLACK DUSK
GRIMY MOORY SWART MORIAN
SWARTH BISTRED BISTERED
SWASH SWIG SWILL SWATCH
SWABBLE SWASHWAY
SWASHBUCKLER SWASH GASCON
SLASHER SWASHER
SWASTIKA FYLFOT GAMMADION
SWAT SWOT DEHGAN STRIKE
SWATH SWIPE STADDLE
SWATHE LAP BIND WRAP SWARF
SWADDLE WINDROW
SWATTER FLYSWAT
SWAY NOD WAG BEAR BIAS FLAP
HIKE LILT ROCK ROLL RULE SWAN
SWAG SWIG TILT TOSS WALD WA
CARRY CHARM LURCH POWER
REIGN SHAKE SWALE SWING WAV
WHEEL AFFECT ALLURE CAREEN
DIRECT EMPIRE WAGGLE COMMA
SHOGGIE STAGGER SWABBLE
SWIGGLE
SWAYBACK WARFA LORDOSIS
RENGUERA
SWAYING ASWAY ROLLING
SWAZILAND (**CAPITAL OF** —)
MBABANE
(**LANGUAGE OF** —) SISWATI
(**RIVER IN** —) USUTU KOMATI
MHLATUZE UMBULUZI
(**TOWN IN** —) MANZINI
SWEAR VOW VUM DAMN SINK SNL
SWAN SWOW TAKE CURSE ADJUF
AFFIRM BEDAMN DEPONE DEPOSI
OBJURE CONJURE DEJERATE
EXECRATE FORSWEAR
(— **FALSELY**) RAP MOUNT
FORSWEAR MONSWEAR

WEARING JURATION
(FALSE —) PERJURY
WEARWORD CUSS
WEAT DEW WET STEW WASH
BREAN MADOR SUDOR SUDATE
LAUNDER PARBOIL SWELTER
SWIVVET TRANSUDE
(— SKINS) STALE
(DYNAMITE —) LEAK
WEATBOX HOTBOX
WEATER FROCK GANSEY JUMPER
WOOLLY CARDIGAN SLIPOVER
WEATHOUSE TEMESCAL
WEATING TUB ASWEAT SWELTRY
SUDATION SUDATORY
WEATY PUGGY ASWEAT PERSPIRY
SUDOROUS SWEATFUL

SWEDEN

CAPITAL: STOCKHOLM
COIN: ORE KRONA SKILLING
DIVISION: AMT LAEN SKANE
  OREBRO UPPSALA GOTALAND
  JAMTLAND SWEALAND
GULF: BOTHNIA
ISLAND: OLAND GOTALAND
LAKE: SILJAN VANERN MALAREN
  VATTERN DALALVEN HJALMREN
  STORAVAN
MEASURE: AM ALN FOT MIL REF
  TUM FAMN STOP FODER KANNA
  KAPPE LINJE NYMIL SPANN
  STANG TUNNA FATHOM JUMFRU
  KOLLAST OXHUVUD TUNLAND
  FJARDING KAPPLAND KOLTUNNA
MOUNTAIN: SARV AMMAR OVIKS
  HELAGS SARJEK
PROVINCE: KALMAR OREBRO
  GOTLAND HALLAND UPPSALA
  ALVSBORG BLEKINGE ELFSBORG
  JAMTLAND MALMOHUS
  WERMLAND
RIVER: DAL UME GOTA KLAR LULE
  KALIX PITEA RANEA LAINIO
  LJUSNE TORNEA WINDEL
  ANGERMAN
TOWN: UMEA BODEN BORAS
  EDANE FALUN GAVLE LULEA
  MALMO PITEA VISBY YSTAD
  ARVIKA OREBRO LUDVIKA
  UPPSALA GOTEBORG NYKOPING
  VASTERAS
WEIGHT: ASS LOD ORT MARK
  PUND STEN UNTZ NYLAST
  LISPUND SKEPPUND

WEEP BUCK DUST RAFF SOOP
SWAY TILT BESOM BROOM DIGHT
DRIFT FETCH SCOPE SKIRL SWIPE
SWOOP BREADTH CLEANSE
PICOTAH SHADOOF STRICKLE
(— A NET) BEAT
(— MAJESTICALLY) SWAN
(— OF SCYTHE) SWATH SWATHE
(— OFF) SLIPE
(— ON CULTIVATOR) SKIN
(CHIMNEY —) CHUMMY SWEEPY
RAMONEUR

(HAY —) BUCK
SWEEPBOARD STRICKLE
SWEEPER BUNGY SWEEP TOPAZ
BHANGI BHUNGI MEHTAR PRYLER
ROADER SOOPER TOPASS
BROOMER TUBEMAN BHUNGINI
MATRANEE SCRUBBER
SWEEPING SURGE RASANT SWEEPY
(— FOR FISH) DRAFT DRAUGHT
(PL.) DUST FULVIE FULZIE RIFFRAFF
SWEET DOUX DUMP FOOL SOOT
SUCK CREAM DILIS DOUCE DULCE
FRESH HONEY MERRY SOOTH SPICY
SPLIT DULCET FRUITY GENTLE
SILKEN SILVER SIRUPY SUGARY
DARLING FAIRING HONEYED INSIPID
MUSICAL PANDROP SUGARED
SWEETLY WINNING WINSOME
AROMATIC ENGAGING FLUMMERY
LIEBLICH LUSCIOUS NECTARED
PLEASANT
(SLIGHTLY —) SEC
SWEET BAY BREWSTER MAGNOLIA
SWEETBREAD BUR BURR
(— OF DEER) INCHPIN
SWEETBRIER BEDEGUAR EGLANTINE
SWEET CALABASH KURUBA
SWEET CASSAVA AIPI AIPIM
SWEET CICELY MYRRH
SWEET CLOVER LOTUS MELILOT
SWEET COLTSFOOT LAGWORT
SWEETEN CANDY HONEY SUGAR
SWEET PURIFY ADDULCE CLEANSE
DULCIFY FRESHEN MOLLIFY
PERFUME MITIGATE
SWEET FENNEL FINOCHIO
FLORENCE
SWEET FERN FERNGALE
SWEETFISH AYU
SWEET FLAG SEDGE BEEWORT
CALAMUS
SWEET GALE GOLD GAGEL
BAYBUSH FLEAWOOD GALEWORT
GALLBUSH
SWEET GUM AMBER COPALM
STORAX BILSTED
SWEETHEART JO BOY GRA HON
JOE LAD PUG SIS AGRA BABY BEAU
DEAR DOLL DOXY FAIR GILL GIRL
JILL LADY LASS LIEF LOVE MASH
MORT POUT AGRAH BULLY BUSSY
CHERI COOKY DOLLY DONAH
DONEY DRURY FLAME LEMAN
LOVER PUGGY SPARK SWEET
COOKIE EMILIA FELLOW FRIEND
MOPSEY PIGEON STEADY WAHINE
AMOROSA BELOVED PHYLLIS
PIGSNEY QUERIDA SPRUNNY
SWEETIE TOOTSIE DOWSABEL
DULCINEA FOLLOWER LADYBIRD
LADYLOVE LIEBCHEN LOVELASS
MISTRESS SWEETING TRUELOVE
SWEETLEAF DYELEAVES
SYMPLOCOS
SWEET MARJORAM OREGANO
SWEETMEAT DUMP KISS DULCE
GOODY PLATE SPICE TOFFY
BUCAYO COMFIT DRAGEE DREDGE
JUNKET BANQUET CARAWAY

CLAGGUM LOUKOUM PENUCHE
SUCCADE CONSERVE HARDBAKE
MARZIPAN
(PL.) BALUSHAI CONFETTI
SWEETNESS DULCE HONEY SIRUP
SYRUP DULCOR DOUCEUR DULCITY
SUAVITY FLORIMEL WORDNESS
SWEET ORANGE CHINA CHINO
SWEET PEA CATGUT LATHYRUS
SWEET PEPPERBUSH CLETHRA
SOAPBUSH
SWEET POTATO YAM SWEET
BATATA CAMOTE KUMARA
SWEET RUSH SQUINANT
SWEET-SMELLING AROMATIC
SWEETSOP ANON ATES ATIS ATTA
CORAZON SWEETING
SWEET-SOUNDING MERRY
SWEET VIOLET FINELEAF
SWEET WILLIAM DIANTHUS
SWELL BAG NIB NOB BEAL BELL
BLAB BLOW BLUB BOLL BULB BULK
BUMP BUOY DOME FILL GROW
HOVE HUFF HUSH PINK PLIM RISE
TOFF TONY WAVE BELLY BLOAT
BULGE BUNCH FLASH PLUFF SMART
STOCK STRUT SURGE TULIP BILLOW
BOWDEN DILATE EXPAND GROWTH
LOVELY SPRING STROUT TUMEFY
UPRISE AUGMENT BLUBBER
BURGEON DISTEND INFLATE
SWAGGER OVERBLOW TURGESCE
(— OF GUN MUZZLE) TULIP
(— OF WATER) HUSH SURF FLOOD
SURGE
(— OUT) BAG POD BUNT DRAW
POUT BOSOM BILLOW SPONGE
BALLOON BLADDER
(HEAVY —) RUN SEA
SWELLDOODLE EGGFISH
SWELLED BIAS
SWELLFISH BLOWER PUFFER
TAMBOR
SWELLING BIG BUR NOB PAP PIN
BLAB BUBO BUMP BURR CLAP
COWL CURB FROG FULL GALL KNOB
KNOT NODE POKE PONE AMPER
BLAIN BOTCH BOUGE BULGE BUNCH
BUNNY EDEMA JETTY MOUSE
SURGE SWELL TUMOR ANCOME
ASWELL BOSOMY BUNCHY CALLUS
FLATUS GIBBER GROWTH KERNEL
PIMPLE STRUMA SWELTH WARBLE
AMPULLA BOSSING CAPELET
CHAGOMA CUSHION GOUNDOU
TURGENT UREDEMA UROCELE
APOSTEME BULLNECK CHEMOSIS
DACRYOMA FURUNCLE GLANDULE
GOURDING HAPTERON HEMATOMA
MUCOCELE NODOSITY PUMPKNOT
QUELLUNG STYLOPOD VESSICON
(— IN HORSE'S CHEST) ANTICOR
(— OF PLANT TISSUE) GALL
(— OF THE CHEEK) HONE
(— ON ANIMAL'S JOINTS) BUNNY
(— ON HEAD) COWL
(EYE —) STY STYE
SWELTER STEW SWELT

SWELTERING STEWY SULTRY SWELTRY

SWERVE BOW CUT LUG BIAS FADE JOUK SKEW VARY WARP SHEER STRAY DEPART DEVIATE DIGRESS DIVERGE

SWIDDEN CAINGIN KAINGIN

SWIFT CRAN FAST FLIT MAIN VITE FLEET HASTY LIGHT QUICK RAPID SNELL SWITH WIGHT WINDY ARROWY MARLET NIMBLE RAKING SOUPLE SPEEDY STRICT SUDDEN SWIFTY TOTTER WINGED COLLIER DEVELIN FLIGHTY POSTING SWALLOW TANTIVY DEVELING HEPIALID PEGASEAN SCREAMER SCUTTLER SQUEALER SWIFTLET

SWIFTLY FAST SWAP APACE SNELL SNELLY LIGHTLY STEEPLY TANTIVY

SWIFTNESS FOOT HASTE SPEED CELERITY FASTNESS VELOCITY

SWIG SCOUR SWILL SWING SWIGGLE

SWILL SOSS SLOSH SLUICE HOGWASH PIGWASH SWILLING

SWIM COWD SAIL SOOM SPAN TEEM BATHE CRAWL FLEET FLOAT GLIDE SWARM OVERFLOW
(— IN NEW DIRECTION) MILL
(— TOGETHER) SCHOOL

SWIMMER BATHER NATATOR

SWIMMING ASWIM NATANT FLOTANT NATATION
(— STUNT) MARLIN WALKOVER

SWIMMING POOL POOL THERM PLUNGE THERME PISCINA NATATORY

SWINDLE DO CON GIP GYP JOB RIG BILK FLAP HAVE MACE PULL RAMP ROOK ROPE SWIZ BUNCO BUNKO CHEAT FLING FOIST GOUGE LURCH PLANT ROGUE SHARK SHARP SHAVE SLANG SPOOF SWIZZ UNCLE BOODLE BUCKET DIDDLE FIDDLE HUSTLE INTAKE NOBBLE SUCKER TREPAN FINAGLE THIMBLE VERNEUK FLIMFLAM

SWINDLER DO FOB GYP LEG BILK FYNK HAWK SKIN CHEAT CROOK FAKER GREEK HARPY KNAVE MACER ROGUE CHIAUS GOUGER INTAKE RINGER ROOKER SALTER SHAVER VERSER MACEMAN MAGSMAN NOBBLER SHARPER SLICKER SPIELER BARNACLE BLACKLEG FINAGLER GILENYER LUMBERER PIGEONER SHELLMAN TRAMPOSO
(DECOY —) BARNARD

SWINDLING MACE BUNCO BUNKO ROOKY SHARK GYPPERY JOUKERY CHEATERY JOOKERIE

SWINE HOG OIC PIG SOW BOAR GALT GILT PORK SUID YILT DUROC ESSEX SWIPE WHITE GUSSIE POLAND PORKER PORKET BUSHPIG PECCARY SUFFOLK SUIDIAN CHESHIRE HYOTHERE LANDRACE TAMWORTH
(— AND FOOD) PANNAGE

(— AND MAN) OMNIVORA

SWINEHERD GURTH HOGMAN EUMAEUS HOGHERD HOGWARD

SWINE-LIKE GADARENE

SWING GO HIKE JUMP LILT SCUP STOT SWAY SWEE TURN SHAKE SHOWD SLING SWALE TREND DANGLE GYRATE HANDLE SWINGE SWITCH SWIVEL TOTTER JUMPING SHOGGIE SWINGEL WAMPISH BRANDISH FLOURISH
(— A SHIP) SPRING
(— AROUND) JIB SLEW SLUE SLOUGH
(— BY BATTER) CUT
(— FROM POSITION) CANT
(— FROM SIDE TO SIDE) JOW
(— FROM THE TIDE) TEND
(— OF PENDULUM) BEAT
(— OF SAIL) GYBE JIBE
(— OF SWORD) MOULINET
(— OUT OF LINE) SWAG
(— THE FOREFEET) DISH
(RHYTHMICAL —) LILT
(WILD —) HAYMAKER

SWINGING BANK ASWING SWINGY

SWINGLE SWORD SCUTCH SWIPPLE

SWING SEAT TRANSOM

SWINISH SOWISH HOGGISH PORCINE

SWIPE COP CHOP GLOM WIPE SNAKE STEAL VULTURE

SWIRL BOIL GULF HURL PURL WALM GURGE SWALE SWEEL SWORL SWOOSH WREATHE
(— OF SALMON) BULGE

SWIRLING VORTICAL

SWISH HISH WHIP SMART SWILL WHISH

SWISS MUFF SWISSER
(— PINE) MUGHO

SWITCH GAD TAN TWIG WAND AZOTE BIRCH BREAK SHUNT SWISH CHANGE CUTOUT DERAIL DIPPER FERULA FERULE LARRUP RATTAN SCUTCH SILENT SPRING HICKORY KIPPEEN SCOURGE SQUITCH HAIRWORK POSTICHE
(— FOCUS) FADE
(ELECTRIC —) KEY
(RAILROAD —) GATE POINT

SWITCH ENGINE GOAT

SWITCHMAN SHUNTER SWITCHER

SWITZERLAND

BAY: URI
CANTON: URI ZUG BERN VAUD BASEL AARGAU GENEVA GLARUS LUZERN SCHWYZ TICINO VALAIS ZURICH GRISONS THURGAU FRIBOURG OBWALDEN
CAPITAL: BERN BERNE
COIN: FRANC RAPPE RAPPEN ANGSTER DUPLONE BLAFFERT
LAKE: URI ZUG THON AGERI LEMAN MORAT BIENNE BRIENZ GENEVA LUGANO SARNEN WALLEN ZURICH HALLWIL LUCERNE LUNGERN VIERVALD

MEASURE: POT AUNE ELLE FUSS IMMI MUID PIED SAUM ZOLL LIEVE LIGNE LINIE MAASS MOULE POUCE SCHUH STAAB TOISE PERCHE SETIER STRICH JUCHART KLAFTER VIERTEL
MOUNTAIN: JURA RIGI ROSA BLANC CENIS KARPF LINARD PIZELA BERNINA BEVERIN GRIMSEL PILATUS ROTONDO BALMHORN JUNGFRAU MATTERHORN
MOUNTAIN PASS: CENIS FURKA ALBERG MALOJA BRENNER GRIMSEL SIMPLON SPLUGEN LOTSCHEN
NAME: HELVETIA
RIVER: AAR INN AARE THUR BROYE DOUBS LINTH REUSS RHINE RHONE MAGGIA SARINE TICINO PRATIGAU
TOWN: BALE BERN BIEL BRIG CHUR SION BASEL VEVEY GENEVA GLARUS LUZERN SCHWYZ ZURICH FYZABAD HERISAU LUCERNE LAUSANNE MONTREUX
VALLEY: AAR ZERMATT ENGADINE
WEIGHT: PFUND CENTNER QUINTAL

SWIVEL LOPER SWAPE SWIPE CASTER FIDDLE TIRRET TOGGLE TONGUE TRAVERSE TRUNNION

SWOLLEN BLUB FULL PLIM RANK BLOWN CHUFF GOUTY GREAT GUMMY POBBY PROUD TUMID BOLLEN BRAWNY BULLED GOURDY TURGID BESTRUT BLOATED BLUBBER BULBOUS GIBBOSE GIBBOUS GOURDED GOUTISH TURGENT BEPUFFED BLADDERY TUMOROUS

SWOON KEEL SWEB SWIM DROWN DWALM FAINT SLOOM SOUND SWARF SWELT STOUND SWOUND TRANCE ECSTASY SWITHER SYNCOPE SWOONING

SWOONING ASWOON SYNCOPE

SWOOP CHOP JOUK SWAP SWOP SOUSE STOOP SWOPE POUNCE SOURCE DESCEND

SWOOPING SOUSE

SWORD FOX SAX BILL DIRK FALX GRAM IRON PATA SAEX SPIT TOOL TURK BILBO BLADE BRAND DEGEN DIEGO ESTOC GULLY KNIFE KUKRI PRICK RIPON SABER SABRE SHARP STEEL ANDREW BARONG BILBOA CATTAN DAMASK DUSACK FLORET GLAIVE HANGER KHANDA KUKERI MIMING PARANG PINKER PORKER RAPIER SMITER SPATHA TILTER TIZONA TOLEDO WAFTER BALMUNG BRANDON CURTANA CUTLASH CUTLASS ESPADON ESTOQUE FERRARA FLEURET IMPALER JOYEUSE MALCHUS MORGLAY

SHABBLE SLASHER SNICKER
SPURTLE TOASTER WHIFFLE
WHINGER ACINACES BASELARD
CAMPILAN CLAYMORE DAMASCUS
DURENDAL FALCHION FLAMBERG
SCHLAGER SPADROON SPITFROG
WACADASH WHINYARD
(— OF CHARLEMAGNE) JOYEUSE
(— OF CID) TIZONA
(— OF HERMES) HARPE
(— OF LANCELOT) ARONDIGHT
(— OF ROLAND) DURENDAL
(— OF SIEGFRIED) GRAM BALMUNG
(— OF SIR BEVIS) MORGLAY
(— OF ST. GEORGE) ASCALON
ASKELON
(— USED BY ST. PETER) MALCHUS
(BLUNT —) WAFTER SCHLAGER
(CELTIC —) SAX SAEX
(DOUBLE-EDGED —) KEN PATA
KHANDA SPATHA
(DUELLING —) EPEE SHARP
(DYAK —) PARANG
(FENCING —) EPEE FOIL SABER
SABRE RAPIER
(HALF OF —) FORTE
(JAPANESE —) CATAN CATTAN
KATANA WACADASH
(LONG —) SPATHA WHIFFLE
(MATADOR'S —) ESTOQUE
(MORO —) BARONG CAMPILAN
(NARROW —) TUCK
(NORMAN —) SPATHA
(PERSIAN —) ACINACES
(POINTLESS —) CURTANA
(RUSTY —) SHABBLE
(SHORT —) DIRK ESTOC KUKRI
SKEAN WHINGER WHINYARD
(THRUSTING —) ESTOC STOCK
(TWO-HANDED —) ESPADON
CLAYMORE
(WOODEN —) WASTER STRICKLE
SWORD-BEARER VERGER SELICTAR
PORTGLAVE
(PL.) ENSIFERI
SWORD DANCER MATACHIN
SWORDFISH AU ESPADA ESPADON
XIPHIAS ALBACORA BILLFISH
BOATBILL FORKTAIL XIPHIOID
SCOMBROID
SWORDPLAY SPADROON
SWORD-SHAPED ENSATE ENSIFORM
GLADIATE
SWORDSMAN BLADE BLADER
FENCER SLASHER SWORDER
THRUSTER
SWORDTAIL HELLERI
SWORN AVOWED
SYAGUSH SHARGOSS
SYBARITE EPICURE
SYBARITIC SENSUOUS
SYCAMORE MAY DAROO COTONIER
LACEWOOD PLANTAIN
SYCEE SHOE
SYCOPHANCY FAWNERY
SYCOPHANT TOADY COGGER
FAWNER GNATHO HANGBY TAGTAIL
CLAWBACK PARASITE
SYCOPHANTIC FAWNING SERVILE

SLAVISH OBEDIENT TRENCHER
SYCOSIS MENTAGRA
SYENITE APPINITE TRACHYTE
SYLLABARY KANA IROFA IROHA
SYLLABIC SONANT CENTROID
SONANTIC
SYLLABLE ARSIS BREVE GROUP
SHORT DISEME SYLLAB THESIS
TRISEME ASSONANT
(— DENOTING ASSENT) OM
(BOBIZATION —) BO CE DI GA GE
LO MA NI
(LAST — BUT ONE) PENULT
(LAST —) ULTIMA
(LONG —) LONG
(MUSICAL —) DI DO FA FI LA LE LI
ME MI RA RE RI SE SI SO TA TE TI
TO UT SOL
(REFRAIN —) DILDO
(SHORT —) MORA SHORT
(STRONG —) STRESS
(UNACCENTED —S) THESIS
SYLLABUS PROGRAM VIDIMUS
HEADNOTE SYNOPSIS
SYLLOGISM BARBARA ABDUCTION
ENTHYMEME
(SERIES OF —S) SORITES
SYLPH ARIEL SYLPHID
SYLVAN WOODY FOREST SILVAN
WOODEN WOODISH SYLVATIC
SYLVITE HARDSALT
SYMBIOSIS LICHENISM MUTUALISM
NUTRICISM
SYMBOL KEY CODE FISH FOUR ICON
IDOL IKON MARK NEUM SEAL SIGN
TYPE CREST CROSS EAGLE IMAGE
INDEX CARACT CIPHER EMBLEM
ENSIGN FIGURE LETTER PNEUME
SHADOW SIGNAL FACIEND MANDALA
PALATAL CEREMONY CONSTANT
DIRECTOR EXPONENT GUTTURAL
IDEOGRAM LOGOGRAM OPERATOR
SWASTIKA SYMBOLUM TRISKELE
(— FOR WAVELENGTH) LAMBDA
(— OF DISTINCTION) BELT HONOR
(— OF FAITHFUL DEAD) ORANT
(— OF FRANCE) LILY
(— OF MONK) COWL
(— OF PHYSICIAN) CADUCEUS
(— OF RAILROAD) HERALD
(— OF SPRING) KARPAS
(— OF STRENGTH) HORN
(— OF SUN) DISC DISK
(— ON UNCHANGEABLENESS)
LEOPARD
(— REPRESENTING THE ABSOLUTE)
TAIKIH
(ALGEBRAIC —) EXPONENT
(CRICKET —) ASHES
(CRUSADERS' —) CROSS
(CURVED —) HOOK
(KOREAN —) TAHGOOK
(MAGIC —) CARACT
(MATHEMATICAL —) KNOWN
FACTOR FACIEND OPERAND
(PHALLIC —) LINGA LINGAM
(PICTOGRAPHIC —) ISOTYPE
(PRINTING —) DIAGONAL
(PRONUNCIATION —) ENG

(RELIGIOUS —) LABRYS
(PL.) KATAKANA
SYMBOLIC GRAPHIC SHADOWY
ANICONIC
SYMBOLICAL ALLUSIVE MYSTICAL
SYMBOLISM CONOLOGY
SYMBOLIZE BODY SIGN TOKEN
FIGURE SAMPLE SHADOW SYMBOL
TYPIFY EXPRESS PORTEND SIGNIFY
RESEMBLE
SYMMETRICAL FORMAL DIMERIC
REGULAR SHAPELY SPHERAL
BALANCED
(NOT —) SKEW
SYMMETRY MEASURE
SYMPATHETIC AKIN FERE SOFT
WARM HUMAN FELLOW KINDLY
TENDER PIETOSO SIMPATICO
SYMPATHIZER FABIAN BLACKNEB
SHAYSITE
SYMPATHY PITY RUTH FLESH PHILIA
CONSENT EMPATHY AFFINITY
KINDNESS
SYMPHONY SINFONIA
SYMPOSIUM POTATION
SYMPTOM MARK NOTE SIGN
SHOWER STIGMA INSTANCE
PRODROME
SYNAGOGUE SHUL SCHUL ALJAMA
PROSEUCHA
SYNAPSIS PAIRING
SYNAPTE ECTENE EKTENE
SYNARTHROSIS SUTURE
SYNCHRO SELSYN
SYNCHRONIZER SPEEDGUN
SYNCLINE DOWNFOLD ISOCLINE
SYNCOPATED ZOPPA ABRIDGED
SYNCOPE SWOON COTYPE FAINTING
SYNDICATE HUI GROUP
SYNDICATED CANNED
SYNECDOCHE MERISM
SYNERGIST BOOSTER SESAMIN
SYNOD SOBOR
SYNODAL SENAGE
SYNONYM ANTONYM HOMONYM
EUPHONYM POLYONYM
SYNOPSIS BRIEF TABLE EPITOME
SUMMARY ABSTRACT SCENARIO
SYLLABUS
SYNSACRUM SACRARY
SYNTACTICAL FORMAL
SYNTHESIS SUMMA FUSION
SYSTASIS
SYNTHETIC ERSATZ SYSTATIC
SYPHILIS POX LUES SYPH CRINKUM
GRINCOME

SYRIA

CAPITAL: DAMASCUS
COIN: POUND TALENT PIASTER
DISTRICT: ALEPPO HAVRAN
LAKE: DJEBOID TIBERIAS
MEASURE: MAKUK GARAVA
MOUNTAIN: HERMON LIBANUS
NAME: ARAM
NATIVE: DRUSE ANSARIE
SARACEN ANSARIEH
RIVER: ASI BARADA JORDAN

KNABUR ORONTES EUPHRATES
TOWN: ALEP HAMA HOMS NAWA
BUSRA CALNO DERRA HALAB
HAMAH IDLIB JERUD RAQQA
ALEPPO BALBEL BIERUT
LATAKIA SELEUCIA
WEIGHT: COLA ROTL ARTAL
ARTEL RATEL TALENT

SYRINGE GUN HYPO ENEMA SCOOT
DOUCHE FILLER SQUIRT SCOOTER
SERRING
SYRINGIN LILACIN
SYRNIUM STRIX
SYRYENIAN SYRYAN ZYRIAN
(PL.) KAMI KOMI
SYRUP DIBS LICK SIRUP ORGEAT
ANTIQUE ECLEGMA FALERNUM
QUIDDANY
(STARCH —) GLUCOSE
SYRUPY FRUITY
SYSTEM ISM AREA CREDO FRAME
ORDER CIRCLE METHOD SCHEME
STEREO SYNTAX COMPLEX DUALISM
ECONOMY FAGGERY NAVARHO
REGIMEN ENSEMBLE GALENISM
RELIGION UNIVERSE
(— OF BARS) LATTICE
(— OF BELIEFS) FAITH
(— OF BELL CHANGES) CATERS
QUATERS STEDMAN
(— OF CORDS) BRIDLE
(— OF CROSSING THREADS) LEASE
(— OF ETHICS) SELFISM

(— OF EXCHANGE) KULA
(— OF FAITH) CREED
(— OF GEARS) COMPOUND
(— OF JOINTS) CLEAT
(— OF LANGUAGE SIGNS) SIGNARY
(— OF LAW) EQUITY
(— OF LINES IN EYEPIECE) RETICLE
RETICULE
(— OF MANUAL TRAINING) SLOJD
SLOYD
(— OF MEANING) SEMANTIC
(— OF MEDICINE) AYURVEDA
(— OF NUMERALS) ALGORISM
(— OF OCCULT THEOSOPHY)
CABALA
(— OF PHILOSOPHY) HUMISM
HOBBISM SAMKHYA SANKHYA
STOICISM
(— OF PHONETIC NOTATION) ROMIC
(— OF PRINCIPLES) CODE
(— OF RAYS) ASTER
(— OF ROCKS) CENOZOIC
DEVONIAN SILURIAN
(— OF RULE) REGIME
(— OF RULES) ART
(— OF SOLMIZATION) FASOLA
(— OF SPACES) LACUNOME
(— OF SYMBOLS) CODE
(— OF TENANCY) CROFTING
(— OF TRANSPORTATION) AIRLINE
AIRMAIL
(— OF TRUSSING) CABANE
(— OF VALUES) ETHOS
(— OF WEIGHTS) TROY

(— OF WIRES) HARNESS
(— OF WORSHIP) CULT CULTUS
(— OF WRITING) KANJI BRAILLE
ALPHABET
(ACOUSTICAL —) SODAR
(AGRICULTURAL —) KOLKOZ
KOLKHOS
(ALARM —) BUG
(BETTING —) ALEMBERT
(COLLOIDAL —) SOL
(COMMUNICATION —) BLOWER
CIRCUIT
(CULTURAL —) ISLAM
(DEFENSE —) SAGE
(DISPERSE —) GEL
(ELECTRICAL —) SELSYN
(GEOLOGICAL —) KEEWATIN
TERTIARY
(HAULING —) DILLY
(IRRIGATION —) KAREZ
(LANGUAGE —) LATINXUA
(NAVIGATION —) GEE LANAC
SHORAN
(RELIGIOUS —) LAW CULT CULTUS
SHIISM SUNNISM DRUIDISM
(RHYTHMIC —) STROPHE GLYCONIC
(SOCIAL —) CASTE
(STAR —) GALAXY
(TECHNOLOGICAL —) FORDISM
(TELEVISION —) SCOPHONY
(TRUCK —) TOMMY
SYSTEMATIC ORDERLY REGULAR
METHODIC
SYSTEMATIZE CODIFY ORGANIZE

TEE TARE TANGO
AAL AFRIKAANS
AB JAG PAN TAG BILL COST CHECK
FLASH PRICE TALLY WATCH EARTAB
EARTAG SIGNAL TOEPLATE
ABANID GADFLY
ABERNACLE PIX PYX HOVEL
SACRARY
ABES WASTING
ABETIC MARCID
ABLATURE LYRAWAY PICTURE
PAINTING
ABLE KEY PIE PYE RUN BANK BUCK
DAIS DESK FORM MESS BELLY
BENCH BOARD CANON CHART PINAX
PLANK SCALE STALL STAND STONE
WAGON COMMON SCHEME TABLET
TABULA TARIFF TRIPOD VANNER
CABARET CAMBIST CONSOLE
COUNTER DIAGRAM DIPTYCH
DRESSER PROJECT SHAMBLE
TABLEAU TESSERA TROLLEY
WHIRLER CALENDAR CREDENCE
GUERIDON PEDIGREE PEMBROKE
REGIMENT SPECULUM STILLAGE
TOILETTE VANITORY
(— FOR BOWING HAT-BODY) HURL
(— FOR GLAZING LEATHER) BANK
(— FOR ORNAMENT) CARTOUCH
(— FOR PHOTOGRAPHIC PLATES)
WHIRLER
(— FURNISHED WITH MEAL) SPREAD
(— IN STORE) COUNTER
(— OF ANCESTORS) PEDIGREE
(— OF CONTENTS) INDEX METHOD
(— OF DECLINATIONS) REGIMENT
(— TOP) AMOEBA
(— USED IN FELTING A HAT) BASON
(— WITH BRAZIER BENEATH)
TENDOOR TENDOUR
(ARITHMETIC —) TARIFF
(ASTROLOGICAL —) SPECULUM
(BOTANIC —) KEY
(CIRCULAR —) ROUNDEL
(COMMUNION —) ALTAR
(DINING —) MAHOGANY
(DRESSING —) TOILET VANITY
TOILETTE
(FOLDING —) SERVETTE
(INNER —) HOME
(MASSAGE —) PLINTH
(MUSICAL —) DIAGRAM
(NIGHT —) SOMNO
(PRINCIPAL —) DAIS
(PROFUSELY ORNAMENTED —)
PEMBROKE
(SERVING —) WAGON
(SHAKING —) SLIMER
(SMALL —) KURSI STAND TABORET
TABOURET
(TEA —) TEAPOY
(WRITING —) DESK
TABLEAU LAYOUT PAGEANT
TABLECLOTH CLOTH COVER
TABLE D'HOTE DINNER
TABLELAND PLAT PUNA PUNO
KAROO TABLE KARROO PLATEAU
BALAGHAT
TABLET PAX BRED ALBUM FACIA

PIECE PINAX SLATE TABLE TABULA
TABULE TROCHE ASPIRIN CODICIL
DIPTYCH PALETTE PREFORM
TABLING CARTOUCH CHURINGA
TABULATE TRIPTYCH
(— BEARING SYMBOL OF CHRIST)
PAX
(— FOR PUBLISHING LAWS)
PARAPEGM
(— OVER SHOP FRONT) FACIA
FASCIA
(MEDICATED —) ASPIRIN JELLOID
TABELLA
(MEDICINAL —) DISC DISK TROCHE
(MEMORIAL —) BRASS TABUT
(PAINTER'S —) PALETTE
(SQUARE —) ABACK
(UPRIGHT —) STELA STELE
(VOTIVE —) PINAX
(WRITING —) CODICIL TRIPTYCH
TABLEWARE CHINA FLATWARE
HAVILAND
TABOO KAPU TABU TAPU
FORBIDDEN INEFFABLE
TABOR ATABAL TABRET TIMBRE
TABORIN TIMBREL
TABULATION SCALE SCHEME
TABLING
TABUT TAZIA TAZEEA
TACHOMETER CUTMETER
TACHYGLOSSUS ECHIDNA
TACIT SILENT IMPLICIT
TACITURN DUMB STILL SILENT
RESERVED
TACK LAY BEAT CAST STAY BASTE
BOARD FETCH ENTAIL LAVEER
TACKET TINGLE SADDLERY
(GLAZIERS' —) BRAD
TACKER GUN SPREADER
TACKLE CAT RIG TAW SWIG TACK
YOKE ANGLE FALLS ATTACK
BURTON COLLAR GARNET JIGGER
LEDGER RUNNER STEEVE TAGLIA
TEAGLE DERRICK HALYARD
HARNESS RIGGING FISHFALL
PURCHASE TACKLING
(— FOR RAISING BOAT) FALLS
(— TO HOIST ANCHOR) CAT
(COMBINATION OF —S) JEER JEERS
(FISHING —) TEW LEGER OTTER
LEDGER
TACT TOUCH ADDRESS CONDUCT
DELICACY
TACTFUL DISCREET GRACEFUL
TACTFULLY HAPPILY
TACTLESS BRASH
TACTIC GAME
TADPOLE POWHEAD BULLHEAD
POLEHEAD POLLIWOG PORWIGLE
TAEL LIANG
TAENNIN KOSIN KOUSIN
TAFFETA TABBY FLORENCE
TAFFY GUNDY TOFFY TOFFEE
CLAGGUM
TAG HE EAR TAB TIG TAIL TICK
AGLET DAGGE LABEL TALLY TOUCH
AIGLET EARTAB EARTAG FOLLOW
SWATCH TAGGLE TAGRAG TICKET
TIGTAG HANGTAG

(— OF A LACE) AGLET AIGLET
(ANGLING —) TOUCH
(ORNAMENTED —S) FANCY
TAGALOG PULAHAN
TAGESTES MARIGOLD
TAGRAG SHAGRAG
TAHITI (CAPITAL OF —) PAPEETE
(FORMER NAME OF —) OTAHEITE
(MOUNTAIN IN —) OROHENA
TAHR KRAS JHARAL
TAHSILDAR TALUKDAR
TAI LI AHOM SHAM THAI PORGY
KHAMTI
TAIGA URMAN
TAIL BOB BUN CUE BUNT BUSH CLUB
FLAG POLE SCUT BRUSH CAUDA
SNAKE START STERN TRAIN TWIST
FLIGHT FOLLOW RUMPLE SWITCH
TAILET TAILLE FANTAIL FOXTAIL
RATTAIL
(— OF ARTIFICIAL FLY) TOPPING
(— OF BELL CLAPPER) FLIGHT
(— OF BIRD OR ANIMAL) CUE POLE
START
(— OF BIRD) FAN
(— OF BOAR) WREATH
(— OF CART) ARSE
(— OF COAT) DOCK
(— OF COMET) BEARD STREAM
STREAMER
(— OF DEER) FLAG SINGLE SHINGLE
(— OF DOG) FLAG STERN
(— OF FISH) UROSOME
(— OF FLY) WHISK
(— OF FOX) BUSH BRUSH FOXTAIL
(— OF HARE OR RABBIT) BUN FUD
BUNT SCUT
(— OF HORSE) BOB
(— OF MAN'S TIED HAIR) CLUB
(— OF METEOR) TRAIN
(— OF MUSICAL NOTE) QUEUE
(— OF PUG DOG) TWIST
(— OF SQUIRREL) BUN
(— OF STANZA) CODA
(DRAGON'S —) KETU
(STUMP OF —) STRUNT
(TIP OF —) TAG
TAILBAND FOOTBAND
TAILBOARD ENDGATE ENDBOARD
ENDPIECE
TAILED CAUDATE CAUDATED
TAILING CHAT
(PL.) SAND TAIL GRUFFS
TAILLE TALLY
TAILLESS ACAUDAL ANUROUS
ACAUDATE ECAUDATE
TAILOR SLOP SNIP BUILD DARZI
GORER SHRED DARZEE FULLER
SARTOR SNYDER STITCH BOTCHER
CABBAGE SNIPPER TIREMAN
CLOTHIER SEAMSTER SEMPSTER
SHEPSTER
(ITINERANT —) CARDOOER
TAILORBIRD DARZEE
TAILPIECE QUEUE ANQUERA
TAILRACE AFTERBAY
TAILSPIN FLICKER
TAILSTOCK DEADHEAD
TAINO HAITIAN

(— **BELIEFS**) ZEMIISM
TAINT HAUL HOGO MOIL SMUT SPOT
VICE CLOUD STAIN TOUCH DARKEN
INFECT REMORD SMIRCH SMUTCH
ATTAINT BLEMISH CORRUPT
DEBAUCH ENVENOM FLYBLOW
FORRUMP POLLUTE TARNISH
VITIATE EMPOISON TAINTURE
TAINTED OFF GAMY HIGH BLOWN
PINDY SAPPY TAINT WEMMY
ROTTEN SINFUL SMUTTY CORRUPT
FLYBLOWN
TAIWAN (**CAPITAL OF** —) TAIPEI
(**ISLAND GROUP OF** —) MATSU
PENGHU QUEMOY
(**MOUNTAIN IN** —) TZUKAO YUSHAN
HSINKAO
(**OTHER NAME OF** —) FORMOSA
(**RIVER IN** —) WUCHI TACHIA
CHOSHUI HUALIEN TANSHUI
(**TOWN IN** —) TAINAN TAIPEI
KEELUNG TAICHUNG
TAJIN TOTONAC
TAJ MAHAL (**SITE OF** —) AGRA
TAKE COP HIT NIM NOB BEAR BONE
DRAW FANG GLOM HAVE LEAD
TACK TEEM TOLL ADOPT AFONG
BRING CARRY CATCH CREEL FETCH
GRASP GRIPE LATCH SEIZE SNAKE
ACCEPT CLUTCH COTTON DERIVE
EXTEND FERRET FINGER RECIPE
SNATCH TAKING ATTRACT CABBAGE
CAPTURE RECEIVE UNPURSE
UNDERNIM
(— **A BATH**) TOSH
(— **A CERTAIN POSITION**) SIT
(— **A DIRECTION**) STEER
(— **A DRINK**) SMILE
(— **A LITTLE**) DELIBATE
(— **A NAP**) DOSS
(— **A STAND**) ASSERT
(— **ACTION**) ACT
(— **ADVANTAGE**) DO ABUSE BLUDGE
CLUTCH EXPLOIT
(— **AFTER**) BRAID FOLLOW
(— **AIM**) BEAD
(— **AS ONE'S OWN**) ADOPT
(— **AWAY**) BATE EASE HENT LIFT
TOLL WISP BENIM BLEED HEAVE
REAVE STEAL CONVEY DEDUCE
DEDUCT DEMISE DEPOSE DEVEST
DIVEST ELOIGN EXEMPT REMOVE
UNVEST ABJUDGE BEREAVE
DEPRIVE DETRACT FORTAKE
RETRACT SUBDUCE SUBLATE
ABSTRACT DEROGATE DIMINISH
SUBTRACT
(— **BACK TO ONESELF**) RESUME
(— **BACK**) RECALL RECANT REVOKE
RETRACT
(— **BY FRAUD**) BOB
(— **BY LEVY**) ESTREAT
(— **BY STEALTH**) HOOK SNITCH
(— **BY STORM**) EXPUGN INVADE
SURPRISE
(— **CARE**) FIX SEE GARE KEEP MIND
TEND WARD YEME NURSE BEWARE
GOVERN INTEND CUIDADO HUSBAND
CHAPERON

(— **CENSUS OF**) MUSTER
(— **CHANCE**) DICE RISK
(— **CHARGE OF**) CURE SOLICIT
(— **CHARGE**) ATTEND
(— **COVER**) COOK
(— **DAMAGE**) BANGE
(— **DINNER**) DINE
(— **DOWN**) STOOP STRIKE
(— **EXCEPTION**) DEMUR STRAIN
(— **FOOD**) EAT DINE GRUB
(— **FOR GRANTED**) BEG ASSUME
(— **FOR ONESELF**) CAB
(— **FOR RESALE**) FLOG
(— **FORM**) FORM INFORM
(— **FRAUDULENTLY**) STEAL STRIKE
(— **FRIGHT**) BOOGER
(— **FROM DEPOSIT**) DRAW
(— **FROM**) DETRACT
(— **GOLFING STANCE**) ADDRESS
(— **GREAT DELIGHT**) REVEL
(— **HEART**) BRACE
(— **HEED**) RECK TENT
(— **HOLD**) GET BITE GRAB PINCH
SEIZE ARREST BEGRIPE
(— **HOLIDAY**) LAKE
(— **IN BY LEAKING**) LADE
(— **IN LIVESTOCK**) AGIST
(— **IN SAIL**) BRAIL
(— **IN**) IN EAT SUP BITE HOAX KEEP
DOWSE DRINK ABSORB DEVOUR
ENFOLD GATHER HARBOR INCEPT
INGEST INSORB INSUME INTAKE
MUZZLE BEGRIPE EMBRACE
INCLUDE
(— **INTO HANDS**) TOUCH EMBRACE
(— **LEGALLY**) ATTACH
(— **LEVEL OF**) BONE
(— **LUNCH**) TIFFIN
(— **MEALS**) BOARD
(— **NOTE OF**) NB COUNT SMOKE
NOTICE WITNESS
(— **OATH**) ABJURE
(— **OFF**) OFF DOFF LIFT VAIL DOUSE
SHUCK STRIP DEDUCT
(— **OFFENSE**) DORT HUFF
(— **ON**) MOUNT START
(— **ONE'S LEAVE**) CONGEE
(— **ONESELF**) BETAKE
(— **OUT OF EARTH**) EXTER
(— **OUT**) DELE KILL EXCERPT
AIRBRUSH
(— **PAINS**) BOTHER
(— **PART**) LEAD FIGHT ENGAGE
(— **PLACE**) BE DO GO COME GIVE
PASS ARISE BEFALL HAPPEN
(— **PLEASURE IN**) ENJOY ADMIRE
(— **PORTION OF**) PARTAKE
(— **POSSESSION**) GRIP ANNEX
BESET SEIZE SPOIL EXTEND
CONQUER INHERIT DISTRAIN
(— **REFUGE**) HIDE SOIL EVADE
HAVEN WATCH
(— **ROOT**) MARE MORE ENROOT
STRIKE
(— **SHAPE**) JELL
(— **SHELTER**) HOWF NESTLE
SHROUD
(— **SUPPER**) SUP
(— **THE PLACE OF**) ENSUE SECOND

SUPPLY DISPLACE SUPPLANT
(— **THOUGHT**) ADVISE
(— **TO BE TRUE WITHOUT PROOF**)
PRESUME
(— **TO TASK**) JACK CARPET
(— **TO WING**) FLUSH
(— **UNAWARE**) DECEIVE
(— **UP AGAIN**) RESUME
(— **UP WITH**) ALL
(— **UP**) ENTER MOUNT ADSORB
ASSUME GATHER HANDLE STRIKE
(— **WELL OR ILL**) RESENT
(— **WIND ON OPPOSITE QUARTER**)
JIBE
TAKEN TON TAIN
(— **ABACK**) BLANK
(— **AWAY**) ADEMPT
TAKEOFF SPOOF SCRAMBLE
TAKEOUT STACK
TAKER PERNOR
TAKING HOT TAKY ADOPTION
PERNANCY
(— **EVERYTHING INTO ACCOUNT**)
OVERALL
(— **OF LIFE**) BLOOD
(— **PLACE**) AGATE
TALAK AHSAN
TALARI PATACA PATACOON
TALAUS (**FATHER OF** —) BIAS
(**MOTHER OF** —) PERO
(**SON OF** —) ADRASTUS
(**WIFE OF** —) LYSIMACHE
TALC SPAAD TALCUM AGALITE
STEATITE
TALE SAW DIDO JEST LEED REDE
TELL BOURD CRACK FABLE RECIT
SPELL SPOKE STORY WINDY AITION
FABULA LEGEND PISTLE PURANA
FABLIAU FICTION HISTORY
MARCHEN ROMANCE ANECDOTE
FOLKTALE SPELLING
(— **OF ACHIEVEMENTS**) GEST
GESTE
(— **OF GOLD COAST NEGROS**)
NANCY
(**COMIC COARSE** —) FABLIAU
(**DEVISED** —) AITION
(**EPIC** —) TAIN
(**FALSE** —) VANITY SLANDER
(**FATEFUL** —) WEIRD
(**FOLK** —) NANCY THRENE
(**HUMOROUS** —**S**) FACETIAE
(**MERRY** —) BOURD
(**POETIC NARRATIVE** —) SAGA
(**SHORT** —) LAI CONTE
TALEBEARER BUZZER GOSSIP
TATTLER TALEPYET TELLTALE
TALEBEARING TALEWISE
TALENT GIFT HEAD VEIN DOWER
DOWRY VERVE CICHAR GENIUS
ABILITY CHARISM FACULTY
CAPACITY CHARISMA
TALENTED ABLE CLEVER GIFTED
TALER ORT THALER
TALIPES CLUBFOOT
TALISMAN ANGLE CHARM IMAGE
SAFFI AMULET GRIGRI SAPHIE
SCARAB TELESM ICHTHUS ICHTHYS
GREEGREE

TALK GAB JAW JIB SAW SAY YAP
BUCK BUKH CANT CARP CHAT CHIN
GAFF GIVE GUFF KNAP MEAN TALE
TOVE WORD CRACK FABLE MOUTH
PARLE PITCH SPEAK SPELL SPIEL
SPOKE TUTEL COMMON GAMMON
INDABA KORERO PATTER SERMON
SPEECH STEVEN TOMGUE YABBER
ADDRESS DISCUSS LIPWORK
PALABRA PALAVER PARRALL
PURPOSE WINDJAM CAUSERIE
COLLOQUY CONVERSE LANGUAGE
PARLANCE QUESTION
(— ABOUT) HASH
(— BACK) SASS
(— BIG) BOUNCE
(— BOASTFULLY) GAS
(— BOMBASTICALLY) BEMOUTH
(— CASUALLY) DISH
(— CONFIDENTIALLY) CUTTER
(— CONFUSEDLY) HOTTER
(— DISMALLY) CROAK
(— EMPTILY) BLOW
(— FAMILIARLY) TOVE CONFAB
(— FATUOUSLY) BABBLE
(— FONDLY) COO
(— FOOLISHLY) BLAT FLAP HAVER
BABBLE DRIVEL FOOTER FOOTLE
GABBLE GIBBER SAWNEY TOOTLE
BLATHER BLETHER
(— GLIBLY) PATTER
(— GLIBLY) SCREED
(— IDLY) GAB BLAB CHIN GASH
FABLE GABBLE JANGLE TATTLE
CHATTER GNATTER PRATTLE
(— IMPUDENTLY) SASS
(— INACCURATELY) BLAGUE
(— INARTICULATELY) CHUNNER
CHUNTER
(— INCESSANTLY) YANK BURBLE
CHATTER
(— INCOHERENTLY) BABBLE
HOTTER MITHER MOIDER
(— INCONSIDERATELY) BLAT
(— INFORMALLY) HOBNOB
(— INSOLENTLY) SNASH
(— INTENDED TO DECEIVE)
GAMMON PALAVER
(— IRRATIONALLY) RAVE
(— MONOTONOUSLY) DRONE
(— NEEDLESSLY) PALAVER
(— NOISILY) CLAP BLATTER
BRABBLE
(— NONSENSE) GAS ROT DROOL
FUDGE
(— OFFICIOUSLY) BLEEZE
(— PERTLY) CHELP
(— PRIVATELY) COLLOGUE
(— RAPIDLY) GABBLE JABBER
GNATTER
(— SCANDAL) HORN
(— SNAPPISHLY) KNAP
(— SPORTIVELY) DAFF
(— SUPERFICIALLY) SMATTER
(— TEDIOUSLY) DINGDONG
(— THOUGHTLESSLY) BLAB
(— TOGETHER) DEVISE
(— VAGUELY) WOOZLE
(— VOLUBLY) CHIN PATTER

(— WEAKLY) DRIVEL
(— WITH) CONTACT
(— WITHOUT MEANING) GABBLE
(ABSURD —) BOSH
(ABUSIVE —) HOKER JAWING
(ARROGANT —) GUM BRAG
(BOASTFUL —) BULL GAFF
(BOMBASTIC —) FLASH
(COMMON —) FAME FABLE
HEARSAY
(DECEPTIVE —) GAMMON
(EMPTY —) GAS BOSH GASH FRASE
GLOZE FRAISE BLAFLUM GASSING
PRATTLE BALLYHOO GALBANUM
(ENTHUSIASTIC —) JAZZ
(FALSE —) BALLYHOO
(FAMILIAR —) CONFAB CHITCHAT
(FANTASTIC —) GUYVER
(FOOLISH —) GUP GAFF JIVE BLEAT
CLACK FABLE BLETHERS
(FORMAL —) ADDRESS
(GLIB —) JIVE
(IDLE —) GAB BLAB BUFF CHAT
GAFF GEST GUFF FABLE GESTE
BABBLE CLAVER GOSSIP JANGLE
CHATTER CLATTER PALAVER
TWATTLE BABBLING
(IMPUDENT —) PRATE SLACK
(INCOHERENT —) GABBER JABBER
(INFORMAL —) CAUSERIE
(INSINCERE —) BUNKUM
(JESTING —) CHAFF JAPERY
(LIGHT —) TRIFLING
(MEANINGLESS —) SLIPSLOP
(NONSENSICAL —) BLABBER
BLATHER FOLDEROL
(PIOUS OR SANCTIMONIOUS —) PI
(RAPID —) GABBLE JABBER
CHATTER CLATTER
(SCOLDING —) HARANGUE
(SILLY —) BUFF CLART FOOTLE
TWADDLE
(SMALL —) CHAT BACKCHAT
CHITCHAT
(SMOOTH —) GLOZE BLARNEY
(TRIFLING —) PRATTLE CHITCHAT
(USELESS —) WASTE
(VIOLENT —) BLUSTER
(WEAK —) SLIPSLOP
(WHINING —) BLEAT
TALKATIVE COSY GASH GLIB NAWY
BUZZY TALKY CHATTY CLASHY
CRACKY FLUENT FUTILE VOLUBLE
BIGMOUTH FLIPPANT TELLSOME
TALKATIVENESS FUTILITY
TALKER CAMPER POTGUN CAUSEUR
SPIELER
(IDLE —) WHIFFLER
(PROFESSIONAL —) JAWSMITH
(SENSELESS —) RATTLE
TALKING (LOUD —) NORATION
TALKING-TO EARFUL LECTURE
TALKY GABBY
TALL HIGH LANKY LOFTY STEEP
WANDY CRANEY PROCERE
(— AND FEEBLE) TANGLE
(VERY —) TAUNT
TALLAGE CUTTING
TALLER DOMINANT

TALLOW SUET SEVUM ARMING
TAULCH
TALLY TAB JUMP SUIT AGREE CHECK
COUNT SCORE STICK STOCK
CENSUS STRING SWATCH TAILYE
COMPORT TAILZIE
TALMUD GEMARA
TALON FANG SERE UNCE CLUTCH
POUNCE UNGUIS WEAPON
(— OF TOOTH) HEEL
TALONID HEEL
TALPA TESTUDO
TALTHIB GLAGA GLAGAH
TALUS SCREE RUBBLE ASTRAGAL
TAMANDUA ANTEATER
TAMARACK LARCH LARIX EPINETTE
TAMARIN PINCHE JACCHUS
LEONCITO MARIKINA MARMOSET
TAMARIND SAMPALOC
TAMARISK ATLE JHOW HEATH
TAMASHEK TUAREG
TAMBOURINE RIKK TAAR DAIRA
TAMBO TABOUR TIMBER TABORIN
TIMBREL
TAME MAN DEAD MEEK MILD PACK
ACCOY ATAME BREAK DAUNT MILKY
SPAKE CADISH ENTAME GENTLE
INWARD MEEKEN UNWIFE AFFAITE
CORRECT INSIPID SUBDUED
CICURATE DOMESTIC MANSUETE
(— FALCON) MAN RECLAIM
TAMED BROKE GENTLE
TAMIL VELLALA
TAMMY TAMIS STAMIN
TAMONEA MICONIA
TAM-O-SHANTER TAM TAMMY
TAMP PUG STEM
TAMPER FIX COOK FAKE FOOL GAFF
TOUCH DABBLE FIDDLE MEDDLE
MONKEY POTTER PUDDLE PUTTER
TEMPER FALSIFY TRINKLE
TAMPION TOMKIN TAMPOON
TAM-TAM GONG
TAN FAN ARAB BARK ADUST ASCOT
DRESS TANKA TAWNY ORIOLE
COCONUT EMBROWN LEATHER
SUNBURN
(BEACH —) SEDGE
(TROTTEUR —) BAY
TANACETYL THUJYL
TANAGER YENI LINDO REDBIRD
WARBIRD CARDINAL EUPHONIA
FIREBIRD ORGANIST
TANBARK BARK TAWN AVARAM
TURWAR ALGERIAN ALGERINE
TANDAN EELFISH
TANEKAHA TOATOA
TANG NIP TING VEIN SHANK STRAP
TASTE TWANG RELISH TANGLE
TONGUE SEATANG FAREWELL
TANGELO UGLI
TANGENCY CONTACT
TANGENT SLOPE
TANGERINE NAARTJE MANDARIN
TANGIBLE ACTUAL TACTILE
CONCRETE MATERIAL PALPABLE
TANGLE COT ELF TAT FANK FOUL
HARL SHAG TAUT HARLE KNURL
SNARL SNIRL THRUM TWINE WOPSE

BALTER ENTRAP HANGER JUNGLE
MOMBLE MUCKER RAFFLE SLEAVE
TAFFLE TARDLE TAUGHT TEIHTE
BRANGLE TAISSLE THICKET
FURBELOW SCROBBLE
(PL.) COBWEB
TANGLED AFOUL TOUSY MESHED
SNARLY TAUTED IMPLICIT INTORTED
INVOLVED
(— **UP**) HAYWIRE
TANGLEHEAD PILI
TANGY BRISK
TANHA TRISHNA
TANK DAM DIP TAL BOSH SUMP
BASIN MIXER STANK STEEP TRUNK
BLOWUP BOILER HOPPER PANZER
TROUGH BATTERY BLOWPIT
BREAKER CISTERN FLUSHER
PISCINA PLUNGER POACHER
SETTLER STEEPER BLEACHER
DIGESTOR LANDSHIP SUBSIDER
(— **FOR DYE OR SOAP**) BECK
(— **FOR FISH**) STEW TRUNK
AQUARIUM STEWPOND
(— **IN SHIP**) FOREPEAK
(**ARMORED** —) FLAIL WHIPPET
LANDSHIP
(**PAPER MANUFACTURING** —)
POACHER
(**PHOTOGRAPHIC** —) CUVETTE
(**POTTER'S** —) PLUNGER
(**RECTANGULAR** —) BOWLY
(**SALT MANUFACTURING** —)
GRAINER
(**STORAGE** —) CHEST
(**SUGAR REFINING** —) TIGER
BLOWUP
(**TANNING** —) FLOATER
(PL.) HEAVIES
TANKAGE AMMONATE
TANKARD GUN JACK FACER STOOP
STOUP PEWTER POTTLE TANKER
GODDARD
TANNED BROWN RUDDY TAWNY
BRONZED
(**NOT** —) RAW
TANNER EGGER SAMAR BARKER
STAKER PERCHER
TANNING PASTING
(— **SOLUTION**) PLUMPER
TANSY COSTMARY
TANSY MUSTARD FLIXWEED
FLUXWEED
TANSY RAGWORT RAGWEED
TANTALIZE GRIG JADE TEASE
HARASS
TANTALUS (DAUGHTER OF —) NIOBE
(**FATHER OF** —) JUPITER THYESTES
(**MOTHER OF** —) PLUTO
(**SON OF** —) PELOPS
(**WIFE OF** —) DIONE
TANTAMOUNT SAME
TANTRA AGAMA
TANTRUM HISSY TIRRIVEE WINGDING

TANZANIA
CAPITAL: DARESSALAM
LAKE: RUKWA

NATIVE: BANTU SUKUMA
MAKONDE SWAHILI
RIVER: RUVU WAMI RUAHA
KAGERA RUFIJI RUVUMA
PANGANI MBENKURU
TOWN: WETE KILWA MOSHI TANGA
ARUSHA DODOMA KIGOMA
MWANZA TABORA MTAWARA
MOROGORO
WEIGHT: FARSALAH

TAO MAN PEASANT
(— **PRACTICE**) WUWEI
TAP BOB DAB PAT TAT TIP TIT TOP
BEAT COCK DRUB FLIP JOWL PENK
TICK TIRL TUNK APPEL FLIRT QUILL
SNOCK START ALETAP BROACH
CANNEL DABBLE FAUCET NATTLE
TAPLET DRAWOFF HEELTAP
PERCUSS
(— **A CASK**) QUILL STRIKE
(— **A DRUM**) TUCK
(— **FOR A LOAN**) TIG
(— **ON SHOE**) CLUMP UNDERLAY
(— **ON THE SHOULDER**) FOB
(— **REPEATEDLY**) DRUM
(— **THE GROUND**) BEAT
(**FENCING** —) BEAT
(**MASTER** —) HOB HUB
(**SMART** — **OF THE FOOT**) APPEL
TAPA KAPA SIAPO KIKEPA
TAPACOLA TURCO
TAPE LEAR FERRET GARTER SCOTCH
TAPERY YNKELL BINDING MEASURE
TAPELINE TELETAPE
(**FISH** —) SNAKE
(**LAMP** —) WICK
(**LINEN** —) INKLE
(**METALLIC** —) GALLOON
(**NARROW** —) TASTE
(**RED** —) WIGGERY
TAPE GRASS EELGRASS
TAPEMAN CHAINMAN
TAPER DRAW RISE DRAFT GAUDY
SCARF SNAPE SWAGE CIERGE
DRAUGHT LIGHTER PRICKET
TRINDLE DIMINISH
(— **OF A SPRING**) DRAW
(— **OF PATTERN**) STRIP
(— **OFF**) CEASE TONGUE
TAPERED BARRELED BOATTAIL
GRADUATED
TAPERING SHARP SPIRAL SPIRED
TERETE SPIRING FUSIFORM
SUBULATE
TAPER ROD PODGER
TAPESTRY ARRAS TAPET TAPIS
COSTER DORSER DOSSER CEILING
GOBELIN HANGING SUSANEE
VERDURE AUBUSSON MORTLAKE
TAPEWORM TAPE LIGULA TAENIA
COENURE HYDATID PLATODE
BANDWORM COENURUS DAVAINEA
FLATWORM HELMINTH
(PL.) CYSTICA
TAPHOLE TAP FLOSS MOUTH
TAPIR ANTA KUDA DANTA TENNU
TAPIROID

TAPPED ABROACH
TAPPET WIPER
TAPROOM TAP SALOON BARROOM
BUVETTE TAPHOUSE
TAPSTER NICKPOT SKINKER
TAPUYAN GE GES GHES BUGRE
GESAN JUYAS CAYAPO GOYANA
CAMACAN CARAHOS COROADO
TIMBIRA APINAGES BOTOCUDO
CAINGANG CHAVANTE
TAR PAY BREA BINDER ALKITRAN
(**BIRCH** —) DAGGETT
(**MINERAL** —) MALTHA
TARA DOLMA
TARANTULA HUNTER JAYHAWK
MYGALID
TARBOOSH FEZ
TARDIGRADA ARCTISCA
TARDILY SLOWLY
TARDINESS SLOTH TARDITY
TARDY LAG LAX DREE LATE SLOW
SLACK DREIGH LAGGED REMISS
LAGGING DILATORY LATESOME
TARE VETCH LEAKAGE
(PL.) FILTH
TARES ZIZANY
TARGET AIM MOT BUTT MARK WANE
CLOUT LEVEL PRICK ROVER SCOOP
SCOPE TARGE WHITE BANNER
NIVEAU OBJECT SLEEVE COCKSHY
INCOMER OUTGOER SARACEN
POPINJAY
(— **OF KNEELING FIGURE**) SQUAW
(— **OF LEVELING STAFF**) VANE
(— **OF RIDICULE**) GAME
(— **RING**) SOUS
(**EASY** —) SITTER
(**PIECE OF** —) SCAB
(**RAILROAD SWITCH** —) BANNER
(**STRIKE A** —) KEYHOLE
(**THROWN** —) COCKSHY COCKSHUT
(**TOWED** —) DROGUE
(**UNIDENTIFIED** —) SKUNK
TARHEEL STATE NORTHCAROLINA
TARIFF AVERAGE TRIBUTE
TARNISH DIM BLOT SMIT SOIL
CLOUD DIRTY STAIN SULLY TACHE
BREATH DARKEN DEFILE INJURE
SMIRCH ASPERSE BEGRIME
BESMEAR OBSCURE BESMIRCH
DISCOLOR
TARO COCO DALO EDDO GABE KALO
MASI TALO COCCO KAROU TANIA
TANYA COCKER TARROW YAUTIA
DASHEEN MALANGA COCOROOT
EDDYROOT
TAROT NAIB TAROCCO
TARPON SABALO
TARRAGON TARCHON ESTRAGON
TARRY BIDE STAY STOP ABIDE
DALLY DEMUR PAUSE ARREST
LINGER REMAIN SOJOURN
TARSIER LEMUR
TARSOMETATARSUS SHANK
TARSUS HAND ANKLE DIGITAL
(**BIRD'S** —) SHANK
TART ACID FLAN SOUR BOWLA
CUPID EAGER SHARP SNIPPY
SUNKET PIQUANT POLYNEE

PUNGENT SUBACID TARTLET
TURNOVER
TARTAN PLAID
(— **PATTERN**) SETT
TARTAR ARGAL ARGOL CALCULUS
TARTNESS ACRITY ACIDITY
VERDURE ACERBITY ASPERITY
VERJUICE
TASK FAG JOB TAX CHAR DARG TOIL
CHARE CHORE GRIND KNACK
LABOR NULLO STINT CHARGE
DEVOIR NIYOGA PENSUM RAMSCH
TOURNE FATIGUE SWEATER
TRAVAIL BUSINESS EXERCISE
TRAUCHLE
(— **AS PSYCHOLOGICAL TEST**)
AUFGABE
(**ASSIGNED** —) STENT STINT DEVOIR
(**EASY** —) PIPE SNAP SETUP
(**ONEROUS** —) CORVEE
(**ROUTINE** —) DRUDGE
TASKMASTER DRIVER TASKER
RAWHIDER
TASMANIA (**CAPITAL OF** —) HOBART
(**LAKE IN** —) ECHO SORELL
(**MOUNTAIN IN** —) DROME NEVIS
BARRON CRADLE LOMOND
HUMBOLDT
(**RIVER IN** —) ESK HUDN TAMAR
GORDON JORDAN PIEMAN DERWENT
(**TOWN IN** —) BURNIE HOBART
TASMANIAN DEVIL DASYURID
TASMANIAN WOLF HYENA
THYLACINE
TASSEL TAG TUFT LABEL THRUM
TARCEL TARGET TOORIE CORDELLE
(PL.) ZIZITH
TASTABLE GUSTABLE
TASTE EAT GAB GOO LAP SIP CAST
DASH GOUT GUST HINT PREE RASA
SALT TANG TEST TINT WAFT ASSAY
DRINK FANCY GUSTO HEART PROVE
RELES SAVOR SHADE SKILL SMACK
SNACK SPICE TOOTH TOUCH
DEGUST FLAVOR GENIUS LIKING
PALATE RELISH SAMPLE SMATCH
ATTASTE PREGUST SOUPCON
THOUGHT APPETITE JUDGMENT
PENCHANT SAPIDITY
(— **COMBINED WITH APTITUDE**)
FLAIR
(— **IN MATTERS OF ART**) FANCY
(**BAD** —) GOTHISM
(**DECIDED** —) PENCHANT
(**DELICATE** —) BREED
(**DISCRIMINATING** —) SKILL
(**GOOD** —) DECORUM
(**STRONG** —) GOO
(PL.) MERIDIAN
TASTEFUL NEAT ELEGANT GUSTOSO
TASTELESS DEAF FLAT FLASH
MALMY VAPID WERSH WALLON
FATUOUS INSIPID INSULSE WEARISH
UNSAVORY
TASTER TRIER
TASTING ASSAY
(— **OF MALT**) CORNY
TASTY GUSTABLE TASTEFUL
TATAR KIN JUNG KITAN SOYOT

CHAZAR KHAZAR KHITAN KHOZAR
SHORTZY MELETSKI
(PL.) HU
TATOUAY CABASSOU
TATTER JAG RAG TAG SHRED
FITTER LIBBET TAGRAG TARGET
FLITTER TROLLOP
(PL.) DUDS TAVERS FITTERS
RIBBONS TAIVERS FLITTERS
TATTERED DUDDY BEATEN TAGGED
FORWORN TATTERY TOTTERED
TATTLE BLAB GASH CHEEP CLASH
CLYPE PEACH SNEAK TUTEL GOSSIP
QUATCH SNITCH TATTER TITTLE
CLATTER
TATTLER LAB CLASH SNIPE FABLER
GAMBET GOSSIP TUTLER YELPER
TITTLER TELLTALE
TATTLING LEAKY FUTILE
TATTOO TAT MOKO PINK POUNCE
TATTOOED PINKED
(— **MAN**) YUN
TATTOOING MOKO
TAUGHT MAK TEACHED INSTRUCT
(**EASILY** —) DOCIBLE
TAUNT BOB MOB CHIP GIBE JAPE
JEER JEST MOCK PROG SKIT TWIT
CHECK FRUMP GLAIK JAUNT SCOFF
SCORN SLANT SLARE SLART DERIDE
SNEEST UPCAST SARCASM TWITTER
RIDICULE
TAUNTING RAIL
TAUPE MOLESKIN
TAUROTRAGUS OREAS ORIAS
TA-URT THOUERIS
TAUT SNUG TORT STIFF TIGHT
CORDED
TAUTEN SNUB STIFFEN SWIFTER
TENSION
TAUTOG CHUB MOLL LABROID
TAVERN INN BUSH HOWF VENT
MITER MITRE TAMBO BISTRO
CABACK BUVETTE CABARET
OSTERIA TABERNA GASTHAUS
ORDINARY POTHOUSE TAPHOUSE
TAW TER SCORE MARBLE GLASSIE
SHOOTER
TAWDRY CHEAP GAUDY GILDED
TINSEL
TAWNY FUSC BRUSK DUSKY FULVID
TANNED FULVOUS JACINTH
TAW-SUG SULU
TAX LAY LOT CAST CESS DUTY GELD
GELT GILD LEVY POLL RATE SCAT
SCOT SESS TAIL TASK TOLL ABUSE
AGIST DONUM FINTA HANSA HANSE
LEKIN MAILL OBROK QUINT SCATT
STENT TOUST VERGI WATCH ZAKAH
ZAKAT ABKARI ASSESS AVANIA
BURDEN CEDULA DEMAND EXCISE
EXTENT HIDAGE IMPOST JEZIAH
KHARAJ MURAGE OCTROI OCTROY
PAVAGE PURVEY SENSUS STRAIN
SURTAX VINAGE BOOMAGE
BOSCAGE CHANCER CHEVAGE
CHIVAGE CONDUCT FINANCE
GABELLE LASTAGE PATENTE
PENSION POLLAGE PONTAGE
SCUTAGE STIPEND TAILAGE

TERRAGE TRIBUTE ALCABALA
AUXILIUM BONAUGHT CARUCAGE
CORNBOLE DANEGELD EXACTION
EXERCISE KERNETTY MALTOLTE
OBLATION PESHKASH ROMESCOT
ROMESHOT STACKAGE SUPERTAX
TAXATION WHEELAGE
(— **AT HARVESTTIME**) CORNBOLE
(— **FOR STORING LOGS**) BOOMAGE
(— **OF ONE-FIFTH**) QUINT
(— **ON EVERY PLOW**) CARUCAGE
(— **ON HERRING CATCH**) LASTAGE
(— **ON LIQUOR**) ABKARI
(— **ON SALT**) GABELLE
(— **ON UNBELIEVERS**) KHARAJ
(— **CN WALLS**) MURAGE
(— **ON WOOD**) BOSCAGE
(— **ON WOOL**) MALETOTE
MALTOLTE
(— **TO PETTY PRINCES**) KERNETTY
(— **TO SYNAGOGUE**) FINTA
(— **TO TENTH AMOUNT**) TITHE
(— **UNDULY**) STRAIN
(**CAPITATION** —) JIZYA JIZYAH
(**CHINESE** —) LEKIN LIKEN LIKIN
(**EXTRAORDINARY** —) AUXILIUM
(**IRISH** —) BONAGHT
(**MOHAMMEDAN** —) JEZIAH
(**PARISH** —) PURVEY
(**PHILLIPINES** —) CEDULA
(**POLL** —) TOLL CENSUS
(**RUSSIAN** —) OBROK
(**SPANISH** —) ALCABALA ALCAVALA
(**TURKISH** —) VERGI AVANIA
TAXABLE LISTABLE
TAX COLLECTOR TITHER GABELLER
TAXGATHERER POLLER TAXMAN
TAXI JIXIE CRAWLER
TAXICAB CAB HACK CRUISER
MOTORCAB
TAXIDERMY NASSOLOGY
TAXING SEVERE GRUELING
TAXON MONERA
TAXONOMIST LUMPER SPLITTER
TAYASSU PECARI
TAYRA GALERA
TCHAMBULI CHAMBERI
TEA CHA CHIA TCHA THAM TSIA
ASSAM CAPER CHAIS CONGO
FAHAM HYSON MIANG PEKOE STEEP
CONGOU KEEMUN OOLONG PTISAN
SUNGLO REDROOT TWANKAY
AUTUMNAL GOWIDDIE SOUCHONG
WORMSEED
(**AFRICAN** —) CAT KAT QAT KHAT
QUAT
(**BLACK** —) BOHEA CONGO OOPAK
OOPACK SYCHEE
(**COARSE** —) BANCHA
(**HIGH-GRADE** —) GYOKURO
(**INFERIOR** —) BOHEA
(**MEDICINAL** —) TISANE
(**MEXICAN** —) BASOTE APASOTE
(**POOR** —) BLASH
TEA BOWL CHAWAN
TEACAKE LUNN SCONE
TEACH ARAL LEAR READ SHOW
TECH TENT CARRY COACH EDIFY
ENDUE LEARN SPELL TRAIN TUTOR

WISSE INFORM PREACH SCHOOL
BITECHE EDUCATE EXAMPLE
EXPOUND GRAMMAR AMAISTER
DISCIPLE DOCUMENT INSTRUCT
PUPILIZE
(— TO FIGHT) SPAR
TEACHABLE DOCILE DOCIBLE
TEACHABLENESS DOCITY DOSSETY
TEACHER RAB ALIM GURU AKHUN
BIDDY CADET GUIDE MOLLA RABBI
REBBE TUTOR USHER AKHUND
AMAUTA DOCENT DOCTOR DOZENT
FATHER MADRIH MAULVI MENTOR
MULLAH PANDIT PUNDIT RABBAN
READER REGENT RHETOR SUPPLY
ACHARYA ALFAQUI DOMINIE
MAESTRA MAESTRO MUNCHEE
MURSHID PEDAGOG SHASTRI
SOPHIST SPONSOR STARETS
TRAINER ALFAQUIN AYUDANTE
DIRECTOR EDUCATOR EXTENDER
GAMALIEL MAGISTER MELAMMED
MISTRESS MOONSHEE MUJTAHID
(— OF ELOQUENCE) RHETOR
(— OF EMINENCE) MAESTRO
(— OF HIGH LEARNING) SOPHIST
(— OF KORAN) ALFAKI ALFAQUIN
(— OF PAUL) GAMALIEL
(INCA —) AMAUTA
(MOHAMMEDAN —) COJA HODJA
KHOJA KHOJAH
TEACHING LAW DHARMA DOCENT
LESSON LORING ACROAMA TUITION
BUDDHISM DIDACTIC DOCTRINE
DOCUMENT TUTELAGE
(PL.) ACOUSMA BROWNISM
CACODOXY DIDACTICS
TEAK SAJ DJATI EBONY
TEAKETTLE SUKE SUKEY CHAFER
KETTLE POURIE CRESSET
TEAL CRICK BLUEWING GARGANEY
SARCELLE
TEAM SET FIVE PLOW SIDE SPAN
YOKE DRAFT SWING PLOUGH
SEXTET DRAUGHT CARTWARE
(— 2 ABREAST, 1 LEADING) SPIKE
UNICORN
(— HARNESSED ONE BEFORE
ANOTHER) TANDEM
(— OF 3 HORSES ABREAST) TROIKA
(— OF GLASSWORKERS) SHOP
CHAIR
(— THAT FINISHES LAST) DOORMAT
(2-HORSE —) PODANGER
(3-HORSE —) RANDEM
(ATHLETIC —) CLUB
(BASEBALL —) NINE
(BASKETBALL —) FIVE
(FOOTBALL —) ELEVEN
TEAMSTER CARTER TEAMEO
CARTMAN SKINNER TEAMMAN
TEAPOT TRACK TRACKPOT
TEAR RIP RIT RUG TUT CLAW PILL
PULL RACE RASE RAVE REND RIVE
RUGG SKAG SNAG STUN BREAK
CLAUT LARME PEARL SHARK SLENT
SPALT SPLIT TOUSE CLEAVE
HARROW RANCHE RIPPLE SCHISM
SCREED WRENCH CHATTER

CONVELL DISCIND EYEDROP
SCRATCH DISTRAIN FRACTURE
LACERATE LACHRYMA TEARDROP
(— APART) REND TEASE DISCERP
DIVULSE
(— ASUNDER) DIVEL
(— AWAY) AVULSE
(— DOWN) UNPILE DESTROY
DEMOLISH
(— IN NEGATIVE) SLUG
(— INTO PIECES) DRAW TOLE DEVIL
SHRED TEASE LANIATE
(— INTO SHREDS) HOG DEVIL
TATTER
(— INTO) LAMBAST LAMBASTE
(— OFF) STRIP ABRUPT DISCERP
(— OPEN) PROSCIND
(— UP BY THE ROOTS) ARACHE
(PL.) DEW BRINE RHEUM EYEWATER
TEARDROP EYEWATER
TEARFUL SOFT TEARY WEEPY
LIQUID WATERY WEEPLY FLEBILE
MAUDLIN SHOWERY SNIVELY
SNIVELLY
TEARING SCREED
(— AWAY) AVULSION
TEARPIT LARMIER
TEASE COD FUN ROT TAR TRY TUM
BAIT DRAG FASH FRET HARE HOCK
JADE JIVE JOSH LARK NARK RAZZ
TARR TOUT WORK CHAFF CHEEK
CHEVY DEVIL FEEZE TARIE TAUNT
TOOSE WRACK BANTER BOTHER
CADDLE CHIVVY HARASS HOORAY
HURRAH MOLEST MURDER PESTER
PLAGUE HATCHEL TERRIFY
TORMENT WHERRET
TEASEL KING TASSEL TEASLE
MANWEED
TEASELER GIGGER TEASER
TEASELING MOZING
TEASER TIZEUR
TEASING CHAFF MERRY BANTER
DEVILING QUIZZING
TEAT DUG PAP TIT DIDDY SPEAN
NIPPLE SUCKLE
TEA TREE TI MANUKA
TECHNICIAN SWITCHER
TECHNIQUE FEAT GATE WRINKLE
COQUILLE INDUSTRY SPICCATO
(BILLIARD —) FOLLOW
(DANCE —) HEELWORK
(DECORATION —) IKAT
(JUMPING —) SCISSORS
(WRESTLING —) GLIMA
(WRITING —) CUBISM
TECHNOLOGY FISHERY TECHNIC
CERAMICS
TECMESSA (FATHER OF —)
TELEUTAS
(HUSBAND OF —) AJAX
(SON OF —) EURYSACES
TECOMIN LAPACHOL
TECTRIX COVERT
TEDDER KICKER
TEDIOUS DEAD DREE DULL LATE
POKY PROSY ALENGE BORING
DREECH DREIGH ELENGE MORTAL
IRKSOME PREACHY PROSAIC

VERBOSE BORESOME DRAGGING
TIRESOME WEARIFUL
TEDIUM IRK YAWN ENNUI BOREDOM
TEE COCK TIGHT TOZEE WITTER
BULLHEAD
TEEM SNY FLOW SWIM SWARM
ABOUND BUSTLE SCRAWL
TEEMER SHOOTMAN
TEEMING BIG ALIVE TUMID FERTILE
GUSHING TEEMFUL BRAWLING
PREGNANT SWARMING
TEENY SMALL
TEESWATER MUGS MUGGS
TEETER ROCK WAVER JIGGLE
QUIVER SEESAW TREMBLE
TEETH CTENII CHOPPERS CRACKERS
GRINDERS
(HAVING —) IVORIED
(SET OF —) DENTURE
TEETHRIDGE ALVEOLE ALVEOLUS
TEETOTUM TOTUM WHIRLIGIG
TEGETICULA PRONUBA
TEGMENTUM ROOF
TEGULA SQUAMA EPAULET SCAPULA
PATAGIUM SQUAMULA
TEGUMENT COAT TEGMEN
TEHUELCHE PATAGON
TEJU TEIOID JACUARU TEGUEXIN
TELAMON ATLAS
(BROTHER OF —) PELEUS
(FATHER OF —) AEACUS
(MOTHER OF —) ENDEIS
(SON OF —) AJAX TEUCER
(WIFE OF —) GLAUCE HESIONE
TELAMONES ATLANTES
TELEDU BADGER STINKARD
TELEGONUS (FATHER OF —)
ULYSSES
(MOTHER OF —) CIRCE
(SON OF —) ITALUS
(WIFE OF —) PENELOPE
TELEGRAM TAR WIRE FLASH FLIMSY
TELEGRAPH WIRE CABLE BUZZER
TELEGRAM TELOTYPE
TELEMACHUS (FATHER OF —)
ULYSSES
(MOTHER OF —) PENELOPE
(SON OF —) LATINUS
TELENCEPHALON ENDBRAIN
TELEOLOGICAL TELIC FINALIST
TELEOLOGY FINALITY
TELEPHASSA (DAUGHTER OF —)
EUROPA
(HUSBAND OF —) AGENOR
(SON OF —) CADMUS PHOENIX
TELEPHONE PHONE HANDSET
TELEPHOTE DIAPHOTE
TELEPHUS (FATHER OF —)
HERCULES
(MOTHER OF —) AUGE
TELESCOPE TUBE COUDE GLASS
SCOPE TRUNK ALINER FINDER
ALIGNER BINOCLE TRANSIT
PROSPECT SPYGLASS
(SURVEYOR'S —) LEVEL
TELEVISION AIR
TELIOSPORE TELEUTO
TELL SAY DEEM MEAN MOOT READ
SHOW TALE AREAD AREED BREAK

BREVE COUNT NEVEN PITCH SPELL STORY TEACH UTTER AUTHOR DEVISE IMPART INFORM MUSTER QUETHE RECITE RELATE REPEAT REPORT REVEAL CONFESS DIVULGE NARRATE PARTAKE RECOUNT ACQUAINT REHEARSE
(— CONFIDENTIALLY) CONFIDE
(— CONFUSEDLY) SPLATHER
(— EARNESTLY) ASSURE
(— IN ADVANCE) FORESAY
(— LIES) BELY LIGE BELIE
(— OFF) JAR
(— ROMANCES) GEST GESTE
(— SECRETS) CHEEP CLYPE SPILL
(— STRIKINGLY) CRACK
(— TALES) CANT
TELLER SPINNER STORIER TALLIER FABLEIST FABULIST SENACHIE
TELLING REDE PUNGENT POWERFUL
(— OF SECRETS) BLAB
TELLTALE BLAB CLASH TATTLER TITTLER REGISTER
TELLURIDE ALTAITE
TELSON PLEON
TELUGU GENTU GENTOO TELINGA
TEM TUM ATMU ATUM
TEMERITY GALL CHEEK AUDACITY RASHNESS
TEMPER CUE MAD BAIT BATE COOL DASH DRAW MOOD MULL NEAL PADD SCOT TONE ALLOY BIRSE BLOOD CREST DELAY FRAME GRAIN HUMOR IRISH SAUCE SOBER TRAMP ADJUST ANIMUS ANNEAL DANDER MASTER MONKEY SEASON SPLEEN STRAIN SUBMIT CHASTEN CLIMATE COURAGE HACKLES QUALIFY STOMACH EBENEZER GRADUATE MITIGATE MODERATE MOORBURN
(— CLAY) TAMPER
(— METAL) ALLAY
(— OF MIND) CUE SPIRIT
(CAPRICIOUS —) SPLEEN
TEMPERAMENT GEMUT HEART HUMOR CRASIS KIDNEY TEMPER STOMACH SANGUINE
TEMPERAMENTAL FITIFIED
TEMPERANCE MEDIETY SOBRIETY
TEMPERATE CALM COOL MILD SOFT GREEN SOBER TEMPRE MODERATE ORDINATE
TEMPERATURE SUN HEAT TEMP HOTNESS
TEMPERED HARD SOBER SARCENET
TEMPEST GALE THUD WIND ORAGE STORM TUMULT TORMENT TURMOIL WEATHER
TEMPESTUOUS WILD GUSTY STERN WINDY RUGGED STORMY VIOLENT STALWART
TEMPLATE CURB NORMA TEMPLET PADSTONE STRICKLE
TEMPLE VAT WAT DEUL FANE NAOS RATH CANDI GUACA HUACA KIACK KOVIL MARAE RATHA CHANDI HAFFET HERION MANDIR SACRUM SHRINE TEOPAN TJANDI VIHARA HERAEUM HERAION TEMPLET

TEMPLUM VARELLA OLYMPIUM PANTHEON RAMESEUM TEOCALLI VALHALLA
(— AREA) MANDAPA
(CAVE —) SPEOS
(FIJI —) BURE
(HAWAIIAN —) HEIAU
(PART OF —) PRONAOS
(SHINTO —) SHA JINJA JINSHA YASHIRO
(STUDY OF —S) NAOLOGY
(TOWERLIKE —) ZIGGURAT
TEMPLET FORMER
TEMPO TAKT TIME AGOGE MOVEMENT
TEMPORAL CARNAL TIMELY EARTHLY PROFANE SECULAR
TEMPORARY FLYING INTERIM STOPGAP WHILEND EPISODAL EPISODIC TEMPORAL
TEMPORIZER DRIFTER POLITIC
TEMPT EGG FAND FOND LURE TEMP TENT COURT ALLURE ASSAIL ENTICE INVITE SEDUCE ASSAULT ATTEMPT SOLICIT SUGGEST
TEMPTATION TRIAL ATTEMPT TESTING
TEMPTER DEVIL
TEMPTING ALLURING INVITING
TEMPTRESS SIREN DELILAH
TEN ICRE IOTA CHANG DIKER CHEUNG DECADE DENARY DICKER ARTICLE BRISQUE
(— OF TRUMPS) GAME
TEN'A KOYUKON
TENACE FORK
TENACIOUS FAST ROPEY TOUGH CLEDGY DOGGED GRIPPY PLUGGY STICKY STRONG GRIPPLE ADHESIVE GRASPING HOLDFAST
TENACIOUSNESS TENACY FASTNESS
TENACITY LENTOR COURAGE
TENACULUM CLASP
TENANCY CONACRE JOINTURE
TENANT KMET LEUD SAER BARON CEILE DRENG LAIRD BORDAR COTTAR COTTER DRENGH GENEAT HOLDER INMATE LESSEE MOLMAN RADMAN RENTER SOCMAN VASSAL CHAKDAR COTTIER FEODARY FEUDARY GAVELER HOMAGER SOCAGER SOKEMAN VAVASOR COLIBERT CUSTOMER SERGEANT SUCKENER
(LIFE —) LIVIER LIVEYER
(NEW —) INCOME INCOMER
TENCH CYPRINID
TEN COMMANDMENTS DECALOG
TEND HOP NOD RUN SET WRY BABY BEND DRAW GROW KEEP MAKE MIND MOVE TENT DRESS GROOM NURSE OFFER SOUND TREND VERGE WATCH GOVERN INTEND CHERISH CONDUCE DECLINE INCLINE PROPEND
(— A FIRE) STOKE
(— IN A CERTAIN DIRECTION) LEAD
(— TO ONE POINT) CONVERGE

(— TOWARD) AFFECT
(— WHILE AT PASTURE) GRAZE
TENDENCY SET BENT BIAS HAND TONE VEIN DRAFT DRIFT DRIVE HABIT KNACK TENOR TREND TWIST ANIMUS COURSE EONISM GENIUS MOTION APTNESS CONATUS DRAUGHT IMPULSE LEANING NITENCY SAMKARA APTITUDE INSTINCT STEERING VERGENCY
(— IN NATURE) KIND
(— TO APPROACH) ADIENCE
(— TO STICK TOGETHER) CLANSHIP
(— TO WITHDRAW) ABIENCE
(— TO WRATH) TIDE
TENDER TID BEAR COCK FINE FOND FRIM FRUM KIND NESH SOFT SORE TAKE TART TENT WARM CAGER DEFER FRAIL GREEN OFFER PAPPY DELATE DRIVER GENTLE GIMPER GINGER HUMANE LOVELY RAISER SILKEN ADVANCE AMABILE AMOROUS CONCHER CRAMPER FLESHLY MASHMAN OBLATIO PATACHE PINNACE PITEOUS PITIFUL PORRECT PROFFER RUTHFUL STENTER CAMELEER COCKBOAT EFFETMAN FEMININE HEATSMAN HERDSMAN LADYLIKE MERCIFUL MORTISER SPREADER
TENDERFOOT DUDE INNOCENT
TENDERHEARTED HUMAN PITIFUL
TENDERLOIN FILET FILLET UNDERCUT
TENDERLY FONDLY GENTLY AMOROSO
TENDERNESS CHERTE TENDER DELICACY FONDNESS KINDNESS SYMPATHY TENERITY YEARNING
(— OF FEELING) FLESH
TENDINOUS SINEWY
TENDON CORD TAIL CHORD NERVE SINEW TENON LEADER STRING
TENDRIL CURL CLASP CROOK TWIST CIRRUS WINDER CAPREOL CIRRHUS TENTACLE
TENEMENT LAND RENT CHAWL DECKER LIVING WARREN HOLDING LETTING BUILDING PRAEDIUM
TENES (FATHER OF —) CYCNUS
(MOTHER OF —) PHILONOME
(SLAYER OF —) ACHILLES
TENET ADOXY CREDO CREED DOGMA BELIEF GNOMON HOLDING MISHNAH PARADOX DOCTRINE
(PL.) FAITH FAMILISM
TENFOLD DENARY DECUPLE
TENNE TAWNY ORANGE HYACINTH

TENNESSEE

CAPITAL: NASHVILLE
COLLEGE: FISK LANE SIENA BETHEL BELMONT LAMBUTH LEMOYNE MILLIGAN TUSCULUM VANDERBILT
COUNTY: DYER KNOX RHEA COCKE GILES MEIGS OBION GRUNDY MCMINN SEVIER UNICOI

TENNESSEE
BLEDSOE FENTRESS
INDIAN: SHAWNEE CHEROKEE CHICKASAW
LAKE: DOUGLAS CHEROKEE REELFOOT WATTSBAR
MOUNTAIN: GUYOT LOOKOUT
MOUNTAIN RANGE: SMOKY
NATIONAL PARK: SHILOH
NATIVE: WHELP
NICKNAME: VOLUNTEER
PRESIDENT: POLK JACKSON
RIVER: ELK DUCK CANEY HOLSTON HIWASSEE CUMBERLAND
STATE BIRD: MOCKINGBIRD
STATE FLOWER: IRIS
STATE TREE: POPLAR
TOWN: ALCOA PARIS CAMDEN SPARTA DICKSON MEMPHIS PULASKI GALLATIN KNOXVILLE

TENNIS (— SHOT) LET LOB DINK
TENON COG PIN COAK STUB TUSK LEWIS TOOTH TABLING DOVETAIL LEWISSON
TENOR PES FECK TONE VEIN COURSE EFFECT TAILLE TENURE CURRENT PURPORT STRENGTH TENDENCY TENORINO
TENOROON FAGOTTINO
TENOR VIOL VIOLET
TENOR VIOLIN ALTO
TENPINS NEWPORT
TENPOUNDER AWA CHIRO MACABI BONEFISH BONYFISH LADYFISH SKIPJACK SPRINGER
TENREC TANGUE CENTETES CENTETID HEDGEHOG HEDGEPIG
TENSE EDGY RAPT TAUT STIFF CORDED FLINCH FUTURE INTENT NARROW STRAIT STRICT BRITTLE INTENSE PRIMARY FRENETIC PRETERIT SYNTONIC
TENSION BENT HEAT DRIVE STEAM SATTVA SPRING STRAIN STRESS TROPPO BALANCE STRAINT TENSURE ISOTONIA
TENT AUL TOP HALE PAWL TAWN TELD TILT CABIN CRAME LODGE TOPEK TUPIK CANNAT CANVAS DOSSIL SEARCH WIGWAM BALAGAN CABINET KIBITKA MARQUEE SPARVER TABERNA TENTLET TENTORY ZDARSKY PAVILION TENTICLE TENTWORK
(— WHERE GOODS ARE SOLD) CRAME
(CIRCULAR —) YURT YOURT YURTA KIBITKA
(INDIAN —) TEPEE WIGWAM
(SAMOYED —) CHUM
(SOUTH AMERICAN —) TOLDO
TENTACLE HORN SAIL PACLE FEELER BRACHIUM
TENTATIVE GINGERLY
TENT CATERPILLAR WEBWORM
TENTERER RACKER RATCHER
TENTH DIME TITHE DECIMA

(— OF CENT) MILL
(— OF LINE) GRY
TENUITY EXILITY DELICACY
TENUOUS FILMY FOGGY FRAIL TENDER FRAGILE GASEOUS SLENDER SUBTILE ETHEREAL GOSSAMER
(TOO —) FINESPUN
TENUOUSNESS FRAILTY
TENURE FEU TAKE TERM GAVEL JAGIR BARONY CAPITE JAGHIR SOCAGE ALMOIGN BONDAGE BORDAGE BURGAGE CENSIVE CURTESY FARMAGE JAGHEER SOCCAGE SOREHON COPYHOLD DRENGAGE FREEHOLD OVERLAND SOCMANRY SUITHOLD VAVASORY VENVILLE
TEPEE CHUM TENT TIPI LODGE TEEPEE WICKIUP
TEPHROSIA CRACCA
TEPID LEW WARM WLACH WLECH LUKEWARM
TEQUISLATEC CHONTAL
TERATOMA EMBRYOMA
TERCET TRISTICH
TEREBINTH TEIL
TEREDO WOODWORM
TERETE CENTRIC
TEREUS (FATHER OF —) MARS
(SON OF —) ITYS
(WIFE OF —) PROCNE
TERGITE TERGUM PYGIDIUM
TERGIVERSATION DECEIT
TERM HALF NAME NOME WORD LEASE RHEMA SPEAK STYLE TRYST ABBACY GNOMON NOTION PARODY EPITHET EXTREME SESSION SUBJECT SUMMAND TERMINE VOCABLE EQUIVOKE HEADWORD MAHALATH POCHISMO SEMESTER TERMTIME
(— IN JAIL) JOLT
(— IN LOGIC) CONSTANT
(— OF ABUSE) CUSSWORD
(— OF ADDRESS) SIRRAH MADONNA
(— OF CONTEMPT) SLIPE PILCHER TITIVIL
(— OF DEFERENCE) AHUNG
(— OF ENDEARMENT) ASTOR CHUCK COCKY HONEY ASTHORE MACHREE STOREEN POSSODIE POWSOWDY
(— OF IMPRISONMENT) LAG LAGGING STRETCH
(— OF PUNISHMENT) JOB
(— OF RATIO) EXTREME
(— OF REPROACH) MINGO
(— OF SYLLOGISM) EXTREME ARGUMENT
(ARITHMETICAL —) NOME GNOMON
(HYPHENED —) COMPOUND
(LITERAL —S) LETTER
(SOCIAL —S) FOOTING
(UNIVERSAL —) CONCEPT
(PL.) LAY MEANS
TERMAGANT JADE SHREW VIXEN VIRAGO
TERMINABLE FINITE

TERMINAL JACK LAST POLE ANODE DEPOT IMPUT INPUT MUCRO CATHODE POTHEAD DESINENT
TERMINATE CUT END ABUT CALL HALT KILL ABORT BLEED CEASE CLOSE ISSUE LAPSE EXPIRE FINISH FOREDO RESULT INCLUDE TERMINE COMPLETE CONCLUDE DISSOLVE
TERMINATED EXPIATE
TERMINATING FINAL
(— ABRUPTLY) BLIND
(SUDDENLY —) ABRUPT
TERMINATION END ISH DATE TERM CLOSE EVENT ISSUE ENDING EXITUS EXPIRY FINALE PERIOD UPSHOT TERMINUS
(— OF CHURCH CHOIR) CHEVET
(— OF FURNITURE LEGS) FOOT
(— OF RIGHT) LAPSE
TERMINATIVE FINITIVE
TERMINOLOGY JARGON
TERMINUS END FLAT
(— IN FINGERPRINT) DELTA
(— OF PERIOD) TIME
TERMITE ANAI ANAY KING NASUTE WORKER POLILLA
TERMITOPHILE SYMPHILE
TERN KIP DARR INCA LARI NOIO PIRL PIRR RIXY LARID NODDY PEARL SCRAY SKEER SKIRR STERN CHIRRE KERMEW PICKET GOELAND MEDRICK PIRRMAW RITTOCK SEAFOWL STRIKER TARRACK TERNLET MANUSINA SPARLING TIRRACKE
TERPENE CARENE PINENE BORNANE SANTENE THUJENE CAMPHENE FENCHENE LIMONENE NOPINENE
TERRA GE GAEA TELLUS
(DAUGHTER OF —) RHEA THEA PHOEBE TETHYS THEMIS MNEMOSYNE
(HUSBAND OF —) URANUS
(SON OF —) OCEANUS
TERRACE POY DAIS PNYX STEP XYST BENCH HEIAU LINCH OFFSET LINCHET CHABUTRA
(LOUNGING —) LANAI
(NATURAL —) MESA
TERRA JAPONICA GAMBIR GAMBIER
TERRAPENE CISTUDO
TERRAPIN EMYD COUNT COODLE POTTER SLIDER TURPIN TURTLE EMYDIAN FEUILLE SKILPOT REDBELLY
(FEMALE —) HEIFER
(MALE —) BULL
TERRARIUM VIVARIUM
TERRELLA EARTHKIN
TERRENE EARTHLY
TERRESTRIAL EARTHY EARTHLY TERRENE PLANETAL SUBLUNAR SUBSOLAR
TERRET CRINGLE
TERRIBLE DIRE UGLY GHAST LURID DEADLY TARBLE TRAGIC TURBLE DIREFUL FEARFUL FERDFUL GHASTLY HIDEOUS ALMIGHTY BHAIRAVA FLEYSOME HORRIBLE

TERRIFIC TIMOROUS TRAGICAL
TERRIBLY FELLY FIERCE GRISLY
CONSARN
TERRIER SKYE LHASA BOSTON
DANDIE RATTER SCOTTY DIEHARD
SCOTTIE ABERDEEN AIREDALE
RATTONER SEALYHAM VERMINER
WIREHAIR
TERRIFIC FINE SWEET GORGON
FEARFUL GORGEOUS
TERRIFIED AFRAID AGHAST
GHASTLY
TERRIFY AWE COW HAG BREE DARE
FEAR FLAY FLEY DREAD GALLY
SCARE ADREAD AFFRAY AGRISE
AWHAPE DISMAY FLIGHT FREEZE
FRIGHTEN
TERRIFYING GHASTLY HIDEOUS
FLEYSOME TERRIBLE
TERRITORIALISM ITOISM
TERRITORY FEE GOA HAN SOC
AREA MARK PALE SOKE BANAT
DUCHY FIELD MARCH STATE TUATH
BORDER COLONY DOMAIN EMPERY
EMPIRE GROUND APANAGE CONFINE
COUNTRY DEMESNE DUKEDOM
EARLDOM ENCLAVE EPARCHY
REGENCY SATRAPY APPANAGE
CASTLERY CONFINES CONQUEST
DISTRICT DOMINION IMPERIUM
LIGEANCE LUCUMONY PARMESAN
PASHALIK REGALITY SEIGNORY
TERROR AWE FEAR FRAY ALARM
APPAL DREAD PANIC AFFRAY
ALARUM APPALL FRIGHT HORROR
DRIDDER DREDDOUR SURPRISE
TERRORISM NIHILISM
TERRORIST GOONDA ALARMIST
SICARIUS
TERRORIZE FRIGHTEN
TERROR-STRICKEN AWFUL
TERSE CURT COMPACT CONCISE
LACONIC POINTED SUMMARY
UNWORDY SUCCINCT
TERSENESS BREVITY LACONISM
TERTIARY NEOZOIC PALAEIC
TESSELLATED MOSAIC
TESSELLATION AREOLE
TESSERA TILETTE ABACULUS
TESSELLA
TEST CON SAY TRY FAND FEEL
FOND TASK TENT ASSAY AVENA
CANON CHECK ESSAY GROPE ISSUE
PROBE PROOF PROVE SENSE
SOUND TASTE TEMPT TESTA TOUCH
TRIAL SAMPLE TIENTA APPROOF
APPROVE AUSSAGE CONTROL
EXAMINE GANTLET PLUMMET
TESTATE BIOASSAY EXERCISE
GAUNTLET SEROLOGY STANDARD
(— EGGS) CANDLE
(— FOR WEIGHT AND FINENESS)
PYX
(— GROUND) BOSE
(— OF COURAGE) SCRATCH
(— OF CRINOID) CALYX
(— OF ORE) VAN
(SEVERE —) CRUCIBLE
(SYPHILIS —) KOLMER

TESTA TEST LORICA EPISPERM
TESTACEOUS SHELLY
TESTAMENT TEST QUETHE
WITWORD
TESTAR TETARD
TESTATOR LEGATOR
TESTED FIRED TRIED WEIGHED
TESTER TRIER CONNER PROVER
SPARVER DENIERER TESTIERE
(BUTTER —) SEARCHER
TESTICLE STONE BALLOCK DIDYMUS
GENITOR
TESTIFY SPEAK SWEAR AFFIRM
DEPONE DEPOSE WITTEN WITNESS
EVIDENCE
(— FALSELY) MOUNT
(— TO) BESPEAK
TESTIMONIAL SCROLL
TESTIMONY TEST ATTEST PROBATE
TESTATE TESTIFY WITNESS
EVIDENCE
TESTING ASSAY CRUCIAL
TESTIS BALL GONAD STONE
BALLOCK CULLION KNOCKER
SPERMARY
(PL.) COBS CODS COJONES
DOWSETS
TEST TUBE PROOF TESTER
PROBATE
TESTUDINATA CHELONIA
TESTUDO SNAIL GALAPAGO
TORTOISE
TESTY DONCY MUSTY TUTTY DONSIE
PATCHY SPUNKY PEEVISH TETTISH
TOUSTIE WASPISH SNAPPISH
TETANIC SPASTIC
TETANUS LOCKJAW HOLOTONY
TETE-A-TETE TWOSOME CAUSEUSE
TETHER BAND STAKE TEDDER
TOGGLE PASTERN CABESTRO
(— A HAWK) WEATHER
TETHYS APLYSIA
(DAUGHTERS OF —) OCEANIDES
(FATHER OF —) URANUS
(HUSBAND OF —) OCEANUS
(MOTHER OF —) TERRA
TETHYUM CYNTHIA
TETRACHORD GENUS HYPATON
LICHANOS
TETRACTYS TETRAD
TETRAD FOURFOLD
TETRADRACHMA OWL
TETRAGONAL DIMETRIC
TETRAHEDRITE FAHLERZ FAHLORE
PANABASE
TETRAHEXAHEDRON FLUOROID
TETRAHYDRIDE GERMANE
STANNANE
TETRASACCHARIDE LUPEOSE
TETTER DARTRE
TETTIX ACRYDIUM
TEUCER (FATHER OF —) TELAMON
SCAMANDER
(MOTHER OF —) HESIONE
TEUTON GOTH LOMBARD
TEUTONIC GOTHIC GERMANIC
GOTHONIC

TEXAS
CAPITAL: AUSTIN
COLLEGE: SMU TCU RICE WILEY
BAYLOR
COUNTY: BEXAR ERATH GARZA
FANNIN GOLIAD YOAKUM
ZAPATA ZAVALA HIDALGO
REFUGIO ATASCOSA
FORTRESS: ALAMO
INDIAN: LIPAN BILOXI KICHAI
SHUMAN HASINAI COMANCHE
TONKAWAN
LAKE: FALCON TEXOMA AMISTAD
NATIVE: TEJANO
NICKNAME: LONESTAR
PRESIDENT: JOHNSON
EISENHOWER
RIVER: RED PECOS BRAZOS
NUECES TRINITY
STATE BIRD: MOCKINGBIRD
STATE FLOWER: BLUEBONNET
STATE TREE: PECAN
TOWN: GAIL VEGA WACO BRYAN
MARFA OZONA PAMPA TYLER
BORGER DALLAS DENTON
ELPASO KILEEN LAREDO
ODESSA QUANAH SONORA
ABILENE HOUSTON LUBBOCK
AMARILLO BEAUMONT
FLOYDADA GALVESTON

TEXAS BUCKTHORN LOTEBUSH
TEXAS FEVER TRISTEZA
TEXT BODY MIQRA PLACE SAKHA
TESTO PURANA SCRIPT SHAKHA
TEXTUS TEXTLET ANTETHEM
PERICOPE VARIORUM
(— OF ADVERTISEMENT) COPY
(— OF OPERA) LIBRETTO
(— SET TO MUSIC) ORATORIO
(SHASTRA —) SRUTI SHRUTI
TEXTBOOK DUNCE TUTOR GENETICS
TEXTILE (ALSO SEE FABRIC) SABA
STUFF GREIGE MOCKADO SAGURAN
SINAMAY TEXTURE TIFFANY
(— MACHINE) WILLOW
(PL.) DRAPE
TEXTURE WEB BONE HAND KNIT
WALE WOOF GRAIN COBWEB
FABRIC WEFTAGE FRACTURE
(— OF SOAP) FIT
THAI LAO SIAMESE

THAILAND
CAPITAL: BANKOK BANGKOK
COIN: AT ATT BAHT FUANG TICAL
PYNUNG SALUNG SATANG
ISLAND: PHUKET
ISTHMUS: KRA
MEASURE: WA KEN NIV NMU RAI
SAT SEN SOK WAH YOT KEUP
NGAN TANG YOTE KWIEN LAANG
SESTI TANAN KABIET KAMMEU
CHAIMEU ROENENG CHANGAWN
MOUNTAIN: KHIEO MAELAMUN
NATIVE: LAO THAI

PLAIN: KHORAT
RIVER: CHI NAN PING MENAM
MEKONG MEPING
TOWN: UBON PUKET RANONG
AYUDHYA AYUTHIA BANGKOK
LOPBURI RAHAENG SINGORA
SONGKLA KHONKAEN KIANGMAI
THONBURI
WEIGHT: HAP PAI SEN SOK BAHT
HAPH KLAM KLOM CATTY
CHANG COYAN PILUL FLUANG
SALUNG SOMPAY TAMLUNG

THALER DALER
THALLOGEN AMPHIGEN
THALLOID FRONDOSE
THALLUS FROND THALAMUS
THAMNIUM
THAMNOPHIS EUTAENIA
THAMYRAS (FATHER OF —)
PHILAMMON
(MOTHER OF —) ARGIOPE
THAN AS NA NE OR TO AND BUT
NOR THEN TILL
THANE THEGN BANQUO GESITH
ABTHAIN MACDUFF
THANK GRACE MERCY REGRACY
REMERCY
THANKFUL GRATEFUL
THANKLESS INGRATE SLOWFUL
THANKS TA GRACE MERCI MERCY
GRAMERCY
THANKSGIVING GLORY DOXOLOGY
THANK-YOU-MA'AM CAHOT
THAT AS AT SE BUT HOW THE THO
WHO YAT LEST THAM THIK THON
WHAT YOND THICK THILK THOUGH
BECAUSE
(— IS TO SAY) NAMELY
(— ONE) ILLE
(— WHICH HAS TO BE PROVED)
IQED
(— YONDER) THON
THATCH NIPA DATCH SIRKI SIRKY
STING THRUM CADJAN
(— OVER BEEHIVE) HOOD
THATCHED THACK REEDED
THATCHER HELER CROWDER
HELLIER THACKER
THAUMAS (DAUGHTER OF —) IRIS
HARPY
(FATHER OF —) NEPTUNE
(MOTHER OF —) TERRA
(WIFE OF —) ELECTRA
THAUMATURGIST(PL.) GOETAE
THAUMATURGY MAGIC
THAW GIVE MELT FRESH UNTHAW
DEFROST
THE LA LE SE TA THI THAM THEY
YARE THERE
THEA CAMELLIA
(FATHER OF —) URANUS
(HUSBAND OF —) HYPERION
(MOTHER OF —) TERRA
THEANO (FATHER OF —) CISSEUS
(HUSBAND OF —) ANTENOR
(SISTER OF —) HECUBA
THEATER CINE GAFF KINO CAVEA

HOUSE LEGIT ODEUM SCENE STAGE
CINEMA OZONER ADELPHI COCKPIT
GUIGNOL ORPHEUM THEATRE
BIOSCOPE COLISEUM PANTHEON
SHOWSHOP SPELLKEN STRAWHAT
THEATRON
THEATRICAL HAMMY STAGY
DRAMATIC SCENICAL SINGSONG
THEATRICALITY HAM
THEBAN LAIUS NIOBE AMPHION
CADMEAN JOCASTA OEDIPUS
PENTHEUS
THECA CUP URN CELL VAGINA
CAPSULE PYXIDIUM VAGINULE
THEELIN ESTRONE FEMININ OESTRIN
THEFT CRIB LIFT HEIST PINCH
SCORE STEAL FURTUM STOUTH
BRIBERY LARCENY MICHERY
PICKING PILFERY ROBBERY
STEALTH BURGLARY STEALAGE
STEALING
(LITERARY —) PIRACY
(PETTY —) CRIB PICKERY
THEIR ARE HER ORE HORE YARE
THEIRS HERN THEIRN
THEM A EM HI UM HEM MUN HEMEN
THEME DUX BASE IDEA TEMA TEXT
DITTY HOBBY MOTIF PLACE SCOPE
TESTO THEMA TOPIC URLAR
MATTER MYTHOS SUBJECT
ANTETHEM
(— OF FUGUE) DUX
(HACKNEYED —) CLICHE
(RECURRING —) BURDEN
THEMIS (DAUGHTER OF —) DICE
IRENE EUNOMIA
(FATHER OF —) URANUS
(HUSBAND OF —) JUPITER
(MOTHER OF —) TERRA
THEMSELVES HEM HEMSELF
THEN SO AND POI THO ANON SYNE
THENCE AWAY THEN THEREFRO
THEOCRACY KHALSA
THEODOLITE TAIPO TRANSIT
TRANSEPT
THEOLOGIAN FAQIH ULEMA DIVINE
MUJTAHID
THEOLOGY KALAM IRENICS DIVINITY
POIMENIC POLEMICS
THEORBO ARCHLUTE
THEOREM DUAL LEMMA CONVERSE
THEORETIC PURE
THEORETICAL BOOK CLOSET
THEORIC ABSTRACT ACADEMIC
ARMCHAIR PLATONIC
THEORIST OPINATOR
THEORIZE SUGGEST
THEORIZING IDEOLOGY
THEORY ISM OVISM EROTIC ETHICS
HOLISM LAXISM SYSTEM AGOGICS
ATOMISM CAMBISM DUALISM
FORMISM HOBBISM PEELISM
PLENISM THEORIC TYCHISM
ACOSMISM AXIOLOGY DITHEISM
DYNAMISM ENERGISM ESTHETIC
ETIOLOGY FEMINISM FINITISM
GHOSTISM GOBINISM HEDONICS
IDEALISM IDEOLOGY MOLINISM
MONADISM PROGRESS SEMANTIC

SEMIOTIC SPERMISM
THEOW SERF THRALL THEWMAN
THERAPEUTICS ACEOLOGY
THERAVADA HINAYANA
THERE ERE YARE ALONG VOILA
WHERE YONDER THEASUM THITHER
THEREABOUTS NEARBY
THEREAFTER UPON THENCE
THEREFORE SO ERGO THEN ARGAL
HENCE FORTHY IGITUR THENCE
THEREON UPON
THEREUPON SO SINCE WITHAL
THEREON THEREUP
THEREWITH MIT WITH
THERIACA GALENA
THERMOMETER GLASS HYDRA
CELSIUS REAUMUR
THERMOPLASTIC SARAN
THERMOSTAT DETECTOR PYROSTAT
THERSANDER (FATHER OF —)
POLYNICES
(MOTHER OF —) ARGIA
(SLAYER OF —) TELEPHUS
THESAURUS TREASURE
THESE THIR THIS THEASUM
THESEUS (FATHER OF —) AEGEUS
(MOTHER OF —) AETHRA
(SON OF —) HIPPOLYTUS
(WIFE OF —) PHAEDRA
THESIS ACT THEMA DOWNBEAT
LOGICISM THESICLE
THESTIUS (DAUGHTER OF —)
ALTHAEA
(FATHER OF —) PARTHAON
(MOTHER OF —) EURYTE
(SON OF —) TOXEUS PLEXIPPUS
THETIS (FATHER OF —) NEREUS
(HUSBAND OF —) PELEUS
(MOTHER OF —) DORIS
(SON OF —) ACHILLES
THEY A HI THO THEI
(— READ) LEG
THIAMINE ANEURIN
THICK FAT SAD HAZY SLAB BLIND
BROAD BURLY BUSHY CLOSE
CRASS DENSE FOGGY GREAT
GROSS MURKY SOLID SQUAB STIFF
STOUT CHUMPY COARSE GREASY
LUBBER SLABBY SPISSY STOCKY
STODGY BLUBBER GRUMOUS
FAMILIAR LUTULENT MOTHERED
(— WITH SMOKE) SMUDGY
(11 POINTS —) HEAVY
(SHORT AND —) SQUAT
THICKEN BODY CLOT FULL BREAK
KEECH LITHE DEEPEN HARDEN
ENGROSS STIFFEN
THICKENED BODIED BULLED
FURRED CALLOUS CLUBBED
THICKENING FALX LEAR ROUX
SWELL CALLUS CLAVATE LIAISON
PLACODE CRASSULA PYCNOSIS
EPHIPPIUM
(— OF COAL SEAM) SWELLY
(— OF LETTER STROKE) STRESS
THICKET COP RONE SHAG SHAW
BLUFF BRAKE CLUMP COPSE DROKE
HEDGE QUICK SHOLA SLICK THICK
BOSKET BUSHET COVERT GREAVE

JUNGLE MALLEE QUEACH SPINNY
BOSCAGE BOSQUET BRUSHET
COPPICE CORYLET SPINNEY
WOODRIS CHAMISAL QUICKSET
SHINNERY THICKSET
THICKHEADED DULL DENSE
THICKHEADED FLY CONOPID
THICK-KNEE CURLEW DIKKOP
BUSTARD
THICKLY STEFLY
THICKNESS PLY BODY LAYER
DIAMETER
(— OF CHIP) CUT FEED
(— OF CLOTH) LAY
(— OF METAL) GRIP
(— OF PAPER) BULK CALLIPER
UNDERLAY
(ONE — OVER ANOTHER) LAYER
(SECOND —) DOUBLING
THICKSET STUB BEEFY PUNCH
SQUAT THICK CHUMPY HUMPTY
PLUGGY STOCKY STUBBY STUGGY
NUGGETY SQUATTY
THIEF GUN NIP CHOR GILT LIFT MILL
PRIG BUDGE CREEP CROOK FAKER
GANEF PIKER SNEAK TAKER TILER
ANGLER CANNON CLOYER DISMAS
GONOPH HOOKER KALLAN LIFTER
MICHER NIMMER NIPPER PICKER
PIRATE RATERO ROBBER SNATCH
TOSHER WASTER BOOSTER
COLLERY FOOTMAN GORILLA
GRIFTER HARRIER HEISTER
LADRONE LURCHER MEECHER
MERCURY PRIGGER PRIGMAN
PROLLER PROWLER SNAPPER
SPOTTER STEALER THIEVER
CLYFAKER CONVEYER CUTPURSE
FINGERER HARROWER PETERMAN
PICAROON PICKLOCK PILFERER
PRIGSTER SNATCHER
(— AT A MINE) CAVER
(CATTLE —) BLOTTER PLANTER
RUSTLER
(CLEVER —) KID CANNON
(CRUCIFIED —) DISMAS
(MOUNTAIN —) CHOAR
(NIGHT —) SCOURER
(PETTY —) HOOKER SLOCKER
(RIVER —) ACKMAN LUMPER
(VAGABOND —) WASTER
(WHARF —) TOSHER
THIEVE NIM
THIEVING LAW SHARK PUGGING
PROGGERY STEALING
THIEVISH STEALY FURTIVE KLEPTIC
SCADDLE PRIGGISH
THIEVISHNESS PRIGGISM
THIGH HAM HOCK FEMUR FLANK
GAMMON
(— PAIN) MERALGIA
THILL FILL SILL BLADE SHAFT
LIMBER
THIMBLE SKEIN BUSHEL GOBLET
SLEEVE CRINGLE
THIMBLEBERRY MULBERRY
THIN HOE LEW FINE FLUE FUSE
LANK LEAN LIMP PRIN RARE SLIM
WEAK WHEY EXILE FRAIL GAUNT

GAUZY LATHY PEAKY SHEER SLINK
SMALL SPARE SWAMP THIRL WASHY
WIZEN AERIAL BLASHY DILUTE
FLUTED HOLLOW MAUGER MEAGER
MEAGRE PEAKED SCRANK SEROSE
SEROUS SHELLY SKINNY SLIGHT
SPINNY SUBTLE TENDER TWIGGY
WATERY WEAKEN COVERED
FOLIOUS FRAGILE GRACILE
HAGGARD SANIOUS SCRAGGY
SCRAILY SCRANKY SCRAWNY
SHALLOW SHILPIT SLENDER
SPINDLY TENUOUS THREADY
ARANEOUS CACHETIC EGGSHELL
HAIRLINE ICHOROUS MACILENT
SCRAGGED SCRANNEL SKINKING
VAPORISH WATERISH SPINDLING
(— AND PINCHED) CHITTY
(— LEATHER) DOLE
(— OUT) HOE CHOP DISBUD
FEATHER
(— SEEDLINGS) SINGLE
(— THE WALLS) IRON
THINE TUUM
THING JOB RES BABY ITEM SORT
WHAT CHEAT CHOSE ANIMAL
DINGUS FELLOW GILGUY MATTER
ARTICLE DINGBAT MINIKEN
SHEBANG WHATNOT THINGLET
(— DONE) FACT ACTUS
(— FOUND) TROVE
(— OF LITTLE ACCOUNT) GEWGAW
(— OF LITTLE VALUE) NIFLE TRIFLE
TRINKET
(— OF LITTLE WORTH) STIVER
(— TO BE REGRETTED) DAMAGE
(— TO EXHIBIT) BRAVERY
(—S PROHIBITED) VETANDA
(ANOTHER —) ALIUD
(CONSECRATED —) ANATHEMA
(ENORMOUS —) MONSTER
(ENTIRE —) INTEGRAL
(EXTRAORDINARY —) ONER
(FAIR —) POTATO
(FIT —) CHECKER
(GOOD —) WELFARE
(HOLY —S) HAGIA KODASHIM
(IMPORTANT —) ACE
(INSIGNIFICANT —) SCRAT
(INSIGNIFICANT —S) SMATTER
(JEWISH —S) JUDAICA
(LITTLE —S) FEWTRILS
(LIVING —S) BIOTA
(MISSHAPEN —) ABORTION
(NEW —) NEWEL
(OUTMODED —) SNUFF
(PETTY —) SHABBLE
(PRECIOUS —) JEWEL
(PRECISE —) POINT
(RIDICULOUS —) MONUMENT
(RIGHT —) POTATO
(ROTTEN —) ROTTOCK
(SAD —) RUTH
(SILLY —) TRIMTRAM
(SINGLE —) UNIT
(SMALL —) SNIPPET
(STRAY —) WAIF
(STUNTED —) SCRUNT SNEESHIN
(SURE —) CERT SNIP

(TERRIFYING —) BOGEYMAN
(UNEXPECTED —) GODSEND
(UNIQUE —) ONER UNICUM
(UNREAL —) NOMINAL
(UNSUBSTANTIAL —) PUFF
(WORLDLY —S) EARTH
(WORNOUT —) SNUFF HUSHEL
(PL.) GEAR REALIA SQUARES
THING-IN-ITSELF THINGY
NOUMENON
THINGUMBOB DODAD DOODAD
JIGGER THINGUM
THINK LET SEE WIS WIT DEEM FEEL
HOLD MAKE MEAN MINT MULL MUSE
READ TROW WEEN ALLOW FANCY
GUESS JUDGE LOUSE OPINE PANSE
SEPAD ESTEEM EXPECT FIGURE
IDEATE RECKON REPUTE BELIEVE
CONCEIT IMAGINE REFLECT
SUPPOSE COGITATE CONSIDER
ENVISAGE
(— BEST) SEEM
(— HARD) YERK
(— OF AS) ACCOUNT
(— OF) MIND PURPENSE
(— OVER) BETHINK
(— UP) INVENT
(— UPON) BROOD
(— WELL OF) APPROVE
THINKER SOPHIST
(CHINESE —) LEGALIST
THINKING CONCEIT THOUGHT
(CLEVER —) HEADWORK
THINLY AIRILY SPARSE SPARSELY
THINNESS RARITY EXILITY FINESSE
TENUITY EXIGUITY
THINNING BALK BAULK CLEANING
THIRD FACE GAMMA TERCE THREE
DITONE TERTIA TIERCE
THIRDLY TERTIO
THIRD-RATE C3 HEDGE
THIRD-RATER PIKER
THIRST DRY ADRY DRYTH APOSIA
DROUTH THRIST DROUGHT DIPSOSIS
THIRSTING SITIENT
THIRSTY DRY ADRY ATHIRST
DROUGHTY
THIS HE SO THIK THILK
THISTLE PUHA HOYLE CARDON
DASHEL DINDLE FISTLE TEASEL
CALTROP CARLINA GUTWEED
RAURIKI WARATAH BEDEGUAR
CALTHROP COMPOSIT ECHINOPS
MILKWEED
THITHER TO YON YOND THERE
YONDER ULTERIOR YONDWARD
THOAS (DAUGHTER OF —)
HYPSIPYLE
(FATHER OF —) BACCHUS
(MOTHER OF —) ARIADNE
(WIFE OF —) MYRINE
THOMIST AQUINIST
THOMSONITE MESOLE MESOTYPE
OZARKITE
THONG RIEM BRAIL GIRTH LASSO
LEASH ROMAL STRAP THUNK
WHANG WHANK LACING LINGEL
STRING TWITCH AMENTUM BABICHE

LANIARD LANYARD LATCHET RIEMPIE
(— ON JAVELIN) AMENTUM
(HAWK'S —) BRAIL
THOR THUNAR THUNOR
THORACIC DORSAL
THORAX CHEST TRUNK BREAST PEREION ALITRUNK CORSELET FOREBODY
THORITE ENALITE ORANGITE
THORN BROD BUSH GOAD PIKE STUG BRIAR BRIER DOORN PRICK SPIKE FUSTIC JAGGER PRICKER STICKER COCKSPUR THORNLET (PL.) SPEAR HAYBOTE
THORN APPLE HAW METEL STAMONY
THORNBACK RAY DORN ROKER
THORNBILL TOMTIT
THORNY HARD SPINY PRICKLY SCROGGY SPINOUS THISTLY THORNED
THORON RADON
THOROUGH RUN DEEP FIRM FULL SOUND ERRANT HOLLOW STRICT HOTSHOT INGOING REGULAR COMPLETE GROUNDLY INTIMATE
THOROUGHBRED HOTBLOOD
THOROUGHFARE BUND DRUM ROAD ALLEY AVENUE STREET HIGHWAY PARKWAY WHITEHALL
THOROUGHGOING PAKKA ARRANT ERRANT HEARTY PROPER PUREDEE RADICAL ABSOLUTE PROFOUND TRUEBRED
THOROUGHLY BUT FULL GOOD INLY CLEAN FULLY PROOF DEEPLY GAINLY KINDLY PROPER RICHLY RIPELY WHOLLY ROUNDLY SOAKING SOBBING SOGGING SOUNDLY DRIPPING GROUNDLY HEARTILY INWARDLY
THOROUGHWORT BONESET
THOSE THEM THEY YOND
THOTH DHOUTI
THOUGH AS AND SET YET ALTHO ALTHOUGH
THOUGHT CARE IDEA MOOD VIEW FANCY TASTE TRACE NOTION PENSEE CONCEIT CONCEPT COUNSEL OPINION SURMISE PEMMICAN RUMINATE
(— OUT) ADVISED
(CAREFUL —) ADVICE ACCOUNT
(HIGHEST —) IDEE
(REASONED —) STUDY
(UNCLEAN —) SEWERAGE
(WELL-EXPRESSED —) STROKE
THOUGHTFUL EARNEST PENSIVE SERIOUS STUDIED THOUGHTY
THOUGHTFULNESS GRACE COUNSEL
THOUGHTLESS RASH DIZZY GLAKY SUPINE GLAIKET RAMSTAM HEEDLESS RECKLESS
THOUSAND CHI MIL GRAND MILLE CHILIAD
(10 —) MYRIAD
(100 —) LAC LAKH

THOUSANDTH (— OF CUBIC CENTIMETER) LAMBDA
(— OF INCH) MIL
(HUNDRED —) SSU
THRACIAN GETE GETAN GETIC THRAX
THRALL SERF GURTH SLAVE CAPTIVE
THRALLDOM BONDAGE SLAVERY THIRLAGE
THRASH DAD LAM PAY TAN BANG BEAT BELT COMB DING DRUB DUST FLAX LACE LICK LOUK MILL PAIL SOLE SOWL SWAP SWOP TOSE WALK WHAP WHIP WHOP YERK BASTE BELAM BLESS CURRY DRASH FLAIL FRAIL LINCH LINGE NOINT SLATE SWACK SWING TABOR TARGE THUMP TOWEL TWINK WHALE WHANG ANOINT BUMFEG CUDGEL FETTLE JACKET MUZZLE RADDLE STOUSH SWINGE TANCEL THREAP THRESH THWACK WALLOP LAMBACK LEATHER SWADDLE TROLLOP TROUNCE BETHWACK BUMBASTE LAMBASTE LAMBSKIN RIBROAST
THRASHER THREAPER THRESHER
THRASHING TOCO BELTING LICKING WARMING WHALING DRUBBING
THRASYMEDES (FATHER OF —) NESTOR
(MOTHER OF —) ANAXIBIA
THREAD BAR END BAVE CHIP CLEW CLUE CORD DOUP FILE FILM GIMP GOLD LACE LINE POIL PURL SILK TRAM WIRE WORM BRIDE CHIVE FIBER FIBRE FLOAT FLOSS HYPHA INKLE REEVE SCREW SETON SHIVE SHOOT SHUTE STEEK TWEER TWIRE TWIST WATAP BOTTOM COBWEB COTTON ENFILE FIBRIL INFILE SINGLE STAMEN STITCH STRAIN STRAND STRING TISSUE BABICHE BASTING DOUPING SLUBBER SPIREME TWITTER WARPING ACONTIUM FILAMENT GOSSAMER LIGATURE PICKOVER RAVELING SPINNING SPIRICLE
(— AROUND BOWSTRING) SERVING
(— IN SEED COATING) SPIRICLE
(— LEGS OF RABBIT) HARL HARLE
(— OF SCREW) WORM
(— OF WAX) SWARF
(—S THAT CROSS WARP) WEFT WOOF
(40 —S) BEER BIER
(BADLY TWINED —) SLUBBER
(BALL OF —) CLEW CLUE CLOWE GLOME
(BUTTONHOLE —S) BAR
(COARSE —) GIRD
(COARSEST — IN LACE) GIMP
(COILED —) COP
(FLOATING —) PICKOVER
(HARD —) LISLE
(LINEN —) LINE INCLE INKLE
(LOOSELY TWISTED —S) BUMP

(METAL —) LAME WIRE
(OAKUM —) PLEDGET
(PULLED —) SNAG
(REFUSE —S) BUR BURR
(SHOEMAKER'S —) END LINGEL LINGLE
(SILK —) TRAM TRAME DOUPIONI
(SOFT SHORT —) THRUM
(STRONG —) GOUNAU
(SURGICAL —) SETON
(WARP —) END STAMEN
(WAXED —) TACKER
(WEFT —) SHOT
(PL.) FLOSS
THREADBARE BARE SEAR SERE TRITE PILLED SHABBY NAPLESS
THREADFIN SEER SEIR SULEA BARBUDO KINGFISH SEERFISH
THREADFISH COBBLER SUNFISH
THREADING SCREW STRINGING
THREADLIKE FILATE FILOSE
THREAT ATTACK MENACE THUNDER (PL.) MINES
THREATEN BRAG FACE BOAST SHORE ATTACK IMPEND MENACE ENDANGER MINATORY
THREATENED FRAUGHT
THREATENING BIG GLUM UGLY ANGRY BOAST SABLE GREASY BANEFUL RAMPANT MINATORY MINITANT
(— TO RAIN) HEAVY
THREE TREY GIMEL LEASH TRIAS TERNARY TERNION
(— CENT PIECE) TRIME
(— IN ONE) TRIUNE
(— MILES) LEAGUE
(— OF A KIND) GLEEK BRELAN TRIPLET
(GROUP OF —) TRIO TRIAD TRIPLE
(SET OF —) PAIRIAL
THREE-DIMENSIONAL CUBIC CUBICAL
THREEFOLD TERN TRINE TERNAL TREBLE TRINAL TRIPLE TERNARY TRIFOLD TRIPLEX THRIBBLE
THREE-FORKED TRISULC
THREEPENCE JOEY TREY THRIP THRUM TICKEY TICKIE
THRENODY HEARSE THRENE
THRESH COB BEAT CAVE LUMP WHIP BERRY FLAIL FRAIL SPELT STAMP THRASH
THRESHEL DRASHEL
THRESHER TASKER
THRESHER SHARK FOX FOXFISH WHIPTAIL
THRESHOLD HEAD SILL SOLE DEARN LIMEN DRASHEL DOORSILL
THRIFT SAVING VIRTUE ECONOMY STATICE THEEDOM
THRIFTILY NEAR
THRIFTLESS WASTEFUL
THRIFTY CANNY FENDY PUIST FRUGAL SAVING CAREFUL SPARING
THRILL JAG BANG DIRL GIRL KICK FLUSH SHOOT THIRL DINDLE STOUND TICKLE TREMOR ENCHANT FRISSON VIBRATE FREMITUS

(SHARP —) ZING
THRILLING VIBRANT TINGLING
THRINTER FRONTER
THRIPID PHYSOPOD
THRIPS BLACKFLY PHYSOPOD
THRIVE DOW GROW LIKE RISE THEE
ADDLE FADGE MOISE PROVE THRAM
BATTEN BATTLE CATTER CHIEVE
PROSPER STORKEN SUCCEED
WELFARE FLOURISH THRODDEN
(— IN) LOVE
THRIVING BIEN GRUSHIE THRIFTY
BLOOMING TOWARDLY
THRIVINGLY GAILY GAYLY BRAVELY
THROAT MAW CRAG CROP GOWL
GULA HALS HASS LANE GORGE
HALSE SWIRE FAUCES GARGET
GULLET GUTTUR GUZZLE RICTUS
CHANNEL JUGULUM STOMACH
SWALLOW WEASAND THRAPPLE
THROPPLE THROTTLE
(— OF ANCHOR) CLUTCH
(— OF COROLLA) FAUCES
(— OF FROG) KNEE
(MOUTH AND —) WHISTLE
(SORE —) HOUSTY
THROATLATCH FIADOR
THROB ACHE BEAT BELK DRUM
DUNT LEAP PANT QUOP WARK
FLACK STANG WARCH STOUND
STRIKE STROKE WALLOP FLACKER
PULSATE VIBRATE FLICHTER
(— IN PAIN) SHOOT
(RAPID —S) FRIMITTS
THROBBING DUNT ATHROB THRILL
PITAPAT
THROE PANG PULL STOUR SHOWER
PAROXYSM
(—S OF DEATH) AGONY
THROMBIN PLASMASE
THROMBOPLASTIN COAGULIN
CYTOZYME
THROMBOSIS SHOCK CORONARY
THRONE GADI ASANA GADDI GADHI
SELLE SIEGE STALL STATE STEAD
STOOL SEGGIO SHINZA TRIBUNE
CATHEDRA SEGGIOLA SINHASAN
(BISHOP'S —) SEE APSE CATHEDRA
THRONE ROOM AIWAN
THRONG CREW HEAP HOST ROUT
CHIRT CROWD FLOCK FRACK POSSE
PRESS SHOAL SWARM RESORT
THRAVE THREAT THRIMP THRUST
COMPANY TEMPEST THRUTCH
SURROUND
(— OF SEAFOWL) SAVSSAT
(CONFUSED —) LURRY
THRONGED ALIVE FREQUENT
NUMEROUS
THROTTLE GUN CHOKE STIFLE
GARROTE STRANGLE THROPPLE
THROUGH BY PER DONE THRU WITH
ROUND AROUND
(RIGHT —) TILL
THROUGHOUT ABOUT ABROAD
BEDENE BIDENE DURING ENTIRE
PASSIM SEMPRE OVERALL THRUOUT
THROW GO DAB HIP HIT PAT PEG
PUT SHY ACES BIFF BUCK BUNG

CALE CAST CHIP COOK CUCK DART
DASH DROW HAIL HANK HIPE HULL
HURL HYPE JERK LACE MILL PECK
PICK SEND SKIM SLAT SOSS TOSS
TURF VANG WARP WURP YEND
CHUCK CHUNK DOUSE FLICK FLING
FLIRT FLURR HEAVE PITCH SLING
SPANG DEVEST ELANCE HAUNCH
HURTLE INJECT LAUNCH SLIGHT
THRILL BLUNDER BUTTOCK
COCKSHY MANGANA UPTHROW
VIBRATE CATAPULT JACULATE
(— ABOUT) BOUNCE
(— ASIDE) DEVEST
(— AWAY) DICE DOFF BANDY WAIVE
PROJECT JETTISON SQUANDER
(— BASEBALL) BURN
(— BY KICKING) WINCE
(— CARELESSLY) COB
(— DICE) JEFF
(— DOWN) EVEN PILE LODGE
DETURB THRING FLATTEN
(— FORTH) EJECT
(— FORWARD) LAUNCH
(— HEAVILY) LOB
(— HEEDLESSLY) SLIGHT
(— IN CRAPS) CRAP CRABS
BOXCARS
(— INTO CONFUSION) CLUB
FLUTTER CONFOUND CONVULSE
(— INTO DISORDER) ADDLE BOLLIX
DERANGE DISRANK DISRUPT
EMBROIL DISARRAY
(— INTO PERPLEXITY) FLUMMOX
(— INTO WASTE) BACK
(— JERKILY) FLIRT
(— LIGHT UPON) ILLUME
(— LIQUID) JAW
(— OF A STEER) DOGFALL
(— OF SHUTTLE) SHOT SHOOT
SHUTE
(— OF THREES) COCKEYES
(— OFF COURSE) EMIT SHED
DERAIL
(— OFF) CANT CAST SPILL SLOUGH
CONFUSE UNBURDEN
(— ONESELF) CLAP
(— OPEN) DISPARK
(— OUT) FIRE HOOF LADE BELCH
EJECT ERUPT SPOUT DETURB
IGNORE EXTRUDE
(— QUICKLY) LASH
(— SIDEWISE) SHY
(— SILK) THROWST
(— SMARTLY) SLAT
(— STEER) BUST
(— STICKS) SQUAIL
(— STONES) ROCK
(— TOGETHER) HUDDLE
(— UNDER) SUBJECT
(— UP) CAVE PICK VOMIT
(— VIOLENTLY) BUZZ DING PASH
SOCK SMASH HURTLE WHITHER
SPANGHEW
(— WITH A JERK) JET CANT SQUIRR
FLOUNCE
(— WITH GREAT FORCE) BUZZ
SWACK
(— WITHOUT VIOLENCE) HURL

(CHEATING — OF DICE) KNAP
(FREE —) FOUL
(LARIAT —) HOOLIAN
(LOWEST — AT DICE) AMBSACE
AMESACE
(WRESTLING —) HANK HIPE HYPE
BUTTOCK BACKHEEL
THROWAWAY DODGER
THROWBACK ATAVISM
THROWER TRAMMER THROWSTER
(SPEAR —) ATLATL
THROWING DARTING
THROWING-STICK ATLATL
WOMMERA WOOMERA HORNERAH
TROMBASH TRUMBASH
THROWN (— AWAY) CASTAWAY
(— DOWN) DEJECTED
THROWSTER TWISTER
THRUM FUM STRUM THUMB
THRUSH POP OMAO SOOR APTHA
BREVE FRUSH GRIVE MAVIS OUZEL
PITTA SABIA SHAMA SHIRL SPREW
UZZLE VEERY APHTHA DRAINE
JAYPIE KICKUP MISSEL OLOMAO
PULISH SHRITE JAYPIET REDWING
WAGTAIL BELLBIRD CHERCOCK
FORKTAIL PRUNELLA SHAGBARK
THRASHER THROSTLE THRUSHEL
THRUSTLE URTICATE WOODCHAT
THRUSHLIKE TURDOID
THRUST DAB DEG DIG DUB JAB JAG
JAM JOB POP PUG BANG BEAR BIRR
BOKE BORE BUCK BUTT CANT CHOP
CRAM DART DASH DUSH FOIN HURL
KICK LICK MURE PASS PICK PILT
POKE PORR POSS POTE PROD PUSH
SEND SINK SPAR STAB STOP TILT
VENY WHAP WHOP BREAK DRIFT
DRIVE EXERT HUNCH LUNGE POACH
POINT PROKE PUNCH SHOOT SPANK
STAVE STICK STOKE STUFF THROW
DARTLE PLUNGE POUNCE STITCH
STRAIN STRESS STRIKE STRIPE
BEARING IMPULSE SHOULDER
STOCCADO
(— A LANCE) AVENTRE
(— ASIDE) DAFF SHUFFLE
(— AWAY) DOFF SHOVE DETRUDE
ABSTRUDE
(— DOWN) THRING DEPULSE
DETRUDE
(— IN) INSERT STRIKE INTRUDE
(— OF ARCH) DRIFT
(— OF EXPLOSION) BLOWOUT
(— ONESELF) CHISEL
(— OUT) REACH STRUT EXSERT
DETRUDE EXTRUDE OBTRUDE
PROTRUDE
(— SUDDENLY) STRIKE
(— THROUGH) ENFILED
(— WITH ELBOW) HUNCH
(— WITH GREAT FORCE) BUZZ
(— WITH NOSE) NUDDLE
(— WITH WEAPON) FOIN SHOVE
(DAGGER —) DAG
(FENCING —) PASS VENY VENUE
REPOST TIMING PASSADO RIPOSTE
STOCCADO STOCCATA
(HOME —) HAI HAY

(MATADOR'S —) ESTOCADA
(SARCASTIC —) GIRD
THUD BAFF DUMP PHUT PLOD SWAG
DOYST FLUMP POUND SQUELCH
THUG GOON GOONDA RODMAN
GORILLA HOODLUM GANGSTER
THUJA BIOTA
THUJONE SALVIOL
THULUTH SOOLOOS
THUMB POLLEX THENAR THROOM
(BALL OF —) THENAR
THUMBSTALL POUCER POUSER
THUMP COB DAD DUB BANG BEAT
DING DIRD DRUB DUNT KNUB LUMP
PAKE POLT SOSS THUD TUNK YARK
YERK BLAFF BLIBE BUNCH CLOUR
CLUNK CRUMP KNOCK POUND
TABOR THACK WHELK BOUNCE
HAMMER PUMMEL THUNGE
THUMPING WHAPPING WHOPPING
THUNDER SULFUR FOULDRE
SULPHUR INTONATE
THUNDERBOLT BOLT FIRE VAJRA
FULMEN FOULDRE ARTIFACT
FIREBOLT
THUNDERSQUALL BAYAMO
VENDAVAL
THUNDERSTONE ARTIFACT
THUNDERSTORM HOUVARI
TEMPEST TORNADO
THURIBLE CENSER
THUS AS SIC DYCE THUSLY
THISWISE THUSGATE
THWACK DUNT CRUMP SOUSE
THWART BALK WART BENCH CROOK
CROSS SPITE THROW ZYGON
BAFFLE SCOTCH STYMIE SNOOKER
CONTRAIR CONTRARY TRAVERSE
THWARTING CROSS CROSSING
THYESTES (BROTHER OF —)
ATREUS
(FATHER OF —) PELOPS
(MOTHER OF —) HIPPODAMIA
THYLACINE YABBI
THYINE THUGA THUYA
THYME MARUM PELETRE HILLWORT
SERPOLET
TI KI TOI TITI
TIARA MITER CIDARIS TIARELLA
TIBBU DAZA TEDA

TIBET
CAPITAL: LASSA LHASA
COIN: TANGA
LAKE: ARU BAM BUM NAM MEMA
TOSU JAGOK TABIA DAGTSE
GARHUR KASHUN SELING
TANGRA YAMDOK KYARING
TERIMAN TSARING ZILLING
JIGGITAI
LANGUAGE: BODSKAD
MOUNTAIN: KAMET SAJUM KAILAS
BANDALA
MOUNTAIN RANGE: KAILAS
KUNLUN HIMALAYA
NATIVE: BHOTIA BHOTIYA
RIVER: NAK NAU SAK SONG INDUS
SUTLEJ MATSANG SALWEEN

TOWN: NOH KARAK LHASA
GARTOK TOTLING GYANGTSE
SHIGATSE

TIBETAN BALTI DRUPA BHOTIA
BHUTIA CHAMPA DROKPA KHAMBA
KHAMBU PANAKA SHERPA TANGUT
BHOTIYA BHUTANI GYARUNG
TIBIA SHIN SHANK CNEMIS SHINBONE
TIBOURBOU CORTEZ
TIC FIXATION
(ONE SUBJECT TO —) TIQUEUR
TICK FAG JAR KEB BEAT KADE NICK
PEAK PICK PIKE CHALK CHICK
CRIKE PIQUE STRAP IXODID PALLET
TALAJE TAMPAN ACARIAN ARGASID
BEDTICK IXODIAN PINOLIA
ARACHNID CARAPATO GARAPATA
GARAPATO TURICATA
TICKED MACKEREL
TICKET LOT TAG BLANK CHECK
DUCAT FICHE TOKEN BALLOT
BILLET COUPON DOCKET PIGEON
POLICY RETURN BENEFIT ETIQUET
CONTRACT DEADHEAD STOPOVER
TRANSFER
(COMMISSION —) SPIFF
(FREE —) PASS
(LOTTERY —) BLANK HORSE
BENEFIT
(SALES —) TRAVELER
(SEASON —) IVORY
(PL.) PAPER
TICKET WINDOW GUICHET
TICKING KISS TICK BEDTICK
TICKLE AMUSE TEASE EXCITE KITTLE
PLEASE THRILL TIDDLE CUITTLE
TICKLISH GOOSEY KITTLE KITTLY
QUEASY TENDER TOUCHY TRICKY
KITTLISH
TICKSEED COREOPSIS
TICK TREFOIL BEDSTRAW SAINFOIN
TICKSEED
TIDBIT SAYNETE BEATILLE
KICKSHAW
TIDDLEYWINK SQUAIL
TIDE FLOW NEAP WAVE AGGER
ROUST SPRING OVERTIDE
SEAFLOOD
(— MOVEMENT) LAKIE
TIDINGS NEWS WORD RUMOR
SOUND UNCOW ADVICE MESSAGE
(GLAD —) GOSPEL
TIDY RID COSH MACK NEAT SIDE
SMUG SNOD SNUG TAUT TOSH TRIG
WEME CHART DONCY DONSY
DOUCE NATTY QUEME TIGHT
DONSIE FETTLE POLITE SPOONY
ALLIGATE MACKLIKE MENSEFUL
TIE BOW LAP TYE BAND BIND BOND
CAST DRAW KILT KNOT LACE LOCK
ROOT WISP YOKE ASCOT BRACE
CADGE LEASH NEXUS POINT THRAP
THROW TRUSS ATTACH BUNDLE
CONNEX COUPLE FASTEN LIGATE
SECURE DOGFALL FOULARD
JAZZBOW NECKTIE SHACKLE
SLEEPER SPANCEL TABLEAU

CROSSTIE INTERTIE LIGATURE
STANDOFF STRINGER VINCULUM
(— BENEATH) SUBNECT
(— IN TENNIS) DEUCE
(— IN WRESTLING) DOGFALL
(— KNOT) CAST
(— LEGS) HOBBLE
(— ONIONS) TRACE
(— SCORE) PEELS
(— THE SCORE) EQUALIZE
(— TOGETHER) KNIT LEASH
HARNESS
(— UP SHORT) SNUB
(— UP) SNUB TRAMMEL LIGATURE
TWITCHEL
(LEATHER —) WANTY
(MADE-UP —) TECK
(NEEDLEWORK —) BRIDE
(PL.) GILLIES
TIED FAST KNIT SQUARE
TIEPIN SCARFPIN STICKPIN
TIE PLATE TURTLE
TIER ROW BANK DECK RANK CHESS
STORY WITHE DEGREE PINAFORE
(— OF CASKS) RIDER
(— OF SEATS) CIRCLE
(— OF SHELVES) STAGE
TIERCE LEASH THIRD
TIFF MIFF TIFT
TIFFIN CONDOR
TIGER SHER SHIR TIGRE TIGERKIN
TIGER CAT CHATI
TIGERFOOT IPOMOEA
TIGER SNAKE ELAPID ELAPOID
TIGHT WET FULL HARD SNUG TAUT
TIDY CLOSE DENSE DRUNK STENT
TENSE STINGY STRAIT STRICT
AIRTIGHT
TIGHTEN JAM CALK FIRM FRAP
CAULK CINCH CLOSE FEEZE SCREW
THRAP WRENCH STRAITEN
TIGHTFISTED STINGY
TIGHT-LIPPED SILENT
TIGHTLY FAST HARD SHORT STRAIT
CLOSELY
TIGHTS MAILLOT LEOTARDS
TIGHTWAD FIST PIKER STIFF
TILDE TIL WAVE TITTLE
(HAVING A —) CURLY
TILE LUMP FAVUS KASHI LATER
SLATE IMBREX LAPPET PAMENT
QUARRY SLATER TEGULA AZULEJO
CARREAU CONDUIT PANTILE
QUARREL STARTER MAINTILE
(— USED IN MOSAIC) ABACULUS
(HEXAGONAL —) FAVUS
(HOLLOW —) BACKING
(LARGE —) DALLE QUARL QUARLE
(MAH JONG —) HONOR SEASON
(ONE-HALF —) HEAD
(PERSIAN —) KASHI
(ROUNDED —) CREASE
(SMALL —) TILETTE
(SQUARE —) QUADREL QUARREL
TILER HELER HELLIER
TILL TO EAR FIT LOB CASH FARM
PLOW TEAL TOIL DRESS LABOR
UNTIL WHILE FURROW MANURE
PLOUGH TILLER WHILST HUSBAND

HUTTLE DUCKFOOT OXHARROW
LABLE EARABLE
LAGE ARABLE GAINOR MANURE
RATION CULTURE TILTURE
LED GEOM TOILED
LER HELM STERN STOOL
USBAND KILLIFER
LING EARTH FALLOW
T DIP TIP TOP BANK CANT CAVE
OCK HEEL LIST SWAG TRAP
RASH HEELD HIELD JOUST STOOP
PUP CASTER TILTER TOPPLE
URRENT TOURNEY COCKBILL
UINTAIN
- BRICK) HACK
- IN WATER) DABBLE
- OF BOWSPRIT) STAVE
- OF NOSE) KIP KIPP
TED ACOCK ASTOOP
T HAMMER OLIVER
TING DIP JOUSTING
BAL DRUM TYMBALON
BER CAP LOG RIB BEAM BIBB
UNK CLOG DRAM FELL FISH FROG
PRT PUMP RAFF SKID SPAR SPUR
REE WOOD CAHUY CAVEL CRUCK
LOOR GRIPE JOIST KEVEL LEDGE
RGUE PLATE RIDER SISSU SPALE
TICK BEARER BRIDGE BUMPER
AMBER CORBEL DAGGER FENDER
OREST KNIGHT LIZARD ROOFER
SSOO SUMMER TIMMER BOLSTER
ARLING DEADMAN DIVIDER
ALLAGE FUTCHEL FUTTOCK
ROUSER PARTNER PITWOOD
BBAND TRANSOM CORDWOOD
OULISSE DOGSHORE FOREHOOK
TRINGER STUMPAGE TRIPSILL
OODFALL
- BETWEEN TRIMMERS) HEADER
- CUT TO LENGTH) JUGGLE
- IN MINE) COG STULL LIFTER
VIDER JUGGLER
- KEPT DRY) BRIGHT
- ON SLED) BUNK
- PIECE) PUTLOG
- SAWED AND SPLIT) LUMBER
- SUPPORTING CAP) LEGPIECE
- SUSTAINING YARDS) MAST
- TO PROP COAL) BROB
CONVEX —) CAMBER
CURVED —) CRUCK
CUT —) FELL
ELLED —) HAG
LOOR —) JOIST SUMMER
LOORING —) BATTEN
RAMING —) PUNCHEON
HORIZONTAL —) REASON
NORWEGIAN —) DRAM
PHILIPPINE —) LAUAN
RINCIPAL — OF VESSEL) KEEL
ROOF —) LEVER RAFTER
ROOFING —S) SILE
HIP'S —) KEEL KNEE RUNG SPUR
EDGE WRONG DAGGER HARPIN
ACING SCROLL BRACKET FUTTOCK
TEMSON DOGSHORE STANDARD
HIPBUILDING —S) STOCKS
EADWOOD HARPINGS

(SLABBED —) CANT
(SUPPORT —) SILL GIRDER LEDGER
STRINGER
(SYSTEM OF —S) BOND
(UNCUT —) STUMPAGE
(WEATHERBEATEN —) DRIKI
TIMBERLAND STICKS WOODLAND
TIMBERMAN BRACER
TIMBO CUBE AJARI
TIMBRE CLANG COLOR KLANG
COLORING
TIMBREL TABOR TABOUR
TIME DAY ELD BELL BOUT HINT
HOUR SELE TIDE WHET ABYSS
CHARE EPOCH FLASH FRIST KALPA
SITHE SPACE STOUN STOUR TEMPO
TEMPS VOLTA WHACK WHILE
COURSE KAIROS PERIOD SEASON
STOUND TEMPUS CADENCE
DEWFALL SESSION MOVEMENT
(— AFTER) POST
(— ALLOWED FOR PAYMENT)
USANCE
(— FOR PAYING) KIST
(— FOR PAYMENT) CREDIT
(— GRANTED) FRIST
(— IN SERVICE) AGE
(— INTERVENING) INTERIM
MEANTIME
(— LONG SINCE PAST) YORE
(— OF BEAUTY) BLOOM
(— OF CRISIS) EXIGENT
(— OF DYING) LAST
(— OF EXPIRY) ISH
(— OF EXUBERANCE) CARNIVAL
(— OF FEASTING) GUTTIDE
(— OF HIGHEST STRENGTH)
HEYDAY
(— OF LIGHT) DAY
(— OF MATURITY OR DECLINE)
AUTUMN
(— OF NEWS STORY) BREAK
(— OF OLD AGE) SUNSET
(— OF QUIET) DEAD
(— OF REST) BREATH SABBATH
(— OF WOE) WOSITH
(— TO COME) FUTURITY
(ANOTHER —) AGAIN
(AT ANOTHER —) ALIAS
(BRIEF —) TINE FLASH THROW
(BY THE —) AGAINST
(EACH —) ONCE
(EXTENDED —) TRAIN
(FIXED —) HOUR STEVEN
(GAY —) FRISK WHOOPEE
(GOOD —) BALL BASH BEANO
JOLLY BARNEY FROLIC HOLIDAY
(HARD —) GYP BUSINESS
(IMMEASURABLY LONG PERIOD OF
—) EON AEON
(INFINITE —) ABYSS
(LONG —) AGE
(OLD —S) ELD
(PAST —) FORETIME
(POINT OF —) MOMENT
(RIGHT —) TID
(SECOND —) YET EFTSOON
EFTSOONS
(SET —) TRYST

(SHORT —) TIFF SPACE START
MINUTE STOUND
(SPARE —) TOOM
(TRIPLE —) TRIPLA
(UNENGAGED —) LEISURE
(WORKING —) CORE
(PL.) SYSE
TIME CLOCK BUNDY TELLTALE
TIMELESS AGELESS ETERNAL
DATELESS
TIMELESSNESS ETERNITY
TIMELY PAT DULY TIDY COGENT
TIMEFUL TIMEOUS TOWARDLY
TIMEPIECE DIAL CLOCK TIMER
VERGE WATCH GHURRY PENDULE
HOROLOGE HOROLOGY
TIMETABLE SCHEDULE
TIMID SHY ARGH EERY NESH SELY
SHAN BAUCH BLATE EERIE FAINT
PAVID SCARE SCARY AFRAID
COWARD ASHAMED BASHFUL
FEARFUL FRIGHTY NERVOUS
RABBITY SCADDLE STRANGE
TREMBLY COWARDLY FEARSOME
GHASTFUL RETIRING TIMOROSO
TIMOROUS
TIMIDITY SHYNESS TIMERITY
FUNKINESS
TIMIDLY SMALL
TIMOR (CAPITAL OF —) DILI
(COIN OF —) AVO PATACA
(ISLAND OF —) MOA LETI LAKOR
(LANGUAGE OF —) TETUM
(TOWN IN —) KUPANG ATAMBUA
TIMOROUS FAINT MILKY TIMID
AFRAID COWISH TREPID FEARFUL
FERDFUL FEARSOME SHEEPISH
TEMEROUS TIMOROSO
TIN SN DIXY JOVE DIXIE KATIN
SWELL TINNY KHATIN JUPITER
PILLION STANNUM PRILLION
TINGLASS
(MESS —) DIXY DIXIE
(ROOFING —) TERNE
(SHEET —) LATTEN LATTIN
(TIE — CAN TO TAIL) TAILPIPE
TINAMOU YUTU MACUCA YNAMBU
TATAUPA MARTINET
TINCAL ALTINCAR
TINCTURE BUFO DRUG COLOR
IMBUE SMACK STAIN TAINT TENNE
TINCT ARGENT ARNICA ELIXIR
DIAMOND ARAMAIZE INFUSION
LAUDANUM TAINTURE
TINDER SPUNK AMADOU TENDRE
FIREBOX
TINE KNAG SNAG TANG GRAIN
OFFER POINT PRONG RIGHT TOOTH
GRAINING TINEWARE TINEWEED
(ANTLER'S —) RIGHT CROCKET
SURROYAL
TIN FOIL TAIN
TINGE DYE EYE HUE CAST DASH
TINT WOAD COLOR FLUSH IMBUE
PAINT SAVOR SHADE STAIN TAINT
TINCT SEASON SMUTCH BEPAINT
DISTAIN GLIMPSE DISCOLOR
TINCTION TINCTURE
TINGED FLORID GILDED

TINGGIAN ITNEG ITANEG
TINGLE SOO BURN DIRL GELL GIRL
THIRL DINDLE SWIDGE TINKLE
PRINGLE PRINKLE TRINKLE
TINKER PRIG TINK CAIRD FIDDLE
FIDGET MUGGER KETTLER PROJECT
TRAVELER
TINKLE TINK DINDLE DINGLE TINGLE
TRINKLE TWINKLE
TINNER TINKER
TINSEL GAUDY TINSY TINNET
TINT DYE EYE COLOR ENNUE GRAIN
TINCT TINGE SPRAING
(— IN HORSE'S COAT) BLOSSOM
(— WITH COSMETICS) SURFLE
(CLANG —) TIMBRE
TINTED TINCT
TINWORKS STANNARY
TINY TINE BITSY BITTY DEENY SMALL
TEENY TIDDY WEENY ATOMIC BITTIE
WEESHY MINIKIN ATOMICAL
TIP CAP DIP END FEE NEB TOP APEX
CANT CAVE COCK HEEL HELD HORN
KEEL LEAD LIST PALM PIKE PILE
SWAG TILT TYPE VAIL GRIFF HEELD
MUCRO POINT POUCH SPIRE SPURE
STEER CAREEN CENTER CENTRE
TICKLE TIPLET TIPPLE TOPPLE
WHEEZE APICULA CUMSHAW
DERTRUM DOUCEUR GRIFFIN
POINTER WRINKLE APICULUS
BONAMANO ENTOMION FOOTHOLD
GRATUITY
(— OF ANTENNA) ARISTA
(— OF BILLIARD CUE) LEATHER
(— OF BIRD'S BILL) DERTRUM
(— OF FOX'S BRUSH) CHAPE
(— OF SKI) SHOVEL
(— OF SPIDER) BULB
(— OF STAMP) SHOE
(— OF TOE) POINTE
(— OF TONGUE) CORONA
(— OF UMBO) BEAK
(— OF WHEAT KERNEL) BRUSH
(— OF WHIP) SNAPPER
(— ON ORGAN PIPE) TOE
(— OVER) TOP PURL
(— UP) CANT
(ABRUPT —) MUCRO
(BOW —) HORN
(INWARD —) BANK
(LARGE —S) LARGESS LARGESSE
TIPCART COUPE COCOPAN
TIPCAT CAT PIGGY PUSSY KITCAT
PIGGIE
TIPPED BANKED
(EASILY —) CRANK
TIPPER DUMPER THROWER TIPPLER
TIPPET FUR AMICE SCARF ALMUCE
SINDON LIRIPIPE LIRIPOOP
TIPPLE BIB NIP POT SOT DRAM GILL
BIBBER BIBBLE FUDDLE PUDDLE
SIPPLE TIPPLER TOOTHFUL
TIPPLER SOUSE TOAST WINER
BIBBER BOLLER BUBBER DRAMMER
PANURGE POTATOR TUMBLER
WHETTER ALESTAKE MALTWORM
TIPPLING POTTING BIBACITY
BIBATION

TIPSY CUT BOSKY DRUNK FRESH
MUSED TIGHT TOZIE BUMPSY
GROGGY SLEWED SPRUNG EBRIOSE
EBRIOUS EXALTED ELEVATED
MUCKIBUS OVERSEEN PLEASANT
TIP-TOP SWELL TIPPY TOPPING
TIRADE SCREED STOUSH JEREMIAD
TIRE DO FAG HAG LAG BORE CORD
FLAT FLOG JADE KILL MOIL SHOE
LABOR SPARE WEARY CASING
HAGGLE HARASS SICKEN TIRING
TUCKER BALLOON EXHAUST
FATIGUE FRAZZLE TRACHLE
CLINCHER FORSPEND
(— OUT) HAG FLOG THEAD BEJADE
HARASS
(WORN —) CARCASS
TIRED SAD TAM BEAT BOEG DEAD
TIRY BLOWN WEARY AWEARY
BLEARY BUSHED PLAYED TAVERT
FORWORN TAIVERT FATIGATE
FORWAKED
TIREDNESS FATIGUE
TIRESOME DRY DREE FAGGY
ALANGE BORING DREICH PROLIX
IRKSOME PROSAIC TEDIOUS
BORESOME BROMIDIC ENNUYANT
LONGSOME
TIRING DRUDGING
TIRL RISP
TIRTHANKARA JINA
TISAMENUS (FATHER OF —)
ORESTES THERSANDER
(MOTHER OF —) HERMIONE
TISANE PTISAN TILLEUL
TISSUE FAT WEB CORK FOIL PITH
TELA TEXT FACIA GLEBA GRAFT
SUBER TRAMA CALLUS DARTOS
DIPLOE FABRIC FASCIA LIGNUM
PANNUS PHLOEM SHEATH TEXTUS
ADENOID ALBUMEN BINDWEB
CAMBIUM CLYPEUS EPITELA
EXPLANT HYDROME KLEENEX
MESTOME NEURINE PHLOEUM
TEXTURE TWITTER ADHESION
BLASTEMA DESMOGEN ECTODERM
ENDODERM EPIPLOON HISTOGEN
HYPODERM ISOGRAFT MERISTEM
OSTEOGEN PERIDERM PERIDESM
STEREOME
(— OF FUNGUS) CENTRUM
(— SURROUNDING TEETH) GUM
(BLACK —) CLYPEUS
(CONNECTING —) STROMA TENDON
LIGAMENT
(CORK —) SUBER
(FATTY —) LARD GREASE
(HARD —) BONE
(HYPOTHETICAL —) COAGULIN
(LYMPHOID —) TONSIL
(NERVE —) GANGLION
(SOFT —) FLAB
(VEGETABLE —) ARMOR
(WOOD —) LIGNUM VITRAIN
(PL.) CHIRATA CHIRETTA MESODERM
TISWIN TESVINO TEXGUINO
TIT TID MESIA TITTY BLUECAP
COLETIT MUFFLIN
TITAN BANA LETO MAIA ASURA

ATLAS COEUS CREUS CRIOS DION
THEIA CRONOS CRONUS PALLAS
PHOEBE TETHYS THEMIS IAPETUS
OCEANUS HYPERION
TITANIC HUGE GREAT TITAN
IMMENSE COLOSSAL GIGANTIC
TITANITE SPHENE GROTHITE
LEDERITE LIGURITE
TITANIUM DIOXIDE ANATASE
TITA ROOT MISHMI MISHMEE
TITHE DIME TEIND TENTH DECIMA
PREBEND TITHING
TITHING BORGH BORROW DECIME
DENARY DECENARY
TITHINGMAN DEAN DECURION
TUTTIMAN
TITHONUS (FATHER OF —)
LAOMEDON
(MOTHER OF —) STRYMO
TITI ORA TEETEE WISTIT SAIMIRI
WISTITI IRONWOOD MARMOSET
ORABASSU OUISTITI
TITILLATE KITTLE TICKLE
TITILLATING GAMY GAMEY
TITLARK PIPIT TEETING
TITLE AGA AYA BAN BEG BEY DAN
DOM DUE FRA JAM LAR MIR PAN
SAG SIR ABBA ABBE AGHA AMIR
ANBA DAME DEVI EMIR FRAY GAC
GRAF HAJI HERR KHAN KNEZ LAR
NAME PANI SIDI SLUG ABGAR
ABUNA AMEER CCOYA CLAIM
CROWN EMEER FRATE GHAZI
GOODY GRACE HADJI HAJJI HAKA
HANUM HONOR KNIAZ KNYAZ MIR
MPRET NAWAB NEGUS NIZAM
PANNA RABBI RIGHT SINGH SOPHI
SOPHY UNWAN BASHAW BEGANI
COUSIN DEGREE DEMAND DESPOT
DOMINE EXARCH HANDLE HUZOOR
LEGEND MADAME MASTER MEHTA
MISTER PESHWA PREFIX SHERIF
SQUIRE SUFFEE TITULE VIDAME
ALFEREZ ALTESSE ALTEZZA
BAHADUR CANDACE CAPTION
CONVITO CRAWLER DIGNITY
EFFENDI EPITHET ESQUIRE FIDALC
GAEKWAR GRAVITY HEADING
HIDALGO INFANTE KHEDIVE
MAHARAO MESSIRE RABBONI
SHAREEF TITULUS VOIVODE
BANNERET BASILEUS COMMENDA
CONVIVIO EMINENCE GOSPODIN
HIGHNESS HOLINESS HOSPODAR
INTEREST LOKINDRA MAGISTER
MAHARAJA MAHARANA MAHARSHI
MISTRESS MONSIEUR PADISHAH
PRINCIPE RAUGRAVE SUBTITLE
TAMBURAN TITULADO
(— ACQUISITION) USUCAPT
(— OF BOOK) QUARE
(— OF MEMBER OF PRIMROSE
LEAGUE) KNIGHT
(— OF RESPECT) SIR SRI COJA LI
MIAN SHRI SIDI BURRA HODJA
KHAJA KHOJA MADAM SAHIB
KHOJAH MADAME MILADY
(BENEDICTINE —) DOM
(MOCK —) IDLESHIP

TMOUSE MAG NUN TIT MAGG
OXEYE PARUS SPICK FUFFIT HEFFEL
PUFFER TOMTIT VERDIN BLUECAP
BUSHTIT COLETIT COLMOSE
GOLDTIT GRIGNET HAGMALL
JACKSAW MUFFLIN PINCHEM
PINNOCK TINNOCK TITMALL
TOMNOUP CHICADEE HACKMALL
OVENBIRD REEDLING SHABROON
SHARPSAW
TTER GIGGLE SNICKER TWITTER
TTLE JOT TITLE MINUTE
TULAR LEGAL HONORARY
TYUS (FATHER OF —) TERRA
JUPITER
(MOTHER OF —) ELARA
U ER EAR TIW TYR ZIO ZIU TIWAZ
SAXNOT
V MUNCHI
ZZY PUCKER SWIVET SWIVVET
AKLIUT ECHE LOOT WISHRAM
EPOLEMUS (FATHER OF —)
HERCULES
(MOTHER OF —) ASTYOCHIA
(SLAYER OF —) SARPEDON
INGIT SITKA KOLUSH SUMDUM
CHILCAT CHILKAT STIKINE
MESIS DIACOPE
NT TROTYL
O A AD FOR INTO TILL UNTO UPON
(— A CONCLUSION) OUT
(— BE SURE) EVEN
(— BE) IBE
(— COME) BEHIND
(— COMPLETION) DOWN
(— IT) TOOT SESSA
(— PRESS) DOWN
(— SUCH DEGREE) EVEN
(— THAT TIME) UNTIL
(— THE END) AF
(— THE OPPOSITE SIDE) ACROSS
(— THE REAR) ABAFT ASTERN
(— THIS PLACE) HERE HITHER
(— THIS) HERETO
(— VICTORY) ABU ABOO
(— WHAT) WHERETO
(— WIT) NAMELY INNUENDO
SCILICET
OAD PAD AGUA BUFO FROG HYLA
PIPA PODE HYLID PADDO PADDY
PIPAL PIPID TOADY ANURAN
CRAPON PEEPER BUFONID CHARLIE
CRAPAUD CRAWLER CREEPER
FROGLET GANGREL HOPTOAD
PADDOCK PODDOCK PUDDOCK
QUILKIN REPTILE SERPENT
GANGEREL
OADFISH SAPO SARPO GRUBBY
SLIMER CABEZON FROGFISH
LORICATE SCORPION
OADFLAX FLAX FLAXWEED
FLAXWORT FLUELLEN GALLWEED
GALLWORT RAMSTEAD
OAD RUSH SALTWEED
OADSTOOL CANKER FUNGUS
OADY FAWN SUCK TOAD ZANY
COTTON EARWIG FAWNER FLUNKY
GREASE LACKEY FLUNKEY LACQUEY
PLACEBO SHONEEN TRUCKLE

BOOTLICK LICKSPIT PARASITE
TOADYING GNATHONIC
TOADYISM FLUNKISM
TOAST WET TOSS BREDE ROUSE
SKOAL TRINQ BIRSLE BUMPER
CHEERS HEALTH PLEDGE PROSIT
BRISTLE CAROUSE CHEERIO
FRIZZLE LEHAYIM PROFACE
PROPINE RESPECT SLAINTE
WASSAIL BRINDISI
(— AND ALE) SWIG
(— ONESELF) LEEP
(JACOBITE —) LIMP
TOBACCO CANE CAPA HAND LEAF
LUGS NAVY POAK POKE QUID ROLL
SHAG WEED BACCO BACCY BACKY
BROKE CUBAN DARKS FOGUS
PETUN REGIE SMOKE SNOUT TABAC
TWIST BACKER BRIGHT BURLEY
COLORY COWPEN FILLER HAVANA
RETURN TOMBAC TUMBAK CAPORAL
CRACCUS GAGROOT GORACCO
KNASTER LATAKIA NAILROD NICOTIA
ORONOKO PERIQUE PIGTAIL
SOTWEED UPPOWOC CANASTER
HONEYDEW MAKHORKA MARYLAND
NICOTIAN ORONOOKO SEEDLEAF
VIRGINIA
(— AND PAPER) MAKINGS
(— CAKED IN PIPE BOWL) DOTTEL
DOTTLE TOPPER
(— HAVING OFFENSIVE SMELL)
MUNDUNGO
(— IN ROPES) BOGIE
(— JUICE) AMBEER PRAISS
(— MOISTENED WITH MOLASSES)
HONEYDEW
(— MOSAIC) WALLOON
(— PASTE) GORACCO
(— ROOM) PRIZERY
(— WORKER) LOOPER LEAFBOY
LEAFGIRL
(CAKED —) HEEL
(COARSE —) SHAG SCRAP CAPORAL
(CUT —) PICADURA
(DRIED —) TABACUM
(HARD-PRESSED —) NAILROD
(INDIAN —) GAGROOT PUKEWEED
EYEBRIGHT
(INFERIOR —) LUGS
(LADIES' —) CUDWEED
(LOWER LEAVES OF —) FLYING
(PERSIAN —) SHIRAZ TUMBEK
TUMBEKI
(PERUVIAN —) SANA
(POOR QUALITY —) DOGLEG
(PULVERIZED —) SNUFF
(QUID OF —) CUD
(RAW —) LEAF
(ROLLED —) CARROT
(SMALL PIECE OF —) FIG
(VIRGINIA —) COWPEN VIRGINIA
TOBACCO WORM HORNWORM
TOBOGGAN CARIOLE CARRIOLE
TOCHARIAN A AGNEAN
TOCHARIAN B KUCHEAN
TODAY DAY NOW NOWADAYS
TODDLE TOT FADGE DADDLE DIDDLE
DODDLE PADDLE TOTTLE WADDLE

TODDLER TROT GANGREL TROTTIE
TODDY TOD TUBA TERRY SAGWIRE
TO-DO ADO FUSS STIR WORK STINK
DOMENT HOOPLA FLUSTER
FOOSTER FOOFARAW TRAVALLY
TODY ROBIN
TOE TER DIGIT DACTYL HALLUX
MINIMUS TOENAIL POULAINE
(— OF BIRD) HEEL
(LITTLE —) MINIMUS
(PL.) TUN TAIS TOON
TOEPLATE SHOD
TOFF NOB
TOGA GOWN ROBE TOGUE TRABEA
TOGETHER ONCE SAME YFERE
BEDENE INSAME JOINTLY ENSEMBLE
(— WITH) AND INTO
TOGGLE COTTAR COTTER TOGGEL
NETSUKE
TOGO (CAPITAL OF —) LOME
(LANGUAGE OF —) EWE TWI MINA
HAUSA KABRAIS LOTOCOLI
(NATIVE OF —) EWE MINA CABRAI
KABRAI OUATCHI
(RIVER IN —) OTI ANIE HAHO MONO
(TOWN IN —) ANECHO PALIME
SOKODE ATAKPAME
TOIL FAG TUG DARG GRUB HACK
MOIL MUCK PLOD TASK WORK
LABOR SCRAT SLAVE SWINK TWEIL
BILDER DRUDGE EFFORT HAMMER
MITHER MOIDER STRIVE UNRUFE
FATIGUE TRAVAIL TURMOIL
DRUDGERY INDUSTRY
TOILER SLAVE MOILER WORKER
TOILET CAN LOO HEAD JOHN BIFFY
CRAPPER BASEMENT BATHROOM
LAVATORY PLUMBING
TOILSOME HARD SWEATY ARDUOUS
TOILFUL MOILSOME SWEATFUL
TOJOLABAL CHANABAL
TOKAY TUCKTOO
TOKEN BUCK CENT HARP SIGN TYPE
BADGE CHECK INDEX SCRIP BEAVER
CASTOR COLLAR COPPER COUPON
DOLLAR EMBLEM JETTON MARKER
OSTENT REMARK SIGNAL TICKET
WITTER AUSPICE COUNTER
EARNEST INDICIA MEMENTO
PRESAGE SYMPTOM TESSERA
BUNGTOWN COINTISE EVIDENCE
FOOTSTEP FORBYSEN INSTANCE
KEEPSAKE MONUMENT SHILLING
SIGNACLE
(— OF LUCK) HANSEL HANDSEL
(— OF RESPECT) SALUTE
(— OF SUPERIORITY) PALM
(— OF VICTORY) LAUREL
(CANADIAN —) HARP
(LOVE —) DRURY AMORET
(PORCELAIN —S) PI
TOKHARI KUCHEAN
TOLERABLE GAY SOSO PRETTY
TARBLE PATIBLE BEARABLE
PASSABLE PORTABLE
TOLERABLY GAIN GEYAN FAIRLY
MEETLY MEETERLY
TOLERANCE MERCY SHERE LEEWAY
REMEDY

TOLERANT SOFT BENIGN
TOLERATE GO BEAR BIDE HACK
HAVE ABIDE ALLOW BROOK SPARE
STAND STICK ACCEPT ENDURE
PARDON PERMIT SUFFER COMPORT
SUPPORT SUSTAIN
TOLERATION WITHGANG
TOLL JOW TAX JOWL PIKE RENT
KNELL PEAGE CAPHAR EXCISE
PEDAGE PESAGE BOOMAGE
KEELAGE LASTAGE LOCKAGE
MULTURE PASSAGE PICCAGE
PONTAGE SCAVAGE SUMMAGE
TERRAGE TOLLAGE TRONAGE
BERTHAGE STALLAGE WEIGHAGE
WHEELAGE
(PL.) CUSTOMS RAHDARI RATTAREE
TOLLHOUSE TOLLERY
TOLLIKER DUMMY
TOLSEN FOOTSTEP
TOLUENE DILUENT
TOLYL CRESYL
TOMAHAWK HATCHET NEOLITH
TOMATO TOM BERRY BURBANK
TOMB PIR CIST MOLE GRAVE GUACA
HUACA MAZAR SPEOS TABUT
THOLE TURBE BURIAL CHULPA
DARGAH DURGAH GALGAL HEARSE
SAMADH SHRINE SYRINX THOLOS
TROUGH TURBEH CHULLPA
MASTABA OSSUARY TOMBLET
TRITAPH CENOTAPH CISTVAEN
CUBICULO HALLCIST KISTVAEN
MARABOUT MASTABAH MONUMENT
TREASURY
(— OF MOSLEM SAINT) ZIARA
ZIARAT
(CAVE —) SPEOS
(PREHISTORIC —) KURGAN
TOMBAC ORSEDE ORSEDUE
TOMBOY GAMINE HOYDEN TOMRIG
TOMBSTONE SLAT TITLE THROUGH
TOMCAT GIB TOMMY PODGER
THOMAS
TOMCOD GADE GADID SMELT
GADOID WHITING TOMMYCOD
TOMENTUM WOOL
TOMFOOLERY HELL HORSE
TOMMY FOOL PODGER REQUIN
TOMMYROT WAHOO
TOMMY TALKER KAZOO
TOMORROW MANANA MORROW
TOMORN
TOMTATE CAESAR
TON TUN TOUN STYLE
TONALAMATL TZOLKIN
TONALITY KEY
TONE A F DO FA LA MI RE SI SO TI
DOH KEY SOH SOL CALL FLAT NOTE
COLOR COUAC DRONE FIFTH FORTE
PRIME SHARP SIXTH SOUND STYLE
TONUS ACCENT DEGREE FOURTH
SECOND FORMANT MEDIANT
PARTIAL DEMITINT ELEVENTH
FORENOTE HARMONIC SONORITY
(— A DRAWING) STUMP
(— DOWN) DRAB TAME SOFTEN
SUBDUE
(BROKEN —) CRACK

(COMPLEX —) KLANG
(DEEP —) BASS
(DOMINANT —) ANIMUS
(DRAWLING —) DRANT DRAUNT
(KEY —) KEYNOTE
(LOUD —) FORTE
(LOW —) SEMISOUN
(MONOTONOUS —) DRONE
(SHARP NASAL —) TWANG
(SIGNIFICANT —) ACCENT
(SINGLE UNVARIED —) MONOTONE
(STRIDENT —) COUAC
(WHINING —) GIRN
TONGA (CAPITAL OF —) NUKUALOFA
(COIN OF —) PAANGA
(ISLAND OF —) ONO TOFUA VAVAU
HAAPAI
(TOWN OF —) NEIAFU
TONGS SNAPS SERVER FORCEPS
GRAMPUS TUEIRON SCISSORS
TONGUE COG GAB CHIB CLAP KALI
NEAP PAWL POLE REED CLACK
IDIOM VOICE GADABA GLOSSA
KABYLE KALIKA LANGUE LINGUA
SPEECH CLAPPER DIALECT FEATHER
ILOKANO LANGUET DOVETAIL
LANGUAGE LORRIKER PLECTRUM
(— IN FLOORING) SPLINE
(— OF BELL) CLAPPER
(— OF JEW'S-HARP) TANG
(— OF LAND) REACH LANGUE
LANGUET
(— OF OXCART) COPE
(— OF SHOE) FLAP KILTY KILTIE
(— OF VEHICLE) NEAP SHAFT
(BELLOWS —) GUSSET
(GIVE —) PRATE
(GOSSIPING —) CLACK CLACKER
(PIVOTED —) PAWL
(ROMANY —) ROMANES
(PL.) GAURA
TONGUEFISH SOLE
TONGUE-LASH SCOLD
TONGUE-LASHING RAT TOCO
BUSINESS
TONGUE-TIED SILENT
TONIC DO DOH ALOE KEEP PICJI
BRACER SAMBUL SONANT SUMBUL
BONESET CALAMUS CALOMBO
CHIRATA COLOMBA DAMIANA
FUMARIA GENTIAN KEYNOTE
NERVINE SALICIN TONICAL
ANTHEMIS BARBERRY BERBERRY
HELONIAS ROBORANT TRILLIUM
TONICITY MYOTONIA
TONKA BEAN GAIAC CUMARU
GUAIAC COUMAROU
TONNA DOLIUM
TONNAGE PORTAGE
TONSIL ALMOND KERNEL ADENOID
AMYGDAL AMYGDALA
TONSILITIS QUINSY
TONSURE CROWN SHAVE SHEAR
CORONA DIKSHA RASURE
TONSURED PEELED PILLED SHAVED
TOO SO ALSO OVER TROP LUCKY
OVERLY LIKEWISE
TOOL (ALSO SEE IMPLEMENT AND
INSTRUMENT) AX ADZ AWL AXE BIT

BUR DIE DIG GIN GUN HOB KEY LA
LOY RIP SAW SAX TAP TIT VOL ZA
ADZE BORE BRAY BURR CLAW
COMB DADO DISC DISK DUPE EDG
FILE FLAY FROE FROG FROW GAG
HACK HAWK HONE LEAF LOOM MIL
PICK ROLL SEAX SLED SNAP SPID
SPUD STOP TAMP TIER VISE AUGE
BLADE BORAL BORER BRAKE
BRAND BREAK BRUSH BURIN DARE
DOLLY DRIFT DRILL DUMMY EDGEI
FLAKE FLOAT FLUTE GAUGE GOUC
GUIDE HARDY HOBBY HOWEL KNIF
KNURL LEVEL MAKER MODEL PLAI
POINT PRUNT PUNCH QUIRK SABE
SABRE SCREW SHAVE SHELL SLIC
SLICK SNIPE SPADE SPEAR SPLIT
STAKE STAMP STING STOCK STRIC
STYLE SWAGE TEWEL TOYLE UPSI
VALET WAGON BEADER BEATER
BIFACE BLADER BODKIN BROACH
BUFFER CALKER CHASER CHISEL
CLEAVE COGGLE COLTER CRADLE
CRANNY CUTTER DEVICE DIBBLE
DIGGER DOCTOR DRIVER ENGINE
FASCET FERRET FILLET FLANGE
FLORET FLUTER FORMER FRAISE
FULLER GIMLET GLAZER GOFFER
GRAVER GUMMER HACKER HAMME
HEMMER HOGGER HOLDER HULLEI
JIGGER JUMPER LADKIN LASTER
LIFTER NIBBER PALLET PARTER
PICKAX PICKER PLIERS PROPER
PUPPET REAMER RIPPER ROCKER
RUNNER SAPPER SCRIBE SEATER
SHAPER SHAVER SHEARS SHOVEL
SKIVER SLATER SOCKET SQUARE
STYLET STYLUS SWIVEL TAGGER
TASTER TONGUE TREPAN TURNER
TURREL TWILLY VEINER WAGGON
WIGWAG WIMBLE WORDLE WORME
YANKEE ABRADER BLOCKER
CALIPER CAULKER CHAMFER
CHIPPER CHOPPER CLEANER
CLEAVER COULTER CREASER
DIAMOND DOLABRA DRESSER
FISTUCA FLANGER FREEZER
FROTTON GRAINER GROOVER
GRUBBER GUDGEON JOINTER
KNOTTER LOGHEAD MITERER
POINTEL POINTER PROFILE RIVETE
ROUGHER ROUNDER SCAUPER
SCORPER SCRIBER SCRIVER
SCURFER SLASHER SLEEKER
SLICKER SPLAYER SPUDDER
STEMMER STRIKER STROKER
TICKLER TREBLET TWIBILL UPRIGH
WRAITHE BIFACIAL BILLHOOK
BOOTJACK BURGOYNE CALLIPER
CREATURE CRIPPLER CROSSCUT
CROWFOOT DUCKFOOT ELEVATOR
EXPANDER FLOUNDER GRAVETTE
GRIFFAUN POLISHER PRITCHEL
PROPERTY PUNCHEON RAVEHOOK
RECAPPER SCRAPPLE SCULPTOR
SPLITTER STIPPLER STRICKLE
STRINGER SURFACER THWACKER
TOLLIKER WARKLOOM WORKLOOM
SCRATCHER

(— A BOOK) FINISH
(PL.) TEW FISH GEAR TRADE
CUTLERY GIBBLES PIONERY
ENGINERY
DOLED GOFFERED
(— WITHOUT GILDING) BLIND
DOLHOLDER TURRET MONITOR
DOLSHED DOGHOUSE
DON LIM CEDAR TOONWOOD
DOT BLOW TOWT BLAST SOUND
TRUMPET
DOTH BIT COG GAM JAG PEG DENS
DENT FANG LEAF RASP SNAG TIND
TINE TUSH TUSK IVORY MOLAR
PEARL PRONG RAKER TENON
BROACH CANINE CUSPID CUTTER
DENTAL INDENT JOGGLE TRIGON
TRITOR DENTILE DIVIDER GRINDER
INCISOR LATERAL SURDENT
UNCINUS ABUTMENT BICUSPID
BLEPHARA DENTICLE EYETOOTH
GAGTOOTH MARGINAL PREMOLAR
SAWTOOTH SPROCKET TOOTHLET
TRIGONID
(— OF A MOSS) BLEPHARA
(— OF HORSE) DIVIDER
(— OF MOLLUSC) MARGINAL
(— OF PINION) LEAF
(— OF RADULA) UNCINUS
(— ON ROTATING PIECE) WIPER
(ARTIFICIAL —) DUMMY PONTIL
(CANINE —) CUSPID HOLDER
LANIARY CYNODONT DOGTOOTH
EYETOOTH
(GEAR —) COG GUB DENT
ADDENDUM SPROCKET
(HARROW —) TINE
(MOLAR —) WANG
(UPPER SURFACE OF —) TABLE
DOTHACHE WORM DENTAGRA
DOTHED SERRATE VIRGATE
SERRATED
DOTHLESS GUMMY
DOTHPICK QUILL ARKANSAN
DOTHWORT CROWTOE COOLWORT
DP CAP COP GIG TAP TIP ACME
APEX BEAT COCK CULM HEAD HELM
ROOF SKIM STOP BLOOM CHIEF
COVER CREST CROWN FANCY
GIGGE RIDGE SPIRE STRIP TOTUM
TRUMP UPPER CALASH CAPOTE
CULMEN SUMMIT UPWARD VERTEX
SPINNER ROUNDTOP SURMOUNT
TEETOTUM
(— FOR CHIMNEY OR PIPE) COWL
HOOD
(— OF ALTAR) MENSA
(— OF AUTOMOBILE) HEAD HOOD
(— OF CAPSTAN) DRUMHEAD
(— OF FURNACE) ARCH
(— OF GLASS) PRETTY
(— OF HEAD) MOLD PATE MOULD
SCALP VERTEX
(— OF HELMET) SKULL
(— OF HILL) KNAG KNAP KNOLL
(— OF INGOT) CROPHEAD
(— OF MOUNTAIN) MAN
(— OF PLANT OR TREE) CROP
(— OF ROOF) DECK

(— OF SPINDLE) COCKHEAD
(— OF THUNDERCLOUD) INCUS
(— OF WOODEN STAND) CRISS
(—S OF CROP) SHAW
(BOOT —) RUFF
(BOX —) COUPON
(CARRIAGE —) CALASH
TOPAZ PYCNITE PYCNIUM
TOPCOAT OVERCOAT SIPHONIA
TOPE DHER DHERI STUPA SOUFFIN
TOPER BOUSER CUPMAN POTMAN
POTTER SIPPER SUPPER TROUGH
BOMBARD POTLING SWILLER
TOSSPOT BLACKPOT DRUNKARD
MALTWORM
TOPI TIANG
TOPIC HARE ITEM TEXT HOBBY
THEMA THEME BURDEN GAMBIT
GROUND MATTER SUBJECT
OCCASION
TOPKNOT ONKOS TOPPING
TOPMAN COB
TOPMINNOW GUPPY LIMIA GULARIS
HELLERI SAILFIN GAMBUSIA
TOPOGRAPHIC TERRAIN
TOPPLE TOP TILT LEVEL TOTTLE
TOPSAIL RAFFE RAFFEE
TOPSOIL KELLY
TOPSTONE CAPSTONE
TOPSWARM TOPCAST
TOPSY-TURVY COCKEYED
REELRALL
TOQUE ZATI MUNGA MACACO
RILAWA MACAQUE
TOQUILLA JIPIJAPA
TORCEL BURN BERNE BORNE
TORCH DUCK JACK LAMP LINK LUNT
PINE WASE WISP BLAZE BRAND
FLARE MATCH FOCKLE LAMPAD
MASHAL MUSSAL BRANDON
CRESSET GRIDDLE LUCIGEN
ROUGHIE TORCHET FLAMBEAU
TORCHBEARER KERYX LINKBOY
LINKMAN DADUCHUS TORCHMAN
TOREADOR TORERO CAPEADOR
TORIL CHIQUERO
TORMENT WO TAW TRY WOE BAIT
BALE FRET MOIL PAIN PANG PINE
RACK TUCK CHEVY CURSE DEVIL
GRILL HARRY SCALD TEASE TWIST
WRING CHIVVY HARASS HARROW
HECTOR INFEST PLAGUE TRAVEL
AFFLICT BEDEVIL CRUCIFY HAGRIDE
HATCHEL MALISON PERPLEX
PINDING TERRIFY TORTURE TRAVAIL
DISTRAIN LACERATE MACERATE
(EXTREME —) AGONY
TORMENTED CRUCIATE
TORMENTIL SEPTFOIL
TORMENTING PLAGUY
TORMINA TORSION
TORN RENT BROKEN BLASTED
TORNADO VORTEX CYCLONE
TRAVADO TWISTER
TORPEDO FISH SHELL SQUIB BATOID
TORPID FOUL NUMB BROSY INERT
SODDEN STUPID TOGGER LANGUID
TORPENT COMATOSE COMATOUS
SLUGGISH

TORPIFY DAZE ETHERIZE
TORPOR COMA SLEEP SWOON
ACEDIA SLUMBER LETHARGY
TORQUE BEE SARPE TWIST
TORRENT FLOW RUSH FLOOD SPATE
STREAM NIAGARA
TORREYA SAVIN TUMION
TORRID HOT SULTRY BOILING
TORSALO BERNE
TORSION STRESS DIDROMY
TORT LIBEL WRONG
TORTE DOBOS
TORT-FEASOR ACTOR
TORTICOLLIS WRYNECK
TORTILLA TOSTADO
TORTOISE EMYD BEKKO GAPER
COOTER GOPHER TURTLE EMYDIAN
HICATEE MUNGOFA TESTUDO
GALAPAGO KASHYAPA SHELLPAD
SHELLPOT TERRAPIN
TORTOISESHELL CAREY
TORTUOUS CRANKY SCREWY
SINUATE WRIGGLY SINUATED
TORTURE TAW BOOT CARD FIRE
PAIN PANG PINE RACK AGONY
SCREW TWIST ENGINE EXTORT
IMPALE MARTYR AFFLICT AGONIZE
BOOTING CRUCIFY PERPLEX
TORMENT
TORTURER BOURREAU
TORUS CORK TORE BASTON BOLTEL
BOUTELL BOWTELL THALAMUS
TORY BANDIT OUTLAW ROBBER
PEELITE TANTIVY LOYALIST
TOSS COB LAB SHY BUNG CANT
CAST CAVE DOSS FLAP FLIP HIKE
PASS SHAG SLAT TOUT CHAFE
CHUCK FLICK FLING FLIRT FLURR
HEAVE TEAVE THROW BETOSS
BOUNCE DANDLE TOTTER WALTER
WELTER WENTLE BLANKET TURMOIL
WAMPISH WHEMMEL
(— A COIN) SKY
(— A JACK) LAG
(— ABOUT) SWAB TAVE POPPLE
THRASH THRESH TORFLE WAMPISH
(— ASIDE) BANDY
(— AWAY) BLOW
(— HEAD) CAVE GECK
(— OF THE HEAD) HEEZE
(— OFF) SWAP SWOP
(— ON WAVES) SURGE
(— TO AND FRO) WALK
(— TOGETHER CONFUSEDLY)
SCRAMBLE
(— WITH THE HORNS) DOSS HIKE
TOSSING SURGING
(— OF BULLFIGHTER) COGIDA
TOSTAO TESTON
TOTAL SUM TOT DEAD MERE TALE
COUNT GROSS MOUNT SUMMA
UTTER WHOLE ENTIRE GLOBAL
OMNIUM SUMMED TOTTLE EMBRACE
FOOTING GENERAL PERFECT
ABSOLUTE COMPLETE ENTIRETY
SURMOUNT TEETOTAL
TOTALITY ALL BODY HEAP BEING
ALLNESS ECOLOGY ETERNITY

HUMANITY INTEGRAL INTERVAL
OMNITUDE
TOTALLY COLD GOOD QUITE
WHOLLY
TOTEM HUACA
TOTTER TOT ROCK TOIT WALT
SHAKE WAVER COGGLE DODDER
DOTTER FALTER JOGGLE STAVER
SWERVE TITTER TOTTLE WAMBLE
WANGLE WAPPER BRANDLE FRIBBLE
STAGGER TREMBLE WHITHER
TITUBATE
TOTTERING SHAKY GROGGY
CRAMBLY PALSIED RICKETY
TOTTERY TITUBANT WAMBLING
TOUCAN TOCO TUCANA ARACARI
TOUCH GET RAP TAG TIG TIP ABUT
BILL DASH FEEL HAND KISS KNEE
MEET PALP PEAL PLAY RAKE RINE
TACT TAKE GLISK GRAZE GROPE
SPICE TAINT TASTE TATTO TINGE
TRAIT TREAT AFFECT ATTAIN
CARESS FINGER GLANCE HANDLE
REGARD SCRUFF SMUTCH STRAIN
TACTUS TWITCH ATTAINT ATTINGE
CONTACT FEELING SOUPCON
TACTION FLOURISH TINCTURE
(— **A KEY**) STRIKE
(— **BRIEFLY**) GLANCE
(— **CARESSINGLY**) FLATTER
(— **CLOSELY**) IMPINGE
(— **GENTLY**) DAB TAT TICK BRUSH
(— **LIGHTLY**) GRAZE SCUFF SKIFF
(— **OF BRUSH**) HAND
(— **OF COLOR**) EYE
(— **OF PAINT**) GLOB
(— **OF PLEASURE**) GLISK
(— **RIGHTLY**) NICK
(**DELICATE** —) STROKE
(**FINISHING** —) HOODER COPESTONE
(**SLIGHT** —) SKIFF SMATCH
TOUCHDOWN ROUGE
TOUCHED FEY DOTTY
TOUCHING ABOUT LIBANT TENDER
AGAINST CONTACT TANGENT
ADJACENT POIGNANT
(— **LIGHTLY**) LAMBENT
TOUCHSTONE TEST TOUCH LYDITE
BASANITE STANDARD
TOUCHWOOD FUNK MONK PUNK
SPUNK PUNKWOOD
TOUCHY HUFFY MIFFY SNAKY
FEISTY KITTLE SNAKEY SNUFFY
SPUNKY TENDER TETCHY GROUCHY
NERVOUS PEEVISH TEMPERY
TICKLISH
TOUGH RUM BHOY HARD TAUT WIRY
CLUNG HARDY STIFF STOUT WITHY
KNOTTY SINEWY STARCH STRONG
HICKORY BULLYBOY LEATHERY
UNTENDER
TOUGHEN TAW ANNEAL ENDURE
HARDEN TEMPER
TOUGHENED CLUNG
TOUGHNESS TUCK FIBER FIBRE
STRENGTH TENACITY
TOUPEE RUG DOILY SCALP
POSTICHE TOPPIECE
TOUR GIRO TURN SWING TOWER

TURUS JUNKET SAFARI JOURNEY
INVASION PROGRESS TOURETTE
(— **OF DUTY**) HERD STATION
(**CANARY** —) GLUCK GLUCKE
TOURACO LORY LOURIE TURAKOO
TOURBILLON KARRUSEL
TOUR DE FORCE STUNT
TOURIST TOURER TRIPPER VISITANT
TOURMALINE SHORL SCHORL
DRAVITE ACHROITE SIBERITE
TOURNAMENT TILT JOUSTS
TOURNEY BONSPIEL CAROUSEL
TOURNEUR DEALER
TOURNEY PLAY
TOURNIQUET GARROT STANCH
TWISTER STANCHER TORCULAR
TOUSLE SOOL SOWL RUMPLE
TOOZLE
TOUSLED TOWZIE TUMBLED
UNKEMPT
TOUT SKIV BRUIT PLIER STEERER
TOW CRIB HAUL PULL HURDS STUPE
TRACK TRACT CODILLA CORDELLE
TOWAGE TRACKAGE
TOWAI BIRCH KAMAHI
TOWARD AD INTO TORT ANENT
ANENST AGAINST FORNENT
ADVERSUS GAINWARD
(— **CENTER OF EARTH**) DOWN
(— **CENTER**) CENTRAD
(— **ONE SIDE**) ASLANT
(— **THE END**) SF
(— **THE HEAD**) ANTERIOR
(— **THE REAR**) ABACK DORSAD
BACKWARD
(— **THE RIGHT**) DEXTRAD
(— **THE SIDE**) LATERAD
(— **THE STERN**) AFTER
TOWEL CLOUT WIPER DIAPER
LAVABO RUBBER
TOWER TOR PEEL PIKE REAR RISE
SOAR SPUR TOUR BABEL BROCH
HEAVE MINAR MOUNT PYLON SIKAR
SPIRE STUPA TEXAS ASCEND
ASPIRE BELFRY CASTLE CHULPA
DOKHMA DONJON GOPURA ROLLER
RONDEL SPRING TURRET BASTIDE
CHULLPA DERRICK GIRALDA
LANTERN MIRADOR NURAGHE
SHIKARA SIKHARA STEEPLE
TALAYOT TORREON TOURNEL
TRACKER TURRION BARBICAN
BASTILLE CLOGHEAD DOMINEER
RONDELLE SCRUBBER TOURELLE
TOWERLET
(— **CONTAINING COKE**) SCRUBBER
(— **FOR SENTINEL**) GUERITE
(— **OF FORT**) SPUR
(— **OF MOSQUE**) MINARET
(— **OF SILENCE**) DAKHMA
(— **ON SUMMIT**) PIKE
(— **OVER**) DROWN BESTRIDE
(**ATTACHED** —) DETAIL
(**BELL** —) CARILLON
(**CONNING** —) SAIL
(**FRACTIONATING** —) STILL
(**PYRAMIDAL** —) SIKAR VIMANA
SHIKARA SIKHARA
(**SIGNAL** —) BANTAYAN

(**WIND** —) BADGIR
TOWERING EMINENT SUPERNAL
AMBITIOUS
TOWERMAN LEVERMAN
TOWER MUSTARD CRUCIFER
TOWHEE JOREE CHEWINK CHEEWIN
TOWING TRACKAGE
TOWLINE CORDELLE
TOWN BY BYE HAM WON CAMP CIT
STAD WENE WICK BAYAN BOURH
BRUGH BURGH DERBY MACHI
PLACE PLECK SIEGE STAND STEAL
VILLE CIUDAD HAMMON ORANGE
PUEBLO STAPLE BASTIDE BOROUC
CHESTER OPPIDUM QUIVIRA
TOWNLET BOOMTOWN BOURGADE
ENCEINTE HOMETOWN TOWNSHIP
(**DESOLATED** —) GUBAT
(**FORTIFIED** —) BURG BURGH
ENCEINTE
(**MYTHICAL** —) QUIVIRA
(**SMALL** —) SHTETL SHTETEL
(**UNFORTIFIED** —) BOURGADE
(**WALLED** —) CHESTER
(PL.) PARGANA
TOWN HALL HALL CABILDO
RATHAUS TOLBOOTH STADHOUSE
TOWNSHIP DEME DORP VILL BAYA
TREEN BOROUGH
TOWNSMAN CAD CIT SNOB TOWN
TOWNEE BURGHER CITIZEN
COCKNEY OPPIDAN
(PL.) BURGWARE
TOWROPE TOW GUNLINE TOWLINE
CORDELLE
TOXALBUMIN ROBIN PHALLIN
TOXEMIA BLACKLEG ECLAMPSIA
TOXIC VENOMOUS
TOXIN BOTULIN EXOTOXIN
TOY DIE GAY TOP COCK DOLL FOC
MOVE PLAY BLOCK DALLY FLIRT
HAPPY KNACK LAKIN PLAID SPOR
TRICK WALLY BAUBLE DANDLE
DOODLE FADDLE FINGER FIZGIG
GEWGAW LAKING PRETTY PUPPET
RATTLE SUCKER BLOWOUT CRICK
DREIDEL PLAYOCK TANGRAM
TRINKET TUMBLER WHIZZER
GIMCRACK KICKSHAW PINWHEEL
SQUAWKER SQUEAKER TEETOTUM
WINDMILL ZOETROPE
(— **AMOROUSLY**) MIRD
(— **WITH**) PADDLE
(**FLYING** —) PIGEON
TOYON TOLLON CHAMISO
TRACE RUN TUG WAD CAST ECHO
HINT LICK MARK RACK SHOW SIG
STEP TANG TINT TROD BRING
GHOST GLEAM GLIFF GRAIN PRINT
SHADE SPOOR STAMP STEAD THE
TINGE TOUCH TRACK TRACT TRAI
TRAIN TRESS DERIVE ENGRAM
HARBOR LACING RESENT SHADOV
SKETCH SMUTCH STRAIN STREAK
SWATHE COCKEYE GLIMPSE
MENTION REMNANT SOUPCON
SURMISE SYMPTOM THOUGHT
UMBRAGE VESTIGE WHISPER
DESCRIBE ENGRAMMA FOOTSTEP

SKERRICK TINCTURE WAINROPE
(— A BEE) COURSE
(— A CURVE) SWEEP
(— A DESIGN) CALK
(— MATHEMATICALLY) GENERATE
(— OF A HARE) FARE
(— ON CHART) PRICK
(— THE COURSE OF) DEDUCE
(HARNESS —) TUG THEAT TREAT
(MEMORY —) ENGRAM ENGRAMME
(SLIGHT —) GHOST STAIN SMATCH
SPARKLE
(SLIGHTEST —) SCINTIL
(PL.) FEUTE
RACER SEEKER OUTLINER
SEARCHER
RACERY FANWORK FROSTING
TRAILERY
RACHEA ARTERY WINDPIPE
(— OF CRANE) TRUMP
RACHEID HYDROID
RACHYANDESITE ARSOITE
VULSINITE
RACHYTE PIPERNO
RACING BAROGRAM POLYGRAM
TRAILING
RACK DOG PUG RAT RUT TAN WAD
WAY CLEW CLUE DRAW FARE FOIL
FOOT HUNT LANE MARK PAGE PATH
PIST RACE RACK RAIK RAIL ROAD
SHOE SLOT SPUR TROD VENT
BLOCK CHUTE DRIFT FEUTE HOUND
LODGE PISTE PLANE SLIDE SPACE
SPOOR STEAD SWATH TRACE
TRACT TRADE TRAIL TRAIN TREAD
BEARER COURSE GROOVE HARBOR
LADDER RETURN RUNWAY SIDING
SLEUTH STRAIN SWATHE CHANNEL
FOILING FOOTING PATHWAY
TANGENT TRAFFIC VESTIGE
BACKBONE FOOTSTEP GUIDEWAY
TRANSFER TRECKPOT TREKPATH
WAGONWAY
(— FOR ROPE) CHANNEL
(— GAME) DRAW
(— OF DEER) SLOT STRAIN
(— OF GAME IN GRASS) FOILING
(— OF HARE) FILE
(— OF WOUNDED BEAST) PERSUE
(— ON PRINTING PRESS) BANK
BEARER
(RAILROAD —) LEAD SPUR STUB
SIDING TANGENT APPROACH
BACKBONE
(RUNNING —) FLAT CINDERS
(SHORT BRANCH —) RETURN
(SIDE —) LIE HOLE
(SKATER'S —) FLAT
(TEMPORARY —) SHOOFLY
(WORM —) NEREITE
RACKER PUGGI PUGGY TRAILER
TRAILMAN
RACKLESS INVIOUS PATHLESS
RACKMAN SPIKER
RACT AREA BEAT DUAR FLAT ZONE
CAMPO COAST DRIVE ESSAY FIELD
GRABE HORST PATCH SWEEP
TRACK BARONY BUNDLE EXTENT
REGION ENCLAVE EURIPUS

QUARTER ROYALTY TERRAIN
TRACTUS BROCHURE CAMPAGNA
CAMPAIGN CINGULUM DISTRICT
FARMHOLD FORESTRY PAMPHLET
PROVINCE TOWNSITE TREATISE
(— KEPT IN NATURAL STATE) PARK
(— OF BARREN LAND) BARREN
DERELICT
(— OF GRASSLAND) PRAIRIE
(— OF LAND) CRU DOAB DUAB
DUAR GORE MARK BLOCK CHASE
CLAIM EJIDO FRITH GRANT LAINE
SCOPE SWELL EIGHTY ESTATE
FOREST GARDEN ISLAND POLDER
STRATH AIRPORT QUILLET RESERVE
TERRAIN BOUNDARY CLEARING
DERELICT FARMHOLD INTERVAL
SCABLAND SLASHING
(— OF MUDDY GROUND) SLOB
(— OF OPEN UPLAND) DOWN
DOWNS
(— OF UNCOVERED ICE) GLADE
(— OF WASTE LAND) HEATH
(BOGGY —) RUNN MORASS
(CLAYEY —) TAKYR
(CLEARED —) JUM JHUM JOOM
(DRY —) SEARING
(FORESTLESS —) STEPPE
(GENITAL —) BEARING
(IRREGULAR —) GORE
(OPEN —) VEGA SLASH
(SANDY —) DEN DENE
(SWAMPY —) FLOW BAYGALL
(UNOCCUPIED AND UNCULTIVATED
—) DESERT
(WATERLESS —) THIRST
TRACTABLE EASY SOFT BUXOM
TAWIE DOCILE GENTLE TOWARD
DUCTILE FLEXIBLE AMENABLE
FLEXIBLE GUIDABLE TOWARDLY
YIELDING
TRACTARIANISM PUSEYISM
TRACTION DRAFT DRAUGHT
TRACTOR CAT MULE DRAGON
BOBTAIL CRAWLER PEDRAIL
(TRAILER —) RIG
TRADE CHAP CHOP COUP DEAL SELL
SWAP CHEAP CRAFT GRAFT PRICE
TREAD TROKE TRUCK BAKERY
BARTER CHANGE EMPLOY HANDLE
MISTER NIFFER OCCUPY SCORCE
SCORSE BARGAIN CALLING
CHAFFER FACULTY MYSTERY
SCIENCE BUSINESS CABOTAGE
EXCHANGE
TRADEMARK CHOP MARK BRAND
COUPON
TRADER SART BANYA PLIER BALIJA
CHETTY DEALER MONGER NEPMAN
TROKER CHAPMAN MARWARI
SANGLEY TRUCKER ASTORIAN
CHANDLER KURVEYOR MERCHANT
OPERATOR
(HORSE —) JOCKEY
(INEXPERIENCED —) LAMB
TRADESMAN CIT BAKAL COOPER
EGGLER SELLER TENSOR FRUITER
GOLADAR OCCUPIER UPHOLDER
TRADESWOMAN WINSTER

TRADITION CABAL STORY SUNNA
CABALA SMRITT SUNNAH THREAP
HALACHA HALAKAH HEREDITY
HERITAGE TRANSFER
(PL.) LEGEND
TRADITIONAL CLASSIC
TRADUCE ILL SLUR ABUSE DEFAME
MALIGN VILIFY ASPERSE DETRACT
TRAFFIC COUP DEAL MANG MART
MONG BROKE TRADE BARTER
PALTER TRAVEL CHAFFER DEALING
BUSINESS CHAFFERY COMMERCE
EXCHANGE
(— IN SACRED THINGS) SIMONY
(— IN SLAVES) MAGONIZE
TRAFFICKER COUPER DEALER
TRAGEDY BUSKIN TRAGIC TROIADES
TRAGIC DIRE DREADFUL THESPIAN
TRAGICOMEDY DRAME
TRAGOPAN MONAL
TRAGUS EARLET
TRAIL PAD PUG DRAG FOIL HARL
HUNT NECK PATH PIST SLOT BLAZE
CRAWL DRAIL PISTE ROUTE SPOOR
STOCK SWEEP TRACE TRADE TRAIN
COMING DAGGLE FOLLOW RUNWAY
SHADOW SLEUTH STRAIN TAIGLE
TRAPES DRAGGLE TRAFFIC
OUTTRAIL STRIGGLE TRAILERY
(— ALONG) STREEL TRAPES
(— OF A FISH) LOOM
(— OUT) STREAM
(— THROUGH MUD) DAGGLE
(DESCENDING —) BAHADA BAJADA
(MOUNTAIN —) CLIMB
(WAGON —) RUDLOFF
TRAILBLAZER HARBINGER
TRAILER SEMI COACH BOXCAR
CARAVAN FLATBED FROGGER
GONDOLA
TRAIN SET DRAG GAIT SECT TILL
TURN ZULU BEARD BREED COACH
DRESS DRILL ENTER FOCUS LOCAL
RANGE TRACE TRACT TRADE TRAIL
TRYNE DIRECT GENTLE GROUND
INFORM MANURE NUZZLE RAPIDE
REPAIR SCHOOL SEASON STRING
SUBWAY AFFAITE BRIGADE
CARAVAN EDUCATE FREIGHT
GEARING LIMITED PEDDLER
RATTLER RETINUE SHUTTLE
VARNISH CIVILIZE DISCIPLE
ELECTRIC EQUIPAGE EXERCISE
HIGHBALL INSTRUCT MANIFEST
REHEARSE
(— AN ANIMAL) BREAK
(— FINE) GAUNT
(— FOR FIGHTING) SPAR
(— OF ANIMALS) COFFLE
(— OF ATTENDANTS) CORTEGE
(— OF COMET) TAIL
(— OF EXPLOSIVE) FUSE
(— OF MINING CARS) JAG RUN TRIP
(FUNERAL —) CONVOY
(PACK —) CONDUCTA
(RAILROAD —) DRAG HOOK LOCAL
PICKUP EXPRESS FREIGHT LIMITED
RATTLER

TRAINED GOOD MADE ADEPT BROKE BROKEN
TRAINEE BOOT CADET
TRAINER FEEDER JINETE LANISTA
TRAINING DRILL THEAT ASCESIS ASKESIS CULTURE NURTURE PAIDEIA BREEDING
(— IN HUMANITIES) CIVILITY
(— OF HORSE) DRESSAGE
(RELIGIOUS —) SADHANA
TRAIT ITEM LEAD MARK VEIN ANGLE CHARM KNACK TRACT AMENITY ELEMENT HALLMARK JAPANISM
(CULTURE —) SURVIVAL
(FOREIGN —) EXOTISM
(GOOD —) THEW
(UNDESIRABLE —) DEMON DAEMON
(WELL-DEFINED —) STREAK
(PL.) CORNERS
TRAITOR JUDAS RUSTY WARLOCK ISCARIOT PRODITOR SQUEALER TRADITOR TREACHER
TRAITOROUS FALSE FELON
TRAJECTORY SPORABOLA
TRA-LA-LA TRALIRA
TRAM TUB DRAM TRAMCAR TRAMMEL TRANVIA
(SET OF —S) JOURNEY
TRAMCAR TRAM DUMMY PICKUP
TRAMMEL TRAM HAMPER STIFLE COTTEREL
TRAMMER PUTTER
TRAMONTANE OVERBERG
TRAMP BO BUM PAD BOOM HAKE HIKE HOBO HUMP PUNK SLOG SWAG VAMP WALK YEGG BURLY CAIRD CLAMP JAVEL PIKER SHACK STIFF STRAG TRAIK TRAIL TRASH TROMP TROUT BAGMAN GAYCAT JOCKER PICARO STODGE STRAMP STROLL TINKER TRANCE TRAPES TRUANT TRUDGE DRUMMER FLOATER RUFFLER SWAGGER SWAGMAN TRAIPSE TRAMPLE TROUNCE TROWANE YEGGMAN FOOTSLOG GANGEREL STROLLER TRAVELER VAGABOND SUNDOWNER
(— ABOUT) WAG
(LONG —) HUMP
(PL.) MONKERY
TRAMPING MONKERY
TRAMPLE HOX JAM PUG FARE FOIL FULL HOOF CHAMP SCAUT SPURN TRAMP TRASH TREAD DEFOIL DEFOUL PADDLE SAVAGE STOACH STRAMP WADDLE OPPRESS OVERRUN SCAMBLE FORTREAD OVERRIDE
TRANCE RAPTUS AMENTIA ECSTASY SAMADHI
TRANQUIL CALM COOL EASY LOWN MILD SOFT EQUAL QUIET STILL GENTLE PACATE PIPING SERENE CALMATO EQUABLE PACIFIC RESTFUL PEACEFUL
TRANQUILIZE CALM LULL QUIET STILL BECALM PACIFY SERENE SETTLE SOFTEN SOOTHE APPEASE COMPOSE

TRANQUILIZING SOOTHING
TRANQUILLITY KEF LEE EASE REST PEACE SATTVA SERENE HARMONY QUIETAGE QUIETUDE SERENITY
TRANS ANTI
TRANSACT DO PASS AGITATE CONDUCT PERFORM
TRANSACTION DEAL GAGE GAGER ACTION AFFAIR MARGIN SPREAD BARGAIN MOHABAT PASSAGE CONTRACT KNOCKOUT
(PL.) ACTA BUSINESS
TRANSCEND PASS SOAR EXCEED OVERTOP SURPASS
TRANSCENDENTAL ACOSMIC
TRANSCENDING EXQUISITE
TRANSCRIBE COPY BRAILLE DESCRIBE EXSCRIBE
TRANSCRIBED CANNED
TRANSCRIBER COPIER COPYIST
TRANSCRIPT COPY SCORE TENOR DOUBLE APOGRAPH EXSCRIPT
TRANSCRIPTION(PL.) PAZAND PAZEND
TRANSEPT PLAGE PORCH
TRANSFER CEDE DEED FLIT GIVE SALE SELL TURN CABLE CARRY CROSS DROGH REFER REMIT SHIFT ASSIGN ATTORN CHANGE DECANT DELATE DONATE REMOVE SWITCH CESSION CONNECT CONSIGN DELIVER DEVOLVE DISPONE MIGRATE TRADUCE ALIENATE ANTEDATE CROCKING DELEGATE DELIVERY DONATION EXCHANGE TRANSACT TRANSUME VIREMENT
(— DYE) EXHAUST
(— HEAT) CONVECT
(— HOMAGE) ATTORN
(— MOLTEN GLASS) LADE
(— OF ENERGY) FLOW
(— OF PROPERTY) DEED GIFT GRANT DISPOSAL
(— PIGMENT) FLUSH
TRANSFERENCE DEMISE EMOTION REMOVAL DELATION DISPOSAL TRANSFER
TRANSFIGURE DEIFY CLARIFY
TRANSFIX FIX DART PITCH STAKE STICK SKEWER THRILL
TRANSFORM TURN SHIFT TOUCH CHANGE STRIKE CONVERT FASHION PERMUTE CATALYZE DISGUISE HETERIZE
(— ENERGY) ABSORB
TRANSFORMATION CHANGE HAIRWORK
TRANSFORMER SET DIMMER JIGGER TEASER VARIAC BALANCE BOOSTER HEDGEHOG
TRANSFUSE ENDUE INDUE
TRANSGRESS ERR SIN BREAK OFFEND OVERGO DIGRESS DISOBEY VIOLATE INFRINGE OVERPASS OVERSLIP OVERSTEP
TRANSGRESSION SIN SLIP CRIME FAULT SCAPE BREACH DELICT ESCAPE MISDEED OFFENSE DELICTUM OVERLOUP TRESPASS

TRANSGRESSOR SINNER OFFENDER
TRANSIENCE FUGACITY
TRANSIENT FLIGHTY PASSING FLEETING FUGITIVE
TRANSIENTLY HOVERLY
TRANSIT BINOCLE PASSAGE TRANSEPT
TRANSITION CUT JUMP LEAP SEGUE SHIFT FERMENT PASSAGE
TRANSITORINESS CADUCITY
TRANSITORY FLEET CADUCE FLYING BRITTLE PASSANT PASSING SLIDING VOLATIC WHILEND CADUCOUS FLEETING FLITTING TEMPORAL VOLATILE
TRANSLATE DRAW MAKE TURN WEND RENDER CONVERT ENGLISH EXPOUND TRADUCE CONSTRUE INTERPRET
TRANSLATION CAB KEY CRIB PONY STEP TROT GLOSS HORSE TARGUM UNSEEN BICYCLE CABBAGE ENGLISH THARGUM TRADUCT VERSION SUBTITLE VERBATIM
(— OF THE CLASSICS) JACK
(LOAN —) CALQUE
TRANSLATOR TURNER
TRANSLUCENT CLEAR LUCID LIMPID LUCENT HYALINE
TRANSMIGRATION SAMARA SAMSARA SANSARA
TRANSMISSION ENTAIL DESCENT GEARBOX SENDING TRANSFER
(— OF SOUND) AUDIO
(— TO OFFSPRING) HEREDITY
TRANSMIT AIR EMIT SEND CARRY CONVEY DEMISE DERIVE ENTAIL EXPORT IMPACT IMPART RENDER CONDUCT FORWARD TRADUCE TRADUCT TRAJECT BEQUEATH DESCRIBE
TRANSMITTER TUBA SLAVE SPARK BEACON JAMMER SENDER VEHICLE RADIATOR
TRANSMITTING ALIVE
TRANSMUTE CHEMIC CHEMICK ENNOBLE PERMUTE EXCHANGE TRANSMUE TRANSUME
TRANSOM PATIBLE TRAVERSE
TRANSPARENCY SLIDE
TRANSPARENT THIN CLEAR FILMY LUCID BRIGHT LIMPID LUCENT CRYSTAL FRAGILE HYALINE HYALOID DIOPTRIC LUCULENT LUMINOUS LUSTROUS PELLUCID
TRANSPIRE HAPPEN
TRANSPLANT SPOT SHIFT DEPLANT
TRANSPORT DAK JOY ROB BEAR BOAT BUSS DAWK DRAY HAUL PORT RAPE RAPT RIDE SHIP CANOE CARRY DROGH FERRY FLUTE GILLY BANISH BARREL CONVEY DEPORT GALLOP WAFTER ECSTASY EXPRESS FRAUGHT ONERARY RAPTURE TRADUCE TROOPER CABOTAGE CARRIAGE DAYDREAM ENRAVISH PALANDER
(— FOR CRIME) LAG
(— LOGS) BOB

(— ORE) SLUSH

TRANSPORTATION AIR DAK FARE
AIRLIFT BOATAGE FREIGHT TRAJECT
TRANSPORT

TRANSPORTED RAPT
(— BY GLACIER) ERRATIC

TRANSPOSE CONVERT REVERSE

TRANSPOSITION SHIFT ANSWER
ANAGRAM

TRANSUBSTANTIATION METUSIA

TRANSVAAL DAISY GERBERA

TRANSVAALER TAKHAAR

TRANSVERSE CROSS FACING
THWART OBLIQUE

TRANSVERSELY ATHWART

TRANSVESTISM EONISM

TRANSVESTITE BERDACHE

TRAP COY GET GIN PIT SET FALL
GIRN GRIN HOOK LACE LIME NAIL
PUTT TIPE TOIL WAIT WEEL BRAKE
BRIKE CATCH LEASH PLANT POUND
SNARE SPELL STALE SWICK SWIKE
TRAIN CRUIVE EELPOT ENGINE
KEDDAH POCKET QUILEZ SNATCH
STAYER WILLOW FLYTRAP PITFALL
PITFOLD PUTCHEN PUTCHER
RATTRAP SETTING SPRINGE
TRAMMEL BIRDLIME COALHOLE
DEADFALL DOWNFALL TRAPROCK
— FOR BIRDS) SCRAPE
— FOR LARGE GAME) HOPO
— FOR RABBITS, MICE, ETC) TIPE
YPE
— FOR RATS) CLAM
— FOR SALMON) PUTT
— FOR SMALL ANIMALS) HATCH
— FOR THE FEET) CALTROPS
— IN POKER) SANDBAG
— INTO SERVICE) CRIMP
FISH —) FYKE KILL LEAP WEEL
WEIR CREEL WILLY CORRAL
WILLOW
SAND —) BUNKER

TRAPDOOR DROP SLOT TRAP
CRUTO VAMPIRE TRAPFALL

TRAPPED CORNERED

TRAPPER WIRER VOYAGEUR

TRAPPINGS GEAR JHOOL ARMORY
LOGGERY BARDINGS EQUIPAGE
HOUSINGS

TRAPSHOOTING SKEET

TRASH ROT BOSH GEAR GOOK JUNK
ELF RAFF TOSH TRAG CLART
RECK DRUSH STUFF SWASH
THROW TRADE TROKE WASTE
WRACK BUSHWA CULTCH KELTER
PALTRY RAMMEL REFUSE RUBBLE
CULCH TROUSE BAGGAGE
EGGARY FULLAGE GARBAGE
MEDLARY RUBBISH TOSHERY
TRAFFIC BLATHERY CLAPTRAP
FLUMMERY MUCKMENT PEDDLERY
KITTLES SMACHRIE TRASHERY
FRUMPERY

TRASHY CHEAP FLASH TOSHY TRIPY
PALTRY SLUSHY BAGGAGE RUBBISH
RIFFRAFF RUBBISHY SIXPENNY
FRUMPERY

TRAVAIL PAIN TASK TOIL AGONY

LABOR TORMENT

TRAVEL GO BAT BUS FLY GIG WAG
FARE GANG HIKE PASS PATH RIVE
TOTE TRIP VAMP WEND COVER
KNOCK SLOPE THROW TRACK
CRUISE TRANCE VOYAGE EXPRESS
JOURNEY TRAVAIL TRUNDLE
WAYFARE PROGRESS TRAVERSE
(— ACROSS SNOW) MUSH
(— AIMLESSLY) SAUNTER
(— ALONG GROUND) TAXI
(— AROUND) TURN COAST CIRCLE
GIRDLE COMPASS
(— AT GOOD SPEED) CRACK
(— AT HIGH SPEED) HELL BARREL
SCORCH
(— AT RANDOM) DRIFT
(— AT SPEED OF) DO
(— BACK AND FORTH) SHUNT
COMMUTE
(— BY AIRCRAFT) AIR FLY AIRPLANE
(— BY OX WAGON) TREK
(— FAST) STREAK
(— IN A VEHICLE) TOOL
(— ON FOOT) HIKE SHANK
KNAPSACK
(— ON WATER) SAIL
(— OVER) TRANCE TRAVERSE
(— THROUGH WOODS) BUSHWACK
(— THROUGH) GO
(— WITHOUT EQUIPMENT) SIWASH
(DAY'S —) JORNADA JOURNAL
JOURNEY

TRAVELER GOER CRAWL FARER
GUEST HORSE BAGMAN GANGER
KILROY POSTER SAILOR VIATOR
CRUISER DRUMMER FOOTMAN
HOWADJI LEEFANG PILGRIM
SWAGGIE TRAILER TREKKER
WAYGOER ARGONAUT EXPLORER
MAGELLAN OUTRIDER VOYAGEUR
WAYFARER
(COMPANY OF —S) CARAVAN

TRAVELER'S JOY HAGROPE
BINDWITH

TRAVELING ERRANT

TRAVELING SALESMAN RIDER
DRUMMER

TRAVERSE DO GO SEE BURN DENY
KNEE LIFT MAKE PASS SPAN WALK
COAST COVER CROSS SHEAR
SWEEP THIRL TRACE TRACK CIRCLE
COURSE DENIAL OVERGO PERCUR
TRAVEL WANDER CHANNEL
JOURNEY MEASURE OVERRUN
PARADOS PERVADE DESCRIBE
OVERPASS OVERWEND SCRAMBLE
UNTHREAD

TRAVERTINE TOPHUS

TRAVESTY EXODE PARODY SATIRE
EXODIUM TRAVEST

TRAVOIS DRAY TRAVOY ALLIGATOR

TRAWL SEINE BOULTER DRAGNET
STOWNET TRAWLNET

TRAWLER PAREJA BRAGOZZO

TRAY HOD CASE TILL TRUG BATEA
BOARD FLOAT SCALE SLICE SUSAN
GALLEY MONKEY SALVER SERVER
SERVET VOIDER WAITER BALANCE

CABARET COASTER CONSOLE
SHALLOW DEJEUNER
(— FOR CRUMBS) VOIDER
(— FOR DRYING FISH) FLAKE
(— FOR MATCH SPLINTS) CAUL
MONKEY
(— FOR SHELLFISH) FLOAT
(— FOR TYPE) GALLEY
(— TO CATCH OVERFLOW) SAFE
(CIRCULAR —) ROUNDEL

TREACHEROUS FOUL CATTY FALSE
PUNIC SNAKY SWACK FELINE
FICKLE HOLLOW YELLOW SNAKISH
FRAUDFUL IMPOSING PLOTTING
SLIDDERY

TREACHERY GUILE SWICK TRAIN
DECEIT FELONY PERFIDY TREASON
UNTRUTH DASTARDY DISTRUST
TRAHISON TRAITORY

TREACLE DIBS CLAGGUM THERIAC

TREAD FIT PAD BEAT FOOT PATH
POST RUNG STEP VOLT CLAMP
TRACK TRADE DEFOIL DEFOUL
PADDLE CRAWLER FEATHER
FOOTING RETREAD TREADER
FOOTSTEP
(— CLUMSILY) CLUMP BALTER
(— DOWN SHOE HEEL) CAM
(— HEAVILY) SPURN TRAMPLE
(— OF FOWL'S EGG) GRANDO
(— ON) FOIL
(— TO MUSIC) FOOT
(TIRE —) COVER

TREADLE PEDAL CHALAZA

TREASON SEDITION

TREASURE POSE ROON HOARD
PRIZE STORE TROVE VALUE
BURSAR COFFER FINDAL GERSUM
WEALTH ASTHORE FINANCE
THESAUR WARISON GARRISON
TREASURY
(— STATE) MONTANA
(LITTLE —) STOREEN
(PL.) CIMELIA

TREASURE BOX HANAPER

TREASURED DEAR CHARY
PRECIOUS

TREASURER BOWSER BURSAR
FISCAL GABBAI BOUCHER HOARDER
SPENDER BHANDARI COFFERER
HAZNADAR PROVISOR RECEIVER

TREASURY FISC FISK KIST CHEST
HOARD PURSE COFFER CORBAN
FISCAL FISCUS BOWSERY BURSARY
CHAMBER CHECKER CHEQUER
HORDARY AERARIUM THESAURY
TREASURE

TREAT RUN USE DEAL DOSE HOCK
LEAD PLAY BEANO BESEE COVER
DIGHT GUIDE LEECH SERVE SETUP
SHOUT TRACT TRAIT WRITE
DEMEAN DOCTOR GOVERN HANDLE
LIQUOR PADDLE REGALO CONDUCT
ENTREAT GARNISH ACTIVATE
AIRBRUSH
(— A HIDE) DRUM
(— AS EQUAL) EVEN
(— BADLY) ILLGUIDE
(— CARELESSLY) BANG BANDY

(— CLOUDS) SEED
(— CONFIDENTIALLY) HUSH
(— CRUELLY) CRUCIFY
(— DAINTILY) PAMPER
(— DIABOLICALLY) BEDEVIL
(— DISCOURTEOUSLY) DISGRACE
(— FIBERS) GILL
(— FLOUR) AGENIZE
(— FONDLY) DANDLE
(— FUR) CARROT
(— GENTLY) FAVOR
(— ILLNESS) POMSTER
(— IMPROPERLY) MISUSE
(— IMPUDENTLY) NOSE
(— LIGHTLY) SCRUFF
(— LOVINGLY) COAX
(— MALICIOUSLY) SPITE
(— MASH) LAUTER
(— OF DRINKS) SETUP
(— OF) DISCOURSE
(— ROUGHLY) BANG MUMBLE
GRABBLE MALTREAT
(— SILK TO RUSTLE) SCROOP
(— SLIGHTINGLY) LIGHTLY
(— STEEL) HARVEY
(— UNFAIRLY) DO
(— UNSKILLFULLY) FOOZLE
(— WITH ACID) SOUR
(— WITH CARE) CODDLE
(— WITH CONTEMPT) HUFF SNUB
BLURT FLIRT FLOCK FLOUT FLAUNT
BAUCHLE
(— WITH HEAT) FOMENT
(— WITH HONOR) RESPECT
(— WITH INATTENTION) FORGET
(— WITH INDULGENCE) FONDLE
(— WITH PARTIALITY) ACCEPT
(— WITH RESPECT) HONOR
(— WITH RIDICULE) SCOUT
(— WITH RUDENESS) FRUMP
(— WITH TAR) BLACK
(— WITH TENDERNESS) CODDLE
(NEW YEAR'S EVE —) HAGMENA
HOGMANAY
TREATISE AGAMA DONET FAUNA
FLORA LIBEL SILVA SUMMA SYLVA
TRACT TREAT BOTANY POETRY
POMONA SERTUM SYSTEM ALGEBRA
ANATOMY BIOLOGY COMMENT
DIETARY GEOLOGY GRAMMAR
HISTORY PANDECT PHYSICS
PINETUM POETICS ZOOLOGY
ALMAGEST BROCHURE CALCULUS
DIDACTIC ECTHESIS EXERCISE
GENETICS GEOMANCY GEOMETRY
GERMANIA HORNBOOK LAPIDARY
MONUMENT PANTHEON PASTORAL
PRACTICE SITOLOGY SPECULUM
TRACTATE
TREATMENT CURE WORK TREAT
USAGE ANIMUS DETAIL FACIAL
QUARTER BEHAVIOR DEMEANOR
ENTREATY
(— BY MASSAGE) SEANCE
(— FOR WOOLLENS) SPONGING
(BAD —) MISUSAGE
(COLD —) FREEZE
(COMPASSIONATE —) MERCY
(CONTEMPTUOUS —) SPURN

(CRUEL —) SEVERITY
(DIRE —) DOLE
(HARMFUL —) ABUSE
(INHUMAN —) CRUELTY
(LUXURIOUS —) DELICACY
(SEVERE —) ROUGH
TREATY MISE ACCORD CARTEL
CONCORD ENTENTE LOCARNO
ALLIANCE TREATISE
TREBLE TRIPLE DESCANT MINIKIN
SOPRANO TRIPLUM
TREBUCHET DONDINE DONDAINE
TREE TI ACH AMA ARN ASH BAY BEL
BEN BUR DAK DAR EBO ELM FIG FIR
GUM HAW KOA KOU LIN OAK SAJ
SAL TAL TUI ULE YEW ACLE AGBA
AKEE ANAM ANAN ANDA ARAR
ASAK ASOK ATIS ATLE AULU AUSU
BAKU BITO BOGO BREA BURI BURR
CADE COLA CRAB DATE DHAK DILO
DITA DOON EBOE IPIL JACK KINO
KOKO LIME MABI MORA OHIA PALA
PINE POLE POON SADR SORB SUPA
TALA TAWA TCHE TEAK TEIL TITI
TOON TREW TUNG TUNO UPAS
VERA WOOD YATE YAYA AALII
ABETO ABURA ACANA ACAPU
ACOMA AFARA AGATI AGOHO AKEKI
ALAMO ALANI ALDER ALGUM ALISO
ALMON ALMUG AMAGA AMAPA
AMBAK ANABO ANJAN APPLE
ARACA ARBOR ARECA ARJAN
ARJUN ARTAR ASOKA ASPEN ATLEE
BABUL BALAO BALSA BALTA BANAK
BEECH BEHEN BETIS BIRCH BONGO
BOREE BOSSE BUMBO CACAO
CARAP CAROB CEBIL CEDAR CEIBO
DADAP DHAVA DHAYA DILLY DURIO
ELDER GABUN GAIAC GENIP GINEP
GINKO HAZEL ICICA IXORA JAMBO
JIQUE JIQUI KAPOR KAPUR KEENA
KOKAN KOKIO KONGU KUSAM
LANSA LARCH LARIX LEHUA LEMON
LICCA LIMBA LINDE LINER LINGO
MAHOE MAHUA MAMIE MAPLE
NARRA NIEPA NURSE OADAL OSAGE
OSIER PACAY PAPAW PECAN PIPER
RAULI ROBLE ROHAN ROWAN SALAI
SAMAN SASSY SCRAG SIMAL SIRIS
SISSU STICK SUMAC TABOG TARFA
TENIO TERAP TIKUR TIMBO TINGI
TOONA TUART ULMUS UMIRI URUCA
URUCU UVITO WAHOO YACAL
YACCA YULAN ZAMAN AHKROT
AKEAKE ALAGAO ALERGE ALERSE
ALFAJE ALMOND ALUPAG AMAMAU
AMBASH AMUGIS AMUYON ANAGAP
ANAGUA ANAQUA ANGICO ANILAO
ARALIA ARANGA ARBUTE AUSUBO
AZALEA BABOEN BACURY BAHERA
BAKULA BALSAM BANABA BANAGO
BANANA BANCAL BANIAN BANYAN
BARBAS BATAAN BIRIBA BOMBAX
BONDUC BONETE BOTONG BRAUNA
BUCARE BUSTIC CALABA CAMARA
CANELA CANELO CAPUMO CARAPA
CASSIA CATIVO CAUCHO CEDRON
CHALTA CHERRY CHICHA CHINAR
CHOGAK CITRON COBOLA COCUYO

CUMBER DATURA DHAMAN DHAURA
DHAURI DRIMYS DURIAN ELCAJA
EMBLIC EMBUIA FEIJOA FILLER
FUSTIC GABOON GINGKO GUAIAC
GURJAN GURJUN IDESIA IDIGBO
ILIAHI ILLIPE ILLUPI JAGUEY JUJUB
KAMALA KEMPAS KINDAL KITTUL
LANSAT LANSEH LAUREL LIGNUM
LINDEN LITCHI LOCUST LONGAN
MAFURA MALLET MAYTEN MEDLAR
MILKER ORANGE PANAMA PAWPAW
PIQUIA POPLAR RAMBEH ROHUNA
RUNNEL SABICU SABINO SANDAN
SANTOL SAPELE SAPOTA SAPOTE
SATINE SAWYER SERAYA SINTOC
SISSOO SOUARI STYRAX SUMACH
SUNDRI TALUTO TARATA TEETEE
TIKOOR TIMBER TINGUY TOATOA
TOTARA TUPELO URUCUM URUSHI
UVALHA WABAYO WAHAHE WALNU
WAMARA WAMPEE WANDOO
WATTLE YACHAN YAGHAN YAMBAN
YOHIME ZAMANG ACHIOTE ACHUET
AILANTO AKEPIRO AMBATCH
AMBOINA AMUGUIS AMUYONG
ANABONG ANNATTO ANONANG
APITONG APRICOT ARARIBA
ARAROBA ARBORET ARBUTUS
AROEIRA ASSAGAI AVOCADO
AVODIRE BANILAD BANKSIA
BECUIBA BENZOIN BILLIAN BOLLIN
BUBINGA BUCKEYE BUISSON
CADAMBA CAJAPUT CANELLA
CARAIPE CASTANA CATALPA
CAUTIVO CERILLO CHAMPAC
CHECHEM CHECKER CHENGAL
COCULLO CONIFER COUMARU
CURUPAY CYPRESS DEADMAN
DESCENT DETERMA DHAMNOO
EPACRID FRUITER GONDANG
GRIBBLE GUMIHAN HICKORY
HOLLONG HOPBUSH HORMIGO
KAMASSI KAMBALA KICKXIA
KITTOOL KOKOONA KOOMBAR
KUMQUAT LOGWOOD MADRONA
MANJACK MARGOSA PARAIBA
PEREIRA PIMENTO PULASAN
PYRAMID RATWOOD REDWOOD
SERINGA SERVICE SHITTAH SPINDI
STOPPER SUNDARI SURETTE
TANGELO TANGHIN TARAIRI
TARATAH TARWOOD TINDALO
TREELET TWISTER URUNDAY
VETERAN WALAHEE WALLABA
WEENONG WONGSHY WONGSKY
YAMANAI YOHIMBI ACEITUNA
ALGAROBA ALLSPICE ALMACIGA
ALMANDER ALMENDRO ALOEWOO
AMARILLO ARAGUANE ARBOLOCO
ARBUSCLE AVELLANO BAKUPARI
BASSWOOD BAYBERRY BELLWOO
BINDOREE BITANHOL BLACKBOX
BOARWOOD BORRACHA BREADNU
CABREUVA CAMELLIA CAMUNING
CARAGANA CARAUNDA CHAMPAC
CHESTNUT CHINCONA CHINOTTO
COPALCHE CRABWOOD CUCUMBO
DEADFALL DOMINANT DOTTEREL
DOVEWOOD DRACAENA DRUMWOO

ETABALLI FIREFALL FORESTER
GAMDEBOO GEELHOUT GENISARO
GUACACOA GUAYROTO HALAPEPE
HARDTACK HARDWOOD HOLDOVER
HORNBEAM HOROPITO IRONWOOD
ISHPINGO ITCHWOOD JELOTONG
JELUTONG KAJUGARU KINGWOOD
KNOBWOOD LACEBARK LEADWOOD
LORDWOOD MAHOGANY MANDARIN
MILKWOOD MOKIHANA OLEASTER
ONEBERRY PEDIGREE PINKWOOD
RAMBUTAN RASAMALA SANDARAC
SANDWOOD SAPUCAIA SASSWOOD
SEBESTEN SHAGBARK SHAVINGS
SILKWOOD SLOGWOOD SOAPBARK
STANDARD SUCUPIRA SWEETSOP
SYCAMORE TAMARACK TAMARIND
TANEKAHA TREELING TURMERIC
ZAPATERO
(— CUT BACK) DOTARD POLLARD
(— FURNISHING SUPPORT TO VINE)
HUSBAND
(— IN STREAM) SAWYER
(— LEFT IN CUTTING) HOLDOVER
(— ON WALL) RIDER
(— OVER 2 FT. DIAMETER) VETERAN
(— SYMBOLIZING UNIVERSE)
YGDRASIL
(— WITH BRANCHES TRIMMED) LOP
LOPSTICK
(—S IN FOREST) STAND
(AROMATIC —) CLUSIA LABIATE
(AUSTRALIAN —) ASH GUM TOON
BELAH BELAR BOREE BUNDY BUNYA
GIDIA HAZEL KARRI NONDA PENDA
SALLY WILGA BAOBAB DRIMYS
GIDGEE GIMLET GYMPIE KOWHAI
MARARA PEROBA SALLEE
DOGWOOD GEEBUNG BEEFWOOD
CARABEEN COOLABAH FLINDOSA
GRAVILEA IRONBARK LACEBARK
QUANDONG ROSEBUSH SANDSTAY
SOAPWOOD TILESEED
(BIG —) SEQUOIA
(CEYLON —) HORA
(CITRUS —) SHADDOCK
(CLOTHES —) COSTUMER
(CLUMP OF —S) TOLL TUMP STELL
(CUBAN —) JIQUE JIQUI GUACACOA
(CURSED —) WARYTREE
(DEAD —) RUNT SNAG RAMPIKE
(DEAD —S) DRIKI
(DECAYED —) DOTTEREL
(DWARF —) SCRUB ARBUSCLE
(EVERGREEN —) FIR YEW PINE SUGI
AWA ABIES ATHEL CAROB CEDAR
CLOVE HOLLY LARCH LEMON OLIVE
THUJA BALSAM BIBIRU COIGUE
OIHUE KANAGI KAPUKA LOQUAT
RANGE SPRUCE ARDISIA BEBEERU
ILIMBI CONIFER HEMLOCK JUNIPER
MADRONA EUCALYPT EUONYMUS
FAMILY —) STEMMA DESCENT
PEDIGREE
(GENEALOGICAL —) ARBOR JESSE
(GROWTH OF —S) SYLVAGE
(GUM —) KARI KINO BABUL BALTA
UMBO ICICA KARRI KIKAR GIMLET
MALLET STORAX TEWART WANDOO

GOMMIER COOLIBAH
(HAWAIIAN —) KOA LEHUA ILIAHI
(INFERNAL —) ZAQQUM
(JAPANESE —) KAYA KIAKI KEYAKI
KADSURA KATSURA
(MANDARIN —) SATSUMA
(MEXICAN —) ULE AMAPA DRAGO
EBANO SERON CAPULI CATENA
CHILTE CAPULIN COPALCHE
(MYTHICAL —) TUBA
(NEW ZEALAND —) AKE KARO KAWA
MIRO PUKA RATA RIMU TAWA TORU
WHAU HINAU KAORI KAURI MAIRE
MANGI MAPAU MATAI TOWAI
AKEAKE KAMAHI KANUKA KAPUKA
KARAKA KARAMU KAWAKA KONINI
MANUKA PURIRI TARATA TITOKI
TOATOA TOTARA WAHAHE AKEPIRO
MANGERO PUKATEA TARAIRI
TARWOOD KAWAKAWA KOHEKOHE
MAKOMAKO
(ORNAMENTAL —) LABURNUM
(PHILIPPINES —) DAO IBA TUA TUI
BOGO DITA IFIL IPIL AGOHO AGOJO
ALMON AMAGA ANABO BAYOG
BAYOK BETIS DANLI GUIJO LAUAN
LIGAS TABOG YACAL ALAGAO
ALUPAG AMUYON ANAGAP ANUBIN
ARANGA BANUYO BATAAN BATETE
BATINO BOTONG DUNGON KATMON
LANETE MABOLO MARANG MOLAVE
SAGING TALUTO AMUGUIS
AMUYONG ANABONG ANOBING
ANONANG APITONG BINUKAU
CAMAGON DANGLIN MANCONO
MAYAPIS TINDALO ALMACIGA
BITANHOL KALIPAYA KALUMPIT
LUMBAYAO MACAASIM MALAPAHO
TANGUILE
(POISONOUS —) GUAO UPAS LIGAS
TANGHIN TANQUEN
(POLYNESIAN —) MACUDA
(SHADE —) ELM DILLY GUAMA
HEVEA CATALPA HALESIA INKWOOD
JOEWOOD SYCAMORE
(SHOWY —) ASAK ASOK ASOKA
(SMALL —) AKE BOX TCHE ALDER
CUMAY DWARF HENNA NGAIO
SERON AKEAKE BLOLLY CHANAR
JOJOBA KOWHAI ARBORET
INKWOOD JOEWOOD KADAMBA
STADDLE TREELET EMAJAGUA
HARDTACK HUISACHE OLEASTER
SNOWBELL SOURWOOD TREELING
(SPINY —) LIME AROMA AROMO
HONEY BOOGUM BUCARE BUMELIA
CATECHU COLORIN LAVANGA
COCKSPUR
(STANDING —) FILLER
(STUNTED —) SCRAB SCRUB
SCRUNT
(THORNY —) BEL BAEL BREA
LEMON AMBACH SAMOHU AMBATCH
(TIMBER —) ASH DAR ENG FIR SAL
ACLE ANDA BAKU COCO CUYA EKKI
IPIL PELU PINE TALA TEAK ACAPU
ALMON AMAPA AMATE AMBAY
ANJAN ARACA BANAK BIRCH CAROB
CEDAR COCOA CULLA EBONY ERIZO

FOTUI HALDU ICICA IROKO KAURI
KHAYA KIAKI KOKAN MANIU MAPLE
NARRA ROBLE TIMBO ALERCE
ALUPAG BABOEN BACURY BANABA
BANCAL CARBON CHUPON CORTEZ
DAGAME DEGAME DUKUMA ESPAVE
FREIJO GAMARI GUMHAR IMBUIA
JACANA LEBBEK MUERMO SANDAN
SATINE AMUGUIS AROEIRA BECUIBA
BILLIAN CARAIPI CYPRESS ESPAVEL
GATEADO GOMAVEL GUARABU
GUAYABI HARPULA HOLLONG
KOOMBAR LAPACHO REDWOOD
AMARILLO BOARWOOD CABREUVA
CARACOLI COCOBOLO CRABWOOD
DONCELLA GUATAMBU GUAYACAN
MAHOGANY SLOGWOOD SUCUPIRA
(TRAINED —) ESPALIER
(TROPICAL —) AKEE AULU DALI
EBOE EKKI GUAO INGA MABA MAHO
MAJO PALM SHEA ACKEE BALSA
BONGO COUMA DALLI FOTUI GUAMA
GUARA ICICA ILAMA JIGUA MARIA
NEPAL NJAVE POOLI TARFA ANUBIN
BAKULA BALATA BANANA CASHEW
CEDRON CHUPON GENIPA HACKIA
ITAUBA LEBBEK LECYTH MAMMEE
PERSEA ANGELIN ANNATTO
CAULOTE COPAIBA DATTOCK
EHRETIA EUGENIA GATEADO
GUACIMO LAPACHO MAJAGUA
MOMBINI SANDBOX SOURSOP
SURETTE BEEFWOOD CALABASA
CAMUNING CORKWOOD FUNTUMIA
MUSKWOOD PATASHTE SWEETSOP
TAMARIND
(UNARMED —) ALBIZZIA
(VARNISH —) DOON THEETSEE
(XEROPHYTIC —) SAXAUL
(YOUNG —) RUNNEL SPRING TILLER
SAPLING SEEDLING SPRINGER
(PL.) BLUFF RINDS SILVA
TREE CREEPER TOMTIT
TREE CYPRESS GILIA
TREE DUCK FIDDLER YAGUAZI
TREE FROG FERREIRO
TREE MOSS USNEA
TREENAIL NOG GUTTA MOOTER
TRUNNEL
TREE PEONY MOUTAN
TREE TOAD HYLA HYLID ANURAN
TREETOP LAP LOP
TREFOIL CANCH LOTUS CLAVER
CROWTOE BEDSTRAW SAINFOIN
TICKSEED
TREHALOSE MYCOSE
TRELLIS TRAIL PERGOLA TARLIES
ESPALIER
TREMATODE FLUKE MARITA
STRIGEID
TREMBLE DARE DIRL RESE BEVER
QUAKE SHAKE SLOWS WIVER
AGRISE DIDDER DINGLE DITHER
DODDER FALTER HOTTLE NITHER
QUAVER QUIVER SHIMMY THRILL
TITTER TOTTER TREMOR TRYMIE
WABBLE WOBBLE FLICKER
SHUDDER STAGGER TWIDDLE
WHITHER THRIMBLE

(PL.) TIRE TIRES
TREMBLER BUZZER HAMMER
VIBRATOR
TREMBLING BEVER SHAKY DITHER
TREMOR TREPID AQUIVER DODDERY
QUAKING QUAVERY QUIVERY
TREMBLY TWITTER
TREMBLY WOOZY
TREMENDOUS BIG AWFUL GIANT
GREAT LARGE TEARING ENORMOUS
HORRIBLE TERRIBLE TERRIFIC
MONSTROUS
TREMOLO HURRY TRILLO
TREMOR RIGOR SHAKE DINDLE
QUIVER THRILL SHUDDER TREMBLE
TREMULOUS ASPEN QUAKY SHAKY
PALSIED SHIVERY TREMBLY
SKIMMERY TINGLING
TRENCH GAW SAP FOSS GRIP GURT
LINE MOAT SICK SIKE TAJO TRIG
BOYAU CHASE DITCH DRAIN DRILL
FLOAT FOSSE GRAFF GRAFT GRAVE
GROOP SEUCH TRINK COFFER
FURROW GUTTER SHEUGH ACEQUIA
CUNETTE OPENCUT SLIDDER
ENCROACH LOCKSPIT SPREADER
THOROUGH TRESPASS
(— **BELOW FOREST FIRE**) GUTTER
(— **FOR BURYING POTATOES**) CAMP
(— **FOR DRAIN TILES**) CHASE
(— **FORMED BY BANKING**
VEGETABLES) GRAVE
(**ARTIFICIAL** —) LEAT
(**IRRIGATION** —) FLOAT SUGSLOOT
TRENCHANT ACID EDGED SHARP
TUANT INCISIVE
TRENCHER PLATTER ROUNDEL
TREND BEND BIAS HAND TONE TURN
BULGE CURVE DRIFT SENSE SLANT
SWING TENOR SQUINT STRIKE
CURRENT DOWNSIDE MOVEMENT
TENDENCY
(**LOWERING PRICE** —) EASE
TREPANG BALATE SWALLO
SWALLOW TITFISH TEATFISH
TREPIDATION FEAR DISMAY
TRESPASS DEBT GILUT POACH
BREACH FURTUM INVADE INTRUDE
OFFENSE ENCROACH ENTRENCH
INFRINGE INTRENCH OVERLOUP
TRESS CURL LOCK TAIL BRAID
SWITCH RINGLET WIMPLER
TRES-TINE TRAY ROYAL
TRESTLE MARE HORSE INRUN
CHEVALET SAWHORSE
TREVALLY TURRUM
TREWS TROUSERS
TRIACETATE ACETIN EUROBIN
TRIAD TRIAS TRINE TRIUNE TERNARY
TERNION TRILOGY TRINARY TRINITY
TRIMURTI TRIRATNA
TRIAL SHY TRY BOUT DOOM FIRE
HACK OYER STAB TEST TURN
ASSAY CROSS ESSAY GRIEF ISSUE
POINT PROOF TASTE TOUCH WHACK
ASSIZE EFFORT EQUITY TRINAL
APPROOF ATTEMPT CALVARY
DISGUST HEARING PROVING
SCRATCH CRUCIBLE EXERCISE

JUDGMENT QUAESTIO TENTAMEN
(— **BY BATTLE**) WAGER
(— **BY ORDEAL**) ORDALIUM
(— **FOR HOUNDS**) DERBY
(— **OF SPEED**) DASH
(**EXPERIMENTAL** —) TENTAMEN
(**SEVERE** —) ORDEAL CRUCIBLE
TRIANGLE APEX CYMBAL OXYGON
TRIGON ISOCELE PYRAMID SCALENE
TRINITY TRIQUET DINGDONG
TRIANGULAR HEATER CUNEATE
HASTATE
(— **AREA**) QUIRK
(— **CLOTH**) GORE
(— **INSET**) GODET
TRIBAL GENTILE GENTLIC TRIBULAR
TRIBE AO GI ATI AUS BOH EVE EWE
GOG KHA KIN KRA ROD SUK YAO
ADAI AKAN AKHA AKIM AKKA BAYA
BONI CLAN DAGO GUHA PURU
QUNG RACE RAVI REKI SAHO SEID
SHIK SHOR SIOL SOGA SUKU SUSU
TOBA TURI TUSH UBII VEPS VILI
VIRA YANA AEQUI ANGKA APTAL
ARAWA BASSI BATAK BESSI CHANG
CINEL DADJO DEDAN DIERI FIRCA
GIBBI HORDE HOUSE ICENI KAJAR
KANDH KEDAR KHOND KIWAI
KONGO KOTAR KREPI LANGO MARSI
MBUBA MENDE MENDI MOSSI MUTER
NANDI PHYLE PONDO QUADI SERER
SOTIK STAMM SUEVI TAIPI TAULI
TCAWI TEKKE TELEI TUATH VEPSE
VOLOF WAKHI WARRI WASHO
WAYAO YOMUD ADIGHE AGAWAM
ANAMIM ANTEVA APAYAO ARAINS
BANYAI BASOGA BUDUMA BUSAOS
CHAMPA CHAWIA CHORAI DOROBO
FAMILY HERULI KARLUK KEREWA
KHAMTI KONYAK KORANA LOBALE
MANGAR MOLALA NATION NERVII
PAHARI PHYLON POKOMO RAMNES
SHAGIA SICULI SIMEON SUKUMA
TAINUI TAMOYO TCHIAM TELEUT
THUSHI TUSHIN TYPEES VENETI
WABENA WABUMA WAGOMA
WAGUHA WAHEHE WARORI WASOGA
WAVIRA ZARAMO ZEGUHA ZENAGA
ABABDEH ABANTES AIAWONG
AKWAPIM AMAKOSA ANOMURA
ANTAIVA ARVERNI BAGIRMI
BAKATAN BAKONGO BAKUNDA
BAMBARA BASONGO CABINDA
CHAOUIA CHAUWIA CHITALI
CHONTAL CHUKCHI COLLERY
DADAYAG DADSCHO ILLANUN
JAZYGES KABINDA KABONGA
KHOKANI KOLDAJI KONIAGA
KOREISH KUBACHI KURUMBA
LLANERO NAIADES PALAUNG PARISII
PIMENTO RAURACI SAMBALA
SAMBARA SEKHWAN SENONES
SEQUANI SHAMMAR SHERANI
SHUKRIA SILIPAN SUIONES SUKKIIM
TAKELMA TARKANI TURKANA
VIDDHAL WAGWENO WAICURI
WAMBUGU WAREGGA WASANGO
ZONGORA AMAFINGO ANDOROBO
ASHANGOS ASSHURIM AWABAKAL

BARKINJI BATETELA BOANBURA
CHERUSCI GEZRITES JICAQUES
KUKURUKU LANDUMAN NEBAIOTH
ORUNCHUN PALLIVAN PHASIRON
PUPULUCA PURUPURU RAHANWIN
SAKALAVA SHINWARI SINGSING
SINTSINK TCHUKCHI TENGGRIS
USTARANA WANGATTA WAPOGOR
WAPOKOMO
(— **OF ISRAEL**) DAN GAD ASHER
REUBEN EPHRAIM ISSACHAR
MANASSEH
(**CHINESE** —**S**) HU
(**PRIVILEGED** —) MAGHZEN
MAKHZAN
(**SEA GYPSY** —) SELUNG
TRIBROMOETHANOL AVERTIN
TRIBULATION AGONY MISERY
SORROW DISTRESS
TRIBUNAL BAR FEME ROTA VEHM
COURT FEHME FORUM JUNTA
VEHME MAJLIS ACUERDO ESGUAR
MEJLISS RIGSRET AREOPAGY
TRIBUNE BEMA VELUTUS
TRIBUTARY ARM BRANCH FEEDER
TYBURN
TRIBUTE AID FEE TAX GELT LEVY
PORT RENT SCAT CANON GAVEL
HANSE MAILL SALVO SCATT
CHAUTH HERIOT HIDAGE HOMAGE
IMPOST CARATCH CHEVAGE
CHIEFRY OVATION PENSION
SYNODAL TREWAGE AUXILIUM
BRENNAGE HEREGELD PESHKASH
ROMESCOT ROMESHOT
TRICE GIRD BLINK THROW INSTAN
TRICHECHUS MANATUS
TRICHINA NEMATODE
TRICHION CRINION
TRICHOME SCALE
TRICHOMONIASIS CANKER
ABORTION
TRICK DO BOB COG CON CUN DA
DOR FOB FOX FUB FUN GIN GUM
JIG JOB PAW BILK BITE BORE CH
CHIP DIDO DIRT DUPE FAKE FIRK
FLAM FLUM FOOL GAFF GAME GA
GECK GULL HAVE HOAX JAPE JE
JINK JOUK JUNT LOCK LURK PAS
PAWK PRAT PULL RORT RUSE SI
SKIT SLUR TURN WILE WIPE WOO
BLEAR BLINK CATCH CHEAT CON
CRAFT CREEK CROOK CULLY
CURVE DODGE DORRE ELUDE FE
FETCH FOURB FRAUD GLEEK GR
GUILE KNACK PAVIE PLANT PRAN
SHIFT SHINE SKITE SLICK STUNT
TRAIN TRUFF TWIST WHEEL WRE
WRINK BAFFLE BANTER BEGUNK
BEJAPE BLENCH BROGUE CAUTE
CHOUSE CRADDY DECEIT DELUD
DOUBLE EUCHRE FOURBE HOCK
HUMBUG JOCKEY JUGGLE MANN
PLISKY POLICY SCONCE SHAVIE
SPRING TREPAN VAGARY WHEEZ
WINNER CANTRIP CHICANE CONG
FICELLE FINESSE FORWARD
GUILERY KNAVERY MARLOCK
PAGEANT SHUFFLE SLEIGHT

WHIZZER ARTIFICE CHALDESE
CLAPTRAP CLOWNADE CONTOISE
CROTCHET DELUSION DOUBLING
FLAGARIE FLIMFLAM GILENYIE
INTRIGUE JEOPARDY PRACTICE
PRANCOME PRESTIGE QUENTISE
SLAMPAMP TRAVERSE TRICKING
(— OUT) FINIFY
(BEGUILING —) WILE
(CARD —) CLUB HEART SPADE
STICH DIAMOND WEAVING
(FRAUDULENT —) RIG TOP
(JUGGLING —) FOIST
(KNAVISH —) DOGTRICK
(LOVE —) AMORETTO
(MEAN —) TOUCH
(MONKEY —) SINGERIE
(OLD —) CONNU
(PETTY —S) CRANS
(SIX —S) BOOK
(SMART —) LIRIPIPE LIRIPOOP
(STUPID —) SHINE
(VEXING —) CHAW
(WRESTLING —) CHIP CLICK FAULX
FORWARD
(PL.) DAGS
RICKER TRUMPER
RICKERY DOLE GAFF SHAM TRAP
TRAY WILE COVIN FRAUD HOCUS
SHARK TRAIN CAUTEL COVINE
DECEIT JAPERY JUGGLE TREGET
DODGERY FALLACY GULLERY
JOUKERY KNAVERY PAWKERY
SLEIGHT ARTIFICE CHEATING
JOOKERIE JUGGLERY PRACTICE
TRICKING TRUMPERY
RICKILY FOXILY
RICKINESS PAWKERY
RICKISH KNAVISH FRAUDFUL
RICKLE DRIP DRILL STILL TRILL
DISTIL DRIVEL SICKER SIGGER
STRAIN ZIGGER DISTILL DRIBBLE
DRIZZLE TRINTLE
RICKSTER GULL SHAM TRAPAN
SLICKER TRICKER SLEEVEEN
TRAMPOSO
RICKSY ELFISH QUIRKSEY
RICKY SLY DEEP BRAID DODGY
RIKIE GAUDY ROWDY SNIDE ARTFUL
CATCHY LUBRIC QUIRKY SHIFTY
SMARTY TWISTY DEVIOUS SLANTER
TRICKLE WINDING FLIMFLAM
JUGGLING LUBRICAL SHIFTFUL
SKITTISH SLIDDERY SLIPPERY
TORTUOUS TRICKING
RICLINIC ANORTHIC
RICOT JERSEY
RICYCLE VELO CYCLE TRIKE
WHEEL TANDEM TRICAR RANTOON
ROADSTER SOCIABLE
RIDENT VAJRA TRISUL TRISULA
RIED TESTED PROBATE WEIGHED
RELIABLE
RIFLE ACE BOB DAB HAW PIN SOU
TOY BEAN COOT DOIT FICO FOOL
HAIR HOOT JAUK MOCK MOTE PLAY
RUSE DALLY FLIRT FLUKE GLAIK
TEMY NIFLE PLACK POINT SCRAT
PORT TRICK TRUFF BAWBEE

BREATH DABBLE DANDLE DAWDLE
DELUDE DIBBLE DOODAD DOODLE
FADDLE FESCUE FIDDLE FOOTER
FOOTLE FRIVOL GEWGAW MONKEY
NIDDLE NIGNAY PADDLE PALTER
PETTLE PICKLE PIDDLE PIGGLE
PINGLE POTTER PUTTER TIFFLE
VANITY WANTON FEATHER FRIBBLE
NOTHING QUIDDLE THOUGHT
TRANEEN TRINKET TRIVIAL WHIFFLE
COQUETTE FALDERAL FLIMFLAM
FOLDEROL GIMCRACK KICKSHAW
MOLEHILL NIHILITY NUGAMENT
RIGMAREE TRANTLUM
(— WITH) JANK DANDLE DELUDE
NIGGLE
(ATTRACTIVE —) CONCEIT
(LITERARY —) TOY
(MERE —) SONG STRAW
(MEREST —) FIG
(PL.) NUGAE TRIVIA GIBLETS
FEWTRILS
TRIFLER DOODLE PLAYER FLANEUR
FOOTLER FRIBBLE NUGATOR
PINGLER TWIDDLER WHIFFLER
TRIFLING AIRY FOND IDLE FUNNY
INANE LIGHT PETTY POTTY SILLY
SMALL FLIMSY FUTILE LEVITY
LIMUTE LITTLE PALTRY SIMPLE
STRAWY TOYISH FOOLISH FRIBBLE
ITEMING TRIVIAL TWATTLE
COQUETRY FIDDLING FLIMFLAM
FRIPPERY IMMOMENT NUGATORY
PIDDLING SNIPPING
TRIFOLIUM CLOVER TREFOIL
TRIG TRIM CHIPPER
TRIGGER VERGE TRICKER
TRIGGERFISH COCUYO TURBOT
OLDWIFE BALISTID FILEFISH
OLDWENCH
TRIGON TRINE SABBEKA SACKBUT
SAMBUCA TRIGONON
TRIGONOMETRY SPHERICS
TRILL BURR FLAP ROLL SHAKE
QUAVER THRILL TRILLO WARBLE
TRILLET
TRILLIUM SARA TRUE SARAH TRUMP
BENJAMIN TRUELOVE
TRILOBITE EODISCID
TRIM AX AXE CUT DUB GIM LIP LOP
NET BARB BEAD BUTT CLIP CROP
DEFT DINK FEAT FUSS GASH GIMP
HACK JIMP LACE NEAT PICK SNAG
SNOD SNUG SPUR STOW TACK
TOSH TRIG BRAID BRUSH CLEAN
COPSE DRESS FITTY GENTY HEDGE
KEMPT KNIFE PREEN PRIME PRUNE
PURGE SAUCY SHAVE SHEAR
SHRAG SHRIP SLEEK SMART SMIRK
SPRIG STUMP TIGHT TRICK VERGE
BARBER DAPPER DONSIE DOUBLE
FETTLE PICKED REFORM SHROUD
SPRUCE SVELTE SWITCH TRIMLY
CHIPPER FEATHER FLOUNCE
SCISSOR MANICURE ORNAMENT
TRIMMING
(— A BOAT) SIT
(— ENDS OF HAIR) SHIRL
(— HEDGE) DUB

(— HIDES) ROUND
(— MEAT) CONDITION
(— SAIL) FILL
(— SEAMS) FETTLE
(— SHOE) FOX
(— TREES) PRIME SWAMP
(— WITH EMBROIDERY) GIMP PANEL
TRIMLY SMARTLY SPRUCELY
TRIMMED PEEKABOO
TRIMMER FINER BRIDLE TACKER
VOLANT ROUNDER SMOCKER
SCRATTER
TRIMMING COQ FUR GIMP LACE
BRAID CHAPE COQUE FRILL GUARD
INKLE JABOT RUCHE ERMINE
LACING OSPREY PURFLE ROBING
BEADING FALBALA FURRING
GALLOON MARABOU PUFFING
BRAIDING EAVESING FALDERAL
FOLDEROL FROSTING FROUFROU
FURBELOW JEWELING PAILETTE
PEARLING PICKADIL PLASTRON
SOUTACHE SPAGHETTI STRAPPING
(PL.) LOP FLOTS SHORTS FIXINGS
LOPPING BRAIDING FRILLIES
TRIMURTI TRINITY
TRINE TRENE TRIGON
TRINIDAD-TOBAGO (CAPITAL OF —)
PORTOFSPAIN
(POINT OF —) GALERA
(RIVER OF —) ORTOIRE
(TOWN OF —) ARIMA LABREA
SIPARIA
TRINITARIAN MATHURIN
TRINITY TRIAD TRIAS TRINE TRIUNE
GODHEAD TERNARY TRIMURTI
TRINUNITY
TRINKET TOY DIDO GAUD BIJOU
HEART KNACK TAHLI BAUBLE
DEVICE DOODAD GEWGAW BIBELOT
TRANGAM TRANKUM GIMCRACK
TRANTLUM TRINKLET WHIMWHAM
(PL.) TRINKUMS
TRINKETRY KNAVERY
TRINITROTOLUENE TOLITE TRITON
TRIO GLEEK TERZET TRIUNE
TERZETTO
TRIOLEFIN TRIENE
TRIONYX AMYDA
TRIOPAS (DAUGHTER OF —)
IPHIMEDIA
(FATHER OF —) NEPTUNE
(MOTHER OF —) CANACE
(SON OF —) ERYSICHTHON
TRIOPS APUS
TRIP HOP JAG JET JOG TIP BOUT
CHIP FOOT GAIT GATE RAKE SKIP
TOUR TROT TURN BROAD DANCE
DRIVE HITCH JAUNT SALLY CRUISE
ERRAND FLIGHT HEGIRA OFFEND
OUTING RAMBLE SAFARI SASHAY
VOYAGE JOURNEY SAILING
SETDOWN STUMBLE TRIPPER
CAMPAIGN PERIPLUS
(— ALONG) CHIP LINK
(— IN WRESTLING) CHIP CLICK
(— INTO COUNTRY) CAMPAIGN
(— UP) SUPPLANT
(HUNTING —) SHOOT

(PLEASURE —) JUNKET
TRIPE PAUNCH ROLPENS TRILLIBUB
TRIPLE TRINE TREBLE TERNARY
TRIFOLD TRIPLEX THRIBBLE
TRIPLET TRIN BRELAN PARIAL
TERCET TRIOLE TRIPLE TERZINA
TRIOLET HEMIOLIA TRILLING
TRIPLING TRISTICH
TRIPLETAIL SAMA CHOBIE FLASHER
GROUPER
TRIPLICITY TRIGON
TRIPOD CAT TRIP SPIDER TEAPOY
TRIPOS TRIVET TRESTLE
TRIPODY HEMIEPES
TRIPOLI SILEX TRIPEL
TRIPPER DECKMAN
TRIPTOLEMUS (FATHER OF —)
CELEUS
(MOTHER OF —) METANIRA
TRISMUS LOCKJAW TETANUS
TRITE FADE HACK WORN BANAL
CONNU CORNY HOARY MUSTY
STALE VAPID BEATEN COMMON
MODERN HACKNEY PERCOCT
TRIVIAL SHOPWORN
TRITENESS BATHOS
TRITERPENOID CERIN
TRITON NEWT TRUMPET
(FATHER OF —) NEPTUNE
(MOTHER OF —) AMPHITRITE
TRITURATE POUND POWDER
TRITURATION TRIPSIS
TRITURUS MOLGE
TRIUMPH WIN PALM INSULT PREVAIL
VICTORY CONQUEST
(— OVER) SCALP
TRIUMPHANT VICTOR JUBILANT
TRIUMPHING OVANT
TRIUNGULIN CRAWLER
TRIVET SPIDER TRIPOD TRESTLE
TRIPPER BRANDISE
TRIVIAL JERK NICE VAIN LEGER
LIGHT PETTY SILLY SMALL TIDDY
FIDFAD FOOTLE SLIGHT TOYISH
COMICAL PIPERLY PUERILE
SHALLOW TIDDLEY DOGGEREL
FEATHERY FOOTLING GIMCRACK
PIDDLING PILULOUS TRIFLING
TRINKETY
(NOT —) SOLID EARNEST
TRIVIALITY FOLLY NIGNAY TRIFLE
INANITY IDLENESS NONSENSE
NUGACITY
TROCHANTER SCAPULA
TROCHE ROTULA TABLET CACHUNDE
PASTILLE
TROCHEE CHOREE CHOREUS
TROCHEUS
TROCHLEA PULLEY
TROCTOLITE GABBRO
TRODDEN TRADED
(MUCH —) BEATEN
TROGLODYTIC SPELEAN
TROGON QUEZAL QUETZAL
TOCORORO
TROILUS (FATHER OF —) PRIAM
(MOTHER OF —) HECUBA
(SLAYER OF —) ACHILLES
TROJAN TROIC DARDAN ANTENOR

(PL.) TEUCRI
TROLL HARL SPIN TROW HARLE
MOOCH TRAWL TROLLOL
TROLLER MOOCHER
TROLLOP CUT DOXY BITCH DOXIE
TROLL TRULL DOLLOP
TROMBONE BONE TRAM BUSINE
POSAUNE SACKBUT SLIPHORN
TRONA URAO
TROOP FARE GING ROUT TURM
ROUTE SOLAK STAND TURMA
WERED CORNET RISALA ROUGHT
SCHOOL THREAT TICHEL TROUPE
COMPANY COMITIVA
(— OF ARMED MEN) CREW
(— OF FOXES) SKULK
(—S ATTACHED TO SOVEREIGN)
GUARDS
(—S IN BATTLE ARRAY) SHELTRON
(—S ON WING OF ARMY) ALARES
(ASSAULTING —S) WAVE
(BOMBAY —S) DUCKS
(CAVALRY —) CORNET
(GIRL SCOUT —) SHIP
(LIGHT-ARMED —S) PSILOI
(SCOTTISH —S) JOCKS
(PL.) PARADE
TROOPER BARGIR RUTTER BARGEER
TROPARION HIRMOS HEIRMOS
TROPARY KATABASIS
TROPE IMAGE EVOVAE
TROPHONEMA VILLUS
TROPHOZOITE CEPHALIN SPORADIN
TROPHY BAG PALM PRIZE SCALP
REWARD LAURELS
TROPIC SOLAR TROPHIC
TROPINE HYOSCINE
TROS (FATHER OF —) ERICTHONIUS
(MOTHER OF —) CALLIRRHOE
(SON OF —) ILUS GANYMEDE
ASSARACUS
TROT JOG SPUD TRIG FADGE HURRY
PIAFFE
TROTH CERTY TROGS TRUTH CERTIE
TROTTER DRIVER CRUBEEN
SPANKER
TROUBADOR MINSTREL SORDELLO
TROUBLE ADO AIL DIK HOE ILL IRK
MAR WOE BEAT BUSY CAIN CARK
EARN FASH FIKE JEEL MASH MOIL
PAIN PINE ROUT SORE STIR TEEN
TINE TRAY UNRO WORK ANNOY
BESET CROSS DROVE DUTCH GRIEF
HAUNT LABOR ROWEL SMITE SPITE
STEER STURT SUSSY THRIE TWEAK
WHILE WORRY BOTHER BURBLE
CADDLE CUMBER DITHER EFFORT
GRIEVE GRUDGE HARASS KIAUGH
MOLEST POTHER RATTLE RUBBER
SORROW TAKING THREAT UNEASE
UNRUFE WORRIT AFFLICT AGITATE
ANXIETY CHAGRIN DISEASE DISTURB
DRUBBLE EMBROIL FASHERY
INFLICT PERTURB PILIKIA SCRUPLE
SPUTTER THOUGHT TRACHLE
TRAVAIL TRIBBLE TURMOIL
BUSINESS DARKNESS DISORDER
DISQUIET DISTRESS NOISANCE
VEXATION WANDRETH

(— ONE'S SELF) PASS
(PL.) CHAGRINS
TROUBLED DRUBLY DRUMLY
GRUMLY QUEASY FRETFUL
HAUNTED HARASSED
TROUBLESOME DIK ILL HARD FIKIE
SHREWD STICKY HARMFUL
TEWSOME UNTOWARD
TROUBLED CAREFUL AGITATED
TROUBLESHOOTER FIXER
TROUBLESOME SAD PLAGUY
UNEASY PESTFUL ANNOYING
FASHIOUS SPITEFUL
TROUBLESOMENESS BOTHER
TROUBLING CHRONIC
TROU-DE-LOUP TRAPHOLE
TROUGH BOX CUP HOD RUN TOM
BACK BOSH BUNK COVE DAIL DALE
DISH DORR SHOE SINK TRAY TROW
BAKIE CHUTE DITCH LAVER SHOOT
SHUTE SLIDE SPOUT STRIP ALVEUS
BACKET BUDDLE GUTTER HARBOR
LAVABO MANGER RUNNER SALTER
SINKER SLUICE STRAKE TROGUE
VALLEY WALLOW CHENEAU
CONDUIT LAUNDER RIFFLER
TRENDLE TROFFER LAVATORY
(— FOR ASHES) BAKIE
(— FOR COOLING INGOTS) BOSH
(— FOR PAPER PULP) RIFFLER
(— FOR WASHING ORE) TOM HUTC
STRIP BUDDLE STRAKE
(— IN MONASTERY) LAVABO
(— OF A WAVE) SULK
(— OF CIDER MILL) CHASE
(— OF ROCK) SYNCLINE
(— OF THE SEA) ALVEUS
(ANNULAR —) CUP
(EAVES —) CANAL CHENEAU
(GLACIAL —) DORR
(SHEEP-DIPPING —) DUP
(WOODEN —) TRUG BAKIE TROGUE
TROUNCE MOP FLOG TRAMP
WHOMP COURSE CUDGEL CANVAS
TROUNCING LACING WARMING
TROUPE SERVANTS CUADRILLA
TROUSER STROSSER
TROUSERING CASINET
TROUSERS BAGS CORDS DUCKS
JEANS KICKS PANTS SLOPS TONGS
TREWS BRAIES DENIMS SHORTS
SKILTS SLACKS WHITES BOTTOMS
BRACCAE BROGUES KERSEYS
NANKINS SHALWAR SLIVERS
STRIDES BLOOMERS BREECHES
FLANNELS KICKSEYS MOLESKIN
NANKEENS OVERALLS SHINTYAN
TROUT CHAR KELT PEAL POGY
BROOK BROWN CHARR LAKER
LUNGE SEWEN SHARD SQUET SQUL
TRUFF FINNOC KIPPER MYKISS
QUASKY SALTER TAIMEN TRUCHA
TULADI BOREGAT BROOKIE
BROWNIE COASTER HERLING
OQUASSA POUNDER RAINBOW
SQUETEE AUREOLUS BODIERON
GILLAROO HARDHEAD KAMLOOPS
SAIBLING SALMONID SISCOWET
(SMALL —) SCURLING SKIRLING

(YOUNG —) WHITLING
ROUVERE BLONDEL
ROW DROW TRUE FAITH BELIEF
COVENANT
ROWEL HAWK LEAF PIPE DARBY
DERBY FLOAT TAPER TREWEL
(HEARTSHAPED —) HEART DOGTAIL
(MOLDER'S —) LEAF TAPER
(PLASTERER'S —) FLOAT
RUANT HOOKY TRONE TROUT
MICHER MEECHER TRIVANT
VAGRANT
RUCE PAX BARLEY TREAGUE
INDUCIAE
RUCK DAN UTE BUNK CORF DRAB
DRAG DUCK DUMP GUNK RACK
WYNN BOGIE BUGGY DILLY DOLLY
GILLY LORRY BARTER BUMMER
CAMION DIESEL DROGUE DRUGGE
DUMPER JITNEY SLOVEN TIPPER
TURTLE CARAVAN FOURGON
GONDOLA SKIDDER SLEEPER
TROLLEY TRUCKLE TRUNDLE
DELIVERY HAULAWAY TRANSFER
(COAL —) DAN
(LOGGING —) BUNK BUMMER
(MINING —) CORF BARNEY
(TIMBER —) DRUG WYNN
RUCKLE FAWN TOADY SLAVER
RUCKLING SERVILE
RUCULENCE BRAG
RUCULENT MEAN CRUEL HARSH
FIERCE SAVAGE SCATHING
RUDGE JOG PAD HAKE PLOD STOG
JAUNT TRACE TRAMP TRASH
STODGE TRAIPSE
RUE SO GOOD JUST LEAL PURE
REAL VERY VRAI PLUMB RIGHT
SOOTH SOUND VERAY FIDELE
LAWFUL DEVOTED GENUINE
GERMANE PRECISE SINCERE
STAUNCH FAITHFUL RELIABLE
RIGHTFUL SOOTHFUL UNERRING
(— TO THE FACT) LITERAL
(QUESTIONABLY —) ALLEGED
RUFFLE TRUB TRUFF EARTHNUT
RUISM SOOTH
RULL DELL BLOWZE CALLET
RULY YEA AWAT EVEN IWIS JUST
QUITE SOOTH SYKER TIGHT ATWEEL
DINKUM INDEED SIMPLY VERILY
INSOOTH SOOTHLY VERAMENT
WITTERLY
RUMP DIS DIX LOW PAM LILY RUFF
BASTA BASTO DEECE TROMBE
MANILLA MATADOR TRIUMPH
SPADILLE
(2ND HIGHEST —) MANILLE
RUMPERY MOCKADO GIMCRACK
PEDDLERY
RUMPET BEME LURE TUBA TRUMP
BOZINE BUCCIN CORNET KERANA
LITUUS TROMBA TULNIC ALCHEMY
BUCCINA CLARINO CLARION
KERRANA SALPINX NARSINGA
SLUGHORN SOURDINE WATERCUP
RUMPET BELL CODON PAVILON
RUMPET CALL DIAN DIANA
SENNET

TRUMPET CREEPER TECOMA
COWHAGE CREEPER FOXGLOVE
HELLVINE
TRUMPETER MOKI AGAMI TRUMP
TOOTER JACAMIN TUBICEN YAKAMIK
TRUMPETER FISH MOKI MOKIHI
TRUMPETER PERCH MADO
TRUMPETS WATERCUP
TRUMPETWOOD IMBAUBA
TRUNCATED STUBBED TRUNKED
TRUNCHEON BATON WARDER
SPONTON PARTISAN SPONTOON
TRUNDLE HURL RUNG TROLL
RUNDLE TRUCKLE WALLOWER
TRUNK BOX BODY BOLE BOOT BULK
KIST LICH RUNT STAM STEM STUD
CABER PETER SHAFT STICK STOCK
TORSO ARIGUE BARREL CAUDEX
COFFER LOCKER CARCASS
CORSAGE STOWAGE TRUNCUS
SARATOGA
(ARTERIAL —) AORTA
(ELEPHANT'S —) SNOUT
(FOSSIL —) CYCAD
(SMALL —) HATBOX
(TREE — OVER 8 INCHES IN
DIAMETER) MAST
(TREE —) BOLE BUTT STICK
(TRIMMED TREE —) LOG
(WORSHIPPED TREE —S) IRMINSUL
TRUNKFISH CHAPIN BOXFISH
COWFISH
TRUSS SPAN WARREN
(— OF STRAW) WAP
(— UP) KILT
TRUST AFFY HOPE LITE POOL RELY
REST TICK TREW TROW FAITH FRIST
GROUP TRUTH BELIEF CARTEL
CHARGE CORNER CREDIT DEPEND
FIANCE LIPPEN OFFICE TICKET
BELIEVE BETRUST CONFIDE
CREANCE CRIANCE JAWBONE
SECRECY VENTURE AFFIANCE
COMMENDA CREDENCE MONOPOLY
RELIANCE
TRUSTED FIDUCIAL
TRUSTEE FEOFEE SINDICO VISITOR
MUTWALLI
TRUSTWORTHINESS HONOR TRUST
HONESTY CREDENCE AXIOPISTY
TRUSTWORTHY SAFE SURE SOOTH
SOUND SYKER TRIED HONEST
SECRET SECURE SICKER STABLE
TRUSTY COCKSURE CREDIBLE
FIDUCIAL RELIABLE TRUSTFUL
TRUSTY TRIG FECKFUL STAUNCH
FAITHFUL RELIABLE
TRUTH TAO UNA SOOTH TROTH
WHITE SATTVA VERITY VERITAS
VERACITY VERIDITY VERIMENT
(— TABLE) MATRIX
(IDEAL —) CHRIST DHARMA
(IN —) CERTES
(RELATING TO —) ALETHIC
(ULTIMATE —) LIGHT SUNYATA
TRUTHFUL TRUE VERY SOOTH
HONEST VERIDIC
TRUTHFULLY GOSPELLY

TRUTHFULNESS HONESTY
VERACITY
TRY GO SHY BURL HACK PENK PREE
SEEK SLAP TEST TIRL TURN AFOND
ASSAY CRACK ESSAY ETTLE FLING
GROPE JUDGE OFFER PROVE SENSE
SOUND TASTE TEMPT TOUCH
WHACK WHIRL APPOSE ASSAIL
FRAIST GRIEVE STRIVE AFFLICT
AFFORCE APPROVE ATTEMPT
DISCUSS ESPROVE IMITATE
STAGGER ENDEAVOR STRUGGLE
(— DESPERATELY) AGONIZE
(— FOR GOAL) SHOT
(— HARD) STRIVE
(— OUT) SAMPLE AUDITION
(— TO ATTAIN) AFFECT
(CASUAL —) FLING
(QUICK —) SLAP
TRYING ARDUOUS CRUCIAL
GRUELING
TRYSAIL SPENCER
TSETSE FLY KIVU GANDI DIPTERAN
GLOSSINA
T-SHAPED TAU
TSILTADEN CHILION
TSUBO BU
TSWANA CHUANA SECHUANA
TUAREG IMOHAGH IMOSHAGH
TUATARA GUANA GUANO IGUANA
HATTERIA
TUB FAT HOD KID KIT SOE SOW TUN
VAT BACK BOWK COOL CORF COWL
GAWN KNOP MEAL TYND TYNE
BOWIE ESHIN KEEVE KIVER SKEEL
STAND BUCKET KEELER KILLER
KIMNEL TROUGH TURNEL BATHTUB
BREAKER SALTFAT TANKARD
TRUNDLE KOOLIMAN LAVATORY
(— FOR ALEWIVES) HOD
(— FOR AMALGAMATING ORES)
TINA
(— FOR BREAD) BARGE
(— OF BUTTER) COOL
(— OF HOGWASH) SWILLTUB
(— USED AS DIPPER) HANDY PIGGIN
(— WITH SLOPING SIDES) SHAUL
(BREWER'S —) BACK KEEVE
(LAUNDRY —) WASHTRAY
(MESS —) KID KIT
(MINING —) CORF
(TANNING —) LEACH
(WATER —) DAN JAILER
(WOODEN —) KIT SOE KIMNEL
TRINDLE
TUBA BASS HELICON BOMBARDON
TUBE TAG BEAK BODY BOOT CANE
CASE CAST CORE DRUM DUCT
HORN HOSE PIPE REED WORM
BATON CANAL CORER CROOK
CRYPT DRAIN GLAND HEART LINER
QUILL SIGHT SLIDE SPILE SPOUT
THECA THIEF TRUMP TUBAL VALVE
AUDION CALCAR CANNEL CANNON
COLUMN CORNET DEWCAP FILTER
GULLET HEADER NOZZLE OCTODE
SLEEVE SUCKER SYRINX THROAT
TRIODE TUBING TUBULE TUNNEL
UPTAKE VESSEL BLOWGUN

CHIMNEY CONDUIT CUVETTE
DROPPER FERRULE FISTULA
HOUSING OOBLAST OVIDUCT
QUILLET ROSTRUM SALPINX
SHALLOT SNORTER SNUFFER
SOXHLET STOPPLE THIMBLE
TUBULUS VENTURI ADJUTAGE
BOMBILLA CORNICLE DIATREME
DRAWTUBE FAIRLEAD GRADUATE
ORTHICON OVARIOLE PENSTOCK
PIPESTEM SAUCISSE SIPHONET
SLEEVING URCEOLUS ZOOECIUM
(— AT BASE OF PETAL) CALCAR
(— CARRYING BASSOON
MOUTHPIECE) CROOK
(— COVERING TRACE CHAIN) PIPING
(— FOR DEPOSITING CONCRETE)
TREMIE
(— FOR DRINKING MATE) BOMBILLA
(— FOR LINING WELL) WELLRING
(— FOR STIFFENING STRING) TAG
(— FOR TRANSFERRING LIQUID)
SIPHON SYPHON
(— FOR WINDING THREAD) COP
(— FROM SHIP'S PUMP) DALE
(— IN ENGINE CYLINDER) LINER
(— OF BALLOON) APPENDIX
(— OF GUN) BORE BARREL
(— OF RETORT) BEAK ROSTRUM
(— OF SPIRIT LEVEL) BUBBLE
(— OF TOBACCO) CIGARET
(— TO LINE A VENT) BOUCHE
(— TWISTED IN COILS) WORM
(— USED IN WHALING) LULL
(AMPLIFIER —) STAGE
(BONE —) SNUFFER
(DISTILLING —) TOWER
(ELECTRO —) BULB
(ELECTRODE —) AUDION
(ELECTRON —) DIODE DRIVER
KLYSTRON PLIOTRON
(FIREWORKS —) LEADER
(GLANDULAR —) CRYPT
(GLASS —) SIGHT MATRASS
(HONEY —) NECTARY SIPHONET
(KNITTED —) STOCKING
(PAPER —) LEADER PASTILLE
(PASTRY —) CORNET
(POLLEN —) SPERMARY
(RECTIFIER —) IGNITRON
(SILK — OF SPIDER) SPIGOT
(SPEAKING —) GOSPORT
(SUCKING —) STRAW
(SURGICAL —) CANNULA
(THERMOMETER —) STEM
(VACUUM —) DIODE KEYER HEXODE
HEPTODE DYNATRON
TUBELET CIRCLET
TUBER ANU SET ANYU BULB CLOG
ROOT SEED SETT YAMP SALEP
JICAMA PIGNUT POTATO WAPATA
WINDER YAUTIA EARTHNUT
MURRNONG
TUBERCLE PEARL NODULE STEMMA
CUSPULE VERRUCA
TUBERCULAR PHTHISIC
TUBERCULOSIS CON CLYERS
DECLINE SCROFULA
TUBING HOSE TUBAGE

TUBMAN DUCKER
TUBULAR PIPY PIPED TUBATE
CANNULAR
(NOT —) FARCTATE
TUBULE TRACHEA TUBULET
TUBULUS
TUCANO BETOYAN
TUCK TOKE STUFF TRUSS FLANGE
(— IN) TRUSS TROUSS
(— UP) FAKE KILT
TUCKER CORDER KILTER PLEATER
TUESDAY (SECOND — AFTER
EASTER) HOCKDAY HOKEDAY
TUFF TRASS PEPERINO PORODITE
SANTORIN
TUFT EAR FAG FOB NOB SOP TOP
COMA DOWN KNOB KNOP MOCK
TUFF TUSK BEARD BUNCH CREST
FLOCK STUPA THRUM WHISK
CIRRUS DOLLOP PAPPUS PENCIL
TASSEL TUFFET CIRRHUS FEATHER
FLOCCUS HOBNAIL PANACHE
SCOPULA TOPKNOT TOPPING
TUSSOCK FLOCCULE
(— OF BRISTLES) BIRSE
(— OF CLOTH) FAG
(— OF DOWN) FRIEZE
(— OF FEATHERS) EAR HORN HULU
EGRET
(— OF FILAMENTS) BYSSUS
(— OF GRASS) FAG SOP MOCK
HASSOCK TUSSOCK
(— OF HAIR ON HORSE'S HOOF)
FETLOCK
(— OF HAIR) TOP TUZZ BRUSH
SWITCH COWLICK FEATHER
FLOCCUS SCOPULA TOPKNOT
IMPERIAL KROBYLOS
(— OF HAY) SOP
(— OF MALE TURKEY) BEARD
(— OF WOOL) FOB TUSK TUZZ
FLOCK
(— ON BIRD'S HEAD) COP CUCK
EGRET
(— ON PINEAPPLE) CROWN
(— ON SEED PLANT) PAPPUS
(— ON SPIDER'S FEET) SCOPULA
(—S OF ROPE YARN) THRUM
(VASCULAR —) GLOMUS
TUFTED COMOSE TAPPET TAPPIT
TUG LUG RUG TIT TOG CHUG DRAG
HALE HAUL PULL TOIL TUCK CHUFF
HITCH PLUCK SHRUG TRACE
RUGGLE TOWBOAT TUGBOAT
TUGBOAT TOW TUG TOWBOAT
TRACKER
TUI POE TUA KOKO TUWI POEBIRD
TUITION CUSTODY
TULIP LILY LILIUM BIZARRE BREEDER
TURNSOLE
TULIP TREE POPLAR BASSWOOD
CUCUMBER
TULIPWOOD AUBURN
TULLE ILLUSION
TUMATAKURU IRISHMAN MATAGORY
TUMBLE TOP COUP WALT LATCH
SPILL THROW TIFLE TRACE COTTON
GROVEL PURLER TIFFLE TOPPLE

WALTER WAMBLE WELTER STUMBL
WHEMMEL
(— OVER) TIPPLE WALLOP
TUMBLE-DOWN RUINOUS
TUMBLER NUT CLICK GLASS LEVER
WIPER ROLLER ACROBAT DRUMME
TIPPLER TOPPLER
TUMID TURGID BLOATED BULGING
FUSTIAN TURGENT INFLATED
TUMOROUS
TUMOR PAP WEN BEAL PIAN WART
AMPER BOTCH MYOMA NEVUS
PHYMA SWELL AMBURY ANBURY
EPULIS GLIOMA GYROMA INCOME
KELOID LIPOMA MYXOMA NUROMA
RISING WARBLE ADENOMA ANGIOM
CYSTOMA DERMOID DESMOID
FIBROID FIBROMA LUTEOMA
MYELOMA OSTEOMA OSTEOME
SARCOMA TESTUDO THYMOMA
ULONCUS ATHEROMA BLASTOMA
CHLOROMA CHORIOMA EMBRYOMA
GLANDULE HEMATOMA HEPATOMA
HOLDFAST LYMPHOMA MELANOMA
MELICERA ODONTOMA PHLEGMON
PLASMOMA PSAMMOMA SCIRRHUS
SEMINOMA TERATOID TERATOMA
WINDGALL
(— OF EYELID) GRANDO
(— ON HORSES'S LEGS) JARDE
(PUSTULAR —) BLAIN
(SKIN —) OUCH
(STUDY OF —S) ONCOLOGY
TUMULT DIN COIL FARE FLAW FRAY
FUSS HURL MUSS REEL RIOT ROUT
VISE BRAWL BROIL HURLY HURRY
LURRY NOISE ROUST STOOR STOU
WHIRL BUSTLE CLAMOR DIRDUM
EMEUTE FRACAS HUBBUB MUTINY
RABBLE RIPPET RUFFLE STEERY
UPROAR UPSTIR BLUSTER BOBBER
FACTION FERMENT GARBOIL
TEMPEST TURMOIL DISORDER
SEDITION STIRRING
TUMULTUOUS HIGH LOUD RUDE
NOISY ROUGH STORMY FURIOUS
HURRIED LAWLESS RIOTOUS
VIOLENT AGITATED CONFUSED
DRAWLING HURTLING
TUMULUS MOTE TUMP MOUND
BARROW BURIAN COTERELL
TUN CASK HAAB
(20 —S) KATUN
(ONE-THIRD —) TERTIAN
TUNA AHI ATUN TUNNY BLUEFIN
PELAMYD ALBACORE KAWAKAWA
TUNE AIR ARIA DUMP FADO LEED
NOTE PORT RANT SONG CHARM
CHORD DRANT POINT ATTUNE
GROUND MAGGOT STRAIN STRING
GUAJIRA HALLING MEASURE
MELISMA SONANCE ANGLAISE
FANDANGO GUARACHA HABANERA
(— A HARP) WREST
(— AN INSTRUMENT) STRING
(DANCE —) FURIANT ANGLAISE
GALLIARD
(FOLK —) FADO
(HILLBILLY —) HOEDOWN

(LIGHT —) TOY
(LITTLE —) CATCH
(LIVELY —) LILT SPRING HORNPIPE
(MELANCHOLY —) DUMP
(SACRED —) CHORAL CHORALE
(TRADITIONAL —) TONE
TUNEBO TAME GUACICO
TUNEFUL TUNY CHANTANT
TUNESOME
TUNEFULNESS MELODY
TUNGSTEN W WOLFRAM SCHEELIN
TUNGUS EVENK LAMUT
TUNIC COAT JAMA JUPE VEST
COTTE FROCK GIPPO JAMAH JUPON
PALLA ACHKAN BLIAUT CAMISE
CHITON CYCLAS FECKET HARDIE
KABAYA KIRTLE TABARD ARISARD
BLEAUNT CAMISIA PALTOCK
SURCOAT TUNICLE COLOBIUM
GANDOURA SUBTUNIC SUBUCULA
SUKKENYE
(— OF MAIL) HAUBERK
(HOODED FUR —) SOVIK
TUNICATE SALP SALPA SALPID
ASCIDIAN TUNICARY UROCHORD
TUNICLE SACCOS
TUNING ANESIS
TUNING FORK EVEL EVIL FORK
TUNER DIAPASE DIAPASON
MODULANT
TUNING HAMMER KEY

TUNISIA

CAPE: BON BLANC
CAPITAL: TUNIS
COIN: DINAR
GULF: GABES TUNIS HAMMAMET
ISLAND: DJERBA
LAKE: ACHKEL DJERID BIZERTE
MEASURE: SAA SAH SAAH CAFIZ
WHIBA METTAR
PORT: SFAX GABES TUNIS SOUSSE
BIZERTE
RIVER: MEDJERDA
TOWN: BEJA SFAX SUSA GABES
GAFSA MATEUR NABEUL
SOUSSE BIZERTE JENDOUBA
TEBOURBA ZAGHOUAN
WEIGHT: SAA ROTL ARTAL ARTEL
RATEL UCKIA KANTAR

TUNNEL ADIT BORE CAVE PUKA
SINK TUBE DRIFT DRIVE KAREZ
STALL BURROW PIERCE
(— INTO AN IGLOO) TOSSUT
TUNNY TUNA ALBACORE SCOMBRID
(YOUNG —) PELAMYD
TUP TIP TRIP MONKEY BLISSOM
TURBAN PAT MOAB PATA SASH
TUFT LUNGI MITER MITRE PATTI
TOWEL TUFFE MANDIL WRAPPER
KAFFIYEH PUGGAREE SEERBAND
TOLIPANE TULIPANT TURBANTO
URBELLARIA APROCTA
URBELLARIAN FLATWORM
URBID FAT RILY DROVY GUMLY
MUDDY ROILY DRUMLY GRUMLY
QUALLY FECULENT LUTULENT

TURBIDITY RILE
TURBOT BRET BRILL WHIFF
FLATFISH
TURBULENCE FURY UPROAR
FERMENT RIOTING
TURBULENT GURL HIGH LOUD RUDE
WILD ROUGH WROTH RUGGED
STORMY UNRULY YEASTY FURIOUS
RABBISH RACKETY TROUBLE
VIOLENT MUTINOUS
TURDUS MERULA
TUREEN DISH TERRINE
TURF SOD VAG CESS DELF FAIL
FALE FEAL FLAG FLAT FLAW PONE
SUNK DELFT SCRAW SPINE SWARD
TRUFF FLAUGHT SHIRREL SODDING
(— CUT BY GOLF STROKE) DIVOT
(— FOR LINING PARAPET) GAZON
(DRIED — FOR FUEL) VAG
(PARED —) BEAT
(ROUGH —) GOR
(SMALL PIECE OF —) TAB
(THIN LAYER OF —) FLAW
TURF SPADE SLANE
TURGID TUMID INFLATED
TURGIDNESS TYMPANY
TURK TURCO TURKO SELJUK
CORSAIR OSMANLI OTTOMAN
TURQUET KONARIOT
TURKANA ELKUMA

TURKEY

CAPE: INCE BAFRA ANAMUR
HINZIR KARATAS KEREMPE
CAPITAL: ANKARA
COIN: PARA AKCHA ASPER ATTUN
REBIA AKCHEH SEQUIN ZEQUIN
ALTILIK BESHLIK PATAQUE
PIASTER MEDJIDIE ZECCHINO
DISTRICT: PERA BEYOGLU CILICIA
GULF: COS ANTALYA
LAKE: TUZ VAN EGRIDIR BEYSEHIR
MEASURE: DRA OKA OKE PIK
DRAA HATT KHAT KILE ZIRA
ALMUD BERRI DONUM KILEH
ZIRAI ARSHIN CHINIK DJERIB
FORTIN HALEBI PARMAK
NOCKTAT
MOUNTAIN: AK ALA KARA HASAN
HINIS HONAZ MURAT MURIT
ARARAT BINGOL BOLGAR
SUPHAN ERCIYAS KARACALI
PROVINCE: SERT SIIRT ANGORA
EYALET
RIVER: DICLE FIRAT GEDIZ HALYS
IRMAK KIZIL MESTA SARUS
SEIHUN SEYHAN SEYLAN TIGRIS
SAKARYA MAEANDER
SEAPORT: ENOS IZMIR MERSIN
SAMSUN TRABZON ISTANBUL
TOWN: URFA ADANA BURSA IZMIR
KONYA MARAS SIIRT SIVAS
AINTAB EDESSA EDIRNE ELAZIZ
MARASH SAMSUN ERZURUM
KAYSERI SCUTARI USKUDAR
ISTANBUL STAMBOUL
WEIGHT: OKA OKE DRAM KILE
ROTL ARTAL ARTEL CEQUI

CHEKE KERAT MAUND OBOLU
RATEL BATMAN DIRHEM KANTAR
MISKAL DRACHMA QUINTAL
YUSDRUM

TURKEY STAG STEG BUSTARD
ERECTER ERECTOR GOBBLER
ALDERMAN
(MALE —) TOM
(YOUNG —) POULT
TURKEY BUZZARD AURA
BROMVOEL BROMVOGEL GALLINAZO
TURKEY-COCK STAG
TURKEY OAK CERRIS
TURKI KAZAK QAZAQ KAZAKH
TURKISH TURK TURCIC OSMANLI
OTTOMAN
TURKISH DELIGHT LOUKOUM
TURKOMAN SEID ERSAR
TURK'S CAP LILY MARTAGON
TURMERIC REA ANGO HALDI OLENA
HULDEE AZAFRAN CURCUMA
TURMIT TURNIP
TURMOIL ADO DIN COIL DUST MOIL
TOIL TOSS BURLE HURLY HURRY
STROW TOUSE WHIRL HASSLE
JABBLE UPROAR WELTER CLUTTER
EMOTION FERMENT GARBOIL
HURLING MAKADOO RUMMAGE
TEMPEST DISPEACE DISQUIET
TURN GO BOW CUT GEE JAR RUN
TON WIN AIRT BEND BOUT BOWL
CALE CAST CHAR CHOP COCK EDDY
GIRO HACK HEAD HINT HURL JAMB
KINK PULL QUIP ROLL ROVE SLEW
TOUR VEER VERT VICE WAFT WELT
WIND AIRTH ANGLE BLANK CHARE
CRANK CRASH CREEK CRICK
CROOK ELBOW FEEZE GLINT PIVOT
PLUCK PRICK QUIRK SHIFT SPELL
SWING SWIRL TARVE TERVE TREND
TRILL TROLL TWINE TWIST VERSE
VOLTI WHEEL WREST ATTURN
BOUGHT CIRCLE COURSE DEPEND
DIRECT DOUBLE GRUPPO GYRATE
INDENT INTEND INTURN POSSET
QUEEVE RESORT RETURN ROTATE
SPIRAL STRAIN SWIVEL TOURNE
TURKEN VOLUME VOLUTE WIMPLE
CONVERT CRANKLE CRINKLE
DEFLECT DISTURB FLEXION
FLEXURE FLOUNCE INCLINE INFLECT
PASSADE REVERSE REVOLVE
SERPENT TWINGLE TWISTER
VERSATE WREATHE CLINAMEN
DOUBLING FLECTION TOURNURE
VOLUTION
(— ABOUT) SLEW SLUE SLOUGH
WINDLASS
(— AGAINST) CROSS
(— AROUND) GYRE WELT WEND
RATCH BEWEND SPHERE
(— ASIDE) ERR WRY DAFF SKEW
WARD ABHOR AVERT BLENK DETER
EVADE FENCE GLENT SHEER WAIVE
BLENCH DEPART DETURN DIVERT
SWERVE SWITCH CRINKLE DECLINE
DEFLECT DEVIATE DIGRESS

DIVERGE PERVERT SCRITHE
(— AT DRINKING) TIRL
(— ATTENTION) ADVERT ADDRESS
(— AWAY) DOFF AVERT CHARE
HIELD REPEL AVERSE DESERT
DETURN DIVERT REVOLT ABANDON
DECLINE REVERSE OVERTURN
WITHTURN
(— AWRY) CONTORT
(— BACK ON) RUMP
(— BACK) KEP ABORT FLIPE FLYPE
RETORT RETURN REVERT REFLECT
UNTWIST RENVERSE
(— BROWN) AUGUST
(— BY TOSSING) FLAP
(— CARD FACE UP) BURN
(— DOWN) DIP DENY
(— FOR BETTER) CRISIS
(— IN ARCHERY) END
(— IN CROQUET) BISK BISQUE
(— IN ROPE) NIP RIDER
(— INSIDE OUT) EVERT INVERT
(— INTO ICE) CONGEAL
(— INTO VINEGAR) ACETIFY
(— LEAVES OF BOOK) LEAF TOSS
(— OF AFFAIRS) GO JOB KICK
(— OF CABLE) BITTER
(— OF DUTY) TOUR SHIFT TRICK
(— OF EVENTS) WENT
(— OF FANCY) GUST
(— OF MIND) FREAK
(— OF TIDE) PINCH
(— OF WIT) FLIRT
(— OF YARN) MOUSING
(— OFF) SHUNT DIVERT
(— ON LATHE) THROW
(— ON) HIT
(— OUT TO BE) PROVE EXFLECT
(— OUT) GO USH BEAR FALL FARE
OUST SORT TAKE CHIVE FUDGE
OUTPUT SUCCEED
(— OUTWARD) EVERT SPLAY
(— OVER) CANT FLAP FLIP KEEL
VETTE VOLVE CLINCH DESIGN
AGITATE CAPSIZE
(— POINT OF) ABATE
(— RAPIDLY) SPIN TIRL GIDDY
(— RIGHT) HAP HUP
(— SAIL YARD) BRACE
(— SKIS) STEM
(— SOUR) FOX BLINK PRILL BLEEZE
CHANGE SOUREN
(— SUDDENLY) FLOP
(— TO NEAR SIDE) HAW
(— TO OFF SIDE) GEE
(— TO ONE SIDE) CORNER GOGGLE
(— TO THE LEFT) HAW PORT WIND
WYND
(— UP NOSE) FLIRT SNURL
(— UP) FACE HAPPEN
(— UPSIDE DOWN) CANT COUP
WHELM INVERT QUELME WHELVE
(— VESSEL IN CIRCLE) CHAPEL
(— WHEELS) CRAMP
(— YELLOW) FIRE
(COMPLETE —) LAP
(DOWNWARD —) SLIDE
(ECCENTRIC —) CRANKUM
(FORTUNATE —) BREAK

(HALF —) CARACOLE
(IN —) AROUND
(SHARP —) DOUBLE WRENCH
ZIGZAG HAIRPIN
(SKI —) SWING CHRISTIE TELEMARK
(SUDDEN —) CURL
(PL.) ALLEGRO
TURNBUCKLE TURNEL TURNBOUT
TURNCOAT APOSTATE RENEGADE
TURNED SOUR VERSED COCKEYED
INFLEXED
(— ABOUT) CONVERSE
(— BACK) EVOLUTE
(— DOWNWARD) ABASED DEFLEXED
(— EDGEWISE) BLIND
(— INWARD) VARUS
(— TOWARD ONE SIDE) AWRY
(— TOWARD) ANODIC
(— UP) ACOCK URVED
(— WRONG WAY) AWK
TURNER SLICE BODGER SLIDER
TWIRLER
TURNING HEAD TWIST VOLTA WRINK
DETOUR ROTARY FLEXION FLEXURE
VOLVENT FLECTION STREPSIS
WHEELERY
(— OF EYE) CAST
(— SOUR) ACESCENT
(— TO RIGHT) DEXTRO
(— TOWARD STEM) ADVERSE
(METAL —S) SWARF
(PL.) SCULL
TURNIP BAGA NAPE NEEP RAPE
NAVEW SWEDE RAPEYE TURMUT
CRUCIFER RUTABAGA
(PL.) KRAUT RAPPINI
TURNIP-SHAPED NAPIFORM
RAPACEUS
TURNIX QUAIL HEMIPOD ORTYGAN
HEMIPODE
TURNKEY SCREW LOCKSMAN
TURNOUT RIG SETOUT EQUIPAGE
TRANSFER
TURNOVER BRAMBLE EMPANADA
FLAPJACK
(PL.) PIROJKI PIROSHKI
TURNPIN TAMPION
TURNSOLE HELIO
TURNSPIT HASTLER
TURNSTILE TIRL STILE TURNGATE
TURNPIKE
TURNSTONE PLOVER REDLEG
CHICARIC CREDDOCK
TURNTABLE RACER ROTARY
NONSYNC PLAYBACK
TURNUS (FATHER OF —) DAUNUS
(MOTHER OF —) VENILIA
(SLAYER OF —) AENEAS
TURPENTINE THUS TURPS SCRAPE
THINNER
(BORDEAUX —) GALIPOT
TURPITUDE FEDITY
TURQUOISE TURKEY TURKIS
CALAITE CALLAIS
TURRET BELFRY CUPOLA GARRET
GAZEBO LOUVER TOURET GUERITE
MIRADOR MONITOR BARTIZAN
GUNHOUSE TURRICLE PEPPERBOX
TURTLE EMYD ARRAU CARET CAREY

TORUP COODLE COOTER JURARA
SLIDER THURGI TURKLE CRAWLER
CREEPER EMYDIAN JUNIATA
LOGHEAD SNAPPER TORTUGA
CHELONID FLAPJACK HAWKBILL
MATAMATA SHAGTAIL STINKPOT
TERRAPIN TORTOISE
(— HAVING COMMERCIAL SHELL)
CHICKEN
(OLD —) MOSSBACK
TURTLEHEAD BALMONY CHELONE
CODHEAD
TUSCANY COLCOTHAR
TUSK CUSK HORN IVORY TOOTH
ELEPHANT
(— OF WILD BOAR) RAZOR
(ELEPHANT'S —) SCRIVELLO
TUSSLE TUG BICKER TASSEL
TOUSLE WARSLE
TUXEDO TUX TUCK
TUSSOCK HASSOCK
TUT HOOT TOOT HOOTS
TUTELAGE TUTELE YEMSEL
NURTURE TEACHING
TUTELARY GENIUS
TUTOR DON TUTE COACH TRACH
DOCENT FEEDER GROUND MASTER
PEDANT SCHOOL GRINDER TEACHE
CRANSIER CREANCER GOVERNOR
PANGLOSS PUPILIZE
TUTTI RIPIENO
TUTU TOOT TUPAKIHI
TWADDLE ROT FUDGE HAVER
BABBLE DRIVEL FOOTLE PIFFLE
TOOTLE TWATTLE NONSENSE
SLIPSLOP
TWANA COLCINE
TWANG TANG PLUCK SNUFFLE
TWANGLE TWANKLE
TWAYBLADE DUFOIL TWIFOIL
(PL.) LISTERA
TWEAK FEAK TWIG
TWEED PATTU PATTOO
TWEEZERS TIT TWIRK TWINGE
TWITCH MULLETS PINCERS
PINCETTE VOLSELLA
TWELFTH TWALT DOZENTH
(— OF INCH) SECOND
(— OF LIGHT PERIOD) INCH
(— PART) UNCIA
TWELVE TWAL DOZEN DICKER
DODECADE
TWELVEMONTH TOWMONT
TWELVER IMAMI
TWELVE-TONE SERIAL
TWELVE-TONE-ROW SET
TWENTIETH VIGESIMAL VINGTIEME
TWENTY KAPH CORGE KAPPA
SCORE COOREE
TWENTY-FIVE QUARTERN
TWENTY-FOURTH CARAT
TWENTY-ONE VANJOHN BLACKJAC
TWICE BIS DOPPIO
(— A DAY) BID
TWIDDLE TWEEDLE TWITTER
TWIG COW CHAT RICE RISP SLIP
WAND YARD BIRCH BRIAR BRIER
SHRAG SHRED SPRAY SPRIG STICK
TWIST VIRGA WAVER WITHE BALEY

FESCUE GREAVE SALLOW SPRING
SWITCH WATTLE WICKER SCOLLOP
TWIGLET ANAPHYTE
(— FOR SNUFF) DIP
(— GROWING FROM STUMP) WAVER
(— IN BIRD SNARE) SWEEK
(— WORN AT SACRIFICES)
INARCULUM
(—S FOR BURNING) CHATWOOD
(—S FOR WATTLING) FRITLES
(—S MADE INTO BROOM) BESOM
(BARE —) COW
(DRIED —) CHAD
(LITTLE —) SURCLE
(THATCHING —) SCOLLOP
(WILLOW —) SALLOW ANAPHYTE
WIGGED VIRGATE
WIGGY SPRAYEY
WILIGHT DIMPS DUMPS GLOAM
TWALE DIMMET DIMMIT UGHTEN
DUCKISH COCKSHUT EVENGLOW
GLOAMING GRISPING CREPUSCLE
(— OF THE GODS) RAGNAROK
(DARKER PART OF —) DUSK
(MORNING —) DAWN
WILL WALE CHINO CADDIS RUSSEL
CADDICE DUNGAREE
WILLED CORDED
WIN DUAL GEMEL SOSIE DIDYMUS
JUMELLE SIAMESE TWINDLE
DIDYMATE DIDYMOID DIDYMOUS
PARASITE TWINLING
(PL.) GEMEL COUPLET
WINE MAT COIL DUNE LACE PIRL
WIND WRAP TWIRL TWIST INFOLD
INTORT ANAMITE ENTWINE
SKEENYIE
(HANK OF —) RAN
(PITCHED —) WHIPPING
WINEBUSH PINBUSH
WINFLOWER LINNAEA
WINGE GIRD PANG PULL SHOOT
TOUCH TWANG STOUND
(— OF CONSCIENCE) SCRUPLE
(— OF PAIN) GLISK
WINKLE WINK BLINK TWEER TWINK
TWIRE SIMPER WINKLE SPARKLE
WINKLING MOMENT TWINKLY
WINLEAF HELMETPOD
WIRL SPIN TIRL DRILL QUERL TRILL
TWIRK TWIST WHIRL TRUNDLE
TWIDDLE TWIZZLE
(— OF BAGPIPE) WARBLER
WIST BOB CUE MAT PLY WIN WIP
CAST COIL CURL DRAW HURL KICK
KINK PIRL RICK SKEW SLEW SLUB
SLUE TURN WARP WIND WISP WORK
CHINK CRANK CRICK CRINK CROOK
CURVE FEEZE GNARL KINCH PLAIT
QUIRK QUIRL REEVE SCREW SKELL
SNAKE SNIRL SNURL SPIRE SWIRL
THROW TWEAK TWIND TWINE TWIRE
TWIRL WINCE WITHE WREST
BOUGHT DETORT EXTORT HANKLE
INTORT QUEEVE SLOUGH SPRAIN
SQUIRL SQUIRM STRAND TWEEZE
WAMBLE WARPLE WASHIN WICKER
WIMBLE WRABBE WRITHE CHIGNON
CONTORT CRANKLE CROOKLE

CRUMPLE DISTORT ENTWINE
ENTWIST FLOUNCE GIMMICK
SQUINCH TORTURE TWISTER
TWISTLE TWIZZLE WREATHE
WRIGGLE CLINAMEN CONVOLVE
ENTANGLE FOREHARD FORETURN
SPRINKLE SQUIGGLE VOLUTION
(— A ROPE) DALLY
(— AWAY) WAIVE
(— BACK) RETORT
(— FORCIBLY) WRING
(— IN A ROPE) GRIND SQUIRM
(— IN GRAIN OF A BOW) BOUGHT
(— IN ONE'S NATURE) KINK
(— OF FACE) STITCH
(— OF HAY) HAYBRAND
(— OF PAPER) SPILL
(— OF PEN IN WRITING) QUIRK
(— OF SPEECH) CRANK
(— OF THE MOUTH) DRAD
(— OF TOBACCO) ROLL
(— OF YARNS) FORETURN
(— OUT OF SHAPE) CONTORT
(— SHARPLY) FEAK
(— TOGETHER) CABLE RADDLE
TWISTED CAM KAM WRY AWRY
TORT KINKY SCREW TORSE WRONG
ATWIST GAUCHE HURLED KNOTTY
SCREWY SKEWED SWIRLY THROWN
TURKEN TWISTY WARPED WRITHE
CRISPED CROOKED GNARLED
KNOTTED SCREWED TORQUED
TORTILE TORTIVE WHELKED
WREATHY COCKEYED IMPLICIT
INTORTED INVOLVED NONPLANE
THRAWART WREATHEN
TWISTING DALLY KNECK AJOINT
TWIRLY TWIDDLY SQUIGGLY
STREPSIS
TWIT TIT CHECK TAUNT ETWITE
TWITTER RIDICULE
TWITCH TIC TIT FEAK FIRK JERK
JUMP PIRN TWIG WINK YANK PLUCK
START THRIP TWEAK TWICK TWIRK
QUATCH QUETCH QUITCH TWINGE
TWITCHEL
TWITCHING TIC JERKS PALMUS
WORKING SACCADIC
TWITTER TWIT CHIRM GARRE TWINK
JARGON WARBLE CHIPPER CHITTER
QUITTER TWITTLE WHITTER
TWO TWA BOTH TWAY TWIN TWAIN
BINARY COUPLE DOUBLE
(— LINES) LONGWAYS
(— OF A KIND) BRACE
(IN —) ATWO
(US —) UNC
TWO-COLORED BICHROME
TWO-FACED JANUS JANIFORM
TWO-FIFTEEN PM TIME
TWOFOLD DUAL DUPLE BACKED
BIFOLD DOUBLE DUPLEX DIGONAL
DIPLOID TWIFOLD DIDYMATE
DIDYMOID DIDYMOUS DIPLASIC
TWEYFOLD
TWO-FOOTED BIPED
TWO-FORKED BIFURCAL
TWO-HANDED BIMANAL BIMANOUS
TWO-HORNED BICORN BICORNED

TWOPENCE TUPPENCE
TWOS POT DEUCE
TWO-UP SWY
TYCOON SHOGUN TAIKUN
TYDEUS (FATHER OF —) OENEUS
(MOTHER OF —) PERIBOEA
(SON OF —) DIOMEDES
TYMPANUM DRUM TYMPAN
EARDRUM EPIPHRAGM
TYNDAREUS (FATHER OF —)
OEBALUS
(WIFE OF —) LEDA
TYPE CUT ILK CAST KIND MAKE
MOLD NORM SORT TAKE BOGUS
IMAGE MOULD STAMP EMBLEM
KICKER LETTER NATURE SHADOW
STRIPE SYMBOL TAKING TIMBER
BATARDE FASHION PARABLE
ANTETYPE EXEMPLAR
(— BLOCK) QUAD
(— OF EXCELLENCE) PARAGON
(— PLACED BOTTOM UP) TURN
(— SET UP) MATTER
(ASSORTMENT OF —) FONT
(DANCE —) LASYA
(DISARRANGED —) PI PIE
(GERMAN —) FRAKTUR
(HEAVY-FACED —) IONIC
(HIGHEST —) PINK
(IDEAL —) CHRIST
(OPPOSITE —) ANTITYPE
(PHYSICAL —) HABIT
(RACIAL —) DEHWAR
(REPRESENTATIVE —) GENIUS
(SET —) STICK
(STYLE OF —) DORIC ELITE GOUDY
GREEK IONIC KABEL ROMAN
BODONI CASLON GOTHIC HEBREW
ITALIC JENSON MODERN BOOKMAN
CENTURY ELZEVIR EMERALD
FULLFACE GARAMOND
TYPEBAR(PL.) BASKET
TYPEFACE FACE BOLDFACE
SANSERIF
TYPEHOLDER PALLET
TYPESETTER MONO
TYPESETTING FAT PHAT
TYPEWRITER MILL TYPER TYPIST
PORTABLE
TYPHON (FATHER OF —) TARTARUS
(MOTHER OF —) TERRA
TYPHOON WIND CYCLONE TUFFOON
TYPICAL FAIR TYPAL TYPIC USUAL
AVERAGE CLASSIC PATTERN
PERFECT REGULAR
TYPIFY TYPE IMAGE SHADOW
EPITOMIZE REPRESENT SYMBOLIZE
TYPIFYING GENERIC
TYR ER EAR TIU TYRR
TYRANNICAL LORDLY SLAVISH
ABSOLUTE DESPOTIC
TYRANNIZE DOMINEER OVERLORD
TYRANNOUS ABSOLUTE
TYRANNY ROD DESPOTISM
TYRANT ANARCH DESPOT NIMROD
FUEHRER PHARAOH PHALARIS
TYRANT FLYCATCHER PEWEE
TYRO HAM COLT PUPIL NOVICE

RABBIT TYRONE BEGINNER
NEOPHYTE
(FATHER OF —) SALMONEUS

(HUSBAND OF —) CRETHEUS
(MOTHER OF —) ALCIDICE
(SON OF —) AESON NELEUS PELIAS

PHERES AMYTHAON
TYRRHENIAN ETRUSCAN
TYTO ALUCO STRIX

J UNCLE UNION
JDDER BAG DUG TID EWER ELDER
SUMEN VESSEL

UGANDA
CAPITAL: KAMPALA
COLLEGE: MAKERERE
FORMER CAPITAL: ENTEBBE
LAKE: KYOGA ALBERT EDWARD
GEORGE VICTORIA
LANGUAGE: ATESO GANDA
LUGANDA SWAHILI
MOUNTAIN: ELGON
NATIVE: ATESO BANTU LANGO
ACHOLI ANKOLE BAGISU BAKIGA
BASOGA BATORO BAGANDA
BUNYORO LUGBARA NILOTIC
SUDANIC
PLATEAU: ANKOLE
PROVINCE: BUGANDA
RIVER: ASWA KAFU PAGER
KATONGA
SEAPORT: MOMBASA
TOWN: JINJA MBALE ENTEBBE
MOMBASA

JGLY FOUL AWFUL OUGLE SNIVY
UNKED CRANKY DREEPY GORGON
HOMELY LAIDLY CRABBED GRIZZLY
HIDEOUS HOUGHLY VICIOUS
GRUESOME UGLISOME UNLOVELY
JGLY-TEMPERED SNARLISH
JGNI BLANC TREBBIANO
JIGHUR JAGATAI
JITOTAN KAIMO WITOTAN
JKE JARANA
JKULELE UKE TAROPATCH
JLCER FRET KYLE SORE WOLF
BOTCH ULCUS MORMAL TETTER
CHANCRE EGILOPS ENCAUMA
AEGILOPS FONTANEL FOSSETTE
ULCUSCLE
(ARTIFICIAL —) ISSUE
JLCERATING EXEDENT
JLCERATION CARIES BEDSORE
HELCOSIS
JLEX LING
JLEXITE TIZA
JLNA CUBIT CUBITAL CUBITUS
JLTIMATE IT DIRE LAST FINAL
ULTIME SUPREME ABSOLUTE
EVENTUAL FARTHEST ULTIMITY
JLTIMATELY FINALLY
JLTIMO PAST
JLTRA EXTREME FANATIC FORWARD
JLTRACONSERVATISM TORYISM
JLTRACONSERVATIVE WHITE
JLTRAFASHIONABLE RITZY SWELL
SWAGGER
JLTRAMONTANISM CURIALISM
JLUA PAPIO PAPIOPIO
JLYSSES (FATHER OF —) LAERTES
(MOTHER OF —) ANTICLEA
(SLAYER OF —) TELEGONUS
(SON OF —) TELEMACHUS
(WIFE OF —) PENELOPE
JMBEL RAY RADIUS SERTULE
UMBELLA SERTULUM UMBELLET

UMBELLIFERONE CUMARIN
COUMARIN
UMBER OMER OMBER PARTRIDGE
UMBILICUS NAVEL
UMBO BEAK UMBONULE
UMBONES NATES
UMBRA DOGFISH MUDFISH NUCLEUS
UMBRINE
UMBRAGE PIQUE SNUFF OFFENSE
UMBRELLA BELL GAMP MUSH
BROLLY CHATTA PAYONG PILEUS
CHATTAH GINGHAM ROUNDEL
FITTISOL KITTYSOL MUSHROOM
TYRASOLE
UMBRELLA BIRD COTINGA
COTINGID
UMBRELLA BUSH MILJEE
UMBRELLA PALM KENTIA
UMBRELLA PLANT SEDGE GLUMAL
UMBRELLA TREE WAHOO
ELKWOOD MAGNOLIA
UMBRETTE UMBRE HOMBRE
UMBRET CICONIID
UMBRIAN IGUVINE
UMBURANA ROBLE
UMLAUT MUTATION METAPHONY
UMPIRE UMP JUDGE TRIER ARBITER
DAYSMAN ODDSMAN STICKLER
UNABASHED BROWLESS
UNABBREVIATED FULL
UNABLE UNHABILE
UNACCENTED GRAVE LIGHT ATONIC
UNACCEPTABLE DREADFUL
UNACCOMPANIED BARE SOLO
ALONE SINGLE
UNACCOUNTABLE STRANGE
UNACCUSTOMED UNUSED
STRANGE INSOLITE WONTLESS
UNACQUAINTED STRANGE
UNCOUTH
UNADORNED DRY BALD STARK
RUSTIC SIMPLE AUSTERE INORNATE
UNADULTERATED NET FRANK
HONEST VIRGIN GENUINE SINCERE
UNADVANTAGEOUSLY ILL
UNAFFECTED EASY REAL PLAIN
HOMELY NATIVE RUSTIC SIMPLE
ARTLESS BUCOLIC SINCERE
SEMPLICE
UNAFRAID BOLD BRAVE DEFIANT
UNAGGRESSIVE AMIABLE
UNALERT SUPINE
UNALLOYED DEEP SOLID VIRGIN
GENUINE
UNALTERABLE IMMUTABLE
UNAMBIGUOUS EXPLICIT
UNANIMATED FLAT VAPID INSIPID
UNANIMITY ATTACK CONSENT
UNANIMOUS SOLID WHOLE
UNANIME UNIVOCAL
UNAPPROACHABLE STATELY
UNARMED BARE INERM UNBARBED
UNASSAILABLE SECURE
UNASSUMED NATURAL
UNASSUMING SHY HUMBLE MODEST
SIMPLE NATURAL RETIRING
UNATTACHED FREE LOOSE SINGLE
UNATTENDED SINGLE
UNATTRACTIVE BLAH UGLY WORSE

HOMELY FRUMPISH UNLIKELY
UNAVAILING VAIN FUTILE GAINLESS
UNAVOIDABLE SHUNLESS
UNAVOWED SECRET
UNAWARE UNWARE WITLESS
HEEDLESS INNOCENT UNBEWARE
WARELESS
UNAWARES ABACK SHORT
UNBALANCED HITE DOTTY NUTTY
FRUITY UNEVEN FANATIC
DERANGED LOPSIDED
UNBAR UNSLOT
UNBARRED UNSTOKEN
UNBECOMING RUDE INEPT INDIGN
UNMEET BENEATH IMPROPER
INDECENT UNSEEMLY UNWORTHY
UNBELIEF UNFAITH
UNBELIEVABLE HOT THIN
UNBELIEVER PAGAN GIAOUR
ATHEIST DOUBTER INFIDEL
SCOFFER SKEPTIC
UNBEND REST THAW FRESE RELAX
UNTIE EXTEND DISBEND UNCROOK
UNBENDING RIGID STARK STERN
STIFF THARF OBDURATE RAMRODDY
RESOLUTE
UNBIASED FAIR JUST DETACHED
UNBIND FREE UNDO UNTIE UNGIRD
UNDRESS
UNBLAMABLE INNOCENT
UNBLEACHED BLAE BLAY ECRU
BEIGE BROWN
UNBLEMISHED FAIR PURE SOUND
ENTIRE SPOTLESS
UNBLOCK REDD
UNBLOODY INCRUENT
UNBOLT OPEN UNBAR UNPIN
UNBOSOM OPEN
UNBOUGHT UNCOFT
UNBOUND FREE LOOSE
UNBOUNDED HUGE
UNBRANDED SLICK NATIVE
UNBROKEN DEAD FLAT FERAL
FLUSH SOLID SINGLE CERRERO
UNRACED STRAIGHT UNBACKED
WAKELESS
UNBUILD DESTROY
UNBUILT UNBIGGED
UNBURDEN EMPTY UNLOAD UNSHIP
UNBURNISHED WHITE MATTED
UNCANNY EERY UNCO EERIE SCARY
UNCOW UNKID WEIRD WISHT
CREEPY SPOOKY UNCOUTH
ELDRITCH POKERISH
UNCASTRATED INTACT
UNCAUGHT UNHENT
UNCEASING ENDLESS ETERNAL
EASELESS MINUTELY
UNCEREMONIOUS CURT BLUFF
BLUNT SHORT ABRUPT FAMILIAR
INFORMAL
UNCERTAIN WAW DARK HAZY WILD
FLUKY SHADY SHAKY WAUGH
CASUAL CLOUDY CRANKY FITFUL
FLUKEY GLEAMY QUEASY CASALTY
CHANCEY COMICAL DUBIOUS
TRICKSY VARIOUS WILSOME
CATCHING DELICATE FLICKERY
FUGITIVE HOVERING INSECURE

SLIPPERY TECHNOUS TICKLISH
UNCERTAINTY MIST WERE DEMUR
DOUBT MAYBE BAFFLE BALANCE
DUBIETY CASUALTY SUSPENSE
UNSURETY
UNCHALLENGED ACCEPTED
UNCHANGEABLE FAST STABLE
DURABLE ETERNAL
UNCHANGING STATIC ETERNAL
UNIFORM STATICAL
UNCHASTE LEWD FRAIL LIGHT
IMPURE WANTON FORLAIN
HAGGARD SCARLET IMMODEST
UNCHASTITY BAWDRY STUPRUM
ADULTERY
UNCHECKED LIBERAL RAMPANT
UNCIFORM HAMATUM
UNCINARIA NECATOR
UNCIVIL RUDE BLUFF ROUGH RUSTY
CRUSTY RUGGED UNFEEL IMPOLITE
UNCIVILIZED RUDE WILD MYALL
INCULT SAVAGE UNCIVIL IGNORANT
SYLVATIC
UNCLAD LOOSE UNDRESSED
UNCLE EME OOM YEME BUNKS
NUNKY NUNCLE
UNCLEAN FOUL TREF VILE BLACK
TARRY TERFA TREFA COMMON
FILTHY IMMUND IMPURE DEFILED
UNCLEANNESS DIRT FOULNESS
UNCLEAR DIM HAZY SHAGGY
UNCLEARLY DIMLY
UNCLENCH UNDOUBLE
UNCLOSE OPE OPEN UNHASP
DISCLOSE
UNCLOTHE TIRL SPOIL UNRIG
DEVEST DESPOIL
UNCLOUDED CLEAR
UNCOIL UNLINK
UNCOLORED FAIR
UNCOMBED UNKAMED UNTEWED
UNCOMBINED FREE FRANK
UNCOMELY INDECENT
UNCOMFORTABLE HOT EVIL POOR
HARSH UNKET UNKID QUEASY
STICKY UNFELE
UNCOMMON MUCH NICE RARE SELD
UNCO BYOUS FORBY UNCOW
VAUDY DAINTY FORBYE SCARCE
SPECIAL STRANGE UNUSUAL
SINGULAR UNWONTED
UNCOMMONLY UNCO BYOUS EXTRA
UNCOW UNCOLY
UNCOMMONNESS SCARCITY
UNCOMMUNICATIVE DUMB SILENT
PRIVATE RESERVED
UNCOMPLICATED RURAL HONEST
SIMPLE
UNCOMPOUNDED SIMPLE SIMPLEX
UNCOMPROMISING ACID FIRM
GRIM RIGID STERN STOUT ULTRA
SEVERE STRICT STRONG EXTREME
UNCONCEALED BARE OPEN
OUVERT APPARENT
UNCONCERN APATHY EASINESS
UNCONCERNED COOL EASY BLAND
CASUAL CARELESS
UNCONCERNEDLY LIGHTLY
UNCONDITIONAL FREE FRANK

UTTER SIMPLE ABSOLUTE EXPLICIT
TERMLESS
UNCONFINED LAX FREE LOOSE
UNCONGENIAL HATEFUL INGRATE
KINDLESS
UNCONNECTED GAPPY DETACHED
UNCONQUERED INVICT INVICTED
UNCONSCIOUS OUT COLD BRUTE
ASLEEP BLOTTO CUCKOO TORPID
UNAWARE COMATOSE IGNORANT
UNCONSTRAINED FREE UNNET
SIMPLE FAMILIAR
UNCONTROLLABLE WILD
UNCONTROLLED FREE LIBERAL
UNBITTED
UNCONVENTIONAL LOOSE CASUAL
DEVIOUS BOHEMIAN INFORMAL
UNCONVINCING FALSE FISHY
UNCOOKED RAW
UNCOUNTABLE SUMLESS
UNCOUPLE CUT DISLINK
UNCOUTH RUDE CRUDE DORIC
GURLY UNKED UNKIT GOTHIC
JUNGLY QUAINT RENISH AWKWARD
BOORISH CUBBISH HIRSUTE
LOUTISH UNGAINLY YOKELISH
(— **PERSON**) TUG
UNCOVER BARE DOFF HUNT ROUT
TIRL TIRR BREAK STRIP TIRVE
UNLAP UNLID UNWRY DETECT
EXHUME SEARCH UNBARE UNCASE
UNHALE UNVEIL UNDRAPE UNEARTH
DISCLOSE DISCOVER UNMANTLE
UNMUFFLE
UNCOVERED BARE OVERT
UNCTION CHRISM OINTMENT
UNCTUOUS FAT OILY SALVY SLEEK
SOAPY SUAVE GREASY COURTLY
PINGUID
UNCULTIVATED RAW BRUT FERAL
DESERT FALLOW INCULT SAVAGE
SLOVEN WILDERN
UNCULTURED RUDE INCULT
ARTLESS
UNCUT RASPED
UNDAMAGED WHOLE
UNDARKENED CLEAR
UNDAUNTED BOLD BRAVE MANLY
SPARTAN FEARLESS INTREPID
UNDE WAVY UNDEE
UNDECAYED GREEN
UNDECEIVE DISABUSE
UNDECIDED MOOT DUBIOUS
PENDING DOUBTFUL WAVERING
UNDECIDEDLY HUMDRUM
UNDECLARED SECRET
UNDEFENDED UNKEPT
UNDEFILED PURE CHASTE INTACT
VIRGIN
UNDEFINED OBSCURE
UNDELIVERABLE DEAD
UNDEMONSTRATIVE COLD ASEPTIC
LACONIC RESERVED
UNDENIABLE BRUTAL
UNDENIABLY INDEED
UNDEPENDABLE CASUAL FLUFFY
UNDER SUB BAJO BELOW INFRA
NEATH SOTTO ANEATH ANUNDER
BENEATH

(— **ORDERS**) SUPPOSED
(— **THE WORD**) IV
(— **THE YEAR**) SA
(— **THIS TITLE**) HT
(— **THIS WORD**) SV SHV
(— **WAY**) AFOOT
UNDERBODICE JUMP BASQUINE
UNDERBRUSH FILTH COVERT
GARSIL MAQUIS RAMMEL ABATURE
UNDERBURNED SOFT
UNDERBUTLER WASHPOT
UNDERCARRIAGE BOGY BOGEY
BOGIE
UNDERCLAY WARRANT
UNDERCLOTHES LININGS
UNDERCOAT PILE ALPACA
SURFACER
UNDERCOVER SECRET
UNDERCRUST ABAISSE
UNDERCURRENT UNDERLAY
UNDERRUN UNDERSET
UNDERCUT JAD HOLE LAME POOL
SUMP KIRVE NOTCH
UNDERDONE RARE
UNDERDRAWERS FLANNELS
UNDERESTIMATE DISPRIZE
MINIMIZE
UNDERFRAME SOLE
UNDERGARMENT BAND SLIP
CYMAR SIMAR SKIRT SMOCK TUNIC
WAIST BODICE CAMISE CILICE
CORSET GIRDLE STAMIN CHEMISE
DOUBLET DRAWERS STAMMEL
TALLITH KNICKERS
(PL.) SMALLS FLANNELS FLIMSIES
SNUGGIES
UNDERGO SERVE ENDURE SUFFER
SUSTAIN
UNDERGRADUATE MAN TASSEL
SERVITOR •
UNDERGROWTH RUSH RAMMEL
SPRING BUSHWOOD
UNDERHAND SLY DERN SHADY
BYHAND SECRET OBLIQUE
INVOLVED SINISTER SNEAKING
UNDERHANDED DERN FUNNY
FILTHY SECRET SINISTER
UNDERIVED ORIGINAL
UNDERLAYER SLASHING
UNDERLIE SUBTEND
UNDERLING MENIAL SEQUEL
UNDERER INFERIOR
UNDERLYING COVERT IMPLICIT
UNDERMINE SAP CAVE HOLE POOL
ERODE KNIFE WEAKEN FOUNDER
SUBVERT ENFEEBLE SUPPLANT
UNDERMINED ROTTEN
UNDERNEATH BELOW BENEATH
UNNEATH
UNDERNSONG TIERCE
UNDERPANTS BRIEFS BLOOMERS
KNICKERS
UNDERPART BELLY
UNDERPASS DIVE SUBWAY
UNDERRATE DECRY DISCOUNT
UNDERRUN BOTTOM
UNDERSACRISTAN CUSTOS
UNDERSHIRT VEST SHIFT SHIRT
CAMISA JERSEY LINDER SEMMIT

SINGLET WRAPPER

UNDERSHRUB HEATH PINKEYE
SEEPWEED SUBSHRUB
UNDERSIDE BOTTOM BREAST
(— **OF CLOUD**) BASE
(— **OF FINGER**) BALL
(— **OF FLOOR**) CEILING
UNDERSIZED DEENY SCRUB STUNT
UNDERSKIRT QUILT CRINOLINE
UNDERSTAND CAN CON GET KEN
SEE GAUM HAVE MAKE TAKE TWIG
BRAIN ENTER GRASP REACH SAVVY
SEIZE SENSE SKILL SPELL ACCEPT
COTTON FIGURE FOLLOW INTAKE
INTEND SUBAUD UPTAKE CONCEIT
DISCERN COMPRISE CONCEIVE
CONSTRUE CONTRIVE FORSTAND
PERCEIVE PERSTAND UNDERNIM
UNDERSTANDING KEN WIT GAUM
HEAD CLASP HEART INWIT SENSE
SKILL ACCORD INTENT NOTION
REASON TREATY UPTAKE COMPACT
CONCEPT ENTENTE INSIGHT
MEANING WITNESS DAYLIGHT
(**IMPERFECT** —) DARKNESS
UNDERSTATEMENT LITOTES
UNDERSTOOD LUCID SUPPOSED
(— **ONLY BY SPECIALLY INITIATED**)
ESOTERIC
(**EASILY** —) EASY CLEAR EXTANT
(**NOT** —) DARKSOME
UNDERSTUDY DOUBLE
UNDERSURFACE SOLE
UNDERTAKE GO TRY DARE FANG
FOND GRANT OFFER ASSUME
INCEPT PLEDGE ATTEMPT EMBRACE
EMPRISE PRETEND UNDERFO
CONTRACT PRESTATE
(— **RESPONSIBILITY**) ACCEPT
ANSWER
UNDERTAKER UPHOLDER
UNDERTAKING JOB AVAL TASK
CAUTIO EFFORT SCHEME VOYAGE
ATTEMPT CALLING PROJECT
VENTURE COVENANT
(— **IN CARDS**) CONTRACT
(**UNPROFITABLE** —) FOLLY
UNDERTEACHER USHER
UNDERTONE INKLING SUBTONE
UNDERTOW SEAPOOSE
UNDERVALUE DECRY DISPRIZE
DISVALUE
UNDERWAIST CAMISOLE
UNDERWATER (— **DEVICE**) OTTER
PARAVANE
UNDERWEAR BRIEFS SHORTS
SKIVVY UNDIES DESSOUS HEAVIES
LINGERIE PRETTIES
UNDERWING CATOCALA
UNDERWOOD FRITH BOSCAGE
COPPICE
UNDERWORLD DUAT DEWAT HADES
ORCUS SHEOL MICTLAN XIBALBA
GANGLAND
UNDERWRITE SIGN INSURE
ENDORSE
UNDERWRITER INSURER
UNDESERVED INDIGN
UNDETERMINED UNSET DUBIOUS

AORISTIC DOUBTFUL INFINITE
UNDEVELOPED CRUDE SLOVEN
GERMING IMMATURE JUVENILE
UNDEVIATINGLY SMACK
UNDIFFERENCED ENTIRE
UNDIFFERENTIATED GLOBAL
AMERISTIC
UNDIGESTED CRUDE
UNDIGNIFIED DOGGREL DOGGEREL
UNDILUTED MERE NEAT PURE
NAKED SHEER SHORT STRAIGHT
UNDIMINISHED ENTIRE
UNDIMMED CLEAR
UNDINE NIX
UNDISCIPLINED WANTON COLTISH
UNDISCLOSED HIDDEN SEALED
UNDISCRIMINATING GROSS
UNDISGUISED BALD PLAIN
UNDISMAYED ONFLEMED
UNDISPUTED LIQUID
UNDISTINGUISHED GROSS
COMMON UNNOBLE FAMELESS
NOTELESS
UNDISTORTED CLEAR
UNDISTURBED SOUND VIRGIN
TRANQUIL
UNDIVIDED WHOLE ENTIRE SINGLE
UNDO COOK SLIP FORDO SPEED
UNPAY DEFEAT DIDDLE FOREDO
UNBIND UNKNIT UNLOCK UNTUCK
UNWORK DEFEISE DESTROY
UNRAVEL UNRIVET UNTWIRL
UNWEAVE UNWREST DECIPHER
DISSOLVE DISTRUSS UNFASTEN
UNDOER ACHAN
UNDOGMATIC AGNOSTIC
UNDOING DEFEAT DOWNFALL
UNDOMESTICATED WILD FERAL
FERINE
UNDOUBTEDLY SURELY FRANKLY
UNDRESS MOB DOFF FLAY TIRR
STRIP UNRAY UNRIG DEVEST
DIVEST UNBUSK UNCASE UNLACE
UNRIND UNROBE UNTIRE DISCASE
UNARRAY UNREADY UNSPOIL
UNTRUSS NEGLIGEE UNATTIRE
UNDRESSED UNDIGHT
UNDUE EXTREME
UNDULATE WAVE WAVY FLOAT
SWING BILLOW GYROSE KELTER
UNDATE UNDOSE FLICKER UNDATED
UNDULATING SURGING FLEXUOUS
INDENTED
UNDULATION FOLD ROLL WAVE
CRIMP TEETER WAVING CRIMPING
UNDULATORY WAVY
UNDUTIFULNESS IMPIETY
UNDYED CORAH
UNDYING IMMORTAL
UNEARTH DIG MOOT EXPOSE
UNCOVER DISCOVER
UNEARTHLY EERY EERIE WEIRD
AWESOME UNCANNY UNGODLY
UNEASINESS ENVY GENE FIDGET
NETTLE SORROW UNEASE AILMENT
ANXIETY DISEASE MISEASE
TROUBLE DISQUIET DISTASTE
UNEASY SICKLY FIDGETY INQUIET

RESTIVE UNQUIET WORRIED
RESTLESS
UNEDUCATED SIMPLE IGNORANT
UNEMBELLISHED DRY PROSE
AUSTERE
UNEMOTIONAL DRY COLD COOL
STOIC STONY STOICAL
UNEMOTIONALLY EVENLY
UNEMPLOYED IDLE ORRA VOID
OTIANT OTIOSE VACANT IDLESET
LEISURE UNBUSIED
UNEMPLOYMENT IDLENESS
UNENCUMBERED VACANT
EXPEDITE
UNENDING ABYSMAL AGELONG
CHRONIC ENDLESS UNDYING
TERMLESS TIMELESS
UNENJOYABLE JOYLESS
UNENLIGHTENED MISTY HEATHEN
IGNORANT
UNENTHUSIASTIC COLD
UNEQUAL IMPAR DISPAR UNEGAL
UNEVEN INEQUAL INFERIOR
(— **TO STRAIN**) FEEBLE
UNEQUALED UNIQUE NONESUCH
UNEQUIVOCAL DIRECT SQUARE
DEFINITE DISTINCT EXPLICIT
UNERRING DEAD TRUE DEADLY
INERRANT
UNERRINGLY CLEAN
UNEVEN EROSE GOBBY HAGGY
JAGGY MEALY ROUGH HOBBLY
PLATTY RAGGED RUGGED SPOTTY
TWITTY UNFAIR UNLIKE DIURNAL
ERRATIC HOTTERY INEQUAL
STREAKY UNEQUAL HUMMOCKY
SCRATCHY SNAGGLED
(— **IN COLOR**) CLOUDY
UNEVENNESS BUMP WAVE FRAZE
ANOMALY ASPERITY
UNEVENTFUL STILL UNDATED
UNEXCITED LEVEL
UNEXCITING DEAD DULL TAME
BORING PROSAIC
UNEXPECTED EERY EERIE ABRUPT
SUDDEN UNWARY INOPINE
UNLOOKED
UNEXPECTEDLY UNWARES
UNAWARES
UNEXPIRED ALIVE
UNEXPLAINED HIDDEN
UNEXPOSED RAW
UNFADABLE FAST
UNFADED FRESH BRIGHT
UNFAILING SURE DEADLY INFALLID
UNERRING
UNFAIR FOUL WRONG BIASED
SHABBY UNEVEN UNJUST DEVIOUS
PARTIAL SLANTER UNEQUAL
UNSEEMLY WRONGFUL
UNFAIRLY HARDLY
UNFAIRNESS INEQUITY
UNFAITHFUL INFIDEL TRAITOR
DISLOYAL RECREANT
UNFALTERING SURE TRUE STEADY
UNERRING
UNFAMILIAR NEW FREMD HEATHER
STRANGE UNKNOWN
UNFASTEN FREE OPEN UNDO

LOOSE UNPIN UNBIND UNHASP
UNLIME UNLINK UNLOCK UNMAKE
UNTINE UNDIGHT UNHITCH UNSTECK
UNTRUSS
UNFATHOMABLE ABYSSAL
PROFOUND
UNFATHOMED COSMIC
UNFAVORABLE BAD ILL FOUL HARD
POOR SHREWD UNFAIR UNKIND
ADVERSE AWKWARD FROWARD
HOSTILE UNHAPPY BACKWARD
CONTRARY INIMICAL SINISTER
UNKINDLY
UNFAVORABLY BADLY CROSS
UNFEELING COLD DULL HARD
CRASS CRUEL HARSH ROCKY
STERN STONY BRUTAL LEADEN
MARBLE STOLID CALLOUS
OBDURATE
UNFEELINGLY HARSHLY
UNFEELINGNESS APATHY
UNFEIGNED OPEN TRUE HEARTY
CORDIAL NATURAL SINCERE
UNFETTERED FREE UNGYVED
UNFILLED BLANK EMPTY VACANT
VACUOUS
UNFINISHED RAW GRAY GREY
KACHA KUTCHA RAGGED KACHCHA
STICKIT IMMATURE
UNFIRED GREEN
UNFIRM UNFAST
UNFIT BAD SICK UNAPT WISHT
WRONG COMMON FAULTY NOUGHT
UNTIDY DISABLE UNFITTY IMPROPER
UNFITTEN UNLIKELY UNLIKING
UNFITTING UNMEETLY
UNFLEDGED SQUAB CALLOW
UNFLINCHING LEVEL STAUNCH
UNFOLD OPEN BREAK BURST SOLVE
UNLAP UNTIE DEPLOY EVOLVE
EXPAND EXPLAT FLOWER SPREAD
UNFURL UNPLAT UNROLL UNTUCK
BLOSSOM DEVELOP DISPLAY
DIVULGE EXPLAIN UNPLAIT
UNRAVEL UNWEAVE UNDOUBLE
UNPLIGHT
UNFOLDED EVOLUTE EXPANDED
UNFOLDING DISPLAY
(— OF EVENTS) ACTION
(— TO VIEW) BURST
UNFORCED EASY GLIB WILLING
UNFORESEEN SUDDEN IMPREVU
UNAWARE
UNFORMED CALLOW INFORM
UNFORTUNATE ILL EVIL POOR
DONCY WEARY SHREWD HAPLESS
UNHAPPY UNLUCKY LUCKLESS
UNTOWARD WANHAPPY
UNFREQUENTED EMPTY UNCOUTH
SOLITARY
UNFRIENDLY ILL COLD FOUL CHILL
BITTER CHILLY FIERCE FROSTY
UNSOME HOSTILE INGRATE
STRANGE INIMICAL
UNFROCK DEFROCK DEGRADE
DISFROCK UNPRIEST
UNFRUITFUL BLUNT BARREN
EFFETE WASTED STERILE USELESS
INFECUND

UNFULFILLMENT BREACH
UNFURL SPREAD UNFOLD DEVELOP
OUTROOL
UNFURNISHED BARE VACANT
UNGAINLY LANKY SPLAY WEEDY
CLUMSY UNGAIN AWKWARD
BOORISH NUNTING UNHEPPEN
UNLICKED UNWIELDY
UNGENEROUS MEAN SHABBY
STINGY GRUDGING
UNGIRDED DISCINCT
UNGODLINESS ATHEISM IMPIETY
IMPIOUS PROFANE
UNGODLY SINFUL WICKED GODLESS
IMPIOUS PROFANE
UNGOVERNABLE WILD UNRULY
FROWARD IMPOTENT
UNGRACEFUL HARD CLUMSY
ANGULAR AWKWARD HALTING
UNTOWARD
UNGRACEFULLY HARSHLY
UNGRACIOUS GRUFF UNFEEL
UNFELE SNAPPISH
UNGRATEFUL UNKIND INGRATE
UNGROOMED UNDRESSED
UNGUARDED STIFF
UNGUENT CEROMA CHRISM PIMENT
POMADE POMATUM UNCTION
OINTMENT
UNGULATE HOG PIG DEER HORSE
TAPIR HOOFED AMBLYPOD
ELEPHANT
UNGUMMED BRIGHT
UNHALLOWED IMPURE UNHOLY
PROFANE
UNHAMPERED FREE DIRECT
EXPEDITE
UNHAPPINESS MISERY SORROW
ILLFARE SADNESS UNBLISS
UNHAPPY SAD DISMAL UNLUCKY
UNLUSTY WANSOME DEJECTED
DOWNBEAT DOWNGONE WOBEGONE
WRETCHED
UNHARMED SAFE UNSHENT
UNHARNESS UNGEAR OUTSHUT
UNHORSE UNTACKLE
UNHEALED GREEN
UNHEALTHY BAD MORBID QUEASY
SICKLY UNHALE NAUGHTY PECCANT
MALADIVE
UNHEATED COLD
UNHEEDED IGNORED UNTENTED
UNHEEDING DEAF CARELESS
UNHESITATING READY UNPOISED
UNHITCH OUTSPAN
UNHOLY IMPURE WICKED IMPIOUS
PROFANE
UNHORSE PURL THROW UNCOLT
DISMOUNT UNSADDLE
UNHURRIED EASY SLOW SOFT
SOBER
UNHURT SAFE HARMLESS HURTLESS
UNHARMED
UNIAT MALKITE MELCHITE
UNICORN LIN REEM KILIN LICORN
LICORNE NARWHAL HOWITZER
UNICORN FISH LIJA UNIE
UNICORN PLANT MARTINOE
UNICUM UNION

UNIDENTIFIED FACELESS
INCOGNITO
UNIFICATION SYSTEM ENSEMBLE
UNIFIED GLOBAL
UNIFIER UMBRELLA
UNIFORM KIT DEAD EVEN FLAT JUST
LIKE SELF SUIT BLUES CLOTH
KHAKI SOLID SUITY GLOBAL
GREENS LIVERY SINGLE STEADY
EQUABLE REGULAR SIMILAR
SUNTANS CONSTANT EQUIFORM
EQUIPAGE MEASURED STANDARD
UNIVOCAL
(— IN HUE) FLAT
(LEATHER —) BUFF
(NOT —) SQUALLY
(PRISONER'S —) STRIPES
UNIFORMITY ONENESS EQUALITY
EVENNESS MONOTONY SAMENESS
UNIFORMLY EVENLY EQUALLY
UNIFY MERGE UNITE CEMENT
COMPACT UNITIZE COALESCE
UNILATERAL SECUND
UNIMAGINATIVE DULL SODDEN
STUPID LIMITED LITERAL PROSAIC
UNIDEAL PEDANTIC
UNIMPAIRED FRESH SOUND ENTIRE
INTACT
(— BY) DEVOID
UNIMPASSIONED SOBER WHOLE
STEADY
UNIMPEDED FREE EXPEDITE
UNIMPORTANT VAIN PETTY CASUAL
SIMPLE TRIVIAL IMMOMENT
TRINKETY
UNINFORMED GREEN UNTOLD
IGNORANT
UNINHABITED WILD EMPTY DESERT
VACANT DESOLATE WASTEFUL
UNINHIBITED LARGE
UNINJURED INTACT SINCERE
UNINSPIRED HACK STODGY
DRYASDUST
UNINSTRUCTED IGNORANT
UNINTELLIGENT DUMB OBTUSE
STUPID ASININE FOOLISH VACUOUS
UNINTELLIGIBLE BLIND MISTY
OPAQUE MYSTICAL
UNINTENTIONAL UNMEANT
UNINTERESTING DRY ARID COLD
DRAB DREE DULL FADE FLAT
DREAR SANDY STALE BORING
DREICH JEJUNE INSIPID BROMIDIC
FRUMPISH
UNINTERMITTENT ITHAND
UNINTERRUPTED SMOOTH STEADY
ENDLESS ETERNAL STRAIGHT
UNINTERRUPTEDLY AWAY
UNIO MUSSEL
UNION ZYG BLOC DUAD ALLOY
GROUP JOINT NONOP UNITY ENOSIS
FUSION GREMIO TAWHID CONCERT
CONTACT MEETING ONENESS
SOCIETY ADHESION ALLIANCE
COHESION ESPOUSAL JOINTURE
JUNCTION JUNCTURE SODALITY
SYSTASIS TRIALISM VINCULUM
(MARITAL —) BED
(SEXUAL —) COPULA COUPLING

(TURKISH —) JETTRU
UNIONIST REFUGEE
UNIQUE ODD SOLE UNIC ALONE
UNION SINGLE SULLEN UNICUM
ALONELY SOLEYNE SPECIAL
STRANGE ISOLATED SINGULAR
UNIQUENESS SOLITUDE
UNISON FIRST HOMOPHONY
UNIT (ALSO SEE MEASURE) ONE
ATOM KLAN FLOOR HUMIT MONAD
NEPER ADDRESS DIOPTER ELEMENT
ENERGID KLAVERN
(— IN COUNTING FISH) MEASE
(— IN EARTHWORK) FLOAT FLOOR
(— OF 100 MEN) CENTURY
(— OF ABSORPTION) SABIN
(— OF ACCELERATION) GAL
(— OF ACTION) EPISODE
(— OF ANGULAR MEASURE)
CENTRAD
(— OF ARCHEOLOGICAL
CLASSIFICATION) ASPECT
(— OF BRIGHTNESS) STILB
LAMBERT
(— OF CAPACITANCE) JAR
(— OF CAPACITY) LAST ARDAB
ARDEB AMPHORA
(— OF COMIC STRIP) BOX
(— OF COUNTING) POINT
(— OF DESIGN) LARME
(— OF DISTANCE) DAY
(— OF ELASTANCE) DARAF
(— OF ELECTRIC CAPACITY) FARAD
(— OF ELECTRIC CONDUCTANCE)
MHO
(— OF ELECTRIC FORCE) VOLT
KILOVOLT STATVOLT
(— OF ELECTRIC INDUCTANCE)
HENRY
(— OF ELECTRIC INTENSITY)
AMPERE OERSTED
(— OF ELECTRIC RELUCTANCE) REL
STATOHM
(— OF ELECTRIC RESISTANCE) OHM
BEGOHM
(— OF ELECTRICITY) ES COULOMB
(— OF ENERGY) ERG JOULE
ATOMERG QUANTUM
(— OF FINENESS) CARAT KARAT
(— OF FLOW) CUSEC
(— OF FLUIDITY) RHE
(— OF FLUX DENSITY) GAUSS
(— OF FORCE) G DYNE STAPP
STHENE POUNDEL
(— OF FREQUENCY) HERTZ
FRESNEL
(— OF GOVERNMENT) DEME LAND
KREIS GEMEINDE
(— OF ILLUMINANCE) LUX
(— OF INTERSTELLAR SPACE)
PARSEC
(— OF LAND AREA) ARE SULUNG
(— OF LANGUAGE) SYLLABLE
(— OF LIGHT INTENSITY) PYR
(— OF LIGHT) LUMEN
(— OF LOUDNESS) SONE DECIBEL
(— OF MACHINERY) STAND
(— OF MAGNETIC FLUX) WEBER

(— OF MAGNETIC FORCE) KAPP
GILBERT
(— OF MAGNETIC INTENSITY)
GAMMA
(— OF MAGNIFICATION) DIAMETER
(— OF MASS) SLUG DALTON
AVOGRAM
(— OF MEMORY) BIT
(— OF METRICAL QUANTITY) MATRA
(— OF MOMENT) DEBYE
(— OF MOMENTUM) BOLE
(— OF NARCOTIC) JOLT
(— OF NYLON FINENESS) DENIER
(— OF ONE INCH) BUTTON
(— OF PAIN INTENSITY) DOL
(— OF PERMEABILITY) DARCY
(— OF PIPE) FOURBLE
(— OF POWER) WATT DYNAM
KILOWATT PONCELET
(— OF PRESSURE) BAR BARAD
BARIE BARYE GWELY CENTIBAR
(— OF PRESSWORK) TOKEN
(— OF RADIATION) LANGLEY
(— OF RADIOACTIVITY) CURIE
(— OF ROCKET) STAGE
(— OF SATURATION) SATRON
(— OF SOCIETY) CLAN HORDE
CHAPTER
(— OF SPEECH) WORD
(— OF SPEED) BAUD KNOT
(— OF THICKNESS) POINT
(— OF TIME) BEAT SVEDBERG
(— OF TRADING) CONTRACT
(— OF VELOCITY) VELO
(— OF VISCOSITY) POISE STOKE
SECONDS
(— OF WAVELENGTH) ANGSTROM
(— OF WEIGHT) SSU TON GRAM
CARAT GRAIN OUNCE POUND STEIN
ARROBA GRAMME
(— OF WIRE MEASUREMENT) MIL
(— OF WORK) ERG CROP HOUR
ERGON JOULE KILERG DINAMODE
(— OF YARN SIZE) CUT
(— OF ZO) CORGE
(ADMINISTRATIVE —) HSIEN AGENCY
BUREAU DISTRICT
(ARBITRARY —) OLFACTY
(ARCHERY —) END
(ARMY —) LEGION BRIGADE
COMPANY MAHALLA
(ARTILLERY —) BATTERY
(AVAILABLE AS —) MARRIED
(BOWLING —) ALLEY
(BOY SCOUT —) SHIP
(BUILDER'S —) SQUARE
(CIGAR-MANUFACTURING —)
BUCKEYE
(COLLECTIVE —) COMMUNE
(COMBAT —) ARMAMENT
(DISCRETE —) FRACTION
(EDUCATIONAL —) COURSE
(ELECTROMAGNETIC —) ABFARAD
ABHENRY MAXWELL ABAMPERE
(FUNDAMENTAL —) BASE
(GRAMMATICAL —) JUNCTION
(HARMONIC —) CELL
(HOUSING —) HUTMENT
(HYPOTHETICAL —) ID IDANT

(LIFE —) BIOPHORE
(LIVING —) BIONT BIOGEN
(LOGARITHMIC —) BEL
(LOGGING —) CHANCE
(MILITARY —) ARMY GOUM CORPS
GROUP LANCE SQUAD BRIGADE
PLATOON SECTION COMMANDO
DIVISION REGIMENT SQUADRON
(NAZI —) FEHME
(ORGANIZATIONAL —) CELL
ACTIVITY
(PHOTOMETRIC —) VIOLLE
(POLITICAL —) SOVIET
(RHYTHMIC —) BASIS COLON
(SELF-PERPETUATING —) BIOSOME
(SOCIAL —) SEPT GROUP KRAAL
SOCIUS
(STORAGE —) BUFFER
(TERRITORIAL —) STAKE STATE
COMMOT CANTRED CANTREF
KINGDOM
(THERMAL —) THERM CALORY
CALORIE
(TRIBAL —) TOWNSHIP
(VOTING —) CENTURY
UNITE ADD MIX ONE OOP PAN SAM
SEW UNE UNY ALLY BAND BIND
CLUB COAK FUSE HASP JOIN KNIT
KNOT LINK SAMM SEAM SOUD UNIT
BANDY CLOSE GRADE GRAFT INONE
JACOB JOINT MERGE NITCH UNIFY
WHOLE ATTACH CEMENT CONCUR
COUPLE EMBODY ENTIRE GATHER
LAUREL LEAGUE SOLDER SPLICE
STRIKE SUTURE ACCRETE AMALGAM
CLUSTER COALITE COMBINE
CONJOIN CONNECT CONSORT
JACOBUS SIAMESE ALLIGATE
ANCYLOSE ANKYLOSE ASSEMBLE
COALESCE COMPOUND CONCRETE
CONSPIRE COPULATE FEDERATE
LAMINATE COLLIGATE
(— BY INTERWEAVING) PLEACH
SPLICE
(— BY THREADS) SEW STITCH
(— CLOSELY) FAY YOT WELD
CEMENT COTTON
(— FOR INTRIGUE) CABAL
(— HOSE) COLLECT
(— IN MARRIAGE) WED SACRE
SACRI SPLICE SPOUSE
(— METALS) WELD SWEAT
UNITED ONE TIED ADDED FUSED
JOINT ALLIED CONNATE ENDLESS
UNIONED COMBINED CONCRETE
CONJOINT CONJUNCT FEDERATE
UNITING SUTURE
UNITY UNION SYSTEM ONENESS
UNITUDE IDENTITY SODALITY
SYMPATHY TOTALITY
(— OF SPIRIT AND NATURE)
ABSOLUTE
UNIVERSAL ALL LOCAL TOTAL
WHOLE WORLD COMMON GLOBAL
PUBLIC VERSAL GENERAL GENERIC
CATHOLIC ECUMENIC
(TRANSCENDENT —) IDEA
UNIVERSALITY ALLNESS OMNITUDE
UNIVERSE ALL LOKA MASS OLAM

WORLD COSMOS SYSTEM
CREATURE EXEMPLAR
(SIDEREAL —) SPACE
UNIVERSITY STUDY CAMPUS
SCHOOL ACADEMY COLLEGE
MADRASA STUDIUM VARSITY
MADRASAH
UNJUST HARD UNFAIR WICKED
UNEQUAL UNRICHT UNRIGHT
WRONGFUL
UNJUSTIFIED INVALID
UNJUSTLY UNDULY FALSELY
UNKEELED RATITE
UNKEMPT FROWZY RUGGED
SHAGGY INCOMPT RAFFISH
RUFFLED SHAGRAG TOUSLED
DRAGGLED SCRAGGLY SLIPSHOD
STRUBBLY UNCOMBED
UNKIND BAD ILL MEAN VILE CRUEL
HARSH STERN SEVERE UNMEEK
UNKINDNESS DISFAVOR
UNKNOWABLE SEALED
UNKNOWN IGN UNCO UNKET UNKID
IGNOTE MUNKAR SEALED SECRET
UNWARE UNWIST FARAWAY
OBSCURE UNCOUTH UNHEARD
IGNORANT UNAWARES UNKENNED
UNWITTING
UNLADEN LEAR LEER
UNLATCH UNSNECK
UNLAWFUL ILLEGAL ILLICIT
NONLICET UNLEEFUL UNLEISUM
UNLEARNED LEWD GROSS
BOOKLESS IGNORANT UNLEARED
UNLESS BUT NIF LESS NISI SAVE
BINNA NOBUT LESSEN ONLESS
WITHOUT
(— BEFORE) NIPR NIPRI
(— OTHERWISE NOTED) NAN
UNLETTERED LEWD BORREL
IGNORANT
UNLIGHTED BLIND LAMPLESS
UNLIKE DIFFORM DISLIKE DIVERSE
(MOST —) OTHEREST
UNLIKELY DUBIOUS
(MOST —) LAST
UNLIMITED VAST SOVRAN
UNTERMED
(— IN POWER) ALMIGHTY
UNLINED SINGLE
UNLOAD TIP DROP DUMP HOVEL
DECANT STRIKE UNLADE UNSHIP
UNSTOW DELIVER DEPLETE
DETRUCK DISLOAD UNTRUSS
DISCHARGE
UNLOCK UNMAKE RESERATE
UNLOUKEN
UNLOOSE OUTWIND UNRIVET
UNLUCKY FAY ILL EVIL FOUL DONSY
DISMAL DONSIE HOODOO HAPLESS
INFAUST UNHAPPY UNCHANCY
UNTOWARD
(— THING) AMBSACE
UNMAN UNDO CRUSH UNNERVE
UNMANAGEABLE ROID DONSY
RANDY RESTIVE CHURLISH
STAFFISH
UNMANLY SOFT MANLESS UNLUSTY
UNMANNERLY RUDE BOORISH

UNCIVIL IMPOLITE UNGENTLE
UNMARKED MAVERICK NOTELESS
UNMARRIED ONE LONE SOLE OLEPI
YOUNG ONLEPY SINGLE
UNMASK EXPOSE UNFACE DISMASK
UNCLOAK
UNMASKING EXPOSURE
UNMEASURED UNMEET MODELESS
UNMELODIOUS SCRANNEL
UNMERCHANTABLE SALABLE
SALEABLE
UNMERCIFUL CRUEL PITILESS
RUTHLESS
UNMETHODICAL CURSORY
UNMINDFUL SLOWFUL CARELESS
HEEDLESS MINDLESS
UNMISTAKABLE FLAT OPEN BROAD
CLEAR FRANK PLAIN PATENT
EXPRESS APPARENT DECISIVE
MANIFEST UNIVOCAL
UNMISTAKABLY SIGNALLY
UNMITIGATED GROSS ARRANT
DAMNED SOVRAN PERFECT
PUREDEE REGULAR ABSOLUTE
UNMIX EXSOLVE
UNMIXED DEEP MERE PURE SELF
SOLE BLANK SHEER UTTER IMMIXT
SIMPLE STRAIGHT
UNMODIFIED BRUTE STRAIGHT
UNMOLESTED SACKLESS
UNMOVED CALM COOL FIRM STONY
TIGHT IMMOTE SERENE ADAMANT
IMMOVED
UNMOVING INERT IMMOBILE
IMMOTIVE
UNMUSICAL NOTELESS SCABROUS
UNNATURAL EERY EERIE CLAMMY
CREEPY UNKIND STRANGE
UNCANNY VIOLENT ABNORMAL
FARCICAL KINDLESS UNKINDLY
UNNECESSARY USELESS NEEDLESS
UNNEEDED WASTE
UNNERVE UNMAN UNMAKE WEAKEN
ENERVATE PARALYZE
UNNERVED SHOOK
UNNOTICED SILENT
UNOBJECTIONABLE VENIAL
UNOBSERVANT HEEDLESS
UNOBSTRUCTED FAIR FREE OPEN
APPARENT
UNOBTRUSIVE SHY MODEST
SEDATE DISCREET RETIRING
UNOCCUPIED IDLE VOID BLANK
EMPTY WASTE VACANT LEISURE
UNSEATED WASTEFUL
UNORGANIZED ACOSMIC INCHOATE
UNORTHODOX HERETIC
UNOSTENTATIOUS SHY QUIET
LENTEN MODEST
UNPACK UNFARDLE
UNPAID DUE UNQUIT UNWAGED
HONORARY WAGELESS
UNPAIRED IMPAR
UNPALATABLE SOD HARD BITTER
BRACKISH
UNPARALLELED ALONE UNIQUE
EPOCHAL PEERLESS SINGULAR
UNPEERED
UNPERTURBED BLAND STILL

UNPLEASANT BAD ACID EVIL HARD
NICE SOUR UGLY AWFUL CRUDE
GRIMY GUMMY HAIRY HARSH
MUCKY ROUGH BRUTAL CRIMPY
RANCID STICKY THRAWN UNFELE
UNGAIN UNLIEF BEASTLY BILIOUS
GHASTLY INGRATE SPINOUS
UNLUSTY UNQUEME UNSONCY
CHISELLY DREADFUL HORRIBLE
INDECENT SCABROUS UNLOVELY
UNPLEASANTLY QUEER HARDLY
UNWINLY
UNPLEASANTNESS ILLNESS
UNPLOWED LEA
UNPOETICAL MUSELESS
UNPOLISHED ILL RUDE BLIND
CRUDE ROUGH COARSE INCULT
RUGGED RUSTIC SAVAGE SHAGGY
UPLAND INCOMPT UNKEMPT
AGRESTIC
UNPOPULARITY ENVY
UNPRACTICED RAW FRESH
UNTRADED
UNPREDICTABLE CHANCY CRANKY
ERRATIC
UNPREJUDICED FAIR
UNPREMEDITATED CASUAL
UNPREPARED TARDY
UNPREPOSSESSING SEEDY
UNPRETENDING LOWLY HOMELY
HUMBLE
UNPRETENTIOUS HOMY HOMEY
PLAIN SOBER COMMON HOMELY
HUMBLE MODEST SIMPLE DISCREET
HOMESPUN
UNPRINCIPLED LIMMER
UNPRODUCTIVE DRY SHY ARID
DEAD DEAF LEAN ADDLE DUSTY
WASTE BARREN GEASON SAPLESS
STERILE WOODSERE
UNPRODUCTIVENESS BORASCO
BORASQUE BORRASCA
UNPROFESSIONAL LAY LAICAL
UNPROFITABLE BAD DRY DEAD
SECK BARREN BOOTLESS GAINLESS
UNGAINLY
UNPROGRESSIVE SLOW DORMANT
BACKWARD
UNPROMISING BLUE DUBIOUS
UNPRONOUNCED MUTE
UNPROPITIOUS ILL EVIL FOUL
THRAW MALIGN SULLEN ADVERSE
AVERTED INFAUST OMINOUS
THRAWART
UNPROTECTED NAKED EXPOSED
HELPLESS
UNPUBLISHED INED INEDITED
UNQUALIFIED NET BARE FULL MERE
PURE BLACK PLUMP SHEER UNFIT
DIRECT ENTIRE UNABLE CLOTTED
PLENARY IMPLICIT INHABILE
UNQUESTIONABLE ASSURED
CERTAIN DECIDED ABSOLUTE
DECISIVE DISTINCT
UNQUESTIONED CLEAR
UNQUESTIONING IMPLICIT
UNRAVEL REDD UNDO BREAK
ENODE FEAZE RAVEL SOLVE TIFFLE

UNFOLD UNKNIT UNLACE ENODATE RESOLVE

UNREAL GOTHIC CHEMICK FANCIED SHADOWY AERIFORM CHIMERIC FARCICAL ILLUSORY NOTIONAL SCENICAL VISIONAL

UNREALISTIC CHIMERIC

UNREALIZED BEHIND

UNREASONABLE ABSURD FANATIC ABSONANT

UNREASONABLENESS ALOGY INSANITY

UNREASONABLY SINFULLY

UNREASONING BRUTE

UNRECOGNIZED UNSUNG CRYPTIC UNWITTED

UNRECOVERABLE DEAD

UNRECTIFIED IMPURE

UNREDEEMED CHEAP

UNREFINED RAW DARK LOUD BRUTE CRUDE DORIC GROSS COARSE COMMON EARTHY JUNGLY VULGAR BOORISH UNCOUTH UNKEMPT DREADFUL SWAINISH

UNREFLECTING GLIB

UNREGENERACY ADAM

UNREGENERATELY MANLY

UNREHEARSED IMPROMPTU

UNRELATED FREMD STRAY UNAKIN UNTOLD EXTREME FRAMMIT POSITIVE

UNRELAXED UNSLAKED

UNRELENTING GRIM HARD IRON CRUEL STERN SEVERE RIGOROUS

UNRELIABLE FISHY SHADY FICKLE GREASY UNSAFE CASALTY STREAKY WILDCAT FECKLESS GLIBBERY SLIPPERY TICKLISH

UNRELIEVED DEAD BRUTE ABJECT EXQUISITE

UNREMITTING BUSY FAST HARD DOGGED

UNREMUNERATIVE HONORARY

UNRESERVED FREE CLEAN FRANK ROUND COMMON UNCLOSE EXPLICIT

UNRESERVEDNESS FREEDOM

UNRESISTING BUXOM

UNRESPONSIVE DEAD DUMB BARREN SILENT STUBBORN

UNREST MOTION AILMENT DISREST WANREST DISQUIET CHEMISTRY PSYCHOSIS

UNRESTRAINED LAX FREE WILD BROAD FANTI FRANK LARGE LOOSE FACILE FANTEE LAVISH UNTIED WANTON FLYAWAY RAMPANT RIOTOUS FAMILIAR FREEHAND LAXATIVE PINDARIC

UNRESTRAINT LICENSE IMMUNITY

UNRESTRICTED FREE GLOBAL SOVRAN UNZONED

UNRETURNED UNYOLDEN

UNREVEALED UNTOLD

UNRIG STRIP

UNRIGHTEOUSNESS ADHARMA

UNRIPE RAW CRUDE GREEN CALLOW UNCURED IMMATURE

UNROBE DISROBE UNDRESS DISARRAY

UNROLL EVOLVE UNCURL DEVELOP OUTROLL TRINDLE UNTREND

UNROOF TIRL TIRR TIRVE DISROOF

UNRUFFLE SMOOTH SOOTHE MOLLIFY

UNRUFFLED CALM COOL EASY EVEN QUIET SOBER STILL ASLEEP PLACID SEDATE SERENE SMOOTH DECOROUS

UNRULY HIGH RAMP ROYT TOUGH HAUNTY WANTON LAWLESS RAMMAGE ROPABLE UNRULED VICIOUS WANRULY WAYWARD INDOCILE MUTINOUS

UNSADDLE UNPANEL

UNSAFE HOT EXPOSED INSECURE PERILOUS

UNSATISFACTORY BAD ILL EVIL CROOK SHREWD WRETCHED

UNSATISFYING DUSTY HOLLOW

UNSAVORY WERSH INSIPID WEARISH

UNSAY WITHDRAW

UNSCHOLARLY BOOKLESS

UNSCRUPULOUS SKIN BRAZEN DEVIOUS DEXTROUS RASCALLY

UNSEASONABLE LAT UNRIPE UNTIDY UNCHANCY UNTIMELY

UNSEASONED RAW GREEN

UNSEAT ADDRESS DISSEAT

UNSEEING BLIND GAZELESS

UNSEEMLY HOIDEN UNFAIR IMPROPER INDECENT SEEMLESS UNMEETLY UNWORTHY

UNSEEN SECRET UNEYED VIEWLESS

UNSERRIED LOOSE

UNSETTLE JAR TURN UNFIX UNSET UPSET COMMOVE DERANGE DISTURB STAGGER UNHINGE UNQUEME DISORDER DISQUIET DISTRACT

UNSETTLED MOOT LIGHT SHAKY UNSAD VAGUE BROKEN FICKLE QUEASY VAGOUS DUBIOUS SHUTTLE UNSTAID RESTLESS UNSTABLE

UNSHAKABLE DOGGED ADAMANT IRONCLAD

UNSHAKEN FIRM STEADY UNMOVED UNSHOOK RESOLUTE

UNSHAPELY DEFORMED UNMACKLY

UNSHARED SOLE

UNSHEATH DISCASE

UNSHEATHED BARE

UNSHOD BAREFOOT DISCALCED

UNSHORN UNPOLLED

UNSIGHTLY UGLY MESSY HOMELY INDECENT

UNSKILLED JAY PUNY GREEN PUISNE UNGAIN UNSEEN STRANGE FECKLESS

UNSKILLFUL ILL EVIL RUDE ARTLESS UNFEATY BUNGLING TINKERLY UNHEPPEN

UNSMILING GLUM AUSTERE

UNSOCIABLE SULLEN INSOCIAL

UNSOILED CLEAN

UNSOPHISTICATE SQUARE

UNSOPHISTICATED JAY NAIF PURE FRANK GREEN NAIVE SILLY CALLOW SIMPLE BUCOLIC VERDANT

HOMEBRED HOMESPUN INNOCENT

UNSOUND BAD ILL EVIL SICK ADDLE CRAZY CRONK DICKY DOTTY DOZED SANDY SHAKY ABSURD FAULTY FLAWED HOLLOW INFIRM INSANE ROTTEN UNHALE INVALID RICKETY UNWHOLE

UNSOUNDNESS CRACK INSANITY

UNSPIRITUAL CARNAL

UNSPOILED RACY UNSHENT

UNSPOKEN TACIT SILENT

UNSPORTSMANLIKE DIRTY

UNSPOTTED CLEAR SPOTLESS

UNSTABLE FLUX BATTY LOOSE SANDY BROTEL CHOPPY FICKLE FITFUL FLITTY LABILE LUBRIC ROTTEN SHIFTY TICKLE UNFIRM WANKLE WANKLY DWAIBLE DWAIBLY DWEEBLE RICKETY SLIDDER SLIDDRY VOLUBLE FEVERISH FIRMLESS FUGITIVE INSECURE LUBRICAL REMUABLE SKITTISH SLIPPERY TICKLISH TOTTLISH VARIABLE (MENTALLY —) BRAINISH

UNSTEADILY GROGGILY

UNSTEADINESS FALTER

UNSTEADY WALT CRANK CRONK DOTTY FLUKY LIGHT NERVY SLACK TIPPY TIPSY TOTTY UNSAD WALTY WONKY COGGLY FICKLE FLICKY FLUFFY GROGGY JIGGLY JOGGLY SWIMMY TOTTIE WAFFLY WAGGLY WAMBLY WANKLE WEEWAW WEEWOW DODDERY GLAIKIT JIGGETY QUAVERY TITTUPY TOTTERY WAYWARD STAGGERY TICKLISH TITUBANT UNSTABLE VARIABLE

UNSTINTED LAVISH ENDLESS

UNSTRESS SLACK

UNSTRESSED SHORT

UNSTRING DISSOLVE

UNSTUDIED GLIB CASUAL CARELESS GLANCING

UNSUBDUED VIRGIN UNBOWED

UNSUBSTANTIAL TOY LIMP THIN WINDY AERIAL CHAFFY FLIMSY SLEAZY SLEEZY SLIGHT UNREAL FOLIOUS FRAGILE INSOLID SHADOWY TENUOUS FILIGREE FINESPUN FOOTLESS GIMCRACK VAPOROUS

UNSUCCESSFUL BAD MANQUE UNSPED STICKIT UNHAPPY ABORTIVE

UNSUITABLE INEPT UNAPT UNDUE UNFIT UNKIND UNMETE UNCOMELY UNGAINLY UNLIKELY

UNSUITABLENESS IMPOLICY

UNSUITED BAD

UNSULLIED FAIR PURE CLEAR VIRGIN INNOCENT SPOTLESS VIRGINAL

UNSUPPLIED HELPLESS

UNSUPPORTED BLIND NAKED BACKWARD STAYLESS

UNSURE TIMID INFIRM DOUBTFUL INSECURE UNSICKER

UNSURPASSED CHAMPION
UNSUSPECTING INNOCENT
UNSWEET UNSOOT
UNSWERVING FIXED FLUSH LOYAL
DIRECT STEADY STRICT STURDY
STAUNCH
UNSWERVINGLY HEADLONG
UNSYMMETRICAL LOPSIDED
UNSYMPATHETIC HARD STONY
FROZEN GLASSY HOSTILE KINDLESS
UNTAINTED FREE GOOD PURE
INNOCENT
UNTAMED WILD FERAL RAMAGE
SAVAGE HAGGARD RAMMISH
WARRAGAL
UNTANGLE FREE SLEAVE UNLACE
UNTAUGHT WASTE UNLERED
IGNORANT
UNTHINKABLE PUERILE
UNTHINKING GLIB BRUTE CASUAL
FECKLESS HEEDLESS
UNTHINKINGLY STUPID
UNTIDINESS JAKES LITTER
UNTIDY DOWDY GAUMY MESSY
ROOKY BUNTING DRAGGLY LITTERY
RUMMAGY UNSIDED DRAGGLED
SLOVENLY STRUBBLY UNHEPPEN
UNTIE UNDO UNBIND UNLASH
UNLATCH UNTRUSS UNTWINE
UNFASTEN
UNTIL AD OR TO GIN HENT INTO
UNTO FORTO TWELL WHILE WHILES
WHILST PENDING
(— THEN) BEFORE
UNTILLED INCULT UNEARED
UNTIMELY UNTIDY IMMATURE
PREVIOUS TIMELESS
UNTIRING BUSY SEDULOUS
TIRELESS
UNTITLED (— MEN) AUMAGA
UNTOLD VAST UNQUOD
UNTOUCHABLE DOM HARIJAN
CHANDALA
(PL.) PANCHAMA
UNTOUCHED FREE INTACT
UNTOWARD ILL UNRULY FROWARD
WAYWARD
UNTRAINED RAW RUDE GREEN
HAGGARD
UNTRAMMELED FREE
UNTRIED MAIDEN UNSOUGHT
UNTRIMMED UNTEWED
UNTRODDEN PATHLESS UNFOOTED
UNTROUBLED CHEERY
UNTRUE FLAM FALSE LEASE WRONG
UNFAST DISLOYAL
UNTRUSTWORTHINESS FALSITY
UNTRUSTWORTHY SHAKY LIMBER
TRICKY UNSURE SLIDDERY
SLIPPERY
UNTRUTH LIE FABLE LEASE SKLENT
FALSITY UNTROTH
UNTRUTHFUL SLANTER
UNTUTORED IGNORANT
UNTWILLED PLAIN
UNTWINE FRESE UNTWIST
UNTWIST FAG FEAZE UNLAY UNSPIN
UNTWIRL
UNTWISTED SLEIDED

UNUSABLE WASTE INUTILE
UNUSED IDLE FRESH WASTE INURED
MAIDEN DERELICT INITIATE
UNWONTED
UNUSUAL ODD EERY RARE SELD
TALL CRAZY EERIE FORBY NOVEL
UTTER WEIRD EXEMPT FORBYE
SCREWY SINGLE UNIQUE STRANGE
ABNORMAL DISTINCT ESPECIAL
INSOLENT KNOCKOUT SELCOUTH
SINGULAR SPANKING UNCOMMON
UNTRADED UNWONTED
UNUSUALLY EXTRA
UNVARIED SAMELY
UNVARNISHED EVERYDAY
UNVARYING FLAT FRANK LEVEL
STABLE UNIFORM
UNVEIL REVEAL UNCOVER UNCROWN
UNDRAPE UNSCREEN UNWIMPLE
UNVERSED STRANGE
UNWANTED STRAY TRAMP FAULTY
UNWARRANTED UNDUE
UNWARY RASH UNAWARE CARELESS
HEEDLESS WARELESS
UNWASHED SOAPLESS
UNWASTEFUL FRUGAL
UNWAVERING FIRM CLEAN LEVEL
SOLID GLASSY STABLE EXPRESS
STAUNCH
UNWAVERINGLY FAST
UNWEAKENED CLEAR
UNWELL ILL EVIL SICK BADLY
CROOK AILING CHIPPY WICKED
COMICAL
UNWHOLESOME ILL EVIL SICK
CAGMAG IMPURE MORBID SICKLY
CORRUPT NOISOME NOXIOUS
UNCLEAN DISEASED
UNWIELDY BULKY CLUMSY UNRIDE
AWKWARD HULKING CUMBROUS
UNGAINLY
UNWILLING CHARY LOATH SWEER
WERSE AVERSE ESCHEW
BACKWARD GRUDGING
UNWILLINGLY MAUGER MAUGRE
UNWILLINGNESS GRUDGE NOLITION
UNWIND UNCLEW UNREEL UNREAVE
UNTWINE
UNWISE FALSE INANE SIMPLE
FOOLISH WITLESS
UNWITTING UNWIST WEETLESS
UNWOMANLY MANKIND
UNWORLDLY WEIRD ASTRAL
UNWORTHY BASE INDIGN BENEATH
UNDIGNE WANWORDY
UNWOUNDED COLD
UNWREATHE UNPLAT
UNWRINKLED BRANT BRENT
UNWROUGHT RAW LIVE
UNYIELDING SET ACID DOUR FAST
FIRM GRIM HARD RIGID STARK
STIFF STITH STONY TOUGH FLINTY
FROZEN GLASSY KNOBBY STEELY
STURDY ADAMANT AUSTERE
COSTIVE FROWARD CHURLISH
OBDURATE OBEDIENT STUBBORN
UNYOKE UNTEAM OUTSHUT
OUTSPAN
UP ON ONE OOP ABOUT ASTIR

DORMY DORMIE
(— AND ABOUT) AFOOT
(— TO THE TIME) UNTIL
(— TO) INTO
(— YONDER) UPBY UPBYE
(FARTHER —) ABOVE
(HIGH —) ALOFT
UPANISHAD ISHA KATHA
UPAS DITA CHETTIK
UPBEAT ARSIS AUFTAKT ANACRUSIS
UP-BOW POUSSE
UPBRAID CHEW RAIL SNUB TUCK
TWIT ABUSE ROUSE SCOLD TAUNT
UPBRAY EMBRAID REPROVE
DISGRACE OUTBRAID
UPCARD STARTER
UPFOLD SADDLE ANTICLINE
UPHEAVAL BOIL UPLIFT RUMMAGE
UPTHROW
UPHILL UPBANK UPWITH
UPHOLD AID TOM ABET BACK FAVOR
AFFIRM ASSERT DEFEND SOOTHE
BOLSTER SUPPORT SUSTAIN
CHAMPION MAINTAIN PRESERVE
UPHOLDER DEFENDER ERASTIAN
FEUDALIST
UPHOLDING BEHIND
UPHOLSTER SQUAB
UPHOLSTERER TAPISER UPHOLDER
UPLAND DOWN DOWNS MAUKA
COTEAU FASTLAND
(PL.) BRAES DOWNS
UPLAND PLOVER QUAILY HILLBIRD
PAPABOTE
UPLIFT TOSS BOOST TOWER
UPTHRUST
UPLIFTED ERECT EXALTEE
UPON ON PON SUR INTO OVER
ABOVE AGAINST
(— THAT) THEREAT
UPPER VAMP SKIVE VAMPEY
SUPERIOR
(PL.) FINISH
UPPERCUT BOLO
UPPER HURONIAN LAWSON
UPPERMOST UMEST UPMOST
OVEREST BUNEMOST OVERMOST
UPPER VOLTA (CAPITAL OF —)
OUAGADOUGOU
(LANGUAGE OF —) BOBO LOBI
SAMO MANDE MOSSI
(MOUNTAIN IN —) TEMA
(NATIVE OF —) BOBO LOBI SAMO
BISSA HAUSA MANDE MARKA MOSSI
PUEHL TUAREG SENOUFO VOLTAIC
YATENGA MANDINGO
(RIVER IN —) VOLTA SOUROU
UPRAISED SUBLIME
UPRIGHT FAIR GOOD HARR JUST
PROP STUD TIDY TRUE ANEND
CHEEK ERECT GUIDE JELLY MORAL
RIGHT ROMAN SETUP STALE STALK
STILE DIRECT ENTIRE HONEST
SQUARE FRIZZEN HOUSING
JANNOCK PITPROP SINCERE
INNOCENT RIGHTFUL STANDARD
STANDING STRAIGHT VERTICAL
VIRTUOUS
(NOT —) BEVEL

(PL.) STUDDING

UPRIGHTNESS HONOR TRUTH EQUITY HONESTY PROBITY JUSTNESS

UPRISING RIOT EMEUTE MUTINY PUTSCH REVOLT TUMULT UPRISE UPRISAL

UPROAR DIN RUT CAIN GILD MOIL RIOT ROUT BURLE CHANG FUROR HURLY RUMOR STOUN STOUR CLAMOR DIRDUM FRACAS HABBLE HUBBLE HUBBUB RANDAN RATTLE RIPPET RUCKUS RUMBLE SHINDY STEVEN STOUND TUMULT CATOUSE FERMENT GAUSTER ORATION OUTROAR RUCTION STASHIE TURMOIL BROUHAHA SCOUTHER STIRRING TINTAMAR

UPROARIOUS FURIOUS ROUTOUS

UPROOT HACK LOUK MORE UNROUT UNPLANT DISPLANT ROOTWALT SUPPLANT

UPROOTED LUMPEN

UPSET ILL TIP TOP TUP CAVE COUP COWP FUSS JUMP PURL TILT TURN WELT EVERT KNOCK ROUSE SHAKE SKELL WHELM BOTHER DISMAY QUELME TIPPLE TOPPLE UPCAST WALTER CAPSIZE DERANGE DISTURB FRAZZLE HAYWIRE OVERSET PERVERT REVERSE SLATTER SUBVERT TEMPEST TURMOIL CAPSIZAL DISTRAIT OVERTILT OVERTURN STREAKED SUPPLANT TURNOVER (EASILY —) FUSSY

UPSHOT ISSUE SHORT UPSET EFFECT SEQUEL UPPING OUTCOME UPSHOOT UPSTROKE

UPSIDE-DOWN CRAZY OVERHAND UPSEDOUN

UPSTAIRS ABOVE

UPSTANDING GRADELY

UPSTART KIP QUAT SNIP SQUIRT UPSKIP DALTEEN PARVENU ARRIVIST MUSHROOM SKIPJACK UPSPRING

UP-TO-DATE ABREAST TODAYISH

UPWARD ALOFT UPLONG UPWAYS UPWITH SKYWARD UPALONG UPWARDS

UPWARD-MOVING ANABATIC

URAEUS ASP

URAMIL MUREXAN

URANUS OURANOS HERSCHEL (WIFE OF —) GAEA

URAO TRONA

URARTAEAN KHALDIAN

URARTU VAN

URATE LITHATE

URBAN TOWN URBIC URBANE BURGHAL

URBANE CIVIL SUAVE POLITE SVELTE AMIABLE GRACIOUS

URBANITY SUAVITY ELEGANCE

URCHIN IMP ELFIN GAMIN KEELIE NIPPER HURCHEON

URD MUNGO

URDEE MATELEY

URDU REKHTA REKHTI MOORISH

URGE ART DUN EGG HIE PLY PUT SIC SUE TAR YEN BROD COAX CRAM EDGE FIRK GOAD MOVE PING SICK SPUR WHIP CROWD DRIVE FILIP FORCE HOOSH IMPEL LABOR PRICK SPANK TREAT COMPEL DEHORT DESIRE ENGAGE EXCITE FILLIP HARDEN HOICKS HUSTLE INCITE INDUCE INVITE MOTION PROPEL STRAIN THREAP THREAT ANIMATE COMMOVE ENFORCE INSTANT OPPRESS PERSIST SOLICIT SUGGEST URGENCY INSTANCE PERSUADE (— IMPORTUNATELY) DUN PRESS (— ON A HORSE) HUP CRAM CHUCK (— ON) EGG ERT HAG SOOL ALARM CHIRK CROWD DRIVE FILIP HASTE HURRY IMPEL YOICK ALARUM FILLIP HARDEN HASTEN INCITE (— STRONGLY) EXHORT SOLICIT (— WITH VEHEMENCE) DING

URGENCY NEED PRESS STRESS URGENCE EXIGENCY INSTANCE INSTANCY

URGENT HOT DIRE RASH ACUTE HASTY STRONG BURNING CLAMANT EXIGENT INSTANT URGEFUL CRITICAL PRESSING PRESSIVE

URGING QUEST

URIAL SHA OORIAL

URINAL DUCK SANITARY

URINATE WET LEAK EMPTY STALE PIDDLE EVACUATE

URINATION MICTION NOCTURIA

URINE MIG SIG LAGE LANT WASH STALE WATER NETTING EMICTION (— USED AS COSMETIC) LOTIUM

URN JAR EWER KIST URNA VASE CAPANNA (— FOR MAKING TEA) KITCHEN SAMOVAR (— IN KENO) GOOSE (BURIAL —) OSSUARY (CINERARY —) DINOS DEINOS (STONE —) STEEN

URN-SHAPED URCEOLAR

UROCHORDA ASCIDIA TUNICATA

UROSTYLE COCCYX

URSA MAJOR OKNARI CHARIOT WAGONER WAGGONER

URSINE ARCTOID

URTICARIA HIVES UREDO CNIDOSIS

URTICASTRUM LAPORTEA

URUGUAY
CAPITAL: MONTEVIDEO
DEPARTMENT: ROCHA SALTO FLORES ARTIGAS SORIANO
ESTUARY: PLATA
LAKE: MERIN MIRIM DIFUNTOS
MEASURE: VARA LEGUA CUADRA SUERTE
RIVER: MALO MIRIM NEGRO ULIMAR CUAREIM QUEGUAY YAGUARON CEBOLLATI
TOWN: MELO MINAS ROCHA

SALTO RIVERA DURAZNO FLORIDA PAYSANDU
WEIGHT: QUINTAL

URUGUAYAN ORIENTAL

URUS TUR URE AUROCHS

US S HIS HIZ HUZ

USABLE FIT UTIBLE SERVABLE

USAGE USE ASAL FORM WONE HABIT HAUNT SUNNA USURE CUSTOM MANNER FASHION HALACHA HALAKAH USATION PRACTICE
(BAD —) ABUSAGE
(HARD —) GRIEF
(RELIGIOUS —) RITUS
(PL.) CEREMONY

USE URE BOOT CALL DUTY HAVE NAIT NOTE USUS WISE APPLY AVAIL GUIDE HABIT SPEND TREAT USAGE WASTE BEHOOF EMPLOY FINISH HANDLE OCCUPY USANCE ACCOUNT ADHIBIT ENTREAT IMPROVE SERVICE UTILITY ACCUSTOM EXERCISE FUNCTION PRACTICE
(— AS WONTED) ADOPT
(— EXPERIMENTALLY) TRY
(— FIGURE OF SPEECH) TROPE
(— IMPROPERLY) ABUSE
(— INDISCRIMINATELY) HACK
(— OF MORE WORDS THAN NECESSARY) PLEONASM
(— OF NEW WORD) NEOLOGY
(— OF SUBTERFUGE) CHICANE
(— UP) EAT TIRE WEAR SHOOT ABSORB DEVOUR EXPEND GUZZLE PERUSE CONSUME EXHAUST OVERWEAR
(— WASTEFULLY) SPILL
(— WITH FULL COMMAND) WIELD
(EXCESSIVE — OF FACE AND HANDS) ABHINAYA
(FOR TEMPORARY —) JURY
(FRUGAL —) SPARE
(GENERAL —) CURRENCY
(LITURGICAL —) RITE
(MUCH IN —) GREAT
(UNRESTRICTED —) FREEDOM

USED WONT
(— CONTINUOUSLY) HOT
(— IN FLIGHT) VOLAR
(— UP) ALL BEAT SHOT SPENT FOREWORN
(MUCH —) GREAT HACKNEY

USEFUL GAIN GOOD UTILE UTIBLE HELPFUL THRIFTY BEHOVELY UTENSILE
(— FOR LONG TIME) HARD

USEFULNESS USE AVAIL VALUE WORTH PROFIT MILEAGE UTILITY

USELESS IDLE LEWD VAIN VOID WIDE EMPTY DOLESS NOUGHT OTIOSE SCREWY TRASHY INUTILE STERILE VAINFUL BOOTLESS FOOTLESS FOOTLING WASTEFUL

USELESSNESS FUTILITY IDLENESS

USER USUS

USHABTI SHAWABTI

USHER BOW USH SHOW HERALD
ISCHAR SEATER CHOBDAR HUISHER
JANITOR MARSHAL STEWARD
USSR (SEE RUSSIA)
USUAL RIFE COMMON FAMOUS
NORMAL SOLEMN VULGAR WONTED
AVERAGE GENERAL NATURAL
REGULAR TYPICAL USITATE
EVERYDAY FREQUENT HABITUAL
ORDINARY ORTHODOX
USURER SHARK GAVELER
HARPAGON
USURP ASSUME INVADE PRESUME
ACCROACH ARROGATE
USURY GAVEL OCKER USURE
USANCE GOMBEEN

UTAH
CAPITAL: SALTLAKECITY
COLLEGE: WEBER
COUNTY: JUAB CACHE PIUTE
SEVIER TOOELE UINTAH
SANPETE
INDIAN: UTE
LAKE: SALT SWAN SEVIER
MOTTO: INDUSTRY
MOUNTAIN: LENA LION WAAS
KINGS PEALE TRAIL FRISCO
NAVAJO SWASEY GRANITE
GRIFFIN HAWKINS PENNELL
LINNAEUS
MOUNTAIN RANGE: CEDAR HENRY
HOGUP UINTA WAHWAH
TERRACE CONFUSION
NATIONAL PARK: ZION
NICKNAME: MORMON BEEHIVE
RIVER: WEBER JORDAN SEVIER
STATE BIRD: SEAGULL
STATE FLOWER: SEGOLILY
STATE TREE: SPRUCE
TOWN: MOAB OREM DELTA HEBER
KANAB LOGAN MAGNA MANTI
NEPHI OGDEN PRICE PROVO
KEARNS TOOELE VERNAL

UTENSIL (ALSO SEE IMPLEMENT AND
TOOL) HOD BOAT IRON MOLD PECK
STEW BAKER FRIER FRYER GRILL
KNIFE MOULD RICER SCOOP SHEET
SHELL SIEVE SLICE ULLER BEATER
BREWER COOKER DABBER FUNNEL
GRATER GRILLE KETTLE LINGEL

MASKER POPPER PUSHER SHAKER
SIFTER BRAZIER BROILER DUSTPAN
FLIPPER GLUEPOT MUDDLER
SCUMMER SKIMMER STEAMER
STIRRER TOASTER CALABASH
GRIDIRON SAUCEPAN SAUCEPOT
SHREDDER SPOUCHER STRAINER
(— FOR COVERING FIRE) CURFEW
(LITURGICAL —) ASTERISK
(PL.) BATTERY COOKWARE
IRONWARE
UTERUS WOMB BELLY METRA
MATRIX BEARING
UTILITARIAN USEFUL ECONOMIC
UTILITY USE AVAIL USAGE PROFIT
BENEFIT SERVICE
UTILIZE USE EMPLOY ENLIST
CONSUME EXPLOIT HARNESS
HUSBAND
UTMOST END BEST LAST MOST
FINAL EXTREME OUTMOST SUPREME
DAMNDEST POSSIBLE UTTEREST
UTOPIA ZION
UTOPIAN IDEAL
UTOPIANISM FUTURISM
UTRAQUIST CALIXTIN
UTRICULUS ALVEUS
UTTER ASK OUT SAY BARK BLOW
BOOM DRIB FAIR GASP GIVE HURL
MAIN MOOT MOVE PASS PURE RANK
SEND VENT VERY BLACK COUGH
CRUDE FETCH FRAME FRANK
GROSS ISSUE MOUTH RAISE SHEER
SOUND SPEAK SPELL STARK THICK
TOTAL VOICE ACCENT BROACH
DAMNED DIRECT INTONE PARLEY
PROFER TONGUE BLUSTER
BREATHE DELIVER ENOUNCE
EXCLAIM EXPRESS OUTMOST
OUTTELL PERFECT PROLATE
UPBRAID ABSOLUTE BLINKING
COMPLETE CRASHING INTONATE
(— ABRUPTLY) BLURT
(— AFFECTEDLY) KNAP MINCE
(— ARGUMENTS) BLAZE
(— CASUALLY) DROP
(— EXPLOSIVELY) BOLT
(— FALSEHOODS) FABLE
(— FOOLISHLY) BLABBER
(— HALTINGLY) BLUBBER
(— HURRIEDLY) CHOP
(— IN HARSH VOICE) GRIT GRATE

(— INADVERTENTLY) SLIP
(— INDISTINCTLY) CHEW
(— LOUD CRY) BRAY BLARE
(— LOUDLY) CRY BLAT CALL HALLO
HALLOO HULLOO PRABBLE
(— LOW SOUNDS) MURMUR
WHISPER
(— MEANINGLESS SOUNDS) BABBLE
(— RAPIDLY) FIRE CHATTER
(— RAUCOUSLY) BLAT
(— REPETITIVELY) CHIME
(— RHETORICALLY) DECLAIM
(— SOLEMNLY) SWEAR
(— STUPIDLY) BLUNDER
(— SUDDENLY) CRACK
(— UNCTUOUSLY) DROOL
(— VIGOROUSLY) FLING
(— WITH EFFORT) HEAVE
UTTERANCE CRY GAB CALL OSSE
DITTY PAROL VOICE ACCENT
ACTION BREATH CHORUS DRIVEL
GIBBER ORACLE PAROLE EXPRESS
INKLING LALLING STATUTE
DELIVERY FOOTNOTE HOMESPUN
JUDGMENT LOCUTION SYLLABIC
(— FROM A DIVINITY) ORACLE
(— OF VOCAL SOUNDS) PHONESIS
(CONDEMNATORY —) INFAMY
(DEFECTIVE —) STAMMER
(FAINT —) INKLING
(FOOLISH —) DRIVEL
(FOOLISH —S) GUFF
(GUSHING —) EFFUSION
(IMPULSIVE —) BLURT
(MALICIOUS —) SLANDER
(OFFENSIVE —) AFFRONT
(PROPHETIC —) OSSE
(PUBLIC —) AIR
(SHORT —) DITTY
(SOLEMN —) EFFATE EFFATUM
(VAPID —) CUCKOO
(PL.) BYRONICS
UTTERED SPOKEN
UTTERLY DOG BONE DEAD BLACK
OUTLY PROOF HOLLOW MERELY
BLANKLY OUTERLY SHEERLY
PROPERLY
UVULA CION UVULE PLECTRUM
STAPHYLE
UVULARIA OAKESIA
UZBEK JAGATAI

V VEE FIVE VICTOR
(INVERTED —) CARET
VACANCY HOLE WANT VACUIT
VACUITY VACATION
VACANT IDLE VOID BLANK EMPTY
FISHY INANE WASTE DEVOID
HOLLOW DORMANT UNFILLED
(BECOME —) FALL
VACATE QUIT TOLL VOID AVOID
EMPTY WAIVE VACANT ABANDON
RESCIND ABROGATE EVACUATE
VACATION OUT REST LEAVE OUTING
RECESS HOLIDAY NONTERM
VACANCY
(SUMMER —) LONG
VACCINE BACTERIN BIOLOGIC
VACCINIA COWPOX
VACILLATE SWAG WAVE DACKER
DITHER HALPER WABBLE WOBBLE
SHAFFLE STICKLE WHIFFLE
HESITATE
VACILLATING INFIRM HALTING
VACILLATION WAVERING
VACUITY BLOW VACANCY FONTANEL
VACUOUS DULL BLANK EMPTY SILLY
VACANT
VACUUM GAPE VOID VACANCY
VACUITY VACATION
VAGABOND BUM VAG HOBO KERN
JAVEL ROGUE SHACK STIFF BRIBER
CANTER HARLOT JOCKEY PICARA
PICARO RODNEY RUNNER TAGRAG
TRUANT WAFFIE ERRATIC FAITOUR
GADLING GANGREL OUTCAST
SCOURER SWAGMAN SWINGER
TINKLER TRUCKER VAGRANT
VAURIEN WASTREL BOHEMIAN
BRODYAGA CURSITOR CUSTROUN
FUGITIVE GLASSMAN PALLIARD
RAPPAREE RUNABOUT RUNAGATE
WHIPJACK
VAGARY WHIM FANCY FREAK VAGUE
CAPRICE CONCEIT CRANKUM
FLAGARIE VAGRANCY
(PL.) HUMORS
VAGINATE SHEATHED
VAGRANCY MOPERY ROGUING
VAGRANT BUM WAFF WAIF CAIRD
PIKER PIKEY ROGUE SKELB STRAG
TRAMP ARRANT CASUAL SHAKER
SHULER TINKER TRUANT VAGROM
VAGUER WAFFIE DEVIOUS DRIFTER
ERRATIC FLOATER GANGREL
ROGUISH SKILDER SWAGMAN
TINKLER TRAMPER TROGGER
BRODYAGA PLANETIC STROLLER
VAGABOND SHACKLING
VAGUE LAX DARK HAZY FOGGY
FUZZY GROSS LOOSE MISTY
CLOUDY DREAMY MYSTIC SHAGGY
BLURRED EVASIVE OBSCURE
SHADOWY UNFIXED CONFUSED
INFINITE NUBILOUS
VAGUELY DIMLY DARKLY DUMBLY
DREAMILY
VAIN MAD IDLE NULL PUFF VOID
WANE EMPTY FLORY PROUD SAUCY
VOGIE WASTE FLIMSY FUTILE
HOLLOW VAUNTY BIGGITY CARRIED

TRIVIAL VAINFUL CONCEITY
NUGATORY PEACOCKY VAPOROUS
WASTEFUL
(NOT —) SOLID
VAINGLORY RUFF GLORY VANITY
ELATION
VAINLY IDLY TOOMLY
VAIR POTENT
VAISRAVANA BISHAMON
VAISYA BAIS BICE
VAJRA DORJE
VALANCE PELMET FRONTLET
PALMETTE
VALE DALE DEAN DELL BACHE
BATCH ENNIS
VALEDICTORY FAREWELL
VALENCE ADICITY ATOMISM
VALERIAN HELIO BENNET SUMBUL
ALLHEAL CUTHEAL SETWALL
CETEWALL
VALERIC PENTOIC
VALET MAN ANDREW SIRDAR
TARTAR WALLIE CRISPIN TIREMAN
VALIANT SAD BRAG PREU PROW
WILD BRAVE LUSTY ORPED PROUD
STOUT WIGHT FIERCE HEROIC
DOUGHTY GAILLARD GALLIARD
INTREPID STALWART VIRTUOUS
VALID FAIR GOOD JUST LEGAL
SOUND COGENT LAWFUL BINDING
ETERNAL WEIGHTY FORCIBLE
VAILABLE VALIDOUS VALUABLE
VALIDATE FIRM SEAL VALID AFFIRM
CONFIRM
VALIDITY FORCE VIGOR STRENGTH
VALISE BAG GRIP MAIL DORLACH
SATCHEL VALLIES SUITCASE
VALKYRIE SHIELDMAY
VALLECULA VALLEY
VALLEY DIB GUT COMB COOM COVE
DALE DELL DENE GILL HOLE HOPE
HOWE HOYA PARK VALE WADI
WADY ATRIO BACHE BREAK CHASM
COMBE COOMB DHOON GHYLL
GLACK GOYAL GOYLE SLACK SLADE
SWALE TEMPE YUNGA BOLSON
BOTTOM CANADA CLOUGH COULEE
DINGLE HOLLOW LAAGTE LEEGTE
RINCON STRATH AIJALON BLOWOUT
GEHENNA VAALITE
(— BETWEEN CONES OF VOLCANO)
ATRIO
(— IN THESSALY) TEMPE
(— ON MOON'S SURFACE) RILL
CLEFT RILLE
(— ON MT BLANC) NANT
(CIRCULAR —) RINCON
(DEEP —) CANON CANYON
(FLAT-FLOORED DESERT —)
BOLSON
(GRASSY MOUNTAIN —) HOLE
(LOWEST PART OF —) SOLE
(MINIATURE —) GULLY GULLEY
(NARROW —) DEAN DENE GLEN
GLACK GOYLE KLOOF CLOUGH
(SECLUDED —) GLEN DINGLE
(TRENCHLIKE —) COULEE
VALOR ARETE MERIT VALUE BOUNTY
VALOUR BRAVERY COURAGE

PROWESS STOMACH CHIVALRY
VALIANCY
VALOROUS BRAVE VIRTUOUS
VALUABLE DEAR COSTLY PRIZED
WORTHY EMINENT WEALTHY
PRECIOUS PRIZABLE SINGULAR
VALUATION PRIZE VALOR VALUE
ESTEEM EXTENT ESTIMATE
TAXATION
VALUE SET COST FECK FOOT HOLD
RATE TELL AVAIL CARAT CHEAP
COUNT FORCE PRICE PRIZE STAMP
STENT STOCK VALOR WORTH
ASSESS ASSIZE EQUITY ESTEEM
EXTENT FIGURE HIDAGE MATTER
MOMENT PRAISE REGARD VALURE
VALUTA VIRTUE ACCOUNT ADVANCE
APPRIZE CAPITAL CHERISH
COMPUTE PRETIUM RESPECT
VALENCY WERGILD ESTIMATE
EVALUATE GOODWILL SPLENDOR
TREASURE VALIDITY VALLIDOM
(— HIGHLY) PRIZE ENDEAR
(— OF ANGLE) EPOCH
(— OF COW) SET
(— OF TIMBER) STUMPAGE
(ABSOLUTE —) MODULUS
(AESTHETIC —) AMENITY
(ESTABLISHED —) PAR
(GOOD —) SNIP
(MATHEMATICAL —) EXTREMUM
(NEGATIVE —) DISVALUE
(STUDY OF —) AXIOLOGY
(TESTED —) ASSAY
VALUED DEAR
VALUELESS BAFF STRAWY
NAUGHTY
VALVE TAP COCK DISC DISK GATE
ORAL STOP CHOKE CLACK MIXER
VALVA WAFER CUTOUT DAMPER
KICKER PALLET POPPET POTLID
SCUTUM SLUICE SUCKER VENTIL
WASHER CLICKET DRAWOFF
PETCOCK REDUCER SCALLOP
SCOLLOP SHUTOFF VALVULA
VALVULE DRAWGATE EPITHECA
EPIVALVE STOPCOCK THROTTLE
(— OF BARNACLE) SCUTUM
(— OF MUSICAL INSTRUMENT)
PISTON VENTIL
(— OF PUMP BOX) FANG
(THIN —) WAFER
(TRIPLE —) KICKER
VAMBRACE BRACELET
VAMOOSE SCRAM CHEESE DECAMP
SKIDDOO
VAMPIRE LAMIA ALUKAH
VAN WAN FORE LEAD SAIL FRONT
TRUCK VAUNT WAGON VAWARD
CARAVAN FOURGON FOREWARD
KHALDIAN
VANADATE UVANITE TURANITE
VANDAL HUN HUNLIKE SARACEN
HOOLIGAN
VANE FAN TEE WEB COCK TAIL WING
FAINE BUCKET TARGET DOGVANE
FLIGHTER VEXILLUM
(— OF ARROW) FEATHER
(— OF CONVEYOR BELT) FLIGHT

(— OF FEATHER) WEB FLUE
VEXILLUM
(— OF SURVEYING STAFF)
TRANSOM
(— OF WINDMILL) FAN FANE TAIL
FAINE
(COOLING — IN BREWING)
FLIGHTER
VANESSA PYRAMEIS
VANGUARD FORLORN
VANISH DIE FLY DROP FADE FLEE
MELT PASS SANT WEDE WEND
CLEAR FLEET SAUNT SLIDE EXHALE
EVANISH SCATTER CONQUEST
DISSOLVE EVANESCE
(— BY DEGREES) DRILL
VANISHED LAPSED EXTINCT
VANITY ABEL POMP VAIN FOLLY
PRIDE EGOISM FEATHER FOPPERY
INANITY SANDUST IDLENESS
IDLESHIP
VANNER SLIMER
VANNIC KHALDIAN
VANQUISH GET WIN BEAT LICK MILL
UTTER EXPUGN MASTER OUTRAY
SUBDUE THRASH CONQUER
OVERWIN SMOTHER CONQUEST
OVERCOME SURMOUNT VENKISEN
VANQUISHED CRAVEN
VAPID DRY DULL FADE FLAT STALE
TRITE JEJUNE INSIPID WATERISH
VAPOR FOG FUME REEK ROKE STEW
BOAST BRUME EWDER HUMOR
SMOKE STEAM STIFE BREATH
VAPOUR EXHAUST HALITUS
(HOT —) LUNT
(NOXIOUS —) DAMP
(PL.) BRUME
VAPORIZATION BURNUP
VAPORIZE DRIVE FLASH STEAM
AERATE AERIFY VAPORATE
VAPOROUS FUMY FUMID HUMID
FUMISH FUMOSE STEAMY VOLATILE
VARANGIAN VARIAG WARING
(PL.) ROS
VARIABILITY HETERISM
VARIABLE FLUX FREE CHOPPY
FICKLE FITFUL KITTLE WRAIST
CEPHEID FACIENT FLUXILE MUTABLE
ROLLING STREAKY UNEQUAL
VARIANT VARIOUS ARGUMENT
FLOATING FLUXIBLE SHIFTING
SKITTISH UNSTABLE VEERABLE
(EXCEEDINGLY —) PROTEAN
VARIANCE ODDS DISCORD DISPUTE
VARIANT STATE
(— IN WHEAT) SPELTOID
(PL.) DIAPHONE
VARIATION REX TURN ERROR
ROGUE SHADE CHANGE DOUBLE
JITTER SWITCH CYCLING DESCANT
EXTREME SHADING VARIETY
WINDING DIVISION DYNAMICS
HETERISM MUTATION
(— IN AIR PRESSURE) ROBBING
(— IN CURRENT) SURGE
(— IN FREQUENCY) SWINGING
(— IN SPEED) HUNTING
(— OF COLOR) ABRASH

(— OF PUPIL OF EYE) HIPPUS
(— OF SHOE) SPRING
(— OF VOWELS) ABLAUT
(ALLOWABLE —) LEEWAY
(BALLET —) ATTITUDE
(TOPOGRAPHICAL —) BREAK
(PL.) PIBROCH
VARICOCELE RAMEX
VARIED SORTY DAEDAL SEVERAL
VARIANT VARIOUS MANIFOLD
VARIED BUNTING PRUSIANO
VARIEGATE DROP FRET FLECK
FREAK SHOOT DAPPLE STRIPE
VARIFY CHECKER
VARIEGATED FAW PIED SHOT JASPE
LYART SHELD DAEDAL MARLED
MENALD MOSAIC SKEWED CHECKED
DAPPLED FREAKED FRETTED
PECKLED SPARKED VARIOUS
DISCOLOR FRECKLED OVERSHOT
PANACHED SKEWBALD
VARIEGATION COLOR
VARIETY FORM KIND MODE SORT
BRAND BREED CLASS SPICE
CHANGE STIRPS STRAIN STRIPE
SPECIES VARIENS
VARIOLA HORSEPOX
VARIOUS MANY SERE DIVERS
SUNDER SUNDRY VARIED DIVERSE
SEVERAL VARIANT MANIFOLD
VARISCITE UTAHITE
VARLET BOY LAD GIPPO JIPPO
PAVISER COISTREL VARLETTO
VARNISH DOPE JAPAN LACKER
MEDIUM PUNDUM FIXATIF LACQUER
VEHICLE VERMEIL FIXATIVE
OVERGILD THEETSEE
VARY HUNT ALTER BREAK DRIFT
SHIFT SPORT CHANGE DIFFER
RECEDE VARIFY CHECKER DEVIATE
DISSENT DIVERGE VARIATE
DISAGREE
VARYING CURRENT
VASE PYX URN OLLA VASA VASO
ASKOS CYLIX DINOS DIOTA KYLIX
PYXIS BASKET BOWPOT COTULA
COTYLA CRATER DEINOS DOLIUM
FILLER HYDRIA KALPIS KOTYLE
KRATER LEKANE SITULA AMPHORA
AMPULLA CANOPUS PATELLA
POTICHE PSYKTER SCYPHUS
SKYPHOS STAMNOS URCEOLE
BOUGHPOT LECYTHUS LEKYTHOS
MURRHINE PROCHOOS
(— FOR PERFUME) CONCH
(— ON PEDESTAL) TAZZA
(—S UNDER THEATER SEATS)
SCHEA
VASODILATOR KELLIN KHELLIN
VASSAL MAN WER BOND LEUD CEILE
LIEGE SLAVE CLIENT GENEAT
SACOPE BONDMAN FEEDMAN
FEODARY HOMAGER RUDIGER
SAMURAI SERVANT SUBJECT
PALATINE
(PL.) MANRED
VASSALAGE MANRED MANRENT
VAST HUGE BROAD ENORM GREAT
LARGE STOUR VASTY COSMIC

IMMANE MIGHTY UNTOLD IMMENSE
VASTITY ENORMOUS INFINITE
MOUNTAIN SPACIOUS
VASTNESS IMMANE GRANDEUR
WIDENESS
VAT ARK BAC DIP FAT PIT TAP TUN
BACK BECK COOM FATE GAAL GAIL
GYLE KEEL KIER TINE APRON
COOMB FETTE FLOAT KEEVE KIEVE
ROUND STAND STEEP KIMNEL
MOTHER BLUNGER DRAINER
GRAINER KEELVAT STEEPER
PRESSFAT
(— USED IN MEASURING SLIPS) ARK
(BREWER'S —) BACK FLOAT KEEVE
UNION CUMMING
(CHEESE —) CHESSEL CHESSET
CHESSART
(COOLING —) KELDER
(DYER'S —) JIG LEAD DYEBECK
(EVAPORATING —) APRON GRAINER
(FERMENTING —) TUN COMB COOM
GYLE KEEL COOMB FLOAT
(TANNER'S —) TAP HANGER
SPENDER
(TEXTILE —) KIER
(WINE —) LAKE
VAUDEVILLE ZARZUELA
VAULT BOUT COPE JUMP LEAP PEND
SKIP TOMB VOLT WOWT AZURE
CROFT CRYPT EMBOW VOLTO
CUPOLA FORNIX SHROUD DUNGEON
TESTUDO VALTAGE CATACOMB
LEAPFROG MONUMENT
(— IN CEILING) LACUNAR
(— OF HEAVEN) WELKIN
(— OF SKY) CONVEX ZENITH
CONCAVE
VAULTED CONCAVE CRYPTED
EMBOWED
VAULTING POMADA POMMADO
VAUNT GAB BRAG BOAST ROOSE
VOUST AVAUNT INSULT GLORIFY
FLOURISH
(— ONESELF) WIND
VAUNTMURE MANURE
VEAL VEAU SLINK FRICANDO
(LIKE —) VITULINE
VECTOR I K PHASOR GRADIENT
VEDDOID PANYAN
VEDIC (— PRINCIPLE) RTA RITA
VEER CUT DIP FLY CAST CHOP SLEW
SLUE SWAY WYRE FETCH SHOFF
SWOOP BROACH CHANGE SLOUGH
SWERVE TUMBLE DEVIATE WHIFFLE
VEERING DRIFT CHOPPY
VEGETABLE PEA YAM BEAN BEET
CORN KALE LEEK OKRA CHARD
GRASS ONION SABZI SALAD
CARROT CELERY LEGUME LENTIL
POTATO RADISH SQUASH TOMATO
TOPEPO TURNIP BLOATER CABBAGE
CELTUCE LETTUCE PARSNIP
PEASCOD RHUBARB SPINACH
VEGETAL BROCCOLI EGGPLANT
RUTABAGA
(— MATTER) SUDD
(—S FOR MARKET) TRUCK
(EARLY —) PRIMEUR

(EARLY —S) HASTINGS
(GARDEN —S) SASS SAUCE
(HYBRID —) GARLION
EGETATION HERB COVER GREEN
SCRUB GROWTH HERBAGE
COVERAGE PLANTAGE PLEUSTON
SMELLAGE
(DECOMPOSED —) STAPLE
(SCRUB —) BRUSH
(UNWANTED —) FILTH
EGETATIVE PLANTAL
EHEMENCE FURY GLOW HEAT
RAGE WARMTH STRENGTH
VIOLENCE
EHEMENT HOT HIGH KEEN LOUD
ANGRY EAGER FIERY HEFTY YEDER
ARDENT BITTER FERVID FIERCE
FLASHY HEARTY HEATED RAGING
STRONG ANIMOSE ANIMOUS
FURIOSO INTENSE JEALOUS
VIOLENT
EHEMENTLY PELLMELL
EHICLE BUS CAB CAR FLY VAN
ARBA AUTO CART DUKE FLAT GOER
JEEP SLED TAXI TEAM WAIN ARABA
BRAKE BREAK BUGGY CARRY DILLY
FLAIL GUIDE HANSA NODDY STAGE
WAGON BLADER CHARET CISIUM
DIESEL HEARSE JITNEY MEDIUM
PEDRAL RANDOM SLEDGE SLEIGH
SURREY TRISHA TROIKA CARRIER
CHARIOT CRUISER HOTSHOT
ICEBOAT KIBITKA MACHINE MINIBUS
OMNIBUS PEDICAB PEDRAIL
SHUTTLE SPEEDER SPRAYER
STEAMER STEERER TARTANA
TAXICAB TRAVOIS TURNOUT UTILITY
AUTORAIL AUTOSLED CARRIAGE
CHARETTE CYCLECAR DEADHEAD
DELIVERY ELECTRIC FILMOGEN
SHOWCASE SOCIABLE UNICYCLE
(— DRAWN BY BULLOCK) EKKA
(— FOR COLORS) MEGILP
(— FOR HAULING) TRACTOR
(— ON RUNNERS) SLED CARRO
SLEDGE SLEIGH ICEBOAT AUTOSLED
(— PULLED BY MAN) BROUETTE
RICKSHAW
(— RUNNING ON RAILS) LORRY
TRAIN
(— WITH 3 HORSES ABREAST)
TROIKA
**(— WITH 3 HORSES BEHIND EACH
OTHER)** RANDOM
(2-WHEELED —) GIG CART SULKY
TONGA CISIUM JINGLE LIMBER
BICYCLE CALECHE CROYDON
RICKSHAW
(AMMUNITION —) CAISSON
(AMPHIBIOUS —) BUFFALO
(AWKWARD —) ARK
(CHILD'S —) PRAM WALKER
SCOOTER STROLLER
(COVERED —) SEDAN LANDAU
CARAVAN KIBITKA
(EARTH-MOVING —) SCOOP
(LITTLE —) HINAYANA
(LUMBERING —) TUG TODE
(OBSOLETE —) CRATE

(POOR-QUALITY —) DOG
(RUDE —) KIBITKA
(SLEDGE-LIKE —) GAMBO
(WHEELLESS —) DRAY
(PL.) PARK
VEIL WRY FALL FILM HIDE MASK
WRAP COVER GLOSS SHADE VELUM
VIMPA VOLET WREIL BUMBLE FAILLE
SHADOW SHROUD VEILER WEEPER
WIMPLE CORTINA CURTAIN
ENDOTYS PARANJA VEILING
ENDOTHYS HEADRAIL MAHARMAH
MANTILLA TELEBLEM
(— IN CHURCH) AER ENDOTYS
ENDOTHYS
(— ON FUNGI) CORTINA
(DOUBLE —) YASHMAK
(HUMERAL —) SUDARY
(WIDOW'S —) WEEPER
VEILED COVERT VELATED
SHROUDED
VEILING PURDAH GOSSAMER
VEIN BAR LOB RIB CAVA LODE MOOD
RAKE REEF VENA AMPER CLOUD
COMES COSTA LEDGE MEDIA NERVE
RIDER SCRIN VARIX LEADER MEDIAL
STRAIN STREAK VENULA VENULE
AXILLAR AZYGOUS CUBITAL
DROPPER JUGULAR NERVURE
PRECAVA PRESTER SAPHENA
VEINLET AXILLARY EMULGENT
PREMEDIA PROFUNDA SUBCOSTA
(— OF LEAF) RIB COSTA MIDRIB
(— OF MINERAL) STREAK STRINGER
(— OF ORE) LODE ROKE LEDGE
RIDER SCRIN LEADER STRING
DROPPER UNDERSET
(— OF WING) CUBIT CUBITAL
CUBITUS SUBCOSTA SUBCOSTAL
(GRANITIC —) ELVAN
(QUARTZ —) SADDLE
(VARICOSE —) AMPER
VEINED MARBLED NERVOSE
VELA SAILS
VELAR GUTTURAL
VELD BUSHVELD SOURVELD
VELELLA SALLYMAN
VELLEITY WOULDING
VELLINCH FLINCHER
VELLUM ORIHON
VELOCIPEDE HOBBY STEED TRICAR
BICYCLE DICYCLE RANTOON
SPEEDER DRAISINE TRICYCLE
VELOCITY DRIFT CELERITY RAPIDITY
STRENGTH
(— OF 1 FOOT PER SECOND) VELO
(— OF FLOW) CURRENT
VELOUR SOLEIL
VELOUTE POULETTE
VELUM VEIL VELAMEN VELARIUM
VELVET PILE YUZEN BIRODO VELURE
FRAYING VELLUTE
VELVETEEN TRIPE
VELVET GRASS FOG
VELVETLEAF DAGGA PAREIRA
VENAL CORRUPT SALABLE HIRELING
SALEABLE VENDIBLE
VEND HAWK SELL UTTER MARKET
PEDDLE

VENDIBLE VENAL SALABLE
SALEABLE
VENDOR FAKER SELLER VENDER
BUTCHER HUSTLER PITCHER
PURLMAN VIANDER PITCHMAN
SAUCEMAN VENDITOR
VENEER BURL BURR JAPAN SHOOK
SKILLET
VENEERER DUSTER
VENERABLE OLD HOAR SAGE
HOARY AUGUST SACRED VETUST
ANCIENT VENERAL VINTAGE
VENERATE FEAR DREAD HALLOW
REVERE VENERE RESPECT WORSHIP
VENERATED HOLY SACRED
HALLOWED
VENERATION AWE CULT DULIA
CULTISM RESPECT DEVOTION
VENETIAN RED SIENA SIERRA
VENETIAN SUMAC SCOTINO

VENEZUELA

CAPITAL: CARACAS
COIN: REAL MEDIO FUERTE
BOLIVAR CENTIMO MOROCOTA
GULF: PARIA
MEASURE: GALON MILLA FANEGA
ESTADEL
MOUNTAIN: PAVA YAVI DUIDA
ICUTU CONCHA CUNEVA PARIMA
IMUTACA MASAITI RORAIMA
NATIVE: CARIB TIMOTE TIMOTEX
GUARAUNO
RIVER: META APURE CAURA
ARAUCA CARONI CUYUNI
GUANARE ORINOCO ORITUEO
PARAGUA SUAPURE VICHADA
GUAVIARE VENTUARI
STATE: LARA APURE SUCRE ZULIA
ARAGUA FALCON MERIDA
BOLIVAR COJEDES GUARICO
MONAGAS TACHIRA YARACUY
CARABOBO TRUJILLO
TOWN: AROA CORO ATURES
CUMANA MERIDA BARINAS
CABELLO GUAWARE MARACAY
MATURIN CARUPANO TACUPITA
VALENCIA
WEIGHT: BAG LIBRA

VENGEANCE WREAK WRECK
AVENGE ULTION WANION ALASTOR
REVENGE VINDICT REQUITAL
VINDICTA
VENILIA (HUSBAND OF —) DAUNUS
(SISTER OF —) AMATA
(SON OF —) TURNUS
VENISON BILTONG
VENOM GALL ATTER VIRUS POISON
SWELTER CROTALIN CROTALUS
VENOMOUS TOXIC ATTERN DEADLY
SNAKEY VENOMY BANEFUL NOXIOUS
SMITTLE SNAKISH POISONED
VIPERINE VIRULENT
VENT EMIT HOLE REEK BELCH DRAIN
FROTH ISSUE TEWEL OUTAGE
OUTLET CHIMNEY EXPRESS
OPENING ORIFICE OUTCAST

OUTFALL OUTTAKE RELEASE
VENTAGE APERTURE BREATHER
DIATREME FONTANEL MOFFETTE
SESPERAL SPIRACLE SUSPIRAL
VENTHOLE VOMITORY
(— IN EARTH'S CRUST) VOLCANO
(VOLCANIC —) BOCCA DIATREME
SOLFATARA
VENTILATE AIR WIND AERATE
EXPRESS
VENTILATION AERAGE AIRING
VENTILATOR BADGIR LOUVER
FEMERELL
VENTING GUST
VENTRAL HEMAL STERNAL
ANTERIOR INFERIOR
VENTRICLE HEART TRICORN
DIACOELE
VENTURE HAB RUN SET CAST DARE
JUMP KITE LUCK MINT REST RISK
WAGE ETTLE FLIER FLYER FROST
RISCO SALLY STAKE TEMPT WAGER
CHANCE DANGER HAZARD SASHAY
FLUTTER IMPERIL JEOPARD
PRESUME ENDANGER GETPENNY
(— AT DICE) THROW
(— TO SAY) DARESAY
VENTURESOME BOLD RASH RISKY
DARING TEMEROUS
VENTURESOMELY CHANCILY
VENUS LOVE VESPER LUCIFER
HESPERUS PHOSPHOR
(FATHER OF —) JUPITER
(HUSBAND OF —) VULCAN
(MOTHER OF —) DIONE
(SON OF —) CUPID AENEAS
VENUSEAN VENEREAN
VERACIOUS TRUE VERY TRUTHY
SINCERE VERIDIC FAITHFUL
TRUTHFUL
VERACITY HSIN TROTH TRUTH
VERITY FIDELITY
VERANDA PYAL LANAI PORCH
STOOP PIAZZA BALCONY GALERIE
GALLERY
VERB RHEMA ACTIVE NOMINAL
DEPONENT
(AUXILIARY —) BE DO CAN MAY
HAVE MUST WILL SHALL
VERBAL ORAL WORDY
VERBATIM DIRECT VERBAL
DIRECTLY
VERBENA ALOYSIA VERVAIN
VERBENALIN CORNIN
VERBIAGE TALK
VERBOSE WINDY WORDY PROLIX
VERBAL DIFFUSE WORDISH
(NOT —) LEAN
VERDANT BOSKY GREEN VIRID
VERDICT WORD VARDI ASSIZE
FINDING OPINION DECISION
JUDGMENT VEREDICT
VERDIGRIS AERUGO CANKER
VERDET
VERDIN GOLDTIT
VERDURE GREENTH GREENERY
VIRIDITY
VERGE TOP EDGE WAND YARD
TOUCH BORDER TRENCH TRIGGER

VERGER WANDSMAN
VERGILIAN MARONIAN MARONIST
VERIFICATION AUDIT AVERRAL
CHECKUP AVERMENT
VERIFY AVER TRUE AUDIT CHECK
PROVE ATTEST RATIFY COLLATE
CONFIRM CONTROL JUSTIFY
SUPPORT
VERILY AMEN FAITH PARDY CERTES
INDEED PARDIE FAITHLY
VERITABLE REAL TRUE VERY
ACTUAL HONEST PROPER GENUINE
VERIMENT
VERITY TROTH TRUTH VERIDITY
VERJUICE VARGE
VERMICULE VAALITE
VERMICULITE KERRITE MACONITE
VERMIFUGE KOSIN HARMAL HARMEL
KAMALA KAMELA KOOSIN HELONIAS
VERMILION RED GOYA MINIUM
PAPRIKA PIMENTO VERMEIL
ZINOBER CARMETTA CINNABAR
TOREADOR
VERMIN FILTH CARRION VARMINT
VERMIS WORM

VERMONT
CAPITAL: MONTPELIER
COLLEGE: BENNINGTON
MIDDLEBURY
COUNTY: ESSEX ORANGE
ORLEANS LAMOILLE
LAKE: CASPIAN DUNMORE
SEYMOUR CHAMPLAIN
MOUNTAIN: BROMLEY HOGBACK
PROSPECT MANSFIELD
MOUNTAIN RANGE: GREEN
TACONIC
PRESIDENT: ARTHUR COOLIDGE
RIVER: SAXTONS NULHEGAN
WINOOSKI
STATE BIRD: THRUSH
STATE FLOWER: CLOVER
STATE TREE: MAPLE
TOWN: BARRE STOWE GRAFTON
NEWFANE RUTLAND
UNIVERSITY: NORWICH

VERMOUTH CINZANO CHAMBERY
VERNACULAR LINGO COMMON
JARGON PATOIS ROMAIC VULGAR
CHALDEE DIALECT SCOTTISH
VERNALIZE IAROVIZE JAROVIZE
YAROVIZE
VERONICA HEBE SUDARIUM
VERNICLE
VERRUCOSE WARTY WARTED
VERSATILE HANDY FICKLE MOBILE
FLEXILE
VERSE FIT EPIC LINE POSE RANN
RICH RIME SONG BLANK IONIC
METER METRE RHYME STAVE STICH
TANKA ADONIC ALCAIC BURDEN
CHIAVE CYWYDD DIPODY HEROIC
JINGLE PANTUN SCAZON STANZA
VERSET ANAPEST DICOLON
DOGGREL ELEGIAC PAEONIC
PENNILL SAPPHIC SAVITRI SOTADIC

STICHOS TRIPODY TROILUS
CHOLIAMB DACTYLIC DINGDONG
DOGGEREL GLYCONIC LEONINES
PRIAPEAN RESPONSE SENTENCE
SINGSONG TERETISM TRIMETER
VERSICLE
(— FORM) VIRELAY KYRIELLE
(— OF 14 LINES) SONNET
(— OF 2 FEET) DIPODY DIMETER
(— OF 6 FEET) CHOLIAMB SENARIAN
SENARIUS
(— WITH LIMPING MOVEMENT)
SCAZON
(DEVOTIONAL —) ANTIPHON
(HINDU —) SLOKA
(JAPANESE —) HAIKAI
(UNMELODIOUS —) TERETISM
(PL.) TRIPOS PINDARICS
VERSED SEEN WITTY BESEEN
TRADED STUDIED FREQUENT
OVERSEEN SCIENCED
(WELL —) SKILLFUL
VERSICLE VERSE VERSET STICHOS
SUFFRAGE
VERSIFIER BARD POET RHYMER
VERSER METERER
VERSIFY METER
VERSION DRAM DRAUGHT EDITION
READING TURNING
(SHORT —) BRIEF
(SIMPLIFIED —) KEY
(TRANSLATED —) CONSTRUE
VERSO REVERSE
VERT VERD POMME VENUS PRASINE
SINOPLE GREENHEW
VERTEBRA AXIS ATLAS DORSAL
LUMBAR SACRAL ACANTHA
CENTRUM CERVICAL METAMERE
PROATLAS RACKBONE SPONDYLE
VERTEBRATA CRANIATA CRANIOTA
VERTEBRATE CRANIATE SAUROPSID
VERTEX APEX COPE POLE CROWN
PITCH SUMMIT VERTICAL
VERTICAL ERECT PLUMB SHEER
WHIRL ORTHAL UPRIGHT COLUMNAR
SHEERING STRAIGHT
VERTICALLY PLUMP ENDLONG
SHEERLY DIRECTLY PALEWISE
VERTICIL WHORL
VERTIGINOUS DIZZY
VERTIGO DINUS TIEGO MEGRIM
MIRLIGO SWIMMING WHIRLING
VERUMONTANUM COLLICLE
VERVAIN GERVAO FROGFOOT
IRONWEED
VERVE DARE DASH BOUNCE ENERGY
PANACHE VITALITY VIVACITY
VERY SO ALL BIG DOG GAY GEY
MUY BRAW DEAD FELL FULL JUST
MAIN MUCH PURE RARE REAL SAME
SELF SUCH TRES UNCO WELL ASSA
AWFUL BLAME BULLY CRAZY
DOOMS JOLLY MOLTO PESKY RIGHT
SOWAN SUPER SWITH UNCOW
VERRA BITTER BLAMED DAMNED
DEUCED FREELY GAINLY LIVING
MAINLY MASTER MIGHTY NATION
POISON PROPER STRONG VERRAY
WONDER AWFULLY BOILING

GALLOWS GREATLY PASSING
SOPPING STRANGE DEUCEDLY
DREADFUL ENORMOUS FAMOUSLY
POWERFUL PRECIOUS SPANKING
SWINGING WHACKING
ESICANT LEWISITE
ESICA PISCIS MANDORLA
ESICATORY BLISTER
ESICLE BLEB CYST APTHA BULLA
BURSE FLOAT APHTHA AMPULLA
BLADDER HYDATID POMPHUS
UTRICLE VACUOLE AEROCYST
MIDBRAIN VESICULA
ESICULAR BULLOSE BULLOUS
ESPERAL TOWEL
ESPERS LYCHNIC PLACEBO
EVENSONG
ESSEL (ALSO SEE BOAT AND SHIP)
GO CAN CAT COG CUP FAT GUM
HOY NEF PIG POT TUB VAS VAT VIA
BARK BOAT BODY BOMB BOOT
BOSS BOWL BRIG BUSH BUSS CASK
CELL COWL DISH DRIP DUCT GAWN
GRAB HORN HULK JACK JUNK LOTA
PINK PINT POST PROW SAIL SHIP
SNOW TING YAWL AMULA BAKIE
BARGE BASIN BIDET BIKIE BOCAL
BOYER CADUS CANNE CHURN
COGUE CRACK CRAER CRAFT
CRARE CRUET CRUSE DIOTA DUBBA
FLASK GLOBE GUIDE JUBBE KETCH
LADLE LAKER LAVER LINER PIECE
PYKAR SCOOP SMACK STEAM STILL
XEBEC YANKY ZABRA BANKER
BARQUE BARREL BILALO BOILER
BOTTLE BOUTRE BUCKET BURNER
CAIQUE CANNER CAPPIE CHARGE
CODMAN COFFIN CONCHA COOLER
COPPER CRATER CRAYER CRUISE
CUTTER DECKER DEINOS DOGGER
DUBBAH ELUTOR FESSEL FIRKIN
FLAGON HOLCAD HOOKER JAGGER
KERNOS KETTLE KRATER LANCHA
LATEEN LEKANE LORCHA MASLIN
MONKEY MULLER PACKET PANKIN
PATERA PICARD PITHOS POURIE
ROLLER SALTER SATTIE SEALER
SERVER SETTEE SHIBAR SITULA
SMOKER TARTAN TENDER TOPMAN
VESICA WHALER BAGGALA BALLOON
BALLOON BLICKEY BLICKIE
BUGGALO CARAVEL CARRIER
CISTERN CLIPPER CORSAIR
COUGNAR CRAGGAN CRESSET
CRISSET CRUISER CUVETTE
DRIFTER DRINKER DROGHER
FELUCCA FLYBOAT FRIGATE
GABBARD GABBART GAIASSA
GALASSA GUNBOAT ORANGER
PATAMAR PINNACE POACHER
POLACRE PSYKTER REDUCER
SALTFAT SCALDER SEEDLIP
SETTLER SPARGER SPOUTER
STEAMER STEEPER TRACHEA
TRENDLE UTENSIL BELANDER
BENITIER BILANDER BILLYBOY
BIRDBATH BLEACHER CORVETTE
CRUCIBLE CRUISKEN CUCURBIT
DECANTER DIGESTER DUTCHMAN

EFFERENT EMISSARY FIREBOAT
FLESHPOT GALLIPOT GALLIVAT
GAROOKUH GAYDIANG HELLSHIP
HONEYPOT INKSTAND INRIGGER
IRONCLAD IRONSIDE KEELBOAT
LATEENER LAVATORY NITRATOR
PICAROON SCHOONER SMUGGLER
SPITTOON WATERPOT
(— **FOR COAL**) GEORDIE
(— **FOR DYE**) TOBY
(— **FOR HEATING LIQUIDS**) ETNA
(— **FOR HOLY WATER**) FAT FONT
STOCK STOOP STOUP
(— **FOR HYPODERMIC USE**) AMPUL
AMPULE AMPOULE
(— **FOR LIQUID WASTE**) DRIP
(— **FOR MEASURING ORE**) HOPPET
(— **FOR MOLTEN METAL**) LADLE
(— **FOR ORE WASHINGS**) LOOL
(— **FOR PERFUMES**) CENSER
(— **FOR SOLDIER'S FOOD**) MESSTIN
(— **FOR WINE SAMPLING**) TASTER
(— **HOLDING CONDIMENTS**) CRUET
CASTER
(— **IN MINE**) CORB
(— **MADE OF HOLLOW LOG**) GUM
(— **OF BARK**) COOLAMAN
COOLAMON COOLIMAN
(— **OF HORN**) BUGLE
(— **ON TRIPOD**) HOLMOS
(— **ROWED BY OARS**) CATUR
GALLEY
(— **STATIONED IN ENGLISH**
CHANNEL) GROPER
(— **USED IN MAKING GLAZE**) HILLER
(**ABANDONED** —) DERELICT
(**ARMORED** —) CRUISER IRONCLAD
IRONSIDE
(**BAPTISMAL** —) FONT
(**BARGELIKE** —) PANGARA
(**BLOOD** —) AORTA ARTERY
BLEEDER EFFERENT
(**BREWER'S** —) ROUND
(**CANDLEMAKING** —) JACK
(**CHEMIST'S** —) BATH FLASK STILL
BEAKER RETORT
(**CHINESE** —) JUNK SAMPAN
(**CIRCULAR** —) KIT
(**CLUMSY** —) CRAY CRARE
HAGBOAT
(**COASTING** —) DHOW DONI GRAB
PONTIN SHEBAR SHIBAR TRADER
COASTER GRIBANE
(**CODFISHING** —) BANKER CODMAN
(**DECORATIVE** —) AIGUIERE
(**DISTILLING** —) BODY STILL RETORT
CUCURBIT
(**DRINKING** —) CAP CUP TIN BOOT
PECE FOUNT GLASS GOURD JORUM
SCALE BICKER CAPPIE CHOPIN
COOPER COOTIE DIPPER DUBBER
FIRLOT GOBLET KITTIE QUAICH
QUAIGH RABBIT RUMKIN BIBERON
CANAKIN CANIKIN GALLIOT
SCYPHUS SKINKER SKYPHOS
TANKARD CANNIKIN CYLINDER
(**DUTCH** —) KOFF YANKY HOOKER
SCHUIT SCHUYT
(**EARTHEN** —) PIG BAYAN PANKIN

TINAGE CRAGGAN
(**ELECTROPLATING** —) TROUGH
(**EUCHARISTIC** —) AMA PYX AMULA
PYXIS FLAGON COLUMBA CHRISMAL
CIBORIUM
(**GLASS** —) VERRE UNDINE BALLOON
(**HERRING-FISHING** —) BUSS
(**HOLLOW METALLIC** —) BELL
(**INVERTED** —) BELL
(**LADLING** —) GAUN
(**LARGE-NECKED** —) JORDAN
(**LATEEN-RIGGED** —) DHOW LATEEN
LATEENER
(**LEATHER** —) BOOT JACK OLPE
GIRBA DUBBER
(**LEVANTINE** —) JERM SAIC
(**LONG-NECKED** —) GOGLET GUGLET
(**LYMPHATIC** —) LACTEAL
(**MALAYAN** —) PROA COUGNAR
(**MELTING** —) GRISSET
(**OPEN** —) LOOM
(**PERFORATED** —) LEACH
(**PINECONE-SHAPED** —) THYRSE
(**PORTUGUESE** —) MULET
(**RARE** —) SNOW
(**SEED** —) POD BUTTON
(**SERVING** —) ARGYLE ARGYLL
SERVER
(**SHALLOW** —) KIVER SKEEL BEDPAN
PANCHION
(**SMALL** —) CAG HOY VIAL PHIAL
VEDET JIGGER LIEPOT PICARD
TINLET YETLIN FLIVVER VEDETTE
YETLING GALLIPOT
(**TOP-HEAVY** —) CRANK
(**TURKISH** —) MAHONE
(**WHALING** —) WHALER SPOUTER
(**WICKER** —) POT
(**WINE** —) AMA AMULA TINAGE
(**WOODEN** —) COG KIT BOSS BAKIE
KIVER BICKER CAPPIE COOTIE
DUDDIE FIRKIN STOUND
(PL.) CRAFT WAFTAGE
VEST GARB GOWN ROBE GILET
ACCRUE ATTACH FECKET INVEST
JACKET JELICK LINDER WESKIT
ENFEOFF CLOTHING
(— **IN**) STATE
VESTA WAX
(**FATHER OF** —) SATURN
(**MOTHER OF** —) RHEA
(**SISTER OF** —) JUNO CERES
VESTED BESTEAD DONATIVE
VESTIBULE HALL ENTRY FOYER
PORCH ATRIUM EPINAOS NARTHEX
PASSAGE ANTEROOM VESTIARY
VESTIGE TAG DREG MARK RACK
SIGN PRINT RELIC SPARK TRACE
TRACK TRACT UMBRA SHADOW
MENTION LEFTOVER TINCTURE
VESTIGIAL REDUCED
VESTING ADITIO
VESTITURE TIRE RAIMENT TUNICLE
VESTMENT ALB CAP ALBE COPE
PALL VEST AMICE COTTA EPHOD
FANON RABAT RASON STOLE
RHASON ROCHET SACCOS SAKKOS
VAKASS MANIPLE ORARION PALLIUM
PILLION PLUVIAL TUNICLE VESTURE

CHASUBLE DALMATIC PHRYGIUM RATIONAL SCAPULAR SURPLICE VESTIARY (PL.) GARB GEAR DRESS CLOTHING

VESTRY SACRISTY VESTIARY

VESUVIANITE EGERAN CYPRINE IDOCRASE VESUVIAN XANTHITE

VETCH DAL ERS AKRA LUCK TARE TINE ERVIL FITCH AXSEED FECCHE THETCH ARVEJON TINETARE TINEWEED

VETERAN VET CHAUVIN EMERITUS HARDENED SEASONED

VETERINARIAN VET LEECH FARRIER

VETERINARY VET FARRIERY

VETIVER BEN KHUS CUSCUS KUSKUS KHASGHAS KHUSKHUS

VETO KILL DISALLOW NEGATIVE

VEUGLAIRE FOWLER

VEX FRY TEW CARK CHAW FASH FAZE FRET FYKE GALL HALE ITCH RILE ROIL RUCK TEEN TOUT YOKE ANGER ANNOY CHAFE FRUMP GRAME GRILL GRIND GRIPE HARRY SCALD SPITE STURT TARRY TEASE WORRY WRACK WRATH YEARN BOTHER BURDEN CORSIE COTTER CUMBER GRIEVE GRUDGE HARASS HARROW INFEST NETTLE OFFEND PLAGUE POTHER RUFFLE THREAT WORRIT BEDEVIL CHAGRIN DESPITE PERPLEX PROVOKE TORMENT BULLYRAG EXERCISE IRRITATE MACERATE

VEXATION VEX CHAW FASH MOIL TEEN TRAY CHAFE CROSS ERROR GRIEF HARRY PIQUE SPITE STEAM WORRY BOTHER REPINE CHAGRIN DISGUST NOISANCE SORENESS

VEXATIOUS SORE TEEN PESKY ACHING FIERCE SHREWD VEXFUL IRKSOME PRICKLY TARSOME ANNOYING CUMBROUS FRAMPOLD PHRAMPEL UNTOWARD VEXATORY WEARIFUL

VEXED DIK MAD RILY SORE TEEN WAXY WILD WRAW ANGRY NARKY RAGGY ROILY MIFFED MUFFED SHIRTY SNUFFY FRABOUS GRIEVED IRKSOME OUTDONE
(EASILY —) CROSS

VEXILLUM WEB VEXIL BANNER STANDARD

VEXING CHRONIC TECHING WAYWARD ANNOYING NETTLING TEACHING

V-GOUGE VEINER

VIABLE VITAL HEALTHY

VIAL AMPUL CRUET PHIAL AMPULE CASTER CASTOR AMPOULE

VIANDS CATE DIET FOOD CHEER VIANDRY VICTUALS

VIBRANT RINGY BRAWLING RESONANT SONOROUS VIGOROUS

VIBRATE JAR WAG BEAT CAST DIRL PLAY ROCK TIRL WHIR PULSE QUAKE SWING THIRL THROB TRILL WAVER DINDLE JUDDER QUAVER QUIVER SHIVER THRILL WARBLE

CHATTER FLUTTER LIBRATE STAGGER TREMBLE TWIDDLE EVIBRATE FLICHTER RESONATE
(— ABNORMALLY) SHIMMY

VIBRATING (— OF AIRPLANE) BUFFET

VIBRATION BUZZ DIRL FLIP TIRL SWING DINDLE QUAVER QUIVER THRILL TREMOR DANCING FLUTTER TEMBLOR DIADROME FREMITUS VIBRANCY
(— OF SAW) CUPPING
(RATTLING —) JAR

VIBRATO TRILL WHINE

VIBRATOR TREMBLER

VIBRISSA FEELER SMELLER

VIBURNUM MAE MAY SNOWBALL

VICAR PROXY DEPUTY STALLAR ALTARIST STALLARY

VICE SIN EVIL CRIME FAULT TAINT ULCER DEFECT DEPUTY INIQUITY

VICE-GERENT EPHOR

VICE-PRESIDENT (— OF SANHEDRIN) ABBETDIN

VICEREGENT VICAR SUBPRIOR

VICEROY EARL VALI NABOB NAWAB NAZIM SUBAH EXARCH KEHAYA PROREX PROVES SATRAP WARDEN PROVOST TSUNGTU SUBAHDAR

VICIA FABA

VICINITY HERE SHADOW ENVIRONS
(— OF MINE SHAFT) COLLAR
(NEAR —) SUBURBS

VICIOUS BAD ILL EVIL LAZY LEWD MEAN UGLY VILE ROWDY TOUGH SINFUL STRONG VITIAL WICKED CORRUPT IMMORAL SKAITHY DEPRAVED DEVILISH FRATCHED INFAMOUS THEWLESS

VICIOUSNESS VICE

VICISSITUDE CHANGE MUTATION
(— OF FORTUNE) WEATHER

VICTIM BUTT DUPE GOAT GULL PREY PATHIC CASUALTY
(— FOR SHARPERS) JAY
(INTENDED —) CHUMP
(SACRIFICIAL —) HOST MERIAH
(UNFORTUNATE —) BASTARD

VICTIMIZATION RIDE

VICTIMIZE HOAX BUNCO BUNKO COZEN

VICTOR COCK CAPTOR MASTER WINNER BANGSTER

VICTORFISH AKU

VICTORIA (FATHER OF —) PALLAS
(MOTHER OF —) STYX

VICTORIAN GENTEEL

VICTORIOUS VICTOR WINNING

VICTORY WIN PALM PRICE BETTER SUBDUE VICTOR SACKING TRIUMPH WINNING CONQUEST DECISION WALKOVER
(EASY —) BREEZE
(OVERWHELMING —) SWEEP

VICTUAL BIT VITE VITTLE
(BROKEN —S) SCRAN
(PL.) KAI BITE CHOW FOOD GRUB PROG SAND VIVERS

VICTUALER PURVEYOR

VIDELICET NAMELY SILICET

VIE ENVY JOSTLE STRIVE COMPETE CONTEND CONTEST EMULATE

VIETNAM (SEE NORTH VIETNAM AN· SOUTH VIETNAM)

VIETNAMESE ANNAMESE

VIEW EYE KEN FACE GLOM MAKE VISE AVIEW BLUSH CATCH MOUTH SCAPE SCENE SIGHT VISTA VIZZY ADVICE ADVISE ASPECT DEVICE GLANCE REGARD SURVEY ALOGISM CONCEIT FEELING GLIMPSE KENNING LOOKOUT OFFLOOK OPINION RESPECT SCENERY SURVIEW THOUGHT AIRSCAPE CONSPECT EYESIGHT OFFSCAPE SEASCAPE SENTENCE
(— ATTENTIVELY) GAZE
(— CLOSELY) INSPECT
(— FROM AFAR) DESCRY
(— FROM ANGLE) SLANT
(— OF MAN) DUALISM
(— WITH SURPRISE) ADMIRE
(BRIEF —) SNAPSHOT
(COMPREHENSIVE —) PANORAMA
(GENERAL —) LANDSKIP
(OPEN —) LIGHT
(PHYSICAL —) INSIGHT
(SATISFYING —) EYEFUL

VIEWPOINT SIGHT LAXISM

VIGIL WAKE WATCH WAKING AGRYPNIA

VIGILANCE WATCH JEALOUSY

VIGILANT AGOG WARE WARY ALER· AWAKE AWARE CHARY SHARP JEALOUS WAKEFUL CAUTIOUS WATCHFUL

VIGOR GO SAP VIM VIR VIS BIRR DASH EDGE ELAN LUST PITH SEVE· SNAP TUCK ARDOR DRIVE FLUSH FORCE GREEN JUICE NERVE POWE· ENERGY ESPRIT FOISON GINGER SPRAWL SPRING STARCH VIGOUR VIRTUS FREEDOM SMEDDUM STAMINA STHENIA FLOURISH STRENGTH TONICITY VITALITY
(FULL OF —) LIFESOME
(MENTAL —) DOCITY SPIRIT
(RENEWED —) REST

VIGOROUS YEP ABLE CANT FRIM HALE LIVE RUDE SPRY YEPE CRAN· EAGER FRACK FRANK JUICY LUST· NIPPY PITHY SASSY SOLID STARK STIFF STOUT TOUGH VIVID FLORID· GOLDEN HEARTY LIVELY POTENT ROBUST RUGGED SINEWY SQUARE· STRONG BUCKISH CHIPPER CORDI· DRASTIC FECKFUL FURIOUS HEALTHY NERVOSE NERVOUS VALIANT VIBRANT ZEALOUS ATHLETIC BOUNCING CHOPPING FORCEFUL MUSCULAR SLAMBANG SLASHING STUBBORN VEHEMENT VIGOROSO YOUTHFUL
(NOT —) GENTEEL

VIGOROUSLY DOWN FELL HARD VERN CRANK SNELL TIGHT VERNE HARDLY SNELLY FRESHLY SMARTL· STOUTLY WIGHTLY HEARTILY

VIGOROUSNESS ENERGY FREEDOM
VIKING DANE WIKING NORSEMAN
VIKRAMADITYA BIKRAM
VILE BAD BASE CLAM FOUL CHEAP
MUCKY POCKY RUSTY SLIMY WILLE
ABJECT CRUSTY DRAFTY DRASTY
FILTHY LECHER NOUGHT PALTRY
SORDID TURPID UNKIND BENEATH
CAITIFF CORRUPT DEBASED
HATEFUL IGNOBLE SLAVISH VICIOUS
BASEBORN DEPRAVED UNKINDLY
VILENESS FEDITY VILITY
VILIFICATION REPROACH
VILIFY ILL VILE ABUSE LIBEL STAIN
DEFAME MALIGN REVILE SLIGHT
ASPERSE BLACKEN DEBAUCH
DETRACT TRADUCE REPROACH
STRUMPET
VILIPEND BELITTLE
VILL HAM TOWN TOWNSHIP
VILLA ALDEA DACHA DATCHA
QUINTA TRIANON
VILLAGE BY AUL BYE GAV HAM KOM
PAH REW BURG DORP HOME MURA
TOWN VILL WICK ALDEA BOURG
CASAL PLACE THORP VICUS ALDEIA
BARRIO BUSTEE CASTLE GOTHAM
HAMLET HAMMON MOUZAH PETTAH
PUEBLO AMBALAM BOROUGH
CAMPODY CASERIO ENDSHIP
MAABARA MISSION OUTPORT
BEREWICK BOURGADE CAMPOODY
CRANFORD TOLDERIA VILLACHE
VILLAGET VILLAKIN
(— IN WHICH BARLEY IS GROWN)
BEREWICK
(— OUTSIDE OF FORT) PETTAH
(AFRICAN —) STAD KRAAL
(ARABIAN —) DOUAR
(ARGENTINE —) TOLDERIA
(FRENCH —) BASTIDE
(IMAGINARY —) CRANFORD
(INDIAN —) CASTLE PUEBLO
CAMPODY CAMPOODY
(JAPANESE —) MURA BUSTI BUSTEE
(JAVANESE —) DESSA
(MALAY —) CAMPONG KAMPONG
(MAORI —) KAIK KAIKA KAINGA
(MEXICAN —) EJIDO
(NEW ZEALAND FORTIFIED —) PA
PAH
(RUSSIAN —) MIR STANITSA
STANITZA
VILLAIN IAGO LOUT SERF BADDY
BRAVO CHURL DEMON DEVIL FAGIN
FELON HEAVY KNAVE ROGUE
SCAMP SHREW BADDIE VILIACO
SCELERAT
VILLAINOUS BAD EVIL GALLUS
GALLOWS KNAVISH VILEYNS
FLAGRANT RASCALLY
VILLAINY CRIME KNAVERY
VILLEIN SERF CHURL COTTER
VILLAR BONDMAN TOWNMAN
VILLAIN COTARIUS
VILLI (HAVING —) ZONARY
VILLOUS SHAGGY
VIM ZIP GIMP ZING FORCE VIGOR

ENERGY GINGER SPIRIT STARCH
VINEGAR
VINA BEN BIN BINA
VINCENTIAN LAZARIST
VINDICATE FREE CLEAR RIGHT
WREAK ACQUIT ASSERT AVENGE
EXCUSE UPHOLD ABSOLVE DERAIGN
JUSTIFY PROPUGN REVENGE
SUSTAIN
VINDICATION APOLOGY THEODICY
VINDICATOR VINDEX ASSERTER
DEFENDER
VINDICTIVE HOSTILE PUNITIVE
SPITEFUL VENGEFUL
VINE AKA FIG HOP IVY IYO BINE
CARO GOGO ODAL SOMA TINE
AKEBI BUAZE BWAZI CAAPI CACUR
GUACO KAIWI KUDZU LIANA PALAY
PRIVY TACSO TIMBO TRAIL TWINE
WITHE WONGA BEJUCO CISSUS
COBAEA COWAGE DERRIS DODDER
ECANDA GERKIN IPOMEA JICAMA
LABLAB RUNNER TURURI TWINER
ULLUCO WINDER APRICOT BIGROOT
BONESET BRAMBLE CALAMUS
CATVINE CERIMAN CLIMBER
COWHAGE COWITCH CUPSEED
EPACRID GHERKIN IPOMOEA
LAVANGA PAREIRA PUMPKIN
TRAILER VINELET YANGTAO
ATRAGENE BINDWEED BOXTHORN
CLEMATIS COMEBACK CUCUMBER
CUCURBIT DECUMARY DOLICHOS
EARDROPS EARTHPEA EVONYMUS
GULANCHA HEARTPEA HEMPWEED
MUSCATEL REDWITHE TINETARE
TINEWEED TRAILERY TRAILING
TREEBINE VINIFERA WINETREE
WISTARIA WISTERIA
VINEGAR EISEL ESILL ACETUM
ALEGAR ASCILL SOURING
BEEREGAR VINAIGRE
VINEGAR EEL EELWORM
VINEGARY ACETOSE ACETOUS
VINEGROWER VINITOR
VINEYARD CRU CLOS COTE VINER
VINERY WINEYARD
VINGT-ET-UN MACAO MACCO
VINOUS WINY
VINTAGE OLD VINT WINE CUVEE
ARCHAIC CLASSIC VENDAGE
OUTMODED
VIOL GUE GIGA LIRA TURR GIGUE
GUDOK TARAU VOYAL VOYOL
CHELYS FIDDLE VIELLE VIOLET
MINIKIN QUINTON SARINDA SULTANA
VIHUELA VIOLONE BARBITON
BASSETTE SERINGHI VIOLETTE
VIOLA ALTO QUINT TENOR TENORE
VIOLET
VIOLA BASTARDA BARITONE
BARYTONE
VIOLA DA BRACCIO QUINT
VIOLA D'AMORE VIOLET
VIOLA DA GAMBA GAMBA
VIOLATE ERR SIN FLAW ABUSE
BREAK CRACK FORCE HARRY
LOOSE VIOLE WRONG BREACH
BROACH DEFILE INVADE OFFEND

RAVISH DEBAUCH DISOBEY FALSIFY
INFRACT OUTRAGE POLLUTE
DEFLOWER DISHONOR FORSWEAR
FRACTURE INFRINGE MISTREAT
STUPRATE SURPRISE TEMERATE
TRESPASS VIOLENCE
VIOLATED FRACTED INFRACT
VIOLATION SIN DEBT ABUSE CRIME
ERROR FAULT SALLY BREACH
INJURY
(HOCKEY —) STICKS
VIOLATOR WRONGER
VIOLENCE FURY NEED RAGE RUFF
BRUNT FORCE RIGOR STORM
BENSIL ESTURE HUBRIS RANDOM
RAPINE STOUSH BENSAIL BENSALL
OUTRAGE FEROCITY SEVERITY
SORENESS
(LETHAL —) DEATH
VIOLENT BIG HOT TEZ DERF HARD
HIGH MAIN RANK RUDE WILD WOOD
ACUTE FIERY HEADY HEAVY HEFTY
RABID SHARP SMART STARK STERN
STIFF STOOR STOUR STOUT WROTH
BROTHE FIERCE HEARTY MANIAC
MIGHTY SAVAGE SEVERE STORMY
STRONG STURDY SUDDEN CRIMSON
FURIOUS HOTSPUR RAMMISH
RAPEFUL RUFFIAN TEARING
VIOLOUS WILSOME CHURLISH
DIABOLIC FLAGRANT FORCEFUL
IMPOTENT MANIACAL RIGOROUS
SEETHING SLAMBANG STALWART
VEHEMENT
VIOLENTLY HARD AMAIN HOTLY
HARDLY SORELY HOPPING SOUNDLY
VIOLET CANON GRAPE MAUVE VIOLA
BLAVER CANYON DAHLIA DAMSON
EVEQUE JOHNNY HOOKERS LOBELIA
OPHELIA PRELATE PRIMULA
PUREAYN CLEMATIS DAMEWORT
FINELEAF IANTHINE ROOSTERS
WISTERIA
VIOLIN GUE KIT ALTO GIGA AMATI
CROWD GEIGE GIGUE REBAB REBEC
STRAD TARAU VIOLA CATGUT
CHORUS CROUTH FIDDLE FITHEL
REBECK TAILLE VIOLON CATLING
CHROTTA CREMONA THEYAOU
VIOLAND VIOLINO GUARNERI
KEMANCHA VIOLOTTA
VIPER ASP HABU ADDER ASPIC
ATHER URUTU WYVER ASPIDE
DABOIA DABOYA JESSUR KATUKA
KUPPER HAGWORM MAMUSHI
VIPERID AMMODYTE CERASTES
JARARACA VIPERINE
VIRAGO RANDY AMAZON BELDAM
CALLET BELDAME TRIMMER VIRAGIN
RIXATRIX
VIREO REDEYE GRASSET TEACHER
GREENLET PREACHER
VIRGATE YOKE VERGE YARDLAND
(HALF —) MANTAL
VIRGIN NEW LIVE MAID PURE FRESH
CHASTE MAIDEN VESTAL INITIAL
PUCELLE DOROTHEA PARAMOUR
(— OF PARADISE) HURI HOURI

VIRGINAL CHERRY INTACT SYMPHONY TRIANGLE

VIRGINIA
CAPITAL: RICHMOND
COLLEGE: AVERETT HOLLINS MADISON RADFORD LONGWOOD
COUNTY: BATH PAGE BLAND FLOYD SMYTH SURRY WYTHE AMELIA LOUISA ACCOMAC HENRICO PULASKI ROANOKE CULPEPER FLUVANNA TAZEWELL
INDIAN: SAPONI TUTELO MONACAN MANAHOAC MEHERRIN NOTTAWAY POWHATAN
LAKE: KERR SMITH
MOUNTAIN: CEDAR ELLIOT ROGERS BALDKNOB
MOUNTAIN RANGE: CLINCH ALLEGHENY BLUERIDGE
PRESIDENT: TYLER MONROE TAYLOR WILSON MADISON HARRISON JEFFERSON WASHINGTON
RIVER: DAN JAMES POTOMAC RAPIDAN
STATE BIRD: CARDINAL
STATE FLOWER: DOGWOOD
STATE TREE: DOGWOOD
TOWN: GALAX LURAY SALEM MARION BEDFORD BRISTOL EMPORIA NORFOLK PULASKI ROANOKE DANVILLE HOPEWELL MANASSAS STAUNTON TAZEWELL

VIRGINIA COWSLIP LUNGWORT
VIRGINIA CREEPER CREEPER WOODBIND WOODBINE
VIRGINIA KNOTWEED JUMPSEED
VIRGINIAN BEAGLE COOHEE CAVALIER TUCKAHOE
VIRGINIA SNAKEROOT SANGREL SNAGREL
VIRGINIA STICKSEED SOLDIERS
VIRGINIA WATERLEAF SHAWNY
VIRGINIA WILLOW ITEA
VIRGINITY HONOR PUCELAGE
VIRGIN MARY DESPOINA THEOTOCOS
VIRGIN'S-BOWER LOVE HONESTY MOONWORT
VIRGULE VIRGULA DIAGONAL
VIRIDIAN EMERAUDE
VIRILE MALE MANLY
VIRILITY LUST GREEN MANHEAD MANHOOD
VIRTUAL IMPLICIT
VIRTUALLY BUT NEARLY MORALLY
VIRTUE JEN HSIN THEW ARETE FAITH GRACE POWER VALOR VERTU WORTH BOUNTY DHARMA CHARISM CHARITY JUSTICE PROBITY QUALITY CHARISMA CHASTITY EFFICACY GOODNESS MORALITY PARAMITA
(CONFUCIAN —) LI
(PL.) CIVISM

VIRTUOSO EXPERT SAVANT ESTHETE LAPIDARY
VIRTUOUS GOOD PURE BRAVE CIVIL MORAL CHASTE HONEST MODEST GODDARD SAINTED SINCERE UPRIGHT VIRTUAL STRAIGHT
VIRULENCE VIRUS
VIRULENT ACRID RABID DEADLY MALIGN VIROSE NOXIOUS VIRIFIC VENOMOUS
(LESS THAN —) MITIS
VIRUS VENOM POISON PATHOGEN SPECIFIC
VIS PEIKTHA
VISAGE FACE CHEER IMAGE VISOR ASPECT FASHION
VISCERA GUTS HASLET INSIDE UMBLES GARBAGE GIBLETS HASSLET INMEATS INNARDS INSIDES NUMBLES ENTRAILS
VISCID SLAB WAXY GOOEY GLAIRY STICKY LENTOUS STRINGY VISCOUS MOTHERED
VISCIDITY LENTOR
VISCOSITY BODY
(— UNIT) POISE
VISCOUS LIMY ROPY SIZY SLAB GOBBY GUMMY ROPEY SLIMY STIFF TARRY SIRUPY SLABBY SMEARY SNOTTY STICKY THONGY VISCID LENTOUS SQUISHY VISCOSE MUCULENT
VISE GEE CHAP JACK SHOP VICE CHEEK CLAMP CRAMP WINCH
VISHNU RAMA VASU KALKI KRISHNA BALARAMA BHAGAVAT
VISIBLE OUT FAIR SEEN CLEAR GROSS EXTANT SIGHTY EVIDENT GLARING OBVIOUS SIGHTLY APPARENT DIOPTRIC EXPLICIT EXTERNAL MANIFEST PROSPECT
(BARELY —) DARK
(SCARCELY —) DIM
VISION EYE RAY DREAM FANCY SIGHT FANTAD SEEING SWEVEN AISLING SHOWING SPECTER SPECTRE EYESIGHT PHOTOPIA
(— IN DIM LIGHT) SCOTOPIA
(BLURRED —) SWIMMING
(DEFECTIVE —) ANOPIA
(IMAGINARY —) SHADOW
(IMPERFECT —) DARKNESS
(MULTIPLE —) POLYOPIA
VISIONARY FEY AERY AIRY WILD IDEAL VIEWY ASTRAL INSANE SHANDY UNREAL DREAMER FANTAST LAPUTAN UTOPIAN ACADEMIC DELUSIVE FANCIFUL FINESPUN IDEALIST NOTIONAL PHANTAST QUIXOTIC ROMANTIC UTOPIAST VISIONER
VISIT DO GAM SEE VIS CALL CHAT STAY APPLY HAUNT TRYST VIZZY COSHER RESORT RETURN CEILIDH CEILIDHE FREQUENT INVASION
(— BETWEEN WHALERS) GAM
(— PERSISTENTLY) INFEST
(— PROFESSIONALLY) ATTEND
(— RELATIVES) COUSIN

(— WRETCHED NEIGHBORHOODS) SLUM
(CEREMONIAL —) SELAMLIK
VISITATION SENE VISIT SENDING
VISITING ACTIVE SOCIAL
VISITOR GUEST LAKER CALLER VISITANT
(MEALTIME —) SCAMBLER
(PL.) COMPANY
VISOR BILL SIGHT UMBER UMBRE VIZOR BEAVER MESAIL UMBRIL VIZARD EYESHADE
VISTA VIEW SCENE OUTLOOK
VISUAL OPTIC OCULAR SCOPIC VISORY VISIBLE
VISUALIZE SEE FANCY IDEATE SYMBOL IMAGINE PICTURE CONCEIVE ENVISAGE
VITAL LIVE BASIC CHIEF FRESH SAPPY LIVELY MOVING VIABLE ZOETIC ANIMATE CAPITAL CORDIAL EXIGENT NEEDFUL ESSENTIAL
VITALITY SAP VIM LIFE COLOR GUSTO JUICE BIOSIS BREATH ENERGY FOISON HEALTH STARCH VIVENCY STRENGTH
(DEFICIENT —) ASTHENIA
(LACKING —) STUFFY TURNIPY
VITALIZE ACTIVATE ENERGIZE
VITAMIN BIOTIN CITRIN NIACIN ADERMIN ANEURIN CHOLINE THIAMIN TORULIN ADVITANT INOSITOL NUTRAMIN ORYZANIN VITAMINE
VITIATE BEAT SPOIL TAINT CANCEL DEBASE POISON CORRUPT DEPRAV[E]
VITIATED PICAL CORRUPT
VITICULTURIST VIGNERON
VITREOUS GLASSY GLAIZIE VITREAN VITROUS
VITRIFY GLAZE
VITRIOL BLUEJACK COPPERAS
(PL.) SORY
VITRIOLIC SHARP BITING BITTER CAUSTIC MORDANT SCATHING
VITUPERATE RAIL ABUSE CURSE SCOLD BERATE REVILE
VITUPERATION ABUSE VITUPER
VITUPERATIVE ABUSIVE REVILING SHAMEFUL
VIVACE VIVO LEBHAFT
VIVACIOUS GAY AIRY BRISK CRISP MERRY SUNNY ACTIVE LIVELY LIVING SPARKY VIVACE ANIMATE JOCULAR ANIMATED SPIRITED SPORTIVE
VIVACITY BRIO FIRE LIFE ZEAL ARDOR VERVE VIGOR ESPRIT GAIETY GAYETY SPIRIT SPRAWL SPARKLE
VIVARIUM STEW VIVARY STEWPOND
VIVAT HOCH
VIVERRINE CIVET GENET FOUSSA MUSANG LINSANG FALANAKA MONGOOSE SURICATE
VIVID DEEP HARD KEEN LIVE RICH VIVE BRISK FRESH GREEN LURID QUICK RUDDY SHARP GARISH LIVELY LIVING STRONG VISUAL

EIDETIC FLAMING FREAKED
GLARING GLOWING GRAPHIC
INTENSE VIOLENT COLORFUL
DISTINCT DRAMATIC SLASHING
STRIKING VIGOROUS
VIVIDNESS COLOR EMPHASIS
VIVIFY LIFE FOMENT ANIMATE
QUICKEN SPARKLE
VIVIPARUS PALUDINA
VIXEN BARD FURY SCOLD SHREW
VIRAGO TAGSTER TRIMMER
VIZIER WAZIR ATABEG ATABEK
VISIER
VLACH WALLACH
V-MAIL AIRGRAPH
VOCABULARY CANT SLANG JARGON
DICTION LEXICON POCHISMO
WORDBOOK
(UNDERWORLD —) ARGOT
VOCAL GLIB ORAL VOWEL FLUENT
TONGUED VOCULAR ELOQUENT
VOCALIST BOPPER SINGER BOPPIST
BOPSTER SONGSTER VOCALLER
VOCATION CALL HOBBY METIER
CALLING SCIENCE
VOCATIONAL BANAUSIC
VOCIFERATION CLAMOR OUTCRY
VOCIFEROUS LOUD NOISY BAWLING
BLATANT BRAWLING STRIDENT
VODKA SAMOGON SAMOGONKA
VOGUE CUT TON CHIC MODE TURN
STYLE CUSTOM FASHION RECLAME
PRACTICE
VOGUL MANSI
VOICE SAY VOX EMIT GIVE HARP
PIPE TONE TURN WISH FROTH
LEDEN RAISE RUMOR SOUND UTTER
ACTIVE CHOICE STEVEN TAISCH
THROAT TONGUE EXPRESS OPINION
SONORIZE DIATHESIS
(— PRAISE) SLAVER
(ARTIFICIAL —) FALSETTO
(FIFTH —) QUINTUS
(HOARSE —) FOGHORN
(LOWEST —) BASS BASSO
(MIDDLE —) MOTETUS
(PRINCIPAL —) CANTUS
(PUBLIC —) CRY
(SINGING —) ALTO BASS TENOR
BREAST SOPRANO BARITONE
FALSETTO
(TENOR —) TAILLE
(UPPER —) DESCANT DISCANT
VOICED SOFT WEAK TONIC MEDIAL
SONANT PHTHONGAL
VOICELESS MUM DUMB HARD MUTE
SURD SHARP ATONIC FLATED
SILENT ANAUDIA APHONIC SPIRATE
APHONOUS BREATHED NOTELESS
VOID NO BAD FREE KORE LEAR LEER
MUTE NULL PASS ABYSS AVOID
BLANK EGEST EJECT EMPTY INEPT
LAPSE PURGE SLICE SPACE WASTE
DEVOID HOLLOW VACANT VACUUM
CONCAVE INVALID VACANCY
VACUITY EVACUATE INDIGENT
NONBEING
(— OF FEELING) BLATE
(— OF SENSE) INANE

(— OF SUBSTANCE) JEJUNE
VOIDED FALSE CLECHE CLECHY
CLECHEE
VOILE NINON
VOLATILE LIGHT FIGENT LIVELY
VOLAGE BUOYANT DARTING
ELASTIC FLIGHTY FLYAWAY
GASEOUS FUGITIVE SKITTISH
VAPOROSE VAPOROUS FUGACIOUS
VOLATILITY LEVITY
VOLCANO APO DOME ETNA ASKJA
PELEE SHASTA VULCAN FURNACE
VULCANO FUMAROLE KRAKATOA
SPITFIRE VESUVIUS
(MUD —) SALSE SALINELLE
VOLE CRABER CRICETID
VOLITATION FLIGHT VOLATION
VOLITION WILL CHOICE INTENT
VOLENCY
VOLLEY CROWD DRIFT VOLEE
FLIGHT BARRAGE PLATOON
BLIZZARD
VOLPLANE GLIDE
VOLSUNG WAELS
VOLT VOLTA REPOLON
(— AMPERE UNIT) VAR
VOLTAGE KICKBACK
VOLTAIC GUR GALVANIC
VOLTE-FACE BACKFLIP
VOLUBILITY FLUENCY
VOLUBLE GLIB WORDY FLUENT
VOLUME MO PEN BAND BOOK BULK
SIZE TOME SPACE CUBAGE
CONTENT DIURNAL MENAION
VOLUMEN CAPACITY CUBATURE
SOLIDITY STRENGTH
(— OF SOUND) STRESS
(— OF WORT) LENGTH
(PATTERN —) DUMMY
VOLUMINOUS FULL AMPLE BULKY
LARGE BOUFFANT
VOLUNTARILY WILLES WILLICHE
VOLUNTARY FREE WILLY SORTIE
WILFUL PRELUDE SORTITA WILLFUL
WILLING ELECTIVE FREEWILL
HONORARY OPTIONAL POSTLUDE
UNFORCED
VOLUNTEER OFFER ENLIST
PROFFER STRANGER
(— STATE) TENNESSEE
VOLUPTUARY SYBARITE
VOLUPTUOUS ADIN LUXIVE LYDIAN
SULTRY WANTON SENSUAL
DELICATE LUSCIOUS SENSUOUS
VOLUPTUOUSNESS DELICE LUXURY
VOLUTE TURN HELIX SCROLL
VOLUTA CILLERY VOLUTION
VOLUTION COIL TWIST WHORL
VOLVA CUP WRAPPER
VOMIT CAT PUT BALK BOCK BOKE
CACK CAST PICK PUKE SICK SPEW
SPUE VOME WOOM BRAKE EVOME
HEAVE REACH RETCH SHOOT
POSSET REJECT VOMITO CASCADE
CASTING REGORGE DISGORGE
PARBREAK SICKNESS VOMITING
VOMITING BOKE EMESIS PYEMESIS
VOMITUS SPEW SPUE
VOODOO HEX OBI CHARM OBEAH

HOODOO SORCERER
(— DESIGN) VERVER
(— SPELL) MOJO
VOODOOISM VODUN WANGA
VORACIOUS GORB GREEDY BULIMIC
ESURINE GLUTTON THROATY
EDACIOUS ESURIENT RAVENING
RAVENOUS
VORACITY EDACITY
VORTEX APEX EDDY GYRE SWIRL
WHIRL
VOTARESS NUN
VOTARY PALMER ZEALOT DEVOTEE
SECTARY ADHERENT DEVOTARY
FOLLOWER
VOTE AYE CON NAY PRO ELECT
FAGOT GRACE VOICE BALLOT
DIVIDE FAGGOT TONGUE APPROVE
PLUMPER SUFFRAGE
(— AGAINST) NAY KNIFE
(— APPROVAL) CONFIRM
(— FOR) AY AYE PRO SUPPORT
(— OF ASSENT) PLACET
VOTER BOLTER POLLER CHOOSER
ELECTOR FLOATER ASSENTOR
VOTIVE VOWED
VOTYAK UDMURT
VOUCH ABLE ASSURE ATTEST
AVOUCH ENDORSE ACCREDIT
VOUCHER CHIT CHALAN POLICY
TICKET WARRANT
VOUCHSAFE GIVE SEND DEIGN
GRANT VOUCH BETEEM PLEASE
WITSAFE
VOUSSOIR QUOIN WEDGE
KEYSTONE SPRINGER
VOW LAY VUM AVOW OATH SNUM
VOTE SWEAR VOUCH BEHEST
PLEDGE BEHIGHT PROMISE
PROTEST
VOWEL SHWA WIDE GLIDE SCHWA
VOCOID AUGMENT GEMINATE
(— POINT) SERE
(CHANGE OF —) UMLAUT
(GROUP OF 2 —S) BROAD DIGRAM
DIGRAPH
(PREFIXED —) AUGMENT
(SHORT —) MATRA
VOYAGE SAIL TRIP VIAGE CRUISE
FLIGHT TRAVEL CARAVAN JOURNEY
PASSAGE SAILING STEAMER
PERIPLUS SHIPPING
VOYAGING SEA NAVIGANT
VULCANITE EBONITE
VULCANIZATION BURNING
VULCANIZE BURN CURE METALIZE
VULCANIZER CEMENTER
VULGAR LOW LEWD LOUD RUDE
FLASH GROSS SLANG SLIMY
COARSE COMMON PORTER RABBLE
VULGUS WOOLEN BOORISH
GENERAL KNAVISH LOWBRED
MOBBISH OBSCENE POPULAR
SECULAR TABLOID VILLAIN
WOOLLEN CHURLISH MECHANIC
PANDEMIC PLEBEIAN PORTERLY
POTHOUSE SOUTERLY
VULGARIAN SLOB RAFFISH

VULGARITY SHODDY FOULNESS
  HARLOTRY
VULGARIZE PLEBIFY PROFANE
VULGARIZED DEGRADED
VULGARLY CHEAPLY
VULNERABILITY GAP EXPOSURE

VULNERABLE LIABLE EXPOSED
VULPINE FOXY ALOPECOID
VULTURE AURA GEIR PAPA AREND
  GRAAP GRAPE GRIPE SWIPE URUBU
  CONDOR CORBIE FALCON GRIPHE
  RAPTOR SNATCH TORGOS GRIFFIN

  GRIFFON GRYPHON NEKHEBT
  AASVOGEL DIRTBIRD GEREAGLE
  NEKHEBET ZOPILOTE GALLINAZO
VULVA DOCK PUDENDUM
VUM SNUM

WAW WHISKEY WILLIAM

A VU KAWA LAWA

ABBLE COCKLE COGGLE HOBBLE WAGGLE WARBLE WAUBLE WOBBLE

ABBLY COGGLE WAGGLY WOBBLY

ABBY LOON WHABBY

ABRON WAYBERRY

ACKY CRAZY INSANE MENTAL ERRATIC

AD BAT BET BOB PAD COLF LINE POKE SWAB SWOB WISP WAGER PLEDGE SCOURER GRAPHITE

ADDLE WAG HODDLE PODDLE TODDLE WALLOP WIDDLE WAUCHLE

ADDY PEG STICK COWBOY RUSTLER WHADDIE

ADE FORD WYDE SLOSH PLODGE PLOUTER PLUTTER

(— IN MUD) LAIR

ADI OUED WASH GULLY RAVINE

ADSET PAWN PLEDGE MORTGAGE

AFER HOST ABRET OBLEY CACHET GAUFRE LAVASH MATZOH OFLETE POPADAM FLATBROD

AFF WAG FLAP GUST ODOR PUFF WAVE WHIFF PALTRY FLUTTER GLIMPSE LOWBORN

AFFIE VAGRANT VAGABOND

AFFLE GOFER WAFER GAUFRE BLATHER

AFT PUFF WHEFT WHIFF BECKON

AG LUG NOD WIG WIT WOG CARD CHAP FLAG WAFF WALK DROLL JOKER SHAKE TROLL FARCER JESTER NICKUM WADDLE WAGGLE WAGWIT WIGWAG HUMORIST SLYBOOTS

AGE FEE PAY WAR HIRE LEVY FIGHT WADGE WEDGE EMPLOY ENGAGE PACKET

(— BATTLE) STRIKE

AGER GO BET LAY SET VIE WED GAGE HOLD PAWN TOSS WOID BOUND PRIZE RAISE REVIE SPORT STAKE STOOP WADGE DEPONE GAMBLE IMPONE LEVANT WEDFEE STOATER QUINELLA

AGES FEE PAY UTU GAGE HIRE MEED GAGES TUNCA REWARD SALARY PENSION SERVICE STIPEND GRATUITY LABORAGE PAYCHECK REQUITAL

AGGISH DROLL JOKEY JOCOSE JESTING JOCULAR ROGUISH WAGSOME HUMOROUS SPORTIVE

AGGLE WAG WIGGLE WOBBLE WOGGLE

AGON CAR FLY VAN CART CHAR DRAY PLOW RACK TEAM TRAM WAIN WANE BUGGY DILLY JERKY RULLY TRUCK CAMION ROLLEY SPIDER TELEGA CAISSON CHARIOT COASTER FOURGON TUMBREL TUMBRIL DEMOCRAT LANDSHIP RUNABOUT WHITETOP

(— WITHOUT SPRINGS) JERKY TELEGA

(BAGGAGE —) FOURGON

(COVERED —) VAN CARAVAN

LANDSHIP CONESTOGA

(LUMBER —) GILLY

(MINING —) TRAM RULLY ROLLEY

(ROUNDUP —) HOODLUM

(RUSSIAN —) TELEGA

(STATION —) SUBURBAN

(TEA —) SERVER

WAGONER AURIGA TREKKER WAINMAN

WAGONLOAD FODDER FOTHER

WAGONMAN FOOTMAN

WAGTAIL MOLLY OATEAR WAGGIE WASHER WATERIE SEEDBIRD WASHDISH WASHTAIL

WAHINE WIFE WOMAN FEMALE VAHINE FEMININE MISTRESS

WAHOO ONO PETO BASSWOOD EUONYMUS GUARAPUCU

WAIF WEFT STRAY FEEBLE PALTRY STRAFE CURRENT IGNOBLE WASTREL

WAIL CRY WOW BAWL GURL HOWL KEEN MOAN RAME YARM CROON MOURN ULULU LAMENT YAMMER EJULATE PLANGOR ULULATE ULLAGONE

WAILING WO WOE LAMENT ULULANT

WAIN CART WAGON WEYNE CHARIOT

WAINSCOT CEIL

WAINSCOTING CEILING PANELING

WAIST JOSIE BASQUE BLOUSE BODICE HALTER MIDDLE TAILLE CORSAGE PIERROT

WAISTCOAT VEST BENJY GILET FECKET JERKIN VESKIT WESKIT SINGLET CAMISOLE

WAISTER TROUNCER

WAIT BIDE HOLD KEEP LITE PARK STAY TEND WHET ABIDE DEFER HOVER TARRY WATCH ATTEND DEPEND EXPECT HARKEN LAYOUT LINGER

(— A WHILE) TAIHOA

(— FOR) KEEP ABIDE AWAIT ATTEND EXPECT

(— ON) HOP SEE SERVE INTEND LACKEY

(— TABLE) HASH SERVE

WAITER MOZO CARHOP DRAWER FLUNKY GARCON HASHER KIDNEY SALVER TENDER THOMAS DAPIFER FLUNKEY KELLNER PANNIER PICCOLO SERVITOR KITMUDGAR

WAITING DORMANT

WAITRESS HASHER PHYLLIS

WAIVE ABEY DEFER EVADE FORGO ABANDON DECLINE FORSAKE POSTPONE RENOUNCE

WAKA CANOE

WAKE WAK CROW NECK PLAY STIR ALERT REVEL ROUSE TANGI TRAIL VIGIL WATCH AROUSE AWAKEN EXCITE FEATHER

WAKEFUL ALERT WACKER RESTLESS VIGILANT WAKERIPE WALKRIFE WATCHFUL

WAKEFULNESS VIGIL WATCH INSOMNIA

WAKE-ROBIN SARA SARAH TRILLIUM

WAKF WAQF VAKUF VACOUF

WALACHIAN RUMAN VLACH ROMANESE

WALAHEE ALAHEE

WALAPAI HUALPAI

WALDENSIAN LEONIST PATARIN SABOTIER

WALE RIB PICK WEAL WELT RIDGE WHELP CHOICE HARPIN STROKE **(PL.)** BEND HARPINS

WALES CYMRU CAMBRIA

WALES

BAY: SWANSEA CARDIGAN TREMADOC

COUNTY: FLINT RADNOR DENBIGH ANGLESEY CARDIGAN MONMOUTH PEMBROKE

HILLS: MALVERN

LAKE: VYRNWY

LANGUAGE: CYMRAEG

MEASURE: COVER CANTRED CANTREF LESTRAD LISTRED CRANNOCK

MOUNTAIN: SNOWDEN

MOUNTAIN RANGE: BERWYN CAMBRIAN

PEOPLE: CYMRY KYMRY WELSH

PORT: CARDIFF

RIVER: DEE USK WYE TAFF TEME TOWY TEIFI SEVERN VYRNWY

TOWN: RHYL ROSS FLINT TOWYN AMLWCH BANGOR BRECON CARDIFF NEWPORT SWANSEA HEREFORD HOLYHEAD PEMBROKE

WALK GO JET MOG FOOT GAIT GANG HIKE HOOF LAMP PACE PAUT REEL STEP TROD ALLEE ALLEY ARBOR LEAVE MARCH PORCH SHANK SLOPE SPACE STALK TRACE TRACK TRADE TRAMP TREAD TROOP ATTEND AVENUE BEHAVE BOUNCE BRIDGE BROGUE DANDER PASEAR SASHAY STROKE TODDLE TRAVEL TRUDGE BERCEAU CRAMBLE FOOTING GALLERY SHUFFLE STRETCH TRACHLE TRAIPSE TURNOUT AMBULATE ARBORWAY FLAGGING FRESCADE NAVIGATE TRAVERSE

(— ABOUT) SLOSH

(— AFFECTEDLY) PRINK

(— AIMLESSLY) PAUP POAP

(— AWKWARDLY) STAUP SHAMBLE

(— BEFORE) PREAMBLE

(— BRISKLY) LEG SKELP

(— CAUTIOUSLY) STALK

(— CLUMSILY) JOLL STUMP LOPPET

(— FOR CATTLE) GANG

(— FOR EXAMINING ENGINE) GALLERY

(— FOR EXERCISE) HIKE GRIND

(— HEAVILY) PLOD STUMP TRAMP LAMPER PLODGE

(— IDLY) DANDER POTTER SAUNTER

(— IN AFFECTED MANNER) MINCE

(— **LAME**) LIMP HIRPLE HOBBLE CRIPPLE
(— **LEISURELY**) AMBLE DANDER STROLL
(— **ON**) BEAT TREAD
(— **OUT**) FLOUNCE
(— **RAPIDLY**) LAMP STAVE
(— **SHAKILY**) DOTTER
(— **SLOWLY**) JET LAG
(— **SMARTLY**) LINK
(— **STEADILY**) SNOVE SNOOVE
(— **UNSTEADILY**) REEL FALTER STAVER STAGGER STUMBLE
(— **WAVERINGLY**) SHEVEL WARPLE
(— **WITH DIFFICULTY**) CRAMBLE CRAMMEL LOUTHER
(— **WITH JERK**) HIRCH
(— **WITH LOFTY GAIT**) JET
(— **WITH OSTENTATION**) PRANCE
(— **WITH SHUFFLE**) COONJINE
(— **WITH STRIDES**) STAG
(— **WITH TREES**) XYST XYSTUS ALAMEDA
(— **WITHOUT LIFTING FEET**) SCUFF
(**BACKSTAGE** —) BRIDGE
(**COOL** —) FRESCADE
(**COVERED** —) CLOISTER
(**COVERED** —) PORCH
(**FOLIAGE-COVERED** —) BERCEAU
(**HARD** —) STRAM SWINGE
(**LIMPING** —) GIMP
(**LONG** —) STRAM
(**POMPOUS** —) STRUT
(**PUBLIC** —) XYST XYSTUS ALAMEDA
(**RAISED** —) GALLERY
(**SHADED** —) MALL ARBOR
(**TEDIOUS** —) TRAIL
WALKER GOER FOOTER FULLER GANGER FOOTMAN TODDLER (PL.) FEET
WALKING HOTFOOT PASSANT AMBULANT GRADIENT TRIPPING
WALKING STICK BAT CANE GIBBY KEBBY STICK WADDY KEBBIE SPECTER ASHPLANT GIBSTAFF WOODHORSE
WALKOUT STRIKE
WALKWAY CATWALK SIDEWALK
WALL WA DAM FIN MUR WAW BAIL BELT CELL CORE CRIB CURB DICK DIKE DRUM DYKE FACE HEAD MURE PACK SKIN SPUR WING WOGE ATTIC BOARD CHEEK CRUST DIGUE EMURE FENCE HEDGE MEURE MURAL PIRCA SHOJI WOGHE WOUGH BAFFLE BAILEY BATTER CUTOFF DOKHMA IMMURE LEADER PARIES PRETIL REBOTE RIPRAP SCREEN SEPTUM SHIELD VALLUM CHEMISE CURTAIN ENCLOSE MIZRACH PARAPET PERPEND PLUTEUS REREDOS TAMBOUR FIREBACK SPANDREL TRAVERSE
(— **ABOVE FACADE**) ATTIC
(— **AROUND**) IMMURE
(— **BEHIND ALTAR**) REREDOS
(— **BETWEEN TWO OPENINGS**) PIER
(— **CARRYING CUPOLA**) DRUM
(— **CARRYING ROOF**) BAHUT

(— **CROSSING RAMPART**) SPUR
(— **IN ROMAN ARENA**) SPINA
(— **IN TRUCK**) HEADER
(— **OF BLAST FURNACE**) DAM INWALL FIREBACK
(— **OF CLAY**) COTTLE
(— **OF HOOF**) CRUST
(— **OF MINE**) FACE
(— **OF MOUTH**) CHEEK
(— **OF TENT**) KANAT CANAUT
(**BODY** —) MANTLE
(**CIRCULAR** —) CASHEL
(**CORE** —) HEARTING
(**CURVED** —) SWEEP
(**DIVIDING** —) SEPTUM
(**END — OF BUILDING**) GABLE
(**FISH** —) LEADER
(**HIGHEST PART OF** —) CRAPWA
(**INNER SLOPE OF** —) BATTER
(**LOG** —) CRIB
(**LOW** —) BAHUT PODIUM PLUTEUS
(**LOWER PART OF** —) DADO
(**OUTER — OF CASTLE**) BAIL BAILEY
(**PEAT** —) COP
(**PUDDLE** —) HEARTING
(**RETAINING** —) CRIB BULKHEAD
(**SCARPED** —) GHAT
(**SECONDARY** —) CHEMISE
(**SUSTAINING** —) RIPRAP
(**THINNED PART OF** —) ALLEGE
(**VENTRAL** —) STERNUM
(**WING** —) AILERON
(PL.) PERICARP
WALLABA APA
WALLABY WURRUP TOOLACH WURRUNG BOONGARY KANGAROO PADMELON WHIPTAIL
WALLACHIAN RUMAN
WALLAROO EURO
WALLBOARD GOBO
WALLET JAG JAGG MAIL POKE BOGET BOUGE BULCH BULGE SCRIP BUDGET READER SACKET ALFARGA ALFORJA LEATHER BILLFOLD NOTECASE
WALLEYE WHALL SAUGER LEUCOMA WATCHEYE EXOTROPIA
WALLEYED PIKE DORE DORY JACK PERCID SALMON WALLEYE PICKEREL
WALLFLOWER CUBA CHEIR GILLY JACKS KEIRI GELOFER WARRIOR GILLIVER
WALL HAWKWEED LUNGWORT
WALLOP BEAT BEER FLOP SLUG SOCK PASTE POUND VALOP GALLOP IMPACT WALLOW FLUTTER TROUNCE FLOUNDER LAMBASTE
WALLOW FADE LAIR ROLL SOIL SLOSH WALWE GROVEL MUDDLE WALTER WELTER WITHER SLUDDER SWELTER FLOUNDER KOMMETJE VOLUTATE
WALLOWISH FLAT WELSH INSIPID
WALLPAPER GROUND SCENIC HANGING TENTURE TAPESTRY
WALL PEPPER SEDUM STONECROP
WALL PLATE PAN RASEN
WALL RUE TENTWORT

WALLY TOY FINE SPOIL PAMPER ROBUST STRONG STURDY SPLENDI VIGOROUS
WALNUT ACAPU NOGAL TRYMA AKHROT BANNUT HEARTNUT (**BRAZILIAN** —) EMBOYA IMBUIA (PL.) JUGLANS
WALNUT SHELL BOLSTER
WALPI HUALPI
WALRUS MORSE WALTRON PELAGIAN PINNIPED ROSMARINE
WALT CRANK UNSTEADY
WALTZ LUG CARRY MARCH VALSE BOSTON BREEZE FLOUNCE
WAMARA CLUBWOOD IRONWOOD PANOCOCO
WAMBLE ROLL SPIN WAMEL NAUSEA REVOLVE
WAMBLY FAINT SHAKY
WAME WEM WAMB WYME BELLY
WAMPUM PEAG FADME HAWOK MONEY PAAGE SEWAN FATHOM SEAWAN ROANOKE
WAMUS JACKET WAMPUS WARMUS
WAN DIM HAW FADE PALE PALY SICH BLAKE FAINT WHITE FEEBLE PALLID SALLOW GHASTLY LANGUID
WANAPUM SOKULK
WAND ROD VARE YARD BATON STAFF STICK VERGE VIRGA FERULA THYRSE WATTLE RHABDOS THYRSUS CADUCEUS
WANDER BAT BUM ERR GAD WAG HAAK HAIK HAKE MAZE MUCK RAVE ROAM ROIL ROLL ROVE WALK WILL RANGE ROGUE SHACK SLOSH STRAY TAVER TRAIK VAGUE WAIVE WAVER CANDER DANDER DAUNER FORAGE LOITER MITHER MOIDER MUCKER PALMER PERUSE RAMBLE RANGLE STRAKE STROLL SWERVE WILDER MEANDER TRAFFIC TRAIPSE VAGRATE VANDYKE CUTICULA SQUANDER STRAGGLE STRAVAGE
(— **ABOUT**) DIVAGATE
(— **ABSTRACTEDLY**) MOON
(— **AIMLESSLY**) SWAN SLOSH TRACE MEANDER
(— **AS A VAGABOND**) SHACK
(— **AS A VAGRANT**) LOITER
(— **AT RANDOM**) SQUANDER
(— **ERRATICALLY**) SWASH
(— **FROM DIRECT COURSE**) STRAGGLE
(— **FROM PLACE TO PLACE**) WAG
(— **IDLY**) HAKE LOUT MAUNDER SHACKLE
(— **IN DELIRIUM**) DWALE DWALL
(— **IN MIND**) DAVER DANDER DELIRE
(— **LEISURELY**) BUMMEL
(— **RESTLESSLY**) FEEK
WANDERER WAIF ROVER VAGUE RANGER PILGRIM RAMBLER FUGITIVE RUNAGATE TRAVELER VAGABOND
WANDERING GAD ROAM ERROR STRAY VAGUE ARRANT ASTRAY

ERRANT MOBILE ROVING VAGANT VAGOUS DEVIOUS NOMADIC ODYSSEY VAGANCY WINDING ABERRANT FLOATING FUGITIVE PELASGIC PLANETAL PLANETIC RAMBLING RESTLESS TRAILING VAGABOND WINDRING

WANDFLOWER GALAX SPARAXIS

WANDOROBO WAASI

WAND-SHAPED VIRGATE

WANE GO EBB SET WELK WILK DECAY UNWAX WANZE REPINE DECLINE DWINDLE DECREASE (— OF MOON) WADDLE

WANGA CHARM SPELL OUANGA WONGAH SORCERY

WANGLE FAKE SHAKE WIGGLE FINAGLE

WANIGAN ARK CHEST COFFER WANGUN

WANT HURT LACK LIKE MISS NEED OONT PINE VOID WANE WONT CRAVE FAULT FORGO BESOIN CHOOSE DEARTH DEFECT DESIRE MISTER PENURY PLIGHT ABSENCE BEGGARY BLEMISH BORASCA DEFAULT MISEASE NEEDHAM POVERTY REQUIRE VACANCY MISCHIEF WANTROKE (— EXCEEDINGLY) DIE (— OF ENERGY) ATONY (— OF GOOD SENSE) FOLLY (— OF REST) UNRO (— OF SUCCESS) FAILURE (— OF VIGOR) DELICACY

WANTAGE ULLAGE

WANTING LACK VOID WANE ALACK MINUS ABSENT LACKING MISSING INDIGENT (— ORIGINALITY) BANAL

WANTON JAY NAG DAFT GOLE IDLE LEWD NICE RAGE SKIT CADGY DALLY LIGHT SAUCY GIGLET GIGLOT HARLOT HAUNTY LACHES LUBRIC RAKISH RIGSBY TICKLE TOYING TOYISH UNRULY COLTISH FULSOME GIGGISH HAGGARD IMMORAL KITTOCK LUSTFUL PAPHIAN RIGGISH RIOTOUS SMICKER WAYWARD FLAGRANT LUSCIOUS MISTRESS PETULANT PLAYSOME RUMBELOW SLIPPERY SPITEFUL SPORTIVE UNCHASTE

WANTONNESS FOLLY PRIDE SPORT RAGERY SUCCUDRY SURQUIDY

WAP BIND BLOW WHOP WRAP BLAST FIGHT KNOCK STORM TRUSS BUNDLE STRIKE

WAPITI ELK ALCE DEER LOSH LUSH STAG MARAL MOOSE CERVID WAMPOOSE

WAR WIN CAMP FEUD MART FIGHT SWORD WORSE WORST BATTLE CONTEND CRUSADE CONFLICT GUERILA OVERCOME (RELIGIOUS —) JEHAD JIHAD

WARBLE SING CAROL CHANT CHIRL CHIRM SHAKE TRILL YODEL JARGON RALISH WARNEL WORMIL DESCANT VIBRATE WOURNIL

WARBLE FLY OXFLY BOTFLY GADFLY OESTRID OESTRIAN

WARBLER CUT KIT CHAT SMEU WREN FITTE CANARY EYSOGE SMEUTH SYLVIA TITIEN CREEPER CROMBEC FANTAIL HAYBIRD HAYSUCK PITBIRD REDPOLL SYLVIID TROCHIL BEAMBIRD BLACKCAP FAUVETTE MALURINE MOCKBIRD OVENBIRD PINCPINC REDSTART REEDBIRD RIRORIRO

WAR CLUB MAR MER MERE MERAI MARREE

WAR CRY ALALA SLOGAN

WARD CARE GUARD MAHAL VICUS WAIRD WATCH ALUMNA BARRIO CALPUL DEFEND ROWENA KEEPING NATUARY CALPOLLI CONTRADA (— OFF) FEND WEAR WERE AVERT AWARD FENCE PARRY REPEL SHIELD BUCKLER EXPIATE FORFEND

WARDAGE WARTH

WARDEN ALCADE DIZDAR PORTER RANGER REGENT ROLAND WARNER ALCAIDE HOGMACE LEATMAN ROWLAND CLAVIGER

WARDER PORTER GUARDER HEIMDAL TURNKEY WATCHMAN BEEFEATER

WARDROBE KAS CLOSET VESTRY ALMIRAH ARMOIRE VESTUARY

WARE CLOTH GOODS SPEND FABRICS SEAWEED SQUANDER (CERAMIC —) SPODE (ENAMELED —) BILSTON COALPORT (INFERIOR —S) SLUM (KIND OF —) RAKU MINTON WHIELDON (MAJOLICA —) DERUTA (PORCELAIN —) CHINA BERLIN (UNGLAZED —) BISQUE (PL.) TROKE CHAFFER TROGGIN

WAREHOUSE GOLA GOLAH STORE BODEGA FONDUK GODOWN STAITH ALMACEN FUNDUCK SPICERY STOWAGE ENTREPOT MAGAZINE SERAGLIO

WARFARE WAR ARMS IRON ARMOR BATTLE PSYWAR MILITIA CONFLICT

WAR-HORSE CHARGER COURSER DESTRER TROOPER DESTRIER

WARILY TIPTOE GINGERLY

WARINESS CAUTEL CAUTION DISTRUST WARESHIP WARIMENT

WARKLOOM TOOL WARKLUME

WARLIKE WARLY MARTIAL FIGHTING MILITARY BELLICOSE (NOT —) IMBELLIC

WARLOCK IMP WITCH SPRITE WARLOW WIZARD CONJUROR SORCERER

WARLORD TUCHUN

WARM HOT LEW LOO RUG BASK BEEK KEEN LEWD MILD CALID CHAFE EAGER FRESH MALMY MUNGY SLACK TEPID TOAST ACHAFE ARDENT DEVOUT DIGEST FOSTER GENIAL HEARTY HEATED RIZZLE TENDER CHERISH CLEMENT CORDIAL GLOWING THERMAL ZEALOUS FRIENDLY SANGUINE (MODERATELY —) LEW SLACK TEPID (— UP) SCORE

WARMHEARTED KIND TENDER FRIENDLY GENEROUS

WARMING FOVENT

WARMOUTH BIGMOUTH FLATFISH SACALAIT

WARMTH GLOW HEAT LIFE ZEAL ARDOR LEWTH ENERGY FERVOR ARDENCY PASSION CALIDITY FERVENCY (INNER —) JUICE

WARN REDE WARD WERN ALERT AREAD WEIRD ADVERT ADVISE EXHORT INFORM CAUTION COMMAND GARNISH PREVISE ADMONISH THREATEN (— OFF) FORBID

WARNING AHEM ITEM ALARM CHECK KNELL CAVEAT LESSON NOTICE OFFICE SAMPLE SIGNAL AVISION CALLING CAUTION JIGGERS MEMENTO MONITOR SUMMONS DOCUMENT GARDYLOO MONITION (— OF DISASTER) DIRE (ARCHERY —) FAST

WARP CUP WEB BIAS CANE CAST LIFT WARF WERP WIND ANGLE CHAIN CHOKE CROOK GEYZE KEDGE PORRY THRAW TWINE WEAVE BUCKLE CHEESE DEFORM WASHIN DEFLECT DISTORT SKELLER (— IN WEAVING) CRAM

WARPED WRY BUCKLED GNARLED HOUSING

WARPER BALLER

WARPING BOW PANDATION

WARRAGAL WILD DINGO HORSE OUTLAW

WARRANT ABLE AMRIT BERAT FIANT SANAD VOUCH AMRITA ASSERT BRANCH BREVET DOCKET ENSURE INSURE PARDON PERMIT PLEVIN POLICY POTENT SUNNUD TICKET BEHIGHT JUSTIFY PRECEPT GUARANTY MITTIMUS

WARRAU GUARANO

WARREN CONYGER WARRANT

WARRIOR TOA WER EARL HERO KEMP RINK WEER BERNE FREIK FREKE HAGEN LLUDD SINGH THANE THEGN OSSIAN WARMAN WEAPON FIGHTER SOLDIER STARKAD WARWOLF ZERBINO CHAMPION RODOMONT SHARDANA STARKATH SWORDMAN WARFARER (— CLASS) MAGANI (— OF NOBLE RANK) EARL (AMERICAN INDIAN —) BRAVE SANNUP (BOASTFUL —) RODOMONT (BRYTHONIC —) LLUDD (BURGUNDIAN —) HAGEN (FEMALE —) AMAZON SHIELDMAY (IRISH —) FENIAN

(KAFFIR —S) IMPI
(MUSLIM —) GAZI GHAZI
(NOTED —) THANE THEGN
(SCANDINAVIAN —) BERSERK
(SCOTTISH —) ZERBINO
(TROJAN —) AGENOR
(VALIANT —) TOA
(VIRGIN —) CAMILLA
(PL.) CHIVALRY GAMMADIM
WARSHIP GUIDE WAFTER CRUISER
MONITOR SULTANA SULTANE
CORVETTE
WART RAT WRAT AMBURY ANBURY
PUSTULE VERRUCA VERRUGA
EPIDERMA PAPILOMA
(POTATO —) CANKER
WART HOG EMGALLA
WARTLIKE PYRENOID
WART SNAKE XENODERM
WARY SHY CAGY WISE CAGEY
CANNY DOWNY HOOLY LEERY
TENDER CAREFUL GUARDED
PRUDENT WAREFUL CAUTIOUS
SKITTISH VIGILANT WATCHFUL
WAS VAS WIS WUZ WYS PAST
WISSHE
(— ABLE) COULD
(— NOT) NAS
(I —) CHWAS
WASH DO BOG FEN LAG LAP NET
TUB BEER BUCK EDDY HOSE HUSH
LAVE SILT SUDS WADI BATHE
CLEAN CLEAR DOLLY DRAFF ERODE
MARSH RINSE SCRUB SLOSH SOUSE
SWILL BUDDLE CRADLE DOLLIE
LOTION PURIFY SLOOSH SLUICE
SOZZLE STREAM ALLUVIO CLEANSE
LAUNDER SHAMPOO ALLUVIUM
EYEWATER LAVAMENT LAVATORY
(— A GAS) SCRUB
(— AWAY) GULL
(— BY TREADING IN WATER) TRAMP
(— DOWN) SIND SOOGEE
(— FOR GOLD) PAN
(— GIVEN TO SWINE) DRAFF
(— GRAVEL) ROCK
(— IN LYE) BUCK
(— LIGHTLY) RINSE
(— OFF) DETERGE
(— ORE) TYE HUTCH BUDDLE
CRADLE STRAKE
(— OUT) SIND ELUTE FLUSH
LAVAGE
(— ROUGHLY) SLUSH
(— THOROUGHLY) SCOUR
(— VIGOROUSLY) SLOSH
(— WITH BROOM) TYE
(— WITH COSMETIC) SURFLE
SURPHUL
(DRY —) ARROYA ARROYO
WASHBASIN LAVER LAVABO
LAVATORY ALJOFAINA
WASHCLOTH FLANNEL
WASHED (— UP) SHOT THROUGH
WASHER BUR BURR DRUM ROVE
CLOUT BUTTON RONDEL SOURER
GROMMET LEATHER RACCOON
COTTEREL LAVENDER RONDELLE
SCRUBBER

WASHERMAN DHOBI DHOBIE
LAVANDERO
WASHERWOMAN LAUNDER
WASHING LAG BATH LAVAGE
SLOOSH LAUNDRY ABLUTION
LAVAMENT LAVATION
(PL.) ELUATE
WASHING MACHINE DASHWHEEL

WASHINGTON

CAPITAL: OLYMPiA
COLLEGE: WHITMAN
COUNTY: ASOTIN KITSAP SKAGIT
YAKIMA CLALLAM KITTITAS
DAM: COULEE
INDIAN: LUMMI MAKAH TWANA
SAMISH SKAGIT YAKIMA
CHINOOK CLALLAM COWLITZ
SANPOIL CHIMAKUM OKANAGON
LAKE: CHELAN
MOUNTAIN: JACK TUNK ADAMS
LEMEI LOGAN MOSES SLOAN
QUARTZ SIMCOE STUART
OLYMPUS RAINIER SHUKSAN
MOUNTAIN RANGE: KETTLE
CASCADE OLYMPIC
NICKNAME: EVERGREEN
RIVER: SNAKE YAKIMA COLUMBIA
SOUND: PUGET
STATE BIRD: GOLDFINCH
STATE FLOWER: RHODODENDRON
STATE TREE: HEMLOCK
TOWN: OMAK PASCO TACOMA
YAKIMA EPHRATA EVERETT
OTHELLO SEATTLE SPOKANE
LONGVIEW

WASHOUT FLOP STUMOR FAILURE
WASHROOM BASEMENT LAVATORY
WASHSTAND COMMODE
WASHTUB FLASKET
WASHY SOFT WEAK LOOSE MOIST
FEEBLE PALLID WATERY DILUTED
WASP MASON SPHEX WHAMP WOPSE
BEMBEX DAUBER DIGGER HORNET
TIPHIA TREMEX VESPID CYNIPID
DRYINID EUMENID MASARID SCOLIID
SERPHID SIRICID SPHECID STINGER
ACULEATE MUTILLID POMPILID
WASPISH TESTY FRETFUL PEEVISH
CHOLERIC SNAPPISH
WASSAIL TOAST PLEDGE CAROUSE
REVELRY CAROUSAL
WASTE EAT FUD GOB TED BURN
GNAW JUNK LOSS PASS ROSS SACK
TEAR TINE WEAR WILD DROSS
EXILE HAVOC SCRAP SLOOM SLOTH
SLOUM SPILL TABID THRUM BANGLE
BEZZLE COMMON DEBRIS DESERT
DEVOUR DIDDLE DRAFFY DRIVEL
ELAPSE EXPEND FOREST GARBLE
GOUSTY LAVISH MOLDER MUDDLE
PADDLE PERISH RAVAGE REFUSE
SPILTH WESTEN CONNACH
CONSUME EXHAUST FRITTER
GARBAGE MULLOCK RUBBISH
SLATTER CONFOUND DEMOLISH
SLATTERN SQUANDER

(— AWAY) BATE MELT DECAY
DWINE SWAIN SWEAL TRAIK TABEI
WINDLE DWINDLE FORPINE MISLIKI
DISSOLVE EMACIATE FORSPEND
MACERATE
(— GRADUALLY) WEAR ABSUME
(— IN DRUNKENNESS) SOT
(— IN RIOT) BEZZLE
(— OF INK) INKSHED
(— OF SILK COCOONS) KNUB
(— TIME) FOOL FRIG IDLE DALLY
DEFER DRILL DAWDLE DIDDLE
FOOTER FOOTLE LOITER DRINGLE
FOOSTER GAUSTER
(COAL —) SLUDGE
(COTTON —) FLUKE SLASHER
SPOOLER
(FOOD —) SLOP
(LIQUID —) DRIPPING EFFLUENT
(MINING —) GOB GOAF
(WOOL —) FUD GARNETT
(YARN —) THRUM EYEBROW
WASTEBASKET HELL HELLBOX
WASTED IDLE FORWORN RAVAGED
DECREPIT
WASTEFUL LAVISH PROFUSE
DESOLATE PRODIGAL SPENDFUL
WASTEFULNESS WAIT UNTHRIFT
WASTELAND CURAGH CURRACH
WASTER THIEF LEISTER WASTREL
PRODIGAL
WASTING FRET DECAY LIGHT
AWASTE ATROPHY CACHEXY
EXEDENT MISLIKE PREYING TABIFIC
CACHEXIA PHTHISIS SYNTEXIS
(— AWAY) SYNTECTIC
WASTREL WAIF REFUSE WASTER
VAGABOND STROYGOOD
WATCH EYE FOB NIT SEE SPY TAB
DIAL ESPY GLIM GLOM HACK HEED
KEEP LOOK MARK MIND PIPE TOUT
TWIG VACH WAIK WAKE WARD
YARD CLOCK GUARD SCOUT SPIAL
SUPER TIMER VERGE VIGIL VIRGE
WAKEN WHEEL BEHOLD DEFEND
DIACLE FOLLOW HUNTER PERDUE
SENTRY SHADOW TICKER TICTIC
TURNIP WAKING YEMING OBSERVE
OVERSEE STRIKER THIMBLE
TOMPION HOROLOGE MEDITATE
SENTINEL SPECTATE TICKTICK
(— FOR) TENT ABIDE AWAIT
(— OF ARMY) BIVOUAC
(— ON THE SLY) FOX
(— OVER) HOLD KEEP TEND TENT
GUARD ATTEND OVERLOOK
(— PEOPLE EATING) GROAK
(— QUIETLY) HINT
(— THAT STRIKES) STRIKER
REPEATER
(— UNIT) LIGNE
(— WITH HINGED COVER) HUNTER
(ALARM —) TATLER TATTLER
(CLOSE —) SCRUTINY
(NAUTICAL —) HACK DOGWATCH
(NIGHT —) LICHWAKE LYKEWAKE
WATCHBAND WRISTER WRISTLET
WATCH CRYSTAL LUNET LUNETTE
WATCHDOG CUR GARM GARMR

MATIN BANDOG KRATIM CERBERUS
WATCHER VEIL WAKER VIEWER
WAITER MUSAHAR SPOTTER
WATCHMAN
WATCHFUL IRA ALERT AWARE
CANNY CHARY ERECT TENTY
WAKER TENTIE WACKER ANXIOUS
GUARDED JEALOUS LIDLESS
WAKEFUL VIGILANT WAKERIFE
WAUKRIFE
WATCHFULNESS OUTLOOK
JEALOUSY
WATCHMAN FLAG MINA WAIT
GUARD SCOOT VIGIL WATCH ASKARI
BANTAY GHAFIR SERENO SHOMER
TOOTER WAITER WARDEN WARDER
BELLMAN CHARLEY GUARDER
TALLIAR WAKEMAN CHOKIDAR
SENTINEL
(NIGHT —) SERENO CHARLIE
WATCHTOWER WARD BEACON
GARRET MIZPAH SENTRY ATALAYA
LOOKOUT MIRADOR SENTINEL
SPECCHIE
WATCHWORD CRY MAXIM ALERTA
ENSIGN PAROLE SIGNAL NAYWORD
PASSWORD
WATCH WORKS MOVEABLE
WATER EAU TJI AGUA AQUA BATH
BRIM BROO BURN LAGE LAKE POND
POOL TIDE WAVE ABYSS BILGE
FLUME LOUGH LYMPH RIVER TABBY
TEARS TUBIG BALLOW BAREGE
CAMLET CONGEE CONJEE PAWNEE
PHLEGM SALIVA STREAM VADOSE
WATHER AQUATIC CRYSTAL
JAVELLE IRRIGATE SNOWMELT
(— AFTER BOILING RICE) CONGEE
CONJEE
(— AS REFUGE FOR GAME) SOIL
(— AT THE MOUTH) DROOL
(— BY CALENDERING) TABBY
(— FOR BREWING) BURN
(— IN SOIL) HOLARD
(— IN WEIR) LASHER
(— REDDISH WITH IRON) RIDDAM
(— RUNNING AGAINST MAIN
CURRENT) EDDY
(— SPIRIT) KELPIE
(— SURROUNDED BY ICE) WAKE
(— UNDER PRESSURE) HUSH
(BAPTISMAL —) LAVER
(BOTTOM — OF SEA) ABYSS
(BUBBLING —) SPRUDEL
(DEEP —) BALLOW
(DIRTY —) SAUR PUDDLE
(FEN —) SUDS
(FROZEN —) ICE FROST
(HOLY —) HYSSOP
(HOT —) SOUP
(LIVING —) RASA
(MINERAL —) VICHY SELTER
SELTZER
(OPEN —) POLYNYA
(RED —) RESP RIDDAM
(ROUGH —) SEA
(SALT —) BRACK BRINE SEAWATER
(SOAPY —) SUDS GRAITH
(SPLASH OF —) FLASH

(STILL —) KELD LOGIN
(SULPHUR —) BAREGE
(SURFACE OF —) RYME
(SWEETENED —) AMRIT AMRITA
(WASHING —) LAVATION
(PL.) APSU
WATER ARUM DRAGON
WATER BAG CHAGUL MATARA
MUSSUK
WATERBIRD ALCATRAS
WATERBRAIN GID
WATERBUCK COB CHUZWI DEFASSA
WATERDOE
WATER BUFFALO KERBAU
WATER CARRIER BHISTI AGUADOR
BHEESTY
WATER CART DILLY
WATER CASK WINGER
WATER CHESTNUT LING CALTROP
SALIGOT
WATER CHINQUAPIN BONNET
NELUMBO WANKAPIN YONCOPIN
RATTLENUT
WATER CLOCK GHURRY
CLEPSYDRA
WATER CLOSET PETTY PRIVY
STOOL SANITARY NECESSARY
WATER COCK KORA
WATERCOLOR GRAPHIC
WATERCOURSE (ALSO SEE STREAM
AND RIVER) RUN URN AGOS DIKE
DYKE GOTE HAHR KHOR LADE LEAT
WADI WADY YORA AUWAI BAYOU
BROOK CANAL CANEL COWAL
DITCH DRAIN ARROYO CANNEL
COURSE FURROW GUTTER KENNEL
NULLAH TRINKET
WATERCRESS EKER KERS CARSE
KERSE BILDERS NOSESMART
WATER DOG OTTER WATERRUG
WATER DRINKER HYDROPOT
WATERED MOIRE
WATERFALL LIN LYN FALL FOSS
LINN SALT FORCE SAULT SPOUT
CATADUPE CATARACT OVERFALL
(FROZEN —) ICEFALL
WATER FENNEL EDGEWEED
WATER FLEA CYCLOPS DAPHNID
WATERFOWL WADER SWIMMER
WATERFRONT PRAYA
WATERGALL WINDDOG WINDGALL
JELLYFISH
WATER GERMANDER SCORDIUM
WATER HEMLOCK CICUTA DEATHIN
JELLICA
WATER HOG BUSHPIG CAPYBARA
WATER HOLE DUB CHARCO TINAJA
ALBERCA
WATER ICE SHERBET
WATERINESS AQUEITY AQUOSITY
WATERING EPIPHORA
WATER JUG GAMLA GOMLAH
GOOLAH
WATERLEAF SHAWNY
WATER LETTUCE QUIAPO
WATER LILY DUCK LOTOS LOTUS
WOCAS WOKAS BOBBIN CANDOCK
NELUMBO CAMALOTE NENUPHAR

WATERLOGGED SOGGY SWAMPY
EDEMATOUS
WATERMAN MERMAN QUENCH
OARSMAN
WATERMARK CROWN TIDEMARK
WATERMARKED LAID
WATERMELON PEPO GOURD MELON
TSAMA CITRUL SANDIA ANGURIA
MILLION CUCURBIT PEPONIDA
PEPONIUM SKIPJACK
WATER MOCCASIN CONGO
WATER NEWT ASK TRITON
WATER OPOSSUM YAPOK YAPOCK
WATER OUZEL PIET OOZEL OWZEL
DIPPER DUCKER
WATER PEPPER LAKEWEED
WATER PLANT LIMU AQUATIC
WATER PLANTAIN ALISMA
THRUMWORT
WATERPOT FONTAL
WATERPROOF RAINCOAT
(— MATERIAL) KERATOL
WATER RAIL RUNNER BILCOCK
MOORHEN OARCOCK
WATER RAT VOLE CRABER
MUSKRAT WATERRUG
WATER SCORPION NEPID
WATERSHED BROW DIVIDE DIVORT
SNOWSHED
WATER SHIELD FANWORT
DEERFOOD FROGLEAF
WATERSKIN MASHAK MATARA
MUSSUK MUSSACK MUSSICK
WATER SOLDIER PONDWORT
WATER SPIRIT ARIEL KELPY KELPIE
UNDINE
WATERSPOUT RONE CANAL SPATE
SPOUT VORTEX PRESTER TWISTER
CATARACT GARGOYLE
WATER STRIDER SKATER SKIMMER
SKIPPER SKETCHER
WATER THRUSH KICKUP WAGTAIL
WATER TIGER DYTISCID
WATERTIGHT THEAT THEET TIGHT
STANCH THIGHT STAUNCH
WATER WALLY BATAMOTE
WATERWAY GUT CASH DOCK HOLE
LODE DITCH INLET ARTERY SEAWAY
CULVERT FAIRWAY HIGHWAY
IGARAPE
(ARTIFICIAL —) LEAD CANAL
(PL.) SCUPPERS
WATERWHEEL NORIA SAGEER
SAKIEH DANAIDE SAKIYEH
TYMPANUM
WATERY WET LASH PALE SICK
WHEY BOGGY MOIST SAMMY
WASHY BLASHY FLASHY LIQUID
PALLID SEROSE SEROUS SWASHY
AQUATIC AQUEOUS CHOROUS
HYDROUS PHLEGMY HUMOROUS
ICHOROUS SKINKING
WATTLE GILL JOWL PLAT SALY TWIG
WAND BOREE COOBA FRITH MULGA
SALLY SALWE STAVE STICK HURDLE
JEWING JOLLOP LAPPET SALLOW
BLUEBUSH CARUNCLE
WATTLEBIRD IAO MOHO MINER
MANUAO MAOMAO GILLBIRD

WATTLE CROW KOKAKO
WAVE FAN FLY JAW SEA WAW BECK
FLAG FLAP GUST LUMP SUFF SULK
SWAY WAFF WAFT WAWE YTHE
BLESS CRIMP FLASH FLOAT PULSE
SHAKE SURGE SWELL SWING
BILLOW COMBER FLAUNT MARCEL
RIPPLE ROLLER WINNOW BREAKER
BRIMMER CRIMPLE FLICKER
FLUTTER TSUNAMI WHIFFLE
ARTEFACT BRANDISH FLOURISH
GRAYBACK UNDULATE UNIPULSE
WHISTLER WHITECAP
(— OF EXCITATION) IMPULSE
(— OF FLAG) DOT DASH
(— OF SHIP) BONE
(ELECTRIC —) STRAY CARRIER
(TIDAL —) EAGER
(PL.) SURF
WAVER HALT REEL SWAG SWAY
VARY CHECK DAKER DOUBT FLOAT
SWALE SWING WIVER DACKER
DAIKER DITHER FALTER MAMMER
QUIVER SWERVE TEETER TOTTER
WABBLE WOBBLE BALANCE FLICKER
FLITTER FLUTTER STAGGER
SWITHER VIBRATE HESITATE
WAVERING WAW WAVY WEAK
WAUCH WAUGH FICKLE GROGGY
WAVERY WIGGLY DUBIOUS
LAMBENT SHUTTLE DOUBTFUL
FLEXUOSE FLEXUOUS FLICKERY
HOVERING WAVEROUS
WAVINESS CRIMP
WAVING UNDE WAFT AWAVE OUNDY
UNDEE WAFTURE FLOURISH
WAVY ONDE UNDE UNDY CRISP
MOIRE SNAKY UNDEE FLECKY
SNAKEY UNDATE WIGGLY BUCKLED
CRINKLY CURVING ENDATED
ROLLING SINUATE UNDULAR
ENRIDGED FLEXUOUS ONDOYANT
SQUIGGLY UNDULATE
(PEOPLE WITH — HAIR) VEDDOID
WAWL HOWL WAIL WOWL SQUALL
WAX WOX CERE CODE GROW RAGE
WACE WOXE SCALE BECOME
CAPPING CERESIN KLISTER
CARNAUBA CERESINE CEROXYLE
COCCERIN EPILATOR INCREASE
(— IN HONEYCOMB) CAPPING
(— STRONG) PREVAIL
(CHINESE —) PELA
(COBBLER'S —) CODE
(KIND OF —) PINSANG
(SKI —) KLISTER
WAXBILL ASTRILD REDBILL
WAXEN WAX PALLID CEREOUS
WAXER GLAZER WAXMAN
WAXFLOWER EPIPHYTE
WAX MYRTLE ARRAYAN
WAX PLANT HOYA
WAXWING WAXBIRD RECOLLET
SILKTAIL
WAXY ANGRY VEXED PLIABLE
YIELDING
WAY LAW PAD TAO VIA WON WYE
FARE FORE FORM GAIT GANG GATE
KIND LANE LARK PACE PATH PAWK

RAKE ROAD SORT TOBY WISE
ALLEY CHANT FORTH GOING GUISE
HABIT MOYEN ROUTE SHEAR STEPS
STYLE TRACT TRADE ACCESS
AVENUE CAREER CHEMIN COURSE
MANNER METHOD STREET TRAJET
CHANNEL FASHION HIGHWAY
PASSAGE SKIDWAY APPROACH
CONTRADA DISTRICT FOOTPATH
THOROUGH VICINITY LAUNCHING
(— OF DEPARTURE) EXIT
(— OF LIFE) LARK TRACE
HEDONISM
(— OF SPEAKING) AMBAGE
(— OF THINKING) DIET
(— OF WALKING) JET
(— OUT) IT EXIT SALVO
(— THROUGH MINEFIELD) BREACH
(CLEVER —) KNACK
(INDIRECT —) AMBAGES
(LONG —) FAR
(MAJOR —) STEM
(NARROW —) DRANG
(ODD —S) JIMJAMS
(PLANK —) BRIDGE
(ROUNDABOUT —) DETOUR CIRCUIT
(SETTLED —) BIAS
(SIDE —) BRANCH
(SLOPING —) RAMP
(UNDEVIATING —) GROOVE
(PL.) DAPS
WAYBILL WILLIE
WAYFARER SHULER VIATOR PILGRIM
SHUILER TRAVELER
WAYFARING TREE WHITTEN
COTTONER VIBURNUM
WAYLAY BELAY BESET BLOCK
BRACE AMBUSH FORLAY FORSET
FORELAY OBSTRUCT SURPRISE
WAYLAYER WAIT
WAYMARK AHU
WEAK DIM LEW COOL DOWY FOND
LAME NESH NICE PALE PUNY SELI
SELY SOFT THIN WASH WAUF WOKE
BAUCH BAUGH CRIMP DICKY FAINT
FLASH FRAIL JERKY LIGHT NAISH
REEDY ROCKY SEELY SILLY SLACK
STANK WASHY WAUGH WEARY
WERSH YOUNG CADUKE DEBILE
DILUTE DOTISH FEEBLE FLABBY
FLAGGY FLIMSY FOIBLE GROGGY
INFIRM LIMBER LITTLE MARCID
SEMMIT SICKLY SINGLE SWASHY
TENDER UNSURE UNWISE WAIRCH
WATERY DWAIBLY DWEEBLE
FLACCID FOOLISH FRAGILE INSIPID
INVALID LANGUID PIMPING PUERILE
REGULAR RICKETY SAUGHEN
SHALLOW SHILPIT SLENDER
SPINDLY TOTTERY UNHARDY
UNLUSTY WEARISH ASTHENIC
CHILDISH DECREPIT DEFINITE
FECKLESS FEMININE FLAGGING
GRIPLESS HELPLESS IMBECILE
IMPOTENT LADYLIKE LANGUENT
PHTHISIC RESOLUTE RUSHLIKE
SACKLESS SCRANNEL UNMIGHTY
UNWIELDY
(— FROM FATIGUE) TANGLE

(— FROM HUNGER) LEER
(— IN RESOLUTION) FRAIL
(MENTALLY —) TOTTY
WEAKEN GO LAG SAP DAMP FAIL
HURT MELT SINK THIN ALLAY
BLUNT BREAK CRAZE DELAY QUAIL
SHAKE SPEND WATER APPALL
DEACON DEADEN DEFEAT DEJECT
DENUDE DILUTE FALTER IMPAIR
INFIRM LABEFY LESSEN REBATE
REDUCE SICKEN SOFTEN CORRODE
CORRUPT CRIPPLE DECLINE
DEPRESS DISABLE MOLLIFY
QUALIFY RESOLVE UNBRACE
UNNERVE CASTRATE DIMINISH
EMBEZZLE ENERVATE ENFEEBLE
ETIOLATE INFRINGE LABEFACT
UNSTRENG
WEAKENED GROGGY ANODYNE
INVALID SHOTTEN DECREPIT
LABEFACT STRAINED
WEAKENING CHRONIC FAILURE
FLAGGING
WEAKEST RECKLING
WEAKFISH DRUM TROUT ACOUPA
SALMON CORBINA CORVINA
DRUMMER SQUETEE TOTOABA
TOTUAVA BLUEFISH CHICKWIT
WEAKLY FEEBLY FEMALE SIMPLY
WEAKLING TOY WRIG DUGON
PULER SLINK SOFTIE RECKLING
SOFTLING
WEAK-MINDED DAFT DOTY DOTED
FOOLISH
WEAKNESS ATONY CRACK CRAZE
FAULT FOLLY TOUCH ATONIA
DEFECT FOIBLE ACRATIA FAILING
FISSURE FRAILTY DEBILITY
DELICACY FONDNESS
(CARNAL —) FLESH
WEAL WHEAL RICHES STRIPE
WEALTH WELFARE
WEALTH WAD WON DHAN GEAR
GOLD GOOD MUCK WONE THING
WORTH GRAITH MAMMON POCKET
PURPLE RICHES TALENT CASHBOX
FORTUNE RICHDOM WARISON
WELFARE CATALLUM OPULENCE
OPULENCY PROPERTY TREASURE
(— OF NATION) STOCK
(PATRON OF —) YAKSHA
WEALTHY FAT FULL OOFY RICH
WELI AMPLE PURSY TINNY OOFIER
COUTHIE MONEYED PURSIVE
ABUNDANT AFFLUENT
WEAN CHILD SPAIN SPANE WAYNE
INFANT ESTRANGE
WEAPON (ALSO SEE SPECIFIC TYPE
OF WEAPON) ARM BOW GUN BILL
BOLA BOLO CLUB COSH DART EDGE
EPEE FALX FOIL IRON MACE PATU
PIKE TOOL WIWI ADAGA ARROW
BILLY CAKRA DEATH FLAIL KNIFE
LANCE ONCIN SHARP SPEAR SQUID
STEEL SWORD VOUGE WAPIN
CANNON CHAKRA DAGGER GLAIVE
MACANA ARCHERY BAZOOKA
FIREARM GISARME HALBERD
HARPOON HURLBAT JAVELIN

LIANGLE POUNAMU SHOTGUN
SLASHER STICKER TICKLER
WHIFFLE ARBALEST BLOWBACK
BLUDGEON CROSSBOW FAUCHARD
HEDGEHOG LEEANGLE PARTISAN
TROMBASH
(DEADLY —) DEATH
(LINE OF —S) RIDGE
(PREHISTORIC —) CELT
(PL.) WAR TACKLE ARCHERY
WEAPONRY
WEAR KIT BEAR FRAY FRET GROW
HAVE PASS CHAFE GUARD SPEND
VOGUE WEARY ABRADE BATTER
BECOME BETHUMB CONSUME
DEFENSE DEGRADE FASHION
FATUGUE FRAZZLE PROCEED
WEATHER PROGRESS
(— AN OPENING) BREACH
(— AND TEAR) GAFF SLITE
GRUELING
(— AWAY) EAT FADE FRET GALL
GNAW GULL PINE ERODE GULLY
SCOUR SPEND ABRADE CORRADE
CORRODE CONTRIVE
(— CLOTHES) DRESS
(— DOWN) BRAY GRIND ABRASE
GRAVEL
(— FURROWS) GUTTER
(— IN PUBLIC) SPORT
(— OFF) FRAY ABRADE
(— OUT) DO BURN COOK FLOG
JADE TIRE TUCK BREAK SLAVE
SLITE SPEND BUGGER HATTER
MAGGLE PERUSE EXHAUST
FORWEAR FORWORK HACKNEY
INVALID SHACHLE OVERFRET
OVERWEAR
(— SHIP) CAST
(— SHOES OUT OF SHAPE)
SHACHLE SHACKLE
(— TIGHT CORSETS) LACE
WEARIED AWEARY FORGONE
FATIGUED WEARIFUL
WEARINESS TIRE FATIGUE
BRAINFAG SICKNESS VEXATION
WEARING DECAY SCUFF BURNING
CLOTHES ABRASION GARMENTS
GRINDING
WEARISOME DRY DULL HARD
WEARY MORTAL PROLIX SODDEN
IRKSOME TEDIOUS SAWDUSTY
TIRESOME TOILSOME
WEARISOMENESS TEDIUM
WEARY FAG IRK SAD BOEG BORE
MOIL PALL PUNY SADE TIRE TIRY
WEAK WORE WORN BORED BREAK
CURSE SPENT HARASS PLAGUE
SICKLY SQUEAL EXHAUST FATIGUE
IRKSOME FATIGATE FORCHASE
GRIEVOUS TIRESOME WRETCHED
FORJASKIT
(BECOME —) JADE
WEARY WILLIE TRAMP
WEASAND WISEN GULLET THROAT
WIZZEN TRACHEA WINDPIPE
WEASEL CANE VAIR VARE WARE
HULDA HURON SNEAK STOAT TAIRA
TAYRA ERMINE FERRET HULDAH

VERMIN ARCTOID VORMELA
FUTTERET MUISHOND MUSTELIN
WHITRACK
WEASEL CAT LINSANG
WEATHER SKY DIRT RAIN TIME
COLLA STORM WINDWARD
(— CONDITION) WHITEOUT
(FAIR —) SHINE
(HOT AND HUMID —) SIZZARD
(INCLEMENT —) SEASON
(INTERVAL OF FAIR —) SLATCH
(UNDER THE —) SEEDY
(VIOLENT —) ELEMENTS
WEATHERBEATEN SEAGOING
WEATHERCOCK COCK FANE VANE
FAINE FANACLE
WEAVE CANE HABI HUCK JOIN LACE
LENO LOOM REED ROCK SPIN WALE
WARP WIND WOOF DOBBY DRAPE
PLAIT TWINE UNITE BROCHE
DAMASK DEVISE DIAPER DOBBIE
FABRIC CANILLE ENTWINE FASHION
INDRAPE SATINET SHUTTLE
VANDYKE DIAGONAL DUCHESSE
OVERSHOT
(— PATTERNS INTO) BROCADE
(BASKET —) BARLEYCORN
(CARPET —) FLOSSA
(HERRINGBONE —) SUMAK SOUMAK
SHEMAKA
(LATTICE —) TEE
(OPEN —) LENO BAREGE
WEAVER KORI TANTI WEBBE
DRAWBOY WEBSTER WOBSTER
PENELOPE TAPESTER
WEAVERBIRD NUN BAYA MAYA
TAHA FINCH MUNIA VIDUA WEBBE
BISHOP CANARY OXBIRD WHIDAH
WHYDAH BENGALI AMADAVAT
AVADAVAT CARDINAL MANNIKIN
WEAVING TANIKO TEXTURE
WEBBING
(— OF WORDS) CONTEXT
(— TOGETHER) PLEXURE
WEAZEN WIZEN SHRINK WIZENED
WEB PLY WOB CAUL FELT MAZE
TENT TOIL VANE WARP WEFT
SNARE THROW TWIST FLEECE
TISSUE ENSNARE FEATHER LAYETTE
TEXTURE SNOWSHOE VEXILLUM
(— IN EYE) HAW
(CRANK —) THROW
WEBBED RINGED PALMATE
WEBBING MAT WEB PALAMA
WEB-FOOTED PALAMATE PALMIPED
WEB SPINNER EMBIID WEBWORM
WED GET BEWED BRIDE MARRY
STAKE WAGER ENGAGE PLEDGE
SPOUSE ESPOUSE WEDLOCK
WEDDING SPLICE NUPTIAL
WEDLOCK ESPOUSAL MARRIAGE
WEDGE KEY COIN FROE FROW GLUT
HORN KYLE PLUG STOB TRIP WAGE
CHOCK CHUCK CLEAT COIGN HACEK
HORSE QUINE SCOTE SLICE THROW
COTTER CUNEUS QUINET SCOTCH
EMBOLUS QUINNET SCHOCHE
VOUSSOIR
(— BETWEEN TWO FEATHERS) KEY

(— IN) JAM JAMB
(— OF OATMEAL) FARL FARLE
(— TO PREVENT MOTION) CHOCK
(CURVED —) CAM
(WOODEN —) COW GLUT JACK
WEDGER SPRINGER
WEDGE-SHAPED CUNEAL SPHENIC
CUNEATED SPHENOID
WEDLOCK WIFE SPOUSAL MARRIAGE
SPOUSAGE
WEDNESDAY MIDWEEK
WEE TINY EARLY SMALL TEENY
YOUNG LITTLE
WEED BUR HOE BURR CHOP CULL
DOCK FORB LOUK SHIM SIDA TARE
WEID CIGAR DRANK DRAWK DRESS
DROKE FLESH DARNEL JIMSON
KNAWEL RIPGUT SARCLE SPURGE
SPURRY STROIL ASHWORT COHITRE
CUCKOLD EGILOPS GARMENT
GOSMORE HOGWORT SANDBUR
TOBACCO VERVAIN VERVINE
CHADLOCK COCKSPUR COWWHEAT
PIRIPIRI PLANTAIN PURSLANE
TOADFLAX ALFILERIA MARIJUANA
(MEXICAN —) BIRDEYE
(TROUBLESOME —) KEX TITTER
(PL.) FILTH WRACK DISMAL SPRING
WEEDAGE TRUMPERY
WEEDER SARCLER
WEEDY FOUL LANKY
WEEK OOK WOK OULK WOKE
SENNET STANZA HEBDOMAD
SENNIGHT
(TWO —S) FORTNIGHT
WEEKDAY FERIA WARDAY
WEEKLY AWEEK
WEEL LEAP POOL TRAP RIGHT
WHIRLPOOL
WEEN MEAN VENE WEND FANCY
GUESS EXPECT BELIEVE IMAGINE
SUPPOSE CONCEIVE
WEENY TINY SMALL WEESHY
WEEP CRY ORP SOB BAWL BEND
GIVE LEAK OOZE PIPE TEAR WAIL
GREET BEWAIL BEWEEP BOOHOO
LAMENT SHOWER BLUBBER
LAPWING SQUINNY COMPLAIN
WEEPER GREETER MOURNER
CAPUCHIN
(PL.) FLENTES
WEEPING WOP GREET MILCH RAINY
LAMENT OOZING PIPING MAUDLIN
TEARFUL DRIPPING LACRIMAL
MADIDANS PLORATION
WEEPING SINEW GANGLION
WEEVER JUGULAR STINGBULL
WEEVIL MAX BOUD POPE WHULE
PICUDO WEEBLE BILLBUG BRUCHUS
VAQUITA CURCULIO WOODWORM
(PLUM —) TURK
WEFT WEB PICK WOOF BLAST
FABRIC FILLING
WEIGH GO SIT HEFT PEIS TARE TELL
COUNT HEAVE HOIST PEIZE POISE
RAISE SCALE BURDEN PONDER
ANALYZE BALANCE DEPRESS
LIBRATE CONSIDER EVALUATE
MEDITATE MILITATE

(— **DOWN**) LADE SWAY SWEE
BESET HEAVY PEISE CADDLE
CHARGE CUMBER PESTER DEPRESS
FREIGHT INGRATE OPPRESS
OVERLAY ENCUMBER
(— **UPON**) SIT GRIEVE
WEIGHER BOXMAN PEISER SCALER
WEIGHING (— **MACHINE**) TRON
SCALE TRONE
WEIGHT (ALSO SEE MEASURE AND
UNIT) BOB FEN FOB MAN NET RAM
SER SIR TOM TUP ABAS ATOM BEEF
CLOG DROP GRAM HEFT IRON KITE
LEAD LOAD MACE MEAL NAIL ONUS
PEIS POND PORT ROTL SEAM SINK
WAIT ABBAS CLOVE CRITH GARCE
MAUND PEASE PEISE POISE POIZE
PRESS RIDER SCALE STAMP
AUNCEL BURDEN CHARGE HAMMER
IMPORT MOMENT MONKEY PASSIR
PONDER PONDUS SINKER STRESS
BALLAST DOLPHIN GRAVITY MILLIER
PLATINE PLUMMET POSIURE
CHALDRON DEMIMARK DUMBBELL
ENCUMBER FARASULA PRESSURE
QUINCUNX STANDARD STRENGTH
(— **AFTER TARE DEDUCTION**)
SUTTLE
(— **CARRIED BY HORSE**) IMPOST
(— **CLOTH**) FLOCK
(— **FOR HURLING**) HAMMER
(— **FOR LEAD**) FOTMAL
(— **FOR PRECIOUS STONE**) CARAT
(— **FOR WOOL**) TOD SARPLER
(— **FOR WOOL, CHEESE, ETC.**)
CLOVE
(— **OF 100 LBS.**) CENTAL CENTENA
CENTNER
(— **OF 1000 LIVRES**) MILLIER
(— **OF 20 OR 21 LBS.**) SCORE
(— **OF 40 BUSHELS**) WEY
(— **OF 5 UNCIAE**) QUINCUNX
(— **OF BROADSIDE**) GUNPOWER
(— **OF COAL**) KEEL
(— **OF COFFEE**) MAT
(— **OF HYDROGEN**) CRITH
(— **OF METAL**) JOURNEY
(— **OF ONE 100TH TAEL**) FEN
(— **OF ONE 10TH TAEL**) MACE
(— **OF PENDULUM**) BOB
(— **OF PILE DRIVER**) TUP
(— **OF RAW SILK**) PARI
(— **OF SILK OR RAYON**) DRAMMAGE
(— **ON MINE SWEEPER**) KITE
(— **ON STEELYARD**) PEA
(— **ON WATCH CHAIN**) FOB
(— **TO BEND HOT METAL**) DUMPER
(— **TO DETECT FALSE COINS**)
PASSIR
(— **TO HINDER MOTION**) CLOG
(— **WHICH VESSEL CAN CARRY**)
TONNAGE
(**ABYSSINIAN** —) FARASULA
(**CARAT** —) SILIQUA
(**CLOCK** —) PEISE
(**FALSE** —) SLANG
(**GREATLY VARYING** —) MAN MAUND
(**HEAVY** —) MONKEY
(**LIGHT** —) SUTTLE

(**MONEYER'S** —) DROIT
(**ORIENTAL** —) CATTY
(**SASHCORD** —) MOUSE
(**SHUFFLEBOARD** —) SHIP
(**SMALL** —) MITE GERAH RIDER
(**SPLINE** —) DOLPHIN
(**UNIT OF** —) SER VIS WEY LAST
ROTL SEER LIANG LIBRA LINGO
MINAL PECUL PERIT PIKOL KANTAR
LINGOE MISKAL POCKET LISPUND
PRICKLE QUINTAL ZOLOTNIK
WEIGHTED BIAS LOADED
WEIGHTER FULLER
WEIGHT-PRODUCING GRAVIFIC
WEIGHTY GRAVE GREAT HEAVY
HEFTY MASSY VALID COGENT
SOLEMN EARNEST MASSIVE
ONEROUS PEISANT SERIOUS
TELLING GRIEVOUS MATERIAL
POWERFUL PREGNANT
WEIR DAM CRIB KEEP LEAP STOP
CAULD DOACH GARTH GORCE
HATCH HEDGE STANK LASHER
WEIRD ODD EERY UNCO UNKO EERIE
UNCOW UNKID CREEPY ELDRICH
ELRITCH UNCANNY UNUSUAL
WIZARDLY
(— **SISTERS**) FATES
WEITSPEKAN YUROK
WEKA RAIL WOODHEN RAILBIRD
WELCOME SEE FAIN GOOD HAIL
ADOPT CHEER GREET RESET TREAT
ACCOIL INVITE SALUTE ACCLAIM
ACCUEIL AMBRACE GRATIFY
BIENVENU GREETING HAEREMAI
PLEASANT
WELD SHUT WELL SWAGE UNITE
WOALD ACACIA
WELDED SHOT
WELDING FUSION SHUTTING
WELFARE SEL GOOD HALE HEAL
SELE WEALTH BENISON BLESSING
WELKIN SKY HEAVENS WALKENE
WELL AIN EYE GAY PIT WEL BENE
FINE FLOW GOOD PANT PUIT PURE
RITE SAFE SINK WINK AWEEL
BOOLY BOWLY GREAT MUSHA
OILER QUELL WISHA BUCKET
CENOTE ENOUGH FAIRLY GASSER
NICELY OFFSET PUMPER TUNNEL
FALLWAY GRADELY HEALTHY
WILDCAT BOREHOLE FOUNTAIN
GRAITHLY POSTHOLE WATERPIT
WEALSOME
(— **AND STRONG**) BUNKUM
(— **THROUGH FLOORS OF**
WAREHOUSE) FALLWAY
(— **UP**) WALL WALM DIGHT
(**AS** —) ALSO
(**NONPRODUCTIVE** —) DUSTER
(**NOT** —) DONNY SOBER INVALID
(**OIL** —) OILER GASSER GUSHER
SPOUTER WILDCAT STRIPPER
(**RECTANGULAR** —) BOOLY BOWLY
(**SACRED** — **AT MECCA**) ZEMZEM
(**TOLERABLY** —) GAYLIES GEYLIES
(**VERY** —) BRAWLY CLEVER
WELL-BALANCED SOBER
WELL-BEHAVED GOOD NICE

MODEST MANNERED
WELL-BEING HEAL SKIN WEAL
HEALTH WEALTH COMFORT
EUCRASY WELFARE EUCRASIA
WELLBORN GENTLE EUGENIC
WELL-BRED GENTIL POLITE
GENTEEL REFINED CULTURED
LADYLIKE
WELL CASING STEANING
WELL-CHOSEN CHOICE
WELL-CONSIDERED THRIFTY
WELL CURB PUTEAL
WELL-DEFINED STRICT
WELL-DISPOSED SIB FAIN GOOD
VAIN
WELL DONE SHABASH
WELL-DRESSED BRAW GASH
BRAWLY
WELL-FED BLOWSY BLOWZY
CHUBBY GAWCEY GAWSIE
WELL-FORMED TIGHT DECENT
PROPER SEEMLY SHAPELY
WELL-FOUNDED FIRM GOOD JUST
SOUND WORTHY
WELL-GROOMED SMUG CRISP
SOIGNE SOIGNEE
WELL-GROUNDED VALID
WELL-GROWN THRODDY
WELL-HUSBANDED THRIFTY
WELL-INFORMED KNOWING
PERFECT
WELL-INTENTIONED AMIABLE
WELL-KEPT SMUG POLITE
WELL-KNIT WIRY
WELL-KNOWN BREEM BREME
BEATEN FAMOUS KENNED FAMILIAR
WELL-LIKED FANCIED POPULAR
WELL-MADE CLEVER
WELL-MANNERED POLITE
COURTEOUS
WELL-NIGH WELLY ALMOST NEARLY
WELLMOST
WELL-ORGANIZED SNOD
WELL-PLEASED FAIN VAIN
WELL-PROPORTIONED SUING
TRETIS HANDSOME
WELL-READ STUDIED LITERARY
WELL-ROUNDED CHUBBY
WELL-SHAPED CLEVER FEATOUS
WELL-TILLED NOT NOTT
WELL-TO-DO ABLE BEIN BIEN EASY
WARM PODDED
WELL-WISHER FRIEND FAVORER
WELS WALLER SHEATFISH
WELSH (ALSO SEE WALES) CYMRY
FUDGE TAFFY CYMRIC KYMRIC
CAMBRIAN
WELSHER QUITTER
WELSHMAN CELT KELT TAFFY
BRYTHON CAMBRIAN
WELSH ONION CIBOL CIBOULE
CHESBOLL
WELT RIDGE STRIP WHELP WELTING
BANDELET TURNOVER
(**SHOE** —**S**) WATTIS
WELTANSCHAUUNG FAITH
IDEOLOGY
WELTER REEL RIOT TOSS WILT
GROVEL TUMBLE WALLOW WRITHE

SMOTHER STAGGER SWELTER
(— OF SOUNDS) DIN
WELWITSCHIA TUMBOA
WEM FLAW SCAR SPOT STAIN
WEN CYST WYNN CLIER CLYER
TALPA TUMOR GOITER
WENCH DELL DILL DOXY DRAB GILL
GIRL JADE MAID MOLL PRIM TRUG
GOUGE KITTY MADAM QUEAN TRULL
WHORE AUDREY BLOUSE BLOWEN
BLOWZE DRAZEL JILLET KITTIE
MOTHER POPLET WOTLINK
POPLOLLY
(CLUMSY —) MODER MODDER
MOTHER MAUTHER
WENCHER DRABBER STRIKER
WEND BOW END SORB VEND STEER
BETAKE DEPART DIRECT TRAVEL
PROCEED SORBIAN LUSATIAN
(— ONE'S WAY) MARK
WENT GODE LANE ROAD YEDE
ALLEY PASSAGE
(— ABOUT) WOLK
WENTLETRAP SCALA
WENZEL JACK
WERE (— IT NOT) SAVE
WEREWOLF TURNSKIN VERSIPEL
WEST STY BEWEST PONENT
OCCIDENT
WESTERN PONENT SCAEAN
HESPERIC SANDWICH
WEST HIGHLAND KYLOE

WEST VIRGINIA
CAPITAL: CHARLESTON
COLLEGE: SALEM BETHANY
  CONCORD MARSHALL
  BLUEFIELD
COUNTY: MINGO ROANE UPSHUR
  BARBOUR KANAWHA
INDIAN: MONETON
LAKE: LYNN
NICKNAME: MOUNTAIN
RIVER: ELK OHIO KANAWHA
  POTOMAC GUYANDOT
STATE BIRD: CARDINAL
STATE FLOWER: RHODODENDRON
STATE TREE: MAPLE
TOWN: ELKINS KEYSER RIPLEY
  VIENNA WESTON BECKLEY
  GRAFTON SPENCER WEIRTON
  FAIRMONT WHEELING

WESTWARD WESSEL OCCASIVE
WESTLINS
WET DEW DIP SOP WAT DAMP DANK
LASH MOIL SLOW SOAK SOFT UVID
BATHE DABBY DROOK DRUNK
HUMID JUICE JUICY LEACH MADID
MOIST MOOTH RAINY SLAKE SNAPY
SOBBY SOPPY SPEWY STEEP TIGHT
WEAKY CLASHY DABBLE DAGGLE
DAMPEN HUMECT IMBRUE JARBLE
LABBER MADEFY MARSHY MOISTY
QUASHY SHOWER SLABBY SOBBED
SPONGY SPOUTY SWASHY WATERY
ARROUSE BLUBBER DRABBLE
FLOTTER MOISTEN SLOPPED
SOBBING SPEWING SPRINGY

IRRIGATE SATURATE SLATTERY
SLOBBERY SLOTTERY WATERISH
(— AND STORMY) FOUL
(— LIGHTLY) SPRINKLE
(— THOROUGHLY) SOUSE DRENCH
(SOFTLY —) SQUASHY
(VERY —) SOPPY
WETHER PUR RAM HAMEL DINMAN
DINMONT
WETNESS DANK
WETTING SOUCE SOUSE SOWSE
MOILING
WHACK DAD LAM TRY BANG BELT
BIFF DEAL HACK SWAK TIME DRIVE
SHARE STATE SWACK WHANG
CHANCE DEFEAT STROKE THWACK
BARGAIN LAMBACK PORTION
WHACKING VERY WHALING
WHOPPING EXTREMELY
WHALE SEI CETE HUEL HULL LASH
ORCA WALL KOGIA POGGY SCRAG
SPERM STUNT BALEEN BELUGA
BLOWER FINNER GIBBAR KILLER
THRASH BOWHEAD DOLPHIN
FINBACK FINFISH GIBBERT
GRAMPUS RIPSACK RORQUAL
SPOUTER ZIPHIAN BALAENID
CACHALOT CETACEAN DOEGLING
GREYBACK HARDHEAD HUMPBACK
JUBARTES MUTILATE THRASHER
ZIPHIOID
(— BUTCHER) LEMMER
(— REFUSE) GURRY
(FINBACK —) GRASO
(SCHOOL OF —S) GAM POD
WHALEBONE BALEEN
WHALER HEADER BUSHMAN
SPOUTER SWAGMAN WHACKER
WHOPPER CETIDIDE
WHALESKIN MUKTUK
WHANG BEAT BLOW FLOG CHUNK
THONG WHACK THRASH RAWHIDE
WHARF KEY POW DOCK GARE PIER
QUAY SLIP BERTH JETTY STADE
STAITH STRAND LANDING PANTALAN
STELLING
WHARVE WARVE WHIRL WHORL
WHAT FAT HOT HOW WET WHO
HOOT HOTE WHEN STUFF WHICH
MATTER PARTLY
WHATA FUTTAH FUTTER
WHATNOT OMNIUM ETAGERE
WHATSOEVER MORTAL
WHEAL HIVE HUEL WALE WELT
URTICA POMPHUS
WHEAT WIT CORN CONES EMMER
FULTZ GRAIN SPELT SPICA TRIGO
BULGUR BURGUL CEREAL KANRED
STAPLE TURKEY EINKORN FORMITY
FRUMETY KUBANKA MARQUIS
POLLARD FRUMENTY SPELTOID
(— BOILED IN MILK) FURMITY
(— MEASURE) TRUG
(BEARDED —) RIVETS
(CRACKED —) GROATS
(GRANULATED —) SUJI SUJEE
(HARD —) DURUM
(PARCHED —) BULGUR
WHEATCAKE PURI

WHEATEAR CHACK ARLING WITTOL
CHACKER ORTOLAN SNORTER
WITTALL CHICKELL
WHEATGRASS BLUESTEM
WHEATLIKE VULGARE
WHEEDLE COG CANT CLAW COAX
CARNY FLUFF GLOSE GLOZE INGLE
JOLLY BANTER CAJOLE FLEECH
GLAVER RADDLE SMOOGE WHILLY
BLARNEY CUITTLE PALAVER
SMOODGE TWEEDLE COLLOGUE
SCROUNGE
WHEEDLING BUTTERY
WHEEL BOB BUR COG FAN NUT ORB
BEAD BUFF GEAR HELM HURL PURL
ROLL RULL STAR TIRL WYLE ATHEY
FLIER FLUFF FLYER IDLER NORIA
REWET RHOMB ROWEL SWING
TRUCK BILOBE CASTER CASTOR
CIRCLE DRIVEN DRIVER FANNER
HORRAL JAGGER KURUMA LEADER
PINION ROLLER ROTATE RUNDLE
RUNNER TRACER BALANCE BICYCLE
CHUKKER GUDGEON LANTERN
PEDRAIL PRICKER REVOLVE
STEPNEY TRAILER TRILOBE TRINDLE
TRUCKLE TRUNDLE UNILOBE
WILDCAT FOLLOWER ODOMETER
SPROCKET
(— A SKIN) FLUFF
(— CHARGED WITH DIAMOND DUST)
SLITTER
(— CONTROLLING RUDDER) HELM
(— FOR EXECUTIONS) RAT
(— IN KNITTING MACHINE) BUR
BURR
(— IN TIMEPIECE) BALANCE
(BUCKET —) LIFTER
(DIAMOND —) SKIVE
(GEAR —) DRIVEN HELICAL
(GRINDING —) SHELL
(GROOVED —) PULLEY SHEAVE
SHIVER
(INTERRUPTER —) TICKER TIKKER
(LOCOMOTIVE —) DRIVER
(METAL —) FILET FILLET
(MILL —) PIRN
(PAIR OF LOGGING —S) CATYDID
KATYDID
(POINTED —) TRACER
(POLISHING —) BOB BUFF SKAIF
SKEIF BUFFER SCAIFE
(POTTER'S —) LATHE THROW
(SPINNING —) TURN CHARKA
CHARKHA
(SPUR —) ROWEL
(TANK —) BOGY BOGEY BOGIE
(TOOTHED —) GEAR PINION
ROULETTE
(TURBINE —) ROTOR
(TWO PAIRS OF —S) CUTS CUTTS
(VANED —) FLIER FLYER
(WATER —) NORIA SAKIA SAKIEH
SAKIYEH TYMPANUM
(PL.) KATYDID
WHEELBARROW GURRY BARROW
CARRIAGE
WHEELER POLER PUSHER
WHEEL-SHAPED ROTATE ROTIFORM

WHEELWORK MOTION
WHEELWRIGHT WHEELER
WOODMAN WHEELMAN
WHEEZE JOKE HOOSE HOOZE TRICK
COGHLE
WHELK FILK GRUB WELT BUCKIE
MAGGOT PAPULE PIMPLE WINKLE
PUSTULE
WHELP CUB PUP SON CHIT FAWN
PUPPY YELPER KITLING SPROCKET
WHEMMEL UPSET FUMMEL FUMMLE
WHAMBLE OVERTURN
WHEN AS BUT FAN FRO GIN THO
WON THAN THEN THOA TILL SINCE
UNTIL ENOUGH ALTHOUGH
WHENEVER ONCE
WHERE AS FAR FUR FAUR FEAR
FERRE PLACE QUAIR THERE
WHITHER LOCATION
(— **ABOVE MENTIONED)** US
WHEREFORE WHY CAUSE FORWHY
REASON
WHERENESS UBIETY
WHEREVER THERE
WHEREWITHAL MEANS MONEY
RESOURCES
WHERRET BOX CUFF SLAP HURRY
TEASE WORRY TROUBLE WHIRRICK
WHERRY BARGE ROWBOAT WHIRREY
WHET WET GOAD HONE TIME TURN
GRIND POINT RIFLE ROUSE SLITE
WHILE EXCITE INCITE STROKE
QUICKEN SHARPEN APERITIF
EXACUATE
WHETHER IF GIF GIN WHAR WHERE
EITHER
WHETSTONE BUR RIP RUB BUHR
BURR SLIP STONE RUBBER STRAIK
SHARPER WASHITA WHITTLE
RUBSTONE STRICKLE
WHEY PALE QUAY WHIG SERUM
THRUST WATERY
WHIBA UEBA
WHICH AS THE WHO THAT QUILK
WHILK
(— **SEE)** QV QQV
WHICKER NEIGH WHINNY WIGHER
WHIDAH BIRD VEUVE WEAVER
WHYDAH REDBILL
WHIFF FAN GUF BLOW GUFF GUST
HINT PUFF TIFT WAFT WIFT FLUFF
QUIFF SMOKE EXHALE MAGRIM
MEGRIM WHIFFET
WHIFFLE FIFE SWAY FLICKER
FLUTTER
WHIFFLETREE HEELTREE
SWINGLEBAR
WHIG JOG QUIG WHEY
WHILE AS BIT GAM THO YET FILE
FYLE TIDE TILL WHEN WHET WOLE
FILIE PIECE SPACE STEAD STOUN
THROW UNTIL STOUND WHENAS
WHILOM BEGUILE TROUBLE
EXERTION OCCASION
(— **AWAY)** AMUSE FLEET DIVERT
DECEIVE
(**LITTLE** —) AWEE DRASS WHILEY
WHILEEN WHILOCK
WHILES UNTIL SOMETIMES

WHILLY GULL CAJOLE WHEEDLE
WHILST TILL UNTIL
WHIM BEE FAD GIG GIN TOY FIKE
FLAM KINK CRANK FANCY FLISK
FOLLY FREAK HUMOR QUIRK THRUM
FEGARY FITTEN MAGGOT MEGRIM
SPLEEN VAGARY WHIMSY BOUTADE
CAPRICE CONCEIT WRINKLE
CROTCHET
WHIMBREL JACK SPOW SPOWE
CURLEW MAYBIRD MAYFOWL
TITTEREL
WHIMPER GIRN MEWL PULE WAIL
WEAK BLEAT WHINE SIMPER
WHINGE YAMMER GRIZZLE SNIFFLE
SNUFFLE WHINDLE WHINNEL
WHITTER WHINNOCK
WHIMSICAL FANCY COCKLE FLISJY
NOTION QUAINT BIZARRE GIGGISH
BIZZARRO FANCIFUL FREAKISH
HUMOROUS NOTIONAL SINGULAR
WHIMSY WHIM FREAK VAGARY
CAPRICE WHIMWHAM
WHIN FUN ULEX FURZE WHINCOW
WOODWAX
WHINCHAT TICK UTICK WHEATEAR
WHINE WOW GIRN GOWL MEWL
PULE TIRM TOOT YARM YIRN BLEAT
CROON MEECH QUINE TWINE
WHAUP WHEWT SNIVEL TREBLE
WHINGE WINNEL YAMMER WHIMPER
WHINDLE
WHINNY HINNY NEIGH PLAIN
SNICKER WHICKER
WHINSTONE TRAP WHIN SCURDY
WHINYARD SWORD HANGER
POCHARD WHINGER SHOVELER
WHIP CAT EEL FAN GAD ROD TAW
BEAT CAST COIL DICK DUST FLOG
FOAM GOAD HIDE JERK LASH LICK
LOUK PLET TAWS URGE WHUP
ABUSE AZOTE BIRCH CRACK FLAIL
FLICK FLISK IMPEL KNOUT LEASH
PLETE QUILT ROMAL SLASH STRAP
SWEPE SWING SWISH TAWSE
THONG THUMP AROUSE BREECH
CHABUK DEFEAT FEAGUE INCITE
LAINER LARRUP LICKER MAIDEN
NETTLE PIZZLE QUIPPE SCUTCH
SNATCH SWITCH TICKLE CHABOUK
CHICOTE COWHIDE COWSKIN
CURBASH KURBASH LAMBAST
LAYOVER NAGAIKA RAWHIDE
SCOURGE SHINGLE SJAMBOK
SLASHER TICKLER CHAWBUCK
COACHMAN CONFOUND FLAGELLA
KOURBASH PEPPERER
(— **EGGS)** CAST
(— **HANDLE)** CROP
(— **IN PIANO ACTION)** WIPPEN
(— **WITH 3 LASHES)** PLET PLETE
(**HORSE** —) WAND
(**JOCKEY'S** —) BAT
(**RIDING** —) CROP DICK QUIRT
(**RUSSIAN** —) KNOUT
WHIPLASH COSAQUE CRACKER
WHIPPED BEATEN BROKEN
DEFEATED FOUETTEE CHANTILLY
WHIPPER TICKLER THONGMAN

THRASHER THREAPER
WHIPPER-IN PRICKER
WHIPPERSNAPPER SQUIRT
WHIFFET WHIPSTER
WHIPPING LICK TOCO TOKO HIDING
CLANKER FANNING SERVING
BIRCHING BROWSING SKELPING
WHIPPING POST FORK PILLAR
WHIP SCORPION GRAMPUS
PHRYNID PEDIPALP WHIPTAIL
WHIPSOCKET SNEAD
WHIPSTITCH MINUTE INSTANT
OVERCAST
WHIR BIRR ZIZZ WHIRRY
WHIRL BIRL EDDY FURL GYRE HURL
PURL RUSH SPIN TIRL DRILL GIDDY
SKIRL SQUIR SWIRL THIRL THROW
TWIRL TWIST WALTZ WHORL
BUSTLE CIRCLE GYRATE HURTLE
SWINGE VORTEX WHORLE WINDLE
WIRBLE MIZMAZE REVOLVE
TRUNDLE TURMOIL VERTICIL
(— **ABOUT)** DOZE GURGE
(— **IN THE AIR)** WARP
WHIRLIGIG GIG SPIN TURN WHEEL
FIZGIG FISHGIG
WHIRLING GIDDY WHEELY
GYRATION GYRATORY VORTICAL
WHIRLPOOL EDDY GULF SUCK WELL
WIEL GORCE GOURD BULLER
GORGES SWELTH VORTEX GURGLET
SWALLOW SWILKIE SUCKHOLE
MAELSTROM
WHIRLWIND OE DEVIL VORTEX
PRESTER TORNADO
WHISHT HUSH SILENCE
WHISK ZIP FISK TUFT WHID WHIP
WISP CAURI FLICK FLISK HURRY
SPEED SWISH CHAURI CHOWRY
SWITCH COWTAIL WHISKER
WHISKER HAIRLINE VIBRISSA
(PL.) BEARD ZIFFS WEEPER
GALWAYS VIBRISSA MOUSTACHE
SIDEBURNS
WHISKY RYE BOND CORN CIDER
IRISH USQUE POTEEN REDEYE
SCOTCH BOURBON BLOCKADE
BUSTHEAD CREATURE POPSKULL
USQUABAE
(**GLASS OF** —) RUBDOWN
(**RAW** —) DRUDGE
WHISPER BUZZ HARK HINT ROUN
RUNE ROUND RUMOR TRACE TUTEL
BREATH BREEZE HARKEN MURMUR
SUSURR TITTLE WHISHT HEARKEN
SUSURRUS
WHIST MORT VINT QUIET BOSTON
SILENT WHEESHT
WHISTLE BLOW CALL FUTE PIPE
WHEW QUILL WHAUP WHEEP WHUTE
BUZZER CUCKOO FUSSLE HOOTER
SIFFLE SISTLE SQUEAL YELPER
TWEEDLE BIRDCALL
WHISTLE FLUTE SIFFLOT
WHISTLER PIPER MARMOT ROARER
FLUTIST LAPWING SIFFLEUR
WHISTLING PIPY PIPEY ROARING
SIFFLET RHONCHUS
WHIT BIT JOT ATOM DOIT HATE

HOOT IOTA QUAT QUIT BODLE GROAT POINT QUITE SPECK CIVITE PARTICLE TWOPENNY

WHITE CUT WAN BAWN FITE HOAR LILY PALE QUAT QUIT ASHEN BLOND HOARY LABAN LINEN SNOWY ALBINO ARGENT BLANCH BRIGHT BUCKRA CANDID CIVITE ERMINE SILVER WINTRY CANDENT LEUCOUS NIVEOUS WHITTLE FAVORITE INNOCENT LACTEOUS

(— AND SMOOTH) IVORINE
(— OF EGG) GLAIR ALBUMEN
(— PERSON) OFAY
(POOR —) YAHOO CRACKER

WHITE ALDER CLETHRA

WHITE ANT ANAY NASUTE TERMITE

WHITEBAIT SMELT ICEFISH SALANGID SALMONID

WHITEBEAM ARIA SERVICE MULBERRY

WHITEBOY PET LEVELER

WHITE BRYONY COWBIND

WHITE CEDAR JUNIPER

WHITE CLOVER SHAMROCK

WHITEFISH BLOAT CISCO PILOT POWAN BELUGA CHIVEY POLLAN TULIPI VENDIS BLOATER BOWBACK LAVARET VENDACE BLACKFIN GREYBACK HUMPBACK MENOMINI SALMONID SCHNABEL TULLIBEE

WHITEFLY HOMOPTER MEALYWING

WHITE GUM TUART

WHITE-HEADED GOLDEN FAVORED FORTUNATE

WHITE HELLEBORE ITCHREED ITCHWEED

WHITE IPECAC ITOUBOU

WHITE LEAD CERUSE

WHITE MAPAU PIROPIRI

WHITE MUSTARD KEDLOCK SINAPIS CRUCIFER

WHITEN SCURF ALBIFY BLANCH BLANCO BLEACH BLENCH DEALBATE EMBLANCH ETIOLATE

WHITENESS IVORY ALBEDO ARGENT CANDOR PURITY CANITIES PALENESS

WHITE OAK ROBLE

WHITE POPLAR ABELE ABELTREE

WHITE SNAKEROOT STEVIA POOLWORT RICHWEED WHITETOP

WHITE STURGEON BELUGA

WHITETHROAT JACK MUFF MUFTY MUGGY PEGGY EYSOGE MILLER MUFFET WHISKY WINNEL HAYSUCK WHEYBIRD

WHITEWASH LIME GLASS BLANCH PARGET CHICAGO LIMEWASH PALLIATE

WHITEWEED DAISY

WHITE WHALE BELUGA

WHITHER GUST HURL RUSH WHIZ HURRY SHAKE WHERE FLURRY BLUSTER WHERETO

WHITING BARB HAKE CORBINA CORVINA KINGFISH MOONFISH

WHITING-POUT BIB KLEG BLENS

WHITISH BAWN PALE DILUTE SUBALBID

WHITLOW FELON ANCOME FETLOW BREEDER PANARIS RUNROUND

WHITLOW GRASS DRABA NAILWORT SHADBLOW

WHITRACK WEASEL FUTTERET WHITTRET

WHITSUNDAY TERM

WHITSUNTIDE PINXTER PINGSTER PINKSTER

WHITTLE CUT PARE CARVE KNIFE STEEL TWITE EXCITE MANTLE THWITE BLANKET

WHIZ BUZZ DEAL GIRL PIRR QUIZ SING WHIR ZIZZ SOUGH WHISH WHIZZ WIZARD BARGAIN SWITHER WHINNER

WHIZ-BANG EXPERT NOTABLE

WHO AS HOW THE WHA WHAT WHICH

WHOA WO WAY WHO STOP

WHOEVER WHATSO EVERWHO

WHOLE ALL HOW SUM BODY COOL EVEN HALE HALF HOLY HULL BLOCK GREAT GROSS HAILL SOUND TOTAL TOTUM TUTTA UNCUT CORPSE ENTIRE HEALED INTACT GENERAL INFRACT INTEGER PERFECT SINCERE SOLIDUM COMPLETE ENSEMBLE ENTIRETY GLOBULAR INTEGRAL LIVELONG OUTRIGHT UNBROKEN

(— OF ANY ORGANISM) SOMA
(— OF REALITY) ABSOLUTE
(ORGANIC —) SYSTEM

WHOLEHEARTED HEARTY SINCERE ZESTFUL COMPLETE IMPLICIT

WHOLESALE MASSIVE SWEEPING

WHOLESALER JOBBER EXPORTER

WHOLESOME GOOD CLEAN SOUND SWEET BENIGN SAVORY HEALTHY PRUDENT CURATIVE HALESOME HEALSOME HOMELIKE REMEDIAL SALUTARY HEALTHFUL

WHOLE-SOULED SINCERE

WHOLLY ALL FAIR FLAT HALE ONLY BLACK CLEAR FULLY QUITE STARK ALGATE BODILY FLATLY HOLLOW PURELY SOLELY ALGATES ROUNDLY SOLIDLY TOTALLY DIRECTLY ENTIRELY

WHOOP BOOM HOOP HOOT BOOST RAISE SHOUT EXCITE HALLOO HOOPOE

WHOOPING COUGH KINKHOST CHINCOUGH PERTUSSIS

WHOP WAP BEAT THUD THUMP STRIKE THRASH

WHOPPER LIE SIZER BOUNCER CRUMPER SLAPPER SNAPPER SWAPPER SWINGER STRAPPER WALLOPER

WHOPPING VERY LARGE BANGING RAPPING WAPPING WHALING SWINGING WHACKING

WHORE DRAB JILT FILTH WENCH HARLOT PUTAIN DEBAUCH STRUMPET SUCCUBUS

WHOREMONGER HOLOUR

WHORL TURN CYCLE SPIRE SWIRL WHIRL THWORL VOLUTE WHARVE WREATH ANNULUS GYRATION VERTICIL VOLUTION

WHORTLEBERRY HOT HURT FRAWN HOOTE FRAGHAN BILBERRY

WHY HOW QUI ENIGMA FORWHY

WICK BAD EVIL FARM TOWN ANGLE CREEK DAIRY MATCH QUICK SNAST CORNER LIVING WICKED VILLAGE FARMSTEAD

(— CLOGGED WITH TALLOW) ROUGHIE
(LONG WAXED —) TAPER

WICKED BAD SAD DARK EVIL FAST FOUL IRON LAZY LEWD MEAN PIKY VILE BLACK CURST FELON SHREW SORRY WRONG WROTH CURSED GUILTY LITHER LUTHER NEFAST PERDIT PITCHY SEVERE SHREWD SINFUL UNHOLY UNJUST UNLEAD UNLEDE UNWELL CAITIFF DARKSUM GODLESS HEINOUS HELLISH IMMORAL NAUGHTY NINETED NOXIOUS PRAVOUS PROFANE ROGUISH UNGODLY UNSEELY UNSOUND UNWREST VICIOUS VILLAIN CRIMINAL DARKSOME DEPRAVED DEVILISH DIABOLIC ENORMOUS FELONOUS FIENDISH FLAGRANT MESCHANT OBDURATE TERRIBLE UNKINDLY

WICKEDNESS ILL SIN EVIL HARM VICE CRIME FOLLY GUILT BELIAL FELONY NOUGHT UNGOOD ATHEISM DEVILRY ILLNESS DARKNESS DEVILTRY INIQUITY MISCHIEF SATANISM WANGRACE

WICKERWORK WEB WEEL TWIGGEN BASKETRY

WICKET GATE HOOP HATCH PITCH STUMP GUICHET

(FALLING OF —S) ROT

WICKETKEEPER STUMP STUMPER

WICKIUP HUT WAKIUP SHELTER

WIDDRIM FIT FURY

WIDDY NOOSE WIDOW WITHY HALTER

WIDE FAR LAX DEEP ROOM SIDE AMPLE BROAD LARGE ROOMY SHARP SLACK WRONG ASTRAY ROOMWARD SPACEFUL SPACIOUS

(— OF THE MARK) AWRY ABROAD
(— OF) BESIDE
(LONG AND —) SIDE

WIDE-AWAKE FLY FOXY KEEN LIVE ALERT FLASH LEERY SLIPPY KNOWING WAKEFUL WATCHFUL

WIDELY FAR BROAD ABROAD GREATLY LARGELY

WIDEN FLAN REAM DILATE EXPAND EXTEND FLANGE FUNNEL BROADEN

WIDENESS WIDTH BREADTH

WIDESPREAD RIFE DIFFUSE GENERAL CATHOLIC EXTENDED SWEEPING

WIDGEON SMEE WHIM GOOSE WHEWER ZUIZIN POACHER

POTCHER BALDPATE BLUEBILL WHISTLER
WIDOW VID BALO DAME SKAT BLIND KITTY VEUVE WEEDA WIDDY MATRON RELICT TERCER DOWAGER EMPRESS BARONESS DOWERESS (PL.) VIDUAGE
WIDOWHOOD VIDUAGE VIDUITY
WIDTH GAPE SIDE RANGE SCOPE BREADTH OPENING FRONTAGE FULLNESS LARGEOUR LATITUDE WIDENESS
(— OF CUT) KERF
(— OF HORSESHOE) COVER
(— OF PALM) HAND
(— OF PAPER) FILL
(— OF PULLEY) FACE
(— OF SHIP'S BAND) STRAKE
(— OF SHIP) BEAM
(— OF TYPE) SET
(— OF WEB) DECKLE
WIELD PLY RUN BEAR WALT WIND EXERT SWING VELDE EMPLOY GOVERN HANDLE MANAGE STRAIN CONTROL
WIFE UX FEM HEN MRS RIB WYF BABY BIBI DAME DORA ENID FEME FERE FRAU FROW JAEL LADY MAKE MATE RANI UXOR DIRCE DONNA DUTCH FEMME LUCKY MATCH MUJER SQUAW WOMAN ELMIRE EMILIA GAMMER KEEPER MATRON MISSIS MULIER SPOUSE VENDER WAHINE BEDMATE DIONYZA EMPRESS PARTNER WEDLOCK DEIANIRA DEIDAMIA ERIPHYLE HELPMATE HELPMEET MISTRESS PECULIAR
(— OF COTTER) COTQUEAN
(— OF KNIGHT OR BARONET) DAME
(— OF MOHAMMEDAN) KHADIJA
(AFFIANCED —) FUTURE
(INDIAN'S —) WEBB
(OLD —) GAMMER
(PL.) PUNALUA
WIG BOB JIZ RUG TIE FRIZ GIZZ JANE JIZZ LOCK TETE TOUR BUSBY CAXON FLASH JASEY MAJOR SCALP SCOLD ADONIS BRUTUS FROWZE PERUKE REBUKE TOUPEE TOUPET COMBING RAMILIE SCRATCH SHEITEL SPENCER BOBJEROM CHEDREUX CHEWELER NIGHTCAP PERUKERY POSTICHE ROGERIAN VALLANCY
(— WITH ROUGHLY CROPPED HAIR) BRUTUS
(18TH CENTURY —) ADONIS GEORGE
(BUSHY —) BUSBY
(GRAY —) GRIZZLE
(WORSTED —) JASEY
WIGGLE JET HOTCH JIGGLE WABBLE WANGLE
WIGGLER PUPA LARVA WRYER
WIGHT MAN SWIFT STRONG VALIANT CREATURE STALWART
WIGMAKER WIGGER PERUKER PERUKIER

WIGWAG SIGNAL
WIGWAM LODGE WEEKWAM WICKIUP
WIKENO NIKENO HEILTSUK
WILD REE SHY FAST RUDE SCAR WOWF CRAZY FANTI FELON FERAL GIDDY MYALL RANDY RANTY ROUGH ROYET SKEER WASTE DESERT FANTEE FERINE FIERCE LAVISH MADCAP NATIVE RAMAGE RANDOM RENISH SAVAGE SHANDY STORMY UNRULY BERSERK BREACHY ERRATIC FRANTIC GALLOUS GALLOWS HAGGARD HOWLING MADDING OUTWARD RIOTOUS SKADDLE SKEERED WILDING ABERRANT AGRESTAL BARBARIC DESOLATE FAROUCHE FRENETIC HALUCKET HELLICAT RECKLESS UNTILLED WARRAGAL WILLYARD
(— CARD) FREAK
WILD ASS GOUR KIANG KULAN COTULA KOULAN ONAGER QUAGGA CHIGETAI
WILD BALSAM APPLE CREEPER
WILD BEE KARBI
WILD BOAR APER SUID TUSKER SOUNDER SUIDIAN WILRONE SANGLIER
WILD BUFFALO ARNA ARNEE
WILD BUSH BEAN PHASEMY
WILD CABBAGE YELLOWS
WILD CARDAMOM RUEWORT KNOBWOOD
WILD CARROT DILL ELTROT FIDDLE BIRDNEST HILLTROT
WILDCAT CAT BALU EYRA CHATI CHAUS MANUL TIGER MARGAY SERVAL WAGATI COLOCOLA
WILD CELERY ACHE ECHE EELGRASS SMALLAGE
WILD CHERRY GEAN
WILD CHERVIL KECK COWWEED HONEWORT MILKWEED
WILD CYCLAMEN SOWBREAD
WILD DOG ADJAG DHOLE DINGO GUARA AGUARA AGOUARA CIMARRON WARRAGAL
WILDEBEEST GNU
WILDERNESS BUSH WILD WASTE DESERT FOREST WESTERN SOLITUDE
WILD-EYED HAGGARD RADICAL
WILDFOWL VOLATILE
WILD GARLIC MOLY
WILD GERANIUM ALUMROOT DOVEFOOT FLUXWEED
WILD GOAT TUR IBEX TAHR EVECK PASAN MAZAME MARKHOR AEGAGRUS MARKHOOR
WILD HORSE BRUMBY KUMRAH TARPAN BRUMBIE WARRAGAL WARRIGAL
WILD HYACINTH CUCKOO CROWTOE GREGGLE BRODIAEA CROWFOOT
WILD INDIGO SHOOFLY
WILD LETTUCE FIREWEED

WILD MAN SAVAGE WOODMAN WOODSMAN
WILD MANGOSTEEN SANTOL
WILD MARJORAM ORGAN ORGAMY ORGANY ORIGAN ORGAMENT
WILD MULBERRY YAWWEED
WILD MUSTARD CHARLOCK
WILDNESS FERITY HEYDAY HEYDEY FEROCITY SAVAGERY SAVAGISM
WILD OAT DRANK DRAWK DROKE HAVER HEVER EGILOPS
WILD ONION UMBEL UMBELLA
WILD OX BUF YAK ANOA BUFF REEM UNICORN
WILD PARSLEY ELTROT HILLTROT
WILD PEAR DOGBERRY
WILD PLUM SLOE ISLAY
WILD POTATO MANROOT WAPATOO
WILD RADISH RUNCH
WILD RICE MANOMIN
WILD SAGE EYESEED
WILD SARSAPARILLA SHOTBUSH
WILD SERVICE TREE SORB SORBUS
WILD SHEEP SHA URIAL AOUDAD ARGALI BHARAL NAYAUR BIGHORN MOUFLON
WILD SWAN ELK
WILD THYME HILLWORT SERPOLET
WILD TOBACCO GAGROOT SOURBUSH MARIJUANA SALVADORA
WILD TURNIP NAVEW
WILD VANILLA LIATRIS
WILE PAUK PAWK RUSE FRAUD GUILE TRICK ALLURE BLENCH DECEIT ENGINE ENTICE BEGUILE ARTIFICE TRICKERY
WILGA WILLOW
WILL EGO MAY ULL FATE LIST TEST WISH LEAVE OUGHT SHALL WORST ANIMUS CHOICE DESIRE DEVICE DEVISE LEGATE LIKING QUETHE SCRIPT APETITE CODICIL PASSION WITWORD AMBITION BEQUEATH PLEASING PLEASURE VOLITION
(— NOT) WONT WINNA WONNA WUNNA WONNOT
(— OF DEITY) DECREE
(— OF GOD) LAW
(— OF LEGISLATURE) ACT
(— TO LIVE) TANGHA
(FREE —) ACCORD
(GOOD —) GREE
(I —) CHILL
(ILL —) ARR ENVY HEST ANIMUS ENMITY UNTHANK AMBITION
WILLET TATLER TATTLER
WILLFUL HEADY WILLY FEISTY UNRULY HAGGARD WAYWARD WILSOME CAMSTRARY
WILLFULLY WOLDES SCIENTER
WILLIES JUMPS CREEPS
WILLING BAIN FAIN FREE GLAD LIEF RATH PRONE READY MINDED TOWARD CONTENT UNFORCED
WILLINGLY LIEF SOON FREELY GLADLY LIEFLY FRANKLY READILY
WILLINGNESS HEART FREEDOM FAINNESS

(— TO FIGHT) DEFIANCE
WILLIWAW STORM WOOLLY
TEMPEST
WILLOW DULY ITEA SALE WYLW
OSIER SALEW SALIX WIDDY WITHY
WOODY DUSTER SALLOW TEASER
TWILLY WITHEN WUDDIE
(— FOR THATCHING) SPRAYS
(— IN TEXTILES) WOLF
(NATIVE —) COOBA COOBAH
(SIMPLE —) WHIPPER
WILLOWER DULER DUSTÉR TEASER
WILLIER
WILLOW HERB WICOPY EPILOBE
FIRETOP PIGWEED ROSEBAY
BURNWEED FIREWEED
WILLOW WARBLER SMEU SMEUTH
MUDDLER TROCHIL OVENBIRD
WILLOW WREN PEGGY
WILLOWY SUPPLE SLIPPER
DELICATE
WILLY-NILLY PERFORCE
WILSON'S PLOVER COLLIER
WILSON'S SNIPE JACK SHADBIRD
WILSON'S TERN MEDRICK
WILSON'S THRUSH VEERY
WILT EBB SAG DROP FADE FLAG
WELK DROOP SUCCUMB COLLAPSE
WILTED EMARCID
WILY SLY FOXY CANNY SLICK
ARTFUL ASTUTE CLEVER CRAFTY
QUAINT SHREWD STALKY SUBTLE
CUNNING POLITIC VERSUTE
WINDING
WIMBLE BORE BRISK ACTIVE GIMLET
LIVELY NIMBLE WIBBLE WUMMEL
WIMPLE BEND WIND CURVE TWIST
GORGET RIPPLE MEANDER
WIMLUNGE
WIN BAG COP HIT DRAW GAIN HAVE
LAND LICK FORCE SCORE ATTACH
CLINCH OBTAIN ACHIEVE CONQUER
DESERVE HARVEST POSSESS
TRIUMPH DECISION OVERCOME
STRAIGHT
(— AGAINST) BREAK SCOOP
(— AWAY) STEAL DEBAUCH
(— BACK) RECOVER
(— BY GUILE) GET POT BEAR
CARRY RAISE TRAIN GATHER
CAPTURE INVEIGLE PROMERIT
(— NARROWLY) SQUEEZE
(— OVER) DEFEAT DISARM
(— OVERWHELMINGLY) SWEEP
WINCE KICK CHECK QUECH CRINGE
FLINCH QUATCH QUINCH QUITCH
RECOIL SHRINK
WINCH CRAB JACK REEL WINK
GIPSY WINZE ROLLER WHIMSY
WINDLE CATHEAD TRAVELER
VARIABLE WINDLASS
WIND AIR COP LAP BALL BIRR BISE
BIZE COIL CONE CURL EAST FIST
FLAW FOHN GALE GUST KINK PUFF
PUNO ROLL WEST WRAP BATCH
BLAST BLORE CRANK CREEK
CROOK FOEHN QUILL SPOOL
STORM TRADE TREND TWINE TWIST
WEAVE WITHE BOTTOM BOUGHT

BREEZE BUSTER CAURUS COLLAR
KECKLE SANSAR SHAMAL SPIRAL
SPIRIT SQUALL WAMPLE WESTER
ZEPHYR BREATHE CRANKLE
CRINKLE CYCLONE ENTWINE
EQUINOX ETESIAN GREGALE
INVOLVE MEANDER MISTRAL
SERPENT SINUATE TEMPEST
TWINGLE TWISTER WEATHER
WHIRLER WINDILL ARGESTES
DOWNWARD EASTERLY FAVONIUS
(— ABEAM) LASK
(— ABOUT) WIRE SNAKE
(— AFTER DYEING) BATCH
(— FROM THE ANDES) PAMPERO
(— IN AND OUT) INDENT WINGLE
(— MAGNETS) COMPOUND
(— OF ARGENTINA) ZONDA
PAMPERO
(— OF HAWAII) KONA
(— OF OREGON AND WASHINGTON)
CHINOOK
(— OF TUNISIA) CHILE CHILI CHILLI
(— ROPE) WORM WOOLD
(— THREAD OR YARN) QUILL
CHEESE
(— TO PREVENT CHAFING) KECKLE
(— WOOL) TREND
(— YARN) BEAM SERVE WINDLE
(—S OF CHILE AND PERU) SURES
(ADRIATIC —) BORA
(BREAKING —) FIST
(BROKEN —) HEAVES
(COLD —) BISE BIZE BORA SARSAR
BLIZZARD
(COOLING —) IMBAT
(DEAD —) NOSER
(DESERT —) SAMUM GIBLEH SAMIEL
SIMOOM SIMOON SIROCCO
(DRYING —) TRADE
(EASTERLY —) LEVANT LEVANTER
(FIERCE —) BUSTER
(GUST OF —) FLAN FLAW
(HIGH —) RIG
(HOT —) GIBLEH SOLANO CHAMSIN
KHAMSIN SIROCCO
(LIGHT GENTLE —) BREEZE
(MOUNTAIN —) PUNA
(NORTH —) BISE AQUILO BOREAS
AQUILON MISTRAL
(NORTHEAST —) BURAN GREGALE
(NORTHWEST —) CAURUS
(PERIODICAL —) ETESIAN MONSOON
(PERSIAN GULF —) SHAMAL SHARKI
SHIMAL
(PERUVIAN —) PUNO
(ROARING —) BLORE
(SEVERE —) SNIFTER
(SOUTH —) NOTUS AUSTER
(SOUTHEAST —) EURUS SOLANO
(SOUTHEASTERLY —) SHARKI
SHURGEE
(SOUTHWEST —) CHINOOK LIBECCIO
(STRONG —) BIRR
(VIOLENT —) BUSTER SQUALL
SNORTER
(WARM —) FOHN FOEHN CHINOOK
SANTANA

(WEST —) ZEPHYR FAVONIUS
ZEPHYRUS
WINDAGE DRIFT
WINDER REEL WINCH DRUMMER
PLUGGER SKEINER SPOOLER
TENDRIL
WINDFALL VAIL GRAVY MANNA
FALLING BLOWDOWN BUCKSHEE
WINDGALL PUFF WINDDOG
WINDING LINK MAZY CRANK LACET
SPIRE GYRATE SCREWY SPIRAL
TWISTY WANLAS CRINKLE DEVIOUS
MEANDER SINUOUS SNAKING
WRIGGLY WRINKLE
(PL.) RADDLINGS
WINDING-SHEET SHROUD SUDARY
CEREMENT
WINDING STAIR COCKLE COCLEA
WINDER COCHLEA
WINDLASS CRAB WINK FEARN
WINCH STOWCE STOWSE TACKLE
TURNEL WINDLE TWISTER WILDCAT
ARTIFICE DRAWBEAM MANEUVER
WINDMILL JUMBO MOTOR COPTER
PINWHEEL
(— BAR) UPLONG
(— SAIL) AWE EIE EIGHE FLIER
FLYER SWEEP SWIFT
WINDOW BAY EYE ROSE SASH SLIT
SLOT CHAFF GLAZE GRILL INLET
LIGHT SIGHT THURL AWNING
DORMER GRILLE LANCET PEEPER
SPLITE THURLE WICKET BALCONE
COUPLET DORMANT FENSTER
GUICHET LUTHERN MIRADOR
ORIFICE TRANSOM VENTANA
WINNOCK CASEMENT FANLIGHT
FENESTER FENESTRA JALOUSIE
VENETIAN
(— OF TWO LIGHTS) COUPLET
(BAY —) ORIEL MIRADOR
(BLANK —) ORB
(DORMER —) DORMANT LUCARNE
LUTHERN
(HIGH NARROW —) LANCET
(OVAL —) OXEYE
(ROUND —) OXEYE OCULUS
ROUNDEL
(SEMICIRCULAR —) FANLIGHT
(TICKET —) GRILLE GUICHET
(TWIN —) AJIMEZ
(PL.) STORMS
WINDOW DRESSING TRIM FRONT
FACADE
WINDOW FRAME SASH REVEAL
WINDOW OYSTER COPIS
WINDOWPANE LIGHT LOZEN QUIRK
LOZENGE
WINDOWSILL SOLE
WINDPIPE HALS ARBER ARBOR
ERBER HALSE WIZEN ARTERY
GUGGLE STROUP WEEZLE KEACORN
THACHEA WEASAND THRAPPLE
THROPPLE THROTTLE
WINDROW BANK HEAP RIDGE
SWATH SWATHE
WINDSOR CHAIR FANBACK
WINDSTORM BLOW BURA THUD
BURAN BOURRAN

WINDWARD ALOOF WEATHER
(— **SIDE**) KOOLAU
WINDY BLOWY EMPTY GASSY GUSTY
HUFFY PROUD STARK SWALE
FLIMSY STORMY WONDIE BREATHY
FEARFUL GUSTFUL NERVOUS
VENTOSE VIOLENT
(— **CITY**) CHICAGO
WINE CUP VIN BOIS BUAL CUIT CUTE
DEAL PALM PORT RAPE ROSE ROSY
TENT TYRE CAPRI GRAPE KRAMA
LUNEL PETER PORTO SCIAN SHRAB
TINTO VINUM WHITE BARSAC
CORTON COUTET GRAVES KIJAFA
LISBON MASDEU PIMENT ROCHET
SAUMUR SHIRAZ SOLERA TIVOLI
ALICANT AMBONNA BACCHUS
BANYULS BARBERA BASTARD
CATAWBA CHACOLI CHATEAU
DEZALEY FALERNO MARSALA
MISSION MOSELLE ORVIETO
PALERMO PIGMENT RHENISH
ROSOLIO SERCIAL SILLERY
VERNAGE VIDONIA VINTAGE
APERITIF BORDEAUX BURGUNDY
CHARNECO DELAWARE LACHRYMA
LIBATION MALVASIA MARSALLA
RIESLING ROCHELLE RULANDER
RUMBOOZE SPARKLER
(— **BOILED WITH HONEY**) MULSE
(— **CHEST**) TANTALUS
(— **FROM VINEGAR**) ESILL
(— **MIXED WITH WATER**) KRASIS
(— **OF EXCELLENT QUALITY**)
VINTAGE
(— **OF SACRAMENT**) BLOOD
(— **SELLER**) ABKAR BISTRO WINARE
(— **SERVING**) VOIDEE
(**AROMATIZED** —) DUBONNET
(**BULK** —) CUVEE
(**CONSECRATED** —) CUP
(**FIRST-GROWTH** —) LAFITE LAFITTE
(**FRANCONIAN** —) STEIN LEISTEN
(**GREEK** —) RUMNEY
(**HEATED** —) WHITEPOT
(**JAPANESE** —) SAKI
(**LIGHT** —) BUAL CAPRI BAROLO
CANARY
(**MULLED** —) GLUHWEIN
(**NEW — BOILED DOWN**) CUIT CUTE
(**NEW** —) MUST
(**PALM** —) SAGWIRE
(**RED** —) MACON TINTA BEAUNE
CLARET CHIANTI HOLLOCK
ALICANTE BURGUNDY CABERNET
FLORENCE
(**REVIVED** —) STUM
(**RHINE** —) HOCK SYLVANER
(**SPANISH** —) SACK TENT DULCE
OPORTO SHERRY ALIKANT BASTARD
(**STILL** —) PONTAC PONTACQ
(**SWEET** —) TYRE DULCE CANARY
BASTARD MALMSEY CHARNECO
MUSCATEL
(**TENT** —) TINTO
(**TOKAY** —) ESSENCE
(**TUSCAN** —) VERDEA CHIANTI
FLORENCE
(**WHITE** —) HOCK SACK CAPRI

CASEL FORST BARSAC MALAGA
BROMIAN CATAWBA CHABLIS
CONTHEY LANGOON BUCELLAS
RIESLING SAUTERNE VERMOUTH
(PL.) PALUS
WINEBERRY MAKO MAKOMAKO
WINEGLASS FLUTE
WINEGROWER WINER VIGNERON
WINESHOP BISTRO BODEGA
WINE-VAULT SHADE
WING ALA ARM ELL FAN FLY OAR
RIB VAN FORE JAMB SAIL TAIL
ALULA BLOCK FLANK JAMBE PINNA
POINT SHEAR VOLET BRANCH
FLETCH FLIGHT HALTER PENNON
PINION POISER DEMIVOL ELYTRON
ELYTRUM BALANCER DISPATCH
(— **OF ARMY**) HORN
(— **OF BUILDING**) ELL JAMB JAMBE
ALETTE FLANKER
(— **OF SHELL**) AURICLE
(— **OF THEATER**) COULISSE
TORMENTOR
(— **OF TRIPTYCH**) VOLET
(—**S DISPLAYED**) VOL
(**BASTARD** —) ALULA
(**BIRD'S** —) FLAG
(PL.) PENS FEATHERS
WINGED AILE ALATE LOFTY RAPID
SWIFT ALATED PENNED PENNATE
ELEVATED
WINGED DISK FEROHER
WING-FOOTED FLEET SWIFT ALIPED
WINGLESS APTERAL
WING-LIKE ALARY ALIFORM
PTEROID
WING SHELL STROMB ELYTRON
STROMBUS
WINK BAT NAP PINK BLINK DEATH
FLASH PRINK SLEEP TWINK
CONNIVE FLICKER INSTANT NICTATE
SPARKLE TWINKLE
WINKER EYE BLINKER EYELASH
WINKING BLINK
WINKLE PERIWIG TWINKLE
WINNER VICTOR FACEMAN
BANGSTER
WINNING GAIN SWEET PROFIT
GAINING VICTORY WINSOME
CHARMING
(— **OF ALL TRICKS**) CAPOT
SCHWARZ
(PL.) WIN VELVET
WINNOW FAN WIM CHAR SIFT WIND
DIGHT SIEVE DELETE REMOVE
SELECT WINDER SEPARATE
WINNOWER VAN WINDER DIGHTER
WINSOME GAY SWEET CHARMING
CHEERFUL PLEASANT
WINTER BISE SNOW YEAR HIEMS
DECEMBER HIBERNATE
(— **OVER**) HOG
WINTERBERRY PRINOS HOOPWOOD
WINTERBLOOM AZALEA
WINTERGREEN JINKS CHINKS
PYROLA DRUNKER BOXBERRY
DRUNKARD EYEBERRY GAYWINGS
IVYBERRY LIMONIUM RATSBANE
SHINLEAF TEABERRY

WINTERLIKE BRUMAL
WINTRY AGED COLD WHITE BOREAL
HIEMAL STORMY CHILLING
HIBERNAL
WINTUN COPEHAN
WINY VINOUS DRUNKEN
WIPE BEAT BLOW DRUB DUST GIBE
DIGHT SWIPE CANCEL SPONGE
SPUNGE STRIKE ABOLISH CLEANSE
SQUEEGEE
(— **BEAK OF HAWK**) FEAK
(— **NOSE**) SNITE
(— **OFF**) SCUFF
(— **OUT**) ERASE SCRUB SWEEP
EFFACE DESTROY
(— **UP**) SWAB SWOB
WIPER DUSTER TRIPPET
WIRE GUY TAP BINE CORE DENT
DRAG FILE FUSE PURL CABLE
OUTER RISER SNAKE SWEEP TAPER
BRIDGE FESCUE FINGER HEATER
JUMPER NEEDLE STAPLE STOLON
STRAND DROPPER HAYWIRE
LAMETTA LASHING PRICKER
SHIFTER SNUFFER FILAMENT
LIGATURE PALISADE PULLDOWN
STRINGER TELEGRAM
(— **BETWEEN TWO VESSELS**) SWEEP
(— **FOR CUTTING CLAY**) SLING
(— **FOR SUSTAINING HAIR**)
PALISADE
(— **IN BLASTING CAP**) BRIDGE
(— **IN CATHETER**) STYLET
(— **IN WEAVING LOOM**) DENT
(— **OF GOLD,SILVER OR BRASS**)
LAMETTA
(— **TO ADJUST WICK**) SNUFFER
(— **TO CLOSE A BREAK**) JUMPER
(— **TO REMOVE TUMORS**) LIGATURE
(— **USED AS POINTER**) FESCUE
(— **USED IN SPLICING CABLES**)
TAPER
(—**S BOUND TOGETHER**) SELVAGE
(4 —**S TWISTED TOGETHER**) QUAD
(**ENAMELED** —) LITZ
(**FENCE** —) DROPPER
(**FRAYED** —) JAGGER
(**GOLD** —) KINSEN
(**PALLET** —) PULLDOWN
(**PRIMING** —) PICKER EPINGLETTE
(**SURGICAL** —) STYLET
(**TWISTED** —) HEADLE HEDDLE
(**VENT** —) PRICKER
WIRE CUTTER SECATEUR
WIREDRAW WREST OUTWIT
DEFRAUD DISTORT ELONGATE
WIREGLASS FLUTE
WIRE GRASS POA
WIRELESS RADIO
WIRE ROPE JACKSTAY
WIRETAP BUG
WIREWORM ELATER ELATRID
MILLIPEDE
WIRY THIN HARDY STIFF WITHY
FEEBLE KNOTTY SINEWY STRINGY
THREADY
WIS KNOW THINK SURELY SUPPOSE

WISCONSIN

CAPITAL: MADISON
COLLEGE: RIPON BELOIT ALVERNO CARROLL VITERBO CARTHAGE
COUNTY: DOOR VILAS JUNEAU CALUMET SHAWANO WAUSHARA
INDIAN: FOX SAUK KICKAPOO WINNEBAGO
LAKE: POYGAN MENDOTA WISSOTA
MOUNTAIN: TIMSHILL SUGARBUSH
NATIVE: BADGER
NICKNAME: BADGER
RIVER: FOX CHIPEWA STCROIX
STATE BIRD: ROBIN
STATE FLOWER: VIOLET
STATE TREE: MAPLE
TOWN: ANTIGO BELOIT RACINE WAUSAU ASHLAND BARABOO KENOSHA MADISON OSHKOSH PORTAGE SHAWANO LACROSSE SUPERIOR WAUKESHA MILWAUKEE

WISDOM WIT LORE SABE SABBY SAVEY SENSE SOPHY ADVICE GNOSIS HOKMAH POLICY SATTVA SOPHIA WISURE CUNNING MINERVA SAGESSE SLEIGHT AFTERWIT JUDGMENT PRUDENCE SAPIENCE **(DIVINE —)** WORD THEOMAGY **(ESOTERIC —)** GNOSIS **(SUPREME —)** PRAJNA
WISE HEP SLY DEEP GASH GOOD KIND SAGE SANE SEND TURN CANNY FRESH GUIDE SMART SOUND WITTY ADVISE CRAFTY DIRECT QUAINT WITFUL WITTER ANCIENT ERUDITE GNOSTIC KNOWING LEARNED POLITIC PRUDENT SAPIENT THRIVEN PERSUADE PROFOUND SENSIBLE SPACIOUS **(— MAN)** AMAUTA
WISEACRE SAGE DUNCE GOTHAM SOLONIST WISEHEAD WISELING
WISECRACK JOKE QUIP
WISENT BISON AUROCH UROCHS BONASUS
WISH CARE GIVE GOAL HOPE LIST LUST MIND VOTE WANT WILL BOSOM COVET CRAVE DREAM HEART TASTE VOICE DESIRE UTINAM FAREWELL GODSPEED PLEASURE **(DEATH —)** DESTRUDO **(SLIGHT —)** VELLEITY
WISHBONE FURCULA FOURCHET FURCULUM
WISHFUL EAGER HOPEFUL LONGING ALLURING
WISHING ANXIOUS DESIROUS
WISHY-WASHY PALE THIN WEAK BLAND VAPID FEEBLE DILUTED INSIPID SLIPSLOP
WISKET BASKET WHISKET
WISP WUSP SCRAP SHRED SKIFF

SKIFT TWIST RUMPLE CRUMPLE MASSAGE **(— OF HAY)** RISP **(— OF STRAW)** WAP WASE DOSSIL **(— OF THATCH)** TIPPET
WISPY FRAIL NEBULOUS
WISTERIA FUJI KRAUNHIA
WISTFUL INTENT PENSIVE WISHFUL MOURNFUL YEARNING
WISTITI WISTIT MARMOSET
WIT VAT VYT WAG KNOW NOUS SALT BRAIN HUMOR IRONY SENSE THINK WHITE WOTTE ACUMEN ESPRIT POLICY SANITY SATIRE WISDOM CUNNING PICADOR SARCASM SUPPOSE THINKER WITWORM BADINAGE REPARTEE **(BITING —)** DICACITY **(PL.)** BUTTONS
WITCH ALP ANI HAG HEG HEX MARE SAGA TRAT WYCH BRUJA BUTCH GREBE LAMIA WIGHT ASUANG CARLEY CARLIN CUMMER DOWSER DUESSA HECATE KIMMER PILWIZ WIZARD AGANICE CANIDIA HAGGARD HELLCAT SYCORAX BABAJAGA CAROLINE ERICHTHO SORCERER SPAEWIFE VERSIERA WALKYRIE **(PL.)** COVEN
WITCHCRAFT CHARM GOETY CUNNING HEXEREI SORCERY BRUJERIA DEVILTRY PISHOGUE WIZARDRY
WITCH DOCTOR BOCOR BOKOR GOOFER GUFFER
WITCHERY CHARM SPELL SORCERY SORTIARY
WITCHES'-BROOM STAGHEAD
WITCHGRASS COUCH PANIC PANICLE
WITE WAT BLAME FAULT WAYTE CENSURE REPROACH HAMESOKEN
WITH BY CUM MID MIT WUD AVEC CHEZ DOWN AMONG ANENT WIGHT AGAINST **(— HAND ON HIP)** AKIMBO **(— REGARD TO)** ABOUT **(— SPEED)** TIVY
WITHDRAW GO COY DROP TAKE AVOID DEMIT LOOSE REVEL SHIFT START UNSAY CHANGE DECEDE DESERT DETACH DETRAY DEVOID EFFACE FLINCH MINISH RECALL RECANT RECEDE RETIRE REVOKE ROGATE SECEDE SHRINK SINGLE SYPHON ABSCOND CONCEAL DESCEND DETRACT FORSAKE INVEIGH RETRACT RETREAT SCRATCH SCUTTLE SECLUDE SUBDUCE SUBDUCT UNSCREW SEPARATE SUBTRACT **(— FROM POKER POT)** DROP **(— FROM)** VAIK **(— SUPPORT)** ABANDON
WITHDRAWAL DRAIN FLIGHT HIDING OFFLAP RETIRE SHRINK ABSENCE PULLOUT REGRESS RETIRAL RETREAT SCUTTLE

(— OF BUILDING FACE) SETBACK
WITHDRAWN SHY ASOCIAL INGROWN SECLUSE DISTRAIT ISOLATED SECLUDED
WITHE HANK ROPE TIER TWIG WITHY WATTLE WICKER CRINGLE
WITHER BURN DAZE FADE MIFF PINE RUST SEAR STUN WARP WELK BLAST CLING DAVER DECAY QUAIL WIZEN COTTER SHRINK WALLOW WELTER WILTER WINDER AREFACT DECLINE FORWELK SENESCE SHRIVEL LANGUISH PARALYZE
WITHERED DRY ARID SEAR SERE CORKY SCRAM MARCID BLASTED UNGREEN WIZENED
WITHHELD DEFERRED SUSPENSE
WITHHOLD CURB DENY HIDE KEEP STOP CHECK SCANT ABSENT DEPORT DETAIN REFUSE ABSTAIN BOYCOTT DEFORCE FORBEAR OUTHOLD REPRESS RESERVE SUSPEND RESTRAIN SUBTRACT **(— CONSENT)** DECLINE
WITHHOLDING DETAINER **(— OF DUES)** CHECKOFF
WITHIN IN ON BEN BIN INBY INLY INTRA HEREIN INSIDE INWITH INDOORS ENCLOSED INCLUDED INWARDLY
WITHOUT EX BUT OUT SEN BOUT FREE OHNE SANS SINE MINUS SENZA FAILING OUTSIDE WANTING INNOCENT OUTDOORS **(— A FLANGE)** BALD **(— A MATE)** ODD **(— ACTION)** DEEDLESS **(— BEGINNING OR END)** ETERNAL **(— BLEMISH)** CHOICE **(— CONTENTS)** INANE **(— DELAY)** AWAY FOOTHOT SUMMARY **(— DELIBERATION)** HEADLONG **(— EMOTION)** DRYLY DULLY **(— EXCEPTION)** ALWAYS **(— FEET)** APOD **(— FUNDS)** CLEAN **(— HORNS)** ACEROUS **(— INTEREST)** BARREN **(— LIGHT)** APHOTIC **(— LIMITS OF DURATION)** AGELESS **(— ORDER)** ANYHOW **(— POWER)** ADRIFT **(— QUESTION)** EASILY SECURELY **(— REALITY)** AIRY **(— REASON)** BLINDLY **(— REMEDY)** BOOTLESS **(— ROADS)** INVIOUS **(— RULE OR LAW)** ANARCHIC **(— SADDLES)** ASELLATE **(— TEETH, TONGUE OR CLAWS)** MORNE **(— WINGS)** APTEROUS
WITHSTAND BIDE DEFY TAKE ABIDE OPPOSE OPPUGN RESIST CONTAIN CONTEST FORBEAR SUSTAIN CONFRONT WITHSTAY
WITHY WIRY AGILE OSIER WOODY WILLOW WOODIE WINDING

WITLESS MAD GROSS INSANE STUPID FATUOUS FOOLISH UNWITTY HEEDLESS SLAPHAPPY
WITLOOF ENDIVE CHICORY
WITNESS SEE TAKE TEST PROOF ATTEST BEHOLD MARTYR RECORD TESTIS TESTOR CURATOR TESTATE TESTIFY EVIDENCE RECORDER SUFFRAGE
(FALSE —) JUROR
(PL.) SECTA
WITNESS-BOX STAND
WITOTO HUITOTE
WITTICISM WIT JEER JEST JOKE SLENT WHEEZE
WITTING NEWS TIDINGS
WITTOL FOOL CUCKOLD WITTALL
WITTY GASH WILY WISE DROLL LEPID SHARP SMART CLEVER FACETE JOCOSE JOCULAR KNOWING CONCEITY HUMOROUS
(NOT —) INFICETE
WIVERN DRAGON WYVERN
WIZARD SEER SHIZ FIEND DOCTOR EXPERT PELLAR WARLOW CHARMED MAGICAL SPAEMAN WARLOCK WISEMAN CONJUROR MAGICIAN SORCERER TROLLMAN WITCHMAN
(PL.) GOETAE
WIZARDRY SORCERY
WIZEN DRY WITHER SHRIVEL
WIZENED GIZZEN WEAZEN
WOAD DYE NIL ODE ANIL KERS NILL OADE CRESS ANILLA INDICO INDIGO PASTEL
WOADWAXEN ALLELUIA ALLELUJA
WOBBLE COCKLE COGGLE HOBBLE QUAVER TITTER WABBLE WIGGLE TREMBLE
WOBBLY LOOSE SHAKY COGGLY DRUNKEN DOUBTFUL
WOE WA WEI BALE BANE PAIN PINE WAWE GRIEF MISERY SORROW TROUBLE WILLAWA CALAMITY DISTRESS WELLADAY WELLAWAY
WOEBEGONE WAFF UNHAPPY DEJECTED DESOLATE DOWNCAST
WOEFUL MEAN DISMAL PALTRY RUEFUL DIREFUL DOLEFUL RUTHFUL DOLOROUS PITIABLE WRETCHED
WOLF GLUT LOBO CANID FREKI YABBI CHANCO COYOTE FAMINE FENRIR ISGRIN KABERU LOAFER MASHER SIGRIM THOOID POVERTY ISENGRIM
(FOX —) ZORRO
WOLFBERRY BUCKBUSH
WOLFHOUND ALAN BORZOI PSOVIE
WOLFISH LUPINE RAVENOUS
WOLFLIKE THOOID
WOLFRAMITE CAL TUNGSTEN
WOLFSBANE ACONITE DOGBANE FOXBANE
WOLF SPIDER HUNT JAGER HUNTER JAEGER JAYHAWK LYCOSID TARANTULA
WOLVERINE PIG GLUT GORB MIKER GLOTUM HELLUO GLUTTON GUTLING LURCHER MOOCHER

RAVENER SWILLER CARCAJOU DRAFFMAN GOURMAND GULLYGUT
(— STATE) MICHIGAN
WOMAN BIM DAM EVE HEN HER JUG MEG SHE TEG TIT BABE BABY BINT BOSS CONY DAME FAIR FEME FLAG FROW JADE JANE LADY MARY MORT PERI SLUT WIFE BIDDY BIMBO BLADE BROAD CHINA DONAH FEMME JATNI LUBRA LUCKY MUJER QUEAN SKIRT SMOCK SQUAW TAGGE TWIST UMMAN VROUW BURDIE CALICO CARLIN CUMMER FEMALE GIMMER HEIFER KIMMER LUCKIE MANESS SISTER TOMATO VIRAGO WAHINE CARLING CHANGAR DISTAFF PARTLET PINNACE PLACKET QUAEDAM MISTRESS
(— DESERTED BY HUSBAND) AGUNAH
(— OF CONSEQUENCE) HERSELF
(— OF LOW CASTE) DASI
(— OF RANK) DOMINA
(— OF UNSTEADY CHARACTER) FLAP
(— OF WEALTH) FORTUNE
(— WHO ACTS AS ADVISER) EGERIA
(— WITH 3 CHILDREN) TRIPARA
(— WITH ONE CHILD) UNIPARA
(ABORIGINAL —) GIN LUBRA
(ABUSIVE —) FISHWIFE
(ALLURING —) DISH
(ATHENIAN — OF HIGH RANK) GERARA GERAERA
(ATTRACTIVE —) DOLLY SHEBA DOLLIE CHARMER
(AUSTRALIAN —) BINT
(AWKWARD —) ROIL
(BEAUTIFUL —) HURI PERI BELLE HOURI SIREN SPARK CHERUB EYEFUL MUSIDORA
(BOISTEROUS —) HOYDEN
(BOLD —) RAMP
(CLEANING —) CHAR
(COARSE —) BEAST BLOWZE RULLION
(COOLIE —) CHANGAR
(COY —) HAGGARD
(CREMATED —) SATI SUTTEE
(DEAR —) PEAT
(DUTCH OR GERMAN —) FRAU FROW FROKIN FRAULEIN
(ENGAGED —) BONDAGER
(ENTICING —) SIREN
(EVIL OLD —) HAG HELLHAG
(FASHIONABLE —) MILADY GALLANT ELEGANTE
(FAT —) BOSS FUSTILUGS
(FINE —) SCREAMER
(FIRST —) EMBLA
(FLIRTING —) FIZGIG
(FORWARD —) STRAP
(GAUDY —) JAY
(GENTLE —) DOVE
(GOSSIPY —) HAIK HAKE BIDDY TABBY
(GROSS —) SOW
(GYPSY —) ROMI ROMNI GITANA
(ILL-TEMPERED —) VIXEN

(IMMORAL —) RIG GITCH FLAPPER HARLOTRY
(INDIAN —) SQUAW WENCH KLOOCH BUCKEEN
(INSPIRED —) PHOEBAD
(ITALIAN —) DONNA
(LASCIVIOUS —) GIGLET
(LEARNED —) PUNDITA CLERGESS
(LEWD —) REP SLUT BITCH HUSSY HUZZY BROTHEL
(LOOSE —) BAG BIM KIT TIB DRAB FLAP BIMBO TROLL GILLOT HARLOT LIMMER BAGGAGE FRANION TROLLOP
(LOUD-SPOKEN —) RANDY
(LOW OR WORTHLESS —) JADE JURR SLINGDUST
(MARRIED — OF LOWLY STATION) GOODY
(MASCULINE —) AMAZON RULLION CORQUEAN
(MEEK —) GRIZEL
(MYTHOLOGICAL —) HEROINE
(OLD —) GIB HEN BABA TROT CRONE FAGOT FRUMP TROUT BELDAM CARLIN GAMMER GEEZER GRANNY GRANDAM HARRIDAN
(OLD SHRIVELED —) FAGOT FAGGOT
(PEDANTIC —) BLUE
(PERT —) CHIT
(PORTUGESE —) SENHORA
(PREGNANT —) GRAVIDA
(PRIGGISH —) PRUDE
(RUSTIC —) JOAN
(SCOLDING —) SHREW
(SHORT OR STUMPY —) CUTTY
(SHREWISH —) JADE HARPY SKELLAT
(SLATTERNLY —) DRAB FLEABAG
(SLENDER GRACEFUL —) SYLPH
(SLIPSHOD —) MAUX CLATCH TROLLIMOG
(SLOVENLY —) BAG DAW SOW SLUT BESOM TAWPY TROLL TROLLOP SLATTERN
(SPANISH —) DONA GITANA
(SPANISH-INDIAN —) CHOLA
(SPITEFUL —) CAT FURY BITCH
(SQUAT —) TRUB
(SQUEAMISH —) COCKNEY
(STAID —) MATRON
(STATELY —) JUNO
(STORMY VIOLENT —) FURY
(TRACTABLE —) SHEEP
(UGLY —) HAG GORGON
(UNCHASTE —) JILT
(UNMARRIED —) DAME GIRL SPINSTER
(VIXENISH —) HARRIDAN
(WANTON —) MINX TRUB PARNEL
(WICKED —) JEZEBEL
(WISE —) VOLVA ALRUNA ALRUNE
(WITHERED —) CRONE
(YOUNG —) BIT BIRD BURD CHIT DAME DELL DOLL GIRL LASS PUSS BEAST CHICK FILLY FLUFF TOAST DAMSEL HEIFER PIGEON SHEILA SUBDEB BAGGAGE CHICKEN

DAMOZEL FLAPPER WINKLOT
BRISETTE DAUGHTER GRISETTE
WOMAN HATER MISOGYNIST
WOMANISH FEMALE FEMININE
LADYLIKE PETTICOAT
WOMANKIND WOMEN CALICO
MUSLIN FEMINIE
WOMAN'S TONGUE LEBBEK
WOMB BELLY CRADLE UTERUS
WOMBAT KOALA BADGER DIDELPH
VOMBATID
WOMEN DISTAFF
(— OF EARLY CHURCH) SETTERS
AGAPETAE
WON CITY LIVE ROOM ABIDE DWELL
REGION
WONDER AWE MUSE SELI SIGN
TROW UNCO UNKO VERY FARLY
FERLY SELLE SELLY UNCOW
ADMIRE MARVEL MIRATE MAGNALE
MIRABLE MIRACLE PORTENT
PRODIGY STRANGE UNCOUTH
AMERVEIL SELCOUTH SURPRISE
WONDERFUL KEEN SELI FERLY
GRAND GREAT SELLE SWELL
WAKON MIGHTY AMAZING GALLANT
MIRABLE MIRIFIC STRANGE
GLORIOUS MIRABILE WONDROUS
WONDERFULLY AMAZING
WONDER-WORKER THEURGIC
THEURGIST
WONG FIELD GROVE PLAIN MEADOW
WONKY AWRY SHAKY WRONG
UNSTEADY
WONT APT USE FAIN USED VAIN
HABIT USAGE CUSTOM INCLINED
WONTED USUAL HAUNTED
WOO SUE LOVE SEEK SUIT WALE
COURT SPARK SPOON ASSAIL
SPLUNT SUITOR ADDRESS
WOOD (ALSO SEE TREE AND TIMBER)
HAG KIP BOIS BOSK BOWL EKKI
HOLT KIRI MASS MOCK PALO SUPA
TREE WOLE CAHUY CHARK CROWD
EDDER FLOUR GROVE HURST
HYRST RESAK STICK STUFF WEALD
ALMOND ANGILI AUSUBO BRAZIL
EKHIMI FOREST ITAUBA JARANA
LUMBER PALING SPINNY TIMBER
APITONG AVODIRE COPPICE
DADDOCK DUDGEON HAYBOTE
SATINAY VENESIA BAGTIKAN
CRANTARA FIREBOOT
(— BURNT AS PERFUME) AGALLOCH
(— FOR CARPENTRY) STUFF
(— FOR REPAIRING HEDGE) TINING
HAYBOTE
(— OF SMALL EXTENT) GROVE
(— OF THE VERA) VENESIA
(— ON RAFTER) FUR
(— ROTATED ON STRING) ROMBOS
RHOMBOS
(— USEFUL FOR TINDER) PUNK
SPONK TOUCHWOOD
(— YIELDING PERFUME) LINALOA
(BABUL —) SUNT
(BLACK —) EBONY
(CONE-SHAPED PIECE OF —) ACORN
(DARK RED —) RATA

(DENSIFIED —) STAYPAK
(ELASTIC —) SYCAMORE
(FLAT ROUND PIECE OF —)
TRENCHER
(FLEXIBLE —) EDDER
(FOSSIL —) PINITE PEUCITES
(FRAGRANT —) CEDAR
(FUEL —) ESTOVERS
(HARD —) ASH DAO SAL BAKU IPIL
KARI LANA POON ANJAN EBONY
GIDYA KARRI KOKRA MAPLE ZANTE
BANUYO CAMARA FREIJO GIDGEE
KEMPAS SABICU WALNUT CURUPAY
DATTOCK HICKORY GUAIACUM
IRONBARK MAHOGANY
(HEAVY —) DAO EBON EBONY
CHENGAL GUAYABI SUCUPIRA
(LIGHT —) POON BALSA HEMLOCK
(LIMBA —) KORINA
(LOGGED —) CHIP
(LOST —) CHIPPAGE
(LUSTROUS —) LEZA BOARWOOD
(MATCHBOX —) SKILLET
(MOTTLED —) AMBOINA
(NARROW BAR OF —) SLAT
(NUMBER 1 —) DRIVER
(NUMBER 2 —) BRASSIE
(NUMBER 3 —) SPOON
(NUMBER 4 —) CLEEK
(OILY —) BATETE
(OLIVE —) COLLIE
(PETRIFIED —) LITHOXYL
ROCKWOOD
(PINKISH —) BOSSE
(POINTED PIECE OF —) TRIPPET
(REDDISH —) KOA KARI KARRI
ARANGA BANABA CHERRY DUNGON
SATINE KAMBALA
(REDDISH-YELLOW —) GUYO
(ROTTEN —) DADDOCK
(SANDARAC —) ALERCE
(SOFT —) KIRI GABUN GABOON
ELKWOOD AGALLOCH GUATAMBU
(SQUARE LOG OF —) NOG
(STICK OF —) BILLET
(STRIP OF —) LATH STAVE BATTEN
REEPER REGLET
(WATER RESISTING —) AMUBIS
(YELLOWISH —) HALDU FUSTIC
IDIGBO KADAMBA KAMASSI
GUATAMBU
WOOD ANEMONE CYME EMONY
BOWBELLA SNOWDROP
WOODBARK SABLE BLONDINE
WOODBINE BIND WIDBIN EGLATERE
WOODCARVER BODGER
WOODCHUCK CHUG CHUCK MONAX
MARMOT SUSLIK WEJACK MOONACK
GROUNDHOG
WOODCOCK QUIS PEWEE PEWIT
SNIPE SNITE SHRUPS BECASSE
SIMPLETON
WOODCUT BLOCK
WOODCUTTER AXEMAN LOGGER
WOODMAN WOODSMAN
WOOD DUCK SQUEALER BRANCHIER
WOODED BOSKY TREEY HYLEAN
SYLVAN FORESTED
WOODEN DRY DULL STIFF TREEN

CLUMSY STICKY STOLID TIMBER
AWKWARD DEADPAN TIMBERN
LIFELESS
WOOD GUM XYLAN
WOOD HEN WEKA
WOODHEWER PICUCULE
WOOD HOOPOE WHOOP WHOOPE
IRRISOR DUNGBIRD PICARIAN
WOOD HYACINTH SCILLA
CROWTOE GREGGLE HAREBELL
WOOD IBIS STORK GANNET JABIRU
IRONHEAD
WOODLAND DESERT MIOMBO
SPRING
(WASTE —) WEALD
WOODPECKER AWL CHAB JYNX
KATE PEEK ECCLE HECCO HEWEL
ICKLE SPEKT HECKLE NICKLE
PECKER PIANET PICULE SPRITE
TAPPER YAFFLE YUKKEL CLIMBER
CREEPER FLICKER HEWHOLE
HICKWAY LOGCOCK REDHEAD
SAPSUCK SNAPPER SPEIGHT
WHETILE WITWALL WRYNECK
DIRTBIRD KICKWALL PICARIAN
PICUCULE POPINJAY RAINBIRD
RAINFOWL WALLHICK
(LIKE A —) PICIFORM
WOODPILE STRAN STRAND
WOODRICK
WOOD ROBIN MIRO TOMTIT
WOODRUFF HAIROF MUGGET
MUGWET WOODROW HAIRHOOF
WOODS BOSK BUSH BOSQUE
WOODSMAN BUSHY SILVAN SYLVAN
BUSHMAN BUSHWACK
WOOD SORREL OCA COCKOO
HEARTS LUJULA OXALIS TREFOIL
ALLELUIA ALLELUJA SHAMROCK
STABWORT
WOOD THRUSH MAYBIRD
WOODTURNER BODGER
WOODWIND OBOE FLUTE CORNET
BASSOON PIBGORN PICCOLO
CLARINET
WOODWORK CEILING
WOODWORKER JOINER TURNER
MILLMAN
WOODWORM GRIBBLE
WOODY WITHY FRITHY STICKY
SYLVAN XYLOID LIGNOSE LIGNEOUS
WOOER BEAU LOVER WOWER
SUITOR COURTER WOOSTER
COURTIER PARAMOUR
WOOF WEFT WOUGH FILLING
TEXTURE
WOOING SUIT WOHLAC
WOOL OO COT DAG HOG VOL WOW
BEAT BLUE FRIB PULU ROCK FADGE
LAINE MUNGO STUFF TIPPY ALPACA
ARGALI BOTANY BREECH FLEECE
GREASE JACKET JERSEY KERSEY
LUSTER SLIVER WETHER COMBING
HASLOCK KASHMIR MORLING
STUBBLE WIGGING CASHMERE
CLOTHING COMEBACK MORTLING
PICKLOCK TOMENTUM
(— AS IT COMES FROM SHEEP)
GREASE

(— FROM DEAD SHEEP) MORLING MORTLING
(— FROM LEOMINSTER) ORE
(— ON SHEEP'S LEG) GARE BREECH
(— ON SHEEP'S THROAT) HASLOCK
(— WEIGHT) TOD
(COARSE —) ABB SHAG BRAID COWTAIL
(COTTON —) CADDIS CADDICE
(DUNGY BIT OF —) FRIB
(FINE GRADE OF —) PICKLOCK SPINNERS
(GREASY —) TIPPY
(INFERIOR GRADE OF —) HEAD
(KNOT OF —) NOIL
(LAMB'S —) WASSAIL
(LOCK OF —) FLOCK STAPLE
(LONG —) BLUE
(LOW GRADE OF —) LIVERY
(MATTED —) DAG SHAG
(PULLED —) SLIPE
(RECLAIMED —) MUNGO SHODDY
(REFUSE —) COT COTT FLOCK PINION
(ROLL OF —) CARDING
(RUSSIAN —) DONSKY
(SMALL PIECE OF —) TATE
(SPUN —) YARN
(WOUND —) TREND
WOOLCLOTH HODDEN
WOOLEN (ALSO SEE FABRIC) CADDIS CAMLET SUCLAT CADDICE PASHMINA
(PL.) LAINAGE
WOOL FAT LANOLIN
WOOLLY SHEEP LANATE LANOSE COTTONY FLOCCOSE PERONATE
WOOLLY BEAR WOUBIT
WOOLLY CROTON HOGWORT
WOOZY SICK DRUNK TIGHT VAGUE BLURRY WOOLLY
WORD GIG MOT EZEL GULE HAIT NEWS RAFF TERM VERB WHID WHUD ADNEX CHEEP COUCH DERRY DILLY FITCH GLOSS HAPAX HOKEY HYNDE LEMMA MAXIM ORDER PAROL RHEMA RUMOR SPELL ACCENT ADVERB AVOWAL BREATH ETYMON KIBBER LATIVE ONEYER PAROLE PLEDGE QUATCH REMARK REPORT SAYING ACCOUNT ADJUNCT BICCHED COMMAND COMMENT DICTION DUCDAME GENTILE GITTITH HOMONYM INCIPIT MESSAGE PALABRA PRAYFUL PRENZIE PROMISE PROVERB SYNONYM VOCABLE ACROSTIC CATCHCRY CHEVILLE COMPOUND ENCLITIC EQUIVOKE FRABJOUS FRINGENT IDEOGRAM ILLATIVE LATINISM SYLLABLE SYNTAGMA
(— AS CALL TO DUCK) DILLY
(— EXPRESSING COMMAND) JUSSIVE
(— FORMED FROM VOWELS) EUOUAE
(— FROM INITIAL LETTERS) ACRONYM
(— IN A PUZZLE) LIGHT

(— MISPRONOUNCED) BEARD
(— OF CONCLUSION) AMEN EXPLICIT
(— OF HONOR) PAROLE
(— OF MOUTH) FIDELITY
(— OF OPPOSITE MEANING) ANTONYM
(— OF SECONDARY RANK) ADNEX
(— OF UNCERTAIN MEANING) FRINGENT
(— OF UNKNOWN MEANING) KIBBER ONEYER PRAYFUL PRENZIE
(—S IN LOW TONE) ASIDE
(—S OF OPERA) LIBRETTO
(BIBLICAL — OF DOUBTFUL MEANING) EZEL FITCH GITTITH
(CALL —) JINGO
(CHARACTERIZING —) EPITHET
(CODE —) DOG FOX JIG ABLE EASY ECHO GOLF ITEM KING BRAVO DELTA HOTEL INDIA SUGAR GEORGE CHARLIE
(GATHERING —) SLOGAN
(HONEYED —S) MANNA
(HYPHENATED —) SOLID
(IDENTIFYING —) LABEL
(LAST — OF SPEECH) CUE
(MEANINGLESS —) DERRY
(METAPHORICAL —) KENNING
(MNEMONIC —) VIBGYOR
(NONSENSE —) RAFF RAFFE FRABJOUS
(ORIGINAL —) STEM
(PARTING —) ENVOI
(QUOTED —) CITATION
(REDUNDANT —) CHEVILLE
(ROOT —) ETYMON
(SIGNAL —) NAYWORD SECURITY
(SINGLE —) PHRASE
(SOURCE —) ETYMON
(THIEVES' SLANG —) TWAG WHID
(UNEXPLAINED —) DUCDAME
(UTTERED —S) SPEECH
(PL.) LIP TALK SPEECH LANGUAGE DISCOURSE
WORDBOOK LEXICON SPELLER LIBRETTO
WORDINESS VERBIAGE
WORDING LEGEND DICTION PHRASING
WORDLESS DUMB TACIT SILENT TACITURN
WORDPLAY EQUIVOKE
WORDY PROLIX VERBAL DIFFUSE VERBOSE WORDISH
WORK DO GO ACT FAG JOB DIKE DYKE FEND FRET NOTE OPUS TASK TEND TOIL GRAFT GRIND KARMA KNEAD LABOR PRESS YAKKA ARBEIT EFFECT HUSTLE OE1VRE REDUIT RESULT STRIVE THRIFT CALLING EXECUTE EXPLOIT FERMENT HEXAPLA LOUSTER MISSION OPERATE OPIFICE OPUSCLE OUVRAGE OVERAGE PICHERY PURSUIT TRAVAIL ADVOCACY AGENTING BUSINESS CAPONIER DEMILUNE DRUDGERY ENDEAVOR FUNCTION INDUSTRY

LABORAGE OPUSCULE PARERGON RETRENCH EXECUTION
(— ACROSS GRAIN) THURM
(— ACTIVELY) LOUSTER
(— AGAINST) KNIFE ATTACK COMBAT
(— AIMLESSLY) FIDDLE
(— AS REPORTER) HEEL
(— BEYOND ONE'S POWERS) OVERDO
(— CARELESSLY) RABBLE
(— DILIGENTLY) PEG STRIKE BELABOR
(— DONE) WRIHTE
(— FOR) LABOR SERVE BESWINK
(— FREE) START
(— HARD) TEW MOIL SLOG SWOT BULLOCK LEATHER
(— HIDES) BEAM
(— INSIDUOUSLY) WORM
(— INTO A MASS) KNEAD
(— LAND) FLOAT
(— LEISURELY) DAKER DAIKER
(— OCCASIONALLY) SMOOT SMOUT
(— OF ACKNOWLEDGED EXCELLENCE) CLASSIC
(— OF ART) GEM CRAFT ANTIQUE CAPRICE CREATION EPIPHANY EXERCISE
(— OF FICTION) SHOCKER
(— OF HISTORY) STORY
(— OF MENIAL KIND) DRUDGE
(— ONE'S WAY) WISE
(— OUT IN ADVANCE) FOREPLOT
(— OUT) FUDGE SOLVE DESIGN EVOLVE
(— OVER) DIGEST
(— PAID FOR IN ADVANCE) HORSE
(— PERSISTENTLY) HAMMER
(— RESEMBLING PATCHWORK) CENTO
(— SLIPSHOD) MULLOCK
(— STEADILY) PLY
(— TO EXHAUSTION) FAG
(— TO WINDWARD) CLAW
(— TOGETHER) COACT
(— TRIFLINGLY) PIDDLE
(— UNDER ANOTHER NAME) ALLONYM
(— UNFAIRLY OR CRUELLY) HORSE
(— UP) SPUNK
(— UPON) TILL LABOR
(— UPWARD) HIKE
(— VIGOROUSLY) BEND
(ALLEGORICAL —) BESTIARY
(CANVAS —) POINT
(CLEANING —) CHAR
(CLUMSY —) BOTCH
(COMPLETED —) TRAVAIL
(CONTRACT —) GYPPO
(DAMASCENE —) KOFTGARI
(DAY'S —) DARG DARGUE
(DECORATIVE —) FLOCKING
(DIVINE —) THEURGY
(DULL —) DRUDGERY
(EMBOSSED —) CELATURE
(FRAUDULENT —) JERRY
(HAND —) CAMAY
(HARD —) TEW MOIL MUCK SWOT

TWIG YERK SWEAT EFFORT
LEATHER SLAVERY SLOGGING
(JOINER —) FINISH
(LITERARY —) STUDY CHASER
SEQUEL SERIAL CLASSIC DIPTYCH
(LURID —) BLOOD
(MANUAL —) FATIGUE
(METAL —) NIELLO
(MOSAIC —) EMBLEM
(ORNAMENTAL —) BEADWORK
FILIGREE LEAFWORK
(PIECE OF —) JOB
(REFERENCE —) BIBLE SOURCE
(SACRED —) HIERURGY
(SCHOLASTIC —) SUMMA
(SKILLED MECHANICAL —) SLOJD
SLOYD
(SOCIAL —) ALMONING
(WOMAN'S —) DISTAFF
(PL.) CANON PLANT STODGE
FACTORY BUSINESS
WORKABLE YOUNG PLIANT
FEASIBLE
(EASILY —) SWEET
WORKADAY HUMDRUM PROSAIC
ORDINARY
WORKBASKET CABA
WORKBENCH SIEGE DONKEY
TEMPLATE
WORKED INWROUGHT
(— OUT) DEAD
(— UP) ANGRY EXCITED
WORKER (ALSO SEE WORKMAN AND
LABORER) AGER CARL DOER HAND
HIND ICER SCAB AXMAN BOXER
BUTTY DEMAS DRIER EDGER ENDER
FILER FIRER FIXER FLYER FOXER
GLUER GORER HOLER INKER JERRY
LINER LURER MAXIM MINIM NURSE
TAPER TOWER ASHMAN BACKER
BAILER BALLER BANDER BEADER
BENDER BINDER BINMAN BLADER
BLOWER BOILER BONDER BOOKER
BOSHER BRACER BUFFER BUMPER
BURNER BURRER CAPPER CARMAN
CASTER CASUAL CHASER COMBER
COOKER DAYMAN DIPPER DOCKER
DOGGER DOTTER DUMPER ETCHER
FACTOR FAGGER FANMAN FASHER
FEEDER FELLER FILLER FITTER
FLAKER FLAMER FLUTER FLUXER
FOILER FOLDER FORCER FORMER
FRAMER GASSER GOFFER GRADER
GUMMER GUTTER HASHER HEADER
HEELER HELPER HEMMER HOLDER
HOOKER HOOPER HOPPER HUNKIE
INKMAN JOGGER JOINER LEAFER
LEASER LEGGER NOILER PUGGER
READER REEDER SCORER SEAMAN
SEAMER SHAKER SKIVER SOLDER
SLICER SLIDER SLOPER STAVER
STAYER TOILER TOPPER BUILDER
CREATOR EMPLOYE FIELDER
LABORER
(— IN LEATHER) BEAMER CHUMAR
JACKER BLACKER CHUCKLER
(— IN METALS) SMITH FLAPPER
(ADDITIONAL —) EXTRA
(AGRICULTURAL —) ARKIE KISAN

(AIRCRAFT —) BOOTMAN
(ANT —) MAXIM ERGATES REPLETE
(ASBESTOS —) COBBER
(AUTO —) DISKER
(BAKERY —) BRAKER COOLER
DIVIDER BENCHMAN SPREADER
(BLUE-COLLAR —) STIFF
(BREWERY —) HOPPER STEEPER
STILLMAN
(BRICK —) DAUBER CROWDER
(CANNERY —) SLIMER SCALDER
SHEDMAN
(CLOCK —) STAKER
(COAL —) SUMPER GEORDIE
SPRAGGER
(DOCK —) BUNGS HOLDMAN
SHENANGO
(DOMESTIC —) HELP
(FELLOW —) CONFRERE
(FOUNDRY —) FLOGGER SNAGGER
(GARMENT —) FACER SLEEVER
ASSORTER INSEAMER
(GUN —) BLUER
(HARD —) SLOGGER
(HAT —) CURLER BRIMMER
(HIDE —) HEFTER COLORER
(HOSPITAL —) ALMONER
(HOTEL —) SCRUB
(ICEHOUSE —) AIRMAN
(JEWELRY —) ARBORER
(LOGGING —) SNIPER SKIDDER
(MATTRESS —) BEATER
(MIGRATORY —) HOBO
(MILL —) BILLER SPOUTER
(MINE —) BYEMAN FOOTER GOPHER
LANDER DROPPER FACEMAN
SLEDGER SWAMPER DRIFTMAN
(ORCHARD —) SMUDGER
(PACKINGHOUSE —) COOK
(PAPERMILL —) SIZER SIZEMAN
(PIANO —) BELLYMAN
(PLODDING —) GRUBBER
(POTTERY —) CASER BATTER
BEDDER FETTLER JOLLIER JUSTLER
(PRINTING —) FLY FLYBOY
(PUERTO RICAN —) GIBARO JIBARO
(QUARRY —) BREAKER
(RAILROAD —) JERRY HERDER
BRAKEMAN
(SAWMILL —) BOLTER SETTER
BOATMAN DECKMAN CHAINMAN
(SHOE —) CASER FOXER ARCHER
FUDGER HEELER CHALKER
BOTTOMER
(SKILLED —) ARTISTE
(SLAUGHTERHOUSE —) FATTER
SHOVER SINGER SLIMER CHEEKER
CHOPPER KNOCKER LIMEMAN
SCALPER SCRIBER STICKER
SNATCHER
(TANNERY —) GATER STONER
CROPPER CURRIER DELIMER
BEAMSMAN SEASONER
(TEXTILE —) DOFFER DOUPER
DRAWER GIGGER LAPPER LEASER
SINGER CREELER DOUBLER
JACKMAN KETTLER SKEINER
SPINNER SHUTTLER SOFTENER
SPLITTER TEASELER

(THEATER —) FLYMAN STAGEMAN
(TOBACCO —) BULKER SIFTER
STEMMER SCRAPMAN SPRIGGER
STICKMAN STRIPPER
(UNSKILLED —) HELPER DILUTEE
GREENER
(USELESS —) TOOL
(WHITE-COLLAR —) EFFENDI
(YARN —) SOURER CHAINER
(PL.) LABOR
WORKHORSE AVER AIVER TRESTLE
SAWHORSE
WORKHOUSE UNION FACTORY
WORKSHOP
WORKING PLAY GOING OPENCUT
FUNCTION LABORAGE OPENCAST
OPENWORK OPERATIC
(— ALONE) HATTING
(— HARD) HOPPING
(— OF MINE) GWAG CROSSCUT
(— ON) PRACTICE
(MINE —S) SPLIT
WORKMAN (ALSO SEE WORKER AND
LABORER) BOSS HAND MATE ROTO
CAGER CONER EXTRA FINER FLINT
FLUER FROCK LAYER MAJOR MIXER
POLER TONER TRIER TUBER
BLOUSE BOOMER BOWLER BUCKER
BUMMER COATER DIPPER DRIVER
FORKER GAGGER HANGER LASTER
LATHER MASTER NIPPER OILMAN
PUFFER RUNNER SAMMER SCORER
SHAKER SKIVER SLICER SLIDER
SOAKER SPIKER STAGER STAVER
TAPPER TARRER TEEMER TILTER
TIPMAN TIPPER TOPMAN WARMER
WASHER WETTER WRIGHT ARTISAN
DRUMMER HOTSHOT LUDDITE
SHOPMAN
(CHIEF —) BOSS
(CLUMSY —) BUNGLER
(FELLOW —) BULLY BUTTY
(PROFICIENT —) DEACON
(UNSKILLFUL —) BUTCHER
(PL.) VOLK
WORKMANLIKE DEFT ADEPT
SKILLFUL
WORKMANSHIP HAND FABRIC
OVERAGE ARTISANRY
WORKROOM DEN STUDY ATELIER
WORKS HACIENDA
(— OF CLOCK) WATCH
(SALT —) SALINA
WORKSHOP LAB SHED SHOP FORGE
LODGE SMITHY ATELIER BOTTEGA
HOSPITAL OFFICINA PLUMBERY
SKINNERY
WORKTABLE BENCH
WORLD ORB LOKA VALE WARD
EARTH WADRU WARDE CAREER
PUBLIC KINGDOM MONDIAL
CREATION CREATURE UNIVERSE
(— OF BOXING) FISTIANA
(— OF DARKNESS) SHEOL
(— OF DOGS) DOGDOM
(— OF FASHION) STYLEDOM
SWELLDOM
(— OF GODS) DEVALOKA
(— OF THE DEAD) DEEP

(— **OF WOMEN**) FEMINIE
(**ACADEMIC** —) CAMPUS
(**EXTERNAL** —) NONEGO
(**LOWER** —) ORCUS
(**PRIVATE** —) AUTOCOSM
(**THE** —) FOLD
(**TWO-DIMENSIONAL** —) FLATLAND
WORLDLING DIVES
WORLDLY LAY WARLY CARNAL
EARTHY MUNDAL EARTHLY FLESHLY
MUNDANE PROFANE SECULAR
SENSUAL TERRENE
(**NOT** —) INTERIOR
WORLD-WEARY BLASE
WORLDWIDE GLOBAL ECUMENIC
GLOBULAR PLANETAL
WORLD-WISE KNOWING
WORM BOB EEL ESS LOA MAD LURG
NAIS NEMA ARTER CADEW FLUKE
LYTTA PIPER SCREW SNAKE
DRAGON NEREID NEREIS PALMER
PALOLO SHAMIR SYLLID SYLLIS
TEREDO VERMIS WRETCH ANNELID
ASCARID CARBORA ENOPLAN
SABELLA SAGITTA SERPENT
SERPULA SETARID SHUFFLE SPIONID
TAGTAIL TRICLAD WRIGGLE
BRANDLIN CEPHALOB CERCARIA
CHETAPOD CHETOPOD GILTTAIL
HELMINTH LEODICID MEASURER
POLYCLAD STRONGYL TRICHINA
VERMICLE TOOTHACHE
(— **USED FOR BAIT**) TAGTAIL
(**BLOODSUCKING** —) LEECH
(**CADDIS** —) CADEW PIPER CADBAIT
(**FLUKE** —) PLAICE
(**MEASURING** —) LOOPER
(**MUD** —) IPO LOA
(**SHIP** —) BROMA COBRA
(**PL.**) APODA ENTOZOA
WORM-EATEN PITTED DECAYED
VERMOULU WERMETHE
WORMER JAG
WORMHOLE PIQURE
WORMLIKE VERMIAN
WORMSEED AMBROSIA
WORMWOOD MOXA ABSINTH
CUDWEED COMPOSIT MINGWORT
WORMY EARTHY
WORN SEAR SERE USED PASSE
TRITE MAGGED MIZPAH SHABBY
CONTRITE
(— **NEXT TO SKIN**) INTIMATE
(— **OUT**) SHOT BANAL JADED SEELY
SPENT STALE STANK BEATEN
BEDRID BLEARY EFFETE SCREWY
SHABBY CRIPPLE FORWORN
DECREPID FOUGHTEN HARASSED
OBSOLETE STRICKEN
(— **SMOOTH**) BEATEN
WORRICOW DEVIL BUGABOO
BUGBEAR HOBGOBLIN
WORRIED TOEY UNEASY ANXIOUS
FRETTED STREAKED
WORRIT VEX WORRY DISTRESS
WORRY DOG HOE HOW HOX LUG
NAG RUX TEW VEX BAIT BITE CARE
CARK FAZE FIKE FRAB FRET FUSS
HARE MOIL STEW ANNOY CHEVY

CHOKE FEEZE GALLY HARRY HURRY
LURRY PHASE SCALD SHAKE TEASE
TOUSE TOWSE BOTHER CADDLE
COTTER CUMBER FERRET FIDGET
GALLOW HARASS HATTER HECTOR
INFEST MOIDER PESTER PLAGUE
POTHER ANXIETY CHAGRIN
HATCHEL TROUBLE TURMOIL
WHERRET FASHERIE STRANGLE
WORRYING ANXIOUS
WORSE VER WAR SEAMY
WORSEN DESCEND
WORSHIP GOD CULT HERY RANK
ADORE DULIA HONOR NAMAZ
WURTH YAJNA CREDIT PRAISE
REPUTE REVERE BAALISM ELOHISM
ICONISM IDOLISM IDOLIZE IMAGERY
OBSERVE BLESSING HIERURGY
VENERATE
(— **OF SHAKESPEARE**) BARDOLATRY
(**FORM OF** —) RITUAL
(**HIGHEST KIND OF** —) LATRIA
(**INFERIOR KIND OF** —) DULIA
(**SERPENT** —) OPHISM
(**STAR** —) SABAISM
WORSHIPER ISIAC BHAKTA PRAISER
IDOLATER
(— **OF STARS**) AKKUM SABIAN
(**FIRE** —) PARSI GHEBER GUEBER
PARSEE
(**SERPENT** —) SETHIAN SETHITE
WORSHIPFUL GOOD PROUD
NOTABLE
WORST ACE GET BEST LAST OUTDO
SHEND WREST DEFEAT
WORSTED GARN JERRY SERGE
VESSES WHIPCORD
WORT GAIL GYLE SWAT PLANT
LENGTH TUTSAN FILLING KRAUSEN
POTHERB
(**FERMENTED** —) FEED WASH
(**UNFERMENTED** —) GROUT
WORTH FECK MEED CARAT MERIT
PRICE VALOR VALUE BECOME
BOUNTY DESERT ESTEEM REGARD
RICHES VALENT VIRTUE WEALTH
DIGNITY PRETIUM VALIANT WORSHIP
SPLENDOR TREASURE VALIDITY
VALLIDOM
(**NET** —) CAPITAL
WORTHINESS DESERT WORSHIP
WORTHLESS BAD LOW WAF BAFF
BALD BARE BASE EVIL IDLE LEWD
RACA SLIM VAIN VILE WAFF BLANK
BLOWN DUSTY FLASH FOUTY LOSEL
PUTID SLINK SORRY STRAW WASHY
CHAFFY CHEESY CRUMMY DRAFFY
DRASTY DROSSY HOLLOW LIMMER
LITHER LUTHER NAUGHT PALTRY
TRASHY WOODEN BAGGAGE
FUSTIAN NAUGHTY PIPERLY
RAFFISH RUBBISH SCABBED SHILPIT
USELESS FECKLESS HARLOTRY
NUGATORY PRECIOUS RASCALLY
RUBBISHY TRUMPERY VAGABOND
WANWORDY WRETCHED
(— **THING**) AMBSACE
WORTHLESSNESS BELIAL UNTHRIFT
WORTHWHILE TANTI

WORTHY BIG DEAR FAIR GOOD
HOLY TIDY AUGHT CANNY DIGNE
EXALT HONOR JELLY NOBLE PIOUS
GENTLE CONDIGN GRADELY
PAREGAL THRIFTY ELIGIBLE
VALUABLE WAUREGAN
(— **OF BELIEF**) CREDIBLE
(— **OF DEVOTION**) HOLY
(— **OF PRAISE**) LAUDABLE
WOULD WAD WID WANT WISH
COULD SHOULD
(— **NOT**) NOLD WADNA WADDENT
(**I** —) CHUD CHOLD
WOUND ARR CUT HEW WIN BITE
CALK CLAW DUNT FAKE FOIN GALL
GORE HARM HURT MAIM PAIN PINK
RASE RAZE RIST SCAR SKAG SORE
STAB TEAR VULN WING BLESS
BROKE GANCH GRIEF KNIFE KNOCK
SHOOT STICK STING SUGAT THIRL
TOUCH BREACH BRUISE CREASE
ENTAME GRIEVE HARROW INJURE
LAUNCH LESION MARTYR OFFEND
PIERCE PLAGUE SCOTCH TRAUMA
AFFLICT ATTAINT BLIGHTY DIACOPE
GUNSHOT SCRATCH DISTRESS
FLANKARD FLEABITE INCISION
LACERATE SPURGALL
(— **FROM BOAR'S TUSK**) GANCH
GAUNCH
(— **FROM BULL'S HORN**) CORNADA
(— **FROM RUBBING**) GALL
(— **IN DEER'S SIDE**) FLANKARD
(— **MADE BY THRUST**) FOIN
(— **ON FOOT**) FIKE
(— **WITH POINTED WEAPON**) STAB
SWORD
(**DEEP** —) DIACOPE
(**MINUTE** —) PRICK
(**TRIFLING** —) FLEABITE
(**PL.**) NOUNS
WOUNDED HURT WUND VULNED
WINGED VULNOSE STRICKEN
WOUNDWORT BETONY ALLHEAL
HERCULES
WOU-WOU WAWA WAWAH CAMPER
GIBBON
WOVEN BROCHE BROWDEN
DAMASSE
(— **FULL WIDTH**) SEAMLESS
(— **WIDE**) BROAD
(— **WITH RIB**) SOLEIL
WOW HIT MEW BARK HOWL RAVE
WAIL WHINE SUCCESS
WRACK KELP RACK RUIN CUTWEED
DESTROY DOWNFALL EELGRASS
WRECKAGE
WRAITH WAFT FETCH GHOST SPOOK
DOUBLE SHADOW SWARTH
SPECTRE
WRANGLE RAG YED CAMP MOIL
SPAR TIFT ARGLE ARGUE BRAWL
CHIDE DAFER FLITE JOWER PLEAD
STRUT ARGUFY BICKER CAFFLE
CAMPLE CANGLE DACKER FRAPLE
FRATCH HAGGLE HASSLE JANGLE
RAGGLE THREAP BRABBLE
BRANGLE DISPUTE PICKEER

QUARREL SCRAFFLE SQUABBLE
TIRRWIRR
WRANGLER CAMPER COWBOY
GRATER HAFTER WRAGER DEBATER
DEFENDER OPPONENT
WRANGLING JANGLE
WRAP HAP LAP LOT WAP BIND FURL
ROLL WHIP CLASP CLOAK LAMBA
MANTA NUBIA SERVE TWINE WOOLD
AFGHAN BURLAP CLOTHE COCOON
COOLER DOLMAN EMBALE MOIDER
MUFFLE PATTOO SWATHE WRIXLE
ENVELOP INVOLVE SWADDLE
UMBELAP BARRACAN
(— **DEAD BODY**) CERE
(— **ONESELF**) HUDDLE
(— **UP HEAD**) MOB MOP MOBLE
(— **UP**) HAP MAIL ENROL IMPLY
(— **WIRE AROUND FISHING LINE**)
GANGE
(— **WITH BANDAGE**) SWATHE
(PL.) SECRECY RESTRAINT
WRAPPER APRON COVER MOTTO
PILCH SHAWL SMOCK COUPON
FARDEL JACKET ENVELOP OVERALL
SARPLER COVERING MAHARMAH
WOOLPACK
(— **FOR BOOK**) JACKET
(— **FOR CUTLET**) PAPILLOTE
(— **WORN IN EGYPT**) GALABIA
GALABEAH
WRAPPING WAP PACK GELILAH
LAPPING COVERING MANTLING
(— **FOR DEAD**) CEREMENT
(— **OF HEBREW SCROLL**) GELILAH
(— **OF ROPE**) SERVICE
WRASSE COOK BALLAN CONNER
CUNNER LABRID HOGFISH PIGFISH
SEAWIFE CORKWING DONCELLA
JANIZARY LADYFISH SENORITA
WRATH IRE FURY GRIM ANGER
WROTH FELONY PASSION VIOLENCE
WRATHFUL IRY EVIL HIGH ANGRY
IRATE WROTH IREFUL RAGING
FURIOUS JEALOUS CHOLERIC
WREAK CAUSE AVENGE EXPEND
GRATIFY INDULGE INFLICT REVENGE
(— **DESTRUCTION**) ESTREPE
WREATH LEI ORLE PLAY CROWN
GREEN LAURE LORRE OLIVE TORSE
WHORL WRASE ANADEM CRANTS
CREASE LAUREL POTONG TORTIL
CHAPLET CORONET CROWNAL
DOLPHIN FESTOON GARLAND
WRINKLE KELYPHYTE
(**SPIRAL** —) VOLUTION
WREATHE BIND WIND CRISP TWINE
TWIST INTORT WRITHE CONTORT
ENTWINE INTWIST INVOLVE
WREATHED SPIRY TORTIVE
WRITHED INTORTED TORTILLE
WRECK HULK RUIN BLAST CRACK
SHOOT SMASH WRACK DESPOIL
DESTROY FOUNDER GODSEND
SHATTER TORPEDO DEMOLISH
SABOTAGE SHAMBLES
(**HUMAN** —) DERELICT
WRECKAGE FINDAL FLOTSAM
GODSEND WAVESON SHAMBLES

WRECKED NOUGHT
WREN GIRL STAG TOPE CUTTY
JENNY KITTY PEGGY SALLY STAID
TYDIE SCUTTY TIDIFE TIDLEY TINTIE
TOMTIT WRANNY BLUECAP
MALURINE WRANNOCK
WRENCH KEY PIN RUG PULL RACK
RICK RUGG TEAR YERK CRICK
CRINK FORCE THRAW THROW TWIST
WRAMP WREST BEDKEY SPRAIN
STRAIN TWEEZE DISTORT SPANNER
SPANULE SQUINCH TORTURE
TWISTLE
WREST REAR REND EXACT FORCE
TWIST ARREST EXTORT WRENCH
WRITHE ABSTORT WIREDRAW
(— **AWAY**) STRIP DESPOIL
WRESTLE PRAY RASSLE SQUIRM
TUSSLE WRAXLE WRITHE GRAPPLE
SCUFFLE THRIMBLE THRUMBLE
WRESTLER MATMAN WELTER
CLICKER MATSTER GRAPPLER
WRESTLING SUMO PALESTRA
WRAXLING
(— **TECHNIQUE**) GLIMA
WRETCH DOG MIX FILE WARY MISER
SLAVE THING BUGGER PERSON
SQUALL BRETHEL CAITIFF
CAMOOCH CHINCHE GLUTTON
HILDING SCROYLE CREATURE
MESCHANT POLTROON RECREANT
SCULLION
WRETCHED EVIL FOUL MEAN
DAWNY DEENY GAUNT WISHT
WOFUL YEMER CAITIF DISMAL
MEAGER PALTRY SHABBY SICKLY
UNLEAD UNLEDE WOEFUL ABYSMAL
BENEATH FORLORN OUTWORN
SQUALID UNSEELY MESCHANT
(— **PERSON OR ANIMAL**) MISERY
WRIGGLE REG RIG FRIG WIND WRIG
SLIDE WRELE WRING SQUIRM
WAMBLE WANGLE WARPLE WIDDLE
WIMPLE WINTLE WRITHE EYEBROW
SNIGGLE TWIDDLE TWINGLE
WRABILL WRESTLE SCRIGGLE
SQUIGGLE
WRIGGLING EELY SCRIGGLE
SQUIGGLY
WRIGGLY SNAKY SNAKISH
SQUIRMING
WRING RACK DRAIN EXACT SCREW
TWIST WREST EXTORT OPPRESS
SQUEEZE TORMENT TORTURE
(— **THE NECK**) SCRAG
WRINGER RUNG WRUNG SQUEEZER
WRINKLE RUT DRAW FOLD FURL
HINT KNIT LIRK RUCK RUGA SEAM
BREAK CRIMP CRISP DELVE FAULT
FRILL REEVE RIVEL SNIRL BUCKLE
COCKLE CRAVAT CREASE FURROW
METHOD PUCKER RIMPLE RUMPLE
RUNKLE SCRIMP WREATH BLEMISH
CRINKLE CRUMPLE CRUNKLE
FROUNCE FRUMPLE CONTRACT
IRRUGATE RUGOSITY
(— **OF FLESH**) CRAVAT
WRINKLED PURFLY RUGATE
RUGGED RUGOSE RUGOUS SEAMED

COCKLED SAVOYED CRUMPLED
FURROWED PUCKERED WRIZZLED
WRINKLING KNIT KNOT FROWN
WRIST CARPUS SHACKLE
WRISTER MUFFETEE
WRISTLET WRISTER MUFFETEE
WRISTWATCH BAGUET BAGUETTE
WRIT AIEL CAPE MISE PONE TOLT
ALIAS BREVE BRIEF ERROR RECTO
UTRUM BRIEVE CAPIAS ELEGIT
EXTENT VENIRE ACCOUNT DEDIMUS
DETINUE EXIGENT LATITAT PLURIES
PRECEPT PROCESS SUMMONS
WARRANT CESSAVIT COSINAGE
DETAINER DOCUMENT FORMEDON
MANDAMUS MITTIMUS NOVERINT
PRAECIPE QUOMINUS REPLEVIN
SUBPOENA TESTATUM WARRANTY
(— **FOR SUMMONING EXTRA
JURORS**) TALES
WRITE INK PEN BACK BOOK DITE
DRAW READ CLERK DRAFT STYLE
AUTHOR ENFACE INDITE SCRIBE
SCRIVE ADDRESS COMPILE
COMPOSE DICTATE EMPAPER
EXARATE BIOGRAPH INSCRIBE
(— **ADDRESS**) BACK
(— **BRIEFLY**) JOT
(— **CARELESSLY**) DASH SCRAWL
SCRIBBLE
(— **DOWN**) SIGN BREVE DENOTE
RECORD AMORTIZE DESCRIBE
(— **FURTHER**) ADD
(— **HASTILY**) SCRATCH SCRIBBLE
SQUIGGLE
(— **IN A LARGE HAND**) ENGROSS
(— **IN LARGE CHARACTERS**) TEXT
(— **ON FRONT OF BILL**) ENFACE
(— **PASTORAL POEMS**) PHILLIS
(— **WHAT IS NOT TRUE**) FABLE
WRITER PEN BARD HACK PUFF
ALVAR GHOST ODIST SQUIB
AUTHOR FATHER GLOZER HEROIC
LAWYER LETTER MUNSHI NOTARY
PENMAN PRABHU PROSER PURVOE
SCRIBE TRAGIC YEOMAN ADAPTER
ADSMITH ANALYST DIARIST ELOHIST
ESSAYER GLOSSER GNOMIST
HYMNIST IAMBIST JUVENAL LAUDIST
MUNCHEE PENSTER PROPHET
PROSAIC REVUIST SCRIVER STYLIST
SUMMIST TEXTMAN AUGUSTAN
BLURBIST COMEDIAN COMPOSER
DECADENT DECADIST DIDACTIC
EMBOSSER EPISTLER ESSAYIST
FABLEIST FABULIST GROMATIC
HUMORIST IDYLLIST MONODIST
MOONSHEE NOVELIST PARODIST
PENWOMAN PREFACER PRESSMAN
PROSAIST PROSEMAN PSALMIST
REVIEWER SCRIPTER VERSEMAN
(— **OF BURLESQUE**) GABBER
(**FREE-LANCE** —) CREEPER
(**HACK** —) PENSTER
(**INCOMPETENT** —) BOTCHER
WRITHE WRY WIND THROW TWIRL
TWIST WRING SQUIRM TERVEE
WAMBLE WRABBE WRENCH
AGONIZE WRESTLE WRIGGLE

WRINGLE CONVOLVE
WRITHING EELY WRING WRITHY
WRITING BOOK FAIT PAGE POEM
KANJI LIBEL CADJAN GOSSIP
LEGEND LETTER PAGINE SCRIPT
SCRITE SCRIVE UNCIAL ARTICLE
DIPLOMA ESCRIPT SCREEVE
APOCRYPH CONTRACT DOCUMENT
GRAVAMEN HARANGUE KAKEMONO
LETTRURE LIPOGRAM PAMPHLET
SCRIBING SONNETRY
(— **OF LITTLE VALUE**) STUFF
SCRIBBLE
(— **ON PAPER SCROLL**) MAKIMONO
(— **ON SILK**) KAKEMONO
(— **UNDER SEAL**) BOND
(**BITTER** —) DIATRIBE
(**CARELESS** —) SCRAWL
(**CRAMPED** —) NIGGLE
(**CURSIVE** —) JOINHAND
(**HUMOROUS** —**S**) FACETIAE
(**ILLUMINATED** —) FRACTUR
(**MUSICAL** —) GIMEL GYMEL
(**PRETENTIOUS** —) FUSTIAN
(**SACRED** —) ARANYAKA BRAHMANA
SCRIPTURE
(**SHORT** —) SCRIP
(**SYLLABIC** —) KANA
(**VAPID** —) WASH
(**VERBOSE** —) TOOTLE
(PL.) LEGENDA ARANYAKA
POSTHUMA
WRITING CASE STANDISH
WRITTEN KETIB KETHIB KTHIBH
GRAPHIC LITERAL

(— **ABOVE**) SS
(— **AFTER**) ADSCRIPT
(— **HASTILY**) STRAY
WROCLAW BRESLAU
WRONG BAD CAR ILL MIS OUT WET
AWRY HARM HURT SORE SOUR
TORT WITE AGATE AGLEE AGLEY
AMISS CRIME DUTCH FALSE GLEED
GRIEF MALUM UNFIT WATHE WOUGH
AGUILT ASTRAY BLOOEY FAULTY
INJURE INJURY NOUGHT OFFEND
SARAAD SINFUL UNTRUE WICKED
WONDER ABUSION DAMNIFY
DEFRAUD IMMORAL INJURIA
MISBEDE NAUGHTY UNRIGHT
VIOLATE AGGRIEVE COCKEYED
MISTAKEN PERVERSE UNLEEFUL
(**CIVIL** —) TORT
(**IMAGINARY** —) WINDMILL
WRONGDOER ACTOR SINNER
FAULTER MISDOER OFFENDER
WRONGDOING MISS CRIME FAULT
DEFAULT
WRONGHEADED WRY PERVERSE
WRONGFUL UNFAIR UNJUST
TORTIOUS TORTUOUS UNLAWFUL
WRONGLY AMISS BADLY FALSE
NOUGHT UNRICHT UNRIGHT
OVERWART
WROTH ANGRY IRATE IREFUL
WROUGHT BEATEN CARVEN
FORMED SHAPED VROCHT CREATED
HAMMERED
(**ELABORATELY** —) LABORED

WRY ASKEW AVERT TWIST WRING
WRONG WRITHE DEFLECT DISTORT
TWISTED WRITHEN SATURNINE
WRYNECK IYNX JYNX SLAB WEET
LOXIA PEABIRD WEETBIRD
WYCH ELM WITCH WITCHEN
WYLIECOAT WALYCOAT NIGHTGOWN
PETTICOAT
WYND HAW ALLEY CLOSE

WYOMING
CAPITAL: CHEYENNE
COUNTY: TETON UINTA GOSHEN
BIGHORN LARAMIE NIOBRARA
INDIAN: ARAPAHO
LAKE: JACKSON
MOUNTAIN: ELK CLOUD GANNET
HOBACK FREMONT ATLANTIC
SHERIDAN
MOUNTAIN RANGE: TETON
ABSARO BIGHORN LARAMIE
RATTLESNAKE
NICKNAME: EQUALITY
RIVER: GREEN SNAKE PLATTE
POWDER BIGHORN
STATE BIRD: MEADOWLARK
STATE FLOWER: PAINTBRUSH
STATE TREE: COTTONWOOD
TOWN: CODY LUSK CASPER
BUFFALO LARAMIE RAWLINS
WORLAND GREYBULL
KEMMERER SHERIDAN
SUNDANCE

X EX XRAY ERROR MISTAKE
XANTHIC YELLOW
XANTHIPPE (HUSBAND OF —)
  SOCRATES
XANTHIPPUS (SON OF —) PERICLES
XEBEC SHIP CHEBEC CHEBECK
  SHABEQUE
XENIUM GIFT DAINTY DELICACY
XERES JEREZ SHERRY

XHOSA KAFIR KAFFIR
  (PL.) AMAKOSA AMAXOSA
XIPHISTERNUM XIFOID
XIPHOSURUS LIMULUS
X-RAY UROGRAM
XUREL SCAD SAUREL
XUTHUS (ADOPTED SON OF —) ION
  (BROTHER OF —) DORUS AEOLUS
  (FATHER OF —) HELLEN

(WIFE OF —) CREUSA
XYLEM HADROM HADROME XYLOGEN
XYLOID WOODY LIGNEOUS
XYLOPHONE REGAL SARON BALAFO
  GAMBANG GAMELAN MARIMBA
  BALAPHON GAMELANG GIGELIRA
  STICCADO
XYSTUS WALK XYST PORTICO
  TERRACE

Y WY YA WYE YOD YOKE YANKEE
(— **CONNECTION**) SIAMESE
(— **COORDINATE**) SINE
YABBER TALK JABBER LANGUAGE
YABBY CRAWLIE
YACARE CAIMAN CAYMAN JACARE
YACHT SAIL SCOW BRUTE YATCH
DINGHY SONDER YEAGHE KEELBOAT
YAFF YAP BARK YELP
YAFFLE ARMFUL YAFFIL
YAHOO BRUTE CLOWN ROWDY
BUMPKIN
YAHWEH GOD JAVE JAHVAH
YAHWIST JEHOVIST
YAK GAG JOKE LAUGH BULBUL
SARLAK SARLYK YAMMER CHATTER
YAKALA JAGA
YAKKA WORK LABOR
YAKUT SAKHA
YAM HOI UBE UBI UVE JAMB LIMA
RAIL TUGUI IGNAME INAMIA INHAME
POTATO BONIATA
(**TARO** —) KOKO
YAM BEAN KAMAS JICAMA WAYAKA
SINCAMAS
YAMEN COURT YAMUN OFFICE
YAMEO LLAMEO
YAMMER CRY WAIL SCOLD WHINE
YEARN YOMER GRUMBLE WHIMPER
YAMP YAMPA SQUAWROOT
YANAN NOZI
YANG HONK GURJUN
YANK FLOG JERK SLAP HOICK
SNAKE BUFFET
YAP BARK YAWP YELP MOUTH
SCOLD WAFFLE BUMPKIN CHATTER
KYOODLE
YAPOK YAPOCK OPOSSUM OYAPOCK
YAQUI YAKI HIAQUI
YARD HAW YED CREW CROW DUMP
FOLD SKID SPAR TILT COURT
GARTH PATIO STICK CANCHA
HOPPET LOANIN CURTAIN GARSTON
KNACKERY OUTGARTH
(— **OF SAWMILL**) DUMP
(— **WHERE COWS ARE MILKED**)
LOANIN LOANING
(**1-16TH OF A** —) NAIL
(**1-3RD OF CUBIC** —) CARTLOAD
(**20** —**S**) SCORE
(**5 AND A HALF** —**S**) ROD
(**FINAL** —) FELL
(**GRASSY** —) GARSTON
(**PAVED** —) CAUSEY
(**POULTRY** —) BARTON
(**SAIL** —) RAE
YARD GRASS ELEUSINE MANGRASS
YARDLAND VERGE VIRGATE
YARDMASTER DINGER
YARDSTICK VERGE YAIRD METRIC
MEASURE METWAND METEWAND
STANDARD
YARE YAR AYRE YORE BRISK READY
LIVELY NIMBLE PROMPT
YARETA LLARETA
YARM WAIL NOISE OUTCRY SHRIEK
YARN ABB END FOX CORD GARN
GIMP PIRN SILK SLIP WEFT WHIP
DYNEL FLOSS GRAIN INKLE PITCH

ALASKA ANGORA BERLIN BROACH
CADDIS COTTON CREWEL CUFFER
DACRON ESTRON FLORET FRIEZE
MERINO MOTTLE PEELER RATINE
SAXONY SINGLE STRAND THREAD
VINYON WOOLEN ZEPHYR ACETATE
CADDICE FILLING GENAPPE INGRAIN
MELANGE RACKING SCHAPPE
VIGOGNE WORSTED ASBESTOS
BOURETTE CHENILLE FORTISAN
ROUNDING SPINNING VIGOREUX
WHEELING
(— **FOR WARP**) ABB
(— **FROM FLOSS SILK**) FLORET
(— **SIZE**) TYPP
(**BALL OF** —) CLEW CLUE
(**BITS OF ROPE** —) THRUMS
(**BUNDLE OF** —) PAD
(**CONICAL MASS OF** —) COP
(**ELASTIC** —) LASTEX
(**EXAGGERATED** —) STRETCHER
(**FINE SOFT** —) ZEPHYR KASHMIR
CASHMERE
(**LINEN** —) SPINEL
(**ROLL OF** —) PRICK CHEESE
(**ROPE** —**S**) SOOGEE
(**SMALL PIECE OF SPUN** —) RABAND
ROBBIN ROPEBAND
(**UNEVEN** —) BOUCLE
(**PL.**) FOX MENDINGS
YARRAN GIDYA MYALL GIDGEA
GIDGEE
YARROW ALLHEAL CAMMOCK
MAUDLIN MILFOIL
YASHIRO SHA
YASHMAK VEIL ASMACK YAKMAK
YATAGHAN SABER ATAGHAN
SIMITAR
YATTER CHATTER PRATTLE
YAUD MARE YADE
YAUPON ASSI HOLLY YUPON CASINA
CASSINE
YAUTIA COCO TARO TANIA COCKER
TANIER MALANGA
YAW GAPE YAWN LURCH SHEER
BROACH SWERVE
YAWL HOWL DANDY MIZZEN SCREAM
SCHOKKER
YAWN GAP GALP GANE GANT GAPE
YANE ABYSM CHAUM CAVITY
TEDIUM DULLNESS
YAWNING HIANT CHASMA GAPING
OSCITANT
YAWP BAWL GAPE STARE SQUAWK
YAMMER COMPLAIN
YAWS TUBBA TUBBOE
YAWWEED RHUBARB
YAYA COPA
YEA YA YES YOY YIGH TRULY
ASSENT REALLY VERILY
YEAN EAN LAMB
YEANLING KID LAMB EANLING
YEAR EAR SUN AYRE HAAB TIME
ANNUS VAGUE WINTER ZODIAC
TOWMOND TZOLKIN BIRTHDAY
(— **OF EMANCIPATION**) JUBILEE
(**ACADEMIC** —) SESSION
(**IN THIS** —) HA
(**LAST** —) FERNYEAR

(**MANY** —**S**) AGE
(**MAYAN** —) TUN HAAB
(**SABBATICAL** —) JUBILE JUBILEE
(**PL.**) SEASONS
YEARBOOK ANNUAL SERIAL
ANNUARY
YEARLING COLT HORNOTINE
YEARLY ANNUAL SOLEMN
YEARN HO YEN ACHE BURN EARN
GAPE HONE IRNE LONG PANT PINE
SIGH CRAVE GREEN GRIEN ASPIRE
CURDLE GRIEVE HANKER YAMMER
YEARNING EROS DESIRE HANKER
RENNET CRAVING EARNFUL
HOMESICK
YEAST BEE EST BARM BEES EAST
KOJI SOTS FROTH SPUME LEAVEN
NEWING RISING SIZING TORULA
FERMENT SIZZING EMPTINGS
(**FILM** —) FLOR
YEASTY LIGHT FROTHY TRIVIAL
RESTLESS
YEGG ROBBER BURGLAR
YELL CRY CALL GOWL HOWL ROAR
YARM YAUP YOWL YOWT GOLLY
SHOUT TIGER BELLOW GOLLAR
HOLLER SCREAM YAMMER YELLOCH
SCRONACH
YELLOW (ALSO SEE COLOR) OR
GULL AMBER BLAKE BLOND FAVEL
FLAVE JAUNE PALEW SHELL YELWE
ALMOND BANANA FLAVID MELINE
MIMOSA NUGGET OXGALL BISCUIT
JASMINE JONQUIL LEGHORN
MEXICAN MUSTARD NANKEEN
OATMEAL POPCORN SAFFRON
TILLEUL WHEATEN YUCATAN
AUREOLIN GENERALL ICTEROID
LUMINOUS MARIGOLD ORPIMENT
PRIMROSE
(— **AS BUTTER**) BLAKE
(**BROWNISH** —) FULVID FULVOUS
(**GOLDEN** —) FLAVID
(**GREENISH** —) ACACIA
(**INDIAN** —) PURI PURREE
(**LEMON** —) GENERALL
YELLOW ALDER SAGEROSE
YELLOW BEDSTRAW CRUDWORT
CURDWORT FLEAWEED
YELLOW BUGLE IVA IVE IVY
YELLOW CLINTONIA DOGBERRY
YELLOW FOXTAIL STICKERS
YELLOW GENTIAN FELWORT
YELLOWHAMMER SKYT YITE
AMMER GOWDY SKITE GLADDY
GOLDIE VERDIN YORLIN FLICKER
GLADEYE YELDRIN YOLDRING
(— **STATE**) ALABAMA
YELLOW IRIS SEDGE LEVERS
DAGGERS
YELLOWISH SALLOW ICTERINE
SAFFRONY
(— **GREEN**) GLAUCOUS
(— **RED**) FALLOW
YELLOW JACKET VESPA VESPID
YELLOW JASMINE WOODBINE
YELLOWLEGS KILLCU TATLER
WINTER YELPER TATTLER
YELLOW MACKEREL CREVALLE

YELLOWNESS FLAVEDO

YELLOW POND LILY DUCK CLOTE
CLOTS NUPHAR

YELLOW PRICKLE RUBIA
YELLOW RATTLE RATEL
COCKSCOMB LOUSEWORT
YELLOW TOADFLAX RAMSTEAD
YELLOW WAGTAIL OATEAR
YELLOW WATER LILY KELP WOKAS
YELLOWWOOD FUSTIC FUSTOC
MANGWE VIRGILIA
YELP CRY YAP YIP BAFF BARK KIYI
WAFF YAFF YAUP YAWP BOAST
YAMPH AVOCET SQUEAL YAFFLE
YELLOW
YELPING CRY

YEMEN
ANCIENT KINGDOM: SABA SHEBA
CAPITAL: SANA SANAA
COIN: RIYAL
MUSLIM SECT: SHIA SUNNI
PEOPLE: ZAIDI SHAFAI
PORT: MOKA MOCHA
REGION: TIHAMA
RULER: IMAM
TOWN: MOKA DAMAR MOCHA
TAIZZ HODEIDA

YEN EYES LONG URGE YEARN
DESIRE SUCKER LONGING
YEOMAN CHURL CLERK WRITER
GOODMAN GUIDMAN GRAYCOAT
RETAINER BEEFEATER
YERBA SANTA TARBUSH
YERK BEAT GOAD HURL JERK KICK
STAB YARK THUMP EXCITE THRASH
LASHING
YES AY DA IS JA OC SI YA AYE ISS
YAS YAW YEA YEP YIS YUH YUS
YEAH TRULY
YESTERDAY YESTER YESTREEN
(OF —) PRIDIAN
YET AND BUT YIT EVEN STILL
ALGATE HOWEER THOUGH FINALLY
HOWEVER HITHERTO
YETT GATE
YEUK EWK YUK ITCH YUCK ITCHING
YEW YO HEW UGH YOE YOW VIEW
TAXUS TOPIARY CHINWOOD
YEX YOLK
YIDDISH JEWISH
YIELD GO BOW CUT ILD PLY BEAR
BEND CAST CEDE CESS COME CROP
DRAG FOLD GIVE HEAR HELD LOUT
QUIT SELL VAIL WAGE AGREE
ALLOW AMAIN AVALE AWALE BRING
BUDGE CARRY CAUSE DEFER
GRANT HEALD HIELD LEAVE OFFER
SLAKE STOOP ACCEDE AFFORD
BOUNTY BUCKLE COMPLY CONFER
FOLLOW IMPART OUTPUT RELENT
RENDER RETURN SUBMIT SUPPLY
SWERVE UNGIVE UPGIVE ABANDON
ANALYZE CONCEDE DELIVER
FURNISH HARVEST KNUCKLE
OUTTURN PRODUCE PROVIDE
REDOUND RUCKSEY SUCCUMB

BEGRUDGE FRUITAGE OVERGIVE
UNDERLIE
(— FRUIT) ADDLE GRAIN
(— GRASS) GRAZE
(— OF FIELD) BURDEN
(— OF MINE) BONANZA
(— ON BOND) BASIS
(— TO TEMPTATION) FALL
(— TO) INDULGE
(— UP) LET FORLET FORLEIT
(— WELL) HIT BLEED
YIELDING ABLE MEEK NESH SOFT
TALL WAXY NAISH WAXEN BONAIR
FACILE FEEBLE FLABBY LIMBER
OUTPUT PLIANT QUAGGY SUPPLE
BEARING CESSION FINGENT FLACCID
DEDITION LADYLIKE RECREANT
(— IRREGULARLY) BUNCHY
(— OF HORSE) FLEXION
(— STAGE) SEAR
(— TO IMPULSES) ABANDON
YIN SHANG
YIRMILIK METALLIK
YODEL SONG JODEL WARBLE
REFRAIN
YODH IOD JOD
YOGA JOG
YOGI JOGI FAKIR FAKEER
YOKE BOW YOK BAIL CROW DRAG
FORK HOOP PAIR POKE SOLE
BANGY FURCA SHEBA SPANG
BANGHY COUPLE INSPAN DRAGBAR
HARNESS OPPRESS ADJUGATE
(— BAR) SKEY
(— TO HOLD DRILL) CROW
(— TO RAISE CANNON) BAIL
YOKEFELLOW MATE FELLOW
PARTNER YOKEMATE
YOKEL YOB BOOR CLUB FARMER
HAYSEED WAYBACK ABDERITE
CHAWBACON
YOKING BOUT CONTEST MUGGING
YOLDRING YOWLEY
YOLK CENTER YELLOW ESSENCE
LATEBRA VITELLUS
(HAVING A —) LECITHAL
YON YONDER THITHER BACKWARD
YONDER THAT THERE THOSE
THITHER
YORE PAST YARE YEARS
(OF —) OLDEN
YORKER TICE
YORKSHIREMAN TIKE TYKE
LEAROYD
YORUBA NAGO
YOU DU HE IT OW TA TU WE YA YO
ONE OWE SHE SIE YOW YUH THOU
YOUSE YOURSELF
YOUNG FRY JUV BIRD CALF DROP
BIRTH BROOD FETUS FRUIT GREEN
SMALL UNOLD JUNIOR KINDLE
JUVENAL IMMATURE YEANLING
YOUTHFUL
(— OF ANY ANIMAL) FRY BABY
CALF FOAL JOEY LAMB TOTO
(— OF BEAST) SLINK
(— OF BIRD) CHICK
(— OF CAMEL) COLT
(— OF DOG) WHELP

(— OF FISH) FRY
(— OF SEA TROOT) HERLING
(VERY —) SUCKING NEPHIONIC
SHIRTTAIL
YOUNGER KID LESS PUNEE JUNIOR
PUISNE OFFSPRING
YOUNGEST (— OF BROOD)
WALLYDRAG
YOUNGSTER KID BIRD COLT CHILD
YOUTH BUTTON SHAVER URCHIN
YONKER YOUNKER SPALPEEN
YOUNKER DUPE CHILD KNIGHT
NOVICE SQUIRE YUNKER
YOUR OR YO THY YAR YER OURE
OWRE YOURN
YOURSELF ITSELF HERSELF HIMSELF
ONESELF
YOUTH BOY BUD IMP LAD CHAP
PAGE BAHUR CHABO GROOM HYLAS
POULT PRIME SPRIG SWAIN WHELP
BOCHUR BURSCH EPHEBE HOYDEN
INFANT JUVENT KOUROS MASTER
SPRING SQUIRT YONKER CALLANT
EPHEBOS GOSSOON JUVENAL
PUBERTY SAPLING YOUDITH
YOUNGTH ENDYMION JUVENILE
SPRINGAL
(— WHO SERVES LIQUORS)
GANYMEDE
(GODDESS OF —) HEBE
(IMPUDENT —) SQUIRT
(NON-JEWISH —) SHEGETZ
(PERT —) PRINCOX
(RUDE —) HOYDEN
(RUSSIAN — ORGANIZATION)
KOMSOMOL
(SILLY —) CALF SLENDER
(WELLBORN —) CHILD
YOUTHFUL RATH FRESH GREEN
YOUNG BOYISH GOLDEN JUNIOR
MAIDEN NEANIC VIRGIN YOUTHY
LADDISH PUERILE YOUNGLY
IMMATURE JUVENILE SPRINGAL
VIGOROUS
YOUTHFULNESS JEUNESSE
YOWL GOWL HOWL WAIL YELL YELP
YUAN DOLLAR
YUAPIN YARURA
YUCCA LILY PITA YUCA DATIL IZOTE
PALMA JOSHUA LILIAL LILIUM
PALMITO SOAPWEED
YUGA KALI

YUGOSLAVIA
CAPITAL: BEOGRAD BELGRADE
COIN: PARA DINAR
GULF: KVARNER
LAKE: SCUTARI
MEASURE: RIF AKOV RALO DONUM
KHVAT LANAZ STOPA MOTYKA
PALAZE RALICO
MOUNTAIN: TRIGLAV DURMITOR
MOUNTAIN RANGE: DINARIC
PEOPLE: SERB CROAT SLOVENE
PORT: KOTOR SPLIT RIJEKA
NOVISAD BELGRADE DUBROVNIK
REGION: BANAT BOSINA SRBIJA
RIVER: DRIM IBAR KRKA SAVA

683   YELLOWNESS • YUGOSLAVIA

TISA BOSNA CAZMA DRAVA
DRINA RASKA TAMIS VRBAS
DANUBE MORAVA VARDER
VELIKA NERETVA
TOWN: NIS AGRAM BUDVA RTANJ
SPLIT USKUB BITOLA MORAVA
MOSTAR OSIJEK PRILEP

RAGUSA RIJEKA SKOPJE
VARDAR ZAGREB CATTARO
NOVISAD PRIZREN MONASTIR
SARAJEVO SUBOTICA
WEIGHT: OKA OKE DRAMM TOVAR
WAGON SATLIJK

YULE NOEL CHRISTMAS
YUMA CUCHAN
YUMAN PATAYAN
YUNX WRYNECK
YURT TENT

Z ZAD ZED ZEE ZETA ZULU IZARD
ZEBRA IZZARD
(SHAPED LIKE A —) OPENBAND
ZABAGLIONE SABAYON
ZAFFER SMALT SAFFIOR ZAPHARA
ZAGREUS (FATHER OF —) JUPITER
(MOTHER OF —) PROSERPINE

ZAIRE
CAPITAL: KINSHASA
LAKE: KIVU MWERU
LANGUAGE: KIKONGO LINGALA
  SWAHILI TSHILUBA
MONEY: ZAIRE
MOUNTAIN RANGE: MITUMBA
  VIRUNGA RUWENZORI
PROVINCE: KIVU KASAI EQUATOR
  KATANGA ORIENTAL
RIVER: RUKI CONGO DENGU IBINA
  KASAI LINDI ZAIRE LIKATI
  LOMAMI LUKUGA UBANGI
  ARUWIMI LUALABA LULONGA
TOWN: BAYA BOMA LEBO AKETI
  KAMINA KIKWIT BUTEMBO
  KOLWEZI BAKWANGA YANGAMBI

ZAMBIA
CAPITAL: LUSAKA
COIN: KWACHA
CONGO: KINSHASA
FALLS: VICTORIA
LAKE: MWERU BANGWEULU
  TANGANYIKA
LANGUAGE: LOZI BEMBA TONGA
  LUVALE NYANJA AFRIKAANS
MOUNTAIN RANGE: MUCHINGA
RIVER: KAFUE LUANGWA LUAPULA
  ZAMBEZI
TOWN: KITWE NDOLA LUAPULA
  LUANSHYA MUFULIRA

ZAMBO CHINO SAMBO CAFUSO
  CURIBOCA
ZAMIA BANGA CICAD CYCAD
  COONTIE
ZAMINDAR MALIK
ZAMOUSE GAMOUS
ZAMPOGNA BAGPIPE PANPIPE
ZANDER ZANT PERCID SANDER
  SANDRA
ZANTHOXYLUM FAGARA
ZANY FOOL CRAZY TOADY SAWNEY
  BUFFOON IDIOTIC CLOWNISH
  SCREWBALL
ZANZIBAR (SEE TANZANIA)
ZAPARO IQUITO
ZAPATEROL LIMA BOXWOOD
  CERILLO
ZARAH KAZOO
ZEAL FIRE MOOD ARDOR FLAME
  HEART FERVOR WARMTH DEVOTION
  GOODWILL JEALOUSY
(WITH —) DINGDONG
ZEALOT BIGOT VOTARY VOTEEN

ZELANT DEVOTEE FANATIC
  CANANEAN SERAPHIC SICARIUS
  VOTARESS VOTARIST
ZEALOUS HOT HIGH ARDENT FERVID
  STRING CORDIAL DEVOTED
  EARNEST EMULOUS FERVENT
  FORWARD JEALOUS PUSHFUL
  VIGOROUS
(— ABOUT BEAUTY) ESTHETIC
ZEALOUSLY FAST INNERLY
  HEARTILY
ZEBRA DAUW EQUID HORSE QUAGGA
  SOLIPED
ZEBRAWOOD ARAROBA ZINGANA
ZEBU BRAMIN BRAGMAN BRAHMIN
(HYBRID OF — AND CATTLE)
  CATTABU
(HYBRID OF — AND YAK) ZOBO
ZECCHINO SEQUIN
ZEN (— PARADOX) KOAN
(— QUESTIONS) MONDO
ZENANA HAREM HARIM SERAGLIO
ZENICK SURICATE
ZENITH ACME PEAK HIGHT HEIGHT
  SUMMIT VERTEX
ZEOLITE ANALCIME ANALCITE
ZEPHYRUS FAVONIUS
(SON OF —) CARPOS
(WIFE OF —) CHLORIS
ZEPPELIN ZEP ZEPP AIRSHIP
ZERO OH NIL NUL BLOB DUCK NULL
  AUGHT CLOSE EMPTY OUGHT TRAIN
  ABSENT CIPHER NAUGHT LACKING
  NOTHING NULLITY SCRATCH
  NINETEEN
ZEST EDGE ELAN JASM GUSTO
  FLAVOR RELISH STINGO PIQUANCY
ZESTFUL RACY SPICY BREEZY
ZETES (BROTHER OF —) CALAIS
(FATHER OF —) BOREAS
(MOTHER OF —) ORITHYIA
ZETHUS (BROTHER OF —) AMPHION
(FATHER OF —) JUPITER
(SE)(MOTHER OF —) ANTIOPE
ZEUS ZAN SOTER ALASTOR CRONION
  KRONION POLIEUS CRONIDES
(BROTHER OF —) HADES POSEIDON
(FATHER OF —) KRONOS
(MOTHER OF —) RHEA
(SISTER OF —) HERA HESTIA
  DEMETER
(SON OF —) ARES
(WIFE OF —) HERA JUNO METIS
  THEMIS EURYNOME
ZEUXIS UNDERLAY
ZIGZAG BOYAU CRANK BROKEN
  INDENT CRANKLE CHEVONRY
  FLEXUOSE TRAVERSE
ZIMARRA CYMAR SIMAR CASSOCK
ZIMB FLY ZEBUB
ZINC FAR SPELT ZINCUM SPELTER
  TUTENAG EXCLUDER
ZING PEP VIM ZIP DASH SNAP
  ENERGY SPIRIT
ZINGEL PERCID
ZINKE CORNET

ZINNIA CRASSINA
ZION SION ISRAEL UTOPIA
ZIONIST IRGUNIST
ZIOSITE THULITE
ZIP VIM DASH SNAP FORCE WHISK
  BUTTON ENERGY STINGO
ZIPPER FASTENER
ZIRCON JARGON AZORITE MALACON
  HYACINTH STARLITE
ZITHER KIN CANON CANUN GUSLI
  KANOON CITHARA GITERNE GITTERN
  AUTOHARP GALEMPONG
(JAPANESE —) KOTO
ZITHER HARP KOTO
ZIZITH SISITH FRINGES TASSELS
  TSITSITH
ZO DZO ZOH ZOBO
ZOARITE BIMMELER
ZOBO ZO DZO ZOH ZOBU
ZODIAC GIRDLE BALDRIC BAWDRICK
  SIGNIFER
(SIGN OF —) LEO RAM BULL CRAB
  FISH GOAT LION ARIES LIBRA SCALE
  TWINS VIRGO ARCHER CANCER
  GEMINI PISCES TAURUS SCORPIO
  AQUARIUS CAPRICORN
ZONA ZOSTER
ZONE BED AREA BAND BEAM BELT
  HALO PLAGE TRACT CIRCLE REGION
  ZODIAC CLIMATE HORIZON
  ZOMULET CINGULUM FRONTIER
  HABENULA HISTOGEN STRINGER
(— OF CONFLICT) FRONT
(— OF FLAME) MANTLE
(— OF MINERALS) CORONA
(— OF VENUS) CEST CESTUS
(ABYSSAL —) BASSALIA
(PALEONTOLOGIC -—S) ASSISE
(SAFETY —) ISLET ISLAND REFUGE
(STRATOGRAPHIC —) HEMERA
(WELDING —) ROOT
ZOOECIUM AUTOPORE
ZOOID PERSON SIPHON BRYOZOAN
  HYDRANTH POLYPIDE ZOOTHOME
ZOOPHYTE CORAL SPONGE
  HYDROID
ZOOSPORE MONAD SWARMER
  ZOOCARP
ZORIL SKUNK POWCAT CHINCHE
  POLECAT MUISHOND
ZOROASTRIAN GABAR PARSI
  PARSEE
ZOROASTRIANISM MAZDAISM
ZOUAVE ZUZU SCALER ZOUZOU
ZOUNDS OONS WAUNS ZOONS
ZUCCETO CALOTTE SOLIDEO
  SKULLCAP
ZUNI CIBOLAN SHALAKO
ZWINGLIAN TIGURINE
ZYGOMATIC JUGAL
ZYGOSPORE COPULA
ZYGOTE OOSPERM OOSPORE
  SPORONT OOKINETE
ZYME YEAST ZYMIN ENZYME
  FERMENT
ZYRIAN KOMI SYRYAN

ADDENDA

)